KV-577-765

Foreword

THIS *Yearbook of the United Nations* is the thirty-seventh published since the founding of the Organization. During this time, the pages of these volumes have provided a factual record of what the United Nations has done or sought to do. Behind this record lies the whole panorama of the accomplishments and frustrations of humanity in this time of phenomenal change.

We have marvelled as countries rebuilt their lives after the dark night of global war and we have rejoiced as more than a hundred nations gained their independence. We have sought to restrain regional conflicts and we have witnessed with distress the failure of Governments to co-operate in resolving them on a basis of justice and honour. We have struggled to control the spiralling arms race, which can spell doom for the human enterprise. We have laid down standards for the observance of human rights which nevertheless are still violated frequently and on a massive scale. As dramatic advances in communications, knowledge and technology have vastly enriched the human estate, we have striven to reduce the deprivation that still remains the lot of the world's majority. Both triumph and tragedy are writ large in the chronicles of our age.

Our hope is anchored in that constituency of peace which cuts across national frontiers and the divisions of race, culture or ideology. The United Nations represents that constituency. It is not, and was not designed to be, a world government. But it provides structure and continuity to the joint effort to solve international problems which affect peace and impinge on justice and human dignity. If used as its Charter envisioned, with loyalty and commitment by its Member States, it can make all nations good neighbours and give new form and direction to their collective strengths.

The information contained in this volume, and its predecessors, is indispensable to anyone wishing to understand how nations have addressed their common concerns, which have emerged at an ever-increasing rate. Whether reporting progress or set-backs, highlighting success or exposing deficiencies, it furnishes evidence of the fact that there is no alternative to the working of the United Nations for ensuring our survival and the betterment of the human condition.

Javier PÉREZ DE CUÉLLAR
Secretary-General

Contents

Part One: *United Nations*

POLITICAL AND SECURITY QUESTIONS

YEARBOOK OF THE
UNITED NATIONS
1983

Volume 37

YEARBOOK
OF THE
UNITED
NATIONS
1983

Volume 37

Department of Public Information
United Nations, New York

COPYRIGHT © 1987 UNITED NATIONS

ISSN: 0082-8521

ISBN: 92-1-100312-1

STAFFORDSHIRE
COUNTY
LIBRARY

A 8.4.88
C

UNITED NATIONS PUBLICATION

SALES NO. E.86.I.1

08500

ECONOMIC AND SOCIAL QUESTIONS

TRUSTEESHIP AND DECOLONIZATION

LEGAL QUESTIONS

ADMINISTRATIVE AND BUDGETARY QUESTIONS

Part Two: *Intergovernmental organizations related to the United Nations*

Appendices

Indexes

About the 1983 edition of the *Yearbook*

The 1983 *YEARBOOK OF THE UNITED NATIONS* has been designed as a reference tool for use not only by diplomats and other officials but also by writers, researchers, journalists, librarians and students, in fact all who might need readily available information on a particular activity of the United Nations system.

The *Yearbook* covers, during a calendar year, the main activities of the United Nations (Part One) and those of each related organization in the United Nations system (Part Two).

The 1983 edition is subject-oriented like previous editions. Part One (United Nations), containing 50 chapters, is divided into five major sections: political and security questions, economic and social questions, trusteeship and decolonization, legal questions, and administrative and budgetary questions.

Each chapter is divided into a hierarchy of topics, with each level having a heading of distinctive appearance. The assignment of headings implies no editorial judgement about the relative importance of a topic.

Structure and scope of articles

Presented under each topical heading is a summary of pertinent United Nations activities, including those of intergovernmental and expert bodies, major reports, Secretariat activities, and the views of States in written communications. The 1983 edition also gives the position of those States explaining their votes in the principal organs of the Organization. Such explanations are generally given when a recorded vote was taken. At the end of each chapter or subchapter is a list of references, linked by numerical indicators to the text. These references indicate document symbols, previous *Yearbook* pages supplying additional information, and previous resolutions and/or decisions by the principal United Nations organs. The *Yearbook* covers the following:

Activities of United Nations bodies. All resolutions, decisions and other major activities of the principal organs and, where applicable, those of subsidiary bodies, including sub-commissions and sub-committees, are either reproduced or summarized in the respective articles. The texts of all resolutions and decisions adopted by the General Assembly, the Security Council, the Economic and Social Council and the Trusteeship Council, with information on their adoption, are reproduced under the relevant topic. Where relevant provisions of other resolutions and decisions of such bodies are mentioned, the full text can be found by using the INDEX OF RESOLUTIONS AND DECISIONS at the end of this volume.

Major reports. Most 1983 reports of the Secretary-General on which a United Nations body took action during the year, along with selected reports from other United Nations sources such as seminars and working groups, are summarized briefly under the relevant topic(s). The document symbols of all reports cited in an article appear in the references.

Secretariat activities. The operational activities of the United Nations for development and humanitarian assistance are described under the relevant topics. For all major activities financed outside the United Nations regular budget, information is given on contributions by individual countries and on expenditures. Financial data are generally obtained from the audited accounts prepared for each fund, and cover the 1983 calendar year unless otherwise specified.

Views of States. Each written communication sent to the United Nations by a Member State and circulated separately as a document of a principal organ has been summarized under the most relevant topic.

All substantive debates in the Security Council have been analysed by *Yearbook* editors, and their main points can be found under the pertinent topic(s). Users wishing details on the position of individual States in the principal organs of the United Nations or any of their main/sessional committees should refer to the meeting numbers to be found at the end of the summaries of procedural action following all resolution/decision texts.

Related intergovernmental organizations. Part Two of the *Yearbook* describes the 1983 activities of each specialized agency and the International Atomic Energy Agency, based on information prepared by them for the *Yearbook*. Included are data on budgets, contributions by member States and principal officials.

Texts

The *Yearbook* reproduces the texts of all resolutions and substantive decisions adopted in 1983 by the General Assembly, the Security Council, the Economic and Social Council and the Trusteeship Council. These texts, together with the title (if any) of the resolution/decision, are followed by the procedural details giving: date of adoption, meeting number and vote totals (in favour-against-abstaining); information on their approval by a sessional or subsidiary body prior to final adoption, with document symbols of drafts, approved amendments and committee reports; and a list of sponsors. Also given are the document symbols of any financial implications and all relevant meeting numbers of the principal organs and the General Assembly's Main Committees. Details of any recorded or roll-call vote on the resolution/decision as a whole also follow the text.

Terminology

Formal titles of bodies, organizational units, conventions, declarations and officials are given in full on first mention in an article or sequence of articles. They are also used in resolution/decision texts, and in the SUBJECT INDEX under the key word of the title.

Short titles may be used in subsequent references. They employ key words, usually not capitalized, from the formal title, such as "Committee on colonial countries" for "Special Committee on the Situation with regard to the Implementation of the Declaration on the Granting of Independence to Colonial Countries and Peoples". Capital letters are used when the only difference between full and short title is the omission of a term such as "*Ad Hoc*", "International", "Special" or "United Nations" ("Committee against *Apartheid*", for "Special Committee against *Apartheid*"). These short titles have no official standing.

How to find information in the *Yearbook*

The 1983 edition has been designed to enable the user to locate information on United Nations activities in a number of ways.

By subject: Broad subjects may be located in the table of contents on page vi. Each chapter opens with an introduction highlighting the main developments. Where a main topic is subdivided, shorter introductions may precede subchapters. Cross-references give chapters for related information. The SUBJECT INDEX may be used to locate individual topics and specific references to the bodies dealing with each.

By body: Although the *Yearbook* is oriented by subject rather than by body, surveys of the work of many bodies appear under the topic of their main concern. For the principal organs, APPENDIX IV gives the 1983 agenda for each session. The members, officers, and date and place of sessions of each body are given in APPENDIX III. The SUBJECT INDEX lists bodies by the key word(s) of their formal title: "*Apartheid*, Special Committee against".

By resolution and decision number: A numerical list of all resolutions and substantive decisions adopted in 1983 by the principal organs, with page numbers for their text, appears in the final pages of this volume.

Each resolution/decision text appears in an article together with the circumstances of its adoption. Summaries of relevant provisions of other resolutions or decisions may also be added where applicable.

Other information: The annual report of the Secretary-General on the work of the Organization in 1983 is reproduced, beginning on page 3. A list of Member States, with their dates of admission to the United Nations, comprises APPENDIX I. The Charter of the United Nations, including the Statute of the International Court of Justice, is in APPENDIX II. An INDEX OF NAMES follows the SUBJECT INDEX.

ABBREVIATIONS COMMONLY USED IN THE *YEARBOOK*

AALCC	Asian-African Legal Consultative Committee
ACABQ	Advisory Committee on Administrative and Budgetary Questions
ACC	Administrative Committee on Co-ordination
ACPAQ	Advisory Committee on Post Adjustment Questions
ADB	African Development Bank
AMS	Administrative Management Service
ANC	African National Congress of South Africa
APDC	Asian and Pacific Development Centre
ARSAP	Agricultural Requisites Scheme for Asia and the Pacific
ASEAN	Association of South-East Asian Nations
BIS	Bank for International Settlements
CCAQ	Consultative Committee on Administrative Questions
CCIR	International Radio Consultative Committee (ITU)
CCITT	International Telegraph and Telephone Consultative Committee
CCOP/ SOPAC	Committee for Co-ordination of Joint Prospecting for Mineral Resources in South Pacific Offshore Areas
CCSQ	Consultative Committee on Substantive Questions
CDP	Committee for Development Planning
CELADE	Latin American Demographic Centre
CERD	Committee on the Elimination of Racial Discrimination
CFA	Committee on Food Aid Policies and Programmes
CGPRT	coarse grains, pulses, roots and tuber crops
CILSS	Permanent Inter-State Committee on Drought Control in the Sahel
CMEA	Council for Mutual Economic Assistance
COPAC	Joint Committee for the Promotion of Aid to Co-operatives
COPUOS	Committee on the Peaceful Uses of Outer Space
CPC	Committee for Programme and Co-ordination
CSDHA	Centre for Social Development and Humanitarian Affairs (DIESA)
DAC	Development Assistance Committee (OECD)
DIEC	Development and International Economic Co-operation
DIESA	Department of International Economic and Social Affairs
DIS	Development Information System (ISU)
DPI	Department of Public Information
DTA	Democratic Turnhalle Alliance (Namibia)
DTCD	Department of Technical Co-operation for Development
EC	European Community
ECA	Economic Commission for Africa
ECDC	economic co-operation among developing countries
ECE	Economic Commission for Europe
ECLA	Economic Commission for Latin America
ECOWAS	Economic Community of West African States
ECWA	Economic Commission for Western Asia
EEC	European Economic Community
ESA	European Space Agency
ESC	Economic and Social Council
ESCAP	Economic and Social Commission for Asia and the Pacific
EURATOM	European Atomic Energy Community
FADINAP	Fertilizer Advisory, Development and Information Network for Asia and the Pacific
FALPRO	Special Programme on Trade Facilitation
FAO	Food and Agriculture Organization of the United Nations
FICSA	Federation of International Civil Servants' Associations
FRETILIN	Frente Revolucionária de Timor Leste Independente
GA	General Assembly
GAB	General Arrangement to Borrow (IMF)
GATT	General Agreement on Tariffs and Trade
GCO	Greeting Card Operation (UNICEF)
GDP	gross domestic product
GDPS	Global Data-Processing System (WMO)
GEMS	Global Environmental Monitoring System (UNEP)
GNP	gross national product
GOS	Global Observing System (WMO)
GSP	generalized system of preferences
GSTP	global system of trade preferences
GTS	Global Telecommunication System (WMO)
IAEA	International Atomic Energy Agency
IBI	Intergovernmental Bureau of Informatics
ICAO	International Civil Aviation Organization
ICARA	International Conference on Assistance to Refugees in Africa
ICCROM	International Centre for the Study of the Preservation and the Restoration of Cultural Property
ICITO	Interim Commission for the International Trade Organization

ICJ	International Court of Justice
ICM	Intergovernmental Committee for Migration
ICP	International Comparison Project
ICRC	International Committee of the Red Cross
ICRP	International Commission on Radiological Protection
ICSC	International Civil Service Commission
IDA	International Development Association
IDB	Industrial Development Board (UNIDO)
IEFR	International Emergency Food Reserve
IFAD	International Fund for Agricultural Development
IFC	International Finance Corporation
ILC	International Law Commission
ILMAC	Israel-Lebanon Mixed Armistice Commission
ILO	International Labour Organisation
ILPES	Latin American Institute for Economic and Social Planning
IMF	International Monetary Fund
IMO	International Maritime Organization
INCB	International Narcotics Control Board
INFOTERRA	International Referral System for Sources of Environmental Information (UNEP)
INSTRAW	International Research and Training Institute for the Advancement of Women
INTIB	Industrial and Technological Information Bank (UNIDO)
IOB	Inter-Organization Board for Information Systems
IOC	International Oceanographic Commission
IPC	International Pepper Community
IPDC	International Programme for Development of Communication (UNESCO)
IPF	indicative planning figure (UNDP)
IRIRC	International Refugee Integration Resource Centre
IRPTC	International Register of Potentially Toxic Chemicals (UNEP)
ISIP	Integrated Systems Improvement Project (UNDP)
ISU	Information Systems Unit (DIESA)
ITC	International Trade Centre (UNCTAD/GATT)
ITO	International Trade Organization
ITU	International Telecommunication Union
IUCN	International Union for Conservation of Nature and Natural Resources
IYDP	International Year of Disabled Persons
IYC	International Year of the Child
IYY	International Youth Year
JAG	Joint Advisory Group on the International Trade Centre
JIU	Joint Inspection Unit
JUNIC	Joint United Nations Information Committee
LDC	least developed country
LPG	liquefied petroleum gas
MFA	Multifibre Arrangement (Arrangement Regarding Trade in Textiles) (GATT)
MULPOC	Multinational Programming and Operational Centre (ECA)
NATO	North Atlantic Treaty Organization
NEA	Nuclear Energy Agency (OECD)
NGO	non-governmental organization
NPT	Treaty on the Non-Proliferation of Nuclear Weapons
NSGT	Non-Self-Governing Territory
NUSS	Nuclear Safety Standards (IAEA)
OAPEC	Organization of Arab Petroleum Exporting Countries
OAS	Organization of American States
OAU	Organization of African Unity
ODA	official development assistance
OECD	Organisation for Economic Co-operation and Development
OPEC	Organization of Petroleum Exporting Countries
PAC	Pan Africanist Congress of Azania
PADIS	Pan-African Documentation and Information System
PANS	Procedure for Air Navigation Services (ICAO)
PCT	Patent Co-operation Treaty (WIPO)
PHC	primary health care
PLO	Palestine Liberation Organization
POLISARIO	Frente Popular para la Liberación de Saguia el-Hamra y de Río de Oro
POPIN	Population Information Network
PPBB	Programme Planning and Budgeting Board
RCA	Regional Co-operation Agreement for Research, Development and Training Related to Nuclear Science and Technology (IAEA)
RID	International Regulations concerning the Carriage of Dangerous Goods by Rail

SALT	strategic arms limitation talks
SC	Security Council
SDR	special drawing rights
SG	Secretary-General
SIDFA	Senior Industrial Development Field Adviser (UNIDO)
SIS	Special Industrial Services (UNIDO)
SNA	United Nations System of National Accounts
SOLAS	International Convention for the Safety of Life at Sea (IMO)
SPC	Special Political Committee
START	strategic arms reduction talks
SWAPO	South West Africa People's Organization (Namibia)
TC	Trusteeship Council
TCDC	technical co-operation among developing countries
TCP	Technical Co-operation Programme (FAO)
TDB	Trade and Development Board (UNCTAD)
TELECOM-83	World Telecommunication Exhibition
TIR	*transport international routier* (international road transport) (ECE)
TNC	transnational corporation
UN	United Nations
UNCDF	United Nations Capital Development Fund
UNCHS	United Nations Centre for Human Settlements (Habitat)
UNCITRAL	United Nations Commission on International Trade Law
UNCIVPOL	United Nations civilian police (UNFICYP)
UNCTAD	United Nations Conference on Trade and Development
UNDOF	United Nations Disengagement Observer Force (Golan Heights)
UNDP	United Nations Development Programme
UNDRO	Office of the United Nations Disaster Relief Co-ordinator
UNEF	United Nations Emergency Force
UNEP	United Nations Environment Programme
UNESCO	United Nations Educational, Scientific and Cultural Organization
UNFDAC	United Nations Fund for Drug Abuse Control
UNFICYP	United Nations Peace-keeping Force in Cyprus
UNFPA	United Nations Fund for Population Activities
UNHCR	United Nations High Commissioner for Refugees
UNICEF	United Nations Children's Fund

UNIDF	United Nations Industrial Development Fund (UNIDO)
UNIDIR	United Nations Institute for Disarmament Research
UNIDO	United Nations Industrial Development Organization
UNIDROIT	International Institute for the Unification of Private Law
UNIFIL	United Nations Interim Force in Lebanon
UNIPAC	UNICEF Packing and Assembly Centre
UNISPACE-82	Second United Nations Conference on the Exploration and Peaceful Uses of Outer Space
UNITAR	United Nations Institute for Training and Research
UNRFNRE	United Nations Revolving Fund for Natural Resources Exploration
UNRISD	United Nations Research Institute for Social Development
UNRWA	United Nations Relief and Works Agency for Palestine Refugees in the Near East
UNSCEAR	United Nations Scientific Committee on the Effects of Atomic Radiation
UNSDRI	United Nations Social Defence Research Institute
UNSO	United Nations Sudano-Sahelian Office
UNTAG	United Nations Transition Assistance Group
UNTSO	United Nations Truce Supervision Organization (Israel and neighbouring States)
UNU	United Nations University
UNV	United Nations Volunteers
UPU	Universal Postal Union
WAPA	weighted average of post adjustments
WCISP	World Climate Impact Studies Programme
WFC	World Food Council
WFP	World Food Programme
WFS	World Fertility Survey
WHO	World Health Organization
WIPO	World Intellectual Property Organization
WMO	World Meteorological Organization
WTO	World Tourism Organization
WWW	World Weather Watch (WMO)
YUN	*Yearbook of the United Nations*

EXPLANATORY NOTE ON DOCUMENTS

References at the end of each article in Part One of this volume give the symbols of the main documents issued in 1983 on the topic, arranged in the order in which they are referred to in the text. The following is a guide to the principal document symbols:

A/- refers to documents of the General Assembly, numbered in separate series by session. Thus, A/38/- refers to documents issued for consideration at the thirty-eighth session, beginning with A/38/1. Documents of special and emergency special sessions are identified as A/S- and A/ES-, followed by the session number.

A/C.- refers to documents of six of the Assembly's Main Committees, e.g. A/C.1/- is a document of the First Committee, A/C.6/-, a document of the Sixth Committee. The symbol for documents of the seventh Main Committee, the Special Political Committee, is A/SPC/-. A/BUR/- refers to documents of the General Committee. A/AC.- documents are those of the Assembly's *ad hoc* bodies and A/CN.-, of its commissions; e.g. A/AC.105/- identifies documents of the Assembly's Committee on the Peaceful Uses of Outer Space, A/CN.4/-, of its International Law Commission. Assembly resolutions and decisions since the thirty-first (1976) session have been identified by two Arabic numerals: the first indicates the session of adoption; the second, the sequential number in the series. Resolutions are numbered consecutively from 1 at each session. Decisions of regular sessions are numbered consecutively, from 301 for those concerned with elections and appointments, and from 401 for all other decisions. Decisions of special and emergency special sessions are numbered consecutively, from 11 for those concerned with elections and appointments, and from 21 for all other decisions.

E/- refers to documents of the Economic and Social Council, numbered in separate series by year. Thus, E/1983/- refers to documents issued for consideration by the Council at its 1983 sessions, beginning with E/1983/1. E/AC.-, E/C.- and E/CN.-, followed by identifying numbers, refer to documents of the Council's subsidiary *ad hoc* bodies, committees and commissions. For example, E/C.1/-, E/C.2/- and E/C.3/- refer to documents of the Council's sessional committees, namely, the First (Economic), Second (Social) and Third (Programme and Co-ordination) Committees, respectively; E/CN.5/- refers to documents of the Council's Commission for Social Development, E/CN.7/-, to documents of its Committee on Natural Resources. E/ICEF/- documents are those of the United Nations Children's Fund (UNICEF). Symbols for the Council's resolutions and decisions, since 1978, consist of two Arabic numerals: the first indicates the year of adoption and the second, the sequential number in the series. There are two series: one for resolutions, beginning with 1 (resolution 1983/1); and one for decisions, beginning, since 1980, with 100 (decision 1983/100).

S/- refers to documents of the Security Council. Its resolutions are identified by consecutive numbers followed by the year of adoption in parentheses, beginning with resolution 1 (1946).

T/- refers to documents of the Trusteeship Council. Its resolutions are numbered consecutively, with the session at which they were adopted indicated by Roman numerals, e.g. resolution 2175(L) of the fiftieth session. The Council's decisions are not numbered.

ST/-, followed by symbols representing the issuing department or office, refers to documents of the United Nations Secretariat.

Documents of certain bodies bear special series symbols, including the following:

ACC/-	Administrative Committee on Co-ordination
CD/-	Committee on Disarmament
CERD/-	International Convention on the Elimination of All Forms of Racial Discrimination
DC/-	Disarmament Commission
DP/-	United Nations Development Programme
HS/-	Commission on Human Settlements
ID/-	United Nations Industrial Development Organization
ITC/-	International Trade Centre
LOS/PCN/-	Preparatory Commission for the International Sea-Bed Authority and for the International Tribunal for the Law of the Sea
TD/-	United Nations Conference on Trade and Development
UNEP/-	United Nations Environment Programme
UNITAR/-	United Nations Institute for Training and Research

Many documents of the regional commissions bear special symbol series. These are sometimes preceded by the following:

E/CEPAL/-	Economic Commission for Latin America
E/CN.14/-, E/ECA/-	Economic Commission for Africa
E/ECE/-	Economic Commission for Europe
E/ECWA/-	Economic Commission for Western Asia
E/ESCAP/-	Economic and Social Commission for Asia and the Pacific

"L" in a symbol refers to documents of limited distribution, such as draft resolutions; "CONF." to documents of a conference; "INF." to those of general information. Summary records are designated by "SR.", verbatim records by "PV.", each followed by the meeting number.

United Nations sales publications each carry a sales number with the following components separated by periods: a capital letter indicating the language(s) of the publication; two Arabic numerals indicating the year; a Roman numeral indicating the subject category; a capital letter indicating a subdivision of the category, if any; and an Arabic numeral(s) indicating the number of the publication within the category. Examples: E.83.V.7; E/F/R.82.II.E.8; E.84.IX.3.

PART ONE

United Nations

Report of the Secretary-General on the work of the Organization

Following is the text of the report of the Secretary-General on the work of the Organization, submitted to the General Assembly and dated 12 September 1983. [1] *The Assembly took note of the report on 5 December 1983 when it adopted decision 38/410.*

In my annual report last year I commented on the performance of the United Nations in discharging its primary duty of maintaining international peace and security and on ways in which that performance might be improved. I am gratified that those suggestions have been extensively discussed, both in the General Assembly and, in considerable detail and over a long period of time, by the Security Council. Certainly there is an urgent necessity to develop international institutions capable of encompassing the harsh realities of our time. But despite the interest displayed in my last annual report by the General Assembly and the will of the members of the Security Council to enhance and strengthen the performance of the Council, the actual developments of the past year have been far from encouraging. It seems to me that we are more than ever in need of a fresh collective look at some of the major problems of the world. The basic issue continues to be the development of, and commitment to, a working system of international security as an essential complement to progress in disarmament and arms limitation and a renewed effort at the highest level to strengthen international economic co-operation for growth and development.

There are a number of current problems affecting international peace, security and co-operation which cry out for a central instrument of co-operative effort through which Governments can control conflict and work out solutions. Despite the efforts of many, 1983 has, so far, been a frustrating year for the search for peace, stability and justice and for those who believe that the United Nations is the best available international instrumentality to achieve these ends. As I believe that the erosion of multilateralism and internationalism should be arrested and reversed, I propose in this report to concentrate on certain approaches which might make our Organization more effective as a political institution.

* * *

The Charter of the United Nations clearly gives priority to dealing with threats to international peace and security and to the commitment of all nations, especially the permanent members of the Security Council, to co-operate within the framework of the United Nations towards this end. It is the weakening of this commitment that has, perhaps more than any other factor, led to the partial paralysis of the United Nations as the guardian of international peace and security.

Furthermore, when East-West tension is superimposed on regional conflicts and serves to exacerbate them, the already destructive nature of such disputes is likely to be aggravated and the danger of widening strife becomes an ominous prospect. On some occasions this process has gone so far that regional conflicts have been perceived as being wars by proxy among more powerful nations. In situations of this kind, the deliberative organs of the United Nations tend to be bypassed or excluded or, worse yet, to be used solely as a forum for polemical exchanges.

There have been, at any given time in past years, several regional situations with grave potential implications for international peace. At the present time, for example, such situations exist in South-East Asia, Afghanistan, Central America, Namibia and several other parts of Africa including Chad, in the Middle East and Lebanon, Cyprus and in the Iran-Iraq war. I shall be dealing in more detail with most of these situations in separate reports either to the General Assembly or the Security Council.

Neither the Security Council nor any other international organ can in all cases hope to resolve in short order acute international conflict situations that may involve serious clashes of interest between the actual parties as well as between the members of the Council. The Security Council under the Charter has, however, the obligation to assist the parties in the search for solutions to international disputes. But above all it is the Council's duty to ensure that this process should remain peaceful, lest it endanger the wider peace. Even though the members of the Council may be profoundly divided about the merits of a given case, it is their duty to find ways and means of keeping the situation under control, without prejudice to the shape of an eventual settlement. Seen in this perspective, conflict control is a basic element of the primary responsibility of the United Nations for the maintenance of international peace and security.

For their part, States and other parties to international disputes have a primary obligation at all stages to co-operate with the Security Council and the Secretary-General in suitable forms of conflict control. However, the willingness of the parties to co-operate with the United Nations will inevitably be contingent upon the capacity of the Organization to act as an effective and impartial instrument of peace. Only if this essential condition is achieved will Member States come to the realization that in times of trouble they can rely on the United Nations to help to restore or maintain the peaceful conditions in which negotiated solutions of the basic issues can be sought as part of a civilized and rational international order.

Aside from conflict control, the main objective of the Security Council, particularly of its permanent members, should be to develop an effective common approach to potential threats to international peace and security, to assist and, if necessary, to put pressure on the conflicting parties to resolve their differences justly and by peaceful means. Such a concerted approach would dispose of great resources of persuasion and, if necessary, of practical leverage. That, surely, is the approach to important conflict problems which the authors of the Charter had in mind. This approach would go a long way to developing in practice a system for international peace and security designed to supersede arms races, military and other forms of conflict and the inherent risk of ultimate disaster. This is, after all, the basic idea of the Charter.

Unfortunately, we are in danger of becoming accustomed to a very different situation. All too often the members of the Security Council tend to be so divided on the matter at hand and so apprehensive of each other's reaction to it that agreement on how to proceed remains elusive. When we consider how to improve the performance of the United Nations we must give priority to the cohesion and co-operation of the membership in facing threats to international peace. We should recognize that such threats are of an importance which should override the differences of interest and ideology which separate the membership. The Council must be primarily used for the prevention of armed conflict and the search for solutions. Otherwise it will become peripheral to major issues, and in the end the world could pay, as it has before, a heavy price for not learning the lessons of history.

If this analysis seems Utopian, it is certainly preferable to a course of action which risks, through partisanship, the elevating of a local conflict into a world confrontation. Indeed the habit of adopting a concerted approach to problems of international peace and security might lead to the statesmanlike co-operation which will be essential in bridging the great present divisions of our international society and in turning the tide in crucial matters such as disarmament and arms control.

We have this year witnessed some notable efforts to maintain unity and realism in the Security Council on highly charged issues. I am thinking in particular of the Council's proceedings on the complaint of Nicaragua and the Namibia question, which revealed a constructive search for consensus on difficult and controversial problems. This is indeed a step forward, but the next step may be more difficult, namely, to put the necessary leverage and movement into the decisions of the Council.

We must, I believe, firmly persevere in the effort to move from words to action. In this context, and having in mind the views expressed by the members of the Security Council, I have, in the course of this year, kept the Council informed of the responsibilities entrusted to me and of my efforts to discharge them. I have also, within the Secretariat, initiated steps in order to be alerted in advance to incipient problems. I look forward to working with the Council in order to develop a wider and more systematic capacity for fact-finding in potential conflict areas.

As Secretary-General I am the repository of numerous injunctions to use my best efforts, to keep in contact with the parties and to report on a wide variety of problems that no one has been able to solve. Resolutions are passed, on occasion requesting reports which form the basis for new resolutions. This process often becomes the substitute for action, and indeed the antithesis of it. Once again I wish to urge the necessity for realistic and politically effective approaches to problems. I welcome the indications of a trend in this direction.

Naturally, I and my colleagues do our best to follow up on important issues before the Organization. I cannot, however, escape the feeling that decisions of the United Nations on important issues require more than this. As I said last year, I believe that decisions of the various organs should be the beginning, not the end, of governmental concern and action. A continuous effort to contribute to the implementation of United Nations decisions should be an integral part of the foreign policy of Member States to a far greater extent than it is at the present time.

It is deeply disturbing to me as Secretary-General, while pursuing efforts to solve this or that problem, to receive the impression that some Governments sometimes attach little importance to the decisions they themselves have participated in at the United Nations. Conversely it is most encouraging—as I have found in my visits to numerous capitals in the past year—that a basic faith in the purposes and principles of the Charter remains a dominant theme. I wish here to repeat with all possible emphasis the statement in my last report that an essential first step towards strengthening the United Nations would be a conscious recommitment to the Charter by all Governments. With an objective as elusive and as vital as the preservation of peace, a sense of shared purpose and direction is imperative.

* * *

In no area is the need for a recommitment to the principles of the Charter more important and more closely tied to the survival of humanity than in the field of disarmament and arms limitation. The prevention of nuclear war remains the unique challenge of our time, since such a war would be the ultimate negation of all human endeavour. While the international community as a whole is deeply concerned with this vital problem, the key to its solution is in the hands of the two major nuclear Powers.

The current bilateral negotiations on the reduction of strategic and intermediate-range nuclear forces are of vital importance in the face of the destabilizing effects of advancing technology and the continuing arms race. It seems likely that the mood and outcome of these talks will decisively affect the general climate of international relations in the future, as well as the chances of progress on other aspects of disarmament.

The failure so far to achieve real progress in these negotiations can only cause us all profound alarm. If they should fail, we may be faced with another significant escalation in the spiralling arms competition. A development of this kind would inevitably add to the world's burden of insecurity and instability. The situation could well become virtually irreversible if the establishment of viable methods of arms limitation is jeopardized by the development of new weapons systems, and if either side, in search of military advantage, deploys strategic weapons that suggest an attempt to reach out for first-strike capability. Currently, perhaps even more acute is the problem of intermediate-range missiles, which may reach a critical stage unless the present negotiations bear fruit. Beyond all this there looms the longer-term prospect of the militarization of outer space and the computerization and automation of warfare, which could eventually escape political control altogether.

I have no doubt that the responsible leaders on both sides are aware of the ominous prospects, and of the crying need for renewed determination to move the current Geneva talks forward. In this connection, I might venture the observation that in this field there are no bargaining chips. Each side seems determined to respond to any advance achieved by the other side by matching it rather than by making concessions.

In view of the urgency of the situation, especially as regards intermediate-range forces, I hope that the parties will give thought to possible interim measures that would keep open the possibility of negotiations. I further recall that certain promising compromise proposals have been informally discussed in Geneva. It is important to bear in mind that negotiations on one weapons system intended to deter one particular threat are inextricably linked to perceptions of the overall threat and to negotiations on other weapons systems. It is therefore imperative to reduce the totality of mutual threat by moving in the direction of more stable systems. The extension of the mutual observance of current limitations would also be helpful in order to allow consideration of a new longer-term approach. Future limits on qualitative improvements and modernization could provide a useful subject of discussion in both sectors of the Geneva talks. The object, while preserving military parity, should be to promote equal security for all at progressively decreasing levels and under effective international control.

I share the general anxiety about the possible uses of outer space for military purposes, and I welcome recent suggestions to deal with important aspects of this problem. I would strongly urge that comprehensive negotiations should begin at an early date on a peaceful régime for outer space. To improve the atmosphere, it would also be desirable to lend fresh impetus to the talks on banning the production of chemical weapons and destroying existing stocks. Enough work has already been done to provide the basis for the long-awaited convention on this subject. Furthermore, I would urge a renewed effort to conclude negotiations on a comprehensive nuclear-weapon test ban. This would significantly help to halt the nuclear-arms race by impeding the qualitative improvement of nuclear weapons. All these questions are currently under consideration in the Committee on Disarmament at Geneva. In addressing that body earlier this year, I urged its members not to let their vital work fall hostage to lack of progress elsewhere.

The situation relating to conventional arms is a source of increasing concern. It is necessary to bear in mind that the many millions killed in war since Hiroshima and Nagasaki have all died from conventional weapons. This situation has had a corrosively harmful effect not least on the world's developing countries, which feel obliged to spend an increasing proportion of their resources for defence purposes, often to the detriment of essential needs. It is of course the right and duty of all nations to provide for their self-defence. But unresolved disputes tend to provoke regional arms races and the international tensions accompanying competitive arms purchases can no longer be ignored.

In the Final Document of the 1978 special session on disarmament, the General Assembly called for consultations among major arms supplier and recipient countries to limit transfers of conventional weapons, in order to preserve security and promote stability at a lower military level. No concrete action has been taken so far to follow up that appeal. I would therefore suggest that the two Governments concerned give careful thought to the possibility of reviving the bilateral talks on conventional arms transfers, which were suspended in 1978. The scope of these talks could eventually be enlarged, perhaps within the framework of the Committee on Disarmament, to cover multilateral aspects and to provide representation of recipient as well as supplier countries.

The United Nations, as stated in the concluding documents of the two special sessions of the General Assembly devoted to disarmament, has a central role to play in this field. At its thirty-seventh session, the Assembly adopted a record number of resolutions on disarmament matters, including over 20 dealing with nuclear questions. They reflect the deeply felt concern of many Governments with the present situation. World public opinion is increasingly reacting against the constant threat of extinction hanging over humanity, in a world where despite our vaunted advances in science and human knowledge we cannot even assure our children of their future. In this context, I urge all Members to give full support to the World Disarmament Campaign of the United Nations, which was launched at the second special session of the General Assembly devoted to disarmament. In an area hitherto marked by polemics, this campaign will enable the Organization to disseminate objective information worldwide so as to provide a solid, factual basis for constructive public involvement and understanding.

*   *   *

In the common quest to realize the ideals and objectives of the Charter, we must never lose sight of the quality of the world we are seeking to build and of the ultimate *raison d'être* for all our activities: the individual human being, for whom the Universal Declaration of Human Rights proclaims the right to a social and international order in which human rights and fundamental freedoms can be fully realized.

Over the past years, there has developed a growing trend for international co-operation in dealing with human rights issues. In addition to the elaboration of international conventions since the Declaration, I should like to mention the work of the Commission on Human Rights on arbitrary and summary executions and the holding of the Second World Conference to Combat Racism and Racial Discrimination.

However, despite the progress achieved at the international level, gross violations of human rights and restrictions of fundamental freedoms are still taking place in many parts of the world. Racism and racial discrimination in various forms, including the totally unacceptable policy of *apartheid,* have not been eradicated. There are still far too many refugees, uprooted and destitute as a result of political conflicts.

The problem of refugees can be resolved only with a settlement of the root political causes. In the mean time, various United Nations operations and programmes have provided emergency assistance to many refugees and displaced persons and helped to alleviate their plight in some measure. But this is clearly not enough in spite of the effectiveness and devotion of the United Nations personnel involved. The means available to the Organization are grossly inadequate in relation to the actual needs. I earnestly hope that Governments as well as voluntary agencies will intensify their support of the United Nations for this important humanitarian endeavour.

I attach the highest importance to the question of human rights and I believe it my responsibility to consider the most effective means of dealing with specific cases. Taking into account the nature of my office and mindful of the kind of approach necessary to achieve practical results, I have been in contact with a number of Governments regarding particular human rights situations or individual cases. I am heartened by the instances in which co-operation has been extended to me in these contacts, and I am determined to persist in my efforts.

*   *   *

The Preamble of the Charter expresses the determination of the peoples of the United Nations "to promote social progress and better standards of life in larger freedom" and to this end "to employ international machinery for the promotion of the economic and social advancement of all peoples".

I am convinced that the impressive economic progress since the Second World War—in which almost all nations have shared—owes a great deal to multilateral co-operation which the United Nations has helped to bring about and develop. Recent trends and events, however, far from strengthening such co-operation, mark a clear retreat from these efforts. Indeed, while the effects of economic interdependence, due to growing integration in trade, finance and money, are widely acknowledged, obvious opportunities to address the major issues in these areas are being repeatedly missed. There can be no doubt that today more than ever many individual nations are affected—

for good or ill—by trends elsewhere and by the decisions of others. Furthermore, there are categories of problems which can only be dealt with multilaterally or globally. All these developments intensify the need for international mechanisms to bring about greater harmonization of national policies.

Unilateral actions, taken without due regard for their effects on partner countries, would inevitably lead to the weakening of economic co-operation, thereby damaging world growth and development. They would lead to economic nationalism, the evil effects of which we witnessed during the '30s. Unresolved economic conflicts can be, and usually are, a breeding ground for dangerous political tensions.

A major economic imperative of our times is the accelerated development of the developing countries. The eradication of the poverty that continues to be widespread in several parts of the world must remain a collective responsibility. The needs of the least developed and other poor countries require particular attention. The total population of developing countries is projected to increase from around 3 billion to approximately 5 billion by the end of the century, that is, within less than two decades.

The slowing, and sometimes the halt, in the development process that has taken place in recent years should be seen as a temporary phenomenon that must be reversed in the coming years. In the mean time, every effort has to be made to reduce the vulnerability of developing countries to external shocks and to assist them in attaining greater autonomy and freedom of action, both by themselves and in co-operation with other countries—developed and developing.

At the same time, it is necessary to realize a higher level of growth in the industrialized countries. Thirty-two million people are unemployed in the OECD countries alone, and this figure is likely to rise in the immediate future. A burden of this magnitude cannot be economically or politically accepted as a permanent part of the realities of these countries. The need for investment in order to fight unemployment, to ensure structural adjustments and to deal with the needs of underprivileged areas and groups requires higher growth in that region. This would also encourage better prospects for increased trade and transfer of resources from the industrialized countries to the developing countries. Similar considerations call for high growth in socialist economies as well.

I have recently presented, in statements to intergovernmental bodies, my views on ways to revive the world economy and resume the process of development. There is a primary need for action at the national level to correct economic and social imbalances. Such efforts need to be supported by concerted action among nations and the assistance of multilateral institutions. In this connection I have emphasized the need to make additional finance available as part of concerted policies for world recovery and to examine basic reforms in international trade, money and finance. Economic co-operation among developing countries also needs strengthening.

The recently concluded sixth session of UNCTAD provided an important opportunity to counter the present negative trends and to demonstrate the capacity and the will of Governments to overcome difficulties and to act together. Unfortunately, the results of this important Conference are not commensurate with the gravity of the situation in developing countries and the requirements of the world economy in general, and there was a failure to respond to the need for concerted international action. The opportunity of UNCTAD VI was to a large extent allowed to lapse, thus exacerbating political tensions on a range of economic issues. It is regrettable that efforts at flexibility, as evinced, for example, at the Buenos Aires and New Delhi meetings, did not evoke a comparable response. Nevertheless, it is my view that the consensus achieved at Belgrade on several issues could constitute a worthwhile step provided there is a continuing process of dialogue and action. In this context and despite the remaining obstacles, we must activate the process of negotiation between the developed and developing countries on long-term problems in several interrelated areas and at a high political level.

Let me now turn to the role of the United Nations on economic issues. How effective is the United Nations in discharging the responsibilities with which it has been entrusted by its Charter? Contrary to the perceptions of some, the Organization has been successful in anticipating and identifying issues of importance, mobilizing public opinion, researching and analysing critical problems, providing direct assistance within its means and negotiating constructive agreements in various sectors of activity.

The record of performance and accomplishments of the United Nations system in the economic and social fields is varied and substantial. Through a vast network of technical co-operation activities, organizations of the United Nations system continue to assist developing countries in formulating and implementing a large number of specific projects, ranging from the establishment of primary health care centres to highly sophisticated institutions of agronomic research and training, and technology.

However, I am very much aware that much more needs to be done to improve the efficiency and effectiveness of the system and to ensure its responsiveness to changing needs. This requires efforts on the part of the Secretariat as well as of the Member States.

I shall deal elsewhere in this report with issues relating to the improvement of the administration of the Secretariat. There is a need to ensure more concerted action by the organizations of the United Nations system in dealing with the important issues of development and international economic co-operation and in their work at the field level.

As regards Governments, it is important to ensure greater cohesion and consistency in their positions in the different intergovernmental bodies. A greater sense of priority in the deliberations of the General Assembly and of the Economic and Social Council would encourage more effective consideration of issues. It would also strengthen the impact of resolutions. Frequently such resolutions lead to a proliferation of institutions. This can hamper efficiency and add substance to criticism of an ever-expanding bureaucracy. Improvement is also needed in the machinery and methods of negotiation.

Innovative measures should be considered to foster the habit of co-operation. In this connection, I wish to underline the need to strengthen the efforts of the United Nations system to support the initiatives of developing countries to promote co-operation among themselves through the implementation of specific and action-oriented measures.

It is incumbent on us to seize every opportunity to carry forward the development dialogue, setting aside, where necessary, traditional practices or methods which may be obsolete, and testing new means of strengthening the collective effort of Member States to attain their common objectives.

*   *   *

No organization can succeed if its administrative system is inarticulate or unresponsive to its real needs. While there have been criticisms of the United Nations administration as inflated, politicized or extravagant, it is also necessary to understand its fundamental nature and problems. In the full knowledge that much responsible criticism is justified, let me, as chief administrative officer of the United Nations, attempt a brief look at the problems and realities which we face.

The administration of the United Nations is not like the administration of a national Government. For one thing, the Organization has 157 Members, with widely differing notions of administration. For another, it has existed for less than 38 years, a period of great flux in which its membership has more than trebled and the emphasis of its work dramatically changed. The principle of equitable geographical representation, which is essential, nevertheless poses its own considerable problems in the building up of a coherent international civil service. And the fact that there is often on one side of an administrative or budgetary issue a relatively small number of Member States that provide the bulk of the budget, and on the other a majority in the General Assembly that do not, also imposes stresses and strains. These and other factors render the Secretary-General's task as chief administrative officer a complex and sometimes exasperating one, for while all profess their dedication to the principles of independent and objective international administration, few refrain from trying to bring pressure to bear in favour of their own particular interests. This is especially so on the personnel side.

Article 97 of the Charter, which designates the Secretary-General as chief administrative officer of the Organization, gives no precise indication of the functions involved nor of how these functions are to be delimited against those of other principal organs, particularly the General Assembly. I shall not go into detail here about the various fields in which this lack of precision creates problems.

The General Assembly is, of course, pre-eminent. It appoints the Secretary-General under Article 97. It has the power of the purse (Article 17), the power to discuss "any matters . . . relating to the powers and functions of any organs" (Article 10) and to establish regulations for the governance of the Secretariat (Article 101). In other words, the Assembly lays down the general legislative framework within which the Secretary-General performs the executive functions entrusted to him by the Charter. The problem is that there is no defined borderline between the legislative and the executive. This can on occasion have an inhibiting effect on the Secretary-General in instituting and carrying out coherent policies, under the Charter, in recruiting, administering and running the Secretariat and the administration.

Thus in personnel matters, the Charter distribution of functions may be seen as blurred if decisions in respect of individual staff members, or the power to appoint a staff member or part of the staff, are vested in authorities other than the Secretary-General. This is also true of the increasingly detailed directives issued in recent years by the General Assembly concerning various aspects of recruitment, even if these merely reflect its frustration at the administration's failure to achieve, or the slow pace in achieving, goals set in earlier and more general guidelines as to the geographical, gender, linguistic and age distribution of the staff. While it is not my intention to raise constitutional or legal objections to these detailed directives, the fact remains that rigid directives can be counter-productive from a political and administrative point of view and may not always be conducive to the smooth functioning or efficient administration of the Organization. A case in point is the recent decision curtailing the Secretary-General's hitherto unquestioned authority to promulgate Staff Rules, as distinct from the Regulations issued by the General Assembly.

Another, perhaps unintended, consequence is that an effective career development programme is becoming increasingly difficult to work out. A programme of this kind, which I consider essential for the future capacity of the Secretariat as well as for the morale and encouragement of the present staff, presupposes considerable flexibility in conducting an active personnel policy. The current trend seems to be pushing us in the opposite direction.

The Charter is silent as to any explicit financial or budgetary functions of the Secretary-General, although the Financial Regulations and other decisions of the General Assembly assign to him substantial functions in this area. Of these, perhaps the most important is the preparation of the proposed programme budget for each financial period, upon which the General Assembly makes the final decision. The Secretary-General needs to retain the degree of authority necessary to maintain the financial integrity of the Organization and to safeguard the concept of a unified Secretariat. This necessity has, with minor exceptions, by and large been recognized. In the budget adoption process, it is inevitable that differences of opinion will arise at times between the Secretary-General and the Fifth Committee or the Advisory Committee on Administrative and Budgetary Questions. This is completely normal; there is nothing wrong in a process in which the Secretary-General defends his proposals fully and fairly and then implements faithfully whatever decision the Assembly may take thereon.

As regards the structure of the Secretariat, there are, since it is determined by the budget, very considerable restrictions on the Secretary-General's freedom of action. One trend, however, deserves mention here, namely, the tendency to establish more or less autonomous units to carry out certain functions—organs over which the Secretary-General does not have clear control. This trend raises serious questions of organizational responsibility and authority and may sometimes not be altogether consistent with the Charter concept of a unified Secretariat working as a team under a single leadership.

At the same time, critical attention needs to be given to the internal administrative set-up. After nearly four decades of wear and tear it needs a careful overhaul so as to ensure that it meets with increased efficiency the needs of this larger, more complex and more decentralized Organization. To that end I have recently established a high-level advisory group on administrative reform to identify issues and areas in which modification or reform could be effected.

Very often I find myself caught between the directives of the General Assembly, the interests of the staff and the imperatives of good and efficient administration in accordance with the Charter. I believe that it is in the general interest that we act together in full knowledge of the practical difficulties of the enterprise and with the united objective of strengthening the Secretariat and the administration.

This is, admittedly, a formidable task, complicated by the accretion of 38 years of experiment, development and change. I therefore intend to give priority in the coming year to a searching examination and appraisal of the administration with a view to improvement. But I should be less than frank not to pose here the question that often arises in my mind: Does the Secretary-General still have sufficient authority effectively to meet his responsibilities as chief administrative officer of the United Nations?

* * *

Thirty-eight years after the Second World War it would seem that the drive towards an effective, peaceful and more equitable international order has slowed, and the incentive to develop international institutions corresponding to the realities and risks of our time has weakened. Political will to these ends, in its best sense, has been dissipated in a variety of rivalries, confrontations and conflicts. The belief in a common future has been, to a large extent, lost in the anxieties of a divided present. Short-term national interests, old resentments and fears, and ideological differences have obscured the vision of the Charter. The will to compose differences seems weak or absent in most conflict situations, and at the other end of the spectrum the concept of world affairs dominated by concerns for national security or conceived as an open-ended struggle between massive ideological forces seems to have taken the place of the new and enlightened international community envisaged in the Charter. In this connection, the recent tragedy of the downed Korean airliner, and the very serious issues it raises, also points dramatically to the urgent need for more open and ready communications between all sides in the interests of the international community as a whole in order to create an environment in which the use of force would be unthinkable.

Admittedly, we have been through a period of fundamental change in the world—geopolitical change, technological change and a revolutionary change in the nature and scope of war. But all of these things demand more than ever a return to the far-sighted statesmanship of the immediate post-war years, not a retreat from it. Who can possibly believe that a world dominated by the nuclear balance, where $800 billion a year is spent on armaments and where a large proportion of the population lives in destitution and with little real hope, is on the right track? And yet, paradoxically, for the time being at any rate, the United Nations, which was set up to deal with such problems, is too often on the sidelines as far as many major issues are concerned.

We are at present in a period when the value of multilateral diplomacy is being questioned and international institutions are not functioning as they were intended to function. The machinery is running and the wheels are turning, but it is not moving forward as it should. This applies to the United Nations and, in different degrees, to regional organizations and to many international agencies and groupings. Nor is it evident that bilateral diplomacy or unilateral efforts are, in most cases, filling the gap by providing that correlation of national policies which is essential to future stability and the general international interest. We must find means to push the machinery into forward motion again. If we do not do this, we run the risk of being caught, immobile and in the open, in a new international storm too great for us to weather.

Let me here point to a source of real encouragement. It is perhaps best symbolized in the proposal of the Chairman of the seventh non-aligned summit conference, Prime Minister Indira Gandhi, that the United Nations should be strengthened by a meeting of heads of State or Government to give a fresh collective look at some of the major problems of the world. At this critical time in human relations it is encouraging that the non-aligned movement has spoken as a protagonist of the multilateral approach and of the purposes and principles of the Charter. Nor is such a view by any means limited to the non-aligned movement.

In meetings with many leaders throughout the world I have been impressed by the evident desire to see the United Nations function in the manner in which it was intended to function.

It is therefore paradoxical that we should be experiencing, I trust only temporarily, the fragmentation and erosion of the historic effort to build an international system designed to provide peace, security, stability and justice for all. Although in the short term the world may get by without such an effort, in the long term such a system, evolving through a conscious political effort by all States, is indispensable if we are to avoid chaos and disaster on a scale hitherto unknown. At the present time we are witnessing instead the unravelling of many agreements reached by hard and painstaking negotiation over the years. It is absolutely vital that this trend be reversed and that we strengthen our international institutions, not only in order to deal with immediate conflict problems but also to construct a viable framework for the life of future generations on our crowded planet.

Javier PÉREZ DE CUÉLLAR
Secretary-General

GENERAL ASSEMBLY ACTION

Report of the Secretary-General on the work of the Organization

At its 82nd plenary meeting, on 5 December 1983, the General Assembly took note of the report of the Secretary-General on the work of the Organization.

General Assembly decision 38/410

Adopted without vote

Oral proposal by President; agenda item 10.
Meeting number. GA 38th session: plenary 82.

REFERENCE

(1)A/38/1.

Political and security questions

Disarmament

In 1983, most of the United Nations efforts for disarmament and arms limitation, including proposals renewed or initiated, were manifestations of global concern about the current situation and consisted of appeals, rather than implementation of concrete steps, for its improvement.

The Committee on Disarmament—the main intergovernmental negotiating body on disarmament—met at Geneva from 1 February to 29 April and from 14 June to 30 August, with substantially the same agenda as in 1982. It decided to designate itself as the Conference on Disarmament starting in 1984, and agreed to a limited expansion of its membership. The Disarmament Commission, composed of all United Nations Member States, held its 1983 session from 9 May to 3 June at United Nations Headquarters.

At its 1983 regular session, the General Assembly examined 25 disarmament items, including four new items concerning: the 1985 Review Conference of the Parties to the Treaty on the Non-Proliferation of Nuclear Weapons, a proposed treaty on the non-use of force in outer space, condemnation of nuclear war and a nuclear-weapon freeze. In December, 62 resolutions and two decisions were adopted on these items, including an agreement to hold, not later than 1988, the Assembly's third special session devoted to disarmament. As in previous years, all disarmament items were considered by the Assembly's First Committee, where the question of the bilateral nuclear arms negotiations between the USSR and the United States—which were suspended towards the end of 1983—was one of the subjects of intense consideration.

The year 1983 marked the entry into force of the 1980 Convention, and its three Protocols, on Prohibitions or Restrictions on the Use of Certain Conventional Weapons Which May Be Deemed to Be Excessively Injurious or to Have Indiscriminate Effects.

At the beginning of the year, the Centre for Disarmament was transformed into the United Nations Department for Disarmament Affairs, the United Nations Institute for Disarmament Research assumed an autonomous status, and the Secretary-General's Advisory Board on Disarmament Studies was revived with additional functions, as agreed by the Assembly in 1982.

Details on these subjects together with the full texts of the related resolutions or decisions adopted by the General Assembly can be found under the relevant subject headings on the following pages. For resolutions and decisions of major organs mentioned but not reproduced in this chapter, refer to INDEX OF RESOLUTIONS AND DECISIONS.

Topics related to this chapter. Peaceful uses of outer space. International peace and security: implementation of the 1970 Declaration. Arms race and environment. Arms race and social development.

PUBLICATIONS

Disarmament: A Periodic Review by the United Nations, vol. VI: No. 1, Sales No. E.83.IX.6; No. 2, Sales No. E.83.IX.8; No. 3, Sales No. E.83.IX.10. *The United Nations Disarmament Yearbook*, vol. 8, *1983*, Sales No. E.84.IX.3.

General aspects of disarmament

Various aspects of disarmament were discussed in 1983 by the 40-member Committee on Disarmament and by the Disarmament Commission. The General Assembly, in resolutions 38/183 I and E respectively, took note of their activities for the year. Agreement could not be reached on a comprehensive programme of disarmament and, by resolution 38/183 K, the Assembly urged continued efforts for the programme's elaboration.

The Assembly, in resolutions 38/183 H, on implementation of the recommendations and decisions of the tenth special session (the first special session on disarmament), and 38/183 F, on implementation of the 1979 Declaration on International Cooperation for Disarmament, called for progress in disarmament. By resolution 38/73 I, it decided to convene, not later than 1988, the third special session devoted to disarmament.

The Secretary-General, in his 1983 annual report to the General Assembly on the work of the United

Nations (p. 3), stressed the need for a working system of international security as an essential complement to progress in disarmament and arms limitation.

Appeals for peace and disarmament from various sources were transmitted to the Assembly during the year by their respective Governments or those acting as host to the particular meeting. They included appeals from: the Bishops of Austria;[1] the Swedish Ecumenical Council;[2] a meeting of Party and State figures from Bulgaria, Czechoslovakia, the German Democratic Republic, Hungary, Poland, Romania and the USSR (Moscow, 28 June);[3] the Council for Mutual Economic Assistance (thirty-seventh session, Berlin, 18-20 October);[4] and the Committee of Ministers for Foreign Affairs of the States members of the Warsaw Treaty of Friendship, Co-operation and Mutual Assistance (Sofia, Bulgaria, 13 and 14 October).[5] The Assembly also received the text of a letter in support of disarmament, sent by the Standing Committee of the National People's Congress of China to the Senate of the Congress of the Union of the United Mexican States.[6]

A number of other letters circulated under the item on general and complete disarmament also dealt with the Assembly's annual review of its 1970 Declaration on the Strengthening of International Security (see Chapter IV of this section).

Proposed comprehensive programme

Agreement on a comprehensive programme of disarmament was not reached in 1983 despite additional efforts by the Committee on Disarmament to try to elaborate a text. The programme—envisaged in paragraph 109 of the Final Document of the Tenth Special Session of the General Assembly[7] in 1978—had been considered annually by the Committee since 1980. However, it was unable to submit an agreed text to the Assembly's 1982 second special session on disarmament and the Assembly itself, unable to reach a consensus at that session, referred the matter back to the Committee, requesting it to submit a revised draft in 1983.[8]

Consideration by the Committee on Disarmament. The *Ad Hoc* Working Group on the Comprehensive Programme of Disarmament, which had been re-established by the Committee on Disarmament in 1982 at the Assembly's request,[9] held 12 meetings between 16 February and 19 August 1983 under the chairmanship of Alfonso García Robles (Mexico). It set up contact groups to elaborate the various sections of the programme dealing with objectives, principles, priorities, measures and stages of implementation, and machinery and procedures. In addition, informal consultations were held during June, July and August.

Differences of view persisted, however, and in the time available the Working Group was not able to consider the introduction, nor the questions of stages of implementation, time-frames, and the nature of the programme. In a number of areas where it was not possible to agree on new formulations, language similar to that of relevant paragraphs of the 1978 Final Document was used. The resulting texts were annexed to the Working Group's report, with those of a number of paragraphs left pending and the inclusion or placement of others to be decided later.

On 23 August, prior to the Committee's adoption of the Group's report, the Group's Chairman described the proposed programme as much less ambitious than the 1982 draft, but potentially as helpful to Governments in enabling them to gain a clear idea—from a text entirely free of brackets marking passages on which consensus could not be reached—of the most that could currently be aspired to. He suggested that the Assembly could choose either to adopt the text in 1983 or to return it to the Committee; in the latter case, he said, it would be unrealistic to expect any reasonable prospect of success within less than three years.

GENERAL ASSEMBLY ACTION

On the recommendation of the First Committee, the General Assembly, on 20 December 1983, adopted without vote resolution 38/183 K.

Comprehensive programme of disarmament

The General Assembly,

Having examined the report of the *Ad Hoc* Working Group on the Comprehensive Programme of Disarmament, which is an integral part of the report of the Committee on Disarmament on its 1983 session,

Welcoming the progress achieved in the preparation of the programme during the period covered by the report,

Noting, however, that it has not yet been possible to complete the elaboration of a comprehensive programme which, as provided for in paragraph 109 of the Final Document of the Tenth Special Session of the General Assembly, should encompass all measures thought to be advisable in order to ensure that the goal of general and complete disarmament under effective international control becomes a reality in a world in which international peace and security prevail and in which the new international economic order is strengthened and consolidated,

1. *Urges* the Conference on Disarmament, as soon as it considers that the circumstances are propitious for that purpose, to renew its work on the elaboration of the comprehensive programme of disarmament previously requested, to submit to the General Assembly at its thirty-ninth session a progress report on the matter and to submit to the Assembly, not later than at its forty-first session, a complete draft of such a programme;

2. *Decides* to consider at its thirty-ninth session, in the light of the above-mentioned progress report, the advisability of requesting the Disarmament Commission to examine the question further and to make appropriate recommendations to the General Assembly.

General Assembly resolution 38/183 K

20 December 1983   Meeting 103   Adopted without vote

Approved by First Committee (A/38/628) without vote, 25 November (meeting 41); 10-nation draft (A/C.1/38/L.31/Rev.1); agenda item 50.
Sponsors: Algeria, Bangladesh, Brazil, Mexico, Pakistan, Sri Lanka, Sweden, Uruguay, Venezuela, Yugoslavia.
Meeting numbers. GA 38th session: 1st Committee 3-10, 12-31, 34, 35, 41; plenary 103.

The text was based on a draft originally submitted by nine countries, to which Brazil[10] proposed adding a paragraph entrusting the Disarmament Commission, without prejudice to paragraph 1, with the examination in 1984 of approaches that could facilitate progress towards elaborating the programme. Subsequently, Brazil withdrew its amendment and joined the sponsors in the revised text which was approved by the First Committee.

Committee on Disarmament

Activities of the Committee. The 40-member Committee on Disarmament—the main multilateral negotiating body on the subject—met in 1983 at Geneva from 1 February to 29 April and from 14 June to 30 August.[11] Holding 50 formal and 27 informal plenary meetings, it considered—in addition to the proposed comprehensive programme of disarmament (see above)—a nuclear-test ban, cessation of the nuclear-arms race and nuclear disarmament, security assurances to non-nuclear-weapon States, chemical weapons, new types of weapons of mass destruction, and the prevention of an arms race in outer space. Details on developments on these questions during the year can be found elsewhere in this chapter.

On 29 March, the Committee re-established four *ad hoc* working groups: three, first set up in 1980, on security assurances to non-nuclear-weapon States, chemical weapons, and radiological weapons, and a fourth, established in 1982, on a nuclear-test ban.

The Committee accepted, in principle, a limited expansion of its membership, by not more than four States, subject to its agreement on the selection of new members and taking into account the need to maintain balance. Its Chairman was to hold consultations on the selection before the Committee reported to the General Assembly in 1984.

The Committee, taking into account a December 1982 Assembly suggestion,[12] decided to designate itself as the "Conference on Disarmament", effective from commencement of its 1984 annual session. This involved no financial or structural implications and the Committee's rules of procedure remained the same, except for the change of name.

GENERAL ASSEMBLY ACTION

On 20 December, the General Assembly adopted, by recorded vote, resolution 38/183 I, as recommended by the First Committee.

Report of the Committee on Disarmament

The General Assembly,

Recalling its resolutions 34/83 B of 11 December 1979, 35/152 J of 12 December 1980, 36/92 F of 9 December 1981 and 37/78 G of 9 December 1982,

Recalling also the Final Document of the Tenth Special Session of the General Assembly, the first special session devoted to disarmament, and the Concluding Document of the Twelfth Special Session of the General Assembly, the second special session devoted to disarmament,

Having considered the report of the Committee on Disarmament,

Convinced that the Conference on Disarmament, as the single multilateral negotiating body on disarmament, should play the central role in substantive negotiations on priority questions of disarmament and on the implementation of the Programme of Action set forth in section III of the Final Document of the Tenth Special Session,

Reaffirming that the establishment of *ad hoc* working groups offers the best available machinery for the conduct of multilateral negotiations on items on the agenda of the Conference on Disarmament and contributes to the strengthening of the negotiating role of the Conference,

Deploring the fact that, despite repeated requests by the General Assembly and the express wish of the great majority of members of the Committee on Disarmament, the establishment of an *ad hoc* working group to undertake multilateral negotiations on the cessation of the nuclear-arms race and on nuclear disarmament was once again prevented during the session of the Committee in 1983,

Regretting that the Committee on Disarmament has also not been enabled to set up *ad hoc* working groups for negotiations on the prevention of nuclear war and on the prevention of the arms race in outer space, nor to entrust its *Ad Hoc* Working Group under item 1 of its agenda, entitled "Nuclear-test ban", with a new mandate enabling it to undertake substantive negotiations on this question as soon as possible,

Stressing that negotiations on specific disarmament issues conducted outside the Conference on Disarmament should in no way serve as a pretext for preventing the conduct of multilateral negotiations on such questions in the Conference,

1. *Expresses its deep concern and disappointment* that the Committee on Disarmament has not been enabled, this year either, to reach concrete agreements on disarmament issues to which the United Nations has assigned greatest priority and urgency and which have been under consideration for a number of years;

2. *Requests* the Conference on Disarmament to intensify its work, so as to make the utmost effort to achieve concrete results in the shortest possible period of time on the specific priority issues of disarmament on its agenda;

3. *Once again urges* the Conference on Disarmament to continue or to undertake, during its session to be held in 1984, substantive negotiations on the priority questions of disarmament on its agenda, in accordance with the provisions of the Final Document of the Tenth Special Session of the General Assembly and other relevant resolutions of the Assembly on those questions, and, in order to reach that goal, to provide the existing *ad hoc* working groups with appropriate negotiating mandates and to establish, as a matter of urgency, the *ad hoc* working groups on the cessation of the nuclear-arms race and nuclear disarmament, on the prevention of nuclear war and on the prevention of an arms race in outer space;

4. *Urges* the Conference on Disarmament to undertake, without further delay, the elaboration of a draft

international treaty on a nuclear-weapon test ban and to submit a progress report to the General Assembly at its thirty-ninth session;

5.   *Also urges* the Conference on Disarmament to accelerate its work on the elaboration of a draft international convention on the complete and effective prohibition of all chemical weapons and on their destruction and to submit the preliminary draft of such a convention to the General Assembly at its thirty-ninth session;

6.   *Calls upon* the Conference on Disarmament to organize its work in such a way as to concentrate most of its attention and time on substantive negotiations on priority issues of disarmament;

7.   *Calls upon* the members of the Conference on Disarmament that have opposed the negotiation on some substantive issues of disarmament to enable the Conference, by adopting a positive stand, to fulfil effectively the mandate that the international community has entrusted to it in the field of negotiations on disarmament;

8.   *Invites* the members of the Conference on Disarmament involved in separate negotiations on specific priority questions of disarmament to intensify their efforts in order to achieve a positive conclusion of those negotiations without further delay and to submit to the Conference a full report on their separate negotiations and the results achieved in order to contribute most directly to the negotiations in the Conference, in accordance with paragraph 3 above;

9.   *Requests* the Conference on Disarmament to submit a report on its work to the General Assembly at its thirty-ninth session;

10.   *Decides* to include in the provisional agenda of its thirty-ninth session the item entitled "Report of the Conference on Disarmament".

General Assembly resolution 38/183 I

20 December 1983   Meeting 103   129-2-18 (recorded vote)

Approved by First Committee (A/38/628) by recorded vote (104-2-19), 25 November (meeting 40); 27-nation draft (A/C.1/38/L.27); agenda item 50 *(b)*.

Sponsors: Algeria, Argentina, Bangladesh, Brazil, Burma, Congo, Cuba, Egypt, Ethiopia, Ghana, India, Indonesia, Iran, Madagascar, Mexico, Nigeria, Pakistan, Peru, Romania, Sri Lanka, Sudan, Sweden, Upper Volta, Uruguay, Venezuela, Yugoslavia, Zaire.

Meeting numbers. GA 38th session: 1st Committee 3-10, 12-32, 40; plenary 103.

Recorded vote in Assembly as follows:

In favour: Afghanistan, Algeria, Angola, Antigua and Barbuda, Argentina, Austria, Bahamas, Bahrain, Bangladesh, Barbados, Belize, Benin, Bhutan, Bolivia, Botswana, Brazil, Bulgaria, Burma, Burundi, Byelorussian SSR, Cape Verde, Central African Republic, Chad, Chile, China, Colombia, Congo, Costa Rica, Cuba, Cyprus, Czechoslovakia, Democratic Kampuchea, Democratic Yemen, Djibouti, Dominica, Dominican Republic, Ecuador, Egypt, El Salvador, Ethiopia, Fiji, Finland, Gabon, Gambia, German Democratic Republic, Ghana, Guatemala, Guinea, Guinea-Bissau, Guyana, Haiti, Honduras, Hungary, India, Indonesia, Iran, Iraq, Ireland, Ivory Coast, Jamaica, Jordan, Kenya, Kuwait, Lao People's Democratic Republic, Lebanon, Lesotho, Liberia, Libyan Arab Jamahiriya, Madagascar, Malawi, Malaysia, Maldives, Mali, Malta, Mauritania, Mauritius, Mexico, Mongolia, Morocco, Mozambique, Nepal, Nicaragua, Niger, Nigeria, Oman, Pakistan, Panama, Papua New Guinea, Paraguay, Peru, Philippines, Poland, Qatar, Romania, Rwanda, Saint Lucia, Saint Vincent and the Grenadines, Sao Tome and Principe, Saudi Arabia, Senegal, Sierra Leone, Singapore, Somalia, Sri Lanka, Sudan, Suriname, Swaziland, Sweden, Syrian Arab Republic, Thailand, Togo, Trinidad and Tobago, Tunisia, Uganda, Ukrainian SSR, USSR, United Arab Emirates, United Republic of Cameroon, United Republic of Tanzania, Upper Volta, Uruguay, Vanuatu, Venezuela, Viet Nam, Yemen, Yugoslavia, Zaire, Zambia, Zimbabwe.

Against: United Kingdom, United States.

Abstaining: Australia, Belgium, Canada, Denmark, France, Germany, Federal Republic of, Greece, Iceland, Israel, Italy, Japan, Luxembourg, Netherlands, New Zealand, Norway, Portugal, Spain, Turkey.

In explanation of vote on the text, Australia, the Netherlands, the United Kingdom and the United States said the sponsors had not made an attempt to negotiate to make it more generally acceptable, nor shown willingness to respect the views of others. For the United Kingdom, the draft expressed partisan views of the sponsors and the language had become even more objectionable than in the past. Sharing that view, the United States said that the text, instead of reflecting the consensus on the report within the Committee on Disarmament, sought to rewrite it, thus distorting the picture of the work of that body and establishing an unacceptable precedent.

Belgium added that the text gave the impression that the Assembly need only give majority instructions to such a committee in order to produce results; moreover, the sponsors had made no contribution to the Committee on Disarmament, while suggesting that a convention be drafted on a nuclear-test ban. Australia and the Netherlands regretted the resolution's call for a "nuclear-weapon test ban", which departed from the Committee's terminology, "nuclear-test ban".

In 1983, the Assembly adopted a number of other resolutions concerning the Conference on Disarmament (as the Committee on Disarmament would be known in 1984). By resolution 38/183 H, it called on the Conference to start negotiations on nuclear disarmament and on preventing nuclear war, and to elaborate, among others, a draft treaty on a nuclear-weapon test ban. In addition, the Assembly called on the Conference to take up specific topics, in the following resolutions: 38/183 K, on a proposed comprehensive programme of disarmament; 38/183 D, on a proposed working group on nuclear disarmament; 38/73 G, on a draft convention against nuclear weapons; 38/183 G, on preventing nuclear war; 38/62, 38/63 and 38/72, on negotiating a treaty to prohibit nuclear-weapon tests; 38/188 E, on prohibiting production of fissionable material for nuclear weapons; 38/67, on a draft convention on security of non-nuclear-weapon States; 38/183 C, on proposed negotiations to prohibit neutron bombs; 38/70, on the arms race in outer space and anti-satellite systems; 38/80, on outer space; 38/182, on prohibiting new weapons of mass destruction; and 38/187 A and B, on prohibiting chemical weapons.

Disarmament Commission

Disarmament Commission activities. The Disarmament Commission, composed of all United Nations Member States, held its 1983 session from 9 May to 3 June at United Nations Headquarters.[13] It also met on 1 December to organize its work and elect officers for 1984.

Its agenda included items on aspects of the arms race, particularly the nuclear-arms race; reduction of military budgets and expenditures; South

Africa's nuclear capability; follow-up to the 1982 recommendations of the Independent Commission on Disarmament and Security Issues;[14] and guidelines for confidence-building measures. Details on the Commission's discussion of these questions can be found elsewhere in this chapter.

The Commission established informal, open-ended working groups for all these questions except that on aspects of the arms race, for which a Committee of the Whole was established; the Committee subsequently established a contact group on the item to report back to it.

Meeting between 24 May and 1 June, the contact group considered working papers submitted by the Commission Chairman, the German Democratic Republic, the non-aligned countries and Mexico, and letters from the German Democratic Republic, the Federal Republic of Germany and the USSR, but was unable to achieve consensus on a set of recommendations for submission to the Committee and subsequently to the Commission.

GENERAL ASSEMBLY ACTION

On the recommendation of the First Committee, the General Assembly, on 20 December, adopted without vote resolution 38/183 E.

Report of the Disarmament Commission
The General Assembly,
Having considered the report of the Disarmament Commission,
Emphasizing again the importance of an effective follow-up to the relevant recommendations and decisions contained in the Final Document of the Tenth Special Session of the General Assembly, the first special session devoted to disarmament,
Taking into account the relevant sections of the Concluding Document of the Twelfth Special Session of the General Assembly, the second special session devoted to disarmament,
Considering the important role that the Disarmament Commission has played and the significant contribution that it has made in examining and submitting recommendations on various problems in the field of disarmament and in the promotion of the implementation of the relevant decisions of the tenth special session,
Desirous of strengthening the effectiveness of the Disarmament Commission as the deliberative body in the field of disarmament,
Recalling its resolutions 33/71 H of 14 December 1978, 34/83 H of 11 December 1979, 35/152 F of 12 December 1980, 36/92 B of 9 December 1981 and 37/78 H of 9 December 1982,
1. *Takes note* of the report of the Disarmament Commission;
2. *Notes* that the Disarmament Commission has yet to conclude its consideration of some items on its agenda;
3. *Requests* the Disarmament Commission to continue its work in accordance with its mandate, as set forth in paragraph 118 of the Final Document of the Tenth Special Session of the General Assembly, and with

paragraph 3 of resolution 37/78 H, and to that end to make every effort to achieve specific recommendations, at its 1984 substantive session, on the outstanding items on its agenda, taking into account the relevant resolutions of the General Assembly as well as the results of its 1983 session;
4. *Requests* the Disarmament Commission to meet for a period not exceeding four weeks during 1984 and to submit a substantive report, containing specific recommendations on the items inscribed on its agenda, to the General Assembly at its thirty-ninth session;
5. *Requests* the Secretary-General to transmit to the Disarmament Commission the report of the Committee on Disarmament on the work of its 1983 session, together with all the official records of the thirty-eighth session of the General Assembly relating to disarmament matters, and to render all assistance that the Commission may require for implementing the present resolution;
6. *Decides* to include in the provisional agenda of its thirty-ninth session the item entitled "Report of the Disarmament Commission".

General Assembly resolution 38/183 E
20 December 1983   Meeting 103   Adopted without vote

Approved by First Committee (A/38/628) without vote, 21 November (meeting 34); 9-nation draft (A/C.1/38/L.14); agenda item 57 *(a)*.
Sponsors: Bangladesh, Brazil, Czechoslovakia, Germany, Federal Republic of, Romania, Sierra Leone, Sweden, Syrian Arab Republic, Tunisia.
Meeting numbers. GA 38th session: 1st Committee 3-10, 12-31, 34; plenary 103.

In another 20 December resolution (38/183 H), on implementation of the recommendations of the 1978 special session on disarmament, the Assembly called on the Commission to intensify its work with a view to making recommendations on specific items on its agenda. In addition, the Assembly instructed the Commission on specific topics, in the following resolutions: 38/73 A, on confidence-building measures; 38/184 A, on reducing military budgets; and 38/71 B, on disarmament and development.

Special sessions of the General Assembly on disarmament

In 1983, the General Assembly adopted resolutions dealing with its special sessions devoted to disarmament—its first, held in 1978,[15] its second in 1982,[16] and the holding of a third one.

Implementation of the recommendations of the 1978 special session

Sixteen resolutions were adopted by the General Assembly in 1983 on implementation of the recommendations and decisions which had been adopted, in 1978, at its tenth special session—its first such session devoted to disarmament. They were on: bilateral nuclear-arms negotiations between the USSR and the United States (38/183 A, N and P), the non-use of nuclear weapons (38/183 B), prohibiting neutron bombs (38/183 C), nuclear weapons (38/183 D), the work of the Committee on Disarmament (38/183 I) and the Disarmament Commission (38/183 E), international cooperation for disarmament (38/183 F), preventing nuclear war (38/183 G), implementation of the recommendations of the 1978 special session (38/183 H, see below), unilateral disarmament measures (38/183 J), a proposed comprehensive disarmament programme (38/183 K), Disarmament Week (38/183 L), reports by nuclear-weapon States on implementing the 1978 recommendations (38/183 M), and the Advisory Board on Disarmament Studies (38/183 O). Details on these topics can be found in this chapter.

GENERAL ASSEMBLY ACTION

On the recommendation of the First Committee, the General Assembly, on 20 December 1983, adopted by recorded vote resolution 38/183 H.

Implementation of the recommendations and decisions of the tenth special session

The General Assembly,

Having reviewed the implementation of the recommendations and decisions adopted by the General Assembly at its tenth special session, the first special session devoted to disarmament, as well as the Concluding Document of the Twelfth Special Session of the General Assembly, the second special session devoted to disarmament,

Recalling its resolutions S-10/2 of 30 June 1978, 34/83 C of 11 December 1979, 35/46 of 3 December 1980, 35/152 E of 12 December 1980, 36/92 M of 9 December 1981 and 37/78 F of 9 December 1982 and its decision S-12/24 of 10 July 1982,

Deeply concerned that no concrete results regarding the implementation of the recommendations and decisions of the tenth special session have been realized in the course of more than five years since that session, that in the mean time the arms race, particularly in its nuclear aspect, has gained in intensity, that urgent measures to prevent nuclear war and for disarmament have not been adopted and that continued colonial domination and foreign occupation, open threats, pressure and military intervention against independent States and violation of the fundamental principles of the Charter of the United Nations have taken place, posing the most serious threat to international peace and security,

Convinced that the renewed escalation of the nuclear-arms race, in both the quantitative and the qualitative dimensions, as well as reliance on doctrines of nuclear deterrence and of use of nuclear weapons, has heightened the risk of the outbreak of nuclear war and led to greater insecurity and instability in international relations,

Further convinced that international peace and security can only be ensured through general and complete disarmament under effective international control and that one of the most urgent tasks is to halt and reverse the arms race and to undertake concrete measures of disarmament, particularly nuclear disarmament, and that, in this respect, the nuclear-weapon States and other militarily significant States have the primary responsibility,

Noting with great concern that no real progress in disarmament negotiations has been achieved for several years, which has rendered the current international situation even more dangerous and insecure, and that negotiations on disarmament issues are lagging far behind the rapid technological development in the field of armaments and the relentless growth of military arsenals, particularly nuclear arsenals,

Recalling the commitment of States undertaken in various international agreements to negotiate on disarmament measures, in particular on nuclear disarmament,

Considering that it is more than ever imperative in the present circumstances to give a new impetus to negotiations in good faith on disarmament, in particular nuclear disarmament, at all levels and to achieve genuine progress in the immediate future,

Convinced that the success of disarmament negotiations, in which all the people of the world have a vital interest, can be achieved through the active participation of Member States in such negotiations, contributing thereby to the maintenance of international peace and security,

Reaffirming that the United Nations has a central role and primary responsibility in the sphere of disarmament,

Stressing that the Final Document of the Tenth Special Session of the General Assembly, which was unanimously and categorically reaffirmed by all Member States at the twelfth special session as the comprehensive basis for efforts towards halting and reversing the arms race, has retained all its validity and that the objectives and measures contained therein still represent one of the most important and urgent goals to be achieved,

1. *Expresses its grave concern* over the acceleration and intensification of the arms race, particularly the nuclear-arms race, as well as the new, very serious deterioration of relations in the world, and the intensification of focal points of aggression and hotbeds of tension in different regions of the world, which threaten international peace and security and increase the danger of outbreak of nuclear war;

2. *Calls upon* all States, in particular nuclear-weapon States and other militarily significant States, to take urgent measures in order to put an end to the serious aggravation of the international situation, to promote international security on the basis of disarmament, to halt and reverse the arms race and to launch a process of genuine disarmament;

3. *Invites* all States, particularly nuclear-weapon States and especially those among them which possess the most important nuclear arsenals, to take urgent measures with a view to implementing the recommendations and decisions contained in the Final Document of the Tenth Special Session of the General Assembly, as well as to fulfilling the priority tasks set forth in the Programme of Action contained in section III of the Final Document;

4. *Calls upon* all States to refrain from any actions which have or may have negative effects on the outcome of disarmament negotiations;

5. *Once again calls upon* the Conference on Disarmament to concentrate its work on the substantive and priority items on its agenda, to proceed to negotiations on nuclear disarmament and on the prevention of nuclear war without further delay and to elaborate drafts of

treaties on a nuclear-weapon test ban and on a complete and effective prohibition of the development, production and stockpiling of all chemical weapons and on their destruction;

6. *Calls upon* the Disarmament Commission to intensify its work in accordance with its mandate and to continue improving its work with a view to making concrete recommendations on specific items on its agenda;

7. *Calls upon* nuclear-weapon States engaged in separate negotiations on issues of nuclear disarmament to exert the utmost effort with a view to achieving concrete results in those negotiations and thus contribute to the success of multilateral negotiations on nuclear disarmament;

8. *Invites* all States engaged in disarmament and arms limitation negotiations outside the framework of the United Nations to keep the General Assembly and the Conference on Disarmament informed on the status or results of such negotiations, in conformity with the relevant provisions of the Final Document of the Tenth Special Session;

9. *Decides* to include in the provisional agenda of its thirty-ninth session the item entitled "Implementation of the recommendations and decisions of the tenth special session".

General Assembly resolution 38/183 H

20 December 1983   Meeting 103   132-9-8 (recorded vote)

Approved by First Committee (A/38/628) by recorded vote (107-11-7), 25 November (meeting 40); 30-nation draft (A/C.1/38/L.26/Rev.1); agenda item 50 *(g)*.
Sponsors: Algeria, Argentina, Bahamas, Bangladesh, Burma, Colombia, Congo, Cuba, Ecuador, Egypt, Ethiopia, German Democratic Republic, Ghana, India, Indonesia, Iran, Madagascar, Nigeria, Pakistan, Peru, Romania, Sri Lanka, Sudan, United Republic of Cameroon, Upper Volta, Uruguay, Venezuela, Viet Nam, Yugoslavia, Zaire.
Meeting numbers. GA 38th session: 1st Committee 3-10, 12-33, 40; plenary 103.

Recorded vote in Assembly as follows:

In favour: Afghanistan, Algeria, Angola, Antigua and Barbuda, Argentina, Austria, Bahamas, Bahrain, Bangladesh, Barbados, Belize, Benin, Bhutan, Bolivia, Botswana, Brazil, Bulgaria, Burma, Burundi, Byelorussian SSR, Cape Verde, Central African Republic, Chad, Chile, China, Colombia, Congo, Costa Rica, Cuba, Cyprus, Czechoslovakia, Democratic Kampuchea, Democratic Yemen, Denmark, Djibouti, Dominica, Dominican Republic, Ecuador, Egypt, El Salvador, Ethiopia, Fiji, Finland, Gabon, Gambia, German Democratic Republic, Ghana, Greece, Guatemala, Guinea, Guinea-Bissau, Guyana, Haiti, Honduras, Hungary, Iceland, India, Indonesia, Iran, Iraq, Ireland, Ivory Coast, Jamaica, Jordan, Kenya, Kuwait, Lao People's Democratic Republic, Lebanon, Lesotho, Liberia, Libyan Arab Jamahiriya, Madagascar, Malawi, Malaysia, Maldives, Mali, Malta, Mauritania, Mauritius, Mexico, Mongolia, Morocco, Mozambique, Nepal, Nicaragua, Niger, Nigeria, Oman, Pakistan, Panama, Papua New Guinea, Paraguay, Peru, Philippines, Poland, Qatar, Romania, Rwanda, Saint Lucia, Saint Vincent and the Grenadines, Sao Tome and Principe, Saudi Arabia, Senegal, Sierra Leone, Singapore, Somalia, Sri Lanka, Sudan, Suriname, Swaziland, Sweden, Syrian Arab Republic, Thailand, Togo, Trinidad and Tobago, Tunisia, Uganda, Ukrainian SSR, USSR, United Arab Emirates, United Republic of Cameroon, United Republic of Tanzania, Upper Volta, Uruguay, Vanuatu, Venezuela, Viet Nam, Yemen, Yugoslavia, Zaire, Zambia, Zimbabwe.
Against: Canada, France, Germany, Federal Republic of, Luxembourg, Netherlands, Portugal, Turkey, United Kingdom, United States.
Abstaining: Australia, Belgium,[a] Israel, Italy,[a] Japan, New Zealand, Norway, Spain.
[a]Later advised the Secretariat it had intended to vote against.

In explanation of vote on the draft, the United Kingdom said the text reflected not a consensus view but partisan opinions of the sponsors, and the resolution's language had become more extreme than in the past. Australia said that a nuclear-weapon test ban, which the text called for, was far more limited in scope than a comprehensive nuclear-test ban, which it favoured.

Implementation of the recommendations of the 1982 special session

In 1983, the General Assembly adopted 10 resolutions on implementation of the recommendations of its 1982 special session on disarmament. They were on: a third special session on disarmament (38/73 I, see below), a nuclear-weapons freeze (38/73 B and E), regional disarmament (38/73 J), confidence-building measures (38/73 A), disarmament and international security (38/73 H), a draft convention against nuclear weapons (38/73 G), the United Nations fellowships programme on disarmament (38/73 C), and the World Disarmament Campaign (38/73 D and F). Details on these topics can be found in this chapter.

Third special session

GENERAL ASSEMBLY ACTION

As recommended by the First Committee, the General Assembly, on 15 December 1983, adopted resolution 38/73 I without vote.

Convening of the third special session of the General Assembly devoted to disarmament
The General Assembly,

Bearing in mind the decision adopted at its twelfth special session to set, during its thirty-eighth session, the date of the third special session devoted to disarmament,

Desiring to contribute to the furthering and broadening of positive processes initiated through the laying down of the foundations of an international disarmament strategy at its tenth special session,

1. *Decides* that the third special session of the General Assembly devoted to disarmament should be held not later than 1988;

2. *Decides also* to set, not later than at its fortieth session, the date of the third special session of the General Assembly devoted to disarmament and to make appropriate arrangements concerning the establishment of a preparatory committee for that third special session.

General Assembly resolution 38/73 I

15 December 1983   Meeting 97   Adopted without vote

Approved by First Committee (A/38/641) without vote, 21 November (meeting 34); 25-nation draft (A/C.1/38/L.58); agenda item 63.
Sponsors: Algeria, Argentina, Bangladesh, Colombia, Cuba, Democratic Yemen, Ecuador, Egypt, Ethiopia, Ghana, India, Indonesia, Mexico, Nigeria, Pakistan, Romania, Singapore, Sri Lanka, Sudan, Tunisia, Uruguay, Venezuela, Viet Nam, Yugoslavia, Zaire.
Meeting numbers. GA 38th session: 1st Committee 3-10, 12-31, 33, 34; plenary 97.

Implementation of the 1979 Declaration on co-operation for disarmament

In 1983, the General Assembly again called for implementation of its 1979 Declaration on International Co-operation for Disarmament.[17]

GENERAL ASSEMBLY ACTION

On the recommendation of the First Committee, the General Assembly, on 20 December 1983, adopted by recorded vote resolution 38/183 F.

International co-operation for disarmament

The General Assembly,

Stressing again the urgent need for an active and sustained effort to intensify the implementation of the recommendations and decisions unanimously adopted at its tenth special session, the first special session devoted to disarmament, as contained in the Final Document of that session and confirmed in the Concluding Document of the Twelfth Special Session of the General Assembly, the second special session devoted to disarmament,

Recalling the Declaration on International Co-operation for Disarmament of 11 December 1979 and General Assembly resolutions 36/92 D of 9 December 1981 and 37/78 B of 9 December 1982,

Deeply concerned over the growing danger of nuclear war, the continued arms race and the danger of a further, qualitatively new round of the arms race, all of which will have a very negative impact on the international situation,

Stressing the vital importance of eliminating the danger of nuclear war, halting the nuclear-arms race and attaining disarmament, particularly in the nuclear field, for the preservation of peace and the strengthening of international security,

Bearing in mind the vital interest of all nations in the attainment of effective disarmament measures, which would release considerable financial and material resources to be used for the economic and social development of all States, in particular developing countries,

Considering the increased activity of peace and anti-war movements against the arms race and the escalation of the danger of nuclear war,

Convinced of the need to strengthen constructive international co-operation based on the political goodwill of States for successful negotiations on disarmament, in accordance with the Final Document of the Tenth Special Session,

Emphasizing the duty of States to co-operate for the preservation of international peace and security, in accordance with the Charter of the United Nations, as confirmed in the Declaration on Principles of International Law concerning Friendly Relations and Co-operation among States in accordance with the Charter of the United Nations, of 24 October 1970, the obligation to co-operate actively and constructively for the attainment of the aims of disarmament being an indispensable part of that duty,

Expressing the conviction that concrete manifestations of political goodwill, including unilateral measures, such as an obligation not to make first use of nuclear weapons, improve conditions for resolving disarmament issues in a spirit of co-operation among States,

Stressing that proposals, relatively simple in their execution and at the same time effective, such as the proposals aimed at eliminating the use of force, be it on a world-wide or regional scale, contribute considerably to that end,

Bearing in mind that the United Nations bears primary responsibility and plays a central role in unifying efforts to maintain and to develop active co-operation among States in order to resolve the issues of disarmament,

1. *Calls upon* all States, in implementing the Final Document of the Tenth Special Session of the General Assembly, to make active use of the principles and ideas contained in the Declaration on International Co-operation for Disarmament by actively participating in disarmament negotiations, with a view to achieving concrete results, and by conducting them on the basis of equality and undiminished security and the non-use of force in international relations, and to refrain at the same time from developing new directions and channels of the arms race;

2. *Stresses* the importance of strengthening the effectiveness of the United Nations in fulfilling its responsibility for maintaining international peace and security in accordance with the Charter of the United Nations;

3. *Declares* in this context that the elaboration and dissemination of any doctrines and concepts justifying the unleashing of nuclear war endanger world peace, lead to deterioration of the international situation and further intensification of the arms race and are detrimental to the generally recognized necessity of international co-operation for disarmament;

4. *Declares* that the use of force in international relations as well as in attempts to prevent the full implementation of the Declaration on the Granting of Independence to Colonial Countries and Peoples is a phenomenon incompatible with the ideas of international co-operation for disarmament;

5. *Appeals* to States which are members of military groupings to promote, on the basis of the Final Document of the Tenth Special Session, in the spirit of international co-operation for disarmament, the gradual mutual limitation of military activities of these groupings, thus creating conditions for their dissolution;

6. *Calls upon* all Member States to cultivate and disseminate, particularly in connection with the World Disarmament Campaign launched by the General Assembly at its twelfth special session, the ideas of international co-operation for disarmament, *inter alia*, through their educational systems, mass media and cultural policies;

7. *Calls upon* the United Nations Educational, Scientific and Cultural Organization to continue to consider, in order further to mobilize world public opinion on behalf of disarmament, measures aimed at strengthening the ideas of international co-operation for disarmament through research, education, information, communication and culture;

8. *Calls upon* the Governments of all States to contribute substantially, while observing the principle of undiminished security, to halting and reversing the arms race, particularly in the nuclear field, and thus to reducing the danger of nuclear war.

General Assembly resolution 38/183 F

20 December 1983   Meeting 103   109-15-15 (recorded vote)

Approved by First Committee (A/38/628) by recorded vote (84-15-18), 25 November (meeting 40); 22-nation draft (A/C.1/38/L.18), orally revised; agenda item 50.

Sponsors: Afghanistan, Angola, Benin, Congo, Cuba, Czechoslovakia, Democratic Yemen, Ethiopia, German Democratic Republic, Guinea, Guyana, Hungary, Indonesia, Lao People's Democratic Republic, Madagascar, Mongolia, Mozambique, Poland, Syrian Arab Republic, Ukrainian SSR, Viet Nam, Yemen.

Meeting numbers. GA 38th session: 1st Committee 3-10, 12-31, 40; plenary 103.

Recorded vote in Assembly as follows:

In favour: Afghanistan, Algeria, Angola, Antigua and Barbuda, Argentina, Bahamas, Bahrain, Bangladesh, Barbados, Belize, Benin, Bhutan, Bolivia, Botswana, Bulgaria, Burundi, Byelorussian SSR, Cape Verde, Central African Republic, Chad, Chile, Colombia, Congo, Costa Rica, Cuba, Cyprus, Czechoslovakia, Democratic Yemen, Djibouti, Dominica, Dominican Republic, Ecuador, Egypt, El Salvador, Ethiopia, Fiji, Gabon, German Democratic Republic, Ghana, Guinea, Guinea-Bissau, Guyana, Haiti, Hungary, India, Indonesia, Iran, Iraq, Ivory Coast, Jamaica, Jordan, Kenya, Kuwait, Lao People's Democratic Republic, Lesotho, Liberia, Lib-

yan Arab Jamahiriya, Madagascar, Malawi, Malaysia, Maldives, Mali, Maurita-
nia, Mauritius, Mexico, Mongolia, Morocco, Mozambique, Nepal, Nicaragua,
Niger, Nigeria, Oman, Pakistan, Panama, Papua New Guinea, Peru, Poland, Qatar,
Romania, Rwanda, Saint Lucia, Saint Vincent and the Grenadines, Sao Tome
and Principe, Saudi Arabia, Sierra Leone, Sri Lanka, Sudan, Suriname, Syrian
Arab Republic, Thailand, Togo, Trinidad and Tobago, Tunisia, Uganda, Ukrainian SSR, USSR, United Arab Emirates, United Republic of Cameroon, United
Republic of Tanzania, Upper Volta, Vanuatu, Venezuela, Viet Nam, Yemen, Yugo-
slavia, Zaire, Zambia, Zimbabwe.

Against: Australia, Belgium, Canada, France, Germany, Federal Republic of,
Italy, Japan, Luxembourg, Netherlands, New Zealand, Norway, Portugal, Turkey, United Kingdom, United States.

Abstaining: Austria, Brazil, Denmark, Finland, Greece, Guatemala, Honduras,
Iceland, Ireland, Israel, Lebanon, Paraguay, Philippines, Spain, Sweden.

Disarmament negotiations

The General Assembly emphasized the importance of disarmament negotiations in a number
of 1983 resolutions, among them 38/183 F, on implementing the 1979 Declaration on International
Co-operation for Disarmament[17] (see above);
38/183 H and M, on implementing recommendations of its 1978 disarmament special session;[15]
and 38/190, on implementing the 1970 Declaration on the Strengthening of International
Security.[18]

Areas of ongoing and proposed negotiations,
covered elsewhere in this chapter, concerned:
nuclear disarmament, USSR–United States
negotiations, nuclear-war prevention, a draft convention against nuclear weapons, proposed negotiations to prohibit neutron bombs, negotiations for
a treaty against nuclear-weapon tests, international
security of non-nuclear-weapon States, a draft convention on chemical weapons, radiological
weapons, new weapons of mass destruction, naval
armaments, and the arms race in outer space and
anti-satellite systems.

At the 1983 Assembly session, the German
Democratic Republic submitted, and later withdrew, a draft resolution entitled "Obligation of
States to contribute to effective disarmament
negotiations",[19] which, among other things,
would have had the Assembly urge all States, particularly the nuclear-weapon and other militarily
significant States, to intensify their efforts to conclude successfully the negotiations under way in
the Committee on Disarmament and other international forums, to resume suspended negotiations
and to start new ones on effective international disarmament agreements.

Meeting numbers. GA 38th session: 1st Committee 3-10, 12-33.

REFERENCES
[1]A/38/237. [2]A/38/266. [3]A/38/292-S/15862. [4]A/38/537.
[5]A/C.1/38/6. [6]A/38/261. [7]YUN 1978, p. 39, GA res. S-
10/2, 30 June 1978. [8]YUN 1982, p. 19. [9]*Ibid.,* p. 21.
[10]A/C.1/38/L.71. [11]A/38/27 & Corr.1 and CD/421/Appendix
II/vols. I & II (documents compilation). [12]YUN 1982, p. 150,
GA res. 37/99 K, 13 Dec. 1982. [13]A/38/42. [14]YUN 1982,
p. 141. [15]YUN 1978, p. 17. [16]YUN 1982, p. 12. [17]YUN
1979, p. 86, GA res. 34/88, 11 Dec. 1979. [18]YUN 1970,
p. 105, GA res. 2734(XXV), 16 Dec. 1970. [19]A/C.1/38/L.16.

Nuclear weapons

Nuclear disarmament

During 1983, the question of nuclear-arms limitation and disarmament was actively debated in
the Committee on Disarmament, the Disarmament Commission and the General Assembly.

By year's end, the Treaty known as SALT II (a
treaty between the United States and the USSR
on limiting strategic offensive arms), which had
emerged from the second phase of the strategic
arms limitation talks between the two States (1972-
1979), had not entered into force, while further
bilateral negotiations between them had been suspended.

Concern over the possibility of war, specifically
the threat of nuclear conflict, was a recurrent
theme in numerous resolutions adopted by the Assembly in 1983; their texts can be found in this
subchapter.

Activities of the Committee on Disarmament.
The Committee on Disarmament,[1] at its 1983
session, did not reach consensus on the establishment of *ad hoc* working groups for negotiations on
the cessation of the nuclear-arms race and nuclear
disarmament, despite proposals to that effect by
the group of 21 (the non-aligned and neutral States
within the Committee—Algeria, Argentina,
Brazil, Burma, Cuba, Egypt, Ethiopia, India, Indonesia, Iran, Kenya, Mexico, Morocco, Nigeria,
Pakistan, Peru, Sri Lanka, Sweden, Venezuela,
Yugoslavia, Zaire), the group of socialist States
members of the Committee (Bulgaria, Czechoslovakia, German Democratic Republic, Hungary,
Mongolia, Poland, Romania, USSR), and some
States individually. A group of socialist States had
also proposed the setting up of an *ad hoc* working
group on the nuclear neutron weapon. Others,
among them Western European countries, considered it preferable, in the existing circumstances,
to have substantive informal discussions in the
Committee.

In the Committee debate, a number of delegations deplored that the single multilateral negotiating body on disarmament was unable to establish
a working group to initiate negotiations due to the
opposition of certain nuclear-weapon States and
their allies which based their security policy on the
possible use of nuclear weapons. These delegations
maintained that past experience had shown that
exchanges of views in the Committee would not
promote the search for a common approach that
would enable the Committee to fulfil its negotiating role. Other delegations considered informal
meetings to be the most appropriate vehicle to determine such a common approach. A large num-

ber of delegations stated that the security perceptions of some States could not be used as an excuse for opposing the establishment of an *ad hoc* working group on the cessation of the nuclear-arms race
and nuclear disarmament.

Disarmament Commission activities. At its 1983
session, following a general exchange of views on
the nuclear-arms race and nuclear disarmament,
the Committee of the Whole of the Disarmament
Commission[2] established on 20 May an open-
ended contact group, which held 10 meetings between 24 May and 1 June.

The contact group examined a number of working
papers submitted to it, choosing as the basis for its
drafting work a proposal by the non-aligned group,
which contained recommendations dealing with,
among other things, a nuclear-weapon test-ban treaty,
non-use or threat of use of nuclear weapons, declarations by nuclear-weapon States on non-first-use
of such weapons, security assurances to non-nuclear-
weapon States and the establishment of nuclear-
weapon-free zones. It also considered a working
paper prepared by the Commission Chairman, who
suggested that the Commission should adopt concrete
recommendations on specific subjects, rather than
remain on the level of generality as in previous years.
The Commission also had before it working papers
by the German Democratic Republic, Mexico and
the United Kingdom.

As it was unable to achieve consensus on a set
of recommendations for submission to the Committee of the Whole, the contact group suggested
continued consideration of the nuclear-arms race
and nuclear disarmament at the Commission's
1984 session with a view to the formulation of concrete recommendations.

GENERAL ASSEMBLY ACTION

On 20 December, the General Assembly
adopted by recorded vote resolution 38/183 M, the
draft of which had been recommended by the First
Committee.

Implementation of the recommendations and decisions of the tenth special session

The General Assembly,

Recalling the provisions of the Final Document of the
Tenth Special Session of the General Assembly, the first
special session devoted to disarmament, in particular
the following:

(a) That nuclear weapons pose the greatest danger
to mankind and to the survival of civilization,

(b) That it is essential to halt and reverse the nuclear-
arms race in all its aspects in order to avert the danger
of war involving nuclear weapons,

(c) That removing the threat of a world war—a
nuclear war—is the most acute and urgent task of the
present day,

(d) That while disarmament is the responsibility of
all States, the nuclear-weapon States have the primary
responsibility for nuclear disarmament,

(e) That the most effective guarantee against the
danger of nuclear war and the use of nuclear weapons
is nuclear disarmament and the complete elimination
of nuclear weapons,

(f) That pending the achievement of this goal, the
nuclear-weapon States have special responsibilities to undertake measures aimed at preventing the outbreak of
nuclear war,

(g) That, in the task of achieving the goals of nuclear
disarmament, all the nuclear-weapon States, in particular those among them which possess the most important nuclear arsenals, bear a special responsibility,

Deeply regretting that the nuclear-arms race has not yet
been halted and that the danger of nuclear war has been
increasing,

Gravely concerned over the risks of nuclear war inherent in the present world situation,

1. *Solemnly reaffirms* the special responsibilities of the
nuclear-weapon States for nuclear disarmament and for
undertaking measures to prevent nuclear war and to halt
the nuclear-arms race in all its aspects;

2. *Solemnly reaffirms* the vital interest of all the peoples of the world in the success of disarmament negotiations and the consequent duty of all States to contribute to efforts in the field of disarmament;

3. *Solemnly reaffirms* the central role and primary
responsibility of the United Nations in the sphere of disarmament;

4. *Requests* the nuclear-weapon States to submit to
the General Assembly annual reports on the measures
and steps taken by them, jointly or individually, in the
discharge of the special responsibilities incumbent upon
them for the prevention of nuclear war and for halting
and reversing the nuclear-arms race.

General Assembly resolution 38/183 M

20 December 1983   Meeting 103   133-1-14 (recorded vote)

Approved by First Committee (A/38/628) by recorded vote (109-1-15), 23 Novem-
ber (meeting 39); 8-nation draft (A/C.1/38/L.38); agenda item 50 (g).
Sponsors: Argentina, Austria, Brazil, Colombia, Ecuador, Indonesia, Pakistan,
Uruguay.
Meeting numbers. GA 38th session: 1st Committee 3-10, 12-31, 33, 38, 39; ple-
nary 103.

Recorded vote in Assembly as follows:

In favour: Afghanistan, Algeria, Angola, Antigua and Barbuda, Argentina, Aus-
tralia, Austria, Bahamas, Bahrain, Bangladesh, Barbados, Belize, Benin, Bhu-
tan, Bolivia, Botswana, Brazil, Bulgaria, Burma, Burundi, Byelorussian SSR, Cape
Verde, Central African Republic, Chad, Chile, Colombia, Congo, Costa Rica, Cuba,
Cyprus, Czechoslovakia, Democratic Kampuchea, Democratic Yemen, Denmark,
Djibouti, Dominica, Dominican Republic, Ecuador, Egypt, El Salvador, Ethiopia,
Fiji, Finland, Gabon, Gambia, German Democratic Republic, Ghana, Greece,
Guatemala, Guinea, Guinea-Bissau, Guyana, Haiti, Honduras, Hungary, Iceland,
India, Indonesia, Iran, Iraq, Ireland, Ivory Coast, Jamaica, Jordan, Kenya, Kuwait,
Lao People's Democratic Republic, Lebanon, Lesotho, Liberia, Libyan Arab Jama-
hiriya, Madagascar, Malawi, Malaysia, Maldives, Mali, Malta, Mauritania,
Mauritius, Mexico, Mongolia, Morocco, Mozambique, Nepal, New Zealand,
Nicaragua, Niger, Nigeria, Oman, Pakistan, Panama, Papua New Guinea,
Paraguay, Peru, Philippines, Poland, Qatar, Romania, Rwanda, Saint Lucia, Saint
Vincent and the Grenadines, Sao Tome and Principe, Saudi Arabia, Senegal,
Sierra Leone, Singapore, Spain, Sri Lanka, Sudan, Suriname, Swaziland, Sweden,
Syrian Arab Republic, Thailand, Togo, Trinidad and Tobago, Tunisia, Uganda,
Ukrainian SSR, USSR, United Arab Emirates, United Republic of Cameroon,
United Republic of Tanzania, Upper Volta, Uruguay, Vanuatu, Venezuela, Viet
Nam, Yemen, Yugoslavia, Zaire, Zambia, Zimbabwe.
Against: United States.
Abstaining: Belgium, Canada, China, France, Germany, Federal Republic of,
Israel, Italy, Japan, Luxembourg, Netherlands, Norway, Portugal, Turkey, United
Kingdom.

Speaking in explanation of vote on the text, Australia said it interpreted subparagraph (b) in the

preamble as pertaining to both vertical and horizontal proliferation; in that regard, it regretted that the text had selectively quoted paragraph 20 of the 1978 Final Document. It saw paragraph 3 as allowing States to negotiate freely between themselves, and paragraph 4 as merely requesting the international community to be kept broadly informed. India, sharing the beliefs expressed in paragraphs 2 and 3, said the text rightly placed the onus for nuclear disarmament on the nuclear-weapon States. Mongolia viewed the result of the vote as an indication that the majority of nations were committed to the consideration of preventing nuclear war and achieving nuclear disarmament and to drafting international legal instruments on those issues. Oman expressed support for all efforts aimed at preventing nuclear war.

Other 1983 Assembly resolutions containing recommendations to nuclear-weapon States included: 38/63, on nuclear-weapon tests; 38/64, on a nuclear-weapon-free zone in the Middle East; 38/67, on security of non-nuclear-weapon States; 38/73 B, 38/73 E and 38/76, on a nuclear-weapon freeze; 38/183 H, on implementing the recommendations of the 1978 special session; 38/186, on a proposed World Disarmament Conference; and 38/188 F, on naval armaments. Details on these topics can be found elsewhere in the chapter.

USSR–United States negotiations

At the end of 1983, the SALT II Treaty, concluded between the USSR and the United States on 18 June 1979 at Vienna, Austria, had not entered into force, although each party had agreed to adhere to its substantive provisions as long as the other reciprocated. Two further sets of bilateral negotiations, conducted at Geneva, were suspended towards the end of 1983—one on the limitation and reduction of strategic arms, which had begun in June 1982, and the other on intermediate-range systems, which had commenced in November 1981.

As a follow-up to a 1982 General Assembly resolution on the item on implementation of the recommendations of the 1978 special session on disarmament[3], the Secretary-General, in November 1983,[4] transmitted to the Assembly a communication dated 26 October by the USSR concerning disarmament and arms limitation negotiations conducted outside the United Nations framework.

Between August and November, the Secretary-General also received a number of letters dealing with the USSR–United States negotiations in Geneva.

On 31 August,[5] Romania transmitted messages its President had sent on 21 August to the General Secretary of the USSR and to the President of the United States, containing proposals it deemed conducive to the success of the negotiations. Austria transmitted, on 28 October,[6] an appeal it had adopted on 18 October, urging the two parties to reach a political consensus on the basic elements of an agreement on intermediate-range weapons before the time allocated for the talks expired. The USSR transmitted on 28 October[7] an interview its General Secretary had given to the USSR newspaper *Pravda* on the status of the Geneva talks.

Bulgaria transmitted on 17 November[8] an appeal made on 10 November at Sofia by the member States of the Warsaw Treaty Organization to the States participants in the Conference on Security and Co-operation in Europe (November 1980–September 1983), expressing concern over the anticipated United States deployment of nuclear missiles in Europe. Romania transmitted on 22 November[9] a statement made by its President before its Grand National Assembly on 16 November, containing a peace appeal addressed to the parliaments of European States, the United States and Canada in the face of the new missile deployment.

On 25 November,[10] however, the USSR transmitted a statement made the previous day by its General Secretary, declaring that the United States deployment of medium-range missiles—in the Federal Republic of Germany, Italy and the United Kingdom—rendered impossible further USSR participation in the talks. It thereby announced: cancellation of the moratorium on the deployment of its medium-range nuclear weapons in the European part of its territory; acceleration of the deployment of increased-range operational-tactical missiles in Czechoslovakia and the German Democratic Republic; and that, as the United States increased the nuclear threat, corresponding USSR weapons would be deployed in ocean areas.

Bulgaria transmitted on 28 November[11] a declaration by its Government, asserting that the member States of the Warsaw Treaty Organization were forced to respond to the new situation created by the United States action, and calling for mutually acceptable nuclear disarmament agreements in Europe.

Romania transmitted on 29 November[12] a declaration of 25 November, calling on the USSR and the United States to halt the new missile deployment, resume negotiations, convene a summit meeting preceded by a meeting at the Foreign Minister level, and hold consultative meetings of the members of the Warsaw Treaty Organization and the North Atlantic Treaty Organization (NATO).

GENERAL ASSEMBLY CONSIDERATION

Of the 26 resolutions the General Assembly adopted on nuclear questions in 1983, three focused on USSR–United States bilateral nuclear-arms negotiations (see below).

A fourth text on the bilateral negotiations,[13] approved by the First Committee on 22 November by a recorded vote of 65 to 19, with 40 abstentions, was not put to a vote in the Assembly at the request of Bulgaria for the sponsors (Bulgaria, Czechoslovakia, German Democratic Republic, Hungary, Lao People's Democratic Republic, Mongolia, Poland, Viet Nam). That text would have had the Assembly call on the States parties to the bilateral talks to achieve as soon as possible equitable agreement which would provide for the non-deployment of new medium-range nuclear missiles in Europe and for a reduction in the existing nuclear systems of such range without prejudice to anyone's security.

In withdrawing the text on 20 December, Bulgaria stated that the conditions prevailing at the time of the Committee action had subsequently changed radically due to the deployment of new missiles in Western Europe and the suspension of the Geneva talks. The German Democratic Republic stated that the new United States missile deployment had taken away the basis for bilateral nuclear-arms negotiations and had also affected other negotiations and the international situation.

Stating that the emplacement of the United States missiles had removed the possibility of a mutually acceptable agreement at Geneva, the USSR expressed support for the Bulgarian proposal not to vote on the draft submitted by the socialist States.

The United Kingdom expressed doubts about the procedural implications of the Bulgarian proposal, and said that it did not understand which new development was supposed to have rendered the text inappropriate for the Assembly's adoption, since the only intervening event had been the USSR's withdrawal from the bilateral negotiations, while the other party had made perfectly clear its willingness to continue. The United States saw no need to insist on voting on the text, as it did not consider that draft particularly useful; other resolutions expressed better the need for negotiation.

GENERAL ASSEMBLY ACTION

On 20 December 1983, the General Assembly adopted three resolutions (38/183 A, N and P), all of which had been recommended by the First Committee, on the bilateral negotiations.

It adopted resolution 38/183 A by recorded vote.

Bilateral nuclear-arms negotiations

The General Assembly,

Deeply concerned about the possibility of the deployment of new medium-range missiles in Europe and about the development of those already in existence on that continent,

Profoundly alarmed that the bilateral negotiations between the Union of Soviet Socialist Republics and the

United States of America commenced at Geneva on 30 November 1981 have not so far reached results to meet the expectations of peoples,

Deeply concerned that the failure of those negotiations could lead to a significant new escalation in the spiralling arms competition in Europe and in the world, thereby gravely endangering international peace and security,

Firmly convinced that an early successful conclusion of those negotiations by reaching an appropriate agreement, in accordance with the principle of undiminished security at the lowest possible level of armament and military forces, would have crucial importance for the strengthening of international peace and security and for the reduction of the risk of nuclear war,

Convinced also that through negotiations, pursued in a spirit of flexibility and responsibility for the security interests of all peoples, it is still possible to reach an agreement,

1. *Urges* the Government of the Union of Soviet Socialist Republics and the Government of the United States of America to make every effort to reach an agreement at their bilateral negotiations at Geneva, or at least to agree on a provisional basis that no medium-range missiles be deployed and the number of the existing ones be reduced, while the negotiations would continue in order to achieve positive results in conformity with the security interests of all States;

2. *Calls upon* all European States as well as all interested States to do their utmost in order to assist the process of negotiation and promote its successful conclusion;

3. *Calls upon* all States to do their utmost in order to bring the arms race to a halt and to proceed to disarmament, and first of all to nuclear disarmament, as well as to contribute to the relaxation of international tension and to the resumption of the policy of détente, cooperation and respect for the national independence of all peoples;

4. *Requests* the Secretary-General to make the necessary arrangements to transmit the content of the present appeal to the Governments of all States.

General Assembly resolution 38/183 A

20 December 1983   Meeting 103   88-31-24 (recorded vote)

Approved by First Committee (A/38/628) by recorded vote (64-31-21), 22 November (meeting 37); draft by Romania (A/C.1/38/L.3/Rev.2), orally revised; agenda item 50 *(c)*.

Meeting numbers. GA 38th session: 1st Committee 3-10, 12-31, 33, 36, 37; plenary 103.

Recorded vote in Assembly as follows:

In favour: Algeria, Antigua and Barbuda, Argentina, Bahrain, Bangladesh, Belize, Benin, Bhutan, Bolivia, Botswana, Brazil, Burundi, Cape Verde, Central African Republic, Colombia, Congo, Costa Rica, Cyprus, Denmark, Dominica, Dominican Republic, Ecuador, Egypt, El Salvador, Ethiopia, Fiji, Finland, Gabon, Ghana, Greece, Guinea-Bissau, Guyana, Indonesia, Iran, Iraq, Ireland, Jamaica, Jordan, Kenya, Kuwait, Lesotho, Liberia, Libyan Arab Jamahiriya, Madagascar, Malawi, Malaysia, Maldives, Mali, Malta, Mauritania, Mexico, Nicaragua, Niger, Nigeria, Oman, Pakistan, Panama, Papua New Guinea, Paraguay, Peru, Philippines, Qatar, Romania, Rwanda, Saint Lucia, Saudi Arabia, Sierra Leone, Singapore, Somalia, Sri Lanka, Sudan, Sweden, Syrian Arab Republic, Thailand, Togo, Trinidad and Tobago, Tunisia, Uganda, United Arab Emirates, United Republic of Tanzania, Upper Volta, Vanuatu, Venezuela, Yemen, Yugoslavia, Zaire, Zambia, Zimbabwe.

Against: Afghanistan, Australia, Belgium, Bulgaria, Byelorussian SSR, Canada, Cuba, Czechoslovakia, Democratic Yemen, France, German Democratic Republic, Germany, Federal Republic of, Hungary, Iceland, Israel, Italy, Japan, Lao People's Democratic Republic, Luxembourg, Mongolia, Netherlands, New Zealand, Norway, Poland, Portugal, Turkey, Ukrainian SSR, USSR, United Kingdom, United States, Viet Nam.

Abstaining: Angola, Austria, Bahamas, Barbados, Burma, Chad, Chile, Gambia, Guatemala, Haiti, Honduras, India, Ivory Coast, Lebanon, Mauritius, Morocco, Nepal, Saint Vincent and the Grenadines, Senegal, Spain, Suriname, Swaziland, United Republic of Cameroon, Uruguay.

Algeria, Argentina, Bangladesh, Benin, Egypt, Finland, Mexico, Nigeria, Pakistan, Peru, Rwanda, Somalia, Sri Lanka, Sudan, Sweden, Tunisia, Venezuela, Yugoslavia and Zaire indicated that their support for the draft was based mainly on their belief in the need for the negotiations to continue, with a view to seeking meaningful agreement. Some of them, in particular Argentina, Finland and Sri Lanka, added that their vote did not imply taking a position with regard to specific stands on the substance of the bilateral negotiations. Similarly, Mexico stressed that its vote should not be taken as total approval of the text. Along with Sri Lanka, it took a similar position regarding the other drafts on the subject. Venezuela thought that the draft took into consideration the security interests of all the parties concerned in a balanced manner. Peru also viewed it as being balanced, and Algeria thought that it responded to the desires expressed by nearly all States.

Belgium, France, the Federal Republic of Germany, Italy, the Netherlands, Norway and Portugal opposed paragraph 1, saying that it contained the idea of postponing deployment of missiles on the Western side while existing USSR SS-20 missiles would continue to be pointed at Western Europe. That implied, as stated by the Federal Republic of Germany, that negotiations could go on indefinitely, with no incentive for the USSR to alter the situation. Similarly, Italy stated that to advocate a moratorium was tantamount to rewarding the *fait accompli* of the USSR nuclear buildup. Australia felt the text was unbalanced and not likely to enhance the prospect of success of the negotiations.

Austria said that, while it believed that the international community should remind, with one voice, the USSR and the United States of their special responsibilities and urge them to facilitate the successful conclusion of the Geneva talks, the basic political antagonisms between the two had overshadowed all the drafts. India felt that there was lack of clarity in the Romanian draft, which became resolution 38/183 A. The Bahamas, commenting on its abstention on all drafts relating to bilateral nuclear-arms negotiations, stressed that failure to elaborate one single consensus text called into serious doubt the commitment of Member States on the question. Nepal, while supporting the call for unconditional negotiations, did not wish to align itself with any specific position. Similarly, Spain had doubts about the suitability of setting forth guidelines for the behaviour of the negotiating parties.

China explained that its decision not to participate in the vote did not mean that it was not interested in the negotiations; however, after nearly two years, they had not brought about reduc-

tions but had aggravated the nuclear-arms race and increased tensions and were, themselves, in a state of crisis. Albania, which did not participate in the vote on any of the drafts on bilateral nuclear-arms negotiations, also stressed that that was not a sign of its lack of interest, but a way to underscore the fact that, while the super-Powers emphasized their concern over disarmament, it was deeds that mattered.

(See also the explanations of vote following resolutions 38/183 N and P, below.)

The Assembly adopted by recorded vote resolution 38/183 N, as recommended by the First Committee.

Bilateral nuclear-arms negotiations
The General Assembly,

Recalling that at its tenth special session, the first special session devoted to disarmament, it approved by consensus a Declaration, contained in section II of the Final Document of the Tenth Special Session of the General Assembly, in which, *inter alia*, it proclaimed that, in order effectively to discharge the central role and primary responsibility in the sphere of disarmament which belong to the United Nations in accordance with its Charter, the United Nations should be kept appropriately informed of all steps in this field, whether unilateral, bilateral, regional or multilateral, without prejudice to the progress of negotiations,

Recalling also that at its twelfth special session, the second special session devoted to disarmament, Member States reiterated their solemn commitment to implement the Final Document of the Tenth Special Session, the validity of which received their unanimous and categorical reaffirmation,

Noting that the Union of Soviet Socialist Republics and the United States of America have been continuing at Geneva the two series of bilateral nuclear-arms negotiations begun on 30 November 1981 and 29 June 1982 respectively,

Noting with satisfaction that the Union of Soviet Socialist Republics has already submitted the report requested in General Assembly resolution 37/78 A of 9 December 1982,

Hoping that the other major nuclear-weapon State will find it possible to comply also with the request of the General Assembly before the closure of its thirty-eighth session,

Deploring that it has become evident that the bilateral negotiations have not yet produced the desired results,

1. *Urges* the Government of the Union of Soviet Socialist Republics and the Government of the United States of America to examine immediately, as a way out of the present impasse, the possibility of combining into a single forum the two series of negotiations which they have been carrying out and of broadening their scope so as to embrace also the "tactical" or "battlefield" nuclear weapons;

2. *Reiterates its request* to the two negotiating parties that they bear constantly in mind that not only their national interests but also the vital interests of all the peoples of the world are at stake in this question;

3.   *Requests* both parties to keep the United Nations appropriately informed of progress achieved in their negotiations;

4.   *Decides* to include in the provisional agenda of its thirty-ninth session the item entitled "Bilateral nuclear-arms negotiations".

General Assembly resolution 38/183 N

20 December 1983   Meeting 103   122-1-25 (recorded vote)

Approved by First Committee (A/38/628) by recorded vote (104-1-24), 22 November (meeting 37); 7-nation draft (A/C.1/38/L.42); agenda item 50.
Sponsors: Colombia, Ecuador, Mexico, Sweden, Uruguay, Venezuela, Yugoslavia.
Meeting numbers. GA 38th session: 1st Committee 3-10, 12-31, 33, 36, 37; plenary 103.

Recorded vote in Assembly as follows:

In favour: Afghanistan, Algeria, Antigua and Barbuda, Argentina, Austria, Bahrain, Bangladesh, Belize, Benin, Bhutan, Bolivia, Botswana, Brazil, Bulgaria, Burma, Burundi, Byelorussian SSR, Cape Verde, Central African Republic, Chad, China, Colombia, Congo, Costa Rica, Cuba, Cyprus, Czechoslovakia, Democratic Yemen, Denmark, Djibouti, Dominican Republic, Ecuador, Egypt, El Salvador, Ethiopia, Fiji, Finland, Gabon, Gambia, German Democratic Republic, Ghana, Greece, Guatemala, Guinea, Guinea-Bissau, Guyana, Haiti, Hungary, India, Indonesia, Iran, Iraq, Ireland, Ivory Coast, Jamaica, Jordan, Kenya, Kuwait, Lao People's Democratic Republic, Lebanon, Lesotho, Liberia, Libyan Arab Jamahiriya, Madagascar, Malawi, Malaysia, Maldives, Mali, Malta, Mauritania, Mauritius, Mexico, Mongolia, Morocco, Mozambique, Nepal, Nicaragua, Niger, Nigeria, Oman, Pakistan, Panama, Papua New Guinea, Paraguay, Peru, Philippines, Poland, Qatar, Romania, Rwanda, Sao Tome and Principe, Saudi Arabia, Senegal, Sierra Leone, Singapore, Somalia, Sri Lanka, Sudan, Suriname, Swaziland, Sweden, Syrian Arab Republic, Thailand, Togo, Trinidad and Tobago, Tunisia, Uganda, Ukrainian SSR, USSR, United Arab Emirates, United Republic of Cameroon, United Republic of Tanzania, Upper Volta, Uruguay, Vanuatu, Venezuela, Viet Nam, Yemen, Yugoslavia, Zaire, Zambia, Zimbabwe.
Against: United States.
Abstaining: Angola, Australia, Bahamas, Barbados, Belgium, Canada, Chile, Dominica, France, Germany, Federal Republic of, Honduras, Iceland, Israel, Italy, Japan, Luxembourg, Netherlands, New Zealand, Norway, Portugal, Saint Lucia, Saint Vincent and the Grenadines, Spain, Turkey, United Kingdom.

Before acting on the draft that became resolution 38/183 N, the General Assembly took a separate recorded vote on paragraph 1 of the text, which was adopted by 108 to 2 (United Kingdom, United States), with 37 abstentions. The same paragraph had been approved in the First Committee by a recorded vote of 91 to 2 (United Kingdom, United States), with 33 abstentions. In the Committee, separate recorded votes were also taken on the preambular part of the draft and on each of the other operative paragraphs, in which no negative votes were cast.

Algeria, Argentina, Austria, Benin, Cyprus, Finland, India, Pakistan, Peru, Romania, Trinidad and Tobago, and Zaire expressed their support for the goal of the draft. Cyprus, Pakistan, Trinidad and Tobago, and Zaire emphasized their desire to facilitate progress in the negotiations. Algeria saw specifically in the approach of the draft a way out of the existing impasse. Similarly, Peru saw in the text positive aspects which should help overcome the stagnation in the negotiations, while Romania fully agreed with both the letter and spirit of the draft. Argentina stated that the text, in particular paragraph 1, adequately reflected its own views as to how further progress might be made. Austria regarded the draft as being consistent with its belief in the comprehensive approach to disarmament problems. Bangladesh felt that the bilateral negotiations were not only in the national interests of the

two negotiators, but also in the vital interests of all. India, although it would have preferred a single agreed text rather than three drafts, felt the text in question was the clearest on the subject.

Belgium, France and the Federal Republic of Germany expressed appreciation of the fact that the draft had refrained from indicating a stand on the substance of the negotiations; they felt, however, that the technical arrangements put forward should be determined by the two negotiators. Belgium further objected to the implication of paragraph 3 that reports from each should be submitted, feeling that only joint reporting at the opportune moment would allow them to conduct the negotiations freely.

(See also the explanations of vote following resolutions 38/183 A, above, and 38/183 P, below.)

The Assembly adopted by recorded vote resolution 38/183 P, as recommended by the First Committee.

Bilateral nuclear-arms negotiations

The General Assembly,

Deeply regretting that, in their bilateral negotiations, which commenced at Geneva on 30 November 1981, the Union of Soviet Socialist Republics and the United States of America have so far been unable to achieve positive results,

Firmly convinced that an early agreement in those negotiations, in accordance with the principle of undiminished security at the lowest possible level of armaments and military forces, would have crucial importance for the strengthening of international peace and security,

Deeply concerned that a breakdown of the negotiations could impede efforts to strengthen international peace and security and to achieve progress towards disarmament,

Convinced that, through negotiations pursued in a spirit of flexibility and responsibility for the security interests of all States, it is possible to reach an agreement,

1.   *Urges* the Government of the Union of Soviet Socialist Republics and the Government of the United States of America to continue, without pre-conditions, their bilateral negotiations at Geneva as long as is necessary in order to achieve positive results in accordance with the security interests of all States and the universal desire for progress towards disarmament;

2.   *Calls upon* the Government of the Union of Soviet Socialist Republics and the Government of the United States of America to spare no effort in seeking the attainment of the final objective of the negotiations;

3.   *Invites* the Governments of the two States mentioned above to work actively towards the enhancement of mutual trust, in order to create an atmosphere more conducive to disarmament agreements;

4.   *Expresses its firmest possible encouragement and support* to the negotiating parties in their efforts to bring the negotiations to a successful conclusion.

General Assembly resolution 38/183 P

20 December 1983   Meeting 103   99-18-24 (recorded vote)

Approved by First Committee (A/38/628) by recorded vote (85-18-21), 22 November (meeting 37); 9-nation draft (A/C.1/38/L.63); agenda item 50 (c).
Sponsors: Belgium, Canada, Germany, Federal Republic of, Italy, Japan, Netherlands, Norway, Turkey, United Kingdom.
Meeting numbers. GA 38th session: 1st Committee 3-10, 12-31, 33, 36, 37; plenary 103.

Recorded vote in Assembly as follows:

In favour: Algeria, Antigua and Barbuda, Argentina, Australia, Bahrain, Bang-ladesh, Belgium, Belize, Benin, Botswana, Brazil, Canada, Central African Repub-lic, Chad, Chile, Colombia, Congo, Costa Rica, Cyprus, Denmark, Djibouti, Dominica, Dominican Republic, Egypt, Fiji, Finland, France, Gabon, Gambia, Germany, Federal Republic of, Ghana, Greece, Guatemala, Guinea, Guyana, Iceland, Iraq, Ireland, Israel, Italy, Jamaica, Japan, Jordan, Kenya, Lebanon, Lesotho, Liberia, Luxembourg, Madagascar, Malawi, Malaysia, Maldives, Mali, Mauritania, Mexico, Morocco, Netherlands, New Zealand, Nicaragua, Niger, Nigeria, Norway, Oman, Pakistan, Panama, Papua New Guinea, Paraguay, Philip-pines, Portugal, Qatar, Rwanda, Saint Lucia, Saudi Arabia, Senegal, Sierra Leone, Singapore, Somalia, Spain, Sri Lanka, Sudan, Swaziland, Sweden, Thailand, Togo, Trinidad and Tobago, Tunisia, Turkey, Uganda, United Arab Emirates, United Kingdom, United Republic of Tanzania, United States, Upper Volta, Vanuatu, Yemen, Yugoslavia, Zaire, Zambia, Zimbabwe.

Against: Afghanistan, Angola, Bulgaria, Byelorussian SSR, Cuba, Czechoslo-vakia, Democratic Yemen, German Democratic Republic, Hungary, Lao People's Democratic Republic, Mongolia, Mozambique, Poland, Romania, Syrian Arab Republic, Ukrainian SSR, USSR, Viet Nam.

Abstaining: Austria, Bahamas, Barbados, Bhutan, Bolivia, Burma, Cape Verde, China, Ecuador, El Salvador, Guinea-Bissau, Haiti, Honduras, India, Indonesia, Ivory Coast, Mauritius, Nepal, Peru, Saint Vincent and the Grenadines, Suri-name, United Republic of Cameroon, Uruguay, Venezuela.

Although statements by Algeria, Argentina, Aus-tralia, Bangladesh, Benin, Egypt, Finland, the Ivory Coast, Mexico, Nigeria, Pakistan, Portugal, Rwanda, Somalia, Spain, Sri Lanka, Sudan, Sweden, Trinidad and Tobago, Tunisia and Yugoslavia showed some differences in the degree of support for the text, they revealed an equal concern for the outcome of the negotiations. As stated by Yugoslavia, the failure of the Geneva talks would exacerbate the mistrust between the two sides; a dialogue, in its view, was the only alternative to the further buildup of nuclear arms in Europe. Australia, in particular, felt that the text, compared with the others on the same sub-ject, was the least prejudicial to the success of the intermediate-range nuclear-force negotiations. Por-tugal thought it presented an equitable, non-discriminatory solution by recommending the con-tinuation of the talks without pre-conditions. Fin-land, like most others which explained their vote, made clear that it supported the main thrust of all the drafts on bilateral talks, without taking a stand with respect to the specific issues being debated at Geneva. Algeria stated that its support of the drafts should be seen as an appeal to the negotiators to reach an agreement in the interests of all.

Cuba, Democratic Yemen, the German Demo-cratic Republic and Romania felt that the draft that became resolution 38/183 P was an attempt, as the German Democratic Republic stated, to give the deployment of new medium-range weapons in Western Europe the appearance of legitimacy. Cuba held that from the outset one group of countries had tried to prevent the negoti-ations from succeeding and, while Cuba supported the continuation of bilateral negotiations, it be-lieved that they should lead to the dismantling of all nuclear weapons in Europe. Romania stressed that the text's approach was unilateral and rigid; it also stated that some States had negotiated in bad faith during the consultations on its draft (see above).

Austria, the Bahamas, China, India, Nepal, Peru, Venezuela and Zaire believed that there were contradictions between all the drafts, especially be-tween the Western and the Eastern proposals. Some of them stated that they did not want to en-dorse a particular approach.

(See also the explanations of vote following reso-lutions 38/183 A and N, above.)

The USSR and the United States explained their respective positions on the bilateral negotia-tions in the course of the First Committee and the plenary Assembly debate on the subject.

The USSR maintained that it favoured an in-tegrated limitation and reduction of all the com-ponents of strategic potential based on identical security and equality; medium-range nuclear ar-maments in Europe must be radically reduced without disrupting the balance on both sides. It said it had proposed in the Geneva talks the reduc-tion, by some 25 per cent, of the existing arsenals of both sides to equal levels, substantial reductions of nuclear warheads on those armaments, a ban on deploying long-range cruise missiles and other new kinds of strategic systems, and limiting a qualitative upgrading of arms—all subject to verification. It asserted that the United States refusal to take into account British and French missiles in the overall balance of nuclear arms was intended to delay the talks and enable the United States to deploy its missiles in Western Europe by invoking USSR intransigence; that missile deploy-ment would upset the existing regional and global balance in favour of member States of NATO. The USSR believed that the reductions proposed by the United States would affect the USSR strategic arsenal to a considerably greater degree than they would affect that of the United States, and viewed that country's proposal for an increase in reduc-tions or "build-down" as intended to channel the strategic arms race towards a qualitative improve-ment of missiles and bombers rather than to curb it. The USSR, stating that the United States deployment had made impossible further USSR participation in the talks, asserted that they should not be used to camouflage the exacerbation of the arms race, started by certain NATO countries and the United States.

The United States said the security situation in Europe was troubling in view of the continued USSR attempts to alter the balance of forces against the Western alliance; it asserted that, while claiming the existence of balance in Europe, the USSR had increased the number of longer-range "intermediate-range nuclear forces" missile war-heads from 800 to 1,300 in the past few years without a single United States warhead of that category being introduced into the region. The United States said its position in the strategic arms reduction talks in seeking both substantial reductions and increased stability was based on: reducing the current nuclear arsenals of the USSR and itself by almost 50 per cent to 5,000 ballistic missile warheads, a flexible approach to reducing the disparity and destructive capability and potential of ballistic missiles, substantial reductions in deployed ballistic missiles, and effective verification. It had also made build-down proposals which included linking modernization to reductions and a guaranteed annual percentage reduction of nuclear warheads. Asserting that it had been negotiating seriously even though the USSR had at the same time been deploying SS-20 missiles at the rate of one per week, the United States expressed regret that the USSR had broken off the negotiations on intermediate-range nuclear forces and had not set a date for resuming those on reducing strategic arms or on mutual and balanced force reductions.

Proposed working group

GENERAL ASSEMBLY ACTION

On the recommendation of the First Committee, the General Assembly, on 20 December 1983, adopted by recorded vote resolution 38/183 D, calling on the Conference on Disarmament (as the Committee on Disarmament would be known in 1984) to hold negotiations on the cessation of the nuclear-arms race and nuclear disarmament and especially to elaborate a nuclear-disarmament programme, setting up an *ad hoc* working group for that purpose.

Nuclear weapons in all aspects
The General Assembly,

Recalling that at its twelfth special session, the second special session devoted to disarmament, it expressed its profound preoccupation over the danger of war, in particular nuclear war, the prevention of which remains the most acute and urgent task of the present day,

Reaffirming once again that nuclear weapons pose the most serious threat to mankind and its survival and that it is therefore essential to proceed with nuclear disarmament and the complete elimination of nuclear weapons,

Reaffirming also that all nuclear-weapon States, in particular those which possess the most important nuclear arsenals, bear a special responsibility for the fulfilment of the task of achieving the goals of nuclear disarmament,

Stressing again that existing arsenals of nuclear weapons alone are more than sufficient to destroy all life on Earth, and bearing in mind the devastating results which nuclear war would have on belligerents and non-belligerents alike,

Recalling that at its tenth special session, the first special session devoted to disarmament, it decided that effective measures of nuclear disarmament and the prevention of nuclear war had the highest priority and that it was essential to halt and reverse the nuclear-arms race in all its aspects in order to avert the danger of war involving nuclear weapons,

Stressing that any expectation of winning a nuclear war is senseless and that such a war would inevitably lead to the destruction of nations, to enormous devastation and to catastrophic consequences for civilization and life itself on Earth,

Recalling further that, in its resolution 35/152 B of 12 December 1980, it noted with alarm the increased risk of a nuclear catastrophe associated both with the intensification of the nuclear-arms race and with the adoption of the new doctrines of limited or partial use of nuclear weapons, which are incompatible with its resolution 110(II) of 3 November 1947, entitled "Measures to be taken against propaganda and the inciters of a new war", and give rise to illusions of the admissibility and acceptability of a nuclear conflict,

Noting with alarm that to the doctrine of a limited nuclear war was later added the concept of a protracted nuclear war and that these dangerous doctrines lead to a new twist in the spiral of the arms race, which may seriously hamper the reaching of agreement on nuclear disarmament,

Gravely concerned about the renewed escalation of the nuclear-arms race, in both its quantitative and qualitative dimensions, as well as reliance on the doctrine of nuclear deterrence, which in fact is heightening the risk of the outbreak of nuclear war and leads to increased tensions and instability in international relations,

Taking note of the relevant deliberations of the Disarmament Commission in 1983 with regard to item 4 of its agenda, as contained in its report,

Stressing the urgent need for the cessation of the development and deployment of new types and systems of nuclear weapons as a step on the road to nuclear disarmament,

Stressing again that priority in disarmament negotiations should be given to nuclear weapons and referring to paragraphs 49 and 54 of the Final Document of the Tenth Special Session of the General Assembly,

Recalling its resolutions 33/71 H of 14 December 1978, 34/83 J of 11 December 1979, 35/152 B and C of 12 December 1980, 36/92 E of 9 December 1981 and 37/78 C of 9 December 1982,

Noting that the Committee on Disarmament, at its session held in 1983, discussed the question of the cessation of the nuclear-arms race and nuclear disarmament and, in particular, the establishment of an *ad hoc* working group for negotiations on that question,

Regretting, however, that the Committee on Disarmament was unable to reach agreement on the establishment of an *ad hoc* working group for the purpose of undertaking multilateral negotiations on the question of the cessation of the nuclear-arms race and nuclear disarmament,

Considering that efforts will continue to be made in order to enable the Conference on Disarmament to fulfil its negotiating role with regard to the cessation of the nuclear-arms race and nuclear disarmament, bearing in mind the high priority accorded to this question in the Final Document of the Tenth Special Session,

Convinced that the Conference on Disarmament is the most suitable forum for the preparation and conduct of negotiations on nuclear disarmament,

1. *Calls upon* the Conference on Disarmament to proceed without delay to negotiations on the cessation of the nuclear-arms race and nuclear disarmament in accordance with paragraph 50 of the Final Document of

the Tenth Special Session of the General Assembly and especially to elaborate a nuclear-disarmament programme, and to establish for this purpose an *ad hoc* working group on the cessation of the nuclear-arms race and on nuclear disarmament;

2. *Decides* to include in the provisional agenda of its thirty-ninth session the item entitled "Cessation of the nuclear-arms race and nuclear disarmament: report of the Conference on Disarmament".

General Assembly resolution 38/183 D

20 December 1983   Meeting 103   108-19-16 (recorded vote)

Approved by First Committee (A/38/628) by recorded vote (91-19-8), 23 November (meeting 39); 16-nation draft (A/C.1/38/L.13); agenda item 50.
Sponsors: Afghanistan, Angola, Bulgaria, Byelorussian SSR, Cuba, Czechoslovakia, German Democratic Republic, Hungary, Lao People's Democratic Republic, Mongolia, Poland, Romania, Ukrainian SSR, USSR, Viet Nam, Zimbabwe.
Meeting numbers. GA 38th session: 1st Committee 3-10, 12-31, 39; plenary 103.

Recorded vote in Assembly as follows:

In favour: Afghanistan, Algeria, Angola, Antigua and Barbuda, Argentina, Austria, Bahrain, Bangladesh, Barbados, Belize, Benin, Bhutan, Bolivia, Botswana, Brazil, Bulgaria, Burma, Burundi, Byelorussian SSR, Cape Verde, Central African Republic, Chile, Colombia, Congo, Costa Rica, Cuba, Cyprus, Czechoslovakia, Democratic Yemen, Dominican Republic, Ecuador, Egypt, El Salvador, Ethiopia, Fiji, Finland, Gabon, German Democratic Republic, Ghana, Greece, Guinea, Guinea-Bissau, Guyana, Hungary, India, Indonesia, Iran, Iraq, Ireland, Jamaica, Jordan, Kenya, Kuwait, Lao People's Democratic Republic, Lebanon, Lesotho, Liberia, Libyan Arab Jamahiriya, Madagascar, Malawi, Malaysia, Maldives, Mali, Mauritania, Mauritius, Mexico, Mongolia, Mozambique, Nepal, Nicaragua, Niger, Nigeria, Oman, Pakistan, Panama, Papua New Guinea, Peru, Poland, Qatar, Romania, Rwanda, Sao Tome and Principe, Saudi Arabia, Sierra Leone, Singapore, Sri Lanka, Sudan, Suriname, Sweden, Syrian Arab Republic, Thailand, Togo, Trinidad and Tobago, Tunisia, Uganda, Ukrainian SSR, USSR, United Arab Emirates, United Republic of Cameroon, United Republic of Tanzania, Upper Volta, Vanuatu, Venezuela, Viet Nam, Yemen, Yugoslavia, Zambia, Zimbabwe.
Against: Australia, Belgium, Canada, Denmark, France, Germany, Federal Republic of, Iceland, Israel, Italy, Japan, Luxembourg, Netherlands, New Zealand, Norway, Portugal, Spain, Turkey, United Kingdom, United States.
Abstaining: Bahamas, Chad, Dominica, Gambia, Guatemala, Haiti, Honduras, Ivory Coast, Paraguay, Philippines, Saint Lucia, Saint Vincent and the Grenadines, Senegal, Swaziland, Uruguay, Zaire.

Speaking in explanation of vote on the draft, Austria and Finland stated that, despite certain reservations on some of the preambular parts of the text, their votes reflected their concern that the escalating nuclear-arms race be halted and reversed. Austria also supported stronger involvement by the Conference on Disarmament in nuclear disarmament efforts and said it would welcome establishing a working group on the subject. Oman supported all efforts aimed at preventing nuclear war. Brazil understood that the nuclear disarmament programme referred to in paragraph 1 corresponded to the "comprehensive, phased programme" mentioned in paragraph 50 *(c)* of the Final Document of the Tenth Special Session[14] and that the elaboration of such a programme must not be a substitute or condition for priority negotiations on the cessation of the nuclear-arms race and on nuclear disarmament, which the Conference on Disarmament should act upon urgently.

Australia regarded the proposal as among those which were put forward for propaganda purposes. Belgium considered the text's approach as unproductive and its reference to doctrines of the use of nuclear weapons as unrealistic, when it was war itself that should be prevented; Belgium wished

to ensure common security by deterrence at lower levels of both conventional and nuclear weapons.

A call for the establishment of an *ad hoc* working group on the cessation of the nuclear-arms race and nuclear disarmament was also made in Assembly resolution 38/183 I (see below, under PREVENTION OF NUCLEAR WAR).

Experts' study

GENERAL ASSEMBLY ACTION

On the recommendation of the First Committee, the General Assembly, by resolution 38/183 J, adopted by recorded vote on 20 December 1983, requested the Secretary-General to prepare, with the assistance of governmental experts, a report on unilateral nuclear disarmament measures.

Unilateral nuclear disarmament measures

The General Assembly,

Having examined the various concrete proposals submitted to the Disarmament Commission at its 1983 session and reproduced by the Commission in its report to the General Assembly,

Considering that one of these proposals, intended to expedite negotiations on nuclear disarmament through the preparation of a study on unilateral measures, would be of particular value at present in view of the impasse existing in both the bilateral and the multilateral negotiations,

Requests the Secretary-General to prepare, with the assistance of qualified governmental experts* and applying the methods customary in these cases, a report, to be submitted to the General Assembly at its thirty-ninth session, on ways and means that seem advisable for stimulating the adoption of unilateral nuclear disarmament measures which, without prejudice to the security of States, would come to promote and complement bilateral and multilateral negotiations in this sphere.

---

*Subsequently referred to as the Group of Governmental Experts on Unilateral Nuclear Disarmament Measures.

General Assembly resolution 38/183 J

20 December 1983   Meeting 103   132-2-14 (recorded vote)

Approved by First Committee (A/38/628) by recorded vote (109-1-15), 23 November (meeting 39); 3-nation draft (A/C.1/38/L.30); agenda item 50.
Sponsors: Colombia, Ecuador, Mexico.
Financial implications. ACABQ, A/38/7/Add.21; 5th Committee, A/38/762; S-G, A/C.1/38/L.72, A/C.5/38/83.
Meeting numbers. GA 38th session: 1st Committee 3-10, 12-31, 33, 39; 5th Committee 68; plenary 103.

Recorded vote in Assembly as follows:

In favour: Afghanistan, Algeria, Angola, Antigua and Barbuda, Argentina, Austria, Bahamas, Bahrain, Bangladesh, Barbados, Belize, Benin, Bhutan, Bolivia, Botswana, Brazil, Bulgaria, Burma, Burundi, Byelorussian SSR, Cape Verde, Chad, Chile, China, Colombia, Congo, Costa Rica, Cuba, Cyprus, Czechoslovakia, Democratic Kampuchea, Democratic Yemen, Denmark, Djibouti, Dominica, Dominican Republic, Ecuador, Egypt, El Salvador, Ethiopia, Fiji, Finland, Gabon, Gambia, German Democratic Republic, Ghana, Greece, Guatemala, Guinea, Guinea-Bissau, Guyana, Haiti, Honduras, Hungary, Iceland, India, Indonesia, Iran, Iraq, Ireland, Ivory Coast, Jamaica, Jordan, Kenya, Kuwait, Lao People's Democratic Republic, Lebanon, Lesotho, Liberia, Libyan Arab Jamahiriya, Madagascar, Malawi, Malaysia, Maldives, Mali, Malta, Mauritania, Mauritius, Mexico, Mongolia, Morocco, Mozambique, Nepal, Nicaragua, Niger, Nigeria, Oman, Pakistan, Panama, Papua New Guinea, Paraguay, Peru, Philippines, Poland, Qatar, Romania, Rwanda, Saint Lucia, Saint Vincent and the Grenadines, Sao Tome and Principe, Saudi Arabia, Senegal, Sierra Leone, Singapore, Somalia, Spain, Sri Lanka, Sudan, Suriname, Swaziland, Sweden, Syrian Arab

Republic, Thailand, Togo, Trinidad and Tobago, Tunisia, Uganda, Ukrainian SSR, USSR, United Arab Emirates, United Republic of Cameroon, United Republic of Tanzania, Upper Volta, Uruguay, Vanuatu, Venezuela, Viet Nam, Yemen, Yugoslavia, Zaire, Zambia, Zimbabwe.

Against: United Kingdom,[a] United States.

Abstaining: Australia, Belgium, Canada, France, Germany, Federal Republic of, Israel, Italy, Japan, Luxembourg, Netherlands, New Zealand, Norway, Portugal, Turkey.

[a]Later advised the Secretariat it had intended to abstain.

China said it was necessary to explore all channels for the prohibition of nuclear weapons and had itself unilaterally announced, upon acquiring such weapons, that it would not be the first to use them nor would it use them against non-nuclear-weapon States.

The Netherlands recalled a recent announcement by NATO on the withdrawal of 1,400 nuclear warheads from Europe over a number of years, as a step that could inspire Governments to follow suit; it doubted, however, whether the study would contribute much to the success of current arms control negotiations.

Oman and the USSR said they supported any efforts to prevent nuclear war and achieve nuclear disarmament.

Prevention of nuclear war

At the United Nations, the debate on nuclear war prevention continued to focus in 1983, as in recent years, on whether a declaration on the non-use or non-first-use of nuclear weapons, or an international convention outlawing the use of such weapons, would effectively reduce the threat of such war. The supporters of a declaration continued to maintain that a declaration by all nuclear-weapon States would strengthen the relevant principle of the Charter of the United Nations, while the Western States felt such a measure would undermine the wider principle of the non-use of force—in any form—enshrined in the Charter.

At its 1983 session, the Committee on Disarmament[1] had before it a number of working papers on the prevention of nuclear war. In papers submitted by the group of 21 neutral and non-aligned States[15] and by a group of socialist States,[16] the necessity of urgent negotiations on measures to prevent nuclear war was emphasized and, to achieve this end, an *ad hoc* working group was proposed (see below). The socialist States also called for the renunciation by all nuclear-weapon States of the first use of nuclear weapons and the conclusion of a world-wide treaty on the non-use of force in international relations. These calls were repeated in a paper put forward by the German Democratic Republic,[17] which also listed as relevant several items such as a freeze on the production and deployment of nuclear weapons and a moratorium on all nuclear explosions.

The Federal Republic of Germany submitted a working paper[18] on preventing all armed conflict, beginning with the prohibition of the threat or use of force as embodied in Article 2 of the Charter. Belgium's working paper[19] was on confidence-building measures within the framework of the prevention of nuclear war. Further, Australia, Belgium, the Federal Republic of Germany, Italy, Japan and the Netherlands, in a joint paper,[20] outlined how preventing nuclear war might be explored in informal meetings.

GENERAL ASSEMBLY ACTION

In December, the General Assembly adopted resolutions 38/75 and 38/183 B on nuclear war prevention, the former under an item entitled "Condemnation of nuclear war", included in the agenda of the Assembly's 1983 regular session at the request of the USSR.

In transmitting that proposal by a letter of 4 October,[21] the USSR stated that any designs for unleashing nuclear war were criminal and should receive the most severe universal condemnation. The letter carried the text of a draft resolution which, with the addition of the fourth preambular paragraph and after revision by the additional sponsors and approval by the First Committee, was adopted by recorded vote on 15 December as Assembly resolution 38/75.

Condemnation of nuclear war

The General Assembly,

Expressing its alarm at the growing threat of nuclear war, which can lead to the destruction of civilization on earth,

Drawing the attention of all States and peoples to the conclusions arrived at by the most eminent scientists and military and civilian experts to the effect that it is impossible to limit the deadly consequences of nuclear war if it is ever begun and that in a nuclear war there can be no victors,

Convinced that the prevention of nuclear catastrophe is the most profound aspiration of billions of people on earth,

Reaffirming its call for the conclusion of an international convention on the prohibition of the use of nuclear weapons with the participation of all the nuclear-weapon States,

1. *Resolutely, unconditionally and for all time condemns* nuclear war as being contrary to human conscience and reason, as the most monstrous crime against peoples and as a violation of the foremost human right—the right to life;

2. *Condemns* the formulation, propounding, dissemination and propaganda of political and military doctrines and concepts intended to provide "legitimacy" for the first use of nuclear weapons and in general to justify the "admissibility" of unleashing nuclear war;

3. *Calls upon* all States to unite and redouble their efforts aimed at removing the threat of nuclear war, halting the nuclear-arms race and reducing nuclear weapons until they are completely eliminated.

General Assembly resolution 38/75

15 December 1983   Meeting 97   95-19-30 (recorded vote)

Approved by First Committee (A/38/648) by recorded vote (72-19-23), 23 November (meeting 39); 10-nation draft (A/C.1/38/L.1/Rev.1); agenda item 143.
Sponsors: Bulgaria, Byelorussian SSR, Czechoslovakia, German Democratic Republic, Hungary, Mongolia, Poland, Ukrainian SSR, USSR, Viet Nam.
Meeting numbers. GA 38th session: General Committee 4; 1st Committee 3-10, 12-31, 38, 39; plenary 97.
Recorded vote in Assembly as follows:

In favour: Afghanistan, Algeria, Angola, Antigua and Barbuda, Argentina, Bahrain, Bangladesh, Barbados, Belize, Benin, Bhutan, Bolivia, Botswana, Brazil, Bulgaria, Burma, Burundi, Byelorussian SSR, Cape Verde, Central African Republic, Chile, Congo, Cuba, Cyprus, Czechoslovakia, Democratic Yemen, Ecuador, Egypt, El Salvador, Ethiopia, Gabon, German Democratic Republic, Ghana, Greece, Grenada, Guinea, Guyana, Hungary, India, Indonesia, Iran, Iraq, Jamaica, Jordan, Kenya, Kuwait, Lao People's Democratic Republic, Lesotho, Libyan Arab Jamahiriya, Madagascar, Malaysia, Maldives, Mali, Mauritania, Mauritius, Mexico, Mongolia, Mozambique, Nepal, Nicaragua, Niger, Nigeria, Oman, Pakistan, Panama, Peru, Poland, Qatar, Romania, Sao Tome and Principe, Saudi Arabia, Seychelles, Sierra Leone, Sri Lanka, Sudan, Swaziland, Syrian Arab Republic, Thailand, Togo, Tunisia, Uganda, Ukrainian SSR, USSR, United Arab Emirates, United Republic of Cameroon, United Republic of Tanzania, Upper Volta, Uruguay, Vanuatu, Venezuela, Viet Nam, Yemen, Yugoslavia, Zambia, Zimbabwe.

Against: Australia, Belgium, Canada, Denmark, France, Germany, Federal Republic of, Iceland, Israel, Italy, Japan, Luxembourg, Netherlands, New Zealand, Norway, Portugal, Spain, Turkey, United Kingdom, United States.

Abstaining: Austria, Bahamas, Chad, China, Colombia, Costa Rica, Dominican Republic, Fiji, Finland, Gambia, Guatemala, Haiti, Honduras, Ireland, Ivory Coast, Lebanon, Liberia, Malawi, Morocco, Papua New Guinea, Paraguay, Philippines, Rwanda, Saint Lucia, Senegal, Singapore, Solomon Islands, Suriname, Sweden, Zaire.

In explanation of vote, Greece, India, Indonesia, Mongolia, Oman, Pakistan, Sri Lanka, the Sudan and Togo expressed support for the text's main thrust.

Austria, Belgium, Greece and the Sudan asserted that the condemnation should cover both conventional and nuclear wars.

Sri Lanka held that the mere condemnation of war was inadequate to ensure its prevention, and asserted that some of the language in paragraphs 1 and 2 did not help towards realizing an international convention with the participation of all the nuclear-weapon States. While in agreement with a number of ideas in the resolution, Ireland considered paragraphs 1 and 2 as being rhetorical and as ignoring fundamental problems inherent in nuclear deterrence as a means of maintaining international security. India and Indonesia said, with regard to paragraph 2, that the best way to prevent the outbreak of nuclear war was to forswear the use or threat of use of nuclear weapons under any circumstances. Togo also had reservations on paragraph 2, and Indonesia said that, had a separate vote been taken on that paragraph, it would have abstained.

Recalling a 1982 NATO declaration (Bonn, Federal Republic of Germany) that no NATO weapons would ever be used except in response to attack, the United Kingdom objected to what it called unwarranted implications in paragraph 2, that those not agreeing with the USSR sought to justify the unleashing of a nuclear war; the text diverted attention from practical arms control measures and other real dangers that arose daily from conventional war. For the United States, paragraph 2 reflected the sponsors' aversion to free public discussion of nuclear and other military issues; it would continue to negotiate for concrete and verifiable disarmament measures rather than support

such unenforceable resolutions that might lull people into a false sense of security. Austria also emphasized the need for early agreement between the two major Powers on nuclear arms limitations and reductions. China said the international community expected the two Powers to take practical action instead of verbally condemning nuclear war.

Australia thought that the text promoted propagandistic aims. The Federal Republic of Germany called the text a new version of the perennial USSR proposal on nuclear non-first-use, a concept which it maintained neither met Charter obligations nor provided effective means for preventing nuclear war.

Malta, which did not participate in the vote, said the international community should be proposing, instead, the dissemination of positive, well-argued and thoroughly researched stances that would demolish doctrines and concepts that attempted to justify nuclear war.

On 20 December 1983, the Assembly adopted by recorded vote resolution 38/183 B, as recommended by the First Committee.

Non-use of nuclear weapons and prevention of nuclear war

The General Assembly,

Alarmed by the threat to the survival of mankind posed by the existence of nuclear weapons and the continuing arms race,

Recalling that, in accordance with the Final Document of the Tenth Special Session of the General Assembly, the first special session devoted to disarmament, effective measures of nuclear disarmament and the prevention of nuclear war have the highest priority,

Recalling also that this commitment was reaffirmed by the General Assembly at its twelfth special session, the second special session devoted to disarmament,

Bearing in mind its resolutions 36/81 B, 36/92 I and 36/100 of 9 December 1981 and 37/78 J of 9 December 1982,

Reaffirming that the most effective guarantee against the danger of nuclear war and the use of nuclear weapons is nuclear disarmament and the complete elimination of nuclear weapons,

Recalling also paragraph 58 of the Final Document of the Tenth Special Session, in which it is stated that all States should actively participate in efforts to bring about conditions in international relations among States in which a code of peaceful conduct of nations in international affairs could be agreed upon and which would preclude the use or threat of use of nuclear weapons,

Reaffirming also that the nuclear-weapon States have special responsibilities to undertake measures aimed at preventing the outbreak of nuclear war,

1. *Considers* that the solemn declarations by two nuclear-weapon States made or reiterated at the twelfth special session of the General Assembly, the second special session devoted to disarmament, concerning their respective obligations not to be the first to use nuclear weapons offer an important avenue to decrease the danger of nuclear war;

2. *Expresses the hope* that those nuclear-weapon States which have not yet done so would consider making similar declarations with respect to not being the first to use nuclear weapons.

General Assembly resolution 38/183 B

20 December 1983   Meeting 103   110-19-15 (recorded vote)

Approved by First Committee (A/38/628) by recorded vote (87-19-8), 23 November (meeting 39); 4-nation draft (A/C.1/38/L.10); agenda item 50.

Sponsors: Cuba, German Democratic Republic, Mongolia, Romania.

Meeting numbers. GA 38th session: 1st Committee 3-10, 12-31, 38, 39; plenary 103.

Recorded vote in Assembly as follows:

In favour: Afghanistan, Algeria, Angola, Antigua and Barbuda, Argentina, Bahrain, Bangladesh, Barbados, Belize, Benin, Bhutan, Bolivia, Botswana, Brazil, Bulgaria, Burma, Byelorussian SSR, Cape Verde, Central African Republic, Chad, Chile, Colombia, Congo, Costa Rica, Cuba, Cyprus, Czechoslovakia, Democratic Yemen, Dominican Republic, Ecuador, Egypt, El Salvador, Ethiopia, Fiji, Finland, Gabon, Gambia, German Democratic Republic, Ghana, Greece, Guinea, Guinea-Bissau, Guyana, Hungary, India, Indonesia, Iran, Iraq, Ireland, Jamaica, Jordan, Kenya, Kuwait, Lao People's Democratic Republic, Lebanon, Lesotho, Liberia, Libyan Arab Jamahiriya, Madagascar, Malaysia, Maldives, Mali, Mauritania, Mauritius, Mexico, Mongolia, Morocco, Mozambique, Nepal, Nicaragua, Niger, Nigeria, Oman, Pakistan, Panama, Papua New Guinea, Peru, Poland, Qatar, Romania, Rwanda, Sao Tome and Principe, Saudi Arabia, Senegal, Sierra Leone, Sri Lanka, Sudan, Suriname, Swaziland, Sweden, Syrian Arab Republic, Thailand, Togo, Trinidad and Tobago, Tunisia, Uganda, Ukrainian SSR, USSR, United Arab Emirates, United Republic of Cameroon, United Republic of Tanzania, Upper Volta, Vanuatu, Venezuela, Viet Nam, Yemen, Yugoslavia, Zaire, Zambia, Zimbabwe.

Against: Australia, Belgium, Canada, Denmark, France, Germany, Federal Republic of, Iceland, Israel, Italy, Japan, Luxembourg, Netherlands, New Zealand, Norway, Portugal, Spain, Turkey, United Kingdom, United States.

Abstaining: Austria, Bahamas, China, Dominica, Guatemala, Haiti, Honduras, Ivory Coast, Malawi, Paraguay, Philippines, Saint Lucia, Saint Vincent and the Grenadines, Singapore, Uruguay.

In explanation of vote, Australia stated that the text attempted to "score points", rather than improve the atmosphere for negotiations. Belgium said that the scope of the text was limited to the renunciation of the first use of nuclear weapons by those States possessing such weapons, while States should ban all uses of force, as required by the United Nations Charter.

Czechoslovakia felt that a commitment on non-first-use would be an important step towards preventing nuclear war, and Mongolia viewed the non-first-use obligation as acquiring greater relevance and immediacy. While Bulgaria rejected allegations that the text was propagandistic, and deplored attempts to place nuclear and other wars on an equal footing, Hungary believed that the search for nuclear war prevention would create better conditions for preventing any kind of war. The USSR said it had taken several unilateral actions, one being its commitment never to be the first to use nuclear weapons.

Finland and India expressed agreement with the thrust of the proposal, with the latter adding that the use or threat of use of nuclear weapons should be forsworn completely pending nuclear disarmament. Similarly, Indonesia considered that any use of nuclear weapons should be condemned. The Sudan stated that it welcomed any declaratory measure on the non-use of nuclear weapons, provided that such measures were not viewed as effective disarmament measures or in isolation

from the Charter principle. Sweden, which viewed the concept of non-first-use of nuclear weapons as important, stressed that a rough parity in both conventional and nuclear forces must be established at lower levels in order to facilitate undertakings by nuclear-weapon States not to be the first to use nuclear weapons.

Other 1983 Assembly resolutions dealing with nuclear war prevention included 38/183 F, on implementation of the 1979 Declaration on International Co-operation for Disarmament; 38/183 H, on implementation of recommendations of the 1978 special session on disarmament; and 38/183 M, on nuclear disarmament. (For texts of these resolutions, refer to INDEX OF RESOLUTIONS AND DECISIONS).

On 14 October, Czechoslovakia transmitted to the Secretary-General the text of an appeal[22] adopted by the World Assembly for Peace and Life, against Nuclear War (Prague, 21-26 June).

Proposed working group

The idea of establishing a working group to negotiate measures for preventing nuclear war was suggested in working papers submitted to the 1983 session of the Committee on Disarmament[1] by the group of 21[15] and by a group of socialist States.[16] The Committee considered the suggestions but was not able to reach a consensus on them.

GENERAL ASSEMBLY ACTION

On 20 December, the General Assembly, as recommended by the First Committee, adopted by recorded vote resolution 38/183 G, requesting the Conference on Disarmament (as the Committee on Disarmament would be known in 1984) to establish a working group on the prevention of nuclear war. That request was repeated in resolution 38/183 I, adopted the same day.

Prevention of nuclear war

The General Assembly,

Alarmed by the threat to the survival of mankind posed by the existence of nuclear weapons and the continuing arms race,

Recalling that removal of the threat of nuclear war is the most acute and urgent task of the present day,

Reiterating that it is the shared responsibility of all Member States to save succeeding generations from the scourge of another world war, which would inevitably be a nuclear war,

Recalling the provisions of paragraphs 47 to 50 and 56 to 58 of the Final Document of the Tenth Special Session of the General Assembly regarding the procedures designed to secure the avoidance of nuclear war,

Recalling also its resolution 36/81 B of 9 December 1981 and, in particular, its resolution 37/78 I of 9 December 1982, in which it requested the Committee on Disarmament to undertake, as a matter of the highest priority, negotiations with a view to achieving agreement on appropriate and practical measures for the prevention of nuclear war,

Having considered the report of the Committee on Disarmament,

Noting with concern that the Committee on Disarmament was not able to start negotiations on the question during its 1983 session,

Taking into account the deliberations on this item at its thirty-eighth session,

Convinced that the prevention of nuclear war and the reduction of the risks of nuclear war are matters of the highest priority and of vital interest to all the peoples of the world,

1.   *Again requests* the Conference on Disarmament to undertake, as a matter of the highest priority, negotiations with a view to achieving agreement on appropriate and practical measures for the prevention of nuclear war, taking into account the documents referred to in General Assembly resolution 37/78 I as well as other existing proposals and future initiatives;

2.   *Further requests* the Conference on Disarmament to establish for that purpose an *ad hoc* working group on the subject at the beginning of its 1984 session;

3.   *Decides* to include in the provisional agenda of its thirty-ninth session the item entitled "Prevention of nuclear war: report of the Conference on Disarmament".

General Assembly resolution 38/183 G

20 December 1983   Meeting 103   128-0-20 (recorded vote)

Approved by First Committee (A/38/628) by recorded vote (107-0-18), 23 November (meeting 39); 18-nation draft (A/C.1/38/L.19); agenda item 50 *(h)*.

Sponsors: Algeria, Argentina, Bangladesh, Brazil, Colombia, Congo, Ecuador, Egypt, German Democratic Republic, India, Indonesia, Mexico, Pakistan, Romania, Sudan, Uruguay, Venezuela, Yugoslavia.

Meeting numbers. GA 38th session: 1st Committee 3-10, 12-31, 38, 39; plenary 103.

Recorded vote in Assembly as follows:

In favour: Afghanistan, Algeria, Angola, Antigua and Barbuda, Argentina, Austria, Bahamas, Bahrain, Bangladesh, Barbados, Belize, Benin, Bhutan, Bolivia, Botswana, Brazil, Bulgaria, Burma, Burundi, Byelorussian SSR, Cape Verde, Central African Republic, Chad, Chile, China, Colombia, Congo, Costa Rica, Cuba, Cyprus, Czechoslovakia, Democratic Kampuchea, Democratic Yemen, Djibouti, Dominica, Dominican Republic, Ecuador, Egypt, El Salvador, Ethiopia, Fiji, Finland, Gabon, Gambia, German Democratic Republic, Ghana, Greece, Guatemala, Guinea, Guinea-Bissau, Guyana, Honduras, Hungary, India, Indonesia, Iran, Iraq, Ireland, Israel, Jamaica, Jordan, Kenya, Kuwait, Lao People's Democratic Republic, Lebanon, Lesotho, Liberia, Libyan Arab Jamahiriya, Madagascar, Malawi, Malaysia, Maldives, Mali, Malta, Mauritania, Mauritius, Mexico, Mongolia, Morocco, Mozambique, Nepal, Nicaragua, Niger, Nigeria, Oman, Pakistan, Panama, Papua New Guinea, Paraguay, Peru, Philippines, Poland, Qatar, Romania, Rwanda, Saint Lucia, Saint Vincent and the Grenadines, Sao Tome and Principe, Saudi Arabia, Senegal, Sierra Leone, Singapore, Sri Lanka, Sudan, Suriname, Swaziland, Sweden, Syrian Arab Republic, Thailand, Togo, Trinidad and Tobago, Tunisia, Uganda, Ukrainian SSR, USSR, United Arab Emirates, United Republic of Cameroon, United Republic of Tanzania, Upper Volta, Uruguay, Vanuatu, Venezuela, Viet Nam, Yemen, Yugoslavia, Zaire, Zambia, Zimbabwe.

Against: None.

Abstaining: Australia, Belgium, Canada, Denmark, France, Germany, Federal Republic of, Haiti, Iceland, Italy, Ivory Coast, Japan, Luxembourg, Netherlands, New Zealand, Norway, Portugal, Spain, Turkey, United Kingdom, United States.

In explanation of vote, Belgium said the text prejudged the form that the work of the Conference on Disarmament should take; consensus might have been possible had the language been less confining. The United Kingdom emphasized that it continued to set the prevention of nuclear war in the context of preventing war in general, because the causes of war, whether conventional or nuclear, were the same; the unwillingness of cer-

tain delegations to accept that fact had delayed reaching agreement on an agenda for the Committee on Disarmament in 1983, and contributed to that body's failure to agree to a thorough discussion on the subject, as an essential first stage for identifying areas where negotiation might be possible. Mongolia expressed the hope that, at the 1984 session of the Conference on Disarmament, the Western members would display a spirit of co-operation and a willingness to negotiate on the prevention of nuclear war and on nuclear disarmament. Oman said it supported any efforts to prevent nuclear war.

Proposed nuclear-weapon freeze

GENERAL ASSEMBLY ACTION

In December 1983, the General Assembly adopted three resolutions (38/73 B, 38/73 E and 38/76) on nuclear-weapon freeze proposals.

Resolution 38/76 was based on a draft which had accompanied a USSR proposal of 4 October[23] for inclusion of a new item entitled "Nuclear-weapon freeze" in the agenda of the Assembly's thirty-eighth (1983) session.

On 15 December, the General Assembly adopted by recorded vote resolution 38/73 B, as recommended by the First Committee.

Freeze on nuclear weapons

The General Assembly,

Recalling its resolution 37/100 A of 13 December 1982,

Convinced that in this nuclear age lasting world peace can be based only on the attainment of the goal of general and complete disarmament under effective international control,

Further convinced that the highest priority objectives in the field of disarmament have to be nuclear disarmament and the elimination of all weapons of mass destruction,

Recognizing the urgent need to halt the arms race, particularly in nuclear weapons,

Recognizing further the urgent need for a negotiated reduction of nuclear-weapon stockpiles leading to their complete elimination,

Noting with deep concern that nuclear-weapon States have not so far taken any action in response to the call made in resolution 37/100 A,

1.   *Once again calls upon* all nuclear-weapon States to agree to a freeze on nuclear weapons, which would, *inter alia,* provide for a simultaneous total stoppage of any further production of nuclear weapons and a complete cut-off in the production of fissionable material for weapons purposes;

2.   *Decides* to include in the provisional agenda of its thirty-ninth session the item entitled "Freeze on nuclear weapons".

General Assembly resolution 38/73 B

15 December 1983   Meeting 97   124-15-7 (recorded vote)

Approved by First Committee (A/38/641) by recorded vote (101-15-7), 22 November (meeting 37); 2-nation draft (A/C.1/38/L.34); agenda item 63 *(a)*.

Sponsors: India, Mali.

Meeting numbers. GA 38th session: 1st Committee 3-10, 12-33, 36, 37; plenary 97.

Recorded vote in Assembly as follows:

In favour: Afghanistan, Algeria, Angola, Antigua and Barbuda, Argentina, Austria, Bahamas, Bahrain, Bangladesh, Barbados, Belize, Benin, Bhutan, Bolivia, Botswana, Brazil, Bulgaria, Burma, Burundi, Byelorussian SSR, Cape Verde, Central African Republic, Chad, Chile, Colombia, Congo, Costa Rica, Cuba, Cyprus, Czechoslovakia, Democratic Yemen, Denmark, Djibouti, Dominican Republic, Ecuador, Egypt, El Salvador, Ethiopia, Fiji, Finland, Gabon, Gambia, German Democratic Republic, Greece, Grenada, Guatemala, Guinea, Guyana, Haiti, Honduras, Hungary, India, Indonesia, Iran, Iraq, Ireland, Ivory Coast, Jamaica, Jordan, Kenya, Kuwait, Lao People's Democratic Republic, Lebanon, Lesotho, Liberia, Libyan Arab Jamahiriya, Madagascar, Malawi, Malaysia, Maldives, Mali, Mauritania, Mauritius, Mexico, Mongolia, Morocco, Mozambique, Nepal, Nicaragua, Niger, Nigeria, Oman, Pakistan, Panama, Papua New Guinea, Paraguay, Peru, Philippines, Poland, Qatar, Romania, Rwanda, Sao Tome and Principe, Saudi Arabia, Senegal, Seychelles, Sierra Leone, Singapore, Solomon Islands, Sri Lanka, Sudan, Suriname, Swaziland, Sweden, Syrian Arab Republic, Thailand, Togo, Trinidad and Tobago, Tunisia, Uganda, Ukrainian SSR, USSR, United Arab Emirates, United Republic of Cameroon, United Republic of Tanzania, Upper Volta, Uruguay, Vanuatu, Venezuela, Viet Nam, Yemen, Yugoslavia, Zambia, Zimbabwe.

Against: Belgium, Canada, France, Germany, Federal Republic of, Israel, Italy, Luxembourg, Netherlands, New Zealand, Norway, Portugal, Spain, Turkey, United Kingdom, United States.

Abstaining: Australia, China, Ghana,[a] Iceland, Japan, Saint Lucia, Zaire.

[a]Later advised the Secretariat it had intended to vote in favour.

On the recommendation of the First Committee, the General Assembly, on 15 December, adopted by recorded vote resolution 38/73 E.

Nuclear-arms freeze

The General Assembly,

Recalling that in the Final Document of the Tenth Special Session of the General Assembly, the first special session devoted to disarmament, adopted in 1978 and unanimously and categorically reaffirmed in 1982 during the twelfth special session of the General Assembly, the second special session devoted to disarmament, the Assembly expressed deep concern over the threat to the very survival of mankind posed by the existence of nuclear weapons and the continuing arms race,

Recalling also that, on those occasions, it pointed out that existing arsenals of nuclear weapons are more than sufficient to destroy all life on Earth and stressed that mankind is therefore confronted with a choice: halt the arms race and proceed to disarmament, or face annihilation,

Noting that the conditions prevailing today are a source of even more serious concern than those existing in 1978 because of several factors such as the deterioration of the international situation, the increase in the accuracy, speed and destructive power of nuclear weapons, the promotion of illusory doctrines of "limited" or "winnable" nuclear war and the many false alarms which have occurred owing to the malfunctioning of computers,

Noting also that at the Seventh Conference of Heads of State or Government of Non-Aligned Countries, held at New Delhi from 7 to 12 March 1983, it was declared that the renewed escalation in the nuclear-arms race, both in its quantitative and qualitative dimensions, as well as reliance on doctrines of nuclear deterrence, has heightened the risk of the outbreak of nuclear war and led to greater insecurity and instability in international relations,

Believing that it is a matter of the utmost urgency to stop any further increase in the awesome arsenals of the two major nuclear-weapon States, which already have ample retaliatory power and a frightening overkill capacity,

Believing also that it is equally urgent to activate negotiations for the substantial reduction and qualitative limitation of nuclear arms,

Considering that a nuclear-arms freeze, while not an end in itself, would constitute the most effective first step for the achievement of the above-mentioned two objectives, since it would provide a favourable environment for the conduct of the reduction negotiations while, at the same time, preventing the continued increase and qualitative improvement of existing nuclear weaponry during the period when the negotiations would take place,

Firmly convinced that at present the conditions are most propitious for such a freeze, since the Union of Soviet Socialist Republics and the United States of America are now equivalent in nuclear military power and it seems evident that there exists between them an overall rough parity,

Conscious that the mere application of the systems of surveillance, verification and control already agreed upon in some previous cases would be sufficient to provide a reasonable guarantee of faithful compliance with the undertakings derived from the freeze,

Convinced that it would be to the benefit of all other States possessing nuclear weapons to follow the example of the two major nuclear-weapon States as soon as positive results derived from the freeze agreed by them have been obtained,

1. *Urges once more* the Union of Soviet Socialist Republics and the United States of America, as the two major nuclear-weapon States, to proclaim, either through simultaneous unilateral declarations or through a joint declaration, an immediate nuclear-arms freeze, which would be a first step towards the comprehensive programme of disarmament and whose structure and scope would:

   (a) Embrace:

   (i) A comprehensive test ban of nuclear weapons and of their delivery vehicles;

   (ii) The complete cessation of the manufacture of nuclear weapons and of their delivery vehicles;

   (iii) A ban on all further deployment of nuclear weapons and of their delivery vehicles;

   (iv) The complete cessation of the production of fissionable material for weapons purposes;

   (b) Be subject to all the relevant measures and procedures of verification which have already been agreed by the parties in the case of the SALT I and SALT II treaties, as well as those agreed upon in principle by them during the preparatory trilateral negotiations on the comprehensive test ban held at Geneva;

   (c) Be of an initial five-year duration, subject to prolongation in the event of other nuclear-weapon States joining in such a freeze, as the General Assembly expects them to do;

2. *Requests* the above-mentioned two major nuclear-weapon States to submit a joint report or two separate reports to the General Assembly, prior to the opening of its thirty-ninth session, on the implementation of the present resolution;

3. *Decides* to include in the provisional agenda of its thirty-ninth session an item entitled "Implementation of General Assembly resolution 38/73 E on a nuclear-arms freeze".

General Assembly resolution 38/73 E

15 December 1983   Meeting 97   124-13-8 (recorded vote)

Approved by First Committee (A/38/641) by recorded vote (101-14-7), 22 November (meeting 37); 7-nation draft (A/C.1/38/L.43); agenda item 63 *(a)*.
Sponsors: Colombia, Ecuador, Indonesia, Mexico, Pakistan, Sweden, Uruguay.
Meeting numbers. GA 38th session: 1st Committee 3-10, 12-33, 36, 37; plenary 97.

Recorded vote in Assembly as follows:

In favour: Afghanistan, Algeria, Angola, Antigua and Barbuda, Argentina, Austria, Bahrain, Bangladesh, Barbados, Belize, Benin, Bhutan, Bolivia, Botswana, Brazil, Bulgaria, Burma, Burundi, Byelorussian SSR, Cape Verde, Central African Republic, Chad, Chile, Colombia, Congo, Costa Rica, Cuba, Cyprus, Czechoslovakia, Democratic Yemen, Denmark, Djibouti, Dominican Republic, Ecuador, Egypt, El Salvador, Ethiopia, Fiji, Finland, Gabon, Gambia, German Democratic Republic, Ghana, Greece, Grenada, Guatemala, Guinea, Guyana, Haiti, Honduras, Hungary, India, Indonesia, Iran, Iraq, Ireland, Ivory Coast, Jamaica, Jordan, Kenya, Kuwait, Lao People's Democratic Republic, Lebanon, Lesotho, Liberia, Libyan Arab Jamahiriya, Madagascar, Malawi, Malaysia, Maldives, Mali, Malta, Mauritania, Mauritius, Mexico, Mongolia, Morocco, Mozambique, Nepal, Nicaragua, Niger, Nigeria, Oman, Pakistan, Panama, Papua New Guinea, Paraguay, Peru, Philippines, Poland, Qatar, Romania, Rwanda, Sao Tome and Principe, Saudi Arabia, Senegal, Seychelles, Sierra Leone, Singapore, Solomon Islands, Sri Lanka, Sudan, Suriname, Swaziland, Sweden, Syrian Arab Republic, Togo, Trinidad and Tobago, Tunisia, Uganda, Ukrainian SSR, USSR, United Arab Emirates, United Republic of Cameroon, United Republic of Tanzania, Upper Volta, Uruguay, Vanuatu, Venezuela, Viet Nam, Yemen, Yugoslavia, Zambia, Zimbabwe.

Against: Belgium, Canada, France, Germany, Federal Republic of, Israel, Italy, Japan, Luxembourg, New Zealand, Portugal, Turkey, United Kingdom, United States.

Abstaining: Australia, Bahamas, Iceland, Netherlands, Norway, Saint Lucia, Spain, Zaire.

On 15 December, the General Assembly adopted by recorded vote resolution 38/76, the draft of which was recommended by the First Committee.

Nuclear-weapon freeze

The General Assembly,

Expressing its alarm that the continuing nuclear-arms race seriously increases the risk of the outbreak of a nuclear war,

Taking into account the great responsibility of nuclear States for the preservation of universal peace and the prevention of nuclear war,

Recalling its resolution 37/100 B of 13 December 1982, in which it expressed the firm conviction that the existing conditions were most propitious for a nuclear-weapon freeze,

1. *Urges* all nuclear-weapon States to proceed to freeze, under appropriate verification, all nuclear weapons in their possession both in quantitative and qualitative terms, namely:

(a) To cease the buildup of all components of nuclear arsenals, including all kinds of nuclear-weapon delivery systems and all kinds of nuclear weapons;

(b) Not to deploy nuclear weapons of new kinds and types;

(c) To establish a moratorium on all tests of nuclear weapons and on tests of new kinds and types of their delivery systems;

(d) To stop the production of fissionable materials for the purpose of creating nuclear weapons;

2. *Calls upon* the Union of Soviet Socialist Republics and the United States of America, which possess the largest nuclear arsenals, to freeze, in the first place and simultaneously, their nuclear weapons on a bilateral basis by way of example to the other nuclear States;

3. *Believes* that all the other nuclear-weapon States should subsequently and as soon as possible freeze their nuclear weapons;

4. *Stresses* the urgent need to intensify efforts aimed at the speedy achievement of agreements on substantial limitations and radical reductions of nuclear weapons with a view to their complete elimination as the ultimate goal.

General Assembly resolution 38/76

15 December 1983   Meeting 97   108-18-20 (recorded vote)

Approved by First Committee (A/38/649) by recorded vote (84-19-17), 22 November (meeting 37); 9-nation draft (A/C.1/38/L.2); agenda item 144.

Sponsors: Angola, Bulgaria, Byelorussian SSR, German Democratic Republic, Hungary, Mongolia, Poland, Ukrainian SSR, USSR.

Meeting numbers. GA 38th session: General Committee 4; 1st Committee 3-10, 12-33, 36, 37; plenary 97.

Recorded vote in Assembly as follows:

In favour: Afghanistan, Algeria, Angola, Antigua and Barbuda, Argentina, Austria, Bahamas, Bahrain, Bangladesh, Barbados, Belize, Benin, Bhutan, Bolivia, Botswana, Brazil, Bulgaria, Burma, Burundi, Byelorussian SSR, Cape Verde, Central African Republic, Chile, Colombia, Congo, Cuba, Cyprus, Czechoslovakia, Democratic Yemen, Ecuador, Egypt, El Salvador, Ethiopia, Fiji, Finland, Gabon, Gambia, German Democratic Republic, Ghana, Greece, Grenada, Guinea, Guyana, Haiti, Hungary, India, Indonesia, Iran, Iraq, Ireland, Jamaica, Jordan, Kenya, Kuwait, Lao People's Democratic Republic, Lesotho, Libyan Arab Jamahiriya, Madagascar, Malaysia, Maldives, Mali, Mauritania, Mauritius, Mexico, Mongolia, Mozambique, Nepal, Nicaragua, Niger, Nigeria, Oman, Pakistan, Panama, Papua New Guinea, Peru, Poland, Qatar, Romania, Rwanda, Sao Tome and Principe, Saudi Arabia, Senegal, Seychelles, Sierra Leone, Singapore, Solomon Islands, Sri Lanka, Sudan, Suriname, Syrian Arab Republic, Thailand, Togo, Trinidad and Tobago, Tunisia, Uganda, Ukrainian SSR, USSR, United Arab Emirates, United Republic of Cameroon, United Republic of Tanzania, Upper Volta, Vanuatu, Venezuela, Viet Nam, Yemen, Yugoslavia, Zambia, Zimbabwe.

Against: Belgium, Canada, Denmark, France, Germany, Federal Republic of, Iceland, Israel, Italy, Japan, Luxembourg, Netherlands, New Zealand, Norway, Portugal, Spain, Turkey, United Kingdom, United States.

Abstaining: Australia, Chad, China, Costa Rica, Dominican Republic, Guatemala, Honduras, Ivory Coast, Lebanon, Liberia, Malawi, Morocco, Paraguay, Philippines, Saint Lucia, Somalia, Swaziland, Sweden, Uruguay, Zaire.

A number of States explained in single statements their positions on the three texts which became resolutions 38/73 B and E and 38/76.

Belgium, France, the Federal Republic of Germany, the Netherlands and the United States maintained that a freeze at existing levels was tantamount to expecting the Western States to acquiesce in a codification of the existing imbalances and USSR superiority and to live in a position of destabilizing military vulnerability under threat, unable to resort to adequate countermeasures. Similarly, Norway asserted that ongoing nuclear disarmament efforts should not be complicated by a call for a freeze that would result in the preservation of serious military imbalances; it emphasized the need to attain agreed substantial reductions and reduce imbalances in nuclear arsenals. The United States added that nuclear-freeze proposals, however well-intentioned, would decrease international stability and ultimately increase the danger of war; along with France, it asserted that a freeze would be difficult to verify and that the relevant negotiations would be lengthy and complex. Belgium also felt that negotiations on a freeze would add to the difficulties in the existing negotiations in the area of verification. The Federal Republic of Germany asserted that any freeze, to be acceptable, needed adequate verification embodied in firm contractual commitments. The Netherlands considered that the sponsors had grossly underestimated the verification problems. Australia did not believe that the three texts provided the balance and verifiability crucial to maintaining stability and confidence.

Norway found some positive elements in the text which became resolution 38/73 E, including, though somewhat insufficient, a reference to verification and the provisions on a comprehensive test ban. Costa Rica said its support for the drafts which became resolutions 38/73 B and E was based, in part, on their recognition of the need for verification and control; it did not support the other draft for lack of guarantees for verification. Zaire said a freeze, in the absence of effective verification measures, would seemingly consist of keeping nuclear weapons ready for use; its votes were aimed at inciting all negotiators to provide evidence of greater flexibility in their discussions.

France, the Federal Republic of Germany and the United States maintained that a Power might benefit from a freeze, and thus it could have a negative effect on that Power's readiness to negotiate seriously for reductions. France added that negotiations should begin by defining and establishing a balance satisfactory to both sides. The Netherlands said a declaratory type of freeze could undermine the current bilateral negotiations, as did the United States, which believed that a freeze would make significant arms control more difficult. For Costa Rica, however, the text which became resolution 38/73 E recognized the freeze as the most effective first step for stopping the nuclear-arms race and encouraging negotiations for reductions. The Netherlands rejected the fourth preambular paragraph in that text for what it considered unwarranted mention of nuclear-deterrence strategy.

The German Democratic Republic, which supported all the texts, viewed as unfounded allegations of USSR superiority in the nuclear field and of difficulties regarding verification.

The USSR regarded the sixth preambular paragraph of the text which became resolution 38/73 B as relating to nuclear-weapon States that spoke against a freeze. It asserted that the countries possessing the largest nuclear arsenals—the USSR and the United States—should set an example to other nuclear-weapon Powers; it added that a call it had made in June 1983 to nuclear Powers to freeze all existing stockpiles had not met a positive response.

Indonesia, supporting the three texts, stressed that a freeze was a means and not an end in itself, and that the importance of such a measure should be judged in conjunction with the last paragraph of resolution 38/76. Greece expressed support for all efforts aimed at reducing nuclear weapons to the lowest possible level; it also felt that conventional weapons should be dealt with on an equal footing, since modern technology had made them weapons of mass destruction.

Draft convention against nuclear weapons

GENERAL ASSEMBLY ACTION

On the recommendation of the First Committee, the General Assembly, on 15 December 1983, adopted by recorded vote resolution 38/73 G concerning a possible convention banning the use of nuclear weapons, a draft of which was annexed to the resolution to serve as a basis for negotiations in the Conference on Disarmament.

Convention on the Prohibition of the Use of Nuclear Weapons

The General Assembly,

Alarmed by the threat to the survival of mankind and to the life-sustaining system posed by nuclear weapons and by their use, inherent in concepts of deterrence,

Conscious of an increased danger of nuclear war as a result of the intensification of the nuclear-arms race and the serious deterioration of the international situation,

Convinced that nuclear disarmament is essential for the prevention of nuclear war and for the strengthening of international peace and security,

Further convinced that a prohibition of the use or threat of use of nuclear weapons would be a step towards the complete elimination of nuclear weapons leading to general and complete disarmament under strict and effective international control,

Recalling that, in paragraph 58 of the Final Document of the Tenth Special Session of the General Assembly, it is stated that all States should actively participate in efforts to bring about conditions in international relations among States in which a code of peaceful conduct of nations in international affairs could be agreed upon and which would preclude the use or threat of use of nuclear weapons,

Reaffirming that the use of nuclear weapons would be a violation of the Charter of the United Nations and a crime against humanity, as declared in its resolutions 1653(XVI) of 24 November 1961, 33/71 B of 14 December 1978, 34/83 G of 11 December 1979, 35/152 D of 12 December 1980 and 36/92 I of 9 December 1981,

Noting with regret that the Committee on Disarmament, during its session in 1983, was not able to undertake negotiations with a view to achieving agreement on an international convention prohibiting the use or threat of use of nuclear weapons under any circumstances, taking as a basis the text annexed to General Assembly resolution 37/100 C of 13 December 1982,

1. *Reiterates its request* to the Conference on Disarmament to commence negotiations, as a matter of priority, in order to achieve agreement on an international convention prohibiting the use or threat of use of nuclear weapons under any circumstances, taking as a basis the text of the draft Convention on the Prohibition of the Use of Nuclear Weapons annexed to the present resolution;

2. *Further requests* the Conference on Disarmament to report to the General Assembly at its thirty-ninth session on the results of those negotiations.

ANNEX
Draft Convention on the Prohibition of the Use of Nuclear Weapons

The States Parties to this Convention,

Alarmed by the threat to the very survival of mankind posed by the existence of nuclear weapons,

Convinced that any use of nuclear weapons constitutes a violation of the Charter of the United Nations and a crime against humanity,

Convinced that this Convention would be a step towards the complete elimination of nuclear weapons leading to general and complete disarmament under strict and effective international control,

Determined to continue negotiations for the achievement of this goal,

Have agreed as follows:

Article 1

The States Parties to this Convention solemnly undertake not to use or threaten to use nuclear weapons under any circumstances.

Article 2

This Convention shall be of unlimited duration.

Article 3

1. This Convention shall be open to all States for signature. Any State which does not sign the Convention before its entry into force in accordance with paragraph 3 of this article may accede to it at any time.

2. This Convention shall be subject to ratification by signatory States. Instruments of ratification or accession shall be deposited with the Secretary-General of the United Nations.

3. This Convention shall enter into force on the deposit of instruments of ratification by twenty-five Governments, including the Governments of the five nuclear-weapon States, in accordance with paragraph 2 of this article.

4. For States whose instruments of ratification or accession are deposited after the entry into force of this Convention, it shall enter into force on the date of the deposit of their instruments of ratification or accession.

5. The depositary shall promptly inform all signatory and acceding States of the date of each signature, the date of deposit of each instrument of ratification or accession and the date of the entry into force of this Convention, as well as of the receipt of other notices.

6. This Convention shall be registered by the depositary in accordance with Article 102 of the Charter of the United Nations.

Article 4

This Convention, of which the Arabic, Chinese, English, French, Russian and Spanish texts are equally authentic, shall be deposited with the Secretary-General of the United Nations, who shall send duly certified copies thereof to the Governments of the signatory and acceding States.

IN WITNESS WHEREOF, the undersigned, being duly authorized thereto by their respective Governments, have signed this Convention, opened for signature at _____, on the _____ day of _____ one thousand nine hundred and _____.

General Assembly resolution 38/73 G

15 December 1983   Meeting 97   126-17-6 (recorded vote)

Approved by First Committee (A/38/641) by recorded vote (104-17-6), 23 November (meeting 39); 16-nation draft (A/C.1/38/L.55); agenda item 63 *(c)*.

Sponsors: Algeria, Argentina, Bahamas, Bangladesh, Bhutan, Congo, Ecuador, Egypt, Ethiopia, India, Indonesia, Madagascar, Nigeria, Romania, Viet Nam, Yugoslavia.

Meeting numbers. GA 38th session: 1st Committee 3-10, 12-31, 33, 39; plenary 97.

Recorded vote in Assembly as follows:

In favour: Afghanistan, Algeria, Angola, Antigua and Barbuda, Argentina, Bahamas, Bahrain, Bangladesh, Barbados, Belize, Benin, Bhutan, Bolivia, Botswana, Brazil, Bulgaria, Burma, Burundi, Byelorussian SSR, Cape Verde, Central African Republic, Chad, Chile, China, Colombia, Congo, Costa Rica, Cuba, Cyprus, Czechoslovakia, Democratic Kampuchea, Democratic Yemen, Djibouti, Dominican Republic, Ecuador, Egypt, El Salvador, Ethiopia, Fiji, Finland, Gabon, Gambia, German Democratic Republic, Ghana, Grenada, Guatemala, Guinea, Guyana, Haiti, Honduras, Hungary, India, Indonesia, Iran, Iraq, Ivory Coast, Jamaica, Jordan, Kenya, Kuwait, Lao People's Democratic Republic, Lebanon, Lesotho, Liberia, Libyan Arab Jamahiriya, Madagascar, Malawi, Malaysia, Maldives, Mali, Malta, Mauritania, Mauritius, Mexico, Mongolia, Morocco, Mozambique, Nepal, Nicaragua, Niger, Nigeria, Oman, Pakistan, Panama, Papua New Guinea, Paraguay, Peru, Poland, Qatar, Romania, Rwanda, Saint Lucia, Sao Tome and Principe, Saudi Arabia, Senegal, Seychelles, Sierra Leone, Singapore, Solomon Islands, Somalia, Sri Lanka, Sudan, Suriname, Swaziland, Sweden, Syrian Arab Republic, Thailand, Togo, Trinidad and Tobago, Tunisia, Uganda, Ukrainian SSR, USSR, United Arab Emirates, United Republic of Cameroon, United Republic of Tanzania, Upper Volta, Uruguay, Vanuatu, Venezuela, Viet Nam, Yemen, Yugoslavia, Zaire, Zambia, Zimbabwe.

Against: Australia, Belgium, Canada, Denmark, France, Germany, Federal Republic of, Iceland, Italy, Luxembourg, Netherlands, New Zealand, Norway, Portugal, Spain, Turkey, United Kingdom, United States.

Abstaining: Austria, Greece, Ireland, Israel, Japan, Philippines.

In explanation of vote, Australia considered that a convention prohibiting the use of nuclear weapons could lull the international community into a false sense of security and was an implausible way of seeking to prevent nuclear war; what was needed was a stable, mutual deterrence and viable measures of preventing all war. It was joined by Sweden in favouring balanced reductions of nuclear weapons, leading to their elimination. Sweden, while sharing the text's objectives, expressed reservations on the sixth preambular paragraph which, it said, provided a legally contestable interpretation of the United Nations Charter.

Proposed negotiations on the neutron bomb

For the third consecutive year, the General Assembly requested, in its 1983 resolution 38/183 C, that the Conference on Disarmament (as the Committee on Disarmament would be known in 1984) start without delay negotiations with a view to concluding a convention prohibiting the development, production, stockpiling, deployment and use of nuclear neutron weapons, also known as enhanced radiation weapons.

The Democratic People's Republic of Korea, in a letter of 16 May 1983, asserted that the United States planned to deploy neutron weapons in the Republic of Korea; this charge was refuted as propaganda by the Republic of Korea in a letter of 23 May (see Chapter VI of this section).

GENERAL ASSEMBLY ACTION

As recommended by the First Committee, the General Assembly, on 20 December 1983, adopted by recorded vote resolution 38/183 C.

Prohibition of the nuclear neutron weapon

The General Assembly,

Recalling paragraph 50 of the Final Document of the Tenth Special Session of the General Assembly, in which it is stated that the achievement of nuclear disarmament will require urgent negotiation of agreements, *inter alia*, for the cessation of the qualitative improvement and development of nuclear-weapon systems, which is especially emphasized in paragraph 50 *(a)* of that Document,

Stressing that the nuclear neutron weapon represents a further step in the qualitative arms race in the field of nuclear weapons,

Reaffirming its resolutions 36/92 K of 9 December 1981 and 37/78 E of 9 December 1982,

Sharing the world-wide concern expressed by Member States, as well as by non-governmental organizations, about the continued and expanded production and introduction of the nuclear neutron weapon in military arsenals, which escalates the nuclear-arms race and significantly lowers the threshold of nuclear war,

Aware of the inhuman effects of that weapon, which constitutes a grave threat, particularly to the unprotected civilian population,

Noting the consideration by the Committee on Disarmament at its session in 1983 of issues connected with the cessation of the nuclear-arms race and nuclear disarmament, as well as the prohibition of the nuclear neutron weapon,

Regretting that the Committee on Disarmament was not able to reach agreement on the commencement of negotiations on the cessation of the nuclear-arms race and on nuclear disarmament or on the prohibition of the nuclear neutron weapon in an appropriate organizational framework,

1. *Reaffirms its request* to the Conference on Disarmament to start without delay negotiations within an appropriate organizational framework with a view to concluding a convention on the prohibition of the development, production, stockpiling, deployment and use of nuclear neutron weapons as an organic element of negotiations, as envisaged in paragraph 50 of the Final Document of the Tenth Special Session of the General Assembly;

2. *Requests* the Secretary-General to transmit to the Conference on Disarmament all documents relating to the consideration of this question by the General Assembly at its thirty-eighth session;

3. *Requests* the Conference on Disarmament to submit a report on this question to the General Assembly at its thirty-ninth session;

4. *Decides* to include in the provisional agenda of its thirty-ninth session the item entitled "Prohibition of the nuclear neutron weapon".

General Assembly resolution 38/183 C

20 December 1983   Meeting 103   74-12-57 (recorded vote)

Approved by First Committee (A/38/628) by recorded vote (56-12-47), 23 November (meeting 39); 20-nation draft (A/C.1/38/L.12); agenda item 50 *(f)*.

Sponsors: Afghanistan, Angola, Bulgaria, Byelorussian SSR, Cuba, Czechoslovakia, Democratic Yemen, Ethiopia, German Democratic Republic, Hungary, Lao People's Democratic Republic, Mongolia, Mozambique, Poland, Romania, Sao Tome and Principe, Syrian Arab Republic, Ukrainian SSR, Viet Nam, Zimbabwe.

Meeting numbers. GA 38th session: 1st Committee 3-10, 12-31, 38, 39; plenary 103.

Recorded vote in Assembly as follows:

In favour: Afghanistan, Algeria, Angola, Antigua and Barbuda, Bahrain, Barbados, Belize, Benin, Botswana, Bulgaria, Burundi, Byelorussian SSR, Cape Verde, Central African Republic, Congo, Cuba, Cyprus, Czechoslovakia, Democratic Yemen, Ecuador, Ethiopia, Fiji, Finland, German Democratic Republic, Ghana, Guinea, Guinea-Bissau, Hungary, India, Indonesia, Iran, Iraq, Jordan, Kenya, Lao People's Democratic Republic, Lesotho, Libyan Arab Jamahiriya, Madagascar, Malaysia, Mali, Mauritania, Mauritius, Mexico, Mongolia, Mozambique, Nicaragua, Nigeria, Panama, Papua New Guinea, Poland, Qatar, Romania, Rwanda, Sao Tome and Principe, Saudi Arabia, Sierra Leone, Syrian Arab Republic, Togo, Trinidad and Tobago, Tunisia, Uganda, Ukrainian SSR, USSR, United

Arab Emirates, United Republic of Cameroon, United Republic of Tanzania, Upper Volta, Uruguay, Vanuatu, Viet Nam, Yemen, Yugoslavia, Zambia, Zimbabwe.

Against: Belgium, Canada, France, Germany, Federal Republic of, Israel, Italy, Japan, Luxembourg, Portugal, Turkey, United Kingdom, United States.

Abstaining: Argentina, Australia, Austria, Bahamas, Bangladesh, Bhutan, Bolivia, Brazil, Burma, Chad, Chile, Colombia, Costa Rica, Denmark, Djibouti, Dominica, Dominican Republic, Egypt, El Salvador, Gambia, Greece, Guatemala, Guyana, Haiti, Honduras, Iceland, Ireland, Ivory Coast, Jamaica, Lebanon, Liberia, Malawi, Maldives, Morocco, Nepal, Netherlands, New Zealand, Niger, Norway, Oman, Pakistan, Paraguay, Peru, Philippines, Saint Lucia, Saint Vincent and the Grenadines, Senegal, Singapore, Spain, Sri Lanka, Sudan, Suriname, Swaziland, Sweden, Thailand, Venezuela, Zaire.

Explaining their votes, Bangladesh, Brazil, Egypt, Guyana, Ireland, Oman, Pakistan, the Sudan, Sweden and Zaire generally condemned the development and production of nuclear neutron weapons, but at the same time had serious reservations about the idea of prohibiting only one specific nuclear weapon or adopting a selective approach to the nuclear-arms race and nuclear disarmament. Denmark further stated that, while it would not accept nuclear neutron weapons on its territory, it considered the text as an undisguised attempt to split the Western allies in an important area of defence policy. Similarly, the Netherlands viewed the text as having been politically inspired and not genuinely serving the cause of disarmament.

Australia, which favoured the elimination of all nuclear weapons through negotiations, interpreted the text as lending credence to the view that the neutron weapon could be prohibited only as an organic element of negotiations on nuclear weapons as a whole; it did not agree that the neutron weapon could be the subject of a separate disarmament treaty, and it opposed the establishment in the Conference on Disarmament of a working group on that weapon. Sweden considered the reference to the Final Document, in paragraph 1, as an improvement on the previous year's resolution on the same subject.

India supported the text, saying that the nuclear neutron weapon was the manifestation of one of the particularly dangerous consequences of the nuclear-arms race, whose reversal should be negotiated by the Conference on Disarmament without delay.

Nuclear non-proliferation

In 1983, the General Assembly continued efforts to prevent the spread of nuclear weapons to countries other than known nuclear-weapon Powers, as reflected in resolutions 38/62 and 38/188 E (see below).

Throughout the year, the International Atomic Energy Agency (IAEA) continued its efforts concerning nuclear safeguards, particularly in relation to the 1968 Treaty on the Non-Proliferation of Nuclear Weapons (NPT) (see PART TWO, Chapter I). States were urged, in Assembly resolution 38/8, to ensure the effectiveness of the Agency's safeguards system.

Nuclear-weapon-free zones

The establishment of nuclear-weapon-free zones in various parts of the world was discussed in 1983 by the Disarmament Commission, the Committee on Disarmament and the General Assembly. A number of delegations considered that the 1967 Treaty for the Prohibition of Nuclear Weapons in Latin America (Treaty of Tlatelolco) should serve as a model for possible zones in other parts of the world. Along with the debate on the establishment of zones in Africa, the Middle East and South Asia, proposals were made for such zones in the Balkans and Northern and Central Europe, but no formal initiatives were taken on these proposals at the United Nations.

Group of Experts

Pursuant to a December 1982 General Assembly resolution,[24] the Secretary-General set up in 1983 the Group of Governmental Experts on Nuclear-Weapon-Free Zones to review and supplement a 1975 expert study entitled *Comprehensive study of the question of nuclear-weapon-free zones in all its aspects.*[25] The 21-member Group met twice during 1983. At an organizational session (14-18 March), it agreed on the study's structure and outline, and decided that the experts would submit written contributions to the Secretariat which would then produce a draft. This draft was discussed at the second session (25 July–5 August), and it was decided that further work would be carried out in 1984, before submission of the study to the Assembly later that year.

The Group consisted of experts from Algeria, Argentina, Australia, Bulgaria, China, Cuba, Egypt, Finland, France, the Federal Republic of Germany, India, Japan, Mexico, Pakistan, Poland, Romania, the USSR, the United Kingdom, the United Republic of Tanzania, the United States and Yugoslavia.

GENERAL ASSEMBLY ACTION

On the recommendation of the First Committee, the General Assembly, on 20 December 1983, adopted by recorded vote resolution 38/188 I.

Review of and supplement to the *Comprehensive study of the question of nuclear-weapon-free zones in all its aspects*

The General Assembly,

Recalling its resolution 37/99 F of 13 December 1982, in which it decided that a study should be undertaken to review and supplement the *Comprehensive study of the question of nuclear-weapon-free zones in all its aspects* in the light of information and experience accumulated since 1975,

Recalling also that in paragraph 61 of the Final Document of the Tenth Special Session of the General Assembly it was determined that the process of establishing nuclear-weapon-free zones should be encouraged, with the ultimate objective of achieving a world entirely free of nuclear weapons,

Considering that the documents submitted to the General Assembly at its thirty-eighth session on the question of nuclear-weapon-free zones, as well as the views expressed in the general debate on this particular subject, provide additional elements relevant to the updating of the study,

Requests the Secretary-General to transmit to the Group of Governmental Experts on Nuclear-Weapon-Free Zones, established by resolution 37/99 F, for its consideration and analysis all the relevant documents submitted to the General Assembly at its thirty-eighth session, as well as the records of the debate on the question of nuclear-weapon-free zones.

General Assembly resolution 38/188 I

20 December 1983   Meeting 103   146-0-3 (recorded vote)

Approved by First Committee (A/38/640) by recorded vote (125-0-3), 23 November (meeting 38); 9-nation draft (A/C.1/38/L.60); agenda item 62.

Sponsors: Argentina, Brazil, Colombia, Ecuador, Indonesia, Mexico, Uruguay, Venezuela, Yugoslavia.

Meeting numbers. GA 38th session: 1st Committee 3-10, 12-31, 33, 38; plenary 103.

Recorded vote in Assembly as follows:

In favour: Afghanistan, Algeria, Angola, Antigua and Barbuda, Argentina, Australia, Austria, Bahamas, Bahrain, Bangladesh, Barbados, Belgium, Belize, Benin, Bhutan, Bolivia, Botswana, Brazil, Bulgaria, Burma, Burundi, Byelorussian SSR, Canada, Cape Verde, Central African Republic, Chad, Chile, China, Colombia, Congo, Costa Rica, Cuba, Cyprus, Czechoslovakia, Democratic Kampuchea, Democratic Yemen, Denmark, Djibouti, Dominica, Dominican Republic, Ecuador, Egypt, El Salvador, Ethiopia, Fiji, Finland, France, Gabon, Gambia, German Democratic Republic, Germany, Federal Republic of, Ghana, Greece, Guatemala, Guinea, Guinea-Bissau, Guyana, Haiti, Honduras, Hungary, Iceland, Indonesia, Iran, Iraq, Ireland, Israel, Italy, Ivory Coast, Jamaica, Japan, Jordan, Kenya, Kuwait, Lao People's Democratic Republic, Lebanon, Lesotho, Liberia, Libyan Arab Jamahiriya, Luxembourg, Madagascar, Malawi, Malaysia, Maldives, Mali, Malta, Mauritania, Mauritius, Mexico, Mongolia, Morocco, Mozambique, Nepal, Netherlands, New Zealand, Nicaragua, Niger, Nigeria, Norway, Oman, Pakistan, Panama, Papua New Guinea, Paraguay, Peru, Philippines, Poland, Portugal, Qatar, Romania, Rwanda, Saint Lucia, Saint Vincent and the Grenadines, Sao Tome and Principe, Saudi Arabia, Senegal, Sierra Leone, Singapore, Somalia, Spain, Sri Lanka, Sudan, Suriname, Swaziland, Sweden, Syrian Arab Republic, Thailand, Togo, Trinidad and Tobago, Tunisia, Turkey, Uganda, Ukrainian SSR, USSR, United Arab Emirates, United Republic of Cameroon, United Republic of Tanzania, Upper Volta, Uruguay, Vanuatu, Venezuela, Viet Nam, Yemen, Yugoslavia, Zaire, Zambia, Zimbabwe.

Against: None.

Abstaining: India, United Kingdom, United States.

India said that, while its position on nuclear-weapon-free zones remained unchanged, it abstained in the vote as the text was merely of a procedural character. While voting in favour, the Federal Republic of Germany considered the text unnecessary and felt that resolutions should not interfere with the orderly transaction of United Nations studies, according to their mandate.

Africa

The Declaration on the Denuclearization of Africa was adopted in 1964 by the Organization of African Unity (OAU).[26] The General Assembly in 1983 again called on all States to regard the continent as a nuclear-weapon-free zone.

GENERAL ASSEMBLY ACTION

On 20 December, the Assembly adopted by recorded vote resolution 38/181 A.

Implementation of the Declaration

The General Assembly,

Bearing in mind the Declaration on the Denuclearization of Africa adopted by the Assembly of Heads of State and Government of the Organization of African Unity at its first ordinary session, held at Cairo from 17 to 21 July 1964,

Recalling resolution 1652(XVI) of 24 November 1961, its earliest on the subject, as well as its resolutions 2033(XX) of 3 December 1965, 32/81 of 12 December 1977, 33/63 of 14 December 1978, 34/76 A of 11 December 1979, 35/146 B of 12 December 1980, 36/86 B of 9 December 1981 and 37/74 A of 9 December 1982, in which it called upon all States to consider and respect the continent of Africa and its surrounding areas as a nuclear-weapon-free zone,

Recalling that in its resolution 33/63 it vigorously condemned any overt or covert attempt by South Africa to introduce nuclear weapons into the continent of Africa and demanded that South Africa refrain forthwith from conducting any nuclear explosion in the continent of Africa or elsewhere,

Recalling its resolution 35/146 A of 12 December 1980, by which it, *inter alia*, expressed its appreciation to the Secretary-General for his report on South Africa's plan and capability in the nuclear field and expressed its deep alarm that the report of the Secretary-General had established South Africa's capability to manufacture nuclear weapons,

Reaffirming that South Africa's continued development of a nuclear capability seriously jeopardizes the realization of the objective of the Declaration and poses a grave threat not only to the security of African States but also to international peace and security,

Recalling also its resolution 37/100 F of 13 December 1982, by which it, *inter alia*, requested the Secretariat, in particular the Department for Disarmament Affairs, and the United Nations Institute for Disarmament Research to lend assistance to States and regional institutions which may request it in the context of regional disarmament measures taken at the initiative and with the participation of all the States concerned,

Taking note of the report of the Director of the United Nations Institute for Disarmament Research,

Taking note of the report of the Secretary-General on the activities of the Advisory Board on Disarmament Studies,

Taking note with concern of the report of the Disarmament Commission, in particular its paragraph 24 dealing with the question of the nuclear capability of South Africa,

Convinced of the urgent need for the international community to consider practical measures for the realization of the objective of the Declaration,

1. *Strongly reiterates* its call upon all States to consider and respect the continent of Africa and its surrounding areas as a nuclear-weapon-free zone;

2. *Reaffirms* that implementation of the Declaration on the Denuclearization of Africa adopted by African heads of State and Government would be a significant measure to prevent the proliferation of nuclear weapons and to promote international peace and security;

3. *Condemns* South Africa's continued pursuit of a nuclear capability and all forms of nuclear collaboration by any State, corporation, institution or individual

with the racist régime which enable it to frustrate the objective of the Declaration which seeks to keep Africa free from nuclear weapons;

4. *Calls upon* all States, corporations, institutions and individuals to terminate forthwith any form of collaboration with the racist régime of South Africa which enables it to frustrate the objective of the Declaration;

5. *Demands once again* that the racist régime of South Africa refrain from testing, manufacturing, deploying, transporting, storing, using or threatening to use nuclear weapons;

6. *Demands once again* that South Africa submit forthwith all its nuclear installations and facilities to inspection by the International Atomic Energy Agency;

7. *Requests* the United Nations Institute for Disarmament Research, in co-operation with the Department for Disarmament Affairs and in consultation with the Organization of African Unity, to provide data on the continued development of South Africa's nuclear capability;

8. *Requests* the Secretary-General to provide the necessary support to the United Nations Institute for Disarmament Research to enable it to carry out the task entrusted to it under the present resolution and for the Institute to submit a report to the Assembly at its thirty-ninth session;

9. *Decides* to include in the provisional agenda of its thirty-ninth session the item entitled "Implementation of the Declaration on the Denuclearization of Africa".

General Assembly resolution 38/181 A

20 December 1983   Meeting 103   142-0-6 (recorded vote)

Approved by First Committee (A/38/624) by recorded vote (121-0-6), 25 November (meeting 41); draft by Sierra Leone, for African Group (A/C.1/38/L.67/Rev.2); agenda item 46.

Financial implications. ACABQ, A/38/7/Add.21; 5th Committee, A/38/762; S-G, A/C.1/38/L.79, A/C.5/38/88.

Meeting numbers. GA 38th session: 1st Committee 3-10, 12-31, 33, 41; 5th Committee 68; plenary 103.

Recorded vote in Assembly as follows:

In favour: Afghanistan, Albania, Algeria, Angola, Antigua and Barbuda, Argentina, Australia, Austria, Bahamas, Bahrain, Bangladesh, Barbados, Belize, Benin, Bhutan, Bolivia, Botswana, Brazil, Bulgaria, Burma, Burundi, Byelorussian SSR, Canada, Cape Verde, Central African Republic, Chad, Chile, China, Colombia, Congo, Costa Rica, Cuba, Cyprus, Czechoslovakia, Democratic Kampuchea, Democratic Yemen, Denmark, Djibouti, Dominica, Dominican Republic, Ecuador, Egypt, El Salvador, Ethiopia, Fiji, Finland, Gabon, Gambia, German Democratic Republic, Germany, Federal Republic of, Ghana, Greece, Guatemala, Guinea, Guinea-Bissau, Guyana, Haiti, Honduras, Hungary, Iceland, India, Indonesia, Iran, Iraq, Ireland, Italy, Ivory Coast, Jamaica, Japan, Jordan, Kenya, Kuwait, Lao People's Democratic Republic, Lebanon, Liberia, Libyan Arab Jamahiriya, Luxembourg, Madagascar, Malawi, Malaysia, Maldives, Mali, Malta, Mauritania, Mauritius, Mexico, Mongolia, Morocco, Mozambique, Nepal, Netherlands, New Zealand, Nicaragua, Niger, Nigeria, Norway, Oman, Pakistan, Panama, Papua New Guinea, Peru, Philippines, Poland, Qatar, Romania, Rwanda, Saint Lucia, Saint Vincent and the Grenadines, Sao Tome and Principe, Saudi Arabia, Senegal, Sierra Leone, Singapore, Somalia, Spain, Sri Lanka, Sudan, Suriname, Swaziland, Sweden, Syrian Arab Republic, Thailand, Togo, Trinidad and Tobago, Tunisia, Turkey, Uganda, Ukrainian SSR, USSR, United Arab Emirates, United Republic of Cameroon, United Republic of Tanzania, Upper Volta, Uruguay, Vanuatu, Venezuela, Viet Nam, Yemen, Yugoslavia, Zaire, Zambia, Zimbabwe.

Against: None.

Abstaining: Belgium, France, Israel, Portugal, United Kingdom, United States.

On 25 November, the First Committee, before approving the draft as a whole, approved paragraph 8 of the twice-revised draft which became resolution 38/181 A by a recorded vote of 103 to 1 (United States), with 22 abstentions. On 20 December, the Assembly also voted separately on that paragraph and adopted it by a recorded vote of 123 to 1 (United States), with 22 abstentions.

In explanation of vote on paragraph 8, the United Kingdom and the United States asserted that the study should be financed within the budgetary limits of the United Nations; Canada agreed and said it preferred the original wording of the paragraph simply requesting the Director of the United Nations Institute for Disarmament Research (UNIDIR) to submit a report. The Federal Republic of Germany had similar reservations and considered the amounts contained in the financial implications to be exaggerated. Japan also felt that the paragraph lacked conclusive, supporting evidence. The USSR said that the paragraph implied a departure from the established practice of financing UNIDIR activities by voluntary contributions. The Netherlands reserved its position on the financial implications.

On the text as a whole, a number of countries, among them Australia and Portugal, expressed support for the denuclearization of Africa, or for calls to South Africa to become a party to NPT and for it to place all its nuclear installations under IAEA safeguards.

Bulgaria called for the immediate cessation of the support given to South Africa by certain Western countries, particularly in the military and nuclear field, which, it said, was the main obstacle to the denuclearization of Africa. Canada and the Netherlands welcomed the deletion from the 1983 text, as compared to its predecessors, of reference to the nuclear collaboration of certain Western countries and Israel with South Africa. While sharing that view, the Federal Republic of Germany had reservations on the second preambular paragraph and paragraph 1 which, in its view, ambiguously defined the confines of the future nuclear-weapon-free zone. The USSR said the call in paragraph 1 should not be allowed to affect the norms of international law, including the principle of freedom of navigation on the high seas.

As regards paragraphs 3 and 4, the Federal Republic of Germany saw need for their careful interpretation, while Malawi said it would have abstained had a separate vote been taken on those paragraphs because of their implicit call for sanctions. Spain also had reservations about paragraph 4. The United Kingdom, asserting that all States had the right to the peaceful uses of nuclear energy, said it was wrong to seek to limit that right in individual cases for political reasons. Belgium, France and Ireland also regretted the text's failure to distinguish between the uses of nuclear energy for peaceful or for military purposes, and between the corresponding types of co-operation. Portugal considered as excessive the wording relating to nuclear collaboration. The Netherlands believed,

however, that those paragraphs, read in conjunction with paragraph 6, made an implicit distinction between different types of nuclear collaboration.

The United States considered that the text contained intemperate language, which was unnecessary and potentially harmful to its underlying objective and which discouraged South Africa from implementing a non-proliferation policy. Austria and Japan also had reservations with regard to certain provisions in the text.

Albania said its affirmative vote was in keeping with its position of support for the cause of the African peoples against the racist régime of South Africa, but did not change its position as regards the question of nuclear-weapon-free zones.

The other 1983 disarmament resolution dealing with a nuclear-weapon-free Africa was 38/181 B, on nuclear weapons and South Africa (see below).

Nuclear weapons and South Africa

As in 1982, the Disarmament Commission[2] established in 1983 a working group (Working Group II) to consider, as requested by the General Assembly in a December 1982 resolution,[27] the question of South Africa's nuclear capability.

The Working Group, chaired by Davidson L. Hepburn (Bahamas), held 15 formal meetings and additional informal consultations between 13 May and 1 June, using a text submitted by Mauritius on behalf of the Group of African States members of the Commission as a basis for discussion. However, the consultations conducted by the Chairman revealed divergent positions regarding, *inter alia*, the legal and political interpretation to be placed on South Africa's actions and policy, the verification of its nuclear capability and its eligibility for access to nuclear energy for peaceful purposes. In the absence of a consensus text or recommendations, the Group agreed that two working papers, the one submitted and later revised by the African States and the other submitted by the Federal Republic of Germany, should be annexed to its report and taken as a basis for discussion at the Commission's 1984 session.

In a letter of 20 June[28] to the Secretary-General, Israel stated that various references in the African Group's paper were unfounded and devoid of truth.

In response to the 1982 Assembly resolution,[27] the Secretary-General submitted a report[29] on South Africa's nuclear capability in which he stated that he had followed closely South Africa's activities in that area, but had neither received nor identified any information regarding its nuclear evolution and therefore had nothing to add to his previous reports on the subject.

On the recommendation of the First Committee, the General Assembly, on 20 December 1983, adopted by recorded vote resolution 38/181 B.

Nuclear capability of South Africa

The General Assembly,

Recalling its resolutions 34/76 B of 11 December 1979, 35/146 A of 12 December 1980, 36/86 A of 9 December 1981 and 37/74 B of 9 December 1982,

Bearing in mind the Declaration on the Denuclearization of Africa adopted by the Assembly of Heads of State and Government of the Organization of African Unity at its first ordinary session, held at Cairo from 17 to 21 July 1964,

Recalling that, in the Final Document of the Tenth Special Session of the General Assembly, it noted that the accumulation of armaments and the acquisition of armaments technology by racist régimes, as well as their possible acquisition of nuclear weapons, presented a challenging and increasingly dangerous obstacle to a world community faced with the urgent need to disarm,

Taking note of resolution GC(XXVII)/RES/408 on South Africa's nuclear capabilities, adopted on 14 October 1983 by the General Conference of the International Atomic Energy Agency during its twenty-seventh regular session,

Recalling that, in its resolution 33/63 of 14 December 1978, it vigorously condemned any overt or covert attempt by South Africa to introduce nuclear weapons into the continent of Africa and demanded that South Africa refrain forthwith from conducting any nuclear explosion in the continent of Africa or elsewhere,

Recalling its resolution 35/146 A of 12 December 1980, by which it, *inter alia*, expressed its appreciation to the Secretary-General for his report on South Africa's plan and capability in the nuclear field and expressed its deep alarm that the report of the Secretary-General had established South Africa's capability to manufacture nuclear weapons,

Noting with regret that, despite international concern over the nuclear capability of South Africa and the recognized need to deal concretely and expeditiously with it, the Disarmament Commission failed to conclude consideration of this important item on its agenda with specific recommendations during its 1983 session,

Gravely concerned that South Africa, in flagrant violation of the principles of international law and the relevant provisions of the Charter of the United Nations, has not only continued but has in fact intensified its military attacks and other acts of aggression and subversion against independent States of southern Africa, in particular Lesotho, Mozambique and Angola, part of whose territory still remains occupied by South African forces,

Strongly condemning the military occupation by South African troops of parts of the territory of Angola in violation of its national sovereignty, independence and territorial integrity, and urging the immediate and unconditional withdrawal of South African troops from Angolan soil,

Expressing its grave disappointment that, despite repeated appeals by the international community, certain Western States and Israel have continued to collaborate with the racist régime of South Africa in the military and nuclear fields and that some of the same Western States have, by a ready recourse to the use of the veto, consistently frustrated every effort in the Security Council to deal decisively with the question of South Africa,

1. *Condemns* the massive buildup of South Africa's military machine, including its frenzied acquisition of nuclear-weapon capability for repressive and aggressive purposes and as an instrument of blackmail;

2. *Expresses its full support* for the Governments of the independent States of southern Africa in their efforts to guarantee and safeguard their territorial integrity and national sovereignty;

3. *Reaffirms* that the racist régime's acquisition of nuclear-weapon capability constitutes a very grave danger to international peace and security and, in particular, jeopardizes the security of African States and increases the danger of the proliferation of nuclear weapons;

4. *Requests* the Disarmament Commission to consider substantively and as a matter of priority South Africa's nuclear capability during its session in 1984, taking into account, *inter alia*, the findings contained in the report of the Secretary-General on South Africa's plan and capability in the nuclear field, with a view to adopting concrete recommendations on the question;

5. *Requests* the Security Council, for the purposes of disarmament and to fulfil its obligations and responsibilities for the maintenance of international peace and security, to take enforcement measures to prevent any racist régimes from acquiring arms or arms technology;

6. *Further requests* the Security Council to conclude expeditiously its consideration of the recommendations of its Committee established by resolution 421(1977) concerning the question of South Africa with a view to blocking the existing loopholes in the arms embargo so as to render it more effective and prohibiting, in particular, all forms of co-operation and collaboration with the racist régime of South Africa in the nuclear field;

7. *Condemns* all forms of nuclear collaboration by any State, corporation, institution or individual with the racist régime of South Africa since such collaboration enables it to frustrate, *inter alia*, the objective of the Declaration on the Denuclearization of Africa which seeks to keep Africa free from nuclear weapons;

8. *Condemns*, in particular, recent decisions by some Member States to grant licences to several corporations in their territories to provide equipment and technical and maintenance services for nuclear installations in South Africa;

9. *Calls upon* all States, corporations, institutions and individuals to terminate forthwith all military and nuclear collaboration with the racist régime, including the provision to it of such materials as computers, electronic equipment and related technology;

10. *Demands once again* that South Africa submit forthwith all its nuclear installations and facilities to inspection by the International Atomic Energy Agency;

11. *Requests* the Secretary-General to follow very closely South Africa's evolution in the nuclear field and to report thereon to the General Assembly at its thirty-ninth session.

General Assembly resolution 38/181 B

20 December 1983   Meeting 103   133-4-11 (recorded vote)

Approved by First Committee (A/38/624) by recorded vote (112-4-11), 25 November (meeting 41); draft by Sierra Leone, for African Group (A/C.1/38/L.68/Rev.2), orally revised; agenda item 46.

Meeting numbers. GA 38th session: 1st Committee 3-10, 12-31, 33, 41; plenary 103.

Recorded vote in Assembly as follows:

In favour: Afghanistan, Albania, Algeria, Angola, Antigua and Barbuda, Argentina, Austria, Bahamas, Bahrain, Bangladesh, Barbados, Belize, Benin, Bhutan, Bolivia, Botswana, Brazil, Bulgaria, Burma, Burundi, Byelorussian SSR, Cape Verde, Central African Republic, Chad, Chile, China, Colombia, Congo, Costa Rica, Cuba, Cyprus, Czechoslovakia, Democratic Kampuchea, Democratic Yemen, Denmark, Djibouti, Dominica, Dominican Republic, Ecuador, Egypt, El Salvador, Ethiopia, Fiji, Finland, Gabon, Gambia, German Democratic Republic, Ghana, Greece, Guatemala, Guinea, Guinea-Bissau, Guyana, Haiti, Honduras, Hungary, Iceland, India, Indonesia, Iran, Iraq, Ireland, Ivory Coast, Jamaica, Jordan, Kenya, Kuwait, Lao People's Democratic Republic, Lebanon, Liberia, Libyan Arab Jamahiriya, Madagascar, Malaysia, Maldives, Mali, Malta, Mauritania, Mauritius, Mexico, Mongolia, Morocco, Mozambique, Nepal, Nicaragua, Niger, Nigeria, Norway, Oman, Pakistan, Panama, Papua New Guinea, Peru, Philippines, Poland, Qatar, Romania, Rwanda, Saint Lucia, Saint Vincent and the Grenadines, Sao Tome and Principe, Saudi Arabia, Senegal, Sierra Leone, Singapore, Somalia, Spain, Sri Lanka, Sudan, Suriname, Swaziland, Sweden, Syrian Arab Republic, Thailand, Togo, Trinidad and Tobago, Tunisia, Turkey, Uganda, Ukrainian SSR, USSR, United Arab Emirates, United Kingdom, United Republic of Cameroon, United Republic of Tanzania, Upper Volta, Uruguay, Vanuatu, Venezuela, Viet Nam, Yemen, Yugoslavia, Zaire, Zambia, Zimbabwe.

Against: France, Israel, United Kingdom, United States.

Abstaining: Australia, Belgium, Canada, Germany, Federal Republic of, Italy, Japan, Luxembourg, Malawi, Netherlands, New Zealand, Portugal.

In explanation of vote, a number of countries expressed objection to the singling out of certain Western countries in the text. Denmark, on behalf also of Finland, Iceland, Norway and Sweden, deplored that approach as inappropriate and arbitrary, while the Netherlands considered it unwarranted. Ireland and Spain expressed similar reservations. Portugal considered the language in certain paragraphs to be excessive, particularly those referring to nuclear collaboration.

Bulgaria, on the other hand, urged certain Western countries to cease supporting South Africa immediately, particularly in the military and nuclear field.

France and Denmark (on behalf of the Nordic countries) stated that paragraph 5 was not in conformity with the provisions of the Charter of the United Nations regarding the distribution of responsibilities and powers between the General Assembly and the Security Council. Austria spoke similarly, and Spain had reservations about what it considered the vague language in that paragraph.

The United Kingdom, while believing that South Afica should become a party to NPT, called it wrong to limit, in individual cases for political reasons, the internationally recognized right of all States to apply and develop programmes for the peaceful uses of nuclear energy. Despite its agreement with the fundamental aims of the resolution, France asserted that the text of paragraphs 7 and 8 failed to distinguish between the peaceful and military uses of nuclear energy. Ireland had similar reservations, as did Spain, which felt the language in those paragraphs was also vague.

Australia did not agree with certain elements in the text, but expressed support for those which focused on South Africa's potential to increase the danger of nuclear proliferation. The Netherlands supported the request to the Security Council to look into the existing loopholes in the arms embargo against South Africa.

Albania said its affirmative vote, based on its support for the African cause against the racist régime of South Africa, did not change its position as regards nuclear-weapon-free zones.

For the United States, the draft contained intemperate language, which was unnecessary and potentially harmful to its underlying objectives. Sierra Leone, on behalf of the Group of African States, said the text's language could not be compared to the threat South Africa's *apartheid* policy posed to all African countries.

The question of nuclear weapons and South Africa was also dealt with in 1983 in Assembly resolutions 38/36 A, on the Namibia question; 38/39 G, on military and nuclear relations with South Africa; 38/181 A, on a nuclear-weapon-free zone in Africa; and 38/190, on implementation of the 1970 Declaration on international security (see Chapter IV of this section); and in decision 38/419, on military activity in Non-Self-Governing Territories (for texts, refer to INDEX OF RESOLUTIONS AND DECISIONS).

Throughout 1983, South Africa's military and nuclear relations with other States were kept under consideration by several United Nations bodies (see Chapter V of this section).

Europe

Disarmament Commission consideration. In 1983, the Disarmament Commission[2] established a working group (Working Group III) to deal with a report by the Independent Commission on Disarmament and Security Issues (ICDSI) entitled "Common Security—a programme for disarmament".[30] The report of ICDSI—a body of 17 independent international personalities also known as the Palme Commission—had been transmitted to the Disarmament Commission in response to a December 1982 General Assembly request.[31] Differing views were expressed in the Working Group, which was chaired by Curt Lidgard (Sweden), as regards the principles, proposals and recommendations contained in the report (see below, under REPORT OF THE COMMISSION ON DISARMAMENT AND SECURITY).

Mexico suggested that the Disarmament Commission give priority to the ICDSI proposal for the establishment of a tactical or battlefield nuclear-weapon-free zone in Europe, and urged NATO and the Warsaw Treaty Organization to negotiate without delay the provisions on geographical delimitation, verification machinery and other relevant points for a treaty or convention to be concluded. Those supporting the proposal, including the German Democratic Republic, considered the move an important confidence-building measure, while the Federal Republic of Germany and others rejected it saying that, in view of the conventional superiority of the Warsaw Treaty Organization in Europe, such a zone would actually increase the risk of confrontation.

On the recommendation of the Working Group, the Disarmament Commission noted that in many cases the proposals of ICDSI dealt with efforts under way in the Commission itself, and recommended that the report be duly taken into account in ongoing and future disarmament efforts.

Consideration by the Committee on Disarmament. In the Committee on Disarmament,[1] several delegations, including Mexico, Romania and Yugoslavia, supported a Swedish proposal to create a battlefield nuclear-weapon-free zone in Central Europe as a confidence-building measure; Bulgaria, Czechoslovakia, the German Democratic Republic, Hungary and Poland not only supported the proposal but also advocated enlarging the zone. Several other delegations, including the Federal Republic of Germany, asserted that the proposal did not meet fully the conditions spelt out in the 1978 Final Document,[14] that the decisive question was where the nuclear weapons were aimed at rather than stationed, and that negotiations leading only to a limited geographical disengagement of such arsenals in Europe would not enhance stability, but merely create an illusion of greater security.

In addition, several States, among them Cuba, Hungary, Romania, Sweden and Yugoslavia, supported the creation of a nuclear-weapon-free zone in Northern Europe, with Finland pointing out its long-time interest in the concept. Bulgaria and Romania, supported by Cuba, Hungary and Yugoslavia, reiterated initiatives for the creation of such a zone in the Balkans.

Latin America

Since the signature and ratification of Additional Protocol II of the Treaty for the Prohibition of Nuclear Weapons in Latin America (Treaty of Tlatelolco) by all the five nuclear-weapon States by 1979,[32] only one item concerning that Treaty remained on the General Assembly's agenda: the signature and ratification of Additional Protocol I which concerns the application of the Treaty to territories in the Latin American region for which outside States have *de jure* or *de facto* responsibility, such as the colonial Powers.

By a letter of 3 October,[33] representatives of 12 Latin American and Caribbean countries transmitted to the Assembly President the text of a 19 May resolution adopted by consensus, along with statements made, at the eighth regular session (Jamaica, 16-19 May) of the General Conference of the Agency for the Prohibition of Nuclear Weapons in Latin America, on a report on the United Kingdom's alleged introduction of nuclear weapons into the Falkland Islands (Malvinas) zone

(see also TRUSTEESHIP AND DECOLONIZATION, Chapter IV). Annexed to the letter was a note from the United Kingdom affirming its scrupulous observance of its obligations under Additional Protocols I and II of the Treaty, and a note from Argentina describing that statement as unsatisfactory and insufficient.

GENERAL ASSEMBLY ACTION

On 15 December 1983, the General Assembly adopted by recorded vote resolution 38/61, as recommended by the First Committee.

Implementation of General Assembly resolution 37/71 concerning the signature and ratification of Additional Protocol I of the Treaty for the Prohibition of Nuclear Weapons in Latin America (Treaty of Tlatelolco)

The General Assembly,

Recalling its resolutions 2286(XXII) of 5 December 1967, 3262(XXIX) of 9 December 1974, 3473(XXX) of 11 December 1975, 32/76 of 12 December 1977, S-10/2 of 30 June 1978, 33/58 of 14 December 1978, 34/71 of 11 December 1979, 35/143 of 12 December 1980, 36/83 of 9 December 1981 and 37/71 of 9 December 1982 concerning the signature and ratification of Additional Protocol I of the Treaty for the Prohibition of Nuclear Weapons in Latin America (Treaty of Tlatelolco),

Taking into account that within the zone of application of that Treaty, to which twenty-three sovereign States are already parties, there are some territories which, in spite of not being sovereign political entities, are nevertheless in a position to receive the benefits deriving from the Treaty through its Additional Protocol I, to which the States that *de jure* or *de facto* are internationally responsible for those territories may become parties,

Recalling that the United Kingdom of Great Britain and Northern Ireland, the Kingdom of the Netherlands and the United States of America became parties to Additional Protocol I in 1969, 1971 and 1981, respectively,

1. *Deplores* that the signature of Additional Protocol I by France, which took place on 2 March 1979, has not yet been followed by the corresponding ratification, notwithstanding the time already elapsed and the pressing invitations which the General Assembly has addressed to it;

2. *Once more urges* France not to delay any further such ratification, which has been requested so many times;

3. *Decides* to include in the provisional agenda of its thirty-ninth session an item entitled "Implementation of General Assembly resolution 38/61 concerning the signature and ratification of Additional Protocol I of the Treaty for the Prohibition of Nuclear Weapons in Latin America (Treaty of Tlatelolco)".

General Assembly resolution 38/61

15 December 1983   Meeting 97   135-0-9 (recorded vote)

Approved by First Committee (A/38/621) by recorded vote (118-0-7), 23 November (meeting 38); 21-nation draft (A/C.1/38/L.32); agenda item 43.

Sponsors: Antigua and Barbuda, Bahamas, Barbados, Bolivia, Colombia, Costa Rica, Dominican Republic, Ecuador, El Salvador, Guatemala, Haiti, Honduras, Jamaica, Mexico, Nicaragua, Panama, Paraguay, Peru, Suriname, Trinidad and Tobago, Uruguay.

Meeting numbers. GA 38th session: 1st Committee 3-10, 12-31, 33, 38; plenary 97.

Recorded vote in Assembly as follows:

In favour: Afghanistan, Algeria, Angola, Antigua and Barbuda, Australia, Austria, Bahamas, Bahrain, Bangladesh, Barbados, Belgium, Benin, Bhutan, Bolivia, Botswana, Brazil, Bulgaria, Burma, Burundi, Byelorussian SSR, Canada, Cape Verde, Chile, China, Colombia, Congo, Costa Rica, Cyprus, Czechoslovakia, Democratic Kampuchea, Democratic Yemen, Denmark, Dominican Republic, Ecuador, Egypt, El Salvador, Ethiopia, Fiji, Finland, Gabon, Gambia, German Democratic Republic, Germany, Federal Republic of, Ghana, Greece, Grenada, Guatemala, Guinea, Haiti, Honduras, Hungary, Iceland, India, Indonesia, Iran, Iraq, Ireland, Israel, Italy, Jamaica, Japan, Jordan, Kenya, Kuwait, Lao People's Democratic Republic, Lebanon, Lesotho, Liberia, Libyan Arab Jamahiriya, Luxembourg, Madagascar, Malaysia, Maldives, Malta, Mauritania, Mauritius, Mexico, Mongolia, Morocco, Mozambique, Nepal, Netherlands, New Zealand, Nicaragua, Niger, Nigeria, Norway, Oman, Pakistan, Panama, Papua New Guinea, Paraguay, Peru, Philippines, Poland, Portugal, Qatar, Romania, Rwanda, Saint Lucia, Sao Tome and Principe, Saudi Arabia, Senegal, Sierra Leone, Singapore, Solomon Islands, Somalia, Spain, Sri Lanka, Sudan, Suriname, Swaziland, Sweden, Syrian Arab Republic, Thailand, Togo, Trinidad and Tobago, Tunisia, Turkey, Uganda, Ukrainian SSR, USSR, United Arab Emirates, United Kingdom, United Republic of Cameroon, United Republic of Tanzania, United States, Upper Volta, Uruguay, Viet Nam, Yemen, Yugoslavia, Zaire, Zambia, Zimbabwe.

Against: None.

Abstaining: Argentina, Belize, Cuba, France, Guyana, Ivory Coast, Malawi, Mali, Venezuela.

In explanation of vote, France and the United States expressed regret that the resolution continued to single out one country for not having ratified the Protocol, while there were countries within the region itself which had not ratified or adhered to the Treaty.

Brazil said its affirmative vote was without prejudice to its belief that it had become necessary after the Falkland Islands (Malvinas) conflict to establish in the Treaty a system of verification of compliance by the nuclear-weapon Powers with all the Treaty's provisions. Argentina and Venezuela reaffirmed that their positions remained the same as in 1982.[34]

While expressing its commitment to the establishment of denuclearized zones throughout the world, Mali said it had abstained due to the wording of paragraphs 1 and 2 which, it believed, interfered with the internal procedures followed by States in relation to their security. Cuba reiterated its position that it was not a party to the Treaty since the nuclear Power in its area had been pursuing what it called a hostile and aggressive policy towards Cuba and continued to maintain a military base on its territory.

Middle East

The Secretary-General, in a September 1983 report,[35] submitted at a December 1982 General Assembly request,[36] informed the Assembly of the absence of further development since then with regard to the establishment of a nuclear-weapon-free zone in the Middle East. He expressed the view that, since establishing such a zone would contribute to the improvement of the situation in the area, further efforts to that end deserved strong support.

GENERAL ASSEMBLY ACTION

On the recommendation of the First Committee, the General Assembly, on 15 December 1983, adopted without vote resolution 38/64.

Establishment of a nuclear-weapon-free zone in the region of the Middle East

The General Assembly,

Recalling its resolutions 3263(XXIX) of 9 December 1974, 3474(XXX) of 11 December 1975, 31/71 of 10 December 1976, 32/82 of 12 December 1977, 33/64 of 14 December 1978, 34/77 of 11 December 1979, 35/147 of 12 December 1980, 36/87 of 9 December 1981 and 37/75 of 9 December 1982 on the establishment of a nuclear-weapon-free zone in the region of the Middle East,

Recalling also the recommendations for the establishment of such a zone in the Middle East consistent with paragraphs 60 to 63, in particular paragraph 63 *(d)*, of the Final Document of the Tenth Special Session of the General Assembly,

Emphasizing the basic provisions of the above-mentioned resolutions, which call upon all parties directly concerned to consider taking the practical and urgent steps required for the implementation of the proposal to establish a nuclear-weapon-free zone in the region of the Middle East and, pending and during the establishment of such a zone, to declare solemnly that they will refrain, on a reciprocal basis, from producing, acquiring or in any other way possessing nuclear weapons and nuclear explosive devices and from permitting the stationing of nuclear weapons on their territory by any third party, to agree to place all their nuclear facilities under International Atomic Energy Agency safeguards and to declare their support for the establishment of the zone and deposit such declarations with the Security Council for consideration, as appropriate,

Reaffirming the inalienable right of all States to acquire and develop nuclear energy for peaceful purposes,

Emphasizing further the need for appropriate measures on the question of the prohibition of military attacks on nuclear facilities,

Bearing in mind the consensus reached by the General Assembly at its thirty-fifth session that the establishment of a nuclear-weapon-free zone in the region of the Middle East would greatly enhance international peace and security,

Desirous to build on that consensus so that substantial progress can be made towards establishing a nuclear-weapon-free zone in the region of the Middle East,

Taking note of the report of the Secretary-General,

1. *Urges* all parties directly concerned to consider seriously taking the practical and urgent steps required for the implementation of the proposal to establish a nuclear-weapon-free zone in the region of the Middle East in accordance with the relevant resolutions of the General Assembly and, as a means of promoting this objective, invites the States concerned to adhere to the Treaty on the Non-Proliferation of Nuclear Weapons;

2. *Calls upon* all States of the region that have not done so, pending the establishment of the zone, to agree to place all their nuclear activities under International Atomic Energy Agency safeguards;

3. *Invites* those States, pending the establishment of a nuclear-weapon-free zone in the region of the Middle East, to declare their support for establishing such a zone, consistent with the relevant paragraph of the Final Document of the Tenth Special Session of the General

Assembly, and to deposit those declarations with the Security Council;

4. *Further invites* those States, pending the establishment of the zone, not to develop, produce, test or otherwise acquire nuclear weapons or permit the stationing on their territories, or territories under their control, of nuclear weapons or nuclear explosive devices;

5. *Invites* the nuclear-weapon States and all other States to render their assistance in the establishment of the zone and at the same time to refrain from any action that runs counter to both the letter and spirit of the present resolution;

6. *Requests* the Secretary-General to submit a report to the General Assembly at its thirty-ninth session on the implementation of the present resolution;

7. *Decides* to include in the provisional agenda of its thirty-ninth session the item entitled "Establishment of a nuclear-weapon-free zone in the region of the Middle East".

General Assembly resolution 38/64

15 December 1983   Meeting 97   Adopted without vote

Approved by First Committee (A/38/625) without vote, 23 November (meeting 38); draft by Egypt (A/C.1/38/L.20); agenda item 47.
Meeting numbers. GA 38th session: 1st Committee 3-10, 12-31, 38; plenary 97.

In explanation of its position, Brazil said it did not object to consensus because of the specific characteristics of the situation prevailing in the Middle East. Cuba, India and Zambia asserted that their joining the consensus did not prejudice their positions concerning NPT, mentioned in paragraph 1.

Israel said it joined the consensus despite reservations regarding the modalities included in the text; while it believed that the creation of a zone, modelled after the Treaty of Tlatelolco and based on the initiatives and consultations among the States in the region, would prevent the spread of nuclear weapons to the Middle East, the text omitted mention of the negotiating process, without which such an arrangement was unlikely to come about.

The question of Israeli nuclear armament

In a September 1983 report to the General Assembly,[37] the Secretary-General said he had communicated with both OAU and the League of Arab States with regard to a December 1982 Assembly request[38] for him, in co-operation with those bodies, to follow closely the nuclear and military collaboration between Israel and South Africa. The Secretary-General added that he had continued to follow Israeli nuclear activities, taking into account information published by IAEA, but having received no new information, he had nothing to add to his 1982 report.[39]

Israel, in a 13 September letter to the Secretary-General,[40] expressed the hope that the Assembly would grapple with the establishment of a nuclear-weapon-free zone, rather than deal with the question of attacks on nuclear facilities as in the previous two years (see also Chapter IX of this section). The Libyan Arab Jamahiriya, in a 25 March letter,[41] called for international efforts to halt the danger posed by what it called Israel's nuclear collaboration with South Africa and the United States and by such other measures as Israel's threat to destroy nuclear installations in any Arab country (see also Chapter VIII of this section).

GENERAL ASSEMBLY ACTION

On 15 December 1983, the General Assembly adopted by recorded vote resolution 38/69, as recommended by the First Committee.

Israeli nuclear armament

The General Assembly,

Recalling its previous resolutions on Israeli nuclear armament,

Recalling its relevant resolutions on the establishment of a nuclear-weapon-free zone in the region of the Middle East,

Recalling also its resolution 35/157 of 12 December 1980 on military and nuclear collaboration with Israel,

Recalling its repeated condemnation of nuclear collaboration between Israel and South Africa,

Recalling Security Council resolution 487(1981) of 19 June 1981 and taking note of the special report of the Special Committee against *Apartheid* on recent developments concerning relations between Israel and South Africa,

Noting with concern Israel's refusal to comply with Security Council resolution 487(1981),

Further noting with grave concern Israel's persistent refusal to adhere to the Treaty on the Non-Proliferation of Nuclear Weapons, despite repeated calls by the General Assembly, the Security Council and the International Atomic Energy Agency, and to place its nuclear facilities under Agency safeguards,

Conscious of the grave consequences which endanger international peace and security as a result of Israel's development and acquisition of nuclear weapons and Israel's collaboration with South Africa to develop nuclear weapons and their delivery systems,

Taking note of the report of the Secretary-General,

1. *Condemns* Israel's refusal to renounce any possession of nuclear weapons and to place all its nuclear activities under international safeguards;

2. *Requests* the Security Council to take urgent and effective measures to implement its resolution 487(1981) and to ensure that Israel complies with the resolution and places its nuclear facilities under International Atomic Energy Agency safeguards;

3. *Requests* the International Atomic Energy Agency to suspend any scientific co-operation with Israel which could contribute to Israel's nuclear capabilities;

4. *Reiterates* its condemnation of the Israeli threat, in violation of the Charter of the United Nations, to repeat its armed attack on peaceful nuclear facilities in Iraq and in other countries;

5. *Requests* the Secretary-General to continue to follow closely Israel's nuclear activities and the nuclear and military collaboration between Israel and South Africa and to report to the General Assembly at its thirty-ninth session thereon, as appropriate;

6. *Decides* to include in the provisional agenda of its thirty-ninth session the item entitled "Israeli nuclear armament".

General Assembly resolution 38/69

15 December 1983   Meeting 97   99-2-39 (recorded vote)

Approved by First Committee (A/38/632) by recorded vote (90-2-35), 23 November (meeting 38); 14-nation draft (A/C.1/38/L.51); agenda item 54.

Sponsors: Bahrain, Democratic Yemen, Djibouti, Iraq, Jordan, Kuwait, Libyan Arab Jamahiriya, Mali, Mauritania, Morocco, Qatar, Sudan, United Arab Emirates, Yemen.

Meeting numbers. GA 38th session: First Committee 3-10, 12-31, 33, 38; plenary 97.

Recorded vote in Assembly as follows:

In favour: Afghanistan, Albania, Algeria, Angola, Bahrain, Bangladesh, Barbados, Benin, Bhutan, Bolivia, Botswana, Brazil, Bulgaria, Burundi, Byelorussian SSR, Cape Verde, Central African Republic, Chad, China, Congo, Cuba, Cyprus, Czechoslovakia, Democratic Kampuchea, Democratic Yemen, Djibouti, Ecuador, Egypt, Ethiopia, Gabon, Gambia, German Democratic Republic, Ghana, Greece, Grenada, Guinea, Guyana, Hungary, India, Indonesia, Iran, Iraq, Jordan, Kenya, Kuwait, Lao People's Democratic Republic, Lebanon, Libyan Arab Jamahiriya, Madagascar, Malaysia, Maldives, Mali, Malta, Mauritania, Mexico, Mongolia, Morocco, Mozambique, Nicaragua, Niger, Nigeria, Oman, Pakistan, Papua New Guinea, Peru, Poland, Qatar, Romania, Rwanda, Sao Tome and Principe, Saudi Arabia, Senegal, Seychelles, Sierra Leone, Somalia, Spain, Sri Lanka, Sudan, Suriname, Syrian Arab Republic, Thailand, Togo, Trinidad and Tobago, Tunisia, Turkey, Uganda, Ukrainian SSR, USSR, United Arab Emirates, United Republic of Cameroon, United Republic of Tanzania, Upper Volta, Vanuatu, Venezuela, Viet Nam, Yemen, Yugoslavia, Zambia, Zimbabwe.

Against: Israel, United States.

Abstaining: Argentina, Australia, Austria, Bahamas, Belgium, Burma, Canada, Chile, Colombia, Denmark, Dominican Republic, Fiji, Finland, France, Germany, Federal Republic of, Guatemala, Haiti, Honduras, Iceland, Ireland, Italy, Ivory Coast, Japan, Liberia, Luxembourg, Malawi, Nepal, Netherlands, New Zealand, Norway, Panama, Paraguay, Philippines, Portugal, Swaziland, Sweden, United Kingdom, Uruguay, Zaire.

Prior to adopting the resolution as a whole, the Assembly adopted paragraph 3 by a recorded vote of 79 to 28, with 31 abstentions. The First Committee had approved the same paragraph by a recorded vote—requested by Belgium—of 79 to 26, with 19 abstentions.

In explanation of vote, Israel said the text introduced an imbalance into the international debate on the question and thereby hindered efforts to bring regional problems under control; its alleged nuclear and military co-operation with South Africa was an unsubstantiated speculation, and the text was discriminatory in that it singled out Israel for investigation and was based on a 1981 study by the Group of Experts to Prepare a Study on Israeli Nuclear Armament,[42] whose terms of reference had prejudged the findings.

Peru and the United States also felt that the text was discriminatory in singling out one Member State, while ignoring the number of States which had neither become party to NPT nor placed their nuclear facilities under IAEA safeguards. Venezuela spoke similarly and said it would have abstained had paragraph 1 been put to a vote.

Australia, Belgium, Israel and the United States considered paragraph 3 as interference by the Assembly in the affairs of IAEA, whose Board of Governors and General Conference alone had the competence to act in accordance with the Agency's statutory provisions. Peru expressed similar reservations. In addition, Belgium said scientific co-operation between IAEA and its member States applied to the peaceful uses of nuclear energy, not to armaments. Australia voted against the paragraph and abstained on the text as a whole because of the unconditional call to suspend scientific co-operation with Israel. Costa Rica, which did not participate in the voting on the paragraph or the whole text, added that nuclear weapons should be eliminated not merely in one country but throughout the world.

India said its affirmative votes on the resolution and on paragraph 3 were without prejudice to its stand on full-scale safeguards and on NPT. Peru had reservations about those paragraphs which, it said, contained provisions irreconcilable with the division of responsibilities between the Assembly and the Security Council.

Argentina, recalling its affirmative votes for similar resolutions in past years, said it believed the matter was far more serious at the current session and felt obliged to abstain by virtue of its position of principle.

South Asia

In a 1983 report to the General Assembly,[43] the Secretary-General stated that he had been in contact with States of South Asia with regard to a December 1982 Assembly request[44] that he render assistance required to promote a nuclear-weapon-free zone in that region, but there had been no request by those States for his assistance. In the course of those contacts, a view had been expressed that he should continue to be available for that purpose.

GENERAL ASSEMBLY ACTION

On the recommendation of the First Committee, the General Assembly, on 15 December, adopted by recorded vote resolution 38/65.

Establishment of a nuclear-weapon-free zone in South Asia

The General Assembly,

Recalling its resolutions 3265 B (XXIX) of 9 December 1974, 3476 B (XXX) of 11 December 1975, 31/73 of 10 December 1976, 32/83 of 12 December 1977, 33/65 of 14 December 1978, 34/78 of 11 December 1979, 35/148 of 12 December 1980, 36/88 of 9 December 1981 and 37/76 of 9 December 1982 concerning the establishment of a nuclear-weapon-free zone in South Asia,

Reiterating its conviction that the establishment of nuclear-weapon-free zones in various regions of the world is one of the measures which can contribute most effectively to the objectives of non-proliferation of nuclear weapons and general and complete disarmament,

Believing that the establishment of a nuclear-weapon-free zone in South Asia, as in other regions, will strengthen the security of the States of the region against the use or threat of use of nuclear weapons,

Noting the declarations issued at the highest level by Governments of South Asian States reaffirming their undertaking not to acquire or manufacture nuclear weapons and to devote their nuclear programmes exclusively to the economic and social advancement of their peoples,

Recalling that in the above-mentioned resolutions it called upon the States of the South Asian region, and such other neighbouring non-nuclear-weapon States as might be interested, to make all possible efforts to establish a nuclear-weapon-free zone in South Asia and to refrain, in the mean time, from any action contrary to this objective,

Further recalling that, in its resolutions 3265 B (XXIX), 31/73 and 32/83, it requested the Secretary-General to convene a meeting for the purpose of the consultations mentioned therein and to render such assistance as might be required to promote the efforts for the establishment of a nuclear-weapon-free zone in South Asia,

Bearing in mind the provisions of paragraphs 60 to 63 of the Final Document of the Tenth Special Session of the General Assembly regarding the establishment of nuclear-weapon-free zones, including in the region of South Asia,

Taking note of the report of the Secretary-General,

1. *Reaffirms* its endorsement, in principle, of the concept of a nuclear-weapon-free zone in South Asia;

2. *Urges once again* the States of South Asia, and such other neighbouring non-nuclear-weapon States as may be interested, to continue to make all possible efforts to establish a nuclear-weapon-free zone in South Asia and to refrain, in the mean time, from any action contrary to this objective;

3. *Calls upon* those nuclear-weapon States that have not done so to respond positively to this proposal and to extend the necessary co-operation in the efforts to establish a nuclear-weapon-free zone in South Asia;

4. *Requests* the Secretary-General to render such assistance as may be required to promote the efforts for the establishment of a nuclear-weapon-free zone in South Asia and to report on the subject to the General Assembly at its thirty-ninth session;

5. *Decides* to include in the provisional agenda of its thirty-ninth session the item entitled "Establishment of a nuclear-weapon-free zone in South Asia".

General Assembly resolution 38/65

15 December 1983   Meeting 97   94-3-46 (recorded vote)

Approved by First Committee (A/38/626) by recorded vote (81-2-42), 23 November (meeting 38); draft by Pakistan (A/C.1/38/L.6); agenda item 48.
Meeting numbers. GA 38th session: 1st Committee 3-10, 12-31, 38; plenary 97.

Recorded vote in Assembly as follows:

In favour: Angola, Antigua and Barbuda, Bahrain, Bangladesh, Barbados, Belgium, Bolivia, Botswana, Burundi, Canada, Chad, Chile, China, Colombia, Costa Rica, Democratic Kampuchea, Djibouti, Dominican Republic, Ecuador, Egypt, El Salvador, Finland, Gabon, Gambia, Germany, Federal Republic of, Ghana, Greece, Guatemala, Guyana, Haiti, Honduras, Iran, Iraq, Ireland, Ivory Coast, Jamaica, Japan, Jordan, Kenya, Kuwait, Lebanon, Lesotho, Liberia, Libyan Arab Jamahiriya, Luxembourg, Malawi, Malaysia, Maldives, Mali, Malta, Mauritania, Mexico, Morocco, Nepal, Netherlands, New Zealand, Niger, Nigeria, Oman, Pakistan, Panama, Paraguay, Peru, Philippines, Portugal, Qatar, Romania, Rwanda, Saint Lucia, Saudi Arabia, Senegal, Sierra Leone, Singapore, Somalia, Spain, Sri Lanka, Sudan, Swaziland, Thailand, Togo, Trinidad and Tobago, Tunisia, Turkey, Uganda, United Arab Emirates, United Republic of Cameroon, United Republic of Tanzania, United States, Uruguay, Venezuela, Yemen, Zaire, Zambia, Zimbabwe.

Against: Bhutan, India, Mauritius.

Abstaining: Afghanistan, Algeria, Argentina, Australia, Austria, Bahamas, Belize, Benin, Brazil, Bulgaria, Burma, Byelorussian SSR, Cape Verde, Congo, Cuba, Cyprus, Czechoslovakia, Democratic Yemen, Denmark, Ethiopia, Fiji, France, German Democratic Republic, Guinea, Hungary, Iceland, Indonesia, Israel, Italy, Lao People's Democratic Republic, Madagascar, Mongolia, Mozambique,

Nicaragua, Norway, Papua New Guinea, Poland, Sao Tome and Principe, Seychelles, Sweden, Ukrainian SSR, USSR, United Kingdom, Upper Volta, Viet Nam, Yugoslavia.

In explanation of vote, India said that a draft on a nuclear-weapon-free zone in South Asia had become an annual and pointless ritual for the First Committee, that there was no consensus among the countries in the region on setting up such a zone, and that the proposal only introduced a discordant note into the process of fostering beneficial regional co-operation.

Those explaining their affirmative votes or abstentions all expressed support for the establishment of nuclear-weapon-free zones, with some of them listing requirements for their success. Unanimity on the issue based on close consultations among the countries of the region was stressed by Bangladesh, Brazil, Indonesia, Japan and Sri Lanka. For Bangladesh, consensus on the delimitation of the zone was important, and for Sri Lanka, full recognition of the characteristics of the zone. Indonesia and Japan stressed the importance of the initiatives of the countries of the region. The United States believed that effective zones, negotiated and supported by the States of the region, could enhance the security of States and reinforce non-proliferation goals on a regional basis. Zambia reserved its position regarding the second preambular paragraph because of its reference to non-proliferation.

Brazil said the text did not reflect adequately its concerns regarding the requirements for the establishment of a nuclear-weapon-free zone, among them a commitment by the nuclear-weapon States to respect the status of the zone and to refrain from interfering in the negotiating process, and provisions on verification of compliance by those Powers with commitments under the instrument establishing a zone. Indonesia and Sweden observed that the resolution did not enjoy unanimous regional support. The Lao People's Democratic Republic felt that it was impossible to establish such a zone in South Asia because there were military bases of imperialist States in the region in which nuclear weapons were stationed.

Preparations for the 1985 Review Conference on the Treaty on the Non-Proliferation of Nuclear Weapons

In 1983, the General Assembly considered, at the request of a group of 59 Member States,[45] a new agenda item entitled "Implementation of the conclusions of the Second Review Conference of the Parties to the Treaty on the Non-Proliferation of Nuclear Weapons and establishment of a preparatory committee for the Third Review Conference".

The second quinquennial Review Conference of the Parties to NPT, which had entered into force on 5 March 1970, had been held in 1980[46] to review the operation of the various articles of the instrument. It was not able to agree on a substantive final document, but recommended that a third conference be held in 1985.

GENERAL ASSEMBLY ACTION

On the recommendation of the First Committee, the General Assembly, on 15 December 1983, adopted by recorded vote resolution 38/74.

Implementation of the conclusions of the Second Review Conference of the Parties to the Treaty on the Non-Proliferation of Nuclear Weapons and establishment of the Preparatory Committee for the Third Review Conference of the Parties to the Treaty

The General Assembly,

Recalling its resolution 2373(XXII) of 12 June 1968, the annex to which contains the Treaty on the Non-Proliferation of Nuclear Weapons,

Noting the provisions of article VIII, paragraph 3, of that Treaty concerning the holding of successive review conferences,

Noting that in the Final Document of the Second Review Conference of the Parties to the Treaty on the Non-Proliferation of Nuclear Weapons, held at Geneva from 11 August to 7 September 1980, the Conference proposed to the Depositary Governments that a third conference to review the operation of the Treaty be convened in 1985 and noting that there appears to be a consensus among the parties that the Third Review Conference should be held at Geneva in August/September of that year,

1. *Notes* that, following appropriate consultations, an open-ended Preparatory Committee for the Third Review Conference of the Parties to the Treaty on the Non-Proliferation of Nuclear Weapons was formed of parties to the Treaty serving on the Board of Governors of the International Atomic Energy Agency or represented on the Committee on Disarmament as well as any party to the Treaty which may express its interest in participating in the work of the Preparatory Committee;

2. *Requests* the Secretary-General to render the necessary assistance and to provide such services, including summary records, as may be required for the Third Review Conference of the Parties to the Treaty on the Non-Proliferation of Nuclear Weapons and its preparation.

General Assembly resolution 38/74

15 December 1983   Meeting 97   134-0-7 (recorded vote)

Approved by First Committee (A/38/645) by recorded vote (115-0-6), 23 November (meeting 39); 48-nation draft (A/C.1/38/L.50); agenda item 139.

Sponsors: Australia, Austria, Bangladesh, Belgium, Bolivia, Bulgaria, Canada, Czechoslovakia, Democratic Yemen, Denmark, Egypt, Ethiopia, Fiji, Finland, German Democratic Republic, Germany, Federal Republic of, Greece, Honduras, Hungary, Iraq, Ireland, Italy, Japan, Liberia, Madagascar, Mali, Mexico, Mongolia, Netherlands, New Zealand, Nigeria, Norway, Philippines, Poland, Portugal, Romania, Samoa, Sudan, Sweden, Thailand, Togo, Tunisia, Turkey, Uganda, USSR, United Kingdom, United States, Uruguay.

Meeting numbers. GA 38th session: 1st Committee 3-10, 12-31, 33, 39; plenary 97.

Recorded vote in Assembly as follows:

In favour: Afghanistan, Angola, Antigua and Barbuda, Australia, Austria, Bahamas, Bahrain, Bangladesh, Barbados, Belgium, Belize, Benin, Bhutan, Bolivia, Botswana, Bulgaria, Burundi, Byelorussian SSR, Canada, Cape Verde, Central African Republic, Chad, Chile, Colombia, Congo, Costa Rica, Cyprus, Czechoslovakia, Democratic Kampuchea, Democratic Yemen, Denmark, Dominican Republic, Ecuador, Egypt, Ethiopia, Fiji, Finland, Gabon, Gambia, German Democratic Republic, Germany, Federal Republic of, Ghana, Greece, Grenada, Guatemala, Guinea, Guyana, Haiti, Honduras, Hungary, Iceland, Indonesia, Iran, Iraq, Ireland, Israel, Italy, Ivory Coast, Jamaica, Japan, Jordan, Kenya, Kuwait, Lao People's Democratic Republic, Lebanon, Lesotho, Liberia, Libyan Arab Jamahiriya, Luxembourg, Madagascar, Malawi, Malaysia, Maldives, Mali, Malta, Mauritania, Mauritius, Mexico, Mongolia, Morocco, Nepal, Netherlands, New Zealand, Nicaragua, Niger, Nigeria, Norway, Oman, Panama, Papua New Guinea, Paraguay, Peru, Philippines, Poland, Portugal, Qatar, Romania, Rwanda, Saint Lucia, Sao Tome and Principe, Saudi Arabia, Senegal, Seychelles, Sierra Leone, Singapore, Solomon Islands, Somalia, Spain, Sri Lanka, Sudan, Suriname, Swaziland, Sweden, Syrian Arab Republic, Thailand, Togo, Trinidad and Tobago, Tunisia, Turkey, Uganda, Ukrainian SSR, USSR, United Arab Emirates, United Kingdom, United Republic of Cameroon, United States, Upper Volta, Uruguay, Vanuatu, Venezuela, Viet Nam, Yemen, Yugoslavia, Zaire.

Against: None.

Abstaining: Argentina, Brazil, Cuba, India, Pakistan, United Republic of Tanzania, Zambia.

The recorded vote in the First Committee was taken at the request of Brazil.

Review Conference on the 1971 Treaty against weapons of mass destruction on the sea-bed

The Second Review Conference of the Parties to the Treaty on the Prohibition of the Emplacement of Nuclear Weapons and Other Weapons of Mass Destruction on the Sea-Bed and the Ocean Floor and in the Subsoil Thereof (sea-bed Treaty), met at Geneva from 12 to 23 September 1983,[47] with the participation of 45 of the 73 States parties, four signatories and two observer States, as well as two non-governmental organizations. It adopted by consensus a Final Document, which contained the Final Declaration consisting of a preamble and the Conference's article-by-article review of the Treaty, including affirmations and requests concerning its operation and a call for additional States to become parties. The other two parts of the Document dealt with the organization and work of the Conference, and summary records of the plenary meetings.

The Treaty, which was concluded in 1970 by a non–United Nations conference and commended to Member States by the General Assembly,[48] was opened for signature on 11 February 1971 and entered into force on 18 May 1972. Its parties included three nuclear-weapon States—the USSR, the United Kingdom and the United States—whose Governments were designated as depositaries of the Treaty. The first Review Conference took place in 1977.[49]

Preparations for the Second Review Conference, including agreements on date, venue and the provisional agenda, had been made by its Preparatory Committee, which held one session at Geneva from 2 to 5 May 1983, with the participation of 42 States parties to the Treaty as well as four non-parties who were signatories (Greece, Lebanon, Madagascar, Senegal).

In the Committee on Disarmament,[1] Sweden reiterated in 1983 its proposal for consideration by the Committee of the major technological developments which affected the operation of the sea-bed Treaty, believing that such developments might lead to increased military use of the sea-bed within either the current scope of the Treaty or an enlarged one.

At the invitation of the Conference Preparatory Committee, the Committee on Disarmament, in an informal meeting on 9 August, considered follow-up measures to the conclusions of the first Review Conference, and provided the Chairman of the Preparatory Committee with summaries of statements by Sweden, the USSR, the United Kingdom and the United States. While Sweden reiterated its views and urged all States to submit relevant information to the Second Review Conference, the three nuclear-weapon States, each urging the widest possible adherence to the Treaty, said they either had received no official communications on the Treaty or were unaware of any technological developments that affected its operation.

GENERAL ASSEMBLY ACTION

On 20 December 1983, the General Assembly adopted without vote resolution 38/188 B, as recommended by the First Committee.

Review Conference of the Parties to the Treaty on the Prohibition of the Emplacement of Nuclear Weapons and Other Weapons of Mass Destruction on the Sea-Bed and the Ocean Floor and in the Subsoil Thereof

The General Assembly,

Recalling its resolution 2660(XXV) of 7 December 1970, in which it commended the Treaty on the Prohibition of the Emplacement of Nuclear Weapons and Other Weapons of Mass Destruction on the Sea-Bed and the Ocean Floor and in the Subsoil Thereof,

Convinced that the Treaty constitutes a step towards the exclusion of the sea-bed, the ocean floor and the subsoil thereof from the arms race,

Recalling that the States parties to the Treaty met at Geneva from 12 to 23 September 1983 to review the operation of the Treaty with a view to assuring that the purposes of the preamble and the provisions of the Treaty were being realized,

Noting with satisfaction that the Review Conference of the Parties to the Treaty on the Prohibition of the Emplacement of Nuclear Weapons and Other Weapons of Mass Destruction on the Sea-Bed and the Ocean Floor and in the Subsoil Thereof concluded that the obligations assumed under the Treaty had been faithfully observed by the States parties,

Noting that in its Final Declaration the Review Conference affirmed its belief that universal adherence to the Treaty would enhance international peace and security,

Noting furthermore that the States parties to the Treaty reaffirmed their strong support for and continued dedication to the principles and objectives of the Treaty, as well as their commitment to implement effectively its provisions,

Recognizing that in the Final Declaration the States parties to the Treaty reaffirmed the commitment undertaken in article V to continue negotiations in good faith concerning further measures in the field of disarmament for the prevention of an arms race on the sea-bed, the ocean floor and the subsoil thereof,

1. *Welcomes with satisfaction* the positive assessment by the Review Conference of the Parties to the Treaty on the Prohibition of the Emplacement of Nuclear Weapons and Other Weapons of Mass Destruction on the Sea-Bed and the Ocean Floor and in the Subsoil Thereof of the effectiveness of the Treaty since its entry into force, as reflected in its Final Declaration;

2. *Reiterates* its expressed hope for the widest possible adherence to the Treaty;

3. *Affirms* its strong interest in avoiding an arms race in nuclear weapons or any other types of weapons of mass destruction on the sea-bed, the ocean floor or the subsoil thereof;

4. *Calls again upon* all States to refrain from any action which might lead to the extension of the arms race to the sea-bed and the ocean floor;

5. *Requests* the Conference on Disarmament, in consultation with the States parties to the Treaty, taking into account existing proposals and any relevant technological developments, to proceed promptly with consideration of further measures in the field of disarmament for the prevention of an arms race on the sea-bed, the ocean floor and the subsoil thereof;

6. *Requests* the Secretary-General to transmit to the Conference on Disarmament all documents of the thirty-eighth session of the General Assembly relevant to further measures in the field of disarmament for the prevention of an arms race on the sea-bed, the ocean floor and the subsoil thereof;

7. *Requests* the Conference on Disarmament to report on its consideration of further measures in the field of disarmament for the prevention of an arms race on the sea-bed, the ocean floor and the subsoil thereof to the General Assembly at its fortieth session.

General Assembly resolution 38/188 B

20 December 1983   Meeting 103   Adopted without vote

Approved by First Committee (A/38/640) without vote, 21 November (meeting 34); 26-nation draft (A/C.1/38/L.9); agenda item 62.
Sponsors: Afghanistan, Argentina, Australia, Austria, Belgium, Canada, Cyprus, Denmark, Finland, German Democratic Republic, Ghana, Iceland, India, Italy, Japan, Malta, Mongolia, Netherlands, Norway, Portugal, Romania, Singapore, Ukrainian SSR, USSR, United Kingdom, United States.
Meeting numbers. GA 38th session: 1st Committee 3-10, 12-31, 34; plenary 103.

Cessation of nuclear-weapon tests

Negotiations for a treaty against nuclear-weapon tests

The Committee on Disarmament[1] re-established on 29 March 1983 an *Ad Hoc* Working Group on a Nuclear-Test Ban, based on the Group's 1982 mandate, to continue to discuss and define issues relating to verification and compliance with a view to making further progress towards a nuclear-test ban. At the same time, the Committee decided to consider with urgency the question of the Group's mandate, including the possibility of revising it.

The Working Group, chaired by Gerhard Herder and later by Harald Rose (both of the German Democratic Republic), held 17 meetings between 8 April and 16 August. As in 1982, two nuclear-weapon States (China, France) did not participate. The Group considered documents submitted by, among others, Australia on proposals for the scope of a comprehensive nuclear-test ban, Sweden on a draft treaty banning any nuclear-weapon-test explosion in any environment, the USSR on basic provisions of a treaty on the complete and general prohibition of nuclear-weapon tests, and the United Kingdom on peaceful explosions in relation to a nuclear-test ban.

The Working Group reported to the Committee that a large number of delegations felt that the Group had fulfilled its mandate by discussing and defining, in 1982 and 1983, all issues relating to verification and compliance of a nuclear-test ban (see below), and that the Group's mandate should be changed so that it could proceed to negotiate without further delay on a nuclear-test-ban treaty. However, some delegations maintained that consideration of the subject was not exhausted and that a number of views expressed during the discussions required further examination. In the absence of consensus, a large number of delegations requested that the question of the mandate be taken up at the beginning of the 1984 session of the Conference on Disarmament (as the Committee would then be known).

Verification measures

During the 1983 meetings of the *Ad Hoc* Working Group on a Nuclear-Test Ban, of the Committee on Disarmament,[1] it was generally recognized that a verification system of a nuclear-test ban should be based on a combination of national and international measures and could include national technical means, international exchange of seismic data, procedures and mechanisms for consultation and co-operation, a multilateral organ or organs of States parties, procedure for complaints and on-site inspection. As regards an international exchange of seismic data, there was general recognition that such an exchange should be based on the future recommendations of the *Ad Hoc* Group of Scientific Experts to Consider International Co-operative Measures to Detect and Identify Seismic Events (see below); and that it could consist of a network of seismic stations, use of the Global Telecommunication System of the World Meteorological Organization (WMO), and international data centres.

A number of delegations, including that of one nuclear-weapon State, reaffirmed that the existing means of verification were sufficient to provide reasonable assurance of compliance with a nuclear-test-ban treaty (see above). Others, including two nuclear-weapon States, reiterated that the question of adequacy of means of verification could be defined only by each State individually on the basis of its national requirements. Some delegations believed that, apart from a seismic monitoring network, means of verifying a nuclear-test ban should include a similar network for the monitoring of airborne radioactivity; others, however, questioned the need for such a network.

Documents before the Committee on the subject were submitted by, among others: Australia, on institutional arrangements, and a proposal for an international management panel; Japan, on verification and compliance, and an international seismic data exchange system; Sweden, on international surveillance of airborne radioactivity; and the United Kingdom, on verification aspects.

In 1983, the *Ad Hoc* Group of Scientific Experts on seismic events, composed of experts from 20 countries and a representative from WMO, held its fifteenth and sixteenth sessions (7-18 February and 11-22 July, respectively). Its Chairman noted that the Group needed one more meeting in 1984 to complete its work, particularly with regard to the detailed technical instructions to be annexed to its report to the Conference on Disarmament.

On 15 June, the WMO Secretary-General responded to an August 1982 communication by the Chairman of the Committee on Disarmament concerning the regular use of the WMO Global Telecommunication System of the World Weather Watch for transmission of data for the detection and identification of seismic events. The WMO Secretary-General stated that the WMO Executive Council (thirty-fifth session, Geneva, May/June) had approved inclusion of seismic bulletins in the global exchange programme, for implementation not later than 1 December 1983.

GENERAL ASSEMBLY ACTION

In December 1983, the General Assembly adopted three resolutions (38/62, 38/63 and 38/72) dealing with the cessation of nuclear-weapon tests.

The question of a nuclear-weapon test ban was also touched upon in other 1983 Assembly resolutions: 38/73 E, on a nuclear-arms freeze; 38/76, on a nuclear-weapon freeze; 38/183 H, on implementation of the recommendations and decisions of the tenth special session; and 38/183 I, on the report of the Committee on Disarmament. (For texts of these resolutions, refer to INDEX OF RESOLUTIONS AND DECISIONS.)

On 15 December, the General Assembly adopted by recorded vote resolution 38/62, as recommended by the First Committee.

Cessation of all test explosions of nuclear weapons
The General Assembly,
Bearing in mind that the complete cessation of nuclear-weapon tests, which has been examined for more than twenty-five years and on which the General Assembly has adopted more than forty resolutions, is a basic

objective of the United Nations in the sphere of disarmament, to the attainment of which it has repeatedly assigned the highest priority,

Stressing that on seven different occasions it has condemned such tests in the strongest terms and that, since 1974, it has stated its conviction that the continuance of nuclear-weapon testing will intensify the arms race, thus increasing the danger of nuclear war,

Reiterating the assertion made in several previous resolutions that, whatever may be the differences on the question of verification, there is no valid reason for delaying the conclusion of an agreement on a comprehensive test ban,

Recalling that since 1972 the Secretary-General has declared that all the technical and scientific aspects of the problem have been so fully explored that only a political decision is now necessary in order to achieve final agreement, that when the existing means of verification are taken into account it is difficult to understand further delay in achieving agreement on an underground-test ban, and that the potential risks of continuing underground nuclear-weapon tests would far outweigh any possible risks from ending such tests,

Taking into account that the three nuclear-weapon States which act as depositaries of the Treaty Banning Nuclear Weapon Tests in the Atmosphere, in Outer Space and under Water undertook in that Treaty, twenty years ago, to seek the achievement of the discontinuance of all test explosions of nuclear weapons for all time and that such an undertaking was explicitly reiterated in 1968 in the preamble to the Treaty on the Non-Proliferation of Nuclear Weapons, article VI of which further embodies their solemn and legally binding commitment to take effective measures relating to cessation of the nuclear-arms race at an early date and to nuclear disarmament,

Bearing in mind the growing negative influence that the total lack of compliance with those undertakings had on both the first and the second Review Conferences of the Parties to the Treaty on the Non-Proliferation of Nuclear Weapons, held at Geneva from 5 to 30 May 1975 and from 11 August to 7 September 1980 respectively,

Convinced that the maintenance of such a situation would not augur well for the third review conference of that Treaty, which is to take place in 1985, and even for the future of the Treaty itself,

Deploring that, due to the persistent obstruction of a very small number of its members, the Committee on Disarmament—which henceforth will be designated as the Conference on Disarmament—has been unable to initiate multilateral negotiation of a treaty for the prohibition of all nuclear-weapon tests, as it was specifically requested to do in General Assembly resolution 37/72 of 9 December 1982,

Noting that the Conference on Disarmament has already received various concrete proposals on this question, including a complete draft for the eventual text of the treaty as a whole,

1.   *Reiterates once again its grave concern* that nuclear-weapon testing continues unabated, against the wishes of the overwhelming majority of Member States;

2.   *Reaffirms its conviction* that a treaty to achieve the prohibition of all nuclear-test explosions by all States for all time is a matter of the highest priority;

3.   *Reaffirms also its conviction* that such a treaty would constitute a contribution of the utmost importance to the cessation of the arms race and an indispensable element for the success of the Treaty on the Non-Proliferation of Nuclear Weapons, since it is only through the fulfilment of the obligations under the Treaty that its three depositary Powers may expect all other parties to comply likewise with their respective obligations;

4.   *Urges once more* the three depositary Powers of the Treaty Banning Nuclear Weapon Tests in the Atmosphere, in Outer Space and under Water and of the Treaty on the Non-Proliferation of Nuclear Weapons to abide strictly by their undertakings to seek to achieve the discontinuance of all test explosions of nuclear weapons for all time and to continue negotiations to this end;

5.   *Urges also* all States that have not yet done so to adhere to the Treaty Banning Nuclear Weapon Tests in the Atmosphere, in Outer Space and under Water and, meanwhile, to refrain from testing in the environments covered by that Treaty;

6.   *Reiterates its appeal* to all States members of the Conference on Disarmament to initiate immediately the multilateral negotiation of a treaty for the prohibition of all nuclear-weapon tests and to exert their best endeavours in order that the Conference may transmit to the General Assembly at its thirty-ninth session the complete draft of such a treaty;

7.   *Calls upon* the States depositaries of the Treaty Banning Nuclear Weapon Tests in the Atmosphere, in Outer Space and under Water and the Treaty on the Non-Proliferation of Nuclear Weapons, by virtue of their special responsibilities under those two Treaties and as a provisional measure, to bring to a halt without delay all nuclear-test explosions, either through a trilaterally agreed moratorium or through three unilateral moratoria;

8.   *Decides* to include in the provisional agenda of its thirty-ninth session the item entitled "Cessation of all test explosions of nuclear weapons".

General Assembly resolution 38/62

15 December 1983   Meeting 97   119-2-26 (recorded vote)

Approved by First Committee (A/38/622) by recorded vote (100-2-28), 22 November (meeting 37); 15-nation draft (A/C.1/38/L.48); agenda item 44.

Sponsors: Bangladesh, Colombia, Costa Rica, Ecuador, Indonesia, Kenya, Mali, Mexico, Pakistan, Sri Lanka, Sudan, Sweden, Uruguay, Venezuela, Yugoslavia.

Meeting numbers. GA 38th session: 1st Committee 3-10, 12-31, 32, 37; plenary 97.

Recorded vote in Assembly as follows:

In favour: Afghanistan, Algeria, Angola, Antigua and Barbuda, Austria, Bahamas, Bahrain, Bangladesh, Barbados, Belize, Benin, Bhutan, Bolivia, Botswana, Bulgaria, Burundi, Byelorussian SSR, Cape Verde, Central African Republic, Chad, Colombia, Congo, Costa Rica, Cuba, Cyprus, Czechoslovakia, Democratic Yemen, Djibouti, Dominican Republic, Ecuador, Egypt, El Salvador, Ethiopia, Fiji, Finland, Gabon, Gambia, German Democratic Republic, Ghana, Grenada, Guatemala, Guinea, Guyana, Haiti, Honduras, Hungary, Indonesia, Iran, Iraq, Ireland, Ivory Coast, Jamaica, Jordan, Kenya, Kuwait, Lao People's Democratic Republic, Lebanon, Lesotho, Liberia, Libyan Arab Jamahiriya, Madagascar, Malawi, Malaysia, Maldives, Mali, Malta, Mauritania, Mauritius, Mexico, Mongolia, Morocco, Mozambique, Nepal, Nicaragua, Niger, Nigeria, Oman, Pakistan, Panama, Papua New Guinea, Paraguay, Peru, Philippines, Poland, Qatar, Romania, Rwanda, Saint Lucia, Sao Tome and Principe, Saudi Arabia, Senegal, Seychelles, Sierra Leone, Singapore, Somalia, Sri Lanka, Sudan, Suriname, Swaziland, Sweden, Syrian Arab Republic, Thailand, Togo, Trinidad and Tobago, Tunisia, Uganda, Ukrainian SSR, USSR, United Arab Emirates, United Republic of Cameroon, United Republic of Tanzania, Upper Volta, Uruguay, Venezuela, Viet Nam, Yemen, Yugoslavia, Zaire, Zimbabwe.

Against: United Kingdom, United States.

Abstaining: Argentina, Australia, Belgium, Brazil, Burma, Canada, Chile, China, Denmark, France, Germany, Federal Republic of, Greece, Iceland, India, Israel, Italy, Japan, Luxembourg, Netherlands, New Zealand, Norway, Portugal, Solomon Islands, Spain, Turkey, Zambia.

In explanation of vote, the United Kingdom stated that the text referred only to nuclear-weapon tests and avoided the issue of nuclear explosions for peaceful purposes in the context of a comprehensive test ban; the text also proposed a moratorium, which the United Kingdom had consistently rejected.

New Zealand could not accept that the text was restricted to the prohibition of nuclear-weapon testing and objected to the call for a moratorium limited to the three original parties to the 1963 Treaty Banning Nuclear Weapon Tests in the Atmosphere, in Outer Space and under Water (partial test-ban Treaty).[50] Similarly, Samoa believed that a test ban should be general and complete. Argentina, Brazil, India and Zambia explained their abstentions on the grounds of the linkage established in the text between a test-ban treaty and NPT.

Fiji had a reservation because the text was limited to weapon tests, but voted in favour because of its policy of general support for such initiatives. Algeria shared the concerns expressed in the resolution, despite some reservations. Ireland agreed with the general thrust of the text but would not draw the conclusions contained in paragraph 3 which, it said, detracted unfairly from the value of NPT. The USSR agreed with the appeal contained in the text for an immediate initiation of negotiations on a nuclear-test-ban treaty, expressed willingness to examine proposals submitted by other States on the subject, and said it had proposed a moratorium on nuclear tests until the conclusion of an agreement. Mongolia said it regarded paragraph 5 as particularly important and expressed concern that not all the nuclear Powers were represented in the Working Group of the Committee on Disarmament. Cuba stated that its affirmative vote should not be interpreted as a change in its position with respect to the partial test-ban Treaty.

France explained its position on all three drafts (see below under resolution 38/72).

On the recommendation of the First Committee, the General Assembly, on 15 December, adopted by recorded vote resolution 38/63.

Urgent need for a comprehensive nuclear-test-ban treaty

The General Assembly,

Convinced of the urgent need for a comprehensive nuclear-test-ban treaty capable of attracting the widest possible international support and adherence,

Reaffirming its conviction that an end to nuclear-weapon testing by all States in all environments would be a major step towards ending the qualitative improvement, development and proliferation of nuclear weapons, a means of relieving the deep apprehension concerning the harmful consequences of radioactive contamination for the health of present and future generations and a measure of the utmost importance in bringing the nuclear-arms race to an end,

Recalling that the parties to the Treaty Banning Nuclear Weapon Tests in the Atmosphere, in Outer Space and under Water undertook not to carry out any nuclear-weapon-test explosion, or any other nuclear explosion, in the environments covered by that Treaty, and that in that Treaty and in the Treaty on the Non-Proliferation of Nuclear Weapons the parties expressed their determination to continue negotiations to achieve the discontinuance of all test explosions of nuclear weapons for all time,

Recalling also its previous resolutions on this subject,

Taking into account that part of the report of the Committee on Disarmament concerning consideration of the item entitled "Nuclear-test ban" during its session in 1983,

Noting, in particular, that Sweden submitted to the Committee on Disarmament a draft treaty banning any nuclear-weapon-test explosion in any environment which took into account both the report on the trilateral negotiations submitted to the Committee in 1980 and the basic provisions of a treaty on the complete and general prohibition of nuclear-weapon tests proposed by the Union of Soviet Socialist Republics in 1982,

Recognizing the important role of the Conference on Disarmament in the negotiation of a comprehensive nuclear-test-ban treaty,

Recognizing the importance to such a treaty of the work assigned by the Committee on Disarmament to the *Ad Hoc* Group of Scientific Experts to Consider International Co-operative Measures to Detect and Identify Seismic Events on a global network of stations for the exchange of seismological data,

Recalling paragraph 31 of the Final Document of the Tenth Special Session of the General Assembly, relating to verification of disarmament and arms control agreements, which stated that the form and modalities of the verification to be provided for in any specific agreement depend on, and should be determined by, the purposes, scope and nature of the agreement,

1. *Reiterates its profound concern* that, despite the express wishes of the majority of Member States, nuclear-weapon testing continues;

2. *Reaffirms its conviction* that a treaty to achieve the prohibition of all nuclear-test explosions by all States for all time is a matter of the greatest importance;

3. *Expresses the conviction* that such a treaty would constitute a vital element for the success of efforts to halt and reverse the nuclear-arms race and the qualitative improvement of nuclear weapons, and to prevent the expansion of existing nuclear arsenals and the spread of nuclear weapons to additional countries;

4. *Notes* that the Committee on Disarmament, in the exercise of its responsibilities as the multilateral disarmament negotiating forum, re-established at its session in 1983 an *Ad Hoc* Working Group under item 1 of its agenda, entitled "Nuclear-test ban", and that the *Ad Hoc* Working Group considered the issues under its mandate;

5. *Also notes* that the Committee on Disarmament agreed that the mandate of the *Ad Hoc* Working Group on a Nuclear-Test Ban may thereafter be revised as decided by the Committee, which will consider this question with appropriate urgency, and that the Committee discussed the matter;

6. *Requests* the Conference on Disarmament:

(a) To resume its examination of issues relating to a comprehensive test ban, with a view to the negotiation of a treaty on the subject and, in accordance with that part of the report of the Committee concerning this item, to take up the question of a revised mandate for the *Ad Hoc* Working Group during its 1984 session;

(b)　To determine, in the context of its negotiations on such a treaty, the institutional and administrative arrangements necessary for establishing, testing and operating an international seismic monitoring network as part of an effective verification system;

(c)　To initiate investigation of other international measures to improve verification arrangements under such a treaty, including an international network to monitor atmospheric radioactivity;

7.　*Urges* all members of the Conference on Disarmament, in particular the nuclear-weapon States, to cooperate with the Conference in fulfilling these tasks;

8.　*Calls upon* the Conference on Disarmament to report on progress to the General Assembly at its thirty-ninth session;

9.　*Decides* to include in the provisional agenda of its thirty-ninth session the item entitled "Urgent need for a comprehensive nuclear-test-ban treaty".

General Assembly resolution 38/63

15 December 1983　　　　Meeting 97　　　　117-0-29 (recorded vote)

Approved by First Committee (A/38/623) by recorded vote (99-0-31), 22 November (meeting 37); 23-nation draft (A/C.1/38/L.35); agenda item 45.
Sponsors: Australia, Bahamas, Canada, Colombia, Denmark, Ecuador, Fiji, Finland, Japan, Kenya, Netherlands, New Zealand, Norway, Papua New Guinea, Philippines, Samoa, Sierra Leone, Singapore, Solomon Islands, Spain, Sweden, Thailand, Uruguay.
Meeting numbers. GA 38th session: 1st Committee 3-10, 12-31, 32, 37; plenary 97.

Recorded vote in Assembly as follows:

In favour: Algeria, Angola, Antigua and Barbuda, Australia, Austria, Bahamas, Bahrain, Bangladesh, Barbados, Belgium, Benin, Bhutan, Bolivia, Botswana, Brazil, Burma, Burundi, Canada, Cape Verde, Central African Republic, Chad, Chile, Colombia, Congo, Costa Rica, Cyprus, Democratic Kampuchea, Denmark, Djibouti, Dominican Republic, Ecuador, Egypt, El Salvador, Ethiopia, Fiji, Finland, Gabon, Gambia, Germany, Federal Republic of, Ghana, Greece, Grenada, Guatemala, Guinea, Guyana, Haiti, Honduras, Iceland, Indonesia, Iraq, Ireland, Italy, Ivory Coast, Jamaica, Japan, Jordan, Kenya, Kuwait, Lebanon, Lesotho, Liberia, Libyan Arab Jamahiriya, Luxembourg, Madagascar, Malawi, Malaysia, Maldives, Mali, Malta, Mauritania, Mauritius, Morocco, Nepal, Netherlands, New Zealand, Niger, Norway, Oman, Pakistan, Panama, Papua New Guinea, Paraguay, Philippines, Portugal, Qatar, Romania, Rwanda, Saint Lucia, Sao Tome and Principe, Saudi Arabia, Senegal, Seychelles, Sierra Leone, Singapore, Solomon Islands, Somalia, Spain, Sri Lanka, Sudan, Suriname, Swaziland, Sweden, Syrian Arab Republic, Thailand, Togo, Trinidad and Tobago, Tunisia, Turkey, United Arab Emirates, United Republic of Cameroon, United Republic of Tanzania, Upper Volta, Uruguay, Yemen, Yugoslavia, Zaire, Zimbabwe.
Against: None.
Abstaining: Afghanistan, Argentina, Bulgaria, Byelorussian SSR, China, Cuba, Czechoslovakia, Democratic Yemen, France, German Democratic Republic, Hungary, India, Israel, Lao People's Democratic Republic, Mexico, Mongolia, Mozambique, Nicaragua, Nigeria, Peru, Poland, Uganda, Ukrainian SSR, USSR, United Kingdom, United States, Venezuela, Viet Nam, Zambia.

In explanation of their positions, the German Democratic Republic and the USSR said the text did not provide for practical negotiations on the issue and the request to the Conference on Disarmament in paragraph 6 *(a)* was insufficient. The USSR also objected to paragraph 6 *(c)*, as did India, which saw it as unnecessary, and held that by including such issues the text would impede progress in the Conference on Disarmament.

Brazil supported the procedural recommendations contained in paragraph 6 as representing a positive trend towards starting negotiations; its affirmative vote was not to be taken as an endorse-

ment of paragraphs dealing with the future scope of a test-ban treaty. Along with India, which considered the existing means of verification to be adequate, Indonesia felt that the request to the Conference on Disarmament for resumed examination constituted a retrogression from the previous stance of the Assembly, and called for the immediate start of negotiations and the revision of the Group's mandate.

Argentina, while supporting the banning of weapons tests, found the scope of the text to be too general. Ireland regretted that the text did not convey a greater sense of urgency. Algeria felt that the text was not in conformity with the consensus established in the 1978 Final Document, and said its support for the text was limited to those aspects which were in keeping with the provisions of that Document.

On 15 December, the General Assembly adopted by recorded vote resolution 38/72, as recommended by the First Committee.

Immediate cessation and prohibition of nuclear-weapon tests

The General Assembly,

Deeply concerned over the continuing nuclear-arms race and the growing danger of nuclear war,

Convinced that the conclusion of a multilateral treaty on the prohibition of nuclear-weapon tests by all States would constitute a vital element for the success of efforts to halt and reverse the nuclear-arms race and the qualitative improvement of nuclear weapons, and to prevent the expansion of existing nuclear arsenals and the spread of nuclear weapons to additional countries,

Convinced also that the elaboration of such a treaty is a task of the highest priority and should not be made dependent on the attainment of any other measure in the field of disarmament,

Deploring that the Committee on Disarmament has to date been unable to carry out negotiations with a view to reaching agreement on such a treaty,

Recalling its previous resolutions on this subject,

1.　*Urges* all States to exert every effort for the speediest elaboration of a multilateral treaty on the prohibition of nuclear-weapon tests by all States;

2.　*Urges* the Conference on Disarmament to proceed promptly to negotiations with a view to elaborating such a treaty as a matter of the highest priority, taking into account all existing drafts and proposals and future initiatives, and for that purpose to assign to its subsidiary body a negotiating mandate under an appropriate item of its agenda;

3.　*Decides* to include in the provisional agenda of its thirty-ninth session an item entitled "Implementation of General Assembly resolution 38/72 on the immediate cessation and prohibition of nuclear-weapon tests".

General Assembly resolution 38/72

15 December 1983　　　　Meeting 97　　　　118-4-24 (recorded vote)

Approved by First Committee (A/38/635) by recorded vote (98-4-26), 22 November (meeting 37); 12-nation draft (A/C.1/38/L.29); agenda item 57.

Sponsors: Angola, Bulgaria, Byelorussian SSR, Czechoslovakia, German Democratic Republic, Hungary, Lao People's Democratic Republic, Mongolia, Poland,
Ukrainian SSR, USSR, Viet Nam.

Meeting numbers. GA 38th session: 1st Committee 3-10, 12-31, 32, 37; plenary 97.

Recorded vote in Assembly as follows:

In favour: Afghanistan, Algeria, Angola, Antigua and Barbuda, Argentina, Austria,
Bahamas, Bahrain, Bangladesh, Barbados, Belize, Benin, Bhutan, Bolivia, Bo-
tswana, Brazil, Bulgaria, Burma, Burundi, Byelorussian SSR, Cape Verde, Cen-
tral African Republic, Chad, Chile, Colombia, Congo, Costa Rica, Cuba, Cyprus,
Czechoslovakia, Democratic Yemen, Djibouti, Dominican Republic, Ecuador, Egypt,
El Salvador, Ethiopia, Fiji, Finland, Gabon, Gambia, German Democratic Republic,
Ghana, Greece, Grenada, Guinea, Guyana, Haiti, Honduras, Hungary, India, In-
donesia, Iran, Iraq, Ireland, Ivory Coast, Jamaica, Jordan, Kenya, Kuwait, Lao
People's Democratic Republic, Lesotho, Liberia, Libyan Arab Jamahiriya, Madagascar,
Malaysia, Maldives, Mali, Mauritania, Mauritius, Mexico, Mongolia, Mozambique,
Nepal, Nicaragua, Niger, Nigeria, Oman, Pakistan, Panama, Papua New Guinea,
Philippines, Poland, Qatar, Romania, Rwanda, Sao Tome and Principe, Saudi Arabia,
Senegal, Seychelles, Sierra Leone, Singapore, Somalia, Sri Lanka, Sudan, Suri-
name, Swaziland, Sweden, Syrian Arab Republic, Thailand, Togo, Trinidad and
Tobago, Tunisia, Uganda, Ukrainian SSR, USSR, United Arab Emirates, United
Republic of Cameroon, United Republic of Tanzania, Upper Volta, Uruguay, Vanuatu,
Viet Nam, Yemen, Yugoslavia, Zaire, Zambia, Zimbabwe.

Against: China, France, United Kingdom, United States.

Abstaining: Australia, Belgium, Canada, Denmark, Germany, Federal Republic of, Guatemala, Iceland, Israel, Italy, Japan, Lebanon, Luxembourg, Malawi,
Netherlands, New Zealand, Norway, Paraguay, Peru, Portugal, Saint Lucia, Solomon Islands, Spain, Turkey, Venezuela.

The United Kingdom stated that it cast a negative vote because the text referred only to nuclear-
weapon tests, avoiding the issue of nuclear explosions for peaceful purposes on which there were
fundamental differences to be resolved. New
Zealand, for that reason and for lack of mention
in the text about the need for verification, abstained. Samoa abstained because of its conviction
that a test ban should be general and complete.

Fiji felt that the text, despite its unnecessary, politically motivated tone, addressed the urgency of
the immediate prohibition of nuclear-weapon tests.
Ireland said it voted affirmatively with some hesi-
tation in view of what it considered as the restricted nature of the scope of the proposals contained in the text. Argentina believed the
resolution referred satisfactorily to the complete
prohibition of nuclear-weapon tests.

Explaining its position on all three drafts,
France held that any test ban should be placed
within the framework of an effective nuclear disarmament process. It could not, therefore, associate itself with such proposals until the two main
nuclear Powers, by reducing their arsenals, had
created conditions that would, in turn, permit
France to enter into commitments, including those
relating to its own nuclear testing.

Fissionable materials for nuclear weapons

At the General Assembly's 1983 regular session,
the question of prohibiting the production of fissionable materials for nuclear explosive devices
was taken up under the item on general and complete disarmament.

GENERAL ASSEMBLY ACTION

On the recommendation of the First Committee, the General Assembly, on 20 December 1983,
adopted by recorded vote resolution 38/188 E.

Prohibition of the production of fissionable
material for weapons purposes

The General Assembly,

Recalling its resolutions 33/91 H of 16 December 1978,
34/87 D of 11 December 1979, 35/156 H of 12 December 1980, 36/97 G of 9 December 1981 and 37/99 E of
13 December 1982, in which it requested the Committee on Disarmament, at an appropriate stage of the implementation of the Programme of Action set forth in
section III of the Final Document of the Tenth Special
Session of the General Assembly and of its work on the
item entitled "Nuclear weapons in all aspects", to consider urgently the question of adequately verified cessation and prohibition of the production of fissionable
material for nuclear weapons and other nuclear explosive devices and to keep the Assembly informed of the
progress of that consideration,

Noting that the agenda of the Committee on Disarmament for 1983 included the item entitled "Cessation
of the nuclear arms race and nuclear disarmament" and
that the Committee's programme of work for both parts
of the session held in 1983 contained this item,

Recalling the proposals and statements made in the
Committee on Disarmament on that item,

Considering that the cessation of the production of fissionable material for weapons purposes and the progressive conversion and transfer of stocks to peaceful uses
would be a significant step towards halting and reversing the nuclear-arms race,

Considering that the prohibition of the production of
fissionable material for nuclear weapons and other explosive devices also would be an important measure in
facilitating the prevention of the proliferation of nuclear
weapons and explosive devices,

Requests the Conference on Disarmament, at an appropriate stage of its work on the item entitled "Nuclear
weapons in all aspects", to pursue its consideration of
the question of adequately verified cessation and prohibition of the production of fissionable material for
nuclear weapons and other nuclear explosive devices and
to keep the General Assembly informed of the progress
of that consideration.

General Assembly resolution 38/188 E

20 December 1983   Meeting 103   124-0-23 (recorded vote)

Approved by First Committee (A/38/640) by recorded vote (106-0-25), 22 November (meeting 37); 19-nation draft (A/C.1/38/L.37); agenda item 62 *(h)*.

Sponsors: Australia, Austria, Bahamas, Bangladesh, Canada, Denmark, Finland,
Greece, Indonesia, Ireland, Japan, Netherlands, New Zealand, Norway, Philippines, Romania, Singapore, Sweden, Uruguay.

Meeting numbers. GA 38th session: 1st Committee 3-10, 12-31, 33, 37; plenary 103.

Recorded vote in Assembly as follows:

In favour: Algeria, Antigua and Barbuda, Australia, Austria, Bahamas, Bahrain,
Bangladesh, Barbados, Belgium, Belize, Benin, Bhutan, Bolivia, Burma, Burundi,
Canada, Cape Verde, Central African Republic, Chad, Chile, Colombia, Congo,
Costa Rica, Cyprus, Democratic Kampuchea, Democratic Yemen, Denmark,
Djibouti, Dominica, Dominican Republic, Ecuador, Egypt, El Salvador, Ethiopia,
Fiji, Finland, Gabon, Gambia, Germany, Federal Republic of, Ghana, Greece,
Guatemala, Guinea, Guinea-Bissau, Guyana, Haiti, Honduras, Iceland, Indonesia,
Iran, Iraq, Ireland, Israel, Italy, Ivory Coast, Jamaica, Japan, Jordan, Kenya,
Kuwait, Lebanon, Lesotho, Liberia, Libyan Arab Jamahiriya, Luxembourg,
Madagascar, Malawi, Malaysia, Maldives, Mali, Malta, Mauritania, Mauritius,
Mexico, Morocco, Nepal, Netherlands, New Zealand, Niger, Nigeria, Norway,
Oman, Pakistan, Panama, Papua New Guinea, Paraguay, Peru, Philippines, Por-
tugal, Qatar, Romania, Rwanda, Saint Lucia, Saint Vincent and the Grenadines,
Saudi Arabia, Senegal, Sierra Leone, Singapore, Somalia, Spain, Sri Lanka,
Sudan, Suriname, Swaziland, Sweden, Syrian Arab Republic, Thailand, Togo,
Trinidad and Tobago, Tunisia, Turkey, Uganda, United Arab Emirates, United
Republic of Cameroon, United Republic of Tanzania, Upper Volta, Uruguay, Vanu-
atu, Venezuela, Yemen, Yugoslavia, Zaire, Zambia, Zimbabwe.

Against: None.
Abstaining: Afghanistan, Angola, Argentina, Brazil, Bulgaria, Byelorussian SSR, China, Cuba, Czechoslovakia, France, German Democratic Republic, Hungary, India, Lao People's Democratic Republic, Mongolia, Mozambique, Nicaragua, Poland, Ukrainian SSR, USSR, United Kingdom, United States, Viet Nam.

In explanation of vote, Algeria said that, while all opportunities for dialogue and negotiation should be encouraged, its support for the text was limited to those aspects that were in conformity with the consensus established in the 1978 Final Document.[14] Argentina asserted that, although some objectionable elements contained in previous drafts on the subject had been mitigated, it still had reservations about the scope of the proposal. India maintained that attempts to separate the question of fissionable material for weapons purposes from other aspects of the nuclear disarmament process were inconsistent with the consensus in paragraph 50 of the Final Document; it felt that simultaneous cessation of the production of both nuclear weapons and fissionable materials for weapons purposes would facilitate universal acceptance of equitable and non-discriminatory safeguards on all nuclear facilities. The USSR believed that prohibiting the production of fissionable material for weapons purposes should be examined, but as one of the first steps in nuclear disarmament leading to the elimination of nuclear weapons.

The Assembly's call for stopping the production of fissionable material for weapons purposes was also contained in its 1983 resolutions 38/73 B, 38/73 E and 38/76, concerning a freeze on nuclear weapons. (For texts of these resolutions, refer to INDEX OF RESOLUTIONS AND DECISIONS.)

Strengthening of the security of non-nuclear-weapon States

The Committee on Disarmament[1] continued to consider in 1983 an agenda item entitled "Effective international arrangements to assure non-nuclear-weapon States against the use or threat of use of nuclear weapons", arrangements also known as negative security assurances. Discussion took place in the Committee and in an *ad hoc* working group set up in 1979 and re-established on 29 March 1983 under the chairmanship of Mansur Ahmad (Pakistan).

The Working Group held nine meetings between 26 and 29 April and between 16 June and 22 August. Among documents submitted to the Working Group in 1983 was one by the Group of 21, in which Group members reaffirmed adherence to principles they had set out in 1982.[51] They stated that the inflexibility of the concerned nuclear-weapon States to remove the limitations, conditions and exceptions contained in their unilateral declarations ran counter to their obligations to extend credible security assurances to

the non-nuclear-weapon States. The Group of 21 urged them to display the necessary political will so as to enable the Working Group to resume its work.

In its conclusions and recommendations, the Working Group reaffirmed the need for effective security guarantees to non-nuclear-weapon States, and stated that no progress had been achieved on a common formula acceptable to all nor on an international convention, due to specific difficulties related to differing perceptions of security interests of some States and to the complexity of the issues. The Working Group recommended to the Committee on Disarmament that ways should be explored to overcome the difficulties, that a working group be re-established in 1984 and that consultations take place to determine the most appropriate course of action.

GENERAL ASSEMBLY ACTION

In December 1983, the General Assembly adopted two resolutions, 38/67 and 38/68, on security assurances for non-nuclear-weapon States against the use or threat of use of nuclear weapons.

On 15 December, the General Assembly adopted by recorded vote resolution 38/67, as recommended by the First Committee.

Conclusion of an international convention on the strengthening of the security of non-nuclear-weapon States against the use or threat of use of nuclear weapons

The General Assembly,

Convinced of the need to take effective measures for the strengthening of the security of States and prompted by the desire shared by all nations to eliminate war and prevent nuclear conflagration,

Taking into account the principle of non-use of force or threat of force enshrined in the Charter of the United Nations and reaffirmed in a number of United Nations declarations and resolutions,

Considering that, until nuclear disarmament is achieved on a universal basis, it is imperative for the international community to develop effective measures to ensure the security of non-nuclear-weapon States against the use or threat of use of nuclear weapons from any quarter,

Recognizing that effective measures to assure non-nuclear-weapon States against the use or threat of use of nuclear weapons can constitute a positive contribution to the prevention of the spread of nuclear weapons,

Noting with satisfaction the desire of States in various regions to prevent nuclear weapons from being introduced into their territories, including through the establishment of nuclear-weapon-free zones, on the basis of arrangements freely arrived at among the States of the region concerned, and being anxious to contribute to the attainment of this objective,

Concerned at the continuing escalation of the arms race, in particular the nuclear-arms race, and the increased danger of recourse to use or threat of use of nuclear weapons,

Desirous of promoting the implementation of paragraph 59 of the Final Document of the Tenth Special Session of the General Assembly, the first special session devoted to disarmament, in which it urged the nuclear-weapon States to pursue efforts to conclude, as appropriate, effective arrangements to assure non-nuclear-weapon States against the use or threat of use of nuclear weapons,

Recalling its resolutions on this subject as well as the relevant part of the special report of the Committee on Disarmament, submitted to the General Assembly at its twelfth special session, the second special session devoted to disarmament,

Noting that the Committee on Disarmament considered in 1983 the item entitled "Effective international arrangements to assure non-nuclear-weapon States against the use or threat of use of nuclear weapons" and the work done by its *Ad Hoc* Working Group on this item, as reflected in the report of the Committee on Disarmament,

Noting the proposals submitted under that item in the Committee on Disarmament, including the drafts of an international convention, and the widespread international support for the conclusion of such a convention,

Wishing to promote an early and successful completion of the negotiations in the Conference on Disarmament, aimed at the elaboration of a convention on the item,

Further noting that the idea of interim arrangements as a first step towards the conclusion of such a convention has also been considered in the Committee on Disarmament, particularly in the form of a Security Council resolution on this subject, and reaffirming the calls made in that respect in General Assembly resolutions 35/154 of 12 December 1980, 36/94 of 9 December 1981 and 37/80 of 9 December 1982,

Convinced that abandoning policies of first use of nuclear weapons would, *inter alia*, constitute a substantive contribution to the efforts to achieve progress towards effective strengthening of the security guarantees for non-nuclear-weapon States,

Welcoming once again the solemn declarations made by some nuclear-weapon States concerning non-first-use of nuclear weapons, in particular the obligation not to be the first to use nuclear weapons, assumed at the highest political level or confirmed at the twelfth special session of the General Assembly,

Convinced further that, if all nuclear-weapon States were to assume obligations not to be the first to use nuclear weapons, that would be tantamount, in practice, to banning the use of nuclear weapons against all States, including all non-nuclear-weapon States,

Considering that, in the search for a solution to the problem of security assurances, priority should be given to the legitimate security concerns of the non-nuclear-weapon States which, by virtue of their forgoing the nuclear option and of not allowing nuclear weapons to be stationed on their territories, have every right to expect to be most effectively guaranteed against the use or threat of use of nuclear weapons,

1. *Reaffirms once again* the urgent need to reach agreement on effective international arrangements to assure non-nuclear-weapon States against the use or threat of use of nuclear weapons;

2. *Notes with satisfaction* that in the Committee on Disarmament there is once again no objection, in prin-ciple, to the idea of an international convention on this subject, although the difficulties involved have also been pointed out;

3. *Expresses its regret* that the difficulties as regards evolving a common approach acceptable to all, related to differing perceptions of security interests of some nuclear-weapon States and non-nuclear-weapon States, have once again prevented the Committee on Disarmament from making substantive progress towards the achievement of an agreement;

4. *Considers* that the Conference on Disarmament should continue to explore ways and means to overcome the difficulties encountered in the negotiations to reach an appropriate agreement on effective international arrangements to assure non-nuclear-weapon States against the use or threat of use of nuclear weapons;

5. *Requests* the Conference on Disarmament to continue the negotiations, as recommended in the report of the Committee on Disarmament on its 1983 session, with a view to concluding an international instrument of a legally binding character to assure non-nuclear-weapon States against the use or threat of use of nuclear weapons;

6. *Decides* to include in the provisional agenda of its thirty-ninth session the item entitled "Conclusion of an international convention on the strengthening of the security of non-nuclear-weapon States against the use or threat of use of nuclear weapons".

General Assembly resolution 38/67

15 December 1983   Meeting 97   108-17-18 (recorded vote)

Approved by First Committee (A/38/630) by recorded vote (70-16-15), 23 November (meeting 38); 9-nation draft (A/C.1/38/L.47); agenda item 52.

Sponsors: Angola, Bulgaria, Byelorussian SSR, Czechoslovakia, Democratic Yemen, Ethiopia, Mongolia, USSR, Viet Nam.

Meeting numbers. GA 38th session: 1st Committee 3-10, 12-32, 38; plenary 97.

Recorded vote in Assembly as follows:

In favour: Afghanistan, Algeria, Angola, Antigua and Barbuda, Bahrain, Bangladesh, Barbados, Benin, Bolivia, Botswana, Bulgaria, Burundi, Byelorussian SSR, Cape Verde, Central African Republic, Chad, Chile, Colombia, Congo, Costa Rica, Cuba, Cyprus, Czechoslovakia, Democratic Yemen, Djibouti, Dominican Republic, Ecuador, Egypt, El Salvador, Ethiopia, Fiji, Finland, Gabon, Gambia, German Democratic Republic, Ghana, Greece, Grenada, Guatemala, Guinea, Guyana, Haiti, Honduras, Hungary, Indonesia, Iran, Iraq, Jamaica, Jordan, Kenya, Kuwait, Lao People's Democratic Republic, Lebanon, Lesotho, Liberia, Libyan Arab Jamahiriya, Madagascar, Malawi, Maldives, Mali, Malta, Mauritania, Mauritius, Mexico, Mongolia, Mozambique, Nepal, Nicaragua, Niger, Nigeria, Oman, Pakistan, Panama, Papua New Guinea, Peru, Poland, Qatar, Romania, Rwanda, Sao Tome and Principe, Saudi Arabia, Senegal, Seychelles, Sierra Leone, Sri Lanka, Sudan, Suriname, Swaziland, Syrian Arab Republic, Thailand, Togo, Trinidad and Tobago, Tunisia, Uganda, Ukrainian SSR, USSR, United Arab Emirates, United Republic of Cameroon, United Republic of Tanzania, Upper Volta, Vanuatu, Venezuela, Viet Nam, Yemen, Yugoslavia, Zaire, Zambia, Zimbabwe.

Against: Australia, Belgium, Canada, Denmark, France, Germany, Federal Republic of, Iceland, Italy, Luxembourg, Netherlands, New Zealand, Norway, Portugal, Spain, Turkey, United Kingdom, United States.

Abstaining: Argentina, Austria, Bahamas, Belize, Brazil, Burma, India, Ireland, Israel, Ivory Coast, Japan, Malaysia, Paraguay, Philippines, Saint Lucia, Singapore, Sweden, Uruguay.

On 15 December, the General Assembly adopted by recorded vote resolution 38/68, as recommended by the First Committee.

Conclusion of effective international arrangements to assure non-nuclear-weapon States against the use or threat of use of nuclear weapons

The General Assembly,

Bearing in mind the need to allay the legitimate concern of the States of the world with regard to ensuring lasting security for their peoples,

Convinced that nuclear weapons pose the greatest threat to mankind and to the survival of civilization,

Deeply concerned at the continuing escalation of the arms race, in particular the nuclear-arms race, and the possibility of the use or threat of use of nuclear weapons,

Convinced that nuclear disarmament and the complete elimination of nuclear weapons are essential to remove the danger of nuclear war,

Taking into account the principle of the non-use of force or threat of force enshrined in the Charter of the United Nations,

Deeply concerned about the possibility of the use or threat of use of nuclear weapons,

Recognizing that the independence, territorial integrity and sovereignty of non-nuclear-weapon States need to be safeguarded against the use or threat of use of force, including the use or threat of use of nuclear weapons,

Considering that, until nuclear disarmament is achieved on a universal basis, it is imperative for the international community to develop effective measures to ensure the security of non-nuclear-weapon States against the use or threat of use of nuclear weapons from any quarter,

Recognizing that effective measures to assure the non-nuclear-weapon States against the use or threat of use of nuclear weapons can constitute a positive contribution to the prevention of the spread of nuclear weapons,

Recalling its resolutions 3261 G (XXIX) of 9 December 1974 and 31/189 C of 21 December 1976,

Bearing in mind paragraph 59 of the Final Document of the Tenth Special Session of the General Assembly, in which it urged the nuclear-weapon States to pursue efforts to conclude, as appropriate, effective arrangements to assure non-nuclear-weapon States against the use or threat of use of nuclear weapons,

Desirous of promoting the implementation of the relevant provisions of the Final Document of the Tenth Special Session,

Recalling its resolutions 33/72 of 14 December 1978, 34/85 of 11 December 1979, 35/155 of 12 December 1980, 36/95 of 9 December 1981 and 37/81 of 9 December 1982,

Further recalling paragraph 12 of the Declaration of the 1980s as the Second Disarmament Decade, contained in the annex to its resolution 35/46 of 3 December 1980, which states, *inter alia*, that all efforts should be exerted by the Committee on Disarmament urgently to negotiate with a view to reaching agreement on effective international arrangements to assure non-nuclear-weapon States against the use or threat of use of nuclear weapons,

Welcoming the in-depth negotiations undertaken in the Committee on Disarmament and its *Ad Hoc* Working Group on Effective International Arrangements to Assure Non-Nuclear-Weapon States against the Use or Threat of Use of Nuclear Weapons, with a view to reaching agreement on this item,

Noting the proposals submitted under that item in the Committee on Disarmament, including the drafts of an international convention,

Taking note of the decision of the Seventh Conference of Heads of State or Government of Non-Aligned Countries, held at New Delhi from 7 to 12 March 1983, as well as the relevant recommendations of the Organization of the Islamic Conference reiterated at the Thirteenth Islamic Conference of Foreign Ministers, held at Niamey from 22 to 26 August 1982, calling upon the Committee on Disarmament to elaborate and reach an agreement on an international basis to assure non-nuclear-weapon States against the use or threat of use of nuclear weapons,

Further noting the support expressed in the Committee on Disarmament and in the General Assembly for the elaboration of an international convention to assure non-nuclear-weapon States against the use or threat of use of nuclear weapons, as well as the difficulties pointed out in evolving a common approach acceptable to all,

1. *Reaffirms* the urgent need to reach agreement on effective international arrangements to assure non-nuclear-weapon States against the use or threat of use of nuclear weapons;

2. *Notes with satisfaction* that in the Committee on Disarmament there is no objection, in principle, to the idea of an international convention to assure non-nuclear-weapon States against the use or threat of use of nuclear weapons, although the difficulties as regards evolving a common approach acceptable to all have also been pointed out;

3. *Appeals* to all States, especially the nuclear-weapon States, to demonstrate the political will necessary to reach agreement on a common approach and, in particular, on a common formula which could be included in an international instrument of a legally binding character;

4. *Recommends* that further intensive efforts should be devoted to the search for such a common approach or common formula and that the various alternative approaches, including in particular those considered in the Committee on Disarmament, should be further explored in order to overcome the difficulties;

5. *Recommends* that the Conference on Disarmament should actively continue negotiations with a view to reaching early agreement and concluding effective international arrangements to assure non-nuclear-weapon States against the use or threat of use of nuclear weapons, taking into account the widespread support for the conclusion of an international convention and giving consideration to any other proposals designed to secure the same objective;

6. *Decides* to include in the provisional agenda of its thirty-ninth session the item entitled "Conclusion of effective international arrangements to assure non-nuclear-weapon States against the use or threat of use of nuclear weapons".

General Assembly resolution 38/68

15 December 1983   Meeting 97   141-0-6 (recorded vote)

Approved by First Committee (A/38/631) by recorded vote (91-0-5), 23 November (meeting 38); draft by Pakistan (A/C.1/38/L.7); agenda item 53.

Meeting numbers. GA 38th session: 1st Committee 3-10, 12-32, 38; plenary 97.

Recorded vote in Assembly as follows:

In favour: Afghanistan, Algeria, Angola, Antigua and Barbuda, Australia, Austria, Bahamas, Bahrain, Bangladesh, Barbados, Belgium, Belize, Benin, Bolivia, Botswana, Bulgaria, Burma, Burundi, Byelorussian SSR, Canada, Cape Verde, Central African Republic, Chad, Chile, China, Colombia, Congo, Costa Rica, Cuba, Cyprus, Czechoslovakia, Democratic Kampuchea, Democratic Yemen, Denmark, Djibouti, Dominican Republic, Ecuador, Egypt, El Salvador, Ethiopia, Fiji, Finland, France, Gabon, Gambia, German Democratic Republic, Germany, Federal Republic of, Ghana, Greece, Grenada, Guatemala, Guinea, Guyana, Haiti, Honduras, Hungary, Iceland, Indonesia, Iran, Iraq, Ireland, Israel, Italy, Ivory Coast, Jamaica, Japan, Jordan, Kenya, Kuwait, Lao People's Democratic Republic, Lebanon, Lesotho, Liberia, Libyan Arab Jamahiriya, Luxembourg, Madagascar, Malawi, Malaysia, Maldives, Mali, Malta, Mauritania, Mauritius, Mexico, Mongolia, Morocco, Mozambique, Nepal, Netherlands, New Zealand, Nicaragua, Niger, Nigeria, Norway, Oman, Pakistan, Panama, Papua New Guinea, Paraguay, Peru, Poland, Portugal, Qatar, Romania, Rwanda, Saint Lucia, Sao Tome and

Principe, Saudi Arabia, Senegal, Seychelles, Sierra Leone, Singapore, Somalia, Spain, Sri Lanka, Sudan, Suriname, Swaziland, Sweden, Syrian Arab Republic, Thailand, Togo, Trinidad and Tobago, Tunisia, Turkey, Uganda, Ukrainian SSR, USSR, United Arab Emirates, United Republic of Cameroon, United Republic of Tanzania, Upper Volta, Uruguay, Vanuatu, Venezuela, Viet Nam, Yemen, Yugoslavia, Zaire, Zambia, Zimbabwe.

Against: None.

Abstaining: Argentina, Brazil, India, Philippines, United Kingdom, United States.

Speaking in explanation of vote on both drafts, Brazil said the attitude of the nuclear-weapon States had compelled it to revise its position and to withdraw support it had previously extended to such proposals. Argentina spoke similarly and said it was increasingly convinced of an impasse having been reached; new ways needed to be found to make progress towards a truly satisfactory solution.

Japan explained that it had reservations on parts of the text which became resolution 38/67 concerning a specific procedure of negative security assurances, since it would prejudice the work of the Conference on Disarmament; despite similar reservations, it believed the text which became resolution 38/68 reflected the trend of the work of the Working Group, in particular reference to a common formula, and hoped the Conference would continue efforts in that direction.

Ireland felt that the first text did not take into account the possibility of different approaches to the achievement of international arrangements and favoured the idea of an international convention which would seem to imply further obligations for non-nuclear-weapon States. Sharing that view, Sweden added that that text specifically underlined the importance of a convention, which had a direct bearing on Sweden's policy of neutrality. The Netherlands said that although it saw some positive changes in the text's wording compared with those of previous years, it could not condone the accusations against some countries of having prevented the Committee on Disarmament from making progress towards an agreement; it considered the non-first-use of weapons, rather than of nuclear weapons, as the fundamental pledge; and it maintained its reservations about a convention as the form of agreement.

REFERENCES

[1]A/38/27 & Corr.1. [2]A/38/42. [3]YUN 1982, p. 27, GA res. 37/78 F, 9 Dec. 1982. [4]A/38/562. [5]A/38/375. [6]A/C.1/38/7. [7]A/C.1/38/8. [8]A/C.1/38/11. [9]A/C.1/38/12. [10]A/38/607-S/16182. [11]A/C.1/38/13. [12]A/C.1/38/14. [13]A/C.1/38/L.65/Rev.1. [14]YUN 1978, p. 39, GA res. S-10/2, 30 June 1978. [15]CD/341. [16]CD/355. [17]CD/406. [18]CD/357. [19]CD/380. [20]CD/411. [21]A/38/243. [22]A/C.1/38/5. [23]A/38/244. [24]YUN 1982, p. 64, GA res. 37/99 F, 13 Dec. 1982. [25]*Comprehensive study of the question of nuclear-weapon-free zones in all its aspects*, Sales No. E.76.I.7. [26]YUN 1964, p. 69. [27]YUN 1982, p. 68, GA res. 37/74 B, 9 Dec. 1982. [28]A/38/279. [29]A/38/196. [30]A/CN.10/38. [31]YUN 1982, p. 141, GA res. 37/99 B, 13 Dec. 1982. [32]YUN 1979, p. 46. [33]A/38/496. [34]YUN 1982, p. 69. [35]A/38/197. [36]YUN 1982, p. 70, GA res. 37/75, 9 Dec. 1982. [37]A/38/199. [38]YUN 1982, p. 72, GA res. 37/82, 9 Dec. 1982. [39]Ibid., p. 71. [40]A/38/411. [41]A/38/127. [42]YUN 1981, p. 51. [43]A/38/198. [44]YUN 1982, p. 74, GA res. 37/76, 9 Dec. 1982. [45]A/38/192 & Add.1,2. [46]YUN 1980, p. 51. [47]*The Sea-Bed Treaty: Results of the Second Review Conference of the States Parties, 12-23 September 1983* (Disarmament Fact Sheet, No. 32), DPI/798. [48]YUN 1970, p. 18, GA res. 2660(XXV), annex, 7 Dec. 1970. [49]YUN 1977, p. 44. [50]YUN 1963, p. 137. [51]YUN 1982, p. 88.

Other weapons of mass destruction

Efforts continued in 1983 in the Committee on Disarmament and the General Assembly to agree on measures for prohibiting the use and development of chemical, biological, radiological and other weapons of mass destruction.

In December, the Assembly adopted resolutions 38/187 A and B in which it urged the Conference on Disarmament in 1984 (as the Committee on Disarmament would then be known) to continue negotiations on, or submit to the Assembly, a draft convention prohibiting chemical weapons. In resolution 38/187 C, the Assembly requested the Secretary-General to complete the task it had entrusted to him in 1982 to devise, with the assistance of consultant experts, procedures for investigating possible chemical weapons use. It also asked the Conference, in resolution 38/188 D, to conclude a draft convention banning radiological weapons and to continue searching for a solution to prohibit attacks on nuclear facilities.

The Assembly further requested the Conference, in resolution 38/182, to intensify negotiations for a draft comprehensive agreement on the prohibition of new types and systems of weapons of mass destruction, and called on militarily significant States to declare their refusal to create such weapons.

Chemical and biological weapons

Implementation of the 1925 Protocol

Communications. In 1983, the Secretary-General received a number of communications on the implementation of a December 1982 General Assembly resolution[1] calling for compliance with the 1925 Geneva Protocol for the Prohibition of the Use in War of Asphyxiating, Poisonous or Other Gases, and of Bacteriological Methods of Warfare. By that resolution, the Assembly had decided, among other things, to establish procedures to investigate possible violations of the Protocol, and requested the Secretary-General to devise procedures for such investigation, compile lists of experts and laboratories that could be called on, and conduct investigations with the assistance of experts.

The USSR, in a 30 March 1983 letter,[2] said the 1982 Assembly resolution was illegal and contradicted the 1969 Vienna Convention on the Law of Treaties,[3] as it increased the scope of obligations assumed by States parties to the Protocol, with the participation of non-parties to that instrument. The USSR also objected that the resolution attempted to give the Secretary-General the functions, not assigned to him under the Charter of the United Nations, of monitoring the implementation of a disarmament agreement.

Similarly, by a letter of 18 April,[4] Viet Nam said the resolution had widened the commitments of the States parties to the 1925 Protocol without their approval; those wishing to amend and revise it should do so at the ongoing Geneva talks on a new convention on the prohibition of chemical weapons.

The United States, on 27 April,[5] stated that the prohibition contained in the 1925 Protocol had become part of customary international law and was thus binding on all States; the 1982 Assembly resolution allowed States to work together and with the Secretary-General in investigating possible violations and constituted an important step forward in helping to bring about an end to the use of chemical and toxin weapons.

Similar views were expressed by three States. The Federal Republic of Germany, on 13 June,[6] added that the procedures envisaged represented a confidence-building measure in the efforts to free mankind from the threat of the use of chemical weapons. The United Kingdom, on 24 June,[7] also considered the mechanism envisaged by the Assembly as temporary until an effective chemical weapons convention came into operation. France, the sole depositary of the 1925 Protocol, in a 26 August letter,[8] spoke in like manner and observed that Article 11 of the Charter allowed the Assembly to make recommendations on disarmament, and hence it could, subject to conditions laid down in Article 98, entrust the Secretary-General with specific functions within the framework thereby established. The Federal Republic of Germany, the United Kingdom and the United States also affirmed their commitment to the early conclusion of a comprehensive and verifiable ban on the development, production and stockpiling of chemical weapons. France and the United Kingdom expressed regret over the USSR declaration that it did not intend to carry out the recommendations contained in the 1982 Assembly resolution.

On 10 October,[9] Democratic Kampuchea transmitted three letters from its Prime Minister—two of 28 and 29 January to France and another of 26 September to the Secretary-General—stating that it had decided to recognize the 1925 Protocol as *ipso facto* binding; the 28 January letter added that Democratic Kampuchea

reserved the right to consider the Protocol no longer binding when the prohibitions laid down in it ceased to be respected by any enemy's armed forces.

Report of the Secretary-General. In October 1983, the Secretary-General submitted a report[10]—containing two annexes—to the Assembly, as requested in 1982.[1]

Annex I contained the replies of 25 Member States to his request for the names of qualified experts and laboratories whose services they might be in a position to provide. While a number of Western and other States submitted lists of experts and laboratories, three Eastern European States explained their reasons for opposing the implementation of the 1982 resolution.

Annex II contained the report of the Group of Consultant Experts, which held two sessions in New York from 9 to 20 May and from 22 August to 2 September 1983. The Group comprised experts from Austria, Ecuador, Egypt, France, Sweden and the United States, acting in their personal capacities. The report consisted of three main chapters: organization of work and summary of proceedings, procedures devised by the Group, and the assembling and systematic organization of documentation. The chapter on procedures dealt with criteria to guide the Secretary-General in deciding whether or not to initiate an investigation, follow-up actions related to the initiation of an investigation, and guidance for, and tasks relating to, the organization and conduct of an investigation. The Group's report also contained four appendices dealing with various aspects of an investigation.

The Group pointed out that, because of the complexity of the subject-matter and the short time available, it had not been possible to review thoroughly certain aspects, particularly those concerning the assembling and organization of documentation and some parts of main sections dealing with procedures.

GENERAL ASSEMBLY ACTION

On the recommendation of the First Committee, the General Assembly, on 20 December 1983, adopted by recorded vote resolution 38/187 C.

Chemical and bacteriological (biological) weapons
The General Assembly,

Recalling the provisions of the Protocol for the Prohibition of the Use in War of Asphyxiating, Poisonous or Other Gases, and of Bacteriological Methods of Warfare, signed at Geneva on 17 June 1925,

Recalling also its resolution 37/98 D of 13 December 1982,

1. *Takes note* of the report submitted by the Secretary-General on the implementation of resolution 37/98 D;

2. *Requests* the Secretary-General to pursue his action to this end and, in particular, to complete during

1984, with the assistance of the Group of Consultant Experts established by him, the task entrusted to him under the terms of paragraph 7 of resolution 37/98 D and to submit his report on the work of the Group;

3. *Requests* the Secretary-General to keep the General Assembly regularly informed on the implementation of resolution 37/98 D.

General Assembly resolution 38/187 C

20 December 1983   Meeting 103   97-20-30 (recorded vote)

Approved by First Committee (A/38/639) by recorded vote (77-20-29), 23 November (meeting 39); 11-nation draft (A/C.1/38/L.53); agenda item 61.
Sponsors: Australia, Belgium, Colombia, Costa Rica, Ecuador, France, Netherlands, Norway, Sweden, Uruguay, Zaire.
Financial implications. ACABQ, A/38/7/Add.21; 5th Committee, A/38/761; S-G, A/C.1/38/L.75, A/C.5/38/70.
Meeting numbers. GA 38th session: 1st Committee 3-10, 12-31, 33, 39; 5th Committee 68; plenary 103.

Recorded vote in Assembly as follows:

In favour: Antigua and Barbuda, Australia, Austria, Bahamas, Bangladesh, Belgium, Belize, Bhutan, Bolivia, Botswana, Burundi, Canada, Central African Republic, Chad, China, Colombia, Costa Rica, Democratic Kampuchea, Denmark, Djibouti, Dominica, Dominican Republic, Ecuador, Egypt, El Salvador, Fiji, France, Gabon, Gambia, Germany, Federal Republic of, Ghana, Greece, Guatemala, Guinea, Guyana, Haiti, Honduras, Iceland, Indonesia, Ireland, Israel, Italy, Ivory Coast, Jamaica, Japan, Kenya, Lebanon, Lesotho, Liberia, Luxembourg, Malawi, Malaysia, Maldives, Mali, Malta, Mauritania, Mauritius, Morocco, Nepal, Netherlands, New Zealand, Niger, Nigeria, Norway, Oman, Pakistan, Papua New Guinea, Paraguay, Peru, Philippines, Portugal, Romania, Rwanda, Saint Lucia, Saint Vincent and the Grenadines, Saudi Arabia, Senegal, Sierra Leone, Singapore, Somalia, Spain, Sudan, Suriname, Swaziland, Sweden, Thailand, Togo, Trinidad and Tobago, Tunisia, Turkey, United Kingdom, United Republic of Cameroon, United States, Uruguay, Zaire, Zambia, Zimbabwe.
Against: Afghanistan, Bulgaria, Byelorussian SSR, Congo, Cuba, Czechoslovakia, Democratic Yemen, Ethiopia, German Democratic Republic, Hungary, India, Lao People's Democratic Republic, Libyan Arab Jamahiriya, Mongolia, Mozambique, Poland, Syrian Arab Republic, Ukrainian SSR, USSR, Viet Nam.
Abstaining: Algeria, Angola, Argentina, Bahrain, Barbados, Benin, Brazil, Burma, Cape Verde, Chile, Cyprus, Finland, Guinea-Bissau, Iraq, Jordan, Kuwait, Madagascar, Mexico, Nicaragua, Panama, Qatar, Seychelles, Sri Lanka, Uganda, United Arab Emirates, United Republic of Tanzania, Upper Volta, Venezuela, Yemen, Yugoslavia.

In explanation of vote, Chile and Mexico maintained that a treaty could be amended only with the participation of all the States parties. Similarly, the Byelorussian SSR, Poland, the USSR and Viet Nam said the setting up of verification machinery under the 1982 Assembly resolution, and its continued implementation under the 1983 text, either violated the Protocol or the norms of international law. Argentina and India considered that move a bad precedent. Afghanistan said the 1983 resolution followed the same line as that of the 1982 text. Algeria, although considering the 1983 proposal to be purely procedural, and Yugoslavia, favouring effective systems of verification and control, abstained as the text advocated further continuation of the action begun earlier.

Poland and Viet Nam added that they viewed the text as undermining the Secretary-General's neutral status by forcing him to become involved in highly sensitive, controversial political issues. The Lao People's Democratic Republic said the United States used the initiative to interfere in the internal affairs of other countries on the pretext that chemical weapons were being used in South-East Asia.

Democratic Kampuchea supported the renewing of the mandate so that the Secretary-General

and the Group of Consultant Experts could complete the work entrusted to them.

Canada believed the terms of the Vienna Convention on the Law of Treaties were in harmony with those of the Protocol and, moreover, regarded the text as a procedural one based on the concept that it was important for the United Nations to continue work already begun. New Zealand welcomed that a number of countries had participated in implementing the 1982 resolution which provided for interim procedures to uphold the authority of the 1925 Protocol; it rejected the argument that the procedures involved extended the scope of an obligation under the Protocol. Indonesia said its affirmative vote should not be interpreted as in any way contrary to its position that the objectives of the text would be met more appropriately by a comprehensive convention on chemical weapons, such as that being sought by the Committee on Disarmament (to be known as the Conference on Disarmament in 1984).

A draft resolution,[11] entitled chemical and bacteriological (biological) weapons, was withdrawn by the sponsors (Somalia, Swaziland, United Kingdom, United States, Uruguay), citing the heavy work-load of the First Committee and the Chairman's desire to minimize the number of proposals before that body. The draft would have had the Assembly call anew for strict observance of existing legal constraints on chemical and bacteriological weapons and condemn contrary actions, welcome the ongoing efforts to ensure the most effective constraints on such weapons, and urge the Conference on Disarmament to accelerate its negotiations aimed at eliminating such weapons.

Draft convention on chemical weapons

Activities of the Committee on Disarmament. In 1983, negotiations on a convention banning chemical weapons continued in the Committee on Disarmament[12] which re-established on 29 March an *Ad Hoc* Working Group on Chemical Weapons under the chairmanship of D. S. McPhail (Canada). The Working Group held 23 meetings between 6 April and 22 August; in addition, the Chairman held a number of informal consultations. The Group's report was incorporated into the Committee's report to the General Assembly.

In an effort to resolve the remaining areas of disagreement and to record those of agreement, the Working Group set up, on the Chairman's proposal, four contact groups to deal with specific spheres of the convention: existing stockpiles, compliance provisions and verification issues, prohibition of use, and definitions. The remaining two major issues—destruction of existing means of production and non-production, and other issues requiring attention, such as the prohibition of transfers and non-development—were considered by the Working Group itself.

The Working Group's report consisted of four chapters and two annexes: annex I, containing the substantive provisions which it considered should be included in a convention; and annex II, containing the mandates of the co-ordinators of the four contact groups and their reports submitted to the Working Group.

The Committee on Disarmament accepted the recommendations made by the *Ad Hoc* Working Group: that the views set forth in annex I to its report be used as a basis for the Group's future work; that the views in annex II, including the draft formulations for possible use in a future convention, together with other relevant reports and documents of the Committee, also be utilized in the further elaboration of a convention; and that the Working Group resume negotiations in 1984 aimed at the final elaboration of a convention at the earliest date.

The Committee decided on 26 August that the Working Group on Chemical Weapons should resume its activities on 16 January 1984.

GENERAL ASSEMBLY ACTION

In December 1983, the General Assembly adopted two resolutions, 38/187 A and B, on a convention banning chemical weapons.

The call on the Committee (Conference) on Disarmament for a speedy elaboration of such a convention was also repeated in Assembly resolutions 38/183 H and I.

On 20 December, the General Assembly adopted by recorded vote resolution 38/187 A, as recommended by the First Committee.

Prohibition of chemical and bacteriological weapons
The General Assembly,

Recalling paragraph 75 of the Final Document of the Tenth Special Session of the General Assembly, the first special session devoted to disarmament, which states that the complete and effective prohibition of the development, production and stockpiling of all chemical weapons and their destruction represents one of the most urgent measures of disarmament,

Referring to the unanimous and categorical reaffirmation by all Member States at the twelfth special session of the General Assembly, the second special session devoted to disarmament, of the validity of the Final Document of the Tenth Special Session,

Convinced of the need for the earliest conclusion of a convention on the prohibition of the development, production and stockpiling of all chemical weapons and on their destruction, which would significantly contribute to general and complete disarmament under effective international control,

Recalling its resolutions 36/96 B of 9 December 1981 and 37/98 A of 13 December 1982,

Expressing profound concern at the intended production and deployment of binary chemical weapons,

Taking into consideration the decision by the Committee on Disarmament on the mandate for the *Ad Hoc* Working Group on Chemical Weapons, as well as the work of this Group during the session of the Committee on Disarmament in 1983,

Deeming it desirable for States to refrain from taking any action that could delay or further complicate negotiations,

Aware that the qualitative improvement and development of chemical weapons complicate ongoing negotiations on the prohibition of chemical weapons,

Taking note of proposals on the creation of chemical-weapon-free zones aimed at facilitating the complete prohibition of chemical weapons,

1. *Reaffirms* the necessity of the speediest elaboration and conclusion of a convention on the prohibition of the development, production and stockpiling of all chemical weapons and on their destruction;

2. *Appeals* to all States to facilitate in every possible way the conclusion of such a convention;

3. *Urges* the Conference on Disarmament to intensify the negotiations in the *Ad Hoc* Working Group on Chemical Weapons in fulfilment of its present mandate, to achieve accord on a chemical weapons convention at the earliest possible date and, for this purpose, to proceed immediately to drafting such a convention for submission to the General Assembly at its thirty-ninth session;

4. *Reaffirms its call* to all States to refrain from any action that could impede negotiations on the prohibition of chemical weapons and specifically to refrain from the production and deployment of binary and other new types of chemical weapons, as well as from stationing chemical weapons on the territory of other States.

General Assembly resolution 38/187 A

20 December 1983   Meeting 103   98-1-49 (recorded vote)

Approved by First Committee (A/38/639) by recorded vote (73-1-49), 23 November (meeting 39); 12-nation draft (A/C.1/38/L.11/Rev.1); agenda item 61.

Sponsors: Afghanistan, Angola, Bulgaria, Byelorussian SSR, Czechoslovakia, German Democratic Republic, Hungary, Lao People's Democratic Republic, Mongolia, Poland, Ukrainian SSR, Viet Nam.

Meeting numbers. GA 38th session: 1st Committee 3-10, 12-31, 39; plenary 103.

Recorded vote in Assembly as follows:

In favour: Afghanistan, Algeria, Angola, Antigua and Barbuda, Bahrain, Bangladesh, Barbados, Belize, Benin, Bhutan, Bolivia, Botswana, Bulgaria, Burundi, Byelorussian SSR, Cape Verde, Central African Republic, Chad, Congo, Cuba, Cyprus, Czechoslovakia, Democratic Yemen, Dominica, Ecuador, Egypt, Ethiopia, Fiji, Gabon, Gambia, German Democratic Republic, Ghana, Guinea, Guinea-Bissau, Guyana, Hungary, Indonesia, Iran, Iraq, Jamaica, Jordan, Kenya, Kuwait, Lao People's Democratic Republic, Lesotho, Liberia, Libyan Arab Jamahiriya, Madagascar, Malawi,[a] Malaysia, Maldives, Mali, Mauritania, Mauritius, Mexico, Mongolia, Mozambique, Nepal, Nicaragua, Niger, Nigeria, Oman, Pakistan, Panama, Papua New Guinea, Peru, Poland, Qatar, Romania, Rwanda, Saint Lucia, Saint Vincent and the Grenadines, Sao Tome and Principe, Saudi Arabia, Senegal, Sierra Leone, Singapore, Swaziland, Syrian Arab Republic, Thailand, Togo, Trinidad and Tobago, Tunisia, Uganda, Ukrainian SSR, USSR, United Arab Emirates, United Republic of Cameroon, United Republic of Tanzania, Upper Volta, Vanuatu, Venezuela, Viet Nam, Yemen, Yugoslavia, Zaire, Zambia, Zimbabwe.

Against: United States.

Abstaining: Argentina, Australia, Austria, Bahamas, Belgium, Brazil, Burma, Canada, Chile, China, Colombia, Costa Rica, Democratic Kampuchea, Denmark, Djibouti, Dominican Republic, El Salvador, Finland, France, Germany, Federal Republic of, Greece, Guatemala, Haiti, Honduras, Iceland, India, Ireland, Israel, Italy, Ivory Coast, Japan, Lebanon, Luxembourg, Netherlands, New Zealand, Norway, Paraguay, Philippines, Portugal, Seychelles, Somalia, Spain, Sri Lanka, Sudan, Suriname, Sweden, Turkey, United Kingdom, Uruguay.

[a]Later advised the Secretariat it had intended to abstain.

In explanation of vote, New Zealand said it could not support the text because it lacked balance in its approach and threatened to hinder rather than advance the work of the Conference on Disarmament; there was no justification for singling out one kind of chemical weapon while ignoring the existing large arsenals of other kinds. Similarly, Brazil said the convention should encompass all types of chemical weapons and expressed reservations as regards the concept of chemical-weapon-free zones. Those views were shared by Australia, which added that the scope of a future chemical weapons convention failed to include a ban on use, and that the measure called for in paragraph 4 was not verifiable. India was unable to support the setting up of such zones as an interim measure, holding that all efforts should be directed towards the early conclusion of a multilateral convention that would eliminate chemical weapons. The Netherlands regarded the text as an unbalanced and one-sided document which affected the consensus on a chemical weapons ban and which, while criticizing the possible resumption of the production of such weapons by a Power which had long respected a unilateral moratorium, did not effectively refute the continuing reports of their use, with which the text's sponsors would be associated.

On the recommendation of the First Committee, the General Assembly adopted without vote on 20 December resolution 38/187 B.

Chemical and bacteriological (biological) weapons
The General Assembly,

Recalling its previous resolutions relating to the complete and effective prohibition of the development, production and stockpiling of all chemical weapons and to their destruction,

Reaffirming the necessity of strict observance by all States of the principles and objectives of the Protocol for the Prohibition of the Use in War of Asphyxiating, Poisonous or Other Gases, and of Bacteriological Methods of Warfare, signed at Geneva on 17 June 1925, and of the adherence by all States to the Convention on the Prohibition of the Development, Production and Stockpiling of Bacteriological (Biological) and Toxin Weapons and on Their Destruction, signed in London, Moscow and Washington on 10 April 1972,

Having considered the report of the Committee on Disarmament, which includes, *inter alia,* the report of its *Ad Hoc* Working Group on Chemical Weapons,

Considering it necessary that all efforts be exerted for the resumption and successful conclusion of negotiations on the prohibition of the development, production and stockpiling of all chemical weapons and on their destruction,

1. *Takes note* of the work of the Committee on Disarmament during its session in 1983 regarding the prohibition of chemical weapons and, in particular, appreciates the work of its *Ad Hoc* Working Group on Chemical Weapons and the progress achieved therein;

2. *Expresses its regret* that an agreement on the complete and effective prohibition of the development, production and stockpiling of all chemical weapons and on their destruction has not yet been elaborated;

3. *Urges* the Conference on Disarmament, as a matter of high priority, to intensify, during its session in 1984, the negotiations on a convention on the prohibition of the development, production and stockpiling of all chemical weapons and on their destruction, taking into account all existing proposals and future initiatives with a view to the final elaboration of a convention at the earliest possible date, and to re-establish its *Ad Hoc* Working Group on Chemical Weapons for this purpose;

4. *Requests* the Conference on Disarmament to report on the results of its negotiations to the General Assembly at its thirty-ninth session.

General Assembly resolution 38/187 B

20 December 1983   Meeting 103   Adopted without vote

Approved by First Committee (A/38/639) without vote, 23 November (meeting 39); 17-nation draft (A/C.1/38/L.41); agenda item 61.
Sponsors: Argentina, Australia, Belgium, Canada, German Democratic Republic, Germany, Federal Republic of, Indonesia, Ireland, Japan, Kenya, Mongolia, Norway, Poland, Spain, Sweden, Ukrainian SSR, Viet Nam.
Meeting numbers. GA 38th session: 1st Committee 3-10, 12-31, 39; plenary 103.

Democratic Kampuchea said that Viet Nam's sponsorship of the drafts that became resolutions 38/187 A and B demonstrated that country's hypocrisy and cynicism.

Alleged uses of chemical and bacteriological (biological) weapons

In 1983, the Secretary-General received a series of communications relating to alleged uses of chemical weapons in various parts of Asia (see also Chapter VI of this section).

By a letter of 4 February,[13] the USSR submitted a critique prepared by Soviet experts, evaluating a November 1982 United States report[14] which alleged chemical weapons use by the USSR and its allies in South-East Asia and Afghanistan. The critique declared that the so-called new evidence supporting the allegation did not stand up to scientific scrutiny: it was a mixture of slanderous conjecture and distortion, and, to give the report a semblance of objectivity, made references to an on-site study[14] in Thailand by Dr. H. Bruno Schiefer, whose work in that country, however, was devoted to lecturing on mycotoxins and distributing information on trichothecene mycotoxicoses and various questionnaires.

Finding the USSR critique to contain what it termed an attack on the scientific integrity of Dr. Schiefer's study and on Canada's motive in commissioning the study, Canada said by a letter of 18 March[15] that it found it necessary to provide an assessment of the critique as it applied to the study. The assessment stated that the critique, by not identifying Dr. Schiefer as a national of Canada, gave the impression that he was working for the United States Department of State, and tried to undercut the study's objectivity by ascribing a motive, namely, to train the reported victims and witnesses of chemical poisoning to give false testimony; the assessment concluded that the attempt to mislead by omission, misquotation, quotation out of context and misinterpretation had destroyed whatever credibility the USSR critique might otherwise have had.

Viet Nam, by a letter of 18 April,[16] transmitted the documents of the International Symposium on Herbicides and Defoliants in War: The long-term effects on man and nature (Ho Chi Minh City, Viet Nam, 14-19 January). According to its report, the Symposium was attended by more than 160 scientists and experts from 21 countries, as well as observers from the Food and Agriculture Organization of the United Nations, the United Nations Environment Programme and the United Nations Educational, Scientific and Cultural Organization, to discuss the effects of what Viet Nam called the United States chemical warfare in Viet Nam between 1961 and 1975.

Democratic Kampuchea transmitted on 23 February[17] and on 12 April[18] lists of incidents which it claimed represented the uses of chemical and bacteriological weapons against it by Viet Nam, between December 1982 and March 1983. On 21 March,[19] Democratic Kampuchea transmitted a 16 March statement by its Ministry of Foreign Affairs denouncing what it called the intensified chemical weapons use by Viet Nam against the Kampuchean civilian population. It requested that the letter, accompanied by photographs, be also brought to the attention of the Group of Consultant Experts on the implementation of the 1925 Geneva Protocol (see above).

On 4 August,[20] the United States submitted a further report on the use of chemical and toxin weapons, based on the scientific analysis of what it said were blood samples drawn from victims in Kampuchea and in the Lao People's Democratic Republic.

By a letter dated 3 November,[21] Iran informed the Security Council, through the Secretary-General, of what it called the chemical weapons attacks by Iraq; Iran said it would be helpful if the Secretary-General's representative were given a mandate to examine the relevant medical and military evidence. On 9 November,[22] Iran reported what it called further Iraqi attacks on Iranian civilian targets, involving the use of chemical weapons in some cases. It further reported, on the same date,[23] that its Mission to the United Nations had received samples of what it claimed as evidence of Iraq's chemical weapons attack against Iran on 25 October, and that they were available for inspection by any expert who might be assigned by the Secretary-General. Asserting that Iraq persisted in its chemical attacks on Iranian civilian targets, Iran expressed the hope, on 16 November,[24] that the Secretary-General would dispatch a team of experts to the sites of attacks which it claimed had occurred on 21 and 30 October, to verify the use of chemical weapons by Iraq, before the traces of the chemicals disappeared.

By a letter of 29 November,[25] Iraq rejected the allegations by Iran as diversion and procrastination tactics aimed at disengagement from international obligations to halt the war and to abide by the relevant Security Council resolutions. It also rejected any response to the Iranian proposals for the dispatch of a representative of the Secretary-General or an expert or a team of experts.

Iran, in a letter of 27 December,[26] held the Security Council responsible for obstructing the acquisition of evidence of what it called Iraq's chemical attacks, by having remained aloof while much of the evidence faded away due to the lapse of time. The Council's failure to deal constructively with the Iran-Iraq war did not reduce that body's responsibility towards Iraq's violations of international humanitarian law, Iran added.

Radiological weapons

The General Assembly, in 1983, requested the Conference on Disarmament (as the Committee on Disarmament would be known in 1984) to conclude the elaboration of a convention banning radiological weapons and to seek a speedy solution to prohibiting attacks on nuclear facilities.

Consideration by the Committee on Disarmament. The agenda item on "New types of weapons of mass destruction and new systems of such weapons; radiological weapons" was considered by the Committee on Disarmament[12] at its 1983 session from 11 to 15 and from 25 to 29 April. In addition, the Committee re-established on 29 March the *Ad Hoc* Working Group on Radiological Weapons—initially established in 1980[27]—under the chairmanship of Curt Lidgard (Sweden).

The Working Group held six meetings between 8 and 29 April and between 13 June and 17 August. It established two groups on 8 April, at the Chairman's suggestion: Group A, co-ordinated by the representative of the United States, to consider questions relating to traditional radiological weapons subject-matter; and Group B, co-ordinated by the USSR representative, to examine issues relating to the prohibition of attacks against nuclear facilities. The Working Group itself devoted two meetings to the question of linkage between the two issues.

In its report to the Committee, the Working Group concluded that, although certain outstanding issues remained, the discussion in Group A had further clarified many of the problems involved and would pave the way for future work on the subject. Group A had forwarded to the Working Group a consolidated negotiating text of a treaty prohibiting radiological weapons, which was prepared by its Co-ordinator on his own responsibility, reflecting the state of the negotiations, including areas of agreement and disagreement. In spite of differences on specific matters, the substantive discussion in Group B—focusing on such issues as scope, legal aspects, zones, and compliance and verification—was also considered useful, having led to a better comprehension of the problems and contributed to the examination of common approaches and possible activities of the Group in the future. The Working Group recommended to the Committee that a similar group be established at the beginning of the 1984 session to continue its work and to assess how best to make progress on the subject. On 23 August, the Committee adopted the Working Group's report as part of its own report to the General Assembly.

GENERAL ASSEMBLY ACTION

On the recommendation of the First Committee, the General Assembly, on 20 December 1983, adopted without vote resolution 38/188 D.

Prohibition of the development, production, stockpiling and use of radiological weapons
The General Assembly,

Recalling the resolution of the Commission for Conventional Armaments of 12 August 1948, which defined weapons of mass destruction to include atomic explosive weapons, radioactive material weapons, lethal chemical and biological weapons and any weapons developed in the future which have characteristics comparable in destructive effect to those of the atomic bomb or the other weapons mentioned above,

Recalling its resolution 2602 C (XXIV) of 16 December 1969,

Recalling paragraph 76 of the Final Document of the Tenth Special Session of the General Assembly, in which it is stated that a convention should be concluded prohibiting the development, production, stockpiling and use of radiological weapons,

Reaffirming its resolution 37/99 C of 13 December 1982 on the conclusion of such a convention,

Convinced that such a convention would serve to spare mankind the potential dangers of the use of radiological weapons and thereby contribute to strengthening peace and averting the threat of war,

Noting that negotiations on the conclusion of an international convention prohibiting the development, production, stockpiling and use of radiological weapons have been conducted in the Committee on Disarmament,

Taking note of that part of the report of the Committee on Disarmament on the work of its 1983 session which deals with those negotiations, including the report of the *Ad Hoc* Working Group on Radiological Weapons,

Recognizing that, notwithstanding the progress achieved in those negotiations, divergent views continue to exist in connection with various aspects,

Taking into consideration that the peaceful applications of nuclear energy involve the establishment of a large number of nuclear installations with a high concentration of radioactive materials, and bearing in mind that attacks against such nuclear facilities could have disastrous consequences,

Noting with satisfaction the wide recognition of the need to reach agreement on the comprehensive prohibition of radiological weapons,

1. *Requests* the Conference on Disarmament to continue negotiations with a view to a prompt conclusion of the elaboration of a convention prohibiting the development, production, stockpiling and use of radiological weapons in order that it may be submitted to the General Assembly at its thirty-ninth session;

2. *Further requests* the Conference on Disarmament to continue its search for a prompt solution to the question of prohibition of attacks on nuclear facilities, including the scope of such prohibition, taking into account all proposals submitted to it to this end;

3. *Takes note* of the recommendation of the *Ad Hoc* Working Group on Radiological Weapons, in the report adopted by the Committee on Disarmament, to re-establish an *Ad Hoc* Working Group at the beginning of its 1984 session to continue its work and in that context to review and assess how best to make progress on the subject-matter;

4. *Requests* the Secretary-General to transmit to the Conference on Disarmament all documents relating to the consideration by the General Assembly at its thirty-eighth session of the prohibition of the development, production, stockpiling and use of radiological weapons and on the question of prohibition of attacks on nuclear facilities;

5. *Decides* to include in the provisional agenda of its thirty-ninth session the item entitled "Prohibition of the development, production, stockpiling and use of radiological weapons".

General Assembly resolution 38/188 D

20 December 1983   Meeting 103   Adopted without vote

Approved by First Committee (A/38/640) without vote, 21 November (meeting 34); 4-nation draft (A/C.1/38/L.23/Rev.1); agenda item 62 *(f)*.
Sponsors: Germany, Federal Republic of, Hungary, Japan, Sweden.
Meeting numbers. GA 38th session: 1st Committee 3-10, 12-31, 33, 34; plenary 103.

In explanation of its position, France expressed a reservation, saying that the text dealt with two subjects, one of which was not covered by the agenda item under which it was submitted; it would have preferred the text to deal solely with that item, which corresponded to the mandate of the Working Group on that question in the Committee on Disarmament.

In a similar vein, the United States maintained that the conclusion of the negotiations on radiological weapons must not be held up because of the discussions which involved issues essentially independent of the traditional radiological weapons subject-matter; it stressed the complexity of the question of military attacks on nuclear facilities and the need for continued evaluation of the existing prohibitions and rules, as well as for gathering expert opinion on the adequacy of existing legal protection.

The question of prohibiting attacks on nuclear facilities was also dealt with in 1983 General Assembly resolutions 38/9, on an armed incident involving Iraqi nuclear facilities and Israel; and 38/69, on nuclear weapons and Israel. (For texts of these resolutions, refer to INDEX OF RESOLUTIONS AND DECISIONS.)

New weapons of mass destruction

Divergent approaches towards the prohibition of the development and manufacture of new weapons of mass destruction continued to persist in 1983. In December, the General Assembly, in resolution 38/182, requested the Conference on Disarmament to intensify negotiations on preparing a draft agreement on the ban, and called on militarily significant States to make declarations, to be subsequently approved by the Security Council, on the' refusal to create such weapons.

Activities of the Committee on Disarmament. Discussion on the question of new types and systems of weapons of mass destruction continued in 1983 in the Committee on Disarmament, at plenary meetings.

The exchange of views, as summarized in the Committee's annual report to the General Assembly,[12] showed the continued presence of two differing approaches. One group of delegations favoured a general agreement prohibiting the development and manufacture of all new types of weapons of mass destruction, to be exemplified in a list, and which would also provide for the conclusion of separate agreements to ban specific weapons. Expressing concern over the development of the nuclear neutron weapon, they maintained that the permanent members of the Security Council and other militarily significant States should declare their refusal to develop new weapons of mass destruction and that an *ad hoc* group of governmental experts be established to draft agreements.

Another group of delegations believed it more appropriate to negotiate agreements case by case as such weapons might be identified. They observed that no such weapons had been identified and asserted that a general prohibitory agreement would be too ambiguous to be useful in concrete situations and would not permit the definition and implementation of verification measures. They added that the so-called nuclear neutron weapon could not be considered as a new weapon of mass destruction nor was it based on new scientific principles, and that any consideration of that subject belonged under another agenda item of the Committee, namely, the cessation of the nuclear-arms race and nuclear disarmament and all related matters.

GENERAL ASSEMBLY ACTION

On the recommendation of the First Committee, the General Assembly, on 20 December 1983, adopted by recorded vote resolution 38/182.

Prohibition of the development and manufacture of new types of weapons of mass destruction and new systems of such weapons

The General Assembly,

Recalling its resolutions 3479(XXX) of 11 December 1975, 31/74 of 10 December 1976, 32/84 A of 12 December 1977, 33/66 B of 14 December 1978, 34/79 of 11 December 1979, 35/149 of 12 December 1980, 36/89 of 9 December 1981 and 37/77 A of 9 December 1982 concerning the prohibition of new types of weapons of mass destruction,

Bearing in mind the provisions of paragraph 39 of the Final Document of the Tenth Special Session of the General Assembly, according to which qualitative and quantitative disarmament measures are both important for halting the arms race and efforts to that end must include negotiations on the limitation and cessation of the qualitative improvement of armaments, especially weapons of mass destruction, and the development of new means of warfare,

Recalling the decision contained in paragraph 77 of the Final Document to the effect that, in order to help prevent a qualitative arms race and so that scientific and technological achievements might ultimately be used solely for peaceful purposes, effective measures should be taken to prevent the emergence of new types of weapons of mass destruction based on new scientific principles and achievements, and that efforts aimed at the prohibition of such new types and new systems of weapons of mass destruction should be appropriately pursued,

Expressing once again its firm belief, in the light of the decisions adopted at the tenth special session, in the importance of concluding an agreement or agreements to prevent the use of scientific and technological progress for the development of new types of weapons of mass destruction and new systems of such weapons,

Noting that in the course of its session in 1983 the Committee on Disarmament considered the item entitled "New types of weapons of mass destruction and new systems of such weapons; radiological weapons",

Convinced that all ways and means should be utilized to prevent the development and manufacture of new types of weapons of mass destruction and new systems of such weapons,

Taking into consideration the part of the report of the Committee on Disarmament relating to this question,

1. *Requests* the Conference on Disarmament, in the light of its existing priorities, to intensify negotiations, with the assistance of qualified governmental experts, with a view to preparing a draft comprehensive agreement on the prohibition of the development and manufacture of new types of weapons of mass destruction and new systems of such weapons, and to draft possible agreements on particular types of such weapons;

2. *Once again urges* all States to refrain from any action which could adversely affect the talks aimed at working out an agreement or agreements to prevent the emergence of new types of weapons of mass destruction and new systems of such weapons;

3. *Calls upon* the States permanent members of the Security Council as well as upon other militarily significant States to make declarations, identical in substance, concerning the refusal to create new types of weapons of mass destruction and new systems of such weapons, as a first step towards the conclusion of a comprehensive agreement on this subject, bearing in mind that such declarations would be approved thereafter by a decision of the Security Council;

4. *Calls again upon* all States to undertake efforts to ensure that ultimately scientific and technological achievements may be used solely for peaceful purposes;

5. *Requests* the Secretary-General to transmit to the Conference on Disarmament all documents relating to

the consideration of this item by the General Assembly at its thirty-eighth session;

6. *Requests* the Conference on Disarmament to submit a report on the results achieved to the General Assembly for consideration at its thirty-ninth session;

7. *Decides* to include in the provisional agenda of its thirty-ninth session the item entitled "Prohibition of the development and manufacture of new types of weapons of mass destruction and new systems of such weapons: report of the Conference on Disarmament".

General Assembly resolution 38/182

| 20 December 1983 | Meeting 103 | 116-1-26 (recorded vote) |

Approved by First Committee (A/38/627) by recorded vote (94-1-28), 23 November (meeting 39); 28-nation draft (A/C.1/38/L.25); agenda item 49.

Sponsors: Afghanistan, Angola, Benin, Bulgaria, Burundi, Byelorussian SSR, Congo, Cuba, Czechoslovakia, Democratic Yemen, Ethiopia, German Democratic Republic, Guinea, Hungary, Lao People's Democratic Republic, Libyan Arab Jamahiriya, Mongolia, Mozambique, Poland, Romania, Sao Tome and Principe, Syrian Arab Republic, Ukrainian SSR, USSR, Upper Volta, Viet Nam, Yemen, Zimbabwe.

Meeting numbers. GA 38th session: 1st Committee 3-10, 12-31, 39; plenary 103.

Recorded vote in Assembly as follows:

In favour: Afghanistan, Algeria, Angola, Antigua and Barbuda, Argentina, Bahamas, Bahrain, Bangladesh, Barbados, Belize, Benin, Bhutan, Bolivia, Botswana, Brazil, Bulgaria, Burma, Burundi, Byelorussian SSR, Cape Verde, Central African Republic, Chad, Chile, Colombia, Congo, Costa Rica, Cuba, Cyprus, Czechoslovakia, Democratic Yemen, Dominican Republic, Ecuador, Egypt, El Salvador, Ethiopia, Fiji, Finland, Gabon, Gambia, German Democratic Republic, Ghana, Guinea, Guinea-Bissau, Guyana, Haiti, Honduras, Hungary, India, Indonesia, Iran, Iraq, Jamaica, Jordan, Kenya, Kuwait, Lao People's Democratic Republic, Lebanon, Lesotho, Liberia, Libyan Arab Jamahiriya, Madagascar, Malawi, Malaysia, Maldives, Mali, Mauritania, Mauritius, Mexico, Mongolia, Morocco, Mozambique, Nepal, Nicaragua, Niger, Nigeria, Oman, Pakistan, Panama, Papua New Guinea, Peru, Philippines, Poland, Qatar, Romania, Rwanda, Saint Lucia, Saint Vincent and the Grenadines, Sao Tome and Principe, Saudi Arabia, Senegal, Sierra Leone, Singapore, Sri Lanka, Sudan, Suriname, Syrian Arab Republic, Thailand, Togo, Trinidad and Tobago, Tunisia, Uganda, Ukrainian SSR, USSR, United Arab Emirates, United Republic of Cameroon, United Republic of Tanzania, Upper Volta, Uruguay, Vanuatu, Venezuela, Viet Nam, Yemen, Yugoslavia, Zaire, Zambia, Zimbabwe.

Against: United States.

Abstaining: Australia, Austria, Belgium, Canada, Denmark, France, Germany, Federal Republic of, Greece, Iceland, Ireland, Israel, Italy, Ivory Coast, Japan, Luxembourg, Netherlands, New Zealand, Norway, Paraguay, Portugal, Somalia, Spain, Swaziland, Sweden, Turkey, United Kingdom.

In explanation of vote, Greece, on behalf of the 10 States members of the European Community (EC), asserted that the approach presented in the text was unrealistic, and that those weapons and their technology could be effectively and permanently prohibited only if they were subject to concrete and verifiable controls. By giving special importance to a single blanket prohibition on the development and manufacture of such weapons, the text failed to emphasize the difficulty in distinguishing the precise delimitation of civilian and military research; it was not clear how such a prohibition could be verified, particularly in view of the need for international supervision of civil research activities. A non-verifiable comprehensive prohibition, EC maintained, would not strengthen confidence in the area. It recognized, however, the continued need for international discussions to identify potentially dangerous developments in science and technology, so that necessary control could be introduced early.

Sweden, while convinced of the importance of early prevention of the use of scientific and tech-

nological achievements for the development of new weapons of mass destruction, continued to have doubts about the idea of a general prohibition but noted with satisfaction that the text included a request to the Conference on Disarmament to prepare specific agreements on particular types of such weapons.

REFERENCES

[1]YUN 1982, p. 94, GA res. 37/98 D, 13 Dec. 1982. [2]A/38/131. [3]YUN 1969, p. 734. [4]A/38/162. [5]A/38/184. [6]A/38/281. [7]A/38/285. [8]A/38/370. [9]A/C.1/38/3. [10]A/38/435. [11]A/C.1/38/L.64. [12]A/38/27 & Corr.1. [13]A/38/86. [14]YUN 1982, p. 103. [15]A/38/120. [16]A/38/161 & Corr.1. [17]A/38/96-S/15622. [18]A/38/156-S/15702. [19]A/38/121-S/15650. [20]A/38/326. [21]S/16128. [22]S/16139. [23]S/16140. [24]S/16154. [25]A/38/650-S/16193. [26]S/16235. [27]YUN 1980, p. 27.

Conventional weapons

The year 1983 marked the entry into force of the 1980 Convention on Prohibitions or Restrictions on the Use of Certain Conventional Weapons Which May Be Deemed to Be Excessively Injurious or to Have Indiscriminate Effects, and its three Protocols.[1] The General Assembly, in resolution 38/66, noted with satisfaction their entry into force and urged all States which had not done so to become parties to them.

The Assembly, in resolution 38/188 A, extended by one year the deadline for completion of a study by the Group of Experts on All Aspects of the Conventional Arms Race and on Disarmament relating to Conventional Weapons and Armed Forces. In resolution 38/188 G, the Assembly initiated a comprehensive study on the naval arms race and, in resolution 38/188 F, invited Member States to submit their views on the holding of negotiations on naval disarmament.

Group of Experts

The Group of Experts on All Aspects of the Conventional Arms Race and on Disarmament relating to Conventional Weapons and Armed Forces—the 23-member body which had held its first two sessions in 1982[2] to prepare a study on the subject—met again in 1983, from 11 to 22 April and from 18 to 29 July. In an effort to maintain the timetable by which the Secretary-General had been asked to submit a final report to the thirty-eighth (1983) session of the General Assembly, a fifth session was held from 5 to 16 September, but there was insufficient progress to permit completion of the study.

In a 16 September letter annexed to the Secretary-General's report to the Assembly,[3] the Chairman explained that, owing to the wide area embraced and the sensitivity and complexity of the issues involved, the Group needed further time to complete its work. The Chairman reported that the Group, striving for consensus, had almost completed the substantive part of the study and had begun work on the conclusions and recommendations. He also pointed out that the two years the Assembly had envisaged for the study had been reduced to some 15 months by the time the Disarmament Commission had reached agreement in May 1982 on guidelines and the Group had commenced work in July of that year.

GENERAL ASSEMBLY ACTION

On 20 December 1983, the General Assembly, on the recommendation of the First Committee, adopted resolution 38/188 A by recorded vote.

Study on conventional disarmament

The General Assembly,

Recalling its previous resolutions in which, *inter alia*, it approved the carrying out of a study on all aspects of the conventional arms race and on disarmament relating to conventional weapons and armed forces, to be undertaken by the Secretary-General with the assistance of a group of qualified experts appointed by him on a balanced geographical basis,

Recalling the discussions at the 1981 and 1982 substantive sessions of the Disarmament Commission on the general approach to the study and its structure and scope, which resulted in the establishment of agreed guidelines for the study,

1. *Takes note* of the report of the Secretary-General to which is annexed a letter from the Chairman of the Group of Experts on All Aspects of the Conventional Arms Race and on Disarmament relating to Conventional Weapons and Armed Forces informing the Secretary-General that, owing to the very wide area embraced by the study and the sensitivity and complexity of the issues involved, the Group of Experts needs further time in order to complete its work;

2. *Requests* the Secretary-General to continue the study and to submit the final report to the General Assembly at its thirty-ninth session.

General Assembly resolution 38/188 A

20 December 1983   Meeting 103   138-0-8 (recorded vote)

Approved by First Committee (A/38/640) by recorded vote (107-0-9), 21 November (meeting 34); draft by Denmark (A/C.1/38/L.4/Rev.1); agenda item 62 (c).

Financial implications. ACABQ, A/38/7/Add.21; 5th Committee, A/38/762; S-G, A/C.1/38/L.69, A/C.5/38/65.

Meeting numbers. GA 38th session: 1st Committee 3-10, 12-31, 34; 5th Committee 68; plenary 103.

Recorded vote in Assembly as follows:

In favour: Afghanistan, Algeria, Angola, Antigua and Barbuda, Argentina, Australia, Austria, Bahamas, Bangladesh, Barbados, Belgium, Belize, Benin, Bhutan, Bolivia, Brazil, Bulgaria, Burma, Burundi, Byelorussian SSR, Canada, Cape Verde, Central African Republic, Chad, Chile, China, Colombia, Congo, Costa Rica, Cuba, Cyprus, Czechoslovakia, Democratic Kampuchea, Democratic Yemen, Denmark, Djibouti, Dominica, Dominican Republic, Ecuador, Egypt, El Salvador, Ethiopia, Fiji, Finland, France, Gabon, Gambia, German Democratic Republic, Germany, Federal Republic of, Greece, Guatemala, Guinea, Guinea-Bissau, Guyana, Haiti, Honduras, Hungary, Iceland, Indonesia, Iran, Ireland, Israel, Italy, Ivory Coast, Jamaica, Japan, Kenya, Lao People's Democratic Republic, Lebanon, Lesotho, Liberia, Luxembourg, Madagascar, Malawi, Malaysia, Maldives, Mali, Malta, Mauritania, Mauritius, Mexico, Mongolia, Morocco, Mozambique, Nepal, Netherlands, New Zealand, Nicaragua, Niger, Nigeria, Norway, Oman, Pakistan, Panama, Papua New Guinea, Paraguay, Peru, Philippines, Poland, Portugal, Romania, Rwanda, Saint Lucia, Saint Vincent and the Grenadines, Sao Tome and Principe, Saudi Arabia, Senegal, Sierra Leone, Singapore, Somalia, Spain, Sri Lanka, Sudan, Suriname, Swaziland, Sweden, Syrian Arab Republic, Thailand, Togo, Trinidad and Tobago, Tunisia, Turkey, Uganda, Ukrainian SSR, USSR, United Kingdom, United Republic of Cameroon, United Republic of Tanzania, United States, Upper Volta, Uruguay, Vanuatu, Venezuela, Viet Nam, Yugoslavia, Zaire, Zambia, Zimbabwe.

Against: None.

Abstaining: Bahrain, India, Iraq, Jordan, Kuwait, Qatar, United Arab Emirates, Yemen.

In explanation of vote, India, while not objecting to granting more time for completing the study, said attention should not be diverted nor should the time and energies of the international community be wasted on non-priority issues, when measures for nuclear disarmament commanded the highest priority.

The United States considered that the study should be funded within existing resources. Sharing that view, the United Kingdom expressed disappointment that, despite an additional session, the Group of Experts had been unable to complete its work.

Ratification of the 1980 Convention and Protocols

The Convention on Prohibitions or Restrictions on the Use of Certain Conventional Weapons Which May Be Deemed to Be Excessively Injurious or to Have Indiscriminate Effects, along with its three Protocols, which had been concluded in 1980,[1] entered into force on 2 December 1983.

The Convention and Protocols provided new rules for the protection of military personnel, civilians and civilian objects from injury or attack by means of incendiary weapons, land-mines, booby traps and other devices, as well as fragments that cannot be easily detected in the human body by X-rays.

In the course of the year, Australia, Austria, Guatemala, the Lao People's Democratic Republic, Norway, Poland and Yugoslavia ratified or acceded to the Convention, thus bringing the total number of States parties to 23[4] and enabling the Convention's entry into force, which required a lapse of six months after 20 States had notified their consent to be bound by the instrument. These States also accepted the Convention's Protocol on Non-Detectable Fragments (Protocol I), the Protocol on Prohibitions or Restrictions on the Use of Mines, Booby Traps and Other Devices (Protocol II) and the Protocol on Prohibitions or Restrictions on the Use of Incendiary Weapons (Protocol III).

The Secretary-General's report[5] to the General Assembly contained a list of signatories and parties to the Convention and Protocols as at 31 August 1983.

GENERAL ASSEMBLY ACTION

On the recommendation of the First Committee, the General Assembly, on 15 December 1983, adopted resolution 38/66 without vote.

Convention on Prohibitions or Restrictions on the Use of Certain Conventional Weapons Which May Be Deemed to Be Excessively Injurious or to Have Indiscriminate Effects

The General Assembly,

Recalling its resolutions 32/152 of 19 December 1977, 35/153 of 12 December 1980, 36/93 of 9 December 1981 and 37/79 of 9 December 1982,

Recalling with satisfaction the adoption, on 10 October 1980, of the Convention on Prohibitions or Restrictions on the Use of Certain Conventional Weapons Which May Be Deemed to Be Excessively Injurious or to Have Indiscriminate Effects, together with the Protocol on Non-Detectable Fragments (Protocol I), the Protocol on Prohibitions or Restrictions on the Use of Mines, Booby Traps and Other Devices (Protocol II) and the Protocol on Prohibitions or Restrictions on the Use of Incendiary Weapons (Protocol III),

Reaffirming its conviction that general agreement on the prohibition or restriction of use of specific conventional weapons would significantly reduce the suffering of civilian populations and of combatants,

Taking note with satisfaction of the report of the Secretary-General,

1. *Notes with satisfaction* that an increasing number of States have either signed, ratified, accepted or acceded to the Convention on Prohibitions or Restrictions on the Use of Certain Conventional Weapons Which May Be Deemed to Be Excessively Injurious or to Have Indiscriminate Effects, which was opened for signature in New York on 10 April 1981;

2. *Further notes with satisfaction* that, upon the fulfilment of the conditions set out in article 5 of the Convention, the Convention and the three Protocols annexed thereto entered into force on 2 December 1983;

3. *Urges* all States which have not yet done so to exert their best endeavours to become parties to the Convention and the Protocols annexed thereto as early as possible, so as to obtain ultimately universal adherence;

4. *Notes* that, under article 8 of the Convention, conferences may be convened to consider amendments to the Convention or any of the annexed Protocols, to consider additional Protocols relating to other categories of conventional weapons not covered by the existing annexed Protocols, or to review the scope and operation of the Convention and the Protocols annexed thereto and to consider any proposal for amendments to the Convention or to the existing annexed Protocols and any proposals for additional protocols relating to other categories of conventional weapons not covered by the existing annexed Protocols;

5. *Requests* the Secretary-General, as the depositary of the Convention and its three annexed Protocols, to inform the General Assembly from time to time of the state of adherence to the said Convention and its Protocols;

6. *Decides* to include in the provisional agenda of its thirty-ninth session the item entitled "Convention on Prohibitions or Restrictions on the Use of Certain Conventional Weapons Which May Be Deemed to Be Excessively Injurious or to Have Indiscriminate Effects".

General Assembly resolution 38/66

15 December 1983   Meeting 97   Adopted without vote

Approved by First Committee (A/38/629) without vote, 21 November (meeting 34); 20-nation draft (A/C.1/38/L.21/Rev.1); agenda item 51.

Sponsors: Austria, Belgium, Costa Rica, Cuba, Denmark, Ecuador, Finland, France, German Democratic Republic, Greece, Ireland, Italy, Netherlands, New Zealand, Nigeria, Norway, Sweden, United Kingdom, Viet Nam, Yugoslavia.
Meeting numbers. GA 38th session: 1st Committee 3-10, 12-31, 34; plenary 97.

Explaining its position, the USSR recalled that it had proposed prohibiting other types of excessively injurious weapons, such as phosphorus munitions; with the entry into force of the Convention, no obstacles remained to talks on further additional protocols to that instrument.

Naval armaments

In 1983, the General Assembly adopted two resolutions dealing with naval disarmament. In resolution 38/188 F, the Assembly invited Member States to submit their views on the holding of negotiations on limiting and reducing naval armaments; in resolution 38/188 G, it requested the Secretary-General, with the assistance of governmental experts, to carry out a comprehensive study on the naval arms race.

Proposed negotiations

GENERAL ASSEMBLY ACTION

On 20 December 1983, the General Assembly adopted by recorded vote resolution 38/188 F on proposed negotiations on naval armaments, as recommended by the First Committee.

Curbing the naval arms race: limitation and reduction of naval armaments and extension of confidence-building measures to seas and oceans

The General Assembly,

Convinced that all channels of the arms race, and in particular the nuclear-arms race, should be effectively covered by the efforts to halt and reverse it,

Disturbed by the growing threat to international peace and security posed by the continuing escalation of the naval arms race, especially in its nuclear aspects,

Aware that the growing military presence and naval activities of some States in conflict areas or far from their own shores increase the tension in these regions and could adversely affect the security of the international sea lanes through these areas and the exploitation of marine resources,

Alarmed by the ever more frequent use of naval formations (units, fleets, forces) for the demonstration of force and as an instrument of pressure against sovereign States or of interference in their internal affairs, thus threatening their vital security interests, independence and territorial integrity,

Firmly convinced that the undertaking of urgent practical steps to curb military confrontation at sea would serve the interests of international peace, security and prevention of nuclear war,

Convinced that the progress at the ongoing bilateral negotiations on limitation and reduction of strategic armaments could, *inter alia*, facilitate the efforts to restrict dangerous destabilizing naval activities and the naval arms race,

Aware of the numerous initiatives and concrete proposals to undertake agreed measures aimed at limiting naval activities, limiting and reducing naval armaments and extending confidence-building measures to seas and oceans,

Believing that measures in this field would be a significant contribution to the efforts to strengthen international security and prevent war, especially nuclear war,

Reaffirming that seas and oceans, being of vital importance for mankind, should be used exclusively for peaceful purposes,

1. *Appeals* to all Member States, in particular the major naval Powers, to refrain from enlarging their naval activities in areas of conflict or tension, or far from their own shores;

2. *Recognizes* the urgent need to start negotiations with the participation of the major naval Powers, the nuclear-weapon States in particular, and other interested States on the limitation of naval activities, the limitation and reduction of naval armaments, taking into due account the nuclear aspect of the naval arms race, and the extension of confidence-building measures to seas and oceans, especially to regions with the busiest sea lanes or regions where the probability of conflict situations is high;

3. *Invites* the Member States to communicate to the Secretary-General, not later than June 1984, their views concerning modalities for holding such negotiations;

4. *Requests* the Secretary-General to submit to the General Assembly at its thirty-ninth session a report based on the replies of Member States called for under paragraph 3 above;

5. *Decides* to include in the provisional agenda of its thirty-ninth session an item entitled "Curbing the naval arms race: limitation and reduction of naval armaments and extension of confidence-building measures to seas and oceans".

General Assembly resolution 38/188 F

20 December 1983   Meeting 103   73-19-44 (recorded vote)

Approved by First Committee (A/38/640) by recorded vote (57-20-35), 25 November (meeting 40); 8-nation draft (A/C.1/38/L.45/Rev.1); agenda item 62.

Sponsors: Bulgaria, Democratic Yemen, German Democratic Republic, Lao People's Democratic Republic, Libyan Arab Jamahiriya, Poland, Syrian Arab Republic, Viet Nam.

Meeting numbers. GA 38th session: 1st Committee 3-10, 12-31, 33, 40; plenary 103.

Recorded vote in Assembly as follows:

In favour: Afghanistan, Algeria, Antigua and Barbuda, Argentina, Bahrain, Benin, Bolivia, Brazil, Bulgaria, Burundi, Byelorussian SSR, Cape Verde, Colombia, Congo, Cuba, Cyprus, Czechoslovakia, Democratic Yemen, Ecuador, Ethiopia, Finland, Gambia, German Democratic Republic, Ghana, Guinea, Guinea-Bissau, Guyana, Honduras,[a] Hungary, Iran, Iraq, Jamaica, Jordan, Kenya, Kuwait, Lao People's Democratic Republic, Lesotho, Libyan Arab Jamahiriya, Madagascar, Malaysia,[a] Mali, Malta, Mauritania, Mexico, Mongolia, Mozambique, Nicaragua, Niger, Nigeria, Papua New Guinea, Peru, Poland, Qatar, Romania, Rwanda, Sao Tome and Principe, Saudi Arabia, Sierra Leone, Syrian Arab Republic, Uganda, Ukrainian SSR, USSR, United Arab Emirates, United Republic of Cameroon, United Republic of Tanzania, Upper Volta, Vanuatu, Venezuela, Viet Nam, Yemen, Yugoslavia, Zambia, Zimbabwe.

Against: Australia, Belgium, Canada, Denmark, France, Germany, Federal Republic of, Iceland, Israel, Italy, Japan, Luxembourg, Netherlands, New Zealand, Norway, Portugal, Spain, Turkey, United Kingdom, United States.

Abstaining: Angola, Austria, Bahamas, Bangladesh, Barbados, Belize, Bhutan, Chad, Chile, Costa Rica, Djibouti, Dominica, Dominican Republic, Egypt, El Salvador, Fiji, Gabon, Greece, Guatemala, Haiti, India, Indonesia, Ireland, Ivory Coast, Lebanon, Liberia, Malawi, Maldives, Mauritius, Morocco, Nepal, Oman, Pakistan, Paraguay, Philippines, Saint Lucia, Saint Vincent and the Grenadines, Sri Lanka, Sudan, Suriname, Swaziland, Sweden, Togo, Zaire.

[a]Later advised the Secretariat it had intended to abstain.

Explaining their votes, Costa Rica, India, Oman and Somalia found the text selective in approach. Somalia, which abstained in the First Committee vote, said international peace and security was endangered not solely by the escalation of the naval arms race but also by developments such as the introduction of massive foreign forces into the territories of non-aligned States and the use of extra-regional surrogate troops for the purpose of destabilizing the militarily weak countries. Sharing that view, Costa Rica also expressed concern about the reference in the preamble to confidence-building measures, saying that the perception of what inspired confidence depended on which Power was deploying its military forces and where. Oman found the text unbalanced and not conducive to achieving disarmament. India did not feel that the singling out of naval activities was the right approach for disarmament; efforts should focus on nuclear disarmament.

Argentina felt it appropriate for the United Nations to concern itself with what it called the disturbing issue of the recent buildup in naval deployments and their consequences for international peace and security. Also considering the issue to be timely, the Congo said the world was witnessing in all its oceans not merely an increase in naval forces, but also many military manoeuvres carried out by air and sea forces.

Experts' study

GENERAL ASSEMBLY ACTION

By resolution 38/188 G, adopted by recorded vote on 20 December 1983 on the recommendation of the First Committee, the General Assembly requested the Secretary-General, assisted by governmental experts, to carry out a study on the naval arms race.

Study on the naval arms race

The General Assembly,

Concerned about the naval buildup and the development of naval arms systems,

Mindful of the paramount importance for the security and well-being of all nations, for international trade and shipping and for the economic exploitation of marine resources of preserving freedom of the high seas and of keeping open international sea communications for trade and shipping in a manner consistent with the Charter of the United Nations and with the principles of international law,

Mindful also of recent developments in the law of the sea,

Noting that some naval units constitute integral parts of the strategic nuclear forces of the two major nuclear-weapon Powers and are therefore included in the strategic arms negotiations while other naval nuclear-weapons systems are not the subject of any disarmament negotiations,

Recalling paragraph 96 of the Final Document of the Tenth Special Session of the General Assembly, which stated that taking further steps in the field of disarmament and other measures aimed at promoting international peace and security would be facilitated by the carrying out of studies by the Secretary-General in this field with appropriate assistance from governmental or consultant experts,

Convinced that a broad study carried out by the United Nations on the naval arms race, as well as on the development of naval forces and systems and their deployment, would enhance international understanding of the issues involved,

1. *Requests* the Secretary-General, with the assistance of qualified governmental experts,* to carry out a comprehensive study on the naval arms race, on naval forces and naval arms systems, including maritime nuclear-weapons systems, as well as on the development, deployment and mode of operation of such naval forces and systems, all with a view to analysing their possible implications for international security, for the freedom of the high seas, for international shipping routes and for the exploitation of marine resources, thereby facilitating the identification of possible areas for disarmament and confidence-building measures;

2. *Invites* all Governments to submit to the Secretary-General, not later than 1 April 1984, their views on the content of such a study and to co-operate with him by making relevant material available in order to achieve the objectives of the study;

3. *Requests* the Secretary-General to submit the final report to the General Assembly at its fortieth session.

---

*Subsequently referred to as the Group of Governmental Experts to Carry Out a Comprehensive Study on the Naval Arms Race, Naval Forces and Naval Arms Systems.

General Assembly resolution 38/188 G

20 December 1983   Meeting 103   113-1-32 (recorded vote)

Approved by First Committee (A/38/640) by recorded vote (93-1-31), 25 November (meeting 40); 7-nation draft (A/C.1/38/L.57/Rev.2); agenda item 62.
Sponsors: Austria, Finland, Iceland, Indonesia, Mexico, Sweden, Yugoslavia.
Finanicial implications: ACABQ, A/38/7/Add.21; 5th Committee, A/38/762; S-G, A/C.1/38/L.77/Rev.1; A/C.5/38/73.
Meeting numbers. GA 38th session: 1st Committee 3-10, 12-31, 40; 5th Committee 68; plenary 103.

Recorded vote in Assembly as follows:

In favour: Algeria, Antigua and Barbuda, Argentina, Australia, Austria, Bahamas, Bahrain, Bangladesh, Barbados, Belize, Benin, Bhutan, Bolivia, Brazil, Burma, Burundi, Cape Verde, Chad, Chile, China, Colombia, Congo, Costa Rica, Cyprus, Democratic Kampuchea, Democratic Yemen, Denmark, Djibouti, Dominican Republic, Ecuador, Egypt, El Salvador, Ethiopia, Fiji, Finland, Gabon, Gambia, Ghana, Greece, Guatemala, Guinea, Guinea-Bissau, Guyana, Haiti, Honduras, Iceland, Indonesia, Iran, Iraq, Ireland, Ivory Coast, Jamaica, Jordan, Kenya, Kuwait, Lebanon, Lesotho, Libyan Arab Jamahiriya, Madagascar, Malawi, Malaysia, Maldives, Mali, Malta, Mauritania, Mauritius, Mexico, Morocco, Nepal, Netherlands, Nicaragua, Niger, Nigeria, Norway, Oman, Pakistan, Panama, Papua New Guinea, Paraguay, Peru, Philippines, Qatar, Romania, Rwanda, Saint Vincent and the Grenadines, Saudi Arabia, Senegal, Sierra Leone, Singapore, Somalia, Spain, Sri Lanka, Sudan, Suriname, Swaziland, Sweden, Syrian Arab Republic, Thailand, Trinidad and Tobago, Tunisia, Uganda, United Arab Emirates, United Republic of Cameroon, United Republic of Tanzania, Upper Volta, Uruguay, Vanuatu, Venezuela, Yemen, Yugoslavia, Zaire, Zambia, Zimbabwe.

Against: United States.

Abstaining: Afghanistan, Angola, Belgium, Bulgaria, Byelorussian SSR, Canada, Cuba, Czechoslovakia, Dominica, France, German Democratic Republic, Germany, Federal Republic of, Hungary, India, Israel, Italy, Japan, Lao People's Democratic Republic, Liberia, Luxembourg, Mongolia, Mozambique, New Zealand, Poland, Portugal, Saint Lucia, Togo, Turkey, Ukrainian SSR, USSR, United Kingdom, Viet Nam.

The United States, speaking in explanation of vote, viewed the study's terms of reference and underlying concepts to be broad and imprecise, finding it difficult to see how a small number of experts could deal in a meaningful way with the vast array of issues to be covered; despite consultations with the sponsors, the text failed to indicate that the study would be financed within existing United Nations resources.

Sharing the concern over financial implications and the setting up of an expert group capable of studying the subject in a balanced manner, the United Kingdom said that, by postulating a naval arms race, the study seemed disposed to produce a set of conclusions with which the United Kingdom found it hard to agree; it could not condone the attempt by a few Governments to have a United Nations expert group endorse their own views. The Federal Republic of Germany regarded the proposed study as a regrettable example of a proliferation of United Nations disarmament studies without an adequate preparatory stage.

The USSR felt the study dealt purely with technical aspects and was not aimed at taking practical measures to reduce naval activity and armaments. India said that the singling out of naval activities was not the right approach, and that the international community should focus on nuclear disarmament, rather than divert its resources and energies to activities which did not seem to have any utility.

Argentina asserted that the recent buildup in naval deployments was a timely issue, with which the United Nations should concern itself. Malta considered the text to be a valuable initiative in tackling what it called an increasingly threatening problem; however, it had hoped the text would have given equal importance to the implications of naval forces and their armaments for the security of coastal States.

REFERENCES

[1]YUN 1980, p. 76. [2]YUN 1982, p. 113. [3]A/38/437. [4]*Multilateral Treaties Deposited with the Secretary-General, Supplement: Actions from 1 January to 31 December 1983* (ST/LEG/SER.E/2/Add.1), Sales No. E.84.V.4 (p. XXVI.2-1). [5]A/38/405.

Other aspects of disarmament and related matters

In 1983, the General Assembly had on its agenda for the tenth year an item concerning the reduction of military budgets. It also continued to discuss measures for building confidence among States and for facilitating a better flow of information on military capabilities so as to avoid misperceptions and thus contribute to disarmament. The United Nations system endeavoured to reflect in its activities the interrelationship between disarmament and development.

In its continuing efforts to prevent an arms race in outer space, the Assembly considered in 1983 a new agenda item on a draft treaty on the non-use of force in that sphere. The Assembly again addressed questions of regional disarmament but, as in previous years, no agreement was reached on the convening of a Conference on the Indian Ocean. The Assembly continued consideration of its item on a World Disarmament Conference.

The World Disarmament Campaign entered its second year of implementation under United Nations auspices, and the United Nations disarmament fellowship programme provided training to 25 participants.

The Secretary-General's Advisory Board on Disarmament Studies was revived in 1983, with an additional function as the Board of Trustees of the United Nations Institute for Disarmament Research which, in turn, assumed an autonomous status at the beginning of the year. The Centre for Disarmament was transformed into the United Nations Department for Disarmament Affairs.

Military budgets and expenditures

The United Nations continued to grapple in 1983 with the problems involved in limiting and reducing military budgets and with the related objective of diverting resources from the arms race to promote economic and social development. The Disarmament Commission strove to reach agreement on the principles that should govern the further actions of States in freezing and reducing military expenditure; however, discussions revealed irreconcilable differences. Meanwhile, the Group of Experts on the Reduction of Military Budgets proceeded to construct price indices and purchasing-power parities for military expenditures.

Disarmament Commission consideration. As in previous years, the Disarmament Commission[1] considered two aspects of the reduction of military budgets: harmonization of views on their gradual, agreed reduction and the reallocation to economic and social development of resources thus saved; and examination and identification of ways to achieve verifiable agreements to freeze, reduce or otherwise restrain military expenditures in a balanced manner.

As in the two previous years, the Commission, on 9 May, established an informal, open-ended working group (Working Group I) to consider the question. The Working Group held 14 meetings between 12 and 31 May under the chairmanship of Ion Diaconu (Romania).

The Group based its deliberations on a background paper[2] annexed to the Commission's report to the General Assembly's 1982 special session on disarmament. The Group also referred to a 1982 working paper by India[2] and one by Romania and Sweden submitted in 1981.[3] Two new working papers were submitted in 1983: one by

Australia, Belgium, Canada, France, Italy, Japan, the Netherlands and the United Kingdom, stressing the need for transparency and comparability of data; and another by Bulgaria, Czechoslovakia, the German Democratic Republic, Hungary and Poland, which concluded that curbing and subsequently reducing military expenditure could not be achieved by abstract discussions on data.

During the Group's meetings, suggestions were made to reconcile conflicting positions, but no consensus was reached and, at the end of the discussion, the Chairman submitted a working paper containing a set of suggestions for formulating several of the proposals and ideas that had been considered.

On 2 June, the Commission adopted by consensus the report of the Working Group, in which it was suggested, among other things, that the Commission should continue in 1984 considering proposals and ideas, including the Chairman's suggestions, in order to identify and elaborate the principles which should govern further actions of States on freezing and reducing military expenditures.

GENERAL ASSEMBLY ACTION

On the recommendation of the First Committee, the General Assembly, on 20 December 1983, adopted without vote resolution 38/184 A, under the item on reduction of military budgets.

The General Assembly,

Deeply concerned about the ever-spiralling arms race and growing military expenditures, which constitute a heavy burden for the economies of all nations and have extremely harmful effects on world peace and security,

Reaffirming once again the provisions of the Final Document of the Tenth Special Session of the General Assembly, the first special session devoted to disarmament, according to which the gradual reduction of military budgets on a mutually agreed basis, for example in absolute figures or in terms of percentage, particularly by nuclear-weapon States and other militarily significant States, would contribute to curbing the arms race and would increase the possibilities for the reallocation of resources now being used for military purposes to economic and social development, particularly for the benefit of the developing countries,

Recalling that at its twelfth special session, the second special session devoted to disarmament, all Member States unanimously and categorically reaffirmed the validity of the Final Document of the Tenth Special Session, as well as their solemn commitment to it,

Recalling also the Declaration of the 1980s as the Second United Nations Disarmament Decade, in which it is provided that during this period renewed efforts should be made to reach agreement on the reduction of military expenditures and the reallocation of resources thus saved to economic and social development, especially for the benefit of developing countries,

Recalling further the provisions of its resolution 34/83 F of 11 December 1979, subsequently reaffirmed in its resolutions 35/142 A of 12 December 1980, 36/82 A of 9 December 1981 and 37/95 A of 13 December 1982, in which it considered that a new impetus should be given to the endeavours to achieve agreements to freeze, reduce or otherwise restrain, in a balanced manner, military expenditure, including adequate measures of verification satisfactory to all parties concerned,

Aware of the various proposals submitted by Member States and of the activities carried out so far within the framework of the United Nations in the field of the reduction of military budgets,

Convinced that identification and elaboration of the principles which should govern further actions of States in freezing and reducing military budgets could contribute to harmonizing the views of States and create confidence among them conducive to achieving international agreements on the reduction of military budgets,

Considering that the identification and elaboration of the principles which should govern further actions of States in freezing and reducing military budgets and the other current activities within the framework of the United Nations related to the question of the reduction of military budgets should be regarded as having the fundamental objective of reaching international agreements on the reduction of military expenditures,

Taking note of the report of the Disarmament Commission on the work accomplished during its session in 1983 on the question of the reduction of military budgets,

1. *Declares once again its conviction* that it is possible to achieve international agreements on the reduction of military budgets without prejudice to the right of all States to undiminished security, self-defence and sovereignty;

2. *Reaffirms* that the human and material resources released through the reduction of military expenditures could be reallocated to economic and social development, particularly for the benefit of the developing countries;

3. *Calls upon* all Member States, in particular the most heavily armed States, to reinforce their readiness to co-operate in a constructive manner with a view to reaching agreements to freeze, reduce or otherwise restrain military expenditures;

4. *Appeals* to all States, in particular to the most heavily armed States, pending the conclusion of agreements on the reduction of military expenditures, to exercise self-restraint in their military expenditures with a view to reallocating the funds thus saved to economic and social development, particularly for the benefit of developing countries;

5. *Requests* the Disarmament Commission to continue, at its 1984 substantive session, the consideration of the item entitled "Reduction of military budgets", including consideration of the suggestions of the Chairman of the working group, as well as other proposals and ideas on the subject-matter, with a view to further identifying and elaborating the principles which should govern further actions of States in the field of freezing and reduction of military expenditures, keeping in mind the possibility of embodying such principles in a suitable document at an appropriate stage;

6. *Decides* to include in the provisional agenda of its thirty-ninth session the item entitled "Reduction of military budgets".

General Assembly resolution 38/184 A

20 December 1983   Meeting 103   Adopted without vote

Approved by First Committee (A/38/636) without vote, 25 November (meeting 40); 16-nation draft (A/C.1/38/L.44); agenda item 58.
Sponsors: Austria, Bangladesh, Colombia, Costa Rica, Ecuador, Indonesia, Ireland, Malta, Nigeria, Peru, Romania, Rwanda, Senegal, Sudan, Sweden, Uruguay.
Meeting numbers. GA 38th session: 1st Committee 3-10, 12-32, 40; plenary 103.

Stating that it would have abstained had a vote been taken on the text, the Netherlands said a mutually agreed, gradual reduction of military budgets would be meaningful only if it were adequately verifiable; accordingly, it regretted that States of one particular group—including Romania, a sponsor of the text—continued to refuse to report their military expenditures. Similarly, France hoped that Romania would participate in the reporting system. The United States said it interpreted the text's reference to activities on military budgets reduction to include participation in the reporting system and in the efforts for resolving problems associated with data evaluation. India, which also would have abstained had there been a vote, could not endorse the premise that all States, rather than a few militarily significant ones, were responsible for rising military expenditures.

In related action (resolution 38/71 B), the Assembly also considered the contribution a reduction in arms and military expenditures could make to development and invited Member States to comment in that regard (see below, under DISARMAMENT AND DEVELOPMENT).

Reporting procedures

Report of the Group of Experts. Responding to a December 1982 General Assembly resolution,[4] the Group of Experts on the Reduction of Military Budgets met twice in 1983, from 7 to 11 March and from 8 to 19 August, holding 26 formal meetings as well as a number of informal ones. In a progress report[5] on the construction of price indices and purchasing-power parities for military expenditures, the Group stated that it had examined replies received as at 19 August to the Secretary-General's earlier inquiry regarding Member States' willingness to assist the Group in its work.

Ten of the 21 responding countries (Australia, Austria, Canada, Finland, Federal Republic of Germany, Italy, Norway, Sweden, United Kingdom, United States) indicated their willingness to exchange data. Although the Group felt it desirable to obtain wider participation, including countries in all geographic regions and with different accounting and budgeting systems, it considered the number of participants sufficient to proceed with its task and prepared initial requests for information from them. The Group observed that additional resources would be needed for the successful completion of its task.

Reports of the Secretary-General. In 1983, the third annual report by the Secretary-General containing information on military expenditures supplied on a voluntary basis by Member States was issued.[6] Of the 23 countries submitting information as at 2 November, 20 had used the standard reporting instrument, consisting of a matrix designed to show how much each force group (such as land, naval and air forces) spent in each resource category (such as personnel, procurement and operations). The Secretary-General submitted a further report[7] containing the views of 10 States on practical means of promoting the wider participation of States in the international system of standardized reporting of military expenditures.

Both reports were submitted in response to the Assembly's December 1982 resolution.[4]

GENERAL ASSEMBLY ACTION

As recommended by the First Committee, the General Assembly, on 20 December 1983, adopted by recorded vote resolution 38/184 B, under the item on reduction of military budgets.

The General Assembly,

Deeply concerned about the arms race and present tendencies to increase further the rate of growth of military expenditures, the deplorable waste of human and economic resources and the potentially harmful effects on world peace and security,

Considering that a gradual reduction of military expenditures on a mutually agreed basis would be a measure that would contribute to curbing the arms race and would increase the possibilities of reallocating resources now being used for military purposes to economic and social development, particularly for the benefit of the developing countries,

Convinced that such reductions could and should be carried out on a mutually agreed basis without detriment to the national security of any country,

Reaffirming its conviction that provisions for defining, reporting, comparing and verifying military expenditures will have to be basic elements of any international agreement to reduce such expenditures,

Recalling that an international system for the standardized reporting of military expenditures has been introduced in pursuance of General Assembly resolution 35/142 B of 12 December 1980, and that annual reports on military expenditures are now being received from a number of Member States,

Considering that a wider participation in the reporting system of States from different geographic regions and representing different budgeting systems would promote its further refinement and would, by contributing to greater openness in military matters, increase confidence between States,

Noting, in this connection, the proposal to convene an international conference on military expenditures,

Recalling its resolution 37/95 B of 13 December 1982, in which it requested the Secretary-General, with the assistance of a group of qualified experts and with the voluntary co-operation of States, to undertake the task

of constructing price indices and purchasing-power parities for the military expenditures of participating States,

Considering that a wide participation in this exercise is essential for achieving the most useful results possible,

Noting that in the progress report of the Secretary-General the Group of Experts on the Reduction of Military Budgets established that a direct contact between its members and the voluntarily participating Member States is vital for the work of the Group,

Emphasizing that all the above-mentioned activities and initiatives, as well as other ongoing activities within the United Nations relating to the reduction of military budgets, should have the fundamental objective of facilitating future negotiations aimed at the conclusion of international agreements on the reduction of military expenditures,

1. *Takes note with appreciation* of the report of the Secretary-General containing the replies received in 1983 from Member States in the framework of the above-mentioned reporting system and with the submitted data arranged by the Secretariat according to statistical practice, and of the report of the Secretary-General containing views and suggestions of States on practical means of promoting the wider participation of States in the international system of standardized reporting of military expenditures;

2. *Stresses* the need to increase the number of reporting States with a view to the broadest possible participation of States from different geographic regions and representing different budgeting systems;

3. *Reiterates its recommendation* that all Member States should report annually, by 30 April, to the Secretary-General, using the reporting instrument, their military expenditures for the latest fiscal year for which data are available;

4. *Also takes note with appreciation* of the progress report of the Secretary-General on the ongoing exercise undertaken in pursuance of paragraph 5 of General Assembly resolution 37/95 B;

5. *Reiterates its invitation* to all Member States to participate in the above-mentioned exercise;

6. *Requests* the Secretary-General to provide the Group of Experts on the Reduction of Military Budgets with sufficient financial and other resources to carry out its complex tasks as outlined in the progress report of the Secretary-General;

7. *Decides* to include in the provisional agenda of its thirty-ninth session the item entitled "Reduction of military budgets".

General Assembly resolution 38/184 B

20 December 1983   Meeting 103   116-13-8 (recorded vote)

Approved by First Committee (A/38/636) by recorded vote (78-12-8), 25 November (meeting 40); 18-nation draft (A/C.1/38/L.49); agenda item 58.

Sponsors: Australia, Austria, Belgium, Canada, Costa Rica, Ecuador, Finland, France, Germany, Federal Republic of, Ireland, Italy, Malta, New Zealand, Norway, Romania, Sudan, Sweden, Uruguay.

Financial implications. ACABQ, A/38/7/Add.21; 5th Committee, A/38/759; S-G, A/C.1/38/L.74, A/C.5/38/69.

Meeting numbers. GA 38th session: 1st Committee 3-10, 12-31, 33, 40; 5th Committee 68; plenary 103.

Recorded vote in Assembly as follows:

In favour: Angola, Antigua and Barbuda, Australia, Austria, Bahamas, Bahrain, Bangladesh, Barbados, Belgium, Belize, Benin, Bhutan, Bolivia, Botswana, Burundi, Canada, Cape Verde, Central African Republic, Chad, Chile, Colombia, Congo, Costa Rica, Cyprus, Democratic Kampuchea, Denmark, Djibouti, Dominica, Dominican Republic, Ecuador, Egypt, El Salvador, Fiji, Finland, France, Gabon, Gambia, Germany, Federal Republic of, Ghana, Greece, Guatemala,

Guinea, Guinea-Bissau, Guyana, Haiti, Honduras, Iceland, Indonesia, Iraq, Ireland, Israel, Italy, Ivory Coast, Jamaica, Japan, Jordan, Kenya, Lebanon, Lesotho, Liberia, Luxembourg, Madagascar, Malawi, Malaysia, Maldives, Mali, Malta, Mauritania, Mauritius, Mexico, Morocco, Nepal, Netherlands, New Zealand, Niger, Nigeria, Norway, Oman, Pakistan, Panama, Papua New Guinea, Paraguay, Peru, Philippines, Portugal, Qatar, Romania, Rwanda, Saint Lucia, Saint Vincent and the Grenadines, Senegal, Sierra Leone, Singapore, Somalia, Spain, Sri Lanka, Sudan, Suriname, Swaziland, Sweden, Thailand, Togo, Trinidad and Tobago, Tunisia, Turkey, Uganda, United Arab Emirates, United Kingdom, United Republic of Cameroon, United States, Uruguay, Vanuatu, Venezuela, Yemen, Yugoslavia, Zaire.

Against: Afghanistan, Bulgaria, Byelorussian SSR, Cuba, Czechoslovakia, German Democratic Republic, Hungary, Lao People's Democratic Republic, Mongolia, Poland, Ukrainian SSR, USSR, Viet Nam.

Abstaining: Argentina, Brazil, China, India, Mozambique, Syrian Arab Republic, United Republic of Tanzania, Zambia.

In explanation of vote, Brazil said the text did not stress the special responsibility borne by the nuclear-weapon States, whose military expenditures, it said, accounted for almost 90 per cent of the overall resources diverted to armaments. Sharing that view, India felt that exercises such as that endorsed by the text served to deflect attention from the principal political issues in disarmament. Yugoslavia said the text would be useful and effective only if all countries, primarily the militarily significant States, participated in the reporting system.

The German Democratic Republic, asserting that agreements on freeze or reduction could be readily attained given the necessary political will, said insistence on transparency and agreement on reporting, comparison and verification prevented negotiations leading to that end.

The United Kingdom and the United States welcomed the text's emphasis on the need for wider participation in the reporting system, saying that greater openness and comparison of military expenditures helped strengthen international confidence. The United Kingdom was disappointed, however, that no State member of the Warsaw Treaty Organization had participated in that exercise. According to the Netherlands, the negative votes showed that those States were not serious about reducing military budgets. France hoped that Romania, a sponsor of the text, would participate, and stressed the need for comparability of data for the drawing of valid conclusions.

The United Kingdom believed that, because of the limited participation in the exercise, additional support should be found within the existing resources.

Arms race in outer space and anti-satellite systems

In 1983, the General Assembly considered a new agenda item and the text of a draft treaty, both proposed by the USSR, on the non-use of force in outer space. At the same time, it continued to discuss whether to concentrate on reaching a general agreement on preventing an arms race in outer space in all its aspects, or on a verifiable agreement prohibiting anti-satellite systems.

Activities of the Committee on Disarmament. The Committee on Disarmament[8] considered the item on preventing an arms race in outer space, from 18 to 22 April and from 8 to 12 August 1983, in both plenary and informal meetings. The debate centred on an appropriate mandate for an *ad hoc* working group on the question. Despite the setting up of a contact group, which held a number of meetings under the guidance of the Committee Chairman to formulate a mandate, no consensus was reached.

Two proposals submitted to the Committee in 1983 dealt with an *ad hoc* working group. Mongolia[9] believed that the mandate should provide a possibility for negotiating an agreement on preventing an arms race in outer space in all its aspects and for initially identifying the questions of immediate concern. The 10 Western States in the Committee[10] would have had the working group identify, through substantive examination, issues relevant to preventing such an arms race, taking into account all existing agreements and proposals as well as future initiatives.

In the Committee, the group of 21 and the socialist States reiterated their previous separate proposals[11] for setting up a working group. The socialist States also indicated that they could support the proposal of the group of 21—that a working group be established immediately with a mandate to negotiate an agreement or agreements for preventing an arms race in outer space in all aspects—which China also supported.

A working paper, submitted by France,[12] dealt, *inter alia*, with possible future technological developments and the inadequacy of existing legal instruments in ensuring the immunity of satellites. The USSR also submitted a document,[13] stating its commitment not to be the first to put into outer space any type of anti-satellite weapon as long as other countries, including the United States, reciprocated.

Consideration by the Committee on outer space. The Committee on the Peaceful Uses of Outer Space (Committee on outer space),[14] in 1983, urged all nations, particularly those with major space capabilities, to contribute actively to preventing an arms race in outer space, declaring that objective to be essential for international cooperation in the peaceful uses of that sphere. Some delegations called for the early preparation of legal instruments to prevent further militarization of outer space; some also felt that the two major space Powers should resume the arms control negotiations on anti-satellite systems. Some considered the Conference on Disarmament (as the Committee on Disarmament would be known in 1984) to be the appropriate forum to deal with the question; others spoke of the legitimate interest of the Committee on outer space, believed that body should give priority consideration to the question, and felt that the Conference should take the Committee's views into account in its negotiations.

Subsequently, the General Assembly, in resolution 38/80, called for prompt negotiations under United Nations auspices on agreement(s) on halting the militarization of outer space; it requested the Committee on outer space to consider, as a priority, the questions relating to such militarization, taking also into account the need to co-ordinate its efforts with those of the Conference (see Chapter II of this section).

GENERAL ASSEMBLY CONSIDERATION

In 1983, the General Assembly considered the question of outer space and its uses under the previous two items of its agenda—"Prevention of an arms race in outer space: report of the Committee on Disarmament" and "General and complete disarmament", the latter including a sub-item entitled "Prevention of an arms race in outer space and prohition of anti-satellite systems: report of the Committee on Disarmament"—and a third item entitled "Conclusion of a treaty on the prohibition of the use of force in outer space and from space against the Earth", which was included in the 1983 agenda at the request of the USSR.[15] In proposing the item, the USSR stated that it was seeking to avoid the militarization of outer space, being particularly concerned about the plans to create and deploy various space-weapon systems capable of destroying targets both in space and on the Earth. A draft treaty was annexed to the proposal.

Three draft resolutions were submitted to the First Committee. Two of them—one sponsored by 12 Western and other States, and one by Mongolia—were not pressed to a vote; the other, sponsored by 20 States, was approved.

The draft sponsored by the Western and other States, entitled "Prevention of an arms race in outer space and prohibition of anti-satellite systems",[16] would have had the Assembly request the Conference on Disarmament to continue consideration of negotiating effective and verifiable agreements on that subject, including ways of strengthening the outer-space legal régime for protecting satellites.

Mongolia's draft,[17] submitted under the new agenda item on concluding an outer space treaty, would have had the Assembly request the Conference, in co-operation with the Committee on outer space, to consider elaborating a relevant international agreement, and to consider, *inter alia*, establishing an *ad hoc* working group to negotiate an agreement or agreements to prevent an arms race in outer space in all aspects. In announcing that it would not press its draft to a vote, Mongolia joined the sponsors of the text that became resolution 38/70 (see below).

GENERAL ASSEMBLY ACTION

By decision 38/421 of 15 December, the Assembly, on an oral proposal by its President, took note of the First Committee's report[18] on the disposition of the Mongolian draft.

Conclusion of a treaty on the prohibition of the use of force in outer space and from space against the Earth
At its 97th plenary meeting, on 15 December 1983, the General Assembly took note of the report of the First Committee.

General Assembly decision 38/421

Adopted without vote

Oral proposal by President; agenda item 141.
Meeting numbers. GA 38th session: 1st Committee 3-10, 12-31, 33, 41; plenary 97.

On 15 December, the Assembly, on the recommendation of the First Committee, adopted resolution 38/70 by recorded vote.

Prevention of an arms race in outer space
The General Assembly,

Inspired by the great prospects opening up before mankind as a result of man's entry into outer space twenty-six years ago,

Recognizing the common interest of all mankind in the exploration and use of outer space for peaceful purposes,

Reaffirming that the exploration and use of outer space, including the Moon and other celestial bodies, shall be carried out for the benefit and in the interest of all countries, irrespective of their degree of economic or scientific development, and shall be the province of all mankind,

Reaffirming further the will of all States that the exploration and use of outer space, including the Moon and other celestial bodies, shall be exclusively for peaceful purposes,

Recalling that the States parties to the Treaty on Principles Governing the Activities of States in the Exploration and Use of Outer Space, including the Moon and Other Celestial Bodies, have undertaken, in article III, to carry on activities in the exploration and use of outer space, including the Moon and other celestial bodies, in accordance with international law and the Charter of the United Nations, in the interest of maintaining international peace and security and promoting international co-operation and understanding,

Reaffirming, in particular, article IV of the above-mentioned Treaty, which stipulates that States parties to the Treaty undertake not to place in orbit around the Earth any objects carrying nuclear weapons or any other kinds of weapons of mass destruction, install such weapons on celestial bodies or station such weapons in outer space in any other manner,

Reaffirming also paragraph 80 of the Final Document of the Tenth Special Session of the General Assembly, in which it is stated that, in order to prevent an arms race in outer space, further measures should be taken and appropriate international negotiations held in accordance with the spirit of the Treaty,

Recalling its resolutions 36/97 C and 36/99 of 9 December 1981, 37/83 of 9 December 1982 and 37/99 D of 13 December 1982,

Gravely concerned at the danger posed to all mankind by an arms race in outer space,

Mindful of the widespread interest expressed by Member States in the course of the negotiations on and following the adoption of the above-mentioned Treaty in ensuring that the exploration and use of outer space should be for peaceful purposes, and taking note of proposals submitted to the General Assembly at its tenth special session and at its regular sessions and to the Committee on Disarmament,

Noting the grave concern expressed by the Second United Nations Conference on the Exploration and Peaceful Uses of Outer Space over the extension of an arms race into outer space and the recommendations made to the competent organs of the United Nations, in particular the General Assembly, and also to the Committee on Disarmament,

Convinced that further measures are needed for the prevention of an arms race in outer space,

Recognizing that, in the context of multilateral negotiations for preventing an arms race in outer space, the resumption of bilateral negotiations between the Union of Soviet Socialist Republics and the United States of America could make a significant contribution to such an objective,

Taking note of the report of the Committee on Disarmament,

Noting that in the course of its session in 1983 the Committee on Disarmament considered this subject both at its formal and informal meetings, as well as through informal consultations,

Aware of the various proposals submitted by Member States to the Committee on Disarmament, particularly concerning the establishment of a working group on the subject and its draft mandate, which had been considered extensively by a contact group,

Taking note of the draft Treaty on the Prohibition of the Use of Force in Outer Space and from Space against the Earth, submitted by the Union of Soviet Socialist Republics, as well as views and comments expressed during the discussion of that draft at its thirty-eighth session,

Expressing its deep concern and disappointment that, although there was no objection, in principle, to the establishment without delay of such a working group, the Committee on Disarmament has not thus far been enabled to reach agreement on an acceptable mandate for the working group during its 1983 session,

1. *Reaffirms* that general and complete disarmament under effective international control warrants that outer space shall be used exclusively for peaceful purposes and that it shall not become an arena for an arms race;

2. *Emphasizes* that further effective measures to prevent an arms race in outer space should be adopted by the international community;

3. *Calls upon* all States, in particular those with major space capabilities, to contribute actively to the objective of the peaceful use of outer space and to take immediate measures to prevent an arms race in outer space;

4. *Reiterates* that the Conference on Disarmament, as the single multilateral disarmament negotiating forum, has a primary role in the negotiation of an agreement or agreements, as appropriate, on the prevention of an arms race in all its aspects in outer space;

5. *Requests* the Conference on Disarmament to consider as a matter of priority the question of preventing an arms race in outer space;

6. *Also requests* the Conference on Disarmament to intensify its consideration of the question of the prevention of an arms race in outer space in all its aspects, taking into account all relevant proposals, including the consideration of the proposal referred to in the preambular part of the present resolution;

7. *Further requests* the Conference on Disarmament to establish an *ad hoc* working group at the beginning of its session in 1984, with a view to undertaking negotiations for the conclusion of an agreement or agreements, as appropriate, to prevent an arms race in all its aspects in outer space;

8. *Requests* the Conference on Disarmament to report on its consideration of this subject to the General Assembly at its thirty-ninth session;

9. *Requests* the Secretary-General to transmit to the Conference on Disarmament all documents relating to the consideration of this subject by the General Assembly at its thirty-eighth session;

10. *Decides* to include in the provisional agenda of its thirty-ninth session the item entitled "Prevention of an arms race in outer space".

General Assembly resolution 38/70

15 December 1983   Meeting 97   147-1-1 (recorded vote)

Approved by First Committee (A/38/633) by recorded vote (121-1-1), 25 November (meeting 41); 20-nation draft (A/C.1/38/L.36/Rev.1), orally revised; agenda item 55.
Sponsors: Bangladesh, Bulgaria, Byelorussian SSR, Cuba, Czechoslovakia, Egypt, German Democratic Republic, Hungary, India, Indonesia, Ireland, Maldives, Mongolia, Pakistan, Poland, Sri Lanka, Sudan, Sweden, Ukrainian SSR, Viet Nam.
Meeting numbers. GA 38th session: 1st Committee 3-10, 12-31, 33, 41; plenary 97.
Recorded vote in Assembly as follows

In favour: Afghanistan, Algeria, Angola, Antigua and Barbuda, Argentina, Australia, Austria, Bahamas, Bahrain, Bangladesh, Barbados, Belgium, Belize, Benin, Bhutan, Bolivia, Botswana, Brazil, Bulgaria, Burma, Burundi, Byelorussian SSR, Canada, Cape Verde, Central African Republic, Chad, Chile, China, Colombia, Congo, Costa Rica, Cuba, Cyprus, Czechoslovakia, Democratic Kampuchea, Democratic Yemen, Denmark, Djibouti, Dominican Republic, Ecuador, Egypt, El Salvador, Ethiopia, Fiji, Finland, France, Gabon, Gambia, German Democratic Republic, Germany, Federal Republic of, Ghana, Greece, Grenada, Guatemala, Guinea, Guyana, Haiti, Honduras, Hungary, Iceland, India, Indonesia, Iran, Iraq, Ireland, Israel, Italy, Ivory Coast, Jamaica, Japan, Jordan, Kenya, Kuwait, Lao People's Democratic Republic, Lebanon, Lesotho, Liberia, Libyan Arab Jamahiriya, Luxembourg, Madagascar, Malawi, Malaysia, Maldives, Mali, Malta, Mauritania, Mauritius, Mexico, Mongolia, Morocco, Mozambique, Nepal, Netherlands, New Zealand, Nicaragua, Niger, Nigeria, Norway, Oman, Pakistan, Panama, Papua New Guinea, Paraguay, Peru, Philippines, Poland, Portugal, Qatar, Romania, Rwanda, Saint Lucia, Sao Tome and Principe, Saudi Arabia, Senegal, Seychelles, Sierra Leone, Singapore, Solomon Islands, Somalia, Spain, Sri Lanka, Sudan, Suriname, Swaziland, Sweden, Syrian Arab Republic, Thailand, Togo, Trinidad and Tobago, Tunisia, Turkey, Uganda, Ukrainian SSR, USSR, United Arab Emirates, United Republic of Cameroon, United Republic of Tanzania, Upper Volta, Uruguay, Vanuatu, Venezuela, Viet Nam, Yemen, Yugoslavia, Zaire, Zambia, Zimbabwe.

Against: United States.

Abstaining: United Kingdom.

In explanation of vote, the United Kingdom said the text prejudged a number of important issues and ignored or dismissed unsolved problems, whereas the withdrawn Western draft had offered a realistic and balanced approach.

Italy said that paragraph 7 on the mandate did not fully respect the autonomy of the Conference on Disarmament; Belgium, the Federal Republic of Germany and Japan expressed similar reservations. Norway felt that the proposed mandate was broader than what was currently acceptable to all members of that body. Mexico and the USSR stressed the need for an *ad hoc* working group with an appropriate mandate. Brazil and Mexico hoped that the State casting the sole negative vote would honour the wishes of the majority, while India hoped the adoption of a consensus text would be reflected in the Conference's deliberations.

The Federal Republic of Germany and Turkey expressed reservations about the phrase "exclusively for peaceful purposes", in paragraph 1. Similarly, Australia said this should not be interpreted as contrary to its interest in stable deterrence, and Belgium rejected concepts linked to the demilitarization of outer space in so far as that affected security.

Italy, Japan and Norway considered it inappropriate that the text singled out from other proposals the draft treaty proposed by the USSR; the Federal Republic of Germany further expressed doubts about whether that draft proposal formed a suitable basis for negotiations. Japan also felt the various terms of the text lacked precise definition. The Federal Republic of Germany added that it should be left to the parties of former bilateral discussions to decide when to renew their efforts.

Regional disarmament

The General Assembly's 1983 consideration of regional disarmament measures focused on implementing its 1971 Declaration of the Indian Ocean as a Zone of Peace[19] and on the possibility of establishing a zone of peace in South-East Asia.

Report of the Secretary-General. In connection with the Assembly's consideration of regional disarmament, the Secretary-General submitted in early October a report, with later addenda,[20] prepared in response to a December 1982 Assembly resolution,[21] containing the views of, or measures taken by, Belgium, Bulgaria and the USSR in regard to regional disarmament. Information was also provided by the United Nations Institute for Disarmament Research (see below) which stated that it had received no specific requests to assist States and regional institutions concerning regional disarmament.

GENERAL ASSEMBLY ACTION

Acting on the recommendation of the First Committee, the General Assembly, on 15 December 1983, adopted without vote resolution 38/73 J.

Regional disarmament

The General Assembly,

Recalling its resolution 37/100 F of 13 December 1982 on regional disarmament,

1. *Takes note* of the report of the Secretary-General;

2. *Takes note also* of the fact that, at the request of the States having participated in the Madrid meeting of representatives of the participating States of the Conference on Security and Co-operation in Europe, held from 11 November 1980 to 9 September 1983, on the basis of the provisions of the Final Act relating to the follow-up to the Conference, the Government of Spain has transmitted the Concluding Document of this meeting to the Secretary-General;

3. *Expresses its satisfaction,* in this connection, at the convening at Stockholm of the Conference on Confidence- and Security-building Measures and Disarmament in Europe, commencing on 17 January 1984, as a substantial and integral part of the multilateral process initiated by the Conference on Security and Co-operation in Europe;

4. *Takes note also* of the proposals made in the context of regional disarmament since the adoption of its resolution 37/100 F;

5. *Requests* the Secretary-General to keep the General Assembly regularly informed on the implementation of resolution 37/100 F, as well as on the activities carried out by the Secretariat, in particular the Department for Disarmament Affairs, and the United Nations Institute for Disarmament Research, in the field of the regional approach to disarmament;

6. *Decides* to include in the provisional agenda of its thirty-ninth session the item entitled "Regional disarmament: report of the Secretary-General".

General Assembly resolution 38/73 J

15 December 1983   Meeting 97   Adopted without vote

Approved by First Committee (A/38/641) without vote, 21 November (meeting 34); 35-nation draft (A/C.1/38/L.62); agenda item 63 (e).

Sponsors: Austria, Bahamas, Bangladesh, Belgium, Bulgaria, Canada, Costa Rica, Czechoslovakia, Denmark, Ecuador, Egypt, Finland, France, Germany, Federal Republic of, Greece, Guatemala, Ireland, Italy, Liberia, Netherlands, Nigeria, Norway, Pakistan, Peru, Poland, Portugal, Romania, Singapore, Spain, Sudan, Sweden, Turkey, United Kingdom, Uruguay, Zaire.

Meeting numbers. GA 38th session: 1st Committee 3-10, 12-32, 34; plenary 97.

Zones of peace

Indian Ocean region

Activities of the Committee on the Indian Ocean. In 1983, the *Ad Hoc* Committee on the Indian Ocean, established by the General Assembly in 1972[22] to study practical measures for achieving the objectives of the 1971 Declaration of the Indian Ocean as a Zone of Peace,[19] held three sessions in New York—31 January to 9 February, 11 to 22 April and 12 to 22 July—with two additional meetings on 15 and 30 November; at this last meeting the Committee adopted its annual report to the Assembly.[23] Thirty-two formal meetings were held in addition to a number of informal ones.

Membership of the *Ad Hoc* Committee rose to 47, with the appointment of the United Arab Emirates by the Assembly President on 11 May 1983; the Committee was unable, in the time available, to reach consensus on the applications for participation in its work made by Czechoslovakia, Democratic Kampuchea, Hungary, Mongolia and Viet Nam.

As in previous years, two different approaches continued to be advocated in the Committee as it continued efforts to harmonize views relevant to the convening of the proposed Conference on the Indian Ocean—as first decided by the Assembly in 1979[24]—as a necessary step for implementing the Declaration. Most of the non-aligned and Eastern European members asserted that the continued deterioration of the political and security climate in the area had established the urgency for the Conference, and urged the Committee to begin practical preparations for convening the Conference no later than the first half of 1984, a timing indicated in a December 1982 Assembly resolution.[25] Other Committee members asserted that the lack of progress in harmonizing views, and the political and security climate in the region, were not currently conducive for such an undertaking.

In July, Sri Lanka introduced a draft resolution, on behalf of the non-aligned States members of the Committee, calling for the convening of the Conference at Colombo on 4 June 1984 for a period of three weeks.[26]

Among working papers submitted to the Committee in 1983 were those by: Bulgaria and the German Democratic Republic on the Conference's structure and agenda;[27] Egypt on safeguards governing the *Ad Hoc* Committee's work;[28] and Australia, also on behalf of the United States, on the views of the ANZUS Council partners—the third party being New Zealand—on peace proposals for the Indian Ocean, referred to in a July 1983 Council communiqué.[29] In addition, the German Democratic Republic submitted an excerpt from a January 1983 Prague declaration of the States parties to the Warsaw Treaty Organization,[30] and the USSR submitted an excerpt from the statement made in 1982 to the General Assembly by its Minister for Foreign Affairs.[31]

On 30 November, the Committee adopted parts I and II of its report by consensus, and then proceeded to consider part III, containing a draft resolution put together by an open-ended drafting group for recommendation to the General Assembly (the draft being subsequently adopted by the Assembly, see below). During the discussion on the text, the USSR stated that since paragraphs 5 and 6 failed to provide a sufficiently reliable basis for the preparatory work of the Conference, it could not support the adoption of the text by consensus.

Related action. In an October 1983 communiqué,[32] the Meeting of Foreign Ministers and Heads of Delegations of the Non-Aligned Countries to the General Assembly's thirty-eighth (1983) session (New York, 4-7 October) expressed concern over the increasing military presence of the major Powers in the Indian Ocean area, and reaffirmed their determination to ensure that the Conference be held in 1984.

GENERAL ASSEMBLY ACTION

On 20 December 1983, the General Assembly adopted without vote resolution 38/185, the draft of which had been recommended by the *Ad Hoc* Committee on the Indian Ocean and approved by the First Committee.

Implementation of the Declaration of the Indian Ocean as a Zone of Peace

The General Assembly,

Recalling the Declaration of the Indian Ocean as a Zone of Peace, contained in its resolution 2832(XXVI) of 16 December 1971, and recalling also its resolutions 2992(XXVII) of 15 December 1972, 3080(XXVIII) of 6 December 1973, 3259 A (XXIX) of 9 December 1974, 3468(XXX) of 11 December 1975, 31/88 of 14 December 1976, 32/86 of 12 December 1977, S-10/2 of 30 June 1978, 33/68 of 14 December 1978, 34/80 A and B of 11 December 1979, 35/150 of 12 December 1980, 36/90 of 9 December 1981 and 37/96 of 13 December 1982, and other relevant resolutions,

Recalling further the report of the Meeting of the Littoral and Hinterland States of the Indian Ocean,

Reaffirming its conviction that concrete action for the achievement of the objectives of the Declaration of the Indian Ocean as a Zone of Peace would be a substantial contribution to the strengthening of international peace and security,

Recalling its decision, taken at its thirty-fourth session in resolution 34/80 B, to convene a Conference on the Indian Ocean at Colombo during 1981,

Recalling also its decision to make every effort, in consideration of the political and security climate in the Indian Ocean area and progress made in the harmonization of views, to finalize, in accordance with its normal methods of work, all preparations for the Conference, including the dates for its convening,

Recalling further its decision, taken at the thirty-seventh session in resolution 37/96, concerning the consideration of the convening of the Conference not later than the first half of 1984,

Recalling the exchange of views in the *Ad Hoc* Committee on the Indian Ocean in 1983,

Noting the exchange of views on the adverse political and security climate in the region,

Noting further the various documents before the *Ad Hoc* Committee,

Convinced that the continued military presence of the great Powers in the Indian Ocean area, conceived in the context of their confrontation, gives urgency to the need to take practical steps for the early achievement of the objectives of the Declaration of the Indian Ocean as a Zone of Peace,

Considering that any other foreign military presence in the area, whenever it is contrary to the objectives of the Declaration of the Indian Ocean as a Zone of Peace and the purposes and principles of the Charter of the United Nations, gives greater urgency to the need to take practical steps towards the early achievement of the objectives of the Declaration,

Considering also that the creation of a zone of peace in the Indian Ocean requires the active participation of and full co-operation among the littoral and hinterland States, the permanent members of the Security Council and the major maritime users to ensure conditions of peace and security based on the purposes and principles of the Charter, as well as on the general principles of international law,

Considering further that the creation of a zone of peace requires co-operation and agreement among the States of the region to ensure conditions of peace and security within the area, as envisaged in the Declaration of the Indian Ocean as a Zone of Peace, and respect for the independence, sovereignty and territorial integrity of the littoral and hinterland States,

Calling for the renewal of genuinely constructive efforts through the exercise of the political will necessary for the achievement of the objectives of the Declaration of the Indian Ocean as a Zone of Peace,

Deeply concerned at the danger posed by the grave and ominous developments in the area and the resulting sharp deterioration of peace, security and stability which particularly seriously affect the littoral and hinterland States, as well as international peace and security,

Convinced that the continued deterioration of the political and security climate in the Indian Ocean area is an important consideration bearing on the question of the urgent convening of the Conference and that the easing of tension in the area would enhance the prospect of success being achieved by the Conference,

1. *Takes note* of the report of the *Ad Hoc* Committee on the Indian Ocean and the exchange of views in the Committee;

2. *Regrets* that the *Ad Hoc* Committee has failed to reach consensus on the finalization of dates for the convening, during 1984, of the Conference on the Indian Ocean;

3. *Emphasizes* its decision to convene the Conference at Colombo as a necessary step for the implementation of the Declaration of the Indian Ocean as a Zone of Peace, adopted in 1971;

4. *Takes note* of the work of the *Ad Hoc* Committee during 1983;

5. *Requests* the *Ad Hoc* Committee to make decisive efforts in 1984 to complete preparatory work relating to the Conference on the Indian Ocean, in consideration of the political and security climate in the region and with a view to enabling the opening of the Conference at Colombo in the first half of 1985, it being understood that such preparatory work would comprise organizational matters, including the provisional agenda for the Conference, rules of procedure, documentation and consideration of appropriate arrangements for any international agreement that may ultimately be reached for the maintenance of the Indian Ocean as a zone of peace, and substantive issues;

6. *Requests* the *Ad Hoc* Committee at the same time to make determined efforts in 1984 for the necessary harmonization of views on the remaining relevant issues;

7. *Renews* the mandate of the *Ad Hoc* Committee as defined in the relevant resolutions and requests the Committee to intensify its work with regard to the implementation of its mandate;

8. *Requests* the *Ad Hoc* Committee to hold three further sessions in 1984 of a duration of two weeks each, with the possibility of holding a fourth session to be considered as required;

9. *Requests* the Chairman of the *Ad Hoc* Committee to continue his consultations on the participation in the work of the Committee by States Members of the United Nations which are not members of the Committee, with the aim of resolving this matter at the earliest possible date;

10. *Requests* the *Ad Hoc* Committee to submit to the General Assembly at its thirty-ninth session a full report on the implementation of the present resolution;

11. *Requests* the Secretary-General to continue to render all necessary assistance to the *Ad Hoc* Committee, including the provision of summary records.

General Assembly resolution 38/185

20 December 1983   Meeting 103   Adopted without vote

Approved by First Committee (A/38/637) without vote, 2 December (meeting 48); draft by Committee on Indian Ocean (A/38/29); agenda item 59.
Financial implications. 5th Committee, A/38/729; S-G, A/C.1/38/L.85, A/C.5/38/84.
Meeting numbers. GA 38th session: 1st Committee 3-10, 12-31, 48; 5th Committee 62; plenary 103.

Prior to the text's approval in the First Committee, roll-call votes, requested by Poland, were taken on two paragraphs. Paragraph 5 was approved by 97 votes to none, with 16 abstentions; paragraph 6 was approved by 94 votes to none, with 20 abstentions. Among those abstaining were the Eastern European and some other socialist countries, as well as the United States.

In explanation of position, the USSR stated that among the obstacles impeding implementation of the Declaration was the absence, in annual Assembly resolutions, of precise indications concerning the Conference preparatory tasks and the inclusion of pre-conditions for its convening; paragraphs 5 and 6 served to substitute what it called pointless discussion for actual preparation. Similar views were expressed by Madagascar. Viet Nam expressed disappointment at the further postponement of the Conference.

Ethiopia, while supporting the paragraphs, felt that paragraph 5 contained a thinly veiled attempt to hold the Conference hostage to the strategic objectives of extra-regional Powers; it considered the harmonization of views, referred to in paragraph 6, as a process already commenced and continuing through the Conference. Cuba deplored what it called the stalling tactics used by those wishing to maintain their military presence in the region. Bulgaria accepted the draft as a whole as a compromise for the continued mandate of the Committee, even though it felt that the pre-conditions threatened to reduce the text's general positive thrust.

Democratic Yemen said the lack of progress in the *Ad Hoc* Committee had influenced the voting on the paragraphs; members of that body should, therefore, strive in 1984 to complete preparations, including organizational matters, for the Conference.

The United States said that, because it respected the long-standing consensus procedure in the *Ad Hoc* Committee, it had reluctantly agreed to what it considered was the text's less than satisfactory language, however, since it deplored the decision by some delegations to depart from that procedure by calling for votes on two paragraphs, it was not participating in either the First Committee or the Assembly action.

South-East Asia

In 1983, the General Assembly, in resolution 38/3 on the situation in Kampuchea, urged the countries of South-East Asia to exert renewed efforts to establish a zone of peace, freedom and neutrality in the region, once a comprehensive political solution to the Kampuchean conflict was achieved (see Chapter VII of this section).

Confidence-building measures

In 1983, the Disarmament Commission began elaborating guidelines for confidence-building measures as elements beneficial for international peace and security and for disarmament. The Secretary-General reported on the views of Member States concerning information exchange on their military capabilities as a possible confidence-building measure, and also made a number of observations on the requirements for setting up an international satellite agency to monitor the implementation of disarmament agreements.

Disarmament Commission consideration. In pursuance of a December 1982 General Assembly resolution,[33] the Disarmament Commission[1] established on 9 May 1983 an informal, open-ended working group (Working Group IV) to elaborate guidelines for appropriate types of confidence-building measures and for their global or regional implementation. The Working Group held 11 meetings between 13 and 27 May, under the chairmanship of Henning Wegener (Federal Republic of Germany); additional informal consultations were held through the Chairman. Proceeding on the understanding that the Commission would have two years to complete its task, the Group held a first reading of papers presented to it by the Bahamas, the Federal Republic of Germany, India and the Netherlands, as well as one by the Chairman dealing with definitions of the concept, and his compilation of issues which had evolved during the general debate on the question. The 1981 study by the Group of Governmental Experts on Confidence-building Measures[34] was also before the Working Group.

In summarizing its work, the Working Group noted that all participants agreed that confidence-building measures should not be a substitute or pre-condition for disarmament or disarmament negotiations; at the same time, they observed that disarmament measures which limited or reduced military potential had a high confidence-building value. There were varying views in the Group about: the relative importance or effectiveness of various approaches and kinds of confidence-building measures; the focus of future guidelines and the usefulness of a precise definition of confidence-building measures; and the value of openness in the military sphere—such as availability of reliable information on military activities and expenditures (see below).

The Commission recommended that the work be continued in 1984.

GENERAL ASSEMBLY ACTION

On the recommendation of the First Committee, the General Assembly, on 15 December 1983, adopted without vote resolution 38/73 A.

Confidence-building measures

The General Assembly,

Recalling its resolution 37/100 D of 13 December 1982, in which it requested the Disarmament Commission to consider the elaboration of guidelines for appropriate types of confidence-building measures and for the implementation of such measures on a global or regional level and to submit a progress report on its deliberations on this item to the General Assembly at its thirty-eighth session,

Having considered the report of the Disarmament Commission on the work accomplished during its session in 1983 on the item "Elaboration of guidelines for appropriate types of confidence-building measures and for the implementation of such measures on a global or regional level",

Expressing its concern about the deterioration of the international situation and the further escalation of the arms race, which both reflect and aggravate the unsatisfactory international political climate, tension and mistrust,

Desirous of strengthening international peace and security and, at the same time, creating and improving conditions conducive to further measures of disarmament,

Noting again the findings of the *Comprehensive Study on Confidence-building Measures* and in particular the important role that confidence-building measures can play with regard to regional and world-wide stability as well as to progress in disarmament,

Mindful of the fact that, while confidence-building measures cannot serve as a substitute for concrete disarmament measures, they play a very significant role in achieving disarmament, whether they are taken unilaterally, bilaterally or multilaterally,

Convinced of the usefulness of confidence-building measures freely arrived at by the States concerned and agreed upon, taking into account the particular conditions and requirements of the regions concerned,

Convinced of the need to reduce mistrust and fear among States through the realization of confidence-building measures, such as those recommended by consensus in the *Comprehensive Study on Confidence-building Measures*, including pertinent and timely information on military activities and other matters pertaining to mutual security, and measures concerning the peacetime military conduct of States, as well as through progress on concrete measures of disarmament,

Recalling that confidence reflects a set of interrelated factors of a military as well as of a non-military character and that a plurality of approaches is needed to overcome fear, apprehension and mistrust between States and to replace them by confidence,

Welcoming the convening at Stockholm on 17 January 1984 of the Conference on Confidence- and Security-building Measures and Disarmament in Europe, of which the first stage will be devoted to the negotiation and adoption of a set of mutually complementary confidence- and security-building measures designed to reduce the risk of military confrontation in Europe as characterized in the Concluding Document of the Madrid meeting of representatives of the participating States of the Conference on Security and Co-operation in Europe, held from 11 November 1980 to 9 September 1983,

1. *Urges* all States to encourage and assist all efforts designed to explore further the ways in which confidence-building measures can strengthen international peace and security;

2. *Invites* all States to consider the possible introduction unilaterally, bilaterally or multilaterally of confidence-building measures in their particular regions and, where possible, to negotiate on them in keeping with the conditions and requirements prevailing in their respective regions;

3. *Requests* the Disarmament Commission to continue and conclude at its l984 session the consideration of the item entitled "Elaboration of guidelines for appropriate types of confidence-building measures and for the implementation of such measures on a global or regional level";

4. *Further requests* the Disarmament Commission to submit a report on its deliberations on this item, containing such guidelines, to the General Assembly at its thirty-ninth session;

5. *Recommends* that all States consider the inclusion of a reference to, or an agreement on, confidence-building measures, as appropriate, in any joint statements or declarations of a political nature;

6. *Decides* to include in the provisional agenda of its thirty-ninth session the item entitled "Consideration of guidelines for confidence-building measures".

General Assembly resolution 38/73 A

15 December 1983   Meeting 97   Adopted without vote

Approved by First Committee (A/38/641) without vote, 21 November (meeting 34); 42-nation draft (A/C.1/38/L.5); agenda item 63 *(d)*.

Sponsors: Austria, Bahamas, Bangladesh, Belgium, Bolivia, Canada, Chile, Colombia, Congo, Costa Rica, Denmark, Ecuador, Egypt, Finland, France, Germany, Federal Republic of, Ghana, Greece, Indonesia, Ireland, Italy, Japan, Mali, Mauritania, Netherlands, New Zealand, Norway, Pakistan, Peru, Philippines, Romania, Samoa, Spain, Sudan, Sweden, Turkey, United Kingdom, United Republic of Cameroon, Upper Volta, Uruguay, Yemen, Zaire.

Meeting numbers. GA 38th session: 1st Committee 3-10, 12-31, 34; plenary 97.

In explanation of position, the USSR said that talks on confidence-building were being used to create the illusion that such measures could be achieved at the same time as an arms buildup, provided they were accompanied by, among other things, measures to establish transparency and predictability; confidence-building measures had to be established along with military détente, arms limitation and disarmament, rather than in isolation from them—a requirement, not reflected adequately in the text, which must be taken into account in the Commission's future work.

A number of delegations expressed reservations on paragraph 5. Nigeria would have abstained had a separate vote been taken on it, as the recommendation raised the status of confidence-building

measures—a mere collateral of disarmament—to that of an article of faith. Argentina added that the measures should not receive the special treatment given. Mexico felt that the wording was broader than had been intended by the sponsors. Albania also said it had difficulty with that text and the final preambular paragraph. Algeria would have preferred a procedural draft in view of the ongoing work in the Disarmament Commission; it felt the text failed to mention many other measures conducive to building confidence.

A need for confidence-building measures was also mentioned in 1983 General Assembly resolutions 38/188 F, on curbing the naval arms race and extension of confidence-building measures to seas and oceans (see above, under NAVAL ARMAMENTS), and 38/196, on confidence-building in international economic relations (see ECONOMIC AND SOCIAL QUESTIONS, Chapter I).

Proposed information exchange on armaments and armed forces

Report of the Secretary-General. In pursuance of a December 1982 General Assembly resolution,[35] the Secretary-General submitted to the Assembly in September 1983 a report[36] with later addenda containing 16 replies of Member States to an invitation to communicate their views on additional measures to facilitate the provision of objective information on military capabilities, thereby removing misperceptions and contributing to disarmament.

Three of the responding States did not think it useful to take special measures and involve the United Nations in the endeavour, while most of the others, including the Federal Republic of Germany on behalf of the 10 member States of EC, spoke of the possible use of existing United Nations machinery and the benefit that could be drawn from the Organization's experience.

The Secretary-General stated that, in view of the complexity of the subject-matter, a greater number of replies would be needed to analyse the United Nations role.

GENERAL ASSEMBLY ACTION

As recommended by the First Committee, the Assembly, on 20 December, adopted by recorded vote resolution 38/188 C.

Measures to provide objective information on military capabilities

The General Assembly,

Recalling its resolution 37/99 G of 13 December 1982,

Deeply concerned about the continuing escalation of the arms race, in particular the nuclear-arms race, its extremely harmful effects on world peace and security and the deplorable waste of human and material resources for military purposes,

Recalling paragraph 105 of the Final Document of the Tenth Special Session of the General Assembly, which encourages Member States to ensure a better flow of information with regard to the various aspects of disarmament to avoid dissemination of false and tendentious information concerning armaments and to concentrate on the danger of escalation of the arms race and on the need for general and complete disarmament under effective international control,

Noting that misperceptions of the military capabilities and the intentions of potential adversaries, which could be caused, *inter alia*, by the lack of objective information, could induce States to undertake armaments programmes leading to the acceleration of the arms race, in particular the nuclear-arms race, and to heightened international tensions,

Aware that objective information on the military capabilities, in particular among nuclear-weapon States and other militarily significant States, could contribute to the building of confidence among States and to the conclusion of concrete disarmament agreements and, thereby, help to halt and reverse the arms race,

1. *Takes note* of the report of the Secretary-General;
2. *Calls once more upon* all States, in particular nuclear-weapon States and other militarily significant States, to consider additional measures to facilitate the provision of objective information on, as well as objective assessments of, military capabilities;
3. *Invites* all States that have not communicated to the Secretary-General their views and proposals concerning such measures to do so as soon as possible, and those States that have already communicated such views and proposals to supplement them, as appropriate;
4. *Requests* the Secretary-General to ask the Advisory Board on Disarmament Studies to consider the modalities of studying the question of measures to facilitate objective information on, and objective assessments of, military capabilities, in particular among nuclear-weapon States and other militarily significant States;
5. *Further requests* the Secretary-General to report to the General Assembly at its thirty-ninth session on the implementation of the provisions of the present resolution.

General Assembly resolution 38/188 C

20 December 1983　　　Meeting 103　　　119-0-21 (recorded vote)

Approved by First Committee (A/38/640) by recorded vote (77-0-17), 25 November (meeting 40); 17-nation draft (A/C.1/38/L.22); agenda item 62 *(i)*.

Sponsors: Australia, Austria, Bahamas, Bangladesh, Belgium, Colombia, Costa Rica, Ecuador, France, Germany, Federal Republic of, Indonesia, Ireland, Nigeria, Pakistan, Romania, Sudan, Sweden.

Meeting numbers. GA 38th session: 1st Committee 3-10, 12-31, 40; plenary 103.

Recorded vote in Assembly as follows:

In favour: Algeria, Antigua and Barbuda, Argentina, Australia, Austria, Bahamas, Bahrain, Bangladesh, Barbados, Belgium, Belize, Benin, Bhutan, Bolivia, Brazil, Burma, Burundi, Canada, Cape Verde, Central African Republic, Chad, Chile, Colombia, Costa Rica, Cyprus, Democratic Kampuchea, Denmark, Djibouti, Dominica, Dominican Republic, Ecuador, Egypt, El Salvador, Fiji, Finland, France, Gabon, Gambia, Germany, Federal Republic of, Ghana, Greece, Guatemala, Guinea, Guinea-Bissau, Haiti, Honduras, Iceland, Indonesia, Iran, Iraq, Ireland, Israel, Italy, Ivory Coast, Jamaica, Japan, Jordan, Kenya, Kuwait, Lebanon, Lesotho, Liberia, Luxembourg, Madagascar, Malawi, Malaysia, Maldives, Mali, Malta, Mauritania, Mauritius, Mexico, Morocco, Nepal, Netherlands, New Zealand, Niger, Nigeria, Norway, Oman, Pakistan, Panama, Papua New Guinea, Paraguay, Peru, Philippines, Portugal, Qatar, Romania, Saint Lucia, Saint Vincent and the Grenadines, Saudi Arabia, Senegal, Sierra Leone, Singapore, Somalia, Spain, Sri Lanka, Sudan, Suriname, Swaziland, Sweden, Thailand, Togo, Trinidad and Tobago, Tunisia, Turkey, Uganda, United Arab Emirates, United Kingdom, United Republic of Cameroon, United States, Upper Volta, Uruguay, Vanuatu, Venezuela, Yemen, Yugoslavia, Zaire.

Against: None.

Abstaining: Afghanistan, Angola, Bulgaria, Byelorussian SSR, Congo, Cuba, Czechoslovakia, German Democratic Republic, Guyana, Hungary, India, Lao People's Democratic Republic, Mongolia, Mozambique, Poland, Syrian Arab Republic, Ukrainian SSR, USSR, United Republic of Tanzania, Viet Nam, Zambia.

In explanation of vote, the USSR said the information exchange on military capabilities was desirable and possible in a general climate of international confidence; such an exchange, however, should be linked directly to concrete disarmament measures, rather than being a separate, preliminary step as was envisaged in the text. India considered that progress in disarmament depended on the exercise of political will by the major Powers, rather than on information on military expenditures or an adequate format for collecting such information.

Proposed intergovernmental body for satellite monitoring of disarmament agreements

In 1983, the Secretary-General submitted, in pursuance of a December 1982 General Assembly resolution,[37] a report[38] on the institutional aspects involved in establishing an international satellite monitoring agency (ISMA)—an idea originally proposed by France in 1978 at the Assembly's first special session devoted to disarmament.[39] Two other studies, prepared by the Secretary-General with the assistance of the Group of Governmental Experts on the Question of the Establishment of an International Satellite Monitoring Agency, had been submitted to the Assembly in 1979[40] and 1981.[41]

The Secretary-General noted the Group's observation that ISMA would have to be established by a treaty or convention in view of its highly sensitive mission, affecting the security interests of States. Consequently, he observed that the Assembly would have to decide on a process and a legal framework leading to such establishment; that some institutional aspects would have to be negotiated between the participating States; and that, should the Assembly decide to establish ISMA, it could also identify his specific responsibilities in the framework of the negotiations.

Disarmament and international security

In its 1983 consideration of disarmament and international security, the General Assembly, in resolution 38/73 H, requested the Security Council to render operative the collective security system provided for in the Charter of the United Nations and thereby facilitate disarmament negotiations. It recommended, in resolution 38/188 H, that the 1982 report of the Independent Commission on Disarmament and Security Issues (ICDSI)[42]—a private group of individuals, also known as the Palme Commission—be taken into account in disarmament efforts, and requested the

Secretary-General, with the assistance of governmental experts, to study the concepts of security.

The question of disarmament and international security was also taken up by the Assembly in resolutions 38/183 F (see above, under IMPLEMENTATION OF THE 1979 DECLARATION ON CO-OPERATION FOR DISARMAMENT) and 38/183 H (see above, under IMPLEMENTATION OF THE RECOMMENDATIONS OF THE 1978 SPECIAL SESSION).

GENERAL ASSEMBLY ACTION

On 15 December 1983, the General Assembly, on the recommendation of the First Committee, adopted by recorded vote resolution 38/73 H.

Disarmament and international security
The General Assembly,

Recalling its resolutions 34/83 A of 11 December 1979, 35/156 J of 12 December 1980, 36/97 K of 9 December 1981 and 37/100 E of 13 December 1982,

Deeply concerned over the continuing stagnation in the disarmament negotiating efforts and the ever-escalating arms race, particularly the nuclear-arms race, which make the survival of mankind extremely precarious,

Gravely concerned over the present state of international affairs characterized by the continued resort to violence and the use of force, in violation of the Charter of the United Nations,

Firmly convinced that a closely interdependent world composed of many sovereign nations cannot possibly function towards peace, security and survival in a nuclear and space age without an effectively functioning organization,

Noting that the fundamental function of the United Nations in its primary purpose is the security system provided for in the Charter and that the principles of disarmament embodied in Article 11 of the Charter and flowing from it are an integral part of the system of security,

Convinced that restoring to the United Nations its essential function in accordance with the provisions of the Charter would be a significant factor in creating the conditions conducive to the cessation of the arms race, particularly the nuclear-arms race, and for productive negotiations on disarmament measures,

Bearing in mind that recent events have brought into sharp focus the reality that consecutive decisions of the Security Council, adopted unanimously, were ignored and bypassed by those required to comply with them and in consequence the chain of events that followed further aggravated the situation,

Determined to avert the danger of an approaching nuclear war in a world of insecurity and anarchy in which the continuing lack of collective security through the United Nations is an essential factor,

Having regard to the warning in the report of the Secretary-General on the work of the Organization, submitted to the General Assembly at its thirty-seventh session, that "it was the lack of an effective system of collective security through the League of Nations that . . . led to the Second World War",

1. *Requests* the Security Council to expedite the conclusion of the agreements making armed forces available to the Security Council, as required by the Charter of the United Nations, to render operative the collective security system provided for in the Charter and thereby facilitate productive negotiations for the cessation of the arms race, particularly the nuclear-arms race, and for progress on disarmament;

2. *Further requests* the Security Council to submit a report, through the Secretary-General, to the General Assembly at its thirty-ninth session.

General Assembly resolution 38/73 H

15 December 1983   Meeting 97   133-0-13 (recorded vote)

Approved by First Committee (A/38/641) by recorded vote (109-0-14), 25 November (meeting 40); 12-nation draft (A/C.1/38/L.56/Rev.1); agenda item 63.
Sponsors: Bahamas, Colombia, Costa Rica, Cyprus, Ecuador, Egypt, Greece, Malta, Panama, Sri Lanka, Sudan, Yugoslavia.
Meeting numbers. GA 38th session: 1st Committee 3-10, 12-31, 40; plenary 97.

Recorded vote in Assembly as follows:

In favour: Afghanistan, Algeria, Angola, Antigua and Barbuda, Argentina, Australia, Austria, Bahamas, Bahrain, Bangladesh, Barbados, Belize, Benin, Bhutan, Bolivia, Botswana, Brazil, Bulgaria, Burma, Burundi, Byelorussian SSR, Cape Verde, Central African Republic, Chad, Chile, China, Colombia, Congo, Costa Rica, Cuba, Cyprus, Czechoslovakia, Democratic Kampuchea, Democratic Yemen, Denmark, Djibouti, Dominican Republic, Ecuador, Egypt, El Salvador, Ethiopia, Fiji, Finland, Gabon, Gambia, German Democratic Republic, Ghana, Greece, Grenada, Guatemala, Guinea, Guyana, Haiti, Honduras, Hungary, Iceland, India, Iraq, Ireland, Ivory Coast, Jamaica, Jordan, Kenya, Kuwait, Lao People's Democratic Republic, Lebanon, Lesotho, Liberia, Libyan Arab Jamahiriya, Madagascar, Malawi, Malaysia, Maldives, Mali, Malta, Mauritania, Mauritius, Mexico, Mongolia, Morocco, Mozambique, Nepal, Nicaragua, Niger, Nigeria, Norway, Oman, Pakistan, Panama, Papua New Guinea, Paraguay, Peru, Philippines, Poland, Qatar, Romania, Rwanda, Saint Lucia, Sao Tome and Principe, Saudi Arabia, Senegal, Seychelles, Sierra Leone, Singapore, Solomon Islands, Somalia, Spain, Sri Lanka, Sudan, Suriname, Swaziland, Sweden, Syrian Arab Republic, Thailand, Togo, Trinidad and Tobago, Tunisia, Uganda, Ukrainian SSR, USSR, United Arab Emirates, United Republic of Cameroon, United Republic of Tanzania, Upper Volta, Uruguay, Vanuatu, Venezuela, Viet Nam, Yemen, Yugoslavia, Zaire, Zambia, Zimbabwe.
Against: None.
Abstaining: Belgium, Canada, France, Germany, Federal Republic of, Israel, Italy, Japan, Luxembourg, Netherlands, New Zealand, Portugal, United Kingdom, United States.

Report of the Commission on disarmament and security

Disarmament Commission consideration. In 1983, the Disarmament Commission[(1)] established an informal, open-ended working group (Working Group III), which held 11 meetings as well as informal consultations between 12 May and 1 June under the chairmanship of Curt Lidgard (Sweden), to consider the disarmament-related recommendations and proposals contained in the 1982 ICDSI report, entitled "Common security—a programme for disarmament".[(42)]

Established at Vienna in September 1980 under the chairmanship of Olof Palme of Sweden, ICDSI, consisting of prominent individuals from various parts of the world, had presented its report to the Assembly at its second (1982) special session devoted to disarmament. Its recommendations concerned the nuclear challenge and East-West relations, curbing the qualitative arms competition, assuring confidence among States, strengthening the United Nations security system, regional approaches to security and economic security. Also, ICDSI recognized the United Nations as the most valuable tool for common security, which should be used in a more determined way.

While differing views were expressed—particularly with regard to the ICDSI recommendations for establishing a tactical or battlefield nuclear-weapon-free zone in Europe (see above, under NUCLEAR-WEAPON-FREE ZONES)—the Disarmament Commission found the report noteworthy in that it reflected agreement among prominent individuals of different political convictions on a concrete programme aimed at halting the arms race and creating a downward spiral in armaments. The Commission also regarded the report as a timely and constructive contribution to international efforts to strengthen peace and security, and recommended that it be taken into account in disarmament efforts.

GENERAL ASSEMBLY ACTION

As recommended by the First Committee, the Assembly adopted resolution 38/188 H by recorded vote on 20 December 1983.

Independent Commission on Disarmament and Security Issues

The General Assembly,

Recalling its resolution 37/99 B of 13 December 1982, in which it noted the report of the Independent Commission on Disarmament and Security Issues entitled "Common security—a programme for disarmament", submitted to the General Assembly at its twelfth special session, the second special session devoted to disarmament,

Recalling also that the Disarmament Commission, in accordance with resolution 37/99 B, considered the recommendations and proposals in the report of the Independent Commission, and that the Disarmament Commission recommended that the report be taken into account in ongoing and future disarmament efforts,

Regretting the lack of trust and confidence between States, especially between the nuclear-weapon Powers, reflected, *inter alia*, in the concepts of security adopted by Governments,

Bearing in mind that the Disarmament Commission held a broad discussion of the concept of common security which it found a valuable approach in the search for lasting peace and security,

Emphasizing the need for creating concepts enhancing political and economic confidence between nations and policies arrived at not against, but in co-operation with other nations, as, for instance, in the *Comprehensive Study on Confidence-building Measures,*

Recalling paragraph 96 of the Final Document of the Tenth Special Session of the General Assembly, in which it was stated that taking further steps in the field of disarmament and other measures aimed at promoting international peace and security would be facilitated by the carrying out of studies by the Secretary-General in this field with appropriate assistance from governmental or consultant experts,

1. *Welcomes* the report of the Independent Commission on Disarmament and Security Issues as a timely and constructive contribution to international efforts to achieve disarmament and to maintain and strengthen international peace and security;

2. *Recommends* that the report of the Independent Commission on Disarmament and Security Issues be duly taken into account in ongoing and future disarmament efforts;

3. *Requests* the Secretary-General, with the assistance of qualified governmental experts,* to carry out a comprehensive study of concepts of security, in particular security policies which emphasize co-operative efforts and mutual understanding between States, with a view to developing proposals for policies aimed at preventing the arms race, building confidence in relations between States, enhancing the possibility of reaching agreements on arms limitation and disarmament and promoting political and economic security;

4. *Invites* all States to submit to the Secretary-General, not later than 1 April 1984, their views on the content of such a study and to co-operate with him in order to achieve the objectives of the study;

5. *Requests* the Secretary-General to submit the final report to the General Assembly at its fortieth session.

---

*Subsequently referred to as the Group of Governmental Experts to Carry Out a Comprehensive Study of Concepts of Security.

General Assembly resolution 38/188 H

20 December 1983   Meeting 103   132-1-15 (recorded vote)

Approved by First Committee (A/38/640) by recorded vote (110-1-14), 25 November (meeting 40); 11-nation draft (A/C.1/38/L.59); agenda item 62 (e).

Sponsors: Austria, Bahamas, Colombia, Costa Rica, Ecuador, Finland, Mexico, Nigeria, Romania, Sweden, Yugoslavia.

Financial implications: ACABQ, A/38/7/ Add.21; 5th Committee, A/38/762; S-G, A/C.1/38/L.76, A/C.5/38/68.

Meeting numbers. GA 38th session: 1st Committee 3-10, 12-31, 33, 40, 41; 5th Committee 68; plenary 103.

Recorded vote in Assembly as follows:

In favour: Afghanistan, Algeria, Angola, Antigua and Barbuda, Argentina, Australia, Austria, Bahamas, Bahrain, Bangladesh, Barbados, Belize, Benin, Bhutan, Bolivia, Botswana, Brazil, Bulgaria, Burma, Burundi, Byelorussian SSR, Cape Verde, Central African Republic, Chad, Chile, Colombia, Congo, Costa Rica, Cuba, Cyprus, Czechoslovakia, Democratic Kampuchea, Democratic Yemen, Denmark, Djibouti, Dominica, Dominican Republic, Ecuador, Egypt, El Salvador, Ethiopia, Fiji, Finland, Gabon, Gambia, German Democratic Republic, Ghana, Greece, Guatemala, Guinea, Guinea-Bissau, Guyana, Haiti, Honduras, Hungary, Iceland, Indonesia, Iran, Iraq, Ireland, Ivory Coast, Jamaica, Jordan, Kenya, Kuwait, Lao People's Democratic Republic, Lebanon, Lesotho, Liberia, Libyan Arab Jamahiriya, Madagascar, Malawi, Malaysia, Maldives, Mali, Malta, Mauritania, Mauritius, Mexico, Mongolia, Morocco, Mozambique, Nepal, Nicaragua, Niger, Nigeria, Norway, Oman, Pakistan, Panama, Papua New Guinea, Paraguay, Peru, Philippines, Poland, Qatar, Romania, Rwanda, Saint Lucia, Saint Vincent and the Grenadines, Sao Tome and Principe, Saudi Arabia, Senegal, Sierra Leone, Singapore, Spain, Sri Lanka, Sudan, Suriname, Swaziland, Sweden, Syrian Arab Republic, Thailand, Togo, Trinidad and Tobago, Tunisia, Uganda, Ukrainian SSR, USSR, United Arab Emirates, United Republic of Cameroon, United Republic of Tanzania, Upper Volta, Uruguay, Vanuatu, Venezuela, Viet Nam, Yemen, Yugoslavia, Zaire, Zambia, Zimbabwe.

Against: United States.

Abstaining: Belgium, Canada, France, Germany, Federal Republic of, India, Israel, Italy, Japan, Luxembourg, Netherlands, New Zealand, Portugal, Somalia, Turkey, United Kingdom.

In explanation of vote, the Federal Republic of Germany, Japan, the Netherlands, New Zealand, Turkey and the United States expressed doubts on the wisdom of carrying out a study, the outline of which they found vague; on the absence of sufficient consultations before the presentation of the proposal; or on discussing, in the United Nations, reports prepared by private persons. The Federal Republic of Germany also felt that the Advisory Board on Disarmament Studies (see below) should have been asked to review study projects, and the United States asserted that the study should be carried out within existing United Nations resources.

India did not favour any alternative security doctrine other than that of collective security as embodied in the United Nations Charter; further, it had reservations about some of the ICDSI recommendations.

Disarmament and development

In 1983, efforts were made to incorporate the disarmament-development perspective into United Nations activities, as recommended by the Group of Governmental Experts on the Relationship between Disarmament and Development in its 1981 study.[43]

The Group had viewed the relationship as a two-way street wherein development not only benefited from but also contributed towards disarmament, and had recommended, *inter alia*, that the Secretary-General take appropriate action, through the existing inter-agency consultative mechanism of the Administrative Committee on Co-ordination (ACC) and its Consultative Committee on Substantive Questions (Programme Matters) (CCSQ (PROG)), to foster and co-ordinate the incorporation of the disarmament-development perspective in the programmes and activities of the United Nations system. The Department for Disarmament Affairs (formerly the Centre for Disarmament) and the Office of the Director-General for Development and International Economic Co-operation (DIEC) had been identified by the Group as having lead functions in that endeavour.

The Secretary-General's October 1983 report,[44] submitted to the Assembly in pursuance of a December 1982 resolution,[45] contained information received from within the United Nations system. It mentioned that the Department for Disarmament Affairs had received a growing number of requests for an elaboration of the reasoning of the 1981 study, for further investigation of the problems covered therein, and for additional information and expert advice for incorporating the disarmament-development perspective. The Secretary-General also reported that the Department, in consultation with the Office of the DIEC Director-General, planned to convene in early 1984 an *ad hoc* group of technical experts to act on the decisions taken by CCSQ (PROG) (first regular session, Geneva, 10-15 March 1983),[46] including a recommendation that the organs within the United Nations system should designate focal points to facilitate contacts with the Department—a proposal also made by ACC in its 1983 annual report to the Economic and Social Council.[47]

The Committee for Development Planning pointed out in its 1983 report[48] that the world's arms expenditures—over \$650 billion in 1982—were greater than the combined incomes of over 2 billion people living in the world's 50 poorest countries. It said the continuing increase in armaments and military expenditure threatened world security and survival, that the grotesque cost impeded development, and that the resources released through disarmament would contribute to the economic and social advancement of all nations.

By resolution 1983/18, the Economic and Social Council requested the Secretary-General to report every three years on the adverse effects of the arms race on social progress and development. The Council also called on States to reallocate the resources being spent for military purposes, in order to ensure social progress (see ECONOMIC AND SOCIAL QUESTIONS, Chapter XIII).

The Trade and Development Board of the United Nations Conference on Trade and Development[49] decided, on 20 October 1983, to defer until 1984 the question of including an item on trade and economic aspects of disarmament in the provisional agenda of a subsequent session.

GENERAL ASSEMBLY ACTION

On 15 December 1983, the General Assembly adopted two resolutions—38/71 A and B—under the item on the relationship between disarmament and development, both on the recommendation of the First Committee.

Resolution 38/71 A was adopted by recorded vote.

The General Assembly,

Recalling the conclusions contained in the study entitled *The Relationship between Disarmament and Development,*

Recalling also its resolution 37/84 of 9 December 1982,

1. *Takes note with appreciation* of the report of the Secretary-General on measures taken within the United Nations system in implementation of resolution 37/84;

2. *Requests* the Secretary-General to submit a report to the General Assembly at its fortieth session based on appropriate measures taken by Member States and within the United Nations system in accordance with resolution 37/84.

General Assembly resolution 38/71 A

15 December 1983   Meeting 97   137-0-12 (recorded vote)

Approved by First Committee (A/38/634) by recorded vote (112-0-13), 25 November (meeting 40); 20-nation draft (A/C.1/38/L.15); agenda item 56.

Sponsors: Bahamas, Bangladesh, Colombia, Denmark, Ecuador, Egypt, Finland, Greece, Iceland, Indonesia, Mali, Nigeria, Norway, Pakistan, Romania, Senegal, Sri Lanka, Sweden, Uruguay, Yugoslavia.

Meeting numbers. GA 38th session: 1st Committee 3-10, 12-31, 33, 40, 46; plenary 97.

Recorded vote in Assembly as follows:

In favour: Algeria, Angola, Antigua and Barbuda, Argentina, Australia, Austria, Bahamas, Bahrain, Bangladesh, Barbados, Belgium, Belize, Benin, Bhutan, Bolivia, Botswana, Brazil, Burma, Burundi, Canada, Cape Verde, Central African Republic, Chad, Chile, China, Colombia, Congo, Costa Rica, Cuba, Cyprus, Democratic Kampuchea, Democratic Yemen, Denmark, Djibouti, Dominican

Republic, Ecuador, Egypt, El Salvador, Ethiopia, Fiji, Finland, France, Gabon, Gambia, Germany, Federal Republic of, Ghana, Greece, Grenada, Guatemala, Guinea, Guyana, Haiti, Honduras, Iceland, India, Indonesia, Iran, Iraq, Ireland, Israel, Italy, Ivory Coast, Jamaica, Japan, Jordan, Kenya, Kuwait, Lebanon, Lesotho, Liberia, Libyan Arab Jamahiriya, Luxembourg, Madagascar, Malawi, Malaysia, Maldives, Mali, Malta, Mauritania, Mauritius, Mexico, Morocco, Mozambique, Nepal, Netherlands, New Zealand, Nicaragua, Niger, Nigeria, Norway, Oman, Pakistan, Panama, Papua New Guinea, Paraguay, Peru, Philippines, Portugal, Qatar, Romania, Rwanda, Saint Lucia, Sao Tome and Principe, Saudi Arabia, Senegal, Seychelles, Sierra Leone, Singapore, Solomon Islands, Somalia, Spain, Sri Lanka, Sudan, Suriname, Swaziland, Sweden, Syrian Arab Republic, Thailand, Togo, Trinidad and Tobago, Tunisia, Turkey, Uganda, United Arab Emirates, United Kingdom, United Republic of Cameroon, United Republic of Tanzania, United States, Upper Volta, Uruguay, Vanuatu, Venezuela, Yemen, Yugoslavia, Zaire, Zambia, Zimbabwe.

Against: None.

Abstaining: Afghanistan, Bulgaria, Byelorussian SSR, Czechoslovakia, German Democratic Republic, Hungary, Lao People's Democratic Republic, Mongolia, Poland, Ukrainian SSR, USSR, Viet Nam.

The Assembly adopted resolution 38/71 B without vote.

The General Assembly,

Deeply concerned by the arms buildup and trends in military expenditures, the consequent waste of human and economic resources and the resulting risks for world peace and security,

Also concerned by the extent of the crisis affecting the world economy, particularly the developing countries,

Considering that the magnitude of military expenditures is now such that their various implications can no longer be ignored in the efforts pursued in the international community to secure the recovery of the world economy and the establishment of a new international economic order,

Also considering that a reduction of arms expenditures, especially by nuclear-weapon States and other militarily important States, on a mutually agreed basis would be a measure that would curb the arms buildup and would make it possible to release additional resources for use in economic and social development, particularly for the benefit of the developing countries,

Bearing in mind the conclusions of the study entitled *The Relationship between Disarmament and Development,* as well as General Assembly resolutions 36/92 G of 9 December 1981 and 37/84 of 9 December 1982, in which the Assembly took note of those conclusions,

Noting that an investigation of the modalities of an international disarmament fund for development was undertaken in 1983 by the United Nations Institute for Disarmament Research, as requested by the General Assembly in its resolution 37/84,

Recalling the recommendation of the General Assembly in that resolution that the question of the conversion of resources from military to civilian purposes and the reallocation to economic and social development of the resources released by disarmament measures should be included in the provisional agenda of the Assembly at intervals to be decided upon,

Convinced that the time has come to study measures that could be taken on the basis of the conclusions and recommendations of existing studies or studies being prepared on the question,

Noting that the envisaged initiatives include, in particular, a proposal for a conference on the various implications of the relationship between disarmament and development and a proposal on the establishment of an international disarmament fund for development,

1. *Expresses its conviction* that increased solidarity in the field of development would serve the cause of international peace and security and that the resources released by the reduction of arms expenditures would contribute to the growth and stability of the world economy, and particularly the economies of developing countries;

2. *Invites* Member States to communicate to the Secretary-General, by 1 April 1984, their views and proposals concerning the relationship between disarmament and development, in particular with regard to the following:

(a) The evaluation of the burden of armaments in the world;

(b) The impact of military expenditures on the world economic situation and development;

(c) The contribution that a reduction in arms and military expenditures, in particular by nuclear-weapon States and other militarily important States, or a contribution by those States, as appropriate, would make to development tasks;

(d) The ways and means that would enable this contribution to be made, in particular in the interests of the economic and social progress of the developing countries;

(e) The consideration of proposals relating to the convening of a conference;

3. *Requests* the Secretary-General to transmit the replies of Member States to the Disarmament Commission in good time;

4. *Requests* the Disarmament Commission to include this item in the agenda of its session to be held in 1984, to consider the replies received and to make appropriate recommendations to the General Assembly at its thirty-ninth session.

General Assembly resolution 38/71 B

15 December 1983   Meeting 97   Adopted without vote

Approved by First Committee (A/38/634) without vote, 30 November (meeting 46); 6-nation draft (A/C.1/38/L.54/Rev.2); agenda item 56.
Sponsors: Djibouti, France, Ivory Coast, Mali, Togo, Zaire.
Meeting numbers. GA 38th session: 1st Committee 3-10, 12-31, 33, 40, 46; plenary 97.

In explanation of position, the USSR said that, while not opposed to adopting the text which contained certain ambiguities, its position remained unchanged as regards the 1982 resolution, including its opposition to the idea of creating a disarmament-for-development fund.

The Federal Republic of Germany said the successful implementation of the text depended in part on agreements among Member States on the importance of transparency and comparability of data for achieving a reduction of military expenditures; it felt it wise for the Commission to complete the current tasks on its agenda before taking on additional work.

In resolution 38/113 on human rights and use of scientific and technological developments, the Assembly stressed the importance of implementing practical measures of disarmament and the use of resources thus released for social and economic development (for text, refer to INDEX OF RESOLUTIONS AND DECISIONS).

Military research and development

The Secretary-General, in pursuance of a December 1982 General Assembly resolution,[50] established in 1983 a group of experts to carry out a comprehensive study on the scope, role and direction of the military use of research and development, the mechanisms involved, its role in the overall arms race, and its impact on arms limitation and disarmament, with a view to preventing a qualitative arms race and to ensuring that scientific and technological achievements might ultimately be used solely for peaceful purposes.

With the participation of experts from Argentina, China, Egypt, France, the German Democratic Republic, India, Japan, Peru, Sweden, the USSR, the United Kingdom and the United States, the group, known as the Group of Governmental Experts on Military Research and Development, held its first session from 21 to 25 March in New York. Experts from Czechoslovakia and Ghana later joined the Group. At the first session, Rolf Björnerstedt (Sweden) was elected as Chairman and the discussion centred on the organization of work and a preliminary exchange of views on the content of the study.

The second session (New York, 5-15 July), attended by all 14 experts, focused on detailed discussion of the subject-matter, taking into account views of 28 Governments as submitted to the Secretary-General. The Group decided to ask the Secretariat to prepare a working draft of its report for consideration at the third session, due to be held in February 1984.

Parties and signatories to disarmament agreements

In October 1983, the Secretary-General submitted to the General Assembly his annual report on the status of multilateral disarmament agreements,[51] based on information received from the States depositaries of those agreements. Listing the parties to and signatories of agreements as at 31 August 1983, the report also contained similar information on the Convention on the Prohibition of Military or Any Other Hostile Use of Environmental Modification Techniques, the Agreement Governing the Activities of States on the Moon and Other Celestial Bodies, and the Convention on Prohibitions or Restrictions on the Use of Certain Conventional Weapons Which May Be Deemed to Be Excessively Injurious or to Have Indiscriminate Effects, of which the Secretary-General was the depositary. The last Convention, which entered into force in 1983, was also the sub-

ject of a separate report to the Assembly (see above, under CONVENTIONAL WEAPONS).

As at 31 December 1983, the following numbers of States had become parties to the agreements covered in the Secretary-General's report (listed in chronological order, with the years in which they were initially signed or opened for signature in parentheses):[52]

(Geneva) Protocol for the Prohibition of the Use in War of Asphyxiating, Poisonous or Other Gases, and of Bacteriological Methods of Warfare (1925): 105 parties

The Antarctic Treaty (1959): 28 parties

Treaty Banning Nuclear Weapon Tests in the Atmosphere, in Outer Space and under Water (1963): 111 parties

Treaty on Principles Governing the Activities of States in the Exploration and Use of Outer Space, including the Moon and Other Celestial Bodies (1967):[53] 84 parties

Treaty for the Prohibition of Nuclear Weapons in Latin America (1967): 31 parties

Treaty on the Non-Proliferation of Nuclear Weapons (1968):[54] 120 parties

Treaty on the Prohibition of the Emplacement of Nuclear Weapons and Other Weapons of Mass Destruction on the Sea-Bed and the Ocean Floor and in the Subsoil Thereof (1971):[55] 73 parties

Convention on the Prohibition of the Development, Production and Stockpiling of Bacteriological (Biological) and Toxin Weapons and on Their Destruction (1972):[56] 98 parties

Convention on the Prohibition of Military or Any Other Hostile Use of Environmental Modification Techniques (1977):[57] 42 parties

Agreement Governing the Activities of States on the Moon and Other Celestial Bodies (1979):[58] 4 parties

Proposed World Disarmament Conference

The concept of a world disarmament conference was first endorsed by the General Assembly in 1965[59] and had been discussed each year since 1971. In 1983, no further progress was made towards the covening of such a conference, as the basic positions of nuclear-weapon States remained largely unchanged.

***Ad Hoc* Committee activities.** The 40-member *Ad Hoc* Committee on the World Disarmament Conference held two sessions in New York in 1983: three meetings between 4 and 7 April and four others between 5 and 8 July. Its 1983 annual report[60] to the Assembly contained the updated views of the five nuclear-weapon States regarding the holding of such a conference. The Committee, which had been discussing the question since it first met in 1974,[61] also informed the Assembly that, through its Chairman, it had maintained close contact with those States so as to remain currently informed of their attitudes.

According to the report, the USSR continued to support the convening of a conference, rejected what it viewed as attempts by some nuclear-weapon States to justify their unconstructive attitudes by allusions to the deteriorating international situation, and called for a decision on specific preparatory measures.

China continued to hold that, since the super-Powers had escalated their arms race and had not shown sincerity towards disarmament, the time was not ripe for a conference. France observed the absence of consensus on the question; it had no objection, therefore, to the *Ad Hoc* Committee's studying the possibility of spacing its meetings in view of the continuing deadlock. The United Kingdom maintained that, in the current international climate, consideration of the matter was not useful; it also doubted the usefulness of further Committee meetings. The United States continued to believe it premature to convene a conference in view of the insufficient political agreement on the fundamental disarmament issues; an unsuccessful conference would impede future efforts towards concrete and verifiable measures.

The *Ad Hoc* Committee reiterated its previous conclusions: that the idea of a world disarmament conference had wide support, though with varying degrees of emphasis and differences regarding conditions and aspects relevant to its convening, including the deteriorating international situation; and that no consensus on convening a conference under current conditions had been reached among the nuclear-weapon States, whose participation was widely deemed essential. It suggested that the General Assembly might renew the Committee's mandate and request the Committee to maintain close contact with the nuclear-weapon and all other States and to consider any relevant comments and observations which might be made to it.

GENERAL ASSEMBLY ACTION

On the recommendation of the First Committee, the General Assembly, on 20 December 1983, adopted without vote resolution 38/186.

World Disarmament Conference

The General Assembly,

Recalling its resolutions 2833(XXVI) of 16 December 1971, 2930(XXVII) of 29 November 1972, 3183(XXVIII) of 18 December 1973, 3260(XXIX) of 9 December 1974, 3469(XXX) of 11 December 1975, 31/190 of 21 December 1976, 32/89 of 12 December 1977, 33/69 of 14 December 1978, 34/81 of 11 December 1979, 35/151 of 12 December 1980, 36/91 of 9 December 1981 and 37/97 of 13 December 1982,

Reiterating its conviction that all the peoples of the world have a vital interest in the success of disarmament negotiations and that all States should be in a position to contribute to the adoption of measures for the achievement of this goal,

Stressing anew its conviction that a world disarmament conference, adequately prepared and convened at an appropriate time, could provide the realization of such an aim and that the co-operation of all nuclear-weapon Powers would considerably facilitate its attainment,

Taking note of the report of the *Ad Hoc* Committee on the World Disarmament Conference,

Recalling that, in paragraph 122 of the Final Document of the Tenth Special Session of the General Assembly, it decided that, at the earliest appropriate time, a world disarmament conference should be convened with universal participation and with adequate preparation,

Recalling also that, in paragraph 23 of the Declaration of the 1980s as the Second Disarmament Decade, the General Assembly considered it pertinent also to recall that in paragraph 122 of the Final Document of the Tenth Special Session it had stated that at the earliest appropriate time a world disarmament conference should be convened, with universal participation and with adequate preparation,

1. *Notes with satisfaction* that in its report to the General Assembly the *Ad Hoc* Committee on the World Disarmament Conference stated, *inter alia*, the following:

"Having regard for the important requirements of a world disarmament conference to be convened at the earliest appropriate time, with universal participation and with adequate preparation, the General Assembly should take up the question at its thirty-eighth regular session for further consideration, bearing in mind the relevant provisions of resolution 36/91, adopted by consensus, in particular paragraph 1 of that resolution, and resolution 37/97, also adopted by consensus";

2. *Renews* the mandate of the *Ad Hoc* Committee;

3. *Requests* the *Ad Hoc* Committee to continue to maintain close contact with the representatives of the States possessing nuclear weapons, in order to remain currently informed of their attitudes, as well as with all other States, and to consider any relevant comments and observations which might be made to the Committee, especially having in mind paragraph 122 of the Final Document of the Tenth Special Session of the General Assembly;

4. *Requests* the *Ad Hoc* Committee to report to the General Assembly at its thirty-ninth session;

5. *Decides* to include in the provisional agenda of its thirty-ninth session the item entitled "World Disarmament Conference".

General Assembly resolution 38/186

20 December 1983   Meeting 103   Adopted without vote

Approved by First Committee (A/38/638) without vote, 21 November (meeting 34); 8-nation draft (A/C.1/38/L.17); agenda item 60.

Sponsors: Burundi, Congo, Mali, Mongolia, Peru, Poland, Spain, Sri Lanka.

Financial implications. ACABQ, A/38/7/ Add.21; 5th Committee, A/38/762; S-G, A/C.1/38/L.70, A/C.5/38/90.

Meeting numbers. GA 38th session: 1st Committee 3-10, 12-31, 34; 5th Committee 68; plenary 103.

In explanation of position, the United States said it had noted the understanding reflected in the text that such a conference should be adequately prepared and convened at an appropriate time.

Public information

Efforts to generate public understanding and support for the United Nations disarmament objectives continued in 1983, as the World Disarmament Campaign entered its second year of implementation. The first United Nations Pledging Conference for the World Disarmament Campaign was held in New York during Disarmament Week, and the Assembly decided, in resolution 38/73 D, to hold another pledging conference in 1984.

World Disarmament Campaign

The World Disarmament Campaign, aimed at informing, educating and generating public understanding and support for the disarmament objectives of the United Nations, was launched by the General Assembly on 7 June 1982, at the start of its second special session devoted to disarmament.[62] In December that year, the Assembly approved[63] the general framework for the Campaign and a 1983 programme of activities.[64]

The August 1983 report of the Secretary-General[65] on the Campaign's implementation outlined the co-ordinating role of the Department for Disarmament Affairs and the participation of others, particularly the Department of Public Information. It also described: United Nations information materials, including the introduction in June of a *Disarmament Newsletter*; interpersonal communication, seminars and training, among them a regional conference for non-governmental organizations (NGOs) held at New Delhi, India (August), and a regional seminar for educators at Caracas, Venezuela (October); special events, such as panel discussions, exhibits and film-making activities; a publicity programme; and activities of the United Nations information centres and other field offices.

The Secretary-General pointed to the need for additional resources, and reported that Member States' pledges to the World Disarmament Campaign Voluntary Trust Fund from the launching of the Campaign until the issuance of his current (August) report totalled some $2.9 million; in addition, various NGOs and individuals had contributed over $1 million. The Secretary-General proposed strengthening the Department for Disarmament Affairs through provision of two permanent posts for the Campaign for 1984-1985.

The Advisory Board on Disarmament Studies (see below),[66] mandated by the Assembly to advise the Secretary-General on the implementation of the Campaign,[67] expressed the view that the Campaign's effectiveness should be appraised by such means as questionnaires, and that NGOs should be asked to meet and discuss with it the Campaign's implementation, starting at its 1984 session. Support was expressed for the recommendation contained in the Secretary-General's report to strengthen the staff of the Department for Disarmament Affairs.

The first United Nations Pledging Conference for the World Disarmament Campaign was held at United Nations Headquarters on 27 October, during the 1983 Disarmament Week, and was attended by 61 States.[68]

The Conference President, Alfonso García Robles (Mexico), stated at the closing of the meeting that the pledges totalled $3,103,516—18 pledges amounting to the equivalent of $3,000,899 announced before, and 12 new pledges amounting to $102,617 made during, the 1983 Pledging Conference. He observed that the $3 million pledged represented less than what the world spent on arms in three minutes; in view of that enormous disparity, he anticipated the convening of a second pledging conference with the participation of all Member States.

Either during the Pledging Conference or at other times in the course of the year, the following pledges to the Campaign were made: Australia ($A 30,000), Bangladesh (25,000 taka), Burma ($1,500), Canada ($Can 100,000), Cuba (5,000 pesos), Czechoslovakia (300,000 koruny), Democratic Yemen ($2,000), Denmark (250,000 kroner), Egypt (40,000 pounds), Greece ($10,000), India ($100,000), Indonesia ($5,000), Japan ($50,000), Libyan Arab Jamahiriya (5,000 dinars), Nigeria (10,000 naira), Norway ($25,000), Poland (100,000 zlotych), Sri Lanka ($5,000), Tunisia ($10,000 equivalent), Uganda (300,000 shillings), Viet Nam (50,000 dong).

GENERAL ASSEMBLY ACTION

On 15 December 1983, the General Assembly, on the recommendation of the First Committee, adopted two resolutions, 38/73 D and F, concerning the World Disarmament Campaign.

Resolution 38/73 D, providing for a second pledging conference, was adopted without vote.

World Disarmament Campaign

The General Assembly,

Recalling that, in paragraph 15 of the Final Document of the Tenth Special Session of the General Assembly, the first special session devoted to disarmament, it declared that it was essential that not only Governments but also the peoples of the world recognize and understand the dangers in the present situation and stressed the importance of mobilizing world public opinion on behalf of disarmament,

Recalling also its resolutions 35/152 I of 12 December 1980, 36/92 C of 9 December 1981 and 37/100 I of 13 December 1982, as well as the reports of the Secretary-General of 17 September 1981, 11 June 1982 and 3 November 1982,

Having examined the report of the Secretary-General of 30 August 1983 on the implementation of the programme of activities of the World Disarmament Campaign,

Having also examined the part of the report of the Secretary-General dealing with the activities of the Advisory Board on Disarmament Studies relating to the programme of activities of the World Disarmament Campaign, as well as the final act of the 1983 United Nations Pledging Conference for the Campaign held on 27 October 1983,

1. *Notes with satisfaction* the implementation of the programme of activities of the World Disarmament Campaign for 1983 as described in the report of the Secretary-General;

2. *Notes also with satisfaction* the voluntary contributions made by Member States to the World Disarmament Campaign Voluntary Trust Fund, prior to and during the 1983 United Nations Pledging Conference for the Campaign;

3. *Decides* that at its thirty-ninth session there should be a second United Nations Pledging Conference for the World Disarmament Campaign, in order that all those Member States that have not yet announced their voluntary contributions may have an opportunity to do so;

4. *Recommends* that the voluntary contributions made by Member States to the World Disarmament Campaign Voluntary Trust Fund should not be earmarked for specific activities inasmuch as it is most desirable that the Secretary-General may enjoy full freedom to take the decisions he deems fit within the framework of the Campaign previously approved by the General Assembly and in exercise of the powers vested in him in connection with the Campaign;

5. *Requests* the Secretary-General to instruct the United Nations information centres and regional commissions to give wide publicity to the World Disarmament Campaign and, whenever necessary, to adapt, as far as possible, United Nations information materials into local languages;

6. *Also requests* the Secretary-General to submit to the General Assembly at its thirty-ninth session a report covering both the implementation of the programme of activities of the World Disarmament Campaign by the United Nations system during 1984 and the programme of activities contemplated by the system for 1985;

7. *Decides* to include in the provisional agenda of its thirty-ninth session the item entitled "World Disarmament Campaign".

General Assembly resolution 38/73 D

15 December 1983   Meeting 97   Adopted without vote

Approved by First Committee (A/38/641) without vote, 25 November (meeting 40); 9-nation draft (A/C.1/38/L.40); agenda item 63 *(g)*.
Sponsors: Bangladesh, Egypt, Indonesia, Mexico, Romania, Sri Lanka, Sweden, Venezuela, Yugoslavia.
Meeting numbers. GA 38th session: 1st Committee 3-10, 12-32, 40; plenary 97.

In explanation of position, the Federal Republic of Germany and the Netherlands expressed reservations concerning paragraph 3, saying that too much emphasis on pledging conferences might erroneously suggest that the Campaign's success depended merely on fund-raising rather than on free, unencumbered flow of information.

The USSR said it understood paragraph 4 to mean that the Secretary-General would consult donor countries about concrete Campaign measures in their countries. For the German Democratic Republic, that paragraph meant that the Secretary-General's Campaign-related decisions would be based on the Charter of the United Nations, the Final Document of the Tenth Special Session of the General Assembly,[69] and relevant United Nations resolutions.

As recommended by the First Committee, the Assembly adopted, by recorded vote on 15 December, resolution 38/73 F.

World Disarmament Campaign: actions and activities

The General Assembly,

Aware of the growing public concern at the dangers of the arms race, particularly the nuclear-arms race, and its negative social and economic consequences,

Noting with satisfaction the successful beginning of the implementation of the World Disarmament Campaign and its positive impact on the mobilization on a large scale of world public opinion on behalf of peace and disarmament,

Recalling its resolutions 36/92 J of 9 December 1981 and 37/100 H of 13 December 1982, as well as the report of the Secretary-General on world-wide action for collecting signatures in support of measures to prevent nuclear war, to curb the arms race and for disarmament,

Welcoming the voluntary contributions made to the World Disarmament Campaign Voluntary Trust Fund to carry out the objectives of the Campaign,

Taking into account the report of the Secretary-General on the implementation of the programme of activities of the World Disarmament Campaign,

Convinced that the United Nations system, Member States, with respect for their sovereign rights, and other bodies, in particular non-governmental organizations, all have their role to play in achieving the objectives of the World Disarmament Campaign,

Taking into account the great number of various activities carried out within the framework of the World Disarmament Campaign, including action for collecting signatures in support of measures to prevent nuclear war, to curb the arms race and for disarmament,

1. *Reaffirms* the usefulness of further carrying out actions and activities which are an important manifestation of the will of world public opinion and which contribute effectively to the achievement of the objectives of the World Disarmament Campaign and thus to the creation of a favourable climate for making progress in the field of disarmament with a view to achieving the goal of general and complete disarmament under effective international control;

2. *Invites once again* Member States to co-operate with the United Nations to ensure a better flow of accurate information with regard to the various aspects of disarmament as well as actions and activities of the world public in support of peace and disarmament, and to avoid dissemination of false and tendentious information;

3. *Requests* the Secretary-General to report annually to the General Assembly on the implementation of the provisions of the present resolution.

General Assembly resolution 38/73 F

15 December 1983   Meeting 97   112-1-29 (recorded vote)

Approved by First Committee (A/38/641) by recorded vote (88-1-30), 25 November (meeting 40); 5-nation draft (A/C.1/38/L.46); agenda item 63 *(g)*.
Sponsors: Bulgaria, German Democratic Republic, Mongolia, Romania, Viet Nam.
Meeting numbers. GA 38th session: 1st Committee 3-10, 12-32, 40; plenary 97.

Recorded vote in Assembly as follows:

In favour: Afghanistan, Algeria, Angola, Antigua and Barbuda, Australia, Bahrain, Bangladesh, Barbados, Belize, Benin, Bhutan, Bolivia, Botswana, Bulgaria, Burundi, Byelorussian SSR, Cape Verde, Central African Republic, Chad, Colombia, Congo, Costa Rica, Cuba, Cyprus, Czechoslovakia, Democratic Yemen, Djibouti, Dominican Republic, Ecuador, Egypt, El Salvador, Ethiopia, Fiji, Gabon, Gambia, German Democratic Republic, Ghana, Grenada, Guatemala, Guinea, Guyana, Haiti, Hungary, India, Indonesia, Iran, Iraq, Ivory Coast, Jamaica, Japan, Jordan, Kenya, Kuwait, Lao People's Democratic Republic, Lebanon, Lesotho, Liberia, Libyan Arab Jamahiriya, Madagascar, Malawi, Malaysia, Maldives, Mali, Mauritania, Mauritius, Mexico, Mongolia, Mozambique, Nepal, Nicaragua, Niger, Nigeria, Oman, Pakistan, Panama, Papua New Guinea, Peru, Philippines, Poland, Qatar, Romania, Rwanda, Saint Lucia, Sao Tome and Principe, Saudi Arabia, Senegal, Seychelles, Sierra Leone, Solomon Islands, Sri Lanka, Sudan, Suriname, Swaziland, Syrian Arab Republic, Thailand, Togo, Trinidad and Tobago, Tunisia, Uganda, Ukrainian SSR, USSR, United Arab Emirates, United Republic of Cameroon, United Republic of Tanzania, Upper Volta, Vanuatu, Venezuela, Viet Nam, Yemen, Yugoslavia, Zambia, Zimbabwe.

Against: Brazil.

Abstaining: Argentina, Austria, Bahamas, Belgium, Canada, Chile, Democratic Kampuchea, Denmark, Finland, France, Germany, Federal Republic of, Greece, Honduras, Iceland, Ireland, Israel, Italy, Luxembourg, Netherlands, New Zealand, Norway, Paraguay, Portugal, Spain, Sweden, Turkey, United Kingdom, United States, Uruguay.

In explanation of vote, Brazil said activities such as collecting signatures did not conform to the function and purpose of the United Nations. France also had serious reservations regarding the reference to that measure, and was joined by the United Kingdom in adding that paragraph 2 was an invitation to censorship and posed the question of who would judge what was false and tendentious information. Expressing regret that a second text on the Campaign had been thought essential, the United Kingdom added that, on a subject as important as disarmament, every facet should be explored fully and debated publicly. Australia said it supported the text at face value but did not endorse State censorship or control of information available to citizens.

In 1983, in its resolution 38/183 F, the Assembly also called on Member State and the United Nations Educational, Scientific and Cultural Organization to disseminate the ideas of international co-operation for disarmament (see above, under IMPLEMENTATION OF THE 1979 DECLARATION ON CO-OPERATION FOR DISARMAMENT).

Observance of Disarmament Week (24-30 October)

Disarmament Week—proclaimed by the General Assembly in 1978[69] to start on United Nations Day, 24 October—was marked in 1983 at United Nations Headquarters at a special meeting on that day of the Assembly's First Committee, where statements were made by the Assembly President and the Secretary-General as well as by representatives of regional groups.

The President, stating that relations between societies could never be peaceful if they were based on terror, called for a bold, imaginative step to reduce tensions, to improve international relations and to promote development as well as international economic co-operation.

The Secretary-General stressed the importance of the USSR–United States bilateral negotiations on arms limitation and expressed hope that provisional measures would be adopted to give them more time to achieve positive results; at the same time, he urged that the negotiations within the United Nations framework should continue with greater determination.

The Secretary-General submitted to the Assembly in an annual report[70] the replies received from 17 Governments and from several programmes and agencies within the United Nations system concerning activities in connection with Disarmament Week 1982. A number of international NGOs also submitted information.

GENERAL ASSEMBLY ACTION

On the recommendation of the First Committee, the General Assembly, on 20 December, adopted by recorded vote resolution 38/183 L.

Disarmament Week

The General Assembly,

Gravely concerned over the escalating arms race,

Emphasizing the urgent need for and the importance of wide and continued mobilization of world public opinion in support of halting and reversing the arms race, especially the nuclear-arms race in all its aspects,

Mindful of the world-wide mass anti-war and anti-nuclear movement,

Noting with satisfaction the broad and active support by Governments and international and national organizations of the decision taken by the General Assembly at its tenth special session, the first special session devoted to disarmament, regarding the proclamation of the week starting 24 October, the day of the foundation of the United Nations, as a week devoted to fostering the objectives of disarmament,

Recalling the recommendations concerning the World Disarmament Campaign contained in annex V to the Concluding Document of the Twelfth Special Session of the General Assembly, the second special session devoted to disarmament, in particular the recommendation that, in view of the fact that Disarmament Week has played a useful role in fostering the objectives of disarmament, the week starting 24 October should continue to be widely observed as Disarmament Week,

Recalling also its resolutions 33/71 D of 14 December 1978, 34/83 I of 11 December 1979 and 37/78 D of 9 December 1982,

1. *Takes note with satisfaction* of the report of the Secretary-General on the follow-up measures undertaken by governmental and non-governmental organizations in holding Disarmament Week;

2. *Expresses its appreciation* to all States and international and national governmental and non-governmental organizations for their energetic support of and active participation in Disarmament Week;

3. *Invites* all States, in carrying out appropriate measures at the local level on the occasion of Disarmament Week, to take into account the elements of the model programme for Disarmament Week, prepared by the Secretary-General;

4. *Also invites* the relevant specialized agencies and the International Atomic Energy Agency to intensify activities, within their areas of competence, to disseminate

information on the consequences of the arms race and requests them to inform the Secretary-General accordingly;

5. *Requests* Governments, in accordance with General Assembly resolution 33/71 D, to inform the Secretary-General of activities undertaken to promote the objectives of Disarmament Week;

6. *Invites* international non-governmental organizations to take an active part in Disarmament Week and to inform the Secretary-General of the activities undertaken;

7. *Requests* the Secretary-General, in accordance with paragraph 4 of resolution 33/71 D, to submit to the General Assembly at its thirty-ninth session a report containing the information referred to in paragraph 7 of resolution 37/78 D, as well as paragraphs 4 to 6 above.

General Assembly resolution 38/183 L

20 December 1983   Meeting 103   136-0-12 (recorded vote)

Approved by First Committee (A/38/628) by recorded vote (107-0-13), 25 November (meeting 40); 12-nation draft (A/C.1/38/L.33/Rev.1); agenda item 50 *(e)*.

Sponsors: Afghanistan, Bulgaria, Byelorussian SSR, Cuba, Czechoslovakia, German Democratic Republic, India, Lao People's Democratic Republic, Mongolia, Mozambique, Ukrainian SSR, Viet Nam.

Meeting numbers. GA 38th session: 1st Committee 11, 33, 40; plenary 103.

Recorded vote in Assembly as follows:

In favour: Afghanistan, Algeria, Angola, Antigua and Barbuda, Argentina, Austria, Bahamas, Bahrain, Bangladesh, Barbados, Belize, Benin, Bhutan, Bolivia, Botswana, Brazil, Bulgaria, Burma, Burundi, Byelorussian SSR, Canada, Cape Verde, Central African Republic, Chad, Chile, Colombia, Congo, Costa Rica, Cuba, Cyprus, Czechoslovakia, Democratic Yemen, Denmark, Djibouti, Dominica, Dominican Republic, Ecuador, Egypt, El Salvador, Ethiopia, Fiji, Finland, Gabon, Gambia, German Democratic Republic, Ghana, Greece, Guatemala, Guinea, Guinea-Bissau, Guyana, Haiti, Honduras, Hungary, Iceland, India, Indonesia, Iran, Iraq, Ireland, Ivory Coast, Jamaica, Japan, Jordan, Kenya, Kuwait, Lao People's Democratic Republic, Lebanon, Lesotho, Liberia, Libyan Arab Jamahiriya, Madagascar, Malawi, Malaysia, Maldives, Mali, Malta, Mauritania, Mauritius, Mexico, Mongolia, Morocco, Mozambique, Nepal, New Zealand, Nicaragua, Niger, Nigeria, Norway, Oman, Pakistan, Panama, Papua New Guinea, Paraguay, Peru, Philippines, Poland, Portugal, Qatar, Romania, Rwanda, Saint Lucia, Saint Vincent and the Grenadines, Sao Tome and Principe, Saudi Arabia, Senegal, Sierra Leone, Singapore, Somalia, Spain, Sri Lanka, Sudan, Suriname, Swaziland, Sweden, Syrian Arab Republic, Thailand, Togo, Trinidad and Tobago, Tunisia, Uganda, Ukrainian SSR, USSR, United Arab Emirates, United Republic of Cameroon, United Republic of Tanzania, Upper Volta, Uruguay, Vanuatu, Venezuela, Viet Nam, Yemen, Yugoslavia, Zaire, Zambia, Zimbabwe.

Against: None.

Abstaining: Australia, Belgium, Democratic Kampuchea, France, Germany, Federal Republic of, Israel, Italy, Luxembourg, Netherlands, Turkey, United Kingdom, United States.

In explanation of vote, Australia regretted the inclusion of paragraph 4, which invited IAEA, in particular, to undertake activities which, it believed, were outside the scope of the Agency's statute. France also considered the paragraph to be contrary to the balance of responsibilities and competence established within the United Nations system, and Canada also expected the agencies involved to remain within their mandates.

Peace and disarmament movements

GENERAL ASSEMBLY CONSIDERATION

In 1983, a draft resolution entitled "Peace and disarmament movements"[71] was submitted—but later withdrawn—in the General Assembly's First Committee by Australia, the Bahamas, Costa Rica, the Federal Republic of Germany, Indonesia,

Jamaica, Japan, Kenya, the Netherlands, Norway, Portugal, Singapore, Sweden, the United Kingdom, the United States and Uruguay.

The proposal would have had the Assembly call on Member States to permit their citizens free public expression of their own views on disarmament and the exchange of such views with the Secretary-General, express regret that some groups had had difficulty in engaging in activities promoting peace and disarmament, and encourage Member States and NGOs to provide the Secretary-General with information pertinent to monitoring compliance with the commitment to further free debate on disarmament.

Czechoslovakia proposed amendments[72] to the draft consisting of an additional preambular paragraph, by which the Assembly would have emphasized that Governments should take into account the will of the peoples as reflected by the mass movements for the prevention of nuclear war and the arms race, and a new operative paragraph 1, by which it would have urged Governments of nuclear-weapon and other militarily significant States to harmonize their policies with the demands of such movements. The United States proposed sub-amendments[73] to those amendments which referred to the wishes of all people concerned, rather than the mass movements, being taken into account by Governments and, in paragraph 1, urged Governments, especially of nuclear-weapon and other militarily significant States, to redouble their efforts to achieve general disarmament and prevent nuclear and any other type of war.

The sponsors subsequently submitted a revised text[74] in which they deleted references to free exchange of disarmament-related information between citizens and the Secretary-General. Thereafter, Bulgaria and Czechoslovakia submitted amendments to the revised draft, both further modifying paragraph 1. Bulgaria's amendment[75] would have had the Assembly renew its call on Member States to facilitate the flow of accurate information on disarmament matters, both governmental and non-governmental, to and among citizens. The amendment proposed by Czechoslovakia[76] would have had the Assembly urge Governments to harmonize their policies with the demands of the mass peace and disarmament movements.

The United States, on behalf of the sponsors, withdrew the draft, stating that the proposed amendments sought to redirect the draft resolution to such an extent that they perverted the text's basic objective.

Meeting numbers. GA 38th session: 1st Committee 3-10, 12-31, 33, 46.

Disarmament research

In 1983, the General Assembly initiated three new disarmament studies on the following subjects: unilateral nuclear disarmament measures (resolution

38/183 J), the naval arms race (resolution 38/188 G) and concepts of security (resolution 38/188 H). In addition, three studies were in progress, on conventional disarmament (see above, under CONVENTIONAL WEAPONS), nuclear-weapon-free zones (see above, under NUCLEAR-WEAPON-FREE ZONES), and military research and development (see above, under MILITARY RESEARCH AND DEVELOPMENT).

UN Institute for Disarmament Research

Activities of the Institute. On 1 January 1983, the United Nations Institute for Disarmament Research (UNIDIR), established in 1980[77] within the United Nations Institute for Training and Research,[78] became a Geneva-based autonomous institution, in pursuance of a December 1982 General Assembly resolution.[67]

Reporting to the Assembly through the Secretary-General,[79] the UNIDIR Director said the Institute, financed by voluntary contributions, received assistance from Australia, Canada, France and Norway, which had responded to the Assembly invitation in that regard.[67] In 1983, UNIDIR established, in accordance with a December 1982 Assembly recommendation,[80] a six-member steering group, which met at Geneva on 21 and 22 June and agreed on guidelines for investigating the modalities of an international disarmament fund for development; the group also indicated that the study would be completed by June 1984 for submission to the Assembly. Among a number of ongoing UNIDIR studies, many of which were to be completed in 1984, were those dealing with international law of disarmament, disarmament and the right to security, denuclearization of the Balkans, chemical weapons prohibition, and new technologies in the conventional armaments field. Work continued on studies on the lowering of the level of armaments.

UNIDIR also provided information to the General Assembly in connection with its 1983 consideration of regional disarmament (see above).

Activities of the Board of Trustees. The Secretary-General reported to the General Assembly that the Advisory Board on Disarmament Studies (see below),[66] meeting for the first time as the UNIDIR Board of Trustees (New York, 6-13 September 1983), adopted research guidelines and project proposals, along with the Institute's draft statute.

The draft statute, annexed to the Secretary-General's report, covered the Institute's purposes, functions, Board of Trustees and other institutional arrangements such as finance and administrative support. It reflected the view of the Board that UNIDIR's activities should be financed partly from the regular budget of the United Nations, as far as basic operating and administrative costs were

concerned, and partly from voluntary contributions and special-purpose grants which, it envisaged, should cover the main study programme.

ACABQ consideration. The Advisory Committee on Administrative and Budgetary Questions (ACABQ), in a November 1983 report,[81] observed that UNIDIR's administrative and financial arrangements should be defined clearly from the outset; it called for removing the ambiguities arising from an attempt to make the draft statute cover both the UNIDIR financing on a voluntary basis and the possibility of an Assembly decision to fund certain expenditures from the United Nations regular budget.

GENERAL ASSEMBLY CONSIDERATION

In the light of the ACABQ observations, a 33-nation draft resolution[82] in the First Committee, which would have had the Assembly approve the draft statute, was withdrawn. As orally proposed by its Chairman, the Committee decided, without objection, to recommend that the Assembly act in 1984 after the UNIDIR Board of Trustees submitted clarifications on the statute's provisions.

Subsequently, the Fifth (Administrative and Budgetary) Committee, which had been asked by the First Committee Chairman to consider the administrative implications of the draft on the question,[83] also decided without objection to defer action on the ACABQ report until 1984.[84]

GENERAL ASSEMBLY ACTION

On 20 December, the General Assembly adopted decision 38/447, as recommended by the First Committee.

Draft statute of the United Nations Institute for Disarmament Research

At its 103rd plenary meeting, on 20 December 1983, the General Assembly, on the recommendation of the First Committee, decided that the draft statute of the United Nations Institute for Disarmament Research should be returned to the Board of Trustees of the Institute with a request that the Board spell out the meaning of the provisions of the draft statute, so that the Assembly could take a decision on that draft statute at its thirty-ninth session.

General Assembly decision 38/447

Adopted without vote

Approved by First Committee (A/38/640) without vote, 25 November (meeting 41); draft orally proposed by Chairman, agenda item 62 *(j)*.
Meeting numbers. GA 38th session: 1st Committee 3-10, 12-31, 41; 5th Committee 51; plenary 103.

In 1983, the Assembly made other requests to UNIDIR: under resolution 38/181 A, to provide data on the development of South Africa's nuclear capability; and under resolution 38/73 J, to keep the Assembly informed, through the Secretary-General, on its activities relating to the regional approach to disarmament (for texts of these resolutions, refer to INDEX OF RESOLUTIONS AND DECISIONS).

Advisory Board on Disarmament Studies

The Advisory Board on Disarmament Studies, revived by the Secretary-General pursuant to a December 1982 General Assembly resolution,[67] held its eighth and ninth sessions in New York from 6 to 13 September and from 12 to 16 December 1983.

The Board was established in 1978 to advise the Secretary-General on various aspects of United Nations studies on disarmament and arms limitation,[85] and had last met in 1981.

Its 1983 sessions focused on United Nations studies on disarmament, the implementation of the World Disarmament Campaign (see above), and the work and draft statute of UNIDIR, for which it acted for the first time in 1983 as Board of Trustees (see above).

GENERAL ASSEMBLY ACTION

On 20 December, the General Assembly, on the recommendation of the First Committee, adopted without vote resolution 38/183 O.

Advisory Board on Disarmament Studies

The General Assembly,

Recalling paragraph 124 of the Final Document of the Tenth Special Session of the General Assembly,

Recalling further its resolution 37/99 K of 13 December 1982, by section III of which it requested the Secretary-General to revive the Advisory Board on Disarmament Studies,

1. *Expresses its satisfaction* that the Secretary-General has revived the Advisory Board on Disarmament Studies;

2. *Takes note with appreciation* of the report of the Secretary-General on the activities of the Advisory Board in 1983;

3. *Requests* the Secretary-General to report annually to the General Assembly on the work of the Advisory Board.

General Assembly resolution 38/183 O

20 December 1983   Meeting 103   Adopted without vote

Approved by First Committee (A/38/628) without vote, 21 November (meeting 35); 13-nation draft (A/C.1/38/L.52); agenda item 50 *(j)*.

Sponsors: Algeria, Argentina, Cuba, German Democratic Republic, Germany, Federal Republic of, India, Mali, Mexico, Pakistan, Romania, Sri Lanka, United Kingdom, Yugoslavia.

Meeting numbers. GA 38th session: 1st Committee 3-10, 12-31, 33, 35; plenary 103.

In other 1983 action, the Assembly, by resolution 38/188 C, requested the Advisory Board, through the Secretary-General, to consider studying the measures to facilitate objective information and assessments of military capabilities (see above, under PROPOSED INFORMATION EXCHANGE ON ARMAMENTS AND ARMED FORCES).

Fellowships

The Secretary-General reported to the General Assembly that the 1983 United Nations programme of fellowships on disarmament (29 June–30 November)[86] consisted of lectures, seminars, research, observation of the Committee on Disarmament at Geneva and the Assembly's First Committee in New York, and a one-week course at IAEA in Vienna. Twenty-five fellows from as many countries participated in the programme, which also included study visits in the Federal Republic of Germany, Japan, Sweden, the USSR and the United States, at the invitation of those countries.

The Secretary-General noted that the programme, which the Assembly established in 1978 at its first special session on disarmament[69] to promote expertise in disarmament, especially in developing countries, had trained 104 public officials from 67 countries in its first five years of existence.

GENERAL ASSEMBLY ACTION

On the recommendation of the First Committee, the General Assembly, on 15 December, adopted without vote resolution 38/73 C.

United Nations programme of fellowships on disarmament

The General Assembly,

Recalling its decision, contained in paragraph 108 of the Final Document of the Tenth Special Session of the General Assembly, to establish a programme of fellowships on disarmament, as well as its decisions contained in annex IV to the Concluding Document of the Twelfth Special Session of the General Assembly, in which it, *inter alia*, decided to continue the programme and to increase the number of fellowships from twenty to twenty-five as from 1983,

Noting with satisfaction that the programme has already trained one hundred and four public officials from sixty-seven countries, most of whom are now in positions of responsibility in the field of disarmament affairs within their Governments or Permanent Missions to the United Nations, or representing their Governments at international disarmament meetings,

Bearing in mind the growing interest which continues to be manifested in the programme by an ever-increasing number of States,

Recognizing the fact that the programme of studies and activities as outlined in the report of the Secretary-General on the United Nations programme of fellowships on disarmament has continued to expand,

Having considered the report of the Secretary-General,

1. *Decides* to continue the United Nations programme of fellowships on disarmament;

2. *Requests* the Secretary-General to continue to apply the same criteria of objectivity and balance in drawing up the future programme of activities as he has done so far, in accordance with the guidelines established by the General Assembly at its thirty-third session;

3. *Expresses its appreciation* to the Governments of Germany, the Federal Republic of, Japan, Sweden, the Union of Soviet Socialist Republics and the United States of America for inviting the fellows to their countries in 1983 to study selected activities in the field of disarmament, thereby contributing to the fulfilment of the overall objectives of the programme, as well as

providing additional information sources and practical knowledge for the fellows, and, in this connection, expresses the hope that other Member States will extend similar support to the programme;

4. *Takes note* of the decision of the Secretary-General to relocate the fellowship programme and its staff at Geneva as from 1 May 1983;

5. *Notes* that the expansion of the programme has led to an increase in the level of its activities;

6. *Commends* the Secretary-General for the diligence with which the programme has continued to be carried out;

7. *Requests* the Secretary-General to make the necessary arrangements for the implementation of the programme for 1984, in accordance with the guidelines established for it;

8. *Also requests* the Secretary-General to report to the General Assembly at its thirty-ninth session on the implementation of the provisions of the present resolution.

General Assembly resolution 38/73 C

15 December 1983   Meeting 97   Adopted without vote

Approved by First Committee (A/38/641) without vote, 21 November (meeting 34); 35-nation draft (A/C.1/38/L.39), orally revised; agenda item 63 *(f)*.
Sponsors: Algeria, Bahamas, Bangladesh, Colombia, Congo, Costa Rica, Cuba, Democratic Yemen, Ecuador, Egypt, Ethiopia, France, Greece, Haiti, Indonesia, Kenya, Liberia, Mali, Mexico, Nigeria, Philippines, Senegal, Somalia, Sri Lanka, Sudan, Sweden, Togo, Tunisia, Uganda, United Republic of Cameroon, Uruguay, Venezuela, Yugoslavia, Zaire, Zambia.
Meeting numbers. GA 38th session: 1st Committee 3-10, 12-34; plenary 97.

Organizational aspects

Co-ordination in the UN system

Responding to a 1982 General Assembly request,[80] the Administrative Committee on Coordination in 1983 studied the question of coordinating disarmament activities in the United Nations system (see above, under DISARMAMENT AND DEVELOPMENT).

GENERAL ASSEMBLY ACTION

As recommended by the First Committee, the General Assembly, on 20 December, adopted by recorded vote resolution 38/188 J.

Institutional arrangements relating to the process of disarmament

The General Assembly,

Convinced that the United Nations, in accordance with the Charter, has a central role and primary responsibility in the sphere of disarmament and should, accordingly, play a more active role in this field,

Reaffirming that the international machinery should be utilized more effectively to promote the cause of disarmament,

Reaffirming also the role of the Conference on Disarmament as the single multilateral disarmament negotiating forum,

Stressing that the Department for Disarmament Affairs of the Secretariat should take full account of the possibilities offered by specialized agencies and other organizations and programmes of the United Nations system with regard to studies and information on disarmament,

Stressing again the close relationship between matters concerning international security and disarmament and the interest in close co-operation between the units in the Secretariat dealing with them,

Convinced that all possible avenues should be effectively utilized for the cause of preventing war, in particular nuclear war, and achieving disarmament,

Reaffirming further the close link existing between disarmament and development,

Convinced that disarmament would contribute over the long term to the effective economic and social development of all States, in particular developing countries, by contributing to reducing the economic disparities between developed and developing countries and establishing the new international economic order on the basis of justice, equity and co-operation, and towards solving other global problems,

Convinced also that there is a close relationship between the development of international co-operation in various fields, such as trade, economic development, environmental protection and health and the prevention of war, in particular nuclear war, and the achievement of arms limitation and disarmament,

Reaffirming its invitation to the relevant specialized agencies to intensify activities within their areas of competence to disseminate information on the consequences of the arms race,

Taking note with appreciation of various activities carried out by United Nations organizations and agencies within the framework of the World Disarmament Campaign,

Commending the report of the World Health Organization entitled "Effects of nuclear war on health and health services", as well as appropriate efforts undertaken by other specialized agencies,

1. *Invites* the specialized agencies and other organizations and programmes of the United Nations system to broaden further their contribution, within their areas of competence, to the cause of arms limitation and disarmament;

2. *Reaffirms* the necessity of ensuring constant coordination of activities carried out in the field of disarmament by various entities of the United Nations;

3. *Invites* the specialized agencies and other organizations and programmes of the United Nations system to report to the General Assembly at its thirty-ninth session on the activities carried out by them in implementation of the present resolution;

4. *Recommends* to the Secretary-General that, in the agenda of his periodic meetings with the executive heads of the specialized agencies, he include an item relative to disarmament, in the consideration of which the Under-Secretary-General for Disarmament Affairs would participate;

5. *Decides* to include in the provisional agenda of its thirty-ninth session an item entitled "Contribution of the specialized agencies and other organizations and programmes of the United Nations system to the cause of arms limitation and disarmament".

General Assembly resolution 38/188 J

20 December 1983   Meeting 103   114-17-12 (recorded vote)

Approved by First Committee (A/38/640) by recorded vote (80-16-15), 21 November (meeting 35); 4-nation draft (A/C.1/38/L.66), orally revised; agenda item 62 *(j)*.
Sponsors: Cuba, Czechoslovakia, German Democratic Republic, Mongolia.
Meeting numbers. GA 38th session: 1st Committee 3-10, 12-31, 33, 35; plenary 103.

Recorded vote in Assembly as follows:

In favour: Afghanistan, Algeria, Angola, Antigua and Barbuda, Argentina, Bahrain, Bangladesh, Belize, Benin, Bhutan, Bolivia, Botswana, Brazil, Bulgaria, Burundi, Byelorussian SSR, Cape Verde, Chad, Chile, Colombia, Congo, Costa Rica, Cuba, Cyprus, Czechoslovakia, Democratic Yemen, Dominica, Dominican Republic, Ecuador, Egypt, El Salvador, Ethiopia, Fiji, Gabon, Gambia, German Democratic Republic, Ghana, Guatemala, Guinea, Guinea-Bissau, Guyana, Honduras, Hungary, India, Indonesia, Iran, Iraq, Ivory Coast, Jamaica, Jordan, Kenya, Kuwait, Lao People's Democratic Republic, Lebanon, Lesotho, Liberia, Libyan Arab Jamahiriya, Madagascar, Malawi, Malaysia, Maldives, Mali, Mauritania, Mauritius, Mexico, Mongolia, Morocco, Mozambique, Nepal, Nicaragua, Niger, Nigeria, Oman, Pakistan, Panama, Papua New Guinea, Peru, Philippines, Poland, Qatar, Romania, Rwanda, Saint Lucia, Sao Tome and Principe, Saudi Arabia, Senegal, Sierra Leone, Singapore, Somalia, Sri Lanka, Sudan, Suriname, Swaziland, Syrian Arab Republic, Thailand, Togo, Trinidad and Tobago, Tunisia, Uganda, Ukrainian SSR, USSR, United Arab Emirates, United Republic of Cameroon, United Republic of Tanzania, Upper Volta, Uruguay, Vanuatu, Venezuela, Viet Nam, Yemen, Yugoslavia, Zaire, Zambia, Zimbabwe.

Against: Australia, Belgium, Canada, France, Germany, Federal Republic of, Iceland, Israel, Italy, Japan, Luxembourg, Netherlands, New Zealand, Norway, Portugal, Turkey, United Kingdom, United States.

Abstaining: Austria, Bahamas, Barbados, China, Denmark, Finland, Greece, Ireland, Paraguay, Saint Vincent and the Grenadines, Spain, Sweden.

In explanation of vote, Sweden felt that unqualified recommendations to international organizations to broaden their activities to political issues could seriously disturb and hamper the support for, as well as the work in, those agencies. Similarly, Canada felt it ill-advised to introduce political issues into United Nations functional bodies, and stressed that the division of labour be respected.

Sharing these views, the United States said the text would also impede progress towards adopting concrete, effective and verifiable measures of arms control and disarmament in the competent bodies which, according to the understandings enshrined in the 1978 Final Document,[69] were the General Assembly's First Committee, the Disarmament Commission and the Committee on Disarmament. Canada agreed that arms control and disarmament matters should be discussed in those specific bodies and in IAEA. Speaking on behalf of the 10 States members of EC, Greece observed that, although the work of the specialized agencies involved certain aspects of disarmament which fell within their areas of competence, the text could detract from the United Nations central role in disarmament and the Secretary-General's responsibility for co-ordinating disarmament-related activities undertaken within the United Nations system.

Department for Disarmament Affairs

The Secretary-General reported to the General Assembly in 1983[87] that, in accordance with a December 1982 Assembly request,[67] the Centre for Disarmament had been transformed into the United Nations Department for Disarmament Affairs as of 1 January 1983, and that he had appointed Under-Secretary-General Jan Martenson as its head.

The Department, whose functions included assisting the Secretary-General in discharging his disarmament-related responsibilities, consisted of the Office of the Under-Secretary-General, the Committee and Conference Services Branch, the Information and Studies Branch, and the Geneva Branch.

At its inception, the Department had at its disposal the 26 established Professional posts of its predecessor, occupied by staff members representing 23 nationalities from all geographical regions. In view of the priority attached to disarmament questions and the increased scope and volume of relevant Secretariat activities, the Secretary-General proposed measures that would result in a net growth in 1984-1985 of two established Professional posts.

In 1983 action, the Assembly requested the Secretary-General, under resolution 38/73 J, to keep it informed of the activities carried out by the Department for Disarmament Affairs concerning the regional approach to disarmament; and, under resolution 38/181 A, called on UNIDIR, in co-operation with the Department and in consultation with OAU, to provide data on the continued development of South Africa's nuclear capability (for texts of these resolutions, refer to INDEX OF RESOLUTIONS AND DECISIONS).

REFERENCES

[1]A/38/42. [2]YUN 1982, p. 115. [3]YUN 1981, p. 90. [4]YUN 1982, p. 119, GA res. 37/95 B, 13 Dec. 1982. [5]A/38/354 & Corr.1. [6]A/38/434. [7]A/38/353 & Corr.1 & Add.1. [8]A/38/27 & Corr.1. [9]CD/410. [10]CD/413. [11]YUN 1982, p. 122. [12]CD/375. [13]CD/420. [14]A/38/20. [15]A/38/194. [16]A/C.1/38/L.28. [17]A/C.1/38/L.24 & Rev.1,2. [18]A/38/647. [19]YUN 1971, p. 34, GA res. 2832(XXVI), 16 Dec. 1971. [20]A/38/376 & Add.1,2. [21]YUN 1982, p. 128, GA res. 37/100 F, 13 Dec. 1982. [22]YUN 1972, p. 29, GA res. 2992(XXVII), 15 Dec. 1972. [23]A/38/29. [24]YUN 1979, p. 67, GA res. 34/80 B, 11 Dec. 1979. [25]YUN 1982, p. 130, GA res. 37/96, 13 Dec. 1982. [26]A/AC.159/L.57. [27]A/AC.159/L.53, annex. [28]A/AC.159/L.54. [29]A/AC.159/L.58, annex. [30]A/AC.159/L.50. [31]A/AC.159/L.51. [32]A/38/495-S/16035. [33]YUN 1982, p. 133, GA res. 37/100 D, 13 Dec. 1982. [34]YUN 1981, p. 102. [35]YUN 1982, p. 134, GA res. 37/99 G, 13 Dec. 1982. [36]A/38/368 & Add.1,2. [37]YUN 1982, p. 138, GA res. 37/78 K, 9 Dec. 1982. [38]A/38/404. [39]YUN 1978, p. 34. [40]YUN 1979, p. 94. [41]YUN 1981, p. 104. [42]YUN 1982, p. 141. [43]YUN 1981, p. 96. [44]A/38/436. [45]YUN 1982, p. 145, GA res. 37/84, 9 Dec. 1982. [46]ACC/1983/5. [47]E/1983/39. [48]E/1983/16. [49]A/38/15 (vol. II). [50]YUN 1982, p. 135, GA res. 37/99 J, 13 Dec. 1982. [51]A/38/524. [52]*The United Nations Disarmament Yearbook,* vol. 8, *1983,* Sales No. E.84.IX.3. [53]YUN 1966, p. 41, GA res. 2222(XXI), annex, 19 Dec. 1966. [54]YUN 1968, p. 17, GA res. 2373(XXII), annex, 12 June 1968. [55]YUN 1970, p. 18, GA res. 2660(XXV), annex, 7 Dec. 1970. [56]YUN 1971, p. 19, GA res. 2826(XXVI), annex, 16 Dec. 1971. [57]YUN 1976, p. 45, GA res. 31/72, annex, 10 Dec. 1976. [58]YUN 1979, p. 111, GA res. 34/68, annex, 5 Dec. 1979. [59]YUN 1965, p. 62, GA res. 2030(XX), 29 Nov. 1965. [60]A/38/28. [61]YUN 1974, p. 52. [62]YUN 1982, p. 31. [63]*Ibid.,* p. 35, GA res. 37/100 I, 13 Dec. 1982. [64]*Ibid.,* p. 33; *World Disarmament Campaign: General Framework and Programme of Activities for 1983* (Disarmament Fact Sheet No. 28), DPI/742. [65]A/38/349. [66]A/38/467. [67]YUN 1982, p. 150, GA res. 37/99 K, 13 Dec. 1982. [68]A/CONF.123/1 & Corr.1. [69]YUN 1978, p. 39, GA res. S-10/2, 30 June 1978. [70]A/38/144. [71]A/C.1/38/L.61. [72]A/C.1/38/L.73. [73]A/C.1/38/L.78. [74]A/C.1/38/L.61/Rev.1. [75]A/C.1/38/L.82. [76]A/C.1/38/L.81. [77]YUN 1980, p. 113. [78]A/38/14. [79]A/38/475. [80]YUN 1982, p. 145, GA res. 37/84, 9 Dec. 1982. [81]A/38/7/Add.11. [82]A/C.1/38/L.8/Rev.1. [83]A/C.5/38/45. [84]A/38/760. [85]YUN 1978, p. 109. [86]A/38/533. [87]A/38/401.

Chapter II

Peaceful uses of outer space

Questions relating to international co-operation in the peaceful uses of outer space continued to be discussed during 1983 in the Committee on the Peaceful Uses of Outer Space (Committee on outer space), in its two sub-committees—the Legal Sub-Committee and the Scientific and Technical Sub-Committee—and in the General Assembly.

In December, the Assembly considered a number of recommendations made by the Committee and adopted a resolution (38/80) on international co-operation in the peaceful uses of outer space in which, among other things, it called on States to negotiate promptly to halt the militarization of outer space.

Topics related to this chapter. Disarmament: arms race in outer space. Other administrative and management questions: communications satellite.

Space science and technology

The Scientific and Technical Sub-Committee of the Committee on outer space held its twentieth session in New York from 7 to 17 February 1983.[1] The Sub-Committee proposed steps to implement the recommendations of the 1982 Second United Nations Conference on the Exploration and Peaceful Uses of Outer Space (UNISPACE-82),[2] recommended approval of the 1984 United Nations Programme on Space Applications and reviewed the co-ordination of space activities in the United Nations system. It again considered the use of nuclear power sources in outer space and related safety requirements, examined technical aspects of the geostationary orbit, and reviewed progress in remote sensing of the Earth by satellites and space transportation systems. The Sub-Committee's recommendations were acted on by the Committee on outer space in June/July.

Implementation of the recommendations of the 1982 Conference on outer space

Plans were prepared during 1983 to carry out a number of the recommendations made by UNISPACE-82 for promoting international co-operation in the exploration and peaceful uses of outer space.[2]

Preliminary suggestions were presented in a January report[3] by the United Nations Expert on Space Applications. The Expert recalled that in 1982 the General Assembly had decided to create an International Space Information Service, initially consisting of a directory of sources of information and data services.[4] It was expected that the first directory would be available in 1984.

Meeting in February, the Scientific and Technical Sub-Committee, while noting that primary responsibility for establishing and operating space technology programmes in developing countries lay with the countries concerned, invited developed nations to assume greater responsibility in making contributions for implementing UNISPACE-82 recommendations. It recommended that all States should have access to the appropriate space technology they required. After reviewing a list of studies suggested by the Conference, the Sub-Committee suggested that priority be given to studies by the United Nations on remote sensing needs, the use of broadcasting satellites for educational purposes, and the possibility of closer spacing of satellites in the geostationary orbit. It proposed that groups of experts from Member States help prepare the studies. The Sub-Committee also recommended that the Secretary-General consult with funding agencies and bodies with operational activities on their plans for implementing the UNISPACE-82 recommendations and report to the Committee on outer space at its June/July session. The Sub-Committee requested the Secretary-General to support the establishment and strengthening of regional mechanisms of co-operation.

In a June report with later addenda,[5] the Secretary-General gave the plans of 12 United Nations bodies for implementing the UNISPACE-82 recommendations.

In July,[6] the Committee on outer space endorsed an agreement reached in the Sub-Committee that it was important to carry out the recommendations of UNISPACE-82 as early as possible. It also endorsed the Sub-Committee's recommendation on the studies to be given priority, and its request that the Secretary-General support more vigorous regional co-operation.

Referring to those studies which fell within its competence, the International Telecommunication Union (ITU) submitted in October a note[7] annexing additional information on direct broadcasting satellites for educational purposes and on the spacing of satellites in the geostationary orbit. An ITU World Administrative Radio Conference, to be held in two sessions in 1985 and 1988, was to cover all aspects of the question leading to optimum use of the orbit, including the optimum spacing practicable.

During 1983, three regional or interregional seminars[8] focused on implementing UNISPACE-82 recommendations. They were held in Brazil (São José dos Campos, 2-6 May), Thailand, (Bangkok, 30 May–3 June) and Ethiopia (Addis Ababa, 4-8 July), for the member States of the Economic Commission for Latin America, the Economic and Social Commission for Asia and the Pacific, and the Economic Commissions for Africa and Western Asia, respectively. Participants in each seminar asked that a regional meeting of experts be convened. At São José dos Campos, the participants proposed that such a meeting take up the current state of space science and the extent of co-operation. At Bangkok, they agreed that the meeting should consider the funding of a central data bank and the teaching of space science. At Addis Ababa, it was suggested that the meeting examine questions of space technology and its applications, research and education.

The Secretary-General reported to the General Assembly in October[9] on the progress made in implementing the UNISPACE-82 recommendations. He summarized the recommendations by the Committee on outer space, described activities planned under the Programme on Space Applications and listed nine voluntary contributors to the expanded Programme (see below).

UN activities

UN Programme on Space Applications

In addition to regional/interregional seminars (see above), training courses were given and fellowships and grants were awarded as part of the United Nations Programme on Space Applications during 1983.

Two international training courses were offered. The first international seminar on the applications of remote sensing to operational agrometeorology in semi-arid countries (Niamey, Niger, 11-29 July)[10] was organized jointly by the United Nations, the World Meteorological Organization (WMO), the European Space Agency (ESA), and the Food and Agriculture Organization of the United Nations (FAO). It was attended by 22 senior technical personnel from 20 countries in Africa and Western Asia. The participants recommended that training courses give more time to practical exercises, urged intensifed research in remote sensing as applied to agrometeorology, and called for similar courses in places with different climates.

The eighth United Nations international training course on the applications of satellite remote sensing to water resources (Rome, Italy, 19 September–7 October) was organized in co-operation with FAO, the United Nations Educational, Scientific and Cultural Organization and Italy.[11] One participant from each of 21 developing countries attended. Participants expressed the desire to spend more time on: fundamentals of remote sensing and its applications for drainage-basin morphology, surface-water monitoring and flood mapping; erosion and sedimentation; ground-water search; and remote sensing for decision-making in management and field work.

Austria awarded two training fellowships in microwave technology for a year's study at the Technical University of Graz, Austria. Consultations were conducted on fellowships to be presented to candidates from developing countries by Egypt, Greece, Indonesia, the USSR and ESA.

The United Nations Expert on Space Applications, in his January report to the Committee on outer space,[3] outlined future activities under the Programme to translate the space-applications–related recommendations of UNISPACE-82[12] into operational programmes. These included developing indigenous capabilities for education and training; promoting co-operation among Member States in space science and technology and their applications; providing technical advisory services to Member States, on request; and disseminating information on every aspect of outer space.

The Expert's report on the 1983 Programme,[8] submitted in December to the Committee on outer space, included an evaluation of the effectiveness of the Programme for 1981. It was based on 59 replies to a questionnaire sent in May 1983 to 150 individuals who had taken part in seminars and training courses. The replies indicated that a high percentage of participants had continued to work in remote sensing, communications and meteorology, and that the knowledge they gained had subsequently enabled them to initiate, establish or direct study groups, national programmes, regional/international co-operation and other activities.

The Scientific and Technical Sub-Committee had noted in February[1] that voluntary contributions amounting to $459,000 would be required to finance the Programme on Space Applications in 1984. The Secretary-General reported to the General Assembly in October[9] that contributions had been offered by Bulgaria, China, Egypt, the Federal Republic of Germany, Greece, Indonesia, Sweden, the USSR and ESA.

The Programme for 1984—proposed by the Expert on Space Applications,[13] and recommended by the Sub-Committee and the Committee—included seminars on the application of remote sensing to forestry and to agrometeorology, and a workshop to help educators in developing countries to introduce space science into their curricula.

The Committee on outer space expressed appreciation at its June/July session for offers of contributions, seminars and fellowships.

Co-ordination in the UN system

Noting the progress achieved in co-ordinating programmes on space activities among organizations within the United Nations system, the Scientific and Technical Sub-Committee in February 1983[1] continued to stress the necessity of effective consultations to avoid duplication of activities.

The Committee on outer space, which met in June/July,[6] commented that the reports submitted by United Nations bodies had helped the Committee and its subsidiary bodies to fulfil their role as a focal point for international co-operation, especially in regard to the practical application of space technology in developing countries.

The fifth Inter-Agency Meeting on Outer Space Activities, convened by the Administrative Committee on Co-ordination (ACC), was held at Geneva from 4 to 6 October.[14] The Meeting found that the machinery for co-ordinating practical applications of space technology had worked satisfactorily; consequently, there were no major organizational or procedural questions to bring before ACC. A draft report of the Secretary-General to the Scientific and Technical Sub-Committee on the co-ordination of outer space activities for 1984, 1985 and future years was discussed. The report covered information dissemination, education, expert services and the provision of equipment related to remote sensing by satellites, communications, meteorology and navigation.[15] On other matters, the Meeting agreed that organizations should submit information for a possible paper on training in space technology and that a 1977 publication on space activities and resources should be updated. It proposed that a further Inter-Agency Meeting be held in 1984.

Remote sensing of the Earth by satellites

In February 1983, the Scientific and Technical Sub-Committee[1] continued to consider remote sensing of the Earth by satellites. It noted that a supplementary list of remote sensing applications had been prepared and said that updating of the catalogue should be continued. It also noted that a seminar on rural disaster preparedness, hosted by Colombia and sponsored by ESA, FAO, the Office of the United Nations Disaster Relief Co-ordinator and WMO, was to be held in June. In addition, a training course on remote sensing applied to land resources, sponsored by the Federal Republic of Germany and FAO, was to be held at Munich and a training course on flood monitoring, sponsored by FAO and ESA, in co-operation with WMO, was to be held at Rome, both in October.

The Committee on outer space, at its June/July session,[6] commented on the importance of the

compatibility and complimentarity of remote sensing systems. It emphasized the need for continuity of data availability in a form compatible with current systems, given the investments made by many countries in ground stations, processing equipment, data archiving and software. It suggested that system operators keep this in mind when planning future systems.

Nuclear power sources and safety in spacecraft

The Scientific and Technical Sub-Committee in February 1983[1] discussed technical aspects and safety measures relating to the use of nuclear devices as power sources for spacecraft. Several delegations referred to the conclusion reached in 1981 by the Sub-Committee's Working Group on the Use of Nuclear Power Sources in Outer Space[16] that nuclear power sources could be used safely, provided that the necessary safety requirements were met. Others referred to the re-entry into the earth's atmosphere between December 1982 and February 1983 of COSMOS-1402, which had a nuclear reactor on board. In the light of that event, they felt, international safety regulations concerning the use of nuclear power sources in outer space were needed. They urged that the Legal Sub-Committee expedite its work in that area (see below). Some of these delegations said that a moratorium on the launching of nuclear reactors into orbit should be observed until international regulations were adopted. Others said that the Working Group had provided sufficient guidelines.

Meeting in June/July,[6] the Committee on outer space recommended that the Working Group be reconvened to do further work during the 1984 session of the Scientific and Technical Sub-Committee. The Committee endorsed a recommendation by its Sub-Committee that the use of nuclear power sources in outer space be kept as a priority item on the Sub-Committee's agenda.

Space transportation

Progress being made in space transportation systems was noted by the Scientific and Technical Sub-Committee at its February 1983 session.[1] Referring to activities by China, India, Japan, the USSR, the United States and ESA, the Sub-Committee observed that their progress was providing the international community with much wider possibilities for the launching of payloads. A decision by the Sub-Committee that it continue in 1984 to consider space transportation systems was endorsed by the Committee on outer space in June/July.[6]

Technical aspects of the geostationary orbit

The Scientific and Technical Sub-Committee, in February 1983,[1] continued examining the physical nature and technical attributes of the geostationary orbit, in which communications satellites and other satellites maintain a position 36,000 kilometres above a selected location on the Equator. In accordance with recommendations made by UNISPACE-82,[17] the Sub-Committee said that future ITU conferences should seek to develop criteria, planning methods and arrangements for the equitable use of the geostationary orbit and the radio frequency spectrum. Their use should be based on the genuine needs of each country and the specific needs of developing countries. The Sub-Committee noted that ITU was preparing technical studies for the World Administrative Radio Conference scheduled for 1985 and 1988 to consider the use of the geostationary orbit. The Sub-Committee decided to continue examining the question at its 1984 session, a decision endorsed by the Committee on outer space at its June/July session.[6]

Space law

The Legal Sub-Committee of the Committee on outer space, during its twenty-second session in New York from 21 March to 8 April 1983,[18] considered three substantive items: the legal implications of remote sensing of the Earth from space, with the aim of formulating draft principles; the possibility of supplementing the norms of international law relevant to the use of nuclear power sources in outer space; and the definition and/or delimitation of outer space and outer space activities.

At its June/July session,[6] the Committee on outer space noted the report of the Sub-Committee and recommended that it continue in 1984 to consider the substantive items before it.

Legal aspects of remote sensing of the Earth from space

A working group re-established on 22 March 1983 by the Legal Sub-Committee continued to consider from then until 7 April[18] the legal implications of remote sensing of the Earth from space, with the aim of formulating draft principles. The group, open to all members of the Sub-Committee, reviewed the 17 draft principles as they appeared at the end of the Sub-Committee's 1982 session,[19] and then discussed principles XI to XV which concerned State responsibility, access to data by a State whose territory was being sensed, notification to the United Nations of planned sensing activities, consultation with sensed States, and the need for prior approval by a sensed State before data on its natural resources could be disseminated by a sensing State. The draft principles as they appeared at the conclusion of the group's session were set out in an annex to the Sub-Committee's report. They contained notes and passages within brackets indicating the need for further consideration.

The Committee on outer space noted at its June/July session[6] that a number of issues required resolution before a final text could be prepared. It recommended that the Legal Sub-Committee retain the matter as a priority item for its 1984 session and make every effort to finalize the draft principles.

Legal aspects of nuclear power sources in spacecraft

A working group to consider supplementing the norms of international law relevant to the use of nuclear power sources in outer space was re-established by the Legal Sub-Committee on 22 March 1983 and met between that date and 7 April.[18]

The group examined the question of notification in a case where a spacecraft with nuclear power sources on board was malfunctioning with the risk of re-entry of radioactive materials to the earth. It concentrated on the procedure and format of notification and, following discussions and informal consultations, agreed that in the event of malfunctioning the State that launched the spacecraft should inform States concerned and the Secretary-General. The group specified in general terms the parameters of the information to be furnished about the spacecraft and the radiological risk.

Working papers by Canada and the Federal Republic of Germany were submitted to the group and were annexed to the Sub-Committee's report. The Canadian paper consolidated papers previously presented by that country dealing with the submission of information by launching States, safety measures regarding radiological protection, notification prior to re-entry, assistance to States in cases of uncontrolled re-entry into the atmosphere, and State responsibility. The Federal Republic of Germany's paper discussed the uncertainty connected with the re-entry of COSMOS-1402 into the earth's atmosphere (see above) and offered recommendations for notification prior to the re-entry of a nuclear-powered satellite following malfunction.

The Committee on outer space at its June/July session[6] endorsed the procedure for notification in case of the malfunction of a nuclear-powered spacecraft, as agreed on by the Sub-Committee's working group. The Committee recommended that the Sub-Committee continue seeking to elaborate the norms of international law relevant to the use of nuclear power sources in outer space.

Legal aspects of the geostationary orbit and definition of outer space

The Legal Sub-Committee, at its March/April 1983 session,[18] continued considering the definition and/or delimitation of outer space and outer space activities, including questions relating to the geostationary orbit. Some delegations said that the definition of outer space was an urgent issue and ought to be established through a multilateral agreement. They spoke of the different legal régimes that applied to airspace and outer space and the desirability of a global and easily determinable boundary. Some of these delegations expressed support for a USSR proposal, presented in a working paper annexed to the Sub-Committee's report,[18] which would fix the boundary at 110 kilometres above sea-level. Other delegations said they believed that a definition of outer space was currently neither necessary nor feasible, that there was no scientific basis for it, and that an arbitrary definition could give rise to difficulties and might impede technological development.

Discussing the geostationary orbit, some delegations said that the Sub-Committee should begin formulating regulations governing its use. They contended that, if the orbit was to continue being used on a first come, first served basis, the technologically less developed countries would be at a disadvantage. Others expressed the view that the technological capacity of the orbit would continue to increase and keep pace with the demand for services. They said that management of the orbit through ITU was required.

The Committee on outer space, at its June/July session,[6] recommended that the Legal Sub-Committee keep matters related to the definition of outer space and the geostationary orbit on the agenda of its 1984 session.

Scientific and technical aspects of the geostationary orbit were discussed in February by the Scientific and Technical Sub-Committee (see above).

Action by principal UN organs

GENERAL ASSEMBLY ACTION

On the recommendation of its Special Political Committee, the General Assembly, on 15 December 1983, adopted by recorded vote resolution 38/80.

International co-operation in the peaceful uses of outer space

The General Assembly,

Recalling its resolutions 37/89 and 37/90 of 10 December 1982,

Deeply convinced of the common interest of mankind in promoting the exploration and use of outer space for peaceful purposes and in continuing efforts to extend to all States the benefits derived therefrom, and of the importance of international co-operation in this field, for which the United Nations should continue to provide a focal point,

Reaffirming the importance of international co-operation in developing the rule of law for the advancement and preservation of the exploration and peaceful uses of outer space,

Gravely concerned at the extension of the arms race into outer space,

Aware of the need to increase the benefits of space technology and its applications and to contribute to an orderly growth of space activities favourable to the socio-economic advancement of mankind, in particular the peoples of developing countries,

Taking note with satisfaction of the progress achieved in the further development of peaceful space exploration and application as well as in various national and co-operative space projects, which contribute to international co-operation in this field,

Taking note of the report of the Secretary-General on the implementation of resolution 37/90,

Having considered the report of the Committee on the Peaceful Uses of Outer Space on the work of its twenty-sixth session,

1.   *Endorses* the report of the Committee on the Peaceful Uses of Outer Space;

2.   *Invites* States that have not yet become parties to the international treaties governing the use of outer space* to give consideration to ratifying or acceding to those treaties;

3.   *Notes* that the Legal Sub-Committee of the Committee on the Peaceful Uses of Outer Space at its twenty-second session continued:

(*a*)   Its efforts to formulate draft principles relating to the legal implications of remote sensing of the Earth from space;

(*b*)   Its consideration of the possibility of supplementing the norms of international law relevant to the use of nuclear power sources in outer space through its working group;

(*c*)   Its discussion of matters relating to the definition or delimitation of outer space and outer space activities, bearing in mind, *inter alia*, questions relating to the geostationary orbit;

4.   *Notes with satisfaction* the successful efforts of the Legal Sub-Committee of the Committee on the Peaceful Uses of Outer Space in elaborating an agreed text concerning the format and the procedure for notification in case of malfunction of a spacecraft carrying a nuclear power source on board;

5.   *Decides* that the Legal Sub-Committee at its twenty-third session should:

(*a*)   Continue, on a priority basis, its detailed consideration of the legal implications of remote sensing of the Earth from space, with the aim of formulating draft principles relating to remote sensing;

(*b*)   Continue its consideration of the possibility of supplementing the norms of international law relevant to the use of nuclear power sources in outer space through its working group;

(*c*)   Establish a working group to consider, on a priority basis, matters relating to the definition and delimitation of outer space and to the character and utilization of the geostationary orbit, including the elaboration of general principles to govern the rational and equitable use of the geostationary orbit, a limited natural resource, and, to that end, requests Member States to submit draft principles; in doing so, it would have to take account of the different legal régimes governing airspace and outer space, respectively, and the need for technical planning and legal regulation of the geostationary orbit;

6. *Notes* that the Scientific and Technical Sub-Committee of the Committee on the Peaceful Uses of Outer Space at its twentieth session continued:

(a) Its consideration of the United Nations Programme on Space Applications and the co-ordination of space activities within the United Nations system;

(b) Its consideration of questions relating to remote sensing of the Earth by satellites;

(c) Its examination of the physical nature and technical attributes of the geostationary orbit;

(d) Its consideration of technical aspects and safety measures relating to the use of nuclear power sources in outer space;

(e) Its consideration of questions relating to space transportation systems and their implications for future activities in space;

(f) Its consideration of the implementation of the recommendations of the Second United Nations Conference on the Exploration and Peaceful Uses of Outer Space;

7. *Endorses* the recommendation of the Committee on the Peaceful Uses of Outer Space that the Scientific and Technical Sub-Committee at its twenty-first session should:

(a) Consider the following items on a priority basis:

(i) United Nations Programme on Space Applications and the co-ordination of space activities within the United Nations system;

(ii) Implementation of the recommendations of the Second United Nations Conference on the Exploration and Peaceful Uses of Outer Space;

(iii) Questions relating to remote sensing of the Earth by satellites;

(iv) Use of nuclear power sources in outer space;

(b) Consider the following items:

(i) Questions relating to space transportation systems and their implications for future activities in space;

(ii) Examination of the physical nature and technical attributes of the geostationary orbit;

8. *Endorses further* the recommendation of the Committee on the Peaceful Uses of Outer Space that, during the twenty-first session of the Scientific and Technical Sub-Committee, the Working Group on the Use of Nuclear Power Sources in Outer Space should be reconvened to conduct additional work on the basis of the report of the Working Group on the work of its third session;

9. *Endorses* the United Nations Programme on Space Applications for 1984, as proposed to the Committee on the Peaceful Uses of Outer Space by the Expert on Space Applications;

10. *Emphasizes* the urgency and importance of implementing fully the recommendations of the Second United Nations Conference on the Exploration and Peaceful Uses of Outer Space as early as possible;

11. *Reaffirms* its approval of the recommendation of the Conference regarding the establishment and strengthening of regional mechanisms of co-operation and their promotion and creation through the United Nations system;

12. *Expresses its appreciation* to all Governments that made or expressed their intention to make contributions towards carrying out the recommendations of the Conference;

13. *Invites* all Governments to take effective action for the implementation of the recommendations of the Conference;

14. *Calls upon* all States, in particular those with major space capabilities, to undertake prompt negotiations, under the auspices of the United Nations, with a view to reaching agreement or agreements designed to halt the militarization of outer space and to prevent an arms race in outer space, thus contributing to the achievement of the internationally accepted goal of ensuring the use of outer space exclusively for peaceful purposes;

15. *Requests* the Committee on the Peaceful Uses of Outer Space to consider, as a matter of priority, the questions relating to the militarization of outer space, taking into account that, in General Assembly resolution 37/83 of 9 December 1982, the Committee on Disarmament† was requested to consider as a matter of priority the question of preventing an arms race in outer space, and also taking into account the need to co-ordinate the efforts of the Committee on the Peaceful Uses of Outer Space and the Committee on Disarmament;

16. *Requests* the Committee on the Peaceful Uses of Outer Space to report to the General Assembly at its thirty-ninth session on the outcome of its consideration of the subject referred to in paragraph 15 above;

17. *Endorses* the recommendation of the Committee on the Peaceful Uses of Outer Space that, of the study projects proposed by the United Nations Conference on the Exploration and Peaceful Uses of Outer Space, the following three studies be carried out on a priority basis:

(a) Assistance to countries in studying their remote-sensing needs and assessing appropriate systems for meeting such needs (United Nations, United Nations Environment Programme, United Nations Development Programme and Food and Agriculture Organization of the United Nations);

(b) The feasibility of using direct broadcasting satellites for educational purposes and of internationally or regionally owned space segments (United Nations, United Nations Educational, Scientific and Cultural Organization and International Telecommunication Union);

(c) The feasibility of obtaining closer spacing of satellites in the geostationary orbit and their satisfactory coexistence, including a closer examination of techno-economic implications, particularly for developing countries, in order to ensure the most effective utilization of this orbit in the interest of all countries (United Nations, International Telecommunication Union and other organizations);

18. *Approves* the recommendations of the Committee on the Peaceful Uses of Outer Space concerning the procedures for carrying out these studies;

19. *Decides* that the United Nations should bear the travel and per diem expenses of the experts to be appointed by the Secretary-General for carrying out the studies referred to in paragraph 17 above;

20. *Affirms* that the interference that satellite systems to be newly established may cause to systems already registered with the International Telecommunication Union shall not exceed the limits specified in the relevant provision of the International Telecommunication Union radio regulations applicable to space services;

21. *Requests* all organs, organizations and bodies of the United Nations system and other intergovernmental organizations working in the field of outer space or on space-related matters to co-operate in the implementation of the recommendations of the Conference;

22. *Requests* the Secretary-General to report to the General Assembly at its thirty-ninth session on the implementation of the recommendations of the Conference;

23.   *Requests* the specialized agencies and other inter-national organizations to continue and, where appropriate, enhance their co-operation with the Committee on the Peaceful Uses of Outer Space and to provide it with progress reports on their work relating to the peaceful uses of outer space;

24.   *Takes note* of the invitation by the Government of Austria to hold the twenty-seventh session of the Com-mittee on the Peaceful Uses of Outer Space at Vienna;

25.   *Decides* to convene the twenty-seventh session of the Committee on the Peaceful Uses of Outer Space at Vienna from 11 to 22 June 1984;

26.   *Requests* the Committee on the Peaceful Uses of Outer Space to continue its work, in accordance with the present resolution, to consider, as appropriate, new projects in outer space activities and to submit a report to the General Assembly at its thirty-ninth session, in-cluding its views on which subjects should be studied in the future.

---

*Treaty on Principles Governing the Activities of States in the Exploration and Use of Outer Space, including the Moon and Other Celestial Bodies (resolution 2222(XXI), annex); Agreement on the Rescue of Astronauts, the Return of As-tronauts and the Return of Objects Launched into Outer Space (resolution 2345(XXII), annex); Convention on International Liability for Damage Caused by Space Objects (resolution 2777(XXVI), annex); Convention on Registration of Objects Launched into Outer Space (resolution 3235(XXIX), annex); Agreement Governing the Activities of States on the Moon and Other Celestial Bodies (resolution 34/68, annex).

†From 7 February 1984, the date of commencement of its annual session, the Committee on Disarmament is to be known as the "Conference on Disarmament".

General Assembly resolution 38/80

15 December 1983   Meeting 98   124-12-8 (recorded vote)

Approved by SPC (A/38/714) by recorded vote (98-12-8), 1 December (meeting 43); draft by Austria (A/SPC/38/L.28), amended by Mexico (A/SPC/38/L.29) and by Mexico for Group of 77 (A/SPC/38/L.30); agenda item 70.
Financial implications. 5th Committee, A/38/716; S-G, A/SPC/38/L.33 & L.34, A/C.5/38/74.
Meeting numbers. GA 38th session: SPC 18, 19, 21, 25-27, 39, 43; 5th Committee 58; plenary 98.

Recorded vote in Assembly as follows:

In favour: Afghanistan, Algeria, Angola, Argentina, Austria, Bahamas, Bahrain, Bangladesh, Barbados, Belize, Benin, Bhutan, Bolivia, Botswana, Brazil, Bulgaria, Burma, Burundi, Byelorussian SSR, Cape Verde, Chad, Chile, China, Colombia, Congo, Cyprus, Czechoslovakia, Democratic Kampuchea, Democratic Yemen, Djibouti, Dominica, Dominican Republic, Ecuador, Egypt, El Salvador, Equatorial Guinea, Ethiopia, Fiji, Gabon, Gambia, German Democratic Republic, Ghana, Greece, Guinea, Guinea-Bissau, Guyana, Honduras, Hungary, India, Indonesia, Iran, Iraq, Ireland, Ivory Coast, Jamaica, Jordan, Kenya, Kuwait, Lao People's Demo-cratic Republic, Lebanon, Lesotho, Liberia, Libyan Arab Jamahiriya, Madagas-car, Malawi, Malaysia, Maldives, Mali, Malta, Mauritania, Mauritius, Mexico, Mon-golia, Morocco, Mozambique, Nepal, Nicaragua, Niger, Nigeria, Oman, Pakistan, Panama, Papua New Guinea, Paraguay, Peru, Philippines, Poland, Qatar, Romania, Rwanda, Saint Lucia, Sao Tome and Principe, Saudi Arabia, Senegal, Seychelles, Sierra Leone, Singapore, Somalia, Sri Lanka, Sudan, Suriname, Swaziland, Syrian Arab Republic, Thailand, Togo, Trinidad and Tobago, Tunisia, Turkey, Uganda, Ukrainian SSR, USSR, United Arab Emirates, United Republic of Cameroon, United Republic of Tanzania, Upper Volta, Uruguay, Vanuatu, Venezuela, Viet Nam, Yemen, Yugoslavia, Zaire, Zambia, Zimbabwe.
Against: Australia, Belgium, France, Germany, Federal Republic of, Israel, Italy, Japan, Luxembourg, Netherlands, New Zealand, United Kingdom, United States.
Abstaining: Canada, Denmark, Finland, Iceland, Norway, Portugal, Spain, Sweden.

Three amendments were put forward in the Spe-cial Political Committee: two by Mexico—one on behalf of the Group of 77 developing countries— and one by the German Democratic Republic.

The Mexican amendment, approved by a recorded vote of 92 to 16, with 9 abstentions, be-came paragraph 14. By the original, Member States, particularly those with major space capabilities, would have been urged to contribute actively to the goal of preventing an arms race in outer space, as an essential condition for promoting international co-operation in the exploration and uses of outer space for peaceful purposes.

The amendment proposed by Mexico for the Group of 77 was in two parts, both approved by recorded votes. The first—approved by 92 votes to 16, with 9 abstentions—constituted paragraph 5 *(c)*, which originally called for consideration of mat-ters relating to the definition and/or delimitation of outer space and outer space activities, bearing in mind questions relating to the geostationary orbit, and for the establishment of a working group to give those matters deeper consideration. The sec-ond part, approved by 91 votes to 17, with 8 ab-stentions, made up paragraphs 15 and 16; these replaced a paragraph in which the Committee on outer space would have been requested, in its dis-cussion on preventing an arms race in outer space, to take into account that the Committee on Dis-armament had been asked, in a 1982 Assembly reso-lution,[20] to consider the question as a matter of priority and that the views expressed on it should be reflected more adequately in the report of the Committee's 1984 session.

The amendment sponsored by the German Democratic Republic[21] was withdrawn. It sought to add a paragraph by which the Assembly would have decided to establish an *ad hoc* working group of the whole to assist the Committee on outer space in its consideration of the prevention of an arms race in outer space.

In explaining their votes in the Special Political Committee, almost all speakers regretted that it had proved impossible to reach a consensus. Finland, Italy, Sweden and the United Kingdom felt that this departure from the Assembly's tradition of deal-ing with outer space matters by consensus might negatively affect the future work and ability of the Committee on outer space. The United States said the Committee's work programme as outlined would not lead to any significant progress. The USSR felt that, had it not been for one delegation's attitude, the situation concerning consensus would have been different.

Most of those voting negatively or abstaining could not accept the text as amended.

Some States which voted against, namely, Aus-tralia, the Federal Republic of Germany, Italy, the Netherlands, the United Kingdom and the United States—along with Canada, Finland and Sweden, which abstained—were opposed to the request made to the Committee on outer space to consider ques-tions relating to the militarization of outer space.

They were unanimous in asserting that the Committee on Disarmament was the only body competent to discuss such issues. Sweden pointed out that the request was at variance with a provision of the Final Document of the Tenth Special Session of the General Assembly[22] naming that Committee as the single multilateral disarmament negotiating forum. Discussion by any other body of so specialized and complex a subject as arms control in outer space would be inappropriate, the United Kingdom and the United States felt. Pointing also to the existence of international agreements limiting military activities in outer space— among them the Treaty on Principles Governing the Activities of States in the Exploration and Use of Outer Space, including the Moon and Other Celestial Bodies[23]—the United Kingdom believed that it would be for the Committee on Disarmament to consider, in the first instance, the desirability of supplementing those agreements.

These same countries were further opposed to the establishment of a working group to consider the utilization of the geostationary orbit. They believed that the appropriate forum for the subject was ITU, which, Australia said, enjoyed its fullest confidence in that regard. The United Kingdom was of the opinion that there was no scientific basis or practical need for the definition or delimitation of outer space—an opinion shared by Turkey, which voted in favour. Canada felt that the proposed working group, besides interfering with ITU, would seriously affect the Legal Sub-Committee's work of supplementing the norms of international law on the use of nuclear power sources in outer space, a view similarly voiced by Italy and Sweden.

Australia and the United Kingdom also objected to the decision that the United Nations pay the expenses of experts to carry out certain study projects specified in the text. In accordance with usual practice, those expenses, the United Kingdom said, should be borne by the States nominating the experts.

Among those voting in favour but voicing reservations, Cuba said that it could not accept the priority accorded to satellite systems already registered with ITU rather than to newly established systems, a question it would take up with ITU. Egypt, although it voted for the amendments, would have preferred a reaffirmation of the mandate of the Committee on Disarmament as the sole forum for questions relating to the militarization of outer space. Despite its abstention on the two-part amendment, Ireland voted for the text as a whole in the belief that the Committee on outer space would continue working constructively.

Turkey abstained on the amendments because it felt that the meaning of the phrase "exclusively for peaceful purposes" in paragraph 14 was not sufficiently clear, and paragraph 15, apart from being worded ambiguously, called for work already being performed by other bodies.

The USSR said that it had voted for the resolution and for all the amendments because they reflected the interests of the majority.

Spacecraft launchings

During 1983, four countries and an intergovernmental organization provided information to the United Nations on the launching of objects into orbit or beyond, in accordance with a 1961 General Assembly resolution[24] and the Convention on Registration of Objects Launched into Outer Space.[25]

Twenty-two notifications of objects launched during 1983 and the latter part of 1982 were received in 1983 and distributed as United Nations documents.[26]

Information was submitted by India on 2 launchings, by Japan on 2 launchings, by the USSR on 95 launchings, by the United States on 9 launchings and by the European Space Agency (ESA) on 4 launchings. (Some of the launchings involved multiple space objects sent aloft by a single carrier rocket. Launchings during 1983 but not reported to the United Nations until 1984 are excluded from the above count.)

In January and February the USSR also furnished information on the re-entry of COSMOS-1402 (see above) and in January ESA submitted data on its geostationary satellites.

There were a total of 32 States parties to the Convention on Registration as at 31 December 1983, including Japan, which acceded during 1983.

REFERENCES

[1]A/AC.105/318. [2]YUN 1982, p. 162. [3]A/AC.105/313. [4]YUN 1982, p. 163, GA res. 37/90, 10 Dec. 1982. [5]A/AC.105/L.136 & Add.1,2. [6]A/38/20. [7]A/AC.105/327. [8]A/AC.105/330. [9]A/38/412. [10]A/AC.105/328. [11]A/AC.105/329. [12]YUN 1982, p. 164. [13]A/AC.105/310. [14]ACC/1983/27. [15]A/AC.105/325. [16]YUN 1981, p. 117. [17]YUN 1982, p. 171. [18]A/AC.105/320 & Corr.1. [19]YUN 1982, p. 175. [20]*Ibid.*, p. 124, GA res. 37/83, 9 Dec. 1982. [21]A/SPC/38/L.31. [22]YUN 1978, p. 39, GA res. S-10/2, 30 June 1978. [23]YUN 1966, p. 41, GA res. 2222(XXI), annex, 19 Dec. 1966. [24]YUN 1961, p. 35, GA res. 1721 B (XVI), 20 Dec. 1961. [25]YUN 1974, p. 63, GA res. 3235(XXIX), annex, 12 Nov. 1974. [26]A/AC.105/INF.393 & Corr.1; ST/SG/SER.E/72/Add.1-4, ST/SG/SER.E/73, 75-78, 80-94.

Chapter III

Law of the sea

The first steps were taken during 1983 towards implementing the United Nations Convention on the Law of the Sea.

By the end of 1983, there were 132 signatories to the Convention, while eight States and the United Nations Council for Namibia, on behalf of Namibia, had ratified it.

The Preparatory Commission for the International Sea-Bed Authority and for the International Tribunal for the Law of the Sea held its first session and the Secretary-General assumed his responsibilities under the Convention through the Office of his Special Representative.

By resolution 38/59 A, adopted in December, the General Assembly called on States that had not done so to consider signing and ratifying the Convention and appealed to States to refrain from any action that would undermine it. Also in December, the Assembly, by resolution 38/59 B, paid tribute to Bernardo Zuleta, Special Representative of the Secretary-General for the Law of the Sea from 1974 until his death on 2 December 1983.

Topics related to this chapter. Disarmament: naval disarmament. Transport: maritime transport. Natural resources: marine resources. Environment: marine ecosystems. International Court of Justice: continental shelf boundary between the Libyan Arab Jamahiriya and Malta; Canada–United States boundary in the Gulf of Maine.

UN Convention on the Law of the Sea

Signatures and ratifications

As at 31 December 1983,[1] signatories to the United Nations Convention on the Law of the Sea totalled 132. The Convention had been adopted in April 1982 by the Third United Nations Conference on the Law of the Sea[2] and welcomed by the General Assembly in December 1982.[3] Those signing in 1983 were: Afghanistan, Antigua and Barbuda, Benin, Democratic Kampuchea, Dominica, Guatemala, Japan, Madagascar, Mali, Oman, Republic of Korea, Sao Tome and Principe, Zaire.

In 1983, the number of ratifications to the Convention—which was to enter into force 12 months after receipt of the sixtieth instrument of ratification or accession—rose to nine with the addition of: Bahamas, Belize, Egypt, Ghana, Jamaica, Mexico, Namibia (United Nations Council for Namibia), Zambia.

During 1983, statements relating to participation in the Convention were made by the Group of 77 developing countries and the USSR. In April,[4] at the first session of the Preparatory Commission (see below), the Group of 77, appealing to States which had not done so to expedite the signing of the Convention, declared its opposition to attempts by those States to apply provisions selectively while continuing to reject those relating to the international sea-bed "Area" (the sea-bed beyond national jurisdiction). In a letter of 28 April to the Secretary-General,[5] the USSR transmitted a Government statement of 23 April criticizing the United States for not signing the Convention and for announcing its intention of using discretion in matters relating to the resources of the world's oceans.

Preparatory Commission

The Preparatory Commission for the International Sea-Bed Authority and for the International Tribunal for the Law of the Sea held its first session at Kingston, Jamaica, from 15 March to 8 April 1983 with 99 members and 17 observers in attendance. Informal meetings were held at United Nations Headquarters on 26 and 27 May. The Commission reconvened the session at Kingston from 15 August to 9 September with 82 members and 16 observers attending. An account of its proceedings was given by the Secretary-General in a November report to the General Assembly.[6]

The Commission—established by resolution I of the Conference on the Law of the Sea, adopted in April 1982[7]—was to convene between 60 and 90 days after 50 States had signed the Convention on the Law of the Sea, a requirement met on 10 December 1982 when the Convention was opened for signature.[8] Signatories to the Convention became members of the Commission; others could participate as observers if they had signed the Final Act of the Conference.

On 8 April 1983, the Commission adopted a "consensus statement of understanding"[9] on the general features of its structure. This statement provided that the Commission would consist of the Plenary as the principal organ and four Special Commissions of equal status. In the Plenary, the Commission would deal with preparation of rules on administrative and financial matters for the organs of the International Sea-Bed Authority;

implementation of resolution II of the Conference, governing investment in pioneer activities related to polymetallic nodules in the international sea-bed Area; presentation of a report on practical arrangements for establishment of the International Tribunal for the Law of the Sea; and all matters not specifically assigned to the Special Commissions or other subsidiary bodies. The Commission would also take up the reports of the Special Commissions.

Special Commission 1 was to consider problems that might be encountered by developing land-based producer States affected by the production of minerals from the Area. Special Commission 2 would examine the measures necessary for early entry into effective operation of the Enterprise (the organ of the Authority which was to carry out mining and other activities in the Area). Special Commission 3 was to prepare a sea-bed mining code, and Special Commission 4 would recommend practical arrangements for establishing the International Tribunal.

On 8 September, the Commission adopted a package of three suggestions by its Chairman,[10] concerning the structure and functions of the Commission and its organs, procedures and guidelines for registration of pioneer sea-bed investors (see below, under SEA-BED MINING), and rules of procedure.

Before these suggestions were adopted, the Chairman said it was the Commission's understanding that the adoption of procedures for the implementation of Conference resolution II would be a matter of high priority for the Commission in 1984.

Under the rules of procedure,[11] each member of the Commission was to have one vote. Decisions on procedural matters were to be taken by a majority of those present and voting. Certain decisions on substantive matters were to be taken by consensus, defined as absence of any formal objection. These decisions concerned all matters which required consensus under the Convention;[12] rules and procedures for the implementation of resolution II and for the establishment of adequate machinery to protect pioneer investors; regulations for exploration and exploitation of the Area; the final report on matters within the Commission's mandate for submission to the Assembly of the Authority; and cases where financial obligations not provided for in the United Nations budget were imposed on States. On other matters of substance, decisions would be taken by a two-thirds majority.

The rules of procedure also provided for the participation of observers, and established a General Committee and secretariat. In addition to observers representing States which had signed only the Final Act of the Conference, observers might include the specialized agencies of the United Nations and the International Atomic Energy Agency, intergovernmental and non-governmental organizations, and national liberation movements. The General Committee was to consist of the Chairman and other officers of the Commission and its Special Commissions. The administrative duties of the secretariat would include publishing the reports of the Commission and a journal of the decisions taken by it, its Special Commissions and other subsidiary bodies. The United Nations Secretary-General, in agreement with the Commission, would promulgate procedures for handling confidential data on sea-bed sites.

The Chairman of the Group of Western European and Other States said the Group would have preferred to entrust questions on pioneer investments protection to a Special Commission; nevertheless, in a spirit of compromise, it agreed that such questions might be referred to the Plenary.[13] The Group also favoured creating an *ad hoc* body to draw up procedures for implementing resolution II and a working group to draft procedures concerning the Authority.

The Commission decided that it would hold one regular four-week session a year at the seat of the Authority (Kingston) and one four-week session of its Plenary, Special Commissions and other subsidiary bodies at Kingston, New York or Geneva.

Functions of the Secretary-General

Office of the Special Representative

During 1983, the Office of the Special Representative of the Secretary-General for the Law of the Sea began work on the activities resulting from the adoption in 1982 of the Convention on the Law of the Sea.[2] The responsibilities thus assumed by the Secretary-General had been approved by the General Assembly later that year.[3]

Among the main activities of the Office, as described by the Secretary-General,[6] were preparation of the introduction for the publication containing the texts of the Convention, the related resolutions and the Final Act of the Conference on the Law of the Sea, together with an index; the continued publishing of Conference records, projected to total 20 volumes; investigating the technical aspects of receiving charts and lists of co-ordinates delimiting maritime zones as required under the Convention; collecting national maritime legislation as a guide to the evolution of State practice in the law of the sea; and initiating studies in co-operation with the International Civil Aviation Organization and the International Maritime Organization.

The Office began publishing the *Law of the Sea Bulletin*; the first issue[14] contained information about the status of the Convention, recent treaties, national legislation and other international developments related to the law of the sea.

Meetings of the Preparatory Commission at Kingston (see above) were serviced by the Office, which negotiated with the Government of Jamaica a draft agreement for the cost of using the conference complex and office space there.

An interdepartmental mechanism to review follow-up actions to the Conference was established by the Secretary-General in January 1983. A task force, convened at head-of-department level by the Director-General for Development and International Economic Co-operation, carried out the review.

The review included examination of the approved plans of Secretariat units concerned with marine affairs (see ECONOMIC AND SOCIAL QUESTIONS, Chapter IX) and the existing activities of the Office of the Special Representative. The task force concluded that the first follow-up action to the Conference would be to present to the Committee for Programme and Co-ordination (CPC) a proposal for a major marine affairs programme in the United Nations medium-term plan for 1984-1989.

This proposal was submitted to CPC at the first part of its 1983 session (May/June).[15] The major programme contained two central programmes, on law of the sea affairs and on economic and technical aspects of marine affairs. Programme 1 included subprogrammes on the uniform and consistent application of the Convention, the provision of information, advice and assistance to States on implementation of the Convention, and co-operation in the United Nations system to achieve a cohesive approach to the Convention. CPC recommended adoption of the major programme, with a few revisions, to the Economic and Social Council and the General Assembly. The Council endorsed the major programme when it adopted resolution 1983/48 on 28 July and the Assembly endorsed it on 20 December when it adopted resolution 38/227 B.

The Secretary-General recommended that the Office of the Special Representative be continued, that it be designated the core office in the Secretariat for the law of the sea and that it be responsible for implementing programme 1.

On 13 December,[16] the Fifth Committee approved by 75 votes to 2, with 18 abstentions, a net appropriation of $6,314,300 for the Office's 1984-1985 activities. The appropriation represented the sum of $5,427,300 initially proposed by the Secretary-General and an additional $887,000 which he requested in the form of revised estimates.[17] The addition reflected adjustments in staff, office, conference, travel and miscellaneous costs. The Advisory Committee on Administrative and Budgetary Questions noted[18] that the

Office was to have 55 posts (30 established, 25 temporary) and that the number approved for 1982-1983 had also been 55, but all had been temporary.

Sea-bed mining

Procedures and guidelines for registering pioneer investors in sea-bed mining under resolution II, adopted by the Third United Nations Conference on the Law of the Sea in 1982,[19] were adopted by the Preparatory Commission on 8 September 1983.[10] The guidelines covered the submission of the application for registration, its content, its examination by the General Committee, and the allocation of sea-bed areas for exploration.

In deciding on the structure of its work (see above, under PREPARATORY COMMISSION), the Commission designated three of its four Special Commissions to deal with various aspects relating to the sea-bed, including arrangements for the International Sea-Bed Authority to be established under the Convention on the Law of the Sea.

Prospects for sea-bed mining were discussed in an April report[20] on mineral resources development submitted by the Secretary-General to the Economic and Social Council's Committee on Natural Resources (see ECONOMIC AND SOCIAL QUESTIONS, Chapter IX). Minerals in the sea-bed beyond national jurisdiction included polymetallic nodules containing nickel, copper, cobalt and manganese, and minor amounts of molybdenum, vanadium and titanium. Interest also had been expressed in polymetallic sulphides, rich in zinc or copper, the report added. There was virtually no current production of non-fuel minerals beyond the territorial sea.

According to the report, the development of sea-bed mining was difficult to forecast. There was no immediate or urgent industrial need for the metals, and decisions to go ahead with prototype operations were at least as dependent on economic factors as on legal arrangements. Currently, dates after 1990 were being suggested for the first venture into commercial production, the report concluded.

Pioneer investors

A number of communications relating to pioneer sea-bed investors were addressed to the Chairman of the Preparatory Commission in 1983. Pioneer investors were States and private consortia interested in exploring the international sea-bed Area before entry into force of the Convention on the Law of the Sea. Two prospective pioneer investors, India[21] and the USSR,[22] stated that they had met at New Delhi on 29 and 30 April and assured themselves that the areas in respect of which they intended to apply for registration did not overlap. Other prospective certifying

States, members or observers—Belgium,[23] Canada,[24] France,[25] the Federal Republic of Germany,[26] Indonesia,[27] Italy,[28] Japan,[29] the Netherlands[30] and the United Kingdom[31]—reserved their position regarding the communications by India and the USSR with most insisting that before submitting any application the Commission should be functioning effectively and that all prospective pioneer investors should negotiate in order to identify and resolve possible conflicts arising from the overlapping of areas.

The first application for registration was submitted on 20 July[32] by the USSR which said that the location of the area to be explored and its co-ordinates were being transmitted in a sealed packet to preserve their confidentiality. Receipt of the application was acknowledged by the Chairman on 25 August,[33] who stated that the packet would be deposited for safe keeping with the Secretary-General.

Other communications received by the Chairman were from India[34] and the USSR[35] announcing that they were prepared to exchange geographical co-ordinates with other prospective certifying States; from the USSR[36] stating its readiness to negotiate towards resolving conflicts arising over boundaries of the sea-bed areas; and from Canada[37] transmitting a draft "memorandum of understanding on the settlement of conflicting claims with respect to sea-bed areas" on the basis of which other prospective investors were conducting consultations with a view to reaching agreement.

On 8 September 1983, the Commission adopted proposals concerning procedures and guidelines for registering pioneer investors, as part of a package relating to the Commission's structure and functions (see section above).

Action by principal UN organs

GENERAL ASSEMBLY ACTION

On 14 December 1983, the General Assembly adopted two resolutions concerning the law of the sea. It adopted resolution 38/59 A by recorded vote and resolution 38/59 B unanimously.

Third United Nations Conference on the Law of the Sea

A

The General Assembly,

Recalling its resolution 37/66 of 3 December 1982 regarding the Third United Nations Conference on the Law of the Sea,

Noting that the Conference was concluded at Montego Bay, Jamaica, on 10 December 1982, that the United Nations Convention on the Law of the Sea was opened for signature and that one hundred and nineteen signatures were affixed to it on that date,

Taking further note of the increasing and overwhelming support for the Convention, as evidenced, *inter alia*, by the one hundred and thirty-two signatures and nine ratifications by States and by the United Nations Council for Namibia, on behalf of Namibia, as at 31 October 1983,

Concerned at any attempt to undermine the Convention and its related resolutions,

Recognizing that, as stated in the third preambular paragraph of the Convention, the problems of ocean space are closely interrelated and need to be considered as a whole,

Convinced that it is important to safeguard the unified character of the Convention and its related resolutions and to refrain from any action to apply their provisions selectively, in a manner inconsistent with their objectives and purposes,

Noting the increasing needs of countries, especially developing countries, for information, advice and assistance in their developmental process for the full realization of the benefits of the comprehensive legal régime established by the Convention, as also recognized by the Economic and Social Council in its resolution 1983/48 of 28 July 1983,

Recalling that the Convention provides that the seat of the International Sea-Bed Authority shall be in Jamaica and the seat of the International Tribunal for the Law of the Sea shall be at Hamburg, Federal Republic of Germany,

Recalling also that in paragraph 12 of Conference resolution I of 30 April 1982, establishing the Preparatory Commission for the International Sea-Bed Authority and for the International Tribunal for the Law of the Sea, it is expressly provided that the Commission shall meet at the seat of the Authority if facilities are available and as often as necessary for the expeditious exercise of its functions,

Noting also that the Preparatory Commission held its first session at Kingston, at which it elected its Bureau, concluded the elaboration of its organizational framework by allocating functions between the Plenary and Special Commissions and requested the secretariat to prepare background information and working papers in respect of the work allocated to these organs, and decided, *inter alia*, to hold its next regular session at Kingston from 19 March to 13 April 1984 and a session for its working groups during the summer of 1984, in New York or Geneva, as it may decide,

Recalling its approval of the assumption by the Secretary-General of the responsibilities entrusted to him under the Convention and its related resolutions and the approval of the stationing of an adequate number of secretariat staff in Jamaica for the purpose of servicing the Preparatory Commission, as required by its functions and programme of work,

Taking note also of the major programme on marine affairs, set forth in chapter 25 of the medium-term plan for the period 1984-1989,

Recalling the extensive functions entrusted to the Preparatory Commission, including the administration of the scheme governing preparatory investments in pioneer activities relating to polymetallic nodules,

Recalling its approval of the financing of the expenses of the Preparatory Commission from the regular budget of the United Nations,

Taking special note of the report of the Secretary-General prepared in response to paragraph 10 of General Assembly resolution 37/66,

1. *Recalls* the historic significance of the United Nations Convention on the Law of the Sea as an important contribution to the maintenance of peace, justice and progress for all peoples of the world;

2. *Expresses its satisfaction* at the large number of signatures affixed to the Convention as well as at the number of ratifications deposited with the Secretary-General during the year following the opening of the Convention for signature;

3. *Calls upon* States that have not done so to consider signing and ratifying the Convention at the earliest possible date to allow the effective entry into force of the new legal régime for the uses of the sea and its resources;

4. *Calls upon* all States to safeguard the unified character of the Convention and its related resolutions;

5. *Appeals* to all States to refrain from taking any action directed at undermining the Convention or defeating its objectives and purposes;

6. *Requests* the Secretary-General to accord due consideration to the activities outlined in his report, special emphasis being placed on the work of the Preparatory Commission for the International Sea-Bed Authority and for the International Tribunal for the Law of the Sea;

7. *Expresses its appreciation* for the report of the Secretary-General and approves the recommendations contained therein;

8. *Requests* the Secretary-General to report to the General Assembly at its thirty-ninth session on developments relating to the Convention and on the implementation of the present resolution;

9. *Decides* to include in the provisional agenda of its thirty-ninth session an item entitled "Law of the sea".

General Assembly resolution 38/59 A

14 December 1983   Meeting 96   136-2-6 (recorded vote)

54-nation draft (A/38/L.18/Rev.1 & Rev.1/Add.1); agenda item 31.
Sponsors: Antigua and Barbuda, Australia, Austria, Bahamas, Bangladesh, Barbados, Belize, Bhutan, Canada, Cape Verde, Chad, Chile, Cuba, Denmark, Dominica, Egypt, Fiji, Finland, Gabon, Gambia, Greece, Guyana, Haiti, Iceland, India, Indonesia, Ireland, Jamaica, Kenya, Kuwait, Madagascar, Malaysia, Mali, Mauritania, Mongolia, New Zealand, Nigeria, Norway, Papua New Guinea, Philippines, Saint Christopher and Nevis, Saint Lucia, Saint Vincent and the Grenadines, Senegal, Singapore, Solomon Islands, Sri Lanka, Sweden, Togo, Trinidad and Tobago, Uganda, United Republic of Cameroon, United Republic of Tanzania, Uruguay.
Financial implications. 5th Committee, A/38/760 & Corr.1.
Meeting numbers. GA 38th session: 5th Committee 63; plenary 96.

Recorded vote in Assembly as follows:

In favour: Afghanistan, Algeria, Australia, Austria, Bahamas, Bahrain, Bangladesh, Barbados, Belize, Benin, Bhutan, Botswana, Brazil, Bulgaria, Burma, Burundi, Byelorussian SSR, Canada, Cape Verde, Central African Republic, Chile, China, Colombia, Congo, Costa Rica, Cuba, Cyprus, Czechoslovakia, Democratic Kampuchea, Democratic Yemen, Denmark, Djibouti, Dominican Republic, Ecuador, Egypt, El Salvador, Equatorial Guinea, Ethiopia, Fiji, Finland, France, Gabon, Gambia, German Democratic Republic, Ghana, Greece, Grenada, Guatemala, Guinea, Guinea-Bissau, Guyana, Haiti, Honduras, Hungary, Iceland, India, Indonesia, Iran, Iraq, Ireland, Ivory Coast, Jamaica, Japan, Jordan, Kenya, Kuwait, Lao People's Democratic Republic, Lebanon, Lesotho, Liberia, Libyan Arab Jamahiriya, Madagascar, Malawi, Malaysia, Maldives, Mali, Malta, Mauritania, Mauritius, Mexico, Mongolia, Morocco, Mozambique, Nepal, Netherlands, New Zealand, Nicaragua, Niger, Nigeria, Norway, Oman, Pakistan, Panama, Papua New Guinea, Paraguay, Peru, Philippines, Poland, Portugal, Qatar, Romania, Rwanda, Saint Lucia, Sao Tome and Principe, Saudi Arabia, Senegal, Seychelles, Sierra Leone, Singapore, Solomon Islands, Somalia, Spain, Sri Lanka, Sudan, Suriname, Swaziland, Sweden, Syrian Arab Republic, Thailand, Togo, Trinidad and Tobago, Tunisia, Uganda, Ukrainian SSR, USSR, United Arab Emirates, United Republic of Cameroon, United Republic of Tanzania, Upper Volta, Uruguay, Vanuatu, Viet Nam, Yemen, Yugoslavia, Zaire, Zambia.

Against: Turkey, United States.
Abstaining: Belgium, Bolivia, Germany, Federal Republic of, Israel, Italy, United Kingdom.

B

The General Assembly
Pays tribute to His Excellency Mr. Bernardo Zuleta, Special Representative of the Secretary-General for the Law of the Sea, recently deceased, whose services to the Third United Nations Conference on the Law of the Sea were decisive for the elaboration of the United Nations Convention on the Law of the Sea and for the progressive development of international law and international co-operation.

General Assembly resolution 38/59 B

14 December 1983   Meeting 96   Adopted unanimously

Draft by Guatemala (A/38/L.47); agenda item 31.
Meeting numbers. GA 38th session: plenary 81, 96.

In explaining its negative vote on resolution 38/59 A, Turkey said that, as it had not signed either the Convention on the Law of the Sea or the Final Act of the Conference, it objected to financing the Preparatory Commission from the United Nations regular budget and reserved its right not to contribute to, and provide payments for expenditures emanating from, the Convention's implementation. The United States spoke in like manner and said that the reference in the text to the unity of the Convention and the appeal to States to refrain from taking action which would selectively apply its provisions was neither good law nor good policy since it was inconsistent with a basic purpose of multilateral treaties—the codification of and development of customary law; States not signatories to such treaties should not be discouraged from complying with important provisions.

Several States explained their abstentions. The Federal Republic of Germany said that, since it had not made a decision on signing the Convention, it could not agree to any Assembly decision which would prejudice that position; many paragraphs of the resolution would have that effect. Speaking similarly, the United Kingdom also expressed reservations on the text's financial aspects and reiterated that the Convention's provisions regarding deep-sea mining, including the transfer of technology, were unacceptable in their current form. Although Bolivia believed that the rules set forth in the Convention were an important contribution to the law of the sea, it was unable to support the resolution as it had not signed the Convention. Belgium said it, too, had not signed the Convention and therefore could not accept the resolution's sixth preambular paragraph; it also had reservations on the fourth preambular paragraph and on paragraph 5 which, it felt, suggested that initiatives for international co-operation taken outside the Convention undermined its effectiveness; any interpretation which confused customary law and the Convention were also unacceptable. Belgium also objected to the financial considerations of continuing the law of the sea secretariat on an established basis. Italy spoke in like vein and also said it had reservations on paragraphs 3 and 4.

Albania, not participating in the vote, said that the resolution contained provisions it could not support and cited particularly the sixth preambular paragraph and paragraphs 1, 4 and 5. Argentina said its non-participation was because of the link that some States were seeking to establish between the Convention and the declaration in Conference resolution III relating to disputes between States over the sovereignty of a territory.

France said its positive vote did not alter its stand on the Convention and its various parts which was submitted at the time of its 1982 signature.

REFERENCES

[1]*Multilateral Treaties Deposited with the Secretary-General, Status as at 31 December 1984* (ST/LEG/SER.E/3), Sales No. E.85.V.4. [2]YUN 1982, p. 178. [3]*Ibid.*, p. 180, GA res. 37/66, 3 Dec. 1982. [4]LOS/PCN/5. [5]A/38/175. [6]A/38/570 & Corr.1. [7]YUN 1982, p. 242. [8]*Ibid.* [9]LOS/PCN/3. [10]LOS/PCN/27. [11]LOS/PCN/28 & Corr.1,2. [12]YUN 1982, p. 223. [13]LOS/PCN/29. [14]*Law of the Sea Bulletin*, No. 1. [15]A/38/38. [16]A/38/760 & Corr.1. [17]A/38/570/Add.1 & Add.1/Corr.1. [18]A/38/7/Add.17. [19]YUN 1982, p. 216. [20]E/C.7/1983/8. [21]LOS/PCN/21. [22]LOS/PCN/19. [23]LOS/PCN/14 & 16. [24]LOS/PCN/15. [25]LOS/PCN/8, 12 & 22. [26]LOS/PCN/9. [27]LOS/PCN/20. [28]LOS/PCN/10. [29]LOS/PCN/11. [30]LOS/PCN/18. [31]LOS/PCN/13. [32]LOS/PCN/30. [33]LOS/PCN/31. [34]LOS/PCN/7. [35]LOS/PCN/4. [36]LOS/PCN/17. [37]LOS/PCN/24.

PUBLICATION

A Quiet Revolution: The United Nations Convention on the Law of the Sea, Sales No. E.83.V.7.

Chapter IV

International peace and security

Several resolutions adopted by the General Assembly in 1983 dealt with international peace and security. In resolution 38/190, the Assembly put forward suggestions to improve international security. By resolution 38/191, it established an *Ad Hoc* Committee to seek ways to implement the collective security provisions of the Charter of the United Nations. In resolution 38/81, the Assembly, urging full co-operation in United Nations peace-keeping operations, expressed concern about their difficult financial situation. By resolution 38/56, it requested the Secretary-General to set up a fund for the programme of the International Year of Peace (1986) and called for voluntary contributions. In other action, the Assembly abolished the Peace Observation Commission.

The Secretary-General, in his annual report to the Assembly (p. 3), reviewed current problems affecting international peace and security which, he said, cried out for a central instrument of co-operative effort through which Governments could control conflict and work out solutions.

Topics related to this chapter. Disarmament: general aspects of disarmament; international security of non-nuclear-weapon States; disarmament and international security. Human rights: human rights and international security. Legal aspects of international political relations: force in international relations; good-neighbourliness among States; dispute settlement; draft code of offences against peace and security. International organizations and international law: strengthening the role of the United Nations.

Implementation of the 1970 Declaration on international security

In December 1983, following its annual review of the implementation of its 1970 Declaration on the Strengthening of International Security,[1] the General Assembly adopted resolution 38/190 in which it urged States and the Security Council to take several steps to reduce international tension.

Communications. During 1983, letters were received from Member States in connection with the review of the implementation of the Declaration.

A 5 January declaration by the Political Consultative Committee of the States Parties to the 1955 Warsaw Treaty of Friendship, Co-operation and Mutual Assistance (Prague, Czechoslovakia, 4 and 5 January), transmitted by Czechoslovakia on 7 January,[2] gave the Committee's ideas on ways of averting nuclear war, détente, solving disarmament problems, buttressing security and developing international co-operation.

By a letter of 8 April,[3] Czechoslovakia transmitted a communiqué adopted by the Warsaw Treaty States Parties' Committee of Ministers for Foreign Affairs (Prague, 6 and 7 April) giving details of the meeting's discussion relating to the implementation of the initiatives advanced by the Political Consultative Committee in January. That Committee's conclusions regarding the development of the international situation were confirmed in a joint statement issued at a 28 June meeting (Moscow) of leading Party and State figures of Bulgaria, Czechoslovakia, the German Democratic Republic, Hungary, Poland, Romania and the USSR; the statement, expressing concern at the increasing tension and further destabilization of relations between States, was transmitted by the USSR on 8 July.[4] A communiqué of the regular meeting of the Foreign Ministers Committee (Sofia, Bulgaria, 13 and 14 October) was forwarded by Bulgaria on 18 October;[5] the Ministers discussed the evolution of the situation in Europe, including the deployment of nuclear weapons, and other States' responses to the Prague declaration.

Several communications by the USSR dealt with its foreign policy and that of the United States. Three letters contained statements by the General Secretary of the Central Committee of the Communist Party: one of 29 March[6] transmitted his replies to questions from *Pravda* (USSR), published on 27 March; a second dated 27 April[7] transmitted an interview given to the magazine *Der Spiegel* (Federal Republic of Germany); and a third, of 29 September,[8] forwarded a statement he had made the previous day. The transcript of a 2 April press conference given by the USSR Minister for Foreign Affairs was transmitted on 5 April.[9] A 29 December resolution of the USSR Supreme Soviet concerning the international situation and USSR foreign policy was transmitted by a letter of 30 December.[10]

Annexed to a 14 September letter[11] from the Minister for Foreign Affairs of the German Democratic Republic was a statement by the General

Secretary of the Central Committee of its Socialist Unity Party and Chairman of the Council of State delivered at a Council session (Berlin, 12 September); the statement emphasized the United Nations role, particularly in the current international situation, with regard to maintaining world peace.

On 10 October,[(12)] Mongolia transmitted a memorandum regarding its 1981 proposal for a convention on non-aggression and non-use of force in Asia and the Pacific,[(13)] which, it stated, would serve as a guarantee to strengthen mutual co-operation in relations among countries of the region.

On 4 November,[(14)] Bulgaria transmitted a 27 October speech made at Sofia by the General Secretary of the Central Committee of its Communist Party and President of its State Council at an international trade union meeting and dialogue on the topic of peace and the trade unions.

On 5 December,[(15)] Romania transmitted a letter from a 12 November meeting entitled "Romania's youth wants peace", held at Bucharest, appealing to the United Nations to make greater efforts to stop the arms race, avert the danger of nuclear war and guarantee international peace.

Other 1983 letters received under this subject heading dealt with general disarmament (see Chapter I of this section) or specific situations, such as: Afghanistan, Central America, the Falkland Islands (Malvinas), Kampuchea, Mozambique–South Africa, and South-East Asia (see SUBJECT INDEX).

GENERAL ASSEMBLY ACTION

On the recommendation of its First Committee, the General Assembly, on 20 December 1983, adopted by recorded vote resolution 38/190.

Review of the implementation of the Declaration on the Strengthening of International Security

The General Assembly,

Having considered the item entitled "Review of the implementation of the Declaration on the Strengthening of International Security",

Recalling the duty of States not to intervene in the internal or external affairs of any State, in accordance with the Charter of the United Nations,

Recalling the provisions of the Declaration on Principles of International Law concerning Friendly Relations and Co-operation among States in accordance with the Charter of the United Nations,

Noting the provisions of the Declaration on the Inadmissibility of Intervention and Interference in the Internal Affairs of States,

Alarmed by increasing tensions in international relations, the resurgence of great-Power confrontations, the revival of the cold war accompanied by the policy of competition for spheres of influence, domination and exploitation in more and more parts of the world and the intensified escalation to new levels of the arms race,

particularly in nuclear weapons, all of which pose a grave threat to global peace and security,

Profoundly disturbed by the increasing recourse to the use or threat of use of force, military intervention and interference, aggression and foreign occupation; the aggravation of existing crises in the world and the outbreak of new ones; continued infringement of the independence, sovereignty and territorial integrity of countries; the denial of the right to self-determination of peoples under colonial and foreign occupation, and attempts to characterize erroneously the struggles of peoples for independence and human dignity as falling within the context of East-West confrontation, thus denying them the right to self-determination, to decide their own destiny and realize their legitimate aspirations; the persistence of colonialism, racism and *apartheid* supported by growing use of military force; the intensification and expansion in scope and frequency of manoeuvres and other military activities conceived within the context of big-Power confrontation and used as means of pressure, threat and destabilization; and the lack of solutions to the world economic crisis in which the deeper underlying problems of a structural nature have been compounded by cyclical factors and which has further aggravated the inequalities and injustices in international economic relations,

Aware of the increasing interdependence among nations and of the fact that in the present-day world there is no alternative to a policy of peaceful coexistence, détente and co-operation among States on the basis of equality, irrespective of their economic or military power, political and social systems or size and geographic location,

Noting with concern that the United Nations system of collective security has not been used effectively,

Stressing the need for the main organs of the United Nations responsible for the maintenance of peace and security, particularly the Security Council, to contribute more effectively to the promotion of international peace and security by seeking solutions to the unresolved problems and crises in the world,

1. *Reaffirms* the validity of the Declaration on the Strengthening of International Security and calls upon all States to contribute effectively to its implementation;

2. *Again calls upon* all States, in particular the nuclear-weapon States and other militarily significant States, to take immediate steps aimed at promoting and using effectively the system of collective security as envisaged in the Charter of the United Nations, together with measures for the effective halting of the arms race and for the achievement of general and complete disarmament under effective international control;

3. *Reiterates* that the current deterioration of the international situation requires an effective Security Council and, to that end, emphasizes the great urgency of examining all existing mechanisms and working methods in order to enhance the authority and enforcement capacity of the Council, in accordance with the Charter;

4. *Emphasizes*, in particular, the need to consider holding periodic meetings of the Security Council in specific cases to consider and review outstanding problems and crises, thus enabling the Council to play a more active role in preventing conflicts;

5. *Takes note* of the fact that the Security Council has thus far failed to report to the General Assembly on steps

taken to implement the provisions of paragraphs 3 and 4 above, which have been adopted since 1980, and expresses the firm hope that the Council will do so at the thirty-ninth session of the Assembly;

6. *Urges* all States to abide strictly, in their international relations, by their commitment to the Charter and, to this end:

(a) To refrain from the use or threat of use of force, intervention, interference, aggression, foreign occupation and colonial domination or measures of political and economic coercion which violate the sovereignty, territorial integrity, independence and security of other States or their right freely to dispose of their natural resources;

(b) To refrain from supporting or encouraging any such act for any reason whatsoever and to reject and refuse recognition of situations brought about by any such act;

7. *Invites* all States, in particular the major military Powers and States members of military alliances, to refrain, especially in critical situations and in crisis areas, from actions, including military activities and manoeuvres, conceived within the context of big-Power confrontation and used as a means of pressure on, threat to and destabilization of other States and regions;

8. *Urges* all States, in particular the permanent members of the Security Council, to take all necessary measures to prevent the further deterioration of the international situation and, to this end:

(a) To seek, through the means provided for in the Charter, the peaceful settlement of disputes and the elimination of the focal points of crisis and tension which constitute a threat to international peace and security;

(b) To proceed without delay to a global consideration of ways and means for bringing about a revival of the world economy and for the restructuring of international economic relations within the framework of the global negotiations with a view to establishing the new international economic order;

(c) To accelerate the economic development of developing countries, particularly the least developed ones;

9. *Considers* that respect for and the promotion of human rights and fundamental freedoms in their civil, political, economic, social and cultural aspects, on the one hand, and the strengthening of international peace and security, on the other, mutually reinforce each other;

10. *Reaffirms* the legitimacy of the struggle of peoples under colonial domination, foreign occupation or racist régimes and their inalienable right to self-determination and independence, and urges Member States to increase their support for and solidarity with them and their national liberation movements and to take urgent and effective measures for the speedy completion of the implementation of the Declaration on the Granting of Independence to Colonial Countries and Peoples and for the final elimination of colonialism, racism and *apartheid;*

11. *Calls upon* all States, particularly the members of the Security Council, to take appropriate and effective measures to promote the fulfilment of the objective of the denuclearization of Africa in order to avert the serious danger which the nuclear capability of South Africa constitutes to the African States, in particular the frontline States, as well as to international peace and security;

12. *Welcomes* the successful conclusion of the Madrid meeting of representatives of the participating States of the Conference on Security and Co-operation in Europe,

held from 11 November 1980 to 9 September 1983, which has demonstrated that political will to negotiate is necessary as a contribution to the strengthening of peace and security not only in Europe but also internationally, and expresses the hope that the conference to be held at Stockholm, beginning on 17 January 1984, the Conference on Confidence- and Security-Building Measures and Disarmament in Europe, the continent with the greatest concentration of armaments and military forces, will achieve significant and positive results;

13. *Affirms* that the democratization of international relations is an imperative necessity, under conditions of interdependence, for the full development and independence of all States, as well as the attainment of genuine security, peace and co-operation in the world;

14. *Calls upon* the great Powers to engage in constructive negotiations in good faith and to abandon policies of confrontation which have hitherto given rise to tension and mistrust;

15. *Decides* to include in the provisional agenda of its thirty-ninth session the item entitled "Review of the implementation of the Declaration on the Strengthening of International Security".

General Assembly resolution 38/190

20 December 1983   Meeting 103   135-0-12 (recorded vote)

Approved by First Committee (A/38/643) by roll-call vote (108-0-12), 9 December (meeting 54); 24-nation draft (A/C.1/38/L.87/Rev.1), orally revised; agenda item 66.

Sponsors: Algeria, Bahamas, Congo, Ecuador, Egypt, Ethiopia, Ghana, Guyana, India, Indonesia, Madagascar, Mali, Nigeria, Pakistan, Romania, Senegal, Sierra Leone, Sri Lanka, Sudan, Togo, Tunisia, Uruguay, Yugoslavia, Zambia.

Meeting numbers. GA 38th session: 1st Committee 49-54; plenary 103.

Recorded vote in Assembly as follows:

In favour: Afghanistan, Algeria, Angola, Antigua and Barbuda, Argentina, Australia, Austria, Bahamas, Bahrain, Bangladesh, Barbados, Belize, Benin, Bhutan, Bolivia, Botswana, Brazil, Bulgaria, Burma, Burundi, Byelorussian SSR, Cape Verde, Central African Republic, Chad, Chile, China, Colombia, Congo, Costa Rica, Cuba, Cyprus, Czechoslovakia, Democratic Kampuchea, Democratic Yemen, Denmark, Djibouti, Dominica, Dominican Republic, Ecuador, Egypt, El Salvador, Ethiopia, Fiji, Finland, France, Gabon, Gambia, German Democratic Republic, Ghana, Greece, Guatemala, Guinea, Guinea-Bissau, Guyana, Honduras, Hungary, Iceland, India, Indonesia, Iran, Iraq, Ireland, Ivory Coast, Jamaica, Jordan, Kenya, Kuwait, Lao People's Democratic Republic, Lebanon, Lesotho, Liberia, Libyan Arab Jamahiriya, Madagascar, Malawi, Malaysia, Maldives, Mali, Malta, Mauritania, Mauritius, Mexico, Mongolia, Morocco, Mozambique, Nepal, Netherlands, Nicaragua, Niger, Nigeria, Norway, Oman, Pakistan, Panama, Papua New Guinea, Peru, Philippines, Poland, Qatar, Romania, Rwanda, Saint Lucia, Saint Vincent and the Grenadines, Sao Tome and Principe, Saudi Arabia, Senegal, Sierra Leone, Singapore, Somalia, Spain, Sri Lanka, Sudan, Suriname, Swaziland, Sweden, Syrian Arab Republic, Thailand, Togo, Trinidad and Tobago, Tunisia, Uganda, Ukrainian SSR, USSR, United Arab Emirates, United Republic of Cameroon, United Republic of Tanzania, Upper Volta, Uruguay, Vanuatu, Venezuela, Viet Nam, Yemen, Yugoslavia, Zaire, Zambia, Zimbabwe.

Against: None.

Abstaining: Belgium, Canada, Germany, Federal Republic of, Israel, Italy, Japan, Luxembourg, New Zealand, Portugal, Turkey, United Kingdom, United States.

In the First Committee, Yugoslavia, at the request of the majority of the sponsors, orally revised paragraph 5 of the draft. At the beginning, "Takes note of" replaced "Regrets", and added at the end was the phrase "and expresses the firm hope that the Council will do so at the thirty-ninth session of the Assembly".

REFERENCES

[1]YUN 1970, p. 105, GA res. 2734(XXV), 16 Dec. 1970. [2]A/38/67-S/15556 & Corr.1. [3]A/38/151-S/15696. [4]A/38/292-S/15862. [5]A/C.1/38/6. [6]A/38/129-S/15663. [7]A/38/171. [8]A/38/459-S/16017. [9]A/38/139. [10]A/39/61. [11]A/38/425. [12]A/38/509. [13]YUN 1981, p. 141. [14]A/C.1/38/9 & Corr.1. [15]A/C.1/38/15.

Implementation of the security provisions of the UN Charter

As it had decided in 1982,[1] the General Assembly continued in 1983 its consideration of the implementation of the collective security provisions of the Charter of the United Nations for the maintenance of international peace and security, and by resolution 38/191 established an *Ad Hoc* Committee to explore ways of implementing those provisions.

In the First Committee, Cyprus put forward and subsequently withdrew a draft resolution[2] which would have had the Assembly call on the two major Powers to hold a high-level meeting in an effort to overcome current tensions, and call on other Member States, particularly those of the two major military alliances, to support such a meeting and exert efforts to relax international tension.

GENERAL ASSEMBLY ACTION

On the recommendation of the First Committee, the General Assembly, on 20 December 1983, adopted by recorded vote resolution 38/191.

Implementation of the collective security provisions of the Charter of the United Nations for the maintenance of international peace and security

The General Assembly,

Recalling its resolution 37/119 of 16 December 1982 on the implementation of the collective security provisions of the Charter of the United Nations for the maintenance of international peace and security,

Reaffirming that the primary function of the United Nations, in particular through the Security Council, is the maintenance of international peace and security,

Renewing its commitment to the fundamental principle of the Charter that all States have the duty not to threaten or use force against the sovereignty, political independence or territorial integrity of other States,

Stressing that the purposes of the United Nations can be achieved only under conditions in which States comply fully with their obligations assumed under the Charter,

Alarmed over the growing tendency of States to resort to the use of force, interference and intervention in international relations, thus ignoring the Charter and the Declaration on Principles of International Law concerning Friendly Relations and Co-operation among States in accordance with the Charter of the United Nations,

Concerned that the Security Council has not always been able to take decisive action for the maintenance of international peace and for resolving international problems,

Recognizing that fundamental approaches to genuine security include, *inter alia*, the strengthening of the Charter system of collective security,

Conscious of the important role with which the Security Council is entrusted in enhancing the collective security provisions of the Charter for the promotion and maintenance of international peace and security, in accordance with the Charter,

Regretting that the provisions of the Charter relating to collective security measures have not been fully implemented,

Taking into account, in this connection, the reports of the Secretary-General on the work of the Organization to the General Assembly at its thirty-seventh and thirty-eighth sessions,

Also taking into account the note by the President of the Security Council of 12 September 1983,

Recalling the views of the Governments of the five Nordic countries on the strengthening of the United Nations,

Also recalling the Political Declaration adopted by the Seventh Conference of Heads of State or Government of Non-Aligned Countries, held at New Delhi from 7 to 12 March 1983,

Having considered the item entitled "Implementation of the collective security provisions of the Charter of the United Nations for the maintenance of international peace and security",

1. *Decides* to establish an *Ad Hoc* Committee on the Implementation of the Collective Security Provisions of the Charter of the United Nations for the purpose of exploring ways and means of implementing the said provisions;

2. *Requests* the Secretary-General urgently to invite the views and comments of Member States on the matter not later than 30 May 1984 and to transmit them to the *Ad Hoc* Committee as soon as possible;

3. *Requests* the *Ad Hoc* Committee, in considering the matter, to take due account of the views and comments of Member States, including their recommendations, and to submit a progress report to the Security Council for its consideration and comments and to the General Assembly at its thirty-ninth session, and a final report to the Assembly at its fortieth session;

4. *Decides* to include in the provisional agenda of its thirty-ninth session the item entitled "Implementation of the collective security provisions of the Charter of the United Nations for the maintenance of international peace and security".

General Assembly resolution 38/191

20 December 1983   Meeting 103   109-20-18 (recorded vote)

Approved by First Committee (A/38/644) by roll-call vote (75-19-18), 9 December (meeting 54); 20-nation draft (A/C.1/38/L.83/Rev.3); agenda item 67.

Sponsors: Bahamas, Bangladesh, Cyprus, Ecuador, Ghana, Indonesia, Kenya, Liberia, Malawi, Malaysia, Mali, Nigeria, Qatar, Sierra Leone, Sri Lanka, Togo, Trinidad and Tobago, Uganda, Uruguay, Zambia.

Financial implications. 5th Committee, A/38/737; S-G, A/C.1/38/L.89, A/C.5/38/91.

Meeting numbers. GA 38th session: 1st Committee 47, 49-54; 5th Committee 66; plenary 103.

Recorded vote in Assembly as follows:

In favour: Algeria, Angola, Antigua and Barbuda, Argentina, Bahamas, Bahrain, Bangladesh, Barbados, Belize, Benin, Bhutan, Bolivia, Botswana, Brazil, Burma, Burundi, Cape Verde, Central African Republic, Chad, Chile, China, Colombia, Congo, Costa Rica, Cyprus, Democratic Kampuchea, Djibouti, Dominica, Dominican Republic, Ecuador, Egypt, El Salvador, Ethiopia, Fiji, Gabon, Gambia, Ghana, Greece, Guatemala, Guinea, Guinea-Bissau, Guyana, Honduras, India, Indonesia, Iran, Iraq, Ivory Coast, Jamaica, Jordan, Kenya, Kuwait, Lebanon, Lesotho, Liberia, Libyan Arab Jamahiriya, Madagascar, Malawi, Malaysia, Maldives, Mali, Mauritania, Mauritius, Mexico, Morocco, Nepal, Nicaragua, Niger, Nigeria, Oman, Pakistan, Panama, Papua New Guinea, Paraguay, Peru, Philippines, Qatar, Romania, Rwanda, Saint Lucia, Saint Vincent and the Grenadines, Sao Tome and Principe, Saudi Arabia, Senegal, Seychelles, Sierra Leone, Singapore, Somalia, Sri Lanka, Sudan, Suriname, Swaziland, Thailand, Togo, Trinidad and Tobago, Tunisia, Uganda, United Arab Emirates, United Republic of Cameroon, United Republic of Tanzania, Upper Volta, Uruguay, Vanuatu, Venezuela, Yemen, Yugoslavia, Zaire, Zambia, Zimbabwe.

Against: Belgium, Bulgaria, Byelorussian SSR, Cuba, Czechoslovakia, France, German Democratic Republic, Germany, Federal Republic of, Hungary, Italy, Luxembourg, Mongolia, Netherlands, Poland, Portugal, Turkey, Ukrainian SSR, USSR, United Kingdom, United States.
Abstaining: Afghanistan, Australia, Austria, Canada, Democratic Yemen, Denmark, Finland, Iceland, Ireland, Israel, Japan, Lao People's Democratic Republic, New Zealand, Norway, Spain, Sweden, Syrian Arab Republic, Viet Nam.

Several States explained their negative votes on the draft which had been revised three times. The USSR said that the text contradicted the Assembly's 1982 resolution[1] on the same subject, as the Security Council had been requested to study implementing the Charter's collective security provisions; paragraph 1 of the text violated the Charter as such questions were the prerogative of the Council. For Italy, the *Ad Hoc* Committee would be redundant and overlap the Council's responsibility. France felt that the Committee would have only a partial view of the matter which should be put before either the Council or the Special Committee on the Charter of the United Nations and on the Strengthening of the Role of the Organization whose mandate gave priority to all aspects of maintaining international peace and security. Speaking in like manner, the German Democratic Republic pointed out that the Committee on the Charter had dealt with the issue time and again, and that it was not the lack of an institutional framework for implementing the Charter provisions but the lack of political will by certain countries which had prevented full application of the collective security system.

On the other hand, Guyana, which voted positively, saw the *Ad Hoc* Committee as a first step towards establishing an effective collective security system within the Charter's framework and a first attempt to give small States the confidence that their sovereignty, independence and territorial integrity were secure. Introducing the revised text, Sierra Leone pointed out that the pre-eminent role of the Security Council had been acknowledged in the text and that the sponsors had tried to make clear that implementing the Charter's collective security provisions would enhance the Council's role; setting up an *ad hoc* rather than a special committee emphasized the matter's urgency while demonstrating that the body was not intended to be permanent.

REFERENCES
[1]YUN 1982, p. 252, GA res. 37/119, 16 Dec. 1982. [2]A/C.1/38/L.86/Rev.1.

Review of peace-keeping operations

Concern about the difficult financial position of United Nations peace-keeping operations was expressed by the General Assembly in December 1983 when it adopted resolution 38/81.

The Special Committee on Peace-keeping Operations, established by the Assembly in 1965,[1] met three times during 1983.[2] On 23 June, the Committee asked its officers to serve for another year and, on 1 August, it authorized its Working Group to discuss and elaborate on its mandate. The Working Group, meeting on 17 and 29 August, took up an informal paper which included a proposed organization of work for the Committee. However, no consensus was reached on the matter. On 1 September, the Committee, in considering its report to the Assembly, concluded that the United Nations should continue to work for a comprehensive review of peace-keeping operations. Some members felt that the Committee's work required reactivation and that its mandate should be renewed, while others believed that the question of renewing the mandate should be decided by the Assembly.

At the second part of its 1983 session (August/September),[3] the Committee for Programme and Co-ordination (CPC) expressed the view that the Special Committee on Peace-keeping Operations might streamline its work.

On the recommendation of the Special Political Committee, the General Assembly, on 15 December 1983, adopted resolution 38/81 by recorded vote.

Comprehensive review of the whole question of peace-keeping operations in all their aspects
The General Assembly,

Recalling its resolutions 1874(S-IV) of 27 June 1963, 2006(XIX) of 18 February 1965, 2053 A (XX) of 15 December 1965, 2249(S-V) of 23 May 1967, 2308(XXII) of 13 December 1967, 2451(XXIII) of 19 December 1968, 2670(XXV) of 8 December 1970, 2835(XXVI) of 17 December 1971, 2965(XXVII) of 13 December 1972, 3091(XXVIII) of 7 December 1973, 3239(XXIX) of 29 November 1974, 3457(XXX) of 10 December 1975, 31/105 of 15 December 1976, 32/106 of 15 December 1977, 33/114 of 18 December 1978, 34/53 of 23 November 1979, 35/121 of 11 December 1980, 36/37 of 18 November 1981 and 37/93 of 10 December 1982,

Taking account of the views expressed and issues raised on the question of peace-keeping during the debate on the item,

Reaffirming the primary responsibility of the Security Council for the maintenance of international peace and security,

Conscious of the vital role played by United Nations peace-keeping forces in support of decisions of the Security Council in discharging its primary responsibility in accordance with the Charter of the United Nations,

Recognizing that the presence of United Nations peace-keeping forces authorized by the Security Council in conflict areas demonstrates the common concern of Members of the United Nations in the preservation of stability and easing of tension in those areas,

Aware of the extremely difficult financial situation of the United Nations peace-keeping forces in the light of the heavy burden incurred by troop contributors, especially those from developing countries,

Stressing the collective responsibility of Member States, in accordance with the Charter, to share equitably the financial burdens of such operations established by the Security Council, which should continue to be conducted with maximum efficiency and economy,

Urging, at the same time, that other areas of co-operation with and support for United Nations peace-keeping forces should be encouraged,

Recognizing the need to enhance the efficiency and effectiveness of United Nations peace-keeping forces,

Commending the Secretary-General for the way he is carrying out peace-keeping operations of the United Nations decided upon by the Security Council,

Convinced that the importance of the issue of United Nations peace-keeping is such that the United Nations should continue to work for a comprehensive review of the whole question of peace-keeping operations in all their aspects,

Taking note of the report of the Special Committee on Peace-keeping Operations,

1. *Expresses its conviction* that peace-keeping operations of the United Nations, conducted with the consent of the host country and with respect for its sovereignty and territorial integrity, in accordance with the Charter of the United Nations, are an essential function of the United Nations, though not a substitute for the peaceful settlement of disputes and therefore of a temporary nature;

2. *Urges* all concerned to co-operate fully in the implementation of United Nations peace-keeping operations;

3. *Reaffirms and renews* the mandate given to the Special Committee on Peace-keeping Operations by relevant resolutions of the General Assembly;

4. *Expresses concern* about the difficult financial situation of United Nations peace-keeping operations;

5. *Urges again* the Special Committee on Peace-keeping Operations, in accordance with its mandate, to renew its efforts to work towards the completion of agreed guidelines that will govern the conduct of United Nations peace-keeping operations in accordance with the Charter of the United Nations, and to devote further attention to specific questions relating to the practical implementation of peace-keeping operations;

6. *Requests* the Special Committee on Peace-keeping Operations to submit a status report on its present situation, to determine the areas of possible progress and other areas where progress would be difficult to achieve or is still pending, and to consider proposals to reactivate and rationalize its work;

7. *Decides* to include in the provisional agenda of its thirty-ninth session the item entitled "Comprehensive review of the whole question of peace-keeping operations in all their aspects".

General Assembly resolution 38/81

15 December 1983   Meeting 98   125-16-5 (recorded vote)

Approved by SPC (A/38/719) by roll-call vote (96-14-4), 9 December (meeting 48); 10-nation draft (A/SPC/38/L.48/Rev.1); agenda item 71.
Sponsors: Australia, Canada, Egypt, Fiji, France, Italy, Japan, Netherlands, Philippines, United Kingdom.
Meeting numbers. GA 38th session: SPC 5-7, 46-48; plenary 98.

Recorded vote in Assembly as follows:

In favour: Algeria, Argentina, Australia, Austria, Bahamas, Bahrain, Bangladesh, Barbados, Belgium, Belize, Bhutan, Bolivia, Botswana, Brazil, Burma, Burundi, Canada, Cape Verde, Central African Republic, Chad, Chile, China, Colombia, Congo, Costa Rica, Cyprus, Democratic Kampuchea, Denmark, Dominica, Dominican Republic, Ecuador, Egypt, El Salvador, Equatorial Guinea, Ethiopia, Fiji, Finland, France, Gabon, Gambia, Germany, Federal Republic of, Ghana, Greece, Grenada, Guatemala, Guinea, Guinea-Bissau, Guyana, Honduras, Iceland, India, Indonesia, Iraq, Ireland, Israel, Italy, Ivory Coast, Jamaica, Japan, Jordan, Kenya, Kuwait, Lebanon, Lesotho, Liberia, Luxembourg, Madagascar, Malawi, Malaysia, Maldives, Mali, Malta, Mauritania, Mauritius, Mexico, Morocco, Nepal, Netherlands, New Zealand, Nicaragua, Niger, Nigeria, Norway, Oman, Panama, Papua New Guinea, Paraguay, Peru, Philippines, Portugal, Qatar, Romania, Rwanda, Saint Lucia, Sao Tome and Principe, Saudi Arabia, Senegal, Sierra Leone, Singapore, Solomon Islands, Somalia, Spain, Sri Lanka, Sudan, Suriname, Swaziland, Sweden, Thailand, Togo, Trinidad and Tobago, Tunisia, Uganda, United Arab Emirates, United Kingdom, United Republic of Cameroon, United Republic of Tanzania, United States, Upper Volta, Uruguay, Vanuatu, Venezuela, Yugoslavia, Zaire, Zambia, Zimbabwe.

Against: Afghanistan, Albania, Bulgaria, Byelorussian SSR, Cuba, Czechoslovakia, German Democratic Republic, Hungary, Lao People's Democratic Republic, Mongolia, Mozambique, Poland, Turkey, Ukrainian SSR, USSR, Viet Nam.

Abstaining: Democratic Yemen, Pakistan, Seychelles, Syrian Arab Republic, Yemen.

A separate vote on the seventh preambular paragraph, stressing the responsibility of sharing equitably the financing of peace-keeping operations, was taken in both the Special Political Committee and the Assembly.

In the Committee, after Algeria, Mexico and the Syrian Arab Republic had requested the vote, the preambular paragraph was approved by a roll-call vote of 76 to 14, with 21 abstentions. The Assembly adopted the paragraph by a recorded vote of 97 to 16, with 24 abstentions.

The 10-nation draft—a revised version of a text sponsored by the same nations together with Bangladesh and Pakistan—was generally based on a draft, sponsored by Australia, Canada, Egypt, France, Italy, Japan, the Netherlands, the Philippines and the United Kingdom, which had been withdrawn.[4] The 10-nation draft differed from that withdrawn in a number of its provisions, some of which were either reformulated or omitted. The withdrawn text would have had the Assembly: stress that peace-keeping operations must be supplemented by sustained diplomatic efforts; recommend that the Secretary-General continue promoting the peaceful settlement of disputes; stress prerequisites for effective peace-keeping—political support and co-operation, respect for the host country's national sovereignty, and agreements between the United Nations and the host country to grant peace-keeping forces privileges and immunities and provide them with facilities necessary for their task; express regret that the Special Committee on Peace-keeping Operations had not fulfilled its mandate; reaffirm that mandate; and recommend that its future renewal be determined in the light of a status report on the Committee's current situation.

In the Special Political Committee, a number of States explained their votes, with the majority expressing concern that they had not been adequately consulted by the sponsors during the preparation of the draft. Among issues raised was the Security Council's role in peace-keeping operations and the question of financing those operations.

Several States gave their reasons for voting against the text as a whole. The German Democratic Republic said the text prejudged the work of the Special Committee on Peace-keeping Operations with regard to completing guidelines governing such operations, and felt that its adoption would compromise that body's effectiveness. Poland spoke similarly, but stressed that it did not question the appropriateness of peace-keeping operations conducted according to the United Nations Charter, or the usefulness of Poland's contribution to those operations. According to the USSR, the draft's sponsors had introduced many provisions not conforming to the Charter and wished to thwart the Special Committee's work on the guidelines since those guidelines would enable the Security Council to maintain the security of States, particularly small ones. For Turkey, several preambular paragraphs, including the seventh, raised problems: according to the fourth, peace-keeping forces would be called on to support Council decisions, whereas those forces had a precise mandate; the eighth and ninth were vague and involved sweeping judgements about the forces' efficiency and effectiveness. Concerning paragraph 1, Turkey was not certain that the prerequisites were appropriate in all cases or the only ones and also did not cover all situations. Albania said it opposed the dispatch of United Nations forces as, it believed, experience had shown that they could not defend peoples' freedom and independence or international peace and security. Hungary, stressing that a resolution on Charter principles relating to the international situation should be adopted by consensus, suggested that a procedural draft be formulated which could be approved in that manner, and which also would renew the Special Committee's mandate.

Pakistan, which abstained, said it had withdrawn its sponsorship of the draft as it believed that no modification could be made to the mandate, character or duration of peace-keeping operations authorized by the Security Council unless the Council decided; the revised draft had changed the spirit of the original by including paragraph 1, making peace-keeping operations dependent on the host country's consent.

Explaining its abstention on the preambular paragraph, Iraq said the aggressor should pay for the entire cost of peace-keeping operations. Tunisia thought that the aggressor should at least pay a major portion of costs. Also abstaining was Algeria which felt that the paragraph's wording was imprecise and represented a bold interpretation of Charter provisions, especially Article 43. Jordan noted

that some delegations had expressed confusion over the interpretation of the wording of the paragraph.

The Libyan Arab Jamahiriya, speaking in the Assembly, said it had not participated in either vote because it felt that the aggressor should pay the price for its aggression and therefore bear the entire costs.

Several States explained their postive votes on the the text as a whole and on the preambular paragraph. Ireland said it was in favour of sharing the financial burden equitably, a view supported by Norway which would, however, have preferred to have had that obligation mentioned in an operative paragraph of the text. The United States said the question of guidelines was a non-issue; attempts to resurrect an issue which had been solved were aimed at distracting the Assembly from the real problem, the financing of the forces and practical organizational measures to be taken on them. Stressing the serious financial situation facing peace-keeping operations, the United Kingdom said a mere procedural resolution would indicate a lack of interest and conviction by Member States; the current position imposed an unfair burden on troop contributors, particularly the least wealthy. France agreed and said it was surprising that some States which said they regretted that the Organization was unable to face its responsibilities had voted against a text calling for submission of proposals to remedy that situation. Nepal felt that the revised text placed the whole question in a proper perspective. Greece spoke similarly but added that it preferred the text prior to its revision. Mexico was among those which said that it would have been better had consultations been held on drafting the text. The Sudan said its positive vote should not be interpreted as placing aggressor and victim on the same footing. Lebanon spoke similarly but added that the seventh preambular paragraph derived from a general principle, that of collective security, to which it subscribed.

An oral amendment to the draft resolution introduced by the Syrian Arab Republic was withdrawn at the request of Mexico. The amendment would have added a preambular paragraph stating that aggressors should pay the whole costs of peace-keeping operations. Cyprus, which had voted positively in both instances, said it would have been better had this provision been included.

For its consideration of the item, the Special Political Committee also had before it two notes verbales addressed to the Secretary-General. In the first, dated 20 September,[5] Canada gave its suggestions on questions related to the practical implementation of peace-keeping operations, particularly the authority of the Security Council and the role of the Secretary-General, financing, preparations by troop contributors, standardizing United Nations practice, and training aspects. In the second, dated 7 October,[6] the United Kingdom—expressing regret that certain Member States which professed support for maintaining peace and international security were withholding their assessed contributions for peacekeeping—urged that the matter be drawn to the Assembly's attention.

(For information on the financing of specific peace-keeping operations, see POLITICAL AND SECURITY QUESTIONS, Chapters VIII and IX.)

REFERENCES
[1]YUN 1964, p. 59, GA res. 2006(XIX), 18 Feb. 1965. [2]A/38/381. [3]A/38/38. [4]A/SPC/38/L.46. [5]A/38/499. [6]A/38/489.

International Year of Peace (1986)

Following up its 1982 decision,[1] declaring 1986 as the International Year of Peace, the General Assembly decided in December 1983 by resolution 38/56 to establish a voluntary fund for the programme of the Year.

Responding to the Assembly's request,[1] the Secretary-General, in October 1983,[2] submitted to the Assembly a draft programme for the observance of the Year. As at 6 December, 13 Member States and one non-member State had transmitted proposals to the Secretary-General for the programme; 19 United Nations organizations had declared their interest in participating, several of which had initiated preparations; 123 nongovernmental organizations in consultative status with the Economic and Social Council had expressed interest and two consultative meetings were held in New York and Geneva (6 and 13 June); and 28 academic and research institutions had also responded to an invitation to participate. Proposed activities included publications, lectures, seminars, conferences, research projects, television and radio programmes, and contests, and the issuance of commemorative stamps and a peace medal. The activities would be carried out by the United Nations, its specialized agencies, States, non-governmental organizations and academic institutions.

The Secretary-General noted that no voluntary contributions to finance the programme had been offered.

GENERAL ASSEMBLY ACTION

On 7 December 1983, the General Assembly adopted resolution 38/56 without vote.

International Year of Peace

The General Assembly,

Recalling its resolution 37/16 of 16 November 1982, in which it declared 1986 to be the International Year of Peace,

Taking note with appreciation of the report of the Secretary-General, containing the draft programme of the International Year of Peace,

Taking into account the guidelines for international years and anniversaries adopted by the General Assembly in its decision 35/424 of 5 December 1980,

Recognizing that the International Year of Peace, which will be linked with the fortieth anniversary of the United Nations, is especially important and will permit the United Nations and its Member States to concentrate their efforts towards promoting the ideals of peace, as evidence of their dedication to serve peace by all possible means,

Considering also that the preparations for the International Year of Peace must be carried through to ensure positive results in international co-operation for the promotion of peace during the Year,

1. *Endorses* the principal objectives of the International Year of Peace indicated in the report of the Secretary-General;

2. *Invites* all States, all organizations within the United Nations system and interested non-governmental organizations to co-operate with the Secretary-General in achieving the objectives of the International Year of Peace;

3. *Requests* the Secretary-General to establish a voluntary fund for the programme of the International Year of Peace and urges all States and interested organizations to contribute to that fund;

4. *Also requests* the Secretary-General to carry out during 1984-1985 the necessary preparations for the observance of the International Year of Peace, including the organization of regional seminars devoted to promoting the objectives of the Year;

5. *Further requests* the Secretary-General to report to the General Assembly at its thirty-ninth session on the draft programme of the International Year of Peace and on the arrangements for financing it;

6. *Decides* to include in the provisional agenda of its thirty-ninth session an item entitled "International Year of Peace".

General Assembly resolution 38/56

7 December 1983   Meeting 87   Adopted without vote

32-nation draft (A/38/L.16 & Add.1); agenda item 12.
Sponsors: Argentina, Bahamas, Bangladesh, Bolivia, Chile, Colombia, Costa Rica, Cyprus, Dominican Republic, Ecuador, Egypt, El Salvador, Equatorial Guinea, Guatemala, Honduras, Malta, Nepal, Nicaragua, Nigeria, Pakistan, Panama, Peru, Philippines, Poland, Romania, Saint Lucia, Senegal, Singapore, Swaziland, Thailand, Uruguay, Zaire.
Financial implications. 5th Committee, A/38/658; S-G, A/C.5/38/60.
Meeting numbers. GA 38th session: 5th Committee 55; plenary 83, 87.

An amendment by the United States[3] to paragraph 4 of the 32-nation draft was rejected by a recorded vote of 64 to 16, with 35 abstentions. By the amendment, the Assembly would have requested the Secretary-General "to utilize the voluntary fund" to carry out the preparations for the Year.

REFERENCES
[1]YUN 1982, p. 254, GA res. 37/16, 16 Nov. 1982. [2]A/38/413 & Add.1,2. [3]A/38/L.41.

Peace Observation Commission

In a September 1983 note[1] to the General Assembly concerning the appointment of members of the Peace Observation Commission, the Secretary-General pointed out that CPC had recommended in 1982[2] that the mandate of the Commission should be terminated and consequently that reference to it should be deleted from the proposed medium-term plan for 1984-1989. By a 1982 resolution,[3] the Assembly had adopted the medium-term plan as revised by CPC, but made no specific reference to the Commission. Therefore, the Secretary-General stated, it would be desirable to determine conclusively whether the Assembly intended formally to abolish that organ.

The Commission was abolished on 23 September when the General Assembly adopted a recommendation[4] by the General Committee (decision 38/402) calling for a clarification of the Assembly's intention. (For further details, see APPENDIX III, under Peace Observation Commission.)

REFERENCES
[1]A/38/402. [2]YUN 1982, p. 1626. [3]*Ibid.*, p. 1430, GA res. 37/234, 21 Dec. 1982. [4]A/38/250.

Chapter V

Africa

In the political sphere, much of the work of the United Nations in 1983 pertaining to Africa focused on southern Africa, in particular on ways to end the *apartheid* policies of South Africa. In a series of resolutions adopted in December, the General Assembly took action on ways to bring about the end of *apartheid*. It requested the Security Council to consider action against South Africa under Chapter VII of the Charter of the United Nations which deals with action with respect to threats to the peace, breaches of the peace and acts of aggression. The Assembly requested that the Council consider comprehensive and mandatory sanctions against South Africa, and called for a strengthening of the mandatory arms embargo imposed since 1977. Recommendations for international action against *apartheid* were also made by the Special Committee against *Apartheid*, the Commission on Human Rights, the United Nations Council for Namibia and the Second World Conference to Combat Racism and Racial Discrimination, among others. Such activities included drafting a convention against *apartheid* in sports, special aid programmes for *apartheid* victims and promoting the international campaign against *apartheid* by informing the public. Special attention was given to political prisoners, in particular to the three members of the African National Congress of South Africa (ANC) who were executed in 1983, and women and children.

A related area of concern for the United Nations was South Africa's relations with the other States of the region, especially its aggression against Angola, Lesotho and Mozambique, which the Assembly condemned. In December, the Security Council, acting on Angola's complaint, demanded that South Africa withdraw its occupying forces from Angola. By a June resolution, the Council took action on Lesotho, requesting special economic assistance for that country for those needs (mainly security and health services, food supplies and construction) identified by a Council mission sent there in January.

In 1983, both Chad and Egypt claimed that the Libyan Arab Jamahiriya had violated their territories. Chad twice brought its complaint to the Security Council, and in April the Council urged the two sides to work towards a settlement and to use the mechanism of the Organization of African Unity (OAU) for that purpose.

The Assembly in November reaffirmed the sovereignty of the Comoros over the Indian Ocean island of Mayotte. In October, it called for further co-operation between OAU and the United Nations system. The Security Council concluded its mission to investigate the origin and damages of a 1981 attack on Seychelles. During 1983, the United Kingdom and Mauritius disputed each other's claims to sovereignty over the Chagos Archipelago, a group of islands in the Indian Ocean. The United Nations Educational and Training Programme for Southern Africa continued to provide scholarships and, in December, the Assembly appealed for increased contributions to the Programme.

Topics related to this chapter. Mediterranean: Libyan Arab Jamahiriya–United States dispute. Transnational corporations. Regional economic and social activities: Africa. Environment: environment and *apartheid*. Human rights: human rights violations—South Africa and Namibia. Refugees: Africa. Namibia.

South Africa and *apartheid*

In 1983, several United Nations bodies continued to consider ways to end *apartheid*—the system of laws and policies based on racial separation imposed by the Government of South Africa in 1948.

The General Assembly on 5 December adopted 11 resolutions on the issue, repeatedly condemning South Africa and calling for an end to *apartheid*. In a resolution on the situation in South Africa (38/39 A), the Assembly recognized the right of the oppressed people to use all means, including armed struggle, to resist the illegitimate régime of South Africa, called for assistance to liberation movements, condemned collaboration with South Africa, reiterated its appeal to the Security Council to impose comprehensive and mandatory sanctions against that country, urged the International Monetary Fund (IMF) and the International Atomic Energy Agency (IAEA) to refrain from assisting it, and called for promoting the international campaign against *apartheid*.

By another resolution (38/39 B), the Assembly commended the Programme of Action against

Apartheid, adopted by the Special Committee against *Apartheid* in October. The Programme included recommendations for action by Governments, the United Nations system and other organizations.

In a resolution on sanctions against South Africa (38/39 D), the Assembly requested the Security Council to take measures to reinforce the arms embargo, ban military and nuclear co-operation with South Africa, impose an oil embargo and prohibit loans to and new investments in South Africa. Three further resolutions defined possible Council action in regard to military and nuclear collaboration (38/39 G), investments in South Africa (38/39 I) and an oil embargo (38/39 J). The Assembly demanded that Israel desist from its collaboration with South Africa (38/39 F), especially in the military and nuclear fields, and called for further work on drafting a convention against *apartheid* in sports (38/39 K).

A resolution on the effects of *apartheid* on southern Africa (38/39 C) included a condemnation of South Africa's aggression against Angola, Lesotho and Mozambique and its threats against other States (see subchapter below).

The Assembly endorsed the work of the Special Committee against *Apartheid* (38/39 E), in particular the recommendations on its work and that of the Secretariat's Centre against *Apartheid*. Most of the Assembly's actions were based on recommendations of the Committee, which submitted its annual report to the Assembly in September. The Committee called on Governments to terminate all economic collaboration with South Africa, including direct and indirect trade, loans and investments. States were called on to prohibit their transnational corporations from dealing with South Africa and to ban air and shipping services to and from that country. The Economic and Social Council, in a July resolution (1983/74), also called for the termination of assistance by transnational corporations to South Africa. In its report to the Assembly, the United Nations Council for Namibia described economic relations with South Africa and affirmed that economic sanctions would be effective in bringing a halt to *apartheid* if implemented by South Africa's major Western trading partners.

The Commission on Human Rights as well as the Second World Conference to Combat Racism and Racial Discrimination also formulated measures to end *apartheid*.

The Commission in February appealed for action by the international community to save the lives of three members of ANC who had been sentenced to death by South Africa; the Security Council (in resolution 533(1983) adopted in June) called for commutation of the death sentences; and the Assembly (in resolution 38/17 adopted in November) expressed its indignation at the execution of the three men on 9 June. Other measures were taken on the situation in regard to political prisoners. The Assembly (in resolution 38/11 adopted in November), the Commission and the Committee against Apartheid rejected as unacceptable a new Constitution adopted by South Africa in November because it continued to deny political rights to the black majority.

In his annual report to the Assembly (p. 3), the Secretary-General stressed that the policy of *apartheid* was totally unacceptable.

A number of United Nations organizations co-operated in special aid programmes for the oppressed people of South Africa, including assistance to national liberation movements. The Assembly called for further inter-agency co-operation (resolution 38/39 A) in providing such assistance. Another source was the United Nations Trust Fund for South Africa, and the Assembly called for increased contributions to it (38/39 H).

Other United Nations action aimed at promoting the international campaign against *apartheid* was through dissemination of information to the public, co-operation with non-governmental organizations, and holding meetings, missions and observances.

General aspects

In 1983, both the Special Committee against *Apartheid* and the Second World Conference to Combat Racism and Racial Discrimination recommended ways for the United Nations, States and others to eradicate *apartheid*. The General Assembly endorsed the Committee's report in resolution 38/39 A and commended its Programme of Action in resolution 38/39 B; it also outlined policies and activities to achieve *apartheid*'s eradication.

Activities of the Committee against *Apartheid*. The Special Committee against *Apartheid*, in its annual report[1] to the General Assembly and the Security Council unanimously adopted in September, emphasized that Governments, organizations and individuals had a duty to take all action in their power to eradicate *apartheid* and to enable the South African people, through self-determination, to establish a democratic society. At stake were peace in southern Africa, the lives of the people in the region and their legitimate aspirations for political, economic and social development, as well as the commitment of the United Nations to promote international peace and security, international co-operation and human rights, and to eliminate colonialism and racism. As a result of the position taken by its Western permanent members, the Security Council had proved powerless to implement its resolutions calling for an end to *apartheid*, the release of South African political prisoners and the cessation of aggression by the *apartheid* régime against neighbouring States. In the Committee's view, the system of collective security, enshrined in the Charter of the United Nations, had been seriously undermined in relation to southern Africa.

The Committee considered it essential that the United Nations review the implementation of its resolutions on *apartheid* and South Africa's aggression and identify the causes of non-implementation, particularly the policies of States which failed to co-operate in international action, and consider measures to secure respect for the Organization's decisions. The Committee remained convinced that the United Nations had the power and was the most appropriate course to ensure an end to *apartheid*. The main obstacle had been the attitude of certain Western Powers and Israel which failed to implement United Nations resolutions and provided protection and assistance to South Africa. The Committee rejected the contention of certain Western Powers that their collaboration with that country and hostility to the national liberation movement was justified by their concern for a peaceful solution of the problems posed by *apartheid*.

The overwhelming majority of States, the Committee found, were committed to sanctions against South Africa and to support for the national liberation movement. International action to eliminate *apartheid*, it said, would require: recognition that *apartheid* could not be reformed but must be destroyed, that the régime was the sole enemy of peace and freedom in southern Africa, and that the struggle against *apartheid* contributed to the objectives of the United Nations; readiness by committed States, organizations and individuals to increase moral, political and material assistance to the liberation struggle; action to ensure that collaborators with *apartheid* desisted from such collaboration; and full commitment of the United Nations agencies. A more action-oriented approach should be adopted by the United Nations, following three main lines: total isolation of the *apartheid* régime; support to the oppressed people of South Africa and their national liberation movement; and encouragement of public action in support of United Nations efforts. In addition, it suggested that efforts be made to expose and dissuade collaboration with *apartheid*.

In view of South Africa's efforts to deprive the African majority of citizenship rights, the Committee considered it essential that the Council and the Assembly reconsider South Africa's membership in the United Nations and the legal status of the illegitimate *apartheid* régime, and called for an immediate suspension of its United Nations privileges.

According to the Committee, a few Western Governments and Israel as well as many transnational corporations which sought to profit from *apartheid* had hindered its eradication. The Committee

welcomed the intention of OAU to strengthen its offices in the major Western countries with the aim of persuading them to co-operate in action against *apartheid*. It commended the Secretary-General's statement to the press in Luanda, Angola, on 26 August, affirming his intention to further the objective of peace in southern Africa.

The Committee proposed to the Assembly a new Programme of Action against *Apartheid*,[2] outlined a work programme for itself and the United Nations Centre against *Apartheid*, and adopted a special report on relations between Israel and South Africa (see below).[3] Recommendations were made concerning relations with South Africa, sanctions and boycotts, military and nuclear relations, an oil embargo, transnational corporations in South Africa, the relations of IMF with South Africa, political prisoners and detained persons, the new South African constitution, women and children in South Africa, *apartheid* in sports, aid programmes for national liberation movements, inter-agency co-operation to help eradicate *apartheid*, public information, and South Africa's relations with front-line States of southern Africa (see below for further information on these subjects).

The Committee held meetings on 30 and 31 March in observance of its twentieth anniversary.

By a letter of 6 July,[4] India forwarded to the Council and the Assembly a communiqué on the situation in South Africa, adopted by the Co-ordinating Bureau of the Movement of Non-Aligned Countries on 28 June. The Bureau condemned the South African Government for its increased acts of internal repression and terrorism, destabilization and aggression against neighbouring States, and for the hanging on 9 June of three ANC members (see below).

Action by the Conference against racial discrimination. The Second World Conference to Combat Racism and Racial Discrimination,[5] held at Geneva from 1 to 12 August (see ECONOMIC AND SOCIAL QUESTIONS, Chapter XVIII), formulated measures aimed at ensuring the full and universal implementation of United Nations resolutions against racism, racial discrimination and *apartheid*. Convened in accordance with a 1980 General Assembly resolution,[6] it reviewed activities undertaken to achieve the goals of the Decade for Action to Combat Racism and Racial Discrimination (1973-1983), launched by the Assembly in 1973,[7] at the national, regional and international levels, and implementation of the Programme of Action adopted at the first World Conference in 1978.[8]

Although consensus was not achieved, the Second Conference adopted a Declaration and a Programme of Action for a new decade by a large majority. The Declaration stressed the need for national, regional and international action to eliminate *apartheid*, racism and racial discrimination, and recommended that the Assembly declare a Second Decade for Action to Combat Racism and Racial Discrimination, extending until 1993. Condemning *apartheid* as an institutionalized form of racism and a crime against humanity, the Conference stated that those who contributed to the maintenance of that system were accomplices in the perpetuation of that crime. The Programme of Action, approved by the Assembly in resolution 38/14, provided a set of proposals for international and national action against *apartheid* (see below for recommendations in specific areas) and for increased political and material assistance to the oppressed people of South Africa and Namibia.

The Conference affirmed that United Nations sanctions against South Africa must be implemented by all States in order to isolate it further. It requested the Security Council to consider imposing mandatory sanctions, under Chapter VII of the United Nations Charter. Assistance to and collaboration with the régime in the economic, military, nuclear and other fields constituted an impediment to the struggle against *apartheid*, it added.

Reaffirming the legitimacy of the struggle of the oppressed people of South Africa and Namibia and their national liberation movements for the elimination of *apartheid* by all available means, including armed struggle, the Conference stressed the special responsibility of the United Nations to provide them with moral, political and material assistance. It reiterated the commitment of the United Nations to the total eradication of *apartheid* and the establishment of a democratic society. It reaffirmed the international community's rejection of measures of the *apartheid* system which denied the black majority their legitimate rights to their land and to their citizenship of South Africa.

GENERAL ASSEMBLY ACTION

On 5 December, the General Assembly adopted resolution 38/39 A by recorded vote.

Situation in South Africa

The General Assembly,

Recalling and reaffirming its resolution 37/69 of 9 December 1982,

Having considered the report of the Special Committee against *Apartheid*, as well as its special report on recent developments concerning relations between Israel and South Africa,

Taking note of the declarations of conferences organized or co-sponsored by the Special Committee, namely, the International Conference of Trade Unions on Sanctions and Other Actions against the *Apartheid* Régime in South Africa, held at Geneva on 10 and 11 June 1983, the International Conference for Sanctions against *Apartheid* in Sports, held in London from 27 to 29 June 1983, the International Non-Governmental Organizations Conference of Action against *Apartheid* and Racism, held at

Geneva from 5 to 8 July 1983, the International Conference on the Alliance between South Africa and Israel, held at Vienna from 11 to 13 July 1983, and the Latin American Regional Conference for Action against *Apartheid*, held at Caracas from 16 to 18 September 1983,

Gravely concerned over the threat to international peace and security, and repeated breaches of the peace and acts of aggression, caused by the policies and actions of the racist minority régime of South Africa,

Condemning the racist minority régime of South Africa for its repeated defiance of the United Nations, its oppression of the great majority of the people of South Africa and its ruthless repression of all opponents of *apartheid*,

Strongly condemning the execution of Simon Mogoerane, Jerry Mosololi and Thabo Motaung, members of the African National Congress of South Africa, in defiance of appeals by the General Assembly and the Security Council,

Reaffirming that *apartheid* is a crime against humanity,

Strongly convinced that peace and stability in southern Africa require the total eradication of *apartheid* and the exercise of the right of self-determination by all the people of South Africa, irrespective of race, colour or creed,

Convinced that the racist minority régime of South Africa has been encouraged to perpetrate those criminal acts by the protection accorded to it by major Western Powers against international sanctions and by their continued collaboration with it,

Recognizing that the policies and actions of certain Western Powers and Israel are the main obstacles that have frustrated international efforts for the elimination of *apartheid*,

Condemning, in particular, the increased collaboration by the Government of the United States of America with the racist régime of South Africa, in pursuance of its policy of so-called "constructive engagement", which has encouraged the racist régime to entrench *apartheid*, intensify repression and escalate aggression against and destabilization of independent African States,

Condemning the increasing collaboration by Israel with the racist minority régime of South Africa, particularly in the military and nuclear fields,

Rejecting the so-called "constitutional proposals" by the racist minority régime of South Africa as designed to entrench *apartheid*,

Commending the unity of the oppressed people of South Africa in their opposition to the constitutional proposals as well as in their struggle for the elimination of *apartheid* and for the establishment of a democratic and non-racial society in a non-fragmented South Africa,

Taking note of the advance of the armed struggle for liberation undertaken by the national liberation movements in the face of brutal repression of peaceful protest,

Recognizing that the legitimate struggle of the South African people for liberation from *apartheid* is a contribution to the objectives of the United Nations,

Reaffirming that the elimination of *apartheid* constitutes a major objective of the United Nations,

Considering that all the organizations of the United Nations system have a duty to make a maximum contribution, within their mandates, to the international campaign against *apartheid*,

1.   *Endorses* the annual report of the Special Committee against *Apartheid* and its special report on recent developments concerning relations between Israel and South Africa;

2. *Declares* that the United Nations and the international community have a special responsibility towards the oppressed people of South Africa and their national liberation movements in their legitimate struggle for the elimination of *apartheid* and the establishment of a nonracial democratic society assuring human rights and fundamental freedoms to all the people of the country, irrespective of race, colour or creed;

3. *Again proclaims* that the national liberation movements of South Africa are the authentic representatives of the people of South Africa in their just struggle for national liberation;

4. *Recognizes* the right of the oppressed people and their national liberation movements to resort to all the means at their disposal, including armed struggle, in their resistance to the illegitimate racist minority régime of South Africa;

5. *Demands* that the racist minority régime of South Africa:

 (a) Release persons imprisoned or restricted for their opposition to *apartheid;*

 (b) Allow those who have been exiled for their opposition to *apartheid* to return unconditionally to their country;

 (c) Rescind bans on political and other organizations and media opposed to *apartheid;*

 (d) Terminate all political trials and all repressive measures against opponents of *apartheid;*

6. *Commends* the people of South Africa and their national liberation movements for the great advance in their struggle for national liberation;

7. *Commends* the oppressed people of South Africa and their national liberation movements, particularly the African National Congress of South Africa, for intensifying the armed struggle against the racist régime of South Africa;

8. *Calls upon* all States and organizations to provide all necessary moral, political and material assistance to the South African liberation movements recognized by the Organization of African Unity at this crucial stage in their struggle for liberation;

9. *Reaffirms* that freedom fighters of South Africa should be treated as prisoners of war in accordance with Additional Protocol I to the Geneva Conventions of 12 August 1949;

10. *Strongly condemns* the *apartheid* régime of South Africa for its brutal repression of all opponents of *apartheid*, its torture and killing of detainees, its execution of freedom fighters and its repeated acts of aggression, subversion and terrorism against independent African States;

11. *Condemns* as an international crime the policy of "bantustanization" designed to dispossess the African majority of its inalienable rights and to deprive it of citizenship, as well as the continuing forced removal of black people;

12. *Condemns* the policies of certain Western States, especially the United States of America, and Israel, and of their transnational corporations and financial institutions that have increased political, economic and military collaboration with the racist minority régime of South Africa despite repeated appeals by the General Assembly;

13. *Again urges* the Security Council to determine that the situation in South Africa and in southern Africa as a whole, resulting from the policies and actions of the *apartheid* régime of South Africa, constitutes a grave and growing threat to international peace and security, and to impose comprehensive and mandatory sanctions against the racist minority régime under Chapter VII of the Charter of the United Nations;

14. *Urgently calls upon* the International Monetary Fund to terminate credits or other assistance to the racist minority régime of South Africa;

15. *Again requests* the International Atomic Energy Agency to refrain from extending to South Africa any facilities which may assist it in its nuclear plans and, in particular, to exclude South Africa from all its technical working groups;

16. *Calls upon* all States that have not yet done so to accede to the International Convention on the Suppression and Punishment of the Crime of *Apartheid;*

17. *Decides* to continue the authorization of adequate financial provision in the regular budget of the United Nations to enable the South African liberation movements recognized by the Organization of African Unity—namely, the African National Congress of South Africa and the Pan Africanist Congress of Azania—to maintain offices in New York in order to participate effectively in the deliberations of the Special Committee and other appropriate bodies;

18. *Commends* the anti-*apartheid* and solidarity movements, religious bodies, trade unions, youth and student organizations and other groups engaged in campaigns for the isolation of the *apartheid* régime and assistance to the South African liberation movements recognized by the Organization of African Unity;

19. *Urges* all Governments to lend all appropriate assistance, including financial assistance, to such groups, especially in countries which continue to collaborate with the *apartheid* régime;

20. *Appeals* to journalists, writers, artists and other professionals working in the mass media, as well as their professional associations, to foster the role of the mass media in the dissemination of information commensurable with the urgent need to eradicate *apartheid;*

21. *Requests* the Secretary-General:

 (a) To instruct all relevant units of the Secretariat and all United Nations offices to promote the international campaign against *apartheid* in co-operation with the Special Committee;

 (b) To take all necessary measures to deny any facilities to, and to refrain from any investment in, corporations operating in South Africa;

 (c) To enter into urgent consultations with the International Monetary Fund and the International Atomic Energy Agency to secure their full co-operation in action against *apartheid*, in accordance with the resolutions of the General Assembly;

 (d) To prepare, in consultation with the executive heads of the organizations of the United Nations system, proposals for concerted action by all the agencies in the international campaign against *apartheid;*

22. *Requests* the Special Committee:

 (a) To prepare a report reviewing the implementation of the resolutions of the General Assembly and the Security Council on the problem of *apartheid* and the acts of aggression by the racist régime of South Africa, and the policies and actions of States which have failed to co-operate in international action;

 (b) To review developments concerning collaboration by the United States of America, Israel and other States

with the racist régime of South Africa, and to report from time to time, as appropriate;

(c) To pay special attention to mobilizing public opinion and encouraging public action against collaboration with South Africa.

General Assembly resolution 38/39 A

5 December 1983   Meeting 83   124-16-10 (recorded vote)

34-nation draft (A/38/L.20 & Corr.1); agenda item 32.

Sponsors: Afghanistan, Algeria, Angola, Benin, Bulgaria, Byelorussian SSR, Cuba, Czechoslovakia, Democratic Yemen, German Democratic Republic, Ghana, Guinea, Guyana, Hungary, Kenya, Lao People's Democratic Republic, Libyan Arab Jamahiriya, Madagascar, Malaysia, Mauritania, Mongolia, Mozambique, Nigeria, Poland, Sao Tome and Principe, Sierra Leone, Syrian Arab Republic, Uganda, Ukrainian SSR, United Republic of Cameroon, United Republic of Tanzania, Viet Nam, Zambia, Zimbabwe.

Financial implications. 5th Committee, A/38/654; S-G, A/C.5/38/53 & Corr.1.

Meeting numbers. GA 38th session: 5th Committee 51; plenary 60-63, 69-71, 83.

Recorded vote in Assembly as follows:

In favour: Afghanistan, Albania, Algeria, Angola, Antigua and Barbuda, Argentina, Bahamas, Bahrain, Bangladesh, Barbados, Belize, Benin, Bhutan, Bolivia, Botswana, Brazil, Bulgaria, Burma, Burundi, Byelorussian SSR, Cape Verde, Central African Republic, Chad, China, Colombia, Comoros, Congo, Costa Rica, Cuba, Cyprus, Czechoslovakia, Democratic Kampuchea, Democratic Yemen, Djibouti, Dominican Republic, Ecuador, Egypt, El Salvador, Equatorial Guinea, Ethiopia, Fiji, Gabon, Gambia, German Democratic Republic, Ghana, Guinea, Guinea-Bissau, Guyana, Haiti, Honduras, Hungary, India, Indonesia, Iran, Iraq, Jamaica, Jordan, Kenya, Kuwait, Lao People's Democratic Republic, Lebanon, Lesotho, Libyan Arab Jamahiriya, Madagascar, Malaysia, Maldives, Mali, Malta, Mauritania, Mauritius, Mexico, Mongolia, Morocco, Mozambique, Nepal, Nicaragua, Niger, Nigeria, Oman, Pakistan, Panama, Papua New Guinea, Peru, Philippines, Poland, Qatar, Romania, Rwanda, Saint Lucia, Saint Vincent and the Grenadines, Samoa, Sao Tome and Principe, Saudi Arabia, Senegal, Seychelles, Sierra Leone, Singapore, Solomon Islands, Somalia, Sri Lanka, Sudan, Suriname, Syrian Arab Republic, Thailand, Togo, Trinidad and Tobago, Tunisia, Turkey, Uganda, Ukrainian SSR, USSR, United Arab Emirates, United Republic of Cameroon, United Republic of Tanzania, Upper Volta, Uruguay, Vanuatu, Venezuela, Viet Nam, Yemen, Yugoslavia, Zaire, Zambia, Zimbabwe.

Against: Australia, Belgium, Canada, France, Germany, Federal Republic of, Iceland, Italy, Japan, Luxembourg, Netherlands, New Zealand, Norway, Paraguay, Portugal, United Kingdom, United States.

Abstaining: Austria, Denmark, Finland, Greece, Guatemala, Ireland, Ivory Coast, Malawi, Spain, Sweden.

Paragraph 12 was adopted by a recorded vote of 71 to 22, with 44 abstentions.

After the Assembly voted on resolution 38/39 A and the 10 others concerning *apartheid*, States explained their votes, giving reservations on the resolutions in general as well as on specific areas of disagreement.

Many countries objected to paragraphs in the various texts which singled out individual Member States. Some believed that those provisions were discriminatory, others mentioned the need to uphold the principle of universality, and still others objected on the grounds that the States mentioned were countries with which they had friendly relations. Countries expressing such reservations included: Canada, France, the Federal Republic of Germany, the Netherlands, New Zealand, the United Kingdom and the United States, which all voted against resolution 38/39 A; Greece, speaking for the 10 European Community (EC) members, Guatemala, Ireland and Lesotho, which abstained; Denmark (for the five Nordic countries, which either voted against or abstained); and the Bahamas, Bolivia, Burma, Colombia, Costa Rica, the Dominican Republic, Honduras, Morocco, Oman, Panama, Peru, the

Philippines, Singapore, Sri Lanka, Thailand, Turkey, Uruguay and Zaire, which voted in favour.

Chile, which did not participate in the vote on resolution 38/39 A, said that while it supported most of the resolutions on *apartheid*, it objected to singling out certain States, a practice which did not contribute to the support of the international community in the struggle against *apartheid* and undermined the credibility of Assembly resolutions on the subject.

Also expressing support for measures to eradicate *apartheid*, the Bahamas expressed the same reservations, adding that the practice would not enhance the chances of achieving the elimination of *apartheid*. Bolivia believed mentioning third parties by name was contrary to the friendly relations which it maintained with them. In Costa Rica's view, this practice might be discriminatory, and Morocco considered that it was not always justified. The Dominican Republic believed that the practice introduced extraneous counter-productive factors, that those paragraphs robbed the various resolutions of balance and objectivity, and that such action was at variance with the principle of universality. The Federal Republic of Germany agreed with the main thrust of the resolutions, but opposed singling out individual States and rejected the unfounded criticism directed against Western countries, suggesting that they encouraged South Africa to undertake criminal acts against its neighbours and assisted its pursuit of *apartheid*. According to New Zealand, singling out individual countries limited the effectiveness of the resolutions and might make them counter-productive. Having voted for all the resolutions concerning *apartheid*, Turkey believed that the ninth to eleventh preambular paragraphs and paragraphs 12 and 22 (b) of resolution 38/39 A, which mentioned certain States, were not balanced.

A number of States would have preferred calling for change in the *apartheid* system by peaceful means, rather than recognizing the right of the oppressed people to resort to armed struggle, as mentioned in paragraph 4. Austria, Canada, Denmark (for the Nordic countries) Greece (for the EC members), Honduras, Ireland, Italy, the Netherlands, Peru, Portugal and Uruguay expressed opposition to that provision. Honduras said its positive votes for the resolutions on *apartheid* did not signify support for the call for violent struggle, which dismissed any possibility of a peaceful solution and the duty of the international community to promote the exercise of the right of all peoples to self-determination by means of peaceful change leading to representative democracy.

Ethiopia supported paragraph 4 as appropriate and timely because it believed that a call on the masses of South Africa to give up the option of armed struggle, especially when the avenues for peaceful change had been blocked, would only be a call for their continued subjection. Similarly, Vanu-atu said that the world should not be deceived by talking of peaceful change in South Africa since *apart-heid* by its very nature was not peaceful.

Among those objecting to the language of the resolutions were Australia, Brazil, Burma, France, Guatemala, Malawi, Portugal and the United Kingdom. Australia, for example, said that it preferred practical measures rather than extravagant rhetoric to eradicate *apartheid*. Brazil voted in favour of all the resolutions on *apartheid* despite reservations about the language in some which did not seem to be conducive to the achievement of the common goals in respect of South Africa. Guatemala also felt that certain paragraphs could be improved. Despite its opposition to *apartheid*, the United Kingdom could not support resolution 38/39 A because of its extravagant language and extreme proposals which, it felt, debased the currency of the United Nations, making it easier for the proponents of *apartheid* to refuse to take account of the Assembly's views.

Ireland, Italy and the Netherlands opposed having the Assembly call on the Security Council to impose mandatory sanctions; Botswana and Lesotho expressed reservations on that paragraph. Ireland said that the formulation was inappropriate. Australia, Canada, Denmark (for the Nordic countries) and Uruguay believed that some provisions of the resolution went beyond the Assembly's responsibilities. Denmark said the Nordic countries adhered to the United Nations Charter and therefore had reservations with regard to formulations which failed to take into account that only the Council could adopt decisions binding on Member States.

In this connection, Canada objected to some recommendations in the resolutions which went beyond the competence of the Assembly, such as those calling for South Africa's exclusion from multilateral organizations. The Federal Republic of Germany, the United States and Uruguay regretted that efforts were being made to interfere with the work of independent international organizations. In particular, the United States objected to the attempt to politicize such technical bodies as IMF and IAEA. In addition, Botswana expressed reservations about paragraph 14 of resolution 38/39 A.

Greece, speaking for the EC countries, did not support calls to cut off all relations with South Africa; it said existing channels of communication should be used to permit free expression of views on all political, social and economic matters of concern to the people. Speaking similarly, Portugal believed that the total isolation of South Africa was unlikely to lead to a consensus, which must be the basis of effective international pressure to allow the South African majority to exercise fully its lawful rights.

The Netherlands did not recognize the national liberation movement of South Africa as the authentic representative of the people. Uruguay said all peoples must determine their own representation in accordance with the principle of self-determination, and added that United Nations efforts should aim at eradicating *apartheid* in South Africa and creating a democratic society without discrimination where the people might freely decide their own destiny.

In addition to the 11 resolutions on various aspects of *apartheid*, the Assembly, in resolution 38/17 on self-determination of peoples, condemned the policy of "bantustanization", the South African policy of confining homes of blacks to specific areas, and reiterated its support for the oppressed people of South Africa in its just and legitimate struggle against the racist régime.

In accordance with an Assembly decision that those having a special interest in the *apartheid* policies of South Africa should be heard, the Assembly's Special Political Committee, on 4 and 8 November, heard statements by 33 persons. Most of them represented non-governmental organizations and had submitted written requests to speak.[9] They were:

Arnold Braithwaite, United States Peace Council; Gordon Molyneux, American–South African Peoples' Friendship Association; Philip Oke, Christian Peace Conference; Wilfrid Grenville-Grey, International Defence and Aid Fund for Southern Africa; Jeanne M. Woods, Deborah Jackson, Wendy R. Brown and Emily M. Bass, National Conference of Black Lawyers; Vera Michelson, Capital District Coalition against *Apartheid* and Racism; Kaleem Shabazz; Ira L. Williams, Social Service Employees' Union Local 371; Tarig Iddinn, International Relations Committee of the National Association of Black Social Workers; Albie Sachs; Indris Naidoo; Vicki Erenstein, National Lawyers Guild; Beatrice von Roemer, International Confederation of Free Trade Unions; John R. Carlisle, Freedom in Sport; Robert Brown, All African People's Revolutionary Party; Lennox S. Hinds, International Association of Democratic Lawyers; Larry Holmes, People's Anti-War Mobilization; Elombe Brath, Patrice Lumumba Coalition; Pierre Sutton, National Association of Black-Owned Broadcasters; David Lampel, Inner City Broadcasting Corporation and the Radio Television News Directors Association; Enrique Kirved, Chile Democrático; William Booth, American Committee on Africa; Gay J. McDougall, Lawyers' Committee for Civil Rights Under Law; Stephen Paganuzzi, National Alliance against Racist and Political Repression; Romesh Chandra and James Lamond, World Peace Council; Una G. Mulzac, Liberation Bookstore, Inc.; Peter Sluiter, Holland Committee on Southern Africa and Working Group Kairos; Joseph Lowery, Southern Christian Leadership Conference; and Sylvia Hill, Southern Africa Support Project.

Chile, in a letter to the Committee Chairman of 31 October,[10] questioned the validity of the request of Chile Democrático to speak as an organization with "a special interest" in *apartheid*. Consequently, the Committee on 1 November referred the request to the Legal Counsel. However, on 8 November, the Chairman read out a subsequent letter from Chile, in which it said it had no objection to the granting of the request.

These events were reported to the Assembly by the Committee on 10 November.[11] The Assembly, on an oral proposal of its President, adopted decision 38/407 without vote.

Policies of *apartheid* of the Government of South Africa

At its 60th plenary meeting, on 17 November 1983, the General Assembly took note of the report of the Special Political Committee.

General Assembly decision 38/407

Adopted without vote

Oral proposal by President; agenda item 32.
Meeting numbers. GA 38th session: SPC 2, 17, 18, 20, 22, 23; plenary 60.

Programme of Action against *Apartheid*

The Special Committee against *Apartheid* adopted on 25 October 1983 a Programme of Action against *Apartheid*, which the Chairman transmitted on 26 October to the Secretary-General for the attention of the General Assembly.[2] The Programme was aimed at isolating the *apartheid* régime and assisting the oppressed people of South Africa and their liberation movements to eliminate *apartheid* and establish a democratic society with equal rights. It called for specific action by Governments, specialized agencies and other intergovernmental organizations, trade unions, churches, anti-*apartheid* and solidarity movements, other non-governmental organizations, individuals, the Secretary-General and the Centre against *Apartheid*, as well as by the Committee itself. Measures recommended in the Programme to implement United Nations resolutions concerned: official relations with South Africa; sanctions and boycotts; military and nuclear relations; the arms embargo; economic relations; an oil embargo; transnational corporations; relations between South Africa and IMF; political prisoners and other detained persons; women and children; *apartheid* in sports; national liberation movements; inter-agency co-operation; public information; non-governmental organizations; special meetings, missions and observances; the work programme of the Committee against *Apartheid;* and South Africa's relations with southern African States (see below under specific topics).

In its annual report to the Assembly,[1] the Committee recommended that the Programme be endorsed by the Assembly and disseminated as widely as possible. The Committee urged the Assembly and the Security Council to endorse the declarations of conferences it organized or co-sponsored during 1983: the International Conference of Trade Unions on Sanctions and other Ac-

tions against the *Apartheid* Régime in South Africa (Geneva, 10 and 11 June), the International Conference for Sanctions against *Apartheid* in Sports (London, 27-29 June), the International Non-Governmental Organizations Conference on Action against *Apartheid* and Racism (Geneva, 5-8 July), and the International Conference on the Alliance between South Africa and Israel (Vienna, Austria, 11-13 July).

GENERAL ASSEMBLY ACTION

The General Assembly took action on the Programme in resolution 38/39 B of 5 December, which it adopted by recorded vote.

Programme of Action against *Apartheid*

The General Assembly,

Seriously concerned over the grave situation in southern Africa resulting from the policies and actions of the racist régime of South Africa,

Anxious to promote more effective action by the international community to secure the speedy eradication of *apartheid* and the establishment of a non-racial democratic State in South Africa,

Recognizing the importance of concerted action by Governments, as well as intergovernmental and non-governmental organizations and individuals, for this purpose,

Taking note of the proclamation of the Second Decade to Combat Racism and Racial Discrimination, beginning on 10 December 1983,

Having considered the Programme of Action against *Apartheid*, adopted by the Special Committee against *Apartheid* on 25 October 1983,

1. *Commends* the Programme of Action against *Apartheid* to the attention of all Governments, intergovernmental and non-governmental organizations and individuals;

2. *Invites* all Governments, organizations and individuals to take effective action in the light of the Programme of Action, in close co-operation with the Special Committee against *Apartheid* and the Centre against *Apartheid* of the Secretariat;

3. *Requests* the Secretary-General, through the Department of Public Information of the Secretariat, to ensure the widest publicity for the Programme of Action and to instruct all United Nations offices to take appropriate action to promote its implementation.

General Assembly resolution 38/39 B

5 December 1983   Meeting 83   128-2-22 (recorded vote)

49-nation draft (A/38/L.21 & Add.1); agenda item 32.
Sponsors: Afghanistan, Algeria, Angola, Benin, Burundi, Byelorussian SSR, Cape Verde, Cuba, Democratic Yemen, Djibouti, Gabon, Gambia, German Democratic Republic, Ghana, Guinea, Guinea-Bissau, Guyana, Hungary, India, Indonesia, Kenya, Lao People's Democratic Republic, Libyan Arab Jamahiriya, Madagascar, Malaysia, Mali, Mauritania, Mongolia, Morocco, Mozambique, Nicaragua, Nigeria, Pakistan, Poland, Qatar, Rwanda, Sao Tome and Principe, Senegal, Sierra Leone, Somalia, Syrian Arab Republic, Togo, Uganda, Ukrainian SSR, United Republic of Cameroon, United Republic of Tanzania, Viet Nam, Zambia, Zimbabwe.
Financial implications. 5th Committee, A/38/654; S-G, A/C.5/38/53 & Corr.1.
Meeting numbers. GA 38th session: 5th Committee 51; plenary 60-63, 69-71, 83.
Recorded vote in Assembly as follows:

In favour: Afghanistan, Albania, Algeria, Angola, Antigua and Barbuda, Argentina, Bahamas, Bahrain, Bangladesh, Barbados, Belize, Benin, Bhutan, Bolivia,

Brazil, Bulgaria, Burma, Burundi, Byelorussian SSR, Cape Verde, Central African Republic, Chad, Chile, China, Colombia, Comoros, Congo, Costa Rica, Cuba, Cyprus, Czechoslovakia, Democratic Kampuchea, Democratic Yemen, Djibouti, Dominican Republic, Ecuador, Egypt, El Salvador, Equatorial Guinea, Ethiopia, Fiji, France, Gabon, Gambia, German Democratic Republic, Ghana, Guatemala, Guinea, Guinea-Bissau, Guyana, Haiti, Honduras, Hungary, India, Indonesia, Iran, Iraq, Ivory Coast, Jamaica, Jordan, Kenya, Kuwait, Lao People's Democratic Republic, Lebanon, Liberia, Libyan Arab Jamahiriya, Madagascar, Malawi, Malaysia, Maldives, Mali, Malta, Mauritania, Mauritius, Mexico, Mongolia, Morocco, Mozambique, Nepal, Nicaragua, Niger, Nigeria, Oman, Pakistan, Panama, Papua New Guinea, Peru, Philippines, Poland, Qatar, Romania, Rwanda, Saint Lucia, Saint Vincent and the Grenadines, Samoa, Sao Tome and Principe, Saudi Arabia, Senegal, Seychelles, Sierra Leone, Singapore, Solomon Islands, Somalia, Sri Lanka, Sudan, Suriname, Syrian Arab Republic, Thailand, Togo, Trinidad and Tobago, Tunisia, Turkey, Uganda, Ukrainian SSR, USSR, United Arab Emirates, United Republic of Cameroon, United Republic of Tanzania, Upper Volta, Uruguay, Vanuatu, Venezuela, Viet Nam, Yemen, Yugoslavia, Zaire, Zambia, Zimbabwe.

Against: United Kingdom, United States.

Abstaining: Australia, Austria, Belgium, Botswana, Canada, Denmark, Finland, Germany, Federal Republic of, Greece, Iceland, Ireland, Italy, Japan, Lesotho, Luxembourg, Netherlands, New Zealand, Norway, Portugal, Spain, Swaziland, Sweden.

In explanation of vote, Botswana said that it was obliged to abstain because of its geopolitical circumstances in southern Africa. Expressing its desire to continue its excellent relations with the Special Committee, France said that the non-binding terms of the resolution left it free to act on certain judicious proposals and to refrain from acting on a number of others that it deemed unacceptable.

Japan regretted that the Programme of Action was proposed without having been discussed in depth and despite the fact that a similar programme was adopted, after painstaking negotiations, at the Second World Conference to Combat Racism and Racial Discrimination (see ECONOMIC AND SOCIAL QUESTIONS, Chapter XVIII); however, it appreciated the fundamental philosophy of the resolution and some elements of the Programme.

The Netherlands found some formulae in the Programme unacceptable, but believed that its policy was in consonance with the resolution. Although there was much in the Programme that it supported, New Zealand was unable to go along with the calls for legislative and other action. Ireland spoke similarly and added that the text included inappropriate proposals which did not take into account the status of the specialized agencies or which were aimed specifically at some permanent members of the Security Council. Portugal found some of the language of the Programme unacceptable, in the light of its support for peaceful change in South Africa.

Relations with South Africa

During 1983, the General Assembly continued to press for breaking off all relations between South Africa and other States as a means of isolating that country and forcing it to abandon *apartheid*. In addition to the Assembly's calls for strengthening the arms embargo and ending various forms of economic assistance, several other United Nations bodies called for such action, including a halt to military and nuclear relations, an oil embargo, breaking off foreign investments and loans, and ending collaboration of transnational corporations (TNCs).

Activities of the Committee against *Apartheid*. The Special Committee against *Apartheid*, in both its annual report to the General Assembly[1] and its October 1983 Programme of Action against *Apartheid*[2] (see above), made recommendations regarding relations with South Africa. During the year, it also continued to follow developments concerning military, nuclear, economic and other collaboration with that country.

The Committee repeatedly condemned the continued collaboration of certain Western States and Israel, as well as TNCs, with South Africa as an essential cause for the escalation of that country's aggression against independent African States, and the continuation of its oppression against the South African people and its illegal occupation of Namibia. The Committee emphasized that the international campaign against *apartheid* had been undermined by the three Western permanent members of the Security Council which had prevented effective Council action in this regard, as well as by the States which had continued collaborating with South Africa and paid little heed to Assembly resolutions. In the Committee's view, those Council members had failed to be guided by their responsibilities under the United Nations Charter for the maintenance of international peace and security.

The Committee stated that the United States policy of "constructive engagement" with South Africa negated the limited measures it had previously undertaken to dissociate itself from *apartheid*, and that policy—diametrically opposed to United Nations action—had facilitated South Africa's obstructive manoeuvres as regards implementation of the Security Council's 1978 resolution outlining a plan for Namibia's independence.[12] This policy of "constructive engagement" was seen by South Africa as encouragement of its aggression.

Certain Western States had tried to resolve the situation in southern Africa by securing the South African Government while encouraging adjustments in its racial policies calculated to offset growing national and international opposition, thereby enabling it to gain time to entrench *apartheid*. The Committee rejected the contention of those States that South Africa was militarily and economically so powerful that peace could be secured only through accommodation, and rejected as well the United States policy in favour of "co-operation and peaceful coexistence" between southern African States and the régime, purportedly in the interest of South Africa's legitimate security concerns.

The Committee drew attention to the responsibility of the main trading partners of South Africa, namely, the United Kingdom, the United States, the Federal Republic of Germany, Japan, Italy and France, and to the involvement of TNCs, mainly from those countries. Israel, it said, had continued to collaborate with South Africa, especially in the military and nuclear fields (see below), while the local authorities in Taiwan had also developed military and other relations.

In the Committee's view, the *apartheid* régime could not have survived but for the fact that certain countries and vested interests had blocked international action and assisted it in all serious crises. The international community should insist that the Western Powers concerned respect United Nations decisions, recognize the legitimacy of the struggle for liberation from *apartheid*, and cease providing comfort and encouragement to the régime. The Committee's efforts to inform public opinion in the countries concerned had contributed to solidarity, as evidenced by the fact that the large majority of States which had not supported the Assembly's 1962 call for sanctions against South Africa[13] currently favoured such measures. As part of the pursuit to eliminate *apartheid*, the Committee said, the collaboration of certain States and foreign economic interests with South Africa should be publicized more widely, concerted action by committed States was required to end such collaboration, and it was necessary to isolate the régime totally.

In its Programme of Action,[2] the Committee called on Governments to persuade those countries which were collaborating to desist and to implement United Nations resolutions. It stated its intention to promote an international campaign against collaboration by Governments, banks and TNCs with South Africa.

Activities of the Council for Namibia. The United Nations Council for Namibia, in its annual report to the Assembly covering the period from 1 September 1982 to 31 August 1983,[14] stated that the United Kingdom, the United States, the Federal Republic of Germany, Japan, Switzerland, France, Israel and the local authorities in Taiwan continued to increase their collaboration with South Africa. (The Federal Republic of Germany, Japan and Switzerland had rejected those allegations.) That collaboration had contributed to the survival of *apartheid*, South Africa's occupation of Namibia and its aggression against African States.

As requested by the Assembly in 1982,[15] the Council continued to monitor the comprehensive boycott which in 1981 the Assembly had urged States to impose against South Africa in order to isolate it politically, economically, militarily and culturally.[16] Also in 1981, the Assembly had called on States to co-operate with the Council in fulfilling that task and to supply such information as it might

need.[17] Having sent communications to all States, the Council reported that, as of 24 January 1983, it had received replies from 31 States: 17 asserted they had never had any relations with South Africa; 8 stated that they had had some but had severed them in compliance with United Nations resolutions; 4 indicated their support for the relevant resolutions; and 2 indicated that when those resolutions had been adopted, they had reserved their position on some paragraphs because of geopolitical constraints. As of 30 June 1982, 24 States had diplomatic missions in South Africa and 36 had consular and/or honorary missions; South Africa had diplomatic missions in 25 States and consular and/or honorary missions in another 33. According to the Council, most countries which had political and diplomatic relations with South Africa prior to adoption of the 1981 resolutions had made little or no effort to discontinue them. A small number of those States had taken measures to terminate such contacts.

While an overwhelming majority of States, by boycotting South Africa, had demonstrated their adherence to the principle of self-determination and independence for the Namibian people, the support accorded to the South African Government by certain States not only militated against those efforts, but encouraged the régime to step up its *apartheid* policies and entrench its illegal occupation of Namibia (see TRUSTEESHIP AND DECOLONIZATION, Chapter III). The Council called for action by the international community to avert the threat to world peace and security resulting from the situation in southern Africa. If collaboration with South Africa continued, it said, the result would be violence between the forces of oppression, racism and colonialism and those seeking justice, equality and national independence.

In its annual report, the Council reproduced the Paris Declaration on Namibia, adopted by the International Conference in Support of the Struggle of the Namibian People for Independence. The Conference, held in Paris from 25 to 29 April 1983, was organized by the United Nations in consultation with OAU in accordance with a 1982 Assembly resolution.[18] It called for an end to the assistance rendered to South Africa by certain countries in the political, economic, military, nuclear and other fields, in defiance of the international community. It noted that the United States policy of "constructive engagement" with South Africa had further encouraged it to intensify repression of the people of South Africa and Namibia, aggression against the front-line States and intransigence over Namibian independence.

Action by the Commission on Human Rights. In a resolution of 15 February,[19] the Commission on Human Rights strongly condemned all collaboration, particularly in the nuclear, military and economic fields, with South Africa and called on the States concerned to cease such collaboration. It condemned the policies of those Western and other countries whose political, economic, military, nuclear, strategic, cultural and sports relations with the régime encouraged it to persist in suppressing the aspirations of peoples to self-determination and independence.

The General Assembly, in several 1983 resolutions, condemned relations with South Africa.

In resolution 38/39 A on the situation in South Africa, the Assembly on 5 December condemned the policies of certain Western States, especially the United States, and Israel, and of their TNCs and financial institutions that had increased collaboration with South Africa, and requested the Special Committee against *Apartheid* to report on such collaboration.

The Assembly, in resolution 38/36 A of 1 December, condemned the increased assistance by major Western countries and Israel to South Africa in several fields, which, the Assembly said, constituted hostile action against the people of Namibia and the front-line States since it was bound to strengthen the military capability of the régime. It requested States to take measures to isolate South Africa politically, economically, militarily and culturally, and asked the Council for Namibia to continue to follow such steps. The Council was also requested to report all contacts with South Africa.

In resolution 38/17 of 22 November, the Assembly condemned the policy of those Western States, Israel and others whose relations with South Africa encouraged its suppression of the aspirations of peoples to self-determination and independence.

In resolution 38/50 of 7 December, the Assembly called on States, particularly certain Western States, to take measures to terminate collaboration with South Africa and to refrain from entering into other relations with it in violation of resolutions of the United Nations and OAU. States were also requested to isolate South Africa politically, economically, militarily and culturally.

In resolution 38/14 of 22 November approving the Programme of Action for the Second Decade to Combat Racism and Racial Discrimination as recommended by the Second World Conference to Combat Racism and Racial Discrimination, the Assembly called for the termination of relations with South Africa. It approved the Conference's call to refrain from action that might imply recognition of or support for the illegal occupation of Namibia.

The Assembly also took action on sanctions and boycotts against South Africa, an arms embargo, economic sanctions, an oil embargo and *apartheid* in sports (see below).

Communications. Several 1983 letters to the Secretary-General from Member States dealt with specific relations with South Africa. On 3 November,[20] Turkey forwarded a letter of the same date from Nail Atalay, described as the representative of the Turkish Federated State of Cyprus, stating that a diplomat from the South African Embassy at Athens, Greece, was refused permission to enter the Turkish-controlled area of Cyprus because of South Africa's *apartheid* policy and alleging that he had been holding contacts in southern Cyprus with Greek Cypriot officials. Rejecting the allegations on 9 December,[21] Cyprus said it had not held contacts with anyone from the South African régime and had no relations with it. Iraq, on 16 December,[22] claimed that Iran, although denouncing South Africa for its *apartheid* policy, maintained diplomatic relations and collaborated in other ways with that régime.

Sanctions and boycotts

Activities of the Committee against *Apartheid*. The Special Committee against *Apartheid* stressed the importance of comprehensive and mandatory sanctions against South Africa, to be instituted by the Security Council under Chapter VII of the United Nations Charter, as a means to isolate the *apartheid* régime. In its annual report to the General Assembly,[1] the Committee gave priority to an embargo on all military and nuclear co-operation with South Africa, an oil embargo and other economic measures (see below). It also recognized the importance of sports, cultural, consumer and other boycotts, campaigns against TNCs operating in South Africa and related actions which enabled large segments of the public to reinforce governmental action.

Since the Western permanent members of the Security Council had prevented mandatory sanctions, the Committee called on countries which had not done so to end collaboration with the régime and to exercise their influence to persuade those Council members to fulfil their responsibilities regarding the threat to international peace and security resulting from South Africa's *apartheid* and aggression. The Committee welcomed the decision of the Assembly of Heads of State and Government of OAU, at its June 1983 session at Addis Ababa, Ethiopia, to seek a Council meeting to strengthen the arms embargo and impose comprehensive and mandatory sanctions. The Committee recommended that the General Assembly call on Governments to implement United Nations resolutions on boycotts against South Africa, terminate cultural agreements with that country, and take appropriate action with respect to persons visiting there for sports and cultural activities who were named in lists prepared by the Committee.

In its October 1983 Programme of Action against *Apartheid*,[2] the Committee called on Governments to support and facilitate the Council's imposition of sanctions against South Africa, and to implement all measures to isolate it politically, economically, militarily and culturally, pending mandatory sanctions by the Council. The Committee urged corporations and employers to persuade employers' organizations to work for a policy of sanctions against South Africa. With the assistance of the Centre against *Apartheid*, the Committee intended to promote an international campaign for sanctions.

With regard to educational, cultural, sporting and other collaboration, the Committee stated that Governments should suspend such exchanges with the régime and with organizations or institutions in South Africa which practised *apartheid*. Governments were urged to: abrogate arrangements with South Africa in such areas; cease cultural and academic collaboration, including research and the exchange of scientists, students and academic personalities; prevent promotion of tourism to South Africa; terminate visa-free entry privileges to South Africans; and take appropriate action with respect to those sportsmen, entertainers and others who had been named by the Committee. Noting that public organizations could contribute to strengthening the sporting and cultural boycott of South Africa, the Committee recommended that those organizations: persuade artists, musicians and entertainers to boycott South Africa; encourage authors, painters and film-makers to refuse to allow their works to be performed or exhibited in South Africa; support measures against individuals and institutions which defied the cultural boycott; and co-operate with the Committee in compiling and publicizing registers of collaborators with South Africa in the cultural field and in securing action against those violating the boycott. Writers, artists and musicians were called on not to participate in cultural events in South Africa, to ensure that their trade union supported the cultural boycott, and to give performances for assistance to South African refugees or their national liberation movement.

In this connection, the Committee, in order to facilitate appropriate action by Governments, organizations and individuals committed to ending *apartheid*, published on 26 October a register of entertainers, actors and others who had performed since 1981 in South Africa. The Committee intended to keep the list up to date. The Chairman of its Sub-Committee on the Implementation of United Nations Resolutions and Collaboration with South Africa, James Victor Gbeho (Ghana), met with members of the United States–based Coalition to End Cultural Collaboration with South Africa to consult on ways to promote the cultural boycott. They agreed that a hearing on a cultural boycott organized by the Committee would be desirable in order to maximize public-

ity, bring together activist organizations and organizers of boycotts, and launch the cultural boycott of South Africa in the United States. The Committee, having promoted the establishment in 1982 of a Committee of Artists of the World against *Apartheid*, supported an international art exhibit against *apartheid* organized by those artists in Paris from 22 November to 30 December 1983. An exhibition by 15 artists who contributed to the Committee of Artists was held in Paris on 21 March.

The Committee against *Apartheid* and the Workers' Group of the Governing Body of the International Labour Organisation (ILO), in co-operation with the United Nations Council for Namibia, OAU and the Organization of African Trade Union Unity, organized at Geneva on 10 and 11 June the International Conference of Trade Unions on Sanctions and Other Actions against the *Apartheid* Régime in South Africa. In addition to supporting international action to eliminate *apartheid* through sanctions, its objective was to promote solidarity with, and assistance to, the black trade-union movement of South Africa. The Conference, in a declaration transmitted to the Secretary-General on 11 June,[23] requested the United Nations to expand sanctions against South Africa and make them mandatory. It called on Governments to promote mandatory economic sanctions and, pending Security Council action, to take unilateral and regional measures by severing political, cultural, sports, commercial and diplomatic relations. The Conference urged all workers and their trade-union organizations to bring pressure to bear on Governments to end relations and called for specific sanctions and boycotts (see below). The report of the Special Committee's representatives to the Conference was adopted by the Committee on 27 July.

A mission sent by the Committee to the front-line States of Angola, Botswana, the United Republic of Tanzania, Zambia and Zimbabwe to gather information on South Africa's aggression (see below) issued a report in May[24] in which it recommended that the Council adopt effective measures, under Chapter VII of the United Nations Charter, to prevent further aggression by that country. In its view, comprehensive or selective mandatory sanctions would be the most appropriate and effective means to do so, and all States must be called on to end collaboration with South Africa in the political, diplomatic, economic, trade, military, nuclear and other fields. In addition, those permanent members of the Council which supported South Africa should be urged to cease their opposition to sanctions.

Action by the Conference for Namibia's independence. In its Paris Declaration on Namibia, reproduced by the United Nations Council for Namibia in its annual report to the General Assembly,[14] the International Conference in Support of the Struggle of the Namibian People for Independence expressed concern that Namibia's independence continued to be obstructed by South Africa's refusal to comply with the independence plan for Namibia endorsed by the Security Council in 1978[12] (see TRUSTEESHIP AND DECOLONIZATION, Chapter III). Expressing dismay at the Council's failure to discharge its responsibilities for the maintenance of international peace and security owing to the opposition of its Western permanent members, the Conference affirmed that sanctions under Chapter VII of the Charter were the only available means to ensure South Africa's compliance with United Nations decisions and to prevent further armed conflict in the region. Therefore, the Conference called on the Council to consider further action to implement its 1978 resolution. Pending the imposition of comprehensive and mandatory sanctions by the Council, the Conference urged States to adopt economic measures against South Africa and commended those that had already done so.

The Conference's Committee of the Whole, meeting from 26 to 28 April, supported the decisions of the OAU Co-ordinating Committee for the Liberation of Africa (Arusha, United Republic of Tanzania, 10-12 February), the Seventh Conference of Heads of State or Government of Non-Aligned Countries (New Delhi, India, 7-11 March) and the International Conference in Solidarity with the Front-line States (Lisbon, Portugal, 25-27 March) to urge the Council urgently to resume full responsibility for the speedy implementation of the 1978 resolution. According to the Committee of the Whole, the Council should respond to the overwhelming demand of the international community by immediately imposing sanctions, including an arms embargo (see below). In the mean time, the Committee requested Governments to apply sanctions unilaterally and collectively.

Activities of the Council for Namibia. The Council for Namibia, having considered the conclusions of the International Conference and the Committee of the Whole, concluded that it was of the utmost importance that the Security Council proceed without delay to impose comprehensive and mandatory sanctions against South Africa. The Security Council, it said, had been repeatedly thwarted from taking that action by its three Western permanent members, which should bring their policies into accord with the wish of the international community.

Action by the Conference against racial discrimination. The need for sanctions against South Africa was also stressed in the Declaration and Programme of Action for the Second Decade to Combat Racism and Racial Discrimination (1983-1993) adopted by the Second World Conference to Combat Racism and Racial Discrimination.[5]

In the Declaration, the Conference reaffirmed that United Nations sanctions against South Africa must be implemented strictly and faithfully by all States in order to isolate it further. Assistance and collaboration in the economic, military, nuclear and other fields constituted an impediment to the struggle against *apartheid*. The Conference believed that it was the obligation of all Governments to develop legislation that would prevent TNCs from following those practices which assisted and supported the régime or which exploited the natural resources and people of South Africa and Namibia.

In the Programme of Action for the new decade, approved by the General Assembly (resolution 38/14), the Conference called on the Security Council to consider urgently the imposition of mandatory sanctions, in particular a ban on nuclear collaboration, an arms embargo, termination of foreign investments and loans, an oil embargo and a trade boycott (see below). The Conference called on States to refrain from any relations with South Africa which could contribute to the continuance of *apartheid*, and specifically to sever all sporting, cultural and scientific links.

GENERAL ASSEMBLY ACTION

On 5 December, the General Assembly adopted resolution 38/39 D by recorded vote.

Sanctions against South Africa

The General Assembly,

Considering that the policies and actions of the racist régime of South Africa, its military buildup and its nuclear plans constitute a grave threat to international peace and security,

Reaffirming its conviction that comprehensive and mandatory sanctions imposed by the Security Council under Chapter VII of the Charter of the United Nations, universally applied, are the most appropriate and effective means by which the international community can assist the legitimate struggle of the oppressed people of South Africa and discharge its responsibilities for the maintenance of international peace and security,

Recalling the Paris Declaration on Sanctions against South Africa,

Considering that political, economic, military and any other collaboration with the *apartheid* régime of South Africa encourages its persistent intransigence and defiance of the international community and its escalating repression, aggression and destabilization,

Recognizing the urgent need for the termination of military, nuclear, economic and technological collaboration with the racist régime of South Africa, as well as the cessation of sports, cultural and other relations with South Africa,

Gravely concerned that the racist régime of South Africa has continued, despite the mandatory arms embargo imposed by the Security Council in resolution 418(1977)

of 4 November 1977, to obtain military equipment and ammunition, as well as technology and know-how to develop its armaments industry, and to acquire nuclear-weapon capability,

Deploring the attitude of those Western permanent members of the Security Council that have so far prevented the Council from adopting comprehensive sanctions against South Africa under Chapter VII of the Charter,

Deploring also the attitude of those States, in particular the United States of America and Israel, which have continued and increased their political, economic and other collaboration with South Africa,

Gravely concerned over the activities of those transnational corporations that continue to collaborate with the *apartheid* régime and of those financial institutions that have continued to provide loans and credits to South Africa, and over the failure of the States concerned to take effective action to prevent such collaboration,

Expressing serious concern over the greatly increased trade with, investments in, and loans to South Africa by the United Kingdom of Great Britain and Northern Ireland, the United States of America, the Federal Republic of Germany and Switzerland,

Commending all States that have taken effective measures, in accordance with relevant resolutions, for the elimination of *apartheid* in South Africa,

Expressing great appreciation to intergovernmental and non-governmental organizations, in particular anti-*apartheid* and solidarity movements, trade unions and religious bodies, as well as city and other local authorities, that have taken action to isolate the racist régime of South Africa and to promote support for comprehensive sanctions against that régime,

Commending athletes, entertainers and others who demonstrated solidarity with the oppressed people of South Africa by complying with the boycotts of South Africa,

Commending the Special Committee against *Apartheid* for its activities, with the assistance of the Centre against *Apartheid* of the Secretariat and the co-operation of Governments and organizations, in promoting the widest possible support for sanctions against South Africa,

Taking note of the decision of the Assembly of Heads of State and Government of the Organization of African Unity at its nineteenth ordinary session, held at Addis Ababa from 6 to 12 June 1983, calling for an early convening of the Security Council for the purpose of strengthening the arms embargo and imposing comprehensive and mandatory sanctions against South Africa under Chapter VII of the Charter,

1. *Again requests* the Security Council to consider action under Chapter VII of the Charter of the United Nations towards comprehensive and mandatory sanctions against South Africa and, in particular, to take measures:

(a) To monitor effectively and to reinforce the mandatory arms embargo against South Africa;

(b) To prohibit all co-operation with South Africa in the military and nuclear fields by Governments, corporations, institutions and individuals;

(c) To prohibit imports of any military equipment or component parts from South Africa;

(d) To prevent any co-operation or association with South Africa by any military alliances;

(e) To impose an effective embargo on the supply of oil and oil products to South Africa and on all assistance to the oil industry in South Africa;

(f) To prohibit financial loans to and new investments in South Africa, as well as all promotion of trade with South Africa;

2. *Requests* all States to take all appropriate measures to facilitate such action by the Security Council;

3. *Requests* all States concerned to take action against corporations and other interests that violate the mandatory arms embargo against South Africa or that are involved in the illicit supply to South Africa of oil from States that have imposed an embargo against South Africa;

4. *Invites* all Governments and organizations to assist, in consultation with the national liberation movements of South Africa and Namibia, persons compelled to leave South Africa because of their objection, on the grounds of conscience, to serving in the military or police force of the *apartheid* régime;

5. *Encourages* action by Governments, organizations and individuals in support of sports, cultural, consumer and other boycotts of South Africa;

6. *Requests and authorizes* the Special Committee against *Apartheid* to intensify its activities for the total isolation of the racist régime of South Africa and for promoting comprehensive and mandatory sanctions against South Africa.

General Assembly resolution 38/39 D

5 December 1983   Meeting 83   122-10-18 (recorded vote)

36-nation draft (A/38/L.23 & Corr.1); agenda item 32.

Sponsors: Afghanistan, Algeria, Angola, Benin, Bulgaria, Byelorussian SSR, Cape Verde, Cuba, Democratic Yemen, German Democratic Republic, Ghana, Guinea, Guinea-Bissau, Guyana, Hungary, Kenya, Lao People's Democratic Republic, Libyan Arab Jamahiriya, Madagascar, Malaysia, Mauritania, Mongolia, Mozambique, Nigeria, Qatar, Sao Tome and Principe, Senegal, Sierra Leone, Syrian Arab Republic, Uganda, Ukrainian SSR, United Republic of Cameroon, United Republic of Tanzania, Viet Nam, Zambia, Zimbabwe.

Meeting numbers. GA 38th session: plenary 60-63, 69-71, 83.

Recorded vote in Assembly as follows:

In favour: Afghanistan, Albania, Algeria, Angola, Antigua and Barbuda, Argentina, Bahamas, Bahrain, Bangladesh, Barbados, Belize, Benin, Bhutan, Bolivia, Brazil, Bulgaria, Burma, Burundi, Byelorussian SSR, Cape Verde, Central African Republic, Chad, China, Colombia, Comoros, Congo, Costa Rica, Cuba, Cyprus, Czechoslovakia, Democratic Kampuchea, Democratic Yemen, Djibouti, Dominican Republic, Ecuador, Egypt, El Salvador, Equatorial Guinea, Ethiopia, Fiji, Gabon, Gambia, German Democratic Republic, Ghana, Guinea, Guinea-Bissau, Guyana, Haiti, Honduras, Hungary, India, Indonesia, Iran, Iraq, Jamaica, Jordan, Kenya, Kuwait, Lao People's Democratic Republic, Lebanon, Libyan Arab Jamahiriya, Madagascar, Malaysia, Maldives, Mali, Malta, Mauritania, Mauritius, Mexico, Mongolia, Morocco, Mozambique, Nepal, Nicaragua, Niger, Nigeria, Oman, Pakistan, Panama, Papua New Guinea, Peru, Philippines, Poland, Qatar, Romania, Rwanda, Saint Lucia, Saint Vincent and the Grenadines, Samoa, Sao Tome and Principe, Saudi Arabia, Senegal, Seychelles, Sierra Leone, Singapore, Solomon Islands, Somalia, Sri Lanka, Sudan, Suriname, Syrian Arab Republic, Thailand, Togo, Trinidad and Tobago, Tunisia, Turkey, Uganda, Ukrainian SSR, USSR, United Arab Emirates, United Republic of Cameroon, United Republic of Tanzania, Upper Volta, Uruguay, Vanuatu, Venezuela, Viet Nam, Yemen, Yugoslavia, Zaire, Zambia, Zimbabwe.

Against: Belgium, Canada, France, Germany, Federal Republic of, Japan, Luxembourg, Netherlands, Portugal, United Kingdom, United States.

Abstaining: Australia, Austria, Botswana, Denmark, Finland, Greece, Guatemala, Iceland, Ireland, Italy, Ivory Coast, Lesotho, Malawi, New Zealand, Norway, Spain, Swaziland, Sweden.

The eighth and tenth preambular paragraphs were adopted by recorded votes of 71 to 22, with 40 abstentions, and 72 to 22, with 40 abstentions, respectively.

Speaking in explanation of vote, Canada, the Federal Republic of Germany, Maldives, Morocco,

Sri Lanka, Thailand, Turkey and the United Kingdom said they opposed those paragraphs singling out particular Member States for their relations with South Africa. Thailand explained that it had reservations on the eighth and tenth preambular paragraphs because they made specific references to countries with which it had diplomatic relations, and it believed that selectively naming countries was not beneficial to positive action. Turkey believed that those paragraphs were not balanced and also had a reservation with regard to the reference to a particular group of countries in the seventh preambular paragraph; a few exceptional provisions of the text also might not conform entirely to existing Turkish laws and it supported those provisions to the extent that they were compatible with those laws.

Taking the opposite view, Ethiopia said it was convinced that this resolution and those on Israel–South Africa relations and military and nuclear relations with South Africa (see below) were factual in their comments regarding the collaboration of certain countries with South Africa.

Malawi, Portugal and the United Kingdom disapproved of certain language in the resolution. Portugal said its negative vote was due to elements of verbal violence, discriminatory references and imprecise language, contradicting its policy of support for peaceful change in South Africa which required channels of communication to facilitate constructive political initiatives. The United Kingdom found the language extravagant and the proposals extreme.

According to Canada and Japan, the resolution went beyond the competence of the Assembly. In particular, Canada mentioned those recommendations involving economic sanctions. Japan believed that the resolution would pre-empt decisions of the Security Council which alone had the authority to impose such sanctions, and it opposed paragraph 1 listing possible sanctions whose implementation Japan could not ensure. In this regard, Costa Rica felt that the Assembly could urge the Council to consider a situation, but it was up to the latter to determine the course it wished to follow.

Ireland, Japan and the Netherlands questioned the effectiveness or the wisdom of imposing mandatory sanctions. Ireland supported applying certain selective measures and would have supported many of those in paragraph 1, but it had doubts over comprehensive sanctions at the current juncture; it preferred a course of steady and graduated pressure for change through carefully chosen, selective sanctions. Sharing the latter view, the Netherlands added that it wished to keep open those channels of communication through which contacts could be made to stimulate forces of peaceful change in South Africa—an approach

which did not allow for the scope of action in the resolution.

Botswana said it abstained because of its own geopolitical circumstances. Speaking on behalf of the five Nordic countries, Denmark cited the reasons it mentioned in explanation of vote on resolution 38/39 A (see above).

The Assembly's call for sanctions against South Africa was reiterated in a number of other 1983 resolutions.

In resolution 38/39 A, it again urged the Security Council to determine that the situation resulting from *apartheid* policies constituted a threat to international peace and security and to impose comprehensive and mandatory sanctions against the South African régime.

The Assembly, in resolution 38/36 A, repeated its call to the Council and requested the Secretary-General to seek to ensure that banks, corporations and other institutions with which the United Nations had contracts were in compliance with sanctions policies.

Besides another call for sanctions in resolution 38/36 B, the Assembly expressed dismay that the three Western permanent members of the Council had prevented measures against South Africa and stated that sanctions would ensure that country's compliance with United Nations decisions.

In resolution 38/50, the Assembly appealed to non-governmental organizations to continue to mobilize international public opinion for the enforcement of sanctions.

By decision 38/419, the Assembly recalled its 1981 resolution[16] urging States to cease all dealings with South Africa in order to isolate it totally.

Military and nuclear relations
Activities of the Committee against *Apartheid*.
The Special Committee against *Apartheid*, in its annual report to the General Assembly,[1] stated that the mandatory arms embargo against South Africa, instituted by the Security Council in 1977,[25] had failed because it was being flouted in letter and spirit by some Governments and vested interests. With the assistance of certain Western States and Israel, South Africa had expanded its military establishment. It had been able to obtain an enormous amount of military equipment and technology, to build up its domestic arms industry and to acquire nuclear capability because of the collusion of those States and a number of TNCs. Assured of protection by certain Western States from effective international action, South Africa had claimed the right to invade or subvert any African State supporting liberation, and it had demanded that neighbouring States deny asylum and humanitarian assistance to refugees from *apartheid* by threatening or using military, eco-

nomic and other actions. In addition, the local authorities in Taiwan had developed extensive military and other relations with South Africa, and the Committee noted that the "Chief of the General Staff of the Armed Forces" of Taiwan had visited South Africa and Namibia in April 1983 and pledged co-operation with the régime.

The Committee urged the Security Council to take action, without delay, on the proposals for strengthening the arms embargo submitted in 1980[26] by the Security Council Committee established by resolution 421(1977)[27] concerning the question of South Africa, and to take mandatory action to stop nuclear collaboration with South Africa. In the Committee's view, such action was necessary in view of the violations of the arms embargo and the inadequacy of monitoring it.

In its Programme of Action adopted in October,[2] the Special Committee called on Governments to implement fully the arms embargo and in this connection outlined specific action that States should take to ensure its effectiveness. In addition to ceasing any provision to South Africa of arms, military equipment and spare parts, States were called on to: abrogate contractual arrangements with South Africa for arms and equipment; prohibit investment in, or technical assistance for, the manufacture of such items; prohibit the transfer of related technology; refrain from providing training for the South African armed forces; refrain from joint military exercises with that country; prohibit military visits and other military communications; prohibit the provision of nuclear equipment or technology that would enable South Africa to acquire nuclear weapon technology; ensure the termination of all co-operation by IAEA with South Africa, except for the inspection of nuclear facilities there under safeguards agreements; and assist persons compelled to leave South Africa because of their objections, on the grounds of conscience, to serving in the military or police forces.

Public organizations were called on to alert the public to the threat posed by South Africa's military and nuclear buildup and to campaign for an end to all forms of military and nuclear collaboration with the régime. They were urged to persuade Governments to enforce the arms embargo and to end nuclear collaboration, to expose all breaches of the embargo, and to protest any governmental action undermining it. Peace organizations were urged to take similar action.

The Committee, with the assistance of the Centre against *Apartheid*, planned to promote international campaigns against all forms of nuclear co-operation with South Africa.

The Sub-Committee on the Implementation of United Nations Resolutions and Collaboration with South Africa, in a report issued by decision of the Committee on 25 October on the development of South Africa's nuclear capability,[28] described flashes in 1979 and 1980 that could be ascribed to nuclear testing by South Africa and reports of co-operation in the nuclear field between that country and Israel. The Sub-Committee noted the policy of the current United States Administration of "constructive engagement" with South Africa in the nuclear field as well as the growing nuclear capability of South Africa. It stated that evidence indicated that the United States had identified its own security interests in southern Africa with those of South Africa. The report also gave updated information on South Africa's nuclear programme and facilities and its role in the world uranium market. Despite the international condemnation of South Africa and its collaborators for the development of its nuclear capability, the Sub-Committee said there was continued assistance to and relations with the nuclear programme by Western States, Israel, Japan and Taiwan, and South Africa remained a supplier of raw uranium in the world market. South Africa persisted in efforts to achieve self-sufficiency in the production of armaments to suit its perception of threats to its security. Given these conditions, the Sub-Committee believed the strategy of denial to be the only logically consistent alternative.

The IAEA Director-General, by a letter of 21 October to the Chairman of the Committee against *Apartheid*,[29] transmitted a 14 October resolution adopted by the IAEA General Conference on South Africa's nuclear capabilities. The Conference demanded that South Africa submit all its nuclear installations to IAEA inspection and called on IAEA member States to end nuclear co-operation with South Africa and, in particular, to terminate all transfer of fissionable material and technology to it which could be used for developing nuclear arms.

The International Conference on the Alliance between South Africa and Israel (Vienna, 11-13 July), organized by the Special Committee, condemned Israel for its collaboration with South Africa, particularly military and nuclear relations (see below).

Activities of the Council for Namibia. The United Nations Council for Namibia, in its 1983 report to the General Assembly,[14] described contacts between Member States and South Africa in the military and nuclear fields since 1981, when the Assembly had requested States to cease any provision to that country of arms and related equipment.[17] It found that such contacts between the régime and the United States, the United Kingdom, France, the Federal Republic of Germany, Belgium, Israel, Japan, the Netherlands, Switzerland and other countries had increased. (Belgium, the Federal Republic of Germany, Japan and Switzerland rejected those allegations.) The Armaments Development and Production Corporation, owned by the South African Government, had been able to produce under licence and acquire through purchases from States which violated the arms embargo a wide range of sophisticated arms and related material. Of particular concern was the growing relationship between South Africa and Israel in the military and nuclear fields. The military collaboration aggravated the instability in southern Africa, resulting from South Africa's *apartheid* policies, illegal occupation of Namibia and aggression against neighbouring States.

According to the Council, the most harmful blow to the international effort to obtaining South Africa's withdrawal from Namibia was the current United States policy of "constructive engagement" with South Africa, entailing a relaxation of the embargo on selling non-military items to South Africa's police and military and of the ban against visits to the United States by high-ranking South African military officers.

The Council said that during the past decade South Africa, with the collaboration of the United States, the United Kingdom, France, the Federal Republic of Germany, Belgium, Israel, Japan, the Netherlands and Switzerland, had been able to become a near-nuclear State. This collaboration had taken various forms, including assistance in extracting and processing Namibian uranium, the supply of nuclear equipment, transfers of technology, provision of training and exchange of scientists.

Action by the Conference for Namibia's independence. The International Conference in Support of the Struggle of the Namibian People for Independence adopted the Paris Declaration on Namibia, which was reproduced in the annual report of the Council.[14] The Conference denounced the massive buildup of South African forces in Namibia, South Africa's recruitment and training of Namibians for tribal armies and its recruitment of mercenaries and other foreign agents in order to carry out its policies of internal repression and external aggression. The Conference called on States to co-operate in preventing the recruitment, training and transit of mercenaries for service in Namibia. It believed that South Africa's acquisition of nuclear weapons capability was intended to intimidate States in the region. The assistance to South Africa by certain Western countries and Israel in this area belied their stated opposition to *apartheid* and made them willing partners of its policies. Expressing concern at reports regarding military agreements between South Africa and other States, the Conference said that such arrangements would constitute a breach of

the Security Council's arms embargo and would pose a threat to the security of Africa. Condemning South Africa's armed aggression and military, political and economic destabilization against States in the region, the Conference said that increased assistance was necessary to enable those States to defend their sovereignty and territorial integrity and to free themselves from economic dependence on South Africa.

The Conference's Committee of the Whole made similar statements in a report adopted on 29 April. It condemned South Africa's massive military buildup in Namibia, its recruitment of Namibians for tribal armies and the use of mercenaries to suppress the Namibian people. It condemned collaboration with South Africa in general, and in particular the nuclear collusion of the United States and Israel, and called on States to refrain from supplying South Africa directly or indirectly with installations that might enable it to produce nuclear materials, reactors or other military equipment.

Action by the Commission on Human Rights. In a resolution of 18 February,[30] the Commission on Human Rights called on States where the banks, TNCs and other organizations named in a report of its Special Rapporteur, Ahmed Mohamed Khalifa, were based to end all technological assistance or collaboration in the manufacture of arms and military supplies in South Africa, and in particular to cease all collaboration with South Africa in the nuclear field (see ECONOMIC AND SOCIAL QUESTIONS, Chapter XVIII).

Action by the Conference against racial discrimination. The Second World Conference to Combat Racism and Racial Discrimination,[5] in its Programme of Action for the Second Decade to Combat Racism and Racial Disrimination (1983-1993), called on the Security Council to consider urgently the imposition of mandatory sanctions, including the cessation of all collaboration with South Africa in the nuclear field, and the prohibition of all technological assistance or collaboration in the manufacture of arms in South Africa and the provision of military supplies to it. The Programme of Action was approved by the General Assembly in resolution 38/14.

GENERAL ASSEMBLY ACTION

By recorded vote on 5 December, the General Assembly adopted resolution 38/39 G.

Military and nuclear collaboration with South Africa
The General Assembly,
Reaffirming its resolutions on military and nuclear collaboration with South Africa, in particular its resolution 37/69 D of 9 December 1982,
Recalling its resolutions concerning the denuclearization of the continent of Africa,

Recalling also Security Council resolutions 418(1977) of 4 November 1977, 421(1977) of 9 December 1977 and 473(1980) of 13 June 1980,

Recalling that the Security Council determined in resolution 418(1977), under Chapter VII of the Charter of the United Nations, that the acquisition by South Africa of arms and related *matériel* constituted a threat to the maintenance of international peace and security,

Having considered the reports of the Special Committee against *Apartheid*, the International Conference on Sanctions against South Africa and the International Conference on the Alliance between South Africa and Israel,

Taking into account the Declarations of the Seventh Conference of Heads of State or Government of Non-Aligned Countries, held at New Delhi from 7 to 12 March 1983, and the resolutions adopted by the Assembly of Heads of State and Government of the Organization of African Unity at its nineteenth ordinary session, held at Addis Ababa from 6 to 12 June 1983,

Gravely concerned that, despite the arms embargo imposed by the Security Council, the racist régime of South Africa has continued to obtain from certain Western States and Israel military equipment and ammunition, as well as technology and know-how to develop its armaments industry and nuclear-weapon capability,

Noting with grave concern that military and nuclear collaboration by certain Western States and Israel with South Africa has enabled the racist régime to develop its arms production and become an arms-exporting country,

Recognizing that the stepped-up arms buildup and nuclear-weapon capability, as well as escalating acts of aggression by the racist régime of South Africa, constitute a grave threat to international peace and security,

Expressing alarm at the growing violation of the arms embargo, as well as the continued nuclear collaboration by the United States of America and some other Western States and Israel with the *apartheid* régime,

Condemning the actions of those transnational corporations that continue, through their collaboration with the racist régime of South Africa, to enhance its military and nuclear capabilities, as well as the failure of the Governments of the home countries of those corporations to take effective action to prevent such collaboration in accordance with the relevant resolutions of the United Nations,

Considering the urgent need for mandatory decisions by the Security Council, under Chapter VII of the Charter, to prohibit any military and nuclear collaboration with the racist régime of South Africa,

1. *Urges* the Security Council to take mandatory decisions, under Chapter VII of the Charter of the United Nations, to ensure the total cessation of all military and nuclear co-operation with the racist régime of South Africa by Governments, corporations, institutions and individuals;

2. *Strongly condemns* the actions of certain Western States and Israel which have provided the racist régime of South Africa with an enormous arsenal of military equipment and technology, as well as assistance in its nuclear plans, and which have allowed corporations under their jurisdiction to invest in the armaments industry in South Africa;

3. *Also condemns* the recent decision of the United States of America approving the request from seven corporations to provide technological and maintenance service to the nuclear installation of racist South Africa;

4. *Further condemns* any manœuvres to create military pacts or arrangements with the participation of the racist régime of South Africa;

5. *Calls upon* all Member States:

(*a*) To monitor effectively and to reinforce the mandatory arms embargo against South Africa;

(*b*) To prohibit all military and nuclear co-operation with South Africa by Governments, corporations, institutions and individuals;

6. *Calls upon* all Governments that have not yet done so to terminate all military and nuclear collaboration with South Africa and to take all necessary measures for preventing corporations and enterprises under their jurisdiction from engaging in any such collaboration.

General Assembly resolution 38/39 G

5 December 1983   Meeting 83   122-9-17 (recorded vote)

37-nation draft (A/38/L.26 & Corr.1); agenda item 32.

Sponsors: Afghanistan, Algeria, Angola, Benin, Botswana, Bulgaria, Byelorussian SSR, Cuba, Czechoslovakia, Democratic Yemen, German Democratic Republic, Ghana, Guinea, Guyana, Hungary, Iraq, Kenya, Lao People's Democratic Republic, Libyan Arab Jamahiriya, Madagascar, Malaysia, Mauritania, Mongolia, Mozambique, Nigeria, Sao Tome and Principe, Senegal, Sierra Leone, Syrian Arab Republic, Uganda, Ukrainian SSR, United Republic of Cameroon, United Republic of Tanzania, Viet Nam, Yugoslavia, Zambia, Zimbabwe.

Meeting numbers. GA 38th session: plenary 60-63, 69-71, 83.

Recorded vote in Assembly as follows:

In favour: Afghanistan, Albania, Algeria, Angola, Antigua and Barbuda, Argentina, Bahamas, Bahrain, Bangladesh, Barbados, Belize, Benin, Bhutan, Bolivia, Botswana, Brazil, Bulgaria, Burma, Burundi, Byelorussian SSR, Cape Verde, Central African Republic, Chad, Chile, China, Colombia, Comoros, Congo, Cuba, Cyprus, Czechoslovakia, Democratic Kampuchea, Democratic Yemen, Djibouti, Dominican Republic, Ecuador, Egypt, Equatorial Guinea, Ethiopia, Fiji, Gabon, Gambia, German Democratic Republic, Ghana, Guinea, Guinea-Bissau, Guyana, Haiti, Hungary, India, Indonesia, Iran, Iraq, Jamaica, Jordan, Kenya, Kuwait, Lao People's Democratic Republic, Lebanon, Lesotho, Libyan Arab Jamahiriya, Madagascar, Malaysia, Maldives, Mali, Malta, Mauritania, Mauritius, Mexico, Mongolia, Morocco, Mozambique, Nepal, Nicaragua, Niger, Nigeria, Oman, Pakistan, Panama, Papua New Guinea, Peru, Philippines, Poland, Qatar, Romania, Rwanda, Saint Lucia, Saint Vincent and the Grenadines, Samoa, Sao Tome and Principe, Saudi Arabia, Senegal, Seychelles, Sierra Leone, Singapore, Solomon Islands, Somalia, Sri Lanka, Sudan, Suriname, Swaziland, Syrian Arab Republic, Thailand, Togo, Trinidad and Tobago, Tunisia, Turkey, Uganda, Ukrainian SSR, USSR, United Arab Emirates, United Republic of Cameroon, United Republic of Tanzania, Upper Volta, Uruguay, Vanuatu, Venezuela, Viet Nam, Yemen, Yugoslavia, Zambia, Zimbabwe.

Against: Australia, Canada, France, Germany, Federal Republic of, Italy, Paraguay, Portugal, United Kingdom, United States.

Abstaining: Austria, Belgium, Denmark, Finland, Greece, Guatemala, Iceland, Ireland, Ivory Coast, Japan, Luxembourg, Malawi, Netherlands, New Zealand, Norway, Spain, Sweden.

The tenth preambular paragraph and paragraph 3 were adopted by recorded votes of 79 to 23, with 33 abstentions, and 72 to 23, with 39 abstentions, respectively.

In explanation of their votes on the resolution as a whole, Burma, Canada, the Federal Republic of Germany, Ireland, Italy, Morocco, Sri Lanka, Turkey and the United Kingdom said they opposed condemning particular Member States. Italy reaffirmed that it did not and would not co-operate with South Africa in the military and nuclear fields, but it opposed the references to Member States in three paragraphs. Ireland favoured calling for an end to military and nuclear collaboration with South Africa, but it found certain references unfair, selective and arbitrary. Turkey said the seventh, eighth and tenth preambular paragraphs and operative paragraphs 2 and 3 had not been drafted in a balanced way; it also noted that certain paragraphs might be incompatible with Turkish laws.

The United States said that the text criticized its Government and ignored the facts, such as the reference in paragraph 3 to the approval by the Government of bidding by United States companies on a contract to provide technical services to a South African firm whose commercial nuclear reactors provided electricity—an approval not violating the arms embargo; the fact that it alone had been cited, although companies from a number of Member States had bid on the same contracts, obliged the United States to conclude that the paragraph was not intended to contribute to the anti-*apartheid* effort, but was an unjustified attempt to single it out for criticism.

Malawi, Portugal and the United Kingdom expressed reservations about some language formulations. Portugal objected to elements of verbal violence and imprecise language. For the United Kingdom, some of the language was extreme.

Speaking on behalf of the five Nordic countries, Denmark referred to the reasons it gave for their votes on resolution 38/39 A (see above).

The Netherlands said it supported strict compliance with the arms embargo and the denial to South Africa of any nuclear capacity with military applications, but rather than asking for the termination of all nuclear co-operation with South Africa, it would have preferred a call on South Africa to accede to the 1968 Treaty on the Non-Proliferation of Nuclear Weapons[31] or to accept full-scope safeguards on all its nuclear activities; in this context, it believed that paragraph 3 was unjustified because the nuclear installations involved were monitored by IAEA.

New Zealand supported the arms embargo against South Africa and the call for the cessation of any nuclear collaboration that could facilitate its development of nuclear weapons, but it believed the resolution included paragraphs that were not justified and did not serve the purposes of the resolution.

Other 1983 Assembly resolutions also dealt with military and nuclear relations with South Africa.

In resolution 38/39 A, the Assembly again requested IAEA to refrain from extending to South Africa any assistance for its nuclear plans and, in particular, to exclude that country from its technical working groups.

In resolution 38/39 D, the Assembly called for Security Council action on sanctions, including measures to prohibit co-operation with South Africa in the military and nuclear fields, to prohibit imports of military equipment or parts from

that country, and to prevent co-operation by military alliances.

The Assembly, in resolution 38/36 A, condemned the military and nuclear collaboration of certain Western States and Israel with South Africa, expressed its concern at South Africa's acquisition of nuclear weapons capability, condemned the collusion by certain Western and other States, particularly the United States and Israel, with it in the nuclear field, and called on France and other States to stop supplying South Africa with installations that might enable it to produce nuclear materials or military equipment.

Again condemning the collusion of certain Western and other States in the nuclear field, the Assembly, by similar wording in resolution 38/50, called on Governments to refrain from such action and condemned States and TNCs which invested in and supplied arms and oil and nuclear technology to South Africa.

In resolution 38/54 on decolonization, the Assembly condemned all collaboration, particularly in the nuclear and military fields, with South Africa and called on States to cease such collaboration. By decision 38/419, it repeated this condemnation and stated that the continuing assistance of certain States belied their stated opposition to the racist practice of the régime and made them willing partners of its hegemonistic and criminal policies.

The Assembly took further related action in resolutions 38/181 A and B on the denuclearization of Africa (see Chapter I of this section).

Arms embargo

Security Council Committee. During 1983, the Security Council Committee established by resolution 421(1977) concerning the question of South Africa,[27] consisting of all Council members, held four closed meetings (on 28 January, 24 June, and 1 and 23 September) to study and recommend means by which the mandatory arms embargo against South Africa, imposed by the Council in 1977,[25] could be made more effective, and to seek from all States information regarding their action concerning the embargo.

In 1983, the Committee had before it two notes verbales from the United Kingdom and from Denmark. On 29 January,[32] the United Kingdom stated that three of its nationals had been convicted in October 1982 on charges relating to the illegal export of rifles and machine-gun spare parts to South Africa and had been sentenced to imprisonment. On 9 May,[33] the United Kingdom stated that it had examined whether the export of certain radar equipment from the United Kingdom to South Africa had involved a breach of the embargo, but determined that no breach was involved since the properly licensed equipment would be used for civil aviation. On 17 February,[34] Denmark, referring to press reports that Danish merchant vessels had violated the arms embargo, informed the Committee that the vessels in question had been time-chartered to a foreign company and were, therefore, not affected by existing law; since then, the relevant law had been amended to make it possible to prosecute any Danish shipowner found guilty of violating the arms embargo, even in cases where the vessel involved was time-chartered to a foreign company for shipping to South Africa. Both the United Kingdom and Denmark affirmed their support for the arms embargo.

Activities of the Committee against *Apartheid*. The Special Committee against *Apartheid*, in its annual report to the General Assembly,[1] urged the Security Council to take action without delay on the proposals for strengthening the arms embargo submitted in 1980 by the Council's Committee on the question of South Africa.[26] Such action, it said, was necessary in view of the frequent violations of the letter and spirit of the arms embargo and the inadequacy of the monitoring procedure.

In its Programme of Action against *Apartheid*,[2] the Committee called on Governments to implement fully the arms embargo against South Africa and outlined measures to ensure implementation (see above, under MILITARY AND NUCLEAR RELATIONS). Public organizations concerned were urged to persuade Governments to ensure that the arms embargo was strengthened and strictly implemented, and to organize campaigns to expose breaches of the embargo. The Committee, with the assistance of the Centre against *Apartheid*, planned to promote international campaigns for an effective arms embargo.

The International Conference of Trade Unions on Sanctions and Other Actions against the *Apartheid* Régime in South Africa, in its 11 June declaration,[23] endorsed the 1980 recommendations of the Security Council Committee on the question of South Africa. The Conference urged the Council to adopt them without delay, extending the embargo to comprise all products that could be used in the manufacture of arms and military equipment. Governments were urged to take measures in line with those recommendations.

Action by the Conference for Namibia's independence. The Committee of the Whole of the International Conference in Support of the Struggle of the Namibian People for Independence, in its Programme of Action on Namibia,[14] called on the Security Council to adopt the necessary measures to tighten the arms embargo against South Africa and to ensure strict compliance with the embargo by all States. In this connection, the Committee called on the Council to implement, as a matter of urgency, the 1980 recommendations of the Council's Committee on the question of South Africa.

Action by the Conference against racial discrimination. The Second World Conference to Combat Racism and Racial Discrimination, in its Programme of Action for the Second Decade to Combat Racism and Racial Discrimination (1983-1993),[5] called on all States to implement strictly the arms embargo and urged the Security Council to strengthen the embargo, in accordance with the 1980 recommendations of the Council's Committee. This Programme of Action was approved by the General Assembly in resolution 38/14.

GENERAL ASSEMBLY ACTION

In five 1983 resolutions, the General Assembly called for measures concerning the arms embargo against South Africa.

In resolution 38/17, it again demanded the immediate application of the embargo by all countries and more particularly by those that maintained military and nuclear co-operation with South Africa and continued to supply it with related *matériel*.

The Assembly, in resolution 38/39 D, requested the Security Council to monitor and to reinforce the embargo, while in resolution 38/39 G, the same call was made to Member States.

Calling on the Council to tighten the embargo and to ensure strict compliance by all States, the Assembly, in resolution 38/36 A, deplored the United Kingdom's decision to supply radar equipment to South Africa, and called on the Council to implement the 1980 recommendations of its Committee on the question of South Africa. In resolution 38/181 B, the Council was requested to conclude expeditiously its consideration of those recommendations with a view to blocking existing loopholes in the arms embargo so as to render it more effective and prohibiting, in particular, all forms of collaboration with South Africa in the nuclear field.

Economic relations

Activities of the Committee against *Apartheid*. The Special Committee against *Apartheid*, in its October 1983 Programme of Action against *Apartheid*,[2] called on Governments to terminate all economic collaboration with South Africa and, in particular, to: cease direct or indirect trade or commercial transactions; refrain from supplying strategic materials; refrain from extending loans, investments and technical assistance to it and companies registered there; prohibit the sale of Krugerrands; prohibit economic and financial interests under their national jurisdiction from co-operating with South Africa and companies registered there; deny tariff and other preferences to its exports and any inducements or guarantees for exports to, or investments in, South Africa; take action in international and regional agencies concerned, such as the European Economic Community, the General Agreement on Tariffs and Trade, IMF and the World Bank, to block assistance to South Africa; and take action, separately or collectively, against TNCs and financial institutions collaborating with it.

In dealing with airlines and shipping lines, Governments were urged to refuse landing and passage facilities to aircraft belonging to South Africa or registered there; close ports to vessels flying the South African flag; prohibit airlines and shipping lines registered in their countries from providing services to and fro; and deny facilities to aircraft or shipping lines proceeding to, or returning from, South Africa. With regard to emigration, the Committee recommended that Governments prohibit or discourage emigration, particularly of skilled and technical personnel, close South African recruitment offices and prohibit advertisements for employment in South Africa.

The Committee called on public organizations to campaign for the boycott of all South African products, an end to the promotion of trade with and tourism to South Africa, the boycott of South African Airways, and stopping airlines and shipping companies from providing services to and fro.

Activities of the Council for Namibia. The United Nations Council for Namibia, in its annual report to the General Assembly,[14] described economic relations and contacts with South Africa. It found that foreign participation in South Africa's economy was extensive, broad-ranging and complex, and that economic relations between South Africa and its traditional Western trading partners had been enhanced. A recent decision by the United States to relax existing restrictions on trade and other economic relations with South Africa apparently had encouraged other countries to take a similar position.

Western support for South Africa was provided in the form of investments, loans, trade, transfers of technology and expertise, according to the Council. Based for the most part on mineral resources, South Africa's economy had attracted Western capital and collaboration, thus enhancing its ability to build up its military, entrench the *apartheid* system and perpetuate its occupation of Namibia. In the Council's view, economic sanctions against South Africa would be effective in combating those South African policies if they were implemented by the major Western trading partners. The Council listed South Africa's main trading partners as (in descending order of trade volume in 1981) the United States, Japan, the United Kingdom, the Federal Republic of Germany, Switzerland, France, Italy, Belgium, the Netherlands and Canada, and described recent reports of large contracts between them and South Africa.

The Council remarked on the slowing growth rate of the South African economy, which had expanded by over 8 per cent in 1980, 4.5 per cent in 1981 and was expected to grow by only 2 to 3 per cent in 1982. In 1981, the Government had devalued the currency and inflation rates climbed to nearly 14 per cent. The bulk of South Africa's imports were industrial and consumer goods and oil, and its main exports were natural resources, on which it depended for foreign exchange.

The Council reported that despite the 1981 General Assembly request that States prevent air and sea services to and from South Africa,[17] Western, Asian and Latin American companies continued those services. Tourism to South Africa continued to increase and provided it with another source of foreign currency. In 1981, 697,228 tourists visited South Africa. Migration to South Africa was also rising, including people with professional and technical skills. Scientific and educational co-operation and exchanges between some countries and South Africa also continued.

Action by the Conference against racial discrimination. The Second World Conference to Combat Racism and Racial Discrimination, in its Programme of Action for the Second Decade to Combat Racism and Racial Disrimination (1983-1993),[5] called on the Security Council to consider the imposition of mandatory sanctions against South Africa, including the interruption of trade relations with that country. The General Assembly approved the Programme by resolution 38/14.

Oil embargo

Activities of the Committee against *Apartheid*. In 1983, the Special Committee against *Apartheid*[1] devoted special attention to consultations on promoting an oil embargo against South Africa. In accordance with a December 1982 General Assembly resolution,[35] the Chairman of the Committee invited 10 countries to nominate individuals to a Group of Experts on the Supply of Oil and Oil Products to South Africa which would prepare a study as a basis for the consideration of national and international measures to implement embargoes imposed or policies declared by oil-producing and oil-exporting countries with regard to South Africa's oil supply. The Group held its first session from 15 to 24 February. The Committee attached great importance to the proposed International Conference on an Oil Embargo against South Africa, authorized by the Assembly in December 1982,[35] for the purpose of considering national and international arrangements to implement embargoes or policies announced by oil-producing and oil-exporting countries. It reiterated that the Security Council should urgently consider a mandatory oil embargo, and called for action by individual Governments, pending Council action. The Committee recommended encouragement of public action in support of an oil embargo, especially in countries whose corporations and tanker fleets were involved in the supply of oil to South Africa.

In its October Programme of Action,[2] the Committee called on Governments to take measures to implement an oil embargo, including: enacting and enforcing "end-users" agreements to stop the supply of oil to South Africa directly or through third parties; prohibiting the transport of oil to it; taking action against suppliers and transporters of oil; seizing tankers owned by their nationals or registered in their countries which were used to transport oil to it; prohibiting assistance to South Africa in the construction of oil-from-coal plants; preventing the efforts of South African corporate interests to maintain or expand their holdings in oil companies or properties outside the country; and banning the participation of corporations and individuals within their jurisdiction in the South African oil industry. Public organizations were urged to campaign for an oil embargo, focusing on the role of the major oil companies supplying South Africa.

The International Conference of Trade Unions on Sanctions and Other Actions against the *Apartheid* Régime in South Africa, in its declaration,[23] urged the Security Council to extend the arms embargo to include raw materials and technology that could be used in the production of nuclear energy and to oil and petroleum products. Governments were called on to adopt an oil embargo against South Africa and, as a first step, to organize under United Nations auspices an international conference of oil-exporting and oil-transporting countries. The Conference requested the Committee against *Apartheid* to produce, on a regular basis, lists of tankers and companies supplying oil to South Africa and to distribute the lists to unions of dock-terminal and oil transport workers.

Action by the Conference against racial discrimination. The Second World Conference to Combat Racism and Racial Discrimination, in its Programme of Action for the Second Decade to Combat Racism and Discrimination (1983-1993)[5] as approved by the General Assembly in resolution 38/14, called on the Security Council to consider the imposition of mandatory sanctions against South Africa, including an embargo on the supply of petroleum, petroleum products and other strategic commodities that would enable South Africa to continue implementing its *apartheid* policy.

GENERAL ASSEMBLY ACTION

On 5 December, the General Assembly adopted resolution 38/39 J by recorded vote.

Oil embargo against South Africa

The General Assembly,

Recalling and reaffirming its resolutions 36/172 G of 17 December 1981 and 37/69 J of 9 December 1982,

Recalling further the Paris Declaration on Sanctions against South Africa,

Convinced of the need to ensure the effective implementation of embargoes imposed or policies declared by most oil-producing and oil-exporting countries with regard to the supply of their oil and oil products to South Africa, and to secure a mandatory oil embargo against South Africa under Chapter VII of the Charter of the United Nations,

Convinced further that such action has become imperative because of increasing repression and acts of aggression by South Africa,

Commending all Governments that have imposed an oil embargo against South Africa,

Commending the Special Committee against *Apartheid* for its efforts, in co-operation with Governments and intergovernmental and non-governmental organizations, to promote an effective oil embargo against South Africa,

Condemning the activities of corporations and other interests engaged in the clandestine supply to South Africa of oil from countries which have imposed an oil embargo,

Noting the need for further consultations among oil-producing and oil-exporting countries committed to the oil embargo against South Africa on national and international arrangements to ensure the effective implementation of the oil embargo against South Africa and on an international conference for that purpose,

1. *Reaffirms its recommendation* to the Security Council to consider urgently a mandatory embargo on the supply of oil and oil products to South Africa under Chapter VII of the Charter of the United Nations;

2. *Urges* all States that have not yet done so to take effective legislative and other measures to ensure the implementation of an oil embargo against South Africa;

3. *Requests* all States concerned to take effective action against corporations and tanker companies involved in the illicit supply of oil to South Africa;

4. *Requests and authorizes* the Special Committee against *Apartheid* to continue its efforts, including the undertaking of missions, the holding of seminars and the publication of studies, to promote an effective oil embargo against South Africa;

5. *Invites* Governments, international and non-governmental organizations, trade unions and other appropriate bodies to lend their full support to the oil embargo against South Africa;

6. *Renews its authorization* to the Secretary-General, in consultation with the Special Committee and in the light of the conclusions reached at the meetings of permanent representatives to the United Nations of the oil-producing and oil-exporting countries committed to the oil embargo against South Africa, to organize an International Conference on an Oil Embargo against South Africa for the purpose of considering national and international arrangements to ensure the implementation of embargoes imposed or policies declared by oil-producing and oil-exporting countries with regard to the supply of oil and oil products to South Africa.

General Assembly resolution 38/39 J

5 December 1983   Meeting 83   130-6-14 (recorded vote)

35-nation draft (A/38/L.30 & Add.1); agenda item 32.

Sponsors: Afghanistan, Algeria, Angola, Bahrain, Burundi, Congo, Cuba, Ecuador, Gabon, Gambia, Guyana, India, Indonesia, Iran, Iraq, Kuwait, Libyan Arab Jamahiriya, Madagascar, Mexico, Nicaragua, Nigeria, Oman, Pakistan, Qatar,

Romania, Saudi Arabia, Senegal, Syrian Arab Republic, Togo, Trinidad and Tobago, Tunisia, USSR, United Arab Emirates, United Republic of Tanzania, Venezuela.

Financial implications. 5th Committee, A/38/654; S-G, A/C.5/38/53 & Corr.1.

Meeting numbers. GA 38th session: 5th Committee 51; plenary 60-63, 69-71, 83.

Recorded vote in Assembly as follows:

In favour: Afghanistan, Albania, Algeria, Angola, Antigua and Barbuda, Argentina, Bahamas, Bahrain, Bangladesh, Barbados, Belize, Benin, Bhutan, Bolivia, Brazil, Bulgaria, Burma, Burundi, Byelorussian SSR, Cape Verde, Central African Republic, Chad, China, Colombia, Comoros, Congo, Costa Rica, Cuba, Cyprus, Czechoslovakia, Democratic Kampuchea, Democratic Yemen, Denmark, Djibouti, Dominican Republic, Ecuador, Egypt, El Salvador, Equatorial Guinea, Ethiopia, Fiji, Finland, Gabon, Gambia, German Democratic Republic, Ghana, Guinea, Guinea-Bissau, Guyana, Haiti, Honduras, Hungary, Iceland, India, Indonesia, Iran, Iraq, Ireland, Jamaica, Jordan, Kenya, Kuwait, Lao People's Democratic Republic, Lebanon, Liberia, Libyan Arab Jamahiriya, Madagascar, Malaysia, Maldives, Mali, Malta, Mauritania, Mauritius, Mexico, Mongolia, Morocco, Mozambique, Nepal, Netherlands, Nicaragua, Niger, Nigeria, Oman, Pakistan, Panama, Papua New Guinea, Peru, Philippines, Poland, Qatar, Romania, Rwanda, Saint Lucia, Saint Vincent and the Grenadines, Samoa, Sao Tome and Principe, Saudi Arabia, Senegal, Seychelles, Sierra Leone, Singapore, Solomon Islands, Somalia, Spain, Sri Lanka, Sudan, Suriname, Sweden, Syrian Arab Republic, Thailand, Togo, Trinidad and Tobago, Tunisia, Turkey, Uganda, Ukrainian SSR, USSR, United Arab Emirates, United Republic of Cameroon, United Republic of Tanzania, Upper Volta, Uruguay, Vanuatu, Venezuela, Viet Nam, Yemen, Yugoslavia, Zaire, Zambia, Zimbabwe.

Against: Belgium, France, Germany, Federal Republic of, Luxembourg, United Kingdom, United States.

Abstaining: Australia, Austria, Botswana, Canada, Greece, Italy, Ivory Coast, Japan, Lesotho, Malawi, New Zealand, Norway, Portugal, Swaziland.

Speaking in explanation of vote, Norway supported the objective of the resolution, but felt the text inappropriate; citing its 1981 initiative to organize a conference of oil-producing and oil-exporting countries which had declared it their policy not to sell oil to South Africa, Norway said that the resolution interfered with the ongoing consultations regarding such a conference and prejudiced its outcome, especially as the text spoke of the illicit transport of oil to South Africa although there was no binding decision by the Security Council in that connection.

The Netherlands explained that its positive vote was, among other things, inspired by the recommendation in paragraph 1 that the Council consider mandatory sanctions; while it hoped that recommendations could be formulated on an oil embargo, it noted that supplies to South Africa could not be labelled illicit as long as they were not prohibited by the Council.

Ireland supported an oil embargo as a means of pressuring South Africa to abandon *apartheid*, but had reservations about paragraphs 2 and 3, which appeared to pre-empt consideration of an oil embargo by the Council.

Botswana said it was obliged to abstain because of its geopolitical circumstances. Malawi said it abstained because it had difficulties with some demands and language formulations.

The Assembly also called for an oil embargo in resolutions on related subjects. In resolution 38/39 D, it requested the Council to consider sanctions, including an embargo on supplying oil to South Africa and on all assistance to its oil industry. In resolution 38/50, it called on oil-producing and oil-exporting countries that had not done so

to take measures against the oil companies concerned so as to terminate the supply of oil and oil products to South Africa.

Foreign investments and loans

Activities of the Committee against *Apartheid*. The flow of foreign capital into South Africa increased in 1982, according to the Special Committee against *Apartheid*. In its 1983 report to the Assembly,[1] the Committee described foreign investments in and loans to South Africa. It reported that in 1982 the inflow of foreign capital totalled $2,397 million, three times the amount in 1981. The net capital outflow during the first quarter of 1983 totalled $591 million, of which 42 per cent represented long-term capital and 58 per cent short-term capital. Approximately 59 per cent of the long-term capital inflow consisted of loans raised in the international financial markets by the South African Treasury, the Transport Services and the Department of Posts and Telecommunications; the rest consisted mostly of loans to public corporations and the private sector.

South African banks borrowed approximately $5,502 million from the international financial markets as of the end of March 1983, an increase of $2,174 million from March 1982, mainly in short-term trade finance and working capital loans from foreign banks and Euromarket institutions. Most of the recipients were domestic companies and South African subsidiaries of TNCs financing their imports or exports or utilizing foreign credit lines instead of domestic overdrafts for general cash. South African banks or South African subsidiaries of foreign banks most often acted as agents for short-term trade finance and working capital loans between the recipients and the financial institution abroad.

On 15 April, the Committee held a hearing of 16 United States legislators who played a role in the campaign against *apartheid*, in particular in legislative action against investments in South Africa.

The Committee, in its October Programme of Action,[2] called on Governments to terminate all economic collaboration with South Africa. Specific measures included an end to loans, investments and technical assistance to that country and companies registered there, and an end to loans by banks or other financial institutions in their countries to South Africa or South African companies. Specialized agencies and other intergovernmental organizations were urged to contribute to the international campaign against *apartheid* by withholding facilities from, or investment of funds in, banks, financial institutions and corporations that gave loans to or invested in South Africa. Among its recommendations for public organizations' participation in the campaign, the Committee called for disinvestment from companies operating in South Africa and an end to loans to it. City and local authorities were urged to withdraw investments held by them in companies with interests in South Africa. Churches and religious organizations were urged to ensure that their institutions divested from corporations with interests in the country and withdrew accounts with banks collaborating with *apartheid*. The Committee said that the Secretary-General should withhold facilities from, or investment of funds in, banks, financial institutions and other corporations that gave loans to or invested in South Africa. With the assistance of the Centre against *Apartheid*, the Committee said it should promote a campaign against collaboration by banks and TNCs (see below, under WORK PROGRAMME OF THE COMMITTEE AGAINST *APARTHEID*).

The International Conference of Trade Unions on Sanctions and Other Actions against the *Apartheid* Régime in South Africa, in its declaration,[23] called on Governments to intensify anti-*apartheid* action in United Nations specialized agencies and intergovernmental organizations to stop dealings with banks co-operating with South Africa. The Conference urged States to pass legislation to end all investment in South Africa, withdraw pension funds and other forms of public investment from banks and companies collaborating with it, put a halt to incentives for exports to South Africa, apply pressure on national and international institutions to end co-operation with South Africa on its overseas borrowing, and refuse to transfer pensions and other State-sponsored benefit schemes to those choosing to emigrate there. Employers' organizations and companies were urged to request foreign companies which had invested in South Africa to withdraw their investments and to refrain from any co-operation in the economic and military field. The Conference urged workers and their trade unions to press Governments to stop all kinds of aid to and investment in South Africa, and take industrial actions against TNCs (see below) investing there.

Action by the Conference against racial discrimination. The Second World Conference to Combat Racism and Racial Discrimination[5] called on the Security Council to consider imposing mandatory sanctions against South Africa, including the cessation of foreign investments in and financial loans to it. This action was included in its Programme of Action for the Second Decade to Combat Racism and Racial Discrimination (1983-1993), approved by the General Assembly in resolution 38/14.

GENERAL ASSEMBLY ACTION

On 5 December, the General Assembly adopted by recorded vote resolution 38/39 I.

Investments in South Africa

The General Assembly,

Recalling its resolution 37/69 H of 9 December 1982,

Taking note of the report of the Special Committee against *Apartheid*,

Convinced that a cessation of all new foreign investments in, and financial loans to, South Africa would constitute an important step in international action for the elimination of *apartheid*, as such investments and loans abet and encourage the *apartheid* policies of that country,

Welcoming the actions of those Governments that have taken legislative and other measures towards that end,

Noting with regret that the Security Council has not yet taken steps towards that end, as requested by the General Assembly in its resolutions 31/6 K of 9 November 1976, 32/105 O of 16 December 1977, 33/183 O of 24 January 1979, 34/93 Q of 12 December 1979, 35/206 Q of 16 December 1980, 36/172 O of 17 December 1981 and 37/69 H of 9 December 1982,

Again urges the Security Council to consider the matter at an early date with a view to taking effective steps to achieve the cessation of further foreign investments in, and financial loans to, South Africa.

General Assembly resolution 38/39 I

5 December 1983   Meeting 83   140-1-9 (recorded vote)

44-nation draft (A/38/L.28 & Add.1); agenda item 32.

Sponsors: Afghanistan, Algeria, Angola, Bangladesh, Barbados, Burundi, Congo, Cuba, Cyprus, Democratic Yemen, Denmark, Finland, Gambia, Guinea, Guinea-Bissau, Guyana, Iceland, India, Indonesia, Ireland, Kenya, Libyan Arab Jamahiriya, Madagascar, Malaysia, Morocco, Mozambique, Netherlands, New Zealand, Nicaragua, Nigeria, Norway, Pakistan, Qatar, Rwanda, Senegal, Sri Lanka, Sweden, Togo, Trinidad and Tobago, Tunisia, Turkey, United Republic of Tanzania, Yugoslavia, Zambia.

Meeting numbers. GA 38th session: plenary 60-63, 69-71, 83.

Recorded vote in Assembly as follows:

In favour: Afghanistan, Albania, Algeria, Angola, Antigua and Barbuda, Argentina, Australia, Austria, Bahamas, Bahrain, Bangladesh, Barbados, Belgium, Belize, Benin, Bhutan, Bolivia, Brazil, Bulgaria, Burma, Burundi, Byelorussian SSR, Cape Verde, Central African Republic, Chad, China, Colombia, Comoros, Congo, Costa Rica, Cuba, Cyprus, Czechoslovakia, Democratic Kampuchea, Democratic Yemen, Denmark, Djibouti, Dominican Republic, Ecuador, Egypt, El Salvador, Equatorial Guinea, Ethiopia, Fiji, Finland, Gabon, Gambia, German Democratic Republic, Ghana, Greece, Guatemala, Guinea, Guinea-Bissau, Guyana, Haiti, Honduras, Hungary, Iceland, India, Indonesia, Iran, Iraq, Ireland, Jamaica, Japan, Jordan, Kenya, Kuwait, Lao People's Democratic Republic, Lebanon, Liberia, Libyan Arab Jamahiriya, Luxembourg, Madagascar, Malaysia, Maldives, Mali, Malta, Mauritania, Mauritius, Mexico, Mongolia, Morocco, Mozambique, Nepal, Netherlands, New Zealand, Nicaragua, Niger, Nigeria, Norway, Oman, Pakistan, Panama, Papua New Guinea, Peru, Philippines, Poland, Portugal, Qatar, Romania, Rwanda, Saint Lucia, Saint Vincent and the Grenadines, Samoa, Sao Tome and Principe, Saudi Arabia, Senegal, Seychelles, Sierra Leone, Singapore, Solomon Islands, Somalia, Spain, Sri Lanka, Sudan, Suriname, Sweden, Syrian Arab Republic, Thailand, Togo, Trinidad and Tobago, Tunisia, Turkey, Uganda, Ukrainian SSR, USSR, United Arab Emirates, United Republic of Cameroon, United Republic of Tanzania, Upper Volta, Uruguay, Vanuatu, Venezuela, Viet Nam, Yemen, Yugoslavia, Zaire, Zambia, Zimbabwe.

Against: United States.

Abstaining: Botswana, Canada, France, Germany, Federal Republic of, Italy, Ivory Coast, Lesotho, Malawi, United Kingdom.

In explanation of vote, Botswana said it was obliged to abstain on account of its geopolitical circumstances. Malawi said it had difficulties with some demands or language formulations.

Ireland believed that the international community had a vital part to play by collectively selecting and implementing measures that would be effective in bringing pressure to bear on South Africa to abandon *apartheid* and, for that reason, it supported ceasing investments and financial loans. Likewise, Portugal felt the resolution would help eradicate *apartheid*.

The Netherlands said it intended to consider in what way investments by Dutch companies in South Africa could be influenced as effectively as possible.

The Assembly took similar action in resolution 38/39 D, in which it requested the Security Council to consider action towards sanctions against South Africa, including the prohibition of financial loans and new investments.

Transnational corporations

Action by the Committee against *Apartheid*. In its annual report to the General Assembly,[1] the Special Committee against *Apartheid* recommended that the Assembly request the Secretary-General to deny facilities to, and to refrain from any investments in, corporations operating in South Africa. The Committee welcomed the actions taken by States and organizations to deny co-operation to TNCs and financial institutions collaborating with *apartheid* and recommended further concerted measures.

The Committee's October Programme of Action[2] included the recommendation that Governments take action, separately or collectively, against TNCs and financial institutions collaborating with South Africa. Specialized agencies and other intergovernmental organizations were urged to deny contracts or facilities to such TNCs and institutions. The Committee said public organizations should intensify the campaign to boycott major banks collaborating with South Africa and direct campaigns at particular companies whose collaboration with it was strategically important. Corporations and employers were urged to withdraw from commercial operations there, persuade employers' organizations to work for a policy of sanctions against South Africa, and implement the 1981 Declaration of ILO concerning the policy of *apartheid* in South Africa.[36] With the assistance of the Centre against *Apartheid*, the Committee said it should promote an international campaign against collaboration by TNCs with South Africa.

Action by the Commission on Human Rights and its Sub-Commission. In July 1983, the Sub-Commission on Prevention of Discrimination and Protection of Minorities of the Commission on Human Rights issued a report listing banks, TNCs and other firms assisting South Africa.[37] Prepared by Special Rapporteur Ahmed Mohamed Khalifa (Egypt), the list updated information in his June 1982 report.[38]

The Commission on Human Rights, in a resolution of 18 February[30] on the consequences for human rights of assistance given to colonial and racist régimes in southern Africa (see ECONOMIC AND SOCIAL QUESTIONS, Chapter XVIII), expressed appreciation to the Special Rapporteur for his 1982 report and called for its wide publicity. The Commission welcomed the Sub-Commission's call for annual updating of the list.[38] By decision 1982/137 of 27 May, the Economic and Social Council endorsed the Commission's action.

In a resolution of 31 August,[39] the Sub-Commission invited the Special Rapporteur to continue to update the list, and the volume and nature of assistance. The Secretary-General was requested to assist and publicize the report.

In another 18 February resolution,[40] the Commission requested, as it had in 1982,[38] the Group of Three Commission members set up under the 1973 International Convention on the Suppression and Punishment of the Crime of *Apartheid*[41] to examine whether the actions of TNCs which operated in South Africa came under the definition of the crime of *apartheid*, and whether legal action could be taken under the Convention (see ECONOMIC AND SOCIAL QUESTIONS, Chapter XVIII).

Report of the Secretary-General. In response to an October 1982 request by the Economic and Social Council,[42] the Secretary-General reported on TNC policies and practices regarding their activities in South Africa and Namibia.[43] The May 1983 report included an annex listing TNCs which operated in strategic sectors of the southern African economy, and of those that had taken measures to terminate their activities in such sectors. It examined investment policies and practices of TNCs in South Africa, their employment practices there, the involvement of TNCs in some strategic sectors of the South African economy, and recent developments regarding TNCs in Namibia. The report was based on information obtained from a questionnaire sent to 303 TNCs with approximately 1,000 affiliates in South Africa and Namibia, selected for the importance of their operations in the area or because they were operating in strategic sectors.

According to the report, foreign involvement in South Africa increased substantially in 1980 and 1981. Many TNCs expanded their activities owing to the strong economic growth experienced by the country and the investment programmes of the Government. Although a few companies had terminated their activities in South Africa, the general trend was not towards divestment. Some TNCs had improved employment practices in South Africa, but progress had not been sufficient to effect any major change in the working conditions of the black population. One of the major effects of TNC activities in South Africa was through the technology those companies supplied, in particular in strategic areas such as the electronics, computer, chemical and energy sectors. The involvement of TNCs in such sectors was helpful in building up the economic and military strength of the country.

The Secretary-General's report was taken note of by the Commission on Transnational Corporations at its June 1983 session.[44]

Action by the Conference against racial discrimination. The Second World Conference to Combat Racism and Racial Discrimination, in its Programme of Action[5] approved by the General Assembly in resolution 38/14, called on States that had not done so to discourage or prevent all business enterprises, including TNCs, from collaborating with South Africa, as such collaboration might contribute towards the continuance of *apartheid*.

ECONOMIC AND SOCIAL COUNCIL ACTION

In 1983, the Economic and Social Council took three separate actions concerning TNC activities in South Africa and Namibia.

Two of these actions (decision 1983/104 and resolution 1983/75) related to preparations for the public hearings on those activities to be held by the Commission in 1985.

In February, the Council adopted decision 1983/104 without vote.

Ad Hoc Committee on the Preparations for the Public Hearings on the Activities of Transnational Corporations in South Africa

At its 2nd plenary meeting, on 4 February 1983, the Council, recalling its resolution 1982/70 of 27 October 1982;

(a) Decided that the membership of the *Ad Hoc* Committee on the Preparations for the Public Hearings on the Activities of Transnational Corporations in South Africa shall include one member from each of the regional groups;

(b) Authorized its President to appoint the members of the *Ad Hoc* Committee on the recommendation of each regional group concerning its representation.

Economic and Social Council decision 1983/104

Adopted without vote

Draft orally proposed by President; agenda item 2.
Meeting number. ESC 2.

On 29 July, the Council, adopted by vote resolution 1983/75, as recommended by its First Committee.

Organization of public hearings on the activities of transnational corporations in South Africa and Namibia

The Economic and Social Council,

Recalling its resolutions on the activities of transnational corporations in southern Africa, in particular resolution 1981/86 of 2 November 1981, in which it called for the organization of public hearings on the activities of transnational corporations in South Africa and Namibia,

Recalling also its resolution 1982/70 of 27 October 1982, according to which public hearings on the activities of transnational corporations in South Africa and Namibia, pursuant to Council resolution 1981/86, shall be conducted by the Commission on Transnational Corporations at its tenth session, which shall, as necessary, be extended for a period of one week for that purpose,

Urges regional groups to nominate their representatives to the *ad hoc* committee established under Council resolution 1982/70, unless they have already done so, to enable it to start work on the organization of the public hearings at the earliest possible time, but not later than the end of the year 1983, and to report to the Commis-

sion at its tenth session, so that it may conduct public hearings at its eleventh session.

Economic and Social Council resolution 1983/75

29 July 1983   Meeting 41   36-0-14

Approved by First Committee (E/1983/125) by vote (32-0-14), 27 July (meeting 25); draft by Commission on TNCs (E/1983/18/Rev.1); agenda item 8.
Meeting number. ESC 41.

Also on 29 July, the Council adopted by vote resolution 1983/74 on the recommendation of its First Committee. It acted after considering the report of the Commission on TNCs (see ECONOMIC AND SOCIAL QUESTIONS, Chapter VII) on its June session[44] and the Secretary-General's report on practices of TNCs regarding their activities in South Africa and Namibia.[43]

Activities of transnational corporations in South Africa and Namibia and collaboration of such corporations with the racist minority régime in South Africa

The Economic and Social Council,

Recalling General Assembly resolutions 3201(S-VI) and 3202(S-VI) of 1 May 1974, containing the Declaration and the Programme of Action on the Establishment of a New International Economic Order, 3281(XXIX) of 12 December 1974, containing the Charter of Economic Rights and Duties of States, and 3362(S-VII) of 16 September 1975 on development and international economic co-operation,

Recalling also General Assembly resolutions 37/39 of 3 December 1982 on the adverse consequences for the enjoyment of human rights of political, military, economic and other forms of assistance given to the racist and colonialist régime of South Africa, 37/40 of 3 December 1982 on the implementation of the Programme for the Decade for Action to Combat Racism and Racial Discrimination, 37/41 of 3 December 1982 on the Second World Conference to Combat Racism and Racial Discrimination, 37/69 of 9 December 1982 on the policies of *apartheid* of the Government of South Africa, 37/74 of 9 December 1982 on the implementation of the Declaration on the Denuclearization of Africa and 37/233 of 20 December 1982 on the question of Namibia,

Reaffirming its previous resolutions on the activities of transnational corporations in southern Africa and the collaboration of such corporations with the racist minority régime in South Africa,

Having considered the report of the Secretary-General on the policies and practices of transnational corporations regarding their activities in South Africa and Namibia, prepared pursuant to Economic and Social Council resolution 1982/69 of 27 October 1982,

Considering that the persistent operations of transnational corporations in Namibia in contravention of various United Nations resolutions continue to reinforce the illegal occupation of Namibia by South Africa and to pose a serious threat to the future political and economic independence of Namibia,

Considering that the role of transnational corporations in the strategic sectors, including military and nuclear sectors of the South African economy, has persisted in violation of United Nations resolutions,

Considering also that the continued collaboration of transnational corporations with the racist minority régime in

South Africa has caused widespread concern in recent years among national and local legislators, non-governmental organizations, trade unions, academic institutions and numerous other groups,

Affirming the need for action at the international level by intergovernmental organizations in order to complement national measures,

1. *Takes note with satisfaction* of the report of the Secretary-General on the policies and practices of transnational corporations regarding their activities in South Africa and Namibia, prepared pursuant to Economic and Social Council resolution 1982/69;

2. *Commends* those groups, bodies and institutions that have exerted pressure on transnational corporations to terminate their investments in South Africa and other forms of collaboration with the racist minority régime, and calls upon such organizations to intensify their efforts in those areas;

3. *Welcomes* as a positive step the policies of Governments directed towards bringing to an end the activities of their transnational corporations in southern Africa;

4. *Condemns* the racist minority régime in South Africa for its perpetuation of the inhuman system of *apartheid* and the illegal occupation of Namibia;

5. *Condemns* those transnational corporations which collaborate with the racist minority régime in South Africa, and calls upon all transnational corporations to respect the various United Nations resolutions concerning southern Africa;

6. *Calls upon* all home countries of transnational corporations to take effective measures to terminate the collaboration of their transnational corporations with the racist minority régime in South Africa, to prevent further new investments and reinvestments and to bring about an immediate withdrawal of all existing investments in South Africa and Namibia;

7. *Calls upon* all countries concerned to re-examine their relations with the transnational corporations operating in their territories which collaborate with the racist minority régime in South Africa;

8. *Calls upon* all anti-*apartheid* movements, religious institutions and bodies, trade unions, universities and other institutions that are shareholders of transnational corporations operating in South Africa and Namibia to contribute to the efforts of the international community to eradicate *apartheid* by withdrawing their shareholdings in such transnational corporations;

9. *Urges* all transnational corporations to comply fully with the relevant United Nations resolutions by terminating all further investments in South Africa and Namibia and by ending their collaboration with the racist minority régime;

10. *Further calls upon* all States Members of the United Nations and all transnational corporations operating in South Africa and Namibia to co-operate with the Secretary-General and the Commission on Transnational Corporations in organizing public hearings on the activities of transnational corporations in South Africa and Namibia;

11. *Reaffirming* Security Council resolution 301(1971) of 20 October 1971, in which the Council called upon States to abstain from entering into economic relations with South Africa in respect of Namibia and declared that rights, titles or contracts granted to individuals or corporations by South Africa after the termination of the mandate were not subject to protection or espousal by their States against the claims of a future lawful Government of Namibia;

12. *Reaffirms* that the code of conduct on transnational corporations should include effective measures against the collaboration of transnational corporations with the racist minority régime in southern Africa;

13. *Requests* the Secretary-General:

(a) To intensify the useful work of the Secretariat in the collection and dissemination of information on the activities of all transnational corporations in southern Africa;

(b) To make arrangements for the organization of public hearings, to be conducted by the Commission on Transnational Corporations, with the assistance of the United Nations Centre on Transnational Corporations, on the activities of transnational corporations in South Africa and Namibia, in accordance with the modalities and procedures to be prescribed by the Commission at its tenth session;

(c) To report to the Commission on Transnational Corporations at its tenth session on the measures taken in pursuance of the present resolution;

(d) To expand the annex to the report of the Secretary-General referred to in paragraph 1 above to include all transnational corporations operating in South Africa and Namibia;

14. *Decides* to include in the provisional agenda for the tenth session of the Commission an item entitled "Responsibilities of home countries with respect to the transnational corporations operating in South Africa and Namibia in violation of the relevant resolutions and decisions of the United Nations".

Economic and Social Council resolution 1983/74

29 July 1983   Meeting 41   36-3-11

Approved by First Committee (E/1983/125) by vote (32-3-11), 27 July (meeting 25); draft by Commission on TNCs (E/1983/18/Rev.1); agenda item 8. *Meeting number.* ESC plenary 41.

Both July texts originated in the Commission on TNCs, where they were sponsored by Bangladesh, on behalf of the members of the Group of 77 which were Commission members. The Commission adopted them on 29 June.

In the First Committee, the United Kingdom requested a separate vote on paragraph 14, which was retained by 31 votes to 4, with 9 abstentions. The Council also held a separate vote on paragraph 14, retaining it by 35 votes to 4, with 10 abstentions.

GENERAL ASSEMBLY ACTION

In resolution 38/39 A of 5 December, the General Assembly requested the Secretary-General to take all necessary measures to deny facilities to, and to refrain from any investment in, corporations operating in South Africa.

The Assembly, in resolution 38/50 of 7 December, took note of the register indicating profits that TNCs derived from their activities in colonial Territories, prepared by the United Nations Centre on Transnational Corporations, and requested the Special Committee on the Situation with regard to the Implementation of the Declaration on the Granting of Independence to Colonial Countries and Peoples to take due account of the register in connection with its consideration of related items.

IMF relations with South Africa

Activities of the Committee against *Apartheid*. The Special Committee against *Apartheid*, in its annual report to the General Assembly,[1] described recent developments in relations between the International Monetary Fund (IMF) and South Africa. Noting a fall in the volume of imports to South Africa and the improvement in gold prices in July 1982, reducing the deficit in the balance-of-payments account, the Committee said that the turn-around in the balance of payments began almost immediately after the formal approval of South Africa's application for a 1.2 billion rand ($1.1 billion) loan from IMF in November 1982.[45] The interest rates on IMF loans were much lower than those on private loans. Despite the protest of the overwhelming majority of United Nations Member States, a loan of 1 billion special drawing rights (SDR) had been approved as a result of the weighted voting system of IMF, thus enabling South Africa to repay some private short-term foreign credits as well as to increase its foreign exchange reserves.

As a result of balance-of-payments deficits in 1981 and during the first three quarters of 1982, South Africa's short-term liabilities to the international financial markets totalled R 3.5 billion as of the end of March 1983. It was expected that South Africa would again use IMF stand-by financial facilities during 1983 to decrease a portion of its short-term foreign financial liabilities.

The Committee expressed concern over IMF assistance to that country despite repeated requests by the Assembly to end such aid. It suggested that the Assembly request the Secretary-General to enter into urgent consultations with IMF in order to secure its full co-operation in action against *apartheid* in accordance with Assembly resolutions.

In its October 1983 Programme of Action against *Apartheid*,[2] the Committee stated that IMF should refrain from granting credits to South Africa and public organizations should campaign and press Governments for an end to IMF loans to that country.

Action of the Commission on Human Rights. The Commission on Human Rights, in a resolution of 18 February[30] on the consequences for human rights of assistance to colonial and racist régimes in southern Africa (see ECONOMIC AND SOCIAL QUESTIONS, Chapter XVIII), requested specialized agencies, particularly IMF and the World Bank, to refrain from granting loans to South Africa.

Action of the Conference for Namibia's independence. The International Conference in Support of the Struggle of the Namibian People for Independence, in its Paris Declaration on Namibia,[14] noted with concern the continued assistance to South Africa by certain international organizations, as exemplified by the IMF loan of SDR 1 billion. The Conference stated that such assistance did not contribute to the welfare of the vast majority of the South African people, but boosted the military capability of the régime and enabled it to continue suppression of the Namibian people and to commit aggression against its neighbours. The Conference called on IMF to terminate co-operation with and assistance to South Africa and urged its States members to take action towards that end.

Action by the Conference against racial discrimination. The Second World Conference to Combat Racism and Racial Discrimination urged the World Bank and IMF, as well as similar institutions, to refrain from extending any credits to South Africa. This action was included in its Programme of Action for the Second Decade to Combat Racism and Racial Discrimination (1983-1993),[5] approved by the General Assembly in resolution 38/14.

ECONOMIC AND SOCIAL COUNCIL ACTION

In resolution 1983/42 of 25 July, the Economic and Social Council deeply deplored the persistent collaboration of IMF with South Africa, in disregard of repeated General Assembly resolutions to the contrary, and called on IMF to put an end to such collaboration.

GENERAL ASSEMBLY ACTION

In several 1983 resolutions, the General Assembly also called for an end to IMF relations with South Africa.

In resolution 38/36 A, it deeply deplored the continued collaboration of IMF with South Africa in disregard of an October 1982 Assembly resolution,[46] and called on IMF to put an end to such collaboration. In resolution 38/39 A, it called on IMF to terminate credits or other assistance and requested the Secretary-General to enter into consultations with IMF to secure its co-operation in action against *apartheid*.

In resolution 38/51, the Assembly regretted that the World Bank and IMF continued to maintain links with South Africa, as exemplified by that country's membership in both, and expressed the view that the two agencies should terminate all links with that Government. Condemning the persistent collaboration between IMF and South Africa, particularly the granting of the November 1982 loan, the Assembly called on IMF to rescind it. The Assembly commended those non-governmental organizations which mobilized public opinion against the IMF assistance to South Africa and called for redoubled efforts by all non-governmental organizations in that respect. The governing bodies of the World Bank and IMF were urged to formulate programmes beneficial to the peoples of colonial Territories, particularly Namibia. The Assembly urged IMF to discuss its relationship with South Africa at its annual meeting in September 1984 and recommended sending a three-member mission to IMF.

Israel–South Africa relations

Activities of the Committee against *Apartheid*. The International Conference on the Alliance between South Africa and Israel, held at Vienna, Austria, from 11 to 13 July 1983, was organized by the Special Committee against *Apartheid*, in cooperation with the Afro-Asian Peoples' Solidarity Organization, the Organization of African Trade Union Unity and the World Peace Council, in response to a December 1982 General Assembly request that the Committee publicize information on relations between Israel and South Africa.[47]

In the Declaration included in its report[48] and transmitted by the Acting Chairman of the Committee to the Secretary-General,[49] the Conference strongly condemned Israel for its collaboration with South Africa, especially in the military and nuclear fields (see above), in defiance of United Nations resolutions. Evidence of Israeli–South African collaboration had increased, the Conference said, and the 1963 declaration of the Organization of African Unity (OAU)[50] that Africa remain a denuclearized zone had been undermined by the development of South Africa's nuclear-weapon capability. The nuclear capabilities of both South Africa and Israel posed an enormous danger to regional and world peace.

The Conference also drew attention to the collaboration by Israel with South Africa in the conventional military field. It expressed concern over the relations of Chile, Paraguay and Uruguay with South Africa, especially in the military field, as well as over any moves for a South Atlantic military pact with the participation of South Africa.

Expressing regret at the opposition of several Western Powers to condemning collaboration by Israel with South Africa, the Conference said it considered that United States policies with regard to those two countries represented support for them against the aspirations of African States to keep the continent free from nuclear weapons, to complete the process of decolonization and to maintain regional peace and security. It urged Governments and organizations to condemn the collaboration between Israel and South Africa and exercise their influence in order to ensure that Israel desist from such collaboration. The Conference expressed the hope that no State would resume relations with Israel so long as it continued its collaboration with South Africa and did not implement United Nations resolutions in that regard.

The Conference emphasized the importance of disseminating all relevant information, especially in the Western countries, in view of the deceitful propaganda by Israel and South Africa on their collaboration and of the attitude of the United States and several other Western countries. The Committee against *Apartheid* was requested to continue monitoring developments in Israeli–South African relations and overseeing implementation of specific requests of the Conference.

The Committee, in its annual report to the Assembly,[1] agreed that Israel had blatantly continued, in contempt of the United Nations, to collaborate with South Africa, especially in the military and nuclear fields. That collaboration had become a serious challenge to the international community.

In September, the Committee transmitted a special report to the Assembly on recent developments concerning relations between the two countries,[3] stating that there was increasing evidence of extensive collaboration between them in the military and nuclear fields, as reported by Western, Israeli and South African media. Regular exchanges of visits between the finance and economic ministers of Israel and South Africa had expanded their economic links. On 3 March, the two countries signed an agreement designed to strengthen trade and investment ties and to provide for a freer flow of currency between them. According to the report, Israeli exports to South Africa increased from $80.75 million in 1980 to $102.93 million in 1981, but Israeli imports from South Africa decreased from $134.43 million in 1980 to $103.17 million in 1981 (excluding military sales, oil, gold and diamonds).

Collaboration had also continued in cultural, academic, scientific, sporting and other fields. Further, there were reports of contacts between Israeli officials and representatives of the so-called independent bantustans of Ciskei and Bophuthatswana.

The Committee concluded that the continued collaboration between Israel and South Africa posed grave dangers to international peace and security. It recommended that the Assembly endorse the Declaration of the Conference and urge Governments and intergovernmental and non-governmental organizations to end that collaboration. Noting with regret that a number of Western countries had continued to oppose any condemnation of the collaboration, and that the United States had provided encouragement to Israel in its defiance of the United Nations, the Committee hoped that those Governments would reassess their positions and persuade Israel to disengage from racist oppression in South Africa. The Committee recommended maximum publicity of the collaboration in support of efforts to end it.

Communications. During 1983, Israel addressed four letters to the Secretary-General protesting United Nations action in regard to the International Conference on the Alliance between South Africa and Israel.

On 25 May,[51] Israel said that the Special Committee against *Apartheid* had not been authorized to organize the Conference and it sought assurances that the event was not a United Nations conference and that United Nations funds, facilities and services would not be misused in connection with it. Again requesting such assurances on 29 June,[52] Israel asked what financial contribution, if any, would be made by the three non-governmental organizations sponsoring the Conference and what expenses would be incurred by the United Nations. On 13 September,[53] Israel said the Conference had been turned into another manifestation of the anti-Israel campaign waged in and through the United Nations by Israel's enemies and their supporters; accordingly, Israel would withhold from its contributions to the United Nations the appropriate amount relative to the expenses incurred by the Conference, and proportionate to Israel's share within the overall contributions of Member States to the Organization. Protesting on 2 November[54] the United Nations publication of the Conference's Declaration, Israel said that the Organization, by disseminating that document, had misused international funds, further compromised the integrity of the Secretariat and exposed the United Nations as a whole to well-justified criticism.

Action by the Conference against racial discrimination. The Second World Conference to Combat Racism and Racial Discrimination,[5] in its Declaration, condemned any form of co-operation with South Africa, notably the increasing relations between Israel and South Africa, in particular those in the economic and military fields, and warned against co-operation between them in the nuclear field. It deplored the expansion of those relations when the international community was exerting efforts towards isolating South Africa completely. The Conference viewed that co-operation as a hostile and deliberate act against the oppressed people of South Africa, as well as defiance of United Nations resolutions and nations' efforts to ensure peace and freedom in southern Africa. In addition, the Conference noted with concern Israeli propaganda against the United Nations and against Governments opposed to *apartheid*.

GENERAL ASSEMBLY ACTION

The General Assembly, on 5 December, adopted by recorded vote resolution 38/39 F.

Relations between Israel and South Africa

The General Assembly,

Reaffirming its resolutions on relations between Israel and South Africa,

Having considered the special report of the Special Committee against *Apartheid* on recent developments concerning relations between Israel and South Africa,

Taking note of the Declaration of the International Conference on the Alliance between South Africa and Israel and the Declaration of the Second World Conference to Combat Racism and Racial Discrimination,

Alarmed at the increasing collaboration by Israel with the racist régime of South Africa, especially in the military and nuclear fields, in defiance of resolutions of the General Assembly and the Security Council,

Considering that such collaboration is a serious hindrance to international action for the eradication of *apartheid*, an encouragement to the racist régime of South Africa to persist in its criminal policy of *apartheid* and a hostile act against the oppressed people of South Africa and the entire African continent, and constitutes a threat to international peace and security,

1. *Again strongly condemns* the continuing and increasing collaboration by Israel with the racist régime of South Africa, especially in the military and nuclear fields;

2. *Demands* that Israel desist from and terminate forthwith all forms of collaboration with South Africa, particularly in the military and nuclear fields, and abide scrupulously by the relevant resolutions of the General Assembly and the Security Council;

3. *Calls upon* all Governments and organizations to exert their influence to persuade Israel to desist from such collaboration and abide by the resolutions of the General Assembly;

4. *Requests* the Special Committee against *Apartheid* to publicize, as widely as possible, information on the relations between Israel and South Africa and especially the Declaration of the International Conference on the Alliance between South Africa and Israel;

5. *Requests* the Secretary-General to render, through the Department of Public Information and the Centre against *Apartheid* of the Secretariat, all possible assistance to the Special Committee in disseminating information relating to the collaboration between Israel and South Africa;

6. *Further requests* the Special Committee to keep the matter under constant review and to report to the General Assembly and the Security Council as appropriate.

General Assembly resolution 38/39 F

5 December 1983   Meeting 83   106-18-17 (recorded vote)

49-nation draft (A/38/L.25 & Corr.1); agenda item 32.

Sponsors: Afghanistan, Algeria, Angola, Benin, Botswana, Bulgaria, Burundi, Byelorussian SSR, Cape Verde, Cuba, Czechoslovakia, Democratic Yemen, Djibouti, Gambia, German Democratic Republic, Ghana, Guinea, Guinea-Bissau, Guyana, Hungary, India, Indonesia, Iraq, Kenya, Lao People's Democratic Republic, Libyan Arab Jamahiriya, Madagascar, Mali, Mauritania, Mongolia, Morocco, Mozambique, Nicaragua, Nigeria, Pakistan, Qatar, Rwanda, Sao Tome and Principe, Senegal, Sierra Leone, Somalia, Syrian Arab Republic, Uganda, Ukrainian SSR, United Republic of Cameroon, United Republic of Tanzania, Viet Nam, Zambia, Zimbabwe.

Financial implications. 5th Committee, A/38/654; S-G, A/C.5/38/53 & Corr.1.

Meeting numbers. GA 38th session: 5th Committee 51; plenary 60-63, 69-71, 83.

Recorded vote in Assembly as follows:

In favour: Afghanistan, Albania, Algeria, Angola, Antigua and Barbuda, Argentina, Bahrain, Bangladesh, Benin, Bhutan, Bolivia, Botswana, Brazil, Bulgaria, Burma, Burundi, Byelorussian SSR, Cape Verde, Central African Republic, Chad, China, Comoros, Congo, Cuba, Cyprus, Czechoslovakia, Democratic Kampuchea, Democratic Yemen, Djibouti, Ecuador, Egypt, Equatorial Guinea, Ethiopia, Gabon, Gambia, German Democratic Republic, Ghana, Greece, Guinea, Guinea-Bissau, Guyana, Hungary, India, Indonesia, Iran, Iraq, Jordan, Kenya, Kuwait, Lao People's Democratic Republic, Lebanon, Lesotho, Libyan Arab Jamahiriya, Madagascar, Malaysia, Maldives, Mali, Malta, Mauritania, Mauritius, Mexico, Mongolia, Morocco, Mozambique, Nepal, Nicaragua, Niger, Nigeria, Oman, Pakistan, Papua New Guinea, Peru, Philippines, Poland, Qatar, Romania, Rwanda, Sao Tome and Principe, Saudi Arabia, Senegal, Seychelles, Sierra Leone, Singapore, Somalia,

Sri Lanka, Sudan, Syrian Arab Republic, Thailand, Togo, Tunisia, Turkey, Uganda, Ukrainian SSR, USSR, United Arab Emirates, United Republic of Cameroon, United Republic of Tanzania, Upper Volta, Uruguay,[a] Vanuatu, Venezuela, Viet Nam, Yemen, Yugoslavia, Zambia, Zimbabwe.

Against: Australia, Austria, Belgium, Canada, Denmark, Finland, France, Germany, Federal Republic of, Iceland, Ireland, Italy, Luxembourg, Netherlands, New Zealand, Norway, Sweden, United Kingdom, United States.

Abstaining: Bahamas, Colombia, Costa Rica, Dominican Republic, Fiji, Guatemala, Haiti, Ivory Coast, Jamaica, Japan, Malawi, Panama, Paraguay, Portugal, Samoa, Solomon Islands, Spain.

[a]Later advised the Secretariat it had intended to abstain.

Speaking in explanation of its refusal to participate in the voting on the resolutions on South Africa's *apartheid* policies, Israel stressed that it rejected any form of racial discrimination but said that the sponsors of some of the texts, particularly of resolution 38/39 F, had relied on unsubstantiated allegations about Israel. In so doing, they sought to divert attention from the real problems of *apartheid*, thus undermining the purpose of the debate and subverting genuine concern for the victims of racial prejudice. The United Nations bodies established to confront the *apartheid* problem had instead abused their responsibilities and were submitting to external interests which pursued their own partisan goals. Israel added that it had again been singled out in the *apartheid* debate as the only country for specific condemnation, based on falsehoods.

Burma, Canada, Colombia, the Dominican Republic, Ireland, Panama and the United Kingdom also expressed reservations about the selective singling out of individual countries in the resolution. The Dominican Republic said that this practice only introduced extraneous factors which would work against the aims of the text.

Malawi and the United Kingdom had problems with some language formulations. Canada said it opposed those recommendations which went beyond the competence of the Assembly.

The Assembly took related action in other 1983 resolutions. In resolution 38/17, it took note of the Declaration of the International Conference on the Alliance between South Africa and Israel. The Assembly, in resolution 38/39 A, endorsed the annual report of the Committee against *Apartheid*[(1)] and its special report on recent developments concerning relations between Israel and South Africa.[(3)] In resolution 38/180 D, it strongly condemned the continuing and increasing collaboration between the two countries, especially in the economic, military and nuclear fields, which, it said, constituted a hostile act against the African and Arab States and enabled Israel to enhance its nuclear capabilities, thus subjecting the States of the region to nuclear blackmail. The Assembly, in resolution 38/69, requested the Secretary-General to continue to follow closely the nuclear and military collaboration between Israel and South Africa.

Situation in South Africa

Activities of the Committee against *Apartheid*.

The Special Committee against *Apartheid* described the current situation in South Africa in its 1983 report to the Assembly.[(1)] According to the report, South Africa had proceeded, despite international condemnation, to proclaim the so-called independence of bantustans—reserves into which African people were forcibly confined on a so-called tribal basis—in an effort to dispossess the African majority and deprive it of citizenship. Since 1976, four bantustans, with a total population of over 8 million blacks, had been established, and South Africa had announced its intention to create another in KwaNdebele in 1984. The Committee agreed with the Director-General of the International Labour Office (the secretariat of ILO), who had pointed out in his annual report on the effect of *apartheid* on labour and employment that the objective of the régime was to create a South Africa with no black citizens.

Racist oppression and exploitation continued unabated behind a smoke-screen of so-called reforms that were in fact manoeuvres to bolster the system, the Committee said. Leaders of black workers' groups and unions had been imprisoned under arbitrary laws. Arrests of Africans under the "pass laws" had increased and the forcible uprooting of black communities continued. Two leaders of African communities were killed by police in April for leading non-violent protests against the eviction of African communities, and several persons died in detention during the year.

The Committee noted the advance of national mobilization for unity and freedom in South Africa, encompassing trade unions, students and youth, religious bodies, community organizations and other segments of the population, despite indiscriminate killing and repression by the régime. It said that the armed struggle by the national liberation movement had advanced, especially under the leadership of ANC. The armed struggle enjoyed the support of the masses of people despite the propaganda of the Government. When the national liberation movement was obliged to resort to armed strugle, the Committee said, it took care to avoid loss of innocent lives, in contrast with the actions of the régime.

In the Committee's view, it was essential that the international community warn South Africa of the serious consequences of its policy and urge it to seek a peaceful solution in accordance with United Nations resolutions, through genuine negotiations with the leaders of the national liberation movement for the elimination of *apartheid* and racism and the establishment of a democratic State. The Committee called for a commitment to universal suffrage in an undivided South Africa and an unconditional amnesty for political prisoners, exiles and combatants, as well as the abrogation of bans on political organizations, so as to facilitate such negotiations.

It also considered it essential that increasing attention be given to solidarity with the struggles of people in South Africa against all manifestations of *apartheid* and to the denunciation of the repression of the régime. In that connection, it drew particular attention to the courage and determination demonstrated by the black workers in independent trade unions and to the repression against them. In its October Programme of Action,[2] the Committee urged trade unions to demonstrate support for black workers' unions in South Africa by mobilizing solidarity with their struggles, refusing to load or unload ships and planes, exposing collaboration between their employers and South Africa and taking industrial action to stop it, refusing to work on military or nuclear projects, ensuring that trade union and pension funds were not invested in companies with South African subsidiaries, and taking disciplinary measures against trade unionists who emigrated to South Africa, including the withdrawal of their union membership cards.

Action by the Commission on Human Rights and its subsidiary bodies. The Commission on Human Rights also considered the human rights situation in South Africa (see ECONOMIC AND SOCIAL QUESTIONS, Chapter XVIII). In a resolution of 15 February on the right to self-determination,[19] the Commission reaffirmed the legitimacy of the struggle of the oppressed people of South Africa and their national liberation movements by all available means, including armed struggle, for the elimination of *apartheid* and the exercise of the right of self-determination. It condemned the régime for its repression and indiscriminate torture and killing of opponents of *apartheid*, including workers and schoolchildren, and the imposition of death sentences on freedom fighters. It also condemned the "bantustanization" policy as contrary to the principle of self-determination. In an 18 February resolution on violations of human rights in southern Africa,[55] the Commission affirmed that any constitutional arrangement in South Africa based on racial segregation constituted a denial of the political rights of the black population. It demanded that South Africa put an end to human rights violations, enact adequate legislation to protect the rights of working children, and cease its military attacks against neighbouring countries. The Commission, in another 18 February resolution,[40] took note of the January report[56] of its Group of Three established under the 1973 International Convention on the Suppression and Punishment of the Crime of *Apartheid*;[41] urged States to accede to the Convention; called on States parties to the

Convention to strengthen their co-operation at the national and international level in order to implement decisions of the Security Council and other United Nations bodies with a view to the prevention, suppression and punishment of the crime of *apartheid*; and noted the importance of measures to be taken by States parties in education for fuller implementation of the Convention.

The Commission's Group of Three and its *Ad Hoc* Working Group of Experts on southern Africa considered various aspects of the situation in South Africa. The former Group (Geneva, 24-28 January) reviewed periodic reports on compliance with the Convention submitted by States parties.[56] The *Ad Hoc* Working Group (Geneva, 3-12 January) issued a study of violations of human rights in South Africa and Namibia and the current situation there, including information on capital punishment, treatment of political prisoners, conditions of detainees, torture, forced removals of populations, the bantustan policy, conditions of black workers, denial of trade union rights, and student movements.[57] Also in January, that Working Group issued a report on *apartheid* as a collective form of slavery.[58]

The Sub-Commission on Prevention of Discrimination and Protection of Minorities, by a resolution of 5 September,[59] recommended that the Commission recognize *apartheid* as a slavery-like practice and endorse the call for mandatory economic sanctions against South Africa (see above).

In 1983, both the Commission and the Economic and Social Council took action on trade union rights in South Africa (see ECONOMIC AND SOCIAL QUESTIONS, Chapter XVIII). In a resolution of 18 February,[55] the Commission, expressing concern regarding infringements of trade union rights and in particular the indiscriminate harassment, arrest and detention of black trade union leaders, demanded that South Africa respect international standards concerning those rights.

ECONOMIC AND SOCIAL COUNCIL ACTION

The Economic and Social Council, by decision 1983/156 of 27 May, noting that the consent of South Africa had been obtained, decided, in conformity with a 1950 Council resolution,[60] to transmit to the Fact-Finding and Conciliation Commission on Freedom of Association of ILO the allegations of infringements of trade union rights in South Africa submitted by the International Confederation of Free Trade Unions on 12 February 1982 and by the World Federation of Trade Unions on 13 July 1982, together with the text of the consent of South Africa. The Council also decided that the Commission's findings should be transmitted to the Council as soon as possible. By another decision (1983/157) of 27 May, the Council took note of the report of the *Ad Hoc* Working Group of Experts of the Commission on Human Rights on allegations regarding infringements of trade union rights in South Africa.

GENERAL ASSEMBLY ACTION

Various aspects of the situation in South Africa were dealt with by the General Assembly in 1983.

In resolution 38/39 A, the Assembly again proclaimed that the national liberation movements of South Africa were the authentic representatives of the people in their just struggle for national liberation and recognized the right of the oppressed people and those movements to resort to all means at their disposal, including armed struggle, in their resistance to the illegitimate racist minority régime. The Assembly demanded that South Africa: release persons imprisoned or restricted for their opposition to *apartheid;* allow those who had been exiled for their opposition to return; rescind bans on political and other organizations and media opposed to *apartheid;* and terminate political trials and repressive measures against opponents of *apartheid.* The Assembly commended the people of South Africa and their national liberation movements for the advance in their struggle for national liberation, also commending them, and particularly ANC, for intensifying the armed struggle. It condemned as an international crime the policy of "bantustanization" designed to dispossess the African majority of its inalienable rights and to deprive it of citizenship, as well as the forced removal of black people.

In a related area, the Assembly, in resolution 38/17, rejected South Africa's so-called reforms, especially the limited parliamentary representation for Coloured people and Asians designed to undermine the unity of the oppressed people of South Africa and buttress the *apartheid* system, and condemned the increasingly widespread massacres of innocent and defenceless people, including women and children, by the régime.

The Assembly, by resolution 38/19, expressed appreciation of the constructive role played by the Group of Three of the Commission on Human Rights in analysing the periodic reports of States and in publicizing the experience gained in the international struggle against *apartheid.*

In resolution 38/21, it condemned *apartheid* in South Africa and Namibia as the most abhorrent form of racial discrimination and urged Member States to adopt effective political, economic and other measures in order to secure the elimination of that policy and to achieve the implementation of United Nations resolutions.

Political prisoners and other detained persons

Action by the Commission on Human Rights and its Sub-Commission. Two 1983 resolutions of the Commission on Human Rights dealt with political prisoners in South Africa (see ECONOMIC AND SOCIAL QUESTIONS, Chapter XVIII). On 15 February,[19] the Commission demanded that South Africa immediately release all people detained or imprisoned as a result of their struggle for self-determination and independence, and demanded full respect for their fundamental rights and the observance of article 5 of the Universal Declaration of Human Rights,[61] under which no one should be subjected to torture or to cruel, inhuman or degrading treatment. The Commission, on 18 February,[55] expressed indignation at the scale and variety of human rights violations in South Africa, in particular the increase in sentences and executions, the torture of political activists during interrogation, the ill-treatment of captured freedom fighters and other detainees, and the deaths of detainees in South African prisons under suspicious circumstances. It requested the *Ad Hoc* Working Group of Experts on southern Africa, in co-operation with the Special Committee against *Apartheid*, to continue investigating cases of torture, ill-treatment and deaths of detainees in South Africa.

In a 5 September resolution,[62] the Sub-Commission on Prevention of Discrimination and Protection of Minorities condemned South Africa's continuing campaign of repressions, detentions and persecution of those opposing *apartheid* and fighting for the establishment of a just, non-racial democratic system. In particular, it condemned the execution in June 1983 of three South African militants (see below) as well as the political trials and imprisonment of political prisoners. The Sub-Commission called on the Commission to investigate the situation and seek action by the General Assembly, and it reaffirmed its support for the world campaign by the Committee against *Apartheid* to secure the release of political prisoners in South Africa and Namibia.

Activities of the Committee against *Apartheid*. The Special Committee against *Apartheid* continued to promote the campaign for the release of political prisoners in South Africa and for an end to repression against *apartheid* opponents.[1] The campaign included support for a declaration initiated by Archbishop Trevor Huddleston, President of the British Anti-*Apartheid* Movement, for the release of Nelson Mandela, the anti-*apartheid* leader serving a life sentence since 1964. The declaration had been signed by over 4,000 leaders of political parties, trade unions, religious bodies, members of Parliament and other leaders of public opinion in many countries. At the proposal of the Chairman of its Task Force on Political Prisoners, the Committee discussed a report on torture and ill-treatment of detainees by South

Africa in 1982 (see ECONOMIC AND SOCIAL QUES-
TIONS, Chapter XVIII). In statements of 13 January and 9 February 1983, the Chairman of the
Committee drew the attention of the international
community to trials under South African security
laws against members of the Pan Africanist Congress of Azania (PAC). On 31 May, he addressed
a cable to the President of the International Red
Cross expressing concern over reports on the conditions under which Mr. Mandela, Walter Sisulu
and their colleagues were being kept in the Polls-
moor prison of South Africa.

The Committee recommended that the General
Assembly invite Governments, organizations and
institutions to lend greater support for the campaign to obtain the release of all political prisoners.
It believed that the Assembly and the Security
Council should urgently consider measures to prevent further executions of patriots in South Africa
and to ensure that captured freedom fighters were
accorded prisoner-of-war status under the 1949
Geneva Conventions and Additional Protocol I of
1977.

In its October Programme of Action against
Apartheid,[2] the Committee called on Governments to act to achieve the release of political
prisoners and an end to repression. It recommended that they: denounce the repression of
apartheid opponents, including torture and ill-
treatment of political prisoners, and demand an
end to repression and an amnesty to those imprisoned, restricted or exiled for their opposition to
apartheid; condemn the execution of freedom
fighters and political prisoners, and exert all influence to prevent such executions; demand that
South Africa grant prisoner-of-war status to captured freedom fighters in accordance with the Additional Protocol I; demand that South Africa
abrogate bans imposed on organizations and the
media for their opposition to *apartheid;* honour the
leaders of the struggle against *apartheid* imprisoned
by South Africa, and publicize their lives; and promote the campaign for the release of South African political prisoners.

The Committee called on public organizations
to intensify the campaign for the release of those
political prisoners and to educate public opinion
about South Africa's repression of *apartheid* opponents. Suggested activities included: urging
Governments to intervene to secure the release of
Nelson Mandela and all political prisoners; giving special attention to the six PAC prisoners sentenced in 1963 and to women and juvenile
prisoners; acting to stop the execution of captured
freedom fighters and to ensure that all such combatants were granted prisoner-of-war status; organizing protests against the inhuman treatment
of detainees, including the use of torture resulting in death; and assisting the victims of South

Africa's laws by contributing to the International
Defence and Aid Fund for Southern Africa.

The Committee, with the assistance of the
Centre against *Apartheid*, pledged to take measures
to promote action against *apartheid* by Governments and intergovernmental and non-
governmental organizations, including action for
the unconditional release of South African political prisoners.

On 11 October, the Committee held two meetings in observance of the Day of Solidarity with
South African Political Prisoners.

**Action by the Conference against racial dis-
crimination.** In a resolution of 12 August,[63] the
Second World Conference to Combat Racism and
Racial Discrimination demanded the immediate
and unconditional release of Mr. Mandela and all
other South African and Namibian political
prisoners. It also expressed its solidarity with Mr.
Mandela and the national liberation movements
of South Africa and Namibia.

GENERAL ASSEMBLY ACTION

The General Assembly took similar action on
5 December in resolution 38/39 A, demanding
that South Africa release persons imprisoned or
restricted for their opposition to *apartheid* and
reaffirmed that freedom fighters of South Africa
should be treated as prisoners of war in accordance
with Additional Protocol I to the 1949 Geneva
Conventions.

Capital punishment of ANC members

On 7 June 1983, the Security Council, having
been alerted to the impending execution of three
members of the African National Congress of
South Africa (ANC), called on the South African
authorities to commute the death sentences.
Despite the appeal, the three men were executed
on 9 June. Three other ANC members sentenced
to death remained in South African prisons. The
General Assembly, the Commission on Human
Rights and the Special Committee against *Apartheid* led international protests against South
Africa's action.

Communications (February/March). In a letter to the Secretary-General of 22 February,[64]
the United States, in response to a December 1982
Security Council resolution[65] urging States to
use their influence to save the lives of the six political prisoners sentenced to death in South Africa
in 1982, reported that it had communicated to that
country its concern regarding their lives.

The Chairman of the Committee against *Apartheid*, on 1 March,[66] forwarded to the Secretary-
General a letter of 28 January from the attorneys
of three of the prisoners, Thelle Simon Mogoerane, Jerry Semano Mosololi and Marcus Thabo
Motaung, who had been charged with high trea-

son by the South African Supreme Court and sentenced to death. The attorneys, refuting charges contained in a letter of 19 October 1982[67] from South Africa concerning the three men, stated that the information about their trials contained in the South African letter was erroneous and misleading.

Action by the Commission on Human Rights. The Commission on Human Rights, in a resolution of 18 February on human rights violations in southern Africa,[55] appealed to the international community to undertake urgent action to save the lives of Bobby Tsotsobe, Johannes Shabangu, David Moise, Mr. Mosololi, Mr. Mogoerane, and Mr. Motaung, sentenced to death in 1982 as a result of their opposition to *apartheid*.

After three of those sentences were carried out in June, the Sub-Commission on Prevention of Discrimination and Protection of Minorities on 5 September condemned those executions (see ECONOMIC AND SOCIAL QUESTIONS, Chapter XVIII).

SECURITY COUNCIL ACTION (June)

In a letter to the President of the Security Council dated 6 June,[68] Morocco, as Chairman of the African Group, called the Council's attention to the confirmation that day by South Africa of the death sentence on the three ANC members to be carried out three days later, despite the Council's December 1982 appeal for clemency.[65] Morocco called for urgent Council action to save their lives.

Meeting on 7 June, the Council unanimously adopted resolution 533(1983), which had been prepared during consultations.

The Security Council,
Having considered the question of the death sentences passed on 6 August 1982 in South Africa on Mr. Thelle Simon Mogoerane, Mr. Jerry Semano Mosololi and Mr. Marcus Thabo Motaung, members of the African National Congress of South Africa,
Recalling its statement of 4 October 1982 as well as its resolution 525(1982) appealing for executive clemency in this case,
Gravely concerned over the decision of the South African authorities on 6 June 1983 to refuse executive clemency in respect of the three men,
Conscious that the carrying out of the death sentences will aggravate the situation in South Africa,
1. *Calls upon* the South African authorities to commute the death sentences imposed on the three men;
2. *Urges* all States and organizations to use their influence and to take urgent measures, in conformity with the Charter of the United Nations, the resolutions of the Security Council and relevant international instruments, to save the lives of the three men.

Security Council resolution 533(1983)

7 June 1983   Meeting 2452   Adopted unanimously

Draft prepared in consultations among Council members (S/15815).
Meeting number. SC 2452.

Following the execution of the three ANC members on 9 June, the Chairman of the Committee against *Apartheid* issued a statement expressing the deepest anguish and indignation and describing the execution as "an international crime". In its annual report to the Assembly and the Council,[1] the Committee stated that the execution was carried out in defiance of appeals by the Assembly, the Council and Governments, organizations and leaders, including leaders of Western Governments which maintained cordial relations with South Africa.

Further communication (June). In June, seven countries protested the death sentences, in communications to either the President of the Security Council or the Secretary-General. India, on 8 June,[69] transmitted a statement issued that day by its Prime Minister appealing for the commutation of the death sentences of the three ANC members and affirming India's support for their cause. Spain made a similar appeal on 9 June,[70] transmitting a telegram of 8 June from its Minister for External Affairs, who requested the Foreign Minister of South Africa to intervene with the South African President so that, for humanitarian reasons, clemency would be extended.

Five countries protested after South Africa carried out the sentences. On 13 June,[71] Viet Nam forwarded a message of 12 June from its Foreign Minister, stating that the executions had aggravated the situation in South Africa, ran counter to the fundamental national rights of the South African people, and violated principles of international law. Brazil sent a telegram on 13 June[72] expressing its repudiation and rejection of South Africa's action. Also on 13 June,[73] Pakistan forwarded a Government statement of 11 June, expressing its anguish and outrage at the action, which it said demonstrated the barbarous and inhuman nature of South Africa's policies, and calling for international support of the South African people's freedom struggle.

The Bahamas, on 30 June,[74] forwarded a letter from its Foreign Minister stating that the execution was a calculated act by South Africa against its citizens who had turned to active resistance in response to its inhumanities and that, by carrying it out, South Africa had again demonstrated its disdain for the sensitivities of the international community. On 28 June,[75] Iraq transmitted a letter of 27 June from its Foreign Minister, who protested and condemned the death sentences as contrary to elementary human principles and customs.

GENERAL ASSEMBLY ACTION

The General Assembly, in resolution 38/17 of 22 November, expressing its indignation at the callous murder of the three ANC freedom fighters, said South Africa had committed the crime with flagrant indifference despite various appeals by the international community, thereby defying the Security Council.

South African Constitution

In 1983, the South African Government proposed changes in its Constitution to expand representation in its Parliament to certain racial groups, but not to the black majority. Despite the protest of the General Assembly, South Africa adopted the new Constitution.

Activities of the Committee against *Apartheid*. The Special Committee against *Apartheid*, in its annual report to the Assembly,[1] said the proposed constitutional changes were being propagated by the *apartheid* régime as reforms. Those changes, offering the Coloureds (persons of mixed race) and Asians (mostly of Indian descent) limited representation in the Parliament, were introduced in that body in May for debate. They envisaged a three-chamber parliament formed by whites, Coloureds and people of Asian origin, but no representation for the African majority. Under the new structure, whites would continue to dominate. The Committee said that the changes were in fact devised to entrench *apartheid* and perpetuate white domination. They had been categorically rejected by Africans as well as by the majority of Coloureds and Asians because they were designed to divide the black people, stifle their political aspirations, conscript Coloureds and Asians into the army, entrench *apartheid* and prolong white domination. The so-called reforms were also rejected by the Opposition Progressive Federal Party. They had also been rejected, although for different reasons, by two far-right Afrikaner parties.

In January, over 300 delegates representing trade-union, civic, student and other organizations met to establish the United Democratic Front and organize opposition to the proposed new system under which, they believed, Coloureds and Asians were meant to become junior partners in *apartheid* and Africans would be divided into designated rural and urban areas so that their movement could be controlled by the Government. The delegates adopted a declaration pledging to fight against the proposals.

At a meeting at Hammanskraal on 11 and 12 June, the National Forum Conference, representing a wide spectrum of black leaders, also rejected the constitutional proposals. Opposition was further expressed at the launching of the United Democratic Front in Cape Town on 21 August. Peaceful demonstrations by blacks in August and September were confronted with violence by the Government, resulting in scores of people killed and hundreds injured, including children.

The new Constitution was adopted by the South African Parliament in September, and on 2 November it was approved by a national whites-only referendum.[76] Elections were planned for 1984, when the Constitution was to go into effect.

In view of the efforts of the Government to deprive the African majority of citizenship rights and its moves for a constitutional amendment excluding the African majority from participation in the Parliament, the Committee considered it essential that the Security Council and the General Assembly reconsider the question of membership of South Africa in the United Nations and the legal status of the illegitimate *apartheid* régime.

Action by the Commission on Human Rights and its Sub-Commission. The Commission on Human Rights, in a resolution of 18 February,[55] affirmed that any constitutional arrangement in South Africa which was based on racial segregation and which denied full citizenship rights to the majority black population as a whole constituted a denial of their political rights, served to perpetuate *apartheid* and was unacceptable.

In a resolution of 5 September,[62] the Sub-Commission on Prevention of Discrimination and Protection of Minorities noted that the South African Constitution put the juridical system and the impartiality of the judiciary into doubt, especially in cases involving the conflicting interests of the white minority and the disenfranchised black majority. Under those circumstances, the Constitution could not be considered as a just basis for a fair judicial system. (See ECONOMIC AND SOCIAL QUESTIONS, Chapter XVIII.)

Action by the Conference against racial discrimination. The Second World Conference to Combat Racism and Racial Discrimination,[5] in its Programme of Action for the Second Decade to Combat Racism and Racial Discrimination (1983-1993), confirmed the international community's rejection of South Africa's so-called reforms, especially the limited parliamentary representation for Coloureds and Asians designed to split the black alliance and buttress the *apartheid* system. The Programme was approved by the General Assembly in resolution 38/14.

On 15 November, the General Assembly adopted resolution 38/11 by recorded vote.

Proposed new racial constitution of South Africa
The General Assembly,

Recalling its many resolutions and those of the Security Council calling on the authorities in South Africa to abandon *apartheid*, end oppression and repression of the black majority and seek a peaceful, just and lasting solution in accordance with the principles of the Charter of the United Nations and the Universal Declaration of Human Rights,

Reaffirming that *apartheid* is a crime against humanity and a threat to international peace and security,

Gravely concerned that the so-called "constitutional proposals" endorsed, on 2 November 1983, by the exclusively white electorate in South Africa further entrench *apartheid*,

Convinced that the aim of the so-called "constitutional proposals" is to deprive the indigenous African majority of all fundamental rights, including the right of citizenship, and to transform South Africa into a country for "whites only", in keeping with the declared policies of *apartheid*,

Aware that the inclusion in the "constitutional proposals" of the so-called "coloured" people and people of Asian origin is aimed at dividing the unity of the oppressed people of South Africa and fomenting internal conflict,

Noting with grave concern that one of the objectives of the so-called "constitutional proposals" of the racist régime is to make the "coloured" people and people of Asian origin in South Africa eligible for conscription into the *apartheid* armed forces for further internal repression and aggression against independent African States,

Welcoming the united resistance of the oppressed people of South Africa against these "constitutional" manœuvres,

Reaffirming the legitimacy of the struggle of the oppressed people of South Africa for the elimination of *apartheid* and for the establishment of a society in which all the people of South Africa as a whole, irrespective of race, colour or creed, will enjoy equal and full political and other rights and participate freely in the determination of their destiny,

Firmly convinced that the implementation of these "constitutional proposals" will further aggravate the already explosive situation prevailing inside *apartheid* South Africa,

1. *Declares* that the so-called "constitutional proposals" are contrary to the principles of the Charter of the United Nations, that the results of the referendum are of no validity whatsoever and that the enforcement of the proposed "constitution" will inevitably aggravate tension and conflict in South Africa and in southern Africa as a whole;

2. *Rejects* the so-called "constitutional proposals" and all insidious manœuvres by the racist minority régime of South Africa further to entrench white minority rule and *apartheid;*

3. *Further rejects* any so-called "negotiated settlement" based on bantustan structures or on the "constitutional proposals";

4. *Solemnly declares* that only the total eradication of *apartheid* and the establishment of a non-racial democratic society based on majority rule, through the full and free exercise of adult suffrage by all the people in a united and non-fragmented South Africa, can lead to a just and lasting solution of the explosive situation in South Africa;

5. *Urges* all Governments and organizations to take appropriate action, in co-operation with the United Nations and the Organization of African Unity and in accordance with the present resolution, to assist the oppressed people of South Africa in their legitimate struggle for a non-racial democratic society;

6. *Requests* the Security Council, as a matter of urgency, to consider the serious implications of the so-called "constitutional proposals" and to take all necessary measures, in accordance with the Charter, to avert the further aggravation of tension and conflict in South Africa and in southern Africa as a whole.

General Assembly resolution 38/11

15 November 1983   Meeting 56   141-0-7 (recorded vote)

19-nation draft (A/38/L.15 & Add.1); agenda item 32.
Sponsors: Bangladesh, Bhutan, Cuba, Democratic Yemen, Guyana, India, Indonesia, Iran, Kuwait, Maldives, Nepal, Nicaragua, Pakistan, Sierra Leone, Sri Lanka, Syrian Arab Republic, Trinidad and Tobago, Viet Nam, Yugoslavia.
Meeting number. GA 38th session: plenary 56.

Recorded vote in Assembly as follows:

In favour: Afghanistan, Albania, Algeria, Angola, Antigua and Barbuda, Argentina, Australia, Austria, Bahamas, Bahrain, Bangladesh, Barbados, Benin, Bhutan, Bolivia, Botswana, Brazil, Bulgaria, Burma, Burundi, Byelorussian SSR, Canada, Cape Verde, Central African Republic, Chile, China, Colombia, Comoros, Costa Rica, Cuba, Cyprus, Czechoslovakia, Democratic Kampuchea, Democratic Yemen, Denmark, Djibouti, Dominican Republic, Ecuador, Egypt, El Salvador, Equatorial Guinea, Ethiopia, Fiji, Finland, France, Gabon, Gambia, German Democratic Republic, Ghana, Greece, Guinea, Guinea-Bissau, Guyana, Haiti, Honduras, Hungary, Iceland, India, Indonesia, Iran, Iraq, Ireland, Italy, Ivory Coast, Jamaica, Japan, Jordan, Kenya, Kuwait, Lao People's Democratic Republic, Lebanon, Lesotho, Liberia, Libyan Arab Jamahiriya, Madagascar, Malawi, Malaysia, Maldives, Mali, Malta, Mauritania, Mauritius, Mexico, Mongolia, Morocco, Mozambique, Nepal, New Zealand, Nicaragua, Niger, Nigeria, Norway, Oman, Pakistan, Panama, Papua New Guinea, Peru, Philippines, Poland, Qatar, Romania, Rwanda, Saint Lucia, Saint Vincent and the Grenadines, Samoa, Sao Tome and Principe, Saudi Arabia, Senegal, Seychelles, Sierra Leone, Singapore, Solomon Islands, Somalia, Spain, Sri Lanka, Sudan, Suriname, Swaziland, Sweden, Syrian Arab Republic, Thailand, Togo, Trinidad and Tobago, Tunisia, Turkey, Uganda, Ukrainian SSR, USSR, United Arab Emirates, United Republic of Cameroon, United Republic of Tanzania, Upper Volta, Uruguay, Vanuatu, Venezuela, Viet Nam, Yemen, Yugoslavia, Zaire, Zambia, Zimbabwe.
Against: None.
Abstaining: Belgium, Germany, Federal Republic of, Luxembourg, Netherlands, Portugal, United Kingdom, United States.

On 22 November, the Assembly took related action, in resolution 38/17 on the self-determination of peoples. It rejected the so-called reforms, especially the limited parliamentary representation for Coloured people and Asians designed to undermine the unity of the oppressed people of South Africa and buttress the *apartheid* system.

South Africa, in a letter to the Secretary-General of 15 November,[77] enclosed a statement made that day by its Foreign Minister, who stated that the overwhelming endorsement of the new Constitution during the recent referendum had alarmed South Africa's enemies at the United Nations because it proposed the continuation of peaceful and evolutionary development in South Africa for the benefit of all rather than confrontation; the country's future would be determined by its peoples and not by the Assembly, he added.

Women and children

Report of the Working Group of Experts. The *Ad Hoc* Working Group of Experts on Southern Africa of the Commission on Human Rights, as requested by the Commission in 1981,[78] had reported in 1982 on the effects of *apartheid* on black women and children,[79] and, after a second mission of inquiry in London in July/August 1982, issued a supplementary report in January 1983.[80] The Working Group concluded that black women and children were the main victims of forced transfer to the "homelands" and resettlement camps. Those women, separated most of the time from their menfolk who were working in different areas, were struggling to survive on barren land and without adequate water, sanitation, housing, food, schools or medical services. Victims of discrimination in education, black women had very few professional opportunities and most were employed in domestic service or agriculture, areas where working conditions were inhumane and wages low.

Children suffered the same effects of forced relocation, including malnutrition and disease. According to estimates, between 30 and 50 per cent of African children in rural areas died before the age of five. Education did not meet their needs even minimally. As a result of the poverty, child labour was widespread, and black children and young people were the victims of detention, interrogation, torture and "disappearances".

The Working Group paid tribute to black women who, despite their living conditions, played a role in their people's struggle for liberation and for the abolition of *apartheid*. United Nations bodies, non-governmental organizations and other groups were requested to give wide publicity to the living conditions of African women and children under *apartheid*. The Working Group called for increased assistance to women and children who were refugees from South Africa, and further research on child labour in South Africa. It denounced the manner in which the police and the courts violated the special status of juveniles and detained, imprisoned, tortured or killed African children and youths.

Action by the Commission on Human Rights. In a resolution of 18 February,[55] the Commission on Human Rights expressed deep indignation at the fact that child labour continued in South Africa, black women and children were exploited and suffered the most from *apartheid*, and young black people suffered discriminatory harassment and imprisonment. The Commission demanded that South Africa put an end to the violations of the rights of the African population, especially women and children, and that it adhere to the 1973 Convention of ILO concerning minimum age for admission to employment and ensure the enactment of adequate legislation to protect the rights of working children.

Activities of the Committee against *Apartheid*. In 1983, the Special Committee against *Apartheid* and its Task Force on Women and Children under *Apartheid* continued to devote special attention to the plight of oppressed women and children in South Africa and Namibia.[1] Following a recommendation of the 1982 International Conference on Women and *Apartheid*,[81] a delegation of women leaders visited Belgium, France, Italy, the Netherlands and Tunisia in January and February 1983 to meet with leaders of Governments and intergovernmental and other organizations in order to promote broader awareness of the plight of women and children under *apartheid* and to urge support for assistance projects for them. Another such delegation visited Denmark, Finland, the Federal Republic of Germany, Norway and Sweden from 13 to 24 June for the same purpose. On 8 March, International Women's Day, the Chairman of the Committee issued a statement drawing the attention of Governments and organizations to the plight of women oppressed by *apartheid*.

The Committee recommended that this plight be given special importance in the agenda of the World Conference to Review and Appraise the Achievements of the United Nations Decade for Women, to be held in 1985, and that action against *apartheid* be given special attention in the programme of International Youth Year (1985). It suggested that the General Assembly support the Committee's efforts to promote assistance to those women and children and stated that it was considering sponsoring a conference on such assistance.

In its October Programme of Action,[2] the Committee urged women's organizations to mobilize women in solidarity with the struggles of the black women of South Africa against *apartheid*, distribute material highlighting the oppression experienced by those women and the role of women in the national liberation struggle, protest the victimization of women engaged in the struggle against *apartheid*, and provide material assistance for South African women refugees and the women's section of the liberation movements recognized by OAU.

On 9 August, the Committee held a meeting in observance of the International Day of Solidarity with the Struggle of Women of South Africa and Namibia.

GENERAL ASSEMBLY ACTION

The General Assembly, in resolution 38/17, condemned the increasingly widespread massacres of innocent and defenceless people, including women and children, by South Africa in its attempt to thwart the legitimate demands of the people, and demanded the immediate release of women and children detained in Namibian and South African prisons.

Apartheid in sports

Activities of the Conference on sports sanctions. The International Conference for Sanctions against *Apartheid* in Sports, organized by the Special Committee against *Apartheid* in co-operation with the South African Non-Racial Olympic Committee (SAN-ROC), was held in London from 27 to 29 June 1983.[82] The Conference reviewed implementation of the General Assembly's 1977 International Declaration against *Apartheid* in Sports,[83] the continued collaboration with *apartheid* sport, and progress in the campaign for the sports boycott of South Africa. In its Declaration, transmitted to the Secretary-General on 15 July by the Acting Chairman of the Special Committee,[84] the Conference expressed support to sportsmen and sportswomen who refused to collaborate with *apartheid* sports, recommended that the reality of *apartheid* and *apartheid* sports be given wide publicity, and requested that SAN-ROC be given maximum assistance to expand the campaign against *apartheid* in sports.

It also recommended that the concept of the third-party principle, which provided for sanctions against those who collaborated with South Africa, be supported by all countries, that sportsmen and women who participated in sports events in South Africa be disqualified from international competition, that States and sports bodies strictly adhere to the Olympic principle of non-discrimination in sports, and that States deny entry to representatives of sports bodies, team members or individual athletes from South Africa. In particular, it recommended that the campaign to expel *apartheid* sports bodies from international sports federations be pursued.

The Conference appealed to sportsmen and women to refuse to tour South Africa, not to compete against South African representatives, to refuse to take part in activities which allowed South African representation, and to support the exclusion of South Africa from international competition and from sports bodies.

Activities of the Committee against *Apartheid*. During the second half of 1982, many Governments and organizations had reaffirmed their commitment to boycott *apartheid* sport, according to the 1983 report of the Special Committee against *Apartheid* to the Assembly,[1] while some sports bodies had continued to provide support for *apartheid* under the pretext of separation of sports and politics. The names of 269 sportsmen and sportswomen were included in the Committee's register of sports contacts with South Africa. After the latest addition to the register was issued on 26 April 1983 (covering July-December 1982), the Chairman of the Committee sent the revised list to Member States for action. On 25 April 1983, the Chairman issued a statement expressing satisfaction at France's decision to cancel the French rugby tour of South Africa, which had been scheduled for June. Together with the Centre against *Apartheid*, the Committee was considering the organization of a meeting to review the progress of the boycott of *apartheid* sports.

In its October Programme of Action,[2] the Committee urged Governments to implement United Nations resolutions on *apartheid* in sports and, in particular, to refrain from contact with sports bodies established on the basis of *apartheid*, withhold support from sporting events in which South African teams were participating, and encourage sports organizations to refrain from exchanges with those teams. Public organizations were encouraged to strengthen the sports boycott by pressing Governments to enforce it, including the cancellation of visa-free entry privileges to South Africans and the refusal of visas to South African sportsmen and women. They were urged to organize campaigns to expel South Africa from international sporting federations, oppose sporting tours of and from that country, persuade sporting organizations to sever relations with *apartheid* sport, stop media publicity of sporting events which included South African teams, counter South African propaganda promoting "multinational" sport, support measures against individuals and organizations which defied the boycott, and co-operate with the Committee in compiling the register of sports contacts with South Africa.

The Committee said that city and local authorities should withhold the use of recreational facilities or other support for sporting or cultural events with South African participation. Sportsmen and women were called on to take those actions recommended by the Conference, protest at the persecution of sportsmen and women who were struggling for non-racial sport, campaign for South Africa's expulsion from international sports federations and competitions, and co-operate with the Committee and SAN-ROC in ensuring the isolation of South Africa from international sport. The Committee affirmed its intention to promote the international campaign for the boycott of racially selected South African sports teams.

Communications. In 1983, four Governments addressed communications to the Secretary-General regarding matters relating to the sports boycott. On 14 January,[85] Jamaica transmitted a 13 January statement by its Minister for Foreign Affairs affirming that the Government condemned the action of a group of Jamaican and other West Indian cricketers who had gone to South Africa to play cricket and adding that the Jamaicans involved would be debarred by the Jamaica Cricket Board of Control for life from playing cricket at all levels; also, the other cricketers would be permanently debarred from playing in Jamaica. On 15 February,[86] Trinidad and Tobago forwarded a 14 January statement by its Minister of Sport, Culture and Youth Affairs noting that one of its nationals had participated in the tour and that similar action had been taken; the Cabinet had decided that any non-national members of the team would not be welcome in Trinidad and Tobago. On 6 May,[87] Venezuela forwarded a Government statement condemning a visit by a Venezuelan sports delegation to South Africa to compete in motor cycle races, which contradicted Venezuela's policy of maintaining no relations with South Africa. The Bahamas transmitted on 28 June[88] a resolution on *apartheid* in sports adopted on 25 May by its House of Assembly, affirming the Government's policy of discouraging contacts by Bahamians with South Africa, ensuring that no support would be given to national sports teams or individuals participating in events with South Africans, and denying entrance to the Bahamas to those having sporting contacts with South Africa.

Statements by Antigua and Barbuda, Barbados, Grenada and Guyana, condemning the cricket tour of South Africa by the West Indians, were issued by the Committee against *Apartheid* on 28 March.[89] The Deputy Prime Minister of Antigua and Barbuda said that his country would not permit those concerned to play cricket there again. The Minister for Foreign Affairs of Barbados, reiterating the Government's policy opposing all sporting contacts with South Africa, said that those who had participated would be disqualified from representing Barbados. In a Government statement, Grenada said that each was declared *persona non grata* and was thereby prohibited from entering Grenada. Guyana's Minister of State for Youth and Sports appealed to sportsmen and sportswomen to condemn the behaviour of the West Indian players and not to be taken in by monetary temptations offered by racists in South Africa.

Draft convention

Activities of the Committee on a convention against *apartheid* in sports. The *Ad Hoc* Committee on the Drafting of an International Convention against *Apartheid* in Sports, established by the General Assembly in 1976,[90] submitted a revised draft Convention to the Assembly in August 1983.[91] A mission, led by the Committee Chairman, visited Algeria, Benin, Kenya, Mozambique, Senegal, the United Republic of Tanzania and Zimbabwe from 14 May to 8 June[92] and the United Kingdom from 27 to 29 June to gather their views in regard to the draft Convention. The Committee's Working Group, set up to finalize the draft, focused its efforts on completing the remaining article.

The Chairman explained the controversy in the Committee concerning the "third-party principle" which would require States parties to the Convention to boycott countries that allowed the participation of their sportsmen, sportswomen and teams with South Africa in the same manner that South

Africa was boycotted. That principle, embodied in article 10 B of the draft Convention, represented the African position. The supporters of that version felt that, without it, the Convention would be very weak. A number of Asian and Latin American States as well as the Eastern European Group expressed difficulties with that version on the grounds that it would lead to either a disruption of international sporting activities or the isolation of States parties to the Convention rather than the isolation of South Africa and its allies. They supported a version (article 10 A) by which States parties would take action to ensure that their nationals refrained from participating in sports events which included representation from a country practising *apartheid*. The Chairman expressed the hope that a compromise could be reached between the supporters of the different versions. The mission determined that there was general support for article 10 B by the African countries it had visited and that article 10 A was not acceptable to them; it supported Algeria's initiative to convene a meeting of African States to consider the alternative proposals concerning article 10 with a view to finding a compromise. The mission took note of the suggestion by the United Republic of Tanzania that, if all other efforts to reach a compromise failed, then the Secretary-General might be invited to join the search for an acceptable solution. In addition, it suggested that the Working Group consider various proposals put forward during the mission.

As a result of the consultations, the Chairman presented for consideration by the Working Group at its 26 July meeting amendments to 5 of the 22 articles of the proposed Convention. Those articles (4, 10, 12, 13 and 20) dealt with measures to prevent sports contact with a country practising *apartheid*, compliance with the Convention and the principle of non-discrimination, monitoring compliance, examination of breaches of the Convention, and amendment of it. Because the members of the Working Group expressed the desire to have time to consult their Governments concerning the proposals, the Committee was unable to complete its drafting work. Therefore, it recommended that its mandate be extended in order to continue negotiations with a view to submitting a draft Convention to the Assembly in 1984.

GENERAL ASSEMBLY ACTION

On 5 December, the General Assembly adopted resolution 38/39 K by recorded vote.

Apartheid in sports

The General Assembly,

Having considered the report of the *Ad Hoc* Committee on the Drafting of an International Convention against *Apartheid* in Sports,

1. *Authorizes* the *Ad Hoc* Committee on the Drafting of an International Convention against *Apartheid* in Sports to continue consultations, as required, with representatives of Governments and organizations concerned and experts on *apartheid* in sports;

2. *Requests* the *Ad Hoc* Committee to continue its work with a view to submitting the draft Convention to the General Assembly at its thirty-ninth session.

General Assembly resolution 38/39 K

5 December 1983   Meeting 83   145-1-6 (recorded vote)

33-nation draft (A/38/L.31 & Add.1); agenda item 32.

Sponsors: Afghanistan, Bahamas, Barbados, Burundi, Congo, Gambia, German Democratic Republic, Guinea, Guyana, Haiti, Hungary, India, Indonesia, Jamaica, Libyan Arab Jamahiriya, Madagascar, Malaysia, Morocco, Nepal, Nicaragua, Nigeria, Pakistan, Poland, Qatar, Senegal, Somalia, Sri Lanka, Syrian Arab Republic, Togo, Trinidad and Tobago, Ukrainian SSR, United Republic of Tanzania, Yugoslavia.

Financial implications. 5th Committee, A/38/654; S-G, A/C.5/38/53 & Corr.1.

Meeting numbers. GA 38th session: 5th Committee 51; plenary 60-63, 69-71, 83;

Recorded vote in Assembly as follows:

In favour: Afghanistan, Albania, Algeria, Angola, Antigua and Barbuda, Argentina, Australia, Austria, Bahamas, Bahrain, Bangladesh, Barbados, Belgium, Belize, Benin, Bhutan, Bolivia, Botswana, Brazil, Bulgaria, Burma, Burundi, Byelorussian SSR, Canada, Cape Verde, Central African Republic, Chad, Chile, China, Colombia, Comoros, Congo, Costa Rica, Cuba, Cyprus, Czechoslovakia, Democratic Kampuchea, Democratic Yemen, Djibouti, Dominican Republic, Ecuador, Egypt, El Salvador, Equatorial Guinea, Ethiopia, Fiji, Finland, France, Gabon, Gambia, German Democratic Republic, Ghana, Greece, Guatemala, Guinea, Guinea-Bissau, Guyana, Haiti, Honduras, Hungary, India, Indonesia, Iran, Iraq, Ireland, Italy, Ivory Coast, Jamaica, Japan, Jordan, Kenya, Kuwait, Lao People's Democratic Republic, Lebanon, Lesotho, Liberia, Libyan Arab Jamahiriya, Luxembourg, Madagascar, Malawi, Malaysia, Maldives, Mali, Malta, Mauritania, Mauritius, Mexico, Mongolia, Morocco, Mozambique, Nepal, Nicaragua, Niger, Nigeria, Norway, Oman, Pakistan, Panama, Papua New Guinea, Peru, Philippines, Poland, Portugal, Qatar, Romania, Rwanda, Saint Lucia, Saint Vincent and the Grenadines, Samoa, Sao Tome and Principe, Saudi Arabia, Senegal, Seychelles, Sierra Leone, Singapore, Solomon Islands, Somalia, Spain, Sri Lanka, Sudan, Suriname, Swaziland, Sweden, Syrian Arab Republic, Thailand, Togo, Trinidad and Tobago, Tunisia, Turkey, Uganda, Ukrainian SSR, USSR, United Arab Emirates, United Republic of Cameroon, United Republic of Tanzania, Upper Volta, Uruguay, Vanuatu, Venezuela, Viet Nam, Yemen, Yugoslavia, Zaire, Zambia, Zimbabwe.

Against: United States.

Abstaining: Denmark, Germany, Federal Republic of, Iceland, Netherlands, New Zealand, United Kingdom.

In explanation of vote, several countries mentioned possible conflicts between the draft Convention and their national jurisdiction.

Canada expressed support for the principle underlying the international effort to draft a convention, but added that national, legal and constitutional obstacles might preclude Canada's adherence to it. Ireland hoped that the terms of the draft would not give rise to such problems for its Government. The Netherlands said that the proposed Convention infringed upon certain constitutionally guaranteed freedoms and was therefore not acceptable; nevertheless, it was attempting to restrict, by visa requirements, the admission of South African sportspersons wishing to participate in events in the Netherlands. While repudiating all discrimination in sports, France reserved its position on the substance of any future draft Convention. Speaking for the 10 members of the European Community, Greece said they rejected *apartheid* in sports and would continue to discourage sporting contacts involving racial discrimination; however, it pointed out that sport was or-

ganized on a private basis in those countries. Portugal felt the resolution was likely to contribute in a balanced way to the eradication of *apartheid*.

Aid programmes and inter-agency co-operation

Throughout 1983, United Nations aid programmes continued to focus on the special needs of the victims of *apartheid*. Some of those programmes channelled aid through national liberation movements of southern Africa, while others provided aid directly to South African refugees or for individual educational and training needs (see also below, under UN TRAINING PROGRAMME FOR SOUTHERN AFRICA). As a means of intensifying the international campaign against *apartheid*, the General Assembly called for concerted action within the United Nations system to aid those concerned, in particular for assistance to the victims of racism and *apartheid* through the national liberation movements recognized by OAU, and for increased contributions to the United Nations Trust Fund for South Africa and agencies providing assistance. In addition, the Assembly requested the Secretary-General to strengthen co-operation between the United Nations and OAU, particularly in regard to assistance to those victims.

National liberation movements

Report of the Secretary-General. In 1983, the United Nations continued to provide assistance to national liberation movements in Africa. Such assistance was described by the Secretary-General in a May report to the General Assembly with three later addenda.[93] The report contained information received from bodies forming part of or associated with the United Nations concerning measures they had taken to implement resolutions pertaining to the 1960 Declaration on the Granting of Independence to Colonial Countries and Peoples.[94] The report, made in accordance with a November 1982 Assembly request,[95] included information from several agencies on their assistance to the national liberation movements recognized by OAU—the African National Congress of South Africa (ANC), the Pan Africanist Congress of Azania (PAC) and the South West Africa People's Organization (SWAPO). In addition, many had invited those movements to participate as observers at meetings.

The Food and Agriculture Organization of the United Nations (FAO), for example, extended material and technical assistance to those movements in an effort to enable the refugee communities administered by them to become self-sufficient in food, and to improve the level of nutrition. Its projects were also intended to provide them with agricultural skills, by providing training or fellowships, so that their members could contribute to the agricultural development of their home countries after independence. The United Nations Educational, Scientific and Cultural Organization (UNESCO), at the request of ANC, organized and funded a workshop on pre-school education in the United Republic of Tanzania.

The World Health Organization (WHO) provided emergency assistance (vaccines, supplies and medicines) to refugees of movements based in Angola, Mozambique, the United Republic of Tanzania, and Zambia. The Office of the United Nations High Commissioner for Refugees (UNHCR) provided assistance in housing, health, education and infrastructure to Namibian refugees, with SWAPO as the operational partner responsible for the execution of projects for the Namibians in Angola. Following specific proposals by ANC, UNHCR provided funds for agricultural equipment and vehicles for an ANC centre in the United Republic of Tanzania; ANC was the implementing agency for programmes for South African refugees in Angola and the United Republic of Tanzania.

UNDP report. The Administrator of the United Nations Development Programme (UNDP), in a March 1984 report to the Governing Council,[96] described UNDP's 1983 programmes of assistance to those national liberation movements recognized by OAU. The Administrator reported that development assistance was aimed at promoting skills and manpower development through education and training, with a view to preparing individuals for eventual administrative, technical and managerial responsibilities, as well as promoting self-reliance in countries of asylum, particularly in agriculture and food production, health care and vocational trades. Four new projects were negotiated with the concerned movements and executing agencies, and approved for financing under the UNDP indicative planning figure (IPF). A joint mission was convened in September to evaluate all projects at midterm, and it visited all 10 ongoing projects of assistance to those movements, located in Angola, the United Republic of Tanzania, and Zambia. The mission determined that the objectives of all projects continued in general to be valid in substance and in terms of beneficiaries, and it made recommendations for improvement.

At the end of 1983, there were 13 projects approved by the Administrator in support of the development activities of all three movements. Eleven were financed from the IPF for a total of $2,071,357 for 1983. The remaining two were financed from the Trust Fund for Assistance to Colonial Countries and Peoples, for a combined budget of $373,889 for the year. Education con-

tinued to be the main sector of UNDP assistance with eight projects accounting for nearly 66 per cent of the budget total ($2,445,246). UNESCO was the executing agency for those projects. Health was the second most important sector, with two projects executed by WHO budgeted at 24 per cent of the total. Food production ranked third in resource concentration, with one project budgeted at nearly 8 per cent of the annual total, executed by FAO.

UNCTAD report. The secretariat of the United Nations Conference on Trade and Development (UNCTAD) reported in April 1983 on UNCTAD assistance to national liberation movements recognized by regional intergovernmental organizations.[97] It had undertaken studies in collaboration with those movements and submitted progress reports to the UNCTAD Trade and Development Board. A study of economic conditions in Namibia and South Africa emphasized, in regard to assistance to national liberation movements, the need for manpower development for future participation in governmental administration and economic management and for further in-depth examination of economic issues that would arise in a transition to majority rule. The study considered international support for transition to majority rule in Namibia to be a matter of urgency, and stressed the need to prepare a comprehensive social and economic survey of Namibia, along the lines of a 1980 study on Zimbabwe conducted by UNCTAD and financed by UNDP.

UNCTAD, by resolution 147(VI) of 2 July,[98] requested its Secretary-General to undertake, in consultation with OAU, a comprehensive survey of the economic and social conditions of the oppressed people of South Africa and urged the UNDP Administrator to provide adequate resources to the UNCTAD secretariat for this purpose. In taking this action, UNCTAD considered the Buenos Aires Platform, the final document of the Fifth Ministerial Meeting of the Group of 77 (Buenos Aires, Argentina, 28 March–9 April), which included a draft resolution on assistance to the peoples of Namibia and South Africa. By that text, UNCTAD would have requested its Secretary-General to intensify work on the survey of the economic and social conditions of the Namibian people and the oppressed people of South Africa, and in that regard to collaborate with the national liberation movements as well as with relevant United Nations bodies and the OAU Liberation Committee. UNDP would have been called on to attach high priority to the UNCTAD programme providing assistance to the national liberation movements recognized by OAU, and the United Nations Council for Namibia would have been requested to collaborate with UNCTAD in preparing the survey.

Activities of the Committee against *Apartheid*.
In its annual report to the General Assembly,[1] the Special Committee against *Apartheid* continued to call for assistance to the oppressed people of South Africa and their national liberation movement. While promoting humanitarian and educational assistance, the Committee stated that there was no substitute for political action for the elimination of *apartheid*. The Committee noted the advance of the armed struggle, which enjoyed the support of the masses, by ANC and PAC, especially under the leadership of ANC. It took note of the resolution, adopted at the nineteenth session of the Assembly of Heads of State and Government of OAU (Addis Ababa, June 1983) on South Africa, which commended ANC as the vanguard of the national liberation movement of South Africa for the intensification of the armed struggle. The Committee condemned the attempts of South Africa and its supporters to label the freedom fighters as "terrorists". Stating that the actions of the national liberation movement were in sharp contrast with the barbarity of the régime because the movement avoided loss of innocent lives, it warned the white community of the consequences if the oppressed people were to retaliate in kind. The Committee believed that assistance to those people and their national liberation movement should include help in acquainting world opinion with their struggle, and moral and political assistance should include recognition of that movement as the authentic representative of the South African people in their struggle for freedom, as well as support for the campaign for the release of South African political prisoners.

At the conclusion of the observance by ANC of the "Year of Unity in Action" (8 January 1982–7 January 1983), the Committee Chairman sent a message of support to the ANC President. Noting that South Africa had continued to execute political prisoners and massacre refugees, he said that the Committee had redoubled its efforts to persuade Governments and public opinion to act against *apartheid*.

In its October Programme of Action,[2] the Committee called on Governments to assist the oppressed people of South Africa and their liberation movements by: providing them with financial and/or material assistance, directly or through OAU; providing broadcasting facilities; providing transit and travel facilities to members of the movements; encouraging public collections for assistance; contributing to the various funds and programmes for South Africa (see below); encouraging judicial organizations and the public to provide assistance to those persecuted by South Africa; granting asylum and educational and employment opportunities to South African refugees; encouraging activities of anti-*apartheid* movements which provided material and political assistance to *apartheid* victims and to liberation movements; and contributing to the projects of the movements and front-line States for assistance to refugee women and children from South Africa.

Specialized agencies and other intergovernmental organizations were urged to assist the oppressed people of South Africa and their liberation movements, and to invite representatives of movements recognized by OAU to attend their conferences and seminars and to make financial provision for their participation. In addition, the Committee called on public organizations to help educate public opinion about the struggle against *apartheid* through such actions as dissemination of information about the liberation struggle, funding projects for South African refugees, mobilizing solidarity with the struggles of the oppressed people, and observing annually the International Day for the Elimination of Racial Discrimination, the International Day of Solidarity with the Struggle of the People of South Africa, the International Day of Solidarity with the Struggle of Women of South Africa and Namibia, and the Day of Solidarity with South African Political Prisoners.

Other consideration. In accordance with a July 1982 Economic and Social Council resolution,[99] the Council President and the Acting Chairman of the Special Committee against *Apartheid* held consultations in 1983 regarding assistance to the national liberation movements by United Nations bodies. Those discussions, which had been held annually since 1980, were described in a June 1983 report to the Council.[100] In view of the frequent acts of destabilization carried out by South Africa against the front-line States—resulting in loss of life, large numbers of refugees and massive destruction—the two officers decided that assistance by the specialized agencies and other organizations to those States and the freedom fighters was critically needed.

ECONOMIC AND SOCIAL COUNCIL ACTION

The Economic and Social Council, in resolution 1983/42 of 25 July, recommended that the secretariats of United Nations bodies and that of OAU consider assistance to national liberation movements recognized by OAU, with a view to strengthening co-ordination of action to ensure the best use of resources for assistance to the peoples of colonial Territories. The Council noted with satisfaction the arrangements made by several United Nations bodies which enabled representatives of those movements to participate as observers during consideration of matters concerning their countries, and called on international institutions to do likewise, including defraying the cost of participation.

In resolution 38/17 of 22 November, the General Assembly called for a substantial increase in all forms of assistance given by States, United Nations organs, specialized agencies and non-governmental organizations to the victims of racism, racial discrimination and *apartheid* through their national liberation movements recognized by OAU. This call was repeated by in resolution 38/39 A of 5 December, when the Assembly pointed out that those movements were at a crucial stage in their struggle for liberation. In the same resolution, the Assembly, acting on the recommendation of the Special Committee against *Apartheid*, authorized the continuation of funds from the regular United Nations budget to enable two movements—ANC and PAC—to maintain New York offices in order to participate in the deliberations of the Committee and other bodies.

UN Trust Fund for South Africa

The United Nations Trust Fund for South Africa, established by the General Assembly in 1965[101] to provide voluntary assistance to persons persecuted under discriminatory legislation in South Africa and Namibia, made six grants totalling $2,370,000 in 1983, according to an October report by the Secretary-General.[102] The Fund received of $1,726,033 in contributions for 1983 (see table below) and a further $221,631 had been pledged. The total income since the Fund's inception, including interest, was $17,961,982, while the total amount of grants was $17,586,828 as at 20 September 1983, leaving a balance of $375,154.

CONTRIBUTIONS TO THE UN TRUST FUND FOR SOUTH AFRICA, 1983
(as at 20 September 1983; in US dollar equivalent)

Country	Amount
Australia	59,364
Austria	34,500
Canada	15,991
China	30,000
Cyprus	182
Denmark	273,523
Finland	92,799
Germany, Federal Republic of	65,679
Ghana	1,650
Greece	4,500
Hungary	2,500
Iceland	2,000
Indonesia	3,000
Jamaica	394
Kuwait	1,000
Liberia	1,000
Malaysia	1,000
Netherlands	123,239
New Zealand	5,244
Norway	382,839
Pakistan	3,000
Republic of Korea	9,000
Saudi Arabia	25,000
Sweden	292,319
United States	257,250
Zimbabwe	39,060
Total	1,726,033

In a report annexed to that of the Secretary-General, the Committee of Trustees said it continued to encourage direct contributions to voluntary organizations providing assistance to victims of *apartheid* and racial discrimination. It expressed concern over the plight of political prisoners, the growing number of political trials and the persecution of *apartheid* opponents, including trade unionists, journalists, religious and community leaders, students and conscientious objectors. It also expressed shock over the 9 June execution by South Africa of three ANC members (see above). In view of the existing conditions, the Committee felt that additional efforts should be made to promote greater contributions to the Fund and to those voluntary organizations.

On 5 December, the General Assembly adopted resolution 38/39 H without vote.

United Nations Trust Fund for South Africa
The General Assembly,

Having considered the report of the Secretary-General on the United Nations Trust Fund for South Africa, to which is annexed the report of the Committee of Trustees of the United Nations Trust Fund for South Africa,

Gravely concerned at the continued and increased repression against opponents of *apartheid* and racial discrimination in South Africa and the institution of numerous trials under arbitrary security legislation, as well as continued repression in Namibia,

Reaffirming that increased humanitarian assistance by the international community to those persecuted under repressive and discriminatory legislation in South Africa and Namibia is appropriate and essential,

Recognizing that increased contributions to the Trust Fund and to the voluntary agencies concerned are necessary to enable them to meet the increased needs for humanitarian and legal assistance,

1. *Commends* the Secretary-General and the Committee of Trustees of the United Nations Trust Fund for South Africa for their efforts to promote humanitarian and legal assistance to persons persecuted under repressive and discriminatory legislation in South Africa and Namibia, as well as assistance to their families and to refugees from South Africa;

2. *Expresses its appreciation* to the Governments, organizations and individuals that have contributed to the Trust Fund and to the voluntary agencies engaged in rendering humanitarian and legal assistance to the victims of *apartheid* and racial discrimination;

3. *Appeals* for generous and increased contributions to the Trust Fund;

4. *Also appeals* for direct contributions to the voluntary agencies engaged in assistance to the victims of *apartheid* and racial discrimination in South Africa and Namibia.

General Assembly resolution 38/39 H

5 December 1983   Meeting 83   Adopted without vote

46-nation draft (A/38/L.27 & Add.1); agenda item 32.

Sponsors: Afghanistan, Algeria, Angola, Austria, Burundi, Canada, Cape Verde, Democratic Yemen, Denmark, Egypt, Finland, France, Gambia, Greece, Guinea, Guinea-Bissau, Guyana, Iceland, India, Indonesia, Ireland, Japan, Kenya, Madagascar, Malaysia, Malta, Morocco, Mozambique, Netherlands, Norway, Pakistan, Qatar, Rwanda, Senegal, Sierra Leone, Sri Lanka, Sweden, Syrian Arab Republic, Togo, Trinidad and Tobago, Tunisia, Turkey, United Republic of Tanzania, Venezuela, Yugoslavia, Zambia.
Meeting numbers. GA 38th session: plenary 60-63, 69-71, 83.

Other UN assistance

The United Nations Educational and Training Programme for Southern Africa (see below) also provided educational and training assistance to South Africans, according to an October 1983 report by the Secretary-General.[103] During the 1982/83 school year, it granted scholarships to 613 South Africans, as compared with 447 for 1981/82. Of the 1982/83 total, 245 were new awards and 368 were extensions of previous grants.

GENERAL ASSEMBLY ACTION

In resolution 38/95, the Assembly called for further assistance to student refugees in southern Africa.

Inter-agency co-operation

Activities of the Committee against *Apartheid*. The Special Committee against *Apartheid*, in its annual report to the General Assembly,[1] stated that in view of the grave situation in southern Africa and the danger of conflict, the international community should consider a strategy for action to secure peace and freedom in the region which would require the full commitment of United Nations agencies. Emphasizing that all agencies should make their maximum contribution to the international campaign against *apartheid*, the Committee expressed its particular appreciation for the co-operation of ILO, FAO, UNESCO and WHO. It noted with concern the assistance provided by IMF to South Africa and expressed concern over South Africa's participation in the activities of IAEA (see above).

The Committee suggested that the Assembly request the Secretary-General: to instruct the Secretariat and United Nations offices to promote the campaign in co-operation with the Committee; to deny facilities to, and to refrain from investments in, corporations operating in South Africa; to enter into consultations with IMF and IAEA in order to secure their full co-operation in action against *apartheid*; and to prepare, in consultation with the executive heads of United Nations agencies, proposals for concerted action by all agencies in the campaign.

In its October Programme of Action against *Apartheid*,[2] the Committee called on all specialized agencies and other intergovernmental organizations to contribute to the maximum, within their mandates, to the campaign, in particular by: excluding South Africa; denying assistance to it; inviting representatives of South African liberation movements recognized by OAU to attend their conferences and seminars and making financial provision for their participation; providing assistance to the oppressed people of South Africa and to those movements; disseminating information against *apartheid* (see below); providing employment within their secretariats as appropriate and assistance for education and training to the oppressed people; withholding facilities from, or investment of funds in, financial institutions and firms that gave loans to or invested in that country; refraining from purchasing South African products; denying contracts or facilities to transnational corporations and financial institutions collaborating with South Africa; prohibiting official travel by South African Airways or South Africa shipping lines; denying assistance to non-governmental organizations which collaborated with the régime and to institutions based on racial discrimination in South Africa; and cooperating with the Committee in the campaign.

The Committee urged IAEA to end all collaboration with South Africa, except with regard to inspection of nuclear facilities.

ECONOMIC AND SOCIAL COUNCIL ACTION

In resolution 1983/42 of 25 July, the Economic and Social Council requested the specialized agencies and other United Nations organizations to intensify their support for the oppressed people of South Africa and to isolate totally the *apartheid* régime and mobilize world public opinion against *apartheid*.

GENERAL ASSEMBLY ACTION

The General Assembly took similar action in resolution 38/51 of 7 December, when it requested those organizations to withhold from South Africa any co-operation and assistance and to discontinue support to its régime until the people of Namibia had exercised their right to self-determination and independence and until *apartheid* had been eradicated.

In resolution 38/39 A of 5 December, the Assembly requested the Secretary-General to prepare, in consultation with the executive heads of the United Nations organizations, proposals for concerted action by all the agencies in the international campaign against *apartheid*.

The Assembly, in resolution 38/5 of 28 October, requested the Secretary-General to strengthen political, economic, cultural and administrative co-operation between the United Nations and OAU, particularly with regard to assistance to the victims of colonialism and *apartheid* in southern Africa, and in this connection drew the attention of the international community to the need to contribute to the OAU Assistance Fund for the Struggle against Colonialism and *Apartheid*.

In a number of other 1983 resolutions, the Assembly called on IMF to terminate credits or other assistance to South Africa and, in resolution 38/39 A, also requested IAEA to refrain from extending to South Africa any facilities which might assist it in its nuclear plans (see above). In that same resolution, the Secretary-General was requested to enter into consultations with those two agencies to secure their co-operation in action against *apartheid*.

Other aspects

Other 1983 activities to promote the international campaign against *apartheid* included encouraging United Nations bodies, intergovernmental and non-governmental organizations as well as the public to disseminate information in this regard. The General Assembly and the Special Committee against *Apartheid* urged Governments and intergovernmental and non-governmental organizations to contribute to the campaign. Organizing special meetings, missions and observances was another means the Committee used for that purpose. The Committee drew up a Programme of Action against *Apartheid* and its work plan, which was approved by the Assembly in December.

Public information

Activities of the Committee against *Apartheid*. The Special Committee against *Apartheid* continued in 1983 to encourage and promote dissemination of information against *apartheid* by the Centre against *Apartheid* and the Department of Public Information, both of the United Nations Secretariat, and by a number of non-governmental organizations, through publications in several languages and audio-visual material. In its annual report to the General Assembly,[1] the Committee noted the importance of the dissemination of information and of the encouragement of public action by parliaments, local authorities, religious bodies, trade unions and other groups in the campaign to isolate the *apartheid* régime and support the liberation struggle.

The Committee stressed the need for a wider mobilization of writers, artists, sportsmen and others in the international campaign against *apartheid*. It recommended that the Assembly: commend anti-*apartheid* movements and other organizations engaged in campaigns for the isolation of the régime and assistance to the national liberation movement of South Africa; urge Governments to lend assistance, including financial assistance, to such groups, especially in countries which continued to collaborate with South Africa; commend cities, local authorities and institutions which boycotted corporations involved in South Africa or

honoured leaders of the national liberation movement, and invite others to consider such measures; and request the Secretary-General, in consultation with UNESCO, to prepare proposals for an information service against *apartheid*. The Committee suggested that the Secretary-General and the UNESCO Director-General be invited to initiate action to honour the memory of leaders of the oppressed peoples in their struggle against *apartheid*, racial discrimination and colonialism.

The Committee stated that it planned to expand the campaigns to promote: an end to military and nuclear collaboration with South Africa; a cessation of loans to South Africa; comprehensive and mandatory sanctions against South Africa; sports, cultural and other boycotts of South Africa; greater assistance to the oppressed people of South Africa and their national liberation movement; the unconditional release of South African political prisoners; treatment of captured freedom fighters as prisoners of war; and action against propaganda by South Africa and its collaborators. Special attention would be given to campaigns in support of front-line States and Lesotho which were subjected to acts of aggression, destabilization and terrorism by South Africa.

The Committee stressed the need for adequate arrangements to ensure the prompt dissemination of information to Governments and organizations concerned, as well as the media, on developments in southern Africa and on anti-*apartheid* activities. It believed that the Centre against *Apartheid* should be equipped to provide increased services in that respect.

On 7 April, the Committee held informal consultations with representatives of the mass media to discuss developments in South Africa.

In its October Programme of Action against *Apartheid*,[2] the Committee called on Governments to: ensure, in co-operation with the United Nations and the national liberation movements of South Africa recognized by OAU, the widest possible dissemination of information on *apartheid* and the struggle for liberation in South Africa; encourage the establishment of national organizations to enlighten public opinion on *apartheid*; encourage information media to contribute to the campaign against *apartheid*; and prevent propaganda by South Africa and private organizations which advocated *apartheid*. Specialized agencies and other intergovernmental organizations were asked to contribute to the campaign by disseminating information against *apartheid* in co-operation with the United Nations.

The Committee suggested that public organizations pursue education programmes aimed at increasing understanding about the realities of *apartheid*, including South Africa's bantustan policies, the consequences of its policies in education, housing, employment, health care and land distribution, and the threat of *apartheid* to international peace and security. Public organizations were also urged to disseminate information about the liberation struggle. Trade unions were called on to distribute information to their officials and members in order to mobilize solidarity with workers' struggles in South Africa.

According to the Programme of Action, city and local authorities should encourage the teaching of the history, culture and struggles of the oppressed people of South Africa and ban South African propaganda from schools and libraries, churches and religious organizations should disseminate information about the inhumanity of the *apartheid* system, and educationalists should encourage the teaching of the anti-*apartheid* struggle and press for banning South African propaganda from educational institutions. In this connection, the Committee stated its intention to promote, with the assistance of the Centre against *Apartheid*, the international campaign against propaganda by South Africa and its collaborators.

The Latin American Regional Conference for Action against *Apartheid* (Caracas, Venezuela, 16-18 September) (see below, under MEETINGS, MISSIONS AND OBSERVANCES) recognized the need for ensuring public awareness of the inhumanity of *apartheid* and of United Nations efforts for its elimination. In its Declaration,[104] the Conference requested the United Nations and other organizations to provide Governments, organizations, institutions and media in Latin America with relevant information in the languages of the region.

The Committee continued to promote and receive voluntary contributions to produce publications in several languages. It reported that the Trust Fund for Publicity against *Apartheid* had received a total of $60,717 from 11 countries between 1 January and 31 May 1983.[1]

GENERAL ASSEMBLY ACTION

The General Assembly, in resolution 38/39 A of 5 December, appealed to those working in the mass media and their professional associations to foster the role of the mass media in the dissemination of information commensurate with the need to eradicate *apartheid*. It requested the Committee against *Apartheid* to pay special attention to mobilizing public opinion and encouraging public action against collaboration with South Africa.

Non-governmental organizations

International NGOs Conference against *Apartheid* and Racism. Non-governmental organizations (NGOs) remained active in the campaign against *apartheid*. The International NGOs Conference of Action against *Apartheid* and Racism, or-ganized by the NGO Sub-Committee on Racism, Racial Discrimination, *Apartheid* and Decolonization in co-operation with the Special Committee against *Apartheid*, was held at Geneva from 5 to 8 July 1983.

In its Declaration, transmitted by the Acting Chairman of the Committee against *Apartheid* to the Secretary-General on 15 July,[105] the Conference condemned racism as a weapon used to divide and exploit people and a major cause of conflict and war; denounced *apartheid* as a crime against humanity and a threat to international peace and security; supported the condemnation by the United Nations and OAU of certain Western and other countries as well as transnational corporations which collaborated with South Africa; and called for comprehensive and mandatory sanctions against that country and urged the Second World Conference for Action to Combat Racism and Racial Discrimination to revitalize international action in this regard.

The Conference urged the United Nations, other intergovernmental organizations and Governments to support the national liberation movements recognized by OAU and to intensify efforts to eliminate discrimination against indigenous peoples and migrant workers. It stressed the need for co-operation between the United Nations and NGOs, including peace, anti-*apartheid* and solidarity movements, religious bodies, trade unions and women's and youth organizations.

Activities of the Committee against *Apartheid*. The Committee against *Apartheid* proposed that the Assembly commend the anti-*apartheid* and solidarity movements, religious bodies, trade unions, youth and student organizations, and other groups engaged in campaigns for the isolation of the *apartheid* régime and assistance to the national liberation movement of South Africa, and urge Governments to lend assistance, including financial assistance, to such groups, especially in countries which continued to collaborate with South Africa.

The Committee, in its October Programme of Action against *Apartheid*,[2] called on specialized agencies and other intergovernmental organizations to deny assistance to NGOs which collaborated with South Africa and to institutions based on racial discrimination in that country.

It called on NGOs, such as trade unions, churches, and anti-*apartheid* and solidarity movements, to contribute to the campaign against *apartheid* by: promoting programmes aimed at educating public opinion about *apartheid;* mobilizing opposition to South Africa's policies of aggression, destabilization and terrorism against neighbouring States; taking action to ensure implementation of the mandatory arms embargo against South Africa and an end to military collaboration with it; becoming involved in the campaign for a mandatory ban on nuclear collaboration with South Africa; urging Governments to desist from collaboration with it and to support mandatory economic sanctions; strengthening the sporting and cultural boycott of South Africa; discouraging individuals from emigrating to South Africa or visiting as tourists; campaigning for the release of South African political prisoners; and mobilizing solidarity with the black workers of South Africa (see above for specific recommendations). The Committee said it would increase co-operation with NGOs in promoting the international campaign against *apartheid*.

GENERAL ASSEMBLY ACTION

The General Assembly, in resolution 38/39 A of 5 December, commended the movements, organizations and other groups engaged in campaigns for the isolation of the régime and assistance to the South African liberation movements recognized by OAU, and urged Governments to assist such groups, especially in countries which collaborated with South Africa.

Meetings, missions and observances

During 1983, the Special Committee against *Apartheid* organized or co-sponsored a number of meetings, missions and observances to promote the international campaign against *apartheid*.[1] (For further details of these events, see under the relevant subject headings in this sub-chapter.)

The Committee supported and participated in the International Conference in Solidarity with the Front-line States and for National Liberation and Peace in Southern Africa, held at Lisbon, Portugal, from 25 to 27 March.

The Committee and the Workers' Group of the Governing Body of ILO organized the International Conference of Trade Unions on Sanctions and Other Actions against the *Apartheid* Régime in South Africa, held at Geneva on 10 and 11 June. In its Declaration, the Conference called for mandatory economic sanctions and condemned employers and investors in South Africa who directly or indirectly helped to maintain the *apartheid* system.

The International Conference on the Alliance between South Africa and Israel, held at Vienna from 11 to 13 July, was organized by the Committee, as was the International Conference for Sanctions against *Apartheid* in Sports, held in London from 27 to 29 June.

The International NGOs Conference of Action against *Apartheid* and Racism, held at Geneva from 5 to 8 July, was organized by the NGO Sub-Committee on Racism, Racial Discrimination, *Apartheid* and Decolonization, in co-operation with the Special Committee.

The Committee organized, in co-operation with Venezuela, the Latin American Regional Conference for Action against *Apartheid*, at Caracas from 16 to 18 September. In the Caracas Declaration for Action against *Apartheid*,[104] the Conference reaffirmed that South Africa's threats to and violations of the territorial integrity and independence of neighbouring States constituted a threat to international peace and security and a serious challenge to the authority of the United Nations, and it declared that *apartheid* was a crime against humanity. It called on the international community to exert pressure on South Africa through sanctions and provide assistance to the victims of *apartheid* and to their national liberation movements. The Conference called for United Nations assistance in promoting public awareness in Latin America of *apartheid*.

In 1983, the Committee sent six missions as part of its activities against *apartheid*. One mission visited the front-line States (Angola, Botswana, United Republic of Tanzania, Zambia, Zimbabwe) from 7 to 21 April[106] to obtain full information on South Africa's aggression, to consult on possible action by the Committee and to promote political and material assistance to those countries. Two other missions, both delegations of women leaders, were concerned with the plight of women and children under *apartheid* and held consultations on providing assistance to projects prepared by the national liberation movements. The first of these missions visited Belgium, France, Italy, the Netherlands and Tunisia in January and February, and the second visited Denmark, Finland, the Federal Republic of Germany, Norway and Sweden from 13 to 24 June.

Three missions were visits of the Committee Chairman to Governments. From 1 to 4 May, he visited Egypt at the invitation of the Afro-Asian Peoples' Solidarity Organization. At the invitation of the Minister for Foreign Affairs, he visited the German Democratic Republic from 23 to 28 May to participate in the observance of Africa Liberation Day and the Week of Solidarity with the Colonial Peoples of Southern Africa. The Chairman visited the USSR from 28 to 31 May, at the invitation of the Soviet Afro-Asian Solidarity Committee, for consultations on further co-operation in the campaign against *apartheid*. In addition, in January and February, the Chairman visited six Nigerian universities to inaugurate Youth Solidarity with South Africa and to launch the campaign for the release of Nelson Mandela.

The Committee organized several special observances in 1983. On 18 February, it held a meeting in memory of the Reverend Canon L.

John Collins, founder and President of the International Defence and Aid Fund for Southern Africa. It held two meetings in observance of the International Day for the Elimination of Racial Discrimination on 21 March (see ECONOMIC AND SOCIAL QUESTIONS, Chapter XVIII). On 30 and 31 March, four meetings were held in observance of the twentieth anniversary of the Committee's first meeting. The Committee, in an April report,[107] issued messages it had received on that occasion from the President of the General Assembly, heads of State and Government, foreign ministers, intergovernmental and non-governmental organizations and individuals.

The Committee held solemn meetings in observance of the International Day of Solidarity with the Struggling People of South Africa on 16 June and the International Day of Solidarity with the Struggle of Women of South Africa and Namibia on 9 August. It observed 11 October as the Day of Solidarity with South African Political Prisoners.

In addition, on 23 May a joint statement was issued by the Acting Chairman of the Committee, the Chairman of the Committee on colonial countries and the President of the Council for Namibia on the occasion of the Week of Solidarity with the Peoples of Namibia and All Other Colonial Territories, as well as those in South Africa, Fighting for Freedom, Independence and Human Rights (23-30 May) (see TRUSTEESHIP AND DECOLONIZATION, Chapter I).

The Committee, in its October Programme of Action against *Apartheid*,[2] called on Governments to observe annually four international days (21 March, 16 June, 9 August and 11 October), and it suggested that public organizations could play a role in educating public opinion about the struggle against *apartheid* by observing them.

Work programme of the Committee against *Apartheid*

Stressing the need to expand its activities with a view to securing greater and more concerted action for the elimination of *apartheid*, the Special Committee against *Apartheid* reported to the General Assembly[1] that it planned to intensify consultations with Governments and intergovernmental organizations and develop its co-operation with parliaments, local authorities, anti-*apartheid* and solidarity movements, peace movements, trade unions, religious bodies and other non-governmental organizations, and educational and other institutions. It would continue to mobilize writers, artists, entertainers, sportsmen, religious leaders and others in support of the struggle for liberation in South Africa

and for the total isolation of that Government. It recognized the need to publicize more widely the collaboration by certain States and foreign economic interests with South Africa. It stated its intention to expand the campaigns to promote an end to military and nuclear collaboration; a cessation of all loans to South Africa; comprehensive and mandatory sanctions against South Africa; sports, cultural and other boycotts of South Africa; greater assistance to the oppressed people there and their liberation movement; the unconditional release of political prisoners and treatment of captured freedom fighters as prisoners of war; and action against propaganda by South Africa and its collaborators. Special attention would be given to support front-line States and Lesotho which were subjected to aggression by South Africa.

The Committee was considering the organization or co-sponsorship of several conferences and seminars. It believed that members of the Committee and the staff of the Centre against *Apartheid* should participate more frequently in anti-*apartheid* events to spread the campaign to regions and segments of public opinion which had not been active. In the Committee's view, the Centre should be equipped to provide increased and better dissemination of information about developments in southern Africa and on anti-*apartheid* activities. The Committee requested that the allocation of $400,000 for special projects be continued in 1984 and that it be authorized to seek and receive voluntary contributions for such projects.

In its October Programme of Action against *Apartheid*,[2] the Committee reiterated its work plan, including its intention to review constantly and publicize the implementation of United Nations resolutions against *apartheid*.

GENERAL ASSEMBLY ACTION

On 5 December, the General Assembly adopted resolution 38/39 E by recorded vote.

Programme of work of the Special Committee against *Apartheid*

The General Assembly,

Having considered the report of the Special Committee against *Apartheid*,

1. *Congratulates* the Special Committee against *Apartheid* for its dedicated efforts since its inception in 1963 in promoting the international campaign against *apartheid*;

2. *Commends* the work of the Centre against *Apartheid* of the Secretariat in assisting the Special Committee;

3. *Endorses* the report of the Special Committee, in particular its conclusions and recommendations on its work and that of the Centre against *Apartheid* contained in paragraphs 354 to 364 of the report, and requests the Secretary-General to take all appropriate

steps to enable the Centre to provide more effective services to the Committee;

4. *Authorizes* the Special Committee to organize or co-sponsor conferences, seminars or other events, to send missions to Governments, organizations and conferences and to assist campaigns against *apartheid* as it may deem necessary in the discharge of its responsibilities, within the financial resources allocated under the present resolution, and requests the Secretary-General to provide the necessary staff and services for such activities;

5. *Decides* to make a special allocation of $400,000 to the Special Committee for 1984 from the regular budget of the United Nations for the cost of special projects to be decided upon by the Committee in order to promote the international campaign against *apartheid;*

6. *Again requests* Governments and organizations to make voluntary contributions or provide other assistance for the special projects of the Special Committee.

General Assembly resolution 38/39 E

5 December 1983   Meeting 83   149-1-2 (recorded vote)

46-nation draft (A/38/L.24 & Add.1); agenda item 32.

Sponsors: Afghanistan, Algeria, Angola, Benin, Botswana, Burundi, Cape Verde, Cuba, Democratic Yemen, Djibouti, Gabon, Gambia, German Democratic Republic, Ghana, Guinea, Guinea-Bissau, Guyana, Hungary, India, Indonesia, Kenya, Libyan Arab Jamahiriya, Madagascar, Malaysia, Mali, Mauritania, Morocco, Mozambique, Nicaragua, Nigeria, Pakistan, Qatar, Rwanda, Sao Tome and Principe, Senegal, Sierra Leone, Somalia, Syrian Arab Republic, Togo, Trinidad and Tobago, Uganda, Ukrainian SSR, United Republic of Cameroon, United Republic of Tanzania, Zambia, Zimbabwe.

Financial implications. 5th Committee, A/38/654; S-G, A/C.5/38/53 & Corr.1.

Meeting numbers. GA 38th session: 5th Committee 51; plenary 60-63, 69-71, 83.

Recorded vote in Assembly as follows:

In favour: Afghanistan, Albania, Algeria, Angola, Antigua and Barbuda, Argentina, Australia, Austria, Bahamas, Bahrain, Bangladesh, Barbados, Belgium, Belize, Benin, Bhutan, Bolivia, Botswana, Brazil, Bulgaria, Burma, Burundi, Byelorussian SSR, Canada, Cape Verde, Central African Republic, Chad, Chile, China, Colombia, Comoros, Congo, Costa Rica, Cuba, Cyprus, Czechoslovakia, Democratic Kampuchea, Democratic Yemen, Denmark, Djibouti, Dominican Republic, Ecuador, Egypt, El Salvador, Equatorial Guinea, Ethiopia, Fiji, Finland, France, Gabon, Gambia, German Democratic Republic, Ghana, Greece, Guatemala, Guinea, Guinea-Bissau, Guyana, Haiti, Honduras, Hungary, Iceland, India, Indonesia, Iran, Iraq, Ireland, Italy, Ivory Coast, Jamaica, Japan, Jordan, Kenya, Kuwait, Lao People's Democratic Republic, Lebanon, Lesotho, Liberia, Libyan Arab Jamahiriya, Luxembourg, Madagascar, Malawi, Malaysia, Maldives, Mali, Malta, Mauritania, Mauritius, Mexico, Mongolia, Morocco, Mozambique, Nepal, Netherlands, New Zealand, Nicaragua, Niger, Nigeria, Norway, Oman, Pakistan, Panama, Papua New Guinea, Peru, Philippines, Poland, Portugal, Qatar, Romania, Rwanda, Saint Lucia, Saint Vincent and the Grenadines, Samoa, Sao Tome and Principe, Saudi Arabia, Senegal, Seychelles, Sierra Leone, Singapore, Solomon Islands, Somalia, Spain, Sri Lanka, Sudan, Suriname, Swaziland, Sweden, Syrian Arab Republic, Thailand, Togo, Trinidad and Tobago, Tunisia, Turkey, Uganda, Ukrainian SSR, USSR, United Arab Emirates, United Republic of Cameroon, United Republic of Tanzania, Upper Volta, Uruguay, Vanuatu, Venezuela, Viet Nam, Yemen, Yugoslavia, Zaire, Zambia, Zimbabwe.

Against: United States.

Abstaining: Germany, Federal Republic of, United Kingdom.

In explanation of vote, Canada questioned the making of a special allocation from the United Nations regular budget without having examined the priority and merits of the issue within the existing programme and budgetary mechanisms for that purpose. The Federal Republic of Germany agreed in principle with the aims of the resolution, but had reservations about certain formulations in the Committee's report, as well as the financial implications of the text.

Ireland said its attitude to the recommendations in the Committee's report must be understood in accordance with its general policy on *apartheid.* Japan also could not accept some of the Committee's conclusions and recommendations and was concerned about paragraph 4 of the resolution which it felt gave that body an excessively wide margin of discretion; it also hoped the Committee would manage its budget efficiently. The Netherlands, New Zealand and Portugal also voiced reservations about the report.

France said its positive vote marked its desire to give expression to the excellent relations which it maintained with the Committee, although it did not approve of all of the work programme.

The Assembly took related action in three other resolutions of 5 December. In resolution 38/39 B, it invited Governments, organizations and individuals to take action in the light of the Committee's Programme of Action against *Apartheid,* in co-operation with the Committee and the Centre against *Apartheid.* The Assembly gave instructions to the Committee in resolution 38/39 A, requesting it to report on implementation of United Nations resolutions on *apartheid* and South Africa's aggression, to review collaboration between South Africa and other States, and to pay special attention to mobilizing public opinion against that collaboration. In resolution 38/39 F, it requested the Committee to publicize information on relations between Israel and South Africa.

REFERENCES

(1)A/38/22.   (2)A/38/539-S/16102.   (3)A/38/22/Add.1.
(4)A/38/294-S/15864. (5)*Report of the Second World Conference to Combat Racism and Racial Discrimination, Geneva (1-12 August 1983)* (A/CONF.119/26 & Corr.1), Sales No. E.83.XIV.4 & Corrigendum. (6)YUN 1980, p. 804, GA res. 35/33, 14 Nov. 1980. (7)YUN 1973, p. 523, GA res. 3057(XXVIII), 2 Nov. 1973. (8)YUN 1978, p. 664. (9)A/SPC/38/L.4 & Add.1-22. (10)A/SPC/38/L.7. (11)A/38/550. (12)YUN 1978, p. 915, SC res. 435(1978), 29 Sept. 1978. (13)YUN 1962, p. 99, GA res. 1761(XVII), 6 Nov. 1962. (14)A/38/24. (15)YUN 1982, p. 1300, GA res. 37/233 A, 20 Dec. 1982. (16)YUN 1981, p. 1153, GA res. ES-8/2, 14 Sep. 1981. (17)*Ibid.,* p. 1157, GA res. 36/121 B, 10 Dec. 1981. (18)YUN 1982, p. 1304, GA res. 37/233 C, 20 Dec. 1982. (19)E/1983/13 (res. 1983/4). (20)A/38/565-S/16112. (21)A/38/723-S/16211. (22)A/38/764. (23)A/38/272-S/15832. (24)A/AC.115/L.593. (25)YUN 1977, p. 161, SC res. 418(1977), 4 Nov. 1977. (26)YUN 1980, p. 200. (27)YUN 1977, p. 162, SC res. 421(1977), 9 Dec. 1977. (28)A/AC.115/L.602. (29)A/AC.115/L.604. (30)E/1983/13 (res. 1983/11). (31)YUN 1968, p. 17, GA res. 2373(XXII), 12 June 1968. (32)S/AC.20/34. (33)S/AC.20/36. (34)S/AC.20/35. (35)YUN 1982, p. 278, GA res. 37/69 J, 9 Dec. 1982. (36)YUN 1981, p. 179. (37)E/CN.4/Sub.2/1983/6 & Add.1,2. (38)YUN 1982, p. 284. (39)E/CN.4/1984/3 (res. 1983/6). (40)E/1983/13 (res. 1983/12). (41)YUN 1973, p. 103, GA res. 3068(XXVIII), annex, 30 Nov. 1973. (42)YUN 1982, p. 285, ESC res. 1982/69, 27

Oct. 1982. (43)*Policies and Practices of Transnational Corporations regarding Their Activities in South Africa and Namibia* (E/C.10/1983/10/Rev.1 & Corr.1), Sales No. E.84.II.A.5. (44)E/1983/18/Rev.1. (45)YUN 1982, p. 287. (46)*Ibid.*, p. 290, GA res. 37/2, 21 Oct. 1982. (47)*Ibid.*, p. 292, GA res. 37/69 F, 9 Dec. 1982. (48)A/AC.115/L.595. (49)A/38/311-S/15883. (50)YUN 1963, p.124. (51)A/38/253. (52)A/38/288. (53)A/38/415. (54)A/38/556. (55)E/1983/13 (res. 1983/9). (56)E/CN.4/1983/25. (57)E/CN.4/1983/10. (58)E/CN.4/1983/37. (59)E/CN.4/1984/3 (res. 1983/13). (60)YUN 1950, p. 539, ESC res. 277(X), 17 Feb. 1950. (61)YUN 1948-49, p. 535, GA res. 217 A (III), 10 Dec. 1948. (62)E/CN.4/1984/3 (res. 1983/25). (63)A/CONF.119/26 & Corr.1 (res. 2(II)). (64)S/15623. (65)YUN 1982, p. 296, SC res. 525(1982), 7 Dec. 1982. (66)A/38/110-S/15634. (67)YUN 1982, p. 294. (68)S/15814. (69)S/15819. (70)S/15821. (71)S/15823. (72)S/15827. (73)S/15829. (74)A/38/286-S/15848. (75)S/15850. (76)A/39/22. (77)A/38/605. (78)YUN 1981, p. 945. (79)YUN 1982, p. 298. (80)E/CN.4/1983/38. (81)YUN 1982, p. 299. (82)A/AC.115/L.594. (83)YUN 1977, p. 173, GA res. 32/105 M, annex, 14 Dec. 1977. (84)A/38/310-S/15882. (85)A/38/74. (86)A/38/95. (87)A/38/181. (88)A/38/289. (89)A/AC.115/L.590 & Corr.1. (90)YUN 1976, p. 136, GA res. 31/6 F, 9 Nov. 1976. (91)A/38/36 & Corr.1. (92)A/AC.192/1. (93)A/38/111 & Add. 1-3 & Add.3/Corr.1. (94)YUN 1960, p. 49, GA res. 1514(XV), 14 Dec. 1960. (95)YUN 1982, p. 1264, GA res. 37/32, 23 Nov. 1982. (96)DP/1984/15. (97)TD/282. (98)*Proceedings of the United Nations Conference on Trade and Development, Sixth Session, Belgrade, 6 June-2 July 1983*, vol. I, *Report and Annexes* (TD/326, vol. I), Sales No. E.83.II.D.6. (99)YUN 1982, p. 1263, ESC res. 1982/47, 27 July 1982. (100)E/1983/106. (101)YUN 1965, p. 115, GA res. 2054 B (XX), 15 Dec. 1965. (102)A/38/455. (103)A/38/469. (104)A/38/451-S/16009. (105)A/38/309-S/15881. (106)A/AC.115/L.593. (107)A/AC.115/L.592.

South Africa and the front-line States of southern Africa

In 1983, several United Nations bodies were concerned with South Africa's relations with its neighbours—Angola, Botswana, Mozambique, the United Republic of Tanzania, Zambia and Zimbabwe. The General Assembly, the Special Committee against *Apartheid*, the Commission on Human Rights, the United Nations Council for Namibia and the Second World Conference to Combat Racism and Racial Discrimination dealt with the effects of those relations, mainly on security issues, but also on the economic development of those countries, the so-called front-line States.

Those bodies expressed concern over the increased aggression and destabilization by South Africa in the region. In resolution 38/39 C of 5 December, the Assembly condemned South Africa's aggression against Angola, Lesotho and Mozambique and its threats against independent States in the region. It demanded that South Africa pay compensation to independent African States for the damage caused by its acts, and called on the international community to provide assistance to countries in the area to enable them to defend themselves.

In late 1983, Angola complained to the Security Council of increased acts of aggression against

its territory by South Africa—charges which were rejected by South Africa. The Council responded by adopting resolution 545(1983) on 20 December in which it demanded that South Africa withdraw unconditionally and immediately. The Council also considered that Angola was entitled to redress for material damage it had incurred. In three 1983 resolutions (38/17, 38/36 A and 38/39 C), the Assembly also condemned South Africa's aggression and occupation of Angola.

A number of times during the year Lesotho complained that South Africa had carried out armed attacks against it, but South Africa rejected those charges. As requested by the Council in 1982, the Secretary-General sent a mission to Lesotho to determine that country's needs for international assistance. In June 1983, the Council, by resolution 535(1983), endorsed the mission's recommendations for international assistance. The Assembly condemned South Africa for its aggression against Lesotho (resolutions 38/17 and 38/39 C) and called for assistance to it (resolutions 38/215 and 38/95).

Mozambique also lodged several complaints about South African attacks. The Assembly (resolution 38/17) and the Economic and Social Council (resolution 1983/42) condemned this aggression.

Activities of the Committee against *Apartheid*. The Special Committee against *Apartheid*, in its annual report to the General Assembly,[1] expressed concern over the escalation of acts of aggression, destabilization and terrorism by South Africa against independent African States since 1975, the year Angola and Mozambique became independent. Evidence of the increased aggression included a sharp rise in military operations by South African forces, especially in Angola, Mozambique and Lesotho, as well as covert activities involving the use of mercenaries and subversive groups, assassination and abduction of individuals, and the destruction of bridges, road and rail lines, oil pipelines, fuel depots and power lines in several neighbouring States. Again condemning those acts, the Committee stressed that the situation in southern Africa was a threat to international peace. It urged the Security Council to take effective measures, under Chapter VII of the United Nations Charter, to force South Africa to end its aggression and terminate its illegal occupation of Namibia. In the Committee's view, South Africa had been encouraged to undertake those acts by the protection afforded by major Western Powers, and even the collusion of some Western interests, against international sanctions (see above).

South Africa continued to rely on the use of force and racist alliances to arrest the process of decolonization, to restore "buffer zones" against the advance of freedom, to entrench racist domination in South Africa and perpetuate illegal occupation in Namibia. The Committee said that South Africa, in an attempt to establish its hegemony in the region, had become more brazen, as evidenced by the attack on Maputo, Mozambique, on 23 May 1983.

The Committee informed the Assembly that it was considering organizing or co-sponsoring an international conference in support of the frontlines States and Lesotho.

In its Programme of Action against *Apartheid*,[2] adopted on 25 October and commended in resolution 38/39 B of 5 December by the Assembly to the attention of Governments, organizations and individuals, the Committee called on Governments to provide, at their request, assistance to the States subjected to South African aggression to enable them to defend their sovereignty and territorial integrity. Governments were also urged to assist the programmes of the Southern African Development Co-ordination Conference (SADCC).

Public organizations were urged to mobilize opposition to South Africa's policies of aggression, destabilization and terrorism against neighbouring States. Such mobilization should involve: publicizing South Africa's aggression and international terrorism, including its assassinations and abductions, its use of mercenaries and support of subversive groups, and its efforts to create political and economic instability in the region; campaigning for solidarity with the front-line States and Lesotho; alerting the public to the threat posed by South Africa's military and nuclear buildup and campaigning for an end to military and nuclear collaboration with that country; providing assistance to victims of South African aggression; and upholding the right of the front-line States and Lesotho to defend their territorial integrity and security, including the securing of military assistance.

In view of the escalating aggression, the Committee decided to send a delegation to southern Africa to obtain information, consult on possible action by the Committee, and promote assistance to front-line States. The mission visited Angola, Botswana, the United Republic of Tanzania, Zambia and Zimbabwe from 7 to 21 April 1983, and also participated in the International Conference in Support of the Struggle of the Namibian People for Independence, held in Paris from 25 to 29 April (see TRUSTEESHIP AND DECOLONIZATION, Chapter III). It held consultations with government officials in those countries and with leaders of the liberation movements of southern Africa— the African National Congress of South Africa (ANC), the South West Africa People's Organization (SWAPO), and the Pan Africanist Congress of Azania (PAC). In its interim report to the Committee of 25 May,[3] the mission said it was unable, for practical reasons, to visit other front-line

and neighbouring States; therefore, it proposed to visit Lesotho, Mozambique and Swaziland, as well as Seychelles, and submit a final report.

Having determined that South Africa was engaged in either military aggression, support of dissident groups or economic and political destabilization in the countries it visited, the mission made recommendations to be transmitted by the Committee for consideration by the General Assembly, calling for political and moral support and material assistance for the oppressed people of South Africa and for the front-line States. It stated that the Security Council must adopt measures, under Chapter VII of the Charter, such as comprehensive or selective mandatory sanctions, to prevent breaches of the peace and acts of aggression by South Africa.

The mission agreed with the Committee that the continuing political, economic and military collaboration of certain Western States and their transnational corporations with South Africa encouraged its defiance of the international community and constituted a major obstacle to eliminating *apartheid*. In particular, the United States policy of "constructive engagement" with South Africa had encouraged the régime's policies. All States, in particular the major supporters of South Africa, should be called on to terminate collaboration with South Africa in accordance with United Nations resolutions. It was incumbent on the international community to demand the immediate and unconditional withdrawal of South African troops from Angolan territory, the mission said. The international community should express indignation over South Africa's acts of aggression, subversion, destabilization and terrorism against all the front-line States, and should condemn South Africa for using Namibia as a base for its aggression against neighbouring States.

In addition, the mission called on the international community to render large-scale assistance, including humanitarian, educational and financial aid, to the front-line States, the oppressed people of South Africa and Namibia and their national liberation movements. Within the United Nations system, the front-line States should be exempted from generalized budgetary cuts. SADCC deserved the support of the international community in its effort to lessen economic dependence of the front-line States on South Africa. Upholding the right of those States to seek and to receive military, financial and material aid to defend their territory, the mission suggested the possibility of rendering assistance in logistics, transportation, clearing of land-mines and training of defence personnel.

The mission, calling on the United Nations to redouble its effort to mobilize world public opinion against South Africa's policies of *apartheid*, aggression, destabilization and terrorism, proposed that consideration be given to assisting front-line States in developing their transmission facilities and broadcasting to counter South African propaganda. News agencies should also be asked to co-operate in that regard.

At a meeting on 19 May, the Committee considered the mission's report and decided to send a second mission to Lesotho and Mozambique. It decided to encourage and assist campaigns in support of front-line States by anti-*apartheid* groups in Western countries.

The Committee participated in the International Conference in Solidarity with the Front-line States and for National Liberation and Peace in Southern Africa (Lisbon, Portugal, 25-27 March).

Action by the Commission on Human Rights. In three resolutions adopted in February,[4] the Commission on Human Rights condemned South Africa's acts of aggression and destabilization against African States, in particular, Angola, Botswana, Lesotho, Mozambique and Zimbabwe. It demanded the cessation of such attacks which were aimed at undermining their economies and destabilizing them (see ECONOMIC AND SOCIAL QUESTIONS, Chapter XVIII, under "Human rights violations—South Africa and Namibia").

Action by the Conference against racial discrimination. The Second World Conference to Combat Racism and Racial Discrimination, held at Geneva from 1 to 12 August 1983, adopted a Declaration and a Programme of Action for the Second Decade to Combat Racism and Racial Discrimination (1983-1993). In its Declaration,[5] the Conference condemned the frequent and unjustified acts of aggression, destruction and sabotage, which South Africa, directly and through the use of mercenaries and armed bandits, continued to perpetrate against the front-line States and other independent African States in the subregion because of their opposition to *apartheid*, assistance to refugees and support for the liberation movements. The Conference called on all States to offer assistance to enable the front-line States and the other independent African States in the area to strengthen their defence capacity and peacefully rebuild their countries.

The Conference took similar action in its Programme of Action as approved by the General Assembly in resolution 38/14 of 22 November. It called for increased international assistance to those States subjected to threats and acts of aggression and destabilization by South Africa to enable them to strengthen their defence capacity, defend their sovereignty and territorial integrity, fight South African and other propaganda that undermined racial harmony and peace, and peacefully develop their countries.

Activities of the Council for Namibia. In its annual report to the General Assembly,[6] the Council for Namibia issued the Paris Declaration on Namibia (see also TRUSTEESHIP AND DECOLONIZATION, Chapter III), adopted by the International Conference in Support of the Struggle of the Namibian People for Independence (Paris, 25-29 April 1983). In that text, the Conference called for increased assistance to the Namibian people and to its liberation movement—SWAPO. It called on States to stop the military buildup in Namibia by South Africa, its recruitment and training of Namibians for tribal armies and its recruitment of mercenaries in order to carry out internal repression and external aggression. The Conference condemned the aggression launched from Namibia against Angola (see below) and the continued military occupation of part of Angola by South African forces.

The Conference considered that the acquisition of nuclear-weapon capability by South Africa constituted an effort to terrorize and intimidate countries in the region. Assistance to South Africa by certain Western countries and Israel in the military and nuclear fields made them willing partners of its hegemonistic policies. Expressing concern at reports regarding the existence of military and security agreements between South Africa and certain countries in other regions, the Conference said such arrangements would constitute a breach of the arms embargo imposed by the Security Council in 1977,[7] greatly aggravate the situation in southern Africa and pose a serious threat to the security of Africa as a whole. It called for vigilance by the international community to prevent any military arrangements with South Africa.

Condemning the increased acts of armed aggression and military, political and economic destabilization by South Africa, the Conference said increased assistance must be rendered to the independent States of southern Africa to enable them to defend their sovereignty and to free them from economic dependence on South Africa. In that connection, the Conference welcomed the establishment of SADCC and called for States to support it.

The Conference's Committee of the Whole, meeting concurrently with the Conference, condemned the terrorist acts by armed groups in the pay of South Africa against Czechoslovak citizens working in Angola and urged the Secretary-General to continue his efforts to obtain the release of those kidnapped. In addition to reiterating the positions taken by the Conference, the Committee specifically condemned South Africa's aggression and destabilization against Botswana, Lesotho, Mozambique, Seychelles, Zambia and Zimbabwe, aimed at intimidating them from supporting the struggle of Namibians and South Africans for independence and at disrupting and destabilizing their economies.

The Committee also called for assistance to the front-line States, including military assistance. United Nations bodies were requested to initiate a major programme of assistance to enable those States to implement United Nations resolutions supporting Namibia's struggle for independence and to withstand the economic sabotage.

GENERAL ASSEMBLY ACTION

On 5 December, the General Assembly adopted resolution 38/39 C by recorded vote.

Effects of *apartheid* on the countries of southern Africa

The General Assembly,

Gravely concerned over the acts of aggression, destabilization and subversion, as well as economic and other pressure, by the *apartheid* régime of South Africa against independent African States in southern Africa,

Convinced of the danger of wider conflict unless effective action is taken by the international community,

Concerned over the safety of South African refugees in neighbouring countries,

Commending the front-line States for their sacrifices in support of the struggle for freedom in South Africa and Namibia,

Condemning the pressure exerted by South Africa to force Lesotho to expel South African refugees in violation of the principles of international law,

Again condemning the racist minority régime of South Africa for its continued occupation of parts of the territory of Angola and its acts of aggression, destabilization and subversion against independent African States, particularly against Lesotho and Mozambique,

Gravely concerned about the economic blockade that South Africa has imposed against Lesotho,

Deploring the pressures exerted by the Government of the United States of America against Angola to impose on it the so-called issue of "linkage" or "parallelism" which encourages the racist minority régime of South Africa to block the negotiations for the independence of Namibia and to continue its illegal occupation of parts of the territory of Angola and escalate its aggression against that country,

1. *Condemns* the acts of aggression by the *apartheid* régime of South Africa against Angola, Lesotho and Mozambique and its threats against independent African States in southern Africa;

2. *Demands* that all troops of the *apartheid* régime of South Africa be immediately and unconditionally withdrawn from Angola and that South Africa respect fully the independence, sovereignty and territorial integrity of independent African States;

3. *Fully supports* the right of the Government of Angola to take measures in accordance with Article 51 of the Charter of the United Nations in order to guarantee and safeguard the territorial integrity and national sovereignty of Angola;

4. *Expresses its full support* for the people and Government of Mozambique in their struggle to preserve their national independence and sovereignty and urges all

States to provide political, diplomatic and material support to Mozambique;

5. *Further strongly condemns* the racist minority régime of Pretoria for its acts of destabilization, armed aggression and economic blockade against Lesotho and strongly urges the international community to extend maximum assistance to Lesotho to enable that country to fulfil its international humanitarian obligations towards refugees, and to use its influence on the racist régime to desist from terrorist acts against Lesotho;

6. *Demands* that the racist régime of South Africa pay full compensation to Angola, Lesotho and other independent African States for the damage to life and property caused by its acts of aggression;

7. *Calls upon* the international community to provide assistance to independent African States in the subregion to enable them to defend their sovereignty and territorial integrity, counter the hostile South African acts of aggression and rebuild their economies;

8. *Urges* the Security Council to consider, as a matter of urgency, the means to ensure peace in southern Africa.

General Assembly resolution 38/39 C

5 December 1983   Meeting 83   146-2-4 (recorded vote)

48-nation draft (A/38/L.22 & Add.1), orally revised; agenda item 32.

Sponsors: Afghanistan, Algeria, Angola, Benin, Botswana, Bulgaria, Burundi, Byelorussian SSR, Cape Verde, Cuba, Czechoslovakia, Democratic Yemen, Gabon, German Democratic Republic, Ghana, Guinea, Guinea-Bissau, Guyana, Hungary, Iraq, Kenya, Lao People's Democratic Republic, Lesotho, Libyan Arab Jamahiriya, Madagascar, Mali, Mauritania, Mauritius, Mongolia, Mozambique, Nigeria, Poland, Qatar, Rwanda, Sao Tome and Principe, Senegal, Sierra Leone, Somalia, Syrian Arab Republic, Togo, Uganda, Ukrainian SSR, United Republic of Cameroon, United Republic of Tanzania, Viet Nam, Yugoslavia, Zambia, Zimbabwe.

Meeting numbers. GA 38th session: plenary 60-63, 69-71, 83.

Recorded vote in Assembly as follows:

In favour: Afghanistan, Albania, Algeria, Angola, Antigua and Barbuda, Argentina, Australia, Austria, Bahamas, Bahrain, Bangladesh, Barbados, Belgium, Belize, Benin, Bhutan, Bolivia, Botswana, Brazil, Bulgaria, Burma, Burundi, Byelorussian SSR, Canada, Cape Verde, Central African Republic, Chad, Chile, China, Colombia, Comoros, Congo, Costa Rica, Cuba, Cyprus, Czechoslovakia, Democratic Kampuchea, Democratic Yemen, Denmark, Djibouti, Dominican Republic, Ecuador, Egypt, El Salvador, Equatorial Guinea, Ethiopia, Fiji, Finland, France, Gabon, Gambia, German Democratic Republic, Ghana, Greece, Guinea, Guinea-Bissau, Guyana, Haiti, Honduras, Hungary, Iceland, India, Indonesia, Iran, Iraq, Ireland, Italy, Ivory Coast, Jamaica, Japan, Jordan, Kenya, Kuwait, Lao People's Democratic Republic, Lebanon, Lesotho, Libyan Arab Jamahiriya, Luxembourg, Madagascar, Malaysia, Maldives, Mali, Malta, Mauritania, Mauritius, Mexico, Mongolia, Morocco, Mozambique, Nepal, Netherlands, New Zealand, Nicaragua, Niger, Nigeria, Norway, Oman, Pakistan, Panama, Papua New Guinea, Peru, Philippines, Poland, Portugal, Qatar, Romania, Rwanda, Saint Lucia, Saint Vincent and the Grenadines, Samoa, Sao Tome and Principe, Saudi Arabia, Senegal, Seychelles, Sierra Leone, Singapore, Solomon Islands, Somalia, Spain, Sri Lanka, Sudan, Suriname, Swaziland, Sweden, Syrian Arab Republic, Thailand, Togo, Trinidad and Tobago, Tunisia, Turkey, Uganda, Ukrainian SSR, USSR, United Arab Emirates, United Republic of Cameroon, United Republic of Tanzania, Upper Volta, Uruguay, Vanuatu, Venezuela, Viet Nam, Yemen, Yugoslavia, Zaire, Zambia, Zimbabwe.

Against: Paraguay, United States.

Abstaining: Germany, Federal Republic of, Guatemala, Malawi, United Kingdom.

Of those countries speaking in explanation of vote, most mentioned reservations they had on the last preambular paragraph or their objection to singling out a particular State. Australia, Austria, Canada, France, the Federal Republic of Germany, Ireland, Italy, Japan, the Netherlands, Portugal, Sri Lanka, Turkey and the United Kingdom made such remarks. Austria believed that the arbitrary singling out of Member States was unjustified and counter-productive. Canada did not wish to be associated with the criticism contained in that paragraph. Italy spoke similarly and expressed reservations concerning other wording but endorsed the basic aim of the text. Turkey said it did not believe that the paragraph reflected accurately the statement made at the most recent Security Council meetings by the country mentioned. While expressing support for the front-line States, the United Kingdom said it could not accept, among other things, what it described as the inaccurate, one-sided and unjustified reference to the United States.

New Zealand had reservations about the language of one of the preambular paragraphs. Malawi objected to some language or wording formulations of the resolution, as did France which deplored the excessive or inaccurate language in a number of paragraphs, particularly the inappropriate use of language that dealt with areas which it said were properly within the Security Council's competence.

Australia opposed the selective naming of States, particularly in instances in which unproved charges were made; it also opposed endorsement of armed struggle. The Federal Republic of Germany expressed reservations on the same provisions—the last preambular paragraph and paragraph 1.

The Assembly called for support to front-line States in other resolutions. In resolution 38/36 A, it condemned the use of Namibian territory by South Africa to launch attacks against neighbouring States, particularly the aggression against and occupation of Angola, in order to intimidate those States and to prevent them from supporting the legitimate struggle of the Namibian and South African peoples for independence. The Assembly called on the international community urgently to extend support, including military support, to the front-line States to enable them to defend themselves against the aggression; called on States to assist SADCC in promoting regional economic cooperation and development; requested the Secretary-General to continue to develop an assistance programme for front-line States; and requested United Nations bodies to co-operate in that programme.

In resolution 38/51, the Assembly urged United Nations bodies to extend material assistance to the front-line States so that they could support the struggle of the people of Namibia for independence and resist the violation of their territorial integrity by South African forces directly or, as in Angola and Mozambique, through puppet traitor groups. The Assembly, in resolution 38/17, condemned South Africa's use of armed terrorist groups to oppose the national liberation movements and

Governments of southern Africa, reaffirmed its solidarity with those movements and countries that were victims of South Africa's aggression and destabilization, and called on the international community to support those countries in strengthening their defence capacity and development.

Angola–South Africa armed incidents and South African occupation of Angola

In August 1983, Angola said that South Africa had carried out more air, artillery and infantry attacks, resulting in loss of lives and destruction of property. In addition, South Africa continued to occupy parts of its territory. South Africa rejected those allegations, but acknowledged that it undertook reconnaissance missions at times to monitor hostile activities since Angola allowed its territory to be used as a springboard for attacks against Namibia. Meeting at Angola's request, the Security Council adopted resolution 545(1983) on 20 December, demanding that South Africa withdraw all its occupation forces from Angola.

The General Assembly also denounced South Africa's action against Angola. In three 1983 resolutions (38/17, 38/36 A and 38/39 C), it condemned the aggression against and occupation of that country.

Activities of the Council for Namibia. The aggression launched from Namibian territory against Angola and the continued military occupation of part of Angolan territory by South African forces was condemned by the International Conference in Support of the Struggle of the Namibian People for Independence in its Paris Declaration on Namibia.[6] The Conference expressed support for the people and Government of Angola in efforts to safeguard their national independence and territorial integrity and demanded the immediate and unconditional withdrawal of South African troops from Angola.

The Council for Namibia reported that, since the invasion of Angola by South Africa in 1975, increasing use had been made of special military units for repeated acts of aggression against that country and Zambia, and it named five units involved in those attacks, the biggest and most active of which operated almost entirely inside Angola. For several years, South Africa had been engaged in a systematic campaign of destabilization of the neighbouring States, the Council stated. Using Namibia as a launching pad, it had repeatedly committed acts of aggression against Angola, causing loss of life and extensive destruction of property. Women and children and other innocent civilians had been its constant victims. Despite numerous United Nations resolutions, an estimated 5,500 South African troops had occupied parts of southern Angola for more than a year, as far as 250 kilometres from the Namibian border.

Action by the Commission on Human Rights.
The Commission on Human Rights, in a resolution of 15 February,[8] demanded that South Africa end its unprovoked acts of aggression and withdraw its occupation forces from Angola. In a resolution of 18 February on human rights violations in southern Africa,[9] the Commission again demanded the immediate withdrawal of those forces (see ECONOMIC AND SOCIAL QUESTIONS, Chapter XVIII).

ECONOMIC AND SOCIAL COUNCIL ACTION (July)

The Economic and Social Council took similar action in resolution 1983/42 of 25 July, condemning South African armed attacks on Namibian refugee camps and settlements in Angola. It requested United Nations organs and international organizations to ensure the protection and safety of those refugees.

Communications (August). In a telegram of 15 August 1983 to the Secretary-General,[10] Angola said that South Africa had carried out more air, artillery and infantry attacks, and had occupied the town of Cangamba; noting the loss of civilian lives and the destruction of public utilities, Angola said that the hypocrisy of certain Western countries, particularly the members of the Security Council, had allowed South Africa to act with impunity. South Africa rejected these allegations in a letter of 22 August,[11] but acknowledged that it undertook reconnaissance flights to monitor hostile activities against Namibia since, South Africa said, Angola allowed its territory to be used as a springboard for armed attacks there; South Africa added that the Angolan civilian population was reacting to atrocities perpetrated against it by Cuban and SWAPO forces and it was the forces of the National Union for the Total Independence of Angola (UNITA), not of South Africa, which had captured Cangamba.

GENERAL ASSEMBLY ACTION (November/December)

The General Assembly, in resolution 38/17 of 22 November, strongly condemned the continued occupation of parts of southern Angola and the aggression carried out by South African troops against Cangamba, 500 kilometres from the Namibian border, and demanded the immediate and unconditional withdrawal of those troops. In resolution 38/36 A of 1 December, the Assembly condemned South Africa for its persistent acts of subversion and aggression against Angola, including occupation, and called on it to cease all such acts and withdraw all troops. The Assembly took similar action in resolution 38/39 C of 5 December, demanding that all troops be immediately and unconditionally withdrawn and that South Africa respect the independence, sovereignty and territorial integrity of independent African States. In addition, the Assembly supported Angola's right to act in accordance with Article 51 of the United Nations Charter (on the right of self-defence) in order to guarantee and safeguard its territorial integrity and national sovereignty.

Communications (December). The Secretary-General or the President of the Security Council received three letters during December 1983 concerning the presence of South African troops in Angola.

Angola, on 5 December,[12] forwarded a copy of a White Paper prepared by its Government, listing and describing acts of aggression against it by South Africa from 1975 to 1982.

On 15 December,[13] South Africa forwarded two letters from its Minister for Foreign Affairs. The first, dated 22 November, dealt with the question of implementation of the Security Council's independence plan for Namibia outlined in resolution 435(1978),[14] in particular the electoral system (see TRUSTEESHIP AND DECOLONIZATION, Chapter III). In the second letter, of 15 December, the Minister said his Government was prepared to begin, on 31 January 1984, a disengagement of forces which from time to time conducted military operations against SWAPO in Angola, on the understanding that this would be reciprocated by Angola, which would assure that its own forces, SWAPO and Cubans there would not exploit the resulting situation.

Angola, on 31 December,[15] transmitted a letter of that date from its President and a list of acts of aggression by South African armed forced against Angola that took place from 16 to 28 December. The President said that, in order to contribute to a peaceful solution to the Namibia problem, Angola would not oppose a 30-day truce beginning 1 February 1984, if the Secretary-General obtained the agreement of SWAPO, and if South Africa withdrew its forces from Angola and promised to initiate the implementation, within 15 days after that period, of resolution 435(1978), without extraneous considerations. As for setting the date for a cease-fire in Namibia between SWAPO and South Africa, the President said the matter involved only those two parties, and the Secretary-General had a mandate from the Council to proceed with the necessary consultations.

SECURITY COUNCIL ACTION (December)

Angola, by a letter of 14 December 1983 to the President of the Security Council,[16] requested an urgent meeting of the Council to deal with the situation resulting from South Africa's occupation since 1981 of parts of southern Angola, including the increase in acts of aggression and violence. The Council held five meetings on Angola's complaint, from 16 to 20 December.

The Council invited Angola, Argentina, Benin, Botswana, Brazil, Canada, Cuba, Egypt, Ethiopia, the German Democratic Republic, India, the Libyan Arab Jamahiriya, Mauritania, Mozambique, Nigeria, Portugal, Somalia, South Africa, Turkey, the United Republic of Tanzania, Yugoslavia and Zambia, at their request, to participate in the discussion without vote. The Chairman of the Special Committee on the Situation with regard to the Implementation of the Declaration on the Granting of Independence to Colonial Countries and Peoples was invited to participate, at his request, in accordance with rule 39 of the Council's provisional rules of procedure.[a]

Addressing the Council on 16 December, Angola said that South Africa's acts of aggression, beginning in 1975, had escalated in 1981 to a full-scale war, and the latest attack had occurred that day. The war was being supported by certain United Nations Members, without whose backing the South African troops would be unable to carry out destabilizing attempts. The Council had acted on Angola's complaints against South Africa five times since 1976 but, due to the negative vote of a permanent member, had failed to take action after a massive invasion in 1981.[(17)] As a result, five South African batallions were occupying southern Angola. In regard to South Africa's 15 December letter (see above), Angola said Pretoria spoke of a disengagement of forces but not withdrawal and linked that withdrawal to other issues, which Angola rejected, stressing that it would not compromise on its territorial integrity and that South African troop withdrawal was a non-negotiable issue.

South Africa said its security operations in Angola had one objective only—the protection of Namibia against terrorist attacks by SWAPO, which had intimidated its political opponents and had been responsible for the assassination of political leaders and the death of others. South Africa would defend the people of Namibia and would not allow SWAPO bands to establish sanctuaries in Angola. After the United Nations had failed to respond to South Africa's proposals for a peaceful solution, South Africa had attempted to resolve the problem directly with Angola at meetings in December 1982 and February 1983 in Cape Verde. South Africa informed Angola of its position that an overall solution to the problems of the region would require the withdrawal of Cubans from Angola. Despite Angola's rejection of this position, South Africa was still prepared to examine the possibility of peaceful coexistence. According to South Africa, the solution could be found by Angola's ensuring that its territory was not used for launching terrorist attacks against its neighbours.

Many speakers in the Council, including Argentina, Brazil, China, the German Democratic Republic, Guyana, India, Mozambique, the Netherlands, Nigeria, Pakistan, Poland, Somalia,

the United Republic of Tanzania, Yugoslavia, Zambia and Zimbabwe, stressed that South Africa's aggression against Angola violated international law and the United Nations Charter. Yugoslavia said that South Africa, by defying Charter principles and international law, posed a direct challenge to the United Nations and the Council. Noting that previous Council action condemning South Africa had not inhibited it from further aggression, Ethiopia said that South Africa should be told that it would not be allowed to violate international law with impunity.

Argentina, China, Guyana, the Netherlands, Portugal, Turkey, the USSR and Yugoslavia expressed concern over the implications of South Africa's aggression for international peace and security. Many of them believed that the situation endangered the security of the region.

Cuba, Guyana, the Libyan Arab Jamahiriya, Mauritania, Nicaragua, Somalia, Turkey, the United Republic of Tanzania, Yugoslavia and Zimbabwe said that South Africa's aggression demonstrated its intention to occupy Angola, destabilize that Government or sabotage its economy.

According to the Libyan Arab Jamahiriya, South Africa had persisted in its aggression, occupying Angolan territory permanently and undermining the country's social and economic progress, and, through its friends, was able to prevent the Council from compelling it to comply with the will of the international community, end its occupation of Namibia and stop its aggression against neighbouring countries. Comparing Angola's situation with its own, Nicaragua said that, in both cases, a major Power was carrying out aggression and destabilization, through its policeman in the area and with the use of mercenary troops; South Africa had steadily increased its aggression, encouraged by statements by the United States. In Turkey's view, South Africa was trying to achieve domination of its neighbours and to eliminate resistance to its policies of racial discrimination and occupation of Namibia. The United Republic of Tanzania believed that the occupation of Angola was intended to destroy its civilian infrastructure and economy and to establish a protective buffer for South Africa's *apartheid* system.

According to Egypt, South Africa, by supporting the terrorists opposing the Angolan Government, was seeking to impose its colonialist and racist policies, and the main reason for South Africa's continued aggression was its dissatisfaction with the policies of the legitimate Government of

[a]Rule 39 of the Council's provisional rules of procedure states: "The Security Council may invite members of the Secretariat or other persons, whom it considers competent for the purpose, to supply it with information or to give other assistance in examining matters within its competence."

Angola. Mozambique believed that South Africa's attacks were due to its view that the attainment of independence by African countries threatened its *apartheid* policies and its very survival.

Botswana said South Africa's attack was an attempt to intimidate Angola and to deny its people the right to choose its political system. Pakistan and Turkey also said South Africa was using intimidation to carry out its policies in southern Africa.

Cuba, Guyana, Nicaragua, the USSR and Zambia expressed the view that the situation was aggravated by the support that the United States or certain other Western countries provided to South Africa. The USSR said that South Africa was benefiting from their patronage and that they were impeding the Council's adoption of effective measures against the aggressor; South Africa and the United States were attempting to cover up their imperialist policy in Africa by claims that the conflict in southern Africa represented an East-West confrontation.

According to the Netherlands, Zambia and Zimbabwe, South Africa had not provided a satisfactory explanation for its action against Angola. Zambia said that South Africa had no valid reason whatsoever for its occupation, but only wanted to perpetuate its occupation of Namibia and the *apartheid* system. In Zimbabwe's opinion, South Africa's explanation was unacceptable to the oppressed masses of Namibia and offensive to the peoples of Africa, since Angola posed no threat to South Africa and the SWAPO freedom fighters were not in Angola but in Namibia.

Many countries, including China, Cuba, Ethiopia, France, the German Democratic Republic, Guyana, India, the Libyan Arab Jamahiriya, Mozambique, Nicaragua, Pakistan, Poland, the United Republic of Tanzania, Yugoslavia and Zimbabwe, believed that the offer of South Africa for a disengagement of its troops in Angola was a manœuvre to link the issue with the removal of Cuban troops from Angola or to disguise its real intentions. China said that South Africa, while stepping up its aggression, had feigned the easing of tension by proposing so-called disengagement in Angola, and was attempting to legitimize its occupation of Namibia. Cuba said that the problem was not the presence of its forces in Angola, which were there under a sovereign agreement between two independent Governments, but the South African occupation of parts of Angola; it added that its forces would remain until there was no longer danger to Angolan security. Also stressing that the problem centred on the occupation of Angola by South African forces, France regretted that South Africa had again linked the independence of Namibia with a matter which was exclusively germane to Angola's sovereignty. Nigeria

said Angola could not legitimately be held hostage to a settlement in Namibia.

The German Democratic Republic said the latest attacks revealed South Africa's intention to deceive world public opinion by statements of alleged readiness to conduct a dialogue with its neighbours and to conclude a non-aggression treaty. India also felt that South Africa was attempting to divert attention to issues that were either fabrications or had no direct bearing on the question under consideration. According to Pakistan, the South African disengagement offer was most likely tactical in nature and limited in objective, and it made conditions which, if accepted, would amount to the United Nations endorsing South Africa's lawless actions.

Malta noted South Africa's record of delay and prevarication, and hoped that its offer marked the beginning of a change of attitude; however, it regretted that the offer coincided with the latest military offensive against Angola. The Netherlands expressed reservations about the wording of South Africa's offer, which it said was imprecise regarding whether South Africa intended to withdraw its forces completely from Angola; if accomplished, that would be a significant step towards avoiding deeper turmoil.

Argentina, Brazil, Cuba, Egypt, Ethiopia, the German Democratic Republic, India, the Libyan Arab Jamahiriya, Poland, Somalia, Turkey, the USSR, the United Republic of Tanzania, and Yugoslavia expressed the view that the Council should adopt measures against South Africa under Chapter VII of the United Nations Charter if it failed to withdraw from Angola.

Calling on the Council to impose comprehensive, mandatory sanctions under Chapter VII, the Libyan Arab Jamahiriya said that South Africa had continuously attempted to fabricate pretexts to justify its aggression and, through its friends, to prevent the Council from adopting measures which might compel it to comply with the will of the international community, end its occupation of Namibia and stop its aggression against neighbouring countries. Noting that the Council's repeated condemnation had been ineffective and its call for compensation to Angola ignored, Somalia called on the Council to fulfil its responsibility for restoring international peace and security by adopting further sanctions against South Africa. Poland said the Council should carry out its primary responsibility for restoring international peace and security, and not remain indifferent in the face of South Africa's threat to continue military actions against Angola.

Mauritania said the Council should call on South Africa's allies to withhold all technological, financial and political support for South Africa's occupation of Angolan territory, and it stressed the responsibility of the Western Powers to restrain South Africa and to help in the reconstruction of Angola.

Portugal and Somalia were among those stressing the responsibility of the United Nations in preserving international peace and security. Portugal said that the need for a just settlement was essential because of the legal, political and moral imperatives of United Nations principles, and it added that the Council needed to reaffirm its belief in those principles by supporting the legitimate demands of Angola.

The Chairman of the Committee on colonial countries said that the latest acts of aggression revealed South Africa's plan to block all avenues towards a negotiated settlement for the independence of Namibia, adding that it was incumbent on the international community to redress and prevent the recurrence of such criminal acts, through the application of the provisions of Chapter VII of the Charter.

On 20 December, the Council adopted resolution 545(1983).

The Security Council,

Having heard the statement of the Permanent Representative of Angola to the United Nations,

Deeply concerned at the continued occupation of parts of southern Angola by the South African military forces in flagrant violation of the principles and objectives of the Charter of the United Nations and of international law,

Gravely concerned at the massive loss of human life and extensive destruction of property brought about by the continuing attacks against and military occupation of the territory of Angola,

Recalling its resolutions 387(1976), 428(1978), 447(1979), 454(1979) and 475(1980),

Bearing in mind that in accordance with Article 2, paragraph 4, of the Charter, all Member States shall refrain in their international relations from the threat or use of force against the territorial integrity or political independence of any State or in any other manner inconsistent with the purposes of the United Nations,

Conscious of the need to take effective measures to maintain international peace and security in view of the continued violation of the Charter by South Africa,

1. *Strongly condemns* South Africa's continued military occupation of parts of southern Angola which constitutes a flagrant violation of international law and of the independence, sovereignty and territorial integrity of Angola;

2. *Declares* that the continued illegal military occupation of the territory of Angola is a flagrant violation of the sovereignty, independence and territorial integrity of Angola and endangers international peace and security;

3. *Demands* that South Africa should unconditionally withdraw forthwith all its occupation forces from the territory of Angola and cease all violations against that State and henceforth scrupulously respect the sovereignty and territorial integrity of Angola;

4. *Considers*, moreover, that Angola is entitled to appropriate redress for any material damage it has suffered;

5. *Calls upon* all Member States to desist from any action which would undermine the independence, territorial integrity and sovereignty of Angola;

6. *Requests* the Secretary-General to monitor the implementation of the present resolution and report to the Security Council accordingly;

7. *Decides* to remain seized of the matter.

Security Council resolution 545(1983)

20 December 1983   Meeting 2508   14-0-1

14-nation draft (S/16226).

Sponsors: Angola, Botswana, Guyana, Jordan, Malta, Mozambique, Nicaragua, Nigeria, Pakistan, Togo, United Republic of Tanzania, Zaire, Zambia, Zimbabwe.

Meeting numbers. SC 2504-2508.

Vote in Council as follows:

In favour: China, France, Guyana, Jordan, Malta, Netherlands, Nicaragua, Pakistan, Poland, Togo, USSR, United Kingdom, Zaire, Zimbabwe.

Against: None.

Abstaining: United States.

In explanation of vote, the United States, stressing its deep concern with the escalating violence in southern Africa, particularly cross-border violence, said that its policy was based on the belief that negotiated solutions were both possible and essential and it would do nothing to jeopardize the delicate point in the ongoing negotiating process, in which the United States was playing an active role; South Africa's commitment to begin a disengagement of its forces from Angola represented a new step in the process which could contribute to negotiations on southern Africa and underscored the validity of the involvement of the Western contact group (Canada, France, the Federal Republic of Germany, the United Kingdom and the United States—which were attempting to open a dialogue with South Africa on Namibian independence).

The United Kingdom, though expressing support for the withdrawal of all foreign forces from Angola, had reservations on the last preambular paragraph and paragraph 2, which it believed did not fall within the provisions of Chapter VII of the Charter or constituted a finding or decision which had specific consequences under the Charter; in addition, the United Kingdom found the wording of paragraph 2 unfortunate and pointed out that it should in no way be taken as a justification for further intervention by foreign forces in the internal affairs of Angola.

Speaking of the resolution as a whole, Guyana said it would have preferred language that was more categorical and unequivocal, and it noted that paragraph 4, in particular, represented a retreat from the terms of Security Council resolution 387(1976),[18] in which South Africa had been called on to meet the just claims of Angola for full compensation for the damage and destruction inflicted on it.

Lesotho–South Africa armed incidents and dispute

In 1983, both the Security Council and the General Assembly considered the situation between Lesotho and South Africa, following a December 1982 attack by South African forces on Lesotho.[19] In response to a December 1982 Council resolution,[20] the Secretary-General sent a mission to Lesotho to determine that country's needs for international assistance. By resolution 535(1983) adopted in June 1983, the Council endorsed the mission's report and requested Member States, international organizations and financial institutions to assist Lesotho in those areas identified in the report (10 projects, including strengthening Lesotho's police services, expansion of hospital and health facilities and a new international airport). Throughout the year, Lesotho and South Africa continued to exchange charges against each other. The Office of the United Nations High Commissioner for Refugees (UNHCR) continued to assist South African refugees living in Lesotho (see ECONOMIC AND SOCIAL QUESTIONS, Chapter XXI).

Communications (February-June). On 8 February 1983,[21] South Africa transmitted a letter of that date from its Foreign Minister, rejecting as one-sided the Security Council's 1982 resolution[20] by which the Council had condemned South Africa for its aggression against Lesotho and demanded that it pay compensation for the damage. Stating that Lesotho pursued a policy of harbouring terrorists and should bear the financial responsibility for damages resulting from that policy, the Minister also expressed his Government's willingness to conclude non-aggression pacts with its neighbours.

Lesotho, in a letter of 28 March,[22] said South Africa had instigated a series of armed attacks and acts of sabotage in Lesotho on 26 and 27 March. On 30 March,[23] South Africa transmitted the text of a message sent by its Foreign Affairs Department to the Foreign Ministry of Lesotho on 28 March, rejecting Lesotho's charges and adding that South Africa would not be held responsible for the actions of dissident elements within Lesotho. In regard to the Council's 29 June consideration of Lesotho's complaint (see below), South Africa, by a letter of that date,[24] forwarded a joint press statement issued on 3 June after a meeting of the Foreign Ministers of the two countries, in which they affirmed their agreement that neither would permit any elements to use their territory to plan subversion against the other and that they expected that unnecessary traffic delays at border posts would be cleared up that day.

Report of the mission to Lesotho. As a first step towards carrying out the Security Council's 1982 resolution,[20] the Secretary-General dispatched a mission to Lesotho from 11 to 16 January 1983. The mission's report,[25] dated 9 February, contained an account of its consultations with the Government concerning Lesotho's need for international assistance. The report listed 10 projects, at an estimated cost of $46 million, for which international assistance was sought. Those projects (including strengthening police services, establishing a fire brigade, improving health care, constructing a maize silo, an afforestation programme and funding for an airport) were aimed at providing for the emergency needs arising directly from the South African attack of 9 December 1982[19] and for the urgent needs arising from Lesotho's vulnerability to political and economic pressures pursuant to its refugee policies (see ECONOMIC AND SOCIAL QUESTIONS, Chapter III, under "Economic assistance—Lesotho").

SECURITY COUNCIL ACTION

When the Security Council met to consider the mission's report on 29 June, Lesotho, addressing the Council at its invitation, expressed appreciation of the report and endorsed its contents. In addition to acts of aggression and destabilization against it, Lesotho had been struggling for a long time under difficult economic circumstances to fulfil its obligation to receive and provide for the welfare of South African refugees, including a number of economic pressures applied by South Africa in an attempt to force Lesotho to close its borders to the victims fleeing *apartheid*. Despite the Council's 1982 resolution, South Africa had continued its attacks against Lesotho in 1983, the most recent of which occurred on 26 June. In addition, a deliberate slow-down in the flow of traffic between the two countries had been engineered by South Africa to exacerbate the economic difficulties of Lesotho and undermine its political stability. Under these circumstances, Lesotho stressed the importance it attached to the new international airport which would provide it with an alternative route to the outside world. Lesotho urged that the United Nations execute the provisions in the mission's report.

On 29 June, the Security Council unanimously adopted resolution 535(1983), prepared during consultations among its members.

The Security Council,

Recalling its resolution 527(1982),

Having examined the report of the Mission to Lesotho appointed by the Secretary-General in accordance with resolution 527(1982),

Having heard the statement of the Chargé d'affaires of the Permanent Mission of the Kingdom of Lesotho expressing the deep concern of his Government at the frequent aggressive acts by South Africa against the territorial integrity and independence of Lesotho,

Reaffirming its opposition to the system of *apartheid* and the right of all countries to receive refugees fleeing from *apartheid* oppression,

Convinced of the importance of international solidarity with Lesotho,

1. *Commends* the Government of Lesotho for its steadfast opposition to *apartheid* and its generosity to the South African refugees;

2. *Expresses* its appreciation to the Secretary-General for having arranged to send a mission to Lesotho to ascertain the assistance needed;

3. *Endorses* the report of the Mission to Lesotho under resolution 527(1982);

4. *Requests* Member States, international organizations and financial institutions to assist Lesotho in the fields identified in the report of the Mission to Lesotho;

5. *Requests* the Secretary-General to give the matter of assistance to Lesotho his continued attention and to keep the Security Council informed;

6. *Decides* to remain seized of the question.

Security Council resolution 535(1983)

29 June 1983   Meeting 2455   Adopted unanimously

Draft prepared in consultations among Council members (S/15846).
Meeting number. SC 2455.

Communications (July-October). On 1 July 1983,[26] South Africa forwarded to the Security Council President a letter of the same date from its Foreign Minister. He stated that South Africa rejected the Council's inferences that South Africa was involved in frequent aggressive acts against Lesotho or that terrorist groups operating from Lesotho were synonymous with refugees fleeing from *apartheid;* in its view, Lesotho was again engaged in a charade calculated to solicit foreign aid to prop up its unelected Government against internal opposition.

From August to October, the Secretary-General received five letters from Lesotho and South Africa. The Foreign Minister of Lesotho appealed to the Secretary-General on 17 August[27] to use his good offices to urge South Africa to exercise restraint on its demands concerning the return of certain refugees whom South Africa claimed were a security threat and to lift restrictions on the movement of people and arms to Lesotho; should those efforts fail, Lesotho would request the international community to help it deal with the refugees, currently estimated at 3,000. On 7 September,[28] Lesotho forwarded a 2 September letter from its Foreign Minister who, thanking the Secretary-General for a visit by his representative, said South Africa continued to cause unacceptable economic suffering for Lesotho's citizens and a deterioration of the security situation; therefore Lesotho and the United Nations High Commissioner for Refugees (UNHCR) had reluctantly agreed to begin resettling in third countries some of those refugees residing in Lesotho, in an attempt to achieve normalization of Lesotho–South Africa relations and to improve the welfare of the refugees.

On 11 October,[29] the South African Foreign Minister denied Lesotho's charges of 2 September and expressed regret that Lesotho had made those charges at a time when the two countries were holding official talks to address certain bilateral problems, especially security issues, including certain border control measures which would be relaxed when South Africa's security concerns were met. On 19 October,[30] South Africa forwarded a message of 18 October from its Foreign Minister to his counterpart in Lesotho, stating that Lesotho's recent address to the General Assembly contained false allegations and inaccuracies, and could further retard progress towards mutually constructive relations.

Lesotho, on 20 October,[31] forwarded its Foreign Minister's reply to South Africa. Lesotho reiterated its allegations that South Africa was allowing its territory to be used for launching attacks against Lesotho and that South African border controls were causing suffering among the peaceful and law-abiding Lesotho citizens, and it denied South African charges concerning the reason some refugees were leaving Lesotho.

GENERAL ASSEMBLY ACTION

In several 1983 resolutions, the General Assembly took action related to the Lesotho–South Africa dispute. In resolutions 38/17 and 38/39 C, it condemned South Africa for its acts of destabilization, armed aggression and economic blockade against Lesotho and urged the international community to extend maximum assistance to Lesotho to enable it to fulfil its international humanitarian obligations towards refugees and to use its influence on South Africa to desist from its terrorist acts.

In resolution 38/215, the Assembly outlined measures for economic assistance to Lesotho and, in resolution 38/95, dealt with assistance to South African student refugees.

Mozambique–South Africa armed incidents

In 1983, Mozambique addressed three letters to the Secretary-General charging South Africa with attacks against its territory. The Economic and Social Council in July (resolution 1983/42) and the General Assembly in November (resolution 38/17) and December (38/39 C) condemned South Africa's actions.

Communications. On 25 May,[32] Mozambique stated that, two days earlier, approximately 16 South African aircraft had bombed an area near Maputo, killing six civilians and wounding 40 others; it added that South Africa was using indiscriminate violence against neighbouring countries to divert the attention of the international community from the conflict in South Africa. On 26 May, the German Democratic Republic[33] and Pakistan[34] forwarded statements by spokesmen of their Foreign Ministries condemning the 23 May air raid. The German Democratic Republic said it was further evidence of South Africa's aggressive destabilization policy against the free peoples of southern Africa. Pakistan called on the international community to ensure that South Africa would not repeat such acts.

On 26 August,[35] Mozambique forwarded a 24 August communiqué in which the Government said that a group of armed bandits, as part of South Africa's destabilization strategy, had attacked a mining installation on 21 August, killing two Soviet geologists and two Mozambican workers, and kidnapping 24 Soviet geologists, two Mozambican women and two Mozambican children. On 18 October,[36] Mozambique said that on the previous day three explosive devices placed by South African agents in a residential building in Maputo had exploded and wounded at least five people; this attack, like most others, had occurred at a time when South Africa was experiencing internal problems.

ECONOMIC AND SOCIAL COUNCIL ACTION

The Economic and Social Council, in resolution 1983/42 of 25 July, strongly condemned the blatant aggression of South Africa in its 23 May bombing attack on Mozambique and the frequent acts of destabilization carried out by it against the frontline States, which had resulted in heavy loss of life, the creation of large numbers of refugees and massive destruction.

GENERAL ASSEMBLY ACTION

In resolution 38/17 of 22 November, the General Assembly also condemned South Africa for that bombing attack and the acts of territorial encroachment and espionage against Mozambique, as well as its attack on 17 October against the office of the African National Congress at Maputo.

REFERENCES

[1]A/38/22. [2]A/38/539-S/16102. [3]A/AC.115/L.593. [4]E/1983/13 (res. 1983/4, 1983/9, 1983/11). [5]*Report of the Second World Conference to Combat Racism and Racial Discrimination, Geneva (1-12 August 1983)* (A/CONF.119/26 & Corr.1), Sales No. E.83.XIV.4 & Corrigendum. [6]A/38/24. [7]YUN 1977, p. 161, SC res. 418(1977), 4 Nov. 1977. [8]E/1983/13 (res. 1983/4). [9]*Ibid.* (res. 1983/10). [10]S/15929. [11]A/38/359-S/15937. [12]S/16198. [13]S/16219. [14]YUN 1978, p. 915, SC res. 435(1978), 29 Sep. 1978. [15]S/16245. [16]S/16216. [17]YUN 1981, p. 218. [18]YUN 1976, p. 178, SC res. 387(1976), 31 Mar. 1976. [19]YUN 1982, p. 313. [20]*Ibid.*, p. 317, SC res. 527(1982), 15 Dec. 1982. [21]S/15598. [22]S/15658. [23]S/15664. [24]S/15847. [25]S/15600. [26]S/15852. [27]S/15931. [28]S/15970. [29]S/16033. [30]S/16054. [31]S/16057. [32]A/38/254-S/15801 & Corr.1. [33]A/38/255-S/15802. [34]S/15794. [35]A/38/371-S/15944. [36]A/38/518-S/16052.

Questions involving the Libyan Arab Jamahiriya

In 1983, the Security Council met for two series of meetings (in March/April and in August) at the request of Chad which claimed that the Libyan Arab Jamahiriya had committed aggression against its territory. The Libyan Arab Jamahiriya rejected the charges on both occasions. After the first series of meetings, the Council on 6 April called on the parties to settle their differences peacefully, based on the United Nations principle of respect for States' political independence, sovereignty and territorial integrity. In that regard, the Council also appealed to both parties to make use of the mechanism of the Organization of African Unity (OAU).

Egypt also claimed that the Libyan Arab Jamahiriya had violated its territory. The latter responded that Egypt was involved in hostile action against it.

Chad-Libyan Arab Jamahiriya dispute

Communications (March). In March 1983, the President of the Security Council received four letters concerning the Chad–Libyan Arab Jamahiriya dispute. On 16 March,[1] Chad requested an urgent meeting of the Council to consider the serious situation prevailing in Chad as a result of what it called the occupation by the Libyan Arab Jamahiriya of the Chadian territory known as the "Aouzou Strip" and of repeated acts of aggression by that country. On 17 March,[2] Chad transmitted a message by its President, Hissein Habré, stating that the Libyan Arab Jamahiriya was stepping up its military attacks on northern Chad with the aim of expanding the occupied zone and of imposing a new government on Chad, and calling on the international community to end the illegal occupation.

Denying Chad's allegations, the Libyan Arab Jamahiriya, also on 17 March,[3] stated that the Aouzou sector was an integral part of its territory, and that the charges constituted interference in its internal affairs and were aimed at diverting world public opinion from the fighting in Chad between the rebel forces controlling the capital, led by Hissein Habré, and the forces of the legitimate Government led by Goukouni Weddey.

Chad responded on 21 March,[4] transmitting the text of a government memorandum concerning what it called the occupation of 150,000 square kilometres of Tibesti (northern Chad) and reviewing its historical claim to the area under dispute.

SECURITY COUNCIL ACTION (March/April)

The Security Council considered Chad's complaint on 22 and 31 March and on 6 April. At their request, Benin, Chad, Democratic Yemen, Egypt, Ethiopia, Gabon, Ghana, Guinea, Iran, the Ivory Coast, the Libyan Arab Jamahiriya, the Niger, Senegal, the Sudan, the Syrian Arab Republic and the United Republic of Cameroon were invited to participate without the right to vote.

On 31 March, Chad submitted a draft resolution,[5] by which the Council would have requested the parties to settle their dispute forthwith and by peaceful means, noted that they were willing to settle the dispute peacefully, appealed to them to make use of the machinery available for doing so, particularly through OAU, and remained seized of the question. Most provisions of the draft were subsequently included in the Council's statement on the matter (see below).

Addressing the Council, the Minister for Foreign Affairs of Chad summarized Chad's historical argument for its claim to the Aouzou sector and said that the Libyan Arab Jamahiriya's occupation had become effective in 1973 and was becoming increasingly flagrant. The situation not only endangered the existence of Chad as a sovereign State, but it could seriously endanger the peace and security of that part of Africa. Chad had called on the Council because it desired to resolve the problem peacefully and to obtain assistance in recovering its territorial integrity. It was requesting that the Libyan Arab Jamahiriya withdraw completely. At a later meeting, Chad said that the problem was of a juridical nature and suggested that the Council refer the parties to the International Court of Justice (ICJ). Both bilateral and regional efforts had proved futile so far to find a peaceful solution because the Libyan Arab Jamahiriya had refused to discuss the substance of the problem, namely the occupation, Chad added.

The Libyan Arab Jamahiriya did not see any reason for convening the Council because, in its view, the letter submitted by the delegation of Hissein Habré did not emanate from the legitimate Government of Chad; the legitimate Government recognized by OAU was that of Goukouni Weddey. Since 1966, the Libyan Arab Jamahiriya had attempted to effect a national reconciliation between warring factions in Chad to protect that country's interests. Mr. Habré had refused to participate in such attempts and had formed an illegal Government which OAU refused to recognize. For the Libyan Arab Jamahiriya, the question of Chad had been resolved by the 1979 Lagos Agreement, which established the Government of National Unity and was signed by most of the Chadian political group leaders including Mr. Habré. In response to Mr. Goukouni, the Libyan Arab Jamahiriya had sent armed forces to assist in putting an end to the rebellion led by Mr. Habré, who received the help of imperialist forces. Affirming that there had never been any sovereignty over the Aouzou sector by Chad, the Libyan Arab Jamahiriya rejected any claim to its land and any consideration of that issue; if there were a border dispute, the Libyan Arab Jamahiriya was not against discussing this with any State, it said. A good-offices commission formed by OAU to negotiate between the two countries on any bilateral dispute was still in existence, the Libyan Arab Jamahiriya pointed out. It affirmed that when there was a national régime in

Chad representing all its people and recognized by OAU, the Libyan Arab Jamahiriya would be ready to consider any dispute with it. It was ready to begin immediate talks with the legitimate Government of Mr. Goukouni.

Chad responded that the Libyan Arab Jamahiriya had evaded the substance of the problem, namely the occupation. In reference to the description of the Chad Government as rebels, it pointed out that the Libyan Arab Jamahiriya had sent a delegation to N'Djamena in March 1983 to discuss State matters with Chad. At that time, the Libyan Arab Jamahiriya had stipulated three conditions to be met before it would hand over political opponents to Chad: Chad must proclaim itself an Arab Islamic Republic, even though it was a non-religious republic; Chad must form a strategic alliance with the Libyan Arab Jamahiriya in order to destabilize the neighbouring countries of the Niger, Nigeria and the United Republic of Cameroon; and the current frontier between the two countries would be obliterated. Those conditions were rejected.

The Libyan Arab Jamahiriya stated that it had never imposed any conditions on Chad or on any other country, and that it respected the territorial integrity of Chad. It warned of a conspiracy by imperialism, joined by Egypt and the Sudan, against the Libyan Arab Jamahiriya.

During the Council's debate, most of the 24 speakers stressed the need to find a peaceful solution. The majority suggested that OAU was the appropriate body for solving the dispute or that a solution could be found within the regional framework. Benin, China, Democratic Yemen, Ethiopia, France, Ghana, Guinea, Jordan, Malta, the Netherlands, Poland, the Syrian Arab Republic and Zimbabwe made such proposals. China, for example, expressed hope that the two countries would settle their differences through peaceful negotiations and it appreciated the efforts made by OAU in that regard. In Ghana's view, the correct modality for addressing disputes between African countries was within OAU, and it believed the Council should refer the issue back to that body. Zimbabwe said it was encouraged by the desire of the parties to seek a peaceful solution to the dispute and by their willingness to avail themselves of the regional mechanisms for settlement.

A group of countries, including Benin, Iran, Jordan, Nicaragua, the Niger and Togo, believed that bilateral negotiations should be initiated as soon as possible. In addition to proposing that the OAU mechanism could be useful, Benin invited the parties to undertake a dialogue and pointed out that they would be given an opportunity to do so in June at the OAU summit (Addis Ababa, Ethiopia, 21-23 June). The Niger was grateful that the two countries had expressed their willingness to resort to dialogue. According to Togo, the territorial dispute could be settled through bilateral negotiations, with or without the mediation of third parties. Jordan hoped that Chad would respond positively to the Libyan Arab Jamahiriya's offer to hold discussions, and it called on the two to exercise restraint in the interest of regional peace and stability. Poland welcomed the statement by the Libyan Arab Jamahiriya expressing its readiness to discuss the border dispute on both a bilateral and regional level. Egypt, on the other hand, said the Libyan Arab Jamahiriya did not demonstrate any readiness to resolve the issue, despite the forthcoming position of Chad.

A number of countries—France, Gabon, Guinea, the Ivory Coast, the Niger, the Sudan, the United Republic of Cameroon, and Zaire—felt that a solution should be in accordance with the principle of respect for the national borders existing at the time the countries achieved independence, a principle that had been adopted by OAU in 1964. Ethiopia, France, Guinea, the Netherlands, Nicaragua and Zaire were among those which said the problem was essentially a territorial or border dispute. In the Netherlands' view, the Council should distinguish between the border dispute and the legitimacy of the Government; the Council could call on the Governments concerned to solve the issue by peaceful means, but the choice of a government was the sole prerogative of the people of the country. Guinea and the United Republic of Cameroon expressed a similar opinion.

Gabon, the Netherlands, Senegal and Zaire called for an end of foreign intervention in Chad. Gabon appealed to the Libyan Arab Jamahiriya to withdraw its troops, thereby enabling Chad to extend its sovereignty over its entire territory. France, Gabon, the Sudan and Zaire said the current situation could lead to a threat to the peace and security of the region.

Several countries—France, Gabon, Guinea, Senegal, the Sudan and the United Republic of Cameroon—supported Chad's claim to the territory under dispute. Senegal said that, as a member of the OAU *ad hoc* committee set up to seek a peaceful solution in the current dispute, it had studied the historical facts and juridical documents left by the colonial Powers and had determined that Chad had legitimate reasons to claim sovereignty over the Aouzou Strip. According to the United Republic of Cameroon, the problem had been clearly presented to the Council by Chad. Democratic Yemen and Iran took the opposite view and supported the claim of the Libyan Arab Jamahiriya to the territory in question.

Among those which stated that the problem had originated through imperialist designs were Benin, Democratic Yemen, Iran, Poland and the Syrian Arab Republic. Benin believed that the Council had been seized of the problem in an attempt by the current leaders in N'Djamena, Chad, to legitimize their authority and as a result of the manoeuvres of international imperialism, which was waging a campaign against the Libyan Arab Jamahiriya. Iran said some countries were trying to undermine the position of the Libyan Arab Jamahiriya in OAU and they desired to see that body weakened; in addition, some countries were trying to justify an increase in military aid to countries in the region. According to the Syrian Arab Republic, imperialist circles, principally the United States, had engaged in political incitement against the Libyan Arab Jamahiriya, to the extent of attempting to cast doubt on its sovereignty over its own territory; the willingness of the Libyan Arab Jamahiriya to enter into consultations with Chad over the issue indicated that the crisis was artificial.

Similarly, Democratic Yemen and Nicaragua felt that the current situation was linked to the United States campaign against the Libyan Arab Jamahiriya. Democratic Yemen added that the move confirmed that the United States had resorted to maligning the Libyan Arab Jamahiriya by prompting its supporters in the region to make groundless complaints, in an attempt to divert the attention of the international community from the main source of tension—imperialism headed by the United States. Nicaragua said the Council did not have a substantive role to play in the territorial dispute because there was no evidence that the situation on the border was posing any threat; the current difficulties could be part of the United States campaign against the Libyan Arab Jamahiriya.

Many speakers made proposals for Council action. Egypt, Senegal, the Sudan and Zaire said it should call on the Libyan Arab Jamahiriya to abide by international law and withdraw its troops from Chadian territory. In the view of the Sudan, the Council needed to take such action in order to fulfil its obligation to maintain international peace and security by safeguarding the independence and sovereignty of Chad. In addition to urging the Council to call for the withdrawal of Libyan troops, Zaire suggested that a neutral force be sent to the Aouzou Strip to preserve peace and security pending a settlement.

Ethiopia and Malta urged the Council to exercise restraint on this issue. Ethiopia said the Council must use caution and respect OAU efforts to find a solution by calling on the parties to settle their disputes by peaceful means. Noting that OAU would discuss the issue in June, Malta said the Council should refrain from taking a definite stand until OAU efforts to find a solution at the regional level had been concluded.

France, the Ivory Coast, the Netherlands and Zaire suggested that the two countries submit the problem to ICJ. The Ivory Coast said the Council could not stand idle in the face of the dispute and adjourn without recommending the use of one of the means for peaceful settlement provided by the Charter, while the Netherlands expressed a preference for an explicit recommendation that the parties submit their dispute to ICJ. France said the Council could play a constructive role by appealing to them through its President; on the basis of that appeal, OAU could resume its mediation efforts with a view to a final settlement.

Following the debate and consultations among Council members, the President, on their behalf, issued the following statement on 6 April.[6]

"The Security Council has heard and taken note of the statements made by the Foreign Minister of Chad, and by the representative of the Libyan Arab Jamahiriya, in the debate on the letter dated 16 March 1983 from the representative of Chad.

"The members of the Council express their concern that the differences between Chad and the Libyan Arab Jamahiriya should not deteriorate and therefore call on the parties to settle these differences without undue delay and by peaceful means, on the basis of the relevant principles of the Charter of the United Nations, and the Charter of the Organization of African Unity, which demand respect for political independence, sovereignty and territorial integrity.

"In this connection, the members of the Council have taken note with appreciation of the willingness expressed by both parties to discuss their differences and to resolve them peacefully and urge both sides to refrain from any actions which could aggravate the current situation.

"The members of the Council also note that the Organization of African Unity, the regional organization, is already seized of this matter. They appeal to both parties to make fullest use of the mechanism available within the regional organization for the peaceful settlement of disputes, including the Good Offices Committee established by the Organization of African Unity and of those provided in Article 33 of the Charter of the United Nations."

Meeting numbers. SC 2419, 2428-2430.

Communications (April-August). During April to August 1983, Chad and the Libyan Arab Jamahiriya exchanged further charges concerning the border dispute, in letters addressed to the President of the Security Council.

On 8 April,[7] Chad said that while the Council was considering its complaint against the Libyan Arab Jamahiriya, Libyan aircraft were overflying Chadian territory near the trail formerly used to supply Libyan troops in northern Chad, in violation of the statement adopted two days earlier by the Council. Responding on 12 April,[8] the Libyan Arab Jamahiriya rejected those allegations and stressed that its aircraft did not over-

fly any part of Chad's territory and that it would continue to work for the achievement of national reconciliation in Chad under the legitimate Government of Goukouni Weddey. Chad made a further similar charge on 19 April,[9] stating that on 16 April Libyan aircraft overflew northern Chad. On 19 May,[10] Chad said that a week earlier Libyan army units attacked the Chad National Armed Forces in the Ounianga-Kébir region causing great loss of life and was extending its attacks throughout the northern region of the country. Reaffirming on 23 May[11] its readiness to cooperate with African States for the achievement of peace and security in Chad, the Libyan Arab Jamahiriya rejected Chad's charges and said it had no connection with events in that country; what was occurring there was a war between the legitimate Government and the rebels under Hissein Habré.

Chad forwarded a 23 June message from its President,[12] who said the Libyan Arab Jamahiriya had launched a large-scale operation against Chad that day, and appealed to the Council President to do everything possible to come to the aid of Chad and to ensure the restoration of its legitimate rights, in particular the right to live in peace. On 27 June,[13] the Libyan Arab Jamahiriya rejected the accusations, reaffirmed its desire to see the security and stability of Chad respected and reiterated that the ongoing conflict in Chad was among nationals of Chad and in Chadian territory.

On 5 July,[14] the Libyan Arab Jamahiriya informed the Council President that its head of State had on 29 June sent a letter to the current OAU Chairman, in which he reaffirmed his country's commitment to neutrality towards the ongoing internal conflict in Chad and proposed that OAU send a fact-finding mission to the town of Faya-Largeau to establish that all allegations about Libyan intervention in Chad were untrue and were but a justification of intervention by certain colonialist Powers and African States in the internal affairs of Chad. In a 20 July statement,[15] a spokesman for the Bureau for Foreign Liaison of the Libyan Arab Jamahiriya asserted that a recent radio statement by the Minister of Information under Mr. Habré revealed the plan of aggression being implemented by him at the behest of imperialists, reactionaries and Zionists, which involved introducing foreign forces into Chad from the United States, France and Zaire, thus posing a threat to the peace, security and territorial integrity of the Libyan Arab Jamahiriya; consequently, it reserved its right to take any measure that would enable it to thwart the plan.

Referring to that statement on 27 July,[16] Chad noted OAU's June endorsement of the Council's 6 April statement by reactivating its *ad hoc* committee on the border dispute, and said that the Libyan Arab Jamahiriya was provoking a new civil war in Chad and was trying to justify itself by asserting that the Aouzou region was an inseparable part of Libyan territory. In a message of 29 July,[17] the Foreign Minister of Chad rejected Libyan charges that Chad was attempting to settle the border dispute by force and stated that Libyan aggression was forcing Chad to defend itself; nevertheless, Chad hoped to obtain a settlement of the dispute, which would require that the Libyan Government put an end to its direct interference in the internal affairs of Chad. In a 31 July message,[18] the President of Chad said that Faya-Largeau had been liberated the previous day from Libyan forces by the Chad National Armed Forces and some 40 Libyan soldiers had been taken prisoner; since then, the Libyan Air Force had bombed the town, causing human and material losses. In two further messages, dated 2 August,[19] the President of Chad charged the Libyan Arab Jamahiriya with stepping up aerial bombing of Chad, specifically of Faya-Largeau which had been razed to the ground, and requested an urgent meeting of the Council to consider the situation.

In a statement of 1 August,[20] the Bureau for Foreign Liaison of the Libyan Arab Jamahiriya, rejecting charges by the United States that the Libyan Arab Jamahiriya was attacking Chad, stated that the extension of fighting to Faya-Largeau as a result of United States intervention and French arms constituted a threat to the Libyan Arab Jamahiriya; it considered that the United States should end its intervention and support to the rebel régime in order to enable OAU to find a settlement to the Chad problem. On 3 August,[21] the Libyan Arab Jamahiriya rejected Chad's 29 and 31 July allegations and charged the United States and France with direct intervention in the affairs of Chad and of supporting the rebellion, thereby endangering peace and security in the region.

The President of Chad, in a 4 August message,[22] stated that the Libyan Arab Jamahiriya had bombed the town of Oum Chalouba that day and the day before, causing loss of human lives, thus escalating its invasion. On 11 August,[23] Chad submitted photographs as evidence of its statements about Libyan intervention.

In addition to Chad and the Libyan Arab Jamahiriya, four other countries sent letters to either the Secretary-General or the President of the Council concerning the situation in Chad.

On 8 August,[24] the USSR transmitted a TASS statement of 4 August stating that the USSR condemned certain acts in the area, such as United States military aircraft bringing forces into Chad, the increased flow of American and French weapons to that country, and the movement of United States vessels to the region in preparation

to intervene. Responding to that letter and the 5 July letter from the Libyan Arab Jamahiriya,[14] the United States on 10 August[25] said that those statements were designed to divert attention from the fact that the Libyan Arab Jamahiriya, which was equipped by the USSR, was primarily responsibile for tension and conflict in Chad and the surrounding area; at the request of Chad, the United States had provided logistical support in monitoring the situation, to help that country defend itself.

The Sudan, on 18 August,[26] said that 116 Sudanese nationals captured by Chad at Oum Chalouba had been victims of Libyan designs and exploitation and had been forced to participate in the war which the Libyan Arab Jamahiriya was waging against Chad.

On 19 August,[27] the Congo transmitted the Declaration of Brazzaville on the situation in Chad, adopted on 16 August by the heads of State and Government of Central Africa. By that text, they requested the OAU Chairman to establish contact with all the parties concerned with a view to achieving a cease-fire, the withdrawal of all foreign troops from Chad, and prohibition of all countries from interfering in its internal affairs.

SECURITY COUNCIL CONSIDERATION (August)

Convening at the request of Chad,[19] the Security Council met on 3, 11, 12, 16 and 31 August 1983. Benin, Chad, the Congo, Egypt, Guinea, Iran, the Ivory Coast, Kenya, Liberia, the Libyan Arab Jamahiriya, the Niger, Senegal, Somalia, the Sudan and the United Republic of Cameroon were invited at their request, to participate in the discussion without the right to vote.

Opening the debate, Chad said that since 31 July the Libyan Arab Jamahiriya had stepped up its aggression against Chad's territory, bombing Faya-Largeau and causing many civilian casualties. Flouting the Council's 6 April statement, the Libyan Arab Jamahiriya had expanded its attacks by occupying successively six eastern towns, which Chadian forces had regained. The Libyan Arab Jamahiriya's covert intention was to destabilize the Government, perpetuate its illegal occupation of the Aouzou Strip, annex the entire country and use it as a base for aggression against other neighbouring States. In order to arrive at a peaceful settlement, Chad reiterated its willingness to maintain talks with the Libyan Arab Jamahiriya which it said had been assisted by the USSR in establishing a large and sophisticated military arsenal. The Libyan Arab Jamahiriya remained a major obstacle to the work of national reconciliation among the people of Chad and to its socio-economic development.

The Secretary of State for Foreign Affairs and Co-operation of Chad, speaking on 11 August, said that over the previous few days Libyan aggression against his country had increased with bombing, artillery and ground attacks, resulting in more than 200 deaths. The Libyan Arab Jamahiriya had never concealed its intention to occupy all of Chad and thus force it to merge with the Libyan Arab Jamahiriya. Its interference in the internal affairs of Chad was demonstrated by its attempts to obstruct Chad's participation in international conferences. Thanks to the defence capacity that had been provided by friendly countries, Chad had been able to shoot down a Libyan bomber in Chadian territory and capture its pilot. The Lagos Agreement of August 1979, cited by the Libyan Arab Jamahiriya as the foundation for the legal Government of Chad, had been rendered invalid. The Secretary reiterated Chad's request that the Council condemn the Libyan Arab Jamahiriya for its armed aggression, order it to cease its attacks and withdraw its forces, and call on it to end its interference in Chad's affairs.

The Libyan Arab Jamahiriya denied that it had intervened in Chad's affairs and that it had sent planes or troops there. It declared its neutrality towards Chad and proposed that OAU send a fact-finding mission there to verify the situation. The Libyan Arab Jamahiriya believed that the best solution was to leave the matter to OAU, whose Chairman was currently undertaking consultations on the matter. Reiterating its commitment to the restoration of peace in Chad and to reconciliation among the various factions in that country, in accordance with the 1979 Lagos Agreement, the Libyan Arab Jamahiriya said that it was ready to settle any problems with the legitimate Government of Chad under Goukouni Weddey. The cause of the deterioration in the situation in Chad was foreign intervention, especially by the United States and France, which were airlifting equipment and military advisers to Hissein Habré's forces. The sending of French troops could not be viewed within the framework of the treaty of co-operation between France (the former colonial Power) and Chad because it was nothing but military intervention in the civil war. In addition, Zaire had sent 2,000 troops to support Mr. Habré and Sudanese forces and Belgian and French mercenaries were transported to Chad with the help of the United States. Stating that the presence of imperialist and colonialist forces in an African country represented a direct threat to itself and its neighbours, the Libyan Arab Jamahiriya called for the immediate termination of intervention in Chad and for the withdrawal of Zairian and other forces and of United States and French military advisers.

Zaire said its forces were in Chad at the request of OAU and the legal Government of Mr. Habré, and were involved because external forces committed aggression against what OAU considered was a legitimate Government. France said it had responded to Chad's request, as provided by the 1976 co-operation agreement between the two countries and in conformity with international law enshrined in the Charter, to assist that country in exercising its right to self-defence. The United States said it had joined some other countries in responding to Chad's appeal for help in its self-defence, but the Sudan denied the Libyan charge that its forces were involved in Chad.

Most speakers acknowledged that the situation had deteriorated, but differing opinions were expressed about the causes and the solution to the problem.

The USSR, remarking on the airlift of military equipment from France and an increasing flow of United States weapons to Chad, said the situation involved ever more interference by certain Western countries which wanted to set up a new imperialist bridgehead in Africa and thus establish their sphere of influence, a policy which had failed. China said the situation had been further complicated as a result of super-Power meddling. According to Benin, the conflict, with the participation of non-African forces, had been foreseeable following Mr. Habré's seizure of power; Chad's problems were those inherited from colonization and the ills of young independence. Iran said that United States and French military assistance to Chad had only contributed to the conflict, and it hoped that some super-Powers that always found it in their interests to create conflicts in the area would refrain from contributing to this one.

Guyana regretted the manner in which developments were being manipulated by outside forces whose interests were unrelated to those of Chad or to Africa as a whole. Similarly, Pakistan believed that external interference, in disregard for respect for Chad's political independence and territorial integrity, was the central issue constituting the international dimension of the crisis, and that this issue, if drawn into the East-West confrontation, would become insoluble. Zimbabwe said the situation had escalated, mainly as a result of the increasing involvement of external factors and forces in the area, and the involvement undermined attempts at national reconciliation and frustrated OAU efforts to bring about a peaceful settlement.

A group of countries, including China, the Congo, France, Guinea, Guyana, Liberia, Pakistan, Senegal, Togo, the United Kingdom and the United Republic of Cameroon, called for the end of foreign intervention in Chad.

Egypt, the Ivory Coast, Kenya, Liberia, the Netherlands, Somalia, the Sudan, the United States and Zaire believed that the Libyan Arab Jamahiriya was involved in the intervention in Chad or aggression against it. In Egypt's view, the Libyan Arab Jamahiriya intended to interfere in the internal affairs of Chad, to impede national reconciliation, to overthrow the legitimate Government, and to assist opponents of that Government. The Ivory Coast believed that the direct participation of the Libyan Air Force in Chad fully justified the presence of friendly States and provision of military assistance.

The Netherlands drew a distinction between the presence of French troops in Chad, which, it said, had been requested by the Government for its self-defence, and the armed intervention of a neighbouring State. Calling on the Libyan Arab Jamahiriya to withdraw its forces unconditionally and to refrain from interfering in Chad's internal affairs, Somalia said that events there demonstrated the Libyan policies of expansionism and destabilization. Questioning the wisdom of certain speakers who believed that the issue should be referred to OAU instead of raised again before the Council, Zaire pointed out that the matter raised in April before the Council concerned a border dispute between Chad and the Libyan Arab Jamahiriya, but since then the problem concerned armed attacks by the latter.

Some countries, including Liberia, Pakistan, Senegal, the Sudan, Togo, the United Kingdom and the United Republic of Cameroon, felt the situation had implications for the security of small countries and/or the region. Liberia stated that failure of the Council to act decisively would not only encourage the Libyan Arab Jamahiriya to intensify its aggression but would also increase the risk that the conflict would spread. The United Republic of Cameroon said that despite the latest OAU efforts to find a solution, the situation had deteriorated to the extent that Chad was experiencing a real war with international ramifications.

A number of speakers expressed support for the current Government of Chad under Mr. Habré, including Egypt, Guinea, Kenya, Liberia, the Netherlands, the Niger, the United Republic of Cameroon, and Zaire.

Among the proposals for a settlement of the situation, many countries urged that OAU be used as a regional framework. Benin, China, France, Iran, the Netherlands, Somalia, the Sudan, the USSR, the United Kingdom and Zimbabwe believed OAU had a role to play in this regard. Iran, the Sudan and Togo believed negotiations between the two countries could be helpful.

The Congo said that the Declaration of Brazzaville on the Chad situation, adopted by the heads of State and Government of Central Africa,[27] was an attempt at diplomatic action aimed at demonstrating Africa's concern with a problem that Africa had the right and duty to solve, and it advocated mutual respect, non-intervention and anti-imperialism. In the view of the Niger, the armed penetration into Chad's territory disturbed the peace and stability of the region and thus called for a counter-offensive, including the assistance of friends. As an alternative to the OAU committee dealing with the problem, the Sudan suggested that the matter be taken up by ICJ. Togo appealed to both countries to apply the Council's April statement, and Zimbabwe said that statement remained valid and relevant.

Stressing the importance of respect for the sovereignty of Chad, Senegal rejected any idea that Chad be partitioned as a solution to the situation.

Many countries called for action by the Security Council. Egypt, France, Guyana, Kenya, the Netherlands, the United Republic of Cameroon and the United States mentioned the Council's responsibility under the Charter to maintain international peace and security. The United States said that, after four weeks of Council meetings without agreement on action, the Council had demonstrated its futility as an effective instrument in that regard and that the Charter had been violated; the Council's response should have been unequivocal and immediate, condemning the Libyan aggression and demanding the immediate withdrawal of its forces.

Guyana, the Ivory Coast, Pakistan, the United Kingdom and the United States urged the Council to call for compliance with international or United Nations principles governing international relations. Speaking at the last 1983 meeting on Chad's complaint, on 31 August, the United Kingdom said the Council should not remain inactive because at stake were the principles of the inadmissibility of external intervention and force, the inviolability of national boundaries, and non-interference in the internal affairs of States; furthermore, there would be implications for the Council's credibility.

Egypt, Liberia, Pakistan, Senegal, the United Kingdom and the United States believed that the Council should call for an end to aggression and the withdrawal of armed forces intervening in Chad, while Benin suggested that it call for the withdrawal of non-African forces. Egypt, Kenya and the United States said the Libyan aggression should be specifically condemned. In addition to that condemnation and a call for withdrawal of Libyan forces, Kenya said the Council should devise ways to bring about a government of national unity in Chad under Mr. Habré. The Council's support for OAU initiatives in solving the problem was proposed by the Netherlands, Pakistan and Zimbabwe.

Several countries—Guyana, the Netherlands, Pakistan and the United Kingdom—felt that the Council should continue to follow the situation. Guyana said this should be done by sending a fact-finding mission to the area, while the Netherlands believed that the Council should at least request the Secretary-General to keep the Council informed of developments.

Speaking at the end of the debate, the Libyan Arab Jamahiriya said that some speakers, led by the United States, had attempted to divert attention from the strife in Chad, presenting it as a conflict between the Libyan Arab Jamahiriya and Chad in order to use the Council as a forum for propaganda against the Libyan Arab Jamahiriya; it would be preferable for the Council to call on the imperialist and colonialist forces to withdraw and allow the people of Chad to solve their problems by themselves or through OAU initiatives.

Also speaking at the conclusion of the debate, Chad said it had submitted a draft resolution to the eight members of the Movement of Non-Aligned Countries which were also members of the Council. However, faced with the lack of political will on the part of the Libyan Arab Jamahiriya, they were unable to arrive at a compromise text. The result was a serious evasion of responsibility by the non-aligned Council members and a grave precedent for the future of the Movement and the Council. Chad agreed in principle with the suggestion that the issue be referred to OAU, but said the suggestion had been made by a group acting as spokesman of the Libyan Arab Jamahiriya, which had blocked the functioning of the OAU *ad hoc* committee on the dispute. As a result, Chad had asked the Council to adopt a suitable text. Despite the Council's inaction, Chad continued to believe in that body's responsibility to restore peace. For this reason, Chad considered that the Council's debate remained open.

France stated that, bearing in mind the current initiative by OAU in regard to Chad, the Council, without evading its responsibilities in the matter, should not take a position at that time.

Meeting numbers. SC 2462, 2463, 2465, 2467, 2469.

Communication (September). The Libyan Arab Jamahiriya, on 13 September,[28] transmitted a letter from its head of State to the President of the Security Council. Drawing a parallel between the situations in Chad and Lebanon, he said that the United States and France were militarily involved in the assault on Muslims in northern Chad and this would make it necessary for Muslims to come to the help of their brothers; he requested that the world conscience, the Council and the General Assembly take action for the withdrawal of United States and French forces from Chad and Lebanon.

Egypt-Libyan Arab Jamahiriya dispute

Three letters concerning a dispute between Egypt and the Libyan Arab Jamahiriya were received by the President of the Security Council in 1983. Egypt, on 25 February,[29] forwarded a message from its Minister for Foreign Affairs, who said that Egypt, having responded to a request by the Sudan to carry out reconnaissance flights over the Sudanese–Libyan border since there were troop movements and concentrations there, had determined that the Libyan Arab Jamahiriya had sent some of its aircraft into Egyptian airspace but had desisted after Egypt had protested. Responding on 7 March,[30] the Libyan Arab Jamahiriya, denying that there were Libyan troop concentrations or movements against the Sudan or other countries, said that the aircraft sent by Egypt were United States reconnaissance aircraft and this emphasized Egypt's involvement in hostile military action in conjunction with a foreign State against the Libyan Arab Jamahiriya. Egypt responded on 10 March,[31] stating that the Libyan Arab Jamahiriya, driven by frustration in finding its efforts to interfere in the internal affairs of a neighbouring State exposed and foiled, was attempting to discredit Egypt by irresponsible allegations.

REFERENCES

[1]S/15643. [2]S/15644. [3]S/15645. [4]S/15649. [5]S/15672. [6]S/15688. [7]S/15693. [8]S/15703. [9]S/15709. [10]S/15775. [11]S/15782. [12]S/15843. [13]S/15844. [14]S/15856. [15]S/15884. [16]S/15889. [17]S/15897. [18]S/15898. [19]S/15902. [20]S/15903. [21]S/15906. [22]S/15907. [23]S/15928. [24]S/15913. [25]S/15920. [26]S/15935. [27]S/15936. [28]S/15981. [29]S/15629. [30]S/15637. [31]S/15641.

Chagos Archipelago

Two 1983 letters addressed to the President of the General Assembly dealt with the question of sovereignty over the Chagos Archipelago, a group of islands in the centre of the Indian Ocean.

The United Kingdom, on 17 November,[1] referred to the address made on 27 September to the Assembly by the Prime Minister of Mauritius, who mentioned his country's "just and legitimate claim over the Chagos Archipelago"; the United Kingdom stated that sovereignty over the Archipelago was vested in its Government which had undertaken to cede those islands to Mauritius when they were no longer required for defence purposes. Responding on 5 December,[2] Mauritius reiterated its claim and said that the United Kingdom, in contradiction to the 1960 Declaration on the Granting of Independence to Colonial Countries and Peoples,[3] had detached the Archipelago from Mauritius in 1965 before Mauritius gained independence in 1968.

REFERENCES

[1]A/38/598. [2]A/38/711. [3]YUN 1960, p. 49, GA res. 1514(XV), 14 Dec. 1960.

Comorian island of Mayotte

In 1983, the General Assembly, in resolution 38/13, reaffirmed the sovereignty of the Comoros over the

Indian Ocean island of Mayotte and invited France to honour its commitment concerning respect for the unity of the Comoros.

As requested by the Assembly in December 1982,[1] the Secretary-General submitted a report, dated 21 October 1983,[2] on the question. In that report, he provided the responses to requests he had addressed to the Comoros, France and the Organization of African Unity (OAU) for information. The Comoros replied that there had been no real change in the situation since the Assembly's 1982 consideration of the subject and added that France was showing a lack of interest and had not taken any concrete measures to return the island to the Comoros. France, on the other hand, said it was pursuing a constructive political dialogue with the Comoros with a view to finding a solution acceptable to all parties. It mentioned that it had appointed at the end of 1982 an individual who would be entrusted with the task of ensuring continuity in that dialogue, in close co-operation with the Comorian authorities. OAU reported that there not been any major development in the search for a solution since the November 1981 meeting of its *Ad Hoc* Committee of Seven.[3] At that time, the Committee had recommended that a mission contact the French authorities in order to consider the modalities for the return of Mayotte to the Comoros.

GENERAL ASSEMBLY ACTION

On 21 November, the General Assembly adopted resolution 38/13 by recorded vote.

Question of the Comorian island of Mayotte
The General Assembly,

Recalling its resolutions 1514(XV) of 14 December 1960, containing the Declaration on the Granting of Independence to Colonial Countries and Peoples, and 2621(XXV) of 12 October 1970, containing the programme of action for the full implementation of the Declaration,

Recalling also its previous resolutions, in particular resolutions 3161(XXVIII) of 14 December 1973, 3291(XXIX) of 13 December 1974, 31/4 of 21 October 1976, 32/7 of 1 November 1977, 34/69 of 6 December 1979, 35/43 of 28 November 1980, 36/105 of 10 December 1981 and 37/65 of 3 December 1982, in which it, *inter alia*, affirmed the unity and territorial integrity of the Comoros,

Recalling, in particular, its resolution 3385(XXX) of 12 November 1975 on the admission of the Comoros to membership in the United Nations, in which it reaffirmed the necessity of respecting the unity and territorial integrity of the Comoro Archipelago, composed of the islands of Anjouan, Grande-Comore, Mayotte and Mohéli,

Recalling further that, in accordance with the agreements between the Comoros and France, signed on 15 June 1973, concerning the accession of the Comoros to independence, the results of the referendum of 22 December 1974 were to be considered on a global basis and not island by island,

Convinced that a just and lasting solution to the question of Mayotte is to be found in respect for the sovereignty, unity and territorial integrity of the Comoro Archipelago,

Bearing in mind the wish expressed by the President of the French Republic to seek actively a just solution to that problem,

Taking note of the talks opened between the Government of the Islamic Federal Republic of the Comoros and the Government of the French Republic,

Taking note also of the wish of the Government of the Comoros to activate the dialogue with the Government of France with a view to encouraging the prompt return of the Comorian island of Mayotte to the Islamic Federal Republic of the Comoros as a whole,

Taking note of the report of the Secretary-General,

Bearing in mind the decisions of the Organization of African Unity, the Movement of Non-Aligned Countries and the Organization of the Islamic Conference concerning this question,

1. *Reaffirms* the sovereignty of the Islamic Federal Republic of the Comoros over the island of Mayotte;

2. *Invites* the Government of France to honour the commitments entered into prior to the referendum on the self-determination of the Comoro Archipelago of 22 December 1974 concerning respect for the unity and territorial integrity of the Comoros;

3. *Calls* for the translation into practice of the wish expressed by the President of the French Republic to see a just solution to the question of Mayotte adopted as soon as possible;

4. *Also invites* the Government of France to open the negotiations with the Government of the Comoros with a view to ensuring the effective and prompt return of the island of Mayotte to the Comoros;

5. *Requests* the Secretary-General of the United Nations to follow developments concerning this question, in conjunction with the Secretary-General of the Organization of African Unity, and to report thereon to the General Assembly at its thirty-ninth session;

6. *Decides* to include in the provisional agenda of its thirty-ninth session the item entitled "Question of the Comorian island of Mayotte".

General Assembly resolution 38/13

21 November 1983   Meeting 65   115-1-24 (recorded vote)

28-nation draft (A/38/L.19); agenda item 30.
Sponsors: Algeria, Bahamas, Benin, Botswana, Cape Verde, Comoros, Congo, Cuba, Ecuador, Gambia, Ghana, Guinea-Bissau, Guyana, Lesotho, Libyan Arab Jamahiriya, Mauritania, Morocco, Nigeria, Oman, Pakistan, Qatar, Senegal, Sierra Leone, Somalia, Swaziland, United Arab Emirates, United Republic of Tanzania, Zambia.
Meeting numbers. GA 38th session: plenary 64, 65.

Recorded vote in Assembly as follows:

In favour: Afghanistan, Albania, Algeria, Angola, Antigua and Barbuda, Argentina, Bahamas, Bahrain, Bangladesh, Barbados, Benin, Bhutan, Bolivia, Botswana, Brazil, Bulgaria, Burma, Burundi, Byelorussian SSR, Cape Verde, Central African Republic, Chad, Chile, China, Colombia, Comoros, Congo, Costa Rica, Cuba, Czechoslovakia, Democratic Kampuchea, Democratic Yemen, Djibouti, Dominican Republic, Ecuador, Egypt, El Salvador, Ethiopia, Fiji, Finland, Gabon, Gambia, German Democratic Republic, Ghana, Guinea, Guinea-Bissau, Haiti, Hungary, India, Indonesia, Iran, Iraq, Ivory Coast, Jamaica, Kenya, Kuwait, Lesotho, Libyan Arab Jamahiriya, Madagascar, Malawi, Malaysia, Maldives, Mali, Malta, Mauritania, Mauritius, Mexico, Mongolia, Morocco, Mozambique, Nepal, Nicaragua, Niger, Nigeria, Oman, Pakistan, Papua New Guinea, Paraguay, Peru, Philippines, Poland, Qatar, Romania, Rwanda, Sao Tome and Principe, Saudi Arabia, Senegal, Sierra Leone, Singapore, Somalia, Sri Lanka, Suriname, Swaziland, Sweden, Syrian Arab Republic, Thailand, Togo, Trinidad and Tobago, Tunisia, Turkey, Uganda, Ukrainian SSR, USSR, United Arab Emirates, United Republic of Cameroon, United Republic of Tanzania, Upper Volta, Uruguay, Vanuatu, Venezuela, Viet Nam, Yemen, Yugoslavia, Zambia, Zimbabwe.

Against: France.

Abstaining: Australia, Austria, Belgium, Canada, Denmark, Germany, Federal Republic of, Greece, Honduras, Iceland, Ireland, Israel, Italy, Japan, Jordan,[a] Lebanon, Luxembourg, Netherlands, New Zealand, Norway, Portugal, Spain, United Kingdom, United States, Zaire.[a]

[a]Later advised the Secretariat it had intended to vote in favour.

France regretted that the question was on the Assembly's agenda because it believed that its consideration undermined the Charter, in particular Article 2, paragraph 7, on the non-intervention by the United Nations in domestic matters within a State's jurisdiction. France believed that the wording of paragraph 1 of the resolution was inaccurate in law, and pointed out that it had adopted a law in 1976 giving the island a special status which did not close the door on any future development regarding its status. Accordingly, France had engaged in constructive dialogue with the Comoros and it intended to work out specific proposals likely to promote a satisfactory solution to the matter. Contacts between the two Governments were being intensified, including a meeting in September between their two Presidents.

The Comoros reaffirmed its sovereignty over Mayotte and outlined the historical origins of the issue. It pointed out that the people of Mayotte had the same language, culture and religion as the other islands of the Comoros. In addition, the Assembly in 1975 had admitted the Comoros to the United Nations as a sovereign State composed of four islands, including Mayotte.[4] Renouncing commitments to carry out the results of a 1974 referendum on self-determination in the Comoros, France had held two referendums in Mayotte in 1976 to give an appearance of legality to its decision to dismember the Comoros and occupy Mayotte. Later that year, the Assembly had declared those results null and void, and affirmed that the French occupation of Mayotte constituted an encroachment on the national unity of the Comoros.[5] Other international organizations had also affirmed the sovereignty of the Comoros over Mayotte.

In later action, on 22 November, the Assembly, in resolution 38/17 on the right of peoples to self-determination, took note of the contacts between the Comoros and France in the search for a solution to the problem of the integration of Mayotte in the Comoros.

REFERENCES

[1]YUN 1982, p. 320, GA res. 37/65, 3 Dec. 1982. [2]A/38/517. [3]YUN 1981, p. 223. [4]YUN 1975, p. 309, GA res. 3385(XXX), 12 Nov. 1975. [5]YUN 1976, p. 183, GA res. 31/4, 21 Oct. 1976.

Malagasy islands question

In 1983, the General Assembly again did not debate the question of the Malagasy islands of Glorieuses, Juan de Nova, Europa and Bassas da India, deciding instead to include the item in the provisional agenda of its 1984 session.

This question, pertaining to the status of four Indian Ocean islands located north and west of Madagascar, had been on the Assembly's agenda each year since 1979, when the Assembly invited France to negotiate with Madagascar on the reintegration of the islands with Madagascar.[1] However, the Assembly had not discussed the question since 1980.

GENERAL ASSEMBLY ACTION

Acting on the Special Political Committee's recommendation, the General Assembly adopted decision 38/422 without vote. The decision was taken after the Committee Chairman had held consultations with the interested delegations, in particular those of France and Madagascar, and in view of talks currently under way between the two countries.

Question of the Malagasy islands of Glorieuses, Juan de Nova, Europa and Bassas da India

At its 98th plenary meeting, on 15 December 1983, the General Assembly, on the recommendation of the Special Political Committee, decided to include in the provisional agenda of its thirty-ninth session the item entitled "Question of the Malagasy islands of Glorieuses, Juan de Nova, Europa and Bassas da India".

General Assembly decision 38/422

Adopted without vote

Approved by SPC (A/38/656) without vote, 1 December (meeting 43); oral proposal by Chairman, based on informal consultations; agenda item 76.
Meeting numbers. GA 38th session: General Committee 2; SPC 43; plenary 98.

REFERENCE
[1]YUN 1979, p. 270, GA res. 34/91, 12 Dec. 1979.

Commission of Inquiry on Seychelles

On 24 June 1983,[1] Seychelles requested the President of the Security Council to terminate the work of the Commission of Inquiry established by the Council in 1981[2] to investigate the mercenary aggression of 25 November 1981 against that country.[3] Seychelles paid tribute to the Council for its assistance in dealing with the attack and requested it to continue operation of the Special Fund, set up in 1982 for the economic reconstruction of Seychelles,[4] and to maintain the item of Seychelles on the Council's agenda.

After holding consultations with the Council members, the President, on 8 July 1983,[5] reported that the Council had agreed that the Commission of Inquiry had fulfilled its mandate.

On 3 August,[6] Seychelles forwarded a press release issued by its President, on 22 July, announcing the pardon and subsequent deportation of the six foreign mercenaries sentenced to death or long prison terms in 1982 for their part in the armed aggression against Seychelles.

REFERENCES

[1]S/15845. [2]YUN 1981, p. 227, SC res. 496(1981), 15 Dec. 1981. [3]*Ibid.*, p. 226. [4]YUN 1982, p. 327, SC res. 507(1982), 28 May 1982. [5]S/15860. [6]S/15908.

UN Educational and Training Programme for Southern Africa

Under the United Nations Educational and Training Programme for Southern Africa, a total of 808 persons held scholarships during the year ended 30 September 1983, according to a report of the Secretary-General dated 19 October.[1] During that period, 263 new awards were granted and 545 were extended. Most of those scholarships, 613, were given to South Africans (see above, under SOUTH AFRICA AND *APARTHEID*, "Other UN assistance"), followed by 159 for persons from Zimbabwe. The remainder were provided to 23 persons from Namibia (see TRUSTEESHIP AND DECOLONIZATION, Chapter III), 8 from Guinea-Bissau, 3 from Sao Tome and Principe and 2 from Cape Verde. New scholarships were granted only to students from Namibia and South Africa. The awards were given for a wide variety of professional, commercial and technical studies. Those receiving scholarships attended educational institutions in many regions: 403 studied in Africa, 285 in North America, 70 in Asia, 46 in Europe and 4 in Latin America and the Caribbean. The Programme was financed by voluntary contributions from States, organizations and individuals; in addition, the Programme received offers of scholarships for training in their own countries from 23 States.

Drawing attention to the increasing demand for educational opportunities by the people of South Africa and Namibia and the rapidly increasing costs of higher education and training, the Secretary-General appealed for greater financial and other support to the Programme.

For the biennium ended 31 December 1983, the Programme had a total income of $8,379,548, of which $7,124,827 was donated by Governments. Expenditures for that period amounted to $7,896,660—$7,727,939 for fellowships and grants and the remainder for operating expenses. The net excess of income over expenditure after adjustments for the previous period was $532,888.

Financial contributions

Thirty-eight States contributed a total of $3,791,427 to the United Nations Educational and Training Programme for Southern Africa in 1983 (see table below). Because of inflation and rising scholarship costs, the 1983 contributions and pledges represented, in real terms, a decline in resources over the previous year when contributions and pledges totalled $3,624,033.

CONTRIBUTIONS TO THE UN EDUCATIONAL AND TRAINING PROGRAMME FOR SOUTHERN AFRICA, 1983
(as at 31 December 1983; in US dollars)

Country	1983 payment
Argentina	7,300
Australia	88,236
Austria	34,500
Bahamas	500
Burma	1,000
Canada	279,850
Cyprus	182
Denmark	300,863
Finland	92,799
France	62,014
Germany, Federal Republic of	64,705
Greece	9,000
Indonesia	3,000
Iran	5,000
Ireland	22,962
Italy	11,001
Japan	200,000
Kuwait	1,000
Malaysia	1,000
Mali	(309)
Netherlands	62,322
New Zealand	10,488
Norway	698,537
Republic of Korea	10,000
Saudi Arabia	25,000
Spain	30,000
Sweden	210,470
Switzerland	118,132
Thailand	1,000
Togo	(31)
Trinidad and Tobago	1,250
Tunisia	20,000
Turkey	5,324
United Kingdom	137,802
United States	1,250,000
Venezuela	5,000
Yugoslavia	2,000
Zimbabwe	19,530
Total	3,791,427

NOTE: Figures in parentheses indicate a loss due to changes in exchange rates; pledges were originally made for the 1982-1983 biennium.

GENERAL ASSEMBLY ACTION

On 7 December 1983, on the recommendation of the Fourth Committee, the General Assembly adopted resolution 38/52 without vote.

United Nations Educational and Training Programme for Southern Africa

The General Assembly,

Recalling its resolutions on the United Nations Educational and Training Programme for Southern Africa, in particular resolutions 36/53 of 24 November 1981 and 37/33 of 23 November 1982,

Having considered the report of the Secretary-General, containing an account of the work of the Advisory Committee on the United Nations Educational and Training Programme for Southern Africa and the operation of the Programme for the period from 1 October 1982 to 30 September 1983,

Recognizing the valuable assistance rendered by the Programme to the peoples of South Africa and Namibia,

Strongly convinced that the continuation and expansion of the Programme is essential in order to meet the increasing demand for educational and training opportunities by the peoples of South Africa and Namibia,

Fully recognizing the need to provide educational opportunities and counselling to student refugees in a wide variety of professional, cultural, technical and linguistic disciplines, particularly in the areas of development and international co-operation,

1. *Endorses* the report of the Secretary-General on the United Nations Educational and Training Programme for Southern Africa;

2. *Commends* the Secretary-General and the Advisory Committee on the United Nations Educational and Training Programme for Southern Africa for their continued efforts to promote generous contributions to the Programme;

3. *Expresses its appreciation* to all those who have supported the Programme by providing contributions, scholarships or places in their educational institutions;

4. *Notes with concern* that, owing to inflation and rising scholarship costs, contributions and pledges have declined, in real terms, in 1983 from the corresponding figure in 1982;

5. *Appeals* to all States, institutions, organizations and individuals to offer greater financial and other support to the Programme in order to ensure its continuation and expansion.

General Assembly resolution 38/52

7 December 1983   Meeting 86   Adopted without vote

Approved by Fourth Committee (A/38/610) without objection, 18 November (meeting 20); 46-nation draft (A/C.4/38/L.5); agenda item 105.

Sponsors: Australia, Bangladesh, Barbados, Brazil, Byelorussian SSR, Canada, Colombia, Congo, Cuba, Cyprus, Democratic Yemen, Denmark, Egypt, Finland, France, German Democratic Republic, Germany, Federal Republic of, Greece, Guyana, Iceland, India, Indonesia, Ireland, Ivory Coast, Japan, Kenya, Lesotho, Liberia, Mali, Mauritania, Netherlands, Nigeria, Norway, Pakistan, Senegal, Sweden, Syrian Arab Republic, Trinidad and Tobago, Tunisia, Turkey, United Republic of Tanzania, United States, Venezuela, Zaire, Zambia, Zimbabwe.

Meeting numbers. GA 38th session: 4th Committee 16, 19, 20; plenary 86.

REFERENCE

[1]A/38/469.

Co-operation between OAU and the UN system

In 1983, co-operation continued in a number of political and economic areas between the United Nations and the Organization of African Unity (OAU), with the General Assembly again calling for a strengthening of those activities.

The Secretary-General, in a report dated 1 August on co-operation between the two organizations,[1] gave a brief account of a meeting between the OAU General Secretariat and the secretariats of organizations within the United Nations system, convened in accordance with a November 1982 Assembly resolution.[2] Held at Addis Ababa, Ethiopia, from 21 to 23 April 1983,

the meeting adopted conclusions and recommendations for co-operation in several areas, including implementation of the Lagos Plan of Action for the Implementation of the Monrovia Strategy for the Economic Development of Africa, adopted by OAU at Lagos, Nigeria, in 1980 as the major framework for the continent's development plans.[3] In regard to the Lagos Plan, the secretariats of the Economic Commission for Africa (ECA) and of OAU concentrated on two areas—the preparation of a treaty establishing an African economic community and the strengthening of the existing regional economic communities and institutions and the establishment of others.

A major achievement in the work of the two secretariats was the establishment of a Preferential Trade Area for eastern and southern African States (PTA), grouping together 18 OAU/ECA member States. The objective of PTA was progressively to establish regional common markets and eventually a continental common market. Recommendations for co-operation were also made in the areas of the use of water resources; human resources development; the role of media and literacy in development; the programme for the Industrial Development Decade for Africa (1980-1990) (see ECONOMIC AND SOCIAL QUESTIONS, Chapter VIII); refugee problems; natural disasters; and assistance to national liberation movements.

In an addendum to his report,[4] dated 18 August, the Secretary-General described the work of 15 United Nations agencies and bodies co-operating with OAU in such areas as the situation in southern Africa, food and agriculture, energy, industrial development, natural and human resources, environment, transport and communications, science and technology, trade and finance, population, development planning and statistics, public administration and management, and health services.

The Niger, in a letter dated 6 July,[5] requested the Secretary-General to circulate to the General Assembly the resolutions adopted by the nineteenth ordinary session of the Assembly of Heads of State and Government of OAU, held at Addis Ababa from 6 to 12 June 1983. Several of the resolutions stressed or called for co-operation with the United Nations, particulary those dealing with Western Sahara, the Palestine question, sanctions against South Africa, preparations for the Second International Conference on Assistance to Refugees in Africa (1984), implementation of the Lagos Plan of Action, realization of the objectives of the International Year of Shelter for the Homeless (1987), and the sixth session of the United Nations Conference on Trade and Development; other resolutions dealt with Namibia, the Chad–Libyan Arab Jamahiriya dispute, the OAU mission to Chad, Lesotho, the Middle East, southern Africa, African candidatures to international organizations, and the OAU budget.

The General Assembly, on 28 October, adopted resolution 38/5 without vote.

Co-operation between the United Nations and the Organization of African Unity

The General Assembly,

Having considered the report of the Secretary-General on co-operation between the United Nations and the Organization of African Unity,

Recalling its previous resolutions on the promotion of co-operation between the United Nations and the Organization of African Unity and the practical measures taken for their implementation, in particular resolution 37/15 of 16 November 1982,

Taking note of the resolutions, decisions and declarations adopted by the Organization of African Unity on the promotion of co-operation between the United Nations and the Organization of African Unity,

Taking note also of the relevant resolutions and decisions adopted by the Assembly of Heads of State and Government of the Organization of African Unity at its nineteenth ordinary session, held at Addis Ababa from 6 to 12 June 1983,

Considering the important message of the current Chairman of the Organization of African Unity, delivered by the Minister for Foreign Affairs of Ethiopia to the General Assembly on 11 October 1983, particularly with regard to matters of concern to the two organizations,

Noting with satisfaction the continued co-operation between the United Nations and the Organization of African Unity in areas of common interest,

Deeply conscious of the special needs of the newly independent African States, particularly with regard to the consolidation of their national independence, their endeavours towards social and economic betterment and the adverse impact on their economies of the current international economic situation,

Gravely concerned about the adverse effect on African economies of the current international economic situation,

Recalling in this connection the Lagos Plan of Action for the Implementation of the Monrovia Strategy for the Economic Development of Africa, adopted by the Assembly of Heads of State and Government of the Organization of African Unity at its second extraordinary session, held at Lagos on 28 and 29 April 1980,

Recognizing the need for closer co-operation between the Organization of African Unity and all specialized organs, organizations and bodies of the United Nations system in realizing the goals and objectives set forth in the Lagos Plan of Action,

Deeply concerned at the gravity of the situation of the refugees in Africa and their increasing needs for international assistance as well as at the heavy social, economic and security burden imposed on African countries of asylum,

Having considered the report of the Secretary-General of 25 October 1983 on the International Conference on Assistance to Refugees in Africa as well as the progress of preparations for the Second International Conference on Assistance to Refugees in Africa,

Gravely concerned also at the need for special economic and emergency assistance programmes for a number of African States affected by serious economic problems, in particular problems of displaced persons, resulting from natural or other disasters, to enable them to pursue effective economic development,

Gravely concerned further at the deteriorating situation in southern Africa arising from the continued domination of the peoples of the area by the minority racist régime of South Africa and conscious of the need to provide increased assistance to the peoples of the region and to their liberation movements in their struggle against colonialism, racial discrimination and *apartheid,*

Conscious of its responsibilities to provide economic, material and humanitarian assistance to independent States in southern Africa to help them to cope with the situation caused by the acts of aggression committed against their territories by the *apartheid* régime of South Africa,

Recognizing the importance of taking effective steps to provide the widest possible dissemination of information relating to the liberation struggle of the peoples of southern Africa,

Recognizing the important role which the various information units and departments of the United Nations system can play in disseminating information to bring about a greater awareness of the social and economic problems and needs of African States and their regional and subregional institutions,

Aware of the need for continuous liaison, exchange of information at the secretariat level and technical co-operation on such matters as training and research between the Organization of African Unity and the United Nations,

Having considered the report of the Secretary-General on the meeting between representatives of the General Secretariat of the Organization of African Unity and the secretariats of the United Nations and other organizations of the United Nations system, held at Addis Ababa from 21 to 23 April 1983, in the context of the co-operation programme,

Noting with satisfaction the useful decisions and proposals which emerged from the conclusions of the Addis Ababa meeting for enhancing co-operation between the United Nations and the Organization of African Unity,

1.   *Takes note* of the report of the Secretary-General on co-operation between the United Nations and the Organization of African Unity and commends his efforts to strengthen such co-operation;

2.   *Notes with appreciation* the increasing participation of the Organization of African Unity in the work of the United Nations and the specialized agencies and its constructive contribution to that work;

3.   *Commends* the continued efforts of the Organization of African Unity to promote multilateral co-operation among African States and to find solutions to African problems of vital importance to the international community and notes with satisfaction the increased collaboration of various United Nations agencies in support of those efforts;

4.   *Reiterates* the determination of the United Nations, in co-operation with the Organization of Afri-

can Unity, to intensify its efforts to eliminate colonialism, racial discrimination and *apartheid* in southern Africa;

5. *Reaffirms* its willingness to co-operate fully with the Organization of African Unity and its organs in the implementation of the relevant resolutions and decisions of that organization;

6. *Approves* the relevant decisions, recommendations, proposals and arrangements contained in the conclusions of the meeting between representatives of the General Secretariat of the Organization of African Unity and the secretariats of the United Nations system and other organizations of the United Nations system, held at Addis Ababa from 21 to 23 April 1983;

7. *Requests* the Secretary-General to implement the relevant decisions, recommendations and proposals contained in the conclusions of the Addis Ababa meeting;

8. *Calls upon* the competent organizations and bodies of the United Nations system to give urgent consideration to the various recommendations and proposals contained in the conclusions of the Addis Ababa meeting, with the objective of enhancing co-operation between the United Nations system and the Organization of African Unity;

9. *Calls upon* the competent organs, specialized agencies and other organizations of the United Nations system to ensure that their personnel and recruitment policies provide for the just and equitable representation of Africa at all levels at their respective headquarters and in their regional and field operations and give due consideration to the various suggestions and proposals in the relevant paragraphs of the conclusions and recommendations of the Addis Ababa meeting;

10. *Requests* the Secretary-General, in consultation with the Secretary-General of the Organization of African Unity, to arrange the date and venue in Africa for the next meeting between representatives of the General Secretariat of that organization and the secretariats of the United Nations and other organizations of the United Nations system, taking into account paragraphs 65 to 67 of the report of the Secretary-General, which relate to the agenda and modalities of the meeting and to suggestions made at the Addis Ababa meeting;

11. *Recognizes* the importance of continued close association by the United Nations and the specialized agencies, where appropriate, with the efforts of the Organization of African Unity to promote social and economic development and to advance intra-African co-operation in that vital field;

12. *Reaffirms* the determination of the United Nations to work closely with the Organization of African Unity towards the establishment of the new international economic order in accordance with the resolutions adopted by the General Assembly and, in that regard, to take full account of the Lagos Plan of Action for the Implementation of the Monrovia Strategy for the Economic Development of Africa in the implementation of the International Development Strategy for the Third United Nations Development Decade;

13. *Reiterates its appreciation* to the Secretary-General for his efforts, on behalf of the international community, to organize and mobilize special programmes of economic assistance for African States experiencing grave economic difficulties, in particular for newly independent African States, the front-line States and other independent States of southern Africa, to help them to cope with the situation caused by the acts of aggression committed against their territories by the *apartheid* régime of South Africa;

14. *Expresses its appreciation* to the World Bank, the United Nations Development Programme and other concerned international financial institutions for their assistance, in response to resolutions of the General Assembly, in the organization of round-table and donor conferences in favour of the least developed countries of Africa, as well as those requiring special programmes of economic assistance;

15. *Calls upon* all Member States, regional and international organizations and organizations of the United Nations system to participate actively in the implementation of those special programmes of economic assistance;

16. *Calls upon* the international community to provide generous assistance to all the African States, particularly those that are affected by natural calamities such as drought and flood, and expresses its appreciation to the Office of the United Nations Disaster Relief Co-ordinator, the World Food Programme, the Food and Agriculture Organization of the United Nations, the World Health Organization and the United Nations Children's Fund for the assistance they have so far rendered to the African States that have suffered those calamities;

17. *Requests* the Secretary-General to keep the Organization of African Unity informed periodically of the response of the international community to those special programmes of economic assistance and to co-ordinate efforts with all similar programmes initiated by that organization;

18. *Also requests* the Secretary-General and the organizations of the United Nations system to ensure that adequate facilities continue to be made available for the provision of technical assistance to the General Secretariat of the Organization of African Unity, as required;

19. *Further requests* the Secretary-General to continue to take the necessary measures to strengthen co-operation at the political, economic, cultural and administrative levels between the United Nations and the Organization of African Unity in accordance with the relevant resolutions of the General Assembly, particularly with regard to the provision of assistance to the victims of colonialism and *apartheid* in southern Africa, and in this connection draws once again the attention of the international community to the need to contribute to the Assistance Fund for the Struggle against Colonialism and *Apartheid* established by the Organization of African Unity;

20. *Calls upon* all Member States and organizations of the United Nations system to increase their assistance to the African States affected by serious economic problems, in particular problems of displaced persons, resulting from natural or other disasters, by mobilizing special programmes of economic and emergency assistance;

21. *Urges* all Member States and regional and international organizations, in particular those of the United Nations system, and non-governmental organizations to continue their support of African refugee programmes and to provide material and economic assistance to help host countries to cope with the heavy burden imposed on their limited resources and weak infrastructures;

22. *Invites* Member States and regional and international organizations, in particular those of the United Nations system, and non-governmental organizations to participate actively in the Second International Conference on Assistance to Refugees in Africa, scheduled to be held in July 1984, and to contribute generously to ensure its success;

23. *Requests* the Secretary-General to draw the attention of the specialized agencies and other organizations of the United Nations system to the need to give increasingly wide publicity to all matters relating to the social and economic development of Africa;

24. *Calls upon* United Nations bodies—in particular the Security Council, the Economic and Social Council, the Special Committee on the Situation with regard to the Implementation of the Declaration on the Granting of Independence to Colonial Countries and Peoples, the Special Committee against *Apartheid* and the United Nations Council for Namibia—to continue to associate closely the Organization of African Unity with all their work concerning Africa;

25. *Urges* the specialized agencies and other organizations concerned within the United Nations system to continue and to expand their co-operation with the Organization of African Unity and, through it, their assistance to the liberation movements recognized by that organization;

26. *Requests* the Secretary-General to report to the General Assembly at its thirty-ninth session on the implementation of the present resolution and on the development of co-operation between the Organization of African Unity and the organizations concerned within the United Nations system.

General Assembly resolution 38/5

28 October 1983   Meeting 39   Adopted without vote

50-nation draft (A/38/L.5 & Corr.1); agenda item 26.

Sponsors: Algeria, Angola, Benin, Botswana, Burundi, Cape Verde, Central African Republic, Chad, Comoros, Congo, Djibouti, Egypt, Equatorial Guinea, Ethiopia, Gabon, Gambia, Ghana, Guinea, Guinea-Bissau, Ivory Coast, Kenya, Lesotho, Liberia, Libyan Arab Jamahiriya, Madagascar, Malawi, Mali, Mauritania, Mauritius, Morocco, Mozambique, Niger, Nigeria, Rwanda, Sao Tome and Principe, Senegal, Seychelles, Sierra Leone, Somalia, Sudan, Swaziland, Togo, Tunisia, Uganda, United Republic of Cameroon, United Republic of Tanzania, Upper Volta, Zaire, Zambia, Zimbabwe.

Meeting number. GA 38th session: plenary 39.

The Assembly dealt with co-operation between the United Nations and OAU in a number of other resolutions. In resolution 38/40 of 7 December, the Assembly urged the two organizations to co-operate with a view to implementing the OAU decisions on Western Sahara (see TRUSTEESHIP AND DECOLONIZATION, Chapter IV), adopted by the OAU June summit at Addis Ababa. The Assembly, in resolution 38/51 of 7 December, recommended that organizations of the United Nations system should broaden contacts with the colonial peoples and their national liberation movements (see above) directly or through OAU, and assist them in their struggle to exercise self-determination and independence.

In resolution 38/55 of 7 December, the Assembly requested the Secretary-General to publicize the work of the United Nations regarding

decolonization through several means, including maintaining a close working relationship with OAU by periodic consultations and by exchanging information. Regarding the implementation of the Declaration on the Denuclearization of Africa (see Chapter I of this section), the Assembly, in resolution 38/181 A of 20 December, requested the United Nations Institute for Disarmament Research, in co-operation with the Department for Disarmament Affairs and in consultation with OAU, to provide data on the development of South Africa's nuclear capability. Concerning industrial development, the Assembly, in resolution 38/192 of 20 December, welcomed efforts by the United Nations Industrial Development Organization (UNIDO) to assist the African countries and intergovernmental organizations in the formulation of national and subregional programmes for the Industrial Development Decade for Africa (1980-1990), which was aimed at mobilizing support for the industrialization of the continent. Also welcomed were UNIDO's efforts in maintaining co-ordination with the OAU secretariat, the Economic Commission for Africa (ECA) and other relevant international organizations.

ECONOMIC AND SOCIAL COUNCIL ACTION

The Economic and Social Council also mentioned co-operation between the United Nations and OAU in two resolutions. In resolution 1983/42 of 25 July, it requested United Nations organizations to continue to co-operate with OAU in implementing the 1960 Declaration on the Granting of Independence to Colonial Countries and Peoples,[6] and to render, in consultation with OAU and the Council for Namibia, increased assistance to the people of Namibia for their liberation struggle. It recommended that a separate item on assistance to national liberation movements (see above) recognized by OAU should be included in the agenda of high-level meetings of the secretariats of OAU and United Nations organizations, with a view to strengthening co-ordination to ensure the best use of available resources for assistance to colonial peoples.

In resolution 1983/70 of 29 July, the Council welcomed UNIDO efforts to assist African countries and intergovernmental organizations in the formulation of national and subregional programmes for the Industrial Development Decade for Africa, and to maintain co-ordination with the secretariats of OAU, ECA and other international organizations.

REFERENCES

[1]A/38/307. [2]YUN 1982, p. 331, GA res. 37/15, 16 Nov. 1982. [3]YUN 1980, p. 548. [4]A/38/307/Add.1. [5]A/38/312. [6]YUN 1960, p. 49, GA res. 1514(XV), 14 Dec. 1960.

Chapter VI

Americas

During 1983, both the Security Council and the General Assembly addressed serious situations in Central America and Grenada.

The Council met in March, May and September to consider Nicaragua's complaints of aggression against it. In May, by resolution 530(1983), the Council urged the Contadora Group—Colombia, Mexico, Panama and Venezuela—to spare no effort to find solutions to the problems affecting the Central American region, while in November, by resolution 38/10, the Assembly urged States to refrain from military operations that might hamper the Group's negotiating efforts.

Following internal political unrest in Grenada and the intervention therein by the United States and several Caribbean countries, the Council considered the question in October; a draft resolution, calling for the withdrawal of foreign troops, was not adopted owing to the negative vote of a permanent member, the United States. However, in November, the Assembly, by resolution 38/7, made that call and requested that free elections be quickly organized.

Details of these subjects as well as a brief account of communications concerning the relations between Nicaragua and several States—Costa Rica, El Salvador, Honduras and the United States—and between Belize and Guatemala can be found in this chapter.

Topics related to this chapter. Disarmament: nuclear-weapon-free zones—Latin America. Regional economic and social activities: Latin America. Human rights: Latin America. Refugees and humanitarian assistance: Americas. Other colonial Territories: Falkland Islands (Malvinas) question.

Central America situation

Communications. Throughout 1983, the Secretary-General and the President of the Security Council received numerous communications on the situation in Central America.

On 11 January,[1] Panama transmitted information on a meeting of the Foreign Ministers of the Contadora Group (Isla Contadora, Panama, 8 and 9 January). The Ministers expressed concern about foreign interference in Central American conflicts, noted that it was undesirable for those conflicts to form part of East-West confrontation, appealed to all Central American countries to negotiate to reduce tension, and reviewed various peace initiatives and their effects.

On 22 February,[2] Nicaragua forwarded the final communiqué of the Ministerial Meeting of the Co-ordinating Bureau of the Non-Aligned Countries (Managua, Nicaragua, 10-14 January), in which the Ministers denounced armed attacks and economic destabilization being carried out against Nicaragua.

El Salvador, in a letter of 8 April,[3] asserted that generalized conflict existed in Central America and that this must be approached through multilateral negotiations on limiting the arms race in Central America, eliminating arms traffic, and strengthening regional economic relations and democratic and pluralist institutions.

On 22 April,[4] Panama transmitted an information bulletin issued on 21 April following consultations by the Foreign Ministers of the Contadora Group with those of Costa Rica, El Salvador, Guatemala, Honduras and Nicaragua, who for the first time had joined in an effort to establish a dialogue.

Panama, on 13 May,[5] transmitted a communiqué of 12 May in which the Contadora Group asked that in its deliberations the Security Council strengthen the principles of self-determination and non-interference in the affairs of other States, the obligation not to allow the territory of a State to be used for committing acts of aggression against other States, the peaceful settlement of disputes and the prohibition of the threat or use of force to resolve conflicts.

The Presidents of the Contadora Group drew up the Cancún Declaration on Peace in Central America (Cancún, Mexico, 17 July), the text of which was transmitted by the Group to the Secretary-General on 19 July.[6] In the Declaration, the Presidents expressed deep concern over the rapidly deteriorating Central American situation and offered general peace proposals, which included controlling the arms race, eliminating foreign advisers, creating demilitarized zones, prohibiting the use of some States' territory for the destabilization of other States, eradicating traffic in arms, prohibiting other forms of aggression or interference in States' internal affairs, and concluding regional peace agreements.

Support for the Declaration was expressed in several communications. It was endorsed at Caracas, Venezuela, on 25 July by the Presidents of Bolivia, Ecuador and Peru and the Foreign Ministers of Argentina and Spain; this information was transmitted by Venezuela on 2 August.[7] On 28 July,[8] India forwarded a communiqué adopted at a 27 July meeting in New York of the Co-ordinating Bureau of the Non-Aligned Countries, welcoming the Declaration, asking the Contadora Group to continue its efforts, and urging the United States not to conduct naval manœuvres off the coasts of Central America. In a letter of 1 August,[9] Panama gave details of a meeting of the Foreign Ministers of the Contadora Group with their counterparts from Costa Rica, El Salvador, Guatemala, Honduras and Nicaragua (Panama City, 28-30 July) at which those countries stated their support for the Declaration. On 10 August,[10] Honduras quoted a note it had sent to the Contadora Group in which it rejected statements by the Foreign Minister of Nicaragua that the Group had continued to press militaristic intentions and paid only lip-service to the Cancún Declaration; Honduras also stated its resolve to achieve regional peace and security.

In a 19 July communiqué annexed to identical letters of 20 and 21 July,[11] Nicaragua called for negotiations to settle the conflicts and put forward a six-point proposal, including a non-aggression agreement between Nicaragua and Honduras, a halt in the supplying of arms by any country to forces fighting in El Salvador, cessation of military support to the forces opposed to any of the Central American Governments, commitments to respect the self-determination of the Central American peoples, ending of acts of aggression and economic discrimination against any Central American country, and suspension of foreign military exercises and the building of foreign military bases in the region.

Panama reported on 12 September[12] a further meeting between the Foreign Ministers of the Contadora Group and those of Costa Rica, El Salvador, Guatemala, Honduras and Nicaragua (Panama City, 7-9 September) at which a Document of Objectives—embodying diverse viewpoints, identifying areas of agreement, and setting out basic commitments for establishing peace, democracy, security and development in Central America—was formulated. The Secretary-General informed the Security Council of his contacts with the representatives of the Contadora Group and the Central American countries, and annexed to a 9 December note to the Council[13] a communication from the Contadora Group's Foreign Ministers to the General Assembly of the Organization of American States (OAS), pointing out that the Document contained 21 basic points for

achieving peace, the co-operation necessary for economic and social development, and the strengthening of democratic institutions in Central America. A proposal embodying norms for implementing the undertakings in the Document, prepared by the Group (Panama City, 20 and 21 December), was transmitted by Panama on 22 December.[14]

On 26 September,[15] Nicaragua transmitted a note sent to the Presidents of the Contadora Group by the co-ordinator of the Governing Junta of National Reconstruction of Nicaragua, saying that, despite aggressive acts against it by the United States, Nicaragua had decided to ratify the Document of Objectives.

On 3 October,[16] Honduras transmitted a 1 September letter it had sent to the countries with which it maintained diplomatic relations; a 29 September letter to the Contadora Group ratifying the Document of Objectives and declaring that Nicaragua, in asking that the United Nations General Assembly discuss the Central American situation (see below), had violated its commitment not to resort to international organizations as long as the Group was searching for a solution; and a statement it had made to the OAS Permanent Council (Washington, D. C., July) charging Nicaragua with numerous attacks on Honduras and throughout the region.

Costa Rica, in a letter of 27 September,[17] said that it was opposed to the inclusion of an item concerning Central America on the agenda of the General Assembly and that it supported the dialogue among Central American Governments in the framework of the Contadora Group.

On 13 October,[18] the Secretary-General informed the Security Council of his endeavours to keep in contact with the Contadora Group, outlined its recent activities and transmitted to the Council the Document of Objectives. The Secretary-General conveyed to the Council on 9 December[13] a resolution on peace efforts in Central America, approved in November by the OAS General Assembly. He observed that there had been developments which, if taken advantage of, would make it possible to have hope for improvement in the region's situation. The OAS resolution had been forwarded by Honduras in a letter of 21 November.[19]

Three other communications on the Central American situation were received during the year. On 26 April,[20] Colombia transmitted the text of a letter it had sent that day to the Libyan Arab Jamahiriya about the overflight of Colombian territory by Libyan aircraft; Colombia repudiated any use of the authority and inviolability of treaties or the principle of good faith among States to further the unauthorized carriage of war *matériel* for unspecified purposes. Nicaragua charged in a letter of 26 October[21] that the United States had ignored all Nicaraguan peace initiatives and that the United States Central Intelligence Agency (CIA) was planning to provoke attacks against both Honduras and Costa Rica in order to blame Nicaragua and have a pretext for unleashing greater aggression against it. In a government statement of 25 October, transmitted the following day,[22] the USSR referred to what it called the aggressive actions of the United States against Nicaragua, said Nicaragua was threatened by a direct invasion of United States forces, and added that the United States showed a lack of interest in a political solution to the problems of Central America.

SECURITY COUNCIL ACTION

On 19 May, the Security Council, appealing urgently to interested States to co-operate with the Contadora Group, commended its efforts to solve the problems affecting Central America and urged the Group to spare no effort in that regard. These actions were incorporated in resolution 530(1983) (see below, under HONDURAS-NICARAGUA DISPUTE AND ARMED INCIDENTS).

GENERAL ASSEMBLY ACTION

The General Assembly took up the Central American situation after the Nicaraguan Foreign Minister had requested, on 28 September,[23] that the subject be placed on the Assembly's agenda. On 21 October,[24] Honduras transmitted a letter of 17 October from its Foreign Minister to those of the Contadora Group, in which he contended that the Assembly's discussion would obstruct that Group's peace efforts.

On 11 November, the Assembly adopted by consensus resolution 38/10.

The situation in Central America: threats to international peace and security and peace initiatives

The General Assembly,

Recalling Security Council resolution 530(1983) of 19 May 1983 in which the Council encouraged the efforts of the Contadora Group and appealed urgently to all interested States in and outside the region to co-operate fully with the Group, through a frank and constructive dialogue, so as to resolve their differences,

Reaffirming the purposes and principles of the Charter of the United Nations relating to the duty of all States to refrain from the threat or use of force against the sovereignty, territorial integrity or political independence of any State,

Also reaffirming the inalienable right of all peoples to decide on their own form of government and to choose their own economic, political and social system free from all foreign intervention, coercion or limitation,

Considering that the internal conflicts in the countries of Central America stem from the economic, political and social conditions obtaining in each of those countries and that they should not, therefore, be placed in the context of East-West confrontation,

Deeply concerned at the worsening of tensions and conflicts in Central America and the increase in outside interference and acts of aggression against the countries of the region, which endanger international peace and security,

Mindful of the necessity of promoting the achievement of peace on a sound basis, which would make possible a genuine democratic process, respect for human rights, and economic and social development,

Noting with deep concern that in recent weeks armed incidents, border clashes, acts of terrorism and sabotage, traffic in arms and destabilizing actions in and against countries of the region have increased in number and intensity,

Noting with great concern the military presence of countries from outside the region, the carrying out of overt and covert actions, and the use of neighbouring territories to engage in destabilizing actions, which have served to heighten tensions in the region,

Deeply concerned at the prolongation of the armed conflict in countries of Central America, which has been aggravated by increasing foreign intervention,

Bearing in mind the progress achieved in the meetings that the Ministers for Foreign Affairs of the Contadora Group have held with the Foreign Ministers of Costa Rica, El Salvador, Guatemala, Honduras and Nicaragua in identifying issues of concern and proposing appropriate procedures for the consideration of those issues,

Recalling the Cancún Declaration on Peace in Central America issued by the Presidents of Colombia, Mexico, Panama and Venezuela on 17 July 1983, which contains an appeal for political commitments on the part of countries situated in and outside the region with the aim of achieving lasting peace in the area,

Bearing in mind the Cancún Declaration and the endorsement by the States of Central America of a Document of Objectives, which provides a basis for an agreement on the negotiations, that should be initiated at the earliest possible date with the aim of drawing up agreements and adopting the necessary procedures for formalizing the commitments and ensuring appropriate systems of control and verification,

Appreciating the broad international support expressed for the efforts of the Contadora Group to secure a peaceful and negotiated settlement of the conflicts affecting the region,

1. *Reaffirms* the right of all the countries of the region to live in peace and to decide their own future, free from all outside interference or intervention, whatever pretext may be adduced or whatever the circumstances in which they may be committed;

2. *Affirms* that respect for the sovereignty and independence of all States of the region is essential to ensure the security and peaceful coexistence of the Central American States;

3. *Condemns* the acts of aggression against the sovereignty, independence and territorial integrity of the States of the region, which have caused losses in human life and irreparable damage to their economies, thereby preventing them from meeting the economic and social development needs of their peoples; especially serious in this context are:

(a) The attacks launched from outside Nicaragua against that country's strategic installations, such as airports and seaports, energy storage facilities and other targets whose destruction seriously affects the country's economic life and endangers densely populated areas;

(b) The continued losses in human life in El Salvador and Honduras, the destruction of important public works and losses in production;

(c) The increase in the number of refugees in several countries of the region;

4. *Urges* the States of the region and other States to desist from, or to refrain from initiating, military operations intended to exert political pressure, which aggravate the situation in the region and hamper the efforts to promote negotiations that the Contadora Group is undertaking with the agreement of the Governments of Central America;

5. *Notes with satisfaction* that the countries of the region have agreed to take measures leading to the establishment and, where appropriate, the improvement of democratic, representative and pluralistic systems which will guarantee effective popular participation in decision-making and ensure the free access of various currents of opinion to honest and periodic electoral processes based on the full observance of civil rights, emphasizing that the strengthening of democratic institutions is closely linked to evolution and advances achieved in the sphere of economic development and social justice;

6. *Expresses its firmest support* for the Contadora Group and urges it to persevere in its efforts, which enjoy the effective support of the international community and the forthright co-operation of the interested countries in or outside the region;

7. *Welcomes with satisfaction* the Cancún Declaration of the Presidents of Colombia, Mexico, Panama and Venezuela and the Document of Objectives endorsed by the Governments of Costa Rica, El Salvador, Guatemala, Honduras and Nicaragua, which contains the basis for the start of negotiations to ensure harmonious coexistence in Central America;

8. *Requests* the Secretary-General, in pursuance of Security Council resolution 530(1983), to keep the Council regularly informed of the development of the situation and of the implementation of that resolution;

9. *Requests* the Secretary-General to submit a report to the General Assembly at its thirty-ninth session on the implementation of the present resolution;

10. *Decides* to keep under review the situation in Central America, threats to security which may occur in the region and the progress of peace initiatives.

General Assembly resolution 38/10

11 November 1983   Meeting 53   Adopted by consensus

6-nation draft (A/38/L.13/Rev.1); agenda item 142.

Sponsors: Congo, Ethiopia, Guyana, Nicaragua, Sao Tome and Principe, Upper Volta.

Meeting numbers. GA 38th session: plenary 47-53.

After the text had been revised during consultations, amendments[25] put forward by Costa Rica were not pressed to a vote. They proposed inserting, after paragraph 4, two paragraphs by which the Assembly would have urged Central American countries to establish democratic systems and to halt the arms race in the region.

Nicaragua, introducing the draft resolution,

said it would make a significant contribution to strengthening the initiative of the Contadora Group, and would make those countries which paid lip-service to peace efforts while leading Central America towards ever more devastating wars give more thought to the situation.

Explanations of position were made by several States. Honduras said that the resolution was not fully in accord with the Document of Objectives, that it overlooked, for example, the aim of slowing down the arms race, failed to give appropriate emphasis to the obligation to refrain from fomenting acts of subversion, and omitted to mention the commitment to guarantee civil and other rights as well as the situation of ethnic minorities that had suffered the violation of their most fundamental rights. Turkey said that, while it supported the efforts of the Contadora Group, it had reservations with respect to paragraph 1, which tended to ignore certain important principles of international law, and to paragraph 8, feeling that the Assembly should not remind the Secretary-General of his duties to the Council. Finland said that it supported the initiatives of the Contadora Group and was particularly concerned about the refugee situation in Central America, and that the principles of non-interference and non-intervention should not be violated.

Nicaragua situation

The situation in Nicaragua was taken up by the Security Council in March, May and September 1983, each time at the request of Nicaragua, which complained of aggressive acts against it.

Nicaragua, in a 5 December letter to the Secretary-General,[26] transmitted the texts of three decree-laws, granting amnesty to Nicaraguans of Miskito Indian origin, promulgating a general amnesty, and setting 1985 as the year for national elections.

The Sub-Commission on Prevention of Discrimination and Protection of Minorities recommended on 31 August[27] that the Commission on Human Rights express its concern about the undeclared war threatening Nicaragua (see ECONOMIC AND SOCIAL QUESTIONS, Chapter XVIII).

Costa Rica-Nicaragua dispute and armed incidents

From May to November 1983, the Secretary-General and/or the President of the Security Council received letters concerning aspects of the situation between Costa Rica and Nicaragua.

Costa Rica, on 6 May,[28] transmitted the text of a message sent on 4 May to the President of the OAS Permanent Council, asking the co-operation of OAS in guaranteeing its neutrality in the current internal Nicaraguan conflict; the text of a declaration of 27 April proclaiming neutrality was appended. On 17 November,[29] Costa Rica transmitted a presidential proclamation made public that day on its permanent, active and unarmed neutrality. Nicaragua, in a letter of 18 November,[30] welcomed Costa Rica's declaration of neutrality as a constructive gesture amid the crisis affecting the Central American region.

On 13 May,[31] Panama transmitted a 12 May communiqué about a meeting of the Foreign Ministers of the Contadora Group (Panama City, 11 and 12 May) at which they considered a Costa Rican request to OAS to set up a peace force to monitor the border between Costa Rica and Nicaragua. The Foreign Ministers decided to send an observer commission to the area to establish the facts, evaluate the circumstances and submit recommendations.

On 31 May,[32] Panama transmitted the text of an information bulletin issued after a meeting held from 28 to 30 May at Panama City by the Foreign Ministers of the Condatora Group and of Costa Rica, El Salvador, Guatemala, Honduras and Nicaragua. The Group heard the report of the observer commission which had visited Costa Rica and Nicaragua the previous week, and agreed that the commission should continue to act as an advisory group on border problems. It also decided to establish a technical group to analyse various proposals for regional coexistence.

In a letter of 16 September,[33] Costa Rica transmitted remarks by its Foreign Minister, who declared that Nicaragua, in a statement to the Security Council on 13 September (see below, under HONDURAS-NICARAGUA DISPUTE AND ARMED INCIDENTS), had sought to discredit Costa Rica by baselessly asserting that aircraft from its territory had made two incursions into Nicaragua on 9 September.

Nicaragua charged in a series of letters that attacks on its territory were being carried out by what it described as mercenary forces based in Costa Rica. On 28 September,[34] it submitted two notes of protest from its Foreign Minister to the Foreign Minister of Costa Rica, denouncing mercenary attacks on the villages of Cárdenas and Sapoá and the customs post of Peñas Blancas. On 30 September,[35] Nicaragua transmitted a communiqué of 29 September by its Foreign Ministry stating that mercenary attacks launched from Costa Rica were increasing and asking that the observer commission revisit the border. A letter from Nicaragua of 6 October[36] transmitted a note to the Foreign Minister of Costa Rica, dated 4 October, calling attention to attacks in which fuel tanks in the port of Benjamín Zeledón had been blown up on 2 October and two high-voltage pylons near the border, one in Nicaragua and the other in Costa Rica, had been destroyed on 27 September.

On 10 October,[37] Nicaragua transmitted a note dated 7 October charging that mercenaries operating from Costa Rica had attacked the Nicaraguan post of El Naranjo; Nicaragua said that, although it was aware that the mercenaries were operating without the authorization of the Costa Rican Government, it could not overlook the increasing seriousness of the attacks. Nicaragua, on 21 November,[38] transmitted a note dated 18 November, reporting a counter-revolutionary attack on the village of Cárdenas and a concentration of counter-revolutionaries in the Peñas Blancas sector who were preparing to attack Nicaraguan positions. On 23 November,[39] Nicaragua transmitted a note dated 22 November, stating that mercenary groups, numbering between 700 and 1,200 individuals, in Costa Rican territory were planning to launch a series of attacks against Nicaraguan villages and frontier posts.

El Salvador-Nicaragua relations

By a letter of 3 October to the Security Council President,[40] Nicaragua transmitted a 28 September note from its Foreign Minister to the Foreign Minister of El Salvador, stating that a crop-spraying plane had been stolen from Nicaragua and flown to El Salvador on 26 September, and asking El Salvador to apprehend the pilot and return the plane.

Honduras-Nicaragua dispute and armed incidents

Communications (January-March). During the early months of 1983, Nicaragua charged, in a number of letters to the President of the Security Council, that it was being attacked by counter-revolutionary units operating from Honduras with the support of the United States. Letters from Honduras during the same period reported alleged attacks by Nicaraguan armed forces on Honduran villages, army patrols and fishing boats. Most of the letters conveyed protest notes that had been ·exchanged between the Foreign Ministers of the two countries.

On 5 January[41] and 10 January,[42] Nicaragua transmitted protest notes of 4 and 8 January to the United States regarding a series of attacks against Nicaragua by armed units from Honduras and reiterating a request for a dialogue to bring about peace in Central America. An announcement of United States-Honduran military manœuvres, scheduled for 1 to 6 February, was denounced as a provocation by Nicaragua in a letter of 19 January.[43]

Attacks which took place between 31 December 1982 and 7 February 1983 and the United States-Honduran manœuvres were reported by Nicaragua in a letter of 16 February.[44] On 25 March,[45] Nicaragua forwarded the texts of three protest notes addressed to Honduras—one dated 22 March and two dated 24 March—a message issued on 21 March to the Nicaraguan people about what was termed a new phase of aggression by the United States against Nicaragua, and a Nicaraguan Defence Ministry communiqué of 23 March. In a letter of 29 March,[46] Nicaragua denounced attacks on 27 March by counter-revolutionaries and the Honduran army on the Nicaraguan observation posts of Loma del Suspiro and Loma el Espino; on a Red Cross ambulance, killing the driver; and on the village of San Fernando. Nicaragua, in a letter of 31 March,[47] reported an attack by counter-revolutionaries on 28 March on the Kum observation post and attacks of 29 March on the village of Teotecacinte, wounding one person, and in the frontier zone, in the sector of Kum; the 29 March attacks were also reported in a Nicaraguan press communiqué dated 30 March, transmitted the next day.[48]

Letters of 6 January,[49] 20 January[50] and 7 February[51] contained protest notes from Honduras to Nicaragua about incursions on 26 December 1982 and 13 January and 3 February 1983, respectively, into Honduran territory by Nicaraguan forces, resulting in the kidnapping of two persons, an attack on an army patrol, and the attempted kidnapping of another person. Replying to the Nicaraguan complaint about joint United States–Honduran military manœuvres,[43] Honduras said in a 21 January letter transmitted three days later[52] that it had invited Nicaragua and the other Central American countries to witness the exercises, which were designed solely to provide training for the Honduran armed forces.

On 9 February,[53] Honduras forwarded a protest note it had sent to Nicaragua concerning a 7 February attack on a Honduran fishing vessel in Honduran territorial waters by a Nicaraguan air force plane; on 25 March,[54] it transmitted a similar protest against the Nicaraguan seizure of two Honduran fishing vessels and their crews on 20 March. The Honduran Foreign Minister invited his Nicaraguan counterpart in a letter of 18 February[55] to visit the frontier area between the two countries and see for himself that no camps of counter-revolutionaries existed there. In a letter of 25 March,[56] Honduras reported a Nicaraguan army buildup along the frontier and termed it a threat to peace.

Other letters on the situation, dated 28 March, were received from Viet Nam[57] and Suriname.[58] Viet Nam condemned the United States and Honduras for what it said were acts of aggression against Nicaragua, while Suriname declared its concern about the infiltration of armed groups into Nicaragua, which it said were aimed at destabilizing the Government.

SECURITY COUNCIL CONSIDERATION (March)

On 22 March,[59] Nicaragua requested that the Security Council meet urgently to consider what it said was a grave increase in aggressive acts against it, thereby endangering international peace. The Council held eight meetings between 23 and 29 March regarding the Nicaraguan complaint.

Meeting numbers. SC 2420-2427.

The following States were invited, at their request, to participate in the deliberations without the right to vote: Algeria, Argentina, Barbados, Belgium, Bolivia, Brazil, Bulgaria, Colombia, Costa Rica, Cuba, Cyprus, Czechoslovakia, Democratic Yemen, Dominican Republic, Ecuador, El Salvador, German Democratic Republic, Federal Republic of Germany, Ghana, Grenada, Guatemala, Honduras, Hungary, India, Iran, Italy, Libyan Arab Jamahiriya, Mauritius, Mexico, Mongolia, Panama, Peru, Philippines, Spain, Syrian Arab Republic, United Republic of Tanzania, Uruguay, Venezuela, Viet Nam, Yugoslavia.

The debate on the item focused on bilateral and multilateral tensions in Central America, the relations between Nicaragua and its neighbours, and the influence of other States on the region's conflicts.

Nicaragua told the Council that it was facing a new escalation of aggression by the United States, which was supporting a massive infiltration of military units into Nicaragua from Honduras. It said the escalation had begun early in the year with the concentration of counter-revolutionary forces previously scattered in camps along the border. It believed that actions in the Nicaraguan Atlantic region might be a diversion, preparatory to a more strategic blow in its Pacific area. It feared that Honduran forces were about to become more directly involved in the conflict, since the Honduran army was massing troops in the Jalapa and Choluteca areas and the troops in Honduran territory had opened fire on the Vado Ancho and Zopilota observation posts in Nicaragua on 22 and 24 March. Nicaragua appealed to the United States to cease its aggressive stance, its threatening military manœuvres and its secret but widely recognized war against Nicaragua, and to reconsider such peace initiatives as those put forward by the Contadora Group, or by the Mexican and Venezuelan Governments which in September 1982 had offered to sponsor negotiations between Nicaragua and Honduras. It declared it was urgent that Nicaragua and Honduras discuss their bilateral problems and then go forward to the more complex regional problems.

Honduras stressed that it was not involved in a dispute with Nicaragua and that the problem was exclusively Nicaraguan and related to increasing internal tensions between its Government and opposition groups. It stated that Honduran forces had been mobilized because of threatening declarations by Nicaragua and armaments currently in Nicaragua, which included two armoured divisions of Soviet origin. It maintained that there were no military camps for counter-revolutionary Nicaraguan forces in Honduran territory, declared that it had an independent policy and was not aligned with the United States, and asked if Nicaragua was prepared for a dialogue under the auspices of any organization to end the tensions in the region. Honduras said it wanted negotiations but, while Nicaragua maintained that those negotiations must be bilateral, Honduras believed the problem to be regional.

The United States said Nicaragua was suffering from an obsession concerning the hostility of the United States towards it, and recalled United States assurances to that country that it had absolutely no intention of engaging in a large-scale military invasion of it. The United States added that the Nicaraguan Government, since its accession to power, had built a military machine unequalled in Central America; sought to destabilize the Government of El Salvador by sending arms into that country, by training and supporting guerrillas there and by directing guerrilla actions from Nicaragua; repeatedly violated Honduran territory with the covert shipment of arms over its borders and fomented guerrilla forces inside Honduras; and systematically violated the rights of Costa Rica by attempts to deny it use of the San Juan River. The United States proposed that peace be achieved in Central America by adherence to the conditions set forth by the democratic States of the region in October 1982 at San José, Costa Rica. Among those conditions in the so-called Final Act were an end to foreign support to terrorists and subversive elements operating for the violent overthrow of other countries; an end to arms trafficking; a limitation of all armaments and forces to those required for defence; the withdrawal of all foreign military advisers and troops under fully verifiable and reciprocal conditions; respect for human rights, including fundamental freedoms such as freedom of speech, assembly and religion and the right to organize political parties; and the establishment of democratic, representative institutions through free and regular elections.

The USSR said the facts demonstrated that armed intervention was being conducted against Nicaragua from Honduran territory and that the United States was the prime mover behind that intervention. The situation that had arisen in the area, it said, posed a threat to international peace and security. It recalled that a year earlier the United States had blocked the adoption of a draft resolution by which the Council, according to the USSR, would have condemned intervention in the internal affairs of the States of Central America and called for a renunciation of the threat or use of force.[60] Thus, the United States had reserved its right to have recourse to armed force in its struggle against the Nicaraguan revolution. The USSR charged that the current invasion of Nicaragua by mercenaries, prepared and instigated by the United States, was a direct consequence of that policy. Moreover, it said it was not talking about an isolated operation against Nicaragua, but the overall policy of the United States of stepping up international tension and escalating threats to independent States in various parts of the world—actions aimed at non-aligned and other developing countries which pursued an independent foreign and domestic policy.

A number of countries expressed fear that the conflict might spread to other States in the region.

Colombia said it was concerned that the region might become the stage for international confrontation. The United Republic of Tanzania appealed to all parties to refrain from further action which could only intensify the conflict in the region. Referring to the rapidly and dangerously deteriorating situation in the Central American and Caribbean regions in particular and in Latin America in general, Zimbabwe said that the least the Council could do was to tell all concerned that interference in Nicaragua's affairs was a grave violation of the United Nations Charter.

Barbados stated that, if only the right formula were discovered, there would be a first-rate opportunity to nip in the bud a situation which, if allowed to escalate, promised almost unlimited tragedy for the immediate region and possibly beyond. Brazil emphasized that there was still time to reverse the escalation of violence in Central America and that the resolution of the current conflict had to follow the path of moderation, constructive dialogue and political understanding.

The crisis was traced by several countries to the interventionist policies of a super-Power.

China said an important cause of the current tension around Nicaragua and the deteriorating situation in the whole of Central America lay in the intervention by a super-Power. Jordan said countries must avoid cold-war policies, promote détente and cease using small States to implement their policies. Guatemala said the problems of armed struggle in Central America were the result of foreign interference, and expressed its desire to take part in a meeting of Central American Foreign Ministers to seek a solution.

According to the Libyan Arab Jamahiriya, Nicaragua and other countries were the victims of United States policy; that policy was supported by its military bases all over the world, which were used for provocation, aggression and intervention. Malta said that, as a small country suffering from the same confrontation-mania that seemed to be the hallmark of present-day super-Power rivalry, it sympathized with Nicaragua, and that the Central American region, like many other parts of the world, cried out for sustained economic and social progress and equally for a new spirit of dialogue, quiet diplomacy and regional initiatives.

Viet Nam said the deteriorating regional situation was due to the efforts of the United States to maintain or reinstate compliant dictatorships in that part of the world which it regarded as its own backyard. Democratic Yemen condemned the exertion by the United States of all kinds of pressure and aggressive acts against the people of Nicaragua. The Syrian Arab Republic called for an end to acts of aggression by the United States aimed at destabilizing the States of the region, particularly Nicaragua. Poland said that an escalation of actions by the United States, reflected in terrorist activities, hostile propaganda, acts of intimidation and the infiltration of foreign-trained mercenaries, was aimed at the destabilization of Nicaragua.

Mongolia contended that current acts of aggression by the United States against Nicaragua were part of its broader strategic aims in Central America and the Caribbean. The German Democratic Republic said the policy of the United States was directed against any progressive development in the area. Bulgaria stated that Nicaragua was the target of an armed attack, organized by United States imperialism, and appealed for its immediate cessation. Czechoslovakia said it had received the reports of the escalating aggression by the United States with deep concern as to its impact on international peace and security. Iran asked if it was not time to let oppressed peoples determine their destiny without inferference by the United States and its lackeys, or by other super-Powers.

Several States held that the dispute was the result of the process of change in developing countries.

Pakistan said attempts by outside parties to distort or thwart that process in the service of their own objectives was a familiar phenomenon of recent times. India observed that the principles of non-alignment laid down that every State had the right to pursue its own political and social system without any interference, and called for a peaceful solution to the conflict.

Yugoslavia declared that it was obvious that the causes of the conflict were to be found in the historical contradictions that affected Central America and the Caribbean as a whole, and that the longer social injustice and direct or indirect foreign domination existed the more exacerbated would be the conditions in which changes occurred.

Ghana recalled that the Movement of Non-Aligned Countries had been set up to help newly independent countries avoid being drawn into the ideological and military conflicts of the super-Powers; it saluted Nicaragua and wished it success in its struggle against poverty, disease and underdevelopment.

Hungary said that social injustice, inequality and poverty in Central America cried out for revolutionary changes, and that the dispute could only be solved by satisfying the demands of the people and putting an end to all outside interference.

Some countries supported the peace initiatives of the Contadora Group.

An increase in tension and a definite deterioration in the political climate in Central America were endangering international peace and security, Panama said. That was why Panama had joined other countries, in particular Colombia, Mexico and Venezuela, in an effort to bring about negotiations. Panama was confident that good judgement would prevail and that the course of negotiations would be followed. It was the only course that could ensure a peaceful and just future for the peoples of the region.

Bolivia, stating the need for respect for the principle of non-interference in the internal affairs of other countries, said it endorsed the Contadora proposals, as did Guyana, which added that it was dangerous, unrealistic and self-serving to seek to explain domestic impulses for change in Central America in terms of East-West confrontation.

Argentina recalled that on various occasions and in different forums it had expressed its agreement with certain peace initiatives, in particular the Mexican-Venezuelan proposal and that of the Contadora Foreign Ministers put forward on 9 January (see above). For more than two years, Mexico said, it had made constant efforts to promote détente and coexistence in Central America and the Caribbean; it again appealed urgently for direct negotiations between the Governments involved, with international participation, to avoid a conflict of grave proportions.

The Contadora initiative was hailed by Cuba as a genuine effort to find a just and lasting solution to the conflicts in the region. Ecuador said that it hoped the steps being taken by the Group would be successful, that the use of force and any foreign interference in Nicaragua would be prohibited, and that the peoples of Central America would be allowed to decide their destinies free of violence and pressure. Appealing for moderation, France said it supported the Contadora principles, particularly the condemnation of interference.

Discussions on a regional basis were urged by other States.

Costa Rica said that it had endeavoured to promote discussion at the regional level and that this was the proper time for such discussion. The Dominican Republic reaffirmed its support for an immediate meeting of all the parties involved in the dispute. El Salvador agreed, and said the situation in Central America did not bode well for stability and that foreign interests were directing ideological groups in support of their own military interests. Grenada said it was committed to the holding of meaningful dialogue at any time.

Peru said it was time every country committed itself to peace. Peru proposed, as a basis for the establishment of a dialogue, that countries undertake to avoid ideological and political polarization; exclude all interests foreign to the area; respect the principles and norms embodied in the United Nations Charter; by decision of the Security Council, bring about an immediate cessation of acts of hostility on the border between Honduras and Nicaragua, while the Council perhaps adopted other helpful measures; and agree to curb the arms race in the area. Mauritius said the way to a solution was through direct dialogue and regional co-operation, which the Council could sanction.

However, Venezuela said that peace in Central America could not be reached through the Council and that the interests of the super-Powers inhibited Council action. It declared that talks among the countries of the region without foreign interference were essential, and offered to assist in their commencement. Zaire said the Council should not decide the substance of the question, which could run the risk of further heightening tension; it should merely take note of the initiatives of the parties and encourage them to co-operate in seeking a solution.

Events currently taking place in Nicaragua underscored the need to seek solutions for the entire area, Spain said. The Netherlands said it attached special importance to the peace initiatives proposed by the countries in the region, adding that in its view OAS might be helpful in finding a solution. Belgium said it supported the peace initiatives made, in particular by the countries of the region, and opposed actions that could only poison a disquieting situation.

The Federal Republic of Germany said the problem was one for the whole region and it wished that Nicaragua was ready to discuss the issues at a regional conference. Italy agreed, adding it was clear that the countries of Central America were confronted with common problems requiring common solutions.

Uruguay noted that Nicaragua had referred to a bilateral dialogue with qualified witnesses, together with a regional dialogue also with qualified witnesses, and that Honduras had referred to a regional dialogue which could include bilateral aspects and to which there could also be qualified witnesses. It concluded that there remained the problem of defining more precisely the machinery and the procedures to be followed, as well as the order and the arrangement of topics.

The United Kingdom proposed that the Council consider asking the Secretary-General to use his good offices to bring about a dialogue on the bilateral and multilateral problems of Central America.

A satisfactory basis for the peaceful resolution of the problems affecting the area was to be found in the 1982 San José Final Act, the Philippines said.

Togo welcomed the statements of the parties with regard to their willingness to negotiate peace in the region. Cyprus said it could not but strongly condemn the resort to violence and intervention, as it too was a victim of aggression and continuing occupation.

Communications (April/May). In April and May 1983, Nicaragua and Honduras addressed a number of letters to the President of the Security Council, each complaining about further armed attacks against its territory.

On 4 April,[61] Nicaragua said that during the previous week counter-revolutionary forces had attempted further penetration of its territory from Honduras and that attacks by Honduran troops were increasing; it charged the United States with directing, supporting and financing these operations.

Notes of protest concerning armed attacks by counter-revolutionaries or Honduran forces were addressed by the Foreign Minister of Nicaragua to the Foreign Minister of Honduras. These charges were contained in notes dated 8 April (transmitted on 11 April),[62] 17 April (21 April),[63] 19 April (21 April),[64] 19 April (25 April),[65] 20 April (21 April),[66] 23 April (25 April),[67] 25 April (26 April),[68] and 27 April (28 April).[69]

The text of a protest note of 2 May from the Foreign Minister of Nicaragua to the Secretary of State of the United States was transmitted on the same date.[70] Nicaragua charged that on 30 April a force of approximately 1,200 mercenaries had invaded Nicaragua and that fighting had been continuing since then with units of the Honduran army providing direct support. It added that it held the United States and Honduras responsible for the consequences flowing from the aggressive policy pursued by the United States against Nicaragua and from its systematic rejection of Nicaragua's proposal for a bilateral dialogue.

A letter from Nicaragua of 9 May[71] enclosed extracts from a 4 May press conference by the United States President and a newspaper article published in *The Washington Post* on 8 May; Nicaragua stated that the President's revelations contained virtually a declaration of war against Nicaragua and the newspaper article revealed the scope of United States assistance to counter-revolutionaries.

Protest notes of 15, 19 and 20 April and 3 May from the Honduran Foreign Minister to his Nicaraguan counterpart were transmitted by Honduras on 15 April,[72] 20 April,[73] 21 April[74] and 4 May,[75] respectively. In them, Honduras charged that on 14 April two Nicaraguan patrol boats shelled two Honduran fishing vessels near the Babel and Media Luna keys in Honduran jurisdictional waters; protested the alleged harassment of a Honduran fishing vessel by a Nicaraguan patrol boat in Honduran territorial waters, which had led to an armed skirmish between Nicaraguan and Honduran patrol boats; charged that on 19 April regular troops of the Nicaraguan army had harassed Honduran communities in the border region; and rejected the allegations against Honduras contained in Nicaragua's note of 2 May to the United States[70] and asserted that the Honduran armed forces had complied strictly with their mandate to defend the territorial integrity of Honduras, despite the intention of contending forces in neighbouring countries to involve them in their internal struggles.

The Lao People's Democratic Republic, on 4 April,[76] transmitted a statement made on 29 March by the spokesman for its Foreign Ministry, strongly condemning alleged military provocations by the Honduran army, with the support of the United States, in the Nicaraguan-Honduran border area and calling on the United States to desist from all intervention in the internal affairs of the countries of Central America. By a letter of 13 May,[77] the German Democratic Republic declared its support for proposals made by Nicaragua, especially the assumption of a role of good offices of the Secretary-General according to a mandate of the Security Council, which could contribute to commencing a bilateral dialogue between Nicaragua and Honduras and between Nicaragua and the United States.

The question of negotiations was also discussed in several other letters. On 4 April,[78] Nicaragua reiterated its call for dialogue at the highest level with the Governments of Honduras and the United States, called on the countries of the Contadora Group to use their good offices to begin that dialogue, declared its support for the role of the Secretary-General and suggested that the dialogue take place at the United Nations. Responding on 8 April,[79] the United States expressed support for regional efforts, including those in OAS, to address the complex, interrelated and multilateral problems in Central America; it commented that the problems did not lend themselves to simple solutions on the basis of bilateral talks and urged members of the Security Council to support ongoing efforts aimed at achieving a regional solution. Also referring to the Nicaraguan letter, Honduras on 11 April[80] reiterated its commitment

first to exhaust regional efforts within the context of the inter-American system. In a letter of 13 April,[81] Nicaragua reaffirmed the right of a Member State to come before the Council for the consideration and settlement of disputes with other States, and stated that Nicaragua had brought its case before the Council under Articles 34 and 35 of the Charter and would continue to do so whenever necessary.

France said in a letter of 6 April[82] that it supported the proposal made in the Council on 29 March by the United Kingdom that the Secretary-General undertake a mission of good offices in Central America with the purpose of recommending a procedure for bringing about a meeting of the parties to the dispute. Replying on 11 April,[83] Honduras pointed out that action was pending with regard to OAS resolutions on its request that the Governments of Costa Rica, El Salvador, Guatemala, Honduras and Nicaragua should hold a meeting as soon as possible for the purpose of initiating a process of global and regional negotiations.

Nicaragua, in a letter of 19 April,[84] informed the Council that it would take part, beginning 20 April, in a round of negotiations with the Contadora Group Foreign Ministers.

SECURITY COUNCIL ACTION (May)

On 5 May,[85] Nicaragua requested an urgent meeting of the Security Council in view of what it said was a new stage of the invasion by counter-revolutionary forces operating out of Honduras and supported by the United States. The complaint was taken up by the Council at seven meetings between 9 and 19 May.

The following States were invited, at their request, to participate in the deliberations without the right to vote: Algeria, Argentina, Colombia, Congo, Costa Rica, Cuba, Dominican Republic, El Salvador, Ethiopia, Greece, Grenada, Guatemala, Honduras, India, Iran, Lao People's Democratic Republic, Libyan Arab Jamahiriya, Mali, Mauritius, Mexico, Panama, Sao Tome and Principe, Seychelles, Spain, Syrian Arab Republic, Uganda, Venezuela, Viet Nam, Yugoslavia.

At the request of Zimbabwe in a letter of 16 May,[86] the Council also extended an invitation under rule 39 of its provisional rules of procedure[a] to the Pan Africanist Congress of Azania.

Opening the debate, Nicaragua said the aggression against it was increasing, and it had come before the Council to appeal for respect for the prin-

---

[a]Rule 39 of the Council's provisional rules of procedure states: "The Security Council may invite members of the Secretariat or other persons, whom it considers competent for the purpose, to supply it with information or to give other assistance in examining matters within its competence."

ciple of non-intervention in the internal affairs of sovereign States. Its declaration that the United States was waging a war against Nicaragua was not a figure of speech, it said, and the war was no less real because it had not been declared. Fearing a loss of credibility, the United States was shielding itself by neither confirming nor denying covert actions. Nicaragua warned that the danger of regionalizing the war was increasing because the United States used some States and affected the neutrality of others in order to attack Nicaragua. It said it would continue to work to strengthen the initiative of the Contadora Group. It appealed to the United States to direct its influence towards negotiated solutions, and reiterated its willingness to hold an immediate, unconditional dialogue with that country in order to find solutions.

Honduras said that once again Nicaragua had given distorted information which, if not analysed correctly, might jeopardize the Council's task. In 1979, upon assuming power, the Sandinist Front of National Liberation had pledged before OAS that it would respect human rights in Nicaragua, promote civil justice and hold free elections. Those promises had become mere words and the people of Nicaragua were suffering under a totalitarian Government maintained by force. To the Nicaraguan Government, OAS was no longer the proper body to deal with differences between nations; Nicaragua was avoiding regional discussions. Honduras pointed out that Nicaragua had not presented any clear evidence to prove its allegations of participation by the Honduran army in acts of aggression. On the other hand, it said, Nicaragua was carrying out an interventionist policy in neighbouring States by promoting traffic in weapons. The problems of Nicaragua were basically internal problems, Honduras said, and were arising from the growing opposition of the Nicaraguan people to the régime. Honduras said it should be noted that Honduras and Nicaragua had agreed not to take steps in the United Nations while the Contadora Group was carrying out its initiative. That agreement had been violated by Nicaragua. Honduras urged the Council to recommend that the Foreign Ministers of Costa Rica, El Salvador, Guatemala, Honduras and Nicaragua, with the participation of other Latin American countries, meet for a dialogue to cover regional problems and reach a solution.

The United States, citing Nicaragua's invocation of the principle of non-intervention, said that, since its current leaders came to power, they had fomented war in the region, destroying the peace in El Salvador, Honduras and other neighbouring States. The United States did not invade small countries on its borders and there was no United States invasion of Nicaragua. There was fighting in Nicaragua, but the problem was not international; Nicaraguans were fighting among themselves for control of their country's destiny. Nicaragua had made a non-substantive response to an eight-point peace proposal offered by the United States in 1982; the proposal had called for an end to Nicaraguan support for guerrillas in neighbouring countries, limits on arms and foreign military advisers, a joint pledge of non-intervention, arms-limit verification measures, resumption of United States economic assistance, implementation of cultural exchange programmes, and the reaffirmation of Nicaraguan commitments to pluralism, free elections and a mixed economy. Nicaragua's insistence on bilateral rather than multilateral talks underlined its desire to resolve its external problems while avoiding the issue of its export of revolution, war and misery, the United States added.

The USSR reiterated that the facts showed that armed intervention against Nicaragua was under way, directed and financed by the United States. Further, the United States had virtually admitted the charges made against it. Although it had stated its preparedness to negotiate with Nicaragua, the United States had put forward pre-conditions to negotiations known to be unacceptable, for example, the demand made of Nicaragua that it confirm its commitment to so-called pluralism and a mixed economy, the USSR added; it was the duty of the Council to follow closely the situation in Nicaragua and to take all necessary measures to safeguard its security and integrity.

A number of countries supported the peace efforts of the Contadora Group, including Argentina, Colombia, Costa Rica, the Dominican Republic, Greece, Guatemala, India, Mali, Spain, Venezuela and Yugoslavia. Argentina felt that the deep-rooted causes of the crisis lay in both the anachronistic political and socio-economic situations and the persistent violations of the principle of non-interference in States' internal affairs; it said the Contadora Group deserved unreserved support. Colombia urged Nicaragua and Honduras to conduct negotiations, using the Contadora framework, and added that to avoid a worsening of the situation the Group had tried to bring all the countries of the region to the bargaining table. Costa Rica said the Council should not weaken regional or subregional mechanisms, and should leave the peace initiative in the hands of the Contadora Foreign Ministers.

Speaking similarly, Guatemala added that the intervention of other countries or organizations could only be counter-productive. Spain said that the Central American crisis was closely related to the processes of change in the region, which stemmed from social and economic imbalances, and that it hoped the Group would find a solution.

Venezuela said that, although it was ready to continue to take part actively in the Group's peace initiatives, it had decided not to take a position on the draft resolution before the Council (see below), which involved matters under discussion and might affect the Group's mediation function.

Several other countries supported the efforts of the Contadora Group, while urging that the Secretary-General also use his good offices to try to achieve a solution. Among them were the Congo, Grenada, the Lao People's Democratic Republic, Mexico, Sao Tome and Principe, the Syrian Arab Republic and Zimbabwe.

Some countries, including China, Cuba, Ethiopia, Grenada, Iran, the Libyan Arab Jamahiriya, Seychelles, Togo, the USSR and Viet Nam, referred to foreign interference in the region and said it was making a solution more difficult to achieve. China opposed any outside interference whatever. Cuba said the United States was using the same weapons against Nicaragua as it used against Cuba—economic aggression, a blockade of international sources of credit, and mercenary bands financed by the CIA; Cuba supported any effort to reach a negotiated solution. Grenada said that it did not comprehend the historic opposition of the United States to any attempts by the peoples of Latin America to liberate themselves, and that real democracy could not be predicated on an imperial creed. The Libyan Arab Jamahiriya said there was no East-West conflict in Central America—the conflict was between United States imperialism and the peoples of the world. Seychelles warned that the current foreign interference from Honduras could lead to a major military confrontation. Togo said the Nicaraguan situation was complicated by rivalries among the great Powers, each of which believed the other was trying to expand its influence in the region and was taking steps to oppose that expansion.

Whether the Security Council should have a role in attempting to settle the crisis was discussed by El Salvador, Panama, Poland and Uganda.

El Salvador felt that the Council was not the appropriate forum in which to try to resolve the situation, that regional problems should be resolved in a regional framework, and that any attempt to compartmentalize interrelated problems with a bilateral approach would distort the region's political reality. The Council had sufficient grounds for taking a decision on the problem, Panama declared, and the seriousness of the situation called for one. Poland said it was essential that the Council act, since the situation constituted a dangerous threat to regional and international security. Uganda said it hoped that the Council would not leave the Contadora Group to carry out alone the task of evolving a viable framework for peace; the responsibility for the maintenance of international peace and security rested primarily with the Council.

The United Kingdom hoped that the Central American nations would be able to discuss their problems in multilateral talks. It observed that there had never been a multilateral international meeting at which bilateral discussions had not taken place on the side. It recalled that Colombia had spoken of bringing all the countries of the region to the table and seeking global solutions, while being in no way opposed to bilateral negotiations. If the region's countries agreed that they were ready for multilateral talks, but found difficulty in agreeing on certain modalities, it might be reasonable to ask the Secretary-General to sort out the modalities, the United Kingdom added. Multilateral talks also were backed by Guatemala.

On 19 May, the Security Council unanimously adopted resolution 530(1983).

The Security Council,

Having heard the statements of the Minister for External Relations of the Republic of Nicaragua,

Having also heard the statements of the representatives of various States Members of the United Nations in the course of the debate,

Deeply concerned, on the one hand, at the situation prevailing on and inside the northern border of Nicaragua and, on the other hand, at the consequent danger of a military confrontation between Honduras and Nicaragua, which could further aggravate the existing critical situation in Central America,

Recalling all the relevant principles of the Charter of the United Nations, particularly the obligation of States to settle their disputes exclusively by peaceful means, not to resort to the threat or use of force and to respect the self-determination of peoples and the sovereign independence of all States,

Noting the widespread desire expressed by the States concerned to achieve solutions to the differences between them,

Commending the appeal of the Contadora Group of countries, Colombia, Mexico, Panama and Venezuela, in its 12 May 1983 communiqué, that the deliberations of the Council should strengthen the principles of self-determination and non-interference in the affairs of other States, the obligation not to allow the territory of a State to be used for committing acts of aggression against other States, the peaceful settlement of disputes and the prohibition of the threat or use of force to resolve conflict,

Considering the broad support expressed for the efforts of the Contadora Group to achieve solutions to the problems that affect Central American countries and to secure a stable and lasting peace in the region,

1. *Reaffirms* the right of Nicaragua and of all the other countries of the area to live in peace and security, free from outside interference;

2. *Commends* the efforts of the Contadora Group and urges the pursuit of those efforts;

3. *Appeals urgently* to the interested States to cooperate fully with the Contadora Group, through a frank

and constructive dialogue, so as to resolve their differences;

4. *Urges* the Contadora Group to spare no effort to find solutions to the problems of the region and to keep the Security Council informed of the results of these efforts;

5. *Requests* the Secretary-General to keep the Council informed of the development of the situation and of the implementation of the present resolution.

Security Council resolution 530(1983)

19 May 1983	Meeting 2437	Adopted unanimously

8-nation draft (S/15770), orally revised.
Sponsors: Guyana, Jordan, Malta, Nicaragua, Pakistan, Togo, Zaire, Zimbabwe.
Meeting numbers. SC 2431-2437.

Following the adoption of the resolution, Nicaragua said it had come before the Council to explain the serious consequences of the invasion of Nicaragua from Honduran territory by mercenaries directed and financed by the United States. It believed that the resolution was important and that, if taken into account, it should succeed in ending the invasion. Nicaragua said it wanted to have normal relations with the United States, but would never bow to pressure, threats or invasions. It hoped the United States would accept the dialogue that Nicaragua had always proposed.

The United States said its policies had been maligned and misrepresented by Nicaragua. It had responded, and stood by its response; when Nicaragua showed a willingness to fulfil its obligations and promises, there need be no further problems between it and the United States.

Honduras supported the efforts of the Council to find a peaceful solution; it urged Nicaragua to participate in the talks of the Contadora Group, and to understand the meaning of dialogue as an opportunity to listen to the other side's arguments and to adopt an attitude of wanting to reach an agreement. Honduras would never be the cause of a military confrontation between Honduras and Nicaragua.

France said that the countries of the region should themselves seek peaceful and negotiated solutions, and that any action should deal particularly with the causes of the problems of Central America, which were of an economic and social nature; everything should be done to prevent tensions from becoming an element of the East-West conflict.

Guyana said that, as the Council had an obligation to make an effective response to the situation, it would have preferred a more forthright and unequivocal response to the aggression against Nicaragua.

Communications (May-September). Between May and September, Nicaragua and Honduras addressed numerous letters to the Security Council President containing allegations of further armed attacks. The allegations were contained in protest notes addressed by the Foreign Minister of one country to the Foreign Minister of the other.

Nicaragua sent notes to Honduras, protesting against alleged acts of aggression by counter-revolutionary forces based in Honduras and expressing readiness to find a solution through bilateral talks, on 13 May (transmitted on 13 May),[87] 16 May (17 May),[88] and 23 May (24 May).[89]

Nicaragua, on 27 May,[90] conveyed the text of a note of 25 May, rejecting Honduran charges that Nicaraguan forces had violated Honduran territory on 24 May, attacked a vehicle between Trojes and Cifuentes, and left five Hondurans dead and one wounded.

On 31 May,[91] Honduras transmitted the text of a note dated 30 May, charging that Nicaraguan troops on 24 May had fired on a Honduran passenger vehicle travelling to Trojes and killed six civilians. Also on 31 May,[92] Panama transmitted information to the Secretary-General about a meeting (Panama City, 28-30 May) held by the Foreign Ministers of the Contadora Group with those of Costa Rica, El Salvador, Guatemala, Honduras and Nicaragua; the Ministers reviewed the regional situation and agreed that the Group's observer commission should continue to act as an advisory group on border problems.

Nicaragua, on 1 June,[93] transmitted the texts of notes of 31 May and 1 June, protesting the alleged harassment of Nicaraguan diplomats accredited to Honduras and rejecting charges by that country of violations of its territory by Nicaraguan forces. In two letters of 7 June,[94] Nicaragua conveyed notes dated 4 and 6 June, protesting the alleged participation on 2 and 5 June, respectively, by Honduran armed forces in attacks on Nicaraguan armed forces in Nicaragua.

Honduras, in two letters of 22 June,[95] submitted notes dated 14 and 21 June, protesting alleged attacks on 8 and 18 June, respectively, by the Nicaraguan army on Honduran territory.

Also on 22 June,[96] Honduras transmitted a press communiqué of 21 June, reporting the deaths of three United States journalists—Richard Cross, William McWhirter and Dial Torgerson—in Honduras when their car was hit by anti-tank grenades fired from Nicaraguan territory and the death of a Honduran civilian who was nearby. Another letter of the same date[97] forwarded the text of a Honduran note of 21 June to Nicaragua, protesting the attack in which the journalists and civilian were killed. Responding that day,[98] Nicaragua said that McWhirter was alive and in the United States, that the Honduran accusation was a pretext for a military attack on Nicaragua, and that it at no time had attacked Honduran territory. Nicaragua, also on 22 June,[99] transmitted a note dated 20 June, adding that it had confined itself to intercepting and expelling those who had invaded its territory.

On 1 July,[100] Honduras transmitted a note dated 30 June in which it said an investigation had shown that the deaths of Cross and Torgerson had been caused not by anti-tank grenades but by anti-tank and anti-personnel mines laid on the highway by Nicaraguan forces.

On 5 July,[101] Nicaragua conveyed a note of 30 June, rejecting Honduran notes dated 20, 21 and 24 June in which Honduras attributed several border incidents to Nicaragua, and, on the same date,[102] transmitted a note of 3 July, protesting against alleged attacks by the Honduran army and mercenaries on 25 and 26 June and 1 July. Nicaragua, on 21 July,[103] transmitted a note of 20 July, charging violations of its airspace on 19 July by aircraft coming from Honduran territory and an attack by two Honduran naval vessels on a Nicaraguan patrol boat on 20 July.

Honduras, on 25 July,[104] transmitted a note of 21 July, alleging that Nicaraguan army units had penetrated Honduran territory on 10 July at a place known as Munguía, in the municipality of Duyure, burning a house, and on 14 July through the El Carao sector, municipality of Concepción de María, causing the death of a civilian, and that a Nicaraguan patrol boat and two aircraft on 20 July had attacked a Honduran patrol boat, wounding a sailor. Nicaragua rejected these charges in a note of 28 July, transmitted on 1 August.[105]

Nicaragua transmitted on 17 August[106] a note dated 15 August, protesting against an alleged violation of its airspace by a Honduran air force plane on 14 August and charging an attack the same day on the frontier post of Las Manos by Honduran soldiers. Nicaragua forwarded on 1 September[107] a note dated 30 August, charging that counter-revolutionaries from Honduran territory had kidnapped from the village of Catarina on 28 August three Nicaraguan citizens, killing two of them, that an aircraft, coming from Honduran territory, flew over the towns of San José de Cusmapa and La Sabana on 29 August and that mercenaries attacked the frontier village of San Pedro de Potrero Grande on 30 August, killing two persons. Nicaragua transmitted on 9 September[108] a note of the same date, reporting that on 8 September a Nicaraguan naval craft came upon a Honduran fishing boat fishing illegally in Nicaraguan waters and, with the assistance of another Nicaraguan vessel, captured it; the note also stated that on the same date three Honduran vessels attacked two Nicaraguan boats in Nicaraguan territorial waters and that Honduran aircraft conducted threatening manoeuvres against the Nicaraguan vessels.

Honduras, on 12 September,[109] transmitted notes of 2 and 9 September, protesting against an alleged attack on 29 August by a Nicaraguan patrol on two Honduran fishermen and the seizure of one of them with his boat, and charging that on 6 September Nicaraguan soldiers had entered Honduran territory and taken 135 head of cattle and 40 horses from a farm.

Nicaragua, on 12 September,[110] transmitted a note of 10 September to the United States, protesting against a 9 September attack on the port of Corinto by two aircraft, originating from Honduras and dropping what it said were bombs made in the United States. A letter of 13 September[111] from Nicaragua annexed what it described as documentary proof that the pilots who allegedly had bombed Managua international airport on 8 September had been provided with facilities by the United States.

SECURITY COUNCIL CONSIDERATION (September)

On 12 September,[112] Nicaragua requested an urgent meeting of the Security Council to consider what it said was a new escalation of aggressive acts against it by counter-revolutionary forces trained and financed by the United States. The Council met on 13 September to consider Nicaragua's complaint.

Meeting number. SC 2477.

Nicaragua, the only speaker, said it was again resorting to the Council to alert the world to the escalation in aggression it had suffered during the preceeding few weeks. Stating that there had been hundreds of attacks and violations of its territory since the Council met to consider the question in May, Nicaragua summarized the incidents, which included bombing attacks and reconnaissance missions by aircraft originating from Honduran and Costa Rican airspace, and said they had led it to conclude that military actions were being staged against it from the north and south, co-ordinated by the CIA. It regretted that war continued to be at the heart of United States policy towards Central America and Nicaragua. Nicaragua observed that, as long as ultra-conservative sectors of the current United States Administration believed that its national interest was incompatible with the independence of the Central American republics, those sectors would pursue misguided policies and place peoples in grave danger. Nicaragua recalled that on 19 July it had put forward a six-point peace proposal[11] (see above), which the United States had described as a positive step; since then, however, there had been no further response.

The Council President announced that the Council would remain seized of the matter.

Communications (September-December). The President of the Security Council received numerous communications from Honduras and Nicaragua between September and December. Most of these transmitted notes which had been exchanged between their respective Foreign Ministers.

In a letter of 20 September,[113] referring to the Council meeting of 13 September, Honduras said Nicaraguan accounts of alleged reconnaissance flights by aircraft from Honduran airspace and of imaginary air-sea engagements between Honduran and Nicaraguan forces testified to a disorientation campaign, designed to give the idea that other Central American countries were intervening in Nicaragua's internal conflict.

Nicaragua transmitted notes of protest dated 26 September (transmitted on 26 September),[114] 4 October (5 October)[115] and 13 October (13 October)[116] from its Foreign Minister to that of Honduras concerning alleged attacks by mercenaries, supported by Honduran forces, on Nicaraguan territory. Nicaragua, on 5 October,[117] conveyed a note dated 4 October in which it reported the shooting down in the Los Cedros sector, north of Rio Blanco, of a twin-engine military plane allegedly carrying 4,000 pounds of supplies for the mercenaries, and, two days later,[118] transmitted a note of 6 October in which it said that, according to three surviving crew members, the plane had taken off from the Honduran base El Aguacate, which had been converted by the CIA into a jumping-off point for operations against Nicaragua. On 10 October,[119] transmitting a note of 7 October, Nicaragua alleged attacks on the latter date on the village of San Fernando and the sector of El Horno and reconnaissance in the sector of Guapinol by unidentified aircraft coming from Honduras. On 11 October,[120] Nicaragua transmitted a note of the same date from its Foreign Minister to the Secretary of State of the United States, charging that mercenaries on 10 October carrying out plans prepared by the CIA had sabotaged a 1.6-million-gallon oil tank in the port of Corinto, causing a fire.

Honduras, on 29 September,[121] rejected Nicaragua's 26 September charges of Honduran army support of attacks on Nicaragua. On 29 September[122] and 4 October,[123] Honduras transmitted notes of 28 and 30 September, respectively, alleging Nicaraguan attacks on Honduran territory on 26 September in the El Espino sector, on 18 September at the village of Tapalchi, on 19 September in the Trojes sector, and on 21 September in the village of Las Vegas. Honduras, by a letter of 18 October,[124] conveying a note of 11 October, rejected Nicaragua's 6 October charge that a twin-engine aircraft shot down in Nicaraguan territory had taken off from a Honduran base. On 20 October,[125] Honduras transmitted a note of 17 October, protesting against an alleged violation of its territorial waters on 15 October by six heavily armed Nicaraguan vessels. Also on 20 October,[126] Honduras forwarded a note of 18 October, charging that on 11 October a Nicaraguan aircraft bombed the village of La Ilaya and killed three persons.

Nicaragua charged in a 20 October note, transmitted on 21 October,[127] that on 18 October mercenaries coming from Honduran territory destroyed the village of Pantasma, killing 47 persons. On 24 October,[128] Nicaragua conveyed a note of 22 October alleging that the day before a high-speed launch coming from Honduras attacked the freighter *Anita*, the dock installations and the district of El Cocal at Puerto Cabezas, and killed one person. On 29 October,[129] Nicaragua transmitted a note of 28 October alleging that on that date Honduran armed forces attacked the observation post of Loma Portobanco in the Santo Tomás del Nance sector and that, in addition, two Nicaraguan coast-guard vessels in Nicaraguan territorial waters were attacked by four Honduran coastguard vessels.

On 2 November,[130] Nicaragua transmitted a note of 31 October protesting against an alleged 30 October attack by Honduran army personnel and mercenaries on the Nicaraguan frontier post of Murrupuchi as well as overflights by unidentified aircraft of the Momotombo geothermal station, the Puerto Corinto sector and the village of El Viejo. Also on 2 November,[131] Nicaragua transmitted a note of 1 November charging that on that date two Honduran patrol boats fired on two Nicaraguan coastguard vessels in Nicaraguan territorial waters.

On 3 November,[132] Nicaragua conveyed a note of 2 November charging that two Honduran coastguard vessels, escorted by a helicopter and protecting three high-speed launches manned by mercenaries, had attacked three Nicaraguan coastguard vessels in Nicaraguan territorial waters and that three aircraft coming from Honduras had penetrated Nicaraguan airspace, the first flying over Ojo de Agua, the second over Jalapa and Murrupuchi and the third towards Wiwilí.

In a letter of 7 November,[133] Nicaragua enclosed notes of 5 and 6 November concerning, respectively, a series of alleged violations of Nicaraguan airspace by aircraft coming from Honduras on 4 November and the seizing and burning of a Nicaraguan fishing boat in its territorial waters by the Honduran navy on 6 November. On 11 November,[134] Nicaragua annexed two notes dated 10 November; in the first, it denied the charges made in a note of 9 November (see below) that its army had attacked the village of La Guaruma on 4 November, and, in the second, it denounced alleged attacks by mercenaries on the border posts of El Kum and Wasla in which six persons were killed on 9 November.

By two letters of 14 November,[135] Nicaragua transmitted, respectively, a note of 11 November protesting against an alleged attack on the frontier post of Murrupuchi that morning by a combined force of Honduran soldiers and mercenaries, and a note of 12 November denying an attack on the Honduran customs post of Cifuentes by the Nicaraguan army on that same day. Also on 14 November,[136] Nicaragua conveyed a note of 12 November protesting the detention on 11 November by Honduran police of two members of the Nicaraguan Embassy in Honduras.

Nicaragua, in a letter of 15 November,[137] sent a note of the same date protesting against an alleged 14 November mortar attack by Honduran troops on the Murrupuchi frontier post. On 16 November,[138] Nicaragua transmitted a note of 15 November charging that a Honduran coastguard vessel on 13 November had attacked a Nicaraguan patrol boat in its territorial waters. On 22 November,[139] Nicaragua submitted a note of 21 November protesting alleged attacks the day before by mercenaries on its frontier posts of Murrupuchi and Santo Tomás del Norte. Nicaragua, on 24 November,[140] transmitted a note of 23 November protesting against the 22 November machine-gunning of three of its frontier posts by a helicopter, which it said came from Honduran territory. On 6 December,[141] Nicaragua conveyed a note of 5 December protesting three alleged Honduran sea and air attacks on 4 and 5 December on Nicaraguan coastguard and fishing vessels in which the captain of one of the fishing boats was killed. On 21 December,[142] Nicaragua transmitted a note of 20 December alleging that mercenaries had attacked the village of Francia-Sirper on the latter date, kidnapping most of the population.

Honduras, on 26 October,[143] transmitted a note of 24 October protesting against the alleged capture on 9 October by Nicaraguan forces of two Honduran citizens who were fishing off Guipo Island, in Honduran territorial waters, and the penetration on the same day by about 80 Nicaraguan soldiers, travelling in four motor boats, of Honduran territory in the district of Guapinol.

On 1 November,[144] Honduras conveyed a note of 30 October protesting an alleged attack on 28 October by two Nicaraguan patrol boats on two Honduran patrol boats in Honduran territorial waters. Honduras, on 2 November,[145] transmitted a letter of protest of 1 November charging that on the latter date two Nicaraguan patrol boats sailing in Honduran waters opened fire on two Honduran patrol vessels, which were obliged to return fire. On 4 November,[146] Honduras transmitted a note of 2 November in which it alleged that on 26 October eight mortar shells fired from Nicaraguan territory hit the village of Quebrada El Oro and that on 29 October a Nicaraguan army

patrol entered the village of El Crique de la Lodoza and kidnapped a citizen.

On 8 November,[147] Honduras transmitted a communication of 7 November alleging that on 2 November Nicaraguan troops burst into the village of Camalotal, firing shots and killing one person, and that on the same day there was an exchange of shots between three Honduran vessels and three Nicaraguan patrol boats in Honduran territorial waters.

Honduras, in two letters of 14 November,[148] transmitted notes of 9 and 11 November, protesting, respectively, against an alleged artillery attack on 4 November by the Nicaraguan army on the Honduran military outpost in the village of La Guaruma and against another alleged attack on 11 November by Nicaraguan forces on the Honduran customs post of Cifuentes.

On 15 November,[149] Honduras transmitted a note of 14 November in which it protested against an alleged violation on 13 November of its territorial waters by six Nicaraguan fishing vessels, one of which, heavily armed, exchanged fire with two Honduran patrol boats. Honduras, on 15 December,[150] conveyed a note of 12 December in which it said that the sea and air incidents of 4 and 5 December to which Nicaragua had referred[141] and which allegedly occurred in Nicaraguan territorial waters had actually taken place in Honduran waters and that Honduran naval and air force units had acted in self-defence.

On 23 December,[151] Honduras transmitted a note of the same date in which it rejected Nicaraguan charges of a 20 December attack by mercenaries on Francia-Sirper[142] as unfounded and said that more than 2,000 Miskito inhabitants of that village had escaped from Nicaraguan repression and fled to Honduras.

Nicaragua-United States relations

From March to November 1983, letters concerning relations between Nicaragua and the United States were sent to the President of the Security Council.

On 24 March,[152] Mongolia transmitted excerpts from a speech by the General Secretary of the Central Committee of the Mongolian People's Revolutionary Party at a 23 March friendship rally between that country and Nicaragua at Ulan Bator, Mongolia, and from a joint Mongolian-Nicaraguan communiqué of 24 March, stating that hostile acts by the United States against Nicaragua and other States of the region had intensified, demanding an end to those acts, and further stating that Nicaraguan proposals were a sound basis for settling problems in Central America and the Caribbean basin.

On 16 June,[153] Nicaragua transmitted a communiqué issued on 15 June after a visit by a

United States Ambassador-at-Large. According to the communiqué, the Ambassador denied the need for bilateral discussions and spoke of United States support for the steps being taken by the Contadora Group. Nicaragua said it found no basis for believing that the Ambassador's travels would be effective; rather, they seemed to form part of a propaganda campaign aimed at neutralizing the Contadora effort and favouring an aggressive approach.

On 16 November,[154] Nicaragua transmitted a communiqué issued after a meeting held the previous day with the United States Ambassador. Nicaragua informed him that, with the danger of larger-scale aggression, it was taking measures to guarantee the safety of all foreign citizens, including those of the United States.

Belize-Guatemala dispute

By a telegram of 7 June,[155] the Prime Minister of Belize transmitted to the Secretary-General a communication sent that day to the Foreign Minister of Guatemala, charging it with a violation of Belizean territory on 5 June when a Guatemalan civilian was murdered by gunmen who had crossed into Belize from Guatemala.

Responding by a letter to the President of the Security Council on 10 June,[156] Guatemala said it did not recognize the independence of Belize or the frontiers with it, and would not recognize them until a solution was found to the territorial dispute between Guatemala and the United Kingdom which, with Belize, had unilaterally fixed those frontiers; consequently, it regarded any incident occurring therein involving Guatemalans as falling under the jurisdiction of Guatemala. The incident might have been a common crime or a public disturbance, it added.

REFERENCES

[1]A/38/68. [2]A/38/106-S/15628. [3]S/15691. [4]A/38/164-S/15727. [5]S/15762. [6]A/38/303-S/15877. [7]A/38/324-S/15904. [8]A/38/321-S/15896. [9]A/38/322-S/15900. [10]S/15987. [11]S/15878 (A/38/308). [12]A/38/407-S/15982. [13]S/16208. [14]A/39/56-S/16231. [15]S/16006. [16]S/16021. [17]A/38/453-S/16011. [18]S/16041. [19]A/38/599. [20]S/15734. [21]S/16082. [22]A/38/535-S/16089. [23]A/38/242. [24]S/16065. [25]A/38/L.14. [26]A/38/693-S/16199. [27]E/CN.4/1984/3 (res. 1983/8). [28]S/15749. [29]A/C.1/38/10. [30]A/38/596-S/16173. [31]A/38/234 (S/15762). [32]A/38/256-S/15809. [33]S/15993. [34]S/16012. [35]S/16018. [36]S/16026. [37]S/16032. [38]S/16176. [39]S/16180. [40]S/16020. [41]S/15551. [42]S/15558. [43]S/15567. [44]S/15611. [45]S/15656. [46]S/15669. [47]S/15671. [48]S/15670. [49]S/15552. [50]S/15568. [51]S/15605. [52]S/15571 & Corr.1. [53]S/15606. [54]S/15710. [55]S/15613. [56]S/15711. [57]S/15662. [58]S/15661. [59]S/15651. [60]YUN 1982, p. 365. [61]S/15676. [62]S/15695. [63]S/15719. [64]S/15721. [65]S/15726. [66]S/15720. [67]S/15725. [68]S/15732. [69]S/15738. [70]S/15742. [71]S/15753. [72]S/15712. [73]S/15716. [74]S/15724. [75]S/15745. [76]S/15679. [77]S/15766. [78]S/15681. [79]S/15694. [80]S/15701. [81]S/15704. [82]S/15705. [83]S/15700. [84]S/15714. [85]S/15746. [86]S/15768. [87]S/15771. [88]S/15780. [89]S/15787. [90]S/15806. [91]S/15808. [92]A/38/256-S/15809. [93]S/15813. [94]S/15816 & S/15817. [95]S/15835 & S/15836. [96]S/15837. [97]S/15838. [98]S/15839. [99]S/15840. [100]S/15855. [101]S/15857. [102]S/15858. [103]S/15879. [104]S/15893. [105]S/15899. [106]S/15930. [107]S/15952. [108]S/15973. [109]S/15980. [110]S/15979. [111]S/15986. [112]S/15975. [113]S/15995. [114]S/16007. [115]S/16025. [116]S/16043. [117]S/16024. [118]S/16030. [119]S/16031. [120]S/16037. [121]S/16013. [122]S/16016. [123]S/16022. [124]S/16058. [125]S/16060. [126]S/16059. [127]S/16062. [128]S/16063. [129]S/16105. [130]S/16110. [131]S/16109. [132]S/16130. [133]S/16134. [134]S/16141. [135]S/16143 & S/16145. [136]S/16144. [137]S/16163. [138]S/16161. [139]S/16177. [140]S/16184. [141]S/16200. [142]S/16229. [143]S/16080. [144]S/16113. [145]S/16123. [146]S/16127. [147]S/16133. [148]S/16166 & S/16167. [149]S/16168. [150]S/16221. [151]S/16234. [152]S/15654. [153]S/15831. [154]S/16160. [155]S/15818. [156]S/15822.

Grenada situation

SECURITY COUNCIL CONSIDERATION

In October 1983, following a period of serious internal political unrest in Grenada, during which the Prime Minister, some members of the Cabinet and a number of civilians were killed, military forces from the United States and several Caribbean countries intervened.

At the request of Nicaragua, the Security Council considered the situation in Grenada at meetings held from 25 to 28 October; a draft resolution,[1] calling for the immediate withdrawal of foreign troops, was not adopted owing to the negative vote of a permanent Council member—the United States. However, this call was upheld by the General Assembly in November when it adopted resolution 38/7.

Meeting numbers. SC 2487, 2489, 2491.

In the early hours of 28 October, the Council voted on the draft resolution sponsored by Guyana, Nicaragua and Zimbabwe. The vote was 11 to 1, with 3 abstentions, as follows:

In favour: China, France, Guyana, Jordan, Malta, Netherlands, Nicaragua, Pakistan, Poland, USSR, Zimbabwe.
Against: United States.
Abstaining: Togo, United Kingdom, Zaire.

By the draft, the Council would have deplored the intervention as a violation of international law and the independence of Grenada; deplored the deaths of civilians caused by the invasion; called for the immediate withdrawal of the foreign troops; and requested the Secretary-General to report to the Council within 48 hours on the implementation of the resolution.

The Council met in response to a letter of 25 October from Nicaragua to the Council President, in which it requested an urgent meeting to consider the situation in Grenada.[2] On the same day, Nicaragua submitted a second letter with the same request,[3] and Grenada[4] and the Libyan Arab Jamahiriya[5] sent letters supporting it.

Several other letters were sent to the Council President on 25 October.

Saint Lucia[6] requested that the Council delay a decision on dealing with the Grenada situation, since OAS was to meet the next day to consider the same subject. Saint Lucia[7] also transmitted a statement by the Organization of Eastern Caribbean States (OECS) secretariat. OECS had met on 21 October to take up the situation arising out of the killing of the Grenadian Prime Minister and several Cabinet ministers. It feared that the situation would worsen. Moreover, it had been concerned that an extensive military buildup in Grenada had created a threat to OECS and neighbouring countries. Under the treaty establishing OECS, member Governments had decided to take action.

The United States[8] pointed out that OECS had called on several countries, including Barbados, Jamaica and the United States, to respond to a deteriorating situation in Grenada, which OECS deemed a threat to peace in the eastern Caribbean. United States forces were to work with OECS and the people of Grenada in "restoring government and order" and to evacuate those United States and other foreign nationals who wished to leave, and would remain only so long as their presence was required.

Belize[9] conveyed a statement from its Prime Minister stating that an emergency meeting of the heads of Government of the 12 Caribbean countries on 22 and 23 October in Trinidad and Tobago had agreed to suspend Grenada from the Caribbean Community (CARICOM), but that four countries—the Bahamas, Guyana, Trinidad and Tobago, and Belize itself—had opposed the call to invade Grenada.

The following States were invited, at their request, to participate in the deliberations of the Council without the right to vote: Afghanistan, Algeria, Angola, Antigua and Barbuda, Argentina, Barbados, Benin, Bolivia, Brazil, Bulgaria, Cape Verde, Chile, Colombia, Cuba, Czechoslovakia, Democratic Yemen, Dominica, the Dominican Republic, Ecuador, Egypt, Ethiopia, German Democratic Republic, Grenada, Guatemala, Guinea-Bissau, Hungary, India, Iran, Jamaica, Lao People's Democratic Republic, Libyan Arab Jamahiriya, Mexico, Mongolia, Mozambique, Nigeria, Peru, Saint Lucia, Saint Vincent and the Grenadines, Sao Tome and Principe, Seychelles, Singapore, Sri Lanka, Syrian Arab Republic, Trinidad and Tobago, United Republic of Tanzania, Venezuela, Viet Nam, Yugoslavia, Zambia.

At the request of Jordan in a letter dated 27 October,[10] the Council also extended an invitation under rule 39 of its provisional rules of procedure[b] to the League of Arab States.

A large majority of the countries taking part in the Council debate condemned the invasion as a violation of the United Nations Charter, under which States were obliged to refrain from the threat or use of force in their international relations. Those countries included: Afghanistan, Algeria, Angola, Argentina, Benin, Bolivia, Bulgaria, China, Colombia, Cuba, Czechoslovakia, Democratic Yemen, Ecuador, Ethiopia, France, German Democratic Republic, Grenada, Guinea-Bissau, Guyana, Hungary, India, Iran, Lao People's Democratic Republic, Libyan Arab Jamahiriya, Malta, Mexico, Mongolia, Mozambique, Netherlands, Nicaragua, Nigeria, Pakistan, Peru, Poland, Sao Tome and Principe, Seychelles, Syrian Arab Republic, USSR, United Republic of Tanzania, Viet Nam, Yugoslavia, Zambia, Zimbabwe.

Algeria said that an invasion undertaken for the purpose of re-establishing order or even democracy presented a frontal attack on the principle of non-intervention and non-interference, and opened the way to breaches of the peace of varying kinds which were completely uncontrollable. China termed the United States intervention an outright act of hegemonism. Once again the marines had struck to subdue a small, weak and developing country, Ethiopia said, the invasion being but the latest manifestation of the policy of domination and force followed by the current United States Administration.

In France's opinion, the justifications put forward for the intervention did not seem admissible; international law authorized intervention only in two eventualities—in response to a request from the legitimate authorities of a country, or upon a decision of the Security Council.

Grenada stated that its current situation was of an entirely internal and domestic nature, and that it had not threatened and was not threatening the use of force against any country. Furthermore, it contended that no danger to United States citizens existed in Grenada, that the OECS treaty provided no justification for the intervention, and that the Council must condemn what had taken place and call for the withdrawal of foreign forces from Grenada.

Speaking similarly, Guyana recalled that the 1970 Declaration on Principles of International Law concerning Friendly Relations and Co-operation among States in accordance with the Charter of the United Nations[11] proclaimed the principle that States should refrain in their international relations from the threat or use of force against the territorial integrity or political independence of any State. The Libyan Arab Jamahiriya

[b]See footnote a, p. 204.

said the United States had committed aggression against a small country and that this aggression must be condemned.

Mexico said the invasion totally lacked justification, and urged the Council to take measures to have foreign troops withdrawn immediately. Nicaragua said the United States by its invasion had violated several treaties and conventions to which it was a party. The Syrian Arab Republic expressed the view that the invasion of Grenada came as no surprise for, ever since Grenada chose a popular, progressive régime, the United States had made it known that it was trying to topple that régime.

The USSR observed that Grenada had for a long time been the object of United States threats, that the invasion violated international law and the Charter, and that, if the Council did not rebuff the aggression, no small nation not to the liking of the United States would find itself safe.

Yugoslavia felt it had to reject any use of force, interference, intervention and the suppression of the rights of peoples freely to decide on the manner of their development.

A number of countries, including Antigua and Barbuda, Barbados, Chile, Dominica, Jamaica, Saint Lucia, Saint Vincent and the Grenadines, and the United States, spoke in favour of the intervention.

Antigua and Barbuda declared that the state of affairs in Grenada had constituted a serious threat to the security and peace of the region, that the OECS countries would ensure that an interim Government was established to carry out free elections, and that, when this was done and the constitutional rights of the people had been restored, assistance would no longer be required and would be withdrawn. The action taken was perfectly legal, Barbados said; the Governor-General of Grenada had formally called on the members of OECS to come to aid it. Chile was certain that the invasion would not have occurred had it not been for an exaggerated arms buildup in Grenada, the establishment of a disproportionate naval and military infrastructure, and the presence of USSR and Cuban advisers and agents, constituting a threat to other nations in the area. The Prime Minister of Dominica said that OECS, Barbados, Jamaica and the United States had undertaken a pre-emptive defensive strike to remove a dangerous threat to peace and security in the area and to restore normalcy to Grenada.

The United States said that the murder of the Prime Minister of Grenada, five Cabinet ministers and 12 other political leaders had created one of the bloodiest struggles for power that the world had seen in some time. United States troops were involved in a joint action to protect its citizens, to facilitate the evacuation of those citizens who

wished to leave, to provide support for eastern Caribbean forces as they assisted Grenada in restoring order and establishing functioning governmental institutions, and to put an end to an acute threat to peace and security in the entire eastern Caribbean. The United States had responded to an urgent appeal by OECS for assistance, and believed that its support was justified and consistent with the United Nations Charter and that of OAS.

During the debate, several other countries presented their views of the situation. Brazil deplored the recourse to armed force, even though internal events in Grenada had provoked disquiet in neighbouring countries. The Dominican Republic agreed and also pointed out that it had suffered at various times the ignominy of occupation by foreign troops. Egypt remarked that experience in other regions—for example, in the Middle East—taught that the use of force and violence could not resolve problems, but only lead to perpetuating and exacerbating them. Guatemala said the main responsibility for what was happening in Grenada fell on those who sought to impose a Government without popular support, who prevented the holding of elections, and who propagated the principle of self-determination in order to extract a country from one sphere of economic influence and place it in another.

Although Barbados, Jamaica, the United States and the member States of OECS were its friends, Singapore found it could not condone the action in Grenada, because in the long run it undermined the moral and legal principles of the Charter. Trinidad and Tobago considered it most unfortunate that a solution involving the non-use of force proposed at the emergency meeting of CARICOM on 22 and 23 October was not pursued. Venezuela reiterated its commitment to the self-determination of peoples, and said therefore that it could not approve any form of intervention by foreign armed forces in the internal affairs of a State.

Three countries—Togo, the United Kingdom and Zaire—abstained in the vote on the resolution.

The United Kingdom said it did not support the military operation carried out in Grenada and had taken no part in it; that it could not, however, go along with a text that did not take adequate account of the concerns of OECS, Barbados, Jamaica and the United States; that it was grateful that the Governor-General of Grenada, the only remaining constitutional authority in the island, had survived the events of recent days; and that the common aim should be the emergence of a constitutional Grenadian Government freely elected by the Grenadian people.

Zaire pointed out that it had always condemned aggression and coups, whatever their origin. Unfortunately, by its passivity and even its division, the Council had sometimes rewarded force and violations of the Charter. Therefore, Zaire was happy that those who in the past had refused on fallacious pretexts to condemn aggression were now asking the Council to condemn it. Against this ambivalence, Zaire rejected aggression by those States which violated the Charter and by those which had divided the world into exclusive zones of influence.

On 27 October, the United States objected to the credentials of the Grenada representative, and requested the Council to seek a report from the Secretary-General on the question. He submitted a report on 31 October.[12] He said a communication dated 26 October had been received from the Governor-General of Grenada stating that no one was authorized to speak before the United Nations without his express permission; currently, he had given no such authorization. The Secretary-General had obtained oral confirmation by radio and had asked for written confirmation. Meanwhile, he would not understand the Governor-General's communication as removing the Permanent Representative from his post but as seeking to limit his authority. He would only be able to formulate an opinion as to who was authorized to speak on behalf of Grenada in the Council after the arrival of the letter which he had requested from the Governor-General.

GENERAL ASSEMBLY ACTION

In November, the General Assembly took up the situation in Grenada after Nicaragua had requested on 31 October[13] that the item be included in the agenda.

On 2 November, the Assembly adopted resolution 38/7 by a recorded vote.

The situation in Grenada

The General Assembly,

Considering the statements made before the Security Council in connection with the situation in Grenada,

Recalling the Declaration on Principles of International Law concerning Friendly Relations and Co-operation among States in accordance with the Charter of the United Nations,

Recalling also the Declaration on the Inadmissibility of Intervention and Interference in the Internal Affairs of States,

Reaffirming the sovereign and inalienable right of Grenada freely to determine its own political, economic and social system, and to develop its international relations without outside intervention, interference, subversion, coercion or threat in any form whatsoever,

Deeply deploring the events in Grenada which led to the killing of the Prime Minister, Mr. Maurice Bishop, and other prominent Grenadians,

Bearing in mind that, in accordance with Article 2, paragraph 4, of the Charter of the United Nations, all Member States are obliged to refrain in their interna-

tional relations from the threat or use of force against the territorial integrity or political independence of any State or in any other manner inconsistent with the principles of the Charter,

Gravely concerned at the military intervention taking place and determined to ensure a speedy return to normalcy in Grenada,

Conscious of the need for States to show consistent respect for the principles of the Charter,

1. *Deeply deplores* the armed intervention in Grenada, which constitutes a flagrant violation of international law and of the independence, sovereignty and territorial integrity of that State;

2. *Deplores* the death of innocent civilians resulting from the armed intervention;

3. *Calls upon* all States to show the strictest respect for the sovereignty, independence and territorial integrity of Grenada;

4. *Calls* for an immediate cessation of the armed intervention and the immediate withdrawal of the foreign troops from Grenada;

5. *Requests* that free elections be organized as rapidly as possible to enable the people of Grenada to choose its government democratically;

6. *Requests* the Secretary-General as a matter of urgency to assess the situation and to report back to the General Assembly within seventy-two hours.

General Assembly resolution 38/7

2 November 1983   Meeting 43   108-9-27 (recorded vote)

3-nation draft (A/38/L.8 & Add.1), amended by Belgium (A/38/L.9); agenda item 145.
Sponsors: Guyana, Nicaragua, Zimbabwe.
Meeting number. GA 38th session: plenary 43.

Recorded vote in Assembly as follows:

In favour: Afghanistan, Algeria, Angola, Argentina, Australia,[a] Austria, Bahamas, Bahrain, Bangladesh, Benin, Bhutan, Bolivia, Botswana, Brazil, Bulgaria, Burma, Burundi, Byelorussian SSR, Cape Verde, Chile, China, Colombia, Comoros, Congo, Costa Rica, Cuba, Cyprus, Czechoslovakia, Democratic Yemen, Denmark, Dominican Republic, Ecuador, Egypt, Ethiopia, Finland, France, German Democratic Republic, Ghana, Greece, Grenada, Guinea, Guinea-Bissau, Guyana, Hungary, Iceland, India, Indonesia, Iran, Iraq, Ireland, Italy, Jordan, Kuwait, Lao People's Democratic Republic, Lesotho, Libyan Arab Jamahiriya, Madagascar, Malaysia, Maldives, Mali, Malta, Mauritania, Mauritius, Mexico, Mongolia, Mozambique, Nepal, Netherlands, Nicaragua, Niger, Nigeria, Norway, Pakistan, Panama, Papua New Guinea, Peru, Poland, Portugal, Qatar, Romania, Sao Tome and Principe, Saudi Arabia, Seychelles, Sierra Leone, Singapore, Somalia, Spain, Sri Lanka, Suriname, Swaziland, Sweden, Syrian Arab Republic, Thailand, Trinidad and Tobago, Uganda, Ukrainian SSR, USSR, United Arab Emirates, United Republic of Tanzania, Upper Volta, Uruguay, Vanuatu, Venezuela, Viet Nam, Yemen, Yugoslavia, Zambia, Zimbabwe.

Against: Antigua and Barbuda, Barbados, Dominica, El Salvador, Israel, Jamaica, Saint Lucia, Saint Vincent and the Grenadines, United States.

Abstaining: Belgium, Belize, Canada, Central African Republic, Chad, Equatorial Guinea, Fiji, Gambia, Germany, Federal Republic of, Guatemala, Haiti, Honduras, Ivory Coast, Japan, Luxembourg, Malawi, New Zealand, Paraguay, Philippines, Samoa, Solomon Islands, Sudan, Togo, Turkey, United Kingdom, United Republic of Cameroon, Zaire.

[a]Later advised the Secretariat it had intended to abstain.

Before adoption of the text as a whole, an amendment by Belgium, adding paragraph 5, was adopted by a recorded vote of 71 to 23, with 41 abstentions.

At the request of the United States, a recorded vote on each operative paragraph was taken: paragraph 1 was adopted by 106 votes to 8, with 25 abstentions; paragraph 2 by 126 to 4, with 8 abstentions; paragraph 3 by 142 to none, with 1 abstention; paragraph 4 by 108 to 9, with 21 abstentions; and paragraph 6 by 122 to 3, with 14 abstentions.

A draft resolution,[14] submitted by the Bahamas and Trinidad and Tobago, was not pressed to a vote. By this draft, in addition to the calls for strict respect for the sovereignty, independence and territorial integrity of Grenada, the immediate withdrawal of foreign troops, and the holding of free elections at an early date, the Assembly would have regretted that force was used as a solution to the problem in Grenada; urged the immediate establishment of a broad-based civilian interim administration, pending elections, the deployment in Grenada of a security presence from members of CARICOM and the Commonwealth, and the setting up of a fact-finding mission which would report to the Secretary-General; called on Member States and the United Nations system to assist in the rehabilitation of Grenada and in the continuation of its social and economic development; requested Member States to co-operate in the above measures; and asked the Secretary-General to use his good offices to secure as a matter of urgency the implementation of the resolution.

Following the adoption of resolution 38/7, many States explained their votes. Several said they voted for the resolution out of respect for the fundamental principles of the Charter, international law, non-intervention and non-use of force. Those countries were Australia, Austria, Finland, Italy, Malaysia, Somalia, Sri Lanka, Sweden, Thailand and Uruguay.

Other States that voted for the resolution, including the Byelorussian SSR, Czechoslovakia, the German Democratic Republic and the USSR, emphasized that they opposed the intervention not only as a violation of international law and the Charter but as a reflection of the aggressive, dangerous, imperialistic policy being followed by the United States.

Cuba said that the vote might help to stop such acts of aggression.

In explanation of its negative vote, Antigua and Barbuda said that foreign forces had been present in Grenada and that the intervention had been carried out to rescue the people from their tyranny. Barbados did not consider its participation in the operation an act of aggression but a response to a request from the sole legal authority remaining in Grenada, the Governor-General, while El Salvador maintained that the root of the problem lay in the intervention by Cuba, the presence of hundreds of Cuban advisers, and the pursuit by Cuba of expansionist aims of an ideological nature. The United States said it was proud to have participated in the liberation of the people of Grenada and in the restoration of their sovereignty, their human rights and their rights to democratic government.

Explaining its abstention, Belgium reaffirmed its attachment to the rules laid down in the United Nations Charter, but said its vote had been influenced by the fact that debate on the draft had been arbitrarily terminated by the adoption, by a recorded vote of 60 to 54, with 24 abstentions, of a motion of closure, made by Democratic Yemen. Canada said the resolution had addressed itself in generally satisfactory form to what had happened but was deficient in regard to such priorities as the full re-establishment of constitutional government and the resumption of economic development in Grenada. The Philippines regretted the military action, but said it had been distressed by the lack of balance in the text and the absence of any mention of the other parties which by their subversive deeds had provoked the United States response.

Some countries explained their position on the Belgian amendment. The Ivory Coast, though supporting free elections, abstained because it felt the amendment did not change the essence of the draft. Albania said it had intended to vote in favour of the resolution as a whole, but in view of the amendment it had decided not to take part in the voting. The Congo said it had voted against the amendment because it seemed to endorse, in a veiled manner perhaps, an act of aggression and military occupation. India, the Upper Volta and Vanuatu indicated that they had voted in favour of the resolution but abstained on the amendment because the elections might be held before the withdrawal of the occupying troops; for a similar reason, the Syrian Arab Republic said it had voted against the amendment.

Report of the Secretary-General. In response to the Assembly's request, contained in resolution 38/7, the Secretary-General submitted a report dated 6 November following a 30-hour visit by Secretariat officials to Grenada.[15] The report pointed out that the most essential aspect of the situation in Grenada was the non-existence of any political machinery for performing the normal functions of government. The Governor-General had informed the Secretary-General's representative that, based on the 1973 Constitution of Grenada, he had decided to provide for an interim arrangement that would enable the country to administer its affairs pending the return to full constitutional government by way of general elections. According to the report, the OECS multinational force, drawn from seven Caribbean countries (Antigua and Barbuda, Barbados, Dominica, Jamaica, Saint Christopher and Nevis, Saint Lucia, and Saint Vincent and the Grenadines), numbered about 300, and the number of United States troops, which had reached 8,000, had been reduced to 5,000.

Grenada continued to maintain relations with Cuba, but the Governor-General had declared all its diplomatic personnel to be *personae non grata* and ordered them to leave Grenada within 24 hours.

The Cuban Government said that 784 Cuban nationals had been in Grenada before the intervention, most of them involved in the construction of an airport at Point Salines.

Communications (October/November). Numerous letters transmitting statements, communiqués, messages and notes on the Grenada situation were received by the President of the Security Council or the Secretary-General during October and November.

The leader of the Libyan Arab Jamahiriya, in a message dated 25 October,[16] stated that the intervention by the United States and reactionary Latin American States was a return to the era of barbarism. Nicaragua, in a communiqué of 25 October from its Ministry of External Relations,[17] condemned the United States invasion as a manifestation of imperial arrogance.

On 26 October,[18] Brazil transmitted a note of the same date deploring the recourse to armed force by some OECS members, the United States, Barbados and Jamaica, which violated the principle of non-intervention embodied in the United Nations and OAS Charters, even though Brazil understood that the internal situation in Grenada could provoke legitimate disquietude in neighbouring countries.

Also on 26 October,[19] India enclosed a statement issued that day by its Government declaring that the invasion of Grenada could not be justified and that it could only aggravate and perpetuate regional instability and conflict. The USSR transmitted on 26 October the text of a TASS statement of the same date[20] condemning the United States aggression against Grenada. Yugoslavia, by a government statement of 26 October, forwarded the same day,[21] said internal upheaval could not be the pretext for foreign, especially military, intervention.

On 27 October, the Democratic People's Republic of Korea transmitted a statement issued that day by its Ministry of Foreign Affairs denouncing the United States intervention in Grenada,[22] and Madagascar transmitted a message by its President dated 26 October condemning it.[23] The German Democratic Republic conveyed on 27 October[24] a statement by its Ministry of Foreign Affairs decrying the long-prepared plot and military action against Grenada. Suriname declared on 27 October[25] that Grenada was the victim of unprovoked armed aggression; it appealed to the international community to take measures to remedy the situation.

Benin, on 28 October,[26] transmitted the text of a statement issued the day before by its National Executive Council, demanding the unconditional withdrawal of the invading troops. Botswana annexed to a letter of 28 October[27] a press release issued on the same date by its Department of External Affairs registering its revulsion at the use

of force against Grenada. Also on 28 October,[28] Democratic Yemen transmitted a 26 October statement by its Ministery of Foreign Affairs condemning the aggression of the United States. Ethiopia annexed to a letter of 28 October[29] a press release issued on 26 October by its Ministry of Foreign Affairs, in which it condemned the action and said it would no doubt exacerbate the tense situation in the area.

Also on 28 October,[30] the Lao People's Democratic Republic transmitted a statement of 27 October by its Ministry of Foreign Affairs demanding the cessation of all acts of interference in Grenada's internal affairs.

India, on 28 October,[31] forwarded the text of a communiqué adopted by the Co-ordinating Bureau of the Non-Aligned Countries meeting in urgent session (New York, 26 and 28 October). The Bureau recalled that the heads of State or Government of non-aligned countries, at their seventh summit at New Delhi in March, had expressed their concern at the continuing colonialist policies in the Caribbean region, condemned the intervention in Grenada and urged the immediate withdrawal of all foreign forces.

On 31 October,[32] Kuwait forwarded a statement of 27 October by its Deputy Prime Minister, Minister for Foreign Affairs and Minister of Information, saying Kuwait found no legal grounds for the invasion of Grenada by the United States and other countries.

On 1 November,[33] Afghanistan transmitted a statement of 27 October in which it condemned the aggression against Grenada. In two letters of 1 November,[34] Venezuela transmitted communiqués dated 25 and 31 October in which it said, respectively, that it could not condone any form of foreign military intervention in the internal affairs of another State and that the presence of foreign armed units in an independent American State on the pretext of maintaining peace was altogether unacceptable.

Cuba, in a letter of 2 November,[35] annexed statements of 28 October and 1 November by its Ministry of External Relations. The first statement denied assertions by the United States that nearly 500 Cubans were fighting in the mountains of Grenada; it added that Cuban workers in Grenada had been building an airport for strictly civilian use. The second statement said that the International Committee of the Red Cross was encountering obstacles in arranging for the evacuation of Cuban dead and wounded from Grenada.

Also on 2 November,[36] Mozambique enclosed a communiqué dated 27 October, declaring that there would be peace in the Caribbean and Central America only when States in and outside the region, big or small, respected other States' independence, sovereignty and territorial integrity.

On 10 November,[37] Iran transmitted a communiqué issued by its Foreign Ministry on 27 October declaring that the United States had once again revealed its aggressive character and calling on the free peoples of the world to resist it.

On 30 November, the USSR complained of criminal acts against its diplomatic mission in Grenada (see LEGAL QUESTIONS, Chapter III).

REFERENCES

[1]S/16077/Rev.1. [2]S/16067. [3]S/16072. [4]S/16075. [5]S/16068. [6]S/16073. [7]S/16070. [8]S/16076. [9]S/16090. [10]S/16091. [11]YUN 1970, p. 789, GA res. 2625(XXV), annex, 24 Oct. 1970. [12]S/16100. [13]A/38/245. [14]A/38/L.10. [15]A/38/568. [16]S/16074. [17]S/16069. [18]S/16084. [19]S/16078. [20]A/38/536-S/16095. [21]S/16086. [22]S/16087. [23]S/16088. [24]S/16093. [25]S/16094. [26]S/16098. [27]S/16124. [28]S/16096. [29]S/16099 & Corr.1. [30]S/16097. [31]A/38/540-S/16103. [32]S/16107. [33]A/38/551-S/16114. [34]S/16111 & A/38/553-S/16116. [35]A/38/554-S/16115. [36]A/38/561-S/16121. [37]A/38/579.

American anniversaries

The General Assembly had decided in December 1982 to take up in 1983 an item on the observance of the quincentenary of the discovery of America.[1]

On 20 December 1983, the General Assembly, in adopting decision 38/456, decided to resume its thirty-eighth session, at a date to be announced, to consider several agenda items, including the observance of the quincentenary.

The Assembly, also in December 1982, had taken note of the decision of the Latin American Group to take measures to commemorate the two hundredth anniversary of the birth of Simón Bolívar on 24 July 1783.[2] Three communications were addressed to the Secretary-General in connection with the observance, each transmitting a Declaration issued at Caracas, Venezuela, on 24 July 1983.

On 2 August,[3] Venezuela transmitted the text of a Declaration made by the heads of State of Bolivia, Colombia, Ecuador, Peru and Venezuela, a representative of the President of Panama, and His Majesty King Juan Carlos I of Spain. Also on 2 August,[4] a "Manifesto to the Peoples of Latin America", examining such matters as Latin American unity, contemporary realities, integration efforts, solidarity, human rights, peace and violence, and democracy, freedom and pluralism, was issued by the Presidents of Bolivia, Colombia, Ecuador, Peru and Venezuela, and a representative of the President of Panama, and transmitted by their representatives to the United Nations. On 4 August,[5] Bolivia, Colombia, Ecuador, Peru and Venezuela conveyed a Declaration on Subregional Integration by their Presidents entitled "The fatherland that is ours: the Americas".

REFERENCES

[1]YUN 1982, p. 375, GA dec. 37/451, 21 Dec. 1982. [2]*Ibid.*, GA dec. 37/443, 20 Dec. 1982. [3]A/38/323. [4]A/38/325-S/15905. [5]A/38/329.

Chapter VII

Asia and the Pacific

Several areas of international tension in Asia and the Pacific occupied the attention of the United Nations during 1983.

The Security Council met in September to consider the shooting down by the USSR of a passenger aircraft belonging to the Republic of Korea; a draft resolution on the incident was not adopted owing to the negative vote of a permanent Council member, the USSR. (See also PART TWO, Chapter X.)

In Korea, the United Nations Command continued to monitor the 1953 Armistice Agreement between the Democratic People's Republic of Korea and the Republic of Korea.

The focus of attention in South-East Asia continued to be the situation in Kampuchea. In pursuance of its mandate to assist in seeking a settlement of that situation, the *Ad Hoc* Committee of the International Conference on Kampuchea sent two missions to five capitals and to Geneva for consultations, and the General Assembly, in October, restated its view of the principal components of a just and lasting solution.

In western Asia, the situation in and around Afghanistan continued to be dealt with by the Secretary-General and the General Assembly. The Secretary-General and his Personal Representative continued contacts with Afghanistan, Iran and Pakistan in a search for a political solution. The Assembly, in November, reiterated its call for an immediate foreign troop withdrawal from Afghanistan and the establishment of conditions to permit the Afghan people to exercise self-determination.

With respect to south-western Asia, the Iran-Iraq conflict, ongoing since 1980, was again taken up by the Security Council. Through its President, the Council in February 1983 called for an immediate cease-fire. In addition, in October, it called for an immediate cessation of all military attacks on civilian targets and of all hostilities in the Gulf region; it requested the Secretary-General to consult with the parties on ways to sustain and verify the cessation of hostilities, including the possible dispatch of United Nations observers.

Topics related to this chapter. Disarmament: zones of peace—Indian Ocean region and South-East Asia. Regional economic and social activities: Asia and the Pacific. Refugees and humanitarian assistance: East Asia; South Asia; Oceania; South-west Asia.

East Asia

Attack on Korean Air Lines aircraft

An incident involving the shooting down by the USSR of a civil airliner of Korean Air Lines (KAL) by a USSR military aircraft, with the loss of all 269 persons on board, was considered by the Security Council at six meetings between 2 and 12 September 1983.

Meeting numbers. SC: 2470-2474, 2476.

The Council convened at the urgent request of the Republic of Korea. The request was made by a letter of 1 September, circulated by the Council President in a note of the same date.[1] The letter reported that KAL flight 007, a Boeing 747 with 240 civilian passengers and a crew of 29, had been shot down by USSR fighter planes at about 1830 hours, Greenwich mean time, on 31 August; the flight was at the time *en route* from New York to Seoul, after refueling at Anchorage, Alaska. The letter strongly condemned what it called an unprovoked barbaric act by the USSR, in violation of basic norms of international law and practice in international civil aviation.

The passengers had included nationals from various States, as follows: United States, 47; China, 44; Japan, 28; Philippines, 15; Canada, 10; Thailand, 8; Australia, 4; India, 1; Sweden, 1; and United Kingdom, 1; and 13 Hong Kong residents.

In association with the Republic of Korea, similar requests for a Council meeting were made, also on 1 September, by the United States,[2] Canada[3] and Japan,[4] and on 2 September by Australia.[5]

The following States were invited, at their request, to participate in the deliberations without the right to vote: Australia, Bangladesh, Belgium, Bulgaria, Canada, Chad, Colombia, Costa Rica, Dominican Republic, Ecuador, Egypt, Fiji, German Democratic Republic, Federal Republic of Germany, Guatemala, Ireland, Italy, Ivory Coast, Japan, Kenya, Liberia, Libyan Arab Jamahiriya, Malaysia, New Zealand, Nigeria, Paraguay, Philippines, Portugal, Republic of Korea, Sierra Leone, Singapore, Spain, Sudan, Sweden, Thailand, Venezuela.

SECURITY COUNCIL CONSIDERATION

On 12 September 1983, at the conclusion of the discussion of the incident, the Security Council voted on a draft resolution[6] sponsored by 17 nations: Australia, Belgium, Canada, Colombia, Fiji, France, Federal Republic of Germany, Italy, Japan, Malaysia, Netherlands, New Zealand, Paraguay, Philippines, Thailand, United Kingdom, United States. The vote was 9 to 2, with 4 abstentions, as follows:

In favour: France, Jordan, Malta, Netherlands, Pakistan, Togo, United Kingdom, United States, Zaire.
Against: Poland, USSR.
Abstaining: China, Guyana, Nicaragua, Zimbabwe.

Owing to the negative vote of a permanent member, the USSR, the draft was not adopted.

By the operative provisions of the text, the Council would have deplored the destruction of the airliner and the tragic loss of civilian life; declared such use of armed force against international civil aviation incompatible with norms governing international behaviour and elementary considerations of humanity; urged compliance with the Convention on International Civil Aviation (Chicago, United States, 1944); and welcomed the decision to convene an urgent meeting of the Council of the International Civil Aviation Organization (ICAO) on the incident. The Security Council would have further urged all States to cooperate with ICAO to strengthen the safety of, and prevent the recurrence of the use of armed force against, international civil aviation, and to facilitate a full investigation of the tragedy, which it would have invited the Secretary-General to conduct and report on within 14 days.

Before its introduction by the Netherlands, the preambular part of the text had been revised to transpose two paragraphs so that the question of appropriate compensation followed, rather than preceded, the mention of a need for an explanation of the facts of the incident based on impartial investigation, and to add a paragraph on the importance of the principle of territorial integrity and the need for applying only internationally agreed procedures in response to airspace intrusions.

Before the vote, the USSR announced its intention to vote against the draft resolution. Having restated what it insisted were the facts surrounding the gross provocation against its sovereignty by United States ruling circles through the KAL aircraft (see below), the USSR asserted that the action to be taken by the Council in this instance should be the prohibition of the use of civil aircraft for intelligence purposes in violation of other countries' airspace.

China said it would abstain because of what it referred to as a serious dispute over certain aspects of the incident. Guyana wished the draft had given consideration to such questions as to how and why the aircraft had come to overfly USSR territory and whether it was exclusively civilian, as well as to the international community's concerns of the need for an impartial approach to the matter and for the truth, the acceptance of responsibility where it properly lay, and the need to reduce tension in super-Power relations and for universal respect for international law. Guyana felt that the draft prejudged the results of the investigation called for, which, to be truly impartial, should have no pre-set time-limit. After the vote, Zimbabwe said it was not satisfied that all the facts had been made known, and that factors not relevant to the incident had been brought to bear on the Council's deliberations.

France stated before the vote that, at the proposed ICAO Council meeting, it would put forward specific measures, including the mandatory requirement that military authorities alert civilian authorities on discovering a civil aircraft in a dangerous situation, speedy installation of compatible civil and military radio equipment, introduction of additional precautionary steps in interception procedures, and an amendment to the Chicago Convention containing a commitment to abstain from the use of force against civil aircraft, within the framework of the Charter of the United Nations. Recalling that, at a diplomatic conference at Rome, Italy, 10 years previously, it had proposed the measure regarding abstention of the use of such force—which had failed to obtain the required majority—France warned that, in the light of the recent air tragedy, those who might again refuse to adopt that rule would have to answer to public opinion.

Jordan said that its vote proceeded solely from the draft's humanitarian and technical aspects, explaining that it found it difficult to support those provisions which it perceived as containing elements beyond the issue at hand, a prejudgement of the proposed investigation, a moral condemnation and an ideological undertone of East-West rivalry. Malta's vote rested on assurances that its primary concern, the protection of civil aviation, would be assiduously pursued at the ICAO meeting.

At the 2 September meeting, the Republic of Korea stated that it was not possible for the USSR authorities to have confused KAL 007 with anything other than a civilian passenger plane; it had been clearly marked as such, flying a route the world knew to be one regularly travelled by KAL Boeing 747s. The shooting down was a criminal act which threatened the very foundation of international order in civil aviation and, if unpunished, could lead to its repetition. Accordingly, the Republic of Korea demanded from the USSR a full account of the incident; an apology and complete compensation for the loss of the aircraft and the persons on board; punishment for those directly responsible; a guarantee of unimpeded access to the crash site for ICAO, other international organizations and KAL, as well as for the Republic of Korea, to which any remains or aircraft debris that might be recovered should be returned; and specific guarantees by the USSR against repetition of its action.

The United States said that, according to irrefutable information available to it, the airliner had strayed into USSR airspace over the Kamchatka Peninsula, the Sea of Okhotsk and Sakhalin Island; it had been under constant tracking from 1600 hours, when it came to the attention of USSR radar personnel, until 1838 hours, when it disappeared from the radar screens—having been shot down at 1826 hours by a USSR pilot who reported that he had fired a missile, destroyed the target (with which he had made visual contact 14 minutes before) and was breaking away; the United States claimed that at least eight USSR fighter planes had reacted to the airliner at one time or another throughout the two-and-a-half-hour period.

The USSR asserted that convening the Council was unjustifiable and unnecessary. For its views on the incident, it quoted a 2 September statement by TASS (the official USSR news agency) to the effect that, on the night of 31 August/1 September, an unidentified plane had intruded into USSR airspace by up to 500 kilometres for more than two hours; it had been flying without navigational lights and had not reacted to radio signals from USSR ground dispatcher services, with which it had at no time tried to make contact; military aircraft ordered aloft had also repeatedly attempted contact by means of generally accepted signals in an effort to escort the plane to the nearest airfield—all of which had been ignored; following warning shots fired on its path over Sakhalin, the plane left USSR airspace and headed towards the Sea of Japan, disappearing from USSR radar screens 10 minutes later.

The USSR questioned why United States monitoring services and those of Japan—which evidently had had the flight under continuous observation—had neither tried to get the plane back to its assigned route nor alerted their USSR counterparts. In the light of these facts and of instances of deliberate violations of its airspace by the United States, the USSR said, it could not regard the intrusion of KAL 007 as other than planned, and part of a major United States intelligence operation. It accused that country of involving the Council in a provocative anti-Soviet spectacle to obtain another pretext to justify its policy aimed at thermonuclear world war.

On 6 September, the United States played a tape recording before the Council of what it claimed were communications between the USSR pilot who downed the airliner and his ground control. According to the United States, the recording established that the USSR had decided to shoot down the airliner, shot it down and then lied about it; that, contrary to USSR statements, the interceptor pilot had seen the airliner's navigation lights, reporting that fact to its ground control on three occasions, and had made no attempt either to communicate with the airliner or to signal it to land in accordance with accepted international practice.

On the same date, Japan said that in view of the regrettable USSR attitude—its failure to offer a satisfactory explanation of the incident, to respond to Japan's requests for co-operation in a search operation and its attempt to shift responsibility for the incident to others including Japan—it was making public a recording of the uncoded communications between the interceptor pilot and his ground control shortly before and after he had fired on the airliner, as recorded by Japan's Air Self-Defence Forces. The portion of the recording played back in the Council quoted the interceptor pilot as saying that the "target" was flashing its navigation lights; he had "fired"; and that the target had been destroyed. That piece of evidence, Japan said, demonstrated the truth of the matter. On 7 September, Japan explained that, because the visibility of its air traffic surveillance radar was limited to airspace over and around Japan, it had been impossible to ascertain that the KAL aircraft was off course.

In subsequent statements, the USSR cast doubt on the authenticity of the tape played by the United States and pointed to discrepancies in the translation from Russian. The USSR also expressed astonishment that no publicity had been given to recorded conversations between the KAL pilot and United States and Japanese navigational services, and stated that this fact indicated that these recordings either contained unpalatable material or were being doctored. It said that an investigation conducted by a USSR governmental commission established that the invasion of USSR airspace by KAL 007 was a carefully planned intelligence operation directed from the United States and Japan.

The facts as established by the commission, the USSR said, were that an unidentified aircraft had come within range of USSR radar stations precisely where United States RC-135 reconnaissance planes were regularly on duty and where one such plane had been observed, some two hours earlier, carrying out manoeuvres at an altitude of 8,000 metres in an area contiguous to the unidentified aircraft's entry point; about the same time three

United States warships were reported to have appeared close to USSR waters. Both planes merged on the radar screen for about 10 minutes, after which one set out towards Alaska and the other towards Petropavlovsk-Kamchatskiy.

At Kamchatka, the plane proceeded directly over the main USSR nuclear strategic base, failing in the process to reply to signals from USSR ground services and interceptor planes that were tracking it, but emitting short, co-ordinated signals characteristic of intelligence transmissions. The plane's behaviour became provocative as it flew over Sakhalin. Besides ignoring signals, it suddenly changed its course, speed and height, flying round extremely sensitive military installations in southern Sakhalin. Since it failed to respond even to four bursts of warning shells and tracer shots of up to 120 rounds, tried to escape and generally moved towards Vladivostok, the interceptors were ordered to abort the flight with missiles—an action fully in keeping with USSR State border regulations.

The USSR observed that the United States, rather than answer questions raised by the incident, was engaging in a noisy concern for human life and security of civil aviation to camouflage its deliberate use of a civil aircraft for intelligence purposes, in disregard for human lives and international law. Its intelligence operation having been stymied, the United States, according to plan, was turning the incident into a major political provocation against the USSR. Responsibility for the tragedy rested with the United States, the USSR insisted.

The 51 States which participated in the debate all expressed sorrow or regret over the heavy loss of life and extended their condolences and sympathy to the bereaved families. The majority voiced outrage at what they called the deliberate destruction of an unarmed, clearly identifiable civil aircraft and condemned the action, with some calling it murder, massacre or sheer lawlessness. Maintaining that no conceivable circumstance could justify such action, they invoked internationally agreed procedures governing airspace intrusions, whether intentional or not, such as those laid down by the 1944 Chicago Convention, to which the USSR was party. They called on the USSR for a full accounting of the circumstances surrounding the incident, for an immediate investigation by the Secretary-General and ICAO so that responsibilities might be determined, and for steps to be taken to improve regulations designed to ensure against similar incidents. Like the Republic of Korea, the majority sought punishment of those directly responsible for the shooting down of the aircraft and demanded compensation for the loss of life and property.

To impress on the USSR the gravity and determination with which it viewed the incident, Canada said it had announced its decision to suspend, for a period of 60 days, the right of the USSR airline,

Aeroflot, to use Canada's Montreal (Quebec) and Gander (Newfoundland) airports. Canada also reserved the right under international law to claim compensation for the loss of Canadian lives—as did the United Kingdom—and believed that the USSR should assist the bereaved families in such humanitarian ways as instituting a co-ordinated search for the victims' remains, organizing memorial services and providing the families with any information available.

In the view of Fiji and the Federal Republic of Germany, the right of a State to enforce respect for its airspace and sovereignty was limited by the principle of proportionality. Sharing that view were Belgium, Canada, Ecuador, Guatemala, the Philippines, Togo, the United States and Zaire, all of which considered the USSR action unjustifiably disproportionate to the cause. The United States said no conceivable assumption of peril posed by a single commercial airliner to USSR security could have justified the action. Similarly, Belgium commented that to accept that certain circumstances justified an action that had cost 269 lives would create a permanent insecurity in international civil aviation. Whatever a State's security requirements might be, Italy said, it was essential that they be fulfilled without endangering the lives of innocent, defenceless civilians.

Elementary considerations of humanity were invoked by the Federal Republic of Germany, Sweden and the United States, which added that, in the view of the International Court of Justice, those considerations were even more exacting in peace than in war. Sweden stated that, in interception of civil aircraft, respect for human life took precedence over protection of territory in times of peace. For Colombia and Zaire, the same held true even in times of conflict.

Sweden drew attention, however, to the well-known fact that the USSR had severe rules to protect its State boundaries, not precluding the use of force even against civilian aircraft—rules which, Sweden added, were not in accordance with generally accepted norms of international law. Singapore demanded that the USSR bring its rules into conformity with those governing international civil aviation.

Pakistan, along with Malaysia, pointed out that, in an age of extensive air travel, passenger safety should be guaranteed not only by technical and legal means but also by exercising compassion and forbearance and by avoiding drastic measures. Since airspace intrusions, especially by accident, could not be ruled out, resorting to irreversible acts of violence—which could have grave consequences—must be.

Egypt and Jordan felt that the current atmosphere of mutual distrust and suspicion and heightened tension could not be excluded from the circumstances leading to the tragedy. Nigeria saw the incident as a symptom of a deeper malaise in the international situation, observing that recently, the super-Powers had appeared to embark on a collision course, thereby endangering the very existence of mankind. The affair was an illustration of the danger of stockpiling deadly armaments, according to Liberia, which felt that the tendency of the two Powers to over-react when provoked should be checked. The Libyan Arab Jamahiriya, recalling that it had lost a civil aircraft under similar circumstances in 1973,[7] pointed to the risk of a recurrence of the tragedy which the use of reconnaissance planes in conjunction with civilian flights could cause. For Sierra Leone, the tragedy demonstrated the need for confidence-building measures to reduce international tension. The United Kingdom hoped that the appalling action by the USSR was not intended to signal its intentions towards international relations as a whole.

Australia believed that attempts by the USSR and others to deny the Republic of Korea its legitimate place in the international community and its rights under international law had contributed to the circumstances leading to the tragedy.

Several States—Costa Rica, the Dominican Republic, Sweden and Zaire—expressed concern over the consequences for détente and international peace and security. Jordan declared its lack of enthusiasm over what it said had become the internationalization of the incident, thus making it part of the East-West cold war. Singapore appealed to the USSR and others not to turn the tragedy into a new bout of such confrontation.

Spain voiced hope that efforts in various forums to achieve détente would continue despite the incident. Instead of using it for casting aspersions on a specific party, the international community should ensure the safety of international aviation, the Libyan Arab Jamahiriya advised. If current Council meetings led to the assurance of such safety, to a restoration of trust and to détente, the sacrifice of life would not have been completely in vain, Colombia said. Paraguay expressed a similar sentiment.

Bulgaria, the German Democratic Republic and Poland were emphatic in stating that, if anyone was responsible for the tragedy, it was the United States. That country, they asserted, had orchestrated the tragedy with cold-blooded calculation, sacrificing innocent lives for political ends, and was currently exploiting the incident for an inflammatory anti-USSR campaign, aimed at exacerbating international tensions and justifying the escalation of United States military build up.

Bulgaria said it could not but conclude that KAL 007 had been deliberately used for intelligence activities over USSR territory of high strategic importance, given the exclusion by *The New*

York Times of 3 September of the possibility of navigational malfunction, the aircraft's unresponsiveness to warnings, and the failure of those who knew of its intrusion to alert it or the USSR. The German Democratic Republic said it was clear why those who had asked the Council to convene failed to explain how an aircraft with the most sophisticated navigational facilities could have deviated so unacceptably from its course and had not reacted to signals; the aircraft's behaviour, the German Democratic Republic asserted, was part of its spying orders.

Like the USSR, Poland doubted the authenticity of the tape played by the United States. No proof had been given of its connection to the incident and only a small portion of the information allegedly monitored had been provided; that information in no way confirmed that the USSR pilot knew KAL 007 was a civilian aircraft, for at no time did he describe it as such. Poland asked why, if the USSR pilot had seen the KAL plane, as the United States claimed, might one not assume that that plane had also seen the USSR pilot and wonder why the KAL plane did not then respond according to generally accepted rules.

The presence of a United States spy plane flying parallel to KAL 007 had had a direct bearing on the incident, Bulgaria stated. In the opinion of the German Democratic Republic, the current Council meeting should contribute to halting United States provocative military manoeuvres along the borders of sovereign States and so cease exposing civil aviation to danger.

Poland urged those who sincerely regretted the incident to do their utmost to create conditions to prevent its repetition and refrain from using the tragedy for the further deterioration of the international atmosphere and from creating even more serious consequences. It hoped that emotions would calm down and sober minds prevail, and that even in the United States a higher concern for peace would prevail over primitive anti-communist and narrow imperialist interests.

Communications. In the course of the Security Council meetings, a number of communications transmitting the official statements of their Governments or stating their position on the incident were addressed to the Council President—or to the Secretary-General requesting their communication to the President—for circulation: from Chile[8] and Thailand[9] on 2 September; Greece[10] and Tunisia[11] on 6 September; Jamaica[12] and Malawi[13] on 7 September; Barbados,[14] India[15] and Indonesia[16] on 8 September; Austria,[17] Belize,[18] Brazil[19] and Nepal[20] on 9 September; and Canada[21] on 13 September. The communications generally reflected the majority position in the Council debate. The letter from Thailand included a call on the USSR to conduct an immediate search for possible survivors. Those from Austria and India stated that, in an atmosphere of international tension charged with mistrust, there was an ever-present risk of error leading to calamity and hence urged the international community to address itself to eliminating the causes of mistrust.

In addition, Japan transmitted on 7 September[22] a statement issued the same day by its Ministry of Foreign Affairs, rebutting the USSR charges that Japanese air traffic controllers, aware that KAL 007 was inside USSR airspace, did nothing to warn or stop the flight. According to the statement, the full radio exchange between the aircraft and Tokyo International Air Control at Narita showed that no warning was possible: no sooner had the air controllers realized the aircraft's identity than it had been shot down. Japan demanded a retraction of the charges, which it concluded were not only groundless but also an attempt to shift part of the blame onto Japan.

Mongolia, by a letter of 9 September,[23] considered it absurd that the USSR should be held responsible for the incident, since it had acted solely to ensure the security of its borders; Mongolia blamed the United States for sending the aircraft into USSR airspace for intelligence purposes and charged the Western press with exploiting the incident for an anti-USSR campaign.

On 16 September,[24] Israel, condemning the downing of the aircraft as wanton and brutal, recalled that an El-Al Israel airliner had experienced a similar fate in 1955 at the hands of Bulgarian Security Forces with the loss of 58 people on board; it also stated that, at the Council meeting of 6 September 1983, the Libyan Arab Jamahiriya had introduced a matter extraneous to the Council's agenda, the correct presentation of which could be found in Israel's March 1973 letter.[7] Responding on 21 September,[25] the Libyan Arab Jamahiriya noted the "Zionist" entity's failure to mention that the extraneous matter was its downing of a Libyan passenger airliner in 1973,[7] causing 108 deaths. On 27 September 1983,[26] in transmitting excerpts of its 1973 letter, Israel said it was astonished that there should have been circulated, as a United Nations document, a letter in which Israel was referred to by other than its official name and requested that, in future, proper caution be exercised in this regard.

Korean question

During 1983, the President of the Security Council received and circulated to the Council several communications from the Democratic People's Republic of Korea and the Republic of Korea concerning military operations in the Korean peninsula. He also received a report of the United

Nations Command concerning maintenance of the 1953 Korean Armistice Agreement.[27]

Communications. By a letter of 8 February 1983,[28] the Democratic People's Republic of Korea transmitted a communiqué of the Supreme Command of the Korean People's Army (KPA) protesting "Team Spirit 83", a joint military exercise that was being conducted by the United States and the Republic of Korea on the Korean peninsula. Denouncing it as an open military provocation and a grave threat to peace in Asia and the world, the communiqué added that the Supreme Command had issued a war alert for the duration of the exercise. Claiming this to be a gross distortion of the facts, the Republic of Korea, in a letter of 11 February,[29] noted that not only had such an exercise been held yearly since 1976 but that prior notification had been provided to the Democratic People's Republic on 15 December 1982, followed by an invitation to send observers, which was quickly rejected.

By a letter of 19 May 1983,[30] the Democratic People's Republic of Korea transmitted a 21 April memorandum from its Ministry of Foreign Affairs, charging the United States with forming a tripartite military alliance with the Republic of Korea and Japan, thereby further aggravating the situation in the Korean peninsula and the Asian region. Replying by a letter of 9 June,[31] the Republic of Korea described the memorandum as replete with distortions and falsehoods; it denied the existence of the so-called tripartite alliance, saying the allegation was a further instance in which the Democratic People's Republic had burdened the Council with propaganda, and reiterated that inter-Korean dialogue was the only practical means of achieving the peaceful unification of Korea.

By a letter of 16 May,[32] the Democratic People's Republic of Korea accused the United States of planning to deploy neutron bombs on the Korean peninsula—quoting *The Washington Post* of 2 May in support of its contention—and converting the Republic of Korea into a nuclear base, in violation of the 1953 Armistice Agreement and international law. That allegation was based on mere speculation, the Republic of Korea said in a letter of 23 May,[33] charging that this latest propaganda manoeuvre was designed to conceal an invasion planned against the Republic of Korea, as reported by two military officers who had defected from the Democratic People's Republic.

Report of the United Nations Command. A report of the United Nations Command concerning maintenance of the 1953 Korean Armistice Agreement between 17 December 1981 and 31 December 1982 was submitted by a letter of 20 April 1983 from the United States,[34] on behalf of the unified command established pursuant to a 1950 Security Council resolution.[35]

The report stated that the KPA/Chinese People's Volunteers side continued to conduct hostile acts against the Command and the Republic of Korea, totalling more than 11,800 violations of the Agreement. An appendix gave details of two 1982 incidents submitted by the Command to the Military Armistice Commission. One was described as occurring on 21 April, in which two guardposts north of the military demarcation line simultaneously opened fire on a guardpost south of it, resulting in one of the most intense fire exchanges across the line in recent years; about an hour later, 15 armed KPA soldiers were observed some 300 metres south of the line. The other incident took place on 15 May: two armed KPA infiltrators, who apparently came in by sea, approached to within 10 metres of a Command observation post; in the ensuing exchange of fire, one of the infiltrators was killed; his body was returned, on request, on 18 May.

The report also stated that Joseph T. White, a private first class (Pfc.) in the Command's military police force, had crossed over north of the demarcation line on 28 August. Repeated requests for an interview with him or for a telephone link with his family in the United States were denied by KPA, which said that he had defected and insisted that the matter not be brought up again.

In June, the Command informed the Democratic People's Republic of Korea that the Commission would periodically call meetings for the sole purpose of negotiating specific tension-reducing measures. The Democratic People's Republic had yet to respond positively to that initiative and to others that had been repeatedly put forward. The report concluded that, for most of the reporting period, KPA had used the Commission to dispense distorted political propaganda; namely, that tension was caused by the United States and the Republic of Korea and that, to remove the tension, United States forces should be withdrawn and the Agreement replaced by a peace treaty.

The Democratic People's Republic of Korea, by a letter of 7 July,[36] described the report as full of fabrications and as slanderous with respect to Pfc. White, maintaining that the Commission was not the forum for arranging contact with him—a matter which was for him alone to decide. The letter reiterated that it was the United States that aggravated tensions in the Korean peninsula, with its provocative military exercises, its reconnaissance flights which regularly violated the airspace of the Democratic People's Republic and other hostile acts.

REFERENCES

[1]S/15948. [2]S/15947. [3]S/15949. [4]S/15950. [5]S/15951. [6]S/15966/Rev.1. [7]YUN 1973, p. 249. [8]S/15955. [9]S/15954. [10]S/15957. [11]S/15958. [12]S/15964. [13]S/15959. [14]S/15967. [15]S/15976. [16]S/15965. [17]S/15968. [18]S/15978. [19]S/15969. [20]S/15984. [21]S/15985. [22]S/15961. [23]S/15972. [24]S/15988. [25]S/15996. [26]S/16008. [27]YUN 1953, p. 136, GA res. 725(VIII), annex, 7 Dec. 1953. [28]S/15602. [29]S/15607. [30]S/15778. [31]S/15820. [32]S/15767. [33]S/15785. [34]S/15728. [35]YUN 1950, p. 230, SC res. 84(1950), 7 July 1950. [36]S/15861.

South-East Asia

Kampuchea situation

The situation in and around Kampuchea and Democratic Kampuchea's representation in the United Nations continued to occupy the attention of the Organization in 1983.

The *Ad Hoc* Committee of the International Conference on Kampuchea dispatched two missions in May and June/July to five capitals and to Geneva for consultations, in pursuance of its mandate to assist in seeking a settlement of the situation. In October, the General Assembly, by resolution 38/3, restated its view of the principal components of a just and lasting solution—withdrawal of all foreign forces, restoration and preservation of the country's independence, sovereignty and territorial integrity, the people's right to determine its destiny, and a commitment by all States to non-interference in Kampuchea's internal affairs.

Numerous communications were received throughout the year on various aspects of the situation and related issues, including the alleged use of chemical weapons, the situation along the common borders of Democratic Kampuchea, Thailand and Viet Nam, general aspects of peace and security in South-East Asia and the China-Viet Nam dispute.

Communications (January-October). A number of the communications received by the Secretary-General between January and October 1983 concerned incidents on the common borders of Democratic Kampuchea, Thailand and Viet Nam, with Democratic Kampuchea claiming Vietnamese attacks on the civilian population in the border areas, calling for humanitarian aid for the victims, and urging the international community to condemn Viet Nam and compel it to withdraw its troops from Kampuchea. Thailand complained of numerous armed incursions into its territory by Vietnamese forces operating from Kampuchea and reaffirmed the right to defend its territory and to protect its nationals. Viet Nam repeatedly rejected Thailand's allegations as fabrications, serving only to undermine the process of dialogue and promote the expansionist schemes of China, which was trying to reimpose the Pol Pot régime on the Kampucheans.

The Viet Nam News Agency, in a statement of 30 December 1982 transmitted on 3 January 1983,[1] referred to a Radio Beijing report quoting Thai newspaper accounts of Thailand's instructions that the Secretary-General be informed of Vietnamese encroachments on Thailand's border, shelling its territory and causing death and injury to civilians; the Agency rejected the report as fabrication aimed at undermining relations between Thailand and Viet Nam when the atmosphere was becoming less strained. By a letter of 7 January,[2] Thailand protested what it claimed to be more than an hour-long artillery barrage on 31 December 1982, 7 kilometres into Thai territory by Vietnamese forces in Kampuchea, killing four Thai children and seriously injuring eight others. Viet Nam also rejected this allegation on 14 January 1983.[3]

By a further letter of 2 February and a later addendum,[4] Thailand charged that Vietnamese forces, in the course of an attack on the Kampuchean civilian encampment at Nong Chan, about a kilometre from the Kampuchea-Thailand border, fired 30 artillery shells into Prachinburi province, killing a Thai civilian, injuring two others, damaging property and killing livestock; the attack on Nong Chan forced some 47,000 Kampucheans to flee to Thailand. Viet Nam, rejecting the charge by two communications—a Viet Nam News Agency statement of 4 February transmitted the same day,[5] and a note verbale of 8 February[6]—countercharged that Khmer reactionary forces, aided by China and the United States, were using Thai territory to stage attacks into Kampuchea in an attempt to reimpose the genocidal Pol Pot régime.

On 7 February,[7] Democratic Kampuchea transmitted two statements dated 3 February, one from President Samdech Norodom Sihanouk and the other from its Ministry of Foreign Affairs, condemning attacks on the Nong Chan refugee camp between 31 January and 2 February, which were said to have reduced the camp to ashes and left its 30,000 inhabitants homeless. In a 21 February statement transmitted on 28 February,[8] President Sihanouk denounced another Vietnamese attack on civilian populations in the Nong Chan area on 4 February and called for the expulsion of Viet Nam from the Movement of Non-Aligned Countries.

The Foreign Ministers of the Association of South-East Asian Nations (ASEAN), in a joint statement of 1 April which Thailand transmitted the same day,[9] condemned what they said were unprovoked and indiscriminate attacks by Vietnamese forces against Kampuchean civilians, and Vietnamese incursions into Thailand; they demanded immediate cessation of the attacks and respect for Thailand's sovereignty and territorial integrity, and called on the international community to assist the Kampuchean victims. President Sihanouk, in a further statement of 1 April transmitted on 5 April,[10] charged that, on 31 March, Vietnamese troops had attacked civilians in the Phnom Chhat area; he urged the international community to condemn such attacks and compel the Vietnamese troops to leave Kampuchea.

A statement of 5 April by Viet Nam's Foreign Ministry, transmitted the same day,[11] denied charges by Thailand, the United States and ASEAN that Vietnamese forces had attacked refugee camps along the border area and had intruded into Thai territory; support given to the armed forces of Kampuchea by the volunteer troops of Viet Nam, the statement continued, was in keeping with a treaty between the two countries, and the tense border situation was due to Thailand's collusion with China in opposing the People's Republic of Kampuchea. Democratic Kampuchea's President Sihanouk, in a 4 April statement transmitted three days later,[12] denounced Viet Nam's 3 April bombardment of the civilian population of O Smach-Sihanouk Borei, near the Kampuchea-Thailand border.

On 14 April,[13] Thailand alleged further violations against its territory: on 1 and 2 April, armed incursions by some 500 and 100 Vietnamese troops into Prachinburi province, resulting in the death of 5 Thai soldiers and injury to 14 others in the skirmish that ensued; and on 3 and 4 April, the shelling of Surin province and attacks on the civilian population of O Smach-Sihanouk Borei in Kampuchea, forcing some 25,000 Kampucheans to take refuge in Surin. Condemning these incursions and attacks, China's Foreign Ministry, in a 5 April statement transmitted the same day,[14] urged the international community to condemn them likewise. Also deploring these events were the Foreign Ministers of the European Community (EC)—in a statement of 25 April transmitted by the Federal Republic of Germany on 28 April[15]—who reiterated the demand made in a joint EC-ASEAN declaration of March that Viet Nam withdraw its troops from Kampuchea and that the Kampucheans' right to self-determination be given effect under relevant United Nations resolutions.

By a letter of 6 May,[16] Thailand reported further Vietnamese violations of its territory: on 8 April, the shooting down of a Thai A-37 reconnaissance aircraft over Thai territory adjacent to the Kampuchea-Thailand border, killing its pilot and co-pilot; and between 5 and 21 April, over 20 violations including seven armed incursions into Thai territory, four clashes with Thai soldiers and over 100 Vietnamese shells landing on Thai territory—resulting in injury to three persons and destruction of property and livestock. Refuting these as distortional allegations, Viet Nam, on 12 May,[17] said that in early April, the forces of the People's Republic of Kampuchea and Vietnamese volunteer troops were forced to counter-attack in the face of Thailand's increased support of sabotage activities and incursions into Kampuchea by the remnants of the Pol Pot clique and other Khmer reactionaries.

On 6 October,[18] Thailand complained that, on over 60 separate occasions between May and August, its land, airspace and waters had been blatantly violated by Vietnamese forces, causing death, serious injuries and destruction of property; these included shelling, armed robbery, firing at a Thai patrol boat and fishing boat and seizing the latter, and two separate attacks on villagers by heavy-calibre machine-gun fire.

Military activity other than border incidents were addressed by Democratic Kampuchea in three communications. A communiqué issued by its Council of Ministers on 30 April and transmitted on 9 May,[19] besides denouncing Viet Nam's attacks on the refugee camps of Nong Chan, Phnom Chhat and O Smach-Sihanouk Borei along the Kampuchea-Thailand border, also denounced a Vietnamese partial troop withdrawal as a manoeuvre to deceive world opinion. A letter of 11 May[20] attached a list of crimes allegedly committed by the Vietnamese army against the Kampuchean civilian population between 2 February and 20 April. A communiqué issued on 9 May by the Military High Command of the National Army of Democratic Kampuchea, transmitted on 20 May,[21] assessed military operations during the dry season (October 1982–April 1983) as being successful and reported 16,600 of the enemy killed or wounded.

Charges concerning chemical weapons use in the conflict between Democratic Kampuchea and Viet Nam continued to be received in 1983, and information was provided for transmittal to the Group of Experts to Investigate Reports on the Alleged Use of Chemical Weapons (see also Chapter I of this section, under CHEMICAL WEAPONS USE).

Democratic Kampuchea sent three such communications. On 23 February,[22] it submitted a list of cases involving the alleged use of chemical toxins and poison-gas shelling by Vietnamese forces in four provinces, on 23 and 29 December 1982 and between 16 January and 12 February 1983. A letter of 12 April[23] cited additional cases involving drinking-water poisoning and aerial spraying of toxic chemicals. Earlier, a Foreign Ministry statement of 16 March, transmitted on 21 March,[24] denounced what it said was the intensifed use of chemical weapons by the Vietnamese against Kampuchean civilians during the 1982-1983 dry season; photographs of Vietnamese soldiers reportedly captured in gas masks were attached.

Democratic Kampuchea also transmitted three statements claiming flagrant violations of its territorial integrity by Viet Nam aimed ultimately at what it referred to as the Vietnamization of Kampuchea.

By the first, issued on 10 January and transmitted on 20 January,[25] the Foreign Ministry of Democratic Kampuchea condemned what it called Hanoi's annexation of parts of Kampuchea's sea waters, as evidenced by a so-called agreement of 7 July 1982 between Viet Nam and its puppet régime in Phnom Penh on the "historical waters of the two countries" and by a 12 November 1982 Vietnamese statement referring to "its territorial sea baseline", which included large tracts of Kampuchean sea waters. Democratic Kampuchea regarded those actions as flagrant violations of its sovereignty and rejected them as null and void. By the second statement, dated 23 July and transmitted two days later,[26] a Foreign Ministry spokesman similarly rejected a so-called treaty between Hanoi and Phnom Penh governing border transit, labelling it a manoeuvre by Hanoi to legalize its occupation of Kampuchea. The third statement, dated 13 October and transmitted a day later,[27] accused Viet Nam of systematically settling its nationals in Kampuchea, whose numbers had reached several hundred thousand; it denounced this population transfer and regarded as null and void any agreement on their settlement in Kampuchea.

On 25 February,[28] the Lao People's Democratic Republic transmitted two statements issued at the end of a conference held at Vientiane on 22 and 23 February with the People's Republic of Kampuchea and Viet Nam; the second statement contained a proposal for the yearly partial but conditional withdrawal of Viet Nam's volunteer forces from Kampuchea in 1983. China's Foreign Ministry, by a statement of 1 March transmitted the same day,[29] denounced the proposal as a hoax and reiterated that the key to a settlement of the Kampuchea situation lay in the total and unconditional withdrawal of Viet Nam's troops. The Ministry summed up China's proposals for a settlement: Viet Nam must declare such withdrawal; the USSR must cease support of Viet Nam's aggression against Kampuchea; on withdrawal of the first batch of troops, China would resume negotiations for improved relations with Viet Nam; after total troop withdrawal, the Kampucheans should choose a government in free elections under United Nations supervision; and, jointly with other countries, China would commit itself to non-interference and to respect Kampuchea's independence and non-aligned status.

The Foreign Ministry of the People's Republic of Kampuchea, in a statement of 6 April transmitted by the Lao People's Democratic Republic on 18 April,[30] charged Thailand with armed provocation against Kampuchea, causing heavy loss of life and property; it also accused China, the United States and the ASEAN leaders of aiding the Pol Pot régime.

The ASEAN Foreign Ministers, in a joint statement released on 21 September at Jakarta and transmitted by Indonesia on the same date,[31] appealed to the international community, particularly to Viet

Nam and the five permanent members of the Security Council, to intensify efforts towards a just solution of the Kampuchea situation so as to restore Kampuchea's status as an independent and sovereign State.

An appeal for humanitarian assistance to Kampucheans was made by the Vice-President of the Council of Ministers and Minister for Foreign Affairs of the People's Republic of Kampuchea in a 25 June message to the Secretary-General; it was transmitted on 13 July[32] by the Lao People's Democratic Republic. That country also transmitted on 7 October[33] an open letter of 12 September from intellectuals and religious people of the People's Republic, appealing for condemnation of international support for the so-called Coalition Government of Kampuchea and for its expulsion from the United Nations; along with the letter was a white paper outlining the policy of the People's Republic towards Vietnamese residents in Kampuchea.

Activities of the Committee of the Conference on Kampuchea. As authorized by the General Assembly in October 1982,[34] the 10-member *Ad Hoc* Committee of the International Conference on Kampuchea held five meetings between 24 January and 20 September 1983. It dispatched a mission on 25 May to Washington, D. C., for consultations with the United States Department of State, and another to Tokyo, Beijing (China), Bangkok (Thailand), London and Geneva from 19 June to 6 July. At Geneva, the mission met with the President of the International Conference on Kampuchea.

The Committee's report on its 1982-1983 activities[35] noted that the missions, in their consultations with the respective Governments, underscored the international community's concern over the continuing Kampuchea conflict and sought the widest possible participation in and support for efforts towards a comprehensive political settlement. They stressed that such a settlement must be based on two principles: the withdrawal of all foreign forces from Kampuchea and the right of the Kampucheans to determine their own destiny. They also reiterated that the settlement should take account of the legitimate security concerns of the region, including a commitment by all States to non-interference in Kampuchea's internal affairs.

The consultations dealt with the partial troop withdrawal announced by Viet Nam, the latest military attacks on Kampuchean civilian encampments along the Kampuchea-Thailand border, a Thai proposal for a 30-kilometre withdrawal of Viet Nam's troops from that border, China's five-point proposal of 1 March,[29] and a declaration adopted by the Conference of Ministers for Foreign Affairs of Non-Aligned Countries (New Delhi, India, 3-5 March), which included a call for foreign troop withdrawal from Kampuchea. The Governments had reaffirmed their support for the objectives laid down by the International Conference and the relevant Assembly resolutions, as well as for initiatives for a negotiated settlement. At Bangkok, the mission was briefed on the results of the ASEAN Ministerial Meeting (Bangkok, 24 and 25 June), with the ASEAN Foreign Ministers reiterating their willingness to engage in consultations with Viet Nam so as to achieve such a settlement.

At Geneva, in addition to reporting to the Conference President on its consultations, the mission discussed current developments in Kampuchea, including reports of Vietnamese measures that could alter the country's demographic character.

Concluding its report, the Committee appealed to those Member States which had not participated in the International Conference to co-operate, and to all parties to pursue the process of dialogue and refrain from actions that could further complicate the situation.

Report of the Secretary-General. In his report to the General Assembly,[36] submitted pursuant to the 1982 Assembly resolution on the Kampuchea situation,[34] the Secretary-General stated that he had maintained close contact with the States most directly concerned and with other interested parties, in the exercise of his good offices. He had held extensive discussions with the Foreign Minister of Viet Nam, as well as with those of Indonesia, Malaysia and Singapore at the March 1983 Conference of Foreign Ministers of non-aligned countries. His Special Representative, Rafeeuddin Ahmed, had visited South-East Asia in June/July to consult with Governments. Thereafter, the Secretary-General had continued discussions in New York with the President of Democratic Kampuchea, the Deputy Prime Minister of Malaysia, the Foreign Ministers of China, Indonesia, the Lao People's Democratic Republic and Viet Nam and with other interested Governments.

In addition, diplomatic exchanges and bilateral consultations had continued among the South-East Asian countries on possible approaches to a dialogue and negotiations. The Secretary-General reported that these had fostered a climate of better understanding. However, despite the emergence of tentative elements of convergence, there remained significant differences. The situation in the region also remained relatively tense, particularly along the Kampuchea-Thailand border.

Reiterating his conviction that continued absence of progress towards genuine negotiations could only generate further tension and thus a deterioration of the situation, the Secretary-General considered it essential that initiatives at various levels be pursued with renewed vigour. He restated his determination to continue to exercise his good offices in this regard.

The Secretary-General also stated that he had continued to implement the humanitarian assistance programme for Kampuchea, which included operations within that country, at the border and within Thailand.

GENERAL ASSEMBLY ACTION

Following consideration of the situation in Kampuchea and the Secretary-General's report, the General Assembly, on 27 October 1983, adopted by recorded vote resolution 38/3.

The situation in Kampuchea

The General Assembly,

Recalling its resolutions 34/22 of 14 November 1979, 35/6 of 22 October 1980, 36/5 of 21 October 1981 and 37/6 of 28 October 1982,

Recalling further the Declaration on Kampuchea and resolution 1(I) adopted by the International Conference on Kampuchea, which offer the negotiating framework for a comprehensive political settlement of the Kampuchean problem,

Taking note of the report of the Secretary-General on the implementation of General Assembly resolution 37/6,

Noting the increasing effectiveness of the coalition with Samdech Norodom Sihanouk as President of Democratic Kampuchea,

Deploring that foreign armed intervention and occupation continue and that foreign forces have not been withdrawn from Kampuchea, thus causing continuing hostilities in that country and seriously threatening international peace and security,

Gravely concerned that the continued deployment of foreign forces in Kampuchea near the Thai-Kampuchean border and the renewed attack on civilians by those forces, in violation of humanitarian principles, have aggravated tension in the region,

Greatly disturbed that the continued fighting and instability in Kampuchea have forced Kampucheans to flee to the Thai-Kampuchean border in search of food and safety,

Recognizing that the assistance extended by the international community has continued to reduce the food shortages and health problems of the Kampuchean people,

Emphasizing that it is the inalienable right of the Kampuchean people who have sought refuge in neighbouring countries to return safely to their homeland,

Emphasizing further that no effective solution to the humanitarian problems can be achieved without a comprehensive political settlement of the Kampuchean conflict,

Seriously concerned about reported demographic changes being imposed in Kampuchea by foreign occupation forces,

Convinced that, to bring about durable peace in South-East Asia, there is an urgent need for a comprehensive political solution to the Kampuchean problem that will provide for the withdrawal of all foreign forces and ensure respect for the sovereignty, independence, territorial integrity and neutral and non-aligned status of Kampuchea, as well as the right of the Kampuchean people to self-determination free from outside interference,

Convinced further that, after the comprehensive political settlement of the Kampuchean question through peaceful means, the countries of the South-East Asian region can pursue efforts to establish a zone of peace, freedom and neutrality in South-East Asia so as to lessen international tensions and to achieve lasting peace in the region,

Reaffirming the need for all States to adhere strictly to the principles of the Charter of the United Nations, which call for respect for the national independence, sovereignty and territorial integrity of all States, non-intervention and non-interference in the internal affairs of States, non-recourse to the threat or use of force and peaceful settlement of disputes,

1. *Reaffirms* its resolutions 34/22, 35/6, 36/5 and 37/6 and calls for their full implementation;

2. *Reiterates its conviction* that the withdrawal of all foreign forces from Kampuchea, the restoration and preservation of its independence, sovereignty and territorial integrity, the right of the Kampuchean people to determine their own destiny and the commitment by all States to non-interference and non-intervention in the internal affairs of Kampuchea are the principal components of any just and lasting resolution of the Kampuchean problem;

3. *Takes note with appreciation* of the report of the *Ad Hoc* Committee of the International Conference on Kampuchea and requests that the Committee continue its work, pending the reconvening of the Conference;

4. *Authorizes* the *Ad Hoc* Committee to convene when necessary and to carry out the tasks entrusted to it in its mandate;

5. *Reaffirms* its decision to reconvene the Conference at an appropriate time, in accordance with Conference resolution 1(I);

6. *Renews its appeal* to all States of South-East Asia and others concerned to attend future sessions of the Conference;

7. *Requests* the Conference to report to the General Assembly on its future sessions;

8. *Requests* the Secretary-General to continue to consult with and assist the Conference and the *Ad Hoc* Committee and to provide them on a regular basis with the necessary facilities to carry out their functions;

9. *Expresses its appreciation once again* to the Secretary-General for taking appropriate steps in following the situation closely and requests him to continue to do so and to exercise his good offices in order to contribute to a comprehensive political settlement;

10. *Expresses its deep appreciation once again* to donor countries, the United Nations and its agencies and other national and international humanitarian organizations that have rendered relief assistance to the Kampuchean people, and appeals to them to continue to provide emergency assistance to those Kampucheans who are still in need, especially along the Thai-Kampuchean border and in the holding centres in Thailand;

11. *Reiterates its deep appreciation* to the Secretary-General for his efforts in co-ordinating humanitarian relief assistance and in monitoring its distribution, and requests him to intensify such efforts as are necessary;

12. *Urges* the countries of South-East Asia, once a comprehensive political solution to the Kampuchean conflict is achieved, to exert renewed efforts to establish a zone of peace, freedom and neutrality in South-East Asia;

13. *Reiterates the hope* that, following a comprehensive political solution, an intergovernmental committee will be established to consider a programme of assistance to Kampuchea for the reconstruction of its economy and for the economic and social development of all States in the region;

14. *Requests* the Secretary-General to report to the General Assembly at its thirty-ninth session on the implementation of the present resolution;

15. *Decides* to include in the provisional agenda of its thirty-ninth session the item entitled "The situation in Kampuchea".

General Assembly resolution 38/3

27 October 1983　　　Meeting 38　　　105-23-19 (recorded vote)

51-nation draft (A/38/L.2 & Add.1); agenda item 23.

Sponsors: Antigua and Barbuda, Bangladesh, Belgium, Canada, Central African Republic, Chad, Chile, Colombia, Comoros, Costa Rica, Denmark, Dominica, Dominican Republic, Fiji, Gambia, Germany, Federal Republic of, Haiti, Honduras, Iceland, Indonesia, Italy, Japan, Liberia, Luxembourg, Malaysia, Maldives, Mauritania, Nepal, Netherlands, New Zealand, Niger, Nigeria, Norway, Oman, Pakistan, Papua New Guinea, Paraguay, Philippines, Saint Lucia, Saint Vincent and the Grenadines, Samoa, Senegal, Singapore, Solomon Islands, Somalia, Swaziland, Thailand, Turkey, United Kingdom, Uruguay, Zaire.

Financial implications. 5th Committee, A/38/531; S-G, A/C.5/38/33.

Meeting numbers. GA 38th session: 5th Committee 16, 17; plenary 35-38.

Recorded vote in Assembly as follows:

In favour: Antigua and Barbuda, Argentina, Australia, Austria, Bahamas, Bahrain, Bangladesh, Barbados, Belgium, Belize, Bhutan, Bolivia, Botswana, Brazil, Burma, Burundi, Canada, Central African Republic, Chad, Chile, China, Colombia, Comoros, Costa Rica, Democratic Kampuchea, Denmark, Djibouti, Dominica, Dominican Republic, Ecuador, Egypt, El Salvador, Equatorial Guinea, Fiji, France, Gabon, Gambia, Germany, Federal Republic of, Greece, Guatemala, Guinea, Haiti, Honduras, Iceland, Indonesia, Ireland, Israel, Italy, Ivory Coast, Jamaica, Japan, Kenya, Kuwait, Lesotho, Liberia, Luxembourg, Malaysia, Maldives, Mali, Malta, Mauritania, Mauritius, Morocco, Nepal, Netherlands, New Zealand, Niger, Nigeria, Norway, Oman, Pakistan, Papua New Guinea, Paraguay, Peru, Philippines, Portugal, Qatar, Rwanda, Saint Lucia, Samoa, Saudi Arabia, Senegal, Sierra Leone, Singapore, Solomon Islands, Somalia, Spain, Sri Lanka, Sudan, Suriname, Swaziland, Sweden, Thailand, Togo, Tunisia, Turkey, United Arab Emirates, United Kingdom, United Republic of Cameroon, United States, Uruguay, Venezuela, Yugoslavia, Zaire, Zambia.

Against: Afghanistan, Albania, Angola, Bulgaria, Byelorussian SSR, Congo, Cuba, Czechoslovakia, Democratic Yemen, Ethiopia, German Democratic Republic, Guyana, Hungary, Lao People's Democratic Republic, Libyan Arab Jamahiriya, Mongolia, Mozambique, Nicaragua, Poland, Syrian Arab Republic, Ukrainian SSR, USSR, Viet Nam.

Abstaining: Algeria, Benin, Cape Verde, Finland, Ghana, Guinea-Bissau, India, Iraq, Lebanon, Madagascar, Malawi, Mexico, Panama, Sao Tome and Principe, Trinidad and Tobago, Uganda, United Republic of Tanzania, Upper Volta, Zimbabwe.

A number of States explained their votes. Mongolia said that the text, in addition to erroneously recognizing the representatives of those responsible for the genocide of the Kampucheans, reflected only the position of one group of countries of South-East Asia; its adoption would constitute not only interference in Kampuchea's internal affairs but an obstacle to dialogue between the parties concerned. That interference, the German Democratic Republic asserted, was the real source of tension and threat to the region's peace and stability, a reality not taken into account in the text.

Nicaragua reaffirmed the position of the Movement of Non-Aligned Countries, which supported a comprehensive political solution of the situation in South-East Asia, the withdrawal of all foreign troops as a guarantee of the independence and sovereignty of the region's States including Kampuchea, and creating a zone of peace, freedom and

neutrality in the region; based on its rejection of forces wanting to establish régimes representing terror, violence and exploitation instead of economic progress, Nicaragua, like the non-aligned Movement, did not recognize the Pol Pot régime as Kampuchea's legitimate Government and rejected any United Nations action that might lead to its acceptance.

On the other hand, a number of States saw the resolution as a confirmation of those principles which they believed essential to a settlement of the Kampuchean conflict—the withdrawal of all foreign forces from Kampuchea, the restoration of the sovereign independence of that country, the right of its people to self-determination, non-intervention in its internal affairs and dispute settlement by negotiation rather than force.

Sierra Leone, which in the past had abstained on every resolution on Kampuchea, voted for the current one because it essentially addressed the various interests at stake; its vote further signified confidence in Samdech Norodom Sihanouk and belief that the Organization could play a constructive role in bringing peace to Kampuchea and to South-East Asia as a whole.

Despite its affirmative vote, Sweden made clear it was not prepared to subscribe to every formulation in the text, in particular to changes in the preambular section from previous formulations. Bolivia, Brazil, Ireland, Mali and Rwanda expressed reservations on the fourth preambular paragraph, believing it prejudged the question of which was the legitimate Government of Kampuchea. That paragraph was neither in keeping with the realities in Kampuchea nor with Mali's policy in recognizing States, Mali observed; had a separate vote been taken on the paragraph, it would have abstained. Rwanda, which also would have abstained on the paragraph, made clear, as did Ireland, that its affirmative vote implied no change in its position on Kampuchean representation. On this point, Sierra Leone reiterated its resolve not to become an accomplice of those responsible for Kampuchea's nightmarish experience nor in its repetition.

Other action. In earlier related action, the Economic and Social Council, by decision 1983/155, endorsed a February resolution of the Commission on Human Rights on self-determination as it applied to Kampuchea (see ECONOMIC AND SOCIAL QUESTIONS, Chapter XVIII, under "Self-determination of peoples").

Further communications. Referring to General Assembly resolution 38/3 on the situation in Kampuchea, a spokesman for the Foreign Ministry of Viet Nam, in a statement of 28 October transmitted the same day,[37] criticized the Assembly for again opposing the Kampuchean people's right to self-determination and interfering in that country's internal affairs, in disregard of the Kampuchean reality. As with past resolutions adopted without the participation and consent of the People's Republic, Viet Nam rejected the resolution as null and void.

A 28 October declaration by the Foreign Ministry of the People's Republic of Kampuchea, transmitted by the Lao People's Democratic Republic on 1 November,[38] called the text ill-judged and worthless and rejected all resolutions which it said guaranteed neither an end to the threat of aggression against the three Indo-Chinese countries— the Lao People's Democratic Republic, the People's Republic of Kampuchea and Viet Nam— nor the independence and sovereignty of all the countries of the region; the declaration stated that the United Nations could play no part in resolving the region's problems as long as it recognized the genocidal Pol Pot criminals hiding behind the flag of the so-called Coalition Government of Democratic Kampuchea.

Participation and representation of Democratic Kampuchea in UN bodies

The question of Democratic Kampuchea's representation in United Nations bodies was again raised in 1983.

In a statement submitted to the President of the Economic and Social Council on 25 July by the German Democratic Republic,[39] 17 States— Afghanistan, Benin, Bulgaria, Byelorussian SSR, the Congo, Cuba, Czechoslovakia, Democratic Yemen, Ethiopia, the German Democratic Republic, Hungary, Mongolia, Poland, the Syrian Arab Republic, the Ukrainian SSR, the USSR and Viet Nam—said they considered illegal the presence of Democratic Kampuchea's delegation at the Council's July session, the only existing Kampuchean State being the People's Republic of Kampuchea.

The Ministry of Foreign Affairs of the People's Republic of Kampuchea, in a declaration of 21 October transmitted by Viet Nam that day,[40] stated that the realities of the Kampuchea situation had proved United Nations decisions on Kampuchea's representation groundless and unjust. Since their deliverance in 1979 from the genocidal régime of "Democratic Kampuchea" imposed by the Pol Pot–Ieng Sary–Khieu Samphan clique, the Kampuchean people under the People's Republic were well on the road to reconstruction and development, with famine suppressed, a national assembly established and order and security throughout the country ensured by an effective and popular government. The declaration demanded restoration of Kampuchea's seat to its rightful representatives, drawing attention in this respect to a provisional solution arrived at in March by the Movement of Non-Aligned Countries to leave vacant Kampuchea's seat in that Movement.

The validity of Democratic Kampuchea's credentials to the 1983 General Assembly session was also questioned at a September meeting of the Credentials Committee. The USSR claimed that there was no such country and that only the State of the People's Republic of Kampuchea existed, set up by free democratic elections and as such was the legitimate representative of the Kampucheans. China, Colombia, Indonesia, Portugal and the United States, on the other hand considered the credentials in question to be in full accord with relevant provisions of the Assembly's rules of procedure.

Democratic Kampuchea's credentials were approved by virtue of General Assembly resolution 38/2, approving the first report of the Credentials Committee (see Chapter XI of this section).

International security in South-East Asia

A number of letters addressed to the Secretary-General during 1983 concerned general aspects of relations among the nations of South-East Asia. Most were circulated as documents under the General Assembly's agenda item on the "Question of peace, stability and co-operation in South-East Asia"—an item which the Assembly considered at three meetings in November.

On 25 February,[28] the Lao People's Democratic Republic transmitted two statements issued jointly with the People's Republic of Kampuchea and Viet Nam at Vientiane on 23 February, the first of which reaffirmed the three countries' solidarity and mutual co-operation and their policy of peace, friendship and good neighbourliness with the rest of South-East Asia, the USSR, the United States and the world at large.

By a statement of 15 March transmitted two days later,[41] the Ministry of Foreign Affairs of Democratic Kampuchea rejected Viet Nam's proposal for a regional conference on Kampuchea, put forward at the Conference of Foreign Ministers of non-aligned countries (New Delhi, 3-5 March).

A spokesman for the Foreign Ministry of Viet Nam, in a statement of 9 April transmitted two days later,[42] condemned the United States for stepped-up military assistance to Thailand, which, according to Western reports, included shipment of anti-aircraft missiles and long-range artillery, to help Thailand resist alleged Vietnamese attacks at the border areas.

The Lao People's Democratic Republic transmitted two communiqués, both issued jointly by its Foreign Minister and those of the People's Republic of Kampuchea and Viet Nam: the first at an extraordinary conference held on 12 April at Phnom Penh and transmitted two days later,[43] and the second at the end of a conference, also at Phnom Penh, on 19 and 20 July and transmitted on 26 July.[44]

By the earlier communiqué, the three Ministers unanimously assessed the solidarity and mutual co-operation reaffirmed in February by their countries[28] as a success and as an important contribution to peace and stability in South-East Asia and the world. Noting the March decision of the Movement of Non-Aligned Countries to leave Kampuchea's seat vacant, the Ministers appealed to the United Nations to rescind its recognition of Democratic Kampuchea. They welcomed the ASEAN proposal for a dialogue put forward by Malaysia on 8 March, insisting, however, that the agenda and participation be based on equality and mutual respect and agreement; announced that the partial withdrawal of Vietnamese voluntary units for 1983 would take place in May; and urged an end to armed conflict at the Kampuchea-Thailand border, reiterating their 1982 proposal[45] for the establishment of a safety zone in the area.

In the later communiqué, the Ministers reiterated their proposal for a dialogue without precondition between their countries and ASEAN; the position of the People's Republic and Viet Nam that the annual partial withdrawal of Vietnamese volunteers from Kampuchea was contingent upon the security and stability in Kampuchea, particularly along the Kampuchea-Thailand border; the imperative that any proposal to reduce tension along that border stemmed from the principle of equal security for both sides; and the proposal for the Red Cross societies of Kampuchea and Thailand to examine, directly or through an intermediary, the humanitarian problem of Kampuchean refugees along the border, based on respect for the two countries' independence, sovereignty and security.

On 15 July,[46] Indonesia transmitted a joint communiqué issued by the ASEAN Ministerial Meeting at Bangkok, on 24 and 25 June, which in part reviewed the Kampuchea situation. By the communiqué, the ASEAN Foreign Ministers reiterated their call for a comprehensive political settlement as provided for by the 1981 Declaration of the International Conference on Kampuchea.[47] They held that Viet Nam's partial troop withdrawal, to be credible, should be part of a total troop withdrawal, expressed concern over reported demographic changes being imposed in eight Kampuchean provinces by the occupying Vietnamese forces, and deplored the attacks by those forces, between January and April, on civilian encampments along the Kampuchea-Thailand border which had caused over 40,000 Kampucheans to flee into Thailand, adding to that country's already heavy burden of providing refuge to some 170,000 Indo-Chinese refugees. The Ministers thus approved of Thailand's proposal for a withdrawal of Viet Nam's forces 30 kilometres from the border.

GENERAL ASSEMBLY ACTION

On an oral proposal of its President, the General Assembly adopted without vote decision 38/406.

Question of peace, stability and co-operation in South-East Asia

At its 59th plenary meeting, on 16 November 1983, the General Assembly decided to include in the provisional agenda of its thirty-ninth session the item entitled "Question of peace, stability and co-operation in South-East Asia".

General Assembly decision 38/406

Adopted without vote

Oral proposal by President; agenda item 37.
Meeting numbers. GA 38th session: plenary 55, 58, 59.

China-Viet Nam dispute

Between February and October 1983, the Secretary-General received several communications from China and Viet Nam, each continuing to charge the other with aggressive acts along their common border and holding the other responsible for the consequences.

A 12 February statement by the Viet Nam News Agency, transmitted four days later,[48] claimed violation of Viet Nam's sovereignty by China which, with United States companies, was exploring and extracting oil and gas from Viet Nam's territorial waters of Oanh Ca, in the Gulf of Bac Bo (Tonkin). Responding by a statement of 18 February transmitted four days later,[49] the New China News Agency (Xinhua) asserted that exploration in China's territorial sea was a matter entirely within its sovereignty. China accused Viet Nam of illegally claiming not only a large portion of the Beibu (Tonkin) Gulf, but also two islands in the area, called Xisha and Nansha by China; China, referring to its Foreign Ministry statement of 28 November 1982,[50] again declared that the maritime boundary in the Gulf as described by Viet Nam was null and void and that the islands which it persistently claimed were an inalienable part of China's territory.

On 11 April,[51] China transmitted a Foreign Ministry note of the day before, protesting more than 70 instances during March of armed provocations by Vietnamese troops along their common border, including three incursions into Chinese territory. Claiming that some 4,000 rounds of shells were fired in the process, killing or wounding 14 of its nationals, China stated that Viet Nam, contrary to its widely publicized intentions to normalize relations with China, had intensified its armed provocations.

By a statement of 29 August, transmitted on the same date,[52] a spokesman for Viet Nam's Foreign Ministry proposed a cessation of armed conflict along the border area from 30 August to 8 October, to allow celebration of Viet Nam's National Day on 2 September and China's on 1 October, thereby contributing to creating a favourable atmosphere for both sides to settle their abnormal relations. In reply, a representative of China's Foreign Ministry, during a visit to the Embassy of Viet Nam at

Beijing on 30 August, stated that what China wanted was a lasting peace at the border, not merely during National Day celebrations or the Lunar New Year festival (Têt). The reply, transmitted by a letter of 7 September,[53] agreed that both sides should celebrate their festivals in peace provided Viet Nam refrained from military provocations and incursions into Chinese territory.

On 17 October, China transmitted a memorandum of 11 October from its Foreign Ministry,[54] protesting to the Vietnamese Embassy against Viet Nam's continued armed intrusions along the border areas and detailing more than 30 separate incidents from the end of August to the end of September, during the period of Viet Nam's proposed cease-fire; the incidents included shelling, direct firing on civilians, intercepting fishing boats in the Beibu Gulf and opening fire on two others in waters near Guangxi, resulting in the death and wounding of many Chinese border inhabitants and property damage.

REFERENCES

[1]A/38/58.   [2]A/38/69-S/15559.   [3]A/38/75-S/15563.
[4]A/38/85-S/15593 & Add.1. [5]A/38/87-S/15594. [6]A/38/90-S/15601. [7]A/38/88-S/15595. [8]A/38/107-S/15631. [9]A/38/134-S/15677.   [10]A/38/136-S/15685.   [11]A/38/137-S/15686.
[12]A/38/140-S/15692. [13]A/38/158-S/15706.   [14]A/38/138-S/15687. [15]A/38/174-S/15740.   [16]A/38/185-S/15751.
[17]A/38/204-S/15759. [18]A/38/486-S/16027. [19]A/38/188-S/15754. [20]A/38/203-S/15758.   [21]A/38/210-S/15786.
[22]A/38/96-S/15622. [23]A/38/156-S/15702. [24]A/38/121-S/15650.   [25]A/38/77-S/15570.   [26]A/38/314-S/15885.
[27]A/38/510-S/16045. [28]A/38/98-S/15626. [29]A/38/109-S/15633.   [30]A/38/159-S/15708.   [31]A/38/441-S/15999.
[32]A/38/300. [33]A/38/490-S/16029. [34]YUN 1982, p. 340, GA res. 37/6, 28 Oct. 1982. [35]A/CONF.109/7. [36]A/38/513.
[37]A/38/544. [38]A/38/552. [39]E/1983/118.   [40]A/38/527.
[41]A/38/119-S/15647. [42]A/38/154-S/15698.   [43]A/38/157-S/15707. [44]A/38/316-S/15891. [45]YUN 1982, p. 346.
[46]A/38/302-S/15875. [47]YUN 1981, p. 242. [48]A/38/94-S/15612. [49]A/38/97-S/15624. [50]YUN 1982, p. 345.
[51]A/38/153-S/15697. [52]A/38/372-S/15945. [53]A/38/396-S/15963. [54]A/38/514-S/16047.

Western and south-western Asia

Afghanistan situation and Afghanistan-Pakistan armed incidents

As it had decided in November 1982,[1] the General Assembly again took up in November 1983 the situation in Afghanistan and its implications for international peace and security. By resolution 38/29, it called anew for immediate foreign troop withdrawal, reaffirmed the Afghan people's right to determine their own form of government, and requested continued efforts by the Secretary-General for a political solution. Meanwhile, the Foreign Ministers of Afghanistan and Pakistan, meeting in another round of discussions at Geneva in April and June through the intermediary of the

Secretary-General's Personal Representative, continued defining the contents of a comprehensive settlement. Throughout the summer, consultations were held with the Office of the United Nations High Commissioner for Refugees (UNHCR) in the light of agreement reached that arrangements for ascertaining the voluntary and unimpeded return of refugees would start without delay.

Communications. In 1983, a majority of the communications addressed to the Secretary-General relating to the situation in Afghanistan concerned allegations and counter-allegations of armed incidents along the Afghanistan-Pakistan border.

Continued violations of its airspace and territory by Afghanistan were reported by Pakistan in letters of 21 January[2] and 26 July[3]. The first cited incidents between August and December 1982, including six instances of shelling of the Chitral and Kurram Agency areas and 22 airspace intrusions, 2 of them serious: on 7 September, when four Afghan helicopters flew 4 miles into Pakistan in the Kurram Agency area and rocketed Afghan refugee camps, injuring two children and killing livestock; and on 29 December, when another Afghan helicopter fired at a border checkpost at Domandai, Baluchistan, subsequently engaging it in an exchange of fire. Similar violations, numbering more than 30, from January to June 1983, were cited by the second letter, the most serious one on 9 April, when 14 shells were fired from Afghanistan on several Pakistani villages some 4 to 8 kilometres inside Pakistan near Chaman, injuring a child and damaging houses. Categorically rejecting these allegations as fabrications, Afghanistan, by a letter of 4 August,[4] said they were intended to cover up Pakistan's aggression against Afghanistan and armed interference in its internal affairs.

By a letter of 2 September,[5] Pakistan reported a violation of its airspace on 30 August, in which two Afghan helicopter gunships flew some 1,000 yards into Pakistan territory and fired on the village of Kotri, injuring a girl and livestock. Likewise rejecting this charge by a letter of 19 September,[6] Afghanistan stated that its Air Force was under strict orders to avoid flights over a 20-mile strip from the Durand line; it countercharged that it was from Pakistan-controlled areas that aggressive acts were repeatedly launched against Afghanistan, citing as an example an incident on 9 April, in which the Afghan village of Jurbaf came under heavy fire from the Pakistan side of the line, while an armed group drove across into Afghan territory for subversive operations.

On 21 September,[7] Pakistan drew attention to what it described as an ominous escalation of violations of its airspace by Afghanistan, listing 10 incidents on 18 and 19 September, involving from one to seven Afghan aircraft, intruding from 16 to 42 nautical miles into Pakistan's airspace. By letters of 5 October[8] and 7 October,[9] Pakistan reported other territorial violations: on 22 September, when Afghan artillery fired 10 shells into Pakistan, injuring seven refugees; and on 4 October, when six Afghan aircraft bombed and strafed an area about a kilometre inside Pakistan, killing three persons and seriously injuring two others—followed by a second airspace violation over the same area some hours later.

Defining these latest allegations as slanderous and baseless, Afghanistan, in a letter of 13 October,[10] explained that it was Pakistan's custom to resort to propaganda campaigns whenever it needed to divert public attention from national problems, to drag the current General Assembly session into yet another unwarranted debate of the so-called Afghanistan question, to cover up what Pakistan had been turned into—a springboard for an undeclared war against Afghanistan—and to justify continued United States military aid to Pakistan. On 22 December, Afghanistan lodged a protest with the Embassy of Pakistan in Kabul against what it claimed to be repeated subversive and provocative acts staged from a Pakistani military outpost, directed at Afghan customs and civil installations in the border area of Torkham; the protest note, an unofficial translation of which was transmitted on 28 December,[11] mentioned an 18 December incident, in which bandits, under cover of heavy-weapons and artillery fire, raided and plundered those installations, causing heavy property damage and some deaths.

Several communications focused on the situation within Afghanistan, including the alleged use of chemical and toxin weapons in that country.

An open letter of 26 March from the National Fatherland Front of the Democratic Republic of Afghanistan, transmitted on 31 March,[12] drew attention to what it called unprecedented interference in Afghanistan's internal affairs by the United States Administration: on its so-called Afghanistan Day, the letter said, that Administration had staged a propaganda campaign aimed at instigating bands of hirelings to commit further crimes against the Afghan people; the letter asked the Secretary-General to use his authority to stop such interference. A statement from the same source, transmitted on 1 November,[13] urged Afghans abroad, particularly those who had been deceived into engaging in subversive activities against their country, to avail themselves of the 1981 general amnesty decree,[14] which allowed them to return in honour.

By a letter of 20 December,[15] Afghanistan transmitted information on the proceedings of a recently held national convention, including messages and a resolution it had adopted. The convention of tribal and religious leaders and retired government officials and generals reaffirmed the objectives of the Afghan revolution, called a halt to the undeclared war against Afghanistan, reaffirmed support for the continued presence of USSR contingents in Afghanistan until all aggression against it had stopped, and, while supporting the talks with Pakistan currently being held at Geneva through the Secretary-General's intermediary, expressed hope for a direct negotiation as the shortest way to a settlement.

Letters were also received from the USSR on 4 February,[16] and Canada on 18 March,[17] concerning a November 1982 United States report[18] alleging chemical weapons use by the USSR in South-East Asia and Afghanistan (see Chapter I of this section, under CHEMICAL WEAPONS USE).

Report of the Secretary-General. Pursuant to a November 1982 General Assembly request, the Secretary-General submitted to the Assembly and the Security Council in September 1983 a report on activities he had undertaken with respect to the Afghanistan situation.[19]

The Secretary-General stated that he had continued promoting a political solution through negotiations. His Personal Representative, Diego Cordovez, had consulted with representatives of Pakistan, Afghanistan and Iran (21 January–7 February), in efforts to define the substantive contents of a comprehensive settlement and to determine the procedural steps required to give impetus to the diplomatic process. The consultations focused on the four items previously identified for consideration: withdrawal of foreign troops, non-interference and non-intervention, international guarantees, and voluntary return of refugees. Understandings were reached on the nature and operation of a policy mechanism to be articulated in the settlement and on provisions to ensure its effective implementation.

The Secretary-General had visited the USSR in March, exchanging views on the situation with President Yuri Andropov and Foreign Minister Andrei Gromyko, who strongly favoured a political settlement.

Through the intermediary of his Personal Representative, a second round of discussions had been held at Geneva in two phases (11-22 April and 12-24 June), in which the Foreign Ministers of Afghanistan and Pakistan had taken part and of which Iran had been kept informed. Substantial progress had been made in defining the contents of a settlement, its principles and objectives, the interrelationship among its four elements and the provisions, including time-frames, for its implementation. It had been agreed that arrangements to ascertain the voluntary and unimpeded character of the return of refugees would start without delay. Consultations for this purpose had accordingly been held throughout the summer with UNHCR.

Concluding, the Secretary-General said that he had not sent his Personal Representative on another visit to Afghanistan, Iran and Pakistan at the end of summer, as requested, because the time had not been suitable for the purposes which the interlocutors had set themselves to achieve. However, the presence in New York of the Foreign Ministers of those countries at the 1983 Assembly session would provide an opportunity for discussions.

GENERAL ASSEMBLY ACTION

Following consideration of the situation in Afghanistan, the General Assembly, on 23 November 1983, adopted by recorded vote resolution 38/29.

The situation in Afghanistan and its implications for international peace and security

The General Assembly,

Having considered the item entitled "The situation in Afghanistan and its implications for international peace and security",

Recalling its resolutions ES-6/2 of 14 January 1980, 35/37 of 20 November 1980, 36/34 of 18 November 1981 and 37/37 of 29 November 1982,

Reaffirming the purposes and principles of the Charter of the United Nations and the obligation of all States to refrain in their international relations from the threat or use of force against the sovereignty, territorial integrity and political independence of any State,

Reaffirming further the inalienable right of all peoples to determine their own form of government and to choose their own economic, political and social system free from outside intervention, subversion, coercion or constraint of any kind whatsoever,

Gravely concerned at the continuing foreign armed intervention in Afghanistan, in contravention of the above principles, and its serious implications for international peace and security,

Noting the increasing concern of the international community over the continued and serious sufferings of the Afghan people and over the magnitude of social and economic problems posed to Pakistan and Iran by the presence on their soil of millions of Afghan refugees, and the continuing increase in their numbers,

Deeply conscious of the urgent need for a political solution of the grave situation in respect of Afghanistan,

Taking note of the report of the Secretary-General, and the status of the diplomatic process initiated by him,

Recognizing the importance of the initiatives of the Organization of the Islamic Conference and the efforts of the Movement of Non-Aligned Countries for a political solution of the situation in respect of Afghanistan,

1. *Reiterates* that the preservation of the sovereignty, territorial integrity, political independence and non-aligned character of Afghanistan is essential for a peaceful solution of the problem;

2. *Reaffirms* the right of the Afghan people to determine their own form of government and to choose their economic, political and social system free from outside intervention, subversion, coercion or constraint of any kind whatsoever;

3. *Calls* for the immediate withdrawal of the foreign troops from Afghanistan;

4. *Calls upon* all parties concerned to work for the urgent achievement of a political solution, in accordance with the provisions of the present resolution, and the creation of the necessary conditions which would enable the Afghan refugees to return voluntarily to their homes in safety and honour;

5. *Renews its appeal* to all States and national and international organizations to continue to extend humanitarian relief assistance with a view to alleviating the hardship of the Afghan refugees, in co-ordination with the United Nations High Commissioner for Refugees;

6. *Expresses its appreciation and support* for the efforts and constructive steps taken by the Secretary-General, especially the diplomatic process initiated by him, in the search for a solution to the problem;

7. *Requests* the Secretary-General to continue those efforts with a view to promoting a political solution, in accordance with the provisions of the present resolution, and the exploration of securing appropriate guarantees for the non-use of force, or threat of force, against the political independence, sovereignty, territorial integrity and security of all neighbouring States, on the basis of mutual guarantees and strict non-interference in each other's internal affairs and with full regard for the principles of the Charter of the United Nations;

8. *Requests* the Secretary-General to keep Member States and the Security Council concurrently informed of progress towards the implementation of the present resolution and to submit to Member States a report on the situation at the earliest appropriate opportunity;

9. *Decides* to include in the provisional agenda of its thirty-ninth session the item entitled "The situation in Afghanistan and its implications for international peace and security".

General Assembly resolution 38/29

23 November 1983   Meeting 69   116-20-17 (recorded vote)

45-nation draft (A/38/L.17 & Add.1); agenda item 29.

Sponsors: Antigua and Barbuda, Bahrain, Bangladesh, Chile, Colombia, Comoros, Costa Rica, Djibouti, Egypt, Fiji, Gambia, Guatemala, Guinea, Haiti, Honduras, Jamaica, Jordan, Kuwait, Liberia, Malaysia, Maldives, Mauritania, Morocco, Nepal, Niger, Oman, Pakistan, Papua New Guinea, Paraguay, Philippines, Qatar, Saint Lucia, Saint Vincent and the Grenadines, Samoa, Saudi Arabia, Senegal, Singapore, Solomon Islands, Somalia, Sudan, Tunisia, Turkey, United Arab Emirates, Uruguay.

Financial implications. 5th Committee report, A/38/597; S-G statement, A/C.5/38/50.

Meeting numbers. GA 38th session: 5th Committee 44; plenary 64, 66-69.

Recorded vote in Assembly as follows:

In favour: Albania, Antigua and Barbuda, Argentina, Australia, Austria, Bahamas, Bahrain, Bangladesh, Barbados, Belgium, Belize, Bolivia, Botswana, Brazil, Burma, Burundi, Canada, Central African Republic, Chad, Chile, China, Colombia, Comoros, Costa Rica, Democratic Kampuchea, Denmark, Djibouti, Dominica, Dominican Republic, Ecuador, Egypt, El Salvador, Fiji, France, Gabon, Gambia, Germany, Federal Republic of, Ghana, Greece, Guatemala, Guinea, Guyana, Haiti, Honduras, Iceland, Indonesia, Iran, Ireland, Israel, Italy, Ivory Coast, Jamaica, Japan, Jordan, Kenya, Kuwait, Lebanon, Lesotho, Liberia, Luxembourg, Malaysia, Maldives, Malta, Mauritania, Mauritius, Mexico, Morocco, Nepal, Netherlands, New Zealand, Niger, Nigeria, Norway, Oman, Pakistan, Panama, Papua New Guinea, Paraguay, Peru, Philippines, Portugal, Qatar, Rwanda, Saint Christopher and Nevis, Saint Lucia, Saint Vincent and the Grenadines, Samoa, Saudi Arabia, Senegal, Sierra Leone, Singapore, Solomon Islands, Somalia, Spain, Sri Lanka, Sudan, Suriname, Swaziland, Sweden, Thailand, Togo, Trinidad and Tobago, Tunisia, Turkey, United Arab Emirates, United Kingdom, United Republic of Cameroon, United Republic of Tanzania, United States, Uruguay, Vanuatu, Venezuela, Yugoslavia, Zaire, Zambia, Zimbabwe.

Against: Afghanistan, Angola, Bulgaria, Byelorussian SSR, Cuba, Czechoslovakia, Democratic Yemen, Ethiopia, German Democratic Republic, Hungary, Lao People's Democratic Republic, Libyan Arab Jamahiriya, Madagascar, Mongolia, Mozambique, Poland, Syrian Arab Republic, Ukrainian SSR, USSR, Viet Nam.

Abstaining: Algeria, Benin, Cape Verde, Congo, Cyprus, Finland, Guinea-Bissau, India, Iraq, Malawi, Mali, Nicaragua, Sao Tome and Principe, Seychelles, Uganda, Upper Volta, Yemen.

As in the past, Afghanistan objected to including the so-called question of Afghanistan in the Assembly's agenda. It stated that, if there was any desire for success of the negotiations with Pakistan through the Secretary-General's good offices, the current harmful exercise should be abandoned once and for all.

Afghanistan described the draft as a gross violation of the Charter of the United Nations and flagrant interference in Afghanistan's internal affairs; the sponsors had arrogated the right to advise on the social, economic and political system the Afghan people should adopt. They had already chosen a system, Afghanistan asserted, under which a comprehensive programme of reforms was resolutely being implemented, despite the undeclared war unleashed on the Afghan revolution. Afghanistan regretted Pakistan's efforts to prevent dissemination of its 1981 amnesty decree[14] to Afghans living in Pakistan, and said that the numbers of so-called refugees had been grossly exaggerated. The limited USSR contingents in Afghanistan were in that country at its request, solely to repel armed aggression from outside. Afghanistan declared that the resolution would in no way be binding on it, reiterating that no realistic and acceptable solution could come from such one-sided resolutions.

Sharing Afghanistan's objection to the Assembly debate, Democratic Yemen said the draft served only to intensify tension rather than create security and stability in south-west Asia. Declaring its recognition of the legitimacy of the Government of Afghanistan, Democratic Yemen condemned action aimed at undermining Afghanistan's independence and sovereignty. It reaffirmed support for Afghanistan's proposals[20] to settle its differences with neighbouring countries and called on them to respond to those proposals.

Malawi and Nicaragua said they were in complete agreement with the principles embodied in the text and focused upon in consultations: non-use of force or threat of the use of force against any State, non-interference in its internal affairs, withdrawal of foreign troops, the right to self-determination and the return of Afghan refugees in safety and honour. Malawi expressed concern, however, at the complete disregard for these principles and doubted the Assembly's ability to give them practical effect with respect to Afghanistan; saying the situation had reached a stalemate, Malawi called for a change in strategy. Nicaragua's concern was that the Assembly debate, rather than facilitate dialogue, had encouraged inflexibility. Both States reiterated their belief in a settlement by negotiation, with Malawi appealing for support of the Secretary-General's efforts in this regard and Nicaragua adding that dialogue should be based on an objective recognition of political realities in the region, including ideological pluralism and social transformation.

Bolivia, Iran, Italy and Mexico, voicing the international community's deep concern over continued USSR occupation of Afghanistan, saw the draft as laying down the principles on which an acceptable solution should be based. Their votes reflected their adherence to the Charter principles and restated their firm belief that the cause of freedom, independence, self-determination and respect for human rights should ultimately prevail.

Clarifying its stand on paragraph 2, Bolivia said its support for the right to self-determination neither prejudged the legitimacy of the Government of Afghanistan nor questioned its programmes for social change and development. Iran said the exercise of that right by the Afghan people required withdrawal of all foreign troops and the return of the Afghan *mujahideen* (freedom fighters). Iran found the text wanting in that it ignored the Islamic nature of the struggle of the Moslem Afghans and shied away from naming the aggressor forces; "restoration" rather than "preservation" was more appropriate in paragraph 1; paragraph 3, if implemented, would make paragraph 4 redundant, since the Afghans, a mature people with a great cultural heritage, were completely capable of handling their own affairs; paragraph 7 provided for an exercise that remained futile as long as negotiations were carried out with the puppet régime of the USSR. Iran restated its rejection of any efforts, including negotiations, in which the true representatives of the Afghan people took no active part.

On 7 December,[21] Afghanistan, referring to its 23 November statement in the Assembly, which it had made in exercise of the right of reply but had been unable to conclude, forwarded the full text of that statement to the Assembly President.

Other action. The Commission on Human Rights, by a resolution of 16 February 1983 on the right of peoples to self-determination as it applied to Afghanistan, reaffirmed the right of the Afghan people to self-determination; it also affirmed the right of the Afghan refugees to return to their homes in safety and honour and appealed for humanitarian relief assistance to be extended to them, in co-operation with UNHCR (see ECONOMIC AND SOCIAL QUESTIONS, Chapter XVIII, under "Self-determination of peoples").

REFERENCES

[1]YUN 1982, p. 354, GA res. 37/37, 29 Nov. 1982.
[2]A/38/79-S/15573. [3]A/38/317-S/15892. [4]A/38/327-S/15911.
[5]A/38/394-S/15960. [6]A/38/432-S/15992. [7]A/38/443-S/16001. [8]A/38/474-S/16023. [9]A/38/488-S/16028.

(10)A/38/507-S/16044. (11)A/39/60-S/16242 & Corr.1.
(12)A/38/135-S/15678. (13)A/38/559-S/16118 & Corr.1. (14)YUN
1982, p. 349. (15)A/38/59-S/16241. (16)A/38/86. (17)A/38/120.
(18)YUN 1982, pp. 103 & 349. (19)A/38/449-S/16005. (20)YUN
1980, p. 303, & 1981, p. 232. (21)A/38/651.

Iran-Iraq armed conflict

During 1983, the Security Council, through a statement issued by its President in February, called for an immediate cease-fire in the continuing armed conflict between Iran and Iraq. In October, by resolution 540(1983), the Council further called for an immediate cessation of all military operations against civilian targets and, affirming the right of free navigation and commerce in international waters, also called for a cessation of hostilities in the Gulf region, including all navigable waterways, offshore installations and ports.

A mission was dispatched to the two countries by the Secretary-General in May to inspect civilian areas reported to have been subjected to military attacks by the other.

In December, the General Assembly deferred consideration of the conflict to its resumed session in 1984.

SECURITY COUNCIL CONSIDERATION (February)

The Security Council met in informal consultations on 21 February 1983 to consider the recent escalation of the conflict between Iran and Iraq, following which the President, on behalf of Council members, made the statement below:[1]

"The members of the Council express their deep concern at the serious situation between Iran and Iraq which gravely endangers international peace and security and at the fact that resolutions 479(1980), 514(1982) and 522(1982) have not yet been implemented.

"The members of the Council continue to urge that all concerned be guided by Member States' obligations under the Charter: to settle their international disputes by peaceful means and in such a manner that international peace and security and justice are not endangered and to refrain in their international relations from the threat or use of force against the territorial integrity or political independence of any State.

"The members of the Council express their profound regret at the continuation and the escalation of the conflict and deplore the grave human losses and the considerable material damage resulting therefrom. They reaffirm the necessity of implementing the Council's previous resolutions on the subject which were unanimously adopted.

"The members of the Council urgently call once again for an immediate cease-fire and an end to all military operations as well as the withdrawal of forces up to internationally recognized boundaries with a view to seeking a peaceful settlement in accordance with the principles of the Charter.

"The Council remains seized of this question and urges all Member States to exert all efforts to assist in the restoration of peace and security in the region.

"The members of the Council request the Secretary-General to continue his efforts, in consultation with the parties concerned, with a view to achieving a peaceful settlement and to keep the Council informed."

Communications (February-June). In communications from Iran and Iraq received during the first half of 1983, each accused the other of deliberately attacking civilian and residential areas, with Iran underscoring what it perceived to be United Nations indifference to Iraq's crimes against humanity, and Iraq insisting on Iran's responsibility for the continuation of the war.

Referring to Iran's 21 December 1982 letter[2] alleging an Iraqi attack on the civilian population of Dezful, Iraq, by a letter of 2 February 1983,[3] rejected the allegation as propaganda and submitted a list of incidents of armed aggression against Iraq from 1 October to 15 November 1982. By a telegram of 7 February 1983, transmitted on the same date,[4] the Deputy Prime Minister and Minister for Foreign Affairs of Iraq drew attention to a large-scale attack launched by Iran against the Iraqi province of Misan, Al-Shib district, on the night of 6 February; the Minister called on the international community to condemn the attack and demand that it stop, and welcomed any United Nations action towards an honourable settlement of the conflict. A 25 January message from the President of Iraq, transmitted on 14 February,[5] drew attention to a communiqué issued jointly by Iran, the Libyan Arab Jamahiriya and the Syrian Arab Republic which, the President said, contained a formal policy seeking the overthrow of his Government.

Iran, in a letter of 24 February,[6] quoted a statement attributed to the Commander of Iraq's Fourth Army, as reported by the 18 February issue of the Lebanese weekly *Al-Hawadeth*, according to which Iraq would redraw the borderline to incorporate the western highlands of Iran into Iraqi territory. Iraq, by a letter of 3 May,[7] described the alleged quotation as but a wretched attempt by Iran to distort the truth and thus evade peaceful settlement of the dispute between them. Iran transmitted, on 27 February,[8] a list of 9,405 Iranian citizens reported missing since the outbreak of the conflict in 1980,[9] with a request that the Secretary-General draw the list to the attention of the Commission on Human Rights at its 1983 session.

By a message of 15 February, transmitted on 2 March,[10] Iraq's President called on the Iranians to give up their quest for Iraq's so-called liberation and conversion to a Moslem State and so end a war Iran could not win. Iraq's Deputy Prime Minister and Minister for Foreign Affairs, in a letter of 11 April transmitted the same day,[11] charged that, against the urgings of the Security

Council President,[1] Iran had launched another large-scale attack at the border area on the night of 10 April; the Minister called on the United Nations to condemn this latest aggression, stating that to remain silent would encourage Iran's aggression.

In a statement to the first extraordinary session of the Regional Organization for the Protection of the Marine Environment, transmitted on 20 April,[12] Iran protested recent Iraqi attacks on Iranian offshore oilfields, causing two oil spillages which had polluted the marine environment. Responding on 5 May,[13] Iraq explained that the spillage from Iran's offshore Noruz 3 oil well occurred on 27 January when a merchant vessel collided with the well and that the other spillage was indeed the result of military action in a war zone so declared by Iraq but in which Iran had nevertheless continued oil explorations; Iraq recalled Iran's rejection of a proposed partial cease-fire under United Nations supervision so that the oil wells might be repaired.

Iran reported, on 22 April[14] and 26 April,[15] that the city of Dezful had come under Iraqi missile attack on 20 and 24 April, resulting in the death of more than 58 civilians, injury to 110 others and destruction of over 200 houses and shops—the last attack having been the forty-eighth on Dezful since the outbreak of hostilities in 1980. Iran further reported on 27 April[16] that the Pol-e-Dokhtar region had been bombarded on 25 April, killing 21 civilians and injuring 100 more. Referring to these charges as hypocrisy and deception, as well as to Iran's statement at a 25 April press conference that it had no intention of retaliating against Iraqi cities, which were within striking range, Iraq countercharged on 2 May[17] that artillery bombardment of its cities of Khanaqin, Mandali, Zurbatiyah, Badra and Al Basrah had been daily occurrences since the withdrawal of its forces in June 1982 to internationally recognized boundaries.

By a letter of 5 May,[18] Iran stated that, as announced on Iraqi television on 2 May, Iraq's Minister of Culture and Information had stated that, in retaliation for shelling its cities, Iraq would bombard those of Iran. Replying on 12 May,[19] Iraq challenged Iran to reaffirm to the United Nations, if it could, that Iranian bombardment of Iraqi cities had not been a daily procedure.

Iran subsequently confirmed, by three letters, that densely populated areas of several cities had been bombarded by Iraq: the first, dated 13 May,[20] described surface-to-surface missile attacks on Andimeshk and Dezful (12 May); the second, dated 25 May,[21] mentioned barrages on civilian targets in Sar-e-Pol-e-Zahab, a town 25 to 30 kilometres from the Iraqi border (18 May) and on residential quarters of the city of Abadan (18 and 21 May); and the third, also of 25 May,[22] told of an attack that day on civilian targets in the town of Baneh. In all, more than 34 people were reported killed, 283 wounded and more than 200 houses and shops destroyed.

On 6 June,[23] Iraq stated that on 10 April an Iranian force of some 120,000 had mounted a two-pronged offensive into Iraqi territory between Al-Tib and Al-Fakkah towards the town of Al-Amarah, but had been pushed back on 16 April, sustaining heavy losses as it withdrew, including 15,000 dead, many prisoners, 41 tanks destroyed, and some 80 armoured carriers captured along with miscellaneous weapons and equipment and many tanks and transport vehicles in working order.

A letter of 7 June from Iraq's President to the people of Iran, transmitted two days later,[24] proposed cessation of hostilities in the Gulf area to allow movement of merchant vessels of both countries and others, the temporary truce to be overseen by a mutually agreed international body. Iraq asserted in a 10 June letter[25] that, as a result of the war imposed by Iran and of its refusal to abide by Security Council decisions, Iran bore responsibility for the tremendous losses Iraq had suffered, both human and economic, and should compensate Iraq accordingly.

Report of the Secretary-General (June). In response to requests made by Iran and Iraq on 2 and 12 May 1983, the Secretary-General dispatched a mission to the two countries in late May to inspect civilian areas which both claimed had been subjected to military attack by the other. The mission's report was transmitted to the Security Council by the Secretary-General, together with his report of 20 June.[26]

The Secretary-General reported that, as agreed with the two Governments, the mission was to determine whether civilian areas had been subjected to damage or destruction by military means, to assess the extent of such damage, and to indicate the type of munitions used. While not instructed to verify casualties and property damage, the mission kept in view the correlation between the extent of damage and the probable extent of loss of life, given the population at the time of damage.

The mission toured war zones in Iran from 21 to 26 May and in Iraq from 28 to 30 May according to itineraries drawn up by the two Governments; the zones included areas which had sustained recent as well as past war damage. The mission relied essentially on government information, supplemented by information ascertained by its own observations. Statistics on casualties provided by the two Governments were included in the mission's report without comment.

In Iran, 12 towns and cities were inspected. The mission observed that in general the extent of damage claimed appeared plausible or reasonably accurate. Evidence examined at Dezful, Andimeshk and Pol-e-Dokhtar, all located some 80 to 85 kilometres from the border, led the mission to conclude that Scud-B surface-to-surface (and, a year earlier, Frog) missiles, aerial bombardment and machine-gun fire had been the instruments of attack. The towns and cities close to the border (between 2 and 35 kilometres from it)—Musian, Dehloran, Abadan, Khorramshahr, Hoveyzeh, Susangerd, Sar-e-Pol-e-Zahab and Qasr-e-Shirin—had been beseiged or occupied by Iraq at the outbreak of hostilities and been retaken in 1982; some had remained under attack. The mission reported large areas as having been razed to the ground, leading it to conclude that, in addition to aerial bombardment (with cluster bombs in three cases), artillery fire, and direct fire when the towns changed hands, high-explosive charges and engineering equipment must have been used to level those areas. Baneh, also close to the border and attacked as recently as the day before the mission's visit, showed evidence of aerial bombardment with cluster bombs, resulting in no major property damage however.

The inspection in Iraq took the mission to seven cities and towns: Zurbatiyah, Mandali, Khanaqin, Kirkuk, Az Zubayr, Al Faw and Abu al Khasib. Aerial bombardment and artillery shelling with BM-21 rockets and 203-mm and 175-mm extended-range artillery were identified as the means of attack. Because the reported attacks on civilian targets in Kirkuk had taken place early in the conflict, physical verification of the munitions used was not possible. Moderate damage was reported for Zurbatiyah and Mandali and light for Al Zubayr. In the mission's opinion, oil installations had been the target in the border towns of Khanaqin and Al Faw, both of which had been heavily damaged, and a fertilizer factory at Abu al Khasib. Kirkuk, Az Zubayr and Abu al Khasib had maintained the same population levels while others had been evacuated. Mandali and Al Faw appeared deserted.

Before its visit to Iraq, the mission had been welcomed and its safety assured by Iraq's Deputy Prime Minister and Minister for Foreign Affairs, in a statement made on 25 May and transmitted two days later.[27] Commenting on the mission's findings in a memorandum transmitted on 29 June,[28] Iran's Foreign Ministry said they showed how much greater had been the damage to Iran. On 14 July,[29] Iraq criticized that memorandum as containing discrepancies, contradictions and deliberate distortions, adding that Iran, by its refusal to abide by the Council's decisions, was to be held solely responsible for the continuation of the war and resultant destruction.

Communications (August-October). Communications from August to October continued to bring to the Secretary-General's attention attacks on civilian targets in Iran and Iraq, with almost every letter from Iran reiterating that the continued indifference of the Security Council and the international community had encouraged Iraq's violations of international humanitarian law. For its part, Iraq felt that Iran was solely to blame for the war's prolongation by its refusal to abide by the international community's will as reflected in the decisions of the Council and the General Assembly.

By a letter of 3 August,[30] Iran cited a statement of the previous day attributed to the Iraqi Minister of Culture and Information that, if Iran continued to bombard civilian targets, Iraq would obliterate Iran's cities—a policy Iraq had pursued to the utmost during its two-year occupation of certain Iranian territories, as witnessed by the mission dispatched to Iran in May. On 4 August,[31] Iraq transmitted excerpts of Iranian military communiqués and official statements attesting to Iran's military offensive begun on 21 July, and quoted an Agence France Presse report of 29 July that large numbers of Iraqi dissidents in Iran had taken part, for the first time.

Subsequent Iraqi attacks during August and early September, mainly on civilian targets, were reported by Iran in five letters, dated as follows: 12 August,[32] an aerial bombardment (10 August) of the town of Gilan Gharb by cluster bombs and strafing; 17 August,[33] a missile attack on Andimeshk (13 August), followed on 1 September by photographs of the resultant destruction; 18 August,[34] an aerial bombardment (13 August) of the villages of Najaf and Karand, and a chemical-bomb attack on the war zone of Val Fajr-2; 26 August,[35] an air raid (23 August) on the village of Vavan-Sardasht in West Azarbaijan; and 7 September,[36] repeated bombardment of the city of Marivan in Kurdestan (27 and 30 August, 1 and 2 September) and an attack on Khanaqah village (28 August) by cluster bombs and napalm dropped from two Mirage fighter planes. The toll was placed at 153 dead, with 1,048 wounded, some 550 houses and shops destroyed, 400 livestock killed, a village harvest burned and four plantations devastated.

Iraq, by a letter of 12 September,[37] referred to these accusations as Iran's futile efforts to gain sympathy for its position, in the face of incontrovertible evidence provided by its own military[31] of its pursuance of the war against Iraq and intervention in Iraq's internal affairs.

On 22 September,[38] Iran stated that Iraqi bombardment of civilian areas had continued unabated and had recently subjected several cities to repeated long-range artillery strikes and air raids: Abadan (6 and 8 September), Sardasht (8 and 11 September), Marivan (7-10 September) and Piranshahr (12 September); casualties included 16 persons killed, more than 46 others injured, 20 houses destroyed and scores damaged, and some 100 livestock killed. Iran emphasized that it reserved the right to resort to retaliatory measures within the limits permitted by Islamic codes. On 29 September,[39] Iran drew attention to a Radio Baghdad announcement, made two days earlier, of Iraq's intention to launch attacks aimed at demoralizing the enemy—a declaration which in Iran's experience meant resuming bombardments of residential targets.

In a communiqué of 13 October, transmitted the next day,[40] Iran's Foreign Ministry said it had successfully stopped the oil spillage from its offshore Noruz oil well, damaged by Iraq in January,[12] and that repair was under way of its other offshore oil installations damaged in subsequent attacks; in the light of recent Iraqi threats on those installations, however, the Ministry felt duty-bound to warn the Gulf States of the grave danger thus posed to the region's marine environment, stressing that Iran should not be expected to compromise in order to remedy the deliberate mischief of others. Another aerial bombardment of the civilian populations of Marivan (11 October) and Baneh (15 October) was reported by Iran on 19 October,[41] which it said had claimed the lives of 23 people, injured 70 and destroyed several residential quarters; Iran added that these crimes against civilians were the main reason for the continuing conflict.

On 20 October,[42] Iraq charged Iran of staging a large-scale attack aimed at occupying Penjween, in northern Iraq, warning that it reserved the right to strike at the aggressor wherever necessary to make it understand that, by prolonging the war against the will of the Security Council and the international community, Iran would not achieve its aims. Responding on 23 October,[43] Iran countercharged that it was Iraq which had totally disregarded the international community's will by starting the war, instead of exhausting every peaceful means possible to settle its dispute; talk about respect for that will was nothing but sheer hypocrisy.

By a letter of 28 October,[44] Iran stated that Iraqi forces, unable to gain the upper hand on the battlefront, had again resorted to inhumane surface-to-surface missile attacks on the civilians of Dezful and Masjid Soleiman, as well as of Marivan, killing more than 120 civilians, wounding some 450 and destroying a large number of houses and shops; Iran invited the Secretary-General to dispatch his representative to the area to witness what it called the realities so that the fact-finding mission's report[26] might be updated.

SECURITY COUNCIL ACTION (October)

Meeting on 31 October 1983, the Security Council adopted resolution 540(1983) below.

The Security Council,

Having considered again the question entitled "The situation between Iran and Iraq",

Recalling its relevant resolutions and statements which, *inter alia,* call for a comprehensive cease-fire and an end to all military operations between the parties,

Recalling the report of the Secretary-General of 20 June 1983 on the mission appointed by him to inspect civilian areas in Iran and Iraq which have been subject to military attacks, and expressing its appreciation to the Secretary-General for presenting a factual, balanced and objective account,

Also noting with appreciation and encouragement the assistance and co-operation given to the Secretary-General's mission by the Governments of Iran and Iraq,

Deploring once again the conflict between the two countries, resulting in heavy losses of civilian lives and extensive damage caused to cities, property and economic infrastructures,

Affirming the desirability of an objective examination of the causes of the war,

1. *Requests* the Secretary-General to continue his mediation efforts with the parties concerned, with a view to achieving a comprehensive, just and honourable settlement acceptable to both sides;

2. *Condems* all violations of international humanitarian law, in particular, the provisions of the Geneva Conventions of 1949 in all their aspects, and calls for the immediate cessation of all military operations against civilian targets, including city and residential areas;

3. *Affirms* the right of free navigation and commerce in international waters, calls on all States to respect this right and also calls upon the belligerents to cease immediately all hostilities in the region of the Gulf, including all sea-lanes, navigable waterways, harbour works, terminals, offshore installations and all ports with direct or indirect access to the sea, and to respect the integrity of the other littoral States;

4. *Requests* the Secretary-General to consult with the parties concerning ways to sustain and verify the cessation of hostilities, including the possible dispatch of United Nations observers, and to submit a report to the Security Council on the results of these consultations;

5. *Calls upon* both parties to refrain from any action that may endanger peace and security as well as marine life in the region of the Gulf;

6. *Calls once more upon* all other States to exercise the utmost restraint and to refrain from any act which may lead to a further escalation and widening of the conflict and, thus, to facilitate the implementation of the present resolution;

7. *Requests* the Secretary-General to consult with the parties regarding immediate and effective implementation of the present resolution.

Security Council resolution 540(1983)

31 October 1983   Meeting 2493   12-0-3

3-nation draft (S/16092).
Sponsors: Guyana, Togo, Zaire.
Meeting number. SC: 2493.

Vote in Council as follows:

In favour: China, France, Guyana, Jordan, Netherlands, Poland, Togo, USSR, United Kingdom, United States, Zaire, Zimbabwe.
Against: None.
Abstaining: Malta, Nicaragua, Pakistan.

Speaking before the vote on the draft resolution, Pakistan said it had hoped that the Council would come up with a text to engage both parties in a process combining immediate containment of hostilities with prospects for a comprehensive peace settlement to follow. Instead, the Council had before it, as in the past, a draft that could hardly have a meaningful impact on the war, thus leaving one of the parties as disenchanted and aggrieved as ever. For that reason and to preserve its impartial role as a member of the Islamic Peace Committee, Pakistan said it would abstain. However, it urged the States of the region, particularly Iran and Iraq, to demonstrate sensitivity to the threat of great-Power confrontation which the war could precipitate, and hasten to make peace in the interests of their own survival and independence.

Malta also believed that a sustained effort during the Council's informal consultations might have succeeded in bringing the two sides together in constructive dialogue—an approach that, although time-consuming, would have offered better possibilities than the mere passage of a draft—especially since one side maintained that the Council had not given it reasonable hearing and that there had not been sufficient consultation. Nicaragua, which had hoped that the Council would be guided by a conciliatory approach to include the stand taken by the Movement of Non-Aligned Countries, felt that the draft lacked a guarantee of effectiveness and even cast doubt on the parties' ability to bring about a relaxation of tension.

The Netherlands—hoping that the resolution would be a first step to meaningful United Nations involvement in the search for a mutually acceptable settlement—reiterated that some co-operation by the conflicting parties was indispensable. The Netherlands believed that if both immediately stopped attacking civilian targets and ceased hostilities in the Gulf region, and if other States refrained from acts which might widen the conflict, favourable conditions for negotiations could be established.

As with previous Council resolutions on the subject, the USSR said its support stemmed from the concern shared by the majority over the continued conflict and from its interest in eliminating hotbeds of tension near its frontiers. The USSR also stressed its continued opposition to exploitation of the conflict by external forces and to armed intervention for whatever reason, even to ensure freedom of navigation in the Gulf. China stated that bringing the parties together to negotiate was of paramount consideration to the Council and that the resolution was consistent with China's position that the conflict be settled peacefully.

Report of the Secretary-General (December). In a report[45] on his efforts to implement Security Council resolution 540(1983), the Secretary-General stated that, in transmitting that resolution to Iran and Iraq, he had informed them of his intention to send, with their concurrence, a small mission of senior Secretariat officials to Teheran and Baghdad for the consultations envisaged in the resolution.

The Secretary-General noted that Iraq, by a letter of 1 November,[46] had welcomed the resolution and had indicated readiness to co-operate in ensuring a cease-fire, but had warned against partial implementation on the premise that the resolution was an integrated and indivisible whole. Iran conveyed its position on 11 December[47] that, while it had decided at the Council consultations to respond positively, the Council's action had remained in the same unbalanced tradition it had followed since the beginning of Iraq's war of aggression, so that Iran had no alternative but to continue to dissociate itself from the resolution; the situation in the region could not be termed "hostilities" as in paragraph 4, but a defensive war of liberation whose purpose was to reverse the consequences of the war initiated by Iraq.

The Secretary-General drew attention to Iran's request[44] for another mission to inspect civilian areas recently subjected to Iraqi military attacks in order to update the first mission's report.[26] Iran had reiterated this request in several letters (see below), three of which reported chemical weapons use by Iraq, and requested that an expert on the subject be included in the proposed mission. Iraq had been unable to accept the proposal for the mission to visit Iraq also, and had addressed letters stating that its own civilian areas had been militarily attacked (see also below) and had rejected allegations of its use of chemical weapons in Iran.

In view of the Iraqi position that Iran's request be considered in the context of paragraph 2 of the resolution—an integrated and indivisible resolution to be implemented as such—the Secretary-General said there were practical difficulties in acceding to Iran's request. Nevertheless, he would continue efforts to bring about a cessation of hostilities. Apart from intensive discussions he and his Special Representative, Olof Palme, had held with the Foreign Ministers of both parties in September, the Secretary-General expected the January 1984 meeting of the Organization of the Islamic Conference to provide him an opportunity to discuss with both countries' heads of State the steps that could facilitate a peaceful solution.

Other communications (November and December). On 2 November,[48] Iran stated that on 29 October the towns of Masjid Soleiman and Behbahan had been bombarded, the latter also having been attacked a few days earlier; casualties totalled some 474 students killed or wounded, 100 household units destroyed, and another 94 people killed (among them 74 students between the ages of 12 and 15). Iraq, by a letter of 3 November,[49] stated that Iran had launched a new large-scale military attack on Penjween for the purpose of occupying it and called this act, occurring only three days after adoption of resolution 540(1983), a flagrant challenge to the will of the Council and the United Nations.

Photographs which Iran said showed the destruction caused by Iraqi attacks on the towns of Dezful, Marivan and Andimeshk in October[41] were transmitted by Iran by a letter of 3 November.[50] On the same date,[51] Iran claimed that on numerous occasions in the past weeks Iraqi forces had used chemical weapons at the front, reiterating in this regard its request for a representative of the Secretary-General to examine the medical and military evidence of such attacks. Continued attacks, including some with chemical weapons, on civilian targets in Andimeshk, Masjid Soleiman, Behbahan, Nahavand and in two villages near Baneh were reported by Iran on 9 November,[52] which, it said, had resulted in 79 dead and 611 injured, a number of them sustaining blindness, severe skin burns and lung injury; more than 240 houses were also damaged or destroyed. Iran issued a reminder that this was not how peace could be achieved and that it was time the Council stopped encouraging Iraq to commit such atrocities. By a further letter of 9 November,[53] Iran stated that shrapnel from two Iraqi artillery rounds fired into the Piranshahr area on 25 October and the injuries caused showed evidence of chemical weapons use, as did several photographs attached. Additional incidents of such use were reported by Iran on 16 November:[54] a chemical bomb dropped on a village near Baneh (21 October), three rounds of chemical shells fired at the front line (30 October) and, in previous attacks, the use of mustard gas and compounds containing arsenic.

On 29 November,[55] Iraq categorically rejected Iran's allegations as a manoeuvre to divert international attention from Iran's refusal to halt its war of aggression and its rejection of Council resolutions. On 27 December,[56] Iran complained that the United Nations had ignored the numerous cases reported to it of Iraqi violation of international humanitarian law; since the evidence, particularly of chemical weapons use, faded with time, Iran charged the Council with obstructing acquisition of such evidence.

By two letters, dated 14 November[57] and 15 November,[58] Iraq transmitted what it said were excerpts of official communiqués, issued by the Iranian military between 20 October and 4 November and by the Iraqi military between 1 October and 6 November, giving evidence of current Iranian occupation of Iraqi territory and attacks, mostly on civilian installations in Iraq. Iran replied on 22 November[59] that it was important for the United Nations to examine whether Iraq had evidence to support those allegations and reiterated its request that another fact-finding mission be dispatched to both countries. Iran transmitted 10 photographs on 25 November[60] showing what it said was damage inflicted by Iraqi missile attacks on civilian sectors of Behbahan, Dezful, Marivan and Masjid Soleiman on 1 September and between 21 and 27 October.

Responding on 28 November[61] to Iran's allegations of Iraqi bombardment of civilian areas and use of chemical weapons, Iraq labelled these as attempts by Iran to use the United Nations for propaganda purposes, deliberately ignoring significant facts and developments which were further elaborated by Iraq.

By three further letters of 28 November, Iraq cited a 26 October speech attributed to the Ayatollah Khomeini exhorting exportation of the Iranian revolution, as well as other Iranian statements which it said were proof of Iran's premeditated aggression against Iraq;[62] reported aerial bombardment of its communications installations, disrupting Iraq's international communications services;[63] and transmitted excerpts of official Iraqi military communiqués between 7 and 25 November attesting to the shelling of civilian targets in Iraq and putting the number of dead at four and wounded at seven, in addition to 6 houses destroyed and a number of civilian installations damaged.[64]

On 5 December,[65] Iran stated that eight Iraqi dissidents had defected to Iran, bringing the number of defectors to 1,589 since 23 October 1982. Referring to an Iraqi television broadcast of 3 December alleging Iranian attacks on Iraqi civilian targets and warning of retaliatory action, Iran stated on 6 December[66] that Iraq was fabricating excuses for a new wave of barbaric attacks on civilian centres in Iran. To correct what it called Iran's distortion of the facts, Iraq, on 14 December,[67] transmitted the full text of the broadcast in question and said that Iran's letters of 22 November,[59] 25 November[60] and 6 December[66] sought to fragment the process adopted by the United Nations for resolving the conflict.

Rejecting Iraqi charges of Iranian involvement in recent bomb attacks in Kuwait, Iran by a letter of 14 December[68] said those allegations were part of an orchestrated attempt by Iraq and its allies, particularly France and the United States, to escalate the war into a regional one and thereby pave the way for super-Power intervention in the Gulf region. On 15 December,[69] Iran accused

Iraq of further atrocities against civilians in the Iranian border towns of Andimeshk, Behbahan, Ramhormoz and Dezful, which had left 33 dead, 287 wounded and some 65 houses destroyed; it was the moral and legal obligation of the United Nations, Iran added, to react strongly and without delay to these atrocities in order to deter Iraq from further carrying out its savage designs. Replying on 23 December,[70] Iraq said its view of such allegations had been set forth in its 29 November letter.[55] Earlier, on 16 December,[71] Iran again accused Iraq of extending the war to the Gulf area by its aerial attack on 8 December of two merchant ships, one Greek and one Cypriot, on approaching Iranian ports, and warned of retaliation in kind.

Following a reported televised announcement on 24 December by Iraq of its intention to strike back at civilian targets in Iran for that country's alleged recent bombardment of Iraqi villages and towns, Iran confirmed on 28 December[72] that its city of Masjid Soleiman had been attacked by ground-to-ground missiles three days earlier, in the early evening to ensure the maximum number of casualties: 32 people were dead, 92 others injured, 50 residential units destroyed, 250 shops or houses damaged and 18 automobiles smashed.

Referring to Iran's communications of 20 April[12] and 14 October[40] alleging Iraqi attacks on its offshore oilfields which had resulted in the pollution of the marine environment—in violation of what Iran cited as article 35 of the Geneva Convention on the safety of the environment and the Kuwait Regional Convention on Co-operation for the Protection of the Marine Environment from Pollution and its protocol—Iraq, on 23 December,[73] challenged the existence of the Geneva Convention cited and contended that the Kuwait Convention did not apply in cases of armed conflict. Also on 23 December,[74] Iraq transmitted excerpts of official communiqués from its military, giving details of Iranian shelling of civilian targets in Iraq between 25 November and 19 December, resulting in one dead and five wounded, destruction of some 26 houses and damage to a number of civilian installations.

GENERAL ASSEMBLY ACTION (December)

Inclusion in the agenda of the 1983 session of the General Assembly of an item entitled "Consequences of the prolongation of the armed conflict between Iran and Iraq" had been requested by Iraq in a letter of 29 July.[75] In an enclosed memorandum, Iraq explained that Iran had stood alone against the will of the international community, which had widely endorsed the Assembly's 1982 resolution[76] affirming the necessity of an immediate cease-fire. As the only body encompassing all members of that community, the Assembly must once again express its view, Iraq stated, and take steps with regard to Iran's policy of prolonging the conflict and rejecting settlement by peaceful means.

The Assembly's action on the request was embodied in decision 38/456 of 20 December, by which it decided to consider that item, among others, at its resumed session in 1984 (see Chapter XI of this section, under GENERAL ASSEMBLY).

Other action. In 1983, other action relating to the Iran-Iraq conflict included a resolution adopted by the West Asian Regional Preparatory Meeting on the International Conference on the Question of Palestine (Sharjah, United Arab Emirates, 25-29 April),[77] by which the Meeting, convinced of the need to bring the conflict to an end without delay, called for redoubled efforts by the international community to restore peace to the region.

The Sub-Commission on Prevention of Discrimination and Protection of Minorities of the Commission on Human Rights, in a 3 September resolution on the exploitation of child labour, recommended for adoption by the Commission a draft resolution among whose provisions was a call on Iran to cease immediately the use of children in its armed forces (see ECONOMIC AND SOCIAL QUESTIONS, Chapter XVIII, under "Rights of the child").

REFERENCES

[1]S/15616. [2]YUN 1982, p. 362. [3]S/15597. [4]A/38/89-S/15596. [5]A/38/91-S/15608. [6]A/38/99-S/15627. [7]A/38/178-S/15744. [8]A/38/108-S/15632. [9]YUN 1980, p. 312. [10]A/38/113-S/15636. [11]A/38/155-S/15699. [12]A/38/163-S/15723. [13]A/38/187-S/15752. [14]A/38/165-S/15729. [15]A/38/167-S/15735. [16]A/38/173-S/15739. [17]A/38/177-S/15743 & Corr.1. [18]S/15747. [19]S/15765. [20]S/15763. [21]A/38/238-S/15796. [22]A/38/239-S/15798. [23]A/38/267-S/15824. [24]A/38/268-S/15825. [25]A/38/269-S/15826. [26]S/15834. [27]S/15804. [28]S/15851. [29]S/15874. [30]S/15909. [31]A/38/330-S/15915. [32]S/15926. [33]S/15932 & Add.1. [34]S/15934. [35]S/15941. [36]S/15962. [37]A/38/408-S/15983. [38]S/16000. [39]S/16019. [40]S/16049. [41]S/16053. [42]A/38/523-S/16061. [43]S/16071. [44]S/16104. [45]S/16214. [46]A/38/560-S/16120. [47]S/16213. [48]S/16117. [49]A/38/564-S/16122. [50]S/16129. [51]S/16128. [52]S/16139. [53]S/16140. [54]S/16154. [55]A/38/650-S/16193. [56]S/16235. [57]A/38/590-S/16156. [58]A/38/591-S/16157. [59]A/38/604-S/16181. [60]S/16185. [61]A/38/616-S/16186. [62]A/38/617-S/16189. [63]A/38/618-S/16190. [64]A/38/619-S/16191. [65]A/38/694. [66]S/16204. [67]A/38/763-S/16225. [68]S/16218. [69]S/16220. [70]A/38/769-S/16240. [71]S/16222. [72]S/16236. [73]A/38/767-S/16238. [74]A/38/768-S/16239. [75]A/38/191. [76]YUN 1982, p. 363, GA res. 37/3, 22 Oct. 1982. [77]A/CONF.114/3.

Chapter VIII

Mediterranean

In 1983, the United Nations focused its attention on several political issues concerning the Mediterranean region: the question of Cyprus, complaints by the Libyan Arab Jamahiriya against the United States, and strengthening security and co-operation in the region.

The Security Council twice extended the stationing of the United Nations Peace-keeping Force in Cyprus (UNFICYP), by resolutions 534(1983) and 544(1983). In May 1983, when it resumed its thirty-seventh (1982) session, the General Assembly adopted resolution 37/253, calling for implementation of United Nations resolutions on Cyprus, in addition to demanding immediate withdrawal of all occupation forces from that country. On 15 November, the Turkish Cypriot community issued a declaration purporting to create an independent State in northern Cyprus, naming it the "Turkish Republic of Northern Cyprus". Meeting on 18 November, the Council adopted resolution 541(1983), deploring the declaration, considering it as legally invalid and calling for its withdrawal. In December, the Assembly, by decision 38/456, deferred consideration of the Cyprus question to its resumed thirty-eighth (1983) session, to be held in 1984.

At the request of the Libyan Arab Jamahiriya, the Council convened in February and in August 1983 to consider complaints by that country of military threats and provocations against it by the United States.

The Assembly, by resolution 38/189 adopted in December, encouraged Mediterranean States to intensify co-operation aimed at reducing tension and strengthening security in that region and urged all other States to co-operate towards that end.

Topics related to this chapter. Africa: questions involving the Libyan Arab Jamahiriya. International Court of Justice: continental shelf delimitation between the Libyan Arab Jamahiriya and Malta.

Cyprus question

Searching for an intercommunal settlement on Cyprus, representatives of the Greek Cypriot and Turkish Cypriot communities continued to meet during 1983, under the mission of good offices of the Secretary-General, entrusted to him by the Security Council, with the last 1983 meeting taking place on 14 April. On his recommendation, the Council in June and again in December extended the stationing of UNFICYP in Cyprus, each time for six months, so that it could continue monitoring the cease-fire lines drawn in 1974[1] between the Cyprus National Guard in the south and the Turkish and Turkish Cypriot forces in the north. On both occasions, the Council requested the Secretary-General to continue his good offices mission.

At the first part of its resumed 1982 session, held in May 1983, the General Assembly considered the Cyprus question for the first time since 1979. The Assembly demanded the immediate withdrawal of all occupying forces from Cyprus and reiterated that the Council should examine the implementation, within a specified time-frame, of its relevant resolutions and, if necessary, adopt measures under the Charter of the United Nations for ensuring implementation of United Nations resolutions on Cyprus.

The major political development of the year, which had negative consequences for the resumption of the intercommunal talks, was the declaration issued on 15 November by the Turkish Cypriot community, purporting to create an independent State within the Republic of Cyprus, naming it "Turkish Republic of Northern Cyprus". The Council deplored the declaration, considered it as legally invalid and called for its withdrawal; it further called on all States not to recognize any Cypriot State other than the Republic of Cyprus and again requested the Secretary-General to continue his good offices mission.

Cyprus and Turkey addressed a number of communications to the Secretary-General on the Cyprus question. Those from Turkey transmitted letters from representatives of the Turkish Cypriot community and were signed by Rauf R. Denktas as "President of the Turkish Federated State of Kibris" (Kibris being the Turkish-language name for Cyprus), by Kenan Atakol as "Minister for Foreign Affairs and Defence of the Turkish Federated State of Kibris" or by Nail Atalay as "representative of the Turkish Federated State of Kibris". As from 15 November, "Turkish Republic of Northern Cyprus" replaced "Turkish Federated State of Kibris" in these designations.

Communications (January-April). Communications from the two sides between January and April concerned property expropriation, with Cyprus reiterating its determination to take legal action against any individual or entity expropriating Greek Cypriot properties; allegations of territorial sea and airspace violations by Turkey; allegations of Cypriot support of Armenian terrorist activities against Turkish diplomats; and Greece's position on the Cyprus question.

On 8 February, Turkey transmitted a letter of the same day from Mr. Atalay,[2] who stated that the alleged violation of the 12-mile territorial sea of Cyprus by Turkish warships on 3 December 1982[3] deserved no reply, since the area in question was under the control and sovereignty of what he referred to as the Turkish Federated State of Kibris; unilateral actions by the Greek Cypriot administration, including extending its territorial sea from 3 to 12 miles, were devoid of legality and hence not binding on the Turkish Cypriot side.

Referring to a Cypriot protest of 29 December 1982[3] against the issuance of "definitive possession certificates" to Turkish Cypriots, Mr. Atalay explained on 22 February[4] that the certificates were aimed at finalizing rehabilitation of the 50 per cent of the Turkish Cypriot population who had moved from the south to the north as a result of past armed conflict in Cyprus and who, under law, were entitled to settlement in property equal in value to property they had left behind. The certificates in no way jeopardized anyone's right to equal property in the south or to compensation in full, and their issuance was without prejudice to a final political solution of the Cyprus question. A statement said to elaborate the legality of the issue was annexed to the letter.

Cyprus, by letters of 17 March[5] and 22 March,[6] further protested the continuing illegal expropriation of properties belonging to non-Turkish Cypriots in occupied Cyprus, drawing attention to a confiscation there of 32 houses owned by Maronite Cypriot families and to the assignment of 27 hotels and other tourist installations to a so-called Tourism Ministry. Responding to the earlier letter—which had also accused Turkey of evading its responsibilities by simply transmitting communications on the Cyprus situation from Mr. Atalay, who served Turkey's interests rather than those of Cyprus—Turkey, on 28 March,[7] said such attacks had no bearing on the issues at hand and should not be allowed if diplomatic discourse was to continue. As to the Cypriot protests against so-called property expropriation, Mr. Atalay, on 19 April,[8] reiterated his position as set forth on 22 February,[4] and, on 25 April,[9] stated that the Maronite houses had been legally requisitioned and renovated for public use, without prejudice to the owners' rights.

On 4 April,[10] Cyprus cited two instances of violations of its airspace by Turkey on 22 March, each involving two F-4 jet fighters originating from southern Turkey; in the second instance, the fighters appeared to have launched air-to-surface rockets and opened machine-gun fire. Such warlike actions and the continued occupation of 40 per cent of Cypriot territory, Cyprus said, was proof of Turkey's interest, not in a political solution of the Cyprus problem, but in expansionist goals. Responding on 18 April,[11] Mr. Atalay stated that the military air exercises referred to had taken place within the Turkish Federated State of Kibris, over which the Greek Cypriot administration had no right of say.

Cyprus drew attention on 5 April[12] to what it described as Turkey's propaganda campaign alleging that Cyprus was aiding and abetting terrorist activities against Turkish diplomats by Armenian organizations in Cyprus. Calling the allegations unfounded and denying the existence of such organizations—as an investigation by UNFICYP had confirmed—Cyprus concluded that the campaign was intended to cover up new aggression planned against it. In reiterating these statements on 19 April,[13] Cyprus stated that the Secretary-General and Member States would doubtless act to end Turkey's threats against the sovereignty and territorial integrity of Cyprus.

Earlier, a letter of 18 April from Mr. Denktas, forwarded the same day by Mr. Atalay through Turkey,[14] had warned that certain developments, including a joint decision by Greece and the Greek Cypriot leadership to resort again to the United Nations, would adversely affect the ongoing intercommunal negotiations. The letter referred to a "destructive statement" by the President of Greece during a recent visit to Athens by the President of Cyprus to the effect that the independence attained by Cyprus would allow it to develop as a State, without dismissing the hope of union with Greece under certain conditions. That visit, the letter said, had again underlined the fact that the expansionist aims of Greece continued to guide the Greek Cypriot leadership.

Report of the Secretary-General (May). In his report on the question of Cyprus[15] to the resumed 1982 session of the General Assembly, held in May 1983, the Secretary-General updated information contained in reports submitted to the Assembly's 1980[16] and 1981[17] sessions. Consideration of the question having been deferred at those sessions, those reports had remained before the Assembly.

The Secretary-General noted that, since January 1982, the intercommunal talks, within the framework of the mission of good offices entrusted to him by the Security Council, had continued regularly under the auspices of his Special

Representative, Hugo J. Gobbi, in an atmosphere that had remained co-operative and constructive. Using the 1981 "evaluation paper" as a method of discussion,[18] the interlocutors of the two sides had systematically discussed the elements identified as "points of coincidence" (on which the positions of the parties largely coincided) and "points of equidistance" (on which substantial differences remained to be bridged). Discussed during 1982 were elements relating to the constitutional aspect; freedom of movement and of settlement and the right of property; organs of the federal Government and transitional provisions, including a re-examination of general constitutional provisions; and the territorial aspect.

The talks had continued into 1983 on various other aspects, with the pace adjusted by consent, in connection with the February presidential elections in Cyprus and thereafter as required. The latest meeting had taken place on 14 April.

With a view to promoting the negotiating process, the Secretary-General had maintained personal contacts with both sides, meeting with President Spyros Kyprianou and Mr. Denktas separately in 1982 on three occasions. He further met with President Kyprianou on 8 March and 24 April 1983, and expected further meetings with Mr. Denktas. The Secretary-General stated his intention to strengthen his personal involvement within the framework of his mission of good offices, in particular to give fresh impetus to the negotiating process and to encourage the parties to develop an overall synthesis covering the remaining major unresolved issues.

UNFICYP had continued to supervise the cease-fire lines, to provide security for civilians in the buffer zone between those lines and to discharge certain humanitarian responsibilities (see below, under PEACE-KEEPING OPERATIONS).

The Secretary-General and his Special Representative had continued efforts to assist in overcoming procedural difficulties that were preventing the Committee on Missing Persons in Cyprus from carrying out its humanitarian task.

GENERAL ASSEMBLY ACTION (May)

Pursuant to a December 1982 decision,[19] the General Assembly took up the question of Cyprus at the first part of its resumed 1982 session, held from 10 to 13 May 1983.

As recommended by its General Committee,[20] the Assembly on 10 May decided to consider the question directly in plenary meeting, on the understanding that it would, when considering the item, invite the Special Political Committee to meet to afford representatives of the two Cypriot communities an opportunity to express their views; the Committee's report on those views would be taken into account by the Assembly.[21]

The Assembly President informed the Committee of that decision, also on 10 May.[22]

Prior to these actions, Mr. Atalay, by a letter of 27 April transmitted by Turkey on the same date,[23] had requested that the item be allocated, not to the plenary Assembly in accordance with past procedure, but to a Main Committee, so as to provide both sides full participation in the debate on an equal footing. Cyprus replied on 6 May[24] that to revise a well-established procedure would disturb the delicate balance struck in 1974 through arduous negotiations and lend support to Turkey's effort to undermine the sovereignty of States Members of the United Nations.

On 10 May,[25] Mr. Atalay said that the procedure decided upon by the Assembly was unacceptable to the Turkish Cypriot side as it was inconsistent with the acknowledged principle of equality between the parties to the Cyprus dispute—a principle which he said had been endorsed and confirmed, respectively, by high-level meetings in 1977[26] and 1979.[27] A debate on the question would be inherently incomplete, since the Assembly would be precluded from becoming fully acquainted with the views of the Turkish Cypriot community.

The Special Political Committee reported[28] to the Assembly that, on 10 May 1983, it had heard a statement by a representative of the Greek Cypriot community, which was reproduced in the meeting record.

Acting on an oral proposal by the President, the Assembly adopted decision 37/455.

Question of Cyprus

At its 117th plenary meeting, on 11 May 1983, the General Assembly took note of the report of the Special Political Committee.

General Assembly decision 37/455

Adopted without vote

Oral proposal by President; agenda item 37.
Meeting numbers. GA 37th session: SPC 50; plenary 116, 117.

On 13 May, at the conclusion of the debate on the Cyprus question held at six meetings, the Assembly adopted resolution 37/253 by recorded vote.

Question of Cyprus

The General Assembly,

Having considered the question of Cyprus,

Recalling its resolution 3212(XXIX) of 1 November 1974 and its subsequent resolutions on the question of Cyprus,

Recalling the high-level agreements of 12 February 1977 and 19 May 1979,

Reaffirming the principle of the inadmissibility of occupation and acquisition of territory by force,

Greatly concerned at the prolongation of the Cyprus crisis, which poses a serious threat to international peace and security,

Deeply regretting that the resolutions of the United Nations on Cyprus have not yet been implemented,

Recalling the idea of holding an international conference on Cyprus,

Deploring the fact that part of the territory of the Republic of Cyprus is still occupied by foreign forces,

Deploring the lack of progress in the intercommunal talks,

Deploring all unilateral actions that change the demographic structure of Cyprus or promote *faits accomplis*,

Reaffirming the need to settle the question of Cyprus without further delay by peaceful means in accordance with the provisions of the Charter of the United Nations and the relevant United Nations resolutions,

1. *Reiterates* its full support for the sovereignty, independence, territorial integrity, unity and non-alignment of the Republic of Cyprus and calls once again for the cessation of all foreign interference in its affairs;

2. *Affirms* the right of the Republic of Cyprus and its people to full and effective sovereignty and control over the entire territory of Cyprus and its natural and other resources and calls upon all States to support and help the Government of the Republic of Cyprus to exercise these rights;

3. *Condemns* any act which tends to undermine the full and effective exercise of the above-mentioned rights, including the unlawful issue of titles of ownership of property;

4. *Welcomes* the proposal for total demilitarization made by the President of the Republic of Cyprus;

5. *Expresses its support* for the high-level agreements of 12 February 1977 and 19 May 1979 and all the provisions thereof;

6. *Demands* the immediate and effective implementation of resolution 3212(XXIX), unanimously adopted by the General Assembly and endorsed by the Security Council in its resolution 365(1974) of 13 December 1974, and of the subsequent resolutions of the Assembly and the Council on Cyprus which provide the valid and essential basis for the solution of the problem of Cyprus;

7. *Considers* the withdrawal of all occupation forces from the Republic of Cyprus as an essential basis for a speedy and mutually acceptable solution of the problem of Cyprus;

8. *Demands* the immediate withdrawal of all occupation forces from the Republic of Cyprus;

9. *Commends* the intensification of the efforts made by the Secretary-General, while noting with concern the lack of progress in the intercommunal talks;

10. *Calls* for meaningful, result-oriented, constructive and substantive negotiations between the representatives of the two communities, under the auspices of the Secretary-General, to be conducted freely and on an equal footing, on the basis of relevant United Nations resolutions and the high-level agreements, with a view to reaching as early as possible a mutually acceptable agreement based on the fundamental and legitimate rights of the two communities;

11. *Calls* for respect of the human rights and fundamental freedoms of all Cypriots, including the freedom of movement, the freedom of settlement and the right to property, and the instituting of urgent measures for the voluntary return of the refugees to their homes in safety;

12. *Considers* that the *de facto* situation created by the force of arms should not be allowed to influence or in any way affect the solution of the problem of Cyprus;

13. *Calls upon* the parties concerned to refrain from any unilateral action which might adversely affect the prospects of a just and lasting solution of the problem of Cyprus by peaceful means and to co-operate fully with the Secretary-General in the performance of his task under the relevant resolutions of the General Assembly and the Security Council as well as with the United Nations Peace-keeping Force in Cyprus;

14. *Calls upon* the parties concerned to refrain from any action which violates or is designed to violate the independence, unity, sovereignty and territorial integrity of the Republic of Cyprus;

15. *Reiterates its recommendation* that the Security Council should examine the question of implementation, within a specified time-frame, of its relevant resolutions and consider and adopt thereafter, if necessary, all appropriate and practical measures under the Charter of the United Nations for ensuring the speedy and effective implementation of the resolutions of the United Nations on Cyprus;

16. *Welcomes* the intention of the Secretary-General, as expressed in his report, to pursue a renewed personal involvement in the quest for a solution of the problem of Cyprus and, in view of this, requests the Secretary-General to undertake such actions or initiatives as he may consider appropriate within the framework of the mission of good offices entrusted to him by the Security Council for promoting a just and lasting solution of the problem and to report to the General Assembly at its thirty-eighth session on the results of his efforts;

17. *Decides* to include in the provisional agenda of its thirty-eighth session the item entitled "Question of Cyprus" and requests the Secretary-General to follow up the implementation of the present resolution and to report on all its aspects to the General Assembly at that session.

General Assembly resolution 37/253

13 May 1983   Meeting 121   103-5-20 (recorded vote)

30-nation draft (A/37/L.63 & Add.1); agenda item 37.

Sponsors: Algeria, Angola, Benin, Botswana, Cape Verde, Congo, Costa Rica, Cuba, Democratic Yemen, Ecuador, Ethiopia, Grenada, Guyana, Haiti, India, Jamaica, Kenya, Lesotho, Mali, Mozambique, Nicaragua, Nigeria, Panama, Saint Lucia, Sao Tome and Principe, Seychelles, Sri Lanka, Togo, Yugoslavia, Zambia.

Meeting numbers. GA 37th session: General Committee 6; SPC 50; plenary 116-121.

Recorded vote in Assembly as follows:

In favour: Afghanistan, Algeria, Angola, Argentina, Australia, Austria, Bahamas, Barbados, Benin, Bhutan, Bolivia, Botswana, Brazil, Bulgaria, Burma, Burundi, Byelorussian SSR, Cape Verde, China, Colombia, Congo, Costa Rica, Cuba, Cyprus, Czechoslovakia, Democratic Yemen, Dominica, Dominican Republic, Ecuador, Egypt, Ethiopia, Fiji, Finland, France, Gambia, German Democratic Republic, Ghana, Greece, Guinea, Guyana, Haiti, Hungary, India, Ireland, Ivory Coast, Jamaica, Kenya, Lao People's Democratic Republic, Lebanon, Lesotho, Liberia, Libyan Arab Jamahiriya, Madagascar, Malawi, Mali, Malta, Mauritius, Mexico, Mongolia, Mozambique, Nepal, New Zealand, Nicaragua, Niger, Nigeria, Panama, Papua New Guinea, Paraguay, Peru, Philippines, Poland, Portugal, Romania, Rwanda, Saint Lucia, Saint Vincent and the Grenadines, Samoa, Sao Tome and Principe, Senegal, Seychelles, Sierra Leone, Spain, Sri Lanka, Sudan, Suriname, Swaziland, Sweden, Syrian Arab Republic, Thailand, Togo, Trinidad and Tobago, Uganda, Ukrainian SSR, USSR, United Republic of Cameroon, Upper Volta, Uruguay, Vanuatu, Venezuela, Viet Nam, Yugoslavia, Zambia, Zimbabwe.

Against: Bangladesh, Malaysia, Pakistan, Somalia, Turkey.

Abstaining: Belgium, Canada, Denmark, Germany, Federal Republic of, Guatemala, Iceland, Indonesia, Israel, Italy, Japan, Jordan, Luxembourg, Maldives, Morocco, Netherlands, Norway, Saudi Arabia, Tunisia, United Kingdom, United States.

Prior to adoption of the draft resolution as a whole, paragraphs 7 and 15 were adopted by recorded votes of 89 to 5, with 27 abstentions, and by 86 to 8, with 25 abstentions, respectively.

In announcing its intention to vote against the draft as a whole, Turkey said it could support only the reaffirmation of the principle of the inadmissibility of acquisition of territory by force, and stressed that its forces in Cyprus were not of occupation but of protection. Turkey explained in detail why the text was unacceptable to the Turkish Cypriot community and why, if adopted, it could not be taken into consideration in the intercommunal negotiations and would lead to a re-evaluation of that community's position.

Turkey's main objections were that: implementation of paragraph 2 could result in the annihilation of the Turkish Cypriot community; paragraphs 3, 4 and 11 were incompatible with provisions of the 1977[26] and 1979[27] high-level agreements; paragraph 7 could be interpreted as making troop withdrawal a condition for continuing the negotiations, thereby offering the Greek Cypriot community and Greece an opportunity to sabotage or prolong those negotiations; the Secretary-General's opening statement at the formal resumption of the intercommunal talks in 1980[29] and the 1981 "evaluation paper"[18] were not cited as part of the basis for the negotiations; paragraph 9 contradicted the Secretary-General's evaluation of the talks; paragraph 13 did not correspond entirely to legal realities—the Secretary-General's mission of good offices had been entrusted to him by a Council resolution and not also by Assembly resolutions, a mission which paragraph 16, owing to its ambiguity, was liable to prejudice; and paragraph 15 contained an inopportune recommendation.

Turkey said the draft was totally defective, for nowhere did it mention the principal objective of the intercommunal talks: a sovereign, independent, territorially integrated and non-aligned Republic of Cyprus, which should also be bicommunal, bizonal and federal, as specified in the high-level agreements and in the Secretary-General's 1980 statement.

Somalia said it cast a negative vote because, apart from believing that more time should have been allowed for the Secretary-General's efforts and the intercommunal talks to bear fruit, it felt that certain provisions with which it disagreed rendered the text unbalanced.

Among those explaining their abstentions, Denmark and Tunisia likewise noted a lack of balance; Denmark added that only direct negotiations between the parties could lead to a settlement. The United Kingdom would have liked the provisions of the 1960 treaties and arrangements (pertaining to the independence of Cyprus) more accurately reflected in paragraph 2, stated that its position regarding paragraph 4 was in accordance with point 7 of the 1979 high-level agreement, and considered paragraph 15 inappropriate; however, it wanted to place on record its support for certain elements, paragraph 16 in particular, remarking that the Secretary-General's intention to strengthen his personal involvement in the negotiating process deserved the international community's whole-hearted support. Japan and Jordan voiced such support, with Jordan saying that the Secretary-General should be given sufficient time to find a formula acceptable to both communities and that in the mean time it was necessary to avoid any course that might prove prejudicial to the negotiations' outcome.

Cyprus, reiterating that the objective of its Government had always been sovereignty, independence and freedom, quoted a paragraph from a resolution recently adopted by its House of Representatives. That paragraph stated, among other things, that the House rejected any solution resulting in the abolition of the Republic of Cyprus, in the annexation of its territory, in whole or in part, by another State, or in the declaration of any part of that territory as a separate State. Cyprus went on to say that the Assembly's vote for the current resolution would be a vote for justice for a small State that had been brutally invaded by a neighbouring State at least 80 times larger in area, population and military power. Although that vote could not undo the injustice done to Cyprus, it would show once more the Assembly's firm stand for the beliefs and principles for which the United Nations had been established and its readiness to continue upholding them until their universal application was realized.

Of the other States explaining their affirmative votes, Barbados said it found nothing in the text that was inconsistent with its commitment to a just settlement through negotiation and to the total demilitarization of Cyprus; nor did it share the pessimistic view that the literal content of the text would seriously damage its fundamental intent. For Colombia, its vote was a demonstration of solidarity with: the principles of sovereign equality of States, non-interference and dispute settlement by means other than force; the efforts of the Secretary-General and his Special Representative; the Cypriot refugees and people; and the Government of Cyprus. Sierra Leone, the Sudan and Venezuela expressed similar views.

Mongolia, Romania and Spain saw the draft as reflecting their belief in the need to solve the Cyprus problem through negotiations based on respect for the independence, sovereignty, territorial integrity and unity of the Republic of Cyprus; Romania, adding the need to respect the non-aligned status of Cyprus, emphasized that it took the reference to troops to mean all foreign armed forces. The Libyan Arab Jamahiriya said its vote signified its desire to help the two communities find a just solution and should in no way be interpreted as favouring either one.

Despite their affirmative votes on the text as a whole, some States expressed certain reservations, among them Austria, the Sudan and Uruguay, all of which had abstained in the separate votes on paragraphs 7 and 15. In the Sudan's view, the international community should lay stress on points of agreement between the two sides rather than on those dividing them.

Uruguay believed that the emphasis on troop withdrawal as essential for a speedy solution might prove a limiting factor to the negotiations. Paragraph 7, containing that provision, seemed ambiguous to France, which noted that, while foreign intervention and occupation existed in Cyprus, that situation should not slow down efforts towards a settlement.

Austria voiced serious misgivings on the Council action recommended in paragraph 15. France, which abstained on that paragraph, questioned the mixing of Council and Assembly jurisdictions, an observation similarly made by Uruguay.

The preambular paragraph on an international conference should have been completely deleted, Uruguay felt, while France wondered whether it was opportune to hold such a conference just when the Secretary-General had announced strengthening his personal involvement in the search for a solution.

Principles governing international relations and essential norms of the functioning of the United Nations, reaffirmed in the resolution, were cited by Portugal in support of the text; they were the same reasons, however, that prevented it from subscribing to certain affirmations in the preambular section and to paragraph 15, against which it had voted. Egypt said its central concern was encouragement of the negotiating process, and therefore it would have preferred the resolution to have been drafted in more conciliatory terms.

Communications (May). On 9 May 1983, the day before the General Assembly resumed its 1982 session to consider the Cyprus question, Mr. Atakol addressed a letter transmitted, also on 9 May, by Mr. Atalay through Turkey,[30] charging that the Greek Cypriot side had sought another recourse to the Assembly in a campaign to internationalize the Cyprus question, to justify its allegation of lack of progress in the intercommunal negotiations. Having summarized developments since the talks resumed in 1980 until their adjournment on 14 April 1983, Mr. Atakol concluded that the lack of progress was due to deleterious tactics by the Greek Cypriot side.

Referring to what it called Turkey's lecture about norms of diplomatic behaviour within the United Nations, as contained in that State's 28 March letter,[7] Cyprus said on 16 May[31] that it was ironic that such a lecture should come from a country which had initiated the practice of circulating, as official documents, communications containing innuendoes about duly accredited representatives of Cyprus to the United Nations, from a fictitious entity set up in contempt of Assembly and Council resolutions.

On 18 May,[32] Cyprus drew attention to what it said was an explicit indication of Turkey's expansionist designs on Cyprus—the issuance by Turkey's Ministry of Culture and Tourism of a museum entrance ticket depicting the territories of Turkey and Cyprus as if they were a single entity.

By a letter of 23 May,[33] Cyprus pointed to a series of what it described as ominous statements by Mr. Denktas, who had made clear his intention to proclaim occupied Cyprus an independent and sovereign "State".

Report of the Secretary-General (June). In his June 1983 report to the Security Council on the United Nations operation in Cyprus covering 1 December 1982 to 31 May 1983,[34] the Secretary-General brought up to date the record of UNFICYP activities, of developments on the resumed intercommunal talks within the framework of the 1979 high-level agreement[27] and of progress regarding his mission of good offices.

The Secretary-General stated, as he had in his report to the General Assembly in May,[15] that he had pursued the good offices mission. The intercommunal talks had continued in Nicosia, with their frequency adjusted to take account of the February presidential elections in Cyprus and thereafter as necessary. The 1981 "evaluation paper"[18] had continued to serve as a structured, substantive method of discussion. An open agenda pattern, adopted at the beginning of 1983, had been helpful in conducting the discussions. The latest meeting of the talks had taken place on 14 April 1983.

The Secretary-General's Special Representative had come to United Nations Headquarters for consultations in December 1982 and May 1983. In addition to a general exchange of views with President Kyprianou on 8 March and 24 April 1983, the Secretary-General had met in New York in May with the Minister for Foreign Affairs of Cyprus, Nicos A. Rolandis, in connection with the Assembly debate on the Cyprus question then in progress, and also with Mr. Atakol, who had conveyed the views of the Turkish Cypriot community.

Following adoption of Assembly resolution 37/253, the leaders of the Turkish Cypriot community announced their decision not to attend the intercommunal meeting scheduled for 31 May.

The Secretary-General continued to hold the view that the intercommunal talks represented the best means of pursuing an effective negotiating process aimed at achieving an agreed, just and lasting settlement. He thus reiterated the hope that talks could be resumed as soon as possible on the existing and mutually accepted basis which remained valid, and appealed to the parties to show the utmost restraint and to assist him in his efforts. As to strengthening his personal involvement in the negotiations, the Secretary-General made clear that his effort was intended to be within the framework of the good offices mission; it would seek to carry forward the work done during the current phase of negotiations without affecting matters previously agreed upon, be inseparable from the intercommunal talks and involve extensive consultations between him and all concerned.

The Secretary-General regretted that, despite renewed efforts by the Committee on Missing Persons in Cyprus, the procedural difficulties preventing it from embarking on its work remained unresolved.

At the Secretary-General's request, the United Nations High Commissioner for Refugees (UNHCR), as Co-ordinator of United Nations Humanitarian Assistance for Cyprus, had continued to assist the displaced and needy in the island (see ECONOMIC AND SOCIAL QUESTIONS, Chapter XXI).

UNFICYP continued to maintain calm and promote normalization in the island (see below, under PEACE-KEEPING OPERATIONS). In the light of the situation on the ground and of political developments, the Secretary-General concluded that the continued presence of UNFICYP remained necessary and recommended to the Council, with the concurrence of the parties, that it extend the UNFICYP mandate for a further period of six months.

SECURITY COUNCIL ACTION (June)

The Security Council met twice on 15 June 1983 to consider the Secretary-General's report and recommendation for the extension of the mandate of UNFICYP. At their request, Canada, Cyprus, Greece and Turkey were invited to participate in the discussion without the right to vote; Mr. Atalay was invited to participate in conformity with rule 39[a] of the Council's provisional rules of procedure.

On the same date, the Council unanimously adopted resolution 534(1983).

The Security Council,

Taking note of the report of the Secretary-General on the United Nations operation in Cyprus of 1 June 1983,

Noting the concurrence of the parties concerned in the recommendation by the Secretary-General that the Security Council should extend the stationing of the United Nations Peace-keeping Force in Cyprus for a further period of six months,

Noting also that the Government of Cyprus has agreed that in view of the prevailing conditions in the island it is necessary to keep the Force in Cyprus beyond 15 June 1983,

Reaffirming the provisions of its resolution 186(1964) and other relevant resolutions,

Reiterating its support of the ten-point agreement for the resumption of the intercommunal talks which was worked out at the high-level meeting on 18 and 19 May 1979 at Nicosia under the auspices of the Secretary-General,

1. *Extends once more* the stationing in Cyprus of the United Nations Peace-keeping Force established under resolution 186(1964) for a further period, ending on 15 December 1983;

2. *Notes with satisfaction* that the parties have resumed the intercommunal talks within the framework of the ten-point agreement and urges them to pursue these talks in a continuing, sustained and result-oriented manner, avoiding any delay;

3. *Requests* the Secretary-General to continue his mission of good offices, to keep the Security Council informed of the progress made and to submit a report on the implementation of the present resolution by 30 November 1983.

Security Council resolution 534(1983)

15 June 1983   Meeting 2453   Adopted unanimously

Draft prepared in consultations among Council members (S/15828).
Meeting numbers. SC 2453, 2454.

In the debate, Cyprus stated that the previous six months had seen a deterioration of the situation in the island. Turkey had further consolidated its incorporation of occupied Cyprus by proceeding with a series of illegal steps initiated the previous year: it had established a so-called central bank, had continued issuing "definitive certificates of ownership" entitling persons to properties belonging to Greek Cypriots and had introduced the Turkish lira, as of 24 May, as the official tender in occupied Cyprus. Turkey had also refused to attend the talks or respond to the Secretary-General's invitation to a meeting to discuss his intention to pursue his renewed personal involvement. Turkey's argument for its refusal was the internationalization of the Cyprus question, which it claimed was contrary to the spirit of the intercommunal talks. Having given its consent to the renewal of the UNFICYP mandate, Cyprus said it extended its full co-operation in the continuation of free and result-oriented negotiations under the Secretary-General's auspices and appealed to Turkey to do likewise.

Greece observed that perpetuation of the Cyprus problem and its development into a major international anomaly had made it ritual for the Council to hear government views twice yearly, at the renewal of the UNFICYP mandate; thus it

[a]Rule 39 of the Council's provisional rules of procedure states: "The Security Council may invite members of the Secretariat or other persons, whom it considers competent for the purpose, to supply it with information or to give other assistance in examining matters within its competence."

was with regret that Greece had asked once again to speak on the matter. Concurring with the consent given by Cyprus, Greece said it was time that an all-out effort be made in the search for a solution and urged that advantage be taken of the continued personal involvement of the Secretary-General. Greece hoped Turkey would co-operate.

Mr. Atalay stated that the Turkish people of Cyprus, for whom he was speaking, had empowered him to consent to extending the mandate of the Force until 15 December 1983, despite certain objections to the enabling resolution, and to pledge continued co-operation for the successful execution of its task. He reiterated the hope for a revision of its mandate and *modus operandi* according to realities in Cyprus. He further hoped that the troop-contributing States which had departed from their traditional posture of impartiality by voting for Assembly resolution 37/253 would return to that posture, so essential to peace-keeping.

Mr. Atalay regretted the references, in the Secretary-General's report, to the Greek Cypriot administration as the "Government of Cyprus". The object of the talks under the Secretary-General's good offices, Mr. Atalay declared, was to establish a government—currently non-existent—that would constitutionally and legitimately represent both the Turkish Cypriot and Greek Cypriot peoples; such references prejudged the outcome of the talks and prejudiced their chance of success. To refer to the Turkish Cypriot component as merely the "Turkish Cypriot community" was an injustice to a people legally and morally entitled to equal status with the Greek Cypriots. Mr. Atalay pointed to the same inequitable attitude with respect to designating leaders of the two Cypriot peoples.

Agreeing with the Secretary-General's assessment that the best means towards a settlement of the Cyprus question were the intercommunal talks, Mr. Atalay stressed the Turkish Cypriots' determination to continue those talks and reiterated their hope that the Greek Cypriot leadership would come to the negotiations with the resolute intention of developing a bizonal federal system in Cyprus, based on the high-level agreements of 1977 and 1979, the Secretary-General's 1980 statement and the 1981 "evaluation paper". The repeated assertion of the Greek Cypriot leadership was that sovereignty belonged exclusively to its people; the Turkish Cypriot people's assertion, however, was that sovereignty in Cyprus could come only from an equal partnership between the two communities.

Turkey agreed to the extension of the UNFICYP mandate and supported the Turkish Cypriot community's request that it be brought into line with prevailing conditions in Cyprus. It held the view

that, unless the troop-contributing States whose impartiality had been called into question reconsidered their action, their contribution could no longer serve the cause of peace and understanding in Cyprus. Turkey echoed the objections to the references and designations in the Secretary-General's report cited by Mr. Atalay, as well as those in the Council resolution just adopted, invoking what it called the principle of equality of the two communities. Turkey said it encouraged the resolve of the Turkish Cypriot community not to leave the negotiating table and emphasized that, whatever the reassessment of its position owing to Assembly resolution 37/253, it would in no way weaken that resolve. Turkey also restated those elements cited by Mr. Atalay on which negotiations must be based.

Canada, though reaffirming its commitment to UNFICYP's extended mandate, was concerned over the failure, for more than 19 years, to achieve the primary objective of the Force: to facilitate achievement of a negotiated settlement and a return to peaceful conditions. Despite stable conditions provided by UNFICYP and maintained by United Nations efforts, Canada said, the two communities and others involved in the dispute had displayed a regrettable lack of will to make the difficult compromises required for a successful political settlement. Making known that its patience and resources were not boundless, Canada called on the parties to enter into serious and fruitful discussions so that progress might become evident before the end of the mandate period.

Communications (June-October). In a series of communications, Cyprus drew attention to accelerated partitionist moves by Turkey and its instruments and called for their speedy arrest. For its part, Turkey claimed that such partition rhetoric was an attempt to cloud the issue of Greece's attempts to annex the whole of Cyprus.

On 21 June 1983,[35] Cyprus denounced new Turkish actions said to be directed against the Maronite Cypriots of Asomatos, one of three Maronite villages in occupied Cyprus where homes had been confiscated to house Turkish officers. Cyprus charged that, as part of a long-term plan to turn the area into a military camp, Turkey's occupation forces had begun levelling a number of houses so as to force the remaining 31 inhabitants to abandon their homes.

By a letter of 22 June,[36] Cyprus drew attention to a 17 June resolution of the so-called Turkish Cypriot Legislative Assembly, affirming the right of the Turkish people in the occupied areas of Cyprus to self-determination. Cyprus called this an affront to the international community's verdict, as contained in the General Assembly's May resolution and the Security Council's June resolution.

Responding by a letter of 1 July, transmitted on 11 July by Mr. Atalay through Turkey,[37] Mr. Atakol asserted that the Turkish Cypriot people, co-founder partner of the Republic of Cyprus and one of two equal parties to the Cyprus dispute, could not be relegated to the position of an ethnic minority in a non-existent Cypriot nation. He reaffirmed that the Turkish Cypriots were ready, as they had always been, to re-establish a binational republic in the form of a bizonal federal one, as agreed in 1977 and 1979.

By a letter of 20 June to the President of the General Assembly, transmitted by Mr. Atalay through Turkey on 5 July,[38] Mr. Denktas expressed the regret of the Turkish people of Cyprus over the Assembly President's exclusion of the Turkish Cypriot zone from his visit to Cyprus between 7 and 9 June, as well as over certain remarks he had made during that visit which were anti–Turkish Cypriot in tone.

On 25 July,[39] Cyprus reported that, while memorial services were being held in Cyprus on the occasion of the ninth anniversary of its invasion, Turkey's envoy, in a speech at Morphou in occupied Cyprus, had declared that Morphou and Lefka would never be returned to their rightful owners. Denouncing this declaration as harmful to the intercommunal talks, Cyprus warned that, unless such interventions ceased, the Secretary-General's quest for a just and lasting solution would be seriously jeopardized. Responding on 22 September,[40] Mr. Atalay emphasized that the focus of the intercommunal talks had never been nor would be the status of any particular piece of territory within northern Cyprus but the fundamental question of the bizonality of a federal republic.

In a letter of 27 July,[41] Cyprus stated that, in addition to his recent secessionist declarations and actions, Mr. Denktas, on instructions from Turkey, had accelerated preparations for a unilateral declaration of independence of occupied Cyprus, including a national flag and anthem. On 17 August,[42] Cyprus protested against what it called new aggressive acts by Turkey on 9 August, when F-4 jet fighters originating from Turkey twice violated Cypriot airspace; in one instance, they had appeared to launch air-to-surface rockets and open machine-gun fire. Those military exercises, Mr. Atalay explained on 22 September,[43] had taken place entirely within the territory and airspace of northern Cyprus, under the sovereignty of the Turkish Federated State of Kibris.

On 26 September,[44] Cyprus stated that, as reported by Turkish Cypriot papers, the so-called cabinet of Ankara's puppet régime in occupied Cyprus had decided to prepare a draft law on a proposed national flag—a decision made to coincide with a meeting between President Kyprianou

and the Secretary-General on 14 September in New York. Mr. Atalay stated in a letter of 10 October, transmitted the following day,[45] that the Turkish Cypriot people were determined not to have the Greek national anthem imposed on them and would never accept the Greek flag as the flag of Cyprus. Refuting allegations that Turkey had designs to annex the island, Mr. Atalay pointed to a 1970 book, *Democracy at Gunpoint: the Greek Front*, by Andreas Papandreou, Prime Minister of Greece, in which the author had admitted that 20,000 Greek troops had been sent to Cyprus in 1964.

Greece agreed on 18 October[46] that it had dispatched the troops, but stressed that it had done so at the request of the legal Government of the Republic of Cyprus, to avert a Turkish invasion that eventually took place in 1974. Had those Greek troops remained in Cyprus, the Turkish invasion might have been thwarted, Greece added.

Report of the Secretary-General (December). In a December 1983 report,[47] submitted to the Security Council in response to its request in resolution 534(1983), the Secretary-General gave an account of the United Nations operation in Cyprus from 1 June to 30 November.

The Secretary-General reported that, during the period under review, the search for a settlement of the Cyprus problem had sustained a set-back, despite intensive efforts on his part in co-operation with the parties. As indicated in his previous report,[34] difficulties had arisen in connection with the adoption of General Assembly resolution 37/253. The Turkish Cypriot community held that the resolution tended to undermine the basis of the intercommunal negotiations, and the Turkish interlocutor declined thereafter to attend the intercommunal talks. Hence, no meeting of the talks had been held during the reporting period.

In order to give fresh impetus to the negotiations, the Secretary-General had met with the leader of the Turkish Cypriot community, Mr. Denktas, on 4 July at Geneva. In further contacts at appropriate levels in New York and, through his Special Representative, at Nicosia, the Secretary-General had conveyed to both sides, on 8 and 9 August, informal and confidential soundings on resuming negotiations on the major outstanding issues arising from the "evaluation paper", within the framework of certain "indicators" designed to narrow the gap between the positions of the two sides; the indicators agreed upon would be referred to the intercommunal talks for negotiation. Following further clarifications with President Kyprianou on 14 and 30 September, the Permanent Representative of Greece to the United Nations and the Foreign Minister of Turkey on 30 September, and Mr. Denktas on 1 October, both sides accepted the Secretary-General's personal involvement in his mission of good offices and declared their readiness to resume the intercommunal negoti-ations on the existing and mutually agreed basis.

The Secretary-General consented to lend his good offices to arrange for a high-level meeting suggested by Mr. Denktas on 3 October, which President Kypri-anou had indicated willingness to attend. The meeting was to clarify the intentions of the two sides for a federal solution and pave the way for a resumption of the talks. Accordingly, the Secretary-General's Special Representative had returned to Cyprus on 14 November to initiate arrangements. The following day, however, Mr. Denktas had informed the Secretary-General of the proclamation by the Turkish Cypriot community of a "Turkish Republic of Northern Cyprus"; at the same time, he expressed readiness to resume negotiations at any time and indicated that his proposal for a high-level meeting remained in effect. (For the Secretary-General's account of his activities following that proclamation and adoption of Security Council resolution 541(1983) on 18 November, see below, under ACTION BY THE TURKISH CYPRIOT COMMUNITY.)

The Secretary-General noted that the Committee on Missing Persons in Cyprus remained unable to overcome the procedural issues which had prevented it from performing its substantive task. One of the three Committee members had travelled to Cyprus on 13 November to try to resolve those issues but left on 30 November, as further progress on the hu-manitarian problem had proved impossible; he would resume his efforts at short notice when circumstances so warranted.

The Secretary-General concluded that the con-tinued presence of UNFICYP remained indispens-able and recommended that its mandate be extended for a further period of six months. He subsequently informed the Council that, as of 15 December, Cyprus, Greece and the United Kingdom had indicated their concurrence in the proposed extension.

SECURITY COUNCIL ACTION (December)

On 15 December 1983, the Security Council met to consider the Secretary-General's report and recom-mendation that the mandate of UNFICYP be fur-ther extended. At their request, Cyprus, Greece and Turkey were invited to participate in the discussion without the right to vote; Mr. Atalay was invited to participate under rule 39[b] of the Council's provi-sional rules of procedure.

On the same date, the Council unanimously adopted resolution 544(1983).

The Security Council,

Taking note of the report of the Secretary-General on the United Nations operation in Cyprus of 1 December 1983,

Noting the recommendation by the Secretary-General that the Security Council should extend the stationing of the United Nations Peace-keeping Force in Cyprus for a further period of six months,

Noting also that the Government of Cyprus has agreed that in view of the prevailing conditions in the island it is necessary to keep the Force in Cyprus beyond 15 De-cember 1983,

Reaffirming the provisions of its resolution 186(1964) and other relevant resolutions,

1. *Extends once more* the stationing in Cyprus of the United Nations Peace-keeping Force established under resolution 186(1964) for a further period, ending on 15 June 1984;

2. *Requests* the Secretary-General to continue his mis-sion of good offices, to keep the Security Council informed of the progress made and to submit a report on the im-plementation of the present resolution by 31 May 1984;

3. *Calls upon* all the parties concerned to continue to co-operate with the Force on the basis of the present mandate.

Security Council resolution 544(1983)

15 December 1983   Meeting 2503   Adopted unanimously

Draft prepared in consultations among Council members (S/16217).
Meeting number. SC 2503.

In the debate, Pakistan stated that extending the UNFICYP mandate required a simple procedural resolution; it regretted, therefore, that the adopted text contained elements having no direct bearing on such an extension. The third and fourth pream-bular paragraphs, to which the Turkish Cypriot representative had objected, remained unaltered. Pakistan had also suggested deletion of "other rele-vant resolutions" in the latter paragraph because the phrase implicitly included Council resolution 541(1983), against which it had voted and which the Turkish Cypriot community had rejected. The text, unlike past resolutions on the mandate's ex-tension, made no reference to the intercommunal talks and to the important agreements which had been reached on the Cyprus issue within and out-side the United Nations. For the first time, the Council had adopted a resolution on UNFICYP which did not enjoy the agreement of all the par-ties, Pakistan stated.

Cyprus stated that it had agreed to the man-date's renewal because it believed the presence of UNFICYP was indispensable to the maintenance of peace and security in Cyprus—conditions in which the search for a just and lasting settlement of the Cyprus problem could best be pursued. Cyprus drew attention to its good faith by its prompt response to the Secretary-General's sound-ings for a resumption of the intercommunal talks, acceptance of his personal involvement in the negotiations and of the methodology proposed for advancing them, and readiness to attend the high-level meeting proposed by Mr. Denktas—all of which had been described in the Secretary-General's report as constructive. In contrast, Cyprus observed, Turkey's attitude after Assem-bly resolution 37/253 had been adopted was one

[b]See footnote a on p. 249.

of delay in meeting with the Secretary-General and refusal to accede to his request for written comments on the methodology proposed for resuming the talks.

Greece welcomed the mandate's extension with particular satisfaction because of what it described as the highly explosive situation created by the presence of 30,000 Turkish troops on Cypriot territory. In expressing appreciation to the Force, the troop-contributing countries and the Secretary-General for their efforts in promoting conditions conducive to a just and viable solution, Greece reiterated that such a solution hinged on Turkish troop withdrawal.

Mr. Atalay said the Turkish people of Cyprus had hoped for a Council resolution that would fulfil two overriding objectives of the moment: to extend the UNFICYP mandate and to support the Secretary-General's good offices mission. He recalled that for the past 20 years they had consistently given consent to such extensions after registering strong reservations on the texts' references to the so-called Government of Cyprus. Not only had the current resolution made those same references, he noted, but had also omitted, on the insistence of the Greek Cypriot side, those paragraphs normally referring to the intercommunal talks. For these reasons, among others, the "Government of the Turkish Republic of Northern Cyprus" rejected the resolution in its entirety. Mr. Atalay said that, henceforth, that "Government" alone would decide on the principle, scope and modalities of its co-operation with UNFICYP.

That rejection was regarded as justified by Turkey, which itself characterized the resolution as not designed to reduce tension and facilitate understanding. Turkey also supported Mr. Atalay's statement concerning future co-operation with UNFICYP. Despite deployment of UNFICYP since 1964, the Turkish Cypriot community had been subjected to severe harassment until the arrival in 1974 of the Turkish peace force, Turkey said, adding that the force would remain in Cyprus until attainment of a final solution guaranteeing the rights and security of the Turkish Cypriot community. While acknowledging that UNFICYP demonstrated United Nations interest in Cyprus and fulfilled a political function to which Turkey and the "Turkish Republic of Northern Cyprus" were not opposed, the manner in which that political interest was expressed and directed, Turkey asserted, was not consistent with basic principles of law and justice.

GENERAL ASSEMBLY ACTION (December)

On 20 December 1983, the General Assembly, by decision 38/456 on the suspension of its thirty-eighth (1983) session, deferred consideration of the Cyprus question, among other agenda items, to its resumed session, at a date to be announced (see Chapter XI of this section).

Shortly before the Assembly convened its 1983 session, Mr. Denktas, by a letter of 16 September, transmitted that day by Mr. Atalay through Turkey,[48] had stated that the intended presence of Mr. Kyprianou at the head of the Greek Cypriot delegation would be unconstitutional and would bear no relevance to the situation in Cyprus, either *de jure* or *de facto;* consequently, everything said or done in the name of the Republic of Cyprus by that delegation would be *ultra vires* and as such considered null and void by the Turkish people of Cyprus and their legitimate representatives.

Other action. The Commission on Human Rights, by a decision of 8 March 1983, postponed the debate on the question of human rights in Cyprus to its 1984 session. On 21 March 1983, the Committee on the Elimination of Racial Discrimination reiterated the hope that the unacceptable state of affairs in Cyprus, due to the foreign occupation of part of its territory, would be brought to an end so that Cyprus would be able to exercise its obligations under the International Convention on the Elimination of All Forms of Racial Discrimination on the whole of its national territory. (See ECONOMIC AND SOCIAL QUESTIONS, Chapter XVIII.)

Action by the Turkish Cypriot community

Communications (November). By a letter of 15 November 1983, transmitted the same day by Mr. Atalay through Turkey,[49] Mr. Denktas announced that the Turkish Cypriot people, exercising their right to self-determination, had proclaimed an independent and non-aligned "Turkish Republic of Northern Cyprus". A declaration embodying the proclamation and explaining why it had become imperative for Turkish Cypriots to take that step, and a resolution approving the declaration and establishment of the "Republic" were enclosed, both adopted by a "Legislative Assembly" on 15 November. The Secretary-General was assured that the proclamation would facilitate, rather than hinder, re-establishment of the partnership between the two peoples within a federal framework, that the Turkish Cypriots desired the continuation of his good offices mission and were ready to resume negotiations, and that Mr. Denktas' proposal for a new summit meeting remained valid.

On 16 November,[50] Turkey transmitted separately to the Secretary-General and the Security Council President a statement made the previous day by its Minister for Foreign Affairs that "President Denktas" had received Turkey's Ambassador to inform him officially of the proclamation, and that, following an examination of the situation, Turkey had decided to recognize the new "Government".

A press release of 17 November, transmitted by Mr. Atalay through Turkey,[51] outlined what was referred to as a peace package of constructive and practical goodwill measures from the "President of the Turkish Republic of Northern Cyprus" to his Greek Cypriot counterpart. These concerned the resettlement of Varosha (a community near the port of Famagusta, just inside the Turkish and Turkish Cypriot forces' cease-fire line) by Greek Cypriots and the reopening of the Nicosia international airport to civilian traffic, each under an interim United Nations administration.

SECURITY COUNCIL ACTION

On 15 November 1983, Cyprus,[52] Greece[53] and the United Kingdom[54] requested the Security Council President to convene an urgent meeting of the Council to consider the situation in Cyprus. Cyprus also asked the Council to take urgent and effective action to deal with the grave development created by the latest secessionist move by Turkey and its instruments in Cyprus.

Accordingly, the Council convened on 17 November. Algeria, Australia, Canada, Cuba, Cyprus, Democratic Yemen, Egypt, Greece, India, Romania, Seychelles, Sri Lanka, Turkey and Yugoslavia were invited at their request to participate without the right to vote; Mr. Denktas was invited to participate in accordance with rule 39[c] of the Council's provisional rules of procedure.

On 18 November, following consideration of the matter at four meetings, the Council adopted resolution 541(1983).

The Security Council,

Having heard the statement of the Foreign Minister of the Government of the Republic of Cyprus,

Concerned at the declaration by the Turkish Cypriot authorities issued on 15 November 1983 which purports to create an independent State in northern Cyprus,

Considering that this declaration is incompatible with the 1960 Treaty concerning the establishment of the Republic of Cyprus and the 1960 Treaty of Guarantee,

Considering, therefore, that the attempt to create a "Turkish Republic of Northern Cyprus" is invalid, and will contribute to a worsening of the situation in Cyprus,

Reaffirming its resolutions 365(1974) and 367(1975),

Aware of the need for a solution of the Cyprus problem based on the mission of good offices undertaken by the Secretary-General,

Affirming its continuing support for the United Nations Peace-keeping Force in Cyprus,

Taking note of the Secretary-General's statement of 17 November 1983,

1. *Deplores* the declaration of the Turkish Cypriot authorities of the purported secession of part of the Republic of Cyprus;

2. *Considers* the declaration referred to above as legally invalid and calls for its withdrawal;

3. *Calls for* the urgent and effective implementation of its resolutions 365(1974) and 367(1975);

4. *Requests* the Secretary-General to pursue his mission of good offices, in order to achieve the earliest possible progress towards a just and lasting settlement in Cyprus;

5. *Calls upon* the parties to co-operate fully with the Secretary-General in his mission of good offices;

6. *Calls upon* all States to respect the sovereignty, independence, territorial integrity and non-alignment of the Republic of Cyprus;

7. *Calls upon* all States not to recognize any Cypriot State other than the Republic of Cyprus;

8. *Calls upon* all States and the two communities in Cyprus to refrain from any action which might exacerbate the situation;

9. *Requests* the Secretary-General to keep the Security Council fully informed.

Security Council resolution 541(1983)

18 November 1983   Meeting 2500   13-1-1

Draft by United Kingdom (S/16149).
Meeting numbers. SC 2497-2500.
Vote in Council as follows:
   In favour: China, France, Guyana, Malta, Netherlands, Nicaragua, Poland, Togo, USSR, United Kingdom, United States, Zaire, Zimbabwe.
   Against: Pakistan.
   Abstaining: Jordan.

Explaining its vote, Pakistan said that certain considerations had determined its position and had motivated it to propose amendments to the provisional text, designed to provide balance and a comprehensive perspective of events since 1963. Those considerations included: preservation of the independence, sovereignty, territorial integrity and unity of Cyprus within a bicommunal, bizonal and federal framework; promotion of the intercommunal talks and support for the Secretary-General's initiatives; and the Council's responsibility, at this current critical turn of events, to promote a united Cyprus within the framework specified—an objective achievable only through reconciliation of the two communities and the intercommunal talks. Pakistan regretted that not only had the amendments been ignored, but an essential element present in the provisional text—namely, the reference to the intercommunal negotiations—had also been omitted from the final text, thus robbing it of an explicit mandate for the Secretary-General to promote the intercommunal talks and conciliation.

Jordan felt that the text failed to take account of the internal aspect of the Cyprus problem, namely, the substance of the dispute between the two communities. Its abstention stemmed from the unacceptability of this continued one-dimensional approach, as well as from the unilateral step taken in northern Cyprus.

For China, the text reflected its consistent support for the preservation of the independence,

[c]See footnote a on p. 249.

sovereignty, territorial integrity and non-aligned status of Cyprus. China believed that, as long as both sides set store by the country's overall interests and continued to negotiate in a spirit of mutual understanding, they should be able to find a just and acceptable solution. The USSR considered the text adequate to meet the situation created by the Turkish Cypriot action. It felt, however, that the Zurich-London agreements (embodied in the treaties cited in the preambular section) that had been imposed on the Republic of Cyprus were a serious curtailment of that State's sovereignty; the guarantees envisaged had been used to serve interests alien to the Cypriot people and had failed to prevent armed intervention and acts aimed at splitting the State.

The Secretary-General informed the Council when it convened on 17 November that, on learning of the proclamation of a "Turkish Republic of Northern Cyprus" from the 15 November letter,[49] he had authorized the United Nations spokesman to issue a statement on his behalf. By the statement, the Secretary-General deeply regretted the move as contrary to Council resolutions on Cyprus and at variance with the high-level agreements of 1977 and 1979; it was bound to affect adversely the Cyprus situation and complicate his efforts to promote an agreed, just and lasting settlement under his good offices mission. He was in consultation on this serious development with all concerned, including the Council President, and appealed to all involved to exercise utmost restraint and refrain from any action that might further aggravate the situation.

Referring to the assurances by Mr. Denktas that his proposal for a high-level meeting remained valid and that he attached importance to the continuance of the negotiations, the Secretary-General said that the chances of success of such efforts depended primarily on the parties' co-operation. He was determined to pursue his search for a settlement, to weather the current crisis and to induce the parties to return to negotiations. To that end, he would take utmost advantage of the current presence in New York of the high-ranking representatives of all concerned.

Cyprus stated that the proclamation of the so-called "Republic" within the territory of the Republic of Cyprus involved international aggression against the territorial integrity, sovereignty and unity of the Republic of Cyprus and interference in its domestic jurisdiction. The declaration, for which Cyprus held Turkey solely responsible, was a nullity, and all States were duty-bound not to recognize any Cypriot State other than the Republic of Cyprus. But for Turkey's military presence, the action would have been impossible. The resultant explosive situation in the eastern Mediterranean posed a threat to international peace and security and a serious challenge to United Nations effectiveness. Cyprus appealed to the Council urgently to discharge its responsibilities under the Charter of the United Nations and adopt effective measures to reverse the unacceptable situation.

Greece called the declaration a breach of the 1960 Treaty of Guarantee signed by Turkey—along with Greece and the United Kingdom—whereby it had undertaken to guarantee the territorial integrity and security of the Republic of Cyprus and its Constitution, article 185 of which expressly excluded separatist independence and provided that the Republic's territory was indivisible. Greece called on all Member States to join in an unequivocal condemnation of Turkey's act and to refrain from recognizing the product of illegality and force. It called on Turkey immediately to withdraw its army of occupation and declared it would continue, with all the means at its disposal, to pursue efforts aimed at re-establishing freedom and legality in Cyprus.

The proclamation, Turkey explained, was to enable the Turkish community to join the Greek community on an equal footing in a bicommunal, bizonal and federal framework that should be the Republic of Cyprus. The only way to achieve that goal was through intercommunal negotiations under the Secretary-General's good offices mission. There were only two possible courses within that context, however: negotiations between the two co-founder communities, or negotiations between two independent States of Cyprus, to be held with their prior consent. In Turkey's view, a Council resolution should call for a resumption of negotiations, without making judgements based on a distortion of historical facts and a prejudiced interpretation of juridical reality, and take account of the Turkish Cypriot community's willingness to negotiate and continue co-operating with UNFICYP. Saying it would always protect the Turkish community, Turkey assured the Council that all that was necessary for a rapid solution was the smallest show of good will by the Greek Cypriot community and Greece: acceptance of the Turkish Cypriot community as an equal partner in an independent, sovereign, bicommunal, bizonal, federal and non-aligned Republic of Cyprus.

Whether the Council accepted it or not, Mr. Denktas said, it was a fact that the Turkish Cypriot people had finally asserted their rights and hoped that the Council would regard them as in full charge of their destiny—because they were. He reiterated their intention to continue negotiations under the Secretary-General's good offices, a process their statehood would help because of the equality of the parties. Claiming that the destruction and denial of its vested partnership had created the Cyprus problem and prevented a solution, he declared that the Turkish Cypriot people did not divide Cyprus; it had been divided when they were thrown out of the Government. He urged the Council to give Cyprus a chance to establish a bizonal, bicommunal federalism by not heeding the demand to condemn and not recognize their statehood. Only with its recognition would the Greek Cypriots feel the need to negotiate for a federal solution, as foreseen by the 1977 and 1979 agreements, the Secretary-General's 1980 opening statement and the 1981 "evaluation paper"—all by which the Turkish Cypriot people stood.

Following adoption of the resolution, Mr. Denktas restated that there existed no Government of the Republic of Cyprus. Rather, the Government in the south represented Greek Cypriots and that in the north, Turkish Cypriots; together, bicommunally, they made up the Government of Cyprus. He reiterated his invitation to the Greek Cypriot side to sit down at the table in order to re-establish a federal system. He insisted that the Turkish Cypriots were not seceding from the Republic and would not do so, if given the chance to re-establish such a system, with the help of the Secretary-General's good offices.

The majority of speakers in the debate—including Algeria, Australia, Cuba, Democratic Yemen, Egypt, France, Guyana, India, the Netherlands, Nicaragua, Poland, Seychelles, Sri Lanka, Togo, the USSR, the United Kingdom, Yugoslavia, Zaire and Zimbabwe—viewed the Turkish Cypriot proclamation with profound concern. They deplored and condemned it as an illegal and unacceptable act that violated the United Nations Charter, contravened the Council and General Assembly resolutions on the Cyprus question and the declarations of the Movement of Non-Aligned Countries, and was incompatible—the United Kingdom and Togo added—with the 1960 Treaties of Establishment and of Guarantee of the Republic of Cyprus and its Constitution. They demanded withdrawal forthwith of the proclamation and asked the Council to declare it null and void. In declaring or urging non-recognition of the entity proclaimed, they reaffirmed their full support for the independence, sovereignty, territorial integrity and non-aligned status of the Republic of Cyprus under President Kyprianou. They held that there could be no alternative to negotiations and peaceful dialogue, and called for a resumption of the intercommunal talks as a matter of urgency and on the two communities to co-operate in good faith with the Secretary-General.

Some States—Algeria, Guyana, the Netherlands and Sri Lanka among them—regarded the action as further complicating the situation in Cyprus and as a set-back in efforts towards a solution. So did the USSR, which also observed, along with

France, that it subverted the foundations of and prospects for a just political settlement. Others, including Algeria, Egypt, India, Poland and Yugoslavia, said the action constituted a new flash-point of tension in the eastern Mediterranean, with far-reaching implications for world peace and security.

There could be no justifying the action, the USSR said, especially as it was taken just when new initiatives were being put forward for resuming the intercommunal talks. India, while granting that the legitimate rights of the Turkish Cypriot community should be respected and defended, failed to see the force of the arguments advanced for the action. Guyana felt that not even past excesses could justify it.

Democratic Yemen called the Turkish community's invocation of the right to self-determination as the legal basis for its proclamation a distortion of the 1960 Declaration on the Granting of Independence to Colonial Countries and Peoples,[55] which declared that all peoples had that right—not on the basis of faction, religion or sect, however, but of national unity and territorial integrity. Moreover, Democratic Yemen pointed out, no people could exercise that right under occupation or foreign domination. Sri Lanka observed that few States could claim ethnic, linguistic and religious homogeneity, or that they were free from problems attendant to their minority populations; thus, the territorial integrity of many States would be in peril if self-determination were interpreted in the colonial context as a right to secede.

Yugoslavia pointed to the increasing use of force and resultant occupation, with every *fait accompli* being forced on the international community and used as justification for another. It advised against coming to terms with such a practice and warned against its consequences for every member of the international community. Guyana, which said the Council had an obligation to discourage the use of force in international relations and be unequivocal in its rejection of such lawlessness, considered the Council's response to the Turkish Cypriot declaration inadequate. It believed that the Council should categorically condemn the action, declare that the United Nations would not accord recognition to the entity created and appeal directly to Member States not to recognize it.

The United Kingdom said the Council's responsibilities required it to address itself to the future. Noting that, amidst the gloom cast by the Turkish Cypriot action, both communities had expressed support for the Secretary-General's mission of good offices and for the 1977 and 1979 agreements, the United Kingdom also said that it was even more necessary to bring the two sides together in resumed talks. The solution in Cyprus lay forward, Guyana stressed, and, while neither side could be expected to forget the past—which could not be invoked in defence of the *status quo* or of ambitions inconsistent with the Charter and United Nations resolutions—both had an obligation to prevent it from influencing their perceptions of current intentions.

Action by Secretary-General. Referring to the suggested measures in the "peace package" offered by Mr. Denktas on 17 November,[51] concerning the resettlement of Varosha and the reopening of the Nicosia international airport, the Secretary-General reported[56] that, in important respects, they followed the line of measures he had discussed with the parties in 1980[57] and 1981,[58] pursuant to points 5 and 6 of the 1979 high-level agreement; under the mandates entrusted to him, he had the authority to take on the suggested responsibilities. The Secretary-General had authorized his spokesman to make a statement to this effect on 18 November.

He had discussed the matter with Mr. Denktas on 19 November and with Turkey's Foreign Minister on 22 November, pointing out that initial steps in respect of Varosha could be worked out between the United Nations and the Turkish Cypriots, since they involved making territory currently under Turkish Cypriot control part of the UNFICYP buffer zone. Following clear signals of encouragement from the Turkish Government to the effect, *inter alia*, that the designated area of Varosha would be placed under provisional United Nations administration, a draft United Nations declaration on Varosha was conveyed to Mr. Denktas on 9 December by the Secretary-General's Acting Special Representative, with the understanding that the area west of Dherinia Avenue would be placed under United Nations administration and settled by Greek Cypriots in two or more successive phases.

Further communications. During the Security Council deliberations in November, a number of communications on the Cyprus situation were addressed to the Council President or to the Secretary-General: on 16 November by France[59] and by Greece, on behalf of the 10 members of the European Community;[60] on 17 November by Nicaragua;[61] on 18 November by Bulgaria,[62] Hungary,[63] Portugal[64] and Sierra Leone;[65] on 21 November by Mongolia[66] and Viet Nam;[67] and on 23 November by Jamaica.[68] The communications transmitted official statements reflecting the majority position in the Council debate—which was staunchly for the rescission of the Turkish Cypriot proclamation, for a united State under the Government of the Republic of Cyprus, and for the resumption of negotiations between the two communities under the Secretary-General's good offices mission.

On 9 December,[69] Cyprus drew attention to statements attributed to the Prime Minister–elect

of Turkey, as reported by *The Christian Science Monitor* of 30 November, which it characterized as provocative; he reportedly had said, among other things, that if a solution based on a loose federation was not achieved, northern Cyprus would irrevocably remain independent and separated from the rest of the island. Mr. Denktas, by a letter of 9 December, transmitted by Mr. Atalay through Turkey on 20 December,[70] quoted a statement attributed to the Greek Prime Minister, and reported on 24 November in an Athens newspaper, *Ethnos*, that Greece's proposal was for a unitary Cyprus—not a federation or confederation—to be negotiated only after the departure of the Turkish force from Cyprus. Mr. Denktas observed that it was such statements that had prevented the intercommunal talks from producing tangible results.

By a letter of 22 December transmitted that day,[71] Mr. Atalay provided certain quotations to refute what he said was the Greek Cypriot administration's protracted misrepresentation of facts as to who had invaded Cyprus, with a request that his letter be annexed to his statement to the Council on 15 December, in the hope that that administration would refrain from displaying indifference to factual accuracy.

Peace-keeping operations

The United Nations Peace-keeping Force in Cyprus (UNFICYP), established by the Security Council in 1964,[72] continued throughout 1983 to monitor, patrol and supervise the cease-fire lines of the Cyprus National Guard and of the Turkish and Turkish Cypriot forces. It also provided security for civilians in the area between the lines; used its best efforts to discharge its functions with regard to the security, welfare and well-being of the Greek Cypriots living in northern Cyprus; continued regular visits to Turkish Cypriots residing in the south; and supported United Nations relief operations.

The Secretary-General reported to the Council that UNFICYP liaison and co-operation with the military authorities of both sides had been excellent at all levels and had been effectively maintained with the civilian authorities. Under new guidelines superseding those issued by the Turkish Cypriot authorities in December 1979, all serious restrictions on the movement of United Nations troops in the north, as identified by a Secretariat Survey Team in 1980,[73] had been removed, thereby increasing the number of routes open for UNFICYP travel. However, a Turkish Cypriot decision on 5 August to deny the Swedish contingent, when in uniform, access to the north had impaired UNFICYP operations until 1 October, when the restriction was lifted. Some minor incidents involving restrictions on the freedom of movement of UNFICYP by both the National Guard and the Turkish and Turkish Cypriot forces had arisen from misunderstandings at the local level.

UNFICYP monitored the buffer zone between the 180-kilometre-long cease-fire lines through a system of 139 observation posts, 71 of them permanently manned (as at 30 November). During 1983, the frequency of shooting incidents diminished significantly and none involved exchanges of fire between the two sides. There continued to be a number of incidents related to attempts by both sides to construct new fortifications forward of the cease-fire lines and to improve existing positions; UNFICYP was successful in restoring the *status quo ante* in all instances where such activities were considered provocative. Adjustments that had been made in August to the perimeter fence in north-western Varosha were withdrawn, following United Nations representations, and the original perimeter fence restored; some houses in the area that had appeared to be under preparation for occupancy remained unoccupied. Overflights of the buffer zone from the north and south of the cease-fire lines by both military and light civil aircraft continued to cause concern; UNFICYP protested all overflights to those concerned. Disputes over delineation of the cease-fire lines were reported; none, however, were of forces from either side crossing the lines.

UNFICYP continued to improve markings and barriers surrounding known or suspected minefields, and undertook three mine-clearing projects, two of them major, during which it received excellent co-operation from both sides.

In the discharge of its humanitarian responsibilities, UNFICYP monitored permanent transfers of Greek Cypriots from north to south and of Turkish Cypriots from south to north, to ensure that such transfers were voluntary. During the 12 months ended 30 November 1983, 53 Greek Cypriots and 11 Maronite Cypriots had transferred to the south—with the number of Greek Cypriots residing in the north falling to 879—while 11 Turkish Cypriots had transferred to the north. Other UNFICYP assistance was in support of such activities as agriculture in the buffer zone, water collection and distribution, anti-mosquito spraying, and what had come to be known as the Nicosia Master Plan project, which was entering its second phase, as well as a country programme covering 1983-1986 and including a variety of projects—both assisted by the United Nations Development Programme (UNDP) and designed to benefit the two communities equitably. Under the Plan's second phase, the United Nations Centre for Human Settlements (Habitat) would continue providing UNDP-financed inputs to the project and technical supervision and back-stopping.

Assistance from the International Labour Organisation, UNDP and UNHCR to the ceramics industry continued, as did assistance from UNDP and the World Health Organization for fellowship training in the prevention and control of thalassemia (Mediterranean anaemia). Continued assistance in the control of animal infertility diseases was envisaged by UNDP.

Relief supplies were distributed or delivered by UNFICYP. During the 12 months ended 30 November 1983, this amounted to 1,275 tons of food, clothing, gas and diesel oil, of which 971 tons went to Greek Cypriots and Maronites and 304 tons to Turkish Cypriots, all in the north. The World Food Programme was a major contributor of food.

The UNFICYP Civilian Police continued to support UNFICYP military units and operated in liaison with both the Cyprus and the Turkish Cypriot police, contributing to maintenance of law and order between the cease-fire lines and to the protection of civilians. It also assisted in the control of civilian movement between the lines.

This information on UNFICYP activities was provided in two 1983 reports by the Secretary-General, covering the periods 1 December 1982 to 31 May 1983[34] and 1 June to 30 November 1983.[47]

In both reports, the Secretary-General concluded that the presence of the Force was necessary to help maintain calm and create conditions for pursuing a peaceful solution. Acting on his recommendations, the Security Council twice in 1983 extended the UNFICYP mandate for a six-month period, first until 15 December 1983 and then until 15 June 1984.

Composition of UNFICYP. As at 30 November 1983, UNFICYP had a strength of 2,348—the same as at 30 November 1982[74]—including 34 civilian police, and was composed of contingents from eight States (see table below).[47]

During the year ended 30 November 1983, two members of the Force died, bringing the total of fatal casualties to 127 since the inception of UNFICYP in 1964.

CONTINGENTS OF UNFICYP
(by country of origin, as at 30 November 1983)

Military personnel

Austria	301
Canada	515
Denmark	341
Finland	10
Ireland	8
Sweden	378
United Kingdom	761
Total	2,314

Civilian police

Australia	20
Sweden	14
Total	34
Grand total	2,348

UNFICYP financing

UNFICYP continued to be financed by voluntary contributions and by troop-contributing Governments. Contributions received in 1983 from 29 Governments totalled $16,715,424 (see table below). Estimated costs totalled $24,100,000, which included the direct cost to the United Nations of maintaining the Force as well as reimbursement by the United Nations of some of the extra costs of Governments providing contingents. The full 12-month cost of the Force was estimated at approximately $101.1 million—excluding regular troops' pay and allowances and normal *matériel* costs—much of which was borne by the troop contributors.

CONTRIBUTIONS RECEIVED IN 1983 FOR UNFICYP
(as at 31 December 1983; in US dollars)

Country	Amount
Australia	106,790
Austria	125,000
Bahamas	2,000
Belgium	405,233
Cyprus	415,000
Denmark	120,000
Finland	37,500
Germany, Federal Republic of	868,472
Greece	800,200
Iceland	10,000
India	10,000
Italy	800,000
Japan	500,000
Kuwait	25,000
Luxembourg	6,498
Malawi	773
Norway	610,000
Pakistan	3,000
Panama	500
Philippines	330
Portugal	4,000
Sweden	200,000
Switzerland	359,155
United Kingdom	2,285,575
United Republic of Cameroon	2,794
United States	9,000,000
Venezuela	5,000
Zambia	10,000
Zimbabwe	2,604
Total	16,715,424

SOURCE: A/39/5.

As at 15 December 1983, the accumulated deficit from the operation's inception in 1964 stood at $111.3 million.[75] Because of that deficit, payments to troop-contributing Governments (which had been absorbing costs in the order of $36.2 million every six-month period) as at that date had met claims only up to the end of June 1977.

Expressing concern over this situation, which placed a disproportionate burden on the troop-contributing countries, the Secretary-General, in his reports of June[34] and December[47] 1983 on the United Nations operation in Cyprus, appealed to Governments for voluntary financial contributions and to those which had not contributed in the past to review their positions and begin contributing.

He repeated that appeal by letters of 24 June[76] and 22 December,[75] sent to all Member States following each renewal of the UNFICYP mandate. In both letters, he explained that in recent years the rate of accumulation of the deficit had been growing, while for each six-month period voluntary contributions had been averaging $8.8 million compared to expenses ranging from $11 million to between $14 million and $15 million.

In a paper on the financing of United Nations peace-keeping operations, submitted on 7 October,[77] the United Kingdom expressed the view that it was reasonable to expect all Member States to share the burden of maintaining UNFICYP; the United Kingdom hoped that those which had not contributed to its cost would review their position and make a positive commitment to peace by contributing generously.

REFERENCES

[1]YUN 1974, p. 275. [2]A/37/792-S/15603. [3]YUN 1982, p. 380. [4]A/37/793-S/15620. [5]A/37/794-S/15648. [6]A/37/795-S/15652. [7]A/37/796-S/15666. [8]A/37/802-S/15722. [9]A/37/803-S/15730. [10]A/37/797-S/15682. [11]A/37/799-S/15715. [12]A/37/798-S/15684. [13]A/37/801-S/15718. [14]A/37/800-S/15717. [15]A/37/805 & Corr.1. [16]YUN 1980, p. 454. [17]YUN 1981, p. 343. [18]Ibid., p. 342. [19]YUN 1982, p. 583, GA dec. 37/452, 21 Dec. 1982. [20]A/37/250/Add.4. [21]A/37/252/Add.4. [22]A/SPC/37/5. [23]A/37/804. [24]A/37/806-S/15750. [25]A/37/810. [26]YUN 1977, p. 344. [27]YUN 1979, p. 421. [28]A/37/808. [29]YUN 1980, p. 453. [30]A/37/809. [31]A/38/205-S/15769. [32]A/38/206-S/15772. [33]A/38/235-S/15788. [34]S/15812 & Corr.1 & Add.1. [35]A/38/283-S/15841. [36]A/38/284-S/15842. [37]A/38/296-S/15866. [38]A/38/290-S/15859. [39]A/38/315-S/15888. [40]A/38/446-S/16004. [41]A/38/319-S/15894. [42]A/38/348-S/15933. [43]A/38/445-S/16003. [44]A/38/452-S/16010. [45]A/38/501-S/16040. [46]A/38/534-S/16079. [47]S/16192 & Add.1. [48]A/38/431-S/15991. [49]A/38/586-S/16148. [50]A/38/602 (S/16152). [51]A/38/594 (S/16159). [52]S/16150. [53]S/16151. [54]S/16147. [55]YUN 1960, p. 49, GA res. 1514(XV), 14 Dec. 1960. [56]S/16519. [57]YUN 1980, p. 450. [58]YUN 1981, p. 341. [59]S/16153. [60]S/16155. [61]S/16158. [62]S/16170. [63]S/16165. [64]S/16175. [65]S/16162. [66]S/16172. [67]S/16174. [68]A/38/606-S/16183. [69]A/38/724-S/16212. [70]A/38/765-S/16227. [71]A/38/766-S/16232. [72]YUN 1964, p. 165, SC res. 186(1964), 4 Mar. 1964. [73]YUN 1980, p. 455. [74]YUN 1982, p. 382. [75]S/16268. [76]S/15870. [77]A/38/489.

Libyan Arab Jamahiriya–United States dispute

In 1983, the Libyan Arab Jamahiriya, by a number of communications to the President of the Security Council, complained of military threats and intensified provocations against it by the United States, conducted along its coastline and close to its borders with neighbouring countries. The Council convened in February and August to consider those complaints. They were rejected by the United States as misrepresentations of the purposes of its naval deployment in international waters, of its joint military exercises with friendly countries, and of its actions to assist Chad, at that country's request (see Chapter V of this section).

Communications (February). By a letter of 18 February 1983,[1] the Libyan Arab Jamahiriya charged that a serious situation was developing as a result of military threats and provocations against it by the United States, referring in particular to the dispatch of AWACS (Airborne Warning and Control System) aircraft to one of its neighbouring States and the stationing of the aircraft-carrier *Nimitz* and other naval vessels near its coastline. A message in support of that complaint was addressed by the President of Benin to the Libyan President and transmitted to the Secretary-General on 22 February.[2] On the same day,[3] the United States rejected the Libyan charge and affirmed its right to free passage in international waters and to conduct training exercises with friendly Governments.

SECURITY COUNCIL CONSIDERATION (February)

In response to the Libyan Arab Jamahiriya's request of 19 February,[4] that the Security Council consider what it described as the deteriorating situation near its shores that could jeopardize the security and peace of the Mediterranean region and the world, the Council convened in four meetings on 22 and 23 February.

Meeting numbers. SC 2415-2418.

Invited, at their request, to participate in the discussions without the right to vote were: Algeria, Benin, Bulgaria, Cuba, Czechoslovakia, Democratic Yemen, Egypt, Ethiopia, German Democratic Republic, Ghana, Hungary, Iran, Libyan Arab Jamahiriya, Madagascar, Sudan, Syrian Arab Republic, Viet Nam. In accordance with rule 39[d] of the Council's provisional rules of procedure, also invited were: the Permanent Observer of the League of Arab States to the United Nations, as requested by Jordan on 22 February;[5] and the Pan Africanist Congress of Azania, as requested by Togo on 23 February.[6]

In its statement to the Council, the Libyan Arab Jamahiriya complained about recent events which it said were the latest in a series of United States provocations and threats against it since the Libyan revolution of 1969, which ended the presence of United States military bases and oil monopolies in that country. Those events included two violations of Libyan territorial waters near Benghazi on 19 January 1983; constant spying activities by United States AWACS in the eastern part of the country, obstructing and jamming civil communications; movement of the aircraft-carrier *Nimitz* and support vessels towards the Libyan coast near the Gulf of Sidra, on 13 February; 13 airspace violations three days later over the Gulf area between Tripoli and Benghazi; and deployment of the Sixth Fleet, on 17 February, at the limit of Libyan territorial waters, 22 kilometres from latitude 32°N. Such actions were illustrative of United States terrorist policy that threatened international peace and security, and peoples' freedom and independence.

Referring to United States official explanations that its naval and air activities were related to a so-called Libyan military buildup near the borders of the Sudan, and that the sending of AWACS to Egypt was part of a joint Egypt–United States manœuvre (see Chapter V of this section), the Libyan Arab Jamahiriya denied any mobilization on its borders with either the Sudan or Egypt, saying it had no desire to interfere in those countries' affairs, and drew attention to Egypt's denial of the alleged joint manœuvre. The Libyan Arab Jamahiriya called on the Council to condemn these acts of aggression by the United States and declared that it would not be intimidated.

The United States said it had been aware for some time of Libyan efforts against the President of the Sudan and of concentrations of Libyan aircraft close to the borders of the Sudan and Egypt. That situation, of concern to those countries, had led the United States to move up the date of an already scheduled AWACS training exercise and to deploy its naval forces in international waters in the eastern Mediterranean, whose presence at times seemed to have proved a deterrence to Libyan adventurism in the region. Citing instances of what it called the long-standing pattern of Libyan misconduct world-wide, the United States charged it was the Libyan foreign policy of subversion and destabilization that posed a continuing threat to peace and security. The United States said it rested its case on the factual record and on its adherence to the principles of the Charter of the United Nations in the cause of international peace and security.

Most speakers in the debate—among them Benin, Bulgaria, China, Czechoslovakia, Democratic Yemen, Ghana, Hungary, Jordan, Madagascar, Poland, the Syrian Arab Republic, the USSR and Zimbabwe—deplored or condemned what they agreed were United States provocations against the Libyan Arab Jamahiriya, interference or meddling in the internal affairs of States, and threats to use force, including, as Zimbabwe said, the dispatch of sophisticated military equipment to northern Africa. They regarded these actions as exacerbating tension in a highly explosive region and seriously jeopardizing international peace and security.

International law entitled no one to threaten or use force to achieve changes in relations between States, Czechoslovakia said. Poland commented

[d]See footnote a on p. 249.

similarly, citing Member States' obligations under the Charter. Only patience and self-restraint by the Libyan Arab Jamahiriya had avoided an open conflict, Hungary said, while Zimbabwe cautioned that, since the United States had only partially withdrawn its sophisticated equipment from the area, the Council should remain seized of the situation until it had changed for the better.

For Madagascar, as also for Algeria, the confrontation was of serious concern to the region because of its potential for precipitating super-Power confrontation.

Nicaragua characterized United States actions against the Libyan Arab Jamahiriya as wide-ranging—from rhetorical denunciations to destabilization measures, constant international propaganda campaigns, economic boycotts, and military threats and aggression. Nicaragua attributed the hasty United States military deployment in the Mediterranean to a foreign policy based on imperial power and military confrontation with third world peoples struggling to achieve or preserve political independence—a policy the United States pursued in other areas as well, Poland added. Those familiar with that policy, Democratic Yemen said, had confirmed that the anti-Libyan campaign, on the eve of the summit conference of the Movement of Non-Aligned Countries, was intended to deflect the conference from confronting United States aggressive policy.

To explain what it called a systematic campaign of threats and intimidation against the Libyan Arab Jamahiriya, the USSR said the United States found unpalatable Libyan anti-imperialistic policy and firm opposition to United States and Israeli attempts to force a capitulationist peace on the Arab peoples.

Viet Nam accused the United States of fabricating a Libyan threat against the Sudan and of pointedly ignoring the 12-mile territorial limit set by the 1982 United Nations Convention on the Law of the Sea[7] in order to engage in hostile activities against the Libyan Arab Jamahiriya. The new acts of provocation were the culmination of a campaign of subversion, intimidation and destruction, intended to divide the Arab States so as to impose United States imperialistic domination throughout the Middle East region.

In Bulgaria's view, the recent events in the Mediterranean Sea were the result of a well-thought-out strategy to paralyse progressive change in the Middle East, to perpetuate exploitation of the region's natural riches by capitalist monopolies and to impose imperialistic supremacy at the crossroads of the three main continents of the old world.

Ethiopia pointed to the high priority that the United States attached to the containment of so-called Libyan adventurism, which Ethiopia took to mean the overthrow of the legitimate Libyan Government; it was pursuit of that objective which had led the United States to deploy its colossal might on the northern shores of Africa, rather than the alleged conflict between two neighbouring African countries. This was not to say that the Libyan Arab Jamahiriya had no differences with some of its neighbours; however, those differences were being exploited to serve as a pretext for United States intervention in and ultimate domination of the region, just as it had previously exploited Ethiopia's strained relations with Somalia.

National sovereignty and security were the responsibility of each State, said Jordan, which also shared Pakistan's view that the maintenance of international peace and security was an international responsibility to be exercised by the United Nations through the Security Council.

It was Malta's belief that the safeguarding of peace and security in the Mediterranean rested with the countries of the region themselves; superimposing extraneous elements, it felt, could exacerbate rather than alleviate local tensions. Ghana suggested that the United States should take friendly cognizance of the sensitivity of all developing countries to strong-arm tactics by the great Powers.

A number of States, among them Bulgaria, Cuba, Ethiopia, the German Democratic Republic, Viet Nam and Zimbabwe, strenuously objected to the United States arrogating to itself the role of world policeman. The German Democratic Republic said the non-aligned countries of Africa, Asia and Latin America had embarked on a road of independent development, were capable of solving their problems, and resolutely opposed interference in their internal affairs by imperialistic Powers through pressure. According to Bulgaria, the ambitions of a large State to assume the role of arbiter in a region thousands of kilometres away was of grave concern to the international community. Cuba said the United States persisted in acting as world policeman, although it neither had the right nor had been asked to do so.

The United States movements in the Gulf of Sidra and the danger they posed to the countries in the area, Algeria stated, confirmed the correctness of its own foreign policy, as endorsed by the non-aligned Movement: to make of the Mediterranean a zone of peace and security. Algeria considered invalid the argument that a Power from outside the region was carrying out manoeuvres jointly with a country within it; that such intervention should have occurred in the Arab world, which was also a part of the African world, was deplorable, because it undermined the regional organizations—the natural forums for examining and peacefully solving the region's problems. In that connection, China hoped that the Organization of African Unity (OAU) and the League of Arab States could play a mediating role.

The Sudan confirmed that, during the previous week, it had witnessed an escalation of armed Libyan presence on its north-western frontier in the form of MIG-23s and long-range bombers; it had also uncovered a Libyan-backed plan to overthrow the Government of the Sudan and impose Libyan hegemony, which was confirmed by reports that suicide squads had been charged with assassinating certain Presidents, including its own. In the face of such a dangerous situation, the Sudan said, it had used every means at its disposal to defend itself, in co-operation with friendly countries and within the context of its defence treaty with Egypt. It was incumbent on the Council to follow the situation closely and put an end to such practices and to the Libyan policy of intervening in the internal affairs of its neighbouring countries. The Sudan stated that it would not have voiced its differences with the Libyan Arab Jamahiriya before the Council had it not been for its concern to place things in proper perspective and to settle those differences—a process which should have been undertaken within the regional organizations to which the two belonged.

Egypt's participation in the debate also proceeded from its concern that matters be put in perspective and the facts clarified. Its statements concerning recent developments had been deliberately made so as not to aggravate matters and raise tensions. Egypt stated that it was fully committed to defending the Sudan in accordance with a mutual defence treaty; it affirmed that both were fully entitled to exercise the right of sovereignty within their respective borders and take defensive measures against aggression or threat of aggression. All they wished from the Libyan Arab Jamahiriya was a commitment to the consolidation of peace and security in the region and to peaceful settlement of disputes.

Israel, by a letter of 25 February,[8] objected to offensive references to it, in the course of the Council deliberations, by no fewer than 14 speakers (see Chapter IX of this section, under MIDDLE EAST SITUATION).

Communications (May-September). By a letter of 10 May,[9] the Libyan Arab Jamahiriya charged that repeated United States violations of Libyan territorial waters and airspace constituted deliberate provocation and a threat to Libyan security and to that of the region. Rejecting this charge on 24 May,[10] the United States asserted that its recent flight operations from its aircraft-carrier *Nimitz*, near the Libyan coast, were entirely routine, conducted only in international airspace and preceded by the filing of a notice to operate within the relevant flight information region; neither the participating vessels nor the aircraft had violated Libyan territorial waters or airspace.

On 18 July,[11] Democratic Yemen, Iran, the Libyan Arab Jamahiriya and the Syrian Arab Republic drew attention to a United States announcement concerning manoeuvres by its rapid intervention forces to be held in the Middle East and Africa in August. They regarded this action to be a serious danger to the security and independence of the region's States and a direct intervention in their internal affairs, and they condemned the existence of those forces, whose goal was to terrorize peoples, to strengthen régimes friendly to the United States, to impose its political and economic hegemony, to support imperialistic monopolies and to sow discord among neighbouring peoples and States so as to facilitate domination over them. To rectify what it called misinformation and baseless allegations, the United States on 22 July[12] stated that the purpose of the joint military exercises, involving military forces of the United States and other nations in the Middle East, was to review and enhance the participants' defensive capabilities, adding that its forces were participating at the invitation of host Governments and would withdraw at the end of the manoeuvres; they did not involve contested land, air or sea space.

The Libyan Arab Jamahiriya again drew the Security Council's attention on 5 August[13] to what it termed the dangerous situation created by the increasing tension provoked by the United States in the Mediterranean and Africa—by publishing threatening official communiqués and by dispatching units of the United States Sixth Fleet to waters near the Libyan coast, military advisers and equipment to Chad, and two AWACS spy aircraft to a country bordering on the Jamahiriya to keep Libyan airspace under observation.

The leader of the Libyan Arab Jamahiriya, in a letter, also of 5 August, transmitted the following day,[14] warned that United States troop landings in Egypt, Oman, Somalia and the Sudan posed a direct threat to Libyan security and a threat of the utmost gravity to the Arab region and the Horn of Africa. Responsibility for any breakdown of international security in the region, he said, lay with the United States and with the Council if it did not call a halt to those landings.

Intensified United States acts of provocation and intimidation were reported on 8 August[15] by the Libyan Arab Jamahiriya, which requested that the Council urgently convene to consider the situation. Responding on 10 August,[16] the United States stated that the purposes and scope of the joint training activities had been clearly set forth in its letter of 22 July[12] and in advance announcements by several participating Governments. It also stated that the exercises threatened no country in Africa or the Middle East and were not in response to any situation or activity that might be taking place in any neighbouring country or countries.

On 13 September,[17] Democratic Yemen transmitted a letter from its Minister for Foreign Affairs protesting United States military manœuvres in Egypt, Oman, Somalia and the Sudan as a breach of the security and stability of those States.

Earlier, the Foreign Minister of the Sudan, in a message transmitted on 11 August,[18] said that the conduct of the joint Sudan–United States training exercises was a sovereign right consistent with international law, the Charter of the United Nations and other international and regional instruments; he called the 5 August letter of the Libyan Arab Jamahiriya[14] a malicious misinterpretation of the intent of those exercises. Somalia, by a letter of 12 August,[19] rejected the Libyan assertion[14] that the military exercises in question constituted a threat to international security; it took exception to the liberty taken by the Libyan Arab Jamahiriya to speak on Somalia's behalf and made clear its opposition to the Council's discussion of Somalia in the context of the Libyan communication. Democratic Yemen's allegations[17] were similarly rejected by Somalia, on 23 September,[20] which added that by permitting a super-Power to establish naval and military bases in Democratic Yemen, that country had endangered the peace and tranquillity of its neighbours and of the region.

On 15 August,[21] referring to what it called the tendentious Libyan misrepresentations concerning the joint military exercises, Egypt stated that they were of limited duration and in no way related to current developments in the region, were not directed towards any State, were intended solely to enhance Egypt's defensive capabilities, and were a legitimate, sovereign right—indeed a duty—that threatened no one. Those misrepresentations were futile attempts by the Libyan Arab Jamahiriya to divert attention from its destabilization designs in the region and continued interference in Chad's internal affairs.

SECURITY COUNCIL CONSIDERATION (August)

In response to the request made by the Libyan Arab Jamahiriya on 8 August 1983,[15] the Security Council convened in three meetings between 11 and 16 August to consider that country's complaint of intensified United States acts of provocation against it.

Meeting numbers. SC 2464, 2466, 2468.

The following were invited, at their request, to participate in the discussions without the right to vote: Afghanistan, Cuba, Czechoslovakia, Democratic Yemen, Egypt, German Democratic Republic, India, Iran, Lao People's Democratic Republic, Libyan Arab Jamahiriya, Sudan, Syrian Arab Republic, Viet Nam.

The Libyan Arab Jamahiriya informed the Council that the United States had recently been engaged in large-scale troop landings in three countries bordering on the Jamahiriya, posing a direct threat to its sovereignty and security. The United States, it asserted, was currently exploiting the civil war in Chad as a pretext to mass its forces in preparation for aggression against the Libyan Arab Jamahiriya. It was ready, as it had always been, to enter into dialogue, but the United States had continually refused. It called on the Council to condemn and put an end to the policy of aggression and provocation relentlessly pursued by the United States against the Jamahiriya.

The United States declared that the issue confronting the Council was unprovoked Libyan aggression against Chad, which the Libyan Arab Jamahiriya, together with the USSR, was attempting to obfuscate with diversionary allegations of United States interference in the affairs of African nations. If that aggression went unpunished, the Council would be revealed as impotent, and a brutal new colonialism would threaten even more urgently the security of north and north-central Africa. The United States accused the Libyan Arab Jamahiriya of conducting a foreign policy of subversion and destabilization that respected no State's independence, territorial integrity and right to peace and security; and of pursuing expansionist goals by providing economic and military aid to radical Governments, bribing officials, helping international terrorists as well as guerrilla groups working to overthrow Governments, and assassinating exiled opponents and officials of target Governments. It was that lawlessness which threatened international peace and security and violated rational, civilized behaviour, and which should be vigorously opposed. The United States reiterated that all of its actions designed to assist Chad to exercise its inherent right of self-defence were consistent with international law and the Charter of the United Nations.

The majority of States speaking in the debate deplored anew what they perceived as a United States campaign of intimidation against the Libyan Arab Jamahiriya and policy of intervention in the internal affairs of States. They called on the Council to end such activities and reiterated their solidarity with the Jamahiriya's firm stand.

Iran demanded that the United States leave the Mediterranean unconditionally and let the people of the region sort out their differences without mediation and observation. It called on the Council to remind the United States that it was neither the United Nations nor a United Nations peacekeeping force and to condemn its provocations against the Libyan Arab Jamahiriya.

The Syrian Arab Republic said the United States allegation of Libyan intervention in Chad was intended to pave the way for sending more AWACS spy planes and other military assistance to that country in an attempt to tighten the vice around the Libyan revolution.

Remarking that tension was being increased around the Libyan Arab Jamahiriya by the daily provocative flights of United States military aircraft in search of a pretext for confrontation, the USSR restated its view that the Libyan Arab Jamahiriya bore the brunt of imperialistic attack because it pursued an independent foreign policy that did not seek advice from Washington. Sharing a similar view were Afghanistan, Democratic Yemen, Poland, Viet Nam and the Lao People's Democratic Republic, which believed that the obvious reason for the heavy-handed tactics of the United States was the pursuit by the Jamahiriya and other progressive countries of a policy of peace, independence, co-operation and non-alignment and the refusal to submit to pressure.

Poland saw the dispatch of military equipment to north Africa and the exercises held there by United States rapid deployment forces as neo-colonialist attempts to interfere in the complicated affairs of countries like Chad. The number of advisers and mercenaries to those countries was increasing, as were the flow of arms and the number of African States being dragged into military or political intervention.

Zimbabwe said charges and countercharges between the Libyan Arab Jamahiriya and the United States were symptomatic of a dangerously escalating situation that could lead to open conflict, with grave consequences for peace and security in north Africa, the Mediterranean and other regions. Both parties should be told in no uncertain terms that the Council, while affirming every nation's right to pursue its own interests, required every United Nations Member to refrain from the threat or use of force against the territorial integrity or political independence of other States in the pursuit of such interests.

Malta said the people of Chad should be left alone to resolve their problems and requested the Council to urge speedy cessation of hostilities, withdrawal of all foreign forces and promotion by OAU of national reconciliation within Chad and good relations with its neighbours. It was only natural for the region's States to take the initiative to safeguard their own peace and security, Malta stressed; the road to peace lay not in the brandishing of military hardware but in dialogue among equals, aided by the relevant regional organization and backed by the Council.

The escalation of tension and conflict in the Mediterranean and north African regions, India said, was the result of increased recourse to the threat or use of force and to military intervention, in violation of the Charter. The non-aligned Movement had always been opposed to all forms of foreign aggression, subjugation, dependence, interference and pressure, as well as to great-Power policies tending to perpetuate world division into blocs or spheres of influence.

The Sudan recalled that the Libyan Arab Jamahiriya, while preparing to launch aggression against the Sudan, hastened to complain to the Council about United States provocations and threats said to jeopardize Libyan security and safety and aimed at toppling its régime. This time, while directly intervening in Chad with flagrant use of force, it had once more come before the Council claiming that Libyan security and safety were being threatened, to divert attention from its armed intervention in Chad. The Sudan explained that its military exercises were aimed solely at enhancing its defence capabilities. It stressed its commitment to a policy of co-operation and good-neighbourliness, as substantiated by its record of good relations with its neighbours, excepting the Libyan Arab Jamahiriya, which it hoped would work for respect for law, principles and international covenants in word and deed.

Zaire agreed with the Sudan's analysis of the complaint by the Libyan Arab Jamahiriya and added that that country, having annexed the Aouzou Strip belonging to Chad, had proceeded to subject Chad to torture, displacement and murder, using internationally prohibited weapons such as phosphorous bombs and napalm, recruiting mercenaries and assisting rebels and insurgents. Zaire concluded that the Libyan complaint was unfounded and a mere ruse to divert attention from the real aggressor, the Libyan Arab Jamahiriya.

REFERENCES

(1)S/15614. (2)S/15618. (3)S/15617. (4)S/15615. (5)S/15619. (6)S/15621. (7)YUN 1982, p. 189. (8)S/15625. (9)S/15755. (10)S/15789. (11)S/15872. (12)S/15887. (13)S/15910. (14)A/38/328 (S/15912). (15)S/15914. (16)S/15919. (17)A/38/417. (18)S/15921. (19)S/15924. (20)A/38/448. (21)S/15925.

International security of the Mediterranean countries

During 1983, the Secretary-General reported to the General Assembly the views of Governments concerning the strengthening of security and co-operation in the Mediterranean region. Recognizing the close link between that region's security and international peace and security, the Assembly, in December, encouraged the Mediterranean States to intensify co-operation aimed at reducing tension and strengthening security in the region, and urged all other States to co-operate towards that end.

By a letter of 25 March,[1] the Libyan Arab Jamahiriya stated that it attached particular importance to the transformation of the Mediterranean region into a zone of peace and co-operation and shared the international community's initiatives in that regard. That objective could not be achieved, however, unless international action was taken to end continued United States naval, air and military presence in the region, aggressive designs against Arab States stemming from a strategic co-operation agreement between the United States and Israel, the development of Israel's nuclear weapons programme, and the threat of Israeli attack on nuclear installations set up for peaceful purposes in any Arab country.

Report of the Secretary-General. In response to a General Assembly request of December 1982,[2] the Secretary-General submitted two 1983 reports on strengthening security and co-operation in the Mediterranean region. The first, dated 22 July, with subsequent addenda,[3] transmitted the replies received during 1983 from eight States containing their views on the subject. The second report, dated 30 September,[4] was an analysis based on six of those replies and on others previously received from 21 other States.[5]

The Secretary-General reported that many States regarded the Mediterranean as strategically significant and therefore its transformation into a zone of peace and co-operation as urgent, given the threat to world peace and stability posed by the crises in that region. While the concept of such a zone needed precise definition, there was agreement that this should not constitute an impediment to strengthening regional security and co-operation. To that end, specific political and security measures were suggested, among them settlement of existing conflicts, co-ordinated reduction of armed forces, non-deployment of nuclear weapons in non-nuclear-weapon States, non-use by nuclear-weapon States of nuclear weapons against States which had renounced such weapons on their territories, withdrawal of foreign fleets and military bases, and non-adherence to military pacts and treaties. Institutional measures were also proposed, and reference was made to economic and technical co-operation. The general view was that strengthened security and co-operation among the Mediterranean States would enhance world stability.

GENERAL ASSEMBLY ACTION

Acting on the recommendation of the First Committee, the General Assembly, on 20 December 1983, adopted resolution 38/189 without vote.

Strengthening of security and co-operation in the Mediterranean region

The General Assembly,

Recalling its resolutions 36/102 of 9 December 1981 and 37/118 of 16 December 1982 on the item entitled "Review of the implementation of the Declaration on the Strengthening of International Security",

Mindful of the importance of strengthening peace and security in the Mediterranean and of the resultant impact on international peace and security,

Noting the provisions relating to the Mediterranean in the Final Act of the Conference on Security and Co-operation in Europe, signed at Helsinki on 1 August 1975, and those of the Concluding Documents of the meetings of representatives of the participating States of the Helsinki Conference, held at Belgrade from 4 October 1977 to 8 March 1978 and at Madrid from 11 November 1980 to 9 September 1983,

Noting the declarations of the successive meetings of the non-aligned countries concerning the Mediterranean, as well as official declarations on, and contributions to, peace and security in the Mediterranean made by individual countries,

Taking note of the analytical report of the Secretary-General,

1. *Recognizes:*

(a) That the security of the Mediterranean is closely linked with international peace and security;

(b) That further efforts are necessary for the reduction of tension and of armaments and for the creation of conditions of security and fruitful co-operation in all fields for all countries and peoples of the Mediterranean, on the basis of the principles of sovereignty, independence, territorial integrity, security, non-intervention and non-interference, non-violation of international borders, non-use of force or threat of use of force, the inadmissibility of the acquisition of territory by force, the peaceful settlement of disputes and respect for sovereignty over natural resources;

(c) The need for just and viable solutions to existing problems and crises in the area, on the basis of the provisions of the Charter and relevant resolutions of the United Nations, the withdrawal of foreign forces of occupation and the right of peoples under colonial or foreign domination to self-determination and independence;

2. *Encourages* efforts to intensify existing and promote new forms of co-operation in various fields, particularly those aimed at reducing tension and strengthening confidence and security in the region;

3. *Urges* Mediterranean States to inform the Secretary-General of any concerted efforts aimed at promoting and strengthening security and co-operation in the Mediterranean;

4. *Urges* all States to co-operate with Mediterranean States in efforts to enhance security and co-operation in the Mediterranean;

5. *Invites* the Secretary-General to give due attention to the question of peace, security and co-operation in the Mediterranean region and, if requested to do so, to render advice and assistance to concerted efforts by Mediterranean countries in promoting peace, security and co-operation in the region;

6. *Requests* the Secretary-General to submit to the General Assembly at its thirty-ninth session, on the basis of all replies received and notifications submitted in the implementation of the present resolution and taking into account the debate on this question during its thirty-eighth session, a comprehensive report on strengthening security and co-operation in the Mediterranean;

7.   *Decides* to include in the provisional agenda of its thirty-ninth session the item entitled "Strengthening of security and co-operation in the Mediterranean region".

General Assembly resolution 38/189

20 December 1983   Meeting 103   Adopted without vote

Approved by First Committee (A/38/642) without vote, 9 December (meeting 54); 12-nation draft (A/C.1/38/L.88/Rev.3); agenda item 65.

Sponsors: Algeria, Bahamas, Cyprus, Egypt, Greece, Libyan Arab Jamahiriya, Malta, Romania, Seychelles, Sierra Leone, Tunisia, Yugoslavia.
Meeting numbers. GA 38th session: 1st Committee 47, 49-54; plenary 103.

REFERENCES

(1)A/38/127. (2)YUN 1982, p. 249, GA res. 37/118, 16 Dec. 1982. (3)A/38/291 & Add.1-3. (4)A/38/395. (5)YUN 1982, p. 384.

Chapter IX

Middle East

In 1983, the situation in the Middle East continued to occupy the attention of the Security Council, the General Assembly and several other United Nations bodies. Aside from the annual debate in the Assembly on the Middle East situation as a whole, the major aspects considered were the Palestine question, the situation in Lebanon and between other individual Arab States and Israel, the situation in the territories occupied by Israel, and Palestine refugees. The United Nations continued to maintain two major peace-keeping operations in the region financed by special assessments on Member States.

Details on these subjects together with the full texts of the related resolutions or decisions adopted can be found under the relevant subject headings on the following pages. For texts of resolutions and decisions of major organs mentioned but not reproduced in this chapter, refer to INDEX OF RESOLUTIONS AND DECISIONS.

Topics related to this chapter. Disarmament: Nuclear-weapon-free zones—Middle East; nuclear weapons and Israel. Africa: Israel–South Africa relations. Mediterranean countries: Libyan Arab Jamahiriya–United States dispute. Disasters and emergency relief: Lebanon. Regional economic and social activities: Western Asia. Human rights. Refugees and humanitarian assistance: Lebanon.

Middle East situation

General aspects

The situation in the Middle East was again considered in 1983 as an item on the agenda of the General Assembly's regular session and, in December, the Assembly adopted five resolutions (38/180 A-E) on different aspects of the situation. Three of these (38/180 A-C) are dealt with elsewhere in this chapter (see INDEX OF RESOLUTIONS AND DECISIONS).

Communications. By a letter of 4 January 1983,[1] Israel drew attention to statements made by Arab and other countries on 20 December 1982, in connection with the Assembly's consideration of the Middle East situation and the Palestine question, and asserted that the statements indicated that the countries in question

maintained their attitude with regard to Israel's right to exist.

By a letter of 14 January,[2] Israel submitted complaints about what it described as terrorist incidents, for which the Palestine Liberation Organization (PLO) had claimed responsibility, in which explosive devices had been used against civilian targets.

By letters of 25 February[3] and 3 November,[4] Israel said that it objected to offensive references made about it by speakers in the Security Council during consideration of the dispute between the Libyan Arab Jamahiriya and the United States (see Chapter VIII of this section), the situation in Grenada (see Chapter VI of this section) and the question of Namibia (see TRUSTEESHIP AND DECOLONIZATION, Chapter III).

On 24 March,[5] the Federal Republic of Germany transmitted the conclusions adopted at a meeting of heads of State and Government of the European Community (EC) at Brussels, Belgium, on 22 March. The meeting expressed concern at the continued lack of progress towards peace between Israel and its neighbours, and reaffirmed EC's previous position on a settlement, built on the right to a secure existence for all States in the region, including Israel, and justice for all the peoples, including the right of the Palestinian people to self-determination. Welcoming the September 1982 peace initiatives[6] of the United States and of the Arab Summit Conference at Fez, Morocco, the EC members expressed regret that no initiatives had succeeded in ending the fighting; they called for a cease-fire, cessation of all military operations and withdrawal of forces to internationally recognized frontiers, and for a just settlement negotiated in accordance with Security Council resolutions and acceptable to both parties.

On 21 April,[7] the Federal Republic of Germany and Thailand transmitted the joint declaration of the Fourth Meeting of the Ministers for Foreign Affairs of the States members of the Association of South-East Asian Nations and EC, held at Bangkok, Thailand, on 24 and 25 March, which stressed the urgency for a Middle East peace settlement and called on all parties to the conflict to seize the opportunity for progress towards that end. The hope for a lasting Middle East peace settlement was reiterated in a letter of 22 June,[8] by which the Federal Republic of Germany transmitted the conclusions adopted at a meeting of the

EC heads of State and Government at Stuttgart on 19 June.

On 21 November,[9] the Sudan transmitted a letter of the same date from the Permanent Observer of the League of Arab States to the United Nations, in reply to a 16 November address to the General Assembly by Chaim Herzog, President of Israel, who had called for negotiations without pre-conditions. The Observer stated that, by annexing Jerusalem, the Golan Heights and Arab lands and cities, it was Israel which had established pre-conditions.

By a letter of 6 December 1983,[10] the Libyan Arab Jamahiriya expressed concern that an agreement between the United States and Israel, reached during the visit of the Israeli Prime Minister to Washington at the end of November, would endanger peace and security in the Arab region.

Report of the Secretary-General. In a September report to the General Assembly and the Security Council,[11] the Secretary-General submitted his observations on the Middle East situation. He noted that developments in the Middle East during the previous year had given little cause for hope for a solution and had made a comprehensive settlement even more difficult. Preoccupation with events in Lebanon (see below, under INCIDENTS AND DISPUTES BETWEEN ARAB COUNTRIES AND ISRAEL) had overshadowed the consideration of other major aspects of the Middle East problem; delay in getting to its roots, he warned, could create a far more fundamental crisis.

Israeli withdrawal from the occupied territories, realization of the rights of the States in the area to live in peace within secure boundaries, and the future and rights of the Palestinians were still the main elements of the conflict, the Secretary-General stated. Lack of mutual recognition and communication had created a dangerous impasse. The June 1982 Israeli invasion of Lebanon[12] and its aftermath had again shown that the use of force could not resolve the Middle East conflict, but only complicate it.

The safety and survival of all the parties, he concluded, could be achieved only through an agreed settlement which took account of the basic aspirations and vital interests of each, based on principles outlined in Security Council resolution 242(1967),[13] and which recognized the rights of the Palestinian people. He hoped that, confronted with the increasing dangers of the conflict which threatened the security of the region and beyond, the major Powers would find it possible to work with each other in the search for a just and durable Middle East peace, with the Council providing a practical framework and becoming a key instrument, and other means of approaching the problem, for example, through the institution of a suitable negotiating process, including, in an appropriate form, an international conference.

GENERAL ASSEMBLY ACTION

Under the agenda item "The situation in the Middle East", the General Assembly, on 19 December 1983, adopted five resolutions, all by recorded vote. Three of them dealt with: the situation in the Syrian Golan Heights (38/180 A) (see below, under INCIDENTS AND DISPUTES BETWEEN ARAB COUNTRIES AND ISRAEL); the Palestinian cultural heritage (38/180 B); and the status of Jerusalem (38/180 C) (see below, under PALESTINE QUESTION).

Resolution 38/180 D, dealing with the Middle East situation in general, was as follows:

The General Assembly,

Having discussed the item entitled "The situation in the Middle East",

Reaffirming its resolutions 36/226 A and B of 17 December 1981, ES-9/1 of 5 February 1982 and 37/123 F of 16 December 1982,

Recalling Security Council resolutions 425(1978) of 19 March 1978, 497(1981) of 17 December 1981, 508(1982) of 5 June 1982, 509(1982) of 6 June 1982, 511(1982) of 18 June 1982, 512(1982) of 19 June 1982, 513(1982) of 4 July 1982, 515(1982) of 29 July 1982, 516(1982) of 1 August 1982, 517(1982) of 4 August 1982, 518(1982) of 12 August 1982, 519(1982) of 17 August 1982, 520(1982) of 17 September 1982 and 521(1982) of 19 September 1982,

Taking note of the report of the Secretary-General of 12 October 1982,

Welcoming the world-wide support extended to the just cause of the Palestinian people and the other Arab countries in their struggle against Israeli aggression and occupation in order to achieve a comprehensive, just and lasting peace in the Middle East and the full exercise by the Palestinian people of its inalienable national rights, as affirmed by previous resolutions of the General Assembly relating to the question of Palestine and to the situation in the Middle East,

Gravely concerned that the Arab and Palestinian territories occupied since 1967, including Jerusalem, still remain under Israeli occupation, that the relevant resolutions of the United Nations have not been implemented and that the Palestinian people is still denied the restoration of its land and the exercise of its inalienable national rights in conformity with international law, as reaffirmed by resolutions of the United Nations,

Reaffirming the applicability of the Geneva Convention relative to the Protection of Civilian Persons in Time of War, of 12 August 1949, to all the occupied Palestinian and other Arab territories, including Jerusalem,

Reiterating all relevant United Nations resolutions which emphasize that the acquisition of territory by force is inadmissible under the Charter of the United Nations and the principles of international law and that Israel must withdraw unconditionally from all the Palestinian and other Arab territories occupied by Israel since 1967, including Jerusalem,

Reaffirming further the imperative necessity of establishing a comprehensive, just and lasting peace in the region, based on full respect for the Charter and the principles of international law,

Gravely concerned also at recent Israeli actions involving the escalation and expansion of the conflict in the region, which further violate the principles of international law and endanger international peace and security,

Recognizing the great importance of the time factor in the endeavours to achieve a comprehensive, just and lasting peace in the Middle East,

1. *Reaffirms its conviction* that the question of Palestine is the core of the conflict in the Middle East and that no comprehensive, just and lasting peace in the region will be achieved without the full exercise by the Palestinian people of its inalienable national rights and the immediate, unconditional and total withdrawal of Israel from all the Palestinian and other occupied Arab territories;

2. *Reaffirms further* that a just and comprehensive settlement of the situation in the Middle East cannot be achieved without the participation on an equal footing of all the parties to the conflict, including the Palestine Liberation Organization, the representative of the Palestinian people;

3. *Declares once more* that peace in the Middle East is indivisible and must be based on a comprehensive, just and lasting solution of the Middle East problem, under the auspices of the United Nations and on the basis of relevant resolutions of the United Nations, which ensures the complete and unconditional withdrawal of Israel from the Palestinian and other Arab territories occupied since 1967, including Jerusalem, and which enables the Palestinian people, under the leadership of the Palestine Liberation Organization, to exercise its inalienable rights, including the right to return and the right to self-determination, national independence and the establishment of its independent sovereign State in Palestine, in accordance with the resolutions of the United Nations relevant to the question of Palestine, in particular General Assembly resolutions ES-7/2 of 29 July 1980, 36/120 A to F of 10 December 1981, 37/86 A to D of 10 December 1982 and 37/86 E of 20 December 1982;

4. *Welcomes* the Arab Peace Plan adopted unanimously at the Twelfth Arab Summit Conference, held at Fez, Morocco, on 25 November 1981 and from 6 to 9 September 1982;

5. *Condemns* Israel's continued occupation of the Palestinian and other Arab territories, including Jerusalem, in violation of the Charter of the United Nations, the principles of international law and the relevant resolutions of the United Nations, and demands the immediate, unconditional and total withdrawal of Israel from all the territories occupied since June 1967;

6. *Rejects* all agreements and arrangements which violate the recognized rights of the Palestinian people and contradict the principles of just and comprehensive solutions to the Middle East problem to ensure the establishment of a just peace in the area;

7. *Deplores* Israel's failure to comply with Security Council resolutions 476(1980) of 30 June 1980 and 478(1980) of 20 August 1980 and General Assembly resolutions 35/207 of 16 December 1980 and 36/226 A and B of 17 December 1981, determines that Israel's decision to annex Jerusalem and to declare it its "capital" as well as the measures to alter its physical character, demographic composition, institutional structure and status are null and void and demands that they be rescinded immediately, and calls upon all Member States, the specialized agencies and all other international organizations to abide by the present resolution and all other relevant resolutions, including Assembly resolutions 37/86 A to E;

8. *Condemns* Israel's aggression, policies and practices against the Palestinian people in the occupied Palestinian territories and outside these territories, particularly Palestinians in Lebanon, including the expropriation and annexation of territory, the establishment of settlements, assassination attempts and other terrorist, aggressive and repressive measures, which are in violation of the Charter and the principles of international law and the relevant international conventions;

9. *Strongly condemns* the imposition by Israel of its laws, jurisdiction and administration on the occupied Syrian Golan Heights, its annexationist policies and practices, the establishment of settlements, the confiscation of lands, the diversion of water resources and the imposition of Israeli citizenship on Syrian nationals, and declares that all these measures are null and void and constitute a violation of the rules and principles of international law relating to belligerent occupation, in particular the Geneva Convention relative to the Protection of Civilian Persons in Time of War, of 12 August 1949;

10. *Considers* that the agreements on strategic cooperation between the United States of America and Israel signed on 30 November 1981, together with the recent accords concluded in this context, would encourage Israel to pursue its aggressive and expansionist policies and practices in the Palestinian and other Arab territories occupied since 1967, including Jerusalem, would have adverse effects on efforts for the establishment of a comprehensive, just and lasting peace in the Middle East and would threaten the security of the region;

11. *Calls upon* all States to put an end to the flow to Israel of any military, economic and financial aid, as well as of human resources, aimed at encouraging it to pursue its aggressive policies against the Arab countries and the Palestinian people;

12. *Strongly condemns* the continuing and increasing collaboration between Israel and the racist régime of South Africa, especially in the economic, military and nuclear fields, which constitutes a hostile act against the African and Arab States and enables Israel to enhance its nuclear capabilities, thus subjecting the States of the region to nuclear blackmail;

13. *Reaffirms* the call for the convening of an international peace conference on the Middle East—as specified in paragraph 5 of the Geneva Declaration on Palestine, adopted on 7 September 1983 by the International Conference on the Question of Palestine—under the auspices of the United Nations and on the basis of relevant resolutions of the United Nations;

14. *Requests* the Secretary-General to report to the Security Council periodically on the development of the situation and to submit to the General Assembly at its thirty-ninth session a comprehensive report covering the developments in the Middle East in all their aspects.

General Assembly resolution 38/180 D

19 December 1983   Meeting 102   101-18-20 (recorded vote)

15-nation draft (A/38/L.46 & Add.1); agenda item 34.

Sponsors: Afghanistan, Bangladesh, Cuba, Guinea, Guyana, India, Indonesia, Lao People's Democratic Republic, Malaysia, Mongolia, Nicaragua, Pakistan, Sri Lanka, Viet Nam, Yugoslavia.

Meeting numbers. GA 38th session: plenary 87-89, 91-95, 102.

Recorded vote in Assembly as follows:

In favour: Afghanistan, Albania, Algeria, Angola, Argentina, Bahamas, Bahrain, Bangladesh, Benin, Bhutan, Bolivia, Botswana, Brazil, Bulgaria, Burundi, Byelorussian SSR, Cape Verde, Central African Republic, China, Colombia, Congo, Cuba, Cyprus, Czechoslovakia, Democratic Kampuchea, Democratic Yemen, Djibouti, Ecuador, Egypt, El Salvador, Ethiopia, Gambia, German Democratic Republic, Ghana, Greece, Guinea, Guinea-Bissau, Guyana, Hungary, India, Indonesia, Iran, Iraq, Jordan, Kenya, Kuwait, Lao People's Democratic Republic, Lebanon, Libyan Arab Jamahiriya, Madagascar, Malaysia, Maldives, Mali, Malta, Mauritania, Mauritius, Mexico, Mongolia, Morocco, Mozambique, Nicaragua, Niger, Nigeria, Oman, Pakistan, Papua New Guinea, Peru, Philippines, Poland, Qatar, Romania, Rwanda, Sao Tome and Principe, Saudi Arabia, Senegal, Seychelles, Sierra Leone, Singapore, Somalia, Sri Lanka, Sudan, Suriname, Syrian Arab Republic, Thailand, Togo, Trinidad and Tobago, Tunisia, Turkey, Uganda, Ukrainian SSR, USSR, United Arab Emirates, United Republic of Cameroon, United Republic of Tanzania, Upper Volta, Venezuela, Viet Nam, Yemen, Yugoslavia, Zambia, Zimbabwe.

Against: Australia, Belgium, Canada, Denmark, France, Germany, Federal Republic of, Haiti, Iceland, Ireland, Israel, Italy, Luxembourg, Netherlands, New Zealand, Norway, Portugal, United Kingdom, United States.

Abstaining: Austria, Barbados, Belize, Burma, Chad, Chile, Dominican Republic, Fiji, Finland, Guatemala, Honduras, Ivory Coast, Jamaica, Japan, Malawi, Saint Lucia, Saint Vincent and the Grenadines, Spain, Sweden, Uruguay.

Israel rejected the resolution as unbalanced, impeding a peaceful solution of the Arab-Israel conflict by presenting that conflict as the root of all Middle East problems and the sole danger in the region to world peace, and contradicting Security Council resolution 242(1967),[13] the only agreed basis for a negotiated settlement. The United States said it opposed resolutions that hindered the peace process, contributed to a continued diplomatic deadlock and eroded confidence in the Assembly's role in solving the Middle East problems.

Portugal dissociated itself from any appeal it considered prejudicial to joint efforts and in particular from any resolution which, because of its language, measures advocated, discriminatory references or legal implications, might harm constructive efforts. Finland regretted especially that the principles of Council resolutions 242(1967) and 338(1973)[14] were not reaffirmed; it particularly reserved its position on elements in the preamble and paragraphs 10 and 11, and voiced reservations on paragraph 13.

Although the text corresponded to a large extent to its position, Austria said it had abstained in view of some formulations. Sweden had strong reservations on paragraphs 10 and 11 and felt that the resolution lacked balance. Spain could not support paragraphs 10, 11 and 12, but believed that paragraphs 4, 6 and 13 did not exclude other ways for a peaceful and negotiated Middle East solution. New Zealand was disappointed that the resolution did not reflect the balance of resolution 242(1967) and was not well calculated to contribute to a negotiated settlement. Honduras found both positive and negative elements in the text.

Though voting in favour, Brazil and the Philippines voiced reservations on some provisions. Mexico and Thailand said they would have abstained had there been separate votes on paragraphs 6 and 10; Thailand felt that they prejudged the outcome of agreements, which a sovereign State had the right to conclude. Peru cautioned that the wording of paragraphs 6, 10 and 11 could be misinterpreted; in its understanding, references to relations between specific States and others were strictly linked to the Palestine question as the core of the Middle East problem. It would also have liked to see specific references to resolutions 242(1967) and 338(1973), as a basis on which the parties could reach an understanding.

Greece said it voted in favour on the basis of its attachment to the principle of the United Nations Charter, Article 2, paragraph 4, stating that Member States should refrain from the threat or use of force against the territorial integrity or political independence of any State. Bolivia and Togo said they voted in favour in keeping with their position on the Middle East situation; its position, Bolivia added, was based on respect for the territorial integrity of all States and the rejection of the forceful acquisition of territory. Malta remarked that its support did not mean that it agreed with every provision.

The Libyan Arab Jamahiriya reaffirmed its opposition to allusions that would give some semblance of legitimacy to Israeli occupation of Palestinian territories or recognize the Zionist entity. Iran spoke similarly, terming that entity an artificially forged State.

By a separately adopted paragraph of resolution 38/6, on co-operation between the United Nations and the League of Arab States, the Assembly requested the Secretary-General to intensify his efforts to implement United Nations resolutions relevant to the Middle East situation and to the Palestine question (see Chapter XI of this section).

Also under the agenda item on the situation in the Middle East, the General Assembly, on 19 December, adopted resolution 38/180 E by recorded vote.

The General Assembly,

Having considered the item entitled "The situation in the Middle East",

Recalling its resolutions 36/226 A of 17 December 1981 and 37/123 F of 20 December 1982, in which it stated, *inter alia,* its concern over certain factors which exacerbate the situation in the Middle East,

Deeply concerned at recent developments in the Middle East and the critical situation confronting the region resulting from the continued escalation of Israel's policy of aggression, expansion and annexation in the region,

Expressing grave concern over the continued supply of modern arms and war materials to Israel, augmented by substantial economic aid, without which Israel's policy of aggression and of flouting United Nations resolutions could not be maintained,

Deeply aware that the recent reported agreements following the memorandum of understanding between the United States of America and Israel will increase Israel's intransigence and its war potential and escalate its expansionist and annexationist policies in the Palestinian and other Arab territories occupied since 1967, including Jerusalem, at a time when it is defying United Nations resolutions,

1. *Declares,* accordingly, the international responsibility of any party or parties that supply Israel with arms or economic aid that augment its war potential;

2. *Expresses deep concern* at and condemns all steps which may result in augmenting the capability of Israel and contributing to its policy of aggression against countries in the region;

3. *Demands* that all States, particularly the United States of America, in the light of the said agreements, refrain from taking any step that would support Israel's war capabilities and consequently its aggressive acts, whether in the Palestinian and other Arab territories occupied since 1967 or against countries in the region;

4. *Calls upon* all States to review, in the light of the present resolution, any agreement, whether military, economic or otherwise, concluded with Israel.

General Assembly resolution 38/180 E

19 December 1983   Meeting 102   81-27-29 (recorded vote)

19-nation draft (A/38/L.50); agenda item 34.
Sponsors: Algeria, Bahrain, Democratic Yemen, Djibouti, Iraq, Jordan, Kuwait, Libyan Arab Jamahiriya, Mauritania, Morocco, Oman, Qatar, Saudi Arabia, Somalia, Sudan, Syrian Arab Republic, Tunisia, United Arab Emirates, Yemen.
Financial implications. 5th Committee, A/38/756; S-G, A/C.5/38/105.
Meeting numbers. GA 38th session: 5th Committee 70; plenary 87-89, 91-95, 102.

Recorded vote in Assembly as follows:

In favour: Afghanistan, Albania, Algeria, Angola, Bahrain, Bangladesh, Benin, Bhutan, Botswana, Bulgaria, Burundi, Byelorussian SSR, Cape Verde, China, Congo, Cuba, Cyprus, Czechoslovakia, Democratic Kampuchea, Democratic Yemen, Djibouti, Egypt, Ethiopia, Gambia, German Democratic Republic, Ghana, Greece, Guinea, Guinea-Bissau, Guyana, Hungary, India, Indonesia, Iran, Iraq, Jordan, Kenya, Kuwait, Lao People's Democratic Republic, Libyan Arab Jamahiriya, Madagascar, Malaysia, Maldives, Mali, Malta, Mauritania, Mongolia, Morocco, Mozambique, Nicaragua, Niger, Nigeria, Oman, Pakistan, Poland, Qatar, Romania, Sao Tome and Principe, Saudi Arabia, Senegal, Seychelles, Sierra Leone, Somalia, Sri Lanka, Sudan, Suriname, Syrian Arab Republic, Tunisia, Turkey, Uganda, Ukrainian SSR, USSR, United Arab Emirates, United Republic of Cameroon, United Republic of Tanzania, Upper Volta, Viet Nam, Yemen, Yugoslavia, Zambia, Zimbabwe.

Against: Australia, Belgium, Canada, Chile, Costa Rica, Denmark, Dominican Republic, Finland, France, Germany, Federal Republic of, Guatemala, Haiti, Honduras, Iceland, Ireland, Israel, Italy, Japan, Luxembourg, Netherlands, New Zealand, Norway, Paraguay, Portugal, Sweden, United Kingdom, United States.

Abstaining: Argentina, Austria, Bahamas, Barbados, Belize, Bolivia, Brazil, Burma, Chad, Colombia, Ecuador, El Salvador, Fiji, Ivory Coast, Jamaica, Malawi, Mexico, Nepal, Papua New Guinea, Peru, Philippines, Saint Lucia, Saint Vincent and the Grenadines, Singapore, Spain, Thailand, Trinidad and Tobago, Uruguay, Venezuela.

Rejecting the resolution, Israel said it was beyond the Assembly's authority to dictate the nature of bilateral relations, which it said were solely within the jurisdiction of the States involved; the sponsors' audacity was heightened by the fact that the Arab States which considered themselves in confrontation with Israel—Iraq, Jordan, the Libyan Arab Jamahiriya, Saudi Arabia and the Syrian Arab Republic—had over the past decade contracted for the delivery of armaments worth over

$100 billion. The United States–Israel understanding had as its sole objective the promotion of peace and security, while the resolution sought to perpetuate regional instability and tension. In a 16 December letter,[15] Israel gave what it said was a breakdown of figures of arms purchases by Arab States. Were they as sincerely interested in mutual disarmament as was Israel, they would have entered into a direct dialogue.

The United States rejected the resolution as an inadmissible intrusion into the right of a State to conduct relations with another; its relationship with Israel was central to the pursuit of peace and not aimed against any State in the region.

Finland said that the arms race in the region was not the sole responsibility of the countries mentioned in the resolution, which was too one-sided and sweeping in order to contribute effectively to the search for a halt to that arms race and for a peaceful settlement. In the opinion of Honduras, the text lacked positive elements. Portugal dissociated itself from any act or appeal prejudicial to joint efforts, and in particular to discriminatory references or legal implications that might harm constructive efforts. Though expressing doubts as to whether the United States–Israel agreement would contribute to a peaceful settlement, New Zealand did not consider it appropriate to judge agreements between sovereign States, a point taken up by Singapore. This latter view was also shared by the Philippines and Thailand, which added that any Assembly action questioning that right might have ramifications beyond the Middle East situation. Colombia said it could not accept a text condemning only one of the parties in the Middle East. Ecuador, too, could not agree to condemning specific agreements or to accepting suggestions to sever relations with Israel. Rather than promoting peace, Venezuela believed that certain paragraphs were disruptive and could lead in the opposite direction. Bolivia did not agree with the drafting style and some of the text's content. Austria had reservations in particular on paragraph 4.

Though voting in favour, Greece dissociated itself from that paragraph. Turkey stressed that its affirmative vote reflected concern over Israel's tendency to use every opportunity to achieve its aggressive aims; the reference to "international responsibility" in paragraph 1 was inappropriate. Seychelles voted in favour for reasons of principle. While concurring with the resolution's thrust, Malta said it did not agree with all provisions.

Though condemnation and denunciation might not be the best way to proceed, Egypt felt that the resolution reflected genuine concern over the developments in the Middle East, including the recent United States–Israel agreement, as a result of which doubts and preoccupations had arisen.

Iran reserved its right with regard to any paragraph which recognized an artificially forged State, the Zionist entity.

The agreement between the United States and Israel was also dealt with by the Assembly in its resolution 38/180 D (see above).

Iran did not press to a vote a draft resolution[16] by which the Assembly would have: considered the strategic alliance between Israel and the United States as a factor of escalation of Middle East tension threatening international peace and security; condemned the recent United States–Israeli aggression in the region, as well as any attempted use or threat of use of force, resulting from the alliance, against the States of the region and aimed at destroying the Palestinians' struggle to regain their rights in their homeland; and requested the Secretary-General to seek Member States' views and to prepare a study on the consequences of the alliance, particularly on the Palestinians.

Persons detained by Israel

In 1983, the General Assembly again took up the case of the Palestinian Ziad Abu Eain, this time in connection with the release of Palestinian prisoners held in Israel and southern Lebanon. The Assembly and the Economic and Social Council had first considered this case in 1981,[17] and in January 1982 the Secretary-General had reported on implementation of the Assembly's demand that Abu Eain be released.[18]

Information on persons detained by Israel in the Israeli-occupied territories was provided by the Special Committee to Investigate Israeli Practices Affecting the Human Rights of the Population of the Occupied Territories (see below, under TERRITORIES OCCUPIED BY ISRAEL). Cases of arrest and detention of staff of the United Nations Relief and Works Agency for Palestine Refugees in the Near East in Lebanon by Israeli authorities were reported on by the Secretary-General (see below, under PALESTINE REFUGEES).

In March 1983,[19] the Commission on Human Rights reaffirmed the human rights of persons detained by Israel (see ECONOMIC AND SOCIAL QUESTIONS, Chapter XVIII).

Communications. On 5 May,[20] Jordan transmitted a letter of 3 May from the PLO observer, to which a letter was attached from the Committee to Defend the Rights of Prisoners at Ansar (Insar) Detention Camp in southern Lebanon, expressing appreciation for the humanitarian role played by the International Committee of the Red Cross (ICRC) and listing a number of violations of prisoners' rights by Israeli authorities.

By a letter of 18 November,[21] the Chairman of the Committee on the Exercise of the Inalienable Rights of the Palestinian People protested the arrest by Israeli authorities of Mohammed Mi'ari and Maysara Sayyid, representatives of two non-governmental organizations based in Israel, on the grounds that they had violated security laws because they had attended the International Conference on the Question of Palestine (see below, under PALESTINE QUESTION).

In a letter of 13 December,[22] Saudi Arabia stated that an ICRC press release issued that day reported that Israel had violated a written agreement, negotiated by ICRC, between PLO and Israel for the simultaneous freeing of six Israeli prisoners and about 100 prisoners detained in Israel itself, as well as all others (some 4,300) in southern Lebanon. Although registered for release, some prisoners from Insar Camp and other military command posts in southern Lebanon had not been freed, among them Ziad Abu Eain, who had been taken to an Israeli prison.

Israel, on 16 December,[23] submitted a press statement of 14 December by its Ministry of Defence pointing out that the Red Cross representative in Israel, in a letter of 29 November to the Ministry, had admitted that the original mistake which prevented the release of Abu Eain, sentenced to life imprisonment for the murder of two Israeli youths in Tiberias in May 1979, derived from an oversight in the Red Cross list by which its representatives at Ben Gurion Airport near Tel Aviv had acted. ICRC claimed that its oversight had been compounded by an error by the Israel Defence Forces (IDF) at the airport. However, due to the absence of Abu Eain's name from the list, the Red Cross and IDF had agreed that another prisoner also sentenced to life imprisonment would be sent to Algeria; thus, Israel had fulfilled its commitment to release 63 prisoners. The Ministry emphasized that the prisoner exchange had at the last moment been moved up by 24 hours; despite the pressures of short notice, IDF had abided by the agreement and, if during the release of 4,500 detainees and 63 prisoners in exchange for six Israeli soldiers some snags had occurred, Israel was not prepared to change what had been implemented.

Speaking on 30 November before the Special Political Committee (SPC), the PLO observer charged that Israeli authorities had kidnapped Abu Eain at the airport as he was about to depart for Algeria. He had been imprisoned again and subjected to torture. Immediate action was required to force Israel to observe the agreement and release him.

GENERAL ASSEMBLY ACTION

Under the agenda item on the report of the Special Committee to Investigate Israeli Practices Affecting the Human Rights of the Population of the Occupied Territories, the General Assembly, on 15 December, adopted resolution 38/79 A by recorded vote. The Assembly took this action on the recommendation of SPC.

The General Assembly,

Having heard the statement of the representative of the Palestine Liberation Organization relative to the fate of Ziad Abu Eain,

Taking note of the report of the International Committee of the Red Cross of 13 December 1983,

1. *Condemns* Israel for the fact that one prisoner, Ziad Abu Eain, who had been registered before embarkation by delegates of the International Committee of the Red Cross at Tel Aviv Airport, was taken at the last minute by the Israeli authorities;

2. *Demands* the immediate release of Ziad Abu Eain, as well as the other prisoners who were duly registered to be freed from Insar Camp and other military command posts in southern Lebanon but have not in fact been released, and the securing of their transfer to Algiers in conformity with the agreement reached through the good offices of the International Committee of the Red Cross;

3. *Requests* the Secretary-General to report on the implementation of the present resolution.

General Assembly resolution 38/79 A

15 December 1983   Meeting 98   110-2-29 (recorded vote)

Approved by SPC (A/38/718) by recorded vote (75-3-30), 7 December (meeting 47); 19-nation draft (A/SPC/38/L.35), amended in Assembly by Saudi Arabia (A/38/L.48); agenda item 69.

Sponsors: Algeria, Bahrain, Cuba, Democratic Yemen, Djibouti, India, Iraq, Jordan, Kuwait, Mali, Mauritania, Nicaragua, Pakistan, Qatar, Saudi Arabia, Sudan, Syrian Arab Republic, United Arab Emirates, Yemen.

Meeting numbers. GA 38th session: SPC 36-42, 45-48; plenary 98.

Recorded vote in Assembly as follows:

In favour: Afghanistan, Albania, Algeria, Angola, Argentina, Austria, Bahrain, Bangladesh, Belgium, Benin, Bhutan, Botswana, Bulgaria, Burundi, Byelorussian SSR, Cape Verde, Central African Republic, Chad, China, Congo, Cuba, Cyprus, Czechoslovakia, Democratic Kampuchea, Democratic Yemen, Denmark, Djibouti, Egypt, Equatorial Guinea, Ethiopia, Fiji, France, Gabon, Gambia, German Democratic Republic, Germany, Federal Republic of, Ghana, Greece, Grenada, Guinea, Guinea-Bissau, Guyana, Hungary, India, Indonesia, Iran, Iraq, Ireland, Italy, Japan, Jordan, Kenya, Kuwait, Lao People's Democratic Republic, Lebanon, Libyan Arab Jamahiriya, Luxembourg, Madagascar, Malaysia, Maldives, Mali, Malta, Mauritania, Mauritius, Mexico, Mongolia, Morocco, Mozambique, Netherlands, New Zealand, Nicaragua, Niger, Nigeria, Oman, Pakistan, Papua New Guinea, Poland, Portugal, Qatar, Romania, Rwanda, Sao Tome and Principe, Saudi Arabia, Senegal, Seychelles, Sierra Leone, Solomon Islands, Somalia, Spain, Sudan, Suriname, Syrian Arab Republic, Togo, Tunisia, Turkey, Uganda, Ukrainian SSR, USSR, United Arab Emirates, United Kingdom, United Republic of Cameroon, United Republic of Tanzania, Upper Volta, Vanuatu, Venezuela, Viet Nam, Yemen, Yugoslavia, Zambia, Zimbabwe.

Against: Israel, United States.

Abstaining: Australia, Bahamas, Barbados, Belize, Bolivia,[a] Brazil, Canada, Colombia, Costa Rica, Dominican Republic, Ecuador, El Salvador, Finland, Iceland, Jamaica, Lesotho, Liberia, Malawi, Nepal, Norway, Panama, Paraguay, Peru, Sri Lanka, Swaziland, Sweden, Trinidad and Tobago, Uruguay, Zaire.

[a]Later advised the Secretariat it had intended to vote in favour.

The draft was amended in the Assembly by Saudi Arabia to add the second preambular paragraph, and to replace the original paragraphs 1 and 2—which would have, respectively, condemned Israel for having kidnapped Ziad Abu Eain, and demanded his immediate release—with those adopted. The amendments were adopted by recorded votes: the second preambular paragraph by 115 to 2, with 17 abstentions; paragraph 2 by 107 to 2, with 24 abstentions; and paragraph 1 by 106 to 2, with 26 abstentions.

Speaking before the Committee vote, Israel said that the release of more than 4,500 prisoners for six Israeli prisoners, not counting the condemned criminals whose names had been on the list given to ICRC at the airport, proved that it had honoured the agreement. Regarding Abu Eain, there had been confusion over the several lists; the definitive one was drawn up by ICRC and he was not included.

The United States said that, since the information provided was diametrically opposed, the Committee needed an independent detailed statement from ICRC.

PLO pointed out that ICRC had confirmed that Abu Eain's name had been on its list; furthermore, *The Jerusalem Post* of 7 December cited numerous sources involved in the exchange, all of which confirmed that he had been listed.

Sri Lanka noted that the draft did not fall within the terms of reference of the Committee on Israeli practices in the occupied territories; since Sri Lanka was a member of that Committee, its vote would have a bearing on the Committee's work and, in the longer term, on the human rights and interests of the inhabitants of the occupied territories.

Austria hoped that not freeing Abu Eain was simply a mistake and requested Israel to free him as soon as possible.

In the Assembly, Argentina explained that its vote was based on the 13 December ICRC press communiqué and on the humanitarian nature of the resolution which it hoped would help ensure the success of the exchange of prisoners; however, paragraph 1 should have confined itself to reflecting the fact that one of the parties had failed to abide by the exchange agreement.

In the absence of full clarification, Canada could not adopt a position on either party and also could not accept the emotive and condemnatory language of paragraph 1.

In other action, also taken on 15 December, the Assembly in resolution 38/83 I called again on Israel to release all detained Palestine refugees.

Credentials of Israel

By a letter of 19 October 1983 to the General Assembly President,[24] 50 States conveyed their reservations on the credentials of Israel, citing the following reasons: Israel was continuing its flagrant and persistent violation of the United Nations Charter and international law and flouted with impunity United Nations resolutions on the Middle East situation and the Palestine question.

On 20 October,[25] Israel responded that the completely unfounded attack on its credentials was an attempt to abuse the credentials procedure and was one more manifestation of the obsessive hatred of States bent on Israel's destruction, in violation of international law and the Charter; the approach by the 50 States was liable to affect adversely the ability of the United Nations to perform its primary functions for maintaining international peace and security.

On 24 October, by a recorded vote, the Assembly decided not to act on an amendment by Iran[26] to reject the credentials of Israel (see Chapter XI of this section).

REFERENCES

[1]A/38/61-S/15549. [2]A/38/73-S/15562. [3]S/15625. [4]S/16119. [5]A/38/124-S/15657. [6]YUN 1982, p. 387. [7]A/38/168-S/15736. [8]A/38/297-S/15867. [9]A/38/601 & Corr.1. [10]S/16201. [11]A/38/458-S/16015. [12]YUN 1982, p. 428. [13]YUN 1967, p. 257, SC res. 242(1967), 22 Nov. 1967. [14]YUN 1973, p. 213, SC res. 338(1973), 22 Oct. 1973. [15]A/38/750-S/16223 & Corr.1. [16]A/38/L.49. [17]YUN 1981, p. 907. [18]YUN 1982, p. 1084. [19]E/1983/13 (res. 1983/27). [20]A/38/179-S/15748. [21]A/38/595-S/16171. [22]A/38/735. [23]A/38/749. [24]A/38/520 & Add.1. [25]A/38/521. [26]A/38/L.4.

Palestine question

The Palestine question continued in 1983 to be a concern of the General Assembly and of its Committee on the Exercise of the Inalienable Rights of the Palestinian People (Committee on Palestinian rights). An International Conference on the Question of Palestine adopted in September a Declaration and a Programme of Action for the Achievement of Palestinian Rights. The Assembly, in one of five December resolutions on the Palestine question, endorsed the Conference's call for an international peace conference on the Middle East (38/58 C). It urged United Nations agencies and organizations to take into account the recommendations of the five regional preparatory meetings of the Conference (38/58 D); again endorsed the 1976 recommendations of the Committee on Palestinian rights (38/58 A); and requested the expansion of United Nations public information activities on the Palestine question (38/58 E). In a fifth resolution (38/58 B), the Assembly dealt with the United Nations Secretariat's Division for Palestinian Rights. The status of Jerusalem and restitution of Palestinian cultural property were the subjects of two other December resolutions (38/180 C and B), adopted under the agenda item on the situation in the Middle East (see above).

United Nations bodies also continued to examine the situation in the territories occupied by Israel (see under TERRITORIES OCCUPIED BY ISRAEL) and to provide and encourage assistance to Palestinians (see below and under PALESTINE REFUGEES).

Communications. By a letter of 4 January 1983,[1] Israel drew attention to statements made on 20 December 1982 by Arab and other countries, during the General Assembly's consideration of the Palestine question and the Middle East situation (see above).

On 16 February,[2] Mongolia transmitted a message of 15 February from its President to the Chairman of the National Council of Palestine, expressing support for the struggle of the Palestinian people for their inalienable rights and for national independence.

By a letter of 26 August,[3] Israel stated that it would withhold from its contributions to the United Nations the amounts proportionate to the expenses incurred by the anti-Israel activities of the Committee on Palestinian rights and the Division for Palestinian Rights which, it said, were designed to exacerbate tensions and polarize the situation in the Middle East.

In connection with the August/September International Conference on the Question of Palestine (see below), several letters were addressed to the Secretary-General. On 11 August,[4] Israel protested against the holding of an exhibition sponsored by the Conference secretariat on United Nations premises in New York. In reply, the Secretary-General informed Israel on 19 August[5] that he had asked for the exhibition's closure because the proper procedures for holding exhibitions at Headquarters had not been fully observed. On 25 August,[6] Israel strongly protested the release of a series of studies prepared for the Conference which, it said, were propaganda serving the cause of international terror, not the cause of international peace. On 27 September,[7] it stated that numerous irregularities had accompanied the preparations for and holding of the Conference, further compounded by placing PLO on an equal footing with participating States.

Two messages to the Conference participants expressed support for the rights of the Palestinians and their struggle for national independence. On 30 August,[8] the USSR transmitted a message of 29 August from the Presidium of the Supreme Soviet of the USSR and the Council of Ministers of the USSR; on 5 September,[9] Bulgaria forwarded a message from the General Secretary of the Central Committee of the Bulgarian Communist Party and President of the State Council.

International Conference on the Question of Palestine. In pursuance of two 1982 General Assembly resolutions,[10] an International Conference on the Question of Palestine was convened at Geneva from 29 August to 7 September 1983.

The Conference[11] adopted the Geneva Declaration on Palestine and the Programme of Action for the Achievement of Palestinian Rights. In the Declaration, the Conference reaffirmed that a just solution to the Palestine question, the core of the Middle East problem, was crucial. It emphasized that the time factor was important in achieving a solution, and expressed its conviction that partial solutions were inadequate and that delays in seeking a comprehensive solution did not eliminate tensions in the region.

The Conference considered that various peace proposals presented in 1982,[12] such as the Arab peace plan adopted by the Twelfth Arab Summit Conference at Fez, should serve as guidelines for concerted international efforts. These guidelines included: attainment by the Palestinians of their legitimate rights, including the rights to return, to self-determination and to establish their own independent State in Palestine; equal participation of PLO, the representative of the Palestinians, in all efforts on the Middle East; the need to end Israel's occupation of and to secure its withdrawal from the territories occupied since 1967, including Jerusalem; the need to reject Israeli policies and practices in those territories and any *de facto* situation created by Israel contrary to international law and United Nations resolutions, particularly the establishment of settlements; the need to reaffirm as null and void all Israeli measures altering the character and status of Jerusalem, including the expropriation of land, and in particular the so-called "Basic Law" on Jerusalem and its proclamation as the capital of Israel; and the right of all States in the region to exist within secure and internationally recognized boundaries, with justice and security for all, the pre-condition of which was the recognition and attainment of Palestinian rights.

To give effect to these guidelines, the Conference considered it essential that an international peace conference on the Middle East be convened (see below).

The Programme of Action enumerated national and international measures to be taken in the political, economic and information fields. It invited the Security Council to establish promptly an independent, sovereign Palestinian State in Palestine through the implementation of United Nations resolutions and by facilitating the organization of an international peace conference.

Reservations and statements of position on the Declaration and the Programme by 17 States were annexed to the Conference report.[11]

The Declaration and the Programme, which were summarized in the Secretary-General's Middle East report,[13] were transmitted to the General Assembly and the Security Council by the Chairman of the Committee on Palestinian rights on 10 October.[14]

As authorized by the Assembly in 1981,[15] that Committee acted as Preparatory Committee for the Conference; its activities in that regard during its second session (13 meetings from 4 February to 27 July 1983 in New York and one meeting on 29 August at Geneva) were summarized in a report to the Assembly.[16] Reviewing the question

of the Conference date and venue, the Preparatory Committee decided on 20 June to change the original dates set in 1982[17] (16-27 August) to 29 August–7 September.

In preparation of the Conference, the Committee organized five regional meetings: for Africa, at Arusha, United Republic of Tanzania (29 March–1 April);[18] for Latin America, at Managua, Nicaragua (12-15 April);[19] for Western Asia, at Sharjah, United Arab Emirates (25-29 April);[20] for Asia, at Kuala Lumpur, Malaysia (3-7 May);[21] and for Europe, at Geneva (4-8 July).[22]

Activities of the Committee on Palestinian rights. The Committee on the Exercise of the Inalienable Rights of the Palestinian People, in 1983, continued to follow developments in the Israeli-occupied territories and action by Israel which the Committee regarded as violations of international law or of United Nations resolutions. The Committee brought such actions, including Israeli settlements in the occupied territories, exploitation by Israeli authorities of Arab-owned lands and other matters affecting the rights of the Palestinians (for details, see below, under TERRITORIES OCCUPIED BY ISRAEL), to the attention of the Secretary-General and the President of the Security Council.

In its annual report to the Assembly,[23] the Committee found that there was abundant evidence that its recommendations made in 1976,[24] endorsed by the Assembly the same year,[25] had been clearly understood by nations and peoples in all regions, and that those recommendations were seen to be fair, legally founded and peaceful, and should therefore be lasting when implemented. The Committee felt that the International Conference had given a new impetus to the attainment of Palestinian rights as a prerequisite for an overall Arab-Israeli settlement. Considering the Conference's Declaration and Programme of Action to be of great value for a settlement of the Palestine question, the Committee appealed to the Assembly and to the Security Council to endorse them and to support their implementation. The Committee endorsed the Conference's recommendation for an international peace conference on the Middle East (see below) and recommended resolute action by all nations, particularly those in the region, through the Council, in the search for durable and comprehensive peace. Among the Committee's recommendations regarding the Secretariat's Division for Palestinian Rights was continued expansion of the Division's efforts concerning seminars.

The Committee met at United Nations Headquarters on 29 November 1983 in observance of the International Day of Solidarity with the Palestinian People, commemorated each year in accordance with a 1977 Assembly resolution.[26] The New York meeting and a similar one at Geneva were addressed by a number of United Nations officials and government representatives.

With the Committee's participation, the Eighth United Nations Seminar on the Question of Palestine, which had as its central theme the inalienable rights of the Palestinians, was held at Jakarta, Indonesia, from 9 to 13 May 1983. The Seminar's comments on various aspects of the question—including restoration of Palestinian rights and Israeli policies in the occupied territories (see below, under TERRITORIES OCCUPIED BY ISRAEL)—were annexed to the Committee's annual report.

The Committee also acted as the Preparatory Committee for the International Conference on the Question of Palestine (see above).

GENERAL ASSEMBLY ACTION

In December, the General Assembly adopted two resolutions (38/58 A and B) dealing with the work of the Committee on Palestinian rights, both under the agenda item on the question of Palestine.

On 13 December, the Assembly adopted resolution 38/58 A by recorded vote.

The General Assembly,

Recalling its resolutions 3376(XXX) of 10 November 1975, 31/20 of 24 November 1976, 32/40 of 2 December 1977, 33/28 of 7 December 1978, 34/65 A and B of 29 November 1979 and 34/65 C and D of 12 December 1979, ES-7/2 of 29 July 1980, 35/169 of 15 December 1980, 36/120 of 10 December 1981, ES-7/4 of 28 April 1982, ES-7/5 of 26 June 1982, ES-7/9 of 24 September 1982 and 37/86 A of 10 December 1982,

Having considered the report of the Committee on the Exercise of the Inalienable Rights of the Palestinian People,

1. *Expresses its appreciation* to the Committee on the Exercise of the Inalienable Rights of the Palestinian People for its efforts in performing the tasks assigned to it by the General Assembly;

2. *Endorses* the recommendations of the Committee contained in paragraphs 94 to 98 of its report and draws the attention of the Security Council to the fact that action on the Committee's recommendations, as repeatedly endorsed by the General Assembly, at its thirty-first session and subsequently, is long overdue;

3. *Requests* the Committee to keep under review the situation relating to the question of Palestine as well as the implementation of the Programme of Action for the Achievement of Palestinian Rights adopted by the International Conference on the Question of Palestine and to report and make suggestions to the General Assembly or the Security Council, as appropriate;

4. *Requests* the United Nations Conciliation Commission for Palestine, established under General Assembly resolution 194(III) of 11 December 1948, as well as other United Nations bodies associated with the question of Palestine, to co-operate fully with the Committee and to make available to it, at its request, the relevant information and documentation which they have at their disposal;

5. *Authorizes* the Committee to continue to exert all efforts to promote the implementation of its recommendations, to send delegations or representatives to international conferences where such representation would be considered by it to be appropriate, and to report thereon to the General Assembly at its thirty-ninth session and thereafter;

6. *Decides* to circulate the report of the Committee to all the competent bodies of the United Nations and urges them to take the necessary action, as appropriate, in accordance with the Committee's programme of implementation;

7. *Requests* the Secretary-General to continue to provide the Committee with all the necessary facilities for the performance of its tasks.

General Assembly resolution 38/58 A

13 December 1983   Meeting 95   126-2-19 (recorded vote)

20-nation draft (A/38/L.36 & Add.1); agenda item 33.

Sponsors: Afghanistan, Bangladesh, Cuba, Egypt, Gambia, German Democratic Republic, Guinea, Guyana, Hungary, India, Indonesia, Lao People's Democratic Republic, Madagascar, Malaysia, Nicaragua, Nigeria, Pakistan, Ukrainian SSR, Viet Nam, Yugoslavia.

Financial implications. 5th Committee, A/38/725; S-G, A/C.5/38/75 & Add.1.

Meeting numbers. GA 38th session: 5th Committee 62; plenary 73, 79-82, 85, 95.

Recorded vote in Assembly as follows:

In favour: Afghanistan, Albania, Algeria, Angola, Argentina, Bahamas, Bahrain, Bangladesh, Belize, Benin, Bhutan, Bolivia, Botswana, Brazil, Bulgaria, Burma, Burundi, Byelorussian SSR, Cape Verde, Central African Republic, Chad, Chile, China, Colombia, Comoros, Congo, Cuba, Cyprus, Czechoslovakia, Democratic Kampuchea, Democratic Yemen, Djibouti, Dominican Republic, Ecuador, Egypt, El Salvador, Equatorial Guinea, Ethiopia, Fiji, Gabon, Gambia, German Democratic Republic, Ghana, Greece, Guinea, Guinea-Bissau, Guyana, Haiti, Honduras, Hungary, India, Indonesia, Iran, Iraq, Ivory Coast, Jamaica, Jordan, Kenya, Kuwait, Lao People's Democratic Republic, Lebanon, Lesotho, Liberia, Libyan Arab Jamahiriya, Madagascar, Malawi, Malaysia, Maldives, Mali, Malta, Mauritania, Mauritius, Mexico, Mongolia, Morocco, Mozambique, Nepal, Nicaragua, Niger, Nigeria, Oman, Pakistan, Panama, Papua New Guinea, Paraguay, Peru, Philippines, Poland, Portugal, Qatar, Romania, Rwanda, Sao Tome and Principe, Saudi Arabia, Senegal, Seychelles, Sierra Leone, Singapore, Solomon Islands, Somalia, Spain, Sri Lanka, Sudan, Suriname, Syrian Arab Republic, Thailand, Togo, Trinidad and Tobago, Tunisia, Turkey, Uganda, Ukrainian SSR, USSR, United Arab Emirates, United Republic of Cameroon, United Republic of Tanzania, Upper Volta, Uruguay, Vanuatu, Venezuela, Viet Nam, Yemen, Yugoslavia, Zaire, Zambia, Zimbabwe.

Against: Israel, United States.

Abstaining: Australia, Austria, Belgium, Canada, Costa Rica, Denmark, Finland, France, Germany, Federal Republic of, Iceland, Ireland, Italy, Japan, Luxembourg, Netherlands, New Zealand, Norway, Sweden, United Kingdom.

Paragraph 2 was adopted separately by a recorded vote of 118 to 5, with 18 abstentions.

Abstaining on that paragraph, Costa Rica said it could not support the whole of the Geneva Declaration. Norway could not endorse the outcome of the Conference and could not accept certain elements in the Declaration and the Programme of Action. In New Zealand's view, the resolution did not adequately reflect the balance of principles embodied in Security Council resolution 242(1967).[27] (See also explanations of vote following resolution 38/58 B, below.)

Also on 13 December, the Assembly adopted resolution 38/58 B by recorded vote.

The General Assembly,

Having considered the report of the Committee on the Exercise of the Inalienable Rights of the Palestinian People,

Noting, in particular, the information contained in paragraphs 86 to 91 of that report,

Recalling its resolutions 32/40 B of 2 December 1977, 33/28 C of 7 December 1978, 34/65 D of 12 December 1979, 35/169 D of 15 December 1980, 36/120 B of 10 December 1981 and 37/86 B of 10 December 1982,

1. *Notes with appreciation* the action taken by the Secretary-General in compliance with General Assembly resolution 37/86 B;

2. *Requests* the Secretary-General to ensure that the Division for Palestinian Rights of the Secretariat continues to discharge the tasks detailed in paragraph 1 of General Assembly resolution 32/40 B, paragraph 2 *(b)* of resolution 34/65 D and paragraph 3 of resolution 36/120 B, in consultation with the Committee on the Exercise of the Inalienable Rights of the Palestinian People and under its guidance;

3. *Also requests* the Secretary-General to provide the Division for Palestinian Rights with the necessary resources to accomplish its tasks and to expand its work programme, *inter alia*, through:

(a) Closer contacts with the media and wider dissemination of the Division's information material, particularly where information on the question of Palestine is inadequate;

(b) Increased contacts with non-governmental organizations and the convening of symposia and meetings for non-governmental organizations in different regions in order to heighten awareness of the facts relating to the question of Palestine;

4. *Further requests* the Secretary-General to ensure the continued co-operation of the Department of Public Information and other units of the Secretariat in enabling the Division for Palestinian Rights to perform its tasks and in covering adequately the various aspects of the question of Palestine;

5. *Invites* all Governments and organizations to lend their co-operation to the Committee on the Exercise of the Inalienable Rights of the Palestinian People and the Division for Palestinian Rights in the performance of their tasks;

6. *Notes with appreciation* the action taken by Member States to observe annually on 29 November the International Day of Solidarity with the Palestinian People and the issuance by them of special postage stamps for the occasion.

General Assembly resolution 38/58 B

13 December 1983   Meeting 95   127-3-17 (recorded vote)

20-nation draft (A/38/L.37 & Add.1); agenda item 33.

Sponsors: Afghanistan, Bangladesh, Cuba, Egypt, Gambia, German Democratic Republic, Guinea, Guyana, Hungary, India, Indonesia, Lao People's Democratic Republic, Madagascar, Malaysia, Nicaragua, Nigeria, Pakistan, Ukrainian SSR, Viet Nam, Yugoslavia.

Financial implications. 5th Committee, A/38/725; S-G, A/C.5/38/75 & Add.1.

Meeting numbers. GA 38th session: 5th Committee 62; plenary 73, 79-82, 85, 95.

Recorded vote in Assembly as follows:

In favour: Afghanistan, Albania, Algeria, Angola, Argentina, Bahamas, Bahrain, Bangladesh, Belize, Benin, Bhutan, Bolivia, Botswana, Brazil, Bulgaria, Burma, Burundi, Byelorussian SSR, Cape Verde, Central African Republic, Chad, Chile, China, Colombia, Comoros, Congo, Costa Rica, Cuba, Cyprus, Czechoslovakia, Democratic Kampuchea, Democratic Yemen, Djibouti, Dominican Republic, Ecuador, Egypt, El Salvador, Equatorial Guinea, Ethiopia, Fiji, Gabon, Gambia, German Democratic Republic, Ghana, Greece, Guinea, Guinea-Bissau, Guyana, Haiti, Honduras, Hungary, India, Indonesia, Iran, Iraq, Ivory Coast, Jamaica, Jordan, Kenya, Kuwait, Lao People's Democratic Republic, Lebanon, Lesotho, Liberia, Libyan Arab Jamahiriya, Madagascar, Malawi, Malaysia, Maldives, Mali, Malta, Mauritania, Mauritius, Mexico, Mongolia, Morocco, Mozambique, Nepal, Nicaragua, Niger, Nigeria, Oman, Pakistan, Panama, Papua New Guinea, Paraguay, Peru, Philippines, Poland, Portugal, Qatar, Romania, Rwanda, Sao Tome and Principe, Saudi Arabia, Senegal, Seychelles, Sierra Leone, Singapore, Solo-

mon Islands, Somalia, Spain, Sri Lanka, Sudan, Suriname, Syrian Arab Republic, Thailand, Togo, Trinidad and Tobago, Tunisia, Turkey, Uganda, Ukrainian SSR, USSR, United Arab Emirates, United Republic of Cameroon, United Republic of Tanzania, Upper Volta, Uruguay, Vanuatu, Venezuela, Viet Nam, Yemen, Yugoslavia, Zaire, Zambia, Zimbabwe.

Against: Canada, Israel, United States.

Abstaining: Australia, Austria, Belgium, Denmark, Finland, France, Germany, Federal Republic of, Iceland, Ireland, Italy, Japan, Luxembourg, Netherlands, New Zealand, Norway, Sweden, United Kingdom.

The United States considered all five resolutions on the Palestine question (38/58 A-E) to be without merit and obstructive to the peace process; it felt that they attempted to dictate the outcome of negotiations and called for costly activities by various United Nations bodies to propagate partial and partisan views of the Palestinian issue.

Finland abstained on both resolutions (38/58 A and B) saying that they lacked balance; it considered the attainment of Palestinian rights to be part of and within the framework of a comprehensive Middle East solution based on Security Council resolutions 242(1967)[27] and 338(1973),[28] a view also shared by Norway.

Speaking for the EC members on all the resolutions on Palestine, Greece reiterated their reservations on elements in the Geneva Declaration, and notably the Programme of Action, which were not in accordance with their position regarding the principles for a comprehensive peace settlement.

Uruguay said its affirmative vote was consistent with its joining in the Conference's consensus; the five resolutions were essentially inspired by the Declaration and Programme of Action, on certain elements of which, however, it had reservations. Such reservations were also voiced by Peru.

Trinidad and Tobago reaffirmed its reservations on the implications of certain language of the Declaration and the Programme of Action. Reservations on parts of the Declaration and the Programme were also voiced by the Libyan Arab Jamahiriya, which affirmed that its positive vote did not alter its position on any references which might be construed as legitimizing the Zionist occupation of Palestine or as recognizing the Zionist entity. A similar position was held by Iran. Albania voiced reservations on the references to some previous United Nations resolutions.

Bolivia stated that its positive vote was in keeping with its desire to co-operate in the efforts to establish conditions for peace. Ecuador declared its support for any measure designed to settle the Palestine question.

In resolution 38/17, the Assembly condemned the constant and deliberate violations of the fundamental rights of the Palestinians, as well as Israel's expansionist activities in the Middle East, which, it determined, constituted an obstacle to the achievement of self-determination and independence by the Palestinians and a threat to peace and stability in the region.

Proposed peace conference

The Geneva Declaration on Palestine, adopted on 7 September by the Conference on the Palestine question (see above),[11] called for an international peace conference on the Middle East based on the Charter of the United Nations and relevant United Nations resolutions, with the aim of achieving a comprehensive, just and lasting solution to the Arab-Israeli conflict. An essential element of a solution would be the establishment of an independent Palestinian State in Palestine. The peace conference should be convened under United Nations auspices, with the participation of all parties to the Arab-Israeli conflict, including PLO, as well as the United States, the USSR and other concerned States, on an equal footing. The Security Council would have primary responsibility to create institutional arrangements on the basis of United Nations resolutions in order to guarantee and carry out the accords of the peace conference.

In its 1983 report,[23] the Committee on Palestinian rights recommended that action be taken to convene a peace conference, and appealed to all parties concerned, the USSR and the United States to co-operate.

GENERAL ASSEMBLY ACTION

Under the agenda item on the question of Palestine, the General Assembly, on 13 December, adopted resolution 38/58 C by recorded vote.

The General Assembly,

Recalling its resolution 36/120 C of 10 December 1981, in which it decided to convene, under the auspices of the United Nations, an International Conference on the Question of Palestine on the basis of its resolution ES-7/2 of 29 July 1980,

Recalling also its resolution 37/86 C of 10 December 1982 in which it, *inter alia*, reiterated the responsibility of the United Nations to strive for a lasting peace in the Middle East through a just solution of the problem of Palestine,

Having considered the report of the International Conference on the Question of Palestine, held at Geneva from 29 August to 7 September 1983,

Convinced that the Conference, in adopting by acclamation the Geneva Declaration on Palestine and the Programme of Action for the Achievement of Palestinian Rights, made an important and positive contribution to the attainment of a comprehensive, just and durable peace in the Middle East through a just solution of the problem of Palestine, the core of the Arab-Israeli conflict,

Conscious of the importance of the time factor in achieving a just solution of the problem of Palestine,

1. *Takes note with satisfaction* of the report of the International Conference on the Question of Palestine;

2. *Endorses* the Geneva Declaration on Palestine, adopted by acclamation on 7 September 1983;

3. *Welcomes and endorses* the call for convening an International Peace Conference on the Middle East in conformity with the following guidelines:

(*a*) The attainment by the Palestinian people of its legitimate inalienable rights, including the right to return, the right to self-determination and the right to establish its own independent State in Palestine;

(*b*) The right of the Palestine Liberation Organization, the representative of the Palestinian people, to participate on an equal footing with other parties in all efforts, deliberations and conferences on the Middle East;

(*c*) The need to put an end to Israel's occupation of the Arab territories, in accordance with the principle of the inadmissibility of the acquisition of territory by force, and, consequently, the need to secure Israeli withdrawal from the territories occupied since 1967, including Jerusalem;

(*d*) The need to oppose and reject such Israeli policies and practices in the occupied territories, including Jerusalem, and any *de facto* situation created by Israel as are contrary to international law and relevant United Nations resolutions, particularly the establishment of settlements, as these policies and practices constitute major obstacles to the achievement of peace in the Middle East;

(*e*) The need to reaffirm as null and void all legislative and administrative measures and actions taken by Israel, the occupying Power, which have altered or purported to alter the character and status of the Holy City of Jerusalem, including the expropriation of land and property situated thereon, and in particular the so-called "Basic Law" on Jerusalem and the proclamation of Jerusalem as the capital of Israel;

(*f*) The right of all States in the region to existence within secure and internationally recognized boundaries, with justice and security for all the people, the *sine qua non* of which is the recognition and attainment of the legitimate, inalienable rights of the Palestinian people as stated in subparagraph (*a*) above;

4. *Invites* all parties to the Arab-Israeli conflict, including the Palestine Liberation Organization, as well as the United States of America, the Union of Soviet Socialist Republics and other concerned States, to participate in the International Peace Conference on the Middle East on an equal footing and with equal rights;

5. *Requests* the Secretary-General, in consultation with the Security Council, urgently to undertake preparatory measures to convene the Conference;

6. *Invites* the Security Council to facilitate the organization of the Conference;

7. *Also requests* the Secretary-General to report on his efforts no later than 15 March 1984;

8. *Decides* to consider at its thirty-ninth session the report of the Secretary-General on the Conference.

General Assembly resolution 38/58 C

13 December 1983   Meeting 95   124-4-15 (recorded vote)

21-nation draft (A/38/L.38 & Add.1); agenda item 33.

Sponsors: Afghanistan, Bangladesh, Cuba, Egypt, German Democratic Republic, Guinea, Guyana, Hungary, India, Indonesia, Lao People's Democratic Republic, Madagascar, Malaysia, Mongolia, Nicaragua, Nigeria, Pakistan, Romania, Ukrainian SSR, Viet Nam, Yugoslavia.

Financial implications. 5th Committee, A/38/725; S-G, A/C.5/38/75.

Meeting numbers. GA 38th session: 5th Committee 62; plenary 73, 79-82, 95.

Recorded vote in Assembly as follows:

In favour: Afghanistan, Albania, Algeria, Angola, Argentina, Austria, Bahamas, Bahrain, Bangladesh, Belize, Benin, Bhutan, Bolivia, Botswana, Brazil, Bulgaria, Burma, Burundi, Byelorussian SSR, Cape Verde, Central African Republic, Chad,

China, Colombia, Comoros, Congo, Cuba, Cyprus, Czechoslovakia, Democratic Kampuchea, Democratic Yemen, Djibouti, Dominican Republic, Ecuador, Egypt, El Salvador, Equatorial Guinea, Ethiopia, Fiji, Finland, Gabon, Gambia, German Democratic Republic, Ghana, Greece, Guinea, Guinea-Bissau, Guyana, Haiti, Hungary, India, Indonesia, Iran, Iraq, Ivory Coast, Jamaica, Jordan, Kenya, Kuwait, Lao People's Democratic Republic, Lebanon, Lesotho, Libyan Arab Jamahiriya, Madagascar, Malawi, Malaysia, Maldives, Mali, Malta, Mauritania, Mauritius, Mexico, Mongolia, Morocco, Mozambique, Nepal, Nicaragua, Niger, Nigeria, Oman, Pakistan, Panama, Papua New Guinea, Paraguay, Peru, Philippines, Poland, Portugal, Qatar, Romania, Rwanda, Sao Tome and Principe, Saudi Arabia, Senegal, Seychelles, Sierra Leone, Singapore, Somalia, Spain, Sri Lanka, Sudan, Suriname, Sweden, Syrian Arab Republic, Thailand, Togo, Trinidad and Tobago, Tunisia, Turkey, Uganda, Ukrainian SSR, USSR, United Arab Emirates, United Republic of Cameroon, United Republic of Tanzania, Upper Volta, Uruguay, Vanuatu, Venezuela, Viet Nam, Yemen, Yugoslavia, Zambia, Zimbabwe.

Against: Australia, Canada, Israel, United States.

Abstaining: Belgium, Costa Rica, Denmark, France, Germany, Federal Republic of, Iceland, Ireland, Italy, Japan, Luxembourg, Netherlands, New Zealand, Norway, Solomon Islands, United Kingdom.

The United States felt that the resolution was unhelpful to the peace process. In Israel's view, the guidelines for the conference were contrary to and undermined Security Council resolution 242(1967),[27] the only basis for a peaceful settlement of the Arab-Israeli conflict. Though acknowledging that Israel's right to exist was implicitly recognized in resolution 38/58 C, Canada said it could not support it because it repeated certain one-sided elements in the Geneva Declaration.

Greece said the EC members had reservations on certain elements in the Programme of Action, also adopted at the Geneva Conference, that were not in accordance with their position on a comprehensive peace settlement. Norway also could not endorse the Declaration and Programme of Action. Supporting in principle the idea of a Palestine settlement under United Nations auspices, New Zealand doubted the practicality of such a proposal until all parties concerned were prepared to participate with realistic expectations. In Costa Rica's opinion, the guidelines for the conference (in paragraph 3) prejudged its results and jeopardized the possibility of the parties to the conflict entering peace negotiations.

Finland, Sweden, and Trinidad and Tobago reiterated their reservations on the Geneva Declaration and Programme of Action.

Brazil would have preferred a more careful and less detailed wording of the conference guidelines, and cautioned that the Secretary-General might not be given enough time to report on the organization of the conference as he was requested in paragraph 7.

Albania did not agree that the United States and the USSR should be invited to participate in the conference; it feared that the super-Powers would try to manipulate it for their own purposes. Jordan believed that paragraph 4 went beyond what was agreed on in the Geneva Declaration.

The Syrian Arab Republic held a similar view and would have preferred paragraph 6 to reflect more explicitly the call in the Declaration on the Security Council to create institutional arrangements based on relevant United Nations resolu-

tions; these were shortcomings, it felt, which weakened the text and attenuated the Geneva Declaration.

Spain stressed that its support for the convening of a conference did not imply exclusion of other peace plans. Portugal expressed the conviction that a peace conference was premature as conditions guaranteeing the presence of all parties did not currently exist.

Uruguay said its affirmative vote was consistent with its participation in the Geneva consensus and its desire for peaceful solutions. Bolivia believed that the resolution complemented Security Council resolutions 242(1967)[27] and 338(1973),[28] which had established the guidelines for a negotiated solution. Reaffirmation of those resolutions, the Dominican Republic believed, would have given resolution 38/58 C greater objectivity and consistency.

Colombia saw in the resolution a contribution to the search for a final settlement but believed that, in order to create the necessary climate for final negotiations, the regional and extraregional causes of the conflict must be borne in mind. Malawi believed that any serious consultations should be encouraged. Ecuador supported any measure designed to settle the Palestine question.

Singapore would have liked to see reflected the recognition of Palestinian rights and the preservation of Israel's right to exist; any action denying the rights of one side or destroying the existence of the other, it believed, would be doomed to failure.

Iran and the Libyan Arab Jamahiriya, on the other hand, rejected any recognition as a party to negotiations of what they called the illegitimate entity of zionism in occupied Palestine.

Honduras explained that it did not participate in the vote in conformity with its principle that the guidelines for and participation in any international peace conference must be based on the free and unanimous consent of the States directly concerned.

PLO regarded the resolution as an encouragement to find a solution through the United Nations.

The call for a conference was repeated in Assembly resolution 38/180 D of 19 December 1983.

Explaining its vote on that resolution, Mexico said it supported the holding of a conference as an important factor for world peace and the appropriate framework for parties to find satisfactory formulae for accommodation, provided there was the necessary political and diplomatic will.

Jerusalem

Communications. On 1 March 1983,[29] Jordan transmitted a letter of 31 January from the

Minister for Occupied Territories Affairs to the Minister of Waqf and Islamic Religious Affairs of Jordan, on the activities of the "Temple Mount Fund" organization which he charged sought the demolition of the Al-Aqsa Mosque in Jerusalem, on the pretext of working on the restoration of the so-called "Third Temple" and restoring Temple Mount to Jewish sovereignty.

By a letter of 14 March,[30] Jordan gave an account of what it described as Israeli assaults on the Al-Aqsa Mosque from June 1967, culminating in an act of desecration on 11 March 1983, when approximately 45 settlers equipped with large amounts of weapons and explosives had attempted to reach the Mosque through a secret tunnel. Jordan alleged that Israel had continually persisted in committing and encouraging such acts against the Mosque and the other Holy Places in Jerusalem.

On 16 March,[31] Iran transmitted a government communiqué condemning what it called Israel's latest attempt to destroy the Mosque.

By a letter of 6 December,[32] Israel gave details of a bomb explosion on a civilian passenger bus in Jerusalem on the same day, for which PLO claimed responsibility; the crime was intended to divert attention from the fighting between PLO rival gangs, it added. On 7 December,[33] Israel pointed out that responsibility for that explosion, which had killed 4 and injured 46 people, was claimed by PLO Chairman Yasser Arafat, as well as by the rival faction of PLO under Abu Musa. Reference to the 6 December explosion was also made by the Israeli Prime Minister in a message of 8 December to the Secretary-General, transmitted by Israel on the same date.[34]

GENERAL ASSEMBLY ACTION

On 19 December 1983, under the agenda item on the situation in the Middle East, the General Assembly adopted resolution 38/180 C by recorded vote.

The General Assembly,

Recalling its resolutions 36/120 E of 10 December 1981 and 37/123 C of 16 December 1982, in which it determined that all legislative and administrative measures and actions taken by Israel, the occupying Power, which had altered or purported to alter the character and status of the Holy City of Jerusalem, in particular the so-called "Basic Law" on Jerusalem and the proclamation of Jerusalem as the capital of Israel, were null and void and must be rescinded forthwith,

Recalling Security Council resolution 478(1980) of 20 August 1980, in which the Council, _inter alia_, decided not to recognize the "Basic Law" and called upon those States that had established diplomatic missions at Jerusalem to withdraw such missions from the Holy City,

1. _Declares once more_ that Israel's decision to impose its laws, jurisdiction and administration on the Holy City of Jerusalem is illegal and therefore null and void and has no validity whatsoever;

2. _Deplores_ the transfer by some States of their diplomatic missions to Jerusalem in violation of Security Council resolution 478(1980);

3. _Calls once again upon_ those States to abide by the provisions of the relevant United Nations resolutions, in conformity with the Charter of the United Nations;

4. _Requests_ the Secretary-General to report to the General Assembly at its thirty-ninth session on the implementation of the present resolution.

General Assembly resolution 38/180 C

19 December 1983   Meeting 102   137-1-3 (recorded vote)

16-nation draft (A/38/L.45 & Add.1); agenda item 34.

Sponsors: Afghanistan, Bangladesh, Cuba, Egypt, Gambia, Guinea, Guyana, India, Indonesia, Lao People's Democratic Republic, Malaysia, Nicaragua, Pakistan, Sri Lanka, Viet Nam, Yugoslavia.

Meeting numbers. GA 38th session: plenary 87-89, 91-95, 102.

Recorded vote in Assembly as follows:

In favour: Afghanistan, Albania, Algeria, Angola, Argentina, Australia, Austria, Bahamas, Bahrain, Bangladesh, Barbados, Belgium, Belize, Benin, Bhutan, Bolivia, Botswana, Brazil, Bulgaria, Burma, Burundi, Byelorussian SSR, Canada, Cape Verde, Central African Republic, Chad, Chile, China, Colombia, Congo, Cuba, Cyprus, Czechoslovakia, Democratic Kampuchea, Democratic Yemen, Denmark, Djibouti, Ecuador, Egypt, El Salvador, Ethiopia, Fiji, Finland, France, Gabon, Gambia, German Democratic Republic, Germany, Federal Republic of, Ghana, Greece, Guinea, Guinea-Bissau, Guyana, Honduras, Hungary, Iceland, India, Indonesia, Iran, Iraq, Ireland, Italy, Ivory Coast, Jamaica, Japan, Jordan, Kenya, Kuwait, Lao People's Democratic Republic, Lebanon, Libyan Arab Jamahiriya, Luxembourg, Madagascar, Malawi, Malaysia, Maldives, Mali, Malta, Mauritania, Mauritius, Mexico, Mongolia, Morocco, Mozambique, Nepal, Netherlands, New Zealand, Nicaragua, Niger, Nigeria, Norway, Oman, Pakistan, Papua New Guinea, Paraguay, Peru, Philippines, Poland, Portugal, Qatar, Romania, Rwanda, Saint Lucia, Saint Vincent and the Grenadines, Sao Tome and Principe, Saudi Arabia, Senegal, Seychelles, Sierra Leone, Singapore, Somalia, Spain, Sri Lanka, Sudan, Suriname, Sweden, Syrian Arab Republic, Thailand, Togo, Trinidad and Tobago, Tunisia, Turkey, Uganda, Ukrainian SSR, USSR, United Arab Emirates, United Kingdom, United Republic of Cameroon, United Republic of Tanzania, Upper Volta, Uruguay, Venezuela, Viet Nam, Yemen, Yugoslavia, Zambia, Zimbabwe.

Against: Israel.

Abstaining: Dominican Republic, Guatemala, United States.

Explaining its vote, Israel said only the Jewish people had regarded Jerusalem as the centre of their national and spiritual life. Reunited since 1967, the city enjoyed unprecedented freedom and prosperity, with the adherents of all faiths guaranteed free access to and worship at their Holy Places.

Ecuador considered null and void Israeli measures which could modify the physical character, demographic composition, institutional structure and status of the Palestinian and Arab territories occupied since 1967, including Jerusalem, a city holy to the three great religions. New Zealand did not recognize Israel's annexation of Jerusalem and did not recognize Jerusalem as the capital of Israel; it supported the principle of the city's internationalization, incorporated in the 1947 Assembly resolution on the future of Palestine.[35] Portugal expressed its support for all provisions that could bring success to a negotiated, comprehensive and peaceful Middle East solution, which it felt applied particularly to resolution 38/180 C.

Speaking on behalf of the EC members, Greece stressed the importance they attached to Security Council resolution 478(1980), by which the Council had decided not to recognize the "Basic Law" on Jerusalem.[36]

Greece said its vote was based on its attachment to the Charter principle that all Members should refrain from the threat or use of force against the territorial integrity or political independence of any State, and to the principles of the Final Act of the Conference on Security and Co-operation in Europe (Helsinki Final Act), signed on 1 August 1975 at Helsinki, Finland. Singapore expressed support for all efforts to restore the rights of the Palestinians and a return to a just and durable Middle East peace. Spain believed that a Middle East solution must be based, among other things, on Israel's withdrawal from all territories occupied since 1967 and on respect for Palestinian rights. Colombia spoke similarly. Bolivia regarded as null and void Israel's actions relating to the occupied territories.

The Libyan Arab Jamahiriya reaffirmed its opposition to all allusions giving some semblance of legitimacy to Israeli occupation of the Palestinian territories or recognizing the Zionist entity. Iran also reserved its position on any paragraphs which constituted recognition of what it called an artificially forged State.

Israel's decision to annex Jerusalem and declare it its capital, as well as the measures to alter its physical character, demographic composition, institutional structure and status, were declared as null and void by the Assembly in another 19 December resolution (38/180 D). The Assembly demanded that they be rescinded immediately and called on Member States, specialized agencies and international organizations to abide by all United Nations resolutions on Jerusalem. Among the guidelines established in the Declaration of the International Conference on the Question of Palestine[11] and endorsed by the Assembly in a 13 December resolution (38/58 C), in relation to the proposed international peace conference on the Middle East (see above), was a guideline stressing the need to reaffirm as null and void all measures by Israel altering the character and status of Jerusalem, including the expropriation of land and property, and in particular the "Basic Law" and the proclamation of Jerusalem as the capital of Israel. By a resolution of 15 December (38/83 K), the Assembly called for the establishment of a university at Jerusalem for Palestine refugees (see below, under PALESTINE REFUGEES).

Other action. Among the recommendations in the Programme of Action for the Achievement of Palestinian Rights, adopted by the Conference on the Palestine question (see above), was that States should fully comply with the relevant resolutions of the United Nations and its specialized agencies, including those rejecting Israel's annexation and declaration of Jerusalem as its capital.[11]

Jerusalem was also discussed at the Eighth United Nations Seminar on the Question of Palestine (see above). The Seminar[23] concluded that the question was among the most difficult to solve. It confirmed that the occupation and Judaization of Jerusalem and Israel's unilateral acts to annex the city should continue to be condemned and declared null and void and without legal effect, and that the Security Council should enforce its decisions. Israeli practices, the Seminar concluded, were impeding the decolonization of Jerusalem which was inseparable from the emergence of Palestine as a State. The status of Jerusalem as envisaged in United Nations resolutions remained the basis of a solution.

Aid programmes for Palestinians

During 1983, United Nations assistance—particularly education and training—continued to be provided to Palestinians in the West Bank and Gaza and neighbouring Arab States, much of it financed by the United Nations Development Programme (UNDP). This was in addition to aid supplied by the United Nations Relief and Works Agency for Palestine Refugees in the Near East (UNRWA) (see below, under PALESTINE REFUGEES) and to humanitarian assistance to Palestinians in Lebanon (see ECONOMIC AND SOCIAL QUESTIONS, Chapters III and XXI).

Action relating to assistance for Palestinians was taken in 1983 by the UNDP Governing Council, the Industrial Development Board of the United Nations Industrial Development Organization (UNIDO) and the United Nations Conference on Trade and Development (UNCTAD). Intensified efforts to provide economic and social assistance to the Palestinians were requested by the Economic and Social Council in resolution 1983/43 of 25 July. A co-ordinated programme of such assistance, taking into account the recommendations of the five regional preparatory meetings of the International Conference on the Question of Palestine and United Nations resolutions, was called for by the General Assembly in resolution 38/58 D of 13 December. Inter-agency co-ordination of assistance to Palestinians was the subject of Assembly resolution 38/145, adopted on 19 December.

UNDP action. Reporting in April 1983[37] to the Governing Council, the UNDP Administrator reviewed the progress in implementing the programme of assistance to the Palestinian people. He reported that, on the basis of regular consultations with the parties concerned, UNDP had developed by the end of 1982 nine new project proposals for the West Bank and Gaza, which were annexed to his report. The proposals, which would involve the private sector to a greater degree than previous projects, included assistance to community centres, specialized training for the glass and ceramics industry, and assistance to private medical institutions. In addition, extensions and new phases of ongoing projects in the fields of health manpower development, the development and strengthening of health institutions, specialized training in agricultural development, and children's institutions were to start in 1983. All but one project under way or envisaged were located in the West Bank and Gaza.

The Governing Council, on 24 June,[38] recommended that urgent efforts be made, with all parties concerned, to meet the economic and social needs of the Palestinians. Following the Administrator's recommendation, the Council reiterated its 1982 appeal[39] to Governments and intergovernmental organizations to provide for that purpose at least an additional $8 million for the 1982-1986 programming cycle to supplement the funds available from UNDP Special Programme Resources. This appeal was endorsed by the General Assembly on 13 December 1983 in resolution 38/145 (see below).

In his annual report for 1983,[40] the Administrator noted that under the assistance programme, which had commenced field operations in 1980, 6 of the 14 projects approved had been completed in 1983, all of them, except one in the Syrian Arab Republic, in the West Bank and Gaza. Five more projects were under implementation at the end of the year. At the end of 1983, all funds available from UNDP central resources for the programme, amounting to $7.5 million, were fully committed. Projects established during the year were in the pipeline, awaiting receipt of contributions from Governments and intergovernmental institutions, following appeals for contributions by the Council and the Assembly.

UNIDO action. Following consideration of a March 1983 report by the UNIDO Executive Director on technical assistance to the Palestinian people,[41] the Industrial Development Board, on 13 May, adopted a conclusion on such assistance.[42] The Board took note of the efforts of UNIDO in approving a number of technical co-operation projects and in finding ways to implement them. It expressed concern at the destruction of Palestinian industrial production capacities by the Israeli army in Lebanon following the Israeli invasion in June 1982,[43] and urged the UNIDO secretariat to assist in reactivating such capacities in the occupied territories and in establishing new capacities for the Palestinians, and to intensify efforts in providing technical assistance to them in co-operation with PLO. The Board called on Israel to give UNIDO access to the Palestinian territories occupied since 1967 to enable it to implement its technical co-operation projects for the Palestinians, and requested the Executive Director to submit in 1984 proposals for expanding its technical assistance programme.

UNCTAD action. On 2 July 1983, at its sixth session, UNCTAD adopted, by a roll-call vote of 84 to 2, with 20 abstentions, resolution 146(VI) on assistance to the Palestinian people.[44] The Conference requested the Secretary-General of UNCTAD to set up a special economic unit to monitor and investigate the policies of the Israeli occupation authorities hampering the economic development of the occupied Palestinian territories (see below, under TERRITORIES OCCUPIED BY ISRAEL), and to report periodically to the Trade and Development Board and the General Assembly, through the Economic and Social Council, on progress in implementing the resolution.

ECONOMIC AND SOCIAL COUNCIL ACTION

In May 1983, the Secretary-General submitted to the Economic and Social Council a report on assistance to Palestinians provided or planned by United Nations organizations and agencies.[45] Acting on the recommendation of its Third (Programme and Co-ordination) Committee, the Council on 25 July adopted by a roll-call vote resolution 1983/43.

Assistance to the Palestinian people
The Economic and Social Council,

Recalling General Assembly resolution 37/134 of 17 December 1982,

Recalling also Council resolution 1982/48 of 27 July 1982,

Noting with deep concern that the continued detention of Palestinian civilians in Al Ansar Camp by the Israeli invasion army has deprived many of their dependants of their sole source of income, in addition to having other adverse economic and social consequences,

Noting also the need to provide economic and social assistance to the Palestinian people,

1. *Takes note* of the report of the Secretary-General on assistance to the Palestinian people;

2. *Expresses its gratitude* to the Governments and United Nations bodies which provided humanitarian assistance to the Palestinian victims of the Israeli invasion of Lebanon;

3. *Takes note with appreciation* of the assistance provided by United Nations bodies to the Palestinian people;

4. *Deplores* the non-compliance of Israel with Economic and Social Council resolution 1982/48;

5. *Calls upon* the Israeli occupation authorities to facilitate the efforts of all United Nations bodies intending to implement assistance projects for the Palestinian people in the occupied Palestinian territories;

6. *Requests* the competent programmes, organizations, agencies and organs of the United Nations system to sustain and intensify their efforts, in co-operation with the Palestine Liberation Organization, in providing economic and social assistance to the Palestinian people;

7. *Also requests* that United Nations assistance to the Palestinians in the Arab host countries should be rendered in co-operation with the Palestine Liberation Organization and with the consent of the Arab host Governments concerned;

8. *Requests* the Secretary-General to report to the General Assembly at its thirty-ninth session, through

the Economic and Social Council, on the progress made in the implementation of the present resolution.

Economic and Social Council resolution 1983/43

25 July 1983   Meeting 39   48-1-1 (roll-call vote)

Approved by Third Committee (E/1983/114) by vote (35-1), 18 July (meeting 12); draft by Bangladesh, for Group of 77 (E/1983/C.3/L.3), orally revised; agenda item 22.
Meeting number. ESC: 39.

Roll-call vote in Council as follows:

In favour: Algeria, Argentina, Austria, Bangladesh, Benin, Botswana, Brazil, Bulgaria, Burundi, Byelorussian SSR, Canada, China, Colombia, Congo, Denmark, Djibouti, Ecuador, France, German Democratic Republic, Germany, Federal Republic of, Greece, India, Japan, Kenya, Lebanon, Luxembourg, Malaysia, Mali, Mexico, Netherlands, New Zealand, Norway, Pakistan, Peru, Poland, Portugal, Qatar, Romania, Saint Lucia, Saudi Arabia, Sudan, Suriname, Swaziland, Thailand, Tunisia, USSR, United Kingdom, Venezuela.

Against: United States.

Abstaining: Liberia.

Before the vote, Israel urged Council members not to adopt the draft, for the following reasons: The third preambular paragraph referred to the continued detention of Palestinian civilians in Al Ansar (Insar) Camp (see above, under PERSONS DETAINED BY ISRAEL), whereas there were only members of the PLO terrorist organization in that camp whose release would threaten Israel's security. It was inappropriate to mention Israel in the context of the reference in paragraph 2 to humanitarian assistance to the Palestinian victims of the Israeli invasion of Lebanon, since there had been civil war in Lebanon for eight years, involving considerable destruction and heavy loss of life. Paragraph 4 deploring Israel's non-compliance with a 1982 Council resolution[46] totally disregarded Israel's position on the matter. The wording of paragraph 5 implied that the Israeli authorities were not facilitating United Nations efforts to provide assistance to the Palestinians; nothing could be further from the truth—Israel had co-operated fully with UNDP, the most important of the agencies.

Speaking for the 10 member States of the European Economic Community (EEC), Greece said they would continue to provide humanitarian assistance to the Palestinians, particularly to those in Lebanon who had suffered from the 1982 Israeli invasion; assistance would be given directly and through the Community, as well as through United Nations agencies and bodies.

Norway stated its support particularly for the activities of the specialized agencies but stressed that its attitude towards PLO remained unchanged.

Speaking also on behalf of Bulgaria, the Byelorussian SSR, Czechoslovakia, Hungary, Mongolia, Poland, the Ukrainian SSR and the USSR, the German Democratic Republic said the resolution should have condemned Israel and its protector, the United States, and should have urged Israel to withdraw its troops from the occupied territories; appealing to Israeli occupation forces to facilitate implementation of assistance projects would not bring liberation of the Palestinians nearer.

Action by the Conference on the Palestine question. In September 1983, taking up recommendations made at the five regional preparatory meetings, the International Conference on the Question of Palestine,[11] in its Programme of Action for the Achievement of Palestinian Rights (see above), called for measures to alleviate the Palestinians' economic and social burdens resulting from continued Israeli occupation of their territories, and for increased contributions to the programmes and projects of United Nations bodies providing humanitarian, economic and social assistance to those people. The Conference referred in particular to: the appeal of the UNDP Governing Council for an additional $8 million during 1982-1986 to help meet the needs of the Palestinians (see above); the proposed establishment within UNCTAD of a Special Economic Unit on Assistance to the Palestinian People; and the setting up of a special legal aid fund to assist them in securing their rights under conditions of occupation.

GENERAL ASSEMBLY ACTION

In December 1983, the General Assembly adopted two resolutions (38/58 D and 38/145) dealing with assistance to the Palestinian people.

Under the agenda item on the question of Palestine, the Assembly, on 13 December, adopted resolution 38/58 D by recorded vote.

The General Assembly,

Having considered the report of the International Conference on the Question of Palestine, held at Geneva from 29 August to 7 September 1983,

Taking note of the Programme of Action for the Achievement of Palestinian Rights,

Bearing in mind its resolution 38/145 of 19 December 1983 on assistance to the Palestinian people,

Urges the meeting of specialized agencies and other organizations of the United Nations system to be convened in 1984, referred to in General Assembly resolution 38/145, to take into account the recommendations of the five regional preparatory meetings of the International Conference on the Question of Palestine and the United Nations resolutions concerning economic and social assistance to the Palestinian people in developing a co-ordinated programme of economic and social assistance to the Palestinian people, and to ensure the implementation of that programme.

General Assembly resolution 38/58 D

13 December 1983   Meeting 95   144-2 (recorded vote)

20-nation draft (A/38/L.39 & Add.1); agenda item 33.
Sponsors: Afghanistan, Bangladesh, Cuba, Egypt, Gambia, German Democratic Republic, Guinea, Guyana, Hungary, India, Indonesia, Lao People's Democratic Republic, Madagascar, Malaysia, Nicaragua, Nigeria, Pakistan, Ukrainian SSR, Viet Nam, Yugoslavia.
Meeting numbers. GA 38th session: plenary 73, 79-82, 95.

Recorded vote in Assembly as follows:

In favour: Afghanistan, Albania, Algeria, Angola, Argentina, Australia, Austria, Bahamas, Bahrain, Bangladesh, Belgium, Belize, Benin, Bhutan, Bolivia, Botswana, Brazil, Bulgaria, Burma, Burundi, Byelorussian SSR, Canada, Cape Verde, Central African Republic, Chad, Chile, China, Colombia, Comoros, Congo, Costa Rica, Cuba, Cyprus, Czechoslovakia, Democratic Kampuchea, Democratic Yemen, Den-

mark, Djibouti, Dominican Republic, Ecuador, Egypt, El Salvador, Equatorial Guinea, Ethiopia, Fiji, Finland, France, Gabon, Gambia, German Democratic Republic, Germany, Federal Republic of, Ghana, Greece, Guinea, Guinea-Bissau, Guyana, Haiti, Honduras, Hungary, Iceland, India, Indonesia, Iran, Iraq, Ireland, Italy, Ivory Coast, Jamaica, Japan, Kenya, Kuwait, Lao People's Democratic Republic, Lebanon, Lesotho, Liberia, Libyan Arab Jamahiriya, Luxembourg, Madagascar, Malawi, Malaysia, Maldives, Mali, Malta, Mauritania, Mauritius, Mexico, Mongolia, Morocco, Mozambique, Nepal, Netherlands, New Zealand, Nicaragua, Niger, Nigeria, Norway, Oman, Pakistan, Panama, Papua New Guinea, Paraguay, Peru, Philippines, Poland, Portugal, Qatar, Romania, Rwanda, Sao Tome and Principe, Saudi Arabia, Senegal, Seychelles, Sierra Leone, Singapore, Solomon Islands, Somalia, Spain, Sri Lanka, Sudan, Suriname, Sweden, Syrian Arab Republic, Thailand, Togo, Trinidad and Tobago, Tunisia, Turkey, Uganda, Ukrainian SSR, USSR, United Arab Emirates, United Kingdom, United Republic of Cameroon, United Republic of Tanzania, Upper Volta, Uruguay, Vanuatu, Venezuela, Viet Nam, Yemen, Yugoslavia, Zaire, Zambia, Zimbabwe.
Against: Israel, United States.

Israel rejected the resolution on the grounds that it sought to accord legitimacy to the International Conference, thus serving the narcissistic excesses of the PLO propagandists and their fellow travellers; if implemented, the proposed recommendations would pour additional money down what appeared to be a bottomless drain.

Speaking for the EC member States, Greece said they understood that the resolution dealt only with economic and social assistance. Even though UNDP was already involved in co-ordinating assistance and a general meeting of specialized agencies seemed unnecessary, Canada said it voted in favour in support of the principle of international assistance to the Palestinians. Finland voted in favour with reservations as it felt the resolution was unbalanced.

Costa Rica believed that the United Nations system must play its part in assisting the Palestinians.

On 19 December, the Assembly, acting on the recommendation of its Second (Economic and Financial) Committee, adopted resolution 38/145 by recorded vote.

Assistance to the Palestinian people
The General Assembly,

Recalling its resolution 37/134 of 17 December 1982,

Recalling also Economic and Social Council resolution 1983/43 of 25 July 1983,

Recalling further the Programme of Action for the Achievement of Palestinian Rights, adopted by the International Conference on the Question of Palestine,

Noting the need to provide economic and social assistance to the Palestinian people,

1. *Endorses* Economic and Social Council resolution 1983/43;

2. *Endorses also* decision 83/11 of 24 June 1983 of the Governing Council of the United Nations Development Programme, in which the Council called upon Governments and intergovernmental organizations to provide additional special contributions to the Programme amounting to at least 8 million dollars during the third programming cycle, so as to ensure the implementation of the United Nations Development Programme assistance programme for the Palestinian people;

3. *Requests* the Secretary-General:

(a) To convene in 1984 a meeting of the relevant programmes, organizations, agencies and organs of the United Nations system to develop a co-ordinated programme of economic and social assistance to the Palestinian people and to ensure its implementation;

(b) To provide for the participation in the meeting of the Palestine Liberation Organization, the Arab host countries and relevant intergovernmental and nongovernmental organizations;

(c) To utilize existing inter-agency mechanisms to prepare proposals for assistance projects to be considered at the meeting;

4. *Requests* that the meeting should look into the most effective inter-agency machinery to co-ordinate and intensify United Nations assistance to the Palestinian people;

5. *Requests* the relevant programmes, organizations, agencies and organs of the United Nations system to intensify their efforts, in co-operation with the Palestine Liberation Organization, to provide economic and social assistance to the Palestinian people;

6. *Also requests* that United Nations assistance to the Palestinians in the Arab host countries should be rendered in co-operation with the Palestine Liberation Organization and with the consent of the Arab host Government concerned;

7. *Requests* the Secretary-General to report to the General Assembly at its thirty-ninth session, through the Economic and Social Council, on the progress made in the implementation of the present resolution.

General Assembly resolution 38/145

19 December 1983   Meeting 102   140-2-1 (recorded vote)

Approved by Second Committee (A/38/701) by recorded vote (131-2), 14 November (meeting 39); 11-nation draft (A/C.2/38/L.24/Rev.1), orally revised; agenda item 12.

Sponsors: Bangladesh, China, Democratic Yemen, Madagascar, Mali, Mauritania, Qatar, Sudan, Tunisia, Viet Nam, Yemen.

Meeting numbers. GA 38th session: 2nd Committee 24, 26-28, 30, 36-37, 39; plenary 73, 79-82, 95, 102.

Recorded vote in Assembly as follows:

In favour: Afghanistan, Albania, Algeria, Angola, Argentina, Australia, Austria, Bahamas, Bahrain, Bangladesh, Barbados, Belgium, Belize, Benin, Bhutan, Bolivia, Botswana, Brazil, Bulgaria, Burma, Burundi, Byelorussian SSR, Canada, Cape Verde, Central African Republic, Chad, Chile, China, Colombia, Congo, Cuba, Cyprus, Czechoslovakia, Democratic Kampuchea, Democratic Yemen, Denmark, Djibouti, Dominican Republic, Ecuador, Egypt, El Salvador, Ethiopia, Fiji, Finland, France, Gabon, Gambia, German Democratic Republic, Germany, Federal Republic of, Ghana, Greece, Guinea, Guinea-Bissau, Guyana, Honduras, Hungary, Iceland, India, Indonesia, Iran, Iraq, Italy, Ivory Coast, Jamaica, Japan, Jordan, Kenya, Kuwait, Lao People's Democratic Republic, Lebanon, Lesotho, Liberia, Libyan Arab Jamahiriya, Luxembourg, Madagascar, Malaysia, Maldives, Mali, Malta, Mauritania, Mauritius, Mexico, Mongolia, Morocco, Mozambique, Nepal, Netherlands, New Zealand, Nicaragua, Niger, Nigeria, Norway, Oman, Pakistan, Panama, Papua New Guinea, Paraguay, Peru, Philippines, Poland, Portugal, Qatar, Romania, Rwanda, Saint Lucia, Saint Vincent and the Grenadines, Sao Tome and Principe, Saudi Arabia, Senegal, Sierra Leone, Singapore, Somalia, Spain, Sri Lanka, Sudan, Suriname, Swaziland, Sweden, Syrian Arab Republic, Thailand, Togo, Trinidad and Tobago, Tunisia, Turkey, Uganda, Ukrainian SSR, USSR, United Arab Emirates, United Kingdom, United Republic of Cameroon, United Republic of Tanzania, Upper Volta, Uruguay, Vanuatu, Venezuela, Viet Nam, Yemen, Yugoslavia, Zaire, Zambia.

Against: Israel, United States.

Abstaining: Ireland.[a]

[a]Later advised the Secretariat it had intended to vote in favour.

Israel, stating that it was endeavouring to help Palestinian Arabs and had improved their standard of living, said it continued to favour legitimate aid to those living in the administered territories and had co-operated with UNDP and other United Nations bodies to assist the Arab populations of Judaea, Samaria and Gaza. Recent UNDP

Governing Council decisions had tended to intensify such co-operation; but it would continue to oppose co-operation with PLO. The international community should dissociate itself from the so-called International Conference.

The United States, pointing out that it would have supported a resolution on humanitarian assistance and that it had contributed more than $1 billion to UNRWA, said the approved text mentioned PLO which the United States did not recognize and which, by refusing to recognize Israel, had impeded the Middle East peace process.

Jordan expressed support for any assistance to the Palestinians in the West Bank and Gaza and to Palestinian refugees, but stressed that this did not imply endorsement of the imbalance in paragraphs 5 and 6; it had sole responsibility for the initiation, planning and organization of social and economic services to all Jordanian citizens, and any assistance to them must be subject to its acceptance.

Expressing support for the resolution because of its substance, Australia voiced reservations to the reference to the Conference, in which it had not participated.

Speaking for the EC members, Greece said they would continue to offer assistance to the Palestinians directly and through the Community, and to the competent United Nations agencies which could best decide on channels through which to assist the Palestinians. Japan stressed that assistance to the Palestinians by UNDP and other United Nations bodies should be provided by the same procedure as that to national liberation movements, in close co-operation with the countries concerned. Norway said it agreed to assisting the Palestinians, but its position towards PLO remained unchanged.

The USSR said its vote was based on its position of principle regarding the need for a just and comprehensive Middle East settlement.

Commenting on the United States statement, the PLO observer said no amount of money contributed to UNRWA could compensate the Palestinians for the occupation of their homeland.

The Assembly's Fifth (Administrative and Budgetary) Committee decided on 17 November,[47] by 75 votes to 2, with 20 abstentions, to include in the 1984-1985 budget $218,000 to establish within the UNCTAD secretariat a Special Economic Unit (Palestinian People). The Secretary-General, in his revised budget estimates,[48] stated that to establish the Unit two new Professional posts were requested, at the P-5 and P-3 levels, together with one General Service post.

Palestinian cultural property

In 1983, the General Assembly took up the question of the restitution of Palestinian cultural property, seized by Israel during its June 1982 invasion of Lebanon,[43] a question first addressed by the Assembly in December 1982.[49]

GENERAL ASSEMBLY ACTION

Under the agenda item on the situation in the Middle East, the Assembly, on 19 December 1983, adopted resolution 38/180 B by recorded vote.

The General Assembly,
Recalling the relevant provisions of the Universal Declaration of Human Rights,
Recalling also the Constitution of the United Nations Educational, Scientific and Cultural Organization and all other relevant international instruments concerning the right to cultural identity in all its forms,
Having learned that the Israeli army, during its occupation of Beirut, seized and took away archives and documents of every kind concerning Palestinian history and culture, including cultural articles belonging to Palestinian institutions—in particular the Palestine Research Centre—archives, documents, manuscripts and materials such as film documents, literary works by major authors, paintings, *objets d'art* and works of folklore, research works and so forth, serving as a foundation for the history, culture, national awareness, unity and solidarity of the Palestinian people,
1. *Condemns* those acts of plundering of the Palestinian cultural heritage;
2. *Calls upon* the Government of Israel to make full restitution, through the United Nations Educational, Scientific and Cultural Organization, of all cultural property belonging to Palestinian institutions, including the archives and documents removed from the Palestine Research Centre and arbitrarily seized by the Israeli forces;
3. *Requests* the Secretary-General to report to the General Assembly at its thirty-ninth session on the implementation of the present resolution.

General Assembly resolution 38/180 B

19 December 1983   Meeting 102   121-1-20 (recorded vote)

15-nation draft (A/38/L.44 & Add.1); agenda item 34.
Sponsors: Afghanistan, Bangladesh, Cuba, Gambia, Guinea, Guyana, India, Indonesia, Lao People's Democratic Republic, Malaysia, Nicaragua, Pakistan, Sri Lanka, Viet Nam, Yugoslavia.
Meeting numbers. GA 38th session: plenary 87-89, 91-95, 102.

Recorded vote in Assembly as follows:

In favour: Afghanistan, Albania, Algeria, Angola, Argentina, Austria, Bahamas, Bahrain, Bangladesh, Barbados, Belize, Benin, Bhutan, Bolivia, Botswana, Brazil, Bulgaria, Burma, Burundi, Byelorussian SSR, Cape Verde, Central African Republic, Chad, Chile, China, Colombia, Congo, Costa Rica, Cuba, Cyprus, Czechoslovakia, Democratic Kampuchea, Democratic Yemen, Djibouti, Ecuador, Egypt, El Salvador, Ethiopia, Fiji, Gabon, Gambia, German Democratic Republic, Ghana, Greece, Guinea, Guinea-Bissau, Guyana, Haiti, Honduras, Hungary, India, Indonesia, Iran, Iraq, Ivory Coast, Jamaica, Japan, Jordan, Kenya, Kuwait, Lao People's Democratic Republic, Lebanon, Libyan Arab Jamahiriya, Madagascar, Malawi, Malaysia, Maldives, Mali, Malta, Mauritania, Mauritius, Mexico, Mongolia, Morocco, Mozambique, Nepal, Nicaragua, Niger, Nigeria, Oman, Pakistan, Papua New Guinea, Paraguay, Peru, Philippines, Poland, Portugal, Qatar, Romania, Rwanda, Sao Tome and Principe, Saudi Arabia, Senegal, Seychelles, Sierra Leone, Singapore, Somalia, Spain, Sri Lanka, Sudan, Suriname, Syrian Arab Republic, Thailand, Togo, Trinidad and Tobago, Tunisia, Turkey, Uganda, Ukrainian SSR, USSR, United Arab Emirates, United Republic of Cameroon, United Republic of Tanzania, Upper Volta, Uruguay, Venezuela, Viet Nam, Yemen, Yugoslavia, Zambia, Zimbabwe.
Against: Israel.
Abstaining: Australia, Belgium, Canada, Denmark, Dominican Republic, Finland, France, Germany, Federal Republic of, Iceland, Ireland, Italy, Luxembourg, Netherlands, New Zealand, Norway, Saint Lucia, Saint Vincent and the Grenadines, Sweden, United Kingdom, United States.

Israel said the resolution ignored the fact that it had returned the files and that the so-called Palestine Research Centre's true function was not research but the production of anti-Israel propaganda and the collection of intelligence data for use by terrorists against Israel and Jewish civilian targets in Israel and throughout the world.

Finland felt that it was unclear whether that property had been returned or not. Sweden spoke similarly. Recalling the support of the EC members for the 1982 resolution,[49] Greece said they also noted that there was now some uncertainty about the facts.

The Philippines had reservations on the formulation of some of the resolution's provisions. Greece explained that it voted in favour on the basis of its attachment to Article 2, paragraph 4, of the United Nations Charter, on the non-use of force against other States, and to the principles in the Helsinki Final Act. Ecuador condemned Israeli policies that violated the rights of the inhabitants of the occupied territories (see below, under TERRITORIES OCCUPIED BY ISRAEL). Singapore said it supported all efforts aiming at restoring legitimate Palestinian rights. Portugal declared its support for any resolution that could bring success to the Middle East peace efforts. Similar positions were taken by Bolivia, Colombia and Spain.

Iran reserved its rights regarding any paragraphs that recognized an artificially forged State, the Zionist entity. The Libyan Arab Jamahiriya also opposed all allusions giving a semblance of legitimacy to Israeli occupation of the occupied Palestinian territories or recognizing that entity.

Public information

Expanded information activities of the United Nations Secretariat, in particular of its Department of Public Information (DPI) relating to the Palestine question, were recommended by the International Conference on the Question of Palestine in September 1983. The General Assembly took up these recommendations in a December resolution.

Conference on the Palestine question. The International Conference on the Question of Palestine,[11] in its Programme of Action (see above), stated that the dissemination of information world-wide and the role of non-governmental organizations (NGOs) remained vital in heightening awareness of the rights of the Palestinians to self-determination and the establishment of an independent Palestinian State. It called on DPI, in co-operation with the Committee on Palestinian rights, to: co-ordinate all United Nations information activities on Palestine through the Joint United Nations Information Committee; expand publications and audio and visual coverage of the Palestine question; publish newsletters and articles on

Israeli violations of human rights in the occupied territories (see below, under TERRITORIES OCCUPIED BY ISRAEL); organize fact-finding missions for journalists to the area; and disseminate information on the Conference results. The Conference also called on United Nations bodies to organize meetings, symposia and seminars on topics relating to specific problems of the Palestinians by establishing closer liaison with NGOs, the media and other interested groups. Organizations were urged to increase international awareness of the economic and social burdens borne by the Palestinians as a result of continued Israeli occupation, to intensify their support of Palestinian rights, to investigate the conditions and Israeli policies in the occupied territories, and to disseminate information.

GENERAL ASSEMBLY ACTION

Under the agenda item on the question of Palestine, the General Assembly, on 13 December 1983, adopted resolution 38/58 E by recorded vote.

The General Assembly,

Having considered the report of the International Conference on the Question of Palestine, held at Geneva from 29 August to 7 September 1983,

Convinced that the world-wide dissemination of accurate and comprehensive information and the role of non-governmental organizations and institutions remain of vital importance in heightening awareness of and support for the inalienable rights of the Palestinian people to self-determination and to the establishment of an independent sovereign Palestinian State,

Requests that the Department of Public Information of the Secretariat, in full co-operation and co-ordination with the Committee on the Exercise of the Inalienable Rights of the Palestinian People, should:

(a) Disseminate all information on the activities of the United Nations system relating to Palestine;

(b) Expand publications and audio-visual coverage of the facts and developments pertaining to the question of Palestine;

(c) Publish newsletters and articles in its relevant publications on Israeli violations of the human rights of the Arab inhabitants of the occupied territories, and organize fact-finding missions to the area for journalists;

(d) Organize regional encounters for journalists;

(e) Disseminate appropriate information on the results of the International Conference on the Question of Palestine.

General Assembly resolution 38/58 E

13 December 1983   Meeting 95   125-3-15 (recorded vote)

20-nation draft (A/38/L.40 & Add.1); agenda item 33.

Sponsors: Afghanistan, Bangladesh, Cuba, Egypt, Gambia, German Democratic Republic, Guinea, Guyana, Hungary, India, Indonesia, Lao People's Democratic Republic, Madagascar, Malaysia, Nicaragua, Nigeria, Pakistan, Ukrainian SSR, Viet Nam, Yugoslavia.

Financial implications. 5th Committee, A/38/725; S-G, A/C.5/38/75.

Meeting numbers. GA 38th session: 5th Committee 62; plenary 73, 79-82, 95.

Recorded vote in Assembly as follows:

In favour: Afghanistan, Albania, Algeria, Angola, Argentina, Austria, Bahamas, Bahrain, Bangladesh, Belize, Benin, Bhutan, Bolivia, Botswana, Brazil, Bulgaria, Burma, Burundi, Byelorussian SSR, Cape Verde, Central African Republic, Chad, China, Colombia, Comoros, Congo, Cuba, Cyprus, Czechoslovakia, Democratic

Kampuchea, Democratic Yemen, Djibouti, Dominican Republic, Ecuador, Egypt, El Salvador, Equatorial Guinea, Ethiopia, Fiji, Finland, Gabon, Gambia, German Democratic Republic, Ghana, Greece, Guinea, Guinea-Bissau, Guyana, Haiti, Honduras, Hungary, India, Indonesia, Iran, Iraq, Jamaica, Jordan, Kenya, Kuwait, Lao People's Democratic Republic, Lebanon, Lesotho, Libyan Arab Jamahiriya, Madagascar, Malawi, Malaysia, Maldives, Mali, Malta, Mauritania, Mauritius, Mexico, Mongolia, Morocco, Mozambique, Nepal, Nicaragua, Niger, Nigeria, Oman, Pakistan, Panama, Papua New Guinea, Paraguay, Peru, Philippines, Poland, Portugal, Qatar, Romania, Rwanda, Sao Tome and Principe, Saudi Arabia, Senegal, Seychelles, Sierra Leone, Singapore, Solomon Islands, Somalia, Spain, Sri Lanka, Sudan, Suriname, Sweden, Syrian Arab Republic, Thailand, Togo, Trinidad and Tobago, Tunisia, Turkey, Uganda, Ukrainian SSR, USSR, United Arab Emirates, United Republic of Cameroon, United Republic of Tanzania, Upper Volta, Uruguay, Vanuatu, Venezuela, Viet Nam, Yemen, Yugoslavia, Zambia, Zimbabwe.

Against: Canada, Israel, United States.

Abstaining: Australia, Belgium, Denmark, France, Germany, Federal Republic of, Iceland, Ireland, Italy, Ivory Coast, Japan, Luxembourg, Netherlands, New Zealand, Norway, United Kingdom.

Canada felt the resolution proposed duplicating machinery already in place for disseminating information on Palestine and implied that DPI, which received its mandate from the Assembly, must submit its programmes to a selective and non-representative Committee; it also stated that it could not support resolutions which took little account of the concerns of one party, and voiced reservations on the objectives of the Conference. Israel rejected the resolution as a drain on United Nations funds and another blow to the credibility of the United Nations Secretariat which, it felt, had been forced to abandon legitimate functions for extraneous interests.

Norway could not endorse the outcome of the Conference. Speaking for the EC member States, Greece said they trusted that DPI would continue to be guided by impartiality and would maintain its normal decision-making process; unnecessary burdens on the United Nations budget should be avoided. Reservations about the cost of information activities were also voiced by New Zealand. Costa Rica abstained on the grounds that Assembly resolution 38/58 B on the Division for Palestinian Rights (see above) already contained the necessary provisions on information.

Sweden, Trinidad and Tobago, and Uruguay reaffirmed their reservations on certain parts of the Declaration and Programme of Action adopted by the Conference, while Finland stated its general reservations on the resolution.

Malawi said it voted in favour to promote the peace-building process. In the opinion of Honduras, the resolution could help achieve Palestinian rights.

The Libyan Arab Jamahiriya affirmed that its positive vote did not alter its position on any references that might be construed as legitimizing the Zionist occupation of Palestine or as recognition of the Zionist entity. Iran held a similar position.

In resolution 38/58 B of the same date, the Assembly requested the Secretary-General to ensure the continued co-operation of DPI and other Secretariat units in enabling the Division of Palestinian Rights to perform its tasks and in covering the various aspects of the Palestine question. It also requested him to expand the Division's work programme through closer contacts with the media and wider dissemination of the Division's information material, increased contacts with NGOs and the convening of symposia and meetings in different regions to heighten awareness of the Palestine question.

Among the recommendations of the Committee on Information, endorsed by the Assembly in resolution 38/82 B of 15 December, was the preparation of a detailed account of the coverage by widely representative world media of developments from June to December 1982 affecting the Palestinians, to be submitted to the Assembly in 1983.

REFERENCES

[1]A/38/61-S/15549. [2]S/15609. [3]A/38/367 & Corr.1. [4]A/38/350. [5]A/38/351. [6]A/38/364 & Corr.1. [7]A/38/454. [8]A/38/373. [9]A/38/398. [10]YUN 1982, p. 420, GA res. ES-7/7, 19 Aug. 1982, and p. 422, GA res. 37/86 C, 10 Dec. 1982. [11]*Report of the International Conference on the Question of Palestine, Geneva, 29 August–7 September 1983* (A/CONF.114/42), Sales No. E.83.I.21. [12]YUN 1982, p. 387. [13]A/38/458-S/16015. [14]A/38/497-S/16038. [15]YUN 1981, p. 271, GA res. 36/120 C, 10 Dec. 1981. [16]A/38/46. [17]YUN 1982, p. 420, GA res. ES-7/7, 19 Aug. 1982. [18]A/CONF.114/1. [19]A/CONF.114/2. [20]A/CONF.114/3. [21]A/CONF.114/4. [22]A/CONF.114/5. [23]A/38/35. [24]YUN 1976, p. 235. [25]*Ibid.*, p. 245, GA res. 31/20, 24 Nov. 1976. [26]YUN 1977, p. 304, GA res. 32/40 B, 2 Dec. 1977. [27]YUN 1967, p. 257, SC res. 242(1967), 22 Nov. 1967. [28]YUN 1973, p. 213, SC res. 338(1973), 22 Oct. 1973. [29]A/38/115-S/15639 & Corr.1. [30]A/38/117-S/15642. [31]A/38/118-S/15646. [32]S/16203. [33]S/16205. [34]A/38/717-S/16209. [35]YUN 1947-48, p. 247, GA res. 181 A (II), 29 Nov. 1947. [36]YUN 1980, p. 426, SC res. 478(1980), 20 Aug. 1980. [37]DP/1983/14. [38]E/1983/20 (dec. 83/11). [39]YUN 1982, p. 423. [40]DP/1984/5/Add.2. [41]ID/B/301. [42]A/38/16 (1983/11). [43]YUN 1982, p. 428. [44]*Proceedings of the United Nations Conference on Trade and Development, Sixth Session, Belgrade, 6 June-2 July 1983*, vol. I, *Report and Annexes* (TD/326, vol. I), Sales No. E.83.II.D.6. [45]E/1983/72 & Add.1. [46]YUN 1982, p. 720, ESC res. 1982/48, 27 July 1982. [47]A/38/760. [48]A/C.5/38/4. [49]YUN 1982, p. 489, GA res. 37/123 B, 16 Dec. 1982.

Incidents and disputes between Arab countries and Israel

The 1981 bombing by Israeli aircraft of a nuclear research centre near Baghdad, Iraq, was again taken up by the General Assembly in December 1983. The Security Council, on several occasions throughout the year, dealt with the situation in Lebanon and in the Syrian Golan Heights and extended the mandate of the United Nations peace-keeping forces there. Israel and the Libyan Arab Jamahiriya exchanged several communications referring to discussions in the Council and the Assembly.

Armed incident involving Iraqi nuclear facilities

The 1981 bombing by Israeli aircraft of a nuclear research centre near Baghdad[1] was again the subject in 1983 of a General Assembly resolution (38/9). The Secretary-General reported on implementation of a November 1982 resolution on the issue and transmitted a study by a Group of Experts reviewing the consequences of the attack.

Communication. On 12 August 1983,[2] Iraq transmitted to the Secretary-General a message from its President to the World Assembly for Peace and Life against Nuclear War (Prague, Czechoslovakia, 21-26 June), stating that the attack by Israel on peaceful Iraqi nuclear installations using conventional weapons must be regarded as equivalent to an attack using nuclear weapons; an attack such as Israel's entailed the risk of exposure to radiation and the possible outbreak of nuclear war.

Report of the Secretary-General. In September 1983,[3] the Secretary-General reported on the implementation of a November 1982 General Assembly resolution on armed Israeli aggression against the Iraqi nuclear installations.[4] In response to a note requesting Israel to inform him of action it had taken, Israel, on 29 June, had replied that it had no policy of attacking nuclear facilities; that the resolution, which demanded that it withdraw its officially declared threat to repeat its armed attack against nuclear facilities, was one-sided and biased; and that it would be regrettable if the Assembly were required to deal once again with the issue since attempts should be made to address essential Middle East issues. The Secretary-General also reported that he had appointed a Group of Experts to study the consequences of the Israeli attack (see below).

Israel reiterated this statement in a 13 September letter.[5]

Study by Group of Experts. In October 1983, the Secretary-General transmitted to the Assembly a study on the consequences of the Israeli attack on the Iraqi nuclear installations,[6] prepared by a six-member Group of Experts appointed in accordance with the Assembly's November 1982 resolution.[4] In meetings held from 18 to 22 April at Vienna and from 11 to 15 July in New York, the Experts reviewed economic, legal, health and other consequences of the attack, carried out by 14 Israeli air force planes. Stating that it had not been possible to assess accurately the extent of the damage, they concluded that the virtual total destruction of the Tammuz-1 reactor and damage to other parts of the Tuwaitha Nuclear Research Centre had resulted in losses of several hundred million dollars of investment and had set back the Iraqi nuclear research and training programme by at least five years. No radiological health problems had been caused, although some could have occurred had the bombs struck the irradiated fuel stored at the site and there could have been an appreciable risk of health consequences had the reactor been operational.

According to the Experts, the more general consequences of the attack included its potentially serious damage to international norms and institutions: it represented a challenge to the 1968 Treaty on the Non-Proliferation of Nuclear Weapons (NPT)[7] and the safeguards system of the International Atomic Energy Agency (IAEA); it undermined international legal constraints on acts of aggression including those of the Charter of the United Nations; it introduced new risks and uncertainties, threatening further peaceful nuclear development and co-operation; and it violated the 1974 Charter of Economic Rights and Duties of States[8] and the 1974 Declaration and the Programme of Action on the Establishment of a New International Economic Order.[9]

Noting that Iraq was a party to NPT, the Experts felt that, if Israel became a party, accepted full-scope safeguards and complied with the Assembly's demand to refrain from its threat to repeat such attacks, the situation would substantially improve. They hoped that the incident would give new impetus to efforts to establish a nuclear-weapon-free zone in the Middle East, to the establishment of additional legal instruments against attacks on peaceful nuclear facilities, and to the improvement of international mechanisms for obtaining redress for damages.

On 31 October 1983,[10] Israel stated that the report was biased, predetermined conclusions having dictated the choice of facts and arguments; also, while Iraq had been invited to make its views known to the Group, Israel had not been invited to do so. The report omitted reference to Israel's statement that it had no policy of attacking nuclear facilities and, in dealing with the issue of the establishment of a nuclear-weapon-free zone in the Middle East, made no reference to the principle of free and direct negotiations among the States of the region. Israel urged that United Nations energies be devoted to supporting positive international initiatives and that an effort be made to prevent Iraq's misuse of the United Nations and IAEA as forums for repeated extraneous political issues.

GENERAL ASSEMBLY ACTION

On 10 November 1983, the General Assembly adopted by recorded vote resolution 38/9.

Armed Israeli aggression against the Iraqi nuclear installations and its grave consequences for the established international system concerning the peaceful uses of nuclear energy, the non-proliferation of nuclear weapons and international peace and security

The General Assembly,

Having considered the item entitled "Armed Israeli aggression against the Iraqi nuclear installations and its grave consequences for the established international system concerning the peaceful uses of nuclear energy, the non-proliferation of nuclear weapons and international peace and security",

Recalling the relevant resolutions of the Security Council and the General Assembly,

Taking note of the relevant resolutions of the International Atomic Energy Agency,

Taking note also with appreciation of the report of the Secretary-General,

Viewing with deep concern Israel's continued refusal to comply with those resolutions,

Reiterating its alarm over the information and evidence regarding the acquisition and development of nuclear weapons by Israel,

Recalling Article 2, paragraph 4, of the Charter of the United Nations, which enjoins all Member States to refrain in their international relations from the threat or use of force against the territorial integrity or political independence of any State, or in any other manner inconsistent with the purposes of the United Nations,

Noting that serious radiological effects would result from an armed attack with conventional weapons on a nuclear installation, which could also lead to the initiation of radiological warfare,

1. *Reiterates its condemnation* of Israel's continued refusal to implement Security Council resolution 487(1981), unanimously adopted by the Council on 19 June 1981;

2. *Notes* that the statements made so far by Israel have not removed apprehensions that its threat to repeat its armed attack against nuclear facilities, as well as any similar action against such facilities, will continue to endanger the role and activities of the International Atomic Energy Agency and other international instruments in the development of nuclear energy for peaceful purposes and in safeguarding against further proliferation of nuclear weapons;

3. *Considers* that any threat to attack and destroy nuclear facilities in Iraq and in other countries constitutes a violation of the Charter of the United Nations;

4. *Reiterates its demand* that Israel withdraw forthwith its threat to attack and destroy nuclear facilities in Iraq and in other countries;

5. *Once again requests* the Security Council to consider the necessary measures to deter Israel from repeating such an attack on nuclear facilities;

6. *Reaffirms its call* for the continuation of the consideration, at the international level, of legal measures to prohibit armed attacks against nuclear facilities, and threats thereof, as a contribution to promoting and ensuring the safe development of nuclear energy for peaceful purposes;

7. *Expresses its deep appreciation* to the Secretary-General and the Group of Experts on the Consequences of the Israeli Armed Attack against the Iraqi Nuclear Installations for their comprehensive study;

8. *Requests* the Secretary-General to report to the General Assembly at its thirty-ninth session on the implementation of the present resolution;

9. *Decides* to include in the provisional agenda of its thirty-ninth session the item entitled "Armed Israeli aggression against the Iraqi nuclear installations and its grave consequences for the established international system concerning the peaceful uses of nuclear energy, the non-proliferation of nuclear weapons and international peace and security".

General Assembly resolution 38/9

10 November 1983   Meeting 52   123-2-12 (recorded vote)

25-nation draft (A/38/L.7/Rev.2); agenda item 28.

Sponsors: Afghanistan, Algeria, Bahrain, Cyprus, Democratic Yemen, Djibouti, Indonesia, Iraq, Jordan, Kuwait, Lebanon, Libyan Arab Jamahiriya, Mali, Mauritania, Morocco, Nicaragua, Oman, Pakistan, Qatar, Saudi Arabia, Syrian Arab Republic, Tunisia, United Arab Emirates, Yemen, Yugoslavia.

Meeting numbers. GA 38th session: plenary 42, 44, 46, 52.

Recorded vote in Assembly as follows:

In favour: Afghanistan, Albania, Algeria, Angola, Argentina, Austria, Bahrain, Bangladesh, Belgium, Benin, Bhutan, Bolivia, Brazil, Bulgaria, Burundi, Byelorussian SSR, Canada, Cape Verde, Central African Republic, Chad, China, Comoros, Congo, Cuba, Cyprus, Czechoslovakia, Democratic Kampuchea, Democratic Yemen, Denmark, Djibouti, Ecuador, Egypt, El Salvador, Ethiopia, Finland, France, Gabon, Gambia, German Democratic Republic, Germany, Federal Republic of, Ghana, Greece, Grenada, Guinea, Guinea-Bissau, Guyana, Hungary, Iceland, India, Indonesia, Iraq, Ireland, Italy, Japan, Jordan, Kenya, Kuwait, Lao People's Democratic Republic, Lebanon, Lesotho, Libyan Arab Jamahiriya, Luxembourg, Madagascar, Malaysia, Maldives, Mali, Malta, Mauritania, Mauritius, Mexico, Mongolia, Morocco, Mozambique, Nepal, Netherlands, New Zealand, Nicaragua, Niger, Norway, Oman, Pakistan, Panama, Papua New Guinea, Peru, Philippines, Poland, Portugal, Qatar, Romania, Rwanda, Samoa, Sao Tome and Principe, Saudi Arabia, Senegal, Sierra Leone, Singapore, Solomon Islands, Somalia, Spain, Sri Lanka, Sudan, Sweden, Syrian Arab Republic, Thailand, Togo, Trinidad and Tobago, Tunisia, Turkey, Uganda, Ukrainian SSR, USSR, United Arab Emirates, United Kingdom, United Republic of Cameroon, United Republic of Tanzania, Upper Volta, Uruguay, Venezuela, Viet Nam, Yemen, Yugoslavia, Zambia, Zimbabwe.

Against: Israel, United States.

Abstaining: Australia, Bahamas, Barbados, Chile, Colombia, Fiji, Guatemala, Haiti, Ivory Coast, Jamaica, Malawi, Paraguay.

The United States said the resolution went far beyond the content of unanimously adopted Security Council resolution 487(1981);[11] to adopt measures two and a half years later was unnecessary and unproductive and detracted from the attention that should be given to a practical and realistic search for a peaceful settlement to the problems of the region. Its negative vote, the United States added, also reflected the view that the Secretary-General's study was superfluous and certain aspects of it were open to question; it treated the existence of a state of war between Israel and Iraq in the most cursory fashion, referred to an Israeli "threat" not mentioned previously and made no reference to specific Israeli declarations on the subject.

Also casting a negative vote, Israel said it would have voted for paragraph 6, had there been a separate vote, in keeping with its position that it had no policy of attacking nuclear facilities and fully supported international efforts to arrive at an early arrangement on the status of such facilities.

Chile believed that many paragraphs went beyond the item under discussion or presupposed intentions that were not sufficiently supported, and that the Security Council should decide whether further action was needed; the item should not be kept permanently on the Assembly's agenda.

Canada felt that the text had improved over the previous year's resolution,[4] in particular by omitting references to "acts of aggression" which, if taken in connection with Chapter VII of the United Nations Charter, could have severe consequences.

The United Kingdom regarded the last preambular paragraph as too categorical in its assertions; it also had reservations on the wording of paragraphs 2 to 6, stressing that it did not regard paragraph 6 as either prejudicing the issue of whether further legal measures to prohibit armed attacks against nuclear facilities were needed, or prejudging the forum for discussion of the subject.

The Federal Republic of Germany considered the text too complex to be constructive and believed other international bodies would be more suitable for discussing the subject. It expressed doubts on the concept of radiological warfare as contained in the last preambular paragraph; as to paragraph 6, it felt that the outcome of the work of the Committee on Disarmament, in seeking a solution to the question of prohibiting military attacks on nuclear facilities, including the scope of such prohibition, should not be prejudged.

Belgium reserved its position in particular on the preamble, saying it referred to problems which had nothing to do with the condemned action. France could not accept the use in the future of certain elements of the resolution's operative part to harm the principle of United Nations universality.

The United Kingdom remarked on the risks of the item's becoming another subject of ritual debate. Belgium, Canada, Denmark, France, the Federal Republic of Germany, the Netherlands and Norway held a similar position. For the Federal Republic of Germany, repeated condemnation of Israel was not likely to promote conditions in which the problems resulting from a two-year-old event could eventually be solved. The Netherlands pointed out that the Security Council was already seized of the question by virtue of paragraph 7 of its resolution 487(1981) and that IAEA was fully competent to deal with the matter.

Iraq responded that the reason behind the request again to include the item in the Assembly agenda was that the Israeli attack had not been an isolated act and that there had been a threat, officially stated a number of times, to repeat that act; it was the Assembly's duty to see to it that that threat was not carried out and was withdrawn in a meaningful way, not in the senseless statement that Israel had no policy of attacking nuclear facilities. Iraq also pointed out that Israel had refused to comply with the Security Council's requests; the point of the resolution was that action must be taken to make Israel realize that it could not with impunity carry out, or threaten to repeat, such an attack.

Other action. The IAEA General Conference decided to withhold Agency research contracts to Israel if it did not withdraw by 1984 its threat to attack nuclear facilities in Iraq and other countries (see also PART II, Chapter I).

Lebanon situation

Military activity in Lebanon, in the aftermath of the June 1982 Israeli invasion, was again a focus of attention in the Security Council in 1983. On 23 November, by resolution 542(1983), the Council repeated its call for strict respect for Lebanon's sovereignty, political independence and territorial integrity, and requested the parties concerned immediately to accept a cease-fire and to observe the cessation of hostilities. As reported by the Secretary-General in December, a cease-fire agreement was reached on 26 November and on 20 December PLO troops were evacuated from Tripoli. In 1983, the mandate of the United Nations Interim Force in Lebanon (UNIFIL) was extended three times, in January, July and October.

Armed incidents and military activity

Communications (February-September). On 16 February 1983,[12] Egypt transmitted excerpts from a statement by its Deputy Prime Minister before the National Security Committee, the Committee on Foreign Relations and the Committee on Arab Affairs of the People's Assembly, expressing concern at Israeli measures being taken against Palestinians in southern Lebanon.

Mongolia, on 18 May,[13] transmitted a statement of 16 May by its Ministry of Foreign Affairs condemning actions of the Israeli military against the Lebanese people and criticizing United States–Israeli proposals for peace with Lebanon, saying they were in fact a gross violation of Lebanon's sovereignty and would lead to that country's dismemberment, transforming it into a United States–Israeli military base.

Concern over the situation in Lebanon was expressed at two meetings of the heads of State and Government of EC (Brussels, Belgium, 22 March; Stuttgart, Federal Republic of Germany, 19 June). In March, they reaffirmed their support for a sovereign and independent Lebanon and for its Government, and called for re-establishment of its unrestricted authority over the whole of its territory. They expressed support for United States efforts to achieve that objective, as well as for the peace-keeping role of the United Nations and multinational forces, and called on all concerned to conclude negotiations without further delay. In June, they called for the complete and prompt withdrawal of foreign forces, except for those whose presence was requested by the Lebanese Government, as a pre-condition for restoring full sovereignty and final peace in Lebanon. In their view, the signing of an Israel-Lebanon agreement on 17 May was a step to be followed by others; they considered, however, that peace would not become a reality unless the security and legitimate interests of the other States and peoples of the region were taken into account. These conclusions were transmitted by the Federal Republic of Germany in letters of 24 March[14] and 22 June.[15]

On 2 September,[16] Lebanon transmitted a letter of the same date from its Minister for Foreign Affairs and Emigration to the Secretary-General of the League of Arab States informing him of Israel's decision to withdraw in the next few days its troops from parts of Mount Lebanon and asking for help in securing the withdrawal of all non-Lebanese forces from Lebanese territory.

By a letter of 9 September,[17] Lebanon stated that since 2 September military action had been escalating and the Lebanese army had had to intervene so as to protect its own positions, maintain law and order in greater Beirut, open international lines of communication and protect the civilian population in various localities from armed elements controlled and directed from abroad. Shelling had been extensive and had spared neither Beirut nor localities in Mount Lebanon. Casualties had been numerous and destruction enormous. The efforts by the League of Arab States, the United Nations and many friendly Governments had not enabled Lebanon to restore its sovereignty and authority over all of its territory, or to prevent the resurgence of hostilities. Stressing that that situation could not be allowed to continue without endangering international peace and security and imperilling its fate, Lebanon urged the Security Council to declare a cease-fire and take whatever measures deemed necessary to implement it, in accordance with the Charter.

On 13 September,[18] the Libyan Arab Jamahiriya transmitted a letter from its head of State stating that the situation in Lebanon had become so explosive as to make peace and security almost impossible; the situation was being aggravated by the internationalization of the conflict and the introduction of extraneous parties under the name of peace-keeping forces from France, the United States and other countries.

Reports of the Secretary-General (September). On 5 September, the Secretary-General reported to the Security Council on the situation in the Beirut area.[19] On the basis of information from the Observer Group Beirut (OGB)—50 United Nations military observers deployed by the Council in August 1982[20] at the request of Lebanon and set up as an arm of the United Nations Truce Supervision Organization (UNTSO) to monitor the situation following intensification of military activities in and around Beirut—he summarized developments relating to the withdrawal of the Israel Defence Forces (IDF) from the area.

Preparations for the withdrawal of IDF had been observed by OGB from late July 1983, and an increasing number of convoys had been noted on the Beirut-Damascus highway, consisting largely of trucks carrying accommodation and heavy equipment, water tanks and stores. On 3 September, OGB had observed heavy IDF traffic moving west on the highway and south towards Khalde and

Damur. That evening, Israeli forces with tanks and armoured personnel carriers had closed off and secured various road junctions in eastern and southern Beirut. No IDF traffic had been observed on the Damascus highway after dawn on 4 September. Early that morning, OGB heard jet aircraft overhead, and it had been reported that IDF had also used other routes to the south. After IDF movement ceased, OGB patrols had sought to verify the situation. Although their task had been made extremely difficult by the hostilities which immediately developed, OGB had been able to confirm that IDF check-points on the main roads around Beirut had been removed.

In the early hours of 4 September, intensive mortar, artillery and automatic weapons fire began east, north and south of Beirut, and in particular on and around the Beirut-Damascus highway. OGB teams observed armed groups operating in some of those areas, especially on the Ridge Line between Alayh and Suq Al-Gharb, in the Shouf mountains. During the daylight hours on 4 September, the north-western edge of the Shouf overlooking Beirut was engulfed by smoke and artillery fire. Similarly, the town of Khalde, to the south of Beirut, was also largely obscured by smoke and fire. Artillery fire from the north and north-east of Beirut continued throughout the evening and night of 4/5 September, the principal targets being Beit Meri, Broummana, Dazi, the western area of Beirut International Airport, Babdun, Aynas and Aley. On the morning of 5 September, heavy shelling was noted around the headquarters of the Lebanese army at Yarze. OGB had not observed any change in deployment of the multinational force, which had come under occasional fire.

OGB had also closely observed the Palestine refugee camps in the Sabra and Shatila areas, where the atmosphere had remained calm, although they were hit by some shells on 5 September.

OGB had maintained close liaison with the Lebanese army, which had deployed throughout Beirut during the preceding week. On 4 September, OGB observed the movement of Lebanese army units, under fire from armed groups, towards Khalde. That evening, OGB was informed that the army had entered Khalde, sustaining light casualties, and had also moved troops and equipment east on the Beirut-Damascus highway.

In his report on the situation in the Middle East, submitted to the Council and the General Assembly on 30 September,[21] the Secretary-General stated that, following the June 1982 Israeli invasion of Lebanon,[22] which had radically altered the situation in which UNIFIL had to function, the Security Council had instructed the Force, as interim tasks, to maintain its positions in its area of deployment and to provide protection and humanitarian assistance to the local population to the extent possible.[23] With the Council's approval, UNIFIL continued to carry out these interim tasks.

The Secretary-General reported that, following the Israeli withdrawal from the Beirut area, fighting had broken out in some areas evacuated by those forces. On 8 September 1983, he had appealed to all concerned to support efforts to achieve a cease-fire and to help restore national unity with the participation and co-operation of all the Lebanese parties. He had also asked the United Nations Co-ordinator of Assistance for the Reconstruction and Development of Lebanon to try to alleviate the suffering of the afflicted people in the area and to help provide them with emergency humanitarian assistance (see ECONOMIC AND SOCIAL QUESTIONS, Chapter III). He had further instructed OGB to continue to follow closely the events in the area and to facilitate such efforts.

Concluding his 5 September report, the Secretary-General stated that, throughout the preceding several days, shells had impacted close to OGB headquarters and its teams had been compelled to limit their patrols, but had been instructed to maintain, to the extent possible, intensified patrolling activity; though being small in numbers and unarmed, the observers were an important independent source of information and their presence represented the concern of the international community.

SECURITY COUNCIL CONSIDERATION (September)

As requested by Lebanon on 9 September,[17] the Security Council convened on 12 September to consider the escalating military action. Lebanon, at its request, was invited to participate in the discussion without the right to vote.

Speaking before the Council, Lebanon again called for a cease-fire, an immediate and effective cessation of all hostilities and the withdrawal of all illegitimate foreign forces. This call was repeated in a draft resolution it submitted to the Council,[24] by which the Council would also have called on all parties to refrain from all acts that violated Lebanon's sovereignty and territorial integrity and endangered its people's safety and unity. It would have authorized the Secretary-General to deploy immediately, in consultation with the Lebanese Government, United Nations observers to monitor the situation, and would have requested all parties to co-operate fully with the observers. The Council would have called on all involved to facilitate the activities of ICRC, the United Nations Co-ordinator of Assistance for the Reconstruction and Development of Lebanon, and United Nations agencies, and to enable them to evacuate the dead and wounded and provide food, medical supplies and humanitarian assistance. It would have called on all States and parties to sup-

port Lebanon in its efforts to ensure the complete and immediate withdrawal of all non-Lebanese forces whose presence did not have the Government's approval. The Secretary-General would have been requested urgently to initiate consultations on additional steps, including possible deployment of United Nations forces, to assist the Government in ensuring peace and public order and securing the full protection of civilians in all areas of hostilities, and to report to the Council on the implementation of the resolution within 72 hours.

As the Council did not act on the draft, Lebanon, by a letter of 19 September,[25] voiced concern that the Council should have been unable, with a tragedy of such magnitude, to respond with a positive contribution to peace in Lebanon. It expressed the hope that the draft would be submitted to a vote at an appropriate time when a positive response was likely or if any Council members felt that further action was necessary in the light of new developments.

Communications (November). On 8 November,[26] the USSR transmitted a TASS statement of 4 November accusing the United States of intending to conduct a large-scale military operation in Lebanon.

On 9 November,[27] the Libyan Arab Jamahiriya transmitted a letter of the same date from its head of State stating that the multinational forces in Lebanon had completed their task and their continued presence only aggravated the already dangerous situation there.

By a letter of 11 November,[28] Iran rejected United States accusations that in October Iran had destroyed the headquarters of the United States Marines in Beirut; those accusations, it said, were a premeditated move to confuse the situation in the region and divert world public opinion from the discontent of the Lebanese people regarding the presence of those forces in their country.

SECURITY COUNCIL ACTION (November)

At two meetings on 11 November, the Security Council, in resuming consideration of the Secretary-General's 12 October report[29] on UNIFIL (see below), returned to the situation in Lebanon. The Council invited Israel, Lebanon, the Sudan and the Syrian Arab Republic, at their request, to participate in the discussion without the right to vote.

At the start of the second meeting, the President made the following statement on behalf of the Council members:[30]

"The members of the Security Council wish to express their profound concern at the recent and current developments in northern Lebanon which have caused and are still causing widespread suffering and loss of human life. The members appeal to all parties concerned to exercise the utmost restraint and seek freely to attain, and to respect, an immediate cessation of hostilities, to settle their differences exclusively by peaceful means and to refrain from the threat or use of force. The members of the Council highly appreciate the work of the United Nations Relief and Works Agency for Palestine Refugees in the Near East and of the International Committee of the Red Cross in providing emergency humanitarian assistance to Palestinian and Lebanese civilians in and around the city of Tripoli. The members of the Council will continue to follow the situation in Lebanon with the greatest attention."

During the Council's discussions, the USSR alleged that Israel, jointly with the United States, was preparing for new aggression in the Near East and a large-scale military operation in Lebanon, thus further exacerbating tension there. Public threats and a new campaign of provocation against the Syrian Arab Republic were being accompanied by an unprecedented concentration of the United States fleet near the coast of Lebanon; the United States intended further to extend its area of interference, in co-operation with the Israeli aggressor which had firmly entrenched itself on Lebanese soil.

The Syrian Arab Republic also stressed that those provocations presaged joint aggression against it, its forces and Lebanon, threatening regional and international security. Israel had isolated southern Lebanon from the rest of the country, thus putting the final touches on its expansionist schemes. With regard to its forces in Lebanon, the Syrian Arab Republic stated that they would not be withdrawn until the last Israeli soldier had been withdrawn unconditionally, and the independence and unity of Lebanon, as an integral part of the Arab nation, had been guaranteed. It also called for withdrawal of the multinational forces from Lebanon and for a rejection of the 17 May agreement imposed on Lebanon under the shadow of occupation.

Rejecting the allegations, the United States said its forces were in Lebanon at the invitation of the Lebanese Government and would remain there until their tasks were discharged; their purpose, along with the forces of three other countries, was to assist that Government in rebuilding its domestic institutions and in extending its sovereignty throughout its territory, which must ultimately involve the withdrawal of all non-Lebanese forces.

Lebanon stated that it held firm to its sovereignty, independence and territorial integrity and to the unity of its people. The events taking place on Lebanese territory were proof that the war that had been raging for nine years was not internal, but one of regional ambitions and conflicting international interests. Confirming that the multinational forces, UNIFIL and the international observers were present at its request, Lebanon reiterated its determination to ensure the withdrawal

of all unauthorized non-Lebanese forces, with the Council being called on to assist.

Israel stated that, since the 18 October Council meeting on UNIFIL (see below), large-scale killings had taken place in Lebanon, affecting primarily innocent civilians; however, when Arabs were killing Arabs, the United Nations had been informed by various Arab representatives over the years that it should not become interested in such events since they were "family affairs". With regard to the 17 May agreement it had signed with Lebanon, Israel pointed out that it provided for full Israeli withdrawal to the international boundary between the two countries, within the context of the agreement and subject to the fulfilment of all its provisions.

In Jordan's view, Israel, in its statement, had avoided the main problem that was threatening international peace and security—it did not respect the Council and its decisions.

At a meeting on 23 November, urgently requested by France in a letter of 22 November,[31] the Council unanimously adopted resolution 542(1983), prepared during Council consultations.

The Security Council,

Having considered the situation prevailing in northern Lebanon,

Recalling the statement made on this question by the President of the Security Council on 11 November 1983,

Deeply concerned by the intensification of the fighting, which continues to cause great suffering and loss of human life,

1. *Deplores* the loss of human life caused by the events taking place in northern Lebanon;

2. *Reiterates its call* for the strict respect for the sovereignty, political independence and territorial integrity of Lebanon within its internationally recognized boundaries;

3. *Requests* the parties concerned immediately to accept a cease-fire and scrupulously to observe the cessation of hostilities;

4. *Invites* the parties concerned to settle their differences exclusively by peaceful means and to refrain from the threat or use of force;

5. *Pays tribute* to the work done by the United Nations Relief and Works Agency for Palestine Refugees in the Near East and by the International Committee of the Red Cross in providing emergency humanitarian assistance to the Palestinian and Lebanese civilians in Tripoli and its surroundings;

6. *Calls upon* the parties concerned to comply with the provisions of the present resolution;

7. *Requests* the Secretary-General to follow the situation in northern Lebanon, to consult with the Government of Lebanon, and to report to the Security Council, which remains seized of the question.

Security Council resolution 542(1983)

23 November 1983   Meeting 2501   Adopted unanimously

Draft prepared in consultations among Council members (S/16179).
Meeting numbers. SC 2475, 2495, 2496, 2501.

As requested by the Council, the Secretary-General reported on 21 December[32] that, on 26 November, a cease-fire agreement had been reached by the parties involved in recent fighting in the Tripoli area and that, on 20 December, PLO Chairman Yasser Arafat and his troops had been evacuated from Tripoli (see below).

Communications (December). On 4 December,[33] the Syrian Arab Republic transmitted a letter of the same date from its Deputy Prime Minister and Minister for Foreign Affairs, complaining of an escalation of military operations by the United States in northern Lebanon and requesting measures to halt hostile United States policy in Lebanon and the Middle East.

Also on 4 December,[34] the United States said that aircraft from its Sixth Fleet had that day carried out air strikes against Syrian anti-aircraft concentrations which had been the source of attacks against United States aircraft on 3 December.

The Syrian Arab Republic replied on 6 December[35] that the air strikes against the positions of its troops in Lebanon had not been carried out in self-defence but were an act of aggression.

On the same date,[36] the USSR transmitted a TASS statement of 5 December condemning the United States 4 December raid.

On 9 December,[37] Viet Nam transmitted a statement of 8 December by the spokesman for its Foreign Ministry, condemning the escalation of United States military operations in Lebanon and the Middle East, carried out as part of a United States–Israel joint plan to bring pressure on Arab countries in the hope of compelling them to accept a solution detrimental to their interests and to the national interests of the Palestinians.

On 12 December,[38] Bulgaria transmitted a declaration of the Bulgarian Telegraph Agency, charging the United States with trying, through its air raid, to force the Lebanese people to accept the Israel-Lebanon agreement, which ran counter to the Lebanese people's interests, and to establish favourable conditions for open armed aggression against the Syrian Arab Republic.

GENERAL ASSEMBLY ACTION

The General Assembly, in resolution 38/17 of 22 November 1983, strongly condemned the massacre of Palestinians and other civilians at Beirut, as well as the Israeli aggression against Lebanon, as endangering stability, peace and security in the region. In resolution 38/83 I of 15 December, on protection of Palestine refugees, the Assembly dealt also with the Palestinian refugees in Lebanon. (For texts of these resolutions, refer to INDEX OF RESOLUTIONS AND DECISIONS.)

Other action. The Commission on Human Rights, on 7 March 1983,[39] adopted a resolution on persons detained by Israel during the conflict in Lebanon. (See also above, under PERSONS DETAINED BY ISRAEL, and ECONOMIC AND SOCIAL QUESTIONS, Chapter XVIII.)

PLO troop withdrawal

Late in December 1983, PLO forces were evacuated from Lebanon.

SECURITY COUNCIL ACTION

In a statement[40] made during consultations of the Security Council on 3 December 1983, the Secretary-General indicated that, on humanitarian grounds, he had authorized the flying of the United Nations flag alongside the national flag of the ships which were to evacuate the armed PLO elements, numbering some 4,000, from Tripoli. The Lebanese Government, which had been fully consulted, had no objection to that practice.

Also on 3 December, the Council President made the following statement:[41]

"With reference to the statement made public by the Secretary-General today, and after consultations with the members of the Council, I confirm, as President of the Security Council, that his statement has the support of the members of the Council."

Communications. By a letter of 7 December,[42] Israel pointed out that responsibility for a bomb explosion on a passenger bus on 6 December at Jerusalem (see above, under JERUSALEM) was claimed by PLO Chairman Yasser Arafat. In this connection, it recalled that Arafat had asked that the United Nations flag be put at his disposal, supposedly on humanitarian grounds, to enable him and his terrorists to escape from Tripoli and that the Security Council had acceded to his request.

On 8 December,[43] Israel transmitted a message of the same date from its Prime Minister to the Secretary-General requesting that he cancel the arrangements to give PLO safe conduct under the United Nations flag, in view of the bomb explosion, for which PLO had claimed responsibility.

By a letter of 17 December,[44] France announced that, in agreement with the Greek Government, it had decided to assist in the evacuation of Palestinian fighters from Tripoli to Yemen and Tunisia.

On 21 December,[45] Greece stated that, as requested by the PLO Chairman and for humanitarian reasons, it had made five vessels available for the evacuation of PLO forces from Tripoli on 20 December. The operation had been carried out in collaboration with France, after consultations with the other Governments concerned, specifically Israel, Italy, Lebanon, the Syrian Arab Republic, the United Kingdom and the United States. The Greek vessels had flown the United Nations flag in addition to the national flag throughout the operation.

By a letter of 23 December,[46] Israel stated that the escape of Yasser Arafat and his troops from Tripoli without assurances that they would abandon the path of terror should be viewed as a dangerous precedent by all those committed to combating international terrorism.

Report of the Secretary-General. As requested by the Security Council in resolution 542(1983) of 23 November (see above), the Secretary-General reported on 21 December[32] that, on 20 December, the United Nations Co-ordinator of Assistance for the Reconstruction and Development of Lebanon and Special Representative of the Secretary-General had received confirmation that Yasser Arafat and his PLO forces had that day sailed from Tripoli in five Greek ships escorted by French naval units. The Greek ships had flown the Greek and United Nations flags and, in the territorial waters of Lebanon, the Lebanese flag. The evacuation had proceeded without incident. On 17 December, 94 seriously wounded PLO armed elements had left for Larnaca, Cyprus, on an Italian ship under the auspices of ICRC.

With regard to the Israeli Prime Minister's 8 December request to cancel the arrangements to give PLO safe conduct under the United Nations flag, the Secretary-General stated that he had not been able to accede to that request since the humanitarian reasons on which his decision was based had remained valid; he had been informed by the Permanent Observer of PLO that on 8 December Arafat had publicly stated that PLO opposed and strongly condemned any action against civilians.

Peace-keeping operation

UNIFIL activities

During 1983, the Security Council extended the mandate of the United Nations Interim Force in Lebanon three times, in January, July and October—by resolutions 529(1983), 536(1983) and 538(1983), respectively—as had been recommended by the Secretary-General in his reports on the activities of the Force. UNIFIL had been established by the Council in 1978.[47]

Report of the Secretary-General (January). In a report of 13 January,[48] the Secretary-General described the activities of UNIFIL since the previous extension of the Force's mandate in October 1982.[49] He stated that UNIFIL had continued to carry out its interim humanitarian and administrative tasks endorsed by the Council[23] after the June 1982 Israeli invasion of Lebanon, and to do its best to maintain peace and order in its area of deployment and prevent activities likely to militate against a peaceful atmosphere. Stressing that it was essential that armed incursions, harassment, arbitrary arrests and other such activities did not

occur, he reported that with the assistance of UNIFIL and the Lebanese battalion attached to it, the Lebanese gendarmerie was playing an increasingly active role in maintaining law and order in the UNIFIL area.

The Secretary-General emphasized that UNIFIL would be able to hand over its responsibilities to the Lebanese authorities only after the withdrawal of all foreign forces from Lebanon. When current negotiations concerning such withdrawal were completed, it would be possible to define in detail UNIFIL's future role. A withdrawal of UNIFIL before the Lebanese Government was in a position to take over with its own security forces would have grave consequences and would be a serious blow to the early restoration of the Government's authority in southern Lebanon, and could lead to violent incidents between the various factions in the UNIFIL area, which would once again jeopardize the safety of the civilian population. In the mean time, UNIFIL's presence was an important factor in ensuring the well-being and prosperity of the civilian population in the area.

For those reasons, the Secretary-General recommended an extension of UNIFIL's mandate, mentioning in that context that Israel had expressed the view that the Force should not be extended for more than two or three months.

Annexed to the report was a letter of 13 January 1983, by which Lebanon asked that UNIFIL's zone of operation be extended to the whole of Lebanese territory for the purpose of confirming the withdrawal of all non-Lebanese forces and armed elements from Lebanon, restoring international peace and security and assisting the Government in re-establishing its effective authority. Lebanon emphasized that it did not wish or envisage any involvement of UNIFIL in any conflict between armed Lebanese elements; it sought a UNIFIL role which would support the Lebanese army in restoring government authority throughout the country.

SECURITY COUNCIL ACTION (January)

The Security Council, by resolution 529(1983) of 18 January, extended UNIFIL's mandate for six months.

The Security Council,

Recalling its resolutions 425(1978) and 426(1978), and all subsequent resolutions on the United Nations Interim Force in Lebanon,

Recalling further its resolutions 508(1982) and 509(1982),

Having taken note of the letter of the Permanent Representative of Lebanon to the President of the Security Council and to the Secretary-General of 13 January 1983, and of the statement he made at the 2411th meeting of the Council,

Having studied the report of the Secretary-General and taking note of his observations,

Responding to the request of the Government of Lebanon,

1. *Decides* to extend the present mandate of the United Nations Interim Force in Lebanon for a further interim period of six months, that is, until 19 July 1983;

2. *Calls upon* all parties concerned to co-operate with the Force for the full implementation of the present resolution;

3. *Requests* the Secretary-General to report to the Security Council on the progress made in this respect.

Security Council resolution 529(1983)

18 January 1983	Meeting 2411	13-0-2

Draft by Jordan (S/15564).
Meeting number. SC 2411.
Vote in Council as follows:

In favour: China, France, Guyana, Jordan, Malta, Netherlands, Nicaragua, Pakistan, Togo, United Kingdom, United States, Zaire, Zimbabwe.
Against: None.
Abstaining: Poland, USSR.

Prior to the vote, the President, with the consent of the Council, invited Israel, Lebanon and the Syrian Arab Republic, at their request, to participate in the discussion without the right to vote. Following adoption of the resolution, the Secretary-General stated that he would do his utmost to make UNIFIL's presence as effective as possible in carrying out its interim tasks. In particular, he said, UNIFIL would assist the Lebanese Government in assuring the security of all inhabitants of its area without discrimination, and would try to prevent local armed groups from operating there unless authorized by the Central Government. He pointed out that, with the departure of the Nigerian contingent in January 1983 and the detailing of 482 men of the French infantry battalion to the multinational force in Beirut,[50] UNIFIL was well below its authorized strength of 7,000.

Lebanon believed that extending UNIFIL's mandate for six months would give it a stability it could not enjoy in a shorter time and allow it to carry out the tasks awaiting it. Reaffirming its 13 January request with regard to UNIFIL's role, Lebanon said it went along with the draft which had been submitted and thus relinquished its initial request in the light of the existing situation, as it wished to facilitate the Council's task and enable it unanimously to extend UNIFIL's mandate, which must not be interrupted or renewed in a spirit of resignation.

Jordan said UNIFIL remained essential in the implementation of the two main purposes for which it had been formed: to ensure the withdrawal of the invading Israeli forces and enable the Lebanese Government to exercise full sovereignty over its territory. In view of Israel's practices in Lebanon, which sought to prolong the Lebanese ordeal and contributed to depriving the country of its sovereignty and independence, and its attempts to prevent UNIFIL from discharging its responsibilities, Jordan considered it necessary for the Council to denounce those practices and

adopt all measures to implement the purposes of the United Nations Charter in order to deter the aggressor and preserve international peace and security.

The Netherlands said that UNIFIL was still a stabilizing element in southern Lebanon; its withdrawal could have grave consequences and be a set-back for the Lebanese Government's efforts to restore peace and reassert its authority. The Netherlands urgently called on Israel to respect UNIFIL's mandate and stop hindering it from performing its duties. Only when the negotiations in progress on the withdrawal of all foreign forces or armed elements from Lebanon were completed, the Netherlands said, would it be possible to define the future role of UNIFIL as envisaged by Lebanon; the Netherlands could not accept any new UNIFIL mandate in which the peace-keeping operations of the Force were not clearly defined and it was of the opinion that any new mandate should be directed to restoring Lebanon's sovereignty and territorial integrity. Based on the belief that a Lebanon once again restored to prosperity and peace with all its neighbours would also advance peace and security in the Middle East, the Netherlands said it would continue its participation in UNIFIL.

Israel emphasized that the resolution did not change UNIFIL's mandate, subject, however, to the Secretary-General's observation in his October 1982 report on UNIFIL[51] in which he stated that the events in Lebanon had radically altered the circumstances in which UNIFIL was established and under which it had functioned since March 1978;[47] in the new circumstances, UNIFIL had outlived its usefulness and its presence was no longer called for in southern Lebanon. Israel believed that security arrangements should be arrived at through the ongoing negotiations between the two countries which were also aimed at ensuring that Lebanon's sovereignty and territorial integrity would be restored within its internationally recognized boundaries, while at the same time permanently precluding the possibility of hostile action against Israel and its citizens from Lebanese soil.

The United States believed that the renewal of UNIFIL's mandate reaffirmed international support for the goal of restoring the Lebanese Government's sovereignty throughout its territory and of securing the withdrawal of all external forces, and that it was a positive element in negotiations between the Government and other parties in the Middle East. It was not yet possible, however, to define precisely the role UNIFIL might be called upon to play in the arrangements under negotiation.

The USSR pointed out that references to resolutions 508(1982)[52] and 509(1982),[53] demanding an end to all military actions in Lebanon and immediate and unconditional Israeli withdrawal, were contained in all Council decisions extending UNIFIL's mandate since June 1982. It was the Council's duty to strive for implementation of those decisions, and it would be inadmissible to depart from previous decisions on the necessity of unconditional withdrawal of the Israeli forces whose presence in Lebanon could not be equated with that of Arab forces under an agreement with the Lebanese Government and in keeping with decisions taken at pan-Arab meetings. It would be illegal to give United Nations forces unaccustomed functions which might lead to their interfering in the internal affairs of Lebanon in contravention of the United Nations Charter.

Nicaragua hoped the resolution would be a positive element in consolidating the role of the United Nations with regard to the Middle East and would lead to alleviating or halting the sufferings of the peoples of Palestine and Lebanon.

Pakistan considered the presence of UNIFIL a critical factor in restoring peace and tranquillity.

Malta hoped that the negotiations under way would reap rapid and positive results and that Israel would start its overdue troop withdrawal.

In Zimbabwe's view, the continuation of Israel's occupation of Lebanon in defiance of the Council's decisions and the presence and activities of its troops made the extension of UNIFIL's mandate necessary.

Report of the Secretary-General (July). In his report to the Council covering UNIFIL activities from 19 January to 12 July 1983,[54] the Secretary-General stated that during the six months under review the UNIFIL area of deployment had been generally quiet. UNIFIL had continued to operate its check-points and to patrol its area, with a view to contributing to maintaining order and ensuring the security of the population. It had continued its interim tasks, protecting and assisting the local population.

After the 1982 invasion, he reported, the capability of UNIFIL to achieve its objectives had been contingent on the co-operation of the Israeli authorities controlling the area. A major problem had been the increased activities of local groups, armed and uniformed by Israel, whose activities led to a number of incidents involving UNIFIL, the worst of which had resulted in the death of a Fijian soldier on 29 May 1983.

The report pointed out that UNIFIL had continued to co-operate with the Lebanese authorities as well as UNRWA, the United Nations Children's Fund (UNICEF) and ICRC in assisting the local population, particularly in implementing vaccination programmes, health and hygiene surveys and training activities. During the reporting period, the UNIFIL hospital in Naqoura had treated more than 4,000 patients.

The Secretary-General observed that, despite the difficulties encountered by the Force, its presence in southern Lebanon was generally recognized as an important element of stability. The situation in the UNIFIL area had been comparatively less tense and disturbed than elsewhere in the region, and the population of the area was increasing and its economy prospering. However, in the existing circumstances, UNIFIL's activities were inevitably in the nature of a holding action, pending further developments and decisions of the Security Council.

Although, as a result of the Israeli invasion, the circumstances under which the Force was established had been radically altered, the task of assisting the Lebanese Government in ensuring the return of its effective authority in southern Lebanon remained especially relevant. A withdrawal of UNIFIL from its area before the Government could assume effective control would be a serious blow to the prospect of an early restoration of the Government's authority in southern Lebanon, as well as to the welfare of the inhabitants. For these reasons, the Secretary-General considered it essential that UNIFIL's mandate be extended on an interim basis for a three-month period, as requested by Lebanon in a letter of 5 July.[55]

SECURITY COUNCIL ACTION (July)

The mandate of UNIFIL was extended for a further three months by the Security Council when it adopted resolution 536(1983) on 18 July.

The Security Council,

Having heard the statement of the Minister for Foreign Affairs of the Republic of Lebanon,

Recalling its resolutions 425(1978) and 426(1978), and all subsequent resolutions on the United Nations Interim Force in Lebanon,

Recalling further its resolutions 508(1982), 509(1982) and 520(1982), as well as all its other resolutions on the situation in Lebanon,

Reiterating its strong support for the territorial integrity, sovereignty and political independence of Lebanon within its internationally recognized boundaries,

Having taken note of the letter of the Permanent Representative of Lebanon to the President of the Security Council of 5 July 1983,

Having studied the report of the Secretary-General and taking note of his observations and recommendation expressed therein,

Responding to the request of the Government of Lebanon,

1. *Decides* to extend the present mandate of the United Nations Interim Force in Lebanon for a further interim period of three months, that is, until 19 October 1983;

2. *Calls upon* all parties concerned to co-operate with the Force for the full implementation of its mandate as defined in resolutions 425(1978) and 426(1978) and the relevant decisions of the Security Council;

3. *Requests* the Secretary-General to report to the Council on the progress made in this respect.

Security Council resolution 536(1983)

18 July 1983   Meeting 2456   13-0-2

Draft prepared in consultations among Council members (S/15871).
Meeting number. SC 2456.
Vote in Council as follows:
    In favour: China, France, Guyana, Jordan, Malta, Netherlands, Nicaragua, Paki-
    stan, Togo, United Kingdom, United States, Zaire, Zimbabwe.
    Against: None.
    Abstaining: Poland, USSR.

Prior to the resolution's adoption, the President, with the consent of the Council, invited Lebanon, at its request, to participate in the discussion without the right to vote.

Lebanon said it was not requesting a change in the nature of UNIFIL's mandate or a new redeployment by asking the Council to renew the Force's mandate for another interim period of three months, during which it hoped that war and destruction would end. By sending troops to serve with UNIFIL, Lebanon had met the commitments required of it by the Council. In addition, it had explored all possibilities to ensure total withdrawal of all unauthorized foreign forces from the country, and was exerting maximum efforts to build a strong army, reform public institutions, maintain internal unity and lay the foundations of a stable and strong State. Lebanon needed the concerted attention of the Council to enable it to disengage from the vortex of political conflicts in the region and thus save not only itself but also the cause of peace in the Middle East. Though the problems facing Lebanon were clearly greater than those addressed by a renewal of UNIFIL's mandate, the Council, by its renewal, would reaffirm its commitment to Lebanon's independence, sovereignty and unity.

The United States also felt that renewal of the mandate would be a reaffirmation of that commitment and one of securing the withdrawal of all unauthorized external forces.

France fully supported Lebanon's request and the Government's attempts to restore its authority throughout the whole of its territory. Expressing concern over the situation of the civilian population—in particular the Palestinians—in Lebanon, especially in the southern part, France urgently appealed to Israel not to limit UNIFIL's opportunities for action.

According to the USSR, the United States and Israel were striving to impose on Lebanon conditions for a settlement aimed at turning the country into an American-Israeli protectorate. A settlement could not be achieved through separate deals such as the one-sided agreement signed on 17 May 1983 or arm-twisting, but by strict compliance with the Council's demands for unconditional Israeli withdrawal. Israel was continuing to provoke incidents with UNIFIL personnel, posing a threat to their life and security. These acts were a violation of previous Council decisions, partic-

ularly resolution 523(1982),[49] which insisted that there should be no interference under any pretext with the operations of UNIFIL and that it should have full freedom of movement in discharging its mandate; it was the Council's duty to ensure respect for its decisions. In the light of the Secretary-General's recommendations and Lebanon's request for renewal of UNIFIL's mandate, and bearing in mind that the goals and functions of UNIFIL would continue to be determined by the 1978 mandate[47] and subsequent Council decisions, the USSR did not object to an extension.

The Netherlands believed that UNIFIL still had a stabilizing effect and played a useful humanitarian role, and its presence indicated that it might be available for duties connected with a future Israeli withdrawal from Lebanon as provided for in the May agreement between the two countries. However, implementation of the agreement was still very much in doubt, for, in order to attain Lebanon's objective that all external forces withdraw from its territory as soon as possible, the co-operation of all concerned was necessary. Bearing in mind that UNIFIL had for more than a year been largely prevented from carrying out its tasks and that it was not likely that it would be able to assume useful functions in the future, the Netherlands concluded that prolongation of UNIFIL based on the current mandate should not be indefinite. Barring entirely new circumstances that would enable it to reconsider its position, the Netherlands said its battalion would be withdrawn from Lebanon as of 19 October.

The United Kingdom believed that the Force was no longer carrying out a conventional or traditional United Nations peace-keeping role; however, it was playing a helpful, protective and humanitarian role. The United Kingdom expressed concern that the troop contributors were being asked to undertake something different from the conventional peace-keeping role, and to do so in difficult and dangerous conditions. It believed that to withdraw UNIFIL would be to remove an element of stability in Lebanon.

Report of the Secretary-General (October). On 12 October,[29] the Secretary-General reported that, during the three months since his 12 July report,[54] the UNIFIL area had continued to be generally quiet and UNIFIL activities had remained essentially unchanged. Events in the Aley and Shouf regions had had no direct impact on the UNIFIL area of deployment, except for an influx of displaced persons from those regions. UNIFIL had continued to carry out its interim tasks, protecting and assisting the local population and trying to prevent activities likely to hamper the restoration of the Lebanese Government's authority in the area. In addition, UNIFIL had continued to co-operate with UNRWA, UNICEF and ICRC.

The activities of local groups armed and uniformed by the Israeli forces had been limited and, with UNIFIL assistance, the Lebanese internal security forces had continued to play an active part in maintaining law and order in the area.

Despite the circumstances, the Secretary-General stated, UNIFIL remained an important stabilizing element in southern Lebanon, its presence also representing the United Nations commitment to support Lebanon's independence, sovereignty and territorial integrity and to help bring about the withdrawal of the Israeli forces. A withdrawal of UNIFIL before the Lebanese national army and security forces were in a position to assume effective control of the area, he added, would seriously harm the prospect of restoring the Lebanese Government's authority there, as well as the security and welfare of the population. It was particularly important to avoid such a development at a time when the Lebanese Government and people, following the recent cease-fire in the Aley and Shouf regions, were exerting their best efforts for national reconciliation.

After quoting a 10 October letter from Lebanon requesting that the UNIFIL mandate be extended for a further six months, the Secretary-General recommended to the Security Council that the mandate be extended for another interim period, stressing the need for all parties to co-operate with the Force in performing its task.

SECURITY COUNCIL ACTION (October)

The Security Council, by resolution 538(1983) of 18 October, extended UNIFIL's mandate for six months, until 19 April 1984.

The Security Council,

Having heard the statement of the representative of Lebanon,

Recalling its resolutions 425(1978) and 426(1978) and all subsequent resolutions on the United Nations Interim Force in Lebanon,

Recalling further its resolutions 508(1982), 509(1982) and 520(1982), as well as all its other resolutions on the situation in Lebanon,

Reiterating its strong support for the territorial integrity, sovereignty and political independence of Lebanon within its internationally recognized boundaries,

Having studied the report of the Secretary-General on the United Nations Interim Force in Lebanon and taking note of the conclusions and recommendations expressed therein,

Taking note of the letter of the Permanent Representative of Lebanon to the Secretary-General,

Responding to the request of the Government of Lebanon,

1. *Decides* to extend the present mandate of the United Nations Interim Force in Lebanon for a further interim period of six months, that is, until 19 April 1984;

2. *Calls upon* all parties concerned to co-operate fully with the Force for the full implementation of its mandate, as defined in resolutions 425(1978) and 426(1978) and the relevant decisions of the Security Council;

3. *Requests* the Secretary-General to report to the Council on the progress made in this respect.

Security Council resolution 538(1983)

18 October 1983	Meeting 2480	13-0-2

Draft prepared in consultations among Council members (S/16046).
Meeting number. SC 2480.
Vote in Council as follows:
In favour: China, France, Guyana, Jordan, Malta, Netherlands, Nicaragua, Pakistan, Togo, United Kingdom, United States, Zaire, Zimbabwe.
Against: None.
Abstaining: Poland, USSR.

Prior to the resolution's adoption, the President, with the consent of the Council, invited Israel, Lebanon and the Syrian Arab Republic, at their request, to participate in the discussion without the right to vote.

Lebanon said the presence of UNIFIL was a consecration of the United Nations commitment to the independence, sovereignty and territorial integrity of Lebanon and to the assurance of the withdrawal of Israeli forces from the south, and constituted a fundamental factor for stability in the region. Renewal of UNIFIL's mandate for a further six months would enable the Lebanese authorities to restore legitimacy in the south up to the internationally recognized boundaries and to find solutions to bring about the withdrawal of all unauthorized forces from all Lebanese territory.

The Netherlands said that, since the June 1982 Israeli invasion,[22] it had become practically impossible for UNIFIL to carry out its original mandate, and its capability to carry out its interim tasks was necessarily contingent on the co-operation of the Israeli authorities who, as the occupying Power, controlled the area. The situation in southern Lebanon had not changed to the extent that the original peace-keeping functions of UNIFIL might be restored within the foreseeable future. However, it still hoped that the Council, in agreement with the Lebanese Government, might devise a more meaningful role for UNIFIL. In view of these considerations, the Netherlands stated that it had decided not to withdraw from UNIFIL altogether as it had indicated in July (see above), but to retain a limited contingent; however, it must be recognized that the international community could not be expected to continue supporting Lebanon indefinitely.

France emphasized that Israel had not withdrawn from southern Lebanon and had an operational battalion in the UNIFIL zone; it hoped that this was only temporary and that there, as everywhere else in Lebanon, the country's unity, integrity and independence would be restored. It believed that the Council would be called upon to give UNIFIL, in addition to the missions it was already carrying out, new tasks in the area. The Force had demonstrated its usefulness by restoring security to the countryside; similarly, it seemed that the observers with UNTSO could be invited to carry out other missions in other areas.

The USSR believed the further extension of the UNIFIL mandate was testimony to the continuing explosive situation in Lebanon. Israel continued to occupy a considerable portion of Lebanese territory and its recent so-called redeployment of its forces was aimed essentially at long-term entrenchment along new lines and at the perpetuation of its occupation, and ultimately annexation, of southern Lebanon. Along with Israel, the so-called multinational force was consolidating its position; on the pretext of ensuring the defence of that interventionist corps, an armada of the United States and its allies of the North Atlantic Treaty Organization (NATO) was lying off the Lebanese coast. The USSR held it imperative that Israel withdraw unconditionally from Lebanon and that neither United States troops nor any foreign troops accompanying them remain on Lebanese soil. With regard to UNIFIL, the USSR agreed with the Secretary-General that, in the difficult circumstances of Israeli occupation, the Force remained an important element of stability in its area of operations.

The United Kingdom felt that it could not be right simply to continue extending the UNIFIL mandate without giving thought to how it could be updated to reflect the changed circumstances.

The Syrian Arab Republic believed that if the Council wished to carry out its duties towards the people of Lebanon, it must without delay fulfil its commitments under resolution 509(1982)[53] and put an end to any attempt to distort that resolution. There were serious attempts to put the Syrian forces, which were part of the Arab peace-keeping forces, on the same level as the Israeli invading forces; these attempts were rejected by Lebanon, the Syrian Arab Republic and the other Arabs, and they had already been rejected by the majority of the Council members.

Israel declared that it was determined to proceed towards implementing the May agreement aimed at restoring Lebanese sovereignty; however, it had now become clear that the Syrian Arab Republic and PLO had no intention of respecting that sovereignty. Israel's withdrawal from the Shouf mountains was a first step towards total withdrawal and had been announced well in advance to give the Lebanese Government and army a chance to extend their control. The Syrian Arab Republic and its proxies had prevented it from doing so, having turned Lebanon into a battleground, exploiting enmity between groups and encouraging all-out war. Israel hoped that the cessation of hostilities and the cease-fire would endure, leading to true recon-

ciliation free of outside intervention. Under no circumstances would Israel agree to return to the state of affairs prevailing 16 months previously, when Lebanese territory had been used as a base for terrorist operations against Israeli citizens.

Composition

As at 12 October 1983, the composition of UNIFIL was as follows:[29]

Infantry battalions	
Fiji	625
Finland	495
France	147
Ghana	550
Ireland	655
Netherlands	731
Norway	605
Senegal	559
Headquarters camp command	
Ghana	154
Ireland	83
Logistic units	
France	793
Italy	41
Norway	199
Sweden	143
	5,780

In addition, the Force was assisted by 73 unarmed military observers of UNTSO. The Lebanese army unit serving with UNIFIL to help maintain order in UNIFIL's area of operation was at a strength of 166 all ranks, following the transfer to Beirut in June of the greater part of the unit for training purposes.

Nigeria discontinued its participation in UNIFIL in January 1983. The French infantry battalion remained at reduced strength, in accordance with a temporary arrangement whereby the greater part of the battalion was released to the French authorities. The Norwegian battalion moved into the area vacated by the Nepalese battalion in November 1982.[50]

Following the departure of the Nigerian battalion, a readjustment of the areas of responsibilities of various units took place. The areas held by the Fijian, Finnish, Irish and Senegalese battalions were enlarged, and the reduced French infantry unit was deployed in the central sector of UNIFIL's area of operation. The military observers of UNTSO continued to man the five observation posts along the armistice demarcation line and to maintain teams at Tyre, Metulla and Château de Beaufort, in addition to four mobile teams.

Between 19 October 1982 and 12 October 1983, 13 members of the Force died, including four as a result of firing. Since UNIFIL's establishment in 1978, 96 members of the Force had died, 41 as a result of firing or mine explosions, 42 in accidents and 13 from natural causes. Also, some 120 had been wounded.

Financing

In December 1983, the General Assembly appropriated $159,421,666 gross ($157,640,833 net) for UNIFIL for the period 19 December 1982 to 18 December 1983. For UNIFIL operation from 19 December 1983 to 18 April 1984, the Assembly appropriated $46,964,000. For the period from 19 April to 18 December 1984, the Secretary-General was authorized to enter into commitments at a monthly rate of $11,741,000 gross ($11,581,000 net), should the Council decide to continue the Force's mandate and subject to the prior concurrence of the Advisory Committee on Administrative and Budgetary Questions (ACABQ).

The Assembly apportioned the expenses for the Force among all Member States in accordance with a special scale used for this purpose since the establishment of the Second United Nations Emergency Force (UNEF II) in 1973.[56] It again invited States to make voluntary contributions and requested the Secretary-General to ensure that UNIFIL be administered with a maximum of efficiency and economy.

The Assembly made these appropriations on the recommendation of ACABQ, which, in a November 1983 report, approved the Secretary-General's cost estimates contained in a report also submitted in November.

On 7 October,[57] the United Kingdom submitted a paper on the financing of United Nations peacekeeping operations, including UNIFIL. The United Kingdom stated that it shared the Secretary-General's concern that the shortfall in the UNIFIL Special Account could jeopardize the functioning of UNIFIL; it noted with particular regret that some members of the Special Committee on Peace-keeping Operations were among the States withholding contributions. In conclusion, the United Kingdom expressed the hope that Member States and in particular the Committee members would give priority to the question of the financing of peace-keeping operations and that States withholding contributions would reconsider their policy.

Report of the Secretary-General. In a 1 November report to the General Assembly,[58] the Secretary-General noted that as at 30 September, contributions totalling $610.7 million had been received for UNIFIL, out of $805.8 million apportioned among Member States for the periods from inception of the Force on 19 March 1978 to 18 October 1983. The balance due of $195.1 million included $154.4 million apportioned among Member States which had stated that they did not intend to pay and $19.5 million transferred to the UNIFIL Special Account. Accordingly, only $21.2 million of the unpaid balance could be considered collectible, leaving a shortfall of $173.9 million. As at 30 September, voluntary contributions to the Suspense Account, established in accordance with a 1979 Assembly resolution[59] to facilitate reimbursement to Governments contributing troops, equipment and supplies to the Force, amounted to only $18,356.

The Secretary-General estimated the costs of UNIFIL for the six-month period from 19 October 1983 to 18 April 1984 inclusive at $70,446,000 gross ($69,486,000 net), based on a Force strength of 5,200 troops. Should the Security Council decide to renew the Force's mandate beyond 18 April 1984 with its existing strength and responsibilities, the Assembly was requested to authorize commitments for UNIFIL for the period to 18 December 1984 at a rate not to exceed $11,741,000 gross ($11,581,000 net) per month.

Expressing concern that the shortfall placed an increasingly heavy burden on the troop-contributing countries, particularly the less wealthy, and, if not remedied, could jeopardize the functioning of the operation, the Secretary-General appealed to all Member States to pay their assessments without delay and to make voluntary contributions.

In his three reports on UNIFIL to the Security Council (see above), the Secretary-General had kept the Council informed of the accumulating shortfall and had also made similar appeals for payment of assessments and voluntary contributions.

ACABQ recommendations. ACABQ, in a report of 17 November 1983,[60] stated that it had no objection to the estimate for UNIFIL for the current six-month period. It recommended that the Assembly authorize $23,482,000 gross ($23,162,000 net) for the operation of UNIFIL for the period 19 October–18 December 1983. For the period 19 December 1983–18 April 1984, ACABQ also concurred with the Secretary-General's estimate and recommended that the Assembly appropriate $46,964,000 gross ($46,324,000 net). In administering this appropriation, the Committee added, the Secretary-General should have the usual flexibility to revise apportionments between objects of expenditure.

With regard to requirements for the period 19 April–18 December 1984, ACABQ recommended approval of the Secretary-General's request that he be authorized to enter into commitments at a rate not to exceed $11,741,000 gross ($11,581,000 net) per month, i.e. on the basis of the cost estimate for the six-month period ending 18 April 1984. The Secretary-General's authority would be subject to obtaining the prior concurrence of ACABQ for the actual level of commitments to be entered into for each mandate period that might be approved subsequent to 19 April 1984.

GENERAL ASSEMBLY ACTION

In December 1983, acting on the recommendation of the Fifth (Administrative and Budgetary) Committee, the General Assembly adopted two resolutions (38/38 A and B) dealing with the financing of UNIFIL.

On 5 December, the Assembly adopted resolution 38/38 A by recorded vote.

The General Assembly,

Having considered the report of the Secretary-General on the financing of the United Nations Interim Force in Lebanon and the related report of the Advisory Committee on Administrative and Budgetary Questions,

Bearing in mind Security Council resolutions 425(1978) and 426(1978) of 19 March 1978, 427(1978) of 3 May 1978, 434(1978) of 18 September 1978, 444(1979) of 19 January 1979, 450(1979) of 14 June 1979, 459(1979) of 19 December 1979, 474(1980) of 17 June 1980, 483(1980) of 17 December 1980, 488(1981) of 19 June 1981, 498(1981) of 18 December 1981, 501(1982) of 25 February 1982, 511(1982) of 18 June 1982, 519(1982) of 17 August 1982, 523(1982) of 18 October 1982, 529(1983) of 18 January 1983, 536(1983) of 18 July 1983 and 538(1983) of 18 October 1983,

Recalling its resolutions S-8/2 of 21 April 1978, 33/14 of 3 November 1978, 34/9 B of 17 December 1979, 35/44 of 1 December 1980, 35/115 A of 10 December 1980, 36/138 A of 16 December 1981, 36/138 C of 19 March 1982 and 37/127 A of 17 December 1982,

Reaffirming its previous decisions regarding the fact that, in order to meet the expenditures caused by such operations, a different procedure from the one applied to meet expenditures of the regular budget of the United Nations is required,

Taking into account the fact that the economically more developed countries are in a position to make relatively larger contributions and that the economically less developed countries have a relatively limited capacity to contribute towards peace-keeping operations involving heavy expenditures,

Bearing in mind the special responsibilities of the States permanent members of the Security Council in the financing of peace-keeping operations decided upon in accordance with the Charter of the United Nations,

I

Decides to appropriate to the Special Account referred to in section I, paragraph 1, of General Assembly resolution S-8/2 an amount of $15,229,666 gross ($15,087,833 net), being the amount authorized and apportioned under the provisions of section V of Assembly resolution 37/127 A for the operation of the United Nations Interim Force in Lebanon from 19 December 1982 to 18 January 1983, inclusive;

II

Decides to appropriate to the Special Account an amount of $80,331,000 gross ($79,466,000 net), being the amount authorized with the prior concurrence of the Advisory Committee on Administrative and Budgetary Questions and apportioned under the provisions of section VI of General Assembly resolution 37/127 A for the operation of the United Nations Interim Force in Lebanon from 19 January to 18 July 1983, inclusive;

III

Decides to appropriate to the Special Account an amount of $40,379,000 gross ($39,925,000 net), being the amount authorized with the prior concurrence of the Advisory Committee on Administrative and Budgetary Questions and apportioned under the provisions of section VI of General Assembly resolution 37/127 A for the operation of the United Nations Interim Force in Lebanon from 19 July to 18 October 1983, inclusive;

IV

Decides to appropriate to the Special Account an amount of $23,482,000 gross ($23,162,000 net), being the amount authorized with the prior concurrence of the Advisory Committee on Administrative and Budgetary Questions and apportioned under the provisions of section VI of General Assembly resolution 37/127 A for the operation of the United Nations Interim Force in Lebanon from 19 October to 18 December 1983, inclusive;

V

1. *Decides* to appropriate to the Special Account an amount of $46,964,000 for the operation of the United Nations Interim Force in Lebanon for the period from 19 December 1983 to 18 April 1984, inclusive;

2. *Decides further*, as an *ad hoc* arrangement, without prejudice to the positions of principle that may be taken by Member States in any consideration by the General Assembly of arrangements for the financing of peace-keeping operations, to apportion the amount of $46,964,000 among Member States in accordance with the scheme set out in Assembly resolution 33/14 and the provisions of section V, paragraph 1, of resolution 34/9 B, section VI, paragraph 1, of resolution 35/115 A, section VI, paragraph 1, of resolution 36/138 A and section IX, paragraph 1, of resolution 37/127 A, in the proportions determined by the scale of assessments for the years 1983, 1984 and 1985;

3. *Decides* that there shall be set off against the apportionment among Member States, as provided in paragraph 2 above, their respective share in the estimated income of $13,333 other than staff assessment income approved for the period from 19 December 1983 to 18 April 1984, inclusive;

4. *Decides* that, in accordance with the provisions of its resolution 973(X) of 15 December 1955, there shall be set off against the apportionment among Member States, as provided for in paragraph 2 above, their respective share in the Tax Equalization Fund of the estimated staff assessment income of $626,667 approved for the period from 19 December 1983 to 18 April 1984, inclusive;

VI

Authorizes the Secretary-General to enter into commitments for the operation of the United Nations Interim Force in Lebanon at a rate not to exceed $11,741,000 gross ($11,581,000 net) per month for the period from 19 April to 18 December 1984, inclusive, should the Security Council decide to continue the Force beyond the period of six months authorized under its resolution 538(1983), subject to obtaining the prior concurrence of the Advisory Committee on Administrative and Budgetary Questions for the actual level of commitments to be entered into for each mandate period that may be approved subsequent to 19 April 1984, the said amount to be apportioned among Member States in accordance with the scheme set out in the present resolution;

VII

1. *Renews its invitation* to Member States to make voluntary contributions to the United Nations Interim

Force in Lebanon both in cash and in the form of services and supplies acceptable to the Secretary-General;

2. *Invites* Member States to make voluntary contributions in cash to the Suspense Account established in accordance with its resolution 34/9 D of 17 December 1979;

VIII

Requests the Secretary-General to take all necessary action to ensure that the United Nations Interim Force in Lebanon shall be administered with a maximum of efficiency and economy.

General Assembly resolution 38/38 A

5 December 1983   Meeting 83   80-11-7 (recorded vote)

Approved by Fifth Committee (A/38/678) by recorded vote (94-12-6), 2 December (meeting 54); 17-nation draft (A/C.5/38/L.14, part A, approved together with part B (see below)); agenda item 119 *(b)*.

Sponsors: Australia, Canada, Denmark, Fiji, Finland, France, Ghana, Ireland, Italy, Lebanon, Nepal, Netherlands, New Zealand, Norway, Panama, Senegal, Sweden.

Meeting numbers. GA 38th session: 5th Committee 49, 54; plenary 83.

Recorded vote in Assembly as follows (resolutions 38/38 A and B together):

In favour: Australia, Austria, Bahrain, Belgium, Bhutan, Bolivia, Brazil, Canada, Chad, Chile, China, Costa Rica, Cyprus, Denmark, Ecuador, Egypt, El Salvador, Ethiopia, Fiji, Finland, France, Gabon, Germany, Federal Republic of, Ghana, Greece, Guatemala, Honduras, Iceland, India, Indonesia, Ireland, Israel, Italy, Ivory Coast, Japan, Jordan, Kuwait, Lebanon, Lesotho, Malaysia, Mali, Malta, Mauritania, Mexico, Nepal, Netherlands, New Zealand, Nicaragua, Nigeria, Norway, Oman, Pakistan, Panama, Philippines, Portugal, Romania, Saint Lucia, Samoa, Saudi Arabia, Singapore, Somalia, Spain, Sudan, Suriname, Swaziland, Sweden, Thailand, Trinidad and Tobago, Tunisia, Turkey, Uganda, United Arab Emirates, United Kingdom, United Republic of Cameroon, United Republic of Tanzania, United States, Uruguay, Venezuela, Yugoslavia, Zambia.

Against: Albania, Bulgaria, Byelorussian SSR, Cuba, German Democratic Republic, Hungary, Mongolia, Poland, Syrian Arab Republic, Ukrainian SSR, USSR.

Abstaining: Afghanistan, Burundi, Cape Verde, Congo, Iraq, Maldives, Yemen.

Also on 5 December, the Assembly adopted resolution 38/38 B by recorded vote.

The General Assembly,

Having regard to the financial position of the Special Account for the United Nations Interim Force in Lebanon, as set forth in the report of the Secretary-General, and referring to paragraph 7 of the report of the Advisory Committee on Administrative and Budgetary Questions,

Mindful of the fact that it is essential to provide the United Nations Interim Force in Lebanon with the necessary financial resources to enable it to fulfil its responsibilities under the relevant resolutions of the Security Council,

Concerned that the Secretary-General is continuing to face growing difficulties in meeting the obligations of the United Nations Interim Force in Lebanon on a current basis, particularly those due to the Governments of troop-contributing States,

Recalling its resolutions 34/9 E of 17 December 1979, 35/115 B of 10 December 1980, 36/138 B of 16 December 1981 and 37/127 B of 17 December 1982,

Recognizing that, in consequence of the withholding of contributions by certain Member States, the surplus balances in the Special Account for the United Nations Interim Force in Lebanon have, in effect, been drawn upon to the full extent to supplement the income received from contributions for meeting expenses of the Force,

Concerned that the application of the provisions of regulations 5.2 *(b)*, 5.2 *(d)*, 4.3 and 4.4 of the Financial

Regulations of the United Nations would aggravate the already difficult financial situation of the United Nations Interim Force in Lebanon,

Decides that the provisions of regulations 5.2 *(b)*, 5.2 *(d)*, 4.3 and 4.4 of the Financial Regulations of the United Nations shall be suspended in respect of the amount of $5,599,876, which otherwise would have to be surrendered pursuant to those provisions, this amount to be entered in the account referred to in the operative part of General Assembly resolution 34/9 E and held in suspense until a further decision is taken by the Assembly.

General Assembly resolution 38/38 B

5 December 1983   Meeting 83   80-11-7 (recorded vote)

Approved by Fifth Committee (A/38/678) by recorded vote (94-12-6), 2 December (meeting 54); 17-nation draft (A/C.5/38/L.14, part B, approved together with part A (see above)); agenda item 119 *(b)*.

Sponsors: Australia, Canada, Denmark, Fiji, Finland, France, Ghana, Ireland, Italy, Lebanon, Nepal, Netherlands, New Zealand, Norway, Panama, Senegal, Sweden.

Meeting numbers. GA 38th session: 5th Committee 49, 54; plenary 83.

(For recorded vote in Assembly, see above under resolution 38/38 A.)

Introducing the drafts, Ireland emphasized that UNIFIL continued to confront very serious financial difficulties. Under the Charter, responsibility for maintaining peace was shared by all Member States and the withholding of contributions was not consistent with the Charter.

Lebanon said the UNIFIL deficit threatened the normal operation of the Force, whose maintenance for the coming six months was particularly important; any withdrawal before the Lebanese army and security services were in a position to assume effective control of the southern part of the country would once again prevent the Lebanese Government from re-establishing its authority and would compromise the peace efforts by certain friendly countries.

The USSR stated that it did not participate in the financing of UNIFIL based on its position of principle that all costs related to the consequences of the armed aggression against Lebanon must be borne by the aggressor. A similar position was held by Democratic Yemen, Mongolia, the Syrian Arab Republic and Yemen. Iraq added that the cost of UNIFIL must under no circumstances be covered by the regular United Nations budget. Hungary said it did not consider itself under any obligation to finance UNIFIL. Albania reiterated its refusal to take part in the Force's financing.

Viet Nam, which did not participate in the vote, also said the peace-keeping forces had not performed their function but on the contrary had exacerbated the situation and added to insecurity in the region and throughout the world.

The Libyan Arab Jamahiriya, explaining its non-participation, said that after the invasion of Lebanon the Force had not deterred the Zionist entity from committing continued acts of aggression, thus proving its ineffectiveness. UNIFIL's presence could not solve the problem in the region;

the solution would be for the aggressor to cease its actions and, with the Power supporting it, shoulder responsibility for its acts.

Algeria, Benin and Iran said they did not participate in the vote in accordance with their established positions.

Voting in favour, Israel expressed the view that peace-keeping operations should be limited in time and could not be a substitute for the peaceful settlement of disputes; the extended presence of UNIFIL was merely the necessary consequence of the hostility of the neighbouring States towards Israel. Cyprus reaffirmed the importance it attached to United Nations peace-keeping forces.

CONTRIBUTIONS TO UNIFIL

(as at 31 December 1983; in US dollars)

Country	Assessments in 1983	Paid in 1983	Total contributions outstanding*	Country	Assessments in 1983	Paid in 1983	Total contributions outstanding*
Afghanistan	2,039	—	7,370	Hungary	95,080	—	536,490
Albania	4,080	—	17,456	Iceland	61,186	40,340	20,846
Algeria	52,902	—	204,567	India	149,875	293,213	71,845
Angola	2,039	—	7,492	Indonesia	53,406	40,695	22,364
Antigua and Barbuda	2,039	—	3,932	Iran	237,468	—	953,338
Argentina	290,494	242,908	188,751	Iraq	48,949	—	191,771
Australia	3,218,546	3,231,569	1,090,930	Ireland	365,858	342,270	23,588
Austria	1,527,146	1,006,001	521,145	Israel	94,070	122,635	31,964
Bahamas	4,080	4,297	4,080	Italy	7,609,644	7,092,156	2,598,776
Bahrain	4,080	2,690	1,390	Ivory Coast	12,238	3,315	24,025
Bangladesh	6,180	18,485	2,994	Jamaica	8,158	5,766	3,991
Barbados	4,080	2,051	4,683	Japan	21,001,539	20,313,096	10,298,018
Belgium	2,606,853	3,487,915	1,306,854	Jordan	4,080	2,690	1,993
Belize	2,039	3,237	695	Kenya	4,080	2,388	7,821
Benin	2,039	—	8,358	Kuwait	101,344	101,344	—
Bhutan	2,039	2,039	—	Lao People's Democratic Republic	2,039	—	8,358
Bolivia	4,080	—	17,456	Lebanon	8,284	42,512	—
Botswana	2,039	891	1,850	Lesotho	2,039	—	6,696
Brazil	565,472	—	1,016,949	Liberia	4,080	—	17,456
Bulgaria	73,171	—	278,338	Libyan Arab Jamahiriya	105,676	—	382,366
Burma	4,080	3,290	1,996	Luxembourg	121,743	80,051	41,692
Burundi	2,039	—	8,358	Madagascar	4,080	—	14,296
Byelorussian SSR	736,140	—	3,389,839	Malawi	2,039	4,548	695
Canada	6,294,496	4,154,327	2,140,169	Malaysia	36,712	35,711	28,819
Cape Verde	2,039	1,093	4,051	Maldives	2,039	891	2,919
Central African Republic	4,080	—	17,456	Mali	2,039	—	5,148
Chad	2,039	—	8,358	Malta	4,080	2,690	1,390
Chile	28,553	18,826	25,014	Mauritania	4,080	—	17,456
China	2,238,154	1,494,606	743,548	Mauritius	4,080	3,290	4,047
Colombia	44,870	69,031	15,287	Mexico	357,440	294,424	122,292
Comoros	2,039	—	8,358	Mongolia	4,080	—	17,456
Congo	4,080	—	17,456	Morocco	20,395	—	54,317
Costa Rica	8,158	—	26,345	Mozambique	2,039	—	10,423
Cuba	36,964	—	184,093	Nepal	2,039	2,775	1,153
Cyprus	4,080	3,486	1,996	Netherlands	3,620,947	2,336,405	1,776,209
Czechoslovakia	1,554,493	—	7,130,015	New Zealand	530,920	431,697	180,664
Democratic Kampuchea	4,080	—	17,456	Nicaragua	4,080	11,371	6,085
Democratic Yemen	2,039	—	8,358	Niger	2,039	—	6,251
Denmark	1,529,041	1,007,896	521,145	Nigeria	77,123	99,742	37,919
Djibouti	2,039	—	5,822	Norway	1,039,547	803,294	236,253
Dominica	2,039	—	8,650	Oman	4,080	2,690	1,390
Dominican Republic	12,238	—	43,603	Pakistan	24,601	24,142	13,128
Ecuador	8,158	5,141	6,638	Panama	8,158	—	30,986
Egypt	28,553	61,601	9,726	Papua New Guinea	2,039	6,272	297
El Salvador	4,080	—	16,429	Paraguay	4,080	—	17,456
Equatorial Guinea	4,080	—	17,456	Peru	28,426	—	102,269
Ethiopia	2,039	—	6,479	Philippines	36,838	21,709	39,220
Fiji	4,080	4,934	1,996	Poland	1,501,345	—	10,130,044
Finland	978,992	790,244	333,533	Portugal	73,550	136	96,338
France	16,121,590	23,334,520	5,500,564	Qatar	12,238	3,620	16,580
Gabon	8,158	—	27,342	Romania	77,755	—	346,109
Gambia	4,080	—	17,456	Rwanda	2,039	1,271	1,674
German Democratic Republic	2,834,993	—	12,002,403	Saint Lucia	2,039	302	6,224
Germany, Federal Republic of	17,403,341	11,469,237	5,934,104	Saint Vincent and the Grenadines	2,039	2,046	695
Ghana	8,284	8,284	—	Samoa	2,039	302	4,463
Greece	162,531	134,917	55,588	Sao Tome and Principe	2,039	—	6,891
Grenada	2,039	4,658	3,043	Saudi Arabia	347,263	297,717	119,515
Guatemala	8,158	7,788	3,991	Senegal	2,039	375	6,315
Guinea	2,039	—	2,643	Seychelles	2,039	1,193	1,148
Guinea-Bissau	2,039	—	5,744	Sierra Leone	4,080	—	17,260
Guyana	4,080	—	4,163	Singapore	36,585	28,905	12,507
Haiti	2,039	—	8,358	Solomon Islands	2,039	—	8,952
Honduras	4,080	—	5,889	Somalia	2,039	—	4,846

Country	Assessments in 1983	Paid in 1983	Total contributions outstanding*	Country	Assessments in 1983	Paid in 1983	Total contributions outstanding*
South Africa	836,853	—	3,647,000	United Kingdom	11,562,616	10,879,690	7,596,233
Spain	784,354	1,631,110	856,646	United Republic of Cameroon	4,080	—	8,947
Sri Lanka	4,206	6,437	1,390	United Republic of Tanzania	2,039	—	8,358
Sudan	2,039	5,186	1,705	United States	62,712,575	41,303,287	21,409,288
Suriname	2,039	1,041	998	Upper Volta	2,039	—	8,358
Swaziland	4,080	—	17,456	Uruguay	16,316	16,648	21,623
Sweden	2,691,592	2,169,521	917,215	Vanuatu	2,039	—	3,932
Syrian Arab Republic	12,238	—	47,945	Venezuela	223,716	78,892	396,505
Thailand	32,886	31,016	9,863	Viet Nam	8,284	—	48,414
Togo	4,080	—	9,799	Yemen	2,039	—	8,358
Trinidad and Tobago	12,238	9,878	4,170	Yugoslavia	187,130	228,909	337,759
Tunisia	12,238	21,903	5,988	Zaire	4,206	—	22,934
Turkey	130,277	120,602	69,849	Zambia	4,206	4,023	1,390
Uganda	2,039	302	7,577	Zimbabwe	4,078	904	6,220
Ukrainian SSR	2,701,070	—	12,624,643				
USSR	26,175,047	—	116,003,777	Total	204,687,820	139,985,300	235,916,612
United Arab Emirates	64,508	—	84,567				

*Covers the period from the inception of UNIFIL (19 March 1978) to 18 April 1984, as at 31 December 1983.

SOURCE: ST/ADM/SER.B/271.

Israel–Libyan Arab Jamahiriya

Communications. By a letter of 16 September 1983,[61] Israel said that the Libyan Arab Jamahiriya had introduced extraneous matters during the Security Council discussion on 6 September of the downing of a Korean airliner (see Chapter VII of this section). Israel added that a correct presentation of those matters was contained in a letter that it had sent in 1973[62] (which referred to an incident that year in which 106 persons died when a Libyan airliner crashed after being shot at by Israeli fighter aircraft over the Sinai).

In a letter of 21 September 1983,[63] the Libyan Arab Jamahiriya said the letter from the Zionist representative had failed to mention the extraneous matter referred to in the Security Council—namely, the iniquitous aggression by the Zionist entity in shooting down the Libyan airliner—because it was ashamed to recall that crime.

In reply, Israel, on 27 September,[64] transmitted excerpts from its 1973 letter. It added that it was astonished that the Libyan letter had been circulated as a United Nations document, since it referred to Israel by a designation other than its official name.

By a letter of 8 December 1983,[65] Israel quoted from a statement made earlier that day by the Libyan Arab Jamahiriya in the General Assembly's debate on the Middle East, describing it as an outburst of racist and religious incitement and asking the Secretary-General to ensure that such an outrage was not repeated.

In response, the Libyan Arab Jamahiriya, in a letter of 14 December,[66] said the Zionist representative had forgotten that the entity he represented continued to disregard all United Nations resolutions and that steps should be taken to ensure that the representative did not repeat his insults against the Arab nation and the United Nations.

Israel–Syrian Arab Republic

Communications. On 19 and 20 January 1983,[67] the Syrian Arab Republic transmitted to the Security Council President and the Secretary-General, respectively, a letter of 19 January from the Vice-Chairman of the Council of Ministers and Minister for Foreign Affairs, drawing attention to the seriousness of repeated hostile declarations by Israel, threatening to use force against anti-aircraft defence facilities on Syrian territory.

Israel, by letters of 21 and 24 January to the Council President and the Secretary-General, respectively,[68] responded that the Syrian Arab Republic had engaged in a deliberate policy of beefing up its military arsenal through the introduction of long-range Soviet missiles, capable of penetrating deep into the airspace of neighbouring countries, and Israel, which over the past decades had been uninterruptedly the target of Syrian hostility, had reasons to be concerned.

By a letter of 27 January,[69] the Syrian Arab Republic stated that Israel was trying to camouflage its military preparations; Israel's huge military arsenal had as its sole objective the pursuit of aggression, occupation, expansion and annexation and the realization of its "strategic interest".

Peace-keeping operation

UNDOF activities

The United Nations Disengagement Observer Force (UNDOF), established by the Security Council in 1974,[70] continued in 1983 to supervise the observance of the cease-fire between Israel and the Syrian Arab Republic in the Golan Heights area and to ensure, in accordance with its mandate, that there were no military forces in the area of separation. On the Secretary-General's recommendation, the Council extended UNDOF's mandate twice during the year, in May and November, by resolutions 531(1983) and 543(1983).

Reports of the Secretary-General. With the mandate of UNDOF expiring on 31 May and 30 November 1983, the Secretary-General submitted to the Security Council two reports on the activities of the Force for the six-month periods from 19 November 1982 to 20 May 1983[71] and 21 May to 21 November 1983.[72]

In both reports, the Secretary-General stated that UNDOF had continued to perform effectively with the co-operation of the parties and that, during the periods under review, the situation in the Israel-Syria sector had remained quiet, without serious incidents.

As at 21 November, UNDOF maintained 34 positions and 14 outposts, and conducted 29 patrols daily and 25 at irregular intervals. It continued to conduct fortnightly inspections of armaments and forces in the area of limitation, and to clear land-mines.

The Secretary-General stated that, despite the prevailing quiet in the sector, the Middle East situation as a whole continued to be potentially dangerous and was likely to remain so without a comprehensive settlement. In the circumstances, he considered the continued presence of UNDOF to be essential and recommended, with the assent of the Syrian Arab Republic and the agreement of Israel, that the Council extend its mandate for further periods of six months each.

SECURITY COUNCIL ACTION

The Security Council renewed UNDOF's mandate twice during 1983. On 26 May, the Council unanimously adopted resolution 531(1983), by which it extended the mandate for six months.

The Security Council,
Having considered the report of the Secretary-General on the United Nations Disengagement Observer Force,
Decides:
  (a) To call upon the parties concerned to implement immediately Security Council resolution 338(1973);
  (b) To renew the mandate of the United Nations Disengagement Observer Force for another period of six months, that is, until 30 November 1983;
  (c) To request the Secretary-General to submit, at the end of this period, a report on the developments in the situation and the measures taken to implement resolution 338(1973).

Security Council resolution 531(1983)

26 May 1983   Meeting 2445   Adopted unanimously

Draft prepared in consultations among Council members (S/15793).
Meeting number. SC 2445.

On 29 November, the Security Council unanimously adopted resolution 543(1983), by which it extended the UNDOF mandate for a further six months.

The Security Council,
Having considered the report of the Secretary-General on the United Nations Disengagement Observer Force,

Decides:
  (a) To call upon the parties concerned to implement immediately Security Council resolution 338(1973);
  (b) To renew the mandate of the United Nations Disengagement Observer Force for another period of six months, that is, until 31 May 1984;
  (c) To request the Secretary-General to submit, at the end of this period, a report on the developments in the situation and the measures taken to implement resolution 338(1973).

Security Council resolution 543(1983)

29 November 1983   Meeting 2502   Adopted unanimously

Draft prepared in consultations among Council members (S/16187).
Meeting number. SC 2502.

Following adoption of each resolution, the President made the following statement on behalf of the Council:[73]

"As is known, the report of the Secretary-General on the United Nations Disengagement Observer Force states, in paragraph 26, that 'despite the present quiet in the Israel-Syria sector, the situation in the Middle East as a whole continues to be potentially dangerous and is likely to remain so, unless and until a comprehensive settlement covering all aspects of the Middle East problem can be reached.' That statement of the Secretary-General reflects the view of the Security Council."

Composition

As at 21 November 1983, the composition of UNDOF was as follows:[72]

Austria	530
Canada	220
Finland	395
Poland	145
United Nations military observers	6
	1,296

In addition, UNTSO observers assigned to the Israel-Syria Mixed Armistice Commission assisted UNDOF as required.

UNDOF financing

The financing of UNDOF from 1 December 1982 to 30 November 1983, totalling $34,372,996, had been dealt with by the General Assembly in November 1982.[74]

In a paper on the financing of United Nations peace-keeping operations, submitted on 7 October 1983,[57] the United Kingdom drew attention to the shortfall in payments (see below) to UNDOF taken together with UNEF until the latter's liquidation in 1980; the policy of certain Member States in withholding contributions to peace-keeping forces was undermining the United Nations ability to carry out its basic tasks, it stated.

Report of the Secretary-General. In an October 1983 report to the General Assembly on the financing of UNDOF,[75] the Secretary-General stated that, as at 30 September, a total of $588.9 million in contributions for UNDOF together with UNEF II had been received for the period from inception in 1974[70] to 30 November 1983. The balance due from Member States amounted to $79.1 million, $15.2 million of which was estimated to be collectible. The balance of $63.9 million comprised the amount of $27.9 million apportioned to Member States which had stated that they did not intend to pay for UNDOF and $36 million of assessed contributions due from China between 25 October 1971 and 31 December 1981, transferred to a special account in accordance with a 1981 Assembly resolution.[76]

According to the Secretary-General, there was a shortfall of approximately $4.3 million in the UNDOF Special Account in respect of the period from 25 October 1979 to 30 November 1983. The shortfall of UNDOF for periods before 24 October 1979, together with UNEF II until its liquidation in 1980, was estimated at $59.6 million. In the circumstances, troop contributors had not been reimbursed fully or on time; they had again conveyed to the Secretary-General their very serious concern over the situation, which placed a heavy burden on them.

Appropriations for UNDOF for the period after 30 November 1983 were estimated at $2,914,916 gross ($2,880,000 net) per month.

ACABQ recommendations. ACABQ, in a report of 17 November 1983,[77] recommended that the Secretary-General's cost estimate for UNDOF for the period from 1 December 1983 to 30 November 1984 be approved; it added that requirements for that period should not exceed $34,979,000 gross, or $34,560,000 net (i.e. $606,000, or 1.7 per cent, higher than the cost for the preceding 12 months). The Committee further recommended that the Secretary-General be permitted the usual flexibility to transfer credits between items of expenditure, should that be necessary in the interest of good management and efficiency.

ACABQ also recommended that the staffing proposals—one new P-3 post and one new local-level post—be approved. It noted the Secretary-General's statement that in the event of a finalization of plans for relocating UNDOF's headquarters before 30 November 1984, the matter would be brought to its attention should additional funds be needed.

GENERAL ASSEMBLY ACTION

In December, the General Assembly, acting on the recommendation of its Fifth (Administrative and Budgetary) Committee, adopted two resolutions (38/35 A and B), dealing with the financing of UNDOF.

On 1 December, the Assembly adopted resolution 38/35 A by recorded vote.

The General Assembly,

Having considered the report of the Secretary-General on the financing of the United Nations Disengagement Observer Force, as well as the related report of the Advisory Committee on Administrative and Budgetary Questions,

Bearing in mind Security Council resolutions 350(1974) of 31 May 1974, 363(1974) of 29 November 1974, 369(1975) of 28 May 1975, 381(1975) of 30 November 1975, 390(1976) of 28 May 1976, 398(1976) of 30 November 1976, 408(1977) of 26 May 1977, 420(1977) of 30 November 1977, 429(1978) of 31 May 1978, 441(1978) of 30 November 1978, 449(1979) of 30 May 1979, 456(1979) of 30 November 1979, 470(1980) of 30 May 1980, 481(1980) of 26 November 1980, 485(1981) of 22 May 1981, 493(1981) of 23 November 1981, 506(1982) of 26 May 1982, 524(1982) of 29 November 1982, 531(1983) of 26 May 1983 and 543(1983) of 29 November 1983,

Recalling its resolutions 3101(XXVIII) of 11 December 1973, 3211 B (XXIX) of 29 November 1974, 3374 C (XXX) of 2 December 1975, 31/5 D of 22 December 1976, 32/4 C of 2 December 1977, 33/13 D of 8 December 1978, 34/7 C of 3 December 1979, 35/44 of 1 December 1980, 35/45 A of 1 December 1980, 36/66 A of 30 November 1981 and 37/38 A of 30 November 1982,

Reaffirming its previous decisions regarding the fact that, in order to meet the expenditures caused by such operations, a different procedure is required from that applied to meet expenditures of the regular budget of the United Nations,

Taking into account the fact that the economically more developed countries are in a position to make relatively larger contributions and that the economically less developed countries have a relatively limited capacity to contribute towards peace-keeping operations involving heavy expenditures,

Bearing in mind the special responsibilities of the States permanent members of the Security Council in the financing of such operations, as indicated in General Assembly resolution 1874(S-IV) of 27 June 1963 and other resolutions of the Assembly,

I

Decides to appropriate to the Special Account referred to in section II, paragraph 1, of General Assembly resolution 3211 B (XXIX) the amount of $17,186,496 gross ($16,983,996 net) authorized and apportioned by section III of Assembly resolution 37/38 A for the operation of the United Nations Disengagement Observer Force for the period from 1 June to 30 November 1983, inclusive;

II

1. *Decides* to appropriate to the Special Account an amount of $17,489,500 for the operation of the United Nations Disengagement Observer Force for the period from 1 December 1983 to 31 May 1984, inclusive;

2. *Decides further,* as an *ad hoc* arrangement, without prejudice to the positions of principle that may be taken by Member States in any consideration by the General Assembly of arrangements for the financing of peace-

keeping operations, to apportion the amount of $17,489,500 among Member States in accordance with the scheme set out in Assembly resolution 3101(XXVIII) and the provisions of section II, paragraphs 2 *(b)* and 2 *(c),* and section V, paragraph 1, of resolution 3374 C (XXX), section V, paragraph 1, of resolution 31/5 D, section V, paragraph 1, of resolution 32/4 C, section V, paragraph 1, of resolution 33/13 D, section V, paragraph 1, of resolution 34/7 C, section V, paragraph 1, of resolution 35/45 A, section V, paragraph 1, of resolution 36/66 A and section V, paragraph 1, of resolution 37/38 A, in the proportions determined by the scale of assessments for the years 1983, 1984 and 1985;

3.   *Decides* that there shall be set off against the apportionment among Member States, as provided in paragraph 2 above, their respective share in the estimated income of $10,000 other than staff assessment income approved for the period from 1 December 1983 to 31 May 1984, inclusive;

4.   *Decides* that, in accordance with the provisions of its resolution 973(X) of 15 December 1955, there shall be set off against the apportionment among Member States, as provided for in paragraph 2 above, their respective share in the Tax Equalization Fund of the estimated staff assessment income of $199,500 approved for the period from 1 December 1983 to 31 May 1984, inclusive;

III

Authorizes the Secretary-General to enter into commitments for the United Nations Disengagement Observer Force at a rate not to exceed $2,914,916 gross ($2,880,000 net) per month for the period from 1 June to 30 November 1984 inclusive, should the Security Council decide to continue the Force beyond the period of six months authorized under its resolution 543(1983), the said amount to be apportioned among Member States in accordance with the scheme set out in the present resolution;

IV

1.   *Stresses* the need for voluntary contributions to the United Nations Disengagement Observer Force, both in cash and in the form of services and supplies acceptable to the Secretary-General;

2.   *Requests* the Secretary-General to take all necessary action to ensure that the United Nations Disengagement Observer Force is conducted with a maximum of efficiency and economy.

General Assembly resolution 38/35 A

1 December 1983   Meeting 79   109-3-14 (recorded vote)

Approved by Fifth Committee (A/38/652) by vote (79-3-12), 30 November (meeting 51); 9-nation draft (A/C.5/38/L.13, part A); agenda item 119 *(a).*
Sponsors: Australia, Austria, Canada, Denmark, Finland, Ireland, New Zealand, Norway, Sweden.
Meeting numbers. GA 38th session: 5th Committee 49, 51; plenary 79.

Recorded vote in Assembly as follows:

In favour: Antigua and Barbuda, Argentina, Australia, Austria, Bangladesh, Barbados, Belgium, Belize, Bhutan, Botswana, Brazil, Burma, Canada, Cape Verde, Central African Republic, Chad, Chile, China, Colombia, Comoros, Costa Rica, Cyprus, Democratic Kampuchea, Denmark, Ecuador, Egypt, El Salvador, Equatorial Guinea, Fiji, Finland, France, Gabon, Germany, Federal Republic of, Ghana, Greece, Guatemala, Guinea-Bissau, Guyana, Honduras, Iceland, India, Indonesia, Ireland, Israel, Italy, Jamaica, Jordan, Kenya, Kuwait, Lebanon, Liberia, Luxembourg, Madagascar, Malawi, Malaysia, Mali, Malta, Mauritania, Mauritius, Mexico, Morocco, Nepal, Netherlands, New Zealand, Niger, Nigeria, Norway, Oman, Pakistan, Panama, Papua New Guinea, Peru, Philippines, Poland, Portugal, Qatar, Romania, Rwanda, Saint Lucia, Samoa, Saudi Arabia, Senegal, Sin-

gapore, Solomon Islands, Somalia, Spain, Sri Lanka, Sudan, Suriname, Sweden, Thailand, Togo, Trinidad and Tobago, Tunisia, Turkey, Uganda, United Arab Emirates, United Kingdom, United Republic of Cameroon, United Republic of Tanzania, United States, Upper Volta, Uruguay, Vanuatu, Venezuela, Yugoslavia, Zaire, Zambia, Zimbabwe.

Against: Albania, Democratic Yemen, Syrian Arab Republic.

Abstaining: Algeria, Bulgaria, Byelorussian SSR, Congo, Cuba, Czechoslovakia, German Democratic Republic, Hungary, Iraq, Ivory Coast, Mongolia, Ukrainian SSR, USSR, Yemen.

Also on 1 December, the Assembly adopted resolution 38/35 B by recorded vote.

The General Assembly,

Having regard to the financial position of the Special Account for the United Nations Emergency Force and the United Nations Disengagement Observer Force, as set forth in the report of the Secretary-General, and referring to paragraph 5 of the report of the Advisory Committee on Administrative and Budgetary Questions,

Mindful of the fact that it is essential to provide the United Nations Disengagement Observer Force with the necessary financial resources to enable it to fulfil its responsibilities under the relevant resolutions of the Security Council,

Concerned that the Secretary-General is continuing to face growing difficulties in meeting the obligations of the Forces on a current basis, particularly those due to the Governments of troop-contributing States,

Recalling its resolutions 33/13 E of 14 December 1978, 34/7 D of 17 December 1979, 35/45 B of 1 December 1980, 36/66 B of 30 November 1981 and 37/38 B of 30 November 1982,

Recognizing that, in consequence of the withholding of contributions by certain Member States, the surplus balances in the Special Account for the United Nations Emergency Force and the United Nations Disengagement Observer Force have, in effect, been drawn upon to the full extent to supplement the income received from contributions for meeting expenses of the Forces,

Concerned that the application of the provisions of regulations 5.2 *(b),* 5.2 *(d),* 4.3 and 4.4 of the Financial Regulations of the United Nations would aggravate the already difficult financial situation of the Forces,

Decides that the provisions of regulations 5.2 *(b),* 5.2 *(d),* 4.3 and 4.4 of the Financial Regulations of the United Nations shall be suspended in respect of the amount of $5,191,637, which otherwise would have to be surrendered pursuant to those provisions, this amount to be entered into the account referred to in the operative part of General Assembly resolution 33/13 E and held in suspense until a further decision is taken by the Assembly.

General Assembly resolution 38/35 B

1 December 1983   Meeting 79   108-12-6 (recorded vote)

Approved by Fifth Committee (A/38/652) by vote (79-12-4), 30 November (meeting 51); 9-nation draft (A/C.5/38/L.13, part B); agenda item 119 *(a).*
Sponsors: Australia, Austria, Canada, Denmark, Finland, Ireland, New Zealand, Norway, Sweden.
Meeting numbers. GA 38th session: 5th Committee 49, 51; plenary 79.

Recorded vote in Assembly as follows:

In favour: Antigua and Barbuda, Argentina, Australia, Austria, Bahrain, Bangladesh, Barbados, Belgium, Belize, Bhutan, Brazil, Burma, Canada, Cape Verde, Central African Republic, Chad, Chile, China, Colombia, Comoros, Costa Rica, Cyprus, Democratic Kampuchea, Denmark, Ecuador, Egypt, El Salvador, Equatorial Guinea, Fiji, Finland, France, Gabon, Germany, Federal Republic of, Ghana, Greece, Guatemala, Guyana, Honduras, Iceland, India, Indonesia, Ireland,

Israel, Italy, Ivory Coast, Jamaica, Jordan, Kenya, Kuwait, Lebanon, Liberia, Luxembourg, Madagascar, Malawi, Malaysia, Mali, Malta, Mauritania, Mauritius, Mexico, Morocco, Nepal, Netherlands, New Zealand, Nicaragua, Niger, Nigeria, Norway, Oman, Pakistan, Panama, Papua New Guinea, Peru, Philippines, Portugal, Qatar, Rwanda, Saint Lucia, Samoa, Saudi Arabia, Senegal, Singapore, Solomon Islands, Somalia, Spain, Sri Lanka, Sudan, Suriname, Sweden, Thailand, Togo, Trinidad and Tobago, Tunisia, Turkey, Uganda, United Arab Emirates, United Kingdom, United Republic of Cameroon, United Republic of Tanzania, United States, Upper Volta, Uruguay, Vanuatu, Venezuela, Yugoslavia, Zaire, Zambia, Zimbabwe.

Against: Albania, Bulgaria, Byelorussian SSR, Cuba, Czechoslovakia, Democratic Yemen, German Democratic Republic, Hungary, Mongolia, Syrian Arab Republic, Ukrainian SSR, USSR.

Abstaining: Algeria, Congo, Iraq, Poland, Romania, Yemen.

Separate votes on the two draft resolutions were taken in the Committee at the request of the USSR. Introducing them, Canada said they took into account the special responsibilities of the permanent members of the Security Council and the ability of developed countries to make relatively larger contributions to the financing of peace-keeping operations; the sponsors felt that broad international participation was essential for the success of those operations.

Explaining its non-participation in the vote, the Libyan Arab Jamahiriya said the presence of such forces in the area would not solve the problems caused by Zionist aggression; the aggressor and the States supporting the Zionist entity in its aggression should bear the responsibility. Iran said the presence of UNDOF in the Middle East was due solely to the Zionist occupation and the refusal to recognize the rights of the Palestinians. International law placed the responsibility for such situations on the aggressor and its supporters. It was the task of the super-Powers and the permanent Council members to lead the struggle for the maintenance of peace. Benin said it did not participate in the vote in accordance with its well-known position of principle on the financing of United Nations peace-keeping forces.

Casting a negative vote on both resolutions, Albania said it objected to the dispatch of United Nations forces, because reality had shown that they could not serve to defend the freedom and independence of people or international peace and security. In the opinion of Democratic Yemen, the

United Nations forces in the Middle East had gone beyond their defined functions and their operations were solely the result of actions by the Zionist entity. The Syrian Arab Republic said UNDOF was a result of that entity, the occupation of Arab territories and the refusal to recognize Palestinian rights; resolution 38/35 A made no distinction between aggressor and victim, which, under international law, must be compensated for damage done by the aggressor.

Abstaining on both texts, Iraq could not support the inclusion in the regular United Nations budget of expenditure which should be borne by the Zionist entity as the party solely responsible.

Abstaining on resolution 38/35 A, the USSR said that, while supporting UNDOF operations, it regarded them only as a step towards the main objective: the complete liberation of Arab territories occupied by Israel. It considered the proposed expenditure for the period from 1 December 1983 to 30 November 1984 too high in relation to that for the previous period; the increase for several expenditures was unjustified and would require an excessive increase in Member States' contributions. Nor was there in the USSR's opinion any justification for the Secretary-General's proposal to assign to additional permanent posts the functions which could be performed by existing staff through better organization. Voting against resolution 38/35 B, the USSR opposed departures from the Financial Regulations of the United Nations, saying that the surplus balances in the Special Account for UNEF and UNDOF should be reimbursed to Member States.

Voting in favour, the United States reaffirmed its support for United Nations peace-keeping operations.

Israel said it voted in favour in view of the importance it attached to UNDOF operations. It could not be seriously claimed that Israel should defray the cost of UNDOF; Israel would pay its share, as it had always done for all United Nations peace-keeping operations whether it approved of them or not.

CONTRIBUTIONS TO UNDOF

(as at 31 December 1983; in US dollars)

Country	Assessments in 1983	Paid in 1983	Total contributions outstanding*	Country	Assessments in 1983	Paid in 1983	Total contributions outstanding*
Afghanistan	513	—	3,354	Barbados	1,025	679	346
Albania	1,025	—	21,296	Belgium	654,249	584,989	454,764
Algeria	13,265	—	51,458	Belize	513	662	173
Angola	513	—	1,768	Benin	513	—	10,457
Antigua and Barbuda	513	—	835	Bhutan	513	340	173
Argentina	73,163	39,638	48,654	Bolivia	1,025	—	13,328
Australia	811,913	540,617	271,296	Botswana	513	—	629
Austria	383,211	253,611	129,600	Brazil	141,781	—	259,533
Bahamas	1,025	2,214	686	Bulgaria	18,335	6,114	119,560
Bahrain	1,025	679	346	Burma	1,025	679	346
Bangladesh	1,568	4,062	1,029	Burundi	513	—	10,457

Country	Assessments in 1983	Paid in 1983	Total contributions outstanding*
Byelorussian SSR	185,333	94,307	802,260
Canada	1,584,024	1,051,800	532,224
Cape Verde	513	—	5,697
Central African Republic	1,025	225	21,071
Chad	513	—	10,457
Chile	7,175	4,755	2,420
China	573,291	388,383	184,908
Colombia	11,275	11,275	—
Comoros	513	—	7,056
Congo	1,025	—	21,296
Costa Rica	2,051	2,051	
Cuba	9,336	—	14,922
Cyprus	1,025	679	346
Czechoslovakia	391,448	261,918	974,883
Democratic Kampuchea	1,025	—	21,296
Democratic Yemen	513	—	5,537
Denmark	384,061	254,461	129,600
Djibouti	513	—	1,512
Dominica	513	—	2,222
Dominican Republic	3,072	1,018	11,608
Ecuador	2,051	1,990	692
Egypt	7,175	16,485	2,420
El Salvador	1,025	—	6,629
Equatorial Guinea	1,025	315	15,063
Ethiopia	513	—	830
Fiji	1,025	994	346
Finland	245,980	163,036	82,944
France	4,046,018	3,197,523	1,367,898
Gabon	2,051	—	9,278
Gambia	1,025	346	679
German Democratic Republic	712,314	589,590	1,871,439
Germany, Federal Republic of	4,369,880	2,894,168	1,475,712
Ghana	2,108	4,198	692
Greece	40,713	26,890	13,823
Grenada	513	7,645	671
Guatemala	2,051	1,311	1,371
Guinea	513	—	513
Guinea-Bissau	513	—	1,216
Guyana	1,025	—	1,025
Haiti	513	—	9,793
Honduras	1,025	—	1,340
Hungary	24,136	—	246,238
Iceland	15,373	10,189	5,184
India	38,254	25,813	12,441
Indonesia	13,492	9,635	12,582
Iran	59,840	—	192,351
Iraq	12,299	—	104,313
Ireland	91,677	60,573	31,104
Israel	23,684	15,213	8,471
Italy	1,908,388	1,806,714	646,272
Ivory Coast	3,072	8,059	1,036
Jamaica	2,051	1,990	692
Japan	5,267,629	3,243,184	3,536,041
Jordan	1,025	679	661
Kenya	1,025	340	1,611
Kuwait	25,340	16,701	8,639
Lao People's Democratic Republic	513	—	2,305
Lebanon	2,108	17,238	21,090
Lesotho	513	—	1,471
Liberia	1,025	—	14,150
Libyan Arab Jamahiriya	26,479	—	214,924
Luxembourg	30,465	20,097	10,368
Madagascar	1,025	—	3,092
Malawi	513	1,323	343
Malaysia	9,223	3,056	7,169
Maldives	513	—	648
Mali	513	—	1,100
Malta	1,025	679	346
Mauritania	1,025	—	11,563
Mauritius	1,025	654	982
Mexico	89,512	59,282	30,412
Mongolia	1,025	679	8,787
Morocco	5,125	3,055	8,635
Mozambique	513	—	8,602
Nepal	513	738	343
Netherlands	907,932	600,348	307,584
New Zealand	133,521	88,593	44,928
Nicaragua	1,025	3,262	1,340
Niger	513	—	1,131
Nigeria	19,304	21,120	13,020
Norway	261,070	172,942	88,128
Oman	1,025	975	908
Pakistan	6,206	4,241	4,112
Panama	2,051	—	20,991
Papua New Guinea	513	934	
Paraguay	1,025	—	21,296
Peru	7,119	—	29,494
Philippines	9,279	3,112	6,167
Poland	383,678	—	579,333
Portugal	18,504	—	18,504
Qatar	3,072	947	7,468
Romania	19,586	—	103,743
Rwanda	513	499	173
Saint Lucia	513	—	1,489
Saint Vincent and the Grenadines	513	498	173
Samoa	513	—	1,482
Sao Tome and Principe	513	—	1,587
Saudi Arabia	86,555	56,835	29,720
Senegal	513	308	205
Seychelles	513	340	173
Sierra Leone	1,025	—	12,437
Singapore	9,166	6,056	3,110
Solomon Islands	513	—	2,222
Somalia	513	—	830
South Africa	210,392	—	2,930,436
Spain	196,504	—	196,510
Sri Lanka	1,082	1,959	346
Sudan	513	6,452	332
Suriname	513	170	911
Swaziland	1,025	—	21,296
Sweden	676,162	223,877	452,285
Syrian Arab Republic	3,072	—	30,214
Thailand	8,311	5,547	2,764
Togo	1,025	—	1,840
Trinidad and Tobago	3,072	2,036	1,036
Tunisia	3,072	6,995	2,054
Turkey	32,681	38,222	14,086
Uganda	513	—	7,531
Ukrainian SSR	680,404	353,041	2,984,834
USSR	6,583,567	3,232,829	27,018,505
United Arab Emirates	16,060	—	19,216
United Kingdom	2,901,400	1,920,128	981,272
United Republic of Cameroon	1,025	—	2,497
United Republic of Tanzania	513	—	7,661
United States	15,748,006	10,434,296	5,313,710
Upper Volta	513	340	2,828
Uruguay	4,099	—	7,248
Vanuatu	513	—	835
Venezuela	56,087	18,682	83,761
Viet Nam	2,108	—	18,134
Yemen	513	—	10,057
Yugoslavia	46,920	58,194	73,427
Zaire	1,082	396	4,751
Zambia	1,082	736	346
Zimbabwe	1,026	1,275	686
Total	**51,424,618**	**32,981,723**	**55,660,900**

*Includes contributions due for UNDOF from its inception on 31 May 1974 through 31 May 1984, as at 31 December 1983, and those due for UNEF II (1973-1979); between 1974 and 1979 there was a single account for the two Forces.

SOURCE: ST / ADM/SER.B/271.

REFERENCES

(1)YUN 1981, p. 275. (2)A/38/341. (3)A/38/342. (4)YUN 1982, p. 427, GA res. 37/18, 16 Nov. 1982. (5)A/38/411. (6)A/38/337. (7)YUN 1968, p. 17, GA res. 2373(XXII), annex, 12 June 1968. (8)YUN 1974, p. 403, GA res. 3281(XXIX), 12 Dec. 1974. (9)*Ibid.*, pp. 324 & 326, GA res. 3201(S-VI) & 3202(S-VI), 1 May 1974. (10)A/38/545. (11)YUN 1981, p. 282, SC res. 487(1981), 19 June 1981. (12)A/38/93-S/15610. (13)S/15773. (14)A/38/124-S/15657. (15)A/38/297-S/15867. (16)A/38/380 (S/15953). (17)S/15974. (18)S/15981. (19)S/15956. (20)YUN 1982, p. 475, SC res. 516(1982),

1 Aug. 1982. [21]A/38/458-S/16015. [22]YUN 1982, p. 428. [23]*Ibid.*, p. 450, SC res. 511(1982), 18 June 1982. [24]S/15990. [25]S/15994. [26]A/38/576-S/16131. [27]S/16138. [28]A/38/581. [29]S/16036. [30]S/16142. [31]S/16178. [32]S/16228. [33]A/38/679 (S/16196). [34]S/16197. [35]A/38/706 (S/16202). [36]A/38/708-S/16207. [37]A/38/721. [38]A/38/728. [39]E/1983/13 (res. 1983/27). [40]S/16194. [41]S/16195. [42]S/16205. [43]A/38/717-S/16209. [44]S/16224. [45]S/16230. [46]A/39/57-S/16233. [47]YUN 1978, p. 312, SC res. 425(1978), 19 Mar. 1978. [48]S/15557. [49]YUN 1982, p. 478, SC res. 523(1982), 18 Oct. 1982. [50]*Ibid.*, p. 491. [51]*Ibid.*, p. 490. [52]*Ibid.*, p. 450, SC res. 508(1982), 5 June 1982. [53]*Ibid.*, SC res. 509(1982), 6 June 1982. [54]S/15863. [55]S/15868. [56]YUN 1973, p. 213, SC res. 340(1973), 25 Oct. 1973. [57]A/38/489. [58]A/38/473 & Corr.1. [59]YUN 1979, p. 352, GA res. 34/9 D, 17 Dec. 1979. [60]A/38/589. [61]S/15988. [62]YUN 1973, p. 249. [63]S/15996. [64]S/16008. [65]A/38/713. [66]A/38/741. [67]S/15566 (A/38/76). [68]S/15569 (A/38/80). [69]A/38/84-S/15576 & Corr.1. [70]YUN 1974, p. 205, SC res. 350(1974), 31 May 1974. [71]S/15777. [72]S/16169. [73]S/15797, S/16188. [74]YUN 1982, p. 501, GA res. 37/38 A, 30 Nov. 1982. [75]A/38/472 & Corr.1. [76]YUN 1981, p. 1299, GA res. 36/116 A, 10 Dec. 1981. [77]A/38/588.

Territories occupied by Israel

During 1983, the situation in the territories occupied by Israel as a result of previous armed conflict in the Middle East was again considered by the General Assembly and its Special Committee to Investigate Israeli Practices Affecting the Human Rights of the Population of the Occupied Territories. The territories consisted of the West Bank of the Jordan River (including East Jerusalem), the Golan Heights and the Gaza Strip.

The Assembly, in December, adopted eight resolutions (38/79 A-H) dealing with specific aspects of the report of the Committee. By the first (38/79 A), it demanded the release of Ziad Abu Eain and other prisoners registered to be freed by Israel (see above, under MIDDLE EAST SITUATION); by another (38/79 E), it demanded that Israel rescind the imprisonment of the Mayors of Hebron and Halhul and the expulsion of the Islamic Judge of Hebron (see below). The Assembly demanded information from Israel about the results of the investigations of the assassination attempts against three Palestinian mayors (38/79 H), and condemned Israeli policies against Palestinian educational institutions (38/79 G). Also censured were Israel's policies on the Syrian Golan Heights (38/79 F). The Assembly strongly condemned a number of Israeli policies and practices and demanded that Israel desist from them (38/79 D). By two other resolutions, the Assembly reprimanded Israel for its failure to comply with the 1949 Geneva Convention relative to the Protection of Civilian Persons in Time of War (fourth Geneva Convention) (38/79 B) and determined that Israel's actions in the occupied territories violated the Convention (38/79 C) (see below).

The situation in the occupied territories was also the subject of the International Conference on the Question of Palestine (see above, under PALESTINE QUESTION), and the Secretary-General dealt with the situation there in his September report on the Middle East and Palestine.[1] The occupation of the territories, in particular Israel's policy of establishing settlements there (see below), was also considered by the Security Council during several meetings in February, May and July/August. Because of the negative vote of a permanent member (United States), a draft resolution to have the Council denounce Israeli measures in the occupied territories, in particular its settlements policy, was not adopted when the Council met in July/August. In April, the Council expressed concern at the alleged mass poisoning of West Bank schoolchildren and requested an inquiry.

Communications. During the year, a number of communications were addressed to the Secretary-General and to the President of the Security Council concerning Israeli measures in the territories, including Jerusalem (see above, under PALESTINE QUESTION).

On 7 January,[2] Jordan transmitted letters of 5 and 6 January from the observer for PLO charging that Israeli authorities had intensified their activities against Palestinians in the West Bank, that Israeli troops had mounted a large-scale arrest campaign and that Palestinian prisoners had been tortured.

On 13 January,[3] Jordan transmitted letters of 10 and 12 January from the PLO observer containing further charges concerning repressive Israeli measures against Palestinians in the West Bank, which included the closing of a number of schools, confiscation of books, arrest of students, imposition of curfews and attacks against Palestinian property.

In a letter of 22 March,[4] the Chairman of the Committee on the Exercise of the Inalienable Rights of the Palestinian People expressed the Committee's deep concern at what he called recent violations by Israel of the legal and human rights of the Palestinians in the occupied territories and Jerusalem, such as the closing of Palestinian schools and universities, firing at Palestinian demonstrators, attacks against the Al-Aqsa Mosque in Jerusalem, curfews and other oppressive measures in refugee camps.

By a letter of 29 March,[5] Iraq, as Chairman of the Arab Group of Member States, drew the Council's attention to what it described as the increasing deterioration of the situation in the occupied territories, including Jerusalem, with an intensified Israeli campaign of repression against Palestinian and Syrian civilians.

On 1 July[6] and 13 July,[7] Jordan transmitted to the Council President letters of 29 June and 12

July, respectively, from the PLO observer complaining about Israeli actions against Palestinians in the occupied territories, including those in refugee camps and under detention.

By a letter of 11 July,[8] Israel stated that there had been various attempts in the past months to disrupt order by violent means in areas it referred to as Judaea and Samaria; to illustrate its point, Israel gave a sample of instances of violence directed against civilian Jewish targets.

Action by the Commission on Human Rights and its Sub-Commission. The Commission on Human Rights (see ECONOMIC AND SOCIAL QUESTIONS, Chapter XVIII) dealt with violations of human rights in the occupied territories in two resolutions adopted on 15 February 1983.[9, 10] In another resolution of the same date, on the right to self-determination,[11] the Commission condemned Israel's continued occupation of the Palestinian and other Arab territories, as well as its aggression and practices against the Palestinians in those territories. The Commission condemned in the strongest terms the September 1982 massacre of Palestinians in the Sabra and Shatila refugee camps[12] and requested the General Assembly to declare 17 September a day to commemorate the victims. It reaffirmed the right of the Palestinians to self-determination, rejected the plan of "autonomy" within the framework of the 1978 Camp David accords (formally called A Framework for Peace in the Middle East, Agreed at Camp David (United States), and Framework for the Conclusion of a Peace Treaty between Egypt and Israel) and declared that those accords had no validity in so far as they purported to determine the future of the Palestinians and of the territories occupied since 1967.

The Sub-Commission on Prevention of Discrimination and Protection of Minorities, by a resolution of 31 August 1983,[13] strongly affirmed that the perpetuation of Israeli occupation of the territories could only be a source of increasing human rights violations and tension. The Sub-Commission recommended that the Commission condemn Israel for its continued occupation of Palestinian and other Arab territories and for its persistence in colonizing those territories aimed at changing their demographic composition, institutional structure and status; and call on Israel to withdraw from them.

Report of the Committee on Israeli practices. In its annual report, approved on 19 August 1983 and transmitted to the General Assembly by the Secretary-General,[14] the Special Committee to Investigate Israeli Practices Affecting the Human Rights of the Population of the Occupied Territories (Committee on Israeli practices), established in 1968,[15] presented information on the situation of the civilian population, on Israeli administra-

tion in the territories, Israel's annexation and settlement policies (see below), and treatment of detainees. The report, with an annexed map showing Israeli settlements established, planned or under construction, covered the situation since the adoption of the Committee's previous report in August 1982.[16] As in previous years, the Committee worked without the co-operation of Israel.

During the reporting period, the Committee held three series of meetings. At the first, from 13 to 15 December 1982 in New York, it reviewed its mandate and decided on the organization of its work. At the second series of meetings, between 30 May and 11 June 1983, beginning at Geneva and moving to Amman (Jordan), Damascus (Syrian Arab Republic) and Rafah (Egypt), the Committee heard the testimony of persons living in the occupied territories and conducted consultations with a representative of the Ministry of Foreign Affairs of the Syrian Arab Republic on the situation in the occupied Syrian territory. At Egypt's request, the Committee visited Rafah for hearings on Israeli practices regarding Palestinian refugees in Egypt. During a third series of meetings, from 8 to 19 August, it examined communications and adopted its report.

In its conclusions, the Committee noted that the imposition of the so-called "civil administration" and "village leagues" had caused serious problems in maintaining public order, and the dissolution of elected municipal councils in the principal towns of the West Bank and their replacement by military governors had further complicated life for the population. The Committee also noted a tendency by the occupation authorities to put pressure on Arabs to leave their homes and emigrate—parallel to a policy of expulsion on other pretexts.

The Committee stated that hardly a day went by in the territories without some incidents involving violence being reported which were, for the most part, directed against the military presence.

Violence by Israeli settlers also had increased considerably, culminating in the events at Hebron (Al-Khalil) (see below). While the settlers, all of whom were armed and subject to no authority other than the Israeli Government, went unpunished, the population of the territories were the subject of severe reprisal measures if they attempted to react to the acts perpetrated against them. The Committee reiterated its conviction that Israel, under the fourth Geneva Convention, remained fully responsible for the acts of the settlers.

The right to freedom of education was impeded by several measures by the authorities, including the requirement established in late 1982 that non-local academics sign a commitment concerning allegiance to PLO—a requirement that had led to the automatic expulsion of some 28 professors and teachers—and the repeated closure of schools and universities. The Committee hoped for urgent action to curtail the cycle of violence provoked by denial of that right.

Information received by the Committee indicated that recourse of the population to judicial remedies had rarely given satisfaction and, other than the granting of temporary injunctions and similarly dilatory remedies, had not provided any firm or long-lasting safeguard of the interests of the population. The Committee felt that the judicial authorities appeared to be completely subjected to the discretion of the military occupation authorities.

As for the treatment of detainees, the Committee noted that a camp for the detention of young persons, mostly arrested for stone-throwing, had been established. The camp, known as Far'a camp, had been the subject of several reports reflecting the inhuman conditions in which detainees were kept. In spite of avowed Israeli intentions to improve those conditions, the Committee noted no improvement; on the contrary, hunger-strikes and other acts of protest had recurred in most prisons and places of detention during the last year.

The overall picture, the Committee stated, reflected a further deterioration of the human rights situation in the territories, with the treatment of the population becoming harsher in all respects. In the West Bank, including Jerusalem, and the Gaza Strip, there was a constant cycle of repressive measures, resistance and reprisals. In the Golan Heights, Israel continued to deny the population their rights. The majority of Syrians expelled after the Israeli occupation in 1967 were still being denied the right to return to their homes, a right they should be given in accordance with international law (see also below, under GOLAN HEIGHTS). In all, the situation of civilians in the territories was more intolerable than ever, a fact which, the Committee noted, had given rise to protest movements in Israel.

The Committee reiterated that the expropriation of Arab land, the establishment of Jewish settlements and the transfer of civilians to the territories violated the fourth Geneva Convention, which remained the principal international instrument in humanitarian law applicable to the territories.

The Committee concluded that Israel's policy was designed to implement its sovereignty over the territories and that the right to self-determination had been disregarded. In certain cases, as in the Golan Heights, outright efforts of annexation were being undertaken. The responsibility of the international community, the Committee believed, was more urgent than ever; it called for urgent action to prevent further deterioration and protect the very basic rights of the civilians in the territories.

In October, following the Assembly's December 1982 request,[17] the Secretary-General reported on the facilities he had continued to provide to the Committee, including coverage of its activities in the form of press releases, news bulletins, and radio and television specials.[18]

Recommendations of the Conference on the Palestine question. The International Conference on the Question of Palestine,[19] in its Declaration on Palestine (see above, under PALESTINE QUESTION), stressed the need to end Israel's occupation of the Arab territories, to secure Israel's withdrawal from them, and to oppose and reject Israeli policies in the occupied territories as major obstacles to peace in the Middle East.

In its Programme of Action for the Achievement of Palestinian Rights, the Conference recommended that all States: consider Israel's continued presence in the territories as exacerbating instability in the region and endangering international peace and security; oppose and reject Israel's expansionist policies in the territories, in particular the alteration of their geographic nature and demographic composition, and the attempt to alter, through domestic legislation, the legal status of those territories; declare null and void such measures as the annexation and expropriation of land and water resources, and the alteration of demographic, geographic, historical and cultural features; alleviate the economic and social burdens borne by the Palestinians as a result of continued Israeli occupation; review the situation of Palestinian women in the territories; review economic, cultural, technical and other relations with Israel, to ensure that the agreements governing them would not be construed as implying recognition of any modification of the legal status of the territories, or an acceptance of Israel's illegal presence there; express concern that the laws applicable in the territories had been totally eclipsed by military orders designed to establish a new "legal régime"; and express concern that Palestinians and other Arabs in the territories were deprived of juridical and other kinds of protection, and that they were victims of repressive legislation, involving mass arrests, torture, destruction of houses and expulsion of people from their homes, flagrantly violating human rights.

The Conference invited the Security Council to ensure Israel's withdrawal from the Palestinian and other Arab territories, including Jerusalem, in accordance with a specific timetable; to guarantee the safety and legal and human rights of the Palestinians pending Israeli withdrawal; and to keep under constant attention Israeli actions against the Palestinians which violated United Nations resolutions, particularly a 1947 General Assembly resolution[20] guaranteeing all persons in Palestine equal and non-discriminatory rights.

GENERAL ASSEMBLY ACTION

Under the agenda item on the report of the Special Committee to Investigate Israeli Practices Affecting the Human Rights of the Population of the Occupied Territories, the General Assembly, on 15 December 1983, adopted by recorded vote resolution 38/79 D. The Assembly took this action on the recommendation of the Special Political Committee.

The General Assembly,

Guided by the purposes and principles of the Charter of the United Nations and by the principles and provisions of the Universal Declaration of Human Rights,

Bearing in mind the provisions of the Geneva Convention relative to the Protection of Civilian Persons in Time of War, of 12 August 1949, as well as of other relevant conventions and regulations,

Recalling all its resolutions on the subject, in particular resolutions 32/91 B and C of 13 December 1977, 33/113 C of 18 December 1978, 34/90 A of 12 December 1979, 35/122 C of 11 December 1980, 36/147 C of 16 December 1981 and 37/88 C of 10 December 1982, and also those adopted by the Security Council, the Commission on Human Rights, in particular its resolution 1983/1 of 15 February 1983, and other United Nations organs concerned and by the specialized agencies,

Having considered the report of the Special Committee to Investigate Israeli Practices Affecting the Human Rights of the Population of the Occupied Territories, which contains, *inter alia*, public statements made by officials of the Government of Israel,

1. *Commends* the Special Committee to Investigate Israeli Practices Affecting the Human Rights of the Population of the Occupied Territories for its efforts in performing the tasks assigned to it by the General Assembly and for its thoroughness and impartiality;

2. *Deplores* the continued refusal by Israel to allow the Special Committee access to the occupied territories;

3. *Demands* that Israel allow the Special Committee access to the occupied territories;

4. *Reaffirms* the fact that occupation itself constitutes a grave violation of the human rights of the civilian population of the occupied Arab territories;

5. *Condemns* the continued and persistent violation by Israel of the Geneva Convention relative to the Protection of Civilian Persons in Time of War, of 12 August 1949, and other applicable international instruments, and condemns in particular those violations which that Convention designates as "grave breaches" thereof;

6. *Declares once more* that Israel's grave breaches of that Convention are war crimes and an affront to humanity;

7. *Strongly condemns* the following Israeli policies and practices:

(a) Annexation of parts of the occupied territories, including Jerusalem;

(b) Imposition of Israeli laws, jurisdiction and administration on the Syrian Golan Heights, which has resulted in the effective annexation of the Syrian Golan Heights;

(c) Establishment of new Israeli settlements and expansion of the existing settlements on private and public Arab lands, and transfer of an alien population thereto;

(d) Evacuation, deportation, expulsion, displacement and transfer of Arab inhabitants of the occupied territories and denial of their right to return;

(e) Confiscation and expropriation of private and public Arab property in the occupied territories and all other transactions for the acquisition of land involving the Israeli authorities, institutions or nationals on the one hand and the inhabitants or institutions of the occupied territories on the other;

(f) Excavation and transformation of the landscape and the historical, cultural and religious sites, especially at Jerusalem;

(g) Pillaging of archaeological and cultural property;

(h) Destruction and demolition of Arab houses;

(i) Collective punishment, mass arrests, administrative detention and ill-treatment of the Arab population;

(j) Ill-treatment and torture of persons under detention;

(k) Interference with religious freedoms and practices as well as family rights and customs;

(l) Interference with the system of education and with the social and economic development of the population in the occupied Palestinian and other Arab territories;

(m) Interference with the freedom of movement of individuals within the occupied Palestinian and other Arab territories;

(n) Illegal exploitation of the natural wealth, resources and population of the occupied territories;

8. *Strongly condemns* the arming of Israeli settlers in the occupied territories to commit acts of violence against Arab civilians and the perpetration of acts of violence by these armed settlers against individuals, causing injury and death and wide-scale damage to Arab property;

9. *Reaffirms* that all measures taken by Israel to change the physical character, demographic composition, institutional structure or status of the occupied territories, or any part thereof, including Jerusalem, are null and void, and that Israel's policy of settling parts of its population and new immigrants in the occupied territories constitutes a flagrant violation of the Geneva Convention and of the relevant resolutions of the United Nations;

10. *Demands* that Israel desist forthwith from the policies and practices referred to in paragraphs 7, 8 and 9 above;

11. *Calls upon* Israel, the occupying Power, to take immediate steps for the return of all displaced Arab and Palestinian inhabitants to their homes or former places of residence in the territories occupied by Israel since 1967;

12. *Urges* the international organizations and the specialized agencies, in particular the International Labour Organisation, to examine the conditions of Arab workers in the occupied Palestinian and other Arab territories, including Jerusalem;

13. *Reiterates its call* upon all States, in particular those States parties to the Geneva Convention, in accordance with article 1 of that Convention, and upon international organizations and the specialized agencies not to recognize any changes carried out by Israel in the occupied territories and to avoid actions, including those in the field of aid, which might be used by Israel in its pursuit of the policies of annexation and colonization or any of the other policies and practices referred to in the present resolution;

14. *Requests* the Special Committee, pending the early termination of Israeli occupation, to continue to investigate Israeli policies and practices in the Arab territories occupied by Israel since 1967, to consult, as appropriate, with the International Committee of the Red Cross in order to ensure the safeguarding of the welfare and human rights of the population of the occupied territories and to report to the Secretary-General as soon as possible and whenever the need arises thereafter;

15. *Requests* the Special Committee to continue to investigate the treatment of civilians in detention in the Arab territories occupied by Israel since 1967;

16. *Condemns* Israel's refusal to permit persons from the occupied territories to appear as witnesses before the Special Committee and to participate in conferences and meetings held outside the occupied territories;

17. *Requests* the Secretary-General:

(a) To provide all necessary facilities to the Special Committee, including those required for its visits to the occupied territories, with a view to investigating the Israeli policies and practices referred to in the present resolution;

(b) To continue to make available additional staff as may be necessary to assist the Special Committee in the performance of its tasks;

(c) To ensure the widest circulation of the reports of the Special Committee, and of information regarding its activities and findings, by all means available through the Department of Public Information of the Secretariat and, where necessary, to reprint those reports of the Special Committee which are no longer available;

(d) To report to the General Assembly at its thirty-ninth session on the tasks entrusted to him in the present paragraph;

18. *Requests* the Security Council to ensure Israel's respect for and compliance with all the provisions of the Geneva Convention relative to the Protection of Civilian Persons in Time of War, of 12 August 1949, in Palestinian and other Arab territories occupied since 1967, including Jerusalem, and to initiate measures to halt Israeli policies and practices in those territories;

19. *Decides* to include in the provisional agenda of its thirty-ninth session the item entitled "Report of the Special Committee to Investigate Israeli Practices Affecting the Human Rights of the Population of the Occupied Territories".

General Assembly resolution 38/79 D

15 December 1983   Meeting 98   115-2-27 (recorded vote)

Approved by SPC (A/38/718) by recorded vote (93-2-20), 5 December (meeting 45); 13-nation draft (A/SPC/38/L.38); agenda item 69.

Sponsors: Afghanistan, Bangladesh, Cuba, Egypt, India, Indonesia, Madagascar, Malaysia, Mali, Mongolia, Pakistan, Qatar, Senegal.

Financial implications. 5th Committee, A/38/730; S-G, A/C.5/38/85, A/SPC/38/L.43.

Meeting numbers. GA 38th session: SPC 36-42, 45-48; 5th Committee 62; plenary 98.

Recorded vote in Assembly as follows:

In favour: Afghanistan, Albania, Algeria, Angola, Argentina, Bahrain, Bangladesh, Belize, Benin, Bhutan, Bolivia, Botswana, Brazil, Bulgaria, Burma, Burundi, Byelorussian SSR, Cape Verde, Central African Republic, Chad, China, Colombia, Congo, Cuba, Cyprus, Czechoslovakia, Democratic Kampuchea, Democratic Yemen, Djibouti, Ecuador, Egypt, Equatorial Guinea, Ethiopia, Fiji, Gabon, Gambia, German Democratic Republic, Ghana, Greece, Grenada, Guinea, Guinea-Bissau, Guyana, Hungary, India, Indonesia, Iran, Iraq, Jamaica, Jordan, Kenya, Kuwait, Lao People's Democratic Republic, Lebanon, Lesotho, Liberia, Libyan Arab Jamahiriya, Madagascar, Malaysia, Maldives, Mali, Malta, Mauritania, Mauritius, Mexico, Mongolia, Morocco, Mozambique, Nepal, Nicaragua, Niger, Nigeria, Oman, Pakistan, Panama, Papua New Guinea, Peru, Philippines, Poland, Portugal, Qatar, Romania, Rwanda, Sao Tome and Principe, Saudi Arabia, Senegal, Seychelles, Sierra Leone, Singapore, Somalia, Spain, Sri Lanka, Sudan, Suriname, Syrian Arab Republic, Thailand, Togo, Trinidad and Tobago, Tunisia, Turkey, Uganda, Ukrainian SSR, USSR, United Arab Emirates, United Republic of Cameroon, United Republic of Tanzania, Upper Volta, Uruguay, Vanuatu, Venezuela, Viet Nam, Yemen, Yugoslavia, Zambia, Zimbabwe.

Against: Israel, United States.

Abstaining: Australia, Austria, Bahamas, Barbados, Belgium, Canada, Costa Rica, Denmark, Dominican Republic, Finland, France, Germany, Federal Republic of, Iceland, Ireland, Italy, Ivory Coast, Japan, Luxembourg, Malawi, Netherlands, New Zealand, Norway, Paraguay, Swaziland, Sweden, United Kingdom, Zaire.

Paragraph 6 was approved in the Committee by a recorded vote of 85 to 20, with 10 abstentions.

The United States considered the text to be of an extremely biased and polemical nature; it objected in particular to what it felt was the extraordinary expense of the Committee's activities.

In Sweden's opinion, the text went beyond the Assembly's competence. Though endorsing the condemnation of Israeli policies and practices, Sweden was not convinced that the language used was in all cases fully justified by established facts. Austria said it had abstained owing to certain unacceptable phrases.

Israel's continued occupation of Palestinian and other Arab territories, including Jerusalem, was also condemned by the Assembly on 19 December in resolution 38/180 D on the Middle East, by which the Assembly demanded the immediate, unconditional and total withdrawal of Israel from all territories occupied since June 1967 and condemned Israel's aggression, policies and practices against the Palestinians in and outside these territories, particularly Palestinians in Lebanon, including the expropriation and annexation of territory, the establishment of settlements, assassination attempts, and other terrorist, aggressive and repressive measures.

In resolution 38/58 C of 13 December, endorsing the call for convening an international peace conference on the Middle East (see above, under PALESTINE QUESTION), the Assembly also acknowledged the need to put an end to Israel's occupation of the Arab territories and the need to secure Israeli withdrawal from the territories occupied since 1967, including Jerusalem.

Settlements policy

Israel's policy of establishing settlements in the occupied territories and incidents involving Israeli settlers were considered by the Security Council during several meetings in February, May, July and August 1983. The International Conference on the Question of Palestine in September, in its Programme of Action (see above, under PALESTINE QUESTION), invited the Council to take urgent action to bring about a cessation of the establishment of settlements, among other Israeli actions. Israel's settlements policy was dealt with also by the General Assembly, the Committee on Israeli practices, the Committee on Palestinian rights and the Commission on Human Settlements (see ECONOMIC AND SOCIAL QUESTIONS, Chapter XVII).

Communications (January). By a letter of 21 January,[21] the Chairman of the Committee on Palestinian rights expressed the Committee's concern at what he called Israel's continuing violation of human rights of the Palestinians in the occupied Arab territories by its persistent establishment of settlements in the West Bank and other repressive measures.

On 24 January,[22] Jordan transmitted a letter of 8 January from its Minister for Occupied Territories Affairs to the Minister for Foreign Affairs detailing what were termed the latest Israeli acts of confiscation and annexation of Palestinian lands in the occupied West Bank and Jerusalem during December 1982.

SECURITY COUNCIL CONSIDERATION (February)

At the urgent request of Jordan, in a letter of 8 February 1983,[23] as Chairman of the Group of Arab States, the Security Council met on 11, 14 and 16 February to resume consideration of the situation in the occupied territories, in particular Israel's settlements policy.

Meeting numbers. SC 2412-2414.

The President, with the consent of the Council, invited Algeria, Cuba, Democratic Yemen, Egypt, the German Democratic Republic, Greece, India, Iran, Kuwait, Lebanon, Morocco, the Niger, Senegal, the Syrian Arab Republic, Turkey, the United Arab Emirates, Yemen and Yugoslavia to participate in the discussion without the right to vote.

At Jordan's request, in a letter of 11 February,[24] the Council that day also decided that an invitation under rule 39 of the Council's provisional rules of procedure[a] should be accorded to the Permanent Observer of the League of Arab States to the United Nations.

Virtually all speakers during the debate expressed concern at Israel's continued settlements policy. They agreed that such policy violated international law—particularly The Hague Convention on the Laws and Customs of War on Land of 1907, and the 1949 fourth Geneva Convention (see below)—defied United Nations resolutions and exacerbated the situation in the occupied territories. The view that Israel's settlements policy could not be reconciled with the principle of the inadmissibility of the acquisition of territory by war, as specified in Council resolution 242(1967),[25] was widely held; that principle was reaffirmed by the Netherlands, Nicaragua, Poland and the United Kingdom, among others.

Opening the debate, the Syrian Arab Republic charged that Israel's settlements policy was accompanied not only by expropriation, expulsion, deportation and oppression, but also by notions of superiority and racial discrimination; it warned

that Israel's persistence in changing the demographic and geographical nature of the occupied territories could only aggravate tension.

Speaking similarly, Turkey added that Israel's policy reduced the chances for a just solution to the Palestine question. The United Kingdom said it opposed the policy as it was against the interests of peace, conflicted with the interests of the Arab inhabitants of the territories and ignored their rights. Each construction or expansion of a settlement, the Netherlands felt, would increase the resentment of the inhabitants; Israel's stated intention further to expand its settlement programme could only undermine the basis for dialogue and trust, which were essential for any constructive negotiations.

In defiance of unanimous condemnation by world opinion, China stated, Israel had accelerated the expansion of settlements in the West Bank, had approved the establishment of four additional settlements and had declared its intention to settle hundreds of thousands of Israelis within five years; in order to realize that wild scheme, Israeli authorities were expropriating large tracts of land, seizing and demolishing civilian dwellings and displacing thousands of Palestinians.

Poland and others said the expanded construction of new settlements, the expropriation of Arab property and such methods as the demolition and sealing of habitations and commercial premises were an integral part of Israel's policy of creeping annexation. Guyana agreed and said such annexation, combined with violent oppression of the rights of the Arab population, was designed to force their acquiescence to perpetual second-class citizenship.

In Zimbabwe's opinion, the policy was part of an overall expansionist plan to settle the Middle East question through extermination and expulsion of the Palestinians. Iran reiterated that Israel intended to annex the West Bank and Gaza, a view shared by Kuwait, which said that this was being achieved by destroying their Palestinian and Arab character. Also, in the opinion of the German Democratic Republic, the growing number of Israeli settlements was an essential part of the de-Arabization of the territories; the process of "creeping annexation" of the West Bank and Gaza had already made considerable headway.

Jordan said that Israel's military attempts and diplomatic manoeuvres could not camouflage the reality of its occupation, or the fact that it was denying the Palestinians their right to self-determination; to legitimize its occupation, it had

[a]Rule 39 of the Council's provisional rules of procedure states: "The Security Council may invite members of the Secretariat or other persons, whom it considers competent for the purpose, to supply it with information or to give other assistance in examining matters within its competence."

created new *faits accomplis* by, among other measures, intensifying its settlement activities.

India charged that all of Israel's actions in the occupied territories were proof that it had every intention to perpetuate its illegal occupation over the West Bank and Gaza, to add to its illegitimate annexation of the Golan Heights (see below), and that it had no desire to contribute to a fair and durable solution of the Palestinian problem.

In Pakistan's view, Israeli policies in the territories had the single objective of annexation in order to build a "greater Israel".

Egypt said Israel had first camouflaged its settlements policy under the pretext of security, then it had used religious arguments and historical claims under the label of "liberated" or "administered" territories; currently it was trying to swallow up the rest of the occupied territories whose inhabitants were being transformed by force from full-fledged to third-class citizens.

The USSR stated that since 1967 Israel had been waging in the territories a campaign of colonial plunder, preparing the ground for final absorption; by its settlements policy, Israel was moving towards converting the land belonging to the Arabs into ghetto-type enclaves or a kind of bantustan reduced to the role of agrarian appendage to the Israeli economy.

Greece said the settlements policy had resulted in untold human suffering and loss of life; the situation in the territories could not be isolated from the problem of the self-determination of the Palestinians and from the realization of their rights, including the right to create their own State.

Israel's settlements policy, a natural corollary of its aggressive and expansionist policy, Democratic Yemen stated, was aimed at creating a new *fait accompli* that made it impossible to implement United Nations resolutions on the Palestinians' rights to return and to self-determination; in addition to the continued occupation of the West Bank, Gaza and the Golan Heights, there was an occupation of what was now called the "North Bank", i.e., Lebanon.

Lebanon, on the other hand, stressed that the situation in the occupied territories could in no way be compared to the situation in some parts of Lebanon.

Several speakers saw in Israel's settlements policy an obstacle to peace prospects in the Middle East. Among those expressing that view were Malta and Turkey. Israel's policies in the West Bank and Gaza might well be considered a time bomb threatening the entire region, said Kuwait. Yugoslavia considered Israel's continued aggression, expansion and annexation of Arab territories to be a threat to peace and security of the region and of the world. A similar position was held by Greece and Jordan, among others.

In Malta's opinion, Israel should be asked to desist from its unacceptable policies and should be persuaded to join the search for justice for the Palestinians, within a settlement of the Arab-Israeli conflict.

Pakistan believed that any progress towards peace in the Middle East was unimaginable unless Israel halted all settlement in the West Bank; even the United States, in putting forward its peace proposals, had acknowledged that a halt to Israeli settlements was indispensable for the continuation of peace efforts. By building further settlements, the United Arab Emirates stated, Israel aimed to disrupt and sabotage all such efforts; from the course taken, it was evident that Israel sought the capitulation of the Palestinians into accepting the occupation of their territories and enslavement by Israel.

France called on Israel not to compromise the chances for peace by regrettable initiatives such as establishing settlements against the unanimous international opinion. The United Kingdom felt an added urgency for appealing to Israel to freeze its settlements and to create no new obstacles to the peace process; it was the common responsibility of the Council members to urge the parties to seize the opportunity for peace that appeared to exist at the moment. Strong support for the call for an immediate settlement freeze, made by the United States President on 1 September 1982, was declared by the Netherlands, which cautioned that a continuation of Israel's policy would constitute one of the most serious obstacles to a peaceful Middle East settlement, the need for which was more pressing than ever.

As a pre-condition for a peace settlement, a number of speakers, among them Greece, Guyana, India, Kuwait, Nicaragua, Poland, the Syrian Arab Republic, Yugoslavia and Zimbabwe, called for complete and immediate Israeli withdrawal from all territories occupied since 1967, including Jerusalem, as requested by the Council in several resolutions. The USSR said the aggressor must comply with the Council's demand for unconditional withdrawal, and the Council must erect a solid barrier to Israel's annexationist designs, as provided for by the United Nations Charter.

In the case of further non-compliance by Israel with the Council's demands, several countries, among them the United Arab Emirates, called for strict Council action. It was the Council's duty to take appropriate measures when an occupying Power failed to meet its obligations under international law, Turkey stated. It was imperative that Israel be restrained without prevarication, India felt. China said the Council must unequivocally condemn Israel's aggressive and expansionist conduct, consider measures to stop Israeli expansion in the occupied territories and compel Israel to withdraw from them. The Council was duty-bound to end the dispersal and continuous violations of the human rights of the Palestinians, said Yugoslavia. In Yemen's view, the Council had no other option but to recognize the rights of the Palestinians.

Israel's recent actions in the occupied West Bank and the annexationist threats hanging over the occupied territories had made effective Council action in accordance with the Charter more urgent, Guyana and others believed. In the face of Israel's open defiance of Council decisions, Pakistan stated, the Council could not escape its responsibilities to act firmly and decisively under the Charter. As long as Israel's allies were not willing to compel Israel to comply with those decisions, Zimbabwe said, the Council had no other option but to implement Chapter VII of the Charter; the existence of a threat to peace by Israel's policy had already been ascertained. Nicaragua pointed out that on 15 February 1983,[9] in a resolution on human rights violations in the occupied territories (see ECONOMIC AND SOCIAL QUESTIONS, Chapter XVIII), the Commission on Human Rights had requested the General Assembly once again to appeal to the Council to adopt against Israel the measures provided for in Chapter VII. Kuwait called on the Council to shoulder its responsibilities and implement the provisions of the Charter.

Cuba, Nicaragua, the Syrian Arab Republic and others called for sanctions against Israel. In addition, the Syrian Arab Republic said, the Council must expel Israel from the United Nations as a non-peace-loving State.

Algeria felt that the time had come for the Council to revise its position and co-ordinate its action with the General Assembly, so that the Palestinians could return to the land from which they had been ousted and recover their property.

Iran condemned any compromise with or concession to what it called the Zionist régime.

PLO said the Council must invoke all the power vested in it by the Charter to compel Israel to accept and carry out the Council's decisions and, in the case of failure, the Council should prescribe the remedies detailed in the Charter.

Communications (March). On 1 March 1983,[26] Jordan transmitted a letter of 16 February from its Minister for Occupied Territories Affairs to the Minister for Foreign Affairs, detailing what were termed Israel's settlement activities in the West Bank and Jerusalem during January, which included confiscation of land, establishment of new settlements and consolidation of the settlement machinery.

By another letter of 1 March,[27] Jordan transmitted a report issued in January by its Ministry of Labour on the effects of Israeli settlements on the situation of Arab workers in the occupied territories.

On 23 March,[28] Jordan transmitted a report by the Minister for Occupied Territories Affairs, detailing what was described as the latest information on Israel's settlement activity during February in the territories, including Jerusalem.

The Security Council considered the situation in the occupied territories at another meeting on 20 May, urgently requested on 13 May by Qatar in its capacity as Chairman of the Arab Group.[29]

Meeting number. SC 2438.

In addition to the States previously invited, the Council invited Mali and Qatar, at their request, to participate in the discussion without the right to vote.

Statements were made by India, Jordan, Qatar (for the Arab Group), the Syrian Arab Republic and PLO.

Opening the debate, Qatar stressed that the situation in the occupied territories continued to deteriorate and said it was the international community's desire for compromise that had encouraged Israel to scorn the United Nations and in particular the Council; the Arab Group maintained that the only way of countering Israel's challenge and intransigence was to remove the restrictions which had prevented the imposition of sanctions under Chapter VII of the Charter.

The Syrian Arab Republic said the latest statistics indicated that Israel had expropriated 60 per cent of the territories on the West Bank; Israel falsely invoked external security as justification for building settlements and moving in alien settlers, while removing Arabs from the area between Nablus and Jerusalem; if the Council wished to regain credibility, it must impose mandatory sanctions or expel Israel from the United Nations as a non-peace-loving country.

As Chairman of the Movement of Non-Aligned Countries, India said that recent events in the territories again documented the increasing number of acts of colonization, brutality and repression by the Israeli authorities which threatened international peace and security; the Co-ordinating Bureau of the Non-Aligned Countries, at a meeting on 19 May in New York, had stated that the Council should take effective action not only to prevent further bloodshed and misery in the territories but also to find a comprehensive, just and lasting settlement of the Palestine question.

In Jordan's opinion, the situation was extremely explosive, with Israel's colonization programme continuing unabated; the Council and particularly its permanent members had a special responsibility to halt that policy.

In disregard of United Nations calls for a settlement freeze, PLO stated, Israel planned 16 additional settlements during the coming year in various parts of Palestine and the Golan Heights; and even if there was a freeze on new settlements, Israel could still expand the population of existing ones and connect them by highways so that they could be converted into big towns and cities. Israel was escalating its genocide and repression, PLO charged, because the Palestinian National Council had reiterated its adherence to United Nations resolutions whose implementation Israel feared.

Communications (May-July). On 25 May,[(30)] Jordan transmitted what it described as the latest information on Israeli settlement activities during March and April.

By a letter of 18 July,[(31)] the Chairman of the Committee on Palestinian rights expressed the Committee's deep concern over the reported intention of Israel to establish Jewish settlers in the centre of Hebron, despite local Arab resistance.

On 26 July,[(32)] Jordan complained about an attack that day against Arab civilians by armed Israeli settlers in Hebron, who had broken into the Islamic University in the city and fired at students and staff, killing three persons and wounding 40 others; the attack, following a similar one on 7 July, confirmed that such acts, prepared by the Israeli occupation authorities, were part of a comprehensive plan to force the Arab population to abandon their homes and land to Israeli settlers.

SECURITY COUNCIL CONSIDERATION (July/August)

Consideration of the situation in the occupied territories was resumed by the Security Council at five meetings held between 28 July and 2 August. In a letter of 27 July,[(33)] Democratic Yemen, as Chairman of the Arab Group, had requested that the Council meet immediately.

Meeting numbers. SC 2457-2461.

In addition to the countries previously invited, the Council invited Afghanistan, Bahrain, Bangladesh, Djibouti, Iraq, Israel, the Libyan Arab Jamahiriya, Malaysia, Mauritania, Oman, Saudi Arabia, Somalia, the Sudan and Tunisia, at their request, to participate in the discussion without the right to vote.

On 2 August, the Security Council voted on a draft resolution,[(34)] sponsored by Algeria, Bahrain, Democratic Yemen, Djibouti, Iraq, Jordan, Kuwait, Lebanon, the Libyan Arab Jamahiriya, Mauritania, Morocco, Oman, Qatar, Saudi Arabia, Somalia, the Sudan, the Syrian Arab Republic, Tunisia, the United Arab Emirates and Yemen. The vote was 13 to 1, with 1 abstention, as follows:

In favour: China, France, Guyana, Jordan, Malta, Netherlands, Nicaragua, Pakistan, Poland, Togo, USSR, United Kingdom, Zimbabwe.
Against: United States.
Abstaining: Zaire.

Owing to the negative vote of a permanent member, the draft was not adopted.

By the draft, the Council would have determined that Israel's settlement policies had no legal validity, were a serious obstacle to Middle East peace and contravened article 49 (6) of the fourth Geneva Convention. It would have called on Israel to abide by that provision, to rescind its previous measures, to desist from any action changing the legal status and geographical nature and materially affecting the demographic composition of the territories and, in particular, not to transfer parts of its own civilian population into the territories and to force transfers of Arab populations from there. It would have strongly deplored Israel's persistence in pursuing those policies and would have called on it to dismantle existing settlements and cease planning and establishing new ones. Further, the Council would have: rejected all Israeli illegal actions, especially those resulting in the expulsion, deportation and forcible transfers of Arabs; condemned the recent attacks against Arab civilians, especially that in Al-Khalil (Hebron); called on all States not to provide Israel with any assistance to be used in connection with its settlements; and reaffirmed its determination, in the event of Israeli non-compliance, to examine ways in accordance with relevant Charter provisions to secure implementation of the resolution.

Introducing the draft on behalf of the League of Arab States, Jordan said that, despite the Council's attempts to deal with the matter, Israel's arbitrary measures against the Arab population had intensified and its settlement activities increased, jeopardizing peace and security in the area and internationally; the elements of the draft, which reflected the past positions of the Council, were basic principles for dealing with the deteriorating situation.

The United States stressed that it shared the anguish about the loss of life and destruction of property in the West Bank and disapproved of Israel's settlements policy; the draft, however, did not adequately address the recent criminal attacks against Israeli settlers and contained unacceptable elements, in particular the implication that Israel had carried out forcible large-scale transfers of the Arab population, an allegation for which there was not sufficient evidence. The future of Israeli settlements was a key issue that needed to be addressed in negotiations; as emphasized by the United States President on 1 September 1982, a settlements freeze would foster the kind of atmosphere needed for peace. The United States, however, did not believe that it was practical or appropriate to call for a dismantling of existing settlements, nor could it accept continuing the sterile argument as to whether the settlements were legal or not, an argument that had dominated discussions to the detriment of the basic issue, namely, how to bring about a just and peaceful solution to the conflict over the occupied territories.

Zaire felt that the text, like previous ones, would not lead to action, which undermined the Council's credibility. The paragraph condemning attacks against the Arab civilian population was not balanced; murder, whether by Israelis or by Arabs, could not be tolerated. The latter view was also shared by the Netherlands.

On the other hand, Guyana saw the draft as a genuine attempt to deal with a deteriorating situation; Israel must be held responsible for the recent incidents in the occupied territories, which could only lead to greater tension.

The USSR said that the United States, by voting against a text representing the united view of all Arab nations and a minimum action, had blocked the path to a just Middle East peace and sanctioned an annexation by Israel of the West Bank. The argument that there was no evidence to support the allegation of mass deportation or forcible transfers was based either on misinformation or misinterpretation, said PLO; Israel's settlements policy was meant to facilitate the acquisition of territory so that it might become a bargaining chip in so-called negotiations.

Condemning the attack of 26 July, France stated that Israel, as the occupying Power responsible for protecting the Palestinian civilian population, must prevent such tragedies. Calling for respect of democratic freedoms and for cessation of the escalation of violence and repression, France noted that Israel's policy of *fait accompli* in the territories was harmful to peace efforts and that its settlements were without legal basis and created an atmosphere of tension.

Malta said there could no longer be any doubt that Israel was embarking on an insidious effort to take over the West Bank and the Gaza Strip; in just three years, the number of both settlements and settlers had more than doubled.

The actions set forth in the draft were urgent and immediate tasks, Nicaragua said. In Poland's opinion, the text constituted the least the Council could do, and an end must be put to the deteriorating situation before the policy of *faits accomplis* in annexing Arab territories achieved its sinister long-range objectives. Among the non-members, Yugoslavia called for adoption of the draft bearing in mind the urgency of the situation. Similarly, Djibouti said the Council, as the guardian of peace and security, must take the necessary measures so that Israel would cease its inhuman and barbaric practices against the Palestinians in the occupied territories.

The Permanent Observer of the League of Arab States remarked that, out of pragmatic considerations and to achieve a compromise, the draft sought not to achieve justice for the Palestinians but to mitigate flagrant injustices; not only was Israel's settlements policy illegal, but it was making Jews cannon-fodder for the expansionist, revisionist objectives of the Government.

Most of the 38 speakers during the debate again denounced Israel's settlements policy as illegal and contrary to international law, as well as an obstacle to a Middle East peace settlement. Israel's claims that, far from constituting an obstacle to peace, the settlements were vital for its security and, as an effective early warning system, a deterrent to war, were rejected by a number of countries, among them Bahrain, Democratic Yemen, Jordan, Kuwait, the Libyan Arab Jamahiriya, Mauritania and Saudi Arabia. Jordan alleged that Israel's settlements policy was a tactic designed to undermine and abort peace efforts. Mauritania said prospects for peace in the Middle East and the rest of the world were threatened if Israel's practices continued with impunity, a position also held by a number of other countries.

The view that Israel's settlements policy was a step towards assimilation and annexation of the occupied territories was reiterated by many speakers, including Afghanistan, Bangladesh, Democratic Yemen, the German Democratic Republic, Guyana, Kuwait, the Libyan Arab Jamahiriya, Morocco, Pakistan, Saudi Arabia and the Permanent Observer of the League of Arab States. Widely held also was the opinion that the establishment or expansion of settlements and the violation of human rights of the Arab population of the territories were two complementary trends. In that context, most speakers condemned the events at Hebron.

Jordan, which opened the debate, charged that those events, as well as systematic Israeli terrorism in the West Bank, Gaza and the Golan Heights, were a step towards emptying those areas. The suppression at Al-Khalil was but the other half of Israel's expansionist policy. As part of the official occupation machinery, the settlers played a central role of organizing and implementing terrorist activities in a deliberate manner conducive to a psychological and social climate in which it was difficult for the Arab citizens to stay, in preparation for a wide-scale evacuation. The incident of 26 July was just one example of Israel's feverish quest to expel indigenous Arabs and replace them with Jewish settlers.

The premeditated and cold-blooded attack against the Islamic University of Hebron and the repression at Bir Zeit, Jerusalem, Nablus and elsewhere were designed to help achieve Israel's openly proclaimed objective of creeping colonization of the West Bank and Gaza, charged Mauritania.

A similar view was expressed by Qatar and others. As the Palestinians had refused to acquiesce to repressive measures, the confiscation of land and limitation of freedoms, and to gradual Judaization, Qatar said, Israel was determined to liquidate them physically.

Nicaragua stated that the situation was becoming more critical day by day; the appeals of the Israeli Government to the settlers not to take the law into their own hands had no credibility, because punishment of the guilty was practically non-existent and the sentences imposed were ridiculously out of proportion to the seriousness of the crimes.

The Sudan said that the recent events in the territories were part of Israel's scheme to drive out indigenous Arabs and to Judaize the territories in full. A similar view was expressed by several others, among them Afghanistan, Bangladesh, Djibouti, the Syrian Arab Republic, Togo and the Permanent Observer of the League of Arab States. The Syrian Arab Republic added that while official Israeli circles and their mouthpieces in the United States were vigorously striving to absolve the ruling classes in Israel of responsibility for the settlers' crimes, each settler was keen on implementing the official settlements policy on which Israel had been based since its beginning.

In the opinion of the Libyan Arab Jamahiriya, the arming of settlers was a concrete expression of the ideas of fanatical Zionists calling for the expulsion of all gentiles from Israel.

The German Democratic Republic said the violence against Palestinian students at Hebron demonstrated anew that the aggressive policy pursued by Israel and its accomplices was aimed at preventing the Palestinians from exercising their inalienable rights, particularly the right to an independent State.

China charged that it was the recent Israeli decision to establish a settlement in Al-Khalil that had further aggravated tension. Facts revealed that the terrorist tactics used by the Israeli authorities to persecute the indigenous inhabitants of the occupied territories were entirely premeditated with the express aim of changing the demographic composition so as to legitimize the Israeli settlements scheme.

A similar position was held by others, including Morocco and Pakistan. Morocco believed that there was an organic relationship between the oppression of Arabs and the establishment of illegal Israeli settlements; the events at Al-Khalil had coincided with the Israeli decision to build settlements in the heart of that city. Pakistan considered that the tragic death of Palestinians in Hebron was a manifestation of the deteriorating situation in the occupied territories for which Israel must assume full responsibility. The settlements had become the main source of violence and conflict; that the settlers were allowed to carry arms was a constant source of harassment and provocation to Arab inhabitants, inevitably leading to tension and clashes.

In Bahrain's opinion, the continuous violence in the occupied territories was an inevitable result of Israel's occupation and aggressive expansionist policy, and of its systematic terrorization of the inhabitants carried out in full view of the Israeli army and security forces.

In Turkey's view, the occurrences in Al-Khalil were yet another manifestation of the fact that Israel was adamant in the pursuit of its policies of repression, thus further aggravating the plight of the Palestinians and the Middle East situation.

Saudi Arabia complained that the Israeli authorities were oblivious to the fact that Al-Khalil and most of the towns of Gaza and the West Bank were under constant curfew; thus, Jewish settlers could rampage through Arab areas, setting fires, engaging in sabotage and committing murder, encouraged and supported by the Israeli authorities.

Afghanistan charged that the Israeli Government did virtually nothing to prevent armed settlers from engaging in cynical attacks. The Israeli authorities had implied that the recent violence against Palestinians was justified because of an attack on a Jewish settler; reports from different sources had indicated that the wounded settler, attacked by unidentified persons, was not attended by the Israeli military, which had thought he was an Arab; had he been taken promptly to the hospital he would have been saved.

Kuwait alleged that the act of aggression at Al-Khalil had been committed by armed Israeli settlers in full view of the Israeli Government, which was not merely content with establishing settlements and importing tens of thousands of Jews to settle therein; it implanted armed bands among the settlers, with whom it co-ordinated action.

Egypt also held Israel directly responsible for the aggression against the students of Al-Khalil University, adding that the ensuing arbitrary measures by the Israeli occupation authorities reaffirmed the plight of Palestinians in the territories and the extent of the danger to which they were exposed. In view of Israel's persistence in building settlements and the terrorism by armed groups of settlers, the Arab inhabitants had no recourse but to exercise their natural right to defend what remained of their properties, territories and homeland.

The killing at Hebron and the building of Israeli settlements was also denounced by Iran.

PLO recalled that on 10 July Israel's Deputy Prime Minister had told reporters that the Israeli cabinet had decided on a two-stage plan for the construction of a Jewish quarter at Hebron, projecting a settlement in the coming three years of 500 Jewish families in the commercial heart of the city, which would entail the eviction or expulsion of the population—or its elimination should it insist on defending its right to stay.

Israel, on the other hand, stressed that the murder at Hebron was unreservedly condemned by its Government and people; it would do everything possible to apprehend the culprits for their crimes. However, while condemning the murder of Arabs, the Council did not condemn the murder of Jews. Referring to its settlements policy, Israel defended the right of Jews to live in any part of the "Land of Israel"; they did not regard themselves as foreigners in Judaea or Samaria or any other part of the "Land of Israel". It could not be accepted that Jews should be prohibited from settling in areas which were the very heart of their homeland; however, it had never been Israel's aim to exercise control over the lives and activities of the Arab inhabitants of Judaea and Samaria, with whom Jews sought to live as equals. It was Israel's policy that no single Palestinian Arab resident of these areas legally holding claim to land should be made homeless by the establishment of Jewish villages, many of which had been established on Jewish-owned land expropriated in 1948 by Jordan or Egypt, land that had been barren for centuries. With regard to article 49 of the fourth Geneva Convention, Israel pointed out that it banned forcible transfers, not voluntary acts of individuals taking up residence; no Arab inhabitants had been displaced by the establishment of Jewish villages.

In the view of the United Kingdom, the latest atrocity at Hebron was one of a series that would not be stopped until the underlying causes had been removed. Israel's settlements policy undermined confidence that it was ready to negotiate freely about the final state of the occupied territories; the United Kingdom called on Israel to put an end to that damaging policy and to declare an immediate settlements freeze.

The call for a settlements freeze was also supported by the Netherlands, which added that the events at Hebron were evidence of the dangerous consequences of Israel's settlements policy, a major source of tension; each construction or expansion of a settlement would only increase the strong and justified resentment of the inhabitants.

In the opinion of the USSR, the Council could not remain indifferent to the illegal acts systematically perpetrated by Israel on Arab soil. The Council should in particular be mindful of the fact that in resolution 465(1980)[35] it had declared that there was no legal validity to the steps taken by Israel to alter the physical character, demographic composition and institutional structure or status of the occupied territories. At that time, the Council had called on Israel to rescind those measures, to dismantle the existing settlements and in particular to cease, on an urgent basis, the establishment, construction and planning of new ones. Israel's response to those minimal demands was the annexation of eastern Jerusalem and the Golan Heights, further aggressive sorties against neighbouring Arab States and the invasion of Lebanon, in addition to the construction of dozens of new settlements on the West Bank and in the Gaza Strip where it continued methodically to carry out plans to locate thousands of new settlers. The United States gave in to every new demand Israel made, at the expense of the Arabs; a further step in that direction was the current United States position that the Israeli settlements on Arab lands were legal.

China said the worsening situation demanded an unequivocal response from the Council, which should strongly condemn the Israeli authorities for engineering the incidents at Al-Khalil, stop all expansionist activities in the occupied territories and compel Israel to withdraw from them.

Jordan believed that Israel would not have gone so far in its expansionist policies had the Council been able to discharge its responsibilities as outlined in the Charter and had the great Powers shouldered their duties with regard to Israel's intransigence and persistence in creating settlements in the territories and in terrorizing the Arab citizens in order to force them to flee their homes, as was the case in Al-Khalil. The credibility of any peace initiative, it added, would depend on a clear acknowledgement of the situation and clear rejection of Israeli settlements.

Pakistan called on the Council to reaffirm that the settlements were illegal and to make yet another effort to compel Israel to respect its resolutions; Israel could be restrained only if the Council could fulfil its responsibility to censure Israel's conduct and condemn its policies of repression and violence.

Poland said the recurrence of acts of terror and violence, such as the ones at Hebron, should be a grim reminder that the Council should fulfil its responsibility and take effective and urgent action by declaring the illegality and inadmissibility of Israeli settlements, which had become a deadly weapon in Israel's annexation policy.

The time had come for the Council, as the primary body for maintaining international peace and security, to take the necessary action under Chapter VII of the Charter, Nicaragua stated.

The call for such action was also supported by several non-members of the Council, including Afghanistan and the Syrian Arab Republic. Unless the Council effectively forced Israel to cease its illegal activities, Afghanistan warned, there would be an increasing danger of violence and armed clashes. The Council's failure to take mandatory action had served to encourage Israel to continue Judaizing the occupied territories, said the Syrian Arab Republic, which called on the United States to enable the Council to take effective steps in accordance with Chapter VII to evacuate the aggressors from the occupied territories, unconditionally, and to enable the Palestinians to exercise their rights to self-determination and to the establishment of an independent State under PLO leadership.

Saudi Arabia called once more on the international community not to permit Israel to disregard United Nations resolutions. As for the latest events at Al-Khalil, it urged the Council to condemn explicitly the Israeli acts and to declare null and void all settlements measures by Israel. There should also be a statement to the effect that the Council would be forced to take measures in accordance with the Charter to implement its resolutions.

Bahrain appealed to the Council to discharge its responsibilities under the Charter and fulfil its obligations to protect the population of the territories from the aggression by armed Israeli bands; it should not be difficult for the Council to compel Israel to implement its resolutions.

Kuwait said the Council must reaffirm its resolutions with regard to the illegality of the Israeli settlements and must exert a new effort to compel Israel to respect those resolutions as well as the international covenants which obliged the occupying Power not just to protect the lives of civilians in their occupied territories but also not to make any changes in their demographic nature and legal status; above all, it was required to put an end to the Israeli occupation and to give the Palestinians the opportunity to exercise their rights. Kuwait called on the countries assisting Israel, foremost the United States, to cease supporting it and to stop putting obstacles in the way of the Council, so that it might carry out its mandate by condemning Israel and imposing the appropriate sanctions.

Qatar urged the Council to give rein to the will of the international community, which Israel had thus far been able to obstruct, and to discharge its responsibility.

The Libyan Arab Jamahiriya called on the Council to shoulder its responsibilities under the Charter and condemn Israeli practices and policies, take concrete steps to deter the aggressor, affirm the illegality of settlements, and condemn the States which assisted Israel in its settlements policy and violation of human rights.

The Sudan said it was incumbent on the Council, which was responsible for the maintenance of international peace and security, to take measures in accordance with the Charter that would put an end to the Israeli practices falling outside international law and United Nations resolutions.

Turkey firmly believed that it was the duty of the international community to remind Israel of its responsibilities under the 1949 Geneva Conventions; it was incumbent on the Council to take measures to prevent Israel from further violating international law and the inalienable rights of the Palestinians.

Democratic Yemen said if the Council was to uphold the seriousness of its resolutions and shoulder its responsibilities under the Charter, it was called upon to condemn Israel's expansionist policies and practices and take immediate steps to deter the aggressor and put an end to Israel's flouting of Council resolutions, especially resolutions 465(1980)[35] and 476(1980),[36] which emphasized the illegality of the Israeli settlements.

Egypt stressed that the Council could not afford to disregard the plight of the Palestinians under Israeli occupation. The terrorists of Al-Khalil should be arrested and brought to trial to prevent the repetition of such actions. The deteriorating situation in the occupied territories required explicit and decisive Council action, with the international community holding Israel completely responsible.

The Council must face up to the explosive situation in the territories and a repetition of the events at Hebron must be prevented, said Mauritania. There must be a thorough examination of the terrorism of which the Palestinians were victims, and the latest cold-blooded crimes—for which the responsibility of the occupying authorities could neither be denied nor even limited—must be vigorously condemned.

Speaking for the non-aligned countries, India called for determined and urgent Council action to prevent further bloodshed and misery. The Council should condemn the recent incidents at Hebron and other cities and fix responsibility for these atrocities on the occupying Israeli forces. It should again declare the illegality and inadmissibility of Israeli settlements practices and secure the annulment of all measures taken by Israel in that direction. Lastly, the Council should strive to find a comprehensive, just and lasting solution to the Palestine question on a priority basis.

Cuba felt that the time had come for the Council to exercise its responsibilities under the Charter and take appropriate action to put a timely end to the misdeeds of the Israeli occupying forces and promote a just and lasting Middle East settlement, especially its root cause—the Palestine problem.

Bangladesh held it imperative for the Council to proceed urgently, with all the authority and resources at its disposal, to implement its resolutions and decisions; recent developments in the occupied territories had demonstrated that a lack of firm and expeditious Council action only aggravated the situation.

In Yugoslavia's view, the Council should reaffirm that the Israeli settlements were illegal and inadmissible, as well as make one more effort and exert pressure to halt such Israeli policy.

Again stressing the importance of implementing the recommendations of the Committee on Palestinian rights, Senegal, speaking on the Committee's behalf, said that the acts of violence in recent months indicated the urgent need to rectify the situation that had continued for too long, a situation whose consequences for international peace and security were more incalculable than ever.

The German Democratic Republic felt that the recent events in the West Bank underscored the urgent need for immediate and unconditional Israeli withdrawal and for a just solution to the Middle East problem, the core of which was the Palestine question; it was time that the Council rose to its responsibility for preserving peace and security and that it took resolute measures for immediate cessation of Israeli aggression and occupation. Several other speakers took a similar position.

According to PLO, the Council had the power under the Charter to ask for an immediate termination of the occupation, on whose illegality there was unanimity. If a Member State refused to comply, the Council could apply the Charter provisions; there was no room in the United Nations for people rejecting the Council's decisions, especially when that rejection brought so much misery and bloodshed. PLO expected from the Council action in very clear-cut language demanding that Israel withdraw immediately and unconditionally from the occupied territories; as stated in a message from its Chairman, PLO called on the international community, represented in the Council, to condemn Israel's racist practices, to seek to put an end to them and to support the inalienable rights of the Palestinians.

The answer lay in the Council and in the collective will to deter Israel from persisting in breaching the Council's resolutions and the United Nations Charter, the Permanent Observer of the League of Arab States said.

Communications (August-November). By a letter of 2 August 1983,[37] Greece transmitted a government statement deploring the attack of 26 July and expressing the hope that Israel would arrest and punish the culprits and ensure that such criminal acts against the Arab population would not be repeated.

By letters of 5 August,[38] 26 August,[39] 20 October[40] and 11 November,[41] Jordan transmitted what it said was information on Israel's settlement activities from May through October.

Recommendations of the Conference on the Palestine question. The International Conference on the Question of Palestine,[19] in its Declaration adopted in September (see above, under PALESTINE QUESTION), considered that the various proposals consistent with international law, such as the Arab peace plan adopted at the Twelfth Arab Summit Conference at Fez in September 1982,[42] should serve as guidelines for concerted international effort to resolve the Palestine question. These guidelines stressed the need to oppose and reject Israeli policies in the occupied territories, including Jerusalem, and any *de facto* situation contrary to international law and United Nations resolutions, in particular the establishment of settlements, as major obstacles to a Middle East peace.

In its Programme of Action, the Conference recommended that States should not encourage migration to the occupied territories until Israel had put a definitive end to its illegal settlements policy. The Conference invited the Security Council to take urgent action to bring about an immediate and complete cessation of the establishment of settlements, to consider urgently the reports of the Security Council Commission established in 1979,[43] which had examined the situation concerning the settlements, and to reactivate that Commission.

Similar recommendations had also been made at the regional preparatory meetings for the Conference.

Activities of the Committee on Palestinian rights. In its 1983 report to the General Assembly,[44] the Committee on the Exercise of the Inalienable Rights of the Palestinian People stated that it had continued to follow closely developments in the occupied territories, in particular the establishment and enlargement of Israeli settlements, the annexation of vast areas of Arab-owned land, and other violations by Israel of the rights of the Palestinians. In communications throughout the year to the Secretary-General and the Security Council President, the Committee had expressed its concern over those Israeli policies. In addition to its letters of protest, the Committee had urged the Council to reactivate, as a matter of priority, its 1979 Commission to examine the situation relating to Israeli settlements. The Committee recalled that the Commission had unanimously adopted its latest report as far back as November 1980,[45] but the report had not been considered by the Council.

The Committee pointed out that, during 1983, Israel had pursued its settlements policy despite international censure, United Nations decisions and public and parliamentary questioning within Israel itself. The Committee stated that the policy constituted a network of settlement programmes and several other administrative and economic procedures designed to force individual and mass transfers from the West Bank and Gaza, with the objective of evacuating the indigenous Arab population. The Committee noted that the number of Israeli settlers in the West Bank and East Jerusalem had increased from 91,000 in April 1979 to some 140,000 in 1982; it was Israel's declared policy to place up to 400,000 non-indigenous, colonial settlers there within five years and 1.4 million Jews over the coming 30 years. By the end of 1982, approximately 153 settlements were estimated to have been established in the West Bank and East Jerusalem; this represented an area of some 2,453 square kilometres, or 44 per cent of the total West Bank territory. Four more new settlements had been approved on 16 January 1983. A close look at Israeli settlement activities revealed that the intention was to fragmentize the demographic, geographic, economic and social unity of the occupied territories.

GENERAL ASSEMBLY ACTION

In two of its 15 December resolutions on the report of the Committee on Palestinian rights, the General Assembly also dealt specifically with Israel's settlements policy. By the first (38/79 C), it deplored Israel's persistence in establishing settlements. By the second (38/79 D), it condemned: the establishment of settlements on Arab lands and transfer of an alien population thereto; and the arming of Israeli settlers and the perpetration of violence by them against Arab civilians. The Assembly also reaffirmed that Israel's measures to change the occupied territories were null and void.

In a 13 December resolution (38/58 C), the Assembly endorsed as a guideline for convening an international peace conference on the Middle East (see above, under PALESTINE QUESTION) the need to oppose Israeli policies and practices, in particular establishing settlements, as one of the major obstacles to achieving Middle East peace. In a resolution of 19 December (38/166), the Assembly rejected Israeli plans and actions to change the demographic composition of the occupied territories, particularly the increase and expansion of settlements, and other actions displacing Palestinians therefrom; and recognized the need for a comprehensive report on the impact of the Israeli settlements on the living conditions of the Palestinians, to be submitted by the Secretary-General in 1984.

Explaining in the Special Political Committee its abstention on the draft which became resolution 38/79 C, the United States said that the text diverted attention from the fundamental question of whether settlements advanced or hindered the peace process; to persist in arguing about the legality of the settlements policy was to embark on an unproductive debate. The immediate adoption of a settlements freeze by Israel could create the confidence needed for wider participation in peace talks; parallel and positive action by the Arabs

would be required if the peace process was to succeed, the United States added.

Sweden, which also abstained, saw in Israel's settlements policy a flagrant violation of international law; the most constructive action Israel could take to improve peace prospects would be to dismantle the settlements.

Fourth Geneva Convention

The applicability of the Geneva Convention relative to the Protection of Civilian Persons in Time of War, of 12 August 1949 (fourth Geneva Convention), to the Israeli-occupied territories was reaffirmed in 1983 by the General Assembly (in resolutions 38/79 B and C) and by the Commission on Human Rights.

Action by the Commission on Human Rights. In one of two resolutions on human rights violations in the occupied Arab territories, adopted on 15 February 1983,[10] the Commission on Human Rights reaffirmed that the fourth Geneva Convention was applicable to all those territories, including Jerusalem. Condemning Israel's failure to acknowledge its applicability, the Commission called on Israel to abide by and respect the obligations arising from that and other international instruments, and urged once more all States parties to ensure respect for and compliance with the Convention in the occupied territories.

In another resolution of 15 February,[46] the Commission reaffirmed that the Convention continued to apply to Syrian territory occupied by Israel. (For further details, see ECONOMIC AND SOCIAL QUESTIONS, Chapter XVIII.)

Recommendations of the Conference on the Palestine question. The International Conference on the Question of Palestine,[19] in its Programme of Action adopted in September (see above, under PALESTINE QUESTION), recommended that all States act in accordance with their obligations under international law, especially with regard to the 1949 Geneva Conventions which required the parties to respect those Conventions in all circumstances, and in particular ensure respect by Israel for the Conventions in the occupied territories; and strive for the adoption of international measures so that Israel would implement in the West Bank and Gaza the provisions of the fourth Geneva Convention, in the light of a 1980 Security Council resolution[35] determining that all Israeli measures to change the character, composition, structure or status of the territories had no legal validity and violated the Convention.

GENERAL ASSEMBLY ACTION

In December 1983, the General Assembly adopted two resolutions (38/79 B and C) demanding that Israel comply with the Convention, both under the agenda item on the report of the Special Committee to Investigate Israeli Practices Affecting the Human Rights of the Population of the Occupied Territories. On 15 December, the Assembly, acting on the recommendation of the Special Political Committee, adopted resolution 38/79 B by recorded vote.

The General Assembly,

Recalling its resolutions 3092 A (XXVIII) of 7 December 1973, 3240 B (XXIX) of 29 November 1974, 3525 B (XXX) of 15 December 1975, 31/106 B of 16 December 1976, 32/91 A of 13 December 1977, 33/113 A of 18 December 1978, 34/90 B of 12 December 1979, 35/122 A of 11 December 1980, 36/147 A of 16 December 1981 and 37/88 A of 10 December 1982,

Recalling also Security Council resolution 465(1980) of 1 March 1980 in which, *inter alia*, the Council affirmed that the Geneva Convention relative to the Protection of Civilian Persons in Time of War, of 12 August 1949, is applicable to the Arab territories occupied by Israel since 1967, including Jerusalem,

Considering that the promotion of respect for the obligations arising from the Charter of the United Nations and other instruments and rules of international law is among the basic purposes and principles of the United Nations,

Bearing in mind the provisions of the Geneva Convention,

Noting that Israel and those Arab States whose territories have been occupied by Israel since June 1967 are parties to that Convention,

Taking into account that States parties to that Convention undertake, in accordance with article 1 thereof, not only to respect but also to ensure respect for the Convention in all circumstances,

1. *Reaffirms* that the Geneva Convention relative to the Protection of Civilian Persons in Time of War, of 12 August 1949, is applicable to Palestinian and other Arab territories occupied by Israel since 1967, including Jerusalem;

2. *Condemns once again* the failure of Israel as the occupying Power to acknowledge the applicability of that Convention to the territories it has occupied since 1967, including Jerusalem;

3. *Strongly demands* that Israel acknowledge and comply with the provisions of that Convention in Palestinian and other Arab territories it has occupied since 1967, including Jerusalem;

4. *Urgently calls upon* all States parties to that Convention to exert every effort in order to ensure respect for and compliance with its provisions in Palestinian and other Arab territories occupied by Israel since 1967, including Jerusalem.

General Assembly resolution 38/79 B

15 December 1983   Meeting 98   146-1-1 (recorded vote)

Approved by SPC (A/38/718) by recorded vote (112-1-1), 5 December (meeting 45); 12-nation draft (A/SPC/38/L.36); agenda item 69.

Sponsors: Afghanistan, Bangladesh, Cuba, Egypt, India, Indonesia, Madagascar, Malaysia, Mali, Pakistan, Qatar, Senegal.

Meeting numbers. GA 38th session: SPC 36-42, 45-48; plenary 98.

Recorded vote in Assembly as follows:

In favour: Afghanistan, Albania, Algeria, Angola, Argentina, Australia, Austria, Bahamas, Bahrain, Bangladesh, Barbados, Belgium, Belize, Benin, Bhutan, Bolivia, Botswana, Brazil, Bulgaria, Burma, Burundi, Byelorussian SSR, Canada, Cape Verde, Central African Republic, Chad, Chile, China, Colombia, Congo, Costa Rica, Cuba, Cyprus, Czechoslovakia, Democratic Kampuchea, Democratic Yemen, Denmark, Djibouti, Dominica, Dominican Republic, Ecuador, Egypt, El Salvador, Equatorial Guinea, Ethiopia, Fiji, Finland, France, Gabon, Gambia, German Democratic Republic, Germany, Federal Republic of, Ghana, Greece, Grenada, Guinea, Guinea-Bissau, Guyana, Hungary, Iceland, India, Indonesia, Iran, Iraq, Ireland, Italy, Ivory Coast, Jamaica, Japan, Jordan, Kuwait, Lao People's Democratic Republic, Lebanon, Lesotho, Liberia, Libyan Arab Jamahiriya, Luxembourg, Madagascar, Malawi, Malaysia, Maldives, Mali, Malta, Mauritania, Mauritius, Mexico, Mongolia, Morocco, Mozambique, Nepal, Netherlands, New Zealand, Nicaragua, Niger, Nigeria, Norway, Oman, Pakistan, Panama, Papua New Guinea, Paraguay, Peru, Philippines, Poland, Portugal, Qatar, Romania, Rwanda, Saint Lucia, Sao Tome and Principe, Saudi Arabia, Senegal, Seychelles, Sierra Leone, Singapore, Solomon Islands, Somalia, Spain, Sri Lanka, Sudan, Suriname, Swaziland, Sweden, Syrian Arab Republic, Thailand, Togo, Trinidad and Tobago, Tunisia, Turkey, Uganda, Ukrainian SSR, USSR, United Arab Emirates, United Kingdom, United Republic of Cameroon, United Republic of Tanzania, Upper Volta, Uruguay, Vanuatu, Venezuela, Viet Nam, Yemen, Yugoslavia, Zaire, Zambia, Zimbabwe.

Against: Israel.

Abstaining: United States.

Also on 15 December 1983, the Assembly, acting on the recommendation of the Special Political Committee, adopted resolution 38/79 C by recorded vote.

The General Assembly,

Recalling its resolutions 32/5 of 28 October 1977, 33/113 B of 18 December 1978, 34/90 C of 12 December 1979, 35/122 B of 11 December 1980, 36/147 B of 16 December 1981 and 37/88 B of 10 December 1982,

Recalling also Security Council resolution 465(1980) of 1 March 1980,

Expressing grave anxiety and concern at the present serious situation in the occupied Palestinian and other Arab territories, including Jerusalem, as a result of the continued Israeli occupation and the measures and actions taken by the Government of Israel, the occupying Power, designed to change the legal status, geographical nature and demographic composition of those territories,

Considering that the Geneva Convention relative to the Protection of Civilian Persons in Time of War, of 12 August 1949, is applicable to all Arab territories occupied since June 1967, including Jerusalem,

1. *Determines* that all such measures and actions taken by Israel in the Palestinian and other Arab territories occupied since 1967, including Jerusalem, are in violation of the relevant provisions of the Geneva Convention relative to the Protection of Civilian Persons in Time of War, of 12 August 1949, and constitute a serious obstruction of efforts to achieve a just and lasting peace in the Middle East and therefore have no legal validity;

2. *Strongly deplores* the persistence of Israel in carrying out such measures, in particular the establishment of settlements in the Palestinian and other occupied Arab territories, including Jerusalem;

3. *Demands* that Israel comply strictly with its international obligations in accordance with the principles of international law and the provisions of the Geneva Convention;

4. *Demands once more* that the Government of Israel, the occupying Power, desist forthwith from taking any action which would result in changing the legal status, geographical nature or demographic composition of the Palestinian and other Arab territories occupied since 1967, including Jerusalem;

5. *Urgently calls upon* all States parties to the Geneva Convention to respect and to exert every effort in order

to ensure respect for and compliance with its provisions in all Arab territories occupied by Israel since 1967, including Jerusalem.

General Assembly resolution 38/79 C

15 December 1983   Meeting 98   147-1-1 (recorded vote)

Approved by SPC (A/38/718) by recorded vote (113-1-1), 5 December (meeting 45); 12-nation draft (A/SPC/38/L.37); agenda item 69.

Sponsors: Afghanistan, Bangladesh, Cuba, Egypt, India, Indonesia, Madagascar, Malaysia, Mali, Pakistan, Qatar, Senegal.

Meeting numbers. GA 38th session: SPC 36-42, 45, 48; plenary 98.

Recorded vote in Assembly as follows:

In favour: Afghanistan, Albania, Algeria, Angola, Argentina, Australia, Austria, Bahamas, Bahrain, Bangladesh, Barbados, Belgium, Belize, Benin, Bhutan, Bolivia, Botswana, Brazil, Bulgaria, Burma, Burundi, Byelorussian SSR, Canada, Cape Verde, Central African Republic, Chad, Chile, China, Colombia, Congo, Costa Rica, Cuba, Cyprus, Czechoslovakia, Democratic Kampuchea, Democratic Yemen, Denmark, Djibouti, Dominica, Dominican Republic, Ecuador, Egypt, El Salvador, Equatorial Guinea, Ethiopia, Fiji, Finland, France, Gabon, Gambia, German Democratic Republic, Germany, Federal Republic of, Ghana, Greece, Grenada, Guinea, Guinea-Bissau, Guyana, Hungary, Iceland, India, Indonesia, Iran, Iraq, Ireland, Italy, Ivory Coast, Jamaica, Japan, Jordan, Kenya, Kuwait, Lao People's Democratic Republic, Lebanon, Lesotho, Liberia, Libyan Arab Jamahiriya, Luxembourg, Madagascar, Malawi, Malaysia, Maldives, Mali, Malta, Mauritania, Mauritius, Mexico, Mongolia, Morocco, Mozambique, Nepal, Netherlands, New Zealand, Nicaragua, Niger, Nigeria, Norway, Oman, Pakistan, Panama, Papua New Guinea, Paraguay, Peru, Philippines, Poland, Portugal, Qatar, Romania, Rwanda, Saint Lucia, Sao Tome and Principe, Saudi Arabia, Senegal, Seychelles, Sierra Leone, Singapore, Solomon Islands, Somalia, Spain, Sri Lanka, Sudan, Suriname, Swaziland, Sweden, Syrian Arab Republic, Thailand, Togo, Trinidad and Tobago, Tunisia, Turkey, Uganda, Ukrainian SSR, USSR, United Arab Emirates, United Kingdom, United Republic of Cameroon, United Republic of Tanzania, Upper Volta, Uruguay, Vanuatu, Venezuela, Viet Nam, Yemen, Yugoslavia, Zaire, Zambia, Zimbabwe.

Against: Israel.

Abstaining: United States.

At the request of the United States, the Special Political Committee adopted paragraph 1 of the draft that became resolution 38/79 B separately, by a recorded vote of 114 to 1. Explaining its support of that paragraph and its abstention on the text as a whole, the United States stressed that it attached great importance to the Convention, which should be applied consistently to all situations of war or military occupation without regard to the nature of the conflict; the text as a whole, however, was a sterile, ritualistic condemnation of Israel.

Israel said the first text was irrelevant and redundant, as the principles of the Convention were applied in practice to the population of the territories; its position, Israel added, was supported by well-known authorities in the field of international law. The second text was in essence a repetition of the first, with encumbering variations.

Sweden expressed its conviction that the Convention was fully applicable to all Israeli-occupied territories.

In resolution 38/79 D of 15 December, the Assembly condemned Israel's continued and persistent violations of the Convention, in particular those designated by the Convention as "grave breaches", which the Assembly declared were war crimes and an affront to humanity.

The Convention's applicability was reaffirmed in two other Assembly resolutions: a 19 December resolution (38/144) on permanent sovereignty over national resources in the occupied territories; and resolution 38/79 G of 15 December, by which the Assembly also condemned Israel's repression against and closing of Palestinian universities, in clear contravention of the Convention, and demanded that Israel comply with it and rescind all measures against educational institutions (see below).

Golan Heights

In 1983, the General Assembly (in resolutions 38/79 F and 38/180 A) and the Commission on Human Rights dealt with the situation in the Syrian Golan Heights. The Golan Heights, a part of the Syrian Arab Republic near the borders with Israel and Lebanon, had been occupied by Israel since 1967.

Action by the Commission on Human Rights. On 15 February 1983,[46] the Commission on Human Rights declared once more that Israel's December 1981 decision to impose its laws, jurisdiction and administration on the occupied Syrian Golan Heights[47] was an act of aggression and that it had no validity. The Commission called on Israel to rescind that decision and emphasized the necessity of total and unconditional Israeli withdrawal from the occupied territories as an essential prerequisite for a Middle East peace. The Commission determined that the continued occupation and effective annexation of the Golan Heights by Israel, as well as the inhuman treatment of the Syrian population, gravely violated the 1948 Universal Declaration of Human Rights,[48] the fourth Geneva Convention and United Nations resolutions. The Commission reaffirmed that the Hague Convention of 1907 and the fourth Geneva Convention continued to apply to Israeli-occupied Syrian territory. It strongly deplored the negative vote of a permanent member of the Security Council which had prevented the adoption of measures under Chapter VII of the United Nations Charter.

Report of the Secretary-General. As requested by the General Assembly, the Secretary-General submitted in October 1983 a report[49] on implementation of a December 1982 resolution[50] in which the Assembly had condemned Israel for refusing to heed demands to rescind its 1981 decision to impose its laws, jurisdiction and administration on the Golan Heights, and calling on Member States not to recognize such measures. He reported that in reply to his note verbale of 10 March 1983, Israel had stated on 27 September that its position was set out fully in December 1981.[51] As at 12 October 1983, eight Member States had replied to the Secretary-General's request for relevant information.

GENERAL ASSEMBLY ACTION

In December 1983, the General Assembly adopted two resolutions dealing with the situation in the Golan Heights. On 15 December, under the agenda item on the report of the Special Committee to Investigate Israeli Practices Affecting the Human Rights of the Population of the Occupied Territories, the Assembly, acting on the recommendation of the Special Political Committee, adopted resolution 38/79 F by recorded vote.

The General Assembly,

Deeply concerned that the Arab territories occupied since 1967 have been under continued Israeli military occupation,

Recalling Security Council resolution 497(1981) of 17 December 1981 and General Assembly resolutions 36/226 B of 17 December 1981, ES-9/1 of 5 February 1982 and 37/88 E of 10 December 1982,

Recalling its previous resolutions, in particular resolutions 3414(XXX) of 5 December 1975, 31/61 of 9 December 1976, 32/20 of 25 November 1977, 33/28 and 33/29 of 7 December 1978, 34/70 of 6 December 1979 and 35/122 E of 11 December 1980, in which it, _inter alia_, called upon Israel to put an end to its occupation of the Arab territories and to withdraw from all those territories,

Reaffirming once more the illegality of Israel's decision of 14 December 1981 to impose its laws, jurisdiction and administration on the occupied Syrian Golan Heights, which has resulted in the effective annexation of that territory,

Reaffirming that the acquisition of territory by force is inadmissible under the Charter of the United Nations and that all territories thus occupied by Israel must be returned,

Recalling the Geneva Convention relative to the Protection of Civilian Persons in Time of War, of 12 August 1949,

1. _Strongly condemns_ Israel, the occupying Power, for its refusal to comply with the relevant resolutions of the General Assembly and the Security Council, particularly Council resolution 497(1981), in which the Council, _inter alia_, decided that the Israeli decision to impose its laws, jurisdiction and administration on the occupied Syrian Golan Heights was null and void and without international legal effect and demanded that Israel, the occupying Power, should rescind forthwith its decision;

2. _Condemns_ the persistence of Israel in changing the physical character, demographic composition, institutional structure and legal status of the occupied Syrian Arab Golan Heights;

3. _Determines_ that all legislative and administrative measures and actions taken or to be taken by Israel, the occupying Power, that purport to alter the character and legal status of the Syrian Arab Golan Heights are null and void and constitute a flagrant violation of international law and of the Geneva Convention relative to the Protection of Civilian Persons in Time of War, of 12 August 1949, and have no legal effect;

4. _Strongly condemns_ Israel for its attempts and measures to impose forcibly Israeli citizenship and Israeli identity cards on the Syrian citizens in the occupied Syrian Arab Golan Heights and calls upon it to desist from its repressive measures against the population of the Syrian Arab Golan Heights;

5. _Calls once again upon_ Member States not to recognize any of the legislative or administrative measures and actions referred to above;

6. _Requests_ the Secretary-General to submit to the General Assembly at its thirty-ninth session a report on the implementation of the present resolution.

General Assembly resolution 38/79 F

15 December 1983   Meeting 98   144-1-1 (recorded vote)

Approved by SPC (A/38/718) by recorded vote (114-1-1), 5 December (meeting 45); 13-nation draft (A/SPC/38/L.40); agenda item 69.

Sponsors: Afghanistan, Bangladesh, Cuba, Egypt, India, Indonesia, Madagascar, Malaysia, Mali, Mongolia, Pakistan, Qatar, Senegal.

Meeting numbers. GA 38th session: SPC 36-42, 45-48; plenary 98.

Recorded vote in Assembly as follows:

In favour: Afghanistan, Albania, Algeria, Angola, Argentina, Australia, Austria, Bahamas, Bahrain, Bangladesh, Barbados, Belgium, Belize, Benin, Bhutan, Bolivia, Botswana, Brazil, Bulgaria, Burma, Burundi, Byelorussian SSR, Canada, Cape Verde, Central African Republic, Chad, Chile, China, Colombia, Congo, Costa Rica, Cuba, Cyprus, Czechoslovakia, Democratic Kampuchea, Democratic Yemen, Denmark, Djibouti, Dominican Republic, Ecuador, Egypt, El Salvador, Equatorial Guinea, Ethiopia, Fiji, Finland, France, Gabon, Gambia, German Democratic Republic, Germany, Federal Republic of, Ghana, Greece, Grenada, Guinea, Guinea-Bissau, Guyana, Hungary, Iceland, India, Indonesia, Iran, Iraq, Ireland, Italy, Ivory Coast, Jamaica, Japan, Jordan, Kenya, Kuwait, Lao People's Democratic Republic, Lebanon, Lesotho, Liberia, Libyan Arab Jamahiriya, Luxembourg, Madagascar, Malawi, Malaysia, Maldives, Mali, Malta, Mauritania, Mauritius, Mexico, Mongolia, Morocco, Mozambique, Nepal, Netherlands, New Zealand, Nicaragua, Niger, Nigeria, Norway, Oman, Pakistan, Panama, Papua New Guinea, Paraguay, Peru, Philippines, Poland, Portugal, Qatar, Romania, Rwanda, Sao Tome and Principe, Saudi Arabia, Senegal, Seychelles, Sierra Leone, Singapore, Solomon Islands, Somalia, Spain, Sri Lanka, Sudan, Suriname, Swaziland, Sweden, Syrian Arab Republic, Thailand, Togo, Trinidad and Tobago, Tunisia, Turkey, Uganda, Ukrainian SSR, USSR, United Arab Emirates, United Kingdom, United Republic of Cameroon, United Republic of Tanzania, Upper Volta, Uruguay, Vanuatu, Venezuela, Viet Nam, Yemen, Yugoslavia, Zambia, Zimbabwe.

Against: Israel.

Abstaining: United States.

Israel said that the text bore witness to the relentless hostility of Syrian leaders and their refusal to contemplate negotiations on the basis of Security Council resolution 242(1967);[25] the text rejected any thought of peace and ignored the causes for Israel's presence in the Golan Heights.

The United States called on Israel to fulfil its obligations to the population in the Golan Heights, but remarked that the resolution went beyond the Security Council's 1981 resolution declaring Israel's decision null and void.[52]

Sweden considered the annexation of the Golan Heights to be a flagrant violation of international law; it stressed that its support for the draft did not alter its opposition to the February 1982 resolution[53] mentioned in the preamble.

The Syrian Arab Republic said that the occupation authorities were imposing Israeli identity by force on the Golan Heights population. Israel's 1981 decision extending its law there was calculated to establish a Greater Israel from the Euphrates to the Nile, and Israeli statements that the Golan Heights were an indivisible part of Israel confirmed those intentions.

On 19 December 1983, under the agenda item "The situation in the Middle East", the General Assembly adopted resolution 38/180 A by recorded vote.

The General Assembly,

Having discussed the item entitled "The situation in the Middle East",

Taking note of the report of the Secretary-General of 30 September 1983,

Recalling Security Council resolution 497(1981) of 17 December 1981,

Reaffirming its resolutions 36/226 B of 17 December 1981, ES-9/1 of 5 February 1982 and 37/123 A of 16 December 1982,

Recalling its resolution 3314(XXIX) of 14 December 1974, in which it defined an act of aggression, *inter alia,* as "the invasion or attack by the armed forces of a State of the territory of another State, or any military occupation, however temporary, resulting from such invasion or attack, or any annexation by the use of force of the territory of another State or part thereof" and provided that "no consideration of whatever nature, whether political, economic, military or otherwise, may serve as a justification for aggression",

Reaffirming the fundamental principle of the inadmissibility of the acquisition of territory by force,

Reaffirming once more the applicability of the Geneva Convention relative to the Protection of Civilian Persons in Time of War, of 12 August 1949, to the occupied Palestinian and other Arab territories, including Jerusalem,

Noting that Israel's record, policies and actions establish conclusively that it is not a peace-loving Member State and that it has not carried out its obligations under the Charter of the United Nations,

Noting further that Israel has refused, in violation of Article 25 of the Charter, to accept and carry out the numerous relevant decisions of the Security Council, in particular resolution 497(1981), thus failing to carry out its obligations under the Charter,

1. *Strongly condemns* Israel for its failure to comply with Security Council resolution 497(1981) and General Assembly resolutions 36/226 B, ES-9/1 and 37/123 A;

2. *Declares once more* that Israel's continued occupation of the Golan Heights and its decision of 14 December 1981 to impose its laws, jurisdiction and administration on the occupied Syrian Golan Heights constitute an act of aggression under the provisions of Article 39 of the Charter of the United Nations and General Assembly resolution 3314(XXIX);

3. *Declares once more* that Israel's decision to impose its laws, jurisdiction and administration on the occupied Syrian Golan Heights is illegal and therefore null and void and has no validity whatsoever;

4. *Declares* all Israeli policies and practices of, or aimed at, annexation of the occupied Palestinian and other Arab territories, including Jerusalem, to be illegal and in violation of international law and of the relevant United Nations resolutions;

5. *Determines once more* that all actions taken by Israel to give effect to its decision relating to the occupied Syrian Golan Heights are illegal and invalid and shall not be recognized;

6. *Reaffirms its determination* that all relevant provisions of the Regulations annexed to the Hague Convention IV of 1907, and the Geneva Convention relative to the Protection of Civilian Persons in Time of War, of 12 August 1949, continue to apply to the Syrian territory occupied by Israel since 1967, and calls upon the parties thereto to respect and ensure respect of their obligations under these instruments in all circumstances;

7. *Determines once more* that the continued occupation of the Syrian Golan Heights since 1967 and their annexation by Israel on 14 December 1981, following Israel's decision to impose its laws, jurisdiction and administration on that territory, constitute a continuing threat to international peace and security;

8. *Strongly deplores* the negative vote by a permanent member of the Security Council which prevented the Council from adopting against Israel, under Chapter VII of the Charter, the "appropriate measures" referred to in resolution 497(1981) unanimously adopted by the Council;

9. *Further deplores* any political, economic, financial, military and technological support to Israel that encourages Israel to commit acts of aggression and to consolidate and perpetuate its occupation and annexation of occupied Arab territories;

10. *Firmly emphasizes once more* its demand that Israel, the occupying Power, rescind forthwith its illegal decision of 14 December 1981 to impose its laws, jurisdiction and administration on the Syrian Golan Heights, which resulted in the effective annexation of that territory;

11. *Reaffirms once more* the overriding necessity of the total and unconditional withdrawal by Israel from all the Palestinian and other Arab territories occupied since 1967, including Jerusalem, which is an essential prerequisite for the establishment of a comprehensive and just peace in the Middle East;

12. *Determines once more* that Israel's record, policies and actions confirm that it is not a peace-loving Member State, that it has persistently violated the principles contained in the Charter and that it has carried out neither its obligations under the Charter nor its commitment under General Assembly resolution 273(III) of 11 May 1949;

13. *Calls once more upon* all Member States to apply the following measures:

(a) To refrain from supplying Israel with any weapons and related equipment and to suspend any military assistance that Israel receives from them;

(b) To refrain from acquiring any weapons or military equipment from Israel;

(c) To suspend economic, financial and technological assistance to and co-operation with Israel;

(d) To sever diplomatic, trade and cultural relations with Israel;

14. *Reiterates its call* to all Member States to cease forthwith, individually and collectively, all dealings with Israel in order totally to isolate it in all fields;

15. *Urges* non-member States to act in accordance with the provisions of the present resolution;

16. *Calls upon* the specialized agencies and other international institutions to conform their relations with Israel to the terms of the present resolution;

17. *Requests* the Secretary-General to report to the General Assembly at its thirty-ninth session on the implementation of the present resolution.

General Assembly resolution 38/180 A

19 December 1983   Meeting 102   84-24-31 (recorded vote)

14-nation draft (A/38/L.43 & Add.1); agenda item 34.

Sponsors: Afghanistan, Bangladesh, Cuba, Guinea, Guyana, India, Indonesia, Lao People's Democratic Republic, Malaysia, Mongolia, Nicaragua, Pakistan, Viet Nam, Yugoslavia.

Meeting numbers. GA 38th session: plenary 87-89, 91-95, 102.

Recorded vote in Assembly as follows:

In favour: Afghanistan, Albania, Algeria, Angola, Bahrain, Bangladesh, Benin, Bhutan, Botswana, Bulgaria, Burundi, Byelorussian SSR, Cape Verde, Central African Republic, China, Congo, Cuba, Cyprus, Czechoslovakia, Democratic Yemen, Djibouti, Ethiopia, Gambia, German Democratic Republic, Ghana, Greece, Guinea, Guinea-Bissau, Guyana, Hungary, India, Indonesia, Iran, Iraq, Jordan, Kenya, Kuwait, Lao People's Democratic Republic, Lebanon, Libyan Arab Jamahiriya, Madagascar, Malaysia, Maldives, Mali, Malta, Mauritania, Mexico, Mongolia, Morocco, Mozambique, Nepal, Nicaragua, Niger, Nigeria, Oman, Pakistan, Poland, Qatar, Rwanda, Sao Tome and Principe, Saudi Arabia, Senegal, Seychelles, Sierra Leone, Somalia, Sri Lanka, Sudan, Suriname, Syrian Arab Republic, Togo, Tunisia, Turkey, Uganda, Ukrainian SSR, USSR, United Arab Emirates, United Republic of Cameroon, United Republic of Tanzania, Upper Volta, Viet Nam, Yemen, Yugoslavia, Zambia, Zimbabwe.

Against: Australia, Belgium, Canada, Chile, Costa Rica, Denmark, Finland, France, Germany, Federal Republic of, Haiti, Iceland, Ireland, Israel, Italy, Japan, Luxembourg, Netherlands, New Zealand, Norway, Portugal, Saint Lucia, Sweden, United Kingdom, United States.

Abstaining: Argentina, Austria, Bahamas, Barbados, Belize, Bolivia, Brazil, Burma, Chad, Colombia, Dominican Republic, Ecuador, Egypt, El Salvador, Fiji, Guatemala, Honduras, Ivory Coast, Jamaica, Malawi, Papua New Guinea, Paraguay, Peru, Philippines, Saint Vincent and the Grenadines, Singapore, Spain, Thailand, Trinidad and Tobago, Uruguay, Venezuela.

Israel said the text was a blatant attempt to harm Israel and legitimize Arab, in particular Syrian, aggression, for which the Golan Heights had served as a launching pad. Instead of condemning the Syrian Arab Republic, Israel was castigated; attempts to vilify it as a non-peace-loving State were ridiculous in the light of the sacrifices it had already made for peace. Instead of calling for negotiations and conciliation, the text grotesquely called on States to refrain from supplying Israel with the necessary means of defence and sought to isolate it so that Arab warmakers were emboldened to strike across its borders.

The United States said such ritualistic exercises failed to make a positive contribution to resolving the Middle East conflict, hardened the positions of the parties and made negotiations between Israel and its Arab neighbours less likely.

In spite of its full support for the text's central theme, Sweden opposed paragraphs 12 to 16, because of their content as well as the fact that they could not be reconciled with the division of responsibilities between the Assembly and the Security Council.

In Finland's view, the text, in particular paragraphs 8 and 12 to 14, did not respect the Charter provisions on the competence of the main organs of the United Nations.

Speaking for the States members of EC, Greece said they had repeatedly stressed the need for a balanced approach; they also could not accept formulations criticizing a permanent Security Council member for exercising its right.

Though stating its support for all provisions which could bring success to peace efforts and its adherence to the rule that nullified any unilateral decision which might change the legal status of territories subjected to military occupation, Portugal dissociated itself in particular from discriminatory references or legal implications that might harm peace efforts.

New Zealand said it was disappointed that the text did not adequately reflect the balance of principles embodied in Council resolution 242(1967) and was not well calculated to contribute to a negotiated settlement.

Although abstaining, Ecuador reiterated support for the condemnation of attempts to legalize the acquisition of territory by force through a unilateral declaration.

Peru believed that certain statements and recommendations in the resolution tended to prejudice the efforts to achieve a Middle East solution within the framework of the United Nations and that the measures proposed were not the best way to begin a peace process but could lead to even greater scorn for international law and an even greater erosion of the Organization's effectiveness.

Brazil felt that Israel's complete isolation would be of no advantage to the peace process, but could, on the contrary, be a pretext for Israel to act with still greater contempt for the rule of law and for the principles of mutually respectful relations among peoples.

Urging Israel to return the Golan Heights to the Syrian Arab Republic, Bolivia said it could not agree with the drafting style and part of the text's content. In Thailand's opinion, the text did not present a complete picture and lacked balance. Speaking similarly, Singapore added it could not support texts which impinged on the sovereign right of third countries having diplomatic relations with Israel. A like view was held by Honduras and the Philippines. Colombia could not accept resolutions that condemned the conduct of only one party. Egypt said it fully supported the view that Israel's decision on the Golan Heights was null and void and that it must withdraw; however, it could not subscribe to certain negative aspects, in particular paragraph 13. Venezuela also voiced serious reservations on certain paragraphs, saying that, rather than promoting peace and understanding, they were disruptive. Though fully supporting the restitution of the Golan Heights to the Syrian Arab Republic, Argentina believed that the areas of competence of the main bodies of the United Nations must be respected. Mexico and Spain had reservations on paragraphs 12 to 14; in Mexico's view, they dealt with questions that might fall under the jurisdiction of another United Nations body. In addition, Spain reserved its position on the eighth preambular paragraph.

Israel's actions in the Golan Heights negated the principles of the 1949 fourth Geneva Convention, Security Council resolution 242(1967) and other United Nations resolutions, Nepal felt. However, Nepal reserved its position on paragraphs 8, 9 and 12 to 14 and on the fourth and eighth preambular paragraphs, adding that the measures called for were a prerogative of the Security Council.

Greece said it would have voted against paragraph 14 and would have abstained on paragraphs 8, 13 *(c)* and 13 *(d)*, had separate votes been taken. Togo would have abstained in separate votes on paragraphs 8 and 12.

The Libyan Arab Jamahiriya reaffirmed its opposition to all direct or indirect allusions that would give a semblance of legitimacy to Israeli occupation. Iran reserved its rights with regard to any provisions that might directly or indirectly constitute recognition of what it called the Zionist entity, an artificially forged State.

West Bank officials

In 1983, the General Assembly again called on Israel to allow the return of three West Bank officials so that they could resume the functions for which they had been elected and appointed. Israel had deported the three Palestinian officials in 1980,[54] on the ground that they had systematically engaged in inciting the local Arab population to acts of violence and subversion, abusing their public offices. The Assembly also considered again the 1980 assassination attempt against the Mayors of Nablus, Ramallah and Al Bireh.[55]

Expulsion of Hebron and Halhul Mayors and of the Islamic Judge of Hebron

Report of the Secretary-General. In June 1983,[56] the Secretary-General informed the General Assembly of Israel's response to its December 1982 demand that Israel rescind the illegal expulsion and imprisonment of the Mayors of Hebron and Halhul and the expulsion of the Sharia (Islamic) Judge of Hebron.[57] He reported that, in reply to his note verbale of 10 March 1983, Israel had stated on 24 May that its position in that matter remained the same as in former years and that it would like to draw the Secretary-General's attention to the fact that the three officials had never recanted their statements and actions and had never committed themselves to desist from inciting anti-Israel hatred. In addition, Israel charged that they were engaged in a continuous anti-Israel propaganda campaign throughout the world, in co-ordination with and with the assistance of PLO.

GENERAL ASSEMBLY ACTION

Under the agenda item on the report of the Special Committee to Investigate Israeli Practices Affecting the Human Rights of the Population of the Occupied Territories, the General Assembly, on 15 December 1983, acting on the recommendation of the Special Political Committee, adopted by recorded vote resolution 38/79 E.

The General Assembly,
Recalling Security Council resolutions 468(1980) of 8 May 1980, 469(1980) of 20 May 1980 and 484(1980) of

19 December 1980 and General Assembly resolutions 36/147 D of 16 December 1981 and 37/88 D of 10 December 1982,

Deeply concerned at the expulsion by the Israeli military occupation authorities of the Mayors of Hebron and Halhul and of the Sharia Judge of Hebron,

Recalling the Geneva Convention relative to the Protection of Civilian Persons in Time of War, of 12 August 1949, in particular article 1 and the first paragraph of article 49, which read as follows:

"Article 1
"The High Contracting Parties undertake to respect and to ensure respect for the present Convention in all circumstances."

"Article 49
"Individual or mass forcible transfers, as well as deportations of protected persons from occupied territory to the territory of the occupying Power or to that of any other country, occupied or not, are prohibited, regardless of their motive . . .",

Reaffirming the applicability of the Geneva Convention to the Palestinian and other Arab territories occupied by Israel since 1967, including Jerusalem,

1. *Demands once more* that the Government of Israel, the occupying Power, rescind the illegal measures taken by the Israeli military occupation authorities in expelling and imprisoning the Mayors of Hebron and Halhul and in expelling the Sharia Judge of Hebron and that it facilitate the immediate return of the expelled Palestinian leaders so that they can resume the functions for which they were elected and appointed;

2. *Requests* the Secretary-General to report to the General Assembly as soon as possible on the implementation of the present resolution.

General Assembly resolution 38/79 E

15 December 1983   Meeting 98   146-1-1 (recorded vote)

Approved by SPC (A/38/718) by recorded vote (115-1-1), 5 December (meeting 45); 12-nation draft (A/SPC/38/L.39); agenda item 69.

Sponsors: Afghanistan, Bangladesh, Cuba, Egypt, India, Indonesia, Madagascar, Malaysia, Mali, Pakistan, Qatar, Senegal.

Meeting numbers. GA 38th session: SPC 36-42, 45-48; plenary 98.

Recorded vote in Assembly as follows:

In favour: Afghanistan, Albania, Algeria, Angola, Argentina, Australia, Austria, Bahamas, Bahrain, Bangladesh, Barbados, Belgium, Belize, Benin, Bhutan, Bolivia, Botswana, Brazil, Bulgaria, Burma, Burundi, Byelorussian SSR, Canada, Cape Verde, Central African Republic, Chad, Chile, China, Colombia, Congo, Costa Rica, Cuba, Cyprus, Czechoslovakia, Democratic Kampuchea, Democratic Yemen, Denmark, Djibouti, Dominican Republic, Ecuador, Egypt, El Salvador, Equatorial Guinea, Ethiopia, Fiji, Finland, France, Gabon, Gambia, German Democratic Republic, Germany, Federal Republic of, Ghana, Greece, Grenada, Guinea, Guinea-Bissau, Guyana, Hungary, Iceland, India, Indonesia, Iran, Iraq, Ireland, Italy, Ivory Coast, Jamaica, Japan, Jordan, Kenya, Kuwait, Lao People's Democratic Republic, Lebanon, Lesotho, Liberia, Libyan Arab Jamahiriya, Luxembourg, Madagascar, Malawi, Malaysia, Maldives, Mali, Malta, Mauritania, Mauritius, Mexico, Mongolia, Morocco, Mozambique, Nepal, Netherlands, New Zealand, Nicaragua, Niger, Nigeria, Norway, Oman, Pakistan, Panama, Papua New Guinea, Paraguay, Peru, Philippines, Poland, Portugal, Qatar, Romania, Rwanda, Saint Lucia, Sao Tome and Principe, Saudi Arabia, Senegal, Seychelles, Sierra Leone, Singapore, Solomon Islands, Somalia, Spain, Sri Lanka, Sudan, Suriname, Swaziland, Sweden, Syrian Arab Republic, Thailand, Togo, Trinidad and Tobago, Tunisia, Turkey, Uganda, Ukrainian SSR, USSR, United Arab Emirates, United Kingdom, United Republic of Cameroon, United Republic of Tanzania, Upper Volta, Uruguay, Vanuatu, Venezuela, Viet Nam, Yemen, Yugoslavia, Zaire, Zambia, Zimbabwe.

Against: Israel.

Abstaining: United States.

Israel said the three Palestinians had openly incited Palestinian Arabs to acts of violence and subversion against Israel. Following expulsion, they had had full recourse to the Israel judicial system and the orders against them had been upheld by the Supreme Court; their belligerent behaviour attested to their total lack of remorse.

The United States said the text omitted any reference to factors contributing to the deportation; that was, however, contrary to the fourth Geneva Convention and they should be allowed to return.

Prosecution in assassination attempts

Report of the Secretary-General. In October 1983,[58] the Secretary-General reported to the General Assembly on implementation of a December 1982 resolution[59] concerning the 1980 assassination attempts against the Mayors of Nablus, Ramallah and Al Bireh. In reply to his note verbale of 10 March 1983, the Secretary-General stated, Israel, on 27 September, had drawn his attention to its statement before the Special Political Committee in December 1982.[60]

GENERAL ASSEMBLY ACTION

Under the agenda item on the report of the Special Committee to Investigate Israeli Practices Affecting the Human Rights of the Population of the Occupied Territories, the General Assembly, on 15 December 1983, acting on the recommendation of the Special Political Committee, adopted by recorded vote resolution 38/79 H.

The General Assembly,

Recalling Security Council resolution 471(1980) of 5 June 1980, in which the Council condemned the assassination attempts against the Mayors of Nablus, Ramallah and Al Bireh and called for the immediate apprehension and prosecution of the perpetrators of those crimes,

Recalling also General Assembly resolutions 36/147 G of 16 December 1981 and 37/88 G of 10 December 1982,

Recalling once again the Geneva Convention relative to the Protection of Civilian Persons in Time of War, of 12 August 1949, in particular article 27, which states, *inter alia:*

"Protected persons are entitled, in all circumstances, to respect for their persons . . . They shall at all times be humanely treated, and shall be protected especially against all acts of violence or threats thereof . . .",

Reaffirming the applicability of that Convention to the Arab territories occupied by Israel since 1967, including Jerusalem,

1. *Expresses deep concern* that Israel, the occupying Power, has failed for three years to apprehend and prosecute the perpetrators of the assassination attempts;

2. *Demands once more* that Israel, the occupying Power, inform the Secretary-General of the results of the investigations relative to the assassination attempts;

3. *Requests* the Secretary-General to submit to the General Assembly at its thirty-ninth session a report on the implementation of the present resolution.

General Assembly resolution 38/79 H

15 December 1983   Meeting 98   145-1-1 (recorded vote)

Approved by SPC (A/38/718) by recorded vote (114-1-1), 5 December (meeting 45); 11-nation draft (A/SPC/38/L.42); agenda item 69.

Sponsors: Afghanistan, Bangladesh, Cuba, Egypt, India, Indonesia, Madagascar, Malaysia, Mali, Pakistan, Qatar.

Meeting numbers. GA 38th session: SPC 36-42; 45-48; plenary 98.

Recorded vote in Assembly as follows:

In favour: Afghanistan, Albania, Algeria, Angola, Argentina, Australia, Austria, Bahamas, Bahrain, Bangladesh, Barbados, Belgium, Belize, Benin, Bhutan, Bolivia, Botswana, Brazil, Bulgaria, Burma, Burundi, Byelorussian SSR, Canada, Cape Verde, Central African Republic, Chad, Chile, China, Colombia, Congo, Costa Rica, Cuba, Cyprus, Czechoslovakia, Democratic Kampuchea, Democratic Yemen, Denmark, Djibouti, Dominican Republic, Ecuador, Egypt, El Salvador, Equatorial Guinea, Ethiopia, Fiji, Finland, France, Gabon, Gambia, German Democratic Republic, Germany, Federal Republic of, Ghana, Greece, Grenada, Guinea, Guinea-Bissau, Guyana, Hungary, Iceland, India, Indonesia, Iran, Iraq, Ireland, Italy, Ivory Coast, Jamaica, Japan, Jordan, Kenya, Kuwait, Lao People's Democratic Republic, Lebanon, Lesotho, Liberia, Libyan Arab Jamahiriya, Luxembourg, Madagascar, Malawi, Malaysia, Maldives, Mali, Malta, Mauritania, Mauritius, Mexico, Mongolia, Morocco, Mozambique, Nepal, Netherlands, New Zealand, Nicaragua, Niger, Nigeria, Norway, Oman, Pakistan, Panama, Papua New Guinea, Paraguay, Peru, Philippines, Poland, Portugal, Qatar, Romania, Rwanda, Saint Lucia, Sao Tome and Principe, Saudi Arabia, Senegal, Seychelles, Sierra Leone, Singapore, Solomon Islands, Somalia, Spain, Sri Lanka, Sudan, Suriname, Swaziland, Sweden, Syrian Arab Republic, Thailand, Togo, Trinidad and Tobago, Tunisia, Turkey, Uganda, Ukrainian SSR, USSR, United Arab Emirates, United Kingdom, United Republic of Cameroon, United Republic of Tanzania, Upper Volta, Uruguay, Vanuatu, Venezuela, Viet Nam, Yemen, Yugoslavia, Zambia, Zimbabwe.

Against: Israel.

Abstaining: United States.

Expressing sympathy for the victims and condemning those responsible, the United States said it could not support a text maligning the Israeli legal process and implying, without offering evidence, that the Israeli authorities were not making any effort to apprehend and prosecute the would-be assassins.

The United Arab Emirates said that the Israeli authorities had ordered that the identity of the criminals not be revealed and the security services had not been empowered to pursue investigations since such acts were fundamental to Israel's settlements policy; it was clear that the military authorities were involved in the affair, since terrorists could not act in the occupied territories without the authorities' consent.

West Bank students

The alleged mass poisoning of Palestinian schoolgirls in the West Bank was the subject of several communications in 1983. Following informal consultations, the President of the Security Council made a statement on 4 April requesting the Secretary-General to inquire into the problem and report on the findings. In pursuance of that request, the World Health Organization (WHO) conducted an independent investigation.

Communications (March/April). On 29 March,[61] Jordan transmitted to the President of the Security Council a letter of the same date from the Deputy Permanent Observer of PLO, alleging that more than 1,000 Palestinian schoolgirls in the West Bank had been poisoned as part of a new phase in Israel's campaign against the Palestinians, and calling on the United Nations to form an international medical committee to investigate, document and report on the poisoning.

The illness among Arab schoolgirls in the West Bank was the subject of a number of other communications.

On 30 March,[62] the Chairman of the Committee on Palestinian rights stated that local residents believed the illness to have been induced by some kind of poison, perhaps gas, in the girls' classrooms. Pending results of investigations, by ICRC and the United Nations, among others, the Chairman urged the Secretary-General to exercise his office to ascertain the full extent, cause and perpetrators of that event.

By a letter dated 31 March,[63] Iraq, as Chairman of the Arab Group, requested an urgent Security Council meeting to discuss the situation.

On 3 April,[64] Israel rejected the charges by Iraq and Jordan as unfounded, and asserted that extensive clinical, laboratory and environmental analyses by Israeli medical authorities had yielded no traces of poisoning. Nevertheless, it added, the Ministry of Health had requested international health authorities, among them WHO, to assess independently the causes of the phenomenon.

SECURITY COUNCIL ACTION

On 4 April, the Security Council President issued the following statement on behalf of the Council members:[65]

"The members of the Security Council have met in informal consultations with great concern on 4 April 1983 to discuss cases of mass poisoning in the occupied Arab territory of the West Bank as referred to in document S/15673.

"The members of the Security Council request the Secretary-General to conduct independent inquiries concerning the causes and effects of the serious problem of the reported cases of poisoning and urgently to report on the findings."

By a letter of 5 April,[66] Israel rejected the Council's statement, asserting that it did not take into account the investigations by Israeli medical authorities and other medical teams, and that it contained an unwarranted reference to cases of mass poisoning; the request for an independent inquiry by the Secretary-General was therefore unjustified.

Report of the Secretary-General. In pursuance of the Security Council's request of 4 April, the Secretary-General submitted on 10 May a report[67] indicating that he had contacted the Director-General of WHO and had requested that an independent inquiry be conducted. In his report annexed to the Secretary-General's report, the Director-General gave an overview of WHO's investigations and findings. In his conclusions, he stated that the WHO inquiry had not been able to indicate any specific cause of the reported health emergency; however, the initial medical records and interviews with cases in the first outbreak and with local health and other authorities suggested that an environmental agent could have provoked at least some cases.

The Director-General recommended that, in view of the anxiety under which the population lived in the occupied territories and given the susceptibility of girls during adolescence, everything possible should be done to protect the local population from unnecessary alarm. For that purpose, WHO presence should be made available in the event of any suspected recrudescence of the ill-defined health emergency, so that all could feel reassured. He added that although it appeared unlikely that the patients would suffer any significant sequelae, there should be provision for clinical follow-up by WHO should any of them or their families so request.

Referring to the Director-General's conclusions as well as to the findings of several other medical authorities, Israel, in a letter of 25 August,[68] stated that they were fully corroborated by the conclusions reached in medical literature on similar phenomena in other countries. Israel noted with regret the Council's silence on the matter since the publication of the Director-General's and other reports.

Economic and social conditions

Both the current and future economic and social conditions of Palestinians in the occupied territories were studied by the Organization in 1983. The living conditions of Palestinians were the subject of reports by the Secretary-General and UNCTAD. The General Assembly, in December, adopted resolution 38/166 on the subject.

Living conditions of Palestinians

Report of the Secretary-General. As requested by the General Assembly in December 1982,[69] the Secretary-General submitted in June 1983 a report on the living conditions of Palestinians in the occupied territories, prepared with the help of three experts.[70] Since permission to visit the occupied territories had not been granted by the Israeli Government, the experts had had to rely on secondary information sources. From 11 February to 24 March, they had visited Egypt, Jordan, Lebanon and the Syrian Arab Republic, where they had had discussions with government and United Nations officials. Discussions had also been held with PLO officials at Damascus and Amman. Meetings had been held with five professors who had been expelled from universities in the West Bank in October 1982, the former Mayors of Halhul and East Jerusalem, the head of the PLO Palestinian Fund, and Palestinians living outside the territories. The experts had also gathered information from several United Nations organizations.

In their report, the experts considered physical factors such as housing, infrastructure, land and settlements, and water resources; economic factors such as employment, income, gross domestic product and gross national product, capital formation, consumption and savings, taxation, sectoral structure of the economy, agriculture and industry; and social and cultural factors, including education and health care.

Summarizing their findings, the experts stated that the shortages of basic facilities in the territories were quite evident and infrastructural facilities were not commensurate with the growing needs of the Palestinian communities. They observed a tendency to segregate services provided to Israeli settlements and Palestinian towns and villages in certain sectors, such as postal services, telecommunications, agriculture and industry. There was pressure on the Palestinian communities to obtain other services, such as water and electricity, from a common network serving the Israeli settlements as well as Israel. The continual expropriation of land by the occupying authorities had reduced the land available to the Palestinian residents; the increase in the establishment of Israeli settlements and their location on the periphery of Arab towns and villages had become an obstacle to the growth and expansion of the latter.

Though the economy of the occupied territories had improved, it continued to be handicapped by lack of long-term planning and programming designed to generate development for the benefit of the indigenous population. The trend had been towards further integration of the economy with that of Israel, thus exposing it to a high rate of inflation. The level of taxation was a burden to the Arab population, as certain elements of the Israeli tax system were not in consonance with the underdeveloped nature of the economy of the territories. Local employment had been falling in the agricultural and industrial sectors and rising in all other sectors. More workers from the territories were commuting to Israel, where their conditions of employment had not shown any appreciable improvement. That almost two thirds of the labour force was in one way or another working in and for the Israeli economy was a deterrent to initiating employment opportunities within the territories that would serve indigenous economic interests.

Agriculture continued to be hindered by loss of land through continuing expropriation, lack of capital for improving production methods and shrinkage in markets. The structure of industry had not shown any significant change over the years of occupation; it was dominated by small enterprises, a high proportion of which were in subsectors executing orders for Israeli enterprises. The industrial sector was handicapped by a lack of capital for improving buildings and equipment, difficulties in importing new technology, export restrictions and competition from Israeli products.

The social and cultural conditions of the Palestinians in the territories had continued to deteriorate. The traditional family pattern was breaking down owing to pressures caused by incomes that were inadequate to meet escalating costs of living. Daily activities had been disrupted by frequent curfews, the ever-present possibility of confrontation with Israeli settlers and restrictions in movement, association and expression. Arab residents were deprived of many Arab-language books and periodicals, and there had been instances where Israeli settlers had interfered with their freedom of worship.

Although school facilities had kept pace with increased enrolment, the content of education did not seem to be progressing along the lines of curricula development in Egypt and Jordan. Many books were revised for or barred from use in the educational system in the territories, which followed the Jordanian system in the West Bank and the Egyptian system in Gaza. West Bank universities had had many set-backs during the preceding years, including the dismissal and deportation of professors and new regulations affecting financial support from abroad. The closing of universities in the wake of demonstrations and frequent arrests and interrogation of students suspected of participating in them also had interfered with the quality of education.

With regard to the health sector, the availability of hospital beds had not kept pace with population growth or the numbers seeking hospital care. Reporting of health data did not follow a uniform pattern for the territories. The efficiency of the health care system continued to be hampered by limitations in equipment, qualified staff and distribution of drugs, with some shortcomings having been remedied to some extent through inputs from international organizations and local voluntary associations as well as the Red Crescent Society.

UNCTAD report and Trade and Development Board action. The economic and social conditions in the occupied territories were also considered in a May 1983 report[71] submitted to the Trade and Development Board of UNCTAD. The report, prepared by P. G. Sadler, former Director of the Institute for the Study of Sparsely Populated Areas, University of Aberdeen, United Kingdom, and Bakir Abu Kishk, Director of Bir Zeit University Research Centre, was a follow-up to a similar one submitted in 1981.[72] Entitled "Palestine: options for development", the 1983 report gave an overview and statistical data on population and manpower, land, water resources, agriculture, industry, foreign trade, balance of payments, housing, education, electricity, transport and health care delivery. In addition, it examined constraints to the economy and future development prospects, concluding that the main preoccupation of an independent Palestinian State would be with the enormous difficulties of providing resources for reconstruction, absorbing a large number of returning exiles and employing the substantial labour force currently employed in Israel but residing in the occupied territories.

In taking note of the report of Sessional Committee I, the Board, on 20 October,[(73)] took note of the consultants' report. It also took note of an oral report by an UNCTAD secretariat representative on action taken to implement UNCTAD resolution 146(VI) on assistance to the Palestinian people (see above, under PALESTINE QUESTION). The representative stated that provision had been made in the proposed United Nations programme budget for 1984-1985 for setting up within UNCTAD a Special Economic Unit on assistance to the Palestinians, as requested by that resolution; the matter was under consideration by the General Assembly.

GENERAL ASSEMBLY ACTION

On 19 December 1983, acting on the recommendation of the Second (Economic and Financial) Committee, the General Assembly adopted by recorded vote resolution 38/166.

Living conditions of the Palestinian people in the occupied Palestinian territories

The General Assembly,

Recalling the Vancouver Declaration on Human Settlements, 1976, and the relevant recommendations for national action adopted by Habitat: United Nations Conference on Human Settlements,

Recalling also resolution 3, entitled "Living conditions of the Palestinians in occupied territories", contained in the recommendations for international co-operation adopted by Habitat: United Nations Conference on Human Settlements,

Recalling further its resolution 37/222 of 20 December 1982,

Taking note of resolution 6/2 adopted by the Commission on Human Settlements on 4 May 1983,

Gravely alarmed by the continuation of the Israeli settlement policies, which have been declared null and void and a major obstacle to peace,

1. *Takes note* of the report of the Secretary-General on the living conditions of the Palestinian people in the occupied Palestinian territories;

2. *Takes note also* of the statement made on 1 November 1983 by the observer of the Palestine Liberation Organization;

3. *Rejects* the Israeli plans and actions intended to change the demographic composition of the occupied Palestinian territories, particularly the increase and expansion of the Israeli settlements, and other plans and actions creating conditions leading to the displacement and exodus of Palestinians from the occupied Palestinian territories;

4. *Expresses its alarm* at the deterioration in the living conditions of the Palestinian people in the Palestinian territories occupied since 1967 as a result of the Israeli occupation;

5. *Affirms* that the Israeli occupation is contradictory to the basic requirements for the social and economic development of the Palestinian people in the occupied West Bank and the Gaza Strip;

6. *Calls upon* the Israeli occupation authorities to give United Nations experts access to the occupied Palestinian territories;

7. *Recognizes* the need for a comprehensive report on the impact of the Israeli settlements on the living conditions of the Palestinian people in the occupied Palestinian territories;

8. *Requests* the Secretary-General to prepare and submit to the General Assembly at its thirty-ninth session, through the Economic and Social Council, a comprehensive report on the current and future impact of the Israeli settlements on the living conditions of the Palestinian people in the occupied Palestinian territories, including a comparison between the living conditions of the latter and those of the residents of the Israeli settlements.

General Assembly resolution 38/166

19 December 1983   Meeting 102   142-2 (recorded vote)

Approved by Second Committee (A/38/702/Add.8) by recorded vote (131-2), 14 November (meeting 39); 9-nation draft (A/C.2/38/L.11), orally revised; agenda item 78 (h).

Sponsors: Bangladesh, Madagascar, Mali, Mauritania, Pakistan, Sudan, Viet Nam, Yemen, Zambia.

Financial implications. 5th Committee, A/38/757; S-G, A/C.2/38/L.25, A/C.5/38/48.

Meeting numbers. GA 38th session: 2nd Committee 16-18, 20, 22-24, 30, 39; 5th Committee 44; plenary 102.

Recorded vote in Assembly as follows:

In favour: Afghanistan, Albania, Algeria, Angola, Argentina, Australia, Austria, Bahamas, Bahrain, Bangladesh, Barbados, Belgium, Belize, Benin, Bhutan, Bolivia, Botswana, Brazil, Bulgaria, Burma, Burundi, Byelorussian SSR, Canada, Cape Verde, Central African Republic, Chad, Chile, China, Colombia, Congo, Cuba, Cyprus, Czechoslovakia, Democratic Kampuchea, Democratic Yemen, Denmark, Djibouti, Dominican Republic, Ecuador, Egypt, El Salvador, Ethiopia, Fiji, Finland, France, Gabon, Gambia, German Democratic Republic, Germany, Federal Republic of, Ghana, Greece, Guinea, Guinea-Bissau, Guyana, Haiti, Honduras, Hungary, Iceland, India, Indonesia, Iran, Iraq, Ireland, Italy, Ivory Coast, Jamaica, Japan, Jordan, Kenya, Kuwait, Lao People's Democratic Republic, Lebanon, Lesotho, Liberia, Libyan Arab Jamahiriya, Luxembourg, Madagascar, Malawi, Malaysia, Maldives, Mali, Malta, Mauritania, Mauritius, Mexico, Mongolia, Morocco, Mozambique, Nepal, Netherlands, New Zealand, Nicaragua, Niger, Nigeria, Norway, Oman, Pakistan, Panama, Papua New Guinea, Paraguay, Peru, Philippines, Poland, Portugal, Qatar, Romania, Rwanda, Saint Lucia, Saint Vincent and the Grenadines, Sao Tome and Principe, Saudi Arabia, Senegal, Sierra Leone, Singapore, Somalia, Spain, Sri Lanka, Sudan, Suriname, Swaziland, Sweden, Syrian Arab Republic, Thailand, Togo, Trinidad and Tobago, Tunisia, Turkey, Uganda, Ukrainian SSR, USSR, United Arab Emirates, United Kingdom, United Republic of Cameroon, United Republic of Tanzania, Upper Volta, Uruguay, Venezuela, Viet Nam, Yemen, Yugoslavia, Zaire, Zambia.

Against: Israel, United States.

Israel rejected the resolution as biased and based on false allegations; by perpetuating lies, the Arab States discredited the significant achievements made by the Palestinian Arab inhabitants of the areas. Rather than the comparative study called for in paragraph 8, a study should be made comparing living conditions in the territories before and after 1967. For example, agricultural production had doubled between 1970 and 1980 and the area under irrigation by Arab farmers had increased by 60 per cent since 1968. Moreover, Israel was encouraging and facilitating industrial development and free trade. Israel said the assertion of a demographic change was ludicrous in view of the fact that in the midst of 1,186,000 Arabs there were only a few thousand Israelis whose presence created the form of coexistence essential to peace between the two peoples.

The United States believed that the text would further exacerbate tensions; the report called for would cost $81,000, not one cent of which would find its way to needy Palestinians. Belgium hoped that implementing paragraph 8 would not involve extra 1983-1985 budget allocations, a view shared by the United Kingdom.

Chile stated that it did not share all views expressed in the text; political matters had no place in a text of a humanitarian nature.

Canada stressed the need to improve living conditions in the territories; it also noted that language which it had had difficulties with in previous years had been omitted from the text.

Norway pointed out that it understood the phrase "occupied Palestinian territories" to mean territories occupied by Israel since 1967.

Speaking on 1 November before the Committee, PLO said that, although the Secretary-General's report was not complete, it illustrated the steady deterioration of the Palestinians' living conditions. Israeli occupation was based on the exploitation of the material and human resources of the territories. The Palestinians were denied their inalienable rights because of Israeli occupation and would not be able to ensure their economic development until they had regained their national rights.

Mediterranean-Dead Sea canal project

In 1983, Israel's plan of March 1981[74] to construct a 67-mile hydraulic structure to channel water from the Mediterranean Sea to the Dead Sea for electric power generation, was the subject of a resolution of the General Assembly (38/85) and a decision of the Governing Council of the United Nations Environment Programme (UNEP). The effects of the project, under which part of the conduit would pass through the Gaza Strip, occupied by Israel since 1967, were studied by experts appointed by the Secretary-General. A report on the environmental consequences of the project was submitted by the UNEP Executive Director.

Report of the UNEP Executive Director. As requested by the UNEP Governing Council in May 1982,[75] the UNEP Executive Director submitted in February 1983 a report on the environmental consequences of Israel's project.[76] Summarizing the findings, which were based on background studies, reports from Jordan and a workshop held at Nairobi, Kenya (31 January and 1 February)—Israel not having replied to the request for technical information—the report enumerated the following possible adverse environmental consequences: accidental contamination of regional aquifers and their water resources; disturbance of

farmland in the coastal lands of the Gaza Strip; and changes in level, stratification and chemistry of the Dead Sea water which would cause inundation of land around its shores and would affect the potash industry.

UNEP Council action. Taking note of the Executive Director's report, the UNEP Governing Council, on 23 May 1983,[77] recalled that the Assembly, in a December 1982 resolution,[78] had demanded that Israel not construct the canal and cease all action or plans towards implementation of the project, and had called on States, specialized agencies and organizations not to assist in the project preparations and execution. The Council requested the Executive Director to facilitate the Secretary-General's work in monitoring and assessing, on a continuing basis, all aspects—especially ecological ones—of the adverse effects on Jordan and the territories occupied since 1967, including Jerusalem, arising from the project's implementation.

Report of the Secretary-General. In accordance with the December 1982 Assembly resolution,[78] the Secretary-General, in October 1983, submitted to the Assembly a report on Israel's decision to build the canal.[79] Annexed was a report of four United Nations experts who, during their visit to Jordan from 28 June to 6 July, had held discussions with government officials and others concerned and had visited various areas around the Dead Sea, particularly the potash works at its southern end. In their report, the experts dealt with the legal dimensions, and the impacts on potash production, agriculture, settlements, infrastructure, recreation and health care facilities, archaeological sites, and environment in Jordan.

The experts observed that, from the evidence available, it appeared that the Israeli proposal to divert water from the Mediterranean into the Dead Sea was, from a strictly technical point of view, feasible. Given engineering techniques already available, safeguards could probably be built into the project to minimize the risk of rupture of the conduit through seismic activity, and consequent leakage into aquifers through which the pipeline would pass.

However, they cautioned, in so far as the proposed route crossed the Gaza Strip, principles of international law relating to belligerent occupation would be applicable; specifically, a permanent installation constructed in an occupied territory for the benefit of the occupying State would encounter "unsurmountable legal obstacles".

In the experts' view, Jordan would suffer appreciable harm, at least with respect to its vital potash industry. Under prevailing legal views, Jordan's consent would be an essential pre-condition for implementing the project. Losses in other sectors appeared very difficult to assess except in broad qualitative terms; however, the experts stated, there were uncertainties relating to such matters as the potential effects of the mixing of the waters of the Mediterranean with those of the Dead Sea and impacts on agriculture. The experts concluded by suggesting that a broader approach to the question would make possible a much higher level of use and the net gains of each co-riparian would be much greater than was likely to result from the current approach.

In reply to the experts' report, Israel submitted on 8 August supplementary material on the project, which was transmitted to the Assembly as an addendum to the Secretary-General's report.[80]

By another addendum, dated 7 December,[81] the Secretary-General confirmed, in answer to the concern expressed in the Special Political Committee, that he had received Israel's answer on 8 August, as a result of his efforts to obtain Israel's co-operation in implementing the December 1982 Assembly resolution demanding that Israel not construct the canal.[78] Israel's response had been received, unfortunately, after the experts had completed their work; the publication of that response had been made without prejudice to the experts' position as reflected in their report, and did not imply any evaluation of the information provided by Israel.

GENERAL ASSEMBLY ACTION

On 15 December, acting on the recommendation of the Special Political Committee, the General Assembly adopted by recorded vote resolution 38/85.

Israel's decision to build a canal linking the Mediterranean Sea to the Dead Sea

The General Assembly,

Recalling its resolutions 36/150 of 16 December 1981 and 37/122 of 16 December 1982,

Recalling the rules and principles of international law relative to the fundamental rights and duties of States,

Bearing in mind the principles of international law relative to belligerent occupation of land, including the Geneva Convention relative to the Protection of Civilian Persons in Time of War, of 12 August 1949, and reaffirming their applicability to all Arab territories occupied since 1967, including Jerusalem,

Taking note of the report of the Secretary-General,

Recognizing that the proposed canal, to be constructed partly through the Gaza Strip, a Palestinian territory occupied in 1967, would violate the principles of international law and affect the interests of the Palestinian people,

Confident that the canal linking the Mediterranean Sea with the Dead Sea, if constructed by Israel, will cause direct, serious and irreparable damage to Jordan's rights and legitimate and vital interests in the economic, agricultural, demographic and ecological fields,

Noting with regret the non-compliance by Israel with General Assembly resolution 36/150,

1. *Deplores* Israel's non-compliance with General Assembly resolution 37/122 and its refusal to receive the team of experts;

2. *Emphasizes* that the canal linking the Mediterranean Sea with the Dead Sea, if constructed, is a violation of the rules and principles of international law, especially those relating to the fundamental rights and duties of States and to belligerent occupation of land;

3. *Demands* that Israel not construct this canal and cease forthwith all actions taken and/or plans made towards the implementation of this project;

4. *Calls upon* all States, specialized agencies and governmental and non-governmental organizations not to assist, directly or indirectly, in the preparation and execution of this project and strongly urges national, international and multinational corporations to do likewise;

5. *Requests* the Secretary-General to monitor and assess, on a continuing basis and through a competent expert organ, all aspects—juridical, political, economic, ecological and demographic—of the adverse effects on Jordan and on the Arab territories occupied since 1967, including Jerusalem, arising from the implementation of the Israeli decision to construct this canal and to forward the findings of that organ on a regular basis to the General Assembly;

6. *Requests* the Secretary-General to report to the General Assembly at its thirty-ninth session on the implementation of the present resolution;

7. *Decides* to include in the provisional agenda of its thirty-ninth session the item entitled "Israel's decision to build a canal linking the Mediterranean Sea to the Dead Sea".

General Assembly resolution 38/85

15 December 1983   Meeting 98   141-2 (recorded vote)

Approved by SPC (A/38/720) by recorded vote (112-2), 7 December (meeting 47); 3-nation draft (A/SPC/38/L.45); agenda item 75.
Sponsors: Iraq, Jordan, Pakistan.
Financial implications. 5th Committee, A/38/732; S-G, A/C.5/38/89, A/SPC/38/L.47.
Meeting numbers. GA 38th session: SPC 45-47; 5th Committee 62; plenary 98.

Recorded vote in Assembly as follows:

In favour: Afghanistan, Albania, Algeria, Angola, Argentina, Australia, Austria, Bahamas, Bahrain, Bangladesh, Barbados, Belgium, Belize, Benin, Bhutan, Bolivia, Botswana, Brazil, Bulgaria, Burma, Burundi, Byelorussian SSR, Canada, Cape Verde, Central African Republic, Chad, Chile, China, Colombia, Congo, Costa Rica, Cuba, Cyprus, Czechoslovakia, Democratic Kampuchea, Democratic Yemen, Denmark, Djibouti, Dominican Republic, Ecuador, Egypt, El Salvador, Equatorial Guinea, Ethiopia, Fiji, Finland, France, Gabon, Gambia, German Democratic Republic, Germany, Federal Republic of, Ghana, Greece, Grenada, Guinea, Guinea-Bissau, Guyana, Hungary, Iceland, India, Indonesia, Iran, Iraq, Ireland, Italy, Jamaica, Japan, Jordan, Kenya, Kuwait, Lao People's Democratic Republic, Lebanon, Lesotho, Liberia, Libyan Arab Jamahiriya, Luxembourg, Madagascar, Malawi, Malaysia, Maldives, Mali, Malta, Mauritania, Mauritius, Mexico, Mongolia, Morocco, Mozambique, Nepal, Netherlands, New Zealand, Nicaragua, Niger, Nigeria, Norway, Oman, Pakistan, Panama, Papua New Guinea, Paraguay, Peru, Philippines, Poland, Portugal, Qatar, Romania, Rwanda, Sao Tome and Principe, Saudi Arabia, Senegal, Seychelles, Sierra Leone, Singapore, Somalia, Spain, Sri Lanka, Sudan, Suriname, Swaziland, Sweden, Syrian Arab Republic, Thailand, Togo, Trinidad and Tobago, Tunisia, Turkey, Uganda, Ukrainian SSR, USSR, United Arab Emirates, United Kingdom, United Republic of Cameroon, United Republic of Tanzania, Upper Volta, Uruguay, Venezuela, Viet Nam, Yemen, Yugoslavia, Zambia, Zimbabwe.

Against: Israel, United States.

Introducing the draft, Jordan stated that it sought to avoid the undesirable effects of implementing the Israeli project, which would seriously damage Jordan's economic, political, ecological and other rights and interests and was contrary to the principles of international law relative to belligerent occupation of territory.

Israel said it could not support a text which gave no indication of any effort having been made to examine objectively the actual situation. Moreover, the Committee had not requested clarifications from Jordan on its project for a canal linking the Red Sea to the Dead Sea, implementation of which would have exactly the same effects as the Israeli project.

Education

As requested by the General Assembly, the Secretary-General submitted in October 1983 a report[82] on implementation of a December 1982 resolution[83] demanding that Israel rescind all measures against educational institutions in the occupied territories. Replying to a note verbale of 10 March 1983, Israel, on 27 September, rejected what it called accusations in that resolution, adding that since 1967 the number of pupils and classes had increased considerably and academic activity on the university campuses and at other educational institutions was conducted without Israeli interference. However, when security was likely to be endangered by virulent demonstrations outside the confines of the campus, authorities were obliged by international law to restore public order and safety; Israel's actions could in no way be interpreted as a "systematic Israeli campaign of repression against and closing of universities".

By a letter of 4 November,[84] the Chairman of the Committee on Palestinian rights expressed the Committee's concern at Israel's decision to close down Bethlehem University in the West Bank, based partly on an exhibition entitled "Palestinian Heritage" held at the University. Israel's repressive policy, the Chairman added, could only aggravate the extremely tense situation in the occupied territories and increase the threat to international peace and security; it was therefore urgent that the strictest respect for United Nations resolutions be ensured, in particular those aimed at enabling Palestinians to exercise their rights.

The Committee on Israeli practices in the occupied territories, in its 1983 report,[14] also provided information on measures affecting the right to freedom of education, including attempts to apply a 1980 Military Order, which required professors and students to obtain a permit to teach and attend universities. The Committee noted that schools and universities in the territories had been repeatedly closed by the authorities, causing serious disruption in the academic life. In its conclusions, the Committee expressed the hope that the attention it had focused in its report on measures affecting the right to freedom of education might lead to a realization of the need for urgent action

by the occupying authorities to curtail the cycle of violence provoked by the denial of that right.

GENERAL ASSEMBLY ACTION

On 15 December 1983, under the agenda item on the report of the Special Committee to Investigate Israeli Practices Affecting the Human Rights of the Population of the Occupied Territories, the General Assembly, acting on the recommendation of the Special Political Committee, adopted by recorded vote resolution 38/79 G.

The General Assembly,

Bearing in mind the Geneva Convention relative to the Protection of Civilian Persons in Time of War, of 12 August 1949,

Deeply shocked by the most recent atrocities committed by Israel, the occupying Power, against educational institutions in the occupied Palestinian territories,

1. *Reaffirms* the applicability of the Geneva Convention relative to the Protection of Civilian Persons in Time of War, of 12 August 1949, to the Palestinian and other Arab territories occupied by Israel since 1967, including Jerusalem;

2. *Condemns* Israeli policies and practices against Palestinian students and faculties in schools, universities and other educational institutions in the occupied Palestinian territories, especially the policy of opening fire on defenceless students, causing many casualties;

3. *Condemns* the systematic Israeli campaign of repression against and closing of universities in the occupied Palestinian territories, restricting and impeding the academic activities of Palestinian universities by subjecting the selection of courses, textbooks and educational programmes, the admission of students and the appointment of faculty members to the control and supervision of the military occupation authorities, in clear contravention of the Geneva Convention;

4. *Demands* that Israel, the occupying Power, comply with the provisions of that Convention, rescind all actions and measures against all educational institutions, ensure the freedom of those institutions and refrain forthwith from hindering the effective operation of the universities and other educational institutions;

5. *Requests* the Secretary-General to submit a report on the implementation of the present resolution before the end of 1984.

General Assembly resolution 38/79 G

15 December 1983   Meeting 98   116-2-28 (recorded vote)

Approved by SPC (A/38/718) by recorded vote (90-2-24), 5 December (meeting 45); 11-nation draft (A/SPC/38/L.41); agenda item 69.

Sponsors: Afghanistan, Bangladesh, Cuba, Egypt, India, Indonesia, Madagascar, Malaysia, Mali, Pakistan, Qatar.

Meeting numbers. GA 38th session: SPC 36-42, 45-48; plenary 98.

Recorded vote in Assembly as follows:

In favour: Afghanistan, Albania, Algeria, Angola, Argentina, Austria, Bahamas, Bahrain, Bangladesh, Belize, Benin, Bhutan, Bolivia, Botswana, Brazil, Bulgaria, Burundi, Byelorussian SSR, Cape Verde, Central African Republic, Chad, China, Congo, Cuba, Cyprus, Czechoslovakia, Democratic Kampuchea, Democratic Yemen, Djibouti, Dominican Republic, Ecuador, Egypt, Equatorial Guinea, Ethiopia, Fiji, Gabon, Gambia, German Democratic Republic, Ghana, Greece, Grenada, Guinea, Guinea-Bissau, Guyana, Hungary, India, Indonesia, Iran, Iraq, Ivory Coast, Jamaica, Jordan, Kenya, Kuwait, Lao People's Democratic Republic, Lebanon, Lesotho, Libyan Arab Jamahiriya, Madagascar, Malawi, Malaysia, Maldives, Mali, Malta, Mauritania, Mauritius, Mexico, Mongolia, Morocco, Mozambique, Nepal, Nicaragua, Niger, Nigeria, Oman, Pakistan, Panama, Papua New Guinea, Peru, Philippines, Poland, Portugal, Qatar, Romania, Rwanda, Sao Tome and Principe,

Saudi Arabia, Senegal, Seychelles, Sierra Leone, Singapore, Somalia, Spain, Sri Lanka, Sudan, Suriname, Syrian Arab Republic, Thailand, Togo, Trinidad and Tobago, Tunisia, Turkey, Uganda, Ukrainian SSR, USSR, United Arab Emirates, United Republic of Cameroon, United Republic of Tanzania, Upper Volta, Vanuatu, Venezuela, Viet Nam, Yemen, Yugoslavia, Zambia, Zimbabwe.
Against: Israel, United States.
Abstaining: Australia, Barbados, Belgium, Burma, Canada, Chile, Colombia, Costa Rica, Denmark, Finland, France, Germany, Federal Republic of, Iceland, Ireland, Italy, Japan, Liberia, Luxembourg, Netherlands, New Zealand, Norway, Paraguay, Solomon Islands, Swaziland, Sweden, United Kingdom, Uruguay, Zaire.

Israel reiterated that since 1967 vast improvements had taken place in the educational system in the areas under its administration. The number of pupils had increased from 200,000 to 400,000. There had been no universities and only a few institutes of higher learning, while there were four university-level institutions in 1983 and vocational training had taken a great leap forward. Terrorist-oriented disruptions in high schools and universities, however, were PLO policy, and Israel would do its utmost to stop them. The text completely ignored all that; its emphasis was not on education but on attempts to sabotage it.

Sweden said that the text, as those adopted in previous years, contained generalizations which were too sweeping. The United States also found the condemnatory language unacceptable, but agreed that there were aspects of Israeli policy towards academic institutions in the territories which were open to criticism.

By two other resolutions of 15 December, pertaining to Palestine refugees, the Assembly appealed for grants and scholarships for higher education and vocational training (38/83 D), and emphasized the need for the establishment of a university at Jerusalem (38/83 K).

Permanent sovereignty over resources

Reports of the Secretary-General. In June 1983, the Secretary-General submitted, in accordance with a December 1982 General Assembly resolution,[85] two reports: one on the permanent sovereignty over national resources in the occupied Palestinian and other Arab territories,[86] and the other on the implications, under international law, of United Nations resolutions on permanent sovereignty over natural resources, on the occupied territories, and on Israel's obligations concerning its conduct in those territories.[87]

Annexed to the first report was another prepared by consultants under the supervision of the Natural Resources and Energy Division, United Nations Department of Technical Co-operation for Development. The consultants' report was based on data in reports of United Nations organs and agencies; information from Governments, PLO and specialized research organizations; and other published material. As efforts to obtain access to the occupied territories had been unsuccessful, the consultants stated, the information presented was limited; every effort had been made, however, also to use Israeli sources and to obtain first-hand information from the territories, through co-operation with and fact-finding missions organized by various United Nations agencies, including UNRWA, and United Nations experts visiting neighbouring countries.

The report dealt with national sovereignty and political institutions; judicial protection; natural resources, including land, water and mineral resources; human resources; economic policies; and cultural resources and values. Concerning follow-up and implementation, the consultants proposed, pending a settlement of basic political issues, certain practical interim measures, among them: land conservation should guide United Nations–sponsored technical co-operation; developments affecting permanent sovereignty over resources in the territories should be monitored; an in-depth study could be made, with a focus on the policies relating to water, but also dealing with the quarrying industry and other resources; and the Assembly could consider ways to increase the opportunities for marketing Palestinian products, could call for a strengthening of bilateral technical co-operation programmes in the territories and could request the United Nations to encourage such assistance and prepare suitable projects.

Annexed to the Secretary-General's second report was one prepared by legal expert Blaine Sloan, Professor of International Law and Organization at Pace University School of Law, White Plains, New York. It examined the development of the principle of permanent sovereignty over natural resources and analysed United Nations resolutions, in particular as they applied to the occupied territories and to Israel's obligations as an occupying Power. Among the implications of United Nations resolutions, the expert considered the following: The primary right of peoples and nations to permanent sovereignty over their natural resources was a right freely to use, control and dispose of such resources; full exercise of that right could take place only with the restoration of control over the occupied territories to the States and peoples concerned; the occupying Power was under an obligation not to interfere with the exercise of permanent sovereignty by the population; under the law of belligerent occupation, natural resources could not be used by the occupying Power beyond the limits imposed by the Regulations respecting the Laws and Customs of War on Land, annexed to Convention IV of The Hague of 1907, and the 1949 fourth Geneva Convention, i.e., land and other resources could not be taken for settlements or be permanently acquired for any purposes; and the right to reparation for any loss or damage to natural resources as a result of violations of the rules of belligerent occupation could be reinforced.

ECONOMIC AND SOCIAL COUNCIL ACTION

By decision 1983/178 of 28 July 1983, adopted without vote, the Economic and Social Council took note of the two reports.

Permanent sovereignty over national resources in the occupied Palestinian and other Arab territories

At its 40th plenary meeting, on 28 July 1983, the Council took note of the reports of the Secretary-General on permanent sovereignty over national resources in the occupied Palestinian and other Arab territories and on the implications, under international law, of the United Nations resolutions on permanent sovereignty over natural resources, on the occupied Palestinian and other Arab territories and on the obligations of Israel concerning its conduct in those territories.

Economic and Social Council decision 1983/178
Adopted without vote

Draft orally proposed by President; agenda item 5.
Meeting numbers. ESC 37, 39, 40.

GENERAL ASSEMBLY ACTION

On 19 December 1983, acting on the recommendation of the Second (Economic and Financial) Committee, the General Assembly adopted by recorded vote resolution 38/144.

Permanent sovereignty over national resources in the occupied Palestinian and other Arab territories

The General Assembly,

Recalling its resolution 37/135 of 17 December 1982,

Recalling also its previous resolutions on permanent sovereignty over natural resources,

Bearing in mind the relevant principles of international law and the provisions of the international conventions and regulations, in particular Convention IV of The Hague of 1907, and the Geneva Convention relative to the Protection of Civilian Persons in Time of War, of 12 August 1949, concerning the obligations and responsibilities of the occupying Power,

Bearing in mind also the pertinent provisions of its resolutions 3201(S-VI) and 3202(S-VI) of 1 May 1974, containing the Declaration and the Programme of Action on the Establishment of a New International Economic Order, and 3281(XXIX) of 12 December 1974, containing the Charter of Economic Rights and Duties of States,

1. *Takes note* of the report of the Secretary-General on permanent sovereignty over national resources in the occupied Palestinian and other Arab territories;

2. *Commends* the report of the Secretary-General on the implications, under international law, of the United Nations resolutions on permanent sovereignty over natural resources, on the occupied Palestinian and other Arab territories and on the obligations of Israel concerning its conduct in these territories;

3. *Condemns* Israel for its exploitation of the national resources of the occupied Palestinian and other Arab territories;

4. *Reaffirms* that Convention IV of The Hague of 1907 and the Geneva Convention relative to the Protection of Civilian Persons in Time of War, of 12 August 1949, are applicable to the occupied Palestinian and other Arab territories;

5. *Emphasizes* the right of the Palestinian and other Arab peoples whose territories are under Israeli occupation to full and effective permanent sovereignty and control over their natural and all other resources, wealth and economic activities;

6. *Also reaffirms* that all measures undertaken by Israel to exploit the human, natural and all other resources, wealth and economic activities in the occupied Palestinian and other Arab territories are illegal, and calls upon Israel to desist immediately from such measures;

7. *Further reaffirms* the right of the Palestinian and other Arab peoples subjected to Israeli aggression and occupation to the restitution of, and full compensation for the exploitation, depletion and loss of and damage to, their natural, human and all other resources, wealth and economic activities, and calls upon Israel to meet their just claims;

8. *Calls upon* all States to support the Palestinian and other Arab peoples in the exercise of their above-mentioned rights;

9. *Calls upon* all States, international organizations, specialized agencies, business corporations and all other institutions not to recognize, or co-operate with or assist in any manner in, any measures undertaken by Israel to exploit the national resources of the occupied Palestinian and other Arab territories or to effect any changes in the demographic composition, the character and form of use of their natural resources or the institutional structure of those territories;

10. *Requests* the Secretary-General to elaborate on his report in order to cover also, in detail, the resources exploited by the Israeli settlements and the Israeli-imposed regulations and policies hampering the economic development of the occupied Palestinian and other Arab territories, including a comparison between the practices of Israel and its obligations under international law;

11. *Also requests* the Secretary-General to submit the detailed report to the General Assembly at its thirty-ninth session, through the Economic and Social Council.

General Assembly resolution 38/144
19 December 1983   Meeting 102   120-2-18 (recorded vote)

Approved by Second Committee (A/38/701) by recorded vote (110-2-20), 14 November (meeting 39); 8-nation draft (A/C.2/38/L.23/Rev.1), orally revised; agenda item 12.
Sponsors: Madagascar, Mali, Mauritania, Senegal, Tunisia, Upper Volta, Yemen, Zimbabwe.
Financial implications. 5th Committee, A/38/751; S-G, A/C.2/38/L.34, A/C.5/38/47.
Meeting numbers. GA 38th session: 2nd Committee 25-30, 34, 37, 39; 5th Committee 44; plenary 102.

Recorded vote in Assembly as follows:

In favour: Afghanistan, Albania, Algeria, Angola, Argentina, Austria, Bahamas, Bahrain, Bangladesh, Barbados, Belize, Benin, Bhutan, Bolivia, Botswana, Brazil, Bulgaria, Burundi, Byelorussian SSR, Cape Verde, Chile, China, Colombia, Congo, Cuba, Cyprus, Czechoslovakia, Democratic Kampuchea, Democratic Yemen, Djibouti, Dominican Republic, Ecuador, Egypt, El Salvador, Ethiopia, Fiji, Gabon, Gambia, German Democratic Republic, Ghana, Greece, Guinea, Guinea-Bissau, Guyana, Honduras, Hungary, India, Indonesia, Iran, Iraq, Jamaica, Japan, Jordan, Kenya, Kuwait, Lao People's Democratic Republic, Lebanon, Lesotho, Liberia, Libyan Arab Jamahiriya, Madagascar, Malaysia, Maldives, Mali, Malta, Mauritania, Mauritius, Mexico, Mongolia, Morocco, Mozambique, Nepal, Nicaragua, Niger, Nigeria, Oman, Pakistan, Panama, Papua New Guinea, Paraguay, Peru, Philippines, Poland, Portugal, Qatar, Romania, Rwanda, Saint Vincent and the Grenadines, Sao Tome and Principe, Saudi Arabia, Senegal, Sierra Leone, Singapore, Somalia, Spain, Sri Lanka, Sudan, Suriname, Swaziland, Syrian Arab Republic, Thailand, Togo, Trinidad and Tobago, Tunisia, Turkey, Uganda, Ukrainian SSR, USSR, United Arab Emirates, United Republic of Cameroon, United Republic of Tanzania, Upper Volta, Uruguay, Vanuatu, Venezuela, Viet Nam, Yemen, Yugoslavia, Zaire, Zambia.

Against: Israel, United States.

Abstaining: Australia, Belgium, Burma, Canada, Denmark, Finland, France, Germany, Federal Republic of, Iceland, Ireland, Italy, Ivory Coast, Luxembourg, Netherlands, New Zealand, Norway, Sweden, United Kingdom.

Israel rejected its condemnation in the text which, it added, presented a distorted picture, sought to impose an irrelevant decision of no practical significance, was motivated solely by hostility to Israel, and was intentionally based on distorted information and a predetermined decision to deny any positive achievements in the territories. The situation there was in complete contrast to what could be inferred from the text, the adoption of which would not affect the existing situation in any way. Paragraph 10 was a further example of the United Nations legal services being abused to produce one-sided reports to satisfy political aims, regardless of the true state of affairs; Israel had been trying to develop the resources of the territories and improve the standard of living there.

The United States considered the expenditure of United Nations resources for a further report to be unjustified, and felt that the text was wholly political and raised issues which could be solved only by direct negotiations between the parties concerned. With regard to the financial implications, the United Kingdom hoped that there would be some offsetting savings.

Chile did not support paragraph 3, saying it would not contribute to co-operation. Zaire also had reservations on that paragraph, stating that it seemed to condemn Israel as a country, whereas the general practice was to condemn the policy of a country. Portugal reserved its position on paragraph 7.

Austria stressed that it supported the text's general thrust but agreed with its specific wording only in so far as it conformed to international law. Japan hoped that the problem of the natural resources in the territories would be solved expeditiously, in conformity with international law. Turkey expressed its support for the text in accordance with its well-known views on the Middle East and Palestine questions. The USSR expressed full support for the Palestinians' and other Arab peoples' right of sovereignty over natural resources in occupied Arab lands.

Introducing the draft, Senegal emphasized that the right of peoples and nations to permanent sovereignty over their natural resources had been accepted as a principle of international law, whose validity had been recognized by the Assembly in 1972.[88]

REFERENCES

[1]A/38/458-S/16015. [2]S/15553. [3]S/15561. [4]A/38/122-S/15653. [5]S/15660. [6]S/15854. [7]S/15869. [8]A/38/295-S/15865. [9]E/1983/13 (res. 1983/1 A). [10]*Ibid.* (res. 1983/1 B). [11]*Ibid.* (res. 1983/3). [12]YUN 1982, p. 481. [13]E/CN.4/1984/3 (res. 1983/9). [14]A/38/409. [15]YUN 1968, p. 555, GA res. 2443(XXIII), 19 Dec. 1968. [16]YUN 1982, p. 524. [17]*Ibid.*, p. 528, GA res. 37/88 C, 10 Dec. 1982. [18]A/38/482. [19]A/CONF.114/42. [20]YUN 1947-48, p. 247, GA res. 181 A (II), 29 Nov. 1947. [21]A/38/78-S/15572. [22]A/38/82-S/15574. [23]S/15599. [24]S/15604. [25]YUN 1967, p. 257, SC res. 242(1967), 22 Nov. 1967. [26]A/38/112-S/15635. [27]A/38/116-S/15640 & Corr.1. [28]A/38/123-S/15655. [29]S/15764. [30]A/38/257-S/15810. [31]A/38/306-S/15880. [32]S/15886. [33]S/15890. [34]S/15895. [35]YUN 1980, p. 427, SC res. 465(1980), 1 Mar. 1980. [36]*Ibid.*, p. 425, SC res. 476(1980), 30 June 1980. [37]S/15901. [38]A/38/331-S/15916. [39]A/38/369-S/15942. [40]A/38/528-S/16066. [41]A/38/592-S/16164. [42]YUN 1982, p. 388. [43]YUN 1979, p. 400, SC res. 446(1979), 22 Mar. 1979. [44]A/38/35. [45]YUN 1980, p. 416. [46]E/1983/13 (res. 1983/2). [47]YUN 1981, p. 307. [48]YUN 1948-49, p. 535, GA res. 217 A (III), 10 Dec. 1948. [49]A/38/481. [50]YUN 1982, p. 516, GA res. 37/88 E, 10 Dec. 1982. [51]YUN 1981, p. 312. [52]*Ibid.*, SC res. 497(1981), 17 Dec. 1981. [53]YUN 1982, p. 515, GA res. ES-9/1, 5 Feb. 1981. [54]YUN 1980, p. 411. [55]*Ibid.*, p. 413. [56]A/38/262. [57]YUN 1982, p. 539, GA res. 37/88 D, 10 Dec. 1982. [58]A/38/484. [59]YUN 1982, p. 540, GA res. 37/88 G, 10 Dec. 1982. [60]YUN 1982, p. 540. [61]S/15659. [62]A/38/128-S/15667. [63]S/15673. [64]S/15674. [65]S/15680. [66]S/15683. [67]S/15756. [68]A/38/365-S/15939. [69]YUN 1982, p. 545, GA res. 37/222, 20 Dec. 1982. [70]A/38/278-E/1983/77. [71]TD/B/960 & Corr.1. [72]YUN 1981, p. 323. [73]TD/B/973. [74]YUN 1981, p. 318. [75]YUN 1982, p. 540. [76]UNEP/GC.11/3/Add.4. [77]A/38/25 (dec. 11/4). [78]YUN 1982, p. 541, GA res. 37/122, 16 Dec. 1982. [79]A/38/502. [80]A/38/502/Add.1. [81]A/38/502/Add.2. [82]A/38/483. [83]YUN 1982, p. 544, GA res. 37/88 F, 10 Dec. 1982. [84]A/38/569-S/16126. [85]YUN 1982, p. 547, GA res. 37/135, 17 Dec. 1982. [86]A/38/282-E/1983/84. [87]A/38/265-E/1983/85. [88]YUN 1972, p. 189, GA res. 3005(XXVII), 15 Dec. 1972.

Palestine refugees

UN Agency for Palestine refugees

In 1983, the United Nations Relief and Works Agency for Palestine Refugees in the Near East (UNRWA) continued to provide assistance to Palestine refugees in Jordan, Lebanon, the Syrian Arab Republic and the Israeli-occupied territories of the West Bank and the Gaza Strip. It maintained its own schools, training establishments, clinics and health centres, and it procured and distributed food rations to needy refugees.

In December, the General Assembly adopted 11 resolutions relating to UNRWA and Palestine refugees. Resolution 38/83 A dealt with assistance to Palestine refugees and resolution 38/83 B with the Working Group on the financing of UNRWA. The other resolutions were on the following topics (for details, see below): assistance to displaced persons (38/83 C); refugee protection (38/83 I); property rights (38/83 H); food aid to Palestine refugees (38/83 F); scholarships for higher education and vocational training (38/83 D); a proposed University of Jerusalem for Palestinian students (38/83 K); proposed repatriation of displaced refugees (38/83 G); and Palestine refugees in the Gaza Strip (38/83 E) and in the West Bank (38/83 J).

UNRWA activities

In the aftermath of the Israeli invasion of Lebanon in June 1982,[1] UNRWA continued in 1983 its emergency relief programme there, providing shelter, food and other supplies to Palestine refugees, regardless of whether or not they were registered with the Agency. During the year, UNRWA started a comprehensive programme of reconstructing UNRWA installations, camp infrastructure and refugee housing.

In addition, the Agency maintained its regular programme, with education and health services as priorities. In 1983, education and training accounted for 64.2 per cent ($125.5 million) of the Agency's total regular programme expenditure. Under an agreement between UNRWA and the United Nations Educational, Scientific and Cultural Organization (UNESCO), the latter was responsible for the professional aspects of the education programme which included general education at elementary and preparatory (lower secondary) levels in Agency schools, vocational and teacher training at Agency centres and a university scholarship programme. In October, a total of 342,245 pupils were enrolled in the Agency's 653 elementary and preparatory schools in Jordan, Lebanon, the Syrian Arab Republic, the West Bank and the Gaza Strip, served by a teaching force of 10,027. A further 98,044 refugee pupils were known to be enrolled in government and private elementary and secondary schools in the same areas, and about 45,100 non-eligible children were in Agency schools.

Expenditure on health services in 1983 totalled almost $40 million, while expenditure on relief services was $19.4 million.

Report of the Commissioner-General. In a report covering UNRWA activities for the period 1 July 1982 to 30 June 1983,[2] the Commissioner-General stated that throughout that period, the situation in Lebanon following the June 1982 Israeli invasion had attracted much of UNRWA's efforts and resources. He added that although the operation in Lebanon had been the major preoccupation of UNRWA, conditions in the occupied territories, particularly in the West Bank (see above), had also been the cause of deep concern. The period was marked by numerous disturbances by Palestinians and Israeli settlers and by security measures taken by the Israeli army. Demonstrations by Palestinians, often accompanied by violence, had caused the occupation authorities to close UNRWA schools and training centres and to impose curfews on refugee camps. Though in general UNRWA had been able, with the co-operation of the Israeli authorities, to maintain minimum essential services to camp inhabitants under curfew, the distress caused to them by prolonged curfews was intense. Clashes between Palestinians and members of the Israeli security forces had been followed by the entry of troops into the three UNRWA training centres in the West Bank.

The Commissioner-General reported that UNRWA had made every effort to limit the interruption of its services and to secure the reopening of training centres and schools. However, he cautioned that as long as the tension in the territories remained high, it had to be feared that incidents involving UNRWA programmes and staff would continue to occur.

The Commissioner-General also recorded Israeli interference with UNRWA building activities in Gaza, which, he said, created serious problems. The Israeli civil administration in Gaza continued to interfere even with minor construction projects in camps and had caused work already started to be halted. Discussions continued with those authorities in the hope of overcoming that obstruction which, in the Agency's view, contravened the agreement concluded between Israel and UNRWA in 1967.

The Commissioner-General stated that, the distribution of foodstuffs to eligible refugees having been suspended in September 1982 with the exception of Lebanon,[3] available resources were devoted to the highest priority programmes, education and health. Before the general ration distribution to the Palestine refugees in all fields could be resumed, as called for by the General Assembly in December 1982,[4] the Agency would have to cover its financial needs for the education and health programmes and for its welfare programmes for the poorest section of the refugee community.

With regard to the financing of regular UNRWA programmes (see below), the Commissioner-General expressed deep concern; the Agency's relatively favourable cash situation in 1983, he stated, was due to exceptional circumstances which would not be repeated in 1984.

GENERAL ASSEMBLY ACTION

On 15 December 1983, on the recommendation of the Special Political Committee, the General Assembly adopted resolution 38/83 A by recorded vote.

Assistance to Palestine refugees
The General Assembly,

Recalling its resolution 37/120 K of 16 December 1982 and all previous resolutions on the question, including resolution 194(III) of 11 December 1948,

Taking note of the report of the Commissioner-General of the United Nations Relief and Works Agency for Palestine Refugees in the Near East, covering the period from 1 July 1982 to 30 June 1983,

1. *Notes with deep regret* that repatriation or compensation of the refugees as provided for in paragraph 11

of General Assembly resolution 194(III) has not been effected, that no substantial progress has been made in the programme endorsed by the Assembly in paragraph 2 of its resolution 513(VI) of 26 January 1952 for the reintegration of refugees either by repatriation or resettlement and that, therefore, the situation of the refugees continues to be a matter of serious concern;

2. *Expresses its thanks* to the Commissioner-General and to all the staff of the United Nations Relief and Works Agency for Palestine Refugees in the Near East, recognizing that the Agency is doing all it can within the limits of available resources, and also expresses its thanks to the specialized agencies and private organizations for their valuable work in assisting the refugees;

3. *Reiterates its request* that the headquarters of the United Nations Relief and Works Agency for Palestine Refugees in the Near East should be relocated to its former site within its area of operations as soon as practicable;

4. *Notes with regret* that the United Nations Conciliation Commission for Palestine has been unable to find a means of achieving progress in the implementation of paragraph 11 of General Assembly resolution 194(III) and requests the Commission to exert continued efforts towards the implementation of that paragraph and to report to the Assembly as appropriate, but not later than 1 October 1984;

5. *Directs attention* to the continuing seriousness of the financial position of the United Nations Relief and Works Agency for Palestine Refugees in the Near East, as outlined in the report of the Commissioner-General;

6. *Notes with profound concern* that, despite the commendable and successful efforts of the Commissioner-General to collect additional contributions, this increased level of income to the United Nations Relief and Works Agency for Palestine Refugees in the Near East is still insufficient to cover essential budget requirements in the present year and that, at currently foreseen levels of giving, deficits will recur each year;

7. *Calls upon* all Governments as a matter of urgency to make the most generous efforts possible to meet the anticipated needs of the United Nations Relief and Works Agency for Palestine Refugees in the Near East, particularly in the light of the budgetary deficit projected in the report of the Commissioner-General, and therefore urges non-contributing Governments to contribute regularly and contributing Governments to consider increasing their regular contributions;

8. *Decides* to extend until 30 June 1987, without prejudice to the provisions of paragraph 11 of General Assembly resolution 194(III), the mandate of the United Nations Relief and Works Agency for Palestine Refugees in the Near East.

General Assembly resolution 38/83 A

15 December 1983   Meeting 98   147-0-1 (recorded vote)

Approved by SPC (A/38/700) by recorded vote (113-0-1), 2 December (meeting 44); draft by United States (A/SPC/38/L.13); agenda item 73.
Financial implications. S-G, A/SPC/38/L.17.
Meeting numbers. GA 38th session: SPC 24, 26-36, 44. plenary 98.

Recorded vote in Assembly as follows:

In favour: Afghanistan, Algeria, Angola, Argentina, Australia, Austria, Bahamas, Bahrain, Bangladesh, Barbados, Belgium, Belize, Benin, Bhutan, Bolivia, Botswana, Brazil, Bulgaria, Burma, Burundi, Byelorussian SSR, Canada, Cape Verde, Central African Republic, Chad, Chile, China, Colombia, Congo, Costa Rica, Cuba, Cyprus, Czechoslovakia, Democratic Kampuchea, Democratic Yemen, Denmark, Djibouti, Dominica, Dominican Republic, Ecuador, Egypt, El Salvador, Equatorial Guinea, Ethiopia, Fiji, Finland, France, Gabon, Gambia, German Democratic Republic, Germany, Federal Republic of, Ghana, Greece, Grenada, Guinea, Guinea-Bissau, Guyana, Honduras, Hungary, Iceland, India, Indonesia, Iran, Iraq, Ireland, Italy, Ivory Coast, Jamaica, Japan, Jordan, Kenya, Kuwait, Lao People's Democratic Republic, Lebanon, Lesotho, Liberia, Libyan Arab Jamahiriya, Luxembourg, Madagascar, Malawi, Malaysia, Maldives, Mali, Malta, Mauritania, Mauritius, Mexico, Mongolia, Morocco, Mozambique, Nepal, Netherlands, New Zealand, Nicaragua, Niger, Nigeria, Norway, Oman, Pakistan, Panama, Papua New Guinea, Paraguay, Peru, Philippines, Poland, Portugal, Qatar, Romania, Rwanda, Saint Lucia, Sao Tome and Principe, Saudi Arabia, Senegal, Seychelles, Sierra Leone, Singapore, Somalia, Spain, Sri Lanka, Sudan, Suriname, Swaziland, Sweden, Syrian Arab Republic, Thailand, Togo, Trinidad and Tobago, Tunisia, Turkey, Uganda, Ukrainian SSR, USSR, United Arab Emirates, United Kingdom, United Republic of Cameroon, United Republic of Tanzania, United States, Upper Volta, Uruguay, Vanuatu, Venezuela, Viet Nam, Yemen, Yugoslavia, Zaire, Zambia, Zimbabwe.

Against: None.

Abstaining: Israel.

Speaking after adoption of the 11 resolutions on UNRWA in the Assembly, Iran said that they were all second-hand approaches to a second-hand problem; the first-hand problem was to remove the Zionist entity in the Middle East.

Before the Assembly votes, Israel said that the drafts reflected the total irrelevance of the decisions to be taken on the subject of the Palestine refugees and disregarded the background facts; the resultant texts made demands on the world to maintain a lopsided policy regarding the Palestinian refugees in continuing contributions 10 times greater per head than the amounts spent on other refugees in Africa, Latin America and Asia.

In the Committee, the Libyan Arab Jamahiriya registered reservations to any direct or indirect reference in the drafts that might imply legitimacy of the Zionist occupation of Palestine.

In resolution 38/201 of 20 December, on the liquidation of the United Nations Emergency Operation Trust Fund, the Assembly decided to allocate 18 per cent of the Fund's remaining balance to UNRWA's educational programme.

UNRWA financing and administration

Financing

In 1983, total UNRWA expenditure amounted to $195.4 million, while income was $174.5 million, resulting in an excess of expenditure over income of $20.9 million. Despite that shortfall, the balance in the working capital as of 31 December 1983 had increased by $10 million as compared with the end of 1982, the reason for this being that the accumulated provision of $30.7 million for termination indemnities had been reverted to working capital at the year-end. The 1983 income for the Lebanon emergency relief, totalling $9.3 million, fell short by $0.8 million in relation to expenditure and commitments of $10.1 million, while income for the Lebanon Reconstruction Programme covered the expenditure and commitments of $5.4 million.

CONTRIBUTIONS TO UNRWA GENERAL FUND, 1983
(as at 31 December 1983; in US dollar equivalent)

Contributor	Payments in kind	Payments in cash	Total	Contributor	Payments in kind	Payments in cash	Total
Argentina	—	21,300	21,300	Netherlands	—	2,093,020	2,093,020
Australia	—	1,268,202	1,268,202	New Zealand	—	79,366	79,366
Austria	—	132,000	132,000	Norway	—	7,688,429	7,688,429
Bahamas	—	500	500	Oman	—	25,000	25,000
Bahrain	—	15,000	15,000	Pakistan	—	16,008	16,008
Belgium	—	347,625	347,625	Panama	—	500	500
Burma	—	1,000	1,000	Philippines	—	5,309	5,309
Canada	1,630,491	3,394,762	5,025,253	Portugal	—	15,000	15,000
Chile	—	5,000	5,000	Republic of Korea	—	5,000	5,000
China	—	50,000	50,000	San Marino	—	5,198	5,198
Cyprus	—	2,010	2,010	Senegal	—	499,678	499,678
Denmark	2,081,363	558,863	2,640,226	Sri Lanka	2,000	—	2,000
Egypt	—	7,299	7,299	Sweden	—	7,914,065	7,914,065
European Economic Community	3,946,008*	—	3,946,008	Switzerland	3,245,153*	780,107	4,025,260
Finland	—	315,516	315,516	Syrian Arab Republic	131,458	—	131,458
France	377,810	780,133	1,157,943	Thailand	—	15,640	15,640
Gaza authorities	103,065	—	103,065	Trinidad and Tobago	—	4,975	4,975
Germany, Federal Republic of	—	3,455,981	3,455,981	Tunisia	—	11,799	11,799
Ghana	—	5,500	5,500	Turkey	—	20,000	20,000
Greece	—	50,000	50,000	United Kingdom	—	7,757,500	7,757,500
Holy See	—	12,500	12,500	United States	—	67,000,000	67,000,000
Iceland	—	9,500	9,500	Venezuela	—	9,983	9,983
Indonesia	—	8,000	8,000	Zimbabwe	—	6,510	6,510
Ireland	—	268,560	268,560	Subtotal	12,610,347	116,496,223	129,106,570
Israel	219,422	—	219,422				
Italy	—	1,220,391	1,220,391	*United Nations and specialized agencies:*			
Jamaica	—	3,000	3,000	United Nations			5,930,000
Japan	—	8,000,000	8,000,000	UNESCO			1,338,032
Jordan	829,077	—	829,077	WHO			417,791
Kuwait	—	1,100,000	1,100,000				
Lebanon	44,500	14,062	58,562	Subtotal			7,685,823
Liberia	—	5,000	5,000				
Libyan Arab Jamahiriya	—	1,431,990	1,431,990	*Organization of Petroleum Exporting Countries*			350,000
Luxembourg	—	7,716	7,716				
Malaysia	—	5,000	5,000	*Non-governmental sources*			3,314,125†
Maldives	—	2,500	2,500				
Malta	—	936	936	*Miscellaneous income and exchange adjustments*			8,183,489
Mauritius	—	1,400	1,400				
Mexico	—	3,024	3,024	Total			148,640,007
Monaco	—	866	866				
Morocco	—	38,000	38,000				

*At donor's valuation.

†Not included in the amount was the balance of $194,391 outstanding at 31 December 1983, of which $39,338 was paid as at June 1984.

NOTE: Contributions include only amounts for 1983 paid as at 31 December 1983.

SOURCE: A/39/5/Add.3

Working Group on financing UNRWA. In November 1983, the Working Group on the Financing of the United Nations Relief and Works Agency for Palestine Refugees in the Near East, established under a 1970 General Assembly resolution,[5] submitted a report on its activities and on UNRWA's financial situation in 1983.[6] The Working Group reported that at a meeting on 28 September, the UNRWA Deputy Commissioner-General had provided it with up-to-date information on UNRWA's financial situation.

In its concluding remarks, the Group expressed concern that UNRWA would again have insufficient funds to finance its budgeted expenditure, even at the revised and reduced levels—$207.5 million—established at the beginning of the year. With expected income in 1983 at $166 million, there would be a shortfall of $41 million. Though recognizing that this gap would be bridged by deferring some non-cash items, the Group expressed concern that the major portion would be met by drawing down cash balances, which would seriously affect the Agency's cash position at the beginning of 1984. The Group considered the shortfall of income during 1983 to be particularly disturbing as income for the regular programme had actually decreased by $16 million as compared with income for 1982, despite some sizeable conversions of contributions in kind into cash. This was due to lower contributions from some of the traditional donors, partly as a result of increases in the value of the United States dollar against the currencies in which they contributed and partly due to the absence of special additional contributions.

In the Group's opinion, the financial outlook for 1984 gave rise to very serious concern. The Commissioner-General had projected expenditures for 1984 at $233 million, an increase of about $25 million over 1983 resulting from expected inflation and additional costs associated with the annual increase in the refugee population served by UNRWA. If income in 1984 did not exceed the level of 1983, there would be a shortfall of $66 million for financing the Agency's activities. The Group agreed that the financial support of UNRWA must be increased.

The willingness of some of the major contributors to convert their contributions in kind into cash or to allow UNRWA to sell their contributions for cash had been a decisive factor in maintaining the educational programme at its current level, the Group found. It expressed the hope that the contributors concerned would continue to assist the Agency in that respect.

The Group also considered the implications of the Agency's contingent liability for termination indemnities to its staff, amounting to $59 million, should UNRWA be forced to close down its operations. During the Group's consideration of that question, it was pointed out that, if the responsibility for termination indemnities could be assumed by the United Nations regular budget, UNRWA would be able to carry on its programmes for several more months during which strenuous attempts could be made to solicit additional contributions. On the other hand, it was pointed out that the proposal represented a financial risk to the United Nations and would also be contrary to the principle of voluntary financing for operational activities.

Stressing the need to ensure a continuation of the Agency's humanitarian assistance to the Palestine refugees, the Group urged for more and generous contributions, and for contributions as early as possible in the calendar year.

JIU recommendations. As requested by the General Assembly in March 1982,[7] the Joint Inspection Unit (JIU) carried out a comprehensive review of the organization, budget and operations of UNRWA, with a view to assisting the Commissioner-General to make the most effective and economical use of the limited funds available to the Agency. In its report, transmitted to the Assembly in August 1983 by a note of the Secretary-General,[8] JIU examined the results of UNRWA's three main programmes on education, health and relief. An examination of operational difficulties and methods led to the problems of budget and finance, personnel, structure and decentralization, and issues related to UNRWA's mandate and institutional setting.

Addressing in particular the Agency's financing problems and the cost effectiveness of the use of its scarce resources, JIU discovered that the financial constraints were the source of serious difficulties for the fulfilment of UNRWA's mandate. In this context, JIU remarked that it seemed obvious that helping UNRWA to have the best pos-

sible management would reinforce the confidence of Member States in its effectiveness, improve its image and credibility, and facilitate regular and stable financing.

In that context, JIU noted that UNRWA's budgetary and financial practices were at variance with the usual practice of the United Nations system. JIU suggested that UNRWA's recurrent financial crisis could be alleviated if the methods used for informing the contributing States on the needs of the Agency were improved. Instead of several presentations of estimated expenditure with different figures during the year, a detailed biennial budget should be established, which would be discussed and approved by Member States. On the basis of the approved budget, Member States could then determine their contributions.

Concluding its review, JIU stated that UNRWA's substantial accomplishments should be measured primarily in humanitarian terms and its shortcomings should be judged against the background of the lack of prospects for a political solution and a just settlement of the question of Palestine refugees. Despite the difficult conditions including increasing financial needs and continued uncertainty concerning the availability of resources, the Agency had developed services of a recurrent, quasi-governmental nature directed towards establishing and maintaining levels of education, health and relief which enabled a large proportion of the Palestine refugees to be socially productive, and also helped in maintaining a Palestinian identity. In that process, UNRWA had acquired specific institutional functions and had given training to thousands of Palestinian staff members; this was the Agency's strongest asset and must be maintained until a just settlement of the Palestinian question was reached, JIU stated.

In spite of the satisfactory nature of UNRWA's operations, JIU noted basic problems such as the deplorable state of many UNRWA installations and buildings, which could be solved only through adequate funding. JIU also felt that improvements in policies and procedures, especially in programming and budgeting, in staffing and in organizing services, were required. The uncertainty of sufficient and stable financing had resulted in the repeated fear of interruption of certain services or discontinuance of entire programmes; this, together with the prolonged displacement of the Agency's headquarters from the area of operations, had led to a weakening of confidence in UNRWA's ability to meet minimum requirements in the future. JIU regarded as urgent the need to redress these weaknesses.

JIU made 15 specific recommendations with regard to UNRWA's programme and operations, management and institutional questions. They concerned in particular: biennial work plans for all programmes; supplementary funding; use of self-help projects; construction and equipment of UNRWA schools, and curricula; strengthening of the education programme, in particular vocational training; new approaches to the relief programme; clearer and more precise budget presentation; review by the Assembly of the question of separation benefits; improvement of recruitment methods for international professionals; comprehensive career planning for area staff and an improved classification system; reorganization of administrative structures, with greater delegation of authority from headquarters to field offices; possible co-operation between UNRWA and the United Nations High Commissioner for Refugees with regard to protection of the Palestinian refugees; and reactivating and strengthening the role of the Advisory Commission of UNRWA. (For further details on individual recommendations, see below.)

In an addendum to the report,[9] the Secretary-General and the Commissioner-General submitted their comments on the JIU recommendations (see below, under specific subsections). The latter commented on several recommendations which, he believed, required qualification, while the Secretary-General took note specifically of JIU's recommendations on liability for separation payment to Agency staff and on refugee protection.

Action by the Conference on the Palestine question. In its Programme of Action for the Achievement of Palestinian Rights (see above, under PALESTINE QUESTION), the International Conference on the Question of Palestine,[10] in September 1983, recommended that all States should ensure that UNRWA could meet the essential needs of the Palestinians without interruption or diminution of services. The Conference also recommended that the Secretary-General convene a meeting of United Nations agencies and organizations, with representatives of PLO and those countries hosting Palestinian refugees, to develop co-ordinated assistance to Palestinians and to look into inter-agency machinery for United Nations assistance.

***Ad Hoc* Committee for the announcement of contributions.** On 22 November 1983, the *Ad Hoc* Committee of the General Assembly for the Announcement of Voluntary Contributions to UNRWA met at United Nations Headquarters. In his closing statement, the Commissioner-General expressed satisfaction that the pledges for 1984 represented an increase over 1983 funding and urged Governments to pay their contributions as early as possible. He added, however, that if those Governments not currently in a position to announce their contributions later pledged at the same level as in 1983, UNRWA would still have far less than the $233 million needed.

GENERAL ASSEMBLY ACTION

On 15 December 1983, on the recommendation of the Special Political Committee, the General Assembly adopted without vote resolution 38/83 B.

Working Group on the Financing of the United Nations Relief and Works Agency for Palestine Refugees in the Near East

The General Assembly,

Recalling its resolutions 2656(XXV) of 7 December 1970, 2728(XXV) of 15 December 1970, 2791(XXVI) of 6 December 1971, 2964(XXVII) of 13 December 1972, 3090(XXVIII) of 7 December 1973, 3330(XXIX) of 17 December 1974, 3419 D (XXX) of 8 December 1975, 31/15 C of 23 November 1976, 32/90 D of 13 December 1977, 33/112 D of 18 December 1978, 34/52 D of 23 November 1979, 35/13 D of 3 November 1980, 36/146 E of 16 December 1981 and 37/120 A of 16 December 1982,

Recalling also its decision 36/462 of 16 March 1982, whereby it took note of the special report of the Working Group on the Financing of the United Nations Relief and Works Agency for Palestine Refugees in the Near East and adopted the recommendations contained therein,

Having considered the report of the Working Group on the Financing of the United Nations Relief and Works Agency for Palestine Refugees in the Near East,

Taking into account the report of the Commissioner-General of the United Nations Relief and Works Agency for Palestine Refugees in the Near East, covering the period from 1 July 1982 to 30 June 1983,

Gravely concerned at the critical financial situation of the United Nations Relief and Works Agency for Palestine Refugees in the Near East, which has already reduced the essential minimum services being provided to the Palestine refugees and which threatens even greater reductions in the future,

Emphasizing the urgent need for extraordinary efforts in order to maintain, at least at their present minimum level, the activities of the United Nations Relief and Works Agency for Palestine Refugees in the Near East,

1. *Commends* the Working Group on the Financing of the United Nations Relief and Works Agency for Palestine Refugees in the Near East for its efforts to assist in ensuring the Agency's financial security;

2. *Takes note with approval* of the report of the Working Group;

3. *Requests* the Working Group to continue its efforts, in co-operation with the Secretary-General and the Commissioner-General of the United Nations Relief and Works Agency for Palestine Refugees in the Near East, for the financing of the Agency for a further period of one year;

4. *Requests* the Secretary-General to provide the necessary services and assistance to the Working Group for the conduct of its work.

General Assembly resolution 38/83 B

15 December 1983   Meeting 98   Adopted without vote

Approved by SPC (A/38/700) without vote, 2 December (meeting 44); 17-nation draft (A/SPC/38/L.14/Rev.1); agenda item 73.

Sponsors: Austria, Bangladesh, Canada, Denmark, Germany, Federal Republic of, India, Indonesia, Liberia, Netherlands, New Zealand, Nigeria, Pakistan, Philippines, Spain, Sri Lanka, Sweden, Yugoslavia.

Financial implications. S-G, A/SPC/38/L.16.

Meeting numbers. GA 38th session: SPC 24, 26-36, 44; plenary 98.

Accounts for 1982

For the year ended 31 December 1982, expenditure and commitments of UNRWA amounted to $234,696,749 under its General Fund.[11] The Board of Auditors noted that UNRWA's financial regulation on the carry forward of funds from one year to another had not been properly complied with and that field offices, prior to their request for headquarters' approval to carry forward funds, had failed to review carefully the need for such action. The Auditors further noted that the new system of remuneration for locally recruited staff, based on comprehensive local surveys of the conditions of service of comparable employees in the public and private sectors, had not been implemented in the field office in Jordan and that budget provisions for salary increases on behalf of the field office's staff had not been properly calculated.

The Auditors also commented on some of the amounts recorded in the accounts, as well as on other budgetary and administrative matters, including procurement, loss of property, inventory, travel and temporary assistance.

In a statement of 5 October 1983 before the General Assembly's Fifth (Administrative and Budgetary) Committee, an UNRWA representative said the Agency had already taken corrective action, or was in the process of doing so, in response to the Auditors' recommendations; there were, however, some differences of opinion with regard to certain recommendations on procurement, contracts, property survey boards and vehicle accidents, which UNRWA intended to discuss further with the Auditors.

The Advisory Committee on Administrative and Budgetary Questions, in its report of September 1983[12] on the financial reports and audited financial statements and reports of the Board of Auditors, stated that it had no comments on the Board's report on the financial statements of UNRWA.

The Assembly, in its resolution 38/30 of 25 November (see ADMINISTRATIVE AND BUDGETARY QUESTIONS, Chapter I), accepted the UNRWA financial reports and accounts and requested remedial action as required by the Board's comments and observations.

Personnel questions

Recommendations with regard to personnel questions were made by JIU in its August 1983 report on UNRWA.[8] Stating that the rules concerning geographical distribution of international professional staff had not been applied to UNRWA and that the academic and professional qualifications of that staff and its knowledge of Arabic were insufficient, JIU recommended that geographical distribution be improved as a matter of urgency; that a recruitment plan be established, and that strict conditions for recruitment be developed.

With regard to area staff, JIU recommended that a comprehensive career planning system be formulated, based on the definition of occupational groups, redefinition of job classifications and the establishment of an internal training system. For all staff, it recommended that an adequate computerized personnel information and management system be set up.

Commenting on JIU's recommendations,[9] the Commissioner-General agreed that the academic qualifications and Arabic knowledge of the international staff should be improved; however, he added that the discussion of academic qualification requirements inadequately reflected UNRWA's nature as an operating rather than an advisory agency, and many occupations did not require high academic qualifications.

Staff security

Report of the Secretary-General. In October 1983, the Secretary-General submitted to the General Assembly a report providing information on arrests and detention of UNRWA staff, with an addendum of 12 November.[13]

The Secretary-General stated that from 1 July 1982 to 30 June 1983, UNRWA had reported 17 cases of arrest and detention in the West Bank and 10 in the Gaza Strip. Of these, one staff member was still in detention in Gaza as at 12 November; another had been arrested there since 30 June and remained in detention. In the West Bank, a staff member had been arrested on 12 September and remained under detention, as did two of three staff members arrested since 1 July in Jordan. In the Syrian Arab Republic, two staff members, one of them arrested after 1 July, were still under detention, and no further information had been given on one detained since September 1980 and another missing since April of that year. In Lebanon, five staff members (of 50 arrested since 1 July 1982) were still detained by the authorities as of 1 November.

Apart from having affected the safety and security of UNRWA staff, the situation in Lebanon also had led to interference with the performance of official functions; the Secretary-General noted that all those cases had been taken up with the Israel Defence Forces as occupying Power or with the Lebanese authorities. UNRWA also had taken up with the Israeli occupation authorities in the Gaza Strip their practice of daily interrogation of some Agency staff on several consecutive days, usually in relation to offences allegedly committed by children or other family members. The Agency also had taken up cases in which UNRWA staff were required by the authorities to serve as guards in government schools.

Annexed were the names and occupations of UNRWA staff members detained in the West Bank and in Gaza, as well as of staff understood to be detained in Lebanon by the Lebanese authorities as of 30 June 1983.

In another October report, on UNRWA staff detained in Lebanon by the Israeli authorities,[14] the Secretary-General noted that, following the June 1982 Israeli invasion of south Lebanon, more than 200 cases of arrest of UNRWA staff had been reported, 29 of whom were arrested in 1983. On 17 October, 68 UNRWA staff members there were still believed to be in detention. The Secretary-General outlined attempts made to obtain information regarding those staff, to secure access to them and to obtain their early release. Such attempts had included contacts between UNRWA and Israeli officials, as well as several communications by the Secretary-General addressed to Israel.

The Secretary-General reported that Israel had stated its position in several replies. On 13 June, it had stated that it had the right to decide unilaterally what constituted an official function of a United Nations official and that it considered that the Organization had no standing with regard to proceedings against its staff members. In his reply of 28 June, the Secretary-General had noted that the Israeli position was not in conformity with international law and practice, and that it was exclusively for the Secretary-General to determine the extent of the duties and functions of the officials. On 12 October, Israel had stated that it had detained certain individuals in Lebanon on account of their involvement in hostile activities and that their detention had no connection with their professional activities but only with actions which had violated their official functions. Israel had added that a number of UNRWA employees would be released as soon as their background and activities had been fully investigated; all detainees were being visited on a regular basis by a representative of ICRC and were permitted to appeal their detention before an Administrative Appeals Board. On 25 October, the Secretary-General had expressed the hope that the release of UNRWA officials would take place without delay. In a related development, he had taken note of a judgement on 13 July in the Supreme Court of Israel sitting as the High Court of Justice; in the Secretary-General's view, the proceedings in the Supreme Court, in so far as they addressed the right of access and legal representation of detainees under the rules of the 1949 fourth Geneva Convention, reinforced the United Nations position which was based on the right of functional protection.

The Secretary-General reiterated his request that the continued detention of UNRWA staff be ur-

gently reconsidered by Israel and that the Organization's right of functional protection be recognized. He added that he would continue to monitor the release of the UNRWA detainees and, in view of Israel's assurance, would provide to the Assembly an updated list of those detainees, taking into account any actions since 30 June 1983.

Annexed to the report was a list of UNRWA staff understood to be detained in Lebanon by the Israeli armed forces as at 17 October.

GENERAL ASSEMBLY ACTION

In resolution 38/230 of 20 December 1983 on privileges and immunities of the international civil service (see ADMINISTRATIVE AND BUDGETARY QUESTIONS, Chapter III), the General Assembly expressed particular concern at the detention of a great number of UNRWA officials and about the cases in which full exercise of the right of functional protection was impossible.

In resolution 38/83 I of 15 December, on protection of Palestine refugees, the Assembly called again on Israel to release all detained Palestine refugees, including the employees of UNRWA.

A draft resolution on the detention of UNRWA personnel by Israeli authorities, sponsored by Bangladesh, Cuba, Egypt, India, Indonesia, Mali, Pakistan and Senegal, was circulated in the Special Political Committee but not submitted for action at the sponsors' request. By the text,[15] the Assembly would have condemned Israel for its persistent violation of the privileges and immunities of personnel of the United Nations and its agencies. It would have demanded the immediate release of the illegally detained UNRWA personnel and would have requested the Secretary-General and the UNRWA Commissioner-General to continue efforts in order to achieve their earliest release.

Organizational structure

In its report on UNRWA,[8] JIU also made recommendations concerning the Agency's administrative structures. It stated that implementation of the recommended reforms in budget, finance and personnel matters required a reorganization of those structures and a greater delegation of authority from headquarters to the field offices.

JIU held it indispensable to entrust the UNRWA Management Division with the monitoring and evaluation of programme implementation; in order to facilitate that task and to guarantee the functioning of the new biennial programme budget system, also recommended by JIU (see above), the Budget Division should be associated with programme formulation. Furthermore, JIU suggested that the Audit Division be attached to the Management Division, to facilitate the modernization of audit methods and the carrying out of more management and programme audits.

Commenting on JIU's recommendation,[9] the Commissioner-General said he accepted the role envisaged for the Management Division, and a close association of the Audit Division with it; he stated that he would give consideration to the combination of the two Divisions, but would not wish to be committed to total integration.

JIU also found that from both the financial and operational point of view it would be highly desirable to have UNRWA headquarters transferred immediately to the region of operations. However, as conditions in Lebanon did not allow a complete transfer, JIU recommended that at least some functions be moved to the Amman section of headquarters or to field offices.

Expressing full support for the General Assembly's requests—reiterated in a December 1982 resolution[16]—to relocate UNRWA headquarters, the Commissioner-General stated that he recognized the desirability of reducing the distance between the Vienna headquarters and the five UNRWA field offices. However, he added, as the Middle East situation remained volatile, it was not possible to determine when it might become feasible to reunite headquarters at Beirut. In his comments on JIU's recommendations, the Commissioner-General stated that, pending implementation of the Assembly's 1982 resolution, he would again review the possibility of transferring certain headquarters functions from Vienna to Amman.

The Assembly, in resolution 38/83 A of 15 December 1983 on assistance to Palestine refugees, reiterated its request that UNRWA headquarters be relocated to its former site within its area of operations as soon as practicable.

Other aspects

Assistance to displaced persons

In 1983, the General Assembly again endorsed the efforts of UNRWA to continue to provide humanitarian assistance, on an emergency basis and as a temporary measure, also to persons displaced as a result of the June 1967 hostilities.

GENERAL ASSEMBLY ACTION

On 15 December 1983, acting on the recommendation of the Special Political Committee, the General Assembly adopted without vote resolution 38/83 C.

Assistance to persons displaced as a result of the June 1967 and subsequent hostilities

The General Assembly,

Recalling its resolution 37/120 B of 16 December 1982 and all previous resolutions on the question,

Taking note of the report of the Commissioner-General of the United Nations Relief and Works Agency for Palestine Refugees in the Near East, covering the period from 1 July 1982 to 30 June 1983,

Concerned about the continued human suffering resulting from the hostilities in the Middle East,

1. *Reaffirms* its resolution 37/120 B and all previous resolutions on the question;

2. *Endorses,* bearing in mind the objectives of those resolutions, the efforts of the Commissioner-General of the United Nations Relief and Works Agency for Palestine Refugees in the Near East to continue to provide humanitarian assistance as far as practicable, on an emergency basis and as a temporary measure, to other persons in the area who are at present displaced and in serious need of continued assistance as a result of the June 1967 and subsequent hostilities;

3. *Strongly appeals* to all Governments and to organizations and individuals to contribute generously for the above purposes to the United Nations Relief and Works Agency for Palestine Refugees in the Near East and to the other intergovernmental and non-governmental organizations concerned.

General Assembly resolution 38/83 C

15 December 1983			Meeting 98			Adopted without vote

Approved by SPC (A/38/700) without vote, 2 December (meeting 44); 18-nation draft (A/SPC/38/L.15); agenda item 73.

Sponsors: Austria, Belgium, Canada, Denmark, Finland, Greece, India, Indonesia, Ireland, Italy, Japan, Mali, Netherlands, Norway, Pakistan, Philippines, Sri Lanka, Sweden.

Meeting numbers. GA 38th session: SPC 24, 26-36, 44; plenary 98.

Education and training

In 1983, the General Assembly called again for measures to establish a univerity at Jerusalem for Palestine refugees and reiterated its appeal for grants and scholarships.

Proposed University of Jerusalem "Al-Quds"

Report of the Secretary-General. As requested by the General Assembly in December 1982,[17] the Secretary-General reported in October 1983 on the question of establishing a university at Jerusalem.[18] As endorsed by the Assembly, he had appointed a group of three experts (Richard Moreton Mawditt, Secretary and Registrar, University of Bath, United Kingdom; Dr. Calvin H. Plimpton, Chairman, Board of Trustees, American University of Beirut; and Abdus Salam, Director, International Centre for Theoretical Physics, Trieste, Italy, and Professor of Theoretical Physics, Imperial College of Science and Technology, London) to prepare a feasibility study, which was annexed to his report. The group held two meetings, one in June and the other in August, during which it visited Jordan to hold consultations with government ministries, university representatives and other officials concerned with higher education in the West Bank, East Jerusalem and the Gaza Strip. Prior to completing its report, the group met with representatives of UNESCO, UNRWA and the United Nations Secretariat; it also corresponded with the United Nations University (UNU).

Summarizing its findings, the group stated that the principal difficulty in establishing the proposed institution lay in the requirement that it should be a university for Palestine refugees. The group added that in all its meetings with officials, it had become clear that they wished to establish a university but not one designed to cater exclusively to the needs of Palestine refugees. During the course of 1983, the group had been informed of several steps taken to create the proposed new University of Al-Quds. In January, an assocation of four colleges had drawn up certain fundamental principles for the University, as a seat of Arab higher learning. As further measures, a Higher Board for the University had been formed of the senior officials and trustees of the constituent colleges, and the Union of Arab Universities had recognized the University as a full member. The University was intended to serve principally the Arab students of the West Bank, the Gaza Strip and East Jerusalem. Forming as it would a part of the system of higher education for those territories, the University would be autonomous, non-exclusive in its admissions and non-sectarian. These measures, the group stated, were the initial steps in establishing the University by drawing into an association existing institutions in and near Jerusalem.

In the group's opinion, UNESCO and other United Nations bodies were mandated to help build the University; also, more vigorous involvement by UNU would be welcomed.

With regard to financing, the group suggested that the endowment for the University should initially be that of UNU, i.e., $100 million. The group endorsed the establishment by the Secretary-General of a trust fund for an advanced fellowship programme for university teachers and scholars. The programme's cost had been estimated by the Secretary-General at $1.7 million, which would enable 20 fellows to receive fellowships for up to four years each over a six-year period.

In conclusion, the group expressed the belief that Israel's hesitations, expressed to the Secretary-General in 1981,[19] had been substantively met and that all concerned might now be able to support the arrangements discussed in the group's report. The group envisaged that the proposed University, together with the associated existing universities co-operating in a common graduate facility, particularly for science and technology, would play the role for the Arab community that the Hebrew University of Jerusalem had played in the development of the Jewish community. Financing from external sources should be found. The new University should be aimed at preserving and enriching the life of the Arab community, nurturing Arab scholarship and reviving science and technology.

GENERAL ASSEMBLY ACTION

On 15 December 1983, on the recommendation of the Special Political Committee, the General Assembly adopted by recorded vote resolution 38/83 K.

University of Jerusalem "Al-Quds" for Palestine refugees

The General Assembly,

Recalling its resolutions 36/146 G of 16 December 1981 and 37/120 C of 16 December 1982,

Having examined the report of the Secretary-General on the question of the establishment of a university at Jerusalem, prepared in pursuance of paragraphs 5 and 7 of resolution 37/120 C,

Having also examined the report of the Commissioner-General of the United Nations Relief and Works Agency for Palestine Refugees in the Near East, covering the period from 1 July 1982 to 30 June 1983,

1. *Commends* the constructive efforts made by the Secretary-General, the Commissioner-General of the United Nations Relief and Works Agency for Palestine Refugees in the Near East, the Council of the United Nations University and the United Nations Educational, Scientific and Cultural Organization, which worked diligently towards the implementation of General Assembly resolution 37/120 C and other relevant resolutions;

2. *Further commends* the close co-operation of the competent educational authorities concerned;

3. *Emphasizes* the need for strengthening the educational system in the Arab territories occupied since 5 June 1967, including Jerusalem, and specifically the need for the establishment of the proposed university;

4. *Takes note* of the various steps recommended in the report of the Secretary-General;

5. *Requests* the Secretary-General to continue to take all necessary measures for establishing the University of Jerusalem "Al-Quds" in accordance with General Assembly resolution 35/13 B of 3 November 1980, giving due consideration to the recommendations consistent with the provisions of that resolution;

6. *Calls upon* Israel, the occupying Power, to co-operate in the implementation of the present resolution and to remove the hindrances which it has put in the way of establishing the University of Jerusalem;

7. *Requests* the Secretary-General to report to the General Assembly at its thirty-ninth session on the progress made in the implementation of the present resolution.

General Assembly resolution 38/83 K

15 December 1983   Meeting 98   146-2 (recorded vote)

Approved by SPC (A/38/700) by recorded vote (116-2), 2 December (meeting 44); 2-nation draft (A/SPC/38/L.27/Rev.1); agenda item 73.

Sponsors: India, Jordan.

Financial implications. 5th Committee, A/38/731; S-G, A/C.5/38/81, A/SPC/38/L.44.

Meeting numbers. GA 38th session: SPC 24, 26-36, 44; 5th Committee 62; plenary 98.

Recorded vote in Assembly as follows:

In favour: Afghanistan, Albania, Algeria, Angola, Argentina, Australia, Austria, Bahamas, Bahrain, Bangladesh, Barbados, Belgium, Belize, Benin, Bhutan, Bolivia, Botswana, Brazil, Bulgaria, Burma, Burundi, Byelorussian SSR, Canada, Cape Verde, Central African Republic, Chad, Chile, China, Colombia, Congo, Costa Rica, Cuba, Cyprus, Czechoslovakia, Democratic Kampuchea, Democratic Yemen, Denmark, Djibouti, Dominican Republic, Ecuador, Egypt, El Salvador, Equatorial Guinea, Ethiopia, Fiji, Finland, France, Gabon, Gambia, German Democratic Republic, Germany, Federal Republic of, Ghana, Greece, Grenada, Guinea, Guinea-Bissau, Guyana, Honduras, Hungary, Iceland, India, Indonesia, Iran, Iraq, Ireland, Italy, Ivory Coast, Jamaica, Japan, Jordan, Kenya, Kuwait, Lao People's Democratic Republic, Lebanon, Lesotho, Liberia, Libyan Arab Jamahiriya, Luxembourg, Madagascar, Malawi, Malaysia, Maldives, Mali, Malta, Mauritania, Mauritius, Mexico, Mongolia, Morocco, Mozambique, Nepal, Netherlands, New Zealand, Nicaragua, Niger, Nigeria, Norway, Oman, Pakistan, Panama, Papua New Guinea, Paraguay, Peru, Philippines, Poland, Portugal, Qatar, Romania, Rwanda, Saint Lucia, Sao Tome and Principe, Saudi Arabia, Senegal, Seychelles, Sierra Leone, Singapore, Somalia, Spain, Sri Lanka, Sudan, Suriname, Swaziland, Sweden, Syrian Arab Republic, Thailand, Togo, Trinidad and Tobago, Tunisia,

Turkey, Uganda, Ukrainian SSR, USSR, United Arab Emirates, United Kingdom, United Republic of Cameroon, United Republic of Tanzania, Upper Volta, Uruguay, Vanuatu, Venezuela, Viet Nam, Yemen, Yugoslavia, Zaire, Zambia, Zimbabwe.

Against: Israel, United States.

Israel said it would continue to do everything it could to improve the existing universities in Judaea, Samaria and Gaza where there were already more students per 100,000 inhabitants than in Afghanistan, Bangladesh, Democratic Yemen, India, Iran, Iraq, Jordan, Saudi Arabia, Sri Lanka, Yemen and other countries. Those who had looked into the matter had made it clear that a project such as establishing a university only for Palestinian refugees was impractical and illogical; the plan was nothing but a political ploy against Israel.

Stating that the text was not a reasonable or practical approach for meeting the educational needs of the Palestine refugees, the United States said its doubts with regard to the text's being purely political had been confirmed by the revised version; the sponsors had apparently dissociated themselves from the Secretary-General's report in which the professional educators had considered the matter in a serious and practical manner.

The United Kingdom welcomed the report as well as the group's proposals which, it believed, were the best available basis for progress.

Scholarships

Report of the Secretary-General. In a report submitted to the General Assembly in August 1983[20] in accordance with a December 1982 request,[21] the Secretary-General presented information on responses by Member States and United Nations agencies to the Assembly's appeal for increased special allocations for grants and scholarships to Palestine refugees. He reported that nine scholarships to graduates of UNRWA vocational training centres had been offered by the Federal Republic of Germany and that two awards by Australia for tertiary studies were being negotiated. UNESCO had granted five fellowships to Palestine refugee education staff of UNRWA for special training courses in overseas countries; more were expected later in the year. The World Intellectual Property Organization had invited the UNRWA Commissioner-General to propose candidates for fellowships. UNRWA had declared its readiness to act as the recipient and trustee of special allocations and scholarships for Palestine refugees.

GENERAL ASSEMBLY ACTION

On 15 December 1983, on the recommendation of the Special Political Committee, the General Assembly adopted by recorded vote resolution 38/83 D.

Offers by Member States of grants and scholarships for higher education, including vocational training, for Palestine refugees

The General Assembly,

Recalling its resolution 212(III) of 19 November 1948 on assistance to Palestine refugees,

Recalling also its resolutions 35/13 B of 3 November 1980, 36/146 H of 16 December 1981 and 37/120 D of 16 December 1982,

Cognizant of the fact that the Palestine refugees have, for the last three decades, lost their lands and means of livelihood,

Having examined with appreciation the report of the Secretary-General on offers of grants and scholarships for higher education for Palestine refugees and on the scope of the implementation of resolution 37/120 D,

Having also examined the report of the Commissioner-General of the United Nations Relief and Works Agency for Palestine Refugees in the Near East, covering the period from 1 July 1982 to 30 June 1983, dealing with this subject,

1. *Urges* all States to respond to the appeal contained in General Assembly resolution 32/90 F of 13 December 1977 in a manner commensurate with the needs of Palestine refugees for higher education and vocational training;

2. *Strongly appeals* to all States, specialized agencies and non-governmental organizations to augment the special allocations for grants and scholarships to Palestine refugees in addition to their contributions to the regular budget of the United Nations Relief and Works Agency for Palestine Refugees in the Near East;

3. *Expresses its appreciation* to all Governments, specialized agencies and non-governmental organizations that responded favourably to General Assembly resolution 36/146 H;

4. *Invites* the relevant organizations of the United Nations system to continue, within their respective spheres of competence, to expand assistance for higher education to Palestine refugee students;

5. *Appeals* to all States, specialized agencies and the United Nations University to contribute generously to the Palestinian universities in the territories occupied by Israel in 1967, including, in due course, the proposed University of Jerusalem "Al-Quds" for Palestine refugees;

6. *Also appeals* to all States, specialized agencies and other international bodies to contribute towards the establishment of vocational training centres for Palestine refugees;

7. *Requests* the United Nations Relief and Works Agency for Palestine Refugees in the Near East to act as the recipient and trustee for such special allocations and scholarships and to award them to qualified Palestine refugee candidates;

8. *Requests* the Secretary-General to report to the General Assembly at its thirty-ninth session on the implementation of the present resolution.

General Assembly resolution 38/83 D

15 December 1983   Meeting 98   147-0-1 (recorded vote)

Approved by SPC (A/38/700) by recorded vote (114-0-1), 2 December (meeting 44); 7-nation draft (A/SPC/38/L.18/Rev.1), orally amended by Lebanon; agenda item 73.

Sponsors: Bangladesh, Egypt, Indonesia, Jordan, Pakistan, Senegal, Yugoslavia.

Meeting numbers. GA 38th session: SPC 24, 26-36, 44; plenary 98.

Recorded vote in Assembly as follows:

In favour: Afghanistan, Algeria, Angola, Argentina, Australia, Austria, Bahamas, Bahrain, Bangladesh, Barbados, Belgium, Belize, Benin, Bhutan, Bolivia, Botswana, Brazil, Bulgaria, Burma, Burundi, Byelorussian SSR, Canada, Cape Verde, Central African Republic, Chad, Chile, China, Colombia, Congo, Costa Rica, Cuba, Cyprus, Czechoslovakia, Democratic Kampuchea, Democratic Yemen, Denmark, Djibouti, Dominica, Dominican Republic, Ecuador, Egypt, El Salvador, Equatorial Guinea, Ethiopia, Fiji, Finland, France, Gabon, Gambia, German Democratic Republic, Germany, Federal Republic of, Ghana, Greece, Grenada, Guinea, Guinea-Bissau, Guyana, Honduras, Hungary, Iceland, India, Indonesia, Iran, Iraq, Ireland, Italy, Ivory Coast, Jamaica, Japan, Jordan, Kenya, Kuwait, Lao People's Democratic Republic, Lebanon, Lesotho, Liberia, Libyan Arab Jamahiriya, Luxembourg, Madagascar, Malawi, Malaysia, Maldives, Mali, Malta, Mauritania, Mauritius, Mexico, Mongolia, Morocco, Mozambique, Nepal, Netherlands, New Zealand, Nicaragua, Niger, Nigeria, Norway, Oman, Pakistan, Panama, Papua New Guinea, Paraguay, Peru, Philippines, Poland, Portugal, Qatar, Romania, Rwanda, Saint Lucia, Sao Tome and Principe, Saudi Arabia, Senegal, Seychelles, Sierra Leone, Singapore, Somalia, Spain, Sri Lanka, Sudan, Suriname, Swaziland, Sweden, Syrian Arab Republic, Thailand, Togo, Trinidad and Tobago, Tunisia, Turkey, Uganda, Ukrainian SSR, USSR, United Arab Emirates, United Kingdom, United Republic of Cameroon, United Republic of Tanzania, United States, Upper Volta, Uruguay, Vanuatu, Venezuela, Viet Nam, Yemen, Yugoslavia, Zaire, Zambia, Zimbabwe.

Against: None.

Abstaining: Israel.

In the Committee, Lebanon proposed an oral amendment, subsequently accepted by the sponsors, to have the wording in paragraph 5 read "the territories occupied by Israel in 1967" rather than "since 1967".

Food aid

The General Assembly, in December 1983, again called for resumption of the general ration distribution to Palestine refugees, which had been suspended in September 1982[3] with the exception of Lebanon.

Report of the Commissioner-General. In his report for the year ended 30 June 1983,[2] the Commissioner-General stated that the general distribution of foodstuffs to eligible refugees had been suspended in September 1982 with the exception of Lebanon where, because of the emergency situation caused by the 1982 Israeli invasion, the distribution of rations had in fact increased. This major change in UNRWA programmes had been undertaken in order to divert available resources to the highest priority programmes—education and health. Before it would be possible to devote resources to the resumption of the general ration distribution, the Commissioner-General added, the Agency would have to be enabled to cover its financial needs for the education and health programmes and for its welfare programmes for the poorest section of the refugee community.

Until March 1983, the emergency ration provided about 2,000 calories per person per day. From 1 April, it was reduced to just over 1,600 calories for all recipients except for some 28,500 persons identified as in special need.

The number of persons receiving emergency rations as a result of the situation in Lebanon was about 178,000, of whom some 7,200 were Palestinians not registered with the Agency and approximately 7,900 had found refuge in the Syrian Arab Republic.

Food rations continued to be distributed to hardship cases, which included widows, orphans, the aged, the physically and mentally handicapped and the chronically sick. In the Syrian Arab Republic, the programme of assistance to hardship cases was introduced from June 1983. At the end of that month, 89,110 persons Agency-wide were benefiting from that assistance. Following cessation of the basic ration programme, there had been a significant and steady increase in the number of applications for hardship assistance.

GENERAL ASSEMBLY ACTION

On 15 December 1983, acting on the recommendation of the Special Political Committee, the General Assembly adopted by recorded vote resolution 38/83 F.

Resumption of the ration distribution to Palestine refugees

The General Assembly,

Recalling its resolutions 36/146 F of 16 December 1981, 37/120 F of 16 December 1982 and all previous resolutions on the question, including resolution 302(IV) of 8 December 1949,

Having considered the report of the Commissioner-General of the United Nations Relief and Works Agency for Palestine Refugees in the Near East, covering the period from 1 July 1982 to 30 June 1983,

Taking note of the report of the Joint Inspection Unit of 1 August 1983,

Deeply concerned at the interruption by the United Nations Relief and Works Agency for Palestine Refugees in the Near East, owing to financial difficulties, of the general ration distribution to Palestine refugees in all fields in the occupied Palestinian territories, Jordan and the Syrian Arab Republic,

1. *Regrets* that resolution 37/120 F of 16 December 1982 has not been implemented;

2. *Calls upon* all Governments, as a matter of urgency, to make the most generous efforts possible and to offer the necessary resources to meet the needs of the United Nations Relief and Works Agency for Palestine Refugees in the Near East, particularly in the light of the interruption by the Agency of the general ration distribution to Palestine refugees in all fields, and therefore urges non-contributing Governments to contribute regularly and contributing Governments to consider increasing their regular contributions;

3. *Requests* the Commissioner-General of the United Nations Relief and Works Agency for Palestine Refugees in the Near East to resume on a continuing basis the interrupted general ration distribution to Palestine refugees in all fields.

General Assembly resolution 38/83 F

15 December 1983　　　Meeting 98　　　123-19-3 (recorded vote)

Approved by SPC (A/38/700) by recorded vote (92-19-3), 2 December (meeting 44); 7-nation draft (A/SPC/38/L.20); agenda item 73.

Sponsors: Bangladesh, Egypt, Indonesia, Mali, Pakistan, Senegal, Yugoslavia.

Meeting numbers. GA 38th session: SPC 24, 26-36, 44; plenary 98.

Recorded vote in Assembly as follows:

In favour: Afghanistan, Algeria, Angola, Argentina, Bahamas, Bahrain, Bangladesh, Barbados, Belize, Benin, Bhutan, Bolivia, Botswana, Brazil, Bulgaria, Burma, Burundi, Byelorussian SSR, Cape Verde, Central African Republic, Chad,

Chile, China, Colombia, Congo, Costa Rica, Cuba, Cyprus, Czechoslovakia, Democratic Kampuchea, Democratic Yemen, Djibouti, Dominican Republic, Ecuador, Egypt, El Salvador, Equatorial Guinea, Ethiopia, Fiji, Gabon, Gambia, German Democratic Republic, Ghana, Greece, Grenada, Guinea, Guinea-Bissau, Guyana, Honduras, Hungary, India, Indonesia, Iran, Iraq, Ivory Coast, Jamaica, Jordan, Kenya, Kuwait, Lao People's Democratic Republic, Lebanon, Lesotho, Liberia, Libyan Arab Jamahiriya, Madagascar, Malawi, Malaysia, Maldives, Mali, Malta, Mauritania, Mauritius, Mexico, Mongolia, Morocco, Mozambique, Nepal, Nicaragua, Niger, Nigeria, Oman, Pakistan, Panama, Papua New Guinea, Paraguay, Peru, Philippines, Poland, Qatar, Romania, Rwanda, Sao Tome and Principe, Saudi Arabia, Senegal, Seychelles, Sierra Leone, Singapore, Somalia, Sri Lanka, Sudan, Suriname, Swaziland, Syrian Arab Republic, Thailand, Togo, Trinidad and Tobago, Tunisia, Turkey, Uganda, Ukrainian SSR, USSR, United Arab Emirates, United Republic of Cameroon, United Republic of Tanzania, Upper Volta, Uruguay, Vanuatu, Venezuela, Viet Nam, Yemen, Yugoslavia, Zambia, Zimbabwe.

Against: Australia, Belgium, Canada, Denmark, Finland, France, Germany, Federal Republic of, Iceland, Ireland, Israel, Italy, Japan, Luxembourg, Netherlands, New Zealand, Norway, Sweden, United Kingdom, United States.

Abstaining: Austria, Portugal, Spain.

The United States said it favoured the gradual elimination of the general ration distribution and did not support the efforts reflected in the text to limit the Commissioner-General's discretionary powers in that regard.

Sweden observed that the Agency's financial situation required the setting of strict priorities. In 1982, the Commissioner-General had decided to grant the highest priority to educational and health needs and to helping the destitute; without sufficient financial resources, the resumption of the ration distribution would endanger those vitally important activities. Because of the categorical way in which the request was formulated, the Commissioner-General would not be able to maintain the necessary order of priority.

Greece, on behalf of the EC member States, said they wished to draw attention to the issues raised in connection with the December 1982 resolution on the subject.[4]

Turkey viewed the request to resume the general ration distribution on a continuing basis in the context of an increase in contributions.

Jordan said it attached great importance and urgency to the resumption of the ration distribution; it rejected some of the options suggested by the Commissioner-General for the distribution of the rations, in reaffirmation of the decision of the Palestine refugees themselves who had also rejected them.

Refugee protection

On 15 December 1983, the General Assembly adopted five resolutions on several other aspects relating to UNRWA and Palestine refugees: protection of the refugees (38/83 I); revenues derived from their properties (38/83 H); the return of refugees displaced since 1967 (38/83 G); and Palestine refugees in the Gaza Strip (38/83 E) and in the West Bank (38/83 J). It also considered the issuance of identity cards for Palestinians, but did not act on a draft resolution appealing to Member States to provide information allowing the Secretary-General to issue such cards to all Palestine refugees and their descendants. Reports on these aspects were submitted by the Secretary-General. Information on Palestine refugee properties was also provided by the United Nations Conciliation Commission for Palestine.

Report of the Secretary-General. In a report submitted to the General Assembly in October 1983,[22] the Secretary-General presented information on the protection of Palestine refugees, as requested in a December 1982 resolution.[23] He reported that the Permanent Observer of PLO had submitted to him and to the President of the Security Council a number of complaints concerning actions said to have been taken by Israeli authorities against Palestinian refugees in occupied territories. The Secretary-General and senior United Nations officials, particularly the UNRWA Commissioner-General, had been in touch with those authorities on the question.

International organizations being obliged to act within a given territory with the consent and cooperation of the authorities in control, it had not been possible for the Secretary-General to undertake the measures requested of him by the Assembly.[23] The Commissioner-General, however, had initiated actions towards the ends specified. In the West Bank and Gaza, he or his representatives had immediately taken up with the authorities any actions, such as the closing of schools and the imposition of camp curfews, interfering with the Agency's education, health and relief services. In south Lebanon, the personal security of refugees continued to be a matter of deep concern. The Commissioner-General had repeatedly drawn the attention of the Lebanese and Israeli Governments, as well as other Governments concerned, to the dangers to the security of Palestine refugees in Lebanon and had urged that adequate measures be taken for their protection.

The Secretary-General reported that on 14 February UNRWA drew Israel's attention to incidents in south Lebanon, particularly in the Sidon area, where unidentified persons had killed Palestine refugees, destroyed or damaged houses and forced refugees to leave their homes. UNRWA had pointed out that in the circumstances existing in south Lebanon, the Israeli armed forces were obliged to ensure the protection of the lives and property of the inhabitants, in accordance with the 1949 fourth Geneva Convention. On 21 March, Israel had replied that it was aware of the responsibilities of the Israel Defence Forces (IDF) for the security of the population, including Palestinians, and that they would do their utmost to provide protection, both in and outside the refugee camps. In this connection, IDF had already adopted a number of measures, such as intensified military presence in the refugee camps and high-level meetings with various authorities and local leaders.

On 1 June, UNRWA had informed the Israeli authorities that since March the situation had deteriorated considerably; several Palestine refugees had been harassed and some killed. The Agency requested that it be informed urgently of such additional steps as the Israeli authorities intended to take to ensure the safety of Palestine refugees in south Lebanon. On 26 August, Israel had informed the Secretary-General that its position remained as stated on 21 March and that the description of the measures taken by IDF to improve the security of all residents of south Lebanon remained valid.

With regard to restoring services to Palestine refugees in Lebanon, the Commissioner-General had supplied the following information: UNRWA education, health and relief services had been gradually re-established in southern Lebanon in late 1982 and all schools had reopened by early 1983; the Agency was in continuous contact with the Lebanese government department responsible for the Palestine refugees in Lebanon and the Commissioner-General had consulted the Government on rehousing the refugees which UNRWA was assisting at a current cost of $8 million; after cessation of hostilities in south Lebanon, UNRWA had commenced a survey of loss and damage to its facilities, which was estimated at $4,610,143.

The Secretary-General added that he and the Commissioner-General had also pursued with the Israeli authorities the question of the continued detention of UNRWA employees by Israel (see above).

JIU recommendations. In its August 1983 report on UNRWA,[8] JIU recommended that, in studying measures to implement the Assembly's December 1982 request for measures to guarantee the safety and security and legal and human rights of the Palestine refugees,[23] the Secretary-General should consult with the United Nations High Commissioner for Refugees (UNHCR) on possible co-operation. JIU felt that the involvement of UNHCR, so far specifically excluded from a role in protecting Palestine refugees, could have a positive effect and that the problem of protection required region-wide consideration.

Commenting on JIU's recommendation,[9] the Secretary-General stated that he shared the concern for legal and physical protection of Palestinian refugees. However, in the absence of a specific mandate from the international community and the consent of the sovereign or occupying Power, an international organ could not assume such responsibility, lacking both legitimacy and the means of carrying out that responsibility. Currently, neither UNHCR nor UNRWA was mandated to provide legal and physical protection to Palestinian refugees in the region.

Report of the Commissioner-General. In his report for the year ended 30 June 1983,[2] the UNRWA Commissioner-General, noting that responsibility for protecting the civilian population lay with the occupying Power, stated that he considered it to be the Agency's moral duty to assist in ensuring the safety of the Palestine refugees. He stated that, although the situation in Beirut and south Lebanon had been at the forefront of attention, UNRWA also feared for the safety of non-combatant Palestine refugees living in the Beqa'a Valley and north Lebanon, where sporadic clashes and the factional fighting from June 1983 among Palestinian forces and their supporters had put at risk the lives of the inhabitants of the Wavel camp and camps close to the town of Tripoli.

GENERAL ASSEMBLY ACTION

On 15 December 1983, acting on the recommendation of the Special Political Committee, the General Assembly adopted by recorded vote resolution 38/83 I.

Protection of Palestine refugees

The General Assembly,

Recalling Security Council resolutions 508(1982) of 5 June 1982, 509(1982) of 6 June 1982, 511(1982) of 18 June 1982, 512(1982) of 19 June 1982, 513(1982) of 4 July 1982, 515(1982) of 29 July 1982, 517(1982) of 4 August 1982, 518(1982) of 12 August 1982, 519(1982) of 17 August 1982, 520(1982) of 17 September 1982 and 523(1982) of 18 October 1982,

Recalling General Assembly resolutions ES-7/5 of 26 June 1982, ES-7/6 of 19 August 1982, ES-7/8 of 19 August 1982, ES-7/9 of 24 September 1982 and 37/120 J of 16 December 1982,

Having considered the report of the Secretary-General of 19 October 1983,

Having also considered the report of the Commissioner-General of the United Nations Relief and Works Agency for Palestine Refugees in the Near East, covering the period from 1 July 1982 to 30 June 1983,

Referring to the humanitarian principles of the Geneva Convention relative to the Protection of Civilian Persons in Time of War, of 12 August 1949, and to the obligations arising from the Regulations annexed to the Hague Convention IV of 1907,

Deeply distressed at the sufferings of the Palestinians resulting from the Israeli invasion of Lebanon,

Reaffirming its support for Lebanese sovereignty, unity and territorial integrity,

1. *Urges* the Secretary-General, in consultation with the United Nations Relief and Works Agency for Palestine Refugees in the Near East, to undertake effective measures to guarantee the safety and security and the legal and human rights of the Palestine refugees in all the territories under Israeli occupation;

2. *Calls once again upon* Israel, the occupying Power, to release forthwith all detained Palestine refugees, including the employees of the United Nations Relief and Works Agency for Palestine Refugees in the Near East;

3. *Also calls upon* Israel to desist forthwith from preventing those Palestinians registered by the United Nations Relief and Works Agency for Palestine Refugees in the

Near East as refugees in Lebanon from returning to their camps in Lebanon;

4. *Further calls upon* Israel to allow the resumption of health, medical, educational and social services rendered by the United Nations Relief and Works Agency for Palestine Refugees in the Near East to the Palestinians in the refugee camps in southern Lebanon;

5. *Requests* the Commissioner-General of the United Nations Relief and Works Agency for Palestine Refugees in the Near East to co-ordinate his activities in rendering those services with the Government of Lebanon, the host country;

6. *Urges* the Commissioner-General to provide housing, in consultation with the Government of Lebanon, to the Palestine refugees whose houses were demolished or razed by the Israeli forces;

7. *Calls upon* Israel to compensate the United Nations Relief and Works Agency for Palestine Refugees in the Near East for the damage to its property and facilities resulting from the Israeli invasion of Lebanon, without prejudice to Israel's responsibility for all damage resulting from that invasion;

8. *Requests* the Secretary-General, in consultation with the Commissioner-General, to report to the General Assembly, before the opening of its thirty-ninth session, on the implementation of the present resolution.

<hr>

General Assembly resolution 38/83 I

15 December 1983   Meeting 98   129-2-15 (recorded vote)

Approved by SPC (A/38/700) by recorded vote (103-2-13), 2 December (meeting 44); 9-nation draft (A/SPC/38/L.23); agenda item 73.

Sponsors: Afghanistan, Bangladesh, Cuba, Egypt, Indonesia, Mali, Pakistan, Senegal, Yugoslavia.

Meeting numbers. GA 38th session: SPC 24, 26-36, 44; plenary 98.

Recorded vote in Assembly as follows:

In favour: Afghanistan, Albania, Algeria, Angola, Argentina, Austria, Bahamas, Bahrain, Bangladesh, Barbados, Belize, Benin, Bhutan, Bolivia, Botswana, Brazil, Bulgaria, Burma, Burundi, Byelorussian SSR, Cape Verde, Central African Republic, Chad, Chile, China, Colombia, Congo, Cuba, Cyprus, Czechoslovakia, Democratic Kampuchea, Democratic Yemen, Djibouti, Dominican Republic, Ecuador, Egypt, El Salvador, Equatorial Guinea, Ethiopia, Fiji, Finland, France, Gabon, Gambia, German Democratic Republic, Ghana, Greece, Grenada, Guinea, Guinea-Bissau, Guyana, Honduras, Hungary, India, Indonesia, Iran, Iraq, Ivory Coast, Japan, Jordan, Kenya, Kuwait, Lao People's Democratic Republic, Lesotho, Liberia, Libyan Arab Jamahiriya, Madagascar, Malawi, Malaysia, Maldives, Mali, Malta, Mauritania, Mauritius, Mexico, Mongolia, Morocco, Mozambique, Nepal, New Zealand, Nicaragua, Niger, Nigeria, Oman, Pakistan, Panama, Papua New Guinea, Paraguay, Peru, Philippines, Poland, Qatar, Romania, Rwanda, Sao Tome and Principe, Saudi Arabia, Senegal, Seychelles, Sierra Leone, Singapore, Somalia, Spain, Sri Lanka, Sudan, Suriname, Swaziland, Sweden, Syrian Arab Republic, Thailand, Togo, Trinidad and Tobago, Tunisia, Turkey, Uganda, Ukrainian SSR, USSR, United Arab Emirates, United Republic of Cameroon, United Republic of Tanzania, Upper Volta, Uruguay, Vanuatu, Venezuela, Viet Nam, Yemen, Yugoslavia, Zaire, Zambia, Zimbabwe.

Against: Israel, United States.

Abstaining: Australia, Belgium, Canada, Costa Rica, Denmark, Germany, Federal Republic of, Iceland, Ireland, Italy, Jamaica,[a] Luxembourg, Netherlands, Norway, Portugal, United Kingdom.

[a]Later advised the Secretariat it had intended to vote in favour.

The United States pointed out that the United Nations Legal Counsel had stated in December 1982[24] that practical and legal problems would arise if the Secretary-General were entrusted with guaranteeing the security and rights of refugees in the occupied territories. Also, the text made Israel solely responsible for damage to UNRWA facilities in Lebanon without attempting to identify other responsible parties as had been the case with the recent fighting in the refugee camps in and around Tripoli. The text called only on Israel to release the detained UNRWA employees, ignoring the fact that Jordan, Lebanon and the Syrian Arab Republic were also detaining UNRWA employees; the paragraph in question did not take account of Israel's recent announcement concerning the release of UNRWA employees detained in southern Lebanon.

Speaking for the EC member States, Greece said they wished to draw attention once again to the issues they had raised in 1982.[25]

Sweden declared that its vote demonstrated its deep concern for the security and rights of the Palestine refugees. Although it considered that the Secretary-General did not have the means to guarantee their security—which was the responsibility of the occupying Power—he should do everything in his power to promote the objectives set forth in paragraph 1.

Finland, voicing strong support for all viable measures to improve the protection of Palestine refugees, nevertheless had grave doubts concerning the practical aspects and effectiveness of paragraphs 1 and 7.

Peru also had reservations on paragraph 1 on the grounds that the responsibility and the mandate entrusted to the Secretary-General were not practical and were questionable from the legal viewpoint.

Property rights

Report of the Secretary-General. In September 1983, the Secretary-General submitted to the General Assembly a report on revenues derived from Palestine refugee properties,[26] as requested by the Assembly in a December 1982 resolution.[27] He reported that on 25 February and 16 March 1983, respectively, he had brought that resolution and the 10 others on UNRWA adopted by the Assembly in December 1982[28] to the attention of the Chairman of the United Nations Conciliation Commission for Palestine and to Israel's attention, requesting the latter to communicate to him—preferably by 30 June 1983—any information on their implementation. Also on 16 March, he had drawn States' attention to the relevant provisions of those resolutions, including the call to Governments concerned, especially Israel, to assist the Secretary-General in implementing the resolution on revenues from Palestine refugee properties.[27]

In the absence of any reply, he had on 26 July again requested information from all States on implementation of that resolution. Israel's reply of 26 August covered various aspects of the 11 resolutions. With regard to that resolution particularly specified, Israel stated that its position had been set out in 1981 before the Special Political Committee.[29]

In a November 1983 addendum[30] to his report, the Secretary-General informed the Assembly that he had received a reply dated 28 October from the Syrian Arab Republic, informing him that the General Administration for Palestinian Arab Refugees (GAPAR), the competent authority dealing with Palestinian refugee affairs in the Syrian Arab Republic, had stated that it did not keep records of Palestinian properties in Palestine and revenues derived therefrom; GAPAR believed that such information on revenues should be provided by the Conciliation Commission for Palestine and by the Secretary-General. The Secretary-General noted that neither he nor the Commission had the required information, and it was for that reason that he had requested information from Israel and other States.

Report of the Conciliation Commission. In its report covering the period from 1 October 1982 to 30 September 1983,[31] the United Nations Conciliation Commission for Palestine also provided information on Palestine refugee properties. The Commission reported that, upon formal request in November 1982 from PLO for a copy of the microfilm on property and land in Palestine, it had decided to grant the Office of the Permanent Observer of PLO access to the relevant records, on the understanding that the materials would continue to be treated confidentially. Early in 1983, the Commission had received an unprecedented request from a representative of certain individual claimants of land and property in Palestine for access to the records in the Commission's custody or to appear before the Commission; therefore, it had sought the opinion of the United Nations Legal Counsel on the matter. In July, in response to a request from Jordan, the Commission had authorized a government official to examine and make extracts from records connected with the immovable properties of the Palestinian refugees.

GENERAL ASSEMBLY ACTION

On 15 December 1983, acting on the recommendation of the Special Political Committee, the General Assembly adopted by recorded vote resolution 38/83 H.

Revenues derived from Palestine refugee properties

The General Assembly,

Recalling its resolutions 35/13 A to F of 3 November 1980, 36/146 C of 16 December 1981, 37/120 H of 16 December 1982 and all its previous resolutions on the question, including resolution 194(III) of 11 December 1948,

Taking note of the reports of the Secretary-General of 2 September and 8 November 1983,

Taking note also of the report of the United Nations Conciliation Commission for Palestine, covering the period from 1 October 1982 to 30 September 1983,

Recalling that the Universal Declaration of Human Rights and the principles of international law uphold the principle that no one shall be arbitrarily deprived of his or her private property,

Considering that the Palestinian Arab refugees are entitled to their property and to the income derived from their property, in conformity with the principles of justice and equity,

Recalling, in particular, its resolution 394(V) of 14 December 1950, in which it directed the United Nations Conciliation Commission for Palestine, in consultation with the parties concerned, to prescribe measures for the protection of the rights, property and interests of the Palestinian Arab refugees,

Taking note of the completion of the programme of identification and evaluation of Arab property, as announced by the United Nations Conciliation Commission for Palestine in its twenty-second progress report, of 11 May 1964, and of the fact that the Land Office had a schedule of Arab owners and file of documents defining the location, area and other particulars of Arab property,

1.　*Requests* the Secretary-General to take all appropriate steps, in consultation with the United Nations Conciliation Commission for Palestine, for the protection and administration of Arab property, assets and property rights in Israel, and to establish a fund for the receipt of income derived therefrom, on behalf of the rightful owners;

2.　*Calls once again upon* the Governments concerned, especially Israel, to render all facilities and assistance to the Secretary-General in the implementation of the present resolution;

3.　*Requests* the Secretary-General to report to the General Assembly at its thirty-ninth session on the implementation of the present resolution.

General Assembly resolution 38/83 H

15 December 1983　　　Meeting 98　　　125-2-20 (recorded vote)

Approved by SPC (A/38/700) by recorded vote (97-2-19), 2 December (meeting 44); 9-nation draft (A/SPC/38/L.22); agenda item 73.

Sponsors: Afghanistan, Bangladesh, Cuba, Egypt, India, Indonesia, Mali, Pakistan, Senegal.

Meeting numbers. GA 38th session: SPC 24, 26-36, 44; plenary 98.

Recorded vote in Assembly as follows:

In favour: Afghanistan, Albania, Algeria, Angola, Argentina, Bahamas, Bahrain, Bangladesh, Barbados, Belize, Benin, Bhutan, Bolivia, Botswana, Brazil, Bulgaria, Burma, Burundi, Byelorussian SSR, Cape Verde, Central African Republic, Chad, Chile, China, Colombia, Congo, Costa Rica, Cuba, Cyprus, Czechoslovakia, Democratic Kampuchea, Democratic Yemen, Djibouti, Dominican Republic, Ecuador, Egypt, El Salvador, Equatorial Guinea, Ethiopia, Fiji, Gabon, Gambia, German Democratic Republic, Ghana, Greece, Grenada, Guinea, Guinea-Bissau, Guyana, Honduras, Hungary, India, Indonesia, Iran, Iraq, Ivory Coast, Jamaica, Jordan, Kenya, Kuwait, Lao People's Democratic Republic, Lebanon, Lesotho, Libyan Arab Jamahiriya, Madagascar, Malawi, Malaysia, Maldives, Mali, Malta, Mauritania, Mauritius, Mexico, Mongolia, Morocco, Mozambique, Nepal, Nicaragua, Niger, Nigeria, Oman, Pakistan, Panama, Papua New Guinea, Paraguay, Peru, Philippines, Poland, Portugal, Qatar, Romania, Rwanda, Sao Tome and Principe, Saudi Arabia, Senegal, Seychelles, Sierra Leone, Singapore, Somalia, Spain, Sri Lanka, Sudan, Suriname, Swaziland, Syrian Arab Republic, Thailand, Togo, Trinidad and Tobago, Tunisia, Turkey, Uganda, Ukrainian SSR, USSR, United Arab Emirates, United Republic of Cameroon, United Republic of Tanzania, Upper Volta, Uruguay, Vanuatu, Venezuela, Viet Nam, Yemen, Yugoslavia, Zambia, Zimbabwe.

Against: Israel, United States.

Abstaining: Australia, Austria, Belgium, Canada, Denmark, Finland, France, Germany, Federal Republic of, Iceland, Ireland, Italy, Japan, Liberia, Luxembourg, Netherlands, New Zealand, Norway, Sweden, United Kingdom, Zaire.

Israel said that no Government would accept outside intervention in administering and regulating public or private property inside its own country. Property rights and income from property were exclusively subject to domestic laws, a proposition not altered by the fact that possible or potential claimants happened to be refugees. For many years, derelict lands and properties in Israel had been managed so as to bring them into productive use.

In the opinion of the United States, the text prejudged questions concerning the repatriation of the refugees and their compensation, which should be settled through negotiations between the parties concerned.

Though supporting in principle the idea that the Palestine refugees were entitled to their property and to compensation for it, Sweden considered that such claims should not be approached in isolation but in the context of a comprehensive Middle East solution.

Speaking on behalf of the EC member States, Greece drew attention to the issues they had raised in 1982.[32]

Proposed repatriation

Report of the Secretary-General. In October 1983, the Secretary-General submitted to the General Assembly a report on population and refugees displaced since 1967,[33] as requested in a December 1982 resolution.[34] He reported that, on 16 March 1983, he had requested information from Israel relevant to the resolution and on 26 August Israel had stated that its position had been set out in successive annual replies, most recently in August 1982.[35] Since the submission of that reply and until the end of March 1983, Israel added, another 5,065 persons had returned to Judaea and Samaria; the total number of those returning since 1967 stood at 61,058 persons.

The Secretary-General reported that he had obtained from the UNRWA Commissioner-General information on the return of refugees registered with the Agency; that information was based on requests by returning registered refugees for transfer of their entitlements for services to the areas to which they had returned. Between 1 July 1982 and 30 June 1983, 139 refugees registered with UNRWA had returned to the West Bank and 47 to the Gaza Strip, bringing the estimated total number of displaced registered refugees who were known by UNRWA to have returned to the occupied territories since June 1967 to about 10,200.

Report of the Conciliation Commission. In its September 1983 report,[31] the United Nations Conciliation Commission for Palestine stated that with regard to implementation of paragraph 11 of the 1948 Assembly resolution[36] resolving that refugees wishing to return to their homes should be permitted to do so and instructing the Commission to facilitate their repatriation, the events in the area had further complicated an already very complex situation and had limited the Commission's possibilities of action.

GENERAL ASSEMBLY ACTION

On 15 December 1983, acting on the recommendation of the Special Political Committee, the General Assembly adopted by recorded vote resolution 38/83 G.

Population and refugees displaced since 1967

The General Assembly,

Recalling Security Council resolution 237(1967) of 14 June 1967,

Recalling also General Assembly resolutions 2252(ES-V) of 4 July 1967, 2452 A (XXIII) of 19 December 1968, 2535 B (XXIV) of 10 December 1969, 2672 D (XXV) of 8 December 1970, 2792 E (XXVI) of 6 December 1971, 2963 C and D (XXVII) of 13 December 1972, 3089 C (XXVIII) of 7 December 1973, 3331 D (XXIX) of 17 December 1974, 3419 C (XXX) of 8 December 1975, 31/15 D of 23 November 1976, 32/90 E of 13 December 1977, 33/112 F of 18 December 1978, 34/52 E of 23 November 1979, ES-7/2 of 29 July 1980, 35/13 E of 3 November 1980, 36/146 B of 16 December 1981 and 37/120 G of 16 December 1982,

Having considered the report of the Commissioner-General of the United Nations Relief and Works Agency for Palestine Refugees in the Near East, covering the period from 1 July 1982 to 30 June 1983, and the report of the Secretary-General of 3 October 1983,

1. *Reaffirms* the inalienable right of all displaced inhabitants to return to their homes or former places of residence in the territories occupied by Israel since 1967 and declares once more that any attempt to restrict, or to attach conditions to, the free exercise of the right of return by any displaced person is inconsistent with that inalienable right and inadmissible;

2. *Considers* any and all agreements embodying any restriction on or condition for the return of the displaced inhabitants as null and void;

3. *Strongly deplores* the continued refusal of the Israeli authorities to take steps for the return of the displaced inhabitants;

4. *Calls once more upon* Israel:

(a) To take immediate steps for the return of all displaced inhabitants;

(b) To desist from all measures that obstruct the return of the displaced inhabitants, including measures affecting the physical and demographic structure of the occupied territories;

5. *Requests* the Secretary-General, after consulting with the Commissioner-General of the United Nations Relief and Works Agency for Palestine Refugees in the Near East, to report to the General Assembly, before the opening of its thirty-ninth session, on Israel's compliance with paragraph 4 above.

General Assembly resolution 38/83 G

15 December 1983   Meeting 98   128-2-17 (recorded vote)

Approved by SPC (A/38/700) by recorded vote (97-2-17), 2 December (meeting 44); 10-nation draft (A/SPC/38/L.21); agenda item 73.

Sponsors: Afghanistan, Bangladesh, Cuba, Egypt, India, Indonesia, Mali, Pakistan, Senegal, Yugoslavia.

Meeting numbers. GA 38th session: SPC 24, 26-36, 44; plenary 98.

Recorded vote in Assembly as follows:

In favour: Afghanistan, Albania, Algeria, Angola, Argentina, Bahamas, Bahrain, Bangladesh, Barbados, Belize, Benin, Bhutan, Bolivia, Botswana, Brazil, Bulgaria, Burma, Burundi, Byelorussian SSR, Cape Verde, Central African Republic, Chad, Chile, China, Colombia, Congo, Costa Rica, Cuba, Cyprus, Czechoslovakia, Democratic Kampuchea, Democratic Yemen, Djibouti, Dominican Republic, Ecuador,

Egypt, El Salvador, Equatorial Guinea, Ethiopia, Fiji, Gabon, Gambia, German Democratic Republic, Ghana, Greece, Grenada, Guinea, Guinea-Bissau, Guyana, Honduras, Hungary, India, Indonesia, Iran, Iraq, Ivory Coast, Jamaica, Japan, Jordan, Kenya, Kuwait, Lao People's Democratic Republic, Lebanon, Lesotho, Liberia, Libyan Arab Jamahiriya, Madagascar, Malawi, Malaysia, Maldives, Mali, Malta, Mauritania, Mauritius, Mexico, Mongolia, Morocco, Mozambique, Nepal, Nicaragua, Niger, Nigeria, Oman, Pakistan, Panama, Papua New Guinea, Paraguay, Peru, Philippines, Poland, Portugal, Qatar, Romania, Rwanda, Sao Tome and Principe, Saudi Arabia, Senegal, Seychelles, Sierra Leone, Singapore, Somalia, Spain, Sri Lanka, Sudan, Suriname, Swaziland, Syrian Arab Republic, Thailand, Togo, Trinidad and Tobago, Tunisia, Turkey, Uganda, Ukrainian SSR, USSR, United Arab Emirates, United Republic of Cameroon, United Republic of Tanzania, Upper Volta, Uruguay, Vanuatu, Venezuela, Viet Nam, Yemen, Yugoslavia, Zaire, Zambia, Zimbabwe.

Against: Israel, United States.

Abstaining: Australia, Austria, Belgium, Canada, Denmark, Finland, France, Germany, Federal Republic of, Iceland, Ireland, Italy, Luxembourg, Netherlands, New Zealand, Norway, Sweden, United Kingdom.

The United States said that the text was simplistic and biased and condemned Israel in a severe manner.

Sweden, although supporting the right of the Palestinians displaced by the 1967 war to return to their homes, considered that the text seemed to rule out the possibility of initiating negotiations or discussing the terms of repatriation.

In another resolution of the same date—38/83 A on assistance to Palestine refugees—the Assembly noted with regret that repatriation or compensation of the refugees had not been effected and that no substantial progress had been made in the reintegration of refugees by repatriation or resettlement. The Assembly requested the Commission to exert continued efforts towards that goal and to report to it not later than 1 October 1984.

Palestine refugees in the Gaza Strip

Report of the Secretary-General. In October 1983, the Secretary-General submitted a report on Palestine refugees in the Gaza Strip,[37] in accordance with a December 1982 General Assembly resolution.[38] He reported that on 16 March 1983 he had requested information from Israel on implementation of that resolution. On 26 August, Israel had replied that its position had been set out in successive annual replies, the latest dated August 1982.[39] With regard to the situation since then, Israel added that it had rehabilitated more than 7,000 families within the refugee rehabilitation programme, while for 1983 the projected number of families involved in that programme was more than 1,000, and during the first half of the year two new rehabilitation projects had been implemented; more than 400 families which had had to transfer their homes from the international boundary between Egypt and Israel near Rafah had been financially compensated and provided with new plots of land, including the necessary infrastructure, in Tel-el-Sultan, and the majority had completed construction of their homes and were residing in them.

The Secretary-General also provided information received from the UNRWA Commissioner-General stating that, in the year under review, Is-

raeli authorities had demolished, on punitive grounds, the housing of 12 families. As a result, some 94 persons had lost their homes and 43 rooms had been destroyed, of which 20 had been built by UNRWA or with its assistance. UNRWA had protested these demolitions, pointing out that such action, amounting to collective punishment, was contrary to Israel's obligations under international law. Claims for compensation had been lodged but not met. The families whose shelters had been demolished in 1979 and 1980 had not been rehoused, although they had found some kind of alternative accommodation. Those whose shelters had been demolished in 1981 had been rehoused by UNRWA. Updating an earlier survey, UNRWA determined that of 440 families regarded as inadequately housed, 126 families remained so and 88 were hardship cases. The Israeli authorities continued to take the position that they had no further obligations with regard to those families. UNRWA had taken up the matter with the Ministry of Foreign Affairs of Israel, but had not received a reply.

From 28 June to mid-July 1983, 73 refugee shelter rooms on the perimeter of Beach camp had been destroyed on the orders of the Israeli authorities, which considered that they had been built without proper authority on State land outside the camp's boundaries. The 35 families (more than 200 persons) affected were virtually homeless. Some had already suffered eviction in 1971 and had then no alternative but to establish rudimentary accommodation on the outskirts of the camps. Individual cases of destruction of "unauthorized" shelters had occurred in former years. UNRWA had made representations to the Israeli authorities to abstain from further demolitions until alternative accommodation could be provided. The authorities, however, had not agreed to that, claiming that the families would be encouraged to squat on State land as a means of obtaining land in a housing project. They had informed UNRWA that the Civil Administration Accommodation (Housing) Branch would determine whether any assistance might be given to those families. Meanwhile, the refugees lived in unsanitary conditions or were an additional burden on other already poorly accommodated refugees.

According to information available to the Commissioner-General, 655 refugee families from the camps had moved into homes built on land purchased in one or another housing project established by the Israeli authorities. During the reporting period, a total of 863 shelter rooms were thus demolished. While the refugees' new accommodation was superior to the shelters, the pressure on housing still remained, partly because of the pre-condition that shelters in the camps be demolished prior to the acquisition of new housing in the housing projects.

A total of 2,932 plots of land in the Gaza Strip had been allocated by the Israeli authorities for housing projects for refugees. On 1,323 of these, houses had been built and were occupied by 1,732 refugee families comprising 10,647 persons. Houses were under construction on 499 plots, and 1,013 plots were still vacant, although it was understood that the majority had already been purchased by refugees. On 97 plots, houses had been built by non-refugee families. In addition, 17,665 refugees had moved to ready-built accommodation in the housing projects.

The three new housing projects at Beit Lahia and Nazleh (near Jabalia camp) and Tel-el-Sultan (near Rafah camp) were still under development; 218, 94 and 443 new houses respectively had been constructed and were occupied. Construction of more new houses was under way.

Since the re-establishment of the border between Egypt and the Gaza Strip, following the return of the Sinai peninsula to Egypt in April 1982, a total of 764 refugee shelter rooms housing 258 families (1,613 persons) had been demolished by, or on the order of, the Israeli authorities to make way for a security zone and border fence. The authorities had paid compensation to all the families concerned, who had availed themselves of the Israeli offer of plots of land in a housing project.

GENERAL ASSEMBLY ACTION

On 15 December 1983, acting on the recommendation of the Special Political Committee, the General Assembly adopted by recorded vote resolution 38/83 E.

Palestine refugees in the Gaza Strip

The General Assembly,

Recalling Security Council resolution 237(1967) of 14 June 1967,

Recalling also General Assembly resolutions 2792 C (XXVI) of 6 December 1971, 2963 C (XXVII) of 13 December 1972, 3089 C (XXVIII) of 7 December 1973, 3331 D (XXIX) of 17 December 1974, 3419 C (XXX) of 8 December 1975, 31/15 E of 23 November 1976, 32/90 C of 13 December 1977, 33/112 E of 18 December 1978, 34/52 F of 23 November 1979, 35/13 F of 3 November 1980, 36/146 A of 16 December 1981 and 37/120 E of 16 December 1982,

Having considered the report of the Commissioner-General of the United Nations Relief and Works Agency for Palestine Refugees in the Near East, covering the period from 1 July 1982 to 30 June 1983, and the report of the Secretary-General of 3 October 1983,

Recalling the provisions of paragraph 11 of its resolution 194(III) of 11 December 1948 and considering that measures to resettle Palestine refugees in the Gaza Strip away from the homes and property from which they were displaced constitute a violation of their inalienable right of return,

Alarmed by the reports received from the Commissioner-General that the Israeli occupying authorities, in contravention of Israel's obligations under international law, persist in their policy of demolishing, on punitive grounds, shelters occupied by refugee families,

1. *Reiterates its demand* that Israel desist from the removal and resettlement of Palestine refugees in the Gaza Strip and from the destruction of their shelters;

2. *Requests* the Secretary-General, after consulting with the Commissioner-General of the United Nations Relief and Works Agency for Palestine Refugees in the Near East, to report to the General Assembly, before the opening of its thirty-ninth session, on Israel's compliance with paragraph 1 above.

General Assembly resolution 38/83 E

15 December 1983   Meeting 98   146-2 (recorded vote)

Approved by SPC (A/38/700) by recorded vote (114-2), 2 December (meeting 44); 9-nation draft (A/SPC/38/L.19); agenda item 73.

Sponsors: Bangladesh, Cuba, Egypt, India, Indonesia, Mali, Pakistan, Senegal, Yugoslavia.

Meeting numbers. GA 38th session: SPC 24, 26-36, 44; plenary 98.

Recorded vote in Assembly as follows:

In favour: Afghanistan, Albania, Algeria, Angola, Argentina, Australia, Austria, Bahamas, Bahrain, Bangladesh, Barbados, Belgium, Belize, Benin, Bhutan, Bolivia, Botswana, Brazil, Bulgaria, Burma, Burundi, Byelorussian SSR, Canada, Cape Verde, Central African Republic, Chad, Chile, China, Colombia, Congo, Costa Rica, Cuba, Cyprus, Czechoslovakia, Democratic Kampuchea, Democratic Yemen, Denmark, Djibouti, Dominican Republic, Ecuador, Egypt, El Salvador, Equatorial Guinea, Ethiopia, Fiji, Finland, France, Gabon, Gambia, German Democratic Republic, Germany, Federal Republic of, Ghana, Greece, Grenada, Guinea, Guinea-Bissau, Guyana, Honduras, Hungary, Iceland, India, Indonesia, Iran, Iraq, Ireland, Italy, Ivory Coast, Jamaica, Japan, Jordan, Kenya, Kuwait, Lao People's Democratic Republic, Lebanon, Lesotho, Liberia, Libyan Arab Jamahiriya, Luxembourg, Madagascar, Malawi, Malaysia, Maldives, Mali, Malta, Mauritania, Mauritius, Mexico, Mongolia, Morocco, Mozambique, Nepal, Netherlands, New Zealand, Nicaragua, Niger, Nigeria, Norway, Oman, Pakistan, Panama, Papua New Guinea, Paraguay, Peru, Philippines, Poland, Portugal, Qatar, Romania, Rwanda, Saint Lucia, Sao Tome and Principe, Saudi Arabia, Senegal, Seychelles, Sierra Leone, Singapore, Somalia, Spain, Sri Lanka, Sudan, Suriname, Swaziland, Sweden, Syrian Arab Republic, Thailand, Togo, Trinidad and Tobago, Tunisia, Turkey, Uganda, Ukrainian SSR, USSR, United Arab Emirates, United Kingdom, United Republic of Cameroon, United Republic of Tanzania, Upper Volta, Uruguay, Vanuatu, Venezuela, Viet Nam, Yemen, Yugoslavia, Zaire, Zambia, Zimbabwe.

Against: Israel, United States.

The United States opposed the text because it felt that it was simplistic and biased and condemned Israel in a severe manner.

Introducing the draft, Pakistan stated that the demand that Israel desist from removing and resettling refugees in the Gaza Strip and from destroying their shelters was necessary in view of the alarming reports from the Commissioner-General that Israel persisted in its policy in contravention of its obligations under international law.

Palestine refugees in the West Bank

Report of the Commissioner-General. In his report on UNRWA activities for the year ended 30 June 1983,[2] the Commissioner-General stated that the conditions in the occupied territories, particularly in the West Bank, had caused concern. The period under review had again been marked by numerous disturbances by Palestinians and Israeli settlers and by security measures by the Israeli army. The continued establishment of Israeli settlements in increasing numbers in the West Bank had led to clashes with and demonstrations by the Palestinians. There had been many instances of harassment of Palestine refugees by armed Israeli settlers. Stone-throwing and other forms of violence had caused the occupation authorities to close UNRWA schools and training centres and to impose curfews on refugee camps.

GENERAL ASSEMBLY ACTION

The resettlement of Palestine refugees in the West Bank was the subject of resolution 38/83 J, adopted by the General Assembly on 15 December 1983 by recorded vote, on the recommendation of the Special Political Committee.

Palestine refugees in the West Bank

The General Assembly,

Recalling Security Council resolution 237(1967) of 14 June 1967,

Having considered the report of the Commissioner-General of the United Nations Relief and Works Agency for Palestine Refugees in the Near East, covering the period from 1 July 1982 to 30 June 1983,

Alarmed by the reports that Israel plans to remove and resettle the Palestine refugees of the West Bank and to destroy their camps,

Recalling the provisions of paragraph 11 of its resolution 194(III) of 11 December 1948 and considering that measures to resettle Palestine refugees in the West Bank away from the homes and property from which they were displaced constitute a violation of their inalienable right of return,

1. *Calls upon* Israel to abandon its plans and to refrain from the removal, and from any action that may lead to the removal and resettlement, of Palestine refugees in the West Bank and from the destruction of their camps;

2. *Requests* the Secretary-General, in co-operation with the Commissioner-General of the United Nations Relief and Works Agency for Palestine Refugees in the Near East, to keep the matter under close supervision and to report to the General Assembly, before the opening of its thirty-ninth session, on any developments regarding this matter.

General Assembly resolution 38/83 J

15 December 1983   Meeting 98   145-2 (recorded vote)

Approved by SPC (A/38/700) by recorded vote (116-2), 2 December (meeting 44); 9-nation draft (A/SPC/38/L.24); agenda item 73.

Sponsors: Bangladesh, Cuba, Egypt, India, Indonesia, Mali, Pakistan, Senegal, Yugoslavia.

Meeting numbers. GA 38th session: SPC 24, 26-36, 44; plenary 98.

Recorded vote in Assembly as follows:

In favour: Afghanistan, Albania, Algeria, Angola, Argentina, Australia, Austria, Bahamas, Bahrain, Bangladesh, Barbados, Belgium, Belize, Benin, Bhutan, Bolivia, Botswana, Brazil, Bulgaria, Burma, Burundi, Byelorussian SSR, Canada, Cape Verde, Central African Republic, Chad, Chile, China, Colombia, Congo, Costa Rica, Cuba, Cyprus, Czechoslovakia, Democratic Kampuchea, Democratic Yemen, Denmark, Djibouti, Dominican Republic, Ecuador, Egypt, El Salvador, Equatorial Guinea, Ethiopia, Fiji, Finland, France, Gabon, Gambia, German Democratic Republic, Germany, Federal Republic of, Ghana, Greece, Grenada, Guinea, Guinea-Bissau, Guyana, Honduras, Hungary, Iceland, India, Indonesia, Iran, Iraq, Ireland, Italy, Ivory Coast, Jamaica, Japan, Jordan, Kenya, Kuwait, Lao People's Democratic Republic, Lebanon, Lesotho, Liberia, Libyan Arab Jamahiriya, Luxembourg, Madagascar, Malawi, Malaysia, Maldives, Mali, Malta, Mauritania, Mauritius, Mexico, Mongolia, Morocco, Mozambique, Nepal, Netherlands, New Zealand, Nicaragua, Niger, Nigeria, Norway, Pakistan, Panama, Papua New Guinea, Paraguay, Peru, Philippines, Poland, Portugal, Qatar, Romania, Rwanda, Saint Lucia, Sao Tome and Principe, Saudi Arabia, Senegal, Seychelles, Sierra Leone, Singapore, Somalia, Spain, Sri Lanka, Sudan, Suriname, Swaziland, Sweden, Syrian Arab Republic, Thailand, Togo, Trinidad and Tobago, Tunisia, Turkey, Uganda, Ukrainian SSR, USSR, United Arab Emirates, United Kingdom, United Republic of Cameroon, United Republic of Tanzania, Upper Volta, Uruguay, Vanuatu, Venezuela, Viet Nam, Yemen, Yugoslavia, Zaire, Zambia, Zimbabwe.

Against: Israel, United States.

Israel termed the text a hysterical, if revealing reaction to the possibility of providing the refugees still living in camps with better housing, not forcibly but on a voluntary basis. The plan so disparaged by the resolution had not even been approved by the Israeli Government; the alarm regarding "plans to remove and resettle" the refugees and destroy the camps was a sad and tragic testimony to the determination of the Arab leaders that refugees remain in misery and squalor so that they could be more easily recruited for the internecine warfare of those leaders.

The United States said the draft was designed to eliminate any programme which might attempt to improve the quality of life for the refugees until an overall political solution was found; no other country sheltering refugees had been requested to take the steps contained in the text.

Though expressing support for the text's general thrust, the United Kingdom had reservations on the wording of the third preambular paragraph and paragraph 1, as it understood that the Israeli Cabinet had not formally approved the plan; it also would have preferred paragraph 1 to state more clearly that the call on Israel was to refrain from removing and resettling Palestinian refugees against their wishes.

Introducing the draft in the Committee, Pakistan said it had been necessitated by the alarming reports about measures which violated the refugees' right to return and which might have grave consequences; it was feared that those policies were part of a calculated Israeli plan to squeeze the Palestinian refugees into areas near the Jordan River and then, in a massive strike, push them across the frontier, thereby creating instability in Jordan.

Jordan said that on 20 November 1983 the Israeli Government had stated that its plan was to demolish Palestinian camps in the West Bank and in the Gaza Strip. For the first time since 1948, Israel was implementing a plan to liquidate the refugees and terminate the existence of the camps.

Identification cards

Report of the Secretary-General. In September 1983, the Secretary-General submitted a report concerning special identification cards for all Palestine refugees,[40] which the General Assembly in a December 1982 resolution had requested that he issue to them.[41] The Secretary-General reported that he had established a team of United Nations experts, including representatives of the Division of Palestinian Rights, the Office of Legal Affairs, the Office for Special Political Affairs, the Department of Political and Security Council Affairs and UNRWA, to assist him in implementing that resolution. The team had considered two broad categories of Palestinians; those registered with UNRWA, numbering some 1.9 million, and those not so registered. With regard to the former category, the team had noted that, prior to the Assembly decision, the UNRWA Commissioner-General had already decided to issue individual registration cards to all refugees registered with the Agency instead of the family cards used (see below). In respect of those not registered with UNRWA, the team had considered the steps to be taken in the process of identifying them, as well as the related issues involved.

Since large numbers of Palestinians were dispersed over many countries, the Secretary-General had sought information from Governments as to the number residing in each country and had solicited views on ways of implementing the resolution. The Permanent Observer of PLO had been asked for similar information. Half of the 20 Governments replying had declared either that there were no Palestinians residing in their countries or that there were none covered by the resolution. Two Governments had replied that the ethnic backgrounds of their resident aliens were unknown. Others provided the numbers of Palestinian residents, but the total of those referred to was fewer than 500. PLO had requested that UNRWA proceed with issuing identity cards to those Palestinian refugees registered with the Agency.

In the circumstances, the Secretary-General stated, he was unable to proceed further with implementing the resolution. However, should significant additional information become available through further replies from Governments, he would reassess the situation and inform the Assembly.

Report of the Commissioner-General. In his report for the year ended 30 June 1983,[2] the Commissioner-General stated that UNRWA had decided in 1982 to issue individual registration cards to Palestine refugees, instead of family registration cards. The preparatory work for the introduction of the new cards had been completed by the end of the period under review, he added, and it was expected that all persons registered with UNRWA who requested an individual card would receive it by June 1984. The decision to issue individual cards had been taken prior to the 1982 Assembly resolution[41] and the procedure was independent of any action to be taken by the Secretary-General in pursuance of that resolution.

Draft resolution. At the request of the sponsors (Afghanistan, Bangladesh, Cuba, Mali, Pakistan, Senegal), a draft resolution circulated in the Special Political Committee was not submitted for action. By the draft,[42] the Assembly would have appealed to Member States to provide the necessary information allowing the Secretary-General, in co-operation with the UNRWA Commissioner-General, to issue identification cards to all Palestine refugees and their descendants, irrespective of whether they were recipients or not of Agency rations and services, as well as to all displaced persons and to those who had been prevented from returning to their home as a result of the 1967 hostilities, and their descendants.

REFERENCES

[1]YUN 1982, p. 428. [2]A/38/13 & Corr.1. [3]YUN 1982, p. 549. [4]*Ibid.*, p. 560, GA res. 37/120 F, 16 Dec. 1982. [5]YUN 1970, p. 280, GA res. 2656(XXV), 7 Dec. 1970. [6]A/38/558. [7]YUN 1982, p. 552, GA dec. 36/462, 16 Mar. 1982. [8]A/38/143. [9]A/38/143/Add.1. [10]A/CONF.114/42. [11]A/38/5/Add.3. [12]A/38/433. [13]A/C.5/38/17 & Corr.1 & Add.1. [14]A/C.5/38/18. [15]A/SPC/38/L.25. [16]YUN 1982, p. 552, GA res. 37/120 K, 16 Dec. 1982. [17]*Ibid.*, p. 563, GA res. 37/120 C, 16 Dec. 1982. [18]A/38/386. [19]YUN 1981, p. 339. [20]A/38/149. [21]YUN 1982, p. 561, GA res. 37/120 D, 16 Dec. 1982. [22]A/38/420 & Corr.1. [23]YUN 1982, p. 481, GA res. 37/120 J, 16 Dec. 1982. [24]*Ibid.*, p. 557. [25]*Ibid.*, p. 558. [26]A/38/361. [27]YUN 1982, p. 559, GA res. 37/120 H, 16 Dec. 1982. [28]*Ibid.*, pp. 481-563, GA res. 37/120 A-K, 16 Dec. 1982. [29]YUN 1981, p. 336. [30]A/38/361/Add.1. [31]A/38/397. [32]YUN 1982, p. 559. [33]A/38/419. [34]YUN 1982, p. 556, GA res. 37/120 G, 16 Dec. 1982. [35]*Ibid.*, p. 555. [36]YUN 1948-49, p. 174, GA res. 194(III), 11 Dec. 1948. [37]A/38/418. [38]YUN 1982, p. 557, GA res. 37/120 E, 16 Dec. 1982. [39]*Ibid.*, p. 556. [40]A/38/382. [41]YUN 1982, p. 558, GA res. 37/120 I, 16 Dec. 1982. [42]A/SPC/38/L.26.

Chapter X

Other political questions

Various aspects of information were considered by the General Assembly and its Committee on Information in 1983. In December, the Assembly made recommendations aimed at building the communications capabilities of developing countries and at improving United Nations public information activities.

Also in December, the Assembly commended the United Nations Scientific Committee on the Effects of Atomic Radiation for its work on the levels, effects and risks of atomic radiation and requested that its work continue.

In other action that month, the Assembly asked the Secretary-General to prepare a study on Antarctica, because of increasing international interest in the region.

Topics related to this chapter. Disarmament: public information. Africa: South Africa and *apartheid*—public information. Middle East: Palestine question—public information. Transport and communications: communications. General decolonization questions: public information. Namibia: public information. Other administrative and management questions: proposed UN communication satellite.

Information

During 1983, United Nations information activities focused on two areas—building up the information gathering and dissemination capabilities of developing countries, thus making them less dependent on outside sources, and achieving a more comprehensive and realistic image of the United Nations throughout the world. The United Nations Educational, Scientific and Cultural Organization (UNESCO) and the Department of Public Information (DPI) of the Secretariat were the main bodies concerned with those activities. Within the United Nations system, the Committee on Information continued to co-ordinate action in the information field and to report to the General Assembly.

The Assembly, on 15 December, adopted two resolutions on information questions, both calling for steps towards the establishment of a new world information and communication order.

By the first resolution (38/82 A), the Assembly called for efforts to make better known the issues underlying the demand for the development of communication capacities in developing countries. It reaffirmed its satisfaction with three UNESCO projects as steps towards a new order—the International Programme for the Development of Communication (a project to help developing countries develop communication infrastructure), the Global Satellite Project for Dissemination and Exchange of Information (planned by UNESCO in co-operation with other organizations), and an appeal for reduction of telecommunication tariffs for news exchanges.

In the second resolution on information (38/82 B), the Assembly approved the recommendations of the Committee on Information and requested it to continue to examine DPI's policies and activities, to promote the establishment of a new order and to seek the co-operation of all United Nations organizations. The Assembly called on DPI and UNESCO to convene a second round table for media representatives in 1985 on a new order. It called for the strengthening of DPI radio and television programmes as well as two United Nations information centres. The Assembly requested that the Joint United Nations Information Committee (JUNIC), the inter-agency co-ordinating body concerned with public information, be strengthened. DPI was requested to cover policies and practices which violated international law relative to belligerent occupation.

The two resolutions were based largely on recommendations by the Committee on Information, established by the Assembly in 1978[1] to examine United Nations public information policies and activities. Having held an organizational session on 28 and 29 March 1983, the Committee convened its fifth substantive session in New York from 20 June to 8 July. In its report on the sessions to the Assembly,[2] the Committee made 62 recommendations on promoting a new order and on United Nations public information activities, all of which were approved by the Assembly.

Mass communication

UNESCO activities. In October, the Secretary-General transmitted to the General Assembly a report by the UNESCO Director-General,[3] describing progress during the period 1981-1983 in implementing the International Programme for the Development of Communication (IPDC), a UNESCO project to help developing countries establish and strengthen communication infrastructure; on activities related to the establishment of a new world information and communication order (see below); and on the impact of technological developments. The report was issued in response to a December 1982 Assembly request.[4]

The IPDC Intergovernmental Council held its fourth session at Tashkent, USSR, from 5 to 12 September 1983. Of 32 projects submitted to the Council, 19 (6 interregional and regional and 13 national) were approved for funding. In addition, the Council recommended that four interregional and regional projects and four national projects which could not be funded at that time be given priority for review at the fifth session, tentatively scheduled for April 1984. The six approved interregional and regional projects were: a refresher course for experienced journalists in the Pool of Non-Aligned News Agencies, a seminar for improving the services of the Pool, an inter-State school for communication systems in African States where Portuguese was the official language, a programme for developing human resources in the graphic arts, a training seminar for news agency journalists belonging to the Latin American Network of National Information Systems, and the creation of a distribution system for Andean television programmes. The 13 national projects approved for funding had been submitted by Benin, Botswana, Burundi, Chad, Ethiopia, Kenya, Madagascar, Mozambique and Zimbabwe for Africa; Somalia and the Sudan for the Arab States; and Jamaica and Mexico for Latin America and the Caribbean.

In order to fund the 19 projects, the IPDC Council approved a supplementary budget of $629,000. That amount, added to the budget of $1,912,000 adopted in December 1982, brought the total IPDC budget for the year ending 31 March 1984 to $2,541,000.

During the triennium 1981-1983, UNESCO implemented 29 other national, regional and interregional projects in communication development, amounting to a total of almost $19 million from extrabudgetary resources. Among those projects, 13 were funded by the United Nations Development Programme (UNDP) in the amount of $7,263,285 and 16 by member States which set up trust funds in the amount of $11,571,439. Trust fund contributions were received from Denmark, Finland, the Federal Republic of Germany, Iceland, Iraq, the Netherlands, Norway, Sweden, Switzerland, the Arab Gulf Programme for the United Nations Development Organizations (comprising Bahrain, Iraq, Kuwait, Oman, Qatar, Saudi Arabia and the United Arab Emirates) and

the African Development Bank. (For other 1983 UNESCO activities related to communications, see PART TWO, Chapter IV.)

Activities of the Committee on Information. In its 1983 report to the General Assembly,[2] the Committee on Information recommended that all countries, the United Nations system and others concerned be called on to give UNESCO support in information and communication activities. It suggested that the Assembly mark the fifth anniversary of the Declaration on Fundamental Principles concerning the Contribution of the Mass Media to Strengthening Peace and International Understanding, to the Promotion of Human Rights and to Countering Racialism, *Apartheid* and Incitement to War,[5] adopted by UNESCO in 1978. It proposed that the Secretary-General present to the Assembly in 1983 a report of the round-table discussion on a new world information and communication order (Innsbruck, Austria, September 1983) (see below). It called for strengthening the information and communication infrastructures of the developing countries and stated that support for IPDC, which constituted an important step in the development of those infrastructures, should be emphasized.

In addition to supporting UNESCO activities, the Committee urged the United Nations to support developing countries with regard to their interests and needs in information. DPI was called on to strengthen its co-operation with the Pool of Non-Aligned News Agencies, as well as with regional news agencies of developing countries. The Committee proposed that DPI activities be strengthened to ensure better coverage of the United Nations and its work, especially in its priority areas (see below, under DPI ACTIVITIES).

GENERAL ASSEMBLY ACTION

Acting on the recommendation of the Special Political Committee, the General Assembly on 15 December adopted resolution 38/82 A without vote. The resolution was adopted under the agenda item on questions relating to information.

The General Assembly,
Recalling its resolutions 34/181 and 34/182 of 18 December 1979, 35/201 of 16 December 1980, 36/149 A of 16 December 1981 and 37/94 A and B of 10 December 1982,
Stressing anew the importance of the establishment of a new world information and communication order and, in this regard, recalling the relevant provisions of the Political Declaration of the Seventh Conference of Heads of State or Government of Non-Aligned Countries, held at New Delhi from 7 to 12 March 1983, as well as the relevant provisions of the Final Declaration of the Sixth Conference of Heads of State or Government of Non-Aligned Countries, held at Havana from 3 to 9 September 1979, of the Declaration of the Conference of Ministers for Foreign Affairs of Non-Aligned Countries,

held at New Delhi from 9 to 13 February 1981, and of the fifth and sixth meetings of the Intergovernmental Council of Ministers of Information of Non-Aligned Countries, held at Georgetown in May 1981 and at Valletta in June 1982,

Recalling the relevant resolutions adopted by the Assembly of Heads of State and Government of the Organization of African Unity at its eighteenth ordinary session, held at Nairobi from 24 to 27 June 1981,

Recalling the relevant provisions of the Final Act of the Conference on Security and Co-operation in Europe, signed at Helsinki on 1 August 1975, and those of the Concluding Document of the meeting of representatives of the participating States of the Conference on Security and Co-operation in Europe, held at Madrid from 11 November 1980 to 9 September 1983,

Recalling, on the occasion of the thirty-fifth anniversary of the Universal Declaration of Human Rights, its article 19, which provides that everyone has the right to freedom of opinion and expression and that this right includes freedom to hold opinions without interference and to seek, receive and impart information and ideas through any media and regardless of frontiers, and article 29, which stipulates that these rights and freedoms may in no case be exercised contrary to the purposes and principles of the United Nations,

Recalling also resolutions 4/19 and 4/21 adopted by the General Conference of the United Nations Educational, Scientific and Cultural Organization at its twenty-first session, held at Belgrade from 23 September to 28 October 1980, and resolution 2/03 adopted by the General Conference at its fourth extraordinary session, held in Paris from 23 November to 3 December 1982,

Recalling also the relevant provisions of the Declaration on the Preparation of Societies for Life in Peace,

Recalling further the relevant resolutions adopted by the Council of Ministers of Information of the members of the League of Arab States at its nineteenth regular session, held at Tunis on 9 and 10 October 1983,

Considering that international co-operation in the field of communication development should take place on the basis of equality, justice, mutual advantage and the principles of international law,

Conscious that, in order progressively to remedy existing imbalances, it is essential to strengthen and intensify the development of infrastructures, networks and resources in the communication field and thus encourage a wider and better balanced dissemination of information,

Conscious that the development of communication infrastructures, including national and regional capacity for indigenous message production and dissemination, is one of the important factors of genuine participation by a large majority of developing countries in international exchanges,

Emphasizing its full support for the International Programme for the Development of Communication of the United Nations Educational, Scientific and Cultural Organization, which constitutes an important step in the development of the infrastructures of communication in the developing countries and the establishment of a new world information and communication order,

Recognizing the central role of the United Nations Educational, Scientific and Cultural Organization in the field of information and communication within its mandate, as well as the progress accomplished by that organization in that field,

1. *Takes note with satisfaction* of the report of the Director-General of the United Nations Educational, Scientific and Cultural Organization on the implementation of the International Programme for the Development of Communication and the establishment of a new world information and communication order, and on the impact of current technological developments and practices and their application in the communication and information sector;

2. *Underlines*, on the occasion of the fifth anniversary of the Declaration on Fundamental Principles concerning the Contribution of the Mass Media to Strengthening Peace and International Understanding, to the Promotion of Human Rights and to Countering Racialism, *Apartheid* and Incitement to War, the importance of efforts made so far for its implementation;

3. *Again calls upon* all Member States and all organizations of the United Nations system, international, governmental and non-governmental organizations and professional organizations in the field of communication to exert every effort to make better known through all means at their disposal the issues underlying the demand for the development of communication capacities in developing countries as a step towards the establishment of a new world information and communication order;

4. *Considers* that the International Programme for the Development of Communication represents a significant step towards the establishment of a new world information and communication order and welcomes the decisions adopted by the Intergovernmental Council of the Programme at its fourth session, held at Tashkent, Union of Soviet Socialist Republics, from 5 to 12 September 1983;

5. *Notes with satisfaction* the co-operation existing between the United Nations, the United Nations Educational, Scientific and Cultural Organization and all other organizations of the United Nations system, particularly the International Telecommunication Union, the Food and Agriculture Organization of the United Nations and the Universal Postal Union, whose projects have been approved by the Intergovernmental Council of the Programme;

6. *Expresses its appreciation* to all Member States that have made or pledged a contribution towards the implementation of the Programme;

7. *Again calls upon* Member States and organizations and bodies of the United Nations system as well as other international governmental and non-governmental organizations and concerned public and private enterprises to respond to the appeals of the Director-General of the United Nations Educational, Scientific and Cultural Organization to contribute to the Programme by making greater financial resources available, as well as more staff, equipment, technologies and training resources;

8. *Notes with satisfaction* the progress made under the Global Satellite Project for Dissemination and Exchange of Information, executed by the United Nations Educational, Scientific and Cultural Organization in co-operation with INTELSAT and INTERSPUTNIK and with the regional radio broadcasting unions in Africa, Asia, Europe and the Arab States and supported by the Programme;

9. *Notes* that very few countries have responded positively to resolution 4/22 concerning the reduction of telecommunication tariffs for news exchanges, adopted by the General Conference of the United Nations Educational, Scientific and Cultural Organization at its twenty-

first session, and calls once again upon Member States to respond positively and effectively to that resolution;

10. *Reaffirms* its strong support for the United Nations Educational, Scientific and Cultural Organization and its efforts to establish a new world information and communication order, as well as for that organization's second medium-term plan for 1984-1989 and its stimulation of research with a view to meeting the challenges of accelerated technological development and the increasing role of communication in societies and cultures;

11. *Requests* the Director-General of the United Nations Educational, Scientific and Cultural Organization to continue his efforts in the information and communication field and to submit to the General Assembly, at its thirty-ninth session, a detailed report on the application of the Programme and the activities relating to the establishment of a new world information and communication order and, in co-operation with the International Telecommunication Union, on the effects of the accelerated development of communication technologies on societies and cultures.

General Assembly resolution 38/82 A

15 December 1983   Meeting 98   Adopted without vote

Approved by SPC (A/38/699) without vote, 1 December (meeting 43); draft by Vice-Chairman, based on Working Group deliberations (A/SPC/38/L.10/Rev.1); agenda item 72.

Meeting numbers. GA 38th session: SPC 10-17, 19, 39, 43; plenary 98.

Proposed new world information and communication order

United Nations efforts during 1983 to promote a new world information and communication order were carried out mainly by UNESCO and DPI.

The Director-General of UNESCO, in an October report,[3] described UNESCO activities aimed at the progressive establishment of the new order. A study on the relationship between a new international economic order and a new world information and communication order was completed in 1982 and scheduled for publication in 1984. It included an analysis of data flow and the role of transnational information industries, particularly in relation to transfers of communication technologies from industrialized to developing countries. A global study was published on the right to communicate and a meeting of experts took place in 1983. Twenty-five studies were commissioned and two consultations of experts were organized in 1982-1983 on the concept of the democratization of communication, dealing with such questions as the threats and promise of communication technologies to the democratization of societies, relationships between communication and power, the contribution of communication to the democratization of culture, education and economy, and the transnationalization of information.

In April 1983, UNESCO organized an international seminar at Nairobi, Kenya, on media and disarmament, which discussed information sources for armament and disarmament matters and the possibility of enhancing disarmament through the mass media.

As part of its programme to enhance circulation and better balanced dissemination of information, a consultation on the establishment of an international network for exchanging television films was held in Paris from 21 to 23 February. A study on the international circulation of television programmes and televised news, currently under way under UNESCO auspices, indicated a tendency towards an increase in regional exchanges, while some exporting countries continued to dominate television exchanges. The increase in regional exchanges was particularly noteworthy in the Arab States and in Latin America.

In regard to UNESCO's call for the reduction of telecommunication tariffs, some countries—Malaysia, the Philippines, Sri Lanka and the USSR—reported reductions. Almost all professional organizations concerned with communication and many news agencies supported tariff reductions. A series of regional meetings between telecommunication and information managers was planned to discuss reduction in tariffs.

Research work initially concentrated on strengthening national or regional research institutions, generally associated with universities or other educational institutions. With regard to theoretical research, the UNESCO secretariat carried out studies on the relationship between advertising and communication and on the self-regulation efforts made by the advertising industry. A preliminary study was carried out on the independence and autonomy of the media, on the basis of studies conducted in Asian and Latin American countries.

Within the United Nations Secretariat, DPI took measures to promote a new world information and communication order, and it co-operated with UNESCO in several projects for this purpose. Those projects included a series of round tables for world mass media leaders, the DPI training programme for broadcasters and journalists and the strengthening of ties with the Pool of Non-Aligned News Agencies. DPI was trying to stimulate the media to co-operate with the United Nations in producing information programmes, as had been done with a consortium of television organizations in producing a television series entitled "Agenda for a Small Planet".

The Committee on Information, in its 1983 report to the General Assembly,[2] recommended that all countries, the United Nations system and all others concerned should collaborate in establishing a new order, based on the free circulation and wider and better balanced dissemination of information, guaranteeing the diversity of sources of information and free access to information, and, in particular, the need to change the dependent status of the developing countries in information and communication. The Committee suggested that the contribution of DPI to UNESCO efforts should be maximized, in particular by disseminating information on UNESCO activities in establishing a new world order and on the Committee's work.

As requested by the Assembly in December 1982,[6] the United Nations and UNESCO jointly organized a Round Table on a New World Information and Communication Order. In October, the Secretary-General issued a report on the Round Table,[7] held at Innsbruck from 14 to 19 September. Twenty-six experts, mostly communications professionals, from 26 countries took part, selected by the host organizations to reflect geographical and cultural diversity. They considered working documents prepared by the United Nations and discussed the current situation of information and communication, inequalities in world communication and the causes of those imbalances, technological progress and its socio-cultural consequences, the one-way flow of information from North to South and ways to rectify the situation, and development of communication infrastructures in third-world countries.

GENERAL ASSEMBLY ACTION

In resolution 38/82 A of 15 December (see above), the Assembly reiterated its call for Member States and United Nations and other organizations in the communications field to make better known the issues underlying the demand for the development of communication capacities in developing countries as a step towards establishing a new world information and communication order. The Assembly considered that UNESCO's IPDC was a step towards that goal. It reaffirmed its support for UNESCO's efforts to establish a new order, for its 1984-1989 medium-term plan and for its stimulation of research with a view to meeting the challenges of accelerated technological development and the increasing role of communication.

Taking similar action in resolution 38/82 B (see below) of the same date, the Assembly expressed satisfaction with the work of the Round Table, and proposed that the United Nations and UNESCO convene a second round table in 1985 to follow up progress made towards establishing a new order. The Assembly requested that JUNIC, as the essential instrument for inter-agency co-ordination in public information, be strengthened and that its secretariat elaborate new work methods and longer-term indicative planning and joint action, especially in the promotion of a new order.

UN public information

The Committee on Information, in its 1983 report to the General Assembly,[2] made a number of recommendations on United Nations public information activities, including specific suggestions for the work of DPI (see below). It proposed that an appeal be addressed to the United Nations system to co-operate, through its information services, in promoting United Nations development activities and, in particular, the improvement of living conditions in developing countries. That appeal should be aimed at achieving a more comprehensive and realistic image of United Nations activities and potential.

Reaffirming the primary role of the Assembly in formulating United Nations information activities and recognizing the important role of UNESCO in information and communications, the Committee suggested that co-operation between the United Nations and UNESCO in promoting a new world information and communication order (see above) take more regular forms, especially at the working level, through the contribution of DPI to UNESCO efforts.

The Committee recommended the following activities to support developing countries in regard to information: assistance in training journalists and technical personnel and in setting up educational and research institutions; granting favourable conditions to provide access to communication technology needed for a national communication system; creation of conditions that would gradually enable developing countries to produce communication technology suited to their needs; and assistance in establishing telecommunication links at subregional, regional and interregional levels, free from conditions.

GENERAL ASSEMBLY ACTION

Under the agenda item on questions relating to information, the General Assembly, on 15 December, adopted resolution 38/82 B by recorded vote. It took this action on the recommendation of its Special Political Committee.

The General Assembly,

Recalling its resolutions 3535(XXX) of 17 December 1975, 31/139 of 16 December 1976, 33/115 A to C of 18 December 1978, 34/181 and 34/182 of 18 December 1979, 35/201 of 16 December 1980, 36/149 B of 16 December 1981 and 37/94 B of 10 December 1982 on questions relating to information,

Recalling article 19 of the Universal Declaration of Human Rights, which provides that everyone has the right to freedom of opinion and expression and that this right includes freedom to hold opinions without interference and to seek, receive and impart information and ideas through any media and regardless of frontiers, and article 29, which stipulates that these rights and freedoms may in no case be exercised contrary to the purposes and principles of the United Nations,

Recalling also articles 19 and 20 of the International Covenant on Civil and Political Rights,

Recalling the relevant provisions of the Political Declaration of the Seventh Conference of Heads of State or Government of Non-Aligned Countries, held at New Delhi from 7 to 12 March 1983, in which the importance of the establishment of a new world information and communication order was stressed anew, as well as the relevant provisions of the Final Declaration of the Sixth Conference of Heads of State or Government of Non-Aligned Countries, held at Havana from 3 to 9 September 1979, of the Declaration of the Conference of Ministers for Foreign Affairs of Non-Aligned Countries, held at New Delhi from 9 to 13 February 1981, and of the fifth and sixth meetings of the Intergovernmental Council of Ministers of Information of Non-Aligned Countries, held at Georgetown in May 1981 and at Valletta in June 1982,

Recalling its resolutions 3201(S-VI) and 3202(S-VI) of 1 May 1974, containing the Declaration and the Programme of Action on the Establishment of a New International Economic Order, 3281(XXIX) of 12 December 1974, containing the Charter of Economic Rights and Duties of States, and 3362(S-VII) of 16 September 1975 on development and international economic co-operation,

Recalling the Declaration on Fundamental Principles concerning the Contribution of the Mass Media to Strengthening Peace and International Understanding, to the Promotion of Human Rights and to Countering Racialism, *Apartheid* and Incitement to War, as well as the relevant resolutions on information and mass communications adopted by the General Conference of the United Nations Educational, Scientific and Cultural Organization at its nineteenth, twentieth, twenty-first and twenty-second sessions,

Recalling the relevant provisions of the Final Act of the Conference on Security and Co-operation in Europe, signed at Helsinki on 1 August 1975, and those of the Concluding Document of the Madrid meeting of representatives of the participating States of the Conference on Security and Co-operation in Europe, held from 11 November 1980 to 9 September 1983,

Recalling also the relevant provisions of the Declaration on the Preparation of Societies for Life in Peace,

Taking note of that part of the Programme of Action on Namibia of the International Conference in Support of the Struggle of the Namibian People for Independence, held in Paris from 25 to 29 April 1983, relevant to the activities requested of the Department of Public Information to develop and further strengthen the dissemination of information regarding the struggle for independence of the people of Namibia, with a view to reaching the broadest possible public by means of a more systematic and better co-ordinated information campaign,

Taking note of the Geneva Declaration on Palestine and the Programme of Action for the Achievement of Palestinian Rights, unanimously adopted by the International Conference on the Question of Palestine, in particular section II.D of the Programme of Action,

Conscious of the need for all countries, the United Nations system as a whole and all others concerned to collaborate in the establishment of a new world information and communication order based, *inter alia*, on the free circulation and wider and better balanced dissemination of information, guaranteeing the diversity of sources of information and free access to information, and, in particular, the urgent need to change the dependent status of the developing countries in the field of information and communication, as the principle of sovereign equality among nations extends also to this field, and intended also to strengthen peace and international understanding, enabling all persons to participate effectively in political, economic, social and cultural life and promoting understanding and friendship among all nations and human rights,

Reaffirming that the establishment of a new world information and communication order is linked to the new international economic order and is an integral part of the international development process,

Emphasizing the important role that public information plays in promoting understanding of and support for the establishment of the new international economic order and international co-operation for development,

Emphasizing the role that public information plays in promoting support for universal disarmament and in increasing awareness of the relationship between disarmament and development among as broad a public as possible,

Reaffirming the primary role which the General Assembly is to play in elaborating, co-ordinating and harmonizing United Nations policies and activities in the field of information and recognizing the central and important role of the United Nations Educational, Scientific and Cultural Organization in the field of information and communication,

Taking note of the statement by the Under-Secretary-General for Public Information, on 1 November 1983, on the question of equitable geographical balance and professional requirements in reinforcing the staff of the Department of Public Information,

Taking note of its resolution 37/234 of 21 December 1982 entitled "Programme planning",

Emphasizing the complementarity of the activities in the field of information and communication and the need to strengthen co-operation and co-ordination between the organs, organizations and bodies of the United Nations system that deal with different aspects of information and communication,

Emphasizing its full support for the International Programme for the Development of Communication, which constitutes an important step in the development of the infrastructures of communication in the developing countries,

Conscious that the transfer of technology to developing countries is vital for the acceleration of the establishment of a new world information and communication order based on justice, freedom and equity,

Taking note of its resolution 37/92 of 10 December 1982 entitled "Principles Governing the Use by States of Artificial Earth Satellites for International Direct Television Broadcasting",

Expressing its satisfaction with the work of the Committee on Information as reflected in its report to the General Assembly at its thirty-eighth session,

Expressing its appreciation to the Joint United Nations Information Committee for its efforts towards improving co-ordination of the public information activities of the various organizations of the United Nations system,

Taking note with satisfaction of the report of the Secretary-General on questions relating to information,

Also taking note with satisfaction of the report of the Director-General of the United Nations Educational, Scientific and Cultural Organization,

1. *Approves* the report of the Committee on Information and all the recommendations contained in paragraph 94 A, annexed to the present resolution, affirms the requests and appeals reproduced therein and urges their full implementation;

2. *Reaffirms* the mandate given to the Committee on Information by the General Assembly in its resolution 34/182;

3. *Requests* the Committee on Information, keeping in mind its mandate, the essential tasks of which are to continue to examine the policies and activities of the Department of Public Information of the Secretariat, to continue to promote the establishment of a new, more just and effective world information and communication order and to continue to seek the co-operation and active participation of all organizations of the United Nations system, particularly the United Nations Educational, Scientific and Cultural Organization and the International Telecommunication Union, while taking all possible steps to avoid any overlapping of activities on this subject;

4. *Reaffirms* its strong support for the United Nations Educational, Scientific and Cultural Organization and for its efforts to promote the establishment of a new world information and communication order;

5. *Reiterates its appeal* to Member States, to the information and communication media, both public and private, as well as to non-governmental organizations, to disseminate more widely objective and better balanced information about the activities of the United Nations and, *inter alia*, about the efforts of the developing countries towards their economic, social and cultural progress and about the efforts of the international community to achieve international social justice and economic development, international peace and security and the progressive elimination of international inequities and tensions, such dissemination being aimed at achieving a more comprehensive and realistic image of the activities and potential of the United Nations system in all its purposes and endeavours;

6. *Requests* that the Joint United Nations Information Committee, as the essential instrument for interagency co-ordination and co-operation in the field of public information, be strengthened and made more effective and that its secretariat elaborate new methods of work and longer-term indicative planning and joint action, especially in the promotion of a new world information and communication order;

7. *Reaffirms* the importance of the rapidly increasing role of United Nations public information programmes in fostering public understanding and support of United Nations activities and requests the Secretary-General to continue to review the current activities of the Department of Public Information with a view to ensuring a better and more efficient use of its available resources in co-operation, as needed, with the Joint Inspection Unit;

8. *Requests* the Department of Public Information to contribute more effectively, through its training programmes, to the development of human, managerial and technical resources of the mass media from developing countries;

9. *Requests* the Secretary-General to take urgent steps, within the next programme budget, to enable the Caribbean Unit in the Radio Service of the Department of Public Information to begin a meaningful work programme, as outlined in the relevant report of the Secretary-General, in particular by the introduction of full programming in French/Creole and limited programming in Dutch/Papiamento;

10. *Requests* the Secretary-General to take the necessary measures to ensure that regional television news magazines are produced for national broadcasting organizations which request them and undertake to broadcast them on a regular basis, taking into account the priorities set by the General Assembly;

11. *Invites* the Department of Public Information, in view of the decision of the Government of Indonesia, to reopen, as a matter of priority, the United Nations Information Centre at Jakarta;

12. *Invites* the Department of Public Information to give a favourable reply to the request of the Government of the United Republic of Cameroon that the United Nations Information Centre at Yaoundé be strengthened and that a full-time director be appointed;

13. *Invites* the Department of Public Information to give a favourable reply to the request of the Government of the Republic of Burundi that the United Nations Information Centre at Bujumbura be strengthened and that a full-time director be appointed;

14. *Invites* the Commission on Transnational Corporations, when exchanging information with the Committee on Information, as encouraged by recommendation 21 of the Committee annexed to the present resolution, to draw the attention of the Committee to documents produced by the Secretariat relevant to the Committee's mandate, in particular those of the United Nations Centre on Transnational Corporations, when they have been considered by the Commission, together with the Commission's comments on them, provided that care is taken to avoid overlapping or duplication of work between the two intergovernmental bodies;

15. *Requests* the Department of Public Information to cover adequately policies and practices which violate the principles of international law relative to belligerent occupation, in particular the Geneva Convention relative to the Protection of Civilian Persons in Time of War, of 12 August 1949, wherever they occur, especially those policies and practices which frustrate the attainment and exercise of the inalienable and national legitimate rights of the Palestinian people in accordance with the relevant resolutions of the United Nations;

16. *Expresses its satisfaction* with the work of the Round Table on a New World Information and Communication Order organized jointly by the United Nations and the United Nations Educational, Scientific and Cultural Organization, held at Innsbruck, Austria, from 14 to 19 September 1983, and its subsequent report;

17. *Requests* the Secretary-General to ensure that the Department of Public Information, jointly with the United Nations Educational, Scientific and Cultural Organization, convenes a second round table in 1985 in order to follow up in more detail the progress made towards the establishment of a new world information and communication order, in which professional journalists, decision-makers and researchers in the various disciplines concerned, representatives of the international media and professional organizations and associations would participate;

18. *Requests* the Secretary-General to report to the Committee on Information, at its substantive session in 1984, on the implementation of all the recommendations contained in the Committee's report;

19. *Requests* the Secretary-General to report to the General Assembly at its thirty-ninth session on the implementation of the present resolution and, in particular, on the implementation of all the recommendations contained in the annex to the present resolution;

20. *Requests* the Committee on Information to report to the General Assembly at its thirty-ninth session;

21. *Decides* to include in the provisional agenda of its thirty-ninth session the item entitled "Questions relating to information".

ANNEX
Recommendations of the Committee on Information

1. The forty-three recommendations of the Committee on Information approved by the General Assembly in resolution 37/94 B of 10 December 1982, as well as all provisions of the resolution, are reiterated. Those recommendations pending implementation should be implemented in full, taking into account the views expressed by delegations at the 100th plenary meeting of the thirty-seventh session of the Assembly on 10 December 1982.

2. The mandate of the Committee on Information should be renewed as set forth in General Assembly resolution 34/182 of 18 December 1979 and reaffirmed in Assembly resolutions 35/201 of 16 December 1980, 36/149 of 16 December 1981 and 37/94 of 10 December 1982.

Promotion of the establishment of a new, more just and more effective world information and communication order intended to strengthen peace and international understanding and based on the free circulation and wider and better balanced dissemination of information

3. All countries, the United Nations system as a whole, and all others concerned, should collaborate in the establishment of a new world information and communication order based, *inter alia*, on the free circulation and wider and better balanced dissemination of information, guaranteeing the diversity of sources of information and free access to information, and, in particular, the urgent need to change the dependent status of the developing countries in the field of information and communication as the principle of sovereign equality among nations extends also to this field, and intended also to strengthen peace and international understanding, enabling all persons to participate effectively in political, economic, social and cultural life, and promoting understanding and friendship among all nations and human rights.

4. An appeal should be addressed to the international media to obtain their support for the efforts of the international community towards global development and, in particular, for the efforts of the developing countries for their own economic, social and cultural progress.

5. An appeal should be addressed to the whole United Nations system to co-operate in a concerted manner, through its information services, in promoting the development activities of the United Nations, in particular the improvement of the conditions of the lives of the people of the developing countries.

6. Such appeals should be aimed at achieving a more comprehensive and realistic image of the activities and potential of the United Nations system, in all its purposes and endeavours, as laid down in the Charter of the United Nations.

7. The need should be noted for the creation of a climate of confidence in relations among States as a means of easing tension and, in this context, an appeal should be addressed to all States and mass media to help promote the purposes of strengthening peace and understanding.

8. Reaffirming the primary role which the General Assembly is to play in elaborating, co-ordinating and harmonizing United Nations policies and activities in the field of information and recognizing the central and important role of the United Nations Educational, Scientific and Cultural Organization in the field of information and communication, the co-operation between that organization and the United Nations in promoting the establishment of a new world information and communication order should take more regular forms, especially at the working level, through which the contribution of the Department of Public Information to the efforts of the United Nations Educational, Scientific and Cultural Organization should be maximized.

9. The Department of Public Information should disseminate as widely as possible information on the activities of the United Nations Educational, Scientific and Cultural Organization in the establishment of a new world information and communication order and on the work of the Committee on Information in that field.

10. The Committee on Information, noting the valuable effort of the United Nations Educational, Scientific and Cultural Organization in the promotion of a new world information and communication order, recommends that the Department of Public Information take steps to avoid any overlapping of its activities on this subject with those of the United Nations Educational, Scientific and Cultural Organization, while stressing at the same time the ever-growing significance of the close working co-operation between the United Nations and the latter organization.

11. All countries, the United Nations system as a whole, and others concerned should be called upon to give the United Nations Educational, Scientific and Cultural Organization adequate support and assistance in the field of information and communication. The fifth anniversary of the Declaration on Fundamental Principles concerning the Contribution of the Mass Media to Strengthening Peace and International Understanding, to the Promotion of Human Rights and to Countering Racialism, *Apartheid* and Incitement to War, should be marked by the General Assembly.

12. The Secretary-General should be requested to present to the General Assembly at its thirty-eighth session the report of the Round Table on a New World Information and Communication Order, held at Innsbruck, Austria, from 14 to 19 September 1983.

13. An appeal should be addressed to the whole United Nations system and the developed countries to co-operate in a concerted manner towards strengthening the information and communication infrastructures of the developing countries in accordance with the priorities attached to such areas by the developing countries. In this regard, full support for the International Programme for Development of Communication of the United Nations Educational, Scientific and Cultural Organization, which constitutes an important step in the development of these infrastructures, should be emphasized.

14. The Department of Public Information should further strengthen its co-operation with the Pool of Non-Aligned News Agencies, as well as with regional news agencies of developing countries, as this co-operation con-

stitutes a concrete step towards a more just and equitable world flow of information, thus contributing to the establishment of a new world information and communication order.

15.   The United Nations system, particularly the United Nations Educational, Scientific and Cultural Organization, should aim at the provision of all possible support and assistance to the developing countries with regard to their interests and needs in the field of information and to actions already adopted within the United Nations system, including, in particular:

(*a*)   Assistance to developing countries in training journalists and technical personnel and in setting up appropriate educational institutions and research facilities;

(*b*)   The granting of favourable conditions to provide developing countries with access to such communication technology as is requisite for the establishment of a national information and communication system and correspondent with the specific situation of the country concerned;

(*c*)   The creation of conditions that will gradually enable the developing countries to produce the communication technology suited to their national needs, as well as the necessary programme material, specifically for radio and television broadcasting, by using their own resources;

(*d*)   Assistance in establishing telecommunication links at subregional, regional and interregional levels, especially among developing countries, free from any kind of conditions.

16.   All the information activities of the Department of Public Information should be guided by, and carried out in conformity with, the principles of the Charter of the United Nations and the aspiration for a new world information and communication order, as well as conform to the consensus reached among States in resolutions 4/19, 4/21 and 4/22 adopted by the General Conference of the United Nations Educational, Scientific and Cultural Organization at its twenty-first session.

17.   The Secretary-General should be requested to ensure that the activities of the Department of Public Information, as the focal point of the public information tasks of the United Nations, should be strengthened, keeping in view the principles of the Charter of the United Nations and along the lines established in the pertinent resolutions of the General Assembly and the recommendations of the Committee on Information, to ensure a more coherent coverage of, and a better knowledge about, the United Nations and its work, especially in its priority areas, such as those stated in section III, paragraph 1, of Assembly resolution 35/201, including international peace and security, disarmament, peace-keeping and peace-making operations, decolonization, the promotion of human rights, the struggle against *apartheid* and racial discrimination, economic, social and development issues, the integration of women in the struggle for peace and development, the establishment of the new international economic order and of a new world information and communication order, the work of the United Nations Council for Namibia and programmes on women and youth.

Continuation of examination of United Nations public information policies and activities, in the light of the evolution of international relations, particularly during the past two decades, and of the imperatives of the establishment of the new international economic order and of a new world information and communication order

18.   The Department of Public Information should ensure that the daily dispatches of the Pool of Non-Aligned News Agencies which it receives are appropriately utilized in the performance of the public information tasks of the United Nations.

(*a*)   With a view to further promotion and development of functional and mutually beneficial co-operation between the Department and the Pool, the existing arrangements in the Department for the conduct of this co-operation should be established on a more regular basis;

(*b*)   In view of the successful joint coverage by the Pool of important conferences and other events within the United Nations system, this practice should be continued and further strengthened;

(*c*)   The Department should consider the possibility of utilizing the dispatches received from the Pool to establish a data base on the information and communication facilities in the non-aligned countries.

19.   In connection with the training programme for journalists and broadcasters from developing countries that the Department of Public Information organizes every year, the possibility should be considered of allocating the last week of the programme for a visit by them to one of the developing countries for the purpose of acquainting themselves with the ways in which information on the United Nations is received and utilized.

20.   The Secretary-General should be requested to make available to the Committee on Information, at its substantive session in 1984, a report on the outcome of the activities conducted by the International Telecommunication Union with regard to the World Communications Year.

21.   The exchange of information between the Committee on Information and the Commission on Transnational Corporations in matters pertaining to the mandate of the Committee should be encouraged.

22.   The Secretary-General should be requested to submit to the General Assembly at its thirty-eighth session the final report on the acquisition of a United Nations communications satellite, in the manner outlined in paragraph 20 of Assembly resolution 37/94 B.

23.   The Secretary-General should be requested to implement fully the request, in paragraph 14 of General Assembly resolution 36/149 B, that present United Nations short-wave broadcasts over rented transmitters should be placed on a daily schedule throughout the year, to the extent that this can be accomplished through more effective utilization of existing resources.

24.   The Secretary-General should be requested to continue the co-operation between the Department of Public Information and the Union of National Radio and Television Organizations of Africa, as well as with radio stations which are members of that Union, in order to broadcast United Nations radio programmes on those radio stations, and further requests the

Secretary-General to co-operate with the national radio broadcasting organizations in Africa for wider broadcasting of United Nations radio programmes.

25. The Secretary-General should be requested to present to the substantive session of the Committee on Information in 1984 a comprehensive report on the viability of a world-wide United Nations short-wave network, taking into account the views expressed at the fifth substantive session of the Committee.

26. The Secretary-General should be requested to implement fully the proposals contained in his report regarding programming in the Portuguese language in the African Unit of the Radio Service and to take immediate steps for the strengthening of programming in the French language.

27. The Secretary-General should be requested to maintain the functions of the Middle East/Arabic Unit as the producer of Arabic television and radio programmes, to strengthen and expand this unit through the redeployment of existing resources to enable it to function in an effective manner, and to report to the Committee on Information at its substantive session in 1984 on the measures taken in implementation of this recommendation.

28. In view of the importance of United Nations broadcasting for the European region, steps should be taken to maintain and enhance the functions of the European Unit in the Radio Service through redeployment of existing resources.

29. The inclusion of Bengali and Indonesian among the languages of the Asian Unit of the Radio Service for the purpose of undertaking programming at a meaningful level, as approved in 1982, should be implemented in full and Bahasa Malaysia (Malay) should also be included among the languages of the unit through redeployment of available resources.

30. Whereas the French Language Production Section of the Press and Publications Division hardly has available the means to provide press releases in sufficient numbers to meet the needs of the numerous delegations from all geographic areas wishing to use French as their working language, the Committee on Information requests that the Secretary-General should provide that Section with the appropriate means through better and more equitable use of available resources. The Committee recommends to the Department of Public Information that it make appropriate use of the official languages of the General Assembly in documents and audiovisual materials, in view of the need to disseminate more broadly and effectively information on the activities of the United Nations to the greatest cross-section of the public, using the greatest number of communications media.

31. United Nations information centres should continue to assist press and information media in their respective countries, and, *inter alia*, promote the establishment of a new world information and communication order.

32. While co-operation between the Department of Public Information and the United Nations Development Programme in the field should be promoted to the maximum extent, it is also important to bear in mind the intrinsic functions of United Nations information centres as distinct from those of United Nations development activities. The United Nations information centres should redouble their efforts to publicize the activities

and achievements of operational activities for development, including those of the Programme, taking into account the priorities determined by the General Assembly.

33. In countries where the size, population, the state of media and non-governmental and other organizations, or the role being played by their Governments in United Nations affairs warrant it, separate United Nations information centres should be established, as and when resources become available. In other cases, the resident representatives or resident co-ordinators of the United Nations Development Programme may be entrusted with being acting directors of United Nations information centres, provided that they are periodically briefed and evaluated by the Department of Public Information with regard to their information tasks and provided that appropriate local staff and equipment can be allocated to them within available resources.

34. The Committee on Information, having considered the report of the Secretary-General on the study on ways and means to enhance the role of the United Nations information centres within the structure of the Department of Public Information recommends that the effectiveness of United Nations information centres should continue to be improved:

(a) Through the continued review of the extent of decentralization which can be achieved within the overall guidance of the Department of Public Information;

(b) Through better training of centre directors and their personnel;

(c) Through an improved feedback and reporting system;

(d) Where appropriate, through reallocation of available resources for local reproduction and other necessary expenditures;

(e) Through appointing the best qualified persons with professional experience from all different geographical regions to the posts of centre directors, in view of the increased importance of the work of the United Nations information centres network, taking into account Article 101, paragraph 3, of the Charter of the United Nations;

(f) Through filling existing vacancies at the level of information centre director without further delay, in order to assure the continuation of the work of the centres under the necessary professional guidance of the Department of Public Information;

(g) Through enabling the External Relations Division of the Department of Public Information to fulfil its important role of management, guidance, supervision and monitoring of United Nations information centres in order to ensure that the universal character of the United Nations and the manifold mandate of the Department be duly reflected in the work of the information centres;

(h) Through strengthening the capacity of and improving the services rendered by the centres within the existing resources of the Department of Public Information, so that the centres can play their indispensable role of fostering an informed public opinion about the United Nations throughout the world.

35. The Department of Public Information should focus on, and give wider coverage to, economic, social and development activities throughout the United Nations system, with the aim of achieving a more comprehensive image of the activities and potential of the

United Nations system, taking into account the priorities set by the General Assembly. The United Nations information centres, among others, should play an important role in this regard. The Department of Public Information should encourage the organization of round-table discussions between chief editors for press, radio and television services of different countries.

36. The Department of Public Information should promote an informed understanding of the work of the United Nations in the area delineated in General Assembly resolutions 34/146 of 17 December 1979, 36/109 of 10 December 1981 and 37/108 of 16 December 1982.

37. The Committee on Information takes note with appreciation of the report of the Secretary-General on the study on ways and means to enhance the role of the United Nations information centres within the structure of the Department of Public Information. The Secretary-General should be requested to submit to the Committee at its substantive session in 1984 a detailed report containing concrete proposals in respect of the suggestions presented in paragraphs 44 to 46 of the report.

38. The Secretary-General should be requested to ensure that United Nations information centres orient their activities to disseminate information on questions according to the mandates and priorities of the Department of Public Information established by the General Assembly.

39. Urgent steps should be taken to ensure that the United Nations Information Service at Vienna give, as a matter of priority, adequate service in the German language in order to act as information centre for Austria and the Federal Republic of Germany. Such steps, which are to be taken within existing resources, may involve redeployment of posts, including those originally assigned to the United Nations Industrial Development Organization–United Nations Information Service. The Committee should be informed about the implementation of this recommendation at its substantive session in 1984.

40. Taking into account the request of the Government of Nicaragua for the opening of a United Nations information centre at Managua, the Secretary-General should be requested to take the appropriate steps for the prompt establishment of the centre, through the redeployment of existing resources.

41. The United Nations information centres should be requested to intensify direct and systematic communication exchange with local information and educational communities in a mutually beneficial way, especially in areas of particular interest to host countries.

42. A detailed and well documented factual summary account of the coverage by widely representative world media of developments affecting the Palestinian people from June to December 1982 should be prepared, within existing resources, and be submitted to the General Assembly at its thirty-eighth session.

43. The Committee on Information, taking note with appreciation of the reports of the Secretary-General on the development of systematic evaluation procedures for the activities of the Department of Public Information and on the in-depth evaluation of the work of the Department of Public Information, encourages the Secretary-General to continue his efforts to develop a system for monitoring and evaluating the effectiveness

of the activities of the Department, particularly in the priority areas determined by the General Assembly. This systematic evaluation process should be pursued and a progress report should be submitted to the Committee at its substantive session in 1984. The Committee looks forward to receiving in due course the progress report on the implementation of decisions taken on the basis of the Secretary-General's report which is to be presented to the Committee for Programme and Co-ordination at its twenty-sixth session.

44. Future reports of the Department of Public Information to the Committee on Information and to the General Assembly, in particular on new programmes or on the expansion of existing programmes, should contain:

(a) More adequate information on the output of the Department in respect of each topic included in its work programme, which forms the basis of its programme budget;

(b) The costs of the activities undertaken in respect of each topic;

(c) More adequate information on target audiences, end-use of the Department's products and an analysis of feedback data received by the Department;

(d) The Department's evaluation of the effectiveness of its different programmes and activities;

(e) A statement detailing the priority level which the Secretary-General has attached to current or future activities of the Department, in documents dealing with such activities.

45. The Committee on Information notes the steps taken by the Department of Public Information in redressing the imbalance in the staff of that Department, particularly in the Radio and Visual Services Division. The Department should continue to intensify its efforts to that end, and, until equitable geographical distribution is achieved, the Secretary-General should take urgent steps to increase the representation of underrepresented groups of countries, in accordance with Article 101, paragraph 3, of the Charter of the United Nations and General Assembly resolutions 33/143, 35/201, 36/149 and 37/94 B; in this regard, the Secretary-General is requested to submit a report to the Committee on Information at its substantive session in 1984.

46. Member States should be called upon to make voluntary contributions to the United Nations Trust Fund for Economic and Social Information.

47. The General Assembly should take note of the report of the Secretary-General on various aspects of the regionalization of the Radio and Visual Services Division of the Department of Public Information and examine it in the light of its resolutions 35/201 and 36/149 B.

48. The World Disarmament Campaign should give full consideration to the role of the mass media as the most effective way to promote in world public opinion a climate of understanding, confidence and co-operation conducive to peace and disarmament, the enhancement of human rights and development. Within the context of the World Disarmament Campaign and Disarmament Week, the Department of Public Information should fulfil the role assigned to it by the General Assembly by utilizing its expertise and resources in public information to ensure maximum effectiveness.

49. The quality, usefulness and coverage of the daily press releases and the weekly news summary issued by the Department of Public Information in all working

languages should be further enhanced and improved in view of the important public information tasks which they can perform. The Department should continue to co-operate closely with and provide assistance to the United Nations Correspondents Association. Services provided at the Press Section of the Department of Public Information booth for the media and delegations should be improved.

50.   The Committee recommends, in view of the importance of graphic presentation for a variety of public information activities, including posters, exhibits and publications, that the Secretary-General should consider redeploying a post of graphic designer from the Department of Conference Services to the Department of Public Information.

51.   The role of the Department of Public Information, as defined by the General Assembly in several relevant resolutions, as the focal point for the formulation and implementation of information activities of the United Nations should be re-emphasized, and the Secretary-General should be requested to study the full implications of this matter and submit a report to the Committee on Information at its substantive session in 1984.

52.   The operations of the Non-Governmental Liaison Services (Geneva and New York), as inter-agency projects reaching specific target audiences in the industrialized countries on international development issues, should be continued on a stable financial basis through United Nations participation in these services. The Committee further recommends that the Secretary-General should be requested to urge all the specialized agencies to make long-term contributions to the financing of these services, thereby stressing their inter-agency character.

53.   The Department of Public Information and the United Nations Development Programme, as important elements of United Nations information and development activities, should be requested to co-operate more closely with each other, both at Headquarters and in the field, in order to concentrate their resources, avoid duplication and effectively foster the process of development.

54.   The Joint United Nations Information Committee, as the essential instrument for inter-agency co-ordination and co-operation in the field of public information, should be enhanced and given more responsibility, thus improving its co-ordination and cost-benefit efficiency of the public information activities of the entire United Nations system.

55.   The Joint United Nations Information Committee should continue to strengthen its activities in the fields of development education and development-support communications.

56.   The recommendations contained in the report of the Joint United Nations Information Committee on public perceptions of the United Nations system should be implemented. An appeal should be addressed to Governments and the mass media to transmit accurate information on major activities of the United Nations, especially those listed in Article I of the Charter of the United Nations.

57.   The Joint United Nations Information Committee should continue to report on its programmes and activities to the Committee on Information for guidance and support.

58.   Since *Development Forum* is the only inter-agency publication of the United Nations system which concentrates on development issues, the Secretary-General should continue, in accordance with pertinent resolutions of the General Assembly, to support its publication from the regular budget while intensifying his efforts to secure a sound and independent financial basis for its continued publication. All the specialized agencies and other organizations of the United Nations system should be urged to contribute to the financing of this system-wide publication, thereby recognizing its inter-agency character.

59.   Having taken note of the report on the relocation of *Development Forum*, the Committee on Information recommends that the Secretary-General should be requested to ensure that *Development Forum* will retain its editorial policy of intellectual independence, thus enabling this publication to continue to serve as a world-wide forum in which diverse opinions on issues related to economic and social development can be freely expressed.

60.   The Secretary-General should be requested to submit a report to the Committee on Information on the current status of financial arrangements for the publication of the *World Newspaper Supplement* project.

61.   In view of the fact that, as is pointed out in the report of the Secretary-General on the in-depth evaluation of the work of the Department of Public Information, the production of the *UN Chronicle* is administratively separate from its distribution and sales, thus adding to the problem of its wider and more effective dissemination, it is recommended that the Secretary-General should consider transferring the sales activity of the *UN Chronicle* to the Department of Public Information.

62.   The importance of the Declaration on the Preparation of Societies for Life in Peace should be noted and Member States called upon to implement it.

General Assembly resolution 38/82 B

15 December 1983   Meeting 98   135-4-9 (recorded vote)

Approved by SPC (A/38/699) by recorded vote (102-4-9), 1 December (meeting 43); draft by Mexico, for Group of 77 (A/SPC/38/L.5/Rev.1 & Rev.1/Corr.1); agenda item 72.

Financial implications. 5th Committee, A/38/715; S-G, A/C.5/38/71, A/SPC/38/L.8/Rev.2.

Meeting numbers. GA 38th session: 5th Committee 58; SPC 10-17, 19, 39, 43; plenary 98.

Recorded vote in Assembly as follows:

In favour: Afghanistan, Algeria, Angola, Argentina, Australia, Bahamas, Bahrain, Bangladesh, Barbados, Belize, Benin, Bhutan, Bolivia, Botswana, Brazil, Bulgaria, Burma, Burundi, Byelorussian SSR, Cape Verde, Chad, Chile, China, Colombia, Congo, Costa Rica, Cuba, Cyprus, Czechoslovakia, Democratic Kampuchea, Democratic Yemen, Denmark, Djibouti, Dominica, Dominican Republic, Egypt, El Salvador, Equatorial Guinea, Ethiopia, Fiji, Finland, Gabon, Gambia, German Democratic Republic, Ghana, Greece, Grenada, Guatemala, Guinea, Guinea-Bissau, Guyana, Honduras, Hungary, Iceland, India, Indonesia, Iran, Iraq, Ireland, Ivory Coast, Jamaica, Jordan, Kenya, Kuwait, Lao People's Democratic Republic, Lebanon, Lesotho, Liberia, Libyan Arab Jamahiriya, Madagascar, Malawi, Malaysia, Maldives, Mali, Malta, Mauritania, Mauritius, Mexico, Mongolia, Morocco, Mozambique, Nepal, Nicaragua, Niger, Nigeria, Norway, Oman, Pakistan, Panama, Papua New Guinea, Paraguay, Peru, Philippines, Poland, Portugal, Qatar, Romania, Rwanda, Saint Lucia, Sao Tome and Principe, Saudi Arabia, Senegal, Seychelles, Sierra Leone, Singapore, Solomon Islands, Somalia, Spain, Sri Lanka, Sudan, Suriname, Swaziland, Sweden, Syrian Arab Republic, Thailand, Togo, Trinidad and Tobago, Tunisia, Turkey, Uganda, Ukrainian SSR, USSR, United Arab Emirates, United Republic of Cameroon, United Republic of Tanzania, Upper Volta, Uruguay, Vanuatu, Venezuela, Viet Nam, Yemen, Yugoslavia, Zaire, Zambia, Zimbabwe.

Against: Ecuador,[a] Israel, United Kingdom, United States.

Abstaining: Austria, Belgium, Canada, France, Italy, Japan, Luxembourg, Netherlands, New Zealand.

[a]Later advised the Secretariat it had intended to vote in favour.

In the Special Political Committee, a United States amendment[8] to add an additional paragraph was rejected by a recorded vote of 70 to 22, with 15 abstentions. By that paragraph, the Assembly would have decided that the resources required to implement the specified activities would be provided through offsetting programmatic or administrative adjustments, and consideration would be given to terminating activities designated lowest priority in the public information section (27) of the programme budget for 1984-1985 (see ADMINISTRATIVE AND BUDGETARY QUESTIONS, Chapter I).

At the request of the USSR, the Committee took recorded votes on paragraphs 9, 11, 12 and 13. They were adopted by votes of 88 to none, with 24 abstentions, 92 to 3, with 16 abstentions, 87 to 2, with 23 abstentions, and 88 to 2, with 23 abstentions, respectively.

Speaking in explanation of vote in the Committee, a number of countries expressed concern over the financial implications of the resolution. Canada, Denmark, Finland, France, the German Democratic Republic, the Federal Republic of Germany, Italy, Mexico, the Netherlands, Poland, the USSR, the United Kingdom and the United States protested additional costs. Canada, for example, felt that DPI should respond to requests for new programmes by redeploying existing resources. France reiterated its commitment to the establishment of a new world information and communication order but felt that, in view of the considerable means available to DPI, it should be able to absorb the new activities proposed each year. Similarly, Italy said that the programme budget of DPI should be sufficient if proper priority were given to the activities to be undertaken.

The Netherlands was convinced of the need for DPI to exercise budgetary restraint, but it understood that exceptions were sometimes inevitable; accordingly it was willing to support some of the paragraphs with financial implications but not those which had been introduced at the last minute or those which had not been previously submitted to the Committee on Information and negotiated. The latter viewpoint was shared by the United Kingdom. Maintaining reservations on the amount of funds to be allocated for the implementation of paragraphs 9, 11, 12 and 13 and desiring austerity measures, Poland nevertheless agreed that exceptions had to be made in certain cases, such as the one described in paragraph 11. The United Kingdom said the text reflected the Special Political Committee's continuing failure to deal effectively with the question of DPI's limited resources, the cost-effectiveness of its activities and the need to set responsible priorities among the recommendations made by the Committee on Information and the Special Political Committee.

In regard to the United States amendment, Finland and Mexico supported the principle of financial restraint but objected to the proposed amendment. Finland said it was arbitrary, while Mexico felt it would call into question the position of the developing countries. Reaffirming support for a new order, the USSR, on the other hand, said that, because considerable financial implications were directed towards activities not of the highest priority, it could not support additional financing for such activities and it supported the United States proposal.

Algeria and the Congo stated that the United Nations should allocate the funds necessary for those activities called for in the resolution. The Congo appealed to those countries which did not support the resolution for financial reasons to reconsider their positions and to try to understand that the requests were fully in keeping with United Nations objectives.

A group of States expressed reservations about the twenty-first preambular paragraph which referred to a December 1982 Assembly resolution on principles for use of satellites for television broadcasting.[9] Austria, Denmark, Finland, the Federal Republic of Germany, the Netherlands and Sweden made similar observations in this regard. Sweden felt that some principles could be interpreted as authorizing government control over television programmes broadcast by satellite, and such control was contrary to Swedish laws, which provided for freedom of the mass media, a position shared by Denmark.

Denmark, Finland, the Federal Republic of Germany, Sweden and the United Kingdom objected to paragraph 15, in which DPI was called on to cover policies and practices violating international law on belligerent occupation. Finland said the paragraph had political elements which were extraneous to questions relating to information and were incompatible with efforts to find a comprehensive settlement to the Middle East problem through negotiations. According to the Federal Republic of Germany, paragraph 15 singled out one particular political item to be covered by DPI and contained unacceptable wording; although the Federal Republic of Germany supported the Palestinian people's right to self-determination, it viewed any interpretation of that right as an anticipation of results which were to be achieved in the framework of a comprehensive settlement. Sweden and Denmark supported the paragraph's main thrust, but believed that the final part did not logically fit with the rest.

The United Kingdom and the United States expressed regret about what they viewed as a tendency to politicize information matters. The United States pointed out that two issues—the question of Namibia and the rights of the Palestinian people—had been selected as threats to international peace and security; it believed that an omnibus resolution on information should deal with generally shared principles regarding the free flow of information and with the efficient, cost-effective operation of DPI. The Netherlands and the United States believed that the resolution should have included a call for evaluation and a system of priorities for DPI activities.

Both Algeria and Canada praised the Group of 77 for the flexibility it had shown in drafting the resolution. In view of that flexibility, Algeria was disappointed that the text had not been adopted by consensus.

Austria felt that consideration might also be given to financing the staffing requirements of the United Nations Information Service at Vienna so as to ensure adequate service in German; it also believed that paragraphs 12 and 13 constituted interference in questions falling within the Secretary-General's competence. The German Democratic Republic said the resolution contained important guidelines for a constructive international exchange regarding information and for the further development of DPI activities, and it believed that resolutions on information should reflect the need for co-operation in the establishment of a new order based on the desire for stronger peace and security and for disarmament measures.

In many other 1983 resolutions, the Assembly called for efforts by the United Nations and others to disseminate information in specific areas, including political, economic and social, and decolonization issues (for texts, refer to INDEX OF RESOLUTIONS AND DECISIONS).

In the political area, the Assembly in resolution 38/73 D called for wide publicity of the World Disarmament Campaign. In resolution 38/183 F, it called for dissemination of the ideas of international co-operation for disarmament. The Assembly, by resolution 38/183 L, invited the relevant specialized agencies and the International Atomic Energy Agency (IAEA) to disseminate information on the consequences of the arms race.

Having commended the Programme of Action against *Apartheid* to the attention of Governments, intergovernmental and non-governmental organizations and individuals by resolution 38/39 B, the Assembly recommended that DPI ensure the Programme's widest publicity. In resolution 38/39 A, the Assembly appealed to writers, artists and others working in the mass media to foster the role of the media in disseminating information commensurate with the need to eradicate *apartheid*. In this connection, the Special Committee against *Apartheid* was requested to pay special attention to mobilizing public opinion and encouraging public action against collaboration with

South Africa. The Assembly, in resolution 38/39 F, requested the Special Committee to publicize information on relations between Israel and South Africa and especially the July 1983 Declaration of the International Conference on the Alliance between South Africa and Israel.

The Assembly also called for dissemination of information on certain Middle East issues. In resolution 38/58 E, it requested DPI to disseminate information on United Nations activities relating to Palestine, including the August/September 1983 International Conference on the Question of Palestine, expand its coverage of Palestine, and publicize Israeli violations of human rights of Arabs living in the occupied territories. The Assembly, in resolution 38/58 B, requested the Secretary-General to provide the Division for Palestinian Rights with the resources to carry out its work through, among other means, closer contacts with the media and wider dissemination of the Division's information material, particularly where information on the question of Palestine was inadequate. The Secretary-General was also requested to ensure the continued co-operation of DPI and other Secretariat units in enabling the Division to perform its tasks and in covering the Palestine question. In resolution 38/79 D, the Assembly requested the Secretary-General to ensure the widest circulation, by means available through DPI, of reports and activities of the Special Committee to Investigate Israeli Practices Affecting the Human Rights of the Population of the Occupied Territories.

The Assembly also called for publicizing economic and social issues. Resolution 38/34 included an appeal to Member States to encourage the mass media and educational and cultural institutions to arouse a greater awareness with regard to the return or restitution of cultural property to its country of origin. In resolution 38/148, the Assembly requested the Secretary-General to ensure that the 1984 International Conference on Population and issues to be discussed there were widely publicized. By resolution 38/14, the Assembly approved the Programme of Action for the Second Decade to Combat Racism and Racial Discrimination (beginning 10 December 1983). That Programme recommended that national institutions inform the public of the nature of their human rights, as provided for in international instruments and national legislation directed towards combating racism, racial discrimination and *apartheid*, and mobilize public opinion against violations of human rights. The Programme also outlined the role the mass media could play in combating racism and racial discrimination and ways to achieve this goal. In resolution 38/19, the Assembly requested the Secretary-General to distribute to States the list compiled by the Commission on

Human Rights of individuals, organizations, institutions and representatives of States deemed responsible for crimes enumerated in article II of the International Convention on the Suppression and Punishment of the Crime of *Apartheid*,[10] and to bring such facts to the attention of the public by all the means of mass communication. The Secretary-General was also requested to intensify efforts to disseminate information on the Convention and its implementation with a view to promoting further ratification or accession.

The Commission on Human Rights, taking action on a related issue by a resolution of 10 March,[11] also called for further promotion and encouragement of human rights and fundamental freedoms, through dissemination of information. In particular, it requested the Secretary-General to report annually on the dissemination of international instruments on human rights and to develop further the promotional and public information activities of the Centre for Human Rights.

In resolution 38/99, the Assembly called for DPI to disseminate information on the fortieth anniversary, in 1985, of the conclusion of the Second World War, exposing totalitarian and other ideologies and practices based on racial or ethnic exclusiveness or intolerance, hatred or denial of human rights. In resolution 38/116, the Secretary-General was urged to ensure that adequate publicity and other arrangements were made to enable the Human Rights Committee and the Economic and Social Council to carry out their functions under the International Covenants on Human Rights.[12]

By resolution 38/118, the Assembly requested the Secretary-General to disseminate widely the 1982 Principles of Medical Ethics[13] and to issue them in the six official United Nations languages. Governments were called on to distribute the Principles widely and intergovernmental and non-governmental organizations were invited to bring them to the attention of the widest possible group of individuals.

By resolution 38/105, the Assembly called on the Secretary-General to disseminate widely in the official United Nations languages the 1982 Declaration on the Participation of Women in Promoting International Peace and Co-operation,[14] and invited Governments to ensure its publicity. The Assembly called for publicity of the International Youth Year (1985) in resolution 38/22. Specifically, it requested the Secretary-General to publicize United Nations activities and other information concerning youth. In resolution 38/120, the Assembly noted with satisfaction the action by the United Nations High Commissioner for Refugees to initiate public information programmes to increase awareness of the refugee situation in Africa and the objectives of the Second (1984) International Conference on Assistance to Refugees in Africa and requested DPI and other competent United Nations bodies to co-operate with the Commissioner to ensure maximum publicity of the African refugee situation and of the Conference.

The Assembly called for publicizing several decolonization issues. Resolution 38/55 dealt with dissemination of information on these questions in general. By that text, the Assembly approved the chapter of the report of the Special Committee on the Situation with regard to the Implementation of the Declaration on the Granting of Independence to Colonial Countries and Peoples, describing dissemination of such information. The Assembly requested the Secretary-General to continue to give publicity to United Nations work in decolonization, and invited States and organizations to disseminate such information.

In resolution 38/50, the Assembly requested the Secretary-General to continue, through DPI, a campaign to inform world public opinion of the pillaging of natural resources in colonial Territories and the exploitation of their indigenous populations by foreign monopolies and, in respect of Namibia, the support they rendered to South Africa. By decision 38/419, the Assembly made a similar request with regard to informing world public opinion of the military activities and arrangements in colonial Territories which were impeding the implementation of the 1960 Declaration on the Granting of Independence to Colonial Countries and Peoples.[15] In resolution 38/53, the Assembly urged the administering Powers of Non-Self-Governing Territories to ensure the widespread dissemination in their Territories of information relating to offers of study and training facilities made by States. Resolution 38/36 D dealt with dissemination of information and mobilization of international public opinion in support of Namibia.

DPI activities

Reports of the Secretary-General. As requested by the General Assembly in December 1982,[6] the Secretary-General reported, in October 1983, on various aspects of the work of DPI. The report[16] described the Secretariat's work in implementing the 1982 resolution, dealing with DPI activities other than those described in separate reports to the Committee on Information.

In order to strengthen the co-operation of DPI with the Pool of Non-Aligned News Agencies, as well as with regional news agencies of developing countries, DPI had established a direct link between United Nations Headquarters and the Pool, through a computerized word-processing system which fed United Nations news dispatches by a telephone line, made available by the Tanjug News

Agency of Yugoslavia, to the Tanjug satellite channel between the United States and Belgrade. A full-time Press Officer sent some 10 to 15 daily dispatches in English, French and Spanish through the line for the Pool. They were retransmitted to the Pool's 84 client agencies, which supplied local and regional redisseminators. DPI invited Pool correspondents from developing countries to cover several United Nations conferences, and four Pool correspondents were invited to participate in the 1983 programme for broadcasters and journalists which took place during the Assembly session.

The report added that, in compliance with an Assembly request[6] that reports of the Secretariat to the Committee on Information and the Assembly contain certain information, DPI began to propose activities in the programme budget for the biennium 1984-1985 along subprogramme lines and priority categories rather than by organizational units. DPI had established a monitoring system which provided its programme managers with comprehensive quarterly reports on DPI activities. It intended to consolidate those reports in its next biennial programme performance report. Two further stages of the evaluation process would be to determine which activities warranted in-depth evaluation and to assess end-users' reactions to those information activities or materials. In response to another request, DPI supplied the Committee on Information with samples of booklets, pamphlets, features, fact sheets and cassettes with radio programmes. Exhibits, posters and books published by external publishers in co-operation with the United Nations were also displayed to Committee members.

By the same 1982 resolution,[6] DPI had been requested to publish the *UN Chronicle*, a magazine on United Nations activities issued 11 times during 1983, in the six official United Nations languages and to expand its coverage. In addition to the existing Arabic, English, French, Russian and Spanish editions, arrangements were being made to produce a Chinese version by late 1983. New sections were added to the publication and its format had been improved, while subscription sales were increasing after a previous decline in circulation.

Other activities reported on were aimed at strengthening the production of United Nations radio programmes (see below).

In a separate report to the Assembly on the World Disarmament Campaign, the Secretary-General described DPI work in regard to an Assembly request[6] that it use its expertise and resources to ensure the maximum effectiveness of the Campaign (see Chapter I of this section).

Activities of the Committee on Information. The Committee on Information, in its annual report to the Assembly,[2] proposed that activities of DPI, as the focal point of the public information tasks of the United Nations, be strengthened to ensure a more coherent coverage of, and a better knowledge about, the United Nations, especially in priority areas, such as those stated by the Assembly in 1980,[17] including international peace and security, disarmament, peace-keeping and peace-making operations, decolonization, the promotion of human rights, the struggle against *apartheid* and racial discrimination, economic, social and development issues, the integration of women in the struggle for peace and development, the establishment of the new international economic order and of a new world information and communication order, the work of the United Nations Council for Namibia and programmes on women and youth. The Committee suggested that DPI focus on United Nations economic, social and development activities in order to achieve a more comprehensive image of the Organization, and that it encourage the organization of round-table discussions between chief editors for press, radio and television services of different countries.

As to co-operation between DPI and the Pool of Non-Aligned News Agencies, as well as with regional news agencies, the Committee called for further co-operation on a more regular basis, including joint coverage by the Pool of United Nations events. It recommended dissemination of information by DPI on UNESCO activities in establishing a new world information and communication order (see above). The Committee stated that the Secretariat had reported some progress in response to 1980,[17] 1981[18] and 1982[6] resolutions calling for an improvement in the geographical balance of DPI staff, and that the Under-Secretary-General for Public Information had noted the need to continue those efforts. DPI should continue efforts to redress the imbalance by increasing representation of underrepresented groups of countries, the Committee said.

Public information activities in connection with International Youth Year (1985) (see ECONOMIC AND SOCIAL QUESTIONS, Chapter XX) were another concern of DPI in 1983; projects included a film on youth, a series of radio programmes, pamphlets and other printed materials. The Under-Secretary-General pointed out that, while DPI had made efforts to promote the Year, there was a limit to what could be done within available resources.

The Committee called on the Secretary-General to report on activities of the International Telecommunication Union with regard to the World Communications Year (1983) (see ECONOMIC AND SOCIAL QUESTIONS, Chapter V). It was also suggested that he present a final report on the acquisition of a United Nations communications satellite, in the manner outlined by the Assembly in 1982.[6]

Regarding the use of official languages in DPI products, the Committee called for the wider use of those languages in documents and audio-visual materials. It also requested the Secretary-General to provide the French Language Production Section of the Press and Publications Division of DPI, through better use of available resources, with the means to produce press releases in sufficient quantity to meet the needs of the numerous delegations using French as their working language.

The Committee also made recommendations on United Nations radio programmes, the functioning of United Nations information centres and on evaluation procedures for information activities (see below under the relevant subject headings). In regard to the World Disarmament Campaign and Disarmament Week (see Chapter I of this section), DPI was called on to fulfil the role assigned to it by the Assembly by utilizing its expertise and resources in public information to ensure the effectiveness of the role of the mass media in promoting a climate conducive to peace and disarmament.

GENERAL ASSEMBLY ACTION

By resolution 38/82 B (see above), the General Assembly approved the Committee's report and recommendations on DPI activities, and urged full implementation of its requests. Reaffirming the importance of the increasing role of United Nations public information programmes in fostering public understanding and support of United Nations activities, the Assembly requested the Secretary-General to continue reviewing DPI activities with a view to ensuring a better use of its resources. It also requested DPI to cover policies and practices which violated the principles of international law relative to belligerent occupation wherever they occurred, especially those relating to the denial of the rights of the Palestinian people (see Chapter IX of this section).

Radio and Visual Services Division

In April 1983, the Secretary-General issued four reports on different aspects of the work of the Radio and Visual Services Division of DPI, in accordance with December 1982 requests by the General Assembly.[6] The reports were submitted to the Assembly through the Committee on Information.

One report dealt with the regionalization of the Division.[19] Regionalization referred to the process of tailoring broadcasting production to the interests of specific regions, a concept which had been debated in the Committee on Information and the Special Political Committee for two years. Regionalized programming dealt with all global issues of special concern to the United Nations as well as with regional interests. As radio, film and

television production required different specialized knowledge, United Nations activities in those areas had been separated into two units: a Radio Service and a Visual Service. The Radio Service consisted of seven regional units (Africa, Asia, the Caribbean, Europe, Latin America/Iberia, North America, and the Middle East/Arabic region) and a News and Central Programmes Section, which provided uniform radio news coverage. The Visual Service was divided into a News Production Section (television), a Feature Production Section (film), a Photographs and Exhibits Section, and a Visual Materials Library.

On the basis of considerations of professionalism and cost-effectiveness, the Secretary-General concluded that: separation of the two Services should be maintained; the output of the regional units of the Radio Service should continue to be balanced by a strong central news and programme element; separation of television and film production should be maintained and all television production should be the responsibility of the Visual Service; efforts should be made to diversify the television news output, within the existing structure and with existing resources; film production should be globally oriented, with more use of qualified outside producers and with due emphasis on adaptations into other languages; and efforts should be made to recruit qualified nationals of developing countries.

A second report by the Secretary-General was on the viability of a world-wide United Nations short-wave network.[20] Because more time was needed to complete the studies for a comprehensive presentation on the subject, the Secretary-General stated that the 1983 report was intended as an interim study, and was confined mainly to the question of viability of such a network and to possible transmission schedules of its regional segments. A 1984 report would deal with construction, staffing and operational requirements, frequencies, and the alternative of continuing to rent broadcasting time on existing national short-wave transmitters.

According to the 1983 report, the United Nations had the legal right to establish and operate short-wave broadcasting facilities at United Nations Headquarters and at the headquarters of the Economic and Social Commission for Asia and the Pacific at Bangkok, Thailand. The possibility of obtaining legal authorization for short-wave facilities at the other regional commissions' headquarters was likely. As for technical questions, the major task of obtaining available and suitable short-wave frequencies could also be overcome. The question of whether a meaningful audience for United Nations programming existed was difficult to assess, however. The report listed possible broadcasting schedules, in terms of hours of broadcasting, languages and target areas, of the four targeted regions of a world-wide United Nations short-wave network—Africa, Asia/Pacific, Latin America and Western Asia/North Africa.

A third report by the Secretary-General concerned the programming of the African Unit of the Radio Service.[21] It described the programmes prepared in English, French, Lingala, Portuguese and Swahili, and listed the staff employed for producing them—currently three Professional staff members to be joined by a fourth after redeployment, three General Service staff and three outside contractors. Most programmes were prepared at Headquarters and distributed on tape to radio stations in the region, and covered current affairs, news bulletins, listener question-and-answer programmes or other short-wave broadcasts.

It had been the experience of the Radio Service that those services did not adequately meet the needs of African listeners and broadcasting organizations, at least as far as United Nations material in English, French and Portuguese was concerned, since demand exceeded what could be supplied with current resources. Over the previous two years, there had been an increase in requests from permanent missions and broadcasting organizations for special reports via radio/telephone circuits; it had not been possible to respond adequately because of staffing constraints. In order to meet the existing demand and considering the need for budgetary restraint, the Secretary-General proposed that a full-time writer/producer at the P-3 level be added for both English and Portuguese production. If this were agreed, the Portuguese-language outside-contractor funds thus released could be used to commence programme production in Hausa, a major regional African language. The additional work of the African Unit would require one more General Service staff member.

The fourth report described the possible expansion of the Caribbean Unit of the Radio Service,[22] which was established to provide United Nations programmes to all except Spanish-speaking audiences and broadcasting organizations in the Caribbean. For the purposes of this Unit, the Caribbean included Belize, French Guiana, Guyana and Suriname. The Spanish-speaking audiences of the Caribbean were served by the Latin American/Iberian Unit.

Current staffing comprised two staff members in the Professional category and two at the General Service level. The Unit's radio programmes, both short-wave broadcasts and taped programmes, were produced in English. In addition to English and Spanish, there were seven languages or dialects used by one or more Caribbean broadcasting stations. The two leading language combina-

tions in terms of population were French/Creole and Dutch/Papiamento, with population figures of 6 million and 650,000 respectively. Therefore, the Secretary-General suggested that any expansion of the Unit's programming concentrate on those two language combinations. As with other regional units of the Radio Service, effective programming was considered to require a combination of short-wave news broadcasts and taped in-depth programmes for medium-wave broadcast by radio stations in the subregion. Accordingly, any meaningful work programme would require one full-time writer/producer at the Professional level and one assistant at the General Service level. In the light of the financial situation, the Secretary-General recommended expanding the Caribbean Unit in phases, introducing both language combinations, but with limited programming and utilizing initially the services of two writer/producers on special service agreements along with a full-time assistant/secretary.

The Secretary-General, in his report to the Assembly[16] dealing with the implementation of the 1982 recommendations of the Committee on Information approved by the Assembly in December 1982,[6] included new radio programming activities. In response to the request for the inclusion of Bengali and Indonesian among the languages of the Asian Unit of the Radio Service, production of a taped weekly 15-minute programme in Bengali and of a monthly programme in Indonesian began in 1983. Also requested by the Committee, production of a similar weekly programme in Lingala, provided to the Congo and Zaire, was begun by the African Unit. The Radio Service at Geneva began production of a similar programme in Serbo-Croat which was sent to seven radio stations in Yugoslavia. In regard to the request that the Spanish Radio Production Officer position at Geneva be filled as soon as possible, the Secretary-General reported that the post was temporarily occupied by a Press Officer but would revert to the Radio Service as soon as possible. Since resources were not available, the recommendation that United Nations short-wave broadcasts over rented transmitters be placed on a daily schedule throughout the year had not been implemented.

Another recommendation had called for co-operation between DPI and the Union of National Radio and Television Organizations of Africa and its member radio stations. DPI had contacted broadcasting organizations in five African countries and was awaiting information concerning the fees, if any, they would charge for the use of their transmitters. Any pilot project would require renting satellite radio circuits to ensure timely delivery. In response to the Assembly's request for balance in the use of all the official United Nations languages in radio programmes covering United

Nations conferences held away from Headquarters, coverage in all six languages was provided at the International Conference in Support of the Struggle of the Namibian People for Independence (Paris, April) (see TRUSTEESHIP AND DECOLONIZATION, Chapter III), and at the International Conference on the Question of Palestine (Geneva, August/September) (see Chapter IX of this section).

The Committee on Information, in its annual report to the Assembly,[2] described its discussions and made recommendations relating to the four reports of the Secretary-General. It proposed that he: implement the Assembly's 1981 request[18] that United Nations short-wave broadcasts over rented transmitters be placed on a daily schedule throughout the year, to the extent possible within existing resources; continue the co-operation between DPI and African broadcasting organizations in order to broadcast United Nations radio programmes; report in 1984 on the viability of a world-wide United Nations short-wave network; implement his proposals regarding United Nations radio programming in Portuguese and immediately strengthen programming in French; strengthen the functions of the Middle East/Arabic Unit as the producer of Arabic television and radio programmes, within existing resources; enhance the broadcasting functions of the European Unit of the Radio Service; and include Bengali, Indonesian and Bahasa Malaysia (Malay) among the languages of the Asian Unit.

Among its recommendations which might have financial implications, the Committee made proposals concerning the Caribbean Unit and regional television news magazines, which were subsequently approved by the Assembly when it adopted resolution 38/32 B.

GENERAL ASSEMBLY ACTION

The Assembly, in resolution 38/82 B on United Nations information activities (see above), approved the Committee's recommendations, affirmed its requests and appeals, and urged their full implementation. The Assembly requested the Secretary-General to enable the Caribbean Unit, within the next programme budget, to begin a meaningful work programme, in particular by introducing full programming in French/Creole and limited programming in Dutch/Papiamento. He was also requested to ensure that regional television news magazines were produced on a regular basis for national broadcasting organizations which requested them.

Yearbook of the United Nations

In the context of revised estimates for the United Nations programme budget for 1984-1985, the Secretary-General proposed in 1983 to the General Assembly's Fifth (Administrative and Budgetary) Committee a small temporary staff increase intended to improve the timeliness of the *Yearbook of the United*

Nations. In a November report to the Committee,[23] the Secretary-General noted that the delay in publication beyond the goal of issuing the book 18 months after the period covered had risen from 8 months in 1974 to 16 months in 1982, dropping to 14 months in 1983 following the redeployment to the *Yearbook* of one editor and the temporary assignment of one General Service post. With the introduction of technological innovations, including word processing and internal typesetting, it was considered feasible to produce the *Yearbook* at 12-month intervals with no increase in the regular staff of the Yearbook Section—five Professional and four General Service posts. However, elimination of the 14-month backlog by 1988, when the 1986 edition was scheduled to be produced, would require the temporary addition, through 1987, of one more editor and one General Service post. The Secretary-General estimated the cost for 1984-1985 at $150,400.

The Advisory Committee on Administrative and Budgetary Questions (ACABQ), in a November report to the Assembly,[24] recalled an observation it had made in 1976[25] that effective means must be devised of ensuring that Secretariat drafts of *Yearbook* articles were well prepared and submitted to the Yearbook Section on time. In view of reported improvements in the submissions, and in order to enable the Section to cope with the resulting increase in work, ACABQ recommended that the Secretary-General's request be approved. It asked him to submit in 1985 a progress report indicating whether the production schedule outlined in his 1983 report had been met, after which it would review the request for continued temporary assistance in 1986-1987.

GENERAL ASSEMBLY ACTION

In resolution 38/234 on the programme budget for 1984-1985, the General Assembly, on 20 December, endorsed the ACABQ conclusions and called for a review of the *Yearbook* format.

On the recommendation of the Fifth Committee, the Assembly adopted section V of resolution 38/234 without vote.

Revised estimates under section 27 (Public information): *Yearbook of the United Nations*

[*The General Assembly . . .*]

1. *Takes note* of the report of the Secretary-General on the *Yearbook of the United Nations* and of the related report of the Advisory Committee on Administrative and Budgetary Questions;

2. *Endorses* the conclusions of the Advisory Committee as contained in its report;

. . .

General Assembly resolution 38/234, section V

20 December 1983   Meeting 104   Adopted without vote

Approved by Fifth Committee (A/38/760 & Corr.1) without vote, 23 November (meeting 46); oral proposal by Chairman; agenda item 109.

Meeting numbers. GA 38th session: 5th Committee 44, 46; plenary 104.

Also on the recommendation of the Fifth Committee, the Assembly adopted section VI of resolution 38/234 without vote.

Yearbook of the United Nations

[*The General Assembly* . . .]

Bearing in mind the desirability of making the *Yearbook of the United Nations* more widely used by the general public,

Recalling the problems which have been encountered in the timely issuance of the *Yearbook of the United Nations*,

Taking note of the paragraphs of the Secretary-General's report which relate to the measures to eliminate the backlog in publication of the *Yearbook of the United Nations* and of the related report of the Advisory Committee on Administrative and Budgetary Questions,

1. *Requests* the Secretary-General to undertake a comprehensive review of the current format of the *Yearbook of the United Nations*, with a view to developing a new format in order to make it more usable and accessible;

2. *Requests* the Secretary-General to report on the implementation of this section of the present resolution to the General Assembly at its fortieth session;

. . .

General Assembly resolution 38/234, section VI

20 December 1983   Meeting 104   Adopted without vote

Approved by Fifth Committee (A/38/760 & Corr.1) without vote, 23 November (meeting 46); draft by United States (A/C.5/38/L.11), orally amended by Morocco; agenda item 109.

Meeting numbers. GA 38th session, 5th Committee 44, 46; plenary 104.

In the Fifth Committee, Morocco orally proposed two amendments to the draft on the *Yearbook* format which were accepted by its sponsor, the United States. The amendments deleted a preambular paragraph recalling a 1982 recommendation of the Committee for Programme and Co-ordination (CPC) that the delay in publication should be reduced to no more than two years, and inserted at the end of paragraph 1 "in order to make it more usable and accessible" in place of "which reduces its complexity, length and cost". The Committee decided, by 76 votes to 17, with 1 abstention, to approve the additional appropriation of $150,400 for the *Yearbook* for 1984-1985.

Speaking in explanation of vote, Belgium said it was willing to accept the United States draft and the Moroccan amendments, which should lead to some improvement in the regrettable situation that had prevailed for some years. Canada felt that merely adding staff to the Yearbook Section was attempting to cope with the results of the problem without getting at its cause and that effective means had to be devised to ensure that drafts from the Secretariat departments concerned were timely and well prepared; it wondered whether the book's current format was the best that could be devised.

UN information centres and services

Report of the Secretary-General. In April 1983, the Secretary-General reported on ways to enhance the role of the United Nations information centres within the structure of DPI.[26] The centres served as the main disseminators of information on the United Nations system in the field. In accordance with a 1982 General Assembly request,[6] the study was aimed at determining measures to increase the centres' functional independence and flexibility, to adjust their work to the needs of countries they served and to assess their financial, material and personnel requirements. The study reviewed the centres' activities, their administration through the DPI External Relations Division, the reporting system and flow of information between Headquarters and the centres, personnel matters, methods of communications and equipment, the kinds of requests for additional funds, and the centres' relationship with non-governmental organizations (NGOs).

The study suggested that an important step to strengthen the capacity of the centres and to develop their relationship with NGOs in their region would be the holding of periodic regional conferences with those organizations, in different areas of the world as often as financially feasible.

In the view of the centre directors, the centres needed a larger degree of discretionary authority in carrying out their work, including production of information material more suited to local needs and interests. More timely delivery of information material from Headquarters was needed, and they believed that a reduction and streamlining of procedural requirements was desirable, and that all communications should be channelled through DPI in order to minimize duplication and confusion. On personnel matters, the directors felt most of their posts needed to be upgraded to levels commensurate with their responsibilities. It was observed that efforts were being made to increase contacts between the centres and Headquarters, and that DPI was trying to bring about more mobility among directors, and between Headquarters and the field. The training programme should be extended to reference assistants. In response to their request, more flexibility was given to the centres to transfer funds among different areas of expenditure within their approved budgets. Most centres requested additional operational funds for purposes such as travel, translation and production of information material, communication, temporary assistance, and organizing seminars and exhibits. DPI would give consideration to all requests for resources and try to satisfy them, on a priority basis, through redeployment whenever possible. Additional funds would enable DPI to satisfy more requests and assist centres in improving their performance, the report concluded.

Activities of the Committee on Information. The Committee on Information considered the Secretary-General's report and made its own recommendations to the Assembly.[2] The Under-

Secretary-General for Public Information informed the Committee that the United Nations Information Centres Manual, which gave guidance for directors, was about to be revised and that DPI had taken action to establish a national information officer category for locally recruited information assistants and to fill vacancies in posts of centre directors. Among its recommendations, the Committee called on the centres to promote the establishment of a new world information and communication order (see above). Noting that field representatives of UNDP frequently also served as centre directors, the Committee said that co-operation between DPI and UNDP in the field should be promoted, while bearing in mind the centres' functions as distinct from those of development activities. The Committee recommended that, in countries where the size, population, the state of the media or the role being played by Governments in United Nations affairs warranted it, separate information centres should be established, as resources became available. In other cases, the UNDP resident representatives might be entrusted with being acting centre directors.

The Committee suggested that the effectiveness of the centres could be improved through: better staff training; improved reporting; reallocation of resources for local reproduction and other necessary expenditures; appointing the best qualified persons as centre directors; filling existing vacancies of directors without delay; enabling the External Relations Division to fulfil its role of management, supervision and monitoring of the centres; and improving the services rendered by the centres. The Committee proposed that the Secretary-General ensure that centres orient their activities according to the mandates and priorities established by the Assembly. It recommended that, within existing resources, the United Nations Information Service in Vienna provide adequate service in German in order to act as the information centre for Austria and the Federal Republic of Germany. Taking into account Nicaragua's request for an information centre at Managua, the Secretary-General should be requested to establish the centre through the redeployment of existing resources. In addition, the Committee proposed that the centres intensify communication exchange with local information and educational communities, especially in areas of particular interest to host countries. The Committee recommended that DPI accept Indonesia's invitation to reopen the Centre at Jakarta, the only recommendation concerning the centres with possible financial implications.

GENERAL ASSEMBLY ACTION

The General Assembly, in resolution 38/82 B (see above), approved the Committee's recommendations not requiring additional financial resources. In addition, it invited DPI: to reopen, as a matter of priority, the Jakarta Information Centre; and to agree to the requests of the United Republic of Cameroon and Burundi that the Yaoundé Centre and the Bujumbura Centre, respectively, be strengthened and full-time directors appointed.

In resolution 38/73 D on the World Disarmament Campaign (see Chapter I of this section), the Assembly requested the Secretary-General to instruct the information centres and regional commissions to give wide publicity to the Campaign and, whenever necessary, to adapt, as far as possible, United Nations information materials into local languages.

Programme evaluation

In April 1983, the Secretary-General submitted an in-depth evaluation of the work of DPI[27] to CPC. The report, covering the period 1971-1982, evaluated DPI's achievement in attaining six objectives of information activities.

The report pointed out that the primary function of DPI was to assist information agencies, educational institutions and NGOs by making available to them services and materials, including physical facilities such as office space, and radio and television studios, and material services such as press releases, press briefings, radio bulletins, live television feeds and documentation. The second objective was to provide information on United Nations activities by relying on redisseminators (mainly correspondents, the press, NGOs, outside authors and publishers, broadcasting organizations, film organizations, educational institutions, students and national information commissions). The third objective—serving the needs of selected groups and institutions with a high opinion-building potential—included efforts to reach target audiences such as the specialized press, schools, universities, professions and NGOs. Fourthly, the report evaluated whether DPI was equipped with the necessary technical facilities to enable it to perform its functions and to provide direct access to the United Nations. Establishment of a mechanism at Headquarters for formulating information policy and activities was another objective. The Planning, Programming and Evaluation Unit (PPEU) was established in 1980 to deal with those and related functions. The sixth objective—establishment of a mechanism at Headquarters for continuous information on the utilization and effectiveness of DPI activities—was currently being performed by PPEU, although there had been some doubt about the locus of the responsibility for the analysis and use of feedback. The data collected continued to be erratic and unreliable, making useful analysis difficult to obtain.

In reviewing the six objectives, the Secretary-General said that some progress had been made during the period under review. At the departmental level, there was commitment to planning, but that was not fully reflected at the operating level. In particular, the separation between production and distribution had been so pervasive that frequently the linkage of particular output to the fulfilment of the basic mandate of DPI had been forgotten. Progress in establishing a programme planning mechanism had been slow, but the current arrangements, namely, directors' meetings, thematic task forces and a planning group serviced by PPEU, should be adequate for that task. Improvement was needed in the means by which management informed itself of DPI activities.

Another area of concern was the means for collection, analysis and sharing of data; quantitative and qualitative data on DPI's production and on the demands for its services were of uneven coverage and utility. The identification of ways to improve the use of existing resources would depend on better feedback, appropriate equipment and the more precise identification of target audiences. In the absence of reliable output statistics and feedback data, it was difficult to assess whether there had been significant improvements in the provision of supporter services. The development of the capacity to make such judgements would be crucial in future attempts to provide such services efficiently and effectively. If support services were to remain accessible to the redisseminators, equipment capable of meeting the technological requirements of the users was needed. When target audiences had been better defined and their interests identified, distribution could be improved and, and in some cases, particular products could be tailored to the needs of specific users.

The Secretary-General stated his intention to take appropriate action on the issues raised by the evaluation, taking into account any comments of CPC and the Committee on Information.

By a note of 28 April,[28] the Secretariat reported to the Committee on Information on progress in the establishment of systematic procedures for monitoring and evaluating DPI activities. The mechanisms for monitoring and evaluation were to be reviewed periodically to improve activities and to ensure that they reflected intergovernmental objectives and the concerns of programme managers and end-users. The procedures consisted of four forms soliciting information on DPI activities—three of the forms required quarterly reports, and the fourth was filled out after every activity was begun or completed. PPEU analysed the data and quarterly reports were provided to the Under-Secretary-General, directors, chiefs of information services and directors of information centres.

In order to evaluate DPI activities, special questionnaires were devised to assess end-user reactions to DPI materials. The assessment was intended to ascertain whether the materials reached intended audiences and were useful to them. This data was supplemented with an analysis of correspondence and other information. Preliminary studies were under way on the annual editors' round tables, the United Nations fellowship programme for educators 1975-1981 and *The World Chronicle*, a weekly television programme produced by the United Nations at which correspondents interviewed United Nations officials.

CPC consideration. In May, CPC considered the Secretary-General's report on evaluation and the Secretariat's note. As stated in its annual report to the Assembly,[29] CPC considered the Secretary-General's report informative and useful, expressed concern about DPI's preoccupation with production and stressed the importance of focusing attention on distribution. Noting that efforts to eliminate the backlog in the publication of the *Yearbook of the United Nations* (see above) had not been effective, and that there had been a decline in demand for certain DPI products and services such as subscriptions to the *UN Chronicle* and visitors taking the guided tour at Headquarters, CPC suggested that DPI reassess the utility of those services as public information tools and define their potential users. CPC requested that further work be done on assessing the impact as well as on the identification and reaction of end-users, and that all future evaluations deal with those aspects.

With respect to DPI activities, CPC recommended that: the imbalance between production and dissemination efforts be corrected; the feedback system be refined and include analysis of the data collected; the target audiences be better identified; the timeliness of the *Yearbook* be improved; and the decline in paid circulation of the *Chronicle* be reversed through proper targeting of the output. The internal evaluation studies planned for 1984-1985 should include distribution of photo materials and radio tapes (in addition to anti-*apartheid* radio programmes, activities to highlight the 1985 Conference on the Achievements of the United Nations Decade for Women, and films on disarmament). CPC decided to consider at its 1986 session a progress report on the action taken by the Secretary-General in regard to the issues raised by the current evaluation.

Consideration by the Committee on Information. The Committee on Information also made recommendations on evaluation procedures for DPI activities.[2] It encouraged the development of the DPI monitoring and evaluating system, particularly in the priority areas determined by the General Assembly, and requested a progress report on the process for its 1984 session. The Committee recommended that future DPI reports, particularly on new or expansion of existing programmes, should contain: information on DPI output on each topic included in its work programme, which formed the basis of its programme budget; the costs of each activity; information on target audiences and end-use of DPI products; an analysis of feedback data received; DPI's evaluation of its effectiveness; and a statement detailing the priority which the Secretary-General attached to current or future activities. The Committee also considered, but not did reach agreement on, other proposals on evaluation procedures.

GENERAL ASSEMBLY ACTION

In resolution 38/82 B adopted in December, the General Assembly approved the recommendations of the Committee on Information (see above) and affirmed its requests and appeals.

Co-ordination in the UN system

JUNIC activities. The inter-agency committee established to co-ordinate information activities in the United Nations system, JUNIC, held a special session as well as its tenth regular session in 1983.

At the special session, held at Geneva from 7 to 9 March,[30] JUNIC drew up proposals on information support for development activities which it presented to its parent body, the Administrative Committee on Co-ordination (ACC), as requested. JUNIC emphasized that the proposals would not be fully effective unless adequate resources were applied. It recommended that *Development Forum*, an inter-agency publication on development questions, be strengthened through assured funding rather than on unpredictable voluntary contributions. JUNIC reached a consensus on the design of a common strategy, by which its members would review existing programmes and activities to stress such themes as the interdependence of economies of developed and developing countries, the need for a global approach to world problems, the complementarity of assistance channelled through the United Nations system, the favourable performance of the system relative to bilateral co-operation and the worsening plight of the least developed countries.

Another recommendation called for units launching new projects with widespread interest to alert information units throughout the system and allocate funds for information activities. As for operational services, JUNIC proposed the establishment of a daily telex news and feature service, to be managed by *Development Forum*, for use by the media. It called for a monthly United Nations system operations report to be added as an insert in *Development Forum*, and for an early warning briefing service to identify important future international issues and provide background

information for the media. JUNIC felt that the Non-Governmental Liaison Services at Geneva and New York could contribute to more regular exchanges of information among NGOs and between NGOs and the United Nations system. It proposed that special materials be prepared on subjects of global importance, such as world economic recovery and the United Nations, aid through the United Nations system, and the United Nations system in the development efforts of the developing countries. JUNIC proposed commissioning an internationally known writer to write a book on the last-mentioned topic. Another proposal called for a fellowship programme offering senior journalists the opportunity to work on *Development Forum* for three months.

At its tenth session held at Vienna from 19 to 22 April,[31] JUNIC discussed its 1982 report to ACC on public perceptions of the United Nations,[32] and noted that action had been initiated on a number of its proposals, including: information programmes of the United Nations system were being co-ordinated, starting with the preparation of the draft JUNIC plan of action for 1984-1985; and UNESCO was requested to initiate contacts with journalism and communications faculties. JUNIC agreed to undertake a common strategy for public information activities related to development assistance within existing resources by reordering and refocusing current projects and activities.

JUNIC approved the relocation of *Development Forum* from Geneva to New York with effect from January 1984. It agreed that the basic costs of the Non-Governmental Liaison Services at Geneva and New York should be assured on a long-term, predictable basis, where possible through regular budgetary support, and that JUNIC members which benefited from their services should ensure funding for special projects.

JUNIC discussed information projects on a number of future international conferences and years, international decades and special observances or campaigns. It accepted an invitation to United Nations organizations to participate in the 1985 international exposition in Japan (Tsukuba Expo) and decided to establish a task force to define guidelines for participation in such expositions in the future. Work was nearly completed on a television series on women and development, JUNIC noted. It agreed that an updated version of *Periodicals of the United Nations and Specialized Agencies* should be prepared.

With regard to its own planning, JUNIC noted that its biennial plan of action served as a framework for co-operation among United Nations organizations, and progress had been achieved as a result of the decision to base the plan on several specific projects related to priority topics, which were conceived, prepared, financed and implemented jointly. It agreed that the plan of action should be more clearly aligned with the programme budget biennium as was done in nearly all United Nations organizations.

In May, the JUNIC secretariat issued a report on its programme and updated plan of activities for 1982-1983.[33] The report identified items for ACC action, including: review of the 1981 and 1982 work of the Committee on Information; the 1982 JUNIC report on public perceptions of the United Nations;[32] and obtaining long-term financing for *Development Forum.*

According to the JUNIC secretariat, the activities of the Non-Governmental Liaison Services at Geneva and New York had enlarged in the light of new trends on the international scene, notably the emergence of the peace movement. The link between environment and development and that between disarmament and development were among the new areas which the Services were addressing. Regarding audio-visual production, the secretariat noted distribution problems and the question of a uniform pricing policy. In preparation for a special meeting of the *Ad Hoc* Working Group on Audio-Visual Matters, JUNIC recommended that an evaluation of United Nations organizations' experience in films and television over the previous 10 years be carried out. It noted that the co-operative venture entitled "Agenda for a Small Planet", a television series on North-South issues co-produced with national broadcasting organizations from 10 developed countries, had been completed in 1980 and was being expanded in a second series.

JUNIC said that the pooling of resources would lead to greater economy and efficiency and that jointly planned and financed projects should be pursued when objectives had been agreed for carefully identified audiences. It cautioned, however, that United Nations organizations needed to sustain separate profiles before the world community and it was possible that few subjects lent themselves to an overall approach. In that context, the JUNIC plan of action, which provided a framework for joint undertakings, needed to be flexible enough to accommodate all members of the system and should reflect efforts to promote a new world information and communication order.

In addition to ongoing joint projects, JUNIC planned new joint projects for 1983 in the areas of *apartheid*, disarmament and environment. Thirteen areas were chosen for individual projects to be co-ordinated through JUNIC: *apartheid*, disarmament, outer space, environment, the United Nations Decade for Women, aging, youth, trade and development, communications, the International Drinking Water Supply and Sanitation Dec-

ade, population, the Industrial Development Decade for Africa, and the world food problem.

CPC consideration. CPC considered the JUNIC programme and plan of activities in June 1983.[29] It recommended that JUNIC present a progress report, including a draft plan of action for 1984-1985, to CPC in 1984, and that JUNIC, together with UNESCO, study ways of strengthening co-operation in development education (see ECONOMIC AND SOCIAL QUESTIONS, Chapter I).

Consideration by the Committee on Information. At its 1983 session,[2] the Committee on Information also considered JUNIC activities. Among its recommendations to the General Assembly, the Committee proposed that JUNIC be enhanced and given more responsibility, thus improving the co-ordination and cost-benefit efficiency of United Nations public information activities, and that it strengthen its activities regarding development education and development-support communications. It proposed that the JUNIC recommendations on public perceptions be implemented, and that an appeal be addressed to Governments and mass media to transmit accurate information on United Nations activities. It called on the Secretary-General to support the publication of *Development Forum* from the regular budget while intensifying efforts to secure a sound and independent financial basis for continued publication. All United Nations organizations should be urged to contribute to financing the publication, which should retain its independent editorial policy. The Committee also recommended that the Secretary-General report on the status of financial arrangements for the publication of the *World Newspaper Supplement.*

GENERAL ASSEMBLY ACTION

The General Assembly, in resolution 38/82 B of 15 December, approved the Committee's recommendations, affirmed its requests and urged their implementation. The Assembly requested that JUNIC be strengthened and made more effective and that its secretariat elaborate new methods of work and longer-term indicative planning and joint action, especially in the promotion of a new world information and communication order.

REFERENCES

[1]YUN 1978, p. 1043, GA res. 33/115 C, 18 Dec. 1978. [2]A/38/21 & Corr.1. [3]A/38/457. [4]YUN 1982, p. 566, GA res. 37/94 A, 10 Dec. 1982. [5]YUN 1978, p. 1101. [6]YUN 1982, p. 567, GA res. 37/94 B, 10 Dec. 1982. [7]A/AC.198/70. [8]A/SPC/38/L.32. [9]YUN 1982, p. 173, GA res. 37/92, 10 Dec. 1982. [10]YUN 1973, p. 103, GA res. 3068(XXVIII), annex, 30 Nov. 1973. [11]E/1983/13 (res. 1983/50). [12]YUN 1966, p. 419, GA res. 2200 A (XXI), annex, 16 Dec. 1966. [13]YUN 1982, p. 1081, GA res. 37/194, annex, 18 Dec. 1982. [14]*Ibid.*, p. 1160, GA res. 37/63, annex, 3 Dec. 1982. [15]YUN 1960, p. 49, GA res. 1514(XV), 14 Dec. 1960. [16]A/38/387. [17]YUN 1980, p. 481, GA res. 35/201, 16 Dec. 1980. [18]YUN

1981, p. 363, GA res. 36/149 B, 16 Dec. 1981. [19]A/AC.198/62. [20]A/AC.198/63.   [21]A/AC.198/64.   [22]A/AC.198/65. [23]A/C.5/38/38. [24]A/38/7/Add.8. [25]YUN 1976, p. 904. [26]A/AC.198/61.   [27]E/AC.51/1983/7.   [28]A/AC.198/60. [29]A/38/38. [30]ACC/1983/13. [31]ACC/1983/19. [32]YUN 1982, p. 575. [33]E/AC.51/1983/8.

Radiation effects

The United Nations Scientific Committee on the Effects of Atomic Radiation (UNSCEAR) continued work on increasing knowledge of the levels, effects and risks of ionizing radiation from all sources. At its thirty-second session (Vienna, 20-24 June 1983),[1] it reviewed a document on dose-response relationships for radiation-induced cancer, which was being revised to include new dosimetry statistics of the survivors of Hiroshima and Nagasaki. It decided to study: the scientific bases for the evaluation of radiation risk and detriment; doses from natural sources of radiation with emphasis on the variability of such doses as a function of time and location; doses to the world population from nuclear explosions; the exposure arising from the nuclear fuel cycle, with emphasis on radioactive wastes; doses from medical use of radiation; the biological effects of pre-natal irradiation; the early effects of high doses of radiation on man; the genetic effects of irradiation; and radiation-induced tumours.

UNSCEAR discussed the type of information it would seek to continue its assessments of radiation exposure and effects, and provided guidance on the format and contents of the Secretariat documents to be produced for its studies. It hoped that United Nations Member States, the specialized agencies and IAEA would continue to assist in its work, especially by providing information relevant to its future programme of study, so that its deliberations could be based on the broadest and most up-to-date scientific and technical information. UNSCEAR believed that the United Nations Environment Programme would continue to support its activities and that the joint relationship would be maintained.

GENERAL ASSEMBLY ACTION

On 15 December 1983, the General Assembly, on the recommendation of the Special Political Committee, adopted resolution 38/78 without vote.

Effects of atomic radiation

The General Assembly,

Recalling its resolution 913(X) of 3 December 1955, by which it established the United Nations Scientific Committee on the Effects of Atomic Radiation, and its subsequent resolutions on the subject, including resolution 37/87 of 10 December 1982, by which the Assembly, *inter alia*, requested the Scientific Committee to continue its work,

Taking note with appreciation of the report of the United Nations Scientific Committee on the Effects of Atomic Radiation,

Reaffirming the desirability of the Scientific Committee continuing its work,

Concerned about the potentially harmful effects on present and future generations, resulting from the levels of radiation to which man is exposed,

Conscious of the continued need to examine and compile information about atomic and ionizing radiation and to analyse its effects on man and his environment,

Taking note of the decision of the Scientific Committee to submit shorter reports with scientific supporting documents on the specialized topics mentioned in its report, as soon as the relevant studies are completed,

1. *Commends* the United Nations Scientific Committee on the Effects of Atomic Radiation for the valuable contribution it has been making in the course of the past twenty-eight years, since its inception, to wider knowledge and understanding of the levels, effects and risks of atomic radiation and for fulfilling its original mandate with scientific authority and independence of judgement;

2. *Notes with satisfaction* the continued and growing scientific co-operation between the Scientific Committee and the United Nations Environment Programme;

3. *Requests* the Scientific Committee to continue its work, including its important co-ordinating activities, to increase knowledge of the levels, effects and risks of ionizing radiation from all sources;

4. *Endorses* the Scientific Committee's intentions and plans for its future activities of scientific review and assessment on behalf of the General Assembly;

5. *Requests* the Scientific Committee to continue at its next session the review of important problems in the field of radiation and to report thereon to the General Assembly at its thirty-ninth session;

6. *Requests* the United Nations Environment Programme to continue providing support for the effective conduct of the Scientific Committee's work and for the dissemination of its findings to the General Assembly, the scientific community and the public;

7. *Expresses its appreciation* for the assistance rendered to the Scientific Committee by Member States, the specialized agencies, the International Atomic Energy Agency and non-governmental organizations, and invites them to increase their co-operation in this field;

8. *Invites* Member States and the organizations of the United Nations system and non-governmental organizations concerned to provide further relevant data about doses, effects and risks from various sources of radiation, which would greatly help in the preparation of the Scientific Committee's future reports to the General Assembly.

General Assembly resolution 38/78

15 December 1983   Meeting 98   Adopted without vote

Approved by SPC (A/38/519) without vote, 7 October (meeting 4); 21-nation draft (A/SPC/38/L.2); agenda item 68.

Sponsors: Argentina, Australia, Austria, Canada, Chile, Czechoslovakia, Denmark, Egypt, Ethiopia, France, Germany, Federal Republic of, Indonesia, Japan, Netherlands, New Zealand, Poland, Sri Lanka, Sweden, USSR, United States, Uruguay.

Meeting numbers. GA 38th session: SPC 3, 4; plenary 98.

REFERENCE

[1]A/38/142.

Antarctica

In a letter dated 11 August 1983 to the Secretary-General,[1] Antigua and Barbuda, and Malaysia, stating that there was a need to examine the possibility for a more positive and wider international concert to ensure that activities carried out in Antarctica were for the benefit of mankind as a whole, requested that the question of Antarctica be included in the agenda of the 1983 General Assembly session. Referring to that letter on 5 October,[2] Australia, on behalf of the consultative parties to the Antarctic Treaty (1959), said that the Treaty, which was open to all countries and was of unlimited duration, served the international community well and had averted international strife and sovereignty disputes over Antarctica; for these reasons, the parties had reservations about the initiative of Antigua and Barbuda and Malaysia and about any attempt to revise or replace the current Treaty system.

GENERAL ASSEMBLY ACTION

On 15 December 1983, the General Assembly adopted resolution 38/77 without vote, on the recommendation of the First Committee.

Question of Antarctica
The General Assembly,

Having considered the item entitled "Question of Antarctica",

Conscious of the increasing international awareness of and interest in Antarctica,

Bearing in mind the Antarctic Treaty and the significance of the system it has developed,

Taking into account the debate on this item at its thirty-eighth session,

Convinced of the advantages of a better knowledge of Antarctica,

Affirming the conviction that, in the interest of all mankind, Antarctica should continue forever to be used exclusively for peaceful purposes and that it should not become the scene or object of international discord,

Recalling the relevant paragraphs of the Economic Declaration adopted by the Seventh Conference of Heads of State or Government of the Non-Aligned Countries, held at New Delhi from 7 to 12 March 1983,

1. *Requests* the Secretary-General to prepare a comprehensive, factual and objective study on all aspects of Antarctica, taking fully into account the Antarctic Treaty system and other relevant factors;

2. *Also requests* the Secretary-General to seek the views of all Member States in the preparation of the study;

3. *Requests* those States conducting scientific research in Antarctica, other interested States, the relevant specialized agencies, organs, organizations and bodies of the United Nations system and relevant international organizations having scientific or technical information on Antarctica to lend the Secretary-General whatever assistance he may request for the purpose of carrying out the study;

4. *Requests* the Secretary-General to report to the General Assembly at its thirty-ninth session;

5. *Decides* to include in the provisional agenda of its thirty-ninth session the item entitled "Question of Antarctica".

General Assembly resolution 38/77

15 December 1983   Meeting 97   Adopted without vote

Approved by First Committee (A/38/646) without vote, 30 November (meeting 46); 12-nation draft (A/C.1/38/L.80); agenda item 140.
Sponsors: Antigua and Barbuda, Bangladesh, Indonesia, Malaysia, Oman, Pakistan, Philippines, Singapore, Sri Lanka, Thailand, Turkey, Uganda.
Meeting numbers. GA 38th session: 1st Committee 42-46; plenary 97.

During the First Committee's consideration of the matter, Sierra Leone, on behalf of the African Group, submitted and subsequently withdrew an amendment[3] to the draft text, by which the Assembly would have expressed concern that the *apartheid* régime of South Africa had been allowed to remain a party to the Treaty.

REFERENCES
[1]A/38/193 & Corr.1. [2]A/38/439/Rev.1. [3]A/C.1/38/L.84.

Chapter XI

Institutional machinery

During 1983, the membership of the United Nations rose to 158 with the admission of Saint Christopher and Nevis.

In addition to its agenda, the Security Council considered ways of enhancing its role as an instrument for the maintenance of international peace and security, focusing on five aspects: preventing conflicts, promoting negotiations and peaceful settlement procedures, implementing its resolutions and decisions and strengthening its peace-keeping operations, giving effect to Article 43 of the Charter of the United Nations including the role envisaged for the Military Staff Committee, and improving procedures for the Council's efficient functioning.

The General Assembly resumed and concluded its thirty-seventh session in 1983. During its thirty-eighth session, the Assembly considered 141 items of its 146-item agenda and decided to consider the remainder in 1984.

Among the major political activities of the Secretary-General in 1983 was the exercise of his good offices on the questions of Cyprus, the Falkland Islands (Malvinas) and Namibia. His annual report to the Assembly on the Organization's work (p. 3) stressed that institutional machinery should be utilized.

The Assembly acted on co-operation between the United Nations and six intergovernmental organizations.

In other action, the Assembly also set in motion preparatory activities for the commemoration of the fortieth anniversary of the United Nations in 1985.

Topics related to this chapter. Africa: co-operation between OAU and the UN system. Regional economic and social activities: co-operation between the Southern African Development Co-ordination Conference and the United Nations. Institutional machinery (economic and social): organization of work of the General Assembly's Second and Third Committees; co-operation between the Agency for Cultural and Technical Co-operation and the United Nations. Intergovernmental organizations and international law: UN institutional machinery; implementation of UN resolutions; rules of procedure of UN conferences. Other legal questions: co-operation between the Asian-African Legal Consultative Committee and the United Nations. Other administrative and management questions: calendar of meetings.

UN Members

During 1983, the number of Member States of the United Nations rose to 158 when Saint Christopher and Nevis was admitted to membership on 23 September. The General Assembly took this action when it adopted resolution 38/1, as recommended by the Security Council in resolution 537(1983).

Saint Christopher and Nevis

Saint Christopher and Nevis, a Caribbean island country formerly administered by the United Kingdom, attained independence on 19 September 1983 and applied for membership by a letter of the same date.[1]

SECURITY COUNCIL ACTION

On 22 September, the Security Council unanimously adopted resolution 537(1983).

The Security Council,
Having examined the application of Saint Christopher and Nevis for admission to the United Nations,
Recommends to the General Assembly that Saint Christopher and Nevis should be admitted to membership in the United Nations.

Security Council resolution 537(1983)

22 September 1983   Meeting 2479   Adopted unanimously

Unanimously recommended by Committee on Admission of New Members (S/15997), 22 September (meeting 70).
Meeting numbers. SC: 2478, 2479.

GENERAL ASSEMBLY ACTION

On 23 September, acting on the recommendation of the Security Council, as transmitted by its President in a letter of 22 September,[2] the General Assembly adopted resolution 38/1 by acclamation.

Admission of Saint Christopher and Nevis to membership in the United Nations

The General Assembly,
Having received the recommendation of the Security Council of 22 September 1983 that Saint Christopher and Nevis should be admitted to membership in the United Nations,
Having considered the application for membership of Saint Christopher and Nevis,
Decides to admit Saint Christopher and Nevis to membership in the United Nations.

General Assembly resolution 38/1

23 September 1983   Meeting 3   Adopted by acclamation

51-nation draft (A/38/L.1 and Add.1); agenda item 19.

Sponsors: Antigua and Barbuda, Australia, Bahamas, Bangladesh, Barbados, Belgium, Belize, Canada, China, Denmark, Dominica, Ecuador, Fiji, Finland, France, Germany, Federal Republic of, Ghana, Greece, Grenada, Guyana, India, Indonesia, Ireland, Italy, Jamaica, Jordan, Kenya, Lesotho, Libyan Arab Jamahiriya, Luxembourg, Mali, Malta, Netherlands, New Zealand, Nigeria, Norway, Pakistan, Papua New Guinea, Saint Lucia, Saint Vincent and the Grenadines, Samoa, Sierra Leone, Singapore, Solomon Islands, Sri Lanka, Togo, Trinidad and Tobago, United Kingdom, United States, Zambia, Zimbabwe.

Meeting number. GA 38th session: plenary 3.

REFERENCES

[1]A/38/424-S/15989. [2]A/38/442.

Security Council

The Security Council held 98 meetings in 1983 and adopted 17 resolutions.

Meeting numbers. SC: 2411-2508.

On 12 September, in accordance with a decision taken during consultations held on 17 August, on the Secretary-General's 1982 report on the work of the Organization,[1] the Council President issued the following note:[2]

"1.   In the context of their constant endeavours to enhance the effectiveness of the Security Council and against the background of a precarious international situation, the members of the Council welcomed the valuable, thought-provoking ideas and observations contained in the report of the Secretary-General on the work of the Organization, which contributed to wide-ranging exchanges of views among members of the Council, carried out in a constructive spirit.

"2.   In order to initiate and facilitate these exchanges in a flexible manner, discussion was structured under five main aspects, as follows:

"*(a)*   The role of the Council in the prevention of conflicts, including both measures by the Council under the relevant Articles of the Charter and its response to situations brought to its attention by Member States or by the Secretary-General under Articles 35 and 99;

"*(b)*   The role of the Council in promoting negotiations or other peaceful settlement procedures between the parties to a dispute, including the part which the Council might itself play in such procedures;

"*(c)*   Implementation of resolutions of the Council, including measures to give effect to its decisions as well as to strengthen United Nations peace-keeping operations and ensure respect for the tasks assigned to peace-keeping forces by the Council;

"*(d)*   Measures for giving effect to Article 43 of the Charter, including the role envisaged for the Military Staff Committee in Articles 43 to 47;

"*(e)*   Procedural improvements designed to facilitate the effective exercise by the Council of its functions under the Charter.

"3.   In the course of the discussion, spread over 18 meetings in informal consultations, many ideas were generated and specific suggestions were also made under each aspect; it was self-evident that most of them required careful analysis and detailed study.

"4.   The members of the Council therefore recognized that the examination of suggestions on possible ways and means to enhance the effectiveness of the Security Council, including those contained in the Secretary-General's report, was an ongoing exercise, not yet completed, that required further detailed consideration.

"5.   Throughout the debate, members stressed the validity and vitality of the purposes and principles of the United Nations and of the Charter and, in the first instance, the duty of all Member States to fulfil in good faith the obligations assumed by them under the Charter, particularly those relating to the peaceful settlement of disputes and the maintenance of international peace and security.

"6.   Within this context, they recalled the obligation of Member States to accept and carry out decisions of the Council, as well as the need for their continuing support to enhance implementation of those decisions.

"7.   Members reaffirmed the need to strengthen the effectiveness of the Security Council in fulfilling its primary responsibility for the maintenance of international peace and security, including procedures for promoting more systematic use of the Council.

"8.   Members considered essential the further development of a 'collegial spirit' among the members of the Council, including adequate working relations among its permanent members.

"9.   Members of the Council noted the clear distinction envisaged in the Charter between the functions and specific powers of the Council and those of the other principal organs of the United Nations and urged all Member States to keep that important distinction in mind.

"10.   Members stressed the option for the establishment of subsidiary organs in accordance with Article 29 as a practical measure when considered necessary.

"11.   Members of the Council also stressed the importance of, and sensed positive prospects in the future for, timely and appropriate action by the Council to prevent, under the relevant provisions of the Charter, aggravation of particular situations or disputes.

"12.   To this end, members of the Council considered measures which would facilitate prompt and effective action by the Council and enable it to recommend appropriate procedures or methods of adjustment.

"13.   In this context, consideration was given to making more effective the existing technical information-gathering capabilities of the Secretariat of the United Nations and the accessibility of this information to members of the Council.

"14.   In the same context, consideration was also given to enhancing the means for the Council to dispatch fact-finding missions or missions of inquiry.

"15.   The members considered the question of holding periodic meetings of the Council and the desirability of holding occasional meetings outside Headquarters, as well as holding meetings at the highest possible level.

"16.   Consideration was also given to strengthening and ensuring respect for United Nations peace-keeping operations.

"17. Members heard suggestions on the possibility of activating the work of the Military Staff Committee in fulfilling the tasks assigned to it under the Charter.

"18. Members considered many other aspects of the work of the Security Council, including suggestions designed to revitalize the concept of collective international security, and other innovative proposals designed to enhance the effectiveness of the Council.

"19. Members sensed that certain elements of convergence in their discussions, which offered greater prospects for progress, merited priority consideration. They are prepared to examine these and all other relevant aspects that may still be raised or brought to their attention."

Acting on the suggestions put forward by the Council President's note, the General Assembly, by resolution 38/73 H on disarmament and international security, requested the Council to expedite the conclusion of agreements making armed forces available to the Council to render operative the collective security system provided for in the Charter and thereby facilitate disarmament negotiations. Also, by resolution 38/190 on the Declaration on the Strengthening of International Security, the Assembly emphasized the urgency of examining all existing mechanisms and working methods to enhance the Council's authority and enforcement capacity, and the need to hold periodic meetings of the Council to review outstanding problems and crises; taking note of the Council's failure to report on its implementation of the foregoing, the Assembly hoped that the Council would do so in 1984.

The question of maintenance of international peace and security was considered in 1983 by a Working Group of the whole of the Special Committee on the Charter of the United Nations and on the Strengthening of the Role of the Organization[3] (see LEGAL QUESTIONS, Chapter IV). The Group discussed a revised draft recommendation on ways to enhance the Council's effectiveness, presented in 1982 by Egypt on behalf of Committee members belonging to the Movement of Non-Aligned Countries[4]—including suggestions made by Japan relating to the principle of unanimity among Council permanent members in non-procedural matters; examined two proposals submitted previously by France[4]—one containing draft amendments to the Assembly's rules of procedure concerning emergency special sessions and the other a proposal for informal hearings by the Council of the views of parties to a conflict; and discussed a draft list of proposals that had been made on the question, prepared by Romania, identifying those of special interest, as requested by the Assembly in December 1982.[5]

Agenda

During 1983—its thirty-eighth year—the Security Council considered 19 agenda items. It continued the practice of adopting at each meeting the agenda for that meeting. (For list of agenda items, see APPENDIX IV.)

Nine of the items were included for the first time in the Council's agenda. They concerned complaints by the Libyan Arab Jamahiriya against the United States (two items), complaints by Chad against the Libyan Arab Jamahiriya (two items), complaints by Nicaragua (three items), the downing of a Korean Air Lines passenger airliner, and the situation in Grenada.

In a 22 September note,[6] the Secretary-General notified the General Assembly, in accordance with Article 12, paragraph 2, of the United Nations Charter, of 15 matters relative to the maintenance of international peace and security which the Council had discussed since his previous annual notification.[7] He listed 94 other matters of which the Council remained seized but which it had not discussed during the period.

In addition, the Council, in fulfilment of its responsibilities for the maintenance of international peace and security, was asked by the Assembly, in resolution 38/69 on Israeli nuclear armament, to implement Council resolution 487(1981)[8] and ensure that Israel complied and placed its nuclear facilities under International Atomic Energy Agency safeguards. The Council was also asked, in resolution 38/181 B on the nuclear capability of South Africa, to take enforcement measures to prevent any racist régimes from acquiring arms or arms technology and to block loopholes in the arms embargo, as recommended by the Committee established by Council resolution 421(1977)[9] concerning the question of South Africa.

GENERAL ASSEMBLY ACTION

On an oral proposal by its President, the General Assembly adopted decision 38/404 without vote.

Notification by the Secretary-General under Article 12, paragraph 2, of the Charter of the United Nations

At its 39th plenary meeting, on 28 October 1983, the General Assembly took note of the note by the Secretary-General dated 22 September 1983.

General Assembly decision 38/404

Adopted without vote

Oral proposal by President; agenda item 7.
Meeting number. GA 38th session: plenary 39.

Members

In 1983, as in the previous year,[10] the question of equitable representation on and increase in the membership of the Security Council was not considered.

On an oral proposal by its President, who stated that no request for consideration of the Council's membership had been made during the session, the General Assembly adopted decision 38/454 without vote.

Question of equitable representation on and increase in the membership of the Security Council

At its 104th plenary meeting, on 20 December 1983, the General Assembly decided to include in the provisional agenda of its thirty-ninth session the item entitled "Question of equitable representation on and increase in the membership of the Security Council".

General Assembly decision 38/454

Adopted without vote

Oral proposal by President; agenda item 39.
Meeting number. GA 38th session: plenary 104.

Security Council report

SECURITY COUNCIL ACTION

At its 2494th meeting, on 11 November 1983, the Security Council considered its draft report to the General Assembly covering the period from 16 June 1982 to 15 June 1983[11] and adopted it unanimously.

GENERAL ASSEMBLY ACTION

On an oral proposal by its President, the Assembly adopted decision 38/424 without vote.

Report of the Security Council

At its 99th plenary meeting, on 16 December 1983, the General Assembly took note of the report of the Security Council.

General Assembly decision 38/424

Adopted without vote

Oral proposal by President; agenda item 11.
Meeting number. GA 38th session: plenary 99.

REFERENCES
[1]YUN 1982, p. 3. [2]S/15971. [3]A/38/33. [4]YUN 1982, p. 1388. [5]*Ibid.*, p. 1389, GA res. 37/114, 16 Dec. 1982. [6]A/38/438. [7]YUN 1982, p. 581. [8]YUN 1981, p. 282, SC res. 487(1981), 19 June 1981. [9]YUN 1977, p. 162, SC res. 421(1977), 9 Dec. 1977. [10]YUN 1982, p. 582. [11]A/38/2.

PUBLICATIONS
Index to Proceedings of the Security Council, Thirty-eighth Year, 1983 (ST/LIB/SER.B/S.20 & Corr.1,2), Sales No. E.84.I.9 & corrigenda. *Resolutions and Decisions of the Security Council, 1983,* S/INF/39.

General Assembly

The General Assembly met in two separate sessions during 1983, to conclude its thirty-seventh regular session and to hold the major part of its thirty-eighth session.

The thirty-seventh session, which had opened on 21 September 1982 and had been suspended on 21 December,[1] was resumed from 10 to 13 May 1983 and on 19 September, closing that day.

The thirty-eighth regular session was opened on 20 September and continued until 20 December, when it was suspended. During the period of the Assembly's general debate, from 26 September to 14 October, 146 statements were made by heads of State or Government and by other heads or members of delegations.

GENERAL ASSEMBLY ACTION

Following a statement by its President that consideration of the agenda had been concluded with the exception of five items and one sub-item, the General Assembly adopted decision 38/456 without vote.

Suspension of the thirty-eighth session

At its 104th plenary meeting, on 20 December 1983, the General Assembly decided to resume its thirty-eighth session, at a date to be announced, for the sole purpose of considering the following agenda items:

Item 15 *(b)*: Election of one member of the Economic and Social Council;

Item 38: Launching of global negotiations on international economic co-operation for development;

Item 40: Observance of the quincentenary of the discovery of America;

Item 41: Question of Cyprus;

Item 42: Implementation of the resolutions of the United Nations;

Item 138: Consequences of the prolongation of the armed conflict between Iran and Iraq.

General Assembly decision 38/456

Adopted without vote

Oral proposal by President; agenda item 8.
Meeting number. GA 38th session: plenary 104.

Agenda

As decided by the General Assembly in December 1982,[2] four items remained on the agenda for consideration at its resumed thirty-seventh session. However, only two were considered, including the substantive one on the question of Cyprus. On the recommendation of its General Committee,[3] the Assembly decided to consider the item directly in plenary meetings.[4] In the Committee, a proposal by Cyprus to allocate the item to the plenary Assembly had been adopted by 21 votes to 1, with 5 abstentions; as a result, no action was taken on a proposal by Turkey to have it allocated to the Special Political Committee. The other two items, on launching global economic negotiations and on implementing United Nations resolutions, were deferred to the thirty-eighth session and included in that session's draft agenda by Assembly decisions 37/456 and 37/457.

The items inscribed in the agenda of the Assembly's thirty-eighth session[5] (annotated by the Secretariat[6]) numbered 146, all of which were recommended by the General Committee without vote. The Committee's action was taken on 21 September on the basis of a provisional agenda of 138 items[7] and a supplementary list of 4 items[8] and a sub-item proposed prior to the session; and on 4, 11 and 31 October and 14 December, of an additional 5 items and a sub-item proposed for inclusion during the session. One item, concerning East Timor (see TRUSTEESHIP AND DECOLONIZATION, Chapter IV), was recommended, also without vote, for deferment to the thirty-ninth (1984) session. The Committee also recommended allocating each of the items, with the exception of the question of Cyprus, to one of the Assembly's Main Committees or directly to plenary meetings.[9]

The additional items recommended for inclusion were on: condemnation of nuclear war, a nuclear-weapon freeze, preparations for the 1985 Review Conference of the Parties to the Treaty on the Non-Proliferation of Nuclear Weapons, and conclusion of a treaty prohibiting the use of force in outer space (see Chapter I of this section); the situations in Central America and in Grenada (see Chapter VI of this section); the Iran-Iraq conflict (see Chapter VII of this section); Antarctica (see Chapter X of this section); and the commemoration of the fortieth anniversary of the United Nations in 1985 (see below). The new sub-items were on the new international human order (see ECONOMIC AND SOCIAL QUESTIONS, Chapter I) and the appointment of a member of the International Civil Service Commission (see APPENDIX III).

GENERAL ASSEMBLY ACTION

Following its examination of the General Committee's recommendations, the General Assembly adopted decision 38/402 without vote.

Adoption of the agenda and allocation of agenda items

At its 3rd, 4th, 21st, 28th, 32nd, 41st and 96th plenary meetings, on 23 September, 6, 11 and 13 October, 1 November and 14 December 1983, the General Assembly, on the recommendations of the General Committee as set forth in its first, second, third, fourth, fifth and sixth reports, adopted the agenda and the allocation of agenda items for the thirty-eighth session.

At its 3rd plenary meeting, on 23 September 1983, the General Assembly, on the recommendation of the General Committee, decided to include in the provisional agenda of its thirty-ninth session the item entitled "Question of East Timor".

General Assembly decision 38/402

Adopted without vote

Approved by General Committee (A/38/250 & Add.1-5), 21 September, 4, 11, 13 and 31 October and 14 December (meetings 1-7); agenda item 8.

Meeting numbers. GA 38th session: General Committee 1-7; plenary 3, 4, 21, 28, 32, 40, 41, 96.

Organization of work

Based on suggestions by the Secretary-General[10] and the Committee on Conferences,[11] the General Committee, in its first report dated 21 September,[12] made a number of recommendations concerning the organization of the thirty-eighth session of the General Assembly.

These organizational arrangements set a daily timetable for meetings, fixed the duration of the general debate, and recommended 20 December as the session's closing date. They called for limits on explanations of vote and on the reproduction of speeches in meeting records, agreement among regional groups on the distribution of Main Committee chairmanships for the following session, setting a deadline of not later than 1 December for submitting draft resolutions with financial implications as well as deadlines for submitting subsidiary organ reports requiring consideration by the Fifth (Administrative and Budgetary) Committee, and providing a 48-hour period between submission of and voting on proposals involving expenditure, to permit preparation of statements of administrative and financial implications. The Assembly was to urge all Member States and subsidiary organs to exercise maximum restraint in requesting circulation of material as official documents.

Also recommended were authorization—subsequently granted by Assembly decision 38/403—for certain subsidiary organs to meet during the session; and for smoking to be prohibited in small conference rooms and discouraged in large ones. The rationalization of work of the Assembly's Second (Economic and Financial) Committee was the subject of Assembly decision 38/429.

Pursuant to a 1982 Assembly request,[13] a Working Group of the whole of the Special Committee on the Charter of the United Nations and on the Strengthening of the Role of the Organization (see LEGAL QUESTIONS, Chapter IV) held eight meetings between 14 and 18 April 1983 to consider Member States' proposals to rationalize existing United Nations procedures. The proposals were contained in working papers submitted by 11 States.

GENERAL ASSEMBLY ACTION

Acting on the General Committee's recommendations, the General Assembly adopted decision 38/401 without vote.

Organization of the thirty-eighth session

At its 3rd plenary meeting, on 23 September 1983, the General Assembly, on the recommendations of the General Committee as set forth in its first report, adopted a number of provisions concerning the organization of the thirty-eighth session.

General Assembly decision 38/401

Adopted without vote

Approved by General Committee (A/38/250) without vote, 21 September (meeting 1); suggestions by Secretary-General (A/BUR/38/1) and by Committee on Conferences (A/38/414 and Add.1); agenda item 8.
Meeting numbers. GA 38th session: General Committee 1; plenary 3.

Credentials

On 12 October 1983, the Credentials Committee examined a memorandum dated the day before from the Secretary-General on the status of credentials of representatives to the General Assembly's thirty-eighth session. The memorandum indicated that formal credentials had been submitted by 115 Member States. At the meeting, the Legal Counsel provided supplementary information that credentials had been received from a further five Members.

Statements in connection with the credentials of Afghanistan, Chile and Democratic Kampuchea were made during the debate.

China and the United States, while not raising formal objection to the credentials of Afghanistan, said their position did not imply acceptance of a régime installed by foreign occupation; the USSR on the other hand considered those remarks inadmissible interference in the internal affairs of a Member State. The USSR also reaffirmed its non-recognition of the credentials of Chile, and reiterated its opposition to those of Democratic Kampuchea (see Chapter VII of this section). Colombia and the United States held that there was no basis for questioning Chile's credentials.

The Committee, acting without vote, adopted a resolution orally proposed by its Chairman by which it accepted the credentials received, taking into account the various reservations expressed during the debate. It also submitted a draft resolution to the Assembly recommending approval of its report.[14]

GENERAL ASSEMBLY ACTION

On 20 October, on the recommendation of the Credentials Committee, the General Assembly adopted resolution 38/2 without vote.

Credentials of representatives to the thirty-eighth session of the General Assembly

The General Assembly

Approves the first report of the Credentials Committee.

General Assembly resolution 38/2

20 October 1983   Meeting 34   Adopted without vote

Approved by Credentials Committee (A/38/508) without vote, 12 October (meeting 1); oral proposal by Chairman; agenda item 3 *(b)*.
Meeting number. GA 38th session: plenary 34.

Before adopting the resolution, the Assembly decided, by a recorded vote of 79 to 43, with 19 abstentions, not to act on an amendment by Iran to reject the credentials of Israel. The formal motion for this action had been made by Norway also on behalf of Denmark, Finland, Iceland and Sweden. Reservations concerning those credentials had been entered by 50 States (see Chapter IX of this section).

Kampuchea's representation in United Nations bodies was also the subject of communications (see Chapter VII of this section).

REFERENCES

[1]YUN 1982, p. 583. [2]*Ibid.*, GA dec. 37/452, 21 Dec. 1982. [3]A/37/250/Add.4. [4]A/37/252/Add.4. [5]A/38/251 & Add.1-4. [6]A/38/100 & Add.1. [7]A/38/150. [8]A/38/200. [9]A/38/250 & Add.1-5. [10]A/BUR/38/1. [11]A/38/414 & Add.1. [12]A/38/250. [13]YUN 1982, p. 1389, GA res. 37/114, 16 Dec. 1982. [14]A/38/508.

PUBLICATIONS

Index to Proceedings of the General Assembly, Thirty-eighth session— 1983/1984, 20 September 1983–17 September 1984 (ST/LIB/SER.B/A.37, Parts I-III), Sales No. E.84.I.17 (Parts I-III). *Resolutions and Decisions adopted by the General Assembly during its Thirty-eighth Session, 20 September–20 December 1983 and 26 June 1984,* A/38/47 & Add.1.

Secretary-General

The urgent necessity of developing and using international institutional machinery was stressed by the Secretary-General in his September 1983 annual report to the General Assembly on the work of the Organization (p. 3).

The Assembly took note of the report when it adopted decision 38/410 in December.

Good offices

During 1983, the Secretary-General pursued several missions of good offices which had been entrusted to him by either the Security Council or the General Assembly. These efforts concerned the questions of Cyprus, the Falkland Islands (Malvinas) and Namibia.

With regard to Cyprus, the Secretary-General's efforts were aimed at bringing about a resumption of the intercommunal negotiating process between the Greek Cypriot and Turkish Cypriot communities (see Chapter VIII of this section).

On the question of Namibia, the Secretary-General held discussions with South African authorities on the urgency of communicating to him their choice of an electoral system for electing the Constituent Assembly of Namibia in order to facilitate the immediate and unconditional implementation of Council resolution 435(1978) embodying the United Nations plan for Namibia's independence (see TRUSTEESHIP AND DECOLONIZATION, Chapter III).

The Secretary-General also undertook a renewed mission of good offices to assist Argentina and the United Kingdom to resume negotiations in order to find a peaceful solution to their sovereignty dispute over the Falkland Islands (Malvinas) (see TRUSTEESHIP AND DECOLONIZATION, Chapter IV).

Co-operation between the United Nations and other intergovernmental organizations

In 1983, the General Assembly adopted without vote five resolutions and a decision on co-operation between the United Nations and the following intergovernmental organizations: the League of Arab States, and the Organization of the Islamic Conference (see below); the Organization of African Unity (see Chapter V of this section); the Southern African Development Co-ordination Conference, and the Agency for Cultural and Technical Co-operation (see ECONOMIC AND SOCIAL QUESTIONS, Chapters VIII and XXIV); and the Asian-African Legal Consultative Committee (see LEGAL QUESTIONS, Chapter VII).

League of Arab States

In accordance with a November 1982 request by the General Assembly,[1] the Secretary-General reported in 1983[2] on the state of co-operation between the United Nations and the League of Arab States, resulting from a meeting which they held from 28 June to 1 July at Tunis, Tunisia.

The Secretary-General noted that, at the meeting, the United Nations system and the League's General Secretariat and specialized organizations considered six main areas of co-operation: international peace and security (disarmament matters and settlement of the Middle East conflict and the Iran-Iraq war, among others); economic, financial and technical co-operation for development (trade and development, development financing, industrial development, energy, minerals, transnational corporations, human settlements, environment, population, civil aviation, maritime transport, postal services), within the framework of the Strategy for Joint Arab Economic Development adopted in 1980;[3] food and agriculture; social development, labour, human resources and cultural affairs; refugees, disaster prevention and emergency relief and human rights promotion; and information and communications.

Proposed general principles for the strategy of co-operation between the two organizations were also considered.

The meeting's Chairman observed that the recommendations agreed upon could be categorized as specific proposals lending themselves to early consideration by competent parties at either the bilateral or multilateral level, and general proposals requiring further elaboration. Certain other proposals were regarded as expressions of intent or interest and

needed to be developed. Follow-up action was also recommended.

Earlier in the year, at the request of the League's Secretariat, Jordan transmitted to the Secretary-General on 28 February[4] a document entitled "Charter of National Economic Action", adopted at the Eleventh Arab Summit Conference (Amman, Jordan, November 1980), for dissemination to Member States.

During the year, the League's Permanent Observer to the United Nations made a statement at four Security Council meetings, to which he had been invited to participate in accordance with rule 39[a] of the Council's provisional rules of procedure. Those meetings dealt with the dispute between the Libyan Arab Jamahiriya and the United States, Namibia, the settlement policy in territories occupied by Israel, and the situation in Grenada.

On 28 October, the General Assembly adopted resolution 38/6 without vote.

Co-operation between the United Nations and the League of Arab States

The General Assembly,

Recalling its previous resolutions on the promotion of co-operation between the United Nations and the League of Arab States, in particular resolutions 36/24 of 9 November 1981 and 37/17 of 16 November 1982,

Having considered the report of the Secretary-General on co-operation between the United Nations and the League of Arab States,

Having heard the statement of the Permanent Observer of the League of Arab States on co-operation between the United Nations and the League of Arab States and having noted the emphasis placed therein on follow-up projects, actions and procedures on the recommendations adopted at the meeting between representatives of the General Secretariat of the League of Arab States and its specialized organizations and the secretariats of the United Nations and other organizations of the United Nations system, held at Tunis from 28 June to 1 July 1983, as well as on various sectoral activities related to development priorities in the Arab region,

Recalling the relevant articles of the Charter of the United Nations which encourage activities through regional arrangements for the promotion of the purposes and principles of the United Nations,

Noting with appreciation the desire of the League of Arab States to consolidate and develop the existing ties with the United Nations in all areas relating to the maintenance of international peace and security, and to co-operate in every possible way with the United Nations in the implementation of United Nations resolutions relating to the question of Palestine and the situation in the Middle East,

---

[a]Rule 39 of the Council's provisional rules of procedure states: "The Security Council may invite members of the Secretariat or other persons, whom it considers competent for the purpose, to supply it with information or to give it other assistance in examining matters within its competence."

Noting that the convening of the Tunis meeting in compliance with General Assembly resolution 37/17 afforded both sides an opportunity to review, in a comprehensive manner, the state of co-operation that has developed during more than three decades between their respective agencies and organizations,

Aware of the vital importance for the countries members of the League of Arab States of achieving a just, comprehensive and durable solution to the Middle East conflict and the question of Palestine, the core of the conflict,

Realizing that the strengthening of international peace and security is directly related, *inter alia*, to disarmament, decolonization, self-determination and the eradication of all forms of racism and racial discrimination,

Convinced that the strengthening and furtherance of co-operation between the United Nations and the organizations of the United Nations system and the League of Arab States contribute to the work of the United Nations system and to the promotion of the purposes and principles of the United Nations,

Noting that the Tunis meeting defined the framework of co-operation between the United Nations and the League of Arab States in certain priority sectors, without determining specific projects that could lend themselves to joint implementation,

Recognizing the need for closer co-operation between the United Nations system and the League of Arab States and its specialized organizations in realizing the goals and objectives set forth in the Strategy for Joint Arab Economic Development adopted by the Eleventh Arab Summit Conference, held at Amman from 25 to 27 November 1980,

1. *Takes note with satisfaction* of the report of the Secretary-General;

2. *Expresses its appreciation* to the Secretary-General for his efforts towards the organization of the meeting between representatives of the General Secretariat of the League of Arab States and its specialized organizations and the secretariats of the United Nations and other organizations of the United Nations system, held at Tunis from 28 June to 1 July 1983, as well as to the specialized agencies and other organizations of the United Nations system for their substantive contributions to that meeting;

3. *Commends* the General Secretariat of the League of Arab States and its specialized organizations for their active involvement in the preparations for the Tunis meeting and for their sustained endeavours towards its success;

4. *Requests* the Secretary-General to intensify his efforts towards the implementation of United Nations resolutions relevant to the question of Palestine and the situation in the Middle East;

5. *Requests* the secretariats of the United Nations and the League of Arab States, within their respective fields of competence, to intensify their co-operation towards the realization of the purposes and principles of the Charter of the United Nations, the strengthening of international peace and security, disarmament, decolonization, self-determination and the eradication of all forms of racism and racial discrimination;

6. *Requests* the Secretary-General to strengthen co-operation and co-ordination between the United Nations and the organizations of the United Nations system and the League of Arab States in order to enhance their capacity to serve the mutual interests of the two organizations in the political, economic, social and cultural fields;

7. *Calls upon* the competent bodies of the United Nations, the specialized agencies and other organizations of the United Nations system to give urgent consideration to the various recommendations contained in the report of the Secretary-General and to inform the Secretary-General of the action taken on them not later than 15 May 1984;

8. *Takes note* of the proposals and recommendations contained in the report of the Secretary-General and requests him to take the necessary steps to ensure their implementation, including the following measures:

(a) Setting up of joint sectoral inter-agency working groups for follow-up of multilateral projects;

(b) Promotion of contacts and consultations regarding projects of a multilateral nature between the counterpart agencies, programmes and bodies concerned;

(c) Promotion of contacts and consultations regarding projects of a bilateral nature between the counterpart agencies, programmes and bodies concerned;

9. *Requests* the Food and Agriculture Organization of the United Nations to consider holding at Rome, not later than 31 August 1984, a meeting on food and agriculture in the Arab region to consider action to be taken and projects to be launched jointly pursuant to the recommendations adopted at the Tunis meeting;

10. *Also recommends* that another sectoral meeting on social development be organized, in January/February 1985, under the aegis of the General Secretariat of the League of Arab States, in a country member of that organization, to give careful consideration to projects prepared for joint implementation, in conformity with the priorities set forth in paragraphs 61 and 62 of the report of the Secretary-General, including joint sectoral meetings;

11. *Requests* the Secretary-General, in close co-operation with the Secretary-General of the League of Arab States, to convene *ad hoc* meetings between representatives of the Secretariat of the United Nations and of the General Secretariat of the League of Arab States for consultations on follow-up policies, projects, actions and procedures;

12. *Further requests* the Secretary-General to submit to the General Assembly, at its thirty-ninth session, a progress report on the implementation of the present resolution;

13. *Decides* to include in the provisional agenda of its thirty-ninth session the item entitled "Co-operation between the United Nations and the League of Arab States".

General Assembly resolution 38/6

28 October 1983   Meeting 39   Adopted without vote

20-nation draft (A/38/L.6/Rev.1); agenda item 27.
Sponsors: Algeria, Bahrain, Democratic Yemen, Djibouti, Iraq, Jordan, Kuwait, Lebanon, Libyan Arab Jamahiriya, Mauritania, Morocco, Oman, Qatar, Saudi Arabia, Somalia, Sudan, Syrian Arab Republic, Tunisia, United Arab Emirates, Yemen.
Meeting numbers. GA 38th session: plenary 39. SC: 2416, 2451, 2461, 2491.

Before adopting the 20-nation revised draft, the General Assembly voted separately on paragraph 4, retaining it by a recorded vote of 90 to 2, with 23 abstentions. The vote had been requested by the United States.

Israel said it had voted against the paragraph and would have voted against the draft as a whole had a vote been taken, to reflect its rejection of the entire text, which ignored the fact that the League, in its hostility to Israel, had consistently and deliberately violated the Charter and, rather than further the cause of peace, had impeded it, emerging as an instrument of warmongering.

The United States, recalling that with others it had opposed some of the resolutions mentioned in the paragraph, said that its inclusion interjected partisan politics into a text which should be apolitical and acceptable to all; it had joined in the consensus in the belief that co-operation between the League and the United Nations could be beneficial.

A similar position was taken by the 10 members of the European Community (EC), on whose behalf Greece stated that it would be better if texts such as that adopted addressed questions of co-operation in terms precluding divisive elements and further burdens on the United Nations budget, and, concerning paragraph 4—on which the EC members except Greece had abstained— without prejudicing the Secretary-General's role. Canada, which welcomed the co-operation promoted by the text, had also abstained on the paragraph, saying that it placed a heavy burden on the Secretary-General in an area of high political sensitivity. Sweden, speaking for the five Nordic countries, said they had participated in the consensus on the understanding that elements with political implications were not relevant to the text's substance and could not prejudice their position on it, hence their abstention on paragraph 4.

The League's Permanent Observer regretted the abstentions on the paragraph, contending that the call for intensified efforts to implement previous resolutions enhanced the text's credibility and the seriousness of United Nations deliberations; that those resolutions were politically sensitive did not warrant attempts to dilute the effectiveness of the majority decisions on Palestinian rights and on the modalities of a just, durable and comprehensive Middle East settlement.

Organization of the Islamic Conference

In a report on the state of co-operation between the United Nations and the Organization of the Islamic Conference,[5] submitted in response to an October 1982 General Assembly request,[6] the Secretary-General stated that his consultations with the Secretary-General of the Islamic Conference on 28 January 1983 emphasized the need for continuous consultations on such issues as the Middle East problem, the Palestine question, the Iran-Iraq war, the Afghanistan situation, and disarmament. Participation and increased representation by both organizations in the meetings of the

other had continued, as had consultations between the Permanent Observer of the Organization of the Islamic Conference to the United Nations and the United Nations Secretariat. The Department of Political Affairs, Trusteeship and Decolonization had remained the focal point for all co-operation issues.

The Secretary-General noted that the first annual meeting of the secretariat of the Islamic Conference and the secretariats of the United Nations system was held at Geneva on 15 July. The meeting considered modalities of co-operation in five priority areas (see below), and specific proposals were put forward.

The meeting designated a lead agency from the United Nations system for each priority area, as follows: the Food and Agriculture Organization of the United Nations (FAO), for food security and agriculture; the Task Force on Science and Technology for Development of the Administrative Committee on Co-ordination, assisted by the Centre for Science and Technology for Development, for science and technology; the United Nations Industrial Development Organization, for investment mechanisms and joint ventures; the United Nations Educational, Scientific and Cultural Organization, for eradication of illiteracy; and the Office of the United Nations High Commissioner for Refugees, for refugee assistance. Designation of focal points to facilitate contact between the two organizations was also recommended.

Co-operation in political matters continued to centre on disarmament, *apartheid*, outer space and decolonization.

Agreements for economic and social co-operation on specific projects continued to be formulated, and one such agreement was signed between the Conference and FAO on 7 April. Consultations and exchange of information also continued in lieu of formal agreements. Forums which provided for such exchanges in 1983 included an expert group meeting on forestry held by the Islamic Conference (Peshawar, Pakistan, 27-29 March), in which FAO participated; the first session of the Standing Committee for the Programme of the Economic Commission for Western Asia (Baghdad, Iraq, May); an Arab Aid Co-ordination Group/World Bank policy meeting (Washington, D. C., 25 September), with the Islamic Development Bank participating; and the Tenth Session of the Islamic Commission for Economic, Cultural and Social Affairs (Jeddah, Saudi Arabia, 2-5 October), at which the Department of Technical Co-operation for Development and the United Nations Conference on Trade and Development (UNCTAD) were represented.

In October, UNCTAD arranged a short training programme for a group of experts from the Islamic

Development Bank on the establishment of a trade information system. With the inception, also in October, of the United Nations Development Programme global project on action-oriented technical co-operation activities among developing countries, Islamic Conference members began benefiting through a trainee-exchange programme. In December, the Islamic Centre for Promotion of Trade completed arrangements for documentation and information exchange with the General Agreement on Tariffs and Trade. The United Nations Fund for Population Activities provided seed money in 1983 for a Muslim scholar congress on health, population and development, to be co-financed with the Islamic Conference.

GENERAL ASSEMBLY ACTION

Acting without vote on 28 October, the General Assembly adopted resolution 38/4.

Co-operation between the United Nations and the Organization of the Islamic Conference

The General Assembly,

Having considered the report of the Secretary-General on co-operation between the United Nations and the Organization of the Islamic Conference,

Taking into account the desire of both organizations to co-operate more closely in their common search for solutions to global problems, such as questions relating to international peace and security, disarmament, self-determination, decolonization, fundamental human rights and the establishment of a new international economic order,

Noting the strengthening of co-operation between the specialized agencies and other organizations of the United Nations system and the Organization of the Islamic Conference,

Expressing its satisfaction at the convening of the first annual meeting between the representatives of the secretariat of the Organization of the Islamic Conference and the secretariats of the United Nations and other organizations of the United Nations system,

Taking into account the high level of representation, the wide degree of participation of specialized agencies and other organizations of the United Nations system, the encouraging results obtained and the imperative necessity of co-ordination and follow-up of the decisions reached at that meeting,

Convinced of the need to strengthen further the co-operation between the United Nations and the Organization of the Islamic Conference,

Recalling its resolution 3369(XXX) of 10 October 1975, by which it granted observer status to the Organization of the Islamic Conference,

Recalling its resolutions 35/36 of 14 November 1980, 36/23 of 9 November 1981 and 37/4 of 22 October 1982,

1. *Takes note with satisfaction* of the report of the Secretary-General;

2. *Approves* the conclusions reached and the recommendations made at the first annual meeting between the representatives of the secretariat of the Organization of the Islamic Conference and the secretariats of

the United Nations and other organizations of the United Nations system, held at Geneva on 15 July 1983;

3. *Requests* the United Nations and the Organization of the Islamic Conference to continue co-operation in their common search for solutions to global problems, such as questions relating to international peace and security, disarmament, self-determination, decolonization, fundamental human rights and the establishment of a new international economic order;

4. *Encourages* the specialized agencies and other organizations of the United Nations system to continue to expand their co-operation with the Organization of the Islamic Conference, *inter alia* by negotiating co-operation agreements, and invites them to designate focal points concerning co-operation in priority areas of interest to the United Nations and the Organization of the Islamic Conference;

5. *Requests* the Secretary-General to continue to take steps to strengthen the co-ordination of the activities of the United Nations system in this field with a view to intensifying co-operation between the United Nations and the Organization of the Islamic Conference;

6. *Requests* the Secretary-General to strengthen co-operation and co-ordination between the United Nations and the organizations of the United Nations system and the Organization of the Islamic Conference to serve the mutual interests of the two organizations in the political, economic, social and cultural fields;

7. *Requests* the Secretary-General to report to the General Assembly at its thirty-ninth session on the state of co-operation between the United Nations and the Organization of the Islamic Conference;

8. *Decides* to include in the provisional agenda of its thirty-ninth session the item entitled "Co-operation between the United Nations and the Organization of the Islamic Conference".

General Assembly resolution 38/4

28 October 1983   Meeting 39   Adopted without vote

Draft by Niger (A/38/L.3/Rev.1); agenda item 22.
Meeting number. GA 38th session: plenary 39.

Other intergovernmental organizations

At the request of the host Governments of several intergovernmental conferences, the main documents of those meetings were transmitted to the Secretary-General during 1983 for circulation as documents of the General Assembly, the Security Council or both, as follows:

—Joint declaration issued at the conclusion of the Fourth Meeting of the Foreign Ministers of the States members of the Association of South-East Asian Nations (ASEAN) and EC (Bangkok, Thailand, 24 and 25 March);[7] joint communiqué of the sixteenth ASEAN ministerial meeting (Bangkok, 24 and 25 June).[8]

—Final communiqué and other documents of the Ministerial Meeting of the Co-ordinating Bureau of the Non-Aligned Countries (Managua, Nicaragua, 10-14 January);[9] final documents of the Seventh Conference of Heads of State or Government of Non-Aligned Countries (New Delhi, India, 7-12 March);[10] final communiqué adopted by the Meeting of Ministers for Foreign Affairs and Heads of Delegations of the Non-Aligned Countries to the thirty-eighth session of the General Assembly (New York, 4-7 October).[11]

—Resolutions adopted by the Seventieth Inter-Parliamentary Conference (Seoul, Republic of Korea, 12 October).[12]

—Conclusions adopted by the heads of State and Government of the 10 EC members, meeting as the European Council (Stuttgart, Federal Republic of Germany, 17-19 June).[13]

—Declaration and other documents of the Commonwealth Heads of Government Meeting (New Delhi, 23-29 November).[14]

REFERENCES

[1]YUN 1982, p. 587, GA res. 37/17, 16 Nov. 1982. [2]A/38/299 & Corr.1. [3]YUN 1982, p. 587. [4]A/38/114. [5]A/38/500. [6]YUN 1982, p. 588, GA res. 37/4, 22 Oct. 1982. [7]A/38/168-S/15736. [8]A/38/302-S/15875. [9]A/38/106-S/15628. [10]A/38/132-S/15675 & Corr.1,2. [11]A/38/495-S/16035. [12]A/38/529. [13]A/38/297-S/15867. [14]A/38/707-S/16206.

PUBLICATION

ASEAN and the United Nations System, UNITAR/RS/9, Sales No. 83.XV.RS/9.

Other institutional questions

Fortieth anniversary of the United Nations (1985)

An item entitled "Commemoration of the fortieth anniversary of the United Nations in 1985" was included in the 1983 agenda of the General Assembly on the recommendation of its General Committee; it was to be considered by the plenary Assembly. Inclusion of the item had been requested by the Secretary-General in a note of 12 December 1983.[1]

In a memorandum annexed to his note, the Secretary-General explained that he considered it appropriate that the occasion be used not only to review the Organization's four decades of performance but also to encourage a rededication to the Charter's principles and purposes, to promote support for the Organization and to reinvigorate international co-operation in all fields of human endeavour. Given the occasion's importance, adequate time was needed to prepare thoughtful proposals. The Secretary-General recommended that the Assembly decide to commemorate the anniversary and establish a mechanism to suggest proposals for suitable activities.

On an oral proposal by its President, the General Assembly adopted decision 38/455 without vote.

Commemoration of the fortieth anniversary of the United Nations in 1985

At its 104th plenary meeting, on 20 December 1983, the General Assembly:

(a) Decided to establish a Preparatory Committee for the Fortieth Anniversary of the United Nations, consisting of the members of the General Committee of the thirty-eighth session and open to the participation of all Member States on an equal basis;

(b) Entrusted the Preparatory Committee with the task of considering and recommending to the Assembly at its thirty-ninth session proposals for suitable activities in connection with the observance of the fortieth anniversary of the United Nations, on the understanding that its decisions would be taken by consensus.

General Assembly decision 38/455

Adopted without vote

Draft orally proposed by President; agenda item 146.
Meeting numbers. GA 38th session: General Committee 7; plenary 104.

Composition of UN organs

In 1983, as in the previous year, consideration of the question of the composition of the relevant organs of the United Nations was deferred.

On the recommendation of its Special Political Committee, the General Assembly adopted decision 38/423 without vote.

Question of the composition of the relevant organs of the United Nations

At its 98th plenary meeting, on 15 December 1983, the General Assembly, on the recommendation of the Special Political Committee, decided to include in the provisional agenda of its thirty-ninth session the item entitled "Question of the composition of the relevant organs of the United Nations".

General Assembly decision 38/423

Adopted without vote

Approved by SPC (A/38/603) without vote, 22 November (meeting 35); oral proposal by Chairman; agenda item 77.
Meeting numbers. GA 38th session: SPC 35; plenary 98.

REFERENCE

[1]A/38/246.

PUBLICATION

Basic Facts about the United Nations (DPI/749), Sales No. E.83.I.8.

Economic and social questions

Development policy and international economic co-operation

The critical world economic situation and the threat it posed to the developing countries continued to be considered in various United Nations bodies during 1983. The need for closer co-operation between developed and developing countries and among developing countries themselves was stressed in several economic reports and during discussions on the subject.

In his annual report on the work of the Organization (p. 3), the Secretary-General, noting the apparent retreat from multilateral economic co-operation, stressed that a major economic imperative was the accelerated development of the developing countries—particularly the least developed—and the eradication of poverty.

The growing interdependence of the world economy was emphasized by the sixth (June/July) session of the United Nations Conference on Trade and Development (UNCTAD VI), which held wide-ranging discussions on the economic situation and adopted a statement highlighting the need for multilateral economic co-operation.

With the approach of the mid-point of the Third United Nations Development Decade (the 1980s), preparations began for the 1984 review and appraisal of the implementation of the Decade's International Development Strategy. Work on contributions for submission to the review and appraisal Committee, which held its first meeting in December, was started by UNCTAD, the United Nations Industrial Development Organization (UNIDO), the Administrative Committee on Co-ordination (ACC) and the Committee for Development Planning (CDP). In December, the General Assembly reaffirmed the need for the review exercise to identify and appraise the real causes for shortfalls encountered in the Strategy's implementation and, if necessary, to adjust the policy measures foreseen in it in order to contribute effectively to the development of developing countries.

Discussion on the launching of global negotiations on international economic co-operation for development, originally scheduled to start in 1980, continued throughout 1983. In December, the Assembly decided to keep the item open after suspension of its 1983 session and to reconvene to consider any agreements that might emerge from informal consultations. Discussions continued throughout the year on various aspects of the proposed new international economic order, including its legal aspects.

Following transmittal by the Economic and Social Council of a draft declaration on a new international human order: moral aspects of development, the Assembly invited Member States to comment on the subject.

Resolutions requesting a study on confidence-building measures in international economic relations and deploring the adoption of economic sanctions against developing countries were adopted for the first time by the Assembly in 1983.

During the year, the question of economic co-operation among developing countries (ECDC) was discussed in several United Nations arenas, including UNCTAD VI, the UNCTAD Trade and Development Board and its Committee on Economic Co-operation among Developing Countries, and CDP. Economic and technical co-operation among developing countries was the main item discussed at the Joint Meetings of the Committee for Programme and Co-ordination and ACC, which agreed that a cross-organizational review should be carried out on the subject. On the question of interregional economic and technical co-operation among developing countries, both the Council and the Assembly agreed that the regional commissions should be provided with resources to meet their responsibilities for their related programmes.

The *World Economic Survey 1983*, which analysed current trends and policies in the world economy, was the background document for the annual discussion in the Council on international economic and social policy. UNCTAD produced the third in its series of annual reports on trade and development issues, the *Trade and Development Report, 1983*, which, in addition to analysing the world economic situation, focused on ECDC with particular reference to trade and finance. A further assessment of the economic situation was also carried out by CDP, which made a number of recommendations to promote world economic recovery.

Broad areas of economic and social development were considered in several United Nations forums during the year. The Assembly repeated its invitation to Governments to provide information on experience acquired in applying a unified approach to socio-economic development. After a report was submitted to the Assembly through the Economic and Social Council on the role of the public sector in economic development, the Secretary-General was invited to submit a further report in 1987.

The improvement of various aspects of development planning, education, administration and information continued to be studied, while support for public administration was given through a programme of technical co-operation.

Rural and regional development activities also continued throughout the United Nations system during 1983.

The Organization's continuing concern for countries particularly affected by the world economic crisis was shown in its adoption of resolutions calling for action on behalf of the developing countries in general and the least developed, land-locked and island developing countries in particular. The Assembly called for immediate measures in favour of the developing countries to ease their economic problems and to promote development. Implementation of the 1981 Substantial New Programme of Action for the 1980s for the Least Developed Countries (LDCs) was considered at UNCTAD VI and by CDP. The United Nations Development Programme (UNDP) reported on action taken with the World Bank in organizing and holding country review meetings for individual LDCs. The status of the UNDP Special Measures Fund for LDCs was reported on as was that of the United Nations Capital Development Fund, whose programme covered 41 countries, 36 of which were LDCs. The particular problems of land-locked countries were discussed at UNCTAD VI, which called for action on their behalf. The Assembly also discussed the issue and made a further request for contributions to the United Nations Special Fund for Land-locked Developing Countries. The problems of island developing countries were also discussed at UNCTAD VI, which urged the international community to provide financial and technical support for them.

Topics related to this chapter. Disarmament: disarmament and development. Operational activities for development. International trade and finance. Regional economic and social activities: economic and social trends—Africa, Asia and the Pacific, Europe, Latin America, Western Asia; development policy and regional economic co-operation—Africa, Asia and the Pacific, Europe, Latin America, Western Asia. Social and cultural development: social aspects of the International Development Strategy; social aspects of development planning; popular participation in development; family in development; social aspects of rural development. Human rights: right to development; proposed new international economic order and human rights; proposed new international humanitarian order. Women: women in development. Statistics: economic statistics.

International economic relations

Development and economic co-operation

During 1983, several United Nations bodies, including UNCTAD VI, discussed the need for greater international co-operation in the light of the economic situation which threatened the developing countries in particular. ECDC was widely discussed, with the UNCTAD Committee on ECDC holding its third session in 1983.

Discussions also took place in various United Nations bodies on preparations for the review and appraisal, scheduled for 1984, of the implementation of the International Development Strategy for the Third United Nations Development Decade. In December, the Committee on the Review and Appraisal held its first meeting to discuss organizational aspects of its work.

The Assembly adopted resolutions calling for confidence-building in international economic relations and deploring economic measures as a means of political and economic coercion against developing countries. Proposals for global economic negotiations, a new international economic order and a new international human order concerned with the moral aspects of development continued to be considered in various United Nations forums throughout the year, with no agreement being reached.

CDP activities. At its April 1983 session,[1] CDP found that the deep crisis and mounting disorder in the world economy called for an urgent response to new initiatives for collaboration. The most serious threats to recovery were the chaotic situation prevailing in international financial relations and protectionist policies in international trade (see also Chapter IV of this section). Referring to countries with large foreign debts, CDP stated that, if recovery was too long delayed and rescheduling done at high interest rates, the need for extensive cancellation would arise.

An overhaul of international co-operation machinery was required for renewed expansion of the international economy. CDP believed that there was justification for a proposed conference on the interrelated areas of trade, money and finance, but that an extensive review of the issues and of the likelihood of securing agreement on new arrangements was necessary. Therefore, it proposed the establishment of an *ad hoc* group of high-level experts to examine proposals for reform and consider modalities for negotiating change.

The Committee believed that large potential gains could be derived from closer co-operation among developing countries in trade and finance, but that realization of such schemes required establishment of a third world secretariat (for further details, see below, under ECONOMIC CO-OPERATION AMONG DEVELOPING COUNTRIES).

Progress towards disarmament was essential to a relaxation of international tension and would also be a great economic relief, CDP said, adding that resources released would assist the advancement of all nations and contribute to bridging the gap between developed and developing countries.

The Committee also considered measures in favour of the least developed and other low-income developing countries (see below).

As a follow-up to a 1981 decision by CDP to study particular aspects of the world economic situation and prospects,[2] the Working Group on Development Patterns and Styles in the Context of Longer-term World Economic Prospects met at Santiago, Chile, from 10 to 14 January 1983.[3]

The Group considered the structural aspects of the world economic situation, including maladjustment among developed market economies, the crisis of the international banking system, and indebtedness of developing countries. In order to indicate some options open to developing countries to accelerate their development, the Group drew a number of conclusions from their experiences with alternative policy approaches and development styles. These related to autonomous decision-making, more equitable patterns of income distribution and effective investment planning. The Group described ways of strengthening developing countries' economic leverage by controlling such key resources as technology, financial resources, markets, non-renewable resources and access to cheap labour, and concluded by considering ways to accelerate progress in ECDC.

In December 1983, the CDP Working Group on the International Monetary and Financial System met at United Nations Headquarters to prepare material for the CDP study of the subject at its 1984 session[4] (see Chapter IV of this section).

ACC activities. In its annual report to the Economic and Social Council,[5] ACC stressed the need for interdependence of countries and groups of countries in finding and implementing solutions to the economic crisis. The economic recovery of developed countries was essential for reactivating and accelerating development in developing countries, which was equally essential to global economic recovery.

Among issues considered by ACC to be of major concern were the global effect of adjustment policies adopted to deal with the economic crisis and expansion of protectionism in international trade. The recession's impact on agriculture, particularly in developing countries, was reviewed, and the relatively good global performance in 1983 was acknowledged. It was observed, however, that agricultural support programmes and protectionism by developed countries posed problems at the international level. Also, developing countries needed to adopt policies to provide incentives to agricultural producers.

Referring to the major role played by the International Monetary Fund (IMF) and the World Bank in assisting developing countries during the crisis, ACC considered it important to maintain, even if at a reduced level, participation of commercial banks. Although there were signs of recovery in some developed countries, that recovery should also benefit developing countries. Action could include strengthening their liquidity and reserve positions and increasing concessional aid flows. Among other areas for possible action were commodities and compensatory financing and the food sector. It was noted that a stable exchange-rate market could also contribute significantly. ACC emphasized that solutions to fundamental problems of developing countries which pre-dated the recession required more than mere correction of transitory imbalances.

ACC concluded that its central objective was to assist Governments in defining and implementing a framework for international economic co-operation and development. If the United Nations system was to succeed in its efforts, Governments had to make full use of the instrumentalities they had created and provide coherent direction and necessary resources.

At its eleventh session, held at Geneva from 2 to 4 March,[6] the ACC Task Force on Long-Term Development Objectives assessed the world economic situation and prospects in the light of development objectives and decided on the organization of its contribution to the 1984 review and appraisal of the International Development Strategy for the Third United Nations Development Decade.[7] The latter topic was also considered at the twelfth session of the Task Force (New York, 10-12 October)[8] (see below).

The Task Force, in an overview of the world economic situation, noted signs of recovery but doubted its strength and duration. It went on to discuss economic interdependence and the need for action at the global level to bring lasting world-wide recovery, adjustment policies and the need for a long-term perspective, the linkage between international and domestic measures for recovery and development, and the need for greater co-operation among developing countries.

In considering the current economic situation and prospects, the Task Force concentrated on the world economic recession and the deteriorating social situation. Economic stagnation aggravated the serious problems faced by many developing countries in providing food, education, health, housing and employment for their rapidly growing populations.

The Task Force observed that the process of adjusting national economies to the crisis took different forms in various groups of countries. The nature of adjustment depended on the degree of integration with the world economy, export structure, debt burden, and availability and cost of external finance. Possible adjustment policies considered by the Task Force included budget retrenchment, cuts in public expenditure, subsidies and imports, and changes in tax systems, salaries and wages. The process should also include consideration of the socio-political environment that would emerge from adjustment policies. The need to make short-term measures development-oriented by allowing a longer period for adjustment was emphasized.

The Task Force discussed several areas in which policy reorientation was required for global recovery and development, paying particular attention to financial and trade issues since they had a strong impact on longer-term development and structural change.

World Economic Survey 1983. During its annual discussion of international economic and social policy, which took place in July (see below), the Economic and Social Council had before it the *World Economic Survey 1983*,[9] prepared by the United Nations Department of International Economic and Social Affairs (DIESA) and based on information available as at 31 March 1983.

The *Survey* stated that, without greater international co-operation, individual countries' efforts to revive output and investment would yield meagre results. Experience had shown that, without some international co-ordination of macro-economic policies, volatility of exchange rates, interest rates and short-term capital flows tended to increase, which heightened uncertainties and deterred investment. Strengthened consultations on exchange rates, resistance to protectionism and dismantling of non-tariff barriers were required for a favourable investment climate.

More broadly-based international co-operation was needed than in past financial emergencies, the *Survey* said, including action by IMF to enable developing countries to draw more resources from it. Revival of investment in developing countries also required increased official development assistance and increased transfers of resources through the World Bank and regional development banks. Lengthening maturities of developing countries' outstanding debt could be decisive in stepping up fixed investment.

Co-operation among developing countries and East-West economic co-operation were important for recovery efforts. ECDC in finance and joint production ventures, explored since the early 1970s, had proved particularly effective and there was scope for further co-operation in those areas as well as in more traditional areas such as trade. UNCTAD VI (see Chapter IV of this section) would provide an opportunity to discuss structural reforms in the international economic system and seek agreement on a wide range of measures to reactivate the world economy and accelerate economic development, the *Survey* indicated.

In the general discussion of international economic and social policy in the Economic and Social Council,[10] there was consensus that the world economy had been passing through a period of difficulty not seen since the end of the Second World War, affecting all groups of countries but particularly the developing ones. There was widespread agreement that economic recovery had been indicated in some industrialized countries but there was also concern that such recovery might not prove strong or lasting, or might not spread, particularly to the developing countries.

Issues of major concern to many speakers were the prospect of grossly inadequate financial flows to developing countries, the debt crisis and protectionism. Support was expressed for high-level international meetings on an improved international monetary system. Attention was also devoted to trends in multilateral co-operation efforts, including international trade and finance, energy, food production and food security, and ECDC.

UNCTAD action. Two documents on the world economic crisis were prepared for UNCTAD VI.

A report by the UNCTAD Secretary-General on development and recovery: the realities of the new interdependence[11] described the critical international economic situation and went on to outline an economic recovery programme requiring mutually reinforcing growth and expansion in both the developed and developing countries.

A further chapter of the report dealt with the longer-term economic perspective and stressed the interdependence of economies. Possible economic scenarios for the 1980s for the developed market-economy countries, the developing countries and the socialist countries of Eastern Europe were discussed.

The report concluded by examining the limitations of multilateral arrangements in the areas of money, finance and trade and described how the "systems" (multilaterally accepted rules, principles, policies and institutions underpinning international economic relations) should adapt to the growing interdependence of the world economy.

A policy paper on the current world economic crisis and perspectives for the 1980s,[12] prepared by the UNCTAD secretariat, described the impact of the crisis on developing countries, developed market-economy countries and the socialist countries of Eastern Europe. Although there were signs that the economies of some major industrial countries were improving, the crisis had caused severe curtailment of growth in developing countries and had impaired their prospects for years to come.

The paper discussed aspects of interdependence in the world economy, some of which involved mainly relations among developed market-economy countries or among developing countries. Many, however, were related to the growing importance of developing countries, as reflected in their rising share of world production, income and trade, their growing role as suppliers of certain key commodities and their rising share of both the deposits and liabilities of the international banking system.

After describing the international economic system's response to the crisis and paying particular attention to weaknesses in monetary and financial systems, the paper devoted chapters to the revival of the world economy and to major areas for long-run reform, such as macro-economic management, money and finance, and trade.

An annex to the paper[13] gave estimates of growth and associated external financial flows based on a number of scenarios, which assumed various rates of growth, patterns of trade, relative prices and terms of finance.

The world economic situation with special emphasis on development: approaches to the current world economic crisis and perspectives for the 1980s, including issues, policies and measures relevant to the attainment of a new international economic order was considered by UNCTAD VI in conjunction with its general debate.

In a statement on the subject adopted on 2 July,[14] the effects of the world economic crisis on multilateral economic co-operation were described. International monetary institutions had not been sufficiently adapted to cope with changes in the world economy and the multilateral trading system had been seriously endangered. The development process required urgent changes in the international economic system.

The United States dissociated itself from the statement because it found the text too negative, one-sided and ideological.

The statement outlined the increasingly important role played by developing countries in the international economy and described how the crisis had brought out growing interlinkages between national economies and between different economic sectors, particularly in raw materials, energy, trade, development, money and finance. Coherent international policies addressing short-term conjunctural problems and longer-term structural problems were called for.

Since the crisis threatened the stability of both developed and developing countries, the launching of a programme of concerted measures to reactivate the global economy was needed. In an increasingly interdependent world, the statement said, the economic future and political stability of all countries were interlinked. The adoption of disarmament measures would release resources for development.

In debating this issue, the Conference had before it, in addition to the documents mentioned above, a Declaration (the Buenos Aires Platform)[14] by the Fifth Ministerial Meeting of the Group of 77 (Buenos Aires, Argentina, 28 March–9 April). Included in the Platform but not in the UNCTAD statement were references to non-fulfilment of commitments and retreat from internationally agreed obligations, erosion by developed countries of accepted norms for international trade by means of retrogressive agreements and policies, and resort by some developed countries to coercive and discriminatory economic measures against developing countries. Reference was also made to the unacceptable concentration of international decision-making power in the developed countries and their lack of positive response to developing countries' attempts to negotiate on global economic issues.

References to international financial and trading institutions in the Platform were reformulated in the UNCTAD statement. The Platform described those institutions as being designed to serve the interests of the developed world and said that efforts to restructure them to support the development process had been to no avail. The institutions were being subordinated to political and other considerations, there was a retreat from multilateralism in both trading and financial co-operation, the official components of the international monetary and financial system had declined in relative importance and the system was being privatized.

The UNCTAD statement contained two paragraphs not included in the Buenos Aires Platform: one stated that developed market-economy countries had taken successful counter-inflationary measures and had agreed to pursue policies to support economic recovery and promote development; and the other indicated that specific regional problems of developing countries, dealt with in such strategies as the 1980 Lagos Plan of Action for the Implementation of the Monrovia Strategy for the Economic Development of Africa,[15] would be included in the programme for reactivating development in developing countries.

At its October/November session, UNCTAD's Trade and Development Board considered the interdependence of problems of trade, development finance and the international monetary system, as well as debt and development problems of developing countries. Annexed to the Board's report[16] was a draft resolution, submitted by Venezuela on behalf of the Group of 77, by which the Board would have decided to convene its thirtieth session in the first half of 1985 at the ministerial level, to review the world economic situation and progress in implementing the UNCTAD VI programme of immediate measures, which incorporated elements contained in the Conference's resolutions on commodities, trade, money and finance, and implementation of the Substantial New Programme of Action for the 1980s for the Least Developed Countries.[17]

Report of the Secretary-General. In his September 1983 report to the General Assembly on the work of the Organization (p. 3), the Secretary-General addressed the international economic situation and the role of the United Nations in economic issues. Recent trends and events marked a clear retreat from multilateral co-operation efforts and, while the effects of economic interdependence were widely acknowledged, opportunities to address the major issues were being repeatedly missed. More than ever, individual nations were affected by trends elsewhere and by decisions of others. International mechanisms were needed to bring about greater harmonization of national policies.

UNCTAD VI had provided an opportunity to demonstrate the capacity and will of Governments to act together, the Secretary-General stated, but there was a failure to respond to the need for concerted international action. There was a need to activate the negotiation process between developed and developing countries on long-term problems in several interrelated areas and at a high political level.

The Secretary-General stated that the United Nations had been successful in various sectors of economic activity. However, there was a need for more concerted action by United Nations organizations in dealing with development and international economic co-operation issues and in their work at the field level.

Communications. Several communications dealing with general aspects of international economic relations were received by the Secretary-General in 1983.

On 6 May,[18] Brazil and Mexico transmitted the text of the "Cancún Declaration", signed by the Presidents of Mexico and Brazil on 29 April at the first meeting of heads of State and Government on international co-operation for development, held at Cancún, Mexico. The Presidents expressed concern over the state of the world economy and its effect on developing countries and on the Latin American region in particular. They called for measures to give the region's exports access to developed countries' markets and for adequate financial resources on appropriate terms. Convinced that conditions were ripe for a new phase of constructive North-South dialogue, the Presidents addressed themselves to heads of State and Government of the industrialized nations, in the hope that they would adopt a decisive stand to bring about international economic co-operation for development and deal effectively with the crisis.

In a communiqué transmitted by Luxembourg on 20 May,[19] the Council of the Organisation for Economic Co-operation and Development, which met at ministerial level on 9 and 10 May, indicated policies to be adopted by member Governments to strengthen the international trading, monetary and financial systems.

On 10 October,[20] Bangladesh transmitted a Declaration adopted by the Foreign Ministers of the Group of 77 at their meeting held in New York on 6, 7 and 10 October. The Declaration covered economic issues of multilateral co-operation for development as well as other issues of concern to the General Assembly.

The communiqué of the thirty-seventh session of the Council for Mutual Economic Assistance[21] (Berlin, 18-20 October) was transmitted by the German Democratic Republic on 27 October. The communiqué included an expression of support for the demands of developing countries regarding the reshaping of international economic relations.

Joint statements by some countries with centrally planned economies (Bulgaria, Byelorussian SSR, Czechoslovakia, German Democratic Republic, Hungary, Mongolia, Poland, Ukrainian SSR, USSR) were transmitted on their behalf on 6 October[22] and 22 November[23] by the Byelorussian SSR and Czechoslovakia, respectively. The former statement dealt with the restructuring of economic relations on a just, equal and democratic basis, while the latter called for measures to be taken against economic coercion.

Bulgaria's economic assistance to developing countries and national liberation movements was outlined in a statement annexed to a letter dated 26 October.[24] On 6 July,[25] Bulgaria had sent an identical text to the President of the Economic and Social Council. A statement annexed to a letter of 5 October[26] described aid provided by the German Democratic Republic to developing countries and national liberation movements. Information on the USSR's economic co-operation with developing countries was annexed to a letter of 8 November.[27]

GENERAL ASSEMBLY ACTION

The General Assembly's Second (Economic and Financial) Committee devoted a major part of its

1983 session to development and international economic co-operation, making recommendations on a large number of specific topics (see APPENDIX IV, agenda item 78). A list of pertinent documents was included in the first part of the Committee's report on this item,[28] which the Assembly took note of when it adopted without vote decision 38/436, as orally proposed by its President.

Development and international economic co-operation

At its 102nd plenary meeting, on 19 December 1983, the General Assembly took note of part I of the report of the Second Committee.

General Assembly decision 38/436

Adopted without vote

Oral proposal by President; agenda item 78.
Meeting numbers. GA 38th session: 2nd Committee 15-24, 38-45; plenary 102.

In its 19 December resolution (38/155) on the report of UNCTAD VI, the Assembly called on countries to implement measures to revitalize the development process of developing countries and deal with structural problems in the global economy. It took note of the UNCTAD VI statement on the world economic situation and called on countries to take action at the national and international levels on UNCTAD VI resolutions and on measures set out in the statement (see Chapter IV of this section).

Proposed global economic negotiations

Discussions on the launching of global negotiations on international economic co-operation for development, originally scheduled to begin in 1980,[29] continued throughout 1983.

On 28 October, the General Assembly President reported that a series of international meetings and conferences had failed to help third world countries to promote their development. He believed that it was the Assembly's duty to alleviate short-term problems leading to negotiations, which would ensure a balanced development of the international economy and of the economies of the developing countries in particular.

On 20 December, when the Assembly again took up the matter, the President described bilateral meetings and high-level multilateral consultations which had taken place during the 1983 regular session. He reported that there had been discernible progress and indicated that most of the elements of doubt or great controversy had been resolved. In the light of this, the President proposed that the consultation process should continue for a concentrated, uninterrupted time period, after which he would convene a multilateral meeting, not later than the end of March 1984, to hear a progress report on the consultations so that the Assembly could adopt appropriate decisions in order to launch the global negotiations.

At the closing meeting of its resumed thirty-seventh session on 19 September, the General Assembly adopted decision 37/456 without vote, as orally proposed by the President.

Launching of global negotiations on international economic co-operation for development

At its 122nd plenary meeting, on 19 September 1983, the General Assembly decided to include in the draft agenda of its thirty-eighth session the item entitled "Launching of global negotiations on international economic co-operation for development".

General Assembly decision 37/456

Adopted without vote

Oral proposal by President; agenda item 38.
Meeting number. GA 37th session: plenary 122.

On 20 December, at its thirty-eighth session, the Assembly adopted decision 38/448 A without vote, as orally proposed by the President.

Launching of global negotiations on international economic co-operation for development

At its 104th plenary meeting, on 20 December 1983, the General Assembly decided to keep the item open in order to allow for the continuation of informal consultations after the suspension of the session and to reconvene on short notice to consider any decisions or agreements that might emerge from the negotiations.

General Assembly decision 38/448 A

Adopted without vote

Oral proposal by President; agenda item 38.
Meeting numbers. GA 38th session: plenary 39, 104.

A number of other 1983 Assembly decisions related to the item. On 20 December, the Assembly decided by decision 38/456 to resume its thirty-eighth session at a date to be announced to consider five agenda items and one sub-item, including the item on the launching of global negotiations.

In a preambular paragraph of its 19 December resolution (38/152) on the review and appraisal of the implementation of the International Development Strategy for the Third United Nations Development Decade,[7] the Assembly expressed regret at the lack of progress in launching the negotiations, which were intended to facilitate the Strategy's implementation.

In a resolution of 20 December (38/190) reviewing the implementation of the 1970 Declaration on the Strengthening of International Security,[30] the Assembly urged States to proceed without delay to a global consideration of ways to revive the world economy and to restructure international economic relations within the framework of global negotiations.

Again on 20 December, by resolution 38/200 on immediate measures for developing countries, the

Assembly urged Governments to pursue effective negotiating efforts, within the United Nations system, with a view to adopting concrete measures in favour of developing countries.

International Development Strategy for the Third UN Development Decade

During 1983, preparations continued for the 1984 review and appraisal of the implementation of the International Development Strategy for the Third United Nations Development Decade (the 1980s), as provided for in the Strategy adopted by the Assembly in 1980[7] and reaffirmed by that body in December 1982.[31]

UNCTAD action. On 28 April, UNCTAD's Trade and Development Board decided[32] to establish an open-ended high-level intergovernmental group to consider the review and appraisal of the Strategy's implementation. The group was to meet before February 1984 and its report was to be submitted to a special session of the Board.

In preparation for the review and appraisal exercise, a report by the UNCTAD secretariat[33] reviewed the basic goals and targets of the Strategy and developments in the world economy. The report also presented the results of a quantitative exercise, which suggested that vigorous policies to foster development together with an improved international economic environment could reverse current unfavourable economic conditions in developing countries. Another UNCTAD secretariat report[34] reviewed progress on specific policy recommendations in the Strategy in areas of interest to UNCTAD.

In resolution 164(VI) on official development assistance,[14] adopted on 2 July, UNCTAD VI urged developed countries to reaffirm commitments undertaken under the Strategy with respect to the target of 0.7 per cent of gross national product as official development assistance, with the target of 1 per cent to be reached as soon as possible thereafter.

UNIDO action. In a 13 May conclusion[35] on follow-up to the Third (1980) General Conference of the United Nations Industrial Development Organization (UNIDO) and the eleventh special session of the General Assembly,[36] held in 1980 to assess progress made by the United Nations system towards establishing a new international economic order, the UNIDO Industrial Development Board (IDB) requested UNIDO's Executive Director to provide suitable material to the Committee on the Review and Appraisal of the Strategy—set up in December 1982 by the Assembly[31]— through IDB or its Permanent Committee.

As requested by IDB on 13 May,[35] the UNIDO secretariat submitted a report[37] to the Permanent Committee's November/December session.[38] The report covered the Strategy's im-

plementation in relation to: the role of industrialization in the Strategy, the Strategy as an instrument of policy for UNIDO programme formulation, progress of industrialization in developing countries, the impact on it of the current world economic crisis and prospects for the remainder of the Decade. In noting efforts to incorporate the Strategy in UNIDO programmes, the Permanent Committee noted with concern not only the lack of progress in attaining the Strategy's industrialization targets but also the real decline in the manufacturing value-added (the value added to manufactures) in developing countries during the Decade's first three years. The Committee requested that its comments and the secretariat's report be transmitted to the Committee on the Review and Appraisal in accordance with the Assembly's December 1982 request.[31]

ACC action. The Consultative Committee on Substantive Questions (Programme Matters) (CCSQ(PROG)) of ACC discussed the review and appraisal of the Strategy at both its first (Geneva, 10-15 March)[39] and second (New York, 7-13 October)[40] regular 1983 sessions. At its first session, it agreed that, because of the relevance of the synthesis and assessment to be carried out by the ACC Task Force on Long-Term Development Objectives (see below), it would review the Task Force's report. In addition, a close working relationship should be maintained between CCSQ(PROG) and the Task Force and a joint meeting would be desirable.

At its second session, CCSQ(PROG) noted that the Committee on the Review and Appraisal would have before it a comprehensive report of the Secretary-General, which would draw, *inter alia*, on the work of the Task Force, sectoral reports from ACC member organizations, a CDP report and a report on progress in social development. The prevailing view in CCSQ(PROG), therefore, was that it would not be necessary to prepare another inter-agency paper. CCSQ(PROG) and the Task Force held a brief joint meeting to exchange views on ACC's role in the review and appraisal process.

At its first session in 1983 (Geneva, 2-4 March),[6] the ACC Task Force discussed its contribution to the Strategy's review and appraisal. It decided that its report would be a synthesis and assessment of contributions of United Nations agencies and organizations and that those contributions would be sectoral, regional or global in scope. The report would be discussed at its second 1983 session, finalized and submitted to ACC and CDP.

At its second session (New York, 10-12 October), the Task Force adopted a consensus report,[8] which reviewed the state of the Strategy's implementation and considered what had to be done to achieve its central objective—the accelerated development of developing countries in the context of an equitable and efficient world order.

The review of the first three years of the Strategy's implementation depicted a period of crisis and economic stagnation, marked also by differences in the performance of regions and groups of countries and by insufficient international economic co-operation. The appraisal of possible future action to reverse negative trends and perspectives stressed the need for active implementation of short- and long-range policies involving the entire international community. The report emphasized that clusters of measures outlined in the Strategy—the creation of a supportive environment for development, stronger international economic co-operation, and greater self-reliance of developing countries—were both important and complementary. It also stressed the crucial role of a favourable overall political context for improving the world economy and the economic and social situation in developing countries, with the central issue of disarmament and development being part of that context.

The report concluded that, three years after the adoption of the Strategy, the Third Development Decade was in serious jeopardy. At stake was not only the achievement of specific targets but the continuation of growth and development and the functioning of the world economy.

CDP consideration. In accordance with the Assembly's December 1982 resolution on the review and appraisal of the Strategy,[31] CDP proposed to focus at its 1984 session on critical problems hampering progress in the Strategy's implementation, particularly those issues on which negotiations had stalled. At its April 1983 session,[1] it proposed convening a working group to assess progress made and identify factors responsible for shortfalls in the Strategy's implementation.

The working group met at United Nations Headquarters from 13 to 18 December. In the overall assessment contained in its report,[41] the group stated that, although the Strategy's purpose remained sound and widely shared, its targets had been overtaken by events. Not only had the advances in developing countries projected in the Strategy not been achieved, but their situation had further deteriorated as the deep recession in the industrialized economies spread hardship to virtually all groups through lowered terms of trade and increased interest rates, compounded by a collapse in net capital flows and growing protectionist trends. The consequences of the critical economic situation were more than economic, the group stated, as the erosion of growth and welfare heightened tensions and raised the potential for turbulence both within and between countries. There was an urgent need to reverse prevailing trends, for which purpose the group proposed adoption of an ambitious but realistic package of immediate measures for recovery and development.

ECONOMIC AND SOCIAL COUNCIL ACTION

In section VI of decision 1983/184 of 29 July, the Economic and Social Council requested the General Assembly, at its 1983 session, to schedule one session of the Committee on the Review and Appraisal of the Implementation of the International Development Strategy for the Third United Nations Development Decade, and decided to consider the Committee's report at the Council's second regular session of 1984.

In a 26 May resolution (1983/9), the Council invited the Committee to examine progress in achieving the Strategy's social goals and objectives (for social aspects of the Strategy, see Chapter XIII of this section). In a 28 July resolution (1983/57), the Council reaffirmed the importance of implementing the 1977 Mar del Plata Action Plan[42] and the objectives of the International Drinking Water Supply and Sanitation Decade (1981-1990) within the context of the Strategy and recommended to the Assembly that the Committee should consider the role played in the Strategy by water resources development.

GENERAL ASSEMBLY ACTION

On 19 December, on the recommendation of the Second Committee, the General Assembly adopted resolution 38/152 without vote.

Review and appraisal of the implementation of the International Development Strategy for the Third United Nations Development Decade

The General Assembly,

Recalling its resolutions 3201(S-VI) and 3202(S-VI) of 1 May 1974, containing the Declaration and the Programme of Action on the Establishment of a New International Economic Order, 3281(XXIX) of 12 December 1974, containing the Charter of Economic Rights and Duties of States, and 3362(S-VII) of 16 September 1975 on development and international economic co-operation,

Recalling its resolution 35/56 of 5 December 1980, the annex to which contains the International Development Strategy for the Third United Nations Development Decade, and reiterating the goals and objectives contained therein,

Recalling also its resolution 37/202 of 20 December 1982, by which it established a committee of universal membership to carry out in 1984 the first overall review and appraisal of the implementation of the International Development Strategy, and provided for the necessary arrangements for fulfilling this task,

Recalling further its resolution 37/203 of 20 December 1982, in which it requested, *inter alia*, that, as part of the preparations for the review and appraisal of the International Development Strategy, an analysis also be made of the negative trends in the world economy which affect international economic co-operation,

Recalling the relevant provisions of Economic and Social Council decision 1983/184 of 29 July 1983,

Deeply conscious that the early part of the Third United Nations Development Decade has been a period of widespread economic stagnation and crisis, particularly in those developing countries where per capita income declined significantly, in marked contrast to the annual growth rate of about 4.5 per cent envisaged in the International Development Strategy,

Expressing its deep regret at the lack of progress in the launching of global negotiations, which are intended to be one of the principal instruments for facilitating the implementation of the International Development Strategy,

Reaffirming, in the context of the International Development Strategy, the continuing need to address the long-term structural economic problems,

Convinced of the urgent need for substantially greater efforts towards the implementation of the goals and objectives of the International Development Strategy in the remaining period of the Decade,

1. *Reiterates* the importance of achieving the goals and objectives of the International Development Strategy for the Third United Nations Development Decade;

2. *Reaffirms* that, in accordance with paragraphs 169 to 180 of the International Development Strategy, the process of review and appraisal of the implementation of the Strategy should consist of systematic scrutiny, within the context of an overall review of the international economic situation, of the progress made towards achieving the goals and objectives of the Strategy, and should ensure its effective implementation and strengthen it as an instrument of policy;

3. *Reaffirms also* the need, in the review and appraisal exercise, to identify and appraise the real causes for shortfalls encountered in the implementation of the International Development Strategy and to carry out, if necessary, the adjustment, intensification or reformulation of the policy measures foreseen in the Strategy in the light of evolving needs and developments, in order for the instrument to contribute effectively to the development of developing countries, with a view to the establishment of a new international economic order;

4. *Urges* all Governments and all concerned to implement fully the provisions of General Assembly resolution 37/202 in order to ensure the successful preparation and conclusion of the review and appraisal exercise;

5. *Recommends* that informal consultations be conducted by the Chairman of the Committee on the Review and Appraisal of the Implementation of the International Development Strategy for the Third United Nations Development Decade, prior to the substantive session of the Committee, to initiate preliminary discussions and an exchange of views on the review and appraisal of the Strategy as envisaged in paragraphs 2 and 3 above, and to review the preparation of documentation for the Committee;

6. *Decides* that documentation to be submitted to the Committee by relevant organs, organizations and bodies of the United Nations system should be concise and brief and should focus on the issues envisaged in paragraphs 2 and 3 above, as well as on questions addressed to them in the relevant provisions of General Assembly resolution 37/202;

7. *Requests* the Secretary-General, in pursuance of General Assembly resolutions 37/202 and 37/203, to prepare and submit to the Committee an analytical, comprehensive, consolidated and synthesized report on the implementation of the International Development Strategy, addressing the issues envisaged in paragraphs 2 and 3 above and drawing on the reports of the relevant organs, organizations and bodies of the United Nations system.

General Assembly resolution 38/152

19 December 1983   Meeting 102   Adopted without vote

Approved by Second Committee (A/38/702/Add.1) without vote, 14 December (meeting 56); draft by Vice-Chairman (A/C.2/38/L.112), based on informal consultations on draft by Mexico, for Group of 77 (A/C.2/38/L.90); agenda item 78 *(a)*.

Meeting numbers. GA 38th session: 2nd Committee 38-45, 52, 56; plenary 102.

In addition to drafting changes, the adopted text differed from that submitted by the Group of 77 in several respects, including the addition of a preambular paragraph recalling Council decision 1983/184 and the addition of operative paragraphs 2 and 5 to 7.

By the Group's text, the Assembly would have expressed deep regret at the failure to tackle long-term structural problems of the world economy, whereas by the final text the Assembly reaffirmed the continuing need to address those problems.

An operative paragraph in the Group's text was reformulated and became paragraph 3. By the former draft, the Assembly would have reaffirmed the need to review progress made towards achieving the Strategy's objectives, to identify causes for lack of compliance with the Strategy's policy measures, goals and objectives, and to propose the necessary corrective measures in order for it to contribute to achieving those goals, the development of developing countries and the strengthening of the United Nations system, with a view to establishing the new international economic order.

Omitted from the final text was a paragraph by which the Assembly would have urged Governments, particularly those of developed countries, to implement paragraphs 10 and 11 of the Assembly's December 1982 resolution[31] (inviting Governments to reflect the Strategy's goals, objectives and policy measures in their policy formulation and developed countries to transmit reports of their development assistance).

A number of other 1983 Assembly resolutions dealt with the review and appraisal process. In resolution 38/195 of 20 December, on implementation of the Substantial New Programme of Action (SNPA) for the 1980s for the Least Developed Countries (see below), the Assembly invited the Committee on the Review and Appraisal of the Strategy to take into account the adoption and implementation process of SNPA and related developments in its review and appraisal exercise at all levels.

In resolution 38/200 on immediate measures in favour of the developing countries, also adopted on 20 December, the Assembly agreed that policy measures of an immediate nature should be taken into account in the review and appraisal of the Strategy.

In resolution 38/179 of 19 December, the Assembly requested the Secretary-General to prepare a report on the application by Governments of a unified approach to development analysis and planning, taking into account the results of the first review and appraisal of the Strategy, and to submit it to the Economic and Social Council and the Assembly in 1985, with a view to using it as input for future reviews and appraisals.

In resolution 38/199 of 20 December, on special measures for the social and economic development of Africa in the 1980s, the Assembly recalled that there was a need for a thorough evaluation of the implementation of those measures during the mid-term review and appraisal of the Strategy.

Committee on the Strategy. The Committee on the Review and Appraisal of the Implementation of the International Development Strategy for the Third United Nations Development Decade, established by the General Assembly in 1982,[31] held an organizational session on 16 December 1983 in New York,[43] at which it decided to hold a substantive session from 7 to 25 May 1984 and agreed that informal consultations would take place in January and towards the end of April and beginning of May. The provisional agenda for the Committee's 1984 session was approved.

Proposed new international economic order

During 1983, the establishment of a new international economic order, called for by the General Assembly in 1974,[44] continued to be considered in several United Nations bodies.

In the statement on the world economic situation adopted at UNCTAD VI on 2 July[14] (see above), it was pointed out that what was needed was an integrated set of policies, encompassing short-term measures in areas of critical importance to developing countries and long-term changes relevant to the attainment of a new international economic order. In drafting this text, UNCTAD VI had considered the Buenos Aires Platform, which called for an integrated set of policies encompassing both immediate measures in areas of critical importance to developing countries and the restructuring of the world economic system and relations needed for the establishment of the new order.

The third and final phase of an analytical study on the progressive development of the principles and norms of international law relating to the new international economic order was to have been prepared by the United Nations Institute for Training and Research (UNITAR) for the Assembly's 1983 regular session. In September, the Secretary-General explained why UNITAR had not completed that phase of the study. On 19 December, in resolution 38/128, the Assembly requested UNITAR to continue preparing the final phase of

the study and a summary and outline of it to facilitate debate. The Secretary-General was requested to submit a report on UNITAR's final study in 1984 (see LEGAL QUESTIONS, Chapter VI).

A study on the new international economic order and the promotion of human rights was prepared for the Sub-Commission on Prevention of Discrimination and Protection of Minorities of the Commission on Human Rights and a resolution on the subject was adopted by the Sub-Commission on 6 September (see Chapter XVIII of this section).

At its May/June session, the United Nations Commission on International Trade Law (UNCITRAL) had before it a report by its Working Group on the New International Economic Order concerning a draft legal guide on drawing up contracts for construction of industrial works. The Group stressed that the guide should be prepared in the context of the new international economic order (see LEGAL QUESTIONS, Chapter VI).

On 19 December, in resolution 38/134, the Assembly called on UNCITRAL to continue to take account of its 1974 and 1975 resolutions concerning the new international economic order and took note of UNCITRAL's work on drafting the legal guide.

In other related action, the Assembly, by resolution 38/5 of 28 October, reaffirmed the determination of the United Nations to work closely with the Organization of African Unity towards the establishment of the new international economic order.

Proposed new international human order

During 1983, a proposal for the drafting of a declaration on a new international human order, concerned with the moral aspects of development, was considered by the Economic and Social Council and the General Assembly. The item had been suggested by the Philippines in August 1982[45] and in December[46] the Assembly had referred the matter to the Council for further study.

The Secretary-General submitted a note[47] to the Council's July 1983 session, summarizing replies from 12 Member States to his request for comments on the question. Also before the Council was a note verbale[48] containing the comments of the Philippines.

ECONOMIC AND SOCIAL COUNCIL ACTION

On 20 July in the Economic and Social Council, the Philippines introduced a draft resolution containing a draft declaration on a new international human order: moral aspects of development. By the draft resolution, the Council would have recommended the declaration for adoption by the Assembly.[49] On the same day, the Philippines, on behalf also of eight other States, introduced a draft decision transmitting the draft resolution to the Assembly.

On 25 July, the Council adopted without vote the nine-nation draft, as decision 1983/171.

A new international human order: moral aspects of development

At its 39th plenary meeting, on 25 July 1983, the Council decided to transmit to the General Assembly at its thirty-eighth session the draft resolution annexed to the present decision, the relevant documents submitted to the Council pursuant to Assembly resolution 37/225 of 20 December 1982, and the comments made thereon by Governments and by the Council during its consideration of the matter at its second regular session of 1983.

ANNEX
Declaration on a new international human order: moral aspects of development

The General Assembly

Adopts the following Declaration:

Declaration on a new international human order: moral aspects of development

We, the Members of the United Nations,

Bearing in mind certain of the principles and objectives enshrined in the Charter of the United Nations, such as reaffirmation of faith in the dignity and worth of the human person, promotion of social progress and better standards of life in larger freedom, and employment of international machinery for the promotion of the economic and social advancement of all peoples,

Recalling that, as stated in Article 55 of the Charter, the United Nations shall promote higher standards of living, full employment, and conditions of economic and social progress and development,

Recognizing that the International Covenant on Economic, Social and Cultural Rights and the Declarations of the Rights of the Child, on Social Progress and Development, on the Elimination of All Forms of Intolerance and of Discrimination Based on Religion or Belief, on the Elimination of Discrimination against Women, on the Rights of Disabled Persons, on the Rights of Mentally Retarded Persons, and the United Nations Declaration on the Elimination of All Forms of Racial Discrimination reflect the concern of the United Nations for all members of the human family,

Also bearing in mind that the Universal Declaration of Human Rights sets a common standard of human rights and obligations to be achieved for all peoples and that everyone is entitled to a social and international order in which the rights and freedoms set forth in the Declaration can be fully realized,

Recalling the Declaration and the Programme of Action on the Establishment of a New International Economic Order, the Charter of Economic Rights and Duties of States and the International Development Strategy for the Third United Nations Development Decade,

Noting that the United Nations has not fully and effectively achieved its objectives, as embodied in the Charter, in the field of economic and social development,

Reaffirming the principles contained in those covenants, conventions and declarations, particularly that:

(a) The recognition of the inherent dignity and of the equal and inalienable rights of all members of the human family is the foundation of freedom, justice and peace in the world,

(b) These rights derive from the inherent dignity of the human person,

(c) The ideal of human beings enjoying freedom from fear and want can be achieved only in conditions in which everyone is guaranteed the enjoyment of economic, social and cultural rights, as well as civil and political rights,

(d) The obligations of States under the Charter of the United Nations include the promotion of universal respect for, and observance of, human rights and fundamental freedoms,

(e) The individual, having duties to other individuals and to the community to which he belongs, has a responsibility to promote and respect the rights of his fellow human beings,

Stressing that the primary responsibility for the development of developing countries rests with them and that it will greatly facilitate their efforts to meet desired development goals under a just and equitable international economic order if economic and social disparities are reduced among peoples and nations,

Recognizing that a contributing factor to the failure of development has been the lack of political will, cooperation and understanding and of a full appreciation of the reality of interdependence and common interest among peoples and States,

Believing that all countries and peoples have to draw from the moral well-springs of equity, justice, mutual understanding and co-operation in the resolution of the economic and social ills that afflict mankind today,

Recognizing that it is in the interest of all States members of the international community that the developing countries should be able to achieve their development goals, and that the developed countries have a moral responsibility to assist in facilitating that process,

Realizing the need to promote the simultaneous attainment of economic and social goals and to create a condition of global growth and prosperity based on a new international human order which emphasizes the moral and humanistic approach to development,

Reaffirming that human beings, as well as States, constitute the membership of the international community,

Solemnly proclaim our common determination to establish and enhance the development and evolution of a new international human order, with emphasis on the moral aspects of development, based on the principles of equity, sovereign equality, common interest and co-operation among all States, regardless of their political and economic systems, and on the principles of equality, mutual respect and co-operation among all peoples,

And to that end

Declare that:

I

1. The growth and progress of societies, and the stability of Governments and States, are inextricably and inseparably linked to the growth, progress and stability of the human being;

2. The growth and development of the human being is the fundamental goal of any society, Government or State;

3. The development of a human being must consist in a balanced development of body and mind and of spiritual faculties;

4. The human being—man, woman or child—is simultaneously the subject and the object of development;

5. As the subject of development, the human being should be the ultimate beneficiary of the development process;

6. The development process must aim at furthering the collective well-being and happiness of all humankind;

7. Governments and States are in the best position to provide the environment that would ensure the balanced development of the human being and his self-realization;

8. In order to provide for such an environment, development must, *inter alia*, aim towards the following goals:

(a) Meeting the basic needs and wants of human beings, which are essential for the sustenance of life under acceptable standards of living;

(b) Furthering the economic betterment of all peoples;

(c) Improving their quality of life by providing the minimum elements in their pursuit of happiness and meaning beyond mere existence and subsistence;

(d) Helping in the fulfilment of the human being in his wholeness and in the total realization of his economic, social and spiritual needs and aspirations;

II

1. In order to achieve a new international human order, development programmes should be designed and carried out at the level of the people, who are the principal instruments and beneficiaries of the development process; development should be carried out to the full extent of popular participation, the people who are the beneficiaries of development being fully involved so as to ensure that their interests are respected, and bearing in mind that popular participation is necessary for the success of development programmes;

2. A new international human order also requires the strengthening and expansion of programmes of assistance to refugees, the disabled, the physically handicapped and the aged; the United Nations should similarly sustain and expand assistance to children; it should extend assistance programmes to human beings in the greatest need, regardless of sex, race or religion, bearing in mind that all humankind is the concern of the United Nations;

3. States, in pursuit of the new international human order, should furthermore work towards the implementation of United Nations declarations on, *inter alia*, the peaceful settlement of international disputes, the granting of independence to colonial countries and peoples, the non-proliferation of nuclear weapons and the prohibition of the use of nuclear and thermonuclear weapons, international co-operation for disarmament, the suppression and punishment of the crime of *apartheid* and the elimination of all forms of racial discrimination, the protection of the human environment and the establishment of a new international economic order;

4. It is in the interest of the international community if nations and peoples in a position to do so assist the less well-endowed among them, and that the former have a moral responsibility to facilitate the process of economic and social development of the latter;

5. In order to achieve a new international human order, all States, Governments, governmental and non-governmental organizations and entities, as well as individuals, are called upon to use all efforts to apply the principles and to attain the goals set forth in the present Declaration.

Economic and Social Council decision 1983/171

Adopted without vote

9-nation draft (E/1983/L.36), orally revised as a result of informal consultations; agenda item 3.
Sponsors: Costa Rica, Ecuador, Indonesia, Malaysia, Philippines, Sierra Leone, Singapore, Thailand, United Republic of Tanzania.
Meeting numbers. ESC 23, 35, 39.

GENERAL ASSEMBLY ACTION

In a letter to the Secretary-General dated 12 August,[50] the Philippines requested that the agenda item on the new international human order: moral aspects of development be inscribed as a sub-item of the item on development and international economic co-operation. The Assembly agreed to this request when it adopted decision 38/402.

On 19 December, on the recommendation of the Second Committee, the Assembly adopted resolution 38/170 without vote.

New international human order: moral aspects of development

The General Assembly,

Recalling its resolution 37/225 of 20 December 1982 entitled "New international human order: moral aspects of development",

Taking note of the report of the Economic and Social Council on its consideration of this question and Council decision 1983/171 of 25 July 1983,

Taking note also of the comments of Governments on the question, as well as statements made during the second regular session of 1983 of the Economic and Social Council and at the current session of the General Assembly,

1. *Invites* Member States that have not yet done so to submit their comments on this question and Member States that have already done so to submit additional comments, particularly on the draft declaration transmitted to the General Assembly by Economic and Social Council decision 1983/171, preferably before 31 July 1985;

2. *Requests* the Secretary-General to submit a report on this question to the General Assembly at its fortieth session;

3. *Decides* to include in the provisional agenda of its fortieth session the sub-item entitled "New international human order: moral aspects of development".

General Assembly resolution 38/170

19 December 1983   Meeting 102   Adopted without vote

Approved by Second Committee (A/38/702/Add.12) without vote, 14 November (meeting 39); draft by Vice-Chairman (A/C.2/38/L.36), based on informal consultations on draft transmitted by Economic and Social Council decision 1983/171 (A/C.2/38/L.6) and on draft by Philippines (A/C.2/38/L.14); agenda item 78 *(n)*.
Meeting numbers. GA 38th session: 2nd Committee 15-24, 30, 39; plenary 102.

In the light of the Committee's approval of the draft which became resolution 38/170, another draft by the Philippines was withdrawn. By this text, the Assembly would additionally have requested the Secretary-General to finalize the draft declaration with the assistance of a small *ad hoc* group of governmental experts, and to report on its preparation in 1984.

The Committee also decided to take no action on the text annexed to Council decision 1983/171.

Confidence-building measures

On 20 December, on the recommendation of the Second Committee, the General Assembly adopted by recorded vote resolution 38/196 on confidence-building in international economic relations.

Confidence-building in international economic relations

The General Assembly,

Taking into account the Charter of the United Nations, article 32 of the Charter of Economic Rights and Duties of States and General Assembly resolutions 3201(S-VI) and 3202(S-VI) of 1 May 1974 and 2625(XXV) of 24 October 1970,

Concerned about the present deterioration in the conditions for the conduct and expansion of international economic relations, and about the increasing departure from the multilateral platform of economic exchanges and negotiations,

Convinced that international economic co-operation should be placed on a long-term stable basis, a basis of broad exchange of relevant information through the United Nations system, and that it should take due account of the principles of equal rights and sovereignty of States,

Conscious that confidence-building in international economic relations can be achieved only through the sustained development of the developing countries,

Convinced also that the protection of economic co-operation among States against the adverse impact of international political tensions, and the reinforcement of confidence among all States in their economic relations, would introduce into those relations desirable elements of stability and reliability, as a valuable contribution to efforts aimed at reviving world trade and consolidating economic recovery, developing peaceful international economic co-operation and establishing a new international economic order,

Requests the Secretary-General to consult all States, as well as the United Nations organizations and bodies concerned, especially the United Nations Conference on Trade and Development and the regional commissions, about the scope of possible confidence-building measures which would lead to the promotion and acceleration of international economic co-operation and to report on his findings to the General Assembly at its thirty-ninth session through the Economic and Social Council.

General Assembly resolution 38/196

20 December 1983   Meeting 104   111-0-24 (recorded vote)

Approved by Second Committee (A/38/702/Add.13) by recorded vote (95-1-27), 28 November (meeting 52); draft by Poland (A/C.2/38/L.41/Rev.1); agenda item 78.
Meeting numbers. GA 38th session: 2nd Committee 41, 52; plenary 104.

Recorded vote in Assembly as follows:

In favour: Afghanistan, Algeria, Angola, Argentina, Bahamas, Bahrain, Bangladesh, Barbados, Benin, Bhutan, Bolivia, Botswana, Bulgaria, Burma, Burundi, Byelorussian SSR, Cape Verde, Central African Republic, Chad, China, Colombia, Congo, Costa Rica, Cuba, Cyprus, Czechoslovakia, Democratic Kampuchea,

Democratic Yemen, Dominican Republic, Egypt, El Salvador, Equatorial Guinea, Ethiopia, Fiji, Gabon, Gambia, German Democratic Republic, Ghana, Guatemala, Guinea, Guinea-Bissau, Guyana, Haiti, Honduras, Hungary, India, Indonesia, Iran, Iraq, Jamaica, Kenya, Kuwait, Lao People's Democratic Republic, Lesotho, Liberia, Libyan Arab Jamahiriya, Madagascar, Malawi, Malaysia, Maldives, Mali, Malta, Mauritania, Mauritius, Mexico, Mongolia, Morocco, Mozambique, Nepal, Nicaragua, Niger, Nigeria, Oman, Pakistan, Panama, Papua New Guinea, Paraguay, Peru, Philippines, Poland, Qatar, Romania, Rwanda, Saint Lucia, Samoa, Sao Tome and Principe, Sierra Leone, Somalia, Sri Lanka, Suriname, Swaziland, Syrian Arab Republic, Thailand, Togo, Trinidad and Tobago, Tunisia, Uganda, Ukrainian SSR, USSR, United Arab Emirates, United Republic of Cameroon, United Republic of Tanzania, Upper Volta, Uruguay, Venezuela, Viet Nam, Yemen, Yugoslavia, Zaire, Zambia, Zimbabwe.

Against: None.

Abstaining: Australia, Austria, Belgium, Canada, Denmark, Finland, France, Germany, Federal Republic of, Greece, Iceland, Ireland, Israel, Italy, Japan, Luxembourg, Netherlands, New Zealand, Norway, Portugal, Spain, Sweden, Turkey, United Kingdom, United States.

Coercive economic measures against developing countries

In 1983, both UNCTAD VI and the General Assembly urged developed countries to refrain from coercive economic actions against developing countries.

UNCTAD action. On 2 July, by a roll-call vote of 81 to 18, with 7 abstentions, UNCTAD VI adopted resolution 152(VI)[14] by which it reiterated that all developed countries should refrain from applying trade restrictions, blockades, embargoes and other economic sanctions against developing countries as a form of political coercion which affected their economic, political and social development.

A similar call had been made in a paragraph on protectionism of a resolution on international trade in goods and services contained in the Buenos Aires Platform—the final document of the March/April Fifth Ministerial Meeting of the Group of 77.[14]

GENERAL ASSEMBLY ACTION

On 20 December, on the recommendation of the Second Committee, the General Assembly adopted by recorded vote resolution 38/197.

Economic measures as a means of political and economic coercion against developing countries

The General Assembly,

Recalling the relevant principles set forth in the Charter of the United Nations,

Recalling also its resolutions 2625(XXV) of 24 October 1970, containing the Declaration on Principles of International Law concerning Friendly Relations and Co-operation among States in accordance with the Charter of the United Nations, 3201(S-VI) and 3202(S-VI) of 1 May 1974, containing the Declaration and the Programme of Action on the Establishment of a New International Economic Order, and 3281(XXIX) of 12 December 1974, containing the Charter of Economic Rights and Duties of States,

Recalling further article 32 of the Charter of Economic Rights and Duties of States, which states that no State may use or encourage the use of economic, political or any other type of measures to coerce another State in order to obtain from it the subordination of the exercise of its sovereign rights,

Bearing in mind the general principles governing international trade relations and trade policies for development contained in its resolution 1995(XIX) of 30 December 1964,

Recalling resolution 152(VI) of 2 July 1983 of the United Nations Conference on Trade and Development, entitled "Rejection of coercive economic measures",

Bearing in mind the principles and rules of the General Agreement on Tariffs and Trade and paragraph 7 (iii) of the Ministerial Declaration adopted on 29 November 1982 by the Contracting Parties of the General Agreement on Tariffs and Trade at their thirty-eighth session,

Recognizing that some developed countries are resorting more and more frequently to threats or the application of coercive and restrictive measures of increasing scope as an instrument for exerting political pressure on some developing countries,

Recognizing also that these measures are at variance with the Charter of the United Nations, the Charter of Economic Rights and Duties of States and the General Agreement on Tariffs and Trade,

Considering that coercive measures have a negative effect on the economies of the developing countries and their development efforts and do not help to create a climate of peace and friendly relations among States,

1. *Deplores* the adoption by certain developed countries, taking advantage of their predominant position in the international economy, of economic measures to exert coercion on the sovereign decisions of developing countries;

2. *Urges* those developed countries, therefore, to refrain from adopting measures aimed at exerting coercion or pressure in order to interfere in the exercise of the sovereign rights of the developing countries;

3. *Reaffirms* that developed countries should refrain from threatening or applying trade restrictions, blockades, embargoes and other economic sanctions, incompatible with the provisions of the Charter of the United Nations and in violation of undertakings contracted multilaterally or bilaterally, against developing countries as a form of political and economic coercion which affects their economic, political and social development;

4. *Requests* the Secretary-General to compile information provided by Governments on the adoption and the effects of the economic measures mentioned in paragraph 3 above, taken by developed countries as a means of political and economic coercion against developing countries, and to submit that information to the General Assembly for consideration at its thirty-ninth session;

5. *Appeals* to Governments to provide the necessary information to the Secretary-General, as requested in paragraph 4 above.

General Assembly resolution 38/197

20 December 1983   Meeting 104   119-19-5 (recorded vote)

Approved by Second Committee (A/38/702/Add.13) by recorded vote (112-19-5), 28 November (meeting 52); draft by Mexico, for Group of 77 (A/C.2/38/L.46); agenda item 78.

Meeting numbers. GA 38th session: 2nd Committee 46, 52; plenary 104.

Recorded vote in Assembly as follows:

In favour: Afghanistan, Albania, Algeria, Angola, Argentina, Bahamas, Bahrain, Bangladesh, Barbados, Benin, Bhutan, Bolivia, Botswana, Brazil, Bulgaria, Burma, Burundi, Byelorussian SSR, Cape Verde, Central African Republic, Chad, China, Colombia, Congo, Costa Rica, Cuba, Cyprus, Czechoslovakia, Democratic Kampuchea, Democratic Yemen, Djibouti, Dominican Republic, Ecuador, Egypt, El Salvador, Equatorial Guinea, Ethiopia, Fiji, Gabon, Gambia, German Democratic Republic, Ghana, Guatemala, Guinea, Guinea-Bissau, Guyana, Haiti, Honduras, Hungary, India, Indonesia, Iran, Iraq, Ivory Coast, Jordan, Kenya, Kuwait, Lao People's Democratic Republic, Lebanon, Lesotho, Liberia, Libyan Arab Jama-

hiriya, Madagascar, Malawi, Malaysia, Maldives, Mali, Malta, Mauritania, Mauritius, Mexico, Mongolia, Morocco, Mozambique, Nicaragua, Niger, Nigeria, Oman, Pakistan, Panama, Papua New Guinea, Paraguay, Peru, Philippines, Poland, Qatar, Romania, Rwanda, Samoa, Sao Tome and Principe, Saudi Arabia, Senegal, Sierra Leone, Singapore, Somalia, Sri Lanka, Sudan, Suriname, Swaziland, Syrian Arab Republic, Thailand, Togo, Trinidad and Tobago, Tunisia, Uganda, Ukrainian SSR, USSR, United Arab Emirates, United Republic of Cameroon, United Republic of Tanzania, Upper Volta, Uruguay, Venezuela, Viet Nam, Yemen, Yugoslavia, Zaire, Zambia, Zimbabwe.

Against: Australia, Belgium, Canada, Denmark, France, Germany, Federal Republic of, Iceland, Ireland, Israel, Italy, Japan, Luxembourg, Netherlands, New Zealand, Norway, Portugal, Turkey, United Kingdom, United States.

Abstaining: Austria, Finland, Greece, Spain, Sweden.

The recorded vote in the Second Committee was requested by the United States. Almost all those who spoke in explanation of vote—Austria, Greece (on behalf of the States members of the European Economic Commission), Israel, Japan, Norway, Spain and Sweden—said they could not support the draft as it referred only to developed countries. Austria and Sweden added that coercive measures should be applied only on the basis of Security Council decisions; furthermore, they did not want to prejudge results of ongoing negotiations in the General Agreement on Tariffs and Trade (GATT).

Japan felt that the Second Committee was not the proper forum to take up political questions. Portugal, Spain and Turkey stated that they held the position which they had set forth at UNCTAD VI on the question of coercive economic measures: Portugal that the resolution was unilateral and essentially political in nature; Spain that it should have been couched in general terms; and Turkey that the subject-matter did not fall within the competence of UNCTAD. Israel subscribed to the relevant provisions of the November 1982 Ministerial Declaration of GATT, which applied to all countries.

In the Assembly, the German Democratic Republic, speaking on behalf of the socialist States of Eastern Europe and Mongolia, pointed out that since the policy of nationalization being followed by developing countries was unfavourable to monopolies, those countries were liable to economic sanctions and other measures which maintained economic dependence.

Economic co-operation among developing countries

During 1983, the United Nations continued to promote economic co-operation among developing countries (ECDC), mainly through UNCTAD. Technical co-operation among developing countries received the support of UNDP (see Chapter II of this section).

UNCTAD activities. On 2 July, in resolution 139(VI) adopted without dissent,[14] UNCTAD VI recognized that ECDC was an integral part of a global development effort and of an interdependent world economy. It decided to continue implementing its resolution 127(V)[51] and to request the Trade and Development Board and the Committee on ECDC to adopt forward-looking decisions and consider effective measures of support, and to call on the Committee to consider ways to give further impetus to ECDC, particularly in relation to continuing work towards establishing the global system of trade preferences among developing countries, co-operation among their State trading organizations, establishing multinational marketing enterprises and promoting multinational production enterprises among developing countries, strengthening subregional, regional and interregional economic co-operation and integration among them, and relevant aspects of their monetary and financial co-operation.

The Conference reiterated the need for appropriate support for ECDC by the UNCTAD secretariat, requested the Committee on ECDC to consider adopting further measures of support by UNCTAD and forward-looking decisions, and to give guidance to the secretariat in that respect, and called on other competent international bodies and on the developed countries to support developing countries' efforts to implement economic co-operation programmes as a contribution towards attaining the objectives of the International Development Strategy for the Third United Nations Development Decade.[7]

In taking this action, the Conference considered the Buenos Aires Platform, the final document of the March/April Fifth Ministerial Meeting of the Group of 77, which included a draft decision on ECDC[14] on which the UNCTAD text was largely based. By that text, UNCTAD would have decided to support full implementation of resolution 127(V), rather than continue implementing it, and would have reiterated the need for a substantial technical and administrative contribution by the UNCTAD secretariat and other competent international organizations, particularly in relation to the areas of ECDC specified in the adopted text.

During its consideration of ECDC, UNCTAD VI had before it a policy paper by the UNCTAD secretariat, reviewing activities in the major programme areas and proposals for future work concerning ECDC.[52]

Also in that context, the Conference, in resolution 142(VI), called on developing countries to provide assistance to the least developed countries (see below, under LEAST DEVELOPED COUNTRIES).

The Trade and Development Board's Committee on ECDC, at its third session (Geneva, 12 September–5 October), adopted by consensus a resolution[53] in which it reiterated the need for the UNCTAD secretariat to continue supporting developing countries' mutual co-operation. The UNCTAD Secretary-General was called on to take further measures in trade expansion and promotion, and monetary and financial co-operation, to report on de-

velopments and present proposals for further work in those areas to the Committee.

The Committee noted the programme for co-operation among economic co-operation and integration groupings of developing countries adopted at the June/July 1982 session of the Working Party on Trade Expansion and Regional Economic Integration among Developing Countries[54] and called on UNCTAD's secretariat to continue programme support activities. The Committee recommended to the Trade and Development Board that a session of the Working Party be held in 1984, took note of support requirements indicated by the Working Party, and requested UNCTAD's Secretary-General to consider convening during 1984 a meeting of secretariats of economic co-operation and integration groupings of developing countries and multilateral development finance institutions to examine problems of promoting and financing integration projects.

Progress achieved in elaborating and establishing the Trade Information System regarding foreign trade of developing countries was welcomed by the Committee. It expressed appreciation to UNDP for financial assistance in support of this work and invited it to consider continuing such assistance. The Committee noted the need for continuing support of related ongoing activities on ECDC in other programme areas, particularly technical co-operation in development and transfer of technology.

In carrying out the ECDC work programme, UNCTAD's Secretary-General was requested to avoid duplication of work and to continue collaborating with international institutions and agencies in support of work in the area of monetary and financial co-operation among developing countries as an integral activity for trade expansion and promotion.

The Committee stressed the importance of technical assistance in achieving the objectives of ECDC and called on donor agencies to consider priorities established by developing countries themselves in this area. Developed countries were urged to contribute to ECDC projects through the United Nations development system.

In other action, the Committee recommended that the Trade and Development Board take into account the Committee's proposals on the global system of trade preferences among developing countries, among others those annexed to the Committee's report.[55]

A three-volume report[56] on economic co-operation and integration among developing countries, reviewing recent developments in subregional, regional and interregional organizations and arrangements, was prepared by the UNCTAD secretariat for the Committee's meeting. The volumes updated a 1976 study and dealt with Latin America, Africa, and Asia and the Pacific, Arab States and interregional.

On 15 October, the Trade and Development Board requested UNCTAD's Secretary-General to provide in the UNCTAD 1984 calendar for up to four weeks of meetings enabling developing countries participating in negotiations on a global system of trade preferences among them to continue working towards establishment of the system (see Chapter IV of this section).

During 1983, several meetings were held in connection with the UNCTAD programme for co-operation among economic co-operation and integration groupings of developing countries, which was established in 1982,[54] including: a meeting of the Informal Contact Group of Secretariats (ICGS) (Geneva, January); and ICGS study team meetings on market integration, industrial integration, and agricultural integration and co-operation (Geneva, 27 January).

A meeting of the Intergovernmental Follow-up and Co-ordination Committee (Tunis, Tunisia, 5-10 September) recommended that: the flow of information should be encouraged between the economic groupings and the Chairman of the Group of 77 in New York; those groupings be encouraged to strengthen ICGS; they be invited to attend technical meetings of the Group of 77 on ECDC, to appoint a liaison officer with the Group's Chairman, and to consider the results of technical meetings under the 1981 Caracas Programme of Action[57] in formulating their work programmes; ICGS be invited to explore capacities of economic groupings for interregional ECDC activities; and those groupings be further encouraged to co-operate among themselves.

Other 1983 meetings under UNCTAD auspices included a meeting enabling the developing countries participating in the negotiations on a global system of trade preferences *inter alia* to define the nature, scope and extent of the support requested from UNCTAD (see Chapter IV of this section); and an expert group meeting on energy co-operation among economic co-operation and integration organizations (see Chapter X of this section).

The UNCTAD *Trade and Development Report, 1983*[58] also considered ECDC and gave a preliminary analysis of trends in and prospects for trade among developing countries, and of financial flows. It concluded: that considerable potential existed for further initiatives in financial co-operation that could underpin future co-operation in trade and related areas, such as the establishment of joint ventures; that further orientation of imports towards greater collective self-reliance in industrial inputs for the agricultural sector would increase the developing countries' aggregate growth rate but, as this growth would accrue mainly to countries with a broad industrial base, specific corrective measures would be required; that closer

mutual trade and financial links could yield indirect benefits in the form of increased bargaining strength *vis-à-vis* Governments and enterprises in developed countries; and that options towards effective collective self-reliance would need to be complemented by far-reaching policy measures to be taken by developing countries as a group to reinforce initiatives in trade and finance, with joint action in transport and communications being necessary in certain cases before trade policy measures could become effective in stimulating mutual trade.

CDP recommendations. Addressing the issue of ECDC or "South-South co-operation" at its April 1983 session, CDP[1] noted that promotion of trade among developing countries seemed to hold special promise in reciprocal intra-industry trade which combined gains from trade with economies of scale. Agreements to allocate new industries in accordance with a pattern of allocation were necessary and could be implemented by lifting import restrictions only for the country to which the product had been assigned and by sharing the cost of protecting infant industries. The number of industries and products allocated among participants should continue to be limited, CDP stated.

Continued and enlarged access to international financial markets would be important in promoting reciprocal trade flows among developing countries. However, regional and subregional financial institutions had a great responsibility in financing trade expansion and should enable multilateral bond flotations and bank borrowing by groups of developing countries which would pool the risks. Payments unions, by which members pooled part of their foreign reserves and settled mutual transactions with minimal use of outside currencies, had renewed appeal in view of current foreign exchange shortages.

CDP was convinced of the large potential gains to be derived from closer co-operation in trade and finance among developing countries but believed that a third world secretariat was necessary for such co-operation and to serve them in international negotiations.

ACTION BY UN PRINCIPAL ORGANS

The question of ECDC was dealt with in several December 1983 Assembly resolutions. In resolution 38/151, the Assembly reaffirmed the need for the United Nations system to support developing countries' efforts to enhance economic and technical co-operation among themselves for the development of energy resources.

The United Nations system was requested to support and assist developing countries' efforts for technical and economic co-operation among themselves regarding new and renewable sources of energy in resolution 38/169 on immediate implementation of the 1981 Nairobi Programme of Action for the Development and Utilization of New and Renewable Sources of Energy.[59]

In its resolution 38/158, the Assembly called on the relevant organizations of the United Nations system to give priority support to economic and technical co-operation among developing countries with regard to food and agriculture. A similar call to the competent entities of the United Nations system had been made by the Economic and Social Council on 29 July (resolution 1983/71).

In resolution 38/201 on liquidation of the United Nations Emergency Operation Trust Fund, the Assembly decided that 12 per cent of the remaining balance of the Fund should be channelled through UNDP for economic and technical co-operation among developing countries.

Co-ordination in the UN system

Joint Meetings of CPC and ACC. Economic and technical co-operation among developing countries was the main item discussed at Joint Meetings of the Committee for Programme and Co-ordination (CPC) and ACC (Geneva, 4 and 5 July).[60] General issues discussed were: the importance of ECDC and technical co-operation among developing countries (TCDC), particularly in the context of the world economic crisis; the role and work of the United Nations in those areas; practical application of concepts; and the obstacles encountered in implementation.

There was widespread agreement on the fundamental importance of ECDC and TCDC for the achievement of developing countries' goals and it was unanimously underlined that they should reinforce other forms of international co-operation.

While it was agreed that the United Nations system had an important role as catalyst, it was generally recognized that the developing countries themselves were responsible for the promotion, support and implementation of ECDC and TCDC concepts. That the regional commissions had an important role to play, particularly regarding regional co-operation, was also agreed.

There was disagreement as to whether additional resources or more efficient use of existing resources would enable more effective implementation of ECDC and TCDC activities in the United Nations system. Other obstacles encountered in the application of ECDC and TCDC included some divergence of interpretation and lack of definitional precision regarding the concepts, and lack of overall perspective defining major issues and providing a framework for coherent planning and programming of activities.

It was agreed that the United Nations organizations would review their work on ECDC and TCDC and that ACC would submit a report thereon to CPC, in order to provide Governments with a comprehensive picture of what was being done.

ECONOMIC AND SOCIAL COUNCIL ACTION

On 28 July, the Economic and Social Council adopted without vote resolution 1983/50, on the recommendation of its Third (Programme and Co-ordination) Committee.

Joint Meetings of the Committee for Programme and Co-ordination and the Administrative Committee on Co-ordination on economic and technical co-operation among developing countries

The Economic and Social Council,

Recalling General Assembly resolution 35/56 of 5 December 1980, containing the International Development Strategy for the Third United Nations Development Decade, in which, *inter alia,* the Assembly stressed that economic and technical co-operation among developing countries based on the principle of collective self-reliance constituted a dynamic and vital component of an effective restructuring of international economic relations,

Recognizing that the primary responsibility for activities in economic and technical co-operation rests with the developing countries and that there is an increasing political commitment on the part of those States towards the implementation of programmes in economic and technical co-operation,

Noting the initiatives taken in this regard within the framework of the Caracas Programme of Action adopted by the High-level Conference on Economic Co-operation among Developing Countries, held at Caracas from 13 to 19 May 1981,

Noting also resolution 139(VI) of 2 July 1983 of the United Nations Conference on Trade and Development concerning economic co-operation among developing countries, which was adopted by consensus,

Reaffirming the role of the organizations of the United Nations system, including the regional commissions, competent regional and subregional organizations of developing countries, as well as the developed countries, to support the full implementation of programmes in economic and technical co-operation as a contribution towards attaining the goals and objectives of the International Development Strategy for the Third United Nations Development Decade,

Emphasizing the importance of enhancing awareness of the considerable potential for activities in economic and technical co-operation, through the exchange of information and the conduct of in-depth social and economic analyses, with a view to highlighting achievements and problems and proposing international policies for dealing with them,

1. *Takes note* of the agreement by the Administrative Committee on Co-ordination at the eighteenth series of Joint Meetings of the Committee for Programme and Co-ordination and the Administrative Committee on Co-ordination to carry out a review of the work in the area of economic and technical co-operation among developing countries, with a view to improving the co-ordination of the activities of the United Nations system in this field and to making them more responsive to the needs of developing countries, and to report thereon to the Committee for Programme and Co-ordination after the nineteenth series of Joint Meetings;

2. *Requests* the Secretary-General to ensure that the cross-organizational programme analysis of the activities of the United Nations system in economic and tech-

nical co-operation, scheduled for review by the Committee for Programme and Co-ordination and the Administrative Committee on Co-ordination in 1985, is carried out with due regard to the support provided by the United Nations system towards the implementation of the Caracas Programme of Action, in accordance with the mandates adopted by the organizations of the United Nations system;

3. *Recommends* that the initial report on the cross-organizational programme analysis requested by the Committee for Programme and Co-ordination should be submitted to the General Assembly at its thirty-ninth session, through the Committee for Programme and Co-ordination;

4. *Further recommends* that the work programmes and plans of the organizations of the United Nations system should be presented in such a manner as to identify clearly activities in economic and technical co-operation carried out by those organizations, in compliance with General Assembly resolutions 31/119 of 16 December 1976, 32/180 of 19 December 1977, 33/195 of 29 January 1979 and 34/202 of 19 December 1979 and that information on activities in economic and technical co-operation should be submitted periodically to Member States;

5. *Invites* the Secretary-General and the specialized agencies and United Nations bodies, in the light of their mandates, to pay particular attention to the assessment of their capacities and potentials for the promotion of economic and technical co-operation among developing countries and to suggest, as appropriate, ways and means of strengthening the activities in this field in their respective organizations, and to play an active role in supporting the efforts of the developing countries to implement economic co-operation programmes among themselves, as a contribution towards the attainment of the objectives of the International Development Strategy for the Third United Nations Development Decade;

6. *Further requests* the Secretary-General to develop, within existing resources, activities in the departments concerned, including the Department of International Economic and Social Affairs, in the field of economic and technical co-operation among developing countries, while avoiding duplication with activities carried out by the United Nations Conference on Trade and Development, the United Nations Development Programme and other competent bodies and organizations of the United Nations system; the *World Economic Survey* should in future contain, on a regular basis, in-depth reviews of activities in economic co-operation among developing countries.

Economic and Social Council resolution 1983/50

28 July 1983   Meeting 40   Adopted without vote

Approved by Third Committee (E/1983/120/Add.1) without vote, 27 July (meeting 19); draft by Vice-Chairman (E/1983/C.3/L.11/Rev.1), based on informal consultations on draft by Bangladesh for Group of 77 (E/1983/C.3/L.11), orally amended by Chairman; agenda item 19.
Meeting number. ESC 40.

The text approved by the Third Committee differed in a number of respects from the draft submitted by the Group of 77.

Changes included the addition of the fourth preambular paragraph and the rewording of several operative paragraphs. By paragraph 1 of the Group's text, the Council would have welcomed the commitment undertaken by ACC to intensify its efforts in economic and technical co-operation. Paragraph 2 had referred to the cross-organizational analysis scheduled for review in 1984 and had omitted the final phrase "in accordance with the mandates adopted by the organizations of the United Nations system". Paragraph 5 was originally two separate paragraphs, in one of which the Secretary-General would have been requested to play a more active role in promoting and co-ordinating economic and technical co-operation activities and reference to the International Development Strategy had been omitted. In paragraph 6 (formerly paragraph 7), the Council would have requested the Secretary-General to strengthen existing activities; omitted were the phrase "within existing resources" and the reference to avoiding duplication of activities with other United Nations bodies.

In another resolution of 28 July (1983/56), the Council requested the Committee on Natural Resources to discuss at its 1985 session the identification of new possibilities for economic and technical co-operation among developing countries concerning natural resources.

GENERAL ASSEMBLY ACTION

In its 20 December resolution (38/227 B) on co-ordination within the United Nations system, the Assembly requested CPC and the Economic and Social Council in 1984 to review the initial report on the cross-organizational programme analysis of economic and technical co-operation among developing countries.

Co-operation among regional commissions

Report of the Secretary-General. In June 1983, the Secretary-General submitted to the Economic and Social Council a report[61] on the promotion of programmes of interregional economic and technical co-operation among developing countries by the United Nations regional commissions. This subject had been recommended for the Council's discussion in 1983 by the executive secretaries of the regional commissions, in compliance with a July 1982 decision[62] by which the Council had decided to identify each year a subject relating to interregional co-operation for consideration under its agenda item on regional co-operation.

In the light of the prevailing international economic situation, the report's conclusions and recommendations included a list of important issues of immediate concern to developing countries, such as food security, food and agricultural production, energy sources development, fair and equitable prices for primary exports, technology exchange, identification of commodities for interregional trade, co-operation in balance of trade and payments adjustments, and operational transport programmes.

There was a need, the report stated, for a facility to develop a portfolio of projects for joint ventures among developing countries and provide training to officials concerned with co-operative projects.

Other recommendations included a proposal that an inter-secretariat meeting of the regional commissions and other United Nations agencies be held to develop further the scope of issues discussed and identify projects for interregional co-operation; the Council might wish to call on potential sources to support immediate steps to be taken by the regional commissions in the areas of priority concern, and might also wish to underscore the need for an adequate and timely response by member Governments and the United Nations system towards meeting the regional commissions' requirements for implementing projects and programmes at the interregional level.

Meeting of executive secretaries of regional commissions. Promotion of interregional economic and technical co-operation among developing countries by the regional commissions was discussed during 1983 at a meeting of the executive secretaries of the five regional commissions (Geneva, 11 and 12 July). Reporting in July to the Economic and Social Council,[63] the Secretary-General said that the executive secretaries agreed unanimously that the inter-secretariat meeting proposed for consideration by the Council,[61] would be essential to achieve optimal co-ordination of activities between different components of the United Nations system.

ECONOMIC AND SOCIAL COUNCIL ACTION

On 29 July, the Economic and Social Council, acting on the recommendation of its First (Economic) Committee, adopted resolution 1983/66 without vote.

Promotion of interregional economic and technical co-operation among developing countries

The Economic and Social Council,

Recalling its decision 1982/174 of 30 July 1982 concerning interregional co-operation, by which it requested the executive secretaries of the regional commissions to submit to the Council at its annual organizational session their joint recommendations for the identification of a subject related to interregional co-operation, of common interest to all regions,

Recalling also that, in its resolution 2043(LXI) of 5 August 1976 concerning the strengthening of the regional commissions, it recognized, without prejudice to the special needs and conditions of each region, that the regional commissions, with their experience in promoting regional and subregional co-operation, were the appropriate institutions within the United Nations to act as centres for the formulation, co-ordination and implementation of programmes for the promotion also of interregional co-operation,

Recalling further the mandate provided for the regional commissions by the General Assembly in section IV of the annex to its resolution 32/197 of 20 December 1977 on the restructuring of the economic and social sectors of the United Nations system, relating to structures for regional co-operation, in which it stated that the regional commissions should be enabled to play their role fully as the main general economic and social development centres within the United Nations system for their respective regions and, as a consequence of that role, *inter alia,* urged the commissions, taking fully into account the relevant global policy decisions of the competent United Nations organs, to intensify their efforts, with the assistance of the competent organizations of the United Nations system and at the request of Governments concerned, to strengthen and enlarge economic co-operation among developing countries at the subregional, regional and interregional levels,

Bearing in mind the special responsibilities of the United Nations Conference on Trade and Development for economic co-operation among developing countries and of the United Nations Development Programme for technical co-operation among developing countries,

Reaffirming the role of the Director-General for Development and International Economic Co-operation as stipulated in General Assembly resolution 32/197,

Having due regard to the Caracas Programme of Action adopted by the High-level Conference on Economic Co-operation among Developing Countries, held at Caracas from 13 to 19 May 1981, which provides the objectives, priorities and framework for activity relating to economic co-operation among developing countries,

Conscious of the fact that the regional commissions, by virtue of their location and multidisciplinary approach, have been called upon to initiate and implement a rapidly expanding range of projects and programmes involving co-operation among developing countries in all regions,

Noting that the Secretary-General, at the Joint Meetings of the Committee for Programme and Co-ordination and the Administrative Committee on Co-ordination, held on 4 and 5 July 1983, stated that the regional commissions had an important role in promoting co-operation among countries at the regional and interregional levels and reaffirmed the commitment of the United Nations bodies and programmes involved to supporting the efforts of developing countries to strengthen and implement their programmes of economic and technical co-operation,

Taking note with appreciation of the report of the Secretary-General on the promotion of programmes of interregional economic and technical co-operation among developing countries by the regional commissions, prepared pursuant to Council decision 1982/174,

1. *Reaffirms* the important role of the regional commissions in the promotion of economic and technical co-operation among developing countries at the subregional, regional and interregional levels, including the identification of areas for practical co-operation and the initiation, co-ordination and implementation of co-operative programmes and projects, as appropriate;

2. *Calls upon* States Members of the United Nations to provide their support to the regional commissions to meet those responsibilities effectively;

3. *Further calls upon* the executive secretaries of the regional commissions, in the light of the responsibility of the commissions for the exercise of team leadership at the regional level, as stipulated by the General Assembly in resolution 32/197, to organize periodic consultations between their respective commissions and United Nations organizations and entities and specialized agencies active at the regional and interregional levels, with a view to ensuring the effective co-ordination of projects and programmes carried out under the auspices of the bodies involved for the promotion of co-operation among developing countries at the subregional, regional and interregional levels, those periodic consultations to take place on the occasion of meetings already scheduled within the United Nations system;

4. *Takes note* of the conclusion in the report of the Secretary-General on the promotion of programmes of interregional economic and technical co-operation among developing countries by the regional commissions that urgent action should be taken, in particular with regard to the areas of immediate concern to the developing countries;

5. *Requests* the Secretary-General to take appropriate steps to ensure co-ordination and co-operation in the preparation and implementation of relevant programmes and activities of the regional commissions for interregional co-operation among developing countries;

6. *Recommends* the General Assembly:

(a) To continue to provide appropriate resources to enable the regional commissions to mobilize and to ensure their existing capability to meet effectively their responsibility for programme formulation, implementation and co-ordination in regard to subregional, regional and interregional economic and technical co-operation among developing countries;

(b) To request the Secretary-General to keep the Assembly informed, through the Economic and Social Council, on a continuing basis, of progress made by the Organization in the promotion of subregional, regional and interregional economic and technical co-operation among developing countries.

Economic and Social Council resolution 1983/66

29 July 1983   Meeting 41   Adopted without vote

Approved by First Committee (E/1983/123) without vote, 27 July (meeting 25); draft by Vice-Chairman (E/1983/C.1/L.31), based on informal consultations on draft by Bangladesh, for Group of 77 (E/1983/C.1/L.20); agenda item 7.
Meeting number. ESC 41.

The text approved by the First Committee differed from the Group of 77 draft in a number of respects. Added to the second preambular paragraph were the phrases "without prejudice to the special needs and conditions of each region" and "with their experience in promoting regional and subregional co-operation". Added to the third preambular paragraph were the phrases "taking fully into account the relevant global policy decisions of the competent United Nations organs" and "with the assistance of the competent organizations of the United Nations system and at the request of Governments concerned". The fourth and fifth preambular paragraphs were also added to the final text.

Paragraph 2 of the earlier draft would have had the Council call on "all" States Members to provide support to the regional commissions. Paragraph 3 did not include the final phrase stating that periodic consultations would take place on the occasion of scheduled meetings. Paragraph 4 would have had the Council endorse the conclusion in the Secretary-General's report rather than take note of it.

By paragraph 5, the Council would have requested the Secretary-General to make appropriate inter-secretariat arrangements to ensure co-ordination and co-operation among the regional commissions in the preparation and implementation of relevant programmes and activities for interregional co-operation among developing countries, including the organization of an inter-secretariat meeting of the regional commissions and other relevant agencies and programmes of the United Nations system.

In paragraph 6, the Council would have recommended that the Assembly provide appropriate resources, rather than continue to provide them, and that it request the Secretary-General to keep the Assembly informed, through the Council, on an ongoing and continuing basis, of progress made.

GENERAL ASSEMBLY ACTION

In December, the General Assembly adopted without vote decision 38/435.

Promotion of interregional economic and technical co-operation among developing countries

At its 102nd plenary meeting, on 19 December 1983, the General Assembly, on the recommendation of the Second Committee, decided to endorse the recommendations made by the Economic and Social Council in its resolution 1983/66 of 29 July 1983.

General Assembly decision 38/435

Adopted without vote

Approved by Second Committee (A/38/701/Add.1) without vote, 14 December (meeting 56); draft orally proposed by Chairman; agenda item 12.
Meeting numbers. GA 38th session: 2nd Committee 25, 26, 56; plenary 102.

REFERENCES

[1]E/1983/16. [2]YUN 1981, p. 381. [3]E/AC.54/1983/L.2. [4]E/AC.54/1984/4. [5]E/1983/39. [6]ACC/1983/14. [7]YUN 1980, p. 503, GA res. 35/56, annex, 5 Dec. 1980. [8]ACC/1983/29. [9]*World Economic Survey 1983: Current Trends and Policies in the World Economy* (E/1983/42), Sales No. E.83.II.C.1. [10]A/38/3. [11]TD/271. [12]TD/272. [13]TD/272/Add.1. [14]*Proceedings of the United Nations Conference on Trade and Development, Sixth Session, Belgrade, 6 June–2 July 1983*, vol. I, *Report and Annexes* (TD/326, vol. I), Sales No. E.83.II.D.6. [15]YUN 1980, p. 548. [16]A/38/15, vol. II. [17]YUN 1981, p. 406. [18]A/38/186 & Corr.1. [19]A/38/209. [20]A/38/494 & Corr.1. [21]A/38/537. [22]A/38/479. [23]A/C.2/38/8. [24]A/C.2/38/5. [25]E/1983/108. [26]A/C.2/38/3. [27]A/C.2/38/6. [28]A/38/702. [29]YUN 1979, p. 468, GA res. 34/138, 14 Dec. 1979. [30]YUN 1970, p. 105, GA res. 2734(XXV), 16 Dec. 1970. [31]YUN 1982, p. 608, GA res. 37/202, 20 Dec. 1982. [32]A/38/15, vol. I (dec. 269(XXVI)). [33]TD/B/AC.36/2 &

Corr.1. (34)TD/B/AC.36/3 & Corr.1. (35)A/38/16 (1983/2). (36)YUN 1980, p. 486. (37)ID/B/C.3/126. (38)ID/B/309. (39)ACC/1983/5. (40)ACC/1983/23. (41)E/AC.54/1984/3. (42)YUN 1977, p. 555. (43)A/AC.219/2. (44)YUN 1974, p. 324, GA res. 3201(S-VI), 1 May 1974. (45)YUN 1982, p. 597. (46)*Ibid.*, GA res. 37/225, 20 Dec. 1982. (47)E/1983/68 & Add.1-3. (48)E/1983/89. (49)E/1983/L.35/Rev.1. (50)A/38/360. (51)YUN 1979, p. 571. (52)TD/281 & Corr.1. (53)TD/B/974 (res. 2(III)). (54)YUN 1982, p. 600. (55)TD/B/974. (56)TD/B/C.7/51 (Parts I-III) (57)YUN 1981, p. 383. (58)*Trade and Development Report, 1983* (UNCTAD/TDR/3/Rev.1 & Corr.1), Sales No. E.83.II.D.13 & Corrigendum. (59)YUN 1981, p. 689. (60)E/1983/98. (61)E/1983/70. (62)YUN 1982, p. 797, ESC dec. 1982/174, 30 July 1982. (63)E/1983/86/Add.1.

Economic and social trends and policy

Economic reports prepared by the United Nations Secretariat in 1983 focused on the elusiveness of world economic recovery and the effect of the continuing recession on the developing countries. In addition to two major reports, which were submitted as background documents for the annual discussion of international economic and social policy in the Economic and Social Council and the Trade and Development Board, the world economic crisis was also discussed in documents prepared for UNCTAD VI (see Chapter IV of this section).

Economic surveys and trends

The *World Economic Survey 1983*,[1] prepared by DIESA and issued in mid-1983, reported that the world economy had remained in the grip of recession during 1982 and, despite prospects of a mild recovery in the main industrial countries, the outlook for developing countries was bleak.

The *Survey*, which was based on information available to the Secretariat as at 31 March, pointed out that the economic performance of most developing countries in 1982 was worse than the poor record of 1981: per capita income fell by close to 3 per cent, growth in agricultural output was weak and the decline in industrial activity was unprecedented. Since 1979, developing countries had seen their growth rates decline. In 1982, however, for the first time in 40 years, their aggregate output actually fell. According to preliminary estimates, average growth rates of gross domestic product (GDP) fell from 0.6 per cent in 1981 to -0.7 per cent in 1982. In the net energy-exporting developing countries, policies veered towards retrenchment as export revenues fell abruptly because of weakened demand for oil. Weakening export receipts and growing cautiousness in international financial markets tightened the balance of payments for most developing countries and, for several of them with large external debts, the

situation became critical in the second half of 1982. Only South and East Asia (particularly the more industrialized exporters of manufactures) increased their per capita output levels, although their aggregate rate of growth slackened. For many developing countries, international reserves were at unprecedented low levels, export earnings were unlikely to recover strongly in the near future and the outlook for 1983 remained bleak.

In 1982, most developed market economies experienced falling or stagnant levels of real output, sharply rising unemployment, very high real interest rates, record numbers of business insolvencies, continuing weak demand for private investment, large fiscal deficits, and a general weakening of currencies *vis-à-vis* the United States dollar. The average growth rate of GDP for these countries for 1982 was estimated at -0.3 per cent. A modest recovery to about 2 per cent was forecast for 1983, making it the fourth successive year of sluggish performance. By the end of 1982, the number of unemployed in this group of countries soared to 32 million—a record average of 8.5 per cent of the civilian labour force, with only Japan maintaining a low rate of 2.3 per cent. The severe reduction in economic activity was felt most by industry. Rigidity of wage costs, together with downward pressures on producer prices and the high cost of financing inventories, reduced corporate profit margins in some developed market economies, particularly the United States. In the major industrial countries there was an average reduction in inflation of 2 to 3 percentage points, measured in terms of consumer prices, while in the smaller countries the decline was only marginal. The difference could be attributed largely to the varying impact of trade price changes.

Although 1982 was the fourth consecutive year of below-plan output levels and slow growth in the centrally planned economies, economic activity in those countries was more buoyant than in other major groups of developed or developing market economies. The growth in aggregate output of this group virtually equalled that of 1981, namely 2.5 per cent. In the Eastern European countries, aggregate economic activity declined marginally; Poland had its fourth consecutive year of negative growth and the USSR's aggregate growth decelerated to 2.6 per cent. Forecasts for 1983 suggested that most of the European centrally planned economies would not fulfil their five-year plan (1981-1985) targets. The Asian planned economies regained substantial growth during 1982 in both industry and agriculture in spite of shortages of skilled workers and materials, the latter being caused partly by import constraints. China achieved a 5 per cent rate of growth because of good grain and cash crops, accelerated coal output and successful adjustment to external constraints. China's 1983 plan envisaged that growth rates of aggregate output, of industry and of agriculture would be 4 per cent.

The *Survey* stated that the prevailing economic situation had reminded countries of how much more interrelated their economies had become. It was not novel for the external environment virtually to eliminate any room for manœuvre in economic policy in individual developing countries, but it was notable that the vigour of recovery in individual developed countries was also severely constrained by external circumstances. If the uncertain recovery could not be translated into sustained growth, the interdependence linking developing and developed countries would increasingly be seen as an impediment to growth and cause for pursuit of alternative patterns of industrialization.

International trade and finance issues (see Chapter IV of this section) and development and economic co-operation (p. 402) were also addressed in the *Survey*.

A supplement to the *Survey*[2] contained articles on recent experience in economic co-operation among developing countries and possibilities for progress in the 1980s, some effects of rising public expenditure in developed market economies, and the impact of workers' remittances on the balance of payments.

In a pessimistic assessment, the *Trade and Development Report, 1983*[3] stated that, despite unmistakable signs of recovery in some major developed market economies, the outlook for the world economy was uncertain at best, and the immediate outlook for the developing countries was grim. This assessment could be altered if the international community adopted and vigorously implemented policy measures to reinforce recovery in those countries where it had already begun and to reactivate the economies of the developing countries.

The *Report*, which was based on information and data available in June 1983, stated that the world economy continued in crisis. The terms of trade of primary commodities remained depressed, prospects for the volume of traded goods remained highly uncertain, interest rates remained high compared to inflation rates, and difficulties of managing external debt increased as access to capital markets worsened.

In the developed market economies, unemployment continued to increase, pressure for increased protectionism had emerged, and government budgets were strained, leading several countries to cut back official development assistance and domestic social programmes. Capital formation growth rates were also sharply reduced, which retarded the restructuring of these countries' economies.

The effect of the world-wide recession on the developing countries had been to bring their growth to a standstill. The growth of debt relative to export earnings, combined with high real interest rates, had progressively reduced the possibility of financing for any significant length of time the large deficits which had emerged. Immediate international measures were needed to allow prompt acceleration of growth in developing countries. This process, together with additional measures in the developed market economies, designed in some cases to reduce fiscal deficits and in others to stimulate further demand, could underpin the fragile world recovery which appeared to be under way.

The world economic crisis had also compounded problems of economic planning in the socialist countries of Eastern Europe. Their efforts to restructure their economies had been set back by the emergence of external financial constraints in a number of them, causing them to reduce their demand for imports by constraining consumption or slowing investment while enlarging the share of investment allocated to export industries.

The *Report* reflected the view that recovery in the developed market economies would continue during 1984. That assessment contained a large element of uncertainty, however, since failure to buttress the incipient recovery could reduce growth prospects for both developed and developing countries, particularly towards the end of 1984. On the other hand, immediate measures in favour of developing countries could increase their growth rates and those measures, combined with domestic policy measures in the developed market economies, could accelerate growth in those countries as well.

Other documents on the world economic crisis included two prepared for UNCTAD VI. A report by UNCTAD's Secretary-General on development and recovery: the realities of the new interdependence[4] gave some economic indicators which it described as alarming. In the developing countries, the growth rate of gross national product for 1982 was even lower than the 1981 rate of only 1.5 per cent, total external debt mounted to over $600 billion, commodity prices plummeted in real terms to the lowest level in 45 years, investment and consumption were being curtailed with consequences for current employment and future growth, and, in 1981 and 1982, apart from the oil exporters, they had lost $34 billion through a decline in their terms of trade. In the developed market economies, growth rates averaged 1 per cent over those two years, and investment and employment declined with the unemployed exceeding 30 million. In the socialist countries of Eastern Europe, growth rates declined to less than 2 per cent.

In 1981 and 1982, the report stated, world trade had stagnated and capital flows contracted. The systems that had sustained international economic relations during the post-war years in the areas of money, finance and trade were themselves in crisis.

A policy paper on the current world economic crisis and perspectives for the 1980s,[5] prepared by the UNCTAD secretariat, stated that the world economic crisis threatened the economic future of all countries and, although there were signs of improvement in some major industrial countries, it was likely to be too slow to alleviate the underlying malaise.

The impact of the crisis on the development of developing countries had been dramatic: output per capita stagnated in 1980, declined by 2 per cent in 1981 and fell by more than 3 per cent in 1982. There was a danger that these countries would face continued difficulties in financing their balance-of-payments deficits, which would prevent them from realizing their growth potential for many years to come. Among major adjustments required to relax external constraint were: the need to overcome low commodity prices, high interest rates, sluggish demand for exports, reduced capital flows and rising protectionism; the need for shifts in the global pattern of resource allocation; and additional investment in developing countries requiring greater mobilization of domestic savings and an increase in external financial assistance. Such efforts, however, had to be accompanied by a swift upturn of the world economy and by an accelerated pace of structural change.

In contrast to the developing countries, slower growth in the developed countries was much more attributable to endogenous factors, including cyclical ones related primarily to policy choices regarding demand and longer-term ones related to the underlying potential for growth. The policy of using demand contraction to deal with cost-push inflation had proved costly to the developed market economies in terms of unemployment, output and investment, and had seriously affected the payments position of developing countries. A change in monetary policy, particularly in the United States, involving an attempt to control the money supply, resulted in an abrupt rise in interest rates for both domestic and foreign borrowers. The change in monetary policy in the United States caused the effective exchange rate of the dollar to rise by one third, which in turn had major consequences for the competitiveness of that country's industry, for energy prices in other countries and for the debt-servicing burden of developing countries.

Slower growth also characterized the economies of the socialist countries of Eastern Europe. Although the external sector of these countries was small, the slower growth of their trade owing to recession in the developed market economies and the growth of protectionism had affected their overall economic performance. Thus, the general trend in their economies had been similar since the mid-1970s to the trend in many other countries. A return to a faster growth trend would require substantial investment

and greater flexibility of the planning system and of sectoral allocation of resources.

Regarding the short-term outlook, the paper said that, despite indications of recovery in the developed market economies, unemployment was likely to continue to rise. The weak recovery could bring about an expansion of world trade of some 1 to 2 per cent—not sufficient to reverse the decline in world market prices. The outlook for socialist countries of Eastern Europe was for a continuation of modest growth. External trade would continue to suffer from weakness of world markets and for some countries servicing of external debt would remain a burden. For the developing countries, the modest growth in the developed market economies was not expected to be sufficient to improve their export performance in 1983. With stagnating or falling export earnings, high debt-service burdens, restraints on fresh borrowing and the need to rebuild international reserves, little growth in import volumes was likely. A continued fall in output and in real income per capita for the third consecutive year was likely—a situation without precedent since the Great Depression.

ECONOMIC AND SOCIAL COUNCIL ACTION

By decision 1983/177, adopted without vote on an oral proposal by its President, the Economic and Social Council took note of the *World Economic Survey* and other reports submitted in connection with its general discussion of international economic and social policy, including those prepared on current economic conditions in Africa, Asia and the Pacific, Europe, Latin America and Western Asia (see Chapter VIII of this section).

Reports considered by the Economic and Social Council in connection with its general discussion of international economic and social policy, including regional and sectoral developments

At its 40th plenary meeting, on 28 July 1983, the Council took note of the following documents:

(a) *World Economic Survey 1983: Current Trends and Policies in the World Economy;*

(b) Report of the Committee for Development Planning on its nineteenth session;

(c) Summary of economic conditions in Africa;

(d) Summary of the economic and social survey of Asia and the Pacific, 1982;

(e) Report on recent economic developments in the region of the Economic Commission for Europe;

(f) Summary of the economic survey of Latin America, 1982;

(g) Summary of the survey of economic and social developments in the region of the Economic Commission for Western Asia, 1983;

(h) Note by the Secretary-General on international co-operation in tax matters.

Economic and Social Council decision 1983/177

Adopted without vote

Oral proposal by President; agenda item 3.
Meeting numbers. ESC 17-30, 38, 40.

By decision 1983/130, the Council also took note of a report of the Secretary-General on some social trends in developing countries and the influence of current economic conditions (see Chapter XIII of this section).

Population, natural resources, environment and development

An Expert Group on Population, Resources, Environment and Development(Geneva, 24-29 April 1983), one of four expert groups convened as part of preparations for the 1984 International Conference on Population, discussed current and projected trends in those areas and made a number of recommendations concerning food and nutrition, resources and the environment, economic and social development, integration in policy, planning and programmes, and research (see Chapter XIV of this section).

In an October report,[6] the Secretary-General informed the General Assembly about progress achieved in implementing the programme of work on interrelationships between resources, environment, people and development, which had been initiated in response to a 1981 Assembly request.[7]

A general trust fund for the programme had been established by the Secretary-General in June 1981[8] to provide financing for co-ordinated research and for the commissioning of specific activities. As at 31 August 1982, three Member States (Sweden, Syrian Arab Republic, United Republic of Cameroon) had contributed a total of $164,080 to the fund. In addition, at the request of Sweden, the fund had transferred to it the balance ($105,195) of the trust fund for the 1979 United Nations symposium on the interactions between resources, environment population and development.[9]

The report gave details of two projects for which financing from the trust fund had been approved: the carrying capacity of Kenya—interactions between population, food, energy and material standards—and the first phase of a project on deforestation of the Himalayan foothills.

The Director-General for Development and International Economic Co-operation, who had been entrusted with management of the trust fund, had decided to postpone the proposed establishment of an advisory body to assist in overall guidance of the programme until the fund's resources became more substantial. Inter-agency co-ordination continued to be arranged through CCSQ(PROG).

Among proposals for future action mentioned in the report were: obtaining increased resources for the trust fund, continuing research studies, and identifying, selecting and screening projects proposed for financing. This last activity would be carried out by CCSQ(PROG), with final approval to remain the prerogative of the Director-General.

On 19 December, in decision 38/442, the Assembly took note of the Secretary-General's report and decided to keep the matter under review.

REFERENCES

[1]*World Economic Survey 1983: Current Trends and Policies in the World Economy* (E/1983/42), Sales No. E.83.II.C.1. [2]*Supplement to World Economic Survey 1983* (ST/ESA/136), Sales No. E.83.II.C.3. [3]*Trade and Development Report, 1983* (UNCTAD/TDR/3/Rev.1 & Corr.1), Sales No. E.83.II.D.13 & corrigendum. [4]TD/271. [5]TD/272. [6]A/38/504 & Corr.1. [7]YUN 1981, p. 393, GA res. 36/179, 17 Dec. 1981. [8]*Ibid.*, p. 391. [9]YUN 1979, p. 480.

Development planning, education, administration and information

During 1983, various aspects of development planning, education, administration and information were considered by United Nations bodies, including CDP, which considered the issue in the context of the world economic crisis.

Preparation of educational materials for the United Nations Decade for Women (1976-1985) continued and consideration was given to preparing a kit for International Youth Year (1985). The Assembly decided to continue the computerized development information system operated by the Information Systems Unit (ISU) of DIESA and took note of a suggestion that ISU be established as a distinct unit within the Dag Hammarskjöld Library.

Development planning

CDP activities. The Committee for Development Planning held its nineteenth session at United Nations Headquarters from 18 to 27 April 1983.[1]

Composed of 24 experts appointed by the Economic and Social Council, CDP examined the state of the world economy and suggested improvements in international economic co-operation. It considered reports by its November 1982 Working Group on Development Prospects[2] and its January 1983 Working Group on Development Patterns and Styles in the Context of Longer-term World Economic Prospects. Ways in which developing countries could attain greater autonomy and freedom of manoeuvre in the international economic arena, including economic co-operation among developing countries, were also considered, as were measures in favour of the least developed and other low-income developing countries and the identification of the least developed among the developing countries (see under relevant subject headings in this chapter).

Unified approach to development planning

Responding to a 1981 General Assembly request,[3] the Secretary-General submitted in

January 1983 a report on a unified approach to development analysis and planning.[4] The Assembly had requested that, based on government information, the Secretary-General report in 1983, through the Commission for Social Development and the Economic and Social Council, on experience acquired in applying such an approach in socio-economic development at the national level as well as in activities of United Nations economic and social bodies. The Secretary-General stated that, by 1 October 1982, six replies had been received from Governments containing their views on the subject, one in the form of official publications and another communicating that no information could be provided. In view of the paucity of replies, it was not considered feasible to prepare a report as requested.

ECONOMIC AND SOCIAL COUNCIL ACTION

On 4 February 1983, the Council, by decision 1983/101 on its basic programme of work for 1983 and 1984, transmitted the Secretary-General's report[4] to the General Assembly without debate. On 11 May, the Chairman of the Council's First Committee stated that the Committee's understanding was that any additional replies received by the Secretariat, as well as any future replies that it might receive on the question, would be brought to the attention of the Assembly. Delegations could return to the question at the Council's July 1983 session in the context of considering the review and appraisal of the International Development Strategy for the Third United Nations Development Decade (see above).

On 26 May, the Council adopted resolution 1983/11, in which it resolved to urge that high priority be given to analysing the interrelationship of social and economic policies, and called for specific action by the United Nations and Member States in this area. Also on 26 May, the Council adopted resolution 1983/13 on the unified approach to development analysis and planning in the field of social integration through popular participation, by which it requested the Secretary-General to arrange a study on the subject and to inform the Commission for Social Development of the results.

GENERAL ASSEMBLY ACTION

On the recommendation of its Second Committee, the Assembly on 19 December adopted resolution 38/179 without vote.

Unified approach to development analysis and planning

The General Assembly,

Recalling its resolutions 2542(XXIV) of 11 December 1969, containing the Declaration on Social Progress and Development, 3409(XXX) of 28 November 1975, concerning a unified approach to development analysis and planning, 3201(S-VI) and 3202(S-VI) of 1 May 1974, containing the Declaration and the Programme of Action

on the Establishment of a New International Economic Order, 3281(XXIX) of 12 December 1974, containing the Charter of Economic Rights and Duties of States, 3362(S-VII) of 16 September 1975 on development and international economic co-operation, 35/56 of 5 December 1980, the annex to which contains the International Development Strategy for the Third United Nations Development Decade, and 37/202 of 20 December 1982, concerning the review and appraisal of the implementation of the International Development Strategy for the Third United Nations Development Decade,

Bearing in mind Economic and Social Council resolution 1747(LIV) of 16 May 1973, which contains recommendations concerning a unified approach to development analysis and planning,

Believing that development is an integral process, embodying both economic and social objectives,

Further believing that a unified approach to analysis and planning of development at the national level is a possible and effective tool for promoting economic, social and human development and for providing increasing opportunities to all people for a better life,

Reaffirming that each State has the sovereign and inalienable right to choose its economic and social system in accordance with the will of its people and without outside interference,

1. *Takes note* of the report of the Secretary-General concerning the status of replies received from Governments on the experience acquired in applying a unified approach to the process of socio-economic development;

2. *Reaffirms* its decision 36/405 of 19 November 1981 to continue consideration of the question of a unified approach to development analysis and planning, taking into account its importance for the process of development, as stressed in the International Development Strategy for the Third United Nations Development Decade;

3. *Invites* interested countries to send information to the Secretary-General on the experience acquired in applying a unified approach to the process of socio-economic development at the national level;

4. *Requests* the Secretary-General:

(a) To continue to study the question of a unified approach to the analysis and planning of development, in order to make available to all States the national and international experience gained in this field;

(b) To prepare, on the basis of the information offered by interested countries, a report on the application by Governments of a unified approach to development analysis and planning, taking into account both the experience gained in this field in the United Nations economic and social organs concerned and the results of the first review and appraisal of the implementation of the International Development Strategy for the Third United Nations Development Decade;

(c) To submit the report to the Economic and Social Council, at its second regular session of 1985, and to the General Assembly for consideration at its fortieth session, with a view to its utilization as an input in the future reviews and appraisals of the International Development Strategy for the Third United Nations Development Decade.

General Assembly resolution 38/179

19 December 1983   Meeting 102   Adopted without vote

Approved by Second Committee (A/38/704) without vote, 28 November (meeting 52); draft by Vice-Chairman (A/C.2/38/L.78), based on informal consultations on draft by German Democratic Republic (A/C.2/38/L.49); agenda item 80 *(c).*

Meeting numbers. GA 38th session: 2nd Committee 31-34, 38, 44, 52; plenary 102.

The text approved by the Second Committee differed in a number of respects from the earlier draft by the German Democratic Republic, which was subsequently withdrawn.

By this text, the Assembly would, in the fourth preambular paragraph, have described the unified approach as "one of the most effective tools" for promoting development. In paragraph 2, it would have reaffirmed its decision, without specifying which one, to continue considering the question regularly. By paragraph 3, the Assembly would have invited Governments that had not done so to submit information to the Secretary-General. In subparagraph 4 *(a)*, "in particular developing countries" would have been added after "all States". In subparagraph 4 *(b)*, the Assembly would have requested that a comprehensive report be prepared on both the application by Governments of a unified approach and the application of that approach in the regional commissions and other United Nations bodies concerned, taking into account the results of the review and appraisal of the implementation of the International Development Strategy. Subparagraph 4 *(c)* would also have referred to a "comprehensive" report and would have omitted reference to future reviews and appraisals of the Strategy.

Two other paragraphs were also included in the earlier text. By these, the Assembly would have requested the Economic and Social Council to include a separate item on a unified approach to development analysis and planning in the provisional agenda of its second regular session of 1985 and decided to include the same item in that of the Assembly's 1985 session.

Other activity. In December, the incorporation of women into development planning and programming was discussed at a seminar organized by the International Research and Training Institute for the Advancement of Women (see Chapter XIX of this section).

Public sector in economic development

Report of the Secretary-General. Responding to a 1979 General Assembly request,[5] the Secretary-General submitted in May 1983, through the Economic and Social Council, the second comprehensive report on the role of the public sector in the economic development of developing countries,[6] the first having been prepared in 1979.

The report dealt with aspects of the role of the public sector specified by the Assembly in 1979: mobilizing national resources for economic and social development; planning, regulating and promoting other sectors; the role of public enterprises as the main instruments of the public sector and ways of increasing their efficacy; ways of strengthening the public sector as a possible means of developing appropriate national and international measures; and the exchange of experience and information among developing countries.

The report's conclusions stated that the public sector played a dominant role in the development of developing countries. It mobilized, in the form of government revenue or loans, a large proportion of a country's economic resources and in allocating them largely determined the main directions of economic and social development. In economies where the major financial institutions were government-owned, mobilization of resources in the private sector occurred through banks that were public enterprises; monetary and credit policies of the public sector contributed to decisions regarding the allocation of those resources.

Planning, laying down economic and social infrastructure, determining critical prices and regulating activities of other sectors comprised a powerful set of policy instruments at the command of the public sector. In many least-developed countries, the public sector constituted the principal institution for structural change, although scarcity of resources, institutional rigidities, domestic management capacity and international conditions substantially circumscribed its power.

With regard to public enterprises, the report noted that they were a source of strength to the public sector and were widely used as instruments of government policy, constituting an effective means of collaborating with other sectors of the economy. Problems concerning their efficacy as instruments of the public sector ranged from the need for clearer definition and articulation of objectives and the institution of systematic and useful methods of control and supervision to improved internal management.

Analysis, discussion and dissemination of information on accumulated experience of the role of the public sector in economic and social development could contribute to a better appreciation of it, the report concluded.

ECONOMIC AND SOCIAL COUNCIL ACTION

As decided in 1981,[7] the Economic and Social Council discussed the report of the Secretary-General at its July 1983 session. On 28 July, it adopted resolution 1983/61 without vote.

Role of the public sector in promoting the economic development of developing countries

The Economic and Social Council,

Recalling its resolutions 1978/60 of 3 August 1978, 1978/75 of 8 November 1978, 1979/48 of 31 July 1979 and 1981/45 of 20 July 1981,

Recalling also General Assembly resolution 34/137 of 14 December 1979, in which the Assembly, *inter alia*, invited the Secretary-General to continue his detailed study of the role of the public sector and to submit, through the Economic and Social Council, a comprehensive report to the Assembly at its thirty-eighth session, paying special attention to several aspects of the matter indicated in that resolution,

Recalling General Assembly resolutions 3201(S-VI) and 3202(S-VI) of 1 May 1974, containing the Declaration and the Programme of Action on the Establishment of a New International Economic Order, and 3281(XXIX) of 12 December 1974, containing the Charter of Economic Rights and Duties of States,

Noting that, in paragraph 31 of section II of the International Development Strategy for the Third United Nations Development Decade, contained in the annex to General Assembly resolution 35/56 of 5 December 1980, it was stated that due account should be taken of the positive role of the public sector in mobilizing internal resources, formulating and implementing overall national development plans and establishing national priorities,

Bearing in mind that every State has the sovereign and inalienable right to choose its economic and social system in accordance with the will of its people, without outside interference,

1. *Takes note* of the report of the Secretary-General on the role of the public sector in promoting the economic development of developing countries;

2. *Invites* the Secretary-General to continue to study the role of the public sector in promoting the economic development of developing countries and to submit, through the Economic and Social Council, a further comprehensive report to the General Assembly at its forty-second session, taking into account information supplied by Member States and comments and suggestions on the subject made by delegations at meetings of intergovernmental bodies, and, *inter alia*, paying special attention to the provisions of paragraph 5 of General Assembly resolution 34/137;

3. *Reaffirms* Council resolution 1978/60, in which it, *inter alia*, invited the regional commissions and other appropriate organizations of the United Nations system to assist the Secretary-General regularly in his continuing study of the role of the public sector in promoting the economic development of developing countries;

4. *Requests* the Secretary-General, while implementing the present resolution, to consider, if necessary, organizing, in close co-operation with competent bodies and organizations of the United Nations system, a seminar on the role of the public sector in promoting the economic development of developing countries;

5. *Invites* the Secretary-General to include reference to the role of the public sector in promoting the economic development of developing countries in the reports called for under General Assembly resolutions 37/202 and 37/204 of 20 December 1982.

Economic and Social Council resolution 1983/61

28 July 1983   Meeting 40   Adopted without vote
7-nation draft (E/1983/L.38/Rev.1); agenda item 3.
Sponsors: Afghanistan, Cuba, German Democratic Republic, India, Madagascar, Mongolia, Syrian Arab Republic.
Meeting number. ESC 40.

GENERAL ASSEMBLY ACTION

On 19 December, the Assembly adopted decision 38/430 without vote.

Role of the public sector in promoting the economic development of developing countries

At its 102nd plenary meeting, on 19 December 1983, the General Assembly, on the recommendation of the Second Committee, took note of the report of the Secretary-General on the role of the public sector in promoting the economic development of developing countries.

General Assembly decision 38/430

Adopted without vote

Approved by Second Committee (A/38/701/Add.1) without vote, 14 December (meeting 56); oral proposal by Chairman; agenda item 12.
Meeting numbers. GA 38th session: 2nd Committee 56; plenary 102.

Development administration

In 1983, the United Nations Department of Technical Co-operation for Development (DTCD) carried out a $10.9-million programme of assistance to Governments in public administration and finance. The programme encompassed personnel administration and training, institution building, administrative reform and improvement and financial management. The main source of funds was UNDP, which provided $8.7 million.

During the year, over 100 technical co-operation projects were executed in 66 developing countries, primarily in the areas of administrative reform, personnel administration and training, and financial and public enterprise management.

A study[8] was issued based on the results of an interregional seminar on regulatory administration for promoting national development (Bangkok, Thailand, 9-13 May), organized by DTCD in collaboration with the Economic and Social Commission for Asia and the Pacific, and on research carried out by DTCD's Development Administration Division.

DTCD also convened an expert working group meeting on modern management and information systems for public administration in developing countries (New York, 12-16 December).[9]

Development education and information

Development education

At its April 1983 session,[10] the Joint United Nations Information Committee (JUNIC) reviewed the work of its *Ad Hoc* Working Group on Development Education, requested it to continue preparing a women and development education kit and continue to explore the possibility of an International Youth Year (1985) development education kit. JUNIC suggested that, in addition to providing its annual report, the Working Group consider focusing on one or two substantive development education issues in its 1984 presentation.

The United Nations Centre for Social Development and Humanitarian Affairs reported that its Advancement of Women Branch had made financial contributions to the JUNIC/Non-

Governmental Organizations Sub-Group on Women and Development and would be the lead organization for preparing the following publications under the aegis of the sub-group: three JUNIC development education kits on the principal objectives of the United Nations Decade for Women (1976-1985) (equality, development and peace); and 10 Decade notes on priority issues of the Programme of Action for the Second Half of the Decade. The Branch had made an allocation to the United Nations Department of Public Information for a television series on women and development, which it hoped could be used by educational institutions as well as television stations.

At its May/June session, CPC recommended[11] that JUNIC, together with the United Nations Educational, Scientific and Cultural Organization, should study ways of strengthening co-operation in the field of development education.

Information Systems Unit

In response to a 1982 request by CPC,[12] the Secretary-General submitted a report[13] on the Information Systems Unit in DIESA to CPC's May/June 1983 session. In 1982, CPC had noted a report submitted to it in response to a 1981 General Assembly resolution[14] and requested additional information on, *inter alia*, the use, value and cost of the computerized Development Information System (DIS) maintained by ISU, and the relationship between ISU and the bibliographic information systems of the regional commissions.

The report described the two major areas of ISU's work as: management and dissemination of unpublished information by means of DIS; and exchange of information through co-operation with the regional commissions and other information systems. DIS activities included collection, selection and analysis of documents and entry of bibliographical data into the computer, preparation of six issues per year of *Development Information Abstracts*, a journal which informed users of the latest items added to the DIS data base, and providing on-line searches, selective dissemination of information services, and copies of documents to users. While the DIS data base had increased by over 30 per cent, ISU costs had shrunk in all areas by 14 to 40 per cent.

Co-operation between ISU and the regional commissions was being carried out in the major areas of compatibility of data structure record format and bibliographical description; maintenance of a common indexing vocabulary—the trilingual (English, French, Spanish) *Macrothesaurus for Information Processing in the Field of Economic and Social Development*; and bibliographical data exchange. Arrangements had been made, the report said, for ISU to serve as a focal point for expanding, merging and distributing development-related data

bases of the regional commissions and maintaining the common indexing vocabulary.

Also in response to the 1981 Assembly resolution,[14] the Secretary-General transmitted a report[15] by the Advisory Committee for the Co-ordination of Information Systems (ACCIS) evaluating the performance and utility of ISU. Annexed to the report was an assessment and review of ISU's programme, prepared by a consultant. ACCIS endorsed the consultant's conclusions and recommendations, in particular: establishing ISU as a distinct unit within the Dag Hammarskjöld Library; identifying ISU as a specific programme with identifiable budgetary support in the Library's programme and budget; continuing all current ISU features and services and the database merger programme and other co-ordination programme elements; and incorporating the *Macrothesaurus* project with the project for revision of the United Nations Bibliographic Information System *Thesaurus*.

In May, CPC noted with satisfaction progress made by ISU in increasing its productivity and advancing its work.[11] It felt that care should be taken that merging data bases of regional commissions and distributing to them the resulting products should contribute to proper co-ordination, information dissemination and strengthening of their information systems. The importance of ISU's continuing to collect valuable unpublished material and to co-operate with other information systems was recognized. CPC proposed that the Secretary-General examine integrating ISU within the Dag Hammarskjöld Library and report to CPC on his decision.

GENERAL ASSEMBLY ACTION

On 20 December, the Assembly, on the recommendation of its Fifth (Administrative and Budgetary) Committee, adopted section XIV of resolution 38/234 without vote:

Evaluation of the performance and utility of the Information Systems Unit of the Department of International Economic and Social Affairs
[*The General Assembly . . .*]
1. *Takes note* of the report of the Advisory Committee for the Co-ordination of Information Systems;
2. *Decides* that the financial arrangements which were applicable to the Information Systems Unit in 1982-1983 should be continued in the biennium 1984-1985;

. . .

General Assembly resolution 38/234, section XIV
20 December 1983   Meeting 104   Adopted without vote

Approved by Fifth Committee (A/38/760) without vote, 8 December (meeting 59); oral proposal by Chairman on ACABQ recommendation; agenda item 109.
Meeting numbers. GA 38th session: 5th Committee 59; plenary 104.

REFERENCES
[1]E/1983/16. [2]YUN 1982, p. 603. [3]YUN 1981, p. 396, GA dec. 36/405, 19 Nov. 1981. [4]A/38/62. [5]YUN 1979, p. 515,

GA res. 34/137, 14 Dec. 1979. [6]A/38/176-E/1983/50. [7]YUN 1981, p. 394, ESC res. 1981/45, 20 July 1981. [8]TCD/SEM.84/4. [9]*Modern Management and Information Systems for Public Administration in Developing Countries* (ST/ESA/SER.E.36), Sales No. E.85.II.H.1. [10]ACC/1983/19. [11]A/38/38. [12]YUN 1982, p. 610. [13]E/AC.51/1983/6. [14]YUN 1981, p. 398, GA res. 36/237, 18 Dec. 1981. [15]A/C.5/38/1.

PUBLICATIONS

Overcoming Economic Disorder: International Action for Recovery and Development; Views and Recommendations of the Committee for Development Planning (ST/ESA/133), Sales No. E.83.II.C.2. *Enhancing Capabilities for Administrative Reform in Developing Countries* (ST/ESA/SER.E/31), Sales No. E.83.II.H.2. *Issues and Priorities in Public Administration and Finance in the Third United Nations Development Decade* (ST/ESA/SER.E/34), Sales No. E.83.II.H.4.

Rural and regional development

Rural and regional development activities continued throughout the United Nations system during 1983.

Rural development

The inter-agency Task Force on Rural Development, a body of ACC, met at Rome, Italy, from 11 to 13 April.[1] The publication that month of the first issue of the Task Force's newsletter was welcomed and improvements suggested for future issues. Since the newsletter contained accounts of each agency's work concerning rural development, the general progress report presented at the Task Force's meeting dealt with areas of common interest, such as the poverty-oriented focus and joint action. Main discussions centred on the three priority areas of work: joint action at the country and regional level; people's participation in rural development; and monitoring and evaluation of rural development.

Regarding inter-agency missions to countries requesting assistance on agrarian reform and rural development policies, several suggestions were made for more effective inter-agency preparation and follow-up and for the use of missions for better inter-agency co-ordination. Progress in establishing national co-ordinating mechanisms had been slow and it was agreed that priority be given to countries visited by inter-agency missions. It was recommended that efforts to establish United Nations working committees at country level be pursued. A 1983-1984 work programme approved by the Task Force included provision for regional inter-agency meetings and missions to individual countries.

An interregional seminar on integrated rural development was organized by DTCD at Shanghai, China, from 16 to 30 August.[2] DTCD also organized an expert group meeting on monitoring and evaluation of rural development programmes

at United Nations Headquarters from 6 to 14 September.[3]

By resolution 1983/10 of 26 May on social aspects of rural development, the Economic and Social Council called on Governments to give special attention to the social impact of democratic land reforms, promotion of co-operative movements, introduction of rural development planning, strengthening the role of qualified national personnel in rural development, and encouragement of popular participation in the development process in rural areas (see Chapter XIII of this section).

Calls for Governments to implement agrarian reform and rural development within national plans and objectives and in accordance with recommendations of the 1979 World Conference on Agrarian Reform and Rural Development were made in Economic and Social Council resolution 1983/71 of 29 July and in General Assembly resolution 38/158 of 19 December, both of which dealt with food problems.

Regional development

Among publications issued during 1983 by the United Nations Centre for Regional Development (UNCRD) (Nagoya, Japan) was *Administration of Regional and Local Development: Studies on Co-ordination.* The periodicals *Regional Development Dialogue,* vol. 4, No. 1, and *UNCRD Newsletter,* No. 15, were also issued during the year.

REFERENCES

[1]ACC/1983/15. [2]TCD/SEM.84/1. [3]TCD/SEM.84/3.

Special economic areas

The General Assembly in 1983 took a number of actions aimed at trying to ease problems in special economic areas.

Addressing the needs of developing countries, the Assembly, in resolution 38/200, urged Governments to adopt immediate measures in specific economic areas and, in resolution 38/195, continued to monitor implementation of the Substantial New Programme of Action for the 1980s for the Least Developed Countries.

The problems of land-locked developing countries, particularly in the transit and transport areas, were considered by UNCTAD. A draft resolution on the subject was referred by the Assembly, in decision 38/437, to its 1984 session. A renewed appeal for resources for the United Nations Special Fund for Land-locked Developing Countries was made in resolution 38/174, while in decision 38/315, the Assembly took note of the Secretary-General's decision not to submit an appointment for the post of Executive Director of the Fund and in decision 38/319 deferred until 1984 the election of members of the Fund's Board of Governors.

The problems of island developing countries were also considered by UNCTAD.

Developing countries

In 1983, the General Assembly again took up the question of immediate measures in favour of developing countries and, among other things, reiterated its call for such measures made in December 1982.[1]

GENERAL ASSEMBLY ACTION

As recommended by the Second Committee, the Assembly, on 20 December 1983, adopted without vote resolution 38/200.

Immediate measures in favour of the developing countries

The General Assembly,

Recalling its resolutions 3201(S-VI) and 3202(S-VI) of 1 May 1974, containing the Declaration and the Programme of Action on the Establishment of a New International Economic Order, 3281(XXIX) of 12 December 1974, containing the Charter of Economic Rights and Duties of States, and 3362(S-VII) of 16 September 1975 on development and international economic co-operation,

Recalling also its resolution 35/56 of 5 December 1980, the annex to which contains the International Development Strategy for the Third United Nations Development Decade, and in particular the policy measures envisaged in the Strategy,

Recalling further its resolution 37/252 of 21 December 1982 on immediate measures in favour of the developing countries,

Taking into account, inter alia, the immediate measures adopted by the United Nations Conference on Trade and Development at its sixth session, and noting related efforts in favour of developing countries by the relevant organs, organizations and bodies of the United Nations system,

Taking note of the Programme of Immediate Measures in Areas of Critical Importance to Developing Countries, contained in section V of the Economic Declaration adopted by the Seventh Conference of Heads of State or Government of Non-Aligned Countries, held at New Delhi from 7 to 12 March 1983, and the proposals contained in the Buenos Aires Platform, adopted at the Fifth Ministerial Meeting of the Group of 77, held from 28 March to 9 April 1983,

Taking note of the proposals on the immediate measures contained in the Declaration of the Ministers for Foreign Affairs of the Group of 77, adopted in New York on 10 October 1983,

Noting that while effective action by the international community is indispensable for the creation of an en-

vironment that is fully supportive of the national and collective efforts of the developing countries for the realization of their development goals, the primary responsibility for the development of developing countries rests with those countries themselves,

Aware that certain economic indicators point to the recovery of some major developed market-economy countries, but that, while the recovery of the developed market-economy countries could be potentially beneficial to the developing countries, by itself it would not be sufficient and could be aborted unless policy measures address both the revitalization of the world economy and the reactivation of the development process in the developing world,

Gravely concerned about the present world economic climate of crisis and its negative impact on the developing countries and their development prospects,

Reiterating, in that context, the need for the immediate adoption of concrete measures in areas of critical importance to the developing countries,

Also aware, in that context, that both immediate and structural problems must be addressed fully and in a coherent manner,

1. *Agrees* that concrete immediate measures in favour of the developing countries should be taken in order to contribute to the easing of current economic problems, to promote the accelerated growth and development of the developing countries on a sustained basis and to promote the reactivation of the world economy;

2. *Agrees* that immediate measures within the organs, organizations and bodies of the United Nations system should include measures directed, *inter alia,* at progress in the following areas:

(a) Food and agriculture, including special food aid measures as required for seriously affected food-deficit countries in Africa;

(b) Money and finance, transfer of resources, including official development assistance, indebtedness and multilateral development activities;

(c) Trade and raw materials, including access to markets for the exports of developing countries, and urgent appropriate action in the area of commodities;

(d) Development of the energy resources of the developing countries;

(e) Implementation of the Substantial New Programme of Action for the 1980s for the Least Developed Countries;

3. *Urges* all Governments, bearing in mind the particular contribution developed countries can make, to pursue effective negotiating efforts, within the organs, organizations and bodies of the United Nations system, with a view to the adoption of concrete measures in the areas described in paragraph 2 above;

4. *Agrees* that policy measures of an immediate nature should be taken into account in the review and appraisal of the International Development Strategy for the Third United Nations Development Decade;

5. *Requests* the relevant organs, organizations and bodies of the United Nations system, in their areas of competence and in accordance with their decisions, to take the appropriate action necessary for the implementation of immediate measures in the areas referred to in paragraph 2 above;

6. *Requests* the Secretary-General, in co-operation with the executive heads of the organs, organizations and bodies of the United Nations system, to submit a

report on the implementation of the present resolution to the General Assembly at its thirty-ninth session.

General Assembly resolution 38/200

20 December 1983   Meeting 104   Adopted without vote

Approved by Second Committee (A/38/702/Add.13) without vote, 14 December (meeting 56); draft by Vice-Chairman (A/C.2/38/L.119), based on informal consultations on draft by Mexico, for Group of 77 (A/C.2/38/L.87); agenda item 78.
Meeting numbers. GA 38th session: 2nd Committee 50, 56; plenary 104.

The draft approved by the Second Committee differed in several ways from that put forward by the Group of 77 and subsequently withdrawn.

In addition to drafting changes, the approved text added the fourth, seventh and eighth preambular paragraphs.

Other revisions included the deletion from the final text of references to continuing the concrete immediate measures within the framework of global negotiations, the establishment of a food security system, action on the international monetary system and assistance by the World Bank in energy resources development. Also deleted from the approved text was a request for a progress report on implementation of the resolution to be submitted to the Committee on the Review and Appraisal of the International Development Strategy.

In another 20 December resolution (38/197), the Assembly dealt with economic measures as a means of political and economic coercion against developing countries (see above).

Least developed countries

The special problems of the 36 officially-designated least developed countries (LDCs) were considered in several United Nations forums during 1983, including UNCTAD, the Governing Council of UNDP, the Industrial Development Board of UNIDO, ACC and the General Assembly.

Programme of Action for the 1980s

During 1983, the United Nations system continued to monitor the implementation of the Substantial New Programme of Action (SNPA) for the 1980s for the Least Developed Countries, adopted in 1981 by the United Nations Conference on the Least Developed Countries[2] and endorsed later that year by the General Assembly.[3]

In response to a December 1982 request,[4] the Secretary-General submitted to the Assembly in October 1983 a report[5] on steps taken to accelerate implementation of SNPA by the United Nations system and others concerned, in the light of the outcome of UNCTAD VI (see Chapter IV of this section) and other developments.

The report contained a brief account of recent economic events in LDCs and the short-term outlook for their economy, including action being taken by them to achieve SNPA targets. The report

also included information on international support measures by organizations of the United Nations system and action outside the system. Follow-up and monitoring of the implementation of SNPA, including individual country review meetings, were reported on, with the importance of these meetings to the success of SNPA being strongly emphasized. One section of the report related to the outcome of UNCTAD VI with respect to SNPA implementation.

Despite the commitment by all concerned to SNPA, the report stated, the general economic situation of LDCs had further deteriorated and their living standards continued to be totally inadequate.

A number of the 36 LDCs[6] had implemented SNPA: they had appointed a governmental focal point to review its implementation at the national level and decided on consultative arrangements required; 11 countries had prepared reports giving details of economic and financial strategies and objectives and external resource requirements, which were presented to country meetings with their development partners; and others were preparing such reports and making arrangements for country meetings. The importance of country review meetings for the implementation of SNPA was stressed and LDCs which had not held first meetings were advised to do so as soon as possible and to prepare for them effectively.

Within the United Nations system, LDCs had been accorded high priority, with the Director-General for Development and International Economic Co-operation being responsible for system-wide mobilization and co-ordination. Operational activities of the system were essential in offsetting some inequalities in distributing official development assistance (ODA) to LDCs.

Attention was drawn to the serious resource situation of UNDP, the main source of multilateral technical co-operation to LDCs. Financial constraints faced by other agencies could also adversely affect their ability to assist LDCs. Therefore there was an urgent need for donor countries to provide substantially greater resources through UNDP, its Special Measures Fund for LDCs and the United Nations Capital Development Fund (UNCDF).

The report noted that, although the 1981 Conference on LDCs had urged donor countries to attain 0.15 per cent of their gross national product as ODA or to double their ODA to LDCs by 1985, a number of major donors had not met either target. Developed donor countries should implement fully and rapidly commitments undertaken in pursuance of Trade and Development Board resolution 165(S-IX)[7] and should respond positively to requests from individual LDCs for alleviation of their debt burden resulting from ODA loans. Noting an upsurge of debt types not covered by that resolution, the report stated in conclusion that urgent attention should be devoted to the problem.

In a report[8] to the Economic and Social Council, CDP stated that, despite commitments made at the Conference on LDCs, little had been done to help them or other low-income developing countries whose position had deteriorated catastrophically in 1982. It observed that action could be taken in both IMF and the World Bank to assist those countries. Although the World Bank had announced a Special Assistance Programme (see PART TWO, Chapter VI) aimed at increasing programme lending in view of the gravity of the situation, the Bank's lending level had virtually stagnated in real terms during the previous three years. Noting that commitment to the International Development Association (IDA) had been weakened by actions and attitudes of some donors, CDP stated that it attached the greatest importance to speedy restoration of IDA to the full operational level previously agreed. In parallel with the eighth quota review of IMF, there was also a need for an early increase in the total capital of the World Bank.

Few bilateral donors had announced increases in levels of ODA, while some had reduced aid in real terms. Many developing countries were unable to secure essential items and their need for short-term balance-of-payments support was compelling.

CDP referred to the need to increase food-aid levels and targets and to the decline in UNDP resources. In connection with the need to improve efficiency of use of most forms of aid, CDP urged renewed international efforts for aid co-ordination, especially in Africa. Trading problems of low-income countries also deserved attention.

In accordance with an Economic and Social Council decision of February 1982,[9] CDP considered the eligibility of Liberia for inclusion in the list of LDCs, based on new data and information supplied by its Government. Reporting to the Council,[8] CDP concluded that Liberia was not eligible for inclusion in the list on the basis of standard criteria relating to per capita gross domestic product (GDP), share of manufacturing output in GDP and the adult literacy rate.

The Committee considered that an overall review of the list of LDCs should be undertaken and reiterated that the criteria used to identify LDCs deserved to be reappraised. It also indicated that no useful purpose would be served by referring further countries to it for identification as LDCs under the existing criteria.

UNDP action. Together with the World Bank, UNDP continued to serve as lead agency in organizing country review meetings, whose aim was to enable individual LDCs to consult with their aid partners on the recipient country's economic sit-

uation, on progress in SNPA implementation, on aid conditions and on needs for additional assistance. During 1983,[10] such round-table review meetings were held, with UNDP assistance, for Benin and Djibouti; for Afghanistan, Bhutan, the Lao People's Democratic Republic, Maldives and Samoa in an Asia/Pacific round-table meeting for each country at Geneva; and for Somalia, organized by the World Bank with UNDP assistance.

Funds for this assistance, and for other activities benefiting LDCs, were provided by the UNDP Special Measures Fund for LDCs. Contributions to the Fund in 1983 totalled $16.1 million and eight Governments pledged $14.1 million for 1984. Expenditures on round-table conferences from the Fund were limited to $100,000 for each LDC.

(For 1983 payments and 1984 pledges to the Special Measures Fund, see Chapter II of this section: table "Contributions to UNDP, 1983 and 1984").

During the year, UNDP continued to give highest priority to assisting the poorest countries (for indicative planning figures and UNDP project expenditures relating to individual countries, see Chapter II of this section). In addition, by the end of the year the UNCDF programme was covering 41 countries comprising the 36 LDCs and five countries which the UNDP Governing Council directed should be given similar consideration. Contributions amounting to $24.2 million were received from UNCDF in 1983. New project commitments in LDCs during the year in the areas of basic needs and productive sector and economic infrastructure development amounted to $30 million, bringing total project commitments since the 1981 Conference on LDCs to $120 million.

In December, the UNDP Administrator established an LDC trust fund for a special contribution of $6,600,660 from the Netherlands.[11] The fund's objectives were to enhance the effectiveness of LDC round-table conferences, to mobilize additional resources to implement projects and programmes identified therein, and to contribute to achieving LDC development goals for which UNDP resources were lacking.

To improve implementation and follow-up of SNPA, the UNDP Governing Council, on 24 June,[12] reiterated its appeal to States to increase assistance to LDCs through contributions to the Special Measures Fund and UNCDF, and through other channels. The Council urged the UNDP Administrator to continue to support SNPA implementation by acting as lead agency, when requested by Governments, in support of national consultation mechanisms. It also urged member States to give careful attention to round-table and donor conferences, contribute to the success of such conferences and follow through on pledges.

UNCTAD action. Following a debate in a sessional committee, UNCTAD's Trade and Development Board took note on 28 April[13] of the report and agreed conclusions of the Second Meeting of Multilateral and Bilateral Financial and Technical Assistance Institutions with Representatives of LDCs, convened by UNCTAD in October 1982.[14]

Responding to a December 1982 request,[4] a report on progress in implementing SNPA[15] was prepared by the UNCTAD secretariat for UNCTAD VI (June/July 1983). It included a short description of the economic situation and prospects of LDCs and went on to describe actions undertaken by LDCs themselves and international support measures required to achieve SNPA objectives. Arrangements for follow-up and monitoring were also discussed. The report's conclusions and recommendations dealt with financial assistance, international commercial policy measures and economic co-operation among developing countries. An appeal was made to donors to fulfil promptly specific commitments made with respect to aid targets while others were urged to accept the SNPA target and implement it by 1985. An addendum to the report contained basic data in tabular form on LDCs.

On 2 July, UNCTAD VI adopted without dissent resolution 142(VI) on progress in implementing SNPA.[16] Most of the provisions of this text were subsequently incorporated into General Assembly resolution 38/195 (see below). The Conference called on developing countries in a position to do so to assist LDCs, in the context of economic co-operation among developing countries (see above) and in the spirit of collective self-reliance, by giving preferential treatment to imports from LDCs; assisting LDCs to develop production potential in food, energy, etc.; providing under preferential terms results of scientific and technological development; providing increased flows of financial and technical assistance and goods; promoting and expanding joint ventures involving transfer of equipment and technology; exploring long-term arrangements to assist LDCs to achieve reasonable sales of products; strengthening subregional and regional co-operation arrangements; and assisting in developing human resources.

UNCTAD VI recognized the dependence of many LDCs on commodity exports for foreign exchange earnings, noted that developed countries' progress reports on ways to help LDCs offset damaging effects of fluctuations in commodity exports, as referred to in SNPA, had not been submitted, and urged submission of such reports by the end of the year. It also welcomed recommendations relating to facilitating trade of LDCs made in a November 1982 Ministerial Declaration by the Contracting Parties to GATT.[17]

The international community was urged to provide substantial financial and material assistance to LDCs in order to mitigate the effects of major man-made and natural disasters.

Stressing the importance of country review meetings, UNCTAD urged lead agencies to assist in preparing and convening them and requested donor and recipient countries to work with agencies to promote their success.

With reference to global monitoring of progress in implementing SNPA, specifically the 1985 mid-term review, the Conference recognized that UNCTAD's role was of great importance and requested its Secretary-General to ensure the effectiveness of the unit responsible.

A recommendation on ODA flows to LDCs was made in UNCTAD resolution 164(VI).

Resolution 142(VI), agreement on which was reached in consultations, was adopted after another draft on implementing SNPA contained in the Buenos Aires Platform—the final document of the Fifth Ministerial Meeting of the Group of 77 (Buenos Aires, 28 March–9 April)—was withdrawn.

The Buenos Aires Platform text[16] differed from the Conference resolution in several respects. The Platform text included a call for donor countries to make substantial contributions to various funds and a request that IMF review principles on which conditionality rested and allocate substantial portions of special drawing rights (SDRs), trust fund facilities and compensatory financial facilities to LDCs, whereas the Conference text reiterated the SNPA call for Governments to make adequate contributions to multilateral development institutions and stressed the critical importance of IDA to LDCs.

A paragraph requesting increased financial transfers to LDCs, including international tax schemes for development, further gold sales by IMF, linking the creation of SDRs to development assistance, and using interest subsidy techniques, was not included in the final text. A further paragraph referring to SNPA paragraph 85, which recommended financial resources for transport infrastructure development, was also not included.

UNIDO action. The progress of industrialization of LDCs was considered by the Industrial Development Board of UNIDO at its April/May session. The Board adopted a conclusion[18] expressing concern about UNIDO's limited resources for technical co-operation for LDCs, and calling for increased contributions to assist them and for immediate implementation of SNPA. The UNIDO secretariat was requested to contribute to the SNPA 1985 mid-term global review and to carry out uncompleted technical co-operation projects in certain LDCs (see Chapter VI of this section).

ACC action. In accordance with a December 1982 General Assembly resolution[4] and a 1981 decision by ACC,[19] a second inter-agency consultation on SNPA follow-up was held at Geneva on 1 and 2 March 1983.[20] The consultation reviewed experience gained from African review meetings and preparations for the round-table meeting of LDCs in the Asia and Pacific region. Action taken by organizations to implement SNPA and arrangements for its global monitoring were discussed, as were measures to be taken concerning the five countries identified by the United Nations as LDCs in December 1982.[6]

GENERAL ASSEMBLY ACTION

On the recommendation of the Second Committee, the General Assembly, on 20 December 1983, adopted resolution 38/195 without vote.

Implementation of the Substantial New Programme of Action for the 1980s for the Least Developed Countries

The General Assembly,

Recalling its resolutions 3201(S-VI) and 3202(S-VI) of 1 May 1974, containing the Declaration and the Programme of Action on the Establishment of a New International Economic Order, 3281(XXIX) of 12 December 1974, containing the Charter of Economic Rights and Duties of States, and 3362(S-VII) of 16 September 1975 on development and international economic co-operation,

Reaffirming the provisions of the International Development Strategy for the Third United Nations Development Decade relating to the least developed countries,

Reaffirming the Substantial New Programme of Action for the 1980s for the Least Developed Countries, adopted unanimously by the United Nations Conference on the Least Developed Countries and endorsed by the General Assembly in its resolution 36/194 of 17 December 1981,

Recalling its resolutions 36/194 of 17 December 1981 and 37/224 of 20 December 1982,

Expressing serious concern at the continued deterioration of the economic and social situation of the least developed countries in spite of their national efforts at development, as well as efforts made by the international community, including donor countries, even two years after the adoption of the Substantial New Programme of Action, and stressing the immediate need for greatly expanded support measures, including a major increase in the transfer of additional resources for the realization of the objectives of the Programme,

Bearing in mind the debt problems faced by the least developed countries,

Reaffirming also that the main objectives of the Substantial New Programme of Action are to transform the economies of the least developed countries towards self-sustaining development, to promote the structural changes necessary to overcome the extreme economic difficulties of the least developed countries, to provide fully adequate and internationally accepted minimum standards of nutrition, health, transport and communications, housing and education, as well as job opportunities, to all their citizens, to identify and support major investment opportunities and priorities and to mitigate the adverse effects of natural disasters,

Recognizing that only a substantial increase in official development assistance in real terms during the present decade will enable the least developed countries to achieve the objectives of their country programmes within the framework of the Substantial New Programme of Action, in accordance with aid targets and modalities contained in the Programme, and emphasizing that external assistance complements and reinforces domestic efforts in the least developed countries themselves,

Alarmed at the negative impact of the current world economic crisis on the least developed countries,

Deeply concerned at the very slow pace at which the Substantial New Programme of Action has been implemented so far,

Recalling resolution 142(VI) of 2 July 1983 of the United Nations Conference on Trade and Development on progress in the implementation of the Substantial New Programme of Action,

Taking note of the report of the Secretary-General on the implementation of the Substantial New Programme of Action for the 1980s for the Least Developed Countries,

1. *Emphasizes* that, in view of their deteriorating socio-economic situation, the least developed countries need the urgent and special attention of the international community and its large-scale support on a continuous basis to enable them to progress towards self-reliant development, consistent with the plans and programmes of each least developed country;

2. *Reaffirms* the commitment of the international community to the Substantial New Programme of Action for the 1980s for the Least Developed Countries and urges all countries, international institutions and others concerned to implement fully and effectively their commitments under the Programme;

3. *Welcomes* the adoption by the United Nations Conference on Trade and Development at its sixth session of resolution 142(VI), reflecting the unanimous support of the international community;

4. *Urges* donor countries, within the overall context of the Substantial New Programme of Action, as adopted, and of progress towards the 0.7 per cent target, to attain 0.15 per cent of their gross national product as official development assistance or to double their official development assistance to the least developed countries by 1985 or as soon as possible thereafter, and recognizes the importance to the least developed countries of flows of official development assistance to them being doubled by 1985, in relation to the transfers to them during the period 1976-1980;

5. *Calls upon* the international community to provide support measures for the efforts of the least developed countries in the priority sectors established by the Governments of the least developed countries in their country programmes and embodied in the Substantial New Programme of Action, particularly food and agriculture, manufacturing industries, exploration and development of energy and natural resources, human resources development, expansion and diversification of exports, development of transport and communications, and improvement in planning, implementation and management capabilities;

6. *Reaffirms* that the least developed countries have primary responsibility for their overall development and that, although international support measures are vitally important, the domestic policies that those coun-

tries pursue will be of critical importance for the success of their development efforts;

7. *Urges* all donor countries to make adequate special allocations to the Special Measures Fund for the Least Developed Countries of the United Nations Development Programme and to the United Nations Capital Development Fund or through other suitable channels for the least developed countries, including other existing funds and resources of the United Nations, to assist in the implementation of the Substantial New Programme of Action, and invites the Administrator of the United Nations Development Programme to continue his efforts to mobilize additional resources for the activities under his administration;

8. *Stresses* the critical importance of the International Development Association to the least developed countries, calls upon Governments to implement speedily their commitments undertaken with regard to the sixth replenishment of the Association and urges that negotiations on the seventh replenishment be completed as soon as possible and at an adequate level;

9. *Urges* developed donor countries that have not yet done so to implement fully and rapidly the commitments undertaken in pursuance of section A of Trade and Development Board resolution 165(S-IX) of 11 March 1978, in respect of least developed countries, and calls upon developed countries to respond in a positive manner to requests from individual least developed countries, taking into account the particular circumstances and the requirements of the situation of the debtor country, for an alleviation of their debt burdens resulting from official development assistance loans provided by the developed country concerned;

10. *Welcomes* the provision by some donors of assistance to least developed countries entirely in the form of grants, as well as in more flexible forms such as local and recurrent-costs financing, maintenance aid, rehabilitation aid and balance-of-payments support, adapted to the special needs of the least developed countries and in response to their deteriorating economic and social situation, and urges other donors to take similar steps as a general rule;

11. *Calls upon* donor countries to provide official development assistance to the least developed countries on an untied basis to the maximum extent possible;

12. *Urges* all donors and all concerned to improve the quality and effectiveness of aid and to reduce, to the maximum extent possible, the time-lag between aid commitment and disbursement;

13. *Also urges* countries and institutions concerned to implement, to the maximum extent possible, the agreed conclusions of the Second Meeting of Multilateral and Bilateral Financial and Technical Assistance Institutions with Representatives of the Least Developed Countries, held at Geneva from 11 to 20 October 1982;

14. *Reaffirms* the decision of the United Nations Conference on Trade and Development at its sixth session relating to assistance to least developed countries in the spirit of collective self-reliance and in the context of economic co-operation among developing countries, in accordance with paragraph 13 of resolution 142(VI) of the Conference;

15. *Strongly recommends* that the first round of review meetings at the national level on the implementation of the Substantial New Programme of Action, to be held in accordance with paragraphs 110 to 116 of the Programme, should be completed by 1983 or soon thereafter, without prejudice to the timing of the global review in 1985;

16. *Requests* the Administrator of the United Nations Development Programme to continue supporting and making arrangements for the round-table meetings for the least developed countries, as required;

17. *Reaffirms* that regular review and monitoring of the progress made in the implementation of the Substantial New Programme of Action at the national, regional and global levels should be undertaken as envisaged in the Programme to maintain the momentum of commitments made by the international community and to promote the implementation of the plans and programmes of the least developed countries;

18. *Urges* all countries, particularly donor countries, and institutions to respond expeditiously, on a regular basis, to the questionnaires of the secretariat of the United Nations Conference on Trade and Development on the steps they are taking to implement the Substantial New Programme of Action to be used in making an objective assessment of the progress made in the implementation process;

19. *Renews its invitation* to the governing bodies of appropriate organs, organizations and bodies of the United Nations system to take the necessary and appropriate measures for effective implementation and follow-up of the Substantial New Programme of Action within their respective spheres of competence and mandates;

20. *Invites* the Committee on the Review and Appraisal of the Implementation of the International Development Strategy for the Third United Nations Development Decade to take into account the adoption and implementation process of the Substantial New Programme of Action and related developments in its review and appraisal exercise at all levels;

21. *Requests* the Trade and Development Board, at its twenty-eighth session, to take a decision on the convening, as part of the preparation for the mid-term global review of the implementation of the Substantial New Programme of Action, of a third meeting of multilateral and bilateral financial and technical assistance institutions with representatives of the least developed countries, taking into account the wish of the least developed countries; the meeting should, *inter alia:*

(a) Undertake a review and assessment of the economic situation of the least developed countries and of assistance requirements for their accelerated progress;

(b) Evaluate and put forward relevant recommendations to improve aid practices and management, notably as regards terms and conditions of aid, adapting assistance criteria to the specific needs of the least developed countries, types of aid and priority areas, administration and management of aid programmes, and technical assistance;

(c) Evaluate the results of the individual country meetings convened in accordance with paragraph 111 of the Substantial New Programme of Action and make recommendations aimed at improving the co-ordination of assistance programmes;

and requests the Secretary-General of the United Nations Conference on Trade and Development to take the necessary action in this regard;

22. *Reaffirms* its decision that the Intergovernmental Group on the Least Developed Countries of the United Nations Conference on Trade and Development,

at its high-level meeting in 1985, should carry out, *inter alia*, the mid-term review of the implementation of the Substantial New Programme of Action, and urges that all necessary steps be taken to ensure appropriate preparations for an in-depth review on that occasion, stressing the importance of the timely preparation of the necessary documentation, including specific recommendations for the full and expeditious implementation of the Substantial New Programme of Action by the United Nations Conference on Trade and Development and other competent organizations, as requested in the Programme;

23. *Requests* the Director-General for Development and International Economic Co-operation, in conformity with paragraph 123 of the Substantial New Programme of Action, to continue, in close collaboration with the Secretary-General of the United Nations Conference on Trade and Development, the executive secretaries of the regional commissions and the lead agencies for the aid consultative groups, to ensure at the secretariat level the full mobilization and co-ordination of the United Nations system for the purpose of implementation and follow-up of the Substantial New Programme of Action, taking into account, in particular, the mid-term global review to be held in 1985;

24. *Requests* the Secretary-General to submit a report to the General Assembly at its thirty-ninth session on the implementation of the present resolution.

General Assembly resolution 38/195

20 December 1983   Meeting 104   Adopted without vote

Approved by Second Committee (A/38/702/Add.11) without vote, 9 December (meeting 55); draft by Vice-Chairman (A/C.2/38/L.96), based on informal consultations on draft by Group of 77 (A/C.2/38/L.74); agenda item 78 *(m)*.
Financial implications. 5th Committee, A/38/738; S-G, A/C.2/38/L.84, A/C.5/38/95.
Meeting numbers. GA 38th session: 2nd Committee 50, 55; 5th Committee 66; plenary 104.

The draft approved by the Second Committee differed in a number of respects from that put forward by the Group of 77 and subseqently withdrawn.

The sixth and seventh preambular paragraphs and the reference in the fifth to efforts made on behalf of LDCs by the international community, including donor countries, were added to the approved text. Also added were paragraphs 6 and 8. A paragraph by which the Assembly would have called for resources for developing transport and communications in LDCs was deleted and other calls for assistance to LDCs in specific areas were reformulated as paragraph 5. By paragraph 9 of the earlier text, the Assembly would have urged developed countries to convert all outstanding bilateral ODA loans into grants for all LDCs without discrimination and to extend relief to LDCs for private debts.

In the Group's text, paragraphs 10 to 13 had formed one paragraph, by which the Assembly would have urged all countries concerned to fulfil immediately their commitment to provide ODA to LDCs fully in the form of grants, to provide highly concessional loans and to fulfil urgently their commitments to provide ODA grants and loans to LDCs on an untied basis without discrimination, to improve the quality and effectiveness of aid and eliminate the time-lag between aid commitment and disbursement, and to implement the recommendations of the Second Meeting of Multilateral and Bilateral Financial and Technical Assistance Institutions with Representatives of LDCs.

The special needs of LDCs were also addressed in several other 1983 resolutions. In resolution 38/171 on a policy review of operational activities for development, the Assembly urged substantial increases in financial resources to United Nations funds and programmes engaged in such activities to enhance implementation of SNPA.

In resolution 38/200 on immediate measures in favour of the developing countries, the Assembly agreed that measures within the United Nations system should include those directed at progress in implementation of SNPA.

Awareness of the need for special measures for LDCs in energy resources development was expressed by the Assembly in resolution 38/151, and a call was made for greater participation by financial institutions in financing energy projects in LDCs.

In resolutions on food problems, both the Assembly (38/158) and the Economic and Social Council (1983/71) expressed concern at expanding food-import requirements in LDCs and called for adequate resources to assist them to increase food production and raise nutritional standards.

Land-locked developing countries

During 1983, the special needs and problems of land-locked developing countries were considered by UNCTAD and the General Assembly. Matters related to the United Nations Special Fund for Land-locked Developing Countries were taken up by the Governing Council of UNDP and the Assembly.

UNCTAD action. The question of land-locked developing countries was considered at UNCTAD VI (June/July 1983) (see Chapter IV of this section).

In resolution 137(VI) on UNCTAD activities on the question,[16] adopted without dissent on 2 July, the Conference requested the international community to provide financial assistance to improve transit-transport infrastructure in land-locked developing countries and their transit countries, and listed areas in which specific action could be taken. Member States were invited to ratify and implement relevant provisions of international conventions on transit trade.

The Conference requested the UNCTAD Secretary-General to pursue the work of the technical advisory services of UNCTAD in order to assist Governments of land-locked developing countries to improve their transit-transport situation and recommended that suitable ways of financing such advisory services be found. The Secretary-General was further invited to appoint a group of experts to study ways of improving transit-transport infrastructures and services, to keep under review progress in implementing specific action related to the needs and problems of those countries and to report annually to the General Assembly through the Trade and Development Board.

Agreement on this resolution was reached after consultations on a draft text contained in the Buenos Aires Platform.

In addition to drafting changes, the Platform resolution[16] had included in the list of agreed areas for further action the granting of benefits to land-locked developing countries by taking their export prices as a basis for levying import duties to compensate for higher transport costs incurred in exporting their products. In its text, UNCTAD VI took note of concerns expressed, particularly by land-locked countries, relating to levying of customs tariffs on a basis which included high transport costs.

Also, whereas in its text the Conference invited UNCTAD's Secretary-General to appoint a small group of experts to study transit-transport infrastructures and services and requested him to review implementation of specific action regarding land-locked developing countries, the Platform resolution had invited him to hold periodic meetings to review such implementation and suggested that they could take place before the regular General Assembly debate on land-locked developing countries.

In considering this item, UNCTAD VI had before it a policy paper[21] which cited specific problems of the countries in question and described current and future activities by UNCTAD and the international community in favour of them.

Technical co-operation assistance to land-locked developing countries during 1983 included inter-regional advisory services in transit transport (financed by the Swedish International Development Authority) and in trade facilitation (financed by UNDP), four UNDP-financed regional projects on transit transport—one for Asian countries and three for African subregions—and UNDP-financed long-term advisers in transit-transport problems for four countries in Africa and Asia. In addition to selecting the most cost-efficient transit corridors and transport modes in order to reduce the cost of access to the sea for these countries, the projects also aimed to promote co-operation between them and their transit neighbours in order to develop infrastructure and facilitate movement of goods in transit.

GENERAL ASSEMBLY ACTION

On 19 December, the Assembly adopted without vote decision 38/437 on the recommendation of its Second Committee.

Specific action related to the particular needs and problems of land-locked developing countries

At its 102nd plenary meeting, on 19 December 1983, the General Assembly, on the recommendation of the Second Committee, decided to refer to its thirty-ninth session for consideration the draft resolution entitled "Specific action related to the particular needs and problems of land-locked developing countries".

General Assembly decision 38/437

Adopted without vote

Approved by Second Committee (A/38/702/Add.2) without vote, 28 November (meeting 52); oral proposal by Chairman, based on informal consultations; agenda item 78 *(b)*.

Meeting numbers. GA 38th session: 2nd Committee 52; plenary 102.

The draft resolution[22] referred to in decision 38/437 had been referred to the Assembly's 1983 session in 1982.[23] By the draft, the Assembly would have reaffirmed the land-locked developing countries' rights to access to the sea and to freedom of transit, urged provision of aid for transport and transit facilities, and invited transit States to co-operate with those countries in transport planning and in promoting joint transport ventures.

UN Special Fund for Land-locked Developing Countries

In September 1983, the Secretary-General submitted a report[24] on implementation of a December 1982 General Assembly resolution[25] on the United Nations Special Fund for Land-locked Developing Countries. The Secretary-General shared the concern for the future of the Fund expressed by the UNDP Administrator in his biennial report[26] to the 1983 session of the UNDP Governing Council. The Administrator had concluded that the Fund's future must be called into question unless substantial increases in contributions were made.

As at 31 December 1983, payments totalling $51,627 were received from 11 States and 15 States pledged $57,834 for 1984[27] (see table below). Most of these States were themselves land-locked. During the year, expenditures from the Fund for projects in Nepal, Rwanda and Swaziland totalled some $179,000.[28]

UNDP action. The UNDP Governing Council, on 24 June,[29] requested the Administrator to submit in 1985 a report on the Fund's resources and activities since its inception, giving reasons for the low level of such resources and making pertinent suggestions. It appealed to all countries to review their position with respect to the Fund and to contribute urgently and generously to it.

UNCTAD action. In resolution 137(VI) on UNCTAD activities in the field of land-locked developing countries[16] (see above), UNCTAD VI requested developed countries and developing countries in a position to do so to pledge substantial contributions to the Special Fund.

GENERAL ASSEMBLY ACTION

On 19 December, on the recommendation of the Second Committee, the Assembly adopted resolution 38/174 by recorded vote.

United Nations Special Fund for Land-locked Developing Countries

The General Assembly,

Recalling its resolution 31/177 of 21 December 1976, by which it approved the statute of the United Nations Special Fund for Land-locked Developing Countries, and its subsequent resolutions on the Fund, including resolution 37/230 of 20 December 1982,

Taking note of resolution 137(VI) of 2 July 1983 of the United Nations Conference on Trade and Development and decision 83/28 of 24 June 1983 of the Governing Council of the United Nations Development Programme,

Recalling the relevant provisions of the International Development Strategy for the Third United Nations Development Decade,

Recalling further the relevant paragraphs of the Substantial New Programme of Action for the 1980s for the Least Developed Countries,

Convinced that access to world markets at the least possible cost is an integral part of the meaningful economic development of land-locked developing countries,

Expressing deep concern at the consistently very low level of contributions that have been pledged to the Fund since its establishment,

Noting that the demands for assistance from the Fund are additional to, and generally different from, the types of activities financed from other sources in the United Nations system,

1. *Expresses concern* at the lack of implementation of its resolutions on the United Nations Special Fund for Land-locked Developing Countries, as noted by the Secretary-General in his report;

2. *Urges* the international community to give full consideration to the special constraints facing the land-locked developing countries in their economic and social development;

3. *Renews its appeal* for adequate resources to be provided to the Fund;

4. *Requests* the Administrator of the United Nations Development Programme, in consultation with the Secretary-General of the United Nations Conference on Trade and Development and the executive heads of the organs, organizations and bodies of the United Nations system, to continue to pursue action in favour of the land-locked developing countries within the framework of the interim arrangements, bearing in mind that each country concerned should receive appropriate technical and financial assistance.

General Assembly resolution 38/174

19 December 1983   Meeting 102   123-0-21 (recorded vote)

Approved by Second Committee (A/38/703) by recorded vote (105-0-22), 9 December (meeting 55); draft by Mexico, for Group of 77 (A/C.2/38/L.103); agenda item 79 *(f)*.

Meeting numbers. GA 38th session: 2nd Committee 48, 54, 55; plenary 102.

Recorded vote in Assembly as follows:

In favour: Afghanistan, Algeria, Angola, Argentina, Austria, Bahamas, Bahrain, Bangladesh, Barbados, Belize, Benin, Bhutan, Bolivia, Botswana, Brazil, Bulgaria, Burma, Burundi, Byelorussian SSR, Cape Verde, Central African Republic, Chad, Chile, China, Colombia, Congo, Costa Rica, Cuba, Cyprus, Czechos-

lovakia, Democratic Kampuchea, Democratic Yemen, Djibouti, Dominican Republic, Ecuador, Egypt, El Salvador, Equatorial Guinea, Ethiopia, Fiji, Gabon, Gambia, German Democratic Republic, Ghana, Guatemala, Guinea, Guinea-Bissau, Guyana, Honduras, Hungary, India, Indonesia, Iran, Iraq, Israel, Ivory Coast, Jamaica, Jordan, Kenya, Kuwait, Lao People's Democratic Republic, Lebanon, Lesotho, Liberia, Libyan Arab Jamahiriya, Madagascar, Malawi, Malaysia, Maldives, Mali, Malta, Mauritania, Mauritius, Mexico, Mongolia, Morocco, Mozambique, Nepal, Nicaragua, Niger, Nigeria, Oman, Panama, Papua New Guinea, Paraguay, Peru, Philippines, Poland, Qatar, Romania, Rwanda, Saint Lucia, Saint Vincent and the Grenadines, Sao Tome and Principe, Saudi Arabia, Senegal, Sierra Leone, Singapore, Somalia, Sri Lanka, Sudan, Suriname, Swaziland, Syrian Arab Republic, Thailand, Togo, Trinidad and Tobago, Tunisia, Turkey, Uganda, Ukrainian SSR, USSR, United Arab Emirates, United Republic of Cameroon, United Republic of Tanzania, Upper Volta, Uruguay, Venezuela, Viet Nam, Yemen, Yugoslavia, Zaire, Zambia.

Against: None.

Abstaining: Australia, Belgium, Canada, Denmark, Finland, France, Germany, Federal Republic of, Greece, Iceland, Ireland, Italy, Japan, Luxembourg, Netherlands, New Zealand, Norway, Portugal, Spain, Sweden, United Kingdom, United States.

CONTRIBUTIONS TO THE UN SPECIAL FUND FOR LAND-LOCKED DEVELOPING COUNTRIES, 1983 AND 1984[27]

(as at 31 December 1983; in US dollar equivalent)

Country	1983 payment	1984 pledge
Afghanistan	5,000	5,000
Bhutan	2,200	1,440
Bolivia	—	500
Botswana	2,830	—
Brazil	—	10,000
Burundi	—	1,720
Lao People's Democratic Republic	1,000	1,000
Lesotho	—	1,500
Malawi	1,697	1,531
Nepal	2,000	—
Philippines	—	2,000
Senegal	2,246	2,000
Thailand	—	1,000
Togo	500	242
Tunisia	2,434	464
Zambia	25,210	23,881
Zimbabwe	6,510	5,556
Total	51,627	57,834

Appointment of an Executive Director

In 1983, the General Assembly considered the question of appointing an Executive Director of the United Nations Special Fund for Land-locked Developing Countries. The Secretary-General submitted a note[30] in which he indicated that he was not submitting for the Assembly's confirmation an appointment for the post. He recalled the circumstances surrounding the setting up of the Fund and the interim arrangements for its management by the UNDP Administrator; he also gave details of the amount pledged for its 1984 operations (see above).

GENERAL ASSEMBLY ACTION

In December, on an oral proposal of its President, the Assembly adopted decision 38/315 without vote.

Confirmation of the appointment of the Executive Director of the United Nations Special Fund for Land-locked Developing Countries

At its 98th plenary meeting, on 15 December 1983, the General Assembly took note of the information contained in the note by the Secretary-General.

General Assembly decision 38/315
Adopted without vote

Oral proposal by President; agenda item 17 *(h)*.
Meeting number. GA 38th session: plenary 98.

Election of a Board of Governors

In December, the Assembly decided to defer action on the election of a Board of Governors of the Special Fund.

GENERAL ASSEMBLY ACTION

On an oral proposal of its President, the Assembly adopted decision 38/319 without vote.

Election of the members of the Board of Governors of the United Nations
Special Fund for Land-locked Developing Countries
At its 98th plenary meeting, on 15 December 1983, the General Assembly decided to defer until its thirty-ninth session the election of the members of the Board of Governors of the United Nations Special Fund for Land-locked Developing Countries, since no candidate had been put forward by the regional groups.

General Assembly decision 38/319
Adopted without vote

Oral proposal by President; agenda item 16 *(e)*.
Meeting number. GA 38th session: plenary 98.

Island developing countries

In 1983, the problems of island developing countries were discussed at UNCTAD VI (June/July) (see Chapter IV of this section), which had before it an UNC-TAD policy paper[31] citing specific problems faced by those countries, such as smallness and remoteness. The paper described priority areas for action in their favour: communications and transport; natural disasters; marine space; self-reliance; environment; and population, manpower and migration. Action by the international community was suggested and UNCTAD's role and work programme in favour of the countries was outlined.

On 2 July, the Conference adopted without dissent resolution 138(VI) on UNCTAD activities concerning island developing countries,[16] by which it urged the international community to provide financial and technical support to them and listed areas for specific action. International financial institutions were urged to increase substantially resource flows by applying policies and credit criteria appropriate to their economic and financial situation.

The UNCTAD Secretary-General was requested to continue in-depth studies of common problems of island economies and of constraints inhibiting their economic development. The UNCTAD secretariat was asked to pursue its role as the focal point for global action in favour of them, and was further requested to continue work on inter-island and feeder transport in collaboration with the United Nations system and other organizations. Efforts were requested to improve methods of mitigating or preventing social and economic damage from natural disasters.

The UNCTAD Secretary-General was invited to study ways of minimizing handicaps resulting from the geographical situation of island developing countries and to report his findings to the Trade and Development Board. He was also asked to review progress in implementing the resolution and to report to the General Assembly through the Board in 1984.

Agreement on this resolution was reached after consultations on a draft text contained in the Buenos Aires Platform.

The Conference resolution differed from the Platform text[16] in several respects. By that text, the Conference would have requested the UNCTAD secretariat, in co-operation with the Office of the United Nations Disaster Relief Co-ordinator and other United Nations agencies to expand activities related to foreign-sector aspects of natural disaster prevention and reconstruction measures, to mitigate their immediate impact on the balance-of-payments of island developing countries, given the openness of their economies. The final text requested efforts to improve methods of mitigating or preventing damage from natural disasters, given the vulnerability of the countries concerned.

The Platform text would also have had UNCTAD request its Secretary-General to hold periodic meetings to review implementation of the programme of specific action suggesting that they take place before the debate on them, normally held every two years in the Assembly.

UN Special Fund

GENERAL ASSEMBLY ACTION

There being no proposal pertaining to women in development or to the United Nations Special Fund,[32] the General Assembly, on 19 December 1983, adopted decision 38/443 without vote.

Effective mobilization and integration of women
in development; United Nations Special Fund
At its 102nd plenary meeting, on 19 December 1983, the General Assembly took note of the report of the Second Committee.

General Assembly decision 38/443
19 December 1983   Meeting 102   Adopted without vote

Oral proposal by President; agenda item 78 *(j)* and *(k)*.
Meeting number. GA 38th session: plenary 102.

REFERENCES

[1]YUN 1982, p. 594, GA res. 37/252, 21 Dec. 1982. [2]YUN 1981, p. 406. [3]*Ibid.,* p. 410, GA res. 36/194, 17 Dec. 1981. [4]YUN 1982, p. 615, GA res. 37/224, 20 Dec. 1982. [5]A/38/471. [6]YUN 1982, p. 616. [7]YUN 1978, p. 429. [8]E/1983/16. [9]YUN 1982, p. 617, ESC dec. 1982/106, 4 Feb. 1982. [10]DP/1984/13. [11]DP/1984/69. [12]E/1983/20 (dec. 83/9). [13]A/38/15, vol. I. [14]YUN 1982, p. 613. [15]TD/276 & Add.1. [16]*Proceedings of the United Nations Conference on Trade and Development, Sixth Session, Belgrade, 6 June-2 July 1983*, vol. I, *Report and Annexes* (TD/326, vol. I), Sales No. E.83.II.D.6. [17]YUN 1982, p. 1598. [18]A/38/16 (1983/7). [19]YUN 1981, p. 408. [20]ACC/1983/12. [21]TD/279 (Part I). [22]A/C.2/38/L.2. [23]YUN 1982, p. 618, GA dec. 37/440, 20 Dec. 1982. [24]A/38/293. [25]YUN 1982, p. 619, GA res. 37/230, 20 Dec. 1982. [26]DP/1983/42 & Corr.1. [27]A/39/5/Add.1. [28]DP/1984/5/Add.6. [29]E/1983/20 (dec. 83/28). [30]A/38/615. [31]TD/279 (Part II). [32]A/38/702/Add.9.

Chapter II

Operational activities for development

Total operational assistance for development by the United Nations system amounted to $4.1 billion in 1983. Of this total, technical co-operation expenditures amounted to approximately $255 million, compared to $303 million in 1982.

Total contributions (exclusive of cost-sharing and other similar contributions) from Governments and other sources to development activities of the United Nations system amounted to $6 billion in 1983, as compared with $7.2 billion in 1982. These figures included contributions to the World Bank and the International Finance Corporation (IFC) and to the International Fund for Agricultural Development (IFAD), which also fell in 1983, to $3.6 billion from more than $4.8 billion in 1982.

The General Assembly, by resolution 38/171 of 19 December 1983, urged that United Nations organizations and bodies continue to attach priority to operational activities for development, noting that, although the outcome of the November United Nations Pledging Conference for Development Activities reflected a positive trend, the overall level of resources remained unsatisfactory.

The share of the United Nations Development Programme (UNDP) in total system-wide grant-financed technical co-operation (i.e., exclusive of World Bank lending operations) was 40 per cent in 1983, as compared with 45 per cent in 1982. Expenditures by UNDP totalled $751 million, almost $120 million lower than forecast. During 1983, there was an $87.2 million surplus of main programme income over expenditure; UNDP's revenue reserve, showing a $5.7 million deficit at the end of 1982, became a surplus of $57.9 million as at 31 December 1983. In June, the UNDP Governing Council adopted measures to improve the Programme's short- and long-term financing, including measures for improving its own work, an action welcomed by the Assembly in December in resolution 38/172; the Assembly also stressed the necessity of significantly increased contributions.

Responsibility for the management and substantive support for the system's technical co-operation activities rested with the United Nations Department of Technical Co-operation for Development (DTCD) which executed in 1983 a programme comprising more than 1,400 projects amounting to $112 million, $15 million less than in 1982. This reduction resulted from a decline in resources and led to a streamlining of DTCD operations.

In 1983, the number of United Nations Volunteers (UNV) serving technical co-operation projects in about 90 countries increased to 1,423, with over 80 per cent of recruits from developing countries themselves. The Assembly, in resolution 38/173 of 19 December, reaffirmed that the programme should continue preparing for the International Youth Year (1985) and its youth-related programmes, and appealed for increased contributions.

The High-level Committee on the Review of Technical Co-operation among Developing Countries, in June, made several recommendations aimed at furthering technical co-operation among developing countries. Measures to further the exchange of skilled manpower among developing countries were suggested in a study by the United Nations Conference on Trade and Development.

With slightly over $24 million in contributions to the United Nations Capital Development Fund in 1983, the Fund did not reach anticipated levels; however, trust fund and cost-sharing contributions enabled it to approve new commitments totalling $30.2 million, over half of which went to drought-stricken African countries.

Topics related to this chapter. Africa: South Africa and *apartheid*—aid programmes and inter-agency co-operation. Middle East: aid programmes for Palestinians. Development policy and international economic co-operation: economic co-operation among developing countries. Disasters, economic assistance and emergency relief. International trade and finance: UNCTAD technical co-operation. Development finance. Regional economic and social activities—technical co-operation. Food: food aid. Refugees: refugee assistance. Namibia: aid programmes.

General aspects

During 1983, operational activities for development, carried out by more than 30 bodies of the United Nations system, comprised the programmes of UNDP, the United Nations Children's Fund (UNICEF), the United Nations Fund for Population Activities (UNFPA) and other funds and programmes covered by the annual United Nations Pledging Conference for Development Activities; the technical co-operation and related operational activities of the specialized agencies and other organizations of the United Nations system; and the food aid provided by the World Food Programme (WFP).

Total United Nations official development assistance (ODA)—expenditures and disbursements from all organizations, including the International Development Association (IDA), IFAD, the refugee, humanitarian and related activities and the programmes of the United Nations Environment Programme (UNEP)—to developing countries amounted to $4,067 million in 1983, or about 12 per cent of total net ODA, about the same proportion as in earlier years. Of this amount, about $2,710 million was channelled through the grant-financed operations of the system; the balance represented disbursements by IDA and IFAD. Total concessional resources (grants and concessional loans) amounted to 58 per cent of the total net transfer of resources through the system, compared with 60 per cent in 1982. Aggregate contributions received by organizations engaged in operational activities declined slightly, from $2,515 million in 1982 to $2,465 million in 1983, while expenditures on operational activities amounted to $2,092 million (exclusive of cost-sharing and similarly financed activities), almost exactly the same level, in nominal terms, as in 1982.

Least developed countries (LDCs) received over one third of resources, about the same as in 1982. The share of resources for country and regional programmes in Africa increased from 30 per cent in 1982 to 37 per cent in 1983. The share of UNDP main programme resources in system-wide grant-financed technical co-operation amounted to 40 per cent in 1983, compared with 45 per cent in 1982.[1]

Report of the Director-General. In his 1983 annual report[2] to the General Assembly through the Economic and Social Council, the Director-General for Development and International Economic Co-operation (DIEC) gave an overview of United Nations operational activities for development. The report, prepared after consultation with the organizations of the system, was submitted in June 1983 to assist the Council and the Assembly in a comprehensive policy review of those activities.

Among issues addressed by the Director-General were: priority areas requiring special attention; mobilization of resources; quality and cost-effectiveness of operational programmes; and intergovernmental reviews of operational activities. He stressed the need to adapt modalities for technical co-operation to the growing capabilities of the developing countries and the availability of qualified national personnel. He also felt that South-South co-operation was a major objective of the developing countries to which United Nations operational activities could make a greater contribution; that linkages among such activities could be enhanced through collaboration among funding and other organizations; and that capital

assistance and technical co-operation could be made more complementary by ensuring better combinations of capital and technical programme and project components and by closer collaboration among technical assistance agencies, other United Nations organizations and multilateral development banks.

Priority areas requiring special attention to ensure that the system remained fully responsive to developing countries' needs included: transfer of know-how and skills in keeping with their growing capabilities; increased support to the development efforts of LDCs; help in mobilizing additional resources for the countries of sub-Saharan Africa; and continued assistance to middle- and high-income developing countries through provision of such things as sophisticated technology.

With regard to mobilizing resources for operational activities, the Director-General held that the period of rapid growth in contributions had ended. Diversification of funding sources for multilateral technical co-operation had continued, marked by the emergence of a number of new modalities for financing technical co-operation, the growth of cost-sharing and similar arrangements whereby developing countries increasingly financed activities from their own resources, and the growth in expenditures on technical co-operation financed through the operations of the World Bank. Addressing the difficulties in mobilizing resources on a more predictable and assured basis, it was recommended that, for the short term, consideration be given to the adoption of targets, greater involvement of members of governing bodies in resource mobilization efforts, and more effective use of annual pledging conferences for consultations among contributors and organizations. For the medium term, it was suggested that more formal arrangements, such as multiyear pledging or negotiated replenishments, be considered.

The Director-General drew attention to the positive aspects of the new modalities for financing technical co-operation which, he said, provided flexibility to both donors and recipients in addressing specific development problems and in improving the system's responsiveness to the particular requirements of developing countries. However, he felt a need to address such issues as the growing trend towards providing contributions tied to the procurement of goods and services in the donor country; in that context, he recommended that contributions made to special purpose funds and programmes be consistent with the principles of multilateralism and remain a proportion of general purpose contributions.

The quality, efficiency and cost-effectiveness of operational programmes as well as action at the country level were also reviewed. It was noted that efficiency and effectiveness of operational activities were to a considerable extent determined by the willingness and capacity of the recipient countries clearly to delineate national priorities, promote co-ordination within national administrations and establish procedures to assess and evaluate the usefulness of operational activities for their development.

The Director-General felt it was necessary to focus attention on ways to implement technical co-operation policies; of particular concern, he believed, was the need to adapt the system to the growing capabilities of developing countries and to the increasing trend towards the use of short-term consultants rather than long-term resident experts. Among options were greater recourse to alternative sources for qualified expertise, greater use of twinning of institutions, and streamlined recruitment procedures.

Progress continued with respect to the further strengthening of evaluation systems within organizations, the Director-General stated; developments included reports by the Joint Inspection Unit (JIU) on co-operation by the United Nations system in developing the evaluation capabilities of Governments and on strengthening the evaluation system of UNDP, the decision to establish a Central Evaluation Office in UNDP, and the decisions of the Administrative Committee on Co-ordination (ACC) to improve the monitoring and evaluation of operational activities at the country level.

The system was improving its coherence of action at that level. ACC had decided to improve complementarity and coherence of programmes and projects (see below). After reviewing the functions of resident co-ordinators and the new arrangements for inter-agency co-operation, ACC had noted the satisfaction expressed by a number of Governments with these arrangements which, it felt, should be allowed to develop in a flexible and pragmatic manner. Other important mechanisms in facilitating co-ordination of external assistance at the country level on a more predictable basis were the round tables of UNDP and the consultative group meetings of the World Bank, which the Director-General suggested should be further developed according to the interests of each particular country.

In the light of the General Assembly's decision to conduct a triennial policy review of operational activities, beginning in 1983, with the Director-General being requested to provide information and statistics, he suggested that the Council and the Assembly might wish to see how best the Assembly might carry out its overview responsibilities for the system's activities, in close conjunction with reviews by other intergovernmental bodies of their activities. The coverage of statistical reporting on operational activities and on overall flows of technical co-operation might be further im-

proved. An *ad hoc* high-level consultation among senior government officials to examine the responsiveness of the system to the changing needs of developing countries could be organized in relation to the review and appraisal of the implementation of the International Development Strategy for the Third United Nations Development Decade (the 1980s) (see Chapter I of this section).

As requested by the Assembly in December 1982,[3] the Director-General initiated in 1983, as a follow-up to his 1982 annual report,[4] a review, in consultation with the organizations of the system, of prospects for harmonizing procedures regarding operational activities, particularly the system's effectiveness and responsiveness. The results were to be placed before ACC which, as also requested by the Assembly, would report on its consideration of the matter in its annual overview report for 1983/84.

ACC action. ACC, on 31 March 1983, adopted a decision[5] approving a number of recommendations by its Consultative Committee on Substantive Questions (Operational Activities) (CCSQ(OPS)) concerning ways to improve country-level action. The recommendations had been made pursuant to a 1982 ACC request.[6] It was stressed that the ACC decisions should be understood within the principle that the sovereign right of countries to determine their own priorities was fundamental to the role and activities of the United Nations system, as well as the most appropriate arrangement for the co-ordination of external aid inputs and their integration with national programmes and activities.

Among measures suggested were: continued assistance to developing countries in enhancing their planning and programming capacity, and in strengthening their central and sectoral planning units and related mechanisms for external inputs, programming and co-ordination; assistance in preparing national programmes and identifying inputs to be financed; adjusting country programming to the specific circumstances of each country and using it as a frame of reference for consultations between national authorities and multilateral and other agencies; strengthening the periodic meetings between the resident co-ordinator and representatives of United Nations organizations, with the results being taken into account when formulating or revising operational plans for programmes and projects; and more systematic selection of specific projects—especially those of an innovative or experimental nature, investment-oriented or involving the establishment or strengthening of national institutions—for subsequent evaluation.

Further measures recommended to improve, monitor and evaluate field-level operations were: improved project format, with well-defined objectives and precise outputs, relevant external assumptions and practical indicators, procedures for periodic monitoring and timely evaluation, and financial provisions; increased involvement of recipient countries in project monitoring and evaluation; specific arrangements for follow-up by Governments after project completion; training of staff in carrying out effective evaluations; improved feedback mechanisms, including establishment of an evaluation memory bank in United Nations organizations to facilitate a synthesis of evaluation results and provide a basis for future programming and project formulation, as well as to refine evaluation methodology, criteria and procedures; more impact studies; and expansion of the exchange of experience among United Nations organizations and between them and bilateral aid agencies.

ACC noted that CCSQ(OPS) would report later on guidelines to influence the direction and flow of bilateral aid, simplification and harmonization of aid modalities to lessen the burden on national administrations, and further strengthening technical backstopping of operational activities.

ECONOMIC AND SOCIAL COUNCIL ACTION

On 29 July 1983, on oral proposals by its President, the Economic and Social Council adopted two decisions in connection with its consideration of a number of reports concerning operational activities for development. The Council adopted decision 1983/186 without vote.

Comprehensive policy review of operational activities for development

At its 42nd plenary meeting, on 29 July 1983, the Council took note of the note by the Secretary-General, to which was annexed the report of the Director-General for Development and International Economic Cooperation on a comprehensive policy review of operational activities for development, and decided to transmit it to the General Assembly for consideration at its thirty-eighth session, together with the summary records of the discussion held by the Council on the question during its second regular session of 1983.

Economic and Social Council decision 1983/186

Adopted without vote

Draft orally proposed by President; agenda item 18.
Meeting numbers. ESC 34-36, 42.

The Council adopted decision 1983/187, also without vote.

Reports considered by the Economic and Social Council in connection with the question of operational activities for development

At its 42nd plenary meeting, on 29 July 1983, the Council took note of the following documents:

(a) Report of the High-level Committee on the Review of Technical Co-operation among Developing Countries on its third session;

(b) Note by the Secretary-General on the review by the Administrative Committee on Co-ordination of the arrangements for the exercise of the function of resident co-ordinator;

(c) Extract from the report of the Governing Council of the United Nations Development Programme on its thirtieth session;

(d) Report of the Executive Board of the United Nations Children's Fund;

(e) Report of the Secretary-General on United Nations technical co-operation activities;

(f) Annual report for 1982 of the Administrator of the United Nations Development Programme on the United Nations Revolving Fund for Natural Resources Exploration.

Economic and Social Council decision 1983/187

Adopted without vote

Draft orally proposed by President; agenda item 18.

Annexed to the Council's report for 1983[7] was a statement, made during its discussion of operational activities for development, by the Group of 77 developing countries, welcoming the Director-General's report and voicing concern at the impact of the world economic crisis on the development process and at the weakening of United Nations operational activities for development. The Group expressed the view that substantially increased resources, including resources for United Nations operational activities, would contribute to world economic recovery, and that activities must be based on universal access to technical assistance and must respond to the priorities determined by the recipient countries themselves.

GENERAL ASSEMBLY ACTION

After considering the Director-General's report,[2] the General Assembly, on the recommendation of the Second (Economic and Financial) Committee, adopted on 19 December 1983 resolution 38/171 without vote.

Comprehensive policy review of operational activities for development

The General Assembly,

Recalling its resolutions 3201(S-VI) and 3202(S-VI) of 1 May 1974, containing the Declaration and the Programme of Action on the Establishment of a New International Economic Order, 3281(XXIX) of 12 December 1974, containing the Charter of Economic Rights and Duties of States, and 3362(S-VII) of 16 September 1975 on development and international economic co-operation,

Recalling also its resolution 35/56 of 5 December 1980, the annex to which contains the International Development Strategy for the Third United Nations Development Decade,

Recalling further its resolutions 2688(XXV) of 11 December 1970 on the capacity of the United Nations development system and 3405(XXX) of 28 November 1975 on new dimensions in technical co-operation,

Reiterating its resolutions 32/197 of 20 December 1977, 33/201 of 29 January 1979 and 35/81 of 5 December 1980 on a comprehensive policy review of operational activities for development, 36/199 of 17 December 1981 and 37/226 of 20 December 1982 on operational activities for development of the United Nations system,

Reaffirming the exclusive responsibility of the Government of the recipient country in formulating its national development plan, priorities and objectives, as set out in the consensus contained in the annex to General Assembly resolution 2688(XXV), and emphasizing that the integration of the operational activities of the United Nations system with national programmes would enhance the impact and relevance of those activities,

Emphasizing the importance that developing countries, through their actions, including increased financial contributions, have attached to the operational activities of the United Nations system, in recognition of the role of those activities in their overall economic development,

Expressing its deep concern about the increasing elements of bilateralism in multilateral economic co-operation and the increased channelling of tied resources through multilateral programmes,

Concerned at the increasingly high cost of experts and consultants and the financial effect on the programmes and projects being implemented, and convinced of the need, as far as possible, to use the services of national experts and consultants and to implement programmes and projects in a cost-effective manner,

Aware that a substantial part of world resources, material as well as human, continues to be diverted to armaments, with detrimental effect on international security and on efforts to achieve the new international economic order, including the operational activities for development of the United Nations system,

Reaffirming that one primary objective of operational activities for development of the United Nations system is to promote the economic self-reliance of developing countries,

Having examined the report of the Director-General for Development and International Economic Co-operation for 1983 on the comprehensive policy review of operational activities for development of the United Nations system,

1. *Takes note with appreciation* of the report of the Director-General for Development and International Economic Co-operation on the comprehensive policy review of operational activities for development of the United Nations system;

2. *Reaffirms* the important contribution that operational activities of the United Nations system make to the development of developing countries and urges the relevant organs, organizations and bodies of the United Nations system to continue to attach priority to operational activities in their plans and programmes;

3. *Notes* that, although the outcome of the 1983 United Nations Pledging Conference for Development Activities reflected a positive trend, the overall level of resources remains unsatisfactory, falling short, in many cases, of the various types of targets set by the relevant intergovernmental bodies, thus hampering the ability of the system to respond to the growing needs of developing countries;

4. *Strongly reiterates* the need for a substantial and real increase in the flow of resources for operational activities on an increasingly predictable, continuous and assured basis, so as to enable the organizations of the system to maintain and, where possible, increase the level of their operational programmes and, in that context, strongly urges all countries, particularly developed countries, whose overall performance is not commensurate with their capacities, to increase rapidly and substantially their voluntary contributions for operational activities for development, taking into account the targets that have been set by relevant intergovernmental bodies;

5. *Reaffirms* that the operational activities of the United Nations system should be in accordance with the national plans, priorities and objectives of the recipient countries in order to enhance their impact on and relevance to the national development process of those countries;

6. *Invites* the World Bank to continue to carry out its country activities in accordance with the national plans and priorities of recipient countries, in order to promote the economic self-reliance of developing countries;

7. *Emphasizes* the need to maintain the multilateral character of the operational activities of the United Nations system and urges all Governments to enhance their commitment in this regard;

8. *Calls upon* all Governments, in the interest of preserving the multilateral principles of the system, to refrain from the practice of tying aid for operational activities of the United Nations system to the procurement of goods and services from the donor countries, restricting it to those funds that have a mandate to accept it on an experimental basis;

9. *Invites* the organs, organizations and bodies of the United Nations system dealing with the flows of concessional resources to developing countries to pay greater attention, in their reviews of these issues, to the funding needs of the United Nations funds and programmes in support of the development plans formulated by the recipient Governments;

10. *Urges* the international community to provide a substantial increase in financial resources to United Nations funds and programmes engaged in operational activities in order to enhance their contributions to the implementation of the Substantial New Programme of Action for the 1980s for the Least Developed Countries, bearing in mind the need of those countries for official development assistance from multilateral sources;

11. *Urges* all Governments concerned to conclude negotiations regarding the seventh replenishment of the International Development Association, with a view to ensuring an appropriate increase in resources, and calls for those negotiations to be completed as soon as possible so that the seventh replenishment may become effective in July 1984;

12. *Urges* all Governments concerned to strengthen the International Fund for Agricultural Development, particularly by releasing their contributions according to agreed schedules and responding positively during the negotiations regarding the second replenishment;

13. *Welcomes* the progress made towards the attainment of the 1983-1984 target for voluntary contributions to the World Food Programme and urges Governments to make every effort to ensure the full attainment of that target, as well as the proposed 1985-1986 target;

14. *Takes note* of the recommendations made in section III of the report of the Director-General for Development and International Economic Co-operation,

designed to enhance the responsiveness of operational activities to the needs and requirements of all developing countries in accordance with their objectives and priorities, as formulated in their national development plans and programmes, and their efforts to promote greater economic and technical co-operation among themselves;

15. *Invites* all organs, organizations and bodies of the United Nations system engaged in operational activities for development, with a view to achieving, *inter alia*, higher cost effectiveness, to make greater use of the capacities of developing countries by:

(a) Engaging national experts and personnel;

(b) Utilizing local or regional sources for the procurement of material, equipment and services;

16. *Decides* that the guidelines on procurement to be issued pursuant to paragraph 7 of decision 81/28 of 30 June 1981 and section II, paragraph 2, of decision 82/34 of 18 June 1982 of the Governing Council of the United Nations Development Programme should govern the procurement activities of organs and bodies under the authority of the General Assembly in their execution of projects financed by the Programme;

17. *Welcomes* decision 82/8 of 18 June 1982 of the Governing Council of the United Nations Development Programme, designed to promote government execution of projects funded by the Programme, the support cost savings that could result therefrom becoming available for programmes and plans, on the basis of the illustrative indicative planning figure;

18. *Reiterates* the set of principles which, in the programming of the resources at the disposal of the different organizations of the United Nations system, should be uniformly applied; those principles, embodied in the consensus of 1970 and decision 80/30 of 26 June 1980 of the Governing Council of the United Nations Development Programme include, *inter alia*, the following:

(a) Equity, particularly in the distribution of resources among developing countries;

(b) Assistance to be provided only in response to the express needs of the recipient countries;

(c) Assistance to be integrated with the overall development objectives and priorities of the country concerned;

(d) Programming to be seen as an integrated process, of which the different phases, such as programming, project formulation, assessment, approval and evaluation, constitute integral parts;

19. *Emphasizes* the important role of the United Nations system in assisting developing countries, upon request, in developing their evaluation capacity and requests the Secretary-General, in consultation with the organs, organizations and bodies of the system, to elaborate, in the light of the conclusions and recommendations of the Joint Inspection Unit contained in its report, proposals to promote the evaluation capacity of recipient Governments;

20. *Recognizes* that, concerning operational activities for development of the United Nations system, evaluation is an important part of the programming process in order to achieve a rational and optimal utilization of the overall resources available;

21. *Reaffirms* the general guidelines embodied in the new dimensions in technical co-operation adopted by the Governing Council in 1975 and urges their full application;

22. *Recommends* improved coherence of action and co-ordination of the operational systems at the country level, under the overall responsibility of the resident co-ordinator and in consultation with the Governments concerned, in order to cut down expenses on administrative and support costs, minimize waste through avoidance of duplication of work and facilitate the task of the host country in co-ordinating external assistance, and considers that further efforts should be undertaken in this regard;

23. *Invites* the Administrator of the United Nations Development Programme and the President of the World Bank, as well as the heads of regional development banks, to examine further possibilities of co-operation between the Programme and those institutions regarding the complementarity of their respective technical co-operation programmes, in order to enhance the implementation of the present resolution and, in so doing, ensure greater utilization of the facilities available in the various organizations of the United Nations system regarding projects financed by those funding agencies, and requests the Administrator to report thereon to the Governing Council of the United Nations Development Programme;

24. *Urges* the relevant organs, organizations and bodies of the United Nations system to increase their support for the process of technical co-operation among developing countries by orienting their programmes and projects, as appropriate, towards strengthening such co-operation;

25. *Urges* the Secretary-General and the executive heads of organs, organizations and bodies of the United Nations system, bearing in mind the need to maintain an appropriate level of support functions, to seek to minimize administrative and other support costs without affecting the field programmes and the network of United Nations Development Programme offices in developing countries, with a view to increasing the proportion of resources available to improve programme delivery to developing countries;

26. *Requests* the organs, organizations and bodies of the United Nations system receiving resources of an extrabudgetary nature to include information on those resources and their utilization in their budgets and reports and to make that information available to the Governments concerned and to the resident co-ordinator in the recipient country;

27. *Recommends* that, in accordance with its resolution 32/197, due consideration should be given to the technical expertise of the Department of Technical Co-operation for Development for its designation as an executing agency for the implementation of projects within its mandate, as well as its role in the execution of technical co-operation activities of the United Nations system, in order to reaffirm the role of the Department within the existing technical and administrative structures and to avoid duplication and accomplish economies of scale;

28. *Urges* all organs, organizations and bodies of the United Nations system, in the light of the recommendations contained in section V of the report of the Director-General for Development and International Economic Co-operation, to take the necessary steps to ensure the harmonization of administrative, financial, personnel, planning and procurement procedures, and requests the Director-General for Development and In-

ternational Economic Co-operation to report annually on specific action taken;

29. *Reiterates* the importance of the co-ordination of multilateral development assistance at the field level, and requests the Director-General for Development and International Economic Co-operation, while preparing his next report on operational activities, to pay particular attention to the need for improved coherence of action and effective integration at the country level, in accordance with section V of the annex to resolution 32/197 and paragraph 11 of resolution 35/81, and to the role of resident co-ordinators in the co-ordination of operational activities of the United Nations system;

30. *Requests* the Joint Inspection Unit to study in depth the structure of the field representation of the organs and organizations of the United Nations system, particularly with regard to the tasks allotted to the resident co-ordinators;

31. *Requests* the Director-General for Development and International Economic Co-operation to include in his report to the General Assembly at its thirty-ninth session:

(a) An examination of the extent and implications of the continuation of the practice of contributions being provided to organizations with conditions attached to their use, taking into account the information to be provided by the heads of the relevant organs, organizations and bodies;

(b) An in-depth analysis of the subject mentioned in paragraph 22 above concerning improved coherence of action and co-ordination of the operational systems at the country level;

(c) A comparative analysis of the relationship between programme delivery and administrative costs pertaining to operational activities for development executed by the organs, organizations and bodies of the United Nations system, as well as an assessment of agency support costs;

32. *Requests* the Director-General for Development and International Economic Co-operation to include in his report for the 1986 comprehensive policy review:

(a) A study, with supporting data, on the progress achieved with respect to the issues identified in paragraph 15 above;

(b) A system-wide review of the activities identified in paragraph 24 above relating to technical co-operation among developing countries as carried out by different organizations, with particular reference to the approaches and methods devised and followed, the kind of activities undertaken by these organizations and the relevant institutional arrangements;

33. *Requests* the Secretary-General, for the purpose of the 1986 comprehensive policy review, as part of the continuous review by the General Assembly, to entrust the Director-General for Development and International Economic Co-operation with the preparation of a report on policy issues pertaining to operational activities for development undertaken by the United Nations system, taking into account the views and comments of delegations at the second regular session of 1983 of the Economic and Social Council and at the thirty-eighth session of the General Assembly, for submission to the Assembly at its forty-first session through the Council at its second regular session of 1986;

34. *Strongly reiterates* its desire for a coherent and co-ordinated United Nations system in the field of opera-

tional activities for development and, in that context, requests the Director-General for Development and International Economic Co-operation to continue to provide effective leadership in the co-ordination of the various components of the United Nations system in that field and in exercising overall co-ordination within the system, as set forth in resolution 32/197, and requests all organs, organizations and bodies of the United Nations system to co-operate fully with the Director-General.

General Assembly resolution 38/171

19 December 1983   Meeting 102   Adopted without vote

Approved by Second Committee (A/38/703) without vote, 14 December (meeting 56); draft by Vice-Chairman (A/C.2/38/L.115), based on informal consultations on draft by Mexico, for Group of 77 (A/C.2/38/L.101); agenda item 79.
Meeting numbers. GA 38th session: 2nd Committee 45-54, 56; plenary 102.

Apart from drafting changes, the adopted text differed from that submitted by the Group of 77 in a number of ways. Paragraphs 6, 20, 30, 32 and 34 were added. Provisions were deleted, by which the Assembly would have: reaffirmed that the country activities by the World Bank group should be in accordance with the national plans and priorities of recipient countries in order to promote the economic self-reliance of the developing countries; reaffirmed that the main objective of United Nations operational activities for development was to promote such self-reliance; called on the governing bodies of UNDP, UNICEF and other programmes to study the effect of the cost of experts and consultants on the various programmes and projects and to propose solutions, in particular the possibility of using national experts and consultants and those from other developing countries; and requested that the next report on a policy review of operational activities should contain a detailed section on the progress by the organizations of the system in making increased use of national experts and institutions and greater procurement in recipient and other developing countries.

Paragraph 24 of the adopted text was shortened; originally, it had enumerated various measures to be taken into account for strengthening technical co-operation among developing countries (TCDC), including: a review of rules and procedures for providing assistance, with a view to removing possible constraints against TCDC-related activities; a system-wide review of such activities, with particular reference to the approaches and methods followed; and a review of arrangements in the system for collecting, generating and disseminating data related to the needs and capabilities of the developing countries. Instead of endorsing and urging full implementation of various recommendations embodied in the new dimensions in technical co-operation adopted by the UNDP Governing Council in 1975,[8] including a number of measures that were detailed in the withdrawn draft, the Assembly (in paragraph 21) simply reaffirmed the general guidelines embodied in those new dimensions and urged their full application. To paragraph 15, inviting United Nations organs and bodies to make greater use of the capacities of developing countries, was added that this should be done with a view to achieving, *inter alia*, higher cost effectiveness. Also added, in paragraph 31, was the request to the Director-General to include in his 1984 report an analysis of the issue of improved coherence of action and co-ordination of the operational systems at the country level, and to include in his comparative analysis of the relation between programme delivery and administrative costs an assessment of agency support costs. To paragraph 22, recommending improved coherence of action and co-ordination at the country level, was added that the Assembly considered that further efforts should be undertaken in that regard.

Financing of operational activities

Contributions (exclusive of cost-sharing and other similar contributions) to the funds and programmes of the United Nations and the operational activities of the specialized agencies and WFP amounted to $2,465 million in 1983, a slight decline in nominal dollar terms from $2,515 million in 1982. Contributions to the World Bank (including IDA), IFC and IFAD also fell in 1983, to $3,586 million from $4,840 million in 1982.

Expenditures on United Nations operational activities in 1983 amounted to $6.5 billion, including concessional and non-concessional loans of $4.4 billion and grants of $2.1 billion; expenditures from cost-sharing and other similar contributions increased to $161 million.

By far the greater share of operational activities went directly to developing countries in support of national development programmes (about 93 per cent). The balance was directed towards operational activities carried out on a regional, interregional and global basis. Operational activities were increasingly concentrated in regions with a large number of low-income countries. Forty per cent of activities took place in LDCs. Nearly 50 per cent was allocated to three sectors: agriculture, health and population. About 20 per cent was allocated to regional, interregional and global programmes. United Nations operational programmes were carried out in about 150 countries and territories, and the number of projects financed partly or wholly by the system was well above 5,000.

Total gross disbursements by the World Bank (including IDA) and IFC amounted to $9.7 billion in 1983, net disbursements to $7.2 billion and net transfers to $4.2 billion. Disbursements by IDA declined, by about 8 per cent compared with 1982. Gross disbursements by the World Bank on tech-

nical co-operation embodied in their lending programmes (i.e., on training and consultants) reached $873 million in 1983, a level more than doubled since 1979. A growing number of World Bank borrowers were beginning to disburse parts of loan funds earmarked for technical co-operation by using services of United Nations organizations. Gross disbursements by IFAD reached $156 million in 1983, a rapid increase over the 1982 level of $110 million, with further increases expected in the light of commitments of over $1.6 billion.

Loans from the World Bank, IFC and IFAD, on a net transfer basis, fell by about 3 per cent in 1983 to $4.4 billion, the result of a drop in IDA disbursements.

The Director-General pointed out that the rapid growth of contributions for operational activities in the 1970s had not been sustained in the first years of the 1980s and that prospects for a significant overall real increase in contributions were not good.[2]

At its April 1983 session,[9] the Committee for Development Planning, calling for a number of measures to remedy the acute crisis in the poorest countries, singled out redressal of the decline in UNDP's resources, an increased level of ODA, a larger aid transfer in rapidly disbursing form, renewed international efforts, and raised food-aid levels and targets.

Expenditures

Total ODA transferred through all United Nations organizations to developing countries amounted to $4,067 million in 1983, or about 12 per cent of net developing country ODA receipts. United Nations ODA comprised exenditures and disbursements from all organizations, including IDA, IFAD, the refugee and humanitarian programmes and related activities and the programmes of the Environment Fund of UNEP, but did not include cost-sharing and self-supporting contributions to organizations and programme expenditures financed therefrom. On a more limited basis, i.e., excluding the concessional funds provided by IDA and IFAD, the share of developing country net ODA receipts channelled through United Nations organizations (excluding IDA and IFAD) had grown from 5.7 per cent in the early 1970s to about 8 per cent in the early 1980s. There was, however, a significant falling off of the rate of increase of net ODA receipts of developing countries channelled through the United Nations system which had grown at an average rate of about 17 per cent over the period 1973 to 1979, but then declined to about 7 per cent.

For operational activities as a whole, the 1983 decline in UNDP main programme expenditures of about $100 million (see below, under TECHNICAL CO-OPERATION THROUGH UNDP) was offset

1983 EXPENDITURES BY THE UN SYSTEM ON OPERATIONAL ACTIVITIES FOR DEVELOPMENT
(in millions of US dollars)

CONCESSIONAL ASSISTANCE

A. *Grants*

1.	Financed from regular budgets	257.8
2.	Financed by UNDP*	485.1
3.	Financed from funds administered by UNDP	64.0
4.	Financed by UNFPA	105.6
5.	Financed by UNICEF	246.2
6.	Financed by specialized agencies and other organizations from extrabudgetary resources†	304.7
7.	Financed by WFP	628.8
	Subtotal (1-7)	2,092.2

B. *Loans*

8.	Disbursed by IDA	
	(a) Gross disbursements	1,429.3
	(b) Net disbursements	1,348.4
	(c) Net transfer	1,232.4
9.	Disbursed by IFAD‡	149.8
	Subtotal (8 *(c)* and 9)	1,382.2
	Total (1-7, 8 *(c)* and 9)	3,474.4

NON-CONCESSIONAL ASSISTANCE

10.	Disbursed by World Bank	
	(a) Gross disbursements	7,777.6
	(b) Net disbursements	5,543.6
	(c) Net transfer	2,835.5
11.	Disbursed by IFC	
	(a) Gross disbursements	365.0
	(b) Net disbursements	166.0
	(c) Net transfer (10 *(c)* and 11 *(b)*)	3,001.5
	Total (1-7, 8 *(c)*, 9, 10 *(c)* and 11 *(b)*)	6,475.9

Other expenditures:

Expenditure financed from cost-sharing contributions to UNDP	68.7
Expenditure financed from government cash counterpart contributions to UNDP	6.3
Expenditure financed from self-financing contributions to specialized agencies and other organizations	92.0
World Bank/IDA technical co-operation§	873.2
Refugee, humanitarian and disaster relief activities	593.0

*Main UNDP programme; excludes expenditures financed from cost-sharing and from cash counterpart contributions.
†From funds not elsewhere specified in the table.
‡Includes a small amount of grants.
§Gross disbursements on training and consultants embodied in World Bank loans and IDA credits to World Bank borrowers.
NOTE: Totals may differ from sum of figures because of rounding.
SOURCE: A/39/417.

UN SYSTEM TECHNICAL CO-OPERATION EXPENDITURES IN 1983, BY EXECUTING AGENCY
(in thousands of US dollars)

Executing agency	UNDP	Other sources	Total
UNIDO	50,200	26,810	77,010
UNCTAD	13,000	2,167	15,167
UN Centre on Transnational Corporations	—	709	709
ECA	4,200	7,479	11,679
ECE	700	397	1,097
ECLA	1,700	5,624	7,324
ECWA	500	975	1,475
ESCAP	6,600	9,632	16,232
UNHCR	—	721	721
UNCHS	12,300	4,398	16,698
Other UN	78,700	36,556	115,256
Subtotal UN	167,900	95,468	263,368
IAEA	3,700	22,351	26,051
ILO	43,100	52,120	95,220
FAO	116,500	143,469	259,969
UNESCO	41,800	52,896	94,696
WHO	15,400	305,388*	320,788
World Bank and IDA	35,200	2,630†	37,830
ICAO	27,600	23,935	51,535
UPU	1,600	1,141	2,741
ITU	21,600	6,426	28,026
WMO	11,300	10,404	21,704
IMO	6,000	3,075	9,075
WIPO	1,200	1,907	3,107
ITC	—	9,544	9,544
UNDP	42,300	32,786	75,086
UNFPA	—	29,354	29,354
UNICEF	—	4,113	4,113
Subtotal other UN system	367,300	701,539	1,068,839
World Tourism Organization	800	—	800
Asian Development Bank	2,900	—	2,900
Arab Fund for Economic and Social Development	300	—	300
Governments	20,900‡	43,540	64,440
Non-governmental organizations	—	242	242
Subtotal non-UN system	24,900	43,782	68,682
Total	560,100	840,789	1,400,889

*Including support costs.
†Excluding $873 million financed by World Bank loans and IDA credits.
‡Including government cash counterpart expenditures of $6,300,000.
NOTE: Figures for UNDP are provisional data covering IPFs, Special Programme Resources, Special Measures Fund for Least Developed Countries, Special Industrial Services, cost-sharing and trust funds established by the Administrator, where applicable; UNDP-administered funds outside the Programme's central resources are included in the "other sources" column.
SOURCE: DP/1984/66.

by increased WFP expenditures by 15 per cent to $629 million and by a 6 per cent growth in UNICEF delivery to $246 million. Technical co-operation expenditures financed from regular budgets also increased in 1983 to $258 million, while expenditures financed from other extrabudgetary sources fell to about $305 million. With the stagnation in overall delivery, per capita expenditures on operational activities declined in 1983 as the population of developing countries grew by about 2 per cent.

Total United Nations system-wide expenditures on technical co-operation amounted to $2,257 million in 1983, compared with $2,166 million in 1982, including the technical co-operation embodied in World Bank lending operations. Grant-financed activities other than those financed by UNICEF and WFP and including cost-sharing and similar expenditures totalled $1,384 million, about 5 per cent less than in 1982. Of that amount, UNDP financed 40 per cent; in 1982, the share of UNDP in total system-wide grant-financed technical co-operation (i.e., exclusive of World Bank lending operations) had been 45 per cent.

Extrabudgetary resources placed directly at the disposal of the specialized agencies and other organizations were the next single most important source of funding, amounting to 29 per cent. WHO (23 per cent) and FAO (19 per cent) accounted for over two fifths of total technical co-operation expenditures, followed by DTCD (8 per cent), UNESCO and ILO (both 7 per cent), UNIDO (6 per cent), and ICAO and the Office for Projects Execution of UNDP (both 5 per cent).

(continued on p. 450)

1983 EXPENDITURES BY THE UN SYSTEM ON OPERATIONAL ACTIVITIES FOR DEVELOPMENT AND NON-DEVELOPMENT ASSISTANCE, BY RECIPIENT COUNTRY AND REGION

(in thousands of US dollars)

RECIPIENT	Development assistance*	Other assistance†
Developing Member States		
Afghanistan	9,655	—
Albania	1,239	—
Algeria	25,045	3,212
Angola	19,270	6,312
Antigua and Barbuda	414	—
Argentina	3,359	2,919
Bahamas	1,417	—
Bahrain	1,179	—
Bangladesh	144,778	—
Barbados	5,615	—
Belize	1,714	—
Benin	11,013	30
Bhutan	9,628	—
Bolivia	(35)	104
Botswana	21,026	1,175
Brazil	788,304	—
Bulgaria	1,241	—
Burma	48,721	—
Burundi	31,121	1,252
Cape Verde	10,482	—
Central African Republic	5,813	—
Chad	25,772	3,947
Chile	674	—
China	61,369	6,730
Colombia	68,545	392
Comoros	7,988	10
Congo	6,065	—
Costa Rica	(2,431)	4,920
Cuba	11,357	—
Cyprus	5,845	5,466
Czechoslovakia	288	—
Democratic Kampuchea	23,314	—
Democratic Yemen	42,597	—
Djibouti	5,046	4,454
Dominica	1,368	—
Dominican Republic	17,580	—
Ecuador	21,158	341
Egypt	247,125	2,806
El Salvador	3,243	—
Equatorial Guinea	4,861	—
Ethiopia	71,792	13,058
Fiji	22,040	10
Gabon	(738)	—
Gambia	10,512	—
Ghana	11,740	30
Greece	(4,979)	796
Grenada	502	—
Guatemala	(2,994)	—
Guinea	9,915	120
Guinea-Bissau	7,196	—
Guyana	4,397	—
Haiti	20,019	—
Honduras	46,573	11,984
Hungary	57,475	—
India	865,886	—
Indonesia	363,101	6,746
Iran	(76,987)	3,562
Iraq	(8,586)	—
Ivory Coast	146,553	—
Jamaica	26,488	—
Jordan	32,001	—
Kenya	81,573	2,576
Kuwait	64	—
Lao People's Democratic Republic	8,132	1,533
Lebanon	36,755	1,248
Lesotho	22,730	907
Liberia	5,618	—
Libyan Arab Jamahiriya	864	—
Madagascar	24,017	—
Malawi	20,427	—
Malaysia	17,435	7,911
Maldives	2,697	—
Mali	39,111	—
Malta	430	—
Mauritania	38,292	25
Mauritius	(27)	—
Mexico	(69,481)	5,420
Mongolia	2,849	—
Morocco	140,788	—
Mozambique	28,701	73
Nepal	57,058	25
Nicaragua	21,365	2,363
Niger	23,654	20
Nigeria	108,546	1,764
Oman	3,152	—
Pakistan	159,381	85,540
Panama	56,013	—
Papua New Guinea	9,741	—
Paraguay	17,415	20
Peru	23,027	1,148
Philippines	438,149	8,609
Poland	1,498	—
Portugal	49,270	813
Qatar	290	—
Romania	155,942	—
Rwanda	24,835	4,162
Saint Lucia	728	—
Saint Vincent and the Grenadines	748	—
Samoa	2,169	—
Sao Tome and Principe	1,438	—
Saudi Arabia	2,198	—
Senegal	31,672	1,304
Seychelles	1,365	—
Sierra Leone	6,470	—
Singapore	(16,122)	—
Solomon Islands	1,058	—
Somalia	54,921	46,558
Spain	(45,848)	1,941
Sri Lanka	70,313	—
Sudan	69,780	31,702
Suriname	843	—
Swaziland	8,625	1,374
Syrian Arab Republic	35,823	—
Thailand	291,497	32,642
Togo	11,701	10
Trinidad and Tobago	(7,119)	—
Tunisia	46,660	—
Turkey	211,236	959
Uganda	36,707	4,804
United Arab Emirates	254	—
United Republic of Cameroon	35,717	1,060
United Republic of Tanzania	64,618	6,345
Upper Volta	25,507	—
Uruguay	5,395	—
Vanuatu	1,021	—
Venezuela	(22,305)	—
Viet Nam	26,156	4,407
Yemen	31,076	—
Yugoslavia	47,270	1,120
Zaire	18,861	13,841
Zambia	(16,606)	3,174
Zimbabwe	47,048	468
Subtotal	**5,925,855**	**356,242**
Developing non-member States/Territories		
Bermuda	12	—
Democratic People's Republic of Korea	2,385	—
Hong Kong	156	4,710
Namibia	4,827	—
Republic of Korea	215,670	—
Tonga	1,382	—
Other countries	(20,330)	—
Subtotal	**204,102**	**4,710**
Total	**6,129,957**	**360,952**
Developed countries	(104,254)	8,921
TOTAL (all countries)	**6,025,703**	**369,873**
Intercountry		
Regional Africa	68,345	121
Regional Americas	43,215	—
Regional Arab States	20,782	544
Regional Asia	70,837	—
Regional Europe	13,712	—
Interregional	162,467	—
Global	67,250	27,406
Total	**446,608**	**28,071**
Not elsewhere classified	3,566	195,028
GRAND TOTAL	**6,475,877**	**592,972**

*Represents the sum of operational activities financed under regular United Nations and agency budgets ($257.8 million), the UNDP main programme ($485.1 million), UNDP-administered funds ($63.9 million), UNFPA ($105.6 million), UNICEF ($246.2 million), other extrabudgetary funds ($304.7 million) and WFP ($628.8 million), plus net transfers from the World Bank ($2,835.5 million), IDA ($1,232.4 million) and IFC ($166 million) and net IFAD disbursements ($149.8 million).

†Represents expenditure financed by UNHCR ($411.1 million), UNRWA ($174.1 million) and UNDRO ($7.8 million).

NOTE: Figures in parentheses are negative.

SOURCE: A/39/417.

1983 CONTRIBUTIONS TO THE UN SYSTEM FOR OPERATIONAL ACTIVITIES
FOR DEVELOPMENT AND FOR OTHER ECONOMIC AND SOCIAL ACTIVITIES
(in thousands of US dollars)

CONTRIBUTOR	Operational activities for development	Other economic and social activities*	CONTRIBUTOR	Operational activities for development	Other economic and social activities*
Member States			Jamaica	1,794	11
Afghanistan	108	1	Japan	830,124	61,785
Albania	31	—	Jordan	958	839
Algeria	1,486	61	Kenya	574	46
Angola	66	—	Kuwait	2,534	1,360
Antigua and Barbuda	203	—	Lao People's Democratic Republic	53	6
Argentina	7,726	168	Lebanon	7,820	69
Australia	133,062	12,320	Lesotho	174	4
Austria	15,273	663	Liberia	68	5
Bahamas	96	8	Libyan Arab Jamahiriya	6,874	1,432
Bahrain	173	15	Luxembourg	1,194	30
Bangladesh	6,530	2	Madagascar	558	—
Barbados	81	4	Malawi	88	—
Belgium	109,778	1,063	Malaysia	16,741	90
Belize	3	—	Maldives	36	4
Benin	92	2	Mali	69	—
Bhutan	32	—	Malta	2,105	4
Bolivia	184	—	Mauritania	33	—
Botswana	94	2	Mauritius	96	23
Brazil	5,179	25	Mexico	5,319	80
Bulgaria	1,392	10	Mongolia	214	1
Burma	2,405	11	Morocco	1,022	48
Burundi	134	—	Mozambique	84	—
Byelorussian SSR	1,152	18	Nepal	85	—
Canada	319,693	19,976	Netherlands	176,718	10,995
Cape Verde	36	—	New Zealand	8,574	317
Central African Republic	42	—	Nicaragua	70	1
Chad	39	—	Niger	42	—
Chile	2,162	40	Nigeria	2,029	296
China	7,794	502	Norway	154,924	21,096
Colombia	2,916	53	Oman	280	41
Comoros	70	6	Pakistan	24,020	30
Congo	85	—	Panama	538	7
Costa Rica	183	—	Papua New Guinea	196	—
Cuba	2,607	—	Paraguay	27	—
Cyprus	2,486	12	Peru	475	—
Czechoslovakia	3,041	49	Philippines	2,395	34
Democratic Kampuchea	27	—	Poland	4,049	32
Democratic Yemen	56	1	Portugal	742	116
Denmark	98,957	13,935	Qatar	1,083	135
Djibouti	28	2	Romania	1,163	—
Dominica	66	—	Rwanda	60	3
Dominican Republic	104	—	Saint Lucia	43	—
Ecuador	879	5	Saint Vincent and the Grenadines	21	—
Egypt	15,534	22	Samoa	23	—
El Salvador	402	—	Sao Tome and Principe	26	—
Equatorial Guinea	26	—	Saudi Arabia	140,647	1,210
Ethiopia	87	—	Senegal	725	8
Fiji	86	—	Seychelles	33	—
Finland	54,495	3,202	Sierra Leone	139	—
France	192,136	3,220	Singapore	414	11
Gabon	964	—	Solomon Islands	2	—
Gambia	62	—	Somalia	152	—
German Democratic Republic	4,284	151	South Africa	2,950	—
Germany, Federal Republic of	538,017	25,000	Spain	7,451	1,598
Ghana	370	16	Sri Lanka	5,767	9
Greece	1,929	185	Sudan	55	2
Grenada	43	—	Suriname	198	—
Guatemala	312	—	Swaziland	62	2
Guinea	306	—	Sweden	161,650	23,009
Guinea-Bissau	34	—	Syrian Arab Republic	560	136
Guyana	83	—	Thailand	1,777	36
Haiti	105	—	Togo	262	—
Honduras	463	—	Trinidad and Tobago	320	7
Hungary	1,746	21	Tunisia	1,061	46
Iceland	2,499	51	Turkey	2,709	31
India	15,013	96	Uganda	55	4
Indonesia	40,481	30	Ukrainian SSR	3,964	44
Iran	1,740	64	USSR	30,202	3,581
Iraq	35,691	—	United Arab Emirates	995	50
Ireland	4,137	531	United Kingdom	372,593	28,364
Israel	696	239	United Republic of Cameroon	420	47
Italy	211,530	3,846	United Republic of Tanzania	2,704	3
Ivory Coast	270	7	United States	1,811,874	200,206
			Upper Volta	101	—

CONTRIBUTOR	Operational activities for development	Other economic and social activities*	CONTRIBUTOR	Operational activities for development	Other economic and social activities*
Member States (cont.)			Switzerland	60,503	9,597
			Tonga	32	—
Uruguay	116	—	Other	2,851	43
Vanuatu	3	—			
Venezuela	53,138	130	Total	65,626	9,656
Viet Nam	107	1			
Yemen	138	—	TOTAL (all countries)	5,792,821	452,915
Yugoslavia	4,956	30			
Zaire	3,140	90	*Inter/non-governmental*		
Zambia	9,310	—	Arab Gulf Programme for		
Zimbabwe	240	40	UN Development Organizations	18,322	—
			European Communities	79,643	54,321
Total	5,727,195	443,259	Other intergovernmental	109,866	9,223
			Non-governmental	50,708	8,904
Non-member States					
			Total	258,539	72,448
Democratic People's Republic of Korea	486	—			
Kiribati	12	—	GRAND TOTAL	6,051,360	525,363
Republic of Korea	1,743	15			

*Includes contributions from Governments and other sources to UNHCR, UNRWA, UNDRO, UNEP and Trust Fund for Special Economic Assistance Programmes.

NOTE: Totals may differ from sum of figures because of rounding.

SOURCE: A/39/417.

Cost-sharing and other similarly financed expenditures reached $161 million in 1983. UNDP cost-sharing expenditures corresponded roughly to the sectoral distribution of country programmes. Unilateral or self-supporting expenditures of the specialized agencies appeared to be concentrated in such sectors as transport and communications, and agriculture, forestry and fisheries. Whereas developing countries with per capita incomes greater than $2,500 accounted for over two thirds of self-supporting expenditures, a wider range of developing countries undertook cost-sharing with UNDP.

United Nations operational activities reflected both universality and a focus on least developed and other low-income countries. Countries with a per capita GNP of less than $500 accounted for 69 per cent of grant-financed expenditures on operational activities, about the same proportion as in earlier years. The proportion reached a high level, over 80 per cent, in the case of UNICEF and funds administered by UNDP. There was a fairly even distribution of resource flows among the developing regions of the world on a per capita basis.

The sectoral distribution of expenditures for technical co-operation was heavily influenced both by the source of funding (i.e., regular or extrabudgetary) and by the organizations involved. Regular budget-financed technical co-operation expenditures tended to be dominated by the health sector (74 per cent), reflecting the size of the regular budget of the World Health Organization (WHO) and its very heavy concentration on technical co-operation. UNDP expenditures financed by indicative planning figure (IPFs) reflected an aggregation of developing country priorities and were concentrated in such sectors as agriculture, forestry and fisheries (23 per cent), natural resources (14 per cent) and general development issues (13 per cent). Two fifths of system-wide expenditures on technical co-operation took place in two sectors—health (23 per cent) and agriculture,

forestry and fisheries (17 per cent). Social sectors other than health, but including education, employment, population and social conditions, absorbed about 17 per cent of total technical co-operation expenditures.

Contributions

Total contributions from Governments and other official and non-official sources to development activities of the United Nations system, amounted to $6 billion in 1983 (see table above) compared with $7.2 billion the previous year. Covered in these totals were all United Nations funds and programmes, the operational activities of the specialized agencies and WFP.

The main features of the pattern of contributions received in 1983 were:

—Aggregate contributions to United Nations funds and programmes amounted to $1,300 million, the same level as in 1982. Most funds and programmes participating in the Pledging Conference experienced a slight decline or no growth at all in the dollar value of contributions in 1983, despite a number of countries increasing the national currency value of their contributions. Most organizations had been adversely affected by exchange rate movements; had exchange rates remained at their end 1982 levels, total 1983 contributions would have amounted to nearly $1,400 million.

—Contributions to the main programme of UNDP (excluding cost-sharing), which represented about 50 per cent of total contributions to the Pledging Conference, stagnated for the fourth consecutive year at around $700 million. UNFPA also experienced no growth in contributions and remained at around $130 million. Contributions to the general resources of UNICEF (i.e., excluding supplementary funding), which had been increasing in the recent past, declined in 1983 by about 5 per cent to $207 million.

—Total contributions (in nominal dollar terms) over the years 1979-1983 to all funds and programmes of the Pledging Conference increased by about 13 per cent, compared with a growth of 5 per cent in total net ODA over the same period.

—Member countries of the Development Assistance Committee of the Organisation for Economic Co-operation and Development (OECD) contributed by far the largest share of resources for operational activities, amounting to nearly 90 per cent in 1983.

—Assessed budget contributions for the technical co-operation activities of the United Nations and specialized agencies reached $257 million in 1983, compared with about $200 million in 1982. Most of that amount was incurred by WHO which allocated 60 per cent of its regular programme budget to technical co-operation and the provision of services to member States.

—Extrabudgetary contributions placed directly at the disposal of specialized agencies and other organizations for their operational activities declined by 10 per cent in 1983 to $247 million, the first time that such a decline had been recorded. In 1983, seven countries (in descending order of total contributions: Italy, Sweden, Netherlands, Norway, Denmark, Belgium, Federal Republic of Germany) provided more than three quarters of total individual country contributions of $168 million. International organizations (particularly the World Bank and IFC and funds associated with OPEC countries) provided a total of $73 million. WHO and FAO received two thirds of total contributions, ILO and UNESCO a further 25 per cent.

Contributions in 1983 to the main programme resources of UNDP, the general resources of UNICEF and the main UNFPA programme amounted to $1,051 million, or 81 per cent of total contributions to United Nations funds and programmes. Other contributions amounting to $249 million were provided to the variety of special-purpose and trust funds administered by UNDP, UNDP third party cost-sharing, supplementary funding through UNICEF, other funds and programmes participating in the annual Pledging Conference and multilateral/bilateral contributions to UNFPA and other United Nations entities. Contributions to all such funding arrangements since 1979 had grown at an annual average rate of about 10 per cent.

Resources provided to developing countries through United Nations organizations were increasingly used to attract supplementary funding from other sources; cost-sharing and other similar contributions from middle- and higher-income developing countries were an important component of that type of financing. In 1983, an increase in such contributions to UNDP was offset by a fall in similar contributions to other organizations.

Contributions for refugee, humanitarian and special economic assistance programmes and disaster relief activities—not included in the above data—amounted to about $500 million in 1983, down from $582 million in 1982.

Contributions to the World Bank and IFC declined in 1983, the result of a slight drop in payments to IDA and in capital subscription payments. The first replenishment agreement payments to IFAD amounted to $1.2 billion for 1981-1983.

In his 1983 report on operational activities,[2] the Director-General submitted several proposals for resource mobilization. He noted that the diversification of funding sources for multilateral technical co-operation had continued, marked by the emergence of a number of new modalities for financing within United Nations agencies and organizations; the growth of cost-sharing and similar arrangements, with developing countries increasingly financing operational activities from their own resources; and the growth in expenditures on technical co-operation financed through the operations of the World Bank.

In the light of those trends, he stated, three areas were identified for consideration: mobilizing sufficient resources; setting desirable and attainable targets to mobilize resources on a more predictable and assured basis; and maintaining a degree of uniformity in distributing resources among the organizations of the system.

The UNDP Governing Council, at its June 1983 session, adopted several measures to improve the longer-term mobilization of resources for UNDP. The General Assembly, on 19 December, adopted resolution 38/172 on the situation of the financial resources of UNDP (see below, under TECHNICAL CO-OPERATION THROUGH UNDP). In resolution 38/171 of the same date, on operational activities for development (see above), the Assembly strongly reiterated the need for and urged a substantial increase in resources, including an increase for IDA and IFAD, and urged for attainment of the 1983-1984 target for contributions to WFP.

By a letter of 17 November,[10] the United States pointed out that on 14 November its President had signed into law a resolution authorizing, for the fiscal year 1984, voluntary contributions to United Nations agencies of $336.7 million, or 16.9 per cent over the previous year.

UN Pledging Conference for Development Activities. The 1983 United Nations Pledging Conference for Development Activities was held at United Nations Headquarters on 8 and 9 November to receive government pledges for 1984 to United Nations funds and programmes concerned with development and related assistance.

Contributions to the funds and programmes participating in the Pledging Conference grew only slightly in 1983, totalling $1,076 million, compared with $1,073 million in 1982. Pledges for 1984, as at 30 June 1984, amounted to $1,046 million, more than half of which was for UNDP.

CONTRIBUTIONS TO FUNDS AND PROGRAMMES INCLUDED IN THE
UN PLEDGING CONFERENCE FOR DEVELOPMENT ACTIVITIES, 1983 AND 1984
*(1983, as at 31 December 1983; 1984, as at 30 June 1984;
in thousands of US dollars)*

FUND OR PROGRAMME	1983 PAYMENT		1984 PLEDGE	
	Amount	Number of donor countries	Amount	Number of donor countries
UN Development Programme	697,835	141	664,071	127
Special Measures Fund for the Least Developed Countries	16,056	11	13,978	11
Energy Account	841	3	33	1
UN Children's Fund	172,372	127	181,014	108
UN Fund for Population Activities	130,257	84	135,087	91
UN Capital Development Fund	24,215	41	21,208	41
UN Industrial Development Fund	13,277	102	14,677	75
UN Fund for Drug Abuse Control	6,425	52	4,096	35
UN Habitat and Human Settlements Foundation	2,427*	48	1,902	41
Voluntary Fund for the UN Decade for Women	2,422	41	2,373	42
UN Revolving Fund for Natural Resources Exploration	2,120	6	2,109	6
UN Trust Fund for African Development Activities	1,754	NA	27	3
UN Institute for Training and Research	1,689	40	1,593	44
Special Voluntary Fund for the UN Volunteers	1,214	23	980	23
Trust Fund for the UN Centre on Transnational Corporations	802	NA	599	8
UN Trust Fund for Social Defence	694	13	500	7
UN Trust Fund for Sudano-Sahelian Activities	536	5	624	9
UN Financing System for Science and Technology for Development	494	27	324	27
UN Trust Fund for the International Research and Training Institute for the Advancement of Women	473	22	492	19
UN Special Fund for Land-locked Developing Countries	52	12	56	16
UN Trust Fund for the Transport and Communications Decade in Africa	43	NA	22	5
Total	1,075,998		1,045,765	

*Amount pledged for 1983, as at 30 June 1983.
NA = Not available.
SOURCES: For 1983, A/39/5/Add.1,2,4,7-9 and unpublished documents; for 1984, A/CONF.122/2.

Inter-agency co-operation

Resident co-ordinators

In 1983, resident co-ordinators continued to be responsible for co-ordinating operational activities for development in individual countries. These arrangements for field representation of the whole United Nations system had become operational in 1980.[11] At the end of 1983, 104 UNDP resident representatives were also acting as co-ordinators.

On 20 June,[12] the Secretary-General transmitted the comments of ACC, submitted in accordance with a December 1982 General Assembly resolution,[3] on the arrangements for the functioning of co-ordinators. ACC's CCSQ(OPS) had prepared the recommendations, based on a synthesis of reports from the co-ordinators resulting from their consultations with Governments as well as comments from United Nations organizations. On 31 March,[5] ACC approved the recommendations of CCSQ(OPS) on improving the complementarity and coherence of programmes and policies at the country level and on improving, monitoring and evaluating operations at the field level;

it decided that the practice of periodic meetings between the co-ordinator and agency representatives should be further strengthened. Also on that date,[13] ACC stated that the co-ordinators, the majority of whom had been in that capacity for 12 to 18 months, had been in place for too brief a period to permit a firm judgement regarding new arrangements. The manner in which they had been exercising their functions varied from country to country, conditioned by the views of the Government concerned and of its own arrangements for co-ordinating external assistance, the extent of agency representation in each country and the nature of operational activities carried out by the organizations of the system in the country concerned. ACC drew attention to the satisfaction expressed by a number of Governments with the arrangements for co-ordinating country-level operational activities and noted with satisfaction the comment by the vast majority of the resident co-ordinators that the procedures followed by the organizations of the system were such as to ensure that the activities conformed with national objectives. Arrangements for inter-agency collaboration at the country level, including those for the functioning of the co-ordinator, should be allowed to develop further in a flexible and pragmatic manner, ACC stated; it would continue to keep the system of resident co-ordinators under review.

Programme and project evaluation

In August 1983, the Secretary-General transmitted to the General Assembly a report of JIU on United Nations system co-operation in developing evaluation by Governments,[14] one of a series of reports on evaluation progress since 1977. The report, prepared by Alfred N. Forde and Earl D. Sohm, dealt with conceptual and policy aspects of the problem, past efforts and constraints, future prospects, United Nations co-operation, and factors influencing evaluation. Concluding, the Inspectors stated that evaluation had been slow to emerge as an integral element of development management, but during the past few years there had been new international policy initiatives, accompanied by a growing interest and understanding of evaluation and increasing co-operative efforts to help develop government evaluation. Encouraging evaluation as a normal development management function on a wide scale would be a long, gradual and challenging task, they added.

They made several recommendations for United Nations action, stressing the potential leadership role of UNDP in strengthening government evaluation. They suggested: assessment by the organizations of their own evaluation systems; arrangements for co-operation and co-ordination in monitoring and evaluation activities with Governments and other development organizations when formulating and implementing projects and programmes; developing data on evaluation needs, resources, skills and contacts; identification and use of institutions in evaluation work; sharing of monitoring and evaluation experience and information through workshops, seminars and reports; and co-operative training in monitoring and evaluation, particularly in developing countries, as part of broader development management training.

Further recommendations were that the United Nations governing bodies might consider issuing a statement of policy to encourage government evaluation; that ACC consider specific areas, roles, arrangements and mechanisms to encourage and co-ordinate joint United Nations and other activities to help strengthen government evaluation; and that the United Nations, under the leadership of the Director-General for DIEC, determine what continuing actions it could take to develop the role of Governments in the internal evaluation system being designed for its economic and social sectors, to include support to government evaluation as a more specific part of its development issues and policies and public administration and finance programmes, and to enlist United Nations enti-

ties in a co-operative network to encourage and strengthen government evaluation.

Commenting on the JIU report in November,[15] ACC supported the thesis that, both within the United Nations system and in Governments, evaluation should be seen as essential and integral to policy formulation, programme planning, budgeting and implementation management. It believed that the report was an excellent basis for further review of the direction which United Nations organizations were taking, in further improving their efforts towards harmonizing their evaluation systems and in supporting government evaluation activities.

ACC expressed full support for the recommendation calling for actions to address various aspects of evaluation on a continuing and co-ordinated basis. With regard to the suggestion that ACC consider specific ways to encourage joint activities to help strengthen government evaluation, ACC stated that it would ensure that information was regularly exchanged among agencies of the system. In addition, it noted that, at its March 1983 session, it had decided to improve monitoring and evaluation of country-level operational activities, through involvement of recipient Governments in United Nations–sponsored projects. With respect to the role of Governments in the internal evaluation system being designed for the economic and social sectors of the United Nations, ACC noted that guidelines for management-oriented evaluation were being developed under which programme managers would be requested to specify in their individual evaluation plans the type and extent of participation by Member States, as a regular feature of medium-term planning. ACC emphasized, however, that for assistance to Governments to be effective, certain pre-conditions must be fulfilled, namely: adequate institutional capability within the United Nations should first be built up; there was a need first to achieve co-ordinated and harmonized planning and implementation of evaluation within the United Nations, in order to secure methodologies appropriate to developing countries' needs and to avoid inconsistent, wasteful and counter-productive assistance; and a more adequate level of technical capability was required, based on a more developed information system. With regard to the proposal to include assistance for evaluation by Governments as a specific part of United Nations programme activities, ACC felt that the rationale for limiting the scope to development issues and policies and public administration and finance was not clear; since assistance for evaluation related essentially to individual developing countries, it added, responsiveness to diverse conditions and specific needs should be emphasized. ACC concluded that the thrust of United Nations support to Governments should come from regional commissions, regional institutions and other entities, with the United Nations Secretariat performing a co-ordinating role.

REFERENCES

[1]A/39/417. [2]A/38/258-E/1983/82. [3]YUN 1982, p. 624, GA res. 37/226, 20 Dec. 1982. [4]*Ibid.*, p. 623. [5]ACC/1983/DEC/1-10 (dec. 1983/1). [6]YUN 1982, p. 624. [7]A/38/3. [8]YUN 1975, p. 411. [9]E/1983/16. [10]A/C.2/38/7. [11]YUN 1980, p. 613. [12]A/38/276-E/1983/103. [13]ACC/1983/DEC/1-10 (dec. 1983/2). [14]A/38/333. [15]A/38/333/Add.1.

Technical co-operation through UNDP

In his annual report for 1983,[1] the UNDP Administrator reported that there had been new developments in Programme management and evaluation, in UNDP's relations with the World Bank, regional development banks and other agency partners. A more solid resource foundation had been established for UNDP, confirmed by modestly improved results at the 1983 United Nations Pledging Conference for Development Activities and evident in new activities for resource mobilization at the developing country level. Additional resources had been mobilized through increased cost-sharing in country projects, in services and funding to LDCs, and in operational activities for increased TCDC.

Highlights of UNDP action following the June 1983 Governing Council session were: involvement in the Secretary-General's initiative for action to meet Africa's food and development crisis, with resident co-ordinators preparing reports on priorities and UNDP field offices providing centres of operational support for large-scale international action; establishment of a new Central Evaluation Office to co-ordinate and oversee all aspects of project and programme evaluation; arrangements with Governments for the provision of additional and complementary funds for UNDP-assisted projects; restoration of programming levels to 80 per cent of illustrative indicative planning levels for some 23 small, mainly island developing countries at a total cost of $4.3 million for the Third Development Co-operation Cycle; further strengthening of UNDP's relationship with the World Bank family and regional development banks, aimed at increasing joint activities; intensified collaboration with the Office of the United Nations High Commissioner for Refugees; continued collaboration with UNFPA and UNICEF under the Joint Consultative Group on Policy, joined in 1983 also by WFP, to achieve more effective co-operation; appointment of a Co-ordinator of Assistance to the Least Developed Countries within the UNDP Planning and Co-ordination Office; continuation of the UNDP Development Study Programme, designed to promote better understanding of operational issues in development policy; establishment, in collaboration with WHO, UNICEF and the United Nations Centre for Social and Humanitarian Affairs, of a joint programme to promote adoption of already proven, low-cost measures to prevent disabilities and impairment of hundreds of millions of people in the developing countries (see Chapter XV of this section); and initiation of a number of administrative actions, including the issuance of updated and consolidated financial management guidelines and instructions to the field network, implementation of revised procedures for government execution of projects, development of model agreements for cost-sharing, trust fund and similar agreements, initiation on a pilot scale of automated systems for financial management and accounting and for project management in field offices, and introduction of new control systems for administrative budgets and appropriations at headquarters, together with the development of new data processing systems for special funds administered by UNDP.

At least partly in response to those activities, UNDP made new special funding arrangements, including the establishment, through transfer of funds from the liquidated United Nations Emergency Operation Trust Fund, of two new UNDP trust funds—one of $34 million for developing countries afflicted by drought, famine and malnutrition, and another of $5.8 million for increased economic and technical co-operation among developing countries. Forty-nine projects—33 in Africa, 10 in Asia and 6 in Latin America—had been approved for $14.3 million in commitments under the drought, famine and malnutrition fund, while project identification and consultation for the second fund was under way. Another arrangement was the allocation, under another trust fund established by the Administrator, of $6.6 million from the Netherlands to strengthen round-table conferences in augmenting development resources for LDCs.

With its growing number of allies and agency partners (the International Trade Centre became the twenty-seventh executing agency of UNDP in 1983) and its new Programme initiatives under way, UNDP was able to pursue more vigorously its co-ordinating role as a central funding organization for technical co-operation, playing a leadership role in each of the priority areas identified by the DIEC Director-General. Priorities for technical co-operation were also discussed in the 1983 development co-operation review of the main donor group, the OECD Development Assistance Committee, which cited the need for more effective evaluation, greater intensity of personnel devoted to rural development projects and projects in low-income countries with weak administrative structures, more careful recruitment and preparation of technical assistance experts, more effective participation of programme representatives in policy dialogues with recipient countries and better participation in co-ordination at the country level, as well as on the governing boards of multilateral organizations.

In its main policy paper, UNDP addressed the need to shift training from pre- and post-entry level courses to in-service training for mid-level personnel, the need to create incentives for greater "bottom-up" responsiveness by planners and the need for more precise terms of reference and selection of project experts. With respect to greater concentration of personnel in rural development and among low-income countries, the emphasis on grass-roots initiatives was especially relevant.

Improved co-ordination at the country level assumed special importance in the context of the Secretary-General's initiative on Africa (see Chapter VIII of this section). He had requested resident co-ordinators in the countries concerned to begin consultations with host Governments, bilateral and multilateral representatives, as well as representatives of non-governmental organizations, in order to identify or update country needs, priorities and gaps in resources.

With regard to strengthening UNDP's field network, during 1983 a number of efforts were taken to improve co-ordination through CCSQ(OPS) and inter-agency consultative meetings at headquarters. Due to resource constraints, many of UNDP's most effective and important field offices had been severely taxed; some of the steps taken in 1983—such as the new financial management guidelines and the pilot programme for field office automation—were projected to ease staffing pressures. Co-ordination remaining only one aspect of their responsibilities, field offices also had to respond to new and evolving technical co-operation requirements, grass-roots initiatives, a growing number of special funds administered by UNDP and country-level resource generation such as cost-sharing, co-financing and parallel financing arrangements.

In 1983, there were many examples of such country-level resource generation. The European Economic Community (EEC) provided $1.6 million for follow-up to the UNDP-supported seed production project for medium and small farms in Yemen. In the Sudan, $9.7 million in co-financing by EEC, France and the Netherlands was being co-ordinated under four UNDP-supported projects for development of the Jonglei Canal. A project for rural access roads in Kenya was being replicated in the Sudan and, with assistance from the Finnish International Development Agency, in Zambia. The UNDP-supported International Centre for Public Enterprises in Developing Countries in Ljubljana, Yugoslavia, had drawn parallel financing of $685,000 from the Netherlands and $461,000 from Sweden. For every dollar contributed by UNDP to various National Household Survey Capability Programmes, two dollars were contributed by bilateral donors. An irrigation project in the United Republic of Tanzania was being co-financed with a $1.3 million food-for-work grant from the World Bank and $1 million for equipment and materials from Australia. In China, 70 per cent of external assistance was provided by multilateral organizations, with UNDP being a leading on-the-scene-representative and with much new bilateral assistance being channelled through UNDP-supported activities.

In its relation with its agency partners, its services to Governments and its managerial and organizational effectiveness, UNDP acted in 1983 to improve the responsiveness and impact of its operational activities.

During 1983, the Inter-Agency Task Force at UNDP headquarters was preoccupied with various responsibilities assigned to it by ACC as a follow-up to the 1982 work by CCSQ(OPS) on the evolution of operational activities for development in the 1980s. The subjects covered by the Task Force included improving complementarity and coherence of United Nations action at the country level; better monitoring, evaluation and impact studies of field operations; strengthening of technical backstopping of operational activities; and making effective use of knowledge and experience of the United Nations development system to influence more effectively the direction and flow of bilateral aid.

Task Force members reviewed the UNDP study on measures to be taken to meet the changing technical co-operation requirements of the developing countries. In addition, UNDP continued to profit from the advice of the Task Force on issues affecting UNDP/agency co-operation, particularly in synthesizing the agencies' comments on the JIU report on UNDP's Office for Projects Execution.

During 1983, the Administrator also consulted with several agencies on ways to strengthen the Task Force. The reduction in the number of full-time permanent members and their substitution by part-time associate members by some agencies was a matter of concern. The Administrator invited the executive heads of the agencies to resume full-time representation and to advise him on ways of ensuring more effective participation by other agencies in the Task Force's activities.

UNDP also searched out other means for strengthening system-wide collaboration. In 1983, WFP joined the Joint Consultative Group on Policy, formed among UNDP, UNFPA and UNICEF, which negotiated an agreement to improve co-ordination in programming—to ensure that staff worked together in the early planning stages to make sure activities of their organizations were mutually reinforcing, to maximize the use of scarce resources and to work out a harmonized strategy within the context of Governments' development priorities. As a first step, the organizations were defining how to attain these objectives in selected countries in Africa, where an increased flow of resources was taking place in response to the drought crisis, with special reference to vulnerable groups, particularly women and children.

Efforts to enhance collaboration between UNDP and the World Bank and regional development banks, begun in 1982, gained momentum in 1983. These efforts were guided by a task force which met periodically to work out modalities for improved collaboration in specific areas, such as UNDP management services for World Bank–funded projects, joint technical co-operation assessment missions, and co-financing or cost-sharing. Other areas of close collaboration in 1983 included joint responsibilities under the Energy Assessment Programme, the Energy Management Assistance Programme, the International Drinking Water Supply and Sanitation Decade (1981-1990), and increased use by UNDP of the Bank's Economic Development Institute.

UNDP and the regional banks also began collaborating along new lines; for example, co-operation with the Asian Development Bank was expanded to include training in pre-investment activities.

In 1983, the Inter-Agency Procurement Services Unit continued inter-agency collaboration in equipment purchases, improvement in delivery and development of new sources of supply, particularly in developing countries, and also published its annual general business guide for potential suppliers of goods and services to the United Nations system.

UNDP stepped up efforts to extend further the usefulness of the field offices and to broaden support for their activities; for the first time, Governments could potentially draw on the services of the central co-ordinating mechanism of the United Nations system as they considered the optimal use and management of external technical inputs. UNDP also improved further field office capabilities. First steps were taken to computerize field office administration; 10 pilot field offices were selected in 1983 for systems development, with initial emphasis on financial management and accounting and Programme project management systems. Updated and consolidated guidelines and instructions for financial management and accounting procedures were issued.

Among steps taken to improve Programme effectiveness were preparations for the establishment of a focal point within UNDP for all matters related to the increased needs for LDCs.

Activities under the UNDP Development Study Programme also continued to expand. Four headquarters lectures were held, and the Istanbul Round

Table, organized jointly with the North-South Round Table of the Society for International Development, brought together some 40 leading financial and development experts, bankers and international policy makers to discuss aspects of world financial and human resources development. Another round table was held jointly with the Development Policy Forum of the German Foundation for Development of the Federal Republic of Germany on technical co-operation in the development process and human resources building. A third seminar, on partnerships for development, was organized jointly with the United Nations Association of the United States at Pittsburgh.

During 1983, there were also further improvements in UNDP's data-based management system. New administrative budget and appropriation control systems were implemented, as were new data systems for the Office for Projects Execution and UNV, while plans were initiated to provide data processing services to UNDP-administered trust funds, including the United Nations Capital Development Fund (UNCDF) and the United Nations and the United Nations Revolving Fund for Natural Resources Exploration (UNRFNRE).

UNDP emergency operations reached an all-time high. The Programme provided emergency/disaster relief assistance to 14 countries, while following up on earlier similar assistance to numerous other countries.

UNDP Council action. In New York, the UNDP Governing Council, held an organizational meeting on 14 February, a special meeting from 14 to 18 February to consider country and intercountry programmes and projects, and its thirtieth session from 6 to 24 June.[2] The Council adopted three decisions in February, on its programme and organization of work during the year; on country and intercountry programmes (see below), and on assistance to Yemen for rehabilitation and reconstruction of the areas affected by an earthquake (see Chapter III of this section).

The 40 decisions adopted by the Council in June dealt with resource mobilization; the Administrator's annual report; recruitment and reduction of the cost of project professional personnel; pre-investment activities; implementation of the Substantial New Programme of Action for the 1980s for LDCs (p. 431); special assistance to Namibia (see TRUSTEESHIP AND COLONIZATION, Chapter III); assistance to the Palestinian people (p. 282); evaluation; illustrative IPFs; country and intercountry programmes and projects; Special Programme Resources; technical co-operation activities; UNFPA (see Chapter XIV of this section); UNV; UNCDF; UNRFNRE; TCDC; United Nations Financing System for Science and Technology for Development (UNFSSTD) (see Chapter XII of this section); energy development programmes (see Chapter X of this section); implementation in the Sudano-Sahelian region of the Plan of Action to Combat Desertification; financial matters concerning the United Nations Sudano-Sahelian Office (UNSO) UNDP/UNEP joint venture (see Chapter XVI of this section); implementation of the recovery and rehabilitation programme in the Sudano-Sahelian region; other assistance to drought-stricken countries in Africa (see Chapter III of this section); United Nations Special Fund for Land-locked Developing Countries; annual review of the financial situation in 1982; revised budget estimates for 1982-1983; budget estimates for 1984-1985; trust funds conditioned on procurement from a donor country; trust funds established by the Administrator; guidelines on procurement; matters on which consensus was not achieved at the Council's 1983 session (concerning financial regulations and other questions); support cost reimbursement arrangements for activities financed from resources of UNCDF and UNSO and for projects executed directly by UNDP; *ex post facto* reporting on agency support costs; audit reports; sectoral support (see below) and financing of technical field advisers in the SIDFA programme (see Chapter VI of this section); measures concerning Governing Council documentation; provisional agenda for the Council's 1984 session; arrangements for Council meetings in 1984; and other reports considered by the Council in 1983.

UNDP operational activities

Country and intercountry programmes

The UNDP Governing Council, on 18 February 1983,[3] approved country programmes and projects for the following: Cape Verde, Ethiopia, Gambia, Mali, Mauritania, Niger, Nigeria, Sao Tome and Principe, Senegal, Sierra Leone, Togo, Upper Volta (Africa); Algeria, Kuwait, Saudi Arabia, Sudan (Arab States); Democratic People's Republic of Korea, Mongolia, Papua New Guinea, Republic of Korea, Tonga, Vanuatu (Asia and the Pacific); Greece (Europe); Uruguay (Latin America). It also approved a country programme for Yemen which exceeded the cost-sharing level established by the Council in June 1982,[4] and took note of a one-year extension of programmes approved by the Administrator for Afghanistan and Benin. It took note with appreciation of an intercountry programme for Latin America and the Caribbean for 1982-1986, presented by the Administrator, and of arrangements for its implementation. The Council authorized him to approve requests for country and regional assistance, keeping expenditures in reasonable conformity with IPFs, with government contributions, and within financial resources; and requested him in implementing programmes to take into account government views.

On 16 June,[5] the Council approved country programmes for: Central African Republic, Chad,

Equatorial Guinea, Ghana, Ivory Coast, Liberia, Uganda, United Republic of Cameroon (Africa); Syrian Arab Republic (Arab States); Iran, Kiribati, Niue, Sri Lanka, Tokelau, Tuvalu (Asia and the Pacific); Cyprus (Europe); Belize, Colombia, Costa Rica, Nicaragua, Trinidad and Tobago (Latin America). The Council authorized the Administrator to approve requests for UNDP country assistance and to approve assistance for Lebanon and Swaziland until new programmes for them had been approved. It decided to extend through 1983 the programmes for Benin, Bolivia and Suriname, and took note of one-year extensions approved by the Administrator for El Salvador and Indonesia, as well as of a regional programme presented by him for the Arab States, 1983-1986, and of arrangements for its implementation.

By the same decision, the Council took note of the Administrator's note on UNDP support to the Technical Advisory Committee of the Consultative Group on International Agricultural Research, of oral explanations and of the comments expressed thereon, and decided that UNDP support to that Committee should continue to be charged against the UNDP biennial budget under a separate appropriation line. It approved supplementary assistance for a global project to increase the fixation of soil nitrogen and the efficiency of soil water use in rainfed agricultural systems in the countries of North Africa and Western Asia, and authorized the Administrator to arrange for its execution.

The Council took note of the Administrator's intention to safeguard the financial integrity of UNDP by approving programmes and projects within the limit of 55 per cent of IPFs and by regulating expenditures accordingly. That action notwithstanding, the Council requested him, subject to available resources, to apply 80 per cent of the respective IPFs to countries to which the supplementary criteria applied and whose IPFs were $1.5 million or less, and a minimum IPF of $1.2 million (80 per cent of $1.5 million) to developing countries with IPFs above $1.5 million. The Council took note of his proposal to issue fact sheets for projects to which the UNDP contribution, including cost-sharing, totalled $400,000 or more.

The General Assembly, in resolution 38/172 of 19 December 1983, also dealt with the financial resources situation of UNDP (see below). In resolution 38/192 of 20 December, the Assembly urged the Governing Council to consider increasing its allocation of financial resources for assistance to African countries and intergovernmental organizations in planning their programmes for the Industrial Development Decade for Africa (1980-1990). In doing so, the Assembly repeated a call by the Economic and Social Council in resolution 1983/70 of 29 July.

UNDP INDICATIVE PLANNING FIGURES AND EXPENDITURES, 1983
(in thousands of US dollars)

	IPFs 1982-1986	Programme expenditures
Africa		
Angola	41,500	4,534
Benin	33,500	2,823
Botswana	8,500	1,715
Burundi	48,500	5,064
Cape Verde	11,250	1,204
Central African Republic	29,500	2,249
Chad	52,000	3,199
Comoros	12,000	1,628
Congo	11,000	2,478
Equatorial Guinea	12,750	987
Ethiopia	112,000	8,276
Gabon	6,000	2,117
Gambia	14,250	1,233
Ghana	40,000	2,946
Guinea	44,500	4,029
Guinea-Bissau	21,750	2,318
Ivory Coast	16,500	1,965
Kenya	52,000	4,903
Lesotho	22,250	2,501
Liberia	13,500	1,976
Madagascar	49,000	3,730
Malawi	53,000	6,268
Mali	65,000	7,411
Mauritania	24,500	2,048
Mauritius	7,000	395
Mozambique	74,000	7,312
Namibia	7,750	1,430
Niger	45,000	4,332
Nigeria	55,000	8,432
Rwanda	45,000	4,406
Sao Tome and Principe	2,000	329
Senegal	33,000	3,366
Seychelles	1,600	180
Sierra Leone	34,900	2,849
Swaziland	5,700	955
Togo	23,550	1,959
Uganda	59,500	5,851
United Republic of Cameroon	27,500	4,171
United Republic of Tanzania	72,000	8,272
Upper Volta	55,000	4,846
Zaire	79,000	5,286
Zambia	21,250	2,278
Zimbabwe	24,250	2,057
Subtotal	1,467,750	146,308
Arab States		
Algeria	20,000	3,932
Bahrain	2,500	1,076
Democratic Yemen	22,250	3,310
Djibouti	5,250	973
Egypt	56,000	7,595
Iraq	15,000	1,984
Jordan	15,000	2,369
Kuwait	—	1,239
Lebanon	10,000	1,276
Libyan Arab Jamihiriya	5,000	2,421
Morocco	27,000	3,668
Oman	4,000	1,701
Qatar	—	535
Saudi Arabia	10,000	6,683
Somalia	48,000	5,676
Sudan	58,500	6,708
Syrian Arab Republic	15,000	1,691
Tunisia	15,000	2,008

	IPFs 1982-1986	Programme expenditures
Arab States (cont.)		
United Arab Emirates	1,000	2,004
Yemen	30,000	6,096
Other*	—	908
Subtotal	359,500	63,853
Asia and the Pacific		
Afghanistan	71,500	5,512
Bangladesh	201,000	22,360
Bhutan	36,500	3,942
Brunei	200	39
Burma	102,000	8,744
China	142,000	19,309
Cook Islands	1,400	369
Democratic Kampuchea	25,500	(504)
Democratic People's Republic of Korea	24,750	1,356
Fiji	5,000	750
Hong Kong	500	73
India	252,000	18,738
Indonesia	106,000	16,814
Iran	20,000	3,977
Kiribati	1,300	119
Lao People's Democratic Republic	52,500	3,344
Malaysia	15,000	2,307
Maldives	7,000	1,325
Mongolia	10,000	1,527
Nauru	60	—
Nepal	98,000	10,166
Niue	1,000	91
Pakistan	118,000	11,253
Papua New Guinea	13,500	1,501
Philippines	46,000	4,450
Republic of Korea	18,000	1,528
Samoa	5,250	656
Singapore	7,500	1,279
Solomon Islands	4,000	497
South Pacific islands	—	136
Sri Lanka	76,000	7,529
Thailand	43,000	4,791
Tokelau	950	140
Tonga	2,500	419
Trust Territory of the Pacific Islands	1,000	285
Tuvalu	1,140	176
Vanuatu	2,000	468
Viet Nam	118,000	10,804
Subtotal	1,630,050	166,270
Europe		
Albania	10,250	967
Bulgaria	6,000	765
Cyprus	5,000	541
Czechoslovakia	2,500	209
Greece	6,000	426
Hungary	3,500	686
Malta	2,500	278
Poland	6,000	768
Portugal	4,000	544
Romania	7,500	1,254
Turkey	20,000	2,517
Yugoslavia	7,500	1,343
Subtotal	80,750	10,298

	IPFs 1982-1986	Programme expenditures
Latin America		
Anguilla	800	2
Antigua and Barbuda	1,765	193
Argentina	20,000	3,220
Bahamas	2,400	453
Barbados	2,500	470
Belize	1,650	334
Bermuda	550	25
Bolivia	19,500	2,682
Brazil	30,000	8,590
British Virgin Islands	300	114
Cayman Islands	560	85
Chile	20,000	2,056
Colombia	22,000	2,662
Costa Rica	5,000	1,151
Cuba	20,500	3,068
Dominica	2,300	419
Dominican Republic	12,000	1,860
Ecuador	15,000	2,460
El Salvador	15,250	1,690
Grenada	2,100	235
Guatemala	13,000	1,596
Guyana	8,500	547
Haiti	38,000	4,093
Honduras	16,000	5,615
Jamaica	7,500	2,396
Mexico	20,000	2,298
Montserrat	700	62
Netherlands Antilles	1,500	645
Nicaragua	9,500	1,133
Panama	7,500	2,163
Paraguay	9,750	1,604
Peru	25,000	3,313
Saint Christopher and Nevis†	1,995	236
Saint Lucia	2,100	207
Saint Vincent and the Grenadines	3,250	498
Suriname	3,500	220
Trinidad and Tobago	5,000	2,661
Turks and Caicos Islands	850	62
Uruguay	10,000	1,159
Venezuela	10,000	2,084
Subtotal	387,820	64,361
Total	3,925,870	451,090
INTERCOUNTRY		
Global	114,800	14,876
Interregional	73,500	13,574
Total	188,300	28,450
Regional		
Africa	283,400	...
Arab States	57,800	...
Asia and the Pacific	296,100	...
Europe	16,200	...
Latin America	76,500	...
Total	730,000	74,365
OTHER		
Multi-island country projects	4,516	841
National liberation movements	15,000	1,820
Unallocated and other	138,264	—
GRAND TOTAL	5,001,950	556,566

*Expenditure for assistance to Palestinian people.
†St. Kitts–Nevis acceded to independence on 19 September 1983 as Saint Christopher and Nevis.
NOTES:
Indicative planning figures: Figures are illustrative; actual figures may vary from those in the table, depending on the total financial resources available to UNDP. Amounts are given as of April 1984.

NOTES *(continued)*:
Programme expenditures: Data cover expenditures financed under IPFs, Special Programme Resources, Special Industrial Services, Special Measures Fund for Least Developed Countries, cost-sharing and trust funds established by the Administrator, when applicable.
Three dots (. . .) indicate that data are not available or are not separately reported.
Regional classification as provided by UNDP.
Totals may differ from sum of figures because of rounding.
SOURCES: DP/1984/5/Add.3, DP/1985/5/Add.3.

Indicative planning figures

On 15 June,[6] the Governing Council approved revised illustrative IPFs for 1982-1986 for the following, in view of their designation as LDCs: Equatorial Guinea, by $1 million to $12,750,000; Sierra Leone, by $2.4 million to $34.9 million; Togo, by $1.8 million to $23.5 million. The Council noted a request by Liberia to be accorded treatment as a least developed country, the third country programme for that country, and that the Committee for Development Planning had concluded that Liberia did not qualify for designation as least developed (p. 431). The Council decided that its 1981 decision concerning an interim IPF for Lebanon[7] should continue until a specific recommendation on a final IPF for the 1982-1986 programming cycle could be submitted. The Council also adopted the Administrator's proposal to establish a separate IPF for Anguilla of $800,000, and authorized the increase of the IPF for 1982-1986 for St. Kitts–Nevis from $1.3 million to $1,995,000, conditional on accession to independence.

In March 1983,[8] the Administrator submitted a report on the use of country IPFs for TCDC during 1980-1982.

Special Programme Resources

On 18 June 1983,[9] the Governing Council approved an allocation of $610,000 from the Special Programme Resources for the 1982-1986 programming cycle for information and communications support for the International Drinking Water Supply and Sanitation Decade (1981-1990) from 1 July 1983 to 31 December 1985 (see Chapter IX of this section). It further approved $600,000 from those Resources for 1982-1986 for promotional activities for TCDC during 1984-1985, subject to consideration of a possible increase as recommended by the High-level Committee on the Review of TCDC, following a mid-term review of the 1982-1986 cycle to take place at the 1984 Council session. The Council decided that $600,000 for the Information Referral System (INRES) for TCDC during 1984-1985 be appropriated separately in the 1984-1985 budget. Further provisions of the decision also related to INRES (see below, under TECHNICAL CO-OPERATION AMONG DEVELOPING COUNTRIES).

UNDP's Budgetary and Finance Committee[10] reviewed the financial aspects of the use of Special Programme Resources for promotional activities for TCDC and for support for the Decade, based on a May note by the Administrator[11] and parts

of the report of the High-level Committee. Introducing the topic, the Deputy Administrator recalled that in 1980 the Governing Council had authorized $83.4 million as a planning figure for the Resources for 1982-1986. Since that amount was subject to an across-the-board reduction to 55 per cent of the established level of resources, the planning level of Special Programme Resources was reduced to $45,879,000 for 1982-1986. Referring to UNDP activities relating to the Water Decade, the Deputy Administrator noted that they had been funded from the programme development portion of the Resources. Under guidelines for the use of funds from that portion, no further amounts could be allocated, nor could intercountry IPFs be utilized given their cut-back to 55 per cent of their levels. Therefore, the Administrator had requested an allocation of $610,000 from the contingency portion of the Resources for support of those activities until the end of 1985. Referring to the May/June session of the High-level Committee (see below, under TECHNICAL CO-OPERATION AMONG DEVELOPING COUNTRIES), the Deputy Administrator reported that the Committee proposed that INRES should continue to be financed from the UNDP budget, rather than from Special Programme Resources, to ensure permanent funding. He remarked, however, that INRES was a compendium of information of countries' capacities and its activities should more appropriately be regarded as a project undertaking. He also stated that the High-level Committee recommended that the Governing Council consider allocating $1 million for promotional work for TCDC for 1984-1985, which meant an additional $400,000 to the $600,000 already recommended by the Administrator.

Training programme for pre-investment studies

As requested by the Governing Council in 1981 and 1982,[12] the Administrator reported in March 1983 on the evaluation of special training in investment development for resident and deputy resident representatives.[13] Under the programme, organized in conjunction with the Economic Development Institute of the World Bank, two seminars were scheduled for April and December 1983. For 1984 and 1985, the Administrator felt, two additional seminars each year would be necessary. By 1986 he expected that one special seminar per year would be sufficient for UNDP to provide Governments with staff trained to assist them effectively in their pre-investment require-ments. Financial resources to implement the proposal for 1984-1985 would amount to $320,000, which had been taken into account in the 1984-1985 budget estimates.

The Governing Council, on 24 June 1983,[14] endorsed the proposal for two seminars in 1984 and 1985.

UNDP programme planning

Among measures approved by the Governing Council on 24 June 1983[15] to mobilize increased resources for UNDP were some for strengthening the role of the Council and participating Govern-ments in programme planning and review. They included: briefing meetings and informal consul-tations between Governments and the UNDP secretariat; better feedback from evaluations and reports on programme implementation into the planning process; greater efforts by the secretariat to provide official documentation to delegations well in advance of Council sessions; and detailed information to help them better understand UNDP's work.

In resolution 38/172 on the financial resources situation of UNDP (see below), the General Assem-bly reiterated recipient Governments' full respon-sibility in preparing country programmes, as well as the Administrator's authority to assist Govern-ments in that process.

Programme evaluation

In 1983, UNDP's system of in-depth evaluation with systematic feedback was reviewed by the Governing Council. On 1 October, the Adminis-trator announced the establishment of a small Central Evaluation Office and a Technical Advi-sory Division within UNDP. The Office was charged with four key functions: further develop-ment and monitoring of evaluation policy; pro-gramme analysis with a view to its improvement and that of the special purpose funds; collabora-tion with agencies and Governments on evalua-tion policies; and provision of evaluation results. The Division was charged with a broad range of technical support activities.

UNDP continued to undertake new thematic evaluations in collaboration with its agency part-ners. Four such evaluations were published in 1983: one with UNIDO, on industrial research and service institutes; one with UNESCO, on educa-tional innovation and reform; one with the Inter-national Trade Centre, on trade promotion; and one on human resources development for primary health care, for which follow-up guidelines pre-pared with WHO were simultaneously issued for field office staff. Other evaluations under way in 1983 included one with FAO on agricultural

research, one with ILO on industrial training, and one on women's participation in development in response to a 24 June 1983 Governing Council de-cision.[16]

Evaluation issues were also discussed at various inter-agency meetings. An inter-agency working group on evaluation was established, with the first meeting scheduled for January 1984. The Ad-ministrator's proposals on evaluation were consid-ered by the UNDP Governing Council's Inter-sessional Committee of the Whole in February 1983 (see below, under FINANCIAL SITUATION), and by the Council at its June session.

Report of the Administrator. In April, the Ad-ministrator submitted to the Governing Council a progress report on UNDP's evaluation pro-gramme,[17] analysing UNDP and agency ex-perience to improve identification, design and im-plementation of future projects. An inquiry had been addressed to all UNDP field offices in Janu-ary 1983. Also reviewed were evaluations in na-tional agricultural research institutes and manufactures industries. Annexed to the report was a summary of a study by UNDP and WHO of human resources development for primary health care (see Chapter XV of this section).

JIU report. In May, the Administrator trans-mitted to the Governing Council a report on the evaluation system of UNDP, prepared by Inspec-tor Earl D. Sohm of JIU.[18] Stressing the impor-tance of evaluation as part of UNDP operations, he stated that new management arrangements were needed to strengthen the evaluation system on an integrated basis. He endorsed the proposal to set up a Central Evaluation Office which, he believed, should also co-operate with evaluation officers from other United Nations organizations in an inter-agency working group.

In addition, he called for further action by the Administrator to: ensure that the evaluation sys-tem's role be clearly defined; revise the 1975 guide-lines for UNDP project evaluation; combine tripar-tite reviews, more disciplined project evaluations, an evaluative component in country programming and a tighter programme of thematic evaluations to determine effectiveness and improve operations; strengthen key linkages of evaluation with the new project design process, with Governments through increased support to their evaluation efforts, and with executing agencies through a new inter-agency working group; ensure effective system operation through revised responsibilities, partic-ularly in the Central Evaluation Office, for evalu-ation planning and oversight, guidelines and train-ing, and analysis of information and its feedback into operations; and co-ordinate these elements at the unit and bureau level for overall assessment of UNDP technical co-operation activities and reporting on Programme effectiveness.

Commenting in December[19] on the JIU report, the Secretary-General observed that there was wide support among the United Nations organizations for the recommendations, especially concerning a Central Evaluation Office. He noted that collaborative action with the agencies had begun, policy guidelines were being revised and the thematic evaluation programme was under review. In particular, he supported the call for an effective tripartite evaluation system with emphasis oh evaluation as an essential element within an integrated management system, and expressed his strong support for the need to clarify and activate UNDP's responsibilities for evaluation.

UNDP Council action. In two decisions of 24 June, one on measures to mobilize increased resources for UNDP,[15] the other on UNDP's evaluation programme,[16] the Governing Council took note with satisfaction of the decision to establish a Central Evaluation Office and to develop a strengthened programme, and noted that the Office's cost in 1983 would be covered from savings in the 1982-1983 budget through redeployment of existing resources. The Council also decided that it should meet as a committee of the whole, to consider, among other things, reports on evaluation studies, and requested the Administrator report in 1984 on the progress made and on the results of the evaluation work. By the latter decision, the Council also dealt with the joint United Nations/UNDP/UNIDO evaluation on manufactures (see Chapter VI of this section).

UNDP financing

Financial situation

In his annual report on the UNDP financial situation in 1983,[20] the Administrator stated that total income amounted to $838.2 million ($4 million lower than forecast), while total expenditure was $751 million. Mainly as a result of the $62.7 million surplus of main programme income over expenditure (as against the forecast of an excess of expenditure over income of $31.9 million), the revenue reserve of UNDP, which had been in deficit to the extent of $5.7 million at 31 December 1982, became a surplus of $57.9 million as at 31 December 1983 (as against the forecast of a negative balance of $37.7 million). Income from voluntary contributions amounted to $697.8 million (including $1 million relating to future years' pledges) which was higher than the forecast by $4.4 million, mainly because most Governments paid their pledges before the end of the year. Miscellaneous income, mainly investment income and gains or losses on exchange and revaluation of currencies, amounted to $17.4 million as against the forecast of $10 million.

Total expenditure in 1983 was $119.9 million lower than forecast. The shortfall occurred mostly in expenditures relating to the main field programme

and cost-sharing. Administrative and programme support costs of $109 million were $5.8 million less than estimated, due to reduced costs (because of a stronger United States dollar), lower than anticipated inflation and the continuation of a recruitment freeze.

Due to improved donor payment patterns and reductions in programme expenditure, the amounts available for short-term investments at year's end were higher than anticipated. The increased level of operating funds held by the agencies was partly the result of unexpected savings realized by the cancellation of some 1982 obligations by some agencies, which had not been reflected in earlier expenditure forecasts.

Cash, letters of credit and investments as at 31 December 1983, exclusive of investments made on behalf of fully funded reserves, totalled $304.9 million, compared to $243.6 million as at 31 December 1982. Cash balances as at 31 December 1983 amounted to $19.2 million (excluding holdings in accumulated non-convertible currencies), of which $2.1 million was held in the central account of UNDP and $17.1 million represented operating cash balances in the field offices.

Inter-sessional Committee of the Whole. The Inter-sessional Committee of the Whole, established in June 1982,[21] reported to the Governing Council in April 1983 on its three sessions,[22] all held at United Nations Headquarters. The first session had been held in September 1982.[23] In 1983, the Committee met for its second and third sessions, from 9 to 11 February and from 6 to 8 April.

The short-term financing situation of UNDP, with particular reference to a one-shot supplementary financing effort, was one of the main subjects considered. Two Governments—Canada and Norway—responded to the appeal for supplementary contributions and, in April, Sweden announced an extraordinary contribution, subject to parliamentary approval, while Switzerland stated that it was seriously considering the question. The Committee's February conclusions on short-term financing, as well as its April recommendations for the long-term mobilization of resources, were taken up by the Governing Council in June (see below).

With regard to additional and alternative ways of financing and providing development assistance through UNDP and the funds administered by it, the Committee recommended that the Administrator's March proposals[24]—which included the conversion of contributions in kind to cash, the provision by UNDP of management and other support services for Governments—be considered further by the Council in the light of additional clarification on the methodology for cost calculation.

Concerning measures to promote better understanding of UNDP's activities and resource requirements, the Committee recognized the need for strengthening information work and recommended that the Administrator be encouraged to explore and implement the proposals he had suggested in that regard in December 1982.[25]

UNDP Council action. Based on the suggestions of the Committee of the Whole, the Governing Council, on 24 June 1983, adopted measures to mobilize more resources on an increasingly predictable, continuous and assured basis.[15] Among those to improve longer-term financing were: informal intergovernmental consultations prior to the annual United Nations Pledging Conference for Development Activities, with Governments able to do so making firm pledges for the pledging year and statements on their pledging for the following two years, expressed in special drawing rights if they so chose; and informal consultations among participating Governments to discuss the growth of UNDP, prior to establishing resource target levels. The Council recommended that Governments maintain the real value of their contributions and inform the Administrator of their intentions at the earliest possible time. It requested him to submit proposals based on the preliminary discussion in the Committee of the Whole on a possible three-year rolling system of pledges and programme implementation.

Concerning UNDP's short-term financing, the Council noted with appreciation that several Governments had provided additional resources, and hoped that others would act similarly. It appealed to all net contributors to transfer to UNDP, at the end of their fiscal years, development assistance resources that could not be disbursed through other channels, and strongly urged Governments to draw attention at international assemblies to UNDP's critical financial situation.

The Council, among additional and alternative ways of financing and providing development assistance through UNDP and UNDP-administered funds, authorized the Administrator to provide management and other support services on behalf of Governments. In providing these services, he was requested to take into account the views expressed by Governments in the Committee of the Whole and in the Council, and to ensure that the central multilateral character of the Programme not be eroded and that the activities remained marginal to government contributions, core resources and the implementation of the UNDP programme. The Council also requested the Administrator to follow the general guidelines set forth by him on further clarification of the proposals on management and other support services in charging donor Governments for such services so as to ensure that they did not entail any financial implications. It further requested him to report annually on the development of those activities, and decided to assess after two years the experience gained.

In order to facilitate longer-term financing, the Council also approved measures to strengthen its role and that of participating Governments (see above, under PROGRAMME PLANNING). The Council recognized the need for strengthening timely information about UNDP. It agreed that the Administrator should explore and implement the proposals made in December 1982[25] and report thereon to the Council.

By another decision of 24 June,[26] the Council, having considered the Administrator's report on the UNDP financial situation in 1982,[27] noted with concern the decline in programme delivery, due to stagnating contributions, and erosion of the Programme's financial reserves. It called on Governments, in particular those whose contributions might have been below their capacity, to increase them. The Council reiterated its concern over delays in payments, urged Governments to make them as early as possible and called on those whose currencies had accumulated and on the Administrator to continue reducing the balance of accumulated non-convertible currencies.

GENERAL ASSEMBLY ACTION

On the recommendation of the Second Committee, the General Assembly on 19 December adopted resolution 38/172 without vote.

Situation of the financial resources of the United Nations Development Programme
The General Assembly,

Recalling its resolutions 3201(S-VI) and 3202(S-VI) of 1 May 1974, containing the Declaration and the Programme of Action on the Establishment of a New International Economic Order, 3281(XXIX) of 12 December 1974, containing the Charter of Economic Rights and Duties of States, and 3362(S-VII) of 16 September 1975 on development and international economic co-operation,

Recalling also its resolution 35/56 of 5 December 1980, the annex to which contains the International Development Strategy for the Third United Nations Development Decade,

Stressing the urgent need to strengthen multilateral co-operation for development as a desirable and effective means for promoting mutually beneficial co-operation between developed and developing countries,

Emphasizing the importance of multilateral technical co-operation in the economic and social development of developing countries and the urgent need for a substantial and real increase in the level of financial resources on an increasingly predictable, continuous and assured basis,

Reiterating the unique and central role of the United Nations Development Programme in the field of technical co-operation for development,

Reaffirming the exclusive responsibility of the Government of the recipient country in formulating its national development plan, priorities and objectives, as set out in the consensus contained in the annex to General Assembly resolution 2688(XXV) of 11 December 1970,

Stressing that the indicative planning figures established for the third programming cycle, 1982-1986, of the United Nations Development Programme should be maintained, to the extent possible, and financed through efforts to increase contributions by the international community,

Having considered the difficult financial situation of the United Nations Development Programme, even in the light of the encouraging outcome of the 1983 United Nations Pledging Conference for Development Activities, and its serious impact on the level of technical assistance provided to developing countries through the Programme,

Aware that, together with efforts to obtain additional voluntary contributions, steps are being taken to increase further the quality, efficiency and effectiveness of the United Nations Development Programme,

Having considered the report of the Governing Council of the United Nations Development Programme for the year 1983,

1. *Takes note* of the report of the Governing Council of the United Nations Development Programme for the year 1983 and the decisions contained therein;

2. *Reaffirms* Economic and Social Council resolution 1982/53 of 29 July 1982, in which the Council, *inter alia*, took note of decision 82/5 of 18 June 1982 of the Governing Council of the United Nations Development Programme, by which the Governing Council reaffirmed its decisions 80/30 of 26 June 1980 and 81/16 of 27 June 1981, including those provisions relating to the indicative planning figures, the assumed overall average annual rate of growth of voluntary contributions and the level of resources envisaged for the third programming cycle, 1982-1986, for the purposes of forward planning;

3. *Welcomes* the adoption by consensus of decision 83/5 of 24 June 1983 of the Governing Council of the United Nations Development Programme;

4. *Notes* that, although the outcome of the 1983 United Nations Pledging Conference for Development Activities has shown that there is a trend towards ending the erosion of the resources of the United Nations Development Programme, greater efforts remain necessary to strengthen that trend in order to lead to a process of growth of resources by increasing significantly the level of contributions on a more equitable basis;

5. *Expresses its appreciation* to those Governments, of both developed and developing countries, which, at the 1983 Pledging Conference, announced their voluntary contributions or their intention to contribute to the United Nations Development Programme for 1984 in amounts approaching, equalling or exceeding an average annual increase of 14 per cent in their contributions, and to those Governments that have consistently maintained their contributions at a high level;

6. *Urges* all other Governments, especially those whose overall performance is not commensurate with their capacities, to renew their efforts, consistent with paragraph 1 *(c)* of section I of decision 83/5 of the Governing Council, to provide the United Nations Development Programme with the resources necessary to establish a sound financial basis for the implementation of its planned activities for the third programming cycle, 1982-1986, which, for the purpose of forward planning, would assume an overall average annual rate of growth of resources of at least 14 per cent;

7. *Expresses its appreciation* to the Administrator of the United Nations Development Programme for his tireless efforts to obtain the necessary level of resources envisaged for the third programming cycle, 1982-1986, in order to secure the financial viability of the Programme and to improve further its quality, efficiency and effectiveness, and encourages the Administrator to continue those efforts, taking into account, *inter alia*, the need to restrain administrative expenditures in order to maximize programme delivery, in accordance with paragraph 4 of Governing Council decision 81/16;

8. *Reaffirms* the mandate of the Governing Council of the United Nations Development Programme, reiterates its confidence in the authority of the Governing Council to consider and approve the programmes formulated by recipient Governments and requests the Governing Council, in accordance with the principles and objectives reflected in the consensus set forth in the annex to General Assembly resolution 2688(XXV), to ensure full implementation, to the extent possible, of the planned activities of the Programme for the third programming cycle, 1982-1986, and beyond;

9. *Reiterates* the full responsibility of recipient Governments in the preparation of country programmes, as well as the authority of the Administrator of the United Nations Development Programme to assist, upon request, those Governments in that process in order to submit the programmes, with his recommendations, to the Governing Council for its consideration and approval;

10. *Requests* the Administrator of the United Nations Development Programme to exercise the utmost vigilance over the financial management of the Programme so that most of the funds are channelled towards programme delivery, with the maximum reduction in expenditure of support and administrative costs, and requests the Administrator to report to the Governing Council in that regard.

General Assembly resolution 38/172

19 December 1983   Meeting 102   Adopted without vote

Approved by Second Committee (A/38/703) without vote, 14 December (meeting 56); draft by Vice-Chairman (A/C.2/38/L.117), based on informal consultations on draft by Mexico for Group of 77 (A/C.2/38/L.102) and orally revised; agenda item 79 (b).

Meeting numbers. GA 38th session: 2nd Committee 45-54, 56; plenary 102.

Apart from drafting changes, the adopted text differed from that submitted by the Group of 77 mainly in the following: in paragraph 2 of the Group's text, the Assembly would have endorsed the July 1982 Economic and Social Council resolution on the report of the UNDP Governing Council;[(28)] in paragraph 3, it would have merely taken note of the Council decision on measures to mobilize increased resources;[(15)] and in paragraph 4, it would have noted that greater efforts remained necessary to strengthen the trend towards ending the erosion of resources in order to lead to a process of growth and renewal of resources, commensurate with the needs of developing countries.

Deciding—in resolution 38/201 of 20 December 1983—to liquidate the United Nations Emergency Operation Trust Fund (see Chapter III of this section), the Assembly allocated 70 per cent of the remaining balance to UNDP-administered funds to finance urgently needed projects; decided that 12 per cent would be channelled through UNDP for economic and technical co-operation among developing countries; and requested the Administrator to report to the Governing Council in 1984 on action taken to implement these decisions.

CONTRIBUTIONS TO UNDP, 1983 AND 1984
(as at 31 December 1983; in US dollar equivalent)

| | 1983 PAYMENT | | | | | | 1984 PLEDGE | | |
CONTRIBUTOR	UNDP Account	Fund for LDCs	Government cost-sharing	Government cash counterpart	Assessed programme costs	Total	UNDP Account*	Fund for LDCs	Total
Afghanistan	33,000	—	—	—	—	33,000	33,000	—	33,000
Albania	5,000	—	—	—	—	5,000	5,714	—	5,714
Algeria	834,000	—	2,013,066	316,700	—	3,163,766	834,000	—	834,000
Argentina	2,662,803	—	2,053,729	—	—	4,716,532	—	—	—
Australia	13,913,043	—	410,916	—	—	14,323,959	—	—	—
Austria	6,800,000	—	—	—	—	6,800,000	7,090,000	—	7,090,000
Bahamas	63,900	—	201,090	—	—	264,990	—	—	—
Bahrain	56,000	—	426,901	—	—	482,901	56,000	—	56,000
Bangladesh	190,000	—	—	—	—	190,000	200,000	—	200,000
Barbados	31,396	—	—	1,637	—	33,033	—	—	—
Belgium	24,982,203	—	—	—	—	24,982,203	10,909,091	—	10,909,091
Benin	10,494	4,000	—	—	—	14,494	—	—	—
Bermuda	—	—	50,000	—	—	50,000	—	—	—
Bhutan	7,560	1,200	—	—	—	8,760	5,000	1,440	6,440
Bolivia	50,000	—	1,083,915	(1,206,915)	—	(73,000)	—	—	—
Botswana	25,001	943	160,990	—	—	186,934	22,345	—	22,345
Brazil	900,000	—	4,797,143	130,231	—	5,827,374	2,503,394	—	2,503,394
British Virgin Islands	7,000	—	75,000	—	—	82,000	7,500	—	7,500
Bulgaria	787,564	—	30,000	—	—	817,564	670,050	—	670,050
Burma	1,162,448	—	—	—	—	1,162,448	111,111	—	111,111
Burundi	—	—	—	—	—	—	3,439	4,299	7,738
Byelorussian SSR	184,426	—	—	—	—	184,426	177,632	—	177,632
Canada	49,593,496	—	1,297,043	—	—	50,890,539	47,967,480	—	47,967,480
Cape Verde	9,000	—	—	—	—	9,000	5,000	—	5,000
Cayman Islands	6,320	—	7,415	—	—	13,735	5,000	—	5,000
Central African Republic	13,055	—	—	—	—	13,055	13,055	—	13,055
Chile	820,000	—	591,147	—	—	1,411,147	970,000	—	970,000
China	1,650,000	—	1,978,591	40,000	—	3,668,591	1,750,000	—	1,750,000
Colombia	2,129,270	—	1,509,389	101,404	—	3,740,063	1,332,000	—	1,332,000
Congo	13,000	—	1,115,315	—	—	1,128,315	12,107	—	12,107
Cook Islands	6,470	—	32,595	—	—	39,065	—	—	—
Costa Rica	102,296	—	249,819	334,122	—	686,237	—	—	—
Cuba	724,330	—	—	—	—	724,330	783,368	—	783,368
Cyprus	149,500	—	23,606	—	—	173,106	—	—	—
Czechoslovakia	567,261	—	—	—	—	567,261	—	—	—
Democratic People's Republic of Korea	364,466	—	150,000	—	—	514,466	182,648	—	182,648
Democratic Yemen	8,987	—	387,770	—	—	396,757	10,600	—	10,600
Denmark	36,784,569	—	—	—	—	36,784,569	—	—	—
Djibouti	—	—	18,330	—	—	18,330	2,000	—	2,000
Dominica	54,938	—	—	—	—	54,938	37,037	—	37,037
Dominican Republic	—	—	352,360	—	—	352,360	—	—	—
Ecuador	298,944	—	503,081	39,608	—	841,633	462,465	—	462,465
Egypt	734,880	21,166	405,997	1,346,190	—	2,508,233	691,979	21,166	713,145
El Salvador	170,410	—	45,100	—	—	215,510	—	—	—
Ethiopia	—	—	—	—	—	—	146,341	—	146,341
Fiji	50,000	—	—	—	—	50,000	43,137	—	43,137
Finland	7,925,929	550,459	46,344	—	—	8,522,732	8,620,690	689,655	9,310,345
France	27,838,235	1,470,588	—	—	—	29,308,823	26,979,552	1,818,182	28,797,734
Gabon	—	—	2,175,516	—	—	2,175,516	—	—	—
German Democratic Republic	378,234	—	—	—	—	378,234	370,370	—	370,370
Germany, Federal Republic of	44,817,926	—	192,883	—	—	45,010,809	42,962,963	—	42,962,963
Ghana	228,661	—	—	14,357	—	243,018	—	—	—
Greece	596,352	—	—	—	—	596,352	1,037,400	—	1,037,400
Grenada	18,403	—	—	—	—	18,403	—	—	—
Guatemala	184,388	—	391,290	—	—	575,678	189,000	—	189,000
Guinea	18,566	—	205,919	—	—	224,485	31,937	—	31,937
Guinea-Bissau	2,877	376	—	—	—	3,253	—	—	—
Guyana	37,716	—	210,000	—	—	247,716	—	—	—
Haiti	7,500	—	181,857	—	—	189,357	5,000	—	5,000
Holy See	—	—	—	—	—	—	2,000	—	2,000
Honduras	55,000	—	2,567,605	125,000	—	2,747,605	37,500	—	37,500
Hong Kong	26,367	—	—	—	—	26,367	—	—	—
Hungary	692,074	—	—	—	—	692,074	662,582	—	662,582
Iceland	217,636	—	—	—	—	217,636	171,000	—	171,000
India	7,035,176	—	244,375	(105,508)	—	7,174,043	7,455,269	—	7,455,269
Indonesia	4,502,394	—	5,087,354	30,000	—	9,619,748	1,100,000	—	1,100,000
Iraq	1,438,710	—	436,024	—	—	1,874,734	—	—	—
Ireland	1,065,650	—	—	—	—	1,065,650	—	—	—
Israel	4,874	—	—	—	—	4,874	70,000	—	70,000
Italy	25,771,069	—	7,122,575	—	—	32,893,644	26,380,368	—	26,380,368
Ivory Coast	61,644	—	170,985	—	—	232,629	—	—	—
Jamaica	60,602	—	3,161,931	1,737	—	3,224,270	58,013	—	58,013
Japan	66,802,000	—	200,000	—	—	67,002,000	—	—	—
Jordan	—	—	773,324	—	—	773,324	—	—	—

CONTRIBUTOR	1983 PAYMENT						1984 PLEDGE		
	UNDP Account	Fund for LDCs	Government cost-sharing	Government cash counterpart	Assessed programme costs	Total	UNDP Account*	Fund for LDCs	Total
Kenya	431,972	—	(186,916)	152,672	—	397,728	88,235	—	88,235
Kiribati	12,174	—	—	—	—	12,174	—	—	—
Kuwait	570,000	—	576,269	—	—	1,146,269	—	—	—
Lao People's Democratic Republic	19,600	—	—	—	—	19,600	19,600	—	19,600
Lebanon	360,000	—	11,400	—	—	371,400	360,000	—	360,000
Lesotho	—	—	—	—	—	—	45,000	—	45,000
Libyan Arab Jamahiriya	—	—	4,225,683	—	—	4,225,683	—	—	—
Luxembourg	79,468	—	—	—	—	79,468	67,909	—	67,909
Madagascar	469,691	—	—	—	—	469,691	205,248	—	205,248
Malawi	34,545	1,695	124,565	—	—	160,805	29,688	1,457	31,145
Malaysia	385,000	—	1,000,000	40,385	—	1,425,385	385,000	—	385,000
Maldives	1,800	—	—	—	—	1,800	1,800	—	1,800
Mali	25,316	—	—	—	—	25,316	—	—	—
Malta	68,781	—	—	—	—	68,781	—	—	—
Mauritania	6,306	—	—	—	—	6,306	—	—	—
Mauritius	58,761	—	—	—	—	58,761	—	—	—
Mekong Committee	—	—	—	39,041	—	39,041	—	—	—
Mexico	953,993	—	910,045	—	—	1,864,038	—	—	—
Monaco	3,824	—	—	—	—	3,824	3,394	—	3,394
Mongolia	179,243	—	—	—	—	179,243	173,900	—	173,900
Montserrat	—	—	—	—	—	—	11,111	—	11,111
Morocco	243,511	—	136,800	236,022	—	616,333	212,199	—	212,199
Mozambique	53,974	—	—	14,564	—	68,538	3,974	—	3,974
Nepal	46,000	—	381,674	—	—	427,674	11,500	—	11,500
Netherlands	50,939,372	—	4,173,214	—	—	55,112,586	42,640,264	—	42,640,264
Netherlands Antilles	62,640	—	520,764	—	—	583,404	—	—	—
New Zealand	960,265	—	—	—	—	960,265	960,265	—	960,265
Nicaragua	40,400	—	194,025	—	—	234,425	—	—	—
Nigeria	733,138	—	2,235,061	—	—	2,968,199	—	—	—
Niue	5,000	—	—	—	—	5,000	—	—	—
Norway	50,915,066	2,857,143	619,058	—	—	54,391,267	48,400,000	2,933,333	51,333,333
Oman	75,000	—	1,876,013	(32,292)	—	1,918,721	75,000	—	75,000
Pakistan	1,890,625	—	21,484	1,772,105	—	3,684,214	1,815,454	—	1,815,454
Panama	435,270	—	1,703,003	(50,568)	—	2,087,705	356,000	—	356,000
Papua New Guinea	162,723	—	27,835	2,439	—	192,997	23,529	—	23,529
Paraguay	—	—	255,902	—	—	255,902	—	—	—
Peru	310,000	—	643,118	—	—	953,118	429,647	—	429,647
Philippines	943,805	—	80,500	14,000	—	1,038,305	700,000	—	700,000
Poland	560,034	—	—	—	—	560,034	583,537	—	583,587
Portugal	179,194	—	75,686	—	—	254,880	—	—	—
Qatar	200,000	—	1,048,645	—	—	1,248,645	—	—	—
Republic of Korea	893,000	—	—	28,075	—	921,075	893,000	—	893,000
Romania	558,000	—	—	—	—	558,000	—	—	—
Rwanda	22,000	—	—	—	—	22,000	15,000	—	15,000
Saint Christopher and Nevis	2,953	—	—	—	—	2,953	—	—	—
Saint Lucia	18,462	—	—	—	—	18,462	—	—	—
Saint Vincent and the Grenadines	15,595	—	—	—	—	15,595	16,765	—	16,765
Sao Tome and Principe	500	—	—	—	—	500	—	—	—
Saudi Arabia	2,500,000	—	10,534,287	204,082	—	13,238,369	3,500,000	—	3,500,000
Senegal	90,670	—	—	—	—	90,670	100,000	—	100,000
Seychelles	—	—	—	—	—	—	1,000	—	1,000
Sierra Leone	101,917	—	—	—	—	101,917	40,000	4,000	44,000
Singapore	220,000	—	43	—	—	220,043	—	—	—
Somalia	2,244	—	4,199	77,405	—	6,443	2,589	—	2,589
Spain	1,417,864	—	—	—	71,528	1,489,392	2,640,000	—	2,640,000
Sri Lanka	751,091	—	147,211	280,966	—	975,707	857,736	—	857,736
Sudan	—	—	589,271	—	—	870,237	200,000	—	200,000
Suriname	165,000	—	3,000	—	—	168,000	—	—	—
Swaziland	13,889	—	399,348	—	—	413,237	25,210	—	25,210
Sweden	49,245,726	6,474,187	372,387	—	—	56,092,300	—	—	—
Switzerland	17,199,576	4,674,341	—	—	—	21,873,917	—	2,431,193	2,431,193
Syrian Arab Republic	283,526	—	—	—	—	283,526	—	—	—
Thailand	1,001,030	—	16,000	64,918	—	1,081,948	1,001,030	—	1,001,030
Togo	194,517	—	—	69,384	—	263,901	2,663	—	2,663
Tokelau	2,000	—	—	—	—	2,000	2,500	—	2,500
Tonga	10,000	—	—	—	—	10,000	10,000	—	10,000
Trinidad and Tobago	166,667	—	5,740,000	—	—	5,906,667	166,667	—	166,667
Trust Territory of the Pacific Islands	—	—	140,000	—	—	140,000	—	—	—
Tunisia	393,581	—	31,817	—	—	425,398	267,826	—	267,826
Turkey	1,097,078	—	294,934	106,743	—	1,498,755	1,150,765	—	1,150,765
Turks and Caicos Islands	2,000	—	3,420	—	—	5,420	2,000	—	2,000
Uganda	476	—	24,550	—	—	25,026	9,174	—	9,174
Ukrainian SSR	461,066	—	—	—	—	461,066	444,079	—	444,079
USSR	2,049,180	—	—	—	—	2,049,180	1,958,225	—	1,958,225
United Arab Emirates	—	—	1,323,081	—	—	1,323,081	—	—	—
United Kingdom	28,536,362	—	250,000	—	—	28,786,362	27,737,226	—	27,737,226
United Republic of Cameroon	260,760	—	—	418,742	—	679,502	—	—	—
United Republic of Tanzania	82,169	—	20,000	—	—	102,169	82,169	—	82,169
United States	139,478,851	—	1,361,190	55,999	—	140,896,040	160,000,000	—	160,000,000

	1983 PAYMENT						1984 PLEDGE		
CONTRIBUTOR	UNDP Account	Fund for LDCs	Government cost-sharing	Government cash counterpart	Assessed programme costs	Total	UNDP Account*	Fund for LDCs	Total
Upper Volta	—	—	—	—	—	—	2,421	—	2,421
Uruguay	—	—	846,085	10,695	—	856,780	—	—	—
Vanuatu	1,000	—	5,883	—	—	6,883	—	—	—
Venezuela	—	—	2,049,071	13,408	—	2,062,479	—	—	—
Viet Nam	10,000	—	—	—	—	10,000	12,000	—	12,000
Yemen	—	—	287,884	703,004	—	990,888	13,110	—	13,110
Yugoslavia	1,129,557	—	—	3,623	—	1,133,180	1,147,805	—	1,147,805
Zambia	201,681	—	—	—	—	201,681	190,299	—	190,299
Zimbabwe	93,750	—	—	—	—	93,750	83,333	—	83,333
Arab Gulf Programme for UN Development Organizations	—	—	150,000	—	—	150,000	—	—	—
Caribbean Development Bank	—	—	34,000	—	—	34,000	—	—	—
Central African Development Bank	—	—	2,794	—	—	2,794	—	—	—
Inter-American Development Bank	—	—	200,000	—	—	200,000	—	—	—
IFAD	—	—	150,000	—	—	150,000	—	—	—
IMF	—	—	135,400	—	—	135,400	—	—	—
ITU	—	—	20,033	—	—	20,033	—	—	—
Latin American Association for Integration	—	—	73,500	—	—	73,500	—	—	—
Latin American Centre for Development Administration	—	—	57,403	—	—	57,403	—	—	—
OPEC Special Fund	—	—	4,846,520	—	—	4,846,520	—	—	—
United Nations	—	—	258,500	—	—	258,500	—	—	—
United Nations Centre for Human Settlements	—	—	(6,481)	—	—	(6,481)	—	—	—
UNICEF	—	—	50,000	—	—	50,000	—	—	—
UNESCO	—	—	10,303	—	—	10,303	—	—	—
World Bank	—	—	66,250	—	—	66,250	—	—	—
Miscellaneous	—	—	113,118	—	—	113,118	—	—	—
Total	697,835,242	16,056,098	94,397,119	5,393,975	71,528	813,753,962	493,352,983	7,904,725	501,257,708

*Includes only those pledges made in 1983.
SOURCE: A/39/5/Add.1.

UNDP EXPENDITURES, 1983
(in US dollars)

UNDP account:

Programme expenditure:
Project costs:

Indicative planning figures	466,595,380
From government cost-sharing contributions	68,660,551
Special Measures Fund for the Least Developed Countries	11,462,587
From government cash counterpart contributions	6,291,238
Special Programme Resources	4,052,558
Special Industrial Services	3,005,559
Subtotal project costs	560,067,873

Other programme expenditure:

Reimbursement of programme support costs to participating and executing agencies	73,146,356
UNDP sectoral support	4,161,898
Expert hiatus financing and extended sick leave	1,127,100
Adjustments to 1982 programme expenditure and programme support costs (net)	(693,781)
Subtotal other programme expenditure	77,741,573
UNDP biennial budget expenditure	108,954,556
UNDP extrabudgetary expenditure	4,213,447
Adjustments for institutional support of UNDP/UNEP joint venture	65,250
Total UNDP account	751,042,699

Trust funds:

UN Capital Development Fund*	30,613,910
UN Financing System for Science and Technology for Development†	9,863,649
UN Trust Fund for Sudano-Sahelian Activities	12,356,552
UN Revolving Fund for Natural Resources Exploration	5,741,059
UNDP Energy Account	3,173,848
UN Volunteers	1,707,708
UNDP Trust Fund for the Nationhood Programme of the Fund for Namibia‡	3,336,907

Trust funds: (cont.)

UNDP Trust Fund for projects financed by the Voluntary Fund for the UN Decade for Women§	2,827,076
UN Trust Fund for Operational Programme in Lesotho	480,671
Trust Fund for Technical Assistance to World Bank Project in Jamaica	1,213,395
Trust Fund for the Training in the USSR of Specialists from Developing Countries	1,236,268
Initial Initiative against Avoidable Disablement (IMPACT)	184,885
UNDP Trust Fund for Action on Development Issues	400,764
UN Trust Fund for Provision of Operational Personnel in Swaziland	138,152
UN Special Fund for Land-locked Developing Countries	192,691
Trust Fund for Assistance to Colonial Countries and Peoples	265,763
UN Korean Reconstruction Agency (residual assets)	7,226
UN Special Relief Office in Bangladesh (residual funds)	1,229,001
UNDP Development Study Programme	41,945
Fund of the United Nations for the Development of West Irian	29,625
Total trust funds	75,041,095

Junior Professional Officers' Programme	7,337,118
GRAND TOTAL	833,420,912

*Includes three sub-trust funds established by the Administrator: Trust Fund for Construction and Maintenance of Priority Feeder Roads ($2,021,779), Trust Fund for Rehabilitation of Rural Water Reservoirs ($748,518) and Trust Fund for the Community Water Supply and Sanitation Project in Nepal ($509,989).

†Includes four sub-trust funds established by the Administrator: Special Purpose Contribution Agreements with Federal Republic of Germany ($1,224,490), Trust Fund for the Establishment of the Beijing Institute for Computer Software ($954,672), Trust Fund for Project Formulation and Design ($92,415) and Goodwill Mission ($9,904).

‡Includes a transfer to the United Nations of $1,085,078 in interest earned by the Fund.

§Includes additional contributions of $121,118 to UNDP in support of such projects and a transfer to the United Nations of $630,217 in interest earned by the Fund.

SOURCE: A/39/5/Add.1.

Expenditures

Field programme expenditure in 1983 was $560.1 million, of which $466.6 million represented expenditure against IPFs, $68.7 million against cost-sharing (exclusive of support costs) and $24.8 million against supplementary programmes in the UNDP account. The reduction of $100.4 million (or approximately 15.2 per cent) from 1982 resulted from a 1982 decision[29] to reduce IPF planning targets to 55 per cent of the illustrative IPFs. In order to provide for smooth transition to a lower level of programming, the Administrator had set progressively declining limitations on IPF expenditures from 1983 to 1985. Thus, the limitations on IPF expenditures for 1983 and 1984 had been set at $530 million and $500 million, respectively. The continued strength of the United States dollar in 1983 had a moderating impact on programme expenditure, as had cautious planning by Governments and resident representatives which resulted in major reductions in project budget approvals in 1983, rather than more gradually as planned. In addition, the savings realized in 1983 from the cancellation of some obligations by executing agencies contributed to the lower levels of expenditure. Cost-sharing expenditures of $68.7 million in 1983 were also influenced by those factors; there was a shortfall of $26.3 million from the forecast of $95 million. Despite the shortfall, however, the amount apportioned to cost-sharing in 1983 showed an increase of $6.5 million, or 10.5 per cent over 1982; cost-sharing expenditure increased from 9.4 per cent in 1982 to 12.2 per cent in 1983. Expenditure chargeable to Special Programme Resources amounted to $4 million, of which $1.5 million was expended for disaster-related projects and $2.5 million for other activities, including assistance to the Palestinian people.

Budgets

Programme support and administrative services costs constitute the UNDP administrative budget, adopted biennially.

Budget for 1982-1983

On 24 June 1983,[30] the Governing Council approved revised appropriations for 1982-1983, covering the administrative costs of the main Programme and of five other activities managed by UNDP: UNV, UNCDF, UNRFNRE, UNSO and the UNSO UNDP/UNEP joint venture (see Chapter XVI of this section).

The Council approved revised appropriations of $301,134,100 gross and resolved that income estimates of $62,718,200 be used to offset the gross appropriations, resulting in net appropriations of $238,415,900 (i.e., $14,128,100 less than it had approved in June 1982).[31] Included in the main Programme allocation of $227,748,000 was $1.5

million authorized for use during the biennium for staff separation costs. The Administrator was authorized to carry forward support cost earnings of the Office for Projects Execution (OPE) at the end of each biennium up to a maximum of 10 per cent of the gross appropriations for the Office for the following biennium, and was asked to report on the use of that authority.

The figures were based on the May 1983 recommendations of the Advisory Committee on Administrative and Budgetary Questions (ACABQ).[32] In April,[33] the Administrator had proposed net appropriations of $238,215,900, or $14,328,100 less than the Council had approved in 1982.[31] Core activities accounted for $12.9 million net ($21.7 million gross) of the decrease, while staff separation costs had been decreased by $1 million. The remainder of the decrease, approximately $1.1 million gross ($400,000 net) was mainly attributable to OPE, the Inter-Agency Procurement Services Unit, UNV and the UNSO UNDP/UNEP joint venture; net decreases in estimates for UNCDF and UNRFNRE were nearly offset by a projected increase in estimates for UNSO.

ACABQ noted that $400,000 was shown as an estimate of income from the United Nations Joint Staff Pension Fund; it pointed out that as a result of the December 1982 General Assembly resolution on improving the Fund's actuarial balance,[34] the estimate for 1983 would have to be deleted, with a consequent increase of $200,000 in the net expenditure budget.

With regard to the Administrator's proposal to allow OPE to carry over savings from one biennium for use in the next, ACABQ noted that, currently, any unused agency support cost earnings in respect of OPE activities reverted to UNDP general resources. It noted the potential difficulties cited by the Administrator involving the rigidity of tying agency support cost earnings to a specific biennium. In the opinion of ACABQ, a system of automatic carry-overs to finance future OPE deficits might also create difficulties and a situation could arise where a series of surpluses over several bienniums could result in a potential cumulative carry-over larger than required. It also saw the possibility that even with the utilization of carry-overs, administrative support might eventually have to be reduced in a situation where delivery rates had not risen to anticipated levels. Therefore, ACABQ believed that the Governing Council should review proposed carry-overs in the light of facts existing when the need was foreseen. Such a review, it added, could take place at the Council's June session in the last year of a biennium. Should the Administrator desire to carry over an OPE support cost surplus, he should be required to seek the Council's prior authority and to justify his request in terms of funds available and anticipated rates of delivery. The Administrator's request should be stated in the context of his proposed biennial budget estimates, where it would be considered by ACABQ before being taken up by the Council.

Budget for 1984-1985

Report of the Administrator. In an April 1983 report,[33] the Administrator proposed budget estimates for 1984-1985 amounting to $355,062,200 (gross) and $276,631,100 (net), an increase of $53.9 million (gross) and $38.4 million (net) over the revised budget estimates for 1982-1983 (see above). The gross increase was composed of currency adjustments of minus $1.5 million, of inflation adjustments of $48.6 million, and of adjustments for other costs of $8.9 million as well as of a volume decrease of $2.1 million. The 1984-1985 budget had been calculated at exchange rates applicable on 1 February 1983, and currency changes were to be reflected in revisions of the estimates; the new budget formulation system allowed for detailed identification of their financial impact.

The inflation forecast for 1984-1985 reflected the decrease in inflation rates, which were expected to continue at substantially higher rates in the developing countries than in the industrialized countries. The forecasts for headquarters and Geneva had been co-ordinated with those of the United Nations, while the forecasts for the field were based on information from resident representatives, co-operating commercial banks and international financial institutions. The new budget format allowed for improved capability to monitor actual price movements against forecasts by country and expenditure category, and the related financial impact on the budget estimates.

The adjustment for other costs in respect of all funds reflected: an increase related to within-grade increment of $12.6 million; an additional $1 million for changes in staff entitlements, which became effective in 1983 and were only partially reflected in the 1982-1983 revised estimates; a $1.5 million decrease in the appropriation for transitionary measures; a $3 million decrease for UNDP core activities due to a 1.5 per cent vacancy rate proposed by the Administrator; and a $0.2 million decrease in respect of reimbursement to UNDP by non-core activities for services rendered.

With respect to volume changes for UNDP core activities, the overall decrease was $1,559,500. Of this, $700,000 referred to the UNDP contribution to the Consultative Group on International Agricultural Research and $521,200 referred to the cost of the INRES project. It was proposed that those items, charged to the UNDP biennial budget, be transferred to other sources of funds. To that extent, it was noted, the volume decrease for core activities represented only the transfer of costs to

other financing sources. Should the Council not agree to that transfer, the amount would be reinstated in the biennial UNDP budget. The remaining volume decrease of $338,300 could be described as marginal.

ACABQ report. In its May 1983 report,[32] ACABQ noted that the new budget format was much better than previous ones and trusted that it would be used in future, thus facilitating comparisons between budgets for different bienniums. ACABQ recommended that information on projection and use of UNDP resources be included in future budgets and that information on temporary posts be incorporated in the tables.

ACABQ recommended approval of the 1984-1985 budget estimates as proposed, taking into account a deletion of $400,000 as income from the Joint Staff Pension Fund, resulting from a December 1982 Assembly resolution;[34] the amounts to be appropriated were therefore $355,062,200 gross and $277,031,100 net, with income estimated at $78,031,100.

UNDP Council action. On 24 June 1983,[35] the Governing Council approved appropriations amounting to $356,603,900 gross for the administrative costs of the main Programme and the five other activities managed by UNDP. It resolved that income estimates of $77,072,800 be used to offset the gross appropriations, resulting in net appropriations of $279,531,100. Noting with appreciation that the Administrator had applied a zero growth rate in real terms in the budget, the Council requested him to reduce administrative costs further. It decided to review in 1984 the extrabudgetary administrative expenditures, to determine how they should be presented in the 1986-1987 budget, and requested the Administrator to report on that matter.

Support costs

In May 1983, the Administrator submitted to the Governing Council a note on *ex post facto* reports on agency support costs,[36] stating that, as part of arrangements agreed between UNDP and the agencies in 1982 on format, content and due dates for such reports,[37] he had conducted a trial report exercise with agencies in late 1982 to identify possible problem areas. The results of that exercise had been discussed with the Consultative Committee on Administrative Questions (Financial and Budgetary Questions) at its March 1983 session. The Administrator also stated his intention to report orally to the Council on those discussions, including a proposal for minor changes in the due dates for submitting *ex post facto* reports.

The Council on 24 June[38] noted with satisfaction the results of the trial reporting exercise. It authorized the Administrator to proceed with the proposed change-over to a biennial *ex post facto* report covering all executing agencies, and requested him to submit his first report in 1984 covering all those agencies for 1982-1983. On the same date,[39] the Council also requested him to examine the feasibility and financial implications of waiving agency support costs for projects financed from the United Nations Fund for Namibia (see TRUSTEESHIP AND DECOLONIZATION, Chapter III).

Support cost reimbursement

Agency support costs reimbursed by UNDP in 1983 were $73.1 million, down from $85.1 million in 1982.[31]

In April 1983,[40] the Administrator reported to the Governing Council on support cost reimbursement arrangements for activities financed by UNCDF and UNSO, and for projects executed directly by OPE. In accordance with a 1982 Council decision,[37] he had carried out a comprehensive review of a 1981/82 study in order to determine the correctness of 11 per cent and 5 per cent support cost rates associated with OPE execution of IPF-funded and UNCDF-funded projects, respectively, and to determine a support cost rate associated with OPE execution of UNSO-funded activities based on more precise calculations for UNSO. Based on the further studies and reviews carried out, the Administrator stated, the validity of the 11 per cent and 5 per cent support cost rates determined in 1982 had been confirmed, and an 8 per cent support cost rate for UNSO-funded projects had been determined.

On 24 June 1983,[41] the Governing Council took note of the Administrator's proposals. Based on his recommendations, it decided that the following rates should apply to the reimbursement of support costs for projects executed by OPE: 11 per cent of project expenditure for technical co-operation activities financed from IPF resources, cost-sharing contributions and any trust fund for activities of a similar nature; 5 per cent for UNCDF-financed activities; and 8 per cent for UNSO-financed activities. The Council decided that reimbursement of support costs to executing agencies for activities financed from UNCDF or UNSO would continue for the time being and would be agreed upon between the funding organization and the agency concerned. It requested the Administrator to keep the matter under review with the agencies and report to the Council whenever significant developments occurred.

Also on 24 June, the financing of institutional support costs of the UNSO UNDP/UNEP joint venture (see Chapter XVI of this section) was dealt with by the Council,[42] as was the question of reimbursement for programme support costs to the World Bank.[43]

Sectoral support

In 1983, $1,150,000 was allocated to 11 executing agencies for sectoral support activities—principally regional advisers and short-term missions of experts—designed to complement similar activities by the agencies from their own resources. This was in addition to $3,693,000 for the largest programme of this type, the Senior Industrial Development Field Advisers (SIDFAs), managed by UNIDO (see Chapter VI of this section).

The 1983 amount for sectoral support was only 64 per cent of the original tentative allocation made in 1981;[44] the amount had been reduced in line with the across-the-board reductions in programming levels for all countries to 55 per cent of illustrative IPFs, to which the sectoral support funds were also subject. In accordance with a June 1982 Governing Council decision,[45] sectoral support financing in 1983 was mainly provided to the smaller agencies.

In an April 1983 report,[46] the Administrator stated that the funds for sectoral support in 1984-1985 would be further reduced; for agencies other than UNIDO, they would decline from $3,192,000 in 1982-1983 to $1,824,000 in 1984-1985. Should the resource situation improve, the allocation would be adjusted upwards as required and the possibility of reinstating sectoral support financing to the larger agencies would be considered. The Administrator believed that the arrangements for distributing individual allocations to agencies, approving these on a case-by-case basis, had worked satisfactorily; he suggested that the Council might again wish to delegate to him the responsibility for distributing the sectoral support allocation among the agencies. For UNIDO's SIDFA programme, an allocation of $4,061,000 for 1984-1985 was suggested.

Following the recommendation of the Budgetary and Finance Committee,[10] the Governing Council on 24 June 1983[47] endorsed the Administrator's proposal and approved the suggested allocation for 1984-1985. It decided to review the question of sectoral support in 1984. Other provisions of the Council decision dealt with the SIDFA programme and its financing.

Contributions

At the November 1983 United Nations Pledging Conference for Development Activities, 10 of UNDP's 18 major donors maintained the real value of their contributions in line with the Governing Council's appeals, while 28 countries (24 of them developing) met or exceeded the 14 per cent growth target set for the 1982-1986 programming cycle in terms of their national currencies. Both the largest developed country donor (United States) and the largest developing country donor

(India) substanitally increased their support level (by 14.8 and 6 per cent, respectively). In response to the Council's appeal for supplementary contributions, Canada, Italy, Norway and Sweden together provided almost $15 million in additional resources for 1983, while Canada, Denmark and the Netherlands pledged a further $14 million in supplementary contributions for 1984.

As a result of these and other developments, voluntary contributions pledged for 1984 rose by almost $20 million, compared with 1983, to a total of $695.2 million, the first substantial increase recorded since the 1979 Pledging Conference. Another $14.1 million was pledged for 1984 to the Special Measures Fund for LDCs.

Total contributions for 1983 amounted to $697.8 million, $22 million more than originally pledged and the highest total ever received. In addition, 1983 marked the first year since 1979 in which total income exceeded total expenditures. Against expenditures of $751 million, total main programme income in 1983 was $838.2 million, including $94.4 million in cost-sharing contributions, $16.1 million in contributions to the Special Measures Fund for LDCs, other contributions of $5.6 million, and miscellaneous income (mostly interest earned) of $24.3 million. Of the cost-sharing contributions, $71.1 million was provided for projects and programmes by recipient Governments and $23.3 million by third parties—18 donor countries and development assistance organizations—of which Italy, the Netherlands and the Organization of Petroleum Exporting Countries supplied almost 70 per cent. Since 1973, such cost-sharing contributions had advanced, on average, by more than 15 per cent a year, and in 1983 they rose by more than 25 per cent compared with 1982.

Income under newly established sub-trust funds rose even more dramatically, from $1.7 million in 1982 to $50.2 million in 1983. During the year, five new sub-trust funds were established under the Administrator's authority, the largest out of contributions from the Netherlands and the United Nations Emergency Operation Trust Fund. In addition, 10 training projects were under implementation in 1983 through the USSR/UNDP Trust Fund, while four new sub-trust funds were also established on behalf of UNCDF and five on behalf of UNFSSTD.

UNDP also administered a number of special purpose funds and programmes, which themselves garnered substantial additional voluntary support totalling $45.5 million, in addition to which another $17.7 million was contributed under cost-sharing and sub-trust-fund arrangements.

Total contributions to UNDP's main programme, the special purpose funds under its administration, sub-trust funds and cost-sharing arrangements amounted to more than $925 million

for 1983, with third-party co-financing and parallel financing generating an additional $186 million, an amount substantially greater than that generated by third-party cost-sharing. Co-financing or parallel financing differed from third-party cost-sharing only in a technical or accounting sense: the funds were provided directly to the project by the participating Government or agency without, as in cost-sharing arrangements, UNDP's own accounting procedures being drawn into play.

In resolution 38/172 (see above), the General Assembly noted that, although the 1983 Pledging Conference had shown a trend towards ending the erosion of UNDP resources, greater efforts were necessary in order to lead to a growth of resources by increasing significantly the level of contributions on a more equitable basis. The Assembly expressed its appreciation to those countries which had announced their contributions or intention to contribute to UNDP in amounts approaching, equalling or exceeding an average annual increase of 14 per cent, and to those that had consistently maintained their contributions at a high level. It urged all others, especially those whose overall performance was not commensurate with their capacities, to renew their efforts to provide UNDP with the resources necessary to establish a sound financial basis for implementing its activities for the 1982-1986 programming cycle.

In resolution 38/145, the Assembly endorsed a Governing Council decision of 24 June calling for additional special contributions to UNDP amounting to at least $8 million during 1982-1986, so as to ensure implementation of the UNDP assistance programme for the Palestinian people (see POLITICAL AND SECURITY QUESTIONS, Chapter IX).

Trust funds

In 1983, the Administrator established 14 trust funds, 5 each on behalf of UNDP and UNFSSTD, and 4 on behalf of UNCDF. In addition, further contributions were received in 1983 to a USSR/UNDP Trust Fund established in 1982, to continue the funding of the training of specialists from developing countries in the USSR. Information on the trust funds established in 1983 was contained in a March 1984 report.[48] Agreements were reached in 1983 on 18 projects financed by contributions on procurement in the donor country, 4 of them for UNCDF, 6 for UNSO and 8 for UNFSSTD.

In April 1983,[49] the Administrator reported to the Governing Council on trust funds he had established in 1982, three on behalf of UNDP and one each for UNCDF and UNFSSTD.

In a June 1983 report to the Council,[50] he noted that the period of one year since the authorization by the Council in 1982[51] had not been sufficient to finalize most negotiations for the establishment of trust funds conditioned on procurement from a donor country and more time was required for assessing the full potential of that new instrument. He added that, from the number and size of the negotiations, it appeared that those trust funds could result in significant, additional aid to developing countries channelled through the United Nations system.

The Governing Council, on 24 June,[52] requested the Administrator to provide each year comprehensive and detailed information on trust funds established by him, as well as on the individual projects financed from those trust funds.

On the same date,[53] the Council authorized him to continue to accept until 30 April 1984 trust funds conditioned on procurement from donor countries; in doing so, he should bear in mind the comments of the Budgetary and Finance Committee at its May/June session. The Council requested him to submit a comprehensive report in 1984 on the results of the experimental period and to present recommendations. The report should include: statistical information on the relation between contributions to general resources and those conditioned on procurement; an analysis of the choices by donors of projects and categories of assistance; an analysis of the effect of those trust funds on the geographical distribution of resources channelled through UNDP and the three organizational entities concerned; an analysis of the effect on sectoral activities of each of those entities; and an estimate of the cost of goods and services purchased from such trust funds in relation to the cost that would have prevailed had the normal UNDP procurement practices been applied.

Accounts and auditing

Reporting procedures

The Governing Council, on 24 June 1983,[43] took note of the Administrator's note transmitting the audit reports of the participating and executing agencies for 1981,[54] as well as of his comments on the substantive observations made by the external auditors and a description of the action taken by the Administrator in response to the Governing Council's June 1982 decision on audit reports.[55] The Council also welcomed the agreement of the panel of external auditors to use a similar reporting style in the various audit reports and to increase the emphasis in its reports on the audit of the effectiveness of financial management. It requested the Administrator to convey to the auditors and to the executing agencies concerned the Council's view that those improvements should be introduced as soon as possible.

The Council noted with appreciation the proposals by the external auditors of the World Bank regarding the estimated additional audit costs involved in expanding the scope of their audit work and their audit report, and agreed with their proposal to prepare, at a total additional cost of approximately $18,500 a long-form audit report which would include their significant findings resulting from a review of: procurement procedures; project performance compared with budgeted performance; internal audit work on UNDP-financed projects; and project progress reports. The Administrator was authorized to reimburse the World Bank for those additional costs and to charge them against the expenditure for reimbursement of programme support costs.

Accounts for 1982

The financial statements of UNDP for the year ended 31 December 1982, together with the report of the Board of Auditors, were submitted to the General Assembly in August 1983.[56] The financial statements also covered the trust funds for which the Administrator had been assigned responsibility.

In its report, the Board observed that due to a sharp decline in voluntary contributions, delays in payment of government contributions, the cumulative and continuing excess of expenditure over income and heavy losses from currency exchange transactions, the financial situation of UNDP as at 31 December 1982 was critical and required action to find new sources of income, reduce expenditures, monitor carefully programme support and administrative costs and improve the role and involvement of executing agencies and staff in implementing UNDP-assisted projects.

The Board noted that its review of programme support and administrative costs had revealed that some consultants and experts had been engaged to carry out administrative work normally performed by UNDP staff members. The audit of projects had revealed that the assistance provided by recipient Governments to UNDP in project implementation had not always been adequate and timely and that there had also been a lack of involvement by participating and executing agencies in project implementation. In the Board's opinion, UNDP field offices needed more substantive and technical backstopping from headquarters as well as active support at critical stages in programme and project cycles. With regard to the Internal Audit Service of UNDP, the Board noted that its terms of reference were not comprehensive and did not cover some areas. Further comments related to, among other things, international agricultural research centres, regional projects, certain field offices, travel and special service agreements.

In response to the Board's observations and recommendations, the Administrator noted that, while the financial statements showed a deficit in the revenue reserve at the end of 1982, a deficit which was likely to increase somewhat in 1983, the programme planning for 1984, 1985 and 1986 was based on reduced programme levels. He expressed his conviction that the measures taken to restrict the 1982-1986 cycle programme to 55 per cent of IPFs, together with the system of annualized forward planning of availability and use of resources, were adequate to control the financial situation; the main thrust of his efforts were accordingly directed towards mobilizing additional contributions. He stated that he had established a Resource Mobilization Advisory Committee and a Resource Mobilization Unit; in addition, country co-ordinators would assist in resource mobilization and collect specific information which might have resource implications. With regard to cuts in expenditure, the Administrator pointed out that careful management of available and projected resources had limited the actual cuts in projects and personnel; thus, no premature termination of expert contracts had been caused by programme reductions, although the total number of recruitments had been reduced due to the decline in new project approvals.

In a September 1983 report,[57] ACABQ expressed agreement with several of the Board's comments and recommendations. It found pertinent the Board's recommendations on further steps to be taken in order to find new sources of income and reduce expenditures, to monitor carefully programme support and administration services costs as well as programme expenditures and to improve involvement by executing agencies as well as by UNDP staff with a view to achieving maximum efficiency and effectiveness in the use of funds. With regard to the nature of the heavy losses from currency exchange transactions stated by the Board, ACABQ said it had been informed that $40.6 million appeared in the financial statements as net losses on exchange and revaluation of currencies—an amount related not only to exchange losses on transactions, but also to losses suffered on the revaluation of UNDP holdings of national currencies. Of the total losses of $40.6 million, $38.9 million resulted from revaluation of holdings, attributable to the increasing strength of the United States dollar in relation to other currencies in the course of 1982, while the remaining $1.7 million related to losses on individual currency exchange transactions.

On the subject of project implementation and evaluation, including monitoring the role of agencies in implementing programmes, the Administrator had referred to proposals made to the UNDP Inter-sessional Committee of the Whole designed to improve current practices in that regard. ACABQ had been informed of some of the specific measures taken by the regional bureaux to achieve better delivery and greater effectiveness, as well as of measures being taken to improve agency backstopping, which would be the subject of interagency discussion in 1984. Concerning the Board's finding that consultants and experts had carried out administrative work normally performed by UNDP staff, ACABQ noted that the Administrator had responded that it had been necessary, in exceptional cases, to recruit individuals temporarily on special service agreements to perform normal staff duties, because the UNDP Appointment and Promotion Board had not been convened to make recommendations on recruitment since July 1981, owing to the continuing recruitment freeze.

Referring to the Board's discussion of global agricultural projects, most of which had been entrusted to international agricultural research centres of the Consultative Group on International Agricultural Research (CGIAR) for execution, ACABQ noted UNDP's description of its sponsorship of CGIAR and the monitoring procedures applied by CGIAR with the involvement of sponsors, including UNDP. However, ACABQ considered that, in view of the high priority given by UNDP to global and interregional projects, UNDP should keep a close watch on its relationships with implementing centres, to ensure that programme implementation, and in particular the need for programme changes, were kept under constant scrutiny.

Referring to the Board's discussion of administrative support to UNDP projects in the form of programme support projects (PSPs) and the recommendation that administrative expenditures not envisaged in the project budget be regularized by charging them to the administrative budget, ACABQ said it had been informed that the purpose of PSPs was to provide administrative and/or logistical support or technical facilities in support of a group of UNDP-financed country projects, but that it was uneconomical to provide on an individual basis. Such projects were established by means of a project document, including a detailed project budget, and they required the approval of the Government concerned.

With regard to the Internal Audit Service, ACABQ considered that it had a significant role to play in the management of UNDP and welcomed its strengthening. ACABQ had been informed that in 1983 internal audit coverage of field activities was expected to represent about 65 per cent of total internal audit work.

As to cases of fraud referred to by the Board, ACABQ said that, according to additional information, 75 cases of fraud were discovered in 1982, involving a total of approximately $190,000. Of these cases, 72 related to a single field office. ACABQ had been informed that, as at 31 July 1983, approximately $65,000 was recovered, while

$28,000 was considered to be uncollectable and the remainder was subject to further collection procedures.

By resolution 38/30 of 25 November 1983 on the 1982 accounts of various United Nations programmes and funds (see ADMINISTRATIVE AND BUDGETARY QUESTIONS, Chapter I), the General Assembly accepted the UNDP accounts for the year ended 31 December 1982, concurred with the ACABQ comments and requested the UNDP Administrator to take such remedial action as might be required by the Board.

Financial regulations

The Governing Council, on 24 June 1983,[58] decided that the revised financial regulations approved in 1981[59] were fully in effect. Existing regulations should apply in the absence of a consensus on certain proposed regulations dealing with the currencies of contributions, until a decision was reached in 1984. The Council also decided that the Budgetary and Finance Committee would consider, within the framework of the provisional agenda for the Council's 1984 session, the parts of the regulations and other questions on which consensus had not been achieved in 1983. The text of the regulations on which there had been no consensus was transmitted in the annex to a January 1983 note of the Administrator.[60]

UNDP administration and staff

Field offices

During 1983, UNDP stepped up efforts to broaden support for field office activities and to improve field office capabilities. First steps were taken to computerize field office administration, and updated financial management guidelines and instructions were issued. In his annual report for 1983,[1] the Administrator stated that implementation of UNDP's reassignment policy, in particular the rotation of international professional staff, also helped strengthen office capabilities.

In May, the Administrator transmitted to the Governing Council a report by JIU on UNDP field offices,[61] prepared by Julio C. Rodríguez-Arias and Earl D. Sohm. The study examined the policy framework governing development co-operation by the United Nations system, and reviewed the main issues of inter-agency country-level co-ordination, including the responsibilities of the offices, their staffing and organization.

The report discussed the functions of the field offices, which included support to host Governments in preparing, implementing, co-ordinating, evaluating and day-to-day management of UNDP-financed projects, as well as co-ordination of the sectoral operations of United Nations organiza-

tions and agencies, and provision to them of central administrative and logistical support. The report did not cover the responsibilities of the resident co-ordinators since they had not been operational long enough; it therefore focused on resident representatives as heads of the field offices while recognizing that they were normally designated as co-ordinators.

The Inspectors found that, although the actual supportive role played by the field offices depended very much on individual country situations and the extent to which Governments involved them in inputs from the United Nations system, that role had, in general, expanded over the past decade well beyond the basic functions of the field offices, particularly in LDCs. The range of activities could in their opinion no longer be viewed in relation to the level of UNDP programme resources, but should be seen in the context of the support provided by these offices to a wide spectrum of activities, notably those funded from special purpose funds, agency regular budgets, some multilateral financial institutions, rapidly increasing cost-sharing arrangements and multi-bilateral funds, all of which had greatly increased demands on the offices.

In view of UNDP's critical resource situation, the Inspectors stated, field office staff had been reduced by 8 per cent and recruitment had been frozen at a time when those offices were barely able to cope with their extensive work-load. In 1982, each office had virtually the same number of budgeted Professional posts (3.6) as 10 years previously, notwithstanding the considerable evolution of activities. Because staff were hard pressed by routine administration, they had been unable to pay adequate attention to programme management, analytical and evaluation functions, and new technical co-operation techniques and concepts were not sufficiently reflected in projects and programmes.

The Inspectors concluded that the offices should be strengthened to enable them to assist host Governments more effectively, and proposed a number of policy options, including increased government contributions to local field costs; redeployment of some posts from UNDP headquarters to the field, especially to LDCs; secondment of government officials; financing some functions from a "core" budget supported by the United Nations regular budget; and the gradual merging of the system's country representation to form United Nations field offices, financed through proportional contributions of United Nations organizations and agencies. Other recommended measures included more systematic field staff assignment, career development and recruitment policies, as well as increased use of local professional officers and system-wide staff secondments and exchanges.

In a decision of 24 June 1983 on the Administrator's annual report,[62] the Governing Council requested him to take into account those JIU recommendations designed to enhance the quality of UNDP-supported programmes and projects and to increase the Programme's overall efficiency and effectiveness.

Commenting in December on the JIU report,[63] the Secretary-General underlined the need, when considering organizations other than UNDP contributing to field offices, to preserve existing authority on staffing, responsibilities and functions and to maintain clearly the lines of command and objectivity. He pointed out that a policy recommendation regarding general contributions to the cost of UNDP field offices could not be considered without full examination of all United Nations field offices. Accordingly, he proposed that a further review of the JIU proposals should await such an examination.

Project professional personnel

In his annual report for 1983,[1] the Administrator stated that the role of local professional staff or national officers had been further strengthened during the year. Through additional salary surveys, the remuneration of those officers was regularized. By the end of 1983, 112 national officers were serving in 47 countries in all the regions serviced by UNDP.

In March, the Administrator submitted, in accordance with a June 1982 Governing Council decision,[64] a report on recruitment and reduction of cost of project professional personnel.[65] The report dealt with improving recruitment of national officers and reducing the cost of internationally recruited officers. It concluded that, while it did not appear possible to reduce the unit cost of internationally recruited project personnel, viable alternatives, such as nationally recruited professional project personnel, should be used to reduce the cost of personnel inputs to UNDP-supported projects. The report called for more careful project design and appraisal to take advantage of a number of alternatives to internationally recruited personnel which were available at lesser cost for similar levels of work, such as United Nations Volunteers.

In an addendum to the report, information was summarized from eight agencies—IAEA, ILO, FAO, UNESCO, WHO, ICAO, ITU and WMO—and from the United Nations Department of Technical Co-operation for Development on measures taken to improve their recruitment policies.

The Governing Council, on 24 June,[66] invited executing agencies to continue improving policies and procedures for recruiting project professional personnel, and requested them to pursue cost-effective recruitment, including the increased use of nationally recruited personnel. It requested the Administrator to arrange for more active UNDP involvement in the clearance process to fill vacant UNDP-supported project posts; to implement the recommendations for reducing the cost of project personnel; and to report in 1985 on progress achieved in reducing those costs.

Guidelines for purchasing equipment and supplies

In a March 1983 note on guidelines for procuring equipment, supplies and services,[67] the Administrator stated that he had continued trying to find a workable solution to the question and that numerous consultations had been held within UNDP and with the executing agencies. A number of steps were being taken which might lead to a solution and he expected to report orally to the Council in June on the progress made.

The Governing Council, on 24 June,[68] expressed appreciation for the Administrator's efforts to evolve practical guidelines, and urged him to pursue vigorously with the executing agencies the study on their procurement practices to be carried out by the Inter-Agency Procurement Working Group with the assistance of the Inter-Agency Procurement Services Unit. The Council requested him to submit a progress report in 1984.

REFERENCES

[1]DP/1984/5 & Add.1-6. [2]E/1983/20. [3]*Ibid.* (dec. 83/2 A). [4]YUN 1982, p. 655. [5]E/1983/20 (dec. 83/14). [6]*Ibid.* (dec. 83/13). [7]YUN 1981, p. 529. [8]TCDC/3/8. [9]E/1983/20 (dec. 83/15). [10]DP/1983/73 & Corr.1. [11]DP/1983/29 & Corr.1. [12]YUN 1982, p. 642. [13]DP/1983/9. [14]E/1983/20 (dec. 83/8). [15]*Ibid.* (dec. 83/5). [16]*Ibid.* (dec. 83/12). [17]DP/1983/16. [18]DP/1983/68. [19]DP/1984/9. [20]DP/1984/53. [21]YUN 1982, p. 659. [22]DP/1983/5. [23]YUN 1982, p. 660. [24]DP/1983/ICW/13. [25]DP/1983/ICW/7. [26]E/1983/20 (dec. 83/29). [27]DP/1983/43. [28]YUN 1982, p. 646, ESC res. 1982/53, 29 July 1982. [29]*Ibid.*, p. 643. [30]E/1983/20 (dec. 83/30). [31]YUN 1982, p. 648. [32]DP/1983/45. [33]DP/1983/44 & Corr.1,2. [34]YUN 1982, p. 1478, GA res. 37/131, 17 Dec. 1982. [35]E/1983/20 (dec. 83/31). [36]DP/1983/53. [37]YUN 1982, p. 649. [38]E/1983/20 (dec. 83/10 B). [39]*Ibid.* (dec. 83/37). [40]DP/1983/54. [41]E/1983/20 (dec. 83/36). [42]*Ibid.* (dec. 83/25). [43]*Ibid.* (dec. 83/38). [44]YUN 1981, p. 450. [45]YUN 1982, p. 650. [46]DP/1983/56. [47]E/1983/20 (dec. 83/39). [48]DP/1984/69 & Corr.1. [49]DP/1983/49. [50]DP/1983/50. [51]YUN 1982, p. 655. [52]E/1983/20 (dec. 83/33). [53]*Ibid.* (dec. 83/32). [54]DP/1983/55 & Add.1. [55]YUN 1982, p. 656. [56]A/38/5/Add.1. [57]A/38/433. [58]E/1983/20 (dec. 83/35). [59]YUN 1981, p. 451. [60]DP/1983/48. [61]DP/1983/67. [62]E/1983/20 (dec. 83/6). [63]DP/1984/7. [64]YUN 1982, p. 657. [65]DP/1983/8 & Add.1 & Add.1/Corr.1. [66]E/1983/20 (dec. 83/7). [67]DP/1983/47. [68]E/1983/20 (dec. 83/34).

Other technical co-operation

UN programmes

The United Nations continued its work in 1983 to further the economic and social progress of the developing countries by supplying experts and advisory services, awarding fellowships and organizing workshops and study tours. These activities covered a broad range of subjects, including development planning and administration, rural and social development, international trade, industrial development, transnational corporations, mineral resources, energy, ocean economics, environment, science and technology, population, women, human rights and statistics.

In 1983, the United Nations delivered a technical co-operation programme of $255 million compared to $303 million in 1982, a 16 per cent decrease in project expenditures. Responsibility for the management and substantive support for the system's technical co-operation activities rested with the United Nations Department of Technical Co-operation for Development (DTCD), a separate organizational entity of the Secretariat. DTCD executed in 1983 a programme amounting to $112 million comprising more than 1,400 projects, compared with $127 million in 1982. This reduction resulted primarily from a decline in resources of its main funding partners—UNDP and UNFPA.

Technical co-operation activities were also carried out under the United Nations regular programme of technical co-operation. Funds from that programme financed activities by a number of United Nations entities, including DTCD, the Centre for Human Rights, the United Nations Centre for Human Settlements (Habitat), the United Nations Conference on Trade and Development (UNCTAD), the regional commissions and the United Nations Industrial Development Organization.

DTCD's catalytic role helped generate new development activities, emphasized TCDC approaches and gave priority to requests for assistance from LDCs. Activities financed under the regular programme were also implemented in close reference with other technical co-operation activities to make maximum use of complementary and innovative efforts.

DTCD's interregional advisory services were made available to nearly all developing countries. Examples of advisory missions included those to Rwanda for assistance in preparing a long-term development plan; to Peru for advice to the National Planning Institute on investment proposals; to Egypt in relation to energy planning; to Guatemala for evaluating the mineral sector's development; to Aruba to help set up administrative government machinery prior to its independence; to China on taxation of offshore oil exploration; to Jamaica on social aspects of reconstruction planning; and to Nicaragua, the Niger and Pakistan in the development of economic statistics.

Training workshops and seminars were organized to respond to specific development needs of developing countries, particularly those of LDCs, in various sectors. The Department followed the TCDC ap-proach wherever possible, using case studies from developing countries as a basis for the exchange of information among those countries on their specific experience and assisting them in establishing guidelines and methodologies particularly responsive to their own needs. Regarding public administration, for example, an interregional workshop on public enterprises in developing countries reviewed different experiences and agreed on criteria, methodology and institutional arrangements for performance evaluation.

UNITED NATIONS TECHNICAL CO-OPERATION PROJECT EXPENDITURES IN 1983, BY ORGANIZATIONAL ENTITY
(in thousands of US dollars)

	Regular programme	UNDP	UNFPA	Trust funds	Total
DTCD	6,725	79,251	11,405	14,880	112,261
Other United Nations	218*	—	—	8,519†	8,737
ECA	1,523	4,245	3,002	3,472	12,242
ECE	—	679	365	114	1,158
ECLA	1,174	1,680	1,790	3,933	8,577
ECWA	623	499	216	688	2,026
ESCAP	779	6,781	1,065	6,784	15,409
UNCHS	378	12,337	—	2,752‡	15,467
UNCTAD	352	13,030	—	1,924	15,306
UNIDO	3,991	50,194	—	9,229	63,414
Total	15,763	168,696	17,843	52,295	254,597

*Comprises $131,379 for Human Rights Division and $86,903 for Centre for Social Development and Humanitarian Affairs portions of the United Nations regular budget administered in Geneva and Vienna, respectively.

†Comprises technical co-operation expenditure incurred against the following trust funds: UN Fund for Drug Abuse Control, $5,421,667; UN Nationhood Programme for Namibia, $1,487,175; Voluntary Fund for the UN Decade for Women, $970,009; Trust Fund for the UN Centre on Transnational Corporations Technical Co-operation Programme, $611,127; and Trust Fund to Provide Advisory Services to Developing Countries in Matters of Policy, Laws, Regulations and Contracts relating to Transnational Corporations, $29,386.

‡Excludes UN Habitat and Human Settlements Foundation activities.

§Excludes UN Industrial Development Fund activities.

SOURCE: DP/1984/42/Add.3.

A project for training statisticians and programmers from developing countries continued to organize on-the-job training in the statistical offices of other developing countries. Started in late 1982, the project had placed about 20 trainees by the end of 1983. A variety of interregional seminars were financed under the regular programme in 1983, such as one on regulatory administration for national development, organized in collaboration with the Economic and Social Commission for Asia and the Pacific, to identify optimal modalities for the public regulation of selected sectors. Another interregional seminar, on integrated rural development, was organized in China.

GENERAL ASSEMBLY ACTION

Following consideration of the Secretary-General's report[1] on United Nations technical co-operation activities in 1982,[2] the General Assembly adopted decision 38/445 without vote, as recommended by the Second Committee.

Report of the Secretary-General on United Nations technical co-operation activities

At its 102nd plenary meeting, on 19 December 1983, the General Assembly, on the recommendation of the Second Committee, took note of the report of the Secretary-General on United Nations technical co-operation activities.

General Assembly decision 38/445

Adopted without vote

Approved by Second Committee (A/38/703) without vote, 14 December (meeting 56); oral proposal by Chairman; agenda item 79 *(i)*.

Meeting numbers. GA 38th session: 2nd Committee 56; plenary 102.

DTCD activities

At the end of 1983, DTCD's programme of technical co-operation amounted to $145 million in approved budgets, with expenditures totalling $112 million. Of these expenditures, $79 million was for UNDP-financed projects, $11 million for UNFPA, $7 million under the United Nations regular programme of technical co-operation and $15 million under trust funds. Budgets fell by 4 per cent as compared with 1982, a decline particularly noticeable in UNFPA funding, where the decrease of 34 per cent was due to a change in resources allocation. Expenditures also fell in 1983 by 11 per cent overall, in the case of UNFPA by 41 per cent. The share of UNDP financing in 1983 budgets, however, rose from 69 per cent in 1982 to 73 per cent in 1983.

Budgets continued to grow in Asia, but declined in all other regions. The distribution of expenditure was little changed from that of 1982, with Africa remaining the most important programme, accounting for $43 million, or 39 per cent of the total, in comparison with $51 million or 40 per cent in 1982, and Asia representing $29 million, or 26 per cent, compared with $30 million or 25 per cent in 1982.

With 46 per cent of DTCD's total budgets, natural resources and energy continued to account for the largest share of the programme. Expenditures in that sector also increased, from 37 per cent ($47 million) in 1982 to 44 per cent ($49 million) in 1983. Development planning was the second most important DTCD activity; although its total budgets had declined, in monetary terms it represented 20 per cent of the total. Expenditures in that sector accounted for 22 per cent, compared with 21 per cent in 1982, but fell by $1.6 million in monetary terms.

The reduction in project expenditures was also reflected in a reduction in DTCD's programme support cost earnings, which amounted to $13.5 million—$10.5 million from UNDP, $1.6 million from UNFPA, $1.2 million from trust funds, and $200,000 from other income. DTCD administrative costs against programme support cost earnings were $16.8 million in 1983, including costs incurred by units outside DTCD in support of its technical co-operation activities. These comprised $15.9 million for staff costs and $900,000 for non-staff costs.

DTCD's financial plan for 1983 envisaged a deficit of $1.5 million at the end of the year, to be offset in 1984 by continued overhead earnings and reduced overhead expenditures, the latter made possible by staff reductions already effected in 1983. Owing to the shortfall in delivery, however, overhead earnings fell by $2.9 million below the expected level of resources. This shortfall, when added to the envisaged $1.5 million deficit, would have increased the total deficit to over $4 million in 1983 had it not been for reductions in expenditures from an estimated $18.6 million to $16.8 million. The savings of approximately $1.8 million were due to various cost-cutting measures as well as to low inflation. By the end of the year, the deficit was $2.6 million, to be offset in 1984-1985.

To counteract the continued decrease in support cost earnings and an increase in salaries and common staff costs, DTCD took measures along the lines of those initiated in 1982; these resulted in a further reduction of nearly one third of the Department's previous manning table.

In 1983, the main substantive areas of DTCD were: development issues and policies, natural resources and energy, development administration and finance, statistics, population, ocean economics and technology, and social development and humanitarian affairs.

DTCD implemented 240 field projects in economic and social development, including integrated rural development, in 75 countries. The 1983 budgets of these projects totalled $35 million. In natural resources and energy, infrastructure, cartography and remote sensing, DTCD executed 490 projects. In the minerals field, it supported 189 projects; some 75 missions were undertaken to more than 60 countries. In the energy sector, including conventional energy, planning, electric power, and new and renewable sources of energy, 117 projects were executed.

The number of projects in the water resources sector was 153; in cartography, 21 technical assistance projects were executed. In the areas of administrative reform, personnel administration and training, and financial and public enterprise management, over 100 projects were executed in 66 developing countries.

The number of fellowship awards in training and upgrading the skills of officials in public services of developing countries was 128. DTCD carried out 43 advisory missions in as many developing countries, dealing with the analysis of problems in administration organization, personnel administration and training, information management and use of computers, tax policy and administration, accounting, budgeting and auditing.

In development planning and programming, 158 projects were under execution; they covered a wide variety of statistical subjects, including general statistical development, national accounts, trade and industrial statistics, demographic and social statistics, censuses, surveys and statistical data processing. Sixteen countries from all regions benefited from on-the-job statistical training. The number of UNFPA-supported demographic projects executed by DTCD was 76.

The Department provided 3,242 fellowships, of which more than 1,500 were in developing countries to further TCDC. DTCD also published the 1983 Directory of Training Courses and Programmes in Europe and Neighbouring Areas, which included more than 400 courses in all fields of DTCD competence.

During 1983, DTCD country programming missions were carried out in Ghana and Uganda, and other missions by both interregional and technical advisers were undertaken to identify project proposals. Draft country programmes were reviewed in detail before their consideration by the UNDP Governing Council. The thrust of DTCD's assistance was to help Governments in undertaking sectoral reviews and financial analysis and to develop rational criteria for selecting programmes and projects that would be implemented by United Nations organizations, as well as to formulate proposals for financing by other sources. DTCD was also involved in the review of country programmes.

As the principal United Nations entity with responsibility for developing and strengthening human and physical infrastructure, DTCD carried out a large number of its field programmes in LDCs. Finance from its regular programme resources continued to be provided on a priority basis in order to meet the requests of LDCs for advisory services and other specific activities. Field projects in LDCs covered a broad range of sectors, including the formulation of development plans and strengthening of project evaluation capability, administrative reform and personnel and financial management, statistics, population and various stages of natural resources exploration and development. For example, assistance was provided to Rwanda and Tonga in intensifying certain aspects of their national planning and to the Sudan for the establishment of a population centre at the University of Gezira. A natural resources exploration project was carried out in Democratic Yemen and Yemen, and rural water supply projects were undertaken in Benin, Guinea-Bissau, Togo and other African LDCs affected by drought.

With regard to the integration of women, the thrust of DTCD's efforts in 1983 was to link activities focusing specifically on women with those in various economic and social sectors in order to promote global priorities, including training.

Special attention was given to relatively new technologies for use by developing countries in meeting some of their priority needs, in particular those that could contribute to a significant increase in energy resources, such as geothermal energy and hydropower. DTCD also attached particular importance to expanding the use of microcomputer technology. It organized in New York in 1983 an expert group on the application of microcomputers in mineral information systems, exploration, geological resources modelling, mining planning and economics as well as management of operations and control. The group recommended that computer training courses be offered to managers and engineers in developing countries, and encouraged the United Nations to increase the application of computer techniques in its technical co-operation projects. This was followed up in Oman with a series of conferences to train nationals in electronic data processing techniques. In Benin, Burundi and other countries, microcomputers were installed to assist government officials in the application of such technology to mineral evaluation.

DTCD participated in missions organized by the United Nations Office for Special Political Questions both with regard to humanitarian assistance programmes and in conjunction with the implementation of special economic assistance programmes (see Chapter III of this section). The Department also provided technical support to the Tenth United Nations Regional Cartographic Conference for Asia and the Pacific (see Chapter IX of this section).

In the areas of pre-investment and investment follow-up, DTCD continued in 1983 to respond to the needs of developing countries. Reported investment commitments relating to DTCD projects totalled $218 million: $134 million in Asia, $41 million in Latin America, $25 million in Africa, and $18 million in Europe and the Middle East. Domestic investments were secured in the Dominican Republic, India, Pakistan, Thailand and Yugoslavia.

DTCD investment seminars initiated in 1982 were continued in 1983 and attended by high-level representatives of the World Bank, as well as by staff from the Asian and African Development Banks. The aim was to assist DTCD in identifying ways of strengthening linkages between technical co-operation and capital assistance. A complete bibliography of all feasibility and United Nations project reports in Africa and Asia was prepared by the Information Systems Unit of the Department of International Economic and Social Affairs (DIESA).

Taking full account of the recommendations of JIU (see below), a major streamling of DTCD's organizational structure was undertaken to accommodate drastic staff cuts, while retaining to the extent possible the wide range of technical and programming services needed for effective programme implementation. Staff were redeployed to promote a more integrated approach to programme management, placing the major emphasis on the substantive aspects of technical co-operation. Managerial and technical personnel were grouped together along sectoral lines, and a merger of recruitment and administrative services was effected to improve the administration of project personnel.

Despite those measures, which were implemented on 1 July 1983, DTCD was able to deliver in 1983 a programme equivalent to nearly 90 per cent of that delivered in 1982.

As part of the streamlining of DTCD during 1983, responsibility for evaluation was assigned to a newly created Country Programming and Evaluation Branch. Internal guidelines were completed but their application was deferred pending revision of UNDP's procedures on evaluation. Projects continued to be evaluated in 1983 under existing UNDP guidelines, and efforts were made to improve project monitoring.

JIU report. By a note of 28 April,[3] the Secretary-General submitted to the General Assembly a JIU report on DTCD, prepared by Mark E. Allen, Earl D. Sohm and Miljenko Vukovic. The report examined the progress made by the Department since its inception in March 1978.[4] The Inspectors' main conclusion was that DTCD had positive achievements to its credit, notably the improvement in its delivery rate, but that it was urgent to re-examine its structure and staffing in order to ensure that operations were cost-effective, to remove uncertainties as to its future and to help provide it with a recognized identity. They noted that DTCD had been operating under temporary terms of reference and had been organized partly on substantive and partly on geographical lines, an arrangement which might not represent an optimum use of resources and was not conducive to giving sufficient attention to the impact of the work. The Inspectors concluded that a structure that emphasized substance and not geography would give the best results most economically; such structure would still require a group of small geographical units with liaison, control and expediting functions and constituting a service for the substantive divisions.

The Inspectors recommended that the Secretary-General ensure the issuance of DTCD's terms of reference and that, in its forthcoming administrative review of the Department, the Administrative Management Service (AMS) look into the question of organization for dealing with technical co-operation and concentrate on its rationalization and streamlining. The Inspectors suggested that part of the resources released through that rationalization be used to set up a small unit within DTCD for central evaluation, reporting to the Under-Secretary-General.

In the Inspectors' opinion, the Department's field work was handicapped to some extent because it had no field representation. However, they did not consider the establishment of field offices, even at the regional level, to be an economical solution. They suggested a series of measures such as: entrusting, on a part-time basis, senior experts with liaison functions on substantive questions between resident representatives/co-ordinators and DTCD headquarters; briefing of resident representatives/co-ordinators to acquaint them with DTCD's needs and activities; establishing direct continuous relations between DTCD headquarters and the offices of the resident representatives/co-ordinators responsible for DTCD; and outposting some of the Development Advisory Services staff to the regional commissions and their subregional offices to assist in country and intercountry programming.

The Inspectors noted that the administration of DTCD field experts had to be referred to the Office of General Services and the Office of Personnel Services for action, since DTCD had no authority to deal with administrative, personnel and financial matters. They recommended that the Department be given more authority to deal with those matters concerning its experts in the field.

They also noted that DTCD suffered from a lack of intergovernmental authority which would give directly the attention required for such issues as the programme of work and policy matters concerning the Department, prior to their examination by the Economic and Social Council and the General Assembly. One solution, they thought, might have been to have DTCD report to a single governing body responsible at the intergovernmental level for United Nations operational activities for development, as suggested by the Assembly in 1977.[5] As such a body had not been established, the Inspectors concluded that the UNDP Governing Council was the most suitable to supervise the work of DTCD. They recommended that the Governing Council consider devoting at least a day once a year to DTCD affairs and take any necessary policy decisions, without infringing on the responsibilities of the Committee for Programme and Co-ordination for policy and programme guidance and direction.

The Inspectors also dealt with DTCD's relationship with other Secretariat entities, noting that the absence of a clear definition of its role had led to some conflict, and that a number of unresolved issues of restructuring, particularly those related to the decentralization and redeployment of resources, continued to add to those difficulties. The Inspectors stated that they had formed the impression that problems flowing from the break-up of the old Department of Economic and Social Affairs were still influencing relations between the two successor Departments (DTCD and DIESA), notably in the areas of statistics and the servicing of joint conferences and seminars.

Comments of the Secretary-General. Commenting in July 1983[6] on the JIU report, the Secretary-General welcomed it as a useful contribution to clarifying and strengthening DTCD's role and that it could serve as a basis for further consideration of issues not yet fully resolved. The Secretary-General believed that further intergovernmental review of DTCD activities was warranted and that, as suggested by JIU, the UNDP Governing Council could devote more time to the review and guidance of United Nations technical co-operation activities. He also noted that his annual report on those activities would be made available in future to the Assembly, through the Economic and Social Council.

The Secretary-General stressed that the following considerations should be kept in mind. Although the Inspectors had taken into account the decline in resources and its effects on DTCD, some of their arguments had become even more acute as a result of further erosion of traditional funding sources. In view of the fact that DTCD staff were financed largely out of overhead earnings on programme delivery, the severe financial constraints were having direct implications on the Department's size and structure and would be a crucial factor in any decision concerning its internal organization; those constraints were also the result of the proliferation and expansion of executing capabilities outside DTCD.

In his comments on specific recommendations, the Secretary-General said he concurred in particular with the need to establish a proper degree of co-ordination and uniformity of approach within the United Nations Secretariat and he intended to address those issues in the following months, including the clustering together in DTCD of relevant functions pertaining to the management of United Nations technical co-operation activities.

With regard to clearly defined terms of reference for DTCD, he noted that, given the context in which the Department had to operate, that question was linked to interrelated issues, including proliferation of execution capabilities within the Secretariat; relationship between DIESA and DTCD and the allocation of activities between the two in such subject areas as statistics and ocean economics; relations of DTCD with its funding partners and criteria for the designation of executing agencies by UNDP, DTCD's main funding partner. These and other areas of concern to DTCD would also be treated in the forthcoming JIU reports on DIESA and UNDP's Office for Projects Execution.

With regard to a rationalization and streamlining of DTCD, the Secretary-General stated that the Department had over the previous year carried out an extensive analysis of its internal organization and that many of JIU's suggestions had already been reflected in DTCD's own streamlining proposals; in his programme budget submission, he would report on measures taken in that regard.

The Secretary-General fully supported the view that current efforts to ensure a more effective field representation of DTCD should be maintained; with regard to the suggestion that regional commissions and their subregional offices could be requested to assist DTCD on specific issues, he pointed out that, for financial and other reasons, no change in existing arrangements could be contemplated.

He fully agreed with the importance attributed to evaluation which, he added, was fully reflected in the various steps taken by DTCD over the previous year to devise methodology, guidelines and procedures for more systematic application in field projects. The setting up of a separate evaluation unit, however, awaited the outcome of decisions on DTCD's structure and also depended on the availability of finances.

Concurring with the thrust of the recommendation on the need of DTCD for greater flexibility in dealing with administrative, personnel and financial matters, the Secretary-General stated that certain measures had already been adopted to increase delegation of authority to the Department in such areas as the establishment and management of trust funds and to streamline administrative systems. He agreed that further steps could be taken, particularly relating to the management of expert personnel and finance in the field, adding that appropriate action was under way.

With regard to a recommendation that Chief Technical Advisers in DTCD-executed projects be authorized to spend up to $10,000 for local or international purchases, the Secretary-General noted that they had the authority to do so, with funds allocated without limit but individual orders not exceeding $5,000.

ACABQ report. In a November 1983 report on DTCD,[7] ACABQ also dealt with the JIU recommendations. It stressed that DTCD's terms of reference, which were being worked out, should be finalized as soon as possible. With regard to the need to establish a proper degree of co-ordination and uniformity of approach within the Secretariat, ACABQ noted the Secretary-General's intention to address the matter in the following months and to provide in the 1984-1985 programme budget the relevant intergovernmental bodies with the opportunity to consider the progress achieved. However, ACABQ questioned whether the revised budget submission[8] could be considered to have fully addressed the issues raised by the Inspectors.

Concerning the forthcoming review of DTCD by AMS, during which AMS should consider the setting up of an organization of substance which integrated backstopping with the work of the substantive specialists, and the Secretary-General's comment that many of JIU's suggestions had already been reflected in DTCD's own proposals for streamlining, ACABQ considered that a more detailed analysis of that streamlining could have been provided in the Secretary-General's revised budget.

Regarding the call for a small evaluation unit, ACABQ noted the Secretary-General's statement that various steps had been taken by DTCD during the year for a more systematic evaluation of field projects and, as stated in the Secretary-General's revised budget report, the country programming and evaluation function would henceforth be carried out in the Policy, Programming and Development Planning Division of the Department. ACABQ said it trusted that DTCD would be able to implement its evaluation activities as an integral part of its operations.

Referring to JIU's observations on DTCD's relations with other Secretariat entities, in particular DIESA, ACABQ noted that the JIU report on DIESA (see Chapter XXIV of this section) recommended that an improved mechanism for co-operation on statistics between the two be worked out.

UNDP Council action. The Governing Council, on 24 June 1983,[9] noted with great concern the impact on DTCD of the decline in availability of resources, particularly with regard to technical co-operation in certain key economic and social areas. It welcomed DTCD's efforts to streamline its operational capabilities so as to maximize the use of limited resources, to strengthen collaboration with UNDP and its field offices as well as with other United Nations entities, and to intensify its co-operation with Governments in order to ensure the responsiveness of its programmes to the needs of developing countries, particularly of the least developed.

The Council recommended that full account be taken of DTCD's technical expertise in decisions to designate executing agencies for the implementation of UNFPA and UNDP projects, as well as projects financed from other funds under the Administrator's authority. It invited the Secretary-General to provide to it in 1984 detailed information on the relationship between programme delivery and administrative costs, the level and use of programme support cost earnings, and expenditures, in particular information on extrabudgetary resources and the associated manning tables, and on United Nations procurement procedures for technical co-operation projects. The Council reiterated its request that action on the restructuring of the economic and social sectors of the United Nations system be completed, to enable DTCD to achieve greater flexibility with regard to administrative, personnel and financial matters related to the implementation of technical co-operation projects, and urged that clearer terms of reference for the Department be issued to avoid duplication of existing structures.

GENERAL ASSEMBLY ACTION

Under the agenda item on questions relating to the proposed programme budget for the biennium 1984-1985, the General Assembly on 20 Decem-

ber 1983 adopted resolution 38/234, section XI, without vote. The Assembly took this action on the recommendation of the Fifth (Administrative and Budgetary) Committee.

Report of the Joint Inspection Unit on the Department of Technical Co-operation for Development

[*The General Assembly . . .*]

Takes note of the report of the Joint Inspection Unit on the Department of Technical Co-operation for Development and the comments thereon by the Secretary-General and of the related report of the Advisory Committee on Administrative and Budgetary Questions;

. . .

General Assembly resolution 38/234, section XI

20 December 1983   Meeting 104   Adopted without vote

Approved by Fifth Committee (A/38/760 & Corr.1) without vote, 1 December (meeting 52); oral proposal by Chairman; agenda item 109.
Meeting numbers. GA 38th session: 5th Committee 52; plenary 104.

In resolution 38/171, the Assembly recommended that due consideration be given to DTCD's technical expertise for its designation as an executing agency for the implementation of projects within its mandate, as well as its role in the execution of technical co-operation activities of the United Nations system, in order to reaffirm the Department's role within the existing technical and administrative structures and to avoid duplication and accomplish economies of scale.

The Fifth Committee, on 1 December 1983,[10] approved without vote revised estimates for DTCD of $17,507,200 for 1984-1985, $89,300 less than the original estimates. The revised estimates were proposed in July 1983 by the Secretary-General[8] and endorsed by ACABQ in October.[11]

In his report, the Secretary-General stated that the decrease of $89,300 was due to reduced requirements for external printing and reduced estimated costs associated with posts being transferred from Geneva to New York in the programme support of field operations. He noted that, as a result of a freeze on appointments to vacant posts at DTCD and to all vacant overhead-financed posts in other Secretariat units, introduced with effect from 1 January 1982, by the end of May 1983 some 115 overhead posts had been abolished and it was expected that during the remainder of 1983 some 40 additional overhead posts would be similarly abolished. Those staff reductions, he added, had required certain organizational modifications to enable DTCD to continue its activities effectively. Consequently, the following organizational modifications were planned to be introduced effective July 1983: the Programming and Implementation Division was to be discontinued, and one D-2 post would be cancelled. DTCD would carry out its functions of policy formulation, programme and project operations and support substantively and managerially through four main divisions, namely: the Policy, Programming and Development Planning Division, which would be concerned with policy co-ordination, resources planning and procedures, and the broad policy aspects of country programming and evaluation, and which would also encompass the Development Advisory Services; two substantive divisions—the Natural Resources and Energy Division and the Development Administration Division—which would be responsible for the operational aspects of all phases of project implementation from design through follow-up, and which would continue all activities required to provide guidance and support for technical co-operation, including training, workshops, seminars and the preparation of studies and publications; and the Programme Support Division, which would, in addition to functions in support of projects with regard to expert recruitment and administration, also carry out project financial management and budgetary control.

In his analysis of overall costs of DTCD, the Secretary-General estimated extrabudgetary resources available during 1984-1985 at $277,740,300, comprising $24,060,000 for services in support of extrabudgetary programmes, $1,420,300 for substantive activities, and $252,260,000 for operational projects, the last figure being identical to the 1982-1983 total for project delivery. An estimated $46,690,000 represented the delivery of projects backstopped by other United Nations units (most notably DIESA), but executed by DTCD. Extrabudgetary resources comprised notably the reimbursement for programme support costs; the Secretary-General added that if support cost income continued to decline in 1984-1985, DTCD would be obliged to make further proposals for remedies to the appropriate bodies.

In its October report,[11] ACABQ stated that it had been informed that "overhead" income would be earned on approximately $242,600,000 of the $252,260,000 expected delivery. The balance of $9.6 million represented projects on which programme support had been waived, such as the United Nations Educational and Training Programme for Southern Africa and certain activities of the United Nations Fund for Namibia. The overhead income earned from actual delivery of projects (normally calculated at 13 per cent of project delivery) was placed in a central fund for programme support of technical co-operation activities. Other offices contributing to that fund included the Centre for Transnational Corporations and the Division of Narcotic Drugs. Provided that the estimated programme delivery was achieved, an amount of $24,060,000, which represented the bulk of the total overhead earnings, was expected to be allocated in 1984-1985 to meet the extrabudgetary costs incurred by DTCD in executing technical co-operation projects. The balance would be apportioned among other offices.

With regard to the number of extrabudgetary posts for DTCD in 1984-1985, estimated at 218 (102 Professional and above and 116 General Service), as compared with the total of 372 originally budgeted for 1982-1983, ACABQ said it had been informed that 364 of those posts had been authorized as at 1 January 1982; by 31 December 1982, that number had decreased to 339. Further reductions in overhead posts had been made during 1983; the number of extrabudgetary posts in 1984-1985 would also depend on the support cost income received during the biennium.

ACABQ also noted that it had been informed that, by 31 July 1983, DTCD had delivered $75 million in technical co-operation in 1983. According to representatives of the Secretary-General, the approved project budgets ($142.7 million as at 31 August 1983) justified the assumption that DTCD could achieve a delivery of $125 million by the end of 1983, despite the disruption brought about by the streamlining of DTCD's organizational structure. The Department also expected to maintain that level of delivery in 1984 and 1985, which would generate an estimated $16.3 million in overhead earnings in each year of the biennium. However, ACABQ cautioned that those expectations might be somewhat optimistic when viewed in the context of a number of factors, including the budget/delivery ratio of previous years. It considered it essential that the Secretary-General keep DTCD's delivery situation under constant scrutiny, with a view to anticipating additional remedial measures, both in DTCD and other Secretariat units, should the Department fail to achieve the projected level of support cost income.

United Nations Volunteers

In 1983, the United Nations Volunteers (UNV) programme continued to respond to the expressed needs for cost-effective middle and higher level operational expertise from some 90 developing countries, including the 36 LDCs where more than half of all serving volunteers were assigned. Demands for that expertise continued to increase; the total number of UNV posts requested in 1983 was 1,423, compared with 1,356 in 1982. The increase was possible because of certain recipient countries funding volunteers through cost-sharing, additional contributions from bilateral donors, and the increase in the number of posts fully funded by United Nations agencies. Information on UNV activities was provided by the UNDP Administrator in his annual reports for 1983 on the programme[12] and on UNDP.[13]

With over 80 per cent of its recruits from developing countries themselves, technical co-operation among those countries (see below) remained an important feature of the programme.

As requested by the UNDP Governing Council in June 1982,[14] new efforts were made in 1983 to increase the participation in the programme and to develop further working relations with United Nations organizations and agencies. Additional measures were taken to increase the programme's monitoring capacity and the conditions of service for the volunteers were revised.

Efforts continued to broaden participation in UNV. Co-operation agreements were concluded with four new countries: New Zealand, Poland, the Republic of Korea and Yugoslavia.

A UNV Consultative Meeting on international volunteer service and development—the first convened in accordance with the 1982 Sana'a Declaration[15]—was held at Geneva from 6 to 8 April 1983, with 41 representatives and six observers of Governments and co-operating organizations from developed and developing countries participating.

During the year, UNV undertook efforts to further programme development and fulfilment of its mandate, both as the focal point for international volunteerism in the United Nations system and as a major contributor of operational expertise for multilateral technical co-operation activities. In particular, it put into practice a programme development strategy involving missions to Bhutan, Chad, China, Fiji, Indonesia, Madagascar, Papua New Guinea and Singapore. UNV also participated in tripartite reviews of technical co-operation projects and in donor round-table meetings for LDCs to present more fully UNV's capabilities as a technical co-operation instrument.

Closely related to those programme development initiatives was a new emphasis on quality of UNV operations and on internal analysis through such mechanisms as project reviews, visits to volunteers in the field and the introduction of a revised and improved UNV periodic reporting system.

Parallel to those activities, more active information and media programmes provided fuller and more timely information about UNV. In addition, numerous publications were prepared. A totally revised edition of the *World Statistical Directory* was published containing information on the activities of over 1,000 volunteer and development service organizations. A briefing kit summarizing living and working conditions in China was completed for the use of serving volunteers and potential candidates for that country. A new information kit specifically designed for UNV use was under preparation, and priority was to be given to such kits for Bhutan, Papua New Guinea and the Upper Volta.

In 1983, a new focus was the question of changing requirements for TCDC. There was a trend towards financing technical co-operation from loan assistance. Governments were also beginning to programme volunteers in activities executed by themselves which contained technical assistance components financed by credits of development banks.

UNV also stepped up contacts with the World Bank and the regional development banks, all of which had begun to employ volunteers in projects executed by them. Fifty-three volunteers were provided to UNHCR, UNICEF and WFP.

During 1983, interest in community-based development activities—"grass-roots" rural development—increased rapidly, with UNV being widely involved. Its youth and domestic development services (DDS) programme—aimed at establishing networks among rural grass-roots level activities, for the purpose of sharing experience in technical co-operation—continued to develop.

A new phase of the regional Asia and Pacific DDS project began in January 1983; Fiji, Solomon Islands, Tonga and Vanuatu were to join the six other countries already receiving teams of volunteers. The new project phase included a subproject of assistance to groups of young people to start income-generating activities in rural areas. A modest DDS project was approved for Africa. A programming workshop for that project was cohosted by the Ministry of Culture, Sports and Arts of Mali and was organized at Bamako in December 1983; the workshop resulted in a work plan to make the pilot project operational in the first quarter of 1984.

DDS also provided on-the-job training, technology training and advisory services. Technical co-operation between DDS organizations was stimulated through study visits, workshops, publications and short-term personnel exchanges.

UNV also participated in ILO-executed labour-intensive public works projects and other, particularly agricultural, activities whose common denominator was the provision of additional assistance in the form of technical skills.

The preparatory work of UNV at the local level in relation to the International Youth Year (1985) continued (see Chapter XX of this section).

Despite repeated appeals to donor countries, contributions to the UNV Special Voluntary Fund decreased to $1.2 million in 1983; project expenditures totalled $1.8 million. The deficit between income and expenditure during 1983 was to some extent offset by investment income of approximately $300,000 and by income expected from a scheme established in May to finance part of the external costs from IPF allocations, cost-sharing arrangements, etc. Those arrangements would be reviewed annually, taking into account the level of contributions to the Fund for that year and making the necessary adjustment. The status of the Fund forced the Administrator to resort to other resources to meet part of UNV's external costs.

UNV PROJECT EXPENDITURES, 1983
(as at 31 December 1983; in thousands of US dollars)

Country	Amount	Country	Amount	Country	Amount
Afghanistan	3	Ivory Coast	7	Sri Lanka	172
Bahrain	4	Jamaica	7	Sudan	45
Bangladesh	15	Kenya	20	Swaziland	17
Belize	3	Lao People's Democratic Republic	8	Syrian Arab Republic	57
Benin	37	Lesotho	59	Togo	5
Bhutan	23	Liberia	31	Tonga	13
Botswana	32	Malawi	1	Trust Territory of the Pacific Islands	33
Burundi	3	Maldives	8	Tuvalu	9
Cape Verde	10	Mali	2	Uganda	23
Central African Republic	30	Mauritania	16	United Republic of Cameroon	7
Chad	5	Morocco	2	United Republic of Tanzania	78
China	3	Mozambique	36	Upper Volta	21
Comoros	47	Namibia	2	Vanuatu	13
Congo	3	Nepal	4	Yemen	172
Cook Islands	74	Nicaragua	2	Zimbabwe	9
Democratic Yemen	28	Niger	26		
Djibouti	5	Niue	4	Total	1,630
Dominica	2	Oman	1		
Dominican Republic	4	Pakistan	2	*INTERCOUNTRY*	
Equatorial Guinea	7	Panama	2	*Global*	143
Ethiopia	15	Papua New Guinea	21	*Regional*	
Fiji	2	Paraguay	3		
Gabon	1	Rwanda	1	Africa	5
Gambia	5	Saint Christopher and Nevis	9	Arab States	10
Ghana	6	Saint Lucia	4	Asia and the Pacific	13
Guinea	5	Samoa	47	Latin America and the Caribbean	10
Guinea-Bissau	68	Sao Tome and Principe	33		
Guyana	5	Seychelles	5	Total	181
Haiti	15	Sierra Leone	13		
Honduras	15	Solomon Islands	13	GRAND TOTAL	1,811
Indonesia	12	Somalia	80		

SOURCE: DP/1984/5/Add.6.

UNDP Council action. Taking note of the Administrator's report on UNV for 1982, submitted in April 1983,[16] the UNDP Governing Council on 23 June[17] decided not to change the financial arrangements for the programme, and appealed to Governments to solve the problem of financing the Special Voluntary Fund.

In his report, the Administrator concluded that, in response to increasing requests for assistance, it would be necessary to formulate and support proposals that would enable the programme to assume its increased responsibilities. He recommended that the Council decide that support costs should be charged in respect of UNDP-financed, UNV-executed projects.

On 24 June,[18] the Council approved revised budget appropriations for UNV for 1982-1983 of $5,720,700 gross ($4,771,900 net). For 1984-1985, it approved[19] $6,680,100 gross ($5,572,200 net).

GENERAL ASSEMBLY ACTION

On 19 December, on the recommendation of the Second Committee, the General Assembly adopted resolution 38/173 without vote.

United Nations Volunteers programme
The General Assembly,

Recalling its resolution 2659(XXV) of 7 December 1970 and its subsequent resolutions on the United Nations Volunteers programme, including resolution 37/229 of 20 December 1982,

Taking note of decision 83/18 of 23 June 1983 of the Governing Council of the United Nations Development Programme,

Bearing in mind the recommendations of the Sana'a Declaration, adopted at the High-level Symposium on International Volunteer Service and Development,

1. *Notes with satisfaction* the continued achievements of the United Nations Volunteers programme during the past year;

2. *Reaffirms* that the United Nations Volunteers programme continues to be an effective instrument of multilateral technical co-operation programmes responding to the needs of the developing countries, particularly to those of the least developed among them;

3. *Expresses the hope* that full consideration will be given to the use of United Nations Volunteers, as requested in decision 83/7 of 24 June 1983 of the Governing Council of the United Nations Development Programme on recruitment and reduction of the cost of project professional personnel;

4. *Considers* that the use of United Nations Volunteers offers particular advantages for community development activities in rural areas;

5. *Notes* the expanding activities of the United Nations Volunteers programme in the field of youth and domestic development services;

6. *Reaffirms* that the United Nations Volunteers programme should continue its involvement in the preparations for the International Youth Year and its activities in the implementation of programmes relating to youth;

7. *Appeals again* to Governments, organizations and individuals to contribute or to increase their contributions to the Special Voluntary Fund for the United Nations Volunteers programme to enable the programme to meet the external cost of volunteers recruited from developing countries.

General Assembly resolution 38/173

19 December 1983   Meeting 102   Adopted without vote

Approved by Second Committee (A/38/703) without vote, 9 December (meeting 55); 30-nation draft (A/C.2/38/L.95); agenda item 79 *(e)*.

Sponsors: Australia, Austria, Bangladesh, Barbados, Belgium, Bhutan, Botswana, China, Costa Rica, Democratic Yemen, Denmark, Egypt, Guinea-Bissau, Italy, Lebanon, Liberia, Maldives, Nepal, Norway, Oman, Pakistan, Philippines, Singapore, Sudan, Suriname, Thailand, Tunisia, United States, Yemen, Yugoslavia.

Meeting numbers. GA 38th session: 2nd Committee 45-53, 55; plenary 102.

CONTRIBUTIONS TO THE SPECIAL VOLUNTARY FUND
FOR THE UN VOLUNTEERS, 1983 AND 1984
(as at 31 December 1983; in US dollar equivalent)

Country	1983 payment	1984 pledge
Austria	7,700	9,211
Bangladesh	1,000	1,100
Belgium	290,538	181,818
Bhutan	1,265	820
Botswana	472	367
Brazil	—	10,000
China	20,000	20,000
Denmark	58,661	51,020
Germany, Federal Republic of	115,385	—
Guinea-Bissau	376	—
India	5,000	5,000
Indonesia	1,000	—
Italy	125,786	122,699
Lesotho	200	1,000
Liberia	2,000	—
Morocco	—	5,000
Netherlands	169,493	165,017
Norway	71,429	133,333
Philippines	—	1,000
Republic of Korea	10,000	10,000
Sri Lanka	2,765	3,000
Sudan	—	1,000
Switzerland	169,323	137,615
Syrian Arab Republic	5,064	—
Thailand	1,500	1,500
Tunisia	5,132	4,043
United States	150,000	—
Total	1,214,089	864,543

SOURCE: A/39/5/Add.1.

Technical co-operation among developing countries

In 1983, UNDP, with other United Nations organizations, continued to carry out its special responsibility for technical co-operation among developing countries (TCDC)—a major effort by developing countries to promote their collective self-reliance. Those activities paralleled action in favour of economic co-operation among developing countries (ECDC), taken by UNCTAD and others (p. 413).

At its May/June session, the High-level Committee on the Review of TCDC made several recommendations to further active support for and promotion of TCDC, most significant among them one on strengthening the TCDC multisectoral Information Referral System (INRES), and another

on the use of Special Programme Resources for supporting TCDC activities. Both recommendations were considered favourably by the UNDP Governing Council, which decided on 24 June to provide during 1984-1985 $600,000 (net) from UNDP's administrative budget for the support of INRES and another $600,000 from Special Programme Resources for TCDC operational and promotional activities.

With this support, UNDP continued to develop INRES, listing institutional capacities of developing countries in education and training, research, technological development, consultancy and expert services, together with the bilateral and multilateral project experiences of those institutions. UNDP's Special Unit for TCDC also co-operated with the Inter-Agency Procurement Services Unit to support a pilot study on additional information concerning the suppliers of equipment from developing countries for the use of United Nations development organizations and of other developing countries.

During 1983, UNDP also participated in intergovernmental meetings to promote TCDC, notably a technical meeting on the multisectoral information network, convened by the Chairman of the Group of 77 in New York in May; a meeting of experts to draft a model contract for the interchange of experts among developing countries, held at Caracas, Venezuela, in August under the auspices of the Group of 77; a non-aligned meeting of experts on small island developing countries, held in Grenada in September; and the second intergovernmental follow-up and co-ordination committee of the Group of 77 for the follow-up of the 1981 Caracas Plan of Action[20] on ECDC, held at Tunis, Tunisia, in August.

UNDP also pursued TCDC in its field operations. Pursuant to an 18 June Governing Council decision on Special Programme Resources,[21] an interregional project costing $400,000—promotion of action-oriented TCDC activities—was approved. By the end of 1983, 12 activities had been set for implementation under that project, involving TCDC between Haiti and Jamaica, Brazil and Cape Verde, Yemen and Yugoslavia, Brazil and Chile, Somalia and Yugoslavia and the United Republic of Tanzania and Kenya/Ethiopia in such areas as bauxite exploration, public administration, education through television, biological nitrogen fixation and geothermal power.

Along similar lines, Brazil, China and India approved TCDC projects for the 1982-1986 programming cycle under their country programmes. The regional intergovernmental consultations on TCDC, at Beijing, China, in November, provided an example of one such project. During those consultations, 32 TCDC exchanges between China and seven other countries of Asia and the Pacific were identified. Under the Indian project, in addition to various TCDC-oriented workshops and symposia, training was provided to technicians from the United Republic of Tanzania in small-scale industries, and the services of 50 engineers were provided to Sri Lanka to implement the Mahaweli project. Brazil, under its TCDC project, provided training in airline safety to over 80 students from Bolivia, Colombia, Panama, Paraguay and Peru in Latin America, and Angola and Mozambique in Africa.

Action of the Committee on TCDC. The third session of the High-level Committee on the Review of Technical Co-operation among Developing Countries was held in New York from 31 May to 8 June 1983.[22] Its tasks were to review TCDC activities within the United Nations system, to ensure that efforts to strengthen such activities were sustained, to support new policies to further the development of TCDC, to consider the availability of funds and their effective use, and to ensure co-ordination of TCDC activities. These functions had been defined by the Plan of Action for Promoting and Implementing Technical Co-operation among Developing Countries, adopted in 1978 by the United Nations Conference on Technical Co-operation among Developing Countries, held at Buenos Aires, Argentina.[23]

The Committee adopted 12 decisions on 6 June, aimed at promoting TCDC. In one of these,[24] it invited developing countries to strengthen their national focal points for TCDC and to utilize the opportunities provided by the multilateral institutions set up by the developing countries; and invited developed countries to continue their support by increasing their contributions to the operational programmes of the United Nations development system and by accelerating the process of untying their aid resources, as recommended in the Buenos Aires Plan of Action. Progress made by the United Nations in implementing that Plan was the subject of another decision,[25] by which the Committee urged the system to grant adequate importance to TCDC and to support specific projects; it also requested UNDP to increase its support to TCDC, and invited other United Nations bodies to review their procurement policies with a view to increasing procurement in developing countries and to support intergovernmental consultations on the co-ordination of national plans and on arrangements for TCDC. By a third decision,[26] the Committee recommended that the UNDP Governing Council consider subregional and regional intergovernmental organizations in the use of resources established by the regional and interregional IPFs for TCDC activities.

In a decision on measures to facilitate TCDC,[27] the Committee requested the UNDP Administrator to study the possibility of introducing greater flexibility in the use of country IPFs, and to assist Governments and development organizations in pursuing the recommendations on TCDC of the 1981 High-level Conference on Economic Co-operation among Developing Countries,[20] which had recognized the crucial role of TCDC for promoting ECDC. Under the same decision, the Committee noted with deep concern that the activities of UNDP's Special Unit for TCDC were being scaled down and urged the restoration of the Unit's staffing resources.

By another decision,[28] the Committee requested the Governing Council to allow the use of IPFs to cover fully the local currency expenditure on TCDC projects; permit reimbursement, in convertible currency, of local currency expenditure on TCDC projects covered by country IPFs; and ensure procurement of equipment, services and experts from developing countries.

By another decision,[29] the Committee requested the Administrator to provide support in preparing TCDC meetings, and invited the international community to support developing countries' efforts to carry forward TCDC activities by themselves, at all levels.

Other decisions dealt with: INRES (see below); skilled workers (see below); the United Nations Decade for Transport and Communications in Africa, 1978-1988 (see Chapter VIII of this section); rural-urban migration (see Chapter XIV of this section); women in development (see Chapter XIX of this section); and the Committee's provisional agenda for its 1985 session.

The Administrator submitted to the Committee in March 1983 a report[30] on the progress made by United Nations bodies in promoting and supporting TCDC in major areas of activity, namely: information collection and exchange; institution-strengthening and networking; training; legal arrangements; and resource mobilization.

In his conclusions, he stated that efforts by United Nations bodies to promote and support TCDC during 1981-1983 had met with moderate success. Gains were registered particularly in information transfer; in training of developing countries' personnel through fellowship programmes, intercountry workshops and study tours, and improvement of training materials; in the utilization of national experts and advisers to other developing countries in development programmes and training activities; and in expanding institutional networks as a basis for closer intercountry co-operation. He added that some agencies had taken significant new policy decisions designed to increase their effectiveness in promoting TCDC.

The absence of sufficient information on countries' needs and technical capabilities remained a serious constraint to operational TCDC, he observed; greater efforts were needed towards developing simple, cost-effective information systems to provide countries with up-to-date useful information for practical programme purposes. More information on countries' programme and management experiences as well as on available technologies was a particular need. The INRES inquiry service being developed by UNDP was expected to improve the situation, but other organizations also needed to consider how more information directly related to TCDC programming could be built into their sectoral technical information systems; developing countries on their side should consider what mechanisms were needed for effective evaluation and use of TCDC-related information.

While workshops and seminars on general TCDC aspects were still needed in some areas, greater emphasis should be placed on promoting and supporting intergovernmental consultations aimed at identifying operational issues; on co-ordinating national plans and strategies in key development areas of mutual interest; and on negotiating concrete TCDC arrangements.

As promotional efforts by most agencies and organizations had been of a rather *ad hoc* and unco-ordinated nature, efforts should be made to identify development issues and problems within their fields of competence particularly amenable to TCDC approaches; to co-ordinate information, training and promotional activities; and to review mechanisms for collecting information and reporting on TCDC activities. In the current strained financial situation, the Administrator considered that it would be very helpful if more co-operating countries would consider using their country IPFs for TCDC activities.

In another March 1983 report to the Committee,[31] the Administrator gave an account of the status of the use of country IPFs for TCDC during 1980-1982.

UNDP Council action. The Governing Council on 23 June[32] took note of the recommendations of the High-level Committee and urged the Administrator to enable UNDP's Special Unit for TCDC to carry out its functions effectively, paying particular attention to field and action-oriented TCDC activities and having regard to the need to contain administrative costs. It decided to review in 1984 the Unit's staffing pattern in connection with the review of UNDP resources, and requested the Administrator to submit an assessment of the related implications for the Unit's work.

On 18 June, in a decision on Special Programme Resources,[21] the Governing Council approved $600,000 for specific promotional activities for TCDC during 1984-1985.

ECONOMIC AND SOCIAL COUNCIL ACTION

In resolution 1983/50 of 28 July 1983, the Economic and Social Council took note of an agreement reached at Joint Meetings of the Committee for Programme and Co-ordination and the Administrative Committee on Co-ordination to carry out a review of the work in ECDC and TCDC, with a view to improving United Nations co-ordination and making United Nations activities more responsive to the needs of developing countries. It invited the Secretary-General and United Nations bodies to pay particular attention to the assessment of their capacities and potentials for promoting ECDC and TCDC, and requested the Secretary-General to develop ECDC and TCDC activities.

On 29 July, the Council adopted a resolution (1983/66) on promoting interregional ECDC and TCDC; the recommendations made therein were endorsed by the General Assembly in decision 38/435 of 19 December.

In resolution 1983/56 of 28 July, on permanent sovereignty over natural resources, the Council requested the Committee on Natural Resources to identify new possibilities for ECDC and TCDC. In another resolution of the same date (1983/57), on water resources development, the Council called on UNDP and other United Nations organizations to intensify their roles in promoting TCDC.

GENERAL ASSEMBLY ACTION

On 19 December, on the recommendation of the Second Committee, the General Assembly adopted decision 38/441 without vote.

Report of the High-level Committee on the Review of Technical Co-operation among Developing Countries
At its 102nd plenary meeting, on 19 December 1983, the General Assembly, on the recommendation of the Second Committee, took note of the report of the High-level Committee on the Review of Technical Co-operation among Developing Countries.

General Assembly decision 38/441

Adopted without vote

Approved by Second Committee (A/38/702/Add.6) without vote, 14 December (meeting 56); draft orally proposed by Chairman; agenda item 78 *(f)*.
Meeting numbers. GA 38th session: 2nd Committee 56; plenary 102.

Several 19 December Assembly resolutions contained provisions on TCDC.

In resolution 38/171 on a comprehensive policy review of operational activities for development, the Assembly urged United Nations organizations and bodies to increase their support for TCDC by orienting their programmes towards strengthening such co-operation.

In resolution 38/151, the Assembly reaffirmed the need for the United Nations system to support developing countries' efforts to enhance their economic and technical co-operation for the development of their energy resources. In resolution 38/169, the Assembly requested United Nations bodies to support developing countries' efforts for technical and economic co-operation in the field of new and renewable sources of energy. In resolution 38/158, the Assembly called on United Nations organizations and the international community to support economic and technical co-operation among developing countries with regard to food and agriculture.

In a 20 December resolution (38/201) on the liquidation of the United Nations Emergency Operation Trust Fund, the Assembly decided to transfer 12 per cent of the Fund's remaining balance to UNDP for promoting economic and technical co-operation among developing countries, according to the priorities set by them. A UNDP Trust Fund for Economic and Technical Co-operation among Developing Countries was established on 31 December.

Information Referral System for TCDC

In May 1983, the UNDP Administrator submitted to the High-level Committee on the Review of TCDC a report[33] on the status and development of the Information Referral System (INRES), designed to provide comprehensive and up-to-date information on the skills and capacities in developing countries which could be utilized for TCDC. Following its computerization, INRES comprised around 25,000 entries, pertaining to about 1,000 institutions. The Administrator indicated that steps would be taken to facilitate linkages of the INRES data base with national, regional and United Nations information systems. He believed that, with the completion of an initial data base, it would be appropriate to finance the further development and maintenance of INRES as a programme activity from UNDP's Special Programme Resources as distinct from its administrative budget, as had been the case. Accordingly, he proposed that the Governing Council approve $599,200 from Special Programme Resources for INRES for 1984-1985. In addition, he stated that treating INRES as a self-contained project activity promoting programme development in support of TCDC would also facilitate future consideration by developing countries as a group of the possibility of their taking over that activity.

The High-level Committee, on 6 June,[34] requested the Administrator to take immediate measures with regard to a reorientation of INRES and to report in 1985 on its progress and effective use through a multisectoral information network, including the increase of the coverage of institutions and services which could be accessed through a multilingual on-line inquiry service. It urged him to continue to finance the development and expansion of INRES from UNDP's administrative budget.

The Governing Council, in a decision of 18 June on Special Programme Resources,[21] appropriated $600,000 for INRES under a separate appropriation line in the 1984-1985 budget, and requested the Administrator to report in 1984 on its progress.

Skilled workers

In February 1983, the UNCTAD secretariat submitted to the Trade and Development Board a study on institutional and policy issues relating to the cooperative exchange of skills,[35] in accordance with a 1981 Board resolution.[36] In carrying out the study, UNCTAD was assisted by two consultants from India, working in their personal capacity—T. S. Papola, Director of Giri Institute, Lucknow, and K. K. Subrahmanian, Sardar Patel Institute of Economic and Social Research, Ahmedabad.

The study stressed the urgent need for institutionalizing export and import of skilled manpower among developing countries in order to avoid unnecessary costs to migrants and employers as well as imbalances in the labour markets of home and host countries, and to utilize the system of inter-developing country migration as a means of exploiting resource complementarities for the benefit of the national and collective development of developing countries.

To examine the feasibility of such modalities in depth, the study suggested: that a group of experts be convened and that interregional, regional and subregional workshops be organized with the participation of high-level officials in charge of labour and migration; that the High-level Committee and the Committee on Transfer of Technology of UNCTAD review periodically progress made in co-operative exchange of skills and make recommendations; and that national and regional policies for the co-operative exchange of skills and institutional mechanisms to implement them be set up with the assistance of UNDP, UNCTAD and other organizations.

On 22 April, the Board decided to transmit the study to the High-level Committee.[37]

The Committee on 6 June[38] invited the Board to examine the modalities for co-operation and to recommend ways of establishing co-operative policies for the exchange of skills among developing countries, while considering the possibility of entrusting that task to a group of governmental experts. It invited the Board to inform it of implementation of that recommendation and requested the UNDP Administrator to incorporate in his 1985 progress report information on implementation of the recommendation in the 1978 Buenos Aires Plan of Action[23] that, in view of the global nature of the problem of migration of professional and skilled manpower from developing countries and of such manpower's potential as an asset for TCDC, United Nations development organizations should assist developing countries in formulating measures for strengthening their capacities to encourage patterns of voluntary migration between them, but also the return of scientific, professional and technical personnel living outside their countries.

To be able to take a decision on the convening of a group of governmental experts, the Board on

20 October 1983[39] requested the UNCTAD Secretary-General to consult UNCTAD member States, particularly the developing countries concerned.

International skill exchange was also dealt with in an UNCTAD report submitted to the August/September Meeting of Governmental Experts on the Reverse Transfer of Technology (see Chapter XII of this section).

REFERENCES

[1]DP/1983/18 & Add.1,2. [2]YUN 1982, p. 664. [3]A/38/172. [4]YUN 1978, p. 450. [5]YUN 1977, p. 439, GA res. 32/197, annex, 20 Dec. 1977. [6]A/38/172/Add.1. [7]A/38/600. [8]A/C.5/38/2 & Corr.1. [9]E/1983/20 (dec. 83/16). [10]A/38/760 & Corr.1. [11]A/38/7Add.3. [12]DP/1984/43. [13]DP/1984/5/Add.2. [14]YUN 1982, p. 666. [15]*Ibid.*, p. 665. [16]DP/1983/31 & Corr.1. [17]E/1983/20 (dec. 83/18). [18]*Ibid.* (dec. 83/30). [19]*Ibid.* (dec. 83/31). [20]YUN 1981, p. 383. [21]E/1983/20 (dec. 83/15). [22]A/38/39. [23]YUN 1978, p. 467. [24]A/38/39 (dec. 3/1). [25]*Ibid.* (dec. 3/4). [26]*Ibid.* (dec. 3/5). [27]*Ibid.* (dec. 3/8). [28]*Ibid.* (dec. 3/10). [29]*Ibid.* (dec. 3/11). [30]TCDC/3/2. [31]TCDC/3/8. [32]E/1983/20 (dec. 83/21). [33]TCDC/3/9 & Corr.1. [34]A/38/39 (dec. 3/9). [35]TD/B/943 & Corr.1. [36]YUN 1981, p. 464. [37]A/38/15, Vol. I. [38]A/38/39 (dec. 3/6). [39]A/38/15, Vol. II (dec. 279(XXVII)).

UN Capital Development Fund

In his annual report on the United Nations Capital Development Fund (UNCDF) for 1983,[1] the UNDP Administrator described the Fund's programme operations and related activities, as well as its financial situation under the partial funding system.

Programme operations. In 1983, UNCDF approved $29.2 million in commitments for 20 new projects, plus $1 million for increases in existing project budgets, bringing outstanding commitments at year-end to $143.7 million for 193 ongoing projects in 35 LDCs. Of the $30.2 million of approvals in 1983, $23.9 million was funded directly from general resources; the balance was made possible as a result of the conclusion of $6.3 million in trust fund and cost-sharing arrangements.

The situation in Africa, with successive droughts over the previous two or three years, had had a devastating effect on crop and livestock production, resulting in widespread shortages of staple foods and severe economic hardships, particularly for small farmers; the Fund, therefore, identified and developed projects that would help increase food production and food storage and distributions systems. Of the 20 projects approved in 1983, 14 totalling $18 million in UNCDF grant assistance were in that category.

Net project expenditures in 1983 amounted to $24.8 million against outstanding commitments of $148 million for 185 projects carried over from 1982. In addition, approximately $3 million in expenditures was incurred in 1983 against trust fund and cost-sharing contributions.

As authorized by the UNDP Governing Council on 24 June,[2] UNCDF accepted new trust fund contributions conditioned on procurement from donor countries (Austria, Italy) totalling $5.6 million for three projects in Mali, the Niger and Somalia. Another trust fund agreement was formally signed in 1983 for a second project in Mali, covering a contribution of $306,000 from Belgium. A fourth such contribution was for a project urgently requested by Mali in mid-1983, which UNCDF could not approve within the ceiling set for new commitments against its general resources in 1983. Of those trust fund contributions, 36.4 per cent was untied.

In 1983, UNCDF and the Arab Gulf Programme for United Nations Development Organizations concluded cost-sharing agreements, with the latter contributing $700,000 for two projects, bringing its total cost-sharing contributions to $2.1 million for four projects.

During the year, nine programming missions were fielded by the Fund. Following review of project proposals identified by those missions, 24 project preparation missions were sent to 18 countries and,

UNCDF PROJECT EXPENDITURES, 1983

(as at 31 December 1983; in thousands of US dollars)

Country	Amount*	Country	Amount*	Country	Amount*
Afghanistan	8	Gambia	607	Senegal	681
Angola	696	Guinea	1,069	Somalia	748
Bangladesh	919	Guinea-Bissau	168	Sudan	(46)
Benin	793	Haiti	791	Tonga	216
Bhutan	496	Lao People's Democratic Republic	545	Uganda	699
Botswana	(200)	Lesotho	493	United Republic of Tanzania	753
Burundi	2,669	Malawi	739	Upper Volta	1,771
Cape Verde	346	Maldives	93	Viet Nam	20
Central African Republic	18	Mali	1,816	Yemen	1,171
Chad	12	Mauritania	577		
Comoros	784	Nepal	355	Subtotal	27,958
Democratic Yemen	2,220	Nicaragua	257		
Djibouti	456	Niger	3,019	Regional Africa	306
Equatorial Guinea	214	Rwanda	1,771		
Ethiopia	(126)	Samoa	340	Total	28,264

*Figures are estimates not necessarily corresponding to audited figures given in text.

SOURCE: DP/1984/5/Add.6.

CONTRIBUTIONS TO UNCDF, 1983 AND 1984
(as at 31 December 1983; in US dollar equivalent)

Country	1983 payment	1984 pledge	Country	1983 payment	1984 pledge
Afghanistan	2,000	2,000	Mauritius	1,216	—
Algeria	37,000	37,000	Morocco	—	6,337
Argentina	49,500	—	Nepal	1,000	—
Australia	539,220	—	Netherlands	5,120,999	3,828,383
Austria	17,339	15,789	Nicaragua	1,000	—
Bangladesh	3,503	3,750	Norway	4,142,857	2,933,333
Benin	6,000	—	Senegal	27,573	15,410
Bhutan	2,530	1,650	Sierra Leone	—	4,000
Botswana	4,717	4,587	Somalia	—	1,295
Cape Verde	2,000	—	Sweden	4,143,480	—
China	112,245	151,515	Switzerland	2,630,654	1,942,661
Cuba	23,261	23,049	Tunisia	1,846	3,043
Cyprus	500	—	Turkey	152,781	153,153
Democratic Yemen	1,602	1,760	United Republic of Cameroon	829	—
Denmark	2,116,402	2,040,816	United Republic of Tanzania	1,643	1,643
Finland	648,148	991,379	United States	1,900,000	2,000,000
Greece	10,000	10,000	Upper Volta	—	1,211
Guinea-Bissau	376	—	Viet Nam	1,000	1,000
Italy	1,886,792	2,147,239	Yemen	—	3,420
Jamaica	3,200	3,000	Yugoslavia	88,800	88,800
Japan	500,000	—	Zambia	16,807	17,164
Lao People's Democratic Republic	—	1,500	Zimbabwe	6,510	5,556
Lesotho	2,000	1,500			
Malawi	7,273	6,250	Total	24,215,203	16,449,793
Maldives	600	600			

SOURCE: A/39/5/Add.1.

subsequently, 20 projects were put to the UNCDF Projects Committee for approval. At year-end, there were 52 projects in the active pipeline at various stages of preparation, totalling some $77 million.

UNCDF also participated in two round-table donor meetings organized by UNDP for LDCs.

Programme resources. Voluntary contributions received by UNCDF in 1983 amounted to $24.2 million (down from $27.9 million in 1982).[3] In addition, UNCDF received in 1983 $4.2 million in trust fund contributions conditioned on procurement of goods and services in the donor countries (against commitments of $5.6 million), as well as cost-sharing contributions totalling $200,000 (against a commitment of $700,000). As at 31 December, pledges for 1984 amounted to $16.5 million (see table above).

Of the 12 major donors contributing to UNCDF, 10 made their annual pledges in national currencies. Some increased their contributions for 1983 and 1984; those increases, however, were offset by the strength of the United States dollar and also by reduced contributions from two major donors. Although contributions did not reach anticipated levels, trust fund and cost-sharing contributions enabled the Fund to approve $30.2 million in new commitments.

At year-end, total cumulative commitments amounted to $307.4 million, while outstanding commitments under partial funding amounted to $143.7 million (net of amounts related to trust fund and cost-sharing contributions which by their nature required full funding). The Fund's total available resources at year-end amounted to $121.1 million, including the operational reserve of $28.6 million.

Expenditures in 1983 were $27.3 million—$25.3

million in project costs and $2 million for administrative and programme support costs.

UNDP Council action. The Governing Council, on 23 June,[4] took note of the Administrator's report on UNCDF for 1982[5] and in particular of his resource projections for 1983-1986. The Administrator projected annual project approvals of $34 million for 1983, rising to $40 million in 1986. Project commitments in excess of balance of resources and operational reserve were expected to be $52.3 million in 1983, rising to $64.5 million in 1986, while total resources were projected at $101.9 million for 1983, dropping to $91 million in 1986.

On 24 June 1983, in a decision on the Substantial New Programme of Action for the 1980s for LDCs (p. 431), the Council reiterated its appeal for increased contributions to the Special Measures Fund for LDCs and UNCDF. Also on 24 June,[6] the Council took a decision on trust funds conditioned on procurement from a donor country (see above), which also had a bearing on UNCDF's operations. Support cost reimbursement arrangements (see above) for activities financed also from UNCDF resources were dealt with in another decision.[7] The Council decided that a 5 per cent rate should be applied to the reimbursement of support costs for projects financed from UNCDF resources and executed by UNDP's Office for Projects Execution, and that reimbursement of such costs to executing agencies for activities financed from UNCDF resources would continue.

REFERENCES

[1]DP/1984/44. [2]E/1983/20 (dec. 83/32). [3]YUN 1982, p. 671. [4]E/1983/20 (dec. 83/19). [5]DP/1983/33. [6]E/1983/20 (dec. 83/32). [7]*Ibid.* (dec. 83/36).

Chapter III

Economic assistance, disasters and emergency relief

The United Nations continued in 1983 to provide special economic, humanitarian and disaster relief assistance to affected countries, notably in Africa.

The Economic and Social Council, at its second session of 1983, heard the United Nations Joint Co-ordinator for Special Economic Assistance Programmes report on the situation in 14 African countries and Tonga, and took note of oral reports by the United Nations Disaster Relief Co-ordinator on measures to alleviate the effects of disasters, and by the United Nations High Commissioner for Refugees (UNHCR) on assistance to refugees and displaced persons in Africa.

In December, the General Assembly adopted a series of resolutions calling for economic assistance to Benin (resolution 38/210), Cape Verde (38/219), the Central African Republic (38/211), Chad (38/214), the Comoros (38/209), Djibouti (38/213), Equatorial Guinea (38/224), the Gambia (38/212), Ghana (38/203), Guinea-Bissau (38/221), Lesotho (38/215), Mozambique (38/208), Sierra Leone (38/205) and Uganda (38/207). In other regions, the Assembly urged such assistance to Democratic Yemen (38/206), Nicaragua (38/223) and Vanuatu (38/218).

The United Nations system, notably the Office of the United Nations Disaster Relief Co-ordinator (UNDRO), continued to respond to emergency situations arising from natural disasters, and the Assembly urged assistance to countries in the Sudano-Sahelian region (resolution 38/225) and East Africa (38/216), which suffered from drought; Bolivia, Ecuador and Peru (38/222), which were victims of floods; Honduras and Nicaragua (38/217), which coped with the effects of floods and drought; and Yemen (38/204), in its recovery following a 1982 earthquake. The Assembly also adopted resolution 38/202 on strengthening the capacity of the United Nations to respond to natural and other disaster situations.

Emergency humanitarian assistance continued to be provided to displaced persons, as well as Palestinians, in Lebanon, and the Assembly, in resolution 38/220, called for intensified assistance to meet Lebanon's reconstruction and development needs. In other action, the Assembly, by resolution 38/201, dissolved the United Nations Emergency Operation Trust Fund, established in 1974 to help low-income developing countries cope with the economic crisis situation.

Topics related to this chapter. Development policy and international economic co-operation:
special economic areas—developing countries. Regional economic and social activities: Asia and the Pacific—typhoons. Food: food aid. Environment: desertification. Children: emergency relief. Refugees and displaced persons: refugee assistance.

ECONOMIC AND SOCIAL COUNCIL ACTION

The Economic and Social Council, which considered the question of special economic, humanitarian and disaster relief assistance at its second regular session of 1983, adopted decision 1983/172 without vote on 28 July, on the recommendation of its Third (Programme and Co-ordination) Committee.

Special economic, humanitarian and disaster relief assistance

At its 40th plenary meeting, on 28 July 1983, the Council:

(*a*) Took note of:

(i) The oral report made by the Joint Co-ordinator for Special Economic Assistance Programmes, on behalf of the Secretary-General, on assistance to Benin, Botswana, Cape Verde, the Central African Republic, Chad, the Comoros, Djibouti, the Gambia, Guinea-Bissau, Lesotho, Liberia, Mozambique, Sierra Leone, Tonga and Uganda;

(ii) The oral report made by the United Nations High Commissioner for Refugees, on behalf of the Secretary-General, on assistance to refugees in Somalia, assistance to displaced persons in Ethiopia, humanitarian assistance to refugees in Djibouti and assistance to student refugees in southern Africa;

(*b*) Took note further of the statements made by delegations during the discussion of the item entitled "Special economic, humanitarian and disaster relief assistance" at the second regular session of 1983 of the Council;

(*c*) Decided to appeal to all Member States, organs and organizations of the United Nations system, and to other intergovernmental and non-governmental organizations, to continue their efforts to provide the necessary assistance, pursuant to the relevant resolutions of the General Assembly and the Economic and Social Council.

Economic and Social Council decision 1983/172

Adopted without vote

Approved by Third Committee (E/1983/116) without vote, 22 July (meeting 16); oral proposal by Chairman; agenda item 17.
Meeting number. ESC 40.

Economic assistance

The United Nations continued in 1983 to mobilize special economic assistance programmes for a number of developing countries identified by the General Assembly as facing particularly onerous economic difficulties. Often, those difficulties had been aggravated by such unpredictable events as internal strife, natural disasters or an unexpected economic malaise; their fragile economies had been exacerbated by the global recession, foreign exchange position and domestic economic performance, characterized by reduced government revenues and curtailed investment expenditures.

The United Nations Joint Co-ordinator for Special Economic Assistance Programmes, Sotirios Mousouris, told the Assembly's Second (Economic and Financial) Committee on 10 November that although some countries had averted further deterioration in their economies and a few were showing signs of recovery, many others faced heightened economic precariousness and an increased severity in their adjustment programmes. In addition, large population groups were suffering the consequences of adverse climatic conditions, which had sharply reduced food availability and eroded nutritional standards. The influx of refugees, displaced persons or repatriates in some countries was an additional strain.

Reports of the Secretary-General. In October, the Secretary-General reported to the Assembly on the implementation of the Substantial New Programme of Action for the 1980s for the Least Developed Countries (SNPA),[1] adopted by the 1981 United Nations Conference on the Least Developed Countries[2] and endorsed that year by the Assembly.[3] SNPA was aimed at transforming the economies of the least developed countries (LDCs) towards self-sustained development and enabling them to provide their people—particularly the rural and urban poor—with internationally accepted minimum standards of nutrition, health, transport, communication, housing and education. It recognized that only a substantial increase in official development assistance (ODA), in real terms, during the current decade would enable these countries to achieve the objectives of their national programmes.

The report described recent economic performance and national action in the 36 LDCs (see Chapter I of this section), United Nations and other international assistance, follow-up and monitoring of SNPA implementation, and the outcome of the sixth session of the United Nations Conference on Trade and Development (UNCTAD) (see Chapter IV of this section).

Within the United Nations system, the Director-General for Development and International Economic Co-operation, in consultation with the UNCTAD Secretary-General, convened inter-agency consultations on a regular basis to mobilize and co-ordinate all United Nations activities for SNPA implementation. While the system continued to provide to LDCs a high proportion of the grant resources at its disposal—an average of 36 per cent over the 1980-1982 period—its total expenditure in, and the share of concessional loans to, LDCs decreased by 10 per cent in 1982 as compared to 1981, reflecting the stagnating or declining availability of resources. According to the latest estimate, some $45.6 billion in net capital was required for 1981-1985 simply to maintain the dismal growth trend of the past in LDCs. The operational activities of the United Nations system were considered to be essential in offsetting the inequalities in the overall ODA distribution to LDCs.

The Secretary-General warned that, unless greater resources were forthcoming, financial constraints facing the United Nations Development Programme (UNDP)—the main source of multilateral technical co-operation to those countries—and other United Nations agencies could affect their ability effectively to assist LDCs in achieving SNPA objectives.

In a September report,[4] the Secretary-General described special programmes of economic assistance to 12 African countries—Benin, Botswana, Cape Verde, the Central African Republic, the Comoros, Djibouti, the Gambia, Guinea-Bissau, Lesotho, Liberia, Mozambique and Uganda. The report, based on information submitted by the countries concerned, was intended as an interim summary document pending the dispatch of visiting missions in 1984; the countries opted for this measure in the belief that a longer interval between missions would allow for observing sufficiently significant evolution in situations and thus result in reports of greater depth and usefulness than in the past when missions were dispatched annually.

The report noted that those countries had an average per capita income of less than one third of that of oil-importing developing countries, suffered from severe balance-of-payments deficits and precarious reserves, and often depended on one or two commodities for most of their export earnings. Despite compensatory financing provided under the compensatory financing facility of the International Monetary Fund (IMF) and the STABEX scheme of the European Economic Community (EEC), debt-servicing was consuming a substantial proportion of the already reduced export earnings in low-income African countries, rising from 8.8 per cent in 1980 to 28.3 per cent in 1983, including accumulated commercial arrears. Import curtailment to reduce external accounts had seriously affected not only the manufacturing sector but also agriculture, transport and health care; in more than half of the countries concerned, real per capita income had fallen dramatically during the previous decade. While SNPA targeted the ODA flows to LDCs at 0.15 per cent of the gross national product (GNP) of the industrialized countries by 1985, the Organisation for Economic Co-operation and Development estimated the figure in 1982 at 0.09 per cent.

The Secretary-General observed that, in addition to political uncertainties and changes that were not conducive to attracting investment, the combination of negligible past investment, lack of domestic resources from which to generate capital formation and inadequate aid flows augured poorly for economic progress, making it virtually impossible for the countries in question to make significant progress in development on the basis of their own efforts and resources. Often the issue at hand was simply to meet the food requirements and other basic needs of the population.

By an October report,[5] the Secretary-General informed the General Assembly of economic assistance provided by the United Nations to 16 countries—including all those covered in his September report, as well as Chad, Sao Tome and Principe, Sierra Leone and Tonga—in accordance with the 1982 Assembly resolutions adopted on each of them.[6] Such assistance generally focused on food, agriculture, water resources and development of a wide range of basic infrastructures and services.

Africa

The General Assembly, in resolution 38/5 on co-operation between the United Nations and the Organization of African Unity, thanked the Secretary-General for mobilizing special programmes of economic assistance for African States experiencing grave economic difficulties, in particular for newly independent African States, the front-line States and other independent States of southern Africa (see POLITICAL AND SECURITY QUESTIONS, Chapter V). It expressed appreciation to the World Bank, UNDP and other concerned international financial institutions for their assistance to the countries that were least developed or requiring special economic assistance programmes, and called on the international community to provide assistance to these and other African States, including those affected by natural calamities.

In addition, the Assembly, by resolution 38/216, called for assistance to the drought-stricken areas of Djibouti, Ethiopia, Kenya, Somalia, the Sudan and Uganda.

By resolution 38/39 C on the effects of *apartheid* on the countries of southern Africa, the Assembly called for international assistance to enable the independent States in the subregion to defend their sovereignty and territorial integrity, and rebuild their economies.

Benin

The Secretary-General, in his September report on special programmes of economic assistance,[4] observed that Benin, whose economic base rested on a few export commodities, continued to suffer a chronic trade deficit. The Government needed food aid urgently, as the late arrival of the rainy season had set back the planting of the staple crop (maize), and below-average yields were expected; the repatriation of its people from Nigeria in early 1983 had also taken a serious toll.

However, the country's gross domestic product (GDP) had shown a modest growth, the social infrastructure was improving, and administrative reforms had been introduced to facilitate implementation of its second development plan (1983-1987), which incorporated the special programme of economic assistance consisting of 51 projects. The programme's cost, initially estimated at $149.3 million, was revised at $257.2 million after a review in July 1983; in mid-1983, financing amounting to some $96 million had been secured or pledged. A round-table conference, organized by the Government at Cotonou from 1 to 4 March 1983, planned the strategy for 1983-1987 and proposed 138 projects with a total requirement of $822 million in external financial assistance, in such areas as agriculture, water control, animal production, fishing resources, forestry, industrial development, energy, transportation, housing, education and health. At the conference, 10 countries and several organizations and private companies announced interest in providing financial and technical assistance.

GENERAL ASSEMBLY ACTION

On 20 December, the General Assembly, acting on the recommendation of the Second Committee, adopted resolution 38/210 without vote.

Special economic assistance to Benin
The General Assembly,

Recalling its resolutions 35/88 of 5 December 1980, 36/208 of 17 December 1981 and 37/151 of 17 December 1982, in which it appealed to the international community to provide effective and continuous financial, material and technical assistance to Benin so as to help that country overcome its financial and economic difficulties,

Recalling also Security Council resolution 419(1977) of 24 November 1977, in which the Council appealed to all States and all appropriate international organizations, including the United Nations and the specialized agencies, to assist Benin,

Having heard the statement made by the representative of Benin on 10 November 1983 describing his country's serious economic and financial situation and the measures adopted by his Government to address those difficulties,

Having considered the summary report of the Secretary-General,

Noting from that report that, despite a variety of adverse factors, Benin continues to make some progress in its development efforts as a result of the measures adopted by the Government and the assistance provided by the international community,

Deeply concerned, however, by the fact that Benin continues to experience serious economic and financial difficulties, characterized by a severe balance-of-payments disequilibrium, heavy burdens of external debt and a lack of resources to implement its planned economic and social development programme,

Noting also that continued unfavourable climatic conditions in the coastal and northern areas of Benin have entailed losses in agricultural and livestock production,

Having noted the efforts of the Government of Benin to mobilize international support for the country's development plan through the organization of a round-table conference held at Cotonou in March 1983 with the assistance of the United Nations Development Programme,

Bearing in mind that Benin is classified as one of the least developed countries,

1. *Expresses its appreciation* to the Secretary-General for the measures he has taken to organize and mobilize support for the international programme of economic assistance for Benin;

2. *Reiterates its endorsement* of the assessment and recommendations of the review mission dispatched to Benin in July 1982, contained in the annex to the report of the Secretary-General;

3. *Notes with satisfaction* the interest and support for the development plan of Benin expressed by the participants in the round-table conference;

4. *Appeals* to Member States, international financial institutions, the specialized agencies and other organizations of the United Nations system to respond generously and urgently to the needs of Benin, as set out in the country's development plan for 1983-1987;

5. *Expresses its appreciation* for the assistance already given or pledged to Benin by Member States, organizations of the United Nations system and regional, interregional and intergovernmental organizations;

6. *Notes with appreciation* the measures that are being taken by the Government of Benin to strengthen the country's economy through financial and administrative reforms;

7. *Reiterates the appeal* it has addressed to all Member States to provide substantial and appropriate assistance bilaterally and multilaterally, if possible in the form of grants-in-aid or loans granted on favourable terms, in order to enable Benin to carry out fully the recommended special programme of economic assistance;

8. *Requests* the appropriate bodies and programmes of the United Nations—in particular the United Nations Development Programme, the Food and Agriculture Organization of the United Nations, the International Fund for Agricultural Development and the United Nations Children's Fund—to maintain and expand their programmes of assistance to Benin, to co-operate closely with the Secretary-General in organizing an effective

international programme of assistance and to report periodically to him on the measures they have taken and the resources they have made available to help that country;

9. *Requests* the Food and Agriculture Organization of the United Nations, the World Food Programme, the International Fund for Agricultural Development, the United Nations Children's Fund and the World Health Organization to provide all possible assistance to help the Government of Benin to meet the critical humanitarian needs of the population through the provision of food aid, medicines and equipment for areas affected by drought;

10. *Invites* the United Nations Development Programme, the United Nations Children's Fund, the World Food Programme, the World Health Organization, the Food and Agriculture Organization of the United Nations, the World Bank and the International Fund for Agricultural Development to bring to the attention of their governing bodies, for their consideration, the special needs of Benin and to report the decisions of those bodies to the Secretary-General by 15 July 1984;

11. *Requests* the Secretary-General:

(a) To continue his efforts to mobilize the necessary resources for an effective programme of financial, technical and material assistance to Benin;

(b) To ensure that the necessary financial and budgetary arrangements are made to continue the organization of the international programme of assistance to Benin and the mobilization of that assistance;

(c) To keep the situation in Benin under constant review, to maintain close contact with Member States, the specialized agencies, regional and other intergovernmental organizations and the international financial institutions concerned and to apprise the Economic and Social Council, at its second regular session of 1984, of the status of the special programme of economic assistance for Benin;

(d) To arrange for a review of the economic situation in Benin and the status of the special programme of economic assistance and to report thereon to the General Assembly at its thirty-ninth session.

General Assembly resolution 38/210

20 December 1983   Meeting 104   Adopted without vote

Approved by Second Committee (A/38/705 & Corr.1) without vote, 28 November (meeting 52); 22-nation draft (A/C.2/38/L.55); agenda item 81.

Sponsors: Afghanistan, Algeria, Angola, Benin, Botswana, Cape Verde, China, Cyprus, Djibouti, France, Gambia, Guinea, Guinea-Bissau, Libyan Arab Jamahiriya, Madagascar, Mali, Pakistan, Romania, Sao Tome and Principe, Sierra Leone, Viet Nam, Zambia.

Meeting numbers. GA 38th session: 2nd Committee 34-38, 44, 52; plenary 104.

Benin told the Second Committee that the underdeveloped and deteriorating state of the national economy and the negative impact of the international economic crisis, coupled with its efforts to cope with the effects of creeping desertification in the north and the drought in the coastal region, justified continuation of the special economic assistance programme.

Botswana

Three factors adversely affected Botswana's economy in 1983—the volatile political situation in southern Africa and refugee inflows; a recurrent and serious drought in the region threatening the majority of the population dependent on agriculture and livestock production, and necessitating food imports; and weaknesses in world mineral markets, especially diamonds, which affected GDP, government revenue and foreign exchange earnings.[4]

Assistance to refugees was provided by UNHCR, the World Food Programme (WFP), EEC and three non-governmental organizations. In view of the poor harvests caused by drought, the Government appealed in April for international assistance in food aid, seeds, water, drilling equipment and financial support; special relief measures were needed for 445,000 affected persons, almost half the national population. As at mid-1983, additional food assistance pledged amounted to 10,000 metric tons, leaving a gap of 40,000 tons to be met. The livestock sector, producing the second largest revenue after diamonds, needed assistance of $800,000 for the purchase of animal feed.

The Secretary-General reported that Botswana's needs for special economic assistance above and beyond normal international aid flows, because of the economic impact of political tensions in the region since 1977,[7] had largely been met. Donors were financing or had pledged to finance public works construction, but additional funds were needed for telecommunications. Most of the remaining needs related to projects encompassed under the programmes of the Southern African Development Co-ordination Conference.

Cape Verde

In 1983, as in the previous 15 years, drought seriously affected the agricultural sector of Cape Verde—a least developed country—comprised of 10 major and 3 smaller islands.[4] Although 65 per cent of the total population lived in rural areas, the agricultural output accounted for only 17 per cent of GDP. Almost half of the population was less than 15 years old and some 30 per cent of the potential labour force was unemployed.

Cape Verde's balance of payments was characterized by a large and growing trade deficit covered by an inflow of foreign assistance and remittances by its emigrant population. While its regular budget had a small surplus until 1982, a relatively small deficit of $4.6 million was expected for 1983, as a result of greater indebtedness, increased value of the dollar, expansion of government services and absorption of the expenditures previously included in the investment budget. The First National Development Plan (1982-1985), approved in December 1982, proposed the creation of 6,000 to 7,000 permanent jobs and improvements in various sectors, and provided for investments of some $417 million, an amount three times

higher than the investments undertaken during the previous four years.

Due to continued drought, the 1983 production of maize and beans was estimated to meet only 18 per cent of the national requirements; Cape Verde faced a food deficit of 37,830 tons, after taking into account purchases and confirmed food aid expected during the year. The Government negotiated with donors for multiyear commitments tied to selected food security goals and financing for urgent development projects.

The Government informed the first round table of its development partners that about 60 per cent of the financial requirements of its National Development Plan had been mobilized, and that lack of funding affected mainly housing, administration and the investment programme of the national development fund (soil and water conservation, and road networks). Of the 10 biggest projects, funding appeared assured for 6 (Maio cement plant, naval workshop at Sao Vicente, electricity and water for Sal Island, telecommunications, food storage and the National People's Assembly) and discussions continued with the donors for three other major projects (promotion of small and medium-sized enterprises, ports of Fogo and Brava, and Sal airport).

GENERAL ASSEMBLY ACTION

On 20 December, the General Assembly adopted resolution 38/219 without vote, acting on the recommendation of the Second Committee.

Assistance to Cape Verde

The General Assembly,

Recalling its resolutions 32/99 of 13 December 1977, 33/127 of 19 December 1978, 34/119 of 14 December 1979, 35/104 of 5 December 1980, 36/211 of 17 December 1981 and 37/152 of 17 December 1982, in which the international community was requested to provide an appropriate level of resources for the implementation of the programme of assistance to Cape Verde as envisaged in the reports of the Secretary-General,

Recalling resolutions 142(VI) and 138(VI) of 2 July 1983 of the United Nations Conference on Trade and Development on the progress in the implementation of the Substantial New Programme of Action for the 1980s for the Least Developed Countries, and on activities in the field of island developing countries,

Noting that Cape Verde is one of the least developed countries and a small archipelagic State, with a fragile and open economy, aggravated by endemic and severe drought,

Reiterating that increased substantial, continuous and predictable assistance from the international community is needed for the effective implementation of the First National Development Plan (1982-1985),

Gravely concerned at the critical food situation in Cape Verde resulting from the failure of seasonal rains and the continuing recurrence of drought,

Recognizing the strenuous efforts deployed by the Government and people of Cape Verde towards the economic and social development of their country despite existing constraints,

1. *Takes note* of the summary report of the Secretary-General prepared in response to General Assembly resolution 37/152;

2. *Expresses its appreciation* to the Secretary-General for the efforts deployed in mobilizing resources for the implementation of the programme of assistance to Cape Verde;

3. *Expresses its gratitude* to States and to international, regional and interregional organizations and other intergovernmental organizations for their contribution to the programme of assistance to Cape Verde;

4. *Reaffirms* the need for all Governments and international organizations to implement their commitments undertaken within the framework of the Substantial New Programme of Action for the 1980s for the Least Developed Countries, particularly those undertaken at the round table of Cape Verde's partners in development, held in June 1982;

5. *Urges* Governments and international, regional and interregional organizations and other intergovernmental organizations to extend and intensify substantially their assistance with a view to implementing the programme of assistance to Cape Verde as soon as possible;

6. *Invites* the international community, in particular donor countries, to take appropriate and urgent measures to support the realization of the First National Development Plan (1982-1985) of Cape Verde;

7. *Requests* the organs, organizations and bodies of the United Nations system to continue and increase their assistance to Cape Verde, to co-operate with the Secretary-General in his efforts to mobilize resources for the implementation of the programme of assistance and to report periodically to him on the measures they have taken and the resources they have made available to help that country;

8. *Calls upon* the international community to continue to contribute generously to all appeals for food and fodder assistance made by the Government of Cape Verde, or on its behalf by the specialized agencies and other competent organizations of the United Nations system, to help it cope with the critical situation in the country;

9. *Once again draws the attention* of the international community to the special account established at United Nations Headquarters by the Secretary-General, in accordance with General Assembly resolution 32/99, for the purpose of facilitating the channelling of contributions to Cape Verde;

10. *Invites* the United Nations Development Programme, the United Nations Conference on Trade and Development, the United Nations Children's Fund, the World Food Programme, the World Health Organization, the United Nations Industrial Development Organization, the Food and Agriculture Organization of the United Nations, the World Bank and the International Fund for Agricultural Development to continue to consider, through their governing bodies, the special needs of Cape Verde and to report the decisions of those bodies to the Secretary-General by 15 July 1984;

11. *Requests* the Secretary-General:

(a) To continue his efforts to mobilize the necessary resources for implementing the programme of development assistance to Cape Verde;

(b) To keep the situation in Cape Verde under constant review and to apprise the Economic and Social Council, at its second regular session of 1984, of the progress made in the implementation of the present resolution;

(c) To arrange for a review of the economic situation in Cape Verde and to make a substantive report on further progress in organizing and implementing the special programme of economic assistance for that country in time for the matter to be considered by the General Assembly at its thirty-ninth session.

General Assembly resolution 38/219

20 December 1983   Meeting 104   Adopted without vote

Approved by Second Committee (A/38/705 & Corr.1) without vote, 28 November (meeting 52); 45-nation draft (A/C.2/38/L.64), orally revised in informal consultations; agenda item 81.

Sponsors: Afghanistan, Algeria, Angola, Austria, Bangladesh, Benin, Brazil, Canada, Cape Verde, Central African Republic, China, Cuba, Cyprus, Democratic Yemen, Egypt, France, Gambia, Guinea, Guinea-Bissau, Italy, Japan, Liberia, Libyan Arab Jamahiriya, Madagascar, Mauritania, Mozambique, Nepal, Nicaragua, Niger, Nigeria, Pakistan, Panama, Portugal, Sao Tome and Principe, Senegal, Sierra Leone, Sudan, Sweden, Uganda, United Republic of Tanzania, United States, Vanuatu, Yemen, Yugoslavia, Zimbabwe.

Meeting numbers. GA 38th session: 2nd Committee 34-38, 44, 52; plenary 104.

Central African Republic

A drought, lasting from November 1982 until May 1983, had catastrophic effects on the Central African Republic, whose economic slow-down had resulted in loss of fiscal revenues. The landlocked country suffered a loss of food and cash crops, destruction by bush fire of many plantations and forest areas, shortages of electricity, disruption of trade and transport which depended on river navigation, and increased health hazards caused by a shortage of potable water.

The Government appealed for international emergency assistance. As the drought was likely to affect the implementation of the National Programme for 1982-1985, the priorities reflected in the current special economic assistance programme appeared in need of adapting to the new circumstances.

In his September 1983 report on special programmes of economic assistance,[4] the Secretary-General observed that the 1982 production of cotton, the country's major export crop, had amounted to only 40 per cent of the 1977 level, and the coffee crop, another export commodity, was expected to produce in 1983/84 only 30 per cent of the normal yield.

The drought also affected the output and the cost of power supply, which relied on one thermal and two hydroelectric stations. The interruption of river transport led to shortages in the stocks of large volume commodities, and the lack of materials led to a virtual standstill in construction. Industries, particularly the breweries and the factories producing shoes, sheet-metal and aluminium goods, suffered considerable losses.

The losses of government revenue were expected to bring about rising deficits, thus jeopardizing the financial recovery plan prepared with the assistance of IMF. Additional external budgetary support was needed to meet the situation.

Among the United Nations special programmes of economic assistance,[5] an evaluation mission for a hydropower station was planned for late 1983 by the Department of Technical Co-operation for Development.

GENERAL ASSEMBLY ACTION

On 20 December, the General Assembly, acting on the recommendation of the Second Committee, adopted resolution 38/211 without vote.

Assistance for the reconstruction, rehabilitation and development of the Central African Republic

The General Assembly,

Recalling its resolutions 35/87 of 5 December 1980, 36/206 of 17 December 1981 and 37/145 of 17 December 1982, in which it affirmed the urgent need for international action to assist the Government of the Central African Republic in its reconstruction, rehabilitation and development efforts and invited the international community to provide sufficient resources to carry out the programme of assistance to the Central African Republic,

Noting the statement made by the Minister for Foreign Affairs and International Co-operation of the Central African Republic on 10 October 1983, in which he described the serious economic and financial problems of the country and observed that the situation had not improved, owing to the insufficiency of financial resources, and that external assistance continued to be essential,

Noting also the statement made by the representative of the Central African Republic on 10 November 1983, according to which the response of the international community to the urgent appeal of the General Assembly had not been adequate to meet the needs of the situation,

Bearing in mind that the Central African Republic is land-locked and is classified as one of the least developed countries,

Recalling the Substantial New Programme of Action for the 1980s for the Least Developed Countries, which called for increased aid to these countries,

Particularly concerned that the Government of the Central African Republic is unable to provide the population with adequate health, educational and other essential social and public services because of an acute shortage of financial and material resources,

Taking account of the fact that the economic and social situation in the Central African Republic has been further aggravated by an unprecedented drought and a sharp and considerable decrease in export earnings,

Noting with satisfaction the considerable efforts exerted by the Government and people of the Central African Republic for national reconstruction, rehabilitation and development, despite the limitations confronting them,

Having examined the report of the Secretary-General, to which is annexed the report of the mission dispatched to the Central African Republic in June 1982 to carry out a study of the economic situation and the progress being made in organizing and carrying out the special

programme of economic assistance for that country, in accordance with General Assembly resolution 36/206,

Having also examined the summary report of the Secretary-General,

Noting that, according to those reports, the budgetary situation of the Central African Republic continues to make it impossible for the Government to undertake a programme of reconstruction, rehabilitation and development, owing to inadequate external financial assistance,

1. *Expresses its gratification* to the Secretary-General for the efforts he has made to mobilize resources for carrying out the programme of assistance to the Central African Republic;

2. *Expresses its appreciation* to the States, the international, regional and interregional organizations and other intergovernmental organizations for their contribution to the programme of assistance to the Central African Republic;

3. *Notes with concern,* however, that the assistance provided under this heading continues to fall far short of the country's urgent needs;

4. *Urgently draws the attention* of the international community to table 6 of the annex to the Secretary-General's report, which indicates the projects for which financing is partially assured and those for which no financing has been forthcoming;

5. *Reiterates its appeal* to all States to contribute generously, through bilateral or multilateral channels, to the reconstruction, rehabilitation and development of the Central African Republic;

6. *Requests* the appropriate organizations and programmes of the United Nations system—in particular the United Nations Development Programme, the World Bank, the International Monetary Fund, the Food and Agriculture Organization of the United Nations, the International Fund for Agricultural Development, the World Food Programme, the World Health Organization, the United Nations Children's Fund and the United Nations Industrial Development Organization—to maintain their programmes of assistance to the Central African Republic, to co-operate closely with the Secretary-General in his efforts to organize an effective international programme of assistance and to report periodically to him on the steps they have taken and the resources they have made available to help that country;

7. *Calls upon* regional and interregional organizations and other intergovernmental and non-governmental organizations—in particular the European Economic Community, the European Development Fund, the African Development Bank, the Arab Bank for Economic Development in Africa, the Organization of Petroleum Exporting Countries' Fund for International Development, the International Fund for Agricultural Development, the Kuwaiti Fund and the Abu Dhabi Fund—to give urgent consideration to the establishment of a programme of assistance to the Central African Republic or, where one is already in existence, to the expansion and considerable strengthening of that programme with a view to its implementation as soon as possible;

8. *Urges* all States and relevant United Nations bodies—in particular the United Nations Development Programme, the World Food Programme, the United Nations Children's Fund, the World Health Organization, the United Nations Fund for Population Activi-

ties and the United Nations Industrial Development Organization—to provide all possible assistance to help the Government of the Central African Republic to cope with the critical humanitarian needs of the population and to provide, as appropriate, food, medicines and essential equipment for schools and hospitals, as well as to meet the emergency needs of the population in the drought-stricken areas of the country;

9. *Invites* the United Nations Development Programme, the United Nations Children's Fund, the World Food Programme, the World Health Organization, the United Nations Industrial Development Organization, the Food and Agriculture Organization of the United Nations, the World Bank and the International Fund for Agricultural Development to bring to the attention of their governing bodies, for their consideration, the special needs of the Central African Republic and to report the decisions of those bodies to the Secretary-General by 15 July 1984;

10. *Again draws the attention* of the international community to the special account opened by the Secretary-General at United Nations Headquarters, in accordance with General Assembly resolution 35/87, for the purpose of facilitating the channelling of contributions to the Central African Republic;

11. *Requests* the Secretary-General:

(a) To continue his efforts to organize a special emergency assistance programme with regard to food and health, especially medicaments, vaccines, hospital equipment, generating sets for field hospitals, water pumps and food products in order to help the vulnerable populations, whose steadily deteriorating situation is becoming a matter of increasingly serious concern;

(b) To continue also his efforts to mobilize necessary resources for an effective programme of financial, technical and material assistance to the Central African Republic;

(c) To ensure that the necessary financial and budgetary arrangements are made to continue the organization of the international programme of assistance to the Central African Republic and the mobilization of that assistance;

(d) To keep the situation in the Central African Republic under constant review, to maintain close contact with Member States, the specialized agencies, regional and other intergovernmental organizations, and the international financial institutions concerned and to apprise the Economic and Social Council, at its second regular session of 1984, of the status of the special programme of economic assistance for the Central African Republic;

(e) To report on the progress made in the economic situation of the Central African Republic and in organizing and implementing the special programme of economic assistance for that country in time for the matter to be considered by the General Assembly at its thirty-ninth session.

General Assembly resolution 38/211

20 December 1983   Meeting 104   Adopted without vote

Approved by Second Committee (A/38/705 & Corr.1) without vote, 28 November (meeting 52); 28-nation draft (A/C.2/38/L.56); agenda item 81.
Sponsors: Bangladesh, Benin, Burundi, Cape Verde, Central African Republic, Chad, China, Comoros, Congo, Cyprus, Democratic Kampuchea, Djibouti, France, Gabon, Gambia, Guinea-Bissau, Ivory Coast, Liberia, Madagascar, Mauritania, Niger, Pakistan, Panama, Sierra Leone, Thailand, United Republic of Cameroon, Zaire, Zambia.
Meeting numbers. GA 38th session: 2nd Committee 34-38, 44, 52; plenary 26, 104.

Chad

As requested by the General Assembly in December 1982,[8] the Secretary-General reported in June 1983 on the status of special economic assistance for the rehabilitation and reconstruction of Chad.[9] Annexed to the report were the findings of a mission (2-10 May), led by the Director of the United Nations Office for Special Political Questions.

The mission found that nearly 17 years of unrest had taken their toll on Chad (see POLITICAL AND SECURITY QUESTIONS, Chapter V), a situation which had not been made easier by periods of drought and irregular rainfall, a recent outbreak of a cattle disease (*peste bovine*) and lack of trained manpower and of resources for essential education, medical and health services.

Capital flows continued the negative trend of previous years, presumably because of economic conditions in the country, coupled with the high level of external interest rates. Nevertheless, in spite of the decline in exports and a modest growth in imports, there was an overall balance-of-payments surplus at the end of 1982 due to the high level of public transfers. At the end of the first quarter of 1983, only 10 per cent of the Government's revenue budget approved for the year had been received. In the virtual standstill the country's banking system found itself, the Government decreed, in April 1983, the continuation of a credit moratorium to alleviate the burden of previous obligations. With the assistance of UNDP, the Government undertook studies on the possible establishment of a bank for reconstruction and development.

In the five months following a November 1982 international pledging conference on special aid for Chad,[10] there had been a significant response in the form of food and other emergency supplies, as well as commitments to finance projects. While the most immediate emergency situation could thus be dealt with, Chad's continuing need for international assistance was demonstrated, in part, by an estimated food deficit of 192,000 tons in 1983, of which 50,000 tons needed to be distributed before the rainy season in June. UNDRO issued an international appeal in May 1983, urging donors to help avoid disaster by forwarding food aid in time. In connection with food distribution, the Government had received transport equipment, and logistical support pledged by United Nations organizations amounted to a trucking/trailing capacity of 473.5 tons; an additional 337 tons had been provided by non-governmental organizations and a further 762 tons bilaterally. There remained a deficit of some $1.6 million in the logistical resources for food aid distribution. Resources were also needed to increase storage capacity.

The food situation had been made more critical by the return of approximately 400,000 Chadian nationals from neighbouring countries, for whom the Government pursued a policy of economic and social reintegration.

Chad's priority programme, which had been submitted at the 1982 pledging conference to cover medium-term needs for rehabilitation and reconstruction during 1983-1984, consisted of 122 projects in various sectors at a total cost of about $341 million; of those projects, 32 had been funded to the level of $107 million, 59 were in the planning or negotiating stage with interested donors, and 31 were without response.

Among several United Nations organizations providing aid to Chad during 1983,[5] WFP was continuing three development projects valued at $17.5 million and five emergency operations valued at $16.9 million.

GENERAL ASSEMBLY ACTION

On 20 December, the General Assembly adopted resolution 38/214 without vote. It acted on the recommendation of the Second Committee.

Special economic assistance to Chad

The General Assembly,

Recalling its resolution 37/155 of 17 December 1982 and its previous resolutions on the reconstruction, rehabilitation and development of Chad, emergency humanitarian assistance to Chad and special economic assistance to that country,

Having considered the reports of the Secretary-General on special economic assistance to Chad, relating, *inter alia,* to the economic and financial situation of Chad, the status of assistance provided for the rehabilitation and reconstruction of the country and the progress made in organizing and executing the special programme of economic assistance for that country,

Noting that the stability of the situation in Chad enabled the Secretary-General to organize an International Conference on Assistance to Chad, in November 1982 at Geneva, in close co-operation with the Government of Chad,

Aware that the resumption of fighting in Chad has prevented the States and agencies that participated in the International Conference on Assistance to Chad from fully honouring their commitments,

Noting with concern that the resumption of fighting is aggravating the situation of dire need in Chad resulting from the systematic destruction of the economic and social infrastructure during seventeen years of war and from the effects of natural disasters,

Considering that Chad is included in the list of the least developed countries and is therefore entitled to the benefits provided for in the relevant General Assembly resolutions,

Recognizing the need for the provision by the international community of emergency humanitarian assistance, particularly in the areas of food and health, to the population of Chad,

1. *Expresses its gratitude* to the States and organizations that responded to the appeals of the Government of Chad and of the Secretary-General by furnishing assistance to Chad;

2. *Also expresses its gratitude* to the Secretary-General for his efforts to mobilize assistance to Chad;

3. *Again appeals* to the international community to provide, as a matter of urgency, the necessary assistance to the people of Chad, who have suffered from the war;

4. *Renews the request* made to States, appropriate organizations and programmes of the United Nations and international financial institutions to contribute to the rehabilitation and reconstruction of Chad through bilateral or multilateral channels;

5. *Takes note* of the desire of Chad to organize, as soon as circumstances permit, a conference of donors and contributors of funds to consider a general programme of reconstruction and development and to finance detailed projects in the areas of priority;

6. *Requests* the Administrator of the United Nations Development Programme to give all the necessary assistance to Chad for the preparation and organization of the conference, in accordance with the arrangements agreed upon at the International Conference on Assistance to Chad held in November 1982;

7. *Also requests* the Secretary-General:

(*a*) To monitor, in close collaboration with the humanitarian agencies concerned, the humanitarian needs, particularly in the areas of food and health, of the people affected by the war and the drought;

(*b*) To mobilize the humanitarian assistance of the international community for the persons who have suffered as a result of the war in Chad;

(*c*) To pursue his efforts to organize the programme of financial assistance to Chad;

(*d*) To apprise the Economic and Social Council, at its second regular session of 1984, of the situation and to report thereon to the General Assembly at its thirty-ninth session.

General Assembly resolution 38/214

20 December 1983   Meeting 104   Adopted without vote

Approved by Second Committee (A/38/705 & Corr.1) without vote, 28 November (meeting 52); 33-nation draft (A/C.2/38/L.59); agenda item 81.

Sponsors: Burundi, Canada, Central African Republic, Chad, Comoros, Congo, Cyprus, Djibouti, Egypt, France, Gabon, Gambia, Guinea, Guinea-Bissau, Ivory Coast, Lesotho, Liberia, Madagascar, Mali, Mauritania, Pakistan, Rwanda, Senegal, Sierra Leone, Swaziland, Thailand, Togo, Tunisia, Uganda, United Republic of Cameroon, United States, Zaire, Zambia.

Meeting numbers. GA 38th session: 2nd Committee 34-38, 44, 52; plenary 104.

Comoros

The economic situation of the Comoros, a least developed country extremely poor in natural resources, was further aggravated by a cyclone that hit the archipelago in January 1983.[4] The rapid population growth of 3.5 per cent per annum exacerbated an already difficult food situation heavily dependent on imports, and there was widespread malnutrition, especially protein deficiency. The physical infrastructure and basic utilities remained insufficient.

The Comorian economy depended on a few exports crops with large year-to-year fluctuations in the world market: vanilla, ylang-ylang perfume essence, cloves and copra. While agriculture generated some 45 per cent of GDP and was slowly expanding, rice production fell short of national needs, and imports had risen to between 20,000 and 25,000 tons per year; efforts were being made to stimulate maize production as a substitute for rice in the national diet.

An intermediate development plan for 1983-1986 was being finalized for presentation to a donor's conference in early 1984. The plan's six priority areas were: food self-sufficiency; improved inter-island communication; energy production and water supplies; health and population programmes; training; and land and human settlements development. It envisaged an investment programme of $340.6 million, of which $108.5 million had been mobilized as at mid-1983. Of the remainder still being sought, $80.6 million was needed for 1983-1986 and the balance for 1987-1990. From the 98 projects in the investment programme, the Government had selected 19, costing $89.7 million, for inclusion in the special economic assistance programme.

Several United Nations organizations gave such assistance to the Comoros in 1983.[5] Following the cyclone in January, UNDRO launched an appeal for assistance, generating $1.9 million in emergency aid as at mid-February. Among others, WFP had an ongoing project worth $7.75 million and an emergency project costing $1.6 million. A UNDP project on rural development and poultry, worth $3.2 million, was being implemented by the Food and Agriculture Organization of the United Nations (FAO). The International Development Association (IDA), an affiliate of the World Bank, approved a $2.3 million credit to help strengthen the newly created Development Bank of the Comoros by providing it with funds needed for lending during 1983-1986 to small- and medium-scale enterprises and by furnishing it with technical assistance and training.

GENERAL ASSEMBLY ACTION

On 20 December, the General Assembly, acting on the recommendation of the Second Committee, adopted resolution 38/209 without vote.

Assistance to the Comoros

The General Assembly,

Recalling its resolution 37/154 of 17 December 1982 and its previous resolutions on assistance to the Comoros, in which it appealed to the international community to provide effective and continuous financial, material and technical assistance to the Comoros in order to help that country overcome its financial and economic difficulties,

Taking note of the special problems confronting the Comoros as a developing island country and as one of the least developed countries,

Noting that the Government of the Comoros has given priority to the questions of infrastructure, transport and telecommunications,

Noting also the economic difficulties arising from the country's scarcity of natural resources, compounded by the recent drought and cyclones,

Noting further the grave budgetary and balance-of-payments problems facing the Comoros,

Aware of the intention of the Government of the Comoros to convene a donors' conference at the end of the first quarter of 1984,

Having examined the summary report of the Secretary-General,

1. *Expresses its appreciation* to the Secretary-General for the steps he has taken to mobilize assistance for the Comoros;

2. *Notes with satisfaction* the response by various Member States, organizations of the United Nations system and other organizations to its appeals and those of the Secretary-General for assistance to the Comoros;

3. *Notes with concern,* however, that the assistance thus far provided continues to fall short of the country's urgent requirements and that assistance is still urgently required to carry out the projects identified in the annex to the report of the Secretary-General;

4. *Appeals* to those States and organizations invited to the donors' conference to be held in the Comoros early in 1984 to contribute generously to the programme of assistance that will be presented by the Government of the Comoros at that time;

5. *Renews its appeal* to Member States, the appropriate organs, programmes and organizations of the United Nations system, regional and international organizations and other intergovernmental and non-governmental organizations, as well as international financial institutions, to provide the Comoros with assistance to enable it to cope with its difficult economic situation and pursue its development goals;

6. *Requests* the appropriate programmes and organizations of the United Nations system to increase their current programmes of assistance to the Comoros, to co-operate closely with the Secretary-General in organizing an effective international programme of assistance and to report periodically to him on the steps they have taken and the resources they have made available to help that country;

7. *Requests* the Secretary-General:

(a) To continue his efforts to mobilize the necessary resources for an effective programme of financial, technical and material assistance to the Comoros;

(b) To keep the situation in the Comoros under constant review, to maintain close contact with Member States, the specialized agencies, regional and other intergovernmental organizations and international financial institutions concerned and to apprise the Economic and Social Council, at its second regular session of 1984, of the current status of the special programme of economic assistance for the Comoros;

(c) To report on the progress made in the economic situation of the Comoros and in organizing and implementing the special programme of economic assistance for that country in time for the matter to be considered by the General Assembly at its thirty-ninth session.

General Assembly resolution 38/209

20 December 1983   Meeting 104   Adopted without vote

Approved by Second Committee (A/38/705 & Corr.1) without vote, 28 November (meeting 52); 29-nation draft (A/C.2/38/L.54); agenda item 81.

Sponsors: Angola, Benin, Botswana, Burundi, Cape Verde, Central African Republic, Comoros, Cyprus, Djibouti, France, Gambia, Guinea, Guinea-Bissau, India, Indonesia, Japan, Liberia, Madagascar, Malawi, Mauritania, Pakistan, Romania, Rwanda, Senegal, Sierra Leone, Thailand, Turkey, United Republic of Tanzania, Zambia.

Meeting numbers. GA 38th session: 2nd Committee 34-38, 44, 52; plenary 104.

Djibouti

Djibouti, which had been added in 1982[11] to the United Nations list of least developed countries, was faced with chronic water shortages and recurrent drought, according to the Secretary-General's September report on special programmes of economic assistance.[4] The latest population estimate of 382,000 included 42,000 refugees (see Chapter XXI of this section) and 10,000 foreigners. The Government followed a cautious budgetary policy, with income exceeding recurrent expenditures and capital expenditures limited to the available domestic and external resources. Its revenue depended mainly on indirect taxes, largely on products consumed by the expatriate community.

Djibouti, which had received some $478 million in special economic assistance during 1978-1982, organized a donors' conference (21-23 November 1983), at which it presented an investment programme costing $570 million for 1983-1988. In addition to 72 projects for which financing of $310 million was sought at the conference, the investment programme included 45 projects for which $240 million had already been secured or pledged. The balance of $20 million was to be raised domestically for the programme, which aimed at raising the living standards of the low-income groups—directly by assisting herdsmen, fishermen and farmers, and by improving living conditions of the urban poor, and indirectly by increasing employment opportunities and training facilities.

Among United Nations agencies providing special programmes of economic assistance to Djibouti,[5] WFP had ongoing projects with a total value of $13.1 million. A $6.4 million credit had been approved by IDA in support of a three-year road-improvement programme and for transport cost reduction.

GENERAL ASSEMBLY ACTION

On 20 December, the General Assembly, acting on the recommendation of the Second Committee, adopted resolution 38/213 without vote.

Assistance to Djibouti

The General Assembly,

Recalling its resolution 37/153 of 17 December 1982 and its previous resolutions on assistance to Djibouti, in which it drew the attention of the international community to the critical economic situation confronting Djibouti and to the country's urgent need for assistance,

Recalling also its resolution 37/176 of 17 December 1982, in which it called upon the international community to continue to support the efforts made by the Government of Djibouti to cope with the needs of the refugee population,

Recalling further its resolution 36/221 of 17 December 1981, in which it appealed to the international community to contribute generously towards the projects and programmes to help the drought-affected populations,

Having in mind its resolution 37/133 of 17 December 1982, in which it decided to include Djibouti in the list of the least developed countries,

Having examined the summary report of the Secretary-General,

Noting the critical economic situation of Djibouti and the list of urgent and priority projects, formulated by the Government, that require international assistance,

Noting also that the Government of Djibouti convened a donors' conference from 21 to 23 November 1983 in order to seek international support for the country's economic and social development,

1. *Expresses its appreciation* to the Secretary-General for the steps he has taken to organize an international programme of economic assistance for Djibouti;

2. *Notes with appreciation* the assistance already provided or pledged to Djibouti by Member States, organizations of the United Nations system and other organizations;

3. *Again draws the attention* of the international community to the difficult economic situation confronting Djibouti and to the severe structural constraints to its development;

4. *Renews its appeal* to Member States, the appropriate organs, organizations and programmes of the United Nations system, regional and international organizations and other intergovernmental and non-governmental organizations, as well as international financial institutions, to provide assistance bilaterally and multilaterally, as appropriate, to Djibouti in order to enable it to cope with its difficult economic situation and to implement its development strategies;

5. *Requests* the appropriate specialized agencies and other organizations of the United Nations system to maintain and to increase their current and future programmes of assistance to Djibouti, to co-operate closely with the Secretary-General in organizing an effective international programme of assistance and to report periodically to him on the steps they have taken and the resources they have made available to help that country;

6. *Expresses its appreciation* to those States and organizations which participated in the donors' conference, held in Djibouti from 21 to 23 November 1983, and urges them to respond generously to the programme of assistance that was presented by the Government of Djibouti at that time;

7. *Requests* the Secretary-General:

(a) To continue his efforts to mobilize the necessary resources for an effective programme of financial, technical and material assistance to Djibouti;

(b) To continue to ensure that adequate financial and budgetary arrangements are made to mobilize resources and to co-ordinate international assistance to Djibouti;

(c) To keep the situation in Djibouti under constant review, to maintain close contact with Member States, the specialized agencies, regional and other intergovernmental organizations and the international financial institutions concerned and to apprise the Economic and Social Council, at its second regular session of 1984, of the current status of the special programme of economic assistance for Djibouti;

(d) To report on the progress made in the economic situation of Djibouti and in organizing and implementing the special programme of economic assistance for that country in time for the matter to be considered by the General Assembly at its thirty-ninth session.

General Assembly resolution 38/213

20 December 1983   Meeting 104   Adopted without vote

Approved by Second Committee (A/38/705 & Corr.1) without vote, 28 November (meeting 52); 36-nation draft (A/C.2/38/L.58); agenda item 81.

Sponsors: Algeria, Bahrain, Benin, Botswana, Burundi, Cape Verde, Chad, Cyprus, Democratic Yemen, Djibouti, France, Gambia, Guinea, Guinea-Bissau, Japan, Jordan, Lebanon, Lesotho, Liberia, Libyan Arab Jamahiriya, Madagascar, Mali, Oman, Pakistan, Qatar, Rwanda, Sao Tome and Principe, Saudi Arabia, Sierra Leone, Somalia, Tunisia, Uganda, United Arab Emirates, United Republic of Cameroon, United Republic of Tanzania, Zambia.

Meeting numbers. GA 38th session: 2nd Committee 34-38, 44, 52; plenary 104.

Equatorial Guinea

In 1983, Equatorial Guinea's outstanding external public and publicly guaranteed disbursed debt was estimated at $90 million, approximately 50 per cent more than the estimated GDP, and the short-term debt was also growing rapidly. The total debt was about six times the value of exports, while the balance-of-payments deficit for 1983 was estimated at $12.8 million. The Governments's overall budgetary deficit grew by about 35 per cent between 1982 and 1983.

Equatorial Guinea pursued efforts to improve its statistical data base. A demographic census was carried out in 1983 and yielded basic preliminary figures on the national population (estimated at 300,000) and its regional distribution. Projects funded by UNDP in economic planning and statistics were under way to draw up a GDP estimate for the country, which had been added in 1982[11] to the United Nations list of least developed countries. Total GDP for 1982, estimated at $65 million, gave a per capita income of about $216. The decline during the previous decade of cocoa production was halted, and annual production of the leading export crop, stabilized at around 8,000 metric tons, provided a relatively stable annual foreign-exchange inflow of $11 million to $13 million between 1980 and 1983. Timber exports had increased markedly, from 4,530 tons in 1979 to 62,800 in 1982, providing an income of almost $4 million in 1982 as well as in 1983.

Lack of agricultural statistics on food production made the assessment of the food situation difficult. No large-scale food-crop production projects were in operation; several initiatives in the agricultural sector, undertaken with external assistance, had produced limited results. In 1982-1983, food aid totalled 8,236 tons, of which 48 per cent was provided by WFP. Endowed with a rich loam soil, the country, with external assistance, was expected to achieve self-sufficiency in food in the years to come. Major improvements in the supply of goods in domestic markets were expected to result from the country's integration into the Union Douanière des Etats d'Afrique Centrale, formally achieved at the end of 1983. Integration into the Banque des Etats d'Afrique Centrale

monetary and banking system was under way— an action expected to affect all major economic policy decisions.

Equatorial Guinea's capacity to absorb aid effectively had been strengthened by the efforts to reinforce the administrative and planning machinery. Although the majority of the projects previously proposed had been funded, water and sanitation had received practically none and the Government identified eight projects in that sector that were ready for implementation with external assistance, at a total cost of $6.3 million. In addition, food production and fisheries needed substantial support. A follow-up meeting was held in 1983 to review the results of the 1982 International Conference of Donors for the Economic Reactivation and Development of the Republic of Equatorial Guinea,[12] and the Government's Ministry of Planning was conducting a general evaluation of the 1982-1984 programme presented at that Conference.

GENERAL ASSEMBLY ACTION

On 20 December, the General Assembly, acting on the recommendation of the Second Committee, adopted resolution 38/224 without vote.

Assistance for the reconstruction, rehabilitation and development of Equatorial Guinea

The General Assembly,

Recalling its resolutions 35/105 of 5 December 1980 and 36/204 of 17 December 1981, in which, *inter alia,* it recognized the need for the adoption of special measures of assistance to enable Equatorial Guinea to rebuild its economy and to restore to normal the social and public services of the country, and drew the attention of the international community to the critical situation confronting Equatorial Guinea and to the list of urgent short-term and long-term projects required by the Government to carry out its programme of rehabilitation,

Recalling its resolution 37/133 of 17 December 1982, by which Equatorial Guinea was included in the list of the least developed countries,

Recognizing the critical situation still confronting Equatorial Guinea and the difficult task of reconstruction and development facing the Government of that country,

Recognizing also the essential role of both short-term and long-term international assistance in support of the efforts of the Government of Equatorial Guinea,

Noting that the International Conference of Donors for the Economic Reactivation and Development of the Republic of Equatorial Guinea took place at Geneva in April 1982 under the auspices of the United Nations Development Programme and the Government of Equatorial Guinea,

1. *Appeals* to all Member States to respond generously, through bilateral or multilateral channels, to the reconstruction and development needs of Equatorial Guinea as presented at the International Conference of Donors;

2. *Calls upon* regional and interregional organizations and other intergovernmental and non-governmental organizations, as well as international financial and development institutions, to give urgent consideration to the establishment of a programme of assistance to Equatorial Guinea or, where one is already in existence, to the expansion of that programme, in response to the International Conference of Donors;

3. *Requests* the appropriate organizations and programmes of the United Nations system—in particular the United Nations Development Programme, the Food and Agriculture Organization of the United Nations, the International Fund for Agricultural Development, the World Bank, the World Food Programme, the World Health Organization, the United Nations Children's Fund and the United Nations Fund for Population Activities—to maintain and expand their programmes of assistance to Equatorial Guinea, to co-operate closely with the Secretary-General in organizing an effective international programme of assistance, to report periodically to the Secretary-General on the steps they have taken and the resources they have made available to help that country and to provide, as appropriate, all possible assistance to meet the critical humanitarian needs of the population and to provide food, medicines and essential equipment for hospitals and schools;

4. *Requests* the Secretary-General:

(a) To continue his efforts to mobilize the necessary resources for an effective programme of financial, technical and material assistance to Equatorial Guinea;

(b) To keep the situation in Equatorial Guinea under review, to maintain close contact with Member States, the specialized agencies, regional and other intergovernmental organizations and international financial institutions concerned and to apprise the Economic and Social Council, at its second regular session of 1984, of the status of assistance to Equatorial Guinea;

(c) To submit to the General Assembly at its thirty-ninth session a report on the economic situation of Equatorial Guinea and the progress made in implementing the present resolution, in particular the response of the international community to the International Conference of Donors.

<hr/>

General Assembly resolution 38/224

20 December 1983   Meeting 104   Adopted without vote

Approved by Second Committee (A/38/705 & Corr.1) without vote, 9 December (meeting 55); 21-nation draft (A/C.2/38/L.99); agenda item 81.

Sponsors: Algeria, Argentina, Bangladesh, Egypt, Equatorial Guinea, Ethiopia, Gabon, Gambia, Ghana, Liberia, Madagascar, Morocco, Nigeria, Pakistan, Senegal, Sierra Leone, Spain, Sudan, Tunisia, United Republic of Cameroon, United Republic of Tanzania.

Meeting numbers. GA 38th session: 2nd Committee 34-38, 55; plenary 104.

Gambia

A recovery took place in ground-nut production and in the tourist industry of the Gambia in 1982/83, according to the Secretary-General's September report on special programmes of economic assistance.[4] The effects of the upturn in those two key sectors, which generated nearly 40 per cent of GDP, however, were limited by various factors, such as a 41 per cent decline in the export prices of ground-nuts, the acute shortage of foreign exchange and some serious budgetary difficulties. A comprehensive five-year tourism marketing plan, included in the special economic assistance programme recommended in 1982,[13] with an estimated $4.9 million required in external funding, had received no assistance as at September 1983.

Although 80 per cent of the population depended on agriculture for livelihood, the extensive cultivation of ground-nuts—the main cash crop accounting for over 90 per cent of export earnings—left the local grains production meeting only 70 per cent of the country's food requirements and about 350,000 tons of cereals were imported annually. The situation was made worse by a severe drought, which resulted in the loss of half of the 1983 cereal production; the Government launched in August an appeal for food assistance and, with an FAO/WFP mission confirming the seriousness of the situation in December, WFP immediately pledged an emergency grant of 7,200 tons of rice.

The Government's budget showed a deficit in 1982/83, after having a small surplus the year before. Budgetary difficulties seriously affected development expenditure; in 1982/83 such expenditure was about 64 per cent of the planned outlay, which meant a reduction in expenditure on the maintenance of essential services and infrastructure, with consequent effects on the welfare of the population. In addition, the Government faced difficulties in meeting the counterpart costs of externally-financed development projects and the costs of projects wholly financed from domestic sources. A one-year credit by IMF provided significant balance-of-payments and budgetary support, and in general the donor community continued to support the Gambia's development effort; some new projects were started during the year in agriculture, forestry, livestock, manufacturing, transport and communications, and tourism. Funding was still needed for the six projects recommended in 1982 for economic assistance.[13] The Government, which in October conducted a mid-term review of its Second Five-Year Plan for Economic and Social Development (1981/82-1985/86), planned to organize a donors' conference in 1984.

GENERAL ASSEMBLY ACTION

On the recommendation of its Second Committee, the General Assembly adopted resolution 38/212 without vote on 20 December.

Assistance to the Gambia

The General Assembly,

Recalling its resolution 37/159 of 17 December 1982, in which it, *inter alia*, noted that the Gambia is a least developed country with acute economic and social problems arising from its weak economic infrastructure and that it also suffers from many of the serious problems common to countries of the Sahelian region, notably drought,

Having heard the statement made by the representative of the Gambia on 11 November 1983 describing her country's serious economic and financial situation and the measures adopted by her Government to deal with these difficulties,

Having considered the summary report of the Secretary-General, in which the recent economic situation in the Gambia is described,

Concerned that the Gambia continues to encounter serious balance-of-payments and budgetary problems and noting that the lack of domestic resources is the most important constraint on development, since the Government lacks the funds to meet the counterpart costs of donor-assisted projects,

Noting that external assistance is still required to enable the Government of the Gambia to implement the six projects recommended by the Secretary-General in his report,

Aware of the intention of the Government of the Gambia to organize, with the assistance of the United Nations Development Programme, a round-table conference of donors in November 1984 to discuss the country's development needs and to consider ways and means of helping the Government in its efforts to meet those needs,

1. *Expresses its appreciation* to the Secretary-General for the steps he has taken to mobilize assistance for the Gambia;

2. *Expresses its appreciation also* to those States and organizations that have provided assistance to the Gambia;

3. *Draws the attention* of the international community to the need for assistance for the projects and programmes identified by the Secretary-General in his reports;

4. *Renews its urgent appeal* to Member States, specialized agencies and other organizations of the United Nations system, regional and interregional organizations and other intergovernmental and non-governmental organizations, as well as international development and financial institutions, to give generous assistance to the Gambia, through bilateral or multilateral channels, and to provide financial, technical and material assistance for the implementation of the projects and programmes recommended by the Secretary-General in his reports;

5. *Urges* donors, as appropriate, to provide financial assistance to the Gambia to help meet the local counterpart costs of externally-assisted projects, bearing in mind that the Gambia is classified as a least developed country;

6. *Urges* Member States, organizations and programmes of the United Nations system, regional and interregional bodies, financial and development institutions and intergovernmental and non-governmental organizations to respond generously to the needs of the Gambia at the round-table conference to be held in November 1984;

7. *Requests* the appropriate organizations and programmes of the United Nations system—in particular the United Nations Development Programme, the United Nations Children's Fund, the World Food Programme, the World Health Organization, the United Nations Industrial Development Organization, the Food and Agriculture Organization of the United Nations and the International Fund for Agricultural Development—

to increase their current and future programmes of assistance to the Gambia, to co-operate closely with the Secretary-General in organizing an effective international programme of assistance and to report periodically to him on the steps they have taken and the resources they have made available to assist that country;

8. *Invites* the United Nations Development Programme, the United Nations Children's Fund, the World Food Programme, the World Health Organization, the United Nations Industrial Development Organization, the Food and Agriculture Organization of the United Nations, the World Bank and the International Fund for Agricultural Development to bring to the attention of their governing bodies, for their consideration, the special needs of the Gambia and to report the decisions of those bodies to the Secretary-General by 15 July 1984;

9. *Requests* the Secretary-General:

(a) To continue his efforts to mobilize the necessary resources for an effective programme of financial, technical and material assistance to the Gambia;

(b) To keep the situation in the Gambia under constant review, to maintain close contact with Member States, the specialized agencies, regional and other intergovernmental organizations and the international financial institutions concerned and to apprise the Economic and Social Council, at its second regular session of 1984, of the status of the special programme of economic assistance for the Gambia;

(c) To report on the progress made in the economic situation of the Gambia and in organizing and implementing the special programme of economic assistance for that country in time for the matter to be considered by the General Assembly at its thirty-ninth session.

General Assembly resolution 38/212

20 December 1983   Meeting 104   Adopted without vote

Approved by Second Committee (A/38/705 & Corr.1) without vote, 28 November (meeting 52); 28-nation draft (A/C.2/38/L.57); agenda item 81.

Sponsors: Algeria, Bangladesh, Cape Verde, Central African Republic, Comoros, Cyprus, Djibouti, Egypt, France, Gambia, Ghana, Guinea-Bissau, Liberia, Madagascar, Mauritania, Morocco, Nigeria, Pakistan, Senegal, Sierra Leone, Thailand, Tunisia, Uganda, United Kingdom, United Republic of Cameroon, United States, Yugoslavia, Zambia.

Meeting numbers. GA 38th session: 2nd Committee 34-38, 44, 52; plenary 104.

Ghana

Report of the Secretary-General. In response to a February 1983 request from Ghana, the Secretary-General sent a multi-agency mission to the country from 10 to 19 May 1983 to assess the need for a short- and medium-term assistance programme geared towards revitalizing the fragile national economy and facilitating the rehabilitation and resettlement of about 1 million returnees from Nigeria.

The mission noted in its report[14] that Ghana's economy, which had been in decline in the last two decades, had been marked by unemployment and underemployment, an acute shortage of foreign exchange, severe strains on the government budget, a high rate of inflation, a major shift in the distribution of income from the poorer working classes to the self-employed in the commercial sector and an exodus from the country, particularly of trained and skilled manpower. In 1982 and 1983, those difficulties were compounded by drought which resulted in reduced food supply at the time the demand for food rose significantly due to the sudden influx of returnees; by mid-1983, Ghana was encountering a serious food shortage.

In early 1983, the Government announced an economic recovery programme for 1983-1986 aimed at reducing the serious financial imbalances in the economy, increasing agricultural and industrial production, reducing inflation, and improving the distribution of goods, services and incomes. In order to bring domestic and external prices into balance, a two-tier structure of bonuses on foreign exchange earnings and surcharges on foreign exchange payments was adopted—a procedure equivalent to using dual exchange rates, or a devaluation of about 810 per cent. Under the 1983 budget, the Government would continue its efforts to reduce public expenditures and improve revenue collection. It was negotiating a balance-of-payments loan with IMF and a general import credit with the World Bank.

The mission recommended 79 projects to be financed by external assistance, at an estimated cost of $188.9 million. The programme comprised emergency-related projects to alleviate immediate problems arising from the influx of returnees (estimated at $49.9 million to be raised in six to eight months), and projects contributing to Ghana's longer-term recovery plan (amounting to $139 million to be implemented from mid-1983 to mid-1985). Forty per cent of the assistance programme fell in the agricultural sector, a further 27 per cent in manufacturing, and 11 per cent in transportation. Those projects were aimed at expanding employment opportunities for the returnees; raising food production for domestic needs and expanding export crops to increase foreign exchange; reviving the manufacturing sector to produce agricultural tools, basic items for construction and certain consumer essentials; and rehabilitating critical transporation arteries to sustain increased economic activity.

ECONOMIC AND SOCIAL COUNCIL ACTION

On 28 July, the Economic and Social Council, on the recommendation of its Third Committee, adopted resolution 1983/44 without vote.

Assistance to Ghana

The Economic and Social Council,

Deeply concerned at the adverse economic conditions in Ghana, exacerbated by the sudden repatriation of over one million Ghanaians and the acute food shortages resulting from unfavourable weather conditions,

Considering the urgent problems of rehabilitating the large number of returnees and reintegrating them in the ailing economy of the country,

Affirming the urgent need for international action to assist the Government and the people of Ghana in their efforts for economic recovery and the rehabilitation of returnees,

Noting with satisfaction the emergency humanitarian assistance rendered by Governments, the United Nations sytem and intergovernmental and non-governmental organizations during the difficult period of the influx of returnees,

Noting with appreciation the response of the Secretary-General to the request of the Government of Ghana and his prompt dispatch of a multi-agency mission to Ghana to consult with the Government on the preparation of short-term and medium-term programmes of assistance geared towards the generation of employment among the returnees,

Having heard the oral report of the Joint Co-ordinator for Special Economic Assistance Programmes on the multi-agency mission to Ghana,

Taking note of the statement made to the Economic and Social Council by the representative of the Government of Ghana,

1. *Takes note* of the efforts made by the Government and the people of Ghana to rehabilitate returnees;

2. *Expresses its appreciation* of the action taken by the Secretary-General;

3. *Takes note* of the oral report on the multi-agency mission and endorses the recommendations of the mission;

4. *Expresses its gratitude* to all States and intergovernmental and non-governmental organizations that have provided emergency humanitarian assistance to Ghana;

5. *Urgently appeals* to all States, intergovernmental and non-governmental organizations and the specialized agencies and programmes of the United Nations system to contribute generously and to provide the further assistance needed to enable Ghana to pursue its economic recovery programme and its efforts to rehabilitate returnees;

6. *Requests* the Secretary-General:

(a)   To submit the report of the multi-agency mission to the General Assembly at its thirty-eighth session and to disseminate it as widely as possible;

(b)   To ensure that adequate financial arrangements are made for the organization of an effective programme of international assistance to Ghana and for the mobilization of international assistance;

(c)   To establish a special account under the United Nations Trust Fund for Special Economic Assistance Programmes for the purpose of facilitating the channelling of contributions to Ghana in accordance with the recommendations of the multi-agency mission;

(d)   To apprise the Economic and Social Council at its second regular session of 1984 of progress made in the implementation of the present resolution.

Economic and Social Council resolution 1983/44

28 July 1983   Meeting 40   Adopted without vote

Approved by Third Committee (E/1983/116) without vote, 15 July (meeting 11); 10-nation draft (E/1983/C.3/L.4), orally revised; agenda item 17.
Sponsors: Bangladesh, Burundi, Congo, India, Kenya, Mali, Saint Lucia, Sierra Leone, Sudan, Tunisia.
Meeting number. ESC 40.

GENERAL ASSEMBLY ACTION

On 20 December, the General Assembly, acting on the recommendation of the Second Committee, adopted resolution 38/203 without vote.

Assistance to Ghana

The General Assembly,

Recalling Economic and Social Council resolution 1983/44 of 28 July 1983, in which the Council expressed its deep concern at the adverse economic conditions in Ghana, exacerbated by the sudden repatriation early in 1983 of over one million Ghanaians,

Having heard the statement made by the Secretary for Foreign Affairs of Ghana on 11 October 1983, in which he expressed appreciation for the humanitarian assistance rendered by Governments, the United Nations system and other organizations during the difficult period of the influx of returnees and his appreciation of the action taken by the Secretary-General, and described his country's serious economic and financial situation,

Having considered the report of the Secretary-General, to which is annexed the report of the multi-agency mission which he dispatched to Ghana in May 1983,

Noting from the report the serious economic and financial problems that confront Ghana and the efforts made by the Government and people of Ghana to cope with these problems and to rehabilitate returnees,

Taking note of the recommended programme of assistance to Ghana, drawn up by the mission in consultation with the Government, concerning short-term emergency-related and medium-term recovery-related assistance,

Affirming the urgent need for international action to assist the Government and the people of Ghana in their efforts towards economic recovery and rehabilitation of returnees,

1. *Takes note* of the efforts made by the Government and people of Ghana to rehabilitate returnees;

2. *Expresses its appreciation* to the Secretary-General for his prompt action and for the report of the multi-agency mission on the economic situation of Ghana and the additional assistance required by that country to cope with the problems exacerbated by the influx of returnees;

3. *Expresses its gratitude* to all States and organizations that have provided emergency humanitarian assistance to Ghana;

4. *Endorses* the assessment and recommendations of the multi-agency mission annexed to the report of the Secretary-General pertaining to assistance to Ghana;

5. *Urgently reiterates the appeal* made by the Economic and Social Council, in its resolution 1983/44, to all States, intergovernmental and non-governmental organizations and the specialized agencies and programmes of the United Nations system to support fully the efforts of the Government of the Ghana to mobilize funds for its special economic assistance programme and respond generously to the short-term and medium-term programmes drawn up by the multi-agency mission in consultation with the Government of Ghana;

6. *Requests* the appropriate organizations and programmes of the United Nations system—in particular the United Nations Development Programme, the World Bank, the Food and Agriculture Organization of the United Nations, the International Fund for Agricultural Development, the World Food Programme, the World Health Organization, the United Nations Children's Fund and the United Nations Industrial Development Organization—to maintain and expand their programmes of assistance to Ghana, to co-operate closely with the Secretary-General in his efforts to organize an effective international programme of assistance and to report periodically to him on the steps they have taken and the resources they have made available to help that country;

7. *Calls upon* regional and interregional organizations and other intergovernmental bodies and non-governmental organizations, as well as international financial institutions, to give urgent consideration to the establishment of a programme of assistance to Ghana or, where one is already in existence, to the expansion of that programme;

8. *Requests* the Secretary-General:

(a) To continue his efforts to mobilize the necessary resources for an effective programme of international assistance to Ghana;

(b) To keep the situation regarding assistance to Ghana under constant review, to maintain close contact with Member States, regional and other intergovernmental organizations, the specialized agencies and international financial institutions concerned, and to apprise the Economic and Social Council, at its second regular sessions of 1984 and 1985, of the current status of the special economic assistance programme for Ghana, including contributions to the United Nations Trust Fund for Special Economic Assistance Programmes, in accordance with Council resolution 1983/44;

(c) To report on the progress made in the economic situation of Ghana and in organizing and implementing the programme of assistance for that country, in time for the matter to be considered by the General Assembly at its fortieth session.

General Assembly resolution 38/203

20 December 1983   Meeting 104   Adopted without vote

Approved by Second Committee (A/38/705 & Corr.1) without vote, 28 November (meeting 52); 20-nation draft (A/C.2/38/L.39), orally revised in informal consultations; agenda item 81.

Sponsors: Afghanistan, Burundi, Congo, Cyprus, Ethiopia, Gambia, Ghana, Guinea-Bissau, Kenya, Madagascar, Mozambique, Pakistan, Romania, Senegal, Sierra Leone, Sudan, Tunisia, Uganda, United Republic of Cameroon, Zambia.

Meeting numbers. GA 38th session: 2nd Committee 34-38, 44, 52; plenary 28, 104.

Guinea-Bissau

The economy of Guinea-Bissau, which suffered a recurrent large food deficit and irregular rainfall, was characterized by a weak economic and social infrastructure and shortages of trained manpower and equipment, according to the Secretary-General's September report on special programmes of economic assistance.[4]

The total government revenue in 1982 showed a 7 per cent decline while total expenditure increased by nearly 23 per cent as compared to 1981. The overall budget deficit of $21 million in 1981 increased to $33.3 million in 1982. The Government expected the deteriorating deficit trend to continue for the coming three or four years. The external debt and debt servicing also increased, and in 1982 debt repayment totalled 59 per cent of export earnings; at the end of 1982, overdue payments on loans and on the trade account had reached $51.8 million. Despite an improvement in agricultural production in 1982/83, the food short-age remained critical, and the Government estimated its 1983 food aid requirements to be about 82,000 metric tons at a cost of $24 million.

In 1983, the Government was finalizing its first national development plan (1983-1986) in time for a donors' round table scheduled for early 1984, at which it expected to seek external assistance for 59 projects costing $177.8 million. The plan dealt with budget management, money and rates of exchange, wages, State enterprises and sectoral investments; those projects in the special economic assistance programme which were still unfunded or partially funded would be included in the plan. The Government also hoped that the creditors would consider rescheduling, converting or cancelling the overdue debt. In anticipation of the 1984 round table, the Government held a preparatory meeting of donors at Lisbon, Portugal, from 17 to 19 November.

Various United Nations organizations provided special economic assistance to Guinea-Bissau in 1983.[5] Among them, WFP's ongoing assistance consisted of three development projects valued at $6.1 million and two emergency operations valued at $1.4 million. Two credits totalling $29.1 million were approved by IDA: $13.1 million in support of an oil-exploration project and a $16 million transportation project to increase the efficiency of Bissau Port.

GENERAL ASSEMBLY ACTION

Acting on the recommendation of the Second Committee, the General Assembly on 20 December adopted resolution 38/221 without vote.

Special economic assistance to Guinea-Bissau
The General Assembly,

Recalling its resolution 35/95 of 5 December 1980, in which it reiterated its appeal to the international community to provide continuous financial, material and technical assistance to Guinea-Bissau to help it overcome its financial and economic difficulties and to permit the implementation of the projects and programmes recommended by the Secretary-General in his report submitted in response to General Assembly resolution 34/121 of 14 December 1979,

Recalling also its resolution 36/217 of 17 December 1981,

Recalling further its resolution 3339(XXIX) of 17 December 1974, in which it invited Member States to provide economic assistance to the then newly independent State of Guinea-Bissau, and its resolutions 32/100 of 13 December 1977 and 33/124 of 19 December 1978, in which it, *inter alia*, expressed deep concern at the serious economic situation in Guinea-Bissau and appealed to the international community to provide financial and economic assistance to that country,

Having examined the summary report of the Secretary-General,

Recalling that Guinea-Bissau is one of the least developed countries,

Noting with concern that Guinea-Bissau continues to be beset by serious economic and financial difficulties,

Also noting with concern that the gross national product has dropped in real terms, that the balance-of-payments deficit continues to increase, that the external debt is imposing a heavy burden on the economy and that the budget deficit has also risen substantially,

Noting that Guinea-Bissau continues to face a serious food shortage and needs more than 82,000 tonnes of foodstuffs,

Noting with satisfaction that the Government of Guinea-Bissau has prepared a comprehensive development strategy aimed at stabilizing the country's finances and ensuring the country's economic recovery within the framework of a four-year development plan (1983-1986),

Noting also that the Government of Guinea-Bissau, in view of the seriousness of the economic situation, has decided to implement a rigorous economic and financial stabilization programme, the main purpose of which is to remedy the economic situation,

Noting further that the Government of Guinea-Bissau had proposed, with the assistance of the United Nations Development Programme, to hold a round table of donors at Geneva in January 1984 and that, to this end, it held a preparatory meeting of donors at Lisbon from 17 to 19 November 1983,

1. *Expresses its appreciation* to the Secretary-General for the steps he has taken to mobilize assistance to Guinea-Bissau;

2. *Draws the attention* of the international community to the requirements for assistance for the projects and programmes identified in the Secretary-General's reports mentioned above;

3. *Expresses its appreciation* to those States and organizations that have provided assistance to Guinea-Bissau in response to appeals by the General Assembly and the Secretary-General;

4. *Calls upon* Member States and the international organizations concerned to be generous in granting Guinea-Bissau the food aid it needs;

5. *Renews its urgent appeal* to Member States, regional and interregional organizations and other intergovernmental organizations to continue providing financial, material and technical assistance to Guinea-Bissau to help it overcome its economic and financial difficulties and to permit the implementation of the projects and programmes identified in the annexes to the reports of the Secretary-General;

6. *Urges* Members States, organizations of the United Nations system, regional and interregional bodies and financial and development institutions, as well as governmental and non-governmental organizations, to respond generously to the needs of Guinea-Bissau at the round table of donors in January 1984;

7. *Appeals* to the international community to contribute to the special account established at United Nations Headquarters by the Secretary-General, in accordance with General Assembly resolution 32/100, for the purpose of facilitating the channelling of contributions to Guinea-Bissau;

8. *Invites* the United Nations Development Programme, the United Nations Children's Fund, the World Food Programme, the World Health Organization, the Food and Agriculture Organization of the United Nations, the World Bank and the International Fund for Agricultural Development to bring to the attention of their governing bodies, for their consideration, the special needs of Guinea-Bissau and to report

the decisions of those bodies to the Secretary-General by 15 July 1984;

9. *Requests* the appropriate specialized agencies and other organizations of the United Nations system to report periodically to the Secretary-General on the steps they have taken and the resources they have made available to assist Guinea-Bissau;

10. *Requests* the Secretary-General:

(a) To continue his efforts to mobilize the necessary resources for an effective programme of financial, technical and material assistance to Guinea-Bissau;

(b) To keep the situation in Guinea-Bissau under constant review, to maintain close contact with Member States, the specialized agencies, regional and other intergovernmental organizations and international financial institutions concerned, and to apprise the Economic and Social Council, at its second regular sessions of 1984 and 1985, as well as the General Assembly at its thirty-ninth session, of the status of the special programme of economic assistance for Guinea-Bissau;

(c) To arrange for a review of the results of the round table of donors scheduled to be held in January 1984, and of the progress made in organizing and implementing the special programme of economic assistance for Guinea-Bissau in time for the matter to be considered by the General Assembly at its fortieth session.

General Assembly resolution 38/221

20 December 1983   Meeting 104   Adopted without vote

Approved by Second Committee (A/38/705 & Corr.1) without vote, 28 November (meeting 52); 49-nation draft (A/C.2/38/L.66); agenda item 81.

Sponsors: Afghanistan, Algeria, Angola, Benin, Brazil, Burundi, Cape Verde, Central African Republic, Chad, China, Comoros, Cyprus, Democratic Yemen, Djibouti, Egypt, Ethiopia, France, Gambia, Ghana, Guinea, Guinea-Bissau, Guyana, Honduras, Lesotho, Liberia, Libyan Arab Jamahiriya, Madagascar, Mali, Mauritania, Mozambique, Nicaragua, Niger, Oman, Pakistan, Panama, Portugal, Qatar, Rwanda, Sao Tome and Principe, Senegal, Sierra Leone, Sudan, Sweden, Thailand, Uganda, United Republic of Tanzania, Vanuatu, Zaire, Zambia.

Meeting numbers. GA 38th session: 2nd Committee 34-38, 44, 52; plenary 104.

Lesotho

In response to a 1982 Security Council resolution[15] following South Africa's attack of 9 December that year on Lesotho's capital, Maseru, the Secretary-General sent a mission from 11 to 16 January 1983 to consult with Lesotho and United Nations agencies on ensuring the welfare of South African refugees in that land-locked country entirely surrounded by South Africa (see Chapter XXI of this section). In its report, transmitted by the Secretary-General to the Council on 9 February,[16] the mission described economic assistance needed to enhance Lesotho's capacity to receive and maintain refugees. The Government's main concerns were the country's inability to defend itself against South African aggression or intimidation, the resultant problem of national security and the growing need to reduce its dependence on South Africa, primarily in economic terms, while strengthening its ties with the international community. The Government maintained that its security needs entailed not only protection from physical harm but safeguards in such areas as food needs, health and education services, employment

opportunities and the development of resources for the benefit of its inhabitants.

The mission reported that Lesotho's economic performance had slackened since 1980, following poor harvests and reduced export earnings from wool and mohair. There was little industrial production, and most food needs were met by imports, with its grain import requirements expected to reach an all-time high of about 200,000 tons in 1983. About 90 per cent of Lesotho's imports came from South Africa, and its exports were either to South Africa or through it to other countries. The income Lesotho received from South Africa under a revenue-sharing formula accounted for about 55 per cent of government revenue in 1982/83; in 1983/84, it was expected to approach 70 per cent. Because Lesotho's currency was based on the South African rand, its payment of foreign financial commitments was guaranteed, but the availability of monetary policy instruments was severely limited, and there were no exchange control restrictions on imports from South Africa. In fiscal 1981/82, the budget deficit amounted to $70 million (almost 20 per cent of GDP), compared to a small surplus in 1978/79. Government borrowing had to be short-term at high rates, resulting in a rapid increase in the debt-service burden.

Lesotho was dependent on South Africa in a number of other areas, including energy (petroleum products, electricity supply) and a labour market. About half of its male labour force and 4 per cent of the female counterpart worked in South Africa; their remittances were the single most important resource in Lesotho's economy. In the event of an expulsion of workers from South Africa, Lesotho would face rising unemployment and a severe reduction in national income.

Lesotho sought international assistance for priority projects directly related to areas where South Africa's actions or pressures added to its vulnerability. The mission consequently identified 10 projects of an immediate nature at an estimated cost of $46 million, addressing the emergency needs arising from South Africa's December 1982 air attack on Maseru and urgent needs arising from the country's vulnerability to political and economic pressures because of its refugee policies. They covered such needs as strengthened police services, an emergency reserve of medical supplies and improved hospital facilities/services, a fire brigade, a silo for grain reserves, afforestation, labour-intensive public works, expansion of industrial estates, construction of a small-scale hydroelectric power plant, and funding for a national airport.

The mission pointed out that the country's fragile economy and weak infrastructure, coupled with the Government's policy of integrating refugees into the community upon their arrival, made it difficult to formulate projects exclusively for refugees. The mission stated that, while Lesotho's economy would continue for the foreseeable future to be heavily dependent on South Africa, there were areas where the dependence could be reduced with international support.

By resolution 535(1983) of 29 June 1983, the Security Council endorsed the mission's findings and requested Member States, international organizations and financial institutions to assist Lesotho in the fields identified in the report (see POLITICAL AND SECURITY QUESTIONS, Chapter V).

The Secretary-General also described the economic situation and assistance to Lesotho in his September report on special economic assistance, giving updated statistics.[4] He noted that Lesotho had complained of new border restrictions affecting the normal movement of people, goods and services. As a result of a severe drought, domestic grain production covered only one fifth of national requirements and the grain shortfall during 1983/84, after taking account of estimated imports and donations amounting to 91,000 tons, was anticipated to reach 119,000 tons. The Government's budget deficit continued to increase and its considerable expenditures on national security diverted funds from development. In support of the national effort to generate employment opportunities and in the context of SNPA, the United Nations was helping the Government prepare a donors' round table, to be held at Maseru in early 1984, on employment creation and income-generating activities for national economic self-reliance.

United Nations assistance to Lesotho in 1983[5] included WFP's ongoing projects with a total value of $42.74 million. Six projects ($4.1 million), funded by UNDP and implemented by FAO, covered rural development, fruit and vegetable cannery, poultry vaccination, forests and veterinary science. Six trust fund projects ($3.5 million) covered storage, land use planning, forestry, seed production and rural development.

GENERAL ASSEMBLY ACTION

On 20 December, the General Assembly, on the recommendation of the Second Committee, adopted resolution 38/215 without vote.

Assistance to Lesotho

The General Assembly,

Recalling Security Council resolution 402(1976) of 22 December 1976, in which the Council, *inter alia*, expressed concern at the serious situation created by South Africa's closure of certain border posts between South Africa and Lesotho aimed at coercing Lesotho into according recognition to the bantustan of the Transkei,

Recalling also Security Council resolution 535(1983) of 29 June 1983, in which the Council endorsed the report

of the mission dispatched to Lesotho in response to resolution 527(1982) of 15 December 1982,

Commending the decision of the Government of Lesotho not to recognize the Transkei, in compliance with United Nations decisions, particularly General Assembly resolution 31/6 A of 26 October 1976,

Also commending the Government of Lesotho for its steadfast opposition to *apartheid* and its generosity to the South African refugees,

Fully aware that the decision of the Government of Lesotho not to recognize the Transkei and its acceptance of refugees from South Africa have imposed special economic burdens upon its people,

Strongly endorsing the appeals made in Security Council resolutions 402(1976) of 22 December 1976, 407(1977) of 25 May 1977 and 535(1983) of 29 June 1983, in General Assembly resolutions 32/98 of 13 December 1977, 33/128 of 19 December 1978, 34/130 of 14 December 1979, 35/96 of 5 December 1980, 36/219 of 17 December 1981 and 37/160 of 17 December 1982, and by the Secretary-General, calling upon all States, regional and intergovernmental organizations and the appropriate organizations of the United Nations system to contribute generously to the international programme of assistance to enable Lesotho to carry out its economic development and enhance its capacity to implement fully the resolutions of the United Nations,

Having examined the summary report of the Secretary-General, prepared in response to General Assembly resolution 37/160, in which the economic situation was reviewed, as well as the progress in the implementation of the special programme of economic assistance for Lesotho,

Noting the priority which the Government of Lesotho accords to raising levels of food production through increased productivity, thus lessening the country's dependency on South Africa for food imports,

Aware that the high prices paid by Lesotho for its imports of petroleum products as a result of the oil embargo on South Africa have become a serious impediment to the development of the country,

Recognizing, in connection with such embargoes, the obligation of the international community to help countries such as Lesotho that act in support of the Charter of the United Nations and in compliance with General Assembly resolutions,

Recalling its resolutions 32/160 of 19 December 1977 and 33/197 of 29 January 1979 concerning the Transport and Communications Decade in Africa and, in this regard, noting Lesotho's geopolitical situation, which necessitates the urgent development of air and telecommunication links with neighbouring countries of Africa and the rest of the world,

Taking account of Lesotho's need for a national network of roads, both for its planned social and economic development and to lessen its dependence on the South African network, to reach various regions of the country affected by the imposition of travel restrictions by South Africa,

Taking note of Lesotho's special problems associated with the employment of large numbers of its able-bodied men in South Africa,

Taking note also of the priority which the Government of Lesotho has accorded to the problem of absorbing into the economy the young generation, as well as migrant workers returning from South Africa,

Welcoming the action taken by the Government of Lesotho to make more effective use of women in the development process by promoting their participation in the economic, social and cultural life of the country,

Taking account also of Lesotho's position as a least developed, most seriously affected and land-locked country,

Recalling its resolution 32/98, in which it, *inter alia*, recognized that the continuing influx of refugees from South Africa imposed an additional burden on Lesotho,

1. *Expresses its concern* at the difficulties that confront the Government of Lesotho as a result of its decision not to recognize the so-called independent Transkei, and of its rejection of *apartheid* and acceptance of refugees from *apartheid* oppression;

2. *Endorses fully* the assessment of the situation contained in the report of the mission to Lesotho, dispatched in response to Security Council resolution 527(1982), and in the summary report of the Secretary-General;

3. *Takes note* of the requirements of Lesotho, as described in the reports of the mission to Lesotho and of the Secretary-General, to carry out the remainder of its development programme, to implement projects necessitated by the present political situation in the region and to lessen its dependence on South Africa;

4. *Expresses its appreciation* to the Secretary-General for the measures he has taken to organize an international programme of economic assistance for Lesotho;

5. *Notes with appreciation* the response made thus far by the international community to the special programme of economic assistance for Lesotho, which has enabled it to proceed with the implementation of parts of the recommended programme;

6. *Reiterates its appeal* to Member States, regional and interregional organizations and other intergovernmental organizations to provide financial, material and technical assistance to Lesotho for the implementation of several projects and programmes that are still unfunded, as identified in the reports of the mission to Lesotho and of the Secretary-General;

7. *Calls upon* Member States and the appropriate agencies, organizations and financial institutions to provide assistance to Lesotho so as to enable it to achieve a greater degree of self-sufficiency in food production;

8. *Also calls upon* Member States to give all possible assistance to Lesotho to ensure an adequate and regular supply of oil to meet its national requirements;

9. *Further calls upon* Member States to assist Lesotho in developing its internal road and air systems and its air communications with the rest of the world;

10. *Commends* the efforts of the Government of Lesotho to integrate women more fully into development efforts and requests the Secretary-General to consult with the Government on the type and amount of assistance it will require to achieve this objective;

11. *Draws the attention* of the international community to the meeting of donors held in Lesotho in November 1979, as well as the agricultural sector conference held in Lesotho in October 1980, and urges Member States and the appropriate agencies and organizations to provide assistance to Lesotho in accordance with the outcome of those meetings;

12. *Also draws the attention* of the international community to the special account which was established at United Nations Headquarters by the Secretary-General, in accordance with Security Council resolution 407(1977), for the purpose of facilitating the channelling of contributions to Lesotho;

13. *Invites* the United Nations Development Programme, the United Nations Children's Fund, the World Health Organization, the United Nations Industrial Development Organization, the Food and Agriculture Organization of the United Nations and the International Fund for Agricultural Development to bring further to the attention of their governing bodies the special needs of Lesotho and to report to the Secretary-General by 15 August 1984 on the steps they have taken;

14. *Requests* the appropriate specialized agencies and other organizations of the United Nations system to co-operate closely with the Secretary-General in organizing an effective international programme of assistance to Lesotho and to report periodically to him on the steps they have taken and the resources they have made available to assist that country;

15. *Requests* the Secretary-General:

   (a) To continue his efforts to mobilize the necessary resources for an effective programme of financial, technical and material assistance to Lesotho;

   (b) To consult with the Government of Lesotho on the question of migrant workers returning from South Africa and to report on the type of assistance which the Government requires in order to establish labour-intensive projects to deal with their absorption into the economy;

   (c) To ensure that adequate financial and budgetary arrangements are made to continue the organization of the international programme of assistance to Lesotho and the mobilization of assistance;

   (d) To keep the situation in Lesotho under constant review, to maintain close contact with Member States, the specialized agencies, regional and other intergovernmental organizations and international financial institutions concerned and to apprise the Economic and Social Council, at its second regular session of 1984, of the current status of the special programme of economic assistance for Lesotho;

   (e) To report on the progress made in the economic situation of Lesotho and in organizing and implementing the special programme of economic assistance for that country in time for the matter to be considered by the General Assembly at its thirty-ninth session.

General Assembly resolution 38/215

20 December 1983   Meeting 104   Adopted without vote

Approved by Second Committee (A/38/705 & Corr.1) without vote, 28 November (meeting 52); 22-nation draft (A/C.2/38/L.60); agenda item 81.

Sponsors: Bangladesh, Botswana, Canada, Chad, China, Cyprus, Djibouti, Guinea-Bissau, Japan, Lesotho, Liberia, Madagascar, Malawi, Mozambique, Pakistan, Sierra Leone, Singapore, Swaziland, Sweden, Uganda, Zambia, Zimbabwe.

Meeting numbers. GA 38th session: 2nd Committee 34-38, 44, 52; plenary 104.

Liberia

The Secretary-General observed in his September 1983 report on special economic assistance[4] that Liberia continued to face serious budgetary deficits, due mainly to rapid increases in wages and salaries and low revenues connected with the stagnant domestic economy and depressed export prices. The situation remained serious even after temporary relief had been provided by the rescheduling, at the Government's request, of some $44 million of debt-service payments by the "Paris Club" of bilateral lenders and about $27 million due by mid-1983 by the "London Club" of commercial creditors.

A short-term stabilization programme, introduced by the Government in collaboration with IMF to reduce the budget deficit and achieve a sustainable balance-of-payments position, aimed at annual GDP growth of 3.3 per cent in real terms, equal to the rate of population growth, and a resource balance improvement from a $76 million deficit in 1983 to a positive $2 million in 1987.

Implementation of the public investment programme 1981-1985, comprising a major element of Liberia's National Socio-Economic Plan for the same period, had been extended to 1987; an additional $698 million was required in external assistance in order to implement fully the Government's overall investment programme. A comprehensive list of development projects and their funding status was presented at a round-table meeting of donors at Geneva in October 1983. The projects, some of which had been recommended for international assistance in 1982 and still needing funding,[17] covered agriculture and rural development, electricity, highways, port rehabilitation, air transport, communications and health; in 1983, the Government identified additional projects requiring funding in those areas and in energy, water supply, and population and housing censuses.

United Nations organizations provided assistance to Liberia in several areas.[5] IMF had granted 177 million special drawing rights (SDR) in credits and loans to Liberia by the end of 1982, while WFP's ongoing assistance, as at April 1983, consisted of four development projects valued at $20 million. As a result of a November 1982 mission to review the current compilation methods of balance-of-payments statistics, publication of such data for Liberia was expected later in 1983, for the first time in 20 years.

Mozambique

Mozambique issued an appeal on 28 May 1983 for international assistance for the victims of South Africa's attack five days earlier on a suburb of Maputo and for reconstruction (see POLITICAL AND SECURITY QUESTIONS, Chapter V). As in the past, it continued to suffer from drought, a foreign exchange shortage and armed disturbances, according to the Secretary-General's September report on special programmes of economic assistance.[4] Those problems were compounded by a 6.9 per cent decline in GNP in 1982.

The drought, which had developed in the southern half of the country early in 1982, had become critical by mid-1983, lasting over two harvest cycles; rainfall in January-April 1983 reached only half the normal level, causing almost total crop failure in the south and severe losses in the central area. Some 4 million people or one third of the national population were affected, and 1.8 million people found themselves totally dependent on external food supplies. Largely because of the drought, the health situation deteriorated, and water shortages for irrigation, drinking and industrial purposes appeared. The United Nations and three countries funded an emergency groundwater development project to meet the critical water shortage in the capital. The continuation of armed disturbances hampered relief operations for rural populations, the distribution of agricultural surpluses from the north and the internal transport system.

With the evident failure of the 1982/83 crop season, the Government appealed in January 1983 for supplemental international assistance amounting to 255,000 tons of grain; as at mid-1983, several donors, including WFP, pledged assistance amounting to almost half of the expressed needs. At the end of August, most of the food shortages directly attributable to the drought were reportedly met, but serious problems existed with internal distribution. In order to establish a food security reserve, a silo was being constructed, with international assistance being sought for two additional silo complexes.

Mozambique's manufacturing and agro-industrial sector was substantial and diversified, but the foreign exchange constraint and economic dislocations had resulted in shortages of certain inputs and replacement parts and machinery, forcing many industries to operate below capacity. The country's rail and port systems, which contributed significantly to its foreign exchange earnings, had been affected in recent years by armed disturbances and sabotage, for which the Government held South Africa responsible.

In early 1983, UNDRO launched an appeal for assistance to the central and southern provinces of Mozambique and the international contribution totalled over $18.8 million.[5] Other United Nations assistance was provided by WFP, with ongoing projects totalling over $74 million and over $9 million in emergency operations. Nine projects, worth more than $16 million in total, were funded by UNDP and implemented by FAO; they concerned livestock, seed and crop production, land and water use, forestry, and fisheries development. Trust fund assistance consisted of 18 similar projects worth $20.5 million.

GENERAL ASSEMBLY ACTION

Acting on the recommendation of the Second Committee, the General Assembly adopted resolution 38/208 on 20 December without vote.

Assistance to Mozambique

The General Assembly,

Recalling Security Council resolution 386(1976) of 17 March 1976, in which the Council appealed to all States to provide, and requested the Secretary-General, in collaboration with the appropriate organizations of the United Nations system, to organize, with immediate effect, financial, technical and material assistance to enable Mozambique to carry out its economic development programme,

Recalling further its resolutions 31/43 of 1 December 1976, 32/95 of 13 December 1977, 33/126 of 19 December 1978, 34/129 of 14 December 1979, 35/99 of 5 December 1980, 36/215 of 17 December 1981 and 37/161 of 17 December 1982, in which it urged the international community to respond effectively and generously with assistance to Mozambique,

Having considered the reports of the Secretary-General on assistance to Mozambique and noting with concern that the economic and financial position of that country remains grave and beset by budgetary and balance-of-payments deficits,

Noting with deep concern the loss of life and the destruction of essential infrastructures such as roads, railways, bridges, petroleum facilities, electricity supply, schools and hospitals, as identified in the reports of the Secretary-General,

Recognizing that the food deficit of over 300,000 tonnes in 1982 has been further exacerbated by continued drought, poor rainfall, severe crop infestation and epidemics of animal diseases, as well as by chronic shortages of production inputs,

Bearing in mind the international appeal, launched by the Government and supported by the Office of the United Nations Disaster Relief Co-ordinator, for urgent food aid for central and southern Mozambique,

Recognizing that substantial international assistance is required for the implementation of a number of reconstruction and development projects,

1. *Strongly endorses* the appeals made by the Security Council and the Secretary-General for international assistance to Mozambique;

2. *Also endorses* the appeals made by the Government and supported by the Office of the United Nations Disaster Relief Co-ordinator for urgent food aid for central and southern Mozambique;

3. *Expresses its appreciation* to the Secretary-General for the measures he has taken to organize an international economic assistance programme for Mozambique;

4. *Also expresses its appreciation* for the assistance provided to Mozambique by various States and regional and international organizations and humanitarian institutions;

5. *Regrets,* however, that the total assistance provided to date falls far short of Mozambique's pressing needs;

6. *Draws the attention* of the international community to the additional financial, economic and material assistance identified in the reports of the Secretary-General as urgently required by Mozambique;

7. *Calls upon* Member States, regional and interregional organizations and other governmental, intergovernmental and non-governmental organizations to provide financial, material and technical assistance to Mozambique, wherever possible in the form of grants,

and urges them to give special consideration to the early inclusion of Mozambique in their programmes of development assistance, if it is not already included;

8. *Urges* Member States and organizations that are already implementing or negotiating assistance programmes for Mozambique to strengthen them, wherever possible;

9. *Appeals* to the international community to provide financial and material assistance to Mozambique to meet its food and other relief requirements arising out of the continued drought;

10. *Also appeals* to the international community to contribute to the special account for Mozambique established by the Secretary-General for the purpose of facilitating the channelling of contributions to Mozambique;

11. *Requests* the appropriate organizations and programmes of the United Nations system—in particular the United Nations Development Programme, the Food and Agriculture Organization of the United Nations, the International Fund for Agricultural Development, the World Food Programme, the World Health Organization and the United Nations Children's Fund—to maintain and increase their current and future programmes of assistance to Mozambique, to cooperate closely with the Secretary-General in organizing an effective international programme of assistance and to report periodically to him on the steps they have taken and the resources they have made available to help that country;

12. *Requests* the Secretary-General:

(a) To continue his efforts to mobilize the necessary resources for an effective programme of financial, technical and material assistance to Mozambique;

(b) To keep the situation in Mozambique under constant review, to maintain close contact with Member States, the specialized agencies, regional and other intergovernmental organizations and international financial institutions and other bodies concerned and to apprise the Economic and Social Council, at its second regular session of 1984, of the current status of the special programme of economic assistance for Mozambique;

(c) To prepare, on the basis of sustained consultations with the Government of Mozambique, a report on the development of the economic situation and the implementation of the special programme of economic assistance for that country in time for the matter to be considered by the General Assembly at its thirty-ninth session.

General Assembly resolution 38/208

20 December 1983   Meeting 104   Adopted without vote

Approved by Second Committee (A/38/705 & Corr.1) without vote, 28 November (meeting 52); 37-nation draft (A/C.2/38/L.53), orally revised in informal consultations; agenda item 81.

Sponsors: Afghanistan, Algeria, Angola, Cape Verde, China, Cuba, Cyprus, Egypt, Gambia, German Democratic Republic, Ghana, Guinea-Bissau, Guyana, India, Italy, Lesotho, Liberia, Madagascar, Mauritania, Mongolia, Mozambique, Nepal, Nicaragua, Pakistan, Portugal, Sao Tome and Principe, Sierra Leone, Sudan, Sweden, Uganda, Ukrainian SSR, United Republic of Cameroon, Vanuatu, Viet Nam, Yugoslavia, Zambia, Zimbabwe.

Meeting numbers. GA 38th session: 2nd Committee 34-38, 44, 52; plenary 104.

In approving the draft, the Second Committee, on the basis of informal consultations, changed the text of the fourth preambular paragraph, which had originally attributed loss of life and destruction to actions of "armed bandits supported by the *apartheid* régime of South Africa".

Sierra Leone

In pursuance of a December 1982 General Assembly request,[18] the Secretary-General dispatched a multi-agency mission to Sierra Leone from 14 to 21 March 1983 to discuss with the Government the additional assistance needed for the country's economic and social development. The mission's findings were annexed to the Secretary-General's June report to the Assembly.[19]

The mission found Sierra Leone, added in 1982[11] to the United Nations list of least developed countries, undergoing economic difficulties. While prices of many imports, especially petroleum, were rising, total revenues from the principal export items—diamonds, bauxite, coffee, cocoa and palm kernels—were declining. Despite reductions in the total import bill, the trade balance remained in substantial deficit, in addition to arrears in external debt payments. The shortage of foreign exchange had depressed activity throughout the economy: trade and commercial credits were drying up, commercial activity and employment had fallen, and the industrial and manufacturing sector accounted for only 5 per cent of GDP. With its budget in serious deficit largely because of reduced revenue from export and import taxes, the Government was unable to improve health and other basic social services or to strengthen the transport infrastructure, on which much of the country's economic and social development depended.

The mission asserted that, given the needed external assistance, Sierra Leone, well endowed with natural resources, had excellent potential for accelerated development. The Second National Development Plan for 1982/83-1985/86, which was in the final stage of preparation, aimed at creating the appropriate economic and financial climate for national development. The Government hoped that the major part of the public investment programme would be financed by external resources and the bulk of the domestic funds would go into the agriculture and energy sectors.

The mission recommended 71 projects for external assistance, costing some $275 million; of those, 27, costing $124 million, were considered especially urgent. The projects concerned agriculture, energy, mining, industry and manufacturing, transportation, health, water and sanitation, housing, education and training, and social welfare.

Preliminary evidence on major crops for 1983 suggested a large increase. The Government abolished in July 1983 the two-tier exchange rate system, which it had adopted in late 1982 to divert foreign resources to the official banking system and consequently reduce parallel market activities.

United Nations assistance[5] included a UNDP grant of $236,000 for 1983 and an additional $100,000 to help organize a donors' conference. Three UNDP projects ($1.96 million), implemented by FAO, covered land and water use, swamp rice development and agricultural data collection. IDA approved a $20 million credit for development of educational programmes. At the end of 1982, Sierra Leone's use of IMF credit stood at some SDR 46 million and Trust Fund loans at SDR 24 million.

GENERAL ASSEMBLY ACTION

On 20 December, the General Assembly, acting on the recommendation of the Second Committee, adopted resolution 38/205 without vote.

Assistance for the development of Sierra Leone
The General Assembly,

Having heard the statement made by the Head of State of Sierra Leone before the General Assembly on 30 September 1983, in which he called for support from the international community for the economic and social development of Sierra Leone,

Recalling its resolution 37/158 of 17 December 1982, in which it appealed to all States, the specialized agencies and international development and financial institutions to provide all possible assistance for the development of Sierra Leone,

Further recalling its resolution 37/133 of 17 December 1982, in which it decided to include Sierra Leone in the list of the least developed countries,

Reiterating that the weak growth rate experienced by the economy of Sierra Leone during the period of the first National Development Plan (1973/74 to 1978/79) and the decline in real terms of per capita gross domestic product during that period have continued to persist,

Having considered the report of the Secretary-General, to which was annexed the report of the multi-agency mission he dispatched to Sierra Leone in March 1983 to consult with the Government on the additional assistance required for the economic and social development of Sierra Leone,

Aware of the need for effective mobilization of international assistance in order to implement fully the programme of assistance outlined in the report of the multi-agency mission,

Noting the intention of the Government of Sierra Leone to organize, with the assistance of the United Nations Development Programme, a round-table conference of donors in 1984 to discuss the country's development needs and to consider ways and means of supplementing the development efforts of the Government,

1. *Expresses its appreciation* to the Secretary-General for his reports on the economic situation of Sierra Leone and the assistance required by that country for its economic and social development;

2. *Endorses* the assessment and recommendations of the multi-agency mission contained in the annex to the report of the Secretary-General pertaining to assistance for the development of Sierra Leone;

3. *Urgently reiterates its appeal* to the international community, including organs, organizations and bodies of the United Nations, to contribute generously, through bilateral or multilateral channels, to the economic and social development of Sierra Leone;

4. *Urges* all States and relevant United Nations bodies—in particular the United Nations Development Programme, the World Food Programme, the United Nations Industrial Development Organization, the United Nations Children's Fund, the World Health Organization, the United Nations Educational, Scientific and Cultural Organization and the United Nations Fund for Population Activities—to provide all possible assistance to help the Government of Sierra Leone meet the critical humanitarian needs of the population and to provide, as appropriate, food, medicines and essential equipment for hospitals and schools;

5. *Invites* the United Nations Development Programme, the United Nations Children's Fund, the World Food Programme, the World Health Organization, the United Nations Industrial Development Organization, the Food and Agriculture Organization of the United Nations, the World Bank, the African Development Bank and the International Fund for Agricultural Development to bring to the attention of their governing bodies, for their consideration, the special needs of Sierra Leone and to report the decisions of those bodies to the Secretary-General by 15 July 1984;

6. *Requests* the Administrator of the United Nations Development Programme and the World Bank to provide all possible assistance to the Government of Sierra Leone in organizing the proposed round-table conference of donors;

7. *Requests* the Secretary-General:

(a) To continue his efforts to mobilize the necessary resources for an effective programme of financial, technical and material assistance to Sierra Leone;

(b) To ensure that adequate financial arrangements are made for the organization of an effective international programme of assistance to Sierra Leone and for the mobilization of international assistance;

(c) To apprise the Economic and Social Council, at its second regular session of 1984, of the assistance granted to Sierra Leone;

(d) To keep the situation regarding assistance to Sierra Leone under review and to report to the General Assembly at its thirty-ninth session on the implementation of the present resolution.

General Assembly resolution 38/205

20 December 1983   Meeting 104   Adopted without vote

Approved by Second Committee (A/38/705 & Corr.1) without vote, 28 November (meeting 52); 23-nation draft (A/C.2/38/L.50), orally revised in informal consultations; agenda item 81.
Sponsors: Bangladesh, Cape Verde, Cyprus, Djibouti, Gambia, Ghana, Guinea-Bissau, Japan, Lebanon, Liberia, Libyan Arab Jamahiriya, Madagascar, Pakistan, Romania, Senegal, Sierra Leone, Singapore, Thailand, Trinidad and Tobago, Tunisia, Uganda, United Republic of Cameroon, Zambia.
Meeting numbers. GA 38th session: 2nd Committee 34-38, 44, 52; plenary 13, 104.

Uganda

The economic recovery of Uganda showed discernible momentum, according to the Secretary-General's September 1983 report on special economic assistance.[4] Real GDP, which had been falling during the previous decade, increased by 7.3 per cent in 1983, and the price incentives given to farmers had led to a substantial increase in agricultural production. Its trade deficit declined sharply from $122.5 million in 1982 to an estimated $51.6 million in 1983. The objectives of the dual exchange-rate system, introduced in August 1982 as a mechanism for allocating scarce foreign exchange, were largely achieved, improving government finances in 1982 and 1983. In contrast to the severe inflation rate of over 100 per cent per annum in 1979 and 1980, the 1982 rate, following 1981 fiscal reforms, had fallen to an estimated 50-60 per cent, with the 1983 rate expected to have fallen further.

Government revenue was heavily dependent on export and import taxes, which contributed a little over half the recurrent revenues in 1982/83; with economic recovery under way and the maintenance of fiscal restraint, its overall deficit was expected to fall substantially in 1982/83; in the first half of that fiscal year, it amounted to 1.5 per cent of GDP.

By mid-1983, a little over 60 per cent of $737 million needed for the Government's Investment Programme (1982-1984)[20] had been mobilized. In November, the Government issued a Revised Recovery Programme for 1983-1985, to be presented to a donors' meeting in 1984.

United Nations economic assistance to Uganda included financing by the World Bank affiliates—IDA and the International Finance Corporation—for projects in agriculture, education, postal services and telecommunications, totalling some $134 million.[5] UNICEF provided assistance valued at $2.4 million, while WFP had ongoing projects with a total value of some $40 million and emergency operations worth $9 million.

GENERAL ASSEMBLY ACTION

On 20 December, the General Assembly, on the recommendation of the Second Committee, adopted resolution 38/207 without vote.

Assistance to Uganda

The General Assembly,

Recalling its resolutions 35/103 of 5 December 1980, 36/218 of 17 December 1981 and 37/162 of 17 December 1982 on assistance to Uganda,

Bearing in mind the enormous economic and social setbacks suffered by Uganda and the resultant precipitous decline in the well-being of its people,

Taking into account the Recovery Programme (1982-1984) presented by the Government of Uganda to the meeting of the Consultative Group on Uganda, held in Paris in May 1982 under the auspices of the World Bank,

Recognizing that Uganda is not only land-locked but also one of the least developed and most seriously affected countries,

Noting the appeals of the Secretary-General for assistance to Uganda,

Taking note of the report of the Secretary-General, submitted in response to General Assembly resolution 36/218, to which was annexed the report on Uganda's needs for assistance,

Taking note also of the summary report of the Secretary-General, in which it is stated that substantial additional assistance is required to finance the remaining projects in the Investment Programme which have not yet attracted the support of the international community,

Reaffirming the urgent need for further international action to assist the Government of Uganda in its continuing efforts for national reconstruction, rehabilitation and development,

Encouraged that the economic policies of the Government of Uganda and the support assistance provided by the donor countries and international organizations have produced positive signs of economic recovery,

1. *Expresses its appreciation* to the Secretary-General for the steps he has taken to mobilize assistance for Uganda;

2. *Further expresses its appreciation* to those States and organizations which have provided assistance to that country;

3. *Reaffirms fully its endorsement* of the assessment and recommendations contained in the annex to the report of the Secretary-General;

4. *Requests* the Secretary-General to ensure that adequate financial and budgetary arrangements are made for the continued mobilization of resources to finance the international programme of assistance to Uganda;

5. *Invites* the international community, in particular the United Nations system and donor countries and organizations, to make available more resources to implement the country's Recovery Programme (1982-1984) and meet the remaining needs described in the annex to the report of the Secretary-General and in his summary report;

6. *Urgently renews its appeal* to all Member States, specialized agencies and other organizations of the United Nations system and international economic and financial institutions to contribute generously, through bilateral and multilateral channels, to the reconstruction, rehabilitation and development needs of Uganda and to its emergency requirements;

7. *Invites* Member States to participate fully in and support effectively the meeting of the World Bank Consultative Group on Uganda, to be held in Paris early in 1984;

8. *Requests* the appropriate organizations and programmes of the United Nations system to maintain and increase their current and future programmes of assistance to Uganda and to report periodically to the Secretary-General on the steps they have taken and the resources they have made available to help that country;

9. *Invites* the United Nations Conference on Trade and Development, the United Nations Industrial Development Organization, the United Nations Children's Fund, the United Nations Development Programme, the World Food Programme, the International Fund for Agricultural Development, the International Labour Organisation, the Food and Agriculture Organization of the United Nations, the United Nations Educational, Scientific and Cultural Organization, the World Health Organization and the World Bank to bring to the attention of their governing bodies, for their consideration, the special needs of Uganda and to report the decisions of those bodies to the Secretary-General by 15 July 1984;

10. *Requests* the United Nations High Commissioner for Refugees to continue his humanitarian assistance programmes in Uganda;

11. *Requests* the Secretary-General:

(*a*) To continue his efforts to mobilize the necessary resources for an effective programme of financial, technical and material assistance to Uganda;

(*b*) To keep the situation in Uganda under constant review, to maintain close contact with Member States, the specialized agencies, regional and other intergovernmental organizations and the international financial institutions concerned, and to apprise the Economic and Social Council, at its second regular session of 1984, of the current status of the special programme of economic assistance for Uganda;

(*c*) To report on the progress made in the economic situation in Uganda and in organizing international assistance for that country in time for the matter to be considered by the General Assembly at its thirty-ninth session.

General Assembly resolution 38/207

20 December 1983   Meeting 104   Adopted without vote

Approved by Second Committee (A/38/705 & Corr.1) without vote, 28 November (meeting 52); 27-nation draft (A/C.2/38/L.52), orally revised in informal consultations; agenda item 81.

Sponsors: Afghanistan, Algeria, Botswana, Cape Verde, Chad, Cyprus, Djibouti, Egypt, Ethiopia, Gambia, Ghana, Guinea-Bissau, Kenya, Lesotho, Liberia, Madagascar, Mozambique, Pakistan, Romania, Rwanda, Sierra Leone, Sudan, Turkey, Uganda, United Republic of Cameroon, United Republic of Tanzania, Zambia.

Meeting numbers. GA 38th session: 2nd Committee 34-38, 44, 52; plenary 104.

Other regions

Democratic Yemen

In pursuance of a December 1982 General Assembly request,[21] the Secretary-General submitted to the Assembly in June 1983 a progress report on assistance to Democratic Yemen,[22] which had suffered an estimated $975 million in damage and loss of 482 lives following serious nation-wide flooding in March 1982.[23]

The international community had responded to calls made in 1982 by the Assembly and the Economic and Social Council,[24] as well as to UNDRO's appeal for rehabilitation and reconstruction assistance. Some donors provided technical and/or financial assistance; others sent missions to draw up aid programmes. Special assistance covered such projects as repairing wells and irrigation systems, rehabilitation of crop production, land reclamation, meteorological forecasting and flood warning systems, housing construction, and road and bridge reconstruction.

The Secretary-General called for further assistance, asserting that the mounting burden of rehabilitation and reconstruction was still beyond the capacity of the Government.

GENERAL ASSEMBLY ACTION

On 20 December, the General Assembly, on the recommendation of the Second Committee, adopted resolution 38/206 without vote.

Assistance to Democratic Yemen

The General Assembly,

Recalling Economic and Social Council resolutions 1982/6 of 28 April 1982 and 1982/59 of 30 July 1982 concerning the extensive devastation caused by the heavy floods in Democratic Yemen,

Recalling also resolution 107(IX) of 11 May 1982 of the Economic Commission for Western Asia, in which the Commission called for the urgent establishment of a programme for the rehabilitation and reconstruction of the flood-stricken areas of Democratic Yemen,

Having considered the report prepared by the Office of the United Nations Disaster Relief Co-ordinator on the extent and nature of the damage caused by the floods,

Taking note of the report of the Secretary-General on assistance to Democratic Yemen,

Recognizing that Democratic Yemen, as one of the least developed countries, is unable to bear the mounting burden of rehabilitation and reconstruction of the affected areas,

Recognizing also the efforts made by Democratic Yemen to alleviate the suffering of the victims of the floods,

1. *Expresses its appreciation* to the Secretary-General for the steps he has taken regarding assistance to Democratic Yemen;

2. *Expresses its gratitude* to those States and international, regional and intergovernmental organizations that have provided assistance to Democratic Yemen;

3. *Requests* the Secretary-General to continue to mobilize the necessary resources for an effective, comprehensive programme of financial, technical and material assistance to Democratic Yemen in order to help mitigate the damage inflicted on it and implement its rehabilitation and reconstruction plans;

4. *Appeals* to Member States to contribute generously through bilateral or multilateral channels to the reconstruction and development process in Democratic Yemen;

5. *Requests* the appropriate organizations and programmes of the United Nations system—in particular the United Nations Development Programme, the World Bank, the World Food Programme, the Food and Agriculture Organization of the United Nations, the International Fund for Agricultural Development, the World Health Organization, the United Nations Fund for Population Activities, the United Nations Children's Fund and the United Nations Industrial Development Organization—to maintain and expand their programmes of assistance to Democratic Yemen and to co-operate closely with the Secretary-General in organizing an effective programme of assistance to that country;

6. *Calls upon* regional and interregional organizations and other intergovernmental and non-governmental organizations to continue their assistance to the development requirements of Democratic Yemen;

7. *Requests* the Secretary-General to keep the situation in Democratic Yemen under review and to report to the General Assembly at its thirty-ninth session on the progress made on the implementation of the present resolution.

General Assembly resolution 38/206

20 December 1983   Meeting 104   Adopted without vote

Approved by Second Committee (A/38/705 & Corr.1) without vote, 28 November (meeting 52); 31-nation draft (A/C.2/38/L.51); agenda item 81.

Sponsors: Afghanistan, Algeria, Angola, Argentina, Bahrain, Bangladesh, Cape Verde, Cuba, Cyprus, Democratic Yemen, Djibouti, Ethiopia, France, Guinea-Bissau, India, Kuwait, Lebanon, Libyan Arab Jamahiriya, Madagascar, Mauritania, Nicaragua, Oman, Pakistan, Qatar, Saudi Arabia, Syrian Arab Republic, Tunisia, United Arab Emirates, Viet Nam, Yemen, Yugoslavia.

Meeting numbers. GA 38th session: 2nd Committee 34-38, 44, 52; plenary 104.

Nicaragua

In response to a December 1982 General Assembly request,[25] the Secretary-General submitted to it in October 1983 a report[26] containing information on assistance to Nicaragua as reported by the country, along with information received from Member States (Czechoslovakia, German Democratic Republic, Federal Republic of Germany, Netherlands, Norway, Spain, Sweden) and from the United Nations system.

Nicaragua reported having received between mid-July 1979 and March 1983 nearly $242 million in grants and about $2 billion in loans and credit. Grants were provided by sources in Western Europe (47 per cent), Latin America (28 per cent), North America (12 per cent) and the United Nations system (10 per cent). About 30 per cent of total credit and loans was provided by multilateral agencies and the remainder by bilateral sources: Latin American countries ($513 million), socialist countries ($461 million), Western European countries ($237 million) and North American countries ($73 million).

The United Nations system provided some $221 million between mid-July 1979 and 30 April 1983. The largest share of resources under technical assistance was approved for security and social justice, followed by health, humanitarian assistance, and agriculture, forestry and fisheries. Other areas of assistance approved dealt with, among others, development policy and planning, education, employment, industry, international trade and development, population, science and technology, and transport and communications.

GENERAL ASSEMBLY ACTION

On 20 December, the General Assembly, acting on the recommendation of the Second Committee, adopted resolution 38/223 without vote.

Assistance to Nicaragua

The General Assembly,

Recalling its resolutions 34/8 of 25 October 1979, 35/84 of 5 December 1980, 36/213 of 17 December 1981 and 37/157 of 17 December 1982 concerning assistance for the reconstruction of Nicaragua,

Recalling also Economic and Social Council decision 1982/168 of 29 July 1982,

Recalling further resolution 982 adopted by the Seventeenth Regional Conference for Latin America of the Food and Agriculture Organization of the United Nations, held at Managua from 30 August to 10 September 1982,

Taking note of the report of the Secretary-General on assistance to Nicaragua,

Noting with satisfaction the support that Member States, the specialized agencies and other organizations of the United Nations system have given to the efforts of the Government of Nicaragua for the reconstruction of the country,

Noting that from June to September 1982 Nicaragua suffered a serious drought that considerably affected the agricultural and livestock sectors, which constitute the most important economic activities of the country,

Considering that, despite the efforts of the Government and people of Nicaragua, the economic situation has not returned to normal and continues to worsen,

Deeply concerned that Nicaragua is experiencing serious economic difficulties directly affecting its development efforts,

1. *Expresses its appreciation* to the Secretary-General for his efforts regarding assistance to Nicaragua;

2. *Expresses its appreciation* to the States and organizations that have provided assistance to Nicaragua;

3. *Urges* all Governments to continue contributing to the reconstruction and development of Nicaragua;

4. *Requests* the organizations of the United Nations system to continue and to increase their assistance in this endeavour;

5. *Recommends* that Nicaragua should continue to receive treatment appropriate to the special needs of the country until the economic situation returns to normal;

6. *Requests* the Secretary-General to report to the General Assembly at its thirty-ninth session on the progress made in the implementation of the present resolution.

General Assembly resolution 38/223

20 December 1983   Meeting 104   Adopted without vote

Approved by Second Committee (A/38/705 & Corr.1) without vote, 28 November (meeting 52); 64-nation draft (A/C.2/38/L.68), orally revised in informal consultations; agenda item 81.

Sponsors: Afghanistan, Algeria, Angola, Argentina, Austria, Bangladesh, Belize, Benin, Bolivia, Brazil, Bulgaria, Burundi, Canada, Cape Verde, China, Colombia, Comoros, Congo, Costa Rica, Cuba, Cyprus, Czechoslovakia, Democratic Yemen, Dominican Republic, Ecuador, Egypt, Ethiopia, France, German Democratic Republic, Greece, Grenada, Guinea-Bissau, Guyana, India, Iran, Lao People's Democratic Republic, Libyan Arab Jamahiriya, Madagascar, Mali, Mauritania, Mexico, Mongolia, Mozambique, Nigeria, Pakistan, Panama, Peru, Romania, Sao Tome and Principe, Seychelles, Spain, Suriname, Sweden, Syrian Arab Republic, Trinidad and Tobago, Tunisia, United Republic of Tanzania, Uruguay, Vanuatu, Venezuela, Viet Nam, Yugoslavia, Zambia, Zimbabwe.

Meeting numbers. GA 38th session: 2nd Committee 34-38, 46, 52; plenary 104.

In related action, the Assembly, in resolution 38/217, focused on special assistance to alleviate the economic and social problems faced in regions of Honduras and Nicaragua as a result of the May 1982 floods and other subsequent natural disasters (see below).

Vanuatu

In 1983, the General Assembly called for international assistance to help Vanuatu, a small archipelagic developing country, meet its development needs.

On the recommendation of the Second Committee, the Assembly, on 20 December, adopted resolution 38/218 without vote.

Economic assistance to Vanuatu

The General Assembly,

Recalling its resolution 3421(XXX) of 8 December 1975 on the implementation of the Declaration on the Granting of Independence to Colonial Countries and Peoples, in which it urged the specialized agencies and other organizations within the United Nations system

to extend assistance to the newly independent and emerging States,

Recalling also its resolutions 31/156 of 21 December 1976, 32/185 of 19 December 1977, 34/205 of 19 December 1979, 35/61 of 5 December 1980 and 37/206 of 20 December 1982, in which it urged all Governments, in particular those of the developed countries, to lend their support, in the context of their assistance programmes, for the implementation of the specific action envisaged in favour of island developing countries, and in which it also called upon all organizations of the United Nations system to implement, within their respective spheres of competence, appropriate specific actions in favour of island developing countries,

Recalling further resolutions 98(IV) of 31 May 1976, 111(V) of 3 June 1979, and 138(VI) of 2 July 1983 of the United Nations Conference on Trade and Development concerning special action related to the particular needs and problems of island developing countries,

Recognizing the difficult problems faced by island developing countries, owing mainly to their smallness, remoteness, constraints in transport, great distances from market centres, highly limited internal markets, lack of natural resources, heavy dependence on a few commodities, shortage of administrative personnel and heavy financial burdens,

Taking into account the fact that Vanuatu is an island developing country and is small and archipelagic, which makes the provision of services difficult and entails very high overhead costs, because of inter-island distances,

Concerned at the severe constraints on the economic development of Vanuatu, particularly those ensuing from its geographical isolation,

Concerned also at the continued structural imbalances in the economy of the country, particularly its overwhelming dependence on imports,

Noting that the disadvantageous demographic and geographic features of Vanuatu, such as its physical remoteness, small area and small population, pose special development problems,

Noting also that, without good transport and communications links, any development will be difficult,

1. *Calls the attention* of the international community to the special problems confronting Vanuatu as an island developing country with a small population;

2. *Appeals* to Member States, regional and interregional organizations and other intergovernmental organizations to provide financial, material and technical assistance to Vanuatu to enable it to establish the social and economic infrastructure that is essential for the well-being of its people;

3. *Invites* the Economic and Social Commission for Asia and the Pacific, the United Nations Conference on Trade and Development, the United Nations Industrial Development Organization, the United Nations Children's Fund, the United Nations Development Programme, the World Food Programme, the International Labour Organisation, the Food and Agriculture Organization of the United Nations, the United Nations Educational, Scientific and Cultural Organization, the International Civil Aviation Organization, the World Health Organization, the World Bank, the International Telecommunication Union, the World Meteorological Organization, the International Maritime Organization and the International Fund for Agricultural Development to bring to the attention of their governing bod-

ies, for their consideration, the special needs of Vanuatu and to report the decisions of those bodies to the Secretary-General by 15 July 1984;

4. *Requests* the Secretary-General to mobilize the financial, technical and economic assistance of the international community, in particular the developed countries and the appropriate organizations of the United Nations system, with a view to meeting the short-term and long-term development needs of Vanuatu;

5. *Requests* the appropriate organizations and programmes of the United Nations system to maintain and increase their current and future programmes of assistance to Vanuatu, to co-operate closely with the Secretary-General in organizing an effective international programme of assistance and to report periodically to him on the steps they have taken and the resources they have made available to help that country;

6. *Requests* the Committee for Development Planning at its twentieth session, as a matter of priority, to give due consideration to the question of the inclusion of Vanuatu in the list of the least developed countries and to submit its conclusions to the Economic and Social Council at its second regular session of 1984;

7. *Calls upon* Member States, pending consideration by the Committee for Development Planning at its twentieth session of the report submitted to it and in view of the critical economic situation of Vanuatu, to accord Vanuatu special measures and, as a matter of priority, to give special consideration to the early inclusion of Vanuatu in their programmes of development assistance;

8. *Also requests* the Secretary-General to keep this matter under review and to report to the General Assembly at its thirty-ninth session on the implementation of the present resolution.

General Assembly resolution 38/218

20 December 1983　　　Meeting 104　　　Adopted without vote

Approved by Second Committee (A/38/705 & Corr.1) without vote, 28 November (meeting 52); 56-nation draft (A/C.2/38/L.63), orally revised in informal consultations; agenda item 81.

Sponsors: Afghanistan, Algeria, Angola, Australia, Bahamas, Belize, Benin, Botswana, Burundi, Cape Verde, China, Comoros, Cyprus, Democratic Yemen, Egypt, Ethiopia, Fiji, Gambia, Greece, Guinea-Bissau, Guyana, Japan, Libyan Arab Jamahiriya, Madagascar, Maldives, Mauritania, Mozambique, New Zealand, Nicaragua, Niger, Nigeria, Pakistan, Panama, Papua New Guinea, Portugal, Romania, Samoa, Sao Tome and Principe, Senegal, Seychelles, Sierra Leone, Solomon Islands, Suriname, Swaziland, Syrian Arab Republic, Thailand, Trinidad and Tobago, Uganda, United Republic of Cameroon, United Republic of Tanzania, Vanuatu, Viet Nam, Yemen, Yugoslavia, Zambia, Zimbabwe.

Meeting numbers. GA 38th session: 2nd Committee 34-38, 46, 52; plenary 104.

REFERENCES

[1]A/38/471. [2]YUN 1981, p. 406. [3]*Ibid.*, p. 410, GA res. 36/194, 17 Dec. 1981. [4]A/38/216. [5]A/38/219. [6]YUN 1982, p. 673. [7]YUN 1977, p. 219. [8]YUN 1982, p. 683, GA res. 37/155, 17 Dec. 1982. [9]A/38/213. [10]YUN 1982, p. 681. [11]*Ibid.*, p. 617, GA res. 37/133, 17 Dec. 1982. [12]*Ibid.*, p. 685. [13]*Ibid.*, p. 686. [14]A/38/215. [15]YUN 1982, p. 317, SC res. 527(1982), 15 Dec. 1982. [16]S/15600. [17]YUN 1982, p. 690. [18]*Ibid.*, p. 695, GA res. 37/158, 17 Dec. 1982. [19]A/38/211. [20]YUN 1982, p. 696. [21]*Ibid.*, p. 698, GA res. 37/150, 17 Dec. 1982. [22]A/38/212. [23]YUN 1982, p. 698. [24]*Ibid.*, p. 711, ESC res. 1982/6, 28 Apr. 1982. [25]*Ibid.*, p. 699, GA res. 37/157, 17 Dec. 1982. [26]A/38/218.

Disasters

During 1983, UNDRO continued to respond to needs arising from natural disasters such as drought, floods, storms and earthquakes, by co-ordinating the relief and assistance activities of the United Nations system. In a series of resolutions, both the General Assembly (38/204, 38/216, 38/217, 38/222 and 38/225) and the Economic and Social Council (1983/45, 1983/46 and 1983/68) dealt with assistance needs resulting from the continuing drought in certain areas of Africa, in particular in the Sudano-Sahelian region and in East Africa; floods in Bolivia, Ecuador and Peru; floods and drought in Honduras and Nicaragua; and an earthquake in Yemen. In addition, the Assembly and the Council, in resolutions 38/202 and 1983/47, respectively, called for the strengthening of the United Nations capacity to respond to disasters.

Office of the United Nations Disaster Relief Co-ordinator

UNDRO activities

In 1983, as in previous years, UNDRO provided comprehensive programmes of disaster management at the request of the Governments concerned, in order to reduce the economic and social impact of natural or man-made disasters such as flood and drought emergencies, cyclones, earthquakes, civil strife, and situations involving displaced persons or a massive influx of returnees from abroad. UNDRO's 1983 activities were described in reports of the Secretary-General to the Economic and Social Council and the General Assembly in June 1983[1] and June 1984.[2]

Between 1 April 1983 and 31 March 1984, UNDRO issued 235 situation reports to inform the international community of relief needs in particular disasters; it helped organize concerted relief programmes through inter-agency consultations, and 23 relief assessment missions were undertaken either by UNDRO alone or jointly with other agencies. An assessment of damage and relief needs was communicated to UNDRO at Geneva, taking into account the data supplied by the Governments concerned.

Revised Disaster Management Guidelines, prepared by UNDRO, were issued by UNDP in October 1983 for the benefit of its resident representatives/co-ordinators, who provided the focal point at the country level for international disaster relief co-ordination.

UNDRO continued to provide technical assistance in disaster preparedness/prevention, and organized seminars or missions dealing with earth-quakes, floods, volcanic eruptions, industrial accidents and health and housing (see below). An UNDRO study on expediting international emergency relief, with particular reference to the principles of relevant international law, was examined at a meeting of an informal group of experts in August at Geneva, attended also by observers from United Nations agencies; the participants prepared a draft international convention on the question[3] for submission to the Economic and Social Council.

Improvements in information-gathering and data-processing capabilities contributed to UNDRO's increased effectiveness. The Country Profile Data Base, established in 1982, had by the end of 1983 been enlarged to contain basic information on more than 100 countries. The preliminary design of the new Suppliers/Stockpiles Profile Data Base was completed in 1983 and input prepared for approximately 75 suppliers of specialized relief items. The design of the Bibliographic Data Base of disaster publications was also initiated. In conjunction with the Centre national d'études spatiales (CNES) in France, UNDRO carried out experiments during 1983 using a portable satellite transmitting beacon supplied by CNES; the beacon contained a keyboard, which allowed on-site entry by an UNDRO relief officer and automatic satellite transmission of detailed information on a disaster and relief requirements.

The bimonthly publication *UNDRO News*, which described UNDRO activities and provided information on technical developments in disaster-related fields, was expanded during 1983.

In several cases of major man-made emergencies, such as those occurring in Angola, Chad, Lebanon (see below) and West Africa, UNDRO organized meetings with relevant United Nations organizations to develop large-scale relief programmes, as follows:

—*Angola.* Relief activities needed as a result of drought and military operations began in 1981 and were completed in February 1983. By that time, contributions to the programme totalled almost $14 million. During a follow-up mission organized by UNDRO that month, Angola was advised of UNDRO's readiness to launch the second phase of the programme, providing relief to displaced persons in the Central Plateau, as soon as the Government viewed it opportune.

—*Chad.* Airlifted food relief was transported to affected areas of Chad, which suffered from drought (see below, under SUDANO-SAHELIAN REGION) and a prolonged civil strife. UNDRO continued to co-ordinate relief efforts of the United Nations system with those of bilateral and international non-governmental organizations. By the end of March, 49,442 tons of food had been received or pledged, and 191 trucks contributed by various donors had been delivered.

—*West Africa.* In mid-January, Nigeria ordered foreign workers illegally in the country to leave (see POLITICAL AND SECURITY QUESTIONS, Chapter V). The majority of those expelled were from Ghana and

to reach their country they had to transit through Benin and Togo. Other countries affected were Benin, the Central African Republic, Chad, Guinea, Mali, the Niger, Togo, the Upper Volta and the United Republic of Cameroon. At the request of the Secretary-General, UNDRO co-ordinated relief to the affected people and sent missions to assess needs and to assist in relief distribution. It convened meetings with donor Governments, United Nations agencies and non-governmental organizations to launch a relief programme, and donations amounted to over $21 million.

In addition to a number of disaster situations concerning which the General Assembly and the Economic and Social Council took action to provide relief assistance (see below, under DISASTER RELIEF), UNDRO took note of several other, mostly natural, disasters, such as those listed below, often responding by launching international appeals at the request of the Governments concerned or by providing cash grants.

—*Afghanistan.* An earthquake, measuring 7.0 on the Richter scale, struck a region on its border with Pakistan, on 31 December, seriously affecting some 27,000 persons.

—*Argentina.* Torrential rains in the north-east during the first six months of the year caused heavy material damage and evacuation of 150,000 people. UNDRO responded to Argentina's appeal with a cash grant of $21,500.

—*Benin.* Severely deficient and erratic rainfall throughout 1983 led to crop failures and a significant lowering of water tables throughout the country.

—*Colombia.* An earthquake on 31 March struck a region 300 kilometres south-west of the capital, causing over 200 deaths and rendering some 30,000 people homeless. UNDRO provided an emergency cash grant of $20,000 and assisted in assessing and co-ordinating relief.

—*Comoros.* A severe cyclone, between 10 and 12 January, caused extensive damage to crops, housing, public buildings, roads and sea walls; 30,000 people were in need of emergency assistance. A cash grant of $10,000 was provided for local purchase of relief supplies.

—*Fiji.* A cyclone, considered to be the most severe in the past decade, hit several islands on 1 and 2 March, causing heavy crop, forestry and housing damage. International emergency relief was provided for 200,000 people, representing one third of the national population.

—*Guinea.* A major earthquake of 22 December killed 275 people, injured 1,436 and rendered 20,000 homeless. Relief was provided to ensure inland transport of supplies.

—*Madagascar.* A cyclone of 8 December and subsequent flooding caused an emergency situation involving crop loss and destruction of communication and transportation systems.

—*Mozambique.* Inadequate rainfall affected the central and southern provinces. Assistance included a water supply project to drill 80 wells in the Maputo area and transport of food.

—*Nepal.* Heavy rains in September resulted in severe flooding affecting some 200,000 persons and causing extensive damage to property, public utilities, communications, crops and livestock. UNDRO released a cash grant of $25,000 for local purchase of emergency relief items.

—*Nicaragua.* Two huge oil tanks exploded in Corinto in October, forcing the Government to evacuate the town. UNDRO provided a cash grant of $30,000.

—*Paraguay.* Continuous heavy rain during the year caused severe flooding, affecting some 120,000 persons, including 36,000 children under five years of age. UNDRO made a $20,000 cash grant for the purchase of essential medicines.

—*Portugal.* Flash floods following storms and heavy rains on 18 and 19 November caused what the Government estimated to be $95 million worth of damage to infrastructure, agriculture, industry, commerce and housing. UNDRO responded with a cash grant of $25,000.

—*Turkey.* A major earthquake of 30 October in the northern provinces caused 1,346 deaths and intensive damage, including destruction of infrastructure and homes, and heavy cattle losses. UNDRO assisted in the relief operation by, among other things, coordinating relief and issuing an international appeal; the donors' response covered all relief needs within one month of the earthquake.

—*Viet Nam.* Four typhoons in late 1983 caused extensive damage in the northern and central provinces, including 658 deaths and food loss of 341,500 tons. UNDRO launched an international appeal for relief aid.

UNDRO finances

The activities of UNDRO in 1983 continued to be financed mainly from the United Nations regular budget and the voluntary UNDRO Trust Fund.[2] The Trust Fund for General Disaster Relief, which supplemented those resources, was used as a reserve fund to guarantee sums pledged by donors for particular relief operations in order to bridge the gap between the date of the pledge and actual receipt of the donation. Net budget appropriations from the regular budget for the biennium 1982-1983, as finalized by the General Assembly in resolution 38/226 A of 20 December 1983, amounted to $5,328,000; for 1984-1985, the Assembly, by resolution 38/236 A of the same date, appropriated $5,236,400.

Expenditures under the Trust Funds during 1983 were $7,147,359, including $6,124,148 to 23 countries. Contributions from 22 Governments and EEC paid to the Trust Funds in 1983 totalled $8,673,758. The UNDRO Trust Fund had three main sub-accounts—for strengthening UNDRO, for disaster relief assistance and for disaster prevention and pre-disaster planning—as well as separate sub-accounts for emergency relief assistance earmarked for given countries (see tables below).

The Advisory Committee on Administrative and Budgetary Questions (ACABQ) reported to the Assembly in October on requests by the United Nations Controller for ACABQ's concurrence on the use of funds from the Working Capital Fund

on unforeseen and extraordinary expenses for the 1982-1983 biennium in connection with UNDRO's emergency assistance grants.[4] Pointing out that the regular budget appropriation of $720,000 for the biennium for such assistance had been expended fully by July 1983, the Controller considered that an advance from the Fund would be required to cover the needs that might arise for the remainder of the year. The Controller therefore sought, on 5 August, commitments up to $100,000, and subsequently revised the figure, on 20 September, to $240,000, adding that, since July, four requests for emergency assistance grants had been received from countries (Argentina, Bolivia, Ecuador, Peru) stricken by major disasters and that, based on recent experience, four additional major disasters could be anticipated before the end of the year. In making the requests, the Controller drew attention to a July 1983 Economic and Social Council recommendation (resolution 1983/47, see below) that the Assembly authorize the Secretary-General to allow UNDRO to respond, within existing resources, to emergency assistance requests up to a maximum of $600,000 in any one year.

ACABQ, having considered the circumstances under which regular budget contributions had been made in the past for emergency disaster assistance grants, concluded that in the case of either the December 1982 Assembly resolution[5] which had raised the ceiling of the total maximum grants allowable per year or the 1983 Council recommendation, responses to requests for such assistance must be made from within the existing appropriation. ACABQ outlined for the Assembly several options for action in response to the 1983 situation.

In December, the General Assembly, in resolution 38/202, authorized the Secretary-General to permit UNDRO to allocate up to a total of $600,000 in any one year for emergency disaster assistance, with a normal ceiling of $50,000 per country in the case of any one disaster, within existing resources as far as possible (see below). It called on States to respond to the Secretary-General's appeals for contributions to meet disaster situations and to make voluntary contributions, channelled through the UNDRO Trust Fund, to help cover UNDRO's unforeseen expenses in connection with disaster relief operations.

Prior to the Assembly action, the Fifth (Administrative and Budgetary) Committee had informed the Assembly that adopting the text entailed no additional appropriations at that time.[6] In related action, the Committee rejected—by 60 votes to 21, with 11 abstentions—a United States proposal,[7] by which the Assembly would have decided to maintain the existing cost-sharing arrangements for grants for emergency assistance.

TRUST FUNDS FOR DISASTER RELIEF ASSISTANCE
EXPENDITURES, 1983
(as at 31 December 1983; in US dollars)

ACCOUNT/PURPOSE	AMOUNT
Disaster relief assistance	
Algeria	755*
Angola	74,982
Benin	29,409
Caribbean	340,365
Chad	1,172,754
Colombia	32,033
Comoros	5,539
Ecuador	48,643
Ethiopia	242,287
Fiji	14,922
Ghana	149,071
Indonesia	144
Lebanon	3,449,613
Nepal	4,387*
Niger	20,000
Paraguay	6,989
Peru	117,412
Saint Lucia	637*
Togo	8,501
Tonga	21,328
Tunisia	30,000
Viet Nam	316,377
Yemen	38,000
General disaster relief operations	53,217
Subtotal	6,177,365
Strengthening of UNDRO	731,158
UNDRO/UNEP projects	34,545
Emergency relief assistance	5,622
Disaster prevention and pre-disaster planning	198,669
Total	7,147,359†

*Adjustment for prior periods.
†Includes adjustment for prior periods of $5,779.

CONTRIBUTIONS TO THE TRUST FUNDS FOR
DISASTER RELIEF ASSISTANCE, 1983
(as at 31 December 1983; in US dollar equivalent)

PURPOSE/CONTRIBUTOR	AMOUNT PAID
Disaster relief in Angola	
Norway	12,000
Subtotal	12,000
Disaster relief in Bolivia	
Australia	44,545
Chile	12,000
Subtotal	56,545
Disaster relief in the Caribbean	
Canada	163,293
European Economic Community	48,010
United States	288,000
Subtotal	499,303
Disaster relief in Chad	
Canada	298,822
Denmark	117,357
European Economic Community	304,472
Germany, Federal Republic of	21,723
Indonesia	25,000
Norway	127,641
Philippines	500
Switzerland	45,673
United States	255,000
Subtotal	1,196,188
Disaster relief in Colombia	
Australia	17,483
Italy	246,914
Subtotal	264,397

PURPOSE/CONTRIBUTOR	AMOUNT PAID
Disaster relief in the Comoros	
Switzerland	15,075
Subtotal	15,075
Disaster relief in Ecuador	
Australia	22,273
Chile	9,000
Italy	298,992
Switzerland	25,126
Subtotal	355,391
Disaster relief in Ethiopia	
Canada	241,410
European Economic Community	101,907
Netherlands	9,600
United Kingdom	109,425
United States	500,000
Subtotal	962,342
Disaster relief in Fiji	
Canada	40,667
Subtotal	40,667
Disaster relief in Ghana	
Italy	33,614
Switzerland	123,153
Subtotal	156,767
Disaster relief in Lebanon	
European Economic Community	3,271,552
Switzerland	125,628
Subtotal	3,397,180
Disaster relief in Mozambique	
Canada	40,323
Germany, Federal Republic of	20,000
Greece	3,000
Norway	67,513
Switzerland	23,474
United Kingdom	150,350
Subtotal	304,660
Disaster relief in Niger	
Canada	60,102
Subtotal	60,102
Disaster relief in Peru	
Australia	39,861
Chile	9,000
Italy	194,198
Switzerland	14,423
Subtotal	257,482
Disaster relief in Turkey	
Australia	367,400
Subtotal	367,400
Disaster relief in Viet Nam	
European Economic Community	283,963
Italy	35,107
Subtotal	319,070
General disaster relief operations	
Cyprus	500
Subtotal	500
Disaster prevention and pre-disaster planning	
Norway	12,500
Subtotal	12,500
Strengthening of UNDRO	
Australia	103,920
Bahamas	1,500
Iceland	5,900
Italy	70,741
Jamaica	3,123
Japan	100,000

PURPOSE/CONTRIBUTOR	AMOUNT PAID
Strengthening of UNDRO (cont.)	
New Zealand	6,429
Nigeria	20,077
Philippines	4,384
Switzerland	72,115
Tunisia	8,000
Subtotal	396,189
Total	8,673,758

Co-ordination in the UN system

In June 1983, the Secretary-General, in response to General Assembly requests of 1981[8] and 1982,[5] submitted to it through the Economic and Social Council a report on strengthening the United Nations capacity to respond to natural and other disaster situations.[9] In addition to describing steps taken by United Nations organizations to that end, the report contained suggestions on ensuring that the needs of people affected by disasters were met through a co-ordinated international effort in which each organization played its specific role.

The Secretary-General observed that, for each emergency, UNDRO drew up a concerted relief programme based on, among other things, an on-the-spot assessment, the request of the country concerned, and a meeting of the concerned United Nations organizations, followed by action by the relevant organization in areas of its competence. In view of the cost and time involved in holding inter-secretariat meetings of the various disaster units and focal points for developing and revising, as necessary, any relief programme, the Secretary-General suggested the use of a teleconferencing system, including video display devices. As regards appeals for resources to respond to emergencies, it was suggested that, following a united appeal, each of the concerned organizations continue its efforts to obtain the necessary funds, while keeping UNDRO as the information focal point informed.

Delivery of relief supplies to and within the affected country continued to be a problem, with an average of a four-month delay between the request for emergency food assistance and delivery. As the few stocks and depots currently maintained by the United Nations and others could meet only a fraction of the immediate emergency needs, it was felt that a small amount of money that could be used in a flexible manner could improve the United Nations capacity to deliver emergency supplies. Programmes had been worked out by FAO to create national and regional food reserves, but little progress had been made. A proposal had also been made to have WFP establish under its control a small stock of strategically located essential supplies; a further approach was to provide it with more cash pledges so that it could use the most appropriate method of meeting emergency food needs, often by commercial purchases in the region.

When local authorities required more than technical advice and requested the United Nations system to assume operational responsibility for transporting and distributing relief supplies, the most appropriate organization needed to be identified on a case-by-case basis and be given the necessary support; this, and the training of officials in disaster-prone countries, were areas in which an UNDRO roster of experts, combined with some general-purpose funding, could contribute to improved United Nations responsiveness to disasters.

Reaffirming the importance of the availability of a general-purpose fund for unearmarked emergency relief, and the UNDRO Trust Fund as the most appropriate channel in that regard, the Secretary-General reiterated that UNDRO's task was to promote, facilitate and co-ordinate international relief efforts, while operational responsibilities rested with other United Nations organizations; the precise funding role for UNDRO, therefore, needed to be spelt out. As regards programme evaluation, the Secretary-General said that, in addition to the existing procedures, assessment should also be made of the way the international community as a whole provided disaster relief in specific cases so as to devise new arrangements, as appropriate. The Secretary-General also considered it helpful to development agencies if UNDRO, in consultation with the Government and the United Nations agencies concerned, included in its report to potential donor countries some reference to the known priority needs for rehabilitation and reconstruction. Donors and development organizations could then pursue matters bilaterally without further UNDRO involvement.

The Secretary-General concluded that a generally satisfactory and workable structure had been set out by the Assembly for promoting, facilitating and co-ordinating relief activities system-wide. Together with the approaches outlined by him, and by the Administrative Committee on Co-ordination (ACC) in 1981[10] and 1982,[11] the relevant Assembly resolutions had provided the basis for continuing collaboration, and the role of the Disaster Relief Co-ordinator was being more clearly defined and appreciated.

ECONOMIC AND SOCIAL COUNCIL ACTION

On 28 July, the Economic and Social Council adopted resolution 1983/47 without vote, on the recommendation of the Third Committee.

Strengthening the capacity of the United Nations system to respond to natural disasters and other disaster situations

The Economic and Social Council,

Recalling General Assembly resolutions 2816(XXVI) of 14 December 1971, by which the Office of the United Nations Disaster Relief Co-ordinator was established, and 36/225 of 17 December 1981, in which the Assembly reaffirmed the mandate of the Office and, *inter alia*, called for the strengthening and improvement of the capacity and effectiveness of the Office,

Recalling also General Assembly resolution 37/144 of 17 December 1982, in which the Assembly recognized that, in order to attain an effective co-ordination system of humanitarian and disaster relief assistance, it was essential to strengthen and improve the capacity and effectiveness of the Office of the United Nations Disaster Relief Co-ordinator and the United Nations system as a whole,

Recognizing that, as a result of those resolutions and other relevant resolutions and decisions, there is now in place a workable system to promote, facilitate and co-ordinate relief activities carried out by the United Nations system, in co-operation with Governments and voluntary agencies,

Noting that the operation of that system has been much improved but that there remains a need for its full application,

Noting further with appreciation the effective responses of the Office of the United Nations Disaster Relief Co-ordinator to recent major disasters,

Recognizing that shortage of resources has been a constraint on an effective response of the United Nations to disaster situations,

1.   *Takes note with appreciation* of the comprehensive report of the Secretary-General on strengthening the capacity of the United Nations system to respond to natural disasters and other disaster situations, which is complemented by his report on the work of the Office of the United Nations Disaster Relief Co-ordinator;

2.   *Notes with particular interest* the observations and conclusions of the Secretary-General relating to the transportation, more rapid delivery and distribution of relief supplies, reconstruction and rehabilitation, and the need for evaluation procedures to assess the way in which the Office of the United Nations Disaster Relief Co-ordinator and the international community as a whole have dealt with the mobilization and provision of disaster relief in particular cases;

3.   *Recognizes* the importance of disaster preparedness and prevention activities, and calls upon the Office of the United Nations Disaster Relief Co-ordinator, Governments and agencies involved to ensure that due priority attention is given to them;

4.   *Reaffirms* the sovereignty of individual Member States, recognizes the primary role of each State in caring for the victims of disasters occurring in its territory, and stresses that all relief operations should be carried out and co-ordinated in a manner consistent with the priorities and needs of the countries concerned;

5.   *Stresses* that the material and other assistance provided by the international community should be appropriate to the particular needs of the populations of disaster-affected areas;

6.   *Repeats* its call to all Governments and competent organs and organizations to co-operate with the Office of the United Nations Disaster Relief Co-ordinator and to improve in particular their flow of information on relief assistance, action, plans and needs;

7.   *Requests* the Office of the United Nations Disaster Relief Co-ordinator to continue and improve further the flow of information to Governments, organizations and agencies concerned, so that a more complete picture of relief activities, assistance received and further requirements may be provided to all concerned;

8.   *Recommends* that the General Assembly should authorize the Secretary-General to permit the Office of the United Nations Disaster Relief Co-ordinator to respond, within existing resources, to requests for emergency disaster assistance up to a total of $600,000 in any one year;

9.   *Appeals* to Governments to consider the possibility of urgent voluntary contributions, channelled directly or through the Trust Fund of the Office of the United Nations Disaster Relief Co-ordinator, to enable the Office to cover, *inter alia*, unforeseen expenses in connection with disaster relief operations;

10.   *Requests* the Secretary-General, in consultation with Governments and appropriate agencies, to submit to the General Assembly at its thirty-ninth session, through the Economic and Social Council at its second regular session of 1984, specific proposals to follow up conclusions and problems identified in his comprehensive report, taking into account the views and observations expressed during the second regular session of 1983 of the Council.

Economic and Social Council resolution 1983/47

28 July 1983   Meeting 40   Adopted without vote

Approved by Third Committee (E/1983/116) without vote, 22 July (meeting 16); 12-nation draft (E/1983/C.3/L.8), orally revised; agenda item 17.
Sponsors: Australia, Austria, Benin, Congo, Ghana, Lebanon, Mali, Pakistan, Qatar, Somalia, Sudan, Tunisia.
Meeting number. ESC 40.

GENERAL ASSEMBLY ACTION

By a recorded vote of 126 to 1, with 15 abstentions, the General Assembly, on 20 December, adopted resolution 38/202 as recommended by the Second Committee.

Strengthening of the capacity of the United Nations system to respond to natural disasters and other disaster situations

The General Assembly,

Recalling its resolutions 2816(XXVI) of 14 December 1971, by which the Office of the United Nations Disaster Relief Co-ordinator was established, and 36/225 of 17 December 1981, by which it reaffirmed the mandate of the Office and, *inter alia*, called for the strengthening and improvement of its capacity and effectiveness,

Recalling also its resolution 37/144 of 17 December 1982, in which the Assembly recognized that, in order to attain an effective co-ordination system of humanitarian and disaster relief assistance, it was essential to strengthen and improve the capacity and effectiveness of the Office of the United Nations Disaster Relief Co-ordinator and of the United Nations system as a whole,

Recalling further Economic and Social Council resolution 1983/47 of 28 July 1983,

Recognizing that, as a result of those resolutions and other relevant resolutions and decisions, there is now in place a workable system to promote, facilitate and co-ordinate relief activities carried out by the United Nations system, in co-operation with Governments and voluntary agencies,

Noting that the operation of that system has been much improved but that there remains a need for its full application,

Noting further with appreciation the effective response of the Office of the United Nations Disaster Relief Co-ordinator to recent major disasters,

Recognizing that shortage of resources has been a constraint on an effective response of the United Nations to disaster situations,

Recognizing also that the primary responsibility for administration, relief operations and disaster preparedness lies with the affected countries and that the major part of the material assistance and human effort in disaster relief comes from the Governments of those countries,

Recognizing further the importance of the contribution of the International Committee of the Red Cross, the League of Red Cross and Red Crescent Societies and appropriate voluntary organizations,

1. *Takes note with appreciation* of the comprehensive report of the Secretary-General on strengthening the capacity of the United Nations system to respond to natural disasters and other disaster situations, as well as of his report on the work of the Office of the United Nations Disaster Relief Co-ordinator and of the statement made by the Co-ordinator on 10 November 1983;

2. *Notes with particular interest* the observations and conclusions of the Secretary-General relating to the transportation, more rapid delivery and distribution of relief supplies, reconstruction and rehabilitation and the need for more effective monitoring and evaluation procedures to assess the way in which the Office of the United Nations Disaster Relief Co-ordinator and the international community as a whole have dealt with the mobilization and provision of disaster relief in particular cases;

3. *Recognizes* the importance of disaster preparedness and prevention activities, and calls upon the Office of the United Nations Disaster Relief Co-ordinator, Governments and agencies involved to ensure that a high level of attention is given to them;

4. *Reaffirms* the sovereignty of individual Member States, recognizes the primary role of each State in caring for the victims of disasters occurring in its territory and stresses that all relief operations should be carried out and co-ordinated in a manner consistent with the priorities and needs of the countries concerned;

5. *Stresses* that the quality and appropriateness of material and other assistance provided by the international community should meet the particular needs of the populations of disaster-affected areas;

6. *Repeats its call* to all Governments and competent organs and organizations to co-operate with the Office of the United Nations Disaster Relief Co-ordinator and to improve, in particular, their flow of information on relief assistance, action, plans and needs;

7. *Requests* the Office of the United Nations Disaster Relief Co-ordinator to continue and improve further the flow of information to Governments, organizations and agencies concerned, so that a more complete picture of relief activities, assistance received and further requirements may be provided to all concerned;

8. *Stresses* the need for the continuance and further strengthening of relations between the Office of the United Nations Disaster Relief Co-ordinator and appropriate voluntary organizations working in the area of disaster relief, including the International Committee of the Red Cross and the League of Red Cross and Red Crescent Societies, and requests the Secretary-

General to consider the establishment of a small consultative group composed of executives of these major relief organizations, in their individual capacity, to provide advice, upon request, to the United Nations Disaster Relief Co-ordinator in the assessment of relief needs and in the preparation and execution of concerted relief programmes;

9. *Authorizes* the Secretary-General to permit the Office of the United Nations Disaster Relief Co-ordinator to respond to requests for emergency disaster assistance up to a total of $600,000 in any one year, with a normal ceiling of $50,000 per country in the case of any one disaster, within existing resources as far as possible;

10. *Once again urgently calls upon* all States to respond positively and expeditiously to the Secretary-General's appeals for contributions to meet natural disasters and other disaster situations;

11. *Appeals* to Governments for urgent voluntary contributions, channelled through the Trust Fund of the Office of the United Nations Disaster Relief Co-ordinator, to enable the Office to cover, *inter alia*, unforeseen expenses in connection with disaster relief operations;

12. *Requests* the Secretary-General, in consultation with the Governments of both donor and recipient countries, as well as with appropriate agencies, to submit to the General Assembly at its thirty-ninth session, through the Economic and Social Council at its second regular session of 1984, specific proposals to follow up the conclusions and problems identified in his comprehensive report, as well as in the present resolution.

General Assembly resolution 38/202

20 December 1983   Meeting 104   126-1-15 (recorded vote)

Approved by Second Committee (A/38/705 & Corr.1) by vote (116-1-15), 28 November (meeting 52); 29-nation draft (A/C.2/38/L.69/Rev.1); agenda item 81.

Sponsors: Algeria, Bangladesh, Benin, Bolivia, Chad, Democratic Yemen, Egypt, Ethiopia, Gambia, Jamaica, Kenya, Lebanon, Liberia, Libyan Arab Jamahiriya, Madagascar, Malawi, Mauritania, Mozambique, Pakistan, Sierra Leone, Sudan, Togo, Trinidad and Tobago, Tunisia, Turkey, United Republic of Cameroon, Yemen, Zambia, Zimbabwe.

Financial implications. ACABQ, A/38/7/Add.16; 5th Committee, A/38/755; S-G, A/C.2/38/L.94, A/C.5/38/57.

Meeting numbers. GA 38th session: 2nd Committee 34-38, 46, 52; 5th Committee 61, 64, 73; plenary 104.

Recorded vote in Assembly as follows:

In favour: Afghanistan, Algeria, Angola, Argentina, Australia, Austria, Bahamas, Bahrain, Bangladesh, Barbados, Belize, Benin, Bhutan, Bolivia, Botswana, Brazil, Burma, Burundi, Cape Verde, Central African Republic, Chad, China, Congo, Costa Rica, Cyprus, Democratic Kampuchea, Democratic Yemen, Denmark, Djibouti, Dominican Republic, Ecuador, Egypt, El Salvador, Ethiopia, Fiji, Finland, Gabon, Gambia, Ghana, Greece, Guatemala, Guinea, Guyana, Haiti, Honduras, Iceland, India, Indonesia, Iran, Iraq, Ireland, Israel, Italy, Ivory Coast, Jamaica, Jordan, Kenya, Kuwait, Lebanon, Lesotho, Liberia, Libyan Arab Jamahiriya, Madagascar, Malawi, Malaysia, Maldives, Mali, Malta, Mauritania, Mauritius, Mexico, Morocco, Mozambique, Nepal, Netherlands, New Zealand, Nicaragua, Niger, Nigeria, Norway, Oman, Pakistan, Panama, Papua New Guinea, Paraguay, Peru, Philippines, Portugal, Qatar, Romania, Rwanda, Saint Lucia, Samoa, Sao Tome and Principe, Saudi Arabia, Senegal, Sierra Leone, Singapore, Somalia, Spain, Sri Lanka, Sudan, Suriname, Swaziland, Sweden, Syrian Arab Republic, Thailand, Togo, Trinidad and Tobago, Tunisia, Turkey, Uganda, United Arab Emirates, United Kingdom, United Republic of Cameroon, United Republic of Tanzania, Upper Volta, Uruguay, Vanuatu, Venezuela, Viet Nam, Yemen, Yugoslavia, Zaire, Zambia, Zimbabwe.

Against: United States.

Abstaining: Belgium, Bulgaria, Byelorussian SSR, Canada, Czechoslovakia, France, German Democratic Republic, Germany, Federal Republic of, Hungary, Japan, Luxembourg, Mongolia, Poland, Ukrainian SSR, USSR.

The Second Committee considered two oral amendments before approving the text. A USSR proposal to delete from paragraph 8 the request for consideration of establishing a consultative group was rejected by 91 votes to 26, with 10 abstentions, and the paragraph in its original form was retained by a recorded vote of 107 to 11, with 11 abstentions. A United States proposal to delete the words "as far as possible" from the end of paragraph 9 was rejected by 97 votes to 21, with 9 abstentions, and the original wording of the paragraph was retained by a recorded vote of 106 to 16, with 8 abstentions.

Several States explained their votes, particularly in relation to paragraphs 8 and 9.

Among those voting for the proposed amendment to paragraph 9 out of concern over budgetary implications, Australia and the United Kingdom said the Organization's regular budget should be kept within certain limits. Sharing that view, the United States felt that the United Nations budget should be kept within zero-growth limits, and the existing funds for disaster relief were adequate. Canada, which supported the proposal to amend paragraph 9, could not vote in favour of paragraph 8; while it did not oppose the idea of a consultative group, that paragraph did not reflect a number of proposals which it had made during informal consultations. France abstained in the vote on paragraph 8, considering it premature to talk of establishing a group before consulting the interested voluntary organizations; it voted against paragraph 9 because UNDRO should not be assigned operational duties, which, it maintained, fell within the competence of Governments and appropriate non-governmental organizations.

Speaking on behalf of the five Nordic countries, Sweden said their support of the text was based on the understanding that the Secretary-General would take account of the views of all interested organizations, when considering the establishment of a consultative group. The USSR objected to paragraph 8, because it felt the proposed group could interfere in the internal affairs of States or weaken the essentially intergovernmental character of UNDRO; it also opposed paragraph 9 for its budgetary implications.

Canada and the USSR expressed concern that the Secretariat had not supplied the Committee with information on the programme implications of the text, as had been called for by the Assembly in 1982.[12]

Disaster relief

Drought-stricken areas of Africa

In 1983, drought again triggered a situation in Africa requiring urgent action and increased aid, particularly in regard to the food situation in the Sudano-Sahelian region and in East Africa. The General Assembly, in resolutions 38/216 and 38/224, and the Economic and Social Council, in resolutions 1983/46 and 1983/68, took action to help overcome the difficulties, and UNDP, the United Nations Sudano-Sahelian Office (UNSO) and WFP were among the United Nations bodies actively assisting in the efforts.

ECONOMIC AND SOCIAL COUNCIL ACTION

On 29 July, the Economic and Social Council, acting on the recommendation of its First (Economic) Committee, adopted resolution 1983/68 without vote.

Climatic situation and drought in Africa

The Economic and Social Council,

Recalling General Assembly resolutions 37/147 of 17 December 1982 on assistance to the drought-stricken areas of Djibouti, Ethiopia, Kenya, Somalia, the Sudan and Uganda, 37/165 of 17 December 1982 on the implementation of the medium-term and long-term recovery and rehabilitation programme in the Sudano-Sahelian region, and 37/216 of 20 December 1982 on the implementation in the Sudano-Sahelian region of the Plan of Action to Combat Desertification,

Recalling also resolution 239(XI) on drought in the Sahelian zone, adopted on 23 February 1973 by the Conference of Ministers of the Economic Commission for Africa,

Aware that drought, which had affected the Sahel region in the 1970s, is now seriously affecting thirty-four African countries, twenty-four of which are among the least developed countries and some of which are located outside the Sudano-Sahelian region and the Kalahari desert region,

Realizing that drought is now a chronic natural phenomenon whose causes, frequency and trends are currently difficult to control and must be studied scientifically,

Conscious of the linear relationship between drought, desertification and underdevelopment,

Recalling further resolution 446(XVII) adopted on 30 April 1982 by the Conference of Ministers of the Economic Commission for Africa,

Deeply concerned about the worsening climatic situation and the dire effects of recurring drought, erosion, cyclones and famine on the peoples of Africa and on the African economy in general,

1. *Urgently requests* the Executive Secretary of the Economic Commission for Africa to organize a special scientific round-table meeting on the problems of the climatic situation in Africa, to which all States members of the Commission should be invited and which should consist of national experts from the countries invited and of international experts on climate, land, water and soil resources, ecology and the environment, with a view to examining the causes, periodicity, trends and effects of drought on the African economy and to proposing measures to be taken in the short, medium and long terms to deal with the problem;

2. *Appeals* to the competent organs, organizations and bodies of the United Nations system, such as the United Nations Environment Programme, the United Nations Development Programme, the United Nations Sudano-Sahelian Office, the Food and Agriculture Organization of the United Nations, the United Nations

Educational, Scientific and Cultural Organization and the World Meteorological Organization, and to the Organization of African Unity and other intergovernmental and non-governmental organizations concerned, to collaborate actively with the Economic Commission for Africa in this urgent task;

3. *Calls upon* African Governments to give high priority, through the allocation of both financial resources and manpower, to the problem of understanding climatic variability in their countries, in order to facilitate advance planning for drought, erosion, cyclones, famine and their related effects;

4. *Requests* the Secretary-General to make available to the Economic Commission for Africa, by redeploying regular resources of the United Nations, adequate financial resources to enable it to undertake this most important task;

5. *Further requests* the Executive Secretary of the Economic Commission for Africa to submit a report on the outcome of the scientific round-table meeting on the climatic situation in Africa to the Economic and Social Council at its second regular session of 1984;

6. *Calls upon* the international community to grant adequate financial resources to the countries affected by drought and desertification and to the institutions engaged in combating those phenomena.

Economic and Social Council resolution 1983/68

29 July 1983   Meeting 41   Adopted without vote

Approved by First Committee (E/1983/123) without vote, 27 July (meeting 25); draft by Benin, for African Group (E/1983/C.1/L.14), orally amended in informal consultations; agenda item 7.
Meeting number. ESC 41.

Sudano-Sahelian region

UNSO, operating within UNDP, continued in 1983 to co-ordinate United Nations efforts to help drought-stricken areas of the Sahel—an arid zone in West and Central Africa south of the Sahara—to implement medium- and long-term recovery and rehabilitation programmes. Those programmes were aimed at mitigating the effects of future droughts, achieving self-sufficiency in food staples and accelerating socio-economic development. The countries assisted—Cape Verde, Chad, the Gambia, Mali, Mauritania, the Niger, Senegal and the Upper Volta—were members of the Permanent Inter-State Committee on Drought Control in the Sahel (CILSS), a non–United Nations body through which the participating States co-ordinated national and regional projects.

Under a separate mandate, UNSO also assisted those and 11 additional countries in Central, East and West Africa to control desertification through a joint venture between UNDP and the United Nations Environment Programme (UNEP) (see also Chapter XVI of this section).

An UNSO assessment of the state of desertification in the Sudano-Sahelian region undertaken in 1983, in pursuance of the 1977 Plan of Action to Combat Desertification,[13] showed that the drought of 1968-1973 not only had continued but had intensified and spread since then, and that the overall desertification situation had generally worsened.

The UNDP Administrator, in a May 1984 report[14] describing the drought's effects during 1983 on the region, also noted the spread of the worsening drought and reported that the level of rainfall in the region in 1983 was comparable to that registered during the disastrous 1972-1973 drought. In addition to causing famine, malnutrition, disease and livestock losses, the drought had almost ruined the already weak economies of the Sahel countries, six of which were among the least developed countries.

The Secretary-General, in reports to the General Assembly in 1983[15] and early 1984,[16] described the activities undertaken in 1983 under the drought-related recovery programme and noted that the number of UNSO-assisted projects reached 136 during the year (33 regional and 103 national), at a total cost of $729 million.

In 1983, UNSO mobilized over $23 million to finance priority projects for drought-related recovery and rehabilitation and an additional $5 million for desertification control for the States members of CILSS; of the former amount, almost $14 million was channelled through the United Nations Trust Fund for Sudano-Sahelian Activities (see below).

The largest of the UNSO-supported regional activities was a $203 million programme for construction, improvement and maintenance of a 5,000-kilometre system of all-weather secondary roads in the Sahel, executed by UNDP. Almost $160 million had already become available for the construction of more than 4,100 kilometres of roads in the CILSS member States, including $117.5 million for UNSO projects. The return of the drought in 1983 emphasized the urgent need for all-weather passable roads in order to guarantee the transport of emergency food supplies to remote areas. Negotiations were conducted with bilateral donors to allow a further, significant expansion of the road programme, while a proposal, prepared by UNSO and UNDP, on the programme's maintenance requirements was finalized at a Paris meeting in February.

UNSO continued to support the programme for the ecological rehabilitation of the Fouta-Djallon massif in Guinea, the watershed area for all the major rivers of West Africa. It also collaborated with States in developing fuel-efficient stoves as a means of reducing the high demand for ligneous materials for domestic energy, as well as of promoting better management, conservation and protection of over-exploited forest resources. It initiated jointly with the West African Economic Community a programme, executed by FAO, for developing village-level storage facilities to reduce post-harvest losses. The Institute of the Sahel—a specialized agency of CILSS—continued to benefit from United Nations assistance in carrying out its operational activities; its training programme in management and conservation of pasture lands, for instance, was supported by UNSO, UNDP and the United Nations Educational, Scientific and Cultural Organization (UNESCO). Other training activities included a regional seminar on the production and commercialization of gum arabic and the role of the gum-producing tree, *Acacia senegal*, as a means of desertification control (Saint Louis, Senegal, April).

JIU report. In a January 1983 report transmitted to the General Assembly by the Secretary-General in May,[17] the Joint Inspection Unit (JIU) recommended that the planning and programming of UNSO projects for drought and desertification control be carried out in such a way that they would be compatible with the priorities and criteria contained in national economic and social development plans. A number of suggestions were made regarding ways to mobilize funds, focusing on increased direct involvement of potential donors in identifying and developing projects, and a recommendation was made for an increase in the unearmarked part of contributions to the United Nations Trust Fund for Sudano-Sahelian Activities in order to enhance UNSO's flexibility and effectiveness in project planning.

Other recommendations called for more frequent project implementation by Governments concerned and more involvement of the local populations; emphasis on on-the job training or training within, rather than outside, the region; strengthening collaboration between UNSO and regional intergovernmental organizations; and assisting interested Governments to establish national committees to co-ordinate drought and desertification control activities. JIU also recommended that UNSO—if its mandate and the geographic area covered remained unchanged—should retain its current staff size (11 Professional and 21 General Service staff members in New York, and 6 Professional and 16 General Service staff members at its Regional Office in Ouagadougou, Upper Volta), while strengthening the Regional Office and diversifying the specialized skills of the Professional staff, thus dispensing with consultants' services.

The Secretary-General, in his June comments[18] on the JIU report, agreed with most of the recommendations, and endorsed the convening, in collaboration with UNEP of an inter-agency task force for a joint strategy on drought and desertification in Africa, whose report would be reviewed subsequently by an UNSO regional seminar. The Secretary-General also agreed to ask ACC to examine the methods used by UNSO in mobilizing financial resources. While agreeing with the JIU

recommendation on UNSO staff, he considered that the staffing should depend on the volume of activities.

UNDP action. During 1983, the UNDP Governing Council[19] adopted a number of decisions related to the Sudano-Sahelian region (see Chapter II of this section).

By a decision of 22 June,[20] it took note with satisfaction of the Secretary-General's April 1983 report[15] on the medium- and long-term recovery and rehabilitation programme in the region, commended the UNDP Administrator for the priority attention given to the drought-affected countries, and appealed to Governments and other donors to strengthen their support for UNSO, including by means of voluntary contributions through the United Nations Pledging Conference for Development Activities, so as to enhance its responsiveness to the needs of the CILSS member States.

The Governing Council, by a 24 June decision,[21] on revised appropriations for the 1982-1983 UNDP budget, approved $3,539,200 (gross) for UNSO projects. In regard to budget estimates for 1984-1985, the Council, by another decision of 24 June,[22] approved appropriations of $3,885,200 for UNSO.

GENERAL ASSEMBLY ACTION

On 20 December, the General Assembly, on the recommendation of the Second Committee, adopted resolution 38/225 without vote.

Implementation of the medium-term and long-term recovery and rehabilitation programme in the Sudano-Sahelian region

The General Assembly,

Recalling its resolutions 3054(XXVIII) of 17 October 1973, 3253(XXIX) of 4 December 1974, 3512(XXX) of 15 December 1975, 31/180 of 21 December 1976, 32/159 of 19 December 1977, 33/133 of 19 December 1978, 34/16 of 9 November 1979, 35/86 of 5 December 1980, 36/203 of 17 December 1981 and 37/165 of 17 December 1982,

Taking note of decision 83/26 of 22 June 1983 of the Governing Council of the United Nations Development Programme concerning the implementation of the medium-term and long-term recovery and rehabilitation programme in the Sudano-Sahelian region,

Noting with satisfaction the important activities of the United Nations Sudano-Sahelian Office in helping to combat the effects of drought and to implement the medium-term and long-term recovery and rehabilitation programme in the Sudano-Sahelian region adopted by the States members of the Permanent Inter-State Committee on Drought Control in the Sahel, as well as in mobilizing the necessary resources to finance priority projects,

Noting also the continued collaboration of the United Nations Educational, Scientific and Cultural Organization with the Permanent Inter-State Committee on Drought Control in the Sahel through its arid and semi-arid zone programmes,

Bearing in mind the statement made before the General Assembly on 28 September 1983 by the President of the Republic of Cape Verde, as current Chairman of the Permanent Inter-State Committee on Drought Control in the Sahel, in which he emphasized the continuing gravity of the drought situation in the countries of the Sahel and its devastating consequences on the development of those countries,

Noting with concern the critical food situation in the countries of the Sahel as highlighted in the statement made by the Director-General of the Food and Agriculture Organization of the United Nations on 27 October 1983,

Noting with satisfaction the collaboration between the Permanent Inter-State Committee on Drought Control in the Sahel and the Club du Sahel and urging that this collaboration be continued and strengthened,

Taking into account the fundamental priorities of the Permanent Inter-State Committee on Drought Control in the Sahel aimed at implementing strategies for rural development and striving to achieve food self-sufficiency and food security, as well as restoration of an ecological balance in the region,

Considering the nature and magnitude of the needs of the States members of the Permanent Inter-State Committee on Drought Control in the Sahel and the need for the continuation and further strengthening of the support of the international community for assisting the recovery efforts and the economic development of those countries,

Taking into account that the First-Generation Programme, adopted by the Biennial Conference of the Heads of State of the Permanent Inter-State Committee on Drought Control in the Sahel, has received only 60 per cent of the financing required,

Having considered the report of the Secretary-General on the implementation of the medium-term and long-term recovery and rehabilitation programme in the Sudano-Sahelian region, as well as the report of the Joint Inspection Unit on the activities of the United Nations Sudano-Sahelian Office,

1. *Takes note* of the report of the Secretary-General on the implementation of the medium-term and long-term recovery and rehabilitation programme in the Sudano-Sahelian region;

2. *Welcomes* the report of the Joint Inspection Unit on the activities of the United Nations Sudano-Sahelian Office, in particular its recommendation that the Office should energetically continue its specific activities, under its first mandate, to combat drought in the countries of the Sahel;

3. *Expresses its gratitude* to the Governments, organizations of the United Nations system, intergovernmental organizations, private organizations and individuals that have contributed to the implementation of the medium-term and long-term recovery and rehabilitation programme in the Sudano-Sahelian region;

4. *Strongly urges* all Governments to make special efforts to increase the resources of the United Nations Sudano-Sahelian Office, including through voluntary contributions to the United Nations Pledging Conference for Development Activities, as well as through bilateral channels, so as to enable it to respond more fully to the priority requirements of the Governments of the States members of the Permanent Inter-State Committee on Drought Control in the Sahel;

5. *Requests* the international community to support the implementation of the Second-Generation Programme of the States members of the Permanent Inter-State Committee on Drought Control in the Sahel, *inter alia*, in regard to:

(a) Development projects already conceived and approved by the respective Governments;

(b) Regional projects for the struggle against desertification;

(c) Basic surveys needed for establishment of the potential for development at national and regional levels;

(d) Strengthening and/or establishment of institutions for research and training, at national and subregional levels, designed to find solutions to the problems confronting the Sahelian countries;

(e) Strengthening of national and subregional capacity for planning, management and evaluation of integrated development actions;

6. *Requests* all Governments and the organs, organizations and programmes of the United Nations system to give special attention to the critical food situation in the countries of the Sahel;

7. *Commends* the Administrator of the United Nations Development Programme for the results achieved, through the United Nations Sudano-Sahelian Office, in assisting the States members of the Permanent Inter-State Committee on Drought Control in the Sahel in the implementation of their medium-term and long-term recovery and rehabilitation programme;

8. *Reaffirms* the role of the United Nations Sudano-Sahelian Office as the co-ordinator of the efforts of the United Nations system to help the countries of the Sahel to implement their recovery and rehabilitation programme;

9. *Invites* the United Nations Sudano-Sahelian Office to continue to strengthen its co-operation with the States members of the Permanent Inter-State Committee on Drought Control in the Sahel and with the Committee itself, with a view to hastening the implementation of the medium-term and long-term recovery and rehabilitation programme in the Sudano-Sahelian region;

10. *Requests* the Secretary-General to continue to report to the General Assembly, through the Governing Council of the United Nations Development Programme and the Economic and Social Council, on the implementation of the medium-term and long-term recovery and rehabilitation programme in the Sudano-Sahelian region.

General Assembly resolution 38/225

20 December 1983   Meeting 104   Adopted without vote

Approved by Second Committee (A/38/705 & Corr.1) without vote, 28 November (meeting 52); 9-nation draft (A/C.2/38/L.70), orally revised in informal consultations; agenda item 81.

Sponsors: Cape Verde, Chad, Gambia, Mali, Mauritania, Niger, Senegal, United Republic of Cameroon, Upper Volta.

Meeting numbers. GA 38th session: 2nd Committee 19, 34-38, 46, 52; plenary 7, 104.

UN Trust Fund for Sudano-Sahelian Activities

Expenditures from the United Nations Trust Fund for Sudano-Sahelian Activities totalled $10,322,000 in 1983. Five Governments paid a total of $535,739 to the Trust Fund during the year (see tables below).

PROGRAMME EXPENDITURES UNDER THE UN TRUST FUND
FOR SUDANO-SAHELIAN ACTIVITIES, 1983
(as at 31 December 1983; in thousands of US dollars)

Country/Region	Amount
Benin	(1)
Cape Verde	743
Chad	228
Ethiopia	78
Gambia	1,005
Mali	1,463
Mauritania	1,679
Niger	2,442
Senegal	1,604
Somalia	126
Sudan	259
Upper Volta	491
Subtotal	10,117
Regional Africa	191
Interregional	14
Subtotal	205
Total	10,322

SOURCE: DP/1984/5/Add.6.

CONTRIBUTIONS TO THE UN TRUST FUND FOR
SUDANO-SAHELIAN ACTIVITIES, 1983 AND 1984
(as at 31 December 1983; in US dollar equivalent)

Country	1983 payment	1984 pledge
Algeria	—	20,000
Chile	—	5,000
Denmark	203,314	—
Italy	314,465	368,098
Philippines	5,000	5,000
Portugal	10,000	10,000
Senegal	—	10,000
Sudan	—	3,000
Yugoslavia	2,960	2,960
Total	535,739	424,058

SOURCE: A/39/5/Add.1.

East Africa

In pursuance of a December 1982 General Assembly request,[23] the Secretary-General reported in July 1983 on assistance provided to six countries of East Africa—Djibouti, Ethiopia, Kenya, Somalia, the Sudan and Uganda—in combating the effects of drought and other natural disasters.[24] He stated that while rainfall had increased in 1982 except in Ethiopia and the Sudan, all six countries continued to receive United Nations and other assistance; the UNDP Governing Council approved respective country programmes, but its assistance was limited due to lack of resources. The Sudan was the only Government of the region to request assistance, as suggested by the Assembly in 1982, for establishing a national drought monitoring office by seeking $935,000 from UNSO.

Assistance to Djibouti included food aid, particularly from WFP, and project implementation or formulation for water resources utilization, construction of an animal feed plant, husbandry and agricultural and rural development. The serious drought situation affecting some 3 million people prompted Ethiopia to launch several international appeals for emergency assistance covering food, medical supplies, clothing, shelter and transport equipment; UNDP projects approved in 1983 included expansion of irrigated areas, soil and water conservation and resettlement of people from drought-affected areas. An inter-agency mission, led by UNDRO, visited Ethiopia from 29 September to 8 October 1983 and submitted its recommendations in December[25] on the relief needs in the drought-stricken northern areas. Although drought in Kenya had ended in 1981, assistance to nomadic peoples affected was continued, while relief distribution was terminated in all but one affected district. In addition to food, United Nations and other assistance to Somalia included strengthening the national machinery for combating drought, and provision of low-cost housing and exploration of the use of renewable energy as part of a scheme to settle nomadic populations from drought-prone areas; future projects approved by UNDP included livestock development. Food aid was also sent to the Sudan, where the pasture and rain-fed cultivation had been affected by the drought of 1982-1983 and the deteriorating grazing potential was combined with an outbreak of rinderpest, a cattle disease. Malnutrition was a problem for Uganda, where inadequate rainfall portended very low harvest yield and potential for famine conditions developing later in the year; United Nations assistance included agricultural development activities, and UNDP continued to assist the Government in strengthening its ability to receive, store and distribute food relief.

By a decision of 24 June,[26] the UNDP Governing Council recommended that reports pertaining to African countries other than the CILSS members (see above) be submitted in the future as warranted.

ECONOMIC AND SOCIAL COUNCIL ACTION

On 28 July, the Economic and Social Council, acting on the recommendation of its Third Committee, adopted resolution 1983/46 without vote.

Assistance to the drought-stricken areas of Djibouti, Ethiopia, Kenya, Somalia, the Sudan and Uganda

The Economic and Social Council,

Recalling General Assembly resolutions 35/90 and 35/91 of 5 December 1980, 36/221 of 17 December 1981 and 37/147 of 17 December 1982 on assistance to the drought-stricken areas of Djibouti, Ethiopia, Kenya, Somalia, the Sudan and Uganda,

Having heard the statement made by the United Nations Disaster Relief Co-ordinator on 11 July 1983,

Noting the statements made by representatives of the States concerned, in which the catastrophic nature of the disaster was highlighted,

Aware of the adverse effects of the drought on the economic and social development of the countries concerned, and on their agricultural and food output,

Conscious of the high costs incurred in the distribution of assistance to the remote areas of the countries concerned,

Noting with deep concern the grave effects in the countries concerned, particularly Ethiopia, of successive years of drought and the resulting shortage of foodstuffs, livestock, fodder and water,

Deeply concerned at the intensity and the permanent and expanding nature of the drought in the subregion,

1. *Notes with appreciation* the measures already taken by the Secretary-General, in co-operation with the Office of the United Nations Disaster Relief Coordinator and other agencies and organizations of the United Nations system, to ensure the speediest and most effective relief aid for the victims of drought in Djibouti, Ethiopia, Kenya, Somalia, the Sudan and Uganda;

2. *Reiterates* its appeal to all States and to international governmental and non-governmental organizations to make generous contributions to assist the affected populations financially, materially and technically;

3. *Requests* the Secretary-General, in close coordination with the countries concerned, the Administrator of the United Nations Development Programme, the competent specialized agencies and other bodies of the United Nations system:

(*a*) To extend all necessary assistance to the Governments of Djibouti, Ethiopia, Kenya, Somalia, the Sudan and Uganda in establishing, within the context of their national development programmes, detailed policies for dealing with drought as a recurring phenomenon;

(*b*) To mobilize international assistance for the affected population in the countries concerned;

4. *Requests* the Secretary-General, in collaboration with the Office of the United Nations Disaster Relief Co-ordinator and other organizations of the United Nations system, to give high priority in their programmes of work to the East African subregion, and to apprise the Economic and Social Council annually, at its second regular session, of the status of this question;

5. *Further requests* the Secretary-General to keep the situation under review and to apprise the General Assembly at its thirty-eighth session of the progress achieved in the implementation of the present resolution.

Eonomic and Social Council resolution 1983/46

28 July 1983   Meeting 40   Adopted without vote

Approved by Third Committee (E/1983/116) without vote, 20 July (meeting 14); 7-nation draft (E/1983/C.3/L.7), orally revised, and orally amended in Council on Secretariat suggestions; agenda item 17.
Sponsors: Bangladesh, Djibouti, Ethiopia, Kenya, Somalia, Sudan, Uganda.
Meeting number. ESC 40.

Prior to adopting the draft, the Council amended paragraphs 4 and 5, thereby asking the Secretary-General to apprise, rather than report to, the Council and the General Assembly.

GENERAL ASSEMBLY ACTION

On 20 December, the General Assembly, on the recommendation of the Second Committee, adopted resolution 38/216 without vote.

Assistance to the drought-stricken areas of Djibouti, Ethiopia, Kenya, Somalia, the Sudan and Uganda

The General Assembly,

Recalling its resolutions 35/90 and 35/91 of 5 December 1980, 36/221 of 17 December 1981 and 37/147 of 17 December 1982 and Economic and Social Council resolution 1983/46 of 28 July 1983,

Taking note of the report of the Secretary-General on assistance to the drought-stricken areas of Djibouti, Ethiopia, Kenya, Somalia, the Sudan and Uganda,

Deeply concerned at the intensity and the permanent and expanding nature of the drought in the subregion,

1. *Reaffirms* its resolutions 36/221 and 37/147 on assistance to the drought-stricken areas of Djibouti, Ethiopia, Kenya, Somalia, the Sudan and Uganda;

2. *Takes note* of the ongoing consultations between the Governments concerned on the establishment of an intergovernmental body to combat the effects of drought and other natural disasters and urges them to finalize, as soon as possible, the necessary arrangements for the establishment of that body;

3. *Requests* the Secretary-General, in close coordination with the Administrator of the United Nations Development Programme and the appropriate specialized agencies and other organizations of the United Nations system, to continue to extend all necessary assistance to those countries in their efforts to combat the effects of drought on the basis of the recommendations of various multi-agency missions, pending the establishment of the intergovernmental body;

4. *Also requests* the Secretary-General, in close coordination with the Administrator of the United Nations Development Programme and the appropriate specialized agencies and other organizations of the United Nations system, to assist the Governments of the region, at their request, in establishing or improving national machinery to combat the effects of drought and other natural disasters, to apprise the Economic and Social Council, at its second regular session of 1984, of the progress achieved in the implementation of the present resolution and to report thereon to the General Assembly at its thirty-ninth session.

General Assembly resolution 38/216

20 December 1983   Meeting 104   Adopted without vote

Approved by Second Committee (A/38/705 & Corr.1) without vote, 28 November (meeting 52); 13-nation draft (A/C.2/38/L.61), orally revised; agenda item 81.
Sponsors: Cyprus, Djibouti, Ethiopia, Guinea-Bissau, Kenya, Lebanon, Madagascar, Mauritania, Pakistan, Somalia, Sudan, Uganda, Zambia.
Meeting numbers. GA 38th session: 2nd Committee 34-38, 46, 52; plenary 104.

Floods and storms

Floods in Bolivia, Ecuador and Peru

The climatic changes associated with disturbances in the ocean current in the South Pacific in 1982-1983, known as the "El Nino" phenomenon, led to flooding in Bolivia (March 1983), Ecuador (December 1982) and Peru (January-May 1983) as well as extensive droughts in highland areas of Bolivia and Peru. The Economic Commission for Latin America (ECLA) estimated the overall losses from disasters at $3,480 million—$840 million for Bolivia, $640 million for Ecuador and $2,000 million for Peru.

In Bolivia, some 1.6 million people in rural areas were directly affected. The drought, in particular, created a situation of national emergency and aggravated existing problems; current and future food production suffered a severe set-back, including a shortage of seeds for future crops due to their diversion for immediate nourishment.[27] Scarcity of some products led to a marked increase in consumer prices, in some cases up to 600 per cent. In both the flood- and drought-stricken areas, mortality increased due to proliferation of disease carriers and consumption of polluted water. In addition to food and seeds, the affected population was in need of water pumps and drilling rigs, as well as cash and spare parts for vehicles for purchase and transport of food supplies from neighbouring countries.

In Ecuador, 950,000 persons were affected, of whom 200,000 were reported in need of emergency assistance. The floods destroyed harvests and widespread food shortages occurred; physical and social infrastructures—including roads and irrigation systems—were damaged. Strong tidal waves and changes in sea-water temperature and salinity levels caused damage to the fishery sector.

The drought, followed by severe frosts and hailstorms, placed a strain on Peru's national resources just when the authorities were engaged in the rehabilitation and reconstruction of the areas earlier affected by floods. Up to 450,000 persons were directly affected by the drought and required emergency assistance, while 83,000 were affected by the floods.[1] The drought caused damage to farming and livestock production; future crops were threatened as food shortages led to the consumption of seed grain. Floods had caused damage to roads, bridges, agricultural fields, houses, and sewage and water evacuation systems.

In addition to appeals launched earlier in the year by UNDRO at the request of the Governments concerned, the Secretary-General issued an appeal, on 10 August, at a donors' meeting he convened in New York. A programme of action was drawn up on the basis of the recommendations of an evaluation mission (30 June–21 July), led by the Secretary-General's Personal Representative for the affected countries, Hugo Navajas-Mogro, with the participation of ECLA, UNDP and UNDRO.[28] The Secretary-General also designated UNDRO as the focal point for co-ordinating international assistance during the emergency phase.

Following the Economic and Social Council's adoption of resolution 1983/45 on 28 July (see below), the Secretary-General dispatched a technical inter-agency mission (22 August–30 September), financed by UNDP and led by an ECLA representative. Observing that the economic deterioration caused by the disasters would have long-term effects until the infrastructure was rehabilitated and production levels restored, the mission, in consultation with the Governments concerned, identified rehabilitation and reconstruction projects totalling $425 million for international funding—$129 million in Bolivia, $97 million in Ecuador, $181 million in Peru and $17 million for subregional projects.

Overall international contributions reported to UNDRO as at 31 January 1984 amounted to: $49,591,996 for Bolivia; $5,073,876 for Ecuador; and $33,109,105 for Peru. In addition to the emergency assistance already provided by FAO, UNDP, UNESCO, UNICEF, WFP and WHO, the United Nations system responded to the Secretary-General's appeal by mobilizing $2.3 million for the three countries.

ECONOMIC AND SOCIAL COUNCIL ACTION

On 28 July, the Economic and Social Council, on the recommendation of its Third Committee, adopted resolution 1983/45 without vote.

Assistance to Bolivia, Ecuador and Peru

The Economic and Social Council,

Deeply concerned about the large-scale devastation wrought by the heavy rain and floods which have recently affected extensive areas of Bolivia, Ecuador and Peru and by the drought being suffered by Bolivia and Peru,

Bearing in mind that those two climatological phenomena have caused destruction in urban and rural areas and serious damage in the agricultural, stock-raising and agro-industrial sectors,

Further bearing in mind that those sectors are important bases of the economies of Bolivia, Ecuador and Peru,

Considering that the urgent problems created require programmes of assistance, rehabilitation and reconstruction,

Affirming the urgent need for prompt and concerted international action to assist the peoples and Governments of Bolivia, Ecuador and Peru to cope with the emergency confronting those countries and to engage in rehabilitation and reconstruction,

Observing with satisfaction the assistance provided by Governments, the United Nations system and governmental and non-governmental organizations during the initial emergency period,

Noting with appreciation the work done by the Office of the United Nations Disaster Relief Co-ordinator,

1. *Expresses its gratitude* to States and organizations that have provided assistance to Bolivia, Ecuador and Peru;

2. *Appeals urgently* to all States, governmental and non-governmental organizations and specialized agencies to co-operate in financing a reconstruction and rehabilitation programme for the affected areas of Bolivia, Ecuador and Peru and to participate actively in its implementation;

3. *Requests* the Secretary-General:

(a) To take the necessary measures to assist the Governments of Bolivia, Ecuador and Peru to prepare a broad programme for the reconstruction and rehabilitation of the areas and sectors affected;

(b) To take appropriate steps to mobilize resources for special international assistance to Bolivia, Ecuador and Peru;

(c) To apprise the General Assembly at its thirty-eighth session and the Economic and Social Council at its second regular session of 1984 of progress made in the implementation of the present resolution.

Economic and Social Council resolution 1983/45

28 July 1983   Meeting 40   Adopted without vote

Approved by Third Committee (E/1983/116) without vote, 19 July (meeting 13); 30-nation draft (E/1983/C.3/L.6), orally revised; agenda item 17.

Sponsors: Algeria, Argentina, Bangladesh, Benin, Bolivia, Brazil, Canada, Chile, China, Colombia, Congo, Cuba, Ecuador, El Salvador, India, Japan, Lebanon, Mexico, Nicaragua, Pakistan, Peru, Portugal, Saint Lucia, Sierra Leone, Spain, Sudan, Suriname, Tunisia, United States, Venezuela.

Meeting number. ESC 40.

GENERAL ASSEMBLY ACTION

On 20 December, the General Assembly, on the recommendation of the Second Committee, adopted resolution 38/222 without vote.

Assistance to Bolivia, Ecuador and Peru to alleviate the effects of natural disasters

The General Assembly,

Recalling Economic and Social Council resolution 1983/45 of 28 July 1983, in which the Council expressed its deep concern about the large-scale devastation wrought by the heavy rain and floods that had recently affected extensive areas of Bolivia, Ecuador and Peru and by the drought suffered by Bolivia and Peru,

Recognizing that those phenomena have devastated urban and rural areas and caused serious damage to agriculture, stock-raising and agro-industry, which are important sectors of economic activity in Bolivia, Ecuador and Peru,

Also recognizing the serious damage to basic services, resulting in impaired living conditions, particularly conditions affecting health, in those areas, and also the serious damage to the transport and communications infrastructure,

Bearing in mind the statements made by the representatives of the Governments of Bolivia, Ecuador and Peru at the special meeting on emergency assistance to Bolivia, Ecuador and Peru, convened by the Secretary-General on 10 August 1983, and the documents submitted to that meeting, containing a preliminary evaluation of the damage caused by the natural phenomena in Bolivia, Ecuador and Peru and the identification of immediate international assistance requirements,

Having received information from the Co-ordinator of the Special Economic Assistance Programmes on the measures taken by the Secretary-General, with particular reference to the findings of the multi-agency mission, which evaluated the damage and proposed a programme of reconstruction and rehabilitation for the affected areas and sectors,

Affirming the urgent need for prompt and concerted international action to assist the peoples and Governments of Bolivia, Ecuador and Peru to cope with the emergency situation resulting from natural disasters and to carry out the rehabilitation and reconstruction of the areas and sectors affected,

Noting with appreciation the work done by the Office of the United Nations Disaster Relief Co-ordinator and

the United Nations Development Programme and the assistance provided by Governments, the programmes and organizations of the United Nations system and governmental and non-governmental organizations during the emergency phase,

Noting with satisfaction the timely action taken by the Secretary-General during the emergency, through the appointment of a personal representative and the dispatch of a multisectoral mission to prepare a special programme of economic assistance for the rehabilitation and reconstruction of the affected areas and sectors in Bolivia, Ecuador and Peru,

1. *Takes note* of the efforts made by the peoples and Governments of Bolivia, Ecuador and Peru to cope with the emergency situation and to initiate rehabilitation and reconstruction;

2. *Expresses its gratitude* to all States, programmes and organizations of the United Nations system and non-governmental organizations that have provided assistance to Bolivia, Ecuador and Peru during the emergency;

3. *Expresses its appreciation* to the Secretary-General for the timely action which he took during the emergency and also for the dispatch of the multisectoral mission to the three countries for the preparation of special programmes of economic assistance for the rehabilitation and reconstruction of the affected areas and sectors in Bolivia, Ecuador and Peru on the basis of their needs;

4. *Urgently reiterates the appeal* of the Economic and Social Council to all States, governmental and non-governmental organizations, specialized agencies and programmes of the United Nations system to co-operate in the financing of programmes for the reconstruction of the infrastructure and for the rehabilitation of the affected areas of Bolivia, Ecuador and Peru and to participate actively in their implementation;

5. *Requests* the appropriate programmes and organizations of the United Nations system to maintain and expand their programmes of assistance to Bolivia, Ecuador and Peru in support of the rehabilitation and reconstruction efforts in those countries;

6. *Also requests* regional and interregional organizations, non-governmental organizations and international financial institutions to give urgent consideration to the establishment of assistance programmes for rehabilitation and reconstruction in Bolivia, Ecuador and Peru or to the expansion of existing programmes;

7. *Invites* the United Nations Development Programme, the Food and Agriculture Organization of the United Nations, the Department of Technical Co-operation for Development of the Secretariat, the United Nations Children's Fund, the World Food Programme, the World Health Organization, the United Nations Industrial Development Organization, the International Labour Organisation, the World Meteorological Organization, the World Bank, the International Fund for Agricultural Development and other appropriate programmes and operational funds, to refer the special needs of Bolivia, Ecuador and Peru to their governing bodies, for their consideration, and to report the decisions of those bodies to the Secretary-General by 15 July 1984;

8. *Requests* the Secretary-General:

(a) To continue his efforts and to take appropriate steps in collaboration with the United Nations Develop-

ment Programme for the mobilization of resources for the implementation of special programmes of economic assistance for rehabilitation and reconstruction in Bolivia, Ecuador and Peru and to disseminate widely the findings of the multisectoral mission;

(b) To keep the situation regarding special economic assistance for the rehabilitation and reconstruction of Bolivia, Ecuador and Peru under constant review, to maintain close contact with Member States, the specialized agencies, regional organizations and the international financial institutions concerned and to apprise the Economic and Social Council, at its second regular session of 1984, of the status of the mobilization of assistance;

(c) To report to the General Assembly at its thirty-ninth session on the implementation of the present resolution.

General Assembly resolution 38/222

20 December 1983   Meeting 104   Adopted without vote

Approved by Second Committee (A/38/705 & Corr.1) without vote, 28 November (meeting 52); 52-nation draft (A/C.2/38/L.67); agenda item 81.
Sponsors: Algeria, Antigua and Barbuda, Argentina, Bahamas, Bangladesh, Belize, Benin, Bolivia, Brazil, Burundi, Canada, Chile, Colombia, Comoros, Costa Rica, Cuba, Cyprus, Dominican Republic, Ecuador, Egypt, El Salvador, Guatemala, Guinea-Bissau, Guyana, Honduras, Italy, Jamaica, Japan, Lebanon, Libyan Arab Jamahiriya, Madagascar, Mexico, Nicaragua, Pakistan, Panama, Paraguay, Peru, Philippines, Portugal, Qatar, Romania, Saudi Arabia, Sierra Leone, Spain, Sudan, Suriname, Trinidad and Tobago, Tunisia, United States, Uruguay, Venezuela, Zaire.
Meeting numbers. GA 38th session: 2nd Committee 34-38, 46, 52; plenary 104.

Floods and drought in Honduras and Nicaragua

Honduras and Nicaragua, which had not recovered from the damage caused by the May 1982 tropical storm and floods,[29] experienced a worsening economic and social situation in parts of the countries as a result of a prolonged drought in 1983.

Further, Nicaragua requested UNDRO, on 14 October, to launch an international appeal for assistance in the aftermath of two oil tank explosions and the subsequent fire that spread to several other tanks.[2] In addition to cash grants from UNDRO, the response of the donor community as at early 1984 amounted to some $156,000.

GENERAL ASSEMBLY ACTION

On 20 December, the General Assembly, on the recommendation of the Second Committee, adopted resolution 38/217 without vote.

Special assistance to alleviate the economic and social problems faced in regions of Honduras and Nicaragua as a result of the May 1982 floods and other subsequent natural disasters
The General Assembly,

Recalling its resolutions 3440(XXX) of 9 December 1975 on assistance in cases of natural disaster and other disaster situations and 37/144 of 17 December 1982 on the Office of the United Nations Disaster Relief Co-ordinator,

Taking note of resolution 419(PLEN.15) on international assistance to alleviate the economic and social problems faced by Honduras and Nicaragua as a result of the May 1982 floods, adopted by the Committee of the Whole

of the Economic Commission for Latin America at its fifteenth special session, held in New York on 22 and 23 July 1982,

Taking into account Economic and Social Council decision 1982/168 of 29 July 1982, by which the Council endorsed resolution 419(PLEN.15) of the Economic Commission for Latin America,

Mindful that by its decision 37/433 of 17 December 1982, adopted in pursuance of Economic and Social Council decision 1982/168, it endorsed resolution 419(PLEN.15),

Bearing in mind that the damage caused by the May 1982 floods in Honduras and Nicaragua has still not been made good,

Bearing in mind also that, during 1983, weather conditions in the south-west region of Honduras and the north-west region of Nicaragua have again been detrimental owing to a prolonged drought, which has caused heavy losses in the production of basic grains and other agricultural products, a phenomenon unprecedented in the past fifty years in Honduras, and which has affected thousands of rural families in those regions in both countries,

Considering that, because of the current drought and despite national efforts in both countries, the economic and social situation of those regions has worsened and the need for assistance from the international community is even greater,

1. *Expresses its gratitude* to the States Members, bodies and organizations of the United Nations system that have provided emergency aid to Honduras and Nicaragua, in order to enable them to cope with the disaster;

2. *Appeals* to the States Members, bodies and organizations of the United Nations system to continue to provide assistance to Honduras and Nicaragua, in order to counter the serious economic and social consequences of the natural disasters experienced during the past two years in the regions referred to above;

3. *Makes an urgent appeal* to the Office of the United Nations Disaster Relief Co-ordinator to take immediate steps to prevent the situation from becoming a state of emergency;

4. *Requests* the Secretary-General to report to the General Assembly at its thirty-ninth session on the progress made in the implementation of the present resolution.

General Assembly resolution 38/217

20 December 1983   Meeting 104   Adopted without vote

Approved by Second Committee (A/38/705 & Corr.1) without vote, 1 December (meeting 53); 15-nation draft (A/C.2/38/L.62/Rev.1); agenda item 81.
Sponsors: Argentina, Bolivia, Brazil, Canada, Colombia, Costa Rica, Dominican Republic, Ecuador, Guinea-Bissau, Madagascar, Pakistan, Panama, Peru, Uruguay, Venezuela.
Meeting numbers. GA 38th session: 2nd Committee 34-38, 50, 53; plenary 104.

In a related action, the Assembly, in resolution 38/223, called for contributions to the reconstruction and development of Nicaragua, which had suffered a drought from June to September 1982.

Storm in Saint Lucia

Saint Lucia, in a note verbale dated 23 September 1983 addressed to the Secretary-General,[30] reported that gale-force winds on 19 September had destroyed up to 90 per cent of the crops in some areas and damaged housing and infrastructural facilities.

Earthquake in Yemen

The Secretary-General, in a June 1983 report,[1] stated that contributions worth more than $41 million had met most of the immediate emergency needs of Yemen, which had been struck in mid-December 1982 by an earthquake measuring 6.0 on the Richter scale. The relief phase was considered over by mid-January, and emphasis shifted to reconstruction and rehabilitation.

At a special meeting for the consideration of country and intercountry programmes and projects, the UNDP Governing Council, by a decision of 18 February 1983,[31] called on the UNDP Administrator, bearing in mind a December 1982 General Assembly request,[32] to consider providing additional assistance to Yemen from the Special Programme Resources beyond the normally authorized amount.

The United Nations Conference on Trade and Development, by resolution 150(VI) of 2 July,[33] appealed to States as well as appropriate United Nations and other organizations to contribute to the relief, rehabilitation and reconstruction of Yemen.

GENERAL ASSEMBLY ACTION

On 20 December, the General Assembly, on the recommendation of the Second Committee, adopted resolution 38/204 without vote.

Assistance to Yemen

The General Assembly,

Recalling its resolution 37/166 of 17 December 1982 and resolution 150(VI) of 2 July 1983 of the United Nations Conference on Trade and Development,

Fully aware of the grave devastation and substantial loss of life and property caused by the earthquake that struck large areas of Yemen on 12 December 1982,

Concerned about the damage caused to infrastructure, which has a far-reaching effect on the implementation of the national development plan in that country,

Taking cognizance of the fact that the cost of the reconstruction of the affected areas is estimated at approximately $622 million,

Recognizing that Yemen, as one of the least developed countries, is unable to bear the mounting burden of the relief efforts and the reconstruction of the affected areas,

Recognizing also the efforts being made by the Government of Yemen to alleviate the effects of the earthquake,

1. *Appeals* to the developed countries and to those developing countries that are in a position to do so to contribute generously to the relief efforts and the reconstruction of the affected areas through financial contributions and the provision of the construction materials and equipment necessary to restore infrastructure and basic services in the affected areas;

2. *Requests* the appropriate organizations and

programmes of the United Nations system to maintain and expand their programmes of assistance to Yemen;

3. *Expresses its gratitude* to the States, the international and regional organizations and the non-governmental organizations that have participated in the ongoing efforts undertaken for the reconstruction of the affected areas in Yemen;

4. *Requests* the Secretary-General to apprise the Economic and Social Council, at its second regular session of 1984, of the progress made in the implementation of the present resolution and to report thereon to the General Assembly at its thirty-ninth session.

General Assembly resolution 38/204

20 December 1983   Meeting 104   Adopted without vote

Approved by Second Committee (A/38/705 & Corr.1) without vote, 28 November (meeting 52); 27-nation draft (A/C.2/38/L.40); agenda item 81.

Sponsors: Afghanistan, Algeria, Bangladesh, Cyprus, Democratic Yemen, Djibouti, Egypt, Guinea-Bissau, India, Iraq, Jordan, Kuwait, Lebanon, Madagascar, Mauritania, Oman, Pakistan, Qatar, Saudi Arabia, Somalia, Sudan, Syrian Arab Republic, United Arab Emirates, Vanuatu, Viet Nam, Yemen, Yugoslavia.

Meeting numbers. GA 38th session: 2nd Committee 34-38, 44, 52; plenary 104.

Disaster preparedness and prevention

In addition to its disaster relief activities, UNDRO continued in 1983 its pre-disaster planning functions by assisting countries so requesting in preparing national emergency plans or strengthening relevant national administrative structures, and organizing or participating in inter-agency missions or international meetings, seminars and training courses on disaster preparedness and prevention.

UNDRO assisted Chad, Indonesia and the United Republic of Tanzania in strengthening their national systems of disaster readiness. In June, an evacuation plan in case of a volcanic eruption was completed for the province of East New Britain in Papua New Guinea, following expert advice provided by UNDRO. Among regional projects, UNDRO in April handed over to the Caribbean Community secretariat the administrative responsibility for the Pan-Caribbean Disaster Preparedness and Prevention Project, covering 28 island countries and territories; work proceeded for establishing an emergency-communications link among the islands and between national meteorological and emergency offices.

UNDRO participated in several programmes on disaster prevention, among them the WMO/ESCAP Panel on Tropical Cyclones (March), the WMO Tropical Cyclone Committee for the South-West Indian Ocean (September), a seminar on disaster-preparedness strategies in the south-west Pacific (Suva, Fiji, March), and an ESCAP/UNDRO seminar on flood plain management for technical personnel from Asian countries (Bangkok, Thailand, October). UNDRO agreed to finance the participation of two disaster relief officials each from Bangladesh, Burma, Pakistan, Sri Lanka and Thailand at a disaster management training programme in India for South Asian countries; the first course was conducted in June. A Disaster Experts Meeting of the Association of South-East Asian Nations (Singapore, 6-8 October) recommended the establishment of an UNDRO-supported regional disaster research and training centre in the Philippines, and requested UNDRO to approach donors for assistance.

An Expert Meeting on Space Applications for the Acquisition and Dissemination of Disaster-Related Data (Geneva, 14-17 June), in which UNDRO participated along with disaster managers from six disaster-prone countries, recommended that the United Nations keep the disaster-management community informed of relevant advances in communications, remote sensing and meteorological satellite application. A training course on satellite applications to flood control and forecasting (Rome, Italy, 7-18 November) acquainted personnel from 24 countries with the use of space technology for those purposes.

Activities relating to disaster preparedness and prevention were also carried out by a number of other United Nations organizations, notably FAO, UNESCO, UNHCR, WFP and WHO. UNCTAD's secretariat conducted, in collaboration with UNDRO, a study on the economic and social effects of natural disasters in island developing countries.[34] Five such countries (Antigua and Barbuda, Cape Verde, Comoros, Maldives, Samoa) were studied in terms of their vulnerability to natural disasters, with particular reference to their effect on the balance of payments.

In resolution 1983/57 of 28 July, the Economic and Social Council recommended that, to mitigate effects from floods and droughts, countries give high priority to early-warning and forecasting systems, and integrate the relevant management projects in overall plans for the development of water resources.

Earthquakes

As in previous years, UNDRO participated in or contributed to several 1983 international and regional seminars on earthquake prediction and risk reduction.

A Balkan Regional Seminar on Earthquake Preparedness (Athens, Greece, 11-14 January), part of a joint UNDP/UNESCO project, stressed the need for greater co-operation between civil authorities and the scientific community, and pointed out the problems of protecting "life-line" systems and cultural/historical property, and providing emergency shelter. Establishment of a permanent international co-ordinating committee on earthquake risk reduction in the region was recommended by a meeting in January (Skopje, Yugoslavia). An UNDRO/UNESCO Seminar on Earthquake Vulner-

ability (Bucharest, Romania, 5-8 December) concluded that a wide gap existed between theoretical and applied vulnerability analysis and that further studies were needed.

An International Earthquake Conference (Los Angeles, California, United States, February), focusing on earthquake disaster management in countries surrounding the Pacific, recommended the setting up of a task force for urban earthquake planning, with UNDRO participation.

A Seminar on Seismicity and Seismic Risk in the Ibero-Maghrebian Region (Córdoba, Spain, November), organized by the Ibero-Maghrebian Working Group of the European Seismological Commission, brought together, for the first time, scientists and civil defence officials from Algeria, Morocco, Portugal, Spain and Tunisia.

A study—funded by UNDRO at the request of the Peruvian Civil Defence and carried out by the National University of Engineering—was completed in March on tsunami hazard zoning of low coastal areas in the vicinity of Lima, for the Government's use in emergency planning.

REFERENCES

[1]A/38/201-E/1983/69 & Corr.1,2. [2]A/39/267-E/1984/96 & Corr.1. [3]A/39/267/Add.2-E/1984/96/Add.2. [4]A/38/476. [5]YUN 1982, p. 703, GA res. 37/144, 17 Dec. 1982. [6]A/38/755. [7]A/C.5/38/L.21. [8]YUN 1981, p. 480, GA res. 36/225, 17 Dec. 1981. [9]A/38/202-E/1983/94. [10]YUN 1981, p. 473. [11]YUN 1982, p. 705. [12]*Ibid.*, p. 1430, GA res. 37/234, 21 Dec. 1982. [13]YUN 1977, p. 509. [14]DP/1984/52 & Add.1. [15]A/38/152-E/1983/38. [16]A/39/211-E/1984/58. [17]A/38/180. [18]A/38/180/Add.1. [19]E/1983/20. [20]*Ibid.* (dec. 83/26). [21]*Ibid.* (dec. 83/30). [22]*Ibid.* (dec. 83/31). [23]YUN 1982, p. 709, GA res. 37/147, 17 Dec. 1982. [24]A/38/214. [25]UNDRO/83/38. [26]E/1983/20 (dec. 83/27). [27]A/39/392. [28]UNDRO/84/8. [29]YUN 1982, p. 711. [30]A/C.2/38/2. [31]E/1983/20 (dec. 83/3). [32]YUN 1982, p. 714, GA res. 37/166, 17 Dec. 1982. [33]*Proceedings of the United Nations Conference on Trade and Development, Sixth Session, Belgrade, 6 June–2 July 1983*, vol. I, *Report and Annexes* (TD/326, vol. I), Sales No. E.83.II.D.6. [34]TD/B/961.

Emergency relief and assistance

The United Nations continued in 1983 its emergency humanitarian assistance to displaced persons, as well as to Palestinians, in Lebanon (Economic and Social Council decision 1983/170). The Council, in decision 1983/112, and the General Assembly, in resolution 38/220, called for intensified international assistance to meet Lebanon's reconstruction and development needs.

In December, the Assembly, in resolution 38/201, liquidated the United Nations Emergency Operation Trust Fund, which had been established in 1974, and decided to allocated the remaining balance to other similarly mandated existing United Nations funds and programmes.

Lebanon

In 1983, the greater part of Lebanon remained outside the Government's control, and the uncertain political situation and the resumption of fighting resulted in a serious decline in production and economic activity and an increase in the number of displaced persons requiring further international emergency humanitarian assistance (see also POLITICAL AND SECURITY QUESTIONS, Chapter IX).

ECONOMIC AND SOCIAL COUNCIL ACTION

In an oral report to the the Economic and Social Council in May, the United Nations Co-ordinator of Assistance for the Reconstruction and Development of Lebanon, Iqbal A. Akhund, said the successful implementation of the reconstruction programme depended on mobilizing the necessary funds, strengthening and modernizing the country's administrative structures and practices, formulating national policies in key sectors and establishing a system for long-term planning. Lebanon informed the Council that the financing of its reconstruction efforts would require a vast mobilization of national and foreign resources for at least 10 years, adding that the success of such efforts depended on the country's political stability, sovereignty and territorial integrity.

On 17 May, the Council, on an oral proposal by its President, adopted decision 1983/112 without vote.

Assistance for the reconstruction and development of Lebanon

At its 7th plenary meeting, on 17 May 1983, the Council decided:

(a) To take note with appreciation of the oral report made by the United Nations Co-ordinator of Assistance for the Reconstruction and Development of Lebanon pursuant to General Assembly resolution 37/163 of 17 December 1982, and of the statement made by the Permanent Representative of Lebanon to the United Nations at the first regular session of 1983 of the Council;

(b) To appeal to all Member States, organs, organizations and bodies of the United Nations system to continue to mobilize all possible assistance for the reconstruction and development of Lebanon, in accordance with the relevant resolutions and decisions of the General Assembly and of the Economic and Social Council.

Economic and Social Council decision 1983/112

Adopted without vote

Draft orally proposed by President; agenda item 1.
Meeting number. ESC 7.

The Secretary-General, in response to a December 1982 General Assembly request,[1] reported to the Assembly, through the Council, that the international community had continued to provide humanitarian assistance to the Palestinian people in Lebanon.[2]

On 25 July, the Council, acting on the recommendation of its Third Committee, adopted decision 1983/170 without vote.

Report of the Secretary-General on assistance to the Palestinian people in Lebanon

At its 39th plenary meeting, on 25 July 1983, the Council took note of the report of the Secretary-General on assistance to the Palestinian people in Lebanon.

Economic and Social Council decision 1983/170

Adopted without vote

Approved by Third Committee (E/1983/114) without vote, 18 July (meeting 12); oral proposal by Chairman; agenda item 22.
Meeting number. ESC 39.

UNCTAD action. The United Nations Conference on Trade and Development (UNCTAD), in resolution 149(VI) of 2 July 1983,[3] urged donors to assist Lebanon in overcoming the economic and social ordeal resulting from eight years of "wars and disturbances", including the 1982 "Israeli invasion". It invited international financial institutions, particularly the World Bank, to consider granting Lebanon financing for reconstruction. It also appealed to the international community to consider appropriate trade measures that would help revive Lebanon's industrial and agricultural commodity exports, and requested the International Trade Centre UNCTAD/General Agreement on Tariffs and Trade to assist the country in regaining its traditional markets.

The text, adopted on a proposal of the UNCTAD President, was based on consultations on a draft originally submitted by Somalia on behalf of the Group of 77 developing countries.

Report of the Secretary-General. The Secretary-General, in a September report on assistance for the reconstruction and development of Lebanon,[4] submitted to the General Assembly at its December 1982 request,[5] stated that most of the United Nations emergency relief assistance to the affected population had been completed by mid-1983.

A World Bank mission, which had visited Lebanon in November 1982 and February 1983 at the Government's request, submitted recommendations in March for a three-year (1983-1985) programme of essential reconstruction projects costing $6 billion, to be financed through external grants, foreign borrowing and domestic fundraising. The programme covered such projects as roads, ports, an airport, power and water supply, sewerage, telecommunications, education, health, urban development, housing and public buildings, and assistance to the private sector; other suggestions concerned improvements in Lebanon's financial management and in public administration. A number of other United Nations bodies also sent special missions in response to the Government's appeal, and made further project proposals in the social and primary sectors, at a total cost of over $68 million. United Nations assistance, by programme and agency for the period from 1 September 1982 to 31 August 1983, was described in an October addendum to the Secretary-General's report.[4] Among them, UNICEF continued its emergency relief operations,[6] assisting in procurement of relief goods in the local market, improvement of water supply, education and rehabilitation projects.

GENERAL ASSEMBLY ACTION

Speaking in the General Assembly's Second Committee in November, the United Nations Co-ordinator observed that the resumption of fighting and systematic violation of the cease-fire since the Secretary-General's report was prepared at the end of August made it necessary to revise the estimated resource and time requirements for Lebanon's reconstruction and development. At the Government's request in early September, the Secretary-General launched an international appeal for emergency relief assistance totalling $10 million for some 150,000 displaced persons; such aid reached the affected population within four days of the Government's request. Among the United Nations bodies responding, the Committee on Assistance for the Reconstruction and Development of Lebanon assisted government authorities in organizing and monitoring the distribution of food and basic household articles to displaced families, and UNDRO and UNHCR distributed rations (see Chapter XXI of this section). In November, Lebanon requested further emergency assistance for 4,000 families—victims of a worsening situation in Tripoli, which had caused displacement of Palestinian refugees and Lebanese citizens. The Co-ordinator observed that since the massive displacement of people had disrupted administrative and social services and had seriously set back productive activity and the economy in general, relief work could not be confined to the provision of basic necessities but must be accompanied by a well-planned and comprehensive programme for the rehabilitation of housing and the physical and social infrastructure.

On 20 December, the Assembly, on the recommendation of the Second Committee, adopted resolution 38/220 without vote.

Assistance for the reconstruction and development of Lebanon

The General Assembly,

Recalling its resolutions 33/146 of 20 December 1978, 34/135 of 14 December 1979, 35/85 of 5 December 1980, 36/205 of 17 December 1981 and 37/163 of 17 December 1982 on assistance for the reconstruction and development of Lebanon,

Recalling also Economic and Social Council resolution 1980/15 of 29 April 1980 and decision 1983/112 of 17 May 1983,

Noting with deep concern the continuing heavy loss of life and the additional destruction of property, which have caused further extensive damage to the economic and social structures of Lebanon,

Welcoming the determined efforts of the Government of Lebanon in undertaking its reconstruction and rehabilitation programme,

Reaffirming the urgent need for further international action to assist the Government of Lebanon in its continuing efforts for reconstruction and development,

Taking note of the report of the Secretary-General and of the statement made by the United Nations Co-ordinator of Assistance for the Reconstruction and Development of Lebanon on 10 November 1983,

1. _Expresses its appreciation_ to the Secretary-General for his report and for the steps he has taken to mobilize assistance to Lebanon;

2. _Commends_ the United Nations Co-ordinator of Assistance for the Reconstruction and Development of Lebanon and his staff for their valuable and unstinting efforts in the discharge of their duties;

3. _Expresses its appreciation_ for the relentless efforts undertaken by the Government of Lebanon in the implementation of the initial phase of the reconstruction of Lebanon, despite adverse circumstances;

4. _Requests_ the Secretary-General to continue and intensify his efforts to mobilize all possible assistance within the United Nations system to help the Government of Lebanon in its reconstruction and development efforts;

5. _Requests_ the organs, organizations and bodies of the United Nations system to intensify their programmes of assistance and to expand them in response to the needs of Lebanon;

6. _Also requests_ the Secretary-General to report to the Economic and Social Council at its second regular session of 1984 and to the General Assembly at its thirty-ninth session on the progress achieved in the implementation of the present resolution.

General Assembly resolution 38/220

20 December 1983   Meeting 104   Adopted without vote

Approved by Second Committee (A/38/705 & Corr.1) without vote, 28 November (meeting 52); 36-nation draft (A/C.2/38/L.65), orally revised in informal consultations; agenda item 81.

Sponsors: Australia, Austria, Bahrain, Bangladesh, Belgium, Brazil, Canada, Cyprus, Democratic Yemen, Djibouti, Egypt, France, Guinea-Bissau, Indonesia, Iraq, Italy, Japan, Jordan, Kuwait, Lebanon, Liberia, Madagascar, Malaysia, Mauritania, Oman, Pakistan, Qatar, Saudi Arabia, Sierra Leone, Spain, Sudan, Tunisia, United Kingdom, United States, Yemen, Yugoslavia.

Meeting numbers. GA 38th session: 2nd Committee 34-38, 44, 52; plenary 104.

Dissolution of the UN Emergency Operation Trust Fund

The Secretary-General, in a November 1983 report to the Assembly,[7] proposed, on the basis of consultations, liquidation of the United Nations Emergency Operation Trust Fund and allocation of its remaining balance to other United Nations funds and programmes.

The Fund had been established by the Assembly in 1974 as part of a special programme of emergency measures to mitigate the difficulties confronting the low-income developing countries most seriously affected by the then economic crisis.[8] As at 31 October 1983, the Fund—whose income had totalled some $309.5 million during its existence—had a balance of $47.8 million, resulting mainly from interest earned from short-term investments.

The Secretary-General proposed that the Fund's balance be used for purposes as close as possible to its original intent, and suggested the ratio of allocation as follows: 70 per cent to the United Nations Capital Development Fund, the UNDP Special Measures Fund for Least Developed Countries and the United Nations Trust Fund for Sudano-Sahelian Activities; 15 per cent to the UNDP Energy Account and the United Nations Revolving Fund for Natural Resources Exploration; and 15 per cent to UNDP for economic and technical co-operation among developing countries. He anticipated reporting to the Assembly in 1985 on the utilization of funds transferred to those programmes.

GENERAL ASSEMBLY ACTION

On 20 December, the General Assembly, on the recommendation of the Second Committee, adopted resolution 38/201 without vote.

Liquidation of the United Nations Emergency Operation Trust Fund and allocation of the remaining balance

The General Assembly,

Taking note of the report of the Secretary-General concerning the need for liquidation of the United Nations Emergency Operation Trust Fund,

Fully aware of the original objectives for which the Fund was created,

Deeply concerned about the exceptional situation faced by many developing countries, in particular African countries, which are afflicted by drought, famine and malnutrition,

Concerned also about the special plight of the Palestine refugees and the financial situation of the United Nations Relief and Works Agency for Palestine Refugees in the Near East,

Taking into account that developing countries, through the Caracas Programme of Action, have taken it upon themselves to implement a series of actions in the field of economic and technical co-operation among developing countries, designed, *inter alia*, to help them face their critical development problems and attain their objectives, giving due regard to the special needs of the least developed among them,

1. *Decides* to liquidate the United Nations Emergency Operation Trust Fund and to allocate the remaining balance to existing funds and programmes of the United Nations as follows:

(a) Seventy per cent shall be channelled through United Nations Development Programme–administered funds to finance urgently needed projects, primarily in the food and agricultural sectors in countries afflicted by famine and malnutrition as a result, particularly, of severe or prolonged drought, with special emphasis on African countries;

(b) Eighteen per cent shall be channelled through the United Nations Relief and Works Agency for Palestine Refugees in the Near East, especially to its educational programme;

(c) Twelve per cent shall be channelled through the United Nations Development Programme for the purpose of economic and technical co-operation among developing countries; these funds shall be allocated to activities in economic and technical co-operation among developing countries of critical importance to developing countries, according to the priorities set by them;

2. *Requests* the Secretary-General to take the necessary action to ensure that the funds are allocated in accordance with the present resolution as soon as possible;

3. *Also requests* the Administrator of the United Nations Development Programme to report to the Governing Council at its thirty-first session on action taken to implement the present resolution;

4. *Further requests* the Secretary-General to monitor closely the implementation of the present resolution, to make available progress reports and to report fully to the General Assembly at its thirty-ninth session.

General Assembly resolution 38/201

20 December 1983   Meeting 104   Adopted without vote

Approved by Second Committee (A/38/702/Add.13) without vote, 14 December (meeting 56); 7-nation draft (A/C.2/38/L.110/Rev.1); agenda item 78.

Sponsors: Algeria, Iran, Kuwait, Netherlands, Saudi Arabia, United Arab Emirates, Venezuela.

Meeting numbers. GA 38th session: 2nd Committee 56; plenary 104.

In the Second Committee, Bangladesh orally proposed, but later withdrew, an amendment to the third preambular paragraph, by which the Assembly would have expressed concern over the situation faced by the least developed countries and other developing countries, rather than by "many developing countries".

REFERENCES

[1]YUN 1982, p. 424, GA res. 37/134, 17 Dec. 1982. [2]A/38/207-E/1983/65. [3]*Proceedings of the United Nations Conference on Trade and Development, Sixth Session, Belgrade, 6 June–2 July 1983*, vol. I, *Report and Annexes* (TD/326, vol. I), Sales No. E.83.II.D.6. [4]A/38/217 & Add.1. [5]YUN 1982, p. 721, GA res. 37/163, 17 Dec. 1982. [6]E/ICEF/1984/11. [7]A/38/566. [8]YUN 1974, p. 326, GA res. 3202(S-VI), 1 May 1974.

Chapter IV

International trade and finance

The major United Nations event concerning international trade and finance for development in 1983 was the sixth (June/July) session of the United Nations Conference on Trade and Development (UNCTAD VI), whose central themes—reflected in an end-of-Conference statement—were development and recovery in the world economy and the complementary character of those two processes. Against the background of the world economic crisis, wide-ranging discussions were held on virtually all major concerns in the area of international co-operation for development—including commodities, international trade, protectionism and structural adjustment, monetary and financial questions, the problems of the least-developed, land-locked and island developing countries, the transfer of technology, shipping, economic co-operation among developing countries, and assistance to individual countries and liberation movements. The Conference adopted 32 resolutions and decisions on these and other issues.

In his annual report on the work of the Organization (p.3), the Secretary-General said that, although UNCTAD VI had provided an important opportunity to counter negative trends in multilateral co-operation, its results were not commensurate with the gravity of the situation in developing countries and the requirements of the world economy in general. The consensus achieved on several issues could, however, constitute a worthwhile step provided there was continuing dialogue and action, in which context the process of negotiation between the developed and developing countries on long-term problems had to be activated at a high political level.

In December, the General Assembly echoed the Secretary-General's views on the results of UNCTAD VI and urged Governments to exercise the necessary political will to reach agreement on the follow-up to the Conference and ensure timely implementation of its results (resolution 38/155).

Following its second annual review of protectionism and structural adjustment, regarded as a key issue for UNCTAD VI, the UNCTAD Trade and Development Board drew attention to new forms of protectionist measures, including discriminatory ones.

UNCTAD VI urged increased contributions to strengthen the commodity-related activities of the International Trade Centre (ITC), which continued to assist developing countries in promoting their exports and facilitating movement of goods in international commerce.

In the area of commodity issues, UNCTAD VI urged early signature and ratification of the Agreement Establishing the Common Fund for Commodities, as did the Assembly in December (resolution 38/156). Although the Agreement was open for signature and ratification at Belgrade during the Conference, it had not received the required number of ratifications by the end of the year for entry into force.

The International Sugar Conference held two sessions in 1983 without reaching agreement. However, the United Nations Conference on Tropical Timber culminated in November in the adoption of the International Tropical Timber Agreement, 1983. Early resumption of the United Nations Conference to Negotiate an International Arrangement to replace the International Wheat Agreement, 1971, as extended, was urged by UNCTAD VI, the Economic and Social Council (resolution 1983/71) and by the General Assembly (resolution 38/158). In March, the Committee on Manufactures reviewed trends, developments and restrictions to trade in manufactures and semi-manufactures.

Both the Council (decision 1983/174) and the Assembly (resolution 38/147) called for finalization and adoption of a set of draft guidelines on consumer protection.

International financial relations, described as chaotic by the United Nations Committee for Development Planning (CDP), were the subject of several resolutions adopted at UNCTAD VI. The question of external debt of developing countries was of particular concern to CDP, the Trade and Development Board and the Conference. With regard to development assistance, the Conference urged developed countries to increase their official development assistance, and multilateral development institutions were invited to expand programme lending.

Trade-related finance was discussed at the March meeting of the Committee on Invisibles and Financing related to Trade, at the Trade and Development Board and at UNCTAD VI. The Conference invited the Board to finalize consideration of a proposed export guarantee facility.

A proposed complementary financing facility for commodity-related shortfalls in export earnings was discussed in the Committee on Commodities and at UNCTAD VI, which invited the UNCTAD Secretary-General to convene an expert group on the subject.

In December, the United Nations *Ad Hoc* Group of Experts on International Co-operation in Tax Matters finalized a set of guidelines for international co-operation against tax evasion.

Topics related to this chapter. Development policy and international economic co-operation. Transport. Industrial development. Regional economic and social activities: international trade and finance—Africa, Asia and the Pacific, Europe, Latin America, Western Asia. Science and technology: technology transfer. International economic law: international trade law.

Sixth session of UNCTAD

The sixth session of the United Nations Conference on Trade and Development (UNCTAD), known as UNCTAD VI, was held at Belgrade, Yugoslavia, from 6 June to 2 July 1983. The Conference was preceded on 2 and 3 June by an organizational meeting of senior officials representing States participating in the Conference.

The Trade and Development Board of UNCTAD had adopted the Conference's provisional agenda in July 1982 and, in September, approved distribution of its items among plenary meetings and four main committees.[1] The twelfth special session of UNCTAD's Trade and Development Board met at Geneva from 25 to 30 April and on 6 May 1983 to complete preparatory work for the Conference. On 6 May, the Board established the composition of the Conference's Bureau and drew up a tentative schedule for the Conference,[2] and also adopted a set of agreed conclusions[3] urging informal consultations on outstanding matters before the pre-Conference meeting of senior officials.

Also in preparation for the Conference, the African, Asian and Latin American regional groups of UNCTAD member States met at the ministerial level during February at Libreville (Gabon), Baghdad (Iraq) and Cartagena (Colombia), respectively, to consider matters proposed for the agenda. The results of these meetings were considered by the Fifth Ministerial Meeting of the Group of 77 developing countries, held at Buenos Aires, Argentina, from 28 March to 9 April. It adopted as its final document the Buenos Aires Platform—the Group's position paper on issues to be discussed at the Conference. In the Platform, the Ministers of the Group of 77 also reviewed the state of the world economy and its functioning in relation to the development of developing countries (see p. 399 *et seq.*). The document was annexed to the report of the proceedings of the Conference.[4]

Preparations were also discussed by Ministers of Foreign Trade of countries members of the Council for Mutual Economic Assistance (Moscow, April) and at the ministerial level by representatives of the Organisation for Economic Co-operation and Development (Paris, May). The Economic Declaration of the Seventh Conference of Heads of State or Government of Non-Aligned Countries (New Delhi, India, 7-12 March) included a section on the Conference.[5]

On 6 June, the Conference established four main open-ended committees, among which the agenda items not handled in plenary meetings were distributed as follows: Committee I—commodities; Committee II—international trade in goods and services; Committee III—financial and monetary issues; Committee IV—UNCTAD activities in technology, shipping, land-locked and island developing countries, trade relations among countries having different economic and social systems, economic co-operation among developing countries, assistance to national liberation movements, and institutional matters.

The Conference was attended by 148 member States of UNCTAD, as well as by representatives of the United Nations Secretariat, the regional commissions and other United Nations organizations, eight specialized agencies, the General Agreement on Tariffs and Trade (GATT) and the International Trade Centre (ITC). Also represented were 36 intergovernmental bodies, 25 non-governmental organizations and four national liberation movements: the African National Congress of South Africa, the Palestine Liberation Organization, the Pan Africanist Congress of Azania and the South West Africa People's Organization.

At its opening meeting on 6 June, the Conference elected as its President Lazar Mojsov (Yugoslavia); it also elected a Rapporteur and 29 Vice-Presidents. (For Conference participants and officers, see APPENDIX III.)

The Conference's inaugural ceremony was addressed by Mr. Mojsov, in his capacity as Federal Secretary for Foreign Affairs of Yugoslavia, who welcomed participants on behalf of his Government, and by Mika Spiljak, President of the Presidency of Yugoslavia, who reviewed the current world economic crisis, stressed the interdependence of the economies of all countries and called for concerted action to revitalize the world economy.

The United Nations Secretary-General, in an address to the opening meeting, felt that four imperative tasks faced the Conference: action on urgent measures to arrest a decline in the economic activity in the developing countries; that those measures should be an integral part of efforts to revive the global economy; that they be supplemented by appropriate domestic policies; and that the basic framework of international economic relations, covering especially the trading, monetary and financial systems, be strengthened. Above all, he stated, action was needed to offer a glimmer of hope to the hundreds of millions who saw no prospect except that of unemployment and continued deprivation.

Referring to the close relationship between economic and social well-being and peace and security, the Secretary-General said that the great challenge for UNCTAD VI was to help develop the spirit of partnership between North and South, on which humanity's economic and political equilibrium greatly depended.

On 2 July, UNCTAD VI concluded by adopting a statement on the main item on its agenda—the world economic situation with special emphasis on development: approaches to the current world economic crisis and perspectives for the 1980s, including issues, policies and measures relevant to the attainment of a new international economic order. The statement's main part described the world economic situation (p. 403) and—in the interrelated fields of commodities, trade, money and finance, and the implementation of the Substantial New Programme of Action for the 1980s for the Least Developed Countries (resolution 142(VI)) (see also p. 430)—UNCTAD VI adopted a programme of immediate measures incorporating elements contained in some of the Conference's resolutions and provided for urgent action on them.

The resolutions on commodities dealt with the Common Fund for Commodities (153(VI)), implementation of the Integrated Programme for Commodities in the area of stabilizing and strengthening commodity markets (155(VI)), implementation of the Integrated Programme for Commodities in the area of processing, marketing and distribution, including transportation (156(VI)), and compensatory financing of export earnings shortfalls (157(VI)). The trade resolution dealt with international trade in goods and services: protectionism, structural adjustment and the international trading system (159(VI)). The money and finance resolutions dealt with external debt (161(VI)), international monetary issues (162(VI)), an international export credit guarantee facility (163(VI)), official development assistance (164(VI)), and multilateral development institutions (165(VI)) (for details of these resolutions, see subject headings below).

Further action by the Conference on the various aspects of trade and financial matters included decisions on UNCTAD activities regarding trade relations among countries having different economic and social systems and all trade flows resulting therefrom (145(VI)), and the work programme on protectionism and structural adjustment (160(VI));

and resolutions on the United Nations Conference to Negotiate an International Arrangement to Replace the International Wheat Agreement, 1971, as extended (154(VI)), and strengthening the International Trade Centre, particularly in relation to commodities (158(VI)) (see subject headings below).

In other action, the Conference adopted resolutions on: rejecting coercive economic measures (152(VI)) (p. 412); UNCTAD activities concerning land-locked (137(VI)) (p. 435) and island (138(VI)) (p. 438) developing countries; economic cooperation among developing countries (139(VI)) (p. 413); the technological transformation of developing countries (143(VI)) (see Chapter XII of this section); UNCTAD activities in shipping (144(VI)) (see Chapter V of this section); assistance to the Palestinian people (146(VI)) (p. 282); assistance to the peoples of Namibia (see TRUSTEESHIP AND DECOLONIZATION, Chapter III) and those of South Africa (147(VI)) (p. 160); provision of assistance for Lebanon (149(VI)) and Yemen (150(VI)); and implementation of the medium- and long-term recovery and rehabilitation programme in the Sudano-Sahelian region (151(VI)) (see Chapter III of this section).

The Conference decided to remit several texts to the October/November session of UNCTAD's Trade and Development Board for further consideration, including two draft texts on institutional matters—one submitted by Somalia on behalf of the States members of the Group of 77 developing countries, and the other by Canada on behalf of the States members of Group B (developed market economies)—as well as an informal text on trade relations among countries having different economic and social systems (see below) and proposals for a work programme on protectionism and structural adjustment.

Trade and Development Board action. At its twenty-seventh session (Geneva, 3-20 October and 2 November),[6] UNCTAD's Trade and Development Board considered several matters arising from UNCTAD VI decisions, including resolutions 146(VI) on assistance to the Palestinian people (p. 282) and 147(VI) on assistance to the peoples of Namibia (see TRUSTEESHIP AND DECOLONIZATION, Chapter III) and those of South Africa (p. 160).

By decision 148(VI), the Conference had remitted two draft texts on institutional matters to the Board (see above). The Board decided to consider the decision further at its twenty-eighth (March/April 1984) session.

The Board also considered Conference resolution 159(VI) on international trade in goods and services: protectionism, structural adjustment and the international trading system, and decision 160(VI) on a work programme on protectionism and structural adjustment (see below) and decided[7] to remit both consideration of the work programme and a draft text on it, submitted by Venezuela for the Group of 77, to its March/April 1984 session.

In resolution 163(VI) on an international export credit guarantee facility, the Conference had requested the Board to finalize its consideration of the issue at its twenty-seventh session. On 20 October, the Board decided to refer a draft text on the subject, submitted by Venezuela for the Group of 77, to its Committee on Invisibles and Financing related to Trade at its eleventh session (see below).

GENERAL ASSEMBLY ACTION

After considering the work of UNCTAD VI and the Trade and Development Board, the General Assembly, on 19 December, adopted resolution 38/155 without vote. It took this action on the recommendation of its Second (Economic and Financial) Committee.

Report of the United Nations Conference on Trade and Development on its sixth session

The General Assembly,

Recalling its resolutions 3201(S-VI) and 3202(S-VI) of 1 May 1974, containing the Declaration and the Programme of Action on the Establishment of a New International Economic Order, 3281(XXIX) of 12 December 1974, containing the Charter of Economic Rights and Duties of States, and 3362(S-VII) of 16 September 1975 on development and international economic cooperation,

Recalling also its resolution 35/56 of 5 December 1980, the annex to which contains the International Development Strategy for the Third United Nations Development Decade,

Recalling further its resolution 37/208 of 20 December 1982,

Having considered the report of the United Nations Conference on Trade and Development on its sixth session, held at Belgrade from 6 June to 2 July 1983, and the report of the Trade and Development Board on its twenty-sixth, twelfth special and twenty-seventh sessions,

Taking note of the Economic Declaration adopted by the Seventh Conference of Heads of State or Government of Non-Aligned Countries, held at New Delhi from 7 to 12 March 1983, and the proposals contained in the Buenos Aires Platform, adopted at the Fifth Ministerial Meeting of the Group of Seventy-seven, held from 28 March to 9 April 1983, as well as the intensive preparations at a high political level by other groups in this regard,

Considering that the sixth session of the United Nations Conference on Trade and Development took place against the background of the harmful effects of the world economic crisis, especially on the economic development of developing countries, and accordingly affirming the importance of achieving a sustained world economic recovery and ensuring a rapid expansion of international trade that is supportive of economic growth and development, in particular that of developing countries,

Recognizing the leading responsibility of developed countries in promoting conditions conducive to world recovery, the need for reviving development momentum in the developing countries and the need for sound policies in both developed and developing countries to restore sustainable development and growth,

Urging accordingly developed countries to take fully into account the international implications of their policy decisions, including their impact on developing countries,

1. *Takes note* of the report of the United Nations Conference on Trade and Development on its sixth session and the report of the Trade and Development Board on its twenty-sixth, twelfth special and twenty-seventh sessions;

2. *Notes with concern* that the Conference was unable to yield results commensurate with the dimension of the problems confronting the developing countries and the world economy as a whole;

3. *Further notes with concern* that the Trade and Development Board was unable, at its twenty-seventh session, to translate into a work programme and action resolutions and decisions of the United Nations Conference on Trade and Development at its sixth session;

4. *Takes note* of resolutions 146(VI), 147(VI), 152(VI) and 157(VI) adopted on 2 July 1983 by the United Nations Conference on Trade and Development at its sixth session;

5. *Endorses* all other resolutions adopted by the United Nations Conference on Trade and Development at its sixth session;

6. *Urges* all Governments, bearing in mind the particular contribution developed countries can make, to exercise the necessary political will so as to enable the Trade and Development Board, at its twenty-eighth session, to reach agreement on the follow-up to the sixth session of the United Nations Conference on Trade and Development and to ensure timely implementation of its results;

7. *Calls upon* all countries to exert every effort to adopt and implement the measures necessary for the revitalization of the development process in the developing countries and for dealing with structural problems in the global economy, and emphasizes the continuing important role of the United Nations Conference on Trade and Development in this regard;

8. *Takes note* of the statement on the world economic situation with special emphasis on development: approaches to the current world economic crisis and perspectives for the 1980s, including issues, policies and measures relevant to the attainment of a new international economic order, adopted at the sixth session of the United Nations Conference on Trade and Development;

9. *Calls upon* all countries to take appropriate action at the national and international levels on the resolutions of the United Nations Conference on Trade and Development at its sixth session and on the immediate measures set out in paragraph 14 of the statement mentioned above;

10. *Requests* the Trade and Development Board, at its twenty-eighth session, and the subsidiary organs of the United Nations Conference on Trade and Development to take the appropriate necessary action on the resolutions and decisions adopted by the Conference at its sixth session;

11. *Invites* all organs, organizations and bodies of the United Nations system to respond positively to the

requests addressed to them in the relevant parts of the resolutions of the United Nations Conference on Trade and Development at its sixth session.

General Assembly resolution 38/155

19 December 1983   Meeting 102   Adopted without vote

Approved by Second Committee (A/38/702/Add.2) without vote, 14 December (meeting 56); draft by Vice-Chairman (A/C.2/38/L.118), based on informal consultations on draft by Mexico, for Group of 77 (A/C.2/38/L.86); agenda item 78 *(b)*.
Meeting numbers. GA 38th session: 2nd Committee 50, 56; plenary 102.

The draft approved by the Second Committee differed in a number of respects from that put forward by the Group of 77 and subsequently withdrawn.

The fifth preambular paragraph of the approved text consolidated two paragraphs in the Group's draft by which the Assembly would have noted the views and recommendations of the Seventh Conference of Heads of State or Government of Non-Aligned Countries relating to global economic problems and, in particular to UNCTAD VI, and noted further the Buenos Aires Platform setting forth the objectives and specific proposals of the developing countries at UNCTAD VI.

By a preambular paragraph of the Group's draft (corresponding to the sixth of the adopted text), the Assembly would have considered that UNCTAD VI had taken place against the background of the continuation of the most pervasive and dangerous crisis experienced since the Great Depression, the burden of which had fallen most heavily on developing countries, particularly the least developed.

By other preambular paragraphs in the Group's draft, the Assembly would have: reiterated that the strategy for surmounting the economic crisis had to recognize developing countries as full partners in world development and that the situation called for a coherent set of international policies addressing short- and longer-term problems; recognized that the revitalization of the development process in the developing countries and the accompanying requirement of structural changes in the global economy had to be central to any programme for its reactivation and for the development of developing countries; and recalled that UNCTAD VI was to deal with important issues of trade, development and related problems, taking fully into account their interrelationship and thus contributing effectively to overcoming grave difficulties facing the world economy, to the economic development of developing countries and to the attainment of a new international economic order.

References in the Group's draft to "continued lack of political will" and "the negative attitude" of some developed countries were omitted from the final text. Also, by that draft, the Assembly would have endorsed all resolutions of UNCTAD VI, rather than the formulation contained in paragraphs 4 and 5 of the final text, and would also have urged

the United Nations system to respond positively to those resolutions.

In a paragraph of the Group's text corresponding to paragraph 6 of the final text, the Assembly would have urged the developed countries (rather than all Governments) to exercise the necessary political will. In a paragraph corresponding to paragraph 9 of the final text, the Group would have had the Assembly call on all countries, "in particular the developed countries," to take appropriate action. The Group's draft would also have had the Assembly endorse the UNCTAD VI statement rather than take note of it.

By the Group's draft, paragraph 10 of the final text would have concluded with the phrase "particularly those in the areas of trade, money and finance and commodities, including the compensatory financing of export earnings shortfalls".

REFERENCES

[1]YUN 1982, p.724. [2]A/38/15, vol. I (dec. 272(S-XII)). [3]*Ibid.* (dec. 273(S-XII)). [4]*Proceedings of the United Nations Conference on Trade and Development, Sixth Session, Belgrade, 6 June–2 July 1983*, vol. I, *Report and Annexes* (TD/326, vol. I), Sales No. E.83.II.D.6. [5]A/38/132-S/15675 and Corr.1,2. [6]A/38/15, vol. II. [7]*Ibid.* (dec. 275(XXVII)).

International trade

During 1983, international trade issues were discussed by various United Nations bodies. Several resolutions dealing with international trade were adopted at UNCTAD VI, where concern was expressed about the lowest non-oil commodity prices in fifty years and shrinking export markets due to the economic recession and protectionist trends in many developed countries. Commodity issues were widely discussed, with the UNCTAD Committee on Commodities holding its tenth session in 1983 and several meetings on individual commodities also taking place. The General Assembly strongly urged States to sign and ratify the Agreement Establishing the Common Fund for Commodities.

The Trade and Development Board conducted its second annual review of protectionism and structural adjustment, which was also a major issue on the agenda of UNCTAD VI. The Assembly also considered this subject and referred a related draft resolution to its 1984 session (decision 38/438).

The generalized system of preferences, the global system of trade preferences among developing countries, and trade among countries having different economic and social systems were all the subjects of UNCTAD VI resolutions.

In the area of trade promotion and facilitation, increased financial support for the International Trade Centre (ITC)—the focal point for United

Nations assistance to developing countries in formulating and implementing trade promotion programmes—was urged by UNCTAD VI, and an intergovernmental group of experts met to discuss restrictive business practices.

A set of draft guidelines on consumer protection was discussed by the Economic and Social Council (decision 1983/174) and by the Assembly (resolution 38/147), which adopted a resolution urging Governments to comment on the draft guidelines and requesting the Secretary-General to extend assistance towards their finalization and adoption.

Trade policy

Although an incipient economic recovery appeared to have set in since the second quarter of 1983, it seemed unlikely to prove strong enough to provide a major boost to non-oil commodity prices, which fell precipitously from 1979 to 1982, said the UNCTAD *Trade and Development Report, 1983*.[1] The UNCTAD combined index of non-oil primary commodities exported by developing countries, measured in United States dollars, dropped by 16.1 per cent in 1982, following a decline of 15.6 per cent in 1981. The two-year fall of more than 30 per cent was the highest for over 20 years. For the first quarter of 1983, the index was about 3 per cent higher than the average for the fourth quarter of 1982, but still lower than the average for the whole year. With a modest economic recovery widely expected, conditions in international commodity markets were likely to improve in 1983 and 1984.

Weakness in world demand was also reflected in the volume of traded goods, which fell in 1982 by about 2 per cent. While the greatest decline occurred in oil exports, the volume of export of manufactured goods fell as well, although exports of agricultural commodities increased slightly.

At its April 1983 session,[2] the Committee for Development Planning, noting the need for order in world trade, said that despite frequent appeals for a halt to protectionism—which was not only disruptive to the world economy, but infused bitter conflicts in international relations—the disruption of the trading system had gathered momentum.

In a February report[3] to the June ministerial session of the World Food Council, the Executive Director, stressing that international trade must contribute to a more rapid recovery of the world economy, said that the results of UNCTAD VI could have a great impact on developing countries' capacity to solve food problems.

UNCTAD VI action. On 2 July, by resolution 159(VI), adopted without dissent, on international trade in goods and services,[4] UNCTAD VI agreed that the Trade and Development Board should review developments in the international trading system. The Board could recommend policies related to international trade and make proposals on strengthening the trading system.

By the Buenos Aires Platform resolution[4] on the same subject, the Conference would have recognized that the existing rules of the trading system were not equitable or effective, and decided that the Board should study them with a view to establishing a new set of rules leading to a universal system. It would also have decided that the special problems of the least developed countries (LDCs) be kept in view while undertaking that task.

Protectionism and structural adjustment

Trade and Development Board activities. The Trade and Development Board at its twenty-sixth session (Geneva, 18-28 April) conducted its second annual review of protectionism and structural adjustment. Several documents were prepared by the UNCTAD secretariat according to guidelines laid down by the Board at its March 1982 session, when it carried out its first review of the issue.[5]

An overview of protectionism and structural adjustment[6] by the UNCTAD secretariat stated that during the second half of the 1970s, trade disputes emerged as a major strain on the international economy. A combination of two broad trends—increased openness in the economies of major trading countries to external influences and increased resistance to structural change—best explained the difficulties facing the international trading system, the report said.

The report attempted broadly to define the terms structural change and structural adjustment and went on to concentrate on some quantifiable aspects of those processes: the direction and extent of structural change, the changes in comparative advantage, and the relationship between the two.

In its final chapter, the report discussed the need for greater transparency in trade relations and the role of public inquiry in that context. Among its proposals for national public inquiry procedures for assistance to industries were that such bodies would: solicit information to determine short- and long-term prospects for industries; consider claims and interests of all parties; and ensure publication of information, including reports on its operations which could facilitate observance of international notification requirements. These bodies would also establish procedures whereby industries could substantiate the need for assistance, and would review evidence on the basis of nationally defined and multilaterally acceptable criteria.

Action proposed at the international level included: establishing internationally agreed criteria for government assistance to industry; gathering and disseminating information on countries' production and trade policies; and co-ordinating industrial policy to reduce the risk of competitive action, other than commercial action, to attain objectives by means not covered in existing trade rules.

Also before the Board was an UNCTAD report[7] on protectionism and structural adjustment in agriculture, which gave the background to policy issues, reviewed trends in agricultural production, employment, consumption and trade, analysed the application of tariffs and non-tariff barriers and the effects and costs of such trade intervention measures, and discussed possible international co-operative action in agricultural production and trade.

Another UNCTAD report[8] submitted to the Board reviewed progress in compiling an inventory of non-tariff barriers affecting the trade of developing countries, and indicated that a comprehensive inventory was an essential step towards securing greater transparency in the international trading system.

An UNCTAD report on production and trade in services, policies and their underlying factors bearing upon international services transactions[9] provided a conceptual overview of the nature of such transactions, discussed some principal determinants of structural patterns in the international services sector, presenting statistical information on production, employment and trade in that sector, and dealt with measures affecting international services activities, including trade- and investment-related measures.

On 28 April, following its discussion of the item, the Trade and Development Board adopted a set of agreed conclusions[10] on protectionism and structural adjustment, in which it referred to the danger of new forms of protectionist measures, including discriminatory ones. The Board reaffirmed the need for an UNCTAD work programme for the Board's future annual reviews of the topic and noted that proposals had been made on some elements for a work programme for consideration by UNCTAD VI. Since the Board could not conclude its consideration of such proposals, the subject, regarded as a key issue for UNCTAD VI, would be dealt with by that Conference.

On 22 March, the UNCTAD Committee on Manufactures adopted a set of agreed conclusions in which it expressed concern about growing protectionism in international trade (see below).

UNCTAD VI action. A policy paper[11] on protectionism, trade relations and structural adjustment was submitted by the UNCTAD secretariat to UNCTAD VI. The report gave an overview of trading conditions and analysed protectionism in its various forms, with an effort to consider all groups of countries, regardless of levels of development or economic and social systems. The report examined policies and practices for international trade relations and the conflicting tendencies that had emerged in their application.

The report also attempted to identify the reasons for protective measures, considering that if those objectives could be accomplished by other measures,—particularly, by structural adjustment policies—the strains on the trading system would be alleviated.

In conclusion, the report recommended a comprehensive approach, combining trade, adjustment and development policies, for the recovery of international trade. Action recommended at the national level included: review of legislation and regulations to remove features leading to harassment of trade; creation of independent bodies, accessible to the public, including representatives of trading partners, to assess whether protective action was justified and to advise on appropriate means of implementing it; and refraining from arbitrary actions by subjecting all decisions affecting trade to those procedures.

Action recommended at the international level included: refraining from unilateral actions adversely affecting trade of other countries; creating an international mechanism to exchange information on trade measures; reviewing policies and practices in international trade relations; establishing criteria for taking protective action in various situations; framing principles and techniques for future multilateral trade negotiations; and providing technical assistance to improve developing countries' understanding of trade-related regulations.

Recommended structural adjustment actions at the national level included: reviewing existing protective measures used in industry, assessing their effects on other producers and consumers, including costs; creating information exchange mechanisms among governments, producers and consumers on production objectives; and adopting structural adjustment policies to encourage less competitive enterprises to move into more viable lines of production.

Recommendations for structural adjustment action at the international level included: reviewing production and trade in various goods and services to prepare the basis for future trade liberalization; giving priority in this context to sectors where protective actions were most prevalent; and framing general principles relating to territorial jurisdiction in respect of investment and business practices.

On 2 July, UNCTAD VI adopted without dissent a four-part resolution (159(VI))[4] on international trade in goods and services. In part I, dealing with protectionism and structural adjustment, the Conference agreed that protectionism harmed trade and development, in particular that of developing countries, and should be resisted. The Conference also agreed that developed countries would: work towards reducing and eliminating quantitative restrictions and periodically review the progress of this process; recognize the role which trade liberalization could play in achieving economic growth and development; fulfil their commitments in international trade and provide more favourable treatment to developing countries; and review their existing procedures relating to anti-dumping and countervailing duties, to assure that there were no unjustifiable impediments to the trade of other countries, especially developing countries, and take remedial action as appropriate.

The Trade and Development Board, in its annual review, was entrusted with monitoring and making recommendations regarding the resolution and continuing its work on non-tariff barriers.

It was also agreed that countries should note the results of the 1982 ministerial session of the General Agreement on Tariffs and Trade (GATT),[12] in particular the decision to examine prospects for increasing trade between developed and developing countries, and that work under way in GATT on a comprehensive understanding based on the Agreement's principles should be continued with a view to reaching results within the agreed time-frame.

With regard to structural adjustment, it was agreed that it was a global and ongoing phenomenon which should be facilitated for optimum overall growth, including developing and diversifying the economies of developing countries to increase their share in production of and trade in processed goods and manufactures. Developed countries were urged to facilitate structural adjustment based on a dynamic pattern of comparative advantage; industrial collaboration arrangements, including international subcontracting, could be employed in that regard.

It was agreed that the Trade and Development Board would continue annually to review patterns of production and trade in the world economy and in that context would provide a forum for discussion of structural adjustment to foster greater transparency and would monitor trade developments and make recommendations to encourage internationally competitive production in the light of comparative advantage. The sessional committee of the Trade and Development Board established in 1981[13] would review progress on structural adjustment and make recommendations to the Board if necessary.

The Conference stressed that particular attention be paid to the special problems of LDCs in dealing with the issues of both protectionism and structural adjustment.

The Conference noted that trade in services was a growing phenomenon worldwide and that the issue needed further study and understanding. The UNCTAD Secretary-General would continue to study the issues involved and UNCTAD would consider the role of the services sector in the development process. The Trade and Development Board was invited to consider at its twenty-ninth (1984) session future work on the subject by UNCTAD.

The resolution also dealt with the international trading system (see above) and the generalized system of preferences (see below).

In addition to the UNCTAD secretariat policy paper,[11] the Conference also had before it a resolution contained in the Buenos Aires Platform[4] on international trade in goods and services. By that text, the Conference would have agreed that developed countries should abstain from imposing new protectionist measures against exports of developing countries, and from unilateral decisions adversely affecting their trade. Developed countries would also eliminate all other measures they were applying to protect their domestic industries which adversely affected the trade of developing countries.

Among other major differences in the two resolutions was the inclusion in the Buenos Aires text of a paragraph by which the Conference would have agreed that developed countries would refrain from applying economic sanctions against developing countries as a form of political coercion. A separate resolution (152(VI)) on rejection of coercive economic measures was adopted by the Conference (see p. 412).

On 2 July, the Conference adopted without dissent decision 160(VI)[4] by which it took note of the agreed conclusions on protectionism and structural adjustment adopted by the Trade and Development Board at its April session (see above) and decided that the Board at its twenty-seventh (October/November) session should establish a work programme taking into account Conference resolution 159(VI) and other proposals by both the Group of 77 and Group B (developed market economies) annexed to the decision.

Follow-up action to UNCTAD VI. The Trade and Development Board at its twenty-seventh session (Geneva, 3-20 October and 2 November) considered UNCTAD VI resolution 159(VI) and decision 160(VI). It also had before it a background note[14] on work being done by the UNCTAD secretariat to facilitate the Board's tasks in complying with Conference resolutions on protectionism and structural adjustment.

On 20 October the Board adopted a decision[15] by which it welcomed the discussion on a work programme on the subject and decided to remit the question to its twenty-eighth (1984) session together with a draft resolution submitted by Venezuela on behalf of the Group of 77, outlining priority areas for attention, on which the Board had been unable to reach agreement. The UNCTAD Secretary-General was requested to assist the deliberations on the subject and the Board reiterated that the review of protectionism and structural adjustment should be based on Conference resolutions 131(V)[16] and 159(VI), a 1981 Board resolution[17] and a 1982 Board decision.[18]

In its December resolution (38/155) on the report of UNCTAD VI (see above), the General Asembly noted with concern that the Board had been unable to translate the resolutions and decisions of UNCTAD VI into a work programme and action.

General Assembly consideration. A draft resolution[19] on protectionism and structural adjustment and the international trading system was submitted to the Second Committee in November by Mexico on behalf of the Group of 77. By this draft the General Assembly would have, among other things: urged States to implement fully UNCTAD resolution 159(VI); emphasized that developed countries should facilitate structural adjustment based on a dynamic pattern of comparative advantage, reiterated the need to accelerate negotiations on protectionism and structural adjustment in the Board; invited the Board to initiate at its March/April 1984 session its annual review of trading developments with a view to formulating trade policies and to make proposals to strengthen the international trading system; and urged the Board to study the generalized system of preferences (see below).

Following withdrawal of the draft text by Mexico on behalf of the sponsors, the Second Committee decided to recommend that the Assembly should refer to its 1984 session a draft resolution contained in a note by the Secretariat.[20]

This draft, originally submitted in 1980[21] and revised in 1981,[22] had been considered in 1982,[23] when it was decided to consider the question again in 1983 in the light of the outcome of UNCTAD VI. The draft resolution, addressed mainly to developed countries, would have the Assembly urge them to limit protectionist policies and facilitate measures to increase the share of developing countries in international trade. A table containing suggestions by some developed countries for changes in the draft was annexed to it.

GENERAL ASSEMBLY ACTION

On 19 December, the Assembly, on the recommendation of the Second Committee, adopted decision 38/438.

Protectionism and structural adjustment

At its 102nd plenary meeting, on 19 December 1983, the General Assembly, on the recommendation of the Second Committee, decided to refer to its thirty-ninth session for consideration the draft resolution entitled "Protectionism and structural adjustment".

General Assembly decision 38/438

Adopted without vote

Approved by Second Committee (A/38/702/Add.2) without vote, 14 December (meeting 56); oral proposal by Chairman; agenda item 78 *(b)*.
Meeting numbers. GA 38th session: 2nd Committee 50, 56; plenary 102.

Multilateral trade negotiations

Trade and Development Board activities. The Trade and Development Board continued in April 1983 its discussion of multilateral trade negotiations, with particular reference to the implementation of agreements reached at the 1979 Tokyo Round of negotiations conducted by the General Agreement on Tariffs and Trade (GATT).[24]

The Board had before it a background note[25] prepared by the UNCTAD secretariat on recent developments in international trade relations, particularly at the 1982 ministerial session of GATT.[26]

On 28 April,[27] the Board expressed satisfaction over the debate at its current session, took note of discussions on the issue at previous sessions of the Board, including statements by the Director of the UNCTAD Manufactures Division, and decided to defer until its October 1983 session negotiations on a draft resolution on developments in the international trading system, submitted in 1981 on behalf of the Group of 77,[28] calling for an annual Board review of international trading system developments, taking into account decisions by UNCTAD VI.

Trade preferences

During 1983, UNCTAD and the United Nations Development Programme (UNDP) continued their joint technical assistance project on the generalized system of preferences. Discussion also continued on a proposed global system of trade preferences among developing countries.

Generalized system of preferences

The UNCTAD Committee on Manufactures, which met at Geneva from 14 to 22 March 1983 (see below), reviewed the report of the Special Committee on Preferences on its eleventh (1982) session,[29] and adopted a set of agreed conclusions in which it reaffirmed the objectives of the generalized system of preferences and agreed that there should be improvements in the system, taking into account the needs of developing countries, particularly LDCs. The Committee invited UNDP to extend beyond 1983 the UNCTAD/UNDP project on assistance to developing countries for the fuller utilization of the generalized system. On 28 April, the Trade and Development Board decided that the report of the Special Committee on its 1982 session should be remitted to the Special Committee's 1984 session.

UNCTAD VI action. In July, UNCTAD VI adopted resolution 159(VI)[4] on international trade in goods and services, part III of which dealt with the generalized system of preferences (GSP). By this resolution, the Conference agreed that developed countries should make improvements in their schemes in accordance with GSP. It was also agreed that special attention be given to products not adequately covered by existing schemes in both the agricultural and industrial sectors and to those of interest to LDCs. The interests of developing countries enjoying special advantages and the need to find ways of protecting their interests should be taken into account.

The Conference further agreed that: preference-giving countries modifying their schemes should afford adequate opportunity for consultations on difficulties or other matters; the Trade and Development Board should study the operation of GSP to assess its stability and effectiveness; the rules of origin should be further liberalized and harmonized and their operation simplified; and the rules for cumulative origin should also be improved. UNDP was invited to continue to support the UNCTAD/UNDP technical assistance programme beyond 1983 to permit developing countries to benefit adequately from the schemes, and the programme's scope should be expanded to cover other laws and regulations of preference-giving countries affecting the exports of developing countries.

The Conference also agreed that special attention be given to LDCs to provide the fullest possible duty-free treatment.

In taking this action, UNCTAD VI considered a resolution on the subject in the Buenos Aires Platform.[4] By that text, the Conference, considering the importance of GSP for the expansion of trade of developing countries and keeping in view the problems being faced by them in the operation of those programmes, would have decided that developed countries should significantly improve GSP, broaden its scope of application and incorporate a greater degree of flexibility into the related procedure.

The Platform text also included a paragraph by which the Conference would have decided that more stability and security should be introduced into GSP schemes, their non-discriminatory nature be ensured and the existing benefits to developing countries be preserved, avoiding the introduction of discriminatory measures such as those applied under the concept of graduation or its use to exert political or economic pressure. The Platform text would have had the Conference decide that the Trade and Development Board should establish a set of multilateral guidelines for the operation of GSP rather than study its operation. Also, whereas the final text called for the UNCTAD/UNDP

technical assistance programme to be expanded to cover laws of preference-giving countries, the Platform text called for the Board to establish a study programme on this issue.

The reference to providing the fullest possible duty-free treatment for LDCs, contained in the last paragraph of the final text, was not included in the Platform resolution.

Technical co-operation

During 1983, assistance to developing countries for fuller utilization of GSP continued through a joint UNCTAD/UNDP technical assistance project. The main objectives of the project were: to promote expansion and diversification of exports from developing countries; to assist preference-receiving countries by providing information on GSP schemes and training officials dealing with GSP and related matters; and to mobilize support from preference-giving countries and preference-receiving countries in a position to do so, in order to enable the latter to derive the fullest possible benefits from GSP.

During the year, the project organized workshops in Burundi, Ethiopia, Paraguay and Tunisia. It also provided assistance to the regional project for Asia and the Pacific for seminars/workshops in Burma, China, India, Malaysia, Nepal and the Republic of Korea. Assistance was also provided for the regional project's advisory missions to Bhutan, Maldives and Viet Nam.

Details on 1982 and 1983 technical co-operation activities were contained in a report[30] to the Special Committee on Preferences.

Global system of trade preferences among developing countries

UNCTAD VI action. UNCTAD VI had before it an UNCTAD secretariat report[31] on economic co-operation among developing countries. In reviewing major programme areas, the report pointed out that developing countries had continued preparations to establish a global system of trade preferences (GSTP) with the technical support of the UNCTAD secretariat.

Following adoption in October 1982 of the Group of 77 Ministerial Declaration on GSTP[32] and of a Trade and Development Board resolution[33] requesting UNCTAD secretariat support for a 1983 meeting on the subject, it was expected that future secretariat work would entail providing support for the negotiations in the form of analytical studies, trade data and meetings servicing. There would also be a need to assist individual countries and groups of developing countries wishing to participate in the negotiations.

On 2 July, in resolution 139(VI)[4] on UNCTAD activities regarding economic co-operation among developing countries (ECDC) (p. 413), UNCTAD VI decided to continue implementing resolution 127(V), [34] to request the Trade and Development Board and the Committee on Economic Co-operation among Developing Countries to adopt forward-looking decisions and to consider effective support measures, and to call on the Committee to consider ways of giving further impetus to ECDC, particularly in relation to establishing GSTP, taking into account a proposal submitted by the Group of 77 (see below).

By the Buenos Aires Platform decision[4] on economic co-operation among developing countries, the Conference would have decided to support full implementation of resolution 127(V) and reiterated the need for a substantial technical and administrative contribution by the UNCTAD secretariat and other international organizations, particularly in establishing GSTP among developing countries, ensuring the participation of interested Group of 77 members.

Action by the Committee on Economic Co-operation among Developing Countries. In 1983, the third session of the UNCTAD Committee on Economic Co-operation among Developing Countries (p. 414) considered the question of GSTP. In a 5 October resolution,[35] the Committee called on the Secretary-General of UNCTAD to continue ECDC activities designed to promote trade expansion, particularly in relation to GSTP. The Committee also recommended that the Trade and Development Board take into account proposals made on GSTP during its third session, including those annexed to the Committee's report, with a view to taking a decision on all outstanding aspects of the matter.

Annexed to the report were a draft resolution on support for the negotiation of GSTP, submitted by Lebanon on behalf of the Group of 77, and two informal texts submitted to the Committee Chairman's informal consultations.

The Committee on ECDC had before it a report[36] of a meeting convened to enable the developing countries participating in the negotiations on GSTP *inter alia* to define the nature, scope and extent of the support requested from UNCTAD (Geneva, 2-11 May), held pursuant to an October 1982 Board resolution. [37] Annexed to the meeting's report was a proposal submitted on behalf of the Group of 77 on support required from the UNCTAD secretariat for negotiation of GSTP.

Trade and Development Board action. On 15 October, after considering the report of the Committee on ECDC,[38] the Trade and Development Board adopted by a roll-call vote of 49 to none, with 9 abstentions, a resolution[39] on provision in the UNCTAD calendar for meetings on GSTP.

By this resolution, the Board requested the UNCTAD Secretary-General to provide in the 1984 calendar for up to four weeks of meetings enabling the developing countries participating in the negotiations on GSTP to continue the necessary work towards the establishment of the system. On 20 October, this resolution was reaffirmed by the Board without vote, following which Group B (developed market economies) reiterated that it dissociated itself from any assertion that a decision to reaffirm the resolution had been taken by consensus.

Trade among countries having different economic and social systems

UNCTAD VI action. In considering trade relations among countries having different economic and social systems and all trade flows resulting therefrom, UNCTAD VI had before it an UNCTAD policy paper[40] on the problems of expansion of trade and intensification of economic co-operation among those groups and suggested possible multilateral action.

On 2 July, UNCTAD VI adopted without dissent decision 145(VI)[4] on UNCTAD activities related to the subject. By that decision the Conference requested member States and the UNCTAD secretariat to further implement UNCTAD IV resolution 95(IV)[41] and decided to remit to the October session of the Trade and Development Board an informal text, which had been remitted to the Conference by the Board in 1982[42] and amended during negotiations.

The four-part informal text, annexed to the decision, called for further expansion of East-West trade and trade between developing countries and the socialist countries of Eastern Europe, called on those socialist countries and the developing countries to give new impetus to their co-operation and expand its volume, requested the UNCTAD Secretary-General to take action in several specific areas, and decided to establish within UNCTAD an advisory service on developing trade between the two country groupings.

The Buenos Aires Platform text[4] on this item contained a number of suggestions regarding trade expansion and increased economic relations between the developing countries and the socialist countries of Eastern Europe. It was recommended that the latter should: contribute to developing countries' efforts to diversify and intensify their trade; embody in their economic plans measures to provide increased imports from developing countries; improve their economic assistance to developing countries and fulfil the targets for transfer of resources set out in the International Development Strategy for the Third United Nations Development Decade (the 1980s)[43] and the 1981 Substantial New Programme of Action for the 1980s for the Least Developed Countries;[44] and take various financial measures to benefit the developing countries. The Platform text also suggested that the UNCTAD secretariat be requested to support member States in strengthening trade and economic relations between the developing countries and the socialist countries of Eastern Europe.

Trade and Development Board action. On 29 October, the Trade and Development Board decided[45] to remit to its 1984 autumn session the informal text annexed to Conference decision 145(VI) (see above). By this decision, the Board also requested the UNCTAD Secretary-General to convene, for one week in 1984, an *ad hoc* group of experts to consider expanding trade and economic relations between countries having different economic and social systems. It further requested him to ensure support for implementing UNCTAD technical assistance projects and programmes concerning trade between developing countries and socialist countries of Eastern Europe, invited UNDP to contribute to their financing and invited voluntary contributions.

For the Board's consideration of this item, the UNCTAD secretariat had prepared a report[46] which reviewed trends and policies in this area, with an addendum containing statistics in tabular form.

Technical co-operation

In 1983, a special trust fund arrangement was set up under the USSR/UNDP Trust Fund for Training in the USSR of Specialists from Developing Countries[47] for UNCTAD activities for development of trade between socialist countries of Eastern Europe and developing countries. For this purpose, the USSR made a contribution to UNDP (75 per cent in rubles and 25 per cent in convertible currency) for a period of 3 years. Under this programme, a seminar was held in Moscow in September/October for officials, trade representatives and economic counsellors from Arab countries to widen their knowledge of trading with socialist countries in Eastern Europe and of the prospects of expanding and diversifying exports.

UNDP-financed regional projects included assistance to African countries in expanding economic relations with the socialist countries of Eastern Europe and studies on economic relations between Latin American countries and countries members of the Council for Mutual Economic Assistance.

Trade promotion and facilitation

During 1983, United Nations bodies continued to assist developing countries to promote their exports and to facilitate the movement of goods in international commerce by harmonizing procedures, standardizing documents and developing new data processing and communication methods for exports, imports and transit. The main origi-

nator of technical co-operation projects in this area was the International Trade Centre (ITC). A resolution on strengthening ITC, particularly in relation to commodities, was adopted by UNCTAD VI. An UNCTAD intergovernmental group of experts met to consider ways of eliminating restrictive business practices as barriers to trade flows.

International Trade Centre

During 1983, the International Trade Centre (ITC), under the joint sponsorship of UNCTAD and GATT, continued its technical co-operation activities, serving as the focal point for United Nations assistance to developing countries in formulating and implementing trade promotion programmes.[48]

ITC reported an overall decrease in expenditures on projects implemented in 1983, citing serious stagnation in financial resources available for multilateral co-operation activities. Trust fund resources had declined during the year, partly due to the appreciation of the dollar in relation to currencies of some donor countries. The number of UNDP-financed projects, however, had increased. Thus, UNDP's share in total resources available increased significantly, reflecting the higher priority given to trade promotion activities by a number of developing countries.

In Africa, country projects increased to 19 from 16 in 1982 and regional projects increased from 5 to 9, with almost all new projects being implemented in LDCs. In Asia and the Pacific, country projects increased to 28 from 23, with 7 regional projects compared to 9 in 1982. In Latin America, country projects rose to 16 from 10 in 1982 and regional projects remained at 12. In Europe, the Mediterranean and the Middle East, technical co-operation activities were again negatively affected in 1983 by scarcity of resources and delays in launching new projects.

Approximately 35.6 per cent of the ITC programme was devoted to export market development, 20.9 per cent to institutional infrastructure for national trade promotion, 16.9 per cent to manpower development, 12.9 per cent to specialized national trade promotion services, 4.4 per cent to import operations and techniques, 3.6 per cent to multinational trade promotion, 2.8 per cent to the special programme of technical co-operation with LDCs, 1.9 per cent to technical co-operation with national chambers of commerce, and 1 per cent to trade promotion oriented to rural development.

ITC activities in 1983 for export market development included expansion of its computerized import and export information systems. Under its import-export contact programme, the Centre increased the number of company profiles on exporters in developing countries and importers in developed and developing countries to almost 15,000. Publication of information began in September with a series of trilingual trade contacts directories, about 15 issues of which were produced in 1983 and 50 planned for 1984. The Centre dealt with about 1,300 requests for special trade information, up 9 per cent over 1982. It added some 7,000 items to its information files by scanning periodicals and other materials, and issued four monographs on trade channels. The first edition of a *World Directory of Trade Promotion Organizations and Other Foreign Trade Bodies* was also published. Market development services included: generic market research for products of interest to several developing countries; programme and project formulation missions; specific marketing research for individual countries and dissemination of the results, including recommended marketing strategies for target markets; development of products showing export potential; lecturing at product-oriented workshops and seminars; and selection and backstopping of experts and advisers. Supply and demand surveys continued in Asia and the Caribbean, as did an interregional UNDP-financed supply and demand survey project.

With regard to institutional infrastructure for trade promotion at the national level, the Centre appointed a senior adviser on institutional aspects of foreign trade promotion to develop an integrated national trade promotion programme planning approach, with special consideration to the needs of LDCs. Programming and consultancy missions were undertaken to Egypt, Ghana, Guatamala and Turkey.

In the area of specialized national trade promotion services, a course was held for packaging designers from Pakistan and the Philippines (Karachi, Pakistan, October) and a package design clinic to improve the graphic designs of Egyptian export packages and labels took place (Amsterdam, the Netherlands, December), followed by a four-day symposium in Cairo on the development of export packages. A two-day workshop was held on the same subject (Manila, the Philippines, July) and included an exhibition of over 300 European consumer and industrial packages. Shorter presentations on packaging were given in various countries.

With regard to multinational trade promotion, ITC continued market promotion projects for jute and jute products in Western Europe and the United States, and completed implementation of a UNDP-financed project to assist the international pepper community in market intelligence. Work also continued on establishing an international spice group.

ITC's special programme of technical co-operation with LDCs attempted to identify critical export problems in programme countries. Fact-finding and programming missions were undertaken to Cape Verde, the Gambia and Guinea-Bissau.

Trade promotion activities oriented to rural development included an advisory mission for a Pakistani national project on exporting fresh fruits and vegetables to some Middle East countries. Fact-finding and programming missions on product selection and assessment of export development needs were carried out for Malawi, Sierra Leone and Zimbabwe.

Total ITC expenditure in 1983 was $27.5 million. Of this amount, technical co-operation activities accounted for $14.9 million compared to $16.1 million in 1982.[49] Trust fund contributions furnished $9.5 million of the 1983 amount for technical co-operation; the remainder, $5.4 million, was provided by UNDP. The Centre's 1983 regular budget of $8.3 million, covering operations at its Geneva headquarters, was contributed in equal parts by the United Nations and GATT. As at 31 December, ITC had a headquarters-based staff of 71 Professionals and 128 in the General Service category. It had 517 experts assigned to projects during the year.

JAG action. The Joint Advisory Group (JAG) on the ITC, at its sixteenth session (Geneva, 21-28 March),[50] endorsed the ITC third medium-term programme (1983-1985). Among recommendations made by the Group on ITC technical co-operation activities were that priority be given to identifying export potential in developing countries and to encouraging development of products for export. It also suggested that ITC activities emphasize: trade problems of LDCs; product adaptation and development in Africa; consideration of level of development in providing assistance; and technical co-operation with the socialist countries of Eastern Europe to expand trade between them and developing countries.

Regarding financing and organization, JAG recommended that the Centre continue to search for new donors and further to develop relations with the World Bank, the regional development banks, bilateral aid programmes and the Commission of the European Communities. The Group unanimously recommended.that ITC should seek, through its parent bodies, executing agency status with UNDP.

As a special topic, JAG discussed a consultant's report on the ITC import operation and techniques programme,[51] and generally endorsed its recommendations.

UNCTAD VI action. On 2 July, UNCTAD VI adopted without dissent resolution 158(VI)[4] on strengthening ITC, particularly in relation to commodities. By this resolution the Conference requested ITC to support the implementation of the Integrated Programme for Commodities (see below), and to this end to co-operate closely with other agencies, particularly UNCTAD and GATT, and to enlarge its programme for providing technical assistance to developing countries, in particular the LDCs, in market research, market development and promotion in the commodity field. The Conference invited the Executive Director of ITC to take action to increase the level of voluntary contributions to ITC to provide for the commodity promotion programme, and urged States members of UNCTAD to consider making such contributions, to strengthen commodity-related ITC activities.

Trade and Development Board action. On 20 October, following its consideration of the JAG report,[50] the Trade and Development Board adopted a resolution[52] on the status of ITC *vis-à-vis* UNDP and strengthening of the Centre. By this resolution, the Board endorsed the JAG recommendation that the Centre should seek executing agency status with UNDP in respect of trade promotion activities and called on the Centre to maintain close collaboration with UNCTAD and GATT. It also invited Governments, in implementing Conference resolution 158(VI) (see above), to announce voluntary contributions to the Centre for its 1984 and 1985 activities at the 1984 session of JAG and to complete such announcements at the twenty-ninth session of the Trade and Development Board in 1984.

Trade facilitation

During 1983, the UNCTAD Special Programme on Trade Facilitation (FALPRO) continued to provide the focal point in an international network of national trade facilitation bodies and interested international organizations. FALPRO's activities included advising Governments on the simplification and harmonization of trade procedures and documentation in order to eliminate technical obstacles to trade. Various manuals, directories and code systems in trade facilitation, established jointly by UNCTAD and the United Nations Economic Commission for Europe (ECE), were maintained and updated during the year. Four issues of *Trade Facilitation News* were issued by ECE and FALPRO in 1983.

Restrictive business practices

The Intergovernmental Group of Experts on Restrictive Business Practices held its second session at Geneva from 21 to 30 November,[53] the first having been held in 1981.[54] The Group was established by the Trade and Development Board as a forum for consultation on matters related to the Set of Multilaterally Agreed Equitable Principles and Rules for the Control of Restrictive Business Practices, approved by a United Nations conference and adopted by the General Assembly in 1980.[55]

The Group had before it two studies by the UNCTAD secretariat on restrictive business practices related to the provisions of the principles and rules: one on collusive tendering,[56] and the other on the effects on international trade transactions of restrictive business practices in the services sector by consulting firms and other enterprises in relation to the design and manufacture of plant and equipment.[57]

Also before the Group was a note by the UNCTAD secretariat[58] which reported on steps taken by States to meet their commitments under the principles and rules, and reviewed legislative and other developments in restrictive business practices, including the technical assistance needs of developing countries.

For its consideration of the revised draft of a model law or laws on restrictive business practices, the Group had before it a paper[59] prepared by the UNCTAD secretariat giving elements for provisions of such a model law.

On 30 November, the Group adopted a resolution[60] by which it decided to consider at its third session, scheduled for November 1984, proposals to develop further the principles and rules for submission to the 1985 United Nations Conference on Restrictive Business Practices. The Group expressed regret that its invitation to UNDP and member States to make financial contributions—for technical assistance and advisory and training programmes on restrictive business practices, particularly for developing countries—had not produced the desired result, reiterated that invitation and invited member States to pursue in the UNDP Governing Council the allocation of resources for such programmes.

The Group recognized the adverse effects of collusive tendering, especially on the trade of developing countries, took note of the UNCTAD report[56] and comments made on it by the Group, requested the UNCTAD secretariat to consider further developing the study in the light of additional information from Governments, and called on States to legislate to control collusive tendering.

The Group also took note of the UNCTAD study on restrictive practices in the services sector[57] and of the Group's comments, requested the UNCTAD Secretary-General to identify restrictive business practices in that field, primarily those faced by prospective new exports, in particular from developing countries, and decided to consider the study in 1984.

The revised draft of the model law(s) on restrictive business practices[59] and the Group's comments thereon were welcomed, and it was decided that the next steps in that work should be: to revise the model law(s), taking into account Government comments, and to submit the new draft to the Group's 1984 meeting; and to compile a handbook on restrictive business practices legislation.

The Group took note of the 1982 Annual Report on Restrictive Business Practices and the quarterly information notes by the UNCTAD secretariat, which were to be continued. It called on States to provide information and asked the UNCTAD secretariat to inform States of information available.

Commodities

Various aspects of commodity issues were considered in UNCTAD's specialized bodies during 1983.

The UNCTAD Committee on Commodities held its tenth session at Geneva from 26 January to 8 February 1983.[61] The Committee reviewed the world commodity situation in general, progress in implementing UNCTAD resolutions relating to commodities, including resolution 93(IV) on the Integrated Programme for Commodities,[62] and international activities outside UNCTAD concerning individual commodities, and discussed liberalization of barriers to trade in primary and processed commodities. The Committee also discussed a policy paper on commodity issues (see below) prepared by the UNCTAD secretariat for UNCTAD VI. No conclusions were reached on issues discussed; the Committee Chairman, however, was asked to prepare a summary of proceedings on his own responsibility.

The Chairman's summary covered all agenda items discussed. He stated that there had been general agreement on the gravity of the world commodity crisis, which was a source of great difficulty for the developing countries in particular, although some countries felt that it was only part of the deep economic recession.

A report[63] prepared by the UNCTAD secretariat reviewed developments in world commodity trade, with emphasis on developing countries, and evaluated the immediate prospects for trade in major primary commodities. The report analysed patterns of world trade in major groups of primary commodities during the two preceding decades, and developments in individual commodity markets were surveyed. In concluding remarks, the growing importance of developing countries in world trade was noted, as was the fact that trade among developing countries had been rising faster than their total world trade. Manufactured goods seemed to be the most dynamic sector of trade among developing countries. Since demand for agricultural raw materials and minerals depended on industrial growth, there was potential for expansion of trade among developing countries in those products, too, if the rate of industrial growth in developing regions was to accelerate. Available information indicated that the granting of mutual tariff preferences within regional integration schemes may have contributed to the rapid expansion of intraregional trade.

The Committee had before it the report of its Permanent Sub-Committee on its third session, held at Geneva from 17 to 26 January.[64] The Sub-Committee had before it five studies prepared by the UNCTAD secretariat on the processing, market-ing and distribution of coffee, copper, jute, sugar and tea. Other reports prepared by the secretariat contained suggestions on a framework of international co-operation on processing, marketing and distribution of primary commodities, and a synthesis of comments of Governments, international organizations and other bodies on the studies discussed at the Sub-Committee's 1982 session.[65]

On 28 April, the Trade and Development Board took note of the Committee's report.[10]

UNCTAD VI action. For its consideration, UNCTAD VI had before it a policy paper[66] prepared by the UNCTAD secretariat on commodity issues. The paper discussed the sharp fall in primary commodity prices between 1980 and 1982 and its implications for the world economy. The paper noted that the fall, which had driven many prices to their lowest levels in half a century, had compounded the burden of developing countries in coping with the severe recession in the developed market-economy countries.

Measures proposed in the report included that Governments ratify the 1980 Agreement Establishing the Common Fund for Commodities[67] by September 1983 for it to become operational by January 1984 (see below), that UNCTAD consider holding an intergovernmental review to identify guidelines to strengthen commodity agreements, and that there should be negotiations on new and more flexible commodity agreements.

Regarding commodity prices, it was proposed that interim agreements be negotiated for commodities listed in Conference resolution 93(IV)[62] but not covered by existing agreements, that interim stocking and/or supply management be considered, that the Common Fund arrange financing for interim commodity agreements, that IMF liberalize its buffer stock financing facility, and that the World Bank and regional development banks increase their assistance to developing countries in meeting transitional costs of internationally agreed supply management measures. It was recommended that IMF expand and liberalize its compensatory financing facility for shortfalls in export earnings and that the socialist countries of Eastern Europe consider a programme of support for shortfalls in developing countries' earnings from commodity exports to those countries.

Proposed longer-term measures included negotiations to establish a complementary facility for commodity-related shortfalls in export earnings and agreement on intergovernmental machinery for those negotiations, commitment by developed market-economy countries to improve market access for primary and processed commodities, and a request to the socialist countries of Eastern Europe to enlarge commitments to purchase primary and processed commodities from developing countries. Regarding processing and marketing of primary commodities, it was recommended that there should be agreement in principle on a facility for financing investment in non-fuel mining, that there should be a commitment to improve market transparency, including monitoring of commodity contracts in international trade, and agreement on increased support for marketing and distribution of commodity exports of developing countries.

The report proposed special measures for commodity exports of LDCs, including special arrangements for those countries as part of the proposed enlargement and liberalization of the IMF compensatory financing facility. Especially advantageous terms for LDCs should be incorporated in any new commodity-related compensatory financing facilities and in a new investment facility to finance mining investment and processing of raw materials in developing countries, should these be established. It was also recommended that special attention be paid to LDCs within a programme of technical support for developing countries in processing and marketing their primary commodities.

On 2 July, the Conference adopted two resolutions on implementing the Integrated Programme for Commodities.

It adopted without dissent resolution 155(VI)[4] on stabilizing and strengthening commodity markets. By this resolution, the Conference, expressing concern about the limited progress in negotiating international commodity agreements under the Integrated Programme and about the vulnerability of commodity markets, urged Governments to reaffirm their commitments made in adopting resolution 93(IV). It urged countries to stabilize commodity markets and join existing commodity agreements to strengthen their effectiveness.

The UNCTAD Secretary-General was requested to convene, at an early date, negotiating conferences on commodities on which preparatory work had reached an advanced stage, to conclude international agreements. The Conference also requested that preparatory work on other commodities be finalized. The Committee on Commodities was requested to provide a forum for interested Governments to consider project proposals or other arrangements on hides and skins within the context of the Integrated Programme.

The Conference decided that the Committee should examine, in the area of commodities of particular export interest to developing countries which were not covered by international arrangements, the feasibility of provisional arrangements to be applied temporarily to mitigate sudden price collapses. It reaffirmed that commodity agreements could be revised only according to their respective provisions and by member countries in their own forums, and requested the Trade and Development Board to convene a special session of the Committee on Commodities to examine the role of international commodity agreements negotiated within UNCTAD in the Integrated Programme.

Countries were requested to participate actively in negotiating a new International Sugar Agreement and the Conference urged that negotiations on an international tropical timber agreement be finalized (see below).

Multilateral and bilateral sources, including UNDP, were requested to consider financing the elaboration into full projects of the summary project proposals on developmental measures approved by preparatory meetings under the Integrated Programme, and the UNCTAD Secretary-General was invited to take action in this regard. These sources were further requested to consider financing activities such as seminars and workshops to promote the objectives of the Integrated Programme.

Governments were urged to minimize disruptions of international commodity markets when disposing of government-held non-commercial reserves, and the Committee on Commodities was requested to review problems in implementing that decision and to report thereon to the Board.

There were several major differences between resolution 155(VI) and the Buenos Aires Platform text on this item.[4] By the Platform resolution, UNCTAD would have recalled its resolution 126(V)[68] on the United Nations Conference to Negotiate an International Arrangement to Replace the International Wheat Agreement, 1971, as extended, and urged all Governments to resume negotiations to conclude a new International Wheat Agreement. The Conference adopted a separate resolution on the International Wheat Agreement (see below). By the Platform text, UNCTAD would have reaffirmed the indicative character of the list of commodities covered by resolution 93(IV)[62] and would have decided to include hides and skins and leather in that list.

The Platform text would also have had UNCTAD request its Secretary-General to explore sources of finance for interim commodity agreements and requested the Committee on Commodities to adopt a set of guidelines or code of conduct for national stockpile operations which disrupted international markets, including establishing arrangements within UNCTAD for international surveillance of such operations.

UNCTAD VI also adopted without dissent resolution 156(VI)[4] on implementing the Integrated Programme for Commodities in the area of processing, marketing and distribution, including transportation. By this resolution, the Conference reaffirmed the need for increased local processing by developing countries and greater participation by them in marketing and distribution, including transportation, of commodity exports. It requested the Permanent Sub-Committee on Commodities to proceed with its consideration of studies on processing, marketing and distribution of individual commodities, decided that a special session of the Committee on Commodities be convened to elaborate frameworks for international co-operation in processing, marketing and distribution of commodities of export interest to developing countries, and requested the Committee to report on that session to the Trade and Development Board not later than 31 December 1984. The Trade and Development Board was requested, preferably at a special session, to decide, on the basis of that report, on further action to be taken.

The Buenos Aires Platform resolution[4] on the same issue differed in a number of respects from resolution 156(VI), including the addition of a paragraph to have UNCTAD urge developed countries to abstain from applying new restrictive measures, to eliminate customs duties and internal taxes levied on commodities imported from developing countries, as well as other restrictions, and in particular to eliminate all forms of tariff escalation affecting exports of semi-processed and processed commodities from those countries. The Platform text would also have had UNCTAD request its Secretary-General to convene a negotiating conference on frameworks for international co-operation in processing, marketing, transportation and distribution of commodity exports of developing countries.

Common Fund for Commodities

Preparations continued in 1983 on arrangements for the Common Fund for Commodities, a mechanism intended to stabilize the commodities market by helping to finance buffer stocks of specific commodities as well as commodity development activities such as research and marketing. Additional States adhered to the 1980 Agreement Establishing the Common Fund for Commodities.[69] Although the Agreement was open for signature and ratification at Belgrade during UNCTAD VI, by the end of the year it had not been ratified, accepted or approved by the required minimum of 90 States necessary for its entry into force.

UNCTAD VI action. After considering a report by the UNCTAD secretariat,[70] submitted in response to a 1982 General Assembly resolution,[71] on progress made towards the entry into force of the Agreement, UNCTAD VI, on 2 July, adopted without dissent resolution 153(VI).[4] It expressed concern at the slow progress in signing and ratifying the Agreement, reaffirmed its support for the Fund and for the entry into force of the Agreement without further delay, and urged

that efforts be made for the Fund's operations to begin as soon as possible after the Agreement entered into force, preferably by 1 January 1984. The Conference hoped that LDCs and other developing countries whose ratification had been delayed by inability to pay their capital subscriptions would be able to ratify by taking advantage of offers by the Organization of the Petroleum Exporting Countries, Norway and the European Economic Community to pay their subscriptions.

Governments parties to commodity agreements providing for either international buffer stocks or internationally co-ordinated national stocks were invited to consider ways of associating their international commodity organizations with the Fund for the purposes of the First Account, and all countries, particularly developed ones, which had not announced pledges to the Second Account were invited to do so at an early date. Governments were further invited to consider projects for financing through that Account.

The UNCTAD Secretary-General was requested to report to the Assembly's 1983 session on progress towards entry into force of the Agreement, and the Preparatory Commission for the Fund was requested to finalize its work.

In addition to drafting changes, the major difference between the Conference text and the Buenos Aires Platform resolution on the same subject[4] was the addition of the invitations to Governments to consider associating international commodity organizations with the Fund and to consider projects for financing through the Second Account.

Signatures and ratifications

As at 31 December 1983, the 1980 Agreement Establishing the Common Fund for Commodities[69] had been signed by 111 States and the European Economic Community, and 68 States had formally adhered by ratifying, accepting or approving it. Of these, 17 States signed the Agreement and 29 adhered during 1983 (italicized in the lists below).

The States which had both signed and adhered to the Agreement as at 31 December were:

Algeria, *Argentina*, Australia, *Austria*, Bangladesh, Benin, Botswana, Burundi, *Canada*, *Central African Republic*, China, Denmark, Ecuador, Egypt, *Equatorial Guinea*, Ethiopia, Finland, France, Gabon, *Gambia*, Ghana, Guinea, *Guinea-Bissau*, Haiti, India, Indonesia, Iraq, Ireland, Japan, Kenya, *Kuwait*, *Lesotho*, Malawi, *Malaysia*, Mali, Mexico, *Netherlands*, New Zealand, Niger, *Nigeria*, Norway, *Pakistan*, Papua New Guinea, Philippines, Republic of Korea, *Rwanda*, Sao Tome and Principe, *Saudi Arabia*, *Senegal*, Sierra Leone, *Singapore*, Sri Lanka, *Sudan*, Sweden, Switzerland, *Syrian Arab Republic*, Tunisia, Uganda, *United Arab Emirates*, United Kingdom, *United Republic of Cameroon*, United Republic of Tanzania, *Upper Volta*, Venezuela, *Yugoslavia*, Zaire, Zambia, Zimbabwe.

In addition, the Agreement had been signed but not adhered to by the following States:

Afghanistan, *Angola*, Belgium, *Bhutan*, Brazil, Cape Verde, Chad, *Colombia*, Comoros, Congo, Costa Rica, *Cuba, Democratic People's Republic of Korea,* Democratic Yemen, *Dominican Republic, El Salvador*, Germany, Federal Republic of, Greece, *Grenada, Guatemala, Guyana, Honduras*, Italy, *Jamaica*, Liberia, Luxembourg, *Madagascar*, Morocco, Mozambique, Nepal, Nicaragua, Peru, Portugal, Samoa, *Saudi Arabia,* Somalia, Spain, *Suriname, Thailand, Togo,* Turkey, United States, Yemen.

Report of the Secretary-General. In accordance with UNCTAD VI resolution 153(VI), a report[72] on the status of the Agreement was submitted to the General Assembly in October 1983. The report recalled that the Agreement was to enter into force after: *(i)* it had been ratified, accepted or approved by a minimum of 90 States, accounting for at least two thirds of the Fund's directly contributed capital of $470 million; and *(ii)* at least 50 per cent of the $280 million target for pledges of voluntary contributions to the Second Account had been met. While the latter requirement had been met by 31 March 1982, the initial deadline for entry into force, the former requirement had not. In June 1982,[73] the deadline had been extended until 30 September 1983.

By 30 September, the Agreement had been signed by 110 States and ratified, accepted or approved by 64 States accounting for 41.47 per cent of the Fund's capital. Conditions for entry into force had, therefore, not been fulfilled.

The report noted that, since the States that had ratified the Agreement were empowered to decide on a new period for fulfilment of requirements for its entry into force, the UNCTAD Secretary-General would be consulting the States concerned.

GENERAL ASSEMBLY ACTION

On 19 December, on the recommendation of the Second Committee, the General Assembly adopted resolution 38/156 without vote.

Signature and ratification of the Agreement Establishing the Common Fund for Commodities
The General Assembly,

Recalling its resolutions 3201(S-VI) and 3202(S-VI) of 1 May 1974, containing the Declaration and the Programme of Action on the Establishment of a New International Economic Order, 3281(XXIX) of 12 December 1974, containing the Charter of Economic Rights and Duties of States, and 3362(S-VII) of 16 September 1975 on development and international economic co-operation,

Recalling also its resolutions 35/56 of 5 December 1980, the annex to which contains the International Development Strategy for the Third United Nations Development Decade, and 37/211 of 20 December 1982 and resolution 153(VI) adopted on 2 July 1983 by the United Nations Conference on Trade and Development at its sixth session,

Noting with appreciation the offer made by the States members of the Organization of Petroleum Exporting Countries, as well as by Norway and the European Economic Community, to pay the full capital subscriptions of the least developed countries and a number of other developing countries concerned,

Having considered the report of the Secretary-General on the status of the Agreement Establishing the Common Fund for Commodities,

Reiterating its concern at the slow rate of progress in the signing and ratification of the Agreement, and regretting that the Agreement did not enter into force on 30 September 1983,

1. *Reaffirms* its strong support for the Agreement Establishing the Common Fund for Commodities and for its early entry into force;

2. *Expresses the hope* that all States that have signed but not yet ratified, accepted or approved the Agreement will expedite the necessary action to that effect and strongly urges all States that have not yet done so to sign and ratify the Agreement without any further delay;

3. *Decides* to review the implementation of the present resolution at its thirty-ninth session.

General Assembly resolution 38/156

19 December 1983   Meeting 102   Adopted without vote

Approved by Second Committee (A/38/702/Add.2) without vote, 14 December (meeting 56); draft by Vice-Chairman, based on informal consultations (A/C.2/38/L.113); agenda item 78 *(b)*.
Financial implications. ACABQ, A/38/7/Add.2; 5th Committee, A/38/760; S-G, A/C.5/38/12.
Meeting numbers. GA 38th session: 2nd Committee 50, 52, 56; 5th Committee 39, 40; plenary 102.

Financial implications for the 1984-1985 budget

In a note of 15 September 1983 to the General Assembly concerning preparatory work for bringing the Common Fund into operation,[74] the Secretary-General requested $942,000 under the UNCTAD section of the 1984-1985 programme budget, representing the unspent balance of an advance of $1,750,500 made by the Assembly in 1980.[75] The amount was to be fully reimbursed by the Common Fund once it was declared operational.

The Advisory Committee on Administrative and Budgetary Questions recommended approval of the Secretary-General's request, also involving an additional provision of $49,000 for staff assessment.[76]

On 17 November, the Assembly's Fifth (Administrative and Budgetary) Committee approved without vote the additional appropriations for 1984-1985.

Individual commodities

Agricultural products

In a policy paper[66] on commodity issues, prepared by the UNCTAD secretariat for UNCTAD VI, it was reported that positive steps had been achieved in the continuing negotiation of agreements for certain agricultural products which focused on commodity development issues, such as research and development, productivity improvement and cost reduction and market promotion. The report noted, however, that a number of the commodities involved also suffered from substantial market instability and/or unfavourable price trends, and that remedial action was an essential element in a longer-term commodity development strategy.

Trade in agricultural products was referred to in identical provisions of resolutions dealing with food problems adopted by the Economic and Social Council in July (1983/71) and by the General Assembly in December (38/158). Both bodies urged that, in implementing food aid policies and programmes, a greater volume of food and agricultural products be acquired from food-exporting developing countries, including through triangular transactions. Additional measures by developed countries to liberalize agricultural trade were called for, as was improved international co-operation by cereal-exporting and -importing countries to avoid instability in the international cereals market adversely affecting developing countries. There was an expression of urgent need to find multilateral solutions to problems of trade, access, competition and supply relating to agricultural products, and relevant institutions were called on to find solutions, taking into account the special needs of developing countries.

Jute. The first session of the Preparatory Committee for the International Jute Council, established in accordance with the International Agreement on Jute and Jute Products, 1982,[77] was held at Geneva from 24 to 27 May 1983. The Agreement was opened for signature from 3 January 1983. As of 31 August, the requirements for entry into force of the Agreement on the part of exporting countries was fulfilled, with four countries representing almost 99 per cent of world exports having signed. Requirements for entry into force would be met when 20 countries, representing 65 per cent of world imports, had deposited instruments of ratification, acceptance, approval or accession. By 31 August, six importing countries accounting for some 8.5 per cent of world imports had deposited such instruments, and a further nine importing countries accounting for some 32 per cent of world imports had notified that they would apply the Agreement provisionally.

Sugar. In 1983, two sessions of a United Nations Sugar Conference were held at Geneva under the auspices of UNCTAD to prepare a successor agreement to the 1977 International Sugar Agreement.[78] The objective of drawing up a new agreement was to stabilize the world price of sugar, which was 6 cents a pound, compared with the range of 13 to 23 cents built into the 1977 Agreement, which was still in force, and with a peak of

28.67 cents in 1980. At the conclusion of the first part of the Conference (2-20 May), a resolution[79] was adopted, by which the Conference, noting the progress made in preparing a successor Agreement, requested the UNCTAD Secretary-General to reconvene the Conference for three weeks later in the year and requested the Conference President to undertake consultations to facilitate its work.

The second session of the Conference (12-30 September) resulted in progress on the regulatory mechanism and price structure of the new Agreement, and on rules for small exporter participants. It also appointed a new working group on the role of medium-sized exporters. The Conference asked the UNCTAD Secretary-General to convene a third session in February 1984 and requested its President to continue consultations with delegations in the mean time.

By resolution 155(VI) (see above), UNCTAD VI requested all producing and consuming countries to participate actively in negotiating a new International Sugar Agreement to stabilize the world sugar market.

Tea. Following the agreement reached at the 1982 Third Preparatory Meeting on Tea[80] on the need to further consider elements of an international tea agreement, the Intergovernmental Group of Experts on Tea held its fourth session at Geneva from 6 to 13 October 1983.[81] The Group decided that the Fourth Preparatory Meeting on Tea would be provisionally scheduled for March 1984, assuming that a meeting of tea-exporting countries planned for January 1984 was successfully concluded. Meanwhile, the UNCTAD secretariat, in consultation with FAO, would prepare an annotated framework for an international tea agreement.

Among documents before the Group was the report of the Meeting of Experts from Tea-Exporting Countries on Minimum Export Standards (Geneva, 3-5 October).[82] Although the experts confirmed that a minimum export standard would be a desirable feature of any tea agreement, some felt that outstanding technical work on tea analysis should be completed before they could commit themselves to specific levels for any parameters.

Tropical Timber. In 1983, pursuant to a request made by the Sixth Preparatory Meeting on Tropical Timber in 1982,[83] the UNCTAD Secretary-General convened the United Nations Conference on Tropical Timber, which culminated on 18 November in the adoption of the International Tropical Timber Agreement, 1983.[84] The Conference was held at Geneva in two parts (14-31 March and 7-18 November).

The Agreement's objectives were to: provide a framework for co-operation between tropical timber-producing and -consuming countries to expand and diversify trade in tropical timber and improve structural conditions in the market; promote research and development to improve forest management and wood utilization; encourage the processing of tropical timber in producing member countries; improve marketing and distribution; and encourage reforestation and forest management, and development of national policies for utilizing and conserving tropical forests and maintaining their ecological balance.

The Agreement was to be opened for signature from 2 January 1984, and would enter into force on 1 October 1984 or any date thereafter, if 12 Governments of producing countries holding at least 55 per cent of the total votes and 16 Governments of consuming countries holding at least 70 per cent of the total votes had signed the Agreement definitively or had ratified, accepted, approved or acceded to it.

The Agreement established an International Tropical Timber Organization, which would function through the International Tropical Timber Council and three permanent committees. The location of the Organization's headquarters would be decided by the Council at its first session. The Council and permanent committees would formulate and implement projects in research and development, market intelligence, processing, and reforestation and forest management, and would monitor trade and ongoing activities in the tropical timber economy. The Organization would seek financing for projects approved by the Council.

A Conference resolution established a Preparatory Committee for the Council, requested the UNCTAD Secretary-General to convene a first meeting of the Preparatory Committee, and to convene the first session of the Council as soon as possible after the entry into force of the Agreement.

By resolution 155(VI) (see above), UNCTAD VI had urged that negotiations on the Agreement be finalized as soon as possible.

Wheat. On 2 July, UNCTAD VI adopted without dissent resolution 154(VI),[4] on the United Nations Conference to Negotiate an International Arrangement to Replace the International Wheat Agreement, 1971, as extended. UNCTAD VI recalled its 1979 resolution 126(V)[85] on the same subject, noted ongoing co-operation between producers and consumers in the International Wheat Council, recalled the Council's extension of the International Wheat Agreement, 1971, to 30 June 1986, upon its expiry on 30 June 1983,[86] noted the commitments of donor countries under the Food Aid Convention, 1980,[87] and the increasing reliance of developing countries on imports of cereals, particularly wheat. UNCTAD VI urged Governments to consider within the Council the early resumption of the Conference, in order to conclude as soon as possible a new agreement to contribute to the efficient operation of the international wheat market, taking into account the interests of developing countries.

A Buenos Aires Platform resolution on implementing the Integrated Programme for Commodities urged resumption of the Conference in order to conclude a new Agreement as soon as possible but no later than 30 June 1984 (see above).

The provision of the UNCTAD VI text was echoed in resolutions by the Economic and Social Council in July (1983/71) and by the General Assembly in December (38/158), with both urging that the International Wheat Council act at its next session.

Minerals and metals

In a policy paper[66] on commodity issues prepared by the UNCTAD secretariat for UNCTAD VI, it was pointed out that for minerals—unlike agricultural commodities, for which Governments were expected to provide solutions to market problems—producers and processers had developed their own means of protection against market instability. Examples were long-term contracts, hedging on commodity exchanges, producer pricings and the maintenance by mining corporations of a favourable ratio of debt to equity. Attempts to stabilize mineral markets by international regulation had thus been seen as unnecessary by large segments of the industry, even in many developing producing countries.

Tungsten. The UNCTAD Committee on Tungsten held its fifteenth session at Geneva from 12 to 16 December 1983 to determine action to enable producing and consuming countries to reach agreement on measures to stabilize the market and convene a negotiating conference.[88] The Committee also reviewed UNCTAD reports on developments in the tungsten market, on tungsten price indicators, and on ways of improving the quality of the quarterly bulletin *Tungsten Statistics*.

The UNCTAD secretariat was asked to continue to follow developments concerning tungsten price indicators, structural and technological change within the industry, and the demand for tungsten in certain sectors, and to report to the Committee at its sixteenth (1984) session.

The Committee suggested establishing a sessional working group to assess the current tungsten situation and the outlook for the next year, as well as certain new statistical issues. The secretariat was requested to prepare a paper outlining the composition, terms of reference and operating procedures of the proposed group.

Regarding the quarterly bulletin *Tungsten Statistics*, the Committee made several suggestions on how to fill gaps in the statistics and improve the timeliness of the publication.

Manufactures

The UNCTAD Committee on Manufactures, at its tenth session (Geneva, 14-22 March 1983), reviewed developments and restrictions of trade in manufactures and semi-manufactures.[89]

Among documents before the Committee was an UNCTAD secretariat report[90] on trade in manufactures and semi-manufactures of developing countries, which noted that developed market-economy countries continued to be the most important export markets for manufactured products of developing countries, accounting for 58 per cent of the total in 1980. However, there had been a marked deceleration in 1981 in the rate of growth of such exports, with many developing countries experiencing actual declines. In contrast, the reverse flow of trade grew at a faster rate in 1981 than in the 1970s, indicating the relative importance of developing countries as markets for the developed countries. Trade among developing countries grew rapidly during the 1970s, and between 1979 and 1980 the increase approached 34 per cent. Exports from those countries to the centrally planned economies increased by more than 70 per cent in 1980 over 1979. However, this still accounted for less than 3 per cent of the developing countries' total exports in 1980.

Following its review, the Committee adopted a set of agreed conclusions expressing concern about growing protectionism in international trade (see above) and stressing that progress in that area could not be attained without restoring confidence in trade relations. The Committee also stressed the importance of continuing to examine trade issues within its mandate, taking into account the interest of all countries, in particular the developing and especially the least developed among them.

Following its consideration of trade-related industrial collaboration arrangements, the Committee adopted a decision[91] by which it requested the UNCTAD secretariat, in co-operation with the United Nations Industrial Development Organization (UNIDO), to continue work on trade-related industrial collaboration between enterprises of developed and developing countries, devoting special attention to new forms of co-operation, including joint ventures to strengthen production of and trade in manufactures of developing countries, including those manufactures involving the use of advanced technology. The secretariat was further requested, in co-operation with UNIDO and other international organizations, to compile and analyse information on industrial collaboration arrangements, to provide the salient features of such arrangements, and to submit recommendations for further work.

The UNCTAD Secretary-General was requested to prepare a report on the secretariat's work in this area for the Committee's eleventh session.

Trade and Development Board action. On 28 April, the Trade and Development Board took note of the agreed conclusions adopted by the Committee on Manufactures and of the Committee decision on trade-related industrial collaboration, and decided that the report of the Special Committee on Preferences on its 1982 session, which had been noted by the Board in 1982, should be remitted to the Special Committee's 1984 session.[10]

Consumer protection

During 1983, the question of elaborating a set of general guidelines for consumer protection, taking particularly into account the needs of developing countries, was considered by the Economic and Social Council and the General Assembly.

In accordance with a 1981 Council request,[92] the Secretary-General submitted a report[93] to the Council's July 1983 session containing a set of draft guidelines based on the conclusions of his 1981 report on consumer protection.[94] The draft guidelines also drew on international legal instruments and the work of international organizations, as well as on the findings of a 1981 intergovernmental regional consultation held at Bangkok, Thailand.[95] They had also been revised in the light of Government comments which were summarized in the 1983 report to the Council.

The draft guidelines focused on the physical safety of consumers and the protection of their economic interests, and the related questions of safety and quality standards, distribution facilities, consumer redress and consumer education and information. Special measures were proposed for food, water and pharmaceutical products because of their importance to developing countries. Finally, the guidelines dealt with international co-operation on consumer protection.

ECONOMIC AND SOCIAL COUNCIL ACTION

The Economic and Social Council adopted without vote decision 1983/174, on the recommendation of its Third (Programme and Co-ordination) Committee.

Consumer protection

At its 40th plenary meeting, on 28 July 1983, the Council decided:

(a) To take note of the report of the Secretary-General on consumer protection and of the statements made on the draft guidelines contained therein by delegations during the discussion of the item entitled "International co-operation and co-ordination within the United Nations system" at the second regular session of 1983 of the Council;

(b) To take note also of the comments made during a preliminary exchange of views on the draft guidelines for consumer protection, conducted at the second regular session of 1983 of the Council;

(c) To transmit the report of the Secretary-General, together with a synopsis of the comments made thereon and any written comments on the guidelines that have been or will be received from Governments, to the General Assembly at its thirty-eighth session;

(d) To urge strongly that those Governments that have not yet provided comments on the draft guidelines do so at the earliest opportunity;

(e) To recommend the General Assembly to determine the procedure for the consideration of the draft guidelines in the light of paragraphs *(c)* and *(d)* above, with a view to their adoption by the Assembly at its thirty-ninth session.

Economic and Social Council decision 1983/174

Adopted without vote

Approved by Third Committee (E/1983/120) without vote, 25 July (meeting 17); draft by Vice-Chairman (E/1983/C.3/L.17); agenda item 19.
Meeting number. ESC 40.

In October, in accordance with the above decision, the Secretary-General transmitted to the General Assembly a note[96] containing a synopsis of Government comments which were both of a general nature and on specific sections of the guidelines.

GENERAL ASSEMBLY ACTION

On 19 December, on the recommendation of the Second Committee, the General Assembly adopted without vote resolution 38/147.

Consumer protection

The General Assembly,

Bearing in mind Economic and Social Council resolution 1981/62 of 23 July 1981, in which the Council requested the Secretary-General to continue consultations on consumer protection with a view to elaborating a set of general guidelines for consumer protection,

Taking note of the report of the Secretary-General on consumer protection, containing the draft guidelines on consumer protection,

Noting Economic and Social Council decision 1983/174 of 28 July 1983, in which the Council, *inter alia*, recommended that the General Assembly should determine the procedure for the consideration of the draft guidelines with a view to their adoption by the Assembly at its thirty-ninth session,

1. *Urges* Governments that have not already provided comments on the draft guidelines in response to the Secretary-General's note verbale dated 17 September 1982 to do so as quickly as possible;

2. *Decides* that the draft guidelines on consumer protection should be considered by the Economic and Social Council during its first and second regular sessions of 1984, perhaps in a sessional working group, with a view to their adoption by the General Assembly at its thirty-ninth session;

3. *Requests* the Secretary-General, in view of the importance of the guidelines for consumers in general and for those in the developing countries in particular, to extend all possible assistance towards the finalization and adoption of the draft guidelines.

General Assembly resolution 38/147

19 December 1983   Meeting 102   Adopted without vote

Approved by Second Committee (A/38/701) without vote, 21 November (meeting 45); draft by Vice-Chairman (A/C.2/38/L.75), based on informal consultations on

5-nation draft (A/C.2/38/L.29); agenda item 12.
Meeting numbers. GA 38th session: 2nd Committee 36, 45; plenary 102.

The text approved by the Second Committee differed from the 5-nation draft (Bangladesh, Ivory Coast, Pakistan, Sudan, Trinidad and Tobago) which was withdrawn. By that text the Assembly would have established a working group to consider the draft guidelines during the Council's 1984 first regular session and agreed that the Council would consider the group's results at its second regular session with a view to finalizing the guidelines and ensuring their adoption by the Assembly in 1984.

REFERENCES

[1]*Trade and Development Report, 1983* (UNCTAD/TDR/3/Rev.1 & Corr.1), Sales No. E.83.II.D.13 & Corrigendum. [2]E/1983/16. [3]WFC/1983/5. [4]*Proceedings of the United Nations Conference on Trade and Development, Sixth Session, Belgrade, 6 June–2 July 1983,* vol. I, *Report and Annexes* (TD/326, vol. I), Sales No. E.83.II.D.6). [5]YUN 1982, p. 727. [6]TD/B/942 & Corr.1. [7]TD/B/939. [8]TD/B/940. [9]TD/B/941 & Corr.1 [10]A/38/15, vol. I. [11]TD/274 & Corr.1. [12]YUN 1982, p. 1598. [13]YUN 1981, p. 541. [14]TD/B/964. [15]A/38/15, vol. II (dec. 275(XXVII)). [16]YUN 1979, p. 560. [17]YUN 1981, p. 541. [18]YUN 1982, p. 727. [19] A/C.2/38/L.85. [20]A/C.2/38/L.3. [21]YUN 1980, p. 627. [22]YUN 1981, p. 542. [23]YUN 1982, p. 727. [24]YUN 1979, p. 1328. [25]TD/B/948. [26]YUN 1982, p. 1598. [27]A/38/15, vol. I (dec. 267(XXVI)). [28]YUN 1981, p. 539. [29]YUN 1982, p. 728. [30]TD/B/C.5/88. [31]TD/281 & Corr.1. [32]YUN 1982, p. 729. [33]*Ibid.*, p. 730. [34]YUN 1979, p. 571. [35]TD/B/974 (res. 2(III)). [36]TD/B/C.7/58. [37]YUN 1982, p. 730. [38]TD/B/974. [39]A/38/15, vol. II (res. 274(XXVII)). [40]TD/280. [41]YUN 1976, p. 400. [42]YUN 1982, p. 730. [43]YUN 1980, p. 503, GA res. 35/56, annex, 5 Dec. 1980. [44]YUN 1981, p. 406. [45]A/38/15, vol. II (dec. 276(XXVII)). [46]TD/B/965 & Add.1. [47]DP/1984/69. [48]ITC/AG(XVII)/90 & Add.1. [49]YUN 1982, p. 732. [50]ITC/AG(XVI)/88. [51]ITC/AG(XVI)/85. [52]A/38/15, vol. II (res. 278(XXVII)). [53]TD/B/976. [54]YUN 1981, p. 545. [55]YUN 1980, p. 626, GA res. 35/63, 5 Dec. 1980. [56]TD/B/RBP/12 & Rev.1. [57]TD/B/RBP/13. [58]TD/B/RBP/14 & Adds.1-3. [59]TD/B/RBP/15 & Rev.1. [60]TD/B/976 (res. 2(II)). [61]TD/B/944. [62]YUN 1976, p. 394. [63]TD/B/C.1/236. [64]TD/B/C.1/246. [65]YUN 1982, p. 733. [66]TD/273 & Corr.1,2. [67]YUN 1980, p. 621. [68]YUN 1979, p. 563. [69]YUN 1980, p. 621. [70]TD/287. [71]YUN 1982, p. 735, GA res. 37/211, 20 Dec. 1982. [72]A/38/487. [73]YUN 1982, p. 734. [74]A/C.5/38/12. [75]YUN 1980, p. 622. [76]A/38/7/Add.2. [77]YUN 1982, p. 737. [78]YUN 1979, p. 477. [79]TD/SUGAR.10/6. [80]YUN 1982, p. 738. [81]TD/B/IPC/TEA/15. [82]TD/B/IPC/TEA/AC.20. [83]YUN 1982, p. 738. [84]*International Tropical Timber Agreement, 1983* (TD/TIMBER/11/Rev.1), Sales No. E.84.II.D.5. [85]YUN 1979, p. 563. [86]YUN 1982, p. 736. [87] YUN 1980, p. 691. [88]TD/B/C.1/250. [89]TD/B/951. [90]TD/B/C.2/214 (Part I). [91]TD/B/951 (res. 13(X)). [92]YUN 1981, p. 557, ESC res. 1981/62, 23 July 1981. [93]E/1983/71. [94]YUN 1981, p. 556. [95]*Ibid.*, p. 557. [96]A/38/498.

PUBLICATIONS

Bulletin of Statistics on World Trade in Engineering Products, 1981, Sales No. 83.II.E.8. *Handbook of International Trade and Development Statistics, suppl. 1981* (TD/STAT/10), Sales No. E/F.82.II.D.11. *Handbook of International Trade and Development Statistics, 1983* (TD/STAT/11), Sales No. E/F.83.II.D.2. *Handbook of State Trading Organizations of Developing Countries* (UNCTAD/ECDC/95), Sales No. A/E/F/S.83.II.D.5. *Juridical Aspects of the Establishment of Multinational Marketing Enterprises Among Developing Countries: Report by the UNCTAD Secretariat* (TD/B/C.7/28/Rev.1), Sales No. 83.II.D.9. *Trends, policies and prospects in trade among countries having different economic and social systems: selected studies* (TD/B/879), Sales No. E.83.II.D.11.

Finance

International financial and monetary issues were discussed in various United Nations bodies during 1983, with the question of external debt of developing countries being of particular concern. At UNCTAD VI, resolutions were adopted calling for assistance to developing countries with debt-servicing difficulties, and for policy decisions by developed countries and IMF to revive development momentum in the developing countries. Developed countries were also urged to reaffirm their commitments under the International Development Strategy for the Third United Nations Development Decade regarding official development assistance (ODA) targets, and adequate funding of multilateral development finance institutions was called for. The Conference also called for the establishment of an expert group to consider the need for an additional complementary financing facility to compensate for the export earnings shortfalls of developing countries and requested the UNCTAD Trade and Development Board to finalize its consideration of a possible international export credit guarantee facility to finance export credits extended by developing countries.

In December, the *Ad Hoc* Group of Experts on International Co-operation in Tax Matters finalized guidelines for co-operation against tax evasion.

Financial policy

The Committee for Development Planning (CDP), meeting in April,[1] considered the most serious threat to world economic recovery to be chaotic international financial relations. Real interest rates remained very high and major exchange rates were still badly out of line. Investment was held back by large excess capacity and pervasive uncertainties.

The CDP Working Group on the International Monetary and Financial System met at United Nations Headquarters on 19 and 20 December to prepare material for CDP's study of the subject at its 1984 session.[2] The Working Group discussed: the international economic situation and monetary and financial obstacles to recovery; measures to be taken within the existing international framework; the need for new arrangements or institutional change; and prospects for negotiations on monetary and financial reform.

The Group noted that lack of effective co-ordination of macro-economic policies was most conspicuous with regard to industrialized countries. While high interest rates were not an absolute deterrent to investment in those countries, they compounded international debt problems,

had a devastating impact on the balance of payments in developing countries and ruled out development projects.

Regarding negotiations on monetary and financial reform, the Group suggested that there was need to oversee the re-examination of the arrangements for international economic co-operation which was under way on many political levels, and in that connection the Group cited a number of high-level economic summits or meetings. It proposed that the Secretary-General appoint a small high-level expert group, assisted by organizations concerned, to monitor these discussions, identify areas of agreement and conflict, and report back within 18 months.

For its consideration of international monetary and financial issues, UNCTAD VI had before it a report on the subject prepared by the UNCTAD secretariat.[3] The paper reviewed external payments problems of developing countries; trends in the international monetary and financial system; adjustment, financing and development; the global dimension of payments adjustment and financing; private finance and development; prospects for multilateral development finance and ODA.

The report stated that the previous decade had seen the international monetary and financial system become increasingly privatized, while the capacity of Governments to influence variables such as exchange and interest rates, and the magnitude and direction of international capital flows had progressively diminished. In the mid-1970s, some developing countries were able to secure substantial external financing but many, such as the least developed and other low-income countries, continued to depend on the Bretton Woods institutions, regional development banks and bilateral donors. Flows from such sources grew in the 1970s but failed to keep abreast of needs, thereby constricting severely the policy choices open to those countries. More recently, private flows had fallen off, accentuating the liquidity and financing shortage and making all groups of developing countries increasingly dependent on official institutions.

The report's proposals for improving the financial position of developing countries included: that IMF should review its conditionality policies, increase its allocations of special drawing rights (SDRs), double its quotas and liberalize its compensatory financing facility; that the World Bank should accelerate its regular lending programme and enlarge its structural adjustment lending programme; that negotiations on the seventh replenishment of IDA, covering the fiscal period 1985-1987, be intensified; that donor countries accelerate progress towards the target of 0.7 per cent of ODA contained in the International Development Strategy for the 1980s;[4] that generalized debt measures be taken regarding developing countries' debt obligations; and that private banks be encouraged to make a full contribution to the financial effort required, including debt rescheduling.

In the longer term, a process of reform was needed to correct structural deficiencies in the international monetary and financial system and should be set in motion swiftly, the report stated.

On 2 July, UNCTAD VI adopted without dissent resolution 162(VI)[5] on international monetary issues. In a preamble to the five-part resolution, the Conference recognized the responsibility of developed countries in promoting conditions conducive to world recovery, urged them to consider the international implications of their policy decisions, recognized the importance for world economic growth and sustained development of promoting convergence of economic performance and greater exchange rate stability and a stable monetary framework, and recognized IMF's responsibility in the world monetary system.

Regarding SDR allocations, the Conference stressed the importance for world economic growth of an adequate, non-inflationary supply of global liquidity, noted that IMF should review allocation of SDRs based on growth trends, inflation and international liquidity, noted the difficult world economic situation and especially the inadequacy of reserves of many developing economies, and invited IMF to consider those factors in its deliberations on allocating SDRs.

With respect to resources, the Conference urged IMF members to recognize the need for the Fund to be adequately provided with resources to meet its members' financing and adjustment needs, and invited the Fund to consider: timely quota increases; activating the general arrangements to borrow; and recourse to other borrowed resources.

Regarding access, the Conference noted the severe impact of external developments on the balance of payments of many IMF members, emphasized the importance of maintaining an adequate level of access to Fund facilities, and invited IMF to complete expeditiously the reviews of its compensatory financing facility and the policy of enlarged access to its resources.

On conditionality, the Conference encouraged IMF members to consult with the Fund at an early stage of emerging difficulties in their balance of payments and invited the Fund to encourage such approaches to establish how it could help, including financing of a suitable programme to restore a sustainable external position and help to maintain external confidence. It invited IMF to keep under review and respond positively and pragmatically to financing and adjustment problems faced by its members, in particular by developing countries, and underlined that, besides sound demand management policies, measures to improve sup-

ply conditions and strengthen the productive base of the economy also needed to be emphasized, having regard to avoiding disruption of the development process of developing countries. IMF was encouraged to maintain its principle of uniform treatment of its members, paying due regard to their domestic social and political objectives, economic priorities and circumstances, including the causes of balance-of-payments problems.

With respect to surveillance, IMF members were urged to co-operate with the Fund to ensure its surveillance of the exchange rate and economic policies of all members. In that connection, the Conference took note of the commitment of several major industrialized countries to co-operate with the Fund in near-term policy actions leading to convergence of economic conditions in the medium term. The Conference invited IMF to give close attention to exchange-rate policies, to improve its monitoring of exchange-rate developments, in particular those of major economies which had wide-ranging impact, and to draw attention to policies that should be pursued by members to reduce exchange-rate instability. It noted the interest of developing countries in further study of the following questions: establishing a link between SDRs and development finance, reviving the IMF Trust Fund, establishing a low-conditional, medium-term facility, and making a special adjustment of small quotas below ten million SDRs.

The Buenos Aires Platform[5] contained a position paper by the Group of 77 on financial and monetary issues which described the development crisis and proposed immediate policy measures in connection with IMF, the World Bank, regional development banks, UNDP, IFAD, export credits, ODA, direct private foreign investment, external debt and the 1981 Substantial New Programme of Action for the 1980s for the Least Developed Countries.[6] Medium- and long-term actions were proposed for international monetary reform, the framework of international financial co-operation for development and institutional arrangements.

Also contained in the Buenos Aires Platform was a resolution on multilateral financial institutions and international monetary reform calling for immediate, medium- and long-term measures. Immediate measures to be taken by IMF included substantial allocations of SDRs, establishment of a link between SDRs and development finance, substantial increase of Fund quotas and expansion and liberalization of its compensatory financing facility with special arrangements for LDCs, a review of the principles of conditionality, and greater participation of developing countries in negotiations on the international monetary system.

Immediate measures to be taken by the World Bank included accelerated disbursement of its

lending programmes, raising the share of programme loans to at least 25 per cent of total lending, revising conditions of structural adjustment
lending and increasing its volume, enlarging its
resources, considering co-financing as a supplement to its regular resources, raising the permissible margin of preference to 25 per cent, ending
its policy of graduation for access to regular capital resources, providing for increased lending to
all recipients in real terms in the seventh replenishment of IDA, and improving the position of developing countries in the World Bank.

The strengthening of multilateral regional development finance institutions through capital increases in real terms was called for, and they were
urged to adopt special programmes to accelerate
disbursements.

Medium- and long-term measures for international monetary reform included negotiations to
correct structural deficiencies in the international
monetary system.

By this resolution, the Conference would also
have invited the UNCTAD Secretary-General to
keep the implementation of the measures under
review and report on progress to the Trade and
Development Board.

On 14 December, a draft decision[7] was introduced in the General Assembly's Second Committee by Mexico on behalf of the Group of 77 developing countries. By this decision, the Assembly
would have requested the Secretary-General to
consult with Governments on an international conference on money and finance for development
and to report to the Assembly not later than at
its thirty-ninth (1984) session. The Committee
Chairman stated that there would be a further exchange of views in due time within the possible
framework of that proposal.

Debt servicing

In a March report[8] to the Trade and Development Board, the UNCTAD secretariat reviewed implementation of a 1980 Board resolution[9] calling
for action relating to the debt problems of developing countries. The report stated that the full potential of the set of detailed features to deal with debt-
servicing problems, annexed to the resolution, had
not been realized. Most debt renegotiation exercises had not attached great importance to the development of debtor countries, but had focused
primarily on restoring debt-servicing capacity in
the short term.

Although IMF conditionality was central to solving a country's debt problems, the Fund's
programmes were primarily short-term in nature
and the associated conditionality was appropriate
primarily to situations of excess demand, which
precluded consideration of a problem before it
manifested itself in a balance-of-payments crisis.

In that the timing of debt-rescheduling exercises
and the length of the consolidation period remained tightly linked to Fund programmes, improvements in some aspects of the procedures for
debt renegotiation appeared to depend on changes
in Fund practices.

There had been a few cases where the central
role of an investment programme supported by aid
donors, multilateral development institutions, IMF
and official and private creditors had been recognized. Those isolated cases suggested that arrangements could be substantially improved.

The report proposed that: least developed and
other low-income countries could consider requesting international consideration of their debt
problems in the context of a donor group, aid consortium or consultative group, which would frame
an action programme including recommendations
on the amount of debt rescheduling required;
middle-income countries, for which official and
officially guaranteed export credits were especially
important, could make use of a special preparatory session of the Paris Club creditor group for
a similar purpose; and countries whose debt-
servicing difficulties involved mainly commercial
banks could benefit by consideration of their
problems by a special tripartite commission involving Governments, bank representatives and international institutions.

In the report on its April session[1] CDP noted
that for countries with large foreign debts the years
ahead would be difficult. If economic recovery was
too long delayed and rescheduling done at high
rates of interest, the need for extensive cancellation would arise. With regard to rescheduling official debt, the Committee stated that more systematic criteria and practices, including
renegotiation, would be in the interest of both creditors and debtors. Establishing an international
banking institute as a clearing-house for information among private banks might serve a stabilizing function. The Committee supported the idea
of a debtors' club or institute with the object of
sharing market experience.

On 22 April, the Trade and Development Board
decided[10] to consider further the subject of debt
at its October session. Although the subject was
discussed at that session, the Board took no
action.[11]

In its report on international financial and
monetary issues[3] prepared for UNCTAD VI, the
UNCTAD secretariat stated that debt-servicing
problems had become widespread and increasingly
unmanageable. Major disruptions during the
preceding decade included large swings in the
prices of primary commodities, food and energy,
rapid increases in prices of manufactured goods
imported by developing countries, slackening of
import demand in developed countries, the deep

and continuing recession that began in 1980, the precipitous rise in interest rates and associated swings in exchange rates, the collapse of primary commodity prices and growing protectionism in developed countries. Current account deficits of non-oil-exporting developing countries had risen threefold from $10 billion in 1972 to $30 billion in 1978, and had then more than doubled, reaching $70 billion in 1981.

On 2 July, UNCTAD VI adopted without dissent resolution 161(VI)[5] on external debt, by which it urged developed countries to implement commitments undertaken under a 1978 Trade and Development Board resolution[12] calling for retroactive adjustment of terms of ODA to relieve the debt problems of developing countries. Developed countries were called on to respond in a positive manner to requests from LDCs for alleviation of debts resulting from ODA loans provided by the developed country concerned. The Conference invited developed countries to consider alleviating immediately the debt service of developing countries resulting from official and officially guaranteed loans.

The Conference invited Governments, within the context of commitments undertaken under a 1980 Board resolution[9] (see above) to continue to improve the functioning of official creditor groups in response to debtor countries in acute debt-servicing difficulties, requested the Board to review implementation of the guidelines contained in that resolution at its twenty-eighth (1984) session, requested the UNCTAD Secretary-General to prepare a report on the issue for the Board at that session and, in that respect, invited him to consult with the Chairman of the Paris Club and with multilateral organizations and Governments, with a view to augmenting the basis for review of the resolution's implementation.

In pursuance of the commitment to implement the Board's 1980 resolution, the Conference: stressed that debt-restructuring operations should contribute to debtor countries' efforts to re-establish their creditworthiness and regain access to financial resources on appropriate terms, thereby restoring their development momentum; stressed the need for continued collaboration between all parties involved in dealing with debt-servicing problems and noted the results achieved through co-operation between debtors, official and private creditors and multilateral institutions; and invited bilateral and multilateral donors to ensure that their actions were based on an adequate assessment of the economic situation and medium-term development objectives of the countries concerned.

The Conference emphasized the desirability of a debtor country's approaching IMF in the early stages of emerging debt difficulties and invited IMF and the World Bank to continue to respond to adjustment problems faced by developing countries in particular. All bilateral official creditors were urged to facilitate debt rescheduling operations on an equitable basis.

The desirability of the competent multilateral institutions improving information on capital market operations and other financial flows was also stressed and debtor countries were invited to collaborate with those institutions to improve external debt data. Multilateral institutions were invited to respond favourably to developing countries' requests for technical support in dealing with debt situations.

The Buenos Aires Platform[5] contained a position paper by the Group of 77 on financial and monetary issues (see above), part of which dealt with external debt. The Group of 77 felt that, at UNCTAD VI, Governments should agree to restructure the external debt of developing countries and review the procedures governing the rescheduling of official debt owed to developed countries. Measures with respect to official debt to be adopted by developed countries would include: rapid implementation of the 1978 Board resolution on debt;[12] and emergency and generalized measures to reduce the debt burden of developing countries for payments on official and officially guaranteed loans.

Principles and procedures governing debt rescheduling would include: for official debt, review and modification of the guidelines contained in the 1980 Board resolution;[9] establishment of a framework for developing countries, prior to debt renegotiations, to convene *ad hoc* meetings of official and private creditors to consider the country's economic situation and development objectives.

Regarding private debt, the position paper noted that the absence of internationally agreed guidelines for their restructuring had seriously undermined developing countries' efforts to reschedule in a manner commensurate with their development requirements. There was need for close monitoring of capital market operations to increase information available to debtor countries. In the light of developments in the institutional framework in which debtors and creditors operated, developing countries needed to formulate appropriate responses to promote their interests, with assistance from international institutions such as UNCTAD.

By a resolution on external debt contained in the Buenos Aires Platform, the Conference would have urged that the following emergency measures be agreed for debt payments on official and officially guaranteed loans: amortization payments on bilateral ODA loans due in 1984-1985 be added to the end of the scheduled repayment period; for official and officially guaranteed export credits from developed countries, a substantial proportion of scheduled interest and amortization payments be consolidated, with the consolidated amount to be repaid over ten years with a five-year grace period; and that multilateral development finance institutions contribute to the emergency relief measures by providing additional programme assistance at least equal to the debt-service obligation of the borrower to the institutions.

By this resolution, the Conference would also have decided to establish a framework for debtor countries to convene meetings with creditors, urged monitoring of capital market operations and called on international institutions to assist developing countries to formulate appropriate responses to promote their interests.

On 20 December, the General Assembly adopted resolution 38/195 on implementing the Substantial New Programme of Action for the 1980s for the Least Developed Countries (LDCs) (p. 433) in which it urged developed donor countries to implement fully and rapidly the commitments undertaken in the 1978 Trade and Development Board resolution[12] in respect of LDCs, and called upon developed countries to respond positively to requests from LDCs for alleviation of their debt burdens resulting from ODA loans provided by the developed country concerned.

Development finance

Official development assistance

The UNCTAD secretariat report[3] on international financial and monetary issues prepared for UNCTAD VI contained a chapter on ODA which stressed that such assistance played a unique role in supporting developing countries' efforts towards structural transformation of their economies through providing concessional finance to activities and sectors that did not normally respond to commercial incentives. However, the flow of concessional finance had failed to respond to the enlarged needs of developing countries, despite efforts by members of the Organization of Petroleum Exporting Countries and some developed donors.

Aid from members of the Development Assistance Committee (DAC) of the Organisation for Economic Co-operation and Development (OECD) in 1981 was still only half of that called for in the International Development Strategies for the Second[13] and Third[4] United Nations Development Decades, and the level of DAC aid was virtually unchanged from the early 1970s. However, the performance of some other donors had improved and a number had adapted their programmes to provide programme assistance and payments support.

On 2 July, UNCTAD VI adopted without dissent resolution 164(VI)[5] on ODA by which it urged

the developed countries to reaffirm their commitment under the current International Development Strategy[4] with respect to the target of 0.7 per cent of gross national product (GNP) as ODA, and recognized the importance to the LDCs that flows of ODA be doubled by 1985. The Conference also recognized that: donor and recipient countries should together ensure that aid was provided in support of development objectives and used with increasing effectiveness; more flexible ODA be provided; improved co-ordination between donors and recipients be encouraged; efforts be made to improve the modalities and quality of aid; ODA be on an increasingly assured, continuous and predictable basis; and ODA loans and grants be untied.

The Conference also instructed the Committee on Invisibles and Financing related to Trade to monitor the above measures, and urged developed donor countries to provide the necessary information for the Committee at its eleventh (1984) session.

A resolution on ODA contained in the Buenos Aires Platform[5] would have had UNCTAD VI urge that developed countries that had not met the 0.7 per cent target do so by 1985, and in any event not later than the second half of the decade, with the target of 1 per cent being reached as soon as possible thereafter, as envisaged in the Strategy.[4]

By this text UNCTAD would also have urged that: interim targets be fixed for achieving the objective over the period; developed donor countries fulfil their commitment to double ODA to LDCs and/or to meeting a 0.15 per cent target by 1985; there be a significant increase in programme lending in ODA flows and ODA not be a vehicle for trade promotion activities by developed countries; and that UNCTAD VI agree on measures to increase ODA flows.

In a 20 December resolution on implementation of the Substantial New Programme of Action (SNPA) for the 1980s for LDCs (p. 433), the General Assembly urged donor countries, within the context of the SNPA and of progress towards the 0.7 per cent target, to attain 0.15 per cent of their GNP as ODA or to double their ODA to LDCs by 1985 or as soon as possible thereafter.

Multilateral development finance

The UNCTAD secretariat report[3] to UNCTAD VI on international financial and monetary issues pointed out that during the previous decade, long-term development finance channelled through multilateral development finance institutions had grown at an average annual rate of 22 per cent. However, the share of multilateral finance in the net flow of long-term financing to developing countries had remained unchanged at about 13 per cent between 1970 and 1981.

On 2 July, UNCTAD VI adopted without dissent resolution 165(VI)[5] by which it agreed that an adequate level of funding of multilateral development finance institutions was essential for continuing growth in their lending in pursuance of their development role. The Conference invited the World Bank to: study the scope for a 5 per cent per annum expansion in real terms of its lending programme, beginning in 1985; review, preferably every six months, its special action programme of accelerated disbursements; consider increases in programme lending; consider, in the design of structural adjustment loans, the burden of adjustment carried by the disadvantaged in recipient countries; pursue its efforts to increase co-financing with public funds and the banking sector; maintain priority on investment in energy development, and review institutional proposals for an energy affiliate and other similar arrangements; continue to apply flexibility in its policy of graduation, avoiding premature phasing out of access by developing countries to ordinary lending, taking into account the availability of alternative sources of long-term development finance; and keep under review the permissible margin of preference.

The Conference called on donors to meet expeditiously their commitments to the sixth replenishment of IDA and urged that all contributions be completed in the Bank's financial year 1984. It stressed the need for negotiations on the seventh replenishment, covering fiscal 1984-1985, to be completed as soon as possible for it to become effective by 1 July 1984 at a substantial level.

Regarding regional development finance institutions, UNCTAD VI noted their important role in development efforts, welcomed their recent capital increase and fund replenishments and urged member countries to meet pledges as committed, and encouraged those institutions to adopt special programmes to accelerate disbursements.

The Conference urged Governments to provide adequate funding for UNDP and invited the UNDP Governing Council to formulate proposals to ensure long-term predictable financing. Member States were also invited to discuss, as early as possible, a second replenishment of IFAD resources.

The Buenos Aires Platform[5] contained both a position paper by the Group of 77 on financial and monetary issues and a resolution on multilateral financial institutions and international monetary reform which included the Group's views on measures to be taken by multilateral institutions to assist developing countries in resuming their development momentum (see above under FINANCIAL POLICY).

Trade-related finance

The second part of the tenth session of the UNCTAD Committee on Invisibles and Financing related to Trade was held at Geneva from 1 to 17 March 1983,[14] the first part having been held in December 1982.[15] The Committee evaluated the operational features of an export credit guarantee facility (see below). It also discussed: requirements of an effective system of international financial co-operation, flow of financial resources to and from developing countries, access to capital markets, international monetary issues, and financial resources for development. The Committee used the report[3] on international financial and monetary issues, prepared by the UNCTAD secretariat for UNCTAD VI, as a basis for its discussions; the Committee Chairman summed up that debate on his own responsibility.

Export credit insurance

At its March meeting,[14] acting in response to a 1982 Trade and Development Board decision,[15] the Committee on Invisibles and Financing related to Trade set up a sessional committee to evaluate the operational features of an export credit guarantee facility. The proposed facility would assist developing countries in refinancing their medium-term export credits in international capital markets. In order to meet the requirements of international competition, those countries had to provide medium-term credits—causing them problems because of the delay in receiving their exchange earnings. The sessional committee had before it the 1982 report of an Intergovernmental Group of Experts on an Export Credit Guarantee Facility[16] and an UNCTAD secretariat report[17] dealing with the financial viability of the proposed facility, the possible implications of international guidelines for the facility, eligibility criteria for the facility's guarantees, and the experts' comments on elements of a draft agreement to establish a facility. Addenda to the report described the rules and guidelines of the International Union of Credit and Investment Insurers (Berne Union) and of the OECD on export credit, analysed the financial and administrative viability of the proposed facility, and discussed eligibility criteria, focusing on the type of export transactions which would be eligible for guarantee.

On 11 March, the Committee on Invisibles and Financing related to Trade took note of the sessional committee's report and requested the Trade and Development Board at its April session to arrange for further consideration of an international export credit guarantee facility with a view to taking an early decision on its establishment.

On 22 April, the Board decided[18] to remit the above decision to UNCTAD VI.

On 2 July, UNCTAD VI adopted without dissent resolution 163(VI)[5] by which it requested the Board, at its October session, to finalize its consideration of the issue.

On 20 October, the Board took note[19] of the report of the Committee on Invisibles and Financing related to Trade on the second part of its tenth session[14] and referred to the Committee's eleventh session a draft resolution on an international export credit guarantee facility. This draft, submitted by Venezuela on behalf of the Group of 77, would have had the Board urge developed countries to increase the volume of export credits available to developing countries, lift country limits on borrowing, and not impose minimum interest rates on export suppliers' credits. It would also have urged an immediate review of the OECD Arrangement on Export Credits, with a view to fully exempting export credits extended to developing countries from its stringent provisions on terms, and invited the UNCTAD Secretary-General to review the international arrangements in that area from the standpoint of their implications for developing countries and to report to the Board at its twenty-eighth (1984) session.

Export earnings

As it had decided in 1982,[20] the UNCTAD Committee on Commodities at its tenth session[21] (26 January–8 February) resumed consideration of a proposed complementary financing facility for commodity-related shortfalls in export earnings. In addition to a 1982 report on the subject,[20] the UNCTAD secretariat also prepared reports on the operation of the IMF compensatory financing facility for temporary shortfalls in export earnings or for excessive increases in cereal import costs,[22] and on the functioning of commodity export earnings stabilization schemes of the 1975 Lomé (Togo) Convention[23] as reinforced in 1979 (a trade co-operation agreement between the EEC and the African, Caribbean and Pacific Group of countries).[24]

On 28 April, the Trade and Development Board took note of the Committee's report.[18]

On 2 July, UNCTAD VI adopted resolution 157(VI)[5] on compensatory financing of export earnings shortfalls by a roll-call vote of 90 to 1 (United States) with 10 abstentions. By this resolution, the Conference invited IMF to complete expeditiously the forthcoming review of its compensatory financing facility and to consider establishing special arrangements for LDCs. The UNCTAD Secretary-General was requested to convene an expert group on the compensatory financing of export earnings shortfalls which was instructed to consider: the need for an additional complementary facility to compensate for the export earnings shortfalls of developing countries, bearing in mind the needs of those countries most dependent on commodity exports, particularly LDCs; the nature, sources of finance and operational rules of such a facility; and the relationship

of such a facility to existing facilities and intergovernmental organizations. In conducting its analysis, the group was to examine the nature and causes of export earnings instability, the role and impact of existing facilities, the impact of export earnings stabilization on commodity markets, the financial and economic costs of stabilizing export earnings, and the possible stabilizing influence of commodity agreements and the Common Fund for Commodities.

Governments were invited to make suggestions on these issues before the end of 1983; the expert group was instructed to complete its work not later than September 1984 and the UNCTAD Secretary-General was requested to transmit its report to a special session of the Trade and Development Board before the end of 1984. The Board was instructed to decide on follow-up action, including the convening of a possible negotiating conference on an additional complementary facility.

The Buenos Aires Platform resolution[5] on the same issue would have requested the UNCTAD Secretary-General to convene, not later than December 1983, a preparatory meeting for a negotiating conference on the complementary facility, and in the light of progress, to convene a conference. It would also have decided that immediate relief be provided to developing countries, pending completion of the negotiation, and to that end would have urged IMF to expand and liberalize its compensatory financing facility and provide special arrangements for the LDCs within that facility, and urged the socialist countries of Eastern Europe to create a special fund to guarantee an annual supply of transferable roubles for the developing countries to compensate for shortfalls in their earnings from commodity exports to those countries.

Taxation

Following a July 1982 decision by the Economic and Social Council[25] to consider in 1983 measures to enable the *Ad Hoc* Group of Experts on International Co-operation in Tax Matters to carry out its future work effectively, the Secretary-General submitted a July note[26] listing the Group's functions: to formulate guidelines for international co-operation to combat tax evasion; to examine the United Nations Model Double Taxation Convention between Developed and Developing Countries, adopted by the Group in 1979, and consider countries' experiences in applying it; and to study possibilities of enhancing the efficiency of tax administrations reducing potential conflicts among tax laws of various countries, and formulating policy and methodology suggestions.

The note stated that a predecessor Group had met for two weeks every two years and for that reason had taken 12 years to complete its work on the

Model Double Taxation Convention; the *Ad Hoc* Group had been working at a similar rhythm. Since the Council had called for expeditious action in solving the problem of international tax evasion, the periodicity of the Group's meetings was highly relevant to the Council's consideration of measures to enable the Group to carry out its future work effectively, the note concluded.

On 28 July, by decision 1983/177, the Council took note of the Secretary-General's note.

Activities of Group of Experts. At its second meeting, held at Geneva from 5 to 16 December 1983,[27] the *Ad Hoc* Group of Experts on International Co-operation in Tax Matters finalized a set of guidelines for international co-operation against tax evasion, with special reference to taxes on income, profits, capital and capital gains.[28]

The guidelines, together with commentaries and background information, were divided into four categories: an introduction on general aspects of information exchange and on co-operation; specific aspects of information exchange, comprising devices used by residents and non-residents, allocation of head office or parent company expenses, remuneration of employees of non-resident employers, artificial transfer prices, adjustment in artificial transfer pricing cases, and other aspects; guidelines on co-operation concerning the use of low-tax countries as tax havens, bank secrecy and the abuse of tax treaties (treaty shopping); and a guideline relating to mutual assistance between tax authorities in implementing tax laws and the recovery of tax.

The introductory guideline noted that international co-operation against tax evasion would most satisfactorily take place under the terms of treaties for the avoidance of double taxation. It could, however, be governed by provisions in a bilateral or multilateral agreement on general mutual assistance by tax authorities, or in other agreements providing for exchange of tax information.

Regarding its future work, the *Ad Hoc* Group proposed, in accordance with a 1982 Economic and Social Council request,[25] to review the experiences of countries in bilateral application of the Model Double Taxation Convention and monitor the Convention's impact. There was consensus that, early in 1984, a questionnaire should be sent to tax authorities of States Members inquiring about their experience in applying the Model Convention.

Also to be studied were possibilities of reducing potential conflicts among the tax systems of countries, enhancing the efficiency of tax administrations, and formulating appropriate policy and methodology suggestions.

REFERENCES

[1]E/1983/16. [2]E/AC.54/1984/4. [3]*Proceedings of the United Nations Conference on Trade and Development, Sixth Session, Belgrade, 6 June–2 July 1983*, vol. III, *Basic documents* (TD/326, vol. III), Sales No. E.83.II.D.8. [4]YUN 1980, p. 503, GA res. 35/56, annex, 5 Dec. 1980. [5]*Proceedings of the United Nations Conference on Trade and Development, Sixth Session, Belgrade, 6 June–2 July 1983*, vol. I, *Report and Annexes* (TD/326, vol. I), Sales No. E.83.II.D.6. [6]YUN 1981, p. 406. [7]A/C.2/38/L.116. [8]TD/B/945. [9]YUN 1980, p. 616. [10]TD/B/957. [11]TD/B/973. [12]YUN 1978, p. 429. [13]YUN 1970, p. 319, GA res. 2626(XXV), 24 Oct. 1970. [14]TD/B/949. [15]YUN 1982, p. 743. [16]*Ibid.*, p. 742. [17]TD/B/C.3/183 & Add.1,2 & Add.2/Corr.1 & Add.3. [18]A/38/15, vol. I. [19]A/38/15, vol. II. [20]YUN 1982, p. 743. [21]TD/B/944. [22]TD/B/C.1/243. [23]TD/B/C.1/237. [24]YUN 1975, p. 330. [25]YUN 1982, p. 746, ESC res. 1982/45, 27 July 1982. [26]E/1983/107. [27]*International Co-operation in Tax Matters: Report of the* Ad Hoc *Group of Experts on International Co-operation in Tax Matters on the Work of its Second Meeting* (ST/ESA/143), Sales No. E.84.XVI.1. [28]*International Co-operation in Tax Matters: Guidelines for International Co-operation Against the Evasion and Avoidance of Taxes (with Special Reference to Taxes on Income, Profits, Capital and Capital Gains)* (ST/ESA/142), Sales No. E.84.XVI.2.

PUBLICATIONS

Annotated Bibliography on Staff Training and Development in the Public Sector and on Public Finance Management, Accounting and Audit (ST/ESA/SER.E/33), Sales No. E.83.II.H.1. *Financial Solidarity for Development, 1983 Review* (TD/B/C.3/187, TD/B/C.7/65), Sales No. E.84.II.D.3. *International Tax Agreements, vol. IX, Supplement No. 39* (ST/ESA/SER.C/9/Suppl.39), Sales No. 83.XVI.2; *Supplement Nos. 40 and 41* (ST/ESA/SER.C/9/Suppls.40 & 41), Sales No. E.83.XVI.3. *Issues and Priorities in Public Administration and Finance in the Third United Nations Development Decade* (ST/ESA/SER.E/34), Sales No. E.83.II.H.4.

Programme and finances of UNCTAD

Since UNCTAD VI adopted a number of resolutions affecting the work programme of UNCTAD for the 1984-1985 biennium, revised estimates for the UNCTAD section of the United Nations programme budget for that biennium were presented to the General Assembly. That section of the 1984-1985 programme budget was also discussed at the October/November meeting of the UNCTAD Working Party on the Medium-term Plan and the Programme Budget.

UNCTAD programme

The Trade and Development Board—the executive body of UNCTAD—held three sessions in 1983, all at Geneva. Its twenty-sixth session was held from 18 to 28 April; its twelfth special session from 25 to 30 April and on 6 May, in conjunction with the Board's twenty-sixth session, in order to consider substantive proposals for action by UNCTAD VI (see above); and its twenty-seventh session from 3 to 20 October and on 2 November.

The Board adopted 2 resolutions and 24 decisions during 1983. Both the resolutions were adopted in October; the first called for provision to be made in the UNCTAD 1984 calendar for meetings on the global system of trade preferences among developing countries, and the second dealt with the status of the International Trade Centre (see subject headings above).

The Board's report for 1983[1] and the report of UNCTAD VI[2] were considered by the General Assembly, which on 19 and 20 December adopted five resolutions dealing with various aspects of the UNCTAD programme. In those resolutions, the Assembly took note of the statement and resolutions of UNCTAD VI,[2] decided to convene a sixth session of the United Nations Conference on an International Code of Conduct on the Transfer of Technology not later than the first half of 1985, called for meetings on the reverse transfer of technology, urged signature and ratification of the 1980 Agreement Establishing the Common Fund for Commodities,[3] and called for implementation of the 1981 Substantial New Programme of Action for the Least Developed Countries.[4]

Programme policy decisions

The seventh session of the Trade and Development Board's Working Party on the Medium-term Plan and the Programme Budget[5] (Geneva, 17 October–2 November 1983) completed only one substantive item of its agenda, namely its review of the UNCTAD section of the United Nations programme budget for the biennium 1984-1985 (see ADMINISTRATIVE AND BUDGETARY QUESTIONS, Chapter I). Other main issues on which work was not completed were UNCTAD's technical assistance activities, and programme evaluation, which it was agreed would be included in the agenda of the Working Party's eighth (1984) session. Meanwhile, the strengthening of UNCTAD programme evaluation was examined by other United Nations bodies during 1983 (see ADMINISTRATIVE AND BUDGETARY QUESTIONS, Chapter II).

On 2 November, the Working Party adopted a set of agreed conclusions submitted by its Chairman, which declared that the proposed 1984-1985 United Nations programme budget relating to UNCTAD should reflect all resolutions and decisions taken by UNCTAD intergovernmental bodies and conferences, particularly UNCTAD VI. While expressing gratitude to the UNCTAD Secretary-General for information provided on the proposed programme budget, the Working Party called for increased clarity in presenting the subprogrammes and programmes when submitting the UNCTAD programme budget for 1986-1987.

A Working Party decision recommended to the Board that it schedule the eighth session of the Working Party for two weeks, before the Board's twenty-eighth (March/April 1984) session, and that it decide on the timing of the Working Party's ninth session at its twenty-eighth session.

On 2 November,[6] the Board took note of the Working Party's report, requested the UNCTAD Secretary-General to transmit it together with comments made thereon to the appropriate United Nations bodies for consideration, and agreed that the matter of scheduling the eighth session be considered at consultations held by the UNCTAD Secretary-General.

On 3 August, the Secretary-General submitted to the General Assembly revised estimates for the UNCTAD section of the proposed programme budget for the biennium 1984-1985,[7] based on a preliminary assessment of the results of UNCTAD VI, which had adopted a number of resolutions giving new direction to the UNCTAD work programme.

On 17 November, the Assembly's Fifth Committee approved by 87 votes to 2, with 7 abstentions, an appropriation of $54,505,500 as well as an additional appropriation of $689,200 for the UNCTAD 1984-1985 proposed programme budget.

Technical co-operation

Total project expenditure incurred by UNCTAD in 1983 for technical co-operation activities amounted to $15.3 million, a decline of $1 million from 1982. Allocations from UNDP totalling $13 million were the main source of funds.

The main sectors in which UNCTAD provided assistance were: shipping, ports and multimodal transport; economic co-operation among developing countries; assistance to the least developed, land-locked and island developing countries; manufactures and semi-manufactures; trade facilitation; money, finance and development; commodities; transfer of technology; trade among countries having different economic and social systems; and assistance to liberation movements.

In addition to these UNCTAD activities, the International Trade Centre (ITC) continued to provide technical co-operation for trade promotion (see above).

The third annual report[8] on UNCTAD technical co-operation activities, prepared by the UNCTAD secretariat for the seventh session of the Working Party on the Medium-term Plan and the Programme Budget, was modified to reflect views expressed at previous sessions and included a description of UNDP programming methods and a list of ongoing projects. The report also focused on the financial crisis in multilateral co-operation and its adverse effects on UNCTAD operational activities.

Organizational questions

Conferences and meetings

Calendar of UNCTAD meetings

On 28 April, the Trade and Development Board approved a calendar of meetings for the remainder of 1983 and a tentative schedule for 1984 and 1985.[9] On 2 July, by decision 166(VI)[2] adopted without dissent, UNCTAD VI approved the 1983 calendar. On 20 October, the Board also approved the 1983 calendar, that for 1984 and the 1985 schedule.[10]

Also on 20 October, the Board adopted a decision[11]—recalling a 1976 UNCTAD resolution[12] which stated that the Board should meet at the ministerial level every two years between sessions of the Conference and noting a proposal contained in a draft resolution submitted by Venezuela on behalf of the Group of 77 that the thirtieth (1985) session be convened at the ministerial level—to postpone a decision on the matter until its twenty-eighth (1984) session and request the UNCTAD Secretary-General to hold consultations on the proposal and report to that session on their outcome.

Scheduling of Trade and Development Board meetings

On 22 April,[13] the Trade and Development Board decided to refer to UNCTAD VI, through the Board's twelfth special session, consideration of Economic and Social Council decision 1983/101 by which the Board was invited to consider rescheduling its meetings so that its report, starting in 1984, could be submitted to the General Assembly through the Council at its second regular session, normally held each July. On 6 May,[13] at its twelfth special session, the Board referred the matter to UNCTAD VI.

On 2 July,[2] UNCTAD VI adopted without dissent resolution 140(VI), by which it decided that the Board should continue to hold two regular sessions annually and considered that it had no possibility of rescheduling Board sessions to conform to a 1980 General Assembly resolution[14] and to Economic and Social Council decision 1983/101.

On 29 July, the Economic and Social Council considered a letter dated 5 July[15] from the President of UNCTAD VI attaching Conference resolution 140(VI), and adopted decision 1983/184 in which it requested the Assembly at its 1983 session to consider scheduling the meetings of the Board so that, starting in 1984, its report could be submitted to the Assembly through the Council at its second regular session.

On 19 December, in decision 38/429 on rationalization of the work of the Second Committee, the Assembly requested the Board to consider scheduling its second regular session so that its reports might be available in all Assembly working languages in time for the Assembly's consideration.

Report of the Trade and Development Board

On 28 April, the Trade and Development Board adopted a decision[16] regarding a November 1982 General Assembly resolution[17] requesting that reports of its subsidiary bodies be no longer than 32 pages. Recalling that in 1982 the Board had approved revised guidelines[18] for its annual report and noting that its 1983 report to the Assembly would be produced in accordance with those guidelines, the Board considered that every effort was being made to comply with the request but that it might not be possible to contain Conference or Board reports within the limit.

On 2 July,[2] UNCTAD VI adopted without dissent resolution 141(VI) by which it noted the Board's 1982 action, invited the Board to attempt to abide by the limit and authorized it to exceed the limit when fuller reporting to the Assembly was indispensable to its understanding of Board matters. The Conference informed the Assembly that it would not be possible to confine the report on its sixth session within the limit. It requested the Board, should it continue preparing the full version of its reports on its sessions, to consider dispensing with the summary records provided for its plenary meetings.

Documentation

On 20 October,[19] the Trade and Development Board established an *Ad Hoc* Working Group on Documentation to identify difficulties encountered with respect to late issuance of UNCTAD documentation and to propose solutions.

Also on 20 October,[6] the Board endorsed continued publication of *Trade and Development: an UNCTAD Review* on the following conditions: it would continue to be published annually and in English only; the number of copies would not exceed 5,000; income from sales would contribute to its financing; it would include original articles; its publication would not interfere with producing documentation for UNCTAD's normal work; and its financing would not come from funds allocated to other purposes.

REFERENCES

[1]A/38/15, vols. I & II. [2]*Proceedings of the United Nations Conference on Trade and Development, Sixth Session, Belgrade, 6 June–2 July 1983*, vol. I, *Report and Annexes* (TD/326, vol. I), Sales No. E.83.II.D.6. [3]YUN 1980, p. 621. [4]YUN 1981, p. 406. [5]TD/B/975. [6]A/38/15, vol. II. [7]A/C.5/38/4. [8]TD/B/WP/26 & Corr.1,2 & Add.1-3. [9]A/38/15, vol. I (dec. 271(XXVI)). [10]A/38/15, vol. II (dec. 281(XXVII)). [11]*Ibid.* (dec. 277(XXVI)). [12]YUN 1976, p. 401. [13]A/38/15, vol. I. [14]YUN 1980, p. 1225, GA res. 35/10 A. [15]E/1983/110. [16]A/38/15, vol. I (dec. 270(XXVI)). [17]YUN 1982, p. 1500, GA res. 37/14 C, 16 Nov. 1982. [18]*Ibid.*, p. 726. [19]A/38/15, vol. II (dec. 280(XXVII)).

Chapter V

Transport, communications and tourism

In 1983, the United Nations Conference on Trade and Development (UNCTAD) continued its work on international transport issues. In addition to reviewing the world situation and UNCTAD activities in regard to maritime transport, UNCTAD subsidiary bodies and its secretariat continued work on providing training assistance, drawing up shipping legislation for marine hull and cargo insurance, investigating sea transport of bulk cargoes, proposing measures to prevent maritime fraud and harmonizing regulations on the transport of dangerous goods.

At its sixth session in June/July, UNCTAD outlined future work for the secretariat. It called for completion of drafting work on an international agreement on conditions for registration of ships, aimed at establishing a genuine link between a vessel and its flag, and jurisdiction of a flag State over ships flying its flag. The Preparatory Committee for a 1984 plenipotentiary conference on the subject adopted a draft text with alternative formulations for the conference's consideration.

In July, the Economic and Social Council adopted resolution 1983/7 calling for amended recommendations for regulations concerning the transport of dangerous goods to be submitted to Governments for their comments.

The 1974 Convention on a Code of Conduct for Liner Conferences entered into force in October 1983; by year's end, 59 countries had become contracting parties. The Code was intended to open up the international shipping trade, organized in a system of liner conferences, to more countries, especially developing ones.

The United Nations marked 1983 as World Communications Year, for which the International Telecommunication Union acted as the lead agency in co-ordinating activities such as conferences, seminars and pilot projects, with special emphasis on stimulating the development of communications infrastructures.

Activities during 1983 to promote tourism included seminars and studies, concentrating on implementation of the 1980 Manila Declaration on World Tourism which provided guidelines for developing tourism, especially in developing countries. In resolution 38/146, the General Assembly urged States to apply the principles of the Declaration when formulating tourism policies and requested the World Tourism Organization to promote tourism along those lines.

Topics related to this chapter. Regional economic and social activities: Africa—Transport and Communications Decade in Africa; Asia and the Pacific—Transport and Communications Decade in Asia and the Pacific. Natural resources. International economic law.

Transport

UNCTAD, the main United Nations body dealing with transport, and its subsidiary bodies, particularly the Committee on Shipping, continued in 1983 to deal with problems of transport.

Maritime transport

In its 1983 annual *Review of Maritime Transport*,[1] the UNCTAD secretariat analysed the main developments in world maritime transport and assessed expected future short-term developments. Emphasis was given to developing countries, in particular to development of their merchant marines. The report, prepared in accordance with the work programme of the Committee on Shipping, stated that, for the fourth consecutive year, the annual total volume of world seaborne trade in 1983 had declined; however, the last quarter of 1983 showed some improvement, as cargo volume was 3 to 4 per cent higher than in the first quarter. Preliminary estimates for 1983 showed that world trade declined to 3.2 billion tons, as compared with 3.3 billion the year before, or a reduction of 3 per cent. The rate of decline was, however, less than in the two previous years—annual seaborne trade had declined by 8 per cent in 1982 and 3.9 per cent in 1981.

Ownership of ships involved in international trade remained concentrated in developed market-economy countries and open-registry country fleets, whose combined tonnage represented 76.1 per cent of the mid-year 1983 world merchant fleet. The share of those vessels from developing countries, however, increased to 15.3 per cent (13.6 per cent in 1982), while that of the socialist countries remained unchanged. The low participation of developing countries in the world merchant fleet continued to be disproportionate to their share of international seaborne trade. Specifically, in 1982 developing countries generated 37.9 per cent of world cargo of international trade but owned only 13.6 per cent of the deadweight tonnage, while developed market-economy countries, either directly or indirectly through open-registry countries, owned 78.4 per cent of world tonnage and generated approximately 55 per cent of world trade.

The world shipping industry continued in 1983 to be over supplied, as reflected in lower levels of the annual average freight rate indices as compared with those for 1982, with the exception of dry cargo tramp trip and crude tanker indices.

The United Nations Convention on a Code of Conduct for Liner Conferences entered into force on 6 October 1983 and, by the end of the year, 59 countries had become contracting parties (see below).

The Preparatory Committee for the United Nations Conference on Conditions for Registration of Ships continued work on the draft text for an international agreement and considered that it had advanced its work sufficiently for the holding of a plenipotentiary conference, scheduled for July/August 1984 (see below).

Shipping

In preparation for the sixth session of UNCTAD (known as UNCTAD VI) (Belgrade, Yugoslavia, 6 June–2 July 1983), the UNCTAD secretariat submitted a report in January on UNCTAD shipping activities.[2] The report provided an overview of maritime transport issues in international trade policy which had been discussed in UNCTAD, particularly those relating to structural adjustment. It described UNCTAD's response since 1965 to shipping issues.

The report noted that the current world economic situation, accompanied by increasing protectionism, had affected the shipping industry. The institutional structure of the liner sector—the conference system—and the economic organization of the bulk market through self-regulated "exchanges" and through controls exercised by transnational corporations gave rise to problems of entry when the developing countries decided to participate in shipping. Consequently, those countries had sought to obtain an equitable and substantial share in shipping within UNCTAD. The importance they attached to shipping was highlighted by the fact that the International Development Strategy for the Third United Nations Development Decade (1981-1990)[3] called for structural change in the industry and for a 20 per cent share of world shipping for developing countries by 1990.

Self-regulation through market forces had not worked in liner shipping owing to market controls exercised by a few large shipowners, as personified in the conference system which inhibited entry into the market and removed price competition.

The high concentration of fleet ownership by traditional maritime countries (developed countries) had impaired the ability of developing countries to compete and increase their shipping operations.

In the report, the UNCTAD secretariat called for a practical approach to current problems and suggested that, to defuse existing tensions, UNCTAD VI reaffirm its faith in the international negotiating processes for settling disputes among States, thereby discouraging the non-observance of international agreements and existing UNCTAD mechanisms for the practical solution of problems. It was also suggested that UNCTAD VI reassert support for shipping activities being implemented by UNCTAD, and call for countries' dedication to United Nations Conventions such as that of 1974 on a Code of Conduct for Liner Conferences (see below),[4] that of 1978 on the Carriage of Goods by Sea (the Hamburg Rules)[5] and that of 1980 on International Multimodal Transport of Goods.[6] The review conferences foreseen in the those Conventions would be useful in addressing problems. Emphasizing a pragmatic approach in negotiations, the report pointed to the work of the 1981 Group of Experts on bulk cargoes (see below), which, while disagreeing on the nature and extent of the barriers to entry in the bulk trades, unanimously adopted several practical recommendations to facilitate the participation of developing countries in relevant markets.

UNCTAD VI, in resolution 144(VI) of 2 July on UNCTAD shipping activities,[7] requested its Secretary-General to review and update the secretariat's 1980 report on ship and port financing for developing countries[8] in order to determine the availability of financial resources and organizational arrangements for those countries to increase their participation in the world seaborne transport of international trade, as envisaged in the International Development Strategy,[3] bearing in mind UNCTAD resolutions on the financing of ships, and paying particular attention to the special problem of the least developed countries. The Secretary-General was also requested to undertake several studies: one on Governments' policies in the world shipping industry which might be detrimental to developing countries' interests, particularly investment and support policies; a preliminary study on the freight rate levels and structures of liner shipping and of selected non-liner commodities, covering dry cargoes of all kinds and liquid cargoes of vegetable origin, and of their possible effects on the exports of developing countries; a preliminary study on a non-mandatory model agreement for feeder services and trans-shipment ports; and an in-depth study on bulk terminals. Furthermore, he was called on to elaborate a standard form and model for multimodal transport documents, guidelines on the application of computer software packages to multimodal transport, and a draft programme of action for co-operation among developing countries in shipping, ports and multimodal transport.

UNCTAD VI also urged the completion of international negotiations on liens and mortgages, and maritime fraud. States not contracting parties to the Convention on International Multimodal Transport of Goods and the Hamburg Rules were invited to ratify or accede to them.

In an April report[9] to the May/June session of the United Nations Commission on International Trade Law, the United Nations Secretary-General described developments regarding the international transport of goods (see LEGAL QUESTIONS, Chapter VI), including UNCTAD's work for the previous several years on marine insurance, transport by container and freight forwarding.

Preparations for the 1984 conference on registration of ships

The question of open registries of ships had been considered within UNCTAD for more than nine years. In resolution 144(VI),[7] UNCTAD VI urged the expeditious completion of work on conditions for the registration of ships, particularly a genuine link between a vessel and the flag it flew and the need for flag States to exercise control over those ships. UNCTAD invited its members to participate in the Preparatory Committee for the United Nations Conference on Conditions for Registration of Ships, set up in pursuance of a December 1982 General Assembly resolution.[10]

The Committee met at Geneva from 7 to 18 November 1983[11] to prepare for the 1984 plenipotentiary Conference and draft an international agreement on conditions for registration of ships. A set of basic principles governing conditions under which vessels should be accepted on national shipping registers had been elaborated in 1982[12] but there remained a number of outstanding issues, in particular relating to manning, management and ownership. Elements taken into consideration by the Committee were: the contribution of the merchant fleet to the national economy of the country, the inclusion of shipping revenues in the national balance-of-payments accounts, the employment of nationals on vessels, and the beneficial ownership of the vessel. The Committee adopted a composite text for transmission to the Conference, which it annexed to its report along with a text proposed by the Chairman on manning, management and equity, and a proposal by the USSR on behalf of States members of Group D (centrally planned economies) for a draft international agreement on ship registration.

The Committee welcomed a 20 October Trade and Development Board decision[13] on the dates

for the Conference (5-23 March 1984). It requested the UNCTAD Secretary-General to prepare draft final provisions for an international agreement concerning the time-frame for the registration of vessels, and procedures for reporting on, and review of, implementation and definitions. The draft text prepared by the Committee contained alternative formulations, reflecting the positions of different groups on such key issues as manning of vessels, equity participation in capital, bareboat charters, and identification and accountability.

In related action concerning the registration of ships, the Economic and Social Council in May adopted resolution 1983/4 on measures to improve international co-operation in the maritime interdiction of illicit drug traffic (see Chapter XXII of this section).

Convention on a Code of Conduct for Liner Conferences

The Convention on a Code of Conduct for Liner Conferences came into force on 6 October 1983, six months after 24 States, the combined tonnage of which amounted to at least 25 per cent of world tonnage, became contracting parties—a requirement which was met in April.

The Convention, adopted by UNCTAD in 1974,[4] provided an internationally accepted regulatory framework for the operations of liner conferences. At the time it came into force, the following 59 countries, accounting for 28.7 per cent of world tonnage, had become contracting parties (those in italics became parties during 1983): Bangladesh, Barbados, Benin, Bulgaria, Cape Verde, Central African Republic, Chile, China, Congo, Costa Rica, Cuba, Czechoslovakia, Egypt, Ethiopia, Gabon, Gambia, German Democratic Republic, *Germany, Federal Republic of*, Ghana, Guatemala, Guinea, Guyana, Honduras, India, Indonesia, Iraq, Ivory Coast, Jamaica, Jordan, Kenya, Lebanon, Madagascar, Malaysia, Mali, Mauritius, Mexico, Morocco, *Netherlands*, Niger, Nigeria, Pakistan, Peru, Philippines, Republic of Korea, Romania, Senegal, Sierra Leone, Sri Lanka, Sudan, Togo, *Trinidad and Tobago*, Tunisia, USSR, United Republic of Cameroon, United Republic of Tanzania, Uruguay, Venezuela, Yugoslavia, Zaire.[1]

The fundamental objectives of the Code were to ensure the right of participation of national lines in trade to entitle them to carry a substantial share of their country's foreign trade, to balance the interests of shippers and shipowners, and to facilitate the orderly expansion of liner trade. To this end, the Code regulated the relationship between member lines of conferences, in particular the rights of admission of national shipping lines to conferences serving their country's foreign trade, and set rules for establishing pools or other types of trade-sharing arrangements in conferences as well as other internal conference activities, such as self-policing. The Code also regulated the relationship between shippers and liner conferences by establishing equitable principles for the use of loyalty arrangements as well as providing that conferences were required to hold consultations with shippers or their representative organizations on matters of concern, such as changes in freight rates and loyalty arrangements.

In resolution 144(VI),[7] UNCTAD VI invited States members which had not become contracting parties to the Convention to consider ratifying or acceding to it and called on those which had already done so to implement it promptly. The UNCTAD Secretary-General was requested to prepare a comprehensive progress report on the Convention's implementation for the Committee on Shipping.

In accordance with the Convention, the UNCTAD Secretary-General convened a meeting of the contracting parties on 13 October to receive their views on the appointment of a Registrar to administer the conciliation process provided for in the Convention. On 29 November,[14] the United Nations Secretary-General informed the General Assembly of the financial implications for the required staff and operating expenses, requesting approval for an appropriation of $250,200 for the 1984-1985 biennium.

The Fifth (Administrative and Budgetary) Committee considered the proposal on 5 December. The United States proposed that the Committee decide that the resources required to implement the activities be provided through offsetting programmatic or administrative adjustments. The Committee rejected that proposal by 64 votes to 24, with 12 abstentions. The Committee then approved without vote an additional appropriation of $142,000 for 1984-1985.

Bulk cargoes

Responding to a 1982 request by the UNCTAD Committee on Shipping,[15] the Group of Experts on International Sea Transport of Liquid Hydrocarbons in Bulk held its first session at Geneva from 25 to 29 April 1983 and submitted an interim report concerning problems faced by developing countries seeking to participate in such transport.[16] The report included a questionnaire for communication through Governments to major importers, exporters, traders and providers of shipping services, concerning their operations in international seaborne transport of crude oil and liquid petroleum products. The Group requested the UNCTAD Secretary-General to submit the questionnaire to UNCTAD member States so that the information thus obtained could be used in

preparation of a final report. This and other information would be assessed to determine whether the operations of the major importers, exporters, traders and providers of shipping services placed any barriers to the ability of shipping companies of developing countries to compete in the international seaborne transportation of those commodities, and, if so, what recommendations could be made to reduce and eliminate such barriers.

In resolution 144(VI),[7] UNCTAD VI requested its Secretary-General to examine the structure of the world shipping industry with the aim of identifying the causes and effects of protectionist policies and monopolistic practices where they might exist, particularly with respect to the carriage of bulk and refrigerated cargo and taking into account the report and recommendations of the Group when they became available (the Group was scheduled to hold its second session in January/February 1984), and those of the 1981 Group of Experts on Problems Faced by the Developing Countries in the Carriage of Bulk Cargoes,[17] with a view to drawing up conclusions and recommendations, if needed, on possible adjustments of those policies and practices and to report thereon to the Committee on Shipping.

International shipping legislation

The Working Group on International Shipping Legislation, at its ninth session held at Geneva from 31 January to 18 February 1983,[18] considered marine hull and cargo insurance. This was the fourth session devoted to marine insurance and was aimed at formulating a set of standard clauses as non-mandatory model legislation, thus creating a more equitable, understandable and internationally acceptable legal base for marine insurance contracts. Composite texts on the two kinds of marine insurance were amended and annexed to the report.

In resolution 144(VI),[7] UNCTAD VI called for the early completion of ongoing international negotiations on maritime legislation, including marine insurance, and the elaboration of model national maritime legislation.

Technical assistance and training

During 1983, the UNCTAD secretariat executed 36 technical assistance projects[1] financed by the United Nations Development Programme (UNDP), recipient countries and funds-in-trust, as compared with 30 in 1982. Those projects were basically concerned with providing advisory services and consultants, training (fellowships and group training), and, to a lesser degree, equipment procurement. In addition, two shipping feasibility studies were completed for two developing countries. Ten projects were initiated and six were completed. A total of 43 experts were engaged in the projects, and 970 fellows/course participants were trained. The total project budget was $2.5 million.

TRAINMAR, the interregional training programme, entered its second phase and expanded its activities to cover eight different projects. The basic objectives of TRAINMAR were: to create and strengthen local training institutions; to develop training materials for use by local instructors; and to exchange training material. By the end of 1983, 10 countries had been associated with TRAINMAR, and 12 courses were completed, attended by 870 participants.

Proposed establishment of the World Maritime University

In 1982, the International Maritime Organization (IMO), UNDP and Sweden had agreed on steps to establish a World Maritime University at Malmö, Sweden.[19] Both UNDP and Sweden had contributed towards its establishment. Resources were being sought to cover the difference between Sweden's pledge of $1 million yearly and the estimated yearly operating costs (an additional $1 million). Those efforts to establish the proposed University, including the hiring of five administrative staff members, were described by the UNDP Administrator in a report to the UNDP Governing Council.[20] By a decision of 18 February,[21] the Governing Council took note of that report.

Maritime fraud

In September 1983, the UNCTAD secretariat concluded a study on possible measures to minimize the occurrence of maritime fraud and piracy,[22] as requested by the Committee on Shipping in 1982.[15] The study was prepared for submission to the *Ad Hoc* Intergovernmental Group to Consider Means of Combating All Aspects of Maritime Fraud, including Piracy, established by the Committee,[15] which was to meet in February 1984. The report dealt with a wide variety of types of fraudulent acts and proposed reforms to minimize fraud. It divided fraudulent activities into six categories: documentary, charter party, marine insurance, deviation, miscellaneous, and piracy. In addition, it reviewed activities of other international organizations involved in combating maritime fraud and piracy, in particular IMO. It noted that the introduction of computerization had vastly expanded capabilities in handling, collating and presenting information in readily usable form and that the shipping community had begun to take advantage of this capability. It cited, as an example, the International Maritime Bureau, a non-governmental non-profit-making organization designed as a central clearing-house for information concerning maritime fraud.

According to the report, various suggestions had been made for international action to combat maritime fraud, but most had not been implemented. They involved some alteration in the existing system of conducting international shipping and trade—some requiring governmental action in the form of altering the applicable law, pursuant to international conventions or otherwise, and others requiring action only by private parties. Among the suggestions was an international convention with provisions to facilitate the exchange of information. Special mention was made of a proposal by Lebanon to IMO for a convention to suppress barratry (wrongful acts committed by the ship's master or crew to the prejudice of the owner or charterer) and unlawful seizure which would provide for broad reciprocal judicial assistance between contracting States in accordance with penal procedures.

Other proposals for further study included: establishing a central registry in which bills of lading would be deposited upon issuance and through which the transfer of title would be effected by communication by the seller and buyer, thus reducing the opportunities for documentation fraud; measures to prevent the forging of bills of lading; co-operation of banks which granted credit in investigating the validity of the documents representing the goods before paying out on the credit; the ongoing work within UNCTAD on conditions for registration of ships to reduce deviation frauds and certain types of marine insurance and charter party frauds, by improving the identifiability and accountability of shipowners and operators, as well as mortgage frauds; improved monitoring of ship movement; governmental procedures concerning the sale of goods by shipowners on voyage termination; and measures to avoid cargo insurance and port-related frauds in handling and storage.

Transport of dangerous goods

In 1983, work continued on harmonizing codes and regulations relating to the transport of hazardous substances such as liquefied gases, radioactive and toxic materials and explosives. The Committee of Experts on the Transport of Dangerous Goods published the third revised edition of its recommendations.[23] In March, the Secretary-General issued a report to the Economic and Social Council describing the Committee's 1981-1982 activities and recommendations on the listing, classification, packaging and labelling of existing and new products and other matters to ensure safety during transport.[24] The report included a recommendation that, in view of the volume and urgency of its work, the Council should increase the staff of the unit for the transport of dangerous goods by one Professional and one General Service post.

In preparation for the Committee's 1984 session, the Group of Rapporteurs of the Committee met from 1 to 12 August 1983 (thirtieth session)[25] and the Group of Experts on Explosives met from 12 to 16 September (twenty-third session),[26] both at Geneva. The Group of Rapporteurs made recommendations on regulations on intermediate bulk containers, multimodal tank containers for refrigerated liquefied gases, specific aspects of packing, classification of dangerous goods and consignment procedures. The Group of Experts discussed test methods and criteria to be included in an explosives test manual, regulations on charging and transport of intermodal freight containers, and new entries or amendments to classification of dangerous goods.

ECONOMIC AND SOCIAL COUNCIL ACTION

On 26 May, the Economic and Social Council, on the recommendation of its First (Economic) Committee, adopted resolution 1983/7 without vote. The text was based on a draft approved by the Committee of Experts and annexed to the Secretary-General's March report.[24]

Work of the Committee of Experts on the Transport of Dangerous Goods

The Economic and Social Council,

Recalling its resolutions 468 G (XV) of 15 April 1953, 645 G (XXIII) of 26 April 1957, 994(XXXVI) of 16 December 1963, 1110(XL) of 7 March 1966, 1488(XLVIII) of 22 May 1970, 1744(LIV) of 4 May 1973, 1973(LIX) and 1974(LIX) of 30 July 1975, 2050(LXII) of 5 May 1977, 1979/42 of 11 May 1979 and 1981/3 of 4 May 1981,

Recognizing the importance of the work of the Committee of Experts on the Transport of Dangerous Goods for the harmonization of codes and regulations relating to the transport of dangerous goods,

Bearing in mind the need to maintain safety standards at all times and to facilitate trade, as well as the importance of this to the various organizations responsible for modal regulations, while meeting the growing concern for the protection of life and property through the safe transport of dangerous goods,

Noting the increasing volume of dangerous goods being introduced into world-wide commerce and the rapid expansion of technology and innovation,

Taking note of the report of the Secretary-General on the work of the Committee of Experts on the Transport of Dangerous Goods,

1. *Takes note with satisfaction* of the work of the Committee of Experts on the Transport of Dangerous Goods and of the recommendations contained in its report with respect to the listing, classification, packaging and labelling of existing and new products, and to other matters that will ensure safety during transport;

2. *Takes note* of the fact that increased importance and reliance is being placed on the work of the Committee of Experts on the Transport of Dangerous Goods by the specialized agencies and other international or-

ganizations and by Member States, which take the recommendations more and more as a guideline for their own recommendations and regulations in order to achieve internationally harmonized laws;

3. *Requests* the Secretary-General, in the light of the contents of the report of the Committee of Experts on the Transport of Dangerous Goods:

(a) To incorporate into a new text all the new and amended recommendations made by the Committee of Experts at its twelfth session, together with any consequential changes to be introduced into existing recommendations;

(b) To publish the resulting revised text of the recommendations of the Committee of Experts in all the official languages of the United Nations as quickly as possible and in the most cost-effective manner, in accordance with the proposal in the report of the Committee;

(c) To circulate the recommendations as soon as possible to the Governments of Member States, the specialized agencies, the International Atomic Energy Agency and other international organizations concerned;

(d) To make available, within existing resources and in order to maintain the standard of work at the requisite level, the improved staffing requested by the Committee for the secretariat unit servicing the Economic Commission for Europe and the Economic and Social Council in their work on the transport of dangerous goods;

4. *Requests* the Secretary-General to examine all the implications of proposals to enlarge the membership of the Committee of Experts on the Transport of Dangerous Goods by, *inter alia*, converting observers into full members in view of their active participation in its work over a continuous period, and, at the same time, of widening the decision-making base of the Committee through broader geographical representation, and to report thereon to the Council;

5. *Invites* all Governments, the specialized agencies, the International Atomic Energy Agency and other international organizations concerned to transmit to the Secretary-General such comments as they may wish to make on the amended recommendations;

6. *Invites* all Governments and international organizations concerned to take account of the recommendations of the Committee of Experts on the Transport of Dangerous Goods when developing appropriate codes and regulations.

Economic and Social Council resolution 1983/7

26 May 1983   Meeting 14   Adopted without vote

Approved by First Committee (E/1983/59) without vote, 16 May (meeting 6); draft by Chairman (E/1983/C.1/L.4), orally revised and orally amended by Netherlands and by Tunisia; agenda item 8.
Financial implications. S-G, E/1983/C.1/L.7.
Meeting number. ESC 14.

Before the draft's approval by the First Committee, two oral amendments were made to the text. The first, by Tunisia, added "in all the official languages of the United Nations" to paragraph 3 *(b);* the second, by the Netherlands, deleted "at its first regular session of 1985" from the end of paragraph 4.

REFERENCES
[1]TD/B/C.4/266. [2]TD/278 & Corr.1. [3]YUN 1980, p. 503,
GA res. 35/56, annex, 5 Dec. 1980. [4]YUN 1974, p. 460.
[5]YUN 1978, p. 956. [6]YUN 1980, p. 1020. [7]*Proceedings of
the United Nations Conference on Trade and Development, Sixth Session, Belgrade, 6 June–2 July 1983*, vol. I, *Report and Annexes* (TD/
326, vol. I), Sales No. E.83.II.D.6. [8]TD/B/C.4/190.
[9]A/CN.9/236. [10]YUN 1982, p. 748, GA res. 37/209, 20
Dec. 1982. [11]TD/RS/CONF/3 & Corr.1. [12]YUN 1982,
p. 747. [13]A/38/15, vol. II (dec. 281(XXVII)). [14]A/C.5/
38/55. [15]YUN 1982, p. 749. [16]TD/B/C.4/257. [17]YUN
1981, p. 567. [18]TD/B/C.4/256. [19]YUN 1982, p. 751.
[20]DP/1983/3. [21]E/1983/20 (dec. 83/2 B). [22]TD/B/C.4/
AC.4/2. [23]*Transport of Dangerous Goods: Recommendations of the
Committee of Experts on the Transport of Dangerous Goods*
(ST/SG/AC.10/1/Rev.3 & Corr.1), Sales No. E.83.VIII.1 & corrigendum. [24]YUN 1982, p. 751 (E/1983/25). [25]ST/SG/
AC.10/C.2/15. [26]ST/SG/AC.10/C.1/10.

PUBLICATIONS
Review of Maritime Transport, 1980 (TD/B/C.4/222/Rev.1), Sales
No. E.83.II.D.4; *1981* (TD/B/C.4/251/Rev.1), Sales No.
E.83.II.D.10. *Multimodal transport and containerization, Guidelines
on the introduction of containerization and multimodal transport and on
the modernization and improvement of the infrastructure of developing
countries* (TD/B/C.4/238/Rev.1), Sales No. E.83.II.D.14. *Census
of Motor Traffic on Main International Traffic Arteries, 1980*, Sales
No. E.83.II.E.27.

Communications

World Communications Year

The United Nations commemorated 1983 as
World Communications Year: Development of
Communications Infrastructures (WCY), in accordance with a 1981 resolution of the General Assembly.[1] As the lead agency for WCY, the International Telecommunication Union (ITU)
co-ordinated United Nations activities and follow-
up action through an inter-agency committee
made up of 17 international organizations. In October, the United Nations Secretary-General transmitted to the Assembly, through the Economic and
Social Council, the report of the ITU Secretary-
General on the Year.[2]

WCY was promoted through three main elements: national committees to co-ordinate communications policies and to serve as a forum for
concerted action, conferences and seminars to provide analytical material on issues relating to communications policies and development, and pilot
projects to stimulate the development of communications infrastructures. The role of UNDP
representatives was stressed with regard to their
continued assistance to national committees. As
at 11 May 1983, 57 countries had created their own
WCY committees. Pilot projects, funded by voluntary contributions, were selected for their applicability to a number of countries. Since the establishment of the WCY secretariat in 1982, five
information bulletins had been published and sent

to hundreds of organizations, companies and individuals wishing to participate in the Year. Two
press kits were prepared and dispatched to 6,000
journalists and editors and to all United Nations
information centres. Within the framework of
WCY, ITU organized the Fourth World Telecommunication Exhibition, known as Telecom 83,
which presented the latest advances in communications technology. A series of seminars covered
key issues highlighting the telecommunications requirements of both industrialized and developing
countries and the efforts to finance national,
regional and world-wide development plans.

The 1982 ITU Plenipotentiary Conference[3] set
up an Independent International Commission for
World-Wide Telecommunications Development,
composed of high-level representatives and
financed by independent non-commercial sources.
In follow-up action on WCY, the Commission was
to examine relationships between countries in
telecommunications involving technical co-
operation and a transfer of resources, to recommend methods for stimulating telecommunications development in the developing world, and
to consider how ITU could stimulate activities to
achieve a more balanced expansion of telecommunications.

Other agencies and organizations carried out
special activities in connection with the Year. The
Universal Postal Union urged postal administrations to issue special commemorative WCY stamps
and to co-ordinate activities with national committees for the Year. It issued three brochures for
postal administrations designed to improve postal
service. The Food and Agriculture Organization
of the United Nations collaborated in producing
a bulletin on telecommunications for agriculture
development. The United Nations Educational,
Scientific and Cultural Organization planned various national, regional and international projects.
Among the international projects, a feasibility
study for the exchange of news and programmes
by satellite was carried out, and a low-cost audio
unit was developed. Publications on various
aspects of telecommunications were issued. The
International Civil Aviation Organization held an
international meeting of experts on aeronautical
communications which discussed ways to improve
the global aeronautical telecommunications network, taking advantage of new technology, including computers and satellites, and emphasizing
meteorological information and other air navigation data.

GENERAL ASSEMBLY ACTION

The General Assembly adopted decision 38/433
without vote, on the recommendation of the Second (Economic and Financial) Committee.

World Communications Year: Development of Communications Infrastructures

At its 102nd plenary meeting, on 19 December 1983, the General Assembly, on the recommendation of the Second Committee, took note of the report of the Secretary-General of the International Telecommunication Union on World Communications Year: Development of Communications Infrastructures.

General Assembly decision 38/433

Adopted without vote

Approved by Second Committee (A/38/701Add.1) without vote, 14 December (meeting 56); draft orally proposed by Chairman; agenda item 12.
Meeting numbers. GA 38th session: 2nd Committee 31, 36, 41, 52, 53, 55, 56; plenary 102.

REFERENCES

[1]YUN 1981, p. 573, GA res. 36/40, 19 Nov. 1981.
[2]A/38/374-E/1983/95. [3]YUN 1982, p. 1576.

Tourism

Implementation of the 1980 Manila Declaration on World Tourism

As requested by the General Assembly in 1981,[1] the Secretary-General of the World Tourism Organization (WTO) reported on progress made in implementing the Manila Declaration on World Tourism, adopted in 1980 by the World Tourism Conference[2] and providing guidelines for the development of national and international tourism, especially in developing countries. The WTO report was transmitted in June 1983 by the United Nations Secretary-General[3] to the Assembly through the Economic and Social Council.

WTO activities included technical meetings at regional and subregional levels, and international seminars on subjects dealt with in the Declaration (including tourism and culture, national and intraregional tourism, and the financing of tourist attractions). Statistics, previously confined to international movements, were expanded by research on national tourism and motivations for travel. Studies were made on the social effects of tourism, the extent to which paid leave was available, national tourism, and new tourist products offered to different economic strata of the population, particularly the less wealthy. It had been found that certain States, in particular the industrialized ones, had provision for the measures called for in the Declaration, such as paid leave assistance to the least privileged strata of the population to enable them to have vacations, cultural activities, measures to protect the environment and facilities for travel. In many States, because of their levels of economic development, the labour legislation did not provide for paid leave for all categories of employees.

Annexed to the WTO report was a document adopted by the World Tourism Meeting, organized by WTO (Acapulco, Mexico, 21-27 August 1982). Attended by 79 countries, the Meeting supported implementation of the Declaration. It stated that the right to rest must be affirmed as a fundamental right in terms of human happiness, which implicitly entailed the right to the use of leisure time and access to holidays. It noted that the development of tourism was closely linked to the social, economic and cultural context of each country. The Meeting recognized that the issue of freedom of movement and of travel, dealt with in the Declaration, was of great importance for the development of world tourism, and said it was incumbent on WTO to foster freedom of movement and of travel within the framework of international cooperation in tourism. The Meeting invited States and all public and private bodies concerned, as well as WTO, to take into account the guidelines and considerations emerging from its work, so as to fulfil the aims proposed for a fresh, more balanced expansion of tourism, within the framework of their development policies and in the spirit of the Declaration.

GENERAL ASSEMBLY ACTION

On 19 December, the General Assembly, on the recommendation of the Second Committee, adopted resolution 38/146 without vote.

World Tourism Organization

The General Assembly,

Recalling its resolutions 32/156 and 32/157 of 19 December 1977, 33/122 of 19 December 1978 and 34/134 of 14 December 1979, concerning the World Tourism Organization,

Recalling also its resolution 36/41 of 19 November 1981, which pertains, *inter alia,* to the Manila Declaration on World Tourism,

Recalling further its resolution 35/56 of 5 December 1980, by which it proclaimed the Third United Nations Development Decade and adopted the International Development Strategy for the Third United Nations Development Decade,

Taking note of paragraph 5 of its resolution 36/41 and of subparagraph *(c)* of Economic and Social Council decision 109(LIX) of 23 July 1975, in which the General Assembly and the Council decided that the World Tourism Organization might participate, on a continuing basis, in the work of the Assembly and the Council in areas of concern to that organization,

Noting that the World Tourism Meeting was convened from 21 to 27 August 1982 at Acapulco, Mexico, and that it adopted the Acapulco Document on World Tourism as a follow-up to the Manila Declaration,

Recognizing the new dimension and role of tourism as a positive instrument towards the improvement of the quality of life for all peoples, as well as a significant force for peace and international understanding,

1. *Welcomes* the report of the Secretary-General of the World Tourism Organization on the progress made in

the implementation of the Manila Declaration on World Tourism;

2. *Urges* Member States to give due attention to the principles of the Manila Declaration and the Acapulco Document on World Tourism while formulating and implementing, as appropriate, their tourism policies, plans and programmes, in accordance with their national priorities and within the framework of the programme of work of the World Tourism Organization;

3. *Requests* the World Tourism Organization, in co-operation with the United Nations system, to continue its efforts towards the future development and promotion of tourism, especially in the developing countries, bearing in mind the principles and guidelines contained in the Manila Declaration and the Acapulco Document;

4. *Requests* the United Nations Development Programme and other relevant United Nations bodies, as well as other international, intergovernmental and non-governmental organizations directly or indirectly interested in tourism, to extend their assistance, in co-operation with the World Tourism Organization and in accordance with the priorities of the Governments concerned, towards the implementation of the Manila Declaration and the Acapulco Document;

5. *Requests* the Secretary-General of the World Tourism Organization to submit to the General Assembly at its fortieth session, through the Economic and Social Council, a report on the progress made in the im-plementation of the Manila Declaration and the Acapulco Document.

General Assembly resolution 38/146

19 December 1983   Meeting 102   Adopted without vote

Approved by Second Committee (A/38/701) without vote, 21 November (meeting 45); draft by Vice-Chairman (A/C.2/38/L.44), based on informal consultations on 3-nation draft (A/C.2/38/L.27); agenda item 12.
Meeting numbers. GA 38th session: 2nd Committee 36, 45; plenary 102.

The resolution was based on a draft text which was submitted to the Second Committee by Bang-ladesh, Jamaica and the Philippines and subsequently withdrawn. Two changes were made to that version. In the last preambular paragraph, tourism was first described as a vital force for peace and international understanding; the adopted text described it as a significant force for that purpose. By the second change, which applied to paragraph 4, an addition was made so that assistance would be extended "in accordance with the priorities of the Governments concerned".

REFERENCES
[1]YUN 1981, p. 574, GA res. 36/41, 19 Nov. 1981. [2]*Ibid.*, p. 573. [3]A/38/182-E/1983/66.

Chapter VI

Industrial development

In 1983, the United Nations Industrial Development Organization (UNIDO) continued to help developing countries raise their share of world industrial production to the target of 25 per cent by the year 2000. This goal was contained in the Lima Declaration and Plan of Action on Industrial Development and Co-operation,[1] adopted in 1975 at the Second General Conference of UNIDO (Lima, Peru). The 1983 UNIDO endeavours were described by its Executive Director in his annual report[2] to the Industrial Development Board, UNIDO's policy-making body.

The 45-nation Board held its seventeenth session at UNIDO headquarters, Vienna, Austria, from 26 April to 13 May 1983.[3] At that session, the Board adopted 17 conclusions on various programme, industrial development and organizational matters; these included technical assistance to the Namibian people (see TRUSTEESHIP AND DECOLONIZATION, Chapter III) and Palestinian people (see POLITICAL AND SECURITY QUESTIONS, Chapter IX, under "Palestine question"), and integration of women in development (see Chapter XIX of this section). In addition, the Board adopted a resolution on the Industrial Development Decade for Africa (see Chapter VIII of this section). The Board's Permanent Committee met twice at Vienna, for its nineteenth (25 and 29 April)[4] and twentieth (28 November–2 December)[5] sessions.

The work of UNIDO and the Board's report were reviewed by the General Assembly, which adopted in December resolution 38/192 on various programme policies for UNIDO, with continued emphasis on the Industrial Development Decade for Africa and preparations for the Fourth (1984) General Conference of UNIDO, for which the Assembly set both place (Vienna) and dates (2-18 August 1984). Revisions made by the Committee for Programme and Co-ordination (CPC) to the 1984-1985 UNIDO work programme and their consequent financial implications were noted by the Economic and Social Council in July (resolution 1983/49) and by the Assembly in December (resolution 38/234).

An evaluation study on technical co-operation activities in manufactures financed by the United Nations Development Programme (UNDP) and executed by UNIDO was completed early in the year. In resolution 1983/49, the Council requested the Secretary-General to submit a report to CPC in 1983 and a comprehensive report in 1984 (which would include comments by UNIDO and UNDRO). The Assembly endorsed that request in resolution 38/227 A.

In May, UNIDO met to conclude arrangements for its conversion into a specialized agency. Steps to accelerate the process were set forth in December by Assembly resolution 38/193. In anticipation of the conversion, modifications to the current arrangements for sharing common services among the International Atomic Energy Agency (IAEA), UNIDO and other United Nations units headquartered at Vienna were outlined by the Secretary-General and noted by the Assembly in December (resolution 38/234).

As a result of the admission of Saint Christopher and Nevis to the United Nations, the Assembly, by its December resolution 38/194, included that country among the States eligible for Board membership.

Topics related to this chapter. Regional economic and social activities: industrial development—Africa; Asia and the Pacific; Europe; Latin America; Western Asia. Energy: industrial uses. Science and technology: technology transfer. Environment: ecosystems—environment and industry. Women: women in development.

Programme and finances of UNIDO

Programme policy

As in the previous two years, UNIDO activities in 1983 focused on the priority areas identified in 1980 by the Industrial Development Board[6] as a follow-up to decisions of UNIDO's Third General Conference,[7] and recommended in 1982 by the Economic and Social Council[8] and the General Assembly[9] for continued priority attention during 1983-1985. Those priorities were: energy-related and other industrial technology, industrial production, human resources development, special measures for the least developed countries (LDCs) and the System of Consultations, established on a permanent basis by the Board in 1980[10] to promote industrialization of developing countries. Other activities included restructuring world industrial production, industrial financing, the Industrial Development Decade for Africa (see Chapter VIII of this section), and monitoring.

Activities were planned and carried out taking into account the International Development Strategy for the Third United Nations Development Decade (the 1980s)[11] and related Assembly decisions and recommendations. Having considered a progress report[12] by the UNIDO Executive Director in follow-up to the Third General Conference and the Strategy, the Board, on 13 May 1983,[13] expressed concern at the lack of progress since the beginning of the Decade in increasing the share of developing countries in world industrial production.

As requested by the Board on the same date, the UNIDO secretariat submitted to the Board's Permanent Committee, for consideration at its November/December session, a report on implementation of the Strategy relevant to industry.[14] In addition to requesting UNIDO to strengthen co-operation with intergovernmental regional and subregional organizations in industrial development, the Committee asked the Executive Director to transmit its comments and the report to the Committee on the Review and Appraisal of the Implementation of the International Development Strategy for the Third United Nations Development Decade (see Chapter I of this section).

GENERAL ASSEMBLY ACTION

On the recommendation of its Second (Economic and Financial) Committee, the General Assembly adopted resolution 38/192 without vote on 20 December 1983.

Industrial development co-operation
The General Assembly,

Recalling its resolutions 3201(S-VI) and 3202(S-VI) of 1 May 1974, containing the Declaration and the Programme of Action on the Establishment of a New International Economic Order, 3281(XXIX) of 12 December 1974, containing the Charter of Economic Rights and Duties of States, 3362(S-VII) of 16 September 1975 on development and international economic co-operation and 35/56 of 5 December 1980, the annex to which contains the International Development Strategy for the Third United Nations Development Decade, in which, *inter alia*, the importance of industrialization in the development of developing countries is stressed,

Recalling also the Lima Declaration and Plan of Action on Industrial Development and Co-operation, in which were laid down the main measures and principles for industrial development and co-operation within the framework of the establishment of the new international economic order, and the New Delhi Declaration and Plan of Action on Industrialization of Developing Countries and International Co-operation for their Industrial Development, in which a strategy was spelt out for the further industrialization of developing countries,

Recalling its resolutions 36/182 of 17 December 1981

and 37/212 of 20 December 1982 on industrial development co-operation,

Recalling Economic and Social Council resolution 1983/50 of 28 July 1983, in which the Council recommended that the work programmes of the relevant organs, organizations and bodies of the United Nations system should be geared towards supporting the full implementation of programmes of economic and technical co-operation among developing countries,

Recognizing that economic co-operation among developing countries is an integral part of a global development effort and of an interdependent world economy,

Stressing that interdependence in all sectors, including the industrial sector, should contribute to the prosperity of all countries, and believing that the industrial development of developing countries should constitute an essential part of the process of reactivation of the world economy,

Expressing its concern at the negative impact of the very difficult world economic situation on the industrialization of the developing countries and reiterating the need for a substantially increased transfer of financial and technical resources to developing countries for their accelerated industrial development,

Conscious of the role of the United Nations Industrial Development Organization as the central co-ordinating organ having primary responsibility within the United Nations system for the promotion of industrial development co-operation, for facilitating the transfer of industrial technology and for the delivery of increased technical assistance to developing countries,

Noting with concern that, in spite of the co-operative efforts of some countries, contributions to the United Nations Industrial Development Fund have remained far below the agreed desirable level of $50 million, and that the value of the Fund has declined in real terms since its establishment,

Recalling paragraph 10 of conclusion 1983/8 of the Industrial Development Board, in which the Board re-emphasized the importance and effectiveness of the Senior Industrial Development Field Advisers Programme in implementing the wide range of programmes and services rendered by the United Nations Industrial Development Organization, noting further the reduction made by the United Nations Development Programme in its allocations for senior industrial development field advisers in the biennium 1984-1985 and expressing concern at the absence of adequate and predictable resources for the Senior Industrial Development Field Advisers Programme,

Bearing in mind the positive effects, *inter alia*, of economic policies of co-operation between different economic sectors—including the public, private, co-operative, social or mixed sectors, as appropriate—as well as of sustained growth and development,

Bearing in mind that, within the framework of the new international economic order, far-reaching changes in the structure of the world economy involve the restructuring of world industry, taking fully into account the capacities and potential of the developing countries,

I

Report of the Industrial Development Board
on its seventeenth session

1. *Takes note* of the report of the Industrial Development Board;

2. *Commends* the Executive Director of the United Nations Industrial Development Organization for his efforts to enhance the role of the organization in promoting the industrialization of developing countries;

3. *Decides* that adequate resources should be provided to enable the United Nations Industrial Development Organization to implement fully its mandate, particularly in support of the activities established in priority areas: industrial technology, energy-related industrial technology, industrial production, development of human resources, special measures for least developed countries, the system of consultations and the Industrial Development Decade for Africa, declared by the Board to be one of the most important programmes of that organization;

4. *Decides* to authorize the Secretary-General to adjust, on the basis of the above agreed priorities, the proposed programme budget for the United Nations Industrial Development Organization for the biennium 1984-1985;

5. *Decides* that adequate resources should be provided from the United Nations regular budget for the United Nations Industrial Development Organization in 1984 to maintain the total staffing of the Senior Industrial Development Field Advisers Programme at the existing level of already appointed senior industrial development field advisers, in addition to the utilization in full of the allocation in the United Nations Development Programme budget, including the carry-over from 1983, as well as voluntary funding through the United Nations Industrial Development Organization;

6. *Appeals* to all States, particularly developed countries, to provide voluntary contributions for the Senior Industrial Development Field Advisers Programme, aimed at maintaining and increasing the number of posts;

7. *Invites* the United Nations Development Programme to finance the maximum possible number of senior industrial development field advisers during the biennium 1984-1985;

8. *Urges* all States, in particular developed countries, to contribute or raise their contributions to the United Nations Industrial Development Fund in order to achieve the agreed desirable annual level of $50 million;

9. *Endorses* the decisions of the Industrial Development Board, contained in its conclusion 1983/4 of 13 May 1983, concerning consultations to be held during the biennium 1984-1985;

10. *Requests* the Executive Director of the United Nations Industrial Development Organization to ensure that experts and expertise from developing as well as developed countries shall be associated with the process of preparation of consultations, having due regard for equitable geographical distribution, and that consultations shall be organized sufficiently in advance so as to allow enough time for a fuller exchange of views among participants, and expresses the hope that future consultations will result in action-oriented recommendations and conclusions;

11. *Reaffirms* its support for strengthening the system of consultations, in the light of experience gained, paying particular attention to measures that could increase the industrial capacities of developing countries;

12. *Requests* the Executive Director of the United Nations Industrial Development Organization to ensure that the documentation submitted to consultations for discussion focuses more narrowly on practical and well-defined subjects directly related to furthering progress in the industrialization of developing countries;

13. *Takes note* of the decision of the Industrial Development Board to begin an appraisal of the system of consultations at its eighteenth session on the basis of material provided by States, drawing on the experiences of their participants in the consultations, and to request the Executive Director of the United Nations Industrial Development Organization also to provide material for that appraisal;

II

Industrial Development Decade for Africa

Recalling its resolution 37/212 of 20 December 1982, and Economic and Social Council resolution 1983/70 of 29 July 1983 emphasizing the Industrial Development Decade for Africa as one of the most important programmes of the United Nations Industrial Development Organization,

Recalling further Industrial Development Board resolution 56(XVII) of 13 May 1983, in which the Board, *inter alia,* expressed its deep concern at the scarcity of resources, including resources made available by the United Nations Development Programme for the Decade, which had contributed to the limited progress achieved in the implementation of the preparatory phase of the Industrial Development Decade for Africa, whereas almost one third of the Decade had already elapsed,

Considering that the attainment of the objectives of the Lagos Plan of Action for the Implementation of the Monrovia Strategy for the Economic Development of Africa and the Final Act of Lagos will, to a large extent, depend on the sustained development of industry and on structural adjustment in the industrial sector, with emphasis on selected strategic core industries,

Noting the deteriorating economic situation in Africa and that the number of the least developed countries in Africa has increased to twenty-six out of the present global total of thirty-six,

Noting also with serious concern the slow progress being made towards the realization of the African regional target of 1.4 per cent of world industrial production by 1990,

Mindful of the high level of investment expenditure required for promoting the objectives of the Industrial Development Decade for Africa,

Noting with appreciation the decision of the African Development Bank to provide increased financing for industrial projects in Africa during its 1982-1986 programme period,

1. *Takes note with appreciation* of the second progress report on the Industrial Development Decade for Africa, prepared jointly by the Executive Director of the United Nations Industrial Development Organization and the Executive Secretary of the Economic Commission for Africa;

2. *Welcomes* the efforts made by the United Nations Industrial Development Organization to assist the African countries and intergovernmental organizations in the formulation of national and subregional programmes for the Decade, as well as in maintaining continuous and harmonious co-ordination with the secretariat of the Organization of African Unity, the Economic Commission for Africa and other relevant international organizations;

3. *Supports* Industrial Development Board resolution 56(XVII) on the Industrial Development Decade for Africa and reiterates the repeated appeals already made to the international community to increase their contributions to the industrial development of Africa within the framework of the programme for the Industrial Development Decade for Africa, with a view to accelerating the pace of industrial development, in order to ensure that the target set by the African Governments of a 1.4 per cent share of world industrial production will be achieved by the African region during the Decade;

4. *Decides* to accord high priority to the Industrial Development Decade for Africa among the programmes of the United Nations Industrial Development Organization and the Economic Commission for Africa and, consequently, requests the Secretary-General to ensure that this priority shall be fully reflected in the programme budgets of those organizations;

5. *Decides further* to increase the allocation to the United Nations Industrial Development Organization, to the extent possible through overall savings from the United Nations regular budget, by $1 million in 1984 for assistance to African countries and to intergovernmental organizations in the implementation of the programme for the Industrial Development Decade for Africa and in the popularization of the Decade, priority being accorded to the formulation of industrial policies, strategies and plans, the development of core industries, industrial manpower, technological capabilities and institutional infrastructures, the development of energy technology and equipment, the promotion of intra-African industrial co-operation, the development of the least developed countries and the mobilization of financial resources;

6. *Appeals* to all countries and institutions to increase their contributions to the United Nations Industrial Development Fund, taking into account the financial requirements of the projects directed towards the implementation of the programme for the Industrial Development Decade for Africa;

7. *Urges* the Governing Council of the United Nations Development Programme to consider increasing its allocation of financial resources for assistance to African countries and intergovernmental organizations in planning and formulating their programmes for the Industrial Development Decade for Africa and to accord high priority to industrial projects, especially for the development of core industries, in its national and regional programmes for Africa;

8. *Appeals* to donor countries, international financial institutions and regional development banks to increase the flow of financial resources for the implementation of national, subregional and regional projects and activities of the Industrial Development Decade for Africa;

9. *Requests* the Executive Director of the United Nations Industrial Development Organization, in co-operation with the Economic Commission for Africa, to submit, through the Industrial Development Board at its eighteenth session and the Economic and Social Council at its second regular session of 1984, a report to the General Assembly at its thirty-ninth session on the progress made in the implementation of the programme for the Industrial Development Decade for Africa;

III
Fourth General Conference of the United Nations Industrial Development Organization

1. *Decides* that the Fourth General Conference of the United Nations Industrial Development Organization shall be held at Vienna, at the seat of the organization, from 2 to 18 August 1984;

2. *Notes with satisfaction* the progress made in the preparations for the Conference;

3. *Recommends* that preparatory meetings should take place at the regional and interregional levels, in order that there might be the fullest possible consultation among all States prior to the convening of the Conference;

4. *Requests* the Secretary-General to invite:

(a) All States to participate actively in the Conference;

(b) Representatives of organizations that have received a standing invitation from the General Assembly to participate in the sessions and the work of all international conferences convened under its auspices, in the capacity of observers, to participate in the Conference in that capacity, in accordance with Assembly resolutions 3237(XXIX) of 22 November 1974 and 31/152 of 20 December 1976;

(c) Representatives of the national liberation movements recognized in its region by the Organization of African Unity to participate in the Conference in the capacity of observers, in accordance with General Assembly resolution 3280(XXIX) of 10 December 1974;

(d) The specialized agencies and the International Atomic Energy Agency, the regional commissions and the interested organs of the United Nations to be represented at the Conference;

(e) Interested intergovernmental organizations to be represented by observers at the Conference;

(f) Directly concerned non-governmental organizations in consultative status with the Economic and Social Council to be represented by observers at the Conference;

5. *Also requests* the Secretary-General to ensure that the necessary arrangements are made for the effective participation in the Conference of the representatives referred to in paragraph 4 (b) and (c) above, including the requisite financial provisions for their travel expenses and per diem;

6. *Requests* the Secretary-General and the Executive Director of the United Nations Industrial Development Organization to seek extrabudgetary resources for the effective participation in the Conference of the representatives of the least developed countries, including the requisite financial provisions for the travel expenses and per diem of two representatives from each of these countries.

General Assembly resolution 38/192

20 December 1983   Meeting 104   Adopted without vote

Approved by Second Committee (A/38/702Add.3) without vote, 9 December (meeting 55); draft by Vice-Chairman (A/C.2/38/L.104), based on informal consultations on draft by Mexico, for Group of 77 (A/C.2/38/L.12/Rev.1); agenda item 78 (c).
Financial implications. 5th Committee, A/38/753; 2nd Committee, A/C.5/38/99; S-G, A/C.2/38/L.32/Rev.1, A/C.2/38/L.111, A/C.5/38/93.
Meeting numbers. GA 38th session: 2nd Committee 15-24, 29, 30, 55, 56; 5th Committee 71, 73; plenary 104.

Evaluation

In 1983, the principal mechanism for reviewing the work of UNIDO as a whole remained the biannual implementation review meeting of senior officers under the chairmanship of the Executive Director. The first meeting, convened in May, reviewed technical co-operation project approvals and implementation targets for 1983 and considered other aspects of the UNIDO work programme; the second, in November, concentrated on the adverse effects of the shortfall in contributions to UNDP and set targets for 1984.

The secretariat reviewed implementation of the 1982-1983 programme budget in December and submitted a report to the Secretary-General for incorporation into his performance report to both CPC and the General Assembly in 1984.

In addition, UNIDO headquarters staff participated in 63 tripartite reviews and evaluation exercises, undertaken jointly by the Government involved, the executing agency and UNDP—the tripartite review being the principal tool for monitoring field projects.

A report describing the operation of UNIDO's new internal evaluation system for field projects, from its inception in May 1982 until February 1983,[15] was prepared by the secretariat and submitted to the Permanent Committee in April. The Committee noted that evaluation reports for 61 per cent of the 142 large-scale projects scheduled for internal evaluation had been received and welcomed the secretariat's continued efforts at increasing the compliance rate in 1983. In requesting a further report on the system's operation, the Committee reiterated that the report should include those elements it had specified in May 1982.[16] It welcomed management's use of evaluations and looked forward to information on how it was using that tool.

The third and final phase of a special joint United Nations/UNDP/UNIDO in-depth evaluation of UNDP-financed and UNIDO-executed technical co-operation activities in manufactures was completed in January 1983. The evaluation was undertaken in response to a 1980 CPC request and had been initiated in 1981[17] (see TECHNICAL CO-OPERATION below).

Institutional machinery

Proposed organizational change

The Constitution to establish UNIDO as a specialized agency, adopted by a United Nations conference in 1979,[18] had been signed by 136 States and ratified, accepted or approved by 113 of them as at 31 December 1983.

The States that had adhered to the Constitution (the 26 in italics acted during 1983) were:

Afghanistan, Algeria, Argentina, Australia, Austria, Bangladesh, Barbados, Belgium, *Benin, Bhutan,* Bolivia, Brazil, Burundi, *Canada,* Central African Republic, Chile, China, Colombia, *Congo,* Cuba, *Cyprus,* Democratic People's Republic of Korea, Democratic Yemen, Denmark, Dominica, *Dominican Republic,* Ecuador, Egypt, Ethiopia, Fiji, Finland, France, Gabon, *Germany, Federal Republic of,* Ghana, *Greece,* Guatemala, Guinea, *Guinea-Bissau,* Haiti, *Honduras, Hungary,* India, Indonesia, Iraq, *Israel,* Ivory Coast, Jamaica, Japan, Jordan, Kenya, Kuwait, Lao People's Democratic Republic, *Lebanon,* Lesotho, Libyan Arab Jamahiriya, *Luxembourg,* Madagascar, Malawi, Malaysia, Mali, Malta, Mauritania, Mauritius, Mexico, *Mozambique, Nepal,* Netherlands, Nicaragua, Niger, Nigeria, Norway, Oman, Pakistan, Panama, Paraguay, Peru, Philippines, Republic of Korea, Romania, *Rwanda,* Saint Lucia, *Senegal,* Seychelles, *Sierra Leone,* Somalia, Spain, Sri Lanka, Sudan, Suriname, Swaziland, Sweden, Switzerland, Syrian Arab Republic, Thailand, Togo, Trinidad and Tobago, Tunisia, Turkey, *Uganda,* United Arab Emirates, *United Kingdom,* United Republic of Cameroon, United Republic of Tanzania, *United States,* Upper Volta, Uruguay, *Venezuela, Viet Nam, Yemen,* Yugoslavia, Zaire, Zambia.

The following 23 States had signed but not formally adhered to the Constitution as at 31 December (the 3 in italics acted during 1983):

Angola, Antigua and Barbuda, Bulgaria, Byelorussian SSR, *Cape Verde,* Chad, Comoros, Czechoslovakia, Djibouti, El Salvador, *Equatorial Guinea,* German Democratic Republic, Iran, Ireland, Italy, Liberia, Mongolia, Morocco, Poland, Portugal, *Sao Tome and Principe,* Ukrainian SSR, USSR.

Action by UNIDO meeting. Pursuant to article 25 of the Constitution and to a December 1982 General Assembly resolution,[19] a formal meeting was convened at Vienna, from 16 to 20 May 1983, on the conversion of UNIDO from an organ of the Assembly into a specialized agency. The meeting adopted a number of conclusions by consensus on the new UNIDO.

Apart from arrangements stipulated by the Constitution, the conclusions included an agreement that ongoing programmes should not be disrupted in the transition period. Existing arrangements governing the United Nations Industrial Development Fund would apply to the new Industrial Development Fund; every effort was to be made to avoid reducing activities financed by the UNIDO regular programme of technical co-operation at the time of transition; and a recommendation was to be made to the Assembly to transfer a share of the Working Capital Fund to the new agency. The agency's structure would be determined by the guiding principles established by the Constitution, Assembly resolutions, the UNIDO General Conferences and the Industrial Development Board; questions relating to staff regulations and conditions of service would continue under existing rules. A provisional agenda of the first General Conference of the new agency was drawn.

A recommendation was made that the Economic and Social Council set out the terms of reference of the Committee on Negotiations with Intergovernmental Agencies, which would draft the text of a relationship agreement between the United Nations and UNIDO as a specialized agency. Documentation was to be prepared by the UNIDO secretariat to permit a speedy decision with regard to the agency's participation in the International Civil Service Commission, the United Nations Joint Staff Pension Fund and the Joint Inspection Unit, and as to whether it should submit to the Administrative Tribunal of the United Nations or of the International Labour Organisation. Arrangements for the administration and management of common services at the United Nations Office at Vienna would be modified and a new headquarters agreement with the host country should be concluded. It was agreed that the date of entry into force of the Constitution should be fixed only when the new agency's financial viability had been ensured.

The formal meeting's report was transmitted to the Assembly by the Secretary-General through a note of 17 August,[20] and to the one-day closing meeting—to be convened in New York at a date to be determined. The closing meeting would execute individual notifications to the Secretary-General of agreement for the Constitution's entry into force.

GENERAL ASSEMBLY ACTION

Acting without vote on the recommendation of its Second Committee, the General Assembly adopted resolution 38/193 on 20 December 1983.

Conversion of the United Nations Industrial Development Organization into a specialized agency

The General Assembly,

Recalling its resolution 34/96 of 13 December 1979,

Bearing in mind the Constitution of the United Nations Industrial Development Organization, which has been ratified, accepted or approved by more than the minimum number of States whose agreement is required for its entry into force,

Recalling its resolution 37/213 of 20 December 1982 in which it laid down the schedule of consultations as required in accordance with article 25, paragraph 1, of the Constitution,

1. *Takes note* of the report of the formal meeting on the conversion of the United Nations Industrial Development Organization into a specialized agency, held at Vienna from 16 to 20 May 1983;

2. *Urges* all States that have not yet done so to ratify the Constitution of the United Nations Industrial Development Organization;

3. *Requests* the Secretary-General:

(a) To undertake consultations with States that have deposited instruments of ratification, acceptance or approval, with a view to determining, *inter alia*, if financial viability is adequately ensured, and, subsequently, to convene the one-day meeting foreseen in paragraph 1 (c) of General Assembly resolution 37/213 to execute individual notifications to the Secretary-General for the entry into force of the Constitution of the United Nations Industrial Development Organization;

(b) To undertake, also, consultations with all interested States with a view to facilitating early ratification of the Constitution of the United Nations Industrial Development Organization by those States that have not yet done so;

4. *Invites* the competent organs of the new United Nations Industrial Development Organization to consider without delay the question of establishing a working capital fund, and to this end the present United Nations Industrial Development Organization secretariat should study possible modalities for that purpose and report thereon to the first General Conference of the United Nations Industrial Development Organization;

5. *Requests* the Secretary-General to initiate the necessary action to implement the recommendations made in paragraphs 27 and 29 of the report of the formal meeting on the conversion of the United Nations Industrial Development Organization into a specialized agency;

6. *Decides* that adequate resources be provided in the regular budget of the United Nations Industrial Development Organization for the biennium 1984-1985 to ensure the provision of the necessary funds, in accordance with paragraph 7 of General Assembly resolution 34/96, for the first General Conference of the United Nations Industrial Development Organization and other costs associated with the conversion of the organization into a specialized agency;

7. *Decides further* that the financial implications pertaining to paragraph 6 above will be considered by the General Assembly at its thirty-ninth session.

General Assembly resolution 38/193

20 December 1983   Meeting 104   Adopted without vote

Approved by Second Committee (A/38/702/Add.3) without vote, 9 December (meeting 55); draft by Vice-Chairman (A/C.2/38/L.105), based on informal consultations on draft by Mexico, for Group of 77 (A/C.2/38/L.13); agenda item 78 (c).
Financial implications. 5th Committee, A/38/753; S-G, A/C.2/38/L.33, A/C.5/38/103.
Meeting numbers. GA 38th session: 2nd Committee 30, 55, 56; 5th Committee 73; plenary 104.

Financial implications for the 1984-1985 budget. In a report of 7 December 1983 to the General Assembly,[21] the Secretary-General described the impact of the conversion of UNIDO into a specialized agency on existing arrangements, on a cost-sharing basis, for the management and administration of common services shared by IAEA, UNIDO and other United Nations units at the United Nations Office at Vienna (UNOV). Under these arrangements—formalized in a March 1977 memorandum of understanding by the Secretary-General, the IAEA Director-General and the UNIDO Executive Director—IAEA was responsible for computer and library services, printing and reproduction, commissary, and medical services; UNIDO for buildings management and operations, catering facilities and language training; and UNOV for security and safety. With the subsequent transfer of other United Nations units to Vienna, UNIDO had been assigned additional responsibility for finance, personnel, public information, and conference and general services; in most cases, it had been provided with resources for the additional work-load.

Emphasizing that the conversion of UNIDO should not alter the premise on which the common services were based, namely, that they should not be duplicated, the Secretary-General suggested modifications entailing revised estimates under the UNIDO and public information sections of the proposed United Nations programme budget for the biennium 1984-1985. He suggested creating separate United Nations services for public information and personnel services, to be initiated forthwith, establishing a joint co-ordinating mechanism for the administration of conference services, and continuing financial and general services by UNIDO on a reimbursable basis.

GENERAL ASSEMBLY ACTION

On the recommendation of its Fifth (Administrative and Budgetary) Committee, the General Assembly adopted resolution 38/234, section XVIII, without vote on 20 December 1983.

Conversion of the United Nations Industrial Development Organization into a specialized agency
[*The General Assembly . . .*]
Takes note of the report of the Secretary-General;
. . .

General Assembly resolution 38/234, section XVIII
20 December 1983   Meeting 104   Adopted without vote

Approved by Fifth Committee (A/38/760) without vote, 19 December (meeting 73); report of Secretary-General (A/C.5/38/87); agenda item 109.
Meeting numbers. GA 38th session: 5th Committee 73; plenary 104.

Appointment of the Committee on Negotiations with Intergovernmental Agencies

On 4 February 1983, the Economic and Social Council agreed to reconstitute the Committee on Negotiations with Intergovernmental Agencies (see also APPENDIX III), to prepare a relationship agreement between the United Nations and UNIDO as a specialized agency.

ECONOMIC AND SOCIAL COUNCIL ACTION

The Council adopted decision 1983/105 without vote.

Arrangements for the negotiation of an agreement between the United Nations and the United Nations Industrial Development Organization
At its 2nd plenary meeting, on 4 February 1983, the Council, pursuant to paragraph 11 of General Assembly resolution 34/96 of 13 December 1979, in which the Assembly requested the Council to arrange for the negotiation with the United Nations Industrial Development Organization of an agreement to constitute it as a specialized agency, in accordance with Articles 57 and 63 of the Charter of the United Nations:

(a) Authorized the President of the Council to appoint from among the States members of the Council, in consultation with the Chairmen of the regional groups, the members of the Committee on Negotiations with Intergovernmental Agencies;

(b) Decided to consider at a subsequent session the programme of the Committee.

Economic and Social Council decision 1983/105
Adopted without vote

Draft orally proposed by President; agenda item 2.
Meeting number. ESC 2.

Eligibility for membership in the Industrial Development Board

As a result of the admission to the United Nations of Saint Christopher and Nevis in September 1983 (see POLITICAL AND SECURITY QUESTIONS, Chapter XI), the General Assembly decided to include that country in the lists of States eligible for membership in the Industrial Development Board.

GENERAL ASSEMBLY ACTION

On the recommendation of its Second Committee, the General Assembly adopted resolution 38/194 without vote on 20 December.

Revision of the lists of States eligible for membership in the Industrial Development Board
The General Assembly,
Recalling section II, paragraph 4, of its resolution 2152(XXI) of 17 November 1966 on the United Nations Industrial Development Organization,
Decides to include Saint Christopher and Nevis in list C of the annex to resolution 2152(XXI).

General Assembly resolution 38/194
20 December 1983   Meeting 104   Adopted without vote

Approved by Second Committee (A/38/702/Add.3) without vote, 9 December (meeting 55); oral proposal by Chairman; agenda item 78 *(c)*.
Meeting numbers. GA 38th session: 2nd Committee 55; plenary meeting 104.

Preparations for the 1984 General Conference

As provided for by the General Assembly in 1982,[9] five high-level expert group meetings were organized in 1983 on the following topics proposed for the Fourth (1984) General Conference of UNIDO: technology, strategies and policies, human resources development, industrial co-operation among developing countries, and energy and industrialization (see Chapter X of this section). The meetings were to examine issues before the Conference and to provide a means for wide participation in the preparatory process. The contribution of United Nations bodies to those expert meetings and towards documentation for the

Conference was discussed at an inter-agency meeting held at Vienna in March. The open-ended working group established by the Board in 1982[22] held its third meeting on 8 July 1983, also at Vienna, to discuss pre-Conference activities.

Acting as the Preparatory Committee for the Fourth General Conference of UNIDO, the Board, on 13 May,[23] took note of a progress report on preparatory arrangements by the Executive Director[24] and recommended that the Assembly, at its 1983 session, determine the dates for the Conference.

The Board's Permanent Committee, at its November/December session,[5] took note of a subsequent report on Conference arrangements by the Executive Director,[25] describing the outcome of the expert meetings. The Committee expressed appreciation for the meetings' reports and requested the Executive Director to ensure completion of all arrangements for the Conference as scheduled. It welcomed Austria's offer to host the Conference and recommended that the Board President arrange informal consultations to identify areas of potential agreement on the items of the provisional agenda.

GENERAL ASSEMBLY ACTION

On 20 December 1983, the General Assembly decided that the Fourth General Conference of UNIDO be held at Vienna from 2 to 18 August 1984. It recommended that preparatory regional and interregional meetings be held to permit the fullest prior consultation among States and requested that extrabudgetary resources be sought for the participation of representatives from LDCs. These actions were contained in section III of Assembly resolution 38/192 on industrial development co-operation (see PROGRAMME POLICY above).

Co-ordination in the UN system

Despite co-ordination efforts and increased inter-agency co-operation, a shortfall in 1983 in UNDP resources for technical co-operation activities resulted in fewer jointly executed projects than in 1982. Co-operation in studies and research programmes fared somewhat better. This assessment was made by a UNIDO secretariat report on co-ordination activities with other United Nations bodies and organizations in industrial development covering November 1982 to October 1983.[26] During that period, seven inter-secretariat co-ordinating meetings and six meetings of joint technical working groups had taken place; for budgetary reasons UNIDO had declined 200 out of 373 invitations to conferences and meetings of other United Nations organizations.

Apart from policy co-ordination, UNIDO maintained co-ordination and close co-operation with the regional commissions and other United Nations bodies through its System of Consultations (see above) and in such areas as industrial manpower training, science and technology for development, and energy, as well as in activities related to the Industrial Development Decade for Africa and to preparations for the Fourth General Conference of UNIDO.

At the close of its November/December session, the Permanent Committee of the Industrial Development Board,[5] having reviewed the report, requested the secretariat to continue co-ordinating industrial development activities within the United Nations system, taking into account the comments made, and to draw up a programme for UNIDO's co-ordinating role. It reiterated its request that future reports on co-ordination include an analysis of costs, benefits and problems encountered, as well as co-ordination efforts in respect of economic co-operation among developing countries.

Financial questions

UN Industrial Development Fund

In 1983, the UNIDO secretariat continued to improve project design and establish more systematic monitoring and reporting of the financial and substantive aspects of projects financed by the United Nations Industrial Development Fund (UNIDF). These measures, together with continued dialogue with current and potential donors, were aimed at producing more effective programming and donor confidence in the Fund's management and use, according to a report by the UNIDO Executive Director.[27]

Approved for UNIDF financing were 160 projects with a total value of $15.3 million, including overheads. Of these, 124 projects, valued at $7.3 million, were financed from the Fund's general-purpose segment, and 36, valued at $8.0 million, from the special-purpose convertible segment.

The nine priority programme components endorsed by the Industrial Development Board continued to be applied to Fund activities. Within that framework, emphasis was given to innovative pilot projects of relevance to the largest number of developing countries. Among these were a global coconut technology consultancy service; a model scheme to utilize *Balanites aegyptiaca* fruits for producing edible oils and pharmaceutical raw materials, based on a 1982 study;[28] and programmes for the production and application of non-metallics in agriculture (activated bentonite and expanded perlite, for soil improvement and as fertilizer carriers and animal feed additives), and for blending alcohols with diesel fuels. Special attention was given to Africa within the context of the Industrial Development Decade for Africa, as well as to LDCs by inviting them to participate in many interregional programmes.

CONTRIBUTIONS TO THE UN INDUSTRIAL DEVELOPMENT FUND, 1983 AND 1984
(as at 31 December 1983; in US dollar equivalent)

Country	1983 payment	1984 pledge	Country	1983 payment	1984 pledge
Afghanistan	3,000	1,500	Malawi	2,273	2,344
Algeria	125,079	40,000	Malta	1,378	—
Angola	20,000	—	Mauritius	914	836
Argentina	59,100	—	Mexico	15,000	—
Australia	294,557	138,889	Mongolia	2,115	2,169
Austria	595,165	655,738	Morocco	8,438	6,417
Bahrain	5,000	5,000	Mozambique	4,872	—
Bangladesh	3,950	2,200	Nepal	700	—
Barbados	4,000	—	Oman	24,000	—
Belgium	984,170	450,704	Pakistan	63,577	75,019
Bhutan	3,066	1,200	Panama	1,000	1,000
Bolivia	5,000	—	Peru	—	20,000
Botswana	—	4,587	Philippines	18,474	13,500
Brazil	—	15,000	Poland	225,568	157,895
Bulgaria	103,627	101,523	Portugal	14,435	15,000
Burma	1,986	1,000	Qatar	30,000	—
Burundi	1,117	—	Republic of Korea	30,000	30,000
Chile	10,000	10,000	Rwanda	4,000	4,000
China	333,334	403,030	Saudi Arabia	1,000,000	—
Colombia	5,708	5,700	Senegal	—	4,000
Congo	2,614	10,000	Sierra Leone	7,200	—
Cuba	23,491	24,202	Sri Lanka	2,882	3,000
Czechoslovakia	163,399	155,763	Sudan	—	11,719
Democratic Yemen	3,637	—	Suriname	4,000	—
Dominica	—	1,852	Swaziland	(183)	—
Ecuador	5,000	5,000	Sweden	325,070	—
Egypt	—	72,492	Switzerland	208,990	2,112,676*
Ethiopia	—	1,122	Syrian Arab Republic	5,372	—
Fiji	1,100	1,050	Thailand	23,084	23,084
France	844,209	1,069,182	Togo	(287)	1,257
German Democratic Republic	526,619	507,692	Trinidad and Tobago	40,000	20,000
Germany, Federal Republic of	2,293,605	2,461,538	Tunisia	50,433	22,101
Ghana	7,273	—	Turkey	200,170	204,082
Greece	22,800	—	Uganda	320	—
Guatemala	5,000	—	USSR	704,225	657,895
Guinea	6,072	—	United Kingdom	77,281	—
Guinea-Bissau	(7)	—	United Republic of Cameroon	6,376	—
Hungary	64,643	68,074	United Republic of Tanzania	1,311	1,643
India	1,000,000	1,000,000	Upper Volta	11,053	2,513
Indonesia	50,000	50,000	Venezuela	20,963	—
Italy	1,933,831	2,515,723	Viet Nam	861	1,000
Ivory Coast	128,928	152,490	Yugoslavia	72,502	161,435
Jamaica	8,000	4,000	Zaire	50,800	3,000
Japan	201,312	135,992	Zambia	12,605	11,194
Jordan	6,000	—	Zimbabwe	13,020	11,538
Kenya	18,143	17,037			
Kuwait	75,000	75,000	Subtotal	13,246,627	13,755,543
Lao People's Democratic Republic	1,500	1,500			
Lebanon	—	2,000	*Organization*		
Lesotho	2,000	2,000			
Liberia	2,500	—	Arab Industrial Development Organization	29,892	—
Luxembourg	4,401	5,446			
Madagascar	2,906	—	Total	13,276,519	13,755,543

*Including $1,056,338 pledged for 1985.

A total of $13,276,519 was paid in voluntary contributions to the Fund in 1983 by 86 countries and one organization, and a total of $13,755,543 was pledged for 1984 by 68 countries, as at 31 December 1983 (see table above).[29]

A review of yearly pledges by Fund components revealed a decline in 1983 in the general-purpose non-convertible segment, attributable in part to exchange rate fluctuations and in part to a switch in pledges from the general- to the special-purpose segment, although the combined total of both segments remained virtually static. Saudi Arabia remained the largest donor to the general-purpose convertible segment, with an annual pledge of $1 million since the Fund's creation in 1976,[30] fol-

lowed by India; together they continued to provide more than 70 per cent of that segment's total resources.

At its 1983 session, the Board, having considered the Executive Director's report on the Fund's programme for 1984 and plan for 1984-1985,[31] approved the proposed programme and plan, including establishment of an operational reserve equal to 5 per cent of the total annual pledge to the general-purpose convertible segment to ensure the Fund's liquidity.[32] The Board agreed to continue delegating authority to the Executive Director to approve projects for financing under the Fund in 1984-1985, and took note of the Special Financial Rules promulgated by the Secretary-

General to be applied to the Fund.[33] Noting the decline in the value of the Fund in real terms since its inception, the Board urged all countries, in particular the industrialized ones, to contribute or raise their contributions with maximum flexibility so as to achieve the agreed desirable annual funding level of $50 million.

This appeal for increased funding was repeated by the General Assembly in resolution 38/192, section I (see PROGRAMME POLICY above).

REFERENCES

[1]YUN 1975, p. 473. [2]ID/B/320. [3]A/38/16. [4] ID/B/307 & Corr.1. [5]ID/B/309. [6]YUN 1980, p. 653. [7]*Ibid.*, p. 644. [8]YUN 1982, p. 757, ESC res. 1982/66 A, 30 Jul. 1982. [9]*Ibid.*, p. 758, GA res. 37/212, sect. I, 20 Dec. 1982. [10]YUN 1980, p. 656. [11]*Ibid.*, p. 503, GA res. 35/56, annex, 5 Dec. 1980. [12]ID/B/295 & Corr.1 & Add.1 & Add.1/Corr.1 & Add.2 & Add.2/Corr.1,2. [13]A/38/16 (conclusion 1983/2). [14]ID/B/C.3/126. [15]ID/B/C.3/120. [16]YUN 1982, p. 759. [17]YUN 1981, p. 580. [18]YUN 1979, p. 618. [19]YUN 1982, p. 760, GA res. 37/213, 20 Dec. 1982. [20]A/38/141. [21]A/C.5/38/87. [22]YUN 1982, p. 761. [23]A/38/16 (conclusion 1983/6). [24]ID/B/306. [25]ID/B/C.3/123 & Add.1. [26]ID/B/C.3/125. [27]ID/B/325. [28]YUN 1982, p. 776. [29]A/39/5/Add.9. [30]YUN 1976, p. 428, GA res. 31/202, 22 Dec. 1976. [31]ID/B/303. [32]A/38/16 (conclusion 1983/9). [33]ST/SGB/UNIDF/Financial Rules/4(1982).

PUBLICATIONS

Industry and Development, No. 8 (ID/SER.M/8 & Add.1), Sales No. E.83.II.B.1 & Add.; No. 9 (ID/SER.M/9 & Add.1 & Erratum), Sales No. E.83.II.B.4 & Add. & Erratum. *Rules of Procedure of the Industrial Development Board* (ID/B/18/Rev.7 & Corr.1, Amend.1), Sales No. E.83.II.B.2 & corrigendum & amendment. *Industry in a Changing World: Special Issue of the Industrial Development Survey for the Fourth General Conference of UNIDO* (ID/CONF.5/2-ID/304), Sales No. E.83.II.B.6.

Industrial development activities

Technical co-operation

In 1983, 1,580 projects were completed or being implemented under the UNIDO programme of technical co-operation. Of these, 122 were of more than $1 million in value, 453 of more than $150,000 and 1,005 below that value. Approved were 509 new projects with a total value of $70.5 million, compared with 717 the previous year with a value of $99.3 million, a 29 per cent drop in technical assistance delivery.

Programme expenditures for the year totalled some $78 million, a decrease from the $91.9 million recorded for 1982.[1] By main programme component, chemical industries accounted for $17.1 million; agro-industries, $10.9 million; institutional infrastructure, $10.4 million; engineering industries, $9.5 million; training, $6.1 million; metallurgical industries, $5.7 million; feasibility studies, $4.5 million; industrial planning, $4.4 million; and factory establishment, $3.2 million. Some $6.2 million represented the share of other related activities.

Africa accounted for $27.5 million (35.2 per cent); Asia and the Pacific, $24.7 million (31.6 per cent); the Americas, $10.0 million (12.8 per cent); the Arab States (excluding those in Africa), $4.8 million (6.2 per cent); Europe, $2.8 million (3.6 per cent); and global and interregional, $8.2 million (10.5 per cent).

By project component, personnel accounted for $42.1 million (53.9 per cent); equipment, $14.7 million (18.9 per cent); fellowships and training, $11.4 million (14.6 per cent); sub-contracts, $7.8 million (10.0 per cent); and miscellaneous, $2.0 million (2.6 per cent).

Notable among UNIDO technical co-operation activities in Africa were the continued formulation of industrial master plans defining priority industrial subsectors, development of agro- and small-scale industries, improvement of repair and maintenance capabilities, and development of national standardization bodies and of new and renewable energy sources, including agricultural wastes. In Asia and the Pacific, as in Africa, emphasis was placed on industrial planning, as well as on development of national management consultancy capacities, particularly for the rehabilitation of existing enterprises, fuller utilization of capacities and improvement of productivity. Activities on behalf of Arab States continued to centre on strengthening industrial institutional infrastructure, developing industrial manpower at all levels, promoting new industries and improving the performance of existing ones. Activities in European countries were aimed at upgrading national institutions for the development of new and advanced technologies for their own needs and eventually to assist other developing countries.

Approximately 67.8 per cent of UNIDO technical co-operation was financed by UNDP, including UNDP-administered trust funds; 27.1 per cent from UNIDF, various trust funds and other sources; and 5.1 per cent from the United Nations regular budget. UNIDO continued to be the third largest executing agency for projects financed by UNDP.

United Nations financing amounted to some $4 million. Almost one half went for personnel training in developing countries through fellowships, group training programmes and study tours, and strengthening training facilities. One fourth of the amount was spent for LDC needs, including national and regional training programmes, establishment and strengthening of small-scale industries, construction of pilot plants and development of institutional infrastructure to explore, exploit and process natural resources.

Tentative allocations of the UNIDO regular programme of technical co-operation for 1984-1985 as proposed by the Executive Director[2] were considered by the Permanent Committee of the Industrial Development Board at its April session.[3] In recommending approval of the proposed allocations, the Committee also proposed that the Board seek to maintain the programme's real value, in particular the component on special needs of LDCs. The Executive Director was to be invited to consider increasing allocations for co-operation among developing countries and group training by redeploying resources within the programme. He was to be asked to report on the programme's real value, taking 1973 as the base year.

Evaluation study

A summary of the conclusions and recommendations of the third and final phase of a special joint United Nations/UNDP/UNIDO in-depth evaluation of UNDP-financed technical co-operation activities of UNIDO in manufactures, together with the comments of UNIDO and UNDP,[4] was submitted by the Secretary-General to CPC at the first part (May/June) of its 1983 session. The evaluation, undertaken in response to a 1980 CPC request, had been completed in January 1983. The full study was distributed shortly thereafter to senior policy-level officials of the participating organizations, as well as to the UNIDO Programme Planning and Budgeting Board in its capacity as the steering committee for evaluation.

The evaluation expressed concern at the lack of definition of responsibilities at the operational level and of results-oriented data from the field. It concluded that, due to the broad and varied nature of UNIDO technical assistance in manufactures—with 1,200 active projects—there were inadequacies in current UNDP and UNIDO staff resources and insufficient participation of the industrial sector in project design. It recommended that UNDP assume the primary responsibility in the tripartite system.

In an October note on the evaluation,[5] UNIDO pointed out two findings of interest: one, that since a high percentage (depending on project category, between 50 and 67 per cent) of the projects examined were found to have achieved the planned degree of impact, the tripartite system, developed pragmatically over the years, could be seen to have its merits; and two, that weaknesses identified at several stages of the project cycle, especially at project identification and design, were generally attributed to difficulties affecting the United Nations development system as a whole rather than to those peculiar to the industrial sector or UNIDO.

The Secretary-General noted that the evaluation raised fundamental policy issues beyond the manufacturing sector. In view of these and the concerns expressed by the UNDP Administrator

and the UNIDO Executive Director—on the evaluating team's approach, its methodology, its conclusions and their implications—the Secretary-General believed that the UNDP Governing Council and the Industrial Development Board should examine the findings before he submitted a comprehensive report to CPC in 1984.

Accepting that opinion, CPC decided on 19 May[6] to transmit the summary and CPC comments to the UNDP Governing Council and the Board's Permanent Committee for consideration. It recommended that the complete evaluation be made available to Member States.

On 24 June,[7] the Governing Council requested the UNDP Administrator to examine further the evaluation's conclusions and recommendations in order to determine those on which action could be taken and to improve project identification and implementation in the industrial sector; the Council decided that a report on the results of this further examination should be prepared for its consideration in 1984 and submission to CPC.

The Permanent Committee asked the UNIDO Executive Director on 2 December[8] to take action on those recommendations he deemed feasible in the light of comments made and to transmit those comments to the Secretary-General, to be taken into account in his comprehensive report on the subject to CPC.

ECONOMIC AND SOCIAL COUNCIL ACTION

By section II of resolution 1983/49 of 28 July, the Economic and Social Council regretted that the comprehensive outcome of the evaluation study had not been submitted formally to CPC as a report of the Secretary-General, whom it therefore requested so to do when CPC resumed its 1983 session (in August/September), on the understanding that his comprehensive report would be submitted in 1984. He was further requested to ensure that the procedure followed in this instance—submitting the evaluation study to organizations covered by it before formally submitting it to CPC—would not constitute a precedent for future evaluations.

GENERAL ASSEMBLY ACTION

The General Assembly, in section IV of resolution 38/227 A of 20 December, endorsed the CPC recommendations and the Council's decisions on the study. The Assembly requested the Secretary-General to submit his comprehensive report on the evaluation to CPC in 1984, taking into account the views of the Industrial Development Board's Permanent Committee at its November/December session and of the UNDP Governing Council at its next (1984) organizational session.

Further action. Pursuant to the Economic and Social Council's request of 28 July, the Secretary-

UNIDO TECHNICAL CO-OPERATION AND SUPPORT EXPENDITURES
BY PROGRAMME COMPONENT, 1983
(as at 31 December 1983; in thousands of US dollars)

Programme component	Technical co-operation	Support
Policy-making organs	—	1,733
Executive direction and management*	4	1,797
Policy co-ordination	578	—
Economic co-operation among developing countries	—	542
Field reports monitoring	—	997
Inter-agency programme co-ordination	—	513
Least developed countries	—	568
Negotiations	—	2,072
New York Liaison Office	—	419
Non-governmental organizations	—	391
Programme development and evaluation	—	1,666
Programme formulation and direction	—	849
Subtotal	578	8,017
Industrial operations		
Agro-industries	10,919	1,081
Chemical industries	17,115	1,678
Engineering industries	9,544	944
Factory establishment and management	3,213	868
Feasibility studies	4,516	656
Industrial planning	4,389	682
Institutional infrastructure	10,402	1,130
Investment co-operative programme	2,774	1,385
Metallurgical industries	5,682	684
Programme formulation and direction	1,150	1,181
Project personnel recruitment†	—	1,516
Purchase and contract	—	1,144
Training	6,060	1,074
Subtotal	75,764	14,023
Industrial studies		
Development and transfer of technology	621	1,056
Global and conceptual studies	40	1,113
Industrial and Technological Information Bank	—	381
Industrial information and information services	11	553
Programme formulation and direction	389	1,315
Regional and country studies	366	1,466
Sectoral studies	59	1,555
Technological advisory services	22	238
Subtotal	1,508	7,677
Conference services, public information and external relations	142	—
Conference service	—	6,826
Governments and intergovernmental organizations relations	—	327
IDB secretariat	—	280
Programme formulation and direction	—	274
Public information	—	621
Subtotal	142	8,328
Administrative and common services		
Electronic data processing	—	1,403
Financial service	—	2,379
General services	—	1,694
Personnel service	—	2,272
Programme direction	—	959
Subtotal	—	8,707
Unspecified	23	—
Total	78,019	50,282

*Including UNIDO representation at Geneva.
†Including Technical Assistance Recruitment Service at Geneva and in New York.
SOURCE: ID/B/320.

General submitted his formal report on the evaluation of the UNDP-financed, UNIDO-executed technical co-operation activities in manufactures[9] to CPC at the second part (August/September) of its 1983 session. In noting this submission,[6] CPC regretted that the report failed to refer to certain points made by the Council regarding the importance it attached to evaluation procedures, the formal submission to CPC of the evaluation as a report of the Secretary-General, and the need to ensure that the procedure followed in this case—submitting the evaluation study to organizations covered by it before formally submitting it to CPC—would not be a precedent for future evaluations.

Training of personnel

In 1983, the UNIDO programme of technical co-operation among developing countries emphasized the training of trainers and organization of training, in an effort to accelerate development of human skills. Increased LDC participation in training activities continued to be a goal. Priority was given to areas with a potential multiplier effect, and emphasis was placed on systematic approaches to curriculum design, training methodologies and techniques, and development of training aids.

Expenditures for the fellowships and training component of all technical co-operation projects implemented by UNIDO in 1983 amounted to $11.4 million, against $12 million in 1982.[10] Of the 1983 amount, fellowships and study tours accounted for $6.7 million, and group training programmes and meetings for $4.7 million.

Compared with 1982, the number of individual training programmes (fellowships) started in 1983 decreased by 2 per cent (1,220, down from 1,246), while the number of placement arrangements by host countries increased by 5.9 per cent (1,949, up from 1,841). Of these, 424 were arranged in developing countries, 177 of the trainees came from LDCs and 150 were women. The trend towards study tours by high-level industrial personnel continued, with a 40:60 ratio between fellowships and study tours.

Among activities undertaken in 1983 were a regional workshop organized for selected African countries on industrial energy management (Zambia); group training programmes in energy conservation in the metallurgical (United Kingdom), ceramic (Czechoslovakia) and cement (France) industries; waste-heat recovery in industrial processes (Australia); maintenance and repair of railway equipment (Belgium, Ivory Coast, Upper Volta) and of ships and smaller craft (Belgium); packaging and conditioning technologies (Italy); environmental assessment and management of air and water pollution by industry (Belgium); computerized maintenance systems in metallurgy at the interregional level, for Asian and Arab countries (Czechoslovakia); and management of public enterprises (Colombia, Tunisia). The concept of energy management was introduced in in-plant group training programmes on: iron and steel, and electric welding (USSR); diesel engine operation and maintenance (China, Czechoslovakia); industrial planning (German Democratic Republic); and cement, iron and steel, and sugar (Turkey).

In keeping with the recommendations of the First (1982) Consultation on the Training of Industrial Manpower,[10] a methodology to assess the training needs of the iron and steel industry was being formulated in 1983. Steps were taken to identify national training needs and to establish an information base on the supply of and demand for training facilities (Nepal, Pakistan); a similar activity aimed at upgrading managerial skills was carried out by a multidisciplinary team in selected LDCs (Mali, Mauritania, Niger, Senegal). In addition, seminars to examine methodologies for the training of trainers were organized (Colombia, Mexico, Tunisia, USSR, Yugoslavia).

A meeting on Accelerated Development of Human Resources for Industrial Development (Yaoundé, United Republic of Cameroon, 30 May–3 June)[11] examined developing countries' problems in this area. One of five expert group meetings convened in 1983 in preparation for the Fourth (1984) General Conference of UNIDO, the meeting was attended by 50 experts from 28 countries.

The meeting concluded that assimilation of modern technology and upgrading of traditional technology depended on developing countries' ability to develop and utilize a range of skilled manpower. National policies and plans for human resources development should be integrated with policies for education and economic development. International organizations, particularly UNIDO, had an important role to play in assisting those countries, especially LDCs, in their development of human resources. Notable among the meeting's recommendations was for each developing country to establish a central body to co-ordinate and oversee the various national, institutional and infrastructural mechanisms for human resources development for industrialization. The need for a national manpower information data base for effective manpower planning was stressed, as was co-operation among developing countries through a network of national training institutions.

SIDFA Programme

In 1983, the Senior Industrial Development Field Advisers (SIDFAs) Programme continued to assist in programming and implementing technical co-operation projects. As focal points of UNIDO activities in countries of their assignment, SIDFAs promoted co-ordination with Governments and UNDP resident representatives, participation in the UNIDO System of Consultations (see below) and project evaluation. They assisted in implementing field projects on energy, investment promotion and

technology transfer, and represented UNIDO at 56 meetings.

A second regional SIDFA meeting for Africa (Douala, United Republic of Cameroon, December) discussed UNIDO programmes in the context of the Industrial Development Decade for Africa (1980-1990) proclaimed by the General Assembly in 1980,[12] with a view to strengthening and harmonizing them. These included industrial planning, rural development, energy, integration of women in industrial development, co-operation among developing countries, and preparations for the Fourth (1984) General Conference of UNIDO. Project implementation was reviewed and sources of financing other than UNDP were studied.

On 13 May,[13] the Industrial Development Board, re-emphasizing the importance of the SIDFA Programme and reiterating that it required strengthening, invited the UNDP Governing Council to finance the maximum number of SIDFAs in 1984-1985 and called on member States, in particular the developed ones, to provide voluntary contributions to permit the number of posts in the Programme to be maintained or increased. It decided to convey to the General Assembly in 1983 the views expressed at the current Board session, including concern over the absence of reliable resources for the Programme in the United Nations budget, and suggestions for such alternative financing sources as the UNDP indicative planning figures, the developing countries themselves and special-purpose contributions.

The UNDP Council, on 24 June,[14] approved $4.06 million to cover the net costs to UNDP for SIDFA services during 1984-1985, subject to resource availability. It reaffirmed that priority be given to those countries which had agreed to finance some or all of the cost of those services from national indicative planning figures and/or other national sources. Like the Board, it called on member States to provide voluntary contributions to the SIDFA Programme.

These actions, as reflected in the reports of the Board and of the Council's Budgetary and Finance Committee,[15] were drawn to the Assembly's attention in an October note by the Secretary-General.[16]

GENERAL ASSEMBLY ACTION

In section I of resolution 38/192 of 20 December, the General Assembly, repeating the appeal for voluntary contributions and the invitation to UNDP to finance the maximum number of SIDFAs in 1984-1985, decided that adequate resources should be provided from the United Nations regular budget for UNIDO in 1984 to maintain the SIDFA Programme's current staffing, in addition to full utilization of the allocation in the UNDP budget, as well as voluntary funding through UNIDO.

The Assembly, in resolution 38/236 on the 1984-1985 budget, appropriated an additional $1 million to UNIDO for 1984 from the United Nations regular budget, thereby financing nine SIDFA posts and operational costs including 18 local staff.

Special Industrial Services

The Special Industrial Services (SIS) programme, funding created to permit action in areas not covered by existing financing methods, was designed primarily to enable UNIDO to meet urgent requirements through the rapid provision of experts to developing countries.

During 1983, 73 requests were received from 53 countries; 34 new projects were approved and 30 projects were extended. Funding for these approvals and extensions amounted to slightly over $1 million. Technical assistance under the programme continued, as in 1982, to be concentrated in the chemical, metallurgical, agro- and engineering industries. There was an increase in assistance in industrial planning, and factory establishment and management.

While the nature of the programme called for quick responses on a first-come, first-served basis, priority was given to LDC needs. Projects for LDCs accounted for about 44 per cent of the value of project approvals and 31.5 per cent of project expenditures during the year.

Industrial co-operation

System of Consultations

In 1983, UNIDO organized three sectoral consultations under its System of Consultations: on wood and wood products (the first on this topic), on the agricultural machinery industry (second) and on the pharmaceutical industry (second), bringing to 21 the number of consultation meetings since 1977.[17] Preparatory and follow-up activities were pursued in other sectors, including leather and leather products, food processing, fisheries, building materials, fertilizers, petrochemicals, iron and steel, non-ferrous metals, and capital goods, with emphasis on energy-related technology and equipment. Follow-up activities were also pursued on two aspects common to all sectors of industry and the subject of previous consultations: training of industrial manpower and industrial financing. The consultations had led to the identification of developing countries' problems, some of which were dealt with through the technical co-operation programmes of UNIDO.

On 13 May 1983, the Industrial Development Board,[18] taking note of the UNIDO Executive Director's report on the 1982 consultations, decided that consultations on the following sectors should be held during 1984-1985: food processing,

with emphasis on vegetable oils and fats; fertilizers; leather and leather products; capital goods, with emphasis on energy-related equipment and technology; petrochemicals; and building materials. The Executive Director was asked to start preliminary preparations for possible consultations during 1986-1987 on the fisheries industry, industrial manpower training, agricultural machinery, non-ferrous metals, iron and steel, and pharmaceuticals.

The Board endorsed the co-sponsorship arrangement between UNIDO and the Food and Agriculture Organization of the United Nations (FAO)[19] for the first consultation on wood and wood products and recommended a similar arrangement for the proposed consultation on the fisheries industry, and with other international organizations in respect of any other sector where there was shared competence between them and UNIDO. The Board hoped that future consultations would result in action-oriented recommendations and decided to begin an appraisal of the System in 1984.

GENERAL ASSEMBLY ACTION

In section I of resolution 38/192 of 20 December, the General Assembly endorsed the consultations proposed for 1984-1985 and echoed the Board's hope. It requested the Executive Director to ensure that experts and expertise from developing as well as developed countries be associated with the preparatory process for those consultations, and that consultations be organized well in advance to allow for a full exchange of views among participants.

Programme of work for 1984-1985

Following examination of the proposed programme budget for the biennium 1984-1985,[20] CPC, at the May/June part of its 1983 session,[6] recommended revisions pertaining to the System of Consultations. The revisions included assigning the highest priority to the consultations proposed for the biennium by the Industrial Development Board; deleting programme elements covering consultations on wood and wood products (since they would be completed in 1983), industrial financing, and trade and trade-related aspects of industrial collaboration arrangements (since no consultations on these sectors were envisioned for the next two bienniums); and merging the elements for consultations on the capital goods industry and on energy-related technology and equipment.

ECONOMIC AND SOCIAL COUNCIL ACTION

By section VI of resolution 1983/49 of 28 July 1983, the Economic and Social Council endorsed the CPC recommendations, on the understanding that UNIDO would carry out follow-up work, if necessary, on the wood and wood products industry, industrial financing, and trade and trade-related aspects of industrial collaboration arrangements, subject to a decision by the Industrial Development Board. The Secretary-General was asked to report to CPC in 1984 on the questions it had raised on various programme elements, to enable it to avoid duplication and achieve a more rational organization of the UNIDO work programme, in anticipation of that organization's conversion into a specialized agency (see above).

GENERAL ASSEMBLY ACTION

On the recommendation of the Fifth (Administrative and Budgetary) Committee, the General Assembly adopted resolution 38/234, section I, without vote on 20 December 1983.

United Nations Industrial Development Organization

[The General Assembly. . .]

Invites the Advisory Committee on Administrative and Budgetary Questions to examine the financial aspects of the recommendations of the Committee for Programme and Co-ordination contained in paragraphs 286 *(c)* and *(d)* of its report, as well as the merger of programme elements 4.9 and 4.15, as recommended by that Committee in paragraph 286 *(a)* of its report, and to report thereon to the General Assembly;

. . .

General Assembly resolution 38/234, section I

20 December 1983   Meeting 104   Adopted without vote

Approved by Fifth Committee (A/38/760) without vote, 3 November (meeting 27); oral proposal by United States; agenda item 109.
Meeting numbers. GA 38th session: 5th Committee 27; plenary 104.

Co-operation among developing countries

During 1983, UNIDO activities to promote economic and technical co-operation among developing countries continued to focus on organizing solidarity meetings in LDCs and round-table ministerial meetings, to bring together developing countries interested in promoting industrialization; following up agreements reached at such meetings and recommendations on technical co-operation reached through the System of Consultations (see above); and developing joint programmes for specific industrial subsectors, and a work programme based on recommendations of various international forums in the context of the action programme adopted by the 1981 High Level Conference on Economic Co-operation among Developing Countries.[21]

Preparatory work was completed for three solidarity meetings scheduled to be held in Burundi, Rwanda and Yemen in 1984. Follow-up activities continued for the fulfilment of commitments made at previous solidarity meetings held in Haiti and the United Republic of Tanzania (1979); Bangladesh (1980); the Sudan and the Upper Volta (1981); and Lesotho, Mauritania and Nepal (1982).

In co-operation with Brazil, UNIDO organized discussions at the First International Latin America/Africa Symposium (Rio de Janeiro,1-5 August 1983), on promoting industrial co-operation between Latin America and Africa. Follow-up activities included an in-plant group training programme in Brazil on the maintenance and repair of railway equipment for participants from Portuguese-speaking African countries. UNIDO arranged for six consultants from other Latin American countries to assist Bolivia in formulating project evaluation, standardization and quality control, small-scale industry, and institutional infrastructure. In addition, a staff mission explored the possibility of a joint economic and technical co-operation programme in five Central American countries.

Subsectors of industry chosen for joint programmes included food processing, a subsector given priority; agricultural machinery; energy, including new and renewable energy sources; and building materials. A project on industrial manpower development, for co-operation among African developing countries, was formulated by UNIDO and the Economic Commission for Africa (ECA) for consideration by UNDP and other financing sources. UNIDO participated in a regional intergovernmental meeting (Beijing, China, November) organized by the Economic and Social Commission for Asia and the Pacific (ESCAP), the purpose of which was to match China's technical co-operation capabilities with those of other developing countries in the region; of 32 projects agreed upon, four (embroidery technology, silverware manufacturing, black tea processing, and bamboo and rattan weaving) were to receive UNIDO support.

An expert group meeting on industrial co-operation among developing countries (Bangkok, Thailand, 18–22 July)[22] reviewed the issues involved in such co-operation and formulated recommendations at all levels, as well as for UNIDO. This meeting, one of five convened in 1983 in preparation for the Fourth (1984) General Conference of UNIDO, was attended by 44 experts from 25 countries. The meeting agreed that this type of co-operation was not a substitute for North-South co-operation, but could help provide an alternative in terms of access to or availability of the requisites of production—human resources, technology, energy and finance. UNIDO was called on to collect and disseminate information on supply and demand of industrial co-operation among developing countries in order to promote the flow of technology, capital and industrial skills, and those countries were urged to establish policies and incentives for promoting industrial co-operation among themselves.

International trade aspects

In 1983, the United Nations Conference on Trade and Development (UNCTAD) and UNIDO continued to review trade and trade-related aspects of industrial collaboration arrangements (see also Chapter IV of this section under TRADE AMONG COUNTRIES HAVING DIFFERENT ECONOMIC AND SOCIAL SYSTEMS). Pursuant to a 1982 decision of the Trade and Development Board of UNCTAD,[23] the Committee on Manufactures, at its March 1983 session, examined the final report[24] of an *Ad Hoc* UNCTAD/UNIDO Group of Experts that had met on the subject in 1979 and 1981.

On 22 March 1983,[25] the Committee requested the UNCTAD secretariat, in co-operation with UNIDO, to continue work on trade-related industrial collaboration between enterprises of developed and developing countries. Attention was to be given to new forms of co-operation, including joint ventures, aimed at strengthening production of and trade in manufactures of developing countries, including manufactures using advanced technology in their production. The Board also requested the secretariat, in co-operation with UNIDO and other international organizations, to compile and analyse information on industrial collaboration arrangements and recommend further work in this area.

UNIDO work during the year centred on the legal and technical aspects of contractual arrangements, ranging from check-lists to model contracts, as drawn up by experts from developed and developing countries representing a variety of interests, notably in the agricultural machinery, fertilizer, leather and leather products, pharmaceutical and petrochemical industries. Various frameworks of international co-operation in agricultural machinery, food processing, and wood and wood products were being elaborated, through which small- and medium-scale enterprises in developed countries and their partners in developing countries could be better informed of conditions governing their co-operation. Such frameworks would include provisions on joint ventures, co-management and repatriation of funds regulated by national laws.

Industrial co-operation contracts

UNCITRAL activities. At its fourth session, held at Vienna, Austria, from 16 to 20 May 1983,[26] the Working Group on the New International Economic Order of the United Nations Commission on International Trade Law (UNCITRAL) began drafting a legal guide on drawing up contracts for sup-

ply and construction of industrial works. The Group considered an outline of the guide's structure and sample chapters on choice of contract types, exemptions and hardship clauses. There was wide support for the inclusion of an index, summaries, check-lists as appropriate, a glossary and model clauses. It was stressed that the guide should carry out the principles laid down by the General Assembly in 1974 in its Declaration on the Establishment of a New International Economic Order[27] and accord with the principles of equality, mutual benefit, equity and reasonableness. The guide's objectives should be to assist developing countries in establishing independent national economies and to promote international economic co-operation.

At its May/June session,[28] UNCITRAL, expressing appreciation for the Group's progress in a complex field, agreed on the need to prepare the legal guide expeditiously.

The General Assembly, in resolution 38/134 on the UNCITRAL report, took note of the Group's commencement of work on drafting the guide, identifying the legal issues involved and suggesting possible solutions to assist parties, in particular from developing countries, in their negotiations. (See also LEGAL QUESTIONS, Chapter VI.)

Industrial development of LDCs

UNIDO efforts to assist LDCs—in line with the Substantial New Programme of Action for the 1980s for the Least Developed Countries,[29] endorsed by the General Assembly in 1981[30]— encountered severe resource constraints in 1983, when a shortfall in contributions caused UNDP to reduce its indicative planning figures for individual countries and financing for the Special Industrial Services programme (see above) to 55 per cent of the levels originally planned. Since the bulk of UNIDO technical co-operation projects was financed from UNDP resources, many projects for which approval had been expected in 1983 had to be curtailed or deferred, and budgets of ongoing projects were either revised downwards or cancelled. Although a reasonable share of UNIDO resources was allocated to LDCs, it was not possible to compensate fully for the shortfall in UNDP resources.

To mobilize financial resources for LDCs, the UNIDO secretariat strengthened its contacts with the United Nations Capital Development Fund, the Voluntary Fund for the United Nations Decade for Women, the United Nations Sudano-Sahelian Office, the World Bank and various regional financial institutions, such as the Islamic Development Bank.

Financial support was provided for LDC participation in the three consultations held during the year (see SYSTEM OF CONSULTATIONS above) and in the regional investment promotion meeting for southern African countries (see INVESTMENT PROMOTION below), as well as for advisory services to 12 African LDCs on pre-investment studies.

Work on the potential for resource-based industrial development in LDCs continued, with studies on Malawi and Somalia completed and similar studies on the Gambia, Guinea-Bissau, Haiti, Lesotho and Nepal in progress. Country reviews were completed for Afghanistan and the United Republic of Tanzania, and were in progress for Bangladesh and the Sudan.

Training programmes designed to meet the special needs of LDCs included seminars on public enterprises management (Guinea-Bissau) and on small-industries development (United Republic of Tanzania), and a workshop to assist small- and medium-scale industrial enterprises. Group training programmes were also organized on such topics as project preparation, small-scale foundry operation and small-business consultancy. Two preparatory missions, covering four African LDCs, were undertaken to establish a long-term programme of co-operation in agro-industries development.

In 1983, UNIDO assisted three more LDCs in preparing for round-table meetings organized with logistic support from UNDP, bringing to nine the LDCs assisted in this manner.

On 13 May 1983,[31] the Industrial Development Board, having examined the progress of the industrial development of LDCs, took note of UNIDO efforts to increase the level of project approvals in 1982 despite financial constraints. The Board expressed concern over the limited resources for the programme of technical co-operation for LDCs, noting that the number of LDCs had increased from 31 to 36,[32] while resources had remained at the same level. The Board called on all countries, in particular the industrialized ones, to increase their contributions to UNIDF with flexibility, so that larger proportions could be applied to LDC assistance within the framework of the Programme. The UNIDO secretariat was asked to continue to contribute to the round-table and consultative group meetings for LDCs prior to the mid-term (1985) global review of the Programme's implementation, and to find ways to carry out technical co-operation projects remaining uncompleted owing to UNDP financial constraints.

Redeployment of industrial production to developing countries

In a report of 28 February 1983[33] to the Industrial Development Board, the Executive Director described the 1982 UNIDO study and research programme on industrial redeployment and restructuring from developed to developing countries

as involving a two-pronged approach: surveillance of structural changes in industry and the driving forces behind them in developed-market economies, centrally planned economies and developing countries; and country analyses of the medium- and long-term policy problems confronting specific industries in developing countries that had requested an assessment of their restructuring prospects.

The report on restructuring of world industrial production indicated a change in the pattern of industrial redeployment which had occurred in the 1960s and 1970s, a period of trade liberalization and internationalization of production. Factors such as the current economic crisis, stagnation in industrial production, increasing trade restrictions, fierce international competition in manufacturing and severe strains on the financial system were forcing both developed and developing countries to reassess policies and seek new ways to secure growth and employment. Thus the processes of redeployment and restructuring were expected to proceed at a slower pace and in a different and more complex pattern than before. During the 1980s, redeployment was expected to decline, be increasingly subject to government interventions, and require increasing financing from the traditional banking system.

The report suggested that UNIDO continue to build its expertise and data base on the subject, and provide direct advisory and analytical services to developing countries. For this purpose, UNIDO should expand its contacts with specialists from private and public industries able to provide pragmatic advice.

On 13 May,[34] the Board reaffirmed its previous decisions on restructuring of world industrial production, including redeployment; it also reaffirmed that those activities should be carried out in accordance with national policies and priorities of member States, in particular the developing ones. The Board noted the report's suggestions and agreed that future studies be action-oriented. It requested the Executive Director to report in 1984 on how UNIDO could strengthen its role regarding participation of all parties in the redeployment of industry from developed to developing countries.

An expert group meeting on industrial development strategies and policies for developing countries (Lima, Peru, 18-22 April)[35] considered studies analysing past strategies and policies, reviewing challenges generated by the current international economic situation for the industrialization of developing countries, and identifying possible reorientations of, and new opportunities for, their long-term industrialization process. This meeting, one of five convened in 1983 in preparation for the Fourth (1984) General Conference of

UNIDO, was attended by some 50 experts from 32 countries. The meeting called for expanded international industrial co-operation as a framework for individual national strategies and policies, and for increased UNIDO participation in the conceptualization and surveillance of such strategies and policies.

Industrial financing

In 1983, UNIDO initiated follow-up action on the recommendations of the 1982 First Consultation on Industrial Financing[36] by testing, at sectoral consultations, such issues as financing to revitalize the leather industry, and for iron and steel projects. In these cases, efforts were directed towards promoting programme lending to cover related services, pre-investment activities, and repair and maintenance. Work was also undertaken to strengthen links between training and establishment of new plants—by linking the financing of training operators and managers to that of plant and equipment costs—and to provide financial support to industry-linked infrastructure in developing countries.

In addition, UNIDO promoted more flexible regulations for the supply of risk capital and more effective lending to small- and medium-scale industries, as well as development of skills in designing financial packages to obtain loans. In this connection, an Expert Group Meeting on Venture Banking was convened by the Organisation for Economic Co-operation and Development in co-operation with UNIDO (Paris, 7-9 November), to examine terms and conditions of financing for risk capital purposes and for the loan portion of financial packages.

Proposed international bank for industrial development

The Industrial Development Board continued, at its April/May session, to consider the UNIDO Executive Director's 1981 proposal for the establishment of an international bank for industrial development.[37] Unable to agree on that proposal, the Board decided to consider the subject again at its 1984 session.[38]

Investment promotion

Under the Investment Co-operative Programme of UNIDO, the Investment Promotion Services continued in 1983 to promote the flow of external financial, technological and managerial resources to developing countries by identifying potential partners in industrialized countries, providing information on the host country and assisting in the preparation of the financial package. The existing network of Services—at Brussels, Belgium;

Cologne, Federal Republic of Germany; New York; Paris; Tokyo; Vienna, Austria; and Zurich, Switzerland—was increased to eight with the opening of a Service at Warsaw, Poland, on 24 November. The Services at Cologne and Vienna were extended to the end of 1987 and of 1985, respectively. Establishment of Services in selected developing countries, including India and one of the Gulf States, remained under consideration.

During the year, the Services promoted some 68 industrial investment projects in 29 countries; 54 of the projects had a known investment value of $322 million. Country presentation meetings were organized for 13 countries—Barbados, Colombia, Egypt, Kenya, Lesotho, Mauritius, Paraguay, Peru, Senegal, Sri Lanka, the United Republic of Tanzania, Zambia and Zimbabwe— to provide them an opportunity to inform entrepreneurs, banks, manufacturers' associations and federations of industry of investment opportunities and the advantages of investing in their countries. The Services accommodated a total of 40 officials from 30 developing countries who were promoting investment in their countries by putting them in contact with potential partners and providing guidance in promotion techniques.

National investment promotion meetings were organized for Pakistan (Karachi, September) and Peru (Lima, November), and a regional meeting for southern African countries (Lusaka, Zambia, October). Held to attract investment from the Gulf Arab countries, the conference in Pakistan, to which 34 investment proposals were submitted, resulted in potential investors signing four letters of intent for projects in the agro-industry, chemicals and engineering sectors. The meeting in Zambia discussed more than 150 proposals and closed with 32 signed letters of intent. The investors' forum in Peru discussed 110 projects with a total investment value exceeding $2 billion; two contracts and six letters of intent were known to have been signed, and 30 projects were selected for future negotiation.

The Investment Promotion Information System became operational in mid-1983. Consisting of two computerized data banks—the Project File and the Investor File—the System contained a summary of over 660 industrial investment project proposals and information on some 2,500 public and private enterprises in industrialized and developing countries that were suitable and willing to participate in specific industrial projects. Other promotional tools included: the Roster of Resources, listing potential partners in industrial investment projects for more than 4,000 products; and a directory of financial resources for industrial projects, covering 313 development institutions and four associations, which was revised and published in four volumes during the year.[39]

Industrial management

In 1983, technical co-operation expenditures for factory establishment and management amounted to $3.2 million, with 93 per cent of total implementation financed from UNDP resources. Of that amount, Africa accounted for 70 per cent; the Americas, 5; the Arab States (excluding those in Africa), 14; and Asia and the Pacific, 13. Completed or under implementation were 54 projects, 6 of them greater than $1 million in value, 19 greater than $150,000 and 29 less than that value.

Consultancy-oriented projects, which received increasing emphasis, together with direct management assistance to industry, made up the bulk of the year's technical assistance activities. Other assistance was in such specialized areas as the introduction of management information systems, and the application and use of computers in administrative, maintenance and energy management.

The preliminary phase of a regional programme for the development of a network of industrial consultancy services in the ESCAP region was completed; a similar project for Africa was in preparation. A large-scale project in Somalia demonstrated the need for effective management, at the institutional and factory levels, to improve capacity utilization and productivity. The project involved management seminars for both middle- and high-level staff; information dissemination through publications; and industrial management assistance to public enterprises in organizational matters, finance and accounting, production and maintenance, and management information systems. In the Sudan, efforts to enhance management techniques focused on three industrial subsectors: textile, leather and food industries.

Demonstrations were held for Government officials from Mauritius, Mexico and Pakistan of the potential applications of computers in management and training in developing countries. Management projects involving the use of computers were in operation in Egypt, Guyana, Iraq and the Syrian Arab Republic.

In the construction industry, a comprehensive programme was being developed to strengthen the management skills and capabilities of project personnel to control the contracting and construction management processes for developing countries. Areas of emphasis included: analysis of project risk factors and development of specific techniques for controlling and monitoring them, strengthening contract management procedures, and design and installation of management information systems to facilitate data collection.

Industrial planning

In 1983, technical co-operation expenditures for industrial planning amounted to $4.4 million, with some 87 per cent of total implementation financed from UNDP resources. Of that amount, Africa accounted for 41 per cent; the Americas, 25; the Arab States (excluding those in Africa), 5; Asia and the Pacific, 27; and Europe, 2. Completed or under implementation were 60 projects, 10 of them greater than $1 million in value, 24 greater than $150,000 and 26 less than that value.

Technical co-operation activities consisted of industrial surveys; formulation of industrial strategies and policies; preparation, monitoring and implementation of national industrial development programmes; planning of capital goods manufacture; and industrial planning at the subregional level on behalf of regional organizations.

For example, UNIDO provided assistance in the formulation of an industrial master plan for Malaysia, for which 14 potential industrial subsectors, 7 of them resource-based, were identified. The first phase of a project to prepare such a plan for the United Republic of Cameroon was also completed. In Mali, UNIDO assisted in developing key industrial branches for the exploitation of natural resources, and similar projects were under way in Benin, Cape Verde and Lesotho.

Special attention was given to key industrial subsectors such as the capital goods industries, as a means of reducing technological dependence. Assistance in this area was provided to Colombia, Ecuador, Mexico, Pakistan, Turkey and Venezuela. In Venezuela, a team of UNIDO and local experts analysed the demand for machinery and equipment in the preceding five years and prepared a study on equipment production for the petroleum industry. In Pakistan, the first phase of a programme for the development of capital goods industries was completed, with an analysis of national suppliers and producers in transport equipment, machine tools, textile machinery, agricultural implements and construction equipment.

Industrial studies

UNIDO industrial studies and research in 1983 continued to analyse the economic development process and map out new approaches to industrial development at the global, regional, country and sectoral levels.

In its work on global restructuring (see above, under REDEPLOYMENT OF INDUSTRIAL PRODUCTION TO DEVELOPING COUNTRIES), UNIDO examined the ongoing process of international industrial restructuring and the impact of protectionism and other trade and finance policies on the strategic options of the developing countries. Studies were completed on trends, action and perspectives in global restructuring, the changing pattern of world production in the automotive industry, and the restructuring process in the European centrally planned economies, with a focus on the implications of the changes for developing countries. Studies were also undertaken on the impact of the world economic crisis on major industries as well as on the industrial output in the developing countries.

New policy-related research included an assessment of recent development strategies and policies in developing countries. An analytical study on regional integration among those countries was published, and a reassessment was made of export-processing zones, the role of multinationals in developing countries, and general trading companies as instruments of development. New studies were also initiated on the impact of foreign exchange constraints on the choice of industrialization strategies and policies, and on the emergence, implications and possible solution of the external debt problem.

Regional and country studies on prospects for industrialization dealt with industrial development strategies. Particular attention was given to servicing both national policy makers and UNIDO operational activities. A study was issued on industrial strategies and policies in developing South, South-east and East Asia and a similar study on Africa was being prepared. A preliminary study was completed on the Southern African Development Co-ordination Conference, highlighting prospects and constraints facing industrial development in the region. A composite document on the changing role of the public industrial sector in development was issued, and a study was completed on performance evaluation in the public sector.

In preparing in-depth country studies, particular attention was given to endogenous resource potentials and trends in the international restructuring process in order to provide an optimal basis for policy-making and industrial strategy formulation. Two studies assessed the potential for resource-based industrial development in Malawi and Somalia; two others on the Gambia and Lesotho were under revision, while work was initiated on a similar study on Guinea-Bissau. Reports were submitted to Thailand on industrial restructuring in the automotive, plastics and chemical industries, together with proposals related to export policy instruments and institutions. Work was nearing completion on a study of the Indonesian industry sector, and a study was undertaken on the potential for resource-based industrial development in Nepal. Work was initiated on a similar study in Haiti, with particular attention to long-term prospects and restructuring of the manufacturing sector. Country reviews providing updated information on the industrial sector were completed on Afghanistan, Argentina, Bangla-

desh, Costa Rica, India, Indonesia, Iran, Kenya, Paraguay, Peru, the Sudan, the United Republic of Cameroon, the United Republic of Tanzania and Uruguay.

Industrial technology

Under the UNIDO industrial technology programme, while work continued on specific technological advances, there was a sharper focus in 1983 on the cumulative impact on developing countries of the interaction of such advances, and on the consequent need of each of those countries to formulate an overall policy integrating national industrial and technological activity. Efforts were aimed at strengthening developing countries' negotiating capacities for technology selection and acquisition. Such activities included assistance in establishing or strengthening government institutions for this purpose, and expanding the UNIDO Technological Information Exchange System (joined in 1983 by Bolivia, Ecuador and Peru), complemented by information provided by the Industrial and Technological Information Bank (see below).

Concerning specific technologies, UNIDO issued papers on problems of software development in developing countries, the impact of micro-electronics on biomedical applications in those countries, and informatics for industrial development. As in the past, UNIDO organized workshops at the national level to stimulate technology policy formulation and technological planning (Malaysia and Trinidad and Tobago).

The International Forum on Technological Advances and Development (Tbilisi, USSR, 12-16 April)[40] helped the secretariat relate the activities on technological advances to measures and policies needed for industrialization. One of five expert group meetings convened in preparation for the Fourth (1984) General Conference of UNIDO, the Forum was attended by experts from 23 countries. The Forum recommended that, in the context of technological advances, developing countries examine individually and collectively their existing state of technological capabilities and take steps to create or reorient national institutions and structures so as to maximize potential benefits and avoid adverse consequences. Each country should assess the socio-economic impact of technological advances, make careful choices of technologies to be imported, and strengthen the negotiating capability for their acquisition.

The Forum reviewed selected technological advances in genetic engineering and biotechnology (see below), micro-electronics, new materials and related technologies, petrochemicals (see below), and energy from biomass and solar photovoltaic cells.

Industrial and Technological Information Bank

The Industrial and Technological Information Bank (INTIB), in its fourth year of operation in 1983, continued to increase and update sources of information, to generate information of relevance to developing countries and to meet end-user requirements. Besides developing further linkages with other data banks and specialized correspondents, efforts were made to promote wider use of INTIB. To that end, UNIDO participated in two seminars (Arusha, United Republic of Tanzania; Bordeaux, France) which helped to focus attention on industrial information needed by developing countries and available INTIB services.

Roughly 1,300 inquiries were received by INTIB's Industrial Inquiry Service during 1983. The inquiries, from industrial enterprises, information sources, research organizations, Governments and consultants, concerned chemicals, food, fabricated metal products, construction and energy.

Publication of four further volumes of the *Industrial Development Abstracts* (IDA)[41] during the year brought the IDA data base up to 13,000 abstracts of UNIDO documents. Preparatory work was begun on a cumulative index for all such abstracts. A revised edition of the *Thesaurus of Industrial Development Terms* in English-French and French-English was published,[42] and the On-Line Information Key (LINK) data base—containing information on institutions, inquiries received by INTIB, subject files and technology suppliers—brought out two directories, one listing institutions engaged in the industrial conversion of biomass and another on acronyms of organizations included in the data base. The monthly *UNIDO Newsletter*[43] generated more than 11,000 requests for some 115,000 documents and publications.

On 13 May,[44] the Industrial Development Board stressed the particular significance of UNIDO work in transferring appropriate and advanced technologies to developing countries (see above). The Board also stressed the utility of INTIB to developing countries, in particular its regional linkages and programmes assisting small- and medium-scale industries. (See also Chapter XII of this section.)

REFERENCES

[1]YUN 1982, p. 764. [2]ID/B/C.3/119. [3]ID/B/307 & Corr.1. [4]E/AC.51/1983/5 & Add.1. [5]ID/B/C.3/122. [6]A/38/38. [7]E/1983/20 (dec. 83/12, sect. IV). [8]ID/B/309. [9]E/AC.51/1983/12. [10]YUN 1982, p. 765. [11]ID/WG.394/8. [12]YUN 1980, p. 662, GA res. 35/66 B, 5 Dec. 1980. [13]A/38/16 (conclusion 1983/8). [14]E/1983/20 (dec. 83/39). [15]DP/1983/73. [16]A/38/516. [17]YUN 1977, p. 493. [18]A/38/16 (conclusion 1983/4). [19]ID/B/299 & Add.1. [20]A/38/6. [21]YUN 1981, p. 383. [22]ID/WG.399/4. [23]YUN 1982, p. 768. [24]ID/B/287 & Add.1 (TD/B/862). [25]TD/B/951 (decision 13(X)). [26]A/CN.9/234. [27]YUN 1974, p. 324, GA res. 3201(S-VI), 1 May 1974. [28]A/38/17. [29]YUN 1981, p. 406. [30]*Ibid.*, p. 410, GA res. 36/194, 17 Dec. 1981. [31]A/38/16 (conclusion 1983/7). [32]YUN 1982, p. 617, GA res. 37/133, 17 Dec. 1982. [33]ID/B/294 & Corr.1. [34]A/38/16 (conclusion 1983/3). [35]UNIDO/IS.431 & Add.1. [36]YUN 1982, p. 770. [37]YUN 1981, p. 591. [38]A/38/16 (conclusion 1983/2). [39]*Financial Resources for Industrial Projects in Developing Countries,* PI/61/Rev.2, vols. 1-4. [40]ID/WG.389/6. [41]*Industrial Development Abstracts: UNIDO Industrial Information System* (INDIS), 11501-11700, ID/295 (UNIDO/LIB/SER.B/48); 11701-12000, ID/301 (UNIDO/LIB/SER.B/49); 12001-12200, ID/303 (UNIDO/LIB/SER.B/50); 12201-12500, ID/305 (UNIDO/LIB/SER.B/51). [42]*Thesaurus of Industrial Development Terms,* ID/172/Rev.1 (UNIDO/LIB/SER.C/4/Rev.1). [43]*UNIDO Newsletter,* Nos. 177-188 (monthly). [44]A/38/16 (conclusion 1983/5).

Development of specific industries

Many of UNIDO's technical co-operation activities, studies and meetings during 1983 related to specific industrial sectors or industries. The major sectors were agro-industries, chemical industries, engineering industries, and metallurgical and mineral industries.

Agro-industries

In 1983, technical co-operation expenditures for activities in the agro-industries amounted to $10.9 million, with some 70 per cent financed from UNDP resources. Of that amount, Africa accounted for 25 per cent; the Americas, 20; the Arab States (excluding those in Africa), 1; Asia and the Pacific, 50; Europe, 1; and interregional and global, 3. A total of 183 projects were completed or being implemented, 16 of them greater than $1 million in value, 61 greater than $150,000 and 106 below that value.

Activities focused on the improvement of industrial production and, as in the past, covered a wide range of light industries including textiles and clothing, food-processing, leather and leather products, packaging, rubber products, and wood and wood products.

Food industry

Work was begun in 1983 on a world-wide study of the vegetable oils and fats industry, a sector to be given special emphasis at a second consultation on the food-processing industry, scheduled for 1984-1985.[1] The study was to give an overview of the vegetable oils and fats industry, describing the developing countries' current and potential contribution to the industry, as well as certain aspects of planning and promotion at the national and subregional levels. Also begun was a study on the integrated development of the industry, based on a new methodology for analysing food production and consumption.

UNIDO contributed to the organization of the International Conference on Co-operative Food-Processing in Developing Countries (Ottawa,

Canada, 22-26 August). The Conference demonstrated the readiness of Canadian co-operatives to co-operate with developing countries. Integrated development of the industry was the subject of an expert group meeting (Alexandria, Egypt, 24-27 October), based on investigations of measures to promote the development of the vegetable oils and fats industry. Surveys of the two industries and of related equipment and spare parts manufacturing were carried out in 19 developing countries to identify and develop specific technical co-operation projects.

In the related area of the fisheries industry, preliminary work was begun in 1983 for a first consultation on this subject, scheduled for 1986-1987.[1] Fish-processing technology and the required industrial equipment and machinery were the topics of concentration. Two country papers on the status of the industry, emphasizing its role in the national economy and constraints on its development, were prepared.

Leather industry

In 1983, activities on the rationalization of world production, marketing and trade in leather and leather products centred on how developing countries could make full use of their existing production capacities and how international co-operation could support this objective.

Two issues were selected for consideration by a third consultation on the industry, scheduled for 1984-1985:[1] revitalization of industrial capacity in this sector in developing countries and development of regional co-operation in the production of basic tanning chemicals and footwear auxiliaries (heels, soles, laces, metallic attachments). Preparations for the consultation included analyses of the prospects of the industry in 40 countries in Africa, 30 in Asia and 15 in Latin America; a case study of the industry's integrated development in the Sudan; and an examination of prospects for regional co-operation in the production of footwear auxiliaries. Two studies on the industry were completed during 1983 for presentation at the consultation—one appraising production, consumption and trade trends since 1977, the other assessing prospects for the production of tanning chemicals in developing countries.

In other action related to the leather industry, UNCTAD VI, on 2 July, requested its Committee on Commodities to take action to provide a forum for interested producer and consumer countries to consider preparing project proposals or other arrangements on hides and skins in the context of the Integrated Programme for Commodities (see Chapter IV of this section).

Wood-using industry

Pursuant to a 1981 decision of the Industrial Development Board,[2] the First Consultation on the Wood and Wood Products Industry was held at Helsinki, Finland, from 19 to 23 September 1983.[3] It was attended by 165 participants from 54 countries and 18 international organizations. The Consultation considered two issues—development of primary and secondary wood-processing industries, and measures to promote the use of wood and wood products—as recommended by a global preparatory meeting (Vienna, Austria, 24-26 January).[4]

On the first issue, it was concluded that the share of developing countries in total world production of wood and wood products was not commensurate with national resources. Contributing factors were difficulty in obtaining financing for processing plants and lack of transportation infrastructure and managerial and skilled labour at all levels. The Consultation recommended that UNIDO develop, in co-operation with a panel of international experts, contractual check-lists for elaborating arrangements in joint ventures, training and marketing; identify specialized research and development institutions in both developed and developing countries and areas of co-operation between them; give priority to a transport study for use at the next consultation; promote collaborative efforts in the preparation and dissemination of training manuals; and develop, in co-operation with FAO and UNCTAD, the regional and global information base necessary for the industry's development.

Concerning the second issue, the Consultation emphasized promotion of commercially less-accepted species of timber, research on the properties and availability of such species, and greater use of such wood for national housing programmes. The Consultation recommended that UNIDO, in collaboration with appropriate organizations, examine the possibility of developing internationally acceptable stress-grading rules and a strength-grouping system for tropical timber and other species from developing countries; compile and disseminate information on existing and new uses of wood in construction; promote education and training in wood technology; and undertake studies on developing countries' participation in world trade of wood and wood products, including technical requirements. The Consultation also recommended that the Board consider convening a second consultation that would emphasize the secondary wood-processing industry.

Chemical industries

In 1983, technical co-operation expenditures for activities in the chemical industries amounted to $17.1 million, with some 51 per cent financed from UNDP resources. Of that amount, Africa accounted for 38 per cent; the Americas, 11; the Arab

States (excluding those in Africa), 3; Asia and the Pacific, 38; Europe, 5; and interregional and global, 5. Completed or under implementation were 321 projects, 27 of them greater than $1 million in value, 93 greater than $150,000 and 201 projects below that value.

Projects were mainly in the sectors of building materials, fertilizers, petrochemicals including pesticides, and pharmaceuticals. Energy-related industrial technology, including biomass processing which involved microbiological processes for producing fuels and chemicals, continued to feature prominently among projects (see Chapter X of this section). Projects were also being implemented in glass and ceramics manufacture, the pulp and paper industry, salt production and pollution control.

Building materials industry

In 1983, a symposium on appropriate building materials for low-cost housing for the African region (Nairobi, Kenya, 7-14 November) was organized with UNIDO co-operation, and a regional project on low-cost construction in the Asian and Pacific region was begun. A project on the development of carbon fibre technology in Brazil, financed by the United Nations Financing System for Science and Technology for Development, made considerable progress in developing materials and components for various applications. An international conference was held (São José dos Campos and Salvador, Brazil, 5-9 December) to demonstrate the project's achievements and to explore possibilities of co-operation among developing countries in acquiring technologies for carbon fibres and carbon fibre composites. Support was provided for the first mechanized brick plant in the Gambia, which started production in 1983, and missions were sent to several countries to provide technical assistance for cement production.

Work continued on the first world-wide study on the construction and building materials industry, for presentation to the first consultation on that industry, scheduled by the Industrial Development Board to take place during 1984-1985.[1] The study would introduce strategies to promote a self-reliant construction sector in developing countries.

Fertilizer industry

In 1983, activities for the development of the fertilizer industry were largely devoted to preparations for a fourth (1984) consultation on the industry, as well as to following up recommendations made by previous consultations.

UNIDO finalized work on the cost-reimbursable and turnkey model contracts for the construction of fertilizer plants, and continued work on drafts of two other model contracts—semi-turnkey contracts and licensing, and engineering services

agreements—for submission to the fourth consultation. Efforts continued towards establishing a programme of co-operation among developing countries in the fertilizer industry. Under the programme, UNIDO carried out a survey on training needs and facilities and began discussions with Indonesia on holding a training course for engineers in the operation and maintenance of fertilizer plants.

Regional meetings were held in April to exchange experiences in the construction and operation of such plants in Asia and the Middle East (New Delhi, India, 4-8 April) and in Latin America and the Caribbean (Salvador, Brazil, 18-23 April). Two other regional meetings—on packaging, storage and distribution systems and on the development of agricultural credit facilities and fertilizer pricing policies—were held as part of a project on fertilizer production and utilization in Arab States.

A draft directory of technological capabilities of developing countries related to the fertilizer industry was prepared on the basis of a 30-country survey; it would be used in preparing UNIDO technical co-operation programmes. A guide on evaluating mini-fertilizer plants was being prepared for use by developing countries in establishing small-scale, modern fertilizer plants. A study was prepared on capital cost control of fertilizer plants in developing countries.

Petrochemical industry

Work continued on updating supply and demand estimates, revising guidelines for joint ventures and developing training schemes related to the petrochemical industry.

A seminar on co-operation among developing countries in petrochemical industries (Vienna, Austria, 7-9 March) was jointly held by UNIDO, the Organization of Petroleum Exporting Countries (OPEC) and the OPEC Fund for International Development; UNIDO submitted to the seminar a study of potential areas for co-operation in building capacities needed to meet demand in 1990 and beyond. An Advisory Panel on Petrochemicals was created to assist those three organizations in implementing the seminar's recommendations, among them the preparation of directories on the technological capabilities and on petrochemical products of developing countries.

A model licensing agreement for the industry was completed by a group of experts from developed and developing countries, and distributed to UNIDO member countries.

In regard to the pesticide industry, a regional network was established for the production, control and use of pesticides in Asia and the Far East. Two expert meetings were held on a pesticide data collection system and pesticide registration requirements.

Pharmaceutical industry

The Second Consultation on the Pharmaceutical Industry, convened at Budapest, Hungary, from 21 to 25 November 1983,[5] was attended by 216 participants from 66 countries and by 18 observers from 12 international organizations. The Consultation discussed four issues: contractual arrangements on the production of drugs; availability, pricing and transfer of technology for bulk drugs and their intermediates; development of drugs based on medicinal plants; and biologicals (production of vaccines).

Differences of opinion were expressed on the documents presented on contractual arrangements for the transfer of technology on the manufacture of bulk drugs, for formulating pharmaceutical dosage forms, and for setting up production plants. It was recommended that those documents be revised and others prepared for submission to a third consultation on the industry. Information on technology holders willing to transfer technology was to be updated. The UNIDO directory of supply sources for 26 essential bulk drugs (deemed suitable for production in developing countries), their chemical intermediates and some raw materials was to be enlarged to include all items in the World Health Organization model list of essential drugs. Other recommendations called for the compilation of a data base and directory of plants used as therapeutic agents; the addition of vaccines, serums and immunoglobulins to the UNIDO illustrative list of biologicals; and a step-by-step approach for establishing infrastructural capabilities for the production of vaccines.

Earlier in the year, at the request of developing countries, a draft report on the establishment of an international centre on information, training and development of pharmaceutical technology for developing countries[6] was presented to a Meeting on Co-operation among Developing Countries on Pharmaceuticals (Tunis, 2-5 September). UNIDO projects in pharmaceuticals included industrial utilization of medicinal plants; establishment of drug factories, training programmes and facilities for quality control; and production of immunologicals and opotherapeutic products.

Engineering industries

In 1983, technical co-operation expenditures for activities in the engineering industries amounted to $9.5 million, with some 80 per cent financed from UNDP resources. Of that amount, Africa accounted for 28 per cent; the Americas, 10; the Arab States (excluding those in Africa), 11; Asia and the Pacific, 44; and Europe, 7. Completed or under implementation were 160 projects, 20 of them greater than $1 million in value, 63 greater than $150,000 and 77 below that value.

Technical assistance continued to be based on appropriate and proven technology, taking into account the recipient country's existing infrastructure and available and potential resources. As in the past, activities focused on industrial production, energy-related technology, and human resources development. Integrated activities aimed at improving the design, manufacture, maintenance and repair of engineering products in five product groups: agricultural machinery and implements, metalworking and machine tools, land-based and water-borne transport equipment, electronic and electrical machinery and equipment, and computers and computer-related equipment.

Some 56 projects were proposed for developing countries in all regions, in response to requests for technical assistance, mostly for development of agricultural machinery, expansion of electronic and related industries, and increased use of computers in industry.

Genetic engineering

At a ministerial-level plenipotentiary meeting held at Madrid, Spain, from 7 to 13 September 1983,[7] the Statutes establishing the International Centre for Genetic Engineering and Biotechnology were adopted. The Centre, through a network of affiliated national, subregional and regional centres, would promote international co-operation in the development and application of the peaceful uses of genetic engineering and biotechnology, especially for developing countries. It would assist those countries in strengthening their scientific and technological capabilities in this field, and stimulate and assist activities at regional and national levels. The Centre would act as a focal point for affiliated research centres and link existing national, subregional, regional and international networks. It would also serve as a forum for information exchange among scientists of member States.

By the end of 1983, 28 countries had signed the Statutes, which would enter into force when at least 24 States, including the host State, had deposited instruments of ratification and after they had ascertained that sufficient financial resources were ensured. A Preparatory Committee consisting of the States which had signed the Statutes was to determine the Centre's location and accelerate work towards making it operational.

At the national and regional levels, UNIDO assisted in organizing workshops in genetic engineering and biotechnology and carried out studies.

Agricultural machinery

The Second Consultation on the Agricultural Machinery Industry was held at Vienna, Austria, from 17 to 21 October 1983.[8] It was attended by 124 participants from 58 countries and observers from 7 international organizations. The Consultation considered three issues: prospects for international co-operation in the agricultural machinery industry; integrated manufacture of agricultural machinery and capital goods; and the main items for inclusion in model contracts for the import, assembly and manufacture of agricultural equipment, including training.

The Consultation proposed convening a group of experts to work out the application of a multiproduct approach and elaborate a framework for co-operation in the industry, with emphasis on small- and medium-scale enterprises. It also suggested that a regional consultation in Latin America, and possibly also in Asia, be convened to promote regional and subregional co-operation. Guidelines were to be drawn up by UNIDO for the elaboration, by a group of experts, of a model licensing agreement for the import, assembly and manufacture of agricultural equipment, and training.

During the year, technical co-operation activities in support of the industry were concerned with improving national capabilities in product design, production, repair and maintenance. In Africa (Ethiopia, Somalia, Uganda, United Republic of Tanzania), assistance was provided in establishing development centres and pilot plants for national design and production technology. In Asia and the Pacific (Bangladesh, China, India, Mongolia, Nepal and Pakistan), assistance was given in establishing national applied research bases, and in Europe (Poland), in strengthening research and design. Other assistance centred on the simultaneous development of the agricultural machinery industry and subsidiary or related industries so as to fully utilize production capacities (Togo, Upper Volta).

Metallurgical and mineral industries

In 1983, UNIDO technical co-operation expenditures for activities in metallurgical industries amounted to $5.7 million, with some 70 per cent financed from UNDP resources. Of that amount, Africa accounted for 40 per cent; the Americas, 15; the Arab States (excluding those in Africa), 8; Asia and the Pacific, 26; Europe, 9; and inter-regional and global, 2. Completed or under implementation were 127 projects, 11 of them greater than $1 million in value, 49 greater than $150,000 and 67 below that value.

As in previous years, the UNIDO programme in the metallurgical sector concentrated on the development, transfer, application and adaptation of metallurgical technology in the following subsectors: light (aluminium, titanium) and heavy (copper, lead, zinc, rare metals) non-ferrous metals; iron and steel industry; ferrous and non-ferrous foundries; and metal transformation processes (rolling, forging, extruding, heat treatment, welding). Units and institutions of metallurgical technology were either established or strengthened.

Technical assistance consisted mainly in providing expertise for the efficient operation of existing metallurgical plants, selection and application of appropriate technologies, standardization of metal products, the introduction of plant maintenance systems, and energy conservation, including utilization of solid wastes. Assistance for setting up new metallurgical plants included not only planning, design and operational know-how, but also techno-economic and market studies.

Reflected in developing countries' requests for technical assistance was the need for foundry and forge pilot plants and demonstration centres, laboratories or evaluation units for developing metallurgical technology and processing methods for metallurgical minerals. Some 11 projects for the development of foundry industries were under implementation in a number of LDCs (Afghanistan, Democratic Yemen, Lesotho, Nepal, Niger, Somalia, Sudan, United Republic of Tanzania).

A fully equipped metallurgical laboratory was installed in Paraguay in 1983, part of a project begun in 1982 to strengthen that country's metallurgical industry. Another such laboratory was under construction in Morocco to assist that country's foundry industry. Centres for metallurgical technology, established with UNDP/UNIDO assistance, became fully operational and self-sufficient, among them the National Welding Research Institute (Tiruchirapalli, India), which had developed into a national centre for research and development, consultancy, training and documentation. In Nigeria, a similar institute was being established, and a nucleus of laboratories was formed for research in mineral beneficiation, coal metallography, refractories and high-temperature furnaces for heat treatment and general laboratory use.

Work proceeded on a development centre for silicon technology in Pakistan, and equipment was shipped to the project site. Preparatory assistance in terms of concept formulation was provided to Mozambique for a technological, metallurgical and non-metallic testing and development laboratory.

A demonstration workshop on maintenance in metallurgical and foundry industries, organized under UNIDO auspices (Cairo, Egypt, 26 March–15 April), was attended by 19 participants from African developing countries. An interregional inplant training programme on computerized maintenance systems in metallurgy was also organized (Czechoslovakia, 17 October–11 November).

Aluminium industry

In the non-ferrous metals subsector, the aluminium industry continued to be the main recipient of UNIDO technical assistance. Although the world economic situation had led to a decline in aluminium production over the last few years—notably in Japan and the United States—there had been a recent improvement in the industry and demands had increased. Events of the preceding two years had accelerated the process of the restructuring of aluminium production from developed to developing countries.

UNIDO continued assistance to the Guangzhou factory in China for a pilot plant manufacturing aluminium alloy door and window frames. It contributed a paper on the aluminium industry in the Arab world to the First International Arab Aluminium Conference (Kuwait, 24-26 October), and undertook a feasibility study for the reconstruction in India of an alumina calciner designed to reduce fuel oil consumption. Also in India, a team of experts examined possibilities for improving anode performance in aluminium smelting, and a detailed project report was prepared on the establishment of an aluminium research, development and design centre in that country.

Assistance was also continued for upgrading the scientific and technological capabilities of the Jamaica Bauxite Institute, and for the Aluminium Project Bureau in Mozambique, with a view to establishing an aluminium smelter. Under the Joint UNIDO/Hungary Aluminium Industry Programme, a number of technical assistance activities were carried out in support of the bauxite/alumina/aluminium industry in developing countries. These included a five-week training programme on alumina production; preparation of two training kits, one on the environmental aspects of bauxite/alumina production and another on possibilities for energy conservation; preparation of a manual on laboratory practice in alumina production; and a study related to establishment of linkages of a vertically integrated aluminium industry. Within the programme, a number of Hungarian experts in the aluminium industry were made available for technical co-operation projects in China, India, Jamaica and Mozambique. Assistance was provided to Zimbabwe for the investigation of prospects for producing lithium salts and alumino-silicate-based products together with potential market outlets.

Iron and steel industry

During 1983, technical co-operation activities in the metallurgical sector were predominantly related to the iron and steel industry.

Whereas in 1982 world output of raw steel totalled some 643.6 million tons (metric), down from 707.7 million in 1981 due largely to reduced output by industrialized countries, the output of developing countries was either maintained or increased. As a result of favourable supply and demand trends, projections for the next 10 years were for the growth of steel production facilities in India, Latin America and the Middle East, based on raw materials. High transportation costs and increased utilization of steel scrap had encouraged establishment of mini-steel plants at centres of consumption. In support of this trend, UNIDO undertook techno-economic studies in this area for some countries (Afghanistan, Democratic Yemen, Yemen), as well as a techno-economic evaluation for the establishment of the iron and steel industry in the United Republic of Tanzania, using domestic coal and iron ore.

A $1.4 million project designed to strengthen a research and development centre for the industry in Argentina became fully operational during the year. Drilling for iron ore deposits in Niger was completed, and some 13 tons of ore samples were being tested to determine ore beneficiation, pelletizing and direct reduction characteristics. A regional programme was prepared for the development of the Arab iron and steel industry, including upgrading the technical manpower skills of the Arab Iron and Steel Union. Jointly with Brazil, UNIDO organized and financed an international seminar on steel standardization (Rio de Janeiro, 21-25 November), which generated awareness of the importance of standards and quality certification.

REFERENCES

[1]A/38/16 (conclusion 1983/4). [2]YUN 1981, p. 588. [3]ID/306. [4]ID/WG.387/10. [5]ID/311. [6]UNIDO/PC.76. [7]ID/WG.397/9 & Add.1. [8]ID/307.

PUBLICATIONS

Formulation of Pesticides in Developing Countries (ID/297), Sales No. E.83.II.B.3. *World Non-Electrical Machinery: An Empirical Study of the Machine-Tool Industry* (ID/290 & Abstract), Sales No. E.83.II.B.5 & Abstract.

Chapter VII

Transnational corporations

The Commission on Transnational Corporations held a special session during March and May 1983 to complete formulation of a code of conduct on transnational corporations (TNCs); significant progress was achieved although not completion. The session's report, containing the agreed provisions and an outline of outstanding issues, was transmitted by the Economic and Social Council (decision 1983/183) in July to the General Assembly. By decision 38/428 of December, the Assembly decided to reconvene the special session in 1984 to continue work on the code.

The Commission's Intergovernmental Working Group of Experts on International Standards of Accounting and Reporting held its first session during February/March 1983. The Commission held its ninth regular session in New York, from 20 to 30 June,[1] and reviewed the work of the United Nations Centre on Transnational Corporations, the main Secretariat unit for TNC-related matters.

In 1983, the Council took several other actions relating to TNCs. Decision 1983/104 and resolution 1983/75 concerned further preparations for the Commission's 1985 public hearings on TNC activities in South Africa and Namibia, while resolution 1983/74 also dealt with those activities and TNC collaboration with the racist régime in South Africa (see POLITICAL AND SECURITY QUESTIONS, Chapter V).

Topics related to this chapter. Africa: transnational corporations. International trade and finance: restrictive business practices and commodity trade.

Draft code of conduct

Special session of the Commission. Pursuant to an October 1982 Economic and Social Council resolution,[2] the Commission on TNCs held a special session in 1983, open to the participation of all States, in order to complete formulation of a draft code of conduct on TNCs. As background, the Centre on TNCs provided an information paper to Governments to brief them on the code's structure and evolution, the status of the negotiations and the major outstanding issues. In addition, during January and February, the Centre organized briefing meetings at Addis Ababa (Ethiopia), Bangkok (Thailand) and New York and in most countries of the Economic Commission for Western Asia.

The special session was held in New York from 7 to 18 March and from 9 to 21 May;[3] the work was conducted in both formal and informal meetings.

In March, the Commission established two working groups to formulate proposals on sections and key issues of the draft code identified as outstanding when the Intergovernmental Working Group on a Code of Conduct had finalized its work in May 1982.[4] Working Group I dealt with the sections on the preamble and objectives, and on definitions and scope of application; Working Group II considered sections on activities of TNCs and on their treatment.

In May, the Commission considered a working paper, submitted jointly by the Chairmen of the working groups, containing a set of proposals relating to the sections on definitions and scope of application, on TNC activities and on TNC treatment; the proposals on each section were presented as a package which, according to the Chairmen, represented a delicate balance among the various positions that was likely to be upset by any major change in a particular text. The Commission reached agreement on the paragraphs concerning adherence to economic goals and development objectives, policies and priorities; ownership and control; balance of payments and financing, accepted *ad referendum* by some delegations; and the treatment of issues relating to competition and restrictive business practices, although the paragraph's placement remained to be resolved.

No final decision was taken on the paragraph on non-collaboration by TNCs with racist minority régimes in southern Africa: many delegations supported the text on the understanding that the paragraph heading formed an integral part of the text; one delegation stated that the text should also include racist régimes in other areas, while others could not arrive at a decision. No agreement was reached on the paragraphs relating to non-interference in internal political affairs and in intergovernmental relations. As to the proposals on definitions and scope of application and on TNC treatment, they were considered as not meeting a number of substantial concerns and therefore were to be amended considerably; in particular, concern was expressed that applicability of the definitions to enterprises and entities of all countries had not been clarified adequately.

A working paper on the preamble and objectives submitted by the Chairman of Working Group I was not considered by the Commission in May. While many delegations supported the proposed text as an adequate expression of the main issues, others felt that, among other modifications, more elements on the positive contribution of TNCs should be included.

Although formulation of the draft code had not been completed, the Commission, on 21 May, adopted the report on its special session, annexing the agreed paragraphs and the texts that had been evolved for further consideration.

ECONOMIC AND SOCIAL COUNCIL ACTION

In July 1983, during consideration of the agenda item on TNCs by the First (Economic) Committee of the Economic and Social Council, Bangladesh introduced a draft resolution on behalf of the Group of 77 developing countries.[5] By that text, the Council would have: reconvened the special session of the Commission on TNCs early in 1984 to complete formulation of the draft code of conduct; had the session submit to the Council in 1984 the completed draft, for transmittal to the General Assembly that year; reaffirmed that the first objective of the code was to embody rules and guidelines addressed to TNCs and that no provision should be construed as indicating acceptance of conduct by corporations not allowed by host country legislation; and urged all concerned to demonstrate the political will and commitment to conclude the draft code without further delay. Following statements on the draft resolution, the Committee decided to transmit it to the Council for further consideration.[6]

At the Council meeting on 29 July, Bangladesh stated that the Group of 77 had decided to withdraw the draft, having concluded that, to avoid repetition of the unsatisfactory outcome of the Commission's March/May special session, the most appropriate step was to take the matter up at the 1983 Assembly session.

Acting on an oral proposal by its President, the Council adopted decision 1983/183 without vote.

Report of the Commission on Transnational Corporations on its special session

At its 41st plenary meeting, on 29 July 1983, the Council decided to transmit the report of the Commission on Transnational Corporations on its special session to the General Assembly at its thirty-eighth session for consideration and action.

Economic and Social Council decision 1983/183

Adopted without vote

Oral proposal by President; agenda item 8.
Meeting number. ESC 41.

In related actions, the Council, in resolution 1983/56 on permanent sovereignty over natural resources, affirmed the importance of the Commission's ongoing work on a code of conduct as it related to natural resources. In resolution 1983/74 on TNC activities in South Africa and Namibia, the Council reaffirmed that the code should include effective measures against TNC collaboration with the racist minority régime in southern Africa.

GENERAL ASSEMBLY ACTION

The General Assembly, acting without vote on a recommendation of the Second (Economic and Financial) Committee, adopted decision 38/428.

Special session of the Commission on Transnational Corporations

At its 102nd plenary meeting, on 19 December 1983, the General Assembly, on the recommendation of the Second Committee, decided to reconvene for one week early in 1984 the special session of the Commission on Transnational Corporations, open to the participation of all States, for the purpose of assessing the work on the draft code of conduct on transnational corporations to facilitate the negotiation of outstanding issues, on the understanding that, if the outcome of that assessment was favourable, the Commission, at the end of its reconvened special session, would recommend the Economic and Social Council, at its organizational session for 1984, to reconvene further the special session for the completion of the code.

General Assembly decision 38/428

Adopted without vote

Approved by Second Committee (A/38/701Add.1) without vote, 28 November (meeting 52); draft by Chairman (A/C.2/38/L.77); agenda item 12.
Financial implications. 5th Committee, A/38/751; S-G, A/C.2/38/L.83, A/C.5/38/61.
Meeting numbers. GA 38th session: 2nd Committee 52; plenary 102.

Definition of TNC

In March 1983, at the first part of the special session of the Commission on TNCs,[3] it was agreed that certain elements of the definition of the term "transnational corporation" would be elaborated in the provisions relating to the scope of the code's application. Accordingly, a set of proposals was evolved that included a paragraph setting out the essential characteristics of a TNC—an enterprise *(a)* comprising entities in two or more countries, regardless of the entities' legal form and fields of activity, that *(b)* operated under a system of decision-making, permitting coherent policies and a common strategy through one or more decision-making centres, *(c)* in which the entities were so linked, by ownership or otherwise, that one or more might be able to exercise significant influence over the activities of others, and, in particular, to share knowledge, resources and responsibilities; a paragraph providing for the code's application to all enterprises having those characteristics regardless of ownership; and a paragraph stipulating that the code was universally applicable in and open for adoption by all countries.

These proposals were also considered in May, at the second part of the special session; however, no agreement was reached on the matter.

On 27 June,[1] during its 1983 regular session, the Commission noted the status of negotiations on the section of the code relating to definitions and scope of application.

Standards of accounting and reporting

The Intergovernmental Working Group of Experts on International Standards of Accounting and Reporting, established by the Economic and Social Council in October 1982,[7] held its first session in New York from 22 February to 4 March 1983.[8] Before it were two studies prepared by the Centre on TNCs: on specific issues of corporate accounting and reporting (information disclosure in relation to user needs, standard-setting approaches, financial accounting concepts, comparability, enforcement of standards); and on efforts to regulate and standardize corporate accounting and reporting in 20 selected countries.

During the general discussion, several delegations, stressing that information disclosure by TNCs was a matter of great importance to developing countries, urged attention to two priority issues: how to meet the information needs of those countries and enforcement of the Group's recommendations.

In accordance with its terms of reference, the Group formulated a programme of work, by which it agreed to review annually issues giving rise to divergent TNC accounting and reporting practices and to identify areas requiring harmonization, based on the work of standard-setting bodies and related studies and reports; to consider regularly accounting and reporting issues arising out of comprehensive information systems maintained by the Centre on TNCs and out of the code of conduct on TNCs currently being formulated; to designate, at each session, the issues to be considered at the following session from among those identified as outstanding by the *Ad Hoc* Intergovernmental Working Group of Experts on International Standards of Accounting and Reporting in 1982;[9] to identify issues arising out of the needs of home and host countries, particularly developing countries; to discuss measures that would give effect to its work, disseminate its results and develop education and training in accounting and reporting in Member States, especially the developing ones; and to discuss any other appropriate business.

The issues considered by the Group in 1983 included the concepts of "true and fair view" and of "accurate and honest" with respect to preparation of financial statements, equity method of accounting for investments, and accounting and reporting of contingent assets and liabilities. Attention was drawn to the importance of an auditor's association with certain financial and non-financial information.

On the Group's recommendation, the Commission on TNCs approved the Group's programme of work on 23 June;[1] it also took note of the Group's report[8] and approved the provisional agenda and documentation recommended for its second (1984) session.

Centre on TNCs

During 1983, the United Nations Centre on TNCs, the main Secretariat unit for matters relating to TNCs, continued to develop a comprehensive information system, carried out research, and conducted and supervised technical co-operation activities. It assisted in work related to the formulation of a code of conduct, and prepared studies for the Intergovernmental Working Group of Experts on International Standards of Accounting and Reporting. It co-operated with other organizations and units inside and outside the United Nations system, in particular with the joint units operated by the Centre and the United Nations regional commissions.

Taking note of the Secretary-General's report summarizing the Centre's activities since mid-1982,[10] together with a report on the financial implications of its 1983 work programme,[11] the Commission on TNCs, on 23 June 1983,[1] requested the Centre to take account in future of delegation views expressed during the discussion of its activities.

Information system

In 1983, the Centre on TNCs continued developing its comprehensive information system on TNCs and responded to a wide variety of requests for information. Collection and analysis of information under the various components of the system continued to expand—trends in TNC activities; policies, laws and regulations relating to TNCs; studies on TNC activities in selected sectors; individual corporations; contracts and agreements between TNCs and host country entities; sources of information; and standards of accounting and reporting. Information collection and analysis also extended to TNC involvement in the manufacture and distribution of toxic or hazardous chemicals and pharmaceuticals, and to TNC activities in colonial Territories, as requested by the General Assembly in December[12] and November[13] 1981.

As in the past, special emphasis was given to those elements accorded priority by the Commission on TNCs: legal information (policies, laws and regulations; contracts and agreements), macro data, industry studies of special importance to host developing countries and corporate profiles of selected individual corporations. The work accomplished was described by the Secretariat in a progress report[14] to the Commission's 1983 regular session, which also described such operational aspects of the system as co-ordination with information systems of other United Nations bodies, information dissemination and the Centre's resources.

According to that report and to a subsequent one covering activities for the remainder of 1983,[15] the Centre continued collecting material on legal enactments, administrative provisions, policy statements and related studies and reports, in addition to a significant number of bilateral and multilateral investment treaties and related agreements. Studies on selected international industries were in progress (see below).

Information on the 382 largest industrial TNCs was updated in respect of original data (on total and foreign components of sales, net assets, earnings, employment, and research and development expenditures) and expanded to cover total and foreign components of earnings before taxes, capital outlay, and wages and salaries. In addition, data on sales, net assets and earnings had been broken down by line of business and geographic areas. Some 170 corporate profiles had been completed and verified by the corporations concerned; another 150 were at various stages of preparation.

The Centre obtained some 90 additional contracts for analysis during the year, bringing the total number of its collection to over 800 contracts, and began a filing and coding system for effective access to them.

The Centre continued to enhance its knowledge of relevant public and private sources of information and their content. Its computer system currently included 13 data bases; it also had on-line access to some 200 data bases through which information could be obtained on developments related to industries in general or in specific countries, on activities of individual corporations and on measures taken by Governments.

Responding to a request from China, the Centre sent a mission there in April to help establish a transnational information centre. Requests for similar assistance had been received from Kenya and the Syrian Arab Republic. A request for assistance from Poland to improve and expand its data base was also received.

In December, the Centre made available the first issue of a list of chemical products deemed toxic or hazardous. It had compiled the list in co-operation with the Food and Agriculture Organization of the United Nations, the International Labour Organisation, the World Health Organization and the United Nations Environment Programme. By resolution 38/149 of 19 December, the Assembly urged the Centre, among other relevant United Nations bodies, to continue to co-operate in providing information for and updating the consolidated list.

In other action, the Centre, in response to a 1982 Assembly request,[16] submitted a register showing profits derived by TNC activities in colonial Territories, which the Assembly took note of by resolution 38/50 of 7 December 1983 (see TRUSTEESHIP AND DECOLONIZATION, Chapter I).

On 28 June,[1] the Commission on TNCs, having considered the Secretariat's progress report[14] on the Centre's information system on TNCs, requested the Centre to continue developing the system, taking account of delegation views.

Joint units with regional commissions

Joint units established between the Centre on TNCs and the United Nations regional commissions in developing areas continued to operate during 1983 in Africa, Asia and the Pacific, Europe, Latin America and Western Asia. Each unit's work programme, tailored to the region's specific needs and to complement the work of the Centre, included research on the economic, social and institutional issues of TNCs, mainly through case-studies, information dissemination, and training and advisory services.

The work of the units during the year was described in two Secretariat reports, one covering May 1982 to April 1983,[17] submitted to the Commission on TNCs at its 1983 session, and another covering May 1983 to March 1984,[18] prepared for its 1984 session.

Research completed or under way included country case-studies on the TNC role in banking and balance of payments and in primary commodity production and exports (Africa); studies on the socio-economic aspects of TNC impact on the food and beverages industry, on primary commodities and on transfer pricing practices, and a project on taxation of natural resource–based industries (Asia and the Pacific); a survey of investment and licensing practices of six European-based transnational bus-and-truck manufacturers in selected industrializing countries, two reports on the TNC role in the industrialization and trade of developing countries, and in relation to economic welfare and public policy (Europe); analysis of TNC impact on economic development in general and on the growth of external debt in particular (Latin America); and two country studies on transnational banks (Western Asia).

Information activities included updating lists or compiling inventories of TNCs operating or based in the region; collecting, analysing and disseminating basic information on them; direct mailing of publications and bibliographic lists; and initiating development of national information systems. In the area of advisory and training services, the joint units organized in co-operation with the Centre, participated in or provided resource persons for a number of meetings, seminars and workshops at which the work of the Commission on TNCs, the Centre and the units themselves were presented; advisory missions were undertaken.

On 23 June,[1] taking note of the 1982/83 Secretariat report,[17] the Commission requested the Centre to take into account the views expressed by delegations, among them that the joint units should undertake additional work on regional investment planning and government policies towards TNCs, to be co-ordinated with the Centre's work in this regard.

Research

Research activities of the Centre on TNCs continued to be aimed at attaining three main objectives: to increase knowledge and understanding of the nature of TNCs and their impact, particularly on developing countries; to strengthen the position of host countries, particularly developing ones, in their dealings with TNCs; and to examine the TNC role in relation to the broader aspects of the development process.

In 1983, the Centre completed work on a comprehensive integrated study on TNCs in world development.[19] The study, the third five-yearly review of the role of TNCs in the world economy, had been the centre-piece of the Centre's research activities in 1981 and 1982. A complementary report to examine the TNC role in implementation of the International Development Strategy for the Third United Nations Development Decade (the 1980s) was in preparation. The second edition of the bibliography of company directories worldwide was also completed and published.[20]

Studies on the following international industries were in progress: armaments, textile and synthetic fibre, construction and engineering, computer and data processing, biotechnology, telecommunications, petrochemicals and pharmaceuticals. An analysis of engineering and industrial consultancy contracts was under way.

Research work also continued on the TNC role in transborder data flows and their impact on home and host countries, particularly developing ones, with the main emphasis on TNCs and remote-sensing data; relationships between TNCs and State-owned enterprises; multilateral, regional and bilateral arrangements related to TNCs; and operations of transnational banks in host developing countries. Other research related to TNCs in South Africa and Namibia, TNCs and the employment of women, and TNCs and the environment.

Following consideration of the Centre's research programme, the Commission on TNCs, on 29 June,[1] orally amended and adopted a draft decision submitted by the Chairman.

By this decision, the Commission, reaffirming that the Centre's research must continue to conform with the objective of avoiding the negative effects of TNC activities on developing countries while maximizing their contribution to development, took note of the Secretariat's report on ongoing and future research[21] and requested the Centre to pay particular attention to: the role of transnational banks as lenders and financial investors in developing countries; the role of TNCs in the commercial, industrial and services sectors in the movements of short-term capital between countries; their contribution to new patterns of production and consumption in developing countries, oriented to conserve energy and other natural resources; their impact on employment in developing countries, and on the development process and international division of labour; conflicts of jurisdiction relating to TNCs; implications and effects of policies on transfer prices of goods and services exported to developing countries by TNCs; and their contribution to investment promotion in the least developed of the developing countries.

Also on 29 June, after considering the agenda item on recent developments related to TNCs and international economic relations, the Commission took note of the Secretariat report[22] presenting an overview of the *Third Survey* and of the publication itself, and decided to discuss further the issues it had raised. At the same meeting the Commission, by 26 votes to 10, postponed consideration of a draft resolution proposed for action by the Economic and Social Council. The text would have had the Council request the Centre to prepare a study on the activities of State-owned enterprises from both market and centrally planned economy countries conducting transnational operations, for presentation to the Commission in 1984, and to include material on such enterprises in all other studies on TNCs.

On the same date, the Commission took note of the Secretariat progress report on TNCs and transborder data flows[23] and requested the Centre to continue work in this area, taking into account the comments made during its discussion.

Technical co-operation

The programme of technical co-operation in advisory and training services of the Centre on TNCs continued in 1983 to respond to a wide variety of requests from developing countries in numerous sectors and areas. The Centre completed or initiated advisory projects in over 40 developing countries and conducted 18 training workshops attended by some 740 participants from 62 developing countries. These activities were described in two Secretariat reports, for the period July 1982 to March 1983[24] and for April to December 1983.[25]

As in the past, the advisory assistance delivered was largely for countries in Africa, Asia and the Pacific, and Latin America, with only a small part for Europe and the Western Asia subregion.

About one third of the projects related to policies, laws and regulations, involving assistance to Governments in *(a)* drafting, revising or evaluating laws and regulations related to TNC activities generally (foreign investment legislation and implementation procedures) or in specific sectors (petroleum, mining, forestry and export processing zones) and issues (technology acquisition); *(b)* examining overall policy options, or options on specific issues (ownership and control, fiscal régimes, performance requirements, incentives and guarantees, access to domestic financial resources, repatriation of capital and investment income); and *(c)* developing guidelines and procedures for projects involving foreign participation, as well as relevant administrative arrangements.

The other two thirds of the projects related to specific arrangements with TNCs in natural resources sectors (petroleum, mining, agriculture, forestry and fisheries) and in manufacturing and service industries (electronics, chemicals, textiles, telecommunications, electric power generation, hotels and airlines). Advisory assistance involved evaluating the merits of alternative forms of contractual arrangements; evaluating legal, financial, economic and operational issues; and providing staff support in preparation for negotiations.

Of the 18 training workshops conducted, seven were general, dealing on a cross-sectional basis with policy matters and specific issues arising from relationships between host countries and TNCs; 11 were specialized, dealing with those same topics in relation to the specific sectors of engineering and construction, fisheries, sugar, mining, petroleum and pharmaceuticals, and to the specific issues of negotiating loans on international capital markets, screening and monitoring industrial projects, and special economic and export processing zones. There were regional and subregional workshops for Asia (nine, including one each for Western Asia, the Pacific islands and the Association of South-East Asian Nations), Africa (one) and Latin America (one); and national workshops for Bangladesh, China, Kenya, Liberia, Mauritius, Namibia (two), Somalia and Zambia.

On 28 June,[1] the Commission took note of the Secretariat report ended March 1983.[24] It

reaffirmed the importance it attached to the Centre's technical co-operation programme and urged the Centre to undertake an evaluation of the usefulness of completed projects and to report to the Commission in 1984. Expressing appreciation to Governments that had made voluntary contributions, the Commission urged others to make similar contributions and recipient Governments to cover local project costs.

Financing

In 1983, the Trust Fund for the United Nations Centre on TNCs, the main source of funding for implementation of the Centre's technical co-operation programme, had an income of $1,740,599.[25] That amount included contributions by three Governments of $436,900 (Finland, $27,700; Norway, $209,300; Sweden, $199,900), interest and miscellaneous income of $114,500 and $139,200 respectively, and a contribution to the programme of $1,049,999 by the United Nations Development Programme (UNDP). Expenditures during the year came to $1,736,699, of which the UNDP share was approximately 60.4 per cent (or $1,049,999), compared to 30 per cent in 1982.[26] Pledged in 1983 for 1984 was a total of $427,170.

Commission on TNCs

Work programme for 1984

ECONOMIC AND SOCIAL COUNCIL ACTION

On the recommendation of its First Committee, the Economic and Social Council adopted decision 1983/182 without vote.

Provisional agenda and documentation for the tenth session of the Commission on Transnational Corporations

At its 41st plenary meeting, on 29 July 1983, the Council approved the provisional agenda and documentation for the tenth session of the Commission on Transnational Corporations, set out below.

Provisional agenda and documentation for the tenth session of the Commission on Transnational Corporations

1. Recent developments related to transnational corporations and international economic relations
   Documentation
      Updated material on the third integrated study on transnational corporations in world development
      Report on the role of transnational corporations in the implementation of the International Development Strategy
2. Activities of the United Nations Centre on Transnational Corporations
   (a) Reports on the activities of the United Nations Centre on Transnational Corporations

Documentation
  Report of the Secretary-General on the activities of the United Nations Centre on Transnational Corporations
  Report on the activities of the joint units with the regional commissions
(b) Allocation of resources among the programme elements of the United Nations Centre on Transnational Corporations
Documentation
  Note on the allocation and use of resources among the programme elements of the United Nations Centre on Transnational Corporations
3 . Work related to the formulation of a code of conduct and other international arrangements and agreements
(a) Code of conduct
Documentation
  Report on the code of conduct on transnational corporations
(b) Bilateral, regional and international arrangements on matters relating to transnational corporations
Documentation
  Report of the Secretariat
4 . International standards of accounting and reporting
Documentation
  Report of the Intergovernmental Working Group of Experts on International Standards of Accounting and Reporting on its second session
5 . Policy analysis and research
(a) Activities of transnational corporations in South Africa and Namibia and collaboration of such corporations with the racist minority régime in that area
Documentation
  Report on the activities of transnational corporations and on measures being taken by Governments to prohibit investments in South Africa and Namibia
  Report of the *ad hoc* committee on the organization of public hearings on the activities of transnational corporations in South Africa and Namibia
(b) Ongoing and future research
Documentation
  Report on ongoing and future research, including a review of the research programme
  Transnational corporations and the production, processing and marketing of primary commodities
(c) The role of transnational corporations in transborder data flows
Documentation
  Report of the Secretariat

6 . Comprehensive information system
Documentation
  Report on the comprehensive information system on transnational corporations
7 . Technical co-operation
Documentation
  Report on the programme of technical co-operation
8 . Work related to the definition of transnational corporations
Documentation
  Report of the Secretariat on the question of the definition of transnational corporations
9 . Question of expert advisers
Documentation
  Note by the Secretariat containing the list of candidates for expert advisers
10 . Responsibilities of home countries with respect to the transnational corporations operating in South Africa and Namibia in violation of the relevant resolutions and decisions of the United Nations
Documentation
  Report of the Secretariat

Economic and Social Council decision 1983/182
Adopted without vote

Approved by First Committee (E/1983/125) without vote, 27 July (meeting 25); draft by Commission on TNCs (E/1983/18/Rev.1); agenda item 8.
Meeting number. ESC 41.

In other action—decision 1983/184 of 29 July—the Council decided to maintain, for a further period of two years, the discontinuance of summary records for the Commission on TNCs.

REFERENCES
[1]E/1983/18/Rev.1. [2]YUN 1982, p. 786, ESC res. 1982/68, 27 Oct. 1982. [3]E/1983/17/Rev.1. [4]YUN 1982, p. 785. [5]E/1983/C.1/L.21. [6]A/38/3. [7]YUN 1982, p. 788, ESC res. 1982/67, 27 Oct. 1982. [8]E/C.10/1983/8. [9]YUN 1982, p. 787. [10]E/C.10/1983/3. [11]E/C.10/1983/5. [12]YUN 1981, p. 825, GA res. 36/166, 16 Dec. 1981. [13]*Ibid*, p. 1108, GA res. 36/51, 24 Nov. 1981. [14]E/C.10/1983/7. [15]E/C.10/1984/15. [16]YUN 1982, p. 1268, GA res. 37/31, 23 Nov. 1982. [17]E/C.10/1983/4 & Corr.1. [18]E/C.10/1984/5. [19]*Transnational Corporations in World Development: Third Survey* (ST/CTC/46 & Corr.1), Sales No. E/F.83.II.A.14 & corrigendum. [20]*List of Company Directories and Summary of Their Contents*, second edition (ST/CTC/33), Sales No. E/F.83.II.A.10. [21]E/C.10/1983/13. [22]E/C.10/1983/2. [23]E/C.10/1983/12 & Corr.1. [24]E/C.10/1983/9. [25]E/C.10/1984/16. [26]YUN 1982, p. 791.

PUBLICATIONS
The CTC Reporter, No. 14, Sales No. E.83.II.A.2; No. 15, Sales No. E.83.II.A.11; No. 16, Sales No. E.83.II.A.20. *Issues in Negotiating International Loan Agreements with Transnational Banks* (ST/CTC/48), Sales No. E.83.II.A.18.

Chapter VIII

Regional economic and social activities

At a time when the global economic situation made it more urgent to increase economic and technical co-operation among themselves, increased efforts were made by all the regional commissions in 1983 to promote interregional co-operation.

In 1983, four of the five regional commissions held their regular intergovernmental sessions at their respective headquarters: the Economic Commission for Africa (ECA) at Addis Ababa, Ethiopia (27 April-3 May); the Economic and Social Commission for Asia and the Pacific (ESCAP) at Bangkok, Thailand (19-29 April); the Economic Commission for Europe (ECE) at Geneva, Switzerland (12-23 April) and the Economic Commission for Western Asia (ECWA) at Baghdad, Iraq (7-11 May). The Economic Commission for Latin America (ECLA) did not meet in regular session during the year.

Among issues of concern to the regional commissions considered by the General Assembly in 1983 were the food and agriculture situation in Africa (resolutions 38/159, 38/198), implementation of the 1980 Lagos Plan of Action for economic development of Africa (38/199), Transport and Communications Decade in Africa (1978-1988) (38/150), Zaire's transport and transit problems (38/143), co-operation between the United Nations system and the Southern African Development Co-ordination Conference (38/160) and administrative questions involving restructuring and decentralization (decision 38/432).

Adequacy of the conference facilities at ECA and ESCAP headquarters was also discussed (sections XXIII and VII of resolution 38/234, respectively), as well as the funding arrangements for the Regional Commissions Liaison Office in New York (section X of resolution 38/234).

The Economic and Social Council, at its second regular session of 1983, took action on: the Europe-Africa permanent link through the Strait of Gibraltar (resolution 1983/62), Zaire's transit problems (1983/64), special measures for the social and economic development of Africa in the 1980s (1983/65), the Transport and Communications Decade in Africa (1983/67), the Transport and Communications Decade in Asia and the Pacific (1983/69), and the Industrial Development Decade for Africa (1980-1989) (1983/70). The Council decided that the provision of summary records should remain discontinued for a number

of its subsidiary bodies, among them ECA, ESCAP, ECE and ECLA ((decision 1983/184)) (see Chapter XXIV of this section).

Summaries of the annual survey of current economic conditions in each region, prepared by commission secretariats, were examined and taken note of by the Council in July during its discussion of the world economic situation (see p. 422). The Council further took note of the report on the meetings of the commissions' executive secretaries on promoting interregional co-operation (decision 1983/180), as well as the Addis Ababa declaration on the occasion of the silver jubilee anniversary celebration of ECA (resolution 1983/63). The Assembly also took note of that declaration (decision 38/434).

Topics related to this chapter. Development and international economic and social policy: economic and social trends and policy. Development assistance. Economic assistance, disasters and emergency relief. Food.

Regional co-operation

Interregional co-operation

In 1983, the regional commissions placed particular emphasis on promoting effective interregional economic and technical co-operation among developing countries.

Reports of the Secretary-General. Reporting to the Economic and Social Council in June 1983, with a July addendum, on the two meetings (New York, 5 November 1982; Geneva, 11 and 12 July 1983)[1] which the executive secretaries of the five regional commissions had held since the Council's July 1982 session, the Secretary-General noted the unanimous endorsement among them of a Council proposal for an inter-secretariat meeting to achieve optimal co-ordination of activities between different components of the United Nations system (see p. 418). The executive secretaries also agreed to establish an intra-secretariat task force that would assist the Secretary-General in preparing a report to the Assembly, as requested in 1982,[2] on progress made in decentralizing United Nations activities. The Secretary-General's report also described the work of the commissions and issues brought by them to the Council for consideration or action.

Another June report, prepared by the regional commissions for submission to the Council by the Secretary-General,[3] stressed the need for the commissions to help establish and strengthen cooperative arrangements among their member countries in order to ensure effective pooling of capabilities in support of interregional economic and technical co-operation. Considering it advisable in the initial stage to concentrate on priority areas based on resource availability and programme impact, the regional commissions identified some of the issues of immediate concern to the developing world, requiring urgent interregional action. The issues included: food security, where developing countries could pledge mutual assistance and establish a progress monitoring mechanism; joint ventures in agro- and marine-based industries; a "safety network" among developing countries ensuring exchange of technology, production and trade in energy other than oil; co-operation for fair and equitable pricing for primary exports, including agreed production and export arrangements; technological exchanges in agriculture; identification of commodities for interregional trade; short-term co-operation in balance-of-trade and payments adjustments; programmes for intercontinental transport links and freight-rate negotiation.

While aware of the need to avoid proliferation of new institutional arrangements, the regional commissions saw need for a facility which would develop a continuously enlarged portfolio of feasible projects for joint ventures among developing countries as well as train officials in all phases of co-operative projects; the commissions felt that a beginning could be made with the creation of a strong joint arrangement among themselves.

ECONOMIC AND SOCIAL COUNCIL ACTION

In July 1983, the Economic and Social Council, acting on the recommendation of its First (Economic) Committee, adopted decision 1983/180.

Meetings of the executive secretaries of the regional commissions

At its 41st plenary meeting, on 29 July 1983, the Council took note of the report of the Secretary-General on the meetings of the executive secretaries of the regional commissions.

Economic and Social Council decision 1983/180

Adopted without vote

Approved by First Committee (E/1983/123) without vote, 27 July (meeting 25); agenda item 7.
Meeting number. ESC 41.

The Council, in resolution 1983/66 of 29 July, called on the executive secretaries to organize peri-

odic consultations between their respective commissions and relevant United Nations bodies with a view to ensuring the effective co-ordination of projects and programmes. That call was subsequently endorsed by the General Assembly in decision 38/435 of 19 December (see p. 418).

Restructuring

In an October 1983 report to the General Assembly,[4] prepared in response to its December 1982 resolution[2] concerning decentralization of resources and responsibilities throughout the United Nations system, the Secretary-General stated that such a policy—aimed at making the Organization more responsive to the needs of the developing countries—was gradually emerging in the administrative but not in the substantive programme areas, where difficulties were encountered in developing and applying consistent approaches and criteria. He reported that arrangements were being made to institute more systematic consultations between United Nations Headquarters and the regional commission secretariats at all stages of programme planning and budgeting, and that senior-level intersecretariat meetings were envisaged to contribute to the most effective distribution of responsibilities for implementing relevant Assembly and Council resolutions.

The decentralization and restructuring efforts continued in the regional commissions, with noteworthy results reported with regard to transport and water resources. A comprehensive review of the public administration programme was undertaken by the Committee for Programme and Co-ordination (CPC) in 1982[5] and modalities were suggested to improve co-operation in that area. A review was being planned for decentralization of activities in such areas as public administration, development issues and policies, social development, science and technology, population, and advisory services.

In the proposed programme budget of the United Nations for 1984-1985,[6] which involved an overall real growth of 0.7 per cent (see ADMINISTRATIVE AND BUDGETARY QUESTIONS, Chapter I), a 3.5 per cent growth was proposed for the four commissions in developing regions, in line with the efforts at decentralization through reinforcing their capacities as major instruments in realizing the potential of economic co-operation among developing countries. That growth was to provide additional posts to sustain the work in the population field in those commissions and to respond to their priority programme needs in such areas as industry and trade. The General Assembly dealt with the question of decentralization and restructuring, as they related to regional commissions, in decision 38/432 (see below, under AFRICA).

In related action, the Assembly, in resolution 38/106, urged the Secretary-General, in consultation with the executive secretaries of the regional commissions, to ensure continuation of senior women's programme officers posts at those commissions (see Chapter XIX of this section).

Regional commissions liaison office

In reviewing the proposed 1984-1985 programme budget for the Economic and Social Commission for Asia and the Pacific (ESCAP), which included the Regional Commissions Liaison Office, CPC[7] concluded that the appropriations for the Office should not be part of the programme budget section of a regional commission, and requested the Secretary-General to make appropriate recommendations to the Assembly.

The Secretary-General subsequently proposed establishing a new section in the proposed budget,[8] adding that the move entailed separation of staff and other associated resources proposed for that office from ESCAP, without additional financial implications or other changes.[9] The Regional Commissions Liaison Office, in operation at Headquarters since 1981, served as a link between the commission secretariats and Headquarters as well as with relevant intergovernmental and non-governmental organizations in New York.

GENERAL ASSEMBLY ACTION

On 20 December, the Assembly, on the recommendation of the Fifth (Administrative and Budgetary) Committee, adopted section X of resolution 38/234 without vote.

Regional Commissions Liaison Office

[*The General Assembly . . .*]

1. *Takes note* of the report of the Secretary-General on the revised estimates under section 11 (Economic and Social Commission for Asia and the Pacific) and on a new section 5C (Regional Commissions Liaison Office);

2. *Decides* to establish a new section 5C of the programme budget entitled "Regional Commissions Liaison Office";

. . .

General Assembly resolution 38/234, section X

20 December 1983   Meeting 104   Adopted without vote

Approved by Fifth Committee (A/38/760) without vote, 30 November (meeting 51); oral proposal by Chairman; agenda item 109.
Meeting numbers. GA 38th session: 5th Committee 51; plenary 104.

REFERENCES
[1]E/1983/86 & Add.1. & Corr.1. [2]YUN 1982, p. 828, GA res. 37/214, 20 Dec. 1982. [3]E/1983/70. [4]A/38/505. [5]YUN 1982, p. 1240. [6]A/38/6. [7]A/38/38/Part II. [8]A/38/505/Add.1. [9]A/C.5/38/52 & Corr.1.

Africa

The critical climatic situation in Africa, with severe drought continuing to affect food production and cause loss of livestock, overshadowed the work of the Economic Commission for Africa (ECA) in 1983.

The twenty-fifth Anniversary of the establishment of ECA, coinciding with the eighteenth session of the Commission and the ninth meeting of its Conference of Ministers (the highest policy body of the Commission), was observed at ECA Headquarters at Addis Ababa, Ethiopia, from 27 April to 2 May 1983.[1] A review of the socio-economic development in Africa, 1958-1983, and a preliminary perspective study of ECA and Africa's development, 1983-2008, highlighted the Silver Jubilee agenda.

Regarding socio-economic development, 1958-1983, a paper prepared by the secretariat stated that, despite progress made, Africa was still faced with a menacing economic crisis challenging its survival. The ECA Executive Secretary told the session that there had, however, been significant progress since the 1960s when many African countries had become politically independent, especially when it was realized that the colonial period did not prepare the Continent for socio-economic development.

On development, 1983-2008, a secretariat preliminary perspective study presented two scenarios: one based on the assumption of continuation of current policies and socio-economic and growth patterns, and the other on the assumption that the goals and objectives of the 1980 Lagos Plan of Action for the Implementation of the Monrovia Strategy for the Economic Development of Africa and the Final Act of Lagos[2] would be achieved. The implication of the first scenario was that, half a century after independence, Africa would still depend on foreign sources of supply in almost all essential areas, which could be expected to have disastrous effects on the food and energy situation and on such social services as education, health and housing. The second scenario supported a radical and substantive transformation of African economies in a desirable change as recommended in the Lagos Plan.

On 29 April, the Addis Ababa Declaration on the Occasion of the Silver Jubilee Anniversary Celebration[1] was adopted. Among other things, it dedicated Commission members to total liberation of Africa; denounced the "linkage proposal" regarding Namibian independence (see TRUSTEESHIP AND DECOLONIZATION, Chapter III); denounced inhuman oppression of the South African people by the Pretoria régime and called for majority rule in that country; reaffirmed the 1980

Lagos Plan of Action; and expressed serious concern over devastating crises of chronic food deficits, pernicious drought, natural disasters, high costs of imports, particularly manufactured goods, capital goods and energy, deteriorating terms of trade, mounting external debts and problems of economic management. It further noted with concern the erroneous belief that development and economic growth depended mostly on external demand and supply factors; consequent neglect of the development of adequate indigenous entrepreneurs, high-level manpower and national, subregional and regional markets; and inappropriate agricultural and industrial policies.

The Declaration further expressed grave concern that, if past and current policies continued, ECA's Golden Jubilee in 2008 would witness a highly marginalized Africa, beset with worse crises of food and energy shortages and balance-of-payments deficits with most factor inputs coming from abroad. It resolved that implementation of the Lagos Plan of Action and the Final Act rested on African Governments and peoples; called, at the same time, on the international community to provide moral, technical and financial support to that endeavour; appealed for immediate initiation of global negotiations for an equitable new order in the international economic and social system; appealed to developed countries to increase official development assistance to developing countries to the target of 0.7 per cent of gross national product and to earmark 0.15 per cent of gross national product for aid to least developed countries (LDCs). Twenty-six of the world's 36 LDCs were among the 50 independent African countries.

The Declaration called for United Nations specialized agencies and African intergovernmental organizations to provide assistance to achieve: food self-sufficiency and security; a physically integrated continent in transport and communications; self-sufficiency in supply of middle- and high-level manpower; the objectives of the Industrial Development Decade for Africa (1980-1990);[3] increased intra-Africa trade and finance co-operation; reinforced transfer, development and adaptation of appropriate development technologies; full knowledge and better exploration, development and utilization of natural resources; and economic co-operation and integration for collective self-reliance.

The Conference of Ministers of ECA, at its 1983 session, adopted 27 resolutions,[1] on various issues of socio-economic development in Africa. Among them were issues brought to the attention of the Economic and Social Council including: support to African land-locked and island countries; United Nations Transport and Communications Decade in Africa (1978-1988); problems of freedoms of the air; the climatic situation and drought; development of cartographic services; and development of resources of the sea.

Other substantive resolutions adopted dealt with: survey of economic and social conditions, situation of food and agriculture, assistance to the livestock sector, implementation of the Industrial Development Decade, establishment of an African Monetary Fund, interregional economic and technical co-operation, statistical services, perspective studies in African countries, Africa and the ongoing international economic negotiations, women in development, strengthening of African capabilities in environmental matters, human settlements, evaluation and harmonization of the activities of African multinational institutions sponsored by ECA and OAU, strengthening of the Multinational Programming and Operational Centres, support to the United Nations Trust Fund for African Development, measures for accelerating the implementation of the Substantial New Programme of Action in African Least Developed Countries, first round of review meetings for the African least developed countries, and activities of the secretariat.

ECA Committee meetings in 1983 were (held at Addis Ababa, unless otherwise specified): Conference of African Ministers of Transport, Communications and Planning (third meeting, Cairo, Egypt, 8-11 March); Follow-up Committee (of the Whole) on Industrialization in Africa (Kigali, Rwanda, 16-19 March); Inter-governmental Committee of Experts of African Least Developed Countries (third meeting, 11-13 April); Meeting of Technical Preparatory Committee of the Whole (fourth meeting, 14-22 April); Conference of Ministers of African Least Developed Countries (third meeting, 25 and 26 April); and Intergovernmental Committee of Experts for Science and Technology Development (second meeting, 14-18 November).

ECONOMIC AND SOCIAL COUNCIL

On 29 July, the Economic and Social Council, acting on the recommendation of its First (Economic) Committee, adopted resolution 1983/63 without vote.

Addis Ababa Declaration on the Occasion of the Silver Jubilee Anniversary Celebration of the Economic Commission for Africa

The Economic and Social Council,

Recalling General Assembly resolutions 32/197 of 20 December 1977, 33/202 of 29 January 1979 and 34/206 of 19 December 1979, concerning the restructuring of the economic and social sectors of the United Nations system, by which the Assembly assigned specific additional tasks to regional commissions, including assuming the role of main general economic and social development centres for their respective regions, providing team leadership and responsibility for co-ordination and co-operation at the regional level and acting as executing agencies,

Mindful of the terms of reference of the Economic Commission for Africa, under which, *inter alia*, the Commission shall participate in measures for facilitating concerted action for the economic development of Africa, including its social aspects, with a view to raising the level of economic activity and levels of living in Africa, and shall assist in the formulation and development of co-ordinated policies as a basis for practical action in promoting economic and technological development in the region,

Noting with satisfaction that in April 1983 the Economic Commission for Africa celebrated the Silver Jubilee Anniversary of its establishment, and noting further that during the past twenty-five years Africa has made noteworthy progress in various aspects of economic and social development, including regional co-operation and integration, as noted in the Addis Ababa Declaration on the Occasion of the Silver Jubilee Anniversary Celebration of the Economic Commission for Africa, adopted on 29 April 1983 by the Conference of Ministers of the Commission,

Expressing its appreciation to the Executive Secretary of the Economic Commission for Africa for his introduction to the general discussion of international economic and social policy, including regional and sectoral developments, in which he apprised the Council of the economic and social conditions prevailing in the African region over the past twelve months,

1. *Takes note with satisfaction* of the report of the Secretary-General on regional co-operation;

2. *Notes* the Addis Ababa Declaration on the Occasion of the Silver Jubilee Anniversary Celebration of the Economic Commission for Africa, particularly the full commitment of the African Governments and peoples to the realization of the goals and objectives of the Lagos Plan of Action for the Implementation of the Monrovia Strategy for the Economic Development of Africa and the Final Act of Lagos, which are an integral part of the International Development Strategy for the Third United Nations Development Decade;

3. *Congratulates* the Economic Commission for Africa on its many positive contributions to Africa in economic and social development and integration during the past twenty-five years;

4. *Encourages* the Commission to intensify its efforts so that the socio-economic development of Africa can be accelerated and national and collective self-reliance at subregional and regional levels can be achieved;

5. *Expresses its confidence* in the dedicated work being undertaken by the secretariat of the Commission and in the ability of the Commission to discharge fully its increased responsibilities for the welfare of the African peoples;

6. *Also expresses its deep concern* with regard to the economic and food prospects for Africa in the year 2000 if the present obstacles to the development of the continent are not quickly removed;

7. *Recommends* the General Assembly to call upon the international community to support the endeavour of the African Governments towards achieving the accelerated development and integration of their continent, by making available to them the necessary moral, technical and financial assistance.

Economic and Social Council resolution 1983/63
29 July 1983   Meeting 41   Adopted without vote

Approved by First Committee (E/1983/123) without vote, 25 July (meeting 23); draft by Mali, for African Group (E/1983/C.1/L.16), orally amended in informal consultations; agenda item 7.
Meeting number. ESC 41.

GENERAL ASSEMBLY ACTION

On the recommendation of the Second (Economic and Financial) Committee, the General Assembly adopted decision 38/434 without vote in December.

Addis Ababa Declaration on the Occasion of the Silver Jubilee Anniversary Celebration of the Economic Commission for Africa

At its 102nd plenary meeting, on 19 December 1983, the General Assembly, on the recommendation of the Second Committee, decided to endorse Economic and Social Council resolution 1983/63 of 29 July 1983 and called upon the international community to support the endeavour of the African Governments towards achieving the accelerated development and integration of their continent by making available to them the necessary moral, technical and financial assistance.

General Assembly decision 38/434
Adopted without vote

Approved by Second Committee (A/38/701Add.1) without vote, 14 December (meeting 56); draft orally proposed by Chairman; agenda item 12.
Meeting numbers. GA 38th session: 2nd Committee 56; plenary 102.

Economic and social trends

Many countries of Africa continued to suffer in 1982 from balance-of-payment difficulties because of lower export revenues originating from lower prices and volume, according to a summary,[4] issued in March 1983, of the ECA survey of economic conditions in Africa. Official development assistance (ODA) flows remained insufficient in real terms to cover the needs of developing countries, while some countries found it necessary to enter into debt rescheduling exercises because of their inability to raise the corresponding revenue. In 1982, world demand remained weak for most of the primary commodities exported by Africa, and export revenues continued to fall; oil production for the year was projected to be 21 per cent less than in 1981, and copper prices reached in mid-1982 their lowest level since the Second World War.

Recovery in 1983 depended on climatic conditions and on the performance of the countries belonging to the Organisation for Economic Co-operation and Development (OECD). If the economy recovered in the OECD area, revived demand for oil and other African exports, along with increased capital outflows, would boost Africa's output, but it was improbable that growth would exceed 3 per cent.

The summary was noted by the Economic and Social Council, in decision 1983/177 of 28 July (see p. 422).

Social and economic development of Africa in the 1980s

In a report,[5] submitted in June 1983 to the Council and the Assembly, the Secretary-General reviewed special measures taken by the international community, in accordance with a 1980 Assembly resolution,[6] for the social and economic development of Africa in the 1980s. The report, the third since the 1980 Assembly action, focused on identifiable measures introduced for facilitating the implementation of the Lagos Plan of Action.[2]

It pointed out that the regional programme for Africa of the United Nations Development Programme, planned at $283,400,000 for 1982-1986, for example, currently stood at $137,208,000. In addition, ECA had witnessed in its negotiations a severe tightening of the purse of traditionally friendly donors of multilateral assistance. At the same time, while 51 non-African countries were invited to the Fourth Biennial Pledging Conference at Addis Ababa on 2 May in connection with the Silver Jubilee Anniversary meetings, not one developed country had made a direct cash contribution to the United Nations Trust Fund for African Development. Contributions were made by China and India.

At the Third Meeting of the Conference of Ministers of African Least Developed Countries (Addis Ababa, 25 and 26 April), it was noted with great concern that the declining trends of overall ODA flows to African LDCs, which started in 1980, had continued.

ECONOMIC AND SOCIAL COUNCIL ACTION

On 29 July, the Economic and Social Council, acting on the recommendation of its Second Committee, adopted resolution 1983/65 without vote.

Special measures for the social and economic development of Africa in the 1980s

The Economic and Social Council,

Recalling General Assembly resolutions 3201(S-VI) and 3202(S-VI) of 1 May 1974, containing the Declaration and the Programme of Action on the Establishment of a New International Economic Order, 3281(XXIX) of 12 December 1974, containing the Charter of Economic Rights and Duties of States, and 3362(S-VII) of 16 September 1975 on development and international economic co-operation,

Recalling General Assembly resolution 35/56 of 5 December 1980, the annex to which contains the International Development Strategy for the Third United Nations Development Decade,

Recalling also section II of General Assembly resolution 36/182 of 17 December 1981 and section II of Assembly resolution 37/212 of 20 December 1982 on the Industrial Development Decade for Africa, as adopted, and Assembly resolutions 37/140 of 17 December 1982 on the Transport and Communications Decade in Africa and 37/245 of 21 December 1982 on the situation of food and agriculture in Africa,

Recalling further General Assembly resolution 37/139 of 17 December 1982, by which the Assembly, *inter alia,* urged donor countries to provide substantial and sustained levels of resources for promoting the accelerated development of African countries and the effective implementation of the Lagos Plan of Action for the Implementation of the Monrovia Strategy for the Economic Development of Africa, and to contribute generously to the United Nations Trust Fund for African Development,

Deeply concerned at the continuing low level of economic activities in Africa and the devastating effects of the current world economic crisis on the particularly vulnerable economies of the countries in the region, twenty-six of which are now classified in the category of the least developed among the developing countries,

Fully aware that the Lagos Plan of Action and the Final Act of Lagos provide a framework of priority action for achieving the rapid overall economic and social development of Africa, as reiterated in the Addis Ababa Declaration on the Occasion of the Silver Jubilee Anniversary Celebration of the Economic Commission for Africa, adopted on 29 April 1983 by the Conference of Ministers of the Commission,

Recognizing the primary responsibility of the African countries for their development and the importance of the mobilization of their national resources for their socio-economic development,

Convinced of the need for increased and sustained external resources in order to achieve the aims and objectives of the Lagos Plan of Action and the Final Act of Lagos,

Recalling that there is a need for a thorough evaluation of the application of special measures for the economic and social development of Africa during the mid-term review and appraisal of the International Development Strategy for the Third United Nations Development Decade,

Having considered the third report of the Secretary-General on special measures for the social and economic development of Africa in the 1980s, which reviews special measures taken by the international community for the social and economic development of Africa in the 1980s,

1. *Takes note* of the third report of the Secretary-General on special measures for the social and economic development of Africa in the 1980s;

2. *Expresses its regret* that, despite efforts undertaken by the international community over the last three years, the resources thus provided are not commensurate with African development requirements;

3. *Notes* the disappointing results of the Fourth Biennial Pledging Conference for the United Nations Trust Fund for African Development, held at Addis Ababa on 2 May 1983;

4. *Renews* its call to the organs, organizations and bodies of the United Nations system to examine measures to increase the resources for the execution of the programmes for the Industrial Development Decade for Africa and the Transport and Communications Decade in Africa and to apply the special measures in a comprehensive and co-ordinated manner;

5. *Urges* donor countries to provide substantial and sustained levels of resources for promoting the accelerated development of African countries and the effective implementation of the Lagos Plan of Action and the

Final Act of Lagos, and to contribute generously to the United Nations Trust Fund for African Development;

6. *Invites* all international financial institutions, particularly the International Bank for Reconstruction and Development, the International Development Association and the International Fund for Agricultural Development, to continue actively to consider increasing substantially their development assistance to Africa and to treat the matter of making a special effort in support of African economic and social development with the urgency it requires;

7. *Stresses* its deep concern at the gravity of the food situation in Africa and the continuing decline in the food self-reliance ratio, and urgently calls upon the African countries to accord due priority to food and agricultural production in their national and subregional plans, and also urges donor countries and international agencies to increase their support for the implementation of the measures contained in the Lagos Plan of Action in the area of food and agriculture;

8. *Requests* the Secretary-General to continue to allocate the necessary resources to the Economic Commission for Africa, taking into account its role as the main economic and social development centre within the United Nations system for the African region, in accordance with General Assembly resolutions 32/197 of 20 December 1977 and 33/202 of 29 January 1979;

9. *Further requests* the Secretary-General to submit to the General Assembly at its thirty-ninth session, through the Economic and Social Council at its second regular session of 1984, a comprehensive report, prepared on a uniform basis and including figures, on the activities throughout the United Nations system in relation to Africa, and on the progress made in the implementation of the present resolution.

Economic and Social Council resolution 1983/65

29 July 1983   Meeting 41   Adopted without vote

Approved by First Committee (E/1983/123) without vote, 27 July (meeting 25); draft by Vice-Chairman (E/1983/C.1/L.30), based on informal consultations on draft by Bangladesh, for Group of 77 (E/1983/C.1/L.19); agenda item 7.
Meeting number. ESC 41.

In related action, the Council, in resolution 1983/63, recommended that the General Assembly call on the international community to support the endeavour of the African Governments towards achieving the accelerated development, by providing moral, technical and financial assistance (see above).

GENERAL ASSEMBLY ACTION

The General Assembly, on the recommendation of the Second Committee, adopted resolution 38/199 without vote on 20 December.

Special measures for the social and economic development of Africa in the 1980s

The General Assembly,

Recalling its resolutions 3201(S-VI) and 3202(S-VI) of 1 May 1974, containing the Declaration and the Programme of Action on the Establishment of a New International Economic Order, 3281(XXIX) of 12 December 1974, containing the Charter of Economic Rights and Duties of States, and 3362(S-VII) of 16 September

1975 on development and international economic cooperation,

Recalling its resolution 35/56 of 5 December 1980, the annex to which contains the International Development Strategy for the Third United Nations Development Decade,

Recalling also its resolutions 35/64 of 5 December 1980 and 36/180 of 17 December 1981, concerning the adoption of a wide range of special measures for the social and economic development of Africa in the 1980s,

Recalling further section II of its resolution 36/182 of 17 December 1981 and section II of its resolution 37/212 of 20 December 1982, on the Industrial Development Decade for Africa, and its resolutions 37/140 of 17 December 1982 on the Transport and Communications Decade in Africa and 37/245 of 21 December 1982 on the situation of food and agriculture in Africa,

Recalling its resolution 37/139 of 17 December 1982, in which it, *inter alia*, urged donor countries to provide substantial and sustained levels of resources for promoting the accelerated development of African countries and the effective implementation of the Lagos Plan of Action for the Implementation of the Monrovia Strategy for the Economic Development of Africa, and to contribute generously to the United Nations Trust Fund for African Development,

Deeply concerned at the negative effects of the current world economic crisis on the economies of African countries and at the scourges that ravage the African continent, which suffers mainly from structural problems, *inter alia* the lowest level of literacy and training and rudimentary structures in the field of health and housing, as well as the extremely precarious living conditions of the largest number of refugees in the world,

Expressing its deep concern at the extreme gravity of the food situation in Africa, which is aggravated by chronic droughts, the continued decrease in food self-reliance and the continued increase in volume of the imports of food products in Africa, particularly in the Sudano-Sahelian and southern regions, and noting that, among other factors, the rate of increase of food production in Africa continues to lag behind population growth,

Recognizing that Africa is the least industrialized region in the world, that this specific situation necessitates the full implementation of the objectives set out in the programme for the Industrial Development Decade for Africa and that, in order to reverse the existing situation, sustained efforts by the international community are required to achieve the effective implementation of the objectives of the Decade,

Recognizing also that Africa is confronted with exceptionally serious economic and social problems, highlighted, *inter alia*, by the fact that it contains three quarters of the least developed countries and half of the land-locked countries of the world,

Convinced of the need for increased and sustained external resources on a predictable and continuous basis in order to achieve in a co-ordinated manner the aims and objectives of the Lagos Plan of Action and the Final Act of Lagos,

Recalling that there is a need for a thorough evaluation of the implementation of special measures for the social and economic development of Africa during the mid-term review and appraisal of the International Development Strategy for the Third United Nations Development Decade,

Having considered the third report of the Secretary-General on special measures for the social and economic development of Africa in the 1980s, which reviews special measures taken by the international community to that end,

1. *Takes note* of the third report of the Secretary-General on special measures for the social and economic development of Africa in the 1980s;

2. *Expresses its regret* that, despite efforts undertaken by the international community over the past three years, the resources thus far provided are not commensurate with African development requirements;

3. *Notes* the disappointing results of the Fourth Biennial Pledging Conference for the United Nations Trust Fund for African Development, held at Addis Ababa on 2 May 1983, particularly for projects aimed at assisting the least developed countries of Africa;

4. *Expresses its gratitude* to all countries which participated and made pledges during that conference;

5. *Strongly urges* all donor countries to implement their commitments, as contained in paragraphs 61 to 69 of the Substantial New Programme of Action for the 1980s for the Least Developed Countries, as adopted, so as to achieve, in that regard, a substantial increase in resources for the development of the least developed countries, twenty-six of which are in Africa;

6. *Welcomes* the steps taken by a number of donor countries to increase their contributions to the United Nations Development Programme, expresses its concern at the decline in real terms in the United Nations Development Programme assistance given to the developing countries through the United Nations system, reflecting a general decrease in multilateral concessional assistance in real terms, which adversely affects the country and regional programmes for Africa of the Programme during the third programming cycle, 1982-1986, and urges all countries, particularly those that have not done so, to increase their annual contributions to the Programme;

7. *Also urges* donor countries to provide substantial and sustained levels of resources for promoting the accelerated development of African countries and the effective implementation of the Lagos Plan of Action for the Implementation of the Monrovia Strategy for the Economic Development of Africa and the Final Act of Lagos, and to contribute generously to the United Nations Trust Fund for African Development;

8. *Recognizes* the important contribution consultative groups and round-table meetings can make to African development by enhancing aid co-ordination and mobilizing additional resources and urges African and donor countries to continue to co-operate to that end;

9. *Invites* all international financial institutions, particularly the World Bank, the International Development Association and the International Fund for Agricultural Development, to continue actively to consider increasing substantially their development assistance to Africa and to treat the matter of making a special effort in support of African economic and social development with the urgency it requires;

10. *Renews its call* to the organs, organizations and bodies of the United Nations system to examine measures to increase the resources for the execution of the programmes for the Industrial Development Decade for Africa and the Transport and Communications Decade in Africa and to apply the special measures in a comprehensive and co-ordinated manner;

11. *Stresses* its deep concern at the gravity of the food situation in Africa and the continuing decline in the food self-reliance ratio, urgently calls upon the African countries to accord due priority to food and agricultural production in their national and subregional plans and also urges donor countries and international agencies to increase their support for the implementation of the measures contained in the Lagos Plan of Action in the area of food and agriculture;

12. *Supports* the urgent appeal launched by the Food and Agriculture Organization of the United Nations in favour of the twenty-two African countries threatened by food shortages and urges the international community to respond generously to that appeal by providing the additional food aid and rehabilitation inputs required;

13. *Requests* the Secretary-General to convene, in co-operation with the Executive Secretary of the Economic Commission for Africa, the Fifth Biennial Pledging Conference for the United Nations Trust Fund for African Development and to take the necessary measures to ensure its success and, in this regard, appeals to donor countries, relevant United Nations organs, international and regional financial institutions and other interested public and private bodies to participate fully and contribute generously to the Fund;

14. *Requests* the Secretary-General to continue to allocate the necessary resources to the Economic Commission for Africa, taking into account its role as the main economic and social development centre within the United Nations system for the African region, in accordance with General Assembly resolutions 32/197 of 20 December 1977 and 33/202 of 29 January 1979;

15. *Further requests* the Secretary-General to submit to the General Assembly at its thirty-ninth session, through the Economic and Social Council at its second regular session of 1984, a comprehensive report, prepared on a uniform basis and including figures, on the activities throughout the United Nations system in relation to Africa and on the progress made in the implementation of the present resolution.

General Assembly resolution 38/199

20 December 1983   Meeting 104   Adopted without vote

Approved by Second Committee (A/38/702/Add.13) without vote, 9 December (meeting 55); draft by Vice-Chairman (A/C.2/38/L.107), based on informal consultations on draft by Sierra Leone, for African Group (A/C.2/38/L.81); agenda item 78.
Meeting numbers. GA 38th session: 2nd Committee 41, 46, 50, 52, 54, 55; plenary 104.

The Assembly, in resolution 38/5 (see p. 192), as well as in decision 38/434 (see above), also called on the international community to provide African countries with necessary assistance.

Activities in 1983

Food and agriculture

Critical situation

The year 1983 was a bad year for agriculture in Africa because of the severe drought both in southern and West Africa.

The worsening food crisis and nutritional status of the African populace at large made it clear that the only option was to promote individual and collective food self-sufficiency as the major objective of agricultural development in the region. Other major activities to implement the objectives of the Lagos Plan of Action and the Regional Food Plan for Africa dealt with livestock development, reduction of food waste and post-harvest losses, and forest resources development and conservation. A region-wide survey of food problems led to publication of *The situation of food and agriculture in Africa.*

Food and agricultural activities were oriented towards helping member States improve their agricultural development policies, planning and programming; promoting integrated rural development, institution building and provision of services; improving market services and facilities; and reducing food losses. Inter-agency consultative meetings were held in 1983 on: food and agriculture technology (May), livestock research and development in Africa (September), and establishment of a subregional maize research centre for Eastern and Southern Africa (September).

The intensity of drought affecting the region was reflected in the drop of gross agricultural output by 2.6 per cent in 1983, the downturn reaching 6.6 per cent in western Africa (see also below, under ENVIRONMENT). The drought created serious dislocations of life in a number of countries, with significant numbers of people migrating in search of food either within or beyond national borders. Emergency measures were required to cope with the situation, despite severe problems of transportation, storage and distribution encountered in relief operations (see p. 523).

On a longer-term basis, African countries were jolted by the drought and the crisis into seeking solutions to their deep-seated problems. Across the Continent, agricultural policies were adjusted to provide more incentives to farmers, and increased amounts of resources were allocated to agriculture to bring about a definite increase in productivity. At the same time, more attention was paid to the initiative of the small producers, with precedence given to decisions at the local level rather than the previous centralized approach.

Reports of the Secretary-General. In a June 1983 report on the state of technology for food and agriculture in Africa,[7] submitted to the General Assembly through the Economic and Social Council, in purusance of a December 1982 Assembly resolution,[8] the Secretary-General noted that total food production in Africa rose by 1.5 per cent against the demographic growth of 2.8 per cent during the 1970s. While other regions of the world succeeded in achieving some notable progress in increasing the production of a number of major crops, Africa continued to witness worsening food production, and its food self-sufficiency ratio dropped from 98 per cent in the 1960s to about 86 per cent in 1980.

The widening food gap had eroded the objective for self-reliance and self-sufficiency in food, subjected millions of people of the region to malnutrition and hunger, and halted development efforts of many African countries by forcing them to resort to imports to cover the deficit, hence draining their badly needed foreign exchange for development.

The importance of agriculture to the economies of African countries remained paramount: in 1981, agriculture in Africa made up to 24 per cent of the gross domestic product (at factor cost) and provided occupation to 67.7 per cent of the active population. Lagging behind in the adoption and development of suitable technology for agriculture, African countries had not been able to make full use of and benefit from the vast natural resources to increase agricultural productivity, which was expected to serve as a base for industrialization; while Africa's potential arable land was estimated at about 1.7 hectares for each person, only about 0.55 hectares per person were being utilized. The factors responsible for the slow growth of the agricultural sector in Africa included droughts and desertification, inadequate investments, poor incentives to farmers through distorted pricing systems, fragmentation and sub-division of holdings, inadequate land tenure systems, limited agricultural research, rural-urban migration and institutional constraints.

The Secretary-General felt that the international community and donor agencies should support the development of research and development capacity in Africa and assist in the design and adaptation of technology appropriate for Africa's factor endowment (factor-supply conditions) and for various ecological zones. Along with a long list of requirements for improvements in the available food and agricultural technology, the Secretary-General observed the need for strengthening national research organizations and for providing greater incentives for African agricultural scientists to stay on in their own countries and play their part in the eradication of hunger and malnutrition. Other recommendations were given in the report for bridging the technology gap.

In his October report to the Assembly, on the food and agriculture situation in Africa,[9] the Secretary-General stated that Africa's total imports of agricultural, forestry and fisheries products were worth some $17.4 billion in 1981; imports of agricultural products alone, which consisted almost entirely of food products, cost the continent $15.7 billion, against export earnings from agricultural products of $9.8 billion.

The Secretary-General concluded that the improvement of the food situation in Africa required, among other things, a strong political will to channel greater volume of resources to agriculture as well as inter-country co-operation, measures to understand and combat drought and desertification, and encouragement by Governments for changes in food habits and consumption patterns, from wheat-based products to those based on locally produced foodstuffs. In the coming few years (1983-1985) a foundation should be laid for the advancement of self-sufficiency in cereals, livestock, and fish production; efforts should focus on reduction of food waste, attainment of a higher degree of food security and a large increase in production of tropical cereals *vis-à-vis* the production of industrial crops. Member States needed to implement more effectively the recommendations of the Lagos Plan of Action through improved project co-ordination, improved research in appropriate fields and the elimination of intra-regional trade barriers for all locally produced raw materials pertaining to food and agriculture.

Concern for the gravity of the food and agriculture situation in Africa was expressed in a number of 1983 resolutions adopted by the Economic and Social Council in July and the General Assembly in December.

ECONOMIC AND SOCIAL COUNCIL ACTION

The Council, in resolution 1983/65 on special measures for the social and economic development of Africa in the 1980s (see above), expressed its deep concern at the gravity of the food situation in Africa and the continuing decline in the food self-reliance ratio, and urgently called on the African countries to give priority to food and agricultural production. In resolution 1983/71 on food problems (see Chapter XI of this section), the Council supported the appeal of the Food and Agriculture Organization of the United Nations (FAO) in favour of the African countries threatened by food shortages, and urged the international community to respond generously to that appeal. Further, in resolution 1983/68 on the climatic situation and drought in Africa (see p. 524), the Council requested the ECA Executive Secretary to organize a special scientific round-table meeting with a view to examining the effects of drought on the African economy.

GENERAL ASSEMBLY ACTION

On 19 December, the General Assembly, acting without vote on the recommendation of the Second Committee, adopted resolution 38/159.

Critical situation of food and agriculture in Africa

The General Assembly,

Recalling its resolutions 3201(S-VI) and 3202(S-VI) of 1 May 1974, containing the Declaration and the Programme of Action on the Establishment of a New International Economic Order, 3281(XXIX) of 12 December 1974, containing the Charter of Economic Rights and Duties of States, and 3362(S-VII) of 16 September 1975 on development and international economic co-operation,

Recalling the International Development Strategy for the Third United Nations Development Decade, contained in the annex to its resolution 35/56 of 5 December 1980, in which the General Assembly emphasized agricultural and rural development and the eradication of hunger and malnutrition as being among the principal objectives of the Decade,

Recalling also the Programme of Action of the World Food Conference, containing the Universal Declaration on the Eradication of Hunger and Malnutrition adopted by the Conference, and the Declaration of Principles and Programme of Action adopted by the World Conference on Agrarian Reform and Rural Development,

Recalling further its resolutions 35/69 of 5 December 1980, 36/186 of 17 December 1981 and 37/245 of 21 December 1982 on the situation of food and agriculture in Africa,

Recognizing the high priority attached to food and agriculture and the commitment and determination of Africa to devote its limited resources on a priority basis to agricultural development, as reflected in and in accordance with the Lagos Plan of Action for the Implementation of the Monrovia Strategy for the Economic Development of Africa,

Noting with grave concern that, over the past two decades, the situation of food and agriculture in Africa has undergone a drastic deterioration, resulting in a decline in food production per capita with detrimental effects on dietary standards, which are well below the minimum requirements, as well as in an alarming increase in the number of people exposed to malnutrition, hunger and starvation,

Gravely concerned at the increasing and painful drain of scarce foreign exchange resulting from the growing dependence of African countries on food imports owing to the critical food shortage, which has had a detrimental effect on their overall development,

Deeply concerned also at the unabated encroachment of the desert and the recurring problem of drought in many countries of Africa, which have continued to accentuate the food problem on that continent,

Recognizing that the food supply crisis has been further exacerbated by such factors as poor rainfall, brush-fires, unusually severe crop infestation, epidemics of animal diseases and chronic shortages of production inputs,

Recognizing that the responsibility for the development of food and agricultural production lies primarily with the developing countries themselves and that there is an increasing effort and growing commitment by the developing countries to accelerate the development of their food and agricultural sectors,

Recognizing the role of food-sector strategies, which emerged from the World Food Council as a means for interested developing countries to adopt an integrated approach for increasing food production, improving consumption and attracting the necessary additional international resources,

Reaffirming the call in the Lagos Plan of Action regarding the application of policies providing incentives for increasing production, particularly for small farmers, while at the same time safeguarding the interests of the poorer consumers,

Convinced that increased international support to combat drought, desertification, epidemics of animal diseases, crop infestation and post-harvest losses, among other problems, is crucial to the attainment of food self-sufficiency in Africa,

Further convinced that international support measures can reinforce the efforts of the African countries to resolve the technological, managerial and financial resource gaps impeding food and agricultural production in Africa,

Noting with serious concern that the findings of the Special FAO/WFP Task Force established by the Director-General of the Food and Agriculture Organization of the United Nations and the Executive Director of the World Food Programme have further highlighted the worsening food supply crisis, which has resulted in increased hunger and malnutrition affecting as many as 150 million people in twenty-two African countries,

Noting with deep concern that the high-level meeting of the African countries concerned and of the potential donor countries, convened by the Director-General of the Food and Agriculture Organization of the United Nations in Rome on 19 October 1983, has not so far resulted in the significant additional food aid resources needed, which have been estimated by the Special FAO/WFP Task Force at 3.2 million tons, of which a minimum of 1 million tons should be provided in the months ahead, including 700,000 tons to be provided on an emergency basis in the next few months in order to maintain supplies to the twenty-two affected countries,

Noting the current unfavourable world economic situation, reflected in, *inter alia*, weak foreign export markets, balance-of-payments deficits and high interest rates, which, together with, in certain cases, a stagnation in aid and other related factors, have seriously undermined the ability of African countries both to sustain a reasonable level of food and agricultural production and to cover food deficits through commercial imports,

1.   *Reaffirms* its resolutions 35/69, 36/186 and 37/245 and calls for their full implementation on an urgent basis;

2.   *Takes note* of the reports of the Secretary-General on the situation of food and agriculture in Africa and on the state of technology for food and agriculture in Africa;

3.   *Welcomes* the conclusions and recommendations of the World Food Council at its ninth ministerial session, in particular those relating to the African region;

4.   *Takes note with appreciation* of the timely and important initiative of the Director-General of the Food and Agriculture Organization of the United Nations in convening a special meeting on the African food supply situation and urges the international community to respond favourably and immediately to the appeal made by the Director-General for alleviation of the present critical food supply situation in Africa;

5.   *Supports* the urgent appeal launched by the Food and Agriculture Organization of the United Nations in favour of the twenty-two African countries threatened by food shortages, and urges the international community to respond generously to that appeal by providing the additional food aid required, which has been estimated by the Special FAO/WFP Task Force at 3.2 million tons, of which a minimum of 1 million tons should be provided in the months ahead, including 700,000 tons to be immediately provided to maintain food supplies in the affected countries, as well as $76 million in agricultural inputs for the rehabilitation of agriculture and animal husbandry;

6.   *Recognizes* the role of the international community, the Food and Agriculture Organization of the United Nations, the World Food Programme, the World Food Council, the International Fund for Agricultural Development and the World Bank in mobilizing food aid and agricultural assistance for Africa, and requests existing and new donor countries to increase the resources required to meet African needs for food aid and agricultural development;

7.   *Urges* all the countries of Africa to continue to accord priority to food and agriculture, in accordance with their national development plans and programmes, and to continue to implement measures to raise substantially their food and agricultural production in keeping with the Lagos Plan of Action for the Implementation of the Monrovia Strategy for the Economic Development of Africa, and in this context reaffirms the important role that national food strategies, plans and programmes could play in this process;

8.   *Urges* the international community to supplement, through increased financial and technical assistance, on a priority and long-term basis, the national efforts of African countries to achieve the goals and objectives set forth in the Lagos Plan of Action relevant to food and agriculture, taking into account the recommendations of the African Ministers for Food and Agriculture at the Twelfth FAO Regional Conference for Africa, in particular the following objectives:

(a)   Significant improvement in their food situation and laying of the foundations for the attainment of self-sufficiency in cereals, livestock and fish;

(b)   Significant progress towards attaining a 50 per cent reduction in post-harvest losses, through, *inter alia*, the construction of storage facilities;

(c)   Improved transport infrastructure to facilitate food distribution at the national, subregional and regional levels;

(d)   Support of indigenous research efforts through expanded and more effective agricultural research, with special emphasis on animal husbandry, improved seeds and an adequate supply of fertilizers, pesticides and other chemicals suitable to African conditions;

9.   *Further urges* all relevant organs, organizations and bodies of the United Nations system to expand their training programmes for the building up of national capabilities for the preparation, execution, monitoring and evaluation of agricultural sector projects;

10.   *Calls upon* the international community to continue to support efforts undertaken by African countries at the national, subregional and regional levels to increase food production through, *inter alia*, the provision, on a priority and long-term basis, of additional financial and technical assistance to Africa by organizations of the United Nations system, such as the International Fund for Agricultural Development, the United Nations Development Programme and other organizations involved in the financing of agriculture development, and through an increase in lending by the World Bank to the agricultural sector in Africa;

11.   *Recognizes* that an international year for the mobilization of financial and technological resources for food and agriculture in Africa would be a useful mechanism for focusing international attention on the problem

and could accelerate the process that would lead to a significant improvement of food and agricultural production in Africa;

12. *Notes* that the report of the Secretary-General on the state of technology for food and agriculture in Africa was incomplete in certain respects and that data are still being gathered, and requests that an updated report be submitted to the General Assembly at its fortieth session, through the Economic and Social Council;

13. *Requests* the Secretary-General to submit to the General Assembly at its thirty-ninth session, through the Economic and Social Council at its second regular session of 1984, a progress report on the implementation of the present resolution.

General Assembly resolution 38/159

19 December 1983   Meeting 102   Adopted without vote

Approved by Second Committee (A/38/702/Add.5) without vote, 21 November (meeting 45); draft by Vice-Chairman (A/C.2/38/L.73), based on informal consultations on draft by Mexico, for Group of 77 (A/C.2/38/L.17); agenda item 78 *(e)*.
Meeting numbers. GA 38th session: 2nd Committee 30, 39, 45; plenary 102.

In related action, the Assembly, in resolutions 38/158 and 38/199, reiterated its support for the FAO appeal in favour of the 22 African countries threatened by food shortages and urged the international community to respond generously; and in resolution 38/200, it agreed that immediate measures taken by the United Nations system in favour of the developing countries should be directed, among other things, at progress in food and agriculture, including special food aid measures as required for seriously affected food-deficit countries in Africa (see Chapter XI of this section). Further, the Assembly, in liquidating the United Nations Emergency Operation Trust Fund, decided in resolution 38/201 to channel 70 per cent of the funds thus available primarily to food and agricultural projects, with special emphasis on African countries (see Chapter III of this section).

Proposed international year

Report of the Secretary-General. In June 1983, the Secretary-General submitted to the Economic and Social Council, for transmittal to the General Assembly in accordance with that body's December 1982 request,[10] a report on the implications of declaring an international year to mobilize financial and technological resources for food and agriculture in Africa.[11] Based on ECA's assessment of various prerequisites for proclaiming and organizing such a year, the Secretary-General observed that, according to past experience, mere declaration of an international year was not likely to result in an appreciable increase in the inflow of resources; without the removal of policy, social, economic, administrative and technical bottlenecks at all levels, availability of additional resources could hardly help to improve the situation.

On 28 July, the Council, in decision 1983/175, took note of the Secretary-General's report.

On 20 December, the General Assembly, on the recommendation of the Second Committee, adopted resolution 38/198 without vote.

International year for the mobilization of financial and technological resources to increase food and agricultural production in Africa

The General Assembly,

Recalling its resolution 37/246 of 21 December 1982 on an international year for the mobilization of financial and technological resources for food and agriculture in Africa,

Noting with great alarm that, since the adoption of its resolutions 35/69 of 5 December 1980, 36/186 of 17 December 1981 and 37/246 of 21 December 1982, the situation of food and agriculture in Africa has worsened, as evidenced by a drastic decline in self-reliance in food,

Recognizing the critical financial gap which seriously hinders the growth of the agricultural sector in African countries,

Recognizing also that the technological gap in Africa has a direct relationship with declining agricultural productivity, which is aggravated by natural factors such as drought and desertification,

Recognizing further that all countries of Africa should implement, in accordance with their national development programmes and priorities, measures to increase substantially their national food and agriculture programmes through, *inter alia*, national, subregional and regional measures, including economic and technical co-operation among developing countries,

Recognizing the role of food-sector strategies, which emerged from the World Food Council as a means for interested developing countries to adopt an integrated approach for increasing food production, improving consumption and attracting the necessary additional international resources,

Having considered the report of the Secretary-General on the implications of declaring an international year for the mobilization of financial and technological resources for food and agriculture in Africa,

1. *Takes note* of the report of the Secretary-General;

2. *Notes* that the year 1991 might be designated international year for the mobilization of financial and technological resources to increase food and agricultural production in Africa, bearing in mind the relevant criteria set forth in the annex to Economic and Social Council resolution 1980/67 of 25 July 1980;

3. *Requests* the Secretary-General, in consultation with the relevant organs, organizations and bodies of the United Nations system, to elaborate action-oriented proposals in respect of the international year for the mobilization of financial and technological resources to increase food and agricultural production in Africa and to report on the implementation of the present resolution to the General Assembly at its fortieth session, through the Economic and Social Council.

General Assembly resolution 38/198

20 December 1983   Meeting 104   Adopted without vote

Approved by Second Committee (A/38/702/Add.13) without vote, 5 December (meeting 54); draft by Vice-Chairman (A/C.2/38/L.98), based on informal consultations on draft by Sierra Leone, for African Group (A/C.2/38/L.76); agenda item 78.
Meeting numbers. GA 38th session: 2nd Committee 50, 54; plenary 104.

Implementation of the programme for the Industrial Development Decade for Africa

Efforts to promote industrial development focused on implementing the programme for the Industrial Development Decade for Africa (IDDA) (1980-1990),[3] with greater emphasis on continuous and closer co-operation with other United Nations agencies and programmes. The Follow-up Committee on Industrialization in Africa (seventh meeting, Kigali, Rwanda, 16-19 March)—including the secretariats of ECA, the Organization of African Unity (OAU) and the United Nations Industrial Development Organization (UNIDO)—reviewed and adopted guidelines for priority action at the national and subregional levels and modalities for implementing IDDA activities. The Joint Committee of the ECA, OAU and UNIDO secretariats concerned with implementing the Decade's programme held its second meeting in June and its third meeting in October to examine issues arising from the Follow-up Committee meeting, the organization of subregional meetings and preparations for the Fourth (1984) General Conference of UNIDO.

Manufacturing output averaged only 1.5 per cent from 1980, as compared to IDDA targets which provided for a growth rate of 12.8 per cent. While government control and planning was stressed in the past, there was an emerging trend towards liberalization and improvement of the climate for foreign investment.

A subregional meeting on promoting intra-African industrial co-operation within the framework of IDDA (Addis Ababa, November) issued its final report regarding co-operation in the Eastern and Southern African subregion.

UNIDO action. On 13 May, the Industrial Development Board of UNIDO adopted a resolution[12] on the Decade. Taking note of a second progress report by the executive heads of UNIDO and ECA,[13] the Board expressed deep concern at the scarcity of resources made available, including UNDP resources, which had contributed to limited progress in implementing the Decade's preparatory phase whereas almost one third of the Decade had elapsed. It appealed to donor countries and institutions for increased contributions to African industrial development so as to achieve the target set by African Governments for a 1.4 per cent share for Africa in world industrial production during the Decade, and reaffirmed its request to UNDP to allocate adequate funds, taking into account the high priority established for the Decade.

In a June 1983 note[14] submitted to the Economic and Social Council through the Industrial Development Board of UNIDO at its April/May session, in pursuance of requests made in 1982 by the Council in July,[15] and by the General As-

sembly in December,[16] the UNIDO Executive Director summarized the activities carried out by the secretariats of ECA, OAU and UNIDO in implementing the programmes for IDDA.

ECONOMIC AND SOCIAL COUNCIL ACTION

Acting on the recommendation of its First Committee, the Council adopted resolution 1983/70 on 29 July by a roll-call vote.

Industrial Development Decade for Africa

The Economic and Social Council,

Recalling its resolution 1982/66 B of 30 July 1982 and section II of General Assembly resolution 37/212 of 20 December 1982, as adopted, in which the Assembly, *inter alia,* recalled that the Industrial Development Decade for Africa was one of the most important programmes of the United Nations Industrial Development Organization,

Recalling further Industrial Development Board resolution 56(XVII) of 13 May 1983, in which the Board, *inter alia,* expressed its deep concern at the scarcity of resources, including resources made available for the Decade by the United Nations Development Programme,

Noting resolution (I) adopted by the Follow-up Committee on Industrialization in Africa at its seventh meeting, held at Kigali, Rwanda, from 16 to 19 March 1983, and resolution 466(XVIII) adopted on 2 May 1983 by the Conference of Ministers of the Economic Commission for Africa, both concerning the implementation of the programme for the Industrial Development Decade for Africa,

Considering that the effective implementation of the Lagos Plan of Action for the implementation of the Monrovia Strategy for the Economic Development of Africa and the Final Act of Lagos will, to a large extent, depend on the sustained development of industry as a supplier and user of goods and services and therefore on the structural adjustment in the industrial sector, with emphasis on selected strategic core industries,

Noting with appreciation the decision of the African Development Bank to provide increased financing for industrial projects in Africa during its 1982-1986 programme period,

Noting further the deteriorating economic situation in Africa and the fact that the number of the least developed countries in Africa has increased from twenty-one to twenty-six, out of the present global total of thirty-six,

1. *Takes note with appreciation* of the second progress report on the Industrial Development Decade for Africa, prepared jointly by the Executive Director of the United Nations Industrial Development Organization and the Executive Secretary of the Economic Commission for Africa;

2. *Welcomes* the efforts made by the United Nations Industrial Development Organization in assisting the African countries and intergovernmental organizations in the formulation of national and subregional programmes for the Decade, and in maintaining continuous and harmonious co-ordination with the secretariats of the Organization of African Unity, the Economic Commission for Africa and other international organizations concerned;

3. *Supports* Industrial Development Board resolution 56(XVII) on the Industrial Development Decade for Africa and reiterates the repeated appeals made to the international community to increase its contribution to African industrial development within the framework of the programme for the Industrial Development Decade for Africa, with a view to ensuring that the target set by the African Governments of a 1.4 per cent share of world industrial production is achieved by the African region during the Decade;

4. *Decides* to accord priority to the Industrial Development Decade for Africa among the programmes of the United Nations Industrial Development Organization and the Economic Commission for Africa and, consequently, requests the Secretary-General to ensure that this priority is fully reflected in the programme budgets of those organizations and that adequate resources will be provided for the co-ordination and monitoring of the Decade, subject to approval by the General Assembly;

5. *Appeals* to all countries and institutions to increase their contributions to the United Nations Industrial Development Fund, taking into account the financial requirements of the projects directed towards the implementation of the programme for the Decade;

6. *Urges* the Governing Council of the United Nations Development Programme to consider increasing its allocation of financial resources for assistance to African countries and intergovernmental organizations in planning and formulating their programmes for the Decade and to accord high priority to industrial projects, especially for the development of core industries, in its national and regional programmes for Africa, taking into account the priorities of the African countries;

7. *Recommends* that the General Assembly, at its thirty-eighth session, should continue to provide the United Nations Industrial Development Organization with adequate funds from the United Nations regular technical assistance programmes for assistance to the African countries and to intergovernmental organizations, necessary for the full implementation of the programme for the Decade and for its popularization, priority being accorded to the formulation of industrial policies, strategies and plans, the development of core industries, industrial manpower, technological capabilities and institutional infrastructures, the development of energy technology and equipment, the promotion of intra-African industrial co-operation, the development of the least developed countries, and the mobilization of financial resources.

Economic and Social Council resolution 1983/70

29 July 1983   Meeting 41   44-1-5 (roll-call vote)

Approved by First Committee (E/1983/126) by vote (32-1-5), 27 July (meeting 25); draft by Bangladesh, for Group of 77 (E/1983/C.1/L.11), orally amended in informal consultations; agenda item 13.
Meeting number. ESC 41.

Roll-call vote in Council as follows:

In favour: Algeria, Argentina, Austria, Bangladesh, Benin, Brazil, Burundi, Canada, China, Colombia, Congo, Denmark, Djibouti, Ecuador, France, Germany, Federal Republic of, Greece, India, Japan, Kenya, Lebanon, Liberia, Luxembourg, Malaysia, Mali, Mexico, Netherlands, New Zealand, Nicaragua, Norway, Pakistan, Peru, Portugal, Qatar, Romania, St. Lucia, Saudi Arabia, Sudan, Suriname, Swaziland, Thailand, Tunisia, United Kingdom, Venezuela.

Against: United States.

Abstaining: Bulgaria, Byelorussian SSR, German Democratic Republic, Poland, USSR.

Prior to adopting the text as a whole, the Council adopted paragraph 4 by a roll-call vote of 42 to 6, with 2 abstentions, the paragraph having been similarly approved by the First Committee by 29 to 7, with 2 abstentions.

Financial considerations—chiefly opposition to measures leading to regular budget increases—were cited in explanation of vote by the United States, which voted against paragraph 4, the German Democratic Republic on behalf also of Bulgaria, the Byelorussian SSR, Poland and the USSR, also against paragraph 4, and Canada, which abstained on that paragraph.

In related action, the Council, in resolution 1983/65, called on the United Nations system to examine measures to increase the resources for the execution of programmes, among others, for IDDA.

GENERAL ASSEMBLY ACTION

Support to the IDDA programme was called for in two 1983 General Assembly resolutions.

In section II of resolution 38/192, the Assembly decided to increase the allocation to UNIDO by $1 million in 1984 for assistance to African countries and to intergovernmental organizations in implementing the programme for the Decade; and appealed to all countries and institutions to increase their contributions to the United Nations Industrial Development Fund (see p. 582). In resolution 38/199 (see above), the Assembly called again on the United Nations system to increase the resources for the execution of the programmes for the Decade.

Environment

The ECA Conference of Ministers, on 2 May 1983, adopted a resolution on the climatic situation and drought in Africa,[1] urging the secretariat to organize a scientific round table, in co-operation with other bodies of the United Nations system, to examine the causes, frequencies and trends, if any, of drought in Africa and to propose ways of dealing with the phenomenon.

A joint ECA/UNEP regional workshop on industrial environment impact assessment and environmental criteria for siting of industry (Addis Ababa, 27-30 June) provided African industrial experts and environmental advisers with an opportunity to discuss applicability of UNEP guidelines to local conditions.

A February 1983 progress report of the Joint Inspection Unit, prepared by Inspectors Toman Hutagalung and Joseph A. Sawe, on the implementation of recommendations on regional programmes in the conservation and management of African wildlife, was submitted to the Economic and Social Council by the Secretary-General in a September note.[17] The report made a number of conclusions and recommendations on support to training programmes in wildlife conservation and on an integrated regional living resources conservation strategy.

In December, the General Assembly, in resolution 38/225, expressed concern for the drought situation in the Sudano-Sahelian region (see p. 526), and, in resolution 38/164, urged all Governments to assist the countries in the region in combating desertification (see Chapter XVI of this section).

International trade and finance

The largest and most serious deterioration in the terms of trade since 1970 was observed in 1982-1983, with a 7.9 per cent decline registered in 1983. While exports declined, particularly because of the fall of oil prices, imports declined faster and the trade and current account positions improved. In 1983, the trade deficit fell to $0.5 billion compared with the 1982 peak of $9.7 billion, and the total current account deficit fell to $13.6 billion compared with $24.7 billion in 1982. The decrease in deficit reflected binding constraints on the availability of external financing rather than a real improvement in the external position. In fact, outstanding external debt had risen to $150 billion at the end of 1983, representing 180 per cent of goods and services exports, while external debt servicing rose to 22.4 per cent of exports of goods and services compared with only 10.7 per cent in 1980. There was a record number of rescheduling exercises in an unprecedented number of countries.

In the area of domestic and intra-African trade, a preliminary study was made of the situation of domestic trade in Africa, focusing on the need to promote such trade and on techniques for rationalizing channels of distribution. Poor performance in developing intra-African trade was attributed, among other things, to lack of clear policies, concentration of trade expansion on long-established links with developed countries and unsatisfactory payment arrangements and credit facilities, coupled with limited production capacity and inadequate transport and communications facilities.

The Preferential Trade Area for Eastern and Southern African States (PTA) became operational on 1 January 1983 and the secretariat prepared studies to help the PTA secretariat in its initial phase. The ECA secretariat also assisted in establishing the Economic Community of Central African States, and the Treaty establishing the Community was signed at Libreville, Gabon, in October, by 10 of its 11 potential members. A feasibility study was prepared for the establishment of an agricultural commodity exchange for Eastern and Southern Africa. Assistance was also given in setting up the African Federation of Chambers of Commerce, and a constitution was adopted at a meeting at Cairo, Egypt, in November.

Steps were taken to convene meetings of the heads of major economic groupings for forging closer links between them, in line with the call of the Lagos Plan of Action for an African economic community by the year 2000. The chief executives of ECA-sponsored institutions (fourth meeting, Dakar, Senegal, December) agreed on the establishment of a buffer fund to tide institutions over in times of temporary financial need.

Regarding South-South collective reliance, a study was undertaken of products of interest to African countries within the framework of the Global System of Trade Preferences among Developing Countries (GSTP), in order to assist ECA members in adopting effective negotiating strategies.

In the field of trade with non-African countries, the major concern was assistance to African countries in finding effective responses to the world trade crisis, particularly resulting from the collapse of commodity prices in the world market, accompanied by higher inflation, interest rates, balance-of-payments deficits and mounting external debt. A study prepared by the secretariat, in collaboration with OAU and the African Development Bank (ADB), on the external indebtedness of African countries analysed, and made recommendations dealing with, the impact of indebtedness on social and economic development, balance-of-payments related issues, debt rescheduling, debt servicing and terms of credit.

Transnational corporations

ECA 1983 activities relating to the role of transnational corporations (TNCs) in African economic development focused on research studies, the implications of the proposed international code of conduct for TNCs (see Chapter VII of this section), technical co-operation and advisory services, and development of comprehensive information on TNCs in Africa. Emphasis was placed on strengthening the negotiating capacity of African countries *vis-à-vis* the corporations, and an integrated paper was prepared on their role in African banking and financial institutions.

The second African regional meeting on a code of conduct on TNCs (Cairo, January and February) recommended that TNCs be called upon to cease investments in South Africa and progressively wind up existing activities and operations, and that the completed code should help strengthen the position of African Governments in their dealings with TNCs.

ACTION BY PRINCIPAL UN ORGANS

A number of 1983 decisions by United Nations major bodies concerned the activities of TNCs in Africa. The Economic and Social Council, in resolution 1983/74, dealt with collaboration with the racist régime of South Africa, and in decision 1983/104 and resolution 1983/75 took action on preparations for 1984 public hearings on TNC activities there (see p. 144). The General Assembly condemned TNCs that had increased collaboration with that régime and requested the Secretary-General to take all measures to deny facilities to and refrain from investment in corporations operating in South Africa (see p. 122); and, in resolution 38/50, took note of a register indicating TNC profits derived from colonial Territories (see TRUSTEESHIP AND DECOLONIZATION, Chapter I).

Natural resources, energy and cartography

In regard to mineral resources, ECA provided technical and administrative assistance to the Eastern and Southern African Mineral Resources Development Centre (Dodoma, United Republic of Tanzania) and hosted the Second Technical Advisory and Fifth Governing Council (Addis Ababa, 9-12 August 1983). The inaugural meeting of the Governing Council of the Central African Mineral Resources Development Centre took place at Brazzaville, Congo (27-30 June), and the ECA secretariat was entrusted with the Centre's day-to-day management until the end of 1984. A workshop on the role of coal in accelerated economic growth in Africa was held at Addis Ababa from 11 to 14 July.

Concerning water resources, a project in progress since July 1980, in co-operation with the World Meteorological Organization, was completed in October 1983. The project, on the planning and development of hydrometeorological networks and related services in Africa, benefited some 29 countries.

Activities began in 1983 for collecting and compiling information on indigenous abilities of ECA member States to explore, exploit, develop and manage marine resources, with a view to recommending a comprehensive agenda for action in the African region.

In respect to energy, technical advisory services were given to a number of countries in: the formulation of national energy policies; the evaluation, development, exploitation and use of energy resources; and the development and use of solar, wind and biogas energy. The secretariat organized a seminar and study tour in China, in August and September, on biomass conversion, solar energy and mini-hydropower; made preparations for establishing an African Regional Centre for Solar Energy; and contributed to making fully operational ECA's solar energy demonstration centre.

Assistance was given in developing two regional cartographic centres—the Regional Centre for Services in Surveying, Mapping and Remote Sensing at Nairobi, Kenya, and the Regional Centre for the Training of Aerial Surveys at Ile-Ife, Nigeria. The secretariat also continued implementing and developing the African Remote Sensing Programme.

Science and technology

A seminar, organized by ECA in collaboration with the USSR, on planning methodologies for the science and technology component in national development plans (Moscow, 22 August–1 September 1983), enabled senior African government officials to learn such methodology, examine the structure and organization of the relevant State machinery in the USSR, pool information and experience, and consider measures for strengthening national capabilities in technological planning in their own countries. The secretariat also organized a meeting of the Intergovernmental Committee of Experts for Science and Technology Development (14-18 November), which reviewed, among other things, the implementation of the science and technology chapter of the Lagos Plan of Action.

Transport

Transport and Communications Decade in Africa (1978-1988)

In 1983, the Third Inter-Governmental Meeting of Experts in Transport, Communications and Planning met at Addis Ababa in January, followed by the Third Conference of African Ministers of Transport, Communications and Planning (Cairo, March). A revised programme for the second phase (1984-1988) of the United Nations Transport and Communications Decade in Africa (1978-1988) was prepared on the basis of the guidelines emerging from that Conference. A round table, held in Paris in June, reviewed the draft programme and advised on methods of presentation.

Reports of the Secretary-General. In June, the Secretary-General reported to the General Assembly, through the Economic and Social Council,[18] that the Conference of transport ministers viewed the estimated cost of $31.7 billion for the draft programme for the second phase as being too large and unrealistic and recommended that individual African countries reduce their programmes to a reasonable level, given the difficulties experienced in financing the programme for the first phase (1980-1983) and continuing turbulent world economic conditions substantially reducing assistance flows. The Secretary-General stated that African countries had made substantial contributions to funding the Decade's programme, much more than was received from external sources. Such funding was mostly from national projects and the only funds for regional and subregional projects came from UNDP. The report concluded that the results of the upcoming second phase depended on a more dynamic role to be played by ECA, backed by funds that were commensurate with the task.

The Secretary-General also noted that the ECA Conference of Ministers had observed in 1983 that less than 50 per cent of the first phase programme had been achieved in financial terms and that the performance of the communication and air transport subsectors had been particularly poor. The Conference was also disturbed that the regional and subregional projects, the most important element in the Decade programme, had fared worse in securing financing than had national projects; feeling that this was contradictory to the order of priority established in the global strategy and plan of action, the Conference urged a reversal of that situation in the second phase. The ECA Conference of Ministers endorsed the call of the Conference of transport ministers for a reduction of the programme in the second phase and the launching of the programme early in 1984. It noted with regret the tendency of donors to introduce unacceptable conditions after pledges had been made so that disbursements were much less than amounts pledged.

In a June note[19] to the Assembly through the Council, the Secretary-General transmitted a report of the ECA Executive Secretary in pursuance of a December 1982 Assembly request,[20] concerning the preparation of a plan of action for the second phase of the Decade. The Executive Secretary concluded that the implementation of the programme for the first phase had been impressive in terms of projects and funds secured (77.5 per cent of some $8,747 million). Projects for the second phase had been successfully carried out and 22.5 per cent of the funds required had been secured.

ECA activities for the Decade since July 1981 were described in a March 1983 report by the UNDP Administrator, submitted to the third session of the High-level Committee on the Review of Technical Co-operation among Developing Countries (New York, 31 May–6 June).[21]

ECONOMIC AND SOCIAL COUNCIL ACTION

On 29 July, the Economic and Social Council, acting on the recommendation of its First Committee, adopted resolution 1983/67 without vote.

Transport and Communications Decade in Africa

The Economic and Social Council,

Recalling resolution 291(XIII) adopted on 26 February 1977 by the Conference of Ministers of the Economic Commission for Africa, Council resolution 2097(LXIII) of 29 July 1977 and General Assembly resolution 32/160 of 19 December 1977, proclaiming the Transport and Communications Decade in Africa,

Recalling also resolution 435(XVII) adopted on 30 April 1982 by the Conference of Ministers of the Economic Commission for Africa,

Referring to Council resolution 1982/54 of 29 July 1982

and General Assembly resolution 37/140 of 17 December 1982,

Considering that the programme for the Decade requires constant adjustment during the remaining period of the Decade,

Having considered the report of the Secretary-General on the Transport and Communications Decade in Africa and the report of the Executive Secretary of the Economic Commission for Africa on the preparation of the plan of action for the second phase (1984-1988) of the Decade,

1. *Expresses its appreciation* to the Secretary-General and the Administrator of the United Nations Development Programme for the financial support they have provided for the organization of the fifth consultative technical meeting to be held from 6 to 8 March 1984, and for the preparation of the plan of action for the second phase of the Transport and Communications Decade in Africa;

2. *Appeals* to donor countries and financial institutions to participate fully and positively in the fifth consultative technical meeting;

3. *Appeals once more* to the donor countries and financial institutions to lend their substantial financial support to the projects of the Decade and to accord particular attention to the programming, financing and implementation of transport and communications projects of special importance to the land-locked developing countries in Africa;

4. *Recommends* that, in view of the success of the consultative technical meetings organized for the mobilization of resources for financing the programme for the first phase, other consultative technical meetings should be organized as soon as possible after the launching of the second phase of the Decade in 1984 and, in any event, not later than the middle of 1985, for the following subsectors of transport and communications:

(a) Broadcasting;
(b) Postal services;
(c) Air transport;
(d) Railways and rail transport;

5. *Requests* the Secretary-General to make available to the Economic Commission for Africa, by redeploying regular resources of the United Nations, adequate financial resources to enable it:

(a) To organize the four consultative technical meetings referred to in paragraph 4 above;

(b) To undertake studies on the harmonization and co-ordination of the various modes of transport and communication;

(c) To prepare, in collaboration with the competent organizations of the United Nations system, a study of the manpower needs of all African countries for all modes of transport and communication;

(d) To draw up urgently programmes on transport and communications of special importance to the land-locked developing countries in Africa;

(e) To organize, in January 1984, the fourth session of the Conference of African Ministers of Transport, Communications and Planning;

6. *Requests* the Executive Secretary of the Economic Commission for Africa to ensure the implementation of the present resolution and to submit regularly to the Economic and Social Council a progress report on the implementation of the programme for the Decade.

Economic and Social Council resolution 1983/67

29 July 1983   Meeting 41   Adopted without vote

Approved by First Committee (E/1983/123) without vote, 27 July (meeting 25); draft by Bangladesh, for Group of 77 (E/1983/C.1/L.12), orally amended in informal consultations; agenda item 7.
Financial implications. S-G, E/1983/C.1/L.26.
Meeting number. ESC 41.

The Council, in resolution 1983/65 (see above), called on the United Nations system to consider measures to increase the resources for executing the programmes for the Decade.

GENERAL ASSEMBLY ACTION

Acting on the recommendation of the Second Committee, the General Assembly, on 19 December, adopted resolution 38/150 by recorded vote.

Transport and Communications Decade in Africa

The General Assembly,

Recalling its resolutions 32/160 of 19 December 1977, 33/197 of 29 January 1979 and 34/15 of 9 November 1979 on the Transport and Communications Decade in Africa and, in particular, its resolutions 35/108 of 5 December 1980 and 36/177 of 17 December 1981, by which it approved the organization of consultative technical meetings for the various African subregions,

Referring to resolution 422(XVI), adopted on 10 April 1981 by the Conference of Ministers of the Economic Commission for Africa, in which the Conference requested the Executive Secretary of the Commission to undertake the preparation of the plan of action for the second phase (1984-1988) of the Decade,

Recalling also its resolution 37/140 of 17 December 1982, in which it, *inter alia*, requested the Executive Secretary of the Economic Commission for Africa to submit to the General Assembly at its thirty-eighth session a report on the state of preparation of the plan of action for the second phase of the Decade,

Recalling Economic and Social Council resolutions 1979/61 of 3 August 1979, 1980/46 of 23 July 1980 and 1981/67 of 24 July 1981 on the Transport and Communications Decade in Africa and Council resolution 1982/54 of 29 July 1982, in which the Council requested the organization of a fifth consultative technical meeting for the countries of North Africa, East Africa and the islands of the Indian Ocean, as endorsed by the General Assembly in its resolution 37/140,

Referring also to resolution 464(XVIII) adopted on 2 May 1983 by the Conference of Ministers of the Economic Commission for Africa, in which the Conference requested the Executive Secretary of the Commission to ensure that the plan of action for the second phase would promote harmonization and co-ordination of the various modes of transport and communication and to organize four consultative technical meetings after the launching of the second phase of the Decade,

Taking note of resolution 465(XVIII) adopted on 2 May 1983 by the Conference of Ministers of the Economic Commission for Africa, in which the Conference requested the Executive Secretary of the Commission to ensure that the resolutions on freedoms of the air in Africa would be implemented,

Recalling also Economic and Social Council resolution 1983/67 of 29 July 1983, in which the Council recom-

mended the organization of consultative technical meetings in 1984 and 1985, as well as the carrying out of required studies and the organization of conferences,

Considering that the programme for the Decade requires updating, as may be necessary, during the entire period of the second phase,

1. *Takes note* of the report of the Secretary-General on the Transport and Communications Decade in Africa;

2. *Takes note also* of the report of the Executive Secretary of the Economic Commission for Africa on the preparation of the plan of action for the second phase (1984-1988) of the Transport and Communications Decade in Africa, as well as the timetable drawn up to adjust the programme with a view to finalizing it for consideration and adoption by the Conference of African Ministers of Transport, Communications and Planning at its fourth session, to be held from 7 to 11 February 1984;

3. *Notes* the financial support provided by the Secretary-General and the Administrator of the United Nations Development Programme to the Economic Commission for Africa for the preparation of the plan of action for the second phase of the Decade;

4. *Notes with interest* the financial resources made available by the Secretary-General to the Economic Commission for Africa for the organization of the fifth consultative technical meeting for the countries of North Africa, East Africa and the islands of the Indian Ocean, to be held from 15 to 17 March 1984;

5. *Also notes with interest* the measure of progress achieved in the implementation of the programme for the first phase of the Decade;

6. *Commends* the efforts undertaken for the preparation of the plan of action for the second phase of the Decade, which should continue to aim at a sound programme, in both its technical and financial aspects, in order to ensure the full realization of the objectives of the Decade;

7. *Requests* the Executive Secretary of the Economic Commission for Africa to organize other consultative technical meetings as soon as possible following the launching of the second phase of the Decade in 1984, and not later than the middle of 1985, for the following subsectors of transport and communications:

   (a) Broadcasting;
   (b) Postal services;
   (c) Air transport;
   (d) Railways and rail transport;

8. *Appeals* to donor countries and financing institutions to participate actively and positively in the fifth consultative technical meeting, as well as in subsequent consultative technical meetings to be organized in 1984 and 1985;

9. *Also requests* the Executive Secretary of the Economic Commission for Africa:

   (a) To undertake studies on the harmonization and co-ordination of various modes of transport and communications;

   (b) To prepare, in collaboration with the relevant organizations of the United Nations system, a study of the training and manpower needs of all African countries for all modes of transport and communications;

   (c) To draw up urgently programmes on transport and communications of special importance to the landlocked developing countries in Africa;

(d)   To organize the fourth session of the Conference of African Ministers of Transport, Communications and Planning, to be held from 7 to 11 February 1984;

(e)   To organize in 1984 a conference of the Governments of African countries and representatives of African airlines with a view to examining ways and means to promote inter-African airlinks;

10.   *Requests* the Secretary-General to provide the Economic Commission for Africa with $1 million from the regular budget of the United Nations to enable it to organize the four consultative technical meetings planned for 1984 and 1985, to elaborate the studies requested in the present resolution, to organize the meetings planned for 1984, such as those specified in paragraphs 7 and 9 above, within the context of the Decade, and to seek additional support from extrabudgetary resources;

11.   *Further requests* the Executive Secretary of the Economic Commission for Africa to explore other approaches for mobilizing financial resources for implementing the programme for the Decade;

12.   *Requests further* the Executive Secretary of the Economic Commission for Africa to continue to present annual progress reports on the implementation of the programme for the Decade;

13.   *Requests* the Secretary-General to submit to the General Assembly at its thirty-ninth session a report on the progress achieved in the implementation of the present resolution.

General Assembly resolution 38/150

19 December 1983   Meeting 102   137-1-8 (recorded vote)

Approved by Second Committee (A/38/701/Add.1) by recorded vote (119-1-8), 9 December (meeting 55); draft by Mexico, for Group of 77 (A/C.2/38/L.30), orally revised in informal consultations; agenda item 12.
Financial implications. 5th Committee, A/38/751; S-G, A/C.2/38/L.42, A/C.5/38/94.
Meeting numbers. GA 38th session: 2nd Committee 36, 55; 5th Committee 68, 69; plenary 102.

Recorded vote in Assembly as follows:

In favour: Afghanistan, Albania, Algeria, Angola, Argentina, Australia, Austria, Bahamas, Bahrain, Bangladesh, Barbados, Belgium, Belize, Benin, Bhutan, Bolivia, Botswana, Brazil, Burma, Burundi, Canada, Cape Verde, Central African Republic, Chad, Chile, China, Colombia, Congo, Costa Rica, Cuba, Cyprus, Democratic Kampuchea, Democratic Yemen, Denmark, Djibouti, Dominican Republic, Ecuador, Egypt, El Salvador, Equatorial Guinea, Ethiopia, Fiji, Finland, France, Gabon, Gambia, Germany, Federal Republic of, Ghana, Greece, Guatemala, Guinea, Guinea-Bissau, Guyana, Haiti, Honduras, Iceland, India, Indonesia, Iran, Iraq, Ireland, Israel, Italy, Ivory Coast, Jamaica, Japan, Jordan, Kenya, Kuwait, Lao People's Democratic Republic, Lebanon, Lesotho, Liberia, Libyan Arab Jamahiriya, Luxembourg, Madagascar, Malaysia, Maldives, Mali, Malta, Mauritania, Mauritius, Mexico, Morocco, Mozambique, Nepal, Netherlands, New Zealand, Nicaragua, Niger, Nigeria, Norway, Oman, Pakistan, Panama, Papua New Guinea, Paraguay, Peru, Philippines, Portugal, Qatar, Romania, Rwanda, Saint Lucia, Saint Vincent and the Grenadines, Sao Tome and Principe, Saudi Arabia, Senegal, Sierra Leone, Singapore, Somalia, Spain, Sri Lanka, Sudan, Suriname, Swaziland, Sweden, Syrian Arab Republic, Thailand, Togo, Trinidad and Tobago, Tunisia, Turkey, Uganda, United Arab Emirates, United Kingdom, United Republic of Cameroon, United Republic of Tanzania, Upper Volta, Uruguay, Vanuatu, Venezuela, Viet Nam, Yemen, Yugoslavia, Zaire, Zambia.
Against: United States.
Abstaining: Bulgaria, Byelorussian SSR, Czechoslovakia, German Democratic Republic, Hungary, Poland, Ukrainian SSR, USSR.

In the Second Committee, approval of the draft followed a decision—by a recorded vote requested by the USSR, of 116 to 9, with 4 abstentions—to retain paragraph 10. The recorded vote on the text as a whole was taken at the request of the United States.

In explanation of vote, the need to control the growth of the United Nations regular budget was cited by the United States, which voted against the

paragraph, the German Democratic Republic, on behalf also of the Eastern European socialist countries, also against the paragraph, and Canada, which abstained in that vote. The United States added that the activities for the Decade should be financed by voluntary contributions. Morocco abstained in the vote on the paragraph, as it believed setting a particular sum in advance could result in a reduction of the activities envisaged.

Mexico, speaking for the member States of the Group of 77 developing countries, expressed regret that some delegations had disregarded the gentleman's agreement which had been reached after lengthy consultations and a large number of concessions had been made by the draft's sponsors in the hope of achieving a consensus. Kenya would have preferred the original version of the draft; it could not support a dangerous tactic whereby a text was limited in scope in the hope of achieving a consensus, only to be voted on and approved in a weakened form.

On 16 December, the Fifth Committee had decided, by recorded vote of 83 to 9, to inform the Assembly that additional appropriations of $1 million would be required under the ECA section of the 1984-1985 programme budget. The Committee took this action on the oral recommendation of the Chairman of the Advisory Committee on Administrative and Budgetary Questions.

In related action, the General Assembly, in resolution 38/199 (see above), called again on the United Nations system to examine measures for increasing the resources for the execution of the programmes for the Decade.

Transport and trade problems of Zaire

The ECA secretariat continued during 1983 to provide technical advice and assistance to help the semi-land-locked State of Zaire with its international trade and transit problems, in response to several past requests by the Economic and Social Council and the General Assembly.

Report of the Secretary-General. In 1983, the Secretary-General submitted to the Council and the Assembly a June report, with an August addendum,[22] focusing on a round-table meeting (Kinshasa, Zaire, 28 and 29 June), on the financing of projects for opening up the land-locked southern and eastern regions of the country. The Secretary-General reported that the meeting considered 59 projects totalling $2.239 billion, of which external sources were expected to provide $1.555 billion. Projects essential to maintaining the potential of existing transport were assigned top priority, with the largest investment being made in railways. It was suggested at the Kinshasa meeting that a second meeting should be organized in 1985 or 1986 to consider the progress made.

ECONOMIC AND SOCIAL COUNCIL ACTION

The Economic and Social Council, acting on the recommendation of its First Committee, adopted resolution 1983/64 without vote on 29 July.

Particular problems facing Zaire with regard to transport, transit and access to foreign markets

The Economic and Social Council,

Referring to General Assembly resolution 32/160 of 19 December 1977, in which the Assembly recalled Council resolution 2097(LXIII) of 29 July 1977 and proclaimed the period 1978-1988 the Transport and Communications Decade in Africa,

Referring also to General Assembly resolutions 34/193 of 19 December 1979, 35/59 of 5 December 1980 and 36/139 of 16 December 1981 on the particular problems facing Zaire with regard to transport, transit and access to foreign markets,

Aware that the internal and external trade and the economy of Zaire will continue to be seriously affected until such time as a durable solution is found to the particular problems facing that country with regard to transport and transit,

Recalling Council resolution 1982/61 of 30 July 1982, by which it approved the organization of a round-table meeting,

1. *Takes note* of the oral report by the Executive Secretary of the Economic Commission for Africa on the results of the round-table meeting organized for the financing of Zaire's transport projects;

2. *Expresses its appreciation* of the contribution made by some donor countries and financing agencies which enabled the round-table meeting to achieve satisfactory results;

3. *Appeals* to donor countries and financing agencies to take prompt action to give effect to the interest which they expressed in financing particular projects;

4. *Requests* the Executive Secretary of the Commission to assist Zaire in order to ensure the follow-up of the results of the round-table meeting;

5. *Also requests* the Executive Secretary of the Commission, in the fulfilment of his tasks, to submit a report on the results of the first round-table meeting to the Economic and Social Council at its second regular session of 1984, together with his views, taking into account the possibility of holding a second round-table meeting in 1985 or 1986.

Economic and Social Council resolution 1983/64

29 July 1983   Meeting 41   Adopted without vote

Approved by First Committee (E/1983/123) without vote, 26 July (meeting 24); draft by Vice-Chairman (E/1983/C.1/L.27), based on informal consultations on 2-nation draft (E/1983/C.1/L.15); agenda item 7.
Meeting number. ESC 41.

GENERAL ASSEMBLY ACTION

On 19 December, the General Assembly, on the recommendation of the Second Committee, adopted resolution 38/143 without vote.

Particular problems facing Zaire with regard to transport, transit and access to foreign markets

The General Assembly,

Referring to its resolution 32/160 of 19 December 1977, in which it recalled Economic and Social Council reso-

lution 2097(LXIII) of 29 July 1977 and proclaimed the period 1978-1988 the Transport and Communications Decade in Africa,

Referring also to its resolutions 34/193 of 19 December 1979, 35/59 of 5 December 1980, 36/139 of 16 December 1981 and 37/205 of 20 December 1982 on particular problems facing Zaire with regard to transport, transit and access to foreign markets, and approving the organization in 1983 of a round-table meeting with donor countries for Zaire's projects in these three fields,

Recalling resolution 110(V) of 3 June 1979 of the United Nations Conference on Trade and Development,

Recalling also Economic and Social Council decision 249(LXIII) of 25 July 1977 and resolution 1981/68 of 24 July 1981, as well as resolution 293(XIII) of 26 February 1977 adopted by the Conference of Ministers of the Economic Commission for Africa,

Having considered the report of the Secretary-General on the outcome of the round-table meeting on the financing of the transport projects of Zaire, held at Kinshasa on 28 and 29 June 1983,

1. *Takes note* of the report of the Secretary-General on the round-table meeting of donors;

2. *Expresses its appreciation* of the contribution made by some donor countries and financing agencies which enabled the round-table meeting to achieve satisfactory results;

3. *Appeals* to donor countries and financing agencies to take prompt action to give effect to the interest which they expressed in financing particular projects;

4. *Requests* the Executive Secretary of the Economic Commission for Africa to assist Zaire in order to ensure follow-up of the results of the round-table meeting;

5. *Approves* the organization in 1985 of a second round-table meeting to review the progress made in financing and implementing the transport projects designed to open up the land-locked regions of Zaire;

6. *Requests* the Secretary-General to provide, within existing resources, the Economic Commission for Africa with the resources required to organize the second round-table meeting.

General Assembly resolution 38/143

19 December 1983   Meeting 102   Adopted without vote

Approved by Second Committee (A/38/701) without vote, 21 November (meeting 45); draft by Vice-Chairman (A/C.2/38/L.43), based on informal consultations on 7-nation draft (A/C.2/38/L.22); agenda item 12.
Meeting numbers. GA 38th session: 2nd Committee 34, 35; plenary 102.

Europe–Africa transport link

In pursuance of a July 1982 request of the Economic and Social Council,[23] representatives of the Economic Commission for Europe (ECE), ECA and Morocco, at a meeting at Addis Ababa in January 1983, agreed on the terms of reference of a consultancy mission for preparing a synthesis and an evaluation of the various reports and studies currently available on the proposed permanent link connecting Africa and Europe across the Strait of Gibraltar. The Executive Secretaries of the two Commissions concerned stated in their joint report to the Council in June[24] that the mission, made up of four consultants, visited Rabat, Madrid and Geneva during March and

April, and orally presented their findings, in April, to ECE and to ECA.

An addendum to the report dealt with issues such as the impact of the project and its integration into the region, technical options, economic soundness of the project and legal questions. In its conclusions and recommendations, the two Commissions noted that the permanent link was technically feasible, that its cost would be high but that the anticipated economic, political and social benefits would probably be considerable. The execution of such a project would radically improve relations between the north and south sides of the Mediterranean and between the African and European continents. While recognizing that the project concerned primarily the two coastal States which had conceived and studied it, the Commissions noted that it was of international and even intercontinental importance and that its execution, therefore, deserved the assistance of the international community.

ECONOMIC AND SOCIAL COUNCIL ACTION

On 29 July, the Economic and Social Council, acting on the recommendation of its Second Committee, adopted resolution 1983/62 without vote.

Europe-Africa permanent link through the Strait of Gibraltar

The Economic and Social Council,

Recalling its resolution 2097(LXIII) of 29 July 1977 and General Assembly resolution 32/160 of 19 December 1977, in which the Assembly proclaimed the period 1978-1988 the Transport and Communications Decade in Africa,

Noting the decision taken by the Conference of African Ministers of Transport, Communications and Planning at its third session, held at Cairo from 8 to 11 March 1983, concerning the Europe-Africa permanent link through the Strait of Gibraltar and the Tangiers-Lagos axis,

Noting also decisions G(XXXVII) of 2 April 1982 and I(XXXVIII) of 22 April 1983 of the Economic Commission for Europe, in which the Executive Secretary of that Commission was requested to continue to co-operate with the secretariats of the Economic Commission for Africa and the Economic Commission for Western Asia on projects of interest to the Mediterranean countries,

Bearing in mind the recommendation adopted at the fifth session of the African Highway Conference, held at Libreville from 6 to 11 February 1983, concerning the Europe-Africa permanent link through the Strait of Gibraltar and the Tangiers-Lagos axis,

Bearing in mind also the results of the seminar on the transport situation in the Mediterranean region, held at Barcelona in June 1983,

Noting with satisfaction the progress made by the Joint Moroccan-Spanish Committee in studies for the project for a Europe-Africa permanent link through the Strait of Gibraltar,

Convinced of the importance of the Europe-Africa permanent link through the Strait of Gibraltar for the Mediterranean region and for the African and European continents with regard to the development of interregional and good-neighbourly relations,

Referring to its resolution 1982/57 of 30 July 1982, in which the Executive Secretaries of the Economic Commission for Europe and the Economic Commission for Africa were requested to evaluate the studies available regarding such a link and to identify, on that basis, the problems related to its establishment,

Taking note with satisfaction of the interim report prepared by the Economic Commission for Europe and the Economic Commission for Africa,

Also taking note of the conclusions of that interim report,

1. *Recommends* the Governments of Morocco and Spain to take account of those conclusions in their further technical, economic and legal studies of the feasibility of such a link and, in particular, to undertake consultations with all the countries of the subregions concerned;

2. *Invites* the Governments and international organizations concerned, as well as research agencies, to co-operate with the Governments of Morocco and Spain in the pursuit of those studies and in the implementation of the conclusions and recommendations contained in the interim report, taking duly into account the international geopolitical, economic and cultural consequences of the project;

3. *Requests* the Executive Secretaries of the Economic Commission for Europe and the Economic Commission for Africa:

(*a*) To continue their efforts in accordance with the recommendations in the interim report, particularly with regard to the choice of the method of construction, the updating of the economic appraisal, the international legal problems deriving from the method of construction selected, and the coherence of the transport infrastructures in Europe and Africa;

(*b*) To report, through the Economic Commission for Europe and the Economic Commission for Africa, to the Economic and Social Council at its second regular session of 1984 on the progress made;

4. *Requests* the Secretary-General to continue the efforts that have already been made to provide, within the limits of the resources available, to the Economic Commission for Africa and the Economic Commission for Europe the resources for the discharge of those tasks.

Economic and Social Council resolution 1983/62

29 July 1983   Meeting 41   Adopted without vote

Approved by First Committee (E/1983/123) without vote, 25 July (meeting 23); draft by Vice-Chairman (E/1983/C.1/L.24), based on informal consultations on 13-nation draft (E/1983/C.1/L.13 & Corr.1) and orally amended by USSR; agenda item 7. *Meeting number.* ESC 41.

Social development

A regional meeting on the 1985 International Youth Year (Addis Ababa, 20-24 June 1983), held in collaboration with the United Nations Centre for Social Development and Humanitarian Affairs (CSDHA), adopted a regional plan of action on youth aimed at promoting substantial participation by young people in all areas of national development. The secretariat also collaborated with CSDHA in organizing the African Regional Preparatory Meeting for the Seventh (1985)

United Nations Congress on Prevention of Crime and Treatment of Offenders (Addis Ababa, 28 November–2 December), where recommendations were adopted on such aspects as new dimensions of criminality and crime prevention in the context of development and the new international economic order.

A workshop on mass media and African society (Tripoli, Libyan Arab Jamahiriya, 1-5 November) was organized by the secretariat, in collaboration with the African Centre for Applied Research and Training in Social Development, to review the role of the mass media in African development.

A report was prepared on a review and appraisal of the United Nations Decade for Women in Africa, and a joint ECA/UNU Expert Group held a meeting on household, gender and age at Addis Ababa in May.

Statistics

Programmes included the African Household Survey Capability Programme, the Statistical Training Programme for Africa, the National Accounts Capability Programme and the development of a statistical data base. The third meeting of Directors of Centres participating in the Statistical Training Programme for Africa was held at Addis Ababa from 31 October to 4 November.

Co-operation between the United Nations and the Southern African Development Co-ordination Conference

Report of the Secretary-General. In an October 1983 report to the General Assembly,[25] submitted in pursuance of its December 1982 request,[26] the Secretary-General described the co-operation between the United Nations and the Southern African Development Co-ordination Conference (SADCC)—a subregional organization, established in 1980 to forge links between member States (Angola, Botswana, Lesotho, Malawi, Mozambique, Swaziland, the United Republic of Tanzania, Zambia, Zimbabwe)—for creating regional integration and harmonizing action to secure international co-operation in the framework of the strategy for economic liberation. The Secretary-General stated that at a summit meeting of SADCC in July 1983 it had been decided that the question of appropriate forms of co-operation would be addressed further at the meeting of the Council of Ministers of SADCC in January 1984.

GENERAL ASSEMBLY ACTION

On 19 December, on the recommendation of the Second Committee, the General Assembly adopted resolution 38/160 without vote.

Co-operation between the United Nations and the Southern African Development Co-ordination Conference

The General Assembly,

Recalling its resolution 37/248 of 21 December 1982, by which it, *inter alia*, requested the Secretary-General to take appropriate measures to promote co-operation between the organs, organizations and bodies of the United Nations system and the Southern African Development Co-ordination Conference,

Having considered the report of the Secretary-General on co-operation between the United Nations and the Southern African Development Co-ordination Conference,

Noting that some progress has been made by some organs, organizations and bodies of the United Nations system in formulating co-operation programmes with the Conference,

Noting that some organs, organizations and bodies of the United Nations system are exploring ways and means of forging co-operation links with the Conference,

1. *Welcomes* the report of the Secretary-General on the progress made in the implementation of General Assembly resolution 37/248;

2. *Commends* the organs, organizations and bodies of the United Nations system that have already established contacts with the Southern African Development Co-ordination Conference, in response to resolution 37/248, and urges them to intensify positively such contacts in order to accelerate the achievement of the objectives envisaged in that resolution;

3. *Appeals* to all organs, organizations and bodies of the United Nations system that have not as yet done so to consult constructively with the secretariat of the Conference to ensure full implementation of resolution 37/248;

4. *Requests* the Secretary-General, in consultation with the Executive Secretary of the Conference, to take appropriate measures to promote and harmonize contacts between the United Nations and the Conference;

5. *Further requests* the Secretary-General to submit to the General Assembly at its thirty-ninth session a report on the implementation of the present resolution.

General Assembly resolution 38/160

19 December 1983   Meeting 102   Adopted without vote

Approved by Second Committee (A/38/702/Add.6) without vote, 5 December (meeting 54); 13-nation draft (A/C.2/38/L.80), orally revised in informal consultations; agenda item 78 *(f)*.

Sponsors: Angola, Benin, Botswana, Comoros, Lesotho, Malawi, Mozambique, Saint Lucia, Swaziland, Uganda, United Republic of Tanzania, Zambia, Zimbabwe.
Meeting numbers. GA 38th session: 2nd Committee, 50-54; plenary 102.

In related action, the Assembly, in resolution 38/36 A, condemned South Africa's attempts to thwart the work of SADCC, and called on all States to assist the Conference in its efforts to promote regional economic co-operation and development.

Programme, organizational and administrative questions concerning ECA

Restructuring

In October 1983, the Secretary-General, following up on a December 1982 General Assembly resolution,[27] reported to the Assembly[28] on the status of the implementation of recommendations made in 1982 by the Joint Inspection Unit (JIU)[29] regarding improving the capacity of the ECA secretariat to programme and manage its activities.

The Secretary-General concluded that a new ECA post (D-2) for programme supervision was not currently required, nor was the establishment of a separate organizational element for management services work; endorsed a recommendation by the Administrative Management Service on increasing the functions delegated to the Deputy Executive Secretary; and reported that most other JIU recommendations had been acted on. Information on the implementation of recommendations on regional programming, operations, restructuring and decentralization issues facing ECA, was also provided in another October report of the Secretary-General.[30]

In the course of 1983, a number of other United Nations bodies examined plans to strengthen Secretariat machinery for programme evaluation, including the possibility of an increase of staff of the ECA evaluation unit (see ADMINISTRATIVE AND BUDGETARY QUESTIONS, Chapter II).

GENERAL ASSEMBLY ACTION

Acting on the recommendation of the Second Committee, the General Assembly adopted decision 38/432 without vote.

Economic Commission for Africa: regional programming, operations, restructuring and decentralization issues

At its 102nd plenary meeting, on 19 December 1983, the General Assembly, on the recommendation of the Second Committee, took note of the report of the Secretary-General on the implementation of Assembly resolution 37/214 of 20 December 1982 and of his intention to submit a further report on the subject to the Assembly at its thirty-ninth session through the Committee for Programme and Co-ordination and the Economic and Social Council, as called for in paragraph 3 of resolution 37/214.

General Assembly decision 38/432

Adopted without vote

Approved by Second Committee (A/38/701 Add.1) without vote, 14 December (meeting 56); draft orally proposed by Chairman; agenda item 12.
Meeting numbers. GA 38th session: 2nd Committee 56; plenary 102.

Expansion of Addis Ababa conference facilities

In pursuance of a December 1982 General Assembly resolution,[31] an architectural and engineering study was conducted in 1983 for the construction of new conference facilities at ECA Headquarters at Addis Ababa. The Secretary-General, in a December report to the Assembly,[32] recommended that it approve, in principle, the construction project—for one large, two medium and four small conference rooms to be built over a seven-year period—at a total estimated cost of $83,200,000.

In addition, an appropriation totalling $320,700 was requested for alterations and improvements ($75,600) and major maintenance ($245,100) of the existing ECA complex.

GENERAL ASSEMBLY ACTION

On 20 December, the General Assembly, on the recommendation of the Fifth (Administrative and Budgetary) Committee, adopted section XXIII of resolution 38/234, concerning the ECA conference facilities.

Adequacy of the conference facilities of the Economic Commission for Africa at Addis Ababa
[*The General Assembly . . .*]

1. *Approves* the programme of major maintenance of and alterations and improvements to the conference facilities of the Economic Commission for Africa at Addis Ababa as reflected in section VII of the report of the Secretary-General;

2. *Defers* until its thirty-ninth session the consideration of the other proposals contained in that report;

3. *Requests* the Secretary-General to submit to the General Assembly at its thirty-ninth session an updated report on this subject.

General Assembly resolution 38/234, section XXIII

20 December 1983   Meeting 104   Adopted without vote

Approved by Fifth Committee (A/38/760) without vote, 18 December (meeting 70); oral proposal by Chairman on ACABQ recommendation and on proposal by Ethiopia; agenda item 109.
Meeting numbers. GA 38th session: 5th Committee 70; plenary 104.

REFERENCES

[1]E/1983/44. [2]YUN 1980, p. 548. [3]*Ibid.*, p. 662, GA res. 35/66 B, 5 Dec. 1980. [4]E/1983/37. [5]A/38/275-E/1983/88. [6]YUN 1980, p. 557, GA res. 35/64, 5 Dec. 1980. [7]A/38/280-E/1983/93. [8]YUN 1982, p. 820, GA res. 37/245, 21 Dec. 1982. [9]A/38/377. [10]YUN 1982, p. 821, GA res. 37/246, 21 Dec. 1982. [11]A/38/277-E/1983/96. [12]A/38/16 (res. 56(XVII)). [13]ID/B/297. [14]E/1983/104. [15]YUN 1982, p. 816, ESC res. 1982/66 B, 30 July 1982. [16]*Ibid.*, p. 758, GA res. 37/212, section II, 20 Dec. 1982. [17]E/1984/3. [18]A/38/259-E/1983/79. [19]A/38/263-E/1983/80. [20]YUN 1982, p. 808, GA res. 37/140, 17 Dec. 1982. [21]TCDC/3/4. [22]A/38/264 & Add.1-E/1983/90 & Add.1. [23]YUN 1982, p. 813, ESC res. 1982/57, 30 July 1982. [24]E/1983/87 & Add.1. [25]A/38/493. [26]YUN 1982, p. 835, GA res. 37/248, 21 Dec. 1982. [27]*Ibid.*, p. 828, GA res. 37/214, 20 Dec. 1982. [28]A/38/505. [29]YUN 1982, p. 826. [30]A/C.5/38/8. [31]YUN 1982, p. 834, GA res. 37/237, section XI, 21 Dec. 1982. [32]A/C.5/38/82.

Asia and the Pacific

The Economic and Social Commission for Asia and the Pacific (ESCAP) held its thirty-ninth session at its headquarters at Bangkok, Thailand, from 19 to 29 April 1983.[1] Food supply and distribution was the session's main theme, accompanied by such other items as the patterns and practices of fiscal policy in the region, the 1984 review and appraisal of the International Development Strategy for the Third United Nations Development Decade (the 1980s) adopted by the General Assembly in 1980,[2] and the Substantial New Programme of Action for the 1980s for the Least Developed Countries (LDCs), adopted in 1981 by the United Nations Conference on LDCs,[3] and consideration of an Asian and Pacific transport and communications decade. The Commission also considered policy matters, including the structure, frequency and duration of its annual sessions, the setting of its programme priorities and the future of its regional institutions.

The Commission's Executive Secretary told the 1983 session that there was need for taking remedial action on commodities and for exploiting opportunities for more trade, joint ventures and economic co-operation in general within the region; he felt it timely for the Governments of the region to consider holding an Asian economic summit and evolving a suitable mechanism for collective decisions aimed at increasing their influence and manoeuvrability on issues of mutual concern. He also drew attention to bleak prospects faced by ESCAP's regional institutions, which had generally failed to assure a permanent character or found themselves without stable funding.

According to the *Economic and Social Survey of Asia and the Pacific, 1982*,[4] a summary of which was noted by the Economic and Social Council in its resolution 1983/177 of 28 July (see p. 422), nearly all economies in the region were recording, by 1982, significantly lower rates of growth, increased payment deficits, intensified unemployment and greater fiscal and monetary policy problems than in preceding years.

Efforts were made in bringing technical co-operation among developing countries (TCDC) into operation by identifying and marketing the needs and capacities of co-operating countries, as exemplified by a November meeting in Beijing, where China and nine other ESCAP member Governments agreed on 32 bilateral TCDC projects. Nevertheless, the vast potential of regional co-operation and collective self-reliance in many areas remained yet to be exploited.

ESCAP, at its 1983 session,[1] adopted four resolutions for attention by the Economic and Social Council, dealing with regional co-operation on programmes for youth development, social aspects of rural development, implementation of the Substantial New Programme of Action for the 1980s for the Least Developed Countries, and the transport and communications decade for Asia and the Pacific (1985-1994).

ESCAP committees meeting in 1983 were: Statistics (June), Population (August), Industry, Technology, Human Settlements and the Environment (September), Natural Resources (October), Agricultural Development (November), and Shipping, and Transport and Communications (November).

Reports of those committees that had met in 1982[5] were endorsed by ESCAP at its 1983 session.

Activities in 1983

Food and agriculture

Overall, rapid population growth surpassed the gains in agricultural production in many countries of Asia and the Pacific, widening the gap between cereal output and requirements. This was especially true of the LDCs of the region (Afghanistan, Bangladesh, Bhutan, Lao People's Democratic Republic, Maldives, Nepal, Samoa) where cereals constituted the major component in people's diet.

A growing consciousness about food security led the Association of South-East Asian Nations (ASEAN) to a reserve of 50,000 tons (metric) of rice. With so many varied needs in the region, it was difficult to find common interests regarding a food security scheme, but an Expert Group Meeting on Food Supply and Distribution in Asia and the Pacific, Food Security, Trade and Investment (Bangkok, January) agreed in principle to establish a food security reserve for the South Asian subregion, as existed in South-East Asia. The Commission, while recognizing the need for further studies, supported the idea; it agreed, however, that foodgrain stockpiling could detract from food self-sufficiency efforts by the countries in the Pacific subregion, and asked the South Pacific Forum to consider the question further. The Commission emphasized that food self-sufficiency through increased domestic production was essential for achieving food security, and called for a study regarding promotion of a greater capital flow for food and agricultural development in the developing countries of the region.

In a March report to the Economic and Social Council,[6] the Secretary-General suggested a number of areas where overlap and duplication in the work of the Food and Agriculture Organization of the United Nations (FAO) and ESCAP appeared to exist and possible improvements could be made, although no major problems were found in co-operation and co-ordination between the two bodies in programme implementation in the region.

An April addendum to the report carried the text of a joint statement by the FAO Director-General and the ESCAP Executive Secretary on harmonization of their respective work programmes in the region, indicating that ESCAP would concentrate on economic and social aspects of selected issues in agriculture in a way complementary to FAO's activities within its broader, global mandate.

Seminars and workshops held in 1983 dealt with such issues as agro-pesticides and fertilizers, and farm broadcasting.

Development planning

In its first review of the International Development Strategy for the 1980s[2] in the ESCAP region, the Commission found that the severe world recession had seriously threatened the achievement of the Strategy's targets and objectives; none of the ESCAP developing countries had achieved the regional strategy targets in the second year of the Decade and immediate prospects for the third year permitted only cautious optimism.

Concern was expressed over lack of progress in restructuring global economic relations and over intensified protectionist and isolationist tendencies. The need for new initiatives for expanding regional co-operation was stressed, together with economic complementarities and the harmonization of national industrialization efforts in the region. A substantial increase in assistance flows was also required.

The Commission endorsed the secretariat's activities in monitoring and evaluating the Strategy's implementation and for a full-scale review in 1984 coinciding with the global review by the General Assembly (see p. 406).

In 1983, ESCAP made a preliminary review of the implementation of the Substantial New Programme of Action for the 1980s for the LDCs.[3] The Commission adopted a resolution on 28 April[1] calling on the Executive Secretary to conduct a comprehensive review of the Programme's implementation and to report to it at its fortieth (1984) session.

The Commission supported creating a comprehensive information service on development planning and endorsed the secretariat's continuing activities in macro-economic modelling and projections.

Among meetings held during the year were a seminar on sectoral planning techniques and the mechanism for intersectoral linkages (Moscow, USSR, October), and the Expert Group on Development Issues and Policies (Bangkok, November).

Transnational corporations

ESCAP, at its 1983 session,[1] noted the significant growth of investment in the region by transnational corporations (TNCs) and the emergence of newer and more complex modes of their participation, and stressed the importance of ensuring that TNCs respected national sovereignty and acted in accordance with the host country's needs and goals. It also drew attention to the emergence of third-world-based TNCs and the trend towards increasing intraregional investments.

An *Ad Hoc* Intergovernmental Meeting on TNCs (Bangkok, January) considered various aspects of TNC involvement in developing Asian and Pacific countries and an *Ad Hoc* Intergovernmental Meeting on Code of Conduct of TNCs (Bangkok, January) briefed ESCAP member countries on the status of a draft code under preparation in view of the special session (March and May) of the United Nations Commission on Transnational Corporations (UNCTC) (see p. 605).

A workshop on the role of TNCs in special economic and export processing zones (Guangzhou and Shenzhen, China, November) provided an opportunity for senior officials from China, India, Pakistan, the Philippines, the Republic of Korea, Sri Lanka and Thailand to discuss ways of maximizing the contribution of such zones to national development. The interregional seminar on TNCs and primary commodity exports (New York, August/September) discussed the ESCAP/ECA/ECLA Interregional Project on the subject. The first workshop on regulating and negotiating with TNCs in the pharmaceutical industry (Bangkok, December), organized by UNCTC, ESCAP's health and development programme and the ESCAP/UNCTC Joint Unit on TNCs, focused on solutions to practical problems.

Industry, technology and human settlements

At its April 1983 session, the Commission agreed that the secretariat should undertake phase II of its studies on industrialization trends in developing ESCAP countries and industrial growth performance and restructuring, which would include a detailed survey of sectoral development. Endorsing the report of its Committee on Industry, Technology, Human Settlements and the Environment, which had met in 1982, the Commission recommended biennial meetings of the ESCAP Club for Industrial Co-operation, establishment of a revolving fund for assistance to member countries, and a study of sick industries in the private sector.

A UNIDO/ESCAP Expert Group Meeting on a Regional Programme for Development of Industrial Consultancy (Kuala Lumpur, Malaysia, January), held in co-operation with the Asian and Pacific Development Centre, discussed ways of strengthening national consultancy capabilities and establishing a regional network for that purpose.

Other meetings held during 1983 included one on industrial co-operation among developing countries (July), and a High-level Expert Group Meeting on Industrialization (December), highlighting the important role of public enterprises especially in financing primarily from domestic sources.

A UNIDO/ESCAP Symposium on Contracts for Construction of Oil and Gas Pipelines (Jakarta,

Indonesia, August-September) discussed contractual arrangements for the construction of international off- and on-shore pipelines, and urged the symposium organizers to prepare a manual or guidelines on preparation and negotiation of such contracts.

An ESCAP/Regional Centre for Technology Transfer regional workshop on management of research and development institutes was held at Seoul, Republic of Korea, in December. A High-level Expert Group on Technology for Development (Bangkok, December) prepared a draft ESCAP plan of action on the subject, for submission to the Intergovernmental Meeting on Technology for Development and to the Commission.

Regarding human settlements, ESCAP drew attention to the urgent need to assist millions of homeless people and refugees through provision of housing facilities, infrastructure and other social services. Other priority areas in its work programme were rural-urban migration, development of small and medium towns, urban land policies, rural settlements, training needs and appropriate technology for human settlements development. The need for self-reliance and enhancing the capacity of communities in housing and infrastructure was emphasized. The Commission also reiterated support for broader utilization of indigenous building materials and construction techniques, urging the secretariat to assess techniques and materials focusing on resource conservation and cost reduction.

Among 1983 meetings were the Expert Group Meeting on a Human Settlement Atlas for the ESCAP region (February) and the Expert Group Meeting on an Integrated Programme for Improvement of Slums and Squatter Settlements with Special Emphasis on Appropriate Infrastructure, Services and Technologies (New Delhi, India, March) which considered policy guidelines developed based on information provided by 10 countries in the region.

Environment

ESCAP, at its 1983 session,[1] endorsed the convening in 1985 of a ministerial-level conference on the environment for Asia, the convening of a Working Group of Experts on the Environment to provide the secretariat with technical and advisory assistance, and the terms of reference of the Environmental Co-ordinating Unit.

Considering the increasing threat of marine pollution in the region, the Commission stressed the need to strengthen the secretariat's programme for the protection of the marine environment. Noting, among other things, that the environment had been and was being polluted in some parts of the ESCAP region in a deliberate effort to endanger human and marine life, and asserting that Iran's repeated attempts to prevent environmental pollution had been stopped in a very persistent manner, the Commission condemned such action resorted to by any State anywhere in the world.

A regional symposium on environmental management of mangrove, coral and island ecosystems in South Asia was held at Dhaka, Bangladesh, in August, and a study tour was organized in September to observe the management of arid and semi-arid lands in China.

Concerning typhoons, the Third Planning Meeting for the Typhoon Operational Experiment (TOPEX) and the seventh session of the TOPEX Management Board took place at Tokyo in February. A working group met in the Philippines in June and prepared a draft medium- to long-term programme for the Typhoon Committee. The second TOPEX was successfully carried out from 1 August to 15 October, and the sixteenth session of the Committee and the eighth session of the Management Board were held at Tokyo in December.

A two-member roving mission on the establishment of a cyclone council for the South Pacific was undertaken jointly by ESCAP and the World Meteorological Organization from October to December to explore with Governments in the subregion the need for, and structure of, the proposed body and the scope of its work.

International trade

At its April 1983 session,[1] ESCAP discussed a number of trade issues, including trade liberalization and effects of protectionist measures, preparations for a future meeting of trade ministers and the need to study policies and institutional arrangements at the national level for counter-trade. It requested the secretariat to assist developing member countries in preparing for their participation in the global system of trade preferences under the programme of economic co-operation among developing countries.

Among the 1983 meetings held at Bangkok were a January/February Expert Group Meeting on Preparations for the sixth (June/July) session of the United Nations Conference on Trade and Development (UNCTAD VI) (see p. 538), a regional seminar on trade policy (September), a workshop on special measures in favour of the least developed land-locked countries (November), and a special body on land-locked countries (seventh session, November).

Meetings on specific commodities included the Governmental Consultation among Jute Producing Countries (seventh session, Bangkok, August), the Second Meeting of the Intergovernmental Consultative Forum of Developing Tropical Timber Producing/Exporting Countries (Jakarta, September) and the Regional Consultative Group on Silk (second session, Bangkok, December).

Representatives of central banks met at Bangkok in December to consider enlargement of the Asian Clearing Union (ACU) and made recommendations.

Natural resources, energy and cartography

The ESCAP Committee on Natural Resources (tenth session, Bangkok, October) endorsed recommendations on implementing the Mar del Plata Action Plan, adopted by the United Nations Water Conference in 1977,[7] and agreed, among other things, on the need for natural water policies and for development of shared water resources in the region. It also endorsed establishment of a regional network for training in water resources development and the setting up of an overall river basin authority as an advisory body to decision-makers.

The ESCAP Committee called for a comprehensive approach for improving irrigation efficiency to include engineering, managerial, agricultural, socio-economic and institutional measures. It recommended the strategies for overcoming pollution and health problems related to low-cost technology applications to water supply and sanitation in the region, and supported convening a seminar on water quality monitoring systems. The Committee also stressed the importance of evolving a regional remote sensing programme as well as a plan of action for joint projects.

At its April 1983 session,[1] ESCAP suggested that a report be prepared on exploration and exploitation of coal in south Asia, looking towards comprehensive development of coal in the region. The steering committee of the regional energy development programme, in May, recommended a future meeting of energy ministers of the region to discuss energy policies and problems.

Meetings held in 1983, at Bangkok, unless otherwise specified, included: a seminar on rural energy planning for the developing countries in Asia (Beijing, April), the second *Ad Hoc* Expert Group Meeting on the Establishment of a Co-operation Mechanism in the Field of Offshore Exploration and Prospecting for Mineral Resources in the Indian Ocean (January), a Meeting on Water Resources Development in the South Pacific (Suva, Fiji, March), the Interagency Task Force on Water for Asia and the Pacific (eleventh session, July), and a seminar on the principles of flood plain management for flood loss prevention (October).

The Tenth United Nations Regional Cartographic Conference for Asia and the Pacific was held in Bangkok, Thailand, in January. In resolution 1983/121 of May, the Economic and Social Council took note of the Secretary-General's report on the Conference. (See Chapter IX of this section.)

Population

The 1983 population of the ESCAP region was calculated at 2,600 million, with current United Nations projections providing a 1.3 per cent average growth rate to the year 2000 and a population then of 3,382 million.

ESCAP endorsed the Asia-Pacific Call for Action on Population and Development—adopted at the Third (1982) Asian and Pacific Population Conference,[8] at Colombo, Sri Lanka—whose overriding theme was the improvement of the quality of life through an integrated approach to population and related programmes of economic and social development. ESCAP called for greater co-operation and collaboration among member countries, especially regarding exchange of information concerning the formulation of plans, programmes and strategies for integrating population elements with the development process. The Commission noted that unless serious consideration were given to population problems, national development efforts would be thwarted, leading to progressive deterioration in the quality of life.

Transport, communications and tourism

Transport and communications continued to be major sectors in the national plans of most ESCAP developing countries, claiming large proportions of total national outlays and often drawing heavily on scarce foreign exchange resources, by using roughly 50 per cent of total consumption of petroleum-based energy. Inadequacies in transport and communications infrastructure were seriously constraining socio-economic growth in various other sectors, creating severe chain reactions.

ESCAP, at its 1983 session,[1] stressed the need for a long-term strategy for integrated development of transport, allowing for an optimum intermodal mix, and commended the secretariat on its realistic and pragmatic approach to the relevant work programme.

Regarding railway transport, a meeting of Ministers Responsible for Railways (Bangkok, 28 February–2 March) adopted a declaration calling for the establishment of an Asian-Pacific railway co-operation group to facilitate closer collaboration among the railway administrations of the region; the meeting called on the ESCAP Executive Secretary to convene the group, and urged the United Nations Development Programme and others to provide financial and technical assistance. The Commission, at its April 1983 session,[1] welcomed the declaration, signed by 16 ESCAP members and associate members, as a historic development in promoting regional co-operation and collective self-reliance in railway transport. The Asia-Pacific Railway Co-operation Group subsequently held its first session at Bangkok in July to formulate its work programme and establish subgroups to deal with specific tasks set out under the declaration.

ESCAP endorsed the strategy for road and road transport development for the 1980s developed by the Intergovernmental Meeting of Highway Experts (Bangkok, February), which had identified 12 crucial areas for action, including the use and potential of alternative sources of energy for road transport, techniques for setting road maintenance priorities, traffic safety, facilitation of international traffic and standardization of vehicle weights and dimensions.

In respect to tourism, the ESCAP region continued to show the highest growth among regions of the world in terms of the volume of international tourist arrivals. In March, the Intergovernmental Meeting on Tourism Development took place in Tokyo to consider the role of Governments in tourism development, economic impact studies in several countries and tourism project formulation and evaluation in member countries.

Among other meetings were: regional seminar on planning and operations in the telecommunications sector (Bangkok, May), seminar/symposium on the post in the 1980s (Bangkok, May/June), seminar-cum-study tour on urban public transportation, with emphasis on integration and co-ordination of various modes of transport (Belgium, June/July), expert meeting on energy audit in the transport sector (Bangkok, July/August), seminars-cum-study tours, on rural road construction and maintenance, and on upgrading of operational efficiency of railway transport (China, September), seminar on promotion of international airfreight transport at international airports of South-East Asia and the Pacific (Federal Republic of Germany, September), and seminar on organization and mechanization of postal services (USSR, October).

Proposed transport and communications decade (1985-1994)

Various meetings held in the region in 1983 recommended proclamation of 1985-1994 as a transport and communications decade for Asia and the Pacific. They included the Intergovernmental Meeting of Highway Experts (February), the Intergovernmental Meeting on Tourism Development (March), and the Meeting of Ministers Responsible for Railways (February/March). The decade aimed at mobilizing political support for an integrated approach regarding the important role of the transport and communications sectors for attaining and sustaining the economic growth and social development of the region and improving the infrastructure and services in those sectors.

ESCAP, in a resolution adopted on 29 April,[1] recommended early proclamation of the proposed decade and asked the Executive Secretary to consider setting up an *ad hoc* intergovernmental group to prepare a phased action programme for the decade, assess the financial implications and ensure United Nations inter-agency co-ordination. A first

meeting of the *ad hoc* group was held at Bangkok in October.

ECONOMIC AND SOCIAL COUNCIL ACTION

On 29 July, the Economic and Social Council, on the recommendation of its First (Economic) Committee, adopted resolution 1983/69 without vote.

Transport and Communications Decade in Asia and the Pacific

The Economic and Social Council,

Noting resolutions 230(XXXVIII) of 1 April 1982 and 234(XXXIX) of 29 April 1983 of the Economic and Social Commission for Asia and the Pacific regarding a transport and communications decade in Asia and the Pacific during the period 1985-1994,

Recalling General Assembly resolution 35/56 of 5 December 1980, the annex to which contains the International Development Strategy for the Third United Nations Development Decade, in particular the development objectives for the transport and communications sectors,

Convinced of the critical role of all modes of transport as enabling elements in economic development and of the importance, therefore, of the improvement and growth of transport infrastructure and services in a manner commensurate with the anticipated growth of various sectors of the economy generating the demand for transport, and also of the importance of communications in modernizing transport and other sectors of the economy,

Taking note of the report of the Secretary-General on regional co-operation, in particular section II.B thereof,

1. *Emphasizes* the urgent need to upgrade the standards of transport and communications infrastructures in Asia and the Pacific region;

2. *Takes account* of the proposal for the proclamation of a transport and communications decade in Asia and the Pacific during the period 1985-1994;

3. *Endorses* resolution 234(XXXIX) of the Economic and Social Commission for Asia and the Pacific, relating, *inter alia*, to the preparation of a phased programme of action for the transport and communications decade in Asia and the Pacific region;

4. *Requests* the Secretary-General to extend all necessary facilities and support to enable the Executive Secretary of the Economic and Social Commission for Asia and the Pacific to prepare a comprehensive programme of action for the decade;

5. *Calls upon* the Economic Commission for Western Asia to take appropriate action to collaborate with the Economic and Social Commission for Asia and the Pacific for the incorporation of the Western Asian region in the programme of action for the decade;

6. *Also requests* the Secretary-General to submit a report on the implementation of the present resolution to the Economic and Social Council at its second regular session of 1984.

Economic and Social Council resolution 1983/69

29 July 1983   Meeting 41   Adopted without vote

Approved by First Committee (E/1983/123) without vote, 27 July (meeting 25); draft by Bangladesh, for Group of 77 (E/1983/C.1/L.18), orally revised, and orally amended in informal consultations; agenda item 7.

Meeting number. ESC 41.

Shipping, ports and inland waterways

ESCAP noted that the difficult situation in the maritime sector had deteriorated further in 1982, with serious setbacks in the oil, bulk and general cargo trades, and an increased tonnage imbalance resulting in large lay-ups, thus depressing freight rates to below break-even point. Shipbuilding activity had slowed down considerably and a further downtrend was expected.

The Commission called for closer and more meaningful co-operation in shipping services, containerization, multimodal transport and related technologies. It also stressed the need for financial assistance to the developing countries in introducing relevant advanced technologies.

Among meetings held were: *Ad Hoc* Intergovernmental Meeting on Maritime Legislation (Bangkok, January), seminar on port development policy (Bangkok, January), meeting of chief executives of port authorities (third session, Hong Kong, February), seminar on modern port management (Hong Kong, February-March), regional workshop on implications of currency fluctuations in shipping (Bangkok, March), Conference on Coastal Port Engineering in Developing Countries (Colombo, Sri Lanka, March), seminar on freight rate making (Bangkok, May), seminar on port containerization for Pacific island countries (Suva, Fiji, May), workshop on shipping policy (Shanghai, China, May), seminar on dredging (Wuhan, China, June), seminar on inland waterways (France, June/July), seminars on seafarers' training and certification and on coastal shipping (Japan, October), seminar on management of the dredging industry (Shanghai, December).

Social development

At its April 1983 session,[1] ESCAP adopted two resolutions relating to social development—one on youth and the other on rural development.

On youth, it appealed to Governments to ensure that youth enjoyed the right of full participation in national development, and recommended that the ESCAP Executive Secretary assist Governments so requesting in increasing public understanding and awareness so as to maximize youth's participation in national development, in promoting programme activities to enhance the potential of youth for rural and urban community work, and in encouraging greater involvement of youth leaders in youth programmes and projects.

On the social aspects of rural development, the Commission invited Governments to give special attention to the social impact of policies relating to integrated rural development programmes, and to present country papers; the Executive Secretary was asked to report to the Commission on the matter at its 1984 session.

Expressing concern over the massive social problems which had existed even before the current economic downturn, ESCAP called for creating more employment opportunities, especially for women, youth and disabled persons; improving essential social services, particularly for the poor and underprivileged; making education more relevant and widely available, as well as extending compulsory education for children and youth; devising special programmes for out-of-school children and youth; extending primary health care, especially to neglected people in rural and remote areas and in urban slums; and extending social security to all.

The Commission endorsed the recommendation of the Intergovernmental Meeting on Health and Development (Bangkok, June), convened jointly with the United Nations Educational, Scientific and Cultural Organization and the World Health Organization, which advised the secretariat on ways to strengthen and co-ordinate its health-related activities for improving the quality of life of the poor.

The Interagency Committee on Women in Development held a special session (Bangkok, January) to consider guidelines for development of indicators on the situation of women in the region. Other meetings, held at Bangkok unless otherwise specified, included: Expert Group Meeting on the Development and Utilization of Local Manpower and Technology for Disability-related Services in Rural and Poverty Areas (Manila, Philippines, February/March), Sixth Regional Seminar on Basic Community Services through Primary Health Care (Seoul, July/August), Regional Preparatory Meeting for the International Youth Year (July), Expert Group Meeting on Social Development Manpower Planning (October), and Expert Group Meeting on Forward-looking Strategies for the Advancement of Women (November/December).

Statistics

ESCAP, at its 1983 session, expressed support for the continuing emphasis of the secretariat's work programme in building statistical capabilities among countries of the region. It noted with satisfaction that a number of countries had initiated action towards participating in the 1983 round of industrial censuses and reiterated its support for the National Household Survey Capability Programme.

Among 1983 activities, the Training Course on Electronic Data Processing (New Delhi, India, July–November) aimed at developing relevant capabilities in the countries in the region, and covered programme languages, systems analysis, statistical data processing and advanced computer concepts.

Mekong river basin development

The Interim Committee for Co-ordination of Investigations of the Lower Mekong Basin held three sessions in 1983: sixteenth, Vientiane, Lao People's Republic, 13-19 January; seventeenth, Bangkok, 2-4 June; and eighteenth, Ho Chi Minh City, Viet Nam, 8-15 September.[9] At its eighteenth session, the Committee, which had held three sessions a year, decided to hold two meetings a year in future, in January and June, in order to achieve savings.

Total investment cost for the Indicative Basin Plan (1970-2000) was estimated in 1983 at $138,080 million. By 1983, 14 tributary projects had been completed at an investment cost of $225 million, and $520 million had been committed to the work programme as a whole.

In 1983, basic needs relating to food production, agricultural development and energy production were covered in the various projects for the inhabitants of the basin, where more than 475,000 million cubic metres of water flowed each year, almost completely unutilized, into the sea. Basic planning was further elaborated, including more effective use of the computerized Lower Mekong Information System and through remote sensing techniques. Programmes were also carried out in navigation improvement, fisheries and agro-industrial development.

Programme, organizational and administrative questions concerning ESCAP

Expansion of ESCAP conference facilities

In an October report to the General Assembly,[10] the Secretary-General recalled the history of United Nations accommodation at Bangkok, and discussed the need to expand the ESCAP conference facilities. He pointed to the unsuitability of current arrangements by which headquarters' office space had been converted to makeshift conference rooms, absence of available facilities in Bangkok that could meet the ESCAP conference requirements, and the resulting fact that close to half the number of 1982 meetings had to be held outside Bangkok. He described his assessment of the possible scope of the proposed expanded conference facilities at ESCAP, related conference support facilities as well as possible future office accommodation requirements.

The Advisory Committee on Administrative and Budgetary Questions (ACABQ) recommended to the Assembly in a November report[11] approval of the Secretary-General's request for $400,000 under the proposed programme budget for 1984-1985 for conducting an independent preliminary architectural and engineering study for the new construction required and retention of an independent quantity surveyor and energy consultant. The results of the study were to be ready for review by the Assembly at its thirty-ninth (1984) session. In view of the Secretary-General's statement that construction of new conference facilities at ESCAP would have no impact on proposed alterations and improvements and major maintenance projects, all relating to the existing ESCAP building complex, ACABQ recommended acceptance of his request for $374,200 under the proposed programme budget for the biennium.

GENERAL ASSEMBLY ACTION

On 20 December, the General Assembly, on the recommendation of the Fifth (Administrative and Budgetary) Committee, adopted section VII of resolution 38/234, relating to the ESCAP conference facilities.

Expansion of the conference facilities of the Economic and Social Commission for Asia and the Pacific at Bangkok

[*The General Assembly . . .*]

1. *Takes note* of the report of the Secretary-General on the expansion of the conference facilities of the Economic and Social Commission for Asia and the Pacific at Bangkok and of the related report of the Advisory Committee on Administrative and Budgetary Questions;

2. *Concurs* with the observations of the Advisory Committee as contained in its report;

3. *Accepts with appreciation* the offer by the Government of Thailand of additional land for the proposed construction of expanded conference facilities for the Commission;

. . .

General Assembly resolution 38/234, section VII

20 December 1983   Meeting 104   Adopted without vote

Approved by Fifth Committee (A/38/760) without vote, 23 November (meeting 46); oral proposal by Chairman; agenda item 109.

Meeting numbers. GA 38th session: Fifth Committee 46; plenary 104.

Restructuring

In the course of 1983, a number of United Nations bodies examined plans to strengthen Secretariat machinery for programme evaluation, including the possibility of an increase of staff of the ESCAP evaluation unit (see ADMINISTRATIVE AND BUDGETARY QUESTIONS, Chapter II).

On 20 December, the General Assembly, in section X of resolution 38/234, decided to finance the Regional Commissions Liaison Office, under a new section of the programme budget for 1984-1985, rather than from funds allocated to ESCAP (see above, under REGIONAL CO-OPERATION).

REFERENCES

[1]E/1983/43. [2]YUN 1980, p. 503, GA res. 35/56, annex, 5 Dec. 1980. [3]YUN 1981, p. 406. [4]*Economic and Social Survey of Asia and the Pacific, 1982* (ST/ESCAP/217), Sales No. E.83.II.F.1 (summary, E/1983/51). [5]YUN 1982, p. 836. [6]E/AC.51/1983/3 & Add.1. [7]YUN 1977, p. 555. [8]YUN 1982, p. 847. [9]E/ESCAP/381. [10]A/C.5/38/34. [11]A/38/7/Add.5.

PUBLICATIONS

Ground Water in the Pacific Region (ST/ESA/121), Sales No. 83.II.A.12. *Statistical Yearbook for Asia and the Pacific, 1983* (ST/ESCAP/285), Sales No. E/F.84.II.F.10. *Statistical Indicators for Asia and the Pacific*, vol. XIII: No. 1 (March 1983) (ST/ESCAP/198), Sales No. E.83.II.F.9; No. 2 (June 1983) (ST/ESCAP/241), Sales No. E.83.II.F.14; No. 3 (September 1983) (ST/ESCAP/250), Sales No. E.83.II.F.18; No. 4 (December 1983) (ST/ESCAP/264), Sales No. E.84.II.F.4. *Economic Bulletin for Asia and the Pacific*, vol. XXXIV: No. 1 (June 1983) (ST/ESCAP/298), Sales No. E.84.II.F.20; No. 2 (December 1983) (ST/ESCAP/308), Sales No. E.85.II.F.3. *Small Industry Bulletin for Asia and the Pacific*, No. 18 (1982), Sales No. E/F.83.II.F.4. *Quarterly Bulletin of Statistics for Asia and the Pacific*, vol. XIII: No. 1 (March 1983) (ST/ESCAP/234), Sales No. E.83.II.F.11; No. 2 (June 1983) (ST/ESCAP/244), Sales No. E.83.II.F.12; No. 3 (September 1983) (ST/ESCAP/255), Sales No. E.83.II.F.19; No. 4 (December 1983) (ST/ESCAP/271), Sales No. E.84.II.F.6. *Foreign Trade Statistics of Asia and the Pacific, 1977-1980*, vol. XIII, Series B (ST/ESCAP/224), Sales No. E.83.II.F.7; *1980*, vol. XIX, Series A (ST/ESCAP/240), Sales No. E.83.II.F.13. *Foreign Trade Statistics of Asia and the Pacific, 1978-1981*, vol. XIV, Series B (ST/ESCAP/245), Sales No. E.83.II.F.15. *Foreign Trade Statistics of Asia and the Pacific, 1981*, vol. XX, Series A (ST/ESCAP/246), Sales No. E.83.II.F.16. *Foreign Trade Statistics of Asia and the Pacific, 1983*, vol. XXII, Series A (ST/ESCAP/399), Sales No. E.86.II.F.6. *ASEAN and Pacific economic co-operation* (ST/ESCAP/228), Sales No. E.83.II.F.18. *Development Papers No. 2, ASEAN and Pacific Economic Co-operation* (ST/ESCAP/228), Sales No. E.83.II.F.17.

Europe

The Economic Commission for Europe (ECE) at its thirty-eighth session (Geneva, 12-23 April 1983)[1] examined the main economic problems facing Europe and North America, reviewed the ECE activities and approved plans for its future work.

In a resolution of 22 April on its work and future activities,[1] ECE called on its members to continue taking full advantage of its potential as an instrument for strengthening regional economic relations and multilateral co-operation, adding that implementation of and respect for the Final Act of the 1975 Helsinki (Finland) Conference on Security and Co-operation in Europe were essential for fostering such activities. The ECE Executive Secretary told the Commission that he considered east-west trade central to ECE programmes and that all Governments might benefit from some confidence-building measures in the economic field as well.

The Commission also invited its subsidiary bodies to pay special attention in their work programmes to the efficiency and effectiveness of their activities, and requested the Executive Secretary to evaluate the activities' impact and usefulness to member Governments.[1]

Several ECE principal bodies met at Geneva during 1983 and reviewed the work of their subsidiary bodies (see under specific topics below).[2]

Among a number of conventions and other instruments, the ECE Convention on Long-range Transboundary Air Pollution entered into force in 1983 (see below, under ENVIRONMENT), as did the European Agreement on Main International Traffic Arteries (see below, under TRANSPORT AND COMMUNICATIONS). The International Convention on the Harmonization of Frontier Control of Goods in the region was opened for signature (see below, under INTERNATIONAL TRADE).

The programme budget for ECE for 1984-1985 was approved by the General Assembly in resolution 38/236 A of 20 December 1983; there were no requests for an increase in personnel resources for the Commission.

Economic trends

The forecasts of recovery in 1982 proved false in western Europe and North America, according to a document[3] prepared by the ECE secretariat on recent economic developments in the region and noted by the Economic and Social Council in decision 1983/177 of 28 July (see Chapter I of this section). In western Europe, growth was a bare 0.1 per cent, with 1982 gross domestic product (GDP) falling in 7 of the 13 more industrialized countries; in the United States, gross national product fell by some 2 per cent between the fourth quarters of 1981 and 1982. Unemployment continued to increase, while there was general decline in the inflation rate. Forecasts for 1983 were modest, with aggregate GDP growth projected at less than 1 per cent.

The survey found that 1982 was another difficult year for the economies of southern Europe, where unemployment continued to be a serious problem, though the agricultural sector contributed positively in all countries to the maintenance of overall output.

In eastern Europe and the USSR, the net material product increased by less than 2 per cent, significantly below the aggregate 2.8 per cent growth implied by the annual plans of the countries concerned. The bulk of adjustment policies fell upon imports, which in most countries contracted in both value and volume, leading to a further decline in overall economic growth and an even more pronounced deceleration in the growth of resources for domestic use.

In 1982, the volume of western exports to, and imports from, the USSR increased by 7 and 13 per cent, respectively, making this an exceptionally dynamic two-way flow. There was a significant swing in the pattern of trade balances between east and west, with a turnaround of about $3 billion in a single year, highlighting the profound adjustment in east-west economic relations under way. Eastern external debt in convertible currencies was estimated to have declined by $8 billion, reversing a decade-long upward trend.

As regards developments in 1983, the *Economic Survey of Europe in 1983*[4] reported a recovery in economic growth throughout the region, with improvement expected to continue in 1984. In western Europe and North America, the recovery of output started in early 1983 against the background of large amounts of unused capacity, both of labour and capital, while inflation rates continued to fall; the outlook for business investment was improving. The upturn in the rate of economic growth in the centrally planned economies of eastern Europe and the USSR continued in 1983, reflecting an easing of supply bottle-necks in several critical sectors, a more efficient use of material inputs, tighter management and planning and, in the case of eastern Europe, a loosening of the balance-of-payments constraint.

Accelerated growth of imports into the ECE region—especially the pronounced recovery of North American imports—contributed to a modest upturn in the volume of world trade, by some 1 to 2 per cent in 1983 following three years of stagnation or decline. In western Europe, trade growth was still weak in 1983, owing to the hesitant recovery of demand. Trade of the east European countries and the USSR grew more strongly, with a marked acceleration in the growth of imports. East-west trade, within the ECE region, was more dynamic than trade with the rest of the world. The upswing in the volume of trade gathered strength in the course of 1983.

The Senior Economic Advisers to ECE Governments (nineteenth session, 21-25 February 1983), in their continuing review of economic developments in the region, agreed to examine further, among other topics, international trade and structural changes in the market and the centrally planned economies of ECE, and a preliminary outline of the overall economic perspective to the year 2000. A seminar on the assessment of the impact of science and technology on long-term economic prospects (Rome, Italy, May) was held jointly with the Senior Advisers to ECE Governments on Science and Technology.

In 1983, ECE requested its Executive Secretary to continue co-operating with the secretariats of ECWA and ECA and other United Nations bodies and to pursue his contacts with all Mediterranean countries not members of ECE, on subjects within ECE competence of common interest to the Mediterranean countries.[1]

Activities in 1983

International trade

On 1 April 1983, the International Convention on the Harmonization of Frontier Control of Goods was opened for signature. The 25-article Convention sought to facilitate international movement of goods—across one or more maritime, air or inland frontiers—by reducing the requirements for completing formalities as well as the number and duration of controls.

The Committee on the Development of Trade (thirty-second session, 5-9 December 1983) focused on obstacles to trade development and on the participation of small- and medium-sized enterprises in intraregional trade; it examined developments in compensation trade on the basis of the report of the Special Experts' Meeting on Compensation Trade (July).

In keeping with the changes taking place in trade facilitation, especially the introduction of automatic interchange of trade data, increased attention was given by the Working Party on Facilitation of International Trade Procedures (March, September) to implementing its recommendations, in particular through co-operation with the Special Programme on Trade Facilitation of the United Nations Conference on Trade and Development (see Chapter IV of this section) and with national facilitation bodies. Co-operation was maintained with other relevant bodies, including the United Nations Commission on International Trade Law (see LEGAL QUESTIONS, Chapter VI).

In 1983, expert groups met on data elements and automatic data interchange (March, September), procedures and documentation (March, September), international contract practices in industry (July, December) and obstacles to trade (September).

In a related field, the Group of Experts on Standardization Policies (Helsinki, Finland, and Stockholm, Sweden, May/June) and a one-day Seminar on Testing (Prague, Czechoslovakia, November) dealt with various standardization issues, including harmonization of standards and technical regulations, consumer protection, conformity certification and testing. ECE decided, on 20 April 1983,[1] to convene prior to its 1984 session the Eighth Meeting of Government Officials Responsible for Standardization Policies.

Industry

The Chemical Industry Committee (sixteenth session, 4-7 October 1983) continued to study trends in feedstocks for organics, low- and non-waste technologies in the production of organics, and the role and place of the chemical industry in the ECE economies. The Committee decided to undertake a sample study on food additives, and to initiate a second Informal Meeting of Experts on Olefins, with a view to preparing world-wide statistics on the production and consumption of specific groups of chemicals.

Among meetings held in 1983 were an *Ad Hoc* Meeting for the Study on the Role and Place of the Chemical Industry in the Economies of ECE Member Countries (November) and a Seminar on Chemicals from Synthesis Gas (June).

The Steel Committee (fifty-first session, 26-28 October 1983), serving as a forum for information exchange between national steel industries representing 85 per cent of world steel production, studied factors influencing the structure of steel production costs, improvement of steel consumption forecasting, and economic problems related to the creation of steel plants using direct reduction.

The Working Party on Engineering Industries and Automation (third session, February) issued studies in 1983 on techno-economic aspects of the international division of labour in the automotive industry and on production and use of industrial robots. Work was under way on various other topics, including engineering equipment for more effective energy use or for water pollution prevention, diffusion of robots in the ECE region, and recent developments in electrical and electronic engineering. Meetings included a Seminar on Innovation in Biomedical Equipment (Budapest, Hungary, May), which focused on the socio-economic consequences of the introduction of sophisticated, mostly micro-electronic, equipment as well as the rapid overall development of national health care systems in the region. On 22 April 1983,[1] ECE agreed to consider in 1984 a possible change in the status of the the Working Party.

Also meeting in 1983 was a Group of Experts on International Contract Practices in Industry (twenty-second and twenty-third sessions, 11-13 July and 12-16 December).

Transport and communications

In 1983, technical studies continued for the Trans-European North-South Motorway, a 10,000-kilometre road transport network that would link the Baltic to the Aegean and the southern parts of the region. On 15 March, the European Agreement on Main International Traffic Arteries came into force, providing a new framework for adapting the European road network to the needs of international traffic. Progress continued to be made in developing a European railway network.

The text of the Consolidated Resolution on the Facilitation of Road Transport, consisting of technical and administrative provisions on such transport in the continent, was completed, as was a major revision of the European Agreement concerning the International Carriage of Dangerous Goods by Road. Ten new Regulations concerning the construction of vehicles were finalized and amendments to 12 of the existing 59 Regulations were elaborated. Recommendations were adopted on technical requirements for the construction and the equipment of new and existing inland naviga-

tion vessels for application on all European waterways. General provisions developed by ECE for packagings were adopted at a world-wide level for the marine and air modes. As regards a Europe-Africa permanent link through the Strait of Gibraltar, the Economic and Social Council, in resolution 1983/62 of 29 July 1983, requested the Executive Secretaries of ECE and ECA to continue their efforts in that regard (see above, under AFRICA).

In addition to the Inland Transport Committee (forty-fourth session, 31 January–4 February 1983), a large number of subsidiary bodies met, also at Geneva, in the course of the year. Among them were groups of rapporteurs on crashworthiness, protective devices, pollution and energy, development of a European railway network, brakes and running gear, customs questions concerning containers, general safety provisions, and safety provisions on motor coaches and buses. Issues discussed by expert groups included transport of dangerous goods, customs questions, transport economics, road traffic safety and construction of vehicles. A seminar on the transport situation in the Mediterranean region (Barcelona, Spain, June) examined the subregion's importance in linking Africa, Asia and Europe. At its April 1983 session,[1] ECE requested its Executive Secretary to continue his efforts in the field of transport in the Mediterranean in co-operation with competent organizations.

ECE also suggested in April 1983 that all Governments which introduced or intended to introduce summer time might determine henceforth that the transition to and from summer time be on the last Sundays in March and September.[1]

Food and agriculture

The Committee on Agricultural Problems (thirty-fourth session, 7-11 March 1983) reviewed recent developments in European trade in agricultural products and the work of its subsidiary bodies. A project on economic, technological, sanitary and environmental aspects of large-scale intensive livestock production was completed with a synoptic report in 1983.

Efforts continued in reaching agreement on, or revising, agricultural products standards. Meetings, held at Geneva unless otherwise specified, included: the Joint FAO/ECE Working Party on Mechanization of Agriculture (September), focusing on energy and environment aspects of its programme; and the Working Party on Standardization of Perishable Produce (October). Expert groups met to discuss standardization of poultry meat (Kulmbach, Federal Republic of Germany, January), co-ordination of standardization of fresh fruit and vegetables (Zurich, Switzerland, February; Geneva, October), standardization of dry and dried produce (fruit) (May), and standardization of egg products (May/June).

Timber

The Timber Committee (forty-first session, 10-14 October 1983) noted some indications of recovery, after three years of declining markets, in the forest products sector of the region. Efforts continued in 1983 on collecting and analysing new data on forest resources, and the Committee collaborated closely with others, including the Executive Body for the Convention on Long-range Transboundary Air Pollution (see below), in assessing the impact of air pollution damage to forests.

Seminars and study tours held during the year dealt with: machines and techniques for forest plant production (Czechoslovakia, June); silvicultural, technological, economic and other problems connected with the mechanization of thinning operations (German Democratic Republic, September); and the Timber Committee's study tour of the United Kingdom.

Subsidiary bodies meeting at Geneva in 1983 included an *Ad Hoc* Meeting on the Impact of Energy Developments on the Forestry and Forest Products Sector (May), the Steering Committee of the Joint FAO/ECE/ILO Committee on Forest Working Techniques and Training of Forest Workers (May) and the Joint FAO/ECE Working Party on Forest Economics and Statistics (June).

Environment

The ECE Convention on Long-range Transboundary Air Pollution, opened for signature in 1979,[5] entered into force on 16 March 1983. It detailed provisions on such matters as information exchange, consultations, research and monitoring. Under the instrument, contracting parties were to develop policies and strategies for combating the discharge of air pollutants, using the best available technology.

The Executive Body created by the Convention (first session, 7-10 June 1983) recognized the need for effective reduction of the total annual emissions of sulphur compounds, or transboundary fluxes, by 1993-1995. It decided to convene a meeting to elaborate a formal instrument to provide for long-term funding of the Co-operative Programme for the Monitoring and Evaluation of Long-range Transmission of Air Pollutants in Europe (EMEP), according to an equitable cost-sharing system. The EMEP steering body (seventh session, 10 and 11 November) discussed various issues, including financing, co-operation with North American projects and plans for the third phase. EMEP, begun in 1978 and carried out by ECE in collaboration with the United Nations Environment Pro-

gramme and the World Meteorological Organization, embraced in mid-1983 more than 75 monitoring stations in 21 ECE countries.

In April 1983, ECE adopted a number of decisions on the environment.[1] On air pollution, it appealed to ECE member countries which had not ratified the Convention to do so at an early date, and stressed the urgent need for action to decrease sulphur emissions. It recognized the significance of intraregional co-operation and co-ordination in water pollution control matters, including transboundary water pollution. It also invited its Senior Advisers to ECE Governments on Environmental Problems to continue their efforts relating to the 1979 Declaration on Low- and Non-waste Technology and Reutilization and Recycling of Wastes,[5] to expand co-operation in protecting flora and fauna and their habitats, and to elaborate a strategy for environmental protection and rational use of natural resources in ECE member countries up to the year 2000 and beyond.

In addition to the Senior Advisers (eleventh session, 14-17 February), bodies meeting at Geneva in 1983 were: National Focal Points for the Compilation of a Compendium on Low- and Non-waste Technology (October), Working Party on Low- and Non-waste Technology and Reutilization and Recycling of Wastes (October) and Group of Experts on Environmental Impact Assessment (November/December).

Natural resources and energy

Natural resources

The Coal Committee (seventy-ninth session, 26-29 September 1983) examined coal-related technical and socio-economic issues and prepared a new ECE industrial classification of medium- and high-rank coals. Expert groups met in 1983, at Geneva unless otherwise specified, to discuss: opencast mines (Ankara, Turkey, May), productivity and management problems in the coal industry (June), coal statistics (June), and utilization and preparation of solid fuels (June). Other activities included: *Ad Hoc* Meeting on the Preparation of a New ECE Classification of Coals (March), Working Party on Coal Trade (June), Symposium on the Utilization of Waste from Coal Mining and Preparation (Tatabánya, Hungary, October), and a Seminar on Integrated Utilization of Low-Calorific-Value Fuels (Moscow, October).

The Committee on Electric Power (forty-first session, 24-28 January 1983), in co-operation with the International Atomic Energy Agency, focused on nuclear power stations and related problems, such as operational conditions and the study of the duration of down-time for checks, maintenance and refueling of such facilities. Issues discussed by expert groups meeting at Geneva in 1983 concerned problems of planning and operating large power systems (May), electric power stations (October), and the relationship between electricity and the environment (November). The ECE region accounted for about 75 per cent of total world electricity consumption in 1982.

The Committee on Gas (twenty-ninth session, 17-21 January 1983) added to its work programme the development of international co-operation in the field of liquefied petroleum gas. Work continued on revising international maps of Europe—one of gas transmission networks and another of natural gas fields. Among expert groups meeting at Geneva in 1983 were those concerned with natural gas resources (May), use and distribution of gas (June), transport and storage of gas (June) and gas statistics and forecasting problems (November).

The Committee on Water Problems (fifteenth session, 14-18 November 1983) completed preparation of, and recommended for adoption by the Commission, an ECE Declaration of Policy on the Rational Use of Water, providing guidelines on water management. It completed a study on techniques and means for industrial and municipal sewage effluent purification, and decided that a set of ECE recommendations should be elaborated. A Seminar on Ground-water Protection Strategies and Practices (Athens, Greece, October) opened the possibility for preparing ECE guiding principles for ground-water management. Meeting at Geneva in 1983 was the Group of Experts on Aspects of Water Quality and Quantity (May).

Energy

A second *ad hoc* Meeting on New and Renewable Sources of Energy (NRSE), convened in November 1983 in pursuance of the Commission's April decision,[1] reviewed the current status and prospects of NRSE in ECE countries and noted that the NRSE supply was expected to grow in the region by some 70 per cent between 1980 and 2000, covering between 11 and 12 per cent of total energy supplies by 2000, compared with about 9 per cent in 1980.

A Symposium on the Rational Utilization of Secondary Forms of Energy in the Economy, particularly in Industry (Bucharest, Romania, October), stressed the topic's importance in enhancing energy economy and efficiency, substituting for oil and reducing the environmental damage of energy use; it recommended the creation of an *ad hoc* group within ECE. An *ad hoc* Meeting on Energy Conservation (November) found that progress had been made in reducing oil imports, improving overall energy efficiency, using more indigenous fuels and substituting other fuels for oil.

A 1983 publication, *An Efficient Energy Future*—prepared by ECE on the basis of its two-year research of energy demand in Europe and North America—suggested that, although energy conservation was the most common policy priority among ECE countries, it was seldom reflected in recent government forecasts, which might have overestimated the needs of industrial countries in the year 2000 by about one fifth.

Science and technology

In 1983, the Senior Advisers to ECE Governments on Science and Technology (eleventh session, 19-23 September) decided to convene in 1985 or 1986 two symposia, one on biotechnology for future economic development, and the other on integrated use of raw materials in industry. Work continued on such issues as NRSE, low-calorific-value fuels and low-calorie coal technology, as well as on science and technology statistics with the aim of describing international flows of technology. Other meetings in 1983 included a seminar on the assessment of the impact of science and technology on long-term economic prospects (Rome, May).

Population

A regional meeting on population (Sofia, Bulgaria, 6-12 October 1983), convened in pursuance of an April 1983 Commission decision[1] as part of the contribution to the preparatory work for the 1984 World Conference on Population, adopted a number of suggestions and recommendations.

Work was started in 1983 on studies on the economic and related aspects of the aging of populations in the region, and on the relationship between population and development in southern Europe.

Human settlements

The Committee on Housing, Building and Planning (forty-fourth session, Ottawa, Canada, 5-9 September 1983) discussed, among other things, problems and policies related to improving postwar housing areas and decided to undertake several projects on urban renewal and modernization policies.

Among the meetings held in 1983 were: Group of Experts on Urban and Regional Research (April), Working Party on Urban and Regional Planning (April), Seminar on Integrated Planning (Rovaniemi, Finland, June), Seminar on Research on Long-term Perspectives for Human Settlements Development (Budapest, October), and Group of Experts on Human Settlements Problems in Southern Europe (Crete and Athens, November).

Social development

At its April 1983 session,[1] ECE requested its Executive Secretary to prepare a revised study on the economic role of women in the ECE region, for presentation to the 1985 World Conference to Review and Appraise the Achievements of the United

Nations Decade for Women (see Chapter XIX of this section), and to convene a seminar in 1984 on that role.

Statistics

The Conference of European Statisticians (thirty-first session, 13-17 June 1983) focused on comparing statistical aggregates and harmonizing economic classifications and nomenclatures. Work continued in economic, social, demographic and environmental statistics, while the European Comparison Programme was finalized. As part of the intercountry project on use of computers for statistical purposes, the secretariat continued to develop a medium-scale computer-based interactive data base for data processing and management.

Subsidiary bodies meeting at Geneva in 1983 included: Working Party on Electronic Data Processing (March), Joint ECE/ILO Meeting on Manpower Statistics (May), Joint FAO/ECE Study Group on Food and Agricultural Statistics in Europe (May), joint *ad hoc* Meeting on Questions of Statistics concerning Engineering Industries and Automation (May/June), and Meeting on Statistical Methodology (November).

REFERENCES

[1]E/1983/22 & Add.1. [2]E/ECE/1066. [3]E/1983/52. [4]*Economic Survey of Europe in 1983*, Sales No. E.84.II.E.1. [5]YUN 1979, p. 710.

PUBLICATIONS

UN/ECE Standards for Fresh Fruits and Vegetables, First Supplement, 1983 (ECE/AGRI/55/Supplement 1), Sales No. E.81.II.E.8/Supp.1. *Guide for Drawing Up International Contracts on Consulting Engineering, including Some Related Aspects of Technical Assistance* (ECE/TRADE/145), Sales No. E.83.II.E.3. *The Improvement of Housing and Its Surroundings: Synthesis Report on the Seminar Held in The Hague (Netherlands), 15-19 October 1979*, Sales No. E.83.II.E.4. *Bulletin of Statistics on World Trade in Engineering Products, 1981*, Sales No. E.83.II.E.8. *Annual Bulletin of General Energy Statistics for Europe, 1981*, vol. XIV, Sales No. E/F/R.83.II.E.9 *Policies and Strategies for Rational Use of Water in the ECE Region* (ECE/WATER/31), Sales No. E.83.II.E.10. *European Handbook of Economic Accounts for Agriculture*, Sales No. E/R.83.II.E.12 & corrigendum. *Techno-economic Aspects of the International Division of Labour in the Automotive Industry* (ECE/ENG.AUT/11), Sales No. E.83.II.E.14. *Agricultural Trade in Europe: Recent Developments* (ECE/AGRI/70), Sales No. E.83.II.E.17. *Catalogue of Building Systems and Components Approved at the National Level and Aimed at International Trade: Agreed Format and Example Catalogue* (ECE/HBP/40), Sales No. E.83.II.E.19. *Energy Transition in the ECE Region* (E/ECE/1063), Sales No. E.83.II.E.21. *Strategy For Energy Use in the Iron and Steel Industry* (ECE/STEEL/41), Sales No. E.83.II.E.22. *Guide to National Building Regulations: Agreed Format and Example Guide* (ECE/HBP/39), Sales No. E.83.II.E.23. *Efficient Use of Energy Sources in Meeting Heat Demand: The potential for energy conservation and fuel substitution in the ECE region* (E/ECE/1064), Sales No. E.83.II.E.25. *Statistics of road traffic accidents in Europe*, Sales No. E/F/R.83.II.E.30. *Prices of Agricultural Products and Selected Inputs in Europe and North America, 1982/83* (ECE/AGRI/75), Sales No. E.84.II.E.4. *Agricultural Trade in Europe, Recent Developments (prepared in 1983) European Trade in Fruit and Vegetables* (ECE/AGRI/77), Sales No. E.84.II.E.9. *Review of the Agricultural Situation in Europe at the End of 1983*, vol. I: *General Review*

and Grain; vol. II: *Livestock, Meat and Dairy Products* (ECE/AGRI/78, vols. I & II), Sales No. E.84.II.E.10. *The Steel Market in 1983* (ECE/STEEL/46), Sales No. E.84.II.E.14. *Annual Bulletin of Coal Statistics for Europe, 1983*, vol. XVIII, Sales No. E/F/R.84.II.E.15. *Annual Bulletin of Housing and Building Statistics for Europe, 1983*, vol. XXVII, Sales No. E/F/R.84.II.E.16. *Statistics of World Trade in Steel, 1983*, Sales No. E/F/R.84.II.E.20. *Annual Bulletin of Electric Energy Statistics for Europe 1983*, vol. XXIX, Sales No. E/F/R.84.II.E.27. *Annual Bulletin of Gas Statistics for Europe 1983*, vol. XXIX, Sales No. E/F/R.84.II.E.28. *Quarterly Bulletin of Steel Statistics for Europe, 1983*, vol. XXXIV, Nos. 1-4. *Annual Bulletin of Trade in Chemical Products, 1983*, vol. X, Sales No. E/F/R.85.II.E.2. *Annual Bulletin of General Energy Statistics for Europe, 1983*, vol. XVI, Sales No. E/F/R.85.II.E.9. *Annual Review of the Chemical Industry, 1983* (ECE/CHEM/55), Sales No. E.85.II.E.19.

Latin America

The economic situation of Latin America in 1983 was characterized by three principal features, a crisis of dimensions not witnessed since the depression of the 1930s, the adjustment effort to reduce the profound disequilibrium of the external sector, and an extraordinary contraction of net capital inflows, with accompanying transfer of resources abroad by Latin American countries. During the year, gross domestic product (GDP) fell, the employment situation worsened and inflation increased markedly.[1]

Faced with the crisis, the Economic Commission for Latin America (ECLA), which did not hold a session in 1983, called a meeting at Bogotá, Colombia (18-21 May), of personalities from a number of Latin American countries to consider its impact and possible solutions.[2] The meeting concluded that the region was facing its most severe economic crisis in the past 50 years as a consequence of the profound imbalances in the international economy and of the accumulation of unresolved problems at the level of its development strategies and internal economic policies.

A Santo Domingo Pledge, based on a document prepared by ECLA and the Latin American Economic System at the request of the President of Ecuador, was adopted at a meeting (1-3 August)[3] in the Dominican Republic, where the nations of the region agreed to hold an economic conference at Quito, Ecuador in 1984.

In another development during 1983, the Secretary-General convened a special meeting at United Nations Headquarters on 10 August and appealed for international emergency relief to Bolivia, Ecuador and Peru, following the disastrous impact of the 1983 climatic situation. ECLA became executing agency for the subsequent United Nations Development Programme (UNDP) multicountry project of assistance. Following a request by the Government, ECLA sent a mission to

Paraguay to assess the damage caused by heavy rains and floods (see p. 519).

Economic trends

In 1982, Latin America suffered its worst economic crisis since the 1930s, according to the *Economic Survey of Latin America*, 1982. The Economic and Social Council took note of a summary of the survey[4] in its decision 1983/177 of 28 July (see p. 422).

The survey stated that the growth rate of GDP fell by almost 1 per cent, the first such decline in 40 years. The loss of dynamism was accompanied by a further rise in urban unemployment, and inflation for the region as a whole reached a record high of 80 per cent. The continued decline in the region's terms of trade led to an unprecedented balance-of-payments deficit of some $14 billion.

During 1983, the region's GDP was estimated to have declined by 2.8 per cent and, given the population growth, the *per capita* product fell by more than 5 per cent and declined in 17 of the 19 countries in the region, for which there were comparable data. This amounted to a *per capita* product almost 9 per cent less than 1980, or equivalent to what the region had already reached six years earlier in 1977. The real standard of living fell even more sharply, with national income *per capita* declining during the previous three years by almost 12 per cent.[1]

At the same time, inflation accelerated spectacularly, reaching unprecedented levels. For the region as a whole, the simple average rate of increase of consumer prices rose from 48 per cent in 1982 to 66 per cent in 1983; the rate weighted by population rose from 86 per cent in 1982 to 130 per cent in 1983. During the year, prices more than quintupled in Argentina, more than quadrupled in Bolivia, tripled in Brazil and more than doubled in Peru. Prices rose by 80 per cent in Mexico, and by more than 50 per cent in Ecuador and Uruguay.

While the overall balance of payments closed with a deficit of almost $2.9 billion, much lower than the $19.6 billion of 1982, the result was a new fall in the level of international reserves of Latin America. The growth rate of external debt fell to 7 per cent as a result of the decline in net flows of capital, a rate well below the 13 per cent of 1982, or the 23 per cent average of 1978-1981. Despite a slight fall in 1983 in the proportion of export earnings absorbed by interest payments, it continued to be very high, at 34.5 per cent.

The fall in net capital flows was so strong that the inflow was inferior to payments of interest and profits on foreign capital. As in 1982, instead of receiving a net transfer of resources from abroad, there was a transfer of resources to the rest of the world. This transfer reached almost $30 billion in 1983, equivalent to 28 per cent of the value of exports of goods and services, or a 36 per cent fall in the terms of trade between 1981 and 1983. The overall result was an extremely severe contraction in the volume of imports, constituting the principal cause of the decline in internal economic activity in the region.

In 11 of the 19 countries for which comparable information was available, GDP dropped and remained virtually at a standstill in two others. Only in Argentina, the Dominican Republic and Nicaragua did the rate of increase of overall economic activity rise above the growth rate of population. In the two largest economies of Latin America, Brazil, which by itself generated around one third of the region's GDP, registered a more than 3 per cent fall in global economic activity, while Mexico's GDP fell by 4.5 per cent.

Inflation was particularly virulent in Argentina, Bolivia, Brazil, Ecuador, Peru and Uruguay and very high in Mexico. It dropped dramatically in Costa Rica and steadily in Colombia and was very low in Barbados, the Dominican Republic and Panama.

Consumer prices continued to rise sharply in Argentina (430 per cent), Bolivia (330 per cent) and Brazil (almost 180 per cent, after rises of 100 per cent in 1980 and 1982). Peru also suffered a seriously accelerated inflation rate (125 per cent, after 70 per cent rises in 1981 and 1982).

By the end of 1983, the total external debt of Latin America, on preliminary estimates, amounted to some $333 billion. The considerably lower rate of growth (7 per cent in 1983) was mainly the result of the restrictive policy adopted by international commercial banks with respect to Latin America; those banks granted virtually no new autonomous loans to the region, channelling their credit through renegotiations of external debt initiated by several Latin American countries. A substantial part of the debt increase was accounted for by banks capitalizing interest payments, partly due to International Monetary Fund (IMF) pressure to refinance part (usually about 50 per cent) of the interest earned, as a contribution to Fund-sponsored adjustment programmes.

In some countries, the percentage of the value of exports devoted to interest payments in 1983 was considerably higher than the region's average of 35 per cent (20 per cent generally being considered an acceptable ceiling): Argentina (51 per cent); Brazil (44 per cent); and Costa Rica (42 per cent).

Report of Bogotá meeting. The economic crisis facing Latin America was discussed by personalities from a number of Latin American countries, at a meeting, called by the ECLA secretariat at Bogotá from 18 to 21 May.[2]

The participants noted that the crisis had been exacerbated by the pincer effect created by the simultaneous drop in export values and sudden increase in interest payments, which had come on top of an abrupt reversal in net capital movements towards the region. The burden of servicing the external debt was debilitating, and it was practically impossible for Latin American countries to obtain trade surpluses and redress the external accounts balance, in view of the slow growth of international trade and the protectionism practised by industrialized countries as a result of the world recession.

They asserted that countries of the region should not deal with the economic situation just by demanding changes in the external sector, but should review their international development policies. There was need to ensure rational conduct of monetary and exchange policies; to bring into greater harmony the objectives of growth and consumption and generation of domestic savings; to base national development strategies increasingly on domestic savings rather than on external indebtedness; to combine import substitution and export promotion policies in a more dynamic and effective way; to confront the industrialization crisis within the context of the current restructuring of world industry; and to make social action and the State apparatus more efficient. At the same time, the lion's share of resources should be allocated to development with consequent reduction in weapons expenditures to the extent politically possible.

Recognizing that the most overwhelming problem confronting the region was the debt-servicing burden, the meeting suggested, among other things, that a regional mechanism be established to provide information on debt management and refinancing, and that IMF modify its loans criteria so that the level of economic activity and employment did not suffer an exaggerated drop in countries entering into agreements with the Fund. It also advocated doubling resources of the Inter-American Development Bank and the World Bank for making loans to Latin America, as well as a new set of international instruments to control the process of creating world financial liquidity.

Regarding regional economic co-operation, it was unanimously considered appropriate to re-examine the potential offered by intra-regional economic co-operation to mitigate the effects of the international recession and to promote adoption of national development strategies. Sharing of markets, promotion of joint action to resolve common problems and co-ordination initiatives *vis-à-vis* third party countries should be a fundamental part of any action programme to overcome the crisis. While various concrete measures were advocated, it was recognized that the most important element for intra-regional co-operation

was the raising of its political profile when formulating the economic policies of the various countries of the region.

The meeting called for an international framework better adapted to the debt renegotiation process. The framework should provide for participation of international financial institutions, private banks and financial authorities of creditor countries, and consideration should be given to providing additional resources both to cover debt-servicing commitments and to meet the minimum financial needs of trade and development. Substantial reductions in interest rates were required and the costs of the international adjustment process should be distributed equitably among creditor countries and banks and debtor countries.

Activities in 1983

Development issues and policies

As in previous years, the Latin American Institute for Economic and Social Planning (ILPES) promoted co-operation among development planning organizations and provided assistance in advisory services, training and research. The Fourth Conference of Ministers and Heads of Planning of Latin America and the Caribbean was held at Buenos Aires, Argentina, on 9 and 10 May.

In the area of advisory assistance, special attention was given to the less developed countries and the less advanced regions of developing countries; assistance was provided to planning bodies in Brazil, Chile, Costa Rica, Colombia, the Dominican Republic, Ecuador, Guatemala, Haiti, Honduras, Nicaragua, Panama and Venezuela.[5]

Research activities concentrated on: planning and co-ordination of economic policy decisions in the short-, medium- and long-term; the region's future standing in the world economy; the territorial effects of global and sectoral economic policies; and the role of the public sector, with special emphasis on social development policy.

ILPES carried out a first mission (September-October) designed to evaluate horizontal co-operation among national planning bodies, involving interviews with more than 100 authorities in Argentina, Brazil, Chile, Colombia, Ecuador, Mexico, Peru and Venezuela. Areas identified by the mission for new services dealing with such co-operation included formulating plans and policies; programming public sector activities; monitoring macro-economic aspects and conjunctional analysis; support for regional development bodies; pre-investment and project activities; science and technology; technical co-operation; and social development. Work continued on the systematic study of the economic evolution of individual countries and the region as a whole, and the analysis and appraisal of the various development policies and strategies applied in the region.

Regarding poverty, a project report found that, unless a significant change was made in development styles, some 30 per cent of the Latin American population would still be living in a state of poverty in the year 2000. Overcoming poverty would call for vigorous State intervention, since economic growth alone could not be expected to satisfy the basic needs of the population.

Food and agriculture

The ECLA programme in food and agriculture focused on such questions as food security, rural poverty and peasant economy, styles of development and agricultural policies, training in agricultural and rural development, and relevant co-operation and integration.[5] Rural poverty research efforts concentrated on the economic and social trends and processes in agricultural and rural activities which determined the state of poverty affecting rural populations.

Meetings held, at ECLA headquarters, included one on the peasantry as a producer of basic food-stuffs and its links to food markets (July), and an ECLA/FAO Expert Meeting on Styles of Development and Agricultural Policies (November).

Environment

Efforts continued in 1983 to strengthen the capacity of the ECLA secretariat and the region to manage the environment and its resources in order to promote regional development and integration and to improve living conditions of the lowest-income groups.[5] Studies—on the economy and the environment and incorporation of the environmental dimension in planning—were presented to the Fourth Conference of Ministers and Heads of Planning of Latin America and the Caribbean (Buenos Aires, May).

Various seminars held during 1983 dealt with the environment and technologies for settlements in arid zones: research and experience in Argentina and Chile (Antofagasta, Chile, March and April), agricultural processes of importance in Latin America from the environmental standpoint (Santiago, Chile, June), and human settlements and development in arid ecosystems (Mendoza, Argentina, November).

Human settlements

ECLA activities were oriented towards analysing traditional criteria for selection of technology, the nature of appropriate technologies as well as their economic and social impact, and their application to the processes of building human settlements and the supply of housing services and infrastructure.[5] Other activities concerned ex-

amination of metropolitanization and social change, particularly in connection with planning and management of large cities and co-operation among metropolitan areas of the region, the role of local governments in promoting and managing municipal development and decentralization, community participation and planning prospects.

Meetings and seminars included one on technologies for human settlements (Bogotá), the *Ad Hoc* Consultative Meeting of Experts in Municipal Planning Methodologies (Cali, Colombia, August), and one on makeshift settlements (Santiago, October).

Industrial development

The High-level Preparatory Meeting for the Fourth General Conference of the United Nations Industrial Development Organization (UNIDO): Strategies and Policies for Industrial Development in the Developing Countries (Lima, Peru, 18-22 April) considered, among other things, a study on the Latin American industrialization strategy, which re-examined the strategy of the 1980s in the light of new factors emerging from the recessive internal situation and the international crisis. The study emphasized correction of extreme forms of technological and social heterogeneity, improvement of production structures, export promotion and correction of intra-regional heterogeneities.[5]

Field work was completed on demand for equipment in the mining sector (metallic minerals and coal) and an analysis began of the industrial significance of that demand; field work began in August on evaluation of the demand for oil prospecting and extraction equipment.

A review of the main industrial sectors indicated that the recessive situation in the region had particularly affected the capital goods production sector, with a large proportion of iron and steel projects suspended or postponed.

Meetings held in 1983 included: a special meeting with senior executives of electricity companies (November); and the ECLA/UNIDO Expert Meeting on Capital Goods Industries in Latin America (Santiago, December), which considered the objectives, results and directions of the regional project on capital goods supply and production in Latin America and identified areas of co-operation.

International trade

ECLA submitted to the May Bogotá meeting of leading Latin American personalities a document on the international economic crisis and Latin America's capacity to respond to it, which analysed the trade problems faced by countries of the region, including the negative impact of the growing tendency towards protectionism at the world level, and suggested possible regional responses.[5]

Another study, presented at the Latin American Ministerial Co-ordination Meeting prior to UNCTAD VI (Cartagena, Colombia, 21-26 February), identified possible policies, programmes and measures for a new Latin American approach to and strategy on basic commodities.

A round-table meeting, on policy options in the external sector: the Latin American case, was held at ECLA headquarters in October. Other meetings and seminars included: special conference on external financing, organized by the Inter-American Economic and Social Council (Caracas, Venezuela, September); Expert Consultation on Commodity Trade, Especially Livestock and Meat, organized by the Food and Agriculture Organization of the United Nations (ECLA headquarters, September); seminar on export promotion (Brasilia, Brazil, September-October); and Meeting of Officials Responsible for External Trade in Latin America (Santiago, March).

Co-operation among developing countries

Co-operation in the field of planning included a meeting on agricultural planning in Trinidad and Tobago, November, in addition to the Third Meeting of Caribbean Heads of Planning, also in Trinidad and Tobago in April-May.[5]

In the transport area, a national subgroup meeting was held in Mexico in September; from this and earlier meetings, a Caribbean maritime search and rescue plan emerged. Also during the year, a subregional workshop on removal of language barriers was held in the Netherlands Antilles, August/September; a regional intensive course in demography was organized in Trinidad and Tobago, June/August; and an *ad hoc* expert group meeting was held in Cuba in October to review draft national trade procedures guides and to recommend future action for facilitating trade.

Natural resources and energy

In 1983, ECLA prepared a report on activities of international agencies in the region in the field of water resources,[5] and began preparations for Latin America's participation in the United Nations Conference for the Promotion of International Co-operation in the Peaceful Uses of Nuclear Energy (see Chapter X of this section).

With the objective of identifying the region's capacity for utilizing the sea and its resources and promoting future co-operation in ocean matters, inventories were under preparation for each country in order to build up an information service.

Meetings included a seminar-workshop on evaluations of the environmental impact on the marine environment and coastal areas in the south-east Pacific (Santiago, November); and the Seventh Latin American Seminar on Irrigation (Santiago, November-December), organized by the Inter-American Institute for Agricultural Co-operation.

Population

In 1983, the Latin American Demographic Centre (CELADE) gave, in Trinidad and Tobago, an intensive demography course for the first time for English-speaking Caribbean countries. Work continued regarding processing, utilization and analysis of the 1980s censuses in the region.[5]

The seventh session of the Committee of High Level Government Experts (CEGAN), within the framework of which the Latin American Regional Preparatory Meeting for the 1984 International Conference on Population was held, met in Havana, Cuba, from 16 to 19 November.

Resolutions adopted concerned the reports of activities and programme of work of the Latin American Demographic Centre and Latin American Regional Population Programme, 1984-1987; support for activities of the Latin American Demographic Centre; and a Latin American proposal to the International Conference on Population.[6]

Science and technology

A report regarding application of biotechnology to solving the region's development problems was examined in 1983 by the ECLA/UNESCO Expert Meeting on Implications for Latin America of Advances in Biotechnology, including Genetic Engineering (Montevideo, Uruguay, November).[5]

Social development and humanitarian affairs

Systematic surveys continued—using the 1960, 1970 and 1980 census series, household surveys and statistical sources—of the changes which had taken place in the occupational structure, education, levels of consumption, and other areas, in order to define the various social groups comprising the Latin American structure and the forms which their demands for development and participation might assume. Particular attention was paid to the peasant sectors and lowest-income urban social groups in order to facilitate their incorporation into the social development process.[5]

Consideration was given to the effects of the economic crisis on styles and forms of development as changes took place in Latin American social structure and stratification as well as in the economy, science and technology and social organization in the developed countries. A seminar on changes in the economies and societies of the developed countries and options for Latin America was held in Rio de Janeiro, Brazil, in October.

The Latin American Regional Preparatory Meeting for the International Youth Year (San

José, Costa Rica, October) adopted a regional plan of action to be submitted in connection with the activities for the Year (1985). In addition, ECLA continued to promote the participation of women within the framework of the International Development Strategy for the Third United Nations Development Decade (the 1980s)[7] and the United Nations Decade for Women (1976-1985).

Statistics

Advance estimates were made towards the end of the year, of the future evolution of domestic external sector economic activity and of the countries of the region, to serve as the basis for preliminary overviews of the Latin American economy.[5]

Technical assistance continued to be provided for household surveys and population censuses.

ECLA participated in the biennial session of the Co-ordinating Board of the Commission for the Improvement of National Statistics at Buenos Aires, in October. Other meetings held included the Latin American Seminar on National Accounts (Lima, October).

Transport

Work by ECLA in the transport area included consideration, at the request of the Latin American Integration Association, of a study on an information system on international transport. To develop this system, a seminar on the uniform system of maritime transport statistics was organized, in conjunction with the Government of Peru and the United Nations Statistical Office, at Lima in November 1983. In co-operation with the International Maritime Organization, ECLA convened the first meeting on regional maritime co-operation among the South American countries, Mexico and Panama (Santiago, October). Other 1983 meetings included the Pan American Transport Congress (Buenos Aires, May/June), and a seminar on road maintenance experience in Latin America (Santiago, August).

Women

The Third Regional Conference on the Integration of Women into the Economic and Social Development of Latin America and the Caribbean (Mexico City, 8-10 August) adopted 12 resolutions, one of which concerned continuation of integration activities beyond the end of the United Nations Decade for Women.[5]

Other resolutions adopted by the Conference concerned guidelines for action to improve the status of women, measures to promote integration of women in development, and financial and technical support for specific programmes.[8]

REFERENCES

[1]E/1984/71. [2]E/CEPAL/G.1250. [3]E/1984/112. [4]E/1983/73. [5]E/1984/22. [6]E/CEPAL/G.1284. [7]YUN 1980, p. 503. [8]E/CEPAL/G.1265.

PUBLICATIONS

Statistical Yearbook for Latin America, 1981 (E/CEPAL/G.1281), Sales No. E./S.83.II.G.1. *CEPAL Review*: No. 19, April 1983 (E/CEPAL/G.1229), Sales No. E.83.II.G.3; No. 20, August 1983, Sales No. E.83.II.G.4; No. 21, December 1983 (E/CEPAL/G.1266), Sales No. E.83.II.G.5. *Measurement of Employment and Income in Rural Areas* (E/CEPAL/G.1226), Sales No. E.83.II.G.10.

Western Asia

The Economic Commission for Western Asia (ECWA) held its tenth session at its headquarters at Baghdad, Iraq, from 7 to 11 May 1983. Its Executive Secretary emphasized the need for co-ordination and co-operation in developmental integration efforts, in view of the economic recession, the consequent decrease in public spending and the rationalization of energy consumption, leading to reduced demand for petroleum.[1]

The Commission adopted nine resolutions, four of which were for consideration by the Economic and Social Council. The four concerned: its programme of work and priorities for 1984-1985, staff and administration questions, international assistance to earthquake-stricken areas of Yemen, and programme of action for the 1980s for the least developed countries (LDCs). One of the texts included a request that the Council propose to the General Assembly assignment of a quota of posts in the ECWA secretariat to the Palestine Liberation Organization (PLO) as a full member of the Commission. Under another, it called on the secretariat to focus its advisory activities on LDCs of the region (Democratic Yemen, Yemen), and to utilize its resources to strengthen infrastructures, expand training opportunities and plan, monitor and implement joint ventures between those countries in line with the Substantial New Programme of Action for the 1980s for LDCs,[2] which was adopted by the 1981 United Nations Conference on LDCs and endorsed the same year by the General Assembly. ECWA also adopted a resolution on a study of the economic and social situation and potential of the Palestinian Arab people (see below).

Survey of economic and social development

The survey of economic and social developments in the ECWA region in 1983,[3] the summary of which was taken note of by the Economic and Social Council in its decision 1983/177 of 28

July (see p. 422), stated that the decline in growth rates had affected both the developed market economies and developing countries, and that, in 1982, a combination of lower oil outputs and a downward shift in the terms of trade had reversed the past trend of consistently high growth rates in oil-exporting countries.

In early 1983, negotiations among countries belonging to the Organization of Petroleum Exporting Countries led to some 15 per cent reduction of official posted prices of oil from $34 to $29 a barrel; it remained to be seen whether that move would help the developed market economies in ending their recession, the survey stated. The decline in oil revenue surpluses of the oil-exporting countries, however, diminished prospects of their continued aid to the non-oil-exporting countries of the region. At the same time, there were signs of a downward trend in many labour-exporting, least developed and other non-oil-exporting countries of the region, whose economies depended on remittances from their workers in Gulf oil countries; problems of return migration, settlement and aggravation of the domestic employment situation could also be expected.

Activities in 1983

Study on Palestinian Arab people

The Final Report on the Economic and Social Situation and Potential of the Palestinian Arab People in the Region of West Asia,[4] a study commissioned by ECWA, was published in May 1983. The decision to carry out the study had been made in 1976, following the acquisition by PLO of a permanent observer status in ECWA in 1975.

The report stated that most Palestinian communities showed the economic, political and social characteristics and attributes of minorities, in terms of both numbers and power relations, and that they tended to be isolated from the mainstream of social change in their area of residence. It observed that the cohesion of the Palestinian communities resulted partly from their 35 years of geographic dispersion, statelessness and minority status.

The report stated that PLO served, among other things, as a force of unity, assertion and cohesion among the Palestinians; they saw PLO as a welfare institution, a source of moral and social authority, a conduit for maintaining family ties, a potential platform for self-realization, a framework for settling grievances and a symbol for asserting national rights. Thus, Palestinians affiliated themselves with PLO as a means of defeating socio-political alienation, and as an act of asserting their Palestinianism, the report stated.

Among recommendations concerning Palestinians made in the report was that there should be a complete release by all States of socio-economic and demographic data on them; a census; and the establishment of a United Nations registry for them, to record such information as demographic changes, land holdings, and other property and cultural treasures. The report also suggested that ECWA enhance the capabilities of the Palestinian Central Bureau of Statistics; that assistance be given to PLO's documentation, research and planning institutions; and that ECWA should encourage intensive research in all its member countries regarding trends in the occupied territories. It called for studies on the disintegration/integration of the Palestinian people, society and economy, as well as on migration, settlement and resettlement.

ECWA, at its 1983 session,[1] referred the report to member States for study, and established a subcommittee to redraft the report in the light of observations to be received, for submission to the August/September International Conference on the Question of Palestine (see p. 274).

In connection with the proposed census, the ECWA secretariat reported that the United Nations Fund for Population Activities planned to send a consultant on a fact-finding mission to determine possibilities for rendering assistance,[5] in accordance with a 1978 General Assembly resolution.[6]

Assistance to flood-stricken areas of Democratic Yemen

High priority was given to obtaining international assistance for Democratic Yemen, which had been struck by severe floods in March 1982[7] (see p. 514).

A rehabilitation and reconstruction programme by the Government, as assessed by ECWA, included examination of needs, rehabilitation of the displaced population, rehabilitation of agricultural land and compensation for livestock and other flood-destroyed property, reconstruction of physical infrastructures, development of a disaster warning system, replacement of development programme resources which had been redeployed to meet immediate relief requirements, and budgetary support to recover losses in production and transport cost and to meet balance-of-payments deficits. Those activities were to be consolidated into ECWA's programme of action for LDCs of the region.

The secretariat proposed that it participate in the assessment and operations of the rehabilitation and reconstruction programme, and assist the country in bringing the programme to the attention of donors.

Earthquake in Yemen

At its May 1983 session, ECWA adopted a resolution[1] on international assistance to the area of

Yemen which had been struck by a December 1982 earthquake (see p. 533), and expressed satisfaction over the joint mission—of ECWA, the Kuwait Fund for Arab Economic Development, the Arab Fund for Economic and Social Development, the World Bank and the Organization of Arab Petroleum Exporting Countries—in preparing a preliminary programme for reconstruction. It also expressed appreciation for relief offers, appealed for further contributions, and asked the Executive Secretary to report on the subject to ECWA at its eleventh session.

Food and agriculture

An Expert Group Meeting on Review of Experiences with Rural Development Projects in the Countries of Western Asia (Baghdad, 29 September–2 October) reviewed national case-studies and submitted its results to the FAO/ECWA Regional Intergovernmental Consultation on Rural Development in the Near East Region (Baghdad, 3-6 October).[8]

An Expert Group Meeting on Constraints in Agricultural Planning and Resource Mobilization for Food Security Programmes in the ECWA Region was held at Baghdad in December.

Several studies and reports were in different stages of preparation in 1983. Among them, a pilot case-study on long-term agricultural development alternatives, efficient resource use and agricultural adjustment in the Syrian Arab Republic was completed in draft form.[9]

A first study on agricultural development in Saudi Arabia—evaluating land and water resources potential, regional cropping patterns, production costs of traditional and commercial farms, and agricultural prices and marketing margins—was discussed at a national in-service workshop at Riyadh, Saudi Arabia, in April. Lebanon was considering a UNDP/FAO study on the reconstruction and development of its agriculture, which included a proposed strategy and policy options for agricultural development, a medium-term reconstruction and development programme and a proposal for reorganization of the agricultural administration.

A case-study on agricultural price policy in Iraq was in progress, while a report on the organization and management of state farms in that country was completed. Rural poverty alleviation in Egypt was the subject of another completed case-study. Papers were prepared dealing with food security issues in Egypt, Iraq and Saudi Arabia, as was one surveying national food grain policies in all ECWA countries.[5]

A joint FAO/ECWA/UNDP mission visited Egypt, Iraq, Kuwait and the Sudan in November to initiate assessment of training needs in agricultural planning and project analysis.[8]

In October, the General Assembly, in resolution 38/6, requested FAO to consider holding at Rome, Italy, not later than 31 August 1984, a meeting on food and agriculture in the Arab region.

Industrial development

A report on the latest industrial development plans of ECWA member countries was issued.[9] Several studies were under way on various aspects of industrial development, including feasibility studies on specific industrial sectors.

The Expert Panel Meeting on Capital Goods and Heavy Engineering Industries (Turbines and Generators), meeting at Baghdad in October, discussed such topics as capacities and skill buildup, technology transfer and development, and technological and manufacturing requirements for components.[8] Steps were taken for the formation of an Arab electric equipment manufacturing company, as recommended by a meeting at Tunis, Tunisia, in November, of the Arab Industrial Development Organization and the Arab Fund.

Natural resources and environment

A draft report was issued on a regional programme for new and renewable sources of energy, with special reference to rural applications.[8] Other reports dealt with electric power generation and distribution opportunities for co-operation in the region, mineral resources development, assessment of skilled manpower needs in the oil and gas sector, and waste-water treatment for reuse.

Meetings held in 1983 included the Expert Group Meeting on Electrical Network Interconnection of the Mesreq Arab Countries (Kuwait, 25-27 October).

ECWA's Environmental Co-ordination Unit continued to assess the state of environment, and provided support to the regional seas programme.

Science and technology

A workshop was held at Baghdad in October on strategic problems involving the importation of technology for industrial advancement.

Reports prepared or published included: development of consulting and engineering design capabilities in selected ECWA countries, proceedings of the ECWA seminar on technology policies in the Arab States, a preliminary outline and plan of action regarding the international movement of highly qualified specialists and technologies with special reference to selected ECWA countries, technological decision-making with the investment process, relations between processes of importing technology and the development of technological capabilities, and education and training of high-level scientific and technological manpower.

Population

Evaluation continued in 1983 of population data provided by censuses and surveys in Jordan, the Syrian Arab Republic, Yemen and the United Arab Emirates.[9]

On population estimates and projections, the revised third issue of the *Demographic and Related Data Sheets* and the *1982 Adjusted Age-Sex Structure of Population in the ECWA region* had been completed. A demographic estimates and projections workshop on the ECWA region was held.

Transport, communications and tourism

A programme on inter-country and regional transport projects was terminated and resources were concentrated, instead, on the training needs of the region, with the ultimate aim of establishing a regional training institution and improving existing centres.

On the question of transport harmonization in the region, difficulties encountered at border crossings were investigated in order to improve the situation and standardize documents.

A report was prepared on the need and potential for developing national merchant marines, and activities for developing inland waterways continued in Egypt and Iraq. A possible maritime information system for monitoring trade and port traffic was investigated. Efforts also continued to improve road maintenance with the aim of preserving a high-standard regional highway network, while a programme on integration and improvement of railways networks was terminated. Continuing also was the programme on monitoring developments in the transport field.

Work was undertaken to formulate a new development strategy for tourism in Western Asia, leading, ultimately, to a master tourism plan for ECWA countries; a report on the strategy, including recommendations, was published in November. Tourism flows were monitored as were payments and policies in the region. A report on a strategy for tourism development in the region was prepared in anticipation of an expert group meeting in 1984.[9]

Contacts were continued with the Economic Commission for Europe in regard to the Trans-European North-South Motorway project, passing through 10 European countries and terminating at the frontiers of the ECWA region. In July, the Economic and Social Council, in resolution 1983/69, called on ECWA to collaborate with the Economic and Social Commission for Asia and the Pacific in incorporating the Western Asia region in the programme of action for a transport and communication decade, which had been proposed for the Asia and the Pacific region (see above, under ASIA AND THE PACIFIC).

Human settlements

Data collection continued for analysis of the human settlement situation, with priority given to profiles of the least developed ECWA member countries (Democratic Yemen, Yemen).[9]

Technical assistance was given to Lebanon on housing policies and schemes. Work was initiated on the assessment and improvement of the building materials and construction industry.

Social development

A regional meeting on International Youth Year (1985) was held at Baghdad in October and a study was made of youth in the region.

ECWA assisted in organizing the Western Asia Regional Preparatory Meeting (Baghdad, December) for the Seventh (1985) United Nations Congress on the Prevention of Crime and the Treatment of Offenders; the meeting adopted a resolution requesting the United Nations Secretary-General to take measures towards establishing a United Nations Arab Regional Institute for the Prevention of Crime.[8]

Other activities dealt with technical or advisory assistance in planning institutions and programmes for the aged, and policies and programmes for the integration of women in development. Among meetings held on the latter was a Regional Expert Group Meeting on Policy Formulation for Developmental Images of Women in the Mass Media (Baghdad, December).

Statistics

Work was initiated on the standardization of national statistics, and assistance was given in developing national accounts and improving the implementation of the United Nations system of national accounts. Publications included: the fourth bulletin of the series *Studies on Prices and Index Numbers in the ECWA Region* (1971-1981), and the *National Accounts Studies.*[9]

The ECWA secretariat participated in, or contributed to, the Technical Committee for Harmonization of the Statistical Classification in the Arab World (Amman, Jordan, August-September), the Statistical Committee of the Council of Arab Economic Unity (Amman, 3-5 September), the Training Workshop on Statistics of the Distributive Trades and Services for Arab Countries (Amman, 3-31 October), and the Statistical Standing Committee of the Arab League (Tunis, 20-24 November).

Technical co-operation

ECWA continued to provide advisory services in public finance, development planning, human resources development, industrial project identification and formulation, financial development, economic statistics and national accounts, household survey design and execution, and transport and communications.[10] Regarding the International Drinking Water Supply and Sanitation Decade (1981-1990), consultancy services were provided to all ECWA member States in support of development plans and programme improvement.

A meeting was held on upgrading the capability of industrial planners to assess imported technologies, and a subregional workshop met on development of skills for organization and participation in training workshops.

Public finance

Assistance was given to UNDP in preparing a project document on establishing a Regional Arab Institute in Banking and Financial Management.[9]

Work on public enterprises and economic development in the countries of Western Asia was completed, while work on financial resources availabilities and needs in ECWA countries was initiated.

REFERENCES

[1]E/1983/45. [2]YUN 1981, p. 406. [3]E/1983/78.
[4]E/ECWA/166/Add.1. [5]E/ECWA/163. [6]YUN 1978, p. 345, GA res. 33/147, 20 Dec. 1978. [7]E/ECWA/164 & Corr.1. [8]E/ECWA/XI/4, part I & Add.1. [9]E/ECWA/162/Add.1. [10]E/ECWA/162/Add.2.

Chapter IX

Natural resources and cartography

During 1983, the United Nations Revolving Fund for Natural Resources Exploration (UNRFNRE) continued its financing activities in developing countries. The Committee on Natural Resources held its eighth session in New York from 8 to 17 June; on the basis of its recommendations, the Economic and Social Council in July adopted resolutions on: developing non-metallic raw materials (1983/52); standardizing terminology for mineral resources (1983/53); applying computer technology in mineral exploration (1983/54); permanent sovereignty over natural resources (1983/56); water resources development (1983/57); utilizing subsurface space (1983/58); co-ordinating United Nations programmes on natural resources (1983/59); and UNRFNRE (1983/55). A resolution on developing the energy resources of developing countries was also adopted (see Chapter X of this section).

The Committee for Programme and Co-ordination again took up the matter of programme co-ordination in mineral resources.

Reformulations of a new major programme in marine affairs, for inclusion in the United Nations medium-term plan for 1984-1989, were adopted by the General Assembly.

The Tenth United Nations Regional Cartographic Conference for Asia and the Pacific was held in January at Bangkok, Thailand.

Topics related to this chapter. Law of the sea: sea-bed mining. Middle East: permanent sovereignty over natural resources in the occupied territories. Operational activities for development: technical co-operation. Regional economic and social activities. Energy. Namibia.

General aspects of natural resources

Exploration

UN Revolving Fund for Natural Resources Exploration

Activities

The United Nations Revolving Fund for Natural Resources Exploration continued to make good progress in all its activities during 1983. Under the administration of the United Nations Development Programme (UNDP), work was carried out in four main areas: pre-investment assistance to countries where mineral finds had been made; management of operational mineral projects; pre-project evaluation and development; and evaluation of projects in the geothermal energy field. UNRFNRE's 1983 activities were outlined in a February 1984 report[1] by the UNDP Administrator.

The Fund provided a number of developing countries with scarce, high-risk financing, expertise and technology for the technical and economic assessment of mineral resources.[2] Eleven exploration projects had been completed by the end of 1983, with seven discoveries recorded. Interest in considering the feasibility of investment was expressed by the mining sector in four of the projects.

To assist Governments, UNRFNRE began to develop documentation which they would be able to use to attract investment. A survey was conducted of private mining groups, the public sector, private and international financing institutions, and regional and national banks to establish a cross-section of opinion on mining development. The survey's results would bring to the attention of user Governments factors critical to obtaining financing and know-how.

Argentina, Benin, the Congo and Ecuador were given assistance in promoting investment follow-up. Activities came to a close in Guyana and Liberia, and were being wound down in Kenya, Suriname and the Upper Volta. The start-up of a project in Haiti and the ratification of a project in Peru were on schedule.

Following a gold-silver discovery in Argentina, UNRFNRE completed a feasibility study which attracted the interest of the country's private mining sector.[3] In Benin, testing showed that a kaolin deposit was suitable for ceramics production and, with treatment, could be applied to various industrial uses for local and export markets. In the Congo, an exploration programme used advanced technological methods to delineate the extent and thickness of sea-bottom phosphate deposits. With the aim of obtaining investment for the development of a silver mine in Ecuador, a reappraisal was made of its end-product concentrate possibilities.

Evaluation was completed of low-grade gold mineralization in Guyana and Liberia. An exploratory study revealed grades of about 3 per cent copper and 3 ounces of silver per ton at a site in Kenya; in addition, kimberlitic rock (host rock for diamonds) was discovered and its potential initially evaluated.

Ore-grade gold was discovered in Suriname, with an average grade well above the economic cut-off level.

Since 1981, more than 33 missions had visited 21 countries to review the development of geothermal energy for electricity production. Installed capacity was continuing to grow in the developing countries, almost doubling from an estimated 670 megawatts (MW) in seven countries at the end of 1981 to 1,200 MW in nine countries at the end of 1983.

The Fund's current financial resources were inadequate, the report stated, and would inhibit its response to new projects. Owing to a depressed mineral market, there was little interest among the industrialized countries in world-wide mining exploration. However, it was important that voluntary contributions to the Fund be increased, given the period necessary to bring projects to the pre-investment stage. Projects would not be ready for implementation if contributions were forthcoming only when the international minerals market improved.

On 23 June 1983, the UNDP Governing Council approved exploration for precious and base metals in northern Haiti and for base metals and gold in Peru, subject to availability of funds.[4]

ECONOMIC AND SOCIAL COUNCIL ACTION

In July 1983, the Economic and Social Council had before it the UNDP Administrator's report on the 1982 activities of UNRFNRE.[5] On 28 July, the Council, acting on the recommendation of its First (Economic) Committee, adopted resolution 1983/55 without vote.

United Nations Revolving Fund for Natural Resources Exploration

The Economic and Social Council,

Recalling General Assembly resolution 3167(XXVIII) of 17 December 1973 and Economic and Social Council resolution 1762(LIV) of 18 May 1973, concerning the establishment of the United Nations Revolving Fund for Natural Resources Exploration,

1. *Takes note* of the report of the Administrator of the United Nations Development Programme on the United Nations Revolving Fund for Natural Resources Exploration;

2. *Welcomes* the efforts of the Fund to identify the requirements for feasibility and post-discovery follow-up work in order to bring successful exploration projects to the production stage;

3. *Takes note also* of the Fund's evaluation of potential geothermal exploration projects;

4. *Recognizes* the need to increase financial support to the Fund in order to meet effectively the exploration requirements of developing countries.

Economic and Social Council resolution 1983/55

28 July 1983   Meeting 40   Adopted without vote

Approved by First Committee (E/1983/122) without vote, 19 July (meeting 17); draft by Committee on Natural Resources (E/1983/19 & Corr.1); agenda item 9.
Meeting number. ESC 40.

The Council also took note of the Administrator's report on the 1982 activities of UNRFNRE when it adopted decision 1983/187 on 29 July.

Contributions and expenditures

Programme expenditures were estimated at $4.8 million in 1983, a decline of $1.6 million from the previous year. Funding availability of about $10 million was sufficient only to cover projects in an advanced stage of development. With only $2.1 million in voluntary contributions having been received in 1983 and a similar amount expected in 1984 (see tables on next page), funding for new projects remained inadequate.

The Fund's cumulative expenditure on completed projects and programme commitments was $32.1 million, which included an estimate on an actuarial basis for subsequent work.

The Fund obtained in 1983 its first co-financing participation from the United States Government for the second phase of offshore phosphate exploration work in the Pointe-Noire sector of the Congo.

On 23 June,[4] the UNDP Governing Council endorsed the efforts by UNRFNRE aimed at promoting follow-up pre-investment work leading to economic development and appealed urgently to Governments to increase their voluntary contributions to the Fund.

New exploration techniques

In March 1983, the Secretary-General presented to the Committee on Natural Resources a report on new techniques, including remote sensing, for identifying, exploring and assessing natural resources,[6] as requested by the Committee in 1981.

The report, a follow-up to one submitted in 1981,[7] concluded that, with the introduction of lower-cost microprocessors, the importance of electronic data processing was growing in ore reserve calculations, geostatistical and simulation studies applied to exploration programmes, and project evaluation. It proposed that current developments be reviewed with the aim of making maximum use of them. Further, in the area of remote sensing, the report said that more sophisticated equipment had become available for the interpretation of satellite imagery. Regarding exploration geophysics and geochemistry, progress had taken place in hardware and programmes for complex interpretation processes and, in diamond-core drilling, a major change had occurred with the increased application of hydraulics in all drilling-rig operations. These new technologies made greater demands, however, in operator skills, maintenance services and initial costs. It was proposed that developing countries be assisted in acquiring new technologies through training seminars, feasibility studies and other catalytic activities, making use of funds available under UNDP country programming. It was also proposed that

CONTRIBUTIONS TO UNRFNRE, 1983 AND 1984
(as at 31 December 1983; in US dollar equivalent)

Country	1983 payment	1984 pledge
Bangladesh	1,067	1,100
Belgium	102,041	90,909
Chile	5,000	5,000
Indonesia	10,000	10,000
Japan	2,000,000	—
Panama	2,000	—
Zambia	—	3,731
Total	2,120,108	110,740

SOURCE: A/39/5/Add.1.

UNRFNRE PROJECT EXPENDITURES, 1983
(as at 31 December 1983; in thousands of US dollars)

Country	Amount
Angola	2
Argentina	53
Benin	26
Bolivia	10
Brazil	1
Burma	5
Burundi	10
Chile	18
Colombia	16
Congo	658
Costa Rica	8
Cyprus	1
Dominican Republic	3
Ecuador	6
Ethiopia	11
Ghana	2
Guatemala	61
Guyana	165
Haiti	310
Honduras	32
Indonesia	3
Iraq	3
Ivory Coast	9
Kenya	834
Liberia	347
Malaysia	6
Mali	665
Mexico	39
Nicaragua	8
Pakistan	5
Panama	(3)
Peru	218
Philippines	(2)
Rwanda	9
Saint Lucia	14
Sierra Leone	112
Suriname	387
Thailand	5
Turkey	17
Uganda	2
Upper Volta	498
Vanuatu	10
Zambia	6
Zimbabwe	6
Total	4,596

SOURCE: DP/1984/5/Add.6.

microcomputer and computer software developments be reviewed to make maximum use of them in mineral-sector training and other technical co-operation activities.

The latest applications of remote sensing technology were being introduced in a number of countries for the exploration of natural resources by the Department of Technical Co-operation for Development (DTCD). The Department also or-ganized in New York in 1983 an expert group on the application of microcomputers in mineral exploration and development (see Chapter II of this section).

ECONOMIC AND SOCIAL COUNCIL ACTION

On 28 July, the Economic and Social Council adopted without vote resolution 1983/54 on the application of computer technology in mineral exploration and development. It followed the recommendation of its First Committee.

Application of computer technology in mineral exploration and development

The Economic and Social Council,

Recognizing the importance of the use of computer processing methods in mineral exploration and development, in particular, but not limited to, remote sensing, geochemistry, ore reserve calculation, mine planning, economic and financial analysis, and data storage and retrieval,

Bearing in mind the advantages that developing countries could derive from a wider application of such techniques,

Taking note of the report of the Secretary-General on new techniques, including remote sensing, for identifying, exploring and assessing natural resources and of the information on the current activities in this field of the Department of Technical Co-operation for Development of the United Nations Secretariat,

Mindful of the importance of the transfer of technology, in particular new technology, that will strengthen the national capabilities of developing countries,

1. *Requests* the Secretary-General to report to the Committee on Natural Resources at its ninth session on the use of computer techniques, particularly in the developing countries, in the exploration and development of natural resources;

2. *Also requests* the Secretary-General to report to the Committee at its ninth session on the progress made in the application of such techniques in the activities of the Department of Technical Co-operation for Development;

3. *Urges* Governments to consider how the application of such techniques can be strengthened in their mineral exploration and development activities and invites Governments and institutions to provide facilities for seminars and symposia on this subject.

Economic and Social Council resolution 1983/54

28 July 1983   Meeting 40   Adopted without vote

Approved by First Committee (E/1983/122) without vote, 19 July (meeting 17); draft by Committee on Natural Resources (E/1983/19 & Corr.1); agenda item 9. *Meeting number.* ESC 40.

Utilization of subsurface space

A report on the utilization of subsurface space for storage of food, water and energy, and for transportation, public utilities and other purposes[8] was submitted in March 1983 by the Secretary-General to the Committee on Natural Resources. The report, responding to a 1981 request by the Economic and Social Council,[9] stated that research on rock mechanics and engineering geology was a prerequisite to the development of subsurface space, that lack of financial resources would continue to limit its utilization in developing countries, and that the United Nations could assist by providing information on the potential of subsurface space, planning, costs and construction techniques. It recommended that the United Nations system encourage subsurface space utilization by providing information and technical assistance and training.

ECONOMIC AND SOCIAL COUNCIL ACTION

On 28 July, the Economic and Social Council adopted without vote resolution 1983/58, as recommended by its First Committee.

Utilization of subsurface space

The Economic and Social Council,

Recalling its resolution 1981/82 of 24 July 1981,

Deeply concerned by the problems of population, urbanization and overcrowding and the need to provide people with food, water and an adequate energy supply,

Recognizing the potential of subsurface space for, *inter alia*, the storage of water, fuel, food and other commodities, as well as for water supply, sewerage and the conservation of energy,

Taking into account the experience in the use of subsurface space already gained in many parts of the world and in specialized international organizations, and the long lead time required for the planning and construction of subsurface facilities,

Having taken note of the report of the Secretary-General on the utilization of subsurface space and its potential in developing countries,

1. *Requests* the Secretary-General to strengthen support mechanisms in the United Nations for making known the scope with respect to the utilization of subsurface space as a potentially important facet of development activity in developing countries;

2. *Also requests* the Secretary-General to prepare a progress report on the development and utilization of subsurface space and the activities of the competent organs, organizations and bodies of the United Nations system in this area, for the consideration of the Committee on Natural Resources at its ninth session.

Economic and Social Council resolution 1983/58

28 July 1983   Meeting 40   Adopted without vote

Approved by First Committee (E/1983/122) without vote, 19 July (meeting 17); draft by Committee on Natural Resources (E/1983/19 & Corr.1); agenda item 9.
Meeting number. ESC 40.

Permanent sovereignty over natural resources

Developments in the exercise of control by developing countries over their natural resources were discussed in an April 1983 report by the Secretary-General to the Committee on Natural Resources.[10] This was the latest in a series of such reports prepared pursuant to a request by the Economic and Social Council in 1977.[11]

According to the report, probably the most important current concern was the impact of the worldwide recession on mineral investment in develop-

ing countries. Growing difficulties in attracting investment funds had led to a re-examination of existing investments and of mining and tax legislation. Current development agreements had assigned a priority to investment promotion, reflecting a change from the 1960s and 1970s when many developing countries were in a stronger position because equity and loan capital for mineral projects were scarce. Much hope was being placed on the development of mineral deposits to overcome the financial and economic effects of the recession.

The report said that developing countries could choose to postpone mineral development, finance a national mining industry with public funds, or encourage foreign investment. It observed that in many countries there was no clear, viable procedure for action after the discovery of mineral deposits, and that experience suggested that countries could increase their bargaining power if, rather than waiting passively for investors, they carried out an active promotion policy. It pointed out that international organizations offered advice to developing countries, covering bargaining strategy, negotiations, contracts, mining, investment and tax legislation; the United Nations Secretariat provided advisory services through interregional advisers, assisted by *ad hoc* consultants. The report added that experience had shown that the elaboration of model agreements could be of considerable use to Governments, both in obtaining expertise and formulating policies.

ECONOMIC AND SOCIAL COUNCIL ACTION

On 28 July, on the recommendation of its First Committee, the Economic and Social Council adopted without vote resolution 1983/56.

Permanent sovereignty over natural resources

The Economic and Social Council,

Recognizing the problems caused by the present international economic situation to most countries, in particular the developing countries,

Noting the importance for all countries, in particular the developing countries, to maximize the benefits from the exploration, exploitation and processing of their natural resources in order to strengthen their economic development,

Having noted the report of the Secretary-General on permanent sovereignty over natural resources and the comments made thereon by the Committee on Natural Resources at its eighth session,

1. *Requests* the Committee on Natural Resources to continue to discuss, at its ninth session, the question of permanent sovereignty over natural resources, including:

(*a*) The strengthening of national capabilities to finance and manage the exploration, exploitation and processing of natural resources for the national benefit;

(*b*) The promotion of investments in natural resources according to basic priorities;

(*c*) The identification of new possibilities for economic and technical co-operation among developing countries in the field of natural resources;

(d) The conservation of natural resources;

(e) The environment and natural resources;

2. *Requests* the Secretary-General to prepare a further report on the subject of permanent sovereignty over natural resources, taking into account the matters referred to in paragraph 1 above and the comments made by the Committee at its eighth session;

3. *Affirms* in this context the importance of the ongoing work of the Commission on Transnational Corporations on a code of conduct for transnational corporations, as it relates to natural resources.

Economic and Social Council resolution 1983/56

28 July 1983	Meeting 40	Adopted without vote

Approved by First Committee (E/1983/122) without vote, 19 July (meeting 17); draft by Committee on Natural Resources (E/1983/19 & Corr.1); agenda item 9. *Meeting number.* ESC 40.

GENERAL ASSEMBLY ACTION

On 19 December 1983, the General Assembly, in resolution 38/144 on permanent sovereignty over national resources in the occupied Palestinian and other Arab territories, condemned Israel for its exploitation of those resources; called on States, international organizations, specialized agencies, business corporations and other institutions not to co-operate with Israel in their exploitation; emphasized the right of the Palestinian and other Arab peoples to sovereignty over those resources; and reaffirmed their right to full compensation (see POLITICAL AND SECURITY QUESTIONS, Chapter IX).

Agenda for the 1985 session of the Committee on Natural Resources

ECONOMIC AND SOCIAL COUNCIL ACTION

Following consideration of the report of the Committee on Natural Resources on its eighth session (New York, 8-17 June 1983),[12] the Economic and Social Council, by decision 1983/176 adopted without vote on 28 July, took note of the report and approved the provisional agenda and documentation for the Committee's ninth session in 1985. The Council acted on the recommendation of its First Committee.

Report of the Committee on Natural Resources on its eighth session and provisional agenda and documentation for the ninth session of the Committee

At its 40th plenary meeting, on 28 July 1983, the Council:

(a) Took note of the report of the Committee on Natural Resources on its eighth session;

(b) Approved the provisional agenda and documentation for the ninth session of the Committee, set out below.

Provisional agenda and documentation for the ninth session of the Committee on Natural Resources

1. Election of officers
2. Adoption of the agenda and organization of work

3. Mineral resources:
   (a) Trends and salient issues
   (b) Prospects for the development of non-metallic raw materials
   Documentation
   Report of the Secretary-General on trends and salient issues in the development of mineral resources
   Report of the Secretary-General on prospects for the development of non-metallic raw materials, with special reference to bentonite, mica, magnesite, feldspar, fluorspar and baryte

4. Energy resources: trends and salient issues
   Documentation
   Report of the Secretary-General on trends and salient issues in the development of energy resources

5. Water resources development: progress in the implementation of the Mar del Plata Action Plan and the International Drinking Water Supply and Sanitation Decade
   Documentation
   Report of the Secretary-General on the progress made by Governments and by international organizations in the implementation of the objectives of the International Drinking Water Supply and Sanitation Decade
   Report of the Secretary-General on the overall progress made by Governments in the implementation of the Mar del Plata Action Plan
   Report of the Secretary-General on the development of integrated approaches and programmes regarding education and training in the field of water resources in developing countries
   Report of the Secretary-General on progress made in the establishment and upgrading of regional and subregional networks for training in the field of water resources

6. New techniques, including remote sensing, for identifying, exploring and assessing natural resources
   Documentation
   Report of the Secretary-General on the application of computer technology in mineral exploration and development

7. United Nations Revolving Fund for Natural Resources Exploration
   Documentation
   Report of the Administrator of the United Nations Development Programme on the United Nations Revolving Fund for Natural Resources Exploration

8. Permanent sovereignty over natural resources
   Documentation
   Report of the Secretary-General on permanent sovereignty over natural resources

9. Utilization of subsurface space
   Documentation
   Progress report of the Secretary-General on the development and utilization of subsurface space

10. Co-ordination of programmes within the United Nations system in the field of natural resources

Documentation
Report of the Secretary-General on co-ordination of programmes within the United Nations system in the field of water resources
11. Draft provisional agenda and documentation for the tenth session of the Committee
12. Adoption of the report of the Committee.

Economic and Social Council decision 1983/176

Adopted without vote.

Approved by First Committee (E/1983/122) without vote, 19 July (meeting 17); draft by Committee on Natural Resources (E/1983/19 & Corr.1), orally amended in Council by Bangladesh, for Group of 77; agenda item 9.
Meeting number. ESC 40.

Before adopting the decision, the Council amended item 4 on energy resources by adding "trends and salient issues", and deleting from the documentation required a report of the Secretary-General on prospects and salient issues in the world energy situation, contained in the draft submitted by the Committee on Natural Resources. At a meeting of the Council's First Committee on 26 July, Bangladesh, on behalf of the Group of 77, had proposed that no decision be taken on a draft resolution entitled "Energy development", submitted by the Committee on Natural Resources; the First Committee adopted the proposal by 24 votes to 11, with 4 abstentions. At the 28 July meeting of the Council, Bangladesh pointed out that the report in question was no longer justified, and proposed the above amendment, which was adopted by a roll-call vote of 32 to 11, with 7 abstentions. The roll-call vote was requested by Greece, on behalf of the members of the European Economic Community.

In another action—decision 1983/184 of 29 July—the Council decided to maintain, for a further period of two years, the discontinuance of the provision of summary records for the Committee on Natural Resources.

REFERENCES

[1]DP/1984/45. [2]DP/1984/5/Add.2. [3]DP/1984/5/Add.1 (Part II). [4]E/1983/20 (dec. 83/20). [5]YUN 1982, p. 877. [6]E/C.7/1983/3. [7]YUN 1981, p. 676. [8]E/C.7/1983/7. [9]YUN 1981, p. 677, ESC res. 1981/82, 24 July 1981. [10]E/C.7/1983/5. [11]YUN 1977, p. 568, ESC res. 2120 (LXIII), 4 Aug. 1977. [12]E/1983/19 & Corr.1.

Mineral resources

Technical co-operation

In 1983, in addition to UNRFNRE activities, DTCD carried out projects in mineral exploration, mining development, institution building, training, mining legislation and contract negotiation, and mineral sector planning. DTCD supported 189 mineral projects, with a comparable number under preparation. Some 75 missions by inter-regional advisers and others were undertaken in more than 60 countries. The projects were described by the Secretary-General in an addendum to his report on United Nations technical co-operation activities in 1983.[1]

Exploration for gold continued, for example: in Benin, where small-scale production of gold was begun for the first time since 1956; in Haiti, where further encouraging results were achieved during continuing exploration; and in Suriname, where feasibility studies were under way. Exploration for tin continued in Thailand, and Colombian geologists and engineers were trained in electronic data-processing techniques.

In Argentina, the Bajo La Alumbrera copper-gold deposit continued to be evaluated, and in Burundi, a promising vanadium occurrence was being investigated. Several projects in India provided technical co-operation in gold mining and exploration for gold and other metals, while a highly successful project in the Philippines was concerned with institution strengthening and regional co-operation. In several countries, including Ethiopia, Gabon, Somalia, the United Republic of Cameroon and the United Republic of Tanzania, activities aimed at strengthening national institutions continued. In Bolivia, the United Nations Financing System for Science and Technology for Development assisted COMIBOL, the national mining company.

Survey of investments

A March 1983 note to the Committee on Natural Resources by the Secretary-General,[2] prepared in accordance with a 1981 Economic and Social Council resolution,[3] commented on the question of investments in mining. The note stated that demand for most major metals and minerals, with the exception of precious metals, had declined during 1981 and 1982. Since output had not been reduced enough, or not early enough, to compensate for the decline in demand, prices had fallen for virtually all minerals. Many mining companies were operating at a loss, the note added. The result was that investment in exploration and production facilities, including maintenance of existing mines and plants, had decreased substantially. Investment in new production capacity had reached a very low level. However, it was expected that with improvement in the economies of the developed market-economy countries, demands for minerals would increase and investment in new production facilities would have to be reconsidered. Therefore, it seemed justified for a survey of planned investment to be undertaken. The guidance of the Committee on Natural Resources was requested.

The Committee on Natural Resources[4] noted with regret that the survey of planned investment in mineral exploration and development, requested by the Council in its 1981 resolution,[3] had not been undertaken. While investment in the international mining industry had declined substantially, investment continued to be made in some developing countries and in centrally planned economies. Investment would be forthcoming if international mineral markets were stabilized and just prices were ensured for producers and exporters, the Committee added.

Phosphates

In March 1983, the Secretary-General submitted a report[5] to the Committee on Natural Resources on new locations for exploration for phosphate rock in developing countries, pursuant to a request by the Economic and Social Council in 1981.[6] The report identified areas in many developing countries that would warrant exploration. The largest new resources of phosphate rock had been found in Egypt, Iraq, Morocco, Peru and Saudi Arabia, while significant discoveries also had been made in India and the Upper Volta. Although excellent world surveys of phosphate rock deposits were available, the report observed, a detailed reassessment was desirable in view of technological and economic changes that had taken place in recent years. It suggested that the Committee on Natural Resources might wish to support efforts by developing countries to increase production of phosphate rock to meet their agricultural needs—a recommendation endorsed by the Committee at its June session[4]—and that additional funds could be made available from UNDP.

Rare metals

Trends and salient issues, with particular reference to rare metals, were the subjects of an April 1983 report,[7] submitted by the Secretary-General to the Committee on Natural Resources in response to a request by the Council in 1981.[8] The report said that 1982 had been the worst year in many decades for the international mineral sector. Consumption and prices had fallen to very low levels owing to a continuing recession in the developed market-economy countries. Several developing countries that were dependent on exports of minerals and metals had experienced difficult times. A threat that other materials might be substituted for metals in many situations was a major long-term consideration. The report discussed tantalum and lithium as rare metals, pointing out that they were "rare" in the sense that production and consumption of them was small. Production was highly concentrated regionally, and consumption was mainly in chemical products (lithium) and electrical components (tantalum). Known reserves were vast in relation to projected consumption levels. The report also examined sea-bed mining, observing that technological developments had virtually stopped in recent years and that metal prices were currently far too low to justify investment.

Non-metallic raw materials

A report dealing with prospects for developing non-metallic minerals for the construction, paper, ceramics and glass industries[9] was presented to the Committee on Natural Resources by the Secretary-General in March 1983, in response to a 1981 Economic and Social Council resolution.[10] Particular attention was paid to cement and its raw materials, mineral aggregates, dimension stone, asbestos, clays, including kaolin, and silica sand. The report said that the trend towards industrialization and higher standards of living provided a basis for increased use of these materials; however, there were barriers to their development. These included limited knowledge of the existence of deposits, their geological variety, limited domestic demand, lack of information on markets, and transportation problems. Geological mapping and basic mineral exploration had so far covered only a small percentage of most developing countries. The report also dealt with potash resources, which, it said, were not widely distributed throughout the world. It pointed out that the delineation of the evaporite basins in which potash deposits might occur was still incomplete, and that all thick evaporate sequences should be investigated in detail for suspected potash mineralization.

ECONOMIC AND SOCIAL COUNCIL ACTION

The Economic and Social Council, acting on the recommendation of its First Committee, adopted without vote on 28 July resolution 1983/52.

Prospects for the development of non-metallic raw materials

The Economic and Social Council,

Pursuant to its resolution 1954(LIX) of 25 July 1975 on problems of availability and supply of natural resources,

Recognizing the importance of natural resources for economic development, in particular non-metallic raw materials,

Taking note of the report of the Secretary-General on prospects for the development of non-metallic minerals,

Requests the Secretary-General to prepare for the Committee on Natural Resources at its ninth session a further report, based on existing literature, on prospects for the development of non-metallic raw materials, with special reference to bentonite, mica, magnesite, feldspar, fluorspar and baryte.

Economic and Social Council resolution 1983/52

28 July 1983   Meeting 40   Adopted without vote

Approved by First Committee (E/1983/122) without vote, 19 July (meeting 17); draft by Committee on Natural Resources (E/1983/19 & Corr.1); agenda item 9.
Meeting number. ESC 40.

Co-ordination of programmes

At its June 1983 session,[4] the Committee on Natural Resources had before it two reports by the Secretary-General, dealing with co-ordination of programmes[11] and programme evaluation within the United Nations system, the latter having been submitted to the Committee for Programme and Co-ordination (CPC) in 1982.[12]

The report on co-ordination of programmes dealt specifically with non-fuel minerals and was submitted in accordance with an Economic and Social Council decision of 1981.[13] Twenty-six main areas of activity were identified, and 14 units of the United Nations and five specialized agencies and organizations were found to have a role in them. In financial terms, the report said, loans were the largest type of activity, with an estimated cost during 1982-1983 of $839.3 million for 51 financial assistance activities. The United Nations also played a dominant role in technical co-operation, with 200 activities costing $57.3 million, and in programme activities, with 46 activities costing $15.1 million. The main financial assistance activities were in direct prospecting, mining production technology and transfer of technology; the main areas most frequently covered by technical co-operation were geological surveys, mineral processing and direct prospecting; and the most numerous programme activities were in geological surveys, policy and planning, and marketing and trade.

Analysed by main area, the report stated that the level of co-operation among United Nations organizations varied widely, ranging from 100 per cent for pollution control to no reported co-operation in 10 of the 26 main areas. It concluded that activities related to mineral resources showed a high degree of concentration in a few organizational units as well as a fairly distinct pattern of main areas of activity, adding that, in such circumstances, the need for highly articulated co-operative arrangements might not be as great as in more diffuse situations.

For co-ordination in the implementation of programmes, the Committee on Natural Resources[4] noted that one recommendation had resulted from the evaluation of mineral activities by CPC in 1982.[14] CPC had recommended that the Administrative Committee on Co-ordination (ACC) seek enhanced co-operation on mineral resources but the recommendation had not been implemented.

Programme evaluation

CPC took up in May 1983[15] the implementation of the recommendations which it had made

in 1982[12] on the United Nations mineral resources programme. It considered a note by the Secretariat on their implementation.[16] The note covered the responses of several United Nations units involved in mineral resources development, including the Department of International Economic and Social Affairs (DIESA), DTCD, the United Nations Conference on Trade and Development (UNCTAD), the Economic and Social Commission for Asia and the Pacific, the Economic Commission for Africa, UNDP and UNRFNRE. The responses related to programme method and to mineral resources activities.

DIESA, for example, indicated that submissions for its proposed 1984-1985 programme budget had been carefully reviewed, as recommended; UNRFNRE reported that it had strengthened its association with other entities in the United Nations system; and UNDP said that problems in procurement, delivery and recruitment had been brought to the attention of the agencies involved but that it was too early to record any significant improvement.

A representative of the Secretary-General explained that the Secretariat, in following up the CPC recommendations, was constrained to depend on reports by the implementing organizations and that, since no objective assessment had been possible, the information had been transmitted as received. CPC requested the Secretariat to provide a more objective analysis in the future.

By section II of resolution 38/227 B, of 20 December 1983, on co-ordination within the United Nations system, the General Assembly endorsed the CPC request.

ECONOMIC AND SOCIAL COUNCIL ACTION

The Economic and Social Council on 28 July, on the recommendation of its First Committee, adopted without vote resolution 1983/59.

Co-ordination of programmes within the United Nations system in the field of natural resources

The Economic and Social Council,

Recalling the terms of reference of the Committee on Natural Resources, as set forth in Council resolution 1535(XLIX) of 27 July 1970,

Bearing in mind the debates held in the Committee on the co-ordination of programmes within the United Nations system in the field of natural resources,

Reaffirming that one of the principal responsibilities of the Committee is to provide the Council with guidance in the programming and implementation of these programmes,

Recognizing that that guidance relates in part to the avoidance of duplication of effort by ensuring that the programmes of the many organizational units of the United Nations are co-ordinated,

Further recognizing the advantages of co-ordinating the efforts of the specialized agencies and organizations of the United Nations system which also carry out work in the natural resources field,

Affirming that the Committee was again unable to discharge this responsibility on the basis of the report submitted by the Secretary-General for consideration at its eighth session,

1. *Requests* the Secretary-General to submit to the Committee on Natural Resources at its future sessions reports that contain an analysis of the level of co-operation and co-ordination among various organs of the United Nations system in the field of natural resources, in order to enable the Committee to identify existing problems, to assess the extent, if any, to which there is duplication of effort, and to formulate appropriate recommendations in this area;

2. *Urges* the organizations of the United Nations system to co-operate fully with the Secretary-General by providing him with the information needed for the elaboration of the reports referred to in paragraph 1 above;

3. *Also requests* the Secretary-General to take full account of the points made in the discussion of this question by the Committee at its eighth session and, in particular, to consider how best to avoid duplication of responsibility and effort within the Secretariat.

Economic and Social Council resolution 1983/59

28 July 1983   Meeting 40   Adopted without vote

Approved by First Committee (E/1983/122) without vote, 19 July (meeting 17); draft by Committee on Natural Resources (E/1983/19 & Corr.1); agenda item 9. *Meeting number*. ESC 40.

Standardization of terminology

Pursuant to a 1979 Economic and Social Council resolution,[17] the Secretary-General submitted to the Committee on Natural Resources in May 1983 a report on the work of the group of experts on the standardization of definitions and terminology for statistics on mineral production and consumption.[18] Meeting in New York from 11 to 19 January 1983, the group stressed that its recommendations on definitions and terminology were not intended to be comprehensive, but should be viewed as an attempt to establish minimum standards for the uniform reporting, compilation and publication of mineral statistics. The definitions and terminology were oriented towards the generation of statistics on mineral production and consumption at the national level. Mineral statistics faced special problems arising out of the large number of mineral forms, the variety of processes for recovery and treatment and the range of uses to which mineral products were put.

The group recommended that mine production should be measured at the stage of first marketable form of a mineral material following its mining. Statistical measurement of metal production should be focused on the production of the final unwrought (unworked) form of a metal, which was frequently the locus of a metal's price formation. Measurement of consumption of a mineral commodity should relate to its use as an industrial raw material or in industrial processes, the group said. Reporting of "apparent" consumption was

preferred at the international level since "reported" consumption data were not readily available from many countries. Furthermore, the group recommended that consumption statistics should refer to the final unwrought form as well as the first marketable form where appropriate.

Confusion would be minimized if countries used a common basis of measurement; therefore, the group recommended that all measurements should be in accordance with the metric system.

Endorsing the group's recommendations, the Secretary-General suggested that the Committee on Natural Resources might want to provide guidance to the Secretariat on how to give those recommendations the widest application, and might wish to request the Economic and Social Council to refer the matter to the Statistical Commission for consideration at its 1985 session.

ECONOMIC AND SOCIAL COUNCIL ACTION

On 28 July, on the recommendation of its First Committee, the Economic and Social Council adopted resolution 1983/53 without vote.

Standardization of definitions and terminology for mineral resources

The Economic and Social Council,

Recognizing the continuing need for internationally consistent and easily understood statistics on mineral production and consumption,

Taking into account the discussions in the Committee on Natural Resources at its eighth session on the report of the Secretary-General on the standardization of definitions and terminology for mineral resources, which summarized the results of the meeting of the group of experts appointed by the Secretary-General in pursuance of Council resolution 1979/72 of 3 August 1979,

1. *Endorses* the report of the Secretary-General on the standardization of definitions and terminology for mineral resources;

2. *Notes* that the Council, in resolution 1979/72, requested that the group of experts should report to the Committee on Natural Resources, and expresses its concern that the report, which was unanimously adopted by the group, had been amended by the Secretary-General before it was issued;

3. *Requests*, therefore, that the action to be taken in response to the requests contained in the paragraphs below be based on the report in its original form;

4. *Requests* the Secretary-General to take into account the recommendations in the report relating to the activities of the United Nations in the reporting, compilation and publication of statistics on mineral production and consumption;

5. *Also requests* the Secretary-General to consider which additional activities would be required to implement those recommendations, including those concerning definitions and terminology for individual minerals and metals, and statistics on the secondary recovery of metals;

6. *Urges* Governments to take into account the recommendations of the group of experts and to give the report the widest possible distribution;

7. *Further requests* the Secretary-General to report the progress made in pursuance of the requests contained in paragraphs 4 and 5 above to the Statistical Commission at its twenty-third session.

Economic and Social Council resolution 1983/53

28 July 1983   Meeting 40   Adopted without vote

Approved by First Committee (E/1983/122) without vote, 19 July (meeting 17); draft by Committee on Natural Resources (E/1983/19 & Corr.1); agenda item 9. *Meeting number.* ESC 40.

REFERENCES

[1]DP/1984/42/Add.1. [2]E/C.7/1983/6. [3]YUN 1981, p. 679, ESC res. 1981/78, 24 July 1981. [4]E/1983/19 & Corr.1. [5]E/C.7/1983/2. [6]YUN 1981, p. 680, ESC res. 1981/79, 24 July 1981. [7]E/C.7/1983/8. [8]YUN 1981, p. 679, ESC res. 1981/77, 24 July 1981. [9]E/C.7/1983/4. [10]YUN 1981, p. 679, ESC res. 1981/76, 24 July 1981. [11]E/C.7/1983/12. [12]YUN 1982, p. 879. [13]YUN 1981, p. 678, ESC dec. 1981/191, 24 July 1981. [14]YUN 1982, p. 880. [15]A/38/38. [16]E/AC.51/1983/4. [17]YUN 1979, p. 688, ESC res. 1979/72, 3 Aug. 1979. [18]E/C.7/1983/9.

Water and marine resources

Water and marine resources were considered by a number of United Nations bodies during 1983. Particular attention was paid to progress and prospects in implementing the 1977 Mar del Plata Action Plan for the development of water resources and the International Drinking Water Supply and Sanitation Decade (1981-1990), in the context of the 1984 review of the International Development Strategy for the Third United Nations Development Decade (the 1980s) (see Chapter I of this section).

The Economic and Social Council in resolution 1983/57 urged developing countries to assign priority to the development of their water resources and called on bilateral and multilateral donors and financing institutions to assist in that regard. In resolution 1983/48 on marine affairs, the Council endorsed a proposed major programme in marine affairs for 1984-1989, which was subsequently adopted by the General Assembly.

Water resources development

In April 1983, the Secretary-General submitted to the Committee on Natural Resources a report[1] on progress in implementing the Mar del Plata Action Plan, adopted by the United Nations Water Conference in 1977,[2] and the International Drinking Water Supply and Sanitation Decade proclaimed by the General Assembly in 1980.[3] The report was intended as a contribution to the 1984 review of the International Development Strategy for the Third United Nations Development Decade, and was prepared in pursuance of a 1981 Economic and Social Council resolution.[4]

The report said that progress in the development of water resources in developing countries had been below the level required to achieve the goals of the International Development Strategy. Regarding agricultural water use, development was not commensurate with the production needed to eliminate hunger; concerning industrial water use, considerable effort was needed in the treatment of waste water, together with mechanisms for the more efficient use of water.

Hydrological and meteorological data were essential for the development of water resources. In addition, attention needed to be given to soil surveys, topographical surveys, mapping and the application of remote-sensing techniques. Efforts to reduce the damage caused by natural disasters needed to be intensified. A basic water policy had to be formulated and the related legal and institutional frameworks established in most countries. The shortage of qualified manpower continued to be critical, and training facilities lacked long-term focus. Above all, there was the ever-growing constraint of lack of adequate financial resources, not only for investment but for feasibility studies; resources ranging from 5 to 10 times the current annual commitments of Governments were needed.

The report pointed out that in future reviews of the water sector, it was necessary for Governments to undertake national assessments, within the framework of their socio-economic plans. Since water was a multisectoral area, a national coordinating organization was required to assess the different sectors.

The Committee on Natural Resources was informed at its June 1983 session[5] that a colloquium on technical co-operation among developing countries for ground-water resources development had been held at Zagreb, Yugoslavia, in May 1982. Participants had agreed that in the development of ground water, there was a need for the establishment of a data base, including a roster of expertise on the subject, and for the dissemination of information. It was also agreed that the Centre for Waters at Zagreb should serve as the international centre to carry out the information function.

UNDP action. At its June 1983 session, the Governing Council of UNDP considered a note by the Administrator on the use of Special Programme Resources for promotional activities for technical co-operation among developing countries (TCDC) and for support for the International Drinking Water Supply and Sanitation Decade,[6] as well as decisions on using those resources[7] and on developing the UNDP Information Referral System for TCDC,[8] adopted by the High-level Committee on the Review of TCDC on 6 June 1983. On 18 June,[9] the Governing Council allocated from Special Programme Resources $610,000 for information and communications support for the Decade from 1 July 1983 to 31 December 1985 and $600,000 for promotional activities for TCDC during 1984-1985. Also for the same period, the Council appropriated $600,000 for the Information Referral System, and requested the Administrator to report in 1984 on the System's progress.

UNEP activities. In keeping with a 24 May 1983 decision[(10)] of the Governing Council of the United Nations Environment Programme (UNEP) (see Chapter XVI of this section), requesting the Executive Director to sharpen the focus of the UNEP water programme, he established an Advisory Group on Water Resources, consisting of four specialists.[(11)] The Group was to advise UNEP on the development of a strategy for its water programme and the implementation of Governing Council decisions concerning water. At its first meeting at Geneva in mid-1983, it made recommendations with regard to the implementation of the water programme during 1984-1985; special emphasis was placed on water pollution control, waste-water management (including recycling of water), rational water management (including river basin management), support for the implementation of the programme for the International Drinking Water Supply and Sanitation Decade and development of inland fisheries and aquaculture.

UNEP was represented at the fourth session of the ACC Inter-Secretariat Group for Water Resources (Rome, Italy, 5-9 December 1983).[(12)] The Group discussed United Nations activities concerning water resources development and considered progress in implementing the Mar del Plata Action Plan and the International Drinking Water Supply and Sanitation Decade, as well as education and training measures. It agreed that an assessment of the co-ordination of field projects would be desirable and must be related to the effects of the decline in project financial resources.

As a member of the Steering Committee for Co-operative Action of the International Drinking Water Supply and Sanitation Decade, UNEP also participated in the eleventh meeting of the Committee at Rome at the end of 1983. It was recognized that co-operative action at the country level was not progressing as well as expected, and agencies were urged to try to remedy the situation.

During 1983, UNEP continued its support to the International Training Centre for Water Resources Management. The project was evaluated with the aim of recommending guidelines on future co-operation. UNEP indicated that it planned to continue support to the Centre for specific training sessions, particularly those held in developing countries, which were given high priority by the

Centre's International Scientific Council. The Council, with the participation of UNEP, held its seventh session in 1983 (Sophia Antipolis, France, 1-3 June).

The first meeting of a working group on large-scale water projects was held on the occasion of the eighteenth General Assembly of the International Union of Geodesy and Geophysics (Hamburg, Federal Republic of Germany, 21-27 August). The group, composed of 10 experts from all regions, together with representatives of the United Nations Educational, Scientific and Cultural Organization and UNEP, analysed the environmental and social impacts of large-scale water transfers, based on case studies in Africa, Asia, Europe and North America. The working group's recommendations were to be published in 1984.

ECONOMIC AND SOCIAL COUNCIL ACTION

The Economic and Social Council on 28 July, on the recommendation of its First Committee, adopted without vote resolution 1983/57.

Water resources development: progress and prospects in the implementation of the Mar del Plata Action Plan and the International Drinking Water Supply and Sanitation Decade

The Economic and Social Council,

Recalling paragraph 4 of section VI of its resolution 1981/80 of 24 July 1981, and other relevant resolutions of the Council and the General Assembly concerning the adoption, implementation and monitoring of the Mar del Plata Action Plan and the International Drinking Water Supply and Sanitation Decade,

Recognizing that water resources development is an interdisciplinary and multisectoral process which cuts across many sectors of economic and social development, such as food production, environment and health, energy, human settlements, desertification, industrialization, transport, economic and technical co-operation among developing countries and disaster relief,

1. *Takes note* of the report of the Secretary-General on the progress achieved and prospects in the implementation by Governments of the Mar del Plata Action Plan and the International Drinking Water Supply and Sanitation Decade, in the context of the review and appraisal of the International Development Strategy for the Third United Nations Development Decade, prepared in consultation with the Inter-Secretariat Group for Water Resources of the Administrative Committee on Co-ordination, in pursuance of paragraph 4 of section VI of Council resolution 1981/80;

2. *Reaffirms* the importance of the implementation, within the context of the International Development Strategy for the Third United Nations Development Decade, of the Mar del Plata Action Plan and the objectives of the International Drinking Water Supply and Sanitation Decade, and notes the progress being made in that context by Governments, with the support of multilateral and bilateral co-operation;

3. *Expresses its concern* that, notwithstanding this progress, the implementation of the Mar del Plata Action Plan has so far been well below the level required

to meet the needs of developing countries, in large part owing to the gap between the need for financial resources and their availability;

4. *Urges* Governments of developing countries to assign high priority in their national development planning to the development of their water resources and to take active steps to formulate proposals for financial and technical assistance;

5. *Urges* bilateral and multilateral donors and financing institutions to respond positively to requests from developing countries and to increase, under favourable terms and conditions, the flow of financial assistance to developing countries for the promotion of the development of water resources;

6. *Stresses* the needs of the least developed countries in this context;

7. *Requests* the Secretary-General, in consultation with the organizations concerned, to compile information on the activities of bilateral aid programmes and international organizations and on present capacities and the terms and conditions under which they provide finances for water resources development, with a view to examining possible measures to increase the flow of resources and to improve the terms and conditions, and to disseminating relevant information to countries and international organizations, and to report thereon to the Committee on Natural Resources at its tenth session;

8. *Reaffirms* the benefits of establishing national mechanisms to co-ordinate all water policies and programmes;

9. *Calls upon* the regional commissions, in co-operation with the organizations of the United Nations system concerned, to examine measures to promote the accelerated development of water resources in their respective regions;

10. *Recommends* to the General Assembly that the Committee on the Review and Appraisal of the International Development Strategy for the Third United Nations Development Decade should, at its session in 1984, give due consideration to the role played by water resources development in the various elements of the Strategy;

11. *Recommends* that Governments should re-evaluate the current status of their respective resources in surface and ground water, with a view to formulating specific programmes for reaching the targets recommended in the Mar del Plata Action Plan and, on the basis of national evaluation of problems, needs and constraints, indicate requirements in respect of technical assistance and advisory services, equipment, expertise and fellowships;

12. *Urges* Governments of developing countries to adopt national targets for drinking water supply and sanitation services, at the highest possible rate commensurate with resource availability, absorptive capacity and ability, and to formulate action plans and programmes for reaching the targets set, taking also into consideration resolution WHA36.13 of 13 May 1983 of the World Health Assembly;

13. *Recommends* that Governments of developing countries should:

(a) Estimate present and future needs for trained manpower for the development and management of water in agriculture, and take concrete steps to formulate plans and programmes to expand training capabilities;

(b) Evolve plans and programmes for improving the efficiency of agricultural water management, including appropriate measures to motivate farmers for this purpose;

(c) Promote the development of medium-scale and small-scale village irrigation schemes, so as to form the pool of experience and expertise necessary for the planning and implementation of large schemes;

14. *Recommends* that Governments should intensify efforts to implement the recommendations on industrial water use made at Mar del Plata and, in particular:

(a) Initiate studies on the present and potential use of water by specific industries;

(b) Integrate industrial water use in overall policies and projects for the development of water resources;

(c) Conduct research on the use, treatment and recycling of water;

(d) Evolve appropriate economic and regulatory mechanisms for more efficient water use in industry and waste-water treatment;

15. *Urges* Governments to consider action to integrate plans for the development of hydropower in overall plans for the development of water resources and electric power systems, and provide for improved co-ordination at the national level between the water-related and energy-related institutional frameworks;

16. *Calls upon* Governments to formulate programmes and projects for the improvement of transport on rivers and lakes, and to promote inter-country co-operation in this field;

17. *Recommends* that, with regard to the mitigation of effects from floods and droughts, countries should give high priority to early-warning and forecasting systems, as well as to structural and other measures, and integrate projects for the management of flood and drought losses in overall plans for the development of water resources;

18. *Urges* Governments to take the steps necessary to intensify efforts to develop and utilize appropriate techniques for the assessment and monitoring of the environmental impact of water projects, and to ensure that environmental and human health considerations will be systematically incorporated in the planning, implementation and operation of water schemes;

19. *Recommends* that Governments should direct their efforts towards developing appropriate hydraulic techniques and systems for the rational utilization and conservation of water resources in rural areas, for example, by means of small-scale dams and ponds, particularly in arid and semi-arid areas;

20. *Calls upon* Governments to co-operate fully in promoting education, training and research in the field of water resources, and to give priority to the teaching of science and technology at secondary and university levels, in particular subjects related to this field;

21. *Calls upon* the United Nations Development Programme and other organizations of the United Nations system concerned to intensify their catalytic roles in the promotion of technical co-operation among developing countries in the field of water resources;

22. *Urges* Governments of developing countries to take appropriate steps to co-operate among themselves and with the United Nations system in compiling, in a systematic manner, information on technical co-operation among developing countries and arranging for its dissemination at periodic intervals, in order to

provide further stimulus to the promotion of technical co-operation in water development;

23. *Welcomes* the conclusions of the colloquium held at the Centre for Waters at Zagreb on support for the establishment within that Centre of a small international technical unit dealing with technical co-operation among developing countries in the water resources sector, and requests the Secretary-General, in co-operation with the United Nations Development Programme and other competent agencies, to study the matter further, especially with regard to a review of possible financial sources for non-local cost components, and to report thereon to the Economic and Social Council at its second regular session of 1984.

Economic and Social Council resolution 1983/57

28 July 1983   Meeting 40   Adopted without vote

Approved by First Committee (E/1983/122) without vote, 19 July (meeting 17); draft by Committee on Natural Resources (E/1983/19 & Corr.1); agenda item 9. *Meeting number.* ESC 40.

Marine resources

As it had decided in 1981,[13] CPC considered in May 1983 a cross-organizational programme analysis of United Nations activities in marine affairs.[14] The analysis showed that 28 United Nations bodies with a multiplicity of mandates and working relationships were active in marine affairs. It suggested that while in specialized fields the relationships among programmes were harmoniously determined, there might be an advantage in keeping the whole range of marine-related activities under review.

CPC also had before it an April report[15] by the Secretary-General containing the replies of six countries to his June 1982 request that all Member States indicate their priorities for action by the United Nations system. The replies were summarized in a working list of activities. Most areas of activity had been given priority by at least one Government. Several areas had been given priority by most of the six, including prevention, reduction and control of pollution; development and transfer of marine technology; environmental monitoring; marine science; marine meteorology and services; and national legislative and administrative development. In addition, one country replied that it was particularly interested in those United Nations activities which had a bearing on the situation of land-locked countries and which encouraged their maritime interests.

A number of recommendations were made by CPC:[16] ACC should review periodically the work of the United Nations system in marine affairs through existing co-ordination mechanisms, with a view to ensuring that the consistent approach demonstrated in the cross-organizational programme analysis continued; the International Maritime Organization and UNCTAD should increase their level of co-operation in the field of maritime transport and should report to CPC in

1984 on their joint efforts; United Nations organizations should co-operate closely in the follow-up to the United Nations Convention on the Law of the Sea,[17] using existing ACC mechanisms, with particular emphasis on joint approaches for assisting developing countries in marine science, technology and ocean service infrastructures; and, as intergovernmental bodies considered new legislative mandates on marine affairs, the servicing secretariat should advise Member States about possible conflict with the mandates of other organizations.

In section I of resolution 38/227 B, dealing with co-ordination, adopted on 20 December 1983, the General Assembly endorsed the conclusions and recommendations of CPC.

The Secretary-General also presented to CPC his proposed reformulations of the new major programme in marine affairs[18] for inclusion in the United Nations medium-term plan for 1984-1989, adopted by the Assembly in 1982.[19] Components included a programme on law of the sea affairs (see POLITICAL AND SECURITY QUESTIONS, Chapter III), a programme on economic and technical aspects of marine affairs, and regional programmes of marine affairs in Africa and Latin America. The reformulations were revised and recommended for adoption by CPC,[16] endorsed by the Economic and Social Council in resolution 1983/48 (see below), and adopted by the Assembly in resolution 38/227 A (see ADMINISTRATIVE AND BUDGETARY QUESTIONS, Chapter II).

Responding to a 1980 request by the Council,[20] the Secretary-General submitted to it in June 1983 a note briefly describing developments in marine resource planning and management, non-living marine resources and ocean science in relation to them, and marine technology.[21]

ECONOMIC AND SOCIAL COUNCIL ACTION

On 28 July, acting on the recommendation of its Third (Programme and Co-ordination) Committee, the Economic and Social Council adopted resolution 1983/48 by vote.

Marine affairs

The Economic and Social Council,

Recalling its long-standing interest in marine affairs and its numerous resolutions on various aspects of the subject dating from 1966,

Recalling also its resolution 1980/68 of 25 July 1980, in response to which the Secretary-General has submitted to the Council a note entitled "Marine affairs: economic and technical developments",

Taking note of the adoption by the Third United Nations Conference on the Law of the Sea at its eleventh session of the United Nations Convention on the Law of the Sea and the related resolutions, as well as the resolution entitled "Development of national marine science, technology and ocean service infrastructures", and of General Assembly resolution 37/66 of 3 December 1982, by which the Assembly, *inter alia*, welcomed the adoption of the Convention and the related resolutions and approved the assumption by the Secretary-General of the responsibilities entrusted to him under the Convention and the related resolutions,

Taking note also of the recommendations, decisions and observations made by the Committee for Programme and Co-ordination at its twenty-third session concerning the cross-organizational programme analysis of activities in marine affairs and the new major programme in marine affairs, particularly the Committee's recommendation that the Economic and Social Council and the General Assembly should adopt the new programme, as revised, for inclusion as chapter 25 in the proposed medium-term plan for the period 1984-1989,

Bearing in mind that the present activities of the Secretary-General relating to marine affairs already contribute to a large extent to the fulfilment of his responsibilities and the exercise of his functions resulting from the adoption of the United Nations Convention on the Law of the Sea and the related resolutions,

Believing firmly that the growing needs of Member States, particularly developing countries, for information, advice and assistance regarding legal, economic and technical aspects of marine affairs warrant an appropriate and commensurate effort on the part of the United Nations and the organizations of the United Nations system to respond to those needs,

1. *Invites* the organizations of the United Nations system, each within its sphere of competence, and with due regard for the efficient co-ordination of activities on a system-wide basis, to continue to make their respective programmes of activities fully responsive to the growing needs of Member States in the field of marine affairs, particularly in the light of the adoption of the United Nations Convention on the Law of the Sea and the related resolutions;

2. *Endorses* the recommendation of the Committee for Programme and Co-ordination regarding the new major programme in marine affairs, as revised;

3. *Requests* the Secretary-General to pursue, within existing budgetary resources, and taking into account the recommendations of the Committee for Programme and Co-ordination at its resumed twenty-third session with regard to the relevant sections of the proposed programme budget for the biennium 1984-1985, the programme of activities, including the collection, analysis and dissemination of information and data, dealing with:

   (*a*) Planning and management, with a view to the national development and utilization of the resources of coastal areas and exclusive economic zones;

   (*b*) Economic and technical issues related to the development of marine mineral resources in connection with the role of non-renewable resources and their impact on the economies of developing countries, as well as on the world economy;

   (*c*) Issues relating to the acquisition and introduction of marine technologies for the development of the resources of the sea, bearing in mind the need to avoid duplication of work in other competent organizations of the United Nations system in their respective areas of competence;

4. *Recommends* to the General Assembly, when it considers the report of the Secretary-General on the implementation of Assembly resolution 37/66, that it should give due consideration to the continuation of activities concerned with information, assistance and advice in matters relating to the new legal régime of the oceans;

5. *Invites* the Secretary-General, in close co-operation with the competent organizations of the United Nations system, to submit to the Council, at its second regular session of 1985, a comprehensive report on economic and technical trends and developments in marine affairs.

Economic and Social Council resolution 1983/48

28 July 1983   Meeting 40   34-0-7

Approved by Third Committee (E/1983/120) by vote (31-0-5), 20 July (meeting 14);
2-nation draft (E/1983/C.3/L.5/Rev.1); agenda item 19.
Sponsors: Colombia, Mexico.
Meeting number. ESC 40.

The revised draft resolution approved by the Third Committee was initially introduced by a Committee Vice-Chairman, on the basis of informal consultations on a draft by Colombia and Mexico.[22] In view of the lack of consensus in the Committee, however, the Vice-Chairman withdrew it and Colombia and Mexico then assumed its sponsorship.

REFERENCES

[1]E/C.7/1983/11. [2]YUN 1977, p. 555. [3]YUN 1980, p. 712, GA res. 35/18, 10 Nov. 1980. [4]YUN 1981, p. 681, ESC res. 1981/80, 24 July 1981. [5]E/1983/19 & Corr.1. [6]DP/1983/29 & Corr.1. [7]A/38/39 (dec. 3/5). [8]*Ibid.* (dec. 3/9). [9]E/1983/20 (dec. 83/15). [10]A/38/25 (dec 11/7). [11]UNEP/GC.12/2. [12]ACC/1984/PG/1. [13]YUN 1981, p. 139. [14]E/AC.51/1983/2 & Corr.1-3. [15]E/AC.51/1983/2/Add.1. [16]A/38/38. [17]YUN 1982, p. 181. [18]A/37/6/Add.1. [19]YUN 1982, p. 1430, GA res. 37/234, 21 Dec. 1982. [20]YUN 1980, p. 714, ESC res. 1980/68, 25 July 1980. [21]E/1983/97. [22]E/1983/C.3/L.5.

PUBLICATIONS

Experiences in the Development and Management of International River and Lake Basins (ST/ESA/120), Sales No. E.82.II.A.17. *Ground Water in the Pacific Region* (ST/ESA/121), Sales No. E.83.II.A.12. *Institutional Arrangements for Marine Resource Development: Report of the Expert Group Meeting on Institutional Arrangements for Marine Resource Development, United Nations Headquarters, 10-14 January 1983* (ST/ESA/144), Sales No. E.84.II.A.9.

Cartography

Standardization of geographical names

The Secretary-General, in a 1983 report[1] to the Economic and Social Council, summarized the recommendations of the Fourth United Nations Conference on the Standardization of Geographical Names, held in 1982.[2] The recommendations dealt with the future work programme of the United Nations Group of Experts on Geographical Names; the standardization of geographical names; writing systems; toponymic guidelines for map and other editors; co-ordination of the preparation of a list of country names; the use of exonyms; and education in cartographic toponymy. The Fourth Conference had also recommended that the Fifth Conference be held in Canada, at that country's invitation, not later than the second half of 1987. The Secretary-General suggested that the Council might wish to request him to implement the recommendations. In an addendum to the report,[3] servicing costs for the Fifth Conference were estimated at $359,300.

ECONOMIC AND SOCIAL COUNCIL ACTION

In May, the Economic and Social Council acted on a recommendation of its First Committee and adopted without vote decision 1983/120.

Standardization of geographical names

At its 14th plenary meeting, on 26 May 1983, the Council decided:

(a) To take note of the report of the Secretary-General on the Fourth United Nations Conference on the Standardization of Geographical Names and to endorse the recommendation to convene the Fifth United Nations Conference on the Standardization of Geographical Names not later than the second half of 1987;

(b) To accept with appreciation the invitation of the Government of Canada to act as host to the Fifth United Nations Conference on the Standardization of Geographical Names, bearing in mind the relevant provisions of General Assembly resolution 31/140 of 17 December 1976;

(c) To request the Secretary-General to take practical measures within existing resources for the implementation of the recommendations addressed to him by the Fourth United Nations Conference on the Standardization of Geographical Names, including the recommendation to investigate the possibility of the provision of funds for the financing of the meetings of the United Nations Group of Experts on Geographical Names.

Economic and Social Council decision 1983/120

Adopted without vote

Approved by First Committee (E/1983/60) without vote, 11 May (meeting 5); draft by Chairman (E/1983/C.1/L.2); agenda item 9.
Meeting number. ESC 14.

Tenth UN Cartographic Conference for Asia and the Pacific

The Tenth United Nations Regional Cartographic Conference for Asia and the Pacific was held at Bangkok, Thailand, from 17 to 28 January 1983.[4] The Conference was attended by 185 representatives and observers from 38 countries and territories and six intergovernmental and international scientific organizations. The Secretary-General submitted his report on the Conference[5] to the Economic and Social Council in March.

The Conference considered the latest techniques and recent developments related to conventional and satellite geodesy; aerial photography, photogrammetry and orthophoto mapping; remote sensing from space for cartography; automated

cartography, computer mapping and digital terrain models; topographic and large-scale mapping; small-scale and thematic mapping, national and regional atlases, the International Map of the World on the Millionth Scale (IMW) and other international map series; cadastral surveying and urban mapping; aeronautical charting; hydrographic surveying and nautical charting; reproduction and printing of maps; and distribution and sale of maps and charts.

In addition, it took up matters dealing with the standardization of geographical names; technical assistance and transfer of technology; education and training; and the feasibility of holding United Nations interregional cartographic conferences.

The Conference adopted 20 resolutions recognizing, in particular, the fundamental importance of surveying, mapping and charting infrastructures, the need for increasing assistance to developing countries in this field, an urgent need for new hydrographic surveys and updated charts of coastal waters of developing countries, the further potential benefits of remote sensing data application for cartography, the necessity of improving the utility of small-scale thematic maps, and the need for an adequate system of land registration and land information as a basis for development. The use of satellites for geodesy and of electronic data processing for cartography were recommended. Member countries were urged to co-ordinate activities among the cartographic services of the region and to co-operate with the United Nations on IMW.

The Tenth Conference had also recommended that the Eleventh Conference be convened in the first half of 1987. The Secretary-General suggested that the Council might wish to request him to implement the other recommendations. In an addendum to the report,[6] servicing costs for the Eleventh Conference were estimated at $598,500.

ECONOMIC AND SOCIAL COUNCIL ACTION

Decision 1983/121 on the Conference was adopted by the Economic and Social Council in May, following the recommendation of its First Committee.

Tenth United Nations Regional Cartographic Conference for Asia and the Pacific

At its 14th plenary meeting, on 26 May 1983, the Council decided:

(a) To take note of the report of the Secretary-General on the Tenth United Nations Regional Cartographic Conference for Asia and the Pacific and to endorse the recommendation that the Eleventh United Nations Regional Cartographic Conference for Asia and the Pacific should be convened in the first half of 1987;

(b) To request the Secretary-General and the executive heads of the specialized agencies concerned to take measures within existing resources to implement the recommendations addressed to them by the Tenth

United Nations Regional Cartographic Conference for Asia and the Pacific.

Economic and Social Council decision 1983/121

Adopted without vote

Approved by First Committee (E/1983/60) without vote, 11 May (meeting 5); draft by Chairman (E/1983/C.1/L.3), orally amended by India; agenda item 9.
Meeting number. ESC 14.

India's oral amendment added to paragraph *(b)* the phrase "and the executive heads of the specialized agencies concerned".

REFERENCES

[1]E/1983/26. [2]YUN 1982, p. 882. [3]E/1983/26/Add.1. [4]*Tenth United Nations Regional Cartographic Conference for Asia and the Pacific, Bangkok, 17-28 January 1983*, vol. I: *Report of the Conference* (E/CONF.75/5), Sales No. E.83.I.18; vol. II: *Technical Papers* (E/CONF.75/5/Add.1), Sales No. E.86.I.11. [5]E/1983/27. [6]E/1983/27/Add.1.

PUBLICATIONS

Ninth United Nations Regional Cartographic Conference for Asia and the Pacific, Wellington, 11-22 February 1980, vol. II: *Technical Papers* (E/CONF.72/4/Add.1), Sales No. E/F.83.I.14. *World Cartography*, vol. XVII (ST/ESA/SER.L/17), Sales No. E.83.I.17.

Chapter X

Energy resources

Throughout 1983, the main thrust of United Nations energy-related activities was aimed at searching for alternatives, nuclear as well as non-nuclear, to reduce world-wide dependence on depletable supplies of petroleum and gas, with particular emphasis on the development of the indigenous energy resources of developing countries. The efforts of various United Nations entities in this sphere, co-ordinated by the inter-agency Administrative Committee on Co-ordination (ACC), were geared towards implementing the Nairobi Programme of Action for the Development and Utilization of New and Renewable Sources of Energy, endorsed by the General Assembly in 1981. Recommendations on specific ways of reaching this goal were worked out at the first session of the Committee on the Development and Utilization of New and Renewable Sources of Energy in April 1983 and endorsed in December by the Assembly in resolution 38/169. Geothermal energy was regarded as a particularly promising source, with the United Nations Revolving Fund for Natural Resources Exploration carrying out extensive work on its research and development.

With regard to the development of energy resources of the developing countries, an effort to assess the prospects of conventional commercial energy sources in energy-deficient countries was undertaken in an analysis by the Secretary-General, while a study of the technological aspects of energy resources development was made by the Secretary-General of the United Nations Conference on Trade and Development (UNCTAD). Upon reviewing their reports in December, the Assembly requested, by resolution 38/151, a comprehensive report on this issue and urged greater international support for the accelerated exploration and development of the energy resources of developing countries. Meanwhile, additional funds in support of energy programmes in developing countries were mobilized by the United Nations Development Programme (UNDP), with total expenditures of $3.1 million under its Energy Account in 1983, representing a substantial increase over the previous year. In view of industry's role as the major single market for energy, the United Nations Industrial Development Organization (UNIDO) pursued an intensive technical co-operation and research and development programme, with particular emphasis on such sources as hydropower and biomass energy, and the ques-

tions of industrial energy management and provision of capital goods for the energy sector. Issues related to technology transfer figured prominently in the activities of UNCTAD.

Concerning nuclear energy, the General Assembly considered in November the annual report of the International Atomic Energy Agency (IAEA), the chief United Nations body carrying out technical work related to nuclear power, and urged, in resolution 38/8, all States to co-operate in promoting the use of nuclear energy and the application of nuclear science and technology for peaceful purposes. In 1983, preparations continued for the United Nations Conference for the Promotion of International Co-operation in the Peaceful Uses of Nuclear Energy. The Assembly endorsed, in December by resolution 38/60, the conclusions of the Preparatory Committee for the Conference and decided to hold it in 1986, with the venue and actual dates to be determined at the 1984 Assembly session.

Topics related to this chapter. Disarmament: nuclear weapons. Peaceful uses of outer space. Regional economic and social activities: energy resources—Africa; Asia and the Pacific; Europe; Latin America. Statistics: energy statistics.

General aspects

In a report submitted in June 1983 to the Committee on Natural Resources,[1] the Secretary-General gave an overview of trends and salient issues in energy resources development, with special emphasis on the problems and policy responses in the medium term, up to 1990. Assessing the current energy balance, the report cited findings contained in the *World Economic Survey 1983*, published by the United Nations Department of International Economic and Social Affairs (DIESA),[2] which showed how the reduced total energy demand affected prices and led to cut-backs in production levels.

While attempting to project the evolution of the energy sector over the remainder of the decade, the report noted the effects of past events and policies, such as the drive for energy conservation and oil substitution, the upsurge in the development of crude oil, the interest in alternative energy sources and the hardening of public attitudes towards nuclear power. Another factor to have a strong impact on the energy supply-demand variables in 1990 was the manner in which some key uncertainties, such as the prospects for economic growth, energy conservation in developing countries, oil production policies and the role of nuclear power, would be resolved. Taking these factors into consideration, the report projected development of energy supply and demand in two different scenarios, characterized respectively by high and low expansion rates in the energy sector.

The report also dealt with some international energy problems, such as financing of energy resources development in developing countries, energy planning and technology transfer. It stressed the important role of UNCTAD and the World Intellectual Property Organization in co-ordinating efforts related to the transfer of technology and technical knowledge. In this context, it reiterated the recommendations of the October/November 1982 Meeting of Governmental Experts on the Transfer, Application and Development of Technology in the Energy Sector.[3] The report also called for increased national and international efforts in such areas as energy conservation and assessment of energy sector investments.

Energy resources development

Report of the Secretary-General. Development of the energy resources of the developing countries was the subject of an analysis presented by the Secretary-General to the Economic and Social Council in June 1983,[4] as requested by the General Assembly in December 1982.[5] In view of the limited time available for preparation of a full report, the submitted document was described as a preliminary analysis, with the main emphasis on the energy-deficient countries and conventional commercial energy sources, especially hydrocarbons in oil and natural gas, which accounted for a major share of total commercial energy use in the developing world.

The report gave an overview of the energy situation in the developing countries, summarizing available information on conventional hydrocarbon and other resources potential and providing commercial energy demand projections. This demand was expected to grow at an average of 5 per cent per annum in the period 1982-2000, alongside of a widening gap between indigenous supply and requirements in the energy-deficient developing countries. On the other hand, the report noted that the vast conventional and unconventional energy resources potential in the developing countries, if adequately exploited, could en-

sure them a significant degree of self-sufficiency by the turn of the century. There were several important factors, however, that hampered the development of energy resources, particularly in the energy-deficient countries, such as the limited knowledge of the resource base, and the lack of necessary technology, skilled manpower and adequate national energy planning. In addition, there was a persistent tendency of directing only a small fraction of exploration efforts towards the developing countries, to the detriment of the productivity of the world's energy economy.

The analysis also dealt with a broad scope of issues related to energy investment requirements and energy development financing. It was estimated that in order to ensure a modest acceleration of energy exploration and development in the energy-deficient developing countries over the period 1982-2000, a fourfold increase over existing levels would be required. Comparing investment needs and current availability of external financing for those countries, the report projected an energy financing gap for 1990 of $20 billion to $25 billion, for the exploration and production side alone.

With regard to possible ways of accelerating the development of energy resources, the report stressed the need for additional funding, particularly for exploratory drilling, and argued for creation of an energy affiliate within the World Bank, an idea already put forward by the Assembly in December 1982.[5] Reviewing several other proposals and mechanisms, the report emphasized that all should have certain common traits, such as a critical minimum size, flexibility to adjust to particular conditions and inclusion of a significant grant element. Most importantly, they should provide concessional financing for the risky, exploratory phases. The report called for concerted action on the part of the international community, urging new initiatives from multilateral, regional and bilateral institutions concerned with financial and technical aspects, as well as from transnational corporations. It was suggested that a more comprehensive report could be submitted to the Economic and Social Council in 1984.

Aspects of energy resources development were also dealt with in the Secretary-General's report on trends and salient issues in energy (see above).

UNCTAD activities. A meeting of the Expert Group on Energy Co-operation among Economic Co-operation and Integration Organizations was held at Quito, Ecuador, from 26 to 30 September 1983, organized jointly by UNCTAD, the Latin American Energy Organization (OLADE) and the Organization of Arab Petroleum Exporting Countries (OAPEC), with support from the Government of Ecuador.[6] Taking part were experts from 19 subregional and regional co-operation and integration organizations, as well as energy research institutions representing the different regions of the developing world. In preparation for the meeting, UNCTAD had compiled two documents, on energy co-operation within and between economic co-operation groupings in trade-related areas and on major issues in the strengthening of the technological capacity of developing countries in the energy sector, which dealt, *inter alia*, with current and future UNCTAD work on energy technology.

Emphasizing the need for an expanded exchange of experiences among subregional and regional groupings and international organizations, the Expert Group adopted a number of conclusions and recommendations related to the development of energy sources and requested OLADE, OAPEC and UNCTAD to work towards their speedy implementation.

UNDP action. During 1983, UNDP made increased efforts to mobilize additional funds from donor countries in support of energy programmes in developing countries, particularly for the joint UNDP/World Bank Energy Sector Assessment Programme and the Energy Sector Management Assistance Programme (ESMAP).[7] Voluntary contributions to the UNDP Energy Account in 1983 totalled $841,335 ($441,250 from Australia, $366,972 from Finland and $33,113 from New Zealand),[8] augmented by another $4 million in cost-sharing contributions. Total expenditures under the Energy Account in 1983 amounted to $3.1 million (see table below), an increase of over $1 million as compared with the previous year.[9]

With regard to the Energy Sector Assessment Programme, aimed at diagnosing the most serious problems and evaluating options for their alleviation, the UNDP Administrator reported in his annual report for 1983[10] completion of 29 assessments, with another 19 under way. Assessment recommendations helped Governments in such areas as energy pricing policies, reorientation of energy sector strategies and improvement of organizational and institutional arrangements. Providing assistance in implementing these recommendations was the goal of ESMAP, which helped developing countries by formulating and justifying high-priority pre-investment and investment projects as well as by rendering management, institutional and policy support. Initiated in April 1983, ESMAP had 26 specific activities completed or in progress in 13 countries by the end of that year. Nearly all projects generated by its reports were under consideration by donor agencies for possible financing.

While the UNDP Energy Account gave priority to financing those Programmes, several other projects were completed in 1983. Among them, a set of training modules for energy management at enterprises was produced and tested in co-operation with the International Centre for Advanced Technical and Vocational Training of the International Labour Organisation (Turin, Italy). In February, a training seminar in energy and power was instituted by the World Bank's Economic Development Institute at Istanbul, Turkey. Two World Bank–executed projects were approved, one global for monitoring biomass gasifiers, the other one regional, to assist Caribbean countries in negotiations on petroleum exploration, contracting, legislation and promotion.

By a decision of 24 June,[11] the UNDP Governing Council expressed satisfaction at the increased support provided by UNDP to developing countries in the development of indigenous energy resources and improvement of the utilization of energy. It recommended that United Nations expertise be taken fully into account in energy assessment studies, and requested the Administrator to report in 1985 on the results of actions taken in respect of energy programmes. In other provisions, the Council dealt with new and renewable energy sources and implementation of the 1981 Nairobi Programme of Action (see below, under NON-CONVENTIONAL ENERGY SOURCES).

UNDP ENERGY ACCOUNT PROJECT EXPENDITURES, 1983[12]
(in thousands of US dollars)

Country/Region	Amount
Barbados	(23)
Bolivia	(4)
Colombia	128
Egypt	(2)
Honduras	7
Jamaica	75
Niger	14
Viet Nam	10
Subtotal	205
Latin America and the Caribbean	5
Interregional	2,433
Global	451
Subtotal	2,889
Total	3,094

UNU activities. Following an agreement concluded with the International Development Research Centre in June 1983 to pursue energy research jointly, the United Nations University (UNU) established a 10-member Energy Research Group of energy analysts and policy-makers from developing countries, to survey the capacity of those countries for energy research and development. At its first meeting in Canada in August, the Group commissioned 120 papers to be submitted to it within a year, to review the field of energy research and technology.

Other UNU activities included training in energy systems and policy. By December 1983, 14 fellows and 1 special fellow completed such training, and 10 other fellows were in training.[13]

ECONOMIC AND SOCIAL COUNCIL ACTION

Following consideration of the report of the Secretary-General on the development of the energy resources of the developing countries (see above), the Economic and Social Council, on the recommendation of its First (Economic) Committee, adopted resolution 1983/60 without vote on 28 July.

Development of the energy resources of the developing countries

The Economic and Social Council,

Recalling General Assembly resolution 37/251 of 21 December 1982, as adopted, on the development of the energy resources of the developing countries,

Reaffirming the importance of continued study and discussion of this question by the international community,

Taking note of the note by the Secretary-General on the development of the energy resources of the developing countries,

Regretting the delay in the submission of the report on this question to the Economic and Social Council,

1. _Requests_ the Secretary-General to submit the completed report, in accordance with the mandate given by the General Assembly in its resolution 37/251, to the Assembly at its thirty-eighth session, to enable it to consider this question in depth and to take action as appropriate;

2. _Further requests_ the Secretary-General to take into account, in completing the report, the preliminary views expressed by Governments at the second regular session of 1983 of the Economic and Social Council.

Economic and Social Council resolution 1983/60

28 July 1983   Meeting 40   Adopted without vote

Approved by First Committee (E/1983/121) without vote, 26 July (meeting 24); draft by Bangladesh, for Group of 77 (E/1983/C.1/L.22), orally revised, and orally amended in informal consultations; agenda item 10.
Meeting number. ESC 40.

In another resolution of the same date (1983/57), the Council urged Governments to integrate plans for the development of hydropower in overall plans for the development of water resources and electric power systems, and to improve national co-ordination between the water-related and energy-related institutional frameworks.

The Council's First Committee, considering the report of the Committee on Natural Resources on its 1983 session,[14] ruled on 26 July that no decision be taken on a draft resolution on energy development approved by that Committee on 17 June. The First Committee action, proposed by Bangladesh on behalf of the Group of 77, was taken by 24 votes to 11, with 4 abstentions.

By that draft, the Council would have requested the Secretary-General to submit to the Committee's 1985 session a report on the world energy situation, prospects and salient issues, including an analysis of progress and of obstacles in implementing policy measures in the energy field, and to improve co-ordination within the United Nations system to promote the most effective and timely development and utilization of energy resources and technologies, in both developing and developed countries.

Consequently, the Council, in decision 1983/176 of 28 July, amended item 4 of the provisional agenda for the 1985 session of the Committee on Natural Resources to read "Energy resources: trends and salient issues", deleting reference to the report on prospects and salient issues in the world energy situation (see Chapter IX of this section).

GENERAL ASSEMBLY ACTION

In accordance with the request of the Council, the Secretary-General presented to the General Assembly supplementary information mainly on new and renewable energy sources, annexed to a note of 26 October 1983 (see below, under NON-CONVENTIONAL ENERGY SOURCES).

On 19 December, on the recommendation of the Second (Economic and Financial) Committee, the Assembly adopted without vote resolution 38/151.

Development of the energy resources of developing countries

The General Assembly,

Recalling the Declaration and the Programme of Action on the Establishment of a New International Economic Order, contained in its resolutions 3201(S-VI) and 3202(S-VI) of 1 May 1974, the Charter of Economic Rights and Duties of States, contained in its resolution 3281(XXIX) of 12 December 1974, and resolution 3362(S-VII) of 16 September 1975 on development and international economic co-operation,

Recalling its resolution 35/56 of 5 December 1980, the annex to which contains the International Development Strategy for the Third United Nations Development Decade, which, _inter alia,_ called for the promotion of the exploration, development, expansion and processing of all energy resources of the developing countries at a rate commensurate with their development objectives and for the provision of adequate financial and technical resources for this purpose,

Recalling its resolution 37/251 of 21 December 1982,

Recalling also the Nairobi Programme of Action for the Development and Utilization of New and Renewable Sources of Energy,

Recalling further section II.A of resolution 112(V) of 3 June 1979 of the United Nations Conference on Trade and Development concerning the strengthening of the technological capacity of the developing countries in the development of their energy resources, including that relating to transition from conventional sources to a more diversified pattern of energy consumption,

Considering that the principal impediments to the realization of the indigenous energy potential of the developing countries are, in addition to inadequate exploration, the scarcity of financial resources, insufficient exploration data, inadequate access to technology and a shortage of skills,

Reaffirming that effective and urgent measures should be taken by the international community to assist and support the efforts of the developing countries for developing the domestic energy resources of those countries, in particular the energy deficient among them, in order to meet their needs through co-operation, assistance and investment in the field of conventional and of new and renewable sources of energy, consistent with their national plans and priorities, as called for in the International Development Strategy,

Aware that special measures are required in this regard for the least developed countries,

Aware that multilateral financial and technical assistance for the exploration, development, expansion and processing of the energy resources of the developing countries continues to be necessary in order to realize their indigenous energy potential and meet their development objectives,

Recognizing the need for an accelerated effort devoted to the exploration and development of the indigenous energy resources of developing countries.

Reaffirming that the developing countries continue to bear the main responsibility for the development of their indigenous energy potential, which would require vigorous measures for a fuller mobilization of their domestic financial and other resources, while external resources, public and private, particularly concessional flows and official development assistance, can constitute an element of support for the developing countries' own efforts,

Emphasizing the importance of intensifying the capabilities of the United Nations in the collection, analysis and dissemination of information relating to all phases of the development of energy resources in the developing countries,

Taking note of the report of the Secretary-General on the development of the energy resources of the developing countries,

Taking note also of the report of the Secretary-General of the United Nations Conference on Trade and Development on the strengthening of the technological capacity of the developing countries in the development of their energy resources.

1. *Requests* the Secretary-General to complete his comprehensive report on the development of the energy resources of the developing countries, as requested by the General Assembly in its resolution 37/251 and the Economic and Social Council in its resolution 1983/60 of 28 July 1983, and to report to the Assembly at its thirty-ninth session;

2. *Also requests* the Secretary-General to explore in his report, in consultation with appropriate international financial institutions, ways and means of mobilizing adequate and additional resources for the development of the energy resources of developing countries and, at the same time, encourages interested Governments, in co-operation with appropriate United Nations bodies, to hold, at an early date, symposia and other similar undertakings in order to explore ways and means of supporting the efforts of developing countries in the exploration and development of their energy resources;

3. *Urges* the international community to mobilize adequate and additional technological resources as well as adequate financial support for the accelerated exploration and development of the energy resources of developing countries;

4. *Urges*, in this connection, accelerated consideration of other possible avenues that would increase energy financing, including, *inter alia*, the mechanisms being examined by the World Bank, such as an energy affiliate, and calls upon Member States to make ap-

propriate efforts to this end in the relevant forums;

5. *Urges* Member States and international bodies and institutions to undertake actions oriented towards the effective implementation of General Assembly resolution 37/251 and stresses that international co-operation in this regard should be focused on developing the indigenous capabilities of developing countries in this field, using domestic resources to the maximum extent possible;

6. *Calls* for greater participation by the international and regional financial institutions in the financing of energy projects in developing countries, in particular those located in the least developed countries, so as to bring about an increase in the flow of resources;

7. *Requests* the Secretary-General of the United Nations Conference on Trade and Development to continue, in consultation with other relevant United Nations bodies and in the context of avoiding duplication, to analyse further the issues contained in his report on the strengthening of the technological capacity of the developing countries in the development of their energy resources;

8. *Reaffirms* the need for the United Nations system to support the efforts of the developing countries to enhance economic and technical co-operation among themselves for the development of their energy resources;

9. *Invites* regional bodies and institutions of economic, technical and financial co-operation to increase their support and assistance to the efforts that the developing countries are making for the development of their energy resources;

10. *Reaffirms also* the significance and importance of the Nairobi Programme of Action for the Development and Utilization of New and Renewable Sources of Energy and urges all Governments, organs, organizations and bodies of the United Nations system, specialized intergovernmental agencies and institutions, as well as nongovernmental organizations concerned with new and renewable sources of energy, to take effective action for the implementation of the Programme of Action.

General Assembly resolution 38/151

19 December 1983   Meeting 102   Adopted without vote

Approved by Second Committee (A/38/701/Add.1) without vote, 9 December (meeting 55); draft by Vice-Chairman (A/C.2/38/L.106), based on informal consultations on draft by Mexico, for Group of 77 (A/C.2/38/L.35); agenda item 12.
Financial implications. 5th Committee, A/38/751; S-G, A/C.2/38/L.109, A/C.5/38/96.
Meeting numbers. GA 38th session: 2nd Committee 41, 55; 5th Committee 67; plenary 102.

In addition to drafting changes, the adopted text differed in a number of respects from that of the Group of 77, which was withdrawn. Added were the eleventh preambular paragraph, regarding the developing countries' continuing to bear the main responsibility for developing their indigenous energy potential, and the last preambular paragraph, on the UNCTAD Secretary-General's report. In paragraph 1, "comprehensive" was added, as was the phrase, in paragraph 2, encouraging interested Governments to support developing countries in exploring and developing their energy resources through symposia and similar undertakings. Paragraph 4 was reformulated—the Group's text would have had the Assembly emphasize the role which an energy affiliate for the development of energy resources of developing countries within the World Bank could play to generate additional resources, urge its early establishment, and stress the importance of other complementary frameworks to mobilize finances in order to assure urgently the needs of developing countries. Paragraph 5 was changed to have the Assembly stress that developing countries' domestic resources should be used to the maximum extent possible in developing indigenous capabilities, instead of stressing that international co-operation not concentrate on creating investment and expert opportunities for developed countries. Also added was the phrase, in paragraph 7, concerning consultation with other United Nations bodies to avoid duplication.

The Assembly adopted a number of other resolutions dealing with the question of energy resources, agreeing in resolution 38/200 that immediate measures within the United Nations system should be directed at progress in the development of the energy resources of the developing countries, and calling on the international community in resolution 38/195 to support the efforts of the least developed countries in exploring and developing energy and natural resources (for texts of these resolutions, refer to INDEX OF RESOLUTIONS AND DECISIONS). Resolution 38/169 also dealt with various aspects of energy resources development (see below, under NON-CONVENTIONAL ENERGY SOURCES).

Technology transfer

In 1983, UNCTAD activities in the field of technology transfer were guided by the recommendations of the 1982 Meeting of Governmental Experts on the Transfer, Application and Development of Technology in the Energy Sector[3] and had two broad orientations: the elaboration of alternative approaches to energy technology policy at the national level in developing countries, and promotion of regional and international co-operation. To examine the technology issues involved in planning the development of the energy sector at the national level, the UNCTAD secretariat was undertaking a research programme, including case studies, with the financial support of the Swedish Government. With respect to regional and international co-operation, it circulated, jointly with the United Nations Department of Technical Co-operation for Development (DTCD), a questionnaire on the technological capacity of developing countries in petroleum resources exploration. A September 1983 meeting of the Expert Group on Energy Co-operation among Economic Co-operation and Integration Organizations (see above, under ENERGY RESOURCES DEVELOPMENT), in which

UNCTAD took part, expressed interest in studying the technology transfer aspects of petroleum contracts negotiated by the developing countries. Focusing on formulation and implementation of concrete policies, UNCTAD called for an agreement by Governments on an international code of conduct on the transfer of technology, which would also facilitate energy technology transfer.

Information on UNCTAD's work related to energy technology, in particular technology transfer, was presented to the General Assembly in an August 1983 report by the UNCTAD Secretary-General,[15] who submitted the information in response to a December 1982 request.[5] Annexed to the report were the conclusions and recommendations of the 1982 Meeting of Governmental Experts.

GENERAL ASSEMBLY ACTION

On 19 December 1983, on the recommendation of the Second Committee, the General Assembly adopted without vote decision 38/439.

Report of the Secretary-General of the United Nations Conference on Trade and Development on the strengthening of the technological capacity of the developing countries in the development of their energy resources

At its 102nd plenary meeting, on 19 December 1983, the General Assembly, on the recommendation of the Second Committee, took note of the report of the Secretary-General of the United Nations Conference on Trade and Development on the strengthening of the technological capacity of the developing countries in the development of their energy resources prepared pursuant to Assembly resolution 37/251 of 21 December 1982.

General Assembly decision 38/439

Adopted without vote

Approved by Second Committee (A/38/702/Add.2) without vote, 14 December (meeting 56); draft orally proposed by Chairman; agenda item 78 (*b*).
Meeting numbers. GA 38th session: 2nd Committee 50, 52, 56; plenary 102.

In resolution 38/151 (see above), also adopted on 19 December, the Assembly requested the UNCTAD Secretary-General to continue to analyse further the issues contained in his report, in consultation with other United Nations bodies.

Energy resources in industry

Having completed in 1982 most of the work to define a comprehensive, integrated and balanced energy programme,[16] UNIDO steered its energy-related activities in 1983 in three main directions: selecting priority areas and implementing projects in those areas; participating in United Nations system-wide developments of new and renewable sources of energy; and intensifying the co-ordination of energy activities with other organizations. Information on UNIDO energy activities in 1983 was contained in the Executive Director's annual report.[17] These activities included 49 technical co-operation projects at various stages of implementation with a total value of $15.8 million; expenditures under these projects were about $5 million during the year. Seventy-eight energy project proposals were under consideration for financing. UNIDO also organized 18 meetings, participated in another 39 meetings and issued some 50 documents and working papers on a variety of energy-related subjects.

With respect to local energy resources for industry, UNIDO devoted particular attention in 1983 to hydropower and biomass energy. As part of its assistance in this sector, it aided Solomon Islands in establishing a micro-hydroelectric power plant. Recognizing the growing significance of small hydropower (SHP) as a source of renewable energy in developing countries, UNIDO participated in the organization of the Third Workshop on SHP, held at Kuala Lumpur, Malaysia, from 7 to 15 March.[18] Attended by representatives from 19 developing countries, five United Nations bodies, the Asian Development Bank and OLADE, and some 45 observers, the Workshop made recommendations on such issues as the policy-planning methodologies of management and feasibility studies for SHP, promotion of local design and manufacturing of SHP equipment, cost reduction techniques, and advancement of SHP development in Africa through a network of experts in that field. UNIDO assisted in organizing a similar workshop at Hangzhou, China, in May/June. It also co-operated with OLADE in publishing a manual for decision makers on mini-hydropower stations. It continued its efforts to assist developing countries in manufacturing capital goods for the energy sector, through studies, expert group meetings and technical co-operation projects such as the regional Latin American project on design and manufacture of axial flow water turbines.

The question of providing the capital goods and other products necessary for energy generation, transmission and distribution was considered at a high-level expert group meeting on energy and industrialization (Oslo, Norway, 29 August–2 September).[19] One of five expert group meetings convened preparatory to the Fourth (1984) General Conference of UNIDO, the meeting was attended by 34 experts from 27 countries and seven observers from international organizations, as well as representatives of United Nations bodies, including UNIDO. Stressing the importance for countries of establishing their own energy capital goods industry, the meeting indicated ways of reaching that goal through such stages as the development of a repair and maintenance capacity for energy equipment and establishment of joint activities with manufacturers in developed countries.

The meeting identified other issues common to the various resource/technology combinations. It called for the creation of an information network to provide developing countries with detailed data on costs, performance specifications, experience in applications and manufactures, emphasized the significance of strategic planning in establishing an integrated national planning capability on a continuous basis, and stressed that social and environmental considerations should become an integral part of energy development strategies and programmes.

Addressing the problem of industrial energy management, the meeting adopted a number of recommendations for specific actions by developing countries, among them: extensive use of energy audits to improve energy savings; strengthening of energy institutions and creation of a scientific technological milieu favourable to the development of energy professionals; and launching of promotion and information campaigns and training programmes to enhance awareness of the benefits of energy savings.

The meeting also worked out a set of specific action-oriented proposals for UNIDO and other international organizations, including extended UNIDO assistance for the manufacture of capital goods and provision of services; extension of UNIDO's project feasibility services by establishing regional centres for project analysis, training and assistance in the preparation of project proposals; and initiating a mini-hydro development programme in Africa.

The meeting recommended that developing countries, with UNIDO assistance, launch a comprehensive—national and regional—energy conservation programme, and that they consider establishing their own corporate entity for that purpose. Industrial energy conservation received a new strong emphasis within UNIDO during 1983, resulting in the formulation of a large-scale regional project for developing countries in Europe and implementation of several small-scale national projects.

Following the reaffirmation in December 1982 by the General Assembly of the importance of new and renewable resources of energy,[20] UNIDO broadened the scope of its activities in this sphere. It participated in the first session of the Committee on the Development and Utilization of New and Renewable Sources of Energy in April 1983 (see below, under NON-CONVENTIONAL ENERGY SOURCES), and prepared specific proposals on upgrading charcoal and solar energy production technologies for industry, the use of industrial and urban waste for energy production, and industrial energy conservation. Nineteen of the projects approved by UNIDO and 47 of the project proposals were related to new and renewable energy sources. UNIDO also worked to improve co-ordination of activities and exchange of information among various agencies, in part making suggestions on the design of a focal point information unit set up within DIESA to deal specifically with multilateral, bilateral and other programmes on new and renewable sources of energy.

In an effort to expand further inter-agency co-operation on energy matters, UNIDO discussed the establishment of new joint committees with the Food and Agriculture Organization of the United Nations (FAO) and DTCD. At the intergovernmental level, UNIDO provided assistance to the Group of 77 for their Meetings on Technical Co-operation in Energy and on Energy Development, Supplies and Rationalization of Energy Consumption, held, respectively, in May and August 1983 at Vienna, Austria, and Bangkok, Thailand. Ways of advancing co-operation in energy training, energy data banks and energy modelling were examined within the framework of the "Vienna Energy Club" comprising members from the Government of Austria, IAEA, UNIDO, the International Institute for Applied Systems Analysis and the Organization of Petroleum Exporting Countries.

REFERENCES

[1]E/C.7/1983/10. [2]*World Economic Survey 1983: Current Trends and Policies in the World Economy* (E/1983/42), Sales No. E.83.II.C.1. [3]YUN 1982, p. 891. [4]E/1983/91 & Corr.1. [5]YUN 1982, p. 890, GA res. 37/251, 21 Dec. 1982. [6]UNCTAD/ST/ECDC/26. [7]DP/1984/5/Add.2. [8]A/39/5/Add.1. [9]YUN 1982, p. 889. [10]DP/1984/5/Add.1 (Part II). [11]E/1983/20 (dec. 83/23). [12]DP/1984/5/Add.6. [13]A/39/31. [14]E/1983/19. [15]A/38/363. [16]YUN 1982, p. 893. [17]ID/B/320. [18]ID/WG.403/33. [19]ID/WG.402/12 & Corr.1. [20]YUN 1982, p. 896, GA res. 37/250, 21 Dec. 1982.

PUBLICATION

Energy Balances 1977-1980 and Electricity Profiles 1976-1981 for Selected Developing Countries and Areas (ST/ESA/STAT/SER.W/1), Sales No. E.83.XVII.4.

Non-conventional energy sources

Implementation of the 1981 Nairobi Programme of Action

In 1983, the United Nations continued its efforts to implement the Nairobi Programme of Action for the Development and Utilization of New and Renewable Sources of Energy, endorsed by the General Assembly in 1981.[1] Most of the activities of various United Nations bodies aimed at implementing the Programme followed recommendations made by the Assembly in December 1982.[2]

As requested by the Assembly, the Secretary-General submitted a report[3] to the April 1983 session of the Committee on the Development and Utilization of New and Renewable Sources of Energy (see below) with proposals regarding guidelines on the preparation and holding of consultative meetings and ways of improving inter-agency co-ordination. With regard to mobilizing additional financial resources, the report pointed out that a number of ways had been envisaged to achieve this end, including establishing an energy affiliate within the World Bank; establishing a new voluntary financing mechanism for new and renewable energy sources; increasing contributions through existing channels; and enhancing private investment. It noted, however, that to formulate specific proposals, more precise information on flows of financial resources and on consultations with donors and recipients was required.

The Secretary General also reported to the Assembly[4] on the implementation of its 1982 resolution[2] concerning the Nairobi Programme of Action. The report summed up the Committee's work and described the steps made to improve secretariat arrangements and co-ordination within the United Nations system. It announced the appointment of a Special Co-ordinator for New and Renewable Sources of Energy in the Office of the Director-General for Development and International Economic Co-operation, and the establishment of a Unit for New and Renewable Sources of Energy in DIESA.

United Nations regional commissions were also involved in activities related to new and renewable energy sources. Among others, the Economic Commission for Europe held an *ad hoc* meeting in November 1983 to review the effects of budgetary restrictions and reduced oil prices and energy demand forecasts on the prospects of those sources.[5] The Economic Commission for Africa focused on technical co-operation activities and assistance to African Governments in the preparation of energy programmes and policies.[6]

Questions related to greater use of new and renewable energy sources in developing countries were considered in a report on the development of the energy resources of those countries, submitted to the Assembly in October as an annex to a note by the Secretary-General.[7] The report was presented in response to a December 1982 Assembly request[8] and supplemented a preliminary report submitted to the Economic and Social Council in June 1983 (see above, under ENERGY RESOURCES DEVELOPMENT). The Secretary-General provided information on the timing of application and investment costs of some 12 different new and renewable energy sources. Covering the near-, medium- and far-term prospects for utilization of modern energy resources, he analysed such solar energy technologies as photovoltaics, photoelectric cells and solar concentrators, and described a variety of biomass energy-producing methods like pyrolysis, anaerobic digestion of organic wastes and cultivation of plants for their energy value. He also examined the possibilities of wind energy systems, ocean thermal-energy conversion and liquid fuel production from oil shale and tar sands.

ACC activities. In accordance with a December 1982 Assembly resolution,[2] ACC established in 1983[9] an *ad hoc* Inter-Agency Group on New and Renewable Sources of Energy, to increase the United Nations responsiveness to the Nairobi Programme of Action and to improve co-ordination within the system. All interested United Nations bodies were invited to participate in the Group. ACC stressed that the Group's programme of work should be prepared in accordance with the recommendations of the Committee on the Development and Utilization of New and Renewable Sources of Energy and decided that the Group should meet as required and report to the Consultative Committee on Substantive Questions (Operational Activities or Programme Matters).

The Group held its first session in New York on 17 and 18 February 1983,[10] concentrating on preparations for the first session of the Committee on new and renewable sources of energy (see below). As a possible input to the Secretary-General's report to the Committee, the Group worked out guidelines for United Nations bodies on the preparation and convening of consultative meetings. It also proposed ways of mobilizing financial resources for new and renewable energy sources and of promoting inter-agency co-ordination. These issues, as well as the formulation and recommendation of action-oriented plans and programmes, were identified as the main areas for contribution by interested United Nations entities.

The Group's second session was held in New York on 19 and 28 April to consider the contributions of those entities to the first session of the Committee on new and renewable sources of energy, which was taking place at the same time, and to plan a co-ordinated follow-up to the Committee's recommendations. The resulting conclusions, which formed a part of the Group's report on its session,[11] stressed the importance of incorporating the May 1982 ACC proposals[12] in the work programmes of United Nations entities and urged mobilization of additional financial resources, *inter alia*, through consultative meetings at the global, regional, subregional and national levels. In the context of inter-agency co-operation, discussions were held on the modalities of operation of the Unit within DIESA set up in December 1982 as a focal point for information on activities concerning new and renewable sources of

energy. The Group made suggestions on formal reporting requirements, the input of the organizations of the system and ways to ensure wider dissemination of the collected information.

Activities of the Committee on new and renewable sources of energy. The Committee on the Development and Utilization of New and Renewable Sources of Energy, established by the General Assembly in December 1982[2] to promote implementation of the Nairobi Programme of Action, held its first session in New York from 18 to 29 April 1983. In its report on the session,[13] the Committee stated that the Programme of Action should be viewed as an integral part of international efforts to accelerate the development of developing countries in accordance with the 1980 International Development Strategy for the Third United Nations Development Decade,[14] and the declarations and resolutions related to the establishment of the new international economic order (see Chapter I of this section). Noting the gradual exhaustion of fossil fuel resources, the Committee called for strengthened commitments and efforts at all levels to implement the Programme of Action.

The Committee reiterated that the primary responsibility for promoting the development and utilization of new and renewable energy sources rested with individual countries. International co-operation, however, was indispensable and should be directed towards supporting national efforts. The developed countries bore a special responsibility for ensuring that both their bilateral and multilateral efforts contributed actively to that end.

With regard to action-oriented plans and programmes, the Committee recommended that the United Nations bodies prepare their detailed projects for immediate implementation based on proposals made in the May 1982 ACC report.[12] These projects were to be accompanied by accurate cost estimates, be consistent with national plans, and give particular attention to the least developed countries and other developing countries whose needs were greatest. The Committee proposed guidelines for the preparation of these projects, emphasizing such aspects as the use of standardized methodologies for resource evaluation, adaptability of energy technologies to local conditions and availability of technical options. The Committee invited UNDP and the World Bank to submit to its next session an updated joint study on the financial requirements for development and utilization of new and renewable sources of energy in developing countries during the 1980s.

In the Committee's view, there was an urgent need for sustained mobilization of financial resources which could be met, in part, by speedy implementation of the June 1982 recommendations of the Interim Committee on New and

Renewable Sources of Energy.[15] All countries were urged to provide adequate financial resources to the relevant United Nations entities, while additional resources should be directed, *inter alia*, through such channels as the general resources of UNDP and its Energy Account, the United Nations Financing System for Science and Technology for Development (see Chapter XII of this section), and the United Nations Revolving Fund for Natural Resources Exploration (see Chapter IX of this section). The consultative meetings were indicated as another effective mechanism for mobilizing additional financial resources. There was also a need for a substantial increase in capital investment and in net flow of non-concessional capital. Noting that the Secretary-General could not submit in his report[3] substantive proposals on ways of mobilizing finances, the Committee requested him to report on that issue at its second session.

The Committee also reaffirmed that interagency co-ordination was essential for effective implementation of the Nairobi Programme of Action and welcomed the organizational arrangements made to ensure greater efficiency of the co-operative effort.

UNDP action. By a decision of 24 June 1983,[16] as called for by the Committee on new and renewable sources of energy, the UNDP Governing Council recommended that developed countries and developing countries in a position to do so provide additional resources for pre-investment and technical assistance activities related to the development of new and renewable sources of energy in developing countries. UNDP's general resources and the Energy Account (see above, under ENERGY RESOURCES DEVELOPMENT) were suggested as possible channels for such support. The Council also invited UNDP to help in implementing the Nairobi Programme of Action and, in particular, to assist interested countries in arranging consultative meetings for consideration of projects and programmes and mobilization of finances.

ECONOMIC AND SOCIAL COUNCIL ACTION

On 25 July 1983, acting on the recommendation of its First Committee, the Economic and Social Council adopted without vote decision 1983/166.

Development and utilization of new and renewable sources of energy

At its 39th plenary meeting, on 25 July 1983, the Council took note of the report of the Committee on the Development and Utilization of New and Renewable Sources of Energy on its first session and decided to transmit it to the General Assembly at its thirty-eighth session for consideration.

Economic and Social Council decision 1983/166

Adopted without vote

Approved by First Committee (E/1983/113) without vote, 19 July (meeting 17); oral proposal by Chairman; agenda item 11.
Meeting number. ESC 39.

GENERAL ASSEMBLY ACTION

On the recommendation of the Second Committee, the General Assembly, on 19 December 1983, adopted without vote resolution 38/169.

Immediate implementation of the Nairobi Programme of Action for the Development and Utilization of New and Renewable Sources of Energy

The General Assembly,

Recalling its resolutions 3201(S-VI) and 3202(S-VI) of 1 May 1974, containing the Declaration and the Programme of Action on the Establishment of a New International Economic Order, 3281(XXIX) of 12 December 1974, containing the Charter of Economic Rights and Duties of States, and 3362(S-VII) of 16 September 1975 on development and international economic co-operation,

Recalling also its resolution 35/56 of 5 December 1980, the annex to which contains the International Development Strategy for the Third United Nations Development Decade,

Recalling further its resolution 36/193 of 17 December 1981, in which it endorsed the Nairobi Programme of Action for the Development and Utilization of New and Renewable Sources of Energy and, in particular, its resolution 37/250 of 21 December 1982 on the immediate implementation of the Nairobi Programme of Action,

Convinced of the importance of developing new and renewable sources of energy in order to contribute to meeting the requirements for continued economic and social development, particularly in the developing countries, through, *inter alia*, the transition from the present international economy based primarily on hydrocarbons to one based increasingly on new and renewable sources of energy,

Reaffirming that, while the primary responsibility for promoting the development and utilization of new and renewable sources of energy rests with individual countries, international co-operation is indispensable and should be directed to assisting and supporting the national efforts of developing countries, that developed countries should play a special role in contributing actively to this end and that other countries in a position to do so should also continue to promote efforts in this regard,

Aware that the present world energy situation should not reverse or halt the efforts of the international community to implement the Nairobi Programme of Action,

Recognizing the need to take urgent and concerted measures for the mobilization of additional and adequate resources necessary for the implementation of the Nairobi Programme of Action,

Recalling that specialized intergovernmental organizations and institutions in the field of new and renewable sources of energy are invited to extend their co-operation in order to strengthen the co-operative action of the international community and to ensure that further resources are made available for the development of new and renewable sources of energy, that national public and private entities in interested countries, as appropriate, have a role to play and that, in certain countries, non-governmental entities will also have a significant role to play,

Recognizing also that the United Nations system has initiated the necessary steps towards its full participation in and support of the implementation of the Nairobi Programme of Action and that it is imperative to increase the responsiveness of the system in this respect, through, *inter alia*, the provision of additional and adequate resources and increased co-ordination of the activities of the organs, organizations and bodies of the United Nations system,

Emphasizing the importance of the subregional, regional and interregional efforts for implementing the Nairobi Programme of Action,

Having considered the report of the Committee on the Development and Utilization of New and Renewable Sources of Energy on its first session, held at United Nations Headquarters from 18 to 29 April 1983,

I

Nairobi Programme of Action for the Development and Utilization of New and Renewable Sources of Energy

1. *Reaffirms* the significance and importance of the Nairobi Programme of Action for the Development and Utilization of New and Renewable Sources of Energy as the basic framework of reference for action by the international community and renews its call for the early and effective implementation of the Programme;

2. *Emphasizes* the importance of the areas for priority action designated in section III.A of the Nairobi Programme of Action and in section V.B of the report of the Committee on the Development and Utilization of New and Renewable Sources of Energy, and calls upon the Committee, at its second session, to make recommendations wherever urgent initiatives are required;

3. *Endorses* the recommendations contained in the report of the Committee on the Development and Utilization of New and Renewable Sources of Energy on its first session;

II

Action-oriented plans and programmes

1. *Reaffirms* that the report of the Administrative Committee on Co-ordination on proposals for action-oriented plans and programmes for carrying out the Nairobi Programme of Action provides a useful framework for agency and inter-agency follow-up to the Programme within the United Nations system; requests, in this connection, the relevant organs, organizations and bodies of the United Nations system to implement as appropriate the set of proposals contained in that report, taking into account the guidelines formulated by the Committee on the Development and Utilization of New and Renewable Sources of Energy at its first session; and calls upon the Administrative Committee on Co-ordination to continue to work in this field;

2. *Notes* that the Administrative Committee on Co-ordination, in its report, presents a useful framework to the international community for identifying, developing and implementing programmes and projects in areas of priority action;

3. *Reaffirms* the importance of international co-operation for the development and utilization of new and renewable sources of energy and stresses that such co-operation should be focused on developing the in-

digenous capabilities of developing countries in this field, using domestic resources to the maximum extent possible;

4. *Requests* the organs, organizations and bodies of the United Nations system to participate fully in and support the implementation of the Nairobi Programme of Action in the short-term, medium-term and long-term context, in particular for the benefit of developing countries in accordance with their national plans and priorities and, in this regard, calls upon relevant organizations of the United Nations system to consider and incorporate in their activities projects arising from the proposals and recommendations made by the Administrative Committee on Co-ordination;

5. *Also requests* the relevant organs, organizations and bodies of the United Nations system to support and assist, to a large extent, the efforts of developing countries for technical and economic co-operation among themselves in the field of new and renewable sources of energy;

III

Mobilization of financial resources

1. *Emphasizes* that the early implementation of the Nairobi Programme of Action requires the mobilization of additional and adequate resources and that each country will continue to bear the main responsibility for the development of its new and renewable sources of energy, which will require vigorous measures for a fuller mobilization of its domestic financial and other resources;

2. *Reaffirms* the importance of the mobilization of financial resources for the early implementation of the Nairobi Programme of Action and, to this end, calls for the urgent implementation of the measures for the mobilization of financial resources enumerated in paragraphs 76 to 95 of the Programme of Action and in paragraphs 75 to 83 of the report of the Committee on the Development and Utilization of New and Renewable Sources of Energy;

3. *Calls upon* all countries, particularly the developed countries and other countries in a position to do so, to provide additional and adequate financial resources to the relevant organs, organizations and bodies of the United Nations system;

4. *Calls* for the preparation and convening of consultative meetings at the national, subregional, regional, interregional and global levels, on a non-discriminatory basis and in accordance with paragraph 81 of the report of the Committee on the Development and Utilization of New and Renewable Sources of Energy;

5. *Requests* the Secretary-General to submit a report to the Committee on the Development and Utilization of New and Renewable Sources of Energy, at its second session, on the progress achieved since its first session in relation to consultative meetings, taking into account, in particular, their contribution to the finalization of and commitment to the programmes and projects aimed at the implementation of the Nairobi Programme of Action and to the mobilization of additional resources;

6. *Reaffirms*, in this context, that specific and additional resources should be directed through such channels as the United Nations Development Programme, the United Nations Revolving Fund for Natural Resources Exploration, the long-term financial arrangements for the United Nations Financing System for Science and Technology for Development, the United Nations Development Programme Energy Account and

others directly or indirectly involved, in accordance with national plans and priorities;

7. *Reiterates* the importance of an appropriate assessment of the financial resources required for the development of new and renewable sources of energy, particularly in the developing countries, and requests the United Nations Development Programme and the World Bank to continue to study this matter;

8. *Requests* the Secretary-General to present to the Committee on the Development and Utilization of New and Renewable Sources of Energy, at its second session, substantive proposals on further ways and means of mobilizing financial resources for new and renewable sources of energy, as requested in General Assembly resolution 37/250;

9. *Urges*, in this connection, all interested parties to accelerate consideration of other possible avenues that would increase financing in this field, including, *inter alia*, the mechanisms being examined by the World Bank, such as an energy affiliate, as stated in paragraph 94 of the Nairobi Programme of Action;

10. *Also requests* the Secretary-General to elicit the views of intergovernmental and non-governmental organizations as to how they can best co-operate in generating additional financial resources for the implementation of the Nairobi Programme of Action;

IV

Inter-agency co-ordination and Secretariat support arrangements

1. *Reaffirms* the importance of the role of the Director-General for Development and International Economic Co-operation in co-ordinating the activities and contributions of the organs, organizations and bodies of the United Nations system in connection with new and renewable sources of energy, including those related to consultative meetings at the national, regional and global levels;

2. *Welcomes* the secretariat arrangements already made and stresses the need for the full implementation of the decisions made in this regard by the General Assembly at its thirty-seventh session;

3. *Welcomes also*, in this regard, the establishment, in the unit on new and renewable sources of energy, of a focal point for information on multilateral, bilateral and other programmes in the field of new and renewable sources of energy and invites Member States and international organizations to facilitate its work by providing appropriate information.

General Assembly resolution 38/169

19 December 1983   Meeting 102   Adopted without vote

Approved by Second Committee (A/38/702/Add.10) without vote, 5 December (meeting 54); draft by Vice-Chairman (A/C.2/38/L.91), based on informal consultations on draft by Mexico, for Group of 77 (A/C.2/38/L.16); agenda item 78 (*l*).
Meeting numbers. GA 38th session: 2nd Committee 34, 54; plenary 102.

Apart from drafting changes, the adopted text differed from that put forward by the Group of 77. A new preambular paragraph was added emphasizing the importance of subregional, regional and interregional efforts for implementing the Nairobi Programme of Action. The Assembly emphasized, in a new paragraph, that early implementation of the Programme required the mobilization of additional and adequate resources,

with each country bearing the main responsibility for the development of its new and renewable energy sources. In addition, it noted that the May 1982 ACC proposals[12] for action-oriented plans and programmes presented a useful framework for developing programmes in areas of priority and stressed the need for the full implementation of the December 1982 Assembly decisions on secretariat arrangements.[2] The adopted version also contained specific references to section III.A on areas for priority action of the Programme of Action and section V.B on action-oriented plans and programmes of the report of the Committee on new and renewable sources of energy, which were absent in the Group of 77's draft. A paragraph calling for consultative meetings was reworded to include reference to paragraph 81 (on consultative meetings) of the Committee's report, rather than calling for financial and technical support by the international community.

Also on 19 December, the Assembly adopted resolution 38/151 reaffirming the significance and importance of the Programme of Action and urging Governments, United Nations entities, specialized intergovernmental agencies and institutions, as well as non-governmental organizations concerned with new and renewable sources of energy, to take effective action for its implementation.

Geothermal exploration

Following a June 1982 decision of the UNDP Governing Council,[17] exploration of geothermal energy became one of the important areas of activities for the United Nations Revolving Fund for Natural Resources Exploration.

In a report on the Fund's activities in 1983,[18] the UNDP Administrator noted that a comprehensive data base had been established as a result of more than 30 missions to 21 countries undertaken by the Fund since 1981 to review the status of high-enthalpy geothermal energy development. Installed capacity continued to grow, reaching an estimated 1,200 megawatts (MW) in nine countries by the end of 1983. There were 38 countries with established and probable high-enthalpy geothermal resources suitable for electricity production, and another 26 with indicated potential where reconnaissance work was in progress.

Project identification was a significant part of the Fund's activities in 1983. Initial evaluation was completed in 8 of the 10 countries which had targets ready for drilling large-diameter exploratory holes and had expressed interest in Fund financing. The most promising prospect appeared to be in Las Planillas, Mexico, with other project possibilities identified in the Philippines, Saint Lucia and Turkey. It was expected that production from a successful project could start within two to three years by means of inexpensive trailer-mounted 5-10 MW turbine-generator units.

The Fund established and maintained contacts, both technical and financial, with national laboratories and research organizations, international and regional banks and funding organizations, and co-operated actively with DTCD and the Energy Office of UNDP in pursuing the Nairobi Programme of Action (see above).

For its part, DTCD[19] was carrying out a major project in China, funded through cost-sharing arrangements by UNDP and Italy. The project involved the provision of training and equipment for production drilling as well as pre-feasibility work, including geological and geophysical investigation, reservoir engineering and assistance in dealing with corrosion problems. Another project, started by DTCD in 1983 in Kenya, focused on reconnaissance, with emphasis on exploratory drilling. Projects were also under implementation in Djibouti, Ethiopia, India, the Philippines, Romania and Thailand.[20]

REFERENCES

[1]YUN 1981, p. 691, GA res. 36/193, 17 Dec. 1981. [2]YUN 1982, p. 896, GA res. 37/250, 21 Dec. 1982. [3]A/AC.218/2. [4]A/38/240-E/1983/76. [5]E/ECE/1073. [6]E/1983/86/Add.1. [7]A/38/512. [8]YUN 1982, p. 890, GA res. 37/251, 21 Dec. 1982. [9]ACC/1983/DEC/1-10 (dec. 1983/4). [10]ACC/1983/PG/5. [11]ACC/1983/PG/6. [12]YUN 1982, p. 894. [13]A/38/44. [14]YUN 1980, p. 503, GA res. 35/56, annex, 5 Dec. 1980. [15]YUN 1982, p. 895. [16]E/1983/20 (dec. 83/23). [17]YUN 1982, p. 901. [18]DP/1984/45. [19]DP/1984/42. [20]DP/1984/42/Add.1.

PUBLICATION

A Guide to Ocean Thermal Energy Conversion for Developing Countries (ST/ESA/134), Sales No. E.83.II.A.21.

Nuclear energy

Most of the United Nations technical work in nuclear energy was carried out by IAEA (for information on IAEA activities in 1983, see PART II, Chapter I). After reviewing the IAEA report for 1982, the General Assembly, in November 1983, urged all States to co-operate in IAEA work and to implement strictly its statute in promoting the use of nuclear energy and the application of nuclear science and technology for peaceful purposes. The Assembly also considered the report of the Preparatory Committee for the United Nations Conference for the Promotion of International Co-operation in the Peaceful Uses of Nuclear Energy, which held its fourth session in 1983. Since the Committee was unable to reach agreement on an agenda or rules of procedure, it decided to recommend to the Assembly not to convene the Conference in 1983. In December, the Assembly requested the Committee to submit a report in 1984, in the light of which it would consider the venue and actual dates for the Conference in 1986.

Nuclear disarmament and nuclear power sources in outer space were dealt with in several other resolutions adopted by the Assembly in 1983 (see POLITICAL AND SECURITY QUESTIONS, Chapters I and II). In his October report to the Assembly on the development of the energy resources of the developing countries (see above, under ENERGY RESOURCES DEVELOPMENT), the Secretary-General also submitted his findings[1] as to nuclear power investment requirements in developing countries where, by the end of 1982, there were nine nuclear power plants in operation and another 19 units under construction. The share of nuclear power in total electricity production in the developing countries was projected to be less than 10 per cent at the end of the century, its rapid growth hindered by such obstacles as the comparatively small size of electricity grids and the array of technical skills required for safe operation of nuclear facilities. Also according to World Bank projections, the investment requirements of developing countries in the nuclear power sector over the 1982-1992 period amounted to $53.1 billion (1982 dollars), or about 8 per cent of their investment requirements in the electric power sector as a whole.

IAEA report

The report of IAEA for 1982 was transmitted to the 1983 General Assembly session by the Secretary-General on 30 August.[2]

Introducing the report to the Assembly on 4 November and updating the information it contained, the IAEA Director General singled out several developments of particular significance for the Agency's efforts in promoting the peaceful uses of nuclear energy and preventing the further proliferation of nuclear weapons. Among such events in 1983 were the resumption in February of United States participation in the Agency's activities; an International Conference on Radioactive Waste Management, held at Seattle, United States, in May; progress at IAEA negotiations with the USSR on that country's offer to submit some of its peaceful nuclear installations to Agency safeguards; and, finally, approval by the IAEA General Conference in October of China's application for membership of the Agency.

In the area of electricity production, the Director General noted a slow but steady progress, with the number of operating reactors in the world passing 300 early in 1983 and continuing to grow. The share of nuclear reactors in world electricity production accounted for about 10 per cent in 1983 and was estimated to reach 20 per cent by 1990, despite the continuing trend in some countries to constrain their plans for construction of nuclear power facilities.

While in several developed countries production of electricity by nuclear power increased to over 30 per cent, the use of nuclear energy in developing countries was hindered by the fact that their electricity demands and grids were too limited for commercially available large nuclear reactors. In its search for a solution to the problem, IAEA initiated a study of small and medium-sized power units.

With regard to safety, the Director General stated that the total radiological impact of the nuclear industry showed a consistent decrease in terms of collective doses per unit of energy generated. To promote nuclear safety further, IAEA had set up operational safety review teams to assist national regulatory bodies in maintaining the required standards and was seeking to establish a world-wide incident reporting system.

Recognizing that practical application of nuclear techniques in such fields as agriculture, medicine and industry was of more immediate importance to the majority of IAEA member States than nuclear power as a source of electricity, the Agency actively promoted these applications through its technical co-operation and assistance programme. With regard to food preservation by radiation processing, for example, the Director General reported that a significant step was made in July when the Codex Alimentarius Commission, a joint body of the World Health Organization and FAO, adopted a revised International Code of Practice for the Operation of Radiation Facilities for the Treatment of Food. Useful results which could lead to large-scale practical application were also achieved in pest eradication and animal husbandry. IAEA joint ventures with other United Nations organizations yielded promising results in medicine, agriculture, energy planning and environment protection, underscoring the need for broader inter-agency co-operation.

Describing activities related to international security, the Director General informed the Assembly that in 1982 IAEA did not detect any diversion of safeguarded nuclear material. He also reported that in 1983 the technical measures necessary to perform fully adequate verification in two cases about which the Agency had had a reservation in 1981 were agreed on and implemented. Stressing the importance of the safeguards system, the Director General called for its further expansion and continued efforts to improve efficiency and cost-effectiveness. Another security-related area in which IAEA had a great responsibility was non-proliferation of nuclear weapons and other disarmament issues (see POLITICAL AND SECU-

RITY QUESTIONS, Chapter I). For example, at the invitation of the Secretary-General, it was taking part in a new study on nuclear-weapon-free zones.

Of vital importance to nuclear security was the problem of attacks on nuclear installations. The IAEA General Conference in October 1983 had called for early conclusion of an international agreement to prohibit attacks such as the 1981 bombing by Israeli aircraft of a nuclear research centre near Baghdad, Iraq (see POLITICAL AND SECURITY QUESTIONS, Chapter IX). It also had urged all member States to work towards the adoption of binding international rules prohibiting armed attacks against any nuclear installation devoted to peaceful purposes (see PART II, Chapter I). The Director General drew attention to Additional Protocol I of 1977 (related to the protection of victims of international armed conflicts) to the Geneva Conventions of 12 August 1949 for the protection of war victims. Protocol I already contained an article prohibiting attacks on nuclear electricity-generating stations, and its early ratification, in the Director General's view, would be conducive to achieving the protection needed in this field.

With regard to South Africa's nuclear capability, the Director General reported that the General Conference in October had demanded that South Africa submit all its nuclear installations and facilities to Agency safeguards. It had also requested the IAEA Board of Governors and the Director General to consider implementing the Assembly's December 1982 request[3] to exclude South Africa from the Agency's technical working groups.

GENERAL ASSEMBLY ACTION

On 4 November 1983, the General Assembly adopted resolution 38/8 without vote.

Report of the International Atomic Energy Agency

The General Assembly,

Having received the report of the International Atomic Energy Agency to the General Assembly for the year 1982,

Taking note of the statement by the Director General of the International Atomic Energy Agency of 4 November 1983, which provides additional information on developments in the Agency's activities during 1983,

Recognizing the importance of the work of and the relevance for the International Atomic Energy Agency to promote further the application of nuclear energy for peaceful purposes, as envisaged in its statute, and to improve further its technical assistance and promotional programmes for the benefit of developing countries,

Conscious of the importance of the work of the International Atomic Energy Agency in the implementation of the safeguards provisions of the Treaty on the Non-Proliferation of Nuclear Weapons and other international treaties, conventions and agreements designed to achieve similar objectives, as well as ensuring, as far as it is able, that the assistance provided by the Agency or at its request or under its supervision or control is not used in such a way as to further any military purpose, as stated in article II of its statute,

Welcoming the decision of the General Conference of the International Atomic Energy Agency of 11 October 1983 to grant membership of the Agency to the People's Republic of China,

Conscious of the useful outcome of the International Conference on Radioactive Waste Management, held at Seattle, United States of America, from 16 to 20 May 1983 by the International Atomic Energy Agency,

Recognizing the importance of the work of the International Atomic Energy Agency on nuclear safety, which increases public confidence in nuclear power,

Bearing in mind resolutions GC(XXVII)/RES/407, GC(XXVII)/RES/408, GC(XXVII)/RES/409 and GC(XXVII)/RES/415, adopted on 14 October 1983 by the General Conference of the International Atomic Energy Agency at its twenty-seventh regular session,

1. *Takes note* of the report of the International Atomic Energy Agency;

2. *Urges* all States to strive for effective and harmonious international co-operation in carrying out the work of the International Atomic Energy Agency and to implement strictly the mandate of its statute in promoting the use of nuclear energy and the application of nuclear science and technology for peaceful purposes; in strengthening technical assistance and co-operation for developing countries; and in ensuring the effectiveness of the Agency's safeguards system;

3. *Expresses its satisfaction* at the prospect of mutual benefit arising from the membership of the People's Republic of China in the International Atomic Energy Agency;

4. *Affirms* its confidence in the role of the International Atomic Energy Agency in the application of nuclear energy for peaceful purposes;

5. *Requests* the Secretary-General to transmit to the Director General of the International Atomic Energy Agency the records of the thirty-eighth session of the General Assembly relating to the Agency's activities.

General Assembly resolution 38/8

4 November 1983   Meeting 46   Adopted without vote

3-nation draft (A/38/L.11); agenda item 14.
Sponsors: Belgium, Bulgaria, Mexico.
Meeting numbers. GA 38th session: plenary 45, 46.

The Assembly adopted a number of other resolutions that also concerned IAEA (for texts, refer to INDEX OF RESOLUTIONS AND DECISIONS). By resolution 38/39 A, it again requested IAEA to refrain from extending to South Africa facilities which might assist it in its nuclear plans and, in particular, to exclude South Africa from its technical working groups. In two other resolutions—38/181 A and B—the Assembly demanded again that South Africa submit its nuclear installations and facilities to inspection by IAEA. By resolution 38/64, it called on States in the Middle East that had not done so to agree to place their nuclear activities under IAEA safeguards. By resolution 38/69, the Assembly requested the Security Council to ensure that Israel placed its nuclear facilities under IAEA safeguards, as the Council had asked Israel to do in 1981,[4] and requested IAEA

to suspend any scientific co-operation with Israel which could contribute to its nuclear capabilities.

Preparations for the Conference on nuclear energy

Preparatory Committee activities. The Preparatory Committee for the United Nations Conference for the Promotion of International Co-operation in the Peaceful Uses of Nuclear Energy, established by the General Assembly in 1980,[5] held its fourth session in New York from 28 March to 8 April 1983 and reported its results to the first part of the Assembly's resumed thirty-seventh session in May.[6]

After intensive discussions during 11 formal and a number of informal group meetings, the Committee was unable, as at previous sessions, to agree on such basic matters as the content and substance of the agenda of the Conference, its rules of procedure and the preparatory work. In an effort to facilitate the task of negotiating outstanding issues, an informal open-ended contact group was set up, which regularly informed the Committee about the progress of its work. In its final statement on 8 April, the group listed 10 proposals made by delegations on the draft provisional agenda and noted several suggestions in respect of the decision-making process, concluding, however, that no agreement was reached.

The Committee recommended that the Assembly should decide not to convene the Conference in 1983 and that it should determine the date and venue of the Committee's fifth session. The Committee also decided that the Conference secretariat should proceed with the Conference preparations in accordance with the relevant Assembly resolutions. Annexed to the report were the Committee's decisions, statements of the Committee Chairman and the Secretary-General of the Conference at the opening of the session, and excerpts from the Political and Economic Declarations of the Seventh Conference of Heads of State or Government of Non-Aligned Countries, held at New Delhi, India, from 7 to 12 March 1983.

GENERAL ASSEMBLY ACTION

The General Assembly took up the question of the Conference on two occasions in 1983: in May when it resumed its thirty-seventh session with four items, including the Conference preparations, remaining from its 1982 agenda;[7] and in December at its thirty-eighth session.

On 10 May, the Assembly adopted without vote decision 37/453.

Arrangements for the United Nations Conference for the Promotion of International Co-operation in the Peaceful Uses of Nuclear Energy and the Preparatory Committee for the Conference

At its 116th plenary meeting, on 10 May 1983, the General Assembly, on the recommendations of the Preparatory

Committee for the United Nations Conference for the Promotion of International Co-operation in the Peaceful Uses of Nuclear Energy as set forth in its decision 5(IV) of 8 April 1983, decided:

(*a*)   Not to convene the United Nations Conference for the Promotion of International Co-operation in the Peaceful Uses of Nuclear Energy in 1983;

(*b*)   To take a decision at its thirty-eighth session on the date and venue of the fifth session of the Preparatory Committee for the Conference.

General Assembly decision 37/453

Adopted without vote

Adopted by Preparatory Committee (A/37/48/Add.1), 8 April; agenda item 27. *Meeting number.* GA 37th session: plenary 116.

Also on 10 May and again without vote, the Assembly adopted decision 37/454.

Preparations for the United Nations Conference for the Promotion of International Co-operation in the Peaceful Uses of Nuclear Energy

At its 116th plenary meeting, on 10 May 1983, the General Assembly took note of decision 6(IV) of 8 April 1983, by which the Preparatory Committee for the United Nations Conference for the Promotion of International Co-operation in the Peaceful Uses of Nuclear Energy had decided that the Conference secretariat should proceed as far as practicable with the preparations for the Conference in accordance with the relevant resolutions of the Assembly.

General Assembly decision 37/454

Adopted without vote

Adopted by Preparatory Committee (A/37/48/Add.1), 8 April; agenda item 27. *Meeting number.* GA 37th session: plenary 116.

On 14 December, the Assembly adopted without vote resolution 38/60.

United Nations Conference for the Promotion of International Co-operation in the Peaceful Uses of Nuclear Energy

The General Assembly,

Reaffirming its resolution 32/50 of 8 December 1977,

Recalling its other resolutions regarding the United Nations Conference for the Promotion of International Co-operation in the Peaceful Uses of Nuclear Energy,

Noting the work carried out so far by the Preparatory Committee for the United Nations Conference for the Promotion of International Co-operation in the Peaceful Uses of Nuclear Energy,

1.   *Decides* that the United Nations Conference for the Promotion of International Co-operation in the Peaceful Uses of Nuclear Energy shall be held in 1986;

2.   *Requests* the Chairman of the Preparatory Committee for the United Nations Conference for the Promotion of International Co-operation in the Peaceful Uses of Nuclear Energy and the Secretary-General of the Conference to undertake immediately appropriate consultations with Member States which could facilitate the resolution of pending issues relating to the Conference, including its provisional agenda and rules of procedure, as well as to the venue and the actual dates of the Conference, and to report thereon to the Preparatory Committee at its fifth session, and decides that the expenses incurred in this regard will be covered from existing budgetary resources;

3.   *Notes with appreciation* that the Conference secretariat is proceeding with the preparations for the Conference and requests the Secretary-General of the Conference to continue those preparations;

4.   *Also decides* that the Preparatory Committee will hold its fifth session at Vienna in June 1984, for a period of up to two weeks, in order to complete its work on an agreed agenda as well as on other outstanding issues related to the Conference;

5.   *Requests* the Preparatory Committee to submit a report to the General Assembly at its thirty-ninth session so that the Assembly may consider, in the light of this report, the venue and actual dates for the Conference in 1986, as also for further meetings of the Committee;

6.   *Urges* the International Atomic Energy Agency, as well as the specialized agencies and other relevant organizations of the United Nations system, to continue to contribute effectively to the preparations for the Conference so as to achieve meaningful results from the Conference, in accordance with the objectives of General Assembly resolution 32/50;

7.   *Urges* all States to co-operate actively in the preparation of the Conference;

8.   *Decides* to include in the provisional agenda of its thirty-ninth session the item entitled "United Nations Conference for the Promotion of International Co-operation in the Peaceful Uses of Nuclear Energy".

General Assembly resolution 38/60

14 December 1983   Meeting 96   Adopted without vote

3-nation draft (A/38/L.35); agenda item 35.
Sponsors: Czechoslovakia, Greece, Mexico.
Financial implications. ACABQ, A/38/7/Add.18; 5th Committee, A/38/734; S-G, A/C.5/38/78 & Corr.1.
Meeting numbers. GA 38th session: 5th Committee 63; plenary 96.

REFERENCES

[1]A/38/512. [2]A/38/346 & Corr.1. [3]YUN 1982, p. 262, GA res. 37/69 A, 9 Dec. 1982. [4]YUN 1981, p. 282, SC res. 487(1981), 19 June 1981. [5]YUN 1980, p. 164, GA res. 35/112, 5 Dec. 1980. [6]A/37/48/Add.1. [7]YUN 1982, p. 583, GA dec. 37/452, 21 Dec. 1982.

Chapter XI

Food

In a year plagued by the continuing uncertainty of the world food economy and chronic hunger and malnutrition in many developing countries, various United Nations bodies stepped up their food-related activities in three main directions: providing emergency aid, rendering development assistance and working to identify priorities and devise policies for solving major food problems in different parts of the world.

The World Food Council (WFC) proposed a number of national and international measures to combat hunger, improve agricultural production, stocking and distribution in developing countries, and upgrade world trade and market stability. These recommendations were welcomed in resolutions of the Economic and Social Council (resolution 1983/71) and the General Assembly (resolution 38/158), which called for urgent action by the international community to improve the world food situation.

While WFC formulated strategies for solving food problems, the World Food Programme (WFP) concentrated on supplying food to those suffering from natural and man-made disasters, and providing financial and technical assistance to developing countries to achieve their national food objectives. Entering its twentieth year of existence, WFP reached its highest level of development and emergency commitments in 1983, with shipments of food exceeding 1.5 million metric tons.

The General Assembly, in December 1983, established a new $1.35 billion pledging target for the Programme's regular resources for the 1985-1986 biennium (resolution 38/176). It acted on the recommendations of the Committee on Food Aid Policies and Programmes (CFA), the governing body of WFP, submitted through the Economic and Social Council (resolution 1983/73). The problem of improving co-ordination of United Nations activities with regard to food and agriculture was addressed by the Economic and Social Council in resolution 1983/77.

Topics related to this chapter. Regional economic and social activities: Africa—food and agriculture. Health and human resources—nutrition. Children—nutrition. Human rights—right to food.

Food problems

World Food Council activities. The ninth ministerial session of WFC was held at United Nations Headquarters from 27 to 30 June 1983,[1] preceded by a preparatory meeting at Rome, Italy, from 10 to 13 May. The 36-member Council—the world's highest-level body dealing solely with food problems—reaffirmed that peace and disarmament were prerequisite to enhanced food security, that food was a universal human right and that it should not be used as an instrument of political pressure. The Council expressed concern over the adverse effect of the world-wide economic recession on the food situation in developing countries. It described ample food supplies in the developed regions as an important resource for helping to eradicate hunger in the food-deficit regions and acknowledged the significance of a mutually reinforcing integration of food aid among the developed and developing countries. The Council also adopted conclusions and recommendations on food trends, strategies and priorities in developing regions, and on food security and trade issues.

While focusing on regional food policies peculiar to Africa, Asia, Latin America and the Caribbean, WFC identified areas of common concern for the developing countries. To combat increasing rural poverty and undernourishment of the population, it called for a greater emphasis on the smallholder traditional farm sector, particularly the role of farm women in the rural family, and reiterated its support for the recommendations of the 1979 World Conference on Agrarian Reform and Rural Development.[2] With regard to low-income, food-deficit countries, WFC reaffirmed the significance of increased food production and said the efforts of the International Development Association, the regional development banks and the International Fund for Agricultural Development (IFAD) were essential in helping the developing countries meet their food objectives. In view of the need for a comprehensive approach to the food problem, WFC reaffirmed its role as a centre for co-ordinating activities of various agencies and expressed satisfaction with the increased technical and economic co-operation among the developing countries.

Reviewing the food situation in Africa, WFC noted growing food deficits, and that racism and neo-colonialism were compounding food problems, especially in the developing countries of southern Africa. It also drew attention to serious outbreaks of livestock-threatening rinderpest. Faced with the challenge to push food production ahead of population growth, African countries needed additional urgent aid from the international community; WFC urged the community to respond generously to appeals. The Council reported that, in an effort to alleviate food deficits, some 30 countries were engaged in policy reform within the framework of the 1980 Lagos Plan of Action for the Implementation of the Monrovia Strategy for the Economic Development of Africa[3]—a plan based on collective self-reliance and self-sustainment. WFC welcomed widespread adoption of food strategies and supported the May 1983 conclusions of the Committee on World Food Security of the Food and Agriculture Organization of the United Nations (FAO) regarding food production constraints in food-deficit countries. In order to increase effectiveness of aid to the African countries, WFC proposed a number of policy adjustments by assistance agencies in such areas as allocation and continuity of aid, integration of food and other aid within the framework of national food strategies, and training, research and institutional development.

Addressing the situation in Asia, WFC stressed that, despite significant gains in production, food remained a top priority concern for most countries, with an estimated 300 million to 500 million people endemically undernourished. It endorsed a number of recommendations urging improvements in such areas as organization and management, utilization of agricultural production potentials, action-oriented research, productivity of smallholders, irrigation, employment of landless workers, family planning programmes and food programmes for vulnerable groups.

Serious economic and political considerations prompted WFC to accord high priority to the food sector in Latin America and the Caribbean, where one third of the population lived in poverty and some 50 million people suffered from malnutrition. Endorsing policy recommendations for the region, WFC stressed that national macro-economic policies should be coherent with food priorities of the national development plans. It also called for increased productivity in the food sector and in the food processing and distribution chains, and urged the improvement of marketing systems. With regard to externally financed projects, WFC stressed the importance of their social component and recommended that international finance institutions contributing to regional food development should increase overall sectoral loans.

Focusing on world food security and trade issues, the Council called for increased international political support for actions aimed at eliminating hunger. It expressed concern over the excessive concentration of food grain supplies in North America and an adverse impact that a rapid depletion of world stocks could have on the balance-of-payments position of developing countries. Two lines of action to attain greater food security emerged from the Council's deliberations. First, WFC urged full utilization of the existing instruments of food security such as the International Emergency Food Reserve, the Food Aid Convention and WFP (see below, under FOOD AID). Secondly, it stressed that improved food production, storage, marketing and distribution were the central objectives of developing countries' national food strategies. WFC also reviewed reports of CFA and the FAO Committee on World Food Security, welcoming the high amounts of pledges to WFP (see below) and the adoption by the FAO Committee of a new integrated concept of food security (see PART TWO, Chapter III).

The Council also reaffirmed its 1982 decision to prepare in 1984 an assessment on progress in meeting the objectives of the 1974 World Food Conference[4] and the priority tasks for the period ahead. In addition, it requested its Executive Director to prepare, in co-operation with United Nations entities and other governmental and non-governmental organizations involved in food issues, a report on progress in improving the world food situation since the 1974 Conference.

The Council's conclusions and recommendations were reiterated by the WFC Executive Director in his statement to the General Assembly's Second (Economic and Financial) Committee on 28 October 1983. Expressing concern over the structural imbalance in the world food economy, he stressed that food strategies should be placed in the context of the development process, with national efforts being the key to a secure future.

ECONOMIC AND SOCIAL COUNCIL ACTION

On 29 July, on the recommendation of its First (Economic) Committee, the Economic and Social Council adopted resolution 1983/71 without vote.

Food problems
The Economic and Social Council,
Recalling the Declaration and the Programme of Action on the Establishment of a New International Economic Order, contained in General Assembly resolutions 3201(S-VI) and 3202(S-VI) of 1 May 1974, the Charter of Economic Rights and Duties of States, contained in Assembly resolution 3281(XXIX) of 12 December 1974, Assembly resolution 3362(S-VII) of 16 September 1975 on development and international economic co-operation, and the International Development Strategy for the Third United Nations Development Decade, contained in Assembly resolution 35/56 of 5 December 1980,

Recalling the Universal Declaration on the Eradication of Hunger and Malnutrition, as adopted by the World Food Conference, and the Programme of Action adopted by the World Conference on Agrarian Reform and Rural Development,

Reaffirming General Assembly resolutions 37/245 on the situation of food and agriculture in Africa, 37/246 on an international year for the mobilization of financial and technological resources for food and agriculture in Africa, and 37/247 on food problems, all of 21 December 1982,

Recognizing the need for keeping food and agriculture issues at the centre of the global agenda,

Concerned that the achievement of the food and agriculture objectives of the developing countries is being severely constrained by the world-wide economic recession and political environment and that those countries are faced with depressed prices in commodity markets, sluggish demand, restricted access to markets, declining concessional flows in real terms and protectionist policies, coupled with the obligations of servicing a large international debt, and with monetary market instability,

Expressing its deep concern at the fact that a substantial part of world resources, material as well as human, continues to be diverted to armaments, which has a detrimental effect on international security and on efforts to achieve the new international economic order, including the solution of food problems, and calling upon Governments to take effective measures in the field of real disarmament that would increase the possibilities of the allocation of the resources now being used for military purposes to economic and social development, especially the development of developing countries, and to improving their food situation,

Emphasizing that food objectives should be pursued within the framework of national food strategies, plans and programmes and that food self-reliance is an essential element of national sovereignty and of political and social policy, that food security should be based, to the maximum extent feasible, on a vigorous domestic food sector and that, consequently, the development of the food sector should be recognized as a dynamic element in the economic development of the developing countries,

Emphasizing the need to adopt, according to priorities identified in the field of food and agriculture, comprehensive national and international measures, with a view to achieving the aims and objectives of the International Development Strategy for the Third United Nations Development Decade concerning the promotion of food and agricultural development in the developing countries,

Recognizing that a substantial increase in the export earnings of developing countries is essential for the adequate financing of their overall economic development, and even for that of their imports of food and agricultural inputs,

Noting the need for all countries, particularly the developed countries, to adopt policies designed to bring about the reduction and elimination of obstacles, in order to avoid the disruption of international trade in agricultural products and to facilitate access to international markets for agricultural exports, especially those of developing countries,

Noting with concern the continuing hunger and malnutrition in many developing countries, especially in Africa and in the least developed countries,

Concerned about the anomaly of large crops and stock accumulation in some developed countries, while many developing countries are facing problems of growing food deficits and hunger,

Stressing that measures taken by certain developed countries to reduce future food and agricultural production should not adversely affect the food problems faced by developing countries,

Further concerned about the uncertainty in the world food economy and the risks of an unstable supply and price situation in the international grain market,

Calling for progressive increases in grain production in developing countries to achieve a better balance in the production and distribution of global stocks,

1. *Welcomes* the conclusions and recommendations of the World Food Council at its ninth ministerial session, in particular those relating to the regions of Africa, Asia and Latin America;

2. *Welcomes* the eighth annual report of the Committee on Food Aid Policies and Programmes;

3. *Emphasizes* the need to consider the food problem in a comprehensive manner, in its technical, economic, commercial, financial and human dimensions;

4. *Reaffirms* that the right to food is a universal human right and that food should not be used as an instrument of political pressure;

5. *Expresses its concern* at the application of economic measures against some developing countries, and urges that those measures be revoked as soon as possible and not be repeated in the future;

6. *Affirms* that peace and disarmament are conducive to improved economic conditions and enhanced food security;

7. *Notes with satisfaction* that integrated national food strategies, plans and programmes, and the comprehensive food security concept are largely accepted by countries and development agencies;

8. *Endorses* the decision of the World Food Council to welcome the adoption by the Committee on World Food Security of the Food and Agriculture Organization of the United Nations of the enlarged and integrated concept of world food security, focusing on the adequacy of food supplies and production, stability in food supplies and markets, and security of access to supplies, and calls for its widest possible implementation by the international community;

9. *Reaffirms* that national food strategies, plans and programmes should play a central role in the process of establishing priorities, in co-ordinating national and international funding and the application of technology, promoting food production and increasing the national food self-reliance of the developing countries;

10. *Emphasizes* the role of women on the farm as part of the rural family, calls for more attention in matters of policy to the role of women in relation to food systems, and stresses the need to involve women in the formulation and implementation of national food strategies, plans and programmes;

11. *Underlines* the role of developing countries in the formulation and implementation of national food and agricultural policies and programmes and the importance of international support measures, including the mobilization of necessary financial resources;

12. *Calls upon* the developed countries, international institutions and others able to furnish development assistance to provide urgently the necessary technical and financial resources to support the efforts of developing countries to achieve the national food objectives that those

countries have themselves defined for the eradication of hunger and malnutrition;

13. *Reaffirms* that increased food production is one of the most important elements in meeting the food needs of the developing countries;

14. *Invites* Governments concerned to adopt direct hunger-reduction measures integrated with productive development within the framework of national strategies and policies, including more assistance to rural development to reach smallholder producers and co-operatives, special attention to the needs of women farmers, investment in human capacities through programmes for mothers and children, the creation of productive employment for poor landless families and an increase in food aid;

15. *Expresses its concern* at the expanding food-import requirements of the developing countries, particularly the least developed, which underlines the gravity of the problem and the importance of food aid both as a temporary relief measure and as a resource for food and agricultural development;

16. *Urges* that, in the implementation of food aid policies and programmes, a greater volume of food and agricultural products be acquired from food-exporting developing countries, where appropriate, including acquisition through triangular transactions;

17. *Calls* for adequate and continuous flows of resources for the World Bank, the International Fund for Agricultural Development and the regional development banks, whose work in food and agricultural development is important and effective in providing to the developing countries, in particular the least developed, additional development assistance to implement more effective incentives and programmes directed towards increasing food production and towards raising nutritional standards;

18. *Stresses* the need for substantial and timely replenishments for the International Development Association, to enable it to increase its assistance to all its recipient countries in the development of food and agriculture;

19. *Calls upon* the competent entities of the United Nations system to accord priority support to economic and technical co-operation among developing countries in food and agriculture;

20. *Emphasizes* the importance of research and exchange of information on scientific research and technological progress for the purposes of the development of food production, and calls upon the international community to provide to the developing countries increased financial and technical assistance in the area of agricultural research and to take appropriate measures to promote the transfer of technology in regard to the improvement of farming methods, including support to activities in these areas relating to technical co-operation among developing countries;

21. *Calls upon* the international community to provide continuing and increasing support towards improving global food security and towards the elimination of hunger and malnutrition;

22. *Recognizes* that the expansion of exports, particularly from developing countries is an important element of food security, and calls for additional measures by developed countries to liberalize agricultural trade;

23. *Calls* for improved international co-operation on the part of countries exporting and importing cereals, in respect of their food trade, production and stocking policies, in order, *inter alia*, to avoid instability in the international cereals market adversely affecting developing countries;

24. *Urges* all Governments concerned to consider, within the International Wheat Council at its next session, the early resumption of the United Nations Conference to Negotiate an International Arrangement to Replace the International Wheat Agreement, 1971, as extended, in order to conclude as soon as possible a new agreement that will contribute to the efficient operation of the international wheat market, taking into account the interests of developing countries;

25. *Calls upon* the international community to support, through the mobilization of financial and other resources, the efforts of developing countries to strengthen their stocking programmes in cases where those countries have expressed the need to build food reserves;

26. *Expresses the urgent need* to find multilateral solutions to the problems of trade, access, competition and supply relating to agricultural products, and calls upon the institutions concerned to find appropriate solutions, taking particularly into account the special needs and circumstances of developing countries;

27. *Endorses* the new target approved by the Committee on Food Aid Policies and Programmes for the biennium 1985-1986 of $1.35 billion for the regular resources of the World Food Programme, and calls upon traditionally and newly contributing countries to ensure its timely achievement;

28. *Supports* the appeal launched by the Food and Agriculture Organization of the United Nations in favour of the African countries threatened by food shortages, and urges the international community to respond generously to that appeal, in particular by increasing on an emergency basis its assistance in food aid and agricultural inputs;

29. *Takes note* of the progress made in the implementation of the Programme of Action as adopted by the World Conference on Agrarian Reform and Rural Development, and looks forward to the comprehensive review to be submitted to the Economic and Social Council in 1984 on progress in agrarian reform and rural development;

30. *Calls upon* the Governments concerned to implement agrarian reform and rural development within the framework of their national plans and objectives and in accordance with the recommendations, as adopted, of the World Conference on Agrarian Reform and Rural Development;

31. *Supports* the establishment of regional mechanisms to reduce food vulnerability, malnutrition and under-nutrition and, in this context, welcomes the recent establishment of the Action Committee for Regional Food Security;

32. *Stresses* the importance of fisheries development for the expansion of food supplies and nutritional improvements, and endorses the initiative by the Food and Agriculture Organization of the United Nations to convene in 1984 a World Conference on Fisheries Management and Development;

33. *Emphasizes* the importance of stock breeding and fisheries development in the food strategies, plans and programmes of developing countries, and calls upon the international community to continue to provide com-

petent international bodies with the necessary resources for the completion of studies in those areas, in order to increase their contribution to the development of the food and agriculture sector;

34. *Takes note with satisfaction* of the preparation by the World Food Council, for its tenth session in 1984, of a special assessment of progress made and the tasks ahead in meeting the objectives of the 1974 World Food Conference;

35. *Urges* the World Food Council, within the context of its mandate, to mobilize and sustain greater efforts in the struggle to overcome hunger, to continue to review and report on major problems and policy issues, and to continue to serve as a co-ordinating mechanism in the field of food and other related policy matters within the United Nations system.

Economic and Social Council resolution 1983/71

29 July 1983	Meeting 41	Adopted without vote

Approved by First Committee (E/1983/124) without vote, 27 July (meeting 25); draft by Vice-Chairman (E/1983/C.1/L.32), based on informal consultations on draft by Bangladesh, for Group of 77 (E/1983/C.1/L.17); agenda item 16.
Meeting number. ESC 41.

The adopted text differed from the draft submitted by the Group of 77 in that the sixth and tenth preambular paragraphs were added, as were operative paragraphs 10, 11, 14, 30 and 34. Also, part of a preambular paragraph in the Group's draft—by which the Council would have expressed concern about the announced intentions of certain developed countries to reduce food production despite the developing countries' food problems—was edited to form the thirteenth preambular paragraph.

On 27 May, the Council, in decision 1983/140, authorized the Sub-Commission on Prevention of Discrimination and Protection of Minorities of the Commission on Human Rights to prepare a study on the right to adequate food as a human right.

GENERAL ASSEMBLY ACTION

On 19 December, on the recommendation of its Second Committee, the General Assembly adopted resolution 38/158 without vote.

Food problems

The General Assembly,

Recalling the Declaration and the Programme of Action on the Establishment of a New International Economic Order, contained in its resolutions 3201(S-VI) and 3202(S-VI) of 1 May 1974, the Charter of Economic Rights and Duties of States, contained in its resolution 3281(XXIX) of 12 December 1974, its resolution 3362(S-VII) of 16 September 1975 on development and international economic co-operation, and the International Development Strategy for the Third United Nations Development Decade, contained in the annex to its resolution 35/56 of 5 December 1980,

Recalling the Universal Declaration on the Eradication of Hunger and Malnutrition, as adopted by the World Food Conference, and the Programme of Action adopted by the World Conference on Agrarian Reform and Rural Development,

Reaffirming its resolutions 37/245 on the situation of food and agriculture in Africa, 37/246 on an international year for the mobilization of financial and technological resources for food and agriculture in Africa and 37/247 on food problems, of 21 December 1982,

Recognizing the need for keeping food and agriculture issues at the centre of the global agenda,

Concerned that the achievement of the food and agriculture objectives of developing countries is being severely constrained by the world-wide economic recession and political environment, and that those countries are faced with depressed prices in commodity markets, sluggish demand, restricted access to markets, declining concessional flows in real terms and protectionist policies, coupled with the obligations of servicing a large international debt and with monetary market instability,

Expressing its deep concern at the fact that a substantial part of world resources, material as well as human, continues to be diverted to armaments, which has a detrimental effect on international security and on efforts to achieve the new international economic order, including the solution of food problems, and calling upon Governments to take effective measures in the field of real disarmament that would increase the possibilities of the allocation of the resources now being used for military purposes to economic and social development, especially development of developing countries, and to improving their food situation,

Emphasizing that food objectives should be pursued within the framework of national food strategies, plans and programmes and that food self-reliance is an essential element of national sovereignty and of political and social policy, that food security should be based, to the maximum extent feasible, on a vigorous domestic food sector and that, consequently, the development of the food sector should be recognized as a dynamic element in the economic development of the developing countries,

Emphasizing the need to adopt, according to priorities identified in the field of food and agriculture, comprehensive national and international measures with a view to realizing the aims and objectives of the International Development Strategy for the Third United Nations Development Decade in the promotion of food and agricultural development in the developing countries,

Recognizing that a substantial increase in the export earnings of developing countries is essential for the adequate financing of their overall economic development, including even their imports of food and agricultural inputs,

Noting the need for all countries, particularly the developed countries, to adopt policies designed to bring about the reduction and elimination of obstacles in order to avoid the disruption of international trade in agricultural products and to facilitate access to international markets for agricultural exports, especially those of developing countries,

Noting with concern the continuing hunger and malnutrition in many developing countries, especially in Africa and in the least developed countries,

Concerned about the anomaly of large crops and stock accumulation in some developed countries while many developing countries are facing problems of growing food deficits and hunger,

Stressing that measures taken by certain developed countries to reduce future food and agricultural production should not adversely affect the food problems faced by developing countries,

Further concerned about the uncertainty in the world food economy and the risks of an unstable supply and price situation in the international grain market,

Calling for progressive increases in grain production in developing countries to achieve a better balance in the production and distribution of global stocks,

1.   *Welcomes* the conclusions and recommendations of the World Food Council at its ninth ministerial session, in particular those relating to the regions of Africa, Asia and Latin America;

2.   *Welcomes* the eighth annual report of the Committee on Food Aid Policies and Programmes;

3.   *Emphasizes* the need to consider the food problem in a comprehensive manner, in its technical, economic, commercial, financial and human dimensions;

4.   *Reaffirms* that the right to food is a universal human right and that food should not be used as an instrument of political pressure;

5.   *Expresses its concern* at the application of economic measures against some developing countries and urges that those measures be revoked as soon as possible and not be repeated in the future;

6.   *Affirms* that peace and disarmament are conducive to improved economic conditions and enhanced food security;

7.   *Notes with satisfaction* that integrated national food strategies, plans and programmes and the comprehensive food security concept are largely accepted by countries and development agencies;

8.   *Endorses* the decision of the World Food Council to welcome the adoption by the Committee on World Food Security of the Food and Agriculture Organization of the United Nations of the enlarged and integrated concept of world food security, focusing on the adequacy of food supplies and production, stability in food supplies and markets, and security of access to supplies, and calls for its widest possible implementation by the international community;

9.   *Reaffirms* that national food strategies, plans and programmes should play a central role in the process of establishing priorities, in co-ordinating national and international funding and the application of technology, promoting food production and increasing the national food self-reliance of the developing countries;

10.   *Emphasizes* the role of farm women as part of the rural family, calls for more policy attention to the role of women in relation to food systems, and stresses the need to involve women in the formulation and implementation of national food strategies, plans and programmes;

11.   *Underlines* the role of developing countries in the formulation and implementation of national food and agricultural policies and programmes and the importance of international support measures, including the mobilization of necessary financial resources;

12.   *Calls upon* the developed countries, international institutions and others able to provide development assistance to provide urgently the necessary technical and financial resources to support the efforts of developing countries to achieve self-defined national food objectives for the eradication of hunger and malnutrition;

13.   *Reaffirms* that increased food production is one of the most important elements in meeting the food needs of the developing countries;

14.   *Invites* Governments concerned to adopt direct hunger-reduction measures integrated with productive development within the framework of national strategies and policies, including, *inter alia*, more assistance to rural development to reach smallholder producers and co-operatives, special attention to the needs of women farmers, investment in human capacities through programmes for mothers and children, the creation of productive employment for poor landless families and an increase in food aid;

15.   *Expresses its concern* at the expanding food-import requirements of the developing countries, particularly the least developed, which underline the gravity of the problem and the importance of food aid both as a temporary relief measure and as a resource for food and agricultural development;

16.   *Urges* that, in the implementation of food aid policies and programmes, a greater volume of food and agricultural products be acquired from food-exporting developing countries, where appropriate, including through triangular transactions;

17.   *Calls* for adequate and continuous flows of resources for the World Bank, the International Fund for Agricultural Development and the regional development banks, whose work in food and agricultural development is important and effective in providing to the developing countries, in particular the least developed countries, additional development assistance to implement more effective incentives and programmes directed towards increasing food production and towards raising nutritional standards;

18.   *Stresses* the need for substantial and timely replenishments of the International Development Association to enable it to increase its assistance to all its recipient countries in the development of food and agriculture;

19.   *Calls upon* the relevant organizations of the United Nations system to accord priority support to economic and technical co-operation among developing countries with regard to food and agriculture;

20.   *Emphasizes* the importance of research and the exchange of information on scientific research and technological progress for the purposes of the development of food production, and calls upon the international community to provide to the developing countries increased financial and technical assistance in the area of agricultural research and to take appropriate measures to promote the transfer of technology in regard to the improvement of farming methods, including support to activities in these areas relating to technical co-operation among developing countries;

21.   *Calls upon* the international community to accord continuing and increasing support towards improving global food security and for the elimination of hunger and malnutrition;

22.   *Recognizes* that the expansion of exports, particularly from developing countries, is an important element of food security and calls for additional measures by developed countries to liberalize agricultural trade;

23.   *Calls* for improved international co-operation by countries exporting and importing cereals, relating to their food trade, production and stocking policies, in order, *inter alia*, to avoid instability in the international cereals market adversely affecting developing countries;

24.   *Urges* all Governments concerned to consider within the International Wheat Council, at its next session, the early resumption of the United Nations Conference to Negotiate an International Arrangement to

Replace the International Wheat Agreement of 1971, as extended, in order to conclude as soon as possible a new agreement that will contribute to the efficient operation of the international wheat market, taking into account the interests of developing countries;

25. *Calls upon* the international community to support, through the mobilization of financial and other resources, the efforts of developing countries to strengthen their stocking programmes in cases where those countries have expressed the need to build food reserves;

26. *Expresses the urgent need* to find multilateral solutions to the problems of trade, access, competition and supply relating to agricultural products and calls upon the relevant institutions to find appropriate solutions, taking particularly into account the special needs and circumstances of developing countries;

27. *Endorses* the new target approved by the Committee on Food Aid Policies and Programmes for the biennium 1985-1986 of $1.35 billion for the regular resources of the World Food Programme, and calls upon traditional and new contributing countries to ensure its timely achievement;

28. *Supports* the appeal launched by the Food and Agriculture Organization of the United Nations in favour of the African countries threatened by food shortages, and urges the international community to respond generously to that appeal, in particular by increasing on an emergency basis its assistance in food aid and agricultural inputs;

29. *Takes note* of the progress made in the implementation of the Programme of Action, as adopted by the World Conference on Agrarian Reform and Rural Development, and looks forward to the comprehensive review to be submitted to the Economic and Social Council in 1984 on progress in agrarian reform and rural development;

30. *Calls upon* the Governments concerned to implement agrarian reform and rural development within the framework of their national plans and objectives and in accordance with the recommendations, as adopted, of the World Conference on Agrarian Reform and Rural Development;

31. *Supports* the establishment of regional mechanisms to reduce food vulnerability, malnutrition and undernutrition and, in this context, welcomes the recent establishment of the Action Committee for Regional Food Security;

32. *Stresses* the importance of fisheries development for the expansion of food supplies and nutritional improvements and endorses the initiative by the Food and Agriculture Organization of the United Nations to convene in 1984 a World Conference on Fisheries Management and Development;

33. *Emphasizes* the importance of stock breeding and fisheries development in the food strategies, plans and programmes of developing countries and calls upon the international community to continue to provide relevant international bodies with the necessary resources for the completion of studies in those areas in order to increase their contribution to the development of the food and agriculture sector;

34. *Takes note with satisfaction* of the preparation by the World Food Council, for its tenth session in 1984, of a special assessment of progress made and the tasks ahead to achieve the objectives of the 1974 World Food Conference;

35. *Urges* the World Food Council, within the context of its mandate, to mobilize and sustain greater efforts in the struggle to overcome hunger, to continue to review and report on major problems and policy issues and to continue to serve as a co-ordinating mechanism in the field of food and other related policy matters within the United Nations system.

General Assembly resolution 38/158

19 December 1983   Meeting 102   Adopted without vote

Approved by Second Committee (A/38/702/Add.5) without vote, 4 November (meeting 30); draft by Vice-Chairman, based on informal consultations (A/C.2/38/L.21); agenda item 78 *(e)*.

Meeting numbers. GA 38th session: 2nd Committee 21, 30; plenary 102.

Two other 1983 Assembly resolutions related to food situations in specific areas. In resolution 38/6 of 28 October, the Assembly requested FAO to consider holding at Rome, not later than 31 August 1984, a meeting on food and agriculture in the Arab region with a view to taking joint action pursuant to recommendations adopted at a June/July 1983 meeting on co-operation between the United Nations and the League of Arab States. On 19 December, the Assembly adopted resolution 38/159 on the critical situation of food and agriculture in Africa.

The Second Committee also dealt with a draft resolution on food and agriculture submitted by the Philippines in 1981. Following 1981[5] and 1982[6] Assembly decisions to refer that text to its next session, the Second Committee in 1983 decided to take no action on it. The Philippine draft would have had the Assembly invite the Secretary-General, together with FAO, WFC, IFAD and others, to develop strategies to solve global food problems.

REFERENCES

[1]A/38/19. [2]YUN 1979, p. 500. [3]YUN 1980, p. 548. [4]YUN 1974, p. 491. [5]YUN 1981, p. 724, GA dec. 36/444, 17 Dec. 1981. [6]YUN 1982, p. 917, GA dec. 37/448, 21 Dec. 1982.

Food aid

World Food Programme

The World Food Programme, a joint undertaking of the United Nations and FAO, marked its twentieth anniversary in 1983 by the highest level of development and emergency commitments in its history.

The anniversary, observed by the Economic and Social Council, the General Assembly and the FAO Conference, and marked by a joint message from the Secretary-General and the FAO Director-General as well as by commemorative stamps, gave WFP an impulse to review its own experience and examine major food aid policy issues at an October seminar at The Hague in co-operation with the Netherlands. There was also a continuous effort by WFP to reassess its policies and working methods, with particular emphasis on in-depth impact studies.

WFP activities

The annual report of CFA,[1] the WFP governing body, stated that development commitments in 1983 totalled $696 million, representing over 1.4 million metric tons of food, with about 80 per cent made to low-income, food-deficit countries. An additional $200 million was allocated to emergency operations. Over the year, total shipments of WFP assistance, for development projects and emergency operations, exceeded 1.5 million tons. The Programme's major emergency effort was directed towards sub-Saharan Africa, which accounted for 34 per cent of its emergency deliveries. WFP also participated in a joint task force with FAO set up in April to monitor the food and agriculture situation in the region. The Programme continued to play a co-ordinating role in major emergency operations on the Thai/Kampuchean border, in Pakistan for Afghan refugees, in Somalia and in Chad. An in-depth evaluation of a food-for-work project in Bangladesh was begun, while preliminary work was started on similar projects in Malawi and Pakistan.

CFA activities. The fifteenth and sixteenth sessions of CFA were held in 1983 at Rome, from 16 to 27 May[2] and from 20 to 28 October.[3]

In May, following its eighth annual review of food aid policies and programmes, CFA submitted its conclusions[4] to the Economic and Social Council, supporting WFP's efforts to integrate food aid into the national plans of developing countries and endorsing its continued emphasis on low-income, food-deficit countries. With regard to food aid targets, no agreement was reached on the figure of 10 million tons; however, there was consensus on the estimate of 20 million tons per year as an indicator of requirements for cereals food aid by 1985. CFA approved a pledging target of $1.35 billion for the regular resources of WFP for the biennium 1985-1986 (see below). It approved 23 projects at a total cost of $282 million and budget increases for 18 previously approved projects, bringing the total of new commitments for approval at the session to $304.4 million. CFA also considered interim evaluation and terminal reports, agreed with the recommendations on a grain sales procedure designed to help meet internal costs in least developed countries and approved the Executive Director's proposals to reduce the size and change the format of reports on WFP emergency operations. In order to strengthen its work, CFA decided to begin, at its October session, reviewing experiences of individual countries with food aid programmes and policies, on a voluntary basis.

In October, CFA took up the first two such reviews—for Bangladesh and Tunisia. It noted the usefulness of these selected analyses, not only for the countries concerned, but also for donors and recipient countries in general, as well as for food aid organizations within and outside the United Nations, and agreed that such reviews should proceed on a continuing basis. With regard to emergency operations, CFA noted an update of their costs and volumes and expressed satisfaction at the effectiveness of co-ordination between WFP and other United Nations agencies and donors in bringing food relief to distressed people. It also reviewed the fee/cost situation in bilateral services and approved a new fee schedule for WFP's bilateral activities from 1 January 1984.

In resolution 38/158 of 19 December 1983, the General Assembly welcomed the CFA report covering 1982,[4] and urged that, in the implementation of food aid policies and programmes, a greater volume of food and agricultural products be acquired from food-exporting developing countries, including through triangular transactions.

Development assistance

In 1983, 67 new development projects valued at $577 million were approved, and a further $119 million was provided in additional commitments for ongoing projects. CFA approved 93 per cent of these new projects by value, while the remainder were approved by the Executive Director[1] (for development projects approved, see table below). WFP continued to concentrate on low-income, food-deficit countries, which received 80 per cent of commitments for development projects. Among the food-deficit countries, those identified by the United Nations as least developed received 36 per cent of the 1983 commitments—five times the amount, for size of population, of WFP assistance to other developing countries. With regard to regional distribution, WFP 1983 commitments in percentage terms showed a substantial increase over 1982 for both the Asia and Pacific region, and the Latin American and Caribbean region, but a decrease for Africa south of the Sahara, which nevertheless had actual deliveries of food aid rise from 405,000 tons in 1982 to 502,000 tons in 1983. However, because of its acute food situation, Africa received a higher share of WFP emergency food aid than other regions (see below).

The various types of WFP development projects approved in 1983 would provide a nutrition supplement to approximately 4 million people, employment to about 800,000 workers and settlement benefits to some 500,000 people, and would generate over $150 million in local currency in five countries to be invested in dairy production.

Emergency operations

In 1983 emergency operations, WFP committed a record $200 million to provide 577,000 tons of food to 12 million people in 38 countries (including additional aid for operations approved earlier). Funds for these operations were provided from the International Emergency Food Reserve (IEFR) and from the $45 million that WFP set aside from its regular resources for this purpose.

Compared with 1982, the distribution of WFP emergency assistance by type of operation underwent considerable changes in 1983, with more than a twofold gain in the share of aid directed to drought-stricken people (43 per cent versus 20 per cent), a drop from 11 to 3 per cent in aid to the victims of natural disasters, and a decrease from 69 to 54 per cent in assistance to refugees and displaced persons following man-made disasters. With respect to geographical distribution, more than half (59 per cent) of the aid went to 42 operations in sub-Saharan Africa, 28 per cent to 11 operations in Asia, 11 per cent to 11 operations in Latin America and the Caribbean, and 2 per cent for 4 operations in North Africa and the Near East (for emergency operations approved, see table below).

As in previous years, in 1983 WFP was involved in a number of large-scale emergency operations. It continued co-ordinating the procurement and delivery of food aid for Kampuchea and relief operations along the Thai/Kampuchean border. By year's end, this aid amounted to $330 million, some two thirds of which had gone to border relief operations in Thailand, and the rest to Kampuchea itself. In total, 237,000 tons of food were provided under IEFR and 565,000 tons bilaterally. Funds were mobilized through five donor meetings, which yielded pledges of nearly $35 million, and a series of special appeals. In Pakistan, WFP provided nearly 200,000 tons of food to 2.2 million Afghan refugees, bringing the total WFP commitment for these refugees to almost 800,000 tons since 1979. In Latin America and the Caribbean, WFP supplied over 22,000 tons of emergency food aid valued at $9 million to displaced persons in El Salvador, Honduras and Mexico, and sent $12.7 million worth of food (more than 24,000 tons) to Cuba and Ecuador, affected by floods, and to Bolivia, Nicaragua and Panama, suffering from drought.

Special emphasis in 1983 was placed on meeting the urgent food needs of Africa, with almost two thirds of WFP emergency operations (42 out of 68) being launched in sub-Saharan Africa. Commitments of emergency food supplies reached all-time highs in that region, both in terms of value ($120 million) and volume (303,000 tons). WFP was the largest provider of food aid in Ghana and in relief efforts for Somalian refugees. It also played a major co-ordinating role in Chad and Mozambique, where low-crop yields and civil strife had left millions of people in extreme distress. In Europe, WFP was a major contributor of food for Greek Cypriot, Maronite and Turkish Cypriot communities as part of the United Nations relief effort in Cyprus.

Twentieth anniversary

ECONOMIC AND SOCIAL COUNCIL ACTION

On 29 July 1983, on the recommendation of its First Committee, the Economic and Social Council adopted resolution 1983/72 without vote.

Twentieth anniversary of the World Food Programme

The Economic and Social Council,

Recalling General Assembly resolutions 1714(XVI) of 19 December 1961, 2095(XX) of 20 December 1965 and 3404(XXX) of 28 November 1975 and resolutions 1/61 of 24 November 1961, 4/65 of 6 December 1965 and 22/75 of 26 November 1975 of the Conference of the Food and Agriculture Organization of the United Nations, setting up the World Food Prgramme as a programme jointly undertaken by the United Nations and the Food and Agriculture Organization of the United Nations and establishing, for the purposes of providing guidance on policy, administration and operations, the Committee on Food Aid Policies and Programmes,

Taking note of the eighth annual report of the Committee on Food Aid Policies and Programmes,

Noting that the World Food Programme is celebrating its twentieth anniversary in 1983,

Noting also the activities of the Programme during the past twenty years in the use of food aid to promote development and to relieve distress, especially in emergencies,

Conscious that the Programme, originally established on an experimental basis, is now an important element in the development activities of the United Nations system,

Noting the versatility of food aid as an instrument for promoting general economic and social development, including rural development,

1. *Expresses its appreciation* to the World Food Programme on its twentieth anniversary and for the initiatives of the Programme to provide added impetus as it enters the third decade of its existence;

2. *Also expresses its appreciation* to Governments and to organs, organizations and bodies of the United Nations system for their support of the Programme;

3. *Calls upon* Governments to intensify their efforts to enable the Programme to fulfil its assigned role in accordance with its mandate even more effectively and for this purpose to channel, to the maximum extent possible and feasible, their food aid through the Programme;

4. *Encourages* the Programme to continue to explore opportunities to improve the constructive use of food aid in support of the economic and social development of the developing countries.

Economic and Social Council resolution 1983/72

29 July 1983   Meeting 41   Adopted without vote

Approved by First Committee (E/1983/124) without vote, 27 July (meeting 25); draft by Chairman (E/1983/C.1/L.23/Rev.1), orally revised and orally amended by Bangladesh; agenda item 16.
Meeting number. ESC 41.

The oral amendment by Bangladesh added the words "possible and" in paragraph 3.

Contributions to WFP

Contributions for 1983-1984

The annual report of CFA[1] pointed out that combined WFP resources stood at a record $1.2 billion for the 1983-1984 biennium. These resources included regular pledges, reported by CFA to be within reach of its $1.2 billion biennium target, as well as contributions made through IEFR and the 1980 Food Aid Convention,[5] as extended in 1981,[6] which established minimum annual contributions of 7.6 million metric tons in grains for each of its parties and had the objective of reaching the 1974 World Food Conference target of at least 10 million metric tons of food aid annually.[7] The Convention had been further extended from 1 July 1983 until 30 June 1986 by the International Wheat Agreement made up of the Food Aid Convention together with the 1971 Wheat Trade Convention. By the end of 1983, 534,121 tons of food, at a value of $149 million, had been contributed to IEFR by 21 donors, the highest number recorded in any one year. Almost the entire quantity of commodities at the disposal of WFP, including both regular pledges and Food Aid Convention contributions of all donors, had been called forward by the end of 1983, and for the most part shipped. Cash pledges and contributions from all sources totalled $127.5 million.

Pledging target for 1985-1986

At its May 1983 session, CFA approved a pledging target of $1.35 billion for WFP's regular resources for 1985-1986. A $1.5 billion target figure had been proposed by the Executive Director and endorsed by the Secretary-General and the FAO Director-General. It was felt by some delegations that the $1.35 billion figure was unrealistic, and by others that it was inadequate in view of the urgent food aid needs of developing countries, particularly the low-income, food-deficit countries. However, it was pointed out that the original figure allowed for an inflation factor which might be too high and that real growth would be possible with a $1.35 billion target. The Committee proposed that the Economic and Social Council and the FAO Council should adopt the relevant draft resolution, annexed to the CFA report.

FOOD AID FOR DEVELOPMENT
(Projects approved in 1983 by CFA)

Country	Field of activity	Amount (in US dollars)	Country	Field of activity	Amount (in US dollars)
Burundi	Secondary school feeding	5,440,200	Lesotho	Roads, soil and water conservation and forestry development	14,421,300
Central African Republic	Multi-purpose rural development	10,262,500	Madagascar	Experimental feeding and development programme for primary schools	5,574,500
China	Dairy development in and around six major cities	60,232,800	Malawi	Feeding in public health centres	9,081,000
	Agricultural development through drainage, irrigation and salinity control in Hebei province	6,350,000	Mali	Multi-purpose project for the development of rural and natural resources	31,166,900
Democratic Yemen	Feeding programme in boarding schools and training institutes	3,902,800	Mauritius	Primary school feeding	4,735,300
	Assistance to mother and child health care (MCH) centres	5,037,400		Feeding of vulnerable groups	2,894,700
Ecuador	Mother and child feeding programme for the lowest-income groups	11,165,000	Niger	Assistance to MCH centres, hospitals and rural health centres	3,354,500
El Salvador	Multi-purpose project for rural and community development	7,299,700	Peru	Assistance to vulnerable groups in small community development self-help schemes	13,395,800
Equatorial Guinea	Vulnerable group feeding	3,853,500	Sri Lanka	Assistance to Mahaweli Ganga development programme	18,082,500
India	Supplementary nutrition for pre-school children, pregnant women and nursing mothers	43,353,900		Assistance to Anuradhapura dry zone agriculture project	5,927,000
	Rural development in Mahendergarh district, Haryana	7,151,100	Sudan	Restocking of the Gum Belt	5,575,700
Jordan	Rangeland and forage development	3,465,500	Total		281,723,600

SOURCE: WFP/CFA:15/20.

EMERGENCY ALLOCATIONS APPROVED IN 1983

Country	Nature of emergency	Amount (in US dollars) IEFR	WFP	Country	Nature of emergency	Amount (in US dollars) IEFR	WFP
Benin	Returnees	188,700	87,000	Comoros	Cyclone	1,328,400	269,400
	Drought	875,000	84,000	Cuba	Floods	1,971,800	—
Bolivia	Drought	3,826,200	618,300	Democratic			
Chad	Returnees	483,800	73,900	Kampuchea	Refugees	2,000,200	—
	Drought	8,164,000	1,395,200		Refugees	1,520,000	—

Country	Nature of emergency	Amount (in US dollars) IEFR	WFP	Country	Nature of emergency	Amount (in US dollars) IEFR	WFP
Democratic				Nicaragua	Drought	2,298,000	1,147,800
Kampuchea *(cont.)*	Refugees	479,000	—	Pakistan	Refugees	19,900,000	3,480,000
	Refugees	1,520,000	—		Refugees	21,150,000	—
	Refugees	1,382,700	—		Refugees	2,147,900	—
Ecuador	Floods	1,944,800	—	Panama	Drought	—	929,600
El Salvador	Displaced persons	2,668,000	—	Rwanda	Refugees/returnees	648,000	778,000
	Displaced persons	—	2,720,800		Refugees	420,000	87,500
Ethiopia	Drought	440,000	88,000	Sao Tome and			
	Drought	727,000	4,196,600	Principe	Drought	203,100	448,300
	Drought	1,822,500	—	Senegal	Drought	1,378,500	715,500
	Returnees	325,000	133,200		Drought	3,167,200	—
Fiji	Drought	1,212,500	745,200	Somalia	Refugees	4,018,000	3,013,100
Gambia	Crop failure	960,000	31,200		Refugees	3,682,800	3,499,000
Ghana	Returnees	—	1,012,300		Refugees	1,860,000	—
	Returnees	2,906,300	1,136,600		Refugees	6,700,200	3,620,500
	Drought/bush fires	2,646,000	1,255,600	Sri Lanka	Displaced persons	—	155,000
	Drought/bush fires	2,860,100	1,231,200	Sudan	Refugees	—	861,500
Guinea	Drought	1,080,000	—		Floods	506,200	140,700
	Earthquake	—	51,540	Swaziland	Drought	432,000	602,100
Guinea-Bissau	Crop failure	750,000	—	Syrian Arab			
Honduras	Refugees	1,097,700	—	Republic	Refugees	516,000	669,500
	Displaced persons	146,500	19,800	Togo	Drought/bush fires	728,000	18,000
	Refugees	1,008,800	398,700		Drought/bush fires	332,800	18,200
Indonesia	Refugees	490,000	—	Uganda	Returnees	990,800	142,100
Lebanon	Civil strife	1,721,800	346,000		Displaced persons	166,200	125,500
Lesotho	Drought	2,590,000	174,800		Displaced settlers	425,000	126,500
Mali	Drought	4,525,300	—		Displaced persons	2,234,100	1,761,200
	Drought	4,530,000	—	United Republic			
Mauritania	Drought	1,427,900	150,000	of Tanzania	Drought	463,700	—
	Drought	7,113,500	2,692,400	Zimbabwe	Drought	4,176,400	—
Mexico	Refugees	452,000	425,600				
Mozambique	Drought	1,085,200	750,800	Total		155,295,600	44,825,540
	Drought	6,480,000	2,397,800				

SOURCE: WFP/CFA:17/9.

CONTRIBUTIONS UNDER THE FOOD AID CONVENTION MADE AVAILABLE TO WFP
(as at 31 December 1983; in US dollars)

CONTRIBUTOR	CROP YEAR 1982/83 Commodity (metric tons)	Value	CASH	CROP YEAR 1983/84 Commodity (metric tons)	Value	CASH
Food Aid Convention net						
Australia	120,000	21,840,000	4,591,944	—	—	—
Belgium	14,000	2,548,000	840,000	—	—	—
Finland	20,000	3,640,000	1,200,000	—	—	—
Germany, Federal Republic of	10,000	1,820,000	600,000	—	—	—
Ireland	4,080	742,560	244,800	—	—	—
Norway	30,000	5,460,000	1,800,000	30,000	4,920,000	1,800,000
Sweden	40,000	7,280,000	2,400,000	40,000	6,560,000	2,400,000
Subtotal	238,080	43,330,560	11,676,744	70,000	11,480,000	4,200,000
Convention through regular programme						
Australia	—	—	—	160,000	26,301,389	6,572,259
EEC	65,000	11,830,000	3,900,000	55,000	9,020,000	3,300,000
Netherlands	16,750	2,965,759	1,005,000	16,750	2,965,759	1,005,000
United Kingdom	50,000	9,100,000	2,773,723	—	—	—
Subtotal	131,750	23,895,759	7,678,723	231,750	38,287,148	10,877,259
*Convention through IEFR**						
Australia	17,925	3,280,275	1,738,725	—	—	—
EEC	40,000	7,320,000	3,880,000	30,000	5,490,000	2,910,000
Germany, Federal Republic of	25,000	4,575,000	2,425,000	—	—	—
Netherlands	8,250	1,509,750	800,250	—	—	—
Switzerland	10,000	1,830,000	970,000	10,000	1,830,000	970,000
United Kingdom	5,000	915,000	485,000	5,000	915,000	485,000
Subtotal	106,175	19,430,025	10,298,975	45,000	8,235,000	4,365,000
Total	476,005	86,656,344	29,654,442	346,750	58,002,148	19,442,259

*Under IEFR, donor countries cover all transportation costs.

SOURCE: WFP:CFA:17/4/Add.1.

CONTRIBUTIONS UNDER THE INTERNATIONAL EMERGENCY FOOD RESERVE
(as at 31 December 1983)

Contributor	Contribution	Quantity (in metric tons)	Estimated value (including costs for transportation) (in US dollars)	Contributor	Contribution	Quantity (in metric tons)	Estimated value (including costs for transportation) (in US dollars)
Multilateral				Sweden	Grain	30,000	9,322,520
					SKr 5,000,000	633	666,667
Argentina	Grain	3,000	580,500		Vegtable oil	1,250	1,270,222
Australia	Rice	13,717	3,444,900	Switzerland	Dried whole milk biscuits	43	231,010
	Wheat flour	4,208	1,178,259		Grain	10,000	2,678,550
Austria	Grain	5,855	1,090,000		Dried whole milk	100	440,000
Canada	$Can 6,500,000	15,310	5,284,553		Dried whole milk	100	450,704
Colombia	Rice	50	17,500	United Kingdom	Grain	5,000	1,400,000
Denmark	DKr 18,000,000	7,072	2,178,913	United States	Various		
EEC	Grain	40,000	11,059,040		commodities	252,219	66,330,900
	Butter oil	500	658,000	Subtotal		474,746	132,571,954
Finland	Fmk 9,250,000	1,117	1,745,283	*Bilateral*			
	Dried skimmed milk	60	192,000	Australia	Grain	32,075	8,981,000
France	Grain	20,000	5,326,200	Austria	Grain	5,000	1,400,000
Germany, Federal				Belgium	Grain	5,500	1,164,230
Republic of	Grain	25,000	5,687,165	France	Grain	3,800	1,064,000
	$US 1,125,000	5,000	1,125,000	Italy	Grain	3,000	975,000
Iceland	$US 8,700	25	8,700	Sweden	Grain	10,000	2,800,000
Japan	$US 1,500,000	6,457	1,500,000	Subtotal		59,375	16,384,230
Netherlands	Grain	8,250	2,350,883				
Norway	NKr 18,000,000	8,730	2,416,107	Total		534,121	148,956,184
	Edible fat	1,050	1,138,378				
Spain	Grain	10,000	2,800,000				

SOURCE: WFP/CFA:17/4 Add.1.

STATEMENT OF PLEDGES TO THE WORLD FOOD PROGRAMME FOR 1983-1984 AND 1985-1986
(as at 31 December 1983; in US dollar equivalent)

	1983-1984			1985-1986		
Contributor	Commodities	Cash and services	Total	Commodities	Cash and services	Total
Afghanistan	—	3,000	3,000	—	3,000	3,000
Algeria	—	—	—	—	132,250	132,250
Angola	—	10,200	10,200	—	—	—
Antigua and Barbuda	—	481	481	—	—	—
Argentina	3,870,000	—	3,870,000	305,529	—	305,529
Australia	68,855,437	22,553,491	91,408,928	56,275,862	28,137,930	84,413,792*
Austria	5,400,000	600,000	6,000,000	6,075,000	675,000	6,750,000
Bangladesh	660,000	—	660,000	990,000	—	990,000
Barbados	—	6,750	6,750	—	6,955	6,955
Belgium	581,818	327,272	909,090	3,277,157	2,100,014	5,377,171
Bhutan	—	1,250	1,250	—	1,500	1,500*
Bolivia	—	10,000	10,000	—	10,000	10,000
Botswana	—	10,984	10,984	—	—	—
Burundi	—	1,675	1,675	—	—	—
Canada	170,731,707	32,520,324	203,252,031	172,463,767	34,352,325	206,816,092*
Central African Republic	—	1,937	1,937	—	—	—
Chile	25,000	—	25,000	—	20,000	20,000
China	—	600,000	600,000	—	1,000,000	1,000,000
Colombia	500,000	22,123	522,123	500,000	11,000	511,000
Cuba	2,500,000	—	2,500,000	1,000,000	—	1,000,000
Cyprus	—	3,744	3,744	—	3,425	3,425*
Democratic Yemen	—	11,000	11,000	—	12,650	12,650
Denmark	20,043,682	10,657,595	30,701,277	22,983,486	10,967,846	33,951,332*
Djibouti	—	2,000	2,000	—	2,000	2,000*
Ecuador	—	50,000	50,000	—	—	—
Egypt	400,000	—	400,000	400,000	—	400,000
Equatorial Guinea	—	—	—	—	1,000	1,000
EEC	110,295,116	19,112,000	129,407,116	79,392,622	16,511,750	95,904,372
Fiji	—	4,000	4,000	—	1,712	1,712
Finland	2,931,034	965,516	3,896,550	17,166,422	5,661,322	22,827,744*
France	2,424,242	2,303,030	4,727,272	—	2,105,263	2,105,263*
Gambia	—	5,000	5,000	—	—	—
Germany, Federal Republic of	25,202,258	12,801,202	38,003,460	26,013,471	11,019,526	37,032,997*
Greece	250,000	—	250,000	250,000	—	250,000
Guatemala	—	—	—	—	11,111	11,111*
Guinea	—	—	—	—	2,000	2,000
Guyana	—	5,000	5,000	—	—	—
Haiti	—	—	—	—	10,000	10,000*
Honduras	—	—	—	—	7,500	7,500*

	1983-1984			1985-1986		
Contributor	Commodities	Cash and services	Total	Commodities	Cash and services	Total
Hungary	440,000	—	440,000	440,000	—	440,000
Iceland	—	40,000	40,000	—	27,600	27,600
India	1,570,000	—	1,570,000	1,760,000	—	1,760,000
Iran	—	—	—	—	40,000	40,000
Ireland	1,630,311	889,699	2,520,010	2,157,055	984,930	3,141,985*
Israel	—	10,000	10,000	10,000	—	10,000
Italy	—	—	—	5,830,904	2,915,451	8,746,355*
Jamaica	—	10,000	10,000	—	10,000	10,000
Japan	10,333,333	5,166,667	15,500,000	14,000,000	7,000,000	21,000,000
Jordan	—	75,000	75,000	—	75,000	75,000
Kenya	—	838	838	—	—	—
Kuwait	—	—	—	—	250,000	250,000
Lao People's Democratic Republic	—	—	—	—	1,000	1,000
Lebanon	—	22,500	22,500	—	—	—
Lesotho	—	13,513	13,513	—	10,000	10,000
Liberia	—	5,000	5,000	—	—	—
Libyan Arab Jamahiriya	—	100,000	100,000	—	—	—
Luxembourg	—	22,909	22,909	—	10,161	10,161*
Malawi	—	1,600	1,600	—	5,000	5,000
Malaysia	17,094	8,583	25,677	16,461	8,036	24,497*
Mali	—	1,470	1,470	—	—	—
Malta	—	2,600	2,600	—	2,600	2,600
Mauritania	—	—	—	—	4,085	4,085
Mauritius	—	—	—	—	1,488	1,488
Mexico	—	—	—	—	100,000	100,000
Morocco	—	20,278	20,278	—	15,645	15,645*
Nepal	—	6,000	6,000	—	7,500	7,500
Netherlands	29,341,773	14,180,810	43,522,583	42,252,021	14,406,132	56,658,153*
New Zealand	355,555	176,600	532,155	306,513	141,093	447,606*
Nicaragua	—	1,000	1,000	—	13,571	13,571
Nigeria	—	250,000	250,000	—	250,000	250,000
Norway	21,485,939	10,910,781	32,396,720	21,763,123	10,146,532	31,909,655*
Pakistan	750,000	—	750,000	750,000	—	750,000
Panama	—	1,000	1,000	—	1,000	1,000
Philippines	—	56,107	56,107	—	46,666	46,666*
Republic of Korea	—	100,000	100,000	—	100,000	100,000
Rwanda	—	1,500	1,500	—	1,500	1,500
Sao Tome and Principe	—	—	—	—	750	750
Saudi Arabia	41,250,000	13,750,000	55,000,000	27,500,000	27,500,000	55,000,000
Seychelles	—	—	—	—	100	100
Sierra Leone	—	—	—	—	471	471*
Somalia	—	575	575	—	204	204
Spain	—	400,000	400,000	—	377,779	377,779*
Sri Lanka	102,417	—	102,417	109,328	—	109,328*
Sudan	—	10,000	10,000	10,000	—	10,000*
Swaziland	—	—	—	—	1,000	1,000*
Sweden	13,000,000	6,562,101	19,562,101	29,899,217	11,628,757	41,527,974*
Switzerland	4,500,352	2,128,994	6,629,346	2,851,675	1,013,097	3,864,772*
Syrian Arab Republic	—	128,205	128,205	—	128,205	128,205*
Thailand	35,000	—	35,000	35,000	—	35,000
Togo	—	3,631	3,631	—	1,044	1,044*
Tonga	—	—	—	—	2,000	2,000
Tunisia	—	55,000	55,000	—	60,500	60,500
Turkey	216,000	—	216,000	216,000	—	216,000
Uganda	—	1,000	1,000	—	5,000	5,000
United Kingdom	9,100,000	4,259,046	13,359,046	16,250,000	9,328,805	25,578,805*
United Republic of Tanzania	—	15,201	15,201	—	13,253	13,253*
United States	188,000,000	62,000,000	250,000,000	188,000,000	62,000,000	250,000,000
Upper Volta	—	—	—	—	1,075	1,075
Venezuela	—	46,728	46,728	—	26,667	26,667
Viet Nam	—	10,000	10,000	—	12,000	12,000*
Yemen	—	—	—	—	10,000	10,000
Yugoslavia	540,000	—	540,000	—	—	—
Zaire	—	—	—	—	2,000	2,000
Zambia	—	—	—	—	517	517*
Zimbabwe	—	32,550	32,550	—	—	—
Total	737,338,068	224,067,060	961,405,128	741,250,613	261,455,293	1,002,705,906

*Pledges announced in local currency.

SOURCE: WFP/CFA:17/4/Add.1, WFP/CFA:21/4/Add.1.

ECONOMIC AND SOCIAL COUNCIL ACTION

On 29 July 1983, on the recommendation of its First Committee, the Economic and Social Council adopted resolution 1983/73 without vote, thereby forwarding the CFA draft to the General Assembly.

Target for World Food Programme pledges for the period 1985-1986

The Economic and Social Council,

Having considered the eighth annual report of the Committee on Food Aid Policies and Programmes,

Noting the comments of the Committee concerning the minimum target for voluntary contributions to the World Food Programme for the period 1985-1986,

Recalling General Assembly resolutions 2462(XXIII) of 20 December 1968 and 2682(XXV) of 11 December 1970, in which the Assembly recognized the experience gained by the World Food Programme in the field of multilateral food aid,

1. *Submits* to the General Assembly for consideration and adoption the draft resolution annexed hereto;

2. *Urges* States Members of the United Nations and members and associate members of the Food and Agriculture Organization of the United Nations to undertake the necessary preparations for the announcement of pledges at the Eleventh Pledging Conference for the World Food Programme.

ANNEX
Target for World Food Programme pledges
for the period 1985-1986

[Text as in General Assembly resolution 38/176 below, except for minor drafting changes.]

Economic and Social Council resolution 1983/73

29 July 1983   Meeting 41   Adopted without vote

Approved by First Committee (E/1983/124) without vote, 27 July (meeting 25); draft by CFA (E/1983/92); agenda item 16.
Meeting number. ESC 41.

GENERAL ASSEMBLY ACTION

On 19 December, on the recommendation of its Second Committee, the General Assembly adopted resolution 38/176 without vote.

Target for World Food Programme pledges for the period 1985-1986

The General Assembly,

Recalling the provisions of its resolution 2095(XX) of 20 December 1965 to the effect that the World Food Programme is to be reviewed before each pledging conference,

Recalling the provisions of paragraph 4 of its resolution 36/202 of 17 December 1981 specifying that, subject to the review mentioned above, the next pledging conference should be convened, at the latest, early in 1984, at which time Governments and appropriate donor organizations should be invited to pledge contributions for 1985 and 1986 with a view to reaching such a target as may be then recommended by the General Assembly and the Conference of the Food and Agriculture Organization of the United Nations,

Noting that the review of the Programme was undertaken by the Committee on Food Aid Policies and Programmes of the World Food Programme at its fifteenth session and by the Economic and Social Council at its second regular session of 1983,

Having considered Economic and Social Council resolution 1983/73 of 29 July 1983, as well as the recommendations of the Committee on Food Aid Policies and Programmes,

Recognizing the value of multilateral food aid as furnished by the World Food Programme since its inception and the necessity for continuing its action both as a form of capital investment and for meeting emergency food needs,

1. *Establishes* for the two years 1985 and 1986 a target for voluntary contributions to the World Food Programme of $1.35 billion, of which not less than one third should be in cash and/or services in aggregate, and expresses the hope that such resources will be augmented by substantial additional contributions from other sources in recognition of the prospective volume of sound project requests and the capacity of the Programme to operate at a higher level;

2. *Urges* States Members of the United Nations and members and associate members of the Food and Agriculture Organization of the United Nations and appropriate donor organizations to make every effort to ensure the full attainment of the target;

3. *Requests* the Secretary-General, in co-operation with the Director-General of the Food and Agriculture Organization of the United Nations, to convene a pledging conference for this purpose at United Nations Headquarters early in 1984;

4. *Decides* that, subject to the review provided for in General Assembly resolution 2095(XX), the subsequent pledging conference, at which Governments and appropriate donor organizations should be invited to pledge contributions for the biennium 1987-1988 with a view to reaching such a target as may be then recommended by the Assembly and the Conference of the Food and Agriculture Organization of the United Nations, should be convened, at the latest, early in 1986.

General Assembly resolution 38/176

19 December 1983   Meeting 102   Adopted without vote

Approved by Second Committee (A/38/703) without vote, 1 December (meeting 53); draft recommended by Economic and Social Council (resolution 1983/73); agenda item 79 *(h)*.
Meeting numbers. GA 38th session: 2nd Committee 53; plenary 102.

In resolution 38/158 of 19 December on food problems, the Assembly also endorsed the $1.35 billion target approved by CFA for 1985-1986 for WFP regular resources, and called on contributing countries to ensure its timely achievement. In resolution 38/171 of the same date, the Assembly welcomed the progress made towards the attainment of the 1983-1984 target for voluntary contributions and urged Governments to make every effort to ensure full attainment of both targets.

REFERENCES

(1)E/1984/117. (2)WFP/CFA:15/20. (3)WFP/CFA:16/19. (4)E/1983/92. (5)YUN 1980, p. 691. (6)YUN 1981, p. 729. (7)YUN 1974, p. 496.

Co-ordination of food activities

Cross-sectoral review

In an effort to enhance its role in co-ordinating economic and social activities of the United Nations system, the Economic and Social Council had decided in 1982[1] to review every six years, beginning in 1983, selected major issues in the proposed medium-term plans of United Nations organizations, and to recommend to the Assembly relative priorities for action. In February 1983, the Council, in decision 1983/101, identified food and agriculture as one of the two areas for such cross-sectoral review in 1983. The other area identified was population (see Chapter XIV of this section).

A June report[2] by the Secretary-General was organized in accordance with the provisions of the International Development Strategy for the Third United Nations Development Decade[3] which required action by United Nations organizations. Accordingly, it concentrated on three major issues: agricultural production, food security, and trade in food and agricultural products. Despite favourable overall statistics of world food production, many countries were suffering from acute food shortages or expecting serious crop shortfalls, while an increasing number relied on grain imports for their survival. In developing countries as a whole, agricultural production had grown at a rate lower than the Strategy's 4 per cent annual target. For low-income countries in general and for a majority of African countries, food production had not kept pace with population growth. The number of people in the world suffering from malnutrition continued to rise and was estimated at 450 million to 500 million. While external assistance in food and agriculture had never reached desirable levels, contributing Governments had reduced their financial support to major multilateral sources of assistance, thus weakening the ability of the United Nations system to fulfil its mandated responsibilities. Continuing along existing lines would not lead to the achievement of the Strategy's goals, the Secretary-General believed.

Among areas which required further strengthening, the Secretary-General named world food security, stressing that access to food should be seen as an issue as vital as that of production. He noted the need for increased activities regarding vulnerable groups in the population, nutritional issues and the role of women in food and agricultural development. He also underscored the importance of protecting the world's natural resource base—soil, water and genetic resources—a problem which transcended developing countries and required special emphasis by the United Nations system.

While noting the increasing programme emphasis on research as an example of sound co-operation among various United Nations entities, the Secretary-General reported absence of progress in initiatives concerned with trade issues, market stability and price structures, and urged improved dialogue among Governments to allow realization of these needed agency programmes.

ECONOMIC AND SOCIAL COUNCIL ACTION

On 29 July 1983, on the recommendation of its Third (Programme and Co-ordination) Committee, the Economic and Social Council adopted resolution 1983/77 without vote.

Cross-sectoral review of food and agriculture

The Economic and Social Council,

Recalling its resolution 1982/50 of 28 July 1982 on the revitalization of the Council, in which, *inter alia,* it decided to review every six years selected major issues in the proposed medium-term plans of the organizations of the United Nations system,

Recalling also its decision 1983/101 of 4 February 1983, by paragraph 2 *(c)* of which it decided that food and agriculture and population would be the two areas for review in 1983,

Bearing in mind its resolution 1983/71 of 29 July 1983 on food problems,

1. *Takes note* of the report of the Secretary-General containing a cross-sectoral review of the food and agriculture sector in the medium-term plans of the organizations of the United Nations system;

2. *Reiterates* the importance of food and agriculture in the development process of the developing countries, and urges the international community to keep this issue as one of its highest priorities, with a view to increasing the food production and agricultural development of those countries, so as to enable them to achieve self-reliance and eliminate hunger and malnutrition;

3. *Requests* the competent entities of the United Nations system to assist, where so requested, in the development and implementation of national food strategies, plans and programmes;

4. *Affirms* that the activities in the food and agriculture sector undertaken by the United Nations system should represent a comprehensive approach towards the issues relating to trade, financial flows and food security questions, and towards efforts covering the whole range of issues concerning production, conservation and storage, processing, marketing, distribution and consumption;

5. *Requests* the entities of the United Nations system to continue and strengthen their efforts to fulfil the objectives of the Programme of Action adopted by the World Food Conference, of the Universal Declaration on the Eradication of Hunger and Malnutrition contained therein, and of the International Development Strategy for the Third United Nations Development Decade;

6. *Emphasizes* the importance of adequate external financial and technical assistance through multilateral

and other channels, to supplement the efforts of the developing countries to achieve their objectives in the field of food and agriculture;

7. *Invites* the competent entities of the United Nations system in the field of food and agriculture to consider appropriate action towards the attainment of the objectives of the enlarged and integrated concept of world food security, in accordance with the decision, as adopted, of the Committee on World Food Security of the Food and Agriculture Organization of the United Nations;

8. *Emphasizes* the responsibilities of the institutions concerned, in accordance with their mandates, to work towards the solution of problems of trade in the food and agriculture sector;

9. *Urges* international organizations, including their respective governing bodies, to make every effort, in close co-operation with each other and keeping each other fully informed, and in accordance with the relevant United Nations resolutions, to ensure that their policies and programmes complement each other and that there is efficient co-ordination of their activities, avoiding duplication and gaps;

10. *Takes note* of the assessment to be carried out by the World Food Council for its tenth session on the progress made and the tasks ahead in meeting the objectives of the 1974 World Food Conference, and requests it to include a complete global assessment of the flow of resources through the United Nations system, broken down by various subsectors in the food and agriculture sector.

Economic and Social Council resolution 1983/77

29 July 1983   Meeting 42   Adopted without vote

Approved by Third Committee (E/1983/128) without vote, 28 July (meeting 20); draft submitted orally by Vice-Chairman, based on informal consultations on draft by Algeria, Bangladesh, Benin, Congo, India, Lebanon, Mali, Pakistan, Qatar, Senegal, Sudan, Tunisia and Yugoslavia (E/1983/C.3/L.16) and orally revised; agenda item 21.

Meeting number. ESC 42.

REFERENCES

[1]YUN 1982, p. 1241, ESC res. 1982/50, 28 July 1982. [2]E/1983/99. [3]YUN 1980, p. 503, GA res. 35/56, annex, 5 Dec. 1980.

Chapter XII

Science and technology

With the 1979 Vienna Programme of Action providing the framework for restructuring international scientific and technological relations, various United Nations entities continued their efforts to strengthen the related capacities of developing countries in 1983 by mobilizing financial resources, enhancing institutional arrangements and improving the balance of technology transfer.

To appraise progress in implementing the Vienna Programme and map ways of strengthening developing countries' endogenous capacities, the Director-General for Development and International Economic Co-operation (DIEC), responsible for overall co-ordination in science and technology within the United Nations system, prepared a first biennial review and a report on the guidelines for future projects. Several *ad hoc* panels of specialists were held to provide expert advice on specific problems such as human resources development, the role of regional organizations, and linkages between research and production.

The United Nations Financing System for Science and Technology for Development (UNFSSTD) played a central role in financing various activities. Despite severe resource constraints, the System contributed to the development of projects financed by donors through trust fund arrangements, increased its portfolio of bankable projects and was instrumental in launching several projects on science and technology policy, planning and information, as well as several conferences promoting international scientific and technological co-operation. At the end of the year, total commitments stood at $44.2 million and its overall income at $45.1 million. In December, the General Assembly decided to convene another pledging conference for UNFSSTD in 1984 and invited Governments to indicate the amounts of their contributions at the earliest possible time (resolution 38/157).

Directing and policy-making functions were carried out by the Intergovernmental Committee on Science and Technology for Development and its Advisory Committee with assistance from the United Nations Centre for Science and Technology for Development. The Intergovernmental Committee held its special session in April/May 1983 to assess the UNFSSTD resource and contribution situation and consider the financing plan and the voting pattern for UNFSSTD's Executive Board. At its regular fifth session in June, it covered a broad range of matters related to institutional arrangements, including the effectiveness of its own work, the role of regional advisory bodies, participation of non-governmental organizations (NGOs), as well as the activities of the Advisory Committee and the Centre for science and technology.

Providing substantive support to the Intergovernmental Committee and co-ordinating United Nations activities at the secretariat level, the Centre proceeded with establishing an advance technology alert system (ATAS), analysed levels of attainment of scientific and technological development and organized specialist panels. On the recommendation of the Intergovernmental Committee, the Assembly noted the revised estimates for a number of activities undertaken by the Centre in addition to the output indicated in the 1984-1985 programme budget (resolution 38/234). The Assembly also recommended that the Committee consider adopting, on an experimental basis, a biennial cycle of meetings, in conformity with the work of the Assembly's Second Committee (decision 38/429). The question of inter-agency co-operation was considered by the Task Force on Science and Technology for Development, which held its fourth session at Geneva in January.

Regulation and promotion of the flow of technology from industrialized to developing countries was another important area of United Nations activities in 1983. At its sixth session, the United Nations Conference for Trade and Development (UNCTAD VI) (see Chapter IV of this section), reiterated the importance of an adequate legal and institutional framework for the transfer, acquisition and development of technology. The United Nations Conference on an International Code of Conduct on the Transfer of Technology at its October/November session made progress in formulating the code but left a number of issues unresolved, prompting the Assembly to decide on convening another conference in 1985 to complete the negotiations (resolution 38/153). The Assembly also addressed the question of the reverse transfer of technology—or brain drain—urging improved co-ordination of United Nations efforts and full participation by all Member States (resolution 38/154).

Topics related to this chapter. Disarmament: peaceful uses of science and technology. Operational activities for development: technical co-operation among developing countries. Industrial development: industrial technology. Human rights: human rights and science and technology. Women: science and technology and women.

Implementation of the Vienna Programme of Action

General aspects

Proceeding in 1983 with its efforts to implement the 1979 Vienna Programme of Action on Science and Technology,[1] the United Nations strove to upgrade further the effectiveness of the Programme's 1981 operational plan[2] which identified eight major programme areas to help make the advantages of science and technology more accessible to developing countries.

As requested by the Intergovernmental Committee on Science and Technology for Development in June 1982,[3] the DIEC Director-General submitted a report proposing guidelines for the formulation of projects and programmes in order to strengthen the endogenous scientific and technological capacities in developing countries. The report was transmitted to the Committee by the Secretary-General on 25 April 1983.[4] The proposed guidelines were based on information provided by 55 countries from the African, Asian, Latin American and other regions in response to a questionnaire sent to Member States, as well as on data from relevant national and international publications.

At a first stage, the guidelines were to assist countries, organizations and institutions at the national, subregional, regional and international levels in identifiying the dimensions of specific programmes and projects and areas in which they could be developed. The Director-General suggested that the Committee might invite Member States to utilize, and United Nations entities to take into account the guidelines, and that it might call on the developed countries to keep the guidelines in view when supporting projects of developing countries.

Another major effort in promoting the Vienna Programme was the preparation of a first biennial review and appraisal of progress in implementing its operational plan, as requested by the Committee in 1981.[2] Submitted by the Secretary-General in May 1983,[5] the DIEC Director-General's review analysed information received from 55 countries in response to a questionnaire. Because the response rate for the African and Asian regions was much lower than the average of the whole response rate

of 35 per cent, the Director-General called for caution in drawing inferences from the review, particularly in regional situations where data had been missing. In addition to testing the received data against other information, a statistical survey of indicators of scientific and technological achievements had been undertaken by the Centre for Science and Technology. Progress was appraised in each of the eight programme areas and some recommendations were made on ways to speed up implementation of the operational plan.

Intergovernmental Committee action. The Intergovernmental Committee welcomed, in a resolution of 17 June,[6] the Director-General's report on the first biennial review. It requested that those Member States which had not responded to his questionnaire to do so not later than the end of 1983 and requested the Advisory Committee on Science and Technology for Development and its 1984 *ad hoc* panels to assist in improving the analytical structure of future biennial reviews.

The Committee took note of the Director-General's report on guidelines for project formulation. Proposing that the report should form a basis for identifying areas for development of such projects, the Committee invited Member States, United Nations entities, and intergovernmental and non-governmental organizations (NGOs) to take the guidelines into account and called on developed countries to keep them in view in assisting developing countries. It further invited the United Nations Financing System for Science and Technology for Development (UNFSSTD) to take into account the guidelines in assisting developing countries in formulating projects to be financed by it. The Committee requested the Director-General to review periodically the guidelines and propose additions when necessary.

In a decision of 20 June,[7] the Committee took note of the Secretary General's April 1983 annual report on 1982 United Nations activities in science and technology for development.[8]

In a further decision of the same date,[9] the Committee called for submission of an analytical report conforming with the United Nations biennial budgetary cycle and decided that from 1984 the report would be submitted at the end of each cycle. It further decided that the report should contain a progress review on implementation of the operational plan and that in alternate years, the Committee should be provided with written information on United Nations activities in science and technology.

Scientific and technological information
Proposed advance technology alert system

Preparation of proposals for the establishment of an advance technology alert system (ATAS) was a major area of activity of the Centre on Science and Technology, following the Intergovernmental Committee's 1981 decision to consider early assessment of new scientific and technological developments as an important element of the operational plan.[10] In 1982, the Centre's proposal had been considered by the Task Force on Science and Technology for Development of the Administrative Committee on Co-ordination (ACC)[11] and by the Advisory Committee's *ad hoc* panel of specialists on the integrated application of emerging and traditional technologies for development.[12]

At its February 1983 session (see below),[13] the Advisory Committee suggested that the Centre proceed with developing ATAS based on an inter-disciplinary, cross-sectoral analysis of existing information and the analysis and packaging of that information in a form most useful to policy makers and planners. The Advisory Committee also suggested that information on the integration of emerging and traditional technologies be taken into account and that developing countries be alerted to the potential of the most advanced technologies and their possible impact on traditional sectors.

Deliberations by these bodies resulted in a progress report and the proposal for the establishment and development of ATAS, which was annexed to a report by the Secretary-General to the Intergovernmental Committee on activities of the Centre.[14] The major objectives of ATAS included alerting developing countries to the implications of new scientific and technological advances; assisting Governments in choosing new technologies and allocating human and financial resources, and assisting Member States in building national ATAS capacities. The expected primary output of ATAS was a semi-annual publication focusing on major scientific and technological breakthroughs and their implication in specific areas. As envisaged, the system was to rely heavily on inputs from a network of specialized research institutions and the international scientific community and to have links with United Nations regional commissions and national decision-making structures. It was proposed to launch ATAS early in 1984 as a four-year pilot project and convene a workshop of experts later in the year to evaluate the first issue of the ATAS publication.

By a decision of 17 June 1983,[15] the Intergovernmental Committee took note of the activities of the Centre with regard to initiating ATAS and welcomed the Advisory Committee's recommendations. It encouraged the Centre to proceed with the planned semi-annual publication and other related activities and recommended that all potential donors give financial support to ATAS during its launching phase in 1984-1985. The Centre was requested to present a progress report in 1984.

Proposed information network

By a decision of 17 June 1983,[16] the Intergovernmental Committee requested the Centre for science and technology, in co-operation with the Advisory Committee, United Nations organizations, the ACC Task Force for science and technology and other intergovernmental institutions, to prepare a study on the long-term plan of action for the establishment of a global scientific and technological information network. It requested the Centre to submit a progress report in 1984 and a final report in 1985. The Committee encouraged United Nations entities to continue strengthening or establishing national scientific and technological information systems and invited the Task Force to review the joint activities in this field in the light of the proposed study.

Scientific research and development

Emerging and traditional technologies

At its February 1983 session,[13] the Advisory Committee endorsed the recommendations of a December 1982 *ad hoc* panel of experts at Los Baños, Philippines, on the integrated application of emerging and traditional technologies for development.[17] It urged Governments and multilateral and bilateral institutions to promote such application through an immediate launching of pioneer and pilot projects in accordance with the criteria established by the panel, and suggested guidelines for compiling a portfolio of United Nations experiments and projects. With a view to wider dissemination of the panel's report, the Committee called for its publication along with the Advisory Committee's comments and supplementary information on United Nations activities. It proposed to organize in 1984 follow-up action on the design, management and implementation of pioneer projects, welcoming the possibility of assistance by China and some Japanese organizations.

The Advisory Committee recommendations were welcomed by the Intergovernmental Committee in a decision of 17 June 1983.[18]

Role of regional associations

At its February 1983 session,[13] the Advisory Committee outlined background documentation for an *ad hoc* panel meeting on the role of regional associations and organizations in strengthening research and development and in the popularization of science and technology in developing countries. The panel was convened in accordance with an Advisory Committee February 1982 decision, subsequently approved by the Intergovernmental Committee.

The panel met at Tunis, Tunisia, from 6 to 9 April 1983.[19] Describing NGOs and associations as an important resource in the use of science and technology, the panel called for their institutional interaction with Governments, full involvement in policy-making and planning and a greater role in promoting research and development and creating a demand for it. The main thrust of their efforts to popularize science and technology, the panel believed, should be directed to the issues concerning people's daily lives, leading to a democratization of knowledge and greater participation in decision-making. The panel also saw NGOs as playing an effective role in developing non-conventional approaches to the dissemination of knowledge on science and technology.

Link between research and production

Following its February 1982 decision[17] to convene an *ad hoc* panel of specialists on linkages between research and development activities and the production system, the Advisory Committee, at its February 1983 session,[13] suggested an outline for preparing background documentation for that panel. It stressed that in accordance with the 1979 Vienna Programme of Action it was useful to explore the role of national research and development corporations as intermediaries between research institutions, entrepreneurs and financing institutions, develop consulting firms and services, and pay greater attention to the demonstration and cost-benefit analysis of research and development. Hosted by the National Council of Science and Technology, the panel met from 11 to 14 October at Lima, Peru.[20] It offered a set of recommendations directed towards three groups of audiences. With regard to research and development institutions, the panel stressed that they should work together with public and private enterprises to assess the needs of the production system, deliver technical information to it and urge its involvement in the creation and management of comprehensive financing systems; extend access to the informal sector; provide technical services correlated with production needs; establish commercial infrastructure within research and development institutions; and urge multinational corporations operating in developing countries to contract the services of local research and development organizations. It also stressed the importance of appropriate management capabilities, training of researchers and industrial staff, mobility-oriented personnel policies and co-operation with consulting engineering organizations.

The panel addressed a number of recommendations to Governments, urging them to ensure representation of the production system in national science and technology bodies; confront the problems of informal urban and traditional rural sectors; expand the use of policy, planning and legal instruments; facilitate execution of joint research and development projects with other countries; and examine the role of external assistance in enhancing research and development links with production. In the panel's view, the United Nations, when giving assistance, should require participation of leaders from the production system in formulating and executing research and development projects; assist the least developed countries (LDCs) through national and sectoral studies and review the impact of new large loans from multilateral and bilateral funding agencies on the research and development sectors in developing countries.

To illustrate some of the concepts of reinforcing linkages between research and development activities and the production system, the panel proposed several pioneer projects in various countries and devised a methodology for their initiation. The suggested projects were grouped into three main categories covering user-oriented technology delivery mechanisms, linkages to improve productivity in under-utilized capacity, and identification of needs in LDCs.

Management training

The question of human resources development for the planning, management and implementation of science and technology programmes in developing countries was considered by an *ad hoc* panel of specialists (Kuwait, 8-11 January 1983), jointly organized by the Centre for Science and Technology and the Kuwait Institute for Scientific Research.[21] The panel made a number of recommendations, directing attention towards the specific course of actions by entities concerned with the development process and application of science and technology to it. It stressed that persons at policy and decision-making levels and middle-level managerial personnel, as well as practioners of science and technology, should be sensitized to various aspects of science and technology management through seminars and flexible training schemes, which would take into account on-the-job experience and specific environmental and organizational factors. The panel recommended organizing inventories of management development schemes, training activities and research programmes to disseminate knowledge on opportunities and experiences and generate new training and research schemes. The United Nations, regional intergovernmental and some non-governmental organizations could be instrumental in promoting those activities and facilitating exchanges of expertise.

The panel suggested that maximum efficiency of those modular-type training schemes could be achieved through a balanced participation of various scientific research and educational institutions, government agencies involved in science and technology regulation and promotion, and productive sector enterprises. It offered guidelines for developing training schemes and proposed maintaining an informal network of their ex-participants. The panel stressed the need for inculcating principles and techniques of science and technology management at the national level and at individual institutions, and called for introducing those topics in university graduation and post-graduation courses in developing countries. It recommended continuous training of tutors and periodic updating of a roster of experts and management research projects for use by interested countries and organizations, and urged the United Nations and other international and regional organizations to promote improvement of science and technology management in developing countries. The panel urged the Advisory Committee on Science and Technology for Development to keep the subject under constant review and called for concrete actions by the Intergovernmental Committee.

At its February 1983 session,[12] the Advisory Committee endorsed the report of the Kuwait panel, noting that concentrated efforts to improve indigenous managerial capacity, through an introduction of various training projects in both developed and developing countries, could bring major benefits to the developing countries over a relatively short period of time. The Advisory Committee specifically underlined the panel's recommendations regarding the development of modular training schemes and compilation of inventories of various management and training activities and research projects at regional and sub-regional levels, and emphasized a need for enlarging national pools of training talent in developing countries. It stressed the important promotional and advisory role of the United Nations, particularly, the ACC Task Force of science and technology. While suggesting several essential prerequisites for fostering successful management systems in developing countries, the Advisory Committee said it would re-evaluate its views and recommendations on an annual basis.

The Advisory Committee's recommendations were welcomed by the Intergovernmental Committee on 17 June.[18]

Assessment of levels of attainment

The activities of the Centre for Science and Technology for Development aimed at analysing the levels of attainment of scientific and technological development among different countries, were summarized in a May 1983 report by the Secretary-General, covering the period from April 1982 to March 1983.[14] To permit the designing of guidelines for programme evaluation, information exchange and the formulation of situation profiles on science and technology strategies, the Centre was establishing a computerized data base

of relevant scientific and technological and socio-economic indicators of a non-sectoral nature. The data, obtained in co-operation with various United Nations entities, were organized in the form of country profiles and covered about 50 variables within the framework of the eight programme areas of the operational plan for implementation of the 1979 Vienna Plan of Action. The information was also analysed to develop alternative indicators for scientific and technological activities.

As a first step in the efforts to study the feasibility of developing suitable indicators, a meeting of nine United Nations entities and agencies— The Centre, UNESCO, UNIDO, UNCTAD, ILO, FAO, UNEP, WHO and UNRISD—was held at UNESCO headquarters in Paris, in November 1983. The Secretary-General's report covering the Centre's activities from March 1983 to February 1984,[22] noted that the participants discussed the purposes and criteria for selecting indicators and the limitations of the existing approaches, and proposed new methodologies to be elaborated under an inter-agency programme. An Advisory Committee panel was scheduled to meet at Vienna in May 1984 to measure the impact of science and technology on selected development objectives, its report to be considered by the Advisory Committee in 1985.

The Intergovernmental Committee, at its June 1983 session, considered the March 1982 report of the DIEC Director-General on the assessment of levels of attainment,[23] along the guidelines suggested by the Secretary-General in a note of 14 April 1983.[24] The Intergovernmental Committee took note of the report in a decision of 17 June.[18]

REFERENCES
[1]YUN 1979, p. 636. [2]YUN 1981, p. 735. [3]YUN 1982, p. 925. [4]A/CN.11/36. [5]A/CN.11/38. [6]A/38/37 (res. 3(V)). [7]Ibid. (dec. 3(V)). [8]YUN 1982, p. 926. [9]A/38/37 (dec. 9(V)). [10]YUN 1981, p. 744. [11]YUN 1982, p. 943. [12]Ibid., p. 934. [13]A/CN.11/34. [14]A/CN.11/40 & Corr.1. [15]A/38/37 (dec. 7(V)). [16]Ibid. (dec. 12(V)). [17]YUN 1982, p. 934. [18]A/38/37 (dec. 10(V)). [19]A/CN.11/AC.1/IV/2. [20]A/CN.11/AC.1/IV/3. [21]A/CN.11/AC.1/III/3. [22]A/CN.11/49. [23]YUN 1982, p. 936. [24]A/CN.11/25/Add.1.

Financing

UN Financing system

Operative since January 1982,[1] the United Nations Financing System for Science and Technology for Development (UNFSSTD) continued during 1983 to help developing countries strengthen their scientific and technological capacities as envisaged by the 1979 Vienna Programme of Action. In June 1983,[2] the Administrator of the United Nations Development Programme (UNDP) and the DIEC Director-General reported to the Intergovernmental Committee that a detailed review of all projects approved by UNFSSTD had been carried out in January to assess the potential for the exchange of results and for follow-up. UNFSSTD also undertook a series of consultations with United Nations agencies and other organizations to clarify legal, financial and operational aspects of increased levels of core and non-core operations.

In a further report on UNFSSTD activities in 1983[3] the Administrator noted that despite severe general resource constraints, the System made progress in developing nine projects to be financed through trust fund arrangements. In February, the first project on this basis, financed by Norway and valued at $1.3 million, was signed to provide for the establishment of the Bejing Institute for Software Research to strengthen the capacity for computer software development and training in China. The other projects, all of them to be financed by Italy, dealt with the application of technologies for rural areas in Indonesia, the strengthening of national capacity for mineral exploration and development in Costa Rica, the utilization of agro-animal wastes for production of energy and chemical products in Malaysia, improvement of technology planning and promotion in Mali, and assessment and planning of rural energy technologies in Mauritania and the Niger. Two other projects in the Niger were concerned with establishing a national centre of agricultural machinery and applied farming research in the country's four major ecological zones. UNFSSTD also entered into negotiations on further projects on food technology and technology management training.

Science and technology policy and planning activities had emerged as a key area within the UNFSSTD programme. In Costa Rica, for example, UNFSSTD assisted the Government in designing a national science and technology system, while in Botswana, Sierra Leone and Zimbabwe it focused on a comprehensive assessment of the state of science and technology. Among a variety of research and development projects, an effort in Malawi centered on developing high-yield, pest-resistant tea clones and in Pakistan on a combined research/production programme in alternative energy. With regard to scientific and technological information, UNFSSTD was instrumental in Kenya in setting up an information and documentation service with a national co-ordinating focal point and helped launch the Andean Technological Information System in the Andean subregion, and an interregional Technological Information Pilot System.

To draw the widest possible range of expertise, resources and linkages, UNFSSTD concluded agreements with a number of non-governmental and private sector organizations, among them the American Chemical Society and Stanford University's Engineering Department, as well as governmental bodies. With a view to promoting international co-operation, UNFSSTD co-sponsored an International Conference on Science and Technology Policy in China, a meeting on International Co-operation for African Technological Development in Senegal and an International Conference on Carbon Fibre Applications in Brazil. It also supported a series of 24 sessions of lectures and discussions in the Arab region attended by leading national and international experts on technology choice, development, acquisition and transfer.

During 1983, the UNFSSTD portfolio of bankable projects increased to 88, with 47 of them fully appraised and internally cleared and the remaining 41 prepared for immediate implementation upon receipt of funds.

Responding to Governments' growing concern about the effectiveness of development assistance projects, UNFSSTD developed, from February to June 1983, evaluation procedures for examining a project's output, design, impact and its administrative and financial soundness. Evaluation operations covered four areas: analysis of existing project concepts, systems and practices; formulation of evaluation procedures; co-ordination with the activities of the UNDP Central Evaluation Office (see Chapter II of this section); and individual project evaluation, used to test the established procedures on four projects, one each in Africa, Asia, Latin America and the Middle East.

Reporting to the UNDP Governing Council on 1983 UNFSSTD operations,[4] the UNDP Administrator noted that its working methods and procedures ensured UNFSSTD's cost-efficiency, responsiveness and self-reliance, and provided for its effective co-operation with UNDP, proper evaluation and dissemination of project results and generation of sizable follow-up investment from public and private sectors. At the end of 1983, the total value of commitments by UNFSSTD was $44.2 million.

Intergovernmental Committee action. As decided by the General Assembly in December 1982,[5] the Intergovernmental Committee held a special session at New York from 25 April to 4 May 1983[6] to assess the resource situation of UNFSSTD and the outlook for the following years. Following consultations, the Chairman submitted a statement of understanding according to which the The Committee agreed that the target for core resources for a period of three years starting in 1983 should be at least $300 million based on a progressive build-up of resources and a joint pattern of contributions by developed and developing countries. The minimum requirement in contributions was set at $50 million for the period from July 1983 to June 1984. The statement also called for immediate consultations to assess the fulfilment of these conditions and work out the voting pattern of the UNFSSTD Executive Board. Assuming agreement on those issues, interested Governments would state their intended contributions during the Committee's June session.

Taking up the institutional and financial issues in June, the Committee reached agreement on the pattern of voting in the Executive Board and incorporated it in a 17 June decision[7] on the establishment of the long-term financial and institutional arrangements for UNFSSTD. Under the same decision, the Committee endorsed the $300 million target for core resources and the $50 million minimum requirement in contributions set at its special session. It requested the Secretary-General to consult with Governments on mobilizing resources and, if appropriate, convene after an informal meeting in October, the Committee's fifth session in early November 1983 to enable Governments to state their intended participation in and pledges to UNFSSTD. Subsequently, the Committee would adopt the financing plan and elect the Executive Board members.

With regard to the pattern of voting, the Committee stated that all Executive Board decisions would be taken on the basis of consensus. If consensus could not be reached, a two-thirds majority with a quorum of a least half the members from developed and developing countries would be needed for cases not concerned with individual national projects. For approval of those projects, a two-thirds majority was required; in other cases, the interested State might raise the matter in the Committee. The Executive Board would adopt conciliation procedures and call attention to unresolved issues when reporting to the Committee.

On 20 June,[8] the Intergovernmental Committee requested the General Assembly and the Committee on Conferences to approve the pledging meetings and make arrangements for their convening as envisaged.

GENERAL ASSEMBLY ACTION

On 19 December, on the recommendation of the Second (Economic and Financial) Committee, the General Assembly adopted resolution 38/157 without vote.

Long-term financial and institutional arrangements for the United Nations Financing System for Science and Technology for Development

The General Assembly,

Recalling the Vienna Programme of Action on Science and Technology for Development and General Assembly resolution 34/218 of 19 December 1979,

Also recalling its resolutions 36/183 of 17 December 1981 and 37/244 of 21 December 1982,

Taking into account the report of the Intergovernmental Committee on Science and Technology for Development on its fifth session, in particular decision 4(V) of 20 June 1983 on the establishment of the long-term financial and institutional arrangements for the United Nations Financing System for Science and Technology for Development,

Noting with appreciation the support provided over the past four years by Governments to the Interim Fund and to the United Nations Financing System for Science and Technology for Development,

Concerned that it has not yet been possible to bring into full effect the provisions of resolution 37/244,

Noting that the informal open-ended meeting, called for by the Intergovernmental Committee in its decision 4(V), indicates that a significant number of countries, developed and developing, are considering making financial contributions to the Financing System in an effort to attain the targets established by the General Assembly,

1. *Decides* that:

(a) The Secretary-General should be authorized to convene, in consultation with Governments, a pledging conference for the United Nations Financing System for Science and Technology for Development prior to the sixth session of the Intergovernmental Committee on Science and Technology for Development to enable interested Governments to announce their pledges for the first year and, if possible, to provide an indication of the amount, they may contribute in the two following years;

(b) Thereafter, the Intergovernmental Committee will, at its sixth session, proceed to adopt decisions as required, including, if appropriate, the financing plan for the Financing System, and to elect the members of the Executive Board of the United Nations Financing System for Science and Technology for Development, as decided by the General Assembly in resolution 37/244;

(c) In the meantime, the existing operating procedures of the present Financing System shall continue;

2. *Decides also* that the period up to the convening of the pledging conference should be fully utilized for all necessary consultations to bring about the successful outcome of the pledging conference and the establishment of the long-term financial and institutional arrangements for the Financing System;

3. *Invites* those Governments that are prepared to do so to indicate to the Secretary-General the amount of their financial contributions to the Financing System at the earliest possible time;

4. *Requests* the Secretary-General to continue to make all efforts to mobilize the support of Governments for the establishment of the long-term arrangements for the Financing System and appeals to all Governments to co-operate with the Secretary-General in this regard.

General Assembly resolution 38/157

19 December 1983   Meeting 102   Adopted without vote

Approved by Second Committee (A/38/702/Add.4) without vote, 14 December (meeting 56); draft by Vice-Chairman (A/C.2/38/L.114), based on informal consultations on 18-nation draft (A/C.2/38/L.100); agenda item 78 (d).

Meeting numbers. GA 38th session: 2nd Committee 55, 56; plenary 102.

Contributions and expenditures

In 1983, 27 countries contributed a total of $494,465 to UNFSSTD, while as of 31 December

1983, 23 countries pledged $249,039 for 1984. UNFSSTD expenditures in 1983 were slightly higher than $7 million; of that amount, $6.3 million were spent on projects in 44 countries, and $881,000 on regional and interregional projects.

CONTRIBUTIONS TO THE UN FINANCING SYSTEM FOR SCIENCE AND TECHNOLOGY FOR DEVELOPMENT, 1983 AND 1984

(as at 31 December 1983- in US dollar equivalent)

Country	1983 payment	1984 pledge
Argentina	15,800	—
Bangladesh	2,000	2,280
Belgium	136,178	54,545
Bhutan	2,200	1,440
Botswana	943	—
Congo	—	2,421
Cuba	31,693	—
Cyprus	382	—
Egypt	6,085	—
Fiji	1,000	980
Guinea-Bissau	2,376	—
Guyana	2,684	—
Honduras	2,000	2,000
Indonesia	12,000	12,000
Jamaica	—	4,396
Kenya	—	67,647
Lesotho	—	500
Malawi	2,000	781
Mauritius	1,026	—
Mongolia	—	295
Pakistan	77,519	—
Panama	2,000	2,000
Papua New Guinea	1,500	—
Philippines	10,000	10,000
Republic of Korea	30,000	30,000
Senegal	—	2,000
Seychelles	—	1,000
Sierra Leone	2,800	800
Thailand	500	242
Togo	4,975	—
Turkey	5,000	5,000
Yugoslavia	91,975	—
Zaire	—	1,000
Zambia	42,017	41,045
Zimbabwe	7,812	6,667
Total	**494,465**	**249,039**

SOURCE: A/39/5/Add.1.

EXPENDITURES OF THE UN FINANCING SYSTEM FOR SCIENCE AND TECHNOLOGY FOR DEVELOPMENT BY COUNTRY OR AREA, 1983

(as at 31 December 1983; in thousands of US dollars)

Country/area	Amount
Bangladesh	3
Botswana	6
Brazil	214
Burundi	45
China	1,150
Cuba	49
Djibouti	44
Ethiopia	1
Fiji	14
Gambia	265
Guinea	164
Guinea-Bissau	56
Haiti	59
Honduras	180
India	769
Indonesia	26
Italy	90
Ivory Coast	30
Jamaica	259
Kenya	75
Lao People's Democratic Republic	64
Lesotho	115

Country/area	Amount
Madagascar	189
Malawi	142
Mauritius	6
Mexico	59
Mongolia	23
Mozambique	20
Nepal	208
Nigeria	293
Pakistan	98
Papua New Guinea	20
Paraguay	52
Philippines	243
Republic of Korea	12
Senegal	75
Seychelles	198
Sierra Leone	33
Sudan	274
Swaziland	152
Thailand	133
United Republic of Tanzania	348
Uruguay	13
Zambia	41
Subtotal	**6,310**
Regional Africa	20
Regional Latin America and the Caribbean	40
Regional Arab States	155
Regional Asia and the Pacific	185
Interregional	481
Global	(90)
Subtotal	**791**
Total	**7,101**

NOTE: Figures in parentheses are negative amounts representing adjustments from prior years' expenditures.

SOURCE: DP/1984/5/Add.6.

REFERENCES

[1]YUN 1982, p. 937. [2]A/CN.11/39. [3]A/CN.11/48. [4]DP/1984/5/Add.1 & 2. [5]YUN 1982, p. 939, GA res. 37/244, 21 Dec. 1982. [6]A/38/37. [7]A/38/37 (dec. 4(V)). [8]*Ibid.* (dec. 5(V)).

Institutional arrangements

National focal points

Further efforts were made in 1983 to encourage the establishment of national focal points—originally set up for the 1979 United Nations Conference on Science and Technology for Development—and to integrate them into the national system for science and technology, as called for by the operational plan for the implementation of the Vienna Programme of Action.

As requested in June 1982 by the Intergovernmental Committee,[1] the Secretary-General, by a note of 31 March 1983,[2] submitted a list of national focal points, which had been reactivated following a 1980 Intergovernmental Committee decision. National focal points had been designated by 22 countries for the first time, the Secretary-General reported.

The Intergovernmental Committee on Science and Technology for Development, by a resolution of 17 June 1983,[3] took note with appreciation of the results of the November 1982 Brazzaville, Congo, meeting on the strengthening of science and technology capacities of African countries,[1] and again recommended organizing such meetings in other regions to promote application of science and technology at the national and regional levels and enhance the interaction of national focal points with the Centre for science and technology. The Committee requested the Centre's Executive Director to submit reports on such meetings and expand, through national focal points, his co-operation with Governments and intergovernmental and non-governmental organizations. It also requested the Secretary-General to submit proposals aimed at strengthening national and regional activities to enable the General Assembly to take these proposals into account when considering the programme budget for 1984-1985.

As requested by the Committee, the Secretary-General submitted to the Assembly in December 1983 revised estimates for the Centre's additional activities recommended by the Committee.[4] Funds required for those activities were estimated at $87,400.

In an oral report before the Fifth (Administrative and Budgetary) Committee, the Chairman of the Advisory Committee on Administrative and Budgetary Questions (ACABQ) recommended that the Assembly take note of the Secretary-General's report.[4] ACABQ noted that the report stated that every endeavour would be made to carry out the additional activities within the 1984-1985 programme budget; to the extent that that was not possible, the related programmatic adjustments and subsequent redeployment of resources would be reported in the context of the budget and programme performance reports on the 1984-1985 biennium. If the resources available were insufficient, the Secretary-General would bring the matter before ACABQ. As emphasized by the Secretary-General, the activities already approved by the Fifth Committee would not be curtailed for those additional activities.

On 16 December, the Fifth Committee decided without objection to recommend that the Assembly take note of the Secretary-General's report and concur with the procedures outlined for obtaining resources for the additional activities.

GENERAL ASSEMBLY ACTION

On 20 December, on the recommendation of the Fifth Committee, the General Assembly adopted section XV of resolution 38/234 without vote.

Revised estimates under section 5B (Centre for Science and Technology for Development) arising from the recommendations of the Intergovernmental Committee on Science and Technology for Development in its resolution 4(V)

[*The General Assembly* . . .]

1. *Takes note* of the report of the Secretary-General;

2. *Concurs* with the procedures outlined in the report;

. . .

General Assembly resolution 38/234, section XV

20 December 1983   Meeting 104   Adopted without vote

Approved by Fifth Committee (A/38/760) without vote, 16 December (meeting 69); oral proposal by Chairman; agenda item 109.
Financial implications. SG, A/C.5/38/64 & Add.1.
Meeting numbers. GA 38th session: 5th Committee 62, 64, 69; plenary 104.

Intergovernmental Committee on science and technology

Review of effectiveness

The Intergovernmental Committee, in a resolution of 20 June 1983,[5] decided to review its organization and methods of work in order to strengthen its role and effectiveness and requested the DIEC Director-General, with the assistance of the Executive Director of the Centre for science and technology, to submit relevant proposals in 1984. The Committee also decided that documentation should be made available six weeks prior to its sessions and agreed to consider in 1984 the possibility of electing at the end of each session the officers for the subsequent session.

NGO participation

By a resolution of 17 June 1983,[6] transmitted from its 1982 session,[7] the Intergovernmental Committee adopted a procedure for the participation of NGOs in its activities, according to which NGOs, in consultative status with the Economic and Social Council and other organizations which had participated in the 1979 United Nations Conference on Science and Technology for Development, might be invited to participate as observers. NGOs, whose names had been submitted by the Secretary-General, might be equally invited if the Committee so approved. Before submitting names of NGOs for approval, the Secretary-General would apply the following criteria: the organization concerned should be a recognized non-profit national or international NGO; as part of its programme, it should be concerned with issues related to the work of the Committee; and its activities related to the Committee's work should be of a nature that made them transferable for use in other countries.

By a decision of the same date,[8] the Committee took note of the report of a March 1983 preliminary consultation meeting at Rome, Italy, on the contribution of NGOs in implementing the 1979 Vienna Programme of Action and encouraged their continued involvement through their co-operation with the Committee.

Work programme

The General Assembly, in decision 38/429, recommended that the Intergovernmental Committee consider adopting, on an experimental basis, a biennial cycle of meetings, in conformity with the biennial programme of work to be established for the Second Committee (see Chapter XXIV of this section).

Report of the Committee

The reports of the Intergovernmental Committee on its special and regular 1983 sessions (New York, 25 April–4 May and 6-20 June)[9] were submitted to the Economic and Social Council at its July session. The Council allocated them to its First (Economic) Committee for consideration and, by decision 1983/167, decided to transmit the reports to the General Assembly.

ECONOMIC AND SOCIAL COUNCIL ACTION

On 22 July, on the recommendation of its First Committee, the Council adopted decision 1983/167 without vote.

Science and technology for development

At its 39th plenary meeting, on 25 July 1983, the Council took note of the reports of the Intergovernmental Committee on Science and Technology for Development on its special session and on its fifth session, and decided to transmit those reports to the General Assembly at its thirty-eighth session for consideration.

Economic and Social Council decision 1983/167

Adopted without vote

Approved by First Committee (E/1983/115) without vote, 22 July (meeting 22); draft orally proposed by Chairman; agenda item 12.
Meeting number. ESC 39.

GENERAL ASSEMBLY ACTION

On 14 December, on the recommendation of the Second (Economic and Financial) Committee, the General Assembly adopted decision 38/440 without vote.

Report of the Intergovernmental Committee on Science and Technology for Development

At its 102nd plenary meeting, on 19 December 1983, the General Assembly, on the recommendation of the Second Committee, took note of the report of the Intergovernmental Committee on Science and Technology for Development on its fifth session.

General Assembly decision 38/440

Adopted without vote

Approved by Second Committee (A/38/702/Add.4) without vote, 14 December (meeting 56); draft orally proposed by Chairman; agenda item 78 *(d).*
Meeting numbers. GA 38th session: 2nd Committee 56; plenary 102.

Advisory Committee on science and technology

The Advisory Committee on Science and Technology for Development held its third session in New York from 1 to 8 February 1983 and submitted a report to the Intergovernmental Committee.[10] The Committee reviewed and endorsed the reports of the December 1982 Los Baños and January 1983 Kuwait panels of specialists, and outlined background documentation for two other panels scheduled to be held in April and October 1983 in Tunis and Peru (see above). It considered the details of organizing in 1983 a panel of experts on science and technology and women (see Chapter XIX of this section) and proposed convening two panels in 1984, in Europe and the African region, on the following subjects: measurement of the impact of science and technology on national development, and a global perspective of science and technology for development and an analysis of obstacles in implementing the Vienna Programme. The Committee also recommended activities for the proposed advance technology alert system (ATAS) (see above) and considered guidelines for improving its collaboration with the international scientific community and the United Nations System for Science and Technology for Development.

By a decision of 17 June,[11] the Intergovernmental Committee took note of the Advisory Committee's report and invited Governments, the United Nations, and organizations to consider its recommendations seriously. It invited Governments to begin formulating and implementing pioneer projects. It recommended that the Advisory Committee be authorized by the General Assembly to establish a maximum of four panels of specialists in 1984 and 1985. Noting the choice of topics for the two 1984 panels, the Intergovernmental Committee proposed that the examination of impact measurement indices should include levels of attainment of scientific and technological development and take into account United Nations initiatives. It requested that a progress report on objective-oriented indices and on the mid-decade review of implementation of the Vienna Programme be submitted to it in 1984 and a final report in 1985. Topics for the 1985 panels were to be submitted to the Intergovernmental Committee at its 1984 session.

Centre for science and technology

During 1983, the United Nations Centre for Science and Technology for Development continued to assist the DIEC Director-General in implementing the 1979 Vienna Programme of Action, particularly in providing substantive support to the Intergovernmental Committee and its subsidiary bodies and promoting and co-ordinating United Nations science and technology activities at the secretariat level.

With regard to policy analysis and research, the Centre's major efforts were aimed at initiating an ATAS identification system, analysing levels of attainment of scientific and technological development, and organizing panels of specialists and follow-up action (see above). The Centre also played a major co-ordinating role in national and regional activities, closely co-operating with the Committee members through a network of national focal points (see above) and promoting systematic interaction with the scientific community and intergovernmental and non-governmental organizations. It continued to publish its newsletter *UPDATE*, which reported on progress in implementing the Vienna Programme.

The Centre maintained consultations with various United Nations entities, especially through the Task Force of Science and Technology for Development of the Administrative Committee on Co-ordination (ACC) (see below). It also promoted mobilization of resources to implement the Vienna Programme and co-operated with the United Nations Financing System in the appraisal of projects.

The Intergovernmental Committee, in a decision of 17 June 1983,[12] took note of the Secretary-General's report on the Centre's activities for the period April 1982–March 1983.[13] It requested the Centre to take into account the following factors, when planning its activities and establishing a multi-annual programme of work: the Centre should work on broad intersectoral disciplines of priority; the ACC Task Force should give high priority to identifying scientific and technological infrastructures and facilitating co-operation between national and regional units or centres; assessments of improvements to national, regional or wider infrastructures in intersectoral disciplines, as well as a list of these disciplines and relevant reports, should be submitted to the Intergovernmental Committee.

Information on the Centre's activities from April 1983 was provided by the Secretary-General in a March 1984 report.[14]

Proposed regional advisory bodies

After examining the Advisory Committee's February 1982 proposals regarding regional advisory bodies,[15] the Intergovernmental Committee, by a decision of 17 June 1983,[16] invited regional commissions to consider the proposed development and strengthening of existing advisory bodies and the establishment, if necessary, of new bodies to assist the commissions in implementing regional strategies within the framework of the Vienna Programme and to facilitate interaction with the Advisory Committee's regional members.

Co-ordination in the system

The Task Force on Science and Technology for Development, set up by ACC as a mechanism of inter-agency co-operation in implementing tasks assigned to the Intergovernmental Committee, held its fourth session at Geneva from 26 to 28 January 1983.[17]

In considering the implementation of the Vienna Programme of Action, the Task Force focused on the recommendations of four working groups established in 1982 to formulate specific proposals for joint activities.[18] Having endorsed the proposed activities, it hoped that United Nations entities would support them from existing as well as extrabudgetary resources, and that support would also come from the United Nations Financing System for Science and Technology for Development (UNFSSTD). The Task Force stressed the importance of informing Member States of the proposed activities and recommended that an *ad hoc* meeting of the working groups' chairmen and UNFSSTD be called by the Centre to make arrangements for effective follow-up. It decided that each joint activity would be implemented by designated lead agencies or through joint management teams in cases involving a sharing of the work by several United Nations entities. The support of non-governmental institutions and organizations was also recognized as valuable. With regard to additional joint activities, the Task Force noted a proposal from the Economic Commission for Latin America concerning mineral development and stated that a detailed examination of the operational plan might be needed to identify other potential projects.

ACC consideration. By a decision of 31 March,[19] ACC took note of the Task Force report and stressed the importance of joint activities as a major inter-agency co-operative undertaking for implementing the Vienna Programme and as a contribution to joint planning and programming in science and technology. The Committee decided that United Nations entities should, to the maximum extent possible, mobilize existing resources for joint activities, that the lead agencies should seek extrabudgetary resources, and that UNFSSTD should consider the possibility of supporting these activities within the applicable policies, procedures and criteria.

Report of the Director-General. Following endorsement of the proposed joint activities by ACC and its Task Force, the DIEC Director-General submitted a report to the Intergovernmental Committee, which was transmitted by the Secretary-General in April 1983.[20] The report described 24 joint activities, their scope and objectives and the lead agencies and participating organizations within the framework of the eight programme areas of the operational plan for the implementation of the Vienna Programme. Representing a collective effort in their formulation, design and execution, those activities encompassed a large number of organizations, covered a wide geographical range and took into account the relevant co-operation among developing countries. The report noted three major aspects of implementing the proposed activities: consultations with Member States, financing and appropriate institutional arrangements. Before submitting the joint activities to appropriate funding bodies, lead agencies would consult with concerned countries to reflect more accurately their needs and priorities.

Even though the Task Force proposals did not cover all activities of the operational plan, the Director-General emphasized that launching another elaborate exercise to identify additional joint activities would be premature without at least securing financing for the proposed activities. In the mean time, the Centre would continue to identify additional areas for joint activities, but submit the results for inter-agency consideration only after the financing for the proposed activities was cleared. It would also continue, in co-operation with individual lead agencies, to co-ordinate efforts to ensure implementation of the joint activities and report annually to the Intergovernmental Committee.

Intergovernmental Committee action. The Intergovernmental Committee, by a decision of 17 June,[21] recommended that all proposed joint activities contained in the Director-General's report should serve as a basis for consultations between lead agencies and Member States, with relevant procedural and project descriptions to be completed before submission of the resulting proposals for financing. The Committee also decided that the mobilization of resources for implementing the joint activities should be based on the existing resources of United Nations entities, the lead agencies' extrabudgetary resources and possible support from UNFSSTD, upon requests by States or groups of States concerned. The Committee requested the DIEC Director-General, with the assistance of the Centre's Executive Director, to monitor the overall implementation of the joint activities and to report to it annually. It also decided that the Centre should continue its efforts to identify additional fields for joint activities and should submit them for inter-agency consideration.

Programme evaluation

As a follow-up to a 1981 study by the Secretary-General of the efficiency of the United Nations in science and technology for development,[22] the ACC Task Force discussed, at its January 1983 session, the assessment of traditional means of assistance to developing countries, on the basis of a paper submitted by the Centre on science and technology in accordance with a 1982 request.[23] The Task Force concluded that, while there was need for reviewing the existing means of assistance, the matter required great care, suitable

methodology and proper selection of functional areas. It requested the Centre to take into account all relevant information available within the United Nations system and draw up proposals for consideration by the *ad hoc* meeting of the working groups' chairmen (see above).

The question of efficiency was also addressed by the Intergovernmental Committee, which endorsed, by a decision of 20 June 1983,[24] the recommendations on evaluation in a March 1982 report by the DIEC Director-General.[25] In conducting these evaluations, the Intergovernmental Committee requested: co-operation by United Nations bodies with the selected recipient countries and the Director-General; biennial reporting by the Director-General on the results of these evaluations; and submission, by the Centre's Executive Director to the Committee in 1984, of proposals for establishing a data base on United Nations scientific and technological activities, geared towards endogenous capacity building of developing countries. The Intergovernmental Committee also invited the Committee for Programme and Co-ordination to consider undertaking at a future session an updated cross-organizational analysis of policies related to science and technology for development.

REFERENCES
[1]YUN 1982, p. 936. [2]A/CN.22/INF.5. [3]A/38/37 (res. 4(V)). [4]A/C.5/38/64 & Add.1. [5]A/38/37 (res. 1(V)). [6]*Ibid.* (res. 2(V)). [7]YUN 1982, p. 945. [8]A/38/37 (dec. 6 (V)). [9]A/38/37. [10]A/CN.11/3∠. [11]A/38/37 (dec. 10(V)). [12]*Ibid.* (dec. 8(V)). [13]A/CN.11/40 & Corr.1. [14]A/CN.11/49. [15]YUN 1982, p. 947. [16]A/38/37 (dec. 11(V)). [17]ACC/1983/3. [18]YUN 1982, p. 943. [19]ACC/1983/DEC/1-10 (dec. 1983/5). [20]A/CN.11/37. [21]A/38/37 (dec. 1(V)). [22]YUN 1981, p. 750. [23]YUN 1982, p. 945. [24]A/38/37 (dec. 3(V)). [25]YUN 1982, p. 944.

Technology transfer

During 1983, United Nations organizations continued to provide advisory services on the choice, acquisition and transfer of technology to developing countries. Those activities were related to programme area III of the operational plan of the Vienna Programme of Action. The bodies most directly concerned with technology transfer were the United Nations Conference on Trade and Development (UNCTAD) and the United Nations Industrial Development Organization (UNIDO) (see below).

UNCTAD activities. In response to a December 1982 request[1] of the Committee on Transfer of Technology, the UNCTAD Secretary-General submitted to the April 1983 session of the UNCTAD Trade and Development Board a report on interregional linkages towards the implementation of strategies for the technological transformation of developing countries.[2]

Noting an imperative need for developing countries to widen the scope of technological options open to them and to improve the conditions for acquiring technology, the report gave three examples of alternative sources of technology that could be explored for joint efforts: the results of research and development financed by the United Nations and by the public sector, and the decommercialization of technologies in the public sector. Following consideration of modalities for establishing interregional linkages in sectors of critical importance to developing countries and among technology centres, the UNCTAD Secretary-General suggested establishing a suitable forum for the discussion of measures and arrangements for co-operation among different regions and emphasized an urgent need to develop within UNCTAD the capacity to deal on a programme basis with sectoral issues.

The Trade and Development Board (TDB), on 28 April,[3] noted that the issues raised in the report would be considered by the 1983 UNCTAD session based on a secretariat report on the UNCTAD work programme in the transfer of technology (see below). TDB also decided to make available the report on interregional linkages, together with the comments by the Board, to the Conference session. The Board further decided that the issue of interregional linkages and strategies for the technological transformation of developing countries be taken up at the 1985 session of the Committee on the Transfer of Technology in the light of the relevant decisions at UNCTAD's 1983 session. Comments by the Board, together with the UNCTAD Secretary-General's proposals, were transmitted to the sixth (June/July) session of UNCTAD (UNCTAD VI) (see p. 539) as an addendum to an UNCTAD policy paper on the work programme of UNCTAD in the development and transfer of technology.[4] The paper gave an overview of UNCTAD's work in that area over the previous decade, outlined the main directions which should be pursued in the following decade to accelerate the technological transformation of developing countries, and summarized the consultations, co-operation and joint activities of UNCTAD with other United Nations bodies. The paper also outlined a strategy for the technological transformation of developing countries.

The session also had before it another policy paper on a strategy for the technological transformation of developing countries with an addendum containing comments by Governments at the 1982 session of the Committee on Transfer of Technology.[5]

On 2 July, UNCTAD VI adopted resolution 143(VI)[6] recognizing the importance of an adequate legal and institutional framework for the transfer, acquisition and development of technology—including international laws, as well as an international code of conduct on the transfer of technology and the Diplomatic Conference on the Revision of the Paris Convention for the Protection of Industrial Property (see PART TWO, Chapter XV). That framework, UNCTAD stated, should increase the technological capacity of developing countries as well as the contribution of technology to social and economic development of all countries. UNCTAD VI noted an October 1982 report by the UNCTAD secretariat on transfer of technology laws and regulations and endorsed the December 1982 resolution on that matter by the Committee on Transfer of Technology.[7]

The Conference requested its Secretary-General to respond to the pressing needs of developing countries, particularly the least developed, and to provide them with technical and operational assistance through the Advisory Service on Transfer of Technology, strongly urging that the Service be provided with sufficient resources to cover increasing requirements. With regard to other activities and initiatives, UNCTAD also expressed its belief that urgent action towards the technological transformation of developing countries was called for; requested the Committee on Transfer of Technology to take up, at its 1984 session, the issues of interregional linkages and co-operative arrangements; and noted the Conference's work in pharmaceuticals and the proposed joint project with other United Nations entities to facilitate pharmaceutical supplies to developing countries. It requested the UNCTAD Secretary-General to: continue work on the transfer, application and development of technology in sectors of critical importance to developing countries and urgently consider issues related to their technological transformation; prepare proposals on possible complementary work by UNCTAD on new and emerging technologies for the 1984 session of the Committee on Transfer of Technology and submit to the same session proposals on ways of improving efficiency of United Nations–funded research and development; examine how developing countries could obtain the fullest and freest possible access to technology in the public domain; and transmit the report on a strategy for the technological transformation of the developing countries to a special session of the Committee on Transfer of Technology to be held before the Board's April 1984 session.

UNIDO activities. The activities of UNIDO, described in the 1983 report of its Executive Director,[8] continued to be aimed at strengthening the negotiating capacity of developing countries. As part of these efforts, assistance was given to Paraguay in negotiations on selected major industrial projects and to Cuba in the negotiation of an export technology. A training workshop to strengthen negotiating capabilities was held in Venezuela. Questions related to further expansion of the UNIDO Technological Information Exchange System and elaboration of an outline for a global review of technological development and transfer were discussed in October at the eighth Meeting of Heads of Technology Transfers Registries in Caracas, Venezuela. The Meeting also considered several studies on the evaluation of transfer of technology agreements and made recommendations on co-operative programmes for training of registry personnel and regional activities.

On 13 May, the Industrial Development Board reiterated the high priority it attached to the development and transfer of technology to developing countries and stressed the significance of the Organization's work in that context.[9] The Board requested early action on strengthening existing institutional arrangements within the UNIDO secretariat and stressed the importance of co-operation among relevant United Nations entities. It also stressed the utility of the Industrial and Technological Information Bank (INTIB) (see p. 599) to the developing countries and requested the Executive Director to submit to its 1984 session a report on UNIDO work relating to the development and transfer of technology, including INTIB.

Draft code of conduct

UNCTAD activities. UNCTAD VI, in resolution 143(VI) of 2 July 1983,[6] urged the United Nations Conference on an International Code of Conduct on the Transfer of Technology, initially convened under UNCTAD auspices in 1978,[10] to complete the formulation of a code of conduct in 1983 so as to enable its adoption by the General Assembly in the same year. Recommending full participation of all countries in this process, UNCTAD strongly urged that the proposals of the Interim Committee of the Conference on a code of conduct, established by the Assembly in 1981,[11] should provide a basis for finding solutions to the outstanding issues.

These issues were considered by the Conference on a code of conduct at its fifth session held at Geneva from 17 October to 4 November 1983.[12] The Conference focused special attention on questions dealing with the scope of application of the code, restrictive practices, responsibilities and obligations of parties to transfer of technology transactions and applicable law and dispute settlement. The Conference was able to finalize the formulation of chapter 5, on responsibilities and obligations of parties, except for the provision on confidentiality, and resolve a number of outstanding provisions on the preamble, as well as chapters 1 and 2. Despite an improved understanding of the complex issues involved, no

consensus was reached on chapters 4 and 9, dealing, respectively, with the regulation of transfer of technology practices and arrangements, and applicable law and settlement of disputes. Since negotiations on these and other outstanding issues could not be concluded, the Conference, by a decision of 4 November, requested the Assembly to authorize the convening of the Conference's next session not later than the first half of 1985. It further invited the UNCTAD Secretary-General to determine the dates of that session and prepare for it the draft international code of conduct and appropriate documentation.

GENERAL ASSEMBLY ACTION

On 19 December 1983, on the recommendation of the Second Committee, the General Assembly adopted resolution 38/153 without vote.

International code of conduct on the transfer of technology

The General Assembly,

Recalling its resolution 37/210 of 20 December 1982 and decision 145(VI) adopted on 2 July 1983 by the United Nations Conference on Trade and Development at its sixth session, held at Belgrade from 6 June to 2 July 1983,

Taking note of the decision adopted on 4 November 1983 by the United Nations Conference on an International Code of Conduct on the Transfer of Technology at its fifth session, held at Geneva from 17 October to 4 November 1983,

1. *Decides* to convene a sixth session of the United Nations Conference on an International Code of Conduct on the Transfer of Technology, under the auspices of the United Nations Conference on Trade and Development, in order to complete successfully the negotiations on the code of conduct not later than the first half of 1985;

2. *Invites* the Secretary-General of the United Nations Conference on Trade and Development, after consultations with regional groups, to determine the precise dates of the sixth session of the United Nations Conference on an International Code of Conduct on the Transfer of Technology;

3. *Also invites* the Secretary-General of the United Nations Conference on Trade and Development to prepare for the sixth session of the United Nations Conference on an International Code of Conduct on the Transfer of Technology the text of the draft international code of conduct as at the end of the fifth session of the Conference, as well as appropriate documentation.

General Assembly resolution 38/153

19 December 1983   Meeting 102   Adopted without vote

Approved by Second Committee (A/38/702/Add.2) without vote, 28 November (meeting 52); draft by Chairman (A/C.2/38/L.82); agenda item 78 (b).
Financial implications. S-G, A/C.2/38/L.89.
Meeting numbers. GA 38th session: 2nd Committee 50, 52; plenary 102.

REFERENCES

[1]YUN 1982, p. 949. [2]TD/B/946 and Corr.1. [3]A/38/15 (dec. 268(XXVI)). [4]TD/284 & Add.1. [5]TD/277/Add.1. [6]*Proceedings of the United Nations Conference on Trade and Development, Sixth Session, Belgrade, 6 June–2 July 1983,* vol. I, *Report and*

Annexes (TD/326, vol. I), Sales No. E.83.II.D.6. [7]YUN 1982, p. 953. [8]ID/B/320. [9]A/38/16 (conclusion 1983/5). [10]YUN 1978, p. 503. [11]YUN 1981, p. 756, GA res. 36/140, 16 Dec. 1981. [12]A/38/580.

Brain drain

During 1983, the negative economic, political and social effects of the reverse transfer of technology—the so-called brain drain of skilled personnel from developing to developed countries—continued to be of major concern for UNCTAD and the General Assembly.

UNCTAD activities. As requested by the General Assembly in December 1982,[1] the UNCTAD Trade and Development Board, by a decision of 28 April 1983,[2] scheduled a Meeting of Governmental Experts on the Reverse Transfer of Technology to be held in August/September 1983. In resolution 143(VI)[3] adopted on 2 July, UNCTAD VI invited its Secretary-General to hold consultations with the regional groups to obtain broadest possible participation at the Meeting.

Following wide regional consultations, the Meeting was held at Geneva from 29 August to 7 September, attended by government experts from 56 Member States. The Meeting had before it a June 1983 UNCTAD study on an integrated approach to international skill exchange.[4] Containing proposals for policy and action on reverse transfer of technology, the study reviewed the existing international consensus on the problem, examined proposals for action by developed and developing countries at bilateral and multilateral levels, and outlined an integrated programme of action, with its basic components ranging from payment schemes to the establishment of norms and standards on skill exchange.

Discussions at the Meeting resulted in a set of conclusions and recommendations, which were annexed to a report it endorsed on 7 September.[5] Stressing the serious negative economic, political and social implications of brain drain, the Meeting concluded that developing countries of origin should receive an equitable share of the benefits accruing to receiving developed countries. It also stated that there was a broad international consensus regarding an urgent need for national, regional and international policies to avoid the reverse transfer of technology and minimize its effects. It recommended that the UNCTAD Secretary-General convene at least two governmental expert meetings before the 1985 session of the Committee on Transfer of Technology, the earliest one to be held before the Committee's 1984 session to define principles and standards concerning brain drain, map up ways to improve the relevant data base and information and outline the terms of

reference for subsequent expert meetings. It also recommended that the Trade and Development Board transmit the Meeting's report to the high-level intergovernmental group set up to consider the review and appraisal of the Implementation of the International Development Strategy for the Third United Nations Development Decade (see p. 406). Further, the Meeting invited the UNCTAD Secretary-General to consult with Governments and regional groups for ensuring full participation at the subsequent meetings of governmental experts and recommended continued study of the brain drain problem by the UNCTAD secretariat.

On 20 October 1983,[6] the Trade and Development Board took note of the Meeting's report. The conclusions and recommendations of the Meeting were described in a November report[7] by the Secretary-General to the General Assembly. The Secretary-General noted that the Meeting's results would benefit an inter-agency meeting requested by the Assembly,[1] which was scheduled to be convened by the UNCTAD Secretary-General prior to the 1984 session of the Committee on Transfer of Technology.

Another UNCTAD secretariat study on institutional and policy issues relating to the co-operative exchange of skills among developing countries (see p. 487) was submitted to the 1983 TDB session.

GENERAL ASSEMBLY ACTION

On 19 December 1983, the General Assembly, on the recommendation of the Second Committee, adopted resolution 38/154 by recorded vote.

Development aspects of the reverse transfer of technology

The General Assembly,

Recalling its resolutions 32/192 of 19 December 1977, 33/151 of 20 December 1978, 34/200 of 19 December 1979, 35/62 of 5 December 1980, 36/141 of 16 December 1981 and 37/207 of 20 December 1982, concerning the development aspects of the reverse transfer of technology,

Reaffirming resolution 102(V) of 30 May 1979 and section II of resolution 143(VI) of 2 July 1983 of the United Nations Conference on Trade and Development and the Vienna Programme of Action on Science and Technology for Development,

1. *Takes note* of the report of the Secretary-General concerning the Meeting of Governmental Experts on the Reverse Transfer of Technology, held at Geneva from 29 August to 7 September 1983;

2. *Regrets* that an inter-agency group to co-ordinate measures on the question of the reverse transfer of technology, as provided for in paragraph 4 of General Assembly resolution 37/207, has not been established;

3. *Requests* the Secretary-General to establish urgently an inter-agency group comprising representatives of the United Nations Conference on Trade and Development, the International Labour Organisation, the United Nations Educational, Scientific and Cultural Organization, the World Health Organization, the United

Nations Development Programme, the Centre for Science and Technology for Development of the Secretariat, the United Nations Institute for Training and Research, the Statistical Office of the Secretariat and other appropriate organs and bodies of the United Nations system to co-ordinate measures on the question of the reverse transfer of technology and, in particular, to examine and enhance the effectiveness of the United Nations system in responding to the complex needs of the countries concerned, as well as any additional measures to that effect;

4. *Requests* the Secretary-General of the United Nations Conference on Trade and Development to convene the meetings of governmental experts on the reverse transfer of technology, at least two of which should be held at an appropriate time before the sixth session of the Committee on Transfer of Technology, scheduled to take place in 1985; the meetings should be based on the terms of reference outlined in General Assembly resolution 37/207 and should take into account the relevant conclusions and recommendations of the Meeting of Governmental Experts on the Reverse Transfer of Technology;

5. *Appeals* to all Member States to participate fully in the meetings of governmental experts on the reverse transfer of technology;

6. *Requests further* the Secretary-General of the United Nations Conference on Trade and Development, in co-operation with the International Labour Organisation and other relevant organizations, to prepare the necessary documentation to assist the next meetings of governmental experts;

7. *Requests* the Trade and Development Board to include, in its reports to the General Assembly at its thirty-ninth and fortieth sessions, the outcome of the meetings of governmental experts on development aspects of the reverse transfer of technology;

8. *Requests* the Secretary-General to submit a report on the results of the meetings of the inter-agency group to the General Assembly at its thirty-ninth session.

General Assembly resolution 38/154

19 December 1983   Meeting 102   122-21-1 (recorded vote)

Approved by Second Committee (A/38/702/Add.2) by recorded vote (109-21-1), 14 December (meeting 55); draft by Mexico, for Group of 77 (A/C.2/38/L.88), orally revised in informal consultations; agenda item 78 *(b)*.

Meeting numbers. GA 38th session: 2nd Committee 50, 56; plenary 102.

Recorded vote in Assembly as follows:

In favour: Afghanistan, Algeria, Angola, Argentina, Bahamas, Bahrain, Bangladesh, Barbados, Belize, Benin, Bhutan, Bolivia, Botswana, Brazil, Bulgaria, Burma, Burundi, Byelorussian SSR, Cape Verde, Chad, Chile, China, Colombia, Congo, Costa Rica, Cuba, Cyprus, Czechoslovakia, Democratic Kampuchea, Democratic Yemen, Djibouti, Dominican Republic, Ecuador, Egypt, El Salvador, Equatorial Guinea, Ethiopia, Fiji, Gabon, Gambia, German Democratic Republic, Ghana, Guatemala, Guinea, Guinea-Bissau, Guyana, Haiti, Honduras, Hungary, India, Indonesia, Iran, Iraq, Ivory Coast, Jamaica, Jordan, Kenya, Kuwait, Lao People's Democratic Republic, Lebanon, Lesotho, Liberia, Libyan Arab Jamahiriya, Madagascar, Malawi, Malaysia, Maldives, Mali, Malta, Mauritania, Mauritius, Mexico, Mongolia, Morocco, Mozambique, Nepal, Nicaragua, Niger, Nigeria, Oman, Pakistan, Panama, Papua New Guinea, Paraguay, Peru, Philippines, Poland, Qatar, Romania, Rwanda, Saint Lucia, Saint Vincent and the Grena-

dines, Sao Tome and Principe, Saudi Arabia, Senegal, Sierra Leone, Singapore, Somalia, Sri Lanka, Sudan, Suriname, Swazi and, Syrian Arab Republic, Thailand, Togo, Trinidad and Tobago, Tunisia, Turkey, Uganda, Ukrainian SSR, USSR, United Arab Emirates, United Republic of Cameroon, United Republic of Tanzania, Upper Volta, Uruguay, Venezuela, Viet Nam, Yemen, Yugoslavia, Zaire, Zambia.

Against: Australia, Austria, Belgium, Canada, Denmark, Finland, France, Germany, Federal Republic of, Iceland, Ireland, Italy, Japan, Luxembourg, Netherlands, New Zealand, Norway, Portugal, Spain, Sweden, United Kingdom, United States.

Abstaining: Greece.

In the opinion of the United States, which had requested the vote in the Second Committee, the text would lead to a waste of UNCTAD resources; instead of compensatory measures for their alleged losses, the developing countries needed to pursue policies aimed at fulfilling their citizens' aspirations. Speaking on behalf of the ten-member European Economic Community (EEC), Greece explained that they had not participated in the Geneva Meeting of governmental experts on the transfer of technology and could not take into account its conclusions; in view of the lack of accurate knowledge on the extent of the problem, any work in that area should begin with studies to determine whether the flow of human resources had measurable economic consequences. The German Democratic Republic, also on behalf of Bulgaria, the Byelorussian SSR, Czechoslovakia, Hungary, Mongolia, the Ukrainian SSR and the USSR, said that the economic imbalance between the developing and the developed capitalist countries caused the reverse transfer of technology, which was used by international capital and corporations to sap the capabilities of the developing countries; stopping the brain drain would help promote the economic and social development of the developing countries with a view to establishing a new international economic order; they regretted that the developed countries had obstructed United Nations efforts by boycotting the Geneva Meeting. Mexico, on behalf of the Group of 77, stated that the reverse transfer of technology required high-priority attention by the international community as a most serious problem facing the developing countries.

REFERENCES

(1)YUN 1982, p. 955, GA res. 37/207, 20 December 1982. (2)A/38/15, dec. 271(XXVI). (3)*Proceedings of the United Nations Conference on Trade and Development, Sixth Session, Belgrade, 6 June–2 July 1983*, vol. I, *Report and Annexes* (TD/326, vol. I), Sales No. E.83.II.D.6. (4)TD/B/AC.35/2. (5)TD/B/969. (6)TDB, A/38/15, vol. II. (7)A/38/557.

Chapter XIII

Social and cultural development

The Commission for Social Development held its twenty-eighth session at Vienna, Austria from 7 to 16 February 1983, at which it recommended to the Economic and Social Council adoption of 16 resolutions and three decisions. Another four decisions adopted by the Commission were brought to the Council's attention.

Following the Commission's recommendations, the Council adopted resolutions on the world social situation (1983/8); economic and social development policies (1983/11); social aspects of the International Development Strategy for the Third United Nations Development Decade (1983/9); the adverse effects of the arms race on social development (1983/18); social welfare policies (1983/22); social integration through popular participation (1983/13); income distribution (1983/12); social aspects of rural development (1983/10); the role of the family in development (1983/23); co-operatives (1983/15); information exchange on the activities of the Centre for Social Development and Humanitarian Affairs (1983/20); and reporting procedures of the Committee on Crime Prevention and Control (1983/25).

Both the Council and the General Assembly—in resolutions 1983/31 and 38/24, respectively—dealt with the issue of popular participation and human rights.

Following consideration of a report of the Secretary-General on national experience in achieving social and economic changes for the purpose of social progress, the Assembly, in resolution 38/25, reaffirmed the right of every State to choose its economic and social system, and requested the Secretary-General to make arrangements for an interregional seminar.

Preparations were made for the Seventh (1985) United Nations Congress on the Prevention of Crime and the Treatment of Offenders; five regional preparatory meetings were held in Europe, Asia and the Pacific, Latin America, Africa and Western Asia. The Committee on Crime Prevention and Control continued to function as the preparatory committee for the Congress. Taking up a March 1982 proposal by the Committee, the Economic and Social Council, in resolution 1983/25, decided that from now on the Committee should report directly to the Council.

The work of the United Nations Educational, Scientific and Cultural Organization (UNESCO) to promote the return or restitution of cultural property to the countries of origin, showed further progress. The Assembly, in resolution 38/34, reaffirmed that the restitution to a country of its cultural property contributed to international co-operation and preservation of cultural values. The Assembly invited States to become parties to the 1970 UNESCO Convention on the Means of Prohibiting and Preventing the Illicit Import, Export and Transfer of Ownership of Cultural Property.

Topics related to this chapter. Disarmament: disarmament and development. Development policy: International Development Strategy for the Third United Nations Development Decade; economic and social trends and policy; rural development. Health: disabled persons. Human rights: migrant workers; rights of detained persons; right to development; right to education and employment.

Social conditions and policy

Social change

In accordance with a 1981 General Assembly request,[1] the Secretary-General submitted to the 1983 Assembly, through the Commission for Social Development and the Economic and Social Council, a report on national experience in achieving far-reaching social and economic changes for social progress.[2] The report was based on 17 replies received by March 1983 to a note verbale sent by the Secretary-General to Member States.

Belgium, Denmark and the Netherlands gave information on their experiences in adapting social policies to changing economic conditions and societal change; Cyprus, Egypt, Kuwait and Pakistan on social welfare services; Ecuador, Mauritius, Nigeria and Tunisia on social guidelines for economic growth; China and Ethiopia on agrarian change; and the Byelorussian SSR, Mongolia, the Ukrainian SSR and the USSR on a political and economic framework for social progress.

The Commission for Social Development took note of the Secretary-General's report on 16 February 1983.[3]

ECONOMIC AND SOCIAL COUNCIL ACTION

On the recommendation of its Second (Social) Committee, the Economic and Social Council adopted decision 1983/129 without vote.

Report of the Secretary-General on national experience in achieving far-reaching social and economic changes for the purpose of social progress

At its 14th plenary meeting, on 26 May 1983, the Council took note of the report of the Secretary-General on national experience in achieving far-reaching social and economic changes for the purpose of social progress.

Economic and Social Council decision 1983/129

Adopted without vote

Approved by Second Committee (E/1983/62), 10 May (meeting 8); agenda item 11.
Meeting number. ESC 14.

In resolution 1983/18, the Economic and Social Council called on States in their national development programmes to reallocate resources for social progress, otherwise spent for military purposes.

GENERAL ASSEMBLY ACTION

On 22 November, on the recommendation of the Third (Social, Humanitarian and Cultural) Committee, the General Assembly adopted resolution 38/25 by recorded vote.

National experience in achieving far-reaching social and economic changes for the purpose of social progress

The General Assembly,

Guided by the desire to promote a higher standard of life, full employment and conditions for economic and social progress and development,

Bearing in mind the Declaration on Social Progress and Development,

Mindful of the provisions of the Declaration and the Programme of Action on the Establishment of a New International Economic Order, as well as the Charter of Economic Rights and Duties of States,

Taking note once again of Economic and Social Council resolutions 1581 A (L) of 21 May 1971, 1667(LII) of 1 June 1972 and 1746(LIV) of 16 May 1973 concerning the importance of fundamental structural socio-economic changes for the strengthening of national independence and the achievement of the ultimate goals of social progress,

Recalling its resolutions 3273(XXIX) of 10 December 1974, 31/38 of 30 November 1976 and 36/19 of 9 November 1981, in which it reaffirmed the importance for every State to exercise its inalienable right to carry out fundamental social and economic changes for the purpose of social progress and the necessity of studying national experience in this field,

Desirous of securing a speedy and complete removal of all obstacles to the economic and social progress of peoples, especially colonialism, neo-colonialism, racism, racial discrimination, *apartheid*, military, political and economic intervention and pressure, foreign aggression and occupation or alien domination, as well as all forms of inequality and exploitation of peoples,

Convinced that peaceful coexistence and co-operation among States, as well as effective measures in the field of disarmament, create favourable international conditions for the socio-economic development of all countries, in particular developing countries,

Desirous also of contributing to the implementation of the International Development Strategy for the Third United Nations Development Decade,

1.   *Takes note* of the report of the Secretary-General on national experience in achieving far-reaching social and economic changes for the purpose of social progress;

2.   *Reaffirms* the sovereign and inalienable right of every State to choose its economic and social system in accordance with the will of its people, without outside interference in whatever form it takes;

3.   *Requests* the Secretary-General to make arrangements for holding in 1984 or 1985 an interregional seminar, as called for in paragraph 4 of General Assembly resolution 36/19, within the resources already requested for sectoral and regional advisory services in the proposed programme budget for the biennium 1984-1985;

4.   *Invites* Member States to submit to the Secretary-General reports on their national experience in achieving far-reaching social and economic changes for the purpose of social progress;

5.   *Also requests* the Secretary-General to prepare, in consultation with Member States, a further report on national experience in achieving far-reaching social and economic changes for the purpose of social progress, taking into account the provisions of General Assembly resolution 36/19, and to submit it to the Assembly at its fortieth session, through the Commission for Social Development and the Economic and Social Council;

6.   *Decides* to include in the provisional agenda of its fortieth session the item entitled "National experience in achieving far-reaching social and economic changes for the purpose of social progress".

General Assembly resolution 38/25

22 November 1983   Meeting 66   131-1-8 (recorded vote)

Approved by Third Committee (A/38/572) by roll-call vote (107-1-9), 4 November (meeting 33); 13-nation draft (A/C.3/38/L.16), orally revised; agenda item 85 *(b)*.
Sponsors: Afghanistan, Angola, Benin, Congo, Cuba, Democratic Yemen, Ethiopia, Lao People's Democratic Republic, Madagascar, Mongolia, Mozambique, Nicaragua, Viet Nam.
Meeting numbers. GA 38th session: 3rd Committee 31, 33; plenary 66.

Recorded vote in Assembly as follows:

In favour: Afghanistan, Albania, Algeria, Angola, Argentina, Austria, Bahamas, Bahrain, Bangladesh, Barbados, Belgium, Bhutan, Bolivia, Botswana, Brazil, Bulgaria, Burma, Burundi, Byelorussian SSR, Cape Verde, Chad, Chile, China, Colombia, Comoros, Congo, Costa Rica, Cuba, Cyprus, Czechoslovakia, Democratic Kampuchea, Democratic Yemen, Denmark, Djibouti, Dominican Republic, Ecuador, Egypt, El Salvador, Ethiopia, Fiji, Finland, France, Gabon, German Democratic Republic, Greece, Guatemala, Guinea, Guinea-Bissau, Guyana, Honduras, Hungary, Iceland, India, Indonesia, Iran, Iraq, Ireland, Jamaica, Jordan, Kenya, Kuwait, Lao People's Democratic Republic, Lebanon, Lesotho, Liberia, Libyan Arab Jamahiriya, Luxembourg, Madagascar, Malawi, Malaysia, Maldives, Mali, Malta, Mauritania, Mauritius, Mexico, Mongolia, Morocco, Mozambique, Nepal, Netherlands, Nicaragua, Nigeria, Norway, Oman, Pakistan, Panama, Papua New Guinea, Peru, Philippines, Poland, Portugal, Qatar, Romania, Rwanda, Saint Lucia, Samoa, Sao Tome and Principe, Saudi Arabia, Senegal, Sierra Leone, Singapore, Solomon Islands, Somalia, Spain, Sri Lanka, Sudan, Suriname, Swaziland, Sweden, Syrian Arab Republic, Thailand, Togo, Trinidad and Tobago, Tunisia, Turkey, Uganda, Ukrainian SSR, USSR, United Arab Emirates, United Republic of Cameroon, United Republic of Tanzania, Upper Volta, Uruguay, Venezuela, Viet Nam, Yemen, Yugoslavia, Zaire, Zambia, Zimbabwe.
Against: United States.
Abstaining: Australia, Canada, Germany, Federal Republic of, Israel, Italy, Japan, New Zealand, United Kingdom.

Introducing the draft that became resolution 38/25, Mongolia said it was a follow-up to a 1981 Assembly resolution[4] affirming the right of every State to choose its economic and social system without outside interference; that was particularly important at a time when the world was witnessing so many flagrant violations of that right.

The United States said the reports on national experience in social and economic changes had produced little of value; in view of the shortage of resources, marginal projects should not be undertaken. Australia doubted whether discussing such vague ideas would produce anything of value. In Canada's view, the text lacked definition and clear focus and its intention was not substantially different from the mandate of the Commission for Social Development. Speaking on behalf of the ten member States of the European Community (EC), Greece said the subject should be considered a subitem under the item on the world social situation; the EC members also had reservations on paragraphs 3 and 5 of the text.

Costa Rica felt it would have been better to add in paragraph 2 "freely expressed" after "in accordance with the will of its people", and to include further changes in the sixth preambular paragraph, such as adding terrorism, as well as ideological intervention and pressure, to the list of obstacles to economic and social progress. Colombia considered that the changes proposed by Costa Rica would have been constructive and positive.

The USSR supported the text whose core it said was the unconditional confirmation of the inalienable right of each State to choose its own social system with no outside interference. Democratic Kampuchea welcomed the adoption of the draft as it attached particular importance to the problems of young people; its own young people were engaged in a desperate fight to protect Kampuchea from its neighbour to the east which had been waging a war of aggression and genocide for nearly five years.

Social survey

By resolution 1983/8 of 26 May 1983, the Economic and Social Council endorsed the conclusions of the Commission for Social Development on the 1982 *Report on the World Social Situation*,[5] and noted that the next report on the world social situation would be made in 1985.

The draft resolution originated in the Commission for Social Development which approved it on 15 February 1983. On 22 September,[6] the Secretary-General noted that the Commission's conclusions were transmitted to the Assembly by the Council resolution.

ECONOMIC AND SOCIAL COUNCIL ACTION

On 26 May 1983, on the recommendation of its Second Committee, the Economic and Social Council adopted resolution 1983/8 without vote.

World social situation

The Economic and Social Council,

Recalling General Assembly resolution 37/54 of 3 December 1982, on the world social situation,

Having considered the report of the Commission for Social Development on its twenty-eighth session,

1. *Endorses* the conclusions reached by the Commission for Social Development on the 1982 *Report on the World Social Situation*, annexed to the present resolution;

2. *Transmits* those conclusions to the General Assembly for its consideration.

ANNEX
Conclusions of the Commission for Social Development on the 1982 *Report on the World Social Situation*

1. The Commission for Social Development notes that recent years have seen a worsening of the social situation. Achievements registered in certain regions and countries or in specific areas of social development do not alter this fact. This general deterioration affects in particular the developing countries. Some long-lasting problems have not been solved. Additionally, new problems have appeared, both in developing and in industrial countries, and much remains to be done to achieve the various objectives adopted by the international community. Some countries appear to remain untouched by this general deterioration.

2. The Commission reaffirms that the ultimate aim of development is the constant improvement of the well-being of the entire population on the basis of its full participation in the process of development and a fair distribution of the benefits therefrom.

3. It is necessary to achieve the rapid and complete elimination of the obstacles to the economic and social progress of peoples. Colonialism, neo-colonialism, racism, racial discrimination, *apartheid*, aggression, occupation and foreign domination and all other forms of inequality and exploitation of peoples constitute major obstacles to the economic and social progress of developing countries and peoples.

4. The existing inequities and imbalances in international economic relations are widening the gap between developed and developing countries, thereby constituting a major obstacle to the development of the developing countries and adversely affecting international relations and the promotion of world peace and security. The arms race and aggravation of international tension continue to contribute to the deterioration of the world social situation. Disarmament would release resources which could be used for the development of developing countries and could contribute to the well-being and prosperity of all.

5. A reduction of social and economic disparities and the adoption of measures to ensure the effective participation of all people in the preparation and execution of national policies for economic and social development are required, based on a full enjoyment of human rights.

6. The adverse social situation reflects the lack of implementation of the Declaration on Social Progress and Development and of the objectives and overall development goals adopted and reaffirmed in the International Development Strategy for the Third United Nations Development Decade.

7. Certain social and economic changes have occurred that have had broad and negative repercussions

on the elements constituting the social sphere. There is a need to adapt governmental policies to the new and urgent needs which have arisen.

8.   Greater attention needs to be accorded to a unified approach to development. The interdependence that exists between economic development and social development is becoming even more noticeable at the present time. The worsening of the social situation has a serious impact in particular areas and countries, notably on employment and income distribution. Even though additional measures are required for social progress, economic development is an essential prerequisite. It has been stressed that social change and development can have a positive influence for pulling societies out of their economic difficulties. The establishment of the new international economic order has become of great importance for social progress.

9.   It is recommended that Governments make a more rational use of various available resources to deal with the worsening social situation, paying greater attention to the most essential and deserving aspects of social development which have experienced the greatest deterioration and have a multiplier effect on such development.

10.   The 1982 *Report on the World Social Situation*, as well as the debate on the report in the Commission, clearly indicate that existing approaches to socio-economic development have not always been able to solve the problems of mass poverty and underdevelopment. Alternative development methods, involving in particular more effective people's participation, are needed.

11.   The social situation should be monitored on a regular and in-depth basis with special attention to the manner in which the Declaration on Social Progress and Development, the International Development Strategy and world plans of action have been implemented.

12.   The 1985 report on the world social situation should retain a global overview while giving special attention to regional and other perspectives in social and overall development. The 1985 report should be focused on issues of international concern mentioned above and should be in line with the priorities established in General Assembly resolutions 34/152 of 17 December 1979 and 37/54 of 3 December 1982. It should fully reflect the crucial importance for social and overall development of all countries of such global international issues as the persisting imbalances in the world economy, the international economic crises particularly affecting the developing world, the relation between development and peace and the need for disarmament.

13.   The 1985 report should emphasize the relationships among various aspects of national, regional and international trends and policies. It should reflect the complex and changing relations between the economic and social, national and international facets of development. It should provide an intersectoral analysis of trends and an intersectoral treatment of issues and policies, bearing in mind different social and cultural traditions.

Economic and Social Council resolution 1983/8

26 May 1983   Meeting 14   Adopted without vote

Approved by Second Committee (E/1983/62) without vote, 10 May (meeting 8); draft by Commission for Social Development (E/1983/14); agenda item 11. *Meeting number.* ESC 14.

In resolution 1983/11, the Council requested that future reports on social aspects of development, especially those on the world social situation, place special emphasis on the interrelationships between social and economic problems.

In resolution 1983/18, the Council requested the Secretary-General to include in his report on the world social situation a section on the adverse effects of the arms race on social progress and development, paying full attention to a redistribution of resources released as a result of disarmament measures for economic and social development.

Social conditions in developing countries

In response to a 1981 Economic and Social Council resolution,[7] the Secretary-General submitted to the Council's first session in 1983 a report on social trends in developing countries and current economic conditions.[8] The Secretary-General found that the world economic recession was straining the already fragile social structure in many developing countries.

The already meagre level of income and consumption had been reduced for large sections of the population, the growth of employment opportunities had slowed down considerably and expenditure on the social sectors, including education and health, had ceased to grow or had actually been reduced, thus further setting back long-term social development.

The Commission for Social Development took note of the report in a decision of 16 February.[3]

ECONOMIC AND SOCIAL COUNCIL ACTION

On the recommendation of its Second Committee, the Economic and Social Council adopted decision 1983/130 without vote.

Report of the Secretary-General on some social trends in developing countries and the influence of current economic conditions

At its 14th plenary meeting, on 26 May 1983, the Council took note of the report of the Secretary-General on some social trends in developing countries and the influence of current economic conditions.

Economic and Social Council decision 1983/130

Adopted without vote

Approved by Second Committee (E/1983/62), 10 May (meeting 8); agenda item 11. *Meeting number.* ESC 14.

Economic and social policies

By a resolution of 26 May 1983 on the interrelationship of social and economic development policies, the Economic and Social Council urged that high priority be given to analysing that interrelationship and requested that future reports on social aspects of development place special emphasis on it. In other provisions, the Council recommended research on income distribution and other social problems, and requested the Secretary-General to report on the conclusions of the project on income distribution (see below).

The draft resolution originated in the Commission for Social Development, which approved it on 14 February.

On 26 May, on the recommendation of its Second Committee, the Economic and Social Council adopted resolution 1983/11 without vote.

Interrelationship of social and economic development policies

The Economic and Social Council,

Considering paragraph 42 of the International Development Strategy for the Third United Nations Development Decade, contained in the annex to General Assembly resolution 35/56 of 5 December 1980, according to which development is an integral process, embodying both economic and social objectives, and the national development plans and targets of the developing countries should be formulated on the basis of a unified approach to economic and social development,

Taking note of paragraph 8 of the International Development Strategy, according to which the ultimate aim of development is the constant improvement of the well-being of the entire population on the basis of its full participation in the process of development and a fair distribution of the benefits therefrom,

Taking note also of the preliminary conclusions of a project on income distribution,

1. *Resolves* to urge that high priority should be given to analysing the interrelationship of social and economic policies;

2. *Calls upon* Governments, when they prepare their national development plans, to have as their main objective the improvement of the quality of life and social conditions of the population, within the context of a unified approach to development;

3. *Recommends* that the Secretary-General should continue to carry out studies and research with a view to arriving at solutions, especially as regards the distribution of income, employment and other basic social problems;

4. *Further recommends* that the Secretary-General should carry out studies and research with a view to extending present knowledge of the interrelationships between economic and social problems;

5. *Urges* that the United Nations should co-operate with countries with a view to elaborating plans based on a unified approach to development;

6. *Calls upon* Member States, in view of the serious economic situation being faced, in particular, by the developing countries, which is also characterized by an increase in the cost of living, to take precautions with respect to the situation of low-income groups;

7. *Requests* the Secretary-General to report on the conclusions of the project on income distribution, including those relating to the adverse effects of the world economic crisis on the level and distribution of income in developing countries;

8. *Further requests* that all future reports on social aspects of development, especially the report on the world social situation, while pursuing a critical analysis of the issues of social problems, should place special emphasis on the interrelationships between economic and social problems.

Economic and Social Council resolution 1983/11

26 May 1983   Meeting 14   Adopted without vote

Approved by Second Committee (E/1983/62) without vote, 10 May (meeting 8); draft by Commission for Social Development (E/1983/14); agenda item 11. *Meeting number.* ESC 14.

In its conclusions on the 1982 report on the world social situation, transmitted to the General Assembly by Council resolution 1983/8, the Commission for Social Development stated that the interdependence between economic and social development was becoming more noticeable; the worsening of the social situation had a serious impact notably on employment and income distribution. The Commission further stated that even though additional measures were required for social progress, economic development was an essential prerequisite.

Social aspects of the International Development Strategy

By a resolution of 26 May 1983, the Economic and Social Council dealt with social aspects of the International Development Strategy for the Third United Nations Development Decade (the 1980s).[9] On the same date, the Council decided that a report should be prepared on progress since 1981 in the area of social development, for submission to the General Assembly for its 1984 review of the implementation of the Strategy (see p. 406). Both the draft resolution and the draft decision originated in the Commission for Social Development which approved them on 15 and 16 February, respectively. A draft resolution introduced in the Commission by the Philippines for adoption by the Council, by which the latter would have decided that the Commission should be convened in 1984 to enable it to participate in the review and appraisal of the implementation of the Strategy, was withdrawn.

On 26 May, on the recommendation of its Second Committee, the Economic and Social Council adopted resolution 1983/9 without vote.

International Development Strategy for the Third United Nations Development Decade

The Economic and Social Council,

Recalling that the Declaration on Social Progress and Development, contained in General Assembly resolution 2542(XXIV) of 11 December 1969, emphasized the interdependence of economic and social development in the wider process of growth and change, as well as the importance of a strategy of integrated development which takes full account at all stages of its social aspects,

Recalling further that the International Development Strategy for the Third United Nations Development Decade called, *inter alia*, for the elimination of hunger and malnutrition, the achievement of full employment by the year 2000, health for all by the year 2000, appropriate population policies, the reduction of the infant mortality rate, the availability of safe water and adequate sanitary facilities by 1990, the attainment of a life expectancy of 60 years as a minimum by the year 2000, universal primary school enrolment by the year 2000 and the securing of the full participation of women in all sectors and at all levels of the development process,

1. *Invites* the Committee on the Review and Appraisal of the Implementation of the International Development Strategy for the Third United Nations Development Decade, established by the General Assembly in its resolution 37/202 of 20 December 1982, to carry out that review and appraisal and to examine fully the progress made towards the achievement of the social goals and objectives of the Strategy;

2. *Invites* Governments to examine ways and means of adjusting, intensifying or reformulating policy measures for achieving the social goals and objectives of the International Development Strategy;

3. *Requests* the Committee for Development Planning to give due attention to the social goals and objectives of the International Development Strategy, as well as to both economic and social policy measures designed to achieve the continuous raising of the material and spiritual standards of living of all members of society;

4. *Requests* the Secretary-General, in preparing the report requested by the General Assembly in resolution 37/202 for submission to the Committee on the Review and Appraisal of the Strategy, to ensure full consideration of the social aspects of development, including measures for future action, and to report on the results of the review and appraisal to the Commission for Social Development at its twenty-ninth session.

Economic and Social Council resolution 1983/9

26 May 1983   Meeting 14   Adopted without vote

Approved by Second Committee (E/1983/62) without vote, 10 May (meeting 8); draft by Commission for Social Development (E/1983/14); agenda item 11.
Meeting number. ESC 14.

Also on the recommendation of its Second Committee, the Council adopted without vote decision 1983/123.

Progress achieved since 1981 in the area of social development

At its 14th plenary meeting, on 26 May 1983, the Council decided, in accordance with paragraph 9 of General Assembly resolution 37/202 of 20 December 1982, that the Department of International Economic and Social Affairs, including the Office for Development Research and Policy Analysis and the Centre for Social Development and Humanitarian Affairs, should prepare a report on the progress achieved since 1981 in the area of social development, for submission to the General Assembly at its thirty-ninth session, for its review, through the Committee on the Review and Appraisal of the Implementation of the International Development Strategy for the Third United Nations Development Decade, established by the Assembly in resolution 37/202, and the Economic and Social Council in 1984.

Economic and Social Council decision 1983/123

Adopted without vote

Approved by Second Committee (E/1983/62), 10 May (meeting 8); draft by the Commission for Social Development (E/1983/14); agenda item 11.
Meeting number. ESC 14.

Arms race and social development

By a resolution of 26 May 1983, the Economic and Social Council requested the Secretary-General to include in his triennial report on the world social situation a section on the adverse effects of the arms race on social progress and development, paying full attention to a redistribution of resources released as a result of disarmament measures for economic and social development. The draft resolution originated in the Commission for Social Development which approved it on 16 February.

ECONOMIC AND SOCIAL COUNCIL ACTION

On 26 May, on the recommendation of its Second Committee, the Economic and Social Council adopted resolution 1983/18 without vote.

Adverse effects of the arms race on social progress and development

The Economic and Social Council,

Having considered the 1982 *Report on the World Social Situation,* as well as the report of the Secretary-General on some social trends in developing countries and the influence of current economic conditions,

Recalling the Declaration on Social Progress and Development, contained in General Assembly resolution 2542(XXIV) of 11 December 1969, which draws attention to the need to achieve general and complete disarmament and to channel the progressively released resources to be used for economic and social progress for the welfare of people everywhere and, in particular, for the benefit of developing countries,

Recalling also the provision of the International Development Strategy for the Third United Nations Development Decade concerning the need to achieve concrete progress towards the goals of general and complete disarmament,

Referring to General Assembly resolutions 32/75 of 12 December 1977, 35/141 of 12 December 1980 and 37/70 of 9 December 1982 on the economic and social consequences of the armaments race and its extremely harmful effects on world peace and security,

Recalling General Assembly resolution 37/189 of 18 December 1982 on human rights and scientific and technological developments, in which the Assembly expressed the firm conviction that all peoples and all individuals have an inherent right to life and that the safeguarding of this foremost right is an essential condition for the enjoyment of the entire range of economic, social and cultural, as well as civil and political, rights,

Recalling also its resolution 1981/19 of 6 May 1981, in which it requested the Secretary-General to pay full attention in his reports on the world social situation to emerging social issues of international concern in connection with the changes in the world situation, giving special attention to the relationship between disarmament and development,

Deeply concerned that the arms race, particularly in nuclear armaments, and military expenditures continue to increase at an alarming speed, constituting a grave danger to world peace and security,

Recalling further the conclusions of the Final Documents of the tenth and twelfth special sessions of the General Assembly, devoted to disarmament, to the effect that the vastly increased military budgets have also contributed to current economic problems in certain States and that existing and planned military programmes constitute a colossal waste of precious resources which might otherwise be used to elevate living standards of all peoples and solve the problems confronting developing countries in achieving economic and social development,

Noting with concern the worsening of social conditions in many countries of the world, a situation which represents a threat to the attainment of the goals and tasks of the Declaration on Social Progress and Development and of the International Development Strategy for the Third United Nations Development Decade,

1. *Requests* the Secretary-General to submit, every three years, through the Commission for Social Development and in the framework of his report on the world social situation, a section on the adverse effects of the arms race on social progress and development in the world;

2. *Further requests* the Secretary-General to pay full attention in his reports on the world social situation to a redistribution of resources released as a result of implementation of disarmament measures for the purpose of economic and social development of all countries, including developing countries, and to contribute to the bridging of the economic gap between developed and developing countries;

3. *Calls upon* States, when preparing their national programmes of social and economic development, to take measures for reallocating the resources which are being spent for military purposes, in the interest of ensuring social progress;

4. *Requests* the Commission for Social Development, at its thirtieth session, to consider the question of the adverse effects of the arms race on social progress.

Economic and Social Council resolution 1983/18

26 May 1983   Meeting 14   Adopted without vote

Approved by Second Committee (E/1983/62) without vote, 10 May (meeting 8); draft by Commission for Social Development (E/1983/14); agenda item 11.
Meeting number. ESC 14.

Social aspects of UN development activities

Pursuant to 1981[10] and 1982[11] Economic and Social Council decisions, the Secretary-General submitted to the Council in April 1983[12] a report reviewing the implementation of recommendations made in 1980 by the *Ad Hoc* Working Group on the Social Aspects of the Development Activities of the United Nations.[13] The Secretary-General pointed out that the Working Group's recommendations on United Nations programme development concerned two complementary matters—integrated social and economic development and the advancement of women, youth, the aging, disabled persons, and international migrant workers and their families.

The main substantive recommendations were reflected in the major programmes in the economic and social sectors of the medium-term plan for 1984-1989, where integrated development, advancement of specific groups, and cross-sectoral development activities were given emphasis.

Since adoption of those recommendations, a number of international instruments had been adopted, the most significant among them the International Development Strategy for the Third United Nations Development Decade (see Chapter I of this section).

On the recommendation of its Second Committee, the Economic and Social Council adopted decision 1983/128 without vote.

Report of the Secretary-General on the feasibility, programme and co-ordination implications, as well as the resource implications, of the main recommendations of the *Ad Hoc* Working Group on the Social Aspects of the Development Activities of the United Nations

At its 14th plenary meeting, on 26 May 1983, the Council took note of the report of the Secretary-General on the feasibility, programme and co-ordination implications, as well as the resource implications, of the main recommendations of the *Ad Hoc* Working Group on the Social Aspects of the Development Activities of the United Nations.

Economic and Social Council decision 1983/128

Adopted without vote

Approved by Second Committee (E/1983/62), 10 May (meeting 8); agenda item 11.
Meeting number. ESC 14.

Social integration and welfare

Social welfare

Report of the Secretary-General. In response to a 1981 Economic and Social Council resolution,[14] the Secretary-General submitted to the February 1983 session of the Commission for Social Development a report on developmental social welfare policies and programmes.[15] The report was based on the preliminary findings of a United Nations Secretariat study on global social welfare trends, in the context of overall development. Reports on social welfare in Ecuador, India, Kuwait, the Netherlands, Nigeria, the Philippines, Poland, the United States and Zambia had been analysed in the course of the study. Those reports were supplemented by analyses of social welfare policies and programmes from national as well as cross-national perspectives and from various sources, including Governments, academic and professional organizations and voluntary bodies.

The Secretary-General's report considered aspects of the changes in national social welfare policies since the 1968 International Conference of Ministers Responsible for Social Welfare,[16] the results of regional and intergovernmental meetings on social welfare and their implications for global action, and key issues in social welfare such as global economic crises, with emphasis on the potential of the family in providing a framework for development and on the need for comprehensive and efficient social welfare delivery systems.

The Secretary-General concluded that there was a need to spell out more clearly the relationship between social welfare provisions and development policies as a basis for national planning, and to study the contribution of social welfare policies to overall development. There was also a need to improve social welfare machineries relevant to development, particularly in rural areas, and to assess the administrative structure of social welfare services. Social welfare policies conceived in industrialized countries and developed in times of economic expansion should be revised, not only for economy's sake but to take into account different societal patterns and economic systems. Due attention should be given to international action through research, increased global and regional consultation, better support of field-oriented projects, and closer integration between broader social welfare and activities specific to different population groups.

ECONOMIC AND SOCIAL COUNCIL ACTION

On 26 May 1983, on the recommendation of its Second Committee, the Economic and Social Council adopted resolution 1983/22 without vote. The draft resolution originated in the Commission for Social Development which approved it on 16 February.

Interregional consultation on developmental social welfare policies and programmes

The Economic and Social Council,

Recalling its resolutions 1979/18 of 9 May 1979 and 1981/20 of 6 May 1981 on strengthening developmental social welfare policies and programmes,

Taking note of the report of the Secretary-General on developmental social welfare policies and programmes,

Aware of the serious consequences of the world-wide economic recession for the welfare of peoples in all countries and for the funding and delivery of social services which are even more essential now than in periods of economic growth,

Bearing in mind the recommendations of the *Ad Hoc* Working Group on the Social Aspects of the Development Activities of the United Nations and of the Second Asian and Pacific Ministerial Conference on Social Welfare and Social Development; held at Bangkok in October 1980,

Recognizing the relevance to social development of the principles and objectives of the Arab Charter for Social Work, as formulated by the first Arab Ministerial Con-

ference on Social Welfare, held at Cairo in 1971, the Lagos Plan of Action for the Implementation of the Monrovia Strategy for the Economic Development of Africa, and the regional programme of action for the implementation of the International Development Strategy for the Third United Nations Development Decade adopted by the Economic Commission for Latin America in its resolution 422(XIX) of 15 May 1981,

1. *Reaffirms* the essential role of social welfare in overall development and in dealing with pressing contemporary social issues, namely, the social aspects of unemployment, rural-urban imbalances, problems of urbanization and decreasing resources for social needs;

2. *Urges* the Secretary-General to continue his efforts in the field of developmental social welfare, in full collaboration with the regional commissions, the specialized agencies and non-governmental organizations;

3. *Requests* the Secretary-General to initiate studies and field-oriented activities, within the limits of available resources, aimed at enhancing welfare services to lessen the problems of poverty and unemployment, at developing rural social welfare for balanced socioeconomic growth, and at promoting better integrated, self-reliant and cost-effective patterns of social welfare administration and delivery of services, particularly involving families and local communities and strengthening training and research in social welfare;

4. *Further urges* the Secretary-General to take steps, within existing budgetary resources, for convening an interregional consultation at an appropriate policy-making level, preferably in 1986, to examine social welfare policies and provisions in relation to present problems and concerns of Governments, and against the background of experience gained since the 1968 International Conference of Ministers Responsible for Social Welfare, with the objective of setting specific goals in the social field for the year 2000;

5. *Further requests* the Secretary-General to report to the Commission for Social Development at its twenty-ninth session on the progress achieved in the above areas, particularly with regard to the preparations for the interregional consultation.

Economic and Social Council resolution 1983/22

26 May 1983   Meeting 14   Adopted without vote

Approved by Second Committee (E/1983/62) without vote, 10 May (meeting 8); draft by Commission for Social Development (E/1983/14); agenda item 11. *Meeting number.* ESC 14.

Popular participation

Social integration through popular participation

The Economic and Social Council, on 26 May 1983, adopted a resolution on a unified approach to development analysis and planning in the field of social integration through popular participation. Popular participation as a factor of change in rural areas was considered by the Secretary-General in a report on social aspects of rural development.

The importance of people's participation in rural development was stressed in another report by the Secretary-General on international experience in promoting the co-operative movement. Popular participation was also the topic of an ongoing research project of the United Nations Research Institute for Social Development (see below).

On 26 May, on the recommendation of its Second Committee, the Economic and Social Council adopted resolution 1983/13 without vote. The draft originated in the Commission for Social Development which approved it on 15 February.

Unified approach to development analysis and planning in the field of social integration through popular participation

The Economic and Social Council,

Mindful of the pledge of Member States to take joint and separate action in co-operation with the United Nations to promote higher standards of living for all segments of the population and to ensure full employment and conditions of economic and social progress for the achievement of social justice and social equality,

Bearing in mind the fact that the Declaration on Social Progress and Development, contained in General Assembly resolution 2542(XXIV) of 11 December 1969, stressed the interdependence of economic and social development in the wider process of growth and change,

Bearing in mind also the fact that in article 2 of the Declaration on Social Progress and Development, the General Assembly proclaimed the necessity for the elimination of all forms of inequality, exploitation of peoples and individuals, colonialism and racism, including nazism and *apartheid*, and other policies and ideologies opposed to the purposes and principles of the United Nations,

Recognizing that social progress and development require the full utilization of human resources, including, in particular, the active participation of all elements of society in defining and achieving the common goals of development, as well as the assurance to disadvantaged population groups of equal opportunities for social and economic advancement in order to achieve an effectively integrated society,

Conscious of the importance of the unified approach to development in the field of social integration through popular participation for the achievement of the social goals proclaimed in the Declaration on Social Progress and Development, as well as in the International Development Strategy for the Third United Nations Development Decade, contained in the annex to General Assembly resolution 35/56 of 5 December 1980,

Convinced that the basic orientation of the activities of the Centre for Social Development and Humanitarian Affairs of the Department of International Economic and Social Affairs, which fell under the mandate of the Commission for Social Development as the concept of "social integration", must be prolonged and reinforced,

1. *Reaffirms* the importance for social progress and development to secure for the less advantaged population groups in society full access to their country's social and economic institutions on the basis of full equality;

2. *Believes* that the application of a unified approach in the field of social integration is connected with social and economic structural changes;

3. *Emphasizes* the role of the Centre for Social De-

velopment and Humanitarian Affairs in the study of popular participation of the specific groups within the broader framework of social development strategies and policies at the international, national and regional levels;

4. *Considers* that strategies and policies for social integration may be regarded as methods and instruments of social change which are aimed at eliminating obstacles and creating the necessary conditions for people, including less integrated population groups, to participate fully in development and to benefit therefrom;

5. *Requests* the Secretary-General, in co-operation with Governments and within the limits of existing resources, to arrange a study on the role of popular participation in the formulation and implementation of strategies and policies for social integration, in order to analyse and compare regional and national experience in this area and make those activities more effective;

6. *Invites* the Secretary-General to inform the Commission for Social Development on the results of those studies;

7. *Requests* the Commission for Social Development, at its twenty-ninth session, to consider recent trends in strategies and policies for the social integration of the less advantaged population groups in developing countries.

Economic and Social Council resolution 1983/13

26 May 1983   Meeting 14   Adopted without vote

Approved by Second Committee (E/1983/62) without vote, 10 May (meeting 8); draft by Commission for Social Development (E/1983/14); agenda item 11.
Meeting number. ESC 14.

The Council, in resolution 1983/10, called on Governments to give special attention to the social impact of, among others, popular participation in the development process in rural areas.

Popular participation and human rights

The Commission on Human Rights, by a resolution of 22 February 1983, noted the report of the May 1982 International Seminar on Popular Participation[17] and recommended to the Economic and Social Council adoption of a draft resolution requesting the Secretary-General to undertake an analytical study of the right to popular participation as an important factor in the full realization of human rights (see Chapter XVIII of this section). Subsequently, by resolution 1983/31 of 27 May 1983, the Council adopted that recommendation.

In response to a December 1982 General Assembly resolution,[18] the Secretary-General submitted to the Assembly in 1983 a report on popular participation in its various forms as an important factor in the development and realization of human rights.[19]

As at 15 December, 13 countries and 11 United Nations organs and six specialized agencies had responded to the request for comments.

On 22 November, the General Assembly requested the Secretary-General to report to it in

1985 on progress in the field and requested the Commission to continue considering the question.

ECONOMIC AND SOCIAL COUNCIL ACTION

On 27 May 1983, on the recommendation of its Second Committee, the Economic and Social Council adopted resolution 1983/31 by a vote.

Question of the realization in all countries of the economic, social and cultural rights contained in the Universal Declaration of Human Rights and in the International Covenant on Economic, Social and Cultural Rights, and study of special problems which the developing countries face in their efforts to achieve these human rights

The Economic and Social Council,

Recalling its resolution 1929(LVIII) of 6 May 1975, in which it noted that, to be effective, popular participation should be consciously promoted by Governments with full recognition of civil, political, social, economic and cultural rights and through innovative measures, including structural changes and institutional reform and development, as well as through the encouragement of all forms of education designed to involve actively all segments of society,

Recalling further General Assembly resolutions 32/130 of 16 December 1977, 34/46 of 23 November 1979 and 37/55 of 3 December 1982,

1. *Requests* the Secretary-General to undertake a comprehensive analytical study on the right to popular participation in its various forms as an important factor in the full realization of all human rights, and to submit a preliminary study to the Commission on Human Rights at its fortieth session and the final study at its forty-first session;

2. *Further requests* the Secretary-General in the preparation of the study, to take account of the work on the concept and practice of popular participation that has been carried out by relevant United Nations organs, specialized agencies and other bodies, as well as of the views expressed at the thirty-ninth session of the Commission on Human Rights and such views on, *inter alia,* relevant national experiences as may be submitted by Governments in response to General Assembly resolution 37/55 and the present resolution.

Economic and Social Council resolution 1983/31

27 May 1983   Meeting 15   49-1

Approved by Second Committee (E/1983/61) by vote (38-1), 23 May (meeting 18); draft by Commission on Human Rights (E/1983/13); agenda item 10.
Meeting number. ESC 15.

GENERAL ASSEMBLY ACTION

On 22 November, on the recommendation of the Third Committee, the General Assembly adopted resolution 38/24 without vote.

Popular participation in its various forms as an important factor in development and in the full realization of all human rights

The General Assembly,

Recalling its resolutions 34/152 of 17 December 1979 and 37/55 of 3 December 1982,

Taking note of Economic and Social Council resolution 1983/31 of 27 May 1983 and of Commission on Human Rights resolution 1983/14 of 22 February 1983,

Having considered the report of the Secretary-General on popular participation in its various forms as an important factor in development and in the realization of human rights,

Recognizing that popular participation, including the participation of workers in management and workers' self-management in countries where they exist, constitutes an important factor of socio-economic development, as well as of respect for human rights and the dignity of the human person,

1. *Takes note with appreciation* of the report of the Secretary-General;

2. *Invites* those Governments, United Nations organs and specialized agencies that have not yet done so to transmit their comments and views to the Secretary-General, as called for in General Assembly resolution 37/55;

3. *Requests* the Commission on Human Rights to continue to consider at its fortieth session the question of popular participation in its various forms as an important factor in the full realization of all human rights;

4. *Requests* the Secretary-General to submit a report to the General Assembly at its fortieth session in order that progress made in this field may be reviewed, taking into account, *inter alia,* the consideration of this question by the Commission on Human Rights at its fortieth and forty-first sessions;

5. *Decides* to continue the consideration of this question at its fortieth session, in the context of the item relating to the world social situation, under the subitem entitled "Popular participation in its various forms as an important factor in development and in the full realization of all human rights".

General Assembly resolution 38/24

22 November 1983   Meeting 66   Adopted without vote

Approved by Third Committee (A/38/572) without vote, 3 November (meeting 32); 16-nation draft (A/C.3/38/L.15); agenda item 85 *(c).*
Sponsors: Algeria, Bangladesh, Benin, China, Cuba, Cyprus, India, Iraq, Libyan Arab Jamahiriya, Madagascar, Mexico, Pakistan, Poland, Romania, Sri Lanka, Yugoslavia.
Meeting numbers. GA 38th session: 3rd Committee 31-32; plenary 66.

Income distribution

Pursuant to a 1981 Economic and Social Council decision,[20] the Secretary-General submitted to the February 1983 session of the Commission for Social Development a note containing preliminary conclusions of a research project on income distribution.[21] The last report on income distribution had been submitted to the Council in 1978.[22] Since then, the Secretary-General pointed out, the deteriorating world economic situation had altered the approach to the main questions. Concern had shifted from those bypassed or hurt by structural changes and institutional transformation accompanying growth to the victims of faltering economies, shrinking employment opportunities, inflation, cuts in public spending and physical shortages. Lowered expectations affected both attitudes and policies towards questions of social justice, including income distribution. Both research and policy were hampered by still inadequate data on income distribution, particularly as to country coverage; improvement in the data base remained a pressing need. The latest estimates for some countries were more than 20 years old and for many others more than 10 years old.

However, in spite of data limitations and limited country coverage, some general observations on trends and patterns could be made, the Secretary-General noted. Despite pronounced fluctuations in income distribution over the short run, there appeared to have been considerable stability over the longer run. Few countries had shown a pronounced trend towards a more equal or a less equal distribution during the past 20 years. The small number of countries in which there had been some modest improvement seemed to be either countries with strong and persistent policies emphasizing equity, or small, higher-income and rapidly developing countries. In many countries, the very high incomes continued to be derived from property, including ownership of natural resources and land. Who owned property was one of the more hazy areas in knowledge about income distribution, except in the case of land which was better documented.

For many developing countries, especially the poorer ones, the basic problem remained of how to mobilize resources, or to save out of current production, in order to make the investments in infrastructure, equipment, public services, education, training and institutions that would improve living conditions. With regard to future research on income distribution and related issues, attention was likely to be concentrated on three critical needs, namely, improved flow and interpretation of basic information, integration of disconnected findings, and enhanced effectiveness of policy measures.

ECONOMIC AND SOCIAL COUNCIL ACTION

On 26 May 1983, on the recommendation of its Second Committee, the Economic and Social Council adopted without vote resolution 1983/12. The draft originated in the Commission for Social Development which approved it on 15 February.

Social policy and the distribution of national income

The Economic and Social Council,

Recalling its resolutions 1086 D (XXXIX) of 30 July 1965, 1322(XLIV) of 31 May 1968, 2074(LXII) of 13 May 1977 and 1979/24 of 9 May 1979 concerning income distribution,

Recalling also the Declaration on Social Progress and Development, contained in General Assembly resolution 2542(XXIV) of 11 December 1969, the Declaration and the Programme of Action on the Establishment of a New International Economic Order, contained in Assembly resolutions 3201(S-VI) and 3202(S-VI) of 1 May 1974, the Charter of Economic Rights and Duties of States, contained in Assembly resolution 3281(XXIX)

of 12 December 1974, and the International Development Strategy for the Third United Nations Development Decade, contained in the annex to General Assembly resolution 35/56 of 5 December 1980,

Taking into account section II of General Assembly resolution 33/48 of 14 December 1978, in which the Assembly affirmed that the social progress of all countries implies, among other things, a just and balanced distribution of income at the national and international levels,

Considering that inequality in living conditions and income levels between the population groups in developed and developing countries is a major obstacle to social and economic progress,

Concerned at the high level of poverty, inflation and unemployment caused by the lack of development of social structures and, in many countries, the improper use of those countries' productive forces, as a result, *inter alia*, of the arms race,

1. *Affirms* the importance of preparing and implementing, with a view to achieving a more equitable distribution of national income, effective measures in the field of property relations, tax policy, the elimination of imbalances between rural and urban areas, and a reduction of the adverse effects of inflation, especially for low-income population groups;

2. *Requests* the Secretary-General to prepare for the twenty-ninth session of the Commission for Social Development a report on the equitable distribution of national income, and to include within the framework of the report on the world social situation information on its distribution between developed and developing countries;

3. *Requests* the Secretary-General to pay special attention in his future surveys and reports relating to the world social situation to the analysis of the national income structure in developed and developing countries;

4. *Invites* the Commission for Social Development to include in the agenda of its thirtieth session an item on the equitable distribution of national income.

Economic and Social Council resolution 1983/12

26 May 1983   Meeting 14   Adopted without vote

Approved by Second Committee (E/1983/62) without vote, 10 May (meeting 8); draft by Commission for Social Development (E/1983/14); agenda item 11.
Meeting number. ESC 14.

In resolution 1983/11, the Council, taking note of the preliminary conclusions of the project on income distribution, requested the Secretary-General to report on the project conclusions, including those relating to the adverse effects of the world economic crisis on the level and distribution of income in developing countries. It recommended that he continue to carry out studies and research regarding income distribution, employment and other basic social problems.

Social aspects of rural development

In response to a 1981 Economic and Social Council request,[23] the Secretary-General submitted to the February 1983 session of the Commission for Social Development a report on the social aspects of rural development.[24] He stated that agrarian reform had been the centre-piece of some of the farthest reaching attempts at rural transformation and development in recent decades. In conditions of extreme rural inequality in land and resource ownership, radical agrarian reform had proved to be vital in relieving the plight of the rural poor. In fostering economic growth among the poor, the provision of irrigated water, fertilizer and extension services had been contingent on giving the poor access to land. When not accompanied by agrarian reform, the targeting of rural development programmes towards low-income groups had been largely ineffective. Even the social welfare components of those programmes such as piped drinking water, electricity and feeder roads had under certain conditions benefitted the rural élite more than the masses. Politically influential landlords had sometimes restricted or diverted to their own ends the implementation of rural projects that would have hurt their interests.

Agrarian reforms, whether they had resulted in collective farming or egalitarian peasant farming, had demonstrated their capacity to break down relations of dependence, reduce exploitation and provide the preconditions for an improved quality of life. In certain cases, beneficiaries of reform had grievances and experienced setbacks. For example, not all production co-operatives had functioned smoothly or profitably, and sometimes timid reforms had ended in failure. Some land reforms had had a negative impact on food production; out of a sense of insecurity, land-owners had sometimes stopped investing in their land even before comprehensive reforms had taken place, as happened in Chile in the early 1970s. The same reaction had occurred in Nicaragua, despite the Government's pledges to maintain private modes of production, with no limit on the size of individual holdings for efficient producers.

The number of agrarian reform programmes currently undertaken in developing countries with a market or mixed economy was small in relation to the 1950s and 1960s, the Secretary-General noted. For developing countries with a socialist development strategy, agrarian reform remained an integral part of structural transformation and egalitarian policies. Other topics considered in the report were the promotion of co-operative endeavours, introduction of development planning, strengthening the role of national personnel in rural development, and encouraging popular participation in rural development.

ECONOMIC AND SOCIAL COUNCIL ACTION

On 26 May, on the recommendation of its Second Committee, the Economic and Social Council adopted resolution 1983/10 without vote. The draft originated in the Commission for Social Development, which approved it on 15 February.

Social aspects of rural development

The Economic and Social Council,

Recalling the Declaration on Social Progress and Development, contained in General Assembly resolution 2542(XXIV) of 11 December 1969,

Recalling also the International Development Strategy for the Third United Nations Development Decade, contained in the annex to General Assembly resolution 35/56 of 5 December 1980,

Stressing the need to implement comprehensive rural development programmes to raise the levels of living of the rural populations, particularly in developing countries,

1. *Takes note* of the report of the Secretary-General on the social aspects of rural development;

2. *Calls upon* Governments to give special attention to the social impact of such important policies as:

   (a) Implementation of democratic land reforms;

   (b) Promotion of co-operative movements;

   (c) Introduction of rural development planning;

   (d) Strengthening of the role of qualified national personnel in rural development;

   (e) Encouragement of popular participation in the development process in rural areas;

3. *Requests* the Secretary-General to give special attention in the 1985 report on the world social situation to the social aspects of rural development;

4. *Also requests* the Secretary-General to prepare a comprehensive analytical study based on the experience of various countries and to submit it to the Economic and Social Council through the Commission for Social Development at its twenty-ninth session;

5. *Further requests* the Secretary-General to consider holding seminars, within existing resources, on the social aspects of rural development, with special emphasis on developing countries;

6. *Requests* the Secretary-General to report to the Commission for Social Development at its twenty-ninth session on the implementation of the present resolution.

Economic and Social Council resolution 1983/10

26 May 1983   Meeting 14   Adopted without vote

Approved by Second Committee (E/1983/62) without vote, 10 May (meeting 8); draft by Commission for Social Development (E/1983/14); agenda item 11.
Meeting number. ESC 14.

Family and development

In accordance with a 1981 Economic and Social Council decision,[20] the Secretary-General presented to the February 1983 session of the Commission for Social Development a report on trends in family and child welfare.[25] The report considered trends in national and international policies towards the family and children, and identified the unmet needs of the family, which needed to be given attention if the family was to be strengthened and thus to contribute to the development process.

The report set out a few of the major problems being encountered by the family—poverty, malnutrition, environment and structural changes.

The Secretary-General stated that significant research had been carried out on family and child welfare policies in developed countries; greater consideration should be given to such policies in developing countries, especially in terms of intent, target groups and scope. Also, efforts were needed to identify parameters, and systematic studies were required on the impact of assistance to families and of the potential application of family policy, as distinct from policies addressed to individuals, in order to provide more effective delivery of services in the face of a scarcity of resources.

With regard to international action, the Secretary-General said while attention had been drawn to the needs of the family through various international policy statements, no such statements or development strategies had systematically set out the basic concerns of the international community in terms of principles, objectives and strategies for strengthening the family. If the impact of international strategies on the family was to be understood, special consideration should be given to the family in international policy reviews.

The family also offered significant opportunities as a unifying theme or conceptual framework for linking international policies regarding specific groups such as children, youth, women, the aging and the disabled. It could also serve as a unifying factor in sectoral policies, such as social welfare, education, family planning and primary health care. Meetings, studies and international events should give importance to the family. The United Nations could, through conceptual analyses and country studies, call attention to common approaches to solving problems and to promoting shared roles and responsibilities, and could identify on a global basis resources of value in meeting family-related problems.

ECONOMIC AND SOCIAL COUNCIL ACTION

On 26 May 1983, on the recommendation of its Second Committee, the Economic and Social Council adopted resolution 1983/23 without vote. The draft resolution originated in the Commission for Social Development which approved it on 16 February.

Role of the family in the development process
The Economic and Social Council,

Recalling General Assembly resolutions 33/48 of 14 December 1978 on world social development, 34/59 of 29 November 1979 on the implementation of the Declaration on Social Progress and Development and 34/152 of 17 December 1979 and 37/54 of 3 December 1982 on the world social situation,

Recalling also General Assembly resolutions 3201(S-VI) and 3202(S-VI) of 1 May 1974, containing the Declaration and the Programme of Action on the Establishment of a New International Economic Order, 3281(XXIX) of 12 December 1974, containing the Charter of Economic Rights and Duties of States, 3362(S-VII) of 16 September 1975 on development and international economic co-operation, and 35/56 of 5 December 1980, the annex to which contains the International

Development Strategy for the Third United Nations Development Decade,

Having considered the 1982 *Report on the World Social Situation,*

Taking note of chapter II of the 1982 *Report on the World Social Situation* dealing with the family, in which is quoted article 4 of the Declaration on Social Progress and Development, where it is stated that the family as a basic unit of society and the natural environment for the growth and well-being of all its members, particularly children and youth, should be assisted and protected so that it may fully assume its responsibilities within the community,

Recognizing that the institution of the family takes many forms and is undergoing important transformations in the process of development,

Concerned that the changes have an impact on the social fabric and the solidarity network, and that ways and means, therefore, need to be evolved to analyse those changes and take them into consideration in social policies,

Taking into account article 16 of the Convention on the Elimination of All Forms of Discrimination against Women, which deals with the rights and responsibilities of women and men in marriage and family matters,

Stressing the fact that the relevant organs, organizations and bodies within the United Nations system should give due attention to the role of the family in the development process,

1. *Invites* Member States to expand their efforts at the national and community levels to consider, examine, identify and evaluate the needs of families and the ways in which those needs may be more effectively met;

2. *Calls upon* Member States to promote economic and social progress through the formulation and implementation of measures addressed to the welfare of the family as a whole, in order to achieve goals and objectives within the framework of national priorities and interests and the development process;

3. *Requests* the Secretary-General to enhance awareness among decision makers and the public of the problems and needs of the family, as well as effective ways of meeting those needs;

4. *Urges* the Secretary-General to continue studies and field-oriented activities, within the limits of available resources, aimed at enhancing the role of the family in development;

5. *Requests* the Secretary-General to study the data available in the reports and action plans developed in the course of recent United Nations activities such as the International Year of the Child and the United Nations Decade for Women: Equality, Development and Peace, as well as the World Assembly on Aging, the International Year of Disabled Persons and others, taking into account the need to strengthen policies for the welfare of the entire society;

6. *Requests* the Secretary-General to study further the impact of development on the family as a fundamental unit of society and to submit a progress report to the Council at its first regular session of 1985, through the Commission for Social Development at its twenty-ninth session, in consultation with the Commission on the Status of Women and the Committee on the Elimination of Discrimination against Women, containing an analysis of policies influencing the role and nature of the

family and its members in the context of development and, in particular, an examination of the changing forms and roles of families.

Economic and Social Council resolution 1983/23

26 May 1983   Meeting 14   Adopted without vote

Approved by Second Committee (E/1983/62) without vote, 10 May (meeting 8); draft by Commission for Social Development (E/1983/14); agenda item 11. *Meeting number.* ESC 14.

Co-operatives

In pursuance of a 1981 General Assembly request,[26] the Secretary-General submitted in January 1983 a report on national experience in promoting the co-operative movement.[27] The term "world co-operative movement" covered a substantial reality, symbolized by the International Co-operative Alliance (ICA) with 360 million individual members in 64 countries; however, the term "national co-operative movement" was often misleading, the Secretary-General stated. There were many instances where the implied unity did not exist or was imperfect, often due to a conflict of interests. Nonetheless, co-operatives could make substantial contribution to implementing the International Development Strategy for the Third United Nations Development Decade (see Chapter I of this section).

An important aspect of co-operative universality was, according to the Secretary-General, that co-operatives could function in any political and economic system where they were not expressly forbidden. As for developing countries, there was no clear-cut relationship between the type of social system and the number of and importance of co-operatives. Many developing countries, particularly in Africa and Asia, retained certain features of the co-operative systems formerly imposed or sponsored by the colonial powers; many of those countries still relied heavily on the export of agricultural raw materials and cash crops to earn foreign exchange and had not given sufficient weight to the importance of increasing production, distribution and consumption of staple food crops and to the potential of co-operative endeavours in those fields.

Major obstacles to the development of co-operatives were inadequate management, lack of participation by co-operators in organizational affairs, and a shortage of credit, stated the report. Combined with those factors was the inhospitable social environment in which co-operatives were sometimes obliged to operate.

The work of co-operatives should be integrated within an overall government plan to promote development programmes that reached the poor, the Secretary-General said. Most co-operatives did not involve the rural poor; their membership was made up largely of the better-off rural people. He concluded that particular attention should be given to promoting people's participation in rural development projects and associations, along the lines adopted by the 1979 World Conference on Agrarian Reform and Rural Development.[28] The development of urban co-operatives should also be encouraged.

In a May 1983 statement to the Economic and Social Council,[29] ICA urged that the Council support the Secretary-General's report and adopt the draft resolution on the subject approved by the Commission for Social Development on 15 February. The Council did so on 26 May by adopting resolution 1983/15 (see below).

ECONOMIC AND SOCIAL COUNCIL ACTION

On 26 May, on the recommendation of its Second Committee, the Economic and Social Council adopted resolution 1983/15 without vote.

National experience in promoting the co-operative movement

The Economic and Social Council,

Recalling General Assembly resolutions 2459(XXIII) of 20 December 1968, 3273(XXIX) of 10 December 1974, 31/37 of 30 November 1976, 33/47 of 14 December 1978 and 36/18 of 9 November 1981, as well as Council resolution 1668(LII) of 1 June 1972,

Desiring to promote the implementation of the International Development Strategy for the Third United Nations Development Decade, contained in the annex to General Assembly resolution 35/56 of 5 December 1980,

Bearing in mind the fact that the establishment and growth of co-operatives is one of the important instruments for the full economic, social and cultural development of all members of society,

Reaffirming that co-operatives play an important role in the socio-economic development of developing countries,

Recognizing the necessity of training and educational programmes at various levels for the growth, diversification and professionalization of the management of co-operatives,

Convinced that the exchange among countries of national experience relating to the co-operative movement plays an essential role in strengthening co-operatives for the benefit of their members and in overcoming difficulties in the development of various co-operatives,

Convinced of the important role that co-operatives in the various sectors of the economy can play in improving the production, marketing and consumption of food, with particular reference to special population groups,

1. *Takes note* of the report of the Secretary-General on national experience in promoting the co-operative movement;

2. *Invites* the regional commissions and specialized agencies concerned to make further efforts with a view to promoting the co-operative movement as an effective instrument for the improvement of the well-being of all people and, in particular, special population groups;

3. *Requests* the Secretary-General to prepare, with particular attention to developing countries, in consultation with Member States and relevant organizations

of the United Nations system and non-governmental organizations, a comprehensive report on national experience in promoting the co-operative movement, paying special attention, *inter alia*, to the following aspects
of the question:

(*a*) The role of co-operatives in overall social and economic development, particularly in rural areas;

(*b*) The role of co-operatives in improving the welfare of their members;

(*c*) The participation of all people, including women,
youth, disabled persons and the aging in co-operatives;

(*d*) The interrelationship between agrarian reform
and agricultural co-operatives;

(*e*) Strengthening of the "movement-to-movement"
activities among co-operatives;

(*f*) The role of co-operatives in the various sectors
in improving the production, marketing and consumption of food;

(*g*) Training and educational programmes to promote the effectiveness of co-operatives and make them
more responsive to the needs of their members;

(*h*) Difficulties faced by countries in the establishment and development of co-operatives in urban, as well
as rural, areas and their experience in overcoming them;

(*i*) The role of Government support in promoting
co-operatives;

4. *Further requests* the Secretary-General to submit
that report, through the Commission for Social Development and the Economic and Social Council, to the
General Assembly at its fortieth session for discussion
under the item entitled "National experience in achieving far-reaching social and economic changes for the
purpose of social progress".

Economic and Social Council resolution 1983/15

26 May 1983   Meeting 14   Adopted without vote

Approved by Second Committee (E/1983/62) without vote, 10 May (meeting 8);
draft by Commission for Social Development (E/1983/14); agenda item 11.
Meeting number. ESC 14.

Institutional machinery

UN Research Institute for Social Development

The United Nations Research Institute for Social Development (UNRISD) continued research in
1983 on food systems and society, improving development data, popular participation in development and refugee settlements. The principal objectives of the food systems project were to suggest
ways of improving food security, which was lacking for large social groups and many countries, to
develop and test methodologies for analysing food
security issues and to act as a catalyst in stimulating further research. The project received crucial
support from the United Nations Development
Programme (UNDP) through a subcontract with
the International Food Policy Research Institute
(IFPRI) for joint research. In September, UNRISD-
IFPRI held a Conference on Sub-Saharan Food
Policy in Zimbabwe. In the framework of a
preliminary assessment of the food situation in
Egypt and the Sudan, financed by the Federal
Republic of Germany, UNRISD funded a mission

to the Sudan in late 1983 to study the role of
women in the food system. During 1983, research
was begun by UNRISD in Chile and in eastern
India.

Work on improving development data continued with projects on measuring and analysing
socio-economic development and on setting up a
methodology for monitoring change in socio-
economic conditions and for examining interrelationships in the development process at local and
national levels.

With regard to the popular participation
project, launched in 1979, the research phase
which had started in 1981 ended in mid-1983. By
the end of the year, 18 draft case-studies on Latin
America had been completed, as well as two on
India and another on Thailand.

The UNRISD studies on refugee settlements
started in 1979 as a series of field evaluations of
refugee settlement conditions in Africa, and were
carried out in close collaboration with the United
Nations High Commissioner for Refugees
(UNHCR). In 1983, the Institute broadened the
scope of its programme by tackling comparative
sociological research projects on refugee social conditions and prospects not only in Africa, but also
in Asia and Latin America.

Income of UNRISD for 1983 amounted to
$1,581,992. Contributions by Governments totalled
$879,812. Special purpose contributions were
received from UNDP/IFPRI ($194,812), WHO
($15,000), UNHCR ($10,000) and UNEP ($8,506).
Expenditures in 1983 were $1,259,764.[30]

By a decision of 15 February 1983,[31] the Commission for Social Development took note of the
UNRISD report on its activities from 1 November
1980 to 31 October 1982.[32]

Commission for Social Development

In its report on its February 1983 session,[33]
the Commission for Social Development recommended to the Economic and Social Council the
adoption of 16 resolutions and three decisions.
Another four decisions adopted by the Commission were brought to the Council's attention.

In May, the Council took note of the report and
approved the provisional agenda and documentation for the Commission's 1985 session. In July,
the Council decided to maintain for another two
years the discontinuance of the provision of several
subsidiary bodies, among them the Commission
for Social Development.

Report of Commission

ECONOMIC AND SOCIAL COUNCIL ACTION

On the recommendation of its Second Committee, the Economic and Social Council adopted decision 1983/126 without vote.

Report of the Commission for Social Development on its twenty-eighth session

At its 14th plenary meeting, on 26 May 1983, the Council took note of the report of the Commission for Social Development on its twenty-eighth session.

Economic and Social Council decision 1983/126

Adopted without vote

Approved by Second Committee (E/1983/62), 10 May (meeting 8); agenda item 11. *Meeting number.* ESC 14.

Agenda for the 1985 session

ECONOMIC AND SOCIAL COUNCIL ACTION

On the recommendation of its Second Committee, the Economic and Social Council adopted decision 1983/124 without vote. The draft originated in the Commission for Social Development which approved it on 16 February.

Provisional agenda and documentation for the twenty-ninth session of the Commission for Social Development

At its 14th plenary meeting, on 26 May 1983, the Council approved the provisional agenda and requested documentation for the twenty-ninth session of the Commission for Social Development as indicated below.

Provisional agenda and documentation for the twenty-ninth
session of the Commission for Social Development

1. Election of officers
2. Adoption of the agenda and other organizational matters
3. Survey of recent and prospective trends and fundamental changes in the field of socio-economic development
   Documentation
   1985 report on the world social situation
   Report by the Secretary-General on the results of the 1984 review and appraisal of the implementation of the International Development Strategy for the Third United Nations Development Decade
   Report of the Secretary-General on co-ordination between the United Nations and the specialized agencies in the collection of social statistics and the preparation of reports on social issues
4. Socio-economic policies related to issues concerning the equitable distribution of national income and the process of institutional development
   Documentation
   Report of the Secretary-General on experiences of countries relating to the social aspects of rural development
   Report of the Secretary-General on the equitable distribution of national income and on the conclusions of a research project on income distribution
5. Policies for social integration, popular participation and social welfare
   Documentation
   Report of the Secretary-General on recent trends in strategies and policies for social integration of less-advantaged groups

Progress report of the Secretary-General on the impact of development on the institution of the family
Progress report of the Secretary-General on the implementation of Economic and Social Council resolution 1983/22
Report of the Secretary-General on national experience in promoting the co-operative movement
Report of the Committee on Crime Prevention and Control on its eighth session

6. Policies related to issues concerning specific groups
   Documentation
   Report of the Secretary-General on the situation of youth in the 1980s
   Report of the Secretary-General on the implementation of the International Plan of Action on Aging
   Report of the Secretary-General on national experiences in implementing the World Programme of Action concerning Disabled Persons and related activities of the United Nations and other international organizations
   Report of the Secretary-General on the situation of migrant workers and their families
7. Other matters
   Documentation
   Progress report for the biennium 1983-1984 on the activities of the Department of International Economic and Social Affairs in the social field
   Progress report on implementation of the social welfare and social development activities of the regional commissions for the biennium 1983-1984
   Report of the Board of the United Nations Research Institute for Social Development
8. Consideration of the draft provisional agenda for the thirtieth session
9. Adoption of the report of the Commission to the Economic and Social Council

Economic and Social Council decision 1983/124

Adopted without vote

Approved by Second Committee (E/1983/62) 10 May (meeting 8); draft by the Commission for Social Development; agenda item 11. *Meeting number.* ESC 14.

Meeting records

ECONOMIC AND SOCIAL COUNCIL ACTION

By decision 1983/184, the Economic and Social Council decided to maintain for another two years the discontinuance of the provision of summary records for several subsidiary bodies, among them the Commission for Social Development.

Centre for Social Development and Humanitarian Affairs

Information on activities of the Centre

As recommended by the Commission for Social Development on 16 February 1983, the Economic and Social Council, in May, adopted a resolution recognizing the need to exchange information on the activities of the United Nations Secretariat Centre for Social Development and Humanitarian Affairs (CSDHA) between the Commission for Social Development and the Commission on the Status of Women.

ECONOMIC AND SOCIAL COUNCIL ACTION

On 26 May, on the recommendation of its Second Committee, the Economic and Social Council adopted resolution 1983/20 without vote.

Exchange of information on the activities of the Centre for Social Development and Humanitarian Affairs between the Commission for Social Development and the Commission on the Status of Women

The Economic and Social Council,

Expressing the view that the Centre for Social Development and Humanitarian Affairs of the Department of International Economic and Social Affairs should, at the same time as it is pursuing its group-specific mandates, pay special attention, *inter alia,* to popular participation, local-level action and social welfare policies, in order to make an appropriate contribution to the work of the United Nations system in the area of the social effects of development for the fulfilment of overall development objectives,

Recalling the responsibilities that have been given to the Centre for Social Development and Humanitarian Affairs in the follow-up to the International Year of Disabled Persons and the World Assembly on Aging, and in the preparations for the International Youth Year, the World Conference to Review and Appraise the Achievements of the United Nations Decade for Women and the Seventh United Nations Congress on the Prevention of Crime and the Treatment of Offenders,

1. *Recognizes* the necessity to exchange information on the activities of the Centre for Social Development and Humanitarian Affairs between the Commission for Social Development and the Commission on the Status of Women;

2. *Reaffirms* the need for an overview of the social aspects of the development activities of the United Nations by the Commission for Social Development;

3. *Endorses* the continuing efforts of the Centre for Social Development and Humanitarian Affairs in developing activities;

4. *Requests* the Secretary-General to include in the progress report to the Commission for Social Development on the biennial work programme information on the activities of the Centre for Social Development and Humanitarian Affairs;

5. *Requests* the Secretary-General to develop and maintain close collaboration between the work of the Commission for Social Development and that of the Commission on the Status of Women through the exchange of their reports in order, in particular, to ensure the social integration of women in society in a way beneficial to both women and society at large.

Economic and Social Council resolution 1983/20

26 May 1983   Meeting 14   Adopted without vote

Approved by Second Committee (E/1983/62) without vote, 10 May (meeting 8); draft by Commission for Social Development (E/1983/14); agenda item 11.
Meeting number. ESC 14.

Location of the Centre

In a report on the Department of International Economic and Social Affairs, the Joint Inspection Unit (JIU) recommended relocation of CSDHA from Vienna, Austria, back to New York (see Chapter XXIV of this section). Taking note of the JIU recommendation, and the comments on it by the Secretary-General and the Advisory Committee on Administrative and Budgetary Questions, the General Assembly, in resolution 38/134, section IX, reaffirmed its previous decision with regard to the Centre's location at Vienna.

REFERENCES

[1]YUN 1981, p. 765, GA res. 36/19, 9 Nov. 1981. [2]A/38/64 & Add.1. [3]E/1983/14 (dec. V). [4]YUN 1981, p. 765, GA res. 36/19, 9 Nov. 1981. [5]YUN 1982, p. 958. [6]A/C.3/38/4. [7]YUN 1981, p. 768, ESC res. 1981/19, 6 May 1981. [8]E/1983/4. [9]YUN 1980, p. 503, GA res. 35/56, annex, 5 Dec. 1980. [10]YUN 1981, p. 763, ESC dec. 1981/176, 23 July 1981. [11]YUN 1982, p. 961, ESC dec. 1982/125, 4 May 1982. [12]E/1983/23. [13]YUN 1980, p. 772. [14]YUN 1981, p. 769, ESC res. 1981/20, 6 May 1981. [15]E/CN.5/1983/8. [16]YUN 1968, p. 505. [17]YUN 1982, p. 961. [18]*Ibid.,* p. 962, GA res. 37/55, 3 Dec. 1982. [19]A/38/338 & Corr.1 & Add.1-4 & Add.4/Corr.1. [20]YUN 1981, p. 771, ESC dec. 1981/121, 6 May 1981. [21]E/CN.5/1983/5. [22]YUN 1978, p. 612. [23]YUN 1981, p. 399, ESC res. 1981/15, 6 May 1981. [24]E/CN.5/1983/4. [25]E/CN.5/1983/9. [26]YUN 1981, p. 767, GA res. 36/18, 9 Nov. 1981. [27]A/38/63. [28]YUN 1979, p. 500. [29]E/1983/NGO/1. [30]E/CN.5/1985/10 & Corr.1. [31]E/1983/14 (dec. II). [32]YUN 1982, p. 963. [33]E/1984/14.

Crime

In 1983, preparations for the Seventh (1985) Congress on the Prevention of Crime and the Treatment of Offenders continued (see below). Other United Nations activities in crime prevention and criminal justice, especially by the Crime Prevention and Criminal Justice Branch of CSDHA, focused on research and training; publication and dissemination of information; and technical assistance, including interregional advisory services to several countries.

United Nations regional and interregional crime institutes conducted seminars, training courses and research.

The United Nations Social Defence Research Institute (UNSDRI) published the third edition of a world-wide *Directory of Criminological Institutes,* containing entries on 404 institutes and units in 60 countries.

UNSDRI was involved in activities related to an institute for Africa, south of the Sahara in the field of crime prevention and the treatment of offenders, which was to be established in accordance with a 1979 Economic and Social Council resolution.[1]

The United Nations Asia and Far East Institute for the Prevention of Crime and the Treatment of Offenders (UNAFEI) organized an international seminar on innovations in the procedural methods and basic structure of criminal justice systems (14 February–19 March), which was attended by 25 public officials from 17 countries. It also held a training course on community-based corrections, including probation, parole, community service order, halfway houses, and residential facilities in the community (19 April–9 July); the course was attended by 26 public officials from 14 countries. In addition, UNAFEI undertook surveys on such topics as the effectiveness of socio-legal preventive and control means in different countries, based on the interaction between criminal behaviour and drug abuse (in collaboration with the United Nations Social Defence Research Institute (UNSDRI), and of arts programmes organized in correctional institutions (in collaboration with the Graduate School and University Center, City University of New York, United States).

The Helsinki Institute for Crime Prevention and Control, affiliated with the United Nations, convened an *ad hoc* meeting of experts on the feasibility of information systems in relation to crime trends and criminal policy (9-10 May). A meeting on victim policy, convened by the Institute (30 October–2 November), brought together some 30 experts from various European countries. Research projects on prosecutorial decision-making and the use of solitary confinement were also carried out.

The United Nations Latin American Institute for the Prevention of Crime and the Treatment of Offenders (ILANUD) organized a number of activities. In April, eight experts from seven countries attended a meeting on victimology and 23 participants from seven countries attended a training course on rehabilitation programmes. A Workshop on Drug Control in the Andean Subregion, held in May in co-operation with the United Nations Fund for Drug Abuse Control, was attended by 20 participants from three Latin American and seven other countries.

Information on United Nations activities in the area was contained in a 1984 report of the Secretary-General.[2]

Preparations for UN congress on crime (1985)

In 1983, the Committee on Crime Prevention and Control continued to function as the preparatory committee for the Seventh (1985) United Nations Congress on the Prevention of Crime and the Treatment of Offenders. Preparation of the Congress included the convening of regional and interregional preparatory meetings; inter-agency consultations; the commissioning of experts to assist in preparing documentation; and a wide public information programme.[3]

Five regional preparatory meetings were held during 1983 as follows: Europe (Sofia, Bulgaria,

6-10 June); Asia and the Pacific (Bangkok, Thailand, 4-8 July); Latin America (San José, Costa Rica, 10-14 October); Africa (Addis Ababa, Ethiopia, 28 November–2 December); and Western Asia (Baghdad, Iraq, 12-16 December). They were attended by representatives of Governments, national liberation movements, specialized agencies and other United Nations bodies, and intergovernmental and non-governmental organizations. The participants exchanged views and experiences on the issues to be discussed by the Congress and identified the main concerns of the countries of the respective regions.

Inter-agency aspects of the preparations were considered in October by the Consultative Committee on Substantive Questions (Programme Matters) of the Administrative Committee on Coordination (ACC).

Several *ad hoc* meetings on different items of the Congress' provisional agenda were held, organized largely by non-governmental organizations. A preliminary meeting of experts on topic 1 (new dimensions of criminality and crime prevention in the context of development) was convened at Siracusa, Italy (10-14 January). An international conference on topic 2 (criminal justice processes and perspectives in a changing world) was organized at Milan, Italy (14-17 June). The Ninth International Congress of Criminology (Vienna, 25-30 September), whose overall theme stressed the relationship between criminology and public policy, dealt also with such issues as new tendencies in research and policy related to victimology (topic 3), and criminal justice and human rights (topic 5), among others. Further input to various Congress topics was provided by meetings held at Ottawa, Canada (28-31 August) on prison health care and at Houston, Texas, United States (25 October–4 November) on the Second United Nations Survey of Crime Trends and the formulation of guidelines for data-base development.

A public information programme, provided by the United Nations Department of Public Information, was to complement the preparatory work for the Congress. The intended target audiences of the programme were government officials; specialists in criminal law and criminal justice; public administrators; parliamentarians and planners active in the areas under discussion; practitioners in probation, parole and social welfare; editors and readers of publications specializing in criminology and penology; and officers and members of professional organizations of judges, law enforcement personnel and other pertinent professional groups.

Committee on crime

The Economic and Social Council, at its May 1983 session, took note of the report of the Committee on Crime Prevention and Control on its 1982 session,[4] which was considered by the Commission for Social Development at its February 1983 session. By the same decision, the Council approved the provisional agenda and documentation for the Committee's 1984 session. The Committee did not meet in 1983, but continued to be involved in preparatory activities for the Seventh (1985) United Nations Congress on the Prevention of Crime and the Treatment of Offenders (see above).

On 16 February 1983, the Commission decided[5] to approve a draft resolution on arbitrary or summary executions (see Chapter XVIII of this section) recommended by the Committee, which was subsequently adopted by the Council (resolution 1983/24). The Commission also decided to forward another draft by the Committee dealing with its reporting procedures, along with the differing views expressed in the Commission; the Council acted on that draft by adopting resolution 1983/25.

Report and agenda

ECONOMIC AND SOCIAL COUNCIL ACTION

The Economic and Social Council, on the recommendation of its Second Committee, adopted decision 1983/125 without vote.

Report of the Committee on Crime Prevention and Control

At its 14th plenary meeting, on 26 May 1983, the Council:

(a) Took note of the report of the Committee on Crime Prevention and Control on its seventh session submitted through the Commission for Social Development;

(b) Approved the provisional agenda and documentation for the eighth session of the Committee on Crime Prevention and Control, to be held in 1984, as contained therein.

Economic and Social Council decision 1983/125

Adopted without vote

Approved by Second Committee (E/1983/62), 10 May (meeting 8); draft by Commission on Crime Prevention and Control; agenda item 11.
Meeting number. ESC 14.

Reporting procedures

Taking up a March 1982 proposal by the Committee on Crime Prevention and Control,[4] the Economic and Social Council decided by resolution 1983/25 that from then on the Committee should report directly to it, instead of following the usual procedure of reporting through the Commission for Social Development. The Commission had considered the proposal at its February 1983 session, but was unable to arrive at a consensus on it. On 16 February,[5] it decided to forward the proposal to the Council, together with views expressed in the Commission.

ECONOMIC AND SOCIAL COUNCIL ACTION

On 26 May 1983, on the recommendation of its Second Committee, the Economic and Social Council adopted resolution 1983/25 without vote.

Functions and long-term programme of work of the Committee on Crime Prevention and Control

The Economic and Social Council,

Recalling its resolution 1584(L) of 21 May 1971 on criminality and social change, in which, *inter alia*, it decided that the members of the Advisory Committee of Experts on the Prevention of Crime and the Treatment of Offenders should be appointed by the Economic and Social Council on the recommendation of the Secretary-General, that the Committee should be renamed the Committee on Crime Prevention and Control and that it should report to the Commission for Social Development and, as appropriate on particular aspects, to the Commission on Human Rights and the Commission on Narcotic Drugs,

Recalling also, however, General Assembly resolution 32/60 of 8 December 1977, in which, *inter alia*, the Assembly decided that the members of the Committee on Crime Prevention and Control should be elected by the Economic and Social Council for a term of four years, with half the membership being elected every two years, on the basis of the principle of equitable geographical distribution, from among experts who possess the necessary qualifications and professional or scientific knowledge in the field and are nominated by Member States, and Economic and Social Council resolutions 1979/19 and 1979/30 of 9 May 1979 on the functions and long-term programme of work and on the enlargement of the Committee on Crime Prevention and Control,

Recalling further its decision 1981/122 of 6 May 1981 and General Assembly resolution 36/21 of 9 November 1981,

Mindful of General Assembly resolution 32/60 and of resolution 35/171 of 15 December 1980, in which the Assembly endorsed the Caracas Declaration adopted by the Sixth United Nations Congress on the Prevention of Crime and the Treatment of Offenders, annexed to that resolution, and the recommendations of the Congress relating to the new perspectives for international co-operation in respect of crime prevention,

Considering that in the Caracas Declaration the General Assembly and the Economic and Social Council were invited to ensure that appropriate measures be taken to strengthen, as necessary, the activities of the competent United Nations organs concerned with crime prevention and the treatment of offenders,

Deeply concerned that crime continues to spread in many parts of the world, requiring continuing and ever-increasing attention on the part of the world community, as demonstrated by the concern expressed by the General Assembly in resolutions 35/171 and 36/21,

Taking note of the important contributions of the Committee on Crime Prevention and Control in elaborating the Code of Conduct for Law Enforcement Officials, the report on methods and ways likely to be most effective in preventing crime and improving the treatment of offenders, and its recommendations on capital punishment and arbitrary or summary executions,

Taking into account the fact that, in paragraph 2 of General Assembly resolution 32/60, the Committee was entrusted with the function of submitting to the Economic and Social Council appropriate proposals concerning the preparation of United Nations congresses on the prevention of crime and the treatment of offenders, and that the composition and the appointment procedures of the Committee were modified in paragraph 4 of the same resolution,

Bearing in mind that the United Nations congresses on the prevention of crime and the treatment of offenders have a comprehensive scope and that their agendas normally cover the main subjects within the functions and programme of the Committee,

Convinced that the magnitude and fundamental importance of the functions entrusted to the Committee require not only the most informed, thoughtful and deliberate consideration by the Committee, but also the timely submission of its recommendations to, and action thereon by, the Economic and Social Council and the General Assembly,

1. *Decides* that henceforth the Committee on Crime Prevention and Control shall report directly to the Council;

2. *Decides also* that the Committee on Crime Prevention and Control will send its report to the Commission for Social Development and, where appropriate, to other relevant United Nations organs.

Economic and Social Council resolution 1983/25

26 May 1983   Meeting 14   Adopted without vote

Approved by Second Committee (E/1983/62) without vote, 10 May (meeting 8); draft by Committee on Crime Prevention and Control (E/CN.5/1983/2), orally amended by Chairman, based on informal consultations; agenda item 11. *Meeting number.* ESC 14.

The draft recommended by the Committee on crime was amended by the Chairman of the Council's Second Committee to include a new paragraph 2. An amendment by the USSR to paragraph 1, by which the Council would have decided that the Committee might report directly to the Council at the Council's request, was not pressed to a vote.[6]

UN Trust Fund for Social Defence

In 1983, the United Nations Trust Fund for Social Defence supplied $457,925 to the United Nations Social Defence Research Institute in Rome, Italy. The Trust Fund was established pursuant to a 1965 resolution of the Economic and Social Council to strengthen United Nations work in social defence.[7]

Contributions to the Trust Fund in 1983 totalled $693,802, from Cyprus ($200), Denmark ($9,420), France ($18,571), Greece ($7,462), Italy ($305,891), Japan ($52,395), Nigeria ($4,510), Norway ($10,960), Saudi Arabia ($240,000), Sweden ($22,749), Switzerland ($10,347), Thailand ($2,000) and Yugoslavia ($9,297). Pledges for future years were received from France ($20,126), Italy ($408,805), Pakistan ($1,000), Switzerland ($10,563) and Thailand ($1,000).

REFERENCES

[1]YUN 1979, p. 781, ESC res. 1979/20, 9 May 1979. [2]E/AC.57/1984/17. [3]E/AC.57/1984/7 & Add.1 & Add.1/Corr.1.
[4]YUN 1982, p. 964. [5]E/1983/14 (dec. VI). [6]E/1983/C.2/L.5. [7]YUN 1965, p. 409, ESC res. 1086 B (XXXIX), 30 July 1965.

Cultural development

Cultural property restitution

Pursuant to a 1981 General Assembly request,[1] the Secretary-General submitted in October 1983 a report on the return or restitution of cultural property to the countries of origin,[2] annexed to which was a report by the Director-General of the United Nations Educational, Scientific and Cultural Organization (UNESCO). Efforts by UNESCO to promote the return of cultural property had progressed steadily, the UNESCO Director-General said.

The subject had been given a prominent place at the 1982 World Conference on Cultural Policies at Mexico City,[3] and measures had been taken by States and the UNESCO secretariat to implement the 1981 recommendations of the Intergovernmental Committee for Promoting the Return of Cultural Property to the Countries of its Origin or its Restitution in Case of Illicit Appropriation.[4] Among those measures were the promotion of bilateral negotiations and of wider awareness of the question and the preparation of national and regional inventories of cultural property.

The necessity of such measures was again stressed by the Intergovernmental Committee at its third session (Istanbul, Turkey, 9-12 May 1983). The Committee reiterated the need for member States to begin bilateral negotiations for the return of cultural property and to reinforce measures to combat illicit traffic in cultural property. The Committee recommended national and international action in that direction. It expressed the belief that the return of cultural property to its countries of origin should be seen as an integral part of international co-operation aimed at improving the understanding of the heritage of each people. With regard to its fourth session, the Committee recommended that the Director-General accept the invitation of Greece to hold the session at Delphi in early 1985.

At the Pacific Science Congress (Dunedin, New Zealand, 1-11 February 1983), a special session on museums in Pacific research was organized with UNESCO assistance. Twenty-nine museum specialists from eight Pacific countries or territories discussed the question of inventorying the dispersed heritage of the region. They proposed that all museums prepare national inventories of cultural property and that once those were completed steps be taken to prepare a selective common and centralized inventory.

The UNESCO secretariat organized a consultation of experts (1-4 March 1983) on the problems of interpretation or implementation encountered by States which had not yet ratified the 1970 Convention[5] on the Means of Prohibiting and Preventing the Illicit Import, Export and Transfer of Ownership of Cultural Property. As of August 1983, the Convention had been ratified or accepted by 52 countries.

A Meeting of Experts on Crimes against the Cultural Patrimony, organized by the United Nations Latin American Institute for the Prevention of Crime and the Treatment of Offenders was attended by 23 experts from seven countries (February 1983). It was aimed at possible legislation to protect pre-Columbian archaeological treasures from theft, unauthorized exportation and wilful damage.

GENERAL ASSEMBLY ACTION

On 25 November 1983, the General Assembly adopted resolution 38/34 by recorded vote.

Return or restitution of cultural property to the countries of origin

The General Assembly,

Recalling its resolutions 3026 A (XXVII) of 18 December 1972, 3148(XXVIII) of 14 December 1973, 3187(XXVIII) of 18 December 1973, 3391(XXX) of 19 November 1975, 31/40 of 30 November 1976, 32/18 of 11 November 1977, 33/50 of 14 December 1978, 34/64 of 29 November 1979, 35/127 and 35/128 of 11 December 1980 and 36/64 of 27 November 1981,

Recalling also the Convention on the Means of Prohibiting and Preventing the Illicit Import, Export and Transfer of Ownership of Cultural Property, adopted on 14 November 1970 by the General Conference of the United Nations Educational, Scientific and Cultural Organization,

Taking note with satisfaction of the report of the Secretary-General submitted in co-operation with the Director-General of the United Nations Educational, Scientific and Cultural Organization,

Aware of the importance attached by the countries of origin to the return of cultural property which is of fundamental spiritual and cultural value to them, so that they may constitute collections representative of their cultural heritage,

Noting with satisfaction that some countries have taken positive steps towards the return or restitution of museum pieces, archives and *objets d'art* to their countries of origin,

Reaffirming the importance of inventories as an essential tool for the understanding and protection of cultural property and for the identification of dispersed heritage and as a contribution to the advancement of scientific and artistic knowledge and intercultural communication,

Deeply concerned at the clandestine excavations and the illicit traffic in cultural property that continue to impoverish the cultural heritage of all peoples,

Supporting the solemn appeal made on 7 June 1978 by the Director-General of the United Nations Educational, Scientific and Cultural Organization for the return of irreplaceable cultural heritage to those who created it,

1. *Commends* the United Nations Educational, Scientific and Cultural Organization and the Intergovernmental Committee for Promoting the Return of Cultural Property to its Countries of Origin or its Restitution in Case of Illicit Appropriation on the work they have accomplished, in particular through the promotion of bilateral negotiations, for the return or restitution of cultural property, the preparation of inventories of movable cultural property, the development of infrastructures for the protection of movable cultural property, the reduction of illicit traffic in cultural property and the dissemination of information to the public;

2. *Reaffirms* that the restitution to a country of its *objets d'art*, monuments, museum pieces, archives, manuscripts, documents and any other cultural or artistic treasures contributes to the strengthening of international co-operation and to the preservation and flowering of universal cultural values through fruitful co-operation between developed and developing countries;

3. *Invites* Member States to draw up, in co-operation with the United Nations Educational, Scientific and Cultural Organization, systematic inventories of cultural property existing in their territory and of their cultural property abroad;

4. *Also invites* Member States engaged in seeking the recovery of cultural and artistic treasures from the seabed, in accordance with international law, to facilitate by mutually acceptable conditions the participation of States having a historical and cultural link with those treasures;

5. *Appeals* to Member States to co-operate closely with the Intergovernmental Committee for Promoting the Return of Cultural Property to its Countries of Origin or its Restitution in Case of Illicit Appropriation and to conclude bilateral agreements for this purpose;

6. *Also appeals* to Member States to encourage the mass information media and educational and cultural institutions to strive to arouse a greater and more general awareness with regard to the return or restitution of cultural property to its country of origin;

7. *Takes note with satisfaction* of the importance accorded by the World Conference on Cultural Policies, held at Mexico City from 26 July to 6 August 1982, to the question of the return or restitution of cultural property during the debate on cultural policies;

8. *Endorses* the opinion expressed at the World Conference on Cultural Policies that the return of cultural property to its country of origin should be accompanied by the training of key personnel and technicians and the provision of the necessary facilities for the satisfactory conservation and presentation of the property restored;

9. *Invites once again* those Member States that have not yet done so to sign and ratify the Convention on the Means of Prohibiting and Preventing the Illicit Import, Export and Transfer of Ownership of Cultural Property;

10. *Requests* the Secretary-General, in co-operation with the Director-General of the United Nations Educational, Scientific and Cultural Organization, to submit

to the General Assembly at its fortieth session a report on the implementation of the present resolution;

11. _Decides_ to include in the provisional agenda of its fortieth session the item entitled "Return or restitution of cultural property to the countries of origin".

General Assembly resolution 38/34

25 November 1983   Meeting 71   123-0-13 (recorded vote)

26-nation draft (A/38/L.29/Rev.1); agenda item 20.

Sponsors: Algeria, Benin, Burundi, Chad, Colombia, Congo, Djibouti, Ecuador, Egypt, Gabon, Greece, Guatemala, Guinea, Guinea-Bissau, Iraq, Ivory Coast, Mali, Malta, Mauritania, Morocco, Niger, Rwanda, Senegal, Togo, United Republic of Cameroon, Zaire.

Meeting number. GA 38th session: plenary 71.

Recorded vote in Assembly as follows:

In favour: Albania, Algeria, Argentina, Australia, Bahrain, Barbados, Benin, Bhutan, Bolivia, Botswana, Brazil, Bulgaria, Burma, Burundi, Byelorussian SSR, Canada, Cape Verde, Central African Republic, Chad, Chile, China, Colombia, Comoros, Congo, Costa Rica, Cuba, Cyprus, Czechoslovakia, Democratic Kampuchea, Democratic Yemen, Djibouti, Ecuador, Egypt, El Salvador, Ethiopia, Fiji, Finland, Gabon, German Democratic Republic, Ghana, Greece, Guatemala, Guinea, Guinea-Bissau, Guyana, Honduras, Iceland, India, Indonesia, Iran, Iraq, Ivory Coast, Jamaica, Japan, Jordan, Kenya, Kuwait, Lao People's Democratic Republic, Lebanon, Liberia, Libyan Arab Jamahiriya, Madagascar, Malawi, Malaysia, Maldives, Mali, Malta, Mauritania, Mauritius, Mexico, Mongolia, Morocco, Mozambique, Nepal, New Zealand, Nicaragua, Niger, Nigeria, Norway, Oman, Pakistan, Panama, Papua New Guinea, Paraguay, Philippines, Poland, Portugal, Qatar, Romania, Rwanda, Saint Lucia, Saint Vincent and the Grenadines, Samoa, Sao Tome and Principe, Saudi Arabia, Senegal, Sierra Leone, Singapore, Solomon Islands, Somalia, Spain, Sri Lanka, Sudan, Syrian Arab Republic, Thailand, Togo, Tunisia, Turkey, Uganda, Ukrainian SSR, USSR, United Arab Emirates, United Republic of Cameroon, United Republic of Tanzania, Uruguay, Vanuatu, Venezuela, Viet Nam, Yemen, Yugoslavia, Zaire, Zambia, Zimbabwe.

Against: None.

Abstaining: Austria, Belgium, Denmark, France, Germany, Federal Republic of, Ireland, Israel, Italy, Luxembourg, Netherlands, Sweden, United Kingdom, United States.

REFERENCES

[1]YUN 1981, p. 777, GA res. 36/64, 27 Nov. 1981. [2]A/38/456. [3]YUN 1982, p. 1534. [4]YUN 1981, p. 775. [5]YUN 1970, p. 915.

Chapter XIV

Population

In 1983, the United Nations system continued efforts to meet needs arising from population-related problems, with the United Nations Fund for Population Activities (UNFPA), the largest source of multilateral assistance, at the forefront. Highlighting those efforts was the presentation of the first United Nations Population Award for outstanding contribution to the awareness of population questions and to their solutions. A system-wide review of population activities was undertaken for the first time. Taking note of the review in July by resolution 1983/76, the Economic and Social Council urged enhanced co-ordination of population programmes.

Preparations for the International Conference on Population (1984) were advanced by four expert group meetings on topics for the Conference. Council resolution 1983/6, adopted in May, fixed the dates and place of the Conference, and specified the categories of participants to be invited and other pre-Conference arrangements to be made. Besides endorsing the Council decisions in December by resolution 38/148, the General Assembly also approved the budgetary resources for the Conference.

Topics related to this chapter. Regional economic and social activities—population: Africa; Asia and the Pacific; Europe; Latin America. Statistics: population and housing censuses.

UN Fund for Population Activities

UNFPA activities

In 1983, UNFPA continued to concentrate on the priority programme areas outlined by the Governing Council of the United Nations Development Programme (UNDP) in 1981:[1] family planning, communication and education, basic data collection, population dynamics, and population policy formulation, implementation and evaluation. Details of these activities and special programmes were described by the Executive Director in his annual report for 1983.[2]

Although UNFPA's total 1983 income of $134.7 million represented a 2.7 per cent increase over its 1982 income of $130.9 million, requests for assistance exceeded resources. Project allocations in 1983 totalled $117.4 million, broken down in the tables below by major function and executing agency, and geographically. Expenditures were $122.6 million, including $69.2 million for country programmes, $31.7 million for intercountry programmes, $4.4 million for the budgets of the UNFPA Deputy Representatives and Senior Advisers on Population, $6.3 million for overhead costs, and $11 million for the administrative budgets.

By the end of the year, UNFPA was assisting 1,831 projects—1,397 country, 189 regional, 85 interregional and 160 global. New projects approved in 1983 numbered 271, amounting to $15.2 million, compared to 290 in 1982, amounting to $15.6 million. Projects completed were 240, bringing the cumulative total to 2,006.

UNFPA assistance for family planning programmes came to $54.1 million, or 46.1 per cent of total allocations, and focused on projects to enhance acceptance of family planning and to expand service delivery. Other projects were to bolster family planning efforts—information, education and communication programmes, and mass-media motivational campaigns; and to improve service quality and accessibility—personnel training and logistic support including transport, medical equipment and contraceptive supplies. UNFPA continued to sponsor the transfer of contraceptive technology and to support research in family planning, contributing $2 million in 1983 to the WHO Special Programme of Research, Development and Research Training in Human Reproduction. UNFPA also continued to integrate family planning with maternal/child health-care and general health services.

Guidelines governing UNFPA assistance for family planning activities were issued in April. These took into account two principles consistently adhered to by UNFPA: a nation's right to determine its own population policies and programmes, and the right of every individual or couple to determine its own family size.

Support for population education and communication activities totalled $16.9 million, or 14.4 per cent of all allocations. The need for such activities continued to grow during the year, outstripping the capacity of the specialized agencies' regional advisers to provide the required technical support. To help meet this rising need, permanent UNFPA mobile teams were established in all regions to operate in close co-operation with executing agency teams.

UNFPA PROJECT ALLOCATIONS, 1983

(in US dollars)

COUNTRY, TERRITORY AND REGIONAL PROJECTS	ALLOCATION	COUNTRY, TERRITORY AND REGIONAL PROJECTS	ALLOCATION	COUNTRY, TERRITORY AND REGIONAL PROJECTS	ALLOCATION
Africa south of the Sahara		*Asia and the Pacific* (cont.)		*Latin America and the Caribbean* (cont.)	
Angola*	279,907	Indonesia*	2,599,148		
Benin*	410,829	Kiribati	177,267	Peru	1,076,923
Botswana	409,734	Lao People's Democratic		St. Kitts–Nevis	32,206
Burundi*	541,829	Republic*	10,250	Saint Lucia	71,287
Cape Verde	261,309	Malaysia	1,087,815	Saint Vincent and the Grenadines	70,208
Central African Republic*	210,651	Maldives*	18,922	Suriname	19,912
Chad*	8,000	Mongolia	336,972	Uruguay	27,002
Comoros*	206,088	Nepal*	2,566,484	Regional	3,443,588
Congo	490,624	Niue	2,500		
Equatorial Guinea*	288,291	Pakistan*	2,953,466	Subtotal	15,507,907
Ethiopia*	2,017,047	Papua New Guinea	37,930		
Gabon	694	Philippines	1,086,541	*Middle East and the Mediterranean*	
Gambia*	320,894	Republic of Korea	505,825		
Ghana*	380,161	Samoa*	218,745	Algeria	12,262
Guinea*	422,724	Singapore	21,825	Bahrain	259,310
Guinea-Bissau	83,632	Solomon Islands*	119,505	Democratic Yemen*	943,594
Ivory Coast	93,535	Sri Lanka*	1,155,461	Djibouti	241,749
Kenya*	511,565	Thailand	1,656,137	Egypt*	1,151,743
Lesotho*	54,649	Tonga	136,377	Iraq	94,989
Liberia*	524,523	Trust Territory of the Pacific		Jordan	554,949
Madagascar*	475,439	Islands	65,841	Kuwait	106,615
Malawi*	349,488	Tuvalu	54,153	Libyan Arab Jamahiriya	4,300
Mali*	439,631	Vanuatu	135,920	Morocco	1,283,893
Mauritania*	671,484	Viet Nam*	2,773,706	Somalia*	806,245
Mauritius	359,269	Regional	5,481,264	Sudan*	1,434,608
Mozambique*	896,840			Syrian Arab Republic	1,098,902
Niger*	490,926	Subtotal	52,245,121	Tunisia	789,902
Nigeria	590,423			Turkey	265,160
Rwanda*	455,684	*Latin America and the Caribbean*		United Arab Emirates	(6,838)
Sao Tome and Principe*	172,134			Yemen*	979,090
Senegal*	860,761	Anguilla	13,046	Regional	1,314,698
Seychelles	61,806	Antigua and Barbuda	15,888		
Sierra Leone*	376,456	Barbados	89,828	Subtotal	11,335,171
Swaziland	185,696	Belize	4,850		
Togo	189,557	Bolivia	635,771	*Europe*	
Uganda*	46,867	Brazil	194,953	Albania	1,828
United Republic of Cameroon	519,246	British Virgin Islands	26,874	Bulgaria	18,200
United Republic of Tanzania*	816,559	Chile	35,632	Czechoslovakia	300
Upper Volta*	636,725	Colombia	215,550	Greece	40,248
Zaire*	445,934	Costa Rica	266,383	Hungary	157,078
Zambia*	495,113	Cuba	1,028,774	Portugal	105,672
Zimbabwe*	390,065	Dominica*	53,637	Romania	46,969
Regional	5,130,923	Dominican Republic	633,976	Yugoslavia	122,639
		Ecuador	1,087,598	Regional	562,651
Subtotal	22,573,712	El Salvador	927,735		
		Grenada	3,504	Subtotal	1,055,585
Asia and the Pacific		Guatemala	704,927		
Afghanistan*	753,410	Guyana	40,175	INTERREGIONAL AND GLOBAL PROJECTS	
Bangladesh*	3,419,998	Haiti*	762,406		
Bhutan*	392,469	Honduras	641,988	*Interregional*	9,210,965
Burma*	231,089	Jamaica	301,580	*Global*	10,523,928
China*	9,159,000	Mexico	1,829,567		
Cook Islands	35,879	Montserrat	4,800	Subtotal	19,734,893
Fiji	703,435	Nicaragua	262,550		
Hong Kong	17,303	Panama	419,645	Total†	122,452,389
India*	14,330,484	Paraguay	565,144		

*Classified as a priority country for UNFPA assistance.

†Includes allocations of $5,148,351 for Deputy Representatives and Senior Advisers on Population, overhead for government-executed projects and infrastructure.

SOURCE: DP/1984/30 & Corr.1 & Add.1 & Add.1/Corr.1.

Assistance for basic data collection was $12.2 million, or 10.4 per cent of all allocations. This amount was substantially less than that shown for 1982,[3] due principally to the phasing out in 1983 of a large number of projects and to the completion of costly census activities which had entailed purchase of data processing equipment. As in the past, population censuses took the largest share ($8.1 million); surveys, the second largest ($2.2 million); and civil registration and vital statistics systems and related activities, the remainder ($1.9 million). Of the 149 developing countries and territories that carried out censuses during 1970-1983, 109 did so with UNFPA support. Forty-six others received support for population surveys, 36 for improvement of civil registration and vital statistics systems, and 11 for related activities.

UNFPA ALLOCATIONS BY MAJOR FUNCTION, 1983

	Amount (in millions of US dollars)	Per cent of total programme
Family planning	54.2	46.1
Communication and education	16.9	14.4
Population dynamics analysis	14.3	12.1
Basic data collection	12.2	10.4
Multisector activities	10.3	8.8
Formulation and evaluation of population policies	6.7	5.7
Special programmes	1.7	1.4
Implementation of policies	1.3	1.1
Total*	117.4	100.0

*Excludes allocations of $5.1 million for Deputy Representatives and Senior Advisers on Population, overhead for government-executed projects and infrastructure; differs from the sum of the figures due to rounding.
SOURCE: DP/1984/28 (Part I).

UNFPA ALLOCATIONS BY EXECUTING AGENCY, 1983

	Amount (in millions of US dollars)	Per cent of total programme
Governments (directly executed)	34.9	29.7
WHO	22.1	18.8
United Nations	16.1	13.7
UNFPA	13.7	11.6
Non-governmental organizations	8.7	7.4
Regional commissions	6.8	5.8
ILO	6.6	5.6
UNESCO	5.6	4.8
UNICEF	1.9	1.6
FAO	0.9	1.0
Total*	117.4	100.0

*Differs from the sum of the figures due to rounding.
SOURCE: DP/1984/28 (Part I).

Some $14.2 million, or 12.1 per cent of all allocations, was devoted to population dynamics, including demographic analyses, projections and studies of the impact of factors affecting population change. Research, training, institution-building, technical backstopping and information exchange remained the main areas of support. Ongoing projects numbered 144 in 1983, of which 89 were at the country level, 20 at the regional and 35 at the interregional and global levels.

Assistance for the formulation and evaluation of population policies and programmes amounted to $6.6 million, or 5.7 per cent of total allocations. This went mostly towards strengthening or setting up national population commissions and units, including wider use of research findings in policy formulation.

Projects in the area of policy implementation—seven country and four interregional and global—totalled $1.2 million, or 1.1 per cent of all allocations. These were aimed at strengthening policy formulation and programme development and at institutionalizing responsibility for implementation.

Under its special programmes, UNFPA continued efforts to enhance the active participation of women and women's organizations in all aspects of population programmes (see Chapter XIX of this section). With UNFPA support, research projects on the potential contribution of the aging segment of the population towards local and national development were begun in selected countries (see Chapter XX of this section). Assistance for special programmes was $1.7 million, or 1.4 per cent of total allocations.

A major portion of the programmes and projects funded by UNFPA and executed by various United Nations bodies and NGOs was executed by the Department of Technical Co-operation for Development (see DTCD ACTIVITIES below).

By a decision of 24 June 1983[4] the UNDP Governing Council, the governing body of UNFPA, requested the Executive Director to continue ensuring co-ordination of population programmes within the United Nations system and urged him to take advantage of United Nations bodies and non-governmental and international organizations as executing agencies for UNFPA programmes.

Country and intercountry programmes

In 1983, UNFPA continued to address the needs of the 53 countries given priority status in 1982,[3] of which 30 were in Africa, 16 in Asia and the Pacific, 2 in Latin America and the Caribbean, and 5 in the Middle East and the Mediterranean. Of the year's total UNFPA project allocations of $117.4 million, those for projects in individual countries amounted to $81.6 million. Intercountry activities accounted for the remainder, consisting of $16.1 million for regional projects, $9.2 million for interregional projects and $10.5 million for global projects.

The $97.7 million for country and regional projects was allocated as follows: $21 million for Africa south of the Sahara; $50.3 million for Asia and the Pacific; $14.9 million for Latin America and the Caribbean; and $11.5 million for the Middle East, the Mediterranean and Europe. The largest proportion of each region's resources was devoted to family planning and related health care activities.

Substantial assistance went to the International Institute for Population Studies (India), and to the Latin American Demographic Centre (Chile) to enable it to provide technical and other support for training, research and dissemination activities for regional demographic programmes. The Centre Démographique ONU-Roumanie (Romania) and Moscow State University (USSR) also received assistance, for offering courses in population and development planning to students from developing countries. Additional future funding for the Population Information Network in Africa, as well as for various African demographic research institutions and the Cairo Demographic

Centre (Egypt), was discussed at a meeting (New York, November).

The year 1983 saw the end of the four-year programme cycle for most UNFPA-supported interregional projects executed by the United Nations, specialized agencies and NGOs. By December, information on project results was being prepared for dissemination to countries for use in programme planning and implementation. Reports on intercountry aspects of the various substantive areas of UNFPA support—completed and presented to the United Nations and specialized agencies during the year—served as the basis for the programming of intercountry activities for the 1984-1987 programme cycle.

On 24 June 1983,[4] the UNDP Governing Council approved recommended assistance to large-scale country programmes for Benin, Malawi, the Niger, Thailand, Zaire and Zimbabwe. It requested the Executive Director to continue efforts to reduce the proportion of assistance to intercountry activities so as not to exceed 25 per cent of total programmable resources by 1984, but at the same time to increase the proportion of regional activities. Increased UNFPA support was encouraged for family planning research at the country level, as was continued assistance for such research at the intercountry level, within 25 per cent of total resources for intercountry programmes.

The Council also approved recommended large-scale assistance to the various intercountry demographic training and research centres for 1984-1987, and asked the Executive Director to report in 1984 on the centres' programmes, taking account of the approved level of support and of the need for adequate support to the African demographic centres.

Family planning research

In response to a June 1982 request of the UNDP Governing Council,[5] the Executive Director presented to it a report on the future role of the United Nations system in family planning research, including contraceptive research and development.[6] Prepared jointly with the WHO Director-General, in consultation with the International Planned Parenthood Federation, the report was based on replies to questionnaires sent to 130 countries and 13 United Nations agencies. Additional information was provided by 34 organizations conducting or directly supporting family planning research and by 30 pharmaceutical firms on the subject of fertility regulating methods.

The report stated that in 1982 about $75 million—15 per cent of the estimated $500 million in global funding of population activities in developing countries—had been used for family planning research. It noted that the United Nations system had unique qualifications that justified its traditionally strong role in family planning research:

it enjoyed wide acceptability and could draw upon a global network of expertise, including from developing countries themselves, NGOs and commercial sources. A United Nations presence in nearly every developing country permitted the system to programme and monitor projects in a way not possible for other development agencies.

The report proposed the following areas be given priority: under programme research—acceptability of programme and methods, programme design and delivery strategy, and programme management, including personnel training, monitoring, logistics and impact evaluation; under biomedical research—contraceptive development and safety testing, improvement and adaptation of current methods to local conditions, and research on infertility; and under social research—research on determinants of fertility affecting acceptance of family planning. To increase research capacity at the country level, it was also proposed that priority be given to expanding research training and strengthening national capabilities for the three categories of research cited.

Accordingly, the Executive Director recommended that the Governing Council approve the priority areas outlined for UNFPA funding. It also recommended approval of a yearly UNFPA allocation to the WHO Special Programme of Research, Development and Research Training in Human Reproduction of $2 million during 1984-1987, provided that overall UNFPA contributions remained at approximately the 1983 level.

On 24 June,[4] the Governing Council endorsed the recommended priorities, approved in principle the four-year funding commitment to the WHO Special Programme, subject to a yearly review by the Council, and decided that the 1984 contribution to the Programme should be $2 million.

Work programmes

The UNFPA work plan for 1984-1987, prepared by the Executive Director,[7] was based on a projected income increase of 7.8 per cent from 1984 to 1985 and of 10 per cent yearly thereafter to 1987. Intercountry activities would account for 25 per cent of total programmable resources, and priority countries would receive two thirds of new programmable resources for country projects. The possibilities of increased shares to family planning and population communication would also be taken into account.

The Executive Director calculated that the programme would cost $631.7 million for the four-year period—$138.2 million for 1984, $149 million for 1985, $164 million for 1986 and $180.5 million for 1987. Following a methodology established by the Governing Council in June 1982,[8] the Council, on 24 June 1983,[4] gave approval authority for 100 per cent of the 1984 figure and smaller proportions

CONTRIBUTIONS TO UNFPA, 1983 AND 1984

(as at 31 December 1983; in US dollar equivalent)

Country or territory	1983 payment	1984 pledge	Country or territory	1983 payment	1984 pledge
Afghanistan	4,000	2,000	Maldives	871	871
Australia	1,960,800	1,041,667	Malta	465	—
Austria	36,200	33,368	Mauritius	3,199	—
Bahamas	2,000	—	Mexico	5,408	—
Bangladesh	36,400	14,500	Mongolia	521	501
Belgium	896,902	345,455	Morocco	—	4,000
Benin	6,000	—	Nepal	3,000	—
Bhutan	2,775	1,810	Netherlands	10,752,406	11,386,139
Botswana	1,132	1,284	New Zealand	229,425	—
British Virgin Islands	500	—	Nigeria	30,675	—
Bulgaria	20,725	—	Norway	11,538,999	12,000,000
Burma	6,219	6,173	Oman	10,000	10,000
Burundi	22,334	4,299	Pakistan	281,955	325,000
Canada	8,333,333	8,333,333	Panama	—	1,000
Chile	5,000	5,000	Papua New Guinea	1,191	1,176
China	330,000	400,000	Paraguay	—	25,000
Colombia	44,000	44,000	Philippines	200,000	118,929
Cook Islands	1,291	—	Poland	—	10,526
Cyprus	—	750	Portugal	—	20,000
Democratic Yemen	5,199	2,000	Qatar	30,000	—
Denmark	4,623,359	4,693,878	Republic of Korea	—	41,000
Ecuador	38,000	20,000	Romania	4,338	4,338
Egypt	254,478	228,921	Rwanda	3,000	1,000
El Salvador	5,000	—	Samoa	633	—
Ethiopia	10,000	—	Saudi Arabia	30,000	30,000
Fiji	2,000	2,000	Senegal	—	7,000
Finland	1,201,923	1,465,517	Seychelles	1,000	500
France	177,033	266,667	Sierra Leone	—	4,000
Germany, Federal Republic of	13,411,911	12,962,963	Somalia	641	1,295
Ghana	17,600	—	Spain	—	88,000
Greece	5,000	5,000	Sri Lanka	7,736	7,500
Guatemala	5,000	—	Sudan	—	25,000
Guinea-Bissau	2,926	—	Suriname	2,500	—
Guyana	333	—	Sweden	6,215,220	6,000,000
Haiti	2,100	—	Switzerland	1,745,192	1,834,862
Honduras	10,000	10,000	Syrian Arab Republic	5,500	5,500
Hungary	11,242	11,346	Thailand	44,000	48,400
Iceland	2,600	2,600	Togo	7,508	—
India	326,198	318,091	Tunisia	15,000	19,130
Indonesia	150,000	150,000	Turkey	—	5,000
Italy	1,886,792	2,147,239	Uganda	—	1,529
Ivory Coast	10,959	—	United Kingdom	3,985,728	4,379,562
Jamaica	561	—	United Republic of Cameroon	3,874	—
Japan	27,350,000	—	United States	33,760,000	—
Jordan	39,938	—	Upper Volta	—	1,211
Kenya	—	3,309	Viet Nam	1,000	1,000
Kuwait	50,000	25,000	Yemen	—	2,850
Lao People's Democratic Republic	—	500	Yugoslavia	10,122	4,440
Lesotho	2,500	1,500	Zaire	—	1,000
Luxembourg	—	4,818	Zambia	—	5,597
Madagascar	310	5,000	Zimbabwe	2,604	2,222
Malawi	1,179	1,297			
Malaysia	10,000	—	Total	130,257,463	68,986,363

SOURCE: A/39/5/Add.7.

(75, 50 and 25 per cent respectively) of total anticipated spending for the three following years. The actual amounts approved were $138.2 million for 1984 ($26.4 million above the amount for that year approved in 1982), $103.6 million for 1985 (a $29.1 million increase), $69.1 million for 1986 (a $31.8 million increase) and $34.5 million for 1987.

Financial and administrative questions

Budget for 1984-1985

In keeping with a June 1982 request of the UNDP Governing Council, the UNFPA Executive Director submitted to it, for the first time in 1983,

biennial budget estimates for UNFPA administrative and programme support services, for the biennium 1984-1985.[9]

On 24 June 1983,[4] the Council, taking note of those estimates, approved net appropriations for the biennium in the amount of $24,577,523. This amount, recommended for approval by the Advisory Committee on Administrative and Budgetary Questions (ACABQ),[10] was to be allocated to finance administrative and programme support services, as follows: $3,109,342 for executive direction and management; $8,255,972 for administration and information support services; and

$13,212,209 for programme planning, appraisal and monitoring. The Council requested the Executive Director to continue to keep the cost of such services to a minimum and agreed that he be authorized to transfer credits between programmes within reasonable limits, with ACABQ concurrence.

Contributions

During 1983, 84 countries and territories paid a total of $130.3 million in voluntary contributions to UNFPA (see table on previous page), compared with $129 million from 67 countries and territories in 1982.[11] This figure, together with additions and adjustments to pledges for prior years, exchange-rate and currency revaluation adjustments, donations and other miscellaneous income, made up a total 1983 income of $134.7 million. Pledges for 1984 from 75 countries and territories totalled $69 million as at 31 December 1983 (see table above), compared with $31.3 from 63 countries and territories at the end of the previous year.[11]

On 24 June 1983,[4] the UNDP Governing Council urged all Governments to support UNFPA's work and to pay their contributions as early in the year as possible. It requested the Executive Director to strengthen his efforts to secure resources from all countries and to explore modalities for securing additional resources from the private sector.

Accounts for 1982

In 1983, following an audit of the UNFPA financial statements for the year ended 31 December 1982, the Board of Auditors made a series of observations and recommendations.[12]

The Board observed that, as recently as April 1983, UNFPA had requested ACABQ concurrence to transfer amounts from the unencumbered balance of one appropriation line in the 1982 administrative and programme support budget to cover excess expenditures incurred under another line. In many projects, expenditures had exceeded, or had been incurred without, allocations. In addition to noting numerous weaknesses in the inventory control system, the Board noted that the UNFPA procurement unit had entered into two leasing agreements, each for over $20,000, without seeking Contract Committee advice, and that the unit's head was not a United Nations staff member. Some projects had their objectives defined only in terms of activities or inputs, and others did not include time-tables for implementation. No clear delineation of functions and responsibilities between UNFPA and UNDP existed, making it difficult to calculate support service costs rendered by each entity.

The Board recommended that requests for credit transfer from one appropriation line to another should be sought prior to incurring expenditures exceeding approved appropriations. It emphasized the need for better control of allocations and expenditures and for more realistic budgets. In its opinion, lease agreements were contracts and as such were subject to the contract clause of the UNDP Policies and Procedures Manual. Project objectives should be clearly defined and a review undertaken of inactive or slow-moving projects. A description of the UNFPA/UNDP working relationship should be made readily accessible and cover areas where a duplication of responsibility was likely to occur.

Commenting on the Board's recommendation on credit transfers, ACABQ noted[13] the Executive Director's reply that the 1982 amounts involved were small ($68,980 and $76,824). In ACABQ's view, prior concurrence should be sought when a significant change in the UNFPA work programme required credit redeployment; otherwise, *post facto* reporting was the most practical approach as long as overall appropriation levels were respected. ACABQ welcomed the Executive Director's response that UNFPA would prepare a description of the UNFPA/UNDP working relationship.

By resolution 38/30 of 25 November 1983, the General Assembly accepted the UNFPA financial reports when it accepted various other 1982 financial reports and audited statements and the Auditors' opinions, concurred with the ACABQ observations, and requested the executive heads to take such remedial action as might be required.

Financial regulations

In accordance with a UNDP Governing Council decision of June 1982,[14] the Executive Director submitted proposed amendments[15] to the UNFPA Financial Regulations resulting from the change to a biennial budgetary cycle beginning with the 1984-1985 biennium and from changes in UNFPA operations that had made some of its financial regulations and rules inapplicable. Once the amendments were approved, the Executive Director would submit revisions to the corresponding UNFPA Financial Rules. The annotated text of the amendments provided a comparison between the current and proposed versions and indicated the comparable UNDP Financial Regulations. ACABQ noted[10] that most of the differences between the revised UNFPA Financial Regulations as proposed and the relevant UNDP regulations were not substantive.

The Council approved the proposed amendments on 24 June 1983,[4] and decided that consequent changes be made to the relevant provisions of the UNDP Financial Regulations. The revised UNFPA regulations were to supersede the current version with effect from 1 January 1984.

Staffing

In a review of UNFPA headquarters and field staffing requirements,[16] the Executive Director proposed that the UNDP Governing Council approve the principle of progressively including UNFPA

Deputy Representatives and their local core staff in the regular manning table, the plan for the proposal's phased implementation to be presented to the Council in 1984. ACABQ was unable to recommend Council acceptance of that proposal:[10] the financial impact of the full transfer to the regular manning table of such posts, currently funded from project funds, would be to increase considerably the budget component on administrative and programme support services, making adjustments more difficult and costly should income and project delivery decline.

On 24 June 1983,[4] the Council requested the Executive Director to submit to it in 1984 a comprehensive report that would enable it to discuss his proposal with a view to encouraging rotation between headquarters and field Professional staff.

REFERENCES

[1]YUN 1981, p. 781. [2]DP/1984/28 (Parts I, II). [3]YUN 1982, p. 968. [4]E/1983/20 (dec. 83/17). [5]YUN 1982, p. 972. [6]DP/1983/21 & Add.1. [7]DP/1983/20. [8]YUN 1982, p. 971. [9]DP/1983/23 & Corr.1,2. [10]DP/1983/26. [11]YUN 1982, p. 973. [12]A/38/5/Add.7. [13]A/38/433. [14]YUN 1982, p. 974. [15]DP/1983/24 & Add.1 & Add.1/Corr.1 & Add.2 & Add.2/Corr.1. [16]DP/1983/25.

UNFPA PUBLICATIONS

Inventory of Population Projects in Developing Countries around the World, 1982/83 (yearly); *1983 Report by the Executive Director of the United Nations Fund for Population Activities*; *Population: UNFPA Newsletter*, vol. 9, Nos. 1-12 (monthly in Arabic, English, French & Spanish; every 2 months in Chinese); *Populi: Journal of the United Nations Fund for Population Activities*, vol. 10, Nos. 1-4 (quarterly).

Preparations for the 1984 Conference on Population

A number of activities in preparation for the International Conference on Population, to be convened in 1984 as decided by the Economic and Social Council in 1981,[1] were organized in 1983 by the United Nations system, at the regional and national levels and by NGOs. These activities were described by the Secretary-General in a November 1983 progress report.[2]

Of note were four expert group meetings on: fertility and the family; population distribution, migration and development; population, resources, environment and development; and mortality and health policy (see below). Another major undertaking, to facilitate Conference deliberations, was a review and appraisal of the implementation of the World Population Plan of Action (see also below), adopted by the 1974 World Population Conference.[3]

Within the United Nations system, a steering committee under the chairmanship of the Director-General for Development and International Economic Co-operation met twice (21 January and 19 October) to review preparatory activities. The *Ad Hoc* Task Force of the International Conference on Population of the Administrative Committee on Co-ordination met (Geneva, 15-20 September) to review two Conference draft documents providing information and comments on population programmes and policies of the regional commissions and specialized agencies.

The United Nations Department of Public Information distributed a Conference brochure and poster to Member States, UNFPA and UNDP field offices, and United Nations information centres. Briefing papers on the topics of the expert group meetings were being prepared for dissemination to the media, NGOs, policy makers, and research and academic institutions. Production of a film on population developments since 1974 was under way and a photo exhibit was being planned. A background paper on the Conference, presented to the annual meeting of the Joint United Nations Information Committee (Geneva, 19-22 April 1983), elicited offers of collaboration from specialized agencies.

At a meeting of the Committee on Population of the Economic and Social Commission for Asia and the Pacific (Bangkok, Thailand, 23-29 August), it was recommended that the regional contribution to the Conference should be the Asia-Pacific Call for Action on Population and Development, adopted by the 1982 Third Asian and Pacific Population Conference.[4] In addition to a meeting on population organized by the Economic Commission for Europe (ECE) (Sofia, Bulgaria, 6-12 October 1983), similar meetings were being planned by the Economic Commission for Africa and the Economic Commission for Western Asia for early 1984.

The Secretary-General of the Conference, who had been appointed in January 1982,[5] visited a number of countries and wrote to Member States: in April 1983, to invite them to organize national committees to co-ordinate preparatory activities; and in November, to set out the objective of such committees as heightening awareness of the importance of population issues and to suggest their composition and seminars they could organize. He also held extensive consultations with NGOs.

A committee created to plan and co-ordinate preparatory activities of the Conference of Non-governmental Organizations in Consultative Status with the Economic and Social Council organized an international consultation (Geneva, 13-15 September). Attended by 62 international and 30 national organizations, the consultation focused on the role of NGOs in furthering the objectives of the Plan of Action and in contributing to renewed Government interest in this area.

As at 1 November 1983, pledges for the Conference totalled $1,045,400—from 22 Governments, including those of developing countries.

ECONOMIC AND SOCIAL COUNCIL ACTION

Having considered an April 1983 report of the Secretary-General of the Conference,[6] the Economic and Social Council, on the recommendation of its First (Economic) Committee, adopted without vote resolution 1983/6 on 26 May 1983.

International Conference on Population, 1984
The Economic and Social Council,

Recalling its resolutions 1981/87 of 25 November 1981, 1982/7 of 30 April 1982 and 1982/42 of 27 July 1982,

1. *Takes note* of the report of the Secretary-General of the Conference on the preparations for the International Conference on Population in 1984 and of his statement to the First (Economic) Committee at its 6th meeting, on 16 May 1983;

2. *Decides* to convene the International Conference on Population at Mexico City from 6 to 13 August 1984, composed of a plenary and one main committee;

3. *Requests* the Secretary-General to invite:

(a) All States to participate in the Conference;

(b) Representatives of organizations that have received a standing invitation from the General Assembly to participate in the sessions and the work of all international conferences convened under its auspices in the capacity of observers to participate in the Conference in that capacity, in accordance with Assembly resolutions 3237(XXIX) of 22 November 1974 and 31/152 of 20 December 1976;

(c) Representatives of the national liberation movements recognized in its region by the Organization of African Unity to participate in the Conference in the capacity of observers, in accordance with General Assembly resolution 3280(XXIX) of 10 December 1974;

(d) The United Nations Council for Namibia to participate in the Conference, in accordance with paragraph 3 of General Assembly resolution 32/9 E of 4 November 1977;

(e) The specialized agencies and the International Atomic Energy Agency, as well as other interested organs of the United Nations, to be represented at the Conference;

(f) Interested intergovernmental organizations to be represented by observers at the Conference;

(g) Interested non-governmental organizations in consultative status with the Economic and Social Council to be represented by observers at the Conference;

(h) Other interested non-governmental organizations that may have a specific contribution to make to the work of the Conference to be represented by observers at the Conference;

4. *Requests* the Secretary-General to make the following arrangements, within the approved regular budgetary resources for the Conference and with available extrabudgetary resources:

(a) To convene, on 5 August 1984, pre-conference consultations on organizational matters regarding the Conference;

(b) To provide the necessary conference facilities for two daily plenary meetings and two daily committee meetings, as well as for evening plenary meetings, if

necessary, and for the possible extension of the Conference for one day, if required;

5. *Decides* that the Population Commission, when acting as the Preparatory Committee for the Conference, should concentrate on the review and appraisal of the World Population Plan of Action and the formulation of specific recommendations to the Conference on the further implementation of that Plan of Action;

6. *Requests* the Secretary-General of the Conference, in the light of the need for thorough preparation for the Conference, to circulate the documentation for the Preparatory Committee for the Conference at an early date, particularly the two basic documents concerning the review and appraisal of the World Population Plan of Action and the recommendations to the Conference on the further implementation of that Plan of Action, as well as the findings of the meetings of the four expert groups;

7. *Recommends* that the General Assembly, at its thirty-eighth session, should approve the regular budgetary resources required for the Conference, as agreed in paragraph 5 of Council resolution 1982/42, and invites the Secretary-General of the Conference to continue his efforts to raise extrabudgetary resources for the Conference.

Economic and Social Council resolution 1983/6

26 May 1983	Meeting 14	Adopted without vote

Approved by First Committee (E/1983/57) without vote, 18 May (meeting 7); draft by Chairman (E/1983/C.1/L.5), orally revised; agenda item 5.
Financial implications. S-G, E/1983/C.1/L.6.
Meeting number. ESC 14.

GENERAL ASSEMBLY ACTION

On 19 December 1983, on the recommendation of its Second (Economic and Financial) Committee, the General Assembly adopted without vote resolution 38/148.

International Conference on Population
The General Assembly,

Recalling its resolutions 3201(S-VI) and 3202(S-VI) of 1 May 1974, containing the Declaration and the Programme of Action on the Establishment of a New International Economic Order, 3281(XXIX) of 12 December 1974, containing the Charter of Economic Rights and Duties of States, and 3362(S-VII) of 16 September 1975 on development and international economic cooperation,

Recalling also its resolution 35/56 of 5 December 1980, to which is annexed the International Development Strategy for the Third United Nations Development Decade, in which the General Assembly declared, *inter alia*, that the implementation of the World Population Plan of Action should be strengthened in the 1980s and that the international community should increase the level of assistance in this field in support of the World Population Plan of Action,

Recalling further its resolution 3344(XXIX) of 17 December 1974 on the World Population Conference,

Recalling Economic and Social Council resolution 1979/32 of 9 May 1979 on the strengthening of actions concerned with the fulfilment of the World Population Plan of Action,

Emphasizing the importance of the population question and its close link to development,

Recalling Economic and Social Council resolutions 1981/87 of 25 November 1981, 1982/7 of 30 April 1982, 1982/42 of 27 July 1982 and 1983/6 of 26 May 1983,

Noting that relevant policies and programmes are being adopted by many States as part of their national plans to implement the provisions of the World Population Plan of Action,

Noting also the programmes adopted by United Nations organs and the activities carried out by the United Nations Fund for Population Activities and by non-governmental organizations concerned with the implementation of the provisions of the World Population Plan of Action,

Noting further that the Population Commission, acting as Preparatory Committee for the International Conference on Population, will hold a session open to the participation of all States in January 1984,

Aware of the necessity of appraising the implementation of the World Population Plan of Action and giving new impetus to its full application,

1. *Endorses* the decisions adopted by the Economic and Social Council in its resolution 1983/6, including the convening of the International Conference on Population at Mexico City from 6 to 13 August 1984;

2. *Welcomes with appreciation* the offer of the Government of Mexico to serve as host to the International Conference on Population in 1984;

3. *Requests* the Population Commission, acting as Preparatory Committee open to the participation of all States, to prepare at its meeting in January 1984 a draft provisional agenda for the Conference, taking into account paragraph 5 of Economic and Social Council resolution 1983/6, and to submit the draft provisional agenda for the approval of the Council at its first regular session of 1984;

4. *Requests* the regional commissions to consider at their annual sessions in 1984 the Preparatory Committee's report on its meeting, to make suggestions and recommendations for the subsequent implementation and updating of the World Population Plan of Action at the regional level, and to transmit their suggestions and recommendations to the Conference for its consideration;

5. *Requests* the Secretary-General to take the appropriate steps to ensure the timely circulation of the preparatory documents for the Conference and, in any event, with strict adherence to the six-week rule, and their availability simultaneously in all the official languages of the United Nations;

6. *Requests* the Secretary-General to take appropriate steps as part of the preparatory process to ensure that the Conference and issues to be discussed at the Conference are widely publicized;

7. *Calls upon* the Secretary-General of the Conference to continue to make every effort to obtain extrabudgetary resources for the Conference;

8. *Urges* all States to participate actively at a high level in the Conference;

9. *Requests* the Preparatory Committee to transmit the report on its meeting in January 1984 to the Economic and Social Council for consideration at its first regular session of 1984;

10. *Requests* the Secretary-General to report to the General Assembly at its thirty-ninth session on the outcome of the Conference.

General Assembly resolution 38/148

19 December 1983   Meeting 102   Adopted without vote

Approved by Second Committee (A/38/701) without vote, 21 November (meeting 45); draft by Vice-Chairman (A/C.2/38/L.45), based on informal consultations on draft by Bangladesh, China, Ecuador, Egypt and Mexico (A/C.2/38/L.31/Rev.1) and orally revised; agenda item 12.

Meeting numbers. GA 38th session: 2nd Committee 3-15, 24-31, 34, 36, 39, 41, 45; plenary 102.

Expert group meetings

As authorized by the Economic and Social Council in 1981,[1] the Secretary-General convened four expert group meetings in preparation for the International Conference on Population (1984). Their purpose was to give the necessary scientific focus to the issues to be considered by the Conference and thus provide an appropriate basis for reassessing the recommendations of the 1974 World Population Plan of Action.

An Expert Group on Fertility and Family met (New Delhi, India, 5-11 January)[7] to discuss fertility response to modernization, the relationship between family structure and fertility, choice in childbearing, reproductive behaviour and economic activities of women, and national demographic policies and family planning programmes in relation to social and economic development objectives.

Among the Group's recommendations was formulation of population policies consistent with national priorities and with the principles of human rights. Such policies should take account of changes in population level, characteristics and trends, incorporate child labour and compulsory education legislation, promote a decline of general mortality, and initiate institutional mechanisms for old-age support and care. Family planning programmes should be integrated into other development programmes, and include safe and legal methods of limiting or spacing births as well as follow-up services. Legislation against child marriage, education and access to viable employment or income-generating activities for women were cited as measures to regulate or reduce fertility. Population policies should be bolstered through information, education and communication. Research on factors impeding and enhancing acceptance of family planning should be undertaken, in addition to biomedical research in contraceptive technology.

On the agenda of the meeting held by an Expert Group on Population Distribution, Migration and Development (Hammamet, Tunisia, 21-25 March)[8] were: conceptual approaches to internal and international migration; migration and rural development; migration, urbanization and development in both developing and developed countries; population distribution policies; and international migration consisting of movements of illegal migrants, skilled groups and refugees.

The Group underlined the need to see internal and international migration in their historical contexts, to make it easier to evaluate various types of migration when formulating, implementing and reviewing migration and population distribution policies. Besides taking account of the fundamental human right to choose one's residence, such policies should help achieve the broader societal goals of greater per capita income, efficiency and inter-group equity. They should seek to balance population distribution and economic activity in strategies for rural, town and city development, and to improve integration of spatial and sectoral planning, as in the spatial allocation of public investments and human settlements. The Group agreed that the Plan of Action overemphasized the adverse effects of urbanization and migration and should be modified to reflect more precise population distribution policies, taking account of the effects that migration and urban development could have on individual migrants and society.

Policies on international migration should respect the individual's fundamental human rights and basic economic and social rights, as set out in ILO conventions. Receiving countries should safeguard the rights of non-nationals and ensure their access to health and social services. Countries affected by significant numbers of migrant workers were urged to conclude agreements to regulate migration and to protect the interests not only of those countries but also of such workers. United Nations Members which had not already done so were also urged to accede to international instruments concerning refugees.

The meeting of the Expert Group on Population, Resources, Environment and Development (Geneva, 25-29 April)[9] discussed trends in population, resources, environment and development and their interrelationships; food and nutrition; resources and environment; the social and economic aspects of development; and integration of population in policy, planning and programmes.

Among the Group's recommendations were measures for expanding agricultural production to meet food requirements of developing countries in the year 2000 and beyond. To protect the resource base and the environment, the Group suggested preparation of environmental impact assessments for large-scale development projects, proper management of hazardous industrial and agricultural wastes, prevention of irreversible changes in resource productivity, establishment of pollution control mechanisms and protection of genetic diversity. Measures to improve social and economic development included modification of national conventions relating to property ownership and inheritance to promote greater equality in land ownership, and increased atten-

tion to infrastructural needs of less developed areas. Governments were urged to adopt population policies to help redress imbalances between population growth and current and projected resource and environmental requirements. Research into long-term demographic projection methods should take account of interrelationships between population, resources, environment and development.

An Expert Group on Mortality and Health Policy was convened (Rome, Italy, 30 May–3 June)[10] to review prospects for mortality reduction through health policies and programmes.

To attain the objective of health care for all by the year 2000, Governments were urged to direct health resources on a multi-sectoral basis towards the most vulnerable groups. Governments were urged to provide clean potable water and regulated waste disposal as a matter of urgency. The Group recommended placing priority on health programmes in national budgets and development plans, orienting medical practice towards prevention, and promoting family planning as part of all maternal and child health programmes. It called for strengthening or creating systems for the collection and processing of data on which to base policy, and for establishing a co-ordinated international data collection and research programme on health and mortality. Noting the need to improve strategies for ensuring health throughout the developing world, the Group strongly urged donor agencies and the United Nations system to increase resources for the formulation, implementation and evaluation of health programmes.

Review and appraisal of the World Population Plan of Action

In December 1983, the Secretary-General reported on the results of the second review and appraisal of the implementation of the 1974 World Population Plan of Action,[11] the first such review having been undertaken in 1979.[12] The review was to facilitate the deliberations of the International Conference on Population (1984), by providing background information on population trends and policies and assessing progress in achieving the objectives of the Plan of Action.

The main input for the review was provided by the four expert group meetings (see above). The review covered the relationship between socio-economic development and population; the formulation and application of population policies; population trends, prospects, goals and policies; promotion of demographic research and information dissemination; the role of Governments and the international community in implementing the Plan; and monitoring and appraising the Plan's effectiveness.

The report, submitted for consideration by the Population Commission, acting as the Preparatory Committee for the International Conference on Population, served as the basis for the Secretary-General's recommendations[13] for further implementation of the Plan.

REFERENCES

[1]YUN 1981, p. 790, ESC res. 1981/87, 25 Nov. 1981. [2]E/CONF.76/PC/2. [3]YUN 1974, p. 552. [4]YUN 1982, p. 847. [5]*Ibid.*, p. 976. [6]E/1983/24. [7]*Fertility and Family: Proceedings of the Expert Group on Fertility and Family, New Delhi, 5-11 January 1983* (ST/ESA/SER.A/88 & Corr.1), Sales No. E.84.XIII.7 & corrigendum. [8]*Population Distribution, Migration and Development: Proceedings of the Expert Group on Population Distribution, Migration and Development, Hammamet (Tunisia), 21-25 March 1983* (ST/ESA/SER.A/89), Sales No. E.84.XIII.3. [9]*Population, Resources, Environment and Development: Proceedings of the Expert Group on Population, Resources, Environment and Development, Geneva, 25-29 April 1983* (ST/ESA/SER.A/90), Sales No. E.84.XIII.12. [10]*Mortality and Health Policy: Proceedings of the Expert Group on Mortality and Health Policy, Rome, 30 May to 3 June 1983* (ST/ESA/SER.A/91), Sales No. E.84.XIII.4. [11]E/CONF.76/PC/10. [12]YUN 1979, p. 787. [13]E/CONF.76/PC/11.

Other population activities

DTCD activities

In 1983, the Department of Technical Co-operation for Development (DTCD), with support from the Statistical Office of the Department of International Economic and Social Affairs (DIESA), executed a number of UNFPA-funded projects in developing countries. Some 82 projects were in population data collection, to provide population data needed for national development plans. More than 100 projects were in demographic activities, including training, analysis of census and survey data, and population policy and development.

DTCD also participated in a number of UNFPA-sponsored missions to assess assistance needs, formulate projects and conduct technical evaluations of ongoing projects. It collaborated with UNFPA and DIESA on arrangements for the International Conference on Population (1984), which included preparation of papers on technical co-operation for the four expert group meetings, and contributed to the review and appraisal of the 1974 World Population Plan of Action (see above).

These activities were described in a report[1] on the work of the agencies and organizations responsible for executing UNFPA-funded projects.

Technical co-operation among developing countries

At the May/June 1983 session of the High-level Committee on the Review of Technical Co-operation among Developing Countries (TCDC) (see Chapter II of this section), the UNDP Administrator presented a report[2] on the role of TCDC in rural-urban migration.

The report reviewed selected interventions by Governments in developing countries aimed at diminishing rural emigration by development programmes, localized projects and special measures to "hold" the potential migrant in an improved rural milieu. Emphasis was placed on drawing conclusions for TCDC activities from examples with identified elements of success. The report's recommendations formed a unified strategy for an international system of TCDC for information exchange to reduce rural-urban migration.

By a decision of 6 June,[3] the Committee took note of the report and invited developing countries to promote TCDC on rural-urban migration issues and to co-operate with other countries wishing to profit from particular country experiences on how to tackle problems arising from such migration. Governments were invited to encourage a subregional or regional intergovernmental organization, or a national institution, to serve as a documentation and referral centre for information exchange. The Committee recommended training courses reducing rural-urban migration. It invited developed countries to provide technical materials on the subject, developed from their own experiences, as well as financial support. It also invited NGO collaboration with Government institutions in project evaluation and migration research.

UN Population Award

On 14 October 1983, the Secretary-General transmitted to the General Assembly a report by the UNFPA Executive Director describing activities related to the United Nations Population Award for 1983.[4]

The Executive Director reported that the Committee for the United Nations Population Award held a series of meetings between 20 January and 8 September to select the recipients of the first annual United Nations Population Award. The Award for 1983 consisted of a diploma, a gold medal and a monetary prize of $12,500.

Two laureates were chosen from 71 nominees for their outstanding contribution to the awareness of population questions and to their solutions: Indira Gandhi, Prime Minister of India; and Qian Xinzhong, Minister-in-Charge, State Family Planning Commission, China. The Award was presented to each in a ceremony held at United Nations Headquarters on 30 September.

In 1983, the Committee also issued invitations for nominations for the 1984 Award.

Reporting on the status of the Trust Fund for the United Nations Population Award, the Executive Director stated that contributions had been received from three countries: China, $100,000; Japan, $200,000; and Mexico, $100,000. The Fund, established by the Secretary-General pursuant to a 1981 Assembly resolution[5] and made up of voluntary contributions, was administered by the Executive Director.

GENERAL ASSEMBLY ACTION

On the recommendation of the Second Committee, the General Assembly adopted decision 38/444 without vote.

Report of the Executive Director of the United Nations Fund for Population Activities on the United Nations Population Award

At its 102nd plenary meeting, on 19 December 1983, the General Assembly, on the recommendation of the Second Committee, took note of the report of the Executive Director of the United Nations Fund for Population Activities on the United Nations Population Award for 1983.

General Assembly decision 38/444

Adopted without vote

Approved by Second Committee (A/38/703) without vote, 14 December (meeting 56); draft orally proposed by Chairman; agenda item 79 *(d)*.
Meeting number. GA 38th session: 2nd Committee 56; plenary 102.

Cross-sectoral review and evaluation

Pursuant to a July 1982 resolution of the Economic and Social Council[6] and to Council decision 1983/101, the Secretary-General submitted a review,[7] dated 15 June 1983, of the population activities proposed in the medium-term plans of United Nations system organizations.

The report noted that, following the 1974 World Population Conference,[8] various United Nations units and specialized agencies had modified the direction of their work to conform to the principles and recommendations of the World Population Plan of Action adopted by the Conference. Expenditures for all international (including bilateral and multilateral) technical co-operation in population had been nearing $500 million yearly, as illustrated by the revised total of $475 million for 1980 and $480 million for 1981. According to UNFPA, total commitments by Governments, the World Bank and private donors exceeded $500 million in 1979 and $550 million in 1980. Despite the sharp drop to $400 million in 1981, such commitment levels were expected to influence favourably the flow of assistance in the next five years, when yearly expenditures were expected to remain at or surpass $500 million.

As a percentage of net official development assistance, population assistance by the Organisation for Economic Co-operation and Development had averaged approximately 2 per cent. Two significant developments in programme funding had emerged in recent years: the growth of multi/bilateral funds and the increase in Government resources allocated to multilateral programmes. A shift from bilateral to multilateral programmes had been equally significant. The share of Government funds for bilateral programmes had declined to 35.5 per cent in 1980 and 1981, from almost 40 per cent in 1977; for multilateral programmes, it had risen from 36 per cent in 1977 to over 39 per cent in 1980 and 1981. The share of Government funds channelled through NGOs remained at approximately 24 per cent.

Since 1969, when its management was entrusted to the UNDP Administrator,[9] UNFPA had become the largest multilateral source of population assistance, its cumulative income adding up to $1 billion, or almost 30 per cent of all Government contributions for the same period.

United Nations activities, as reflected in the medium-term plan for 1984-1985, would emphasize the following aspects of population: improving countries' capabilities to formulate population policies and integrate them into overall development planning; incorporating development strategies into population projections; fertility change and its effects on women and the family; differentials of mortality; and migration at all levels and its impact on development and planning.

As described by the report, the main United Nations bodies engaged in population activities, besides UNFPA, included: the Population Division and Statistical Office of DIESA; DTCD; the United Nations Conference on Trade and Development, which had been concerned with the outflow of skilled manpower from developing to developed countries; the regional commissions, excepting ECE, for the medium-term period 1984-1989; and such specialized agencies as ILO, UNESCO and WHO.

ECONOMIC AND SOCIAL COUNCIL ACTION

Acting without vote on the recommendation of its Third (Programme and Co-ordination) Committee, the Economic and Social Council adopted resolution 1983/76 on 29 July 1983.

Cross-sectoral review of population
The Economic and Social Council,
Recalling its resolution 1982/50 of 28 July 1982 on the revitalization of the Council, in which, *inter alia*, it decided to review every six years selected major issues in the proposed medium-term plans of the organizations of the United Nations system,
Recalling its decision 1983/101 of 4 February 1983, by paragraph 2 *(c)* of which it decided that food and agriculture and population would be the two areas for review in 1983,
Emphasizing the continuing relevance and importance of population policies and programmes in the economic and social development of the developing countries,
Recalling the World Population Plan of Action adopted by consensus at the World Population Conference and

given endorsement by the General Assembly in its resolution 3344(XXIX) of 17 December 1974,

Recalling its resolutions 1981/87 of 25 November 1981, in which it decided to convene an International Conference on Population in 1984, and 1982/7 of 30 April 1982 and 1982/42 of 27 July 1982, concerning preparations for the Conference,

Reaffirming the importance of the Conference,

1. *Takes note* of the report of the Secretary-General, which, *inter alia*, outlines population trends and policies since 1974 and contains a review of the planned programmes and activities of the organizations of the United Nations system concerned in the field of population;

2. *Decides* to continue to attach high priority to population programmes and activities as contributing to the social and economic development of the developing countries, and urges that increased financial support for population activities be made available and that competent entities of the United Nations system take appropriate action accordingly in a co-ordinated manner in their respective programmes of work;

3. *Notes with satisfaction* that the various organizational elements of the United Nations and members of the United Nations system in the area of population are working towards an effective division of labour, and urges them to ensure enhanced co-operation and co-ordination among themselves;

4. *Decides* to consider the matter again at a future session, taking into account the outcome of the International Conference on Population to be held in 1984 in Mexico, and the other developments in the area of population.

Economic and Social Council resolution 1983/76

29 July 1983   Meeting 42   Adopted without vote

Approved by Third Committee (E/1983/128) without vote, 22 July (meeting 16); 4-nation draft (E/1983/C.3/L.10/Rev.1), orally revised; agenda item 21.
Sponsors: Bangladesh, China, India, Pakistan.
Meeting number. ESC 42.

REFERENCES

[1]DP/1984/29.   [2]TCDC/3/5.   [3]A/38/39   (dec. 3/3). [4]A/38/410.   [5]YUN 1981, p. 792, GA res. 36/201, 17 Dec. 1981. [6]YUN 1982, p. 1241, ESC res. 1982/50, 28 July 1982. [7]E/1983/101. [8]YUN 1974, p. 552. [9]YUN 1972, p. 374.

PUBLICATIONS

Courses on Population and Development: Aspects of Technical Co-operation (ST/ESA/SER.E/39), Sales No. E.83.II.A.1. *Computer Software Programs for Demographic Analysis: Aspects of Technical Co-operation*, Sales No. E.83.II.A.5. *Manual X: Indirect Techniques for Demographic Estimation* (ST/ESA/SER.A/81), Sales No. E.83.XIII.2. *Population Bulletin of the United Nations*, No. 15, *1983* (ST/ESA/SER.N/15), Sales No. E.83.XIII.4. *Concise Report on the World Population Situation in 1983* (ST/ESA/SER.A/85), Sales No. E.83.XIII.6. *Population Projections: Methodology of the United Nations: Papers of the United Nations* Ad Hoc *Expert Group on Demographic Projections, United Nations Headquarters, 16-19 November 1981* (ST/ESA/SER.A/83), Sales No. E.83.XIII.7. *Demographic Yearbook 1983* (ST/ESA/STAT/SER.R/13), Sales No. E/F.84.XIII.1. *Recent Levels and Trends of Contraceptive Use as Assessed in 1983* (ST/ESA/SER.A/92), Sales No. E.84.XIII.5. *World Population Trends, Population and Development Interrelations and Population Policies: 1983 Monitoring Report*, vol. I: *Population Trends* (ST/ESA/SER.A/93), Sales No. E.84.XIII.10. *Population Newsletter*, No. 33/34 (Oct. 83).

Chapter XV

Health and human resources

During 1983, many diseases continued to be aggravated in both developed and developing countries by environmental pollution. The United Nations Environment Programme (UNEP) worked with other United Nations bodies in preparing publications on environmental factors influencing human health.

As part of United Nations activities during the United Nations Decade for Disabled Persons (1983-1992), the General Assembly, by resolution 38/28 adopted in November, decided to continue the Trust Fund for the International Year of Disabled Persons (IYDP).

In May, the Economic and Social Council, in resolution 1983/19, called for implementation of the 1982 World Programme of Action concerning Disabled Persons.

Strategies to reduce nutrition-related deaths were considered by the Sub-Committee on Nutrition and the Advisory Group on Nutrition of the Administrative Committee on Co-ordination (ACC).

Despite financial constraints, the United Nations Institute for Training and Research (UNITAR) began a new programme of training for economic and social development. By resolution 38/177 adopted in December, the Assembly agreed to advance $886,000 to UNITAR to cover its 1983 deficit.

The United Nations University (UNU) established its first research and training centre, the World Institute for Development Economics Research at Helsinki, Finland; the Assembly in December appealed for urgent contributions to the UNU Endowment Fund (resolution 38/178).

Topics related to this chapter. Environment: protection against harmful products. Children, youth and aging persons.

Health

Human and environmental health

In 1983, malnutrition, communicable diseases and environmental pollution continued to plague human health, their severity varying according to the regions and countries concerned, the Executive Director of the United Nations Environment

Programme (UNEP) said in his annual report to the UNEP Governing Council.[1] Malnutrition and communicable diseases remained the principal contributors to the high mortality in developing countries; the increasing and uncontrolled use of chemicals in the agricultural sector in those countries also posed a serious threat to human health and life. Even in developed countries, chemical pollution of the environment continued to aggravate many diseases—pulmonary, neoplastic, cardio-vascular and others. The contamination of the soil assumed serious proportions in many areas of the world.

UNEP continued co-operating during the year with ILO, WHO, and the International Agency for Research on Cancer (IARC) in preparing and publishing health criteria documents, providing information to policy-drafters, decision-makers, health personnel and other specialists on a wide spectrum of environmental chemical and physical factors affecting human health. With IARC and WHO, UNEP published the sixth volume of *Environmental Carcinogens: Selected Methods of Analysis*—concerning N-nitroso compounds—which together with five earlier manuals in the series established an information base for control of such carcinogens. Another publication, *Management of Hazardous Waste: Policy Guidelines and Code of Practice*, was jointly financed by UNEP and WHO.

Among the meetings held on human and environmental health was that of the WHO/FAO/UNEP Panel of Experts on Environmental Management for Disease and Vector Control (Rome, Italy, 11-16 September). A meeting on lay reporting of environmental health information (Addis Ababa, Ethiopia, 7-11 March) took up the current procedures for lay reporting in the context of health and social systems in African countries. A training workshop organized by UNEP and WHO on mutagenicity and carcinogenicity testing was held at Nairobi, Kenya, from 24 January to 4 February.

Disabled persons

Three reports about disabled persons were prepared by the Secretary-General during the year.

Pursuant to a December 1982 General Assembly resolution,[2] the Secretary-General, in consultation with Governments, examined the need and possibility of continuing the United Nations

Trust Fund for the International Year of Disabled Persons (IYDP), which had been observed in 1981.[3] In his report to the Assembly on the subject,[4] he stated that, as at 17 October 1983, 27 Governments had responded to an invitation for comments. Views on the Fund also had been expressed at the following meetings: the Commission for Social Development (Vienna, Austria, 7-16 February); the inter-agency meeting on the United Nations Decade of Disabled Persons (Geneva, 30-31 May); and an Expert Group Meeting on Development and Utilization of Local Manpower and Technology in Disability-related Services in the Rural and Poverty Areas of Asia and the Pacific Region (Manila, Philippines, 21 February–1 March). The World Assembly on Youth, the Disabled Peoples' International and the Council of World Organizations Interested in the Handicapped had also submitted their views.

The Secretary-General recalled that the Trust Fund had been established in 1978 in response to a 1977 Assembly resolution[5] in which the Assembly appealed for contributions to IYDP. Thirty-two project proposals had been funded or were in the process of being approved by the Trust Fund at a cost of $856,193, and an additional 14 project proposals had been earmarked for funding; the majority of allocations had been for projects in developing countries.

From 1978 to early 1983, the Trust Fund had provided financial support for: advisory and consultative services concerning the design of national programmes for the prevention of disability, rehabilitation and equalization of opportunities for disabled persons; preparation of technical manuals and documents to assist Governments with statistics and data collection; participation of representatives of least developed countries in meetings and seminars; cultural activities and community programmes; establishment and strengthening of organizations of disabled persons; support services for the exchange of technical information and the transfer of technology, including training courses, seminars and workshops; and development of indigenous capacities to deal more effectively with the prevention of disability, rehabilitation and integration of disabled persons in their societies.

Nineteen of the 27 Governments that submitted views to the Secretary-General recommended continuation of the Trust Fund. However, some Governments felt that assistance regarding disability should be channelled through existing United Nations bodies and connected as closely as possible to the United Nations Development Programme (UNDP), or through bilateral programmes.

The Secretary-General concluded that there was a need to increase the flow of resources to develop-

ing countries for disabled persons, that the Fund had played a catalytic role in supporting activities related to disability, and that, in many cases, it had complemented other available resources. The Trust Fund would provide much-needed assistance, the Secretary-General said, in implementing the World Programme of Action concerning Disabled Persons, adopted by the Assembly in 1982,[6] and in responding to activities for the United Nations Decade of Disabled Persons, which had been proclaimed for 1983-1992.[2]

In a January 1983 report[7] on the implementation of the 1975 Declaration on the Rights of Disabled Persons[8] to the Commission for Social Development at its February session—submitted in response to a 1976 request by the General Assembly[9]—the Secretary-General discussed measures taken during the period 1979-1982 at the national level and by United Nations bodies and non-governmental organizations, as well as the relation of the Declaration to the World Programme of Action and its monitoring system.

Implementation of the Declaration had been greatly enhanced by IYDP and its follow-up, he said. The principle of equalization of opportunities for disabled persons contained in the World Programme of Action could be used for improvement of their rights. Documents and declarations, resolutions and recommendations adopted during IYDP were important instruments for promotion of such rights and a prerequisite for their implementation. Technical assistance to disabled persons, especially in developing countries, and measures for technical co-operation could be among the aims of the Decade of Disabled Persons. To simplify monitoring, future assessment of the Declaration's implementation could be included in and carried out at the same time as the overall evaluation of the Programme of Action.

The Secretary-General, in response to a 1979 Economic and Social Council resolution,[10] reported to the Commission for Social Development's February session on disability prevention and activities concerning disabled persons.[11] An estimated 500 million people in the world were disabled as a result of mental, physical or sensory impairment, he said. Many disabilities could be prevented by measures against malnutrition, environmental pollution, poor hygiene, inadequate pre-natal and post-natal care, water-borne diseases and accidents. Furthermore, the provision of rehabilitation services was essential.

At the national level, activities undertaken included: provision of preventive, treatment and rehabilitation services; examination of current legislation; data collection and research; and information dissemination. It was noted that for a majority of disabled, especially those in developing countries, preventive measures reached only a small proportion of those in need. At the regional level, activities included holding conferences to exchange information, exploring long-term solutions, and technical co-operation. At the international level, the finalization by the Secretariat of the World Programme of Action was cited, together with programmes of the United Nations specialized agencies, interagency co-ordination within the framework of ACC, and activities of intergovernmental and non-governmental organizations.

ECONOMIC AND SOCIAL COUNCIL ACTION

After the Commission for Social Development had considered the Secretary-General's reports on the implementation of the 1975 Declaration,[7] and that on the prevention of disabilities,[11] the Commission recommended a draft resolution[12] for adoption by the Economic and Social Council. On the recommendation of its Second (Social) Committee, the Council adopted resolution 1983/19 on 26 May.

United Nations Decade of Disabled Persons

The Economic and Social Council,

Taking into consideration General Assembly resolutions 37/52 of 3 December 1982, by which the Assembly adopted the World Programme of Action concerning Disabled Persons, and 37/53 of 3 December 1982 on the implementation of the World Programme of Action, in which the Assembly proclaimed the period 1983-1992 United Nations Decade of Disabled Persons,

Taking note with appreciation of the reports of the Secretary-General on the implementation of the Declaration on the Rights of Disabled Persons and on the prevention of disability and on activities concerning disabled persons and of the conclusions reached in those reports,

Concerned with the necessity of keeping alive the momentum generated by the International Year of Disabled Persons in order to ensure the continuous implementation of the Year's main theme of "Full participation and equality",

1. *Requests* the Secretary-General to submit a progress report containing national experiences in the implementation of the World Programme of Action concerning Disabled Persons and the related activities of the United Nations and other international organizations, to be submitted to the Economic and Social Council through the Commission for Social Development at its twenty-ninth session;

2. *Requests* that that report should integrate in one document all other documentation on the subject, such as that requested by the General Assembly in its resolution 31/82 of 13 December 1976 on the implementation of the Declaration on the Rights of Disabled Persons, and by the Economic and Social Council in resolution 1979/14 of 9 May 1979, on prevention of disability, and that it should include a brief account of the progress achieved in developing criteria for monitoring the World Programme of Action;

3. *Calls upon* all governmental and non-governmental organizations interested in disabled persons to take ac-

tion to implement the objectives of the World Programme of Action and the United Nations Decade of Disabled Persons, and invites full and direct participation of disabled persons themselves;

4. *Requests* the Secretary-General to promote these activities, paying special attention to the situation of disabled persons in the developing countries, in accordance with the recommendations of the Vienna Affirmative Action Plan adopted by the World Symposium of Experts on Technical Co-operation among Developing Countries and Technical Assistance in Disability Prevention and Rehabilitation, held at Vienna from 12 to 23 October 1981;

5. *Requests* the Secretary-General to monitor and support the implementation of the World Programme of Action concerning Disabled Persons by enlisting extrabudgetary resources.

Economic and Social Council resolution 1983/19

26 May 1983   Meeting 14   Adopted without vote

Approved by Second Committee (E/1983/62) without vote, 10 May (meeting 8); draft by Commission for Social Development (E/1983/14); agenda item 11. *Meeting number.* ESC 14.

GENERAL ASSEMBLY ACTION

On 22 November, on the recommendation of its Third (Social, Humanitarian and Cultural) Committee, which had considered the Secretary-General's report on the Trust Fund,[4] the General Assembly adopted without vote resolution 38/28.

Implementation of the World Programme of Action concerning Disabled Persons

The General Assembly,

Recalling its resolutions 32/133 of 16 December 1977 and 34/154 of 17 December 1979, in which it appealed to Member States to make generous voluntary contributions to the International Year of Disabled Persons,

Recalling also its resolution 36/77 of 8 December 1981, in which it welcomed the contributions made by Governments and private sources to the United Nations Trust Fund for the International Year of Disabled Persons and appealed for further voluntary contributions which would facilitate the follow-up to the Year,

Deeply concerned that no less than five hundred million persons are estimated to suffer from disability of one form or another, of whom four hundred million are estimated to be in developing countries,

Convinced that the International Year of Disabled Persons gave a genuine and meaningful impetus to activities related to the equalization of opportunities for disabled persons, as well as prevention and rehabilitation at all levels,

Noting the emergence of organizations of disabled persons in all parts of the world and their positive influence on the image and condition of persons with a disability,

Desirous of ensuring effective follow-up to the International Year of Disabled Persons and aware that, if this is to be achieved, Member States, organs, organizations and bodies of the United Nations system, non-governmental organizations and organizations of disabled persons must therefore be encouraged to continue the activities already undertaken and to initiate new programmes and activities,

Stressing that the primary responsibility for promoting effective measures for the prevention of disability, for rehabilitation and for the realization of the goals of "full participation" of disabled persons in social life and development and of "equality" rests with individual countries and that international action should be directed towards assisting and supporting such national efforts in this regard as consultative services in designing national plans and programmes in the field of disability prevention, rehabilitation and the equalization of opportunities for persons with disabilities,

Reiterating its appreciation to the Advisory Committee for the International Year of Disabled Persons for its work, in particular for its contribution to the formulation of the World Programme of Action concerning Disabled Persons,

Recalling its resolution 37/52 of 3 December 1982, by which it adopted the World Programme of Action concerning Disabled Persons, in paragraph 157 of which it is stated that the Trust Fund established by the General Assembly for the International Year of Disabled Persons should be used to meet requests for assistance from developing countries and organizations of disabled persons and to further the implementation of the World Programme of Action and, in paragraph 158, it is indicated that, in general, there is a need to increase the flow of resources to developing countries to implement the objectives of the World Programme of Action, and that, therefore, the Secretary-General should explore new ways and means of raising funds and take the necessary follow-up measures for mobilizing resources, and that voluntary contributions from Governments and from private sources should be encouraged,

Recalling further its resolution 37/53 of 3 December 1982, by which it proclaimed the period 1983-1992 United Nations Decade of Disabled Persons as a long-term plan of action, on the understanding that no additional resources from the United Nations system would be needed for this purpose, and encouraged Member States to utilize this period as one of the means to implement the World Programme of Action concerning Disabled Persons,

Concerned that developing countries are experiencing increasing difficulties in mobilizing adequate resources for meeting pressing needs in the field of disability prevention, rehabilitation and equalization of opportunities for the millions of persons with disabilities, in the face of pressing demands from other high-priority sectors concerned with basic needs,

Convinced that the United Nations Decade of Disabled Persons should give a strong impetus to the implementation of the World Programme of Action and to a broader understanding of its importance,

Taking note of Economic and Social Council resolution 1983/19 of 26 May 1983, in which the Secretary-General was requested to monitor and support the implementation of the World Programme of Action concerning Disabled Persons by enlisting extrabudgetary resources,

Noting with great appreciation the many generous voluntary contributions and pledges already made by Governments, organizations and individuals,

Taking note with appreciation of the report of the Secretary-General concerning the results achieved so far by the United Nations Trust Fund for the International Year of Disabled Persons during the Year and its follow-up activities,

Recognizing that the Trust Fund is an important instrument for the implementation of the World Programme of Action,

1. *Recognizes* the desirability of the continuation of the United Nations Trust Fund for the International Year of Disabled Persons throughout the United Nations Decade of Disabled Persons for the benefit of disabled persons, particularly those in developing countries;

2. *Decides* that the Trust Fund should continue its activities pending a report by the Secretary-General to the General Assembly at its thirty-ninth session, which should include recommendations for the further implementation of the World Programme of Action concerning Disabled Persons, the funding of such activities by voluntary contributions, the possible terms of reference of a trust fund for the United Nations Decade of Disabled Persons, the implementation of the provisions contained in Assembly resolution 36/77 concerning the organization of support services for technical co-operation in favour of disabled persons, as well as the organization of task forces mentioned in Assembly resolution 37/53;

3. *Stresses* the need for the administration of the Trust Fund to continue to be carried out as an integral part of the substantive responsibilities for disability matters discharged by the Secretariat;

4. *Recommends* that the resources of the Trust Fund should be geared, within the framework of the United Nations Decade of Disabled Persons, towards the implementation of the World Programme of Action and towards helping persons with disabilities to organize themselves, towards assisting in implementing support and consultative services for technical co-operation and inter-organizational task forces, as mentioned in resolutions 36/77 and 37/53, and towards strengthening the activities of the regional commissions in the field of disability prevention and the advancement of persons with disabilities;

5. *Requests* the Secretary-General to take the necessary steps to strengthen the Trust Fund and, to this effect, to enlist extrabudgetary resources as indicated in paragraph 158 of the World Programme of Action;

6. *Appeals* to Governments and private sources for continuing generous voluntary contributions to the Trust Fund;

7. *Calls upon* all Member States, all non-governmental organizations concerned and organizations of disabled persons and also calls upon all organs, organizations and bodies of the United Nations system, through a reallocation of existing resources, to continue to ensure the early implementation of the World Programme of Action;

8. *Requests* the Secretary-General to include in his reports to the General Assembly on the implementation of the World Programme of Action a section on the activities of the Trust Fund.

General Assembly resolution 38/28

22 November 1983   Meeting 66   Adopted without vote

Approved by Third Committee (A/38/575) without vote, 3 November (meeting 32); 36-nation draft (A/C.3/38/L.18), orally revised; agenda item 90.

Sponsors: Algeria, Argentina, Bangladesh, Belgium, Chile, Colombia, Costa Rica, Dominican Republic, Ecuador, France, Germany, Federal Republic of, Guinea, Guinea-Bissau, Iraq, Jordan, Libyan Arab Jamahiriya, Madagascar, Malaysia, Mali, Malta, Morocco, Nepal, Nigeria, Oman, Pakistan, Peru, Philippines, Qatar, Romania, Senegal, Sudan, United Republic of Cameroon, United States, Uruguay, Yugoslavia, Zaire.

Meeting numbers. GA 38th session: 3rd Committee 18-20, 22-29, 31-33; plenary 66.

Other UN system activities

An inter-agency meeting on the Decade of Disabled Persons was held by the ACC Consultative Committee on Substantive Questions (Programme Matters) at Geneva on 30 and 31 May.[13] The meeting recommended that interorganizational task forces, as requested by the Assembly in 1982,[2] be established as needed to explore issues of importance to the implementation of the Programme of Action. Further recommendations included: that the Secretariat's Centre for Social Development and Humanitarian Affairs, in consultation with other bodies, should identify issues for further exploration, and that an inter-agency meeting on the Decade be held at Vienna in September 1984. The meeting also agreed that the IYDP Trust Fund was essential for implementation of the Programme of Action and promotion of the Decade.

Recommendations made with the assistance of WHO and ILO on employing disabled persons in United Nations organizations were endorsed by the Consultative Committee on Administrative Questions (CCAQ) (Personnel and General Administrative Questions) at its fifty-eighth session (Vienna, Austria, 28 February–18 March 1983).[14] The Committee agreed: that the organizations should consider indicating in their staff regulations that there would be no discrimination on the grounds of disability in filling vacancies; that the organizations' medical advisers be asked to adopt a common policy on medical clearance for the employment of the disabled; that organizations should acquaint management with the special problems and potential benefits of employing such persons; that recruitment procedures should be the same as for the non-disabled; that organizations might need to modify their premises to facilitate employment of the disabled; that car pools and other *ad hoc* transportation be encouraged; that flexible employment arrangements, emphasizing task-oriented rather than time-oriented work, be considered; and that disabled staff should receive the same health insurance as others.[15] While endorsing the recommendations, the Committee expressed two reservations. The first concerned the text of a proposed personal history form which it thought might diminish the chances of disabled candidates. The second related to a statement on participation of the disabled in the Pension Fund, which it considered irrelevant. The recommendations were made in response to a 1982 CCAQ decision that a study of the question be conducted.[16]

In support of the Decade of Disabled Persons, UNDP, the United Nations Children's Fund (UNICEF) and WHO launched an international programme for the prevention of disability at New Delhi, India, on 2 October. The programme—known as IMPACT—sought to apply proven low-cost techniques for preventing and treating disabilities by incorporating them into health and other development programmes. It was to promote the organization of temporary mass camps for treatment of cataracts and other disabling conditions, the introduction of green leafy vegetables into the diet to prevent nutritional blindness, the addition of iodine to salt to prevent goitre, treatment and reconstructive surgery for leprosy patients, widespread immunization of children against the major childhood diseases, information campaigns and new safety measures to prevent accidents.

In another development related to the rights of the disabled, the Sub-Commission on Prevention of Discrimination and Protection of Minorities of the Commission on Human Rights requested, among other things, that the Commission invite Governments to identify the human rights problems of disabled persons in their jurisdictions (see Chapter XVIII of this section).

Nutrition

The ninth session of the ACC Sub-Committee on Nutrition and its Advisory Group on Nutrition (AGN) (Copenhagen, Denmark, 7-11 March)[17] included a Symposium on Nutrition in Primary Health Care organized by WHO. Five main deficiencies (calories, protein, iron, iodine and vitamin A) were cited as being responsible for the bulk of malnutrition in developing countries. Since causes were complex and varied with location, eradication required collaborative efforts in several sectors over long periods.

It was pointed out that in the shorter term, proven methodologies could reduce nutrition-related deaths, blindness and mental impairment. One such highly cost-effective methodology was nutrient fortification of foods. Another, directly related to primary health care, was the "Road to Health Strategy," utilizing regular contact with families by village health workers throughout pregnancy and childhood, the monitoring of progress with growth charts, and the provision of multiple simple interventions—perinatal care, iron supplementation, immunization, oral rehydration, nutrition education, encouragement of breast-feeding, and improved water and sanitation.

The Sub-Committee decided: that WHO, in consultation with members of AGN and based on the Symposium, would prepare an action statement on nutrition in primary health care; that three countries in the WHO/UNICEF programme on nutrition in primary health care should be selected to test proposals made at the Symposium and be included in the AGN study on roles for international agencies responding to the changing nutritional conditions of the 1980s; and that following this experience, the action statement should be updated for further examination at a future session of the Sub-Committee.

REFERENCES
[1]UNEP/GC.12/2. [2]YUN 1982, p. 983, GA res. 37/53, 3 Dec. 1982. [3]YUN 1981, p. 795. [4]A/38/506. [5]YUN 1977, p. 660, GA res. 32/133, 16 Dec. 1977. [6]YUN 1982, p. 981, GA res. 37/52, 3 Dec. 1982. [7]E/CN.5/1983/13. [7]E/CN.5/1983/13. [8]YUN 1975, p. 691, GA res. 3447(XXX), 9 Dec. 1975. [9]YUN 1976, p. 558, GA res. 31/82, 13 Dec. 1976. [10]YUN 1979, p. 768, ESC res. 1979/4, 9 May 1979. [11]E/CN.5/1983/14. [12]E/1983/14. [13]ACC/1983/PG/8. [14]ACC/1983/9. [15]ACC/1983/PER.12. [16]YUN 1982, p. 984. [17]ACC/1983/16 & Corr.1.

Human resources

Human resources development

The UNDP Governing Council took note[1] at its 1983 meeting in New York of a report that evaluated human resources development for primary health care.[2] The Council had endorsed the study in 1980, following the International Conference on Primary Health Care (Alma-Ata, USSR, 1978)[3] and it was undertaken in 1982. A number of recommendations for strengthening international support in the development of resources for primary health care were given in the report. Among them were increasing basic health personnel, according higher priority to the training of community health and sanitary workers, improving the content and methods of training, upgrading statistics on primary health care needs, promoting the planning of human resources for health, systematically providing in-service and continuing education, and creating better working relations between members of the formal health system and practitioners of traditional medicine.

UN Institute for Training and Research

Activities

The United Nations Institute for Training and Research (UNITAR), an autonomous organization within the United Nations system, restructured its training activities while reappraising its research programme during 1983. A special session of the UNITAR Board of Trustees (New York, 11-14 April) considered the work programme of the Institute in the light of its financial constraints and the need to improve its financial situation. Despite limited resources, a new programme of training for economic and social development was launched during the second half of 1983. The Institute's activi-

ties were described by the Executive Director in annual reports to the General Assembly for the periods from 1 July 1982 to 30 June 1983[4] and from 1 July 1983 to 30 June 1984.[5]

At its special session, the Board of Trustees discussed the future role of the Institute. The Board felt that the Executive Director should be highly selective in the choice of projects that might be implemented, bearing in mind the needs of the Secretary-General, the priority concerns of the developing countries, the problems of peace, disarmament and development, and the improvement of the efficacy of the United Nations. It agreed that the Executive Director should prepare a two-year programme of training and research covering 1984-1985, the cost of which would be about $3 million per year.

A UNITAR Advisory Panel on Training met in New York from 9 to 13 May, and its conclusions were used to restructure UNITAR training activities and prepare its 1984-1985 programme. The Panel discussed the changing training needs of Member States, the relationship between training and research, training methodologies and techniques, the training of international civil servants, advisory assistance and *ad hoc* requests for training. The 1984-1985 programme had to be modified owing to the limited general purpose funds and the implications for staffing. For example, the programme of research on training and training promotion had to be given lower priority than seminars and advisory assistance.

In launching the new programme of training for economic and social development, much time was spent designing the courses, workshops and seminars and making contacts to obtain logistical support and financial assistance. The overall purpose of the programme was to foster the ability of developing countries to design, organize and evaluate training programmes which would enhance their effectiveness in the planning and management of national development. For the biennium 1984-1985, the programme was to concentrate on four areas of training: for development managers, modernization of public administration in African countries, management of public enterprises (state-owned and parastatal), and finance management.

Among the training activities conducted by UNITAR were seminars for members of permanent missions to the United Nations, including: an introduction to the workings of the United Nations system (New York, January); economic development and its international setting (Washington, D. C., 14-26 February); and the activities and special features of the United Nations bodies located at Geneva (Geneva, 28 November–2 December).

Training for other government officials included: the United Nations/UNITAR fellowship programme in international law (The Hague, Netherlands, 3 July–11 August, and other locations, 12 August–4 November) and a regional training and refresher course in international law for Latin American and Caribbean countries (Buenos Aires, Argentina, 26 September–7 October).

In response to *ad hoc* requests, 35 civil servants and foreign service officials from Cape Verde took part in a multilateral diplomacy training programme (Praia, Cape Verde, 7 February–7 May); two high-ranking officials from Qatar attended a training programme in the processes and techniques of multi-lateral diplomacy and international economic co-operation (16 May–3 June); and briefing seminars on the United Nations system and its activities were held for 30 Saudi Arabian diplomats (New York, 6-9 September and 21 November–1 December).

The current and proposed research programme of UNITAR was reviewed at the first session of its Advisory Panel on Research, composed of 13 high-level specialists in international organization, international law, economics, and science and technology (Vienna, Austria, 12-16 September).

The Board of Trustees established a single UNITAR Division of Research which absorbed the activities of the Project on the Future, concentrating on long-term problems of socio-economic and technological transformation. The 1984-1985 research pro-gramme was designed on the assumption that the limited resources of UNITAR would be better uti-lized if the Institute did not engage primarily in basic research, but rather served as a catalyst and synthesizer as well as a monitor of research car-ried out elsewhere. Research financed through the General Fund was to focus on three main areas: peace and security, economic and social develop-ment, and the United Nations system. In addition, UNITAR was to continue research funded by Spe-cial Purpose Grants, covering energy and natural resources and the developing regions of the world.

Research activities in 1983 included: a meeting in March of a Panel of Experts to discuss the results of a study of the development of international law related to the new international economic order; two meetings held jointly with the American So-ciety of International Law on the preparation of a guide to the 1966 International Covenant on Eco-nomic, Social and Cultural Rights[6] (Washington, D. C., February and Paris, March); a seminar on the alternative development of the developing countries and the Mongolian experience (Ulan Bator, Mongolia, September) and a symposium on development strate-gies for the Mediterranean area, attended by some 100 researchers who examined 73 studies concerning the countries of the area (Naples, Italy, 24-26 October).

As part of the Project on the Future, a sympo-sium on the problems of exhaustible resources and North-South trade and development was held at Essex University (United Kingdom, January) and

a programme on strategies for the future of Asia was begun in mid-1983 with an office provided by the University of Chulalongkorn in Bangkok, Thailand.

Among publications issued by UNITAR during the year were *Analytical Papers and Analysis of Texts of Relevant Instruments*, *ASEAN and the United Nations System*, *Creative Women in Changing Societies: A Quest for Alternatives*, and *Law and the Status of the Child*.

Finances of UNITAR

An estimated 1983 deficit of $886,000 in the General Fund budget of $2,720,100 was reported by the UNI-TAR Executive Director to the General Assembly in November. Expenditures had been underestimated by some $300,000 and income over-estimated by about $600,000, he said, pointing out that, infla-tion notwithstanding, the 1983 programme cost was the same as that of 1980. The Institute requested an interest-free loan from the Assembly to cover the deficit.

As at 31 December 1983,[7] the General Fund showed assets of $2,329,929 and liabilities of $3,024,047, a deficit of $694,118. The income of the Special Purpose Grants Fund totalled $920,147 and expenditures $2,071,486; the balance of the Special Purpose Fund was $1,542,565.

In response to a December 1982 Assembly re-quest[8] that the Secretary-General examine all pos-sibilities for funding UNITAR, he submitted a report to the Assembly in November 1983,[9] stating that the new Executive Director was reducing costs and trying to mobilize resources. To enable UNITAR to continue operating until a long-term financial so-lution could be found, the Secretary-General recom-mended that the Assembly advance $886,000 re-quired to balance the 1983 budget. It was expected that UNITAR would be able to repay the advance over several biennia on a non-recurrent reimbursable basis, he said.

The Secretary-General's recommendation was considered by the Advisory Committee on Adminis-trative and Budgetary Questions (ACABQ) in De-cember.[10] It found that the Institute's continuing funding difficulties cast doubts on its future financial viability and ability to repay the proposed advance in the manner indicated. It concluded that the Secretary-General, together with the Executive Director and the Board of Trustees, should re-examine the future role of UNITAR. ACABQ recommended that the Secretary-General, in reporting on the long-term financing of UNITAR in 1984, take into account institutional developments since its inception, in particular, the establishment of the United Nations University and the United Nations Institute for Dis-armament Research.

GENERAL ASSEMBLY ACTION

In December, the General Assembly took three actions concerning UNITAR and its finances.

On 19 December, on the recommendation of the Second (Economic and Financial) Committee, the Assembly adopted by recorded vote resolution 38/177.

United Nations Institute for Training and Research
The General Assembly,
Recalling its resolution 37/142 of 17 December 1982 on the United Nations Institute for Training and Research,
Having considered the report of the Executive Director of the United Nations Institute for Training and Research covering the period from 1 July 1982 to 30 June 1983, and his introductory statement of 7 November 1983,
Recalling the important role assigned to the United Nations Institute for Training and Research in enhancing the effectiveness of the United Nations in achieving its major objectives, particularly in the maintenance of peace and security and the promotion of economic and social development,
Noting with satisfaction the emphasis being placed by the United Nations Institute for Training and Research on the revitalization of its programme, the dissemination of the results of its research, the continuing need for improvement of its management and on the mobilization of adequate resources to enable it to perform its functions satisfactorily,
Sharing the concern of the Executive Director that only a small number of States are contributing to the General Fund of the United Nations Institute for Training and Research, as well as his concern over the inadequacy of the resources available to the Institute for its work,
1. *Takes note with appreciation* of the report of the Executive Director of the United Nations Institute for Training and Research and the measures he has already taken, with the approval of the Board of Trustees of the Institute, with a view to revitalizing the Institute and enhancing its image;
2. *Welcomes* the continuing emphasis of the United Nations Institute for Training and Research on economic and social training and research and the inclusion of specific projects on the problems that exist in the areas identified by the General Assembly at its sixth and seventh special sessions, in the relevant decisions adopted at its twenty-ninth and subsequent sessions, and in the International Development Strategy for the Third United Nations Development Decade, taking into consideration the statements on the programme of work of the Institute made at the current session;
3. *Encourages* the Executive Director, bearing in mind the conclusions reached by the Board of Trustees of the United Nations Institute for Training and Research at its special session held from 11 to 14 April 1983, to continue to evolve clear long-term priorities in the training and research programme of the Institute which would emphasize its role in the promotion and strengthening of the development process and would make the need for that role more obvious;
4. *Notes with satisfaction* the efforts of the Executive Director to strengthen co-operation between the United Nations Institute for Training and Research and other institutions active in the Institute's field of competence;
5. *Urges once again* all States that have not yet contributed to the United Nations Institute for Training and Research to do so, and calls upon all donor countries, especially those that are not contributing at a level commensurate with their capacity, to increase their volun-

tary contributions in order to meet the urgent financial needs of the Institute;
6. *Again requests* all States to continue to announce their contributions to the United Nations Institute for Training and Research early and, if possible, not later than the annual United Nations Pledging Conference for Development Activities, and to speed up the payment of their voluntary contributions to the Institute;
7. *Emphasizes* the necessity for the Institute to intensify its efforts further to improve its management and to develop its programme of activities with a view to balancing its expenses with revenue, on the basis of realistic estimates, and, in this context, notes with satisfaction the steps being taken by the Executive Director to adjust administrative costs and to mobilize resources to ensure avoidance of future deficits in the Institute's budget;
8. *Decides* to support the recommendations of the Secretary-General contained in his interim report on the financing of the United Nations Institute for Training and Research and agrees, on an exceptional basis, that an advance of $886,000 should be given to the Institute to cover the deficit in its budget for 1983; this advance will be non-recurrent and reimbursable, in accordance with the terms set out in the Secretary-General's report, and the repayment will begin after a grace period not exceeding two years;
9. *Decides*, in the light of paragraphs 4 and 5 of the report of the Secretary-General, to consider at its thirty-ninth session the question of long-term financing arrangements for the United Nations Institute for Training and Research.

General Assembly resolution 38/177

19 December 1983   Meeting 102   128-9-6 (recorded vote)

Approved by Second Committee (A/38/704) by recorded vote (115-9-6), 5 December (meeting 54); 14-nation draft (A/C.2/38/L.47/Rev.1), orally revised; agenda item 80 *(a)*.

Sponsors: China, Cyprus, Egypt, Ivory Coast, Lesotho, Liberia, Nigeria, Pakistan, Philippines, Sierra Leone, Sudan, Uganda, United Republic of Cameroon, Zambia.
Financial implications. S-G, A/C.2/38/L.92, A/C.5/38/86.
Meeting numbers. GA 38th session: 2nd Committee 31-35, 44, 46, 54; 5th Committee 69; plenary 102.

Recorded vote in Assembly as follows:

In favour: Afghanistan, Algeria, Angola, Argentina, Austria, Bahamas, Bahrain, Bangladesh, Barbados, Belize, Benin, Bhutan, Bolivia, Botswana, Brazil, Burma, Burundi, Canada, Cape Verde, Central African Republic, Chad, Chile, China, Colombia, Congo, Costa Rica, Cuba, Cyprus, Democratic Kampuchea, Democratic Yemen, Denmark, Djibouti, Dominican Republic, Ecuador, Egypt, El Salvador, Ethiopia, Fiji, Finland, France, Gabon, Gambia, Germany, Federal Republic of, Ghana, Greece, Guatemala, Guinea, Guinea-Bissau, Guyana, Honduras, Iceland, India, Indonesia, Iran, Iraq, Ireland, Israel, Italy, Ivory Coast, Jamaica, Jordan, Kenya, Kuwait, Lao People's Democratic Republic, Lebanon, Lesotho, Liberia, Libyan Arab Jamahiriya, Madagascar, Malawi, Malaysia, Maldives, Mali, Malta, Mauritania, Mauritius, Mexico, Morocco, Mozambique, Nepal, Netherlands, Nicaragua, Niger, Nigeria, Norway, Oman, Pakistan, Panama, Papua New Guinea, Paraguay, Peru, Philippines, Portugal, Qatar, Romania, Rwanda, Saint Lucia, Saint Vincent and the Grenadines, Sao Tome and Principe, Saudi Arabia, Senegal, Sierra Leone, Singapore, Somalia, Spain, Sri Lanka, Sudan, Suriname, Swaziland, Sweden, Syrian Arab Republic, Thailand, Togo, Trinidad and Tobago, Tunisia, Turkey, Uganda, United Arab Emirates, United Republic of Cameroon, United Republic of Tanzania, Upper Volta, Uruguay, Venezuela, Viet Nam, Yemen, Yugoslavia, Zaire, Zambia.
Against: Bulgaria, Byelorussian SSR, Czechoslovakia, German Democratic Republic, Hungary, Poland, Ukrainian SSR, USSR, United States.
Abstaining: Australia, Belgium, Japan, Luxembourg, New Zealand, United Kingdom.

Prior to the adoption of the resolution, the Assembly adopted paragraph 8 by a separate recorded vote of 121 to 15, with 5 abstentions. The Second Committee had approved the paragraph by a recorded vote—requested by the USSR—of 107 to 15, with 5 abstentions; the Committee also approved paragraph

9 by a recorded vote—also requested by the USSR—of 116 to 9, with 3 abstentions.

In the Second Committee, a number of States explained their votes. The United States, which had requested the recorded vote on the draft resolution as a whole, stated that it opposed the draft because of the financial consequences of paragraph 8 and the implication that the Assembly had agreed to a policy of bailing out voluntarily funded organs. The USSR said it had voted against paragraphs 8 and 9 and the draft as a whole since it believed that financing UNITAR's activities through the regular budget was illegal. Brazil, France and Sweden (speaking on behalf of the five Nordic States) stated that they had voted in favour of the resolution because the granting of a loan to UNITAR was to be non-recurrent; Austria said that its decision to vote for the draft should not be viewed as a precedent for the future. Canada declared it had reluctantly supported the resolution on the understanding that UNITAR's financial situation would be thoroughly examined during the next year. The Federal Republic of Germany said that, although it had voted in favour of the resolution as a whole, it had been unable to support the granting of a loan to UNITAR; as an indication of the value it attached to that body, however, it was increasing its voluntary contribution for 1984 and 1985. Belgium and the United Kingdom explained that they had abstained because they opposed the loan procedure.

On the recommendation of the Fifth (Administrative and Budgetary) Committee, the Assembly adopted without vote decision 38/446.

Long-term financing arrangements for the United Nations Institute for Training and Research

At its 102nd plenary meeting, on 19 December 1983, the General Assembly, on the recommendation of the Fifth Committee, endorsed the recommendation of the Advisory Committee on Administrative and Budgetary Questions contained in paragraph 7 of its report.

General Assembly decision 38/446

Adopted without vote

Approved by Fifth Committee (A/38/754) without vote, 16 December (meeting 69); oral proposal by Chairman; agenda items 80 *(a)*, 108 and 109.
Financial implications. ACABQ, A/38/7/Add.20; 5th Committee, A/38/754; S-G, A/C.5/38/86.
Meeting numbers. GA 38th session: 5th Committee 69; plenary 102.

On 20 December, the Assembly, acting without vote, also on the recommendation of the Fifth Committee, adopted section XX of resolution 38/234.

United Nations Institute for Training and Research
[*The General Assembly . . .*]

Endorses the recommendations of the Advisory Committee on Administrative and Budgetary Questions as contained in paragraph 7 of its report;

. . .

General Assembly resolution 38/234, section XX

20 December 1983   Meeting 104   Adopted without vote

Approved by Fifth Committee (A/38/760) without vote, 16 December (meeting 69); oral proposal by Chairman; agenda item 109.
Financial implications. ACABQ, A/38/7/Add.20; 5th Committee, A/38/754; S-G, A/C.5/38/86.
Meeting numbers. GA 38th session: 5th Committee 69; plenary 104.

Accounts for 1982

The Board of Auditors, in examining the 1982 UNITAR accounts,[11] found a need for proper authorization of imprest payments, prompt issuance of receipts and for maintenance of adequate records to ensure effective financial control to improve cash management. Furthermore, it noted that the UNITAR administration was unable to submit the financial statements for 1982 before the deadline of 31 March 1983, as stipulated by the financial regulations. It said that its review indicated, however, that an appreciable effort had been made by the Administration to implement the Board's previous recommendations.[12]

ACABQ had no comments on the Board's report.[13]

In resolution 38/30 of 25 November, the Assembly accepted the Board's financial report and opinions and requested that remedial action be taken by the Executive Director.

CONTRIBUTIONS TO THE UNITAR GENERAL FUND, 1983
(as at 31 December 1983; in US dollar equivalent)

Country	Amount
Algeria	5,000
Argentina	19,600
Australia	40,566
Austria	28,249
Bahamas	500
Barbados	250
Belgium	83,468*
Canada	71,847
Denmark	39,106
Egypt	12,600*
Finland	36,364
France	34,965
Germany, Federal Republic of	177,165
Ghana	8,204
Greece	5,000
Guyana	667
Ireland	10,755
Ivory Coast	32,810
Japan	60,000
Kuwait	20,000
Libyan Arab Jamahiriya	8,750
Luxembourg	2,115
Malawi	1,298
Malta	600
New Zealand	4,588
Norway	69,444
Oman	10,000
Qatar	10,000
Saudi Arabia	20,000
Spain	25,000
Sweden	101,351
Switzerland	73,636
Syrian Arab Republic	10,470
Tunisia	2,700
Uganda	22,838†
USSR	40,000
United Republic of Tanzania	6,276
United States	527,500
Venezuela	60,000
Yugoslavia	5,000
Total	1,688,682

*Pledged and paid for 1982 in 1983 and not previously recorded.
†Pledged and paid for 1980 in 1983 and not previously recorded.
SOURCE: A/39/5/Add.4.

UN University

Activities

The major development in 1983 at the United Nations University (UNU), an autonomous academic institution within the framework of the United Nations, was the establishment of its first research and training centre, the World Institute for Development Economics Research (WIDER). The UNU Council at its twenty-second session (Tokyo, 5-9 December)[14] accepted an offer by the Government of Finland to host the Institute. The offer included $30,000,000 and premises for the centre at Helsinki. WIDER was envisaged as a small, pluralistic, interdisciplinary group of scholars researching aspects of the global economic system that affected the development prospects of the poorest nations. With the establishment of WIDER, moves to develop a network of such centres and broaden the University's institutional links were well under way, the UNU Council said.

Earlier in the year, at its twenty-first session (Tokyo, 27 June–1 July),[15] the Council authorized the Rector of UNU to negotiate agreements with prospective host countries for the setting up of two other centres—the Institute for Natural Resources in Africa and the International Institute for Biotechnology in Venezuela.

The University programme concentrated on broadening the scope of its intellectual and policy concerns. Work was carried out under the five themes of its medium-term perspective, 1982-1987, adopted by the UNU Council in 1981.[16] These themes were: peace, security, conflict resolution and global transformation; the global economy; hunger, poverty, resources and the environment; human and social development and the coexistence of peoples, cultures and social systems; and science and technology and their social and ethical implications.

A brainstorming session was organized (New York, February 1983) with leading scholars from different parts of the world; the subject was the implications for developing countries of the prospects of continued low growth in countries of the Organisation for Economic Co-operation and Development, even following the end of the current recession.

As part of UNU's efforts to increase understanding of global problems, the University and the International Development Research Centre of Canada signed an agreement on 11 June in Tokyo to support an energy research project. Under the project, a 10-member Energy Research Group from developing countries would survey the capacity of those countries to conduct energy research; it was expected to play an innovative role in energy policy formulation. The Group, at its first meeting in Canada in August, commissioned 120 papers to review energy research and technology.

Other UNU activities included a conference on international food data systems (Italy, February); a study and conference tour on food-energy interactions that visited China, France, India and Senegal (September-October); and a workshop to evaluate a Kathmandu-Kakani area base map and mountain hazards maps (Nepal, October).

In the year ended June 1983, UNU held a total of 41 workshops, seminars, symposia and meetings. The number of University fellows in training was 49, 331 having completed training. Moreover, the University had 32 associated institutions and more than 100 research and training units in more than 60 countries carrying out its work.

Preparatory work for the permanent headquarters of the University in Tokyo moved ahead with the allocation of a budgetary provision for the fiscal year 1984-1985 for planning. A working group of an advisory commission of the Japanese Ministry of Education met in December to discuss the draft guidelines for its planning and design.

The activities of UNU were discussed in the annual reports of its Council to the General Assembly, covering 1 July 1982 to 30 June 1983[15] and 1 July 1983 to 30 June 1984.[14]

Implementation of JIU recommendations

Of 15 recommendations put forward by the Joint Inspection Unit (JIU) in a 1981 report assessing UNU and its prospects,[17] only two had not been implemented, the Secretary-General stated in a report to the Assembly.[18]

Whereas it had been recommended that the University Council should normally meet once a year, the Secretary-General noted the Council's conclusion that, because UNU was relatively young, its work demanded periodic policy review, and therefore, the Council should continue to meet twice yearly.

JIU also recommended that to avoid compartmentalization of research activities, there should be only one Vice-Rector (at the Assistant Secretary-General level); current Vice-Rectors should become Programme Directors or Deans and maintain their grades (D-2). The Secretary-General stated that the Council supported the Rector's preference for maintaining the current structure since the proposed reduction in status would make it more difficult to attract distinguished scholars to the positions in question. The medium-term perspective, 1982-1987, had as one of its principal objectives the avoidance of compartmentalization of research activities.

GENERAL ASSEMBLY ACTION

On 19 December 1983, following the recommendation of the Second Committee, the General Assembly adopted without vote resolution 38/178.

United Nations University

The General Assembly,

Recalling its resolutions 2951(XXVII) of 11 December 1972, 3081(XXVIII) of 6 December 1973, 3313(XXIX) of 14 December 1974, 3439(XXX) of 9 December 1975, 31/117 and 31/118 of 16 December 1976, 32/54 of 8 December 1977, 33/108 of 18 December 1978, 34/112 of 14 December 1979, 35/54 of 5 December 1980, 36/45 of 19 November 1981 and 37/143 of 17 December 1982,

Having considered the report of the Council of the United Nations University on the work of the University,

Noting with appreciation the progress being made towards the construction of a permanent headquarters building in Tokyo, with active steps being taken by the Government of Japan,

Also noting with appreciation the dedicated service rendered to the University by the members of the Council whose terms ended in May 1983,

Mindful of the formulation and adoption of the medium-term perspective, 1982-1987,

Noting decision 5.2.2 adopted on 13 October 1983 by the Executive Board of the United Nations Educational, Scientific and Cultural Organization at its one hundred and seventeenth session,

1. *Notes with satisfaction* the further constructive development of the activities of the United Nations University in research, training and the dissemination of knowledge under the medium-term perspective, using multidisciplinary and integrative approaches designed, in accordance with the Charter of the University, to promote greater understanding of urgent and pressing global problems and provide ideas for solving them;

2. *Welcomes* the initiation of a new programme planning process at the University Centre, designed to facilitate the participation of the United Nations University's networks of collaborating scholars, and, as part of this process, the creation of a planning and evaluation services unit;

3. *Also welcomes* the adoption by the Council of the United Nations University of the initial statute of the University, in accordance with its Charter, on the basis of the experience gained by the University since its establishment;

4. *Notes with satisfaction* that progress has been made towards the establishment of the first three research and training centres of the United Nations University, which will be concerned with development economics, natural resources in Africa and biotechnology, respectively, and the further development of the work of the University in helping to strengthen existing institutions in developing countries through the extension of its networks of associate and co-operating institutions and in placing increased emphasis on its post-graduate training through fellowships relevant to the development of research, training and institution-building;

5. *Also notes with satisfaction* the further expansion of the co-operative activities of the United Nations University with the United Nations, its bodies and the specialized agencies, particularly United Nations research and training institutions, and the increasing collaboration of the University with the international academic and scientific community;

6. *Recognizes* that the United Nations University needs to build up its Endowment Fund and other contributions in order to increase its core income, to which end a number of Member States have already extended positive co-operation;

7. *Earnestly appeals* to all Member States to take cognizance of the important developments at the United Nations University and to contribute urgently and generously to its Endowment Fund and, additionally or alternatively, to make operating contributions to the University to enable it to fulfil its mandate effectively, in accordance with its Charter and with the relevant General Assembly resolutions.

General Assembly resolution 38/178

19 December 1983   Meeting 102   Adopted without vote

Approved by Second Committee (A/38/704) without vote, 28 November (meeting 52); 20-nation draft (A/C.2/38/L.48); agenda item 80 *(b)*.

Sponsors: Austria, Bangladesh, China, Colombia, Cyprus, Ecuador, Egypt, France, Ghana, Iceland, India, Indonesia, Ivory Coast, Japan, Jordan, Pakistan, Philippines, Sierra Leone, Singapore, Zaire.

Meeting numbers. GA 38th session: 2nd Committee 31-34, 38, 44, 52; plenary 102.

UNU Council activities

In 1983, the UNU Council held its twenty-first and twenty-second sessions in Tokyo from 27 June to 1 July and from 5 to 9 December, respectively. In June, the Council reviewed the University's progress and the Rector's report on developments since the previous session. In addition to authorizing him to negotiate agreements for establishing UNU research and training centres (see above), the Council considered setting up an institute for advanced studies. It discussed the Rector's proposals for institutional arrangements with the International Centre for Theoretical Physics (Trieste, Italy), a proposed UNU International Centre for Distance Learning, and a proposed joint facility of the International Council on Scientific Unions and its Committee on Science and Technology in Developing Countries (Madras, India). It designated three new associated institutions, namely: Agricultural University of Wageningen, the Netherlands; Instituto de Agroquímica y Technologia de Alimentos, Valencia, Spain; and London School of Tropical Hygiene and Medicine, United Kingdom.

In December, the Council approved the University's biennial programme and budget for 1984-1985, showing the consolidation of activities from 12 sub-programmes in 1982 to nine programme areas in 1983. The budget, which totalled $36.3 million, was the first biennial programme and budget adopted by the Council and brought UNU into line with the United Nations system planning cycle.

The Economic and Social Council, in decision 1983/184 adopted on 29 July, reiterated its request to the UNU Council to consider rescheduling its meetings so that, starting in 1984, its report could be submitted to the General Assembly through the Economic and Social Council at its second regular session.

UNU finances

As at 31 December 1983, the total income available to the UNU General Operating Fund for the 1982-1983 biennium was $33.1 million, including interest income of $28.1 million earned on the Endowment Fund. The total expenditure against the General Operating Fund amounted to $33.7 million, of which $8.4 million comprised unliquidated obligations.

Combined assets of the General Operating Fund, the Endowment Fund, and the UNU External Projects Trust Funds, Housing Assistance Trust Fund and Library Trust Fund amounted to $149.9 million.

In resolution 38/178, the General Assembly recognized that UNU needed to build up its Endowment Fund and other contributions and appealed to Member States to contribute generously.

Fund-raising activities

In 1983, payments to the UNU Endowment Fund by eight countries amounted to $3,622,237 and payments to the General Operating Fund by seven countries amounted to $636,409; as at 31 December 1983, one State had pledged $25,000 to the General Operating Fund for 1984 (see table below). In addition, a number of Governments, institutions and other organizations made indirect contributions in cash and in kind to the work of the University, including extra funds to its associated institutions and major projects in various parts of the world.

Accounts for 1982-1983

In examining the UNU accounts for the biennium ended 31 December 1983, the Board of Auditors[19] found that of $500 million, which was the long-term target figure for contributions to the Endowment Fund, pledges had been made for $140.4 million as at 31 December 1983, of which $117.3 million had been received and approximately $4.2 million was adjusted as cumulative loss in exchange. UNU hoped to raise $100 million during the medium-term period 1982-1987, but had received only about $9.2 million during the first two years. Furthermore, of 21 countries which had pledged contributions to the Endowment Fund, eight had not contributed the full amount. The Board recommended, and the UNU adminis-

tration agreed, that fund-raising efforts should be further intensified.

Although the University issued guidelines and administrative instructions to ensure control of the use of grants, there was no system for rendering accounts regularly to UNU by grant recipients, the Board stated. It recommended, and the UNU administration agreed, that suitable formats be designed for rendering semi-annual or annual statements of expenditures by such recipients.

Examination of the expenditures of ongoing projects revealed that in a number of cases expenditures were made either in excess of or without allotments, while in others allotments remained unutilized or underutilized. The Board recommended that budgetary control be strengthened at all levels and that implementation of projects on schedule be ensured; the UNU administration had confirmed that it was exercising stricter budgetary controls at all levels.

CONTRIBUTIONS TO UNU, 1983 AND 1984
(as at 31 December 1983; in US dollar equivalent)

COUNTRY	1983 payment	1984 pledge
Endowment Fund		
Austria	47,801	—
Germany, Federal Republic of	19,865	—
Ireland	266,361	—
Japan	2,000,000	—
Senegal	(123,622)*	—
Tunisia	4,865	—
United Kingdom	1,406,967	—
Subtotal	3,622,237	—
General Operating Fund		
Cyprus	1,298	—
France	(7,614)*	—
Greece	40,000	—
Honduras	1,000	—
Norway	139,528	—
Sri Lanka	2,000	25,000
Sweden	460,197	—
Subtotal	636,409	25,000
Total	4,258,646	25,000

*Loss on exchange.
SOURCE: A/39/5, vol. III.

REFERENCES

[1]E/1983/20 (dec. 83/12). [2]DP/1983/16. [3]YUN 1978, p. 1107. [4]A/38/14. [5]A/39/14. [6]YUN 1966, p. 419, GA res. 2200 A (XXI), annex, 16 Dec. 1966. [7]A/39/5/Add.4. [8]YUN 1982, p. 988, GA res. 37/142, 17 Dec. 1982. [9]A/38/220. [10]A/38/7/Add.20. [11]A/38/5/Add.4 & Corr.1. [12]YUN 1982, p. 990. [13]A/38/433. [14]A/39/31. [15]A/38/31 & Corr.1, 2. [16]YUN 1981, p. 811. [17]YUN 1982, p. 992. [18]A/C.5/38/8. [19]A/39/5, vol. III.

Chapter XVI

Environment

In 1983, the Governing Council of the United Nations Environment Programme (UNEP) held its eleventh session, and adopted 12 decisions on various environmental questions. The Executive Director of UNEP reported on the Programme's activities for the year in his annual report to the Council.[1]

Forty-four new projects were approved by the Environment Fund in 1983; 37 projects were concluded. During the year, the Fund disbursed $22 million for programme activities; government contributions totalled $28 million.

The Council decided to conduct a detailed assessment of the implementation of the 1977 Plan of Action to Combat Desertification at its 1984 session, while the United Nations Sudano-Sahelian Office (UNSO) continued to mobilize resources for anti-desertification projects. By resolution 38/164, the General Assembly asked the Governing Councils of the United Nations Development Programme (UNDP) and UNEP to continue to provide support for UNSO, which was responsible for implementing the Plan. By resolution 38/163, the Assembly requested Member States that had not yet provided their comments on a plan to establish an international corporation to finance non-commercial desertification measures to do so as soon as possible.

A number of other resolutions and decisions on environmental questions were adopted by the Economic and Social Council and the Assembly. The Assembly, in resolution 38/161, approved the UNEP Governing Council's decision to establish an intergovernmental committee to assist it in preparing an environmental perspective to the year 2000 and beyond, and requested the Secretary-General to appoint the Chairman and Vice-Chairman of a special commission to assist them. In resolution 38/162, it requested the Secretary-General to intensify his efforts to urge States to conduct bilateral consultations and reach an agreement to solve the problems of material remnants of war.

The Global Environmental Monitoring System (GEMS) of Earthwatch, the assessment arm of the environment programme, monitored such things as renewable natural resources, climate, health, the long-range transport of pollutants, and oceans.

Among other UNEP activities were a meeting of its *Ad Hoc* Working Group of Legal and Technical Experts for the Elaboration of a Global Framework Convention for the Protection of the Ozone Layer; implementation of plans to combat desertification, including deforestation control, range management and soil protection; integrated approaches to environment and development and environmental management; and support measures such as environmental education, training and information.

By resolution 38/149 on protection against products harmful to health and the environment, the Assembly requested the Secretary-General to make available and regularly update the consolidated list of products whose consumption and/or sale had been banned, withdrawn, severely restricted, or not approved by Governments. It took note in decision 38/442 of a report of the UNEP Executive Director on international conventions and protocols in the field of the environment.

In addition, the Assembly, in resolution 38/165, took note of the UNEP Governing Council report on its 1983 session[2] and the decisions contained therein; endorsed a decision that there should be no Council session in 1986 and that in 1987 the Council would decide finally on the periodicity of its sessions; and decided to expand the mandate of the Consultative Group for Desertification Control to include information exchange on anti-desertification policies and programmes.

Topics related to this chapter. Africa: cooperation with the Organization of African Unity. Asia: Iran-Iraq armed conflict. Middle East: Mediterranean-Dead Sea canal project. Regional economic and social activities—environment. Natural resources: water resources. Energy resources: nuclear energy. Health and human resources: health. Human settlements.

Programme and finances of UNEP

The Governing Council of the United Nations Environment Programme (UNEP) held its eleventh session at UNEP headquarters at Nairobi, Kenya, from 11 to 24 May 1983.

UNEP Programme

In an introductory report to the Governing Council, submitted in February,[3] the Executive Director presented his views on developments in UNEP during 1982 and made a number of proposals concerning major issues to be dealt with in 1983.

By the first[4] of its six policy decisions, the Council, on 24 May, in addition to providing general policy guidance, dealt with the following subjects: state of the environment and environmental data reports; co-ordination; co-operation with the United Nations Centre for Human Settlements (UNCHS) (Habitat); two proposed conferences, one on industry and environment, the other a parliamentary conference on the environment; the relationship between UNEP and non-governmental organizations (NGOs); and the assessment of progress in implementing the Plan of Action to Combat Desertification adopted by the 1977 United Nations Conference on Desertification.[5] With regard to UNEP's relations with environmental NGOs, the Council encouraged the Executive Director to expand that relationship and to extend it to those organizations which were not directly environmental. It noted the Executive Director's intention to support a global meeting of environmental and developmental NGOs.

The second[6] of the remaining policy decisions, all adopted on 23 May, related to the periodicity and duration of Governing Council sessions. The Council considered it not feasible to meet biennially; it decided that, as of 1984, it would meet for a maximum of eight working days, that on an experimental basis there would be no Council session in 1986, and that it would decide in 1987 on the periodicity of its sessions. It also decided to discontinue forthwith the system of intersessional informal consultations with Governments.

By a third policy decision,[7] the Council recommended to the General Assembly arrangements for the preparation of an environmental perspective. In a fourth decision,[8] the Council stated its views on Israel's decision to build a canal linking the Mediterranean Sea to the Dead Sea (see p. 336). The impacts of apartheid on the environment were the subject of another decision.[9] A sixth decision contained an appeal to Governments to halt the arms race and prevent a major threat to man and his environment.[10]

In an omnibus decision adopted on 24 May 1983,[11] the Governing Council dealt with such matters as programme budget; environment and development; environmental awareness; oceans; water; terrestrial ecosystems; desertification; and regional activities. It requested the Executive Director, in implementing the programme, to be guided by the Governing Council's advice in respect of priorities.

Other programme decisions took up assistance to the South Asia Co-operative Environment Programme[12] and regional programmes in Latin America and the Caribbean.[13]

In a November report to the Council,[14] the Administrative Committee on Co-ordination (ACC)

dealt with environmental issues. To prepare for ACC's discussion of those issues, the Executive Director convened an inter-agency meeting of the Designated Officials for Environmental Matters (Geneva, 21-23 September).

ECONOMIC AND SOCIAL COUNCIL ACTION

In July, on the recommendation of its First (Economic) Committee, the Economic and Social Council adopted decision 1983/168 without vote.

International co-operation on the environment

At its 39th plenary meeting, on 25 July 1983, the Council:

(a) Took note of the reports of the Governing Council of the United Nations Environment Programme on its eleventh session and on the implementation in the Sudano-Sahelian region of the Plan of Action to Combat Desertification, and decided to transmit them, together with the recommendations of the Governing Council, to the General Assembly for consideration and action;

(b) Noted with appreciation Governing Council decision 11/2 of 23 May 1983, concerning the periodicity and duration of Governing Council sessions;

(c) Took note of Governing Council decision 11/3 of 23 May 1983 on the process of preparation of the environmental perspective, and decided to recommend to the General Assembly the adoption of the draft resolution annexed to that decision.

Economic and Social Council decision 1983/168

Adopted without vote

Approved by First Committee (E/1983/111) without vote, 15 July (meeting 14); agenda item 14.

Meeting number. ESC 39.

GENERAL ASSEMBLY ACTION

On 19 December, on the recommendation of the Second (Economic and Financial) Committee, the General Assembly adopted without vote resolution 38/165.

International co-operation in the field of the environment

The General Assembly,

Having considered the report of the Governing Council of the United Nations Environment Programme on the work of its eleventh session,

Taking note of Economic and Social Council decision 1983/168 of 25 July 1983 on international co-operation on the environment,

Noting also the report of the Executive Director of the United Nations Environment Programme on international conventions and protocols in the field of the environment, together with the sixth supplement to the register of such conventions and protocols,

Bearing in mind the involvement of all countries in the protection of the environment with a view to enhancing the quality of life for future generations,

Aware that the continuing increase in the production, stockpiling and risk of use of weapons of mass destruction and the development of new types of weapons not only pose a major threat to the environment and even to life on Earth, but also compete for limited resources that could be better used for constructive purposes, including development,

Reaffirming the need to strengthen international co-operation in the field of the environment, particularly in order to deal with the most serious environmental problems of the developing countries in line with the International Development Strategy for the Third United Nations Development Decade,

Bearing in mind the interrelationships between people, resources, environment and development and convinced of the importance of assessing those interrelationships as they relate to international co-operation for development,

Recalling the catalytic mandate and role of the United Nations Environment Programme with regard to international co-operation in the field of the environment, especially with regard to integrating environmental considerations into the development process,

1.   *Takes note* of the report of the Governing Council of the United Nations Environment Programme on the work of its eleventh session and the decisions contained therein;

2.   *Welcomes* section II of Governing Council decision 11/1 of 24 May 1983, in which it decided, *inter alia*, that the topic to be considered in the 1984 report on the state of the environment would be "The environment in the dialogue between and among developed and developing countries";

3.   *Takes note* of sections V and VI of Governing Council decision 11/1, which relate to the convening of an international conference on world industry and environmental management and a parliamentary conference on the environment;

4.   *Takes note with appreciation* of Governing Council decision 11/2 of 23 May 1983 on the periodicity and duration of Governing Council sessions and endorses the decision that there shall be no session of the Governing Council in 1986, on an experimental basis, and that in 1987 the Governing Council shall decide finally on either of the two options for the periodicity of its sessions in the light of the experience gained in the previous years;

5.   *Also takes note* of Governing Council decision 11/5 of 23 May 1983 on the impacts of *apartheid* on the environment, directed at promoting public awareness of the plight of the victims of *apartheid*;

6.   *Welcomes* part one of Governing Council decision 11/7 of 24 May 1983, by which the Council, while setting priorities for its implementation, approved the programme budget for the first biennium of the system-wide medium-term environment programme, 1984-1985, as an overall framework for activities of the United Nations Environment Programme during that period, and invites Governments participating in relevant governing bodies of specialized agencies and other organizations of the United Nations system to endeavour to take the provisions of the system-wide medium-term environment programme fully into account in their consideration of related issues, so as to achieve the full implementation of the system-wide programme;

7.   *Welcomes* the importance attached by the Governing Council to regional approaches and programmes in the field of international environment co-operation, as reflected in its decisions 11/7, 11/8 and 11/9 of 24 May 1983;

8.   *Welcomes* section VIII of Governing Council decision 11/1, in which the Council decided to devote two days, during its twelfth session, to a detailed assessment of the implementation of the Plan of Action to Combat Desertification, which will include a thorough analysis of the state of implementation of the principal components of the Plan, the lessons learned and the priorities for future action;

9.   *Decides* to expand the mandate of the Consultative Group for Desertification Control to include information exchange on anti-desertification policies and programmes of its participants, in addition to its basic mandate as set out in General Assembly resolution 32/172 of 19 December 1977;

10.   *Welcomes* the progress made in the implementation of the Montevideo Programme for the Development and Periodic Review of Environmental Law and appeals to Governments to participate actively in the Programme and provide adequate financial resources or facilities in order to achieve its full and timely implementation;

11.   *Reaffirms* the need for strengthening the co-ordinating role of the United Nations Environment Programme and the need for additional resources to assist developing countries in dealing with serious environmental problems, and urges the Executive Director of the Programme, in consultation with Governments and international organizations concerned, to accelerate and intensify his efforts in this field;

12.   *Urges* the Executive Director of the United Nations Environment Programme to facilitate the provision of expert assistance to and among developing countries, at their request, in the preparation, monitoring and evaluation of priority environmental programmes and projects, including the application of environmental impact assessment, and in promoting and increasing the exchange of information and experience with respect to the integration of environmental considerations into development activities;

13.   *Expresses its appreciation* to Governments that have contributed to the Fund of the United Nations Environment Programme, particularly to those that have done so for the first time in 1982 and 1983 and those that have increased their contributions for those years, and also to those countries which have changed their yearly payment procedures in order to make their contributions available as early as possible;

14.   *Notes with deep concern*, however, the very meagre pledges to the Fund so far received from Governments and strongly appeals to all Governments to pledge their contributions as soon as possible for 1984, and where possible for 1985, preferably before the end of 1983.

General Assembly resolution 38/165

19 December 1983   Meeting 102   Adopted without vote

Approved by Second Committee (A/38/702/Add.7) without vote, 21 November (meeting 45); draft by Vice-Chairman (A/C.2/38/L.71), based on informal consultations on 22-nation draft (A/C.2/38/L.18); agenda item 78 *(g)*.

Meeting numbers. GA 38th session: 2nd Committee 25, 30, 31, 45, 46; plenary 102.

In addition to drafting changes, the adopted text differed from the 22-nation draft (Western and developing countries) in that the preambular paragraph on weapons of mass destruction and the environment and the paragraph on the impacts of *apartheid* were inserted.

State of the environment

In a February 1983 report to the Governing Council on the state of the environment,[15] the Executive Director highlighted three topics—hazardous wastes, acid rain and environmental aspects of energy farms, selected by the Governing Council in 1982. The Executive Director pointed out that hazardous wastes were generated by chemical processes, by cleaning or closing chemical factories, or by contaminated sites; until recently, many hazardous wastes had been disposed of without evaluating the environmental consequences; however, laws controlling their disposal had become effective in most developed countries, and developing countries could do much to avoid disposal problems by studying those laws.

Acid rain was an environmental problem in parts of Europe and North America. Similarly polluted areas were likely to exist elsewhere, especially around large urban and industrial conglomerations. Rain mixed with pollution from burning fossil fuels, produced by power stations, factories and motor vehicles, and brought down dilute sulphuric and nitric acid. It acidified lakes and rivers, killing fish, accelerated the corrosion of building materials, and damaged historic monuments and other cultural objects. More research was needed to develop advanced control technologies, reduce sulphur and nitrogen oxide emissions, and implement further energy conservation measures.

Other environmental problems could be caused by production of renewable energy sources. The report cautioned that large-scale energy farms—for example, areas of land or water devoted to growing plants for fuel—could cause pollution and other problems that must be assessed at an early stage to make sure that such "green energy" was developed in an environmentally sound way.

UNEP Council action. The UNEP Governing Council on 24 May[4] decided that the topic to be considered in the 1984 report on the state of the environment would be "the environment in the dialogue between and among the developed and developing countries". It requested the Executive Director to ensure that the report included an analysis of emerging global environmental issues, and to make specific proposals on how selected indicators might be published so as to bring environmental trends alive to the world community, and how an index of environmental data and concrete assessment statements of major environmental problems might be produced.

The Council decision was welcomed by the General Assembly in resolution 38/165.

Environmental Perspective

In 1983, the UNEP Governing Council again took up the question of preparing an environmental perspective to the year 2000 and beyond. In a February 1983 report to the Council,[16] the Executive Director summed up government views on the creation of an independent commission of eminent persons representing all regions to report on global environment perspectives and on establishing an intergovernmental process, involving all States, the United Nations system and the world scientific community, to develop the perspective document, and on other possible options.

In his recommendations, the Executive Director stressed that the perspective must provide a framework for activities and a basis for negotiations and agreement on modes of co-operation. The Governing Council should have central responsibility for preparing and recommending action on the perspective. The Executive Director considered establishing an intergovernmental committee of the Council to be the most effective way of preparing the perspective. A special commission, as recommended in 1982,[17] would help develop the perspective and mobilize public opinion. The Executive Director made several recommendations with regard to status and composition of such a commission which, he suggested, should report to the Assembly through the Governing Council. Annexed to the Executive Director's report were terms of reference and financial implications relating to both an intergovernmental committee and a special commission.

The Governing Council, on 23 May,[7] established, subject to Assembly approval of the financial implications, an open-ended intergovernmental inter-sessional preparatory committee and a special commission, to assist it in carrying out its mandate in regard to the environmental perspective. The committee was to hold its first session in May 1984. The Council recommended to the Assembly adoption of a draft resolution on the process of preparing the perspective.

On 25 July, in decision 1983/168 the Economic and Social Council took note of the Governing Council's decision together with its recommendation that the Assembly adopt the draft resolution. The Assembly followed that recommendation by adopting resolution 38/161 (see below).

In a November report,[14] ACC dealt with general environmental matters, among them preparation of the Environmental Perspective. It stated that the process decided on was in keeping with ACC's recommendations in 1981 and 1982.

GENERAL ASSEMBLY ACTION

On 19 December, on the recommendation of the Second Committee, the General Assembly adopted resolution 38/161 without vote.

Process of preparation of the Environmental Perspective to the Year 2000 and Beyond
The General Assembly,
Recalling the importance it has attached at previous sessions to the development of the Environmental Perspective to the Year 2000 and Beyond,
Recalling also its request to the Governing Council of the United Nations Environment Programme at its

eleventh session to make concrete recommendations to the General Assembly at its thirty-eighth session, through the Economic and Social Council at its second regular session of 1983, on the modalities for preparing the Environmental Perspective,

1. *Notes with satisfaction* decision 11/3 of the Governing Council of the United Nations Environment Programme on the process of preparation of the Environmental Perspective to the Year 2000 and Beyond, adopted on 23 May 1983;

2. *Welcomes* the desire of the Governing Council to develop the Environmental Perspective and transmit it to the General Assembly for adoption, benefiting in carrying out that function from its consideration of the relevant proposals made by a special commission;

3. *Approves* the decision of the Governing Council to establish, in order to assist it in fulfilling its mandate in regard to the Environmental Perspective and to report to it in that respect, an intergovernmental inter-sessional preparatory committee to articulate to the special commission at an early stage in its work the Governing Council's expectations regarding the matters which it hopes will, *inter alia*, receive consideration by the commission and, in this connection:

(a) Notes that the commission, at a preliminary stage in the formulation of its conclusions on matters within the mandate and purview of the United Nations Environment Programme, should make them known to the committee with a view to giving consideration to any views of the committee thereon;

(b) Notes from paragraph 41 of the report of the Governing Council on its eleventh session that the cost of the intergovernmental inter-sessional preparatory committee will not result in any net increase in the regular budget of the United Nations;

4. *Also welcomes* the intention of a number of Governments to support the preparation of the Environmental Perspective by facilitating the establishment of the special commission, through the provision of voluntary contributions for its financing;

5. *Requests* the Secretary-General, in consultation with the Executive Director of the United Nations Environment Programme and with Governments, and after such other appropriate consultations as they deem necessary, to appoint the Chairman and Vice-Chairman of the special commission, who will subsequently select the members of that commission and accordingly establish the special commission, which should co-operate closely with the intergovernmental inter-sessional preparatory committee; the Chairman and Vice-Chairman should have experience of policy-making at the highest level, demonstrated interest in environmental and developmental issues and the capacity to attract attention to the work of the commission, and should represent both developed and developing countries;

6. *Expresses its view* that the Chairman and the Vice-Chairman, in selecting the members of the special commission, should take fully into account the need for appropriate geographical distribution and regional balance in membership and the importance of ensuring that at least half of the members of the commission are from the developing countries, as well as the need to consult as appropriate with representatives of Governments, intergovernmental and non-governmental organizations, industry, the scientific community and others concerned with the environment;

7. *Requests* the Executive Director to establish an interim special account under the financial regulations of the United Nations to which voluntary contributions would be credited and from which disbursements would be made for the purposes of the establishment of the special commission, custody over and responsibility for the account to be transferred to that commission, in accordance with its procedures, upon its establishment;

8. *Suggests* that the special commission, when established, should focus mainly on the following terms of reference for its work:

(a) To propose long-term environmental strategies for achieving sustainable development to the year 2000 and beyond;

(b) To recommend ways in which concern for the environment may be translated into greater co-operation among developing countries and between countries at different stages of economic and social development and lead to the achievement of common and mutually supportive objectives, which take account of the interrelationships between people, resources, environment and development;

(c) To consider ways and means by which the international community can deal more effectively with environmental concerns, in the light of the other recommendations in its report;

(d) To help to define shared perceptions of long-term environmental issues and of the appropriate efforts needed to deal successfully with the problems of protecting and enhancing the environment, a long-term agenda for action during the coming decades, and aspirational goals for the world community, taking into account the relevant resolutions of the session of a special character of the Governing Council in 1982;

9. *Further suggests* that, in fulfilling its terms of reference, the special commission should:

(a) Maintain an exchange of views with the scientific community, environmentalists and all other sections of public opinion, particularly youth, concerned with the environment, and those concerned with the relationship between development and environment;

(b) Receive the views of Governments, principally through the Governing Council and its intergovernmental inter-sessional preparatory committee, and through contacts with national leaders, opinion makers and concerned international figures;

(c) Maintain links with other intergovernmental bodies within and outside the United Nations system, while, however, using the Administrative Committee on Co-ordination and the designated officials for environmental matters as the channels of communication with the United Nations system; the willingness of the Administrative Committee on Co-ordination to assist should be communicated to the commission;

(d) Take account of the scope of environmental issues as defined by the United Nations system-wide medium-term environment programme and as reflected in the efforts of the United Nations system, including the United Nations Environment Programme, in the field of the environment;

(e) Make full use of relevant existing reports and material;

10. *Considers* that the special commission should make available a report on environment and the global *problématique* to the year 2000 and beyond, including pro-

posed strategies for sustainable development, within a period of two years from its establishment;

11. *Decides* that, on matters within the mandate and purview of the United Nations Environment Programme, the report of the special commission should in the first instance be considered by the Governing Council of the Programme, for transmission to the General Assembly together with its comments and for use as basic material in the preparation, for adoption by the Assembly, of the Environmental Perspective;

12. *Further decides* that, on those matters which are under consideration or review by the General Assembly itself, the Assembly will consider the relevant aspects of the report of the special commission;

13. *Recognizes* that the special commission may in addition address its report, after consideration by the Governing Council or the intergovernmental intersessional preparatory committee, to other forums, intergovernmental and non-governmental, or to Governments, individuals and the general public, as it sees fit, it being understood that the report of the commission will not be binding on Governments.

General Assembly resolution 38/161

19 December 1983   Meeting 102   Adopted without vote

Approved by Second Committee (A/38/702/Add.7) without vote, 4 November (meeting 30); UNEP draft, recommended by Economic and Social Council decision 1983/168 (A/C.2/38/L.5); agenda item 78 *(g)*.
Meeting numbers. GA 38th session: 2nd Committee 25, 30; plenary 102.

Regional activities

The co-ordination of activities under various regional action plans continued under UNEP throughout 1983. Among its activities were a long-term pollution monitoring and research programme in the Mediterranean which became operational in 1983. The first phase of the Blue Plan was completed, providing a comprehensive picture of the state of the environment and development in the region, and proposals for a second phase were prepared.

In East Africa, a draft regional convention and two protocols were prepared and reviewed by a meeting of government experts in December. The experts also prepared country reports on the status of natural resources and conservation, environmental legislation and socio-economic activities. The reports were collated by FAO, the International Union for Conservation of Nature and Natural Resources (IUCN) and UNEP into regional reviews.

Other regional activities included desertification control, action to combat marine pollution, reforestation, regional seas action programme, information and training (see below).

UNEP Council action. The Governing Council, in its 24 May decision on policy matters,[4] reaffirmed its views expressed at its 1982 session[18] regarding UNEP's regional presence in Africa, Asia and the Pacific, Latin America and the Caribbean and West Asia, and agreed that its presence should continue to be maintained on the current basis in Europe.

In its omnibus decision on programme matters,[11] the Council also dealt with regional activities. It requested the Executive Director to give high priority to assistance to African countries for dealing with the most urgent environmental problems, namely, desertification; safe water supply; protection of forests, reafforestation and soil management; food production systems and prevention of food losses; public awareness of environmental issues; protection of the marine environment; development of alternative energy resources; wildlife conservation; and the environmental aspects of mining and industrial development. The Council invited the Governments of the region to convene an African environmental conference to identify common problems and discuss national environmental priorities.

Referring to Asia and the Pacific, the Council requested the Executive Director to give high priority to assistance to regional activities and to provide financial support, including support for the Environmental Co-ordinating Unit of the Economic and Social Commission for Asia and the Pacific (ESCAP), and to seek further funds.

By the same decision, the Executive Director was invited to continue co-operating closely on environmental issues with the Executive Secretary of the Economic Commission for Europe (ECE), and parties to the ECE Convention on Long-range Transboundary Air Pollution which entered into force in March 1983 were urged to reach agreement on financial arrangements for implementing the Convention at the first meeting of its Executive Body.

The Council also acted on environmental information and environmental education and training in the different regions (see below).

Noting with satisfaction the extent of co-operation among the member countries of the South Asia Co-operative Enviroment Programme, the Council, on 24 May,[12] requested the Executive Director to accord high priority to projects within the framework of that Programme, and to seek additional funds, especially for the priority areas of environment and development, environment and energy, environment and education, and marine ecosystems.

By another decision of 24 May,[13] the Council expressed appreciation to the Executive Director for convening the Meeting of Government-nominated Experts on Regional Environmental Programmes in Latin America and the Caribbean (Buenos Aires, 14-17 March). It decided to support the strengthening of regional and subregional environmental activities and urged Governments and international organizations to strengthen support for the Latin American Environmental Training Network, the Action Plan for the Protection of the Marine Environment and Coastal Areas of the South-East Pacific, and the Action Plan of the Caribbean Environment Programme. It recommended that future intergovernmental meetings in the region be preceded by meetings of high-level government experts to consider the technical aspects of environmental programmes. In addition, the Council invited regional intergovernmental agencies, United Nations organizations and NGOs to participate in the programmes adopted at the meeting and requested the Executive Director to give special consideration to intraregional co-operation.

The General Assembly, in resolution 38/165, welcomed the importance attached to regional approaches and programmes by the Governing Council.

Joint meeting with Habitat

The sixth joint meeting of the Executive Director of UNCHS (Habitat) and the Bureau of the Commission on Human Settlements with the Executive Director of UNEP and the Bureau of its Governing Council was held on 13 and 14 December 1983 at Nairobi.[19] The meeting considered the following areas of collaboration: human settlements planning in relation to population and environmental policies; support of research and training in settlements planning; systems approach to rural settlements planning; global review of human settlements; energy requirements of rural settlements and the urban poor; assessment of environmental conditions in human settlements; environmental aspects of settlements planning and development; environmentally sound technologies; and research, training and information dissemination.

Noting with concern that both UNEP and UNCHS faced a lack of resources for key co-operative projects, the meeting hoped for broader support.

It was further noted that a clearing house mechanism had been established to channel additional resources through UNEP to deal with serious environmental problems in developing countries (see below). The bureaux felt that serious human settlements problems in those countries should be considered for support through that mechanism. It was also suggested that the UNCHS Executive Director might consider establishing a similar procedure.

In a 24 May decision,[4] the UNEP Governing Council expressed satisfaction at the continuing co-operation between UNCHS and UNEP; requested the UNEP Executive Director to invite UNCHS to take part in UNEP's efforts to develop environmental guidelines for solid waste disposal; and asked him to ensure wide dissemination and use of those guidelines, as well as of the guidelines for environmentally sound human settlements. The Council expressed the view that annual joint meetings would no longer be necessary after 1984, because of the expected close proximity of the headquarters of both organizations in Nairobi by the middle of that year, and requested that its view be brought to the attention of the Commission on Human Settlements at its 1984 session.

UNEP Fund and trust funds

During 1983, the UNEP Environment Fund disbursed $21,867,238 for programme activities—not including $244,771 for activities under the programme reserve—in the following areas: human settlements and health, $2,263,006; support, $3,974,758; environment and development, $1,444,555; oceans, $3,370,195; energy, $525,956; environmental management and law, $360,266; terrestial ecosystems, $2,932,105; natural disasters, $88,328; Earthwatch, $4,863,048; environmental data, $136,215; and arid and semi-arid lands, $1,908,806.[20]

Forty-four new projects were approved by the Fund in 1983, compared with 70 in 1982; 37 projects were closed. At the end of 1983, a total of 299 projects were still open. The share of global projects was 57.4 per cent; regional, 30 per cent; and interregional, 12.6 per cent. Projects were shared among the regions as follows: Africa, 11.9 per cent; Asia, 8.1 per cent; Latin America, 7.9 per cent; Europe, 1.7 per cent; and North America, 0.3 per cent.

In 1983, no contributions were paid into the Regional Trust Fund for the Protection and Development of the Marine Environment and Coastal Areas of Bahrain, Iran, Iraq, Kuwait, Oman, Qatar, Saudi Arabia and the United Arab Emirates. Contributions of $2.23 million were received by the Trust Fund for the Protection of the Mediterranean Sea against Pollution; $704,328 by the Regional Trust Fund for the Implementation of the Action Plan for the Caribbean Environment Programme; $464,134 by the Trust Fund for the Convention on International Trade in Endangered Species of Wild Fauna and Flora; and $67,000 by the Regional Trust Fund for the Implementation of the Action Plan for the Protection and Development of the Marine Environment and Coastal Areas of the East Asian Seas.

Procedures for administering the new international Sasakawa Environment Prize were agreed on in 1983, and the Japan Shipbuilding Industry Foundation contributed $1 million to a trust fund to finance the prize. In October 1983, the United Nations Secretary-General announced the establishment of a Prize Selection Committee.

The UNEP Governing Council, on 23 May, adopted three decisions on the Environment Fund and UNEP-administered trust funds. The Council approved for 1984-1985 $70 million for programme activities and $2 million for Fund programme reserve activities;[21] requested the Executive Director to pursue efforts to obtain additional resources for dealing with serious environmental problems in developing countries[22] (see below); and approved revised apropriations for programme and programme support costs—$20,600,000 in 1982-1983 and $26,020,000 in 1984-1985.[23]

The Council reiterated its appeal to Governments that had not yet pledged a contribution to the Environment Fund for 1983 to do so, and again appealed for contributions to be paid as near to the beginning of the year as possible. It reaffirmed the desirability of achieving a Fund programme during the medium-term environment programme 1984-1989, of $42.5 million per annum in 1982 prices.

UNEP administered nine trust funds and a Special Account for financing the implementation of the Plan of Action to Combat Desertification (see below). The Governing Council, on 23 May,[21] extended until 31 December 1985 the following six trust funds: the trust fund for the protection and development of the marine environment and coastal areas of the Gulf States; the trust fund for protec-tion of the Mediterranean Sea; the trust fund for the Convention on international trade in endangered species; the trust fund for the protection and development of the marine environment and coastal areas of the West and Central African region; the trust funds for the Caribbean and the East Asian Seas.

In resolution 38/165, the General Assembly expressed appreciation to those Governments that had contributed to the Environment Fund, but noted with deep concern the meagre pledges so far received. It appealed to all Governments to pledge their contributions as soon as possible for 1984, and where possible for 1985.

The Assembly, in resolution 38/228 A, decided to allocate one half of the net revenues from the sale of postage stamps on the conservation and protection of nature to UNEP for financing projects promoting the protection of nature and endangered species. It also requested the UNEP Executive Director to report to the Governing Council on the results of the projects.

CONTRIBUTIONS TO THE UNEP FUND, 1983 AND FUTURE YEARS

(as at 31 December 1983; in US dollars)

Country	1983 payment	Pledges for future years	Country	1983 payment	Pledges for future years
Algeria	11,000	22,000	Kuwait	200,000	200,000
Argentina	92,200	—	Lesotho	3,648	—
Australia	662,722	—	Luxembourg	13,769	6,009
Austria	300,000	900,000	Malaysia	25,000	30,000
Bahamas	500	—	Malta	1,637	—
Bangladesh	1,999	2,200	Mauritius	3,061	—
Barbados	1,000	—	Mexico	37,109	—
Belgium	213,727	—	Mongolia	906	885
Botswana	2,252	—	Netherlands	555,252	—
Brazil	—	20,000	New Zealand	62,239	—
Bulgaria	10,152	—	Norway	820,205	772,211
Byelorussian SSR	17,760	—	Oman	10,000	10,000
Canada	—	903,000	Pakistan	—	5,000
Chile	5,000	5,000	Panama	6,000	—
China	101,002	—	Philippines	12,814	—
Colombia	35,000	35,000	Poland	32,380	—
Costa Rica	151	—	Portugal	3,000	—
Cyprus	2,000	—	Saudi Arabia	—	1,000,000
Czechoslovakia	48,622	23,364	Seychelles	200	—
Democratic Yemen	1,456	1,840	Singapore	1,000	1,000
Denmark	358,798	—	Somalia	—	1,295
Ecuador	5,000	5,000	Spain	517,752	—
Egypt	15,255	24,340	Sri Lanka	5,500	—
Finland	850,000	584,071	Sudan	—	11,719
France	724,655	849,560	Swaziland	787	901
German Democratic Republic	150,625	413,604	Sweden	2,500,000	2,000,000
Germany, Federal Republic of	1,858,352	1,596,028	Switzerland	480,794	495,413
Ghana	9,570	—	Thailand	10,000	10,000
Guinea-Bissau	—	1,000	Tunisia	20,400	—
Hungary	21,079	21,557	Uganda	1,443	—
Iceland	5,000	4,500	Ukrainian SSR	43,716	—
India	51,206	100,000	USSR	3,581,421	—
Indonesia	12,000	12,000	United Kingdom	1,119,403	—
Iran	64,353	—	United Republic of Cameroon	7,299	—
Ireland	20,812	—	United States	7,831,010	10,000,000
Italy	—	301,887	Venezuela	100,000	—
Ivory Coast	5,479	—	Zaire	90,494	50,000
Jamaica	3,745	—	Zambia	—	11,194
Japan	4,000,000	—	Zimbabwe	6,510	5,769
Jordan	10,000	—			
Kenya	46,430	45,000	Total	27,823,651	20,482,347

SOURCE: A/39/5/Add.6

REFERENCES
[1]UNEP/GC/12/2. [2]A/38/25. [3]UNEP/GC.11/3. [4]A/38/25 (dec. 11/1). [5]YUN 1977, p. 509. [6]A/38/25 (dec. 11/2). [7]*Ibid.* (dec. 11/3). [8]*Ibid.* (dec. 11/4). [9]*Ibid.* (dec. 11/5). [10]*Ibid.* (dec. 11/6). [11]*Ibid.* (dec. 11/7). [12]*Ibid.* (dec. 11/8). [13]*Ibid.* (dec. 11/9). [14]ACC/1983/28. [15]UNEP/GC.11/4 & Add.1. [16]UNEP/GC.11/3/Add.3. [17]YUN 1982, p. 1000. [18]YUN 1982, p. 1004. [19]HS/C/7/2/Add.1. [20]A/39/5/Add.6. [21]A/38/25 (dec. 11/10). [22]*Ibid.* (dec. 11/11). [23]*Ibid.* (dec. 11/12).

Desertification control

Plan of Action to Combat Desertification

In January 1983, the Executive Director submitted a report to the Governing Council,[1] on progress achieved since the Council's 1982 session in implementing the 1977 Plan of Action to Combat Desertification.[2] After reviewing national and international action, he concluded that almost nothing indicated a reversal in the trends leading to more desertification, and that countries affected by it continued to give low priority to its solution. He stressed that among the areas in need of attention, the most important were regional action, financing, and the need to secure for desertification control projects a treatment different from that accorded to standard development projects. Among other measures, the Executive Director suggested that the Council might wish to draw the attention of Governments to the disastrous effects of desertification, and urge serious efforts to implement the Plan.

The Consultative Group for Desertification Control held its fourth meeting at Nairobi, Kenya, from 15 to 17 February.

Expressing deep concern about the slow implementation of the Plan of Action, the Governing Council, on 24 May,[3] invited Governments and international organizations to support and strengthen the role of the Group and enable it to achieve its objectives. The Council invited the Assembly to consider expanding the Group's role to include information exchange, appealed for financial contributions and requested the Executive Director to persuade Governments to make their views known in reasonable time, in particular with reference to providing additional resources.

In an October report[4] to the General Assembly submitted in response to a December 1982 Assembly request,[5] the Secretary-General summarized ten substantive replies from Governments containing views on financing the Plan, in particular on the establishment of an international financial corporation to finance non-commercial desertification measures, proposed in 1981.[6] Concluding, the Secretary-General stated that the response from Member States in 1982[7] and 1983

had been very limited, and the great majority of the countries affected had not replied at all to his invitation for their comments. Therefore, he was not able to submit an objective report in 1983. He suggested that the Assembly might again wish to urge Governments to communicate their views not later than 30 April 1984, so that a final report could be prepared.

The ACC Inter-agency Working Group on Desertification held its eighth and ninth meetings at Geneva in April and September 1983, respectively.

In a November report on environmental issues,[8] ACC again emphasized the need for integrated national action and for increased financial assistance to anti-desertification projects; estimates showed that resources of $2.4 billion annually for a period of 20 years were necessary to halt desertification. ACC suggested that in order to overcome shortage of manpower, indigenous scientific institutions should focus on desertification projects. It considered it important that the assessment of the extent and nature of desertification should continue towards the establishment of a United Nations data base. Concluding, ACC called for intensified international efforts to prevent further deterioration and bring desertification to a halt by the end of the century.

Implementation of the Plan of Action in the Sudano-Sahelian region was also dealt with by the UNEP Council and the Assembly (see below).

GENERAL ASSEMBLY ACTION

On 19 December, on the recommendation of the Second Committee, the General Assembly adopted without vote resolution 38/163.

Study on financing the Plan of Action to Combat Desertification

The General Assembly,

Recalling its resolutions 32/172 of 19 December 1977, 33/89 of 15 December 1978, 34/184 of 18 December 1979, 36/191 of 17 December 1981 and 37/220 of 20 December 1982, dealing with the implementation and financing of the Plan of Action to Combat Desertification,

Having considered the report of the Secretary-General on financing the Plan of Action to Combat Desertification,

1. *Takes note* of the report of the Secretary-General;

2. *Notes* that again very few replies were received from Governments in response to paragraph 3 of General Assembly resolution 37/220, thus not permitting the Secretary-General to prepare, in co-operation with the Executive Director of the United Nations Environment Programme, the report requested in paragraph 5 of that resolution;

3. *Requests again* all Member States that have not yet provided their comments to the Secretary-General on the feasibility studies and concrete recommendations for the implementation of the additional measures of financing, as well as on the modalities for obtaining financial resources, as described in the annex to the report of the

Secretary-General of 1 October 1981, to do so as soon as possible;

4. *Also requests* all Member States that have not yet provided their comments to the Secretary-General on the expert feasibility study and working plan for the establishment of an international financial corporation to finance non-commercial measures to combat desertification, contained in chapter V of the annex to his report, also to do so as soon as possible, particularly with respect to:

(a) The establishment of the corporation;
(b) Their interest in participating financially therein;

5. *Further requests* the Secretary-General, in co-operation with the Executive Director of the United Nations Environment Programme, to report to the General Assembly at its fortieth session on the implementation of the present resolution.

General Assembly resolution 38/163
19 December 1983   Meeting 102   Adopted without vote

Approved by Second Committee (A/38/702/Add.7) without vote, 14 November (meeting 39); draft by Vice-Chairman (A/C.2/38/L.37), based on informal consultations on 3-nation draft (A/C.2/38/L.15); agenda item 78 *(g)*.
Meeting numbers. GA 38th session: 2nd Committee 25, 30, 39; plenary 102.

In paragraphs 3 and 4, instead of requesting, the original draft sponsored by Jamaica, the Sudan and Turkey would have had the Assembly urge and strongly urge Member States to provide their comments; by the original, the Assembly would have also asked that they be submitted no later than 30 April 1985.

Desertification in the Sudano-Sahelian region

In the annex to a January 1983 report to the UNEP Council,[1] on the implementation in the Sudano-Sahelian region of the Plan of Action to Combat Desertification, the Executive Director pointed out that the 19 countries (Benin, Cape Verde, Chad, Djibouti, Ethiopia, Gambia, Guinea, Guinea-Bissau, Kenya, Mali, Mauritania, Niger, Nigeria, Senegal, Somalia, Sudan, Uganda, United Republic of Cameroon, Upper Volta) covered by the desertification control mandate of UNSO—a joint venture of UNEP and UNDP—had an area of 12.4 million square kilometres, of which 80 per cent were arid or semi-arid compared with a world average of some 30 per cent. Over 90 per cent of the rangelands and 85 per cent of the rainfed crop lands of the region were affected by desertification. The Executive Director gave an overview of the main features of UNSO activities which included forestry; range and water management; sand-dune fixation; planning and co-ordination; and other activities involving integrated approaches and alternative or supplementary livelihood systems aimed at easing pressure on the land. The Executive Director's report was transmitted to the General Assembly by a 29 July note of the Secretary-General.[9]

The UNDP Administrator, in his report on 1983 UNDP activities,[10] stated that the countries of the

region affected by desertification had a population of 212 million. Total resources mobilized by UNSO amounted to $62.6 million since the inception of its desertification control mandate in 1979,[11] with funds mobilized in 1983 amounting to $14.6 million.

The Secretary-General transmitted to the Assembly a May report[12] by the Joint Inspection Unit (JIU) on UNSO activities, with his own comments made in June (see p. 526).

In its November 1983 report on environmental matters,[8] ACC agreed with the Executive Director's concluding remarks in his report to the UNEP Council that the year had passed with almost nothing to indicate a reversal in the deteriorating trends leading to further desertification and loss of crop land, and less food-producing capacity. ACC noted the Council's decision of 24 May[3] inviting Governments and international organizations to facilitate the task of the Consultative Group for Desertification Control, and noted that some progress had been accomplished during the year in mobilizing additional resources for Consultative Group projects.

UNEP Council action. The UNEP Council, in its 24 May decision on programme matters,[3] expressed satisfaction at the progress made by UNSO in assisting Governments of the region, and invited the General Assembly to consider expanding UNSO's mandate to include the environmental consequences of drought.

ECONOMIC AND SOCIAL COUNCIL ACTION

The Economic and Social Council, in decision 1983/168, took note of the UNEP Executive Director's report on the implementation in the Sudano-Sahelian region of the Plan of Action to Combat Desertification, and decided to transmit it to the General Assembly.

GENERAL ASSEMBLY ACTION

On 19 December, on the recommendation of the Second Committee, the General Assembly adopted without vote resolution 38/164.

Implementation in the Sudano-Sahelian region of the Plan of Action to Combat Desertification
The General Assembly,
Recalling its resolutions 36/190 of 17 December 1981 and 37/216 of 20 December 1982,
Noting part seven, section B, paragraph 5, of decision 11/7 of 24 May 1983 of the Governing Council of the United Nations Environment Programme on the implementation of the Plan of Action to Combat Desertification in the Sudano-Sahelian region,
Noting also Economic and Social Council resolution 1983/68 of 29 July 1983 on the climatic situation and drought in Africa,
Having considered the report of the Governing Council of the United Nations Environment Programme on the

implementation in the Sudano-Sahelian region of the
Plan of Action to Combat Desertification,

1. *Takes note* of the report of the Governing Council
of the United Nations Environment Programme;

2. *Expresses its satisfaction* with the progress made by
the United Nations Sudano-Sahelian Office, on behalf
of the United Nations Environment Programme, under
a joint venture between the United Nations Environment Programme and the United Nations Development
Programme, to assist the Governments of the region in
implementing the Plan of Action to Combat Desertification;

3. *Requests* the Governing Council of the United
Nations Environment Programme and the Governing
Council of the United Nations Development Programme
to continue to provide adequate support for the United
Nations Sudano-Sahelian Office in order to enable it
to respond more adequately to the pressing needs of the
countries of the Sudano-Sahelian region;

4. *Invites* the Governing Council of the United
Nations Environment Programme to examine, at its
twelfth session, the possibility of including Ghana and
Togo in the list of countries which receive assistance
through the United Nations Sudano-Sahelian Office in
implementing in the Sudano-Sahelian region the Plan
of Action to Combat Desertification and to report on
this matter to the General Assembly at its thirty-ninth
session;

5. *Expresses its gratitude* to the Governments, agencies
of the United Nations system, intergovernmental organizations and other organizations that have contributed
to the implementation in the Sudano-Sahelian region
of the Plan of Action to Combat Desertification;

6. *Urges* all Governments to respond favourably to
requests for assistance from the Governments of the
Sudano-Sahelian region in combating desertification;

7. *Requests* the Governing Council of the United
Nations Environment Programme to continue to report
annually to the General Assembly, through the Economic and Social Council, on the implementation in
the Sudano-Sahelian region of the Plan of Action to
Combat Desertification.

General Assembly resolution 38/164

19 December 1983   Meeting 102   Adopted without vote

Approved by Second Committee (A/38/702/Add.7) without vote, 14 November (meeting 39); draft by Vice-Chairman (A/C.2/38/L.38), based on informal consultations
on 20-nation draft (A/C.2/38/L.20); agenda item 78 (g).
Meeting numbers. GA 38th session: 2nd Committee 25, 30, 39; plenary 102.

Paragraph 4 was added to the draft sponsored
by 20 African States. Also, by that text, the Assembly would have invited the Governing Councils of UNDP and UNEP to strengthen their support for UNSO, rather than requesting them to
continue supporting it.

In resolution 38/225 on the implementation of
the medium-term and long-term recovery and rehabilitation programme in the Sudano-Sahelian region,
the Assembly urged Governments to make special
efforts to increase UNSO resources, through contributions to the annual United Nations Pledging
Conference for Development Activities (see Chapter
II of this section), as well as through bilateral channels.

REFERENCES
[1]UNEP/GC.11/10 & Add.1 & Add.1/Corr.1. [2]YUN 1977, p. 509.
[3]A/38/25 (dec. 11/7). [4]A/38/403. [5]YUN 1982, p. 1017, GA
res. 37/220, 20 Dec. 1982. [6]YUN 1981, p. 827. [7]YUN 1982,
p. 1017. [8]ACC/1983/28. [9]A/38/304. [10]DP/1984/5/Add.2.
[11]YUN 1979, p. 699. [12]A/38/180.

Environmental activities

Environmental monitoring

Protection against harmful products

In accordance with a December 1981 request,[1]
the Secretary-General submitted, in May 1983, a
report on exchange of information on banned
hazardous chemicals and unsafe pharmaceutical
products[2] to both the Economic and Social Council
and the General Assembly. The report summarized
consultations with Member States on their experience
in the exchange of such information, and described
work by United Nations organizations which might
be useful to governmental authorities. Certain conclusions were offered tentatively: the majority of
the responding countries had legislative and other
institutional and technical machinery to keep out
undesired imports of hazardous chemicals and pharmaceutical products; international information systems
available were not being used to the fullest extent.
An unanswered question was whether countries had
an adequate infrastructure to control the import
of hazardous substances and if they did, whether
it was used. Another difficulty was the lack of consistent
product information and the problem of misrepresented
products. An annex to the report described efforts
by United Nations organizations to assist Governments
in information exchange on harmful products.

Speaking on 3 November before the Assembly's
Second Committee, a United Nations Secretariat
representative reported on progress in implementing
the Assembly's December 1982 request[3] that the
Secretary-General prepare a consolidated list of
products whose consumption or sale had been banned,
withdrawn, severely restricted or, in the case of pharmaceuticals, not approved. The list was to be based
on information available within the United Nations
system as well as from Governments. The Secretariat
had collected information from United Nations bodies
and agencies, primarily from the World Health Organization (WHO), UNEP and the United Nations
Centre on Transnational Corporations. A first list,
based on information from both specialized agencies and Governments, was in an advanced stage
of preparation, with the English version expected
to be ready by the end of 1983; the list would be
transmitted directly to Governments. So far, only
25 Governments had replied to the request for additional information; several had underlined the

difficulties involved in preparing a list of the type requested and had indicated the need for more consultations on the subject. Though it was possible to produce the list without assistance from Governments, the result would be rather ineffectual; it was hoped that all Governments would supply the necessary information. A review of the format of the list could be undertaken at the 1984 Assembly session on the basis of the first edition.

The 1983 activities of UNEP concerning the effects of chemicals on human and environmental health were reported on by the UNEP Executive Director in his annual report[4] to the Governing Council (see chapter XV of this section).

On 19 December 1983, on the recommendation of the Second Committee, the General Assembly adopted resolution 38/149 without vote.

Protection against products harmful to health and the environment

The General Assembly,

Recalling its resolutions 36/166 of 16 December 1981 and 37/137 of 17 December 1982,

Bearing in mind the oral report presented by the Secretariat on 3 November 1983 with regard to progress made in the implementation of resolution 37/137,

1. *Takes note* of the report of the Secretary-General on the exchange of information on banned hazardous chemicals and unsafe pharmaceutical products, and of the work being carried out by the organizations of the United Nations system;

2. *Notes with satisfaction* that the work carried out in consultation with organizations of the United Nations system on the consolidated list of products whose consumption and/or sale have been banned, withdrawn, severely restricted or, in the case of pharmaceuticals, not approved by Governments, is in the process of being completed;

3. *Requests* the Secretary-General to make available the consolidated list, as established on the basis of information supplied thus far, in accordance with the objectives of General Assembly resolution 37/137, and to bring it up to date on a regular basis;

4. *Urges* the relevant organs, organizations and bodies of the United Nations system, particularly the Food and Agriculture Organization of the United Nations, the World Health Organization, the International Labour Organisation, the United Nations Environment Programme, the General Agreement on Tariffs and Trade and the United Nations Centre on Transnational Corporations, and other intergovernmental organizations to continue to co-operate fully in providing information for the consolidated list and for its updated versions;

5. *Appreciates* the co-operation extended by Governments and urges all Governments, in particular those that have not yet done so, to provide the necessary information for inclusion in the consolidated list and its updated versions, as well as comments and views that they deem relevant;

6. *Urges* non-governmental organizations to extend co-operation to the Secretary-General regarding the preparation of the consolidated list, particularly in the iden-

tification of potential sources of information among national Governments and in obtaining governmental information on relevant regulatory actions;

7. *Requests* the Secretary-General, for purposes of review by the General Assembly at its thirty-ninth session, to submit a report on the implementation of Assembly resolution 37/137, including the consolidated list, taking into account the latest information and comments collected for possible improvement of the list, as envisaged in paragraph 6 of resolution 37/137;

8. *Requests* the Secretary-General to submit to the General Assembly at its thirty-ninth session, through the Economic and Social Council, a report on the exchange of information on banned hazardous chemicals and unsafe pharmaceutical products identifying elements for possible further work in this area in regard to the needs and capabilities of developing countries to monitor and control those substances in the light of the relevant observations in the report of the Secretary-General;

9. *Requests* the Secretary-General and the competent organs, organizations and bodies of the United Nations system to continue to provide, within available resources, the necessary technical assistance to the developing countries, at their request, for the establishment or strengthening of national systems for better use by those countries of the information provided with regard to banned hazardous chemicals and unsafe pharmaceutical products, as well as for an adequate monitoring of the importation of those products.

General Assembly resolution 38/149

19 December 1983   Meeting 102   Adopted without vote

Approved by Second Committee (A/38/701/Add.1) without vote, 1 December (meeting 53); 10-nation draft (A/C.2/38/L.28/Rev.2); agenda item 12.

Sponsors: Algeria, Bangladesh, Egypt, Ghana, Ivory Coast, Nigeria, Pakistan, Sudan, Trinidad and Tobago, Venezuela.

Meeting numbers. GA 38th session: 2nd Committee 36, 39, 41, 45, 50, 52, 53; plenary 102.

GEMS activities

Environmental assessment and monitoring continued in 1983 to be one of the key tasks of UNEP. Its environment assessment programme Earthwatch was designed as an internationally co-ordinated global system of national facilities and services to study the interaction between man and the environment, provide early warning of potential environmental hazards and determine the state of selected natural resources. The cornerstone of "Earthwatch" was the Global Environmental Monitoring System (GEMS), a collective international effort to acquire, through monitoring, the data needed for the rational management of the environment. The activities of GEMS, which became operational in 1975,[5] were divided in 1983 into five major programmes: renewable natural resource monitoring, climate-related monitoring, health-related monitoring, long-range transport of pollutants monitoring, and ocean monitoring.

Resource monitoring

In 1983, UNEP continued its investigations into the feasibility of establishing a global resource information data base. Sectoral and _ad hoc_ expert working groups examined the desirability and logistics of a global system which would compile, in a geographically referenced form, the many data sets which had been collected within the GEMS monitoring networks. Preliminary designs specified a system by which national and regional planners would be supplied with complex sets of environmental information in easily usable form while building up capabilities for handling environmental data at the national level.

To illustrate how environmental data stored in the global data base might be analysed, data from the GEMS Global Assessment of Tropical Forest Resources were analysed by country to furnish, _inter alia_, a comparison of relative and absolute rates of deforestation. Such analyses were central to the production of environmental assessments.

A pilot project on the inventory and monitoring of Sahelian pastoral ecosystems in Senegal continued to demonstrate the usefulness of GEMS-style ecological monitoring to West Africa. A Workshop on Monitoring of Sahelian Pastoral Ecosystems (Dakar, Senegal, 16-18 November) was attended by rangeland practitioners from throughout the Sahelian region. There was widespread agreement on the soundness and relevance of the theory of rangeland monitoring; it remained to translate the theory into practice.

Two new resource monitoring projects were initiated in Latin America. In Peru, the dynamics of forest and surrounding ecosystems in the High Sierras were studied to gain better understanding of the processes of land degradation. In southern Chile, the behaviour of pollutants in relatively untouched temperate mixed forests was examined, with the assistance of the World Meteorological Organization (WMO) and UNESCO; the results were to be compared to those of similar monitoring projects in the United States.

Climate-related monitoring

More analyses were completed in 1983 of data furnished by the UNEP-WMO Background Air Pollution Monitoring Network. However, the low sampling frequency and the probable contamination of many samples by sea-salt at isolated island stations had led to problems in analysing the data; it appeared that the data were not sufficiently reliable to serve as indicators of long-range atmospheric transport and deposition. Those findings prompted a critical reassessment of sampling procedures within the network.

Health-related monitoring

Analysis of data from the health-related monitoring networks continued during the year. A UNEP-WHO project on the assessment of human exposure to pollutants published findings on or-

ganochlorine compounds. The general observation was that levels of organochlorines, including dichlorodiphenyltrichloroethane (DDT), in human milk, had decreased over a nine-year period in those largely industrialized countries which had restricted or prohibited the use of DDT a decade ago. Industrialized countries tended to have lower levels of DDT, dichlorodiphenyldichloroethylene (DDE) and hexachlorocyclohexane (HCH) in milk fat than more agrarian countries. In the case of polychlorinated biphenyls, however, countries such as the Federal Republic of Germany and Sweden had higher levels than other industrialized countries.

The Monitoring and Assessment Research Centre at the University of London prepared for UNEP and WHO an analysis of air pollution concentrations in selected urban areas between 1973 and 1980. In cities with more than five years' data, the trends for both sulphur dioxide and suspended particulate matter were down. The general decrease in air pollution concentrations was attributed to the installation of emission reduction systems, the use of low-sulphur fuels, the enactment of oil conservation policies and the use of higher chimneys.

An Interregional Expert Review Meeting on Evaluation of Water Quality Data (Burlington, Canada, 17-21 October 1983) examined the status of the GEMS water programme and the integration of water quality monitoring into the activities to be conducted at proposed Health Exposure Assessment Locations, which were to be established to co-ordinate monitoring and assessment of exposure to various sources. The participants agreed that the number of variables collected in the current monitoring programme could be reduced, but at the same time recommended that, in order to achieve comprehensive representation of ranges in climate, urbanization and industrialization, the number of assessment locations should be increased from 15 to 27.

The Economic and Social Council, in resolution 1983/57, urged Governments to develop and utilize techniques to monitor the environmental impact of water projects, and to ensure that environmental and human health considerations would be incorporated in the planning, implementation and operation of water schemes.

Long-range transport of pollutants monitoring

Monitoring the movement of airborne pollutants across national boundaries continued, even though extension of the programme to developing countries, where the extent of the acid rain problem had not yet been ascertained, was hampered by lack of resources.

An expert meeting on the meteorological aspects of the second phase of the European Monitoring and Evaluation Programme (Darmstadt, Federal Republic of Germany, 10-14 October), which monitored the long-range transport of airborne pollutants, examined the results obtained from data collection and modelling of the behaviour of sulphur dioxide by the co-operating Meteorological Synthesizing Centres in Moscow, USSR, and Oslo, Norway. The experts found that model predictions compared well with observed data, but that both needed to be further refined; the programme, developed in conjunction with the Economic Commission for Europe, needed to be expanded, particularly in view of recent damage sustained by European forests.

Ocean monitoring

At an International Symposium on Integrated Global Ocean Monitoring (Tallinn, USSR, 2-10 October) technical reports on the current state of ocean monitoring were reviewed. The importance of global ocean monitoring was highlighted. Participants called in particular for the merging of plans to monitor physical and ecological parameters. The monitoring of sea surface temperatures from co-ordinated satellite and ship observations was also felt to be important. Developing countries asked that special mention be made of the potential usefulness of the UNEP regional seas programme (see below) in relation to global ocean monitoring.

Ecosystems

Atmosphere

Ozone layer depletion

At its sixth session (Geneva, 5-8 April), the UNEP Co-ordinating Committee on the Ozone Layer prepared a new assessment of ozone layer depletion and its impacts, based on the results of national research programmes. The Committee found that current calculations indicated an ultimate reduction of 3 to 5 per cent in the total ozone column, considering only emissions of chlorofluorocarbons 11 and 12 at their current rates. This was a drop from 1981 predictions, resulting from new data on chemical reaction rates.

An assessment carried out by the United States National Aeronautics and Space Administration (NASA) in late 1983 confirmed that estimate. The NASA assessment suggested that ozone column increases would outweigh decreases for the next few decades. One of the reasons was the injection of oxides of nitrogen into the upper troposphere and lower stratosphere by subsonic aircraft. However, the assessment also pointed to major difficulties in predicting the evolution of the ozone column beyond a few decades, arising from uncertainty about future atmospheric methane concentrations.

If atmospheric methane continued to increase at a substantial rate, the combined effect of methane and fluorocarbons might result in no ultimate depletion of column ozone.

Notwithstanding the revised estimate, there were still grounds for concern about the consequences of increased ultraviolet radiation which would occur as a result of ozone depletion, especially with regard to agricultural production, fisheries and human health. The Committee observed that distortion of the vertical ozone profile, as suggested by multiple-scenario models, might become more important than changes in the total amount as far as climatic implications were concerned. Calculations indicated that early next century the combined radiative effect of ozone and other trace gases on the surface temperature might be of the same order as that calculated for carbon dioxide at that time.

A seventh session of the Committee was tentatively planned for 1984.

In 1983, the *Ad Hoc* Working Group of Legal and Technical Experts for the Elaboration of a Global Framework Convention for the Protection of the Ozone Layer held the second part of its second session (Geneva, 11-15 April) and its third session (Geneva, 17-21 October). The Group produced a revised draft text, two draft technical annexes and a separate draft protocol for the control, limitation and reduction of the use and emissions of fully halogenated chlorofluorocarbons.

The revised draft convention[6] included a preamble, 22 articles, and two annexes. The articles covered definitions, general obligations, research and monitoring, scientific and technological co-operation, transmission of information, conference of the contracting parties, secretariat, advisory body, adoption of protocols, amendment of the convention (or protocols), status of annexes, adoption and amendment of annexes, amendment by simplified procedure, settlement of disputes, signature, ratification, accession, entry into force of the convention, reservations, withdrawal, depositary and text languages. The annexes concerned research and monitoring, and information exchange.

UNEP Council action. The UNEP Council, on 24 May,[7] expressed appreciation of the work of the Working Group. It requested the Executive Director to convene a third session in 1983 and if required another in 1984, with a view to having the Group complete its work and transmit an agreed draft convention, through the Executive Director and the UNEP Council, to the General Assembly. It called on Governments and international organizations to participate fully in the Working Group's sessions, appealed to Governments to provide financial resources and facilities, and requested the Executive Director to report in

1984 on progress made on finalizing the draft convention, and to make recommendations with a view to its adoption.

Acid rain

In his report to the UNEP Council on the state of the environment[8] (see above), the Executive Director dealt with acid rain. He stated that the acidification of the environment was a major problem in several regions, particularly in Europe and North America, and might become one in others. The first step towards a solution would be to assess how each regional environment could resist acid fall-out. This would form the basis for implementing pollution control measures to keep deposition at safe levels. In practice, however, that approach would be difficult, as not enough was known about what deposition rates were acceptable, because pollutants were carried for long distances in the air and then distributed unevenly, and because there were uncertainties over the cost-effectiveness of control measures. Nor was enough known about the transport of pollutants to be able to predict, except very broadly, what effects reduced emission in one area would have on deposition rates in another. The Executive Director therefore deemed a stepwise approach to controlling acidification more feasible, both politically and economically.

He also stressed the need for meteorologically and ecologically oriented research topics, and for information on the effects on health of the increasing spread of cadmium and other toxic metals as a result of acidification; among other things, the levels of metals in food, human tissues and body fluids must continue to be monitored. Furthermore, the Executive Director stated, there must be more effort to develop ways of improving energy conservation, environmentally appropriate technologies for producing heat and power, and techniques for removing sulphur from fossil fuels and gaseous emissions.

In its 24 May decision on policy issues,[9] the Council requested the Executive Director to consider UNEP's potential role in facilitating the monitoring of acidity of rainfall in developing countries where the extent of the acid rain problem had not yet been ascertained.

Terrestrial ecosystems

Tropical woodlands and forests ecosystems

The general public became more aware during 1983 of the consequences of unabated deforestation and forest depletion, and Governments responded by implementing programmes to reduce demands on their forest resources to a sustainable level. UNEP assisted by developing the basic information necessary to implement environ-

mentally sound tropical forest management programmes and by training scientists and technicians to continue the programmes.

Training workshops were organized to enable managers and planners to draw up national programmes to conserve tropical forest ecosystems. A workshop was held on the management of indigenous hardwoods in west and central Africa (Abidjan, Ivory Coast, October); participants from eight African countries decided that a research programme should be undertaken to improve the quality and growth rates of west African timber trees. A meeting on reforestation (Wageningen, the Netherlands, September) proposed a world-wide programme to address the basic causes of deforestation and forest degradation; it recommended that the global rate of tree planting be increased fivefold.

In its 24 May decision on programme matters,[7] the UNEP Council commended the initiatives taken by the countries of the South Asia Cooperative Environment Programme to overcome the regional deforestation problem by designating 1988 as Year of the Trees for South Asia. It invited other countries in the region to designate 1988 as Year of the Trees, and asked the Executive Director to support the formulation of projects in connection with the Year.

Mountain, island, coastal and other ecosystems

Awareness grew in 1983 of the fragility of some of the less resilient ecosystems, particularly those associated with coasts and islands. Five projects were being carried out by UNEP in this area; four were regional—two in Latin America and the Caribbean, one in Africa, and one in Europe and the Mediterranean—and one was global, dealing primarily with coastal and freshwater ecosystems.

Soils

During 1983, the international community became increasingly aware that the capacity of land and soil resources for further increases in agricultural production was rapidly diminishing. Increasing demand for food in Africa had resulted in an expansion of crop cultivation to marginal land. In Latin America, farming had encroached on forests, pasture land and bush. The average annual global loss of agricultural land to non-agricultural use was approximately 8 million hectares; erosion had destroyed an additional 3 million hectares and desertification 2 million, while 2 million had been lost to toxification.

A draft plan to implement the World Soils Policy was revised by UNEP. The policy sought to apply scientific management to the soils of the world; draw attention to the extent and importance of soil degradation and loss; monitor changes in soil quality and patterns of land use; slow down the loss of productive land to non-agricultural uses; enlarge the area and improve the quality of the world's agricultural land; and increase production on a sustainable basis.

Draft guidelines for the control of soil degradation were prepared, in co-operation with FAO. Another set of guidelines to improve food production and soil degradation control in the arid, semi-arid and humid tropics was prepared following a UNEP expert group meeting in June at Hyderabad, India; the meeting was attended by representatives of the International Crops Research Institute for the Semi-arid Tropics, the International Institute of Tropical Agriculture and the International Rice Research Institute. The third in a series of meetings on an international reference base for soil classification was held at Sofia, Bulgaria, in October with UNEP support; the meeting was intended to expedite progress towards an international agreement on soil classification.

In another development, the Save our Soils project, sponsored by UNEP and the International Federation of Institutes for Advanced Study, was extended to the end of 1983. A number of case-studies on the social, economic and legislative constraints to soil management were completed. A final report on the steps necessary to secure the application of technologies for soil degradation control was to be published. Implementation of a project on the impact of agricultural management on the environment, sponsored by UNEP and the USSR Commission for UNEP, continued throughout 1983; a map of the world's agroland-scape was prepared.

In its 24 May decision on programme matters,[7] the UNEP Council requested the Executive Director to finalize a draft plan of action for implementation of the World Soils Policy and submit it, together with a financial plan, to the Council in 1984.

Genetic resources

Expressing concern at increasing genetic erosion, the UNEP Council, on 24 May,[7] requested the Executive Director, in co-operation with Governments, and intergovernmental and non-governmental organizations, to continue to promote *in situ* conservation of endangered animal and plant genetic resources and to encourage international organizations to extend coverage of registers and gene banks to include all endangered plant and animal genetic resources.

Marine ecosystems

Marine pollution

An *Ad Hoc* Working Group of Experts on the Protection of the Marine Environment against Pol-

lution from Land-Based Sources held its first session (Geneva, 28 November-2 December 1983),[10] pursuant to a May 1982 decision of UNEP.[11] Experts from 25 countries and a number of United Nations agencies, and intergovernmental and non-governmental organizations attended the session.

The Group considered draft guidelines/principles, and agreed that they should be prepared in the form of a checklist of basic provisions and available options for certain measures, rather than as a model agreement, from which Governments might select, adapt or elaborate to meet the needs of particular marine environments. It also agreed on the importance of preventive action over control measures or remedial action, which should be adequately reflected in the guidelines/principles. Definitions, general provisions, the assessment of inputs, pathways and effects of pollution, its prevention, reduction and control, pollution through media shared by several States, transboundary pollution, liability and compensation, and institutional arrangements were reviewed in relation to the provisions of the 1982 United Nations Convention on the Law of the Sea.[12] Following the first reading of the draft guidelines/principles, the Group agreed that at its next meeting it should draft specific provisions. The Group recommended that UNEP/WHO undertake a study to identify a preferred option and set out definitions, interpretations and implementation requirements.

Annexed to the report were statements by States on the relationship between the draft guidelines/principles and the Convention on the Law of the Sea, as well as an exchange of letters concerning participation in the Working Group of an official of the Federal Environmental Agency of the Federal Republic of Germany which, the USSR stated, was located illegally in West Berlin.

The UNEP Council, in a decision of 24 May,[9] requested the Executive Director to consider reviewing the environmental implications of the disposal of radioactive wastes at sea; the review would be carried out in conjunction with the International Atomic Energy Agency and the Commission of the Convention on the Prevention of Marine Pollution by Dumping of Wastes and Other Matter. In another decision of the same date,[7] the Council appealed to all States to ensure compliance with the international legal obligation to protect and preserve the marine environment.

By the same decision, the Council also noted the co-operation since 1975 between the Intergovernmental Oceanographic Commission (IOC) and UNEP and encouraged further co-operation on such projects as the regional seas programme (see below), the Programme for the Global Investigation of Pollution in the Marine Environment and the Marine Pollution Monitoring System.

In 1983, the armed conflict between Iran and Iraq led to a dispute about pollution of the Persian Gulf from the spillage of oil (see p. 237).

Living marine resources

In 1983, UNEP efforts in regard to living marine resources were concentrated on finalizing a global plan for the conservation of marine mammals. Jointly with FAO, UNEP was developing a world-wide conservation programme for whales, seals and other endangered marine mammals. Specific activities included two expert meetings to formulate research proposals for cetaceans and sirenians, a review of information on the interaction between marine mammals and fisheries, and a compendium of legislative texts on conservation, management and utilization of marine mammals. UNEP also assisted IUCN to continue its biophysical classification of coastal and marine environments based on the natural variability of ecosystems.

The UNEP Council, on 24 May,[7] requested the Executive Director to finalize a financial plan for implementing the draft plan for the conservation of marine mammals.

Regional seas programme

Activities under UNEP regional seas programme included:

Mediterranean. A protocol for the Protection of the Mediterranean Seas against Pollution from Land-based Sources entered into force on 17 June.

Kuwait Action Plan region. UNEP continued to assist the Regional Organization for the Protection of the Marine Environment to co-ordinate the implementation of five major projects in co-operation with FAO, IAEA, IOC, IUCN and UNESCO. The Marine Emergency Mutual Aid Centre in Bahrain convened several technical meetings to formulate surveillance programmes to determine the extent of oil pollution in the region.

Caribbean. Fourteen mainland and island countries and the European Economic Community signed a framework convention and a protocol on co-operation in combating oil spills in the region. At the third meeting of the Caribbean Action Plan Monitoring Committee, several projects were chosen for immediate initiation, with financing from the Caribbean Trust Fund and to be implemented in co-operation with the Economic Commission for Latin America (ECLA), IMO, WHO, IOC, UNESCO, the Caribbean Community, the Caribbean Conservation Association, Cuba and Mexico.

West and Central Africa. Implementation of three priority projects dealing with marine pollution, contingency planning for pollution emergencies and coastal erosion control continued in co-operation with the United Nations Industrial Development Organization (UNIDO), FAO, IAEA, IMO, IOC, UNESCO, WHO,

the United Nations, and national institutions and experts.

Red Sea and Gulf of Aden. UNEP continued its support to marine pollution assessment activities through the Arab League Educational, Cultural and Scientific Organization. Implementation of the action plan continued, with environmental assessment and management activities in a number of the member countries.

South-west Pacific. Two regional meetings of legal and technical experts from 19 Pacific States were held in Nouméa, New Caledonia to revise a draft regional convention and two associated protocols, which were expected to be submitted to the Governments of the region for approval in 1984.

South-east Pacific. In July, plenipotentiaries from the south-east Pacific countries adopted a regional contingency plan to control oil pollution in cases of emergency. They also adopted three regional programmes on research, monitoring and control of marine pollution.

East Asian Seas. Five regional projects became operational in the region.

South Asian Seas. Activities were initiated towards the development of an action plan in the south Asian seas.

UNEP Council action. Welcoming the action plans adopted for the environmental protection of regional seas, the UNEP Council, on 24 May,[7] requested the Executive Director to designate the South Asian Seas as a region to be included in the regional seas programme in collaboration with the South Asia Co-operative Environment Programme and Governments in the region. It urged States to support the adoption and ratification of conventions and protocols for the protection and development of the regional marine environment and coastal areas. The Council urged Governments, United Nations and other organizations to support efforts to combat coastal erosion and marine pollution, and called on the Executive Director to provide funds to the regional seas programme as a high priority.

Freshwater ecosystems

In its 24 May omnibus decision on programme matters,[7] the UNEP Council requested the Executive Director to sharpen the focus of the water programme by promoting water pollution control measures; waste water management, rational water management including river basin management; support for the International Drinking Water Supply and Sanitation Decade (1981-1990) (see Chapter IX of this section); and development of inland fisheries and aquaculture. It also requested the Executive Director to accord high priority in those areas to training workshops, programmes and institution-building.

Biosphere preservation

The first International Biosphere Reserve Congress on conserving key species and ecosystems and enhancing the role of biosphere reserves in regional planning and development was held from 26 September to 2 October at Minsk, Byelorussian SSR, convened jointly by the Byelorussian SSR, the USSR, UNESCO and UNEP.

Solid waste management

An international symposium on solid waste management for developing countries, co-sponsored by the Federal Republic of Germany and UNEP, was held from 23 September to 7 October 1983 at Karlsruhe.

REFERENCES

[1]YUN 1981, p. 825, GA res. 36/166, 16 Dec. 1981. [2]E/1983/67-A/38/190. [3]YUN 1982, p. 1011, GA res. 37/137, 17 Dec. 1982. [4]UNEP/GC.12/2. [5]YUN 1975, p. 463. [6]UNEP/WG.78/10. [7]A/38/25 (dec. 11/7). [8]UNEP/GC.11/4 & Add.1. [9]A/38/25 (dec. 11/1). [10]UNEP/WG.92/4. [11]YUN 1982, p. 1022. [12]*Ibid.*, p. 181.

Environmental aspects of political, economic and other issues

Environmental law

Implementation of the 1981 Montevideo Programme

In his annual report to the UNEP Governing Council,[1] the Executive Director reported a clear shift in UNEP activities in environmental law during 1983 from nature conservation to man-made environmental problems, in particular the management of chemicals. The *Ad Hoc* Working Group of Legal and Technical Experts for the Elaboration of a Global Framework Convention for the Protection of the Ozone Layer and the *Ad Hoc* Working Group of Experts on the Protection of the Marine Environment against Pollution from Land-Based Sources, met separately at Geneva.

Preparatory work was initiated on other priority topics identified in the Montevideo Programme for the Development and Periodic Review of Environmental Law adopted at the 1981 *Ad Hoc* Meeting of Senior Governmental Officials Expert in Environmental Law,[2] particularly on the protection of international water resources against pollution (inter-agency consultations held in December 1983) and on guidelines for environmental impact assessment (working group meeting scheduled for 1984).

The UNEP Council, in a decision of 24 May 1983,[3] noting progress in implementing the environmental law programme, in particular the follow-up to the Montevideo Programme, expressed satisfaction that work had begun on guidelines and principles relating to the protection of the marine environment against pollution from land-based sources; environmentally sound transport, handling (including storage) and disposal of toxic and dangerous wastes; and information exchange on the trade in and use and handling of potentially harmful chemicals, in particular pesticides. The Council also expressed appreciation of the work of the *Ad Hoc* Working Group of Legal and Technical Experts for the Elaboration of a Global Framework Convention for the Protection of the Ozone Layer (see above, under ENVIRONMENTAL MONITORING). It called on Governments and organizations to participate in meetings on those topics, and appealed to them to provide financial resources and facilities to ensure full and timely implementation of the remaining parts of the Montevideo Programme, including the development of national environmental legislation.

In resolution 38/165, the General Assembly welcomed progress made in implementing the Montevideo Programme and appealed to Governments to provide financial resources for its full and timely implementation.

Role of the Group of Experts

The UNEP Council, on 24 May,[3] decided to entrust its Working Group of Experts on Environmental Law with the task of developing principles and guidelines for environmental impact assessment.

International instruments

In response to a 1975 General Assembly resolution,[4] the Secretary-General transmitted in August 1983 a report of the UNEP Executive Director on international conventions and protocols in the field of environment.[5] The Executive Director's report contained information on 14 recent international environment conventions and protocols and changes in the status of existing conventions. It recorded the conventions and protocols for which corrections had been introduced and other conventions pertaining to the environment.

UNEP Governing Council action. The UNEP Governing Council, on 24 May,[3] authorized the Executive Director to forward his report to the Assembly. It requested him to make available to it in 1984 an updated register of international treaties and other agreements on the environment, and to continue collecting and disseminating information on international and national legal machinery.

The Governing Council called on States not yet parties to existing conventions and protocols in the field of the environment to consider early adherence to them, in particular to the conventions on nature conservation. It appealed to contracting parties to promote implementation of those conventions, and appealed to all States to ensure compliance with the international legal obligation to protect and preserve the marine environment.

GENERAL ASSEMBLY ACTION

In December, the General Assembly, on the recommendation of the Second Committee, adopted decision 38/442 without vote.

Environment

At its 102nd plenary meeting, on 19 December 1983, the General Assembly, on the recommendation of the Second Committee:

(a) Took note of the note by the Secretary-General transmitting the report of the Executive Director of the United Nations Environment Programme on international conventions and protocols in the field of the environment;

(b) Took note of the report of the Secretary-General on interrelationships between resources, environment, people and development and decided to keep the matter under review.

General Assembly decision 38/442

Adopted without vote

Approved by Second Committee (A/38/702/Add.7) without vote, 14 December (meeting 56); draft orally proposed by Chairman; agenda item 78 _(g)_.
Meeting numbers. GA 38th session: 2nd Committee 56; plenary 102.

Material remnants of war

In October 1983, the Secretary-General submitted to the General Assembly, pursuant to a December 1982 request,[6] a report on the problem of remnants of war.[7] The report analysed the environmental and economic problems experienced by developing countries affected, the loss of life and property they had suffered, their demands for compensation and the extent to which responsible States were willing to compensate them. It further examined legal aspects and international co-operation required to solve the problem.

Annexed to the report was a study by a high-level group of experts, based on a meeting convened by the UNEP Executive Director (Geneva, 25-28 July 1983). The experts named land, sea and river mines, booby traps and dud munitions as the main remnants of war. They affected ecological balances, impeded socio-economic development, and caused loss of human life and property. Demands of affected countries for compensation had to be seen in the light of the suffering and devastation experienced by them. Some of the Governments responsible had indicated that the question of compensation might delay or jeopardize any practical solution, and therefore should be left aside. The legal aspects of the question were complex and subject to widely different interpretations. It was stated that international co-operation to solve the problem should be considered under two chief headings—how to tackle the existing problem and how to establish preventive measures.

Among the experts' recommendations was that the Assembly might wish to appeal to all States to ratify or accede to the 1980 Convention on Prohibitions or Restrictions on the Use of Certain Conventional Weapons.[8] Technical and historical information about the areas and objects to be cleared was required; similarly, there was an urgent need for a data base on technologies available for mine clearance. Suitable technology for clearing explosive remnants of war must be developed and be made readily available to affected countries. High-explosive munitions should be designed to have built-in mechanisms that rendered them harmless in due course. Clearance of remnants of war that constituted a threat to the environment should be carried out with international co-operation, preferably under the aegis of the United Nations. The experts suggested the convening of an international conference to discuss the problem. They also stressed that the issue of responsibility for damage and compensation should not be minimized or neglected; fair compensation must be considered.

GENERAL ASSEMBLY ACTION

On 19 December, on the recommendation of the Second Committee, the General Assembly adopted resolution 38/162 by recorded vote.

Remnants of war

The General Assembly,

Recalling its resolutions 3435(XXX) of 9 December 1975, 35/71 of 5 December 1980, 36/188 of 17 December 1981 and 37/215 of 20 December 1982 concerning the problem of remnants of war,

Recalling also decisions 80(IV) of 9 April 1976, 101(V) of 25 May 1977, 9/5 of 25 May 1981 and 10/8 of 28 May 1982 of the Governing Council of the United Nations Environment Programme,

Recalling further resolution 32 adopted by the Fifth Conference of Heads of State or Government of Non-Aligned Countries, held at Colombo from 16 to 19 August 1976, and resolution 26/11-P adopted by the Eleventh Islamic Conference of Foreign Ministers, held at Islamabad from 17 to 22 May 1980,

Convinced that the responsibility for the removal of the remnants of war should be borne by the countries that planted them,

Recognizing that the presence of the material remnants of war, particularly mines, in the territories of developing countries seriously impedes their development efforts and causes loss of human life and property,

1. _Takes note_ of the report of the Secretary-General and the study annexed thereto concerning the problem of remnants of war;

2. _Regrets_ that no concrete measures have been taken to solve the problem of remnants of war despite the various resolutions and decisions adopted thereon by the General Assembly and the Governing Council of the United Nations Environment Programme;

3. _Reiterates its support_ of the just demands of the developing countries affected by the implantation of mines and the presence of other remnants of war in their territories for full compensation from the States responsible for those remnants;

4. _Requests_ the Secretary-General, in co-operation with the Executive Director of the United Nations En-

vironment Programme, to continue to seek the views of States on the recommendations contained in section VIII of the study annexed to his report;

5. *Also requests* the Secretary-General to intensify his efforts to urge the States concerned to conduct bilateral consultations immediately, with the aim of concluding, as soon as possible, agreements for the solution of this problem, it being understood that the legitimate right of the affected developing countries to full compensation for damages due to them shall be ensured;

6. *Calls upon* all States to co-operate with the Secretary-General in carrying out the tasks requested of him in paragraphs 4 and 5 above, so as to enable him, in co-operation with the Executive Director of the United Nations Environment Programme, to submit to the General Assembly at its thirty-ninth session a report on the results of his consultations and endeavours with the States concerned.

General Assembly resolution 38/162

19 December 1983   Meeting 102   121-0-23 (recorded vote)

Approved by Second Committee (A/38/702/Add.7) by vote (111-0-23), 14 November (meeting 39); 44-nation draft (A/C.2/38/L.10), orally amended by Venezuela; agenda item 78 (g).

Sponsors: Afghanistan, Algeria, Bahrain, Bangladesh, Benin, Cape Verde, Central African Republic, Comoros, Congo, Cuba, Democratic Yemen, Djibouti, Egypt, Ghana, Guinea, Guinea-Bissau, Iran, Jordan, Kuwait, Lao People's Democratic Republic, Libyan Arab Jamahiriya, Madagascar, Maldives, Mali, Malta, Mauritania, Morocco, Nicaragua, Nigeria, Oman, Pakistan, Peru, Qatar, Rwanda, Saudi Arabia, Sierra Leone, Syrian Arab Republic, Togo, Tunisia, United Arab Emirates, Viet Nam, Yemen, Zambia, Zimbabwe.

Meeting numbers. GA 38th session: 2nd Committee 25, 30, 31, 39; plenary 102.

Recorded vote in Assembly as follows:

In favour: Afghanistan, Albania, Algeria, Angola, Argentina, Bahamas, Bahrain, Bangladesh, Barbados, Belize, Benin, Bhutan, Bolivia, Botswana, Brazil, Bulgaria, Burma, Burundi, Byelorussian SSR, Cape Verde, Central African Republic, Chad, Chile, China, Colombia, Congo, Costa Rica, Cuba, Cyprus, Czechoslovakia, Democratic Kampuchea, Democratic Yemen, Djibouti, Dominican Republic, Ecuador, Egypt, El Salvador, Ethiopia, Fiji, Gabon, Gambia, German Democratic Republic, Ghana, Guatemala, Guinea, Guinea-Bissau, Guyana, Haiti, Honduras, Hungary, India, Indonesia, Iran, Iraq, Ivory Coast, Jamaica, Jordan, Kenya, Kuwait, Lao People's Democratic Republic, Lebanon, Lesotho, Liberia, Libyan Arab Jamahiriya, Madagascar, Malawi, Malaysia, Maldives, Mali, Malta, Mauritania, Mauritius, Mexico, Mongolia, Morocco, Mozambique, Nepal, Nicaragua, Niger, Nigeria, Oman, Pakistan, Panama, Papua New Guinea, Paraguay, Peru, Philippines, Poland, Qatar, Romania, Rwanda, Saint Lucia, Saint Vincent and the Grenadines, Sao Tome and Principe, Saudi Arabia, Sierra Leone, Somalia, Sri Lanka, Sudan, Suriname, Swaziland, Syrian Arab Republic, Thailand, Togo, Trinidad and Tobago, Tunisia, Turkey, Uganda, Ukrainian SSR, USSR, United Arab Emirates, United Republic of Cameroon, United Republic of Tanzania, Upper Volta, Uruguay, Venezuela, Viet Nam, Yemen, Yugoslavia, Zaire, Zambia.

Against: None.

Abstaining: Australia, Austria, Belgium, Canada, Denmark, Finland, France, Germany, Federal Republic of, Greece, Iceland, Ireland, Italy, Japan, Luxembourg, Netherlands, New Zealand, Norway, Portugal, Senegal, Spain, Sweden, United Kingdom, United States.

Arms race and the environment

The UNEP Governing Council, on 23 May 1983,[9] appealed to Governments and the international community to halt the arms race and prevent a major threat to man and his environment. It noted with satisfaction the contribution in that field by United Nations organizations and other intergovernmental and non-governmental organizations. It requested the Executive Director to ensure that the environmental implications of armaments and warfare were taken into account in the documents discussed by the General Assembly and the Committee on Disarmament.

Environmental aspects of *apartheid*

In response to a May 1982 decision of the UNEP Council,[10] the Executive Director submitted in January 1983 a report[11] on impacts of South Africa's *apartheid* and bantustan policies on the environment. Among other social and economic problems, the report considered environmental impacts of border industries within or immediately outside the four "bantustans". It noted that the construction of factories and towns for black workers and their families and the provision of transportation for them were potential sources of environmental degradation. The report cautioned that basic environmental impact requirements which industries would be expected to comply with in the white areas of South Africa might be relaxed in order to attract industries to the bantustans. Specific information on the matter was not available, but there did not appear to be a categorical official statement affirming the Governments's concern with the observance of acceptable environmental safeguards as a condition for the establishment of such industries. The report considered it very important that assurances be clearly given, so that the bantustans were not turned into "pollution havens" where industrial development was rendered cheap at the cost of environmental devastation. The report concluded that the outlook for the black population was still gloomy. Such attempts as the South African Government had made at improvement had not had any real effect, partly because the rapidly growing dimensions of the problems created by its own racial policies had largely nullified those efforts.

By a decision of 23 May,[12] the Governing Council reaffirmed its condemnation of *apartheid* and called on the world community to bring that historical injustice to a quick end. It requested the Executive Director to continue to monitor the environmental impact of *apartheid*, with specific reference to industry in urban townships and in bantustans. It further requested him, in conjunction with other United Nations agencies, to respond to appeals from national liberation movements for assistance to victims of *apartheid*.

The General Assembly, in resolution 38/165, took note of the UNEP Council decision directed at promoting public awareness of the plight of the victims of *apartheid*.

Environment and development

Throughout 1983, UNEP continued its efforts to provide guidance on the integration of environmental considerations into development decision-making. Significant additions were made to the guidance available on the application of social cost-benefit analysis to environmental measures and environmental aspects of development projects.

UNEP published the first volume of a report, *Environmental Decision-Making*, intended to explain the use of social cost-benefit analysis in formulating development projects.

The use of environmental impact assessment methodology spread in the developing countries. To facilitate the exchange of information, UNEP and the Government of China convened a meeting of experts in Guangzhou in March 1983. Discussions focused on the problems and possibilities of applying available methodology in developing countries. In co-operation with the Republic of Korea, UNEP prepared a pilot case-study on Gwachon New Town Development; the study applied to urban development the Environmental Impact Assessment Test Model developed by the UNEP Regional Office for Asia and the Pacific.

Rapid economic development had caused serious congestion and pollution problems in metropolitan areas of several developing countries. A case-study of economic development in the Chubu region of Japan was initiated by UNEP, in co-operation with the United Nations Centre for Regional Development, the United Nations Department of Technical Co-operation for Development and the Government of Japan, the aim of which was to prepare guidelines for integrated physical, environmental, economic and social development in an area with a fragile ecosystem and high population density.

Among projects approved for financing under a general trust fund for a co-ordinated interdisciplinary United Nations programme on interrelationships between resources, environment, people and development (see Chapter I of this section), was the first phase of a project on deforestation of the Himalayan foothills, implemented by UNEP in collaboration with the United Nations, ILO, FAO and UNESCO.

The year also saw the development within UNEP of a clearing-house mechanism for the mobilization of resources over and above regular contributions to meet serious environmental problems in developing countries. The clearing-house concept, which had emerged at the 1982 session of the UNEP Council,[13] incorporated a programming element and a technical assistance element. The UNEP Executive Director reported to the Governing Council in a February 1983 note[14] that the Netherlands and Sweden had pledged $1 million each to the clearing house for 1982-1983 and the Federal Republic of Germany had offered support in kind, in the form of consultants, experts, training and equipment, for the same period. UNEP would provide assistance to developing countries in formulating projects designed to meet their most serious environmental problems.

In a November 1983 report on environmental matters,[15] ACC noted that the preparations by UNEP to establish a clearing-house facility to act as intermediary between donors and recipients in reinforcing the national capacity of developing countries in dealing with their environmental problems, including finding the necessary funds, had progressed to the point where the facility was becoming operational. ACC suggested that United Nations organizations be informed of potential projects.

UNEP Council action. In its 24 May 1983 decision on policy matters,[16] the UNEP Council requested the Executive Director, in co-operation with Governments and intergovernmental and non-governmental organizations, to continue to promote the exchange of information and experience with respect to the integration of environmental considerations in development activities, with a view to better co-ordinating efforts and enhancing general understanding of the concept of sustainable development.

In a decision of 23 May,[17] the Council requested the Executive Director to pursue his efforts to obtain additional resources to deal with serious environmental problems in developing countries.

GENERAL ASSEMBLY ACTION

The General Assembly, in resolution 38/165, reaffirmed the need to strengthen the co-ordinating role of UNEP and the need for additional resources to assist developing countries in dealing with serious environmental problems. It urged the Executive Director to intensify his efforts in this area.

Environment and industry

The environmental impact of industrial activities received continued attention from UNEP in 1983. Interest grew in the role that industry could play in the fight against acid rain, trade in hazardous substances and waste management. A survey of industry experience with environmental management was begun, in preparation for the World Industry Conference on Environmental Management to be held in Paris in 1984. The three-day conference was to identify issues for action by industry, Governments, and intergovernmental and non-governmental organizations.

The UNEP Council, on 24 May,[16] welcomed the Executive Director's call to industry to convene an international conference on ways that industry might contribute more effectively to environmentally sound development and promote an exchange of information on industrial pollution control, waste recycling, and low-waste and non-waste technologies. It requested the widest possible participation in the conference by industry, Governments, international organizations and other groups, as well as geographical balance.

In its decision on programme matters,[3] adopted on the same day, the Council endorsed the general approach proposed by the Executive Director in the industry and transportation component of the programme budget. It encouraged him to maintain a balanced consultative process, involving Governments, the United Nations, industry and relevant international organizations, to ensure that activities in the industrial sector were coherent and sharply focused, efficiently conducted and fully co-ordinated.

Environmental information

In its 24 May omnibus decision on programme matters,[3] the UNEP Council noted that UNEP public information activities were being reformed and the publications programme streamlined to ensure closer co-operation with non-governmental organizations and better communication of information to the regions and media. The Council recommended that the reform be based on a cost-effectiveness analysis to be commissioned from a consultant, whose terms of reference should include examination of target groups, current and projected impact, and current estimated costs and suggested improvements. It urged that UNEP extend its support to regional information activities and requested the Executive Director to ensure that reports on UNEP projects were distributed to Governments and, within available resources, to scientific institutions and non-governmental organizations.

By the same decision, the Council dealt with public information in the different regions. It requested the Executive Director to provide a public information programme to suit the needs of the African and Asian and Pacific regions.

By another decision of the same date,[16] the Council encouraged the Executive Director to continue exploring new information technology and use it in support of the Programme's information role, and requested him to report on the matter in 1984. It also requested the Executive Director to continue to promote the exchange of information on the integration of environmental considerations in development activities.

Environmental education and training

During 1983, environmental training components were part of many UNEP projects: the International Referral System for sources of environmental information (INFOTERRA) organized three training courses, with 40 participants in all; three training courses in desertification control, specifically on ecological studies, soil erosion and water

conservation, and sand dune fixation, were given for 75 technicians from developing countries; 185 participants were trained in eight separate regional training courses under the regional seas programme; and the International Register of Potentially Toxic Chemicals (IRPTC), in conjunction with the USSR Commission for UNEP (UNEP-COM), held an international training course in preventive toxicology for 20 participants from developing countries.

An international post-graduate course on resource management and environmental impact assessment in developing countries organized by UNEP, UNESCO and the German Democratic Republic, began in October 1983 at the Technical University of Dresden with 15 participants. UNEP also continued to co-operate with the International Centre for Training in Environmental Sciences (CIFCA), a major institution providing environmental training for participants from the developing countries of Latin America and the Caribbean.

Twenty-one experts from 13 African countries, as well as Canada and Trinidad and Tobago, met at Nairobi, from 12 to 15 April, to draft a regional programme for environmental education and training. Representatives of UNESCO, the Economic Commission for Africa, the United Nations Children's Fund, UNCHS and seven non-governmental organizations also attended.

UNEP Council action. In its 24 May omnibus decision on programme matters,[3] the UNEP Council requested the Executive Director to assist the countries of Asia and the Pacific region to promote environmental education and training. It also asked him to convene a meeting of experts from Governments and the academic and scientific communities within the region to develop an action programme, as well as public awareness.

The Council commended the Network of Environmental Training Institutions in Latin America and the Caribbean, and recommended that Governments intensify support for it. It requested the Executive Director to disseminate information on the Network and recommended that he continue financial support to it, particularly for environmental training.

REFERENCES
[1]UNEP/GC.12/2. [2]YUN 1981, p. 839. [3]A/38/25 (dec. 11/7). [4]YUN 1975, p. 443, GA res. 3436(XXX), 9 Dec. 1975. [5]A/38/305. [6]YUN 1982, p. 1027, GA res. 37/215, 20 Dec. 1982. [7]A/38/383. [8]YUN 1981, p. 76. [9]A/38/25 (dec. 11/6). [10]YUN 1982, p. 1028. [11]UNEP/GC.11/3/Add.6. [12]A/38/25 (dec. 11/5). [13]YUN 1982, p. 999. [14]UNEP/GC.11/3/Add.5. [15]ACC/1983/28. [16]A/38/25 (dec. 11/1). [17]*Ibid.* (dec. 11/11).

Chapter XVII

Human settlements

The United Nations Centre for Human Settlements (UNCHS), also known as Habitat, continued to make progress in its work programme during 1983, completing 61 technical co-operation projects and beginning 69 new ones. The Centre also made plans for the observance of the International Year of Shelter for the Homeless (1987) (IYSH).

The Commission on Human Settlements, which performs the functions of the governing body of UNCHS, held its sixth session at Helsinki, Finland, from 25 April to 6 May 1983. Items on its agenda included UNCHS activities, its work programme and proposed budget for 1984-1985, land for human settlements, and IYSH. The Commission adopted 14 resolutions and six decisions based on recommendations of two committees of the whole. Two of the resolutions—on human settlements in the Israeli-occupied Palestinian territories and the International Year—required action by the General Assembly.

As recommended by the Commission, the Assembly, in resolution 38/168, endorsed a programme of immediate international action for the International Year. Human settlements were the subject of three other resolutions adopted by the Assembly in December. By resolution 38/167 A, the Assembly reaffirmed its conviction that human settlements activities could play a leading role in stimulating development and in enhancing the quality of life of the poor and the disadvantaged. By resolution 38/167 B, the Assembly took note of the Secretary-General's report summarizing an October decision of the Administrative Committee on Co-ordination (ACC) concerning co-ordination of human settlements programmes within the United Nations system.

Topics related to this chapter. Middle East: territories occupied by Israel—settlements policy, living conditions of Palestinians. Development and international economic and social policy: International Development Strategy. Economic assistance, disasters and emergency relief: disaster preparedness and prevention. Regional economic and social activities. Environment. Refugees.

Programme and finances of UNCHS

Programme policy

Both the Economic and Social Council and the General Assembly took note of the report of the Commission on Human Settlements on its 1983 session.[1]

The Assembly, in resolution 38/167 A of 19 December, expressed appreciation to those who had supported the international effort to promote human settlements development through UNCHS activities, and again appealed to States, particularly the developed countries, to contribute or increase their contributions to the United Nations Habitat and Human Settlements Foundation.

ECONOMIC AND SOCIAL COUNCIL ACTION

In July, the Economic and Social Council, on the recommendation of its First (Economic) Committee, adopted without vote decision 1983/169.

International co-operation in the field of human settlements

At its 39th plenary meeting, on 25 July 1983, the Council:

(*a*) Took note of the report of the Commission on Human Settlements on the work of its sixth session and decided to transmit it, together with the recommendations of the Commission, to the General Assembly for consideration and action;

(*b*) Also took note of the reports of the Secretary-General on the implementation of the Programme for the International Year of Shelter for the Homeless and on the living conditions of the Palestinian people in the occupied Palestinian territories, and decided to transmit those reports to the General Assembly.

Economic and Social Council decision 1983/169

Adopted without vote

Approved by First Committee (E/1983/112) without vote, 15 July (meeting 14); agenda item 15.
Meeting number. ESC 39.

GENERAL ASSEMBLY ACTION

On 19 December 1983, on the recommendation of the Second (Economic and Financial) Committee, the General Assembly adopted without vote resolution 38/167 A.

Report of the Commission on Human Settlements
The General Assembly,

Recalling its resolutions 3201(S-VI) and 3202(S-VI) of 1 May 1974, containing the Declaration and the Programme of Action on the Establishment of a New International Economic Order, 3281(XXIX) of 12 December 1974, containing the Charter of Economic Rights and Duties of States, and 3362(S-VII) of 16 September 1975 on development and international economic co-operation,

Recalling also its resolutions 32/162 of 19 December 1977 on institutional arrangements for international co-operation in the field of human settlements and 34/116 of 14 December 1979 on the strengthening of human settlements activities,

Taking note of Economic and Social Council decision 1983/169 of 25 July 1983 on international co-operation in the field of human settlements,

Having considered the report of the Commission on Human Settlements on the work of its sixth session,

1. *Takes note* of the report of the Commission on Human Settlements;

2. *Commends* the Commission on Human Settlements on the effective manner in which it continues to discharge its mandate in assisting Governments to address the serious problems of human settlements development, as reflected in the various substantive recommendations adopted by it;

3. *Reaffirms its conviction* that human settlements activities can play a leading role in stimulating national economic and social development and in the enhancement of the quality of life of the poor and the disadvantaged, particularly in the developing countries;

4. *Expresses its appreciation* to those Governments and to others that have so far provided financial support for the international effort to promote human settlements development through the activities of the United Nations Centre for Human Settlements (Habitat);

5. *Appeals once again* to Member States, particularly the developed countries and others in a position to do so, to make voluntary contributions, if they have not yet done so, or, as appropriate, to increase their voluntary contributions to the United Nations Habitat and Human Settlements Foundation in support of the activities of the Centre.

General Assembly resolution 38/167 A

19 December 1983   Meeting 102   Adopted without vote

Approved by Second Committee (A/38/702/Add.8) without vote (parts A and B together), 21 November (meeting 45); draft by Vice-Chairman (A/C.2/38/L.72, part A), based on informal consultations on 4-nation draft (A/C.2/38/L.19, part A); agenda item 78 *(h)*.

Meeting numbers. GA 38th session: 2nd Committee 30, 45; plenary 102.

By the original draft, introduced in the Second Committee by the Netherlands, also on behalf of Gabon, Kenya and the Philippines, the Assembly would have commended the Commission on its sound and practical approach to human settlements development, instead of commending it on the effective manner in which it continued to discharge its mandate. In paragraph 3, it would have reaffirmed its conviction that human settlements activities could play a leading role in stimulating national economic and social development, particularly in a period of economic recession.

Work programme for 1984-1985

A draft work programme and programme budget for the biennium 1984-1985,[2] the first to be presented within the framework of the 1984-1989 medium-term plan, was submitted by the UNCHS Executive Director in January 1983. Under a decision adopted by the Commission on Human Settlements in 1981,[3] the programme was organized on the basis of eight subprogramme

areas, instead of the previous six selected at the 1976 Habitat: United Nations Conference on Human Settlements.[4] The eight subprogrammes were: settlement policies and strategies; settlement planning; shelter and community services; development of the indigenous construction sector; low-cost infrastructure for human settlements; land use; mobilization of finance for human settlements development; and institutions and management. Public participation was an integral part of each subprogramme, the Executive Director pointed out. The report provided details of programme elements, outputs, activities and resources.

The Commission, by a decision of 6 May 1983,[5] commended the UNCHS Executive Director for producing a work programme which gave attention to all the high-priority objectives of the medium-term plan, while, at the same time, observing maximum restraint in requesting resources for programme execution. It approved the proposed outputs and activities of the 1984-1985 work programme, endorsing it as a whole as amended, as one that provided the minimum level of activity necessary for UNCHS to achieve the goals fixed by the Commission. It expressed concern that the programme level envisaged was far too low compared to the scale of problems to be addressed, and requested the Executive Director, in implementing the work programme, to take account of the comments by delegations during the debate on the various programme elements.

Administrative and budgetary questions

Extrabudgetary resources

Responding to a May 1982 request of the Commission on Human Settlements,[6] the UNCHS Executive Director submitted a report in January 1983 on the use by the Centre of extrabudgetary resources during 1982-1983, and projections for their use during 1984-1985.[7]

Funds were available to UNCHS from the regular United Nations budget and from the United Nations Habitat and Human Settlements Foundation (see below). Additional extrabudgetary funds for 1982-1983 came primarily from three sources: programme support income from the execution of projects financed by the United Nations Development Programme (UNDP) and trust funds ($4,112,000), a subvention from the World Food Programme ($206,000) and programme support from the United Nations Environment Programme (UNEP) ($114,000). Of the total $4,432,000, an amount of $4,045,000 was spent, mostly ($3,725,000) for substantive and administrative support to field projects.

In addition, UNCHS received funds from two sources: contributions by Governments to trust funds and contributions in support of specific projects. During 1982-1983, trust fund contributions and pledges amounted to $4,931,000, and Belgium, Denmark, France, the Federal Republic of Germany, Italy, the Netherlands, Norway and Sweden provided funds to recruit 36 associate experts for technical co-operation projects. Donors such as Belgium, Denmark, the Netherlands and the World Bank made contributions in support of a number of training projects; UNCHS also entered into agreements with the Libyan Arab Jamahiriya, Somalia and Upper Volta to implement technical co-operation projects in their countries, using earmarked contributions from them. In addition, contributions and pledges were received from several private organizations.

In a decision of 6 May,[5] the Commission appealed to Governments to do their utmost to ensure that extrabudgetary resources were made available to UNCHS.

UN Habitat and Human Settlements Foundation

Expenditures of the United Nations Habitat and Human Settlements Foundation for 1982-1983 totalled $6,718,502, including $199,841 in expenditures for the International Year of Shelter for the Homeless (1987). The excess of income over expenditure was $2,279,375.

Efforts to collect unpaid pledges should be intensified, the Board of Auditors stated in its financial report and audited financial statements on the Foundation.[8] Unpaid pledges receivable as at 31 December 1983 amounted to $2,710,365, out of which $294,799 related to the period prior to the biennium. The Board noted that some unpaid pledges needed adjustment because of fluctuations in exchange rates, and recommended that such adjustments be made. It also recommended that, for effective implementation and monitoring of projects, work plans and reports should be prepared in time and in the prescribed format; experts/consultants should be fielded on schedule, and projects planned appropriately to avoid frequent revisions.

Contributions

The Commission on Human Settlements, by a decision of 6 May,[9] noted with concern that voluntary contributions to the Foundation for 1982-1983 were far lower than for 1980-1981 and that a minimum of $7-$8 million in contributions would be needed to carry out the work programme for 1986-1987. It urgently called on States, particularly the developed countries, to make or increase their contributions.

The General Assembly in resolution 38/167 A reiterated that appeal. In 1983, contributions from 40 countries totalling $3 million were received;

pledges for future years from 38 countries totalled $1.9 million.

CONTRIBUTIONS TO THE UN HABITAT
AND HUMAN SETTLEMENTS FOUNDATION
(as at 31 December 1983; in US dollar equivalent)

Country	1983 payment	Pledges for future years
Algeria	16,560	8,500
Bangladesh	5,000	5,000
Barbados	7,768	1,000
Belgium	393,166	187,793
Bhutan	500	—
Botswana	2,127	1,835
Canada	487,696	616,251
Chile	—	5,000
Colombia	12,000	12,000
Congo	3,572	3,769
Cyprus	781	370
Democratic Yemen	—	500
Denmark	252,387	—
Egypt	—	15,213
Finland	206,153	88,496
France	32,110	77,987
India	101,136	100,000
Indonesia	10,000	10,000
Italy	38,517	—
Jamaica	25,033	10,000
Jordan	3,000	—
Kenya	73,674	45,000
Kuwait	30,000	15,000
Lesotho	6,000	9,000
Liberia	250	—
Madagascar	1,316	—
Malawi	1,000	750
Netherlands	481,183	—
Norway	66,437	108,844
Pakistan	—	5,000
Papua New Guinea	6,000	5,294
Philippines	357,663	50,000
Qatar	30,000	—
Republic of Korea	—	20,000
Somalia	664	1,500
Sri Lanka	4,000	4,000
Sudan	—	2,500
Swaziland	4,070	—
Sweden	224,250	434,538
Trinidad and Tobago	1,000	1,005
Tunisia	24,000	21,044
Turkey	38,835	60,000
Uganda	1,910	1,799
United Republic of Cameroon	—	3,571
United Republic of Tanzania	—	3,287
Venezuela	210,000	—
Zaire	32,000	1,000
Zambia	10	7,463
Total	3,191,768	1,944,309

SOURCE: A/39/5/Add.8/Corr.1.

Budget for 1984-1985

The Executive Director's report on the proposed programme budget for 1984-1985,[10] submitted to the Commission in February 1983, showed projected income of $11,252,700—$8.5 million ($5.5 million in carry-over balance from 1983, plus $3 million in expected contributions and pledges) for the general funds of the Foundation and $2,752,700 for the International Year of Shelter for the Homeless. Expenditures of the Foundation were estimated at $6,794,900, while the cost of activities for the International Year was estimated at $2,134,200.

In a report to the Commission in March 1983,[11] the Advisory Committee on Administrative and Budgetary Questions (ACABQ) stated that it would not object to the Executive Director's estimates for programme and programme support costs. Nevertheless, ACABQ pointed out that the estimate of $896,500 for programme support costs was $187,800, or 26.5%, more than the 1982-1983 estimate. In the light of the financial difficulties being faced by the Foundation, it believed that every effort should be made to reduce programme support costs. ACABQ had no objection to the estimates for the International Year, although those for communications and travel appeared to be on the high side.

The Commission, by a decision of 6 May 1983,[9] approved the proposed allocations for 1984-1985 and the proposed utilization of resources for the International Year.

REFERENCES

[1]A/38/8. [2]HS/C/6/5. [3]YUN 1981, p. 846. [4]YUN 1976, p. 441. [5]A/38/8 (dec. 6/16). [6]YUN 1982, p. 1035. [7]HS/C/6/7 & Corr.1. [8]A/39/5/Add.8 & Corr.1. [9]A/38/8 (dec. 6/17). [10]HS/C/6/6/Rev.1. [11]HS/C/6/6/Add.1.

Human settlements activities

Habitat Centre

In a report to the Commission on Human Settlements on the 1983 activities of UNCHS,[1] the Executive Director described progress made in implementing the 1982-1983 work programme, which was structured on the basis of the six priority areas selected at the 1976 Habitat Conference:[2] settlement policies and strategies; settlement planning; shelter, infrastructure and services; land policy; public participation; and institutions and management.

Reports on human settlements policy options, trends and guidelines and on human settlements policy issues in Asia and the Pacific were completed under the first subprogramme. An outline of the quinquennial *Global Report on Human Settlements* was prepared; the report itself was to be published in 1985. Questionnaires were sent out to determine progress by member States in implementing the recommendations for national action adopted at the 1976 Conference and to collect information on financial and other assistance provided to and among developing countries for human settlements. Theme papers on comprehensive approaches to training and information for human settlements were completed. The Centre participated in expert group meetings to establish the framework for an International Conference on Population which was to be held in Mexico in 1984 (see Chapter XIV of this section).

A forecast of settlement conditions up to the year 2000, with respect to population, economic activities, infrastructure and sanitation strategies, was being prepared under the settlement planning subprogramme. Reports on settlement planning in Latin America and the integration of physical planning with economic and social planning in Asia and the Pacific were being made ready for publication, and reports were completed on data management and urban planning and design of settlements in arid and semi-arid areas. A project was initiated in cooperation with Turkey on environmentally sound regional land-use planning for the metropolitan area of Cukurova, while assistance was provided in the development of Dodoma, the new capital of the United Republic of Tanzania.

Under the subprogramme on shelter, infrastructure and services, case-studies on the decision-making processes in housing programming were completed in Sri Lanka and Zambia. In co-operation with Finland, an expert group meeting on decision-making procedures was held at Nairobi, Kenya, in November. Work continued on upgrading squatter settlements in the Asia and Pacific region. Case-studies on financing human settlements were prepared, based on experiences in Brazil, Egypt, Kenya, India and Indonesia. Research was undertaken on the role played by community-based financial institutions in mobilizing funds for improving low-income settlements; studies were carried out of credit unions and housing co-operatives in Jamaica, Kenya and Zambia. The upgrading of inner-city slums was the subject of an expert group meeting held at Bangkok, Thailand, in November; four films were produced for training purposes on the upgrading of slums, describing experiences in Barrio Escopa (Manila, Philippines), Hann-Dalifort (Dakar, Senegal), Cissin (Ougadougou, Upper Volta) and Maseru (Lesotho). Research was completed on the construction industry in nine countries (Bolivia, Greece, Honduras, Kenya, Mexico, Pakistan, Syrian Arab Republic, Tunisia and Yemen); reports were prepared on the contribution of the construction sector to national development goals and on government guidelines to improve the efficiency of the building industry. Transportation requirements in urban and rural settlements were examined with emphasis on current deficiencies.

Activities under the land policy subprogramme consisted mostly of research on land-resource management and monitoring of trends in land policies and land control measures. Data were collected from technical co-operation projects, government sources, regional commissions, the United Nations system and non-governmental organizations (NGOs).

The main project of the public participation subprogramme was the preparation of a training programme in community participation, conducted in co-operation with the Danish International Development Agency (DANIDA). During the first phase of the project, a reader in community participation was issued, and computer print-outs of a bibliography and a directory of institutions were completed. Another project involved the preparation of a technical report on promoting organized self-help through co-operative modes. Two films on mobilizing public participation in self-help construction were produced.

Four training courses in management of human settlements were held under the institutions and management subprogramme: at Bangkok, from March to May; Rio de Janeiro, Brazil, June; USSR, August; and . Washington, D.C., October/November. Three issues of *Habitat News* were published in 1983 with French and Arabic supplements, bibliographic and technical notes and a regular NGO news supplement. Nine television and 50 radio programmes were produced. A booklet on UNCHS activities in Arabic-speaking countries was issued in Arabic and English, and French and Spanish adaptations of the UNCHS draft *Thesaurus* were published. Some 38 UNCHS publications in several languages were currently available.[3]

Other UNCHS activities involved data-management assistance, including training workshops, special advisory services, project execution, software development, internal management support information and project monitoring. During 1983, workshops were conducted in Jamaica and Finland. An urban data management software package developed by UNCHS for use in human settlements planning received wide circulation. In addition, a new software package on housing finance was developed and installed in the Seychelles, and UNCHS was preparing it for wider distribution.

Special technical advisory services continued to be provided by the Centre to developing countries, with emphasis on the least developed, the land-locked and the island developing countries. In 1983, more than 31 missions were fielded in such areas as innovative use of local building materials, low-cost housing technologies and development of finance institutions.

Technical co-operation

The biennium 1982-1983 started with 122 technical co-operation projects, 61 of which were completed. Sixty-nine new projects were begun, so that at the end of the biennium 130 projects were ongoing.

These ongoing projects were divided among the six subprogrammes as follows: 17 related to national settlement policies and strategies; 27 to settlement planning; 49 to shelter, infrastructure and services; four to national land policy and land control measures; two to public participation; and 31 to institutions and management.

Sectoral support activities, whose main objectives were to identify national technical co-operation needs in the field of human settlements and to assist Governments in formulating project documents and proposals for financing by UNDP and other sources, were also provided by UNCHS. During 1983, missions were fielded to Afghanistan, Argentina, Chad, Costa Rica, Djibouti, Ethiopia, Haiti, Jamaica, Kenya, Panama, Papua New Guinea, the Philippines, Sao Tome and Principe, Tonga, Turkey, Venezuela and Zambia. In 10 cases, one or more project proposals and project documents were prepared and submitted to UNDP and/or Governments concerned. For the 1984-1985 biennium, UNDP funding for sectoral support activities was reduced by half.

International Year of Shelter for the Homeless (1987)

The UNCHS Executive Director reported to the Commission on Human Settlements in February 1983[4] on the International Year of Shelter for the Homeless (1987) (IYSH) which was proclaimed by the General Assembly in 1981.[5] He stated that, in a January 1983 appeal to Governments, he had asked them to pledge a significant financial contribution in support of IYSH. He pointed out that, in order to achieve its goals, a distinctive approach would be required, which would include a commitment by Member States to improve the shelter and neighbourhoods of at least some of the poor before the International Year began. Further, most of the limited funds would be used to support and stimulate national and local action through shelter demonstration projects. An information programme would concentrate not on publicizing problems but on searching for solutions and making successful results more widely known.

The emphasis would be on projects leading to affordable improvements in shelter and neighbourhoods for the many rather than providing conventional houses for a few, the Executive Director stated. Priority would be given to information and training projects related to self-help construction and the use of local skills, methods and building materials. The self-help efforts of the poor would be encouraged. Three major projects were under way with a total investment of $5 million—training for self-help construction, supported by DANIDA; the upgrading of slums and squatter settlements in Karachi, Pakistan, supported by the Bank of Commerce and Credit International Foundation; and a national self-help information and training programme in Sri Lanka, supported by the Netherlands and Sri Lanka.

Guidelines for shelter demonstration projects stated that they should demonstrate new approaches to basic problems such as providing shelter, drinking water, sanitation and waste disposal; improving health conditions; upgrading infrastructure and services for the poor, including roads, public transportation and medical, educational and recreational facilities; generating construction jobs; and using low-cost building techniques and materials. Projects could range from preparing pamphlets or posters showing how to make basic improvements, to conducting training courses in construction skills for local labour, to organizing co-operative and community improvement efforts.

Activities associated with the International Year would take place in three phases. From 1983 to 1986, new ways of improving the shelter and neighbourhoods of at least some of the poor would be devised and tested around the world. Project results would be made widely available so that during 1987 national policy makers could adapt shelter programmes to meet the needs of the majority of the poor. The new methods, policies and programmes would require constant refinement as a part of national development plans between 1988 and 2000.

Countries were asked to designate as soon as possible national focal points to receive and distribute information on the International Year. A budget of $4.9 million for 1983-1987 was proposed; of that total, approximately $4.3 million in voluntary contributions was needed.

In a later report,[6] the Executive Director noted that, as at 31 December 1983, voluntary contributions for the International Year totalling $1.8 million had been pledged by 13 developing and two developed countries; in addition, the Netherlands had pledged $790,000 to the national IYSH project in Sri Lanka. Meanwhile, consultations had been held on the International Year with many United Nations organizations and agencies, as well as NGOs.

Three resolutions on the International Year were adopted by the Commission on Human Settlements on 5 May 1983. The first was a resolution requiring action by the General Assembly.[7] It would appeal to Governments, financial institutions, and intergovernmental and nongovernmental organizations to support the International Year; it included an annex on national action required, the establishment of focal points, assessing needs, implementation of demonstration projects, and progress reports. Expressing deep concern at the increasing magnitude of the refugee problem, the Commission, by a second resolution,[8] declared that no human being should be ejected from his lawful home or land by any foreign Government or as a result of foreign intervention. By a third resolution,[9] the Commission

requested the UNCHS Executive Director to give top priority to recruiting project consultants and experts from the developing countries to identify and implement demonstration projects for IYSH.

Pursuant to a December 1982 Assembly request,[10] the Secretary-General submitted a report in May 1983 on the implementation of the programme for the International Year.[11] He reviewed action by the Commission, the intergovernmental body responsible for organizing IYSH, at its 1983 session. With regard to contributions, he stated that initial support for the International Year had been strong, and that the pledges received were already sufficient to carry the programme to the end of 1984.

By decision 1983/169, the Economic and Social Council took note of the Secretary-General's report and decided to transmit it to the Assembly.

GENERAL ASSEMBLY ACTION

On 19 December, on the recommendation of the Second Committee, the General Assembly adopted resolution 38/168 without vote.

International Year of Shelter for the Homeless
The General Assembly,

Recalling its resolution 37/221 of 20 December 1982, in which it proclaimed the year 1987 International Year of Shelter for the Homeless,

Taking note of the report of the Secretary-General concerning measures and activities to be undertaken prior to and during the International Year of Shelter for the Homeless,

Taking note also of Economic and Social Council decision 1983/169 of 25 July 1983,

Convinced that special efforts need to be made by States and the international community in order to reverse the chronic deterioration in shelter and living conditions suffered by the majority of the poor in urban and rural settlements, especially in developing countries,

Convinced also that national programmes and demonstration projects for the International Year of Shelter for the Homeless should be launched as soon as possible, since most of the action and resources for the Year will be required at the national and local levels,

Noting with appreciation the voluntary contributions and pledges that Governments have so far made for the International Year of Shelter for the Homeless,

1. *Welcomes and endorses* the overall plans for activities before, during and after the International Year of Shelter for the Homeless and the priorities for national and international action during 1983-1984 contained in the report of the Executive Director of the United Nations Centre for Human Settlements (Habitat) to the Commission on Human Settlements at its sixth session;

2. *Calls upon* all Governments, especially those of developing countries, to give renewed political commitment and priority to the improvement of the shelter and neighbourhoods of the poor and to allocate the necessary resources to meet the objectives of the International Year of Shelter for the Homeless;

3. *Endorses* the proposals contained in the annex to the present resolution on national action needed before

April 1984 in order to launch the International Year of Shelter for the Homeless quickly and effectively;

4.　*Urges* all organizations and bodies of the United Nations system and other interested intergovernmental, non-governmental and national organizations to make special efforts through existing and new programmes, including those aimed at involving public-opinion leaders and large groups of the population, to help achieve the objectives of the International Year of Shelter for the Homeless;

5.　*Appeals* to all Governments, especially those of developed countries and others in a position to do so, and to international financial institutions, intergovernmental and non-governmental organizations, to provide effective financial and other support for the programme for the International Year of Shelter for the Homeless.

ANNEX
National action needed before April 1984 for the International Year of Shelter for the Homeless

1.　Most of the action and resources for the International Year of Shelter for the Homeless will be required at the national and local levels. The programme for the Year must be launched quickly and effectively, so that most of the demonstration projects can be completed, or be at a stage where results can be evaluated, by late 1986.

2.　The following national action should be undertaken by countries before the seventh session of the Commission on Human Settlements, to be held in April 1984:

(*a*)　Establish national focal points for the International Year of Shelter for the Homeless;

(*b*)　Assess the existing situation and future needs;

(*c*)　Begin implementation of demonstration projects for the Year.

A. Establishment of national focal points for the International Year of Shelter for the Homeless

3.　All interested countries should designate, as soon as possible, a national focal point for the International Year of Shelter for the Homeless. Although there should be a specific person as a contact point, the national focal point could be an existing agency or a new unit or national committee, including representatives of relevant agencies and non-governmental organizations, specifically established to stimulate and co-ordinate national and local action.

4.　Although the functions of national focal points for the International Year of Shelter for the Homeless will vary from country to country, they could include:

(*a*)　Receiving, producing and exchanging information on the programme and plans for the Year, on relevant activities in other countries and other programme support information;

(*b*)　Developing a national strategy and programme for the Year, including the identification and selection of appropriate demonstration projects;

(*c*)　Encouraging close working relationships with and among non-governmental and community organizations on their projects, plans and possibilities relevant to the Year;

(*d*)　Stimulating and co-ordinating local and national activities and projects for the Year;

(*e*)　Organizing relevant meetings, seminars and training courses;

(*d*)　Reporting periodically on the progress and achievements of activities and projects for the Year in the particular country.

B. Assessment of the existing situation and future needs

5.　In launching a national programme for the International Year of Shelter for the Homeless and before the actual selection of specific demonstration projects, countries should undertake at least a preliminary assessment of the existing situation, taking into account the following questions:

(*a*)　What are the size, distribution and characteristics of the target group in quantitative (for example, those below the poverty line in urban and rural areas) and qualitative terms (for example, access to drinking water, sanitation services, transportation, food, education, energy)?

(*b*)　What previous and existing programmes, or parts of programmes, have successfully provided affordable improvements in the shelter and neighbourhoods of the poor, and how can they best be extended? Why have other programmes failed to do so?

(*c*)　What national and local resources (money, land, labour, materials) are available and needed to improve the shelter and neighbourhoods of the target group? Are there obstacles to the full use of local resources?

(*d*)　What changes are needed in existing programmes, policies and legal, institutional and financing arrangements in order to accelerate the provision of affordable shelter for the poor?

(*e*)　What, based on the answers to the above questions, are the priorities within the national programme for demonstration projects during the Year?

C. Beginning of the implementation of demonstration projects for the International Year of Shelter for the Homeless

6.　Demonstration projects for the International Year of Shelter for the Homeless should test and demonstrate new approaches to basic problems in urban and rural areas, such as providing or improving shelter; providing an improved drinking water supply, sanitation and waste disposal; generating jobs in the formal or informal construction sector; improving environmental and health conditions and services; upgrading infrastructure and services for the poor, including roads, public transportation, energy, and medical, social, educational and recreational facilities; and providing low-cost building techniques and materials, especially through more widespread use of indigenous methods, skills and construction materials.

7.　In addition to projects of a physical character, the national programme and project for the International Year of Shelter for the Homeless should include the review and strengthening of policy, legislative, organizational and financial measures to assist the poor in improving their shelter and neighbourhoods. Areas of special concern might be legislation on land and tenure; building codes and regulations; financing, including credit and loans for shelter for the poor; and institutional arrangements within and between national and local authorities.

8.　In order to meet the objectives for the International Year of Shelter for the Homeless, countries should take the following guidelines into account in the design, selection, implementation and monitoring of demonstration projects for the Year:

(*a*)　Projects must explore, test and demonstrate existing or new ways and means of improving the shelter and neighbourhoods of the poor and disadvantaged, particularly those below the poverty line in urban and rural settlements;

(b) Projects must contribute to or result in a clear and visible improvement in the shelter or neighbourhoods of at least some of the poor and disadvantaged before 1987;

(c) Projects must be replicable, in order for them to reach many more of the poor and disadvantaged, leading to affordable improvements for many rather than major improvements for a few;

(d) Projects must seek a practical balance between what is desirable (in terms, for example, of basic health requirements and structural safety), attainable (technically and administratively, and using local skills, methods and materials), and affordable by the poor themselves and the nation as a whole.

D. Progress report

9. In order that all countries may be informed on the existing situation, priority concerns and activities and plans for the International Year of Shelter for the Homeless in other countries, prior to the seventh session of the Commission on Human Settlements, in April 1984, the national focal points for the Year should submit to the United Nations Centre for Human Settlements (Habitat):

(a) A brief overview (maximum two pages in length) of their national plans, priorities and activities for the Year, including information responding to the questions in paragraph 5 above;

(b) A one-page summary for each of the national demonstration projects for the Year launched to date, using a common format to be prepared by the Centre.

General Assembly resolution 38/168

19 December 1983   Meeting 102   Adopted without vote

Approved by Second Committee (A/38/702/Add.8) without vote, 14 November (meeting 39); draft by Vice-Chairman (A/C.2/38/L.26), based on informal consultations on draft by Commission on Human Settlements (A/C.2/38/L.9); agenda item 78 *(i)*.

Meeting numbers. GA 38th session: 2nd Committee 39; plenary 102.

Settlements planning

In a resolution of 6 May 1983,[12] the Commission on Human Settlements invited Governments to consider adopting policies of local planning for human settlements and incorporating them in their national development plans. The Commission requested the UNCHS Executive Director to work with UNEP and other United Nations bodies to assist countries in local planning by elaborating models and methods for the integral planning of communities, by disseminating information on local participation in developing settlements, by responding to government requests to elaborate policies for local planning, by supporting training programmes for local officials with the collaboration of universities and public administration institutions, and by organizing regional and national seminars to define methods and suggest models of local planning.

Construction

By a resolution of 5 May 1983,[13] the Commission on Human Settlements requested the UNCHS Executive Director to draw up a programme of action to provide assistance to developing countries in using and promoting local materials and assimilating local techniques for the use of those materials, and to report to the Commission in 1984 on progress made in that regard.

By another resolution of the same date,[14] the Commission requested the Executive Director to select, collect and collate technical information relating to experience acquired in the building industry, particularly in developed countries, and to distribute such information to developing countries and others that were interested.

Land use

A report on land for human settlements,[15] which reviewed and analysed the situation and set out a number of recommendations, was submitted to the Commission on Human Settlements by the UNCHS Executive Director in January 1983.

The report largely restricted its review to the problem of residential land for low-income groups which, the report stated, were excluded from legitimate access to land and housing in sufficient proximity to income-earning opportunities. As settlements grew, the housing needs of low-income groups became more serious, but an adequate political response to the challenge of making growing settlements liveable had not yet emerged. Public expenditures on housing programmes had remained much lower than necessary to meet needs; housing targets had rarely been met. Land was becoming the central issue in the housing crisis that faced growing settlements. The inadequacy of land for housing low-income groups was bringing settlements, particularly large cities, under increasing pressures, which reflected the inability of settlements to share the wealth created in them. The settlement process itself created wealth, and it was through the sharing of the value thus created that the issue of land for housing low-income groups could be adequately resolved.

The report also considered "informal" arrangements which low-income groups had used to obtain access to land and housing, such as the occupation of abandoned properties and encroachments on marginal lands; the limited role played by most Governments in providing land for low-income housing; and the increasing market pressures on land availability.

The report suggested a series of possible actions by Governments to make land for housing accessible to low-income groups, such as: increasing the supply of land through public intervention; increasing public participation in land development; increasing and upgrading the supply of land by the private sector; legitimizing informal settlements and preventing their unnecessary destruction; and financing land development. Land for housing low-income groups was primarily a national issue, not an international one, the report concluded. International action could only assist or supplement national initiatives. Action on the issue had to address the unique problems of a particular country. The international community could contribute by accumulating global experience on land issues, developing contacts with professionals, politicians and administrators, and assisting countries in identifying and resolving problems.

Endorsing the report in a decision of 6 May 1983,[16] the Commission recommended that Governments focus increased attention on land development for housing the poor; ensure land availability by renewing decaying urban centres and expanding infrastructure construction; pursue land registration programmes; and monitor speculative practices as a source of undue increase in land costs for housing and related community services.

Natural disasters

By a resolution of 4 May 1983,[17] the Commission requested the UNCHS Executive Director to promote the study of a global plan to make possible immediate technical and financial assistance to areas in developing countries affected by natural disasters such as earthquakes, typhoons, torrential rain and large-scale flooding.

(For further information on other United Nations activities in response to natural disasters, see p. 517.)

Least developed countries

The Commission on Human Settlements, by a resolution of 5 May 1983,[18] took note with appreciation of UNCHS activities for the benefit of the least developed countries (LDCs), in particular, the 49 projects currently being carried out in 35 LDCs in Africa, Asia and Latin America, and of the contribution those activities were making towards realization of the objectives of the 1981 Substantial New Programme of Action (SNPA) for the 1980s of the Least Developed Countries.[19] The Commission appealed to States, the United Nations system, and multilateral development and financial institutions to take measures to accelerate implementation of SNPA in the field of human settlements. It requested the UNCHS Executive Director to continue giving high priority to formulating and implementing human settlements projects for the LDCs.

Financial institution for Asia and the Pacific

The UNCHS Executive Director reported in January 1983[20] to the Commission on Human Settlements on progress made in preparing a feasi-

bility study requested in 1981[21] on the creation of an Asian human settlements bank. To initiate a study on the mobilization of savings and their utilization for human settlements, questionnaires had been sent to all developing countries in the Asia and Pacific region; however, only six replies had been received.

An *Ad Hoc* Group of Experts had met in November/December 1982 at Manila, Philippines, to consider steps to accelerate the feasibility study. In its report annexed to the Executive Director's report, the Group stressed early establishment of such an institution. It was agreed that what was needed was not merely an association of housing institutions but a more active organization whereby share capital would be invested by Governments or their nominated institutions. In its initial stages, it would provide managerial and technical expertise and to a limited extent seed capital, as well as identify projects requiring expertise and potential donor agencies. In the long term, major emphasis should be placed on "self-help", mobilizing domestic capital to alleviate shelter problems. The design and structure of the new body were outlined, and details were provided on the procedures and timetable for its formation.

In a resolution of 4 May,[22] the Commission decided that further steps on the question of a financial institution for Asia and the Pacific should be taken, requested the Executive Director to call a meeting of a small working group of governmental experts, and accepted the offer of the Philippines to host the meeting of the working group.

Human settlements in territories occupied by Israel

Israel's policy of establishing settlements in the territories occupied by it as a result of previous armed conflict in the Middle East (see POLITICAL AND SECURITY QUESTIONS, Chapter IX) was the subject of a resolution adopted by the Commission on 4 May 1983.[23] The Commission condemned the destruction of homes and displacement of their owners by the Israeli authorities in the territories. It also condemned the establishment in their place by Israel of what it described as illegal colonies, and called on the Israeli authorities to stop establishing them. It recommended that the General Assembly request the Secretary-General to set up a team of experts on human settlements to study those colonies and their effects on the indigenous owners, in co-operation with the Palestine Liberation Organization, and to report to the Commission in 1984. It recommended that the Assembly urge the occupying authorities to implement relevant United Nations resolutions and, in the event of their continuing non-compliance, that the Assembly take appropriate action.

Assistance to Africa

Assistance to national liberation movements

In a January 1983 report[24] on UNCHS assistance to the three African national liberation movements recognized by the Organization of African Unity (OAU)—the African National Congress (ANC), the Pan Africanist Congress of Azania (PAC) and the South West Africa People's Organization (SWAPO)—the UNCHS Executive Director stated that three projects were being carried out. They involved training and policy formulation in land use and human settlements development for SWAPO, assistance to self-help community development for ANC at Morogoro, United Republic of Tanzania, and preparatory assistance for the construction of a multi-purpose centre at Bagamoyo, Tanzania, for PAC.

On 5 May 1983, the Commission adopted three resolutions on assistance to Africa. In a resolution on victims of *apartheid* and colonialism in Africa,[25] it strongly condemned South Africa for domestic repression, aggression against neighbouring States, and its illegal occupation of Namibia. It requested the Executive Director to continue his efforts to aid the victims, and to provide additional assistance to those countries in which human settlements had been disrupted by South Africa's régime. It reaffirmed its 1982 request[26] that the national liberation movements recognized by OAU be represented by more than one person at Commission sessions.

By another resolution,[27] the Commission requested the Executive Director to intensify the programme of assistance to Lesotho in the area of human settlements, so as to help it contain its refugees and recover from the December 1982 aggression by South Africa.[28] By a third resolution,[29] the Commission urged increased UNCHS technical assistance for the reconstruction of housing in N'Djamena, Chad, which had been badly damaged during three years of fighting.

Co-operation with Shelter-Afrique

In a January 1983 report,[30] the UNCHS Executive Director traced the creation of Shelter-Afrique, a specialized housing finance institution. UNCHS had been closely involved in its establishment, in co-operation with the African Development Bank.

The first general meeting of Shelter-Afrique, attended by a UNCHS representative, had been held at Nairobi, in December 1982. Its principal officers had been elected, and a Board of Directors appointed. As soon as its permanent secretariat was established, the UNCHS Executive Director would identify specific areas of co-operation and their modalities.

By a resolution of 5 May,[31] the Commission on Human Settlements requested the Executive Director to provide technical, financial and other assistance to Shelter-Afrique and to report on the progress made in 1984.

REFERENCES

[1]HS/C/7/2 & Add.1,2. [2]YUN 1976, p. 441. [3]HS/C/6/INF.5. [4]HS/C/6/4. [5]YUN 1981, p. 855, GA res. 36/71, 4 Dec. 1981. [6]HS/C/7/5. [7]A/38/8 (res. 6/1). [8]*Ibid.* (res. 6/13). [9]*Ibid.* (res. 6/5). [10]YUN 1982, p. 1043, GA res. 37/221, 20 Dec. 1982. [11]A/38/233-E/1983/74 & Corr.1. [12]A/38/8 (res. 6/14). [13]*Ibid.* (res. 6/8). [14]*Ibid.* (res. 6/9). [15]HS/C/6/3 & Corr.1 & Add.1. [16]A/38/8 (dec. 6/15). [17]*Ibid.* (res. 6/3). [18]*Ibid.* (res. 6/12). [19]YUN 1981, p. 406. [20]HS/C/6/2/Add.3. [21]YUN 1981, p. 856. [22]A/38/8 (res. 6/4). [23]*Ibid.* (res. 6/2). [24]HS/C/6/2/Add.1. [25]A/38/8 (res. 6/11). [26]YUN 1982, p. 306. [27]A/38/8 (res. 6/10). [28]YUN 1982, p. 313. [29]A/38/8 (res. 6/6). [30]HS/C/6/2/Add.2. [31]A/38/8 (res. 6/7).

Organizational questions

Co-ordination in the UN system

Pursuant to a December 1982 General Assembly resolution,[1] the Secretary-General reported in November 1983[2] that he had formally proposed that UNCHS take part fully in the work of the Administrative Committee on Co-ordination (ACC), and that informal consultations to that end had followed.

On 27 October,[3] ACC decided that the UNCHS Executive Director should be invited to participate in ACC meetings when questions in which the Centre had a direct interest were under consideration. It further decided to invite UNCHS to participate in meetings of ACC subsidiary bodies when matters of concern to it were taken up.

In December, the sixth joint meeting was held between UNCHS and UNEP (see previous chapter).

GENERAL ASSEMBLY ACTION

On 19 December 1983, on the recommendation of the Second Committee, the General Assembly adopted without vote resolution 38/167 B.

Co-ordination of human settlements programmes within the United Nations system

The General Assembly,

Recalling its resolution 35/77 C of 5 December 1980, in which it invited the Secretary-General to arrange, in consultation with the members of the Administrative Committee on Co-ordination, for the United Nations Centre for Human Settlements (Habitat) to participate in all aspects of the work of that Committee and its subsidiary machinery,

Recalling also its resolution 37/223 C of 20 December 1982, in which it requested the Secretary-General to accelerate his efforts in arranging for such participation and to report thereon to the General Assembly at its thirty-eighth session,

Having considered the report of the Secretary-General summarizing decision 1983/18 of 27 October 1983 of the

Administrative Committee on Co-ordination on the matter, as well as the oral explanation given by the representative of the Secretary-General,

Aware that the decision of the Administrative Committee on Co-ordination does not completely meet the requirement of General Assembly resolutions 35/77 C and 37/223 C,

Takes note of the report of the Secretary-General summarizing decision 1983/18 of the Administrative Committee on Co-ordination and requests him to report to the General Assembly at its thirty-ninth session on the implementation of its resolutions on the question.

General Assembly resolution 38/167 B

19 December 1983   Meeting 102   Adopted without vote

Approved by Second Committee (A/38/702/Add.8) without vote (parts A and B together), 21 November (meeting 45); draft by Vice-Chairman (A/C.2/38/L.72, part B), based on informal consultations on 4-nation draft (A/C.2/38/L.19, part B); agenda item 78 *(h)*.
Meeting numbers. GA 38th session: 2nd Committee 30, 45; plenary 102.

The adopted text was based on informal consultations on a draft introduced by the Netherlands, also on behalf of Gabon, Kenya and the Philippines. By that text, the Assembly would have noted with regret that the ACC October decision did not meet its December 1982 request[1] that UNCHS be enabled to participate in all aspects of the work of ACC and its subsidiary machinery; would have restated its conviction that full participation was essential for UNCHS to fulfil its mandate with respect to co-ordinating United Nations human settlements activities; and would have requested the Secretary-General to intensify his efforts to arrange for full participation without delay.

Cross-organizational programme analysis

In a note submitted to the Commission on Human Settlements in March 1983,[4] the UNCHS secretariat reviewed human settlements activities within the United Nations system during 1982-1983, in accordance with a 1982 decision of the Committee for Programme and Co-ordination (CPC).[5] CPC was to consider that note in preparation for a cross-organizational programme analysis (COPA) of human settlements activities in 1984 (see Chapter XXIV of this section).

The note reviewed 20 areas of action under the six main programme categories set out by the 1976 Habitat Conference,[6] to provide CPC with a basis for expressing its views on whether the current system of activities was responsive to international needs. The note stated that during 1982-1983 the following United Nations bodies were involved in human settlements activities: UNCHS, the United Nations Departments of International

Economic and Social Affairs and of Technical Co-operation for Development, the regional commissions, UNIDO, UNDP, UNEP, UNFPA, UNDRO and UNHCR. Agencies involved included: FAO, ILO, ITU, UNESCO, WHO and WMO. In addition, the United Nations Children's Fund, the World Bank and WFP provided primarily financial and material assistance. The pattern of involvement of United Nations organizations in human settlements activities and the distribution of resources were shown in a table.

The Commission on Human Settlements concluded in a decision of 6 May 1983[7] that the pattern of human settlements activities identified in the note addressed national needs. It requested UNCHS to transmit the note to the United Nations Office of Programme Planning and Co-ordination, Department of International Economic and Social Affairs, for further action.

Work programme of the Commission on Human Settlements

The Commission on Human Settlements decided on 6 May 1983[8] that a special theme for discussion at its 1985 session should be planning and management of human settlements, with emphasis on small and intermediate towns and local growth points. It requested the UNCHS Executive Director to submit for its consideration in 1984 a draft outline of the theme paper and a work plan for its preparation.

Training and information as part of overall human settlements policy were to be the special themes for discussion at the Commission's 1984 session. Information needs and approaches in human settlements development, including UNCHS information activities, were considered by 15 experts at a meeting held in collaboration with the Netherlands Ministry of Housing, Physical Planning and Environment (The Hague, 5-9 September 1983).

In 1983, the Joint Inspection Unit, CPC and the General Assembly examined plans to strengthen Secretariat machinery for evaluating United Nations programmes. These plans included an increase of staff of the UNCHS evaluation unit (see ADMINISTRATIVE AND BUDGETARY QUESTIONS, Chapter II).

REFERENCES

[1]YUN 1982, p. 1045, GA res. 37/223 C, 20 Dec. 1982. [2]A/38/548. [3]ACC/1983/DEC/11-18 (dec. 1983/18). [4]HS/C/6/8 & Add.1. [5]YUN 1982, p. 1240. [6]YUN 1976, p. 441. [7]A/38/8 (dec. 6/18). [8]*Ibid.* (dec. 6/20).

Chapter XVIII

Human rights

In 1983, the United Nations continued to take action against racism, racial discrimination, *apartheid* and other forms of discrimination, to investigate situations involving violations of human rights in several parts of the world, to develop international standards, and to pursue other means of promoting and protecting fundamental rights and freedoms. The Secretary-General stated in his annual report on the Organization's work (p. 3) that he believed it his responsibility to consider ways of dealing with specific cases involving human rights issues. To that end, he had contacted Governments and was determined to persist in his efforts.

Highlighting the year's activities was the Second World Conference to Combat Racism and Racial Discrimination, which convened in August and adopted a Declaration and a Programme of Action for the Second Decade to Combat Racism and Racial Discrimination. The Programme was approved by the General Assembly in November, when it proclaimed the Second Decade, to begin on 10 December, following the close of the first Decade.

The year saw a rise in the number of parties to several human rights instruments—the International Convention on the Elimination of All Forms of Racial Discrimination to 122; the International Covenant on Civil and Political Rights and the International Convention on the Suppression and Punishment of the Crime of *Apartheid*, each to 77; and the International Covenant on Economic, Social and Cultural Rights to 80. Ratification of or adherence to those instruments was again called for in several Assembly resolutions.

The year also marked the commemoration of the thirty-fifth anniversary of the Universal Declararation of Human Rights, whose significance was stressed by the Assembly in December.

Work continued on the elaboration of separate instruments to protect the rights of the child, persons detained or imprisoned, migrant workers, minorities and non-citizens, and against torture and other inhuman treatment. The drafting of guidelines and guarantees for the protection of persons on grounds of mental ill-health or disorder was set in motion. An expert group was reconvened to draft a declaration on the right to development, a right reaffirmed as an inalienable human right by the Assembly in December.

Working groups set up by the Commission on Human Rights and its Sub-Commission on Prevention of Discrimination and Protection of Minorities reviewed developments on detention, on involuntary disappearances, and on slavery and all manner of traffic in persons. A working group on the encouragement of universal acceptance of human rights instruments continued its country-by-country examination.

The right of peoples to self-determination was reaffirmed by the Assembly in November, as it was by the Commission—for Palestinians and for the peoples of Afghanistan, East Timor, Kampuchea, South Africa and Namibia, and Western Sahara—and by the Sub-Commission for the people of Nicaragua.

Alleged violations of human rights on a large scale in several countries continued to be examined, including in Chile, Cyprus, El Salvador, Guatemala, Iran, Poland, South Africa and Namibia, as well as in the territories occupied by Israel. Besides reporting to the Commission on these alleged large-scale violations, the Secretary-General also reported to the Assembly on the question of human rights and mass exoduses. A Special Rapporteur was appointed by the Sub-Commission to update a study on the prevention and punishment of the crime of genocide.

Establishment of a post of United Nations High Commissioner for Human Rights was again discussed by the Commission and its Sub-Commission.

The Commission adopted 54 resolutions and 13 decisions at its thirty-ninth session, held at Geneva from 31 January to 11 March.[1] Its Sub-Commission held its thirty-sixth session, also at Geneva, from 15 August to 9 September, adopting 40 resolutions and 12 decisions.[2] The Economic and Social Council reviewed the Commission's work in May, acting on it and other human rights questions in 12 resolutions and 28 decisions. The Assembly adopted 33 resolutions on various human rights questions between October and December.

Topics related to this chapter. Africa: South Africa and *apartheid*. Americas: Central America situation. Asia and the Pacific: Kampuchea situation; Afghanistan situation; Iran-Iraq armed conflict. Mediterranean: Cyprus question. Middle East: Middle East situation; territories occupied by Israel. Social and cultural development. Health and human resources. Women. Namibia. Other colonial Territories.

Discrimination

Racial discrimination

Decades for Action to Combat Racism and Racial Discrimination

The Decade for Action to Combat Racism and Racial Discrimination (1973-1983)[3] drew to a close in December 1983, immediately following which a Second Decade (1983-1993) began. The Second Decade was proclaimed by the General Assembly on the recommendation of the Second World Conference to Combat Racism and Racial Discrimination.

Second World Conference to
Combat Racism and Racial Discrimination

Pursuant to a programme of activities covering the last four years of the first Decade (1973-1983)—adopted by the General Assembly in 1979[4]—and as decided by the Assembly in December 1982,[5] a Second World Conference to Combat Racism and Racial Discrimination was held towards the end of the Decade, from 1 to 12 August 1983, at Geneva.[6] The first such conference took place in 1978.[7]

The purpose of the Second Conference was to evaluate the work undertaken during the Decade and to chart new measures where necessary. The Conference adopted a Declaration and a Programme of Action; it recommended that a Second Decade be launched with a view to achieving total elimination of racism, racial discrimination and *apartheid*. By resolution 38/14, the Assembly proclaimed a Second Decade to Combat Racism and Racial Discrimination, to begin on 10 December 1983, and approved the Programme of Action for the Second Decade.

Conference preparations

As authorized by the Economic and Social Council in May 1982,[8] the Preparatory Sub-Committee for the Second World Conference held its second session in New York from 21 to 25 March 1983. It was opened by the Secretary-General of the Conference, who had been appointed in keeping with a December 1982 General Assembly request.[9] The Sub-Committee's report,[10] which was submitted to the Council's May 1983 session, supplied information on the status of documentation and other matters pertaining to the Conference preparations, including a draft programme of action containing proposals for activities to be undertaken during the Second Decade.

On 18 February,[11] the Commission on Human Rights, by a roll-call vote of 41 to none, requested the Preparatory Sub-Committee to consider recommending that a study of ways to ensure full and universal implementation of United Nations decisions on racism, racial discrimination and *apartheid* be included in the draft programme of action.

On 10 March,[12] the Secretary-General noted that the Preparatory Sub-Committee would be reporting to the Council in May and that United Nations bodies and intergovernmental and non-governmental organizations would be submitting information on implementation of the 1973 Programme for the Decade for Action to Combat Racism and Racial Discrimination[13] to the Conference. He therefore proposed that the annual report requested of him, containing similar information, should not be submitted.

The Committee on the Elimination of Racial Discrimination (CERD), at its March session (see CONVENTION ON THE ELIMINATION OF RACIAL DISCRIMINATION below), decided to transmit to the Conference two studies, on implementation of article 4 (on promotion of ideas against racial discrimination) and article 7 (calling for measures to combat prejudices leading to racial discrimination) of the International Convention on the Elimination of All Forms of Racial Discrimination. The Committee also designated two of its members to participate in the Conference.

ECONOMIC AND SOCIAL COUNCIL ACTION

On an oral proposal by its President, the Economic and Social Council adopted decision 1983/103 without vote.

Appointment of the members of the Preparatory Sub-Committee for the Second World Conference to Combat Racism and Racial Discrimination

At its 2nd plenary meeting, on 4 February 1983, the Council, after hearing a statement by the President concerning the membership of the Preparatory Sub-Committee for the Second World Conference to Combat Racism and Racial Discrimination, decided that the membership of the Preparatory Sub-Committee should remain at twenty-three, as originally decided by the Council in its decision 1981/130 of 6 May 1981, without prejudice to the respective positions of the regional groups with regard to the equitable geographical distribution of seats, and that the President, in pursuance of Council decision 1981/202 of 25 November 1981, should proceed to appoint, upon nomination by the regional group concerned, the remaining four States, with a view to completing the membership of the Preparatory Sub-Committee.

Economic and Social Council decision 1983/103

Adopted without vote

Oral proposal by President; agenda item 2.
Meeting number. ESC 2.

On an oral proposal by its President, the Council adopted decision 1983/113 without vote.

Decade for Action to Combat Racism and Racial Discrimination

At its 11th plenary meeting, on 24 May 1983, the Council decided:

(a) To take note of the report of the Preparatory Sub-Committee for the Second World Conference to Combat Racism and Racial Discrimination on its second session and of the statements made on the item in the Council during its first regular session of 1983;

(b) To transmit to the Conference the report of the Preparatory Sub-Committee together with the relevant summary records of the Council.

Economic and Social Council decision 1983/113

Adopted without vote

Oral proposal by President; agenda item 2.
Meeting numbers. ESC 8-11, 14.

Conference participation

The Second World Conference was attended by: 128 States and the United Nations Council for Namibia (see APPENDIX III); other United Nations bodies, including the Commission on Human Rights and its Sub-Commission on Prevention of Discrimination and Protection of Minorities, the CERD and the Human Rights Committee; intergovernmental and non-governmental organizations; and four national liberation movements.

On 18 February 1983,[11] the Commission on Human Rights designated its Chairman and the Chairman of the *Ad Hoc* Working Group of Experts on Southern Africa to represent the Commission at the Conference, and expressed support for the General Assembly's December 1982 call[5] for participation by all States.

ECONOMIC AND SOCIAL COUNCIL ACTION

Acting without vote on the recommendation of its Second (Social) Committee, the Economic and Social Council adopted decision 1983/138.

Implementation of the Programme for the Decade for Action to Combat Racism and Racial Discrimination

At its 15th plenary meeting, on 27 May 1983, the Council, noting Commission on Human Rights resolution 1983/13 of 18 February 1983, endorsed the Commission's decision to designate its Chairman and the Chairman of the *Ad Hoc* Working Group of Experts on Southern Africa to represent the Commission at the Second World Conference to Combat Racism and Racial Discrimination, to be held at Geneva from 1 to 12 August 1983.

Economic and Social Council decision 1983/138

Adopted without vote

Approved by Second Committee (E/1983/61) without vote, 23 May (meeting 18); draft by Commission on Human Rights (E/1983/13); agenda item 10.
Meeting number. ESC 15.

Conference action

The Conference set up a General Committee and a Credentials Committee, as well as two committees to prepare a draft Declaration and a draft Programme of Action. The General Committee established a Joint Drafting Committee.

On 12 August, the Conference adopted the Declaration by 101 votes to 12, with 3 abstentions, and the Programme of Action by 104 votes to none, with 10 abstentions.

Declaration. By the Declaration, the Conference, holding all human beings to be born equal in dignity and rights, declared any doctrine of racial superiority to be scientifically false, morally condemnable and socially unjust, and without justification whatsoever. It regarded government policies based on such doctrine as jeopardizing friendly relations among peoples and nations, and thus international peace and security. It singled out *apartheid* as such a policy and an institutionalized form of racism constituting a crime against humanity. Therefore, it condemned any form of co-operation—whether economic, military, nuclear or other—with the racist régime of South Africa, in particular Israel's increasing relations with it, as an impediment to the struggle against *apartheid*.

Deeply concerned over the stepped up activities of many neo-Nazi and Fascist organizations that encouraged tendencies towards racism and racial discrimination, the Conference called for measures against all ideologies and practices—including *apartheid*, nazism, fascism and neo-fascism—based on racial or ethnic exclusiveness or intolerance, hatred, terror or systematic denials of human rights and fundamental freedoms. Likewise concerned over racial discrimination practices against Palestinians and other inhabitants of Arab territories occupied by Israel, the Conference demanded cessation of such practices.

Believing that persons belonging to national, ethnic and other minorities could play a significant role in promoting national and international co-operation and understanding, the Conference stressed that protecting their rights under existing and proposed international instruments and granting them full participation in the national political, economic and social life were essential to the fulfilment of that role. It recognized the rights of indigenous populations to maintain their traditional economic, social and cultural structures and to pursue their development within that context. Other groups affected by various forms of discrimination and cited for special attention in human rights programmes and legislation included women and children, refugees, immigrants and migrant workers.

The Conference called for the development of affirmative action programmes to address racism and racial discrimination inherent in economic, social and cultural systems and to combat racism through education and information. Deeming it the responsibility of Governments to promote awareness of the evils of racism and racial discrimination, the Conference called on them to make clear their condemnation of propaganda and organizations based on theories of superiority of one race or group of persons, and to adopt measures to eradicate all action and incitement to such discrimination. The Conference called for increased moral, political and material support to the South African and Namibian people who, under the leadership of their national liberation movements, were struggling to establish an independent, non-racial and democratic society. It also called for support to national liberation movements.

States, international organizations, governmental and non-governmental organizations, and local, private and religious institutions were called upon to ensure the effective realization of the goals and objectives of the Decade for Action to Combat Racism and Racial Discrimination, reaffirmed by the Declaration thus: to promote human rights and fundamental freedoms for all, without distinction as to race, colour, descent, or national or ethnic origin; to identify, isolate and dispel beliefs, policies and practices contributing to racism, racial discrimination and *apartheid;* and to counteract alliances based on mutual espousal of racism and racial discrimination.

Towards these ends, the Conference, by the Declaration, recommended that a Second Decade to Combat Racism and Racial Discrimination be launched.

Programme of Action. The Programme of Action set forth in detail the legal and administrative measures to be taken at the national, regional and international levels to combat *apartheid,* racism and racial discrimination. The text of the Programme, as approved by General Assembly resolution 38/14, was annexed to that resolution (see below).

Prior to adoption of the Declaration as a whole, paragraph 19, condemning co-operation with South Africa, notably the increasing relations between its racist régime and Israel, was adopted by a roll-call vote, requested by the USSR, of 84 to 15, with 16 abstentions. Paragraph 20, calling for the cessation of practices of racial discrimination against Palestinians and other inhabitants of the occupied Arab territories, was also adopted by a roll-call vote, requested by Egypt, of 87 to 17, with 11 abstentions.

Prior to adoption of the Programme of Action as a whole, the section on action to combat *apartheid* (section A) was adopted by 92 votes to 7, with 12 abstentions, following a vote of 86 to 20, with 2 abstentions, on paragraph 3 (reaffirming the legitimacy of the struggle of the oppressed people of South Africa and Namibia and their national liberation movements for the elimination of *apartheid* by all available means, including armed struggle).

Reservations on the Declaration centred on its two separately adopted paragraphs. It was the unanimous opinion of the participants which voted against both that they introduced elements either divisive or extraneous to the purposes of the Decade and the Conference. Those participants were Australia, Belgium, Canada, Denmark, France, the Federal Republic of Germany, Iceland, Ireland, Italy, Luxembourg, the Netherlands, New Zealand, Norway and Switzerland. Finland and Sweden also voted against paragraph 20 (abstaining on paragraph 19).

Citing inclusion of those paragraphs as the primary reason for their vote against the Declaration as a whole were Canada, Denmark, France, the Federal Republic of Germany and the Netherlands, the same reason for New Zealand's abstention on it. The United Kingdom said it was unable to join in a consensus on the Declaration and the Programme of Action because they included the same unacceptable elements that were in the 1978 texts.[7]

Besides regarding the Middle East situation as beyond the purview of the Conference, Belgium thought it a regrettable error to single out Israel alongside South Africa. Abstaining on the two paragraphs on similar grounds were Austria, Ecuador and Portugal; Austria added that, while it deplored all discriminatory practices in the occupied Arab territories, it did not consider them as practices of racial discrimination. Japan, which also abstained on the paragraphs, said it understood the Middle East problem to be a political one with no direct bearing on the issue of elimination of racial discrimination. Botswana, Lesotho and Spain registered their reservations on the wording of paragraph 19 by abstaining on it.

That *apartheid* was a threat to international peace and security drew reservations from Belgium and Portugal, which noted that, under Chapter VII of the Charter of the United Nations, it was for the Security Council alone to determine the existence of such a threat. France was uncertain whether, from a legal standpoint, there was full justification for characterizing *apartheid* as a crime against humanity—a reservation shared by Belgium, Luxembourg, the Netherlands and Portugal.

Total isolation of South Africa through mandatory sanctions would not lead to the desired goal of eradicating *apartheid*, Belgium, Japan, Luxembourg, the Netherlands and Portugal felt. Such isolation, Belgium claimed, would be extremely harmful to the oppressed majority of South Africans. Along with Denmark and Luxembourg, Belgium also pointed out that sanctions were solely for the Council to impose. In this connection, Colombia noted that Chapter VII of the Charter assigned special functions to the Council which should not be duplicated, exceeded or encroached upon.

France, which abstained on the Programme, said its objections stemmed primarily from its position that sanctions in most cases were ineffective. Lesotho, which supported the Declaration and the Programme of Action, said it had difficulties—as did Botswana—with those provisions calling for trade and economic sanctions or any other measure to isolate South Africa. The United Kingdom could not endorse further economic and cultural sanctions, nor could Portugal endorse the call for termination of all economic and financial collaboration with South Africa. In Japan's opinion, economic assistance and collaboration, as condemned by the Conference, did not include normal trade with South Africa; financial institutions, specifically the World Bank and the International Monetary Fund, which were urged to refrain from extending credits to South Africa, should not be concerned with political issues.

To be effective, sanctions against South Africa must be carefully chosen and co-ordinated and must be imposed by the Council in accordance with the Charter, Ireland said.

Canada explained that, owing to serious reservations on the recommendations in the section on *apartheid*, it could not agree with the Programme as a whole. The Federal Republic of Germany said it abstained on the Programme and voted against that section because it contained certain unacceptable elements. Claiming difficulties with the same section, New Zealand said it was obliged also to abstain on the Programme. The United Kingdom made clear that its vote on the section was without prejudice to its well-known position on negotiations towards an independence settlement for Namibia and to its continuing commitment to an internationally acceptable settlement in accordance with a 1978 Council resolution.[14] Belgium and Luxembourg declared their support for the efforts of Namibians to achieve national independence but believed the situation in South Africa to be fundamentally different in that the campaign against *apartheid* should aim at establishing a democratic and multiracial society.

Switzerland noted that it would take account of the national measures recommended for combating *apartheid* and racial discrimination within the framework of its obligations deriving from the 1965 International Convention on the Elimination of All Forms of Racial Discrimination.[15]

While supporting the anti-*apartheid* efforts of the African National Congress of South Africa and the Pan Africanist Congress of Azania, the Netherlands said it did not recognize them as national liberation movements, since the situation in South Africa was not a colonial one. By the same token, the efforts of the South African people to attain equal political and other rights could not be equated with a presumed right to self-determination. Colombia drew attention to the United Nations practice of recognizing only such movements as were recognized by their respective regional organizations.

Direct and indirect references to armed struggle were rejected by a number of countries, among them Austria, Belgium, Chile, Luxembourg, the Netherlands, Portugal, Spain and Turkey. On behalf of the five Nordic countries, which had voted for the Programme, Norway said their main difficulty lay in the formulation that implied United Nations condonement of armed struggle. France could not advocate it, nor could the United

Kingdom accept proposals for its endorsement. Such endorsement, Ireland pointed out, was contrary to the Charter. Japan said armed struggle should not be considered an appropriate means for eliminating *apartheid*. Colombia reiterated its position in favour of peaceful settlement, and Ecuador its policy of non-recognition of territorial occupation or acquisition by force, support for the defence and protection of human rights, and respect for self-determination of peoples.

As to the call for implementation of Decree No. 1, for the protection of Namibia's natural resources adopted by the United Nations Council for Namibia in 1974,[16] and of the Assembly's December 1982 resolution on the Council's work programme for 1983,[17] Belgium emphasized that the Decree and the resolution were only recommendations.

Voicing reservations on the provisions calling on States to use education as a means of eradicating racism and to apply strictly the principle of non-discrimination and equality in education were Austria and the Federal Republic of Germany. In Iran's view, such use of education should be programmed within the regional cultural, social and economic context, but the role of education should not be so overestimated as to turn action to combat racism and racial discrimination into an academic issue.

The Federal Republic of Germany also reserved its position regarding provisions on the legal status of migrant workers. France's reservations referred specifically to the principle of equality to be accorded to migrant workers and to article 27 (stating that persons belonging to ethnic, religious or linguistic minorities should not be denied the right to enjoy their own culture, practice their own religion or use their own language) of the 1966 International Covenant on Civil and Political Rights.[18]

A number of States—among them Austria, Belgium, Chile, Italy, Japan, Luxembourg, the Netherlands, Spain and the United Kingdom—expressed reservations on references to conventions and other international instruments to which they neither had acceded nor intended to accede, as well as on endorsements of final texts of international conferences in which they had not taken part. The appeal made by the Declaration and the Programme for implementation of those instruments, Austria said, would not prejudge its future decisions on them. Colombia reserved its right of accession as an act of national sovereignty. The United Kingdom stated that its acceptance of section F, on implementation of the 1965 International Convention against racial discrimination[15] and other related instruments, did not change its view regarding the 1973 International Convention on the Suppression and Punishment of the Crime of *Apartheid.*[19] Belgium, Chile, France and Portugal reserved their positions on that Convention mainly on legal grounds.

Conference documents on which reservations were entered included the 1981 Paris Declaration on Sanctions against South Africa[20] and the Programme of Action adopted in April 1983 by the International Conference in Support of the Struggle of the Namibian People for Independence.

The United Kingdom could not accept the language of section G, calling for national legislation and action by national institutions. It noted that the subjects dealt with were already under discussion in an *ad hoc* committee established by the Assembly, and some of the proposals, under certain circumstances, would be unreasonable or incompatible with freedom of speech, association and movement and with other basic freedoms. The United Kingdom could not interfere particularly with freedom of expression; it could neither prescribe curricula and other educational provisions, nor impose strict prohibitions in sports. Italy voiced reservations on parts of the text which, it said, might give rise to interpretations contrary to its Constitution in relation to freedom of the press, expression and thought.

In the opinion of Iran, the Declaration and the Programme of Action, for which it had voted, should have referred explicitly to, among other things, the role of certain Western countries, in particular the United States, as the root cause of South Africa's and Israel's *apartheid* policies and practices and that action must be taken to eliminate that role; to the South African *apartheid* régime as illegal and to any relations with it as a crime against the South African and Namibian people; and to zionism as a form of racism, to be cited in the same manner as racism, racial discrimination, nazism and neo-fascism.

The Conference also adopted two resolutions and a decision without vote. By the first resolution, of 10 August, it approved the report of the Credentials Committee. By the second, of 12 August, the Conference took note with regret that on 5 August Nelson Rolihlahla Mandela had completed 21 years in prison for his leadership in the struggle against *apartheid*, expressed solidarity with him and the national liberation movements of South Africa and Namibia, demanded his immediate and unconditional release and that of all other South African and Namibian political prisoners, and called on the international community to redouble efforts in the campaign for their release. The paragraph expressing solidarity was adopted by 78 votes to none, with 10 abstentions, thereby retaining mention of the national liberation movements. (See also POLITICAL AND SECURITY QUESTIONS, Chapter V.)

By the decision, also of 12 August, the Conference requested its President and Secretary-General, respectively, to submit the Conference report to the Assembly and to assist in the Assembly's consideration of the report, and invited the Secretary-General of the United Nations to make administrative arrangements for that purpose.

Annexed to the Conference report were: the opening addresses by the United Nations Secretary-General, the Conference President and Secretary-General, and the Assembly President; messages from 16 heads of State or Government or other State representatives and from the Chairman of the Palestine Liberation Organization (PLO); and a statement by the Conference President on 9 August, on the occasion of International Day of Solidarity with the Struggle of Women of South Africa and Namibia.

GENERAL ASSEMBLY ACTION

In a September 1983 report to the General Assembly, on the work of the Conference,[21] the Secretary-General expressed satisfaction that Conference participation had been global and noted that, during the deliberations, a constructive spirit had been generally maintained and the Programme of Action had been adopted with no dissenting vote. The successful conclusion of the Conference, he added, had created a favourable atmosphere within which greater efforts could be made for attaining a global consensus on matters relating to racism, racial discrimination and *apartheid*. He hoped that the international community would implement the Conference recommendations effectively so that the Second Decade would yield substantial results.

On 22 November, the Assembly, on the recommendation of the Third (Social, Humanitarian and Cultural) Committee, adopted resolution 38/14 without vote.

Second Decade to Combat Racism and Racial Discrimination

The General Assembly,

Reaffirming its objective contained in the Charter of the United Nations to achieve international co-operation in solving international problems of an economic, social, cultural or humanitarian character, and in promoting and encouraging respect for human rights and fundamental freedoms for all without distinction as to race, sex, language or religion,

Reaffirming its firm determination and its commitment to eradicate totally and unconditionally racism in all its forms, racial discrimination and *apartheid*,

Recalling the Universal Declaration of Human Rights, the International Convention on the Elimination of All Forms of Racial Discrimination, the International Convention on the Suppression and Punishment of the Crime of *Apartheid*, the Convention on the Elimination of All Forms of Discrimination against Women and the Convention against Discrimination in Education, adopted by the United Nations Educational, Scientific and Cultural Organization on 14 December 1960,

Recalling further its resolution 3057(XXVIII) of 2 November 1973, on the first Decade for Action to Combat Racism and Racial Discrimination,

Emphasizing the necessity of attaining the objectives of the Decade,

Recalling the first World Conference to Combat Racism and Racial Discrimination, held at Geneva from 14 to 25 August 1978,

Noting that the Second World Conference to Combat Racism and Racial Discrimination was held at Geneva from 1 to 12 August 1983 pursuant to General Assembly resolution 37/41 of 3 December 1982,

Convinced that the Second World Conference represented a positive contribution by the international community towards attaining the objectives of the Decade, through its adoption of a Declaration and an operational Programme of Action,

Having considered the *Report of the Second World Conference to Combat Racism and Racial Discrimination*,

Noting with concern that, despite the efforts of the international community, the Decade for Action to Combat Racism and Racial Discrimination has not attained its principal objectives and that millions of human beings continue to this day to be the victims of varied forms of racism and of racial discrimination,

Convinced of the need to take continuing and reinforced international measures for the elimination of racism and racial discrimination and the total eradication of *apartheid* in South Africa,

Noting that, in order to attain these objectives, it is imperative, in accordance with the recommendation of the Second World Conference, to declare a second decade at the end of the present Decade, which expires in December 1983,

1. *Proclaims* the ten-year period beginning on 10 December 1983 the Second Decade to Combat Racism and Racial Discrimination;

2. *Takes note* of the results of the Second World Conference to Combat Racism and Racial Discrimination contained in the report of the Conference;

3. *Approves* the Programme of Action for the Second Decade to Combat Racism and Racial Discrimination, which is annexed to the present resolution, and calls upon all States to co-operate in its implementation;

4. *Requests* the Economic and Social Council to take charge, with the help of the Secretary-General, of co-ordinating the implementation of the Programme of Action and of evaluating the activities undertaken during the Second Decade;

5. *Requests* the Secretary-General to submit to the General Assembly at its thirty-ninth session, through the Economic and Social Council, a plan of activities for the period 1985-1989 for implementing the Programme of Action and achieving the objectives of the Second Decade, taking into account the Programme for the Decade for Action to Combat Racism and Racial Discrimination;

6. *Decides* to consider at its thirty-ninth session the plan of activities for the period 1985-1989 to be submitted by the Secretary-General;

7. *Decides further* that the Programme for the first Decade should continue to be applied and implemented until the plan of activities for the period 1985-1989 is adopted;

8. *Invites* Governments, United Nations bodies, the specialized agencies and other intergovernmental organizations, as well as interested non-governmental organizations in consultative status with the Economic and Social Council, to participate in the observance of the Second Decade by intensifying and extending their efforts to ensure the rapid elimination of racism and racial discrimination;

9. *Decides* to consider on an annual basis an item entitled "Implementation of the Programme of Action for the Second Decade to Combat Racism and Racial Discrimination".

ANNEX
Programme of Action for the Second Decade to Combat Racism and Racial Discrimination

A. Action to combat *apartheid*

1. The Conference calls upon all States, United Nations organs and intergovernmental and non-governmental organizations to ensure the full and universal implementation of mandatory Security Council resolutions and to make efforts to implement other United Nations resolutions. Particular attention should be paid to specific measures, including those contained in the present Programme of Action, designed to ensure the implementation of the provisions relating to *apartheid*.

2. The Conference reaffirms that the system of *apartheid* in South Africa is the most extreme form of institutionalized racism, a crime against humanity and an affront to the conscience and dignity of mankind, and that South Africa's policies and practices constitute serious breaches of and threats to regional stability and to international peace and security. The Conference calls upon all States, international organizations, private institutions and non-governmental organizations to render increased political and material assistance to the oppressed peoples of South Africa and Namibia and to accelerate greatly campaigns for obtaining the release of all political prisoners imprisoned for their activities against *apartheid*.

3. The Conference further reaffirms the legitimacy of the struggle of the oppressed peoples of South Africa and Namibia and their national liberation movements for the elimination of *apartheid* by all available means, including armed struggle, and the special responsibility of the United Nations and the international community to provide them with moral, political and material assistance in the realization of their quest to exercise their right to self-determination.

4. The Conference reiterates the commitment of the United Nations to the total eradication of *apartheid* and to the establishment of a democratic society in which all the people of South Africa as a whole, irrespective of race, colour, sex or creed, will enjoy equal and full human rights and fundamental freedoms and participate freely in the determination of their destiny.

5. The Conference reaffirms the international community's rejection of the "bantustanization" policy and similar measures which are an integral part of the discriminatory *apartheid* system and which deny the black majority their legitimate rights to their land and to their citizenship of South Africa.

6. The Conference further confirms the international community's rejection of the régime's so-called reforms, especially the limited parliamentary represen-

tation for the Coloureds and Asians designed to split the black alliance and buttress the *apartheid* system.

7.   The Conference calls upon all States to implement strictly the embargo on the sale and transfer of arms and related military materials imposed against South Africa under Security Council resolution 418(1977) of 4 November 1977. The Conference further urges the Security Council to adopt urgent measures to strengthen the arms embargo, in accordance with the recommendations of the Council's committee established under its resolution 421(1977) of 9 December 1977.

8.   The Conference calls upon the Security Council to consider urgently the imposition of mandatory sanctions, under Chapter VII of the Charter of the United Nations, against the *apartheid* régime of South Africa, and in particular:

   (a)   The cessation of all collaboration with South Africa in the nuclear field, as such collaboration would enhance South Africa's capacity to develop nuclear weapons;

   (b)   The prohibition of all technological assistance or collaboration in the manufacture of arms in South Africa and the provision of military supplies to South Africa;

   (c)   The cessation of foreign investments in, and financial loans to, South Africa;

   (d)   An embargo on the supply of petroleum, petroleum products and other strategic commodities that would enable South Africa to continue implementing its *apartheid* policy;

   (e)   The interruption of trade relations with South Africa.

9.   The Conference strongly condemns the racist régime of South Africa for its systematic oppression of and discrimination against the overwhelming majority of the population of South Africa and for its continuing illegal occupation of Namibia. The Conference also condemns acts of military aggression and acts of political and economic destabilization perpetrated by South Africa against the independent neighbouring States of Angola, Botswana, Lesotho, Mozambique, the Seychelles, Swaziland, Zambia and Zimbabwe, as well as South Africa's activities to recruit, train, finance and arm mercenaries for aggression against and destabilization of the neighbouring States, creating instability in this part of the world.

10.   The Conference calls for increased international assistance and support to the front-line States and other independent States in the subregion that are subjected to threats and acts of aggression and destabilization by the *apartheid* régime of South Africa, in order to enable them to strengthen their defence capacity, defend their sovereignty and territorial integrity, fight the adverse South African and other propaganda that undermines racial harmony and peace in the subregion, and peacefully rebuild and develop their countries.

11.   The Conference calls upon States to sever all sporting, cultural and scientific links with the racist régime and with organizations or institutions in South Africa which practise *apartheid* and to discourage their nationals from having any such contacts.

12.   The Conference calls upon all States that have not yet done so:

   (a)   To refrain from any relations with the *apartheid* régime which could contribute to the continuance of the *apartheid* policy;

   (b)   To discourage or prevent all business enterprises, including transnational corporations, in so far as they are under their jurisdiction or control, from collaborat-

ing in any way with the racist régime of South Africa, as such collaboration may contribute towards the continuance of its *apartheid* policy.

13.   The Conference, reaffirming the direct responsibility of the United Nations for Namibia pending its achievement of genuine self-determination, national independence and territorial integrity, demands the immediate and unconditional implementation of Security Council resolution 435(1978) of 29 September 1978 and calls upon all States, intergovernmental organizations, private institutions and non-governmental organizations to make an active contribution to this aim. The Conference further calls upon all Governments and transnational corporations to implement Decree No. 1 for the Protection of the Natural Resources of Namibia, enacted by the United Nations Council for Namibia on 27 September 1974, and also calls for the implementation of the measures referred to in General Assembly resolution 37/233 C of 20 December 1982 on Namibia.

14.   The Conference calls upon all States, intergovernmental organizations, private institutions and non-governmental organizations to continue to take all necessary measures to ensure the termination of all economic and financial collaboration with the racist régime of South Africa, as such assistance will contribute to the continuance of the policies of *apartheid*, and to refrain from taking any action that might imply recognition of or support for the illegal occupation of the Namibian territory by that régime. In this connection, the Conference cautions against unilateral attempts to relax the application of the sanctions already imposed by the Security Council.

15.   The Conference urges the World Bank and the International Monetary Fund, as well as similar institutions, to refrain from extending any credits to the racist régime of South Africa.

B.   Education, teaching and training

16.   The Conference calls upon all States to use effectively education, teaching and training to create a favourable atmosphere for the eradication of racism and racial discrimination. These media should serve as channels for exposing the myths and fallacies of theories, philosophies, ideas and attitudes that are inherent in discriminatory actions based on differences of race, colour, descent and national or ethnic origin. It is imperative for all States to apply strictly the principle of non-discrimination and equality in the matter of education, as set forth in the Convention against Discrimination in Education adopted by the United Nations Educational, Scientific and Cultural Organization. The Conference invites States:

   (a)   To examine history, geography and social studies textbooks with a view to correcting any erroneous assessment of historical and social data, or their unbalanced presentation, which could give rise to racial prejudice;

   (b)   To ensure that teachers are made conscious of the degree to which they may reflect the prejudices of their society and are instructed to avoid such prejudices;

   (c)   To provide adequate opportunities in schools and institutions of higher learning for the study of the activities of the United Nations in combating racism, racial discrimination and *apartheid;*

   (d)   To provide pupils and students at all levels with access to literature and documentation on racism, racial discrimination and *apartheid;*

   (e)   To ensure that the composition of the teaching staff of institutions reflects, as far as possible, the racial and

ethnic composition of the community; affirmative action programmes should be instituted to facilitate the hiring of teachers who represent the racial, ethnic and linguistic composition of the community;

(*f*) To make available the resources of schools and of teaching and training facilities to persons belonging to all population groups;

(*g*) To take remedial measures in instances where particular racial, ethnic, linguistic or other groups have had a history of being placed at a disadvantage because of their origin and where such a situation has contributed to a lower level of education and a lower standard of living for persons belonging to various population groups; this is the responsibility of society; it might necessitate special educational programmes at all levels of society;

(*h*) To make law enforcement agents aware in their training of the possibility that they may reflect the prejudices of their society;

(*i*) To ensure that school curricula promote a dialogue between persons belonging to the various groups of the society; the curricula should be responsive to the needs and backgrounds of all these persons and foster, where possible, an interchange of cultural experience; in this regard, persons belonging to minority ethnic and racial groups should be allowed to introduce students to the practices and values of the respective cultures; efforts should also be made to allow the topic of human rights to permeate the curricula.

17. National institutions should inform the general public of the nature of their human rights as provided for in the existing international instruments directed towards combating racism, racial discrimination and *apartheid*, as well as in other instruments based on the principles contained in the Universal Declaration of Human Rights or as otherwise covered in national legislation. The general public should be advised by the national institutions on the means of enforcing their rights in accordance with national law. National institutions should ensure that persons are made aware of their own rights and those of others and should assist them in the matter of protecting and enforcing their rights. These institutions should mobilize public opinion in their countries against violations of human rights, especially gross and massive violations, in particular against the practice of *apartheid*, racism and genocide.

18. One of the fundamental objectives of programmes of education and scientific research undertaken in national institutions should be the elimination of racial discrimination and prejudice.

19. It is imperative that all States apply strictly the principle of non-discrimination and equality in the matter of education and adhere to the principles set forth in the Convention against Discrimination in Education. It is important that the right to enter any school should be guaranteed to every child. The availability of special or supplementary education for children belonging to disadvantaged racial and ethnic groups may be appropriate in some cases for their development.

20. International agencies such as the United Nations Educational, Scientific and Cultural Organization should continue their work in the field of human rights education and promote such programmes on a continuing basis as guidelines for textbook analysis, teacher training, curriculum development and other undertakings and, in particular, should develop materials

explaining how discrimination inherent in the system and institutionalized can be addressed through remedial programmes such as affirmative action plans.

21. As was recommended by the International Conference on *Apartheid* and Health, held at Brazzaville from 16 to 20 November 1981, the World Health Organization should continue to implement the Plan of Action in favour of the victims of *apartheid*, in particular in the fields of health, education and training.

C. Dissemination of information and the role of the mass media in combating racism and racial discrimination

22. The mass media should play a vital role in disseminating information on methods and techniques used in combating racism, racial discrimination and *apartheid*. Taking into account the Declaration on fundamental principles concerning the contribution of the mass media to strengthening peace and international understanding, to the promotion of human rights and countering racialism, *apartheid* and incitement to war, adopted by the United Nations Educational, Scientific and Cultural Organization on 28 November 1978, the mass media should regard it as their task, by disseminating information on the aims, aspirations, cultures and needs of all peoples, to contribute to eliminating ignorance and misunderstanding between peoples, to making nationals of a country sensitive to the needs and desires of others, to ensuring respect for the rights and dignity of all nations, all peoples and all individuals without distinction as to race, sex, language, religion or nationality and in that way to contribute to protecting them against the influence of any propaganda supporting racism and racist régimes.

23. The mass media should contribute to making the peoples more aware of the close link between the struggle against *apartheid* and all forms of racism and racial discrimination and the struggle for international peace and security, in accordance with the provisions of the above-mentioned Declaration.

24. Lack of self-expression through the mass media for persons belonging to racial and ethnic minorities in a society can often cause the mass media to become one-sided or distorted. Media of all kinds—radio, television, films, the press, advertising, booklets and public meetings—as well as traditional forms such as drama and story-telling could play a vital role.

25. Events and activities aimed at combating racism and racial discrimination should be given broad coverage by the media. Mention may be made of such activities as the coverage of conferences, seminars, workshops and round tables, as well as of meetings of United Nations organs dealing with a particular question, and the publication and wide distribution of pertinent resolutions and decisions of such bodies. Success stories in combating racial discrimination through legislation, executive action or community action programmes should be given publicity, and the negative and evil side of racism and racial discrimination highlighted. Comic strips, films and magazines for children and adults should be screened with a view to eliminating any form of racial stereotyping, whether favourable or unfavourable. Events having a racial aspect should be presented in their economic and social, cultural and political context; they should not be treated as mere news items.

26. The negative and positive influences exercised by the media in their role as information-conveyors,

entertainers, educators and advertisers should be studied. In addition, the media should seek to raise public consciousness about the positive roles and achievements of racial and ethnic groups from all walks of life throughout history. Efforts should be made to produce radio and television programmes depicting the evils of racial discrimination in a vivid way—for example, by illustrating the plight of individual victims of racial discrimination. Such audio and visual presentations are likely to have great impact, particularly in areas where literacy is not widespread.

27. There should be adequate opportunity within the mass media for persons belonging to groups which are victims of discrimination to express their own points of view, particularly by producing programmes or reports themselves. In addition, persons belonging to such groups should have equal access to the professions within the mass media, especially journalism.

28. National institutions should publicize widely basic texts on the elimination of racism, racial discrimination and *apartheid*, as well as other human rights texts.

D. Measures for the promotion and protection of the human rights of persons belonging to minority groups, indigenous populations and peoples and migrant workers who are subjected to racial discrimination

29. Throughout the various regions of the world there is a diversity of peoples, cultures, traditions and religions that encompasses, in many instances, various minority groups. There is a need for constant effort and continued vigilance on the part of all Governments to obviate any form of discrimination based on race, colour, descent or national or ethnic origin, in accordance with article 1 of the International Convention on the Elimination of All Forms of Racial Discrimination.

30. National and local institutions, as adapted to the needs and conditions of each country, can play an important role in the promotion and protection of human rights, in the prevention of discrimination and the protection of the rights of persons belonging to national and ethnic minorities, of indigenous populations and of refugees. Such national and local institutions could be of varying types, including judicial, administrative, conciliatory, social and educational. Any or all of these types of institutions could be utilized by individual countries according to their own circumstances and needs.

31. In the area of legislation, Governments should abolish and prohibit any discrimination within their jurisdiction. Such legislation should seek to promote and protect the human rights of persons belonging to minority groups, in accordance with the Universal Declaration of Human Rights, the International Covenant on Civil and Political Rights, the International Convention on the Elimination of All Forms of Racial Discrimination and other relevant international instruments. Persons belonging to minorities should enjoy all human rights and fundamental freedoms without any discrimination as to national or ethnic origin, language, religion or sex.

32. Governments should create favourable conditions and take measures that will enable persons belonging to national or ethnic minorities within their jurisdiction to express their characteristics freely and to develop their education, culture, language, traditions and customs and to participate on a non-discriminatory and equitable basis in the cultural, social, economic and political life of the country in which they live. In main-

taining their culture and traditions such persons should be in a position to develop the necessary contacts inside and outside their country, with due respect for the sovereignty, territorial integrity and political independence of the States concerned and for the principle of non-interference by one State in the internal affairs of another State.

33. States should undertake to combat the causes of inter-group antagonism by adopting concrete measures designed to promote understanding, co-operation and harmonious relations among members of population groups. Where tension and friction exist, their elimination cannot be achieved if the realities of political, economic, cultural, religious and linguistic differences between the various components of the society concerned are not taken into account.

34. With respect to indigenous populations, Governments should recognize and respect the basic rights of such populations:

(*a*) To call themselves by their proper name and to express freely their own identity;

(*b*) To have official status and to form their own representative organizations;

(*c*) To maintain within the areas where they live their traditional economic structure and way of life; this should in no way affect their right to participate freely on an equal basis in the economic, social and political development of the country;

(*d*) To maintain and use their own language, wherever possible, for administration and education;

(*e*) To enjoy freedom of religion or belief;

(*f*) To have access to land and natural resources, particularly in the light of the fundamental importance of rights to land and natural resources to their traditions and aspirations;

(*g*) To structure, conduct and control their own educational systems.

35. Indigenous populations should be free to manage their own affairs to the fullest practicable extent, and should be consulted in all matters concerning their interests and welfare, wherever possible through formal consultative arrangements. Special measures should be taken to remedy past dispossession, dispersal and systematic discrimination.

36. Funds should be made available by the national authorities for investments, the uses of which are to be determined with the participation of the indigenous populations themselves, in the economic life of the areas concerned, as well as in all spheres of cultural activity.

37. Governments should allow indigenous populations within their territories to develop cultural and social links with related or similar populations, taking into account the important role of international organizations or associations of indigenous populations, and with due respect for the sovereignty, territorial integrity and political independence of the countries in which indigenous populations live.

38. The Conference further urges States to facilitate and support the establishment of representative nongovernmental international organizations for indigenous populations, through which they can share experiences and promote common interests. The Sub-Commission on Prevention of Discrimination and Protection of Minorities should ensure that the urgent work being carried out by its Working Group on Indigenous Populations is continued so that the complex issues involved

can be analysed and appropriate measures taken at the international and national levels.

39. In view of the vulnerability of indigenous populations to discrimination and violations of their human rights, and of the gravity of the threat faced by indigenous populations in some parts of the world, Governments should pay close attention to situations in which the rights of indigenous populations may be violated or denied, in order to prevent such violations, which should be widely publicized as soon as they are detected.

40. States receiving migrant workers should eliminate all discriminatory practices against such workers and their families by giving them treatment no less favourable than that accorded to their own nationals. Host countries should eliminate from their legislation any type of legal or other provisions which may discriminate against migrant workers on the basis of their nationality. This should pertain, *inter alia*, to vocational training, the type of posts that migrants may occupy, the type of contracts accorded to migrant workers, their right to seek employment in any part of the country, regulations governing working conditions, trade-union activity and access to judicial and administrative tribunals to air grievances concerning discrimination. With a view to combating xenophobia, host countries should develop information campaigns in order to disseminate the idea of equality between nationals and migrant workers.

41. The following measures could also be undertaken by Governments to protect the rights of migrant workers:

(a) The General Assembly should complete, as soon as possible, the elaboration of an international convention on the protection of the rights of all migrant workers and their families; the Conference considers that the conclusion of this convention by the United Nations would constitute an important contribution to its endeavours to protect fundamental human rights, because the convention would be added to the other instruments protecting these rights; the Conference recommends, pending the conclusion of the above-mentioned convention, that a joint consultative mechanism should be established in host countries with a view to contributing to good relations and mutual understanding;

(b) States should ratify, accede to and implement the international instruments aimed at protecting migrant workers from discrimination, including the relevant conventions of the International Labour Organisation;

(c) Migrant workers and members of their families should have the same rights as nationals of the State concerned as regards access to and treatment by the courts and tribunals;

(d) All migrant workers should enjoy treatment no less favourable than that accorded to nationals of the host State in respect of remuneration;

(e) Migrant workers should be ensured equal treatment with national workers in the field of social security, including the right to a retirement pension and similar social rights, while they have lawful residence in the host country;

(f) Host countries should be invited to co-operate with countries of origin to provide migrant workers and their families with the necessary facilities in the fields of education and information to safeguard their cultural identity;

(g) The children of migrant workers should be enabled to receive education in their mother tongue and on different aspects of their cultural heritage with a view to preserving their national identity;

(h) The State of origin and the State of employment should co-operate, as far as possible, with a view to helping to create new job opportunities for migrant workers returning to the State of origin.

E. Recourse procedures for victims of racial discrimination

42. The Conference invites States to take into account, within their domestic recourse procedures, the following considerations:

(a) Access to such procedures should be as broad as possible;

(b) Existing recourse procedures should be publicized within their respective jurisdictions, and victims of racial discrimination should be assisted in utilizing the procedures where appropriate;

(c) In each jurisdiction the rules relating to the initiation of complaints should be made simple and flexible and capable of being entertained in the language of the complainant;

(d) Complaints of racial discrimination should be dealt with as expeditiously as possible and there should be a reasonable time-limit with regard to the length of investigations;

(e) Indigent victims of racial discrimination should receive legal aid and assistance in prosecuting their complaint in civil or criminal proceedings, with the help of an interpreter when necessary.

43. Victims of racial discrimination should have the right to seek from tribunals just and adequate reparation or satisfaction for any damage suffered as a result of such discrimination.

F. Implementation of the International Convention on the Elimination of All Forms of Racial Discrimination and other related international instruments

44. The Conference urges States which have not yet become parties to the International Convention on the Elimination of All Forms of Racial Discrimination to do so as part of their contribution to the objectives of the Decade for Action to Combat Racism and Racial Discrimination and until such States ratify the Convention they should utilize its provisions as guidelines in combating racial discrimination and in securing the realization of the principles of equality at both the national and international levels. The Conference calls upon States parties to the Convention to consider the possibility of making the Declaration provided for in article·14 of the Convention.

45. Those States should enact, as a matter of the highest priority, appropriate legislation and other suitable measures to prohibit and bring to an end racial discrimination, to abrogate, amend, rescind or nullify any policies or regulations that have the effect of creating or perpetuating racial hatred and to declare the dissemination of ideas based on racial superiority and hatred to be an offence punishable by law, taking duly into account the provisions of the International Convention on the Elimination of All Forms of Racial Discrimination.

46. The Conference also appeals to States which have not yet done so to consider ratifying or acceding to as soon as possible other relevant international instruments adopted under the aegis of the United Nations and of the specialized agencies, such as the Convention on the Prevention and Punishment of the Crime of Genocide, the International Covenant on Economic, Social and Cultural Rights, the International Covenant

on Civil and Political Rights, the Convention on the Non-Applicability of Statutory Limitations to War Crimes and Crimes against Humanity, the International Convention on the Suppression and Punishment of the Crime of *Apartheid*, the Convention concerning Discrimination in Respect of Employment and Occupation adopted by the International Labour Organisation on 25 June 1958, the Convention against Discrimination in Education adopted by the United Nations Educational, Scientific and Cultural Organization and the Convention on the Elimination of All Forms of Discrimination against Women; States are urged to comply with the reporting requirements called for by the relevant conventions.

G.   National legislation and institutions

47.   The Conference suggests that States that have not already done so should consider the urgent enactment, as a matter of the highest priority, of appropriate legislation and other suitable measures to prohibit and bring to an end racial discrimination, to abrogate, amend, rescind or nullify any policies or regulations that have the effect of creating or perpetuating racial hatred and, with due regard to the principles embodied in the Universal Declaration of Human Rights, the United Nations Declaration on the Elimination of All Forms of Racial Discrimination, the Declaration on Fundamental Principles concerning the Contribution of the Mass Media to Strengthening Peace and International Understanding, to the Promotion of Human Rights and to Countering Racialism, *Apartheid* and Incitement to War, the Declaration on Race and Racial Prejudice adopted by the United Nations Educational, Scientific and Cultural Organization on 27 November 1978, and the rights set forth in the International Convention on the Elimination of All Forms of Racial Discrimination, to declare the dissemination of ideas based on racial superiority and hatred to be an offence punishable by law.

48.   The Conference calls upon all States that have not yet done so to take effective legislative and other measures, including in the field of penal law, to prevent the recruitment, use, financing and training, transit and transport of mercenaries, in particular when the aim is to assist racist régimes, and to punish such mercenaries as common criminals. The Conference urges the *Ad Hoc* Committee on the Drafting of an International Convention against the Recruitment, Use, Financing and Training of Mercenaries, established by the General Assembly at its thirty-fifth session, to complete, as soon as possible, the draft international convention.

49.   The Conference urges all States to adopt strict legislation to declare any dissemination of ideas based on racial superiority or hatred to be an offence punishable by law and to prohibit organizations based on racial prejudice and hatred, including neo-Nazi and Fascist organizations, and private clubs and institutions established on the basis of racial criteria or propagating ideas of racial discrimination and *apartheid*.

50.   With regard to national legislation, the Conference recommends that:

(*a*)   Governments, where necessary, should guarantee non-discrimination on grounds of race and equal rights for all individuals in their constitutions and legislation;

(*b*)   Governments, where necessary, should undertake to review and update all national legislation and remove from it any discriminatory provisions;

(*c*)   Legislation should be consistent with international standards embodied in relevant international instruments;

(*d*)   Victims of discrimination should be informed and advised of their rights, by all possible means, and given assistance in securing those rights;

(*e*)   Governments should, where necessary, establish appropriate and effective mechanisms, including conciliation and mediation procedures and national commissions, to ensure that such legislation is enforced effectively and thereby to promote equality of opportunity and good race relations.

51.   A system of regular review and appraisal should be continued to enable Member States, all organizations of the United Nations system, including relevant regional bodies, and non-governmental organizations, to assess the measures taken towards achieving the aims and objectives of the Decade.

52.   Within the framework of their national legislation and policy, and according to their means, States should set up national institutions for the promotion and protection of human rights. Those institutions should study legal developments and review the laws and policies of the Government with a view to ensuring the elimination of all discriminatory laws, prejudices and practices based on race, sex, colour, descent and national and ethnic origin.

H.   Seminars and studies

53.   The Conference recommends that, in the context of future activities to combat racism and racial discrimination, consideration should be given to the organization of international and regional seminars on such subjects as:

(*a*)   Political, historical, economic, social and cultural factors leading to racism, racial discrimination and *apartheid;*

(*b*)   International assistance and support to peoples and movements struggling against colonialism, racism, racial discrimination and *apartheid;*

(*c*)   Ways and means of denying support to racist régimes with a view to making them change their policies;

(*d*)   The historical and current dimensions of tribalism;

(*e*)   Main obstacles to the full eradication of racism, racial discrimination and *apartheid;*

(*f*)   The human rights of persons belonging to ethnic groups in countries of immigration;

(*g*)   Equality of treatment for persons belonging to ethnic and racial minorities and disadvantaged groups, such as indigenous populations;

(*h*)   Community relations commissions and their functions.

54.   The Conference also recommends that studies should be continued regarding ways and means of ensuring implementation of United Nations resolutions on *apartheid*, racism and racial discrimination. In particular, the Conference strongly encourages the United Nations Institute for Training and Research to continue to research, study and conduct seminars on racism and racial discrimination.

I.   Action by non-governmental organizations

55.   By virtue of their independent status, non-governmental organizations, individually and collectively, have an important contribution to make to the achievement of the objectives of the Decade for Action to Combat Racism and Racial Discrimination. Through

various activities sponsored by them, non-governmental organizations can be effective in identifying and publicizing areas of racial discrimination which otherwise might not come to light and in helping to create greater practical understanding among young people of the importance of actively combating all forms of discrimination, in their own countries as well as in the international community.

56. Non-governmental organizations have the opportunity to create and sustain awareness among their members and in society at large of the evils of racism and racial discrimination. Such awareness can be transmitted from a national to an international organization with all the added benefits of the concrete experience of a particular country. Governments should therefore ensure that non-governmental organizations shall be enabled to function freely and openly within their societies and thus make an effective contribution to the elimination of racism and racial discrimination throughout the world.

J. International co-operation

57. In order to obtain the full promotion and protection of the human rights of individuals and peoples, it is necessary to intensify national, regional and international action aimed at combating and eliminating the causes of the policies and practices of racism, racial discrimination and *apartheid*.

58. The Conference underlines that the maintenance and strengthening of international co-operation and peace, the implementation of human rights and the combating of *apartheid* and racial discrimination are clearly linked. In order to improve mutual understanding among peoples, exchange visits should be increased and educational, cultural and scientific exchange programmes should be expanded. The free flow of information and ideas with respect to combating racism and racial discrimination should be ensured. The Conference calls on States to exchange information and ideas with respect to combating racism and racial discrimination.

59. The Conference calls upon the World Conference to Review and Appraise the Achievements of the United Nations Decade for Women, to be held in 1985, to contribute to the struggle against racism, racial discrimination and *apartheid* by recommending the adoption of measures aimed at ensuring the active participation of women in the struggle against those evils.

60. The Conference recommends that, in the context of International Youth Year, in 1985, the United Nations and the specialized agencies should undertake activities to encourage the effective contribution of youth to the struggle against racism, racial discrimination and *apartheid*.

61. The Conference calls upon all Governments and international organizations to make every effort to change the economic, political and social conditions on which policies and practices of racism, racial discrimination and *apartheid* are based and to give all their support to the victims of racism, racial discrimination and *apartheid*, and declares that the struggle against the remnants of colonialism and support of the liberation movements recognized by the regional organizations are worthy of particular attention.

62. Article 28 of the Universal Declaration of Human Rights establishes that everyone is entitled to a social and international order in which the rights and freedoms set forth in the Declaration can be fully realized. For this purpose, it is necessary to work for the establishment of a just and fair international order. The establishment of a new international economic order would be an important means of combating the causes which generate racism and racial discrimination.

63. National, regional and international action to combat and eliminate the causes of the policies and practices of racism, racial discrimination and *apartheid* should include measures aimed at improving the conditions of life of peoples and individuals in the economic, political, social and cultural spheres in order that the great inequalities now existing in the fields of employment, nutrition, health, housing and education, among others, may disappear. International development co-operation has an important role to play in securing the resources required by the developing countries to realize these objectives.

64. The Conference urges Governments, with the co-operation of the relevant international organizations, to consider adopting measures to guarantee, through special conventions or other provisions, asylum and transit facilities to those who desert from the armed forces of the racist régime in southern Africa on grounds of conscience or who are forced to leave because of their opposition to *apartheid*.

65. The Conference proclaims that the elimination of all forms of racial discrimination is a matter of high priority to the United Nations and the international community. It proclaims that racism and racial discrimination in all their manifestations are crimes against the conscience and dignity of mankind and must be eradicated by effective and concerted international action. The Conference pays tribute to the United Nations Educational, Scientific and Cultural Organization for its activities during the Decade to Combat Racism and Racial Discrimination and recommends that, within the framework of its Second Medium-term Plan (1984-1989), that organization should continue:

(a) Its work (studies and research) on the factors of influence in the maintenance, transmission and alteration of prejudices and on the causes and effects of the various forms of racism and racial and ethnic discrimination;

(b) Its efforts to ensure that all groups which suffer from discrimination in the fields of education, science, culture and information shall enjoy equal opportunities with others and that the members of such groups shall have full representation and shall be able to exercise their rights in those fields;

(c) Its programme on the appreciation of differing cultures and the promotion and recognition of the equality of cultures and peoples;

(d) Its research and studies on *apartheid*, and the widest possible dissemination of the results of its work.

66. In spite of the efforts of the international community at the national, regional and international levels during the Decade for Action to Combat Racism and Racial Discrimination, racism, racial discrimination and *apartheid* continue unabated and have shown no sign of diminishing. With a view to reaffirming its unalterable determination to mobilize maximum international pressure to attain the objectives of the Decade, the Conference strongly recommends that the General Assembly declare a Second Decade to Combat Racism and Racial Discrimination at the end of the current Decade in December 1983.

General Assembly resolution 38/14

22 November 1983   Meeting 66   Adopted without vote

Approved by Third Committee (A/38/541) by consensus, 26 October (meeting 21); draft by Senegal, for African Group (A/C.3/38/L.8); agenda items 82 and 83.
Meeting numbers. GA 38th session: 3rd Committee 4-18, 21; plenary 66.

Also on 22 November, on the recommendation of the Third Committee, the Assembly adopted resolution 38/15 without vote.

Second World Conference to Combat Racism and Racial Discrimination

The General Assembly,

Recalling its resolution 3057(XXVIII) of 2 November 1973, by which it designated the ten-year period beginning on 10 December 1973 as the Decade for Action to Combat Racism and Racial Discrimination,

Further recalling its resolution 37/41 of 3 December 1982, by which it decided to convene the Second World Conference to Combat Racism and Racial Discrimination at Geneva from 1 to 12 August 1983,

Taking note with appreciation of the *Report of the Second World Conference to Combat Racism and Racial Discrimination* as well as the report of the Secretary-General on the Conference,

Recalling its resolution 38/14 of 22 November 1983, by which the General Assembly proclaimed the ten-year period beginning on 10 December 1983 the Second Decade to Combat Racism and Racial Discrimination,

1. *Expresses its satisfaction* at the serious and constructive work undertaken at the Second World Conference to Combat Racism and Racial Discrimination;

2. *Pays tribute* to the Secretary-General of the Conference for his efforts to promote the aims and objectives of the Conference;

3. *Expresses its firm determination* to continue in the future to attach the highest importance to combating racism and racial discrimination in all their forms;

4. *Appeals* to all Governments, United Nations organs, the specialized agencies and other intergovernmental organizations, as well as the concerned non-governmental organizations in consultative status with the Economic and Social Council, to participate in the observance of the Second Decade to Combat Racism and Racial Discrimination by intensifying and extending their efforts towards ensuring the rapid eradication of racism and racial discrimination;

5. *Decides* to consider at its thirty-ninth session concrete action to be undertaken during the Second Decade.

General Assembly resolution 38/15

22 November 1983   Meeting 66   Adopted without vote

Approved by Third Committee (A/38/541) by consensus, 26 October (meeting 21); draft by Senegal, for African Group (A/C.3/38/L.9), orally revised; agenda items 82 and 83.
Meeting numbers. GA 38th session: 3rd Committee 4-18, 21; plenary 66.

Following adoption of the foregoing resolutions, the United States noted for the record that it had not participated in the consensus on the draft texts in the Third Committee. In a statement of position during the Committee debate, the United States said that only by preserving the universal character of the concern for human rights could abuses of human rights be condemned. If the As-

sembly adopted resolutions against racial persecution only in South Africa, while ignoring political suppression in the USSR, or the terror that had claimed many lives in east Africa and eastern Europe or in the skies over the USSR, one was forced to wonder whether such resolutions arose from a desire to distract attention from such massive violations by Members whose voices were loudest in condemning South Africa. The United States went on to say that although it would not be easy to make changes in South Africa, the white community there was not a monolith; there appeared to be some tendency towards greater racial equity in the economic sphere, implying in some cases a political change as well. The task of bringing about the desired change required formulation of programmes aimed at giving greater impetus to the forces of constructive change. As long as there was hope of change through constructive means, it would be immoral to isolate the world from encouraging that hope.

Also speaking during the Committee debate, Israel said that it had unequivocally supported the 1973 Programme for the Decade for Action to Combat Racism and Racial Discrimination.[13] No lessons had been drawn from the negative experience of the first (1978) World Conference,[7] however, so that, at the Second, Israel had once again been singled out for vicious and groundless accusations, which only harmed the general cause and undermined the consensus necessary for combating racism and racial discrimination. Israel objected in the strongest terms to the selective and unwarranted condemnations of it in the Declaration. Nothing in its attitude towards Arabs or others, Israel asserted, could be characterized as remotely akin to racial discrimination; if there was an element of racism in the Arab-Israeli conflict, it stemmed from the other side.

Other action. Noting that many points in the Programme of Action had a direct bearing on its work, the Sub-Commission on Prevention of Discrimination and Protection of Minorities, by a resolution of 5 September 1983,[22] expressed appreciation for the Conference and the Declaration and Programme of Action. It endorsed the series of studies and seminars proposed in the Programme and recommended to the Commission on Human Rights a draft resolution for adoption by the Economic and Social Council, authorizing the Sub-Commission to entrust Asbjørn Eide (Norway) with a study on achievements made and obstacles encountered during the Decade, to include proposals for new or additional measures. The Sub-Commission took that action by 19 votes to 1, with 3 abstentions.

On 31 August,[23] the Sub-Commission recommended to the Commission adoption of another draft resolution, commending the United Nations

Educational, Scientific and Cultural Organization (UNESCO) for its work in education to combat racism and racial discrimination, and appealing to States to encourage educational institutions to incorporate in their curricula the concept of oneness and biological unity of the human race and the social, economic, cultural and political interdependence of all peoples.

Convention on the elimination of racial discrimination

Accessions and ratifications

As at 31 December 1983, there were 122 parties to the International Convention on the Elimination of All Forms of Racial Discrimination, adopted by the General Assembly in 1965[15] and in force since 1969.[24] In 1983, five States (Afghanistan, Democratic Kampuchea, Dominican Republic, Guatemala, Mozambique) became parties.

In his annual report to the Assembly on the status of the Convention,[25] the Secretary-General listed the States which had signed, ratified or acceded to it as at 1 September.

GENERAL ASSEMBLY ACTION

On 22 November, the General Assembly, on the recommendation of the Third Committee, adopted resolution 38/18 without vote.

Status of the International Convention on the Elimination of All Forms of Racial Discrimination
The General Assembly,

Recalling its resolutions 3057(XXVIII) of 2 November 1973, 3135(XXVIII) of 14 December 1973, 3225(XXIX) of 6 November 1974, 3381(XXX) of 10 November 1975, 31/79 of 13 December 1976, 32/11 of 7 November 1977, 33/101 of 16 December 1978, 34/26 of 15 November 1979, 35/38 of 25 November 1980, 36/11 of 28 October 1981 and 37/45 of 3 December 1982,

Expressing its satisfaction at the entry into force, on 3 December 1982, of the competence of the Committee on the Elimination of Racial Discrimination to accept and to examine communications from persons or groups of persons under article 14 of the International Convention on the Elimination of All Forms of Racial Discrimination,

1. *Takes note* of the report of the Secretary-General on the status of the International Convention on the Elimination of All Forms of Racial Discrimination;

2. *Expresses its satisfaction* at the increase in the number of States that have ratified the Convention or acceded thereto;

3. *Reaffirms once again its conviction* that ratification of or accession to the Convention on a universal basis and implementation of its provisions are necessary for the realization of the objectives of the Decade for Action to Combat Racism and Racial Discrimination;

4. *Requests* those States that have not yet become parties to the Convention to ratify it or accede thereto;

5. *Calls upon* States parties to the Convention to consider the possibility of making the declaration provided for in article 14 of the Convention;

6. *Requests* the Secretary-General to continue to submit to the General Assembly annual reports concerning the status of the Convention, in accordance with Assembly resolution 2106 A (XX) of 21 December 1965.

General Assembly resolution 38/18
22 November 1983   Meeting 66   Adopted without vote

Approved by Third Committee (A/38/543) without vote, 25 October (meeting 20); 26-nation draft (A/C.3/38/L.4), amended by 10 nations (A/C.3/38/L.11); agenda item 87 *(b)*.
Sponsors of draft: Algeria, Argentina, Australia, Bahamas, Bangladesh, Barbados, Belgium, Bulgaria, Cuba, Cyprus, Denmark, Egypt, Germany, Federal Republic of, Hungary, India, Morocco, New Zealand, Nigeria, Pakistan, Portugal, Spain, Syrian Arab Republic, Trinidad and Tobago, Upper Volta, Venezuela, Yugoslavia.
Sponsors of amendments: Costa Rica, Ecuador, France, Iceland, Italy, Netherlands, Norway, Senegal, Sweden, Uruguay.
Meeting numbers. GA 38th session: 3rd Committee 4-18, 20; plenary 66.

Before approving the draft resolution as a whole, the Third Committee adopted, by 58 votes to 3, with 54 abstentions, amendments introduced by Uruguay on behalf of 10 nations. The amendments added the second preambular paragraph and operative paragraph 5.

Implementation of the Convention

Communication. By a letter of 18 October 1983 to the Secretary-General,[26] Israel drew attention to its statement of 16 October concerning the sentencing of Iosif Begun by a USSR court because of his desire to emigrate to Israel and to study and teach the Hebrew language and Jewish culture. Israel called on the USSR to desist from discrimination and repression against Jews and to accord them the human rights to which they were entitled.

CERD activities. The Committee on the Elimination of Racial Discrimination, set up under article 8 of the Convention, held two sessions in 1983, in New York: the twenty-seventh from 7 to 25 March and the twenty-eighth from 11 to 29 July.

Two thirds of the meetings at those sessions were devoted to an examination of reports and additional information submitted by 36 States parties under article 9 of the Convention, on measures to give effect to the Convention's provisions. The annual report of CERD to the Assembly[27] summarized members' views on each country report and statements made by the States parties concerned, and reported on action taken to ensure submission of reports.

As authorized by article 15 of the Convention, also examined were copies of petitions, reports and other information concerning Trust and Non-Self-Governing Territories transmitted by the Trusteeship Council (see TRUSTEESHIP AND DECOLONIZATION, Chapter II) and the Special Committee on the Situation with regard to the Implementation of the Declaration on the Granting of Independence to Colonial Countries and Peoples. In March, CERD approved the membership of its three working groups to examine documentation submitted under article 15 and to report their findings to its July session. On 26 July, CERD adopted the groups' reports with some amendments. On the basis of those reports and other information, it further adopted on the same date opinions and recommendations relating to: African Territories, including Namibia; Pacific and Indian Ocean Territories; and Atlantic Ocean and Caribbean Territories, including Gibraltar.

As a result of the entry into force in December 1982 of article 14[(28)] recognizing CERD's competence to accept and examine communications from individuals or groups of individuals claiming to be victims of a violation of any of the rights under the Convention, CERD, also on 26 July 1983, adopted provisional rules of procedure for considering those communications.

In addition, on 21 March,[(29)] CERD, alarmed at the reported changes in the demographic composition of that territory of Cyprus not under the control of its Government that excluded a considerable segment of the population from enjoyment of their legitimate rights, reiterated its expectation that Cyprus would be enabled, without further delay, to exercise full responsibility for implementing its obligations under the Convention on the whole of its national territory, and that the unacceptable state of affairs in Cyprus due to foreign occupation would be brought to an end.

GENERAL ASSEMBLY ACTION

On 22 November 1983, the General Assembly, on the recommendation of the Third Committee, adopted resolution 38/21 without vote.

Report of the Committee on the Elimination of Racial Discrimination

The General Assembly,

Recalling its resolutions 37/46 of 3 December 1982 on the report of the Committee on the Elimination of Racial Discrimination and 38/18 of 22 November 1983 on the status of the International Convention on the Elimination of All Forms of Racial Discrimination, as well as its other relevant resolutions on the implementation of the Programme for the Decade for Action to Combat Racism and Racial Discrimination,

Having considered the report of the Committee on the Elimination of Racial Discrimination on its twenty-seventh and twenty-eighth sessions, submitted under article 9, paragraph 2, of the International Convention on the Elimination of All Forms of Racial Discrimination,

Emphasizing that it is important for the success of the struggle against all instances of racial discrimination, including vestiges and manifestations of racist ideologies wherever they exist, that all Member States be guided in their internal and foreign policies by the basic provisions of the Convention,

Mindful of the obligation of all States parties to comply fully with the provisions of the Convention,

Welcoming all States that have ratified or acceded to the Convention, including Namibia, which acceded to the Convention on 11 December 1982, represented by the United Nations Council for Namibia,

Welcoming also the continued co-operation of the Committee with the competent specialized agencies, especially with the United Nations Educational, Scientific and Cultural Organization and the International Labour Organisation, and other United Nations bodies,

Taking note of the decisions adopted and the recommendations made by the Committee at its twenty-seventh and twenty-eighth sessions,

1. *Takes note with appreciation* of the report of the Committee on the Elimination of Racial Discrimination on its twenty-seventh and twenty-eighth sessions;

2. *Commends* the Committee for its contribution to the elimination of all forms of discrimination based on race, colour, descent, or national or ethnic origin, wherever it exists;

3. *Strongly condemns* the policy of *apartheid* in South Africa and Namibia as the most abhorrent form of racial discrimination and urges all Member States to adopt effective political, economic and other measures in order to secure the elimination of that policy and to achieve the full implementation of the relevant resolutions of the General Assembly, the Security Council and other United Nations bodies;

4. *Calls upon* the United Nations bodies concerned to ensure that the Committee is supplied with all relevant information on all the Territories to which General Assembly resolution 1514(XV) of 14 December 1960 applies and urges the administering Powers to co-operate with these bodies by providing all the necessary information in order to enable the Committee to discharge fully its responsibilities under article 15 of the International Convention on the Elimination of All Forms of Racial Discrimination;

5. *Commends* the Committee for its continuous endeavours towards the elimination of the policy of *apartheid*, racism and racial discrimination in southern Africa and the implementation of the United Nations resolutions relating to the liberation and independence of Namibia;

6. *Welcomes* the efforts of the Committee aimed at the elimination of all forms of discrimination against national or ethnic minorities, persons belonging to such minorities and indigenous populations, wherever such discrimination exists, and the attainment of the full enjoyment of their human rights through the implementation of the principles and provisions of the Convention;

7. *Welcomes further* the efforts of the Committee aimed at the elimination of all forms of discrimination against migrant workers and their families, the promotion of their rights on a non-discriminatory basis and the achievement of their full equality, including the freedom to maintain their cultural characteristics;

8. *Calls upon* all Member States to adopt effective legislative, socio-economic and other necessary measures in order to ensure the prevention or elimination of discrimination based on race, colour, descent or national or ethnic origin;

9. *Further calls upon* the States parties to the Convention to protect fully, by the adoption of the relevant legislative and other measures, in conformity with the Convention, the rights of national or ethnic minorities and persons belonging to such minorities, as well as the rights of indigenous populations;

10. *Commends* the States parties to the Convention on the measures taken to ensure, within their jurisdiction, the availability of appropriate recourse procedures for the victims of racial discrimination;

11. *Reiterates its invitation* to the States parties to the Convention to provide the Committee, in accordance with its general guidelines, with information on the implementation of the provisions of the Convention, including information on the demographic composition of their population and on their relations with the racist régime of South Africa;

12. *Takes note with appreciation* of the contribution of the Committee towards the achievement of the goals of the Decade to Combat Racism and Racial Discrimination, as well as its contribution to the Second World Conference to Combat Racism and Racial Discrimination in preparing studies on the implementation of particular articles of the Convention;

13. *Appeals* to the States parties to take fully into consideration their obligation under the Convention to submit their reports in due time.

General Assembly resolution 38/21

22 November 1983   Meeting 66   Adopted without vote

Approved by Third Committee (A/38/543) without vote, 27 October (meeting 23); 17-nation draft (A/C.3/38/L.7), orally revised; agenda item 87 *(a)*.
Sponsors: Angola, Bangladesh, Benin, Bolivia, Cape Verde, China, Cuba, Ecuador, Jordan, Madagascar, Nigeria, Pakistan, Sierra Leone, Yemen, Yugoslavia, Zambia, Zimbabwe.
Meeting numbers. GA 38th session: 3rd Committee 4-18, 20-23; plenary 66.

Prior to approving the text as a whole, the Third Committee adopted paragraph 3 by 93 votes to none, with 20 abstentions, and paragraph 11 by 88 votes to none, with 25 abstentions.

Other action. The Second World Conference to Combat Racism and Racial Discrimination in August (see above) called for implementation of the Convention and urged States not parties to it to become parties, or to be guided by its provisions in combating racial discrimination.

Reporting obligations of States parties

As requested by the General Assembly in December 1982,[30] the Secretary-General reported to it in September 1983[31] on the reporting obligations of States parties to the Convention against racial discrimination and other relevant human rights instruments. Based on an analysis of replies received from 22 States in response to his note verbale of 25 January 1983, the Secretary-General put forward several recommendations to improve the situation arising from the high incidence of non-compliance with reporting obligations.

It appeared evident, the Secretary-General stated, that a number of States parties—many of them developing countries—experienced difficulties in submitting not only the periodic report but also the initial one due normally within a year of an instrument's entry into force. The difficulties cited included lack of human and material resources, language difficulties where a reporting country's language was not among the United Nations official languages, the shortness of the interval between reports (two years under article 9 of the Convention), and additional reporting obligations under other instruments that must be met simultaneously. Thus, international monitoring had become difficult and was rendered more so with the increasing number of parties to those instruments.

The Secretary-General recommended that the reporting interval for the Convention be extended from two to four years. With respect to the 1966 International Covenant on Economic, Social and Cultural Rights[32] and the 1973 Convention against *apartheid*,[19] the intervals should be extended by one year. Since the periodic review was one of the main mechanisms of international supervision and control, the Secretary-General stressed a greater degree of co-ordination among the monitoring bodies of human rights instruments. To that end, he suggested periodic meetings of the chairmen of CERD, the Human Rights Committee, the Sessional Working Group of Governmental Experts on the Implementation of the International Covenant on Economic, Social and Cultural Rights, and the Group of Three established under the Convention against *apartheid*. The meetings' objectives would be to: establish flexible mechanisms for information exchange; examine reporting obligations from the substantive and procedural perspectives; and standardize reporting guidelines.

To improve the quality of reports, many of which the Secretary-General noted were utterly inadequate, he also suggested that technical assistance be provided to States parties on request. Such assistance, in the form of seminars, training programmes, follow-up missions, fellowships and advisory services, could be provided by United Nations organizations or States parties with technical and financial facilities.

GENERAL ASSEMBLY ACTION

On 22 November, the General Assembly, on the recommendation of the Third Committee, adopted resolution 38/20 without vote.

Report of the Committee on the Elimination of Racial Discrimination: reporting obligations of States

The General Assembly,

Recalling its resolution 37/44 of 3 December 1982,

Mindful of the obligation of all States parties to comply fully with the provisions of the International Convention on the Elimination of All Forms of Racial Discrimination, including the timely submission of periodic reports under article 9 of the Convention,

Acknowledging once again the burden which reporting obligations under international instruments place upon States parties, especially those with limited technical and administrative resources,

Having examined the report of the Secretary-General on the reporting obligations of States parties under the International Convention on the Elimination of All Forms of Racial Discrimination and other relevant human rights instruments,

Noting that the report of the Secretary-General emphasizes the interrelationship of the problems affecting the reporting system under various human rights instruments,

1. *Takes note with appreciation* of the report of the Secretary-General;

2. *Requests* the Secretary-General to transmit his report, and an analytical summary of the records of the General Assembly's consideration thereof, to the ninth meeting of the States parties to the Convention on the Elimination of All Forms of Racial Discrimination for consideration;

3. *Invites* the Committee on the Elimination of Racial Discrimination to consider the analysis and recommendations contained in the report of the Secretary-General, taking into account the various suggestions made in the General Assembly and at the ninth meeting of the States parties to the Convention, and to transmit its views and recommendations to the Assembly at its thirty-ninth session.

General Assembly resolution 38/20

22 November 1983   Meeting 66   Adopted without vote

Approved by Third Committee (A/38/543) without vote, 26 October (meeting 21); 2-nation draft (A/C.3/38/L.6/Rev.1); agenda item 87 *(a)*.
Sponsors: Australia, Italy.
Meeting numbers. GA 38th session: 3rd Committee 4-18, 20, 21; plenary 66.

Measures against nazism and fascism

Action by the Commission on Human Rights. On 7 March 1983,[33] the Commission on Human Rights again condemned all totalitarian or other ideologies and practices based on racial intolerance, hatred, terror, and systematic denial of human rights and fundamental freedoms. It urged States to draw attention to threats to democratic institutions by such ideologies and practices and called for intensified measures against them. States were invited to enact laws to punish dissemination of ideas based on racial superiority or hatred and of war propaganda, including Nazi, Fascist and neo-Fascist ideologies; and ratify or accede to the 1966 International Covenants on Human Rights,[32] the 1948 Convention on the Prevention and Punishment of the Crime of Genocide,[34] the 1965 Convention against racial discrimination,[15] the 1968 Convention on the Non-Applicability of Statutory Limitations to War Crimes and Crimes against Humanity,[35] and the 1973 Convention against *apartheid*.[19]

The Commission called on States to bring to trial persons suspected of war crimes and crimes against humanity. It noted that 1985 would mark the fortieth anniversary of the end of the Second World War, an event that should serve to mobilize the world community in the struggle against totalitarian and other ideologies and practices.

Report of the Secretary-General. In keeping with a December 1982 General Assembly request,[36] the Secretary-General submitted an April 1983 report with later addenda,[37] summarizing comments and suggestions for measures

to eradicate nazism, fascism and related ideologies, from 21 States, 14 non-governmental organizations (NGOs), 2 intergovernmental organizations and a specialized agency.

Additional comments were transmitted by the USSR on 25 November.[38]

ECONOMIC AND SOCIAL COUNCIL ACTION

Acting without vote on the recommendation of its Second Committee, the Economic and Social Council adopted decision 1983/158.

Report of the Secretary-General on measures to be taken against Nazi, Fascist and neo-Fascist activities and all other forms of totalitarian ideologies and practices based on racial intolerance, hatred and terror

At its 15th plenary meeting, on 27 May 1983, the Council took note of the report of the Secretary-General on measures to be taken against Nazi, Fascist and neo-Fascist activities and all other forms of totalitarian ideologies and practices based on racial intolerance, hatred and terror and decided to transmit it to the General Assembly at its thirty-eighth session.

Economic and Social Council decision 1983/158

Adopted without vote

Approved by Second Committee (E/1983/61) without vote, 23 May (meeting 19); oral proposal by Chairman; agenda item 10.
Meeting number. ESC 15.

GENERAL ASSEMBLY ACTION

On 16 December 1983, the General Assembly, on the recommendation of the Third Committee, adopted resolution 38/99 without vote.

Measures to be taken against Nazi, Fascist and neo-Fascist activities and all other forms of totalitarian ideologies and practices based on racial intolerance, hatred and terror

The General Assembly,

Recalling that the United Nations emerged from the struggle against nazism, fascism, aggression and foreign occupation, and that the peoples expressed their resolve in the Charter of the United Nations to save future generations from the scourge of war,

Bearing in mind the suffering, destruction and death of millions of victims of aggression, foreign occupation, nazism and fascism,

Recalling also the close relationship between all totalitarian ideologies and practices based on racial or ethnic exclusiveness or intolerance, hatred and terror and the systematic denial of human rights and fundamental freedoms,

Considering that the fortieth anniversary of the victory over nazism and fascism in the Second World War will occur in 1985 and should serve to mobilize the efforts of the world community in its struggle against Nazi, Fascist and neo-Fascist and all other totalitarian ideologies and practices based on racial intolerance, hatred and terror,

Reaffirming the purposes and principles laid down in the Charter, which are aimed at maintaining international peace and security, developing friendly relations among nations based on respect for the principle of equal rights and the self-determination of peoples, and achieving international co-operation in promoting and encouraging respect for human rights and fundamental freedoms for all,

Firmly convinced that the best bulwark against nazism and racial discrimination is the establishment and maintenance of democratic institutions, that the existence of genuine political, social and economic democracy is an effective vaccine and an equally effective antidote against the formation or development of Nazi movements and that a political system which is based on freedom and effective participation by the people in the conduct of public affairs, and under which economic and social conditions are such as to ensure a decent standard of living for the population, makes it impossible for fascism, nazism or other ideologies based on terror to succeed,

Emphasizing that all totalitarian or other ideologies and practices, including Nazi, Fascist and neo-Fascist, based on racial or ethnic exclusiveness or intolerance, hatred, terror or systematic denial of human rights and fundamental freedoms, or which have such consequences, may jeopardize world peace and constitute obstacles to friendly relations between States and to the realization of human rights and fundamental freedoms,

Reaffirming that the prosecution and punishment of war crimes and crimes against peace and humanity, as laid down in General Assembly resolutions 3(I) of 13 February 1946 and 95(I) of 11 December 1946, constitute a universal commitment for all States,

Mindful of the principles of international co-operation in the detection, arrest, extradition and punishment of persons guilty of war crimes and crimes against humanity, set forth in General Assembly resolution 3074(XXVIII) of 3 December 1973,

Recalling also its resolutions 2331(XXII) of 18 December 1967, 2438(XXIII) of 19 December 1968, 2545(XXIV) of 11 December 1969, 2713(XXV) of 15 December 1970, 2839(XXVI) of 18 December 1971, 34/24 of 15 November 1979, 35/200 of 15 December 1980, 36/162 of 16 December 1981 and 37/179 of 17 December 1982,

Recalling further the Declaration on Social Progress and Development, the United Nations Declaration on the Elimination of All Forms of Racial Discrimination, the Declaration on the Granting of Independence to Colonial Countries and Peoples and the Declaration on the Elimination of All Forms of Intolerance and of Discrimination Based on Religion or Belief,

Underlining the importance of the Universal Declaration of Human Rights, the International Covenants on Human Rights, the International Convention on the Elimination of All Forms of Racial Discrimination and the Convention on the Prevention and Punishment of the Crime of Genocide,

Acknowledging the fact that a number of States have established legal regulations which are suited to prevent the activities of Nazi, Fascist and neo-Fascist groups and organizations,

Noting again with deep concern that the proponents of Fascist ideologies have, in a number of countries, intensified their activities and are increasingly co-ordinating them on an international scale,

1. *Again condemns* all totalitarian or other ideologies and practices, in particular Nazi, Fascist and neo-Fascist, based on racial or ethnic exclusiveness or intolerance, hatred, terror or systematic denial of human rights and fundamental freedoms, or which have such consequences;

2. *Notes* that the fortieth anniversary of the conclusion of the Second World War will occur in 1985 and should serve to mobilize the efforts of the world community in its struggle against the ideologies and practices described in paragraph 1 above;

3. *Calls upon* States to assist each other in detecting, arresting and bringing to trial persons suspected of having committed war crimes and crimes against humanity and, if they are found guilty, in punishing them;

4. *Urges* all States to draw attention to the threat to democratic institutions by the above-mentioned ideologies and practices and to consider taking measures, in accordance with their national constitutional systems and with the provisions of the Universal Declaration of Human Rights and the International Covenants on Human Rights, to prohibit or otherwise deter activities by groups or organizations or whoever is practising those ideologies;

5. *Calls upon* the appropriate specialized agencies, as well as intergovernmental and international non-governmental organizations, to initiate or intensify measures against the ideologies and practices described in paragraph 1 above;

6. *Invites* Member States to adopt, in accordance with their national constitutional systems and with the provisions of the Universal Declaration of Human Rights and the International Covenants on Human Rights, as a matter of high priority, measures declaring punishable by law any dissemination of ideas based on racial superiority or hatred and of war propaganda, including Nazi, Fascist and neo-Fascist ideologies;

7. *Appeals* to all States that have not yet done so to ratify or to accede or give serious consideration to acceding to the International Covenants on Human Rights, the Convention on the Prevention and Punishment of the Crime of Genocide, the International Convention on the Elimination of All Forms of Racial Discrimination, the Convention on the Non-Applicability of Statutory Limitations to War Crimes and Crimes against Humanity and the International Convention on the Suppression and Punishment of the Crime of *Apartheid;*

8. *Calls once again upon* all States to provide the Secretary-General with their comments on this question;

9. *Requests* the Secretary-General to ensure that the Department of Public Information of the Secretariat pays attention to the dissemination of information on the forthcoming fortieth anniversary of the conclusion of the Second World War, exposing the ideologies and practices described in paragraph 1 above;

10. *Reiterates its request* to the Commission on Human Rights to consider this subject at its fortieth session;

11. *Requests* the Secretary-General to submit a report, through the Economic and Social Council, to the General Assembly at its thirty-ninth session, in the light of the discussion that will take place in the Commission on Human Rights and on the basis of comments provided by States and international organizations.

General Assembly resolution 38/99

16 December 1983   Meeting 100   Adopted without vote

Approved by Third Committee (A/38/680) without vote, 7 December (meeting 67); 15-nation draft (A/C.3/38/L.59), orally revised on suggestions by Netherlands and by United States and following consultations; agenda item 12.

Sponsors: Afghanistan, Angola, Bulgaria, Byelorussian SSR, Cuba, Czechoslovakia, German Democratic Republic, Hungary, Iraq, Lao People's Democratic Republic, Mongolia, Nicaragua, Poland, Ukrainian SSR, Viet Nam.
Meeting numbers. GA 38th session: 3rd Committee 18, 54, 55, 57-67; plenary 100.

In the Committee, following proposals made by the Netherlands and the United States, paragraph 7 was orally revised to appeal to States to accede or to consider acceding to the human rights instruments specified, rather than merely to accede; and, in paragraph 9, the phrase "conclusion of the Second World War, exposing the ideologies and practices described in paragraph 1 above" was substituted for "victory over nazism and fascism in the Second World War, and to the actions taken by the United Nations to combat these evils". Following consultations, paragraph 7 was further orally revised.

Other aspects of discrimination

Implementation of the 1981 Declaration against religious intolerance

Report of the Secretary-General. In a report[39] to the Commission on Human Rights on implementation of the 1981 Declaration on the Elimination of All Forms of Intolerance and of Discrimination Based on Religion or Belief,[40] the Secretary-General stated that, as at 17 February 1983, a specialized agency and two other United Nations bodies responded to his communication of 6 January bringing the Declaration to the attention of appropriate United Nations bodies.

Action by the Commission on Human Rights. By a resolution of 9 March 1983,[41] adopted by a roll-call vote of 39 to none, with 4 abstentions, the Commission on Human Rights requested its Sub-Commission to undertake a comprehensive study of the dimensions of intolerance and discrimination based on religion or belief, using the 1981 Declaration as terms of reference. It requested the Secretary-General to incorporate in his report to the Sub-Commission's 1983 session the views of appropriate United Nations bodies, including UNESCO, and NGOs on measures to implement the Declaration; and to hold, as part of the advisory services programme in 1984-1985, a seminar to encourage tolerance and respect for freedom of religion or belief.

ECONOMIC AND SOCIAL COUNCIL ACTION

On the recommendation of its Second Committee, the Economic and Social Council adopted decision 1983/150 by vote.

Implementation of the Declaration on the Elimination of All Forms of Intolerance and of Discrimination Based on Religion or Belief

At its 15th plenary meeting, on 27 May 1983, the Council, noting Commission on Human Rights resolution 1983/40 of 9 March 1983, endorsed the Commission's request to the Secretary-General to hold within the framework of the advisory services programme in the period 1984-1985 a seminar on the encouragement of understanding, tolerance and respect in matters relating to freedom of religion or belief.

Economic and Social Council decision 1983/150

48-0-4

Approved by Second Committee (E/1983/61) by vote (42-0-4), 23 May (meeting 18); draft by Commission on Human Rights (E/1983/13); agenda item 10.
Meeting number. ESC 15.

Sub-Commission action. As requested in September 1982,[42] the Secretary-General submitted to the Sub-Commission in 1983 a note[43] containing information on the problems of discrimination based on religion or belief, on action taken at the regional level, and on the state of discussions on the question within the United Nations system and by NGOs.

On 6 September,[44] the Sub-Commission recommended that the seminar relating to freedom of religion and belief, to be held during 1984-1985 (see above), should discuss the development of educational programmes to foster religious tolerance and include studies reflecting: the universal spiritual and human rights principles underlying the major world religions; appreciation of the different manifestations of those principles and of the social teachings of different religions; the root causes of religious intolerance and discrimination; the 1981 Declaration; and freedom of atheistic belief. The Sub-Commission appointed Elizabeth Odio Benito (Costa Rica) as Special Rapporteur to undertake the comprehensive study requested by the Commission on Human Rights in March (see above), specifying the various aspects to be covered, and asked the Secretary-General to provide the necessary assistance.

GENERAL ASSEMBLY ACTION

On the recommendation of the Third Committee, the General Assembly, on 16 December 1983, adopted resolution 38/110 without vote.

Elimination of all forms of religious intolerance

The General Assembly,

Reaffirming its resolution 36/55 of 25 November 1981, in which it proclaimed the Declaration on the Elimination of All Forms of Intolerance and of Discrimination Based on Religion or Belief,

Recalling its resolution 37/187 of 18 December 1982, in which it requested the Commission on Human Rights to consider what measures might be necessary to implement the Declaration,

Believing that further efforts are required to promote and protect the right to freedom of thought, conscience, religion or whatever belief,

Taking note of Commission on Human Rights resolution 1983/40 of 9 March 1983, in which the Commission requested the Sub-Commission on Prevention of Discrimination and Protection of Minorities to undertake a comprehensive and thorough study of the current dimensions of the problems of intolerance and of discrimination on grounds of religion or belief, using as terms of reference the Declaration on the Elimination of All Forms of Intolerance and of Discrimination Based on Religion or Belief,

Expressing its satisfaction with the action taken by the Sub-Commission regarding the designation of a Special Rapporteur to undertake this study,

Noting that the Economic and Social Council, in its decision 1983/150 of 27 May 1983, endorsed the request of the Commission on Human Rights to the Secretary-General to hold, within the framework of the advisory services programme in the period 1984-1985, a seminar on the encouragement of understanding, tolerance and respect in matters relating to freedom of religion or belief,

1. *Pledges* its determination to encourage understanding, tolerance and respect in matters relating to freedom of religion or belief and expresses the hope that the seminar will contribute towards the realization of these aims;

2. *Requests* the Commission on Human Rights to continue its consideration of measures to implement the Declaration on the Elimination of All Forms of Intolerance and of Discrimination Based on Religion or Belief and to report, through the Economic and Social Council, to the General Assembly at its thirty-ninth session;

3. *Decides* to include in the provisional agenda of its thirty-ninth session the item entitled "Elimination of all forms of religious intolerance" and to consider the report of the Commission on Human Rights in the context of that item.

General Assembly resolution 38/110

16 December 1983   Meeting 100   Adopted without vote

Approved by Third Committee (A/38/683) without vote, 30 November (meeting 57); 29-nation draft (A/C.3/38/L.30), orally revised; agenda item 93.

Sponsors: Australia, Austria, Barbados, Belgium, Canada, Chad, Colombia, Costa Rica, Dominican Republic, Fiji, Finland, France, Germany, Federal Republic of, Ghana, Ireland, Italy, Japan, Morocco, Netherlands, New Zealand, Norway, Peru, Samoa, Solomon Islands, Suriname, Sweden, Uganda, United States, Uruguay.

Meeting numbers. GA 38th session: 3rd Committee 49-53, 57; plenary 100.

Indigenous populations

The report of the Working Group on Indigenous Populations on its 1982 (first) session, considered by the Sub-Commission in September that year,[45] was before the Commission on Human Rights at its January-March 1983 session. The Group's report on its 1983 (second) session was presented to the Sub-Commission in September. Also before the Sub-Commission was the final report on a study of discrimination against indigenous populations.

Other action on behalf of indigenous populations was taken by the General Assembly and the Second World Conference to Combat Racism and Racial Discrimination.

Action by the Commission on Human Rights. Following consideration of the 1982 report of the Working Group on Indigenous Populations, the Commission on Human Rights, on 4 March 1983,[46] asked its Sub-Commission to suggest ways of making the Group's activities better known to ensure the broadest participation of observers from indigenous populations. It also asked for more specific proposals for establishing a voluntary fund to allow such participation, as requested by the Sub-Commission in September 1982.[45] Suggestions for the fund's administration were asked of the Secretary-General.

On 15 July 1983, the Secretary-General submitted those suggestions[47] to the Sub-Commission, stating that it might wish to submit, for adoption by the Commission, a draft resolution inviting the Economic and Social Council to recommend that the General Assembly establish a trust fund. The draft should annex proposals for the fund's management along the lines he suggested.

Working Group activities. The Working Group on Indigenous Populations held its second session at Geneva from 8 to 12 and on 23 August 1983.[48] Among the participants were observers from five indigenous NGOs and from 18 indigenous population groups and other organizations. The Group reviewed developments in the promotion of human rights and fundamental freedoms of such populations, and in the evolution of standards governing those rights. Establishment of a trust fund was also considered.

The Working Group drew up a future work plan, which included the following items: land and other natural resources; the definition of indigenous populations and registration; and a preliminary list of priorities. The list included the rights of such populations to: develop their own culture; autonomy and self-determination; education, health and legal assistance; association; social security and labour protection; and economic, technological, cultural and social relations. The issue of treaties would be taken up, whenever pertinent.

Sub-Commission action. On 6 September 1983,[49] the Sub-Commission endorsed the Working Group's work plan and requested the Group to examine in 1984 criteria for the administration of the proposed fund.

Also on 6 September,[50] the Sub-Commission, having considered the final report on a study of the problem of discrimination against indigenous populations,[51] undertaken by Special Rapporteur José R. Martínez Cobo (Ecuador), expressed appreciation for a valuable contribution towards clarifying the basic legal, social and cultural problems relating to indigenous populations. It asked that the conclusions and recommendations, which for technical reasons could not be issued in time, be submitted in 1984.

In connection with the final report, the Sub-Commission had before it a letter of 5 September 1983 from Bangladesh,[52] stating that the report contained references to what was described as the situation of "indigenous people" in Bangladesh, which were without foundation. There was no scientific or historical basis for treating the tribal people of Chittagong Hill Tracts as indigenous, the letter asserted, the entire population of Bangladesh being autochthonous.

GENERAL ASSEMBLY ACTION

In resolution 38/21 of 22 November 1983, the General Assembly welcomed CERD efforts to eliminate discrimination against persons belonging to indigenous populations and to secure for them full enjoyment of their human rights. It called on the parties to the 1965 Convention against racial discrimination to protect those rights.

Other action. Section D of the Programme of Action for the Second Decade to Combat Racism and Racial Discrimination—adopted by the Second World Conference to Combat Racism and Racial Discrimination in August and approved by the General Assembly in November (resolution 38/14, annexing the Programme)—recommended specific actions to be taken by Governments and by national and local institutions to prevent discrimination against indigenous populations and to protect their rights. Specific rights which Governments should recognize were also cited.

Migrant workers

Social welfare

Report of the Secretary-General. Pursuant to a 1981 Economic and Social Council request,[53] the Secretary-General submitted to the February 1983 session of the Commission for Social Development a report on legislative and administrative regulations concerning the welfare of migrant workers and their families.[54]

The Secretary-General noted that, despite the growing number of international instruments concerned with migrants, those instruments did not cover all legal aspects of migrants' welfare, and the social provisions were often too general and thus too weak to achieve the intended goals. The instruments were seldom fully applied and not ratified by all States concerned. To remedy that situation, the Secretary-General pointed to the need for international and regional, as well as for bilateral and national, action.

Among the measures suggested were: explicit social welfare provisions—for possible inclusion in a United Nations instrument—on family reunion, housing and other living conditions, education, health services, the preservation of national and cultural identity, and minimum standards of services for migrants in both sending and receiving countries; explicit legal provisions in bilateral and multilateral agreements, to ensure equality of opportunity and treatment, and harmonization of

such agreements; special national legislative and administrative measures to facilitate family reunion, access to social services and transferability of social security rights; and development of comprehensive policies and programmes for the return and reintegration of migrant workers and their families. Regional commissions could conduct research and help draw up and enforce bilateral and multilateral agreements.

ECONOMIC AND SOCIAL COUNCIL ACTION

On 26 May 1983, acting without vote on the recommendation of its Second Committee, the Economic and Social Council adopted resolution 1983/16.

Welfare of migrant workers and their families
The Economic and Social Council,
Recalling its resolutions 1926(LVII) of 6 May 1975, 1979/12 of 9 May 1979 and 1981/21 of 6 May 1981,
Having taken note of the report of the Secretary-General on pertinent regulations concerning the welfare of migrant workers and their families,
Concerned at the fact that bilateral agreements concluded between labour-employing and labour-supplying countries, as well as national legislative and administrative provisions, do not completely exclude the possibility of practices that discriminate against migrant workers and members of their families, particularly with regard to living conditions and access to national systems of social services,
Conscious of the fact that the social situation of migrant workers and their families has deteriorated as a result of present unfavourable economic trends,
Recognizing the need for further efforts to improve the welfare of migrant workers and their families,
1. *Expresses its general agreement* with respect to the need for action at the national, regional and international levels to improve the welfare of migrant workers and their families;
2. *Reaffirms* the need for full implementation of the principle of equal treatment for migrants and their families, in accordance with ratified international agreements, particularly with regard to their living conditions and access to national systems of social services;
3. *Affirms* the need for concerted action by the Governments of both labour-employing and labour-supplying countries to harmonize existing bilateral and multilateral agreements on migrant workers, to extend the coverage of services and benefits provided for them and their families and to eliminate provisions that are either discriminatory or contradictory;
4. *Requests* the Secretary-General to take the necessary steps to ensure the effective co-operation of intergovernmental organizations, specialized agencies and organs of the United Nations system with a view to affirming the rights of migrants and their families and ensuring their full implementation, in accordance with Economic and Social Council resolution 1926 B (LVII);
5. *Welcomes* the progress made by the Working Group on the Drafting of an International Convention on the Protection of the Rights of All Migrant Workers and Their Families, established in accordance with General Assembly resolution 34/172 of 17 December 1979;

6. *Requests* the Secretary-General to use the information received from Member States pursuant to paragraph 2 of Economic and Social Council resolution 1981/21 to prepare, in co-operation with the specialized agencies and other organizations concerned, a report on the situation of migrant workers and their families in which the needs and problems emerging as a result of the changing conditions of international migration will be fully taken into account, and to submit that report to the Commission for Social Development at its twenty-ninth session.

Economic and Social Council resolution 1983/16

26 May 1983   Meeting 14   Adopted without vote

Approved by Second Committee (E/1983/62) without vote, 10 May (meeting 8); draft by Commission for Social Development (E/1983/14), orally amended by Mexico; agenda item 11.
Meeting number. ESC 14.

Draft convention

Action by the Commission on Human Rights. In March 1983, the Commission on Human Rights considered the progress made by the Working Group on the Drafting of an International Convention on the Protection of the Rights of All Migrant Workers and Their Families, as described in the Group's reports on its 1982 May intersessional meeting and October/November session.[55] On 9 March 1983,[56] the Commission invited all Member States to continue co-operating with the Group and reiterated its hope for an early completion of the convention's elaboration.

ECONOMIC AND SOCIAL COUNCIL ACTION

On the recommendation of its Second Committee, the Council, on 27 May 1983, adopted resolution 1983/40 without vote.

Measures to improve the situation and ensure the human rights and dignity of all migrant workers and their families

The Economic and Social Council,

Mindful of the need for international co-operation in solving international problems of an economic, social, intellectual or humanitarian nature and in developing and encouraging respect for human rights and fundamental freedoms for all, without distinction as to race, sex, language or religion,

Recalling in that regard the provisions of the Universal Declaration of Human Rights, of the International Convention on the Elimination of All Forms of Racial Discrimination and of the International Covenants on Human Rights,

Mindful of the contribution made by migrant workers to the economic growth and the social and cultural development of the host countries,

Noting, in particular, that the problems of migrant workers, which are becoming more serious in some regions for political and economic reasons and for social and cultural reasons, constitute a matter of grave concern and continue to be of the greatest importance to certain countries,

Mindful of the important contribution made by the International Labour Organisation in the protection of the rights of all migrant workers,

Appreciating also the efforts of the United Nations Educational, Scientific and Cultural Organization in matters relating to migrant workers,

Deeply concerned at the fact that, despite the general effort made by Member States, regional intergovernmental organizations and various United Nations bodies, migrant workers are still unable fully to exercise their rights in the social field and in the labour field as defined in the Universal Declaration of Human Rights,

Emphasizing, therefore, the efforts that must still be made effectively to protect the rights of all migrant workers and their living conditions,

Recalling its resolutions 1981/21 of 6 May 1981 and 1983/16 of 26 May 1983, and Commission on Human Rights resolution 1983/45 of 9 March 1983,

Recalling also its resolutions 1980/16 of 30 April 1980 and 1981/35 of 9 May 1981,

1. *Welcomes* the progress made by the Working Group on the Drafting of an International Convention on the Protection of the Rights of All Migrant Workers and Their Families, established in pursuance of General Assembly resolution 34/172 of 17 December 1979;

2. *Expresses again its conviction* that the drafting of that convention will further facilitate the exchanges of views needed for protecting the human rights and improving the situation of migrant workers and their families;

3. *Expresses the hope* that substantial progress will be made by the Working Group during the two meetings to be held in 1983 in accordance with General Assembly resolution 37/170 of 17 December 1982, with a view to completing the drafting of the convention during the thirty-eighth session of the General Assembly;

4. *Decides* to consider at its first regular session of 1984 the question of measures to improve the situation and ensure the human rights and dignity of all migrant workers and to monitor the status of work done with a view to protecting the rights of all migrant workers and their families.

Economic and Social Council resolution 1983/40

27 May 1983   Meeting 15   Adopted without vote

Approved by Second Committee (E/1983/61) without vote, 23 May (meeting 19); 11-nation draft (E/1983/C.2/L.12); agenda item 10.
Sponsors: Algeria, Argentina, Benin, Colombia, Jordan, Mali, Mexico, Nicaragua, Pakistan, Philippines, Yugoslavia.
Meeting numbers. ESC 15.

Working Group action. The open-ended Working Group on the Drafting of an International Convention on the Protection of the Rights of All Migrant Workers and Their Families, established by the General Assembly in 1979,[57] convened in New York in 1983 for its third intersessional meeting between 31 May and 10 June[58] and its fourth session from 27 September to 6 October.[59]

At its May/June meeting, the Working Group concluded consideration of part III of the draft convention, with the exception of article 55 (covering migrant workers employed by foreign enterprises or their subsidiaries). That article was to be taken up together with parts IV and I, dealing, respectively, with particular categories of migrant workers and members of their families, and with the convention's scope and definitions. The Group also began consideration of proposals for part V, on promotion of sound, equitable and humane conditions for international migration of workers and their families.

At its September/October session, the Group concluded consideration of part V and of part VII on general provisions. Annexed to the session's report was a working paper submitted by Finland, Greece, Italy, Norway, Portugal, Spain and Sweden on a system for supervising the convention's application.

On 16 December 1983, on the recommendation of the Third Committee, the General Assembly adopted resolution 38/86 without vote.

Measures to improve the situation and ensure the human rights and dignity of all migrant workers

The General Assembly,

Again reaffirming the permanent validity of the principles and standards embodied in the basic instruments regarding the international protection of human rights, in particular in the Universal Declaration of Human Rights, the International Covenants on Human Rights, the International Convention on the Elimination of All Forms of Racial Discrimination and the Convention on the Elimination of All Forms of Discrimination against Women,

Bearing in mind the principles and standards established within the framework of the International Labour Organisation and the United Nations Educational, Scientific and Cultural Organization, and the importance of the task carried out in connection with migrant workers and their families in other specialized agencies and in various organs of the United Nations,

Reiterating that, in spite of the existence of an already established body of principles and standards, there is a need to make further efforts to improve the situation and ensure the human rights and dignity of all migrant workers and their families,

Recalling its resolution 34/172 of 17 December 1979, by which it decided to establish a working group open to all Member States to elaborate an international convention on the protection of the rights of all migrant workers and their families,

Recalling also its resolutions 35/198 of 15 December 1980, 36/160 of 16 December 1981 and 37/170 of 17 December 1982, by which it renewed the mandate of the Working Group on the Drafting of an International Convention on the Protection of the Rights of All Migrant Workers and Their Families and requested it to continue its work,

Having examined the progress made by the Working Group during its third inter-sessional meeting, held from 31 May to 10 June 1983,

Having also examined the reports of the Working Group during the current session of the General Assembly,

1. *Takes note* of the reports of the Working Group on the Drafting of an International Convention on the Protection of the Rights of All Migrant Workers and Their Families and expresses its satisfaction with the substantial progress that the Working Group has so far made in the accomplishment of its mandate;

2. *Decides* that, in order to enable it to complete its task as soon as possible, the Working Group shall again hold an inter-sessional meeting of two weeks' duration in New York, immediately after the first regular session of 1984 of the Economic and Social Council;

3. *Invites* the Secretary-General to transmit to Governments the reports of the Working Group so as to allow the members of the Group to continue their task during the inter-sessional meeting to be held in the spring of 1984, as well as to transmit the results obtained at that meeting in order that the General Assembly may consider them during its thirty-ninth session;

4. *Also invites* the Secretary-General to transmit the above-mentioned documents to the competent organs of the United Nations and to international organizations concerned, for their information, so as to enable them to continue their co-operation with the Working Group;

5. *Decides* that the Working Group shall meet during the thirty-ninth session of the General Assembly, preferably at the beginning of the session, to continue and, if possible, to complete the elaboration of an international convention on the protection of the rights of all migrant workers and their families.

General Assembly resolution 38/86

16 December 1983　　　Meeting 100　　　Adopted without vote

Approved by Third Committee (A/38/680) without vote, 30 November (meeting 57); 28-nation draft (A/C.3/38/L.36); agenda item 12.

Sponsors: Algeria, Argentina, Bolivia, Cape Verde, Colombia, Ecuador, Egypt, France, Greece, India, Italy, Jamaica, Jordan, Mali, Mauritania, Mexico, Morocco, Norway, Pakistan, Philippines, Portugal, Rwanda, Senegal, Spain, Sweden, Turkey, Yemen, Yugoslavia.

Financial implications. 5th Committee, A/38/726; S-G, A/C.3/38/L.49, A/C.5/38/66 & Add.1.

Meeting numbers. GA 38th session: 3rd Committee 18, 54, 55, 57; 5th Committee 61; plenary 100.

Other action. On 31 August 1983,[60] the Sub-Commission on Prevention of Discrimination and Protection of Minorities recommended to the Commission on Human Rights a draft resolution for adoption by the Economic and Social Council, by which the Council would decide that the 1976 report on exploitation of labour through illicit and clandestine trafficking,[61] by Special Rapporteur Halima Embarek Warzazi (Morocco), should be printed, given the widest distribution and transmitted for comment to Governments, United Nations bodies, and governmental and non-governmental organizations.

Section D of the Programme of Action for the Second Decade to Combat Racism and Racial Discrimination—adopted by the Second World Conference to Combat Racism and Racial Discrimination in August and approved by the General Assembly in November (resolution 38/14, annexing the Programme)—recommended specific actions to be taken by Governments to protect the rights of migrant workers.

Protection of minorities

In February/March 1983, the Commission on Human Rights, through an informal working group open to its membership, continued to consider a revised and consolidated draft declaration on the rights of persons belonging to national, ethnic, religious and linguistic minorities, prepared by the Chairman/Rapporteur of the 1980 working group, Ivan Tosevski (Yugoslavia), and submitted to the Commission in 1981.[62] Continuing its first reading of the draft declaration, the group resumed consideration of article 1 and began to consider articles 2 to 6. No text was adopted at the session.

The Commission, on 10 March 1983,[63] after receiving the group's report,[64] decided to set up at its 1984 session an open-ended working group to continue work on the draft.

ECONOMIC AND SOCIAL COUNCIL ACTION

On the recommendation of its Second Committee, the Economic and Social Council adopted without vote decision 1983/151.

Rights of persons belonging to national, ethnic, religious and linguistic minorities

At its 15th plenary meeting, on 27 May 1983, the Council, noting Commission on Human Rights resolution 1983/53 of 10 March 1983, endorsed the Commission's decision to establish at its fortieth session an open-ended working group to continue consideration of the revised draft declaration on the rights of persons belonging to national, ethnic, religious and linguistic minorities proposed by Yugoslavia, taking into account all relevant documents.

Economic and Social Council decision 1983/151

Adopted without vote

Approved by Second Committee (E/1983/61) without vote, 23 May (meeting 18); draft by Commission on Human Rights (E/1983/13); agenda item 10.
Meeting number. ESC 15.

Draft declaration on the human rights of non-citizens

A Working Group established by the General Assembly in December 1982,[65] open to all United Nations Members, with Halima Embarek Warzazi (Morocco) as Chairman/Rapporteur, met between 4 October and 29 November 1983, to continue work on the drafting of a declaration on the human rights of individuals not citizens of the country in which they lived.

Following additional revisions to a revised text of the preambular section of the draft declaration, the Group adopted the preamble. At the second reading of the operative section, it adopted articles 2 and 3, part of article 4 and articles 5 and 6, on the understanding that consideration of those articles was subject for some delegations to elaboration of the part relating to definitions. The adopted texts were contained in the Group's report[66] to the Assembly's Third Committee.

Report of the Secretary-General. Responding to a December 1982 General Assembly request,[65] the Secretary-General submitted a report[67] summarizing the substantive comments received on the draft declaration (see above), based on the reports of each of the working groups set up in the previous three years to work on the draft. As at 15 September 1983, comments were received from nine States, two United Nations organs, three specialized agencies and two intergovernmental organizations. The following stated that they had no comments on the subject: United Nations Industrial Development Organization, Economic Commission for Latin America, Food and Agriculture Organization of the United Nations (FAO), World Bank, Organisation for Economic Co-operation and Development.

GENERAL ASSEMBLY ACTION

On 16 December 1983, on the recommendation of the Third Committee, the General Assembly adopted resolution 38/87 without vote.

Question of the international legal protection of the human rights of individuals who are not citizens of the country in which they live

The General Assembly,

Bearing in mind Economic and Social Council resolutions 1790(LIV) of 18 May 1973 and 1871(LVI) of 17 May 1974 concerning the question of the international legal protection of the human rights of individuals who are not citizens of the country in which they live,

Recalling Commission on Human Rights resolutions 8(XXIX) of 21 March 1973, 11(XXX) of 6 March 1974, 16(XXXV) of 14 March 1979 and 19(XXXVI) of 29 February 1980 on the same subject,

Recalling also resolution 9(XXXI) of 13 September 1978 of the Sub-Commission on Prevention of Discrimination and Protection of Minorities,

Recalling that the Economic and Social Council, by its resolution 1980/29 of 2 May 1980, decided to transmit to the General Assembly at its thirty-fifth session the text of the draft declaration on the human rights of individuals who are not citizens of the country in which they live, prepared by the Special Rapporteur of the Sub-Commission on Prevention of Discrimination and Protection of Minorities and amended by the Sub-Commission, together with the comments on the text received from Member States in response to Council decision 1979/36 of 10 May 1979, and recommended that the Assembly should consider the adoption of a declaration on the subject,

Recalling also its resolutions 35/199 of 15 December 1980, 36/165 of 16 December 1981 and 37/169 of 17 December 1982, by which it decided to establish an open-ended working group for the purpose of concluding the elaboration of the draft declaration on the human rights of individuals who are not citizens of the country in which they live,

Having considered the comments submitted by Governments, specialized agencies, regional and intergovernmental organizations and the competent organs of the United Nations system pursuant to General Assembly resolution 37/169 on the reports of the open-ended working groups established at the thirty-fifth, thirty-sixth and thirty-seventh sessions of the Assembly,

Having considered the report of the Working Group established for the purpose of concluding the elaboration of the draft declaration on the human rights of individuals who are not citizens of the country in which they live,

1. *Takes note* of the report of the Working Group and of the fact that, although the Working Group has done useful work, it has not had sufficient time to conclude its task;

2. *Decides* to establish, at its thirty-ninth session, an open-ended working group for the purpose of concluding the elaboration of the draft declaration on the human rights of individuals who are not citizens of the country in which they live;

3. *Expresses the hope* that a draft declaration on the human rights of individuals who are not citizens of the country in which they live will be adopted by the General Assembly at its thirty-ninth session.

General Assembly resolution 38/87

16 December 1983   Meeting 100   Adopted without vote

Approved by Third Committee (A/38/680) without vote, 2 December (meeting 61); 8-nation draft (A.C.3/38/L.52); agenda item 12.
Sponsors: Costa Rica, Ecuador, Greece, Jamaica, Mexico, Morocco, Pakistan, Venezuela.
Financial implications. 5th Committee, A/38/726; S-G, A/C.3/38/L.53, A/C.5/38/76.
Meeting numbers. GA 38th session: 3rd Committee 18, 54, 55, 57-61; 5th Committee 62; plenary 100.

Discrimination in criminal justice

On 31 August 1983,[68] the Sub-Commission on Prevention of Discrimination and Protection of Minorities recommended that the Commission on Human Rights adopt a draft decision recommending to the Economic and Social Council that the 1982 study by Special Rapporteur Abu Sayeed Chowdhury (Bangladesh) on discriminatory treatment of members of racial, ethnic, religious or linguistic groups at the various levels in the administration of criminal justice, such as police, military, administrative and judicial investigations, arrest, detention, trial and execution of sentences,[69] be printed and given the widest possible distribution, including in Arabic.

On 5 September,[70] the Sub-Commission noted that the South African Constitution, whereby the black majority was denied the franchise and the right to occupy positions as judges, magistrates and prosecutors, put the judicial system and the impartiality of the judiciary into serious doubt and thus could not be considered as a just basis for a fair judicial system (see under HUMAN RIGHTS VIOLATIONS below).

REFERENCES

[1]E/1983/13 & Corr.1. [2]E/CN.4/1984/3 & Corr.1,2. [3]YUN 1973, p. 523, GA res. 3057(XXVIII), 2 Nov. 1973. [4]YUN 1979, p. 806, GA res. 34/24, annex, 15 Nov. 1979. [5]YUN 1982, p. 1057, GA res. 37/41, 3 Dec. 1982. [6]*Report of the Second World Conference to Combat Racism and Racial Discrimination, Geneva (1-12 August 1983)* (A/CONF.119/26 & Corr.1), Sales No. E.83.XIV.4 & corrigendum. [7]YUN 1978, p. 662. [8]YUN 1982, p. 1055, ESC res. 1982/32, 5 May 1982. [9]*Ibid.*, p. 1052, GA res. 37/40, 3 Dec. 1982. [10]E/1983/9 & Corr.1,2. [11]E/1983/13 (res. 1983/13). [12]E/1983/10. [13]YUN 1973, p. 524, GA res. 3057(XXVIII), annex, 2 Nov. 1973. [14]YUN 1978, p. 915, SC res. 435(1978), 29 Sep. 1978. [15]YUN 1965,

p. 440, GA res. 2106 A (XX), annex, 21 Dec. 1965. [16]YUN 1974, p. 152. [17]YUN 1982, p. 1304, GA res. 37/233 C, 20 Dec. 1982. [18]YUN 1966, p. 423, GA res. 2200 A (XXI), annex, 16 Dec. 1966. [19]YUN 1973, p. 103, GA res. 3068(XXVIII), annex, 30 Nov. 1973. [20]YUN 1981, p. 165. [21]A/38/426. [22]E/CN.4/1984/3 (res. 1983/10). [23]*Ibid.* (res. 1983/3). [24]YUN 1969, p. 488. [25]A/38/390. [26]A/C.3/38/8. [27]A/38/18. [28]YUN 1982, p. 1062. [29]A/38/18 (dec. 1(XXVII)). [30]YUN 1982, p. 1061, GA res. 37/44, 3 Dec. 1982. [31]A/38/393. [32]YUN 1966, p. 419, GA res. 2200 A (XXI), annex, 16 Dec. 1966. [33]E/1983/13 (res. 1983/28). [34]YUN 1948-49, p. 959, GA res. 260 A (III), annex, 9 Dec. 1948. [35]YUN 1968, p. 609, GA res. 2391(XXIII), annex, 26 Nov. 1968. [36]YUN 1982, p. 1063, GA res. 37/179, 17 Dec. 1982. [37]A/38/166-E/1983/34 & Add.1-3. [38]A/C.3/38/12. [39]E/CN.4/1983/34 & Add.1. [40]YUN 1981, p. 881, GA res. 36/55, 25 Nov. 1981. [41]E/1983/13 (res. 1983/40). [42]YUN 1982, p. 1064. [43]E/CN.4/Sub.2/1983/29. [44]E/CN.4/1984/3 (res. 1983/31). [45]YUN 1982, p. 1065. [46]E/1983/13 (res. 1983/23). [47]E/CN.4/Sub.2/1983/20. [48]E/CN.4/Sub.2/1983/22. [49]E/CN.4/1984/3 (res. 1983/37). [50]*Ibid.* (res. 1983/33). [51]E/CN.4/Sub.2/1983/21 & Add.1-7. [52]E/CN.4/Sub.2/1983/41. [53]YUN 1981, p. 887, ESC res. 1981/21, 6 May 1981. [54]E/CN.5/1983/10. [55]YUN 1982, p. 1066. [56]E/1983/13 (res. 1938/45). [57]YUN 1979, p. 875, GA res. 34/172, 17 Dec. 1979. [58]A/C.3/38/1. [59]A/C.3/38/5. [60]E/CN.4/1984/3 (res. 1983/7). [61]YUN 1976, p. 607. [62]YUN 1981, p. 883. [63]E/1983/13 (res. 1983/53). [64]E/CN.4/1983/66. [65]YUN 1982, p. 1068, GA res. 37/169, 17 Dec. 1982. [66]A/C.3/38/11 & Corr.1. [67]A/38/147 & Add.1. [68]E/CN.4/1984/3 (res. 1983/4). [69]YUN 1982, p. 1068. [70]E/CN.4/1984/3 (res. 1983/25).

PUBLICATION

Migrant Workers: Pertinent Legislative and Administrative Regulations on the Welfare of Migrant Workers and Their Families (ST/ESA/132), Sales No. E.83.IV.2.

Civil and political rights

Covenant on Civil and Political Rights and Optional Protocol

Accessions and ratifications

As at 31 December 1983, the International Covenant on Civil and Political Rights and the Optional Protocol thereto, adopted by the General Assembly in 1966[1] and in force since 1976,[2] had been ratified or acceded to by 77 and 31 States, respectively. Afghanistan, Belgium, the Congo, Gabon and Luxembourg became parties to the Covenant in 1983. The Congo and Luxembourg also acceded to the Protocol, and Portugal ratified it. Two States—Denmark and Luxembourg—made the declaration under article 41 of the Covenant recognizing the competence of the Human Rights Committee to receive and consider communications to the effect that a State party claimed that another was not fulfilling its obligations under the Covenant.

In a report to the Assembly,[3] the Secretary-General provided information on the status of the Covenant and the Protocol as at 1 September 1983.

Implementation of the
Covenant and the Optional Protocol

Action by the Commission on Human Rights.
In its 22 February resolution on the International Covenants on Human Rights[4] (see under AD-VANCEMENT OF HUMAN RIGHTS below), the Commission on Human Rights expressed appreciation that the Human Rights Committee continued to strive for uniform standards in implementing the Covenant and the Optional Protocol, and urged States to become parties to them and to consider making the declaration under article 41. In emphasizing the importance of the strictest compliance with those instruments, the Commission stressed the obligations of a State party availing itself (in time of public emergency) of the right of derogation from the Covenant's provisions in accordance with article 4, paragraph 1, to inform the other States parties immediately, through the Secretary-General, of the provisions from which it had derogated and the reasons for doing so.

The Commission welcomed the measures taken by the Secretary-General to improve publicity for the work of the Committee and urged him to continue to consider steps for the publication of its documentation. The Commission encouraged Governments and United Nations information centres to give the Covenant and the Protocol the widest publicity. It took note of a December 1982 General Assembly request[5] that the Secretary-General continue to ensure the ability of the Secretariat's Centre for Human Rights to assist the Committee in its functions under the Covenant.

Human Rights Committee activities. The Human Rights Committee, established under article 28 of the Covenant, held three sessions in 1983: the eighteenth, in New York, from 21 March to 8 April; and the nineteenth and twentieth, at Geneva, from 11 to 29 July and from 24 October to 11 November. The Committee set up pre-session working groups to make recommendations on communications under the Optional Protocol.

During the sessions, the Committee considered reports and additional information submitted by 10 States parties—Austria, El Salvador, France, Guinea, Lebanon, New Zealand, Nicaragua, Peru, Sri Lanka and Yugoslavia—under article 40 of the Covenant. The Committee also concluded consideration of and adopted views on 16 communications by individuals claiming that their rights under the Covenant had been violated and that they had exhausted all available domestic remedies. The cases concerned Italy (1), Madagascar (1), Uruguay (12) and Zaire (2). The Committee decided that five other such communications were inadmissible. It took a similar decision on two communications from NGOs.

On 8 April, the Committee adopted a decision recommending the inclusion of Arabic among its official and working languages. On 29 July, it unanimously adopted its seventh annual report[6] to the General Assembly.

Sub-Commission action. By a resolution of 6 September 1983 on the administration of justice and the human rights of detainees,[7] adopted by 19 votes to 1, with 3 abstentions, the Sub-Commission on Prevention of Discrimination and Protection of Minorities decided to include in its agenda an item on implementation of the right of derogation (in states of emergency) provided under the Covenant's article 4 and violation of human rights. Under that item, the Sub-Commission would request its Working Group on Detention (see below) to draw up and update an annual list of countries which proclaimed or terminated a state of emergency. It would also submit an annual report to the Commission on Human Rights containing information on compliance with internal and international rules, guaranteeing the legality of the introduction of a state of emergency.

GENERAL ASSEMBLY ACTION

On 16 December 1983, on the recommendation of the Third Committee, the General Assembly adopted resolution 38/115 without vote.

Arabic language services for meetings of the States parties to the International Covenant on Civil and Political Rights and the Human Rights Committee

The General Assembly,

Aware of the need to achieve greater international co-operation and to promote harmonization of its activities in the field of human rights,

Bearing in mind its resolutions 3190(XXVIII) of 18 December 1973, 34/226 of 20 December 1979 and 35/219 of 17 December 1980 relating to the introduction of Arabic as an official and working language of the General Assembly and its Main Committees,

Authorizes the provision of Arabic language services required for meetings of the States parties to the International Covenant on Civil and Political Rights, as well as of the Human Rights Committee, and requests the Secretary-General to take appropriate measures to that end.

General Assembly resolution 38/115

16 December 1983   Meeting 100   Adopted without vote

Approved by Third Committee (A/38/686 & Corr.1) without vote, 30 November (meeting 57); 23-nation draft (A/C.3/38/L.35), orally revised; agenda item 96.
Sponsors: Algeria, Bahrain, Democratic Yemen, Djibouti, Egypt, Iran, Iraq, Jordan, Kuwait, Lebanon, Libyan Arab Jamahiriya, Mauritania, Morocco, Oman, Qatar, Saudi Arabia, Somalia, Sudan, Syrian Arab Republic, Tunisia, Turkey, United Arab Emirates, Yemen.
Financial implications. 5th Committee, A/38/697; S-G, A/C.3/38/L.50, A/C.5/38/67.
Meeting numbers. GA 38th session: 3rd Committee 49-54, 56, 57; 5th Committee 56; plenary 100.

In resolution 38/116, also adopted on 16 December, the Assembly, taking note of the Human Rights Committee report, expressed satisfaction at the constructive manner in which the Committee continued to perform its functions. It expressed appreciation to those States parties that had co-operated in submitting their reports under article 40, and urged speedy submission of those that were due and compliance with the Committee's request for additional information. Besides repeating the urgings of the Commission on Human Rights for accession, declaration, strictest compliance and assistance (see above), the Assembly requested the Secretary-General to continue to keep the Committee informed of the activities of the Commission and its Sub-Commission, CERD and the Committee on the Elimination of Discrimination against Women, and to expedite arrangements for publishing the Committee's official public records in bound volumes.

Resolution 38/117 of the same date also dealt with the reporting obligations of States parties to the International Covenant on Civil and Political Rights (see under ADVANCEMENT OF HUMAN RIGHTS below).

Self-determination of peoples

In six resolutions adopted at its January-March 1983 session, the Commission on Human Rights dealt with the right of peoples to self-determination (see below). It reaffirmed that right for the following peoples: Palestinians;[8] South Africans as a whole and Namibians;[9] Kampucheans;[10] the people of Western Sahara;[11] Afghans;[12] and the people of East Timor.[13] The Sub-Commission on Prevention of Discrimination and Protection of Minorities adopted a resolution on the right to self-determination of the Nicaraguan people.[14]

The Commission's actions and debate, and actions taken by the Economic and Social Council, were summarized by the Secretary-General in a report to the General Assembly on the universal realization of the right to self-determination.[15] Also summarized were responses to the Assembly's December 1982 resolutions on the topic[16] from 13 Governments, an intergovernmental organization and six NGOs.

On 22 November 1983, the Assembly adopted resolutions 38/16 and 38/17 on the right to self-determination—a right it repeatedly reaffirmed for individual Non-Self-Governing Territories (see TRUSTEESHIP AND DECOLONIZATION, Chapter IV).

Communications. On 27 July 1983,[17] the United States transmitted to the Secretary-General a statement by its President on the occasion of the sixty-first anniversary of the 1922 *de jure* recognition by the United States of the three independent Baltic republics of Estonia, Latvia and Lithuania. Those States, the statement asserted, had been full members of the League of Nations and had signed

non-aggression treaties with the USSR, yet had been forcibly incorporated into the USSR more than 40 years ago. By continuing to occupy them illegally, the USSR was in violation of international law, particularly of the right to self-determination as set forth in the Charter and in United Nations resolutions.

By a letter of 30 September 1983,[18] the USSR transmitted a statement of position on the right to self-determination and on the speedy granting of independence to colonial countries and peoples for the effective observance of human rights. The statement stressed that completion of the decolonization process and ensurance of the realization of the right to self-determination were the urgent tasks confronting the United Nations.

GENERAL ASSEMBLY ACTION

On the recommendation of the Third Committee, the General Assembly adopted on 22 November 1983 two resolutions concerning the right of peoples to self-determination. The first of these—resolution 38/16—was adopted without vote.

Universal realization of the right of peoples to self-determination

The General Assembly,

Reaffirming the importance, for the effective guarantee and observance of human rights, of the universal realization of the right of peoples to self-determination enshrined in the Charter of the United Nations and embodied in the International Covenants on Human Rights, as well as in the Declaration on the Granting of Independence to Colonial Countries and Peoples, contained in General Assembly resolution 1514(XV) of 14 December 1960,

Welcoming the progressive exercise of the right to self-determination by peoples under colonial, foreign or alien occupation and their emergence into sovereign statehood and independence,

Deeply concerned at the continuation of acts or threats of foreign military intervention and occupation, which are threatening to suppress, or have already suppressed, the right to self-determination of an increasing number of sovereign peoples and nations,

Further expressing grave concern that, as a consequence of the persistence of such actions, millions of people have been and are being uprooted from their homes as refugees and displaced persons, and emphasizing the urgent need for concerted international action to alleviate their conditions,

Recalling the relevant resolutions regarding the violation of the right of peoples to self-determination and other human rights as a result of foreign military intervention, aggression and occupation, adopted by the Commission on Human Rights at its thirty-sixth, thirty-seventh, thirty-eighth and thirty-ninth sessions,

Reiterating its resolutions 35/35 B of 14 November 1980, 36/10 of 28 October 1981 and 37/42 of 3 December 1982,

Taking note of the report of the Secretary-General,

1. *Reaffirms* that the universal realization of the right of all peoples, including those under colonial, foreign

and alien domination, to self-determination is a fundamental condition for the effective guarantee and observance of human rights and for the preservation and promotion of such rights;

2. *Declares its firm opposition* to acts of foreign military intervention, aggression and occupation, since these have resulted in the suppression of the right of peoples to self-determination and other human rights in certain parts of the world;

3. *Calls upon* those States responsible to cease immediately their military intervention and occupation of foreign countries and territories, and all acts of repression, discrimination, exploitation and maltreatment, particularly the brutal and inhuman methods reportedly employed for the execution of these acts against the peoples concerned;

4. *Deplores* the plight of the millions of refugees and displaced persons who have been uprooted by the aforementioned acts and reaffirms their right to return to their homes voluntarily in safety and honour;

5. *Requests* the Commission on Human Rights to continue to give special attention to the violation of human rights, especially the right to self-determination, resulting from foreign military intervention, aggression or occupation;

6. *Requests* the Secretary-General to report on this issue to the General Assembly at its thirty-ninth session under the item entitled "Importance of the universal realization of the right of peoples to self-determination and of the speedy granting of independence to colonial countries and peoples for the effective guarantee and observance of human rights".

General Assembly resolution 38/16

22 November 1983   Meeting 66   Adopted without vote

Approved by Third Committee (A/38/542) without vote, 26 October (meeting 21); 18-nation draft (A/C.3/38/L.3); agenda item 86.

Sponsors: Chile, Costa Rica, Djibouti, Ecuador, Jordan, Kuwait, Malaysia, Morocco, Oman, Pakistan, Papua New Guinea, Philippines, Qatar, Saudi Arabia, Singapore, Somalia, Sudan, Thailand.

Meeting numbers. GA 38th session: 3rd Committee 4-18, 21; plenary 66.

The second resolution, 38/17, was adopted by recorded vote.

Importance of the universal realization of the right of peoples to self-determination and of the speedy granting of independence to colonial countries and peoples for the effective guarantee and observance of human rights

The General Assembly,

Reaffirming its faith in the importance of the implementation of the Declaration on the Granting of Independence to Colonial Countries and Peoples contained in its resolution 1514(XV) of 14 December 1960,

Reaffirming the importance of the universal realization of the right of peoples to self-determination, national sovereignty and territorial integrity and of the speedy granting of independence to colonial countries and peoples as imperatives for the full enjoyment of all human rights,

Reaffirming the obligation of all Member States to comply with the principles of the Charter of the United Nations and the resolutions of the United Nations regarding the exercise of the right to self-determination by peoples under colonial and foreign domination,

Recalling its resolutions 2649(XXV) of 30 November 1970, 2955(XXVII) of 12 December 1972,

3070(XXVIII) of 30 November 1973, 3246(XXIX) of 29 November 1974, 3382(XXX) of 10 November 1975, 33/24 of 29 November 1978, 34/44 of 23 November 1979, 35/35 of 14 November 1980, 36/9 of 28 October 1981 and 37/43 of 3 December 1982, and Security Council resolutions 418(1977) of 4 November 1977 and 421(1977) of 9 December 1977,

Recalling also its resolutions 1514(XV) of 14 December 1960, 2465(XXIII) of 20 December 1968, 2708(XXV) of 14 December 1970, 33/44 of 13 December 1978, 35/119 of 11 December 1980, 36/68 of 1 December 1981 and 37/35 of 23 November 1982 concerning the implementation of the Declaration on the Granting of Independence to Colonial Countries and Peoples,

Recalling further its resolutions 3103(XXVIII) of 12 December 1973 and 3314(XXIX) of 14 December 1974, as well as Security Council resolutions 405(1977) of 14 April 1977, 419(1977) of 24 November 1977, 496(1981) of 15 December 1981 and 507(1982) of 28 May 1982, in which the United Nations condemned the recruiting and the use of mercenaries, in particular against developing countries and national liberation movements,

Recalling further its resolutions on the question of Namibia, in particular resolution ES-8/2 of 14 September 1981, and Security Council resolution 532(1983) of 31 May 1983,

Welcoming the holding of the International Conference in Support of the Struggle of the Namibian People for Independence in Paris from 25 to 29 April 1983,

Welcoming also the holding of the International Conference on the Alliance between South Africa and Israel at Vienna from 11 to 13 July 1983,

Recalling resolutions AHG/Res.105 on Namibia, AHG/Res.111 on the policy of destabilization of the racist régime of South Africa and AHG/Res.112 on South Africa, adopted by the Assembly of Heads of State and Government of the Organization of African Unity at its nineteenth ordinary session, held at Addis Ababa from 6 to 12 June 1983,

Recalling further its resolution 37/1 of 1 October 1982 concerning its appeal for clemency on behalf of the freedom fighters of South Africa and Security Council resolution 533(1983) of 7 June 1983 concerning the sentencing to death by South Africa of the three patriots of the African National Congress of South Africa,

Reaffirming that the system of *apartheid* imposed on the South African people constitutes a violation of the fundamental rights of that people, a crime against humanity and a constant threat to international peace and security,

Gravely concerned at the continuation of the illegal occupation of Namibia by South Africa and the continued violations of the human rights of the people in the territory and of the other peoples still under colonial domination and alien subjugation,

Recognizing that the so-called proposals for constitutional reform are an integral part of the policy of "bantustanization", which is incompatible with genuine independence, national unity and sovereignty and has the effect of perpetuating the power of the white minority and the racist system of *apartheid* in South Africa,

Deeply concerned at the continued terrorist acts of aggression committed by the Pretoria régime against independent African States in the region, in particular Angola, Botswana, Lesotho, Mozambique, Seychelles, Swaziland, Zambia and Zimbabwe,

Deeply indignant at the occupation of part of the territory of Angola by the troops of the racist régime of South Africa,

Recalling Security Council resolutions 527(1982) of 15 December 1982 and 535(1983) of 29 June 1983 on Lesotho,

Reaffirming the national unity and territorial integrity of the Comoros,

Recalling the Political Declaration adopted by the First Conference of Heads of State and Government of the Organization of African Unity and the League of Arab States, held at Cairo from 7 to 9 March 1977,

Recalling further its relevant resolutions on the question of Palestine, in particular resolutions 3236(XXIX) and 3237(XXIX) of 22 November 1974, 36/120 of 10 December 1981, ES-7/6 of 19 August 1982 and 37/86 of 10 December 1982,

Recalling the Geneva Declaration on Palestine and the Programme of Action for the Achievement of Palestinian Rights, adopted by the International Conference on the Question of Palestine,

Considering that the denial of the inalienable rights of the Palestinian people to self-determination, sovereignty, independence and return to Palestine and the repeated acts of aggression by Israel against the people of the region constitute a serious threat to international peace and security,

Deeply shocked and alarmed at the deplorable consequences of the Israeli invasion of Lebanon and recalling all the relevant resolutions of the Security Council, in particular resolutions 508(1982) of 5 June 1982, 509(1982) of 6 June 1982, 520(1982) of 17 September 1982 and 521(1982) of 19 September 1982,

1.   *Calls upon* all States to implement fully and faithfully all the resolutions of the United Nations regarding the exercise of the right to self-determination and independence by peoples under colonial and foreign domination;

2.   *Reaffirms* the legitimacy of the struggle of peoples for their independence, territorial integrity, national unity and liberation from colonial domination, *apartheid* and foreign occupation by all available means, including armed struggle;

3.   *Reaffirms* the inalienable right of the Namibian people, the Palestinian people and all peoples under foreign and colonial domination to self-determination, national unity and sovereignty without foreign interference;

4.   *Strongly condemns* those Governments that do not recognize the right to self-determination and independence of all peoples still under colonial domination and alien subjugation, notably the peoples of Africa and the Palestinian people;

5.   *Endorses* the Paris Declaration on Namibia, adopted by the International Conference in Support of the Struggle of the Namibian People for Independence, and the Geneva Declaration on Palestine, adopted by the International Conference on the Question of Palestine, as well as the Programmes of Action adopted by these Conferences, and calls for their immediate implementation;

6.   *Reaffirms* its vigorous condemnation of the illegal occupation of Namibia by South Africa;

7.   *Condemns* the policy of "bantustanization" and reiterates its support for the oppressed people of South Africa in its just and legitimate struggle against the racist minority régime of Pretoria;

8.   *Rejects* the South African régime's so-called reforms, especially the limited parliamentary representation for Coloured people and Asians designed to undermine the unity of the oppressed people of South Africa and buttress the *apartheid* system;

9.   *Condemns* South Africa for its increasing oppression of the Namibian people, for the massive militarization of Namibia and for its armed attacks launched against the States in the region in order to destabilize them politically and to sabotage and destroy their economies;

10.   *Strongly condemns* the establishment and use of armed terrorist groups by South Africa with a view to pitting them against the national liberation movements and destabilizing the legitimate Governments of southern Africa;

11.   *Strongly condemns* the continued occupation of parts of southern Angola and the recent massive aggression carried out by South African troops against the village of Cangamba in the province of Moxico, 500 kilometres from the Namibian border, and demands the immediate and unconditional withdrawal of the South African troops from the Angolan territory;

12.   *Strongly reaffirms* its solidarity with the independent African countries and national liberation movements that are victims of murderous acts of aggression and destabilization by the racist régime of Pretoria, and calls upon the international community to render increased assistance and support to these countries in order to enable them to strengthen their defence capacity, defend their sovereignty and territorial integrity and peacefully rebuild and develop;

13.   *Strongly condemns* the recent bombing of Matola, a suburb of the capital of Mozambique, by South Africa and the acts of territorial encroachment and espionage against Mozambique, as well as the attack on 17 October 1983 against the Office of the African National Congress at Maputo, undertaken by the racist régime of Pretoria;

14.   *Reaffirms* that the practice of using mercenaries against sovereign States and national liberation movements constitutes a criminal act and calls upon the Governments of all countries to enact legislation declaring the recruitment, financing and training of mercenaries in their territories and the transit of mercenaries through their territories to be punishable offences, and prohibiting their nationals from serving as mercenaries, and to report on such legislation to the Secretary-General;

15.   *Strongly condemns* the continued violations of the human rights of the peoples still under colonial domination and alien subjugation, the continuation of the illegal occupation of Namibia, and South Africa's attempts to dismember its territory, the perpetuation of the racist minority régime in southern Africa and the denial to the Palestinian people of their inalienable national rights;

16.   *Further strongly condemns* the racist régime of Pretoria for its acts of destabilization, armed aggression and economic blockade against Lesotho and strongly urges the international community to extend maximum assistance to Lesotho to enable it to fulfil its international humanitarian obligations towards refugees and to use its influence on the racist régime to desist from its terrorist acts against Lesotho;

17.   *Expresses its profound indignation* at the callous murder, on 9 June 1983, of the three freedom fighters

of the African National Congress by the racist régime of South Africa, which committed the crime with flagrant indifference despite various appeals by the international community, thereby defying Security Council resolution 533(1983);

18. *Takes note* of the Declaration of the International Conference on the Alliance between South Africa and Israel;

19. *Strongly condemns* the policy of those Western States, Israel and other States whose political, economic, military, nuclear, strategic, cultural and sports relations with the racist minority régime in South Africa encourage that régime to persist in its suppression of the aspirations of peoples to self-determination and independence;

20. *Again demands* the immediate application of the mandatory arms embargo against South Africa, imposed under Security Council resolution 418(1977), by all countries and more particularly by those countries that maintain military and nuclear co-operation with the racist Pretoria régime and continue to supply it with related *matériel;*

21. *Takes note with satisfaction* of the Paris Declaration on Sanctions against South Africa, the Special Declaration on Namibia and the reports of the technical and political commissions, adopted by the International Conference on Sanctions against South Africa, held under the auspices of the United Nations and the Organization of African Unity;

22. *Demands* the immediate implementation of its resolution ES-8/2 on Namibia;

23. *Urges* all States, specialized agencies, competent organizations of the United Nations system and other international organizations to extend their support to the Namibian people through its sole and legitimate representative, the South West Africa People's Organization, in its struggle to gain its right to self-determination and independence in accordance with the Charter of the United Nations;

24. *Reaffirms* the resolutions on the question of Western Sahara adopted by the Assembly of Heads of State and Government of the Organization of African Unity at its eighteenth and nineteenth ordinary sessions, held at Nairobi from 24 to 27 June 1981, and at Addis Ababa from 6 to 12 June 1983, and calls for their immediate implementation;

25. *Takes note* of the contacts between the Government of the Comoros and the Government of France in the search for a just solution to the problem of the integration of the Comorian island of Mayotte in the Comoros, in accordance with the resolutions of the Organization of African Unity and the United Nations on this question;

26. *Calls* for a substantial increase in all forms of assistance given by all States, United Nations organs, specialized agencies and non-governmental organizations to the victims of racism, racial discrimination and *apartheid* through their national liberation movements recognized by the Organization of African Unity;

27. *Strongly condemns* the increasingly widespread massacres of innocent and defenceless people, including women and children, by the racist minority Pretoria régime in its desperate attempt to thwart the legitimate demands of the people;

28. *Demands* the immediate release of women and children detained in Namibian and South African prisons;

29. *Strongly condemns* the constant and deliberate violations of the fundamental rights of the Palestinian people, as well as the expansionist activities of Israel in the Middle East, which constitute an obstacle to the achievement of self-determination and independence by the Palestinian people and a threat to peace and stability in the region;

30. *Further strongly condemns* the massacre of Palestinians and other civilians at Beirut and the Israeli aggression against Lebanon, which endangers stability, peace and security in the region;

31. *Demands* the immediate and unconditional release of all persons detained or imprisoned as a result of their struggle for self-determination and independence, full respect for their fundamental individual rights and compliance with article 5 of the Universal Declaration of Human Rights, under which no one shall be subjected to torture or to cruel, inhuman or degrading treatment;

32. *Urges* all States, specialized agencies, competent organizations of the United Nations system and other international organizations to extend their support to the Palestinian people through its sole and legitimate representative, the Palestine Liberation Organization, in its struggle to regain its right to self-determination and independence in accordance with the Charter;

33. *Reiterates its satisfaction* at the material and other forms of assistance that peoples under colonial régimes continue to receive from Governments, organizations of the United Nations system and intergovernmental organizations and calls for a substantial increase in this assistance;

34. *Urges* all States, specialized agencies and other competent organizations of the United Nations system to do their utmost to ensure the full implementation of the Declaration on the Granting of Independence to Colonial Countries and Peoples and to intensify their efforts to support peoples under colonial, foreign and racist domination in their just struggle for self-determination and independence;

35. *Requests* the Secretary-General to give maximum publicity to the Declaration on the Granting of Independence to Colonial Countries and Peoples and to give the widest possible publicity to the struggle of oppressed peoples for the achievement of their self-determination and national independence and to report periodically to the General Assembly on his activities;

36. *Decides* to consider this item again at its thirty-ninth session on the basis of the reports that Governments, organizations of the United Nations system and intergovernmental and non-governmental organizations have been requested to submit concerning the strengthening of assistance to colonial territories and peoples.

General Assembly resolution 38/17

22 November 1983   Meeting 66   104-17-6 (recorded vote)

Approved by Third Committee (A/38/542) by recorded vote (105-17-8), 26 October (meeting 21); draft by Senegal, for African Group (A/C.3/38/L.10/Rev.1); agenda item 86.

Meeting numbers. GA 38th session: 3rd Committee 4-18, 21-23; plenary 66.

Recorded vote in Assembly as follows:

In favour: Afghanistan, Albania, Algeria, Angola, Argentina, Bahamas, Bahrain, Bangladesh, Bhutan, Bolivia, Botswana, Brazil, Bulgaria, Burma, Burundi, Byelorussian SSR, Cape Verde, Chile, China, Congo, Cuba, Cyprus, Czechoslovakia, Democratic Kampuchea, Democratic Yemen, Djibouti, Dominican Republic, Ecuador, Egypt, El Salvador, Ethiopia, Fiji, Gabon, German Democratic Republic, Guinea, Guinea-Bissau, Guyana, Hungary, India, Indonesia, Iran, Iraq,

Jamaica, Jordan, Kenya, Kuwait, Lao People's Democratic Republic, Lebanon, Lesotho, Libyan Arab Jamahiriya, Madagascar, Malaysia, Maldives, Mali, Malta, Mauritania, Mauritius, Mexico, Mongolia, Morocco, Mozambique, Nepal, Nicaragua, Nigeria, Oman, Pakistan, Panama, Papua New Guinea, Paraguay,[a] Peru, Philippines, Poland, Qatar, Romania, Rwanda, Saint Lucia, Sao Tome and Principe, Saudi Arabia, Senegal, Singapore, Somalia, Sri Lanka, Sudan, Suriname, Swaziland, Syrian Arab Republic, Thailand, Togo, Trinidad and Tobago, Tunisia, Turkey, Uganda, Ukrainian SSR, USSR, United Arab Emirates, United Republic of Cameroon, United Republic of Tanzania, Upper Volta, Uruguay, Venezuela, Viet Nam, Yemen, Yugoslavia, Zambia.

Against: Australia, Belgium, Canada, Denmark, Finland, France, Germany, Federal Republic of, Iceland, Israel, Italy, Luxembourg, Netherlands, New Zealand, Norway, Sweden, United Kingdom, United States.

Abstaining: Austria, Greece, Ireland, Japan, Portugal, Spain.

[a]Later advised the Secretariat it had intended not to participate.

In the Assembly, Brazil said it supported the resolution's main thrust, but recalled its previously expressed position on certain provisions of the two Declarations endorsed by paragraph 5. Not having been invited to the International Conference on the Alliance between South Africa and Israel, mentioned in paragraph 18, it was not fully aware of the substance of the Conference debates and final documents. Mexico reiterated its reservations in Committee also on those two paragraphs.

Costa Rica did not participate in the vote because the resolution contained paragraphs that it called unilateral. However, it supported those referring to the Declaration on decolonization, the question of Namibia, the struggle of the Namibian people for liberation, the April Conference on Namibia, as well as those rejecting South Africa's policy of *apartheid* and condemning human rights violations, the policy of "bantustanization" and aggression against front-line States.

In the Third Committee, among the States which voted against the draft, the United States said the text was neither universal nor democratic and contained wording on the Arab-Israeli conflict that should be rejected, for it was not possible to support the right to self-determination in favour of one people at the expense of another. It further said it opposed assistance to so-called liberation movements.

Israel observed that it had again been singled out in a draft bearing no relevance to reality and whose wording was yet another proof that some of its initiators denied Israel, a United Nations Member, the very right of existence. Those initiators, it noted, coincidentally belonged to the League of Arab States, which denied self-determination to national minorities living in their midst and wished to deny it to Israel as well. Reaffirming its total rejection of *apartheid*, Israel denied the repeated fabrications about its relations with South Africa.

Greece, speaking on behalf of the 10 European Community members, said they strongly supported the principle of self-determination, but could not accept that to maintain relations with a State was equivalent to approval of its policies—a position shared by Uruguay, which voted affirmatively. They also found it strange for a draft reso-

lution on self-determination to refer to particular situations without mentioning such flagrant and persistent violations as were occurring in Afghanistan and Kampuchea.

Among States abstaining, Portugal voiced reservations on the draft's endorsement of the Declarations in paragraph 5 on which it had previously entered reservations and of armed struggle—which neither Austria nor Spain could endorse and which Uruguay said violated Charter principles—as well as on the draft's references in paragraphs 18 and 21 to conferences in which it had taken no part and to condemning South Africa to isolation. Malawi (which did not participate in the Assembly vote but later advised that it had intended also to abstain) registered its reservations on a number of paragraphs.

Among States which did not participate in the Committee vote, Swaziland said the resolution, if implemented, would enhance the principle of self-determination world-wide, but reiterated its difficulty with sanctions, stressing that its position on the issue remained unchanged.

Of those voting for the draft, Lesotho reaffirmed that it favoured economic sanctions against South Africa, without prejudice to its support for self-determination. Uruguay, along with Turkey, disapproved of the selective wording of paragraph 19, and would have preferred a balanced wording of paragraphs 29 and 30, the latter to mention the need to withdraw foreign forces from Lebanon. Burma voiced reservations on those same paragraphs, and Haiti on paragraph 29. As to paragraph 32, Uruguay believed that the Palestinian people would select their representatives when they could freely exercise self-determination.

Chile entered reservations on those paragraphs that encouraged what it described as unacceptable means for settling conflicts, that condemned certain countries in a selective fashion while ignoring other situations involving violations of the right to self-determination, and that singled out certain Member States—such as Israel—in a discriminatory manner, or were highly subjective. Had separate votes been taken, it would have voted against paragraphs 2, 19, 30 and 32. Chile took the reference to national liberation movements to mean only those recognized by regional organizations. Likewise, it considered that implicit in the endorsement of the Declarations in paragraph 5 was the form in which they had been adopted by the relevant conferences; that is, taking account of the reservations expressed. On the references to the Middle East situation, Chile called for withdrawal of all foreign forces from Lebanon as a prerequisite to that country's exercise of self-determination.

Colombia, pointing to the danger of using the most elemental human aspirations for political purposes, said that many countries denouncing human rights violations in Latin America were themselves guilty of denying peoples' rights—a fact to be kept in mind for more balanced resolutions in the future.

The USSR unconditionally supported the text because it was in favour of freedom and equality of peoples and of eradicating colonialism and neo-colonialism. Condemning United States aggression against Grenada as a crime against peace, the USSR believed that all peace-loving people should make their voices heard in support of the right to self-determination of that country and other sovereign peoples against whom the United States was waging undeclared war.

In the view of Cuba and Nicaragua, a future resolution on self-determination should apply also to other parts of the world, notably Latin America, where Puerto Ricans remained subject to colonial dominion and Grenada had been invaded by United States forces. That invasion underscored the need for strict respect for the right to self-determination, Bulgaria and the Lao People's Democratic Republic observed. The German Democratic Republic, saying the draft resolution had become all the more important in the light of that blatant aggression, accused the United States of suppressing the will of a small country to be its own master. In line with its continued connection with backwardness and reaction, the United States was supporting South Africa's *apartheid* policy and the aggressor in the Israeli-occupied territories; it was trying to destroy the revolution in Nicaragua and to deploy new and dangerous missiles in Western Europe.

Refuting those criticisms in right of reply, the United States asserted that it had acted in Grenada in response to an urgent appeal from the Organization of Eastern Caribbean States, motivated by urgent security concerns stemming from the buildup of Cuban and USSR military forces in Grenada. Referring to what it described as USSR and USSR-sponsored violence in Afghanistan, the United States stated that the people of Grenada would avoid the horrible fate of the Afghans; that was not a violation of the principle of self-determination, it concluded, but a vindication and defence of it.

Afghanistan

By a resolution of 16 February 1983, adopted by a roll-call vote of 29 to 7, with 5 abstentions,[12] the Commission on Human Rights reaffirmed its profound concern that the people of Afghanistan continued to be denied their right to self-determination, to determine their own form of government, and to choose their economic, political and social system free from outside intervention, subversion, coercion or constraint. It called

for a political settlement based on: immediate foreign troop withdrawal from Afghanistan; full respect for that country's independence, sovereignty, territorial integrity and non-aligned status; and strict observance of the principle of non-interference. It urged all concerned to work towards such a settlement, which would also enable the Afghan refugees to return to their homes. The Commission asked the Secretary-General to continue to promote a political solution, urged all concerned to continue to co-operate with him, and appealed for humanitarian relief assistance to alleviate the hardship of Afghan refugees, in coordination with the United Nations High Commissioner for Refugees.

The Sub-Commission, by a resolution adopted on 5 September by 14 votes to 2, with 3 abstentions,[19] requested the Secretary-General to collect information on the human rights situation in Afghanistan for transmittal to the Commission in 1984. It recommended to the Commission a draft resolution for adoption by the Economic and Social Council, by which the Council would request appointment of a special rapporteur to examine that situation and formulate proposals towards ensuring full protection of human rights before, during and after the withdrawal of all foreign forces; and would authorize him to seek information from organizations and specialized agencies.

East Timor

By a resolution of 16 February 1983, adopted by a roll-call vote of 16 to 14, with 10 abstentions,[13] the Commission on Human Rights reaffirmed the inalienable right of the people of East Timor to self-determination and independence and declared that they must be enabled freely to determine their own future on the basis of relevant General Assembly resolutions and human rights instruments. The Commission called on Portugal, as the administering Power, and the representatives of the people of East Timor and Indonesia to co-operate with the United Nations with a view to guaranteeing the people of East Timor free and full exercise of that right. It also called on all concerned to facilitate entry of international aid into the Territory to alleviate the people's suffering due to the situation prevailing there.

The Sub-Commission, by a resolution adopted on 6 September by 10 votes to 7, with 8 abstentions,[20] welcomed the fact that the Assembly, in November 1982,[21] had included the question of East Timor in its 1983 agenda. The Sub-Commission requested the Secretary-General to intensify efforts to encourage the parties to arrive at a stable solution, with due regard for the interests of the people of East Timor, and recommended that the Commission continue to consider the evolution of the situation of human rights there.

On 3 February,[22] during the Commission's consideration of the question, Indonesia transmitted a memorandum of the same date stating that Indonesia categorically opposed United Nations discussion of issues related to the political and juridical status of East Timor. It rejected the draft resolution that was later adopted, stating that the allegations it contained were totally false.

Expressing support of the draft, Portugal stated on 7 February[23] that it could not accept Indonesia's restrictive interpretation, recognizing on the one hand the Commission's competence to deal with human rights and denying on the other its ability to deal with the question of East Timor.

(For further details on the question, see TRUSTEESHIP AND DECOLONIZATION, Chapter IV.)

Kampuchea

The Commission on Human Rights, by a resolution of 15 February, adopted by a roll-call vote of 28 to 9, with 4 abstentions,[10] reaffirmed that the continuing occupation of Kampuchea by foreign forces deprived the people of Kampuchea of the exercise of their right to self-determination, which currently constituted the primary violation of human rights in that country. The Commission emphasized that foreign troop withdrawal, restoration of Kampuchea's independence, sovereignty and territorial integrity, recognition of Kampucheans' right to self-determination and a commitment by all States to non-interference were essential components for a solution to the Kampuchea problem. It reaffirmed its call for a cessation of hostilities and for immediate withdrawal of foreign forces, to enable Kampucheans to exercise their human rights free from foreign interference, aggression and coercion and to determine their own political process through free and fair elections under United Nations supervision; to enable the United Nations to offer its services in the field of human rights; to make possible efforts towards a comprehensive political solution within the framework of the 1981 Declaration on Kampuchea[24] and relevant United Nations resolutions; and to make possible the return of all Kampuchean refugees.

The Commission reiterated its condemnation of the persistent occurrence of gross and flagrant human rights violations in Kampuchea, and deplored violations of the principles of humanitarianism and the Charter, particularly the recent military attack by occupying troops against encampments, including a hospital for Kampucheans, on the Kampuchea-Thailand border.

The Secretary-General was requested to continue to monitor developments in Kampuchea and to intensify efforts towards a political settlement and restoration of human rights. Noting the report

of the *Ad Hoc* Committee of the International Conference on Kampuchea, the Commission requested the Committee to continue its work, pending the reconvening of the Conference. It recommended that the Economic and Social Council continue to take measures to implement recommendations for the achievement by Kampucheans of the full enjoyment of human rights and freedoms, particularly the right to self-determination.

ECONOMIC AND SOCIAL COUNCIL ACTION

On the recommendation of its Second Committee, the Economic and Social Council adopted decision 1983/155 by recorded vote.

Right of peoples to self-determination and its application to peoples under colonial or alien domination or foreign occupation

At its 15th plenary meeting, on 27 May 1983, the Council endorsed Commission on Human Rights resolution 1983/5 of 15 February 1983, by which the Commission, *inter alia*, recognized that the continuing illegal occupation of Kampuchea by foreign forces had compelled a large number of Kampucheans to flee their own homeland; deplored the violations of the fundamental principles of humanitarianism and of the Charter of the United Nations, particularly the recent military attack by occupying troops against border encampments, including a hospital for Kampucheans on the Thai-Kampuchean border; and reaffirmed that the continuing occupation of Kampuchea by foreign forces deprived the people of Kampuchea of the exercise of their right to self-determination and constituted a primary violation of human rights in Kampuchea at present.

In this connection, the Council reaffirmed its decision 1982/143 of 7 May 1982 and once again repeated the call for the withdrawal of all foreign forces from Kampuchea and the exercise of the right to self-determination by the Kampuchean people as contained in the Declaration on Kampuchea adopted by the International Conference on Kampuchea on 17 July 1981 and endorsed by the General Assembly in its resolutions 36/5 of 21 October 1981 and 37/6 of 28 October 1982.

The Council expressed its grave concern at the continuing activities of the foreign forces in Kampuchea, particularly the systematic attacks on other refugee encampments along the Thai-Kampuchean border, resulting in further loss of life and property of Kampucheans and forcing large numbers of Kampuchean civilians to flee into Thailand.

The Council noted with appreciation the role of the Secretary-General and requested him to continue to monitor closely the developments in Kampuchea and to look into the situation, including the violations of humanitarian principles perpetrated against Kampuchean civilian refugees by the foreign-occupying troops along the border, as well as to intensify efforts, including the use of his good offices, to bring about a comprehensive political settlement of the Kampuchean problem and the restoration of fundamental human rights in Kampuchea.

The Council noted with appreciation the efforts of the *Ad Hoc* Committee of the International Conference on Kampuchea and requested that the Committee continue its work, pending the reconvening of the Conference.

Economic and Social Council decision 1983/155

41-9-3 (recorded vote)

Approved by Second Committee (E/1983/61) by recorded vote (34-8-4), 23 May (meeting 19); 23-nation draft (E/1983/C.2/L.13); agenda item 10.
Sponsors: Bangladesh, Belgium, Canada, Costa Rica, Fiji, Gambia, Germany, Federal Republic of, Italy, Japan, Malaysia, Netherlands, New Zealand, Pakistan, Papua New Guinea, Philippines, Saint Lucia, Samoa, Singapore, Solomon Islands, Sudan, Thailand, United Kingdom, Uruguay.
Meeting number. ESC 15.

Recorded vote in Council as follows:

In favour: Argentina, Austria, Bangladesh, Botswana, Brazil, Burundi, Canada, China, Colombia, Denmark, Djibouti, Ecuador, Fiji, France, Germany, Federal Republic of, Greece, Japan, Kenya, Lebanon, Liberia, Luxembourg, Malaysia, Netherlands, New Zealand, Norway, Pakistan, Peru, Portugal, Qatar, Saint Lucia, Saudi Arabia, Sierra Leone, Sudan, Suriname, Swaziland, Thailand, Tunisia, United Kingdom, United Republic of Cameroon, United States, Venezuela.
Against: Benin, Bulgaria, Byelorussian SSR, Congo, German Democratic Republic, India, Nicaragua, Poland, USSR.
Abstaining: Algeria, Mali, Mexico.

Poland, also on behalf of Bulgaria, the Byelorussian SSR, the German Democratic Republic and the USSR, expressed the view that the decision did not help to promote a stable peace in the region and diverted attention from the real reason for tensions along the Kampuchea-Thailand border; it also ignored the fact that armed groups, including those of the Pol Pot régime, were attacking the civilian population.

The Lao People's Democratic Republic said that, as one of the parties directly concerned, it did not believe that the decision would contribute to a solution of the problems of South-East Asia, which should be solved by the two groups of countries in the region—the countries of Indo-China and those of the Association of South-East Asian Nations (ASEAN)—without outside interference. The decision did not take due account of the points of view of the two sides.

Viet Nam rejected the Commission resolution and the Council decision as blatant interference in the domestic affairs of a sovereign State. The Council decision, it said, used human rights to reimpose on Kampucheans, under the guise of a so-called government coalition, the genocidal Pol Pot régime, which had massacred millions and denied normal life to an entire people. What Kampucheans needed was disinterested support from the international community in defence of their human rights—above all of the right to life. Viet Nam asserted that the Kampucheans had exercised self-determination in January 1979 and were determined to defend it, with the help of Vietnamese troops who were in Kampuchea at the request of the People's Republic of Kampuchea. As to the security of refugees along the Kampuchea-Thailand border, Viet Nam pointed to the proposals by the People's Republic to: dissociate refugee camps from armed camps, establish a demilitarized or security zone, and repatriate refu-

gees with the assistance of national Red Cross societies without making such repatriation contingent on reciprocal diplomatic recognition of the countries concerned.

Democratic Kampuchea said the Council decision would encourage Kampucheans under the leadership of the coalition Government to pursue their struggle for the complete liberation of their country. The problem in South-East Asia, it said, was not one between ASEAN and the Indo-Chinese countries, but Viet Nam's aggression against Kampuchea. United Nations response, as reflected in the vote on the decision, was an adequate one to the slanderous allegations by Viet Nam and its supporters.

(For details on the situation in Kampuchea, see POLITICAL AND SECURITY QUESTIONS, Chapter VII.)

Nicaragua

The Sub-Commission on Prevention of Discrimination and Protection of Minorities, by a resolution adopted on 31 August 1983 by 18 votes to 1, with 1 abstention,[14] recommended to the Commission on Human Rights adoption of a draft resolution. That draft would have the Economic and Social Council recommend that all Governments support efforts, especially those of the Contadora Group, towards attainment of peace so that Nicaragua might be assured its right to self-determination and to development without external interference.

This action stemmed from the Sub-Commission's concern, as stated in the resolution's preambular section, over numerous incursions by armed groups from a neighbouring country and sustained by an external force.

(For details on the situation in Nicaragua, see POLITICAL AND SECURITY QUESTIONS, Chapter VI.)

Palestinians

By a resolution of 15 February 1983, adopted by a roll-call vote of 26 to 7, with 10 abstentions,[8] the Commission on Human Rights condemned the continued occupation of Palestinian and other Arab territories by Israel and demanded its immediate, unconditional and total withdrawal. It reaffirmed the right of the Palestinian people to self-determination without external interference and to an independent and sovereign State of Palestine, and called for the return of Palestinians to their homes and property in exercise of that right. It recognized the right of Palestinians to regain their rights by all means in accordance with the purposes and principles of the United Nations Charter and reaffirmed that the future of Palestinians could be decided only with their participation in all efforts through their representative, PLO.

The Commission rejected all partial agreements and separate treaties in so far as they violated the rights of Palestinians and contradicted the principles of just and comprehensive Middle East solutions, as well as the "autonomy" plan proposed in the "Camp David accords", declaring those accords to be without validity. States, United Nations bodies and other international organizations were urged to extend support to Palestinians, through PLO, in the struggle to restore their rights.

The Commission adopted several other resolutions dealing with human rights violations in the occupied Arab territories (see under HUMAN RIGHTS VIOLATIONS below).

As requested by the Commission in the foregoing resolution, the Secretary-General submitted to the Sub-Commission a list of reports, studies and publications prepared by the Division for Palestinian Rights of the United Nations Secretariat,[25] updating a similar list to the Commission.[26]

On 31 August, the Sub-Commission reiterated that the inalienable rights of Palestinians included the rights to self-determination without external interference and to an independent and sovereign State of Palestine (see under HUMAN RIGHTS VIOLATIONS below).

South Africa and Namibia

Information from 14 Governments on the enactment of legislation declaring the recruitment, financing and training of mercenaries to be punishable offences was summarized by the Secretary-General in a report[27] to the Commission on Human Rights at its 1983 session. The report was submitted in response to a February 1982 Commission resolution reaffirming the legitimacy of the struggle of the oppressed people of South Africa and their national liberation movements as well as the right of the Namibian people to self-determination, and calling on Governments to enact legislation against mercenaries (see also LEGAL QUESTIONS, Chapter II).

By a resolution of 15 February adopted by a roll-call vote of 31 to 7, with 4 abstentions,[9] the Commission called on States to take steps to enable the dependent peoples of South Africa and Namibia to exercise fully and without further delay their inalienable right to self-determination. It reaffirmed the right of the Namibian people to freedom and national independence in a united Namibia, including Walvis Bay and the offshore islands, in accordance with the Charter and relevant General Assembly resolutions. It further reaffirmed the legitimacy of their struggle and that of the oppressed people of South Africa by all means, including armed struggle.

The Commission condemned the continued illegal occupation of Namibia by South Africa, in-cluding attempts to dismember its territory, declaring such occupation an act of aggression, a threat to international peace and security, and an affront to the United Nations, which had direct responsibility for the Territory until independence. It demanded the immediate release of all people detained or imprisoned by South Africa because of their struggle for independence, and full respect for their human rights. It condemned the policy of "bantustanization" as contrary to the principle of self-determination and inconsistent with genuine independence and national unity.

The Commission also condemned South Africa's acts of aggression and destabilization against independent African States, in particular Angola, Botswana, Lesotho, Mozambique and Zimbabwe, and demanded an immediate end to such acts and withdrawal of South Africa's forces from Angolan territory. It reaffirmed that the use of mercenaries against national liberation movements and sovereign States was a criminal act and that the mercenaries themselves were criminals, and called on Governments to declare the recruitment, financing and training of mercenaries and transit of mercenaries through their territories punishable offences and to prohibit their nationals from serving as mercenaries.

The Commission reaffirmed that continuation of colonialism in all forms—including racism, racial discrimination, *apartheid*, exploitation by foreign and other interests of economic and human resources, and colonial wars to suppress national liberation movements—was incompatible with the Charter, the 1948 Universal Declaration of Human Rights[28] and the 1960 Declaration on the Granting of Independence to Colonial Countries and Peoples.[29]

In one of two resolutions dated 18 February, the Commission reaffirmed the inalienable right of the oppressed people of South Africa and Namibia to self-determination;[30] in the other,[31] it reaffirmed that the Namibians could legitimately exercise that right only under conditions determined by the Security Council in 1978.[32]

(For further details on the human rights situation in South Africa and Namibia, see under HUMAN RIGHTS VIOLATIONS below.)

Western Sahara

The Commission on Human Rights, by a resolution adopted on 16 February 1973 by 16 votes to 2, with 15 abstentions,[11] reaffirmed the inalienable right of the people of Western Sahara to self-determination and independence. It reiterated its appeal to the two parties to the dispute, Morocco and the Frente Popular para la Liberación de Saguia el-Hamra y de Río de Oro, to enter into direct negotiations for a cease-fire, an indispensable prerequisite for a referendum on self-determination. The Commission decided to follow closely the development of the situation in Western Sahara and to consider the question in 1984 as a matter of high priority. (See also TRUSTEESHIP AND DECOLONIZATION, Chapter IV.)

Rights of detained persons

In 1983, work continued on a draft Body of Principles for the Protection of All Persons under Any Form of Detention or Imprisonment. To expedite its finalization, the General Assembly, by decision 38/426 of 19 December, decided to establish in 1984 an open-ended working group of the Sixth (Legal) Committee.

The human rights of persons subjected to any form of detention or imprisonment were the subject of three reports by the Secretary-General to the Sub-Commission on Prevention of Discrimination and Protection of Minorities. The Sub-Commission's sessional Working Group on Detention met in August; it reviewed developments on detention in certain countries, considered ways to eliminate enforced or involuntary disappearances and made recommendations for the protection of human rights in states of siege or emergency (see below).

In February, the Commission on Human Rights asked the Sub-Commission to propose measures to ensure respect for human rights in states of siege or emergency. In March, it adopted a resolution dealing with persons detained by Israel (see under HUMAN RIGHTS VIOLATIONS below).

Reports of the Secretary-General. In a May 1983 report to the Sub-Commission on the question of human rights of persons subjected to any form of detention or imprisonment,[33] the Secretary-General stated that, in keeping with a September 1982 Sub-Commission resolution,[34] Governments, specialized agencies and intergovernmental and non-governmental organizations had been invited to provide information on the question. As at 1 May, replies had been received from 14 countries, two specialized agencies and two intergovernmental organizations.

In June, the Secretary-General submitted a report containing a synopsis of material received from 10 NGOs.[35] Their comments covered persistent violations of the rights of detainees in the form of such practices as torture, arrest and detention on dubious grounds or without grounds, indefinite detention without trial, preventive detention during a state of emergency, incommunicado detention, death under suspicious circumstances during detention, extraterritorial abduction and forced disappearances. The report included certain features that emerged from the comments and suggestions for international action.

In August, the Secretary-General presented a preliminary survey of maximum detention periods under national laws and of decisions of international organs of investigation and settlement, using information from Governments, specialized agencies, intergovernmental organizations and NGOs.[36] The organs of investigation included the Human Rights Committee, the Committee on Freedom of Association of the International Labour Organisation (ILO), the European Commission of Human Rights and the European Court of Human Rights, and the Inter-American Commission on Human Rights.

Working Group activities. A sessional Working Group on human rights of persons subjected to any form of detention or imprisonment was set up by the Sub-Commission on 16 August 1983. The Group held two meetings during the remainder of the month, with John Carey (United States) as Chairman/Rapporteur. It reviewed developments on detention in certain countries and explored ways of eliminating enforced or involuntary disappearances. It adopted, with some modifications, a series of recommendations put forward by Special Rapporteur Nicole Questiaux (France) in a 1982 study of the implications for human rights of recent developments in situations known as states of siege or emergency.[37] The recommendations, including measures for developing the role of special international surveillance organs and for strengthening substantive guarantees provided for by international law on human rights, were submitted to the Sub-Commission in the Working Group's report.[38]

Sub-Commission action. By a resolution adopted on 6 September 1983 by 19 votes to 1, with 3 abstentions,[39] the Sub-Commission decided to include in its agenda an item on implementation of the right of derogation (in states of emergency), as provided for under article 4 of the International Covenant on Civil and Political Rights,[1] and human rights violations. To be taken up under the item were: a list of countries proclaiming or terminating a state of emergency, to be drawn up and updated each year by the Working Group on Detention; and a report on compliance with rules guaranteeing the legality of a state of emergency, making reference to the principles defined in the 1982 study,[37] for yearly submission by the Sub-Commission to the Commission on Human Rights.

The Sub-Commission also referred proposals to the Working Group, as follows: on the period of imprisonment—to make public without delay or at least enter in a register any arrest followed by remand to custody, to limit the time prescribed by the emergency law itself for holding a person incommunicado, and to make impossible the suspension of the *habeas corpus* procedure or similar remedies in any situation including a state of siege or emergency; on the right to a fair trial—a guarantee of a minimum of communication with a freely chosen defence counsel and the proceedings to be made public; on sentences and on procedure—to abolish capital punishment, particularly where political matters were concerned, and to suspend any provision of penal law permitting retroactive changes in jurisdiction or procedure upon introduction of a state of emergency.

By another resolution of the same date,[40] the Sub-Commission requested one of its members, Louis Joinet (France), to prepare a technical study of amnesty laws and their role in the safeguard and promotion of human rights, including minimum criteria generally accepted by the various legal systems. The findings were to be presented to the Sub-Commission in 1984, for transmission to the Commission.

Arbitrary detention and cruel treatment of prisoners of opinion and other human rights violations, resulting from the state of siege in Paraguay, were dealt with by the Sub-Commission in a 6 September resolution (see under HUMAN RIGHTS VIOLATIONS below).

Human rights in emergency situations

On 22 February 1983,[41] the Commission on Human Rights, noting that the Sub-Commission had endorsed the conclusions of the 1982 study on human rights in states of siege or emergency,[37] requested the Secretary-General to invite comments on the study from Governments, United Nations bodies, and intergovernmental and non-governmental organizations, for forwarding to the Sub-Commission and the Commission. It asked the Sub-Commission to propose measures to ensure respect for human rights in states of siege or emergency for priority consideration by the Commission in 1984.

Taking note of that request on 5 September and expressing concern about the numerous occurrences in many countries of excessive and unwarranted use of force during public gatherings, resulting in civilian loss of life or injury, the Sub-Commission requested the Commission to invite the Committee on Crime Prevention and Control to consider in 1984 how the question of restraints on the use of force by law enforcement officials and military personnel might be effectively examined by the Seventh (1985) United Nations Congress on the Prevention of Crime and the Treatment of Offenders (see Chapter XIII of this section). It requested the Secretary-General to invite the views of the international community and organizations and to prepare an analysis of State policies and practices regarding such restraints.

On 6 September, the Sub-Commission recommended to the Commission adoption of a draft

resolution inviting Paraguay to end the state of siege in force in that country since 1954 (see under HUMAN RIGHTS VIOLATIONS below).

Human rights in states of siege or emergency were also dealt with in connection with the rights of detained persons (see above). In keeping with the Commission's request of 22 February, the Secretary-General transmitted to the Sub-Commission comments on the 1982 study on human rights in states of siege or emergency from six Governments, a United Nations organ, a specialized agency and an NGO.[42]

Draft principles for protection of detainees

In 1983, a Working Group open to all members of the General Assembly's Sixth Committee continued work on a draft Body of Principles for the Protection of All Persons under Any Form of Detention or Imprisonment. The draft originated from a text adopted by the Sub-Commission on Prevention of Discrimination and Protection of Minorities in 1978,[43] work on which had since been carried out by working groups, of the Third Committee in 1980[44] and of the Sixth Committee in 1981[45] and 1982.[46]

Established by the Assembly in December 1982,[47] the 1983 Working Group met in New York between 30 September and 30 November, with Luigi Ferrari Bravo (Italy) as Chairman/Rapporteur. It was agreed at the outset to postpone consideration of definitions and to concentrate on preparation of texts considered generally acceptable. Accordingly, it resumed work on principle 14 of the draft, at which the 1982 working group had left off. Following revisions and amendments, the Group approved principles 14 to 18 (entitlements to: family notification of arrest and place of detention, assistance of and consultations with legal counsel, family visitation, detention near place of residence). The approved provisional texts were annexed to the Group's report.[48]

In a September 1983 report with later addenda,[49] the Secretary-General transmitted the views of six States on the draft text, based on the reports of the three previous working groups, which had been circulated for comment to all Member States.

On the recommendation of the Sixth Committee, the General Assembly adopted decision 38/426 without vote.

Draft Body of Principles for the Protection of All Persons under Any Form of Detention or Imprisonment

At its 101st plenary meeting, on 19 December 1983, the General Assembly, on the recommendation of the Sixth Committee:

(a) Took note with appreciation of the report of the Working Group on the Draft Body of Principles for the Protection of All Persons under Any Form of Detention or Imprisonment, established in accordance with General Assembly decision 37/427 of 16 December 1982 to elaborate a final version of the draft Body of Principles, a task which it had not been able to conclude;

(b) Decided to establish at its thirty-ninth session an open-ended working group of the Sixth Committee with a view to expediting the finalization of the draft Body of Principles for the Protection of All Persons under Any Form of Detention or Imprisonment;

(c) Requested the Secretary-General to circulate to Member States the report of the open-ended Working Group established at the thirty-eighth session;

(d) Decided to include in the provisional agenda of its thirty-ninth session the item entitled "Draft Body of Principles for the Protection of All Persons under Any Form of Detention or Imprisonment".

General Assembly decision 38/426

Adopted without vote

Approved by Sixth Committee (A/38/676) without vote, 8 December (meeting 70); draft by Sweden (A/C.6/38/L.26); agenda item 136.
Meeting numbers. GA 38th session: 6th Committee 3, 70; plenary 101.

Torture and cruel treatment

Work continued in 1983, in the Commission on Human Rights and in a working group, on a draft convention against torture and other cruel, inhuman or degrading treatment or punishment. Following the Commission's recommendation, the Economic and Social Council in May authorized a similar working group for 1984 to complete work on the draft. Its completion in that year as a matter of highest priority was requested of the Commission by the General Assembly in December 1983.

In November, the Secretary-General reported to the Assembly on the status of the United Nations Voluntary Fund for Victims of Torture, to which contributions of $350,882 were made in 1983. Contributions were again called for by the Assembly in December.

On 4 March,[50] the Commission requested that implementation of a September 1982 decision of the Sub-Commission,[51] asking its Working Group on Detention to hear and receive information on torture of detained persons, be deferred until the 1984 Commission session.

Draft convention on the prohibition of torture

Working group activities. A working group with Jan Herman Burgers (Netherlands) as Chairman/Rapporteur and open to all members of the Commission on Human Rights met between 24 January and 24 February 1983 to continue work on a draft convention on the prohibition of torture. The sections considered included: article 3, paragraph 2 (determination of grounds for believing a person to be in danger of being subjected to torture); and article 5, paragraph 2, article 6,

paragraph 4, and article 7 (on universal jurisdiction). Article 16 (State prevention of degrading treatment or punishment) was reconsidered to determine whether the reference to article 14 (redress and compensation) in paragraph 1 should be retained or deleted; since no consensus could be reached, it was decided to maintain the provisional status of the reference by retaining the square brackets around it.

The draft as it emerged at the end of the meetings was annexed to the group's report,[52] to serve as a basis for further discussion. It consisted of a seven-clause preamble adopted in 1983; part I containing 16 substantive articles, decision on 5 of which remained pending; part II containing 8 articles relating to the convention's implementation, 5 of them based on proposals submitted by the Chairman/Rapporteur in 1983 and redrafted in the light of discussions; and part III containing 7 final clauses, 6 of them also based on proposals submitted by the Chairman/Rapporteur.

Action by the Commission on Human Rights. By a resolution of 9 March 1983,[53] the Commission on Human Rights, desirous of expediting work on the draft convention, to which it decided to give priority consideration at its 1984 session, recommended to the Economic and Social Council adoption of a draft resolution authorizing a working group to meet prior to that session to complete work on the draft.

ECONOMIC AND SOCIAL COUNCIL ACTION

On 27 May 1983, the Economic and Social Council, on the recommendation of its Second Committee, adopted resolution 1983/38 without vote.

Question of the human rights of all persons subjected to any form of detention or imprisonment, in particular torture and other cruel, inhuman or degrading treatment or punishment

The Economic and Social Council,

Recalling General Assembly resolution 37/193 of 18 December 1982, by which the Assembly requested the Commission on Human Rights to complete as a matter of the highest priority, at its thirty-ninth session, the drafting of a convention on torture and other cruel, inhuman or degrading treatment or punishment, and Economic and Social Council resolution 1982/38 of 7 May 1982, by which the Council authorized a meeting of an open-ended working group of the Commission on Human Rights for a period of one week prior to the Commission's thirty-ninth session to complete the work on a draft convention against torture and other cruel, inhuman or degrading treatment or punishment,

Considering that it was not found possible to complete the work on the draft convention during the thirty-ninth session of the Commission,

Taking note of Commission on Human Rights resolution 1983/48 of 9 March 1983,

1. *Authorizes* a meeting of an open-ended working group for a period of one week prior to the fortieth ses-

sion of the Commission on Human Rights to complete the work on a draft convention against torture and other cruel, inhuman or degrading treatment or punishment;

2. *Requests* the Secretary-General to transmit to the Commission on Human Rights at its fortieth session all relevant material relating to the draft convention.

Economic and Social Council resolution 1983/38

27 May 1983   Meeting 15   Adopted without vote

Approved by Second Committee (E/1983/61) without vote, 23 May (meeting 18); draft by Commission on Human Rights (E/1983/13); agenda item 10.
Meeting number. ESC 15.

GENERAL ASSEMBLY ACTION

On 16 December 1983, the General Assembly adopted, on the recommendation of the Third Committee, resolution 38/119 without vote.

Torture and other cruel, inhuman or degrading treatment or punishment

The General Assembly,

Recalling the Declaration on the Protection of All Persons from Being Subjected to Torture and Other Cruel, Inhuman or Degrading Treatment or Punishment, adopted by the General Assembly in its resolution 3452(XXX) of 9 December 1975,

Bearing in mind article 7 of the International Covenant on Civil and Political Rights,

Recalling also its resolution 32/62 of 8 December 1977, in which it requested the Commission on Human Rights to draw up a draft convention against torture and other cruel, inhuman or degrading treatment or punishment, in the light of the principles embodied in the Declaration, and its resolution 32/63 of 8 December 1977,

Recalling further that the Sixth United Nations Congress on the Prevention of Crime and the Treatment of Offenders, in its resolution 11 of 5 September 1980, expressed the belief that the draft convention should be finalized at the earliest possible time,

Considering that it was not possible to complete the work on the draft convention during the thirty-ninth session of the Commission on Human Rights,

1. *Welcomes* Economic and Social Council resolution 1983/38 of 27 May 1983, in which the Council authorized a meeting of an open-ended working group of the Commission on Human Rights for a period of one week prior to the fortieth session of the Commission in order to complete the work on a draft convention;

2. *Requests* the Commission on Human Rights to complete, at its fortieth session, as a matter of the highest priority, the drafting of a convention against torture and other cruel, inhuman or degrading treatment or punishment, with a view to submitting a draft, including provisions for the effective implementation of the future convention, to the General Assembly at its thirty-ninth session;

3. *Decides* to include in the provisional agenda of its thirty-ninth session the item entitled "Torture and other cruel, inhuman or degrading treatment or punishment".

General Assembly resolution 38/119

16 December 1983   Meeting 100   Adopted without vote

Approved by Third Committee (A/38/687) without vote, 30 November (meeting 57); 17-nation draft (A/C.3/38/L.32); agenda item 97.
Sponsors: Austria, Bolivia, Canada, Costa Rica, Cuba, Denmark, Finland, Greece, Iceland, Iraq, Italy, Netherlands, Norway, Portugal, Senegal, Spain, Sweden.
Meeting numbers. GA 38th session: 3rd Committee 49-54, 57; plenary 100.

Fund for victims of torture

On 22 February 1983,[54] the Commission on Human Rights, reiterating the need to provide assistance to the victims of torture or to activities on their behalf, called on Governments, organizations and individuals to contribute to the United Nations Voluntary Fund for Victims of Torture, established in 1981.[55] It requested the Secretary-General to transmit its appeal to all Governments and to keep it informed of the Fund's operations.

In his November report on the status of the Fund,[56] the Secretary-General stated that in 1983 its Board of Trustees—at its first session at Geneva from 21 to 25 March and at its second in New York from 24 to 28 October—reviewed the Fund's programme of activities and a number of projects submitted for support. The Board found the needs of torture victims to be considerable and expected requests for assistance, already large in number, to increase. The Board thus decided, as a matter of priority, to solicit contributions from Governments and individuals and other public and private sources.

In keeping with its decision to concentrate initially on supporting programmes providing direct assistance for the rehabilitation of torture victims—a process requiring special medical and psychological care—the Board recommended a number of grants to the Secretary-General for such assistance, including support for medical and psychological training courses and for humanitarian missions by experienced medical personnel. The number of projects reviewed called for a total amount far exceeding the funds available. Nine grants were recommended, amounting to $268,200, which the Secretary-General subsequently made available.

In 1983, eight countries—Canada, Cyprus, Finland, France, the Federal Republic of Germany, Greece, Luxembourg and Sweden—contributed $350,882 to the Fund.

GENERAL ASSEMBLY ACTION

On 16 December 1983, on the recommendation of the Third Committee, the General Assembly adopted resolution 38/92 without vote.

United Nations Voluntary Fund for Victims of Torture

The General Assembly,

Recalling article 5 of the Universal Declaration of Human Rights, which states that no one shall be subjected to torture or to cruel, inhuman or degrading treatment or punishment,

Recalling also the Declaration on the Protection of All Persons from Being Subjected to Torture and Other Cruel, Inhuman or Degrading Treatment or Punishment,

Recalling further its resolution 36/151 of 16 December 1981, in which it noted with deep concern that acts of torture took place in various countries, recognized the need to provide assistance to the victims of torture in a purely humanitarian spirit and established the United Nations Voluntary Fund for Victims of Torture,

Convinced that the struggle to eliminate torture includes the provision of assistance in a humanitarian spirit to the victims and their family members,

Taking note of the report of the Secretary-General on the United Nations Voluntary Fund for Victims of Torture,

1. *Expresses its gratitude and appreciation* to those Governments and individuals that have already contributed to the United Nations Voluntary Fund for Victims of Torture;

2. *Calls upon* all Governments, organizations and individuals in a position to do so to respond favourably to requests for contributions to the Fund;

3. *Expresses its appreciation* to the Board of Trustees of the Fund for the work it has carried out;

4. *Expresses its appreciation* to the Secretary-General for the support given to the Board of Trustees;

5. *Requests* the Secretary-General to make use of all existing possibilities to assist the Board of Trustees of the Fund, *inter alia* through the preparation, production and dissemination of information materials, in its efforts to make the Fund and its humanitarian work better known and in its appeal for contributions.

General Assembly resolution 38/92

16 December 1983   Meeting 100   Adopted without vote

Approved by Third Committee (A/38/680) without vote, 7 December (meeting 67); 12-nation draft (A/C.3/38/L.44); agenda item 12.
Sponsors: Bolivia, Canada, Costa Rica, Denmark, Finland, Germany, Federal Republic of, Iceland, Kenya, Mexico, Netherlands, Norway, Sweden.
Meeting numbers. GA 38th session: 3rd Committee 18, 54, 55, 57-67; plenary 100.

Principles of Medical Ethics

GENERAL ASSEMBLY ACTION

Acting without vote on the recommendation of the Third Committee, the General Assembly, on 16 December 1983, adopted resolution 38/118.

Principles of Medical Ethics

The General Assembly,

Recalling its resolution 37/194 of 18 December 1982, by which it adopted the Principles of Medical Ethics relevant to the role of health personnel, particularly physicians, in the protection of prisoners and detainees against torture and other cruel, inhuman or degrading treatment or punishment,

Alarmed that not infrequently members of the medical profession or other health personnel are engaged in activities which are difficult to reconcile with the Principles of Medical Ethics,

Recognizing the need for the full application of the Principles of Medical Ethics and desiring that the Principles be given wide publicity,

1. *Urges* all Governments to take measures with a view to promoting the application by all health personnel and government officials, in particular those employed in institutions of detention or imprisonment, of the Principles of Medical Ethics relevant to the role of health personnel, particularly physicians, in the protection of prisoners and detainees against torture and other cruel, inhuman or degrading treatment or punishment;

2. *Requests* the Secretary-General to disseminate the Principles of Medical Ethics widely and in as many lan-

guages as possible and to issue a pamphlet containing the text of the Principles in the six official languages of the United Nations;

3. *Calls upon* all Governments to give the Principles of Medical Ethics the widest possible distribution, in particular among medical and paramedical associations and institutions of detention or imprisonment, in an official language of the State;

4. *Invites* all relevant intergovernmental organizations, in particular the World Health Organization, and non-governmental organizations concerned to bring the Principles of Medical Ethics to the attention of the widest possible group of individuals, especially those active in the medical and paramedical field;

5. *Requests* the Secretary-General to report to the General Assembly at its thirty-ninth session on the steps taken by the United Nations and the relevant specialized agencies, as well as by Governments, for the dissemination and implementation of the Principles of Medical Ethics.

General Assembly resolution 38/118

16 December 1983   Meeting 100   Adopted without vote

Approved by Third Committee (A/38/687) without vote, 30 November (meeting 57); 14-nation draft (A/C.3/38/L.31); agenda item 97.
Sponsors: Australia, Austria, Belgium, Canada, Denmark, Fiji, Greece, Ireland, Italy, Netherlands, New Zealand, Norway, Samoa, United States.
Meeting numbers. GA 38th session: 3rd Committee 49-54, 57; plenary 100.

Detention on grounds of mental illness

Following a Commission on Human Rights recommendation of 9 March 1983,[57] the Economic and Social Council adopted resolution 1983/37 on 27 May requesting the Sub-Commission to set up a sessional working group to examine as a matter of highest priority the draft principles, guidelines and guarantees for the protection of persons detained on grounds of mental ill-health or suffering from mental disorder. The draft had been prepared by Special Rapporteur Erica-Irene A. Daes (Greece), who was asked expeditiously to supplement her 1982 report.[58]

Responding, the Special Rapporteur submitted a final report[59] to the Sub-Commission in August. Taking account of comments by Governments, specialized agencies, intergovernmental organizations and NGOs, as well as of judgements of regional and national courts and writings of recognized scholars and scientists, the report summarized the history of the treatment and care of the mentally ill and of mental institutions. It also surveyed the basic contribution to the protection of the patient's human and legal rights by the United Nations and its specialized agencies, the courts, intergovernmental organizations and NGOs.

The report made a series of observations and conclusions. Among them were that: problems created by mental illness varied with such factors as a country's political and legal systems, medical standards, financial resources, and understanding and concern; psychiatry was frequently used to subvert political and legal guarantees of the individual's freedom; psychiatric hospitalization and treatment was forced on individuals who did not support the political régime under which they lived; persons were involuntarily detained and used as guinea pigs for scientific experiments; and patients who should be in the care of an institution because they were a danger to themselves or others were left to live freely without supervision. The definitions of "mental illness", "mentally ill" and "mental disorder" remained to be standardized. While they were sufficiently clarified by science and jurisprudence in some countries, there was no legislative uniformity or harmonization in the definition of those concepts.

Despite economic, social and medical advances, high standards in mental health institutions were not automatically a government priority. Overcrowding, inadequate services and a dearth of trained personnel were serious problems, as were the lack of proper community-care facilities and the tendency to integrate mental health services with services for other illnesses. Evidence pointed to a general pattern of allowing involuntary admission and detention on the grounds of mental illness or through medical discretion, without full judicial hearing. Attention was drawn to some scientific and technological advances with adverse effects which, in certain cases, threatened the patient's physical and intellectual integrity.

The report proposed that the Sub-Commission recommend to the Commission certain measures for consideration by Governments, which should: adapt national legislation to the draft principles; develop programmes for social and community care; ensure respect for the principles of legality, due process of law, fair and public hearing, equality and non-discrimination, and the writ of habeas corpus; recognize the patient's rights to accept or refuse treatment, to rehabilitation and protection, and to be informed of his or her medical diagnosis and report; safeguard confidential information in mental health records; ensure access to appropriate mental health services on a voluntary basis; adopt policy to make involuntary admission to a mental institution unjustifiable where accommodations, food or medical care were below acceptable standards; impose respect for the codes of medical ethics; prohibit psychological and psychiatric abuses in particular on political or other non-medical grounds; and limit restrictions on personal freedom to cases where a patient's condition or treatment so required.

Other measures called for humanizing and individualizing care and treatment, modernizing or upgrading institutional facilities to acceptable standards, developing special services and educational programmes for juvenile patients, rehabilitating former patients and integrating them in commu-

nity life, establishing advocacy systems for patient representation, and disseminating information on the protection of human rights of the mentally ill, in particular against threats arising from certain scientific and technological developments.

On 15 August, the Sub-Commission set up a working group, with Mrs. Daes as Chairman/Rapporteur, to resume the first reading of the draft principles. The group met between 24 August and 1 September and began with article 8, the preliminary consideration of the first seven articles having been completed the previous year. The group also heard statements from representatives of the African National Congress of South Africa and five NGOs.

Following examination of the working group's report[60] and of the Special Rapporteur's final report, the Sub-Commission, on 7 September,[61] expressed appreciation to the Special Rapporteur for a valuable report and requested that it be presented to the Commission. The Sub-Commission recommended to the Commission for adoption by the Economic and Social Council a draft resolution, by which the Council would decide that the Special Rapporteur's study be published and given the widest possible distribution in all the official United Nations languages, and would ask the Sub-Commission to set up a 1984 sessional working group to continue work on the draft principles.

ECONOMIC AND SOCIAL COUNCIL ACTION

The Economic and Social Council, on the recommendation of its Second Committee, adopted resolution 1983/37 without vote on 27 May 1983.

Human rights and scientific and technological developments

The Economic and Social Council,

Mindful of resolution 1982/34 of 10 September 1982 of the Sub-Commission on Prevention of Discrimination and Protection of Minorities, and Commission on Human Rights resolution 1983/44 of 9 March 1983, concerning guidelines, principles and guarantees for the protection of persons detained on grounds of mental ill-health or suffering from mental disorder,

Expressing its deep appreciation to the Special Rapporteur, Mrs. Erica-Irene A. Daes, for her work in preparing her report on this question,

Noting also with appreciation the report of the Sub-Commission's sessional working group on the question of persons detained on the grounds of mental ill-health,

1. *Requests* the Special Rapporteur expeditiously to supplement her final report, containing the body of principles, guidelines and guarantees as well as the summary compilation of replies received from Governments and specialized agencies, taking into account the basic views expressed in the Sub-Commission on Prevention of Discrimination and Protection of Minorities and in the Commission on Human Rights, and to include in the report any new replies from Governments or specialized agencies that may be transmitted in the mean time;

2. *Requests* the Sub-Commission to establish a sessional working group and to allocate to it appropriate time and facilities for a proper examination, as a matter of the highest priority, of the above-mentioned body of principles, guidelines and guarantees, and to submit the revised final report of the Special Rapporteur including the documentation referred to in paragraph 1 above, to the Commission on Human Rights at its fortieth session;

3. *Requests* the Secretary-General to provide the Special Rapporteur with all assistance needed for the completion of her work.

Economic and Social Council resolution 1983/37

27 May 1983   Meeting 15   Adopted without vote

Approved by Second Committee (E/1983/61) without vote, 23 May (meeting 18); draft by Commission on Human Rights (E/1983/13); agenda item 10.
Meeting number. ESC 15.

GENERAL ASSEMBLY ACTION

The General Assembly, on the recommendation of the Third Committee, adopted on 16 December 1983 resolution 38/111 without vote.

Implications of scientific and technological developments for human rights

The General Assembly,

Recalling its resolution 33/53 of 14 December 1978, in which it requested the Commission on Human Rights to urge the Sub-Commission on Prevention of Discrimination and Protection of Minorities to undertake, as a matter of priority, a study of the question of the protection of those detained on the grounds of mental ill-health, with a view to formulating guidelines,

Recalling also its resolutions 35/130 B of 11 December 1980, 36/56 B of 25 November 1981 and 37/188 of 18 December 1982, in which it noted with satisfaction the progress made by the Sub-Commission and urged the Commission on Human Rights and the Sub-Commission to continue and expedite their consideration of this question, so that the Commission could submit its views and recommendations to the General Assembly at its thirty-ninth session, through the Economic and Social Council,

Recalling further Economic and Social Council resolution 1983/37 of 27 May 1983 and Commission on Human Rights resolution 1983/44 of 9 March 1983,

Noting that the Commission on Human Rights will not be in a position to submit a report to the General Assembly at its thirty-ninth session through the Economic and Social Council, as requested in Assembly resolution 37/188, because it was impossible for the Sub-Commission to conclude at its thirty-sixth session its consideration of the draft body of guidelines, principles and guarantees,

Reaffirming its conviction that detention of persons in mental institutions on account of their political views or on other non-medical grounds is a violation of their human rights,

Noting with satisfaction the progress made by the Sub-Commission in its consideration of the draft body of guidelines, principles and guarantees submitted to it,

Again urges the Commission on Human Rights and, through it, the Sub-Commission on Prevention of Discrimination and Protection of Minorities to expedite their consideration of the draft body of guidelines, prin-

ciples and guarantees, so that the Commission can submit its views and recommendations, including a draft body of guidelines, principles and guarantees, to the General Assembly at its fortieth session, through the Economic and Social Council.

General Assembly resolution 38/111

16 December 1983   Meeting 100   Adopted without vote

Approved by Third Committee (A/38/684) without vote, 30 November (meeting 57); 14-nation draft (A/C.3/38/L.29); agenda item 94.
Sponsors: Bolivia, Botswana, Cyprus, Gambia, Italy, Mexico, Morocco, Netherlands, Norway, Sierra Leone, Singapore, Sweden, Togo, United Kingdom.
Meeting numbers. GA 38th session: 3rd Committee 49-54, 56, 57; plenary 100.

Extra-legal executions

In January 1983, Special Rapporteur S. Amos Wako (Kenya) submitted to the Commission on Human Rights a report on questions related to summary or arbitrary executions, which in increasing numbers took place in various parts of the world. The Special Rapporteur had been appointed by the Commission Chairman in August 1982, in accordance with a May 1982 Economic and Social Council resolution.[62] Following the recommendation of the Commission on 8 March 1983,[63] the Council, by resolution 1983/36 of 27 May, decided to continue the Special Rapporteur's mandate for another year, requesting him to review his report in the light of information received from Governments, United Nations bodies, intergovernmental organizations and NGOs. The General Assembly, in resolution 38/96 of 16 December, took note of that decision and again requested the Secretary-General to continue to use his best endeavours in cases where the minimum standard of legal safeguards appeared not to be respected, as provided for in articles 6 (on the right to life), 14 (on minimum guarantees in determining criminal charges) and 15 (on determination of penalty for criminal offence) of the 1966 International Covenant on Civil and Political Rights.[1]

Report of the Special Rapporteur. The report of the Special Rapporteur[64] reviewed international legal standards, national legislation and basic concepts of summary or arbitrary executions in relation to judicial or other proceedings, to those in detention or custody, and to killings resulting from law enforcement; and executions in states of war, armed conflicts and emergency. General patterns of such executions and their targets, and allegations of such executions in specific countries were analysed.

The report stated that summary or arbitrary executions were widespread, indicating a serious erosion of respect for the right to life that was bound to have an effect on international order. In the preceding 15 years, such executions had been practised in a number of countries in a consistent pattern. Conservative estimates had put the known victims at some 2 million persons. Executions were most prevalent in areas with internal disturbances or under states of emergency, and in the wake of government change resulting from war, revolutions or *coups d'état*. In areas of political tension, individuals perceived to be leaders of groups opposed to the Government or simply to be critics of it were targeted for summary execution. Arbitrary executions involving a number of persons usually occurred during demonstrations, strikes or other forms of protest. Governments were found to be reluctant to investigate cases or punish those guilty of carrying out such executions, who in some cases had even been granted immunity from prosecution on the grounds that they had acted in "good faith".

Notable among the Special Rapporteur's recommendations was urgent action by the international community to halt erosion of respect for the right to life by setting up a preventive mechanism that would react speedily to threatened or imminent summary or arbitrary executions. A parallel mechanism should also be set up to monitor such executions and to suggest ways of eliminating them either generally or in specific situations. Among the suggestions received by the Special Rapporteur was to amend the mandate of the Working Group on Enforced or Involuntary Disappearances of the Commission on Human Rights to cover also such executions, or set up a separate working group. An appeal should be made to Governments to ratify international human rights instruments, in particular the International Covenant on Civil and Political Rights, and the 1949 Geneva Conventions and Protocols, and to enforce them. An international campaign should be launched to promote world opinion against summary or arbitrary executions.

Further work on standard-setting should include: clarification of the definition of summary or arbitrary executions, of the minimum guarantees to be observed by military, special or revolutionary tribunals in times of public emergency or of internal disturbance, and of the qualification and tenure of such tribunals; and clarification of the conduct of, and exercise of the powers of arrest by, police or other law enforcement agencies during events such as demonstrations or riots, as well as of safeguards against torture during interrogation. Other recommendations called for: development of minimum standards of investigation and accountability; a study of the specific types or patterns of execution, in order to set national, regional and international standards; and examination of the role of groups other than the Government in acts leading to deprivation of life in a manner equivalent to that from summary or arbitrary executions.

On 14 January, Guatemala invited the Special Rapporteur to visit the country. Responding on 25 January, the Special Rapporteur accepted the invitation in the context of a follow-up to his report, without, however, setting a date.

ECONOMIC AND SOCIAL COUNCIL ACTION

On the recommendation of its Second Committee, the Economic and Social Council adopted two resolutions relating to arbitrary or summary executions. On 26 May, it adopted without vote resolution 1983/24, the draft of which had been prepared by the Committee on Crime Prevention and Control (see Chapter XIII of this section).

Arbitrary or summary executions

The Economic and Social Council,

Recalling General Assembly resolutions 35/172 of 15 December 1980, in which the Secretary-General was requested to report to the Committee on Crime Prevention and Control at its seventh session on arbitrary or summary executions, and 36/22 of 9 November 1981, in which the Committee on Crime Prevention and Control was requested to examine the problem with a view to making recommendations,

Having considered the report of the Secretary-General on the implementation of General Assembly resolution 35/172,

Having regard to the provisions bearing on capital punishment in the International Covenant on Civil and Political Rights, in particular paragraph 1 of article 2 and articles 6, 14 and 15,

Recalling General Assembly resolution 2393(XXIII) of 26 November 1968, in which the Assembly invited Governments of Member States, *inter alia*, to ensure the most careful legal procedures and the greatest possible safeguards for the accused in capital cases in countries where the death penalty obtains,

Mindful that a substantive relationship exists between the issue of human rights, on the one hand, and criminal justice, on the other, which should be further recognized and promoted within the United Nations system,

Concerned about the statement made in the 1980 quinquennial report of the Secretary-General on the question of capital punishment, indicating that extrajudicial executions were increasing in certain countries, retentionist and abolitionist alike,

Taking note of resolution 5 of 5 September 1980 of the Sixth United Nations Congress on the Prevention of Crime and the Treatment of Offenders, in which the Congress deplored and condemned extra-legal executions,

Further recalling the Declaration on the Protection of All Persons from Being Subjected to Torture and Other Cruel, Inhuman or Degrading Treatment or Punishment, the Code of Conduct for Law Enforcement Officials and the Standard Minimum Rules for the Treatment of Prisoners and related recommendations adopted by the United Nations,

Taking account of the work done by the Commission on Human Rights and the Sub-Commission on Prevention of Discrimination and Protection of Minorities in the areas of summary or arbitrary executions, and disappearances of persons, and the more general question of the human rights and protection of persons held under any form of detention and subjected to torture or any other cruel, inhuman or degrading treatment,

Hopeful that work currently undertaken by competent bodies of the United Nations with a view to drafting a convention against torture and other cruel, inhuman or degrading treatment or punishment, a draft body of principles for the protection of all persons under any form of detention or imprisonment and a draft code of medical ethics can be expedited,

1. *Strongly condemns and deplores* the brutal practice of summary executions in various parts of the world, and its apparent increase;

2. *Equally strongly condemns and deplores* the lack or non-observance in certain cases of the minimum legal guarantees and safeguards in respect of the use of capital punishment, which can lead to sham trials and arbitrary executions;

3. *Requests* the Secretary-General to make available to the Committee on Crime Prevention and Control at its eighth session a report on the progress of the work done by the Commission on Human Rights and the Sub-Commission on Prevention of Discrimination and Protection of Minorities;

4. *Decides* that the Committee on Crime Prevention and Control should further study the question of death penalties that do not meet the acknowledged minimum legal guarantees and safeguards, as contained in the International Covenant on Civil and Political Rights and other international instruments, and welcomes the Committee's intention that the issue should be discussed at the Seventh United Nations Congress on the Prevention of Crime and the Treatment of Offenders, under the appropriate item;

5. *Requests* the Secretary-General to continue to obtain information, from Member States and other available sources, on the development of legal provisions, the actual practice relating to the death penalty and the arbitrary character of some executions, and to make his next report on capital punishment available to the Seventh United Nations Congress on the Prevention of Crime and the Treatment of Offenders for consideration.

Economic and Social Council resolution 1983/24

26 May 1983   Meeting 14   Adopted without vote

Approved by Second Committee (E/1983/62) without vote, 10 May (meeting 8); draft by Committee on Crime Prevention and Control (E/CN.5/1983/2); agenda item 11. *Meeting number.* ESC 14.

On 27 May, the Council adopted resolution 1983/36 without vote.

Summary or arbitrary executions

The Economic and Social Council,

Recalling the Universal Declaration of Human Rights, which guarantees the right to life, liberty and security of person,

Having regard to the provisions of the International Covenant on Civil and Political Rights, which states that every human being has the inherent right to life, that this right shall be protected by law and that no one shall be arbitrarily deprived of his life,

Recalling General Assembly resolution 34/175 of 17 December 1979, in which the Assembly reaffirmed that mass and flagrant violations of human rights were of special concern to the United Nations and urged the Commission on Human Rights to take timely and effective action in existing and future cases of mass and flagrant violations of human rights,

Mindful of General Assembly resolutions 36/22 of 9 November 1981 and 37/182 of 17 December 1982, in which the Assembly condemned the practice of summary and arbitrary executions,

Bearing in mind resolution 5 of 5 September 1980 on extra-legal executions adopted by the Sixth United Nations Congress on the Prevention of Crime and the Treatment of Offenders,

Taking note of resolutions 1982/10 and 1982/13 of 7 September 1983 of the Sub-Commission on Prevention of Discrimination and Protection of Minorities, in which the Sub-Commission recommended that effective measures should be adopted to prevent the occurrence of summary and arbitrary executions, including extra-legal executions,

Deeply alarmed about the occurrence on a large scale of summary or arbitrary executions, including extra-legal executions,

Convinced of the need to continue to deal urgently with the question of summary or arbitrary executions, including extra-legal executions,

1. *Strongly deplores*, once again, the increasing number of summary or arbitrary executions, including extra-legal executions, which continue to take place in various parts of the world;

2. *Appeals urgently* to Governments, United Nations bodies, the specialized agencies, regional intergovernmental organizations and non-governmental and humanitarian organizations to take effective action to combat and eliminate summary or arbitrary executions, including extra-legal executions;

3. *Takes note* of the report of the Special Rapporteur, Mr. S. A. Wako, submitted in accordance with Council resolution 1982/35 of 7 May 1982;

4. *Decides* to continue the mandate of the Special Rapporteur, Mr. S. A. Wako, for another year;

5. *Requests* the Special Rapporteur to review his report in the light of the information received, taking particularly into account any new information, including relevant internal legislation, provided by concerned Governments as well as views expressed in the Commission on Human Rights at its thirty-ninth session and to submit a report to the Commission at its fortieth session;

6. *Considers* that the Special Rapporteur, in carrying out his mandate, should continue to seek and receive information from Governments, United Nations bodies, specialized agencies, regional intergovernmental organizations and non-governmental organizations in consultative status with the Economic and Social Council;

7. *Expresses its appreciation* to those Governments that have extended invitations to the Special Rapporteur to visit their respective countries and urges the Special Rapporteur to respond positively to such invitations;

8. *Urges* all Governments and all others concerned to co-operate with and assist the Special Rapporteur;

9. *Requests* the Secretary-General to provide all necessary assistance to the Special Rapporteur;

10. *Decides* that the Commission on Human Rights should consider the question of summary or arbitrary executions as a matter of high priority at its fortieth session under the item entitled "Question of the violation of human rights and fundamental freedoms in any part of the world, with particular reference to colonial and other dependent countries and territories".

Economic and Social Council resolution 1983/36

27 May 1983   Meeting 15   Adopted without vote

Approved by Second Committee (E/1983/61) without vote, 23 May (meeting 18); draft by Commission on Human Rights (E/1983/13); agenda item 10.
Meeting number. ESC 15.

GENERAL ASSEMBLY ACTION

On 16 December 1983, on the recommendation of the Third Committee, the General Assembly adopted resolution 38/96 without vote.

Summary or arbitrary executions

The General Assembly,

Recalling the provisions of the Universal Declaration of Human Rights, which states that every human being has the right to life, liberty and security of person and that everyone is entitled in full equality to a fair and public hearing by an independent and impartial tribunal,

Having regard to the provisions of the International Covenant on Civil and Political Rights, which states that every human being has the inherent right to life, that this right shall be protected by law and that no one shall be arbitrarily deprived of his life,

Recalling also its resolution 34/175 of 17 December 1979, in which it reaffirmed that mass and flagrant violations of human rights are of special concern to the United Nations and urged the Commission on Human Rights to take timely and effective action in existing and future cases of mass and flagrant violations of human rights,

Recalling further its resolution 36/22 of 9 November 1981, in which it condemned the practice of summary and arbitrary executions, and its resolution 37/182 of 17 December 1982,

Deeply alarmed at the occurrence on a large scale of summary or arbitrary executions, including extra-legal executions,

Recalling resolution 1982/13 of 7 September 1982 of the Sub-Commission on Prevention of Discrimination and Protection of Minorities, in which the Sub-Commission recommended that effective measures should be adopted to prevent the occurrence of summary or arbitrary executions,

Convinced of the need for appropriate action to combat and eventually eliminate this practice, which represents a flagrant violation of the most fundamental human right, the right to life,

1. *Welcomes* Economic and Social Council resolution 1982/35 of 7 May 1982, in which the Council decided to appoint for one year a special rapporteur to examine the questions related to summary or arbitrary executions and to submit to the Commission on Human Rights, at its thirty-ninth session, a comprehensive report on the occurrence and extent of the practice of such executions, together with his conclusions and recommendations;

2. *Takes note* of Economic and Social Council resolution 1983/36 of 26 May 1983, in which the Council decided to continue the mandate of the Special Rapporteur, Mr. S. A. Wako, for another year and decided that the Commission on Human Rights should consider the question of summary or arbitrary executions as a matter of high priority at its fortieth session;

3. *Appeals* to all Governments to co-operate with and assist the Special Rapporteur of the Commission on Human Rights in the preparation of his report;

4. *Requests* the Secretary-General to provide all necessary assistance to the Special Rapporteur so that he may effectively carry out his mandate;

5. *Again requests* the Secretary-General to continue to use his best endeavours in cases where the minimum standard of legal safeguards provided for in articles 6, 14 and 15 of the International Covenant on Civil and Political Rights appear not to be respected;

6. *Requests* the Commission on Human Rights at its fortieth session, on the basis of the report of the Special Rapporteur to be prepared in conformity with Economic and Social Council resolutions 1982/35 and 1983/36, to make recommendations concerning appropriate action to combat and eventually eliminate the practice of summary or arbitrary executions.

General Assembly resolution 38/96

16 December 1983   Meeting 100   Adopted without vote

Approved by Third Committee (A/38/680) without vote, 7 December (meeting 67); 18-nation draft (A/C.3/38/L.56); agenda item 12.
Sponsors: Belgium, Costa Rica, Cyprus, Denmark, Finland, France, Gambia, Greece, Iceland, Italy, Japan, Kenya, Morocco, Netherlands, Norway, Portugal, Sweden, Zambia.
Meeting numbers. GA 38th session: 3rd Committee 18, 54, 55, 57-67; plenary 100.

Disappearance of persons

Activities of the Working Group. The five-member Working Group on Enforced or Involuntary Disappearances, established in 1980,[65] held three sessions in 1983: the tenth from 13 to 17 June in New York, and the eleventh and twelfth from 26 to 30 September and from 5 to 9 December, at Geneva.[66]

The Working Group continued to review cases of disappearances submitted to it by relatives, by persons closely connected with the disappeared person, or by organizations acting on their behalf. Information was also submitted by individuals reporting having witnessed the arrest or abduction of missing persons, or stating that they had been detained with them, as well as by one person who claimed knowledge of disappearances from an official position previously held.

Selected for transmission to Governments were only those cases where factual material existed on which to base investigation. During the year, the Group transmitted reports on some 2,390 disappearances to 15 Governments, with requests for information. Some 555 of these had been received between sessions and were thus transmitted by the Chairman in accordance with established procedure. The reply received in a number of cases indicated that the person missing had been released or was being held in officially recognized detention. Such information was sent to the relatives concerned, with their attention drawn to the Commission's request for discretion in its use. Cases not transmitted either required further information from the reporting sources or fell outside the Group's mandate. The Group continued to press Governments for answers to outstanding cases transmitted earlier.

During its 1983 sessions, the Group met with representatives of Argentina, Bolivia, El Salvador, Nicaragua, the Philippines, Uruguay and Zaire, and with representatives of six organizations or associations directly concerned by reports of disappearances. In response to an invitation from the Latin American Federation of Associations for Relatives of Disappeared-Detainees, a Group member attended the Federation's Fourth Congress (Mexico City, 13-19 November), and reported on it at the December session.

Action by the Commission on Human Rights. Taking note of the Working Group's report on its 1982 activities,[67] the Commission on Human Rights, on 22 February 1983,[68] extended the Working Group's mandate for one year, retaining its membership for that period. It requested the Group to submit in 1984 a report on its work and to discharge its mandate with discretion, so as to protect persons providing information, or to limit dissemination of information from Governments. The Commission renewed its request to the Secretary-General to appeal for government co-operation and asked him to continue to provide the Group with necessary assistance. It reminded the Sub-Commission of its request to continue studying the most effective means for eliminating enforced or involuntary disappearances of persons, and asked for recommendations in 1984.

In a resolution of 7 March 1983 on persons detained by Israel, the Commission called on all parties to the conflict in Lebanon to secure for the International Committee of the Red Cross all available information concerning missing and disappeared persons in the wake of the June 1982 invasion of Lebanon. Disappearances of persons in Chile and Guatemala were also dealt with in two Commission resolutions of 8 March. (For details, see under HUMAN RIGHTS VIOLATIONS below). In another resolution, also of 8 March, on the human rights situation in Bolivia (see under ADVANCEMENT OF HUMAN RIGHTS below), the Commission welcomed the creation of a national commission to investigate cases of disappearances.

On 22 February,[69] by 41 votes to none, the Commission postponed until 1984 consideration of a draft resolution recommended by the Sub-Commission in September 1982,[70] requesting the General Assembly to invite the International Law Commission to take into account, when elaborating the draft code of offences against the peace and security of mankind (see LEGAL QUESTIONS, Chapter II), the Sub-Commission's comments on the question of missing and disappeared persons.

ECONOMIC AND SOCIAL COUNCIL ACTION

On the recommendation of its Second Committee, the Economic and Social Council adopted decision 1983/141 without vote.

Question of enforced or involuntary disappearances

At its 15th plenary meeting, on 27 May 1983, the Council, noting Commission on Human Rights resolution 1983/20 of 22 February 1983, approved the Commission's decision to extend for one year the term of the mandate of the Working Group on Enforced or Involuntary Disappearances, as laid down in Commission resolution 20(XXXVI) of 29 February 1980, and requested the Secretary-General to continue to provide the Working Group with all necessary assistance, in particular the staff and resources it required to perform its functions in an effective and expeditious manner, and, if necessary, to make the appropriate arrangements to ensure the continuity of the Secretariat's work.

Economic and Social Council decision 1983/141
Adopted without vote

Approved by Second Committee (E/1983/61) without vote, 23 May (meeting 18); draft by Commission on Human Rights (E/1983/13); agenda item 10.
Financial implications. S-G, E/1983/L.25.
Meeting number. ESC 15.

Sub-Commission action. On 5 September 1983,[71] the Sub-Commission requested its Working Group on Detention to prepare a first draft of a declaration against unacknowledged detention of persons, whatever their condition, for submission in 1984. The Secretary-General was asked to provide any available documentation for that purpose.

GENERAL ASSEMBLY ACTION

On the recommendation of the Third Committee, the General Assembly adopted resolution 38/94 without vote on 16 December 1983.

Question of enforced or involuntary disappearances
The General Assembly,

Recalling its resolution 33/173 of 20 December 1978, entitled "Disappeared persons", and its resolution 37/180 of 17 December 1982 on the question of enforced or involuntary disappearances,

Bearing in mind Commission on Human Rights resolution 1983/20 of 22 February 1983, in which the Commission decided to extend for one year the term of the mandate of the Working Group on Enforced or Involuntary Disappearances, and Economic and Social Council decision 1983/141 of 27 May 1983, in which the Council approved the Commission's decision,

Convinced that the action taken, in consultation with the Governments concerned, to promote the implementation of the provisions of General Assembly resolution 33/173 and other United Nations resolutions concerning the plight of missing or disappeared persons should be continued,

Expressing its emotion at the anguish and sorrow of the families concerned, who should know the fate of their relatives,

1. *Welcomes* the decision of the Commission on Human Rights to extend for one year the term of the mandate of the Working Group on Enforced or Involuntary Disappearances, as laid down in Commission resolution 1983/20;

2. *Expresses its appreciation* to the Working Group for the work it has done and to those Governments that have co-operated with it;

3. *Calls upon* the Commission on Human Rights to continue to study this question as a matter of priority and to take any step it may deem necessary to the pursuit of the task of the Working Group when it considers the report to be submitted by the Group at its fortieth session;

4. *Appeals* to all Governments to provide the Working Group and the Commission on Human Rights with the full co-operation warranted by their strictly humanitarian objectives and their working methods based on discretion;

5. *Renews its request* to the Secretary-General to continue to provide the Working Group with all necessary assistance.

General Assembly resolution 38/94

16 December 1983   Meeting 100   Adopted without vote

Approved by Third Committee (A/38/680) without vote, 7 December (meeting 67); 15-nation draft (A/C.3/38/L.48); agenda item 12.

Sponsors: Bolivia, Colombia, Costa Rica, Cyprus, France, Germany, Federal Republic of, Greece, Italy, Mexico, Morocco, Netherlands, Senegal, Spain, Sweden, United Kingdom.

Meeting numbers. GA 38th session: 3rd Committee 18, 54, 55, 57-67; plenary 100.

Other aspects of civil and political rights

Slavery

The Working Group on Slavery held its ninth session at Geneva from 8 to 12 August 1983. It considered information on slavery and the slave trade, a Sub-Commission mission to Mauritania, female circumcision, debt bondage, traffic in persons and the exploitation of the prostitution of others, exploitation of child labour and the sale of children, and *apartheid* and colonialism.

In July 1983,[72] the Secretary-General informed the Sub-Commission on the steps taken to implement the 1981 Sub-Commission resolution seeking authorization to send a mission to Mauritania to study allegations of slavery-like practices there.[73] The Secretary-General reported that, in response to several communications in 1982 and January/February 1983, Mauritania had indicated that it was prepared to receive the Sub-Commission's delegation in July. However, because of the time needed for preparations, the two delegates appointed in 1982[74]— Marc Bossuyt (Belgium) and Mohamed Yousif Mudawi (Sudan)—felt that the mission could take place after the 1983 Sub-Commission session. At their request, the Secretary-General, on 15 July, transmitted to Mauritania for comment a text with a list of questions dealing with matters on which information was needed.

Following examination of the Group's report on its August session,[75] the Sub-Commission, on 31 August,[76] recommended to the Commission on Human Rights a draft resolution for adoption by the Economic and Social Council, authorizing the Sub-Commission to appoint Halima Embarek Warzazi (Morocco) and Mr. Mudawi to carry out a study on all aspects of the problem of female sexual mutilation, including extent and causes and suggestions on how it might be remedied, with a preliminary report to the Sub-Commission in 1984 and a final one in 1985.

Based on the Group's recommendations, the Sub-Commission on 5 September 1983[77] recommended to the Commission adoption of another draft resolution by which the Commission would: recognize *apartheid* as a slavery-like practice and endorse the call for mandatory economic sanctions against South Africa; appeal to States to become parties to the relevant Conventions or to explain in writing why they felt unable to do so; and request the Secretary-General to call on States parties to the 1926 Slavery Convention, the 1956 Supplementary Convention on the Abolition of Slavery, the Slave Trade and Institutions and Practices Similar to Slavery,[78] and the 1949 Convention for the Suppression of the Traffic in Persons and of the Exploitation of the Prostitution of Others[79] to submit regular reports on the situation in their countries, and to call on other States, United Nations bodies, intergovernmental and non-governmental organizations, and the International Criminal Police Organization (Interpol) to supply relevant information to the Group.

The Commission would also request the Secretary-General to transmit to Governments for comment the statements submitted to the Group in 1981[80] by the Anti-Slavery Society for the Protection of Human Rights, the Minority Rights Group and the International Abolitionist Federation containing allegations on slavery-like practices, and to submit in 1984 a report on how work of the United Nations Development Programme (UNDP) in certain countries could be adapted so as to contribute to the struggle against slavery; request the United Nations system to offer coordinated legal, technical, administrative, educational, financial and other practical assistance to help eliminate conditions conducive to slavery and slavery-like situations; invite ILO, FAO and UNESCO to include in their technical assistance programmes activities designed to eliminate slavery-type problems; invite the Sub-Commission to involve more closely in the Group's work the persons whose names appeared in the list of slavery experts; and ask the Secretary-General to submit to each Group session a résumé of information collected between sessions.

On 6 September, by 17 votes to 4, with 1 abstention,[81] the Sub-Commission deferred until 1984 consideration of a draft resolution recommending that the Council authorize appointment of a Special Rapporteur to carry out a study of gross exploitation of labour leading to slavery-like practices.

Complying with a 1981 Commission request, the *Ad Hoc* Working Group of Experts on Southern Africa examined two 1980 reports[82]—one on *apartheid* as a collective form of slavery by the Secretary-General and another on child labour in South Africa by the Anti-Slavery Society for the Protection of Human Rights—with a view to proposing such measures as it deemed appropriate.

In a report on its findings,[83] submitted to the 1983 Commission session, the Group summarized the main elements of the *apartheid* system, understood as a slavery-like system of labour control and exploitation, as it developed after 1948 and as it currently applied.

Those elements, as identified by the Secretary-General, included: strict controls through a system of identity documents enforced on Africans by penal sanctions introduced in 1952, to control their influx into areas designated for whites and deny them residence there; forcible removal of vast numbers of blacks not qualified to remain in white areas, because they were unemployed or considered redundant, to "reserves" and "group areas" where they faced starvation; progressive enforcement of a migratory labour system on the entire black population to limit their entry into white areas to certain periods and only to sectors requiring their services; enforcement of the colour bar in a way to permit adjustments when needed by the economy, without changing the conditions of exploitation of black workers; physical repression and abusive working conditions of black agricultural workers, including exploitation of child labour; and a discriminatory system of labour relations aimed at undermining autonomous African workers' organizations and facilitating government control over workers' movements.

Child labour was found to be widespread throughout South Africa but in a scale and manner that remained largely hidden. The majority of child labourers, generally offspring of farm workers, were in agriculture. Dating back to the days of slavery, child labour in agriculture was an integral feature of the *apartheid* system. In its recommendations, the Anti-Slavery Society stated that the Government of South Africa should be urged to appoint a commission to examine legislation to protect children and to stop the pernicious system of child labour.

The Group concluded that, owing to its exploitative character and country-wide application, the policy of *apartheid* might be described as a collective form of slavery.

The Group's recommendations called for the abolition of all transit and resettlement camps, and immediate discontinuance of the policy of trans-

ferring African workers involving prolonged separation from their families, as well as of removing populations and splitting up regions in Namibia. The Group reiterated that the Commission should propose revisions to the 1948 Convention on the Prevention and Punishment of the Crime of Genocide,[84] in particular to make inhuman acts resulting from the policies of *apartheid* punishable. Forcible removal of the African population from the Caprivi Strip (a stretch of land in north-east Namibia between Angola and Zambia to the north and Botswana to the south) being an element of genocide, a full investigation of it should be undertaken, as should another to determine whether elements of genocide currently existed in Namibia. The Group should be entrusted by the Commission with the task of looking into elements of genocide arising out of the policy of *apartheid*.

In addition, the Group supported the Sub-Commission's 1980 recommendation[85] calling on Governments, particularly South Africa's, to ratify the 1973 ILO Convention on Minimum Age for Admission to Employment, to implement the relevant Recommendation (No. 146) and to ensure enactment of legislation to protect the rights of working children.

Action by the Commission on Human Rights. On 4 March 1983,[86] the Commission on Human Rights recommended that the Economic and Social Council authorize the printing and widest possible distribution of the 1982 report on slavery.[87]

ECONOMIC AND SOCIAL COUNCIL ACTION

On the recommendation of its Second Committee, the Economic and Social Council adopted decision 1983/143 by vote.

Updating of the *Report on Slavery*
At its 15th plenary meeting, on 27 May 1983, the Council, noting Commission on Human Rights resolution 1983/25 of 4 March 1983, decided that the report prepared by Mr. Benjamin Whitaker, Special Rapporteur of the Sub-Commission on Prevention of Discrimination and Protection of Minorities, entitled "Updating of the *Report on Slavery* submitted to the Sub-Commission in 1966" should be printed and given the widest possible distribution, including distribution in Arabic.

Economic and Social Council decision 1983/143

50-1

Approved by Second Committee (E/1983/61) by vote (45-1), 23 May (meeting 18); draft by Commission on Human Rights (E/1983/13); agenda item 10. *Meeting number.* ESC 15.

Conscientious objectors
Action by the Commission on Human Rights. On 9 March 1983,[88] the Commission on Human Rights emphasized young people's role in their countries' political, economic and social de-

velopment, and especially in the struggle against obstacles to such development—colonialism and neo-colonialism, racial discrimination, *apartheid*, foreign domination and occupation, aggression and threats to national sovereignty and territorial integrity, and denial of human rights and fundamental freedoms and of the rights to self-determination and to full sovereignty over their natural resources.

The Commission called on States, intergovernmental and non-governmental organizations, and United Nations bodies to devote attention to the exercise by young people of human rights, particularly the rights to education and vocational training and to work. It called on States to take legislative, administrative and other action providing for such exercise so as to create conditions for the active participation of young people in formulating and implementing their national economic and social development programmes. The Commission confirmed that it would examine in 1985 the question of youth's exercise of all their rights.

Report of Special Rapporteurs. As requested by the Sub-Commission on Prevention of Discrimination and Protection of Minorities in September 1982,[89] Special Rapporteurs Asbjorn Eide (Norway) and Chama L. C. Mubanga-Chipoya (Zambia) submitted to it in 1983 their final report on the question of conscientious objection to military service.[90] Based on material from governmental, intergovernmental and non-governmental sources, the report analysed the concept of conscientious objection and international standards relating to it, and examined the actual situation with respect to conscientious objection under national laws and practices.

The Special Rapporteurs concluded that State practice varied widely as to the extent to which military service was voluntary or compulsory. Of 152 States and territories surveyed, 66 had no conscription (compulsory military service), 5 had conscription in law but did not enforce it, and 15 had enforced conscription but formally recognized conscientious objection on certain grounds. States in these three categories provided freedom in varying degrees for the individual to decide whether or not to join the armed forces. Grounds for considering an objection valid ranged from "religious" to "moral" to "political". Another 12 States enforcing conscription did not recognize the right of objectors to be exempted, but allowed them noncombatant roles in certain circumstances.

Where conscientious objection was recognized, provision was normally made for alternative service, which related to social development or to promotion of international peace in some countries. In others, it seemed to be considered more as a punishment, consisting of hard work without meaningful content.

The Special Rapporteurs requested the Sub-Commission to consider making several recommendations to the Commission on Human Rights, among them: recognition by law of the right to conscientious objection; setting up of independent decision-making bodies to determine the validity of the objection, with the right to appeal; provision of alternative service for the objector; imposition of penalties by a civilian court if the objector persisted in objection found to be invalid; international standards to ensure favourable attitude towards conscientious objectors requesting asylum; and provisions to prohibit recruitment of children and minors to military service.

Sub-Commission action. On 5 September 1983, the Sub-Commission, by 14 votes to none, with 5 abstentions,[91] transmitted the Special Rapporteurs' report to the Commission, with a request that it study the report's recommendations and in turn make appropriate recommendations to the Economic and Social Council, to include the printing and widest possible distribution of the report.

On 7 September,[92] the Sub-Commission requested the Special Rapporteurs to present their report to the Commission in 1984.

Freedom of movement

On 31 August 1983, by a resolution adopted by 18 votes to 2,[93] the Sub-Commission recommended adoption of a draft resolution by the Commission on Human Rights. That draft would have the Economic and Social Council endorse the Sub-Commission's appointment of Chama L. C. Mubanga-Chipoya (Zambia) to prepare an analysis of trends and developments in respect of the right of everyone to leave any country, including one's own, to return to one's country, and to have the possibility to enter other countries without discrimination or hindrance, especially with regard to the right to employment, taking account of the need to avoid brain drain from developing countries; and to study the extent of restrictions permissible under article 12, paragraph 3, of the International Covenant on Civil and Political Rights.[1]

Independence of the judicial system

On 18 August 1983,[94] the Sub-Commission deferred until 1984 consideration of the question of the independence and impartiality of the judiciary, jurors and assessors, and the independence of lawyers, when Special Rapporteur L. M. Singhvi (India) would submit his final report on the topic.

On 6 September,[95] following consideration of the Special Rapporteur's June progress report,[96] the Sub-Commission broadly approved the tentative synopsis of the study annexed to the report.

It asked the Secretary-General to so inform the Special Rapporteur and to convey the Sub-Commission's gratitude for his thorough work.

In a resolution of the same date, on technical assistance to States for strengthening their legal institutions (see under ADVANCEMENT OF HUMAN RIGHTS below), the Sub-Commission requested the Special Rapporteur to consider in his study the most appropriate means by which the international community could contribute to strengthening legal institutions, especially in developing countries, with a view to promoting full respect for human rights.

REFERENCES

[1]YUN 1966, p. 423, GA res. 2200 A (XXI), annex, 16 Dec. 1966. [2]YUN 1976, p. 609. [3]A/38/392. [4]E/1983/13 (res. 1983/17). [5]YUN 1982, p. 1102, GA res. 37/191, 18 Dec. 1982. [6]A/38/40. [7]E/CN.4/1984/3 (res. 1983/30). [8]E/1983/13 (res. 1983/3). [9]*Ibid.* (res. 1983/4). [10]*Ibid.* (res. 1983/5). [11]*Ibid.* (res. 1983/6). [12]*Ibid.* (res. 1983/7). [13]*Ibid.* (res. 1983/8). [14]E/CN.4/1984/3 (res. 1983/8). [15]A/38//447 & Add.1,2. [16]YUN 1982, pp. 1071 & 1072, GA res. 37/42 & 37/43, 3 Dec. 1982. [17]A/38/318. [18]A/C.3/38/6. [19]E/CN.4/1984/3 (res. 1983/20). [20]*Ibid.* (res. 1983/26). [21]YUN 1982, p. 1349, GA res. 37/30, 23 Nov. 1982. [22]E/CN.4/1983/42. [23]E/CN.4/1983/48. [24]YUN 1981, p. 242. [25]E/CN.4/Sub.2/1983/8. [26]E/CN.4/1983/2 & Add.1. [27]E/CN.4/1983/13. [28]YUN 1948-49, p. 535, GA res. 217 A (III), 10 Dec. 1948. [29]YUN 1960, p. 49, GA res. 1514(XV), 14 Dec. 1960. [30]E/1983/13 (res. 1983/11). [31]*Ibid.* (res. 1983/10). [32]YUN 1978, p. 915, SC res. 435(1978), 29 Sep. 1978; p. 916, SC res. 439(1978), 13 Nov. 1978. [33]E/CN.4/Sub.2/1983/11 & Add.1. [34]YUN 1982, p. 1077. [35]E/CN.4/Sub.2/1983/13. [36]E/CN.4/Sub.2/1983/12. [37]YUN 1982, p. 1139. [38]E/CN.4/Sub.2/1983/14. [39]E/CN.4/1984/3 (res. 1983/30). [40]*Ibid.* (res. 1983/34). [41]E/1983/13 (res. 1983/18). [42]E/CN.4/Sub.2/1983/15. [43]YUN 1978, p. 698. [44]YUN 1980, p. 842. [45]YUN 1981, p. 900. [46]YUN 1982, p. 1080. [47]*Ibid.*, GA dec. 37/427, 16 Dec. 1982. [48]A/C.6/38/L.8. [49]A/38/388 & Add.1-3. [50]E/1983/13 (dec. 1983/104). [51]YUN 1982, p. 1082. [52]E/CN.4/1983/63. [53]E/1983/13 (res. 1983/48). [54]*Ibid.* (res. 1983/19). [55]YUN 1981, p. 906, GA res. 36/151, 16 Dec. 1981. [56]A/38/221. [57]E/1983/13 (res. 1983/44). [58]YUN 1982, p. 1083. [59]E/CN.4/Sub.2/1983/17. [60]E/CN.4/Sub.2/1983/19. [61]E/CN.4/1984/3 (res. 1983/39). [62]YUN 1982, p. 1079, ESC res. 1982/35, 7 May 1982. [63]E/1983/13 (res. 1983/36). [64]E/CN.4/1983/16 & Add.1 & Add.1/Corr.1. [65]YUN 1980, p. 843. [66]E/CN.4/1984/21. [67]YUN 1982, p. 1084. [68]E/1983/13 (res. 1983/20). [69]*Ibid.* (dec. 1983/112). [70]YUN 1982, p. 1085. [71]E/CN.4/1984/3 (res. 1983/23). [72]E/CN.4/Sub.2/1983/26/Rev.1. [73]YUN 1981, p. 914. [74]YUN 1982, p. 1086. [75]E/CN.4/Sub.2/1983/27. [76]E/CN.4/1984/3 (res. 1983/1). [77]*Ibid.* (res. 1983/13). [78]YUN 1956, p. 228. [79]YUN 1948-49, p. 613, GA res. 317(IV), annex, 2 Dec. 1949. [80]YUN 1981, p. 913. [81]E/CN.4/1984/3 (dec. 1983/5). [82]YUN 1980, p. 868. [83]E/CN.4/1983/37. [84]YUN 1948-49, p. 959, GA res. 260 A (III), annex, 9 Dec. 1948. [85]YUN 1980, p. 869. [86]E/1983/13 (res. 1983/25). [87]*Slavery: Report prepared by Benjamin Whitaker, Special Rapporteur of the Sub-Commission on Prevention of Discrimination and Protection of Minorities, updating the Report on Slavery submitted to the Sub-Commission in 1966* (E/CN.4/Sub.2/1982/20/Rev.1), Sales No. E.84.XIV.1; YUN 1982, p. 1087. [88]E/1983/13 (res. 1983/46). [89]YUN 1982, p. 1088. [90]*Conscientious Objection to Military Service* (E/CN.4/Sub.2/1983/30/Rev.1 & Rev.1/Corr.1), Sales No. E.85.XIV.1 & corrigendum. [91]E/CN.4/1984/3 (res. 1983/22). [92]*Ibid.* (dec. 1983/10). [93]*Ibid.* (res. 1983/5). [94]*Ibid.* (dec. 1983/1). [95]*Ibid.* (dec. 1983/6). [96]E/CN.4/Sub.2/1983/16.

Economic, social and cultural rights

Covenant on Economic, Social and Cultural Rights

Accessions and ratifications

As at 31 December 1983, the International Covenant on Economic, Social and Cultural Rights, adopted by the General Assembly in 1966[1] and in force since 1976,[2] had been ratified or acceded to by 80 States. Afghanistan, Belgium, the Congo, Gabon and Luxembourg became parties to it during 1983.

The Secretary-General reported on the status of ratifications or accessions to the Covenant—as at 1 March, in a note to the Economic and Social Council;[3] and as at 1 September, in a report to the General Assembly.[4]

Implementation of the Covenant

The Commission on Human Rights, in a February 1983 resolution on the status of the International Covenants on Human Rights (see below, under ADVANCEMENT OF HUMAN RIGHTS), took note of the May 1982 Economic and Social Council resolution on the review of the composition, organization and administrative arrangements of the Sessional Working Group of Governmental Experts on the Implementation of the International Covenant on Economic, Social and Cultural Rights.[5] The Commission requested the Secretary-General to include, in his 1984 report on the status of the Covenants, information on the work of the Council and its Group of Experts.

In 1983, the Group met in New York from 18 April to 5 May.[6] Established by the Council in 1978[7] and restructured in May 1982,[5] the Group was composed of members elected by the Council in 1982 and 1983 from among the States parties to the Covenant (see APPENDIX III).

Based on the Group's recommendations and suggestions, the Council adopted resolution 1983/41 on the Covenant, its implementation and the reports required from States parties (see below).

ECONOMIC AND SOCIAL COUNCIL ACTION

Acting on the recommendation of the Group of Experts, the Economic and Social Council adopted decision 1983/133 without vote.

Provisional agenda for 1984 of the Sessional Working Group of Governmental Experts on the Implementation of the International Covenant on Economic, Social and Cultural Rights

At its 15th plenary meeting, on 27 May 1983, the Council approved the provisional agenda for 1984 of the Sessional Working Group of Governmental Experts on the Implementation of the International Covenant on Economic, Social and Cultural Rights set out below.

Provisional agenda for 1984 of the Sessional Working Group of Governmental Experts on the Implementation of the International Covenant on Economic, Social and Cultural Rights

1. Consideration of reports submitted in accordance with Council resolution 1988(LX) by States parties to the Covenant concerning rights covered by articles 6 to 9

   Documentation

   Initial report

   Second periodic report
2. Consideration of reports submitted in accordance with Council resolution 1988(LX) by States parties to the Covenant concerning rights covered by articles 10 to 12

   Documentation

   Italy (E/1980/6/Add.31)

   Canada (E/1980/6/Add.32)

   Any other reports received by the Secretary-General
3. Consideration of reports submitted in accordance with Council resolution 1988(LX) by States parties to the Covenant concerning rights covered by articles 13 to 15

   Documentation

   Guyana (E/1982/3/Add.5)
4. Formulation of suggestions and recommendations of a general nature based on the consideration of reports submitted by States parties to the Covenant and by the specialized agencies, in order to assist the Council to fulfil, in particular, its responsibilities under articles 21 and 22 of the Covenant
5. Consideration of the report of the Sessional Working Group of Governmental Experts on the Implementation of the International Covenant on Economic, Social and Cultural Rights.

Economic and Social Council decision 1983/133
Adopted without vote

Approved by Group of Experts on Covenant on Economic, Social and Cultural Rights (E/1983/41) without vote, 5 May (meeting 24); agenda item 4.
Meeting numbers. ESC 14, 15.

Also on the recommendation of the Group of Experts, the Council adopted decision 1983/134 without vote.

Bureau for 1984 of the Sessional Working Group of Governmental Experts on the Implementation of the International Covenant on Economic, Social and Cultural Rights

At its 15th plenary meeting, on 27 May 1983, the Council decided that the bureau for 1984 of the Sessional Working Group of Governmental Experts on the Implementation of the International Covenant on Economic, Social and Cultural Rights should be constituted as follows:

Chairman: Western European and other States;

Vice-Chairmen: African States; Asian States; Eastern European States;

Rapporteur: Latin American States.

Economic and Social Council decision 1983/134
Adopted without vote

Approved by Group of Experts on Covenant on Economic, Social and Cultural Rights (E/1983/41) without vote, 5 May (meeting 24); agenda item 4.
Meeting numbers. ESC 14, 15.

GENERAL ASSEMBLY ACTION

In resolution 38/124 of 16 December 1983, on alternative approaches within the United Nations system for improving the enjoyment of human rights, the Assembly affirmed that all human rights were indivisible and interrelated and that the promotion and protection of one category should not exempt States from promoting or protecting others. It also affirmed its conviction that equal attention and urgent consideration be given to implementing, protecting and promoting both civil and political and economic, social and cultural rights.

Reports under the Covenant

In 1983, the Group of Experts considered reports from 13 States parties on their implementation of specific provisions of the Covenant. On each report, the Group heard statements by, and put questions to, the respective State representative. Under a programme established by the Council in 1976,[8] reports required under the Covenant were to be submitted in three biennial cycles or stages, each stage covering a related group of articles.

The Group considered a report from the Syrian Arab Republic covering articles 6 to 9 of the Covenant (concerning the right to work and to favourable conditions of work, the rights of trade unionists and the right to social security), and a report from Yugoslavia on rights covered by articles 10 to 12 (protection of the family, mothers and children, an adequate living standard, and physical and mental health). It also dealt with reports from: Barbados, Bulgaria, Cyprus, Czechoslovakia, Denmark, German Democratic Republic, Guyana, Libyan Arab Jamahiriya, Poland, Senegal, Spain on rights covered by articles 13 to 15 (education, including compulsory education, and participation in cultural life).

Following consideration of the reports, the Group agreed to bring certain issues to the attention of the Council; based on the Group's suggestions and recommendations, the Council adopted resolution 1983/41 (see below).

In a March note on the status of ratifications and accessions to the Covenant,[3] the Secretary-General listed the reports received from States on rights covered by the three groups of articles. In April, he submitted to the Council the sixth report of ILO on the situation in certain countries with regard to articles 6 to 9.[9]

ECONOMIC AND SOCIAL COUNCIL ACTION

On 27 May 1983, the Economic and Social Council adopted resolution 1983/41 without vote.

Implementation of the International Covenant on Economic, Social and Cultural Rights

The Economic and Social Council,

Bearing in mind its important responsibilities under articles 16 and 17 of the International Covenant on Economic, Social and Cultural Rights,

Recalling its resolutions 1988(LX) of 11 May 1976, 1979/43 of 11 May 1979 and 1982/33 of 6 May 1982 and its decision 1981/158 of 8 May 1981,

Recalling also General Assembly resolution 37/191 of 18 December 1982,

Having considered the report of the Sessional Working Group of Governmental Experts on the Implementation of the International Covenant on Economic, Social and Cultural Rights,

Noting that, as a result of continuing improvements in the work of the Sessional Working Group of Governmental Experts on the Implementation of the International Covenant on Economic, Social and Cultural Rights, consideration of the reports of the States parties is becoming more thorough,

Mindful of the relevant resolutions and decisions adopted by the General Assembly and the Economic and Social Council on the control and limitation of documentation,

1. *Takes note* of the report of the Sessional Working Group of Governmental Experts on the Implementation of the International Covenant on Economic, Social and Cultural Rights;

2. *Invites* States that have thus far neither ratified nor acceded to the International Convenant on Economic, Social and Cultural Rights to do so, pursuant to General Assembly resolution 37/191;

3. *Calls upon* States parties to the International Covenant on Economic, Social and Cultural Rights to submit reports required under article 16 thereof, in accordance with the programme established by Council resolution 1988(LX), and urges States parties that have not yet done so to submit their initial reports as soon as possible and, in those instances in which it is not possible to do so, to inform the Sessional Working Group of Governmental Experts on the Implementation of the International Covenant on Economic, Social and Cultural Rights when those reports will be submitted;

4. *Invites* States parties to the Covenant, in preparing their reports, to comply with the guidelines established by the Secretary-General concerning the form and content of reports;

5. *Urges* States parties to the Covenant which are submitting reports for consideration by the Sessional Working Group of Governmental Experts on the Implementation of the International Covenant on Economic, Social and Cultural Rights, taking into account paragraph 24 *(g)* of its report, to be mindful of the importance of submitting their reports twelve weeks before the session of the Group of Experts in order to permit processing by the Secretariat and adequate study by the members of the Group of Experts;

6. *Requests* the Sessional Working Group of Governmental Experts on the Implementation of the International Covenant on Economic, Social and Cultural Rights to consider including in its report to the Council brief summaries of the consideration of each country report;

7. *Requests* the Secretary-General to ensure that the summary records of the proceedings of the Sessional Working Group of Governmental Experts on the Implementation of the International Covenant on Economic, Social and Cultural Rights are made available to the Council at the time the report of the Group of Experts is considered by the Council;

8. *Requests* the Secretary-General to ensure that the United Nations press service issues press releases on the proceedings of the Sessional Working Group of Governmental Experts on the Implementation of the International Covenant on Economic, Social and Cultural Rights.

Economic and Social Council resolution 1983/41

27 May 1983   Meeting 15   Adopted without vote

8-nation draft (E/1983/L.28/Rev.1), orally revised; agenda item 4.
Sponsors: Denmark, France, Germany, Federal Republic of, Italy, Japan, Jordan, Kenya, Netherlands.
Financial implications. S-G, E/1983/L.30.
Meeting numbers. ESC 14, 15.

GENERAL ASSEMBLY ACTION

In a September 1983 report to the General Assembly on the reporting obligations of States parties under human rights instruments,[10] the Secretary-General noted that 94 reports under the Covenant were overdue at the end of 1982. He suggested that parties requiring assistance in reporting, as well as in implementing the Covenant, might wish to request the expertise of the relevant specialized agencies through the Economic and Social Council, which was authorized under articles 22 and 23 of the Covenant to initiate the granting of such assistance.

Taking note of the Secretary-General's report, the Assembly, in resolution 38/117 on the reporting obligations of the States parties to the International Covenants on Human Rights (see below, under ADVANCEMENT OF HUMAN RIGHTS), requested him to transmit that report to the Council, and asked the Council and its Group of Experts to consider his suggestions with a view to improving the situation.

The right to development and the new international economic order

In 1983, the Commission on Human Rights reconvened the Working Group of Governmental Experts on the Right to Development to elaborate a draft declaration on the topic. The Economic and Social Council, on 27 May, endorsed the Commission's decision to reconvene the Group as well as its request that the Group hold two meetings during the year. On 16 December, the General Assembly reaffirmed the right to development as an inalienable human right.

Action by the Commission on Human Rights. By a resolution adopted on 22 February by a roll-call vote of 40 to none, with 3 abstentions,[11] the Commission on Human Rights expressed concern at the current situation affecting the establishment of a new international economic order (NIEO) and the achievement of human rights, in particular the right to development. It reaffirmed that all nations had the inalienable right to pursue freely their economic and social development and to exercise full and complete sovereignty over all their natural resources; and that foreign occupation, colonialism, *apartheid*, racism and racial discrimination and the denial of the right to self-determination of peoples (see above, under CIVIL AND POLTICIAL RIGHTS) and of universally recognized human rights were serious impediments to economic and social progress.

Noting with satisfaction the recommendations of the Working Group (in its report on sessions held in June/July and November/December 1982),[12] the Commission decided to reconvene the Group with the same mandate to allow it to elaborate a draft declaration on the right to development. It requested the Group to hold two meetings of two weeks each at Geneva, in June and November/December 1983, and to submit proposals for the Commission's consideration in 1984.

By a resolution of the same date, adopted by 42 votes to 1,[13] the Commission took note of the report on the International Seminar on Popular Participation, held in Yugoslavia in May 1982.[14] At the same time, the Commission recommended to the Economic and Social Council adoption of a draft resolution requesting the Secretary-General to undertake a comprehensive analytical study on the right to popular participation in its various forms as an important factor in the full realization of all human rights, and to submit a preliminary study to the Commission in 1984 and a final study in 1985 (see also Chapter XIII of this section). Subsequently, by resolution 1983/31 of 27 May 1983, the Council adopted that recommendation. The Assembly, in resolution 38/24 of 22 November, requested the Secretary-General to report on progress in the field and requested the Commission to continue considering the question.

In a resolution of 9 March on human rights and scientific and technological developments, the Commission called for efforts by all States to use scientific and technological achievements for peaceful economic, social and cultural development and to improve the well-being of peoples, and requested the Sub-Commission to study the use of those achievements to ensure the right to work and development (see below, under OTHER HUMAN RIGHTS QUESTIONS).

ECONOMIC AND SOCIAL ACTION

The Economic and Social Council, on the recommendation of its Second Committee, adopted decision 1983/139.

Question of the realization in all countries of the economic, social and cultural rights contained in the Universal Declaration of Human Rights and in the International Covenant on Economic, Social and Cultural Rights, and study of special problems which the developing countries face in their efforts to achieve these human rights

At its 15th plenary meeting, on 27 May 1983, the Council, noting Commission on Human Rights resolution 1983/15 of 22 February 1983, endorsed the Commission's decision to reconvene the Working Group of Governmental Experts on the Right to Development with its original mandate in order to allow it to elaborate, on the basis of its report and all the documents already submitted or to be submitted, a draft declaration on the right to development. The Council also endorsed the Commission's request to the Working Group to hold two meetings of two weeks each at Geneva, the first in June 1983 and the second in November/December 1983, and requested the Secretary-General to provide all necessary assistance to the Working Group.

Economic and Social Council decision 1983/139
Adopted without vote

Approved by Second Committee (E/1983/61) without vote, 23 May (meeting 18); draft by Commission on Human Rights (E/1983/13); agenda item 10.
Meeting number. ESC 15.

Working Group activities. In 1983, the Working Group of Governmental Experts on the Right to Development held two sessions at Geneva: its sixth from 13 to 24 June and its seventh from 31 October to 11 November.[15] At the sixth session, several drafts and proposals were circulated, on the basis of which the Group requested two experts to prepare a "technical consolidated text", to serve as an informal basis for further work. Following discussions at its seventh session, the Group reached a general understanding on several preambular provisions of the draft declaration.

Reports to the Sub-Commission. In August 1983, Special Rapporteur Raúl Ferrero (Peru) submitted to the Sub-Commission on Prevention of Discrimination and Protection of Minorities a final report on the NIEO and the promotion of human rights,[16] authorized by the Economic and Social Council in 1980.[17] The Special Rapporteur reviewed the background to the current international economic order and its major characteristics; discussed the non-aligned movement and NIEO; the high indebtedness of developing countries; and the link between human rights, economic issues and the national and international orders. He analysed the guiding principles for eliminating disparities in the current economic system; international legislative bases for the establishment of NIEO; NIEO and the right to development; NIEO from the standpoint of human rights based on United Nations instruments; integration of human rights into development strategies; and the North-South dialogue.

The Special Rapporteur considered that the current economic order impeded realization of human rights and fundamental freedoms. The existing system magnified the gap between developing and developed countries, and, burdened by indebtedness, developing countries were making considerable cuts in their development programmes, and unemployment and underemployment were increasing uncontrollably. All this gave rise to a bad social atmosphere affecting the poorest classes and helped generate a dangerous climate of political insecurity.

The Special Rapporteur noted that after the "first generation" of human rights, which included civil and political rights, came economic, social and cultural rights; only in recent times had the right to solidarity—which included the rights to development, quality of the environment, peace and the common heritage of mankind—been recognized. This "third generation" of rights, he stated, had scarcely taken shape and to implement them would take a major effort. NIEO must take into consideration two sets of principles: the sovereignty, territorial integrity and political independence of all States, the sovereign equality of every State, the principles of non-aggression, non-intervention and peaceful coexistence, equal rights and self-determination of peoples, and the peaceful settlement of disputes; and the right of developing countries and of the peoples of territories under colonial and racial domination or foreign occupation to achieve their liberation and regain control over their natural resources and economic activities.

The Special Rapporteur held economic aggression—including the use of threats, commercial sanctions or any other form of blockade, measures of coercion or blackmail, and political pressure aimed at influencing sovereign decisions—by some developed States against developing countries unacceptable. In his view, the concept of "development" should not be interpreted solely in terms of economic and material well-being but in much broader terms covering the physical, moral, intellectual and cultural growth of human beings. If NIEO was to produce a substantial improvement in the extent to which impoverished and oppressed peoples enjoyed human rights, it was important for such a goal to be fully incorporated in national and international development strategies. Disarmament was crucial to the realization of the right to development and to the achievement of NIEO.

In his recommendations, the Special Rapporteur stressed the role that could be played by international organizations in correcting the unjust international relations, and called for a new multilaterism founded on co-ordinated policies in which all countries participated. It was imperative that the global negotiations on international economic co-operation for development be approached with a renewed sense of commitment; the deferral of such efforts could have only an adverse impact on the full realization of human rights, particularly in developing countries.

Noting the importance of regional endeavours to promote economic co-operation, in particular among developing countries, the Special Rapporteur suggested the appointment, possibly within the United Nations regional commissions, of regional advisers on human rights as a means of ensuring that human rights concerns were reflected in regional economic decision-making. Concluding, he emphasized that the basic challenge—to ensure that the establishment of NIEO and the promotion of human rights went hand in hand—could not be resolved simply by focusing on one particular issue such as development assistance, commodity prices or the role of transnational corporations, but required honouring the dignity of the individual and of human solidarity as the guiding principles.

Also in August, the Secretary-General submitted to the Sub-Commission at its September 1982 request,[18] a report on technical assistance available to States in strengthening their legal institutions, including educational facilities,[19] in order to enhance respect for the rule of law in the development process. Summarizing information from three Governments—Bolivia, Equatorial Guinea and Uganda—which had requested advisory services, as well as from nine United Nations bodies and agencies, the report dealt with the United Nations programme of advisory services in the field of human rights (see below, under ADVANCEMENT OF HUMAN RIGHTS) and similar activities, including seminars, fellowships and training.

Sub-Commission action. On 6 September 1983,[20] the Sub-Commission decided to transmit the Special Rapporteur's study to the Commission on Human Rights in 1984, and recommended that the Commission recommend to the Economic and Social Council that it arrange for publication and widest distribution of the study in all official United Nations languages. The Sub-Commission considered it advisable to study in the near future the impact on human rights of the policies and practices of the major international financial institutions, such as the International Monetary Fund and the World Bank, and decided to consider in 1984 the appointment of a Special Rapporteur to undertake such a study.

On 7 September,[21] the Sub-Commission requested the Special Rapporteur to present his report to the Commission in 1984.

Also under the agenda item on NIEO and the promotion of human rights, the Sub-Commission, on 6 September,[22] requested the Secretary-General to prepare and submit in 1984 a report on Governments' expressed need for technical assistance in strengthening their legal institutions with a view to promoting respect for human rights. In that connection, the Sub-Commission called on the Secretary-General to request Governments providing bilateral development assistance to give information on the extent to which such assistance was or could be used in strengthening legal institutions in recipient countries, and to include in his report information on the results achieved in response to requests by the Commission that technical assistance be made available to certain States to assist them in ensuring full respect for human rights. Special Rapporteur L. M. Singhvi (India) was requested to give consideration, in his study on the independence and impartiality of the judiciary, jurors and assessors and the independence of lawyers, to the most appropriate means by which the international community could contribute to strengthening legal institutions, especially in developing countries, with a view to promoting full respect for human rights.

GENERAL ASSEMBLY ACTION

In resolution 38/124 of 16 December 1983, on alternative approaches and ways within the United Nations system for improving the enjoyment of human rights, the General Assembly, by a separately adopted paragraph, reaffirmed that the right to development was an inalienable human right. It requested the Commission on Human Rights to promote the right to development, taking into account the results achieved by the Working Group, and welcomed the Commission's decision that the Working Group should continue its work with the aim of submitting as soon as possible a draft declaration on the topic.

In resolution 38/112 of the same date, on human rights and scientific and technological developments, the Assembly called on all States to use the achievements of science and technology for promoting peaceful social, economic and cultural development and progress.

In resolution 38/24 of 22 November, the Assembly requested the Commission to continue to consider the question of popular participation as an important factor in the full realization of all human rights.

Right to education and employment

In 1983, the General Assembly and the Economic and Social Council dealt with the right to education and employment, particularly in the context of the rights of youth. The right to education was also dealt with by the Secretary-General in two reports, one to the Commission on Human Rights, on implementation of the programme of measures and activities in connection with International Youth Year (1985) (see below, under

OTHER HUMAN RIGHTS QUESTIONS), the other to the Sub-Commission, concerning technical assistance to States in strengthening their legal institutions, including educational facilities (see above).

In his February report to the Commission,[23] the Secretary-General stated that, in establishing national priorities relating to youth, many States had identified unemployment, education and training, among other things, as important problems, and that several countries had enacted national legislation to bring about the enjoyment by youth of human rights, particularly the right to education and to work. Among United Nations bodies and agencies, ILO provided advisory services, collected and disseminated information on national measures, and organized regional or subregional meetings on priority areas of employment policies concerning youth; it had also intensified vocational training for youth, and encouraged increased youth participation in the decision-making process through trade unions. The implementation of several international labour conventions on special youth schemes was to be a major ILO activity for International Youth Year (1985).

The integration of rural youth in the development process was of great concern to FAO, which had sponsored a large number of rural youth programmes in Latin America, Africa and the Near East.

In his report to the Sub-Commission,[19] the Secretary-General described technical assistance and co-operation activities provided by UNESCO in the field of education, as well as those of ILO in strengthening workers' organizations and assisting rural workers' organizations in identifying their educational and other problems.

ECONOMIC AND SOCIAL COUNCIL ACTION

In resolution 1983/17 of 26 May, the Economic and Social Council noted with concern that the growth of unemployment made it increasingly difficult to implement the basic social and economic rights of youth, especially the rights to life, employment and education. The Council strongly urged for measures to ensure implementation of those rights and for provision in national development plans and budgets of specific programmes and resources for that purpose. The Council requested the Secretary-General to take into account the views expressed in the Commission for Social Development (see Chapter XIII of this section) concerning ways and means of realizing the rights of youth when preparing documentation for the 1984 session of the Advisory Committee for the International Youth Year (see Chapter XX of this section). It resolved to consider at the 1985 session of the Commission for Social Development the progress achieved in connection with youth's participation in national development and in realizing and exercising their rights.

In resolution 38/23 of 22 November, on measures for securing implementation and enjoyment by youth of human rights, the General Assembly called on all concerned to pay continuous attention to the implementation of measures aimed at promoting human rights and their enjoyment by youth, particularly the right to education, vocational training and work, with a view to resolving the problem of youth unemployment. The Assembly requested the Advisory Committee for the International Youth Year to give full attention to all relevant human rights instruments in preparing for and during the Year, and invited national coordinating committees or other similar organs for the Year to give priority to the implementation and enjoyment by youth of human rights, particularly the right to education and work.

Right to food

Action by the Commission on Human Rights. Expressing deep concern about the precarious nature of the food situation, particularly in the least developed countries, and about its implications for enjoyment of the fundamental right to food, the Commission on Human Rights, in a resolution adopted on 22 February 1983 by 36 votes to none, with 5 abstentions,[24] recommended to the Economic and Social Council that it authorize the Sub-Commission to entrust Asbjorn Eide (Norway) with preparation of a study on the right to adequate food as a human right.

The Commission acted on a recommendation made by the Sub-Commission in September 1982.[25]

ECONOMIC AND SOCIAL ACTION

On the recommendation of its Second Committee, the Economic and Social Council adopted decision 1983/140 by vote.

The new international economic order and the promotion of human rights

At its 15th plenary meeting, on 27 May 1983, the Council, noting Commission on Human Rights resolution 1983/16 of 22 February 1983, authorized the Sub-Commission on Prevention of Discrimination and Protection of Minorities to entrust Mr. Eide, Special Rapporteur, with the preparation of a study on the right to adequate food as a human right. The Special Rapporteur, in elaborating his study, should take into account all relevant work being done within the United Nations system and should consult with organs and agencies such as the World Food Council, the Food and Agriculture Organization of the United Nations and the United Nations Conference on Trade and Development and

relevant non-governmental organizations in the field. In his study the Special Rapporteur should give special attention to the normative content of the right to food and its significance in relation to the establishment of the new international economic order. The Council requested the Secretary-General to give the Special Rapporteur all the assistance he might require in his work, and requested the Special Rapporteur to submit his preliminary report to the Sub-Commission at its thirty-sixth session and his final report to the Sub-Commission at its thirty-seventh session.

Economic and Social Council decision 1983/140

50-1-1

Approved by Second Committee (E/1983/61) by vote (45-1), 23 May (meeting 18); draft by Commission on Human Rights (E/1983/13); agenda item 10. *Meeting number.* ESC 15.

In related action, the Council, in resolution 1983/71 of 29 July on food problems, reaffirmed that the right to food was a univeral human right and that food should not be used as an instrument of political pressure.

Sub-Commission action. Acknowledging receipt of the Special Rapporteur's preliminary report,[26] providing an outline for the study on the right to food, the Sub-Commission, on 6 September,[27] expressed satisfaction for the approach chosen. It requested the Special Rapporteur to proceed in accordance with the outline and the comments by Sub-Commission members.

The Special Rapporteur believed that the examination of the right to adequate food provided an opportunity to address a number of fundamental questions relating to economic, social and cultural rights; other issues to be dealt with in the study covered the right to food as a human right, the normative content of that right, the relationship between this and other food-related studies, and NEIO and the right to food.

GENERAL ASSEMBLY ACTION

In resolution 38/158 of 19 December on food problems, the General Assembly reiterated the statement made by the Council in resolution 1983/71 (see above).

REFERENCES

[1]YUN 1966, p. 419, GA res. 2200 A (XXI), annex, 16 Dec. 1966. [2]YUN 1976, p. 609. [3]E/1983/36. [4]A/38/392. [5]YUN 1982, p. 1090, ESC res. 1982/33, 6 May 1982. [6]E/1983/41. [7]YUN 1978, p. 727, ESC dec. 1978/10, 3 May 1978. [8]YUN 1976, p. 615, ESC res. 1988(LX), 11 May 1976. [9]E/1983/40. [10]A/38/393. [11]E/1983/13 (res. 1983/15). [12]YUN 1982, p. 1091. [13]E/1983/13 (res. 1983/14). [14]YUN 1982, p. 961. [15]E/CN.4/1984/13 & Corr.1,2. [16]*The New International Economic Order and the Promotion of Human Rights* (E/CN.4/Sub.2/1983/24/Rev.1), Sales No. E.85.XIV.6. [17]YUN 1980, p. 880, ESC dec. 1980/126, 2 May 1980. [18]YUN 1982, p. 1092. [19]E/CN.4/Sub.2/1983/23. [20]E/CN.4/1984/3 (res. 1983/35). [21]*Ibid.* (dec. 1983/11). [22]*Ibid.* (res. 1983/38). [23]E/CN.4/1983/26. [24]E/1983/13 (res. 1983/16). [25]YUN 1982, p. 1094. [26]E/CN.4/Sub.2/1983/25. [27]E/CN.4/1984/3 (res. 1983/29).

Advancement of human rights

Action by the Commission on Human Rights. On 10 March 1983,[1] the Commission on Human Rights requested Governments to facilitate publicity regarding United Nations activities in the field of human rights. It welcomed the establishment of a programme for the dissemination of international human rights instruments and requested the Secretary-General to continue to report each year on the programme's implementation. It recommended again that the United Nations Secretariat develop a compilation of translations of international human rights instruments, particularly the International Covenants on Human Rights (see below), and invited those Governments which had such translations to forward copies to the Centre for Human Rights.

The Commission reiterated its request to the Secretary-General to establish small reference libraries of material in the human rights field in United Nations offices, particularly in developing countries. It requested him, among other things, to enhance and develop further the Centre's promotional and public information activities, and to keep the Commission informed of relevant activities, including the activities of the United Nations information centres in disseminating information on human rights.

Report of the Secretary-General. In October 1983, the Secretary-General submitted to the General Assembly, in pursuance of its December 1982 request,[2] a study on international conditions and human rights,[3] based on information from 19 Governments and 11 NGOs. Their replies raised a broad range of issues, the Secretary-General noted, including the importance of international co-operation in promoting full respect for human rights and of protecting the right to life as the most fundamental human right; the threat posed by the arms race and the buildup of nuclear weapons; the importance of establishing a just and equitable international economic order; the inadmissibility of intervention in the internal affairs of States; the need to accord priority to combating gross and flagrant human rights violations, including *apartheid;* and the need for more effective international machinery to respond to such violations.

In submitting his report, the Secretary-General drew attention to the continued validity of the findings and views expressed in his first report on the topic, submitted in 1981.[4] Among those findings were: the need, at all levels, to integrate the human rights dimension into political, economic, social and cultural policies and programmes; and the inadequate realization of the conditions necessary to bring about the freedom from fear mentioned in the Universal Declaration of Human Rights, or freedom from want, with a large part of the world's peoples lacking basic necessities and suffering conditions far removed from any acceptable level of human decency. Human rights violations were prevalent, and particularly acute in southern Africa where the peoples of South Africa and Namibia were denied their rights to self-determination, equality before the law and equal protection of the law. Further, various patterns of domination and subversion impeded the enjoyment of human rights, and international standards in the human rights field were often flagrantly disregarded in practice.

In connection with his 1981 report, the Secretary-General noted that United Nations approaches for dealing with phenomena—such as torture, disappearances of persons, mass exoduses, and Nazi, Fascist and neo-Fascist activities and other forms of totalitarian ideologies and practices—included the good offices of the Secretary-General, diplomatic and conciliatory approaches, fact-finding, complaints procedures, public consideration in United Nations organs and assistance measures. There was much room for improvement, however, in the way the United Nations responded to urgent situations of mass and flagrant human rights violations.

GENERAL ASSEMBLY ACTION

On 16 December, the General Assembly, acting on the recommendation of the Third Committee, adopted resolution 38/124 by recorded vote.

Alternative approaches and ways and means within the United Nations system for improving the effective enjoyment of human rights and fundamental freedoms

The General Assembly,

Recalling that in the Charter of the United Nations the peoples of the United Nations declared their determination to reaffirm faith in fundamental human rights, in the dignity and worth of the human person and in the equal rights of men and women and of nations large and small and to employ international machinery for the promotion of the economic and social advancement of all peoples,

Recalling also the purposes and principles of the Charter to achieve international co-operation in solving international problems of an economic, social, cultural or humanitarian character, and in promoting and encouraging respect for human rights and for fundamental freedoms for all without distinction as to race, sex, language or religion,

Reaffirming the continued significance and validity of the Universal Declaration of Human Rights and the importance of the International Covenants on Human Rights in promoting respect for and observance of human rights and fundamental freedoms,

Recalling its resolution 32/130 of 16 December 1977, in which it decided that the approach to the future work within the United Nations system with respect to human rights questions should take into account the concepts set forth in that resolution,

Recalling also its resolutions 34/46 of 23 November 1979, 35/174 of 15 December 1980 and 36/133 of 14 December 1981,

Recognizing that the human being is the main subject of development and that everyone has the right to participate in, as well as to benefit from, the development process,

Reiterating once again that the establishment of the new international economic order is an essential element for the effective promotion and the full enjoyment of human rights and fundamental freedoms for all,

Reiterating also its profound conviction that equal attention and urgent consideration should be given to the implementation, protection and promotion of both civil and political and economic, social and cultural rights,

Reaffirming the importance of furthering the activities of the existing organs of the United Nations system in the field of human rights in conformity with the principles of the Charter,

Underlining the need for the creation of conditions at the national and international levels for the promotion and full protection of the human rights of individuals and peoples,

Emphasizing that Governments have the duty to ensure respect for all human rights and fundamental freedoms,

Recognizing that all human rights and fundamental freedoms are indivisible and interrelated and that the right to development is an inalienable human right,

Reaffirming that equality of opportunities for development is a prerogative both of nations and of individuals within nations,

Emphasizing that international peace and security are essential elements for the full realization of human rights, including the right to development,

Recognizing that, through disarmament, resources could be released to contribute in a meaningful way to the development of all States, particularly the developing countries,

Reiterating that co-operation among all nations on the basis of respect for the independence, sovereignty and territorial integrity of each State, including the right of each people to choose freely its own socio-economic and political system, is essential for the promotion of peace and development,

Convinced that the primary aim of such international co-operation must be the achievement by each human being of a life of freedom and dignity and freedom from want,

Reaffirming that nothing in the Universal Declaration of Human Rights may be interpreted as implying for any State, group or person the right to engage in any activity or perform any act aimed at the destruction of any of the rights and freedoms set forth therein,

Affirming that the ultimate aim of development is the constant improvement of the well-being of the entire population, on the basis of its full participation in the process of development and a fair distribution of the benefits therefrom,

1.   *Reiterates its request* that the Commission on Human Rights continue its current work on the overall analysis with a view to further promoting and improving human rights and fundamental freedoms, including the question of the Commission's programme and working methods, and on the overall analysis of the alternative approaches and ways and means for improving the ef-

fective enjoyment of human rights and fundamental freedoms, in accordance with the provisions and concepts of General Assembly resolution 32/130 and other relevant texts;

2.   *Affirms* that a primary aim of international co-operation in the field of human rights is a life of freedom and dignity for all peoples and for each human being, that all human rights and fundamental freedoms are indivisible and interrelated and that the promotion and protection of one category of rights should never exempt or excuse States from the promotion and protection of the others;

3.   *Affirms its profound conviction* that equal attention and urgent consideration should be given to the implementation, protection and promotion of both civil and political and economic, social and cultural rights;

4.   *Reaffirms* that it is of paramount importance for the promotion of human rights and fundamental freedoms that Member States should undertake specific obligations through accession to, or ratification of, international instruments in this field and, consequently, that the standard-setting work within the United Nations system in the field of human rights and the universal acceptance and the implementation of the relevant international instruments should be encouraged;

5.   *Reiterates* that the international community should accord, or continue to accord, priority to the search for solutions to mass and flagrant violations of the human rights of peoples and individuals affected by situations such as those mentioned in paragraph 1 *(e)* of its resolution 32/130, paying due attention also to other situations of violations of human rights;

6.   *Reaffirms* its responsibility for achieving international co-operation in promoting and encouraging respect for human rights and fundamental freedoms for all, and reaffirms that consistent patterns of violations of human rights, wherever they exist, are of concern to the United Nations;

7.   *Expresses concern* at the present situation with regard to the achievement of the objectives and goals for establishing the new international economic order and its adverse effects on the full realization of human rights, in particular, the right to development;

8.   *Reaffirms* that international peace and security are essential elements for the full realization of the right to development;

9.   *Reaffirms also* that the right to development is an inalienable human right;

10.   *Recognizes* that all human rights and fundamental freedoms are indivisible and interrelated;

11.   *Considers* it necessary that all Member States promote international co-operation on the basis of respect for the independence, sovereignty and territorial integrity of each State, including the right of each people to choose freely its own socio-economic and political system, with a view to resolving international problems of an economic, social and humanitarian character;

12.   *Expresses concern also* at the disparity existing between the established principles and the actual situation of all human rights and fundamental freedoms in various parts of the world;

13.   *Urges* all States to co-operate with the Commission on Human Rights in the protection and promotion of human rights and fundamental freedoms;

14.   *Reaffirms also* that, in order to facilitate the full enjoyment of all rights and complete personal dignity,

it is necessary to promote the rights to education, work, health and proper nourishment through the adoption of measures at the national level, including those that provide for workers' participation in management, as well as the adoption of measures at the international level, including the establishment of the new international economic order;

15. *Requests* the Commission on Human Rights to take the necessary measures to promote the right to development, taking into account the results achieved by the Working Group of Governmental Experts on the Right to Development, which is engaged in the study of the scope and content of the right to development, and welcomes the decision of the Commission in its resolution 1982/17 of 9 March 1982, reaffirmed in its resolution 1983/15 of 22 February 1983, to the effect that the Working Group should continue its work with the aim of submitting as soon as possible a draft declaration on the right to development;

16. *Decides* to include in the provisional agenda of its thirty-ninth session the item entitled "Alternative approaches and ways and means within the United Nations system for improving the effective enjoyment of human rights and fundamental freedoms".

General Assembly resolution 38/124

16 December 1983   Meeting 100   132-1-13 (recorded vote)

Approved by Third Committee (A/38/690) by recorded vote (120-1-14), 29 November (meeting 58); 28-nation draft (A/C.3/38/L.25), orally revised on proposal by Djibouti and further orally revised following consultations; agenda item 100.

Sponsors: Algeria, Angola, Argentina, Bangladesh, Benin, Bolivia, Cape Verde, Congo, Cuba, Democratic Yemen, Ethiopia, Guinea-Bissau, Guyana, India, Libyan Arab Jamahiriya, Madagascar, Mali, Mozambique, Nicaragua, Nigeria, Pakistan, Panama, Romania, Sao Tome and Principe, Syrian Arab Republic, Uganda, Viet Nam, Yugoslavia.

Meeting numbers. GA 38th session: 3rd Committee 38-42, 54, 56-59; plenary 100.

Recorded vote in Assembly as follows:

In favour: Afghanistan, Algeria, Angola, Argentina, Australia, Austria, Bahamas, Bahrain, Bangladesh, Belgium, Belize, Benin, Bhutan, Bolivia, Botswana, Brazil, Bulgaria, Burma, Burundi, Byelorussian SSR, Cape Verde, Chad, Chile, China, Colombia, Congo, Costa Rica, Cuba, Cyprus, Czechoslovakia, Democratic Kampuchea, Democratic Yemen, Djibouti, Dominica, Dominican Republic, Ecuador, Egypt, El Salvador, Equatorial Guinea, Ethiopia, Fiji, France, Gabon, Gambia, German Democratic Republic, Ghana, Greece, Grenada, Guatemala, Guinea, Guinea-Bissau, Guyana, Haiti, Honduras, Hungary, India, Indonesia, Iran, Iraq, Italy, Ivory Coast, Jamaica, Jordan, Kenya, Kuwait, Lao People's Democratic Republic, Lebanon, Lesotho, Liberia, Libyan Arab Jamahiriya, Madagascar, Malawi, Malaysia, Maldives, Mali, Malta, Mauritania, Mauritius, Mexico, Mongolia, Morocco, Mozambique, Nepal, Netherlands, New Zealand, Nicaragua, Niger, Nigeria, Oman, Pakistan, Panama, Papua New Guinea, Paraguay, Peru, Philippines, Poland, Portugal, Qatar, Romania, Rwanda, Sao Tome and Principe, Saudi Arabia, Senegal, Sierra Leone, Singapore, Somalia, Spain, Sri Lanka, Sudan, Suriname, Swaziland, Syrian Arab Republic, Thailand, Togo, Trinidad and Tobago, Tunisia, Uganda, Ukrainian SSR, USSR, United Arab Emirates, United Republic of Cameroon, United Republic of Tanzania, Upper Volta, Uruguay, Vanuatu, Venezuela, Viet Nam, Yemen, Yugoslavia, Zaire, Zambia, Zimbabwe.

Against: United States.

Abstaining: Canada, Denmark, Finland, Germany, Federal Republic of, Iceland, Ireland, Israel, Japan, Luxembourg, Norway, Sweden, Turkey, United Kingdom.

As a result of consultations on proposals from Bulgaria, China, Finland, Ireland, Italy, the Netherlands and the USSR, a number of revisions were made to the draft that was to become resolution 38/124. The ninth preambular paragraph was added, as was paragraph 12, which was based on part of an amendment proposed by Italy, by which the Assembly would have expressed concern at the disparity between the established principles and the actual situation of human rights in vari-

ous parts of the world, in particular with regard to the right to life, liberty and security of person.[5]

Paragraph 9 was adopted by a recorded vote, requested by Bulgaria, of 110 to 1, with 22 abstentions.

Voting against the paragraph as well as the text as a whole, the United States, while welcoming the spirit of paragraphs 2, 3, 6, 10 and 12, could not accept the implicit prejudgement of the Working Group's findings, particularly since some States members of the Group responsible for its slow progress were among those supporting the draft. The United States also had misgivings about the implied affirmation in paragraph 9 of the inalienable nature of the right to development and about the notion in the seventh preambular paragraph regarding the establishment of NIEO; the December 1982 Assembly resolution on further promotion and protection of human rights[2] should guide the Committee in its future deliberations.

Japan, abstaining, observed that, while paragraph 9 reaffirmed that the right to development was an inalienable human right, paragraph 14 stated that the Working Group of Governmental Experts was still studying the matter; the Assembly should not pronounce itself definitely on the issue until the Working Group had reached clear conclusions on all questions relating to that right.

Canada said great care must be taken in matters involving the relationship between human rights and development; it felt that the draft gave scant regard to the International Covenants on Human Rights, implied acceptance of a new definition and seemingly asserted certain rights of States which were not human rights, and contained a number of political elements which should be dealt with elsewhere.

Turkey felt that there was no balance in the text between civil and political rights and economic and social rights on the one hand, and between individual and collective rights on the other.

The United Kingdom considered that the draft did not balance the provisions of the December 1982 resolutions—37/199[6] and 37/200[2]—to be acceptable as a single text; nevertheless, it could be seen as a step towards a better future text. Though welcoming the inclusion of elements of one of those resolutions, the Federal Republic of Germany shared the misgivings about the implications of the seventh preambular paragraph and paragraph 9. New Zealand also voiced misgivings about paragraph 9.

Ireland said the text contained no unqualified statement that human rights violations were of concern to the United Nations—an omission all the more significant because paragraph 13 urging Member States to co-operate with the Commission had failed to refer to the latter's study of such violations. It regretted that the sponsors had retained "consistent patterns of" in paragraph 6, despite its request.

The Netherlands said its affirmative vote did not imply acceptance of the entire text. The preambular part and paragraph 9 (on which it abstained) referred to the right to development in a way which prejudged the Working Group's findings; also, the assertion in the seventh preambular paragraph concerning the establishment of NIEO was premature, since the nature and scope of that order had not been defined. With regard to paragraph 13, protection of human rights was a matter for active United Nations involvement.

Portugal, while supporting the draft's stress on the importance of international dialogue for improved enjoyment of human rights, abstained on paragraph 9 which it feared would lead the Assembly to prejudge the outcome of the study; its future vote on similar resolutions would depend on their approach and their capability to reinforce a concept of human rights as one essentially concerning the relationship between State power and the individual.

Among those voting for the draft, the USSR stated that despite its shortcomings and ambiguities, for example in paragraph 6, it none the less hoped that such shortcomings would be overcome in the interest of international co-operation in encouraging respect for human rights. The German Democratic Republic, though not fully satisfied with the text, particularly paragraphs 5 and 6 which, it said, should not be interpreted as authorizing interference in the internal affairs of any State, said it voted in favour in a spirit of compromise and in recognition of the efforts made by the sponsors to take into account a series of ideas and proposals submitted in connection with the draft.

Spain observed that neither the concept of the right to development nor the exerciser of that right was sufficiently clear in the text.

Australia said it failed to see why the text could not reflect the possibility of innovations to United Nations structures aimed at enhancing the promotion and protection of human rights and fundamental freedoms; nevertheless, the spirit of co-operation gave reason to hope that an improved text could be achieved in future. That hope was shared by France which felt that the text reflected efforts at compromise; however, it would have liked the text to reflect better the belief that no category of human rights, particularly civil and political rights, could be subordinated to others.

National institutions for human rights protection

Report of the Secretary-General. In October 1983, the Secretary-General submitted to the General Assembly a report on national institutions for the promotion and protection of human rights,[7] in accordance with a 1981 Assembly request.[8] Following up on a 1981 report on the same topic,[9] the 1983 report was based primarily on information received from 34 countries as at 15 August, in reply to the Secretary-General's 1982 requests. The Secretary-General also took into account information from, among other sources, the United Nations specialized agencies, government reports under various international instruments of concern, and reports and background papers of United Nations seminars.

As in his 1981 study, the Secretary-General understood the concept of national institutions for the promotion and protection of human rights to cover more than the authorities, agencies and procedures established by law; the report encompassed a wide range of organizations, including the media, the churches, professional and workers' unions, women's rights movements and many other voluntary organizations.

Among the national institutions for the protection of human rights, the Secretary-General reviewed judicial institutions and non-judicial organs supervising the observance of the law (such as the "Ombudsman"); human rights commissions and similar public bodies expressly entrusted with such responsibilities; legal counselling and assistance; human rights protection by legislative organs; and the role of NGOs, including trade unions. The Secretary-General also analysed the promotional role of human rights commissions and similar public bodies, and the promotion of those rights through participation in government and the legislative process.

From the data assembled, the Secretary-General considered it possible to observe a trend towards entrenching human rights guarantees in Constitutions and strengthening judicial control in that regard. Also noticeable were the geographical spread of institutions such as the Ombudsman, the creation of human rights commissions and similar bodies, as well as the strengthening of some promotional institutions in the fields of education, employment and labour matters. Those developments, the Secretary-General stated, appeared to reflect a growing awareness of the need for a flexible interplay of diverse approaches—judicial, investigative, conciliatory, legislative, educational—and a wider participation of individuals and groups in normative and implementation processes relating to their human rights.

GENERAL ASSEMBLY ACTION

On 16 December, on the recommendation of the Third Committee, the General Assembly adopted resolution 38/123 without vote.

National institutions for the protection and promotion of human rights

The General Assembly,

Recalling its resolutions 32/123 of 16 December 1977, 33/46 of 14 December 1978, 34/49 of 23 November 1979 and 36/134 of 14 December 1981 concerning national institutions for the promotion and protection of human rights,

Mindful of the guidelines on the structure and functioning of national and local institutions for the promotion and protection of human rights, endorsed by the General Assembly in its resolution 33/46,

Mindful also of the need to create conditions, at the national, regional and international levels, for the protection and promotion of the human rights of individuals and peoples,

Conscious of the significant role which institutions at the national level can play in protecting and promoting human rights and fundamental freedoms and in developing and enhancing public awareness and observance of those rights and freedoms,

Emphasizing the importance of the Universal Declaration of Human Rights, the International Covenants on Human Rights and other international human rights instruments for promoting respect for and observance of human rights and fundamental freedoms,

1. *Takes note with appreciation* of the report of the Secretary-General;

2. *Invites* all Member States to take appropriate steps for the establishment or, where they already exist, the strengthening of national institutions for the protection and promotion of human rights;

3. *Emphasizes* the importance of the integrity and independence of such national institutions, in accordance with national legislation;

4. *Draws attention* to the constructive role that national non-governmental organizations can play in the work of national institutions;

5. *Recommends* that all Member States should take appropriate steps to encourage the exchange of experience in the establishment of national institutions;

6. *Requests* the Secretary-General to transmit his report to Governments and to invite them to submit additional information, comments and observations, with a view to developing further the various types of national institutions for the protection and promotion of human rights;

7. *Also requests* the Secretary-General, in the light of his previous reports and of further information received, to submit to the General Assembly at its thirty-ninth session an updated report providing detailed information on the various types of national and local institutions for the protection and promotion of human rights, taking into account differing social and legal systems and the contributions that national and local institutions can make towards the implementation of international human rights instruments;

8. *Decides* to include in the provisional agenda of its thirty-ninth session the sub-item entitled "National institutions for the protection and promotion of human rights".

General Assembly resolution 38/123

16 December 1983   Meeting 100   Adopted without vote

Approved by Third Committee (A/38/690) without vote, 30 November (meeting 57); 11-nation draft (A/C.3/38/L.26); agenda item 100 *(b)*.

Sponsors: Australia, Costa Rica, Ecuador, India, Iraq, Jamaica, Morocco, New Zealand, Nigeria, Peru, Sri Lanka.

Meeting numbers. GA 38th session: 3rd Committee 38-42, 54, 56, 57; plenary 100.

International human rights instruments

Working Group activities. On 16 August 1983, the Sub-Commission on Prevention of Discrimination and Protection of Minorities, acting in pursuance of a 1979 resolution,[10] established a five-member sessional Working Group on the encouragement of universal acceptance of human rights instruments—such as the 1966 International Covenants on Economic, Social and Cultural Rights and on Civil and Political Rights and the latter's Optional Protocol,[11] the 1965 International Convention on the Elimination of All Forms of Racial Discrimination,[12] the 1948 Convention on the Prevention and Punishment of the Crime of Genocide,[13] the 1973 International Convention on the Suppression and Punishment of the Crime of *Apartheid*,[14] the 1926 Slavery Convention and the 1953 Protocol amending it,[15] the 1956 Supplementary Convention on the Abolition of Slavery, the Slave Trade and Institutions and Practices Similar to Slavery,[16] and the 1949 Convention for the Suppression of the Traffic in Persons and of the Exploitation of the Prostitution of Others.[17]

Meeting on 26 and 31 August, the Working Group considered a report of the Secretary-General[18] containing a summary of information from Governments regarding the circumstances that had so far not enabled them to become parties to the various human rights instruments. In addition, the Working Group continued its country-by-country examination, reviewing information from 17 States and the additional information supplied by four States, and also heard statements from observers for three NGOs.

Sub-Commission action. The Sub-Commission, acting on the Working Group's report and recommendations[19] by a resolution of 6 September,[20] expressed appreciation to Governments which had conveyed information and requested the Secretary-General, among other things, to invite Governments to submit information on the circumstances that had so far not enabled them to become parties to various human rights instruments. The Sub-Commission decided to include the 1979 Convention on the Elimination of All Forms of Discrimination against Women[21] in the list of human rights instruments whose universal acceptance was to be encouraged. It endorsed the Working Group's decision to prepare for the Group's 1984 session a discussion paper analysing types of difficulties preventing States from becoming parties to those instruments and submitting possible suggestions for overcoming them.

Anniversary of the 1948 Universal Declaration of Human Rights

In 1983, the United Nations commemorated the thirty-fifth anniversary of the Universal Declaration of Human Rights, adopted on 10 December 1948.[22] Among several messages addressed to the

Secretary-General on that occasion was one by the President of Austria;[23] messages from nine more Governments were transmitted by the Secretary-General to the General Assembly by a note of 20 December.[24]

In a report to the Assembly,[25] the Secretary-General summarized information from 31 States concerning their annual observance of Human Rights Day, in 1982, in commemoration of the proclamation of the Declaration and in accordance with a 1950 Assembly resolution.[26]

GENERAL ASSEMBLY ACTION

On 9 December, the General Assembly adopted resolution 38/57 without vote.

Thirty-five years of the Universal Declaration of Human Rights: international co-operation for the promotion and observance of civil, political, economic, social and cultural rights

The General Assembly,

Reaffirming the continued significance and the validity of the Universal Declaration of Human Rights,

Welcoming the progress made so far in the promotion and protection of human rights and fundamental freedoms since the proclamation of the Declaration,

Recalling that Member States have pledged themselves to achieve, in co-operation with the United Nations, the promotion of universal respect for and observance of human rights and fundamental freedoms,

Acknowledging that, despite all the efforts made by the international community to promote and protect human rights, there is a need for constant vigilance by the international community in this field,

Recalling also the responsibility of the international community to remove the threat of war from the lives of people, to preserve civilization and to ensure that everyone enjoys the inherent right to life, liberty and security of person,

Underlining the importance of the teaching of human rights at all levels, particularly in primary and secondary schools,

1. *Stresses* the significance of the thirty-fifth anniversary of the Universal Declaration of Human Rights and expresses grave concern at mass and flagrant violations and all other violations of human rights which continue to take place in many parts of the world;

2. *Takes note with satisfaction* of the progress made so far in the field of standard-setting on human rights since the proclamation of the Declaration and reaffirms its commitment to continue to strive for further progress in the field of the promotion and protection of human rights and fundamental freedoms;

3. *Urges* all States to apply the Declaration resolutely, as well as seriously to consider ratifying or acceding to and observing the International Covenant on Civil and Political Rights and the International Covenant on Economic, Social and Cultural Rights, the International Convention on the Elimination of All Forms of Racial Discrimination and instruments relating to *apartheid*, and calls upon all States to ensure greater observance and respect of all other United Nations instruments on human rights;

4. *Urges* the United Nations Educational, Scientific and Cultural Organization, in co-operation with Governments, to undertake rigorous efforts to spread the teaching of human rights in all educational institutions, particularly primary and secondary schools, as well as in the training of relevant professional groups and requests the Director-General of that organization to submit to the General Assembly at its forty-third session, on the occasion of the fortieth anniversary of the Declaration, a report on the efforts made by the United Nations Educational, Scientific and Cultural Organization to those ends.

General Assembly resolution 38/57

9 December 1983   Meeting 91   Adopted without vote

10-nation draft (A/38/L.42/Rev.1); agenda item 21.
Sponsors: Canada, Costa Rica, Mexico, Morocco, Netherlands, Norway, Senegal, Somalia, Spain, Sweden.
Meeting numbers. GA 38th session: plenary 90, 91.

International Covenants on Human Rights

Report of the Secretary-General. In January 1983, the Secretary-General reported to the Commission on Human Rights on the status of the 1966 International Covenants on Human Rights[11] and gave a synopsis of United Nations action taken in that context.[27] Annexed to the report were current lists of States which had signed, ratified or acceded to the Covenants, as well as to the Optional Protocol to the International Covenant on Civil and Political Rights.

Action by the Commission on Human Rights. By a resolution of 22 February,[28] the Commission reaffirmed the importance of the Covenants as major parts of international efforts to promote universal respect for human rights and fundamental freedoms, urged States to become parties and emphasized the importance of strictest compliance. It also emphasized the importance of States parties sending experts to present their reports under the Covenants, as well as nominating experts to serve on the implementation committees set up under them. It encouraged Governments to publish the Covenants' texts in as many languages as possible and to distribute and publicize them widely. It requested the Secretary-General to invite the United Nations information centres to increase their activities to make the Covenants better known and to report to the Commission on action taken in that regard. It further requested him to submit in 1984 a report on the status of the Covenants.

GENERAL ASSEMBLY ACTION

In December 1983, on the recommendation of the Third Committee, the General Assembly adopted two resolutions—38/116 and 38/117—on the International Covenants on Human Rights. On 16 December, it adopted resolution 38/116 without vote.

International Covenants on Human Rights

The General Assembly,

Recalling its resolutions 33/51 of 14 December 1978, 34/45 of 23 November 1979, 35/132 of 11 December 1980, 36/58 of 25 November 1981 and 37/191 of 18 December 1982,

Taking note of the report of the Secretary-General on the status of the International Covenant on Economic, Social and Cultural Rights, the International Covenant on Civil and Political Rights and the Optional Protocol to the International Covenant on Civil and Political Rights,

Noting with appreciation that, following its appeal, more Member States have acceded to the International Covenants on Human Rights,

Recognizing the important role of the Human Rights Committee in the implementation of the International Covenant on Civil and Political Rights and the Optional Protocol thereto,

Taking into account the useful work of the Sessional Working Group of Governmental Experts on the Implementation of the International Covenant on Economic, Social and Cultural Rights,

Bearing in mind the important responsibilities of the Economic and Social Council in relation to the International Covenants on Human Rights,

Taking note of Economic and Social Council decision 1983/184 of 29 July 1983, in which the Council invited the General Assembly to consider at its thirty-eighth session the possibility of scheduling the meetings of the Human Rights Committee so that the Committee's report could be submitted to the Assembly through the Council at its first regular session,

1. *Takes note with appreciation* of the report of the Human Rights Committee on its seventeenth, eighteenth and nineteenth sessions, and expresses its satisfaction at the serious and constructive manner in which the Committee is continuing to perform its functions;

2. *Expresses its appreciation* to those States parties to the International Covenant on Civil and Political Rights that have extended their co-operation to the Human Rights Committee in submitting their reports under article 40 of the Covenant and urges States parties that have not yet done so to submit their reports to the Committee as speedily as possible;

3. *Urges* those States parties to the International Covenant on Civil and Political Rights that have been requested by the Human Rights Committee to provide additional information to comply with that request;

4. *Commends* those States parties to the International Covenant on Economic, Social and Cultural Rights that have submitted their reports under article 16 of the Covenant and urges States that have not yet done so to submit their reports as soon as possible and, in those instances in which it is not possible to do so, to inform the Sessional Working Group of Governmental Experts on the Implementation of the International Covenant on Economic, Social and Cultural Rights as to when those reports will be submitted;

5. *Notes with appreciation* that the majority of States parties to the International Covenant on Civil and Political Rights, and an increasing number of States parties to the International Covenant on Economic, Social and Cultural Rights, have been represented by experts for the presentation of their reports, thereby assisting the Human Rights Committee and the Economic and Social Council in their work, and hopes that all States parties to both Covenants will arrange such representation in future;

6. *Again invites* all States that have not yet done so to become parties to the International Covenant on Economic, Social and Cultural Rights and the International Covenant on Civil and Political Rights, as well as to con-

sider acceding to the Optional Protocol to the International Covenant on Civil and Political Rights;

7. *Invites* the States parties to the International Covenant on Civil and Political Rights to consider making the declaration provided for in article 41 of the Covenant;

8. *Emphasizes* the importance of the strictest compliance by States parties with their obligations under the International Covenant on Economic, Social and Cultural Rights and the International Covenant on Civil and Political Rights and, where applicable, the Optional Protocol to the International Covenant on Civil and Political Rights;

9. *Requests* the Secretary-General to continue to keep the Human Rights Committee informed of the activities of the Commission on Human Rights, the Sub-Commission on Prevention of Discrimination and Protection of Minorities, the Committee on the Elimination of Racial Discrimination and the Committee on the Elimination of Discrimination against Women and also to transmit the annual reports of the Human Rights Committee to those bodies;

10. *Requests* the Secretary-General to submit to the General Assembly at its thirty-ninth session a report on the status of the International Covenant on Economic, Social and Cultural Rights, the International Covenant on Civil and Political Rights and the Optional Protocol to the International Covenant on Civil and Political Rights;

11. *Urges* the Secretary-General to take further positive steps to ensure that adequate publicity and other arrangements are made to enable the Human Rights Committee and the Economic and Social Council to carry out effectively, within existing resources, their respective functions under the International Covenants on Human Rights;

12. *Also urges* the Secretary-General to expedite arrangements for publication of the official public records of the Human Rights Committee in bound volumes, starting with its first session, as indicated in General Assembly resolution 37/191;

13. *Requests* the Secretary-General to continue to take all possible steps to ensure that the Centre for Human Rights of the Secretariat is able to assist effectively the Human Rights Committee and the Economic and Social Council in the implementation of their respective functions under the International Covenants on Human Rights, taking into account General Assembly resolutions 3534(XXX) of 17 December 1975 and 31/93 of 14 December 1976.

General Assembly resolution 38/116

16 December 1983   Meeting 100   Adopted without vote

Approved by Third Committee (A/38/686 & Corr.1) without vote, 30 November (meeting 57); 18-nation draft (A/C.3/38/L.39); agenda item 96.

Sponsors: Australia, Bulgaria, Canada, Costa Rica, Cyprus, Denmark, Ecuador, Finland, Iceland, Italy, Netherlands, Nicaragua, Norway, Peru, Senegal, Spain, Sweden, United Kingdom.

Meeting numbers. GA 38th session: 3rd Committee 49-54, 56, 57; plenary 100.

Also on 16 December, the Assembly adopted resolution 38/117 without vote.

Reporting obligations of the States parties to the International Covenants on Human Rights

The General Assembly,

Recalling its resolution 37/44 of 3 December 1982,

Mindful of the obligation of all States parties to the International Covenants on Human Rights to comply fully with their provisions, including articles 16 and 17 of the International Covenant on Economic, Social and Cultural Rights, which require the submission of periodic reports in accordance with the programme established by the Economic and Social Council,

Having considered the report of the Secretary-General, in which he indicates that a large number of delays occur in the submission of reports on the implementation of the International Covenant on Economic, Social and Cultural Rights,

Noting that the report of the Secretary-General emphasizes the interrelationship of problems affecting the reporting system under various human rights instruments,

1. *Takes note with appreciation* of the report of the Secretary-General;

2. *Reiterates* the importance it attaches to the reporting systems established by the International Covenants on Human Rights;

3. *Requests* the Secretary-General to transmit his report to the Economic and Social Council, which is entrusted with the consideration of the reports of States parties to the International Covenant on Economic, Social and Cultural Rights under article 16 thereof;

4. *Requests* the Economic and Social Council and its Sessional Working Group of Governmental Experts on the Implementation of the International Covenant on Economic, Social and Cultural Rights to consider the suggestions contained in the report of the Secretary-General with a view to improving the situation regarding the submission of reports under the Covenant;

5. *Requests* the Secretary-General to consider the possibility of convening, in accordance with the suggestion contained in the report of the Human Rights Committee and within existing resources, a meeting of the Chairmen of the bodies entrusted with the consideration of reports submitted under the relevant human rights instruments in order to consider the report of the Secretary-General, taking into account the results of General Assembly resolution 38/20 of 22 November 1983 and of the present resolution;

6. *Requests* the Secretary-General to inform the General Assembly at its thirty-ninth session of the views and suggestions expressed at the above-mentioned meeting, if it is convened.

General Assembly resolution 38/117

16 December 1983   Meeting 100   Adopted without vote

Approved by Third Committee (A/38/686 & Corr.1) without vote, 30 November (meeting 57); 6-nation draft (A/C.3/38/L.41); agenda item 96.
Sponsors: Australia, Austria, Canada, Finland, Italy, Netherlands.
Meeting numbers. GA 38th session: 3rd Committee 49-54, 56, 57; plenary 100.

UN machinery

Commission on Human Rights

Organization of work for the 1983 session

In 1983, the Commission on Human Rights held its thirty-ninth session at Geneva from 31 January to 11 March.[29] On 1 February,[30] the Commission decided to set up informal open-ended working groups to consider the following agenda items: torture and other cruel, inhuman or degrading treatment of punishment (see above,

under CIVIL AND POLITICAL RIGHTS); further promotion and encouragement of human rights and fundamental freedoms, including the question of the programme and methods of work of the Commission (see below); convention on the rights of the child (see below, under OTHER HUMAN RIGHTS QUESTIONS); and the rights of persons belonging to national, ethnic, religious and linguistic minorities (see above, under DISCRIMINATION). The Commission also decided to establish a 10-member working group to consider the possibility of rationalizing the agenda of its 1984 session (see below).

By a decision of 2 February, adopted by 23 votes to 7, with 4 abstentions,[31] the Commission requested that the Economic and Social Council authorize 15 additional serviced meetings for the Commission at its 1983 session.

ECONOMIC AND SOCIAL COUNCIL ACTION

On an oral proposal by its President, the Economic and Social Council adopted decision 1983/102 by vote.

Meeting services for the Commission on Human Rights at its thirty-ninth session

At its 2nd plenary meeting, on 4 February 1983, the Council, taking into account the request made by the Commission on Human Rights at the 3rd meeting of its thirty-ninth session, decided to authorize the Commission to hold fifteen extra serviced meetings, without summary records, at its thirty-ninth session.

Economic and Social Council decision 1983/102

41-7-3

Oral proposal by President on request by Commission on Human Rights Chairman (E/1983/8); agenda item 2.
Financial implications. S-G, E/1983/L.15.
Meeting number. ESC 2.

On 27 May, on the recommendation of its Second Committee, the Council adopted decision 1983/154 without vote.

Report of the Commission on Human Rights

At its 15th plenary meeting, on 27 May 1983, the Council took note of the report of the Commission on Human Rights on its thirty-ninth session.

Economic and Social Council decision 1983/154

Adopted without vote

Approved by Second Committee (E/1983/61) without vote, 23 May (meeting 18); draft by Commission on Human Rights (E/1983/13); agenda item 10.
Meeting number. ESC 15.

Programme and work methods

An informal open-ended working group of the Commission on Human Rights, similar to the one established in 1982,[32] held six meetings between 2 February and 3 March 1983 on the question of the programme and work methods of the Commission. Annexed to the group's report[33] were several working papers and an informal listing of relevant issues, including structural and organizational issues.

In a 10 March resolution[34] based on a draft submitted by the group, the Commission noted that, along with a number of ideas which merited consideration, differing views had been expressed in the group on the inter-sessional role of the Bureau, the creation of a post of United Nations High Commissioner for Human Rights (see below), the possible review of the Commission's terms of reference, the Commission's long-term programme of work and the usefulness of the working group. It decided to renew its recommendation to the Economic and Social Council to consider the possibility of rescheduling the Commission's annual session to later in the year, providing for a longer interval following the annual Assembly session.

An informal 10-member Working Group, established under the 1 February 1983 Commission decision (see above), held five meetings between 7 February and 3 March to consider the possibility of rationalizing the agenda for the Commission's 1984 session.

On 10 March, the Commission,[35] having noted with appreciation the Working Group's report,[36] decided to delete from its agenda the item "Communications concerning human rights"; to consider biennially the items "Human rights and scientific and technological developments" (beginning in 1984) and "The role of youth in the promotion and protection of human rights, including the question of conscientious objection to military service" (beginning in 1985); and to consider in 1984 the need to re-establish the Working Group. On 11 March,[37] the Commission took note of the draft provisional agenda for its 1984 session.

By a decision of 10 March, adopted by 29 votes to none, with 9 abstentions,[38] the Commission made several recommendations on the organization of its 1984 session, which were endorsed subsequently by the Economic and Social Council (see below).

ECONOMIC AND SOCIAL COUNCIL ACTION

On the recommendation of its Second Committee, the Economic and Social Council adopted decision 1983/152 by vote.

Organization of the work of the fortieth session of the Commission on Human Rights

At its 15th plenary meeting, on 27 May 1983, the Council, noting Commission on Human Rights decision 1983/109 of 10 March 1983, decided to authorize 20 fully-serviced additional meetings, including summary records, for the Commission's fortieth session and endorsed the Commission's request to the Chairman of the Commission at its fortieth session to make every effort to organize the work of the session within the nor-

mal allotted time, the additional meetings authorized to be utilized only if such meetings prove to be absolutely necessary.

Economic and Social Council decision 1983/152

46-0-7

Approved by Second Committee (E/1983/61) by vote (39-0-7), 23 May (meeting 18); draft by Commission on Human Rights (E/1983/13), orally amended in Council by President; agenda item 10.
Meeting number. ESC 15.

As agreed in 1982,[39] and following the renewed recommendation by the Commission (see above), the Council considered in 1983 the question of rescheduling the annual Commission session. In decision 1983/184 of 29 July, the Council decided to continue for the time being the existing pattern of scheduling the sessions (see Chapter XXIV of this section).

Sub-Commission on Prevention of Discrimination and Protection of Minorities

The Sub-Commission on Prevention of Discrimination and Protection of Minorities had held its thirty-fifth session at Geneva from 16 August to 10 September 1982.[40]

Action by the Commission on Human Rights. By a resolution of 4 March 1983,[41] the Commission on Human Rights called on the Sub-Commission to be guided in its work by relevant resolutions of the Commission, the Economic and Social Council and the General Assembly, adding that it was inappropriate for the Sub-Commission to take decisions affecting its status, role and competence. It invited the Sub-Commission to make recommendations to the Commission on ways to ensure complementarity and co-ordination between the activities of both bodies as well as the undertaking of tasks by the Sub-Commission, which its particular status as a body of individuals elected in an independent and expert capacity best suited it to carry out.

The Sub-Commission was further invited to: examine in 1983 possibilities for rationalizing its method of work, ensure completion on time of studies requested by the Commission and the Council, seek the widest possible measure of agreement when adopting decisions, and be present when its report was considered by the Commission in 1984.

By a resolution of the same date, adopted by a roll-call vote of 31 to 5, with 7 abstentions,[42] the Commission recommended to the Council a draft resolution on the nomination and election of candidates for the Sub-Commission (see below).

ECONOMIC AND SOCIAL COUNCIL ACTION

On 27 May, on the recommendation of its Second Committee, the Economic and Social Council adopted a resolution and a decision relating to the work of the Sub-Commission. Resolution 1983/32 was adopted by vote.

Report of the Sub-Commission on Prevention of Discrimination and Protection of Minorities on its thirty-fifth session

The Economic and Social Council,

Recalling the terms of reference of the Sub-Commission on Prevention of Discrimination and Protection of Minorities, and in particular Commission on Human Rights resolutions 17(XXXVII) of 10 March 1981 and 1982/23 of 10 March 1982,

Recalling in particular that members of the Sub-Commission are elected by the Commission on Human Rights as experts in their individual capacity,

Considering that the same criteria and qualifications should apply to alternates as to members,

Decides that, notwithstanding paragraph 2 of article 13 of the rules of procedure of the functional commissions of the Economic and Social Council, the following rules shall henceforth apply to the Sub-Commission on Prevention of Discrimination and Protection of Minorities:

(a) A nomination of a candidate for membership of the Sub-Commission may be accompanied by a nomination of an expert of the same nationality, who shall be elected simultaneously with the candidate for membership, and who may serve temporarily as an alternate if the member is unable to attend;

(b) The qualifications for alternates shall be the same as for members;

(c) No person may serve as alternate for a member except the expert elected as alternate, pursuant to subparagraph *(a)* above.

Economic and Social Council resolution 1983/32

27 May 1983   Meeting 15   36-6-9

Approved by Second Committee (E/1983/61) by vote (32-6-7), 23 May (meeting 18); draft by Commission on Human Rights (E/1983/13); orally amended in Council by President; agenda item 10.
Meeting number. ESC 15.

Also on 27 May, the Council adopted decision 1983/142 without vote.

Report of the Sub-Commission on Prevention of Discrimination and Protection of Minorities on its thirty-fifth session

At its 15th plenary meeting, on 27 May 1983, the Council, noting Commission on Human Rights resolution 1983/22 of 4 March 1983, endorsed the Commission's invitation to the Sub-Commission on Prevention of Discrimination and Protection of Minorities to be present, through its Chairman or another member it may designate, at the consideration of its report during the fortieth session of the Commission on Human Rights.

Economic and Social Council decision 1983/142

Adopted without vote

Approved by Second Committee (E/1983/61) without vote, 23 May (meeting 18); draft by Commission on Human Rights (E/1983/13); agenda item 10.
Meeting number. ESC 15.

Sub-Commission action. By a 5 September resolution, adopted by 12 votes to 1, with 6 abstentions,[43] the Sub-Commission recommended to the Commission a draft resolution for adoption. By the draft, the Commission would note the Sub-Commission's decision to establish a working group in 1984 to study its working methods, and request the Sub-Commission to authorize a five-day intersessional meeting of the group at Geneva during the Commission's 1985 session for an exchange of views with the Commission. The group was to report back to the Sub-Commission for final consideration of the latter's work programme and methods.

On 7 September,[44] the Sub-Commission adopted a new schedule for its 1984 session and for its pre-session Working Groups on communications alleging human rights violations, on slavery, and on indigenous populations. Also on that date,[45] it decided on the composition of those Working Groups.

By another decision of 7 September,[46] the Sub-Commission requested one of its members, Ivan Tosevski (Yugoslavia), to prepare for its 1984 session a discussion paper on how it could best prepare in future years the report to the Commission on human rights violations.

Proposed UN High Commissioner for Human Rights

The establishment of a post of United Nations High Commissioner for Human Rights, first proposed in 1965 by Costa Rica,[47] was discussed again in 1983 by the Commission on Human Rights and its Sub-Commission.

By a resolution of 10 March, adopted by a roll-call vote of 24 to 11, with 7 abstentions,[48] the Commission took note, and invited resubmission in 1984, of the Sub-Commission's proposals on the possible terms of reference for a High Commissioner, as contained in a September 1982 Sub-Commission resolution.[49] The Commission decided to continue consideration of the question in 1984.

In its 10 March resolution on programme and work methods (see above), the Commission noted that differing views on the creation of such a post had been expressed in its working group.[34]

Following further discussion of the matter, the Sub-Commission, on 6 September, adopted by 16 votes to 3, with 3 abstentions, a resolution spelling out arrangements for the High Commissioner's office if that post were to be established.[50]

Other measures to advance human rights

Advisory services

In 1983, advisory services of experts in the field of human rights were provided to three Governments: Bolivia, Equatorial Guinea and Uganda (see below).

On the thirty-fifth anniversary of the Universal Declaration of Human Rights (see above), an in-

ternational seminar (Geneva, 20 June–1 July) discussed the experiences of different countries in implementing international human rights standards.

In 1983, the Secretary-General received 86
governmental nominations for individual human
rights fellowships; within the financial resources
available, recommendations were made for awarding 26 fellowships to candidates from as many
countries. During the year, no training course was
organized under the programme.[51]

In an August report to the Sub-Commission on
technical assistance to States for the strengthening of their legal institutions (see below), the
Secretary-General also provided information on
the programme.

Bolivia

Following consideration of a second study on the
human rights situation in Bolivia,[52] submitted
by Special Envoy Héctor Gros Espiell (Uruguay),
appointed in 1981,[53] and the observations by the
Government of Bolivia,[54] the Commission on
Human Rights, on 8 March 1983, adopted a resolution which was endorsed subsequently by the
Economic and Social Council in decision 1983/146
(see below).

In the conclusions of his study, the Special
Envoy stated that international assistance, including that of the United Nations, was needed to help
ensure full observance of human rights and to assist in changing the adverse economic and social
circumstances in the country. The campaign
against hunger, poverty, disease and ignorance was
the major basic problem confronting human rights
in Bolivia, since under the democratic constitutional Government, respect for human rights had
been achieved inasmuch as they were no longer
directly violated by government action.

By its resolution of 8 March,[55] the Commission
thanked the Special Envoy and noted with satisfaction his conclusion that, particularly since the
establishment of a constitutional Government on
10 October 1982, Bolivia had demonstrated a complete respect for human rights. It further noted the
Government's determination to ensure a thorough
investigation of past human rights violations, and
welcomed the creation of a national commission
to investigate cases of disappearances, as well as
Bolivia's accession to the International Covenants
on Human Rights and the Optional Protocol to
the Covenant on Civil and Political Rights. It requested the Secretary-General to provide advisory
services and other human rights assistance upon
request and decided to conclude consideration of
the human rights situation in Bolivia.

During the Commission's session, in March,
discussions were held between the Chairman, the
Centre for Human Rights, the Special Envoy and
representatives of the Bolivian Government, on

possible assistance to that country in achieving
economic and political stability. Following a
government request of 7 July, the Special Envoy
visited the country from 8 to 13 December.

ECONOMIC AND SOCIAL COUNCIL ACTION

On the recommendation of its Second Committee, the Economic and Social Council adopted decision 1983/146 without vote.

Situation of human rights in Bolivia

At its 15th plenary meeting, on 27 May 1983, the
Council, noting Commission on Human Rights resolution 1983/33 of 8 March 1983, endorsed the Commission's decision to request the Secretary-General to provide advisory services and other forms of appropriate
human rights assistance as might be requested by the
constitutional Government of Bolivia.

Economic and Social Council decision 1983/146

Adopted without vote

Approved by Second Committee (E/1983/61) by vote (33-1-7), 23 May (meeting 18);
    draft by Commission on Human Rights (E/1983/13); agenda item 10.
Meeting number. ESC 15.

Equatorial Guinea

In 1983, efforts continued to implement the plan
of action for the restoration of human rights in
Equatorial Guinea, which had been proposed by
the Secretary-General in 1981 based on recommendations of a United Nations expert.[56]
Among those activities, meetings were held between the Government and officials of UNDP.

The Secretary-General submitted a report on
advisory services to Equatorial Guinea in 1982 to
the 1983 session of the Commission on Human
Rights.[57]

On 8 March,[58] the Commission recommended to the Economic and Social Council adoption of a draft resolution concerning the situation
in Equatorial Guinea. The Council subsequently
adopted resolution 1983/35 (see below).

ECONOMIC AND SOCIAL COUNCIL ACTION

On 27 May 1983, on the recommendation of its
Second Committee, the Economic and Social
Council adopted resolution 1983/35 without vote.

Situation of human rights in Equatorial Guinea

The Economic and Social Council,

Recalling its resolution 1982/36 of 7 May 1982,

Bearing in mind Commission on Human Rights resolution 1983/32 of 8 March 1983,

Mindful of the role that the United Nations could play
in the promotion, protection and restoration of human
rights and fundamental freedoms in the world,

Conscious of the request of the Government of
Equatorial Guinea for assistance in the restoration of
human rights and fundamental freedoms in that country with a view to ensuring, in particular, the right of
the population to participate in the management of public affairs in the country,

1. *Takes note* of the meetings held between the Permanent Representative of Equatorial Guinea to the United Nations and officials of the United Nations Development Programme;

2. *Takes note* of the report of the Secretary-General and of the report submitted by two constitutional experts, Mr. Rubén Hernández-Valle and Mr. Jorge Mario Laguardia, who were recruited by the Secretary-General, at the request of the Government of Equatorial Guinea, to assist the Equatorial Guinea National Commission to draft a constitution for that country;

3. *Encourages* the Government of Equatorial Guinea to continue to display the same spirit of co-operation in implementing the plan of action prepared by the Secretary-General at the request of the Government of Equatorial Guinea;

4. *Requests* the Secretary-General, in conjunction with the Government of Equatorial Guinea, to consider what further measures could be taken by the United Nations to assist that Government in the continued implementation of the plan of action and to report to the Commission on Human Rights at its fortieth session;

5. *Requests* the Commission on Human Rights, in the light of the Secretary-General's report, to reconsider this question at its fortieth session under the item entitled "Question of the violation of human rights and fundamental freedoms in any part of the world, with particular reference to colonial and other dependent countries and territories".

Economic and Social Council resolution 1983/35

27 May 1983   Meeting 15   Adopted without vote

Approved by Second Committee (E/1983/61) without vote, 23 May (meeting 18); draft by Commission on Human Rights (E/1983/13); agenda item 10.
Meeting number. ESC 15.

Uganda

In accordance with a May 1982 Economic and Social Council decision,[59] approving the Commission on Human Rights's request for the provision of consultative advisory services and other assistance to Uganda, the Secretary-General developed contacts with the Government and with various United Nations sectors and agencies. The Government submitted in January 1983 a statement of needs and projects[60] calling, in particular, for expert assistance in reviewing legislation, for the training of law librarians, legal clerks, penitentiary staff and police officers, and for the supply of books and other legal materials. Information on 1982 advisory services to Uganda was submitted by the Secretary-General[61] to the 1983 session of the Commission on Human Rights.

On 9 March,[62] the Commission requested the Secretary-General to continue his contacts with the Government of Uganda in order to help it continue guaranteeing the enjoyment of human rights. The Commission again invited States, the United Nations system and humanitarian and non-governmental organizations to assist Uganda, and decided to review the question in 1984.

Technical assistance to strengthen legal institutions

In August 1983, the Secretary-General reported to the Sub-Commission on technical assistance currently available to States in strengthening legal institutions to enhance respect for the rule of law.[63] The report also dealt with the United Nations programme of advisory services in the field of human rights and summarized information from the three Governments which had requested such services (see above), as well as from nine United Nations bodies and agencies.

Noting with appreciation the Secretary-General's report, the Sub-Commission on 6 September[64] requested him to invite Governments to indicate whether they felt the need to receive such technical assistance, and request Governments providing bilateral development assistance for information on the extent to which such assistance was or could be used to strengthen legal institutions in recipient countries. Special Rapporteur L. M. Singhvi (India) was requested to give consideration in his study—on the independence and impartiality of the judiciary, jurors and assessors and the independence of lawyers (see above, under DISCRIMINATION)—to the most appropriate means by which the international community could contribute to strengthening legal institutions, especially in developing countries, with a view to promoting full respect for human rights.

Draft declaration on promotion of human rights

On 8 March 1983,[65] the Commission on Human Rights welcomed the 1982 decision of the Sub-Commission to prepare draft principles on the right and responsibility of individuals, groups and organs of society to promote and protect universally recognized human rights, taking into account information from Governments and other sources.[66] The Commission decided to work on a draft declaration in 1985 on the basis of a Sub-Commission report containing the draft principles.

In September 1983, Special Rapporteur Erica-Irene A. Daes (Greece), appointed in 1982, orally presented to the Sub-Commission an outline and the basic elements for possible inclusion in the draft principles. On 7 September,[67] the Sub-Commission recommended to the Commission a draft for adoption by the Economic and Social Council requesting the Special Rapporteur to continue her work with a view to submitting a final report in 1984.

Proposed establishment of a new international humanitarian order

In a September 1983 report to the General Assembly,[68] the Secretary-General stated that no further views had been submitted on the proposal for the promotion of a new international humanitarian order, advanced by Jordan in 1981.[69]

GENERAL ASSEMBLY ACTION

On 16 December, on the recommendation of the Third Committee, the General Assembly adopted resolution 38/125 without vote.

New international humanitarian order

The General Assembly,

Recalling its resolutions 36/136 of 14 December 1981 and 37/201 of 18 December 1982,

Taking note of the reports of the Secretary-General,

Bearing in mind the need for seeking further the views of Governments regarding the proposal relating to a new international humanitarian order,

Noting the establishment in July 1983 of the Independent Commission on International Humanitarian Issues, outside the framework of the United Nations,

Recognizing that the work of the Independent Commission could be useful for further study of the proposal,

1. *Invites* Governments that have not yet done so to communicate to the Secretary-General their views regarding the proposal for the promotion of a new international humanitarian order;

2. *Requests* the Secretary-General to remain in contact with Governments, as well as with the Independent Commission on International Humanitarian Issues, in order to provide a comprehensive report on the subject to the General Assembly at its fortieth session;

3. *Decides* to review at its fortieth session the question of a new international humanitarian order.

General Assembly resolution 38/125

16 December 1983   Meeting 100   Adopted without vote

Approved by Third Committee (A/38/691) without vote, 9 December (meeting 71); 27-nation draft (A/C.3/38/L.55); agenda item 101.

Sponsors: Australia, Austria, Bahrain, Bangladesh, Canada, Chile, Costa Rica, Djibouti, Egypt, Greece, Iraq, Italy, Japan, Jordan, Lebanon, Mauritania, Oman, Pakistan, Qatar, Romania, Senegal, Somalia, Sudan, Tunisia, United Republic of Tanzania, Yemen, Yugoslavia.

Meeting numbers. GA 38th session: 3rd Committee 18, 71; plenary 100.

Regional arrangements

Report of the Secretary-General. In October 1983,[70] the Secretary-General submitted a report on regional arrangements for the promotion and protection of human rights, as requested by the General Assembly in December 1982.[71] In the report, which contained information from a number of intergovernmental and non-governmental organizations, he stated that the United Nations had continued to encourage such arrangements through seminars and other activities.

The Commission on Human Rights had standing arrangements with regional intergovernmental organizations, according to which the latter might submit reports to the Commission on their human rights activities. To enhance this co-operation further, the Secretary-General suggested the mutual exchange of observers on a regular basis, as well as periodic meetings between the Commission Chairman and the heads of regional commissions and regional courts on human rights.

As regards the secretariats, the Secretary-General noted that there were effectively operating informal contacts and co-operation; exchange of information and experience took place at annual informal consultative meetings of the heads of human rights secretariats in the United Nations system as well as of other international organizations, including the regional intergovernmental organizations.

Since regional arrangements had been established or were being discussed, the Secretary-General felt the policy-making organs might consider how United Nations promotional activities could be further developed in the various regions and subregions, including the possibility of having regional advisers on international human rights standards; such a system of advisers, the Secretary-General added, operated successfully within the framework of ILO with regard to international labour standards. More seminars could be held in various regions and subregions to discuss national experiences in the implementation of international human rights standards.

GENERAL ASSEMBLY ACTION

On 16 December, on the recommendation of the Third Committee, the General Assembly adopted resolution 38/97 without vote.

Regional arrangements for the protection of human rights

The General Assembly,

Recalling its resolutions 32/127 of 16 December 1977, 33/167 of 20 December 1978, 34/171 of 17 December 1979, 35/197 of 15 December 1980, 36/154 of 16 December 1981 and 37/171 and 37/172 of 17 December 1982 concerning regional arrangements for the promotion and protection of human rights,

Having considered the report of the Secretary-General on regional arrangements for the promotion and protection of human rights,

1. *Takes note* of the report of the Secretary-General;

2. *Expresses its thanks* to the specialized agencies, the regional commissions and the regional intergovernmental organizations, as well as the non-governmental organizations concerned, which contributed to the preparation of that report;

3. *Invites* the specialized agencies, the regional commissions and the regional intergovernmental organizations which have not yet been able to do so to communicate to the Secretary-General their views on exchanges of information between the United Nations and the regional organizations and bodies for the promotion and protection of human rights, together with their views on ways and means of furthering such exchanges;

4. *Invites* the Secretary-General to submit to the General Assembly at its thirty-ninth session a further report amplifying the report prepared in accordance with resolution 37/172;

5. *Decides* to consider this question further at its thirty-ninth session.

General Assembly resolution 38/97

16 December 1983   Meeting 100   Adopted without vote

Approved by Third Committee (A/38/680) without vote, 7 December (meeting 67); 15-nation draft (A/C.3/38/L.58); agenda item 12.

Sponsors: Australia, Austria, Belgium, Colombia, Costa Rica, Cyprus, Ecuador, France, Gambia, Guinea, Italy, Netherlands, Senegal, Togo, Uruguay.

Meeting numbers. GA 38th session: 3rd Committee 18, 54, 55, 57-67; plenary 100.

Public information activities

In a February 1983 report to the Commission on Human Rights on public information activities in the field of human rights,[72] the Secretary-General stated that activities by the United Nations Department of Public Information (DPI) included coverage of relevant meetings, publications, audio and visual programmes, and special programmes and information dissemination by information centres and services. In accordance with the Commission's March 1982 request to consider establishing in United Nations offices, particularly in developing countries, reference libraries for human rights,[73] preparations were made to set up the basis for a reference facility in the United Nations Centre for Human Rights.

On 10 March,[1] the Commission requested Governments, as well as the Secretary-General, to promote various public information activities in the human rights field (see above).

Human rights education

On 31 August 1983,[74] the Sub-Commission recommended to the Commission on Human Rights adoption of a draft resolution commending UNESCO for its work in the field of education to combat racism and racial discrimination. The Commission would also appeal to States to encourage educational institutions, particularly at the primary level, to incorporate in their curricula, among other things, the concept of the oneness of the human race; the social, economic, cultural and political interdependence of all peoples; and such basic human needs and aspirations as self-identity, the need to belong to and participate in the life of a larger community, and the need of all groups to develop a sense of cultural identity.

The General Assembly, in resolution 38/57 of 9 December, urged UNESCO, in co-operation with Governments, to spread the teaching of human rights in all educational institutions, and requested the Director-General of that organization to report to the Assembly in 1988, on the fortieth anniversary of the Universal Declaration of Human Rights, on efforts made to those ends.

REFERENCES

[1]E/1983/13 (res. 1983/50). [2]YUN 1982, p. 1098, GA res. 37/200, 18 Dec. 1982. [3]A/38/511. [4]YUN 1981, p. 926. [5]A/C.3/38/L.46. [6]YUN 1982, p. 1097, GA res. 37/199, 18 Dec. 1982. [7]A/38/416. [8]YUN 1981, p. 941, GA res. 36/134, 14 Dec. 1981. [9]*Ibid.*, p. 941. [10]YUN 1979, p. 854. [11]YUN 1966, p. 419, GA res. 2200 A (XXI), annex, 16 Dec. 1966. [12]YUN 1965, p. 440,

GA res. 2106 A (XX), annex, 21 Dec. 1965. [13]YUN 1948-49, p. 959, GA res. 260 A (III), annex, 9 Dec. 1948. [14]YUN 1973, p. 103, GA res. 3068(XXVIII), annex, 30 Nov. 1973. [15]YUN 1953, p. 411, GA res. 794(VIII), 23 Oct. 1953. [16]YUN 1956, p. 228. [17]YUN 1948-49, p. 613, GA res. 317(IV), annex, 2 Dec. 1949. [18]E/CN.4/Sub.2/1983/35. [19]E/CN.4/Sub.2/1983/28. [20]E/CN.4/1984/3 (res. 1983/27). [21]YUN 1979, p. 895, GA res. 34/180, annex, 18 Dec. 1979. [22]YUN 1948-49, p. 535, GA res. 217 A (III), 10 Dec. 1948. [23]A/38/710. [24]A/38/733. [25]A/INF/38/2 & Add.1 & Add.1/Corr.1. [26]YUN 1950, p. 535, GA res. 423(V), 4 Dec. 1950. [27]E/CN.4/1983/29. [28]E/1983/13 (res. 1983/17). [29]E/1983/13. [30]*Ibid.* (dec. 1983/101). [31]*Ibid.* (dec. 1983/102). [32]YUN 1982, p. 1099. [33]E/CN.4/1983/64. [34]E/1983/13 (res. 1983/51). [35]*Ibid.* (dec. 1983/108). [36]E/CN.4/1983/65. [37]E/1983/13 (dec. 1983/113). [38]*Ibid.* (dec. 1983/109). [39]YUN 1982, p. 1100, ESC dec. 1982/156, 28 July 1982. [40]E/CN.4/1983/4. [41]E/1983/13 (res. 1983/22). [42]*Ibid.* (res. 1983/21). [43]E/CN.4/1984/3 (res. 1983/21). [44]*Ibid.* (dec. 1983/7). [45]*Ibid.* (dec. 1983/12). [46]*Ibid.* (dec. 1983/9). [47]YUN 1965, p. 494. [48]E/1983/13 (res. 1983/49). [49]YUN 1982, p. 1101. [50]E/CN.4/1984/3 & Corr.2(res. 1983/36). [51]E/CN.4/1984/44. [52]E/CN.4/1983/22. [53]YUN 1981, p. 957. [54]E/CN.4/1983/22/Add.1. [55]E/1983/13 (res. 1983/33). [56]YUN 1981, p. 938. [57]E/CN.4/1983/17. [58]E/1983/13 (res. 1983/32). [59]YUN 1982, p. 1105, ESC dec. 1982/139, 7 May 1982. [60]E/CN.4/1983/31/Add.1. [61]E/CN.4/1983/31. [62]E/1983/13 (res. 1983/47). [63]E/CN.4/Sub.2/1983/23. [64]E/CN.4/1984/3 (res. 1983/38). [65]E/1983/13 (res. 1983/31). [66]YUN 1982, p. 1105. [67]E/CN.4/1984/3 (res. 1983/40). [68]A/38/450. [69]YUN 1981, p. 968. [70]A/38/480. [71]YUN 1982, p. 1106, GA res. 37/172, 17 Dec. 1982. [72]E/CN.4/1983/15. [73]YUN 1982, p. 1107. [74]E/CN.4/1984/3 (res. 1983/3).

PUBLICATIONS

Human Rights: A Compilation of International Instruments (ST/HR/1/Rev.2), Sales No. E.83.XIV.1. *United Nations Action in the Field of Human Rights* (ST/HR/2/Rev.2), Sales No. E.83.XIV.2.

Human rights violations

Situations involving alleged violations of human rights on a large scale in several countries were again examined in 1983 by the General Assembly, the Economic and Social Council and the Commission on Human Rights, as well as by special bodies and officials appointed to examine some of those situations.

In addition, situations of alleged human rights violations involving the self-determination of peoples (see above, under CIVIL AND POLITICAL RIGHTS) were discussed with regard to Afghanistan, East Timor, Kampuchea, South Africa and Namibia, Western Sahara and the Palestinian people. The Commission also dealt with the human rights situation in Bolivia, Equatorial Guinea and Uganda, to which the United Nations provided advisory services (see above, under ADVANCEMENT OF HUMAN RIGHTS).

Under a procedure established in 1970 by the Economic and Social Council to deal with communications alleging denial or violation of human rights,[1] the Commission held closed meetings during its 1983 session to study confidential documents, observations submitted by States and a confidential report by a working group which had examined the material. The Commission maintained all such action confidential. By a decision adopted on 28 February at a closed meeting, and agreed to be made public on 11 March,[2] the Commission decided to set up a working group of five of its members to meet for one week prior to the Commission's 1984 session to examine particular situations referred by the Sub-Commission and those of which the Commission was seized.

On 4 March,[3] the Commission decided to postpone consideration of a draft resolution recommended by the Sub-Commission on Prevention of Discrimination and Protection of Minorities in September 1982,[4] by which the Council would authorize the Sub-Commission to arrange for one or more of its members to visit any country on which reliably attested allegations of gross and consistent human rights violations were received, in order to examine such situations first hand.

At its annual session from 1 to 12 August 1983, the Sub-Commission's five-member Working Group on Communications, established in 1971,[5] also examined on a confidential basis communications alleging human rights violations. After considering the Group's report at four closed meetings, the Sub-Commission adopted, on 7 September, a confidential report communicating its findings to the Commission. On 6 September,[6] the Sub-Commission decided to defer until 1984 consideration of a draft resolution and amendments thereto, concerning possible expansion of the Group's membership in view of the increase in number of communications alleging human rights violations. In related action on 7 September,[7] it requested one of its members, Ivan Tosevski (Yugoslavia), to prepare for its 1984 session a discussion paper on how it could best prepare in future years the report to the Commission on human rights violations.

ECONOMIC AND SOCIAL COUNCIL ACTION

On the recommendation of its Second Committee, the Economic and Social Council adopted decision 1983/153 without vote.

General decision concerning the establishment of a working group of the Commission on Human Rights to examine situations referred to the Commission under Economic and Social Council resolution 1503(XLVIII) and those situations of which the Commission is seized

At its 15th plenary meeting, on 27 May 1983, the Council approved the decision of the Commission on Human Rights, in its decision 1983/110 of 28 February 1983, to set up a working group composed of five of its members to meet for one week prior to the fortieth session to examine such particular situations as might be referred to the Commission by the Sub-Commission on Prevention of Discrimination and Protection of Minori-

ties at its thirty-sixth session under Economic and Social Council resolution 1503(XLVIII) and those situations of which the Commission is seized.

Economic and Social Council decision 1983/153
Adopted without vote

Approved by Second Committee (E/1983/61) without vote, 23 May (meeting 18); draft by Commission on Human Rights (E/1983/13); agenda item 10. *Meeting number.* ESC 15.

GENERAL ASSEMBLY ACTION

In resolution 38/124 of 16 December on alternative approaches for improving the enjoyment of human rights, the General Assembly reiterated that the international community should continue to accord priority to the search for solutions to mass and flagrant violations of the human rights of peoples and individuals. It reaffirmed that consistent patterns of human rights violations, wherever they existed, were of concern to the United Nations.

Africa

South Africa and Namibia

General aspects

In 1983, the *Ad Hoc* Working Group of Experts on Southern Africa submitted to the Commission on Human Rights a progress report on developments concerning policies and practices violating human rights in South Africa and Namibia. Human rights violations there were also dealt with by the Commission in several resolutions. The Economic and Social Council, by decision 1983/135 of 27 May, endorsed the Commission's decision to renew the Working Group's mandate.

Apartheid, racial discrimination and other aspects of the human rights situation in South Africa and Namibia were also dealt with at the Second World Conference to Combat Racism and Racial Discrimination, held at Geneva in August 1983 (see above, under DISCRIMINATION).

As in previous years, the Special Committee against *Apartheid* observed the International Day for the Elimination of Racial Discrimination at two meetings on 21 March,[8] the day when 69 demonstrators against the "pass laws" of the *apartheid* system were killed and 180 others were wounded at Sharpeville, South Africa, in 1960. Further, the Committee observed, on 16 June, the International Day of Solidarity with the Struggling People of South Africa.

Working Group report. The *Ad Hoc* Working Group of Experts on Southern Africa—established in 1967 by the Commission on Human Rights[9] and composed of six members appointed by the Commission and acting in their personal capacities—submitted in January 1983 a report on developments since 1980 concerning policies and practices violating human rights in South Africa and Namibia.[10] The Group had last submitted a report on the topic in 1981.[11] The 1983 report was based mainly on the analysis of published information and on information received in the form of oral testimony and written communications from individuals and organizations during the Group's mission of inquiry (12 July–3 August 1982); 59 witnesses were heard at closed and public meetings.

The report dealt with a wide range of issues, including capital punishment, detainees and political prisoners, forced removals of population and the "homelands" policy, and other serious human rights violations resulting from *apartheid* and racial discrimination. It provided information on persons suspected of being guilty of the crime of *apartheid* or of a serious human rights violation, and summarized the results of conferences, symposia and seminars pertaining to South Africa and Namibia.

In its conclusions, the Group stated that the constitutional developments in South Africa which had in the past ignored the interests of the black population continued to evolve in a discriminatory manner: the blacks were denied any role in the so-called constitutional proposals aimed at establishing three assemblies in which whites, Coloured and Asian population groups were to have representation; without consulting the affected population and contrary to the right to self-determination, the South African Government had planned to cede most of the KaNgwane "homeland" and the Ingwavuma area in Transvaal to Swaziland; and the granting of so-called independence to the homelands contributed to the disruption of national unity and the identity of black South Africans. In the Ciskei, as well as in other so-called independent homelands, security laws were introduced sanctioning *apartheid*. A new law—the Orderly Movement and Settlement of Black Persons Bill—raised the penalty for being in so-called white areas without permission.

The Group also found that: the right to life was violated by South African security forces inside and outside South Africa; the Geneva Conventions of 12 August 1949 for the protection of war victims, to which South Africa was a party, were not applied to captured freedom fighters; torture was used during interrogation of suspects; the number of disappeared persons had increased; the conditions of black workers had not changed fundamentally; strikes by black workers were treated as criminal acts; and the rate of unemployed blacks remained high and unemployed blacks were forcibly removed from urban centres to the so-called homelands.

In Namibia, the Group noted that the human rights situation had not improved—security laws

and measures had been strengthened, resulting in frequent infringements of guaranteed individual freedoms, such as the right to free choice of residence, freedom of movement and freedom of assembly and association. Though noting with satisfaction the beneficial effects of the activities by international organizations in securing a better situation of prisoners and detainees, the Group stated that there was no overall improvement in the situation of political prisoners. Persons disappeared or were indefinitely detained without trial; South African authorities continued to torture political prisoners and captured freedom fighters.

The Group recommended that the Commission denounce as discriminatory and racist the draft constitutional proposals by the South African Government, which denied the black population their birthright as South African citizens. Further recommendations included the strengthening of international campaigns whenever the life of political activists in South Africa was in danger; the study of the question of "sovereignty" of the homelands and the use of that policy to maintain *apartheid;* establishment by ILO of a list of jobs for which an adequate and thorough training for black workers was not guaranteed, and a request to Member States to offer all possible assistance to black South Africans to enable them to acquire professional training particularly in fields where they were denied such training in South Africa. The Group also made recommendations to promote further the 1973 International Convention on the Suppression and Punishment of the Crime of *Apartheid* (see below).

As regards Namibia, the Group recommended that the Commission call on United Nations organs to redouble their efforts to achieve an overall political solution to the Namibia question as rapidly as possible, in accordance with United Nations resolutions. It also invited the Commission to: recommend the adoption of measures on behalf of Namibian refugees, and assist and encourage Governments to take them into their territory; condemn frequent violations of the territorial integrity of the African States adjoining Namibia, recommend measures to avoid their repetition, and call for immediate and unconditional withdrawal of South African forces from Angola; and ensure that the South African authorities granted the captured freedom fighters and political prisoners the status provided for in the 1949 Geneva Conventions and Additional Protocol I thereto.

The Group reaffirmed the need to continue seeking information on the human rights situation in Namibia, especially by collecting evidence from Namibian refugees in the neighbouring countries, and for the Commission to persuade States to ratify the 1973 Convention against *apartheid*. It requested the Commission to encourage all individuals to report any human rights violations by South Africa and recommended the organization of a seminar to investigate ways of securing the rapid elimination of *apartheid*.

Also in January, the Group, in pursuance of a 1981 request by the Commission,[12] gave a brief summary[13] of two 1980 reports: one by the Secretary-General on *apartheid* as a collective form of slavery, and the other on child labour in South Africa, submitted to the Working Group on Slavery by the Anti-Slavery Society for the Protection of Human Rights.

Another January 1983 report provided information on the effects of *apartheid* on black women and children in South Africa (see below).

Action by the Commission on Human Rights. By an 18 February resolution adopted by a roll-call vote of 42 to none,[14] the Commission congratulated the Working Group on the quality of the report and took note of its conclusions and recommendations. It affirmed that any constitutional arrangement in South Africa based on racial segregation constituted a denial of the political rights of the black population, and denounced the policy of "bantustanization".

The Commission expressed profound indignation at the scale and variety of human rights violations in South Africa, in particular: the increased number of sentences and executions; the torture of political activists during interrogation; the ill-treatment of captured freedom fighters and other detainees; and the deaths of detainees in South African prisons under suspicious circumstances. It expressed deep indignation at the continued practice of child labour, exploitation of black women and children, and discriminatory harassment and imprisonment of young blacks. It demanded that South Africa put an end to the policies and practices which violated the rights of the African population, especially women and children, and appealed for urgent action by the international community to save the lives of Bobby Tsotsobe, Johannes Shabangu, Jerry Mosololi, Simon Mogoerane, David Moise and Marcus Motaung, condemned to death as a result of their opposition to *apartheid*. The Commission also condemned South Africa's military attacks against neighbouring countries, such as Angola, Lesotho and Mozambique, and demanded their cessation (see POLITICAL AND SECURITY QUESTIONS, Chapter V).

The Commission decided that the Group should continue to study the policies and practices violating human rights in South Africa and Namibia and asked it to submit its findings in 1985, with a progress report in 1984. The Commission also requested the Group, in co-operation with the Special Committee against *Apartheid*, to continue to investigate the cases of torture, ill-treatment and

deaths of detainees and to bring cases of particularly serious violations to the attention of the Commission Chairman. It authorized the Group to organize in 1984 a seminar on the most effective means of reinforcing the Commission's efforts to eliminate *apartheid*.

The Commission requested the Economic and Social Council to transmit the resolution to the General Assembly, the Security Council, the Committee against *Apartheid* and the United Nations Council for Namibia.

The Economic and Social Council followed that request in decision 1983/136 of 27 May (see below).

By another resolution of 18 February, adopted by a roll-call vote of 37 to none, with 5 abstentions,[15] the Commission reaffirmed the inalienable right of the Namibian people to self-determination and independence, and called on South Africa to comply with all Security Council and Commission resolutions on Namibia. It demanded that South Africa cease all acts of torture and ill-treatment of Namibian political detainees and prisoners, release all Namibian political prisoners, and grant prisoner-of-war status to the captured freedom fighters and treat them in accordance with the 1949 Geneva Conventions and Additional Protocol I.

The Commission requested the *Ad Hoc* Working Group of Experts to study as a priority matter the policies and practices violating human rights in Namibia, and to continue to institute inquiries in respect of any persons suspected of having committed in Namibia the crime of *apartheid* or a serious human rights violation, and to bring the results of those inquiries to the Commission's attention in 1984. It reiterated its request that South Africa allow the Working Group to make an on-the-spot investigation of the prison living conditions and the treatment of prisoners in Namibia and South Africa.

In a resolution of 15 February on the right of the South African and Namibian peoples to self-determination (see above, under CIVIL AND POLITICAL RIGHTS), the Commission strongly condemned the continued violations of the human rights of peoples still under colonial and foreign domination and condemned South Africa for its brutal repression and indiscriminate torture and killing of opponents of *apartheid*.

ECONOMIC AND SOCIAL COUNCIL ACTION

On the recommendation of its Second Committee, the Economic and Social Council adopted decision 1983/136 without vote.

Violations of human rights in southern Africa: transmittal of Commission on Human Rights resolution 1983/9

At its 15th plenary meeting, on 27 May 1983, the Council, noting Commission on Human Rights resolution 1983/9 of 18 February 1983, and pursuant to the Commission's request contained in paragraph 22 of that resolution, decided to transmit that resolution to the General Assembly, the Security Council, the Special Committee against *Apartheid* and the United Nations Council for Namibia.

Economic and Social Council decision 1983/136

Adopted without vote

Approved by Second Committee (E/1983/61) without vote, 23 May (meeting 18); draft by Commission on Human Rights (E/1983/13); agenda item 10.
Meeting number. ESC 15.

Also on the recommendation of its Second Committee, the Council adopted decision 1983/135 without vote.

Violations of human rights in southern Africa: report of the *Ad Hoc* Working Group of Experts

At its 15th plenary meeting, on 27 May 1983, the Council, noting Commission on Human Rights resolution 1983/9 of 18 February 1983, endorsed the Commission's decisions to renew the mandate of the *Ad Hoc* Working Group of Experts, to request the Group to submit a report on its findings to the Commission at its forty-first session at the latest, and to submit a progress report to the Commission at its fortieth session. The Council also endorsed the Commission's decisions to authorize the *Ad Hoc* Working Group to organize in 1984 a seminar to consider the most effective means of reinforcing the Commission's efforts to eliminate *apartheid*, racism and racial discrimination and to authorize the Chairman of the *Ad Hoc* Working Group of Experts to participate in conferences, symposia, seminars or other events connected with the action against *apartheid* organized under the auspices of the Special Committee against *Apartheid* and the United Nations Council for Namibia.

The Council requested the Secretary-General to provide every assistance within available resources to enable the *Ad Hoc* Working Group of Experts to discharge its responsibilities in accordance with paragraphs 17 and 18 of Commission resolution 1983/9 and with its terms of reference.

Economic and Social Council decision 1983/135

Adopted without vote

Approved by Second Committee (E/1983/61) without vote, 23 May (meeting 18); draft by Commission on Human Rights (E/1983/13); agenda item 10.
Meeting number. ESC 15.

Sub-Commission action. On 5 September,[16] the Sub-Commission on Prevention of Discrimination and Protection of Minorities noted with particular concern that the South African Constitution, denying the majority of the black population the franchise as well as the right to occupy judicial posts, put the judiciary and its impartiality as well as the whole judicial system into serious doubt, especially in cases involving the conflicting interests of the ruling white minority and the disenfranchised black majority; under those circumstances, that Constitution did not provide for a fair and just judicial system. The Sub-Commission strongly condemned the South African régime's continuing campaign of repressions, detentions and persecution of those fighting its *apartheid* policies, and condemned in particular the June 1983 execution of three young South African militants for their involvement in the liberation struggle, as well as the continuing spate of political trials and the continued imprisonment of Nelson Mandela and other political prisoners. It called on the Commission to investigate the situation urgently and seek action and intervention by the General Assembly.

Note of the Secretary-General. By a note of 22 September,[17] the Secretary-General drew the General Assembly's attention to the report of the *Ad Hoc* Working Group,[10] as well as two other reports submitted by it, on *apartheid* as a collective form of slavery[13] and on the effects of the policy of *apartheid* on black women and children in South Africa (see below).

GENERAL ASSEMBLY ACTION

In resolution 38/39 A on the situation in South Africa, the General Assembly strongly condemned the South African régime for its brutal repression of opponents of *apartheid*, its torture and killing of detainees, its execution of freedom fighters, and its repeated acts of aggression, subversion and terrorism against independent African States. It demanded that South Africa release persons imprisoned or restricted for their opposition to *apartheid*, terminate all political trials and all repressive measures against opponents of *apartheid*, allow those exiled for their opposition to *apartheid* to return unconditionally to their country, and rescind bans on organizations and media opposed to *apartheid*. The Assembly reaffirmed that freedom fighters should be treated as prisoners of war in accordance with Additional Protocol I to the 1949 Geneva Conventions and condemned the policy of "bantustanization" designed to dispossess the African majority of its rights and to deprive it of citizenship, as well as the continuing forced removal of black people.

In resolution 38/17, on the right of peoples to self-determination, the Assembly strongly condemned the continued human rights violations of peoples under colonial domination and alien subjugation, the continuation of the illegal occupation of Namibia, South Africa's attempts to dismember its territory and the perpetuation of the racist minority régime in southern Africa.

(For further Assembly action on South Africa, see POLITICAL AND SECURITY QUESTIONS, Chapter V; for Assembly action on Namibia, see TRUSTEESHIP AND DECOLONIZATION, Chapter III).

Women and children under apartheid

In January 1983, the *Ad Hoc* Working Group of Experts presented to the Commission on

Human Rights a report,[18] updating a 1982 study,[19] on the effects of *apartheid* on black women and children in South Africa, based on information obtained during a mission of inquiry in July/August 1982 (see POLITICAL AND SECURITY QUESTIONS, Chapter V).

The Commission, on 18 February,[14] expressed deep indignation at the scale and variety of human rights violations in South Africa, including the continued exploitation of black women and children, who suffered the most from the policies and practices of *apartheid* (see above).

1973 Convention against apartheid

As at 31 December 1983, there were 77 parties to the 1973 International Convention on the Suppression and Punishment of the Crime of *Apartheid*.[20] During the year, eight States— Afghanistan, Bolivia, the Congo, China, Lesotho, Mozambique, Venezuela and Zambia—acceded to the Convention.

The Secretary-General annexed to a report to the General Assembly on the status of the Convention a list of States which had signed, ratified or acceded to it as of 1 September.[21]

Activities of the Group of Three. The Group of Three, established under article IX of the Convention to consider reports by States parties on measures taken to implement the Convention's provisions, held its sixth session from 24 to 28 January 1983 at Geneva.[22] As in 1982, the Group consisted of Bulgaria, Mexico and Zaire. The Commission on Human Rights, on 11 March 1983,[23] took note of the Group's composition.

At its 1983 session, the Group considered first (initial) reports from Cape Verde, Ecuador, Peru, and Saint Vincent and the Grenadines. Second periodic reports were filed by Czechoslovakia, India and Yugoslavia, and third periodic reports by Bulgaria, Cuba, Iraq, Poland and the Ukrainian SSR. Representatives of these States, except for Cape Verde and Saint Vincent and the Grenadines, attended the meetings to supplement the information in the reports.

In its conclusions and recommendations, the Group again expressed the opinion that the presence of States' representatives at its meetings in connection with the consideration of reports should be continued. It called on States parties to provide more information on the legislative, judicial and administrative measures adopted to implement article IV of the Convention (on suppression or prevention of encouragement of *apartheid* and prosecution and punishment for the crime of *apartheid*). The Group also called for more information on concrete cases in which measures had been applied to prosecute, bring to trial and punish persons responsible for, or accused of, "crimes of *apartheid*", as defined in article II. It called on

States to identify in their reports individuals, organizations, institutions and representatives of States deemed responsible for such crimes, as well as those against whom legal proceedings were undertaken by the State party, to enable the Commission to continue updating its list under article X. It also drew their attention to the importance of article XI stipulating that "crimes of *apartheid*" should not be considered political crimes for the purpose of extradition.

It requested international organizations to intensify the publication and dissemination of materials concerning problems of racial discrimination, in particular *apartheid*.

Action by the Commission on Human Rights. By a resolution of 18 February,[24] adopted by a roll-call vote of 31 to 1, with 10 abstentions, the Commission on Human Rights took note of the report of the Group of Three. It again requested the Secretary-General to invite States parties to comment on the interim study on ways of ensuring implementation of international instruments, including the establishment of international jurisdiction envisaged by the Convention, submitted in 1981 by the *Ad Hoc* Working Group of Experts on Southern Africa.[25] It called on States parties to strengthen their co-operation to implement United Nations decisions on *apartheid* and stated the desirability of disseminating information on the Convention. It again requested the Group of Three to examine whether the actions of transnational corporations operating in South Africa came under the definition of the crime of *apartheid*, and whether or not some legal action could be taken under the Convention. The Commission decided that the Group should meet for no more than five days before its 1984 session.

GENERAL ASSEMBLY ACTION

On 22 November, on the recommendation of the Third Committee, the General Assembly adopted resolution 38/19 by recorded vote.

Status of the International Convention on the Suppression and Punishment of the Crime of *Apartheid*
The General Assembly,
Recalling its resolution 3068(XXVIII) of 30 November 1973, by which it adopted and opened for signature and ratification the International Convention on the Suppression and Punishment of the Crime of *Apartheid*, and its subsequent resolutions on the status of the Convention,
Reaffirming its conviction that *apartheid* constitutes a total negation of the purposes and principles of the Charter of the United Nations, a gross violation of human rights and a crime against humanity, seriously threatening international peace and security,
Convinced that the Declaration and the Programme of Action adopted by the Second World Conference to Combat Racism and Racial Discrimination and their full implementation will contribute to the final eradi-

cation of *apartheid* and all other forms of racism and racial discrimination,

Strongly condemning South Africa's continued policy of *apartheid* and its continued illegal occupation of Namibia, as well as its repeated acts of aggression against sovereign African States, which constitute a manifest breach of international peace and security,

Condemning the continued collaboration of certain States and transnational corporations with the racist régime of South Africa in the political, economic, military and other fields as an encouragement to the intensification of its odious policy of *apartheid*,

Underlining that the strengthening of the existing mandatory arms embargo and the application of comprehensive mandatory economic sanctions under Chapter VII of the Charter are vital in order to compel the racist régime of South Africa to abandon its policy of *apartheid*,

Firmly convinced that the legitimate struggle of the oppressed peoples in southern Africa against *apartheid*, racism and colonialism and for the effective implementation of their inalienable right to self-determination and independence demands more than ever all necessary support by the international community and, in particular, further action by the Security Council,

Underlining that ratification of and accession to the Convention on a universal basis and the implementation of its provisions without any delay are necessary for its effectiveness and would be a useful contribution towards achieving the complete elimination of *apartheid*,

1. *Takes note* of the report of the Secretary-General on the status of the International Convention on the Suppression and Punishment of the Crime of *Apartheid;*

2. *Commends* those States parties to the Convention that have submitted their reports under article VII thereof;

3. *Appeals once again* to those States that have not yet done so to ratify or to accede to the Convention without further delay;

4. *Expresses its appreciation* of the constructive role played by the Group of Three of the Commission on Human Rights, established in accordance with article IX of the Convention, in analysing the periodic reports of States and in publicizing the experience gained in the international struggle against the crime of *apartheid;*

5. *Requests* States parties to the Convention to take fully into account the guidelines prepared by the Group of Three;

6. *Calls upon* all States parties to the Convention to implement fully article IV thereof by adopting legislative, judicial and administrative measures to prosecute, bring to trial and punish, in accordance with their jurisdiction, persons responsible for, or accused of, the acts enumerated in article II of the Convention;

7. *Requests* the Commission on Human Rights to continue to undertake the functions set out in article X of the Convention and invites the Commission to intensify, in co-operation with the Special Committee against *Apartheid*, its efforts to compile periodically the progressive list of individuals, organizations, institutions and representatives of States deemed responsible for crimes enumerated in article II of the Convention, as well as those against whom or which legal proceedings have been undertaken;

8. *Requests* the Secretary-General to distribute the above-mentioned list among all States parties to the Con-

vention and all Member States and to bring such facts to the attention of the public by all the means of mass communication;

9. *Appeals* to all States, United Nations organs, specialized agencies and international and national non-governmental organizations to step up their activities in enhancing public awareness by denouncing the crimes committed by the racist régime of South Africa;

10. *Requests* the Secretary-General to intensify his efforts, through appropriate channels, to disseminate information on the Convention and its implementation with a view to promoting further ratification of or accession to the Convention;

11. *Requests* the Secretary-General to include in his next annual report under General Assembly resolution 3380(XXX) of 10 November 1975 a special section concerning the implementation of the Convention.

General Assembly resolution 38/19

22 November 1983   Meeting 66   110-1-23 (recorded vote)

Approved by Third Committee (A/38/543) by recorded vote (107-1-23), 25 October (meeting 20); 24-nation draft (A/C.3/38/L.5); agenda item 87 (c).

Sponsors: Afghanistan, Algeria, Angola, Bulgaria, Cape Verde, Congo, Cuba, Czechoslovakia, Ecuador, German Democratic Republic, Guinea-Bissau, Hungary, Iraq, Lao People's Democratic Republic, Madagascar, Mauritania, Mongolia, Mozambique, Nigeria, Rwanda, Ukrainian SSR, Viet Nam, Zambia, Zimbabwe.

Meeting numbers. GA 38th session: 3rd Committee 4-18, 20; plenary 66.

Recorded vote in Assembly as follows:

In favour: Afghanistan, Albania, Algeria, Angola, Argentina, Bahamas, Bahrain, Bangladesh, Bhutan, Bolivia, Botswana, Brazil, Bulgaria, Burma, Burundi, Byelorussian SSR, Cape Verde, Chad, Chile, China, Colombia, Congo, Costa Rica, Cuba, Cyprus, Czechoslovakia, Democratic Kampuchea, Democratic Yemen, Djibouti, Dominican Republic, Ecuador, Egypt, El Salvador, Ethiopia, Fiji, Gabon, German Democratic Republic, Guatemala, Guinea, Guinea-Bissau, Guyana, Honduras, Hungary, India, Indonesia, Iran, Iraq, Jamaica, Jordan, Kenya, Kuwait, Lao People's Democratic Republic, Lebanon, Lesotho, Liberia, Libyan Arab Jamahiriya, Madagascar, Malaysia, Maldives, Mali, Malta, Mauritania, Mauritius, Mexico, Morocco, Mozambique, Nepal, Nicaragua, Nigeria, Oman, Pakistan, Panama, Papua New Guinea, Peru, Philippines, Poland, Qatar, Romania, Rwanda, Saint Lucia, Samoa, Sao Tome and Principe, Saudi Arabia, Senegal, Singapore, Solomon Islands, Somalia, Sri Lanka, Sudan, Suriname, Syrian Arab Republic, Thailand, Togo, Trinidad and Tobago, Tunisia, Turkey, Uganda, Ukrainian SSR, USSR, United Arab Emirates, United Republic of Cameroon, United Republic of Tanzania, Upper Volta, Uruguay, Venezuela, Viet Nam, Yemen, Yugoslavia, Zaire, Zambia.

Against: United States.

Abstaining: Australia, Austria, Belgium, Canada, Denmark, Finland, France, Germany, Federal Republic of, Greece, Iceland, Ireland, Italy, Japan, Luxembourg, Malawi, Netherlands, New Zealand, Norway, Portugal, Spain, Swaziland, Sweden, United Kingdom.

In resolution 38/39 A on the situation in South Africa, the Assembly also called on States to accede to the Convention.

Foreign support of South Africa

Action by the Commission on Human Rights. Having examined a June 1982 report[26] of Special Rapporteur Ahmed Mohamed Khalifa (Egypt) which updated a list of banks, transnational corporations (TNCs) and other organizations assisting South Africa, the Commission on Human Rights, by a resolution of 18 February 1983 adopted by a roll-call vote of 30 to 4, with 8 abstentions,[27] welcomed the September 1982 decision of the Sub-Commission to mandate the Special Rapporteur to continue updating the list, subject to annual review. It called on the Governments of countries where the institutions named were based to stop their activities in South Africa and Namibia and to end all technological assistance or collaboration in the military or nuclear field. It urgently requested all specialized agencies, particularly IMF and the World Bank, to refrain from granting loans to the South African régime.

In a 15 February resolution, on the right to self-determination of the peoples of South Africa and Namibia (see above, under CIVIL AND POLITICAL RIGHTS), the Commission condemned all collaboration, particularly in the nuclear, military and economic fields; the policies of Western and other countries whose relations with South Africa encouraged that régime to persist in suppressing the aspirations of peoples to self-determination and independence; and the continuing activities of foreign economic and other interests impeding the implementation of the 1960 Declaration on the Granting of Independence to Colonial Countries and Peoples[28] with respect to colonial Territories, particularly Namibia.

In a resolution of 18 February on implementation of the Convention against *apartheid*, the Commission again requested the Group of Three to examine whether the actions of TNCs operating in South Africa came under the definition of the crime of *apartheid*, and whether or not legal action could be taken under the Convention (see above).

ECONOMIC AND SOCIAL COUNCIL ACTION

On the recommendation of its Second Committee, the Economic and Social Council adopted decision 1983/137 by vote.

Adverse consequences for the enjoyment of human rights of political, military, economic and other forms of assistance given to colonial and racist régimes in southern Africa

At its 15th plenary meeting, on 27 May 1983, the Council, noting Commission on Human Rights resolution 1983/11 of 18 February 1983, endorsed the Commission's decision to welcome the decision of the Sub-Commission on Prevention of Discrimination and Protection of Minorities to mandate Mr. Ahmed Khalifa, Special Rapporteur, to continue to update the list of banks, transnational corporations and other organizations assisting the racist régime in South Africa, subject to annual review, and to submit, through the Sub-Commission, the revised report to the Commission.

Economic and Social Council decision 1983/137

39-4-10

Approved by Second Committee (E/1983/61) by vote (33-4-10), 23 May (meeting 18); draft by Commission on Human Rights (E/1983/13); agenda item 10.
Meeting number. ESC 15.

Report of the Special Rapporteur. The Special Rapporteur submitted to the Sub-Commission in July an updated report containing a comprehensive list of banks, TNCs and other organizations assisting the South African régime,[29] based on material received as at 10 May 1983.

Sub-Commission action. Having noted with satisfaction the Special Rapporteur's updated report, the Sub-Commission, on 31 August,[30] invited him to continue to update the list, subject to annual review, and to indicate the volume and nature of the assistance given to South Africa. It invited the Secretary-General to issue the updated report as a United Nations publication. Further, the Sub-Commission welcomed the December 1982 General Assembly resolution[31] on adverse consequences for human rights of assistance to South Africa, which affirmed the importance of updating the report.

GENERAL ASSEMBLY ACTION

The General Assembly, in several 1983 resolutions (38/17, 38/36 A, 38/39 A, 38/50), condemned collaboration with South Africa. The Second World Conference to Combat Racism and Racial Discrimination (see above, under DISCRIMINATION), in its Programme of Action approved by the Assembly in resolution 38/14, also called for termination of relations with South Africa.

Violations of trade union rights

Action by the Commission on Human Rights. Expressing concern at infringements of trade union rights and actions against black trade union leaders, the Commission on Human Rights, in a resolution of 18 February 1983 on the report of the *Ad Hoc* Working Group of Experts on Southern Africa (see above), demanded that South Africa respect international standards on trade union rights and adhere to the 1973 ILO Convention concerning Minimum Age for Admission to Employment.

Notes by the Secretariat and the Secretary-General. In March and May 1983, the Economic and Social Council was informed of allegations regarding infringements of trade union rights in South Africa.

In a March note,[32] the Secretariat transmitted extracts from the report of the *Ad Hoc* Working Group of Experts on Southern Africa (see above), concerning in particular the suppression of the right to organize trade unions. The Group had reported that at least 347 arrests of black trade unionists had taken place in South Africa in 1981 and had called for the release of workers and trade unionists arrested as a result of their trade union activities. The names of some trade union leaders persecuted by South Africa were annexed to the report.

In a May note,[33] the Secretary-General transmitted two 1982 communications, one each from the International Confederation of Free Trade Unions on the arrest and continued detention of six South African women trade unionists, and from the World Federation of Trade Unions, calling on the ILO Director-General to make South Africa respect the fundamental trade union rights as set out in ILO Conventions. In so doing, the Secretary-General explained the prescribed procedure he followed in handling those communications, and added that the Economic and Social Council's 1950 resolution on the safeguarding of trade union rights[34] provided that upon receiving consent from a United Nations Member which was not an ILO member, the Council would transmit to the ILO Fact-Finding and Conciliation Commission on Freedom of Association any allegations regarding infringements of trade union rights which it considered suitable for transmittal.

ECONOMIC AND SOCIAL COUNCIL ACTION

On the recommendation of its Second Committee, the Economic and Social Council adopted two decisions relating to infringements of trade union rights in South Africa. Decision 1983/156 was adopted without vote.

Allegations regarding infringements of trade union rights in South Africa

At its 15th plenary meeting, on 27 May 1983, the Council, noting that the consent of the Government of South Africa had been obtained, as required under paragraph 1 *(c)* (i) of Council resolution 277(X) of 17 February 1950, decided, in conformity with paragraph 1 *(c)* (ii) of that resolution, to transmit to the Fact-Finding and Conciliation Commission on Freedom of Association of the International Labour Organisation, through the Governing Body of the International Labour Office, the allegations of infringements of trade union rights in South Africa submitted by the International Confederation of Free Trade Unions on 12 February 1982 and the World Federation of Trade Unions on 13 July 1982, together with the text of the consent of the Government concerned; the Council also decided that, in accordance with the procedure outlined in its resolution 277(X), the Commission's findings should be transmitted to the Council as soon as possible, in keeping with the Commission's established practice.

Economic and Social Council decision 1983/156

Adopted without vote

Approved by Second Committee (E/1983/61) without vote, 23 May (meeting 19); oral proposal by Chairman; agenda item 10.
Meeting number. ESC 15.

Decision 1983/157 was also adopted without vote.

Report of the *Ad Hoc* Working Group of Experts of the Commission on Human Rights on allegations regarding infringements of trade union rights in South Africa

At its 15th plenary meeting, on 27 May 1983, the Council took note of the report of the *Ad Hoc* Working Group of Experts of the Commission on Human Rights on allegations regarding infringements of trade union rights in South Africa.

Economic and Social Council decision 1983/157

Adopted without vote

Approved by Second Committee (E/1983/61) without vote, 23 May (meeting 19); oral proposal by Chairman; agenda item 10.
Meeting number. ESC 15.

Asia and the Pacific

Iran

Reports by the Secretary-General. In a February 1983 report on the human rights situation in Iran,[35] the Secretary-General informed the Commission on Human Rights of the direct contacts he had established with the Government of Iran, in accordance with the Commission's March 1982 request.[36] In his discussion with Iran's Permanent Representative to the United Nations on reported human rights violations, including alleged summary executions of members of the Baha'i religious community, the Secretary-General had been told that there was no religious persecution and that the Government regarded the Baha'is not as a religious group but as a political movement aimed at creating division among the people of Iran. In December 1982, the Permanent Representative had indicated the Government's preparedness to receive an envoy of the Secretary-General in Teheran to discuss human rights matters and to provide the United Nations with relevant information. As a follow-up to those contacts, the Secretary-General's Office contacted the Permanent Mission of Iran to the United Nations on 5 January 1983; the Mission confirmed on 19 January the Iranian authorities' readiness to receive an envoy, and further indicated, on 31 January, that the envoy could travel to Iran in the latter half of March. Details of that visit were being worked out. In addition to his direct contacts, the Secretary-General added, the Under-Secretary-General for Political and General Assembly Affairs and the Director of the Centre for Human Rights had raised with Iranian Government representatives individual cases on a purely humanitarian basis.

Also in February,[37] the Secretary-General transmitted to the Commission a compilation of available information on the human rights situation in Iran. He examined alleged violations of human rights, in particular the rights to life, to physical integrity and freedom from torture, to fair trial and to freedom of conscience and opinion as laid down in the 1966 International Covenant on Civil and Political Rights.[38] Annexed to the note were communications from Iran, one to the Centre for Human Rights and another to the Commission Chairman, listing what it called counter-revolutionary activities and terrorist attacks, and charging the Baha'is with spreading anti-Islamic propaganda and spying. Annexed also was a 14 December 1982 statement by the Baha'i International Community refuting such allegations and inviting the establishment of an impartial body of investigation. Asserting that the Iranian Government persecuted the Baha'is on religious grounds, the Community stated that all nine members of the national governing body of the Baha'i Faith in Iran had disappeared, and eight of their successors had been secretly executed.

Action by the Commission on Human Rights. The Commission adopted on 8 March 1983, by a roll-call vote of 17 to 6, with 19 abstentions, a resolution[39] expressing profound concern at what it called the continuing grave violations of human rights in Iran, particularly at the evidence of summary and arbitrary executions, torture, detention without trial, religious intolerance and persecution, in particular of the Baha'is, and the lack of an independent judiciary and other recognized safeguards for a fair trial. It urged once more that Iran, a State party to the Covenant on Civil and Political Rights, respect the rights recognized under that instrument. It requested the Secretary-General or his representative to continue direct contacts with the Iranian Government and to submit a comprehensive report in 1984.

In accordance with that request, endorsed by the Economic and Social Council (see below), contacts continued at various levels during 1983.[40] By a letter of 12 August, the Secretary-General communicated to the Permanent Representative of Iran his intention to appoint a representative, prior to whose nomination an understanding needed to be reached with the Government of its readiness to receive a visit by that representative. On 17 August, Iran responded that certain members of the Commission had decided to manipulate that body for their own illegitimate interests by taking sheer allegations for facts. By a letter of 23 August to Iran, the Assistant Secretary-General for Human Rights expressed the readiness of the Centre for Human Rights to discuss further details concerning United Nations contacts with the Government.

ECONOMIC AND SOCIAL COUNCIL ACTION

On the recommendation of its Second Committee, the Economic and Social Council adopted decision 1983/147 by recorded vote.

Situation of human rights in the Islamic Republic of Iran

At its 15th plenary meeting, on 27 May 1983, the Council, noting Commission on Human Rights resolution 1983/34 of 8 March 1983, endorsed the Commission's request that the Secretary-General or his representative continue direct contacts with the Government of the Islamic Republic of Iran on the grave human rights situation prevailing in that country, including the situation of the Baha'is, and that the Secretary-General or his representative submit to the Commission at its for-

tieth session a comprehensive report on the direct contacts and the human rights situation in the Islamic Republic of Iran, including conclusions and suggestions regarding the respect for human rights and fundamental freedoms in that country.

Economic and Social Council decision 1983/147

19-3-28 (recorded vote)

Approved by Second Committee (E/1983/61) by recorded vote (17-1-26), 23 May (meeting 18); draft by Commission on Human Rights (E/1983/13); agenda item 10. *Meeting number.* ESC 15.

Recorded vote in Council as follows:

In favour: Austria, Canada, Denmark, Fiji, France, Germany, Federal Republic of, Greece, Japan, Kenya, Luxembourg, Netherlands, New Zealand, Norway, Portugal, Suriname, Swaziland, United Kingdom, United States, Venezuela.

Against: Algeria, Benin, Pakistan.

Abstaining: Argentina, Bangladesh, Brazil, Bulgaria, Burundi, Byelorussian SSR, China, Colombia, Congo, Ecuador, German Democratic Republic, India, Liberia, Malaysia, Mali, Mexico, Nicaragua, Peru, Poland, Qatar, Saint Lucia, Saudi Arabia, Sierra Leone, Sudan, Thailand, Tunisia, USSR, United Republic of Cameroon.

Sub-Commission action. By a resolution adopted on 5 September 1983 by 13 votes to 1, with 7 abstentions,[41] the Sub-Commission on Prevention of Discrimination and Protection of Minorities expressed profound concern at the reports of continuing grave violations of human rights in Iran, and expressed hope that the Secretary-General would succeed through his direct contacts with the Government in bringing about an improvement.

Also on 5 September, the Sub-Commission recommended for adoption by the Commission a draft resolution on the exploitation of child labour, among whose provisions was a call on Iran to cease immediately the use of children in its armed forces (see below, under OTHER HUMAN RIGHTS QUESTIONS).

Sri Lanka

The Sub-Commission, by a 5 September 1983 resolution adopted by 10 votes to 8, with 4 abstentions,[42] requested the Secretary-General to invite Sri Lanka to provide information, for submission to the Commission in 1984, on the recent communal violence, including its efforts to investigate the incidents and to promote national harmony.

Europe and the Mediterranean area

Cyprus

In January 1983, the Secretary-General reported to the Commission on Human Rights on the question of human rights in Cyprus,[43] as requested by it in March 1982.[36] He informed the Commission that procedural difficulties continued to prevent the Committee on Missing Persons, established in 1981,[44] from performing its substantive functions.

The Secretary-General reported that the number of Greek Cypriots living in the north of the island had further diminished; as at 17 January

1983, 942 Greek Cypriots lived in the north, while 186 Turkish Cypriots lived in the south. Contacts remained frequent between members of the Maronite community residing on opposite sides of the cease-fire lines separating the Greek Cypriot and Turkish Cypriot communities.

The Commission, on 8 March 1983,[45] decided to postpone to its 1984 session the debate on the question of human rights in Cyprus, it being understood that action required by previous Commission resolutions on the subject continued to remain operative, including a request to the Secretary-General to report to the Commission on their implementation.

On 21 March,[46] the Committee on the Elimination of Racial Discrimination reiterated the hope that state of affairs in Cyprus—which it considered to be unacceptable—due to foreign occupation of part of its territory, would be brought to an end, so that Cyprus would be able to exercise its obligations under the International Convention on the Elimination of All Forms of Racial Discrimination (see above, under DISCRIMINATION).

(For the political aspects of the situation in Cyrpus, see POLITICAL AND SECURITY QUESTIONS, Chapter VIII).

GENERAL ASSEMBLY ACTION

In resolution 37/253 of 13 May 1983, on the question of Cyprus, the General Assembly called for respect for the human rights of all Cypriots, including the freedom of movement, the freedom of settlement and the right to property, and for urgent measures for the voluntary return of the refugees to their homes in safety.

Poland

In February 1983, Hugo J. Gobbi, designated on 21 December 1982 by the Secretary-General to follow the human rights situation in Poland on his behalf, submitted a report[47] to the Commission on Human Rights, in accordance with its March 1982 request.[36]

Mr. Gobbi reported that, by a letter of 3 January 1983, he had asked for Poland's co-operation in arranging for his visit to the country in the latter half of January. In a reply dated 6 January, Poland reiterated its rejection of the March 1982 Commission resolution as interference in its internal affairs and as illegal, null and void, politically harmful and morally hypocritical. In those circumstances, Mr. Gobbi considered that his visit could not be undertaken at the suggested time.

The report contained a communication of 1 February 1982 from Poland, addressed to the Secretary-General pursuant to article 4 (concerning a state of public emergency) of the 1966 International Covenant on Civil and Political Rights,[38] stating that temporary limitation of certain rights of citizens had been prompted by exigencies of averting civil war, economic anarchy and destabilization of State and social structures; those measures, however, had already been considerably cut back and would be terminated as the situation stabilized. On 16 February 1982, the Secretary-General transmitted the communication to all Member States; he also informed the Human Rights Committee.

On 21 December 1982, Poland informed the Secretary-General that a law had been passed on 18 December terminating as of the end of the year derogation from certain Covenant articles, such as articles 9 (right to liberty and security of person), 12 (freedom of movement), 21 (right to peaceful assembly) and 22 (freedom of association); restrictions of other provisions still derogated from—namely article 14, paragraph 5 (stating that everyone convicted of a crime should have the right to his sentence being reviewed by a higher tribunal), and article 19, paragraph 2 (on the right to freedom of expression)—had been considerably reduced.

The report also gave a description of the main events in Poland since the declaration of martial law on 13 December 1981 (which was approved by the Parliament on 25 January 1982) and summarized allegations contained in information received from non-governmental and other sources, concerning conditions of arrest and internment, treatment of detainees, and infringements of the right to freedom of association and of trade union rights.

Concluding, Mr. Gobbi stated that, as he could not visit Poland to verify the allegations, his analysis of the situation was limited to the normative aspects of the question relating to the application of the relevant international instruments ratified by Poland, namely, the 1966 International Covenants on Human Rights and ILO Conventions. In analysing the law of 8 October 1982, which gave a new trade union structure to the country and abolished all existing organizations, ILO expressed doubts concerning the compatibility of that law and ILO Conventions. Mr. Gobbi felt that some provisions introduced by that law, limiting the capacity to choose new employment, and those modifying articles of the penal code did not conform with the Covenants. With regard to allegations concerning the situation of political prisoners, he could not make any evaluation without verifying them on the site in direct consultation with those concerned and primarily the Polish authorities. Notwithstanding indications of a number of positive steps taken by the Government—such as the adoption of specific legal regulations that limited the competence of military courts with respect to civilians, lifted most of the restrictions on freedom of movement and, in particular, completely lifted internments—Mr. Gobbi hoped that further measures for normalization would be taken in order to satisfy all the requirements established by international instruments ratified by Poland.

By a resolution adopted on 8 March 1983 by a roll-call vote of 19 to 14, with 10 abstentions,[48] the Commission thanked the Secretary-General and his representative for the report, deploring at the same time the attitude of the Polish authorities in not co-operating in the implementation of its March 1982 resolution. It reaffirmed the right of the Polish people to pursue its political, social and cultural development, free from outside interference, and called on the Polish authorities to realize fully and without further delay their stated intention to terminate the restrictive measures imposed on the exercise of human rights, particularly in relation to a review of the severe prison sentences imposed in the context of the state of martial law, the lifting of restrictions on the free flow of information, and the repeal of new restrictions imposed on the people. The Commission requested the Secretary-General to update and complete the study and to present a report in 1984.

ECONOMIC AND SOCIAL COUNCIL ACTION

On the recommendation of its Second Committee, the Economic and Social Council adopted decision 1983/145 by a recorded vote, requested by Poland.

Situation of human rights in Poland

At its 15th plenary meeting, on 27 May 1983, the Council, noting Commission on Human Rights resolution 1983/30 of 8 March 1983, endorsed the Commission's decision to request the Secretary-General or a person designated by him to update and complete the thorough study of the human rights situation in Poland requested in Commission resolution 1982/26 of 10 March 1982, based on such information as he may deem relevant, including comments and materials the Government of Poland may wish to provide, and to present a comprehensive report to the Commission at its fortieth session.

Economic and Social Council decision 1983/145

22-12-18 (recorded vote)

Approved by Second Committee (E/1983/61) by recorded vote (18-10-18), 23 May (meeting 18); draft by Commission on Human Rights (E/1983/13); agenda item 10. *Meeting number.* ESC 15.

Recorded vote in Council as follows:

In favour: Austria, Botswana, Canada, Colombia, Denmark, Fiji, France, Germany, Federal Republic of, Greece, Japan, Lebanon, Luxembourg, Mexico, Netherlands, New Zealand, Norway, Portugal, Saint Lucia, Swaziland, United Kingdom, United States, Venezuela.

Against: Algeria, Argentina, Benin, Bulgaria, Byelorussian SSR, China, German Democratic Republic, India, Nicaragua, Poland, Romania, USSR.

Abstaining: Bangladesh, Brazil, Burundi, Congo, Ecuador, Liberia, Malaysia, Mali, Pakistan, Peru, Qatar, Saudi Arabia, Sierra Leone, Sudan, Suriname, Thailand, Tunisia, United Republic of Cameroon.

Expressing regret at the adoption of the decision, Poland charged that the 1983 Commission resolution completely distorted the actual situation. The Commission called on the Government to repeal "new restrictions", when martial law had been suspended and almost all the associated restrictions had been lifted; by recognizing the right of the Polish people "to pursue its political, social and cultural development, free from outside interference", the resolution represented interference in the internal affairs of a sovereign Member State.

Similarly, the USSR considered the Council decision to be illegal, irrelevant and at variance with the principles of the Charter of the United Nations; the events of the preceding year had shown that the situation could be successfully dealt with by the Polish people themselves.

The United States said the violent suppression of non-violent May Day demonstrations in Polish cities, as well as subsequent acts of violence—including the beating and death of a Solidarity activist's son—made it clear that the crisis brought about by the imposition of martial law remained unresolved. It regretted the refusal by Polish authorities to co-operate in the study, for such co-operation would be taken as a sign of willingness to move towards dialogue and reconciliation.

Latin America

Bolivia

The Commission on Human Rights, on 8 March 1983, decided to conclude its consideration of the human rights situation in Bolivia (see above, under ADVANCEMENT OF HUMAN RIGHTS).

Chile

Report of the Special Rapporteur. In February 1983, Special Rapporteur Abdoulaye Diéye (Senegal) submitted a report on developments in the human rights situation in Chile during the second half of 1982,[49] supplementing a report submitted to the General Assembly in November 1982.[50] The Special Rapporteur stated that Chile had continued to refuse to co-operate; as in past reports, he had relied on official and other communications in the Chilean press, the testimony of witnesses, reports by organizations, and documents and letters from individuals in Chile and elsewhere.

In his conclusions and recommendations, the Special Rapporteur stated that the human rights situation in Chile had not improved; there was no indication of measures designed to restore the enjoyment of human rights, either at the legislative or judicial levels or in the practice of the Executive. Violations of the right to life had increased over 1981 and judicial protection continued to be inadequate. The right to freedom was denied with excessive frequency, particularly in respect of persons attempting to exercise freedom of expression and opinion regarding political matters. While the number of "individual" arrests declined from 646 cases in 1981 to 312 in 1982, arrests in connection with mass demonstrations increased from 263 cases in 1981 to 901 in 1982. Arrests were made without a judicial or administrative warrant and were frequently made by persons not legally authorized to do so. In addition, judicial supervision of the illegal or arbitrary nature of arrests was practically non-existent.

The right to security of Chileans was at times violated by acts of persecution and intimidation in which the State security agencies were implicated; most of the cases appeared to be organized and planned acts against persons associated with organizations for the protection of human rights. With regard to the conditions of detention, there continued to be reports of persecution and intimidation. The fate of persons who had disappeared for political reasons— with the number of unresolved cases since 1973 increased to 662—had not been made clear by the Government, despite repeated appeals of the General Assembly and the Commission.

Concerning the right to freedom of movement, the Special Rapporteur noted that a Special Advisory Commission had been set up in November 1982 to propose to the President of the Republic measures regarding the situation of persons in exile. In that connection, he called for publication of an official list of persons in exile and termination of the double state of emergency, under which the Executive enjoyed discretionary power to prohibit entry into the country or to order expulsions or the assignment of forced residence. According to the Special Rapporteur, the number of persons in political exile might be between 11,000 (unofficial figure given by the authorities) and 38,000 (according to human rights organizations).

The Special Rapporteur stated that procedural guarantees, particularly the exercise of the right to effective remedy upon infringement of right or fundamental freedom, continued to be seriously restricted within the legislative framework of the double state of emergency. Also, such guarantees were extremely difficult to apply under military jurisdiction, particularly in the case of proceedings conducted before military courts, which had been reintroduced. A new procedure for appointing judges also increased the Executive's discretionary powers.

The right to freedom of thought, opinion and expression was also seriously restricted; what had previously been simply "administrative offences" against measures restricting freedom of information were classified as "crimes". During the second half of 1982, restrictions affected, in particular, radio broadcasting, the publication or importation of books and news periodicals, and persecution and intimidation of journalists.

The right of political association had been suspended until 1989 and any breach of that provision was liable to heavy penalties. Humanitarian associations and groups, which were forced to operate outside the law, were subjected to frequent harassment by the authorities. Exercise of the right to participation in public life was impossible, even in regional and communal development councils for which post-constitutional legislation had not always been enacted.

With regard to economic, social and cultural rights, the situation was becoming further removed from the international norm as a result of the special characteristics of Chile's worsening economic and social crisis. Working conditions, particularly with regard to levels of remuneration, were becoming increasingly unfavourable; there had been no improvements in the enjoyment of cultural or trade union rights. A number of leading figures in professional workers'/employers' organizations had been expelled from the country, a situation incompatible with the principle of trade union freedom.

The Special Rapporteur recommended that the Commission once again call on Chile to co-operate with United Nations bodies concerned with human rights protection. In particular, the Government should be requested to put an end to the institutionalization of the state of emergency and to re-establish democratic legal order; in the absence of such a change, the international community should remain concerned with the human rights situation in Chile, using the means it deemed most appropriate to ensure full restoration of those rights.

Annexed to the Special Rapporteur's report was a list of 63 persons subjected to torture and other cruel, inhuman or degrading treatment.

Action by the Commission on Human Rights. Commending the Special Rapporteur for his report, the Commission on Human Rights, by a resolution adopted on 8 March by a roll-call vote of 29 to 6, with 8 abstentions,[51] urged the Chilean authorities to: put an end to the state of emergency under which serious and constant human rights violations were occurring; re-establish the principle of legality, democratic institutions and effective exercise of rights, in accordance with Chile's commitments under various international instruments; investigate and clarify the fate of persons who had disappeared for political reasons, and prosecute and punish those responsible for such disappearances; end intimidation and persecution, arbitrary arrest and detention in secret places and torture and other cruel or degrading treatment which, on occasion, led to unexplained deaths; respect, unconditionally, the rights of Chileans to live in their country and to enter and leave it freely, and put an end to relegation (confinement with forced residence) and forced exile; restore full enjoyment and exercise of labour rights, especially the right to form trade unions, the right of collective bargaining and the right to strike; and respect the rights intended to preserve the cultural identity and to improve the social condition of the indigenous population. It again requested the Chilean authorities to co-operate with the Special Rapporteur and to submit their comments on his report in 1984, when it would consider the question of human rights in Chile as a priority matter.

The Commission extended the Special Rapporteur's mandate for another year, requesting him to report to the General Assembly in 1983 and to the Commission in 1984 on further developments.

ECONOMIC AND SOCIAL COUNCIL ACTION

On the recommendation of its Second Committee, the Economic and Social Council adopted decision 1983/149 by recorded vote.

Question of human rights in Chile

At its 15th plenary meeting, on 27 May 1983, the Council, noting Commission on Human Rights resolution 1983/38 of 8 March 1983, endorsed the Commission's decision to extend the mandate of the Special Rapporteur on the situation of human rights in Chile for a year and requested the Secretary-General to ensure that sufficient financial resources and staff are provided for the implementation of Commission resolution 1983/38.

Economic and Social Council decision 1983/149

38-4-11 (recorded vote)

Approved by Second Committee (E/1983/61) by recorded vote (32-4-10), 23 May (meeting 18); draft by Commission on Human Rights (E/1983/13); agenda item 10.
Meeting number. ESC 15.

Recorded vote in Council as follows:

In favour: Algeria, Austria, Benin, Botswana, Bulgaria, Burundi, Byelorussian SSR, Canada, Congo, Denmark, France, German Democratic Republic, Germany, Federal Republic of, Greece, India, Japan, Kenya, Liberia, Luxembourg, Mali, Mexico, Netherlands, New Zealand, Nicaragua, Norway, Poland, Portugal, Qatar, Romania, Saint Lucia, Saudi Arabia, Sierra Leone, Sudan, Swaziland, Tunisia, USSR, United Kingdom, Venezuela.
Against: Argentina, Brazil, Pakistan, United States.
Abstaining: Bangladesh, China, Colombia, Ecuador, Fiji, Lebanon, Malaysia, Peru, Suriname, Thailand, United Republic of Cameroon.

Speaking after the vote in the Council, the USSR stated that recent events in Chile had shown that people suffered under the yoke of a dictatorship imposed by the United States. Venezuela stated that its affirmative vote was an unequivocal expression of concern for human rights.

Mexico welcomed the adoption of the decision and hoped that a new Special Rapporteur would soon be appointed following the death of Mr. Diéye in March (see below). Denmark and France also stressed the importance of appointing a successor as soon as possible.

Opposing the Council decision as well as the resolution adopted by the Commission on Human Rights, the United States said it would continue to work in the Commission for a resolution reflecting the situation accurately and in a balanced way and providing for equitable and fair procedures aimed at securing Chile's co-operation with the United Nations in its investigation of the human rights situation there.

Sub-Commission action. On 5 September,[52] the Sub-Commission urged the Chilean authorities to put an end to all repressive measures, torture and cruel, inhuman or degrading treatment, and to respect civil, political, economic, social and cultural rights, especially those of the indigenous peoples. It recommended to the Commission that it urge the authorities to respect and promote human rights, in accordance with the international instruments to which Chile was a party, and to co-operate with the Special Rapporteur.

Further report of the Special Rapporteur. In accordance with the request of the Commission, the Secretary-General transmitted to the General Assembly in October 1983 (with a November addendum) the Special Rapporteur's report on further developments of the human rights situation in Chile.[53]

Following the death on 17 March of Mr. Diéye, the Chairman of the Commission had appointed on 1 June Rajsoomer Lallah (Mauritius) as new Special Rapporteur, an action deplored by Chile in a statement of 3 June on grounds of what it called discriminatory procedure. By a reply of 24 June, the Special Rapporteur stressed the importance of the Government's co-operation in presenting the Commission with the most accurate and complete reflection of the human rights situation in Chile, a statement repeated in a letter of 14 July. On 8 July, Chile reiterated its opposition to what it called a discriminatory and selective procedure, established not only without Chile's prior consent, but also departing from universally accepted rules and violating the United Nations Charter; Chile's refusal to recognize the Special Rapporteur's competence and to co-operate was based on a position of principle.

The Special Rapporteur stated in his October report (covering January-June 1983) that, in view of the lack of co-operation, he had largely adopted the method of work followed in former reports. In the November addendum (on developments after 1 July), he stated that between 10 August and 10 October, the Government, under a new Cabinet, had supplied the Secretary-General for the first time with information on its intentions to lift the state of emergency, initiate a dialogue with the opposition parties, achieve democracy and solve the problem of exiles. The Special Rapporteur expressed the hope for closer co-operation with the Government.

Among the improvements in the situation, the Special Rapporteur noted the 28 August government decision not to renew the declaration of the state of emergency, and a decree of 15 September which, for the first time in 10 years, provided for the recognition and exercise of the right of assembly. According to government sources, 3,421 exiles had been permitted to return between September 1982 and October 1983.

Nevertheless, the Special Rapporteur noted, as disturbing elements during July and August 1983: the continuation of the declaration of "a state of danger of disturbance of the peace", under which the Government had exceptional powers affecting the right to liberty, the right of assembly, freedom of information and movement, and the possibility of effective judicial appeal for *amparo* in respect of those rights. Further, there was an increase in violations of the rights to life and to physical and psychological integrity, as well as in breaches of the right to the security of the person; in the first eight months of 1983, 165 acts of persecution and intimidation were recorded. As to freedom of the person, 2,860 arbitrary and/or unlawful arrests were recorded in the first eight months, most of them for public demonstrations; only 274 detainees were brought before a court of justice and only one person was charged with an alleged terrorist offence. On the other hand, 2,586 detainees were released without charge or accused of ordinary misdemeanours. The exercise of civil liberties was made conditional on continuation of the "political truce" which was to last until 1989.

The Special Rapporteur stated that the right of Chileans freely to enter their country could not be subject to arbitrary restrictions and that the Government should make clear the number and identity of the persons to whom some type of prohibition applied. Moreover, freedom of movement within the country had not been respected in a growing number of cases of internal exile (restricted residence) imposed as an administrative measure without the possibility of judicial remedy.

In conclusion, the Special Rapporteur expressed the hope that Chile would take more decisive steps towards re-establishing human rights protection, particularly the exercise of political rights without discrimination, the absence of which appeared to be central to all the human rights problems and the re-establishment of the traditional democratic order in that country.

Appended were lists of 21 persons subjected to torture and other cruel treatment and of 58 persons wounded by gunfire by the security services during July and August 1983.

GENERAL ASSEMBLY ACTION

On 16 December, on the recommendation of the Third Committee, the Assembly adopted resolution 38/102 by recorded vote.

Situation of human rights and fundamental freedoms in Chile

The General Assembly,

Aware of its responsibility to promote and encourage respect for human rights and fundamental freedoms for all and determined to remain vigilant with regard to violations of human rights wherever they occur,

Stressing the obligation of Governments to promote and protect human rights and to carry out the responsibilities they have undertaken by virtue of various international instruments,

Recalling its resolutions 3219(XXIX) of 6 November 1974, 3448(XXX) of 9 December 1975, 31/124 of 16 December 1976, 32/118 of 16 December 1977, 33/175 of 20 December 1978, 34/179 of 17 December 1979, 35/188 of 15 December 1980, 36/157 of 16 December 1981 and 37/183 of 17 December 1982, relating to the situation of human rights in Chile, as well as its resolution 33/173 of 20 December 1978 on disappeared persons,

Recalling also the resolutions of the Commission on Human Rights on the situation of human rights in Chile, in particular resolution 1983/38 of 8 March 1983, in which the Commission decided, *inter alia*, to extend for a year the mandate of the Special Rapporteur on the situation of human rights in Chile,

Deploring once again the fact that the repeated appeals of the General Assembly, the Commission on Human Rights and other international organs to re-establish human rights and fundamental freedoms have been ignored by the Chilean authorities, which continue to refuse to co-operate with the Commission on Human Rights and its Special Rapporteur,

Expressing its profound concern that, according to the conclusions of the Special Rapporteur, the performance of the Chilean authorities with regard to the situation of human rights has been negative in general and that they have not been responsive to the concerns of the international community expressed in resolutions of the General Assembly and the Commission on Human Rights,

Observing that the Chilean authorities have permitted a limited number of nationals to return to the country, but noting that the measures taken to that effect have been arbitrary and restrictive,

1. *Commends* the Special Rapporteur on the situation of human rights in Chile for his report, prepared in accordance with Commission on Human Rights resolution 1983/38;

2. *Reiterates its grave concern* at the persistence of and increase in serious and systematic violations of human rights in Chile, as described in the report of the Special Rapporteur;

3. *Expresses once again its concern* at the disruption of the traditional democratic legal order and its institutions by the maintenance of exceptional legislation, the institutionalization of various states of emergency and the existence of a Constitution in Chile which does not reflect a freely expressed popular will and the provisions of which not only fail to guarantee the enjoyment of human rights and fundamental freedoms but also suppress, suspend or restrict the exercise of those rights and freedoms;

4. *Also reiterates its grave concern* at the inefficacy of recourse to *habeas corpus* or *amparo* and of protection in view of the fact that the judiciary in Chile does not exercise its powers fully in this respect and carries out its functions under severe restrictions;

5. *Once again requests* the Chilean authorities to respect and promote human rights in compliance with the obligations they have assumed under various international instruments and, in particular, to end the régime of exception and especially the practice of declaring states of emergency, under which serious and continuing violations of human rights are committed, and to restore the principle of legality, democratic institutions and the effective enjoyment and exercise of civil and political rights and fundamental freedoms without any discrimination;

6. *Once more urges* the Chilean authorities to investigate and clarify the fate of persons who have disappeared for political reasons, to inform their families of the results of such investigation and to bring to trial and punish those responsible for these disappearances;

7. *Reiterates its appeal* to the Chilean authorities to put an end to intimidation and persecution, as well as arbitrary detentions and imprisonment in secret places and the practice of torture and other forms of cruel, inhuman or degrading treatment which have resulted in unexplained deaths, and to respect the right of persons to life and physical integrity;

8. *Expresses its concern* at the violent suppression of the ever larger and more widespread popular protests in the face of the incapacity of the authorities to restore human rights and fundamental freedoms, as reported by the Special Rapporteur, which have resulted in serious, flagrant and systematic violation of human rights, including mass detentions and numerous deaths;

9. *Once again urges* the Chilean authorities to respect the right of Chileans to live in and freely enter and leave their country, without restrictions or conditions, and to cease the practice of "relegation" (assignment of forced residence) and forced exile;

10. *Renews its appeal* to the Chilean authorities to restore the full enjoyment and exercise of trade union rights, in particular the right to organize trade unions, the right to collective bargaining and the right to strike;

11. *Once more urges* the Chilean authorities to protect and restore the economic, social and cultural rights of the population and, in particular, to respect the rights intended to preserve the cultural identity and improve the social status of the indigenous population;

12. *Concludes*, on the basis of the report of the Special Rapporteur, that it is necessary to keep under consideration the situation of human rights in Chile;

13. *Calls again upon* the Chilean authorities to cooperate with the Special Rapporteur and to submit their comments on his report to the Commission on Human Rights at its fortieth session;

14. *Invites* the Commission on Human Rights to study in depth the report of the Special Rapporteur at its fortieth session and to take the most appropriate steps for the effective restoration of human rights and fundamental freedoms in Chile, including the extension of the mandate of the Special Rapporteur for one more year, and requests the Commission to report, through the Economic and Social Council, to the General Assembly at its thirty-ninth session.

General Assembly resolution 38/102

16 December 1983   Meeting 100   89-17-38 (recorded vote)

Approved by Third Committee (A/38/680) by recorded vote (86-15-32), 9 December (meeting 71); 13-nation draft (A/C.3/38/L.63), orally revised; agenda item 12.

Sponsors: Algeria, Cuba, Denmark, France, Greece, Ireland, Italy, Luxembourg, Mexico, Netherlands, Spain, Sweden, Yugoslavia.

Meeting numbers. GA 38th session: 3rd Committee 18, 54, 55, 57-71; plenary 100.

Recorded vote in Assembly as follows:

In favour: Afghanistan, Algeria, Angola, Australia, Austria, Bahrain, Barbados, Belgium, Benin, Botswana, Bulgaria, Burundi, Byelorussian SSR, Canada, Cape Verde, Congo, Costa Rica, Cuba, Cyprus, Czechoslovakia, Democratic Yemen, Denmark, Ethiopia, Finland, France, Gambia, German Democratic Republic, Ghana, Greece, Grenada, Guinea, Guinea-Bissau, Guyana, Hungary, Iceland, India, Iran, Iraq, Ireland, Italy, Jamaica, Kenya, Kuwait, Lao People's Democratic Republic, Lesotho, Libyan Arab Jamahiriya, Luxembourg, Madagascar, Maldives, Mali, Malta, Mauritania, Mauritius, Mexico, Mongolia, Mozambique, Netherlands, New Zealand, Nicaragua, Nigeria, Norway, Papua New Guinea, Poland, Portugal, Romania, Rwanda, Sao Tome and Principe, Saudi Arabia,[a] Senegal, Seychelles, Sierra Leone, Spain, Sri Lanka, Swaziland, Sweden, Syrian Arab Republic, Togo, Tunisia, Uganda, Ukrainian SSR, USSR, United Arab Emirates, United Republic of Tanzania, Upper Volta, Vanuatu, Viet Nam, Yugoslavia, Zambia, Zimbabwe.

Against: Bangladesh, Brazil, Chile, El Salvador, Guatemala, Haiti, Honduras, Indonesia, Israel, Lebanon, Morocco, Pakistan, Paraguay, Philippines, Thailand, United States, Uruguay.

Abstaining: Bahamas, Belize, Bhutan, Burma, Central African Republic, Chad, China, Colombia, Democratic Kampuchea, Dominica, Dominican Republic, Ecuador, Egypt, Equatorial Guinea, Gabon, Germany, Federal Republic of, Ivory Coast, Japan, Jordan, Liberia, Malawi, Malaysia, Nepal, Niger, Oman, Panama, Peru, Saint Lucia, Singapore, Sudan, Suriname, Trinidad and Tobago, Turkey, United Kingdom, United Republic of Cameroon, Yemen, Zaire.

[a]Later advised the Secretariat it had intended to abstain.

In explanation of vote, opposition or reservation was expressed by a number of delegations to what they considered to be a selective approach of the text; they included Australia, Bhutan, Colombia, Costa Rica, the Dominican Republic, Ecuador, the Federal Republic of Germany, Haiti, Honduras, Jamaica and Portugal.

Declaring itself in favour of protecting human rights in all regions, Bolivia did not participate in the vote. Acting likewise, Venezuela called for a balanced approach to the question of human rights violations.

Morocco considered the draft to be politically suspect and expressed doubts as regards the reliability and impartiality of information used or provided by the Special Rapporteur; it also regretted the retention of the post of the Special Rapporteur.

Indonesia viewed the text as interference in internal affairs under the pretext of protecting human rights. The Federal Republic of Germany felt that certain elements of the draft, in particular the reference to the 1980 Chilean Constitution, were political and had no relevance to human rights; in addition, little was said in the text of the Government's efforts to re-establish democratic institutions. Canada also observed that the text did not refer to the progress made since August 1983, specifically mentioned by the Special Rapporteur, nor did it mention the information provided by the Chilean Government to the Secretary-General or its recent overtures to opposition groups. Honduras also felt the international community should note the Government's efforts to ensure respect for human rights. The United States said the sponsors did not appear to be interested in encouraging the process of reform and transition to democracy which was under way; they no doubt would prefer a violent confrontation which would make more likely the imposition in Chile of a Marxist-Leninist dictatorship.

Singapore and Trinidad and Tobago abstained, stating that the draft's selective approach undermined the United Nations credibility and universality.

Expressing regret that the draft failed to reflect the positive responses Chile had given in certain specific aspects of concern, the United Kingdom hoped that the information provided by the Government would constitute a first step towards re-establishing the co-operation between Chile, the Commission and its Special Rapporteur; it also had reservations with regard to the Assembly's prejudging the decision of the Commission by inviting the latter to extend the Special Rapporteur's mandate.

Australia called on the Chilean Government to establish a dialogue with the opposition to resolve the country's problems and promote basic human rights. Portugal said its support for the text was motivated by its concern at the continuing restrictions on human rights; Chile had twice contacted the Secretary-General on human rights questions and could be expected to co-operate with the United Nations in improving the prevailing human rights situation. Finland felt that a number of provisions of the draft were marked by partiality; it regretted that the Government had refused to co-operate with the Special Rapporteur and appealed to it to change its position in that regard.

Jamaica appealed for the establishment of a High Commissioner for Human Rights, to deal with human rights violations world-wide on an equitable basis.

Chile reiterated its rejection since 1979 of the establishment of what it called selective and arbitrary procedure, and its rejection of the Special Rapporteur, imposed upon it without its prior consent and in violation of the sovereign equality of all Member States. As regards specific provisions in the text, Chile said the reference to the judiciary was made in a perfidious and despicable way, and the denunciation, in paragraph 3, of the "institutionalization of various states of emergency" was ill-considered in view of the fact that the state of emergency had been imposed during what the sponsors' believed was "traditional democratic legal order" under Salvador Allende. Despite assertions made in the seventh preambular paragraph, 3,421 persons had been authorized to return; a special bureau had been set up on 29 October 1983 to deal with their situation. With regard to paragraph 6, Chile said it had been six years since any case of disappearance had been reported; for those who had disappeared before that period, the Government itself had solicited the co-operation of international bodies in the ongoing investigations. As for the charges of violent repression of "the ever larger and more widespread popular protests" at which the Assembly expressed concern in paragraph 8, Chile pointed out that the demonstrations were not spontaneous protests but public meetings announced in advance and authorized by municipal authorities, some of which had given rise to incidents that had resulted in the loss of lives. In so far as the necessary steps had been taken, such incidents were unlikely to recur. Chile added that it would refuse to become involved with any procedure stemming from the Commission or the Assembly, as long as it continued to be subjected to discriminatory treatment; guarantees against such treatment could be provided only by a High Commissioner for Human Rights endowed with the authority to play a universal, apolitical role free from pressure.

El Salvador

Report of the Special Representative. In January 1983, Special Representative José Antonio Pastor Ridruejo submitted to the Commission on Human Rights, in pursuance of its March 1982 request,[54] a report on the human rights situation in El Salvador.[55] The report updated his November 1982 interim report and analysed information gathered during his visit to the country in September 1982,[56] as well as information provided since then in interviews. However, the Special Representative stated that the massive character of human rights violations in El Salvador prevented him from investigating each of the cases brought to his attention. In his opinion, members of the State apparatus, violent groups of the extreme right and armed groups of the extreme left bore responsibility for the violations of civil and political rights. While the situation remained unchanged as regards economic, social and cultural rights, he added that the guerrilla opposition's systematic attacks on the country's economy, although presented as aimed at military targets, seriously affected the future enjoyment of those rights by the Salvadorian people. The situation concerning the activity of the judiciary was still unsatisfactory; despite a slight increase in the punishment of human rights violations, the Special Representative had not heard that any of the proceedings had resulted in a sentence.

Regarding the continued armed clashes between the regular army and the guerrilla forces, he believed that the 1949 Geneva Conventions for the protection of war victims and the 1977 Protocols[57] were still not properly complied with, notwithstanding cases in which both sides had given humanitarian treatment to, and even released, persons captured in combat.

The Special Representative stated that while El Salvador had the right to adopt emergency measures to deal with the existing situation of violence and armed confrontation, nothing justified the use of such measures to violate fundamental and inalienable human rights, including foremost the right to life. He considered the restoration of civil peace a prerequisite for respect for civil, political and other rights, and urged the Government to consider entering into a dialogue with all political forces in the country with a view to ending armed confrontation.

In addition, he recommended to the Government the following measures: the repeal of all legal enactments and other measures that were incompatible with international human rights instruments; institution of real government control over the armed forces, security forces, and all armed organizations and individuals; adoption of legal measures to prevent and punish human rights violations; mass campaigns to promote respect for human rights; and administrative and social reforms.

Action by the Commission on Human Rights. By a resolution of 8 March 1983, adopted by a roll-call vote of 23 to 6, with 10 abstentions,[58] the Commission expressed deepest concern that human rights violations of the most serious nature continued in El Salvador, declared once more that the provisions of the 1949 Geneva Conventions on the laws of war were applicable to the armed conflict in El Salvador, and requested all Salvadorian parties involved to apply a minimum standard of human rights protection and humane treatment to civilians. It reaffirmed the right of the Salvadorian people freely to determine their future without outside interference. It reiterated its appeal to States not to intervene and to suspend all military support, so as to allow the political forces in that country to restore peace and security and the establishment of a democratic system.

The Commission extended the mandate of the Special Representative for another year and requested him to report to the General Assembly in 1983 and to the Commission in 1984.

ECONOMIC AND SOCIAL COUNCIL ACTION

On the recommendation of its Second Committee, the Economic and Social Council adopted decision 1983/144 by recorded vote.

Situation of human rights in El Salvador

At its 15th plenary meeting, on 27 May 1983, the Council, noting Commission on Human Rights resolution 1983/29 of 8 March 1983, endorsed the Commission's decision to extend the mandate of the Special Representative on the situation of human rights in El Salvador for another year and to request him to submit his report on further developments in the situation of human rights in El Salvador to the General Assembly at its thirty-eighth session and to the Commission on Human Rights at its fortieth session, and requested the

Secretary-General to give all necessary assistance to the Special Representative of the Commission.

Economic and Social Council decision 1983/144

29-3-19 (recorded vote)

Approved by Second Committee (E/1983/61) by recorded vote (28-3-15), 23 May (meeting 18); draft by Commission on Human Rights (E/1983/13); agenda item 10. *Meeting number.* ESC 15.

Recorded vote in Council as follows:

In favour: Algeria, Austria, Benin, Bulgaria, Burundi, Byelorussian SSR, Canada, Congo, Denmark, France, German Democratic Republic, Germany, Federal Republic of, Greece, India, Japan, Kenya, Luxembourg, Mexico, Netherlands, New Zealand, Nicaragua, Norway, Poland, Portugal, Suriname, Swaziland, USSR, United Kingdom, Venezuela.

Against: Argentina, Brazil, United States.

Abstaining: Bangladesh, China, Colombia, Djibouti, Ecuador, Fiji, Lebanon, Liberia, Malaysia, Mali, Pakistan, Peru, Qatar, Saint Lucia, Saudi Arabia, Sierra Leone, Sudan, Thailand, Tunisia.

China said foreign intervention, particularly by the super-Powers, was responsible for the unrest in Central America; for peace and stability in the region, the people should decide for themselves on their domestic affairs and their destiny. Venezuela stated that its affirmative vote was an unequivocal expression of concern for human rights.

Sub-Commission action. On 5 September,[59] the Sub-Commission, expressing the belief that efforts to restore human rights protection would be more easily obtained if all States abstained from intervening in the internal situation in El Salvador and from supplying weapons or military assistance to it, suggested that the Special Representative also give attention to the respect, or violation, of humanitarian law in armed conflict. It requested the Secretary-General to report in 1984 on the work of Special Representative and on the Commission's deliberations on it.

Further report. The Special Representative's interim report on the situation in El Salvador, prepared in accordance with the Commission's March request, was transmitted to the General Assembly by a November note of the Secretary-General.[60] As in previous reports, the Special Representative analysed information from Governments and intergovernmental and non-governmental organizations, as well as information gathered during his visit to the country from 11 to 17 September, where he interviewed a number of persons, including political prisoners, and visited places of detention, a hospital where guerrilla fighters were treated and a farming village which had suffered in the conflict. The Special Representative also interviewed, among others, Salvadorians in exile in Mexico.

He reported that the Government extended full co-operation and its senior authorities assured him of their concern to improve the human rights situation in the country. Among the measures taken in that regard were the prohibition, by legislative decree of the Constituent Assembly, of all armed paramilitary groups, left or right; implementation of the Amnesty and Rehabilitation of Citizens Act proclaimed by the Constituent Assembly in May; and the efforts of the governmental Human Rights Commission. According to information given to the Special Representative, the Commission's consideration of 504 complaints during the first six months of 1983 resulted, among other things, in the release of 45 persons detained in military establishments and location of 91 missing persons in various military centres. The Commission also arranged for 152 persons benefiting from the Amnesty Act to be received by Australia, Belgium and Canada; assisted foreigners detained in military establishments; and conducted campaigns in various sectors and institutions—including the armed forces and security bodies—for the promotion and protection of human rights. The Special Representative learned that 1,137 persons—554 political offenders and 583 armed insurgents—had benefited from the Amnesty Act. As regards information on the arrest and murder of some prisoners released under the Act, the authorities told the Special Representative that those were persons released by judicial decision outside the scope of the Act, and that arrest and murder had been carried out by unidentified groups.

The Special Representative concluded that, despite the Government's declared intentions and demonstration of some efforts to improve the human rights situation, serious, massive and persistent violations of civil and political rights continued, including a large number of political murders of non-combatants. The capacity of the judicial system to investigate and punish human rights violations remained inadequate. The Special Representative again recommended that the Government as well as the opposition urgently end attacks on human life, and endeavour to establish a peaceful, democratic and pluralist coexistence. He recommended that the Government adopt measures enabling all parties to participate in future elections, in such a way that in particular the lives, physical integrity and freedom of all candidates, especially those belonging to the left-wing opposition, were safeguarded. In addition, he reiterated the recommendations made in his January report (see above).

GENERAL ASSEMBLY ACTION

The General Assembly, on the recommendation of the Third Committee, adopted resolution 38/101 on 16 December by recorded vote.

Situation of human rights and fundamental freedoms in El Salvador

The General Assembly,

Guided by the principles embodied in the Charter of the United Nations and in the Universal Declaration of Human Rights,

Conscious of its responsibility in all circumstances to promote and encourage respect for human rights and fundamental freedoms for all,

Reiterating that the Governments of all Member States have an obligation to promote and protect human rights and fundamental freedoms and to carry out the responsibilities they have undertaken under various international human rights instruments,

Determined to remain vigilant with regard to violations of human rights wherever they occur and to take measures to restore respect for human rights and fundamental freedoms,

Recalling that, in its resolutions 35/192 of 15 December 1980, 36/155 of 16 December 1981 and 37/185 of 17 December 1982, it expressed deep concern at the situation of human rights in El Salvador, especially in view of the death of thousands of people and the climate of violence and insecurity prevailing in that country, as well as the impunity of paramilitary forces and other armed groups,

Bearing in mind Commission on Human Rights resolutions 32(XXXVII) of 11 March 1981, in which the Commission decided to appoint a Special Representative on the situation of human rights in El Salvador, 1982/28 of 11 March 1982 and 1983/29 of 8 March 1983, whereby the Commission extended the mandate of the Special Representative for another year and requested him to report, *inter alia,* to the General Assembly at its thirty-eighth session,

Taking note with grave concern of the interim report of the Special Representative of the Commission on Human Rights, in which the continuation of a climate of violence and insecurity in El Salvador, characterized by armed clashes, acts of economic sabotage and grave and large-scale violations of human rights, as well as the failure of the Salvadorian authorities to prevent these constant violations of human rights in that country, are confirmed,

Bearing in mind that in its resolution 37/185 the General Assembly observed that the elections which were held in El Salvador in March 1982 had not led to the cessation of violence or to improvement in the situation of human rights and fundamental freedoms in that country,

Noting with satisfaction that the El Salvador Peace Commission, officials and special envoys of other Governments within and outside the region, as well as the representative political forces, have initiated talks in the search for a negotiated comprehensive political solution,

1. *Commends* the Special Representative of the Commission on Human Rights for his interim report on the situation of human rights in El Salvador;

2. *Expresses its deepest concern* at the fact that, as indicated in the report of the Special Representative, the gravest violations of human rights are persisting in El Salvador and that, as a result, the sufferings of the Salvadorian people are continuing, and regrets that the appeals for the cessation of the acts of violence made by the General Assembly, the Commission on Human Rights and the international community as a whole have not been heeded;

3. *Again draws the attention* of the Salvadorian parties concerned to the fact that the rules of international law, as contained in article 3 common to the Geneva Conventions of 12 August 1949 and Additional Protocols I and II thereto, are applicable to armed conflicts not of an international character, such as that in El Salvador, and requests all parties to apply a minimum standard of protection of human rights and of humane treatment of the civilian population;

4.   *Takes note* of resolution 1983/18 of 5 September 1983 of the Sub-Commission on Prevention of Discrimination and Protection of Minorities, in which the Sub-Commission suggested that the Special Representative give attention in his report to respect for or violation of humanitarian law in armed conflict;

5.   *Recommends* that the reforms necessary for the solution of the economic and social problems which are at the root of the internal conflict in El Salvador should be put into effect so as to allow the effective exercise of civil and political rights in that country, and reaffirms the right of the Salvadorian people freely to determine their political, economic and social future without interference from outside and in an atmosphere free from intimidation and terror;

6.   *Calls upon* the Government of El Salvador and other political forces to intensify their talks and to work towards the creation of suitable conditions in the common search for a negotiated comprehensive political solution which will put an end to the internal armed conflict and establish a lasting peace which will allow the full exercise both of civil and political rights and of economic, social and cultural rights by all Salvadorians;

7.   *Once again urges* all States to abstain from intervening in the internal situation in El Salvador and to suspend all supplies of arms and any type of military assistance, so as to allow the restoration of peace and security and the establishment of a democratic system based on full respect for human rights and fundamental freedoms;

8.   *Expresses its deep concern* at reports which prove that government forces regularly resort to bombarding urban areas in El Salvador that are not military objectives, and its concern for the fate of several hundred thousand displaced persons who are currently located in camps in which they are subjected to abuse and in which not even the minimum conditions of internment, in terms of either humane treatment or material needs, are observed;

9.   *Also expresses its deep concern* at the resurgence of disappearances and murders of persons belonging to various sectors of the civilian population, for which the so-called "death squads" claim responsibility, and urges that these activities be investigated with a view to punishing those responsible;

10.   *Expresses its concern* at the consequences of the damage done to the economy of El Salvador as a result of the attacks on the economic infrastructure attributable for the most part, according to the report of the Special Representative, to the opposition forces;

11.   *Reiterates its urgent appeal* to the Government of El Salvador to fulfil its obligations towards its citizens and to assume its international responsibilities in this regard by taking the necessary steps to ensure that all its agencies, including its security forces and other armed organizations operating under its authority, fully respect human rights and fundamental freedoms;

12.   *Urges* the competent authorities of El Salvador to establish the necessary conditions to enable the judiciary to uphold the rule of law, prosecuting and punishing speedily and effectively those responsible for the grave violations of human rights which are being committed in that country;

13.   *Reiterates its appeal* to all Salvadorian parties in the conflict to co-operate fully and not to interfere with the activities of humanitarian organizations dedicated to alleviating the suffering of the civilian population, wherever these organizations operate in the country;

14.   *Deplores* the violent death of Marianela García Villas, President of the Commission of Human Rights of El Salvador, and, given the contradictory reports on the matter, requests the Special Representative of the Commission on Human Rights to investigate the circumstances of her death;

15.   *Renews its appeal* to the Government of El Salvador, as well as all other parties concerned, to continue to co-operate with the Special Representative of the Commission on Human Rights;

16.   *Decides* to keep under consideration, during its thirty-ninth session, the situation of human rights and fundamental freedoms in El Salvador, in order to examine this situation anew in the light of additional elements provided by the Commission on Human Rights and the Economic and Social Council.

General Assembly resolution 38/101

16 December 1983   Meeting 100   84-14-45 (recorded vote)

Approved by Third Committee (A/38/680) by recorded vote (78-13-41), 9 December (meeting 71); 10-nation draft (A/C.3/38/L.62), orally revised on proposal by Morocco and further orally revised; agenda item 12.

Sponsors: Algeria, Denmark, France, Greece, Mexico, Netherlands, Norway, Spain, Sweden, Yugoslavia.

Meeting numbers. GA 38th session: 3rd Committee 18, 54, 55, 57-71; plenary 100.

Recorded vote in Assembly as follows:

In favour: Afghanistan, Algeria, Angola, Australia, Austria, Bahrain, Belgium, Benin, Botswana, Bulgaria, Burundi, Byelorussian SSR, Canada, Cape Verde, Congo, Cuba, Cyprus, Czechoslovakia, Democratic Yemen, Denmark, Ethiopia, Finland, France, Gambia, German Democratic Republic, Ghana, Greece, Grenada, Guinea, Guinea-Bissau, Guyana, Hungary, Iceland, India, Iran, Iraq, Ireland, Italy, Jamaica, Kenya, Kuwait, Lao People's Democratic Republic, Lesotho, Libyan Arab Jamahiriya, Luxembourg, Madagascar, Mali, Malta, Mauritania, Mauritius, Mexico, Mongolia, Mozambique, Netherlands, New Zealand, Nicaragua, Nigeria, Norway, Papua New Guinea, Poland, Portugal, Qatar, Rwanda, Sao Tome and Principe, Saudi Arabia, Senegal, Seychelles, Sierra Leone, Spain, Sweden, Syrian Arab Republic, Togo, Tunisia, Uganda, Ukrainian SSR, USSR, United Arab Emirates, United Republic of Tanzania, Upper Volta, Vanuatu, Viet Nam, Yugoslavia, Zambia, Zimbabwe.

Against: Bangladesh, Brazil, Chile, El Salvador, Guatemala, Haiti, Honduras, Indonesia, Pakistan, Paraguay, Philippines, Saint Lucia, United States, Uruguay.

Abstaining: Bahamas, Barbados, Belize, Bhutan, Burma, Central African Republic, Chad, China, Colombia, Costa Rica, Democratic Kampuchea, Dominica, Dominican Republic, Ecuador, Egypt, Equatorial Guinea, Fiji, Gabon, Germany, Federal Republic of, Ivory Coast, Japan, Jordan, Lebanon, Liberia, Malawi, Malaysia, Maldives, Morocco, Nepal, Niger, Oman, Panama, Peru, Romania, Singapore, Sri Lanka, Sudan, Suriname, Thailand, Trinidad and Tobago, Turkey, United Kingdom, United Republic of Cameroon, Yemen, Zaire.

The draft resolution was revised on an oral proposal by Morocco, deleting, in paragraph 11, the words "or with its permission" after "operating under its authority".

Indonesia considered the text to be an interference in El Salvador's internal affairs under the pretext of protecting human rights. Haiti found it disturbing that consideration was given to the human rights situation in only one part of the world. Singapore and Trinidad and Tobago said the draft's selective approach undermined the United Nations credibility. Honduras rejected a selective approach, and added that mention should be made of the efforts of the Government to ensure respect for human rights. Bhutan asserted that human rights violations occurred in various parts of the world. Colombia, the Dominican Republic and Ecuador also critized selectivity and discriminating criteria. Sharing that view, Jamaica appealed for the establishment of a high commissioner for human rights, to deal with violations world-wide on an equitable basis.

Declaring itself in favour of protection of human rights in all regions, Bolivia did not participate in the vote. Acting likewise, Venezuela called for a balanced approach to the question of human rights violations.

China felt that the instability in El Salvador and the region was due to the hegemonism of a super-Power which intervened in the internal affairs; the question of human rights could be solved only by allowing the peoples themselves to confront the situation.

Canada regarded the draft as unbalanced, in that it did not take account of certain indications demonstrating the Government's genuine concern for human rights. Canada felt that the frequent use in the text of the word "negotiated" conferred the same degree of constitutional legitimacy on the parties engaged in the negotiations in El Salvador which were no longer confined to the Government and opposition forces. Canada recognized the Government as legitimate and thus fully responsible for the administration of the country, including protection of fundamental rights; talk of "negotiations" was likely to undermine the Government's authority and diminish its responsibilities.

Viewing the draft as one-sided and unbalanced, the United States failed to hold the guerrillas responsible for the climate of fear and the acts of economic sabotage in the country. The Government of El Salvador was struggling to attain the institutional authority necessary to eliminate human rights abuses; improvements in that situation had been steady, although not dramatic, and much of the violence would cease with the end of the Marxist-Leninist insurgency. The United States stated further that paragraph 8 was wilfully inaccurate in that there was no proof of regular bombardment of civilian targets, whereas evidence pointed to the guerrillas interfering with military communications so as to direct fire against civilians rather than military targets. Attributing all the human rights problems to the Government served the cause of the insurgent forces whose only purpose, the United States said, was to use violence to create a revolutionary situation in which the Government would have no alternative but to intensify repression.

Costa Rica abstained in order not to prejudice the atmosphere conducive to negotiations by the Contadora Group.

The United Kingdom, while viewing the text as more balanced than in previous years, regarded as unacceptable the appeal for suspension of military assistance in the current circumstances; the

régime, established following the 1982 elections in which 75 per cent of the population were reliably reported to have participated, had the right to defend itself. It deplored the fact that the full cooperation of the Salvadorian authorities with the Special Representative had not been mentioned in the text.

The Federal Republic of Germany said that for the first time an appeal was made to all parties, including the opposition forces, to respect the rules of international law applicable to armed conflict; on the other hand, none of the positive elements noted by the Special Representative in his report appeared in the text. In addition, it had serious reservations on paragraphs 6 and 7. Finland expressed reservations with regard to a number of provisions which, it felt, were marked by partiality. Portugal reserved its position on the wording of the ninth preambular paragraph, as well as paragraphs 6 and 7, adding that the text still stated, in paragraph 5, that the effective exercise of civil and political rights depended on a solution to the economic and social problems, and failed to stress sufficiently the need for the Salvadorians to express their true aspirations in free and democratic elections.

Belgium expressed the hope that no preconditions would be set for the efforts aimed at restoring representative democracy. Cuba considered the draft an appropriate response to the situation in El Salvador.

El Salvador stated that the text was not constructive for the promotion of human rights; it was partisan, interventionist and—like the drafts on Chile and Guatemala—ineffectual and irrelevant because of tendentious and biased wording. In particular, El Salvador objected that the text: indirectly criticized the free and open elections in which all political factions had participated; placed on an equal footing a legitimate Government and opposition minority groups, a point of view no country respecting its own interests could accept; disregarded developments in reform and used language that relegated those events to oblivion; left El Salvador without the means of defence against its opponents who resorted to violence in order to take power; referred, without proof, to regular bombarding of urban areas which were not military objectives, actions which were carried out by the armed opposition groups; and gave the Commission power beyond its established terms of reference.

Guatemala

Action by the Commission on Human Rights. By a note of 4 February 1983,[61] the Chairman informed the Commission on Human Rights that he had appointed in December 1982, in accordance with the Commission's March 1982 request,[62] Elizabeth Odio Benito (Costa Rica) as Special Rapporteur to study the human rights situation in Guatemala. Expressing the desire that the Special Rapporteur should not be a person who had participated as representative of a country in human rights debates, Guatemala, by a letter of 18 January 1983, had requested that another candidate be proposed before the Commission's session.

On 7 February,[63] the Commission decided to continue examination of the situation of human rights in Guatemala and, in view of the wish expressed for information on developments there since March 1982, requested the Secretary-General to prepare a note containing a list of material received by the United Nations Secretariat, together with an indication of its contents. Following that request, the Secretariat, by a note of 15 February,[64] transmitted a list of legislation, communications by the Government, and documents by intergovernmental and non-governmental organizations.

By a resolution of 8 March, adopted by a roll-call vote of 27 to 4, with 12 abstentions,[65] the Commission reiterated its concern at the continuing reports of massive human rights violations in Guatemala, particularly reports of violence against non-combatants, widespread repression, and killing and massive displacement of rural and indigenous people. It urged the Government to ensure that its authorities and agencies, including its security forces, fully respected human rights, suspend immediately any executions ordered by special courts, facilitate the entry of representatives of the International Committee of the Red Cross (ICRC) into the country and investigate the fate of disappeared persons with a view to informing their relatives of their whereabouts. The Commission also called on Governments to refrain from supplying arms and military assistance as long as serious human rights violations in Guatemala continued to be reported.

The Commission again requested the Chairman to appoint a Special Rapporteur to study the human rights situation in Guatemala, and requested the Rapporteur to present an interim report to the General Assembly in 1983 and a final report to the Commission in 1984.

On 11 March, the Chairman announced the appointment of Viscount Colville of Culross (United Kingdom) as Special Rapporteur.

ECONOMIC AND SOCIAL COUNCIL ACTION

The Economic and Social Council, on the recommendation of its Second Committee, adopted decision 1983/148 by recorded vote.

Situation of human rights in Guatemala

At its 15th plenary meeting, on 27 May 1983, the Council, noting Commission on Human Rights resolution 1983/37 of 8 March 1983, welcomed the appointment by the Chairman of the Commission of a Special Rapporteur of the Commission whose mandate will be to make a thorough study of the human rights situation in Guatemala, based on all information which he may deem relevant, including any comments and information which the Government of Guatemala may wish to submit, and endorsed the Commission's decision to request that the Special Rapporteur present an interim report to the General Assembly at its thirty-eighth session and a final report to the Commission at its fortieth session. The Council requested the Secretary-General to give all necessary assistance to the Special Rapporteur.

Economic and Social Council decision 1983/148

31-1-20 (recorded vote)*

Approved by Second Committee (E/1983/61) by vote (25-1-19), 23 May (meeting 18); draft by Commission on Human Rights (E/1983/13), orally amended by Netherlands; agenda item 10.
Financial implications. S-G, E/1983/L.26.
Meeting number. ESC 15.
*Owing to technical difficulties, the result of the voting was not available.

Sub-Commission action. By a letter of 18 August,[66] Guatemala informed the Chairman of the Sub-Commission that it would be inadvisable for the Sub-Commission to take up the question of Guatemala in 1983 while the Special Rapporteur's report was still in preparation. Guatemala stated that it would therefore not participate in the Sub-Commission's 1983 session and rejected any groundless comments about the situation in the country that could interfere with the Special Rapporteur's mandate.

By a resolution adopted on 5 September by 17 votes to none, with 3 abstentions,[67] the Sub-Commission expressed deep concern that the persistent and systematic nature of human rights violations in Guatemala had made the effective exercise of economic, social, cultural, civil and political rights impossible. The Sub-Commission called on the Government to refrain from forced displacement of the Indian communities and their confinement in strategic hamlets, as well as massacres, scorched-earth policies and forced disappearances, and called on all parties to the conflict in Guatemala to assure the application of international norms of humanitarian law in war to protect the civilian non-combatant population. It insisted that the Government ensure compliance of the security forces with humanitarian law, applicable to armed conflicts of a non-international character, and urged it to facilitate the entrance of international humanitarian bodies to assist victims of that conflict. It urged Governments to abstain from providing arms or military assistance to Guatemala as long as reports of serious human rights violations continued.

Guatemala, in a letter of 5 September,[68] protested the manner in which the Sub-Commission dealt with the human rights situation and rejected the resolution as being without foundation, it having ignored the reality and having interfered with the work of the Special Rapporteur.

Report of the Special Rapporteur. By a note of 4 November,[69] the Secretary-General transmitted to the General Assembly a report by the Special Rapporteur on the human rights situation in Guatemala, prepared in accordance with the Commission's March request (see above).

The Special Rapporteur stated that, during his visit to Guatemala from 25 June to 5 July, he had received full co-operation of the Government and the military. The report was based on information collected up to July, with some updating following the change in the Presidency.

In addition to being a party to various international instruments, Guatemala had adopted on 29 March a decree-law approving the 1951 Convention relating to the Status of Refugees[70] and the 1967 Protocol to it.[71] While it had not ratified for technical reasons the 1966 International Covenants on Human Rights,[72] the standards set by them served as the report's foundation. The legal situation in the country had changed since the termination of the state of siege on 23 March, the Special Rapporteur added.

After giving a historical background of the situation in Guatemala, the report dealt with: the current conflict in the country; aspects relating to the indigenous population; current reforms; "model" villages protected by the army against the guerrillas and settlements of internal refugees; religious freedom; special tribunals; and refugees in Mexico.

In his conclusions, the Special Rapporteur stated that the demands and ambitions of the revolutionaries—unlikely to be accepted by the establishment—led to a continuation of the armed conflict which had infringed on civil and political rights. The right to life had unquestionably been violated in circumstances where confrontation in the civil war could not provide an excuse. The new administration had indicated its intention to continue with a credible programme, introduced by the last military Government, that could lead to a genuine improvement. However, time must elapse before any definitive judgement could be formed on the extent to which a comprehensive improvement in the human rights situation had actually been achieved.

The Special Rapporteur considered it desirable that the following policies be actively pursued within Guatemala: practical attempts, using recent experience and the latest amnesty on 8 August, to persuade the internal refugees, whose predicament was increasingly serious, to emerge from hiding in the mountains and forests; encouragement of humane and efficient reception of the returning refugees; and the longer-term plans of public land distribution, opportunities to engage

in agriculture for cash and subsistence foodstuffs, projects for infrastructure, new community buildings, and extension of the road and airstrip network.

With regard to human rights under the Covenant on Civil and Political Rights, he suggested the following: continuation of the work of the newly established Supreme Electoral Tribunal with adherence to the new President's expressed promise of a timetable for the election, free of intrigue or vested interest; urgent decision by the Supreme Court on changes to ensure the proper rights of a defendant in all criminal cases, as instructed by the new Government; prevention of disappearances at the hands of the authorities; and encouragement of the new Confederation of Trade Unions, together with new individual unions, to play their part in the country's economic process. The Special Rapporteur asserted, in connection with freedom of expression and freedom of the independent university, that, possibly, the borderline between freedom of expression and subversion was very narrow in the context of the conflict in the country, and that this area would be of continuing interest in the following months.

The Special Rapporteur, who had had an interview with the President of the Supreme Court, observed: that there had been much criticism of the Court's refusal to grant *amparo* in the case of certain persons sentenced to death earlier in the year by a Special Tribunal; that it was impossible to come to a conclusion on the effectiveness of the Court's powers of supervision if the reasoned judgements were not published; and that, with a fundamental reconstitution of the Supreme Court, it seemed possible that a new series of law reports, bypassing the existing backlog, could be immediately begun. Despite the manifest independence of the Electoral Tribunal, there was a project, in conjunction with the preparation of new electoral registers, to computerize that information under the direction not of the Tribunal but of a senior army officer, a fact that had raised suspicions about the use to which the information might be put.

GENERAL ASSEMBLY ACTION

On 16 December, on the recommendation of the Third Committee, the General Assembly adopted resolution 38/100 by recorded vote.

Situation of human rights and fundamental freedoms in Guatemala

The General Assembly,

Reiterating that the Governments of all Member States have an obligation to promote and protect human rights and fundamental freedoms,

Recalling its resolution 37/184 of 17 December 1982,

Taking note of Commission on Human Rights resolution 1983/37 of 8 March 1983, in which the Commission reiterated its profound concern at the continuing reports of massive violations of human rights in Guatemala,

Noting that the Sub-Commission on Prevention of Discrimination and Protection of Minorities, in its resolution 1983/12 of 5 September 1983, recognized that in Guatemala there existed an armed conflict of a non-international character, which stemmed from economic, social and political factors of a structural nature, and that within that conflict the security forces and government institutions had not respected the norms of international humanitarian law,

Expressing its satisfaction at the appointment of a Special Rapporteur of the Commission on Human Rights and taking note of the co-operation extended to the Special Rapporteur by the Government of Guatemala,

Taking note of the interim report by the Special Rapporteur on the situation of human rights in Guatemala, submitted in accordance with Commission on Human Rights resolution 1983/37,

Welcoming the lifting of the state of siege and the abolition of the special tribunals,

Disturbed at the large number of persons who have disappeared, including those reported to have been tried by the special tribunals, and who, despite appeals from various international organizations, remain unaccounted for,

1. *Expresses its deep concern* at the continuing massive violations of human rights in Guatemala, particularly the violence against non-combatants, and the widespread repression, killing and massive displacement of rural and indigenous populations, which are reported to have increased recently;

2. *Calls upon* the Government of Guatemala to refrain both from forcefully displacing people belonging to rural and indigenous populations and from the practice of coercing people into participation in civilian patrols, leading to human rights violations;

3. *Urges* the Government of Guatemala to take effective measures to ensure that all its authorities and agencies, including its security forces, fully respect human rights and fundamental freedoms;

4. *Requests* the Government of Guatemala to investigate and clarify the fate of persons who have disappeared and are still unaccounted for, including those reported to have been tried by the special tribunals;

5. *Calls upon* the Government of Guatemala to establish a system for the revocation of convictions and sentences passed by the special tribunals, now abolished;

6. *Appeals* to the Government of Guatemala to allow international humanitarian organizations to render assistance in investigating the fate of persons who have disappeared, with a view to informing their relatives of their whereabouts, and to visit detainees or prisoners, and to allow them to bring assistance to the civilian population in areas of conflict;

7. *Appeals also* to all parties concerned in Guatemala to ensure the application of the relevant norms of international humanitarian law applicable in armed conflicts of a non-international character to protect the civilian population and to seek an end to all acts of violence;

8. *Calls upon* Governments to refrain from supplying arms and other military assistance as long as serious human rights violations in Guatemala continue to be reported;

9. *Invites* the Government of Guatemala and other parties concerned to continue co-operating with the Special Rapporteur of the Commission on Human Rights;

10. *Requests* the Commission on Human Rights to study carefully the report of its Special Rapporteur, as well as other information pertaining to the situation in Guatemala, and to consider further steps for securing effective respect for human rights and fundamental freedoms for all in that country;

11. *Decides* to continue its examination of the situation of human rights and fundamental freedoms in Guatemala at its thirty-ninth session.

General Assembly resolution 38/100

16 December 1983   Meeting 100   85-15-44 (recorded vote)

Approved by Third Committee (A/38/680) by recorded vote (80-14-36), 9 December (meeting 71); 9-nation draft (A/C.3/38/L.57); agenda item 12.

Sponsors: Austria, Canada, Denmark, France, Greece, Netherlands, Norway, Spain, Sweden.

Meeting numbers. GA 38th session: 3rd Committee 18, 54, 55, 57-71; plenary 100.

Recorded vote in Assembly as follows:

In favour: Afghanistan, Algeria, Angola, Australia, Austria, Bahrain, Barbados, Belgium, Benin, Botswana, Bulgaria, Burundi, Byelorussian SSR, Canada, Cape Verde, Congo, Cuba, Cyprus, Czechoslovakia, Democratic Yemen, Denmark, Ethiopia, Finland, France, Gambia, German Democratic Republic, Germany, Federal Republic of, Ghana, Greece, Grenada, Guinea-Bissau, Guyana, Hungary, Iceland, Iran, Iraq, Ireland, Italy, Jamaica, Kenya, Kuwait, Lao People's Democratic Republic, Lesotho, Libyan Arab Jamahiriya, Luxembourg, Madagascar, Mali, Malta, Mauritania, Mauritius, Mexico, Mongolia, Mozambique, Netherlands, New Zealand, Nicaragua, Nigeria, Norway, Papua New Guinea, Poland, Portugal, Qatar, Rwanda, Sao Tome and Principe, Saudi Arabia, Senegal, Seychelles, Sierra Leone, Spain, Sweden, Syrian Arab Republic, Togo, Tunisia, Uganda, Ukrainian SSR, USSR, United Arab Emirates, United Kingdom, United Republic of Tanzania, Upper Volta, Vanuatu, Viet Nam, Yugoslavia, Zambia, Zimbabwe.

Against: Bangladesh, Brazil, Chile, El Salvador, Guatemala, Haiti, Honduras, Indonesia, Israel, Morocco, Pakistan, Paraguay, Philippines, United States, Uruguay.

Abstaining: Bahamas, Belize, Bhutan, Burma, Central African Republic, Chad, China, Colombia, Costa Rica, Democratic Kampuchea, Dominica, Dominican Republic, Ecuador, Egypt, Equatorial Guinea, Fiji, Gabon, Guinea, Ivory Coast, Japan, Jordan, Lebanon, Liberia, Malawi, Malaysia, Maldives, Nepal, Niger, Oman, Panama, Peru, Romania, Saint Lucia, Singapore, Sri Lanka, Sudan, Suriname, Thailand, Trinidad and Tobago, Turkey, United Republic of Cameroon, Yemen, Zaire.

Guatemala said the Special Rapporteur had objectively described the human rights situation in the country and had made recommendations for solutions that would gradually enable the Government to overcome the crisis; it deeply regretted that some countries had chosen to pay no heed to the Special Rapporteur's report, thus weakening his mandate.

Guatemala rejected the draft resolution for its selective condemnation, biased and politicized approach to the human rights situation in that country and for not reflecting the Special Rapporteur's conclusions in his report. In this context, Guatemala reiterated its support for the appointment of a high commissioner for human rights so that year by year the Centre for Human Rights could prepare a report on the human rights situation in each Member State.

Referring to specific provisions of the draft, Guatemala found unacceptable the assertion in the fourth preambular paragraph to an armed conflict of a non-international character; it disregarded Guatemala's call to the Sub-Commission to await the Special Rapporteur's conclusions before taking a decision; also, Guatemala had not been allowed to express its point of view during the Sub-Commission's debate. As regards paragraphs 4 and 8, Guatemala said the special tribunals had been abolished on 1 September 1983 and pending cases had been referred back to ordinary courts; no one tried during the existence of the special tribunals had disappeared, many cases had been dropped, and the suspects released. Guatemala rejected paragraphs 1 to 3 and 5 as not in keeping with the Special Rapporteur's conclusions. It also rejected the appeal contained in paragraph 6, saying that the paragraph was incomplete and did not reflect its willingness to co-operate with international humanitarian organizations; the Government had already authorized representatives of such organizations to take note of relevant developments in the country.

Colombia said the draft failed to welcome Guatemala's readiness to agree to a dialogue with the Special Rapporteur, much less recognize that his report encouraged dialogue and enabled the United Nations to exert the necessary pressure for change; the request to the Commission to study the report as well as other information pertaining to the situation in Guatemala meant that the Special Rapporteur's report would be put on an equal footing with often tendentious reports drafted by groups opposing the Government.

The United States said that, by speaking of a non-international conflict in Guatemala, the draft resolution ignored the training of insurgents in Cuba and Nicaragua and the weapons provided by the Soviet bloc; further, the text failed to mention violations of international law by the guerrillas who continued to kill non-combatants and utilize kidnapping as a political weapon. Paragraph 3 urged the Government, but not the guerrillas, to respect human rights, which seemed to suggest that there was no insurgency. No account was taken of the fact recognized by the Special Rapporteur that human rights violations were on a much reduced scale compared to 1981. Paragraph 6 ignored the Government's open-door policy towards responsible human rights groups, and paragraph 8 took no note of the prohibition of covert shipment of arms and military equipment to the guerrillas. The thrust of the draft was that the Government was fully to blame for the situation in the country and did not have the right to use force in opposition to the armed guerrilla insurgency.

Indonesia considered the draft resolution an interference in Guatemala's internal affairs under the pretext of protecting human rights.

Haiti and Honduras found disturbing the selective approach singling out particular countries. Also deploring the text's selectivity, the United Kingdom expressed doubts about the applicability of the references to "non-combatants" and "international humanitarian law" in paragraphs 1 and 7.

The draft's selective approach was rejected by several others, among them Bhutan, the Dominican Republic and Ecuador. Singapore and Trinidad and Tobago stated that they would abstain because of the selective condemnation of human rights, an approach which undermined the United Nations credibility and universality. Similar views were voiced by Bolivia and Venezuela for their non-participation in the vote.

The Federal Republic of Germany had serious reservations particularly as regards the call on Governments, in paragraph 8, to refrain from supplying arms to Guatemala. The text did not take account of the fact that the Government was not alone in using armed force and that military operations were also part of the guerrillas' strategy; it did not acknowledge the positive initiatives such as the lifting of the state of siege and initiation of democratic reforms. Further, the text reflected only partially the Special Rapporteur's conclusions, and the fifth preambular paragraph took note only in a somewhat laconic manner of the Government's co-operation while it had, in fact, fully co-operated. Tunisia welcomed the co-operation between the Special Rapporteur and the Government, as well as such developments as the lifting of the state of siege and the abolition of the special tribunals. Morocco said the draft resolution took no account of the positive strides made by the Government, and mentioned by the Special Rapporteur, in tackling the root causes of discontent and violence.

Expressing alarm at the violence and internal conflict in Guatemala, Portugal deplored that the draft failed to mention that the Government was not solely to blame for it. Finland had reservations with regard to a number of provisions of the draft which, it felt, were marked by partiality. Australia felt that despite such reservations, the international community was duty-bound to express its concern to the Government.

In Cuba's opinion, the draft resolution was an appropriate response to the situation in Guatemala.

Paraguay

The Sub-Commission on Prevention of Discrimination and Protection of Minorities, on 6 September 1983,[73] recommended that the Commission on Human Rights invite Paraguay to consider ending the state of siege in order to encourage the promotion of, and respect for, human rights in the country.

The Sub-Commission made that recommendation taking into account the conclusions of the Special Rapporteur on the status of human rights in situations of a state of siege or emergency (see above, under CIVIL AND POLITICAL RIGHTS). In so doing, the Sub-Commission noted that the state of siege had been used on a permanent basis in Paraguay since 1954 through its renewal every three months, and that recent information pointed to a growing incidence of threats to individual liberty, resulting in arbitrary detention and cruel treatment of prisoners of opinion, as well as of violations of the right to due and equitable process, and serious limitations to the freedom of expression.

Uruguay

By a decision of 31 August 1983,[74] the Sub-Commission requested the Secretary-General to communicate a text to the Chairman of the Commission on Human Rights for transmission by him to the Uruguayan authorities. By that text, the Sub-Commission expressed grave concern over information regarding the health of a mathematician, José Luis Massera, and requested the Government to show an act of clemency and end his detention on humanitarian grounds.

Referring to the Sub-Commission's decision, Uruguay, by a letter of 6 September,[75] stated that the person in question had been imprisoned as a result of regular criminal proceedings. As regards allegations of torture and bad health of the detainee, Uruguay said it had submitted updated reports on the state of his health in accordance with the confidential procedure established by the Economic and Social Council in 1970[1] for dealing with allegations of human rights violations (see above). Contrary to a statement that the detainee was an intellectual of international repute, not a politician, Uruguay said it was well-known that he had served as senator and Secretary-General of the Communist Party.

Middle East

Territories occupied by Israel

During 1983, the question of human rights violations in the territories occupied by Israel as a result of the 1967 hostilities in the Middle East was again considered by the Commission on Human Rights, its Sub-Commission and the General Assembly. This was in addition to the consideration of political and other aspects by the Assembly, its Special Committee to Investigate Israeli Practices Affecting the Human Rights of the Population of the Occupied Territories and other bodies (see POLITICAL AND SECURITY QUESTIONS, Chapter IX).

Action by the Commission on Human Rights. Following consideration of two January 1983 reports of the Secretary-General on human rights violations in the occupied Arab territories, includ-

ing Palestine, the Commission on Human Rights adopted on 15 February four relevant resolutions: two on human rights violations in the territories, and one each on Israeli occupation of the Syrian Golan Heights and on self-determination for the Palestinian people.

In the first report,[76] the Secretary-General stated that, following the Commission's February 1982 decision,[77] a seminar on violations of human rights in the Palestinian and other Arab territories occupied by Israel had been held at Geneva from 29 November to 3 December 1982.[78]

By the second report,[79] the Secretary-General informed the Commission that, in accordance with its February 1982 resolutions,[77] he had brought them to the attention of the General Assembly, the Security Council, Governments, United Nations organs and agencies, and other organizations. He noted that, in response to the Commission's request, DPI had taken steps to ensure wide publicity for the first of the 1982 resolutions.

By the first 15 February 1983 resolution, adopted by a roll-call vote of 29 to 1, with 13 abstentions,[80] the Commission reaffirmed that occupation itself constituted a fundamental violation of the human rights of the civilian population of the territories. It reiterated the alarm expressed by the Committee on Israeli practices that Israel's policy in the territories denied the right to self-determination and was the source of systematic human rights violations; it rejected Israel's decision to annex Jerusalem and change the character and status of the city and of the territories. It declared that Israel's grave breaches of the 1949 Geneva Convention relative to the Protection of Civilian Persons in Time of War (the fourth Geneva Convention) were war crimes and an affront to humanity.

The Commission strongly condemned Israeli measures to promote and expand the establishment of settler colonies, as well as other practices, such as: annexation of parts of the territories, including Jerusalem; continuing establishment and expansion of settlements; arming of settlers and their acts of violence against Arabs; evacuation and displacement of Arabs and the denial of their right to return; confiscation and expropriation of Arab property; destruction and demolition of Arab houses; mass arrests, collective punishments, detention, ill-treatment, torture and inhuman conditions in prisons; pillaging of archaeological and cultural property; interference with religious freedoms and family customs; systematic repression against cultural and educational institutions; illegal exploitation of natural resources; and dismantling of municipal services by dismissing elected mayors and municipal councils and forbidding Arab aid funds.

The Commission called on Israel to take immediate steps for the return of displaced Arabs to their homes and property; to implement Security Council resolutions on the return of the expelled Mayors of Hebron and Halhul; to release all Arabs detained as a result of their struggle for self-determination; and to cease all acts of torture and ill-treatment of prisoners. It reiterated its call to States, international organizations and specialized agencies not to recognize changes carried out by Israel in the territories, including Jerusalem, and to avoid taking action or extending aid which might be used by Israel in its annexation and colonization policies. It urged Israel to refrain from policies and practices violating human rights and to report to it in 1984 through the Secretary-General. It requested the General Assembly, through the Economic and Social Council, to recommend to the Security Council adoption against Israel of measures under Chapter VII of the Charter of the United Nations, for its persistence in violating the human rights of the population of the territories.

By the second resolution, adopted by a roll-call vote of 39 to 1, with 3 abstentions,[81] the Commission expressed deep concern at the consequence of Israel's refusal to apply the fourth Geneva Convention to the territories, including Jerusalem. It reaffirmed that the Convention was applicable to all the territories occupied by Israel since 1967, and condemned Israel's failure to acknowledge its applicability. It called on Israel to abide by and respect the obligations under the United Nations Charter, the Convention and other international instruments, and urged once more all States parties to the Convention to ensure Israel's compliance.

By the third resolution, adopted by a roll-call vote of 27 to 2, with 13 abstentions,[82] the Commission condemned Israel for its failure to comply with Security Council and Assembly resolutions demanding that Israel rescind its 1981 decision to apply Israeli law to the occupied Golan Heights.[83] The Commission reaffirmed the continued applicability to the territory of the Hague Convention of 1907 and the fourth Geneva Convention, and called the continued occupation of the Golan Heights since 1967 and its effective annexation in 1981, as well as the inhuman treatment of the Syrian population, a violation of the 1948 Universal Declaration of Human Rights,[84] the fourth Geneva Convention and United Nations resolutions. It strongly deplored the negative vote of a permanent member of the Security Council which had prevented the Council from adopting against Israel measures under Chapter VII of the Charter. The Commission firmly emphasized the necessity of total and unconditional Israeli withdrawal from all Palestinian and Syrian territories as an essential prerequisite for a comprehensive and just Middle East peace.

In the fourth 15 February resolution, on the right of peoples to self-determination (see above, under CIVIL AND POLITICAL RIGHTS), the Commission condemned Israel's aggression and practices against the Palestinians, condemning in the strongest terms the September 1982 massacre at the Sabra and Shatila refugee camps[85] which, it decided, was an act of genocide. The Commission requested the General Assembly to declare 17 September a day to commemorate the victims, and expressed its grave concern that the Palestinians would be exposed to grave dangers such as the massacre until a just and equitable solution to the Palestine problem had been implemented.

In accordance with the Commission's request,[80] the Secretary-General transmitted to the General Assembly[86] in July 1983 the conclusions, recommendations and appeal adopted by the 1982 seminar (see above).

Sub-Commission action. By a resolution of 31 August, adopted by 15 votes to 1, with 5 abstentions,[87] the Sub-Commission affirmed that the Israeli occupation of the Palestinian and other Arab territories, including Jerusalem, was a source of increasing human rights violations and of tension in the region. It reiterated that the Palestinians had inalienable rights to self-determination without external interference, to return to their homes and property, and to the establishment of a fully independent and sovereign State of Palestine.

The Sub-Commission reaffirmed that the future of the Palestinians could be decided only with its full participation, through PLO as its representative organ. It affirmed that the Palestinian and other freedom fighters detained by Israel were entitled to benefit of the status of prisoner of war, according to the 1949 Geneva Convention relative to the Treatment of Prisoners of War (the third Geneva Convention), and that the Palestinians and other civilians arbitrarily detained by Israel should be immediately released.

The Sub-Commission reaffirmed the applicability of the fourth Geneva Convention to the Israeli-occupied territories and expressed deep concern at the consequences of Israel's refusal to apply that Convention. It also expressed deep concern that, until a just and equitable solution to the Palestine problem had been implemented, the Palestinians would be exposed to grave dangers such as the September 1982 massacre at the Sabra and Shatila refugee camps, which had been qualified as an act of genocide and for which Israel's responsibility had been established.

The Sub-Commission recommended to the Commission the adoption of a draft resolution, condemning Israel for its continued occupation of Palestinian and other Arab territories and for its persistence in colonizing them, reaffirming that such measures violated the 1907 Hague Convention and the fourth Geneva Convention, and calling on Israel to withdraw immediately from the occupied territories, in order to restore to the Palestinians their inalienable national rights.

Persons detained by Israel

By a note of 2 February,[88] the Secretary-General presented to the Commission on Human Rights a report by the International Centre of Information on Lebanese and Palestinian Prisoners, Deportees and Disappeared Persons, transmitted to him on 31 January by PLO.

Expressing alarm at the situation of Palestinian, Lebanese and other detainees held by Israel as a result of the June 1982 invasion of Lebanon (see also POLITICAL AND SECURITY QUESTIONS, Chapter IX), the Commission, by a resolution of 7 March, adopted by a roll-call vote of 40 to none, with 2 abstentions,[89] strongly reaffirmed that the fundamental human rights, as accepted by international law and formulated in international instruments, remained fully applicable in cases of armed conflict. It urged Israel to recognize, according to the third Geneva Convention, the status of prisoners of war to all combatants caught during the war in Lebanon and treat them accordingly; to release immediately all civilians arbitrarily detained since the beginning of that war; to allow ICRC to visit all those in detention centres under its control; and to ensure protection to the Palestinian civilians, including the released detainees, in the areas under its occupation, according to the fourth Geneva Convention and the 1907 Hague Convention. The Commission called on all parties to the conflict to secure for ICRC all available information concerning missing and disappeared persons in the wake of the invasion of Lebanon.

Mass exoduses

Action by the Commission on Human Rights. In January 1983, the Secretary-General submitted to the Commission on Human Rights a report on human rights and mass exoduses.[90] It contained views and communications received, in reply to a December 1982 General Assembly invitation,[91] from 15 Governments, three United Nations bodies, five specialized agencies and 25 NGOs on a 1981 study by the Commission's Special Rapporteur Sadruddin Aga Khan.[92]

Reaffirming its solidarity with the millions of victims of mass exoduses and displacements, the Commission, on 8 March 1983,[93] called on States fully to respect and promote principles of international law and practice guaranteeing such victims protection and assistance. It recognized the contribution the Special Rapporteur's study could

make to the development of international thinking on the pressing problem of mass exoduses and their causes, and acknowledged that his recommendations could possibly contribute to the prevention of further mass movements of population and to the mitigation of their consequences. It again requested Governments to communicate to the Secretary-General their opinions on the Special Rapporteur's study and recommendations, and invited the Secretary-General to propose in his report to the General Assembly international co-operative arrangements to address and alleviate the root causes of mass movements of population related to violations or suppression of human rights, taking in account existing United Nations organs, skills and resources.

Report of the Secretary-General. In a November report to the Assembly,[94] the Secretary-General transmitted further replies—from Austria, Canada, the Central African Republic, Colombia, the Philippines and Venezuela—pursuant to the Commission's resolution (see above). In addition, observations on the study were made orally during the 1982 Assembly session and the 1982 and 1983 Commission sessions.

The Secretary-General stated in the report that the international community recognized the urgent need to examine ways to solve the root causes of and the problems resulting from mass exoduses. Recognizing the importance of an early-warning system on potential mass exoduses, as recommended by the Special Rapporteur, the Secretary-General reported having initiated steps within the Secretariat in order to be alerted in advance to incipient problems. He expressed his intention to work closely with the Security Council in order to develop a wider and more systematic capacity for fact-finding in potential conflict areas. With respect to situations which could lead to mass exoduses, he expected to utilize existing United Nations machinery to obtain information at an early stage concerning the possibility of impending mass flows of refugees.

The Secretary-General expressed interest in learning further the attitude of Member States towards the proposal of appointing a special representative for humanitarian questions; in that connection, he had on many occasions designated special representatives on humanitarian issues on an *ad hoc* basis and was prepared to expand that practice where such an appointment would be helpful in identifying or resolving situations involving a potential mass exodus. The Commission, for its part, had designated special rapporteurs, special envoys or experts to deal with situations in human rights and humanitarian fields; in many cases, persons appointed by the Commission had exercised functions similar to those of his special representatives.

With regard to the establishment of a corps of "humanitarian observers", the Secretary-General considered that it would require the concurrence of the Governments concerned, as well as the legislative authority of the Assembly. Accordingly, the Assembly and the Group of Governmental Experts on International Co-operation to Avert New Flows of Refugees might wish to consider that proposal further.

GENERAL ASSEMBLY ACTION

On 16 December, on the recommendation of the Third Committee, the General Assembly adopted resolution 38/103 without vote.

Human rights and mass exoduses
The General Assembly,

Mindful of its general humanitarian mandate under the Charter of the United Nations and its mandate to promote and encourage respect for human rights and fundamental freedoms for all,

Deeply disturbed by the continuing scale and magnitude of exoduses and displacements of populations in many regions of the world and by the human suffering of millions of refugees and displaced persons in all regions of the world,

Conscious that human rights violations are among the principal factors in the complex and multiple causes of mass exoduses of population,

Deeply preoccupied by the increasingly heavy burden being imposed, particularly upon developing countries with limited resources of their own, and upon the international community as a whole, by these sudden and mass exoduses and displacements of population,

Recalling its resolution 32/130 of 16 December 1977 and Commission on Human Rights resolution 4(XXXIII) of 21 February 1977 on the full realization of economic, social and cultural rights,

Recalling also its resolutions 35/124 of 11 December 1980, 36/148 of 16 December 1981 and 37/121 of 16 December 1982 on international co-operation to avert new flows of refugees, 35/196 of 15 December 1980 and 37/186 of 17 December 1982 on human rights and mass exoduses and Commission on Human Rights resolutions 29(XXXVII) of 11 March 1981, 1982/32 of 11 March 1982 and 1983/35 of 8 March 1983,

Convinced that there is an urgent need to improve co-ordination within the existing international machinery to deal with mass exoduses and displacements of population,

Recognizing that the study on human rights and massive exoduses prepared by the Special Rapporteur of the Commission on Human Rights can make an important contribution to the development of international thinking on the present problem of mass exoduses and their causes, and thus help in the prevention of further mass movements of population and the mitigation of their consequences,

1. *Takes due note* of the report of the Secretary-General on human rights and mass exoduses;

2. *Invites* Governments to intensify their co-operation and assistance in world-wide efforts to address the increasingly serious problem of mass exoduses;

3. *Requests* those Governments that have not yet done so to communicate to the Secretary-General their opinions on the study prepared by the Special Rapporteur and the recommendations made therein with a view to the General Assembly taking a decision on those recommendations;

4. *Notes* the Secretary-General's request to the agencies and organizations of the United Nations system to make recommendations and to take whatever steps possible, within their mandates and existing resources, to improve international co-operation in these fields;

5. *Considers it desirable* for the Secretary-General to utilize to the greatest extent possible relevant United Nations machinery to analyse promptly information on situations which might cause mass exoduses;

6. *Notes with interest* that the Secretary-General has on many occasions designated special representatives on humanitarian issues on an *ad hoc* basis, and his readiness to continue and expand this practice;

7. *Requests* the Secretary-General to follow closely developments on this question, to take into consideration all the further comments of Member States, including those expressed at the thirty-eighth session of the General Assembly and at the fortieth session of the Commission on Human Rights, and to keep under review the recommendations of the Special Rapporteur;

8. *Recalls* that, in its resolution 36/148, the General Assembly requested the Group of Governmental Experts on International Co-operation to Avert New Flows of Refugees to undertake a comprehensive review of the problem of massive flows of refugees and, in accordance with paragraph 7 of that resolution, invited the Group of Governmental Experts to consider the recommendations of the Special Rapporteur which fall within its mandate;

9. *Decides* to consider the question of human rights and mass exoduses at its thirty-ninth session.

General Assembly resolution 38/103

16 December 1983   Meeting 100   Adopted without vote

Approved by Third Committee (A/38/680) without vote, 9 December (meeting 71); 14-nation draft (A/C.3/38/L.61), amended by 14 nations (A/C.3/38/L.64, orally revised by draft's sponsors), and orally revised on proposals by Bulgaria and by Byelorussian SSR; agenda item 12.

Sponsors of draft: Australia, Canada, Colombia, Costa Rica, Gambia, Germany, Federal Republic of, Japan, Jordan; joined by Bangladesh, Pakistan, Philippines, Senegal, Somalia, Sudan, following acceptance of amendments.

Sponsors of amendments: Afghanistan, Algeria, Angola, Bangladesh, Benin, Cuba, Democratic Yemen, Ethiopia, India, Indonesia, Nicaragua, Nigeria, Philippines, Yugoslavia.

Meeting numbers. GA 38th session: 3rd Committee 18, 54, 55, 57-71; plenary 100.

In related action, the Assembly, on 15 December, adopted resolution 38/84 on international co-operation to avert new flows of refugees.

Genocide

As recommended on 4 March 1983 by the Commission on Human Rights,[95] following a September 1982 recommendation of the Sub-Commission on Prevention of Discrimination and Protection of Minorities,[96] the Economic and Social Council in May 1983 (see below) requested the Sub-Commission to appoint a Special Rapporteur to revise and update the 1978 study on the prevention and punishment of the crime of genocide.[97] The Sub-Commission, on 18 August,[98] appointed Benjamin Charles George Whitaker (United Kingdom) as Special Rapporteur.

The *Ad Hoc* Working Group on Southern Africa, in a report on *apartheid* as a form of slavery (see above, under CIVIL AND POLITICAL RIGHTS), called for an investigation to determine whether elements of the crime of genocide existed in South Africa and Namibia. The Group recommended that it be entrusted by the Commission to pay attention to the elements of genocide arising out of the policy of *apartheid*. It also renewed its recommendation that the Commission make specific proposals concerning revision of the 1948 Convention on the Prevention and Punishment of the Crime of Genocide[99] with a view to making "inhuman acts resulting from the policies of *apartheid*" punishable under that Convention.

ECONOMIC AND SOCIAL COUNCIL ACTION

On 27 May, on the recommendation of its Second Committee, the Economic and Social Council adopted resolution 1983/33 without vote.

Updating of the study on the question of the prevention and punishment of the crime of genocide

The Economic and Social Council,

Mindful of resolution 1982/2 of 7 September 1982 of the Sub-Commission on Prevention of Discrimination and Protection of Minorities and Commission on Human Rights resolution 1983/24 of 4 March 1983, related to the revision and updating of the study on the question of the prevention and punishment of the crime of genocide,

1. *Requests* the Sub-Commission on Prevention of Discrimination and Protection of Minorities to appoint one of its members as Special Rapporteur with the mandate to revise, as a whole, and update the study on the question of the prevention and punishment of the crime of genocide, taking into consideration the views expressed by the members of the Sub-Commission and the Commission on Human Rights, as well as replies of Governments, specialized agencies and other organizations of the United Nations system, regional organizations and non-governmental organizations to a questionnaire to be prepared by the Special Rapporteur;

2. *Further requests* the Sub-Commission to consider and to submit to the Commission on Human Rights at its fortieth session the aforementioned revised and updated study.

Economic and Social Council resolution 1983/33

27 May 1983   Meeting 15   Adopted without vote

Approved by Second Committee (E/1983/61) without vote, 23 May (meeting 18); draft by Commission on Human Rights (E/1983/13); agenda item 10.
Meeting number. ESC 15.

REFERENCES

[1]YUN 1970, p. 530, ESC res. 1503(XLVIII), 27 May 1970. [2]E/1983/13 (dec. 1983/110). [3]*Ibid.* (dec. 1983/105). [4]YUN 1982, p. 1108. [5]YUN 1971, p. 419. [6]E/CN.4/1984/3 (dec. 1983/4). [7]*Ibid.* (dec. 1983/9). [8]A/38/22. [9]YUN 1967, p. 509. [10]E/CN.4/1983/10. [11]YUN 1981, p. 943. [12]*Ibid.*, p. 945. [13]E/CN.4/1983/37. [14]E/1983/13 (res. 1983/9). [15]*Ibid.*

[16]E/CN.4/1984/3 (res. 1983/25). [17]A/38/422. [18]E/CN.4/1983/38. [19]YUN 1982, p. 298. [20]YUN 1973, p. 103, GA res. 3068(XXVIII), annex, 30 Nov. 1973. [21]A/38/391. [22]E/CN.4/1983/25. [23]E/1983/13 (dec. 1983/111). [24]*Ibid.* (res. 1983/12). [25]YUN 1981, p. 947. [26]YUN 1982, p. 1111. [27]E/1983/13 (res. 1983/11). [28]YUN 1960, p. 49, GA res. 1514(XV), 14 Dec. 1960. [29]E/CN.4/Sub.2/1983/6 & Add.1. [30]E/CN.4/1984/3 (res. 1983/6). [31]YUN 1982, p. 1112, GA res. 37/39, 3 Dec. 1982. [32]E/1983/28. [33]E/1983/49. [34]YUN 1950, p. 539, ESC res. 277(X), 17 Feb. 1950. [35]E/CN.4/1983/52. [36]YUN 1982, p. 1117. [37]E/CN.4/1983/19. [38]YUN 1966, p. 423, GA res. 2200 A (XXI), annex, 16 Dec. 1966. [39]E/1983/13 (res. 1983/34). [40]E/CN.4/1984/32. [41]E/CN.4/1984/3 (res. 1983/14). [42]*Ibid.* (res. 1983/16). [43]E/CN.4/1983/23. [44]YUN 1981, p. 345. [45]E/1983/13 (dec. 1983/107). [46]A/38/18 (dec. 1(XXVII). [47]E/CN.4/1983/18. [48]E/1983/13 (res. 1983/30). [49]E/CN.4/1983/9. [50]YUN 1982, p. 1119. [51]E/1983/13 (res. 1983/38). [52]E/CN.4/1984/3 (res. 1983/19). [53]A/38/385 & Add.1. [54]YUN 1982, p. 1123. [55]E/CN.4/1983/20. [56]YUN 1982, p. 1124. [57]YUN 1977, p. 706. [58]E/1983/13 (res. 1983/29). [59]E/CN.4/1984/3 (res. 1983/18). [60]A/38/503. [61]E/CN.4/1983/43. [62]YUN 1982, p. 1128. [63]E/1983/13 (dec. 1983/103). [64]E/CN.4/1983/47. [65]E/1983/13 (res. 1983/37). [66]E/CN.4/Sub.2/1983/37. [67]E/CN.4/1984/3 (res. 1983/12). [68]E/CN.4/Sub.2/1983/40. [69]A/38/485. [70]YUN 1951, p. 520. [71]YUN 1967, p. 477. [72]YUN 1966, p. 419, GA res. 2200 A (XXI), annex, 16 Dec. 1966. [73]E/CN.4/1984/3 (res. 1983/28). [74]*Ibid.* (dec. 1983/3). [75]E/CN.4/Sub.2/1983/42. [76]E/CN.4/1983/8. [77]YUN 1982, p. 1130. [78]*Ibid.*, p. 1131. [79]E/CN.4/1983/7. [80]E/1983/13 (res. 1983/1 A). [81]*Ibid.* (res. 1983/1 B). [82]*Ibid.* (res. 1983/2). [83]YUN 1981, p. 309. [84]YUN 1948-49, p. 535, GA res. 217 A (III), 10 Dec. 1948. [85]YUN 1982, p. 481. [86]A/38/270. [87]E/CN.4/1984/3 (res. 1983/9). [88]E/CN.4/1983/5. [89]E/1983/13 (res. 1983/27). [90]E/CN.4/1983/33 & Corr.1 & Add.1. [91]YUN 1982, p. 1134, GA res. 37/186, 17 Dec. 1982. [92]YUN 1981, p. 966. [93]E/1983/13 (res. 1983/35). [94]A/38/538. [95]E/1983/13 (res. 1983/24). [96]YUN 1982, p. 1134. [97]YUN 1978, p. 723. [98]E/CN.4/1984/3 (dec. 1983/2). [99]YUN 1948-49, p. 959, GA res. 260 A (III), annex, 9 Dec. 1948.

Other human rights questions

Additional Protocols I and II to the 1949 Geneva Conventions

A list of parties as at 21 September 1983 to the two 1977 Protocols Additional to the Geneva Conventions of 12 August 1949 for the protection of war victims,[1] was submitted by the Secretary-General to the General Assembly.[2]

As at 31 December 1983, 37 States and the United Nations Council for Namibia had ratified or acceded to Protocol I (on protection of victims of international armed conflicts), as follows (those adhering in 1983 are italicized):

Austria, Bahamas, Bangladesh, *Bolivia*, Botswana, *China*, *Congo*, Costa Rica, Cuba, Cyprus. Denmark, Ecuador, El Salvador, Finland, Gabon, Ghana, Jordan, Lao People's Democratic Republic, Libyan Arab Jamahiriya, Mauritania, Mauritius, *Mexico*, *Mozambique*, Niger, Norway, Republic of Korea, Saint Lucia, *Saint Vincent and the Grenadines*, Sweden, Switzerland, *Syrian Arab Republic*, Tunisia, *United Arab Emirates*, *United Republic of Tanzania*, Viet Nam, Yugoslavia, Zaire; *United Nations Council for Namibia.*

All of these parties, except Cuba, Cyprus, Mexico, Mozambique, the Syrian Arab Republic, Viet Nam and Zaire, had also adhered to Protocol II (on protection of victims of non-international conflicts).

Rights of the child

The General Assembly, the Economic and Social Council and the Commission on Human Rights continued work in 1983 on a draft convention on the rights of the child. The Sub-Commission on Prevention of Discrimination and Protection of Minorities recommended for adoption by the Commission two draft resolutions on child labour. The Assembly also adopted a resolution on a draft Declaration on Social and Legal Principles relating to the Protection and Welfare of Children, with Special Reference to Foster Placement and Adoption Nationally and Internationally (see Chapter XX of this section).

Draft convention

Working Group action. An open-ended Working Group of the Commission on Human Rights, chaired by Adam Lopatka (Poland), held meetings from 24 to 28 January and on 7 and 9 March to continue work on a draft convention on the rights of the child, begun in 1979.[3] At those meetings, the Group adopted article 6, paragraphs 3 and 4 (concerning the rights of a child separated from its parents); part of article 6 *bis* (rights to reunification of children and parents residing in different States); article 6 *ter* (measures to combat illicit transfer and non-return of children abroad); and article 12, paragraphs 2-4 (rights and special needs of disabled children). The articles adopted in 1983 and prior years were annexed to the Working Group's report to the Commission.[4]

Action by the Commission on Human Rights. On 10 March 1983,[5] the Commission decided to continue in 1984, as a matter of highest priority, its work on a draft convention. It requested the Economic and Social Council to authorize prior to the Commission's 1984 session a one-week session of an open-ended working group to facilitate and speed up completion of the draft instrument. It also recommended to the Council that it request the Secretary-General to transmit to the Commission documents relating to the draft convention and to extend all facilities to the working group.

In accordance with a May 1982 Council request,[6] the Secretary-General submitted to the Commission in 1983 a report on the protection of the rights of children and parents in cases of removal or retention of children[7]—a question which the Council had invited the Commission to take into account in drafting a convention. The report summarized replies from 17 Governments.

ECONOMIC AND SOCIAL COUNCIL ACTION

On 27 May 1983, on the recommendation of its Second Committee, the Economic and Social Council adopted resolution 1983/39 without vote.

Question of a convention on the rights of the child
The Economic and Social Council,

Recalling General Assembly resolution 37/190 of 18 December 1982, by which the Assembly requested the Commission on Human Rights to continue to give the highest priority at its thirty-ninth session to the question of completing the draft convention on the rights of the child, and Economic and Social Council resolution 1982/37 of 7 May 1982, by which the Council authorized a meeting of an open-ended working group for a period of one week prior to the thirty-ninth session of the Commission to facilitate the completion of the work on the draft convention on the rights of the child,

Considering that it was not found possible to complete the work on the draft convention during the thirty-ninth session of the Commission,

Taking note of Commission on Human Rights resolution 1983/52 of 10 March 1983,

1. *Authorizes* a meeting of an open-ended working group for a period of one week prior to the fortieth session of the Commission on Human Rights to facilitate and speed up the completion of the work on a draft convention on the rights of the child;

2. *Requests* the Secretary-General to transmit documents relating to the draft convention on the rights of the child to the Commission on Human Rights at its fortieth session and to extend all facilities to the open-ended working group during its meeting prior to the fortieth session of the Commission.

Economic and Social Council resolution 1983/39

27 May 1983   Meeting 15   Adopted without vote

Approved by Second Committee (E/1983/61) without vote, 23 May (meeting 18); draft by Commission on Human Rights (E/1983/13); agenda item 10.
Meeting number. ESC 15.

GENERAL ASSEMBLY ACTION

On 16 December 1983, on the recommendation of the Third Committee, the General Assembly adopted resolution 38/114 without vote.

Question of a convention on the rights of the child
The General Assembly,

Recalling its resolutions 33/166 of 20 December 1978, 34/4 of 18 October 1979, 35/131 of 11 December 1980, 36/57 of 25 November 1981 and 37/190 of 18 December 1982,

Recalling also Commission on Human Rights resolutions 20(XXXIV) of 8 March 1978, 19(XXXV) of 14 March 1979, 36(XXXVI) of 12 March 1980, 26(XXXVII) of 10 March 1981, 1982/39 of 11 March 1982 and 1983/52 of 10 March 1983 as well as Economic and Social Council resolutions 1978/18 of 5 May 1978, 1978/40 of 1 August 1978, 1982/37 of 7 May 1982 and 1983/39 of 27 May 1983 and Council decisions 1980/138 of 2 May 1980 and 1981/144 of 8 May 1981,

Bearing in mind that children's rights are basic human rights and call for continuous improvement of the situation of children all over the world, as well as their development and education in conditions of peace,

Mindful of the need to keep up the momentum of positive action for the sake of children generated by the International Year of the Child,

Noting the important role of the United Nations Children's Fund and the United Nations in promoting the well-being of children and their development,

Aware of the importance of an international convention on the rights of the child for a more effective protection of children's rights, as well as of the widespread interest in the elaboration of such an international instrument displayed by a growing number of Governments and international organizations,

Considering that the year 1984 will mark the twenty-fifth anniversary of the Declaration of the Rights of the Child,

Reaffirming that mankind owes to the child the best it has to give,

Noting with appreciation that further progress was made in the elaboration of a draft convention on the rights of the child prior to and during the thirty-ninth session of the Commission on Human Rights,

1. *Welcomes* Economic and Social Council resolution 1983/39, in which the Council authorized a meeting of an open-ended working group of the Commission on Human Rights for a period of one week prior to the fortieth session of the Commission to facilitate and speed up the completion of the work on a draft convention on the rights of the child;

2. *Requests* the Commission on Human Rights to give the highest priority at its fortieth session to the question of completing the draft convention and to make every effort to submit it, through the Economic and Social Council, to the General Assembly at its thirty-ninth session, as the Commission's tangible contribution to the commemoration of the twenty-fifth anniversary of the Declaration of the Rights of the Child;

3. *Invites* all Member States to offer their effective contribution to the completion without delay of the draft convention on the rights of the child;

4. *Requests* the Secretary-General to provide all necessary assistance to the working group to ensure its smooth and efficient work;

5. *Decides* to include in the provisional agenda of its thirty-ninth session the item entitled "Question of a convention on the rights of the child".

General Assembly resolution 38/114

16 December 1983   Meeting 100   Adopted without vote

Approved by Third Committee (A/38/685) without vote, 30 November (meeting 57); 85-nation draft (A/C.3/38/L.23); agenda item 95.

Sponsors: Afghanistan, Algeria, Angola, Argentina, Australia, Bahamas, Bangladesh, Benin, Bhutan, Bolivia, Bulgaria, Byelorussian SSR, Canada, Cape Verde, China, Colombia, Congo, Costa Rica, Cuba, Cyprus, Czechoslovakia, Democratic Yemen, Denmark, Ecuador, Egypt, Ethiopia, Fiji, France, Gambia, German Democratic Republic, Ghana, Greece, Guinea, Guinea-Bissau, Guyana, Hungary, India, Iran, Iraq, Ivory Coast, Jamaica, Jordan, Kenya, Lao People's Democratic Republic, Lesotho, Liberia, Libyan Arab Jamahiriya, Madagascar, Mali, Malta, Mauritania, Mexico, Mongolia, Morocco, Mozambique, New Zealand, Nicaragua, Nigeria, Norway, Pakistan, Peru, Philippines, Poland, Rwanda, Sao Tome and Principe, Senegal, Sierra Leone, Spain, Sri Lanka, Suriname, Syrian Arab Republic, Togo, Ukrainian SSR, USSR, United Republic of Cameroon, United Republic of Tanzania, Upper Volta, Uruguay, Venezuela, Viet Nam, Yemen, Yugoslavia, Zaire, Zambia, Zimbabwe.

Meeting numbers. GA 38th session: 3rd Committee 49-53, 57; plenary 100.

In related action, the Assembly, on 19 December, adopted resolution 38/142 on a draft Declaration on Social and Legal Principles relating to the Protection and Welfare of Children, with Special Reference to Foster Placement and Adoption Nationally and Internationally.

Child labour

In 1983, the Sub-Commission recommended to the Commission for adoption two draft resolutions on child labour. The first draft, recommended on 31 August,[8] would have the Commission recommend that the Economic and Social Council request the Secretary-General to organize a seminar on measures to eliminate the exploitation of child labour, within the framework of the programme of advisory services in human rights. By the second, recommended by a 5 September resolution adopted by 12 votes to none, with 6 abstentions,[9] the Commission would call on the Government of Iran to cease immediately the use of children in the armed forces, especially in time of war; and would invite international organizations to offer all possible aid for the welfare of the children prisoners of war in Iraq, especially with regard to their education and physical and mental health, or to assist those children so desiring to settle in another Islamic country until their return to Iran became feasible.

Child labour was also dealt with by the *Ad Hoc* Working Group of Experts on Southern Africa (see above, under HUMAN RIGHTS VIOLATIONS, and "Slavery" under CIVIL AND POLITICAL RIGHTS).

Youth and human rights

In February 1983,[10] the Secretary-General presented to the Commission on Human Rights, in pursuance of its March 1982 request,[11] a report on the implementation—by Member States, the United Nations system and others—of the Specific Programme of Measures and Activities in connection with International Youth Year (1985) (see Chapter XX of this section). He noted that a growing awareness had been observed in several countries of the need to establish mechanisms for co-ordinating youth-related activities; in establishing national priorities relating to youth, many had identified, as important problems, unemployment, education and training (see above, under ECONOMIC AND SOCIAL RIGHTS), population, environment and housing, health and crime prevention.

Another youth-related issue dealt with by the Commission and its Sub-Commission was conscientious objection to military service (see above, under CIVIL AND POLITICAL RIGHTS).

The General Assembly, in resolution 38/23 of 22 November, called on States, governmental and non-governmental organizations, and United Nations bodies and agencies to pay continuous attention to efforts and measures aimed at the promotion of human rights and their enjoyment by youth.

Women's rights

On 9 March 1983, the Commission on Human Rights adopted a resolution[12] on communications concerning the status of women (see Chapter XIX of this section).

Human rights of disabled persons

In August 1983, the Secretary-General submitted to the Sub-Commission, in pursuance of its September 1982 request,[11] a note[13] summarizing information provided as at 18 August by five Governments, two United Nations bodies and a specialized agency, and three NGOs concerning measures for realizing the rights of disabled persons. The report also contained information drawn from the report of the Advisory Committee for the International Year of Disabled Persons (1981), specifically with regard to the objectives of the 1982 World Programme of Action concerning Disabled Persons,[14] the current situation of the disabled, and national and international measures (see Chapter XV of this section).

The Sub-Commission, on 5 September,[15] requested that the Secretary-General again invite NGOs to investigate human rights problems of disabled persons and submit the findings in 1984. It also urged him to continue seeking views of the United Nations system, regional intergovernmental organizations, ICRC and NGOs on ways of preventing violations of human rights of disabled persons, as well as ways to prevent disabilities, especially those caused by violations of humanitarian norms governing armed conflict.

The Sub-Commission welcomed the General Assembly's December 1982 decision[16] to proclaim 1983-1992 as United Nations Decade of Disabled Persons. It requested the Commission to invite Governments, in consultation with disabled persons, to identify human rights problems of such persons in their jurisdictions and to provide descriptions of those problems, along with plans to alleviate them, to the Sub-Commission for consideration in 1984. It recommended that the Commission request Governments to pay particular attention to ways to strengthen procedures whereby disabled persons could bring alleged human rights violations to an authoritative body or to the Government, as recommended by the Sub-Commission in 1982.[11]

Questions related to disabled persons were also dealt with by the General Assembly and the Economic and Social Council (see Chapter XV of this section).

Human rights of the individual and international law

Work continued in 1983 on a study of the status of the individual and international law, mandated by the Commission on Human Rights in 1981[17] and authorized by the Economic and Social Council the same year.[18]

On 4 March 1983,[19] the Commission recommended to the Council adoption of a draft submitted in 1982[20] by its Sub-Commission.

ECONOMIC AND SOCIAL COUNCIL ACTION

On 27 May 1983, on the recommendation of its Second Committee, the Council adopted resolution 1983/34 without vote.

Status of the individual and contemporary international law

The Economic and Social Council,

Mindful of resolution 1982/35 of 10 September 1982 of the Sub-Commission on Prevention of Discrimination and Protection of Minorities and Commission on Human Rights resolution 1983/26 of 4 March 1983,

Expressing its deep appreciation to the Special Rapporteur, Mrs. Erica-Irene A. Daes, for the work she has thus far accomplished in connection with the important study in progress on the status of the individual and contemporary international law,

1. *Requests* the Special Rapporteur to continue her work on the above-mentioned study with a view to submitting, if possible, her final report to the Sub-Commission on Prevention of Discrimination and Protection of Minorities at its thirty-sixth session;

2. *Requests* the Secretary-General to transmit a reminder with the relevant questionnaire to Governments, specialized agencies, regional organizations, intergovernmental organizations and non-governmental organizations that have not yet replied, to submit if they so wish their comments on and replies to the questionnaire of the Special Rapporteur;

3. *Further requests* the Secretary-General to give the Special Rapporteur all the assistance she may require in her work.

Economic and Social Council resolution 1983/34

27 May 1983	Meeting 15	Adopted without vote

Approved by Second Committee (E/1983/61) without vote, 23 May (meeting 18); draft by Commission on Human Rights (E/1983/13); agenda item 10.
Meeting number. ESC 15.

Sub-Commission action. Following consideration of a preliminary report by the Special Rapporteur,[21] the Sub-Commission, on 5 September 1983,[22] expressed appreciation for the work so far accomplished. It recommended that the Commission recommend to the Council adoption of a draft resolution requesting the Special Rapporteur to submit her final report in 1984.

Human rights and science and technology

Action by the Commission on Human Rights. On 9 March 1983, the Commission on Human Rights adopted two resolutions on human rights and scientific and technological developments. By the first,[23] it invited Member States and international organizations to submit to the Secretary-General their views on the most effective ways of using the results of scientific and technological developments for promoting and realizing human rights, and requested him to present to it in 1984 a report, prepared on the basis of those comments and other sources.

By the second resolution,[24] adopted by 32 votes to none, with 9 abstentions, the Commission stressed the importance of the implementation by all States of the provisions and principles contained in the 1975 Declaration on the Use of Scientific and Technological Progress in the Interests of Peace and for the Benefit of Mankind,[25] in order to promote human rights under conditions of scientific and technological progress. It requested its Sub-Commission to undertake, as a priority matter, a study on the use of those achievements to ensure the right to work and development.

In related action, the Commission adopted on the same date, and under the same agenda item, a resolution on human rights and peace (see below).

Sub-Commission action. On 7 September,[26] the Sub-Commission approved the conclusions and recommendations contained in the final report on guidelines in the field of computerized personnel files,[27] which had been presented by Special Rapporteur Louis Joinet (France) in June, in accordance with a 1980 Sub-Commission request.[28] The Sub-Commission decided to submit the report to the Commission on Human Rights in 1984.

The report dealt with human rights affected by the computerization of personal data, reviewed international and regional measures to protect those rights and examined specific problems posed by the use of computerized personnel files. The Special Rapporteur recommended, among other things, that United Nations bodies adopt guidelines to encourage States to promote protective regulations in their domestic legislation and to help avoid excessive discrepancies between differing legislations. As an immediate step, he suggested that one of the Sub-Commission members be appointed to study draft internal regulations governing United Nations computerized files.

Report of the Secretary-General. Also in September, the Secretary-General submitted to the General Assembly a report summarizing substantive replies from Governments[29] concerning implementation of the 1975 Declaration on the Use of Scientific and Technological Progress in the Interests of Peace and for the Benefit of Mankind.[25] The Assembly, in December 1982, had again invited States and United Nations agencies and organizations to submit such information.[30] The Secretary-General stated that as at 5 August 1983, substantive replies had been received from eight Governments.

GENERAL ASSEMBLY ACTION

On 16 December 1983, on the recommendation of the Third Committee, the General Assembly adopted resolution 38/112 by recorded vote.

Human rights and scientific and technological developments

The General Assembly,

Noting that scientific and technological progress is one of the important factors in the development of human society,

Noting once again the great importance of the Declaration on the Use of Scientific and Technological Progress in the Interests of Peace and for the Benefit of Mankind, adopted by the General Assembly in its resolution 3384(XXX) of 10 November 1975,

Considering that implementation of the said Declaration will contribute to the strengthening of international peace and the security of peoples and to their economic and social development, as well as to international co-operation in the field of human rights,

Seriously concerned that the results of scientific and technological progress could be used for the arms race, to the detriment of international peace and security and social progress, human rights and fundamental freedoms and the dignity of the human person,

Recognizing that the establishment of the new international economic order calls in particular for an important contribution to be made by science and technology to economic and social progress,

Bearing in mind that the exchange and transfer of scientific and technological knowledge is one of the important ways to accelerate the social and economic development of the developing countries,

Taking note with satisfaction of the report of the Secretary-General on human rights and scientific and technological developments,

1. *Stresses* the importance of the implementation by all States of the provisions and principles contained in the Declaration on the Use of Scientific and Technological Progress in the Interests of Peace and for the Benefit of Mankind in order to promote human rights and fundamental freedoms;

2. *Calls upon* all States to make every effort to use the achievements of science and technology in order to promote peaceful social, economic and cultural development and progress;

3. *Requests* the specialized agencies and other organizations of the United Nations system to take into account in their programmes and activities the provisions of the Declaration;

4. *Invites* those Member States, specialized agencies and other organizations of the United Nations system that have not yet done so to submit their information pursuant to General Assembly resolution 35/130 A of 11 December 1980;

5. *Requests* the Commission on Human Rights to pay special attention, in its consideration of the item entitled "Human rights and scientific and technological developments", to the question of the implementation of the provisions of the Declaration, taking into consideration the information submitted by Member States, specialized agencies and other organizations of the United Nations system pursuant to General Assembly resolution 35/130 A;

6. *Decides* to include in the provisional agenda of its thirty-ninth session the item entitled "Human rights and scientific and technological developments".

General Assembly resolution 38/112

16 December 1983   Meeting 100   125-0-22 (recorded vote)

Approved by Third Committee (A/38/684) by recorded vote (114-0-22), 30 November (meeting 57); 29-nation draft (A/C.3/38/L.40); agenda item 94.

Sponsors: Afghanistan, Algeria, Angola, Argentina, Bangladesh, Benin, Bolivia, Bulgaria, Byelorussian SSR, Cuba, Cyprus, Czechoslovakia, Democratic Yemen, Ecuador, German Democratic Republic, Guinea, Guinea-Bissau, Hungary, Lao People's Democratic Republic, Madagascar, Mali, Mauritania, Mongolia, Morocco, Nicaragua, Poland, Viet Nam, Zambia, Zimbabwe.

Meeting numbers. GA 38th session: 3rd Committee 49-54, 56, 57; plenary 100.

Recorded vote in Assembly as follows:

In favour: Afghanistan, Algeria, Angola, Argentina, Bahamas, Bahrain, Bangladesh, Belize, Benin, Bhutan, Bolivia, Botswana, Brazil, Bulgaria, Burma, Burundi, Byelorussian SSR, Cape Verde, Central African Republic, Chad, Chile, China, Colombia, Congo, Costa Rica, Cuba, Cyprus, Czechoslovakia, Democratic Kampuchea, Democratic Yemen, Djibouti, Dominica, Dominican Republic, Ecuador, Egypt, El Salvador, Equatorial Guinea, Ethiopia, Fiji, Gabon, Gambia, German Democratic Republic, Ghana, Greece, Grenada, Guatemala, Guinea, Guinea-Bissau, Guyana, Haiti, Honduras, Hungary, India, Indonesia, Iran, Iraq, Ivory Coast, Jamaica, Japan, Jordan, Kenya, Kuwait, Lao People's Democratic Republic, Lebanon, Lesotho, Liberia, Libyan Arab Jamahiriya, Madagascar, Malaysia, Maldives, Mali, Malta, Mauritania, Mauritius, Mexico, Mongolia, Morocco, Mozambique, Nepal, Nicaragua, Niger, Nigeria, Oman, Pakistan, Panama, Papua New Guinea, Peru, Philippines, Poland, Qatar, Romania, Rwanda, Saint Lucia, Sao Tome and Principe, Saudi Arabia, Senegal, Sierra Leone, Singapore, Somalia, Sri Lanka, Sudan, Suriname, Swaziland, Syrian Arab Republic, Thailand, Togo, Trinidad and Tobago, Tunisia, Turkey, Uganda, Ukrainian SSR, USSR, United Arab Emirates, United Republic of Cameroon, United Republic of Tanzania, Upper Volta, Uruguay, Vanuatu, Venezuela, Viet Nam, Yemen, Yugoslavia, Zaire, Zambia, Zimbabwe.

Against: None.

Abstaining: Australia, Austria, Belgium, Canada, Denmark, Finland, France, Germany, Federal Republic of, Iceland, Ireland, Israel, Italy, Luxembourg, Netherlands, New Zealand, Norway, Paraguay, Portugal, Spain, Sweden, United Kingdom, United States.

Also on 16 December and under the agenda item on science and technology and human rights, the Assembly adopted resolution 38/111, concerning the preparation of a draft body of guidelines, principles and guarantees for persons detained on grounds of mental illness (see above, under CIVIL AND POLITICAL RIGHTS), and resolution 38/113, on human rights and peace (see below).

Human rights and peace

Action by the Commission on Human Rights.
By a resolution of 9 March 1983,[31] adopted by a roll-call vote of 32 to none, with 11 abstentions, the Commission on Human Rights reaffirmed that all peoples and individuals had an inherent right to life, and that the safeguarding of that right was an essential condition for the enjoyment of economic, social and cultural as well as civil and political rights. It stressed once again the urgent need for the international community to strengthen peace, halt the arms race and achieve general and complete disarmament under international control, and to implement practical measures of disarmament for releasing resources for social and economic development, particularly for the benefit of the developing countries.

The Commission urged all States to ensure that in matters relating to the right to life, everyone should have the right to freedom of expression, peaceful assembly and freedom of association, and to take part in public affairs. It called on States to prohibit propaganda for war and again called on them, as well as on the United Nations system and others, to ensure that scientific and technological achievements were used exclusively in the interests of peace, for the benefit of mankind and for promoting human rights.

On 8 March,[32] the Commission decided that a draft resolution, concerning the effects of gross human rights violations on international peace and security, which had been recommended by the Sub-Commission in September 1982,[33] should be sent back to that body for further consideration in the light of the comments made by the Commission at its 1983 session.

Sub-Commission action. On 6 September,[34] the Sub-Commission reaffirmed the need, in order to obtain peaceful and friendly relations among nations, to create conditions of stability and well-being, promote economic and social progress, find solutions to international problems, achieve universal respect for human rights and establish equal rights and self-determination of peoples. It reaffirmed the obligation of States to refrain from the threat or use of force in international relations, and expressed the hope that they would avoid threats to peace by promoting human rights, including releasing all persons detained for their views who had not used or advocated violence. The Sub-Commission requested the Secretary-General to ask Governments, specialized agencies and organizations for their views and comments and to present to the Sub-Commission in 1984 an analysis of the subject.

GENERAL ASSEMBLY ACTION

On 16 December 1983, on the recommendation of the Third Committee, the General Assembly adopted resolution 38/113 by recorded vote.

Human rights and use of scientific and technological developments

The General Assembly,

Reaffirming the determination of the peoples of the United Nations to save succeeding generations from the scourge of war, to reaffirm faith in the dignity and worth of the human person, to maintain international peace and security and to develop friendly relations among peoples and international co-operation in promoting and encouraging universal respect for human rights and fundamental freedoms,

Recalling the relevant provisions of the Universal Declaration of Human Rights, the International Covenant on Economic, Social and Cultural Rights, and the International Covenant on Civil and Political Rights,

Recalling also the Charter of Economic Rights and Duties of States and the Declaration and the Programme of Action on the Establishment of a New International Economic Order,

Recalling further the Declaration on the Strengthening of International Security, the Declaration on the Use of Scientific and Technological Progress in the Interests of

Peace and for the Benefit of Mankind, the Declaration on the Preparation of Societies for Life in Peace, the Declaration on the Prevention of Nuclear Catastrophe and General Assembly resolutions 36/92 I of 9 December 1981, on the non-use of nuclear weapons and prevention of nuclear war, and 37/100 C of 13 December 1982, on a convention on the prohibition of the use of nuclear weapons,

Taking note with appreciation of Commission on Human Rights resolutions 1982/7 of 19 February 1982 and 1983/43 of 9 March 1983,

Reaffirming the inherent right to life,

Profoundly concerned that international peace and security continue to be threatened by the arms race in all its aspects, particularly the nuclear arms race, as well as by violations of the principles of the Charter of the United Nations regarding the sovereignty and territorial integrity of States and the self-determination of peoples,

Aware that all the horrors of past wars and all other calamities that have befallen people would pale in comparison with what is inherent in the use of nuclear weapons capable of destroying civilization on Earth,

Noting the pressing need for urgent measures towards general and complete disarmament, particularly nuclear disarmament, for the sake of life on Earth,

Bearing in mind that, in accordance with the International Covenant on Civil and Political Rights, any propaganda for war shall be prohibited by law,

Recalling the historic responsibility of the Governments of all countries of the world to remove the threat of war from the lives of people, to preserve civilization and ensure that everyone enjoys his inherent right to life,

Convinced that for no people in the world today is there a more important question than that of the preservation of peace and of ensuring the cardinal right of every human being, namely, the right to life,

1. *Reaffirms* that all peoples and all individuals have an inherent right to life and that the safeguarding of this cardinal right is an essential condition for the enjoyment of the entire range of economic, social and cultural, as well as civil and political, rights;

2. *Stresses once again* the urgent need for the international community to make every effort to strengthen peace, remove the growing threat of war, particularly nuclear war, halt the arms race and achieve general and complete disarmament under effective international control, and prevent violations of the principles of the Charter of the United Nations regarding the sovereignty and territorial integrity of States and self-determination of peoples, thus contributing to ensuring the right to life;

3. *Stresses further* the foremost importance of the implementation of practical measures of disarmament for releasing substantial additional resources, which should be utilized for social and economic development, particularly for the benefit of the developing countries;

4. *Calls upon* all States, appropriate organs of the United Nations, specialized agencies and intergovernmental and non-governmental organizations concerned to take the necessary measures to ensure that the results of scientific and technological progress are used exclusively in the interests of international peace, for the benefit of mankind and for promoting and encouraging universal respect for human rights and fundamental freedoms;

5. *Again calls upon* all States that have not yet done so to take effective measures with a view to prohibiting by law any propaganda for war;

6. *Looks forward* to further efforts by the Commission on Human Rights with a view to ensuring the inherent right of all peoples and all individuals to life;

7. *Decides* to consider this question at its thirty-ninth session under the item entitled "Human rights and scientific and technological developments".

General Assembly resolution 38/113

16 December 1983   Meeting 100   123-0-23 (recorded vote)

Approved by Third Committee (A/38/684) by recorded vote (110-0-23), 30 November (meeting 58); 29-nation draft (A/C.3/38/L.38), orally revised on proposal by Pakistan and further orally revised; agenda item 94.

Sponsors: Angola, Benin, Bulgaria, Byelorussian SSR, Cape Verde, Congo, Cuba, Czechoslovakia, Democratic Yemen, Ethiopia, German Democratic Republic, Guinea, Guinea-Bissau, Hungary, India, Lao People's Democratic Republic, Madagascar, Mali, Mauritania, Mongolia, Mozambique, Nicaragua, Nigeria, Poland, Syrian Arab Republic, Ukrainian SSR, USSR, Viet Nam, Zambia.

Meeting numbers. GA 38th session: 3rd Committee 49-54, 56-58; plenary 100.

Recorded vote in Assembly as follows:

In favour: Afghanistan, Algeria, Angola, Argentina, Bahamas, Bahrain, Bangladesh, Belize, Benin, Bhutan, Bolivia, Botswana, Brazil, Bulgaria, Burma, Burundi, Byelorussian SSR, Cape Verde, Central African Republic, Chad, Chile, China, Colombia, Congo, Costa Rica, Cuba, Cyprus, Czechoslovakia, Democratic Kampuchea, Democratic Yemen, Djibouti, Dominica, Dominican Republic, Ecuador, Egypt, El Salvador, Equatorial Guinea, Ethiopia, Fiji, Gabon, Gambia, German Democratic Republic, Ghana, Greece, Grenada, Guatemala, Guinea, Guinea-Bissau, Guyana, Haiti, Honduras, Hungary, India, Indonesia, Iran, Iraq, Ivory Coast, Jamaica, Jordan, Kenya, Kuwait, Lao People's Democratic Republic, Lebanon, Lesotho, Liberia, Libyan Arab Jamahiriya, Madagascar, Malaysia, Maldives, Mali, Malta, Mauritania, Mauritius, Mexico, Mongolia, Morocco, Mozambique, Nepal, Nicaragua, Niger, Nigeria, Oman, Pakistan, Panama, Papua New Guinea, Peru, Philippines, Poland, Qatar, Romania, Rwanda, Saint Lucia, Sao Tome and Principe, Saudi Arabia, Senegal, Sierra Leone, Singapore, Somalia, Sri Lanka, Sudan, Suriname, Swaziland, Syrian Arab Republic, Thailand, Togo, Trinidad and Tobago, Tunisia, Uganda, Ukrainian SSR, USSR, United Arab Emirates, United Republic of Cameroon, United Republic of Tanzania, Upper Volta, Uruguay, Vanuatu, Venezuela, Viet Nam, Yemen, Yugoslavia, Zaire, Zambia, Zimbabwe.

Against: None.

Abstaining: Australia, Austria, Belgium, Canada, Denmark, Finland, France, Germany, Federal Republic of, Iceland, Ireland, Israel, Italy, Japan, Luxembourg, Netherlands, New Zealand, Norway, Portugal, Spain, Sweden, Turkey, United Kingdom, United States.

In resolution 38/190 of 20 December, concerning the review of the implementation of the 1970 Declaration on the Strengthening of International Security, the Assembly considered that respect for and the promotion of human rights in their civil, political, economic, social and cultural aspects, on the one hand, and the strengthening of international peace and security, on the other, reinforced each other.

REFERENCES

[1]YUN 1977, p. 706. [2]A/INF/38/6. [3]YUN 1979, p. 863. [4]E/CN.4/1983/62. [5]E/1983/13 (res. 1983/52). [6]YUN 1982, p. 1137, ESC res. 1983/39, 7 May 1982. [7]E/CN.4/1983/32 & Add.1-4. [8]E/CN.4/1984/3 (res. 1983/2). [9]*Ibid.* (res. 1983/11). [10]E/CN.4/1983/26. [11]YUN 1982, p. 1138. [12]E/1983/13 (res. 1983/39). [13]E/CN.4/Sub.2/1983/36 & Add.1-3. [14]YUN 1982, p. 980. [15]E/CN.4/1984/3 (res. 1983/15). [16]YUN 1982, p. 983, GA res. 37/53, 3 Dec. 1982. [17]YUN 1981, p. 975. [18]*Ibid.*, p. 976, ESC dec. 1981/142, 8 May 1981. [19]E/1983/13 (res. 1983/26). [20]YUN 1982, p. 1139. [21]E/CN.4/Sub.2/1983/31. [22]E/CN.4/1984/3 (res. 1983/17). [23]E/1983/13 (res. 1983/41). [24]*Ibid.* (res. 1983/42). [25]YUN 1975, p. 631, GA res. 3384(XXX), 10 Nov. 1975. [26]E/CN.4/1984/3 (dec. 1983/8). [27]E/CN.4/Sub.2/1983/18. [28]YUN 1980, p. 862. [29]A/38/195. [30]YUN 1982, p. 1140, GA res. 37/189 B, 18 Dec. 1982. [31]E/1983/13 (res. 1983/43). [32]*Ibid.* (dec. 1983/106). [33]YUN 1982, p. 1140. [34]E/CN.4/1984/3 (res. 1983/32).

Chapter XIX

Women

In 1983, Governments and the United Nations system worked for the implementation of the Programme of Action for the Second Half of the United Nations Decade for Women and addressed issues concerned with preparations for the 1985 Conference to review the Decade. The Commission on the Status of Women, meeting as the preparatory body for the Conference, made recommendations on the preparations which were endorsed by the Economic and Social Council in May (decision 1983/132) and the General Assembly in December (resolution 38/108).

The Voluntary Fund for the United Nations Decade for Women continued its work to augment the flow of resources to rural and poor urban women. During 1983, the Fund spent almost $5 million on projects, the majority to expand employment of women in new income-generating activities to stimulate self-reliance in rural communities and urban slums.

The International Research and Training Institute for the Advancement of Women (INSTRAW) completed the first phase of a programme to improve statistics on the situation of women and co-operated with other United Nations bodies to support related programmes.

The need for greater participation of women in development was further recognized throughout the United Nations system and the Commission cited the problems faced by rural women as deserving particular attention.

After considering a synthesis of studies on traffic in persons and prostitution, the Economic and Social Council recommended in May that States draw up policies to prevent prostitution (resolution 1983/30); in December, the General Assembly urged States to take humane measures, including legislation, to that end (resolution 38/107).

The Committee on the Elimination of Discrimination against Women considered initial reports of States parties to the 1979 Convention on the Elimination of All Forms of Discrimination against Women and approved general guidelines on the form and contents of such reports. In May, the Council welcomed the beginning of the work of the Committee (resolution 1983/1), as did the Assembly in December (resolution 38/109).

Following a review by the Commission on Human Rights, the Council in May reaffirmed the mandate of the Commission on the Status of Women to consider confidential and non-

confidential communications regarding the status of women (resolution 1983/27).

Topics related to this chapter. Africa: women and children under *apartheid*.

Advancement of women

Decade for Women (1976-1985)

Implementation of the Programme for 1981-1985

In 1983, Governments and the United Nations system continued their activities to implement the Programme of Action for the Second Half of the United Nations Decade for Women—adopted in 1980 by the World Conference of the United Nations Decade for Women: Equality, Development and Peace and endorsed by the General Assembly the same year.[1] In September 1983, the Secretary-General reported to the Assembly on the activities by four intergovernmental and 18 non-governmental organizations (NGOs) which had given particular attention to the need for technical co-operation to ensure women's full and equal participation in all sectors of development.[2]

A December report by the Secretary-General[3] to the Commission on the Status of Women focused on United Nations activities during 1982-1983, which included technical co-operation, fellowships and advisory services provided by, among others, the United Nations Department of Technical Co-operation for Development, United Nations Fund for Population Activities, United Nations Children's Fund and United Nations Industrial Development Organization. Work by the United Nations Secretariat focused on elaborating and reviewing international standards, research, data collection and analysis, and the dissemination of information and experience. The Secretariat had prepared a compendium of international conventions and recommendations covering women, with notes on their respective current status. It started work on a series of inventories of national legislation on sex equality, to assist countries considering their own legislation; research concentrated on various international instruments and on deviations from standards adopted under the 1979 Convention on the Elimination of All Forms of Discrimination against Women.[4]

Preparations for the Conference on the Decade for Women (1985)

The Commission on the Status of Women, meeting for its first session as the preparatory body for the 1985 World Conference to Review and Appraise the Achievements of the United Nations Decade for Women, made recommendations for the Conference's preparation which were endorsed by the Economic and Social Council in May and by the General Assembly in December. The Council also decided that the programme budget implications of those recommendations be revised to reflect the views expressed by delegations, and requested the Secretary-General to submit the revised proposals to the Assembly. Revised appropriations for preparations for the Conference were approved by the Assembly's Fifth (Administrative and Budgetary) Committee. Kenya's offer to host the Conference was accepted by the Assembly.

Also in May, the Council requested the Secretary-General to invite NGOs to participate in the preparations and to submit their views on the progress made and on the obstacles towards attaining the objectives of the Decade, as well as on priorities and strategies. Governments were urged to invite NGOs to do the same on a national level and to co-operate in national reports to be submitted; and regional commissions were requested to ensure that NGOs participated in regional preparatory meetings.

Pursuant to a May 1982 Economic and Social Council resolution,[5] the Commission on the Status of Women met at Vienna, Austria, from 23 February to 4 March 1983. In its report on its first session as the preparatory body for the 1985 World Conference,[6] the Commission set priorities for the Conference, placing emphasis on identifying practical measures to ensure that existing programmes be effectively and rapidly carried out. It was the unanimous view of the Commission that both the objectives of the United Nations Decade for Women, "equality, development and peace", and the sub-theme "employment, health and education", remained valid and should constitute the framework of the Conference.

Recommendations for the provisional agenda included a critical appraisal of progress achieved at the national, regional and international levels, and of the obstacles encountered in attaining the objectives of the Decade; as well as strategies and measures to overcome those obstacles.

Concerning preparatory meetings and activities, the Commission urged that steps be taken at the national level—including the ratification of the 1979 Convention on the Elimination of All Forms of Discrimination against Women and the realization of the Declaration on the Participation of Women in Promoting Peace and Co-operation, proclaimed by the General Assembly in December 1982[7]—and that national committees, together with NGOs, participate in or promote preparatory activities. At the regional level, the Commission recommended that the regional commissions, in co-operation with Governments, organize meetings to review progress and obstacles; and that the Secretary-General convene an interregional seminar to consider measures for improving the situation of rural women, with emphasis on developing countries. It recommended that resources be provided from the existing 1983 budget and the regular budget for 1984-1985, with voluntary contributions to be channelled to a special trust fund for Conference preparations, set up under the Secretary-General.

To create public awareness and highlight preparatory activities for the Conference, the Commission recommended that the information programme aim to reach women and men particularly at the grass-roots level through national commissions, media, information agencies, intergovernmental organizations and NGOs. Special attention should be given to information activities to reach rural and poor urban women. A photo exhibit should be held depicting the objectives of the Decade.

The Commission also recommended that its title as preparatory body for the Conference be amended to Commission on the Status of Women, Acting as the Preparatory Body for the World Conference to Review and Appraise the Achievements of the United Nations Decade for Women: Equality, Development and Peace.

Following the Council's invitation in May 1982, the Secretary-General submitted to the Commission a report on the results of consultations held by the regional commissions on Conference issues and themes.[8]

An Inter-Agency Meeting on the Preparations for the World Conference to Review and Appraise the Achievements of the United Nations Decade for Women[9] was convened at Vienna, on 21 and 22 February 1983, under the auspices of the Administrative Committee on Co-ordination. The Meeting agreed that following the first meeting of the Commission on the Status of Women, acting as the preparatory body, the collaborating agencies would determine the need for technical and lead agencies to ensure efficient co-ordination and analysis. It recommended that a second inter-agency meeting be convened at Vienna, in conjunction with the second session of the Commission as the preparatory body, in February-March 1984. It also made a recommendation with regard to the world survey on the role of women in development (see below).

ECONOMIC AND SOCIAL COUNCIL ACTION

On 26 May 1983, on the recommendation of its Second (Social) Committee, the Economic and Social Council adopted decision 1983/132 without vote.

Report of the Commission on the Status of Women Acting as the Preparatory Body for the World Conference to Review and Appraise the Achievements of the United Nations Decade for Women

At its 14th plenary meeting, on 26 May 1983, the Council:

(a) Took note of the report of the Commission on the Status of Women Acting as the Preparatory Body for the World Conference to Review and Appraise the Achievements of the United Nations Decade for Women;

(b) Decided to endorse the recommendations contained therein and to transmit the report to the General Assembly for consideration at its thirty-eighth session.

Economic and Social Council decision 1983/132

26 May 1983   Meeting 14   Adopted without vote

Approved by Second Committee (E/1983/63), 19 May (meeting 15). Proposal by Chairman; agenda item 12.
Meeting number. ESC 14.

GENERAL ASSEMBLY ACTION

In accordance with the Council's decision, the report of the Commission was transmitted to the the General Assembly's Third (Social, Humanitarian and Cultural) Committee by a 7 October note of the Secretary-General.[10] On 16 December, the Assembly adopted by recorded vote resolution 38/108 as approved by the Committee.

Preparations for the World Conference to Review and Appraise the Achievements of the United Nations Decade for Women

The General Assembly,

Recalling its resolution 3520(XXX) of 15 December 1975, in which it endorsed, *inter alia*, the action proposals contained in the World Plan of Action for the Implementation of the Objectives of the International Women's Year,

Recalling its resolution 3490(XXX) of 12 December 1975, in which it expressed its conviction that a comprehensive and thorough review and appraisal of progress made in meeting the goals of the World Plan of Action was of crucial importance for the success of the Plan and recognized that the results of the implementation of the Plan would contribute to the consideration of the review and appraisal of the International Development Strategy for the Second United Nations Development Decade and would consequently promote the role of women in the development process,

Recalling its resolution 35/136 of 11 December 1980, in which it endorsed the Programme of Action for the Second Half of the United Nations Decade for Women as adopted at the World Conference of the United Nations Decade for Women, and decided to convene in 1985, at the conclusion of the Decade, a World Conference to Review and Appraise the Achievements of the United Nations Decade for Women,

Recalling also that the International Development Strategy for the Third United Nations Development Decade stressed that the important set of measures to improve the status of women contained in the World Plan of Action adopted at Mexico City in 1975, and the important agreed measures relating to the International Development Strategy in the Programme of Action for the Second Half of the United Nations Decade for Women, adopted at Copenhagen in 1980, should be implemented,

Recalling further its resolution 37/60 of 3 December 1982, in which it welcomed the decision of the Economic and Social Council that the Commission on the Status of Women should act as the preparatory body for the Conference and noted that the Commission would hold its first session in that capacity at Vienna from 23 February to 4 March 1983,

Taking into consideration Economic and Social Council decision 1983/132 of 26 May 1983 on the recommendations of the Commission on the Status of Women as the preparatory body for the Conference as set forth in its report, and Council resolution 1983/28 of 26 May 1983 on the participation of non-governmental organizations in the preparations for the Conference,

Bearing in mind all its relevant resolutions and decisions regarding preparations for special conferences,

Having considered the report of the Commission on the Status of Women on the work of its first session as the preparatory body for the Conference,

1. *Decides* to accept with appreciation the offer of the Government of Kenya to act as host at Nairobi, in 1985, to the World Conference to Review and Appraise the Achievements of the United Nations Decade for Women;

2. *Takes note* of the report of the Commission on the Status of Women on the work of its first session as the preparatory body for the Conference;

3. *Endorses* the recommendations contained in the report of the Commission;

4. *Considers* that, within the framework of item 7 of the provisional agenda proposed by the Commission at its first session as the preparatory body for the Conference, particular attention will be paid to the problems of women in Territories under racist colonial rule and in Territories under foreign occupation, on the basis of appropriate documentation from the international conferences on women, held at Mexico City and Copenhagen, with the theme equality, development and peace;

5. *Welcomes* the decision of the Economic and Social Council, in its resolution 1983/28, to invite non-governmental organizations to participate in the preparations for the Conference;

6. *Decides* to include in the provisional agenda of its thirty-ninth session the item entitled "United Nations Decade for Women: Equality, Development and Peace".

General Assembly resolution 38/108

16 December 1983   Meeting 100   141-2-7 (recorded vote)

Approved by Third Committee (A/38/681) by roll-call vote (122-2-7) following a separate vote on operative paragraph 4 (107-8-14), 1 December (meeting 59); draft by Mexico, for Group of 77 (A/C.3/38/L.27); agenda item 91 *(b)*.
Financial implications. ACABQ, A/38/7/Add.19; 5th Committee, A/38/736; S-G, A/C.3/38/2/Add.1, A/C.5/38/77.
Meeting numbers. GA 38th session: 3rd Committee 55, 59; plenary 100.

Recorded vote in Assembly as follows:

In favour: Afghanistan, Albania, Algeria, Angola, Argentina, Australia, Austria, Bahamas, Bahrain, Bangladesh, Belize, Benin, Bhutan, Bolivia, Botswana, Brazil, Bulgaria, Burma, Burundi, Byelorussian SSR, Cape Verde, Central African Republic, Chad, Chile, China, Colombia, Congo, Costa Rica, Cuba, Cyprus, Czechoslovakia, Democratic Kampuchea, Democratic Yemen, Denmark, Djibouti, Dominica, Dominican Republic, Ecuador, Egypt, El Salvador, Equatorial Guinea, Ethiopia, Fiji, Finland, France, Gabon, Gambia, German Democratic Republic, Ghana, Greece, Grenada, Guatemala, Guinea, Guinea-Bissau, Guyana, Haiti, Honduras, Hungary, Iceland, India, Indonesia, Iran, Iraq, Ireland, Ivory Coast, Jamaica, Japan, Jordan, Kenya, Kuwait, Lao People's Democratic Republic, Lebanon, Lesotho, Liberia, Libyan Arab Jamahiriya, Madagascar, Malawi, Malaysia, Maldives, Mali, Malta, Mauritania, Mauritius, Mexico, Mongolia, Morocco, Mozambique, Nepal, New Zealand, Nicaragua, Niger, Nigeria, Norway, Oman, Pakistan, Panama, Papua New

Guinea, Paraguay, Peru, Philippines, Poland, Portugal, Qatar, Romania, Rwanda, Saint Lucia, Sao Tome and Principe, Saudi Arabia, Senegal, Seychelles, Sierra Leone, Singapore, Somalia, Spain, Sri Lanka, Sudan, Suriname, Swaziland, Sweden, Syrian Arab Republic, Thailand, Togo, Trinidad and Tobago, Tunisia, Turkey, Uganda, Ukrainian SSR, USSR, United Arab Emirates, United Republic of Cameroon, United Republic of Tanzania, Upper Volta, Uruguay, Vanuatu, Venezuela, Viet Nam, Yemen, Yugoslavia, Zaire, Zambia, Zimbabwe.

Against: Israel, United States.

Abstaining: Belgium, Canada, Germany, Federal Republic of, Italy, Luxembourg, Netherlands, United Kingdom.

In the Committee, a number of States spoke in explanation of vote. The United States regretted that it upset the delicate balance of the text, since it highlighted situations which were bound to be divisive and detracted from the substantive concerns of the Conference; it also expressed concern on the financial implications. Israel also objected to paragraph 4, which referred to questions which would enable the parties concerned to engage in procedures used at the 1980 Conference. The Federal Republic of Germany felt that the paragraph introduced unrelated political questions. The Netherlands believed that the specific problems of Palestinian women refugees and of women in South Africa, while important, ought not to be the primary issue; the Conference should confine itself to the agenda drafted by the Commission, which was sufficiently flexible to cover any questions without repeating the mistakes of previous conferences. Similarly, the United Kingdom also felt that the Assembly should not direct the Conference's attention to politically controversial issues, and Italy said polemic subjects should be avoided. In Canada's view, the text provided a poor basis for the Conference since it prevented the achievement of consensus.

Explaining its abstention on paragraph 4, the Ivory Coast said that creating a division with regard to the programme of the Conference could doom it to failure. Japan regarded it as inadvisable for the Assembly to adopt a position on the direction to be taken by the Conference debates. Australia said it abstained because it objected to any attempt to give the agenda a contentious political focus. New Zealand spoke in like manner. France would have preferred the agenda proposed by the Commission—whereby it was possible to consider equally the problems of women in all difficult situations. Austria believed that problems arising in that context were not related exclusively to women. Denmark, speaking on behalf of the five Nordic countries, said the Conference's objectives would be fully achieved only if it focused on improving the status of women.

Among those voting for the paragraph, Kenya felt that the raising of controversial issues would be settled during the Conference. Iraq felt that some States opposing the draft were responsible for preventing solutions to the question of Namibia and lending support to South Africa.

Bulgaria hoped the Conference would attend to the link between the problems of the inequality of women and the issues of peace, racism, *apartheid*, foreign occupation and the right of peoples to self-determination. The USSR considered the draft useful for the preparatory work and also supported it because it was based on extensive consultations. Algeria regretted that the efforts of the Group of 77 and the African States had not achieved a consensus, and, viewing paragraph 4 as the product of considerable negotiation, it felt that the attitude of those who opposed it did not augur well for the Committee's future work.

Introducing the draft on behalf of the Group of 77, Mexico said that the concerns in the draft were not exclusive to any country or region and it was only in that spirit that the status of women could be improved.

Financing

ECONOMIC AND SOCIAL COUNCIL ACTION

On 26 May, on the recommendation of its Second Committee, the Economic and Social Council adopted decision 1983/131 without vote.

Programme budget implications of the recommendations contained in the report of the Commission on the Status of Women Acting as the Preparatory Body for the World Conference to Review and Appraise the Achievements of the United Nations Decade for Women

At its 14th plenary meeting, on 26 May 1983, the Council decided that the programme budget implications of the recommendations of the Commission on the Status of Women Acting as the Preparatory Body for the World Conference to Review and Appraise the Achievements of the United Nations Decade for Women should be revised to adequately reflect the views expressed by delegations at the first session of that body and at the first regular session of 1983 of the Economic and Social Council, and requested the Secretary-General to submit those revised proposals to the General Assembly at its thirty-eighth session.

Economic and Social Council decision 1983/131

26 May 1983   Meeting 14   Adopted without vote

Approved by Second Committee (E/1983/63), 19 May (meeting 15); draft by United States (E/1983/C.2/L.11); agenda item 12.
Meeting number. ESC 14.

By a note of 6 May 1983,[11] the Secretary-General presented to the Economic and Social Council programme budget implications of the Commission's recommendations. Total cost of Conference preparations during 1984-1985 were estimated at $1,501,200.

Following the Council's decision on 26 May that the programme budget implications should be revised, the Secretary-General submitted in December to the General Assembly's Fifth Committee revised estimates totalling $1,405,000 for 1984-1985.[12] The Advisory Committee on Administrative and Budgetary Questions (ACABQ), in December,[13] recommended reductions of $364,400— $47,800 less for regional activities, $20,000 less for travel, and reductions of $213,000 and $83,600 for Secretariat support and public information activities, respectively. Following ACABQ's recommendations, the Fifth Committee, on 14 December, approved total appropriations of $1,040,600, comprising $183,000 for regional activities, $71,900 for the interregional seminar, $423,200 for Secretariat support and $362,300 for public information activities. The Committee took that action by 81 votes to 2, with 14 abstentions.

In addition to the appropriations of $1,040,600, the Fifth Committee noted that conference servicing costs of $889,400 would arise. However, much of this amount was absorbed through utilization of conference services already available.

NGO participation

The Commission on the Status of Women, acting as the preparatory body for the 1985 World Conference, made several recommendations at its first session pertaining to the participation of NGOs in the Conference.

A Council resolution of 26 May, inviting NGOs to participate in the Conference preparations, was welcomed by the General Assembly in resolution 38/108 of 16 December (see above).

Following the Council's invitation in May 1982, the Secretary-General presented to the Commission a report containing the views of NGOs on their contributions to the Conference and on possible issues and themes.[14]

ECONOMIC AND SOCIAL COUNCIL ACTION

On 26 May 1983, acting on the recommendation of its Second Committee, the Economic and Social Council adopted resolution 1983/28 without vote.

Participation of non-governmental organizations in the preparations for the World Conference to Review and Appraise the Achievements of the United Nations Decade for Women

The Economic and Social Council,

Taking note of the report of the Commission on the Status of Women Acting as the Preparatory Body for the World Conference to Review and Appraise the Achievements of the United Nations Decade for Women,

Bearing in mind the valuable contributions that non-governmental organizations have made to the advancement of women, particularly during the United Nations Decade for Women and especially in the preparation for and follow-up of the World Conference of the International Women's Year, held at Mexico City from 19 June to 2 July 1975, and the World Conference of the United Nations Decade for Women: Equality, Development and Peace, held at Copenhagen from 14 to 30 July 1980,

1. *Requests* the Secretary-General to invite the interested non-governmental organizations in consultative status

with the Economic and Social Council to participate actively in the preparations for and in the World Conference to Review and Appraise the Achievements of the United Nations Decade for Women, to be held in 1985;

2. *Further requests* the Secretary-General to invite interested non-governmental organizations in consultative status with the Economic and Social Council to submit to the Commission on the Status of Women Acting as the Preparatory Body for the 1985 World Conference, information, including their views on the progress made and the obstacles still to be overcome towards the attainment of the goals of the Decade, as well as their views on priorities and strategies looking to the year 2000;

3. *Urges* Governments to invite interested non-governmental organizations in their respective countries also to submit views on the progress made at the national level, obstacles remaining and goals to be attained, and to co-operate in the preparation of the national reports to be submitted by them to the Secretary-General;

4. *Requests* the regional commissions to ensure that the interested non-governmental organizations in consultative status with the Economic and Social Council participate in their respective regions in the preparations for and in the intergovernmental preparatory regional meetings for the 1985 World Conference.

Economic and Social Council resolution 1983/28

26 May 1983   Meeting 14   Adopted without vote

Approved by Second Committee (E/1983/63) without vote, 19 May (meeting 16); 10-nation draft (E/1983/C.2/L.8/Rev.1), orally revised by Kenya; orally amended in Council by United Kingdom; agenda item 12.

Sponsors: Japan, Kenya, Lesotho, Mali, New Zealand, Nicaragua, Nigeria, Rwanda, Thailand, United Kingdom.

Meeting number. ESC 14.

Voluntary Fund

In 1983, the Voluntary Fund for the United Nations Decade for Women continued to provide financial and technical assistance to promote economic growth, employment and social equity, with special attention to rural and poor urban woman.

In 1983, contributions to the Fund by Governments totalled $2.4 million; in addition, non-governmental contributions amounted to $92,000. Savings from cancelled or completed projects and interest income allowed commitments of $4.9 million for new projects and additions to existing projects. Average costs per project increased to $95,000 in 1982-1983. Since a large number of projects were assigned to Governments and national NGOs as executing agencies, full-time international experts were employed in less than 10 per cent of country projects.

The Fund's activities from October 1982 to September 1983, its financial situation and needs, and a summary of the Consultative Committee's recommendations at its thirteenth (21-25 March) and fourteenth (29 August–2 September) sessions were detailed in an October report of the Secretary-General to the General Assembly.[15]

The Committee proposed policy guidelines for the use of Fund resources and reviewed requests for support. In view of the multiplying demands on the Fund and the critical need for increasing women's access to development resources, it expressed the view that the Fund should have a sound financial basis for its future activities and that this could be accomplished through an endowment, with the target date set for 1985. The Committee also expressed the view that senior posts for women programme officers at the regional commissions should be financed from the regular United Nations budget.

Of about 200 projects for which Fund support was requested, 92 were approved on the recommendation of the Fund's Technical Advisory Group and Consultative Committee. Of those 92 projects, including programming missions, 37 were in Africa, 25 in Latin America and the Caribbean, 20 in Asia and the Pacific, and 9 in Western Asia, plus one global project. Fifty-two of the projects totalled $4.6 million; others were small-scale projects valued at less than $20,000, or additional inputs to ongoing activities. During 1982-1983, 42 per cent of all projects related to expanding employment in new income-generating activities such as animal husbandry, clothes production, pottery making, and fish smoking and marketing. An additional 30 per cent of projects involved human development, including the training of rural trainers and pilot projects to stimulate self-reliance in rural communities and urban slums. Other projects included training of development planners, and training for identification, execution and evaluation of programmes (17 per cent), as well as activities for energy production (7 per cent), such as promotion of fuel-saving cooking stoves, forest industries and re-forestation. National and regional information activities, including research on electronics and other industries, and on law, as well as the publication and dissemination of action-oriented research, accounted for 4 per cent.

In 1983, the proportion of country-level projects—all of which were administered by the United Nations Development Programme (UNDP)—was some 90 per cent.[16] The use of funds from UNDP's Individual Planning Figures for follow-up activities initially assisted by the Fund also increased, for example in Bangladesh, Bolivia and Burundi. Two out of four joint UNDP/Voluntary Fund programming missions undertaken in 1983 and intended to reorient large-scale activities to ensure consideration of women, had already produced positive results in Guinea-Bissau and Sierra Leone. One of the missions recommended that round-table donors' conferences should adopt a guideline that all appropriate projects involve women. Adoption of a similar guideline for World Bank projects was proposed by the Fund's Consultative Committee.

As at 31 December 1983, contributions and pledges to the Fund were as follows:

CONTRIBUTIONS TO THE VOLUNTARY FUND FOR THE UNITED NATIONS DECADE FOR WOMEN, 1983 AND 1984
(as at 31 December 1983; in US dollar equivalent)

Country	1983 payment	For future years
Afghanistan	—	500
Algeria	—	10,000
Australia	95,744	113,695
Austria	21,000	20,109
Bangladesh	2,000	—
Belgium	148,012	75,117
Botswana	4,464	4,587
Brunei	5,000	—
Canada	16,260	32,520
Chile	5,000	—
China	20,000	20,000
Congo	—	7,537
Democratic Yemen	—	1,600
Denmark	91,028	100,000
Egypt	1,000	—
Finland	90,620	88,496
France	19,353	27,673
Germany, Federal Republic of	(1,926)	19,231
Greece	3,500	3,500
Guinea	—	1,000
Guinea-Bissau	(7)	
Honduras	1,000	1,000
Iceland	6,000	6,000
India	—	20,000
Indonesia	—	3,000
Italy	(45,573)	220,126
Jamaica	—	344
Japan	584,474	—
Lesotho	2,000	1,000
Madagascar	(225)	
Maldives	1,200	—
Mexico	2,448	
Netherlands	360,915	165,017
New Zealand	7,866	—
Nigeria	7,215	
Norway	835,804	816,327
Pakistan	5,651	7,502
Philippines	5,261	3,300
Portugal	3,500	3,500
Qatar	5,000	
Republic of Korea	2,000	2,000
Senegal	—	1,500
Sweden	102,171	102,564
Thailand	—	3,000
Togo	(369)	1,256
Trinidad and Tobago	4,008	1,000
Tunisia	4,719	—
United Republic of Cameroon	(696)	
Zaire	—	500
Zambia	—	3,731
Zimbabwe	6,510	—
Total	2,421,927	1,888,232

NOTE: Figures in parentheses indicate negative exchange rate adjustments.

SOURCE: Interim United Nations financial statements for the biennium ended 31 December 1983: schedules of individual trust funds.

GENERAL ASSEMBLY ACTION

On 16 December 1983, on the recommendation of the Third Committee, the Assembly adopted resolution 38/106 without vote.

Voluntary Fund for the United Nations Decade for Women

The General Assembly,

Recalling its resolution 31/133 of 16 December 1976, containing the criteria and arrangements for the management of the Voluntary Fund for the United Nations Decade for Women,

Recalling also its resolution 36/129 of 14 December 1981, in which it decided that the Fund should continue its activities beyond the United Nations Decade for Women: Equality, Development and Peace,

Recalling further its resolution 37/62 of 3 December 1982 and, in particular, its view that the appointment of senior women's programme officers at the regional commissions represents a valuable contribution to the implementation of the goals of the Decade,

Reaffirming that questions concerning women should be approached and dealt with as an integral part of overall policies and programmes in the field of social and economic development,

Noting with appreciation the effective management and continuing expansion of the activities of the Fund and the co-operation extended by relevant bodies of the United Nations, including the United Nations Children's Fund, the United Nations Development Programme and the regional commissions, and by non-governmental organizations,

Welcoming the contributions made by Member States and non-governmental organizations towards the implementation of the goals of the Decade,

Taking note with appreciation of the report of the Secretary-General on the activities of the Fund,

1. *Takes note with satisfaction* of the recommendations of the Consultative Committee on the Voluntary Fund for the United Nations Decade for Women at its thirteenth and fourteenth sessions, referred to in the report of the Secretary-General;

2. *Expresses its concern* that the question of senior women's programme officers posts at the regional commissions is still unresolved and that lack of progress in this regard is seriously impeding work on the women's programmes in several regions;

3. *Urges* the Secretary-General, in consultation with the executive secretaries of the regional commissions, to give priority to solving the question of senior women's programme officers and to take urgently appropriate measures to ensure that all temporary and permanent senior women's programme officers posts at the regional commissions should be continued within the regular budget resources available to them;

4. *Notes with satisfaction* the continuing increase in the number of projects submitted to and financed by the resources of the Fund and their contribution to promoting the involvement of women in development;

5. *Considers* that the Fund has a unique contribution to make in the technical assistance field to the implementation of the goals of the United Nations Decade for Women: Equality, Development and Peace;

6. *Stresses* that the Fund also has a unique contribution to make to the achievement of the goals of the Third United Nations Development Decade, and even beyond it;

7. *Expresses its appreciation* for the voluntary support given to the Fund by Member States, national committees for the Fund, national United Nations associations and other non-governmental organizations;

8. *Notes with concern* that contributions to the Fund have not been sufficient to enable it to take on all the worthwhile projects submitted to it;

9. *Notes* that contributions by Governments have a vital role to play in maintaining and increasing the financial viability and effectiveness of the work of the Fund;

10. *Urges* Governments, accordingly, to continue and increase, where possible, their contributions to the Fund and calls upon those Governments that have not yet done so to consider contributing to the Fund;

11. *Decides* that, when considering the reports of the Secretary-General to be submitted to the General Assembly at its thirty-ninth session pursuant to Assembly resolution 36/129, all possible options for continuing the Fund's activities beyond the end of the Decade will be reviewed in depth;

12. *Requests* that the results of the forward-looking assessment that is being undertaken on the activities assisted by the Fund be reflected in the reports of the Secretary-General on the Fund to be submitted to the General Assembly at its thirty-ninth session;

13. *Takes note with appreciation* of the measures taken by the Secretary-General, in response to resolution 37/62, to improve and streamline the administration of the Fund;

14. *Commends* the United Nations Development Programme on its continuing technical and resource assistance to the Fund;

15. *Requests* the Secretary-General:

(*a*) To continue to report annually on the management of the Fund and on the progress of its activities and to include in his report to the General Assembly at its thirty-ninth session information on the implementation of measures taken in response to paragraph 3 above;

(*b*) To continue, on an annual basis, to include the Fund among the programmes for which funds are pledged at the United Nations Pledging Conference for Development Activities.

General Assembly resolution 38/106

16 December 1983   Meeting 100   Adopted without vote

Approved by Third Committee (A/38/681) without vote, 28 November (meeting 57); 5-nation draft (A/C.3/38/L.22), orally revised; agenda item 91 *(d)*.
Sponsors: German Democratic Republic, India, Jamaica, Kenya, Norway.
Financial implications. S-G, A/C.3/38/L.42, A/C.5/38/80.
Meeting numbers. GA 38th session: 3rd Committee 53, 57; plenary 100.

1979 Convention on Discrimination against Women

As at 31 December 1983, there were 53 States parties to the Convention on the Elimination of All Forms of Discriminiation against Women, adopted in 1979.[4] The Committee on the Elimination of Discrimination against Women, established in 1982 under the Convention,[17] held its second session in New York from 1 to 12 August 1983, to consider reports of States parties submitted under article 18 of the Convention. At that session, the Committee also adopted general guidelines regarding the form and contents of those reports. The Economic and Social Council in May urged States to become parties. The General Assembly in December extended a similar invitation.

Implementation of the Convention

The Committee on the Elimination of Discrimination Against Women, at its second session,[18] considered initial reports of seven States parties on measures they had adopted to give effect to the Convention, out of 13 reports received since the Convention entered into force in 1981.[19] On each report, the Committee heard a statement by, and put questions to, the respective States. General guidelines regarding the form and contents of reports from States parties to be submitted under article 18 of the Convention were elaborated by an informal working group and adopted by the Committee as orally revised.

With regard to participation of specialized agencies, the Committee decided by consensus to invite, in accordance with article 22 of the Convention, those whose activities were relevant to the Convention to prepare reports on such programmes which might promote implementation of the Convention and to provide the Committee with additional information.

The Committee agreed to hold its third session in New York from 26 March to 6 April 1984, while the second meeting of States parties to the Convention would be convened on 9 April 1984. The fourth Committee session would be held at Vienna in March 1985. The Committee also agreed to hold its sessions in New York when States parties met for the election of half of the Committee members every second year, and at Vienna in those years when no meeting of States parties was foreseen.

ECONOMIC AND SOCIAL COUNCIL ACTION

Following consideration of the report of the Committee[20] on its 1982 session,[17] the Economic and Social Council adopted resolution 1983/1 without vote on 17 May 1983.

Convention on the Elimination of All Forms of Discrimination against Women

The Economic and Social Council,

Recalling General Assembly resolution 34/180 of 18 December 1979, by which the Assembly adopted the Convention on the Elimination of All Forms of Discrimination against Women contained in the annex thereto,

Recalling also General Assembly resolutions 35/140 of 11 December 1980, 36/131 of 14 December 1981 and 37/64 of 3 December 1982,

Taking into account Economic and Social Council decision 1982/123 of 4 May 1982,

Having considered the report of the Committee on the Elimination of Discrimination against Women on the work of its first session,

1. *Notes with appreciation* the increasing number of Member States which have ratified or acceded to the Convention on the Elimination of All Forms of Discrimination against Women;

2. *Urges* States that have not yet become parties to the Convention to consider ratifying it or acceding to it;

3. *Takes note* of the report of the Committee on the Elimination of Discrimination against Women and welcomes the beginning of the work of the Committee;

4. *Requests* the Secretary-General to transmit the report of the Committee on the Elimination of Discrimination against Women to the General Assembly at its thirty-eighth session for consideration, as well as to the Commission on the Status of Women for information.

Economic and Social Council resolution 1983/1

17 May 1983	Meeting 6	Adopted without vote

10-nation draft (E/1983/L.24); agenda item 14.
Sponsors: Bulgaria, Byelorussian SSR, Canada, China, Congo, Denmark, German Democratic Republic, Mexico, Norway, Portugal.
Meeting numbers. ESC 5-7.

GENERAL ASSEMBLY ACTION

On 16 December 1983, acting on the recommendation of the Third Committee, the General Assembly adopted resolution 38/109 without vote.

Elimination of all forms of discrimination against women

The General Assembly,

Considering that one of the purposes of the United Nations, as stated in Articles 1 and 55 of the Charter, is to promote universal respect for human rights and fundamental freedoms without distinction of any kind, including distinction as to sex,

Reaffirming that women and men should, on a basis of equality, participate in and contribute to the social, economic and political processes of development and should share equally in improved conditions of life,

Recalling its resolution 34/180 of 18 December 1979, by which it adopted the Convention on the Elimination of All Forms of Discrimination against Women,

Recalling also its resolutions 35/140 of 11 December 1980, 36/131 of 14 December 1981 and 37/64 of 3 December 1982, as well as Economic and Social Council resolution 1983/1 of 17 May 1983,

Taking note of the report of the Secretary-General on the status of the Convention,

Having considered the report of the Committee on the Elimination of Discrimination against Women on its first session,

1. *Notes with appreciation* the increasing number of Member States that have ratified or acceded to the Convention on the Elimination of All Forms of Discrimination against Women;

2. *Invites* States that have not yet done so to become parties to the Convention by ratifying or acceding to it;

3. *Takes note* of the report of the Committee on the Elimination of Discrimination against Women on its first session;

4. *Welcomes* the fact that the Committee on the Elimination of Discrimination against Women has successfully started its work and, *inter alia*, has adopted general guidelines regarding the form and contents of reports received from States parties under article 18 of the Convention;

5. *Requests* the Secretary-General to submit to the General Assembly at its thirty-ninth session a report on the status of the Convention.

General Assembly resolution 38/109

16 December 1983	Meeting 100	Adopted without vote

Approved by Third Committee (A/38/682) without vote, 30 November (meeting 57); 34-nation draft (A/C.3/38/L.19); agenda item 92.
Sponsors: Australia, Austria, Bhutan, Bulgaria, Canada, China, Congo, Costa Rica, Cuba, Denmark, Dominican Republic, Ecuador, Egypt, Finland, German Democratic Republic, Germany, Federal Republic of, Greece, Guinea, Hungary, Iceland, Mexico, Mongolia, Netherlands, Norway, Philippines, Poland, Portugal, Rwanda, Sri Lanka, Sweden, USSR, Uruguay, Viet Nam, Yugoslavia.
Financial implications. S-G, A/C.3/38/7.
Meeting numbers. GA 38th session: 3rd Committee 30-38, 53, 55-59; plenary 100.

Ratifications and accessions

As at 31 December 1983, the following 53 States had ratified or acceded to the Convention (the eight in italics acted in 1983):

Australia, Austria, Barbados, Bhutan, Bulgaria, Byelorussian SSR, Canada, Cape Verde, China, Colombia, Congo, Cuba, Czechoslovakia, *Denmark*, Dominica, Dominican Republic, Ecuador, Egypt, El Salvador, Ethiopia, *France*, *Gabon*, German Democratic Republic, *Greece*, Guatemala, Guinea, Guyana, Haiti, *Honduras*, Hungary, Lao People's Democratic Republic, Mexico, Mongolia, Nicaragua, Norway, Panama, Peru, Philippines, Poland, Portugal, Romania, Rwanda, Saint Lucia, Saint Vincent and the Grenadines, Sri Lanka, Sweden, *Togo*, Ukrainian SSR, USSR, Uruguay *Venezuela*, Viet Nam, Yugoslavia.

In a report to the General Assembly, the Secretary-General listed the States which had signed, ratified or acceded to the Convention as at 1 August 1983.[21] Annexed to the report were reservations made since 31 December 1982 by three States.

UN Research and Training Institute for the Advancement of Women (INSTRAW)

The permanent headquarters of the International Research and Training Institute for the Advancement of Women (INSTRAW), at Santo Domingo in the Dominican Republic, were officially inaugurated on 11 August 1983. By a note of 21 October,[22] the Secretary-General transmitted a report on the programme activities of INSTRAW, as invited by the General Assembly in December 1982.[23] The report covered the objectives, mode of operation and organizational structure, as well as the staffing, financial arrangements and programme of INSTRAW. It cited as the Institute's objectives to stimulate and assist, through research, training, and collection and exchange of information, the efforts of intergovernmental, governmental and non-governmental organizations aimed at the advancement of women and their integration in development, both as participants and beneficiaries.

The INSTRAW Board of Trustees held its third session in New York from 24-28 January. After reviewing the progress report of the Director, the Board examined a proposal for launching the Institute's fellowship programme and approved an allocation of $50,000 for 1983 for its implementation. It welcomed the proposals of the regional commissions for collaboration with INSTRAW and approved a decentralized system for implementing research and training. Examining the financial provisions for the Institute, the Board asked the Secretary-General to continue providing administrative, legal and other assistance, and urged the Economic and Social Council to continue to invite all Member States to contribute to the Institute trust fund. It authorized the Director to obtain supplementary funding, including inviting Board members to establish national support teams in their respective countries.

The Board decided that the 1984-1985 programme budget should focus on research, training and information activities to include follow-up of the current programme, development of new programmes with other United Nations bodies and agencies, and a contribution of the Institute to the 1985 World Conference to Review and Appraise the Achievements of the United Nations Decade for Women.

The Board endorsed the proposal to conduct a series of research studies on the role of women in international economic relations. It invited the United Nations Institute for Training and Research (UNITAR) to continue co-operating with INSTRAW in that area and also invited other United Nations bodies, such as the Centre for Science and Technology for Development, to co-operate in this undertaking.

The Board approved INSTRAW's commitment to the International Drinking Water Supply and Sanitation Decade (1981-1990), and recommended that it organize a seminar on the role of women and the Decade.

The Board also adopted rules of procedure which were annexed to its report to the Economic and Social Council.[24]

Following the Board's decision, collaboration was initiated with the United Nations Conference on Trade and Development (UNCTAD) regarding research studies on the role of women in international economic relations, the first series of those studies dealing with the transfer, development and choice of technology and its impact on women.

The first phase of a programme to improve statistics on the situation of women, undertaken jointly with the United Nations Statistical Office, was completed during the year. Within the framework of that programme, an expert group meeting was convened in New York from 11 to 15 April, at which 17 organizations both within and outside the United Nations system participated.

An interregional Seminar on the Incorporation of Women into Development Planning was held at the Institute's headquarters (Santo Domingo, Dominican Republic, 5-11 December) in order to exchange experience among high-level experts in development planning and women's issues and to raise awareness of the need to increase the involvement of women in development planning.

INSTRAW also continued its co-operation with UNDP's Special Unit for Technical Co-operation among Developing Countries and started a series of publications on women and technical co-operation among developing countries.

In co-operation with other United Nations bodies, the Institute carried out a number of projects integrating concerns affecting women into development planning and worked with UNDP on implementing the policy of collective self-reliance in developing countries. In co-operation with the United Nations Industrial Development Organization (UNIDO), a study of methods for mobilizing women in small-scale and rural industry was conducted. As part of a project to train women entrepreneurs, an exploratory mission was sent to the United Republic of Tanzania, and possibilities of joint training programmes between UNIDO and INSTRAW were being further explored.

Focusing on training programmes, in co-operation with FAO, the Institute examined the role of women in relation to food production strategies and post-harvest food preservation, especially in Africa. It followed the United Nations staff training activities as these related to women. An Institute fellowship programme was launched for implementation through the regional commissions and academic institutions. Advocacy activities to raise public awareness of action for the advancement of women included university lectures and seminars and the identification of a network of contact points for information on research and training activities. Serving as a clearing-house, INSTRAW responded to many requests for information on means available and institutions involved in improving women's conditions world-wide.

ECONOMIC AND SOCIAL COUNCIL ACTION

On 26 May 1983, following the recommendation of its Second Committee, the Economic and Social Council adopted resolution 1983/29 without vote.

International Research and Training Institute for the Advancement of Women

The Economic and Social Council,

Recalling its resolution 1982/27 of 4 May 1982 on the International Research and Training Institute for the Advancement of Women,

Bearing in mind the goals of the United Nations Decade for Women: Equality, Development and Peace,

Having considered the report of the Board of Trustees of the International Research and Training Institute for the Advancement of Women on its third session,

1. *Expresses its satisfaction* with the activities thus far accomplished in the programme of work of the International Research and Training Institute for the Advancement of Women;

2. *Takes note* of the decisions and recommendations made by the Board of Trustees of the Institute at its third session;

3. *Notes with satisfaction* the completion of the first phase of the programme on statistics and indicators on the situation of women and the launching of training and fellowship programmes of the Institute;

4. *Emphasizes* that the work programme of the Institute for the biennium 1984-1985 should continue to focus on research, training and information that would lead to the integration of women in mainstream developmental activities;

5. *Reiterates* the need for support and close co-operation between the Institute and the regional commissions, specialized agencies and other United Nations bodies;

6. *Calls upon* all Member States to contribute to the United Nations Trust Fund for the International Research and Training Institute for the Advancement of Women and to ensure regular and effective financing for its progress and development.

Economic and Social Council resolution 1983/29

26 May 1983   Meeting 14   Adopted without vote

Approved by Second Committee (E/1983/63) without vote, 19 May (meeting 16); 31-nation draft (E/1983/C.2/L.9), orally revised; agenda item 12.

Sponsors: Algeria, Angola, Argentina, Bangladesh, Bolivia, Colombia, Congo, Costa Rica, Cuba, Denmark, Dominican Republic, Ecuador, Egypt, France, Greece, Guinea, India, Japan, Jordan, Kenya, Mali, Mexico, Morocco, Nicaragua, Norway, Pakistan, Saint Lucia, Suriname, Venezuela, Yugoslavia, Zaire.

Meeting number. ESC 14.

GENERAL ASSEMBLY ACTION

On 16 December 1983, the General Assembly adopted resolution 38/104 without vote, as approved by the Third Committee.

International Research and Training Institute for the Advancement of Women

The General Assembly,

Recalling its resolution 37/56 of 3 December 1982, in which it invited the Secretary-General to submit to the General Assembly at its thirty-eighth session a report on the programme activities of the International Research and Training Institute for the Advancement of Women,

Taking note of the report of the Institute on its programme activities,

Recalling Economic and Social Council resolution 1983/29 of 26 May 1983 concerning the programme of work of the Institute for the biennium 1984-1985,

Bearing in mind that the operation of the Institute depends solely on voluntary contributions,

1. *Expresses its satisfaction* at the official inauguration of the International Research and Training Institute for the Advancement of Women at its permanent headquarters at Santo Domingo;

2. *Takes note with satisfaction* of the programme of work of the Institute and requests that the Institute continue activities that contribute to the full integration of women in the mainstream of development and that due attention be given to the interdependence of micro and macro economy and its impact on the role of women in the development process;

3. *Requests* the Secretary-General to take into account, when preparing the statute of the Institute, all relevant factors, including the fact that the Institute and its work are funded from voluntary contributions, as well as the principle of equitable geographical distribution applicable to the membership of the Board of Trustees;

4. *Similarly requests* the Economic and Social Council, when considering the statute of the Institute, to take the above-mentioned elements into account;

5. *Urges* the Secretary-General to continue to provide support to the Institute through the various depart-

ments of the Secretariat and to secure office space at United Nations Headquarters for liaison purposes in order to ensure prompt execution of the Institute's programme of work, as well as to maintain channels of communication between the Institute and the United Nations in conformity with the decision of the Board of Trustees;

6. *Invites* Governments and intergovernmental and non-governmental organizations to contribute to the United Nations Trust Fund for the International Research and Training Institute for the Advancement of Women to meet the urgent need for financial resources in order to implement the programme of work of the Institute;

7. *Decides* to include in the provisional agenda of its thirty-ninth session a separate item entitled "International Research and Training Institute for the Advancement of Women".

General Assembly resolution 38/104

16 December 1983   Meeting 100   Adopted without vote

Approved by Third Committee (A/38/681) without vote, 30 November (meeting 57); 45-nation draft (A/C.3/38/L.20); agenda item 91 *(c)*.

Sponsors: Afghanistan, Algeria, Angola, Argentina, Austria, Bahamas, Bangladesh, Belgium, Bolivia, Colombia, Congo, Costa Rica, Cuba, Cyprus, Denmark, Dominican Republic, Ecuador, Egypt, France, Greece, Guatemala, Guinea, Guinea-Bissau, India, Jamaica, Japan, Jordan, Madagascar, Mali, Mexico, Morocco, Nicaragua, Nigeria, Norway, Pakistan, Paraguay, Peru, Philippines, Sudan, Trinidad and Tobago, United Republic of Cameroon, Uruguay, Venezuela, Yugoslavia, Zaire.

Meeting numbers. GA 38th session: 3rd Committee 53, 57; plenary 100.

INSTRAW finances

Expenditures from the United Nations Trust Fund for INSTRAW in 1983 totalled $998,462, exceeding income for 1983—which amounted to $854,606—by $143,856. For the biennium 1982-1983, however, there was an excess of income over expenditure of $160,615 as at 31 December 1983.

CONTRIBUTIONS TO INSTRAW, 1983 AND 1984

(as at 31 December 1983; in US dollar equivalent)

Country	1983 payment	1984 pledge
Afghanistan	—	500
Austria	7,000	6,721
Chile	5,000	—
China	3,000	5,000
Cuba	1,441	1,153
Cyprus	300	300
Denmark	25,180	50,000
Egypt	—	500
France	58,058	83,019
Ghana	2,750	—
Greece	2,000	2,500
Indonesia	—	5,000
Jamaica	1,123	344
Madagascar	—	523
Mexico	5,758	—
Nicaragua	200	—
Nigeria	3,174	—
Norway	347,047	340,136
Pakistan	2,825	3,751
Philippines	3,000	3,000
Sudan	—	3,906
Trinidad and Tobago	4,000	—
Yugoslavia	1,600	—
Zaire	—	500
Zambia	—	3,731
Total	473,442	510,584

SOURCE: Interim United Nations financial statements for the biennium ended 31 December 1983: schedules of individual trust funds.

Contributions to the Institute in 1983 totalled $473,449, compared to $409,270 in 1982.[25] Pledges for 1984 were $510,584.

A call for contributions to the Fund was made both by the Economic and Social Council, in resolution 1983/29, and by the General Assembly, in resolution 38/104 (see above).

REFERENCES

[1]YUN 1980, p. 905, GA res. 35/136, 11 Dec. 1980. [2]A/38/146. [3]E/CN.6/1984/2. [4]YUN 1979, p. 895, GA res. 34/180, annex, 18 Dec. 1979. [5]YUN 1982, p. 1145, ESC res. 1982/26, 4 May 1982. [6]A/CONF.116/PC/9. [7]YUN 1982, p. 1159, GA res. 37/63, 3 Dec. 1982. [8]A/CONF.116/PC/3 & Corr.1. [9]ACC/1983/PG/3. [10]A/C.3/38/2 & Add.1. [11]A/CONF.116/PC/9/Add.1. [12]A/C.5/38/77. [13]A/38/7/Add.19. [14]A/CONF.116/PC/6 & Corr.1 & Add.1. [15]A/38/530. [16]DP/1984/5/Add.2. [17]YUN 1982, p. 1149. [18]A/39/45. [19]YUN 1981, p. 994. [20]A/38/45. [21]A/38/378. [22]A/38/406. [23]YUN 1982, p. 1151, GA res. 37/56, 3 Dec. 1982. [24]E/1983/31. [25]YUN 1982, p. 1152.

Status of women

Elimination of prostitution and illicit traffic in women

As requested by the Economic and Social Council in May 1982,[1] the Secretary-General appointed in October 1982 a Special Rapporteur to prepare a synthesis of the surveys and studies on traffic in persons and the exploitation of prostitution. In a January 1983 report to the Council,[2] the Special Rapporteur discussed economic factors and social attitudes underlying prostitution and its causes—poverty, emotional deprivation, trickery and coercion. The Rapporteur stated that it was not necessary to invoke any kind of mental weakness or supposed vicious inclination to explain why women fell into prostitution, and that, once there, prostitution became a form of slavery from which it was very difficult to escape. Few regions and countries were free of international traffic in women, which was far from confined to a flow from less developed to more developed regions, but rather involved the traffic of poor women towards rich men. Also discussed were the exploitation of prostitution for tourist purposes, its destructive effects on the identity of women and means available to combat this practice.

The Special Rapporteur felt that there would be no lasting change with regard to prostitution until collective attitudes changed concerning sexist discrimination in general and discrimination which placed prostitutes in a marginal situation, treating them as criminals and maintaining their dependence. The Rapporteur proposed the rehabilitation of prostitutes and prosecution of procurers through State action backed by private associations, both humanitarian groups and self-help organizations. He recommended that Governments co-operate openly with the competent international agencies to identify international procurers' networks and reconvert the sectors of their economies where poverty and indebtedness were recognized as the most common reason that women and children (often with the complicity of parents) fell into prostitution. He also identified organizations within and outside the United Nations system which were best suited for specific action in that regard. Concluding, the Rapporteur expressed the hope that his report would provide the Economic and Social Council with elements that would enable it to proclaim clear principles and inspire a coherent programme of action.

Annexed to the report were excerpts pertaining to prostitution from two reports: one on slavery, submitted to the Commission on Human Rights in 1982,[(3)] and another on child labour, presented to the Sub-Commission on Prevention of Discrimination and Protection of Minorities in 1981.[(4)]

ECONOMIC AND SOCIAL COUNCIL ACTION

On 26 May 1983, on the recommendation of its Second Committee, the Economic and Social Council adopted resolution 1983/30 without vote.

Suppression of the traffic in persons and of the exploitation of the prostitution of others

The Economic and Social Council,

Recalling that the enslavement of women and children subjected to prostitution is incompatible with the dignity and fundamental rights of the human person,

Recalling its resolution 1982/20 of 4 May 1982,

Having taken note of the report prepared by the Special Rapporteur in pursuance of that resolution,

1. *Again invites* Member States to sign, ratify and implement the Convention for the Suppression of the Traffic in Persons and of the Exploitation of the Prostitution of Others;

2. *Also invites* Member States to sign, ratify and implement the International Convention for the Suppression of the Circulation of and Traffic in Obscene Publications, concluded at Geneva on 12 September 1923, as amended by the Protocol signed at Lake Success, New York, on 12 November 1947;

3. *Recommends* that Member States should take account of the report of the Special Rapporteur and draw up, subject to their constitutions and legislation and in consultation with the parties concerned, policies aimed, to the extent possible, at:

(a) Preventing prostitution by moral education and civics training, in and out of school;

(b) Increasing the number of women among the State's personnel having direct contact with the populations concerned;

(c) Eliminating discrimination that ostracizes prostitutes and makes their reabsorption into society more difficult;

(d) Curbing the pornography industry and the trade in pornography and penalizing them very severely when minors are involved;

(e) Punishing all forms of procuring in such a way as to deter it, particularly when it exploits minors;

(f) Facilitating occupational training for and the reabsorption into society of persons rescued from prostitution;

4. *Further invites* Member States to co-operate closely with one another in the research for missing persons and in the identification of international networks of procurers and, if they are members of the International Criminal Police Organization, to co-operate with that organization, requesting it to make the suppression of the traffic in persons one of its priorities;

5. *Invites* the regional commissions to help Member States and United Nations bodies wishing to organize regional expert meetings, seminars or symposia on the traffic in persons;

6. *Suggests* to the Secretary-General that he designate as a focal point the Centre for Human Rights, specifically the secretariat of the Working Group on Slavery, in close co-operation with the Centre for Social Development and Humanitarian Affairs of the Department of International Economic and Social Affairs;

7. *Requests* the Sub-Commission on Prevention of Discrimination and Protection of Minorities to consider the possibility of inviting the Commission on the Status of Women to designate a representative to participate in all sessions of the Working Group on Slavery, in accordance with Economic and Social Council resolution 48(IV) of 29 March 1947;

8. *Requests* the Centre for Human Rights to prepare, in liaison with the United Nations agencies and organs concerned and with the competent non-governmental organizations, two complementary studies: one on the sale of children and the other on the legal and social problems of sexual minorities, including male prostitution, and to submit those studies as soon as possible to the Sub-Commission on Prevention of Discrimination and Protection of Minorities;

9. *Encourages* the Centre for Social Development and Humanitarian Affairs of the Department of International Economic and Social Affairs to utilize the available resources of all its branches with a view to undertaking interdisciplinary studies, and to co-operate with the Division of Narcotic Drugs;

10. *Invites* all the organs, organizations and agencies of the United Nations system concerned, particularly the United Nations Children's Fund, the Office of the United Nations High Commissioner for Refugees, the International Labour Organisation and the World Health Organization, to bring the traffic in persons to the notice of their representatives and experts and to transmit their observations and their studies to the focal point designated by the Secretary-General;

11. *Encourages* the United Nations Educational, Scientific and Cultural Organization to draw up, with member States, programmes for use in schools and in the media concerning the image of women in society;

12. *Invites* the World Tourism Organization to place the question of sex-oriented tourism on its agenda;

13. *Requests* the Secretary-General to take the necessary steps to have the report prepared by the Special Rapporteur in pursuance of Council resolution 1982/20 reproduced as a United Nations publication so that it may be widely disseminated;

14. *Also requests* the Secretary-General to report to the Economic and Social Council, at its first regular session of 1985, on the steps taken to implement the present resolution;

15. *Decides* that the activities recommended in the present resolution will be carried out within the limits of the resources provided for by the Secretary-General in the proposed programme budget for the biennium 1984-1985.

Economic and Social Council resolution 1983/30

26 May 1983   Meeting 14   Adopted without vote

Approved by Second Committee (E/1983/63) without vote, 19 May (meeting 16); draft by France (E/1983/C.2/L.10/Rev.1); agenda item 12.
Meeting number. ESC 14.

GENERAL ASSEMBLY ACTION

On 16 December 1983, following the recommendation of the Third Committee, the General Assembly adopted resolution 38/107 by recorded vote.

Prevention of prostitution

The General Assembly,

Reaffirming the objectives of the United Nations Decade for Women: Equality, Development and Peace,

Taking into account the resolutions, declarations, conventions and recommendations of the United Nations, the specialized agencies and international conferences designed to eliminate all forms of discrimination against women, as well as those relating to the suppression of traffic in persons and the exploitation of the prostitution of others, including Economic and Social Council resolution 1983/30 of 26 May 1983,

Convinced of the importance of the full integration of women in the social, political and economic activities of their community,

Bearing in mind the essential role of women in the welfare of the family and the development of society,

Considering that prostitution and the accompanying evil of the traffic in persons for the purpose of prostitution are incompatible with the dignity and worth of the human person and endanger the welfare of the individual, the family and the community,

Further considering that women and children are still all too often victims of physical abuse and sexual exploitation,

Mindful that the prevailing economic and social conditions are largely responsible for the continued existence of the social problems of prostitution and traffic in persons,

1. *Urges* Member States to take all appropriate humane measures, including legislation, to combat prostitution, exploitation of the prostitution of others and all forms of traffic in persons;

2. *Appeals* to Member States to provide special protection to victims of prostitution through measures including education, social guarantees and employment opportunities for those victims with a view to their rehabilitation;

3. *Requests* the Economic and Social Council, the Commission on Human Rights, the Commission on the Status of Women, the regional commissions and other concerned bodies of the United Nations system to devote greater attention to the problem of prostitution and the means for its prevention;

4. *Requests* the Economic and Social Council to consider this question at its first regular session of 1985, together with the reports requested by the Council in its resolution 1983/30, and to transmit its comments to the General Assembly at its fortieth session.

General Assembly resolution 38/107

16 December 1983   Meeting 100   121-0-25 (recorded vote)

Approved by Third Committee (A/38/681) by recorded vote (106-0-28), 30 November (meeting 58); 8-nation draft (A/C.3/38/L.28/Rev.1), orally revised on suggestions by Canada, Costa Rica and Ethiopia and further orally revised; agenda item 91.
Sponsors: Iran, Kuwait, Libyan Arab Jamahiriya, Malaysia, Morocco, Pakistan, Sudan, Turkey.
Meeting numbers. GA 38th session: 3rd Committee 55, 57, 58; plenary 100.

Recorded vote in Assembly as follows:

In favour: Afghanistan, Albania, Algeria, Angola, Argentina, Bahamas, Bahrain, Bangladesh, Belize, Benin, Bhutan, Bolivia, Botswana, Brazil, Bulgaria, Burma, Burundi, Byelorussian SSR, Cape Verde, Central African Republic, Chad, Chile, China, Colombia, Congo, Costa Rica, Cuba, Cyprus, Czechoslovakia, Democratic Kampuchea, Democratic Yemen, Djibouti, Dominica, Dominican Republic, Ecuador, Egypt, El Salvador, Equatorial Guinea, Ethiopia, Fiji, Gabon, German Democratic Republic, Ghana, Grenada, Guatemala, Guinea, Guinea-Bissau, Guyana, Haiti, Honduras, Hungary, India, Indonesia, Iran, Iraq, Ivory Coast, Jamaica, Japan, Jordan, Kenya, Kuwait, Lao People's Democratic Republic, Lebanon, Lesotho, Libyan Arab Jamahiriya, Madagascar, Malawi, Malaysia, Maldives, Mali, Malta, Mauritania, Mauritius, Mexico, Mongolia, Morocco, Mozambique, Nepal, Nicaragua, Niger, Oman, Pakistan, Panama, Papua New Guinea, Paraguay, Peru, Philippines, Poland, Qatar, Romania, Rwanda, Saint Lucia, Sao Tome and Principe, Saudi Arabia, Sierra Leone, Singapore, Somalia, Sri Lanka, Sudan, Suriname, Swaziland, Syrian Arab Republic, Thailand, Togo, Turkey, Uganda, Ukrainian SSR, USSR, United Arab Emirates, United Republic of Cameroon, United Republic of Tanzania, Upper Volta, Uruguay, Vanuatu, Venezuela, Viet Nam, Yemen, Yugoslavia, Zaire, Zambia, Zimbabwe.

Against: None.

Abstaining: Australia, Austria, Belgium, Canada, Denmark, Finland, France, Germany, Federal Republic of, Greece, Iceland, Ireland, Italy, Liberia, Luxembourg, Netherlands, New Zealand, Nigeria, Norway, Portugal, Seychelles, Spain, Sweden, Trinidad and Tobago, United Kingdom, United States.

Women and racism

The Declaration and Programme of Action adopted by the Second World Conference to Combat Racism and Racial Discrimination in August 1983 (see Chapter XVIII of this section) also addressed the issue of women and racism. The Declaration stated that, whenever there was racial discrimination, women were often doubly discriminated against and that, consequently, further special efforts were called for to eliminate the effects of racial discrimination on women, and to ensure conditions promoting women's equal participation in the political, economic, social and cultural life of their societies. In that context, the Declaration drew attention to the particular importance of the 1979 International Convention on the Elimination of All Forms of Discrimination against Women.[5]

In its Programme of Action, approved by the General Assembly in resolution 38/14, the Conference appealed to States which had not yet done so to consider ratifying or acceding to the Convention. It also called on the World Conference to Review and Appraise the Achievements of the United Nations Decade for Women, to be held in 1985, to contribute to the struggle against racism and *apartheid* by recommending measures aimed at ensuring the active participation of women in the struggle against those evils.

On 9 August, on the occasion of the International Day of Solidarity with the Struggle of Women in South Africa and Namibia, the President made a statement on behalf of the Conference recalling the plight of women suffering particular indignities under *apartheid* and extending solidarity to the oppressed women of South Africa and Namibia.

The situation of women and children under *apartheid* was also considered by the Commission on Human Rights and its *Ad Hoc* Working Group of Experts on Southern Africa, as well as by the Task Force on Women and Children under *Apartheid* of the Special Committee against *Apartheid* (see POLITICAL AND SECURITY QUESTIONS, Chapter V).

Women in rural areas

At the February/March 1983 session of the Commission on the Status of Women, meeting as the preparatory body for the 1985 World Conference (see above), one of the most frequently cited issues was that of problems faced by rural women—a high proportion of women in most developing countries—for whom, even in developed countries, difficult problems were caused by rapid societal change. A number of delegations pointed out that such issues as health and nutrition, family planning, education and training, access to water, sanitation and shelter, services and infrastructure, energy and technology took on a particularly difficult character for rural women.

Concerning a December 1982 General Assembly request[6] for a report on national experience in improving the situation of women in rural areas, the Secretary-General stated, in December 1983,[7] that a questionnaire had been sent to Member States as part of the preparations for a comprehensive report requested by the Commission for submission to the 1985 World Conference. The questionnaire covered policy-making and planning at the national level, institutional arrangements and programmes, and legislative and other provisions to facilitate the advancement of women. The review of national experience on improving the situation of women in rural areas would be part of a comprehensive review and appraisal by the Secretary-General for the 1985 World Conference.

The Economic and Social Council in July 1983 (resolution 1983/71) and the General Assembly in December (resolution 38/158) emphasized the role of women on the farm, called for more attention in matters of policy to the role of women in relation to food systems and stressed the need to involve women in the formulation and implementation of national food programmes (see Chapter XI of this section).

REFERENCES
[1]YUN 1982, p. 1154, ESC res. 1982/20, 4 May 1982. [2]E/1983/7 & Corr.1,2. [3]YUN 1982, p. 1087. [4]YUN 1981, p. 971. [5]YUN 1979, p. 895, GA res. 34/180, annex, 18 Dec. 1979. [6]YUN 1982, p. 1155, GA res. 37/59, 3 Dec. 1982. [7]A/39/58-E/1984/5.

Women and society

Women in development

The need for greater participation of women in development was further recognized in 1983. In the Commission on the Status of Women, acting as the preparatory body for the 1985 World Conference to Review and Appraise the Achievements of the United Nations Decade for Women (see above), a number of delegations reported that national machinery had been established to improve women's conditions and to integrate them in the development process. Plans for a world survey on the role of women in development were reviewed in February by an inter-agency meeting on preparations for the World Conference, which recommended using an analytical structure to include specific ways to improve women's role and examine the potential impact of such improvements on overall development goals. Among the Commission's recommendations was that the world survey constitute one of the Conference's basic documents. That recommendation was endorsed by the Economic and Social Council in its decision 1983/132 of 26 May. In December,[1] the Secretary-General reported that the world survey would contain seven sections prepared by different United Nations bodies, providing an overview and sections on the role of women in relation to agriculture, industry, trade, energy, money and finance, and science and technology. The survey would be prepared for submission to the General Assembly in 1984 and would be considered in 1985 by the Commission as the Conference's preparatory body.

At the April 1983 session of the Joint United Nations Information Committee (JUNIC) (see Chapter I of this section), the Advancement of Women Branch of the United Nations Centre for Social Development and Humanitarian Affairs (CSDHA) reported plans for development education kits on the objectives of the Decade and notes on priority issues for action. In addition, the Branch had allocated $50,000 to the United Nations Department of Public Information for its television series "Women and Development".

In his October report to the General Assembly on the Voluntary Fund for the United Nations Decade for Women (see above), the UNDP Administrator stated that giving rural and poor urban women access to resources tended to have considerable spill-over effects on their families and communities—since women generally invested their earnings in family nutrition and in improving their homes, schools and communities—and the impact of projects benefiting women on their self-esteem and the attitudes of others towards them tended to increase their involvement in community and national activities.

A forward-looking assessment being undertaken by the Voluntary Fund, in co-operation with the regional commissions and the UNDP regional bureaux for presentation to the Assembly in 1984, sought to identify improved strategies of technical co-operation for increasing women's participation in development as both agents and beneficiaries. On 24 June 1983, the UNDP Governing Council decided that its evaluation of the involvement of women in technical co-operation should be available before the end of 1984.[2]

The Board of the United Nations Industrial Development Organization (UNIDO), on 13 May 1983,[3] stressed the contribution made by women to the industrialization of developing countries and reaffirmed its strong support for the increased involvement of women in the development process. The Board urged the UNIDO secretariat to give attention in its training programmes to the upgrading of women's skills and to provide information on projects integrating women in industrialization. The Board called for strengthening the work of the Interdivisional Working Group on Integration of Women in Industrial Development and its co-operation with the Advancement of Women Branch of CSDHA.

The United Nations Fund for Population Activities (UNFPA) continued its efforts to integrate women and women's organizations in all aspects of population programmes. To this end, it organized two seminars in 1983: one on women, family and development (Tunis, Tunisia, October), attended by Arab and Islamic delegations from 15 countries; the other, on population and development (Basseterre, Saint Christopher and Nevis, November), attended by women leaders from the English-speaking Caribbean region.

In 1983, UNFPA assistance to activities relating exclusively to women's concerns totalled almost $2 million. It covered a wide range of projects but did not include women's components of projects concerned with family planning. Larger projects included one in Senegal aimed at promoting the situation of women in family and community, with planned allocations of $529,000, and a project for skills development and training for women in Mexico amounting to $509,581 for a four-year period. There were 41 ongoing country projects in this sector in 1983; the Asia and Pacific region accounted for 18 projects, followed by Africa with

11, the Middle East and Mediterranean with 6, and Latin America and the Caribbean also with 6. In addition, there were 7 regional and 6 interregional and global projects.[4]

The work of UNESCO concerning women concentrated in 1983 on promoting equal educational opportunities for girls and women; training women, particularly those in communications; fellowships, with 23 per cent of 1983 fellowships awarded to women; studies and research; and public information.[5]

FAO continued to promote a broad socioeconomic approach to rural development by focusing on the small farmer, assisting women's co-operatives, training women extension workers and employing women advisers in an effort to counter attitudes which marginalized rural women. An Inter-Divisional Working Group on Women in Development within FAO advised on policies and programmes to integrate women into FAO's agricultural and rural development efforts and co-ordinated these policies with those of other agencies. Specific activities included community action for disadvantaged rural women, projects on women and food systems in Africa, on participation in local rural organizations, on household energy and technology, and on food policy and nutrition. Beginning in mid-1983, national consultants from 17 countries were asked to identify and prepare small-scale grass-roots projects of around $5,000 to promote women's activities in marketing. Other activities included national and regional seminars, research papers and studies, with special attention to women in food systems.[6]

The United Nations Department of Technical Co-operation for Development continued to link activities specifically for women with those carried out in other sectors. Training in practical skills—for example, in the operation and maintenance of water pumps—was found to increase the integration of women in development. Other projects provided training in public administration to improve the status of women in management positions and training for women statisticians.[7]

By a June decision,[8] the High-Level Committee on the Review of Technical Co-operation among Developing Countries (TCDC) (see Chapter II of this section) invited developing countries to strengthen links with women's organizations, to facilitate women's incorporation into development processes and to give due consideration to women's participation when identifying operational issues. United Nations agencies and organizations were invited to include specific references to women in their activities for TCDC, and the UNDP Administrator was requested to continue to support the incorporation of women's issues in all such activities.

GENERAL ASSEMBLY ACTION

The General Assembly, on 19 December, adopted decision 38/443 without vote (p. 438), by which it took note of a Second Committee report[9] stating that there was no specific proposal pertaining to women in development.

In resolution 38/104 of 16 December on IN-STRAW, the Assembly requested that the Institute continue activities contributing to the full integration of women in the mainstream of development and that due attention be given to the interdependence of micro and macro economy and its impact on women's role in the development process. By resolution 38/106 of the same date, the Assembly noted with satisfaction the continuing increase in the number of projects financed by the Fund and their contribution to promoting women's involvement in development.

Women and science and technology

At its June 1983 session, the Intergovernmental Committee on Science and Technology for Development (see Chapter XII of this section) decided to review at its 1984 session progress in implementing the 1979 Vienna Programme of Action as it related to women, science and technology, taking into account the outcome of a 1983 panel of experts on that subject. The panel of experts[10] met at South Hadley, Massachusetts, United States, from 12 to 16 September under the joint sponsorship of the United Nations Advisory Committee on Science and Technology for Development and the American Association for the Advancement of Science. It recommended that Governments appoint women to science and technology bodies, take account of the use of technology to relieve women from time-consuming and underproductive work, and increase educational and training facilities for girls and women. It also recommended that the United Nations system include women in its science and technology bodies, and that scientific and professional societies and funding agencies should increase the participation of women scientists and engineers on their staffs and in their projects, provide leadership opportunities for women, and assess the impact of new technical information on women.

Participation of women in promoting peace and co-operation

In considering preparations for the 1985 World Conference, a number of delegations in the Commission on the Status of Women drew attention to the 1982 Declaration on the Participation of Women in Promoting International Peace and Co-operation.[11] Some indicated the importance of enhancing women's role in decision-making on peace, international co-operation and disarma-

ment, acknowledging that women were frustrated by being extremely underrepresented in forums on such subjects. A number of delegations emphasized that only in conditions of peace was it possible to attain equality and development, and it was noted that in time of war women and children suffered most.

GENERAL ASSEMBLY ACTION

On 16 December, on the recommendation of the Third Committee, the General Assembly adopted resolution 38/105 without vote.

Participation of women in promoting international peace and co-operation

The General Assembly,

Reaffirming its resolution 37/63 of 3 December 1982, by which it proclaimed the Declaration on the Participation of Women in Promoting International Peace and Co-operation,

Believing that further efforts are required to eliminate discrimination against women in all its forms and in every field of human endeavour,

Wishing to encourage the active participation of women in promoting international peace and security and co-operation,

Conscious of the need to implement the provisions of the Declaration,

Desiring that publicity be given to the Declaration,

1. *Calls upon* the Secretary-General to disseminate widely the Declaration on the Participation of Women in Promoting International Peace and Co-operation in the six official languages of the United Nations;

2. *Invites* all Governments to take the necessary measures to ensure wide publicity for the Declaration;

3. *Requests* the Secretary-General to bring the Declaration to the attention of the appropriate specialized agencies, including the United Nations Educational, Scientific and Cultural Organization, the International Labour Organisation, the World Health Organization and other appropriate bodies within the United Nations system, for the consideration of measures to implement the Declaration;

4. *Requests* the Commission on the Status of Women to consider what measures may be necessary in order to implement the Declaration and to report, through the Economic and Social Council, to the General Assembly at its thirty-ninth session;

5. *Decides* to consider at its thirty-ninth session the report of the Commission on the Status of Women under the item entitled "United Nations Decade for Women: Equality, Development and Peace", together with the preparations for the World Conference to Review and Appraise the Achievements of the United Nations Decade for Women, to be held in 1985.

General Assembly resolution 38/105

16 December 1983   Meeting 100   Adopted without vote

Approved by Third Committee (A/38/681) without vote, 30 November (meeting 57); 24-nation draft (A/C.3/38/L.21); agenda item 91.

Sponsors: Afghanistan, Algeria, Angola, Cape Verde, Congo, Cuba, Czechoslovakia, Democratic Yemen, Ethiopia, German Democratic Republic, Guinea-Bissau, Hungary, Iraq, Lao People's Democratic Republic, Madagascar, Mali, Mongolia, Mozambique, Nicaragua, Nigeria, Poland, Sao Tome and Principe, Ukrainian SSR, Viet Nam.

Meeting numbers. GA 38th session: 3rd Committee 53, 57; plenary 100.

REFERENCES
[1]A/CONF.116/PC/14. [2]E/1983/20 (dec. 83/12). [3]A/38/16 (conclusion 1983/12). [4]DP/1984/28 (Part II). [5]E/CN.6/1984/7. [6]E/CN.6/1984/6. [7]DP/1984/42. [8]A/38/39 (dec. 3/7). [9]A/38/702/Add.9. [10]A/CN.11/AC.1/IV/4. [11]YUN 1982, p. 1159, GA res. 37/63, annex, 3 Dec. 1982.

Organizational questions

Procedures for communications received

On 9 March 1983,[1] the Commission on Human Rights decided, in pursuance of a May 1982 request by the Economic and Social Council,[2] to submit the following view for consideration by the Council: that implementation in the Commission on the Status of Women of a procedure to consider communications concerning the status of women would be a useful complement to procedures in the Commission on Human Rights for considering communications on human rights violations. In implementing such a procedure, efforts should be made to encourage co-ordination between the various United Nations organs receiving communications, and to avoid unnecessary duplication. The Commission on Human Rights should continue to consider all communications concerning human rights violations; the Commission on the Status of Women, for its part, could, on the basis of those communications which specifically affected the status of women, submit recommendations to the Council on issues relating to women's rights. The Commission on Human Rights also declared its readiness to continue to co-operate with the Commission on the Status of Women to ensure co-ordination of communications procedures.

The resolution was transmitted to the Council's Second Committee by a Secretariat note of 27 April.[3]

ECONOMIC AND SOCIAL COUNCIL ACTION

On 26 May 1983, on the recommendation of its Second Committee, the Economic and Social Council adopted resolution 1983/27 by recorded vote.

Communications concerning the status of women

The Economic and Social Council,

Recalling its resolutions 76(V) of 5 August 1947 and 304 I (XI) of 14 and 17 July 1950, which continue to form the basis for the mandate of the Commission on the Status of Women to receive at each of its regular sessions a list of confidential and non-confidential communications relating to the status of women,

Recalling also its resolution 1980/39 of 2 May 1980,

Recognizing the desirability of strengthening the capacity of the Commission on the Status of Women to deal with communications and, in this respect, taking note of paragraph 274 of the Programme of Action for the Second Half of the United Nations Decade for Women, in which it was emphasized that the Commission's ability to consider communications should be improved,

Considering that, since the beginning of the United Nations Decade for Women, the volume of communications on the status of women has increased substantially,

Affirming that discrimination against women is incompatible with human dignity and that women and men should participate on the basis of equality, irrespective of race or creed, in the social, economic and political processes of their countries,

1. *Reaffirms* the mandate of the Commission on the Status of Women to consider confidential and non-confidential communications on the status of women;

2. *Requests* the Secretary-General to submit to the Commission, beginning at its thirtieth session, a report on confidential and non-confidential communications on the status of women, which shall include:

(a) Communications received under Council resolutions 76(V) and 304 I (XI), including the comments of Governments thereon, if any;

(b) Communications received by the specialized agencies, regional commissions and other United Nations bodies, together with information on action that may have been taken following the receipt of such communications;

3. *Also requests* the Secretary-General to solicit the co-operation of the specialized agencies, regional commissions and other United Nations bodies in compiling the report called for under paragraph 2 above;

4. *Authorizes* the Commission on the Status of Women henceforth to appoint a working group consisting of not more than five of its members, selected with due regard for geographical distribution, to meet in closed meetings during each session of the Commission in order that it may perform the following functions:

(a) Consideration of all communications, including the replies of Governments thereon, if any, with a view to bringing to the attention of the Commission those communications, including the replies of Governments, which appear to reveal a consistent pattern of reliably attested injustice and discriminatory practices against women;

(b) Preparation of a report, based on its analysis of the confidential and non-confidential communications, which will indicate the categories in which communications are most frequently submitted to the Commission;

5. *Requests* the Commission on the Status of Women to examine the report of the working group and to avoid duplication of the work undertaken by other organs of the Economic and Social Council, the Commission being, in this respect, empowered only to make recommendations to the Council, which shall then decide what action may appropriately be taken on the emerging trends and patterns of communications;

6. *Decides* that all actions envisaged in the implementation of the present resolution by the Commission on the Status of Women shall remain confidential until such time as the Commission may decide to make recommendations to the Economic and Social Council;

7. *Decides* to authorize the Secretary-General to provide, within existing budgetary resources, the services and facilities necessary for the implementation of the present resolution.

Economic and Social Council resolution 1983/27

26 May 1983   Meeting 14   34-5-9 (recorded vote)

Approved by Second Committee (E/1983/63) by recorded vote (34-5-10), 19 May (meeting 16); draft by Commission on the Status of Women as submitted by Secretariat (E/1983/C.2/L.6); agenda item 12.

Meeting numbers. ESC 14-16.

Recorded vote in Council as follows:

In favour: Austria, Bangladesh, Botswana, Brazil, Canada, Denmark, Djibouti, Ecuador, Fiji, France, Germany, Federal Republic of, Greece, Japan, Lebanon, Liberia, Luxembourg, Malaysia, Mali, Mexico, Netherlands, New Zealand, Norway, Portugal, Qatar, Saint Lucia, Sierra Leone, Sudan, Suriname, Swaziland, Thailand, Tunisia, United Kingdom, United States, Venezuela.

Against: Bulgaria, Byelorussian SSR, German Democratic Republic, Poland, USSR.

Abstaining: Algeria, Argentina, China, Congo, Kenya, Nicaragua, Pakistan, Romania, United Republic of Cameroon.

In the Committee, the Byelorussian SSR, also on behalf of Bulgaria, introduced a draft decision[4] requesting the Secretary-General to transmit to Member States the views of the Commission on the Status of Women and the Commission on Human Rights on procedures concerning communications relating to the status of women for their consideration and possible comments, which the Council would discuss at its first regular session in 1984.

The Committee considered that draft decision together with the text that became resolution 1983/27. Following the rejection, by 20 votes to 16 with 13 abstentions, of a proposal by Kenya that the Committee first take action on the draft decision, Kenya proposed that no decision be taken on both texts. The Committee also rejected that proposal, by a recorded vote of 20 to 14 with 14 abstentions. The Committee then voted on the draft resolution, after which the Byelorussian SSR and Bulgaria indicated that they would not insist on having their draft decision put to the vote.

Following the vote in the Council, Romania said it had abstained because it considered that, from a legal point of view, a Council resolution could not establish procedures governing consideration of communications valid for all Member States. The Byelorussian SSR had voted against because it saw the resolution as at variance with Council resolutions on procedures for dealing with human rights communications, which should only be changed after consultations with all Member States. The USSR stated that confidential communications on the status of women were not within the mandate of the Commission on the Status of Women but were rightly dealt with by the Commission on Human Rights; the resolution would lead to duplication and would divert the attention of the former Commission from other issues.

Other organizational matters

On 26 May, the Council adopted resolution 1983/20 on the exchange of information on the activities of CSDHA between the Commission for Social Development and the Commission on the Status of Women. In that resolution, the Council recognized the necessity to exchange such information, and requested the Secretary-General to develop and maintain close collaboration between the two bodies to ensure the integration of women in society.

By decision 1983/184 of 29 July, the Economic and Social Council decided to discontinue for another two years the provision of summary records for several bodies, among them the Commission on the Status of Women (see Chapter XXIV of this section).

REFERENCES

[1]E/1983/13 (res. 1983/39). [2]YUN 1982, p. 1162, ESC dec. 1982/122, 4 May 1982. [3]E/1983/C.2/L.1. [4]E/1983/C.2/L.7.

Chapter XX

Children, youth and aging persons

As in previous years, 1983 United Nations programmes for children were primarily carried out by the United Nations Children's Fund (UNICEF), which helped almost 1.3 billion children through programmes in Africa, Asia, Latin America and the Mediterranean area. Support was provided for water supply and sanitation, primary health care, education, food and nutrition, social services and emergency relief. UNICEF continued to promote simple, inexpensive techniques to improve children's health and reduce child mortality; in comparison to those techniques, providing food supplements, promoting family spacing and extending education were either more costly or more difficult. The General Assembly reaffirmed the importance of UNICEF's basic-services approach for children. It called for comments by States on a draft declaration relating to children's protection and welfare, especially foster placement and adoption.

Activities during the year relating to youth—persons aged between 15 and 24 years—focused on preparations for International Youth Year (1985) and on strengthening communication between youth and the United Nations. The Assembly and the Economic and Social Council called for further preparations for the Year, while the Assembly also called for promoting the human rights of youth.

Following the Assembly's endorsement in 1982 of the Vienna International Plan of Action on Aging—concerning people over 60 years of age—both the Assembly and the Council in 1983 followed up on its implementation.

Topics related to this chapter. Africa: women and children under *apartheid*; Health and human resources. Human Rights: rights of the child; youth and human rights.

Children

Assistance for children in 113 countries—in Africa, Asia, Latin America and the Mediterranean area—was provided by UNICEF during 1983, frequently in co-operation with other United Nations bodies, in the areas of water supply and sanitation, primary health care, education, food and nutrition, social services and emergency relief. As part of the health programme, UNICEF continued to promote four techniques aimed at reducing child mortality and morbidity. The General Assembly, in resolution 38/175, reaffirmed the paramount importance of the basic-services approach for children in the delivery of UNICEF programmes, and appealed to Governments to increase their contributions so that UNICEF could strengthen its co-operation with developing countries and respond to the needs of children in those countries. Concerning the legal aspects of child adoption, the Assembly, in resolution 38/142, took action on the draft Declaration on Social and Legal Principles relating to the Protection and Welfare of Children, with Special Reference to Foster Placement and Adoption Nationally and Internationally, which was being prepared by the Commission on Human Rights. It requested the Secretary-General to report in 1984 on comments by Member States on that text.

UN Children's Fund

In 1983, UNICEF co-operated in programmes in 113 countries, with a total population under 16 years of age of approximately 1.3 billion. Total programme expenditure was $246.1 million. The average expenditure per child in 1983 for countries where UNICEF was co-operating in long-term programmes was 31 cents—21 cents from general UNICEF resources and 10 cents from supplementary funds. Support was given to basic maternal and child health services and nutrition in 105 countries, to social welfare services in 98 countries, water supply and sanitation in 97 countries, formal education in 96 countries, non-formal education in 87 countries and emergency relief in 33 countries. Of the total programme expenditure, 28 per cent was spent for water supply and sanitation, 24 per cent for basic child health, 16 per cent for formal and non-formal education, 12 per cent for planning and project support, 8 per cent for nutrition, 7 per cent for social services and 5 per cent for emergency relief.

The UNICEF Executive Board held its regular 1983 session from 9 to 20 May.[1] It also met on 20 May and 30 June to elect officers for the period 1 August 1983 to 31 July 1984.[2] The Programme Committee, sitting as a committee of the whole, met from 12 to 16 May, and the Committee on Administration and Finance, sitting likewise, met from 17 to 19 May.

According to the UNICEF Executive Director,[3] programme and support activities had become more clearly focused on the priorities of child survival and development through primary health care and basic services programmes approved in 1983 by the Executive Board. At its May 1983 regular session, the Board considered a report on the state of the world's children which highlighted four low-cost, simple-to-use techniques for achieving significant gains in child well-being. Those techniques were: oral rehydration therapy—a method of preventing dehydration caused by diarrhoea, a leading cause of child death; growth monitoring of infants by plotting their weight on charts—a technique which, when used with back-up advice, could prevent up to half of the deaths due to malnutrition in the developing world; expanded immunization, using improved vaccines to prevent six communicable diseases from killing an estimated 5 million children annually; and breast-feeding, which has nutritional and sanitary benefits for children. The UNICEF programme was endorsed by the Board.

The Executive Director pointed out that the world recession had had grave consequences for children and mothers in the developing world, and the situation in sub-Saharan Africa was so serious that it was singled out as a special case. During 1983, a special study on the impact of the world recession on children was prepared by UNICEF with the assistance of economists. In spite of data deficiencies, the evidence confirmed that children in poor societies were measurably suffering from the recession's effects. In northern Zambia, for example, there were indications that children's height-for-age was falling; in São Paolo, Brazil, the proportion of low-birth-weight babies was rising; and in one area of Costa Rica, the number of children being treated for severe malnutrition doubled between 1981 and 1982. The impact of the world recession, however, differed considerably in different parts of the world.

Programme policy decisions

At its May 1983 session,[1] the UNICEF Executive Board reviewed UNICEF's performance in 1982, endorsed new programme initiatives to accelerate child health and survival, reviewed the situation of children, and approved the programmatic and financial objectives of the medium-term plan for 1982-1986, as well as several budget estimates, including the budget for the 1984-1985 biennium, which had been formulated based on zero growth of Professional posts. As approved by the Board in its endorsement of programme approaches, the infant mortality rate, along with gross national product per capita and child population, would be used to guide the content and level of UNICEF programmes for individual countries.

The Board approved general resource commitments totalling $109.4 million and "noted" projects (for which funds had not been obtained) in the amount of $136.1 million for financing through specific-purpose contributions. It noted UNICEF's policy review on supplementary funding and specific-purpose contributions, stressing that general resources should continue to be the mainstay of funding. Following a debate on external relations, the Board endorsed a policy of improving and extending UNICEF external relations activities and encouraged the Executive Director to make full use of the National Committees for UNICEF.

The Board also endorsed the aims of a programme, to be undertaken jointly with the United Nations Educational, Scientific and Cultural Organization (UNESCO), to foster primary education and literacy, and "noted" education projects in four countries.

By decision 1983/187 of 29 July, the Economic and Social Council took note of several documents on operational activities for development (see Chapter II of this section), including the report of the UNICEF Executive Board.[1]

GENERAL ASSEMBLY ACTION

On 19 December, the General Assembly, on the recommendation of the Second (Economic and Financial) Committee, adopted resolution 38/175 without vote.

United Nations Children's Fund

The General Assembly,

Taking note of Economic and Social Council decision 1983/187 of 29 July 1983,

Having considered the report of the Executive Board of the United Nations Children's Fund on its session held at United Nations Headquarters from 9 to 21 May 1983,

Reaffirming the principles and guidelines for programme activities established by the Executive Board of the United Nations Children's Fund in its efforts to reach the most disadvantaged in order to bring about a major improvement in child survival and child development, taking special advantage of developments in primary health care techniques and communications,

Acutely aware that the present global economic situation adversely affects vulnerable groups such as children and therefore makes the need for those efforts all the more critical,

1. *Commends* the policies and activities of the United Nations Children's Fund;

2. *Endorses* the conclusions and recommendations contained in the report of the 1983 session of the Executive Board of the United Nations Children's Fund;

3. *Reaffirms* the role of the United Nations Children's Fund as the lead agency in the United Nations system responsible for co-ordinating the follow-up activities of the International Year of the Child related to the goals and objectives concerning children set forth in the International Development Strategy for the Third United Nations Development Decade;

4. *Reaffirms* the paramount importance of the basic-services approach for children in the delivery of the programmes of the United Nations Children's Fund, while also urging the Executive Director to continue and intensify his efforts on the basis of recent developments in the social and biological sciences which present a new opportunity to bring about a virtual revolution in child survival and child development, at a low cost and in a relatively short time, in accordance with the relevant decisions of the Executive Board of the Fund;

5. *Commends* the Executive Director of the United Nations Children's Fund for his efforts to enlarge the income of the Fund so that the Fund may respond effectively to the needs of the developing countries, in continued pursuance of its mandate;

6. *Expresses its appreciation* to Governments that have responded to the needs of the United Nations Children's Fund and expresses the hope that more States will come forward with positive responses;

7. *Appeals* to all Governments to increase their contributions so that, in the light of the current economic situation, the Fund may be able to strengthen its co-operation with developing countries and respond to the urgent needs of children in those countries.

General Assembly resolution 38/175

19 December 1983   Meeting 102   Adopted without vote

Approved by Second Committee (A/38/703) without vote, 9 December (meeting 55); draft by Vice-Chairman (A/C.2/38/L.108), based on informal consultations on 31-nation draft (A/C.2/38/L.93); agenda item 79 *(g)*.
Meeting numbers. GA 38th session: 2nd Committee 46-53, 55; plenary 102.

The 31-nation draft—by developing and Western States—which was withdrawn in view of the adoption of resolution 38/175, was identical to that text except for paragraphs 4 and 5. Paragraph 4 of the multi-nation draft read: "Urges the Executive Director and the secretariat of the United Nations Children's Fund to continue and intensify their efforts based on recent developments in the social and biological sciences which present a new opportunity to bring about a virtual revolution in child survival and child development, at a low cost and in a relatively short span of time, thereby adapting the basic-services approach for children in the light of current developments in accordance with the relevant decisions of the Executive Board of the Fund". Under paragraph 5 of the original text, the Assembly would have commended both the UNICEF Executive Director and the secretariat for efforts to enlarge UNICEF's income.

Medium-term plan for 1982-1986

At its May 1983 session,[1] the Executive Board approved the programme objectives of the medium-term plan for 1982-1986 as prepared by UNICEF,[4] which were to promote child survival and reduce infant and child mortality and to improve the situation and welfare of children and poorer women. Such objectives were sought through a basic-services strategy, with special em-

phasis on policies and programmes having the potential to achieve more benefits at proportionately less cost. In the report on the plan, the Executive Director recommended that the Board approve the plan as a framework of projections for 1983-1986, including the preparation of up to $215 million in programme commitments from general resources to be submitted to the 1984 Board session. That amount was subject to the condition that estimates of income and expenditure continued to be valid. The Board approved the financial objectives contained in the medium-term plan projecting that UNICEF income would increase from $410 million in 1983 to $495 million in 1986, while annual expenditure would increase from $356 million to $465 million.

Maurice Pate Memorial Award

In February, the Executive Director recommended that the 1983 Maurice Pate Memorial Award, established to commemorate the first Executive Director of UNICEF, be awarded to the Pan-African Institute for Development.[5] The Executive Board, by approving the 1983 commitments at its May session, approved the recommendation. The Institute was recognized for its efforts to train middle- and upper-level personnel involved with rural development in Africa, particularly in nutrition. The Insitute planned to use the $15,000 award to research and produce a guide for training village-level nutrition workers.

UNICEF programmes by region

In 1983, programme expenditures for Africa increased by 16 per cent over 1982; for the Americas, by 22.5 per cent; for East Asia and Pakistan, by 2 per cent; and for the Eastern Mediterranean, by 57 per cent. Programme expenditures for South Central Asia decreased by 3 per cent, and there were no expenditures for Europe in 1983 (in 1982, Poland and Turkey were recipients of UNICEF programmes).

The tables on the following pages show expenditures and commitments for 1983,[6] and commitments and "notings" (for projects awaiting funding) approved by the Executive Board in May.[1]

Africa

In 1983, UNICEF reinforced its programmes in eastern Africa,[7] an area that suffered from the global economic situation and from food shortages, notably in Ethiopia and Mozambique due to long-lasting drought (see Chapter III of this section). Large essential drug and nutrition programmes were launched in Africa. The essential drug programme in the United Republic of Tanzania moved from the planning stage to implementation.

1983 UNICEF EXPENDITURE AND MULTIYEAR COMMITMENTS BY COUNTRY AND REGION

(as at 31 December 1983; in US dollars)

COUNTRY	Expenditure	Approved new commitment	COUNTRY	Expenditure	Approved new commitment
Africa			*Americas* (cont.)		
Angola	2,948,477	—	Mexico	907,070	—
Benin	867,095	—	Nicaragua	521,774	—
Botswana	212,411	486,000	Panama	83,162	77,000
Burundi	1,149,182	—	Paraguay	328,498	—
Cape Verde	415,212	—	Peru	1,487,493	—
Central African Republic	771,489	—	Saint Lucia	24,980	75,000
Chad	1,901,015	—	Saint Vincent and the Grenadines	4,383	—
Comoros	149,943	—	Suriname	1,752	—
Congo	97,828	334,000	Regional projects	1,264,086	1,450,000
Djibouti	1,012,213	245,452			
Equatorial Guinea	122,385	—	Subtotal	13,615,391	9,311,000
Ethiopia	12,550,613	27,956,000	*East Asia and Pakistan*		
Gambia	111,655	389,000	Asian Institute for Training		
Ghana	1,266,741	—	and Research	—	240,000
Guinea	733,693	—	Bangladesh	12,610,634	—
Guinea-Bissau	327,447	—	Burma	7,039,260	—
Ivory Coast	509,529	—	China	6,131,977	—
Kenya	636,507	—	Democratic Kampuchea	3,790,180	1,488,000
Lesotho	178,917	—	Indonesia	9,586,736	—
Liberia	443,874	—	Kampuchean relief	3,566,120	—
Madagascar	1,053,019	—	Lao People's Democratic Republic	897,728	—
Malawi	1,043,375	—	Malaysia	536,591	—
Mali	1,314,494	—	Pacific island Territories	578,717	—
Mauritania	713,323	—	Pakistan	11,520,005	—
Mauritius	120,945	420,000	Papua New Guinea	166,120	591,000
Mozambique	1,920,328	—	Philippines	3,284,721	10,827,000
Niger	1,028,908	—	Republic of Korea	582,503	—
Nigeria	4,719,312	11,746,000	Thailand	2,664,422	—
Rwanda	1,252,209	2,186,000	Viet Nam	3,672,616	—
Sao Tome and Principe	94,988	—	Regional projects	252,049	1,164,000
Senegal	962,293	1,230,000			
Seychelles	25,245	30,000	Subtotal	66,880,377	14,310,000
Sierra Leone	314,329	—	*South Central Asia*		
Somalia	4,026,323	—	Afghanistan	2,466,465	—
Swaziland	85,578	—	Bhutan	1,233,183	—
Togo	269,679	—	India	33,213,008	—
Tunisia	—	1,507,000	Maldives	242,324	—
Uganda	6,113,295	5,169,697	Mongolia	22,878	—
United Republic of Cameroon	422,719	—	Nepal	4,023,175	—
United Republic of Tanzania	6,478,802	—	Sri Lanka	2,621,373	3,313,000
Upper Volta	1,695,820	3,935,000			
Zaire	1,957,974	—	Subtotal	43,822,406	3,313,000
Zambia	384,663	—	*Eastern Mediterranean*		
Zimbabwe	1,446,428	4,260,000	Algeria	76,793	—
Regional projects	1,134,915	466,000	Bahrain	680,482	—
			Democratic Yemen	479,614	—
Subtotal	64,985,193	60,360,149	Egypt	6,218,431	—
Americas			Iran	108,993	—
Antigua	5,992	70,000	Jordan	128,151	—
Barbados	1,000	—	Lebanon	19,631,270	—
Belize	48,086	168,000	Lebanon rehabilitation	7,597,695	—
Bolivia	1,589,781	—	Morocco	1,526,819	—
Brazil	1,122,482	477,000	Oman	295,478	—
Chile	61,685	—	Sudan	6,593,547	—
Colombia	2,047,725	5,790,000	Syrian Arab Republic	456,583	—
Costa Rica	89,119	110,000	Tunisia	205,822	—
Cuba	50,532	178,000	Turkey	209,155	—
Dominica	39,567	—	Yemen	3,854,218	—
Dominican Republic	401,052	—	Palestine children and mothers	345,305	—
Ecuador	537,797	916,000	Regional projects	363,656	—
El Salvador	257,008	—			
Grenada	27,422	—	Subtotal	48,772,013	—
Guatemala	576,356	—	*Interregional*	—	22,074,075
Guyana	143,180	—			
Haiti	1,396,704	—	Savings (cancellation)	—	(32,381)
Honduras	346,568	—			
Jamaica	250,137	—	Total	238,075,380	109,335,843

NOTE: Approved new commitments include the following to cover over-expenditures incurred in previous commitments: Djibouti, $21,452; and Uganda, $67,697.

Totals may differ from sum of figures because of rounding.

COMMITMENTS AND "NOTINGS" APPROVED BY THE UNICEF
EXECUTIVE BOARD IN 1983 FOR INTERREGIONAL PROJECTS
(in US dollars)

	Period	Approved commitments	Approved for "notings"
Maurice Pate Memorial Award	1984	15,000	—
Interregional fund for programme preparation	1984-1985	14,418,000	—
Interregional commitments for additional support to various programme fields	1984-1988	7,600,000	30,000,000
Commitment to cover over-expenditure		41,075	—
Total		22,074,075	30,000,000

NOTE: No regional projects were considered in 1983.

Joint World Health Organization (WHO)/UNICEF nutrition support programmes were begun in Ethiopia and the United Republic of Tanzania and were near implementation in Mozambique and Somalia. Training and staff development continued to receive considerable attention. A second regional programme workshop, held in August, was attended by national and international staff of various functions, including programme, supply, finance and audit. Efficient programme delivery continued to be a concern within each country, and a study of the periodic progress report system resulted in some changes and the addition of a programme officer to oversee and co-ordinate feedback.

Primary health care (PHC)—including training health workers, monitoring infants' growth, diarrhoeal-disease control by oral rehydration therapy, promotion of breast-feeding, and immunization—continued to be emphasized in eastern Africa by many Governments (Botswana, Kenya, Lesotho, Malawi, Swaziland, United Republic of Tanzania, Zambia and Zimbabwe), non-governmental organizations and professional groups, with UNICEF support. Education was another priority area, and in some countries, such as Ethiopia, Rwanda and the United Republic of Tanzania, major reforms had been implemented to provide an educational system more relevant to the population's needs. In about one third of the countries, universal primary education had been achieved and emphasis turned to improving the quality of education and reaching minority groups. Other areas of work in the region included water supply and sanitation, child-related social statistics, technology to improve the home environment, and transport assistance.

In west and central Africa,[8] a region affected by political upheaval as well as the world economic recession and food shortages in 1983, UNICEF focused on providing food for the malnourished, child health and anti-epidemic measures. Infant mortality rates for the region were among the highest in the world and there was a high incidence of disease. UNICEF co-operation continued to be structured around health, nutrition and child survival; water and sanitation (particularly in Benin, the Central African Republic, Chad, Mali, Mauritania and the Niger); education (particularly in Angola, Benin, the Central African Republic, Chad, the Congo, Guinea-Bissau, Mali, the Niger, Senegal and the Upper Volta); social and community development (through aiding Governments, including Benin, the Central African Republic, Guinea, the Niger and Senegal, to foster community developments); and response to emergencies (aiding Benin, Ghana and Togo—when their nationals were suddenly expelled from Nigeria—and Angola and Chad).

Americas

The basic services strategy continued to be the guide-post for the UNICEF country programmes in Latin America in 1983,[9] with special attention given to the most disadvantaged geographical areas, especially where the infant mortality rate was high. The region did not experience the expected economic recovery predicted for that year, but was facing an economic crisis after many years of growth. Some countries were hit by major natural disasters (see Chapter III of this section).

UNICEF provided assistance in PHC (in Colombia, Ecuador, Haiti, Mexico and Nicaragua), a national care plan for young children in Bolivia, an inter-agency workshop in Chile on early childhood development programmes, community child care in Colombia, early childhood development (preschool education in the Dominican Republic, health and nutrition services in Haiti and in the English-speaking Caribbean islands, and a regional seminar on pre-school education in Peru), primary education (Colombia and Jamaica), abandoned children (through developing community-based models and interventions in collaboration with Brazil, Colombia, Ecuador and Mexico), support for economic activities for women (Belize, Costa Rica, Guatemala, Honduras, Mexico and Nicaragua), and urban basic services in low-income areas (through active community involvement in Ecuador, Haiti and Mexico, and a regional project for Central America).

Asia

In East Asia and Pakistan,[10] UNICEF continued to concentrate its programmes on less privileged areas, with full participation and contribution of resources by local communities as well as by Governments and other agencies. The need to ensure national coverage of the techniques endorsed by UNICEF to promote better child care (see above) was generally recognized by Governments. In better-off countries where child survival was no longer the prime concern, greater attention was given to pre-school education, especially in Malaysia, the Republic of Korea and, to a certain degree, in the Philippines. Although several countries still had to import food, no famine had been reported in the region in the previous few years.

Many programmes focused on PHC. Indonesia was being considered for a joint UNICEF/WHO programme, as had been implemented in Burma and Papua New Guinea. The Philippines, with UNICEF support for training, expanded its infrastructure in this area and mobilized community groups for improved delivery of health services. In Thailand, emphasis was placed on community action for providing basic services. Because growth monitoring had become village-based, programmes in Burma, Indonesia, the Philippines and Thailand were more effective. Immunization had been expanded in Pakistan and Viet Nam, and immunization programmes were audited in Indonesia, the Philippines and Thailand. National codes to control the marketing of breast-milk substitutes were adopted by Pakistan, Papua New Guinea, the Philippines and Thailand. A UNICEF-supported seminar on infant feeding in the Pacific Islands gave rise to a recommendation for Cabinet action on national codes. In Bangladesh, Burma, Indonesia and the Republic of Korea, UNICEF was involved in promoting such national codes.

UNICEF assistance was also provided for water and sanitation, and increasing attention was given to training, including construction, repair and maintenance of water systems (Papua New Guinea and Thailand). In Burma, Pakistan and Thailand, oral rehydration salts, a treatment for diarrhoeal disease, were produced. Seven countries of the region (Bangladesh, Indonesia, Malaysia, Pakistan, the Philippines, the Republic of Korea and Thailand) had projects in basic services in urban areas. PHC, nutrition, and non-formal education for women were the core services.

In South Central Asia,[11] despite the shrinkage of aid resources and foreign earnings, major health projects with UNICEF and WHO collaboration—such as maternal and child health, family planning and goitre control—received more financial support than in 1982. Improved infant feeding was emphasized. Afghanistan and Sri Lanka adopted national codes on marketing of breast-milk substitutes, and India actively promoted breast-feeding. Immunization was expanded in cooperation with Governments (India, Nepal, Pakistan and Sri Lanka). UNICEF promoted local manufacture of oral rehydration salts by women's groups (India) and by government companies (Afghanistan, Nepal and Sri Lanka), and responded to an epidemic of meningitis in Nepal and of diarrhoea in Maldives and Sri Lanka.

After studies revealed severe iodine deficiency, special nutritional programmes were initiated in

Bhutan and India. Regional co-operation was expanded in large-scale production and distribution of iodated salt, with UNICEF funding provided for setting up plants in India and for iodinated oil injections in India and Nepal. It also provided vitamin A tablets. Other programmes focused on education and literacy (Nepal and Sri Lanka), and water and sanitation (Bhutan, India and Nepal). Urban slum improvement (Afghanistan, India and Sri Lanka) was another area of concern.

Middle East and North Africa

In 1983, political confrontation continued to be the main factor affecting the lives of children and their families in the Mediterranean area. The situation had a major impact on regional institutional structures, which were not fully available to provide critical linkage, communication and technical support. The Gulf area UNICEF office in the United Arab Emirates, which was given a new mandate to provide leadership and support to the country offices in the Gulf, became fully operational in 1983. Throughout the conflict in Lebanon, the UNICEF office in Beirut continued to operate, despite a major disruption of its regional support functions when the Beirut airport was closed for the month of September. The uncertain political and economic climate was reflected in the reduced number of UNICEF Executive Board submissions for 1983. The Arab Gulf Programme for the United Nations Development Organizations (AGFUND) remained the best regional supporter of UNICEF. By the end of the fiscal year ending 31 August 1983, AGFUND had allocated $46.9 million to UNICEF.

The WHO regional office carried out in 1983 an assessment of the implementation of PHC activities in 23 Eastern Mediterranean countries, according to which achievements were far behind the targets set for the year 2000. The adult literacy rate was 36 per cent compared to the target of 70 per cent, and the immunization rate remained low. About 52 per cent of the population was within easy reach of safe drinking water and 40 per cent was within easy reach of waste disposal facilities, compared to targets of 100 per cent. Most countries of the region had responded to those problems and were implementing one or more of the strategies outlined by UNICEF to achieve a better state of child welfare (see above). UNICEF provided support for many of those programmes, for example: supplying oral rehydration salts for Jordan, supporting a vaccination campaign in Lebanon and an evaluation of infant care in the Syrian Arab Republic, providing instructional aids on nutrition to Jordan, and organizing workshops in Saudi Arabia on breast-feeding. Public information activities centred on advocating UNICEF policies at both the country and regional levels, with special efforts to mobilize the mass media to support those strategies aimed at reducing infant mortality rates. In the Sudan, a conference on nomadic groups was being organized to identify methodologies to provide for their special needs.

UNICEF responded to emergencies caused by both man-made and natural disasters, providing assistance to Lebanon, Turkey and Yemen (see Chapter III of this section). During relief operations in Lebanon, UNICEF took the opportunity to introduce oral rehydration therapy and to emphasize the importance of breast-feeding. In Turkey, which was struck by an earthquake in 1983, UNICEF supplemented the relief assistance of other organizations by providing clothing and shoes for 1,800 children.

UNICEF programmes by sector

As in the previous five years, child health, including nutrition, accounted for the largest portion of UNICEF's expenditures in 1983, followed by water supply and sanitation. Other major programmes were social welfare services and education. The table below gives UNICEF expenditures[12] and commitments[1] by sector.

1983 UNICEF EXPENDITURE AND COMMITMENTS,
BY MAIN FIELD OF CO-OPERATION
(in thousands of US dollars)

	1983 expenditure	*Approved commitments*
Child health	77,590	36,006
Water supply/sanitation	67,842	19,945
Social welfare services for children	17,667	7,219
Formal education	29,972	14,371
Non-formal education	10,409	6,806
Emergency relief	13,393	—
General	29,292	24,891
Programme support services	44,684	—
Total	290,849	109,238

Child welfare in urban areas

During 1983, UNICEF continued to expand support to community-based activities in the slums and shanty towns of third world cities,[3] according to policy guidelines approved by the Executive Board in 1982.[13] Nearly 50 countries were receiving urban basic services assistance. Priority programme areas included reducing infant and child mortality and malnutrition, increasing women's income-earning potential, providing day-care facilities, improving water supplies and environmental sanitation, and reintegrating abandoned children into society. Slum and shanty dwellers represented a growing proportion of city populations, and UNICEF field offices reported an alarming increase in malnutrition among urban children. A contributing factor was the decline in the duration and incidence of breast-feeding. Other health problems occurring in high-density urban areas, where sanitation facilities and refuse disposal services were all but non-existent, included diarrhoea, measles, parasitic infestation and respiratory infections. UNICEF's approach to the problems of abandoned, refugee and abused children and those working under intolerable conditions—a problem in urban areas throughout developing countries—was to back non-conventional and non-institutional activities for street children and help Governments and voluntary organizations learn from such experiences.

An example of UNICEF assistance in this sector was support for the Davao Medical Foundation in Davao City, the Philippines, in a programme to reduce illness and malnutrition. In the light of the number of child minders in slum areas who were themselves children, "child-to-child" instruction was an important feature of the programme. In Peru, UNICEF-assisted PHC and pre-school services covered an urban community of 500,000 and included growth monitoring and oral rehydration. A project in Brazil to help reintegrate street children into their communities was expanded to include 120 state and local organizations. The urban basic services programme in Mexico, being initiated in four pilot communities, included activities focused on child health, low-cost water and sanitation technology, housing, food production and income-generation.

At its May session,[1] the Executive Board welcomed the continued expansion of UNICEF urban activities as consistent with its 1982 urban programme strategy.[13] More comprehensive support for urban children was called for, including special shelter facilities, sanitation and nutrition programmes, job preparation, organized community involvement, action against child labour, prevention of juvenile delinquency and help for abandoned children.

Education

In absolute terms, UNICEF's annual expenditure on education increased over previous years, but the proportion spent on education declined from an average of 21 per cent during 1975-1979 to 14.5 per cent during 1979-1982. In 1983, 16 per cent of expenditure was for education (both formal and non-formal), for a total of $40.4 million, compared with 14 per cent, or $29.1 million, in 1982. A growing share was being devoted to non-formal community activities for early childhood care and education. UNICEF, during 1983, co-operated in primary and non-formal education in 101 countries: 43 in Africa, 26 in Asia, 21 in the Americas and 11 in the Middle East and North Africa region. Its programmes included: providing stipends for training teachers, equipping primary schools and teacher-training institutions with teaching aids, and assisting countries to prepare textbooks locally by funding printing, bookbinding and paper.

UNICEF's support for basic and primary education focused on disadvantaged children, especially those living in remote and underdeveloped areas. According to estimates, 86 per cent of primary age children in developing countries were enrolled in schools in 1980, compared to 57 per cent in 1960, but of those, one in two did not complete the full primary education cycle. The low literacy rate among women in developing countries (50 per cent of women over 15 years of age) was particularly disturbing because of its negative implications for child welfare. Studies had found that the higher the level of the mother's education, the lower the mortality rate of infants. UNICEF's efforts to improve child education were included in activities designated as necessary for child survival, and emphasis was placed on participation of girls and women in primary education and literacy programmes. Support was given to special education projects for women in "family life training centres" in Chad, Ethiopia and Haiti, for example. In Bangladesh, Ethiopia, the Sudan and Zimbabwe, assistance was given to pre-service and in-service training for primary school teachers. In remote areas of Indonesia and the Syrian Arab Republic, UNICEF assisted in the development of one-room multi-grade schools. In Ethiopia and Oman, UNICEF supported the production of literacy and post-literacy materials, and in the Lao People's Democratic Republic, the production and distribution of basic school supplies. Reading materials on health, hygiene and nutrition for use in schools and literacy classes were distributed to rural areas in Egypt.

In addition to the regular programme, in 1983 the Executive Board[1] approved a $30 million joint programme with UNESCO,[14] to be financed through special contributions, to support universal primary education and literacy, initially in five countries: Bangladesh, Ethiopia, Nepal, Nicaragua and Peru. In approving the programme, the Board endorsed the UNICEF initiative to collaborate with UNESCO, Governments and others in efforts to achieve education for all by the end of the century. Countries to be assisted were low on the socio-economic scale, with high infant mortality and low per capita income.

Nutrition

In 1983, UNICEF co-operated in nutrition programmes in 93 countries—39 in Africa, 25 in Asia, 20 in the Americas and 9 in the Middle East and North Africa region—with a total expenditure of $19.2 million, an increase of $200,000 over 1982. Its activities included expanding nutrition programmes in over 19,000 villages, equipping nutrition centres and demonstration areas, provid-

ing stipends to train nutrition workers, and delivering some 24,438 metric tons of food. A five-year joint UNICEF/WHO nutrition support programme, approved by the Executive Board in 1982[15] and financed by a contribution of $85.3 million from Italy, had its first full year of operation in 1983, a year devoted to planning and project preparation. The programme aimed to combine dietary and non-dietary measures within the broad context of PHC, in order to reduce child mortality and morbidity, and improve child development and maternal nutrition. At a meeting on 1 and 2 February in Geneva,[16] the UNICEF/WHO Joint Committee on Health Policy noted with satisfaction the progress on this project—three countries (Mali, the Sudan and the United Republic of Tanzania) had formulated plans at that time, and funding had been approved.

Nutrition programmes included supplementary feeding in areas where drought or civil disturbance had caused crop failure. High priority was given to the control of dietary deficiency diseases by the distribution of iodized salt, vitamin A and other food supplements in many countries, including Angola, Egypt, Haiti, Indonesia, Lebanon and Zimbabwe. The use of appropriate weaning foods was another UNICEF concern, and it co-operated in home and community production of such foods, based on locally available ingredients, in Brazil, Ethiopia, Indonesia, Iraq and the United Republic of Tanzania. UNICEF also supported the industrial production of supplementary weaning foods, mostly for urban areas, in Algeria, China and the Lao People's Democratic Republic. Gardening and preservation of home-grown foodstuffs were supported in many countries, including Guatemala, Jamaica, Mexico, the Republic of Korea and Uganda.

Infant feeding

UNICEF and WHO continued to co-operate in 1983 with countries to promote breast-feeding, a practice beneficial to child health. Studies published in 1983—confirming that breast-feeding still predominated in the rural areas of almost all developing countries, but that in metropolitan areas bottle-feeding was on the rise—reinforced the arguments against bottle-feeding. Efforts were continued to strengthen the application in individual countries of the 1981 International Code on Marketing of Breast-milk Substitutes.[17] By the end of 1983, more than 20 countries had adopted the Code, and close to 1,000 more were engaged in actions related to the Code; however, most national regulations were legally weak, and there was little monitoring of violations.

The media were used to promote breast-feeding in many countries. UNICEF provided assistance for a multi-media national campaign for breast-feeding in Brazil and for distribution of breast-feeding booklets and posters in Egypt, the Philippines and Saudi Arabia.

Primary health care

UNICEF continued in 1983 to emphasize primary health care (PHC), and its expenditures in this sector totalled $58.4 million for the year. As the infant mortality rate remained high in many countries, UNICEF attempted to expand PHC through four low-cost techniques: monitoring child growth, oral rehydration for the treatment of diarrhoea, the promotion of breast-feeding, and universal childhood immunization (see above). It co-operated in child health programmes in 102 countries—43 in Africa, 27 in Asia, 21 in the Americas and 11 in the Middle East and North Africa region. Its activities included: providing grants for training health workers; providing technical supplies and equipment for health centres, especially in rural areas; and supplying medicines and vaccines against tuberculosis, diphtheria, tetanus, typhoid, measles, polio and other diseases.

Diarrhoea, acute respiratory infections, communicable diseases and malnutrition continued to be the major causes of death in children in developing countries. In general, PHC services expanded, although they were far from universal in their practical application. UNICEF played an important advocacy role in several countries and supported national seminars and reviews of PHC strategy. It recognized that PHC problems could only be tackled by better community services and involvement, incorporating education and nutrition.

Major initiatives on communication programmes for health were undertaken in the Arab Gulf countries, Central America, Liberia, Mauritius, the Syrian Arab Republic and the United Republic of Tanzania. The Philippines taught organization and communication skills to Government health workers, and Kenya and Malawi trained district teams to mobilize community leaders for planning and managing PHC. Swaziland set up community health councils.

In many countries, maternal and child health were strengthened by training traditional birth attendants, who carried out the majority of deliveries. Programmes were expanded in Djibouti, Malawi, Nepal, Pakistan, Papua New Guinea, Sudan and Yemen.

For several years, UNICEF and WHO had been co-operating in a programme on the supply of essential drugs. In 1983, UNICEF increased the level of its co-operation, giving special attention to a number of African countries, including Ethiopia, Guinea-Bissau, Mozambique, Somalia, the United Republic of Tanzania, and the Upper Volta. The UNICEF/WHO Joint Committee on Health Policy (Geneva, 1-2 February)[16] considered how to support the implementation and development of PHC in countries with a clear commitment to that approach. It decided that progress reports should be made to the Committee every two years. It recommended that the two organizations pay particular attention to: strengthening community involvement, improving health information systems in order to monitor implementation, adapting health manpower planning to PHC objectives, increasing resources for PHC, and facilitating the exchange of experience among countries. The recommendations were endorsed by the Executive Director of UNICEF.[18]

A study by UNDP and WHO of human resources development for primary health care was completed in 1983 (see Chapter XV of this section).

UNICEF finances

The financial position of UNICEF continued to be sound in 1983, despite the continuing effects of global economic recession.[12] Income, excluding funds for emergencies, was $332 million, compared with $328 million in 1982. Emergency funds provided another $10 million. Voluntary contributions from Governments continued to make up 75 per cent of the total, but contributions from private sources increased slightly to 17 per cent of the total; the remaining 8 per cent came from United Nations organizations and from other miscellaneous income. Income for general resources was $241 million, virtually the same level as in 1982, excluding contributions for Lebanon relief operations. It was estimated that the effects of the strengthening exchange rate for the United States dollar had reduced income by $19 million.

Total expenditure in 1983 was $332 million, which was $24 million, or 6 per cent, less than estimated. Expenditure of $236 million was from general resources and $96 million from supplementary funds. The higher purchasing power of the United States dollar reduced the cost of goods and services paid in other countries by $12 million.

Financial plan for 1983-1986

The UNICEF financial plan for 1983-1986, set out in the medium-term work plan, projected an income of $270 million for 1983, and $290 million, $315 million and $338 million for the following three years. Projected expenditures for the same period were $263 million, $288 million, $313 million and $335 million.

At its May meeting,[1] the Executive Board approved the medium-term plan as a framework of projections, including the preparation of up to $215 million in programme commitments from general resources to be submitted to the Board in 1984. That amount was subject to the condition that estimates of income and expenditure made in the plan continued to be valid. The Board considered that the income projections were realistic, while recognizing that exchange rate fluctuations and other economic uncertainties continued to prevail.

Budget for 1984-1985

In a report to the Executive Board at its May session, the UNICEF Executive Director presented budget estimates for the 1984-1985 biennium.[19] The budget proposal, based on the medium-term plan (see above), suggested that UNICEF goals could be achieved with zero growth in the number of professional and national officer posts.

UNICEF budget estimates for the biennium amounted to $218 million (gross), a 9.8 per cent annual increase over the 1982-1983 budget. The comparable annual increase of total UNICEF expediture, bóth programme and budgetary, was about 14 per cent, from $657 million in 1982-1983 to $847 million in 1984-1985. The annual increase was mainly due to anticipated inflation estimated at a global rate of 6 to 7 per cent, mandatory salary increments, investment in electronic data processing equipment, staff consolidations and additional general service posts. Consolidation and integration of units and organizational changes in the secretariat were taking place to cope with the increased work-load anticipated for 1984-1985. The budget allocated $124.5 million for programme activities, $55.4 million for general administration,

$26.8 million for external relations and $13.1 million for policy-making, direction, co-ordination and control.

In May, the Board approved a commitment of $219.8 million (gross) for the 1984-1985 budget, including expenditure and income ($38.1 million) estimates.[l] The budget of the UNICEF Packing and Assembly Centre at Copenhagen, Denmark, was approved as part of the regular budget on a provisional basis, on the understanding that the unit would remain self-financing. The Board found the projections to be realistic but expressed concern over the build-up of general resources liquidity, which had been slower than planned in 1982.

The Board, having considered the report of the Advisory Committee on Administrative and Budgetary Questions (ACABQ) on the 1984-1985 budget estimates, decided to consider adopting a revised format for the UNICEF budget estimates and to request the Executive Director to submit a revised budget format more in line with the organizational structure of the secretariat. In December, the Director submitted a mock-up of the proposed format, using information from the 1984-1985 budget for presentation.[20]

Contributions

Contributions to UNICEF received in or pledged for 1983 totalled $295,808,588, after a deduction of $752,917 in adjustments to prior years' income (see table below).

CONTRIBUTIONS TO UNICEF
(INCLUDING GENERAL RESOURCES AND SUPPLEMENTARY FUNDS)
(as at 31 December 1983; in US dollar equivalent)

Country or organization	Received in or pledged for 1983 Governmental	Received in or pledged for 1983 Non-governmental	Pledged for 1984 Governmental	Country or organization	Received in or pledged for 1983 Governmental	Received in or pledged for 1983 Non-governmental	Pledged for 1984 Governmental
Afghanistan	30,000	—	30,000	China	300,000	—	350,000
Algeria	142,500	—	142,000	Colombia	396,927	—	385,000
Angola	10,201	—	—	Congo	16,097	—	16,667
Antigua	300	—	—	Cook Islands	649	—	—
Argentina	136,400	—	—	Costa Rica	21,928	10,000	—
Australia	6,997,270	290,119	2,026,800	Cuba	117,350	—	116,988
Austria	1,235,264	91,936	722,912	Cyprus	—	810	—
Bahamas	3,000	—	—	Czechoslovakia	81,037	—	77,882
Bahrain	15,000	403	15,000	Democratic Yemen	6,401	—	7,040
Bangladesh	6,000	824	7,200	Denmark	19,187,430	79,320	5,165,417
Barbados	5,000	—	5,000	Djibouti	2,000	—	2,000
Belgium	1,244,917	372,167	666,667	Dominica	1,479	—	1,000
Belize	495	—	—	Dominican Republic	20,000	—	—
Benin	8,824	—	—	Ecuador	51,051	—	25,407
Bhutan	2,876	—	3,630	Egypt	77,279	—	82,202
Bolivia	16,000	—	—	Ethiopia	49,756	279	49,275
Botswana	9,174	47	8,696	Fiji	2,000	—	1,863
Brazil	100,000	11,308	100,000	Finland	4,121,238	673,010	6,005,773
British Virgin Islands	150	—	150	France	4,183,007	3,000,340	4,074,074
Bulgaria	50,761	5,181	60,914	Gambia	2,769	—	—
Burma	204,087	—	44,456	German Democratic Republic	116,667	—	102,941
Burundi	2,965	—	1,732	Germany, Federal Republic of	6,148,105	6,309,520	5,000,000
Byelorussian SSR	78,125	—	70,225	Ghana	21,000	—	—
Canada	11,770,036	7,865,036	12,368,323				
Chile	150,000	—	50,000				

Country or organization	Received in or pledged for 1983		Pledged for 1984	Country or organization	Received in or pledged for 1983		Pledged for 1984
	Governmental	Non-governmental	Governmental		Governmental	Non-governmental	Governmental
Greece	135,000	21,882	135,000	San Marino	1,386	2,537	—
Guatemala	53,375	433	30,000	Saudi Arabia	1,000,000	136	1,000,000
Guinea	—	—	1,000	Senegal	2,877	—	6,000
Guyana	—	3,333	—	Sierra Leone	—	—	24,000
Haiti	11,750	—	—	Singapore	—	668	—
Holy See	1,000	—	1,000	Solomon Islands	500	—	—
Honduras	20,000	—	—	Somalia	3,452	—	—
Hong Kong	17,305	—	9,712	Spain	282,715	820,360	440,000
Hungary	21,079	13,418	21,041	Sri Lanka	9,825	—	10,265
Iceland	12,068	—	11,370	Sudan	32,065	4,158	35,000
India	1,814,475	41,532	1,671,362	Swaziland	6,019	—	5,078
Indonesia	557,732	1,885	300,000	Sweden	26,615,343	200,457	21,118,012
Ireland	344,432	76,841	—	Switzerland	8,117,070	1,701,936	4,061,614
Israel	50,000	—	50,000	Syrian Arab Republic	25,641	—	—
Italy	34,224,842	1,803,658	15,748,503	Thailand	292,400	5,437	203,101
Ivory Coast	23,663	213	63,636	Togo	—	—	1,190
Jamaica	5,484	—	4,416	Tonga	—	—	5,900
Japan	10,421,362	2,625,149	12,428,087	Trinidad and Tobago	10,365	—	10,417
Jordan	27,435	—	26,490	Tunisia	44,240	—	35,973
Kenya	19,259	—	10,000	Turkey	151,780	648	91,463
Kuwait	200,000	—	200,000	Uganda	1,529	2	3,058
Lao People's				Ukrainian SSR	153,689	—	140,449
Democratic Republic	5,000	—	5,000	USSR	843,750	—	758,427
Lebanon	7,314,936	2,029	50,000	United Arab Emirates	694,575	1,615	—
Lesotho	2,500	—	2,500	United Kingdom	9,192,574	376,714	8,447,143
Liberia	20,000	—	—	United Republic of			
Libyan Arab Jamahiriya	9,174	—	—	Cameroon	66,914	—	—
Liechtenstein	2,000	48,077	—	United Republic of			
Luxembourg	15,455	20,947	14,912	Tanzania	23,418	—	23,418
Madagascar	—	—	6,151	United States	42,510,000	6,567,644	52,500,000
Malawi	3,909	—	3,185	Upper Volta	1,817	—	2,857
Malaysia	184,267	539	84,330	Venezuela	199,651	—	6,000
Maldives	3,000	—	3,000	Viet Nam	4,858	—	6,000
Malta	4,788	—	—	Yemen	14,410	—	12,915
Mexico	136,933	19,952	—	Yugoslavia	205,402	16,831	250,000
Monaco	3,564	—	3,304	Zaire	—	—	2,000
Mongolia	3,612	—	3,529	Zambia	54,519	—	14,465
Morocco	100,000	272	100,000	Zimbabwe	26,042	—	22,936
Nepal	—	—	5				
Netherlands	10,840,985	2,182,792	5,708,051	Subtotal	237,090,962	35,310,269	181,474,782
New Zealand	457,516	17,471	460,526				
Niger	—	—	75	*Intergovernmental*			
Nigeria	402,685	—	362,416	*agencies*			
Norway	20,724,885	11,102	16,028,421	Arab Fund for Economic			
Oman	50,000	—	50,000	and Social			
Pakistan	113,840	2,208	54,088	Development	106,250	—	—
Panama	44,000	—	22,000	Arab Gulf Programme			
Peru	—	30	120,000	for the UN Develop-			
Philippines	496,518	28	413,700	ment Organizations	14,601,035	6,051,323	—
Poland	78,930	—	64,432	European Community	2,764,633	—	—
Portugal	16,500	6,891	15,000	OPEC	635,000		
Qatar	200,000	—	—				
Republic of Korea	147,000	64	147,000	Subtotal	18,106,918	6,051,323	—
Romania	10,846	—	10,965				
Rwanda	4,017	—	4,000	*United Nations system*	—	2,033	
St. Kitts–Nevis–Anguilla	750	—	—	Adjustments to prior			
Saint Vincent and the				years' income	(684,640)	(68,277)	—
Grenadines	750	—	750	Total	254,513,240	41,295,348	—
Samoa	—	—	1,000				

SOURCES: A/39/5/Add.2 and A/CONF.122/2.

Accounts

1981

At its May 1983 session,[1] the Executive Board reviewed and noted the observations on the 1981 UNICEF financial report and the financial report of the Greeting Card Operation (GCO) for the 1980/1981 season by the United Nations Board of Auditors and ACABQ,[21] and the comments made and action taken by the Executive Director in response to those observations.[22] The Board welcomed the improved format of the financial report, which presented for the first time the observations in one composite document organized by subject.

The Board acted on the recommendation of its Committee on Administration and Finance, which met in New York from 17 to 19 May.[23]

1982

In June 1983, following an audit of UNICEF accounts, the United Nations Board of Auditors submitted to the General Assembly the financial statements of UNICEF, including GCO, for 1982.[24]

The Board made recommendations for improving financial management and control systems, and noted that the necessary data for banking and investment purposes had not been computerized in Geneva. Its examination of the balances in the advances recoverable locally and in accounts to Governments indicated the need for further streamlining of the existing follow-up and reporting procedures. The Board also found that consultants had been engaged in the field without authorization by headquarters and performance evaluation of their work had not been carried out. On procurement matters, it noted that occasionally competitive bids had not been submitted and delivery dates were not kept by suppliers. It recommended that the existing procedure for repeat orders be reviewed in order to effect more economy in procurement, and that project monitoring and evaluation be strengthened by headquarters.

Regarding GCO, the Board said that budgetary control could be made more effective by earmarking certain authorizations to clearly identifiable objects of expenditure and by instituting appropriate authorization control procedures. In addition, it said that further efforts were necessary to make GCO more profitable.

In its September 1983 report on audited financial statements,[21] ACABQ commented on the Board's suggestions and noted that UNICEF income for 1982 rose by 30 per cent over 1981. ACABQ, having inquired about a scheme of zero-balance bank accounts that the Board said would be introduced on an experimental basis, learned that the scheme had been partially implemented, with 23 accounts included. UNICEF estimated that, as a result of the procedure, it had been able to reduce its non-interest-bearing balances by 25 per cent. With the consolidation of UNICEF's supply, procurement and shipping services in Copenhagen, a number of procedures relating to procurement were being examined. ACABQ hoped that the re-examination would result in meeting some of the problems observed by the Board. On the issue of standardization, ACABQ was informed by UNICEF that the current system allowed for competitive bidding. Regarding its own 1982 recommendation that penalty clauses for late delivery be included in standard UNICEF procurement contracts,[25] ACABQ noted that this was being considered on a contract-by-contract basis.

In statements to the General Assembly's Fifth (Administrative and Budgetary) Committee, the UNICEF Executive Director and administration also commented on the 1982 financial statements, and on the recommendations of the Board of Auditors and ACABQ. These comments and recommendations were included in a January 1984 report to the Economic and Social Council.[26] Regarding the recommendation on cash management, UNICEF noted that all its accounts earned interest and therefore, balances, which were kept at low levels, could not be considered idle cash. As a result of previous recommendations regarding consultancy services, UNICEF had taken corrective action when instructions had not been followed, including a reporting system on the performance of consultants. Procurement and shipping services were being improved by consolidation in the International Supply Centre in Copenhagen, and procedures were being re-examined, including redefinition of standardization concepts and review of the reordering process.

The UNICEF Committeee on Administration and Finance, during its May 1983 meeting,[23] noted that UNICEF's financial position had improved in 1982. It was pointed out that total current account balances at the end of 1982 were at about the same level as the previous year and represented about two weeks of average expenditures. Balances of restricted currencies at that time were at about the same level as the previous year, indicating that such currencies were turned over with no accumulation, although it had not been possible to reduce such holdings.

At its May 1983 session,[1] the UNICEF Board reviewed and noted the financial report and statements for 1982. On 25 November, the General Assembly—in resolution 38/30, on a number of financial reports audited by the Board of Auditors, including UNICEF's—accepted those reports and concurred with the ACABQ comments. It requested the executive heads of the organizations concerned to take remedial action as required by the Auditors.

Organizational questions

Greeting Card Operation

During the 1982 GCO season (1 May 1982–30 April 1983), 115 million cards, 441,000 calendars, 314,000 packs of stationery and other items were sold in 139 countries.[3] The sales generated $46.9 million in gross revenues, compared to $46.8 million the previous year, yielding a net operational income of $18.1 million to UNICEF general resources. According to a May 1983 UNICEF report on GCO,[27] the net proceeds were $40 million, or $5 million (14 per cent) more than in 1981/1982. The cost of goods delivered increased to $9 million, up $1 million (12 per cent), due to larger quantities produced and inflationary factors. The fixed costs amounted to $13 million, or $2 million (18 per cent) more than in the previous year, partly due to a one-time expenditure for the automation of the production plant in New York.

The UNICEF Executive Board, at its May session,[1] approved the 1983/1984 work plan for GCO, in which planned card production ranged from 115 million to 135 million, expenditure from $24.6 million to $28.4 million and corresponding revenue projections from $42.9 million to $59 million. The work plan for 1 May 1983–30 April 1984 had been recommended by the UNICEF Executive Director.[28] He noted that there was no increase in planned expenditures for the 1983 season due to improved internal efficiency and currency changes.

NGO relations

UNICEF continued in 1983 to foster contacts with non-governmental organizations (NGOs).[3] Several international NGOs working in developing countries adopted proposals to reduce infant mortality by supporting priority action measures, and possibilities for global and regional programmes were explored. A collaborative project with the International Paediatric Association called for three regional meetings to focus on the major avoidable causes of childhood mortality and morbidity, including discussion of how to expand immunization, oral rehydration therapy and growth monitoring, and promote breast-feeding and safe weaning (see above). Similarly, the League of Red Cross Societies was planning, in co-operation with UNICEF, to support information and health programmes of national societies in diarrhoea control, promotion of breast-feeding and nutritional awareness.

In its efforts to increase co-operation between UNICEF and NGOs, the NGO Committee on UNICEF asked its members for information on their activities in countries which were preparing programmes for the UNICEF Executive Board in 1984 and 1985. The information would be shared with programme staff as a basis for furthering co-operation at the country level. The Committee issued a report in April on UNICEF/NGO co-operation at intermediate and local levels.[29]

Draft declaration on adoption and foster placement

In an October 1983 report with three later addenda,[30] the Secretary-General submitted to the General Assembly replies he had received from 22 Governments concerning the draft Declaration on Social and Legal Principles relating to the Protection and Welfare of Children, with Special Reference to Foster Placement and Adoption Nationally and Internationally.

The draft declaration had been prepared by a group of experts in response to a 1975 Economic and Social Council resolution,[31] and was submitted to the Council in 1979.[32] In December 1982,[33] the Assembly requested the Secretary-General to circulate the draft text to Member States to obtain their views.

On 19 December, the General Assembly, acting on the recommendation of the Sixth (Legal) Committee, adopted resolution 38/142 without vote.

Draft Declaration on Social and Legal Principles relating to the Protection and Welfare of Children, with Special Reference to Foster Placement and Adoption Nationally and Internationally

The General Assembly,

Recalling its resolution 36/167 of 16 December 1981, whereby it decided, *inter alia,* that appropriate measures should be taken to finalize the draft Declaration on Social and Legal Principles relating to the Protection and Welfare of Children, with Special Reference to Foster Placement and Adoption Nationally and Internationally,

Noting, in this connection, the current efforts of the Commission on Human Rights to elaborate a draft Convention on the Rights of the Child,

Recalling the action taken by the Economic and Social Council on the draft Declaration,

Bearing in mind the reports of the Secretary-General of 8 September 1980, 19 October 1982 and 6 October 1983, containing the views of Member States on the text of the draft Declaration,

Noting that the first of the above-mentioned reports contains, in section VI, some proposed amendments and reformulations of certain articles based on comments by Member States,

Fully aware of the sovereign right of Governments to define their national and international policies as regards the protection and welfare of children, including foster placement and adoption,

Bearing in mind the existence of different national legislation in the field of the protection and welfare of children,

Recognizing that it is the responsibility of Governments to determine the adequacy of their national services for children and to recognize those children whose needs are not being met by existing services,

Noting the usefulness of regional co-operation in matters regarding the well-being of children,

Recognizing that the best child welfare is good family welfare and that, when family care is unavailable or inappropriate, substitute family care should be considered, in conformity with national legislation,

Convinced that adoption of the draft Declaration will promote the well-being of children with special needs,

1. *Requests* the Secretary-General to invite Member States to comment on the most appropriate procedure for completing work on the draft Declaration on Social and Legal Principles relating to the Protection and Welfare of Children, with Special Reference to Foster Placement and Adoption Nationally and Internationally and the forum for future discussion, bearing in mind the suggestions and proposals made in the Sixth Committee;

2. *Also requests* the Secretary-General to submit to the General Assembly at its thirty-ninth session a report containing the comments and observations received pursuant to paragraph 1 above, with a view to taking a final decision on the procedure to be followed;

3. *Decides* to include in the provisional agenda of its thirty-ninth session an item entitled "Consideration of the draft Declaration on Social and Legal Principles

relating to the Protection and Welfare of Children, with Special Reference to Foster Placement and Adoption Nationally and Internationally".

General Assembly resolution 38/142

19 December 1983   Meeting 101   Adopted without vote

Approved by Sixth Committee (A/38/675) without vote, 9 December (meeting 72); 7-nation draft (A/C.6/38/L.25/Rev.1); agenda item 135.

Sponsors: Colombia, Finland, Iceland, Netherlands, Norway, Sweden, Uruguay.
Meeting numbers. GA 38th session: 6th Committee 72; plenary 101.

REFERENCES

[1]E/1983/21. [2]E/ICEF/702. [3]E/ICEF/1984/2. [4]E/ICEF/699. [5]E/ICEF/P/L.2189(REC). [6]A/39/5/Add.2. [7]E/ICEF/1984/5. [8]E/ICEF/1984/6 & Add.1. [9]E/ICEF/1984/7. [10]E/ICEF/1984/8. [11]E/ICEF/1984/9. [12]E/1984/19. [13]YUN 1982, p. 1170. [14]E/ICEF/Misc.401. [15]YUN 1982, p. 1171. [16]E/ICEF/L.1456 & Corr. 1. [17]YUN 1981, p. 1419. [18]E/ICEF/L.1457. [19]E/ICEF/AB/L.249. [20]E/ICEF/1984/AB/L.1. [21]A/38/433. [22]E/ICEF/AB/L.246. [23]E/ICEF/AB/L.254. [24]A/38/5/Add.2. [25]YUN 1982, p. 1175. [26]E/ICEF/1984/AB/L.3. [27]E/ICEF/AB/L.253. [28]E/ICEF/AB/L.250. [29]E/ICEF/NGO/210. [30]A/38/389 & Add.1-3. [31]YUN 1975, p. 684, ESC res. 1925(LVIII), 6 May 1975. [32]YUN 1979, p. 769, ESC res. 1979/28, 9 May 1979. [33]YUN 1982, p. 1177, GA res. 37/115, 16 Dec. 1982.

PUBLICATION

Law and the Status of the Child, Sales No. E.83.XV.RR/29.

Youth

Activities during the year relating to youth—persons 15 to 24 years old—focused on preparations for International Youth Year (1985) (IYY) and on strengthening communication between youth and the United Nations. The Assembly, in resolutions 38/22 and 38/26, and the Economic and Social Council, in resolution 1983/14, called for further preparations for the Year. While the Council, in resolution 1983/26, acted to improve co-ordination and information relating to youth, the Assembly requested the Secretary-General to publicize United Nations–related activities and also called for promoting the human rights of youth (resolution 38/23), particularly the right to education and vocational training and to work.

The Council, in resolutions 1983/14 and 1983/17, took note of a 1982 report of the Secretary-General on the situation of youth in the 1980s,[1] in which he stated that the youth population—20 per cent of that of the world—would continue to rise in developing countries and decline in developed nations. According to the report, young people in the 1980s faced economic recession and rising unemployment, coupled with social changes of family disintegration, rapid urbanization and industrialization. The Council called for measures to ensure the employment of young people, and for the implementation of their rights to social and economic development, education and employment.

ECONOMIC AND SOCIAL COUNCIL ACTION

On 26 May 1983, the Economic and Social Council, acting on the recommendation of its Second (Social) Committee, adopted two resolutions concerning the development of youth.

It adopted resolution 1983/14 without vote.

Youth in the contemporary world

The Economic and Social Council,

Noting with great interest the importance attached by the General Assembly and other United Nations bodies to the concerns of youth,

Recalling its resolutions 1979/16 of 9 May 1979 and 1981/16 of 6 May 1981 on youth in the contemporary world, as well as General Assembly resolutions 35/126 of 11 December 1980, 36/28 of 13 November 1981 and 37/48 of 3 December 1982 on the International Youth Year: Participation, Development, Peace, and 36/17 of 9 November 1981 and 37/50 of 3 December 1982 on channels of communication between the United Nations and youth and youth organizations,

Noting with satisfaction that the Declaration on the Promotion among Youth of the Ideals of Peace, Mutual Respect and Understanding between Peoples, contained in General Assembly resolution 2037(XX) of 7 December 1965, continues to provide a useful basis and incentive for further action in the field of youth, at the national, regional, interregional and international levels,

Convinced that the preservation and strengthening of international peace and security are prerequisites for a secure and happy future for the youth of all countries,

Recognizing the importance of integrating young people in the overall life of society and of taking fully into account their special needs when formulating national plans and programmes,

Emphasizing the need to increase the quantity and quality of opportunities for young people for their active and productive participation in the general development of society,

Reaffirming the necessity of intensifying and consolidating the efforts of the United Nations so as to give effect to a co-ordinated and practical approach to the youth programmes of all the United Nations agencies involved, as well as strengthening co-operation with non-governmental youth organizations or organizations dealing directly with youth,

Noting the views on the question of youth in the contemporary world expressed in the report of the Secretary-General on the situation of youth in the 1980s and in the report of the Commission for Social Development on its twenty-seventh session,

1. *Takes note with appreciation* of the report of the Secretary-General on the situation of youth in the 1980s;

2. *Requests* the Secretary-General to bring to the attention of the General Assembly at its thirty-eighth session all relevant documents on the question of youth prepared for the Commission for Social Development;

3. *Also requests* the Secretary-General to take into account the views expressed on youth in the Commission for Social Development in the preparation of the documentation to be submitted to the Advisory Committee for the International Youth Year: Participation, Development, Peace;

4. *Further requests* the Secretary-General to submit the present resolution to the five regional meetings devoted

to the International Youth Year and to take all necessary organizational measures to ensure their success as provided by the General Assembly in paragraph 4 of its resolution 37/48;

5. *Decides* to include the item entitled "Youth in the contemporary world" in the agenda of the twenty-ninth session of the Commission for Social Development; decides also that the Commission should consider under that item a report of the Secretary-General on the situation of youth in the 1980s in connection with the International Youth Year: Participation, Development, Peace; and decides further that the report should be transmitted to the General Assembly through the Economic and Social Council.

Economic and Social Council resolution 1983/14

26 May 1983   Meeting 14   Adopted without vote

Approved by Second Committee (E/1983/62) without vote, 10 May (meeting 8); draft by Commission for Social Development (E/1983/14); agenda item 11. *Meeting number.* ESC 14.

The Council also adopted resolution 1983/17 without vote.

Youth participation in social and economic development and their exercise of the rights to life, employment and education

The Economic and Social Council,

Drawing attention to the exceptional importance of all forms of assistance in the large-scale integration of young people into the social and economic development of their respective countries for ensuring the economic, social, cultural, political and civil rights of youth, in particular the rights of youth to life, education and employment in conditions of peace,

Convinced that youth can make a valuable contribution to efforts to create a new international economic order,

Considering that States should take measures at the domestic level to create conditions for young persons in which they can play an effective and active role in the social and economic development of their respective countries,

Recalling General Assembly resolutions 36/28 of 13 November 1981, by which the Assembly endorsed the Specific Programme of Measures and Activities to be undertaken prior to and during the International Youth Year, 37/48 of 3 December 1982 on the International Youth Year: Participation, Development, Peace, and 37/49 of 3 December 1982 on efforts and measures for securing the implementation and the enjoyment by youth of human rights, particularly the right to education and to work in conditions of peace,

Recalling also its resolutions 1979/16 of 9 May 1979 and 1981/16 of 6 May 1981, in which, in particular, it recognized the importance of integrating young people into the overall life of society and of taking fully into account their special needs when formulating national plans and programmes,

Recognizing the fact that insufficient education and unemployment among young people limit their opportunities for participating in the process of development, and in this context emphasizing the importance of secondary and higher education, and also of the access of youth to suitable programmes of vocational and technical training,

Considering that in many countries the majority of young people, under the prevailing conditions of social and economic crisis, are facing serious problems in the exercise of their rights, mainly as regards employment and education,

1. *Takes note with satisfaction* of the report of the Secretary-General on the situation of youth in the 1980s;

2. *Notes with concern* that at present there is a rapidly growing number of unemployed young people in the world, many of whom have never had work, and that with the growth of unemployment it is becoming increasingly difficult to implement the basic social and economic rights of youth, especially the rights to life, employment and education;

3. *Strongly urges* all Governments, all governmental and non-governmental organizations and interested United Nations bodies to give priority to the formulation and implementation of effective measures for ensuring the employment of young people, for the implementation of their rights to social and economic development, education and employment in conditions of peace, and also to make provision in national development plans and country budgets for the adoption of specific programmes and for allocation of the necessary resources for ensuring the employment, education and vocational training of youth;

4. *Invites* all interested United Nations bodies to take an active part in the implementation of the Specific Programme of Measures and Activities which has been developed in the United Nations and is to be implemented during the International Youth Year and in the preceding period;

5. *Requests* the Secretary-General to take into account the views expressed in the Commission for Social Development concerning ways and means of realizing the rights of youth, in particular the rights to employment and education, and also the provisions of the present resolution, in the preparation of documentation for the third session of the Advisory Committee for the International Youth Year: Participation, Development, Peace;

6. *Resolves* to consider at the twenty-ninth session of the Commission for Social Development the progress achieved in connection with the participation of young people in the development of their respective countries and in the realization and exercise of their rights to life, employment and education.

Economic and Social Council resolution 1983/17

26 May 1983   Meeting 14   Adopted without vote

Approved by Second Committee (E/1983/62) without vote, 10 May (meeting 8); draft by Commission for Social Development (E/1983/14); agenda item 11. *Meeting number.* ESC 14.

In recommending the draft resolutions to the Council, the Committee approved drafts submitted by the Commission for Social Development in its report to the Council on its twenty-eighth session (7-16 February).[2]

Activities of the UN system

The Secretary-General, in a March 1983 report to the Economic and Social Council,[3] described action by the United Nations system and other organizations to facilitate co-ordination and information with regard to youth (see also POLITICAL AND SECURITY QUESTIONS, Chapter X). The report, prepared in accordance with a May 1982 request by the Council,[4] was based on information received from United Nations bodies and other organizations, on the co-ordination of information on youth, in the context of implementing the 1981 Specific Programme of Measures and Activities to be undertaken prior to and during International Youth Year (1985).[5]

United Nations activities emphasized improving co-ordination and increasing dissemination of information about youth. New programmes were being developed and implemented. Networks at the regional and national levels were being strengthened or established. Informational and promotional activities within the context of IYY had been expanded to promote awareness and mobilize public opinion. Activities of the regional commissions included: special conferences, meetings, workshops and seminars; research and studies; co-operation with other United Nations bodies and NGOs; informational and promotional activities; and advisory services and preparations for regional meetings related to IYY. Within the Secretariat, the Centre for Social Development and Humanitarian Affairs (Department of International Economic and Social Affairs) served as the United Nations lead entity for the Year, and provided information on policy measures and strategies for bringing young people into the mainstream of development. In addition to providing support to youth organizations to help them convene meetings, the Organization also provided advisory services to Member States, through an interregional adviser. Five regional meetings on IYY were held in 1983 (see below, under PREPARATIONS FOR INTERNATIONAL YOUTH YEAR (1985)). At the national level, the United Nations encouraged Governments to establish national co-ordinating committees.

The Secretary-General urged that channels of communication between the United Nations and youth and their organizations be strengthened. Because of the importance of information activities to the success of IYY, the Joint United Nations Information Committee would review the guidelines on information activities recommended by the IYY Advisory Committee.

ECONOMIC AND SOCIAL COUNCIL ACTION

On 26 May 1983, the Economic and Social Council, on the recommendation of its Second Committee, adopted resolution 1983/26 without vote.

Co-ordination and information in the field of youth
The Economic and Social Council,

Recalling its resolutions 1979/27 of 9 May 1979, 1980/25 of 2 May 1980, 1981/25 of 6 May 1981 and 1982/28 of 4 May 1982 on co-ordination and information in the field of youth,

Recalling also General Assembly resolutions 34/151 of 17 December 1979, 36/28 of 13 November 1981 and 37/48 of 3 December 1982 on the International Youth Year: Participation, Development, Peace,

Noting that the Advisory Committee for the International Youth Year will hold its third session at Vienna during the first half of 1984,

Considering that the implementation of the Specific Programme of Measures and Activities to be undertaken prior to and during the International Youth Year, as well as the recommendations endorsed by the General Assembly in its resolution 37/48, will contribute to intensifying and improving the co-ordination of the activities of the United Nations and specialized agencies relating to youth,

Convinced of the importance of giving widespread publicity to the activities of the United Nations in the field of youth and of increasing the dissemination of information about youth, especially in the context of the preparations for the International Youth Year,

Noting that the inter-agency consultations have proved to be a useful tool in planning, initiating, promoting and implementing activities in the field of youth in the context of the implementation of the Specific Programme of Measures and Activities to be undertaken prior to and during the International Youth Year,

Taking note of the report of the Secretary-General on co-ordination and information in the field of youth,

1. *Endorses* the conclusions contained in the report of the Secretary-General on co-ordination and information in the field of youth;

2. *Requests* the Secretary-General to take all necessary organizational measures to ensure the success of the regional meetings devoted to the International Youth Year, in accordance with paragraph 4 of General Assembly resolution 37/48;

3. *Requests* the Secretary-General to take into account the ideas expressed in the Economic and Social Council on ways and means for improving the activities of co-ordination and information in the field of youth in the preparation of the documentation to be submitted to the Advisory Committee for the International Youth Year at its third session;

4. *Invites* all United Nations bodies, specialized agencies, regional commissions and other international intergovernmental organizations, as well as non-governmental organizations concerned, to pay particular attention to the improvement of co-ordination and information in the field of youth in the context of the implementation of the Specific Programme of Measures and Activities to be undertaken prior to and during the International Youth Year, as well as of the recommendations endorsed by the General Assembly in its resolution 37/48;

5. *Decides* to consider at its first regular session of 1984, on the basis of a report of the Secretary-General, the progress achieved in co-ordination and information in the field of youth.

Economic and Social Council resolution 1983/26

26 May 1983   Meeting 14   Adopted without vote

Approved by Second Committee (E/1983/62) without vote, 11 May (meeting 9); 31-nation draft (E/1983/C.2/L.4); agenda item 11.

Sponsors: Algeria, Argentina, Bangladesh, China, Costa Rica, Cuba, Djibouti, Dominican Republic, Ecuador, Egypt, France, Germany, Federal Republic of, Greece, India, Indonesia, Kenya, Mali, Mexico, Morocco, Nigeria, Pakistan, Peru, Philippines, Romania, Rwanda, Saint Lucia, Sudan, Tunisia, Venezuela, Yugoslavia, Zaire.

Meeting number. ESC 14.

GENERAL ASSEMBLY ACTION

In resolution 38/22 on IYY (see below), the General Assembly requested the Secretary-General to continue, within existing resources, using all communications media at his disposal, to publicize widely United Nations youth activities and to increase the dissemination of related information.

Strengthening channels of communication between youth and the United Nations

In a September 1983 report to the General Assembly,[6] the Secretary-General, as requested in December 1982,[7] reviewed the implementation of the 1977[8] and 1981[9] guidelines for improving communication channels between the United Nations and youth and youth organizations. He described developments to implement the guidelines. At the international level, for example, the IYY secretariat initiated a three-phase project to improve channels of communication within the context of IYY—a study on strengthening such channels, an expert group to elaborate on the measures proposed, and a technical publication based on the study due for completion in 1983.

While noting that innovative approaches had been suggested by Member States with greater emphasis on the developmental aspects of the socio-economic situation of various population groups, the Secretary-General said that new approaches were subject to the constraints of limited resources and disparities in the communication of countries. Existing channels required strengthening and needed to be extended to reach more people with relevant information.

In view of the recognized potential of public opinion in the development process, young people should be informed about United Nations activities and urged to participate in the elaboration of its programmes, according to the report. The main channels used to communicate with youth and their organizations were publications, radio and television programmes, exhibitions, correspondence, and briefings for individuals and groups. During IYY, those activities should be expanded, which would require extrabudgetary resources. Efforts needed to be made in public information to bring about awareness of the IYY objectives.

The following measures were suggested to expand the flow of information: Governments could assign higher priority to acting on information received from the United Nations; NGOs could make increased efforts to bring that information to their membership; mass media representatives should be encouraged to publicize United Nations activities; the role of the family in the education of young people should be strengthened; and

Governments and concerned organizations could develop programmes to heighten public awareness of the role that families had as the principal informal educators of young people. The Secretary-General emphasized that proper information was a prerequisite for a successful IYY.

GENERAL ASSEMBLY ACTION

On 22 November, the General Assembly, acting on the recommendation of the Third (Social, Humanitarian and Cultural) Committee, adopted resolution 38/26 without vote.

Channels of communication between the United Nations and youth and youth organizations

The General Assembly,

Recalling its resolutions 32/135 of 16 December 1977 and 36/17 of 9 November 1981, in which it adopted guidelines for the improvement of the channels of communication between the United Nations and youth and youth organizations, and its resolution 37/50 of 3 December 1982,

Bearing in mind the importance of the existence of effective channels of communication between the United Nations and youth and youth organizations for the proper information of young people and their effective participation in the work of the United Nations and the specialized agencies at the national, regional and international levels,

Taking note of the report of the Secretary-General,

Also taking note of the efforts in inter-agency co-operation to promote and strengthen channels of communication between the United Nations and youth and youth organizations within the context of the International Youth Year,

Convinced that the existence and proper functioning of channels of communication between the United Nations and youth and youth organizations form a basic prerequisite of the active involvement of young people and thus of the successful preparation for, observance of and follow-up to the International Youth Year at all levels,

1. *Requests* the Secretary-General to continue to give full co-operation and support to inter-agency co-operation and co-ordination in promotional and information activities within the context of the International Youth Year;

2. *Calls upon* Member States, specialized agencies and other intergovernmental organizations, in co-operation with youth and with youth organizations in consultative status with the Economic and Social Council and other youth organizations concerned, to continue to promote actively the full and effective implementation of the guidelines and additional guidelines adopted by the General Assembly in its resolutions 32/135 and 36/17, in particular through informing young people of relevant policies and programmes and encouraging them to participate in the preparation and implementation of these policies and programmes;

3. *Requests* the Advisory Committee for the International Youth Year at its third session to monitor and evaluate the measures taken with respect to the implementation of the guidelines on the basis of the relevant reports of the Secretary-General and other rele-

vant information provided to it and to make recommendations for the full and effective implementation and the further elaboration of the guidelines as an integral part of the preparation for, observance of and follow-up to the International Youth Year;

4. *Decides* to review at its thirty-ninth session the question of the channels of communication between the United Nations and youth and youth organizations, on the basis of the report of the Advisory Committee for the International Youth Year.

General Assembly resolution 38/26

22 November 1983   Meeting 66   Adopted without vote

Approved by Third Committee (A/38/573) without vote, 3 November (meeting 32); 35-nation draft (A/C.3/38/L.14); agenda item 88.

Sponsors: Bangladesh, Belgium, Bolivia, Chile, Costa Rica, Denmark, Dominican Republic, Ecuador, Egypt, El Salvador, Ethiopia, Fiji, Germany, Federal Republic of, Greece, Guatemala, Indonesia, Kenya, Mali, Malta, Morocco, Netherlands, Nigeria, Norway, Pakistan, Philippines, Romania, Rwanda, Spain, Sudan, Sweden, United Republic of Cameroon, United States, Uruguay, Venezuela, Zaire.

Meeting numbers. GA 38th session: 3rd Committee, 18-20, 22-29, 31-33; plenary, 66.

Preparations for International Youth Year (1985)

In October 1983, the Secretary-General submitted a report[10] to the General Assembly on progress made in implementing the Specific Programme of Measures and Activities for IYY (1985). The report described trends and activities of Member States, the United Nations system and other bodies in preparing for the Year and, in particular, in implementing the Programme endorsed by the Assembly in 1981.[11] As requested by the Assembly in 1982,[12] the Secretary-General had transmitted to States and organizations concerned the recommendations of the Advisory Committee for IYY in 1982.

In general, the Secretary-General found there was an increasing awareness among Governments that youth policies should be aimed at the full participation of youth in the development process. As at 1 July 1983, 42 Governments had established, or were establishing, national co-ordinating committees or mechanisms, to assess the situation of youth within the country, to develop a national plan of action and to act as liaison between the United Nations and youth and their organizations, as well as to encourage IYY at the national level.

The concerned United Nations bodies had demonstrated their support for IYY by: co-operating with the Secretariat in expanding information and promotional activities; establishing new programmes and strengthening regular programme activities; strengthening networks at the regional and national levels; and identifying focal points for the Year, with a view to strengthening inter-agency co-ordination and co-operation (see above). The secretariat for the Year had participated in numerous youth meetings within and outside the United Nations system to disseminate IYY information and promote interest. Technical support to youth organizations had been provided to help them convene meetings on youth. The *Youth*

Information Bulletin, a United Nations quarterly publication produced in English, French and Spanish, continued to serve as a channel of communication.

Five regional meetings were held in 1983 to assess the situation of youth and propose recommendations to implement the Programme: for Africa, at Addis Ababa, Ethiopia, 20-24 June; for Asia and the Pacific, at Bangkok, Thailand, 26-30 July; for Europe, at Costinesti, Romania, 5-9 September; for Latin America, at San José, Costa Rica, 3-7 October; and for Western Asia, at Baghdad, Iraq, 9-13 October. These meetings made similar recommendations and adopted regional action plans. They encouraged the establishment of national committees, and four meetings called for an international conference on youth under United Nations auspices. The meetings recommended that technical co-operation projects and implementation of IYY activities be promoted, possibly through voluntary contributions to the Trust Fund for IYY. In addition, each meeting made suggestions specific to its individual region.

The Secretary-General suggested further action to ensure successful preparations for the Year, particularly at the national level. He called for world-wide publicity, as well as the Programme's implementation, and urged States to establish national committees. In addition to assessing the situation of youth, they should prepare a national agenda for action identifying their needs within the context of IYY. The capability of the committees needed to be enhanced through their composition and location within the governmental structure and through provision of necessary resources. He also suggested that the regional commissions co-ordinate regional and national organizations, promoting exchange of views and experiences between countries and ensuring that all youth organizations would be closely involved in IYY preparations. The United Nations system should ensure joint planning at the field level to supplement national and regional action, particularly concerning technical co-operation activities, as well as promotional and information activities (see also POLITICAL AND SECURITY QUESTIONS, Chapter X). Improvements should be made in channels of communication between the United Nations and youth, and public information should be increased at all levels to generate awareness of the objectives of the Year, the Secretary-General said.

In February, the Secretary-General reported to the Commission on Human Rights on the implementation of the programme of activities in connection with IYY (see Chapter XVIII of this section).

GENERAL ASSEMBLY ACTION

On 22 November, the General Assembly adopted two resolutions dealing with youth and

IYY; both were adopted on the recommendation of the Third Committee.

The Assembly adopted resolution 38/22 without vote.

International Youth Year: Participation, Development, Peace

The General Assembly,

Recalling its resolutions 34/151 of 17 December 1979, 35/126 of 11 December 1980, 36/28 of 13 November 1981 and 37/48 of 3 December 1982,

Recognizing the profound importance of the direct participation of youth in shaping the future of mankind and the valuable contribution that youth can make in the implementation of the new international economic order based on equity and justice,

Considering it necessary to disseminate among youth the ideals of peace, respect for human rights and fundamental freedoms, human solidarity and dedication to the objectives of progress and development,

Convinced of the imperative need to harness the energies, enthusiasms and creative abilities of youth to the tasks of nation-building, the struggle for self-determination and national independence, in accordance with the Charter of the United Nations, against foreign domination and occupation, and for the economic, social and cultural advancement of peoples, the implementation of the new international economic order, the preservation of world peace and the promotion of international co-operation and understanding,

Emphasizing again that the United Nations should pay more attention to the role of young people in the world of today and to their demands for the world of tomorrow,

Recalling the topicality of assessing the needs and aspirations of youth, and reaffirming the importance of current and projected United Nations activities designed to increase the opportunities for youth and for its active participation in national development activities,

Believing that it is urgently desirable to intensify the efforts of all States in carrying out specific programmes concerning youth and to improve the activities of the United Nations and the specialized agencies in the field of youth, including youth exchanges in the cultural, sporting and other fields,

Reaffirming the importance of better co-ordination of efforts in dealing with specific problems confronting young people and in examining the manner in which those problems are being treated by the specialized agencies and by various United Nations bodies,

Aware of the valuable contribution which the United Nations Educational, Scientific and Cultural Organization is making to the promotion of international co-operation in the field of youth,

Convinced that the preparation for and observance in 1985 of the International Youth Year with the motto "Participation, Development, Peace" will offer a useful and significant opportunity for drawing attention to the situation and specific needs and aspirations of youth, for increasing co-operation at all levels in dealing with youth issues, for undertaking concerted action programmes in favour of youth and for involving young people in the study and resolution of major national, regional and international problems,

Confident that the International Youth Year will serve to mobilize efforts at the local, national, regional and international levels in order to promote the best educational, professional and living conditions for young people, to ensure their active participation in the overall development of society and to encourage the preparation of new national and local policies and programmes, in accordance with each country's experience, conditions and priorities,

Recognizing that the preparation for and observance of the International Youth Year will contribute to the reaffirmation of the goals of the new international economic order and to the implementation of the International Development Strategy for the Third United Nations Development Decade,

Recalling also in this connection its decision 35/424 of 5 December 1980 and Economic and Social Council resolution 1980/67 of 25 July 1980 on the question of guidelines for international years and anniversaries,

Aware that, for the International Youth Year to be successful and to maximize its impact and practical efficiency, adequate preparation and the widespread support of Governments, all specialized agencies, international intergovernmental and non-governmental organizations and the public will be required,

Recognizing the important role of United Nations bodies, the specialized agencies and the regional commissions in promoting international co-operation in the field of youth and the necessity of strengthening their role in the effective implementation of the Specific Programme of Measures and Activities to be undertaken prior to and during the International Youth Year,

1. *Takes note* of the report of the Secretary-General on the implementation of General Assembly resolution 37/48;

2. *Commends* the five regional meetings devoted to the International Youth Year held during 1983 and requests the Secretary-General to bring the regional plans of action and the recommendations adopted by the regional meetings to the notice of all States with a view to their implementation;

3. *Again invites* all States that have not already done so to establish national co-ordinating committees or other forms of co-ordination for the International Youth Year;

4. *Stresses again* the importance of active and direct participation of youth organizations in the activities organized at the local, national, regional and international levels for the preparation for and observance of the International Youth Year;

5. *Requests* the Secretary-General to use all means at his disposal, within existing resources, to ensure the implementation of and follow-up to the Specific Programme of Measures and Activities to be undertaken prior to and during the International Youth Year, including the provision of information;

6. *Decides* that the third session of the Advisory Committee for the International Youth Year shall be convened at Vienna from 2 to 11 April 1984;

7. *Requests* the Advisory Committee to make every effort to implement the tasks entrusted to it by decisions of the General Assembly and by recommendations of the five regional meetings devoted to the International Youth Year and to submit the report on its third session to the General Assembly at its thirty-ninth session with practical proposals on specific ways and means for the observance, in 1985, of the International Youth Year in an appropriate organizational framework within the United Nations;

8. *Requests* the Secretary-General to continue to take concrete measures, within existing resources, using all the communications media at his disposal, to give widespread publicity to the activities of the United Nations system in the field of youth and to increase the dissemination of information on youth;

9. *Welcomes* the voluntary contributions made so far for the International Youth Year, expresses its appreciation to all contributors and again appeals to all States, to international governmental and non-governmental organizations and to the public to make in due time generous voluntary contributions to supplement funds provided under the regular budget of the United Nations for the costs of the Specific Programme of Measures and Activities and requests the Secretary-General to take all appropriate measures for obtaining such voluntary contributions;

10. *Decides* to include in the provisional agenda of its thirty-ninth session the item entitled "International Youth Year: Participation, Development, Peace" and to grant it high priority.

General Assembly resolution 38/22

22 November 1983   Meeting 66   Adopted without vote

Approved by Third Committee (A/38/571) without vote, 3 November (meeting 32); 87-nation draft (A/C.3/38/L.12/Rev.1); agenda item 84.

Sponsors: Algeria, Angola, Argentina, Bahamas, Bangladesh, Benin, Bhutan, Bolivia, Burundi, Cape Verde, Central African Republic, Chad, Chile, China, Colombia, Congo, Costa Rica, Cuba, Cyprus, Democratic Yemen, Djibouti, Dominican Republic, Ecuador, Egypt, El Salvador, Ethiopia, Gambia, Greece, Guatemala, Guinea, Guinea-Bissau, Guyana, Indonesia, Iran, Iraq, Ivory Coast, Jamaica, Japan, Kenya, Lesotho, Liberia, Madagascar, Malawi, Mali, Malta, Mauritania, Mexico, Morocco, Mozambique, Nepal, Netherlands, Nicaragua, Niger, Nigeria, Pakistan, Panama, Peru, Philippines, Qatar, Romania, Rwanda, Saint Lucia, Sao Tome and Principe, Senegal, Sierra Leone, Singapore, Spain, Sri Lanka, Sudan, Suriname, Syrian Arab Republic, Thailand, Togo, Trinidad and Tobago, Turkey, Uganda, United Republic of Cameroon, United Republic of Tanzania, United States, Upper Volta, Uruguay, Venezuela, Viet Nam, Yemen, Yugoslavia, Zaire, Zambia.

Meeting numbers. GA 38th session: 3rd Committee 18-20, 22-29, 31, 32; plenary 66.

The Assembly adopted resolution 38/23 without vote.

Efforts and measures for securing the implementation and the enjoyment by youth of human rights, particularly the right to education and to work

The General Assembly,

Recalling its resolutions 36/29 of 13 November 1981 and 37/49 of 3 December 1982, in which it, *inter alia*, recognized the need to adopt appropriate measures for securing the implementation and the enjoyment by youth of human rights, particularly the right to education and to work,

Recalling also its resolution 34/151 of 17 December 1979, by which it decided to designate 1985 as International Youth Year: Participation, Development, Peace,

Convinced that it is necessary to ensure full enjoyment by youth of the rights stipulated in the Universal Declaration of Human Rights, the International Covenant on Economic, Social and Cultural Rights and the International Covenant on Civil and Political Rights, with special regard for the right to education and to work,

Aware of the fact that insufficient education and the unemployment of young people limits their ability to participate in the development process, and, in this regard, emphasizing the importance of the secondary and higher education of young people, as well as of access for them to appropriate technical, vocational guidance and training programmes,

Expressing its serious interest in the success of the International Youth Year which should, *inter alia*, promote increasing participation of young people in the socio-economic life of their country,

1. *Calls upon* all States, all governmental and non-governmental organizations and the interested bodies of the United Nations and specialized agencies to pay continuous attention to the implementation of General Assembly resolutions 36/29 and 37/49 relating to efforts and measures aimed at the promotion of human rights and their enjoyment by youth, particularly the right to education and vocational training and to work, with a view to resolving the problem of youth unemployment;

2. *Requests* the Advisory Committee for the International Youth Year to give full attention to resolutions 36/29 and 37/49 and to all relevant international human rights instruments in the preparation for and in the course of the International Youth Year, in particular in elaborating its recommendations concerning the Year;

3. *Invites* national co-ordinating committees or other organs of co-ordination for the International Youth Year to give appropriate priority in activities to be undertaken prior to and during the Year to the implementation and the enjoyment by youth of human rights, particularly the right to education and to work.

General Assembly resolution 38/23

22 November 1983   Meeting 66   Adopted without vote

Approved by Third Committee (A/38/571) without vote, 3 November (meeting 32); 21-nation draft (A/C.3/38/L.13), orally amended by Djibouti; agenda item 84.

Sponsors: Afghanistan, Algeria, Angola, Bulgaria, Byelorussian SSR, Congo, Cuba, Czechoslovakia, Democratic Yemen, Ethiopia, German Democratic Republic, Lao People's Democratic Republic, Madagascar, Mali, Mongolia, Mozambique, Nicaragua, Syrian Arab Republic, Venezuela, Viet Nam, Zimbabwe.

Meeting numbers. GA 38th session: 3rd Committee 18-20, 22-29, 31-33; plenary 66.

In resolution 38/27 on the question of aging (see below), the Assembly requested the Secretary-General to continue promoting, in co-operation with national committees, joint activities concerning aging and youth, particularly as they related to intergenerational matters, especially during IYY.

The Assembly, in resolution 38/173, reaffirmed that the United Nations Volunteers programme should continue its involvement in the IYY preparations and its activities in programmes relating to youth.

ECONOMIC AND SOCIAL COUNCIL ACTION

In resolution 1983/17 on youth participation in social and economic development and their exercise of the rights to life, employment and education, the Economic and Social Council invited all interested United Nations bodies to take part in implementing the Specific Programme for IYY, and requested the Secretary-General to take into account the views of the Commission for Social Development on ways of realizing the rights of youth, in particular the rights to employment and education, in preparing documentation for the third (1984) session of the Advisory Committee for IYY.

REFERENCES

[1]YUN 1982, p. 1177. [2]E/1983/14. [3]E/1983/29. [4]YUN 1982, p. 1178, ESC res. 1982/28, 4 May 1982. [5]YUN 1981, p. 1019. [6]A/38/339. [7]YUN 1982, p. 1179, GA res. 37/50, 3 Dec. 1982. [8]YUN 1977, p. 801, GA res. 32/135, annex, 16 Dec. 1977. [9]YUN 1981, p. 1017, GA res. 36/17, annex, 9 Nov. 1981. [10]A/38/460 & Add.1. [11]YUN 1981, p. 1021, GA res. 36/28, 13 Nov. 1981. [12]YUN 1982, p. 1181, GA res. 37/48, 3 Dec. 1982.

Aging persons

Following the General Assembly's 1982 endorsement of the Vienna International Plan of Action on Aging, pertaining to people aged 60 and over, both the Assembly (in resolution 38/27) and the Economic and Social Council (in resolution 1983/21) called for follow-up on its implementation. In particular, Governments were urged to establish or maintain national machinery to promote the Plan. According to the Secretary-General, the response by Member States had been positive.

Implementation of the Plan of Action

Following the adoption of the Vienna International Plan of Action on Aging by the July/August 1982 World Assembly on Aging,[1] and its subsequent endorsement by the General Assembly in December,[2] the United Nations took action in 1983 to follow up on its implementation. The basic aims of the Plan were to strengthen countries' capacities to deal with the aging of their populations and with the needs of the elderly. It attempted to promote understanding of the social, economic and cultural implications of aging and of related humanitarian and developmental issues; to encourage an international exchange of skills and knowledge; and to promote the education and training required to respond to the aging of the world's population.

ECONOMIC AND SOCIAL COUNCIL ACTION

On 26 May, the Economic and Social Council, acting on the recommendation of its Second Committee, adopted resolution 1983/21 without vote.

Aging

The Economic and Social Council,

Recalling General Assembly resolution 37/51 of 3 December 1982 by which the General Assembly endorsed the International Plan of Action on Aging,

Convinced that the International Plan of Action on Aging should be considered an integral component of major international, regional and national strategies and should be implemented at the international, regional and national levels in order to enhance the quality of life of aging individuals and to respond effectively to the economic and social impact of the aging of populations on development,

Recognizing that the General Assembly, in its resolution 37/51, has requested the Economic and Social Council, through the Commission for Social Development, to review the implementation of the Plan of Action every four years, beginning in 1985, and transmit its findings to the General Assembly,

Reaffirming General Assembly resolution 37/51, in which the Assembly requested the Secretary-General to make use of the United Nations Trust Fund for the World Assembly on Aging to meet the rapidly increasing needs of the aging in developing countries,

Acknowledging the efforts of the United Nations and the specialized agencies in the field of aging and the need to strengthen and co-ordinate these activities to ensure the effective implementation of the Plan of Action,

Aware that the exchange of information and experience at the international level is an effective means for stimulating progress and encouraging the adoption of measures to respond to the economic and social implications of the aging of populations and to meet the needs of older persons,

1. *Calls upon* Governments to make continuous efforts to implement the International Plan of Action on Aging at the national level and to encourage, where appropriate, the maintenance of the national machinery established for the World Assembly on Aging and the co-operation of those committees with the United Nations through the Centre for Social Development and Humanitarian Affairs, for the exchange of information at the international and regional levels;

2. *Requests* the Secretary-General to take such steps as may be appropriate for the necessary strengthening of activities in the field of aging at the central and regional levels of the United Nations, as set forth in the Plan of Action;

3. *Also requests* the Secretary-General, in promoting the exchange of information and experience at the international level, as mandated by General Assembly resolution 37/51, to include, *inter alia*, the publication of an international review on aging and to continue research activities on the prospects and challenges of the aging of the world's population, to be financed from either voluntary contributions or existing resources;

4. *Further requests* the Secretary-General, in implementing General Assembly resolution 37/51 concerning the assessment, review and appraisal of the implementation of the International Plan of Action on Aging, to convene an expert group meeting on the topic for the purpose of establishing guidelines and format for the preparation of the review, to be financed from voluntary contributions;

5. *Invites* the intergovernmental and non-governmental organizations concerned to continue and strengthen their efforts in this field, in co-operation with the United Nations.

Economic and Social Council resolution 1983/21

26 May 1983   Meeting 14   Adopted without vote

Approved by Second Committee (E/1983/62) without vote, 10 May (meeting 8); draft by Commission for Social Development (E/1983/14); agenda item 11. *Meeting number.* ESC 14.

During the consideration of the topic at the Commission for Social Development's February session,[3] a representative of the Secretary-

General indicated that publishing an international review, provided it was printed at Headquarters, would have no financial implications for the regular budget.

In a note of 25 March,[4] the Secretary-General referred to the Council's 1981 request[5] that he report to the Assembly in 1983, through the Council and the Commission for Social Development, on further actions to implement the recommendations adopted by the World Assembly. In view of the short time since the Plan of Action had been endorsed by the Assembly—in December 1982— he said, there had not been time to prepare a meaningful report for submission to the Commission in February. Consequently, the Secretary-General suggested that, as his report to the 1983 session of the Assembly in pursuance of the Assembly's 1982 request[2] would deal with the implementation of the Plan of Action (see below), the Council might wish to inform the Assembly that that report might also be considered as the response to the 1981 Council request.

On 26 May, the Council acted on the Secretary-General's suggestion by adopting decision 1983/127.

Implementation of the International Plan of Action on Aging

At its 14th plenary meeting, on 26 May 1983, the Council decided to inform the General Assembly that the report to be submitted by the Secretary-General to the Assembly at its thirty-eighth session on the implementation of the International Plan of Action on Aging in pursuance of Assembly resolution 37/51 of 3 December 1982, should also be considered as the response to Council resolution 1981/23 of 6 May 1981.

Economic and Social Council decision 1983/127

Adopted without vote

Approved by Second Committee (E/1983/62), 10 May (meeting 8); agenda item 11. *Meeting number.* ESC 14.

Secretary-General's report. In October 1983, the Secretary-General submitted a report[6] to the Assembly on implementation of the Vienna International Plan of Action on Aging, giving a brief account of activities regarding the exchange of knowledge, skills and experiences; research; international co-operation; and the Trust Fund for Aging (see below).

Following the Assembly's endorsement of the Plan of Action,[2] the United Nations in early 1983 wrote to all national committees concerned with the Plan's implementation, indicating the Secretary-General's desire to continue to provide substantive support to them, and urging the continuation of the committees to ensure that the momentum generated by the World Assembly was not lost. Responses were positive, indicating a willingness to develop national priority plans. As part of its programme to promote the exchange of knowledge, skills and experiences, the United

Nations continued to publish and disseminate the periodical *Bulletin on Aging.* The *International Directory of Organizations Concerned with Aging* was updated to include the newly established organizations concerned with aging, particularly in developing regions. The network of information exchange had a membership of about 50 research and training institutions. Among its own activities, the United Nations was undertaking the standardization of definitions, terms and research methodologies to facilitate the exchange and use of information. It had begun two research studies—a comparative analysis of the situation of the world's aging and a study of the impact of the aging of populations on selected economic and social institutions.

In response to the request that specialized agencies concerned co-operate in implementing the Plan of Action, an *Ad Hoc* Inter-Agency Meeting on Aging was convened on 17 and 18 February at Vienna to establish a mechanism for joint action. At the meeting, the United Nations Fund for Population Activities (UNFPA), which continued to provide assistance with regard to aging, agreed to work with other organizations responsible for international population assistance, within the limitations of its mandate and resources.

Within the context of the Plan of Action, which noted that aging was a population issue affecting development, UNFPA provided support for three research projects begun in 1983 in Colombia, India and the Philippines.[7] Designed to develop a better understanding of the aged and their potential contribution to development, the projects were intended to be completed for the 1984 International Conference on Population (see Chapter XIV of this section).

As for co-operation with NGOs concerned with aging, the Secretary-General remarked that they had always been active in promoting related United Nations work. Two NGO committees on aging had played a major role in preparations for the 1982 World Assembly on Aging and had decided to continue to work for implementation of the Plan of Action. At all levels, NGOs were undertaking activities such as holding conferences, seminars and workshops to promote the Plan's implementation. They were also ensuring that aging was considered in the context of forthcoming United Nations international events, in particular, the Population Conference, International Youth Year (1985) (see above) and the World Conference to Review and Appraise the Achievements of the United Nations Decade for Women (1985) (see Chapter XIX of this section).

In a note verbale of 28 October to the Secretary-General,[8] the USSR submitted information concerning implementation in that country of the Plan and measures it had adopted concerning social welfare and services for the aged.

On 22 November, the General Assembly, on the recommendation of the Third Committee, adopted resolution 38/27 without vote.

Question of aging

The General Assembly,

Reaffirming its resolution 37/51 of 3 December 1982, in which it endorsed the International Plan of Action on Aging adopted by the World Assembly on Aging, and called upon Governments and the Secretary-General to make continuous efforts to implement the principles and recommendations of the Plan of Action,

Recalling Economic and Social Council resolution 1981/87 of 25 November 1981, in which the Council decided to convene in 1984 an International Conference on Population, and also recalling the International Plan of Action on Aging, in which it is acknowledged that aging is a population issue that affects development and requires increasing international assistance and co-operation,

Recognizing the significant contributions of the World Assembly on Aging and the United Nations Trust Fund for the World Assembly on Aging in the promotion and strengthening of international co-operation in this field,

Conscious of the positive response of many countries to the World Assembly on Aging and to the recommendations contained in the Plan of Action and of the need to provide national authorities, at their request, with assistance in their efforts to implement the Plan,

Noting with satisfaction that many Governments have retained or established national mechanisms to facilitate the planning, implementation and co-ordination of the activities recommended in the Plan of Action,

Recognizing the role played by the United Nations and the specialized agencies through their efforts in the field of aging and the need to strengthen this role, especially at the regional level, in order to ensure the implementation of the Plan of Action and the systematic and efficient functioning of the technical advisory and co-ordination services of the United Nations,

Acknowledging the role played by the international network of existing information, research and training centres in exchanging information and experience at the international level and in stimulating progress and encouraging the adoption of measures to respond to the economic and social implications of the aging of populations and to meet the needs of older persons,

Noting that the relationship between aging and youth, particularly as it relates to intergenerational matters, is recognized in the Plan of Action,

Recognizing that women have a longer life expectancy than men and that they will increasingly constitute the majority of the older population,

1. *Takes note* of the report of the Secretary-General on the question of aging;

2. *Affirms* that the question of aging should be considered in the context of economic development, political, social and cultural systems and social values and changes;

3. *Calls upon* Governments to continue to make efforts to implement the principles and recommendations contained in the International Plan of Action on Aging in accordance with the economic, social and cultural circumstances of each country;

4. *Invites* Governments to retain or establish, in a suitable form, mechanisms at the national level to promote the implementation of the Plan of Action;

5. *Urges* the Secretary-General to continue his efforts to ensure effective implementation of and follow-up action to the Plan of Action and to maintain the impetus generated by the United Nations Trust Fund for the World Assembly on Aging at the national, regional and international levels;

6. *Requests* the Secretary-General to continue to promote the Trust Fund so as to assist countries in formulating and implementing policies and programmes for aging;

7. *Requests* the Secretary-General to continue his information exchange activities through, *inter alia*, the international network of existing information, research and training centres and to convene, using voluntary contributions, meetings of the members of this network, as appropriate, to strengthen these activities and to promote technical co-operation among developing countries;

8. *Urges* the Secretary-General to include advisory services to developing countries that request them in technical co-operation programmes, to the extent feasible under the funding of those programmes;

9. *Requests* the Secretary-General to ensure, as requested in the Plan of Action, that the question of aging of populations is brought to the attention of the appropriate United Nations bodies responsible for the preparation of the International Conference on Population and that the question of aging is considered under the appropriate agenda items of the Conference itself;

10. *Also requests* the Secretary-General to continue to promote, in co-operation with the national committees concerned, joint activities in the field of aging and youth, particularly as they relate to intergenerational matters, especially during the International Youth Year, to be observed in 1985;

11. *Further requests* the Secretary-General to examine the gender-based difference in longevity and the impact of the increasing number and proportion of older women on living arrangements, income, health care and other support systems, and to bring the question of older women to the attention of the preparatory body for the World Conference to Review and Appraise the Achievements of the United Nations Decade for Women, to be held in 1985, for its consideration;

12. *Urges* the United Nations Fund for Population Activities, in co-operation with all organizations responsible for international population assistance, to continue its assistance, within its mandate, in the field of aging, particularly in developing countries;

13. *Invites* the regional commissions to review the objectives of the Plan of Action and contribute to their realization and to organize and conduct the regional periodic review and appraisal of the Plan in coordination with that at the international level;

14. *Invites* the specialized agencies and other intergovernmental and non-governmental organizations concerned to continue to be actively involved, in a coordinated manner, in the implementation of the Plan of Action;

15. *Requests* the Secretary-General to submit to the General Assembly at its thirty-ninth session a report on the measures taken to implement the present resolution;

16. *Decides* to include in the provisional agenda of its thirty-ninth session the item entitled "Question of aging".

General Assembly resolution 38/27

22 November 1983   Meeting 66   Adopted without vote

Approved by Third Committee (A/38/574) without vote, 3 November (meeting 32); 24-nation draft (A/C.3/38/L.17), orally revised; agenda item 89.
Sponsors: Austria, Bangladesh, Chile, Colombia, Costa Rica, Cyprus, Dominican Republic, Egypt, France, Greece, Guatemala, Jordan, Malta, Morocco, Nepal, Pakistan, Philippines, Romania, Samoa, Spain, Suriname, United States, Uruguay, Venezuela.
Meeting numbers. GA 38th session: 3rd Committee 18-20, 22-29, 31-33; plenary 66.

UN Trust Fund

The Trust Fund for the World Assembly on Aging, set up in pursuance of a 1980 General Assembly resolution[9] to provide supplementary funds for preparations for the 1982 World Assembly, had been used since then to meet the increasing needs of the aging in developing countries, in particular in the least developed countries, as requested by the General Assembly in 1982.[2] In order to reflect this extended mandate, the Secretary-General changed the name of the Fund, which was financed by voluntary contributions, to the Trust Fund on Aging and reported on its use in an October 1983 report[6] on implementation of the 1982 Plan of Action on Aging.[1] To ensure that responses were made to the most urgent needs, priority areas of assistance were established for the use of Fund resources. Priority was given to selected developing countries, taking into account their level of development, demographic trends and the status of their aging population. Resources were used for housing, income security, health, education and social welfare. Resources were also used to finance activities concerned with the effect of the aging of populations on the economic and social development of society, including rural development, migration, and production, consumption and savings patterns. Governments were helped to develop national policies, including census analysis, surveys, research and seminars for the exchange of knowledge and experience.

Contributions to the Fund during 1981-1982 amounted to $991,986. The balance of available resources as at 31 December 1982 was $741,041. In 1983, additional pledges and contributions amounting to $70,000 had been received. During the first half of 1983, the United Nations approved $344,000 from the Fund's resources for support to 28 countries. In addition, one project at the level of $60,000 was to be financed multilaterally. Because the Plan of Action stressed national-level activities, 88 per cent of resources were to be used at that level. Project requests from all developing regions were under review, including requests from 15 countries.

In resolution 38/27 on the question of aging (see above), the General Assembly urged the Secretary-General to continue ensuring implementation of and follow-up action to the International Plan of Action on Aging and to maintain the impetus generated by the Trust Fund for the World Assembly on Aging at all levels. He was also requested to continue promoting the Fund so as to assist countries in formulating and implementing policies and programmes for aging.

REFERENCES

[1]YUN 1982, p. 1182. [2]*Ibid.*, p. 1186, GA res. 37/51, 3 Dec. 1982. [3]E/1983/14. [4]E/1983/35. [5]YUN 1981, p. 1026, ESC res. 1981/23, 6 May 1981. [6]A/38/470. [7]DP/1984/28 (Part II). [8]A/C.3/38/10. [9]YUN 1980, p. 1019, GA res. 35/129, 11 Dec. 1980.

Chapter XXI

Refugees and displaced persons

In 1983, with some large-scale refugee situations showing relative stability, the Office of the United Nations High Commissioner for Refugees (UNHCR) continued to promote durable solutions and provide care and maintenance to refugees. Despite the absence of large new refugee influxes, however, more than $5 million was obligated from the Emergency Fund on 12 occasions.

Major assistance programmes continued, notably in Pakistan, which remained host to the world's largest refugee population; the Horn of Africa, where programmes benefited returnees as well as refugees; South-East Asia, which saw a decrease of over 37,000 in camp populations during 1983; and Central America and Mexico, where emergency assistance was coupled with local integration initiatives. New programmes in 1983 included aid to Afghan refugees in Iran; repatriations to Argentina and Chile; and emergency relief for Angolans in Zaire, Mozambicans in Zimbabwe and Sudanese in Ethiopia.

As in previous years, assistance to Palestine refugees was provided by the United Nations Relief and Works Agency for Palestine Refugees in the Near East (UNRWA).

The High Commissioner told the Executive Committee of the UNHCR Programme, at its thirty-fourth session (Geneva, 10-20 October), that there were currently some 10 million refugees, as against 1.5 million when UNHCR started its activities in 1951.

In his annual report to the General Assembly on the work of the Organization (p. 3), the Secretary-General stressed that the refugee problem could be resolved only with a settlement of the root political causes; the means available to the United Nations to help alleviate the problem were grossly inadequate.

In December, the Assembly called on all States to promote durable solutions and to contribute generously to the High Commissioner's humanitarian programmes in order to assist refugees, displaced persons and returnees in a spirit of international solidarity and burden-sharing (resolution 38/121).

The Assembly approved the arrangements for the Second (1984) International Conference on Assistance to Refugees in Africa and appealed to the international community to make it a success (38/120). It also called for assistance to refugees in Djibouti (38/89), Somalia (38/88) and the Sudan (38/90) as well as to displaced persons in Ethiopia (38/91) and student refugees in southern Africa (38/95).

The Group of Governmental Experts on International Co-operation to Avert New Flows of Refugees met for the first time in 1983, and the Assembly asked it to continue working towards developing recommendations to that end (38/84).

The Nansen Medal for the year—awarded since 1955 in honour of Fridtjof Nansen, the first League of Nations High Commissioner for Refugees—went to President Julius Nyerere of the United Republic of Tanzania in recognition of his personal contribution and that of his country to the cause of refugees. The President announced that the $50,000 prize accompanying the award would be used to build schools for refugee children in his country.

Topics related to this chapter. Middle East: Palestine refugees. Economic assistance, disasters and emergency relief.

Programme and finances of UNHCR

Programme policy

Executive Committee action. In 1983, the Executive Committee of the UNHCR Programme,[1] while noting as a positive development the absence of new large-scale refugee outflows, expressed concern at the continued severity of refugee problems, notably in Africa, Asia and Central America, and requested UNHCR to continue providing assistance and international protection. It reaffirmed the principle of international solidarity and burden-sharing as well as the fundamental humanitarian character of UNHCR activities, and drew attention to the vital need for the international community to deal in appropriate forums with the root causes of refugee flows (see below).

The Committee noted with satisfaction the High Commissioner's renewed efforts, and progress made, in reorienting many major assistance activities from emergency or relief phase to the promotion of self-reliance and durable solutions through voluntary repatriation, local integration and resettlement. It welcomed the workshops and seminars held to further these objectives as well as the Commissioner's support of the international refugee integration resource centre.

However, the Committee expressed concern at decreasing resettlement rates and urged Governments, in accordance with the principle of international burden-sharing, to meet the needs of those refugees with no other durable solution immediately in prospect; it requested the Commissioner to co-ordinate and facilitate the planning of resettlement programmes by Governments through updated assessments of needs and priorities.

The Committee recommended that States seriously consider supporting UNHCR efforts to promote the Rescue at Sea Resettlement Offers scheme and providing the necessary quotas and other undertakings to enable UNHCR to initiate the scheme on a trial basis; welcomed the support given to the Disembarkation Resettlement Offers scheme; and commended the initiatives taken by UNHCR and the International Maritime Organization, including an October joint appeal, for facilitating the rescue of asylum-seekers in distress at sea.

UNHCR continued to co-operate with other United Nations organizations in its programme implementation. Such co-operation included the International Labour Organisation (ILO) promoting vocational training and income-generating activities in refugee settlements, and the United Nations Children's Fund (UNICEF) providing care and maintenance and supporting community development. Agreement was reached with the United Nations Development Programme (UNDP) on future co-operation in situations requiring longer-term assistance to refugees and involving development projects. The World Food Programme (WFP) continued to meet most of the basic food needs of refugees and displaced persons in many affected areas.

UNHCR also co-operated with other intergovernmental organizations, liberation movements and non-governmental organizations (NGOs). As a result of NGO interest in greater involvement in the annual meeting of the Executive Committee, the Commissioner convened in October 1983 the first pre–Executive Committee meeting for NGOs, which was attended by the representatives of 66 agencies.

The Executive Committee welcomed the Commissioner's co-operation with other members of the United Nations system, in particular with WFP in providing relief assistance and with the World Bank and ILO in promoting self-sufficiency and income-generating or employment opportunities.

ECONOMIC AND SOCIAL COUNCIL ACTION

By decision 1983/101 of 4 February 1983, the Economic and Social Council decided to transmit, without debate, the UNHCR report[2] to the General Assembly.

Therefore, it did not consider the item at its second regular session of 1983, but adopted decision 1983/172 on 28 July, thereby taking note of the High Commissioner's oral report in the Council on assistance to refugees in Djibouti and Somalia, to displaced persons in Ethiopia, and to student refugees in southern Africa.

GENERAL ASSEMBLY ACTION

In the General Assembly's Third (Social, Humanitarian and Cultural) Committee, High Commissioner Poul Hartling reviewed the activities of his Office and pointed out that the presence of a large number of refugees in a country could create social, economic or political difficulties which were compounded if there was little prospect for refugees to become an asset and not a burden. UNHCR could act only as a catalyst; it was up to Governments to create conditions leading to solutions.

On 16 December 1983, the General Assembly, acting on the recommendation of the Third Committee, adopted resolution 38/121 without vote.

Report of the United Nations High Commissioner for Refugees

The General Assembly,

Having considered the report of the United Nations High Commissioner for Refugees on the activities of his Office, as well as the report of the Executive Committee of the Programme of the High Commissioner on the work of its thirty-fourth session, and having heard the statement made by the High Commissioner on 14 November 1983,

Recalling its resolution 37/195 of 18 December 1982,

Reaffirming the eminently humanitarian and non-political character of the activities of the Office of the High Commissioner,

Noting with deep concern that problems of refugees and displaced persons of concern to the High Commissioner remain acute in all parts of the world, notably in Africa, Asia and Latin America,

Stressing the fundamental importance of the High Commissioner's international protection function and the need for States to co-operate with the High Commissioner in the exercise of this essential function,

Expressing serious concern over the difficulties encountered by the High Commissioner in the exercise of his international protection function in the face of continued violations of the basic rights of persons of concern to his Office,

Deeply concerned that in various regions the safety and welfare of refugees and asylum-seekers have been seriously jeopardized on account of military or armed attacks, acts of piracy and other forms of brutality,

Acknowledging with appreciation the note of the Executive Committee on the strengthening of the management policy of the Office of the United Nations High Commissioner for Refugees, submitted by the High Commissioner, and the High Commissioner's efforts to strengthen the management of his Office,

Noting that the Executive Committee has requested the High Commissioner to undertake a comprehensive study of the full financial and practical implications of the inclusion of Arabic, Chinese and Spanish among the official and working languages of the Executive Committee,

Noting with deep appreciation the valuable support extended by many Governments to the High Commissioner in carrying out his duties,

Welcoming the increasing number of accessions by States to the 1951 Convention and the 1967 Protocol relating to the Status of Refugees,

Emphasizing that voluntary repatriation is the most desirable and durable solution to problems of refugees and displaced persons of concern to the High Commissioner,

1. *Commends* the United Nations High Commissioner for Refugees and his staff for the valuable work they perform on behalf of refugees, returnees and displaced persons of concern to the Office of the High Commissioner;

2. *Reaffirms* the fundamental nature of the High Commissioner's function to provide international protection and the need for Governments to co-operate fully with him to facilitate the effective exercise of this essential function, in particular by acceding to and fully implementing the relevant international and regional instruments and by scrupulously observing the principles of asylum and *non-refoulement;*

3. *Deplores* all violations of the rights and safety of refugees and asylum-seekers, in particular through military or armed attacks against refugee camps and settlements, other forms of brutality and failure to rescue asylum-seekers in distress at sea;

4. *Urges* States, in co-operation with the Office of the High Commissioner and other competent international bodies, to take all necessary measures to ensure the safety of refugees and asylum-seekers;

5. *Reaffirms* the principle of international solidarity and burden-sharing in responding to the refugee problem, particularly in view of the heavy burden borne by receiving countries on account of the presence of large numbers of refugees and asylum-seekers;

6. *Expresses its deep appreciation* for the valuable material and humanitarian response of receiving countries, in particular of many developing countries that give asylum to or accept on a temporary basis large numbers of refugees;

7. *Commends* all States that facilitate the attainment of durable solutions, accept refugees for resettlement and contribute generously to the High Commissioner's programmes;

8. *Urges* all States to support the High Commissioner in his efforts to find durable solutions to refugee problems, primarily through voluntary repatriation, including assistance to returnees, as appropriate, or, wherever appropriate, through integration in countries of asylum or resettlement in third countries;

9. *Notes with appreciation* the continuing support given to the High Commissioner by organizations of the United Nations system, as well as intergovernmental and non-governmental organizations, in carrying out his humanitarian task and requests the High Commissioner to continue to co-ordinate his efforts with those agencies and organizations;

10. *Calls upon* all States to promote durable solutions and to contribute generously to the High Commissioner's humanitarian programmes in order to assist refugees, displaced persons and returnees in a spirit of international solidarity and burden-sharing.

General Assembly resolution 38/121

16 December 1983   Meeting 100   Adopted without vote

Approved by Third Committee (A/38/688) without vote, 30 November (meeting 57); 39-nation draft (A/C.3/38/L.34); agenda item 98 *(a)*.

Sponsors: Algeria, Argentina, Australia, Austria, Belgium, Bolivia, Canada, Congo, Costa Rica, Denmark, Djibouti, Dominican Republic, Egypt, Finland, France, Germany, Federal Republic of, Greece, Honduras, Iceland, Italy, Japan, Lesotho, Madagascar, New Zealand, Nicaragua, Norway, Pakistan, Peru, Portugal, Senegal, Sierra Leone, Somalia, Sudan, Swaziland, Sweden, Thailand, United States, Venezuela, Zaire.

Meeting numbers. GA 38th session: 3rd Committee 42-46, 54, 56, 57, 59; plenary 100.

In a related action, the Assembly, by resolution 38/16 on the universal realization of the right of peoples to self-determination, deplored the plight of refugees and displaced persons and reaffirmed their right to return to their homes voluntarily in safety and honour (see Chapter XVIII of this section).

Financial and administrative questions

UNHCR's overall voluntary funds expenditure in 1983 amounted to $398 million, including $316.2 million under General Programmes and $81.5 million under Special Programmes. Additional expenditure of $13.5 million represented administrative costs under the United Nations regular budget.

Total income for 1983 was $377.8 million.

Contributions

Contributions from governmental and private sources totalled some $312 million in 1983. In addition to Governments, intergovernmental organizations provided contributions amounting to $31.2 million, principally in food, and NGOs contributed in cash and kind valued at $5.3 million.

The establishment of a programme for voluntary repatriation of Ethiopian refugees in Djibouti required a special appeal in June, and later in the year it became necessary to reiterate the need for additional funding for the Programme of Orderly Departures from Viet Nam. In August, a special appeal was issued to promote contributions for a major income-generating project established by the World Bank for Afghan refugees in Pakistan, for which $1.6 million was received by year's end. (See below, for specific projects.)

At its October 1983 session, the Executive Committee of the UNHCR Programme[1] approved a target of $368,460,000 for General Programmes in 1984. At the same time, it thanked donor Governments and NGOs for their generosity, reaffirmed the need for more equitable and widespread financial support within the international community for UNHCR programmes, and urged Governments to make early contributions and payments to the 1984 General Programmes so as to ensure early availability of funds and effective implementation of programmes.

Governmental contributions were announced at the 18 November 1983 meeting of the *Ad Hoc* Committee of the General Assembly for the Announcement of Voluntary Contributions to the 1984 Programme of UNHCR.[3]

Contributions paid or pledged in 1983, were as follows:

CONTRIBUTIONS PAID OR PLEDGED TO UNHCR ASSISTANCE PROGRAMMES, 1983

(as at 31 December 1983; in US dollar equivalent)

Country	1983 payment or pledge	Country	1983 payment or pledge	Country	1983 payment or pledge
Algeria	50,000	Italy	2,302,129	Sudan	2,344
Argentina	70,900	Ivory Coast	2,296	Swaziland	1,330
Australia	12,616,154	Jamaica	550	Sweden	12,272,667
Austria	233,416	Japan	47,855,960	Switzerland	4,693,763
Bahamas	4,500	Kuwait	60,000	Syrian Arab Republic	1,000
Barbados	500	Lao People's Democratic Republic	6,000	Thailand	10,000
Belgium	982,225	Lebanon	10,000	Togo	3,737
Benin	2,000	Liechtenstein	9,615	Trinidad and Tobago	2,073
Brazil	15,000	Luxembourg	7,957	Tunisia	19,069
Burma	10,000	Malawi	260	Turkey	11,000
Burundi	1,675	Malaysia	20,000	Uganda	2,500
Canada	12,432,548	Malta	892	United Arab Emirates	50,000
Chile	20,000	Mexico	40,000	United Kingdom	17,699,773
China	350,505	Monaco	1,142	United Republic of Cameroon	4,843
Colombia	18,015	Morocco	20,000	United Republic of Tanzania	3,287
Cyprus	3,685	Netherlands	8,033,340	United States	107,696,787
Denmark	9,566,124	New Zealand	143,180	Upper Volta	3,613
Djibouti	2,000	Nigeria	276,109	Venezuela	19,965
El Salvador	1,000	Norway	12,203,371	Viet Nam	1,000
Finland	1,938,473	Oman	6,000	Yugoslavia	30,000
France	1,300,905	Pakistan	3,906	Zimbabwe	26,042
Gambia	333	Panama	500		
Germany, Federal Republic of	19,409,645	Philippines	6,000	Subtotal	273,268,974
Greece	90,000	Portugal	97,960		
Guyana	833	Qatar	35,000	*Intergovernmental contributions*	
Holy See	2,500	Republic of Korea	10,000	European Economic Community	31,011,201
Iceland	30,200	Rwanda	2,548	United Nations Trust Fund for	
India	10,493	San Marino	11,968	Southern Africans	200,000
Indonesia	25,000	Saudi Arabia	10,000	Subtotal	31,211,201
Iran	80,000	Senegal	3,000		
Ireland	235,869	Spain	30,000	Total	304,480,175

SOURCE: A/39/5/Add.5.

Accounts of voluntary funds for 1982

The audited financial statements for the year ended 31 December 1982 on the voluntary funds administered by UNHCR showed a total expenditure of $407 million, and total income of $444 million.

After examining the financial statements, the Board of Auditors recommended in its report[4] to the General Assembly that administrative budget monitoring and cash management of UNHCR field offices should be improved. It noted lack of adequate control in some cases over project implementation, particularly as regards expenditures in relation to allotments, and observed that inadequate feasibility studies, insufficient project budgets, or lack of control over the non-expendable property of projects, among other things, had resulted in cost overruns or substantial losses. Moreover, monitoring of some project activities was unsatisfactory due either to non-submission of periodic reports by the implementing agencies or to lack of co-ordination between them and the UNHCR field offices. Accordingly, it called for improved procurement planning and incorporation in agreements of specific penalty/liquidated damage clauses, as well as establishment of appropriate reporting procedures between headquarters and field offices, in order to protect the interests of UNHCR.

The Advisory Committee on Administrative and Budgetary Questions (ACABQ), commenting on the Board's audit in a September report,[5] stressed the importance of proper planning and of careful examination of procurement agreements in keeping losses to a minimum. It expected that UNHCR would introduce procedures for better financial control, and that the experience gained to date would lead to further improvements in project management.

The Executive Committee of the UNHCR Programme, in October,[1] took note of the 1982 financial accounts and the reports of the Board and ACABQ, as well as the report of its Sub-Committee on Administrative and Financial Matters (see below).

In November, the General Assembly, by resolution 38/30, accepted the financial reports, audited financial statements and the audit opinion of the Board of Auditors; concurred with the ACABQ observations; and requested the High Commissioner to take remedial action as called for by the Board.

Administrative and organizational questions

The Sub-Committee on Administrative and Financial Matters of the Executive Committee, at its third meeting (Geneva, October 1983),[6] discussed the strengthening of UNHCR's management policy as well as personnel issues such as the geographical composition of UNHCR staff, recruitment policies, career development, promotion, staff rotation and training.

Taking note of the Sub-Committee's report, the Executive Committee,[1] in October, urged continued efforts towards improved management of the UNHCR Office—particularly regarding devolution of authority, staffing policy and effective programme delivery—and asked the High Commissioner to report periodically on the question. Among a series of personnel questions, it commended the Commissioner for the proposed net zero growth in the established staffing level of his Office in 1984, and stressed the importance of continuing efforts to meet additional needs through redeployment of posts. The Committee also noted that the proposed voluntary funds programmes and budget for 1984 reflected part of the reapportionment of UNHCR's administrative costs between the United Nations regular programme budget and voluntary funds which were subject to General Assembly approval in 1983.

Noting the absence of consensus on a proposal made at the session by the Sudan on behalf of a number of other countries, the Executive Committee requested the High Commissioner to study the full financial and practical implications of including Arabic, Chinese and Spanish among its official and working languages—an action subsequently noted by the General Assembly in resolution 38/121.

REFERENCES

[1]A/38/12/Add.1. [2]A/38/12. [3]A/AC.221/SR.1 & Corr.1.
[4]A/38/5/Add.5. [5]A/38/433. [6]A/AC.96/628.

Activities for refugees

Assistance

Because of the relative stabilization of major refugee situations and the absence of massive new movements, UNHCR expenditure in assistance programmes continued to fall for the third consecutive year, totalling $398 million in 1983 as compared with $497 million in 1980. The higher proportion of expenditures under General Programmes—$316.2 million as against $81.5 million under Special Programmes—reflected the trend away from purely emergency operations.

While the promotion of durable solutions—through voluntary repatriation, local integration in the country of first asylum or resettlement in a third country—remained the long-term goal, UNHCR responded to requests for emergency assistance to new arrivals and continued to pursue

care and maintenance programmes (food, shelter, water, health services, education) for refugees for whom no immediate solution could be implemented. Whenever possible, relief programmes also included measures aimed at promoting self-reliance among refugees.

The largest single care and maintenance programme continued to be for Afghan refugees in Pakistan ($83.9 million), followed by Indo-Chinese refugees in South-East Asia pending a more durable solution ($58 million). Intermediate care and maintenance assistance amounted to some 55 per cent of total UNHCR 1983 General Programmes expenditure.

Some $5,455,000 was obligated from the Emergency Fund, of which $1.1 million was allocated to help 10,000 Sudanese refugees in Ethiopia and $1 million for the purchase and airlift of 5,000 family-size tents for an influx of Afghan refugees in Iran. Allocation of $1.2 million from the Fund assisted persons of concern to UNHCR in Lebanon as well as needy Lebanese who, due to events in their country, were unable to return and needed temporary assistance; of that amount, $685,000 was for assistance inside Lebanon, $250,000 for assistance to Lebanese displaced persons in the Syrian Arab Republic, $135,000 for Lebanese in Cyprus and $173,000 for those in various European countries. Further, $600,000 from the Fund was used to meet emergency needs of a new influx of Angolans in Zambia, $350,000 to assist illegal immigrants expelled from Nigeria, $675,000 for Nicaraguan refugees in Costa Rica, and $500,000 to assist a group of refugees and displaced persons in Uganda.

Various social services continued in the form of community services and counselling, education and aid to handicapped refugees. Disabled refugees and their families, totalling about 1,000 persons, were admitted to new countries of asylum under special resettlement programmes. Scholarship assistance programmes worth $12.7 million helped nearly 14,300 refugee students to study at the secondary and tertiary levels, an increase of 12 per cent over 1982; approximately 66 per cent of the students were in secondary school, 19 per cent in technical training courses and 15 per cent at universities.

A number of assistance projects, as in the Sudan, the United Republic of Tanzania and Zaire, were phased out and responsibilities for further assistance transferred to host Governments.

The UNHCR *Handbook for Emergencies*, published in English in 1982, was issued in French in 1983, and managerial and technical innovations as well as practical lessons learned in the field were being collated for the second edition.

The following table shows 1983 programme expenditure by country or area.

UNHCR EXPENDITURE IN 1983 BY COUNTRY OR AREA*
(in thousands of US dollars)

Country or area	Local settlement	Resettlement	Voluntary repatriation	Relief*and other assistance	Total
AFRICA					
Algeria	3,179.0	0.4	—	13.0	3,192.4
Angola	5,087.8	1.1	1.0	558.4	5,648.3
Botswana	831.7	4.0	32.0	92.7	960.4
Burundi	871.8	—	25.0	83.5	980.3
Djibouti	3,281.6	10.1	353.1	169.7	3,814.5
Egypt	2,234.4	227.6	0.7	133.0	2,595.7
Ethiopia	1,630.1	100.5	3,556.9	5,347.9	10,635.4
Kenya	1,663.8	30.7	5.3	515.5	2,215.3
Lesotho	586.3	26.7	0.5	145.2	758.7
Nigeria	865.1	—	0.7	382.5	1,248.3
Rwanda	3,445.1	4.7	—	368.5	3,818.3
Senegal	547.6	148.5	—	88.0	784.1
Somalia	28,625.1	4.1	—	16,563.8	45,193.0
Sudan	28,436.5	224.7	110.0	1,189.6	29,960.8
Swaziland	1,092.6	12.0	—	81.7	1,186.3
Uganda	1,895.5	3.6	512.9	1,878.6	4,290.6
United Republic of Cameroon	630.0	2.8	0.4	—	633.2
United Republic of Tanzania	5,801.8	—	0.3	159.2	5,961.3
Zaire	12,392.9	22.3	310.2	9.0	12,734.4
Zambia	1,595.5	2.6	0.5	1,104.1	2,702.7
Zimbabwe	231.1	—	—	58.8	289.9
Other	3,329.1	9.1	1,302.4	521.6	5,162.2
Follow-up on recommendations of Pan-African Conference on Refugees	—	—	—	120.5	120.5
Subtotal	108,254.4	835.5	6,211.9	29,584.8	144,886.6
AMERICAS					
Argentina	1,794.8	91.6	30.0	575.2	2,491.6
Costa Rica	1,334.1	10.0	55.0	2,922.7	4,321.8
Honduras	3,536.4	—	10.0	8,127.7	11,674.1
Mexico	454.4	10.0	154.7	4,499.3	5,118.4
Nicaragua	885.8	—	—	1,170.0	2,055.8
Peru	374.0	12.0	3.3	58.0	447.3
Other northern Latin America	1,341.4	115.0	90.3	302.0	1,848.7
Other north-western South America	398.9	—	11.8	159.5	570.2
Other southern Latin America	508.3	345.0	41.7	802.8	1,697.8
North America	2.7	4.8	4.3	80.4	92.2
Subtotal	10,630.8	588.4	401.1	18,697.6	30,317.9
EAST AND SOUTH ASIA AND OCEANIA					
Australia	0.1	—	3.0	—	3.1
China	6,532.9	70.8	—	1.1	6,604.8
Hong Kong	—	746.2	0.3	3,613.8	4,360.3
Indonesia	—	2,174.6	—	4,251.5	6,426.1
Lao People's Democratic Republic	208.6	1.5	1,164.8	—	1,374.9
Malaysia	1,146.6	618.3	—	5,451.5	7,216.4
Philippines	78.6	743.0	—	7,536.2	8,357.8
Thailand	109.1	2,526.3	0.9	28,919.8	31,556.1
Viet Nam	1,020.0	2,800.0	—	—	3,820.0
Other	586.4	606.7	—	8,249.4	9,442.5
Subtotal	9,682.3	10,287.4	1,169.0	58,023.3	79,162.0
EUROPE					
Austria	234.6	83.2	8.0	90.9	416.7
Belgium	216.6	7.5	17.5	77.6	319.2
France	250.0	57.7	33.0	110.0	450.7
Germany, Federal Republic of	162.6	0.6	11.3	1,801.4	1,975.9
Greece	258.3	36.4	2.1	310.0	606.8
Italy	316.1	99.8	1.3	783.0	1,200.2
Portugal	539.3	3.3	4.0	122.0	668.6
Spain	1,107.9	2.0	76.3	555.0	1,741.2
Turkey	61.5	397.6	—	24.9	484.0
United Kingdom	65.6	4.4	11.1	199.1	280.2
Yugoslavia	15.0	130.1	—	900.4	1,045.5
Other	110.9	18.0	28.2	131.3	288.4
Subtotal	3,338.4	840.6	192.8	5,105.6	9,477.4
MIDDLE EAST AND SOUTH-WEST ASIA					
Cyprus	4,666.0	—	—	581.7	5,247.7
Iran	2,500.0	6.9	—	1,050.0	3,556.9
Lebanon	751.5	8.8	—	15.0	775.3

Country or area	Local settlement	Resettlement	Voluntary repatriation	Relieft / and other assistance	Total
MIDDLE EAST AND SOUTH-WEST ASIA (cont.)					
Pakistan	243.9	240.3	—	83,940.9	84,425.1
Western Asia	182.6	81.4	—	267.0	531.0
Subtotal	8,344.0	337.4	—	85,854.6	94,536.0
GLOBAL AND REGIONAL	724.9	288.3	44.3	701.1	1,758.6
Total	140,974.8	13,177.6	8,019.1	197,967.0	360,138.5

*Not including expenditure for programme support and administration.
†Including donations in kind, such as food.
SOURCE: A/39/12.

Africa

In 1983, preparations were made for the Second (1984) International Conference on Assistance to Refugees in Africa (see below), and joint technical teams—comprising UNDP, UNHCR and, in some cases, the Organization of African Unity (OAU)—visited 14 countries to help them prepare requests for assistance to meet additional needs and the increased infrastructural requirements caused by the refugees' presence.

The 1983 UNHCR expenditures in Africa totalled over $153 million, of which some $114.8 million was obligated under General Programmes and $38 million under Special Programmes. Activities in the region featured formulating comprehensive plans of action for refugee self-sufficiency, income generation, education, and phasing-out of activities upon attainment of self-sufficiency.

In Chad, the repatriation operation which had started in 1981 was virtually completed by year's end, as remaining groups from the Central African Republic, Nigeria, the Sudan and the United Republic of Cameroon returned home; some 200,000 persons received UNHCR assistance under the operation. In order to complete UNHCR activities in Chad, a six-month agreement was concluded with UNDP in N'Djamena to phase out rehabilitation assistance.

A tripartite agreement on voluntary repatriation, reached in April between Djibouti, Ethiopia and UNHCR, led to the return of some 12,000 Ethiopian refugees from Djibouti. The Special Programme of Assistance to Ethiopian Returnees, originally scheduled for completion by June 1983, had to be extended owing to delays in various programme sectors; half of the total programme valued at $20 million had been obligated in cash, and $6.3 million in kind, by year's end. A new influx of some 21,000 refugees into south-western Ethiopia in the latter half of 1983 necessitated an emergency response, and a UNHCR review mission in October/November recommended some programme modifications.

The Sudan saw new refugee arrivals in its southern and eastern regions, due partly to the severe drought. WFP assisted in improving food transportation in the south, while ILO, which concluded in April a study with UNHCR on income-generating activities for refugees in eastern and central Sudan, developed activities to benefit some 10,000 families. Discussions began with UNDP to examine the longer-term needs of the refugee-affected area in the south.

Somalia continued to host a large number of refugees, where insufficient availability of food continued to pose difficulties; self-sufficiency schemes were implemented in most of the 35 refugee camps with the co-operation of voluntary agencies. With the Government's consent, agreement was reached on setting up a Steering Committee—chaired by the National Refugee Commission and comprising the Ministry of Planning, UNDP and UNHCR—to co-ordinate the local settlement programme for those refugees not wishing to repatriate; a specialist mission was undertaken in October/November to study the proposed settlements.

There were signs that Ugandan refugees were prepared to repatriate from the Sudan and Zaire, and frequent homeward movements, particularly to the West Nile region, had been observed. The programme in that region was implemented under a tripartite agreement between the Government, the Lutheran World Federation and UNHCR, with WFP, UNICEF and Médecins sans frontières co-operating in the effort. Other developments included a programme mission in September, and the appointment of a liaison officer to the UNHCR African Bureau to ensure co-ordinated action in the countries of asylum and origin.

The United Republic of Tanzania expressed its willingness to grant nationality to a large group of Burundi refugees once a programme to naturalize some 36,000 Rwandese refugees was completed. In Uganda, the right to citizenship was recognized for a group of long-time residents internally displaced during the previous year.

The situation remained largely unchanged for more than 27,000 South African refugees in Angola, Botswana, Lesotho, Mozambique,

Swaziland, the United Republic of Tanzania, Zambia and Zimbabwe, where UNHCR assistance continued to comprise subsistence allowances, scholarships and the promotion of self-sufficiency either in rural settlements or through individual income-generating activities. UNHCR continued to assist some 75,000 Namibian refugees in Angola, Zambia and other African countries. At the United Nations, the question of Namibian refugees was taken up by the General Assembly, the Security Council and the Economic and Social Council (see TRUSTEESHIP AND DECOLONIZATION, Chapter III).

At its October 1983 session, the Executive Committee of the UNHCR Programme[1] noted increased assistance needs in Africa, welcomed UNHCR efforts in preparing for the 1984 International Conference and invited the Office to collaborate with other organizations for its success.

In October, the Assembly, in resolution 38/5 on co-operation between the United Nations and OAU, urged Member States and various organizations to continue their support of African refugee programmes and to assist host countries in coping with the burden imposed on their limited resources and weak infrastructures (see POLITICAL AND SECURITY QUESTIONS, Chapter V). The Assembly also adopted, at its 1983 session, resolutions dealing with: the 1984 Conference; refugee situations in Djibouti, Somalia and the Sudan; the situation of displaced persons in Ethiopia; and South African student refugees (see below).

Second International Conference on Assistance to Refugees in Africa

Preparations were under way during 1983 for the Second (1984) International Conference on Assistance to Refugees in Africa, which the General Assembly in 1982[2] had decided to convene for the purpose of: reviewing the results of the first (1981) Conference;[3] considering the assistance needs for the relief, rehabilitation and resettlement of refugees and returnees; and assessing the need for strengthening the economic and social infrastructure of the affected countries to cope with the problem. The 1981 Conference, while resulting in pledges and contributions amounting to some $570 million, could not meet the additional assistance needs of the affected countries.

Report of the Secretary-General. In his October report,[4] submitted in response to a December 1982 Assembly request,[2] the Secretary-General noted that most African countries affected by refugee situations were among the least developed in the world and, despite generous international assistance given to meet the emergency requirements of refugees, more resources were needed for the authorities concerned to implement durable solutions, such as land settlement

schemes, strengthening the relevant infrastructure of the affected countries, and the creation of income-generating activities.

Recommending that the Assembly convene the Second Conference at Geneva from 9 to 11 July 1984, the Secretary-General stated that a Steering Committee—composed of his representative, as well as those of the OAU Secretary-General, the High Commissioner and the UNDP Administrator—had been established to maintain liaison with African Governments and to direct preparatory work, along with a United Nations Technical Team to assist in preparing country reports. Inclusion of UNDP in the Steering Committee underscored the emphasis of the Conference on the role of development in support of ongoing programmes and in the search for durable solutions. A public information campaign took place in 1983 to publicize the objectives of the Conference (see below).

The Executive Committee of the UNHCR Programme, at its October 1983 session,[1] recognized the importance and timeliness of the Second Conference in pursuing durable solutions to refugee problems in Africa, and reiterated the need for carefully prepared and realistic project submissions so as to help ensure the Conference's success. It also welcomed UNHCR efforts in its preparations and invited the Office to collaborate in that regard with other organizations.

GENERAL ASSEMBLY ACTION

On 16 December, the General Assembly, on the recommendation of the Third Committee, adopted resolution 38/120 without vote.

Second International Conference on Assistance to Refugees in Africa

The General Assembly,

Having considered the report of the Secretary-General concerning preparations for the Second International Conference on Assistance to Refugees in Africa and the sections on Africa contained in the report of the United Nations High Commissioner for Refugees,

Recalling its resolutions 37/197 of 18 December 1982, entitled "International Conference on Assistance to Refugees in Africa", and 38/5 of 28 October 1983 on co-operation between the United Nations and the Organization of African Unity,

Bearing in mind resolution AHG/Res.114(XIX) on the Second Conference, adopted by the Assembly of Heads of State and Government of the Organization of African Unity at its nineteenth ordinary session, held at Addis Ababa from 6 to 12 June 1983,

Gravely concerned at the persistent and serious problem of large numbers of refugees on the African continent,

Aware of the economic and social burden borne by African countries of asylum on account of the presence of these refugees and its consequences for their national development and of the heavy sacrifices made by them, despite their limited resources,

Recognizing the universal collective responsibility of sharing the urgent and overwhelming burden of the problem of African refugees through effective mobilization of resources to meet the urgent and long-term needs of the refugees and to strengthen the capacity of countries of asylum to provide adequately for the refugees while they remain in those countries, as well as to assist the countries of origin in the rehabilitation of voluntary returnees,

Recognizing that the achievement of durable solutions to refugee problems, in particular voluntary repatriation and local integration, calls for generous humanitarian and developmental assistance to the affected countries, as well as for efforts to address the causes of refugee situations,

1. *Takes note with appreciation* of the report of the Secretary-General concerning preparations for the Second International Conference on Assistance to Refugees in Africa;

2. *Approves* the proposed Conference arrangements contained in paragraph 17 of the report of the Secretary-General;

3. *Requests* the Secretary-General to invite all States to participate in the Conference at the ministerial level and to invite also the relevant organs, organizations and bodies of the United Nations system and intergovernmental and non-governmental organizations to participate in the Conference at a high level;

4. *Appeals* to the international community, all States, specialized agencies and regional intergovernmental and non-governmental organizations to provide the utmost support for the Conference with a view to offering maximum financial and material assistance to refugees in Africa and to ensuring the success of the Conference;

5. *Expresses its deep appreciation* to the countries of asylum for the generous contribution and the sacrifices that they are making to alleviate the plight of refugees;

6. *Commends* those countries that are supporting programmes for refugees and returnees for their continued assistance and calls upon them, as well as other States and international organizations, to assist and cooperate with the United Nations High Commissioner for Refugees in the promotion of durable solutions;

7. *Requests* the Secretary-General, in close cooperation with the Organization of African Unity and the Office of the United Nations High Commissioner for Refugees, to ensure that, in the period leading up to the Conference, all appropriate measures are taken so that Member States, in particular principal donors, are kept fully informed of the priority needs of the affected countries and that contacts are established in the capitals concerned to mobilize the necessary support and resources;

8. *Notes with satisfaction* the action taken by the United Nations High Commissioner for Refugees to initiate public information programmes to increase public awareness of the refugee situation in Africa and the objectives of the Conference;

9. *Requests* the Department of Public Information of the Secretariat and other competent bodies of the United Nations system to co-operate closely with the United Nations High Commissioner for Refugees to ensure that the maximum amount of publicity is given to the refugee situation in Africa, as well as to the Conference and its objectives;

10. *Requests* the Secretary-General to report to the General Assembly at its thirty-ninth session on the implementation of the present resolution.

General Assembly resolution 38/120

16 December 1983   Meeting 100   Adopted without vote

Approved by Third Committee (A/38/688) without vote, 30 November (meeting 57); draft by Sierra Leone, for African Group (A/C.3/38/L.24), orally revised; agenda item 98 *(b)*.

Meeting numbers. GA 38th session: 3rd Committee 42-46, 54, 56, 57, 59; plenary 100.

In a related action, the General Assembly, in resolution 38/5 on co-operation between the United Nations and OAU, invited Member States and various organizations to participate actively in the 1984 Conference and to contribute generously to ensure its success.

Djibouti

In view of developments in the refugee situation in Djibouti during 1983, especially the tripartite agreement on voluntary repatriation by the Governments of Djibouti and Ethiopia, and UNHCR, an inter-agency mission concentrating on relief and rehabilitation, as requested by the General Assembly in 1982,[5] was deemed inopportune. Instead, an internal UNHCR mission was undertaken in February 1983 to review with the Government an assistance programme for 1983 and 1984.

In a September 1983 report to the Assembly,[6] the Secretary-General observed that voluntary repatriation appeared to be the only viable durable solution for refugees in Djibouti, in view of the country's arid climate, sparse natural resources and lack of infrastructure. The refugee population in 1982 was estimated at 35,000—half of them children under the age of 15 and most with pastoral background—which represented more than 10 per cent of the local population. Under the voluntary repatriation programme, some 1,500 refugees had returned spontaneously to Ethiopia by the end of June 1983, and as many as 10,000 refugees were expected to repatriate by year's end. The UNHCR branch office in Djibouti was strengthened through the assignment of two repatriation officers.

In June, the High Commissioner appealed to the international community to support an additional special programme of immediate relief and assistance in Ethiopia to voluntary repatriates from Djibouti (see also below, under ETHIOPIA).

At its October 1983 session, the Executive Committee of the UNHCR Programme[1] commended the High Commissioner's efforts, in co-operation with the Governments concerned, to launch the voluntary repatriation programme.

GENERAL ASSEMBLY ACTION

On 16 December, the General Assembly, acting on the recommendation of the Third Committee, adopted resolution 38/89 without vote.

Humanitarian assistance to refugees in Djibouti

The General Assembly,

Recalling its resolutions 35/182 of 15 December 1980, 36/156 of 16 December 1981 and 37/176 of 17 December 1982 on humanitarian assistance to refugees in Djibouti,

Having heard the statement made on 14 November 1983 by the United Nations High Commissioner for Refugees,

Having considered with satisfaction the reports of the United Nations High Commissioner for Refugees on humanitarian assistance to refugees in Djibouti,

Appreciating the determined efforts made by the Government of Djibouti, despite its limited economic resources, to cope with the pressing needs of the refugees,

Aware of the social and economic burden placed on the Government and people of Djibouti as a result of the presence of refugees and of the consequent impact on the development and infrastructure of the country,

Deeply concerned about the continuing plight of the refugees and displaced persons in the country, which has been aggravated by the devastating effects of the prolonged drought,

Noting with appreciation the steps taken by the Government of Djibouti, in close co-operation with the High Commissioner, to achieve adequate, appropriate and lasting solutions in respect of the refugees,

Also noting with appreciation the concern and unremitting efforts of the Office of the United Nations High Commissioner for Refugees, the United Nations Development Programme, the United Nations Children's Fund, the World Health Organization, the World Food Programme, the Food and Agriculture Organization of the United Nations, the intergovernmental and non-governmental organizations and the voluntary agencies which have worked closely with the Government of Djibouti in the relief and rehabilitation programme for the refugees in that country,

1. *Takes note with appreciation* of the reports of the United Nations High Commissioner for Refugees on humanitarian assistance to refugees in Djibouti;

2. *Appreciates* the efforts made by the High Commissioner to keep the situation of the refugees in Djibouti under constant review;

3. *Welcomes* the steps taken by the Government of Djibouti, in close co-operation with the High Commissioner, to achieve adequate, appropriate and lasting solutions in respect of the refugees in Djibouti;

4. *Calls upon* the High Commissioner to mobilize the necessary resources to implement lasting solutions in respect of the refugees in Djibouti;

5. *Urges* the High Commissioner to continue to take the necessary measures to ensure that adequate, appropriate and lasting solutions are achieved in respect of the refugees in Djibouti and to maintain close contact with the Member States, intergovernmental and non-governmental organizations and voluntary agencies concerned with a view to mobilizing the necessary assistance to enable the Government of Djibouti to cope effectively with the refugee situation, which has been aggravated by the debilitating effects of the prolonged drought;

6. *Appreciates* the assistance provided thus far by Member States, the specialized agencies, intergovernmental and non-governmental organizations and voluntary agencies to the relief and rehabilitation programmes for the refugees and displaced persons in Djibouti;

7. *Calls upon* all Member States, the organizations of the United Nations system, the specialized agencies, intergovernmental and non-governmental organizations and voluntary agencies to continue to support the efforts being made by the Government of Djibouti to cope with the current needs of the refugee population and the other victims of drought in that country;

8. *Requests* the High Commissioner, in close co-operation with the Secretary-General, to report to the General Assembly at its thirty-ninth session on the implementation of the present resolution.

General Assembly resolution 38/89

16 December 1983   Meeting 100   Adopted without vote

Approved by Third Committee (A/38/680) without vote, 7 December (meeting 67); 60-nation draft (A/C.3/38/L.43/Rev.2); agenda item 12.

Sponsors: Algeria, Bahrain, Bangladesh, Botswana, Cape Verde, Chad, China, Comoros, Congo, Democratic Yemen, Djibouti, Ethiopia, France, Gambia, Ghana, Guinea-Bissau, India, Indonesia, Iraq, Italy, Ivory Coast, Jordan, Kenya, Kuwait, Lesotho, Liberia, Libyan Arab Jamahiriya, Madagascar, Malawi, Mali, Mauritania, Morocco, Niger, Nigeria, Oman, Pakistan, Panama, Qatar, Saint Lucia, Saudi Arabia, Senegal, Sierra Leone, Singapore, Somalia, Sri Lanka, Sudan, Swaziland, Syrian Arab Republic, Thailand, Togo, Tunisia, Turkey, United Arab Emirates, United Republic of Cameroon, United Republic of Tanzania, United States, Yemen, Zaire, Zambia, Zimbabwe.

Meeting numbers. GA 38th session: 3rd Committee 6, 67; plenary 100.

Ethiopia

In an October 1983 report,[7] submitted in pursuance of a December 1982 General Assembly request,[8] the Secretary-General noted that the Government of Ethiopia had extended its 1980 amnesty proclamation to the end of 1983, that the tripartite commission had agreed on principles governing voluntary repatriation, and that refugees wishing to remain in Djibouti would be permitted to do so while durable solutions were explored by Djibouti and UNHCR in co-operation with the international community (see above). The UNHCR regional liaison office had been expanded to include a protection officer and a logistics officer.

In June, the High Commissioner appealed for international support for a special programme—estimated to require some $8 million for the 12-month period beginning on 15 August 1983—aimed at providing voluntary repatriates from Djibouti with basic relief assistance as well as improving two irrigated agricultural sites. This organized voluntary repatriation programme differed in target population and geographic coverage from the separate ongoing returnees programme in the Eritrea and Hararghe regions for an estimated 110,000 to 126,000 persons of Ethiopian origin returning mainly from Somalia and the Sudan (see below).

GENERAL ASSEMBLY ACTION

On 16 December, the General Assembly, on the recommendation of the Third Committee, adopted resolution 38/91 without vote.

Assistance to displaced persons in Ethiopia

The General Assembly,

Recalling its resolutions 35/91 of 5 December 1980, 36/161 of 16 December 1981 and 37/175 of 17 December 1982 and Economic and Social Council resolutions 1980/54 of 24 July 1980 and 1982/2 of 27 April 1982,

Recalling also the report of the Secretary-General on assistance to displaced persons in Ethiopia, prepared pursuant to Economic and Social Council resolution 1980/8 of 28 April 1980,

Taking note of the report of the Secretary-General on assistance to displaced persons in Ethiopia,

Recalling further the appeal of the Secretary-General contained in his note verbale of 11 November 1980 as well as those of the General Assembly and the Economic and Social Council,

Having heard the statement made on 14 November 1983 by the United Nations High Commissioner for Refugees,

Recognizing the number of voluntary returnees in Ethiopia,

Deeply concerned that the repeated appeals of the Secretary-General, the General Assembly and the Economic and Social Council have yet to receive an adequate response,

Aware of the heavy burden placed on the Government of Ethiopia in caring for displaced persons and victims of natural disasters,

1. *Endorses once again* the appeals of the Secretary-General, the General Assembly and the Economic and Social Council concerning assistance to displaced persons and voluntary returnees in Ethiopia;

2. *Commends* the efforts made by various organs of the United Nations and the specialized agencies in mobilizing humanitarian assistance to the displaced persons and voluntary returnees in Ethiopia;

3. *Appeals once again* to the Governments of Member States and to intergovernmental and non-governmental organizations and all voluntary agencies to contribute generously to assist the Government of Ethiopia in its efforts to provide relief and rehabilitation to the displaced persons and voluntary returnees in Ethiopia;

4. *Requests* the United Nations High Commissioner for Refugees to intensify his efforts in mobilizing humanitarian assistance for the relief, rehabilitation and resettlement of numbers of voluntary returnees, as well as for displaced persons;

5. *Requests* the Secretary-General, in co-operation with the High Commissioner, to apprise the Economic and Social Council, at its second regular session of 1984, of the implementation of the present resolution and to report thereon to the General Assembly at its thirty-ninth session.

General Assembly resolution 38/91

16 December 1983   Meeting 100   Adopted without vote

Approved by Third Committee (A/38/680) without vote, 7 December (meeting 67); 34-nation draft (A/C.3/38/L.51/Rev.1); agenda item 12.

Sponsors: Afghanistan, Algeria, Angola, Bangladesh, Bulgaria, Cape Verde, Congo, Cyprus, Democratic Yemen, Djibouti, Egypt, Ethiopia, Gambia, Ghana, Guinea-Bissau, India, Ivory Coast, Kenya, Lao People's Democratic Republic, Lesotho, Liberia, Madagascar, Malawi, Mali, Mauritania, Mongolia, Morocco, Nicaragua, Nigeria, Senegal, Sierra Leone, Zaire, Zambia, Zimbabwe.

Meeting numbers. GA 38th session: 3rd Committee 67; plenary 100.

Lesotho

Following a December 1982 attack by South African forces on Lesotho,[9] the Secretary-General had been requested by the Security Council[10] to consult with Lesotho and United Nations agencies to ensure the welfare and security of refugees there. In February 1983, he reported to the Council[11] the conclusions of a mission sent to the country in January (see POLITICAL AND SECURITY QUESTIONS, Chapter V, and Chapter III of this section).

While the Government of Lesotho had not established verifiable refugee statistics, 2,000 were formally registered as refugees and some 9,000 persons concentrated in the national primary and secondary schools were believed to be eligible for refugee status.

On the basis of consultations with the Government and UNHCR, the mission was satisfied that current refugee programmes adequately met the needs of identified refugees, and that the policy of local integration offered the best arrangement for their security. However, the mission felt that the Government should process expeditiously the large number of unregistered refugees, so as to provide them with legal protection and qualify them for assistance.

Somalia

The High Commissioner,[12] in pursuance of a December 1982 General Assembly request,[13] reported in September 1983 on the findings of a mission—led by UNHCR and including a representative of WFP—which had visited Somalia from 12 to 28 March to review the refugee situation. Due to difficulties in conducting a census in the 35 refugee camps spread over four different regions, the mission recommended, for programme planning purposes, the use of 700,000 as a camp population, as had been agreed in 1982.[14] About 50 per cent were estimated to be children.

While an organized programme of voluntary repatriation was viewed as the best durable solution for Ethiopian refugees in the country, there was a need to give greater emphasis to self-help activities and land settlement, as refugees were likely to remain in Somalia for the time being. In 1983, Somalia developed a local settlement programme for those unable to attain self-sufficiency under prevailing camp conditions, and reviewed the programme with a United Nations technical interagency mission (19 October–9 November); pending the outcome of the mission, a provision of $12 million had been made to establish the settlements, with the initial aim of accommodating up to 40,000 refugees. Considerable material and financial assistance was required to sustain and strengthen Somalia's fragile economic infrastructure, particularly in refugee-affected areas, to enable it to support the increased population, the report stated.

Most of the refugees' basic care and maintenance needs were being met with external assistance, and some 30 voluntary agencies from Western Europe and North America operated in the camps. As-

sistance requirements for 1983 were estimated at
$124 million, including $94.5 million for 150,000
metric tons of food.

In October, the Executive Committee of the
UNHCR Programme[1] welcomed the initiatives of
Somalia and the High Commissioner in im-
plementing the rural settlement schemes.

Acting on the recommendation of the Third
Committee, the General Assembly, on 16 December, adopted resolution 38/88 without vote.

Assistance to refugees in Somalia

The General Assembly,

Recalling its resolutions 35/180 of 15 December 1980,
36/153 of 16 December 1981 and 37/174 of 17 December 1982 on the question of assistance to refugees in
Somalia,

Recalling also Economic and Social Council resolutions
1981/31 of 6 May 1981 and 1982/4 of 27 April 1982,

Having considered the report of the United Nations High
Commissioner for Refugees on the conditions of the
refugees in Somalia, particularly paragraph 6 of the
report,

Deeply concerned that the refugee problem in Somalia
has not yet been resolved,

Recognizing from the recommendations contained in
the report of the High Commissioner that there remains
an urgent need for increased assistance in the provision
of food, water and medicines, the strengthening of health
and educational facilities in the refugee camps, and the
expansion of the number of self-help schemes and small-
scale farming and fruit-growing projects necessary for
the promotion of self-reliance among the refugees,

Noting the decision of the Government of Somalia to
facilitate a programme of local settlement of the refugees,

Aware of the consequences of the social and economic
burden placed on the Government and people of Somalia as a result of the continued presence of refugees and
the consequent impact on the national development and
the infrastructure of the country,

1. *Takes note* of the report of the United Nations High
Commissioner for Refugees;

2. *Expresses its appreciation* to the High Commissioner
for his continued efforts to mobilize international assistance on behalf of the refugees in Somalia;

3. *Takes note with satisfaction* of the assistance rendered
to refugees in Somalia by various Member States, the
Office of the United Nations High Commissioner for
Refugees, the World Food Programme, the United
Nations Children's Fund and other concerned inter-
governmental and non-governmental organizations;

4. *Appeals* to Member States, international organizations and voluntary agencies to render maximum
material, financial and technical assistance to the
Government of Somalia in its efforts to provide all necessary assistance to the refugees;

5. *Notes with satisfaction* the visit of the United
Nations technical inter-agency mission to Somalia from
19 October to 9 November 1983 to review with the
Government a comprehensive settlement programme for
refugees who wish to be settled in the country;

6. *Notes* that the Government of Somalia will indicate to the Second International Conference on Assistance to Refugees in Africa, to be held at Geneva in
July 1984, its additional needs for material and financial help to assist the refugees in that country;

7. *Requests* the High Commissioner to make a further comprehensive review of the overall needs of the
refugees, taking into account those aspects relating to
their rehabilitation and settlement;

8. *Also requests* the High Commissioner, in consultation with the Secretary-General, to apprise the Economic and Social Council, at its second regular session
of 1984, of the proposed review of the refugee situation
in Somalia;

9. *Further requests* the High Commissioner, in consultation with the Secretary-General, to submit a report
to the General Assembly at its thirty-ninth session on
the progress achieved in the implementation of the
present resolution.

General Assembly resolution 38/88

16 December 1983   Meeting 100   Adopted without vote

Approved by Third Committee (A/38/680) without vote, 7 December (meeting 67);
35-nation draft (A/C.3/38/L.37/Rev.2); agenda item 12.
Sponsors: Bahrain, Bangladesh, Barbados, Botswana, Cape Verde, China, Comoros,
Djibouti, Egypt, Indonesia, Iraq, Ivory Coast, Jordan, Kenya, Kuwait, Lesotho,
Liberia, Malaysia, Mali, Mauritania, Morocco, Nepal, Oman, Pakistan, Philippines,
Qatar, Senegal, Sierra Leone, Singapore, Somalia, Sudan, United States, Yemen,
Zaire, Zambia.
Meeting numbers. GA 38th session: 3rd Committee 65, 67; plenary 100.

Sudan

The Secretary-General, in a September 1983
report[15] submitted in response to a December
1982 General Assembly request,[16] stated that the
Sudan hosted an estimated refugee population of
670,000—of whom 465,000 were from Ethiopia,
200,000 from Uganda and 5,000 from Zaire. Some
22,000 Chad refugees had repatriated, either with
UNHCR assistance or spontaneously.

A continuing refugee influx was noted, however,
with a monthly average of 1,000 to 1,500 arriving
in the east, and some 4,500 in the southern border
area. As at August 1983, 22 settlements in eastern
Sudan accommodated 100,000 refugees and 25 in
southern Sudan sheltered as many as 140,000; in
addition, the transit centres in the south held
21,150 people as at July.

During a mission undertaken in February,
UNHCR arranged with the Sudan's Office of the
Commissioner for Refugees for implementation of
the recommendations made by an inter-agency
review mission in November 1982.[17] Major
follow-up action being taken included international
protection, co-ordination of assistance, delivery of
social and technical services, access to land and
water, housing, wage-earning settlements, refugee
participation, and the phasing-out of UNHCR activities. In order to ensure improved co-ordination
of assistance provided from various sources, an advisory body comprising the Sudan's Commissioner
for Refugees, UNHCR, WFP and several voluntary
agencies had been established.

In view of the uncertain general situation in the region, a contingency plan was being worked out by UNHCR for possible large-scale emergency assistance. It was suggested that, in addition to the participation of WFP and ILO, consideration should be given to further UNDP involvement in refugee-affected areas of the Sudan and in developmental initiatives involving refugee settlements.

GENERAL ASSEMBLY ACTION

Acting on the recommendation of the Third Committee, the General Assembly adopted resolution 38/90 without vote on 16 December.

Situation of refugees in the Sudan

The General Assembly,

Recalling its resolutions 35/181 of 15 December 1980, 36/158 of 16 December 1981 and 37/173 of 17 December 1982 on the situation of refugees in the Sudan,

Having considered the report of the Secretary-General on the situation of refugees in the Sudan,

Taking note of the ever-increasing number of refugees arriving in the Sudan,

Recognizing the heavy burden placed on the Government of the Sudan and the sacrifices it is making in caring for the refugees and the need for adequate international assistance to enable it to continue its efforts to provide assistance to the refugees,

Expressing its appreciation for the assistance rendered to the Sudan by Member States and intergovernmental and non-governmental organizations in support of refugee programmes,

1. *Takes note* of the report of the Secretary-General and the recommendations of the inter-agency technical follow-up missions contained therein;

2. *Expresses its appreciation* to the Secretary-General, the United Nations High Commissioner for Refugees, donor countries and voluntary agencies for their efforts to assist the refugees in the Sudan;

3. *Commends* the efforts of the High Commissioner and the International Labour Office to create income-generating activities for refugees in the Sudan;

4. *Appreciates* the measures which the Government of the Sudan is taking to provide shelter, food, education and health and other services to the refugees;

5. *Requests* the Secretary-General to mobilize the necessary financial and material assistance for the full implementation of the recommendations of the various inter-agency missions;

6. *Appeals* to Member States, the appropriate organs, organizations and programmes of the United Nations, other intergovernmental and non-governmental organizations and the international financial institutions to provide the Government of the Sudan with the necessary resources for the implementation of development assistance projects in regions affected by the presence of refugees, as envisaged in the reports of the various inter-agency missions, and to strengthen its social and economic infrastructure so that essential services and facilities for refugees can be strengthened and expanded;

7. *Requests* the High Commissioner to continue co-ordination with the appropriate specialized agencies in order to consolidate and ensure the continuation of essential services to the refugees in their settlements;

8. *Also requests* the High Commissioner, in co-operation with the Secretary-General, to submit a comprehensive report to the General Assembly at its thirty-ninth session on the progress made in the implementation of the recommendations of the inter-agency technical follow-up missions as well as on the implementation of the present resolution.

General Assembly resolution 38/90

16 December 1983   Meeting 100   Adopted without vote

Approved by Third Committee (A/38/680) without vote, 7 December (meeting 67); 54-nation draft (A/C.3/38/L.47); agenda item 12.

Sponsors: Algeria, Australia, Bahrain, Bangladesh, Canada, Cape Verde, China, Comoros, Cyprus, Djibouti, Egypt, France, Gambia, Germany, Federal Republic of, Greece, India, Indonesia, Iraq, Italy, Ivory Coast, Jamaica, Jordan, Kenya, Kuwait, Lebanon, Lesotho, Liberia, Madagascar, Malawi, Malaysia, Mali, Mauritania, Morocco, Nepal, Nigeria, Oman, Pakistan, Philippines, Qatar, Romania, Saudi Arabia, Senegal, Singapore, Somalia, Sudan, Swaziland, Thailand, Tunisia, Turkey, United Arab Emirates, United States, Zaire, Zambia, Zimbabwe.

Meeting numbers. GA 38th session: 3rd Committee 67; plenary 100.

Student refugees in southern Africa

In a September 1983 report,[18] submitted in pursuance of a December 1982 General Assembly request,[19] the Secretary-General noted that all of the originally proposed projects designed to alleviate the burden which the presence of Namibian and South African student refugees posed on asylum countries had been completed, and that ongoing assistance to such refugees in Botswana, Lesotho, Swaziland, Zambia and Zimbabwe had been fully incorporated into the UNHCR regular programme.

Government contributions received by July 1983, in response to the High Commissioner's 1977 appeal and earmarked for Botswana, Lesotho, Swaziland and Zambia, amounted to some $16 million, with various other contributions of $8.7 million and additional scholarships.

At different times during the year, the number of South African student refugees or school-age refugees were reported as: 154 in Botswana; 11,500 in Lesotho; 728 in Swaziland; 68 in Zambia; and 32 in Zimbabwe. The Namibian counterparts were estimated at: 121 in Botswana; one in Swaziland; and 3,500 in Zambia.

GENERAL ASSEMBLY ACTION

On 16 December, the General Assembly, on the recommendation of the Third Committee, adopted resolution 38/95 without vote.

Assistance to student refugees in southern Africa

The General Assembly,

Recalling its resolution 37/177 of 17 December 1982, in which it, *inter alia,* requested the Secretary-General, in co-operation with the United Nations High Commissioner for Refugees, to continue to organize and implement an effective programme of educational and other appropriate assistance for student refugees from Namibia and South Africa who had taken asylum in Botswana, Lesotho, Swaziland and Zambia,

Having considered the report of the Secretary-General containing the review by the High Commissioner of assistance programmes for student refugees from South Africa and Namibia,

Noting with appreciation that some of the projects recommended in the report on assistance to student refugees in southern Africa have been successfully completed,

Noting with concern the continued influx into Botswana, Lesotho, Swaziland and Zambia of student refugees from South Africa, as well as from Namibia,

Convinced that the discriminatory policies and repressive measures being applied in South Africa and Namibia will lead to a further exodus of student refugees from those countries,

Conscious of the burden placed on the limited financial, material and administrative resources of the host countries by the increasing number of student refugees,

Appreciating the efforts of the host countries to deal with their student refugee populations, with the assistance of the international community,

1. *Endorses* the assessments and recommendations contained in the report of the Secretary-General and commends him and the United Nations High Commissioner for Refugees for their efforts to mobilize resources and organize the programme of assistance for student refugees in the host countries of southern Africa;

2. *Expresses its appreciation* to the Governments of Botswana, Lesotho, Swaziland and Zambia for granting asylum and making educational and other facilities available to the student refugees, in spite of the pressure which the continuing influx of those refugees exerts on facilities in their countries;

3. *Also expresses its appreciation* to the Governments of Botswana, Lesotho, Swaziland and Zambia for the co-operation which they have extended to the Secretary-General and to the High Commissioner on matters concerning the welfare of those refugees;

4. *Notes with appreciation* the financial and material support provided for the student refugees by Member States, the Office of the United Nations High Commissioner for Refugees, other bodies of the United Nations system and intergovernmental and non-governmental organizations;

5. *Requests* the Secretary-General, in co-operation with the High Commissioner, to continue to organize and implement an effective programme of educational and other appropriate assistance for student refugees from Namibia and South Africa who have taken asylum in Botswana, Lesotho, Swaziland and Zambia;

6. *Urges* all Member States and intergovernmental and non-governmental organizations to continue contributing generously to the assistance programmes for student refugees, through financial support of the regular programmes of the High Commissioner, of the projects identified in the report of the Secretary-General and of the projects and programmes, including unfunded projects, which will be submitted to the Second International Conference on Assistance to Refugees in Africa, to be held at Geneva in July 1984;

7. *Also urges* all Member States and all intergovernmental and non-governmental organizations to assist the countries of asylum materially and otherwise to enable them to continue to discharge their humanitarian obligations towards refugees;

8. *Appeals* to the Office of the United Nations High Commissioner for Refugees, the United Nations Development Programme and the United Nations Educational, Scientific and Cultural Organization, as well as other international and non-governmental organizations, to continue providing humanitarian and development assistance to expedite the settlement of student refugees from South Africa who have been granted asylum in Botswana, Lesotho, Swaziland and Zambia;

9. *Calls upon* all agencies and programmes of the United Nations system to continue co-operating with the Secretary-General and the High Commissioner in the implementation of humanitarian programmes of assistance for the student refugees in southern Africa;

10. *Requests* the High Commissioner, in co-operation with the Secretary-General, to continue to keep the matter under review, to apprise the Economic and Social Council, at its second regular session of 1984, of the current status of the programmes and to report to the General Assembly at its thirty-ninth session on the implementation of the present resolution.

General Assembly resolution 38/95

16 December 1983　　　　Meeting 100　　　　Adopted without vote

Approved by Third Committee (A/38/680) without vote, 7 December (meeting 67); 30-nation draft (A/C.3/38/L.54), orally revised; agenda item 12.

Sponsors: Algeria, Angola, Botswana, China, Congo, Djibouti, Egypt, Ethiopia, Gambia, Ghana, Kenya, Lesotho, Liberia, Madagascar, Malawi, Mali, Morocco, Senegal, Sierra Leone, Singapore, Somalia, Sudan, Swaziland, Togo, Trinidad and Tobago, Uganda, United Republic of Tanzania, Yugoslavia, Zaire, Zambia.

Meeting numbers. GA 38th session: 3rd Committee 64, 65, 67, 69; plenary 100.

The Americas and Europe

UNHCR obligations in the Americas and Europe totalled $44 million in 1983, of which $40 million was under General Programmes and $4 million under Special Programmes.

The Americas

A major development in Latin America in 1983 included a continued increase in the number of refugees in Central America and Mexico—from some 312,000 to over 330,000, due mainly to new influxes of Nicaraguan and Salvadoran refugees in Costa Rica and Honduras and of Guatemalan refugees in Mexico. There was a proportional increase in the number of refugees assisted by UNHCR, which totalled some 96,500 by year's end.

The year also marked the beginning of significant voluntary repatriation movements to Argentina, Bolivia and Chile—following developments in the respective countries, including publication by the Chilean authorities in September 1983 of lists of exiles authorized to return. In response to a request by Bolivia, UNHCR used its good offices to solicit contributions to a rehabilitation fund for needy returnees facing difficulties in their economic and social reintegration; $200,000 was made available in May to assist up to 1,250 returnees.

In Honduras, some 17,500 Salvadorian and 500 Guatemalan refugees were regrouped in camps near the western border. Approximately 15,000 Nicaraguan refugees of Miskito origin, who began arriving in Honduras in 1982, were placed in rural villages where self-sufficiency projects were started;

some 2,800 other Nicaraguan refugees had benefited from UNHCR assistance since the latter part of 1982. In Mexico, nearly 43,000 Guatemalan refugees, settled in 89 sites along the border, continued to receive care and maintenance assistance.

In Central America and the Caribbean, there were some 85,500 refugees—mostly Salvadorians, with the balance from Guatemala, Haiti, Nicaragua and other countries—in Belize (7,000), Cuba (2,000), the Dominican Republic (5,000), Guatemala (70,000) and Panama (1,500). Those receiving UNHCR assistance totalled some 3,700 in the region.

Many refugees and displaced persons continued to benefit from resettlement in Canada and the United States, where over 12,000 and 62,000 persons, respectively, were resettled, the majority being from South-East Asia and Europe, with the rest from Africa, the Middle East and Latin America. As in previous years, most assistance in North America was provided by voluntary agencies and government sources, with special help available from UNHCR on a case-by-case basis.

The Executive Committee of the UNHCR Programme, at its October 1983 session,[1] expressed concern over the refugee situation in Central America and appealed to Governments in the region to support the High Commissioner in implementing self-sufficiency projects and durable solutions.

Europe

In Europe in 1983, the total number of refugees was estimated at 600,000. The flow of asylum-seekers continued unabated, particularly from developing countries, with the number reaching 100,000. The countries receiving the most asylum-seekers continued to be France and the Federal Republic of Germany, although the latter's intake was greatly reduced in 1983. In relation to its population, Switzerland received the highest percentage of refugees in Europe; increases were also registered in Austria, Italy, Sweden and Turkey.

Many European Governments, preoccupied by economic recession and the heavy financial burden posed by asylum-seekers, indicated a growing reluctance to accept such applicants, while traditional resettlement countries also decreased their refugee intake; UNHCR was called on to increase its contribution to a number of projects, particularly in legal assistance. Some Governments introduced deterrents to discourage economic migrants from utilizing the asylum procedure, such as a ban on employment and a reduction in social benefits during examination of applications. As a result of such measures, accumulation of cases was noted in first-asylum countries such as Austria, Greece, Italy, Turkey and Yugoslavia.

UNHCR assistance was also given to needy Lebanese stranded in Europe.

The Executive Committee, at its October 1983 session,[1] noted the increased assistance requirements in Europe, welcomed the High Commissioner's initiative in convening a seminar on the integration of refugees in Europe (Geneva, September)—attended by 19 Governments and by non-governmental organizations—and expressed the hope that there would be an appropriate follow-up to the seminar's conclusions.

East and South Asia and Oceania

In 1983, refugees of Indo-Chinese origin remained the largest refugee group in East and South Asia and Oceania. By year's end, those awaiting durable solutions in camps and centres in the region's asylum countries numbered some 167,000, of whom 42,237 were so-called boat people. In addition, there were 276,000 Indo-Chinese refugees settled on 257 state farms in China and some 26,000 Kampuchean refugees in Viet Nam, the majority of whom also benefited from UNHCR assistance.

Among the first-asylum countries in the region, Thailand accommodated the largest number of Indo-Chinese refugees—some 133,000, including 68,000 Lao, 56,300 Kampucheans and 8,600 Vietnamese. Other countries and areas providing temporary asylum to significant numbers of Indo-Chinese refugees included Hong Kong, Indonesia, Japan, Macau, Malaysia, the Philippines and Singapore. In addition, there were two refugee processing centres—one each in Indonesia and the Philippines—which provided temporary accommodation to some 21,000 Indo-Chinese who had already been accepted for resettlement by third countries.

During the year, some 68,000 Indo-Chinese refugees—35,000 Vietnamese, 27,000 Kampucheans and 6,000 Lao—were resettled in third countries, and an additional 19,000 Vietnamese, departing directly from Viet Nam under the Orderly Departure Programme, joined family members abroad. Over 16,400 refugees, mostly Indo-Chinese, were accepted for resettlement by Australia.

Voluntary repatriation candidates and groups of spontaneous returnees to countries of origin also benefited from UNHCR assistance, including provision of resettlement kits and, when appropriate, rice. Beneficiaries included 2,236 Kampuchean repatriates from the Lao People's Democratic Republic under a bilateral arrangement, and 2,397 Lao refugees from Thailand, who had repatriated voluntarily with UNHCR assistance since the programme's inception in 1980. While negotiations continued regarding the voluntary return of Kampuchean refugees in Thailand, 1,200 Kampucheans in the Lao People's Democratic Republic and 21,000 more in Viet Nam benefited from UNHCR assistance.

Other groups of concern to UNHCR in the region included some 8,000 Afghans and Iranians in India; asylum-seekers from Irian Jaya, Indonesia, in Papua New Guinea; and other individual refugees, mostly Iranians, in several other countries.

The High Commissioner told the Executive Committee in October[1] that new initiatives must be provided to cope with the special problem of some 4,000 unaccompanied minors in refugee camps in the region, many of whom had no relatives in third countries and might not qualify for current resettlement programmes.

During 1983, $74.2 million was obligated for assistance to refugees in East and South Asia and Oceania under General Programmes and $9.5 million under Special Programmes. Of this amount, $58 million was spent on multi-purpose assistance for Indo-Chinese refugees in the region.

At its October 1983 session, the Executive Committee drew attention to the difficulties that the ongoing refugee problems entailed for the affected countries in South-East Asia, noted with concern that the size of the Indo-Chinese refugee camp population remained stable despite a significant reduction in arrivals, and called on the High Commissioner to promote durable solutions to those problems. It welcomed the continuing co-operation between Governments concerned and UNHCR, which had facilitated the operation of the Orderly Departure Programme from Viet Nam. In addition, the Executive Committee commended the High Commissioner for his efforts to secure the disembarkation and resettlement of refugees rescued at sea, called on Governments of both coastal and flag States to facilitate disembarkation, and appealed to the latter to give guarantees for the resettlement of those rescued at sea by ships flying their flags.

Middle East and South-west Asia

The largest single UNHCR assistance programme continued in 1983 for an estimated caseload of 2.3 million Afghan refugees in Pakistan, where a $20 million joint project with the World Bank was finalized in the North-West Frontier Province and Baluchistan for income-generating activities through repairing damage to forest areas and improving irrigation systems and roads, all of which had been adversely affected by refugees and their livestock. UNHCR programmes incorporated some of the employment-generating and skills-training projects recommended by ILO after a mission to the country in late 1982; a vocational training project, funded by UNHCR and implemented by ILO, was started in Baluchistan. Under Pakistan's ongoing refugee relocation pro-

gramme, some 40,000 refugees were transferred out of the North-West Frontier Province.

On top of its traditional assistance for refugees in the Middle East, events in Lebanon necessitated UNHCR emergency assistance to some 98,000 persons including displaced Lebanese and refugees, in addition to 38,000 Lebanese and Palestinians (not registered with UNRWA) who had taken refuge in the Syrian Arab Republic (see POLITICAL AND SECURITY QUESTIONS, Chapter IX). UNHCR also provided monthly subsistence grants to some 200 needy Lebanese in Cyprus.

Elsewhere in the region, UNHCR continued discussions with Iran on local integration of Afghan refugees, and co-ordinated the United Nations humanitarian assistance for Cyprus for the displaced and needy there (see POLITICAL AND SECURITY QUESTIONS, Chapter VIII). It obligated a total of $96 million for these programmes, of which $68.8 million was under General Programmes and $27.2 million under Special Programmes. Of this amount, $3.5 million was for an initial programme of assistance to Afghan refugees in Iran, including $1 million made available from the Emergency Fund to provide some 5,000 family-size tents to meet the urgent needs of new arrivals.

The Executive Committee of the UNHCR Programme, at its October 1983 session,[1] noted and encouraged the continued efforts of Pakistan and the High Commissioner in promoting employment and self-sufficiency activities for Afghan refugees in Pakistan.

In November, the General Assembly, in resolution 38/29 on the situation in Afghanistan and its implications for international peace and security, called on all parties concerned to create the necessary conditions for Afghan refugees to return voluntarily to their homes in safety and honour, and renewed its appeal for humanitarian relief assistance (see POLITICAL AND SECURITY QUESTIONS, Chapter VI).

Public information

UNHCR's public information activities in 1983 were aimed at promoting greater public awareness of the plight of refugees and of the objectives of the Second (1984) International Conference on Assistance to Refugees in Africa (see above).

In addition to the monthly newspaper *Refugees*, its quarterly supplement, *Refugees* magazine, focused on Afghan refugees in Pakistan, Indo-Chinese refugees, attacks on refugee camps, and refugees in Africa; the newspaper was published in English and French, with one special issue in German, while the magazine was published in English and French, with special issues in Arabic, Italian and Spanish. Other publications included a catalogue of information materials, posters, a refugee map and calendar, and country fact sheets.

The UNHCR photo library distributed some 45,000 photographs to the media, schools and NGOs. The film department prepared three documentary films: "The Camp on Lantau Island" (boat people in Hong Kong), "The Lost Tribes" (Afghan refugees in Pakistan) and "Beyond Emergency" (Ethiopian refugees in Somalia). UNHCR also continued film co-productions with major television networks on refugee situations around the world.

In the course of the year, journalists, television crews and photographers participated in itinerant media seminars, one of which visited South-East Asia and another the refugee asylum countries of Central America. Two other seminars travelled through a number of African countries on information-gathering programmes for the 1984 International Conference.

In resolution 38/120, the General Assembly noted with satisfaction the UNHCR public information programmes aimed at increasing public awareness of the refugee situation in Africa and the objectives of the 1984 Conference, and requested the United Nations Department of Public Information and other United Nations bodies to co-operate closely with the High Commissioner in ensuring maximum publicity.

Refugee protection

UNHCR continued to provide various measures of protection to refugees, who often lived in insecurity, fearful even of their lives and basic safety. Despite almost universal respect in recent years for the principle of *non-refoulement*—whereby asylum-seekers were not forcibly returned to countries where they faced persecution or death—cases of expulsion had been reported and large numbers of refugees and asylum-seekers everywhere were subjected to various forms, and harsh conditions, of detention.

In addition, States showed an increasing unwillingness to recognize the distinction between refugees and ordinary migrants, as well as a tendency to regard as temporary the predicament, and admission, of refugees for the reason that most of them were fleeing armed conflicts or internal disturbances in their home country.

The climate of economic austerity in various parts of the world had an adverse effect on the range of economic and social rights granted to refugees and asylum-seekers. The fact that most of them were found in countries with a high unemployment rate among local populations also compounded their difficulties in seeking economic independence.

In May, UNHCR hosted a two-day seminar on international protection, attended by legal experts from NGOs and academic institutions. A Meeting of Experts on Refugee Aid and Development, held in August, called for a review of policies for refugee assistance in low-income countries with a major refugee problem and for a new approach to solving such problems. Government officials from some 30 countries attended the Second Refugee Law Course, organized jointly by UNHCR and the International Institute of Humanitarian Law at San Remo, Italy; the Institute also organized a Round Table on Movements of Populations (Florence, Italy, June). In Asia, a Seminar on Refugee Law (Colombo, Sri Lanka, June), held jointly by UNHCR and the Sri Lanka Foundation Institute, enabled government officials from southern and central Asian countries to discuss principles of international protection and problems relating to their practical application in the region.

The Executive Committee of the High Commissioner's Programme, at its October 1983 session,[1] noted the restrictive trends relating to the granting of asylum and the determination of refugee status, the burden that the problem of manifestly unfounded or abusive applications for refugee status or asylum placed on the affected countries as well as its detrimental effect on the interests of legitimate applicants, and recommended procedures for safeguarding the interests of both parties.

The Executive Committee also noted with profound concern the violation of the physical safety of refugees and asylum-seekers through military or armed attacks, acts of piracy and other forms of brutality and the failure to rescue asylum-seekers in distress at sea, and began consideration of a draft statement of principles on the prohibition of military attacks on refugee camps and settlements, taking into account a report by former High Commissioner Felix Schnyder (Switzerland) and the proposals made by its Sub-Committee of the Whole on International Protection (eighth meeting, Geneva, 3-6 and 11 October).[20]

In 1983, UNHCR furnished Governments with some 9,500 Convention Travel Documents, provided for under the 1951 United Nations Convention relating to the Status of Refugees;[21] printed 250,000 refugee identity cards at the request of various Governments; and contributed to the cost of providing cards in several other countries.

In resolution 38/121, the General Assembly reaffirmed as fundamental the High Commissioner's function to provide international protection and the need for Governments to co-operate in the effective exercise of that function, deplored violations of the rights and safety of refugees and asylum-seekers, and urged States to ensure their safety.

International refugee instruments

As at 31 December 1983, the 1951 Convention relating to the Status of Refugees[21] and the 1967

Protocol[22] had been ratified or acceded to by 94 and 93 States, respectively, as a result of 1983 accession to the Convention by El Salvador, Guatemala and Mozambique, and to the Protocol by El Salvador, Guatemala and Peru.[23] Bolivia and Kiribati adhered to the 1954 Convention relating to the Status of Stateless Persons, as well as to the 1961 Convention on the Reduction of Statelessness, bringing to 34 and 12, respectively, the number of States parties to those instruments.[23]

The 1951 Convention, which described the various rights and obligations of refugees, was complemented by the 1950 UNHCR statute,[24] which defined the persons of concern to the High Commissioner and the action he was required to take on their behalf.

Other intergovernmental legal instruments of benefit to refugees included: the 1969 OAU Convention Governing the Specific Aspects of Refugee Problems in Africa, the 1957 Agreement relating to Refugee Seamen and its 1973 Protocol, the 1959 European Agreement on the Abolition of Visas for Refugees, the 1980 European Agreement on Transfer of Responsibility for Refugees, and the 1969 American Convention on Human Rights Pact of San José, Costa Rica.

UNHCR expressed concern that, in two regions of the world where large-scale refugee problems existed and continued to arise, the international refugee instruments had been accepted by only a small number of States. The Executive Committee of the UNHCR Programme,[1] in October, stressed the importance for further States to accede to the 1951 Convention and the 1967 Protocol.

In resolution 38/121 on the report of UNHCR, the General Assembly reaffirmed the need for Governments to facilitate the effective exercise of the High Commissioner's function to provide international protection, in particular by acceding to and fully implementing the relevant international and regional instruments and by scrupulously observing the principles of asylum and *non-refoulement*.

REFERENCES

[1]A/38/12/Add.1. [2]YUN 1982, p. 1203, GA res. 37/197, 18 Dec. 1982. [3]YUN 1981, p. 1039. [4]A/38/526. [5]YUN 1982, p. 1206, GA res. 37/176, 17 Dec. 1982. [6]A/38/399 & Corr.1. [7]A/38/428 & Corr.1. [8]YUN 1982, p. 1207, GA res. 37/175, 17 Dec. 1982. [9]*Ibid.*, p. 313. [10]*Ibid.*, p. 317, SC res. 527(1982), 15 Dec. 1982. [11]S/15600. [12]A/38/400 & Corr.1. [13]YUN 1982, p. 1210, GA res. 37/174, 17 Dec. 1982. [14]*Ibid.*, p. 1208. [15]A/38/427 & Corr.1. [16]YUN 1982, p. 1211, GA res. 37/173, 17 Dec. 1982. [17]*Ibid.*, p. 1210. [18]A/38/429 & Corr.1. [19]YUN 1982, p. 1213, GA res. 37/177, 17 Dec. 1982. [20]A/AC.96/629. [21]YUN 1951, p. 520. [22]YUN 1967, p. 769. [23]*Multilateral Treaties Deposited with the Secretary-General, Supplement: Actions from 1 January to 31 December 1983* (ST/LEG/SER.E/2/Add.1), Sales No. E.84.V.4. [24]YUN 1950, p. 585, GA res. 428(V), annex, 14 Dec. 1950.

International co-operation to avert new refugee flows

In 1983, the Group of Governmental Experts on International Co-operation to Avert New Flows of Refugees, established by the General Assembly in 1981[1] to review the problem and develop recommendations, held its first two sessions in New York (12-15 April and 6-10 June). In its report, transmitted by a July note of the Secretary-General,[2] the Group informed the Assembly that it had agreed on a programme of work, to be conducted, as a general rule, in closed meetings. The work programme covered, among other things, examination of circumstances causing new massive flows of refugees, both natural (catastrophes, emergencies) and man-made (political, economic, other); analysis of existing relevant international instruments, machinery and practices; and consideration of political, juridical, economic and other means for improved international co-operation to avert refugee flows.

The Group requested that the Assembly renew its mandate, adding that, in view of the magnitude and complexity of the task, it would require two 2-week sessions in 1984, with one session meeting in New York and the other elsewhere. The Group recognized the need to have all experts present at its future sessions.

The Secretary-General, in a September report,[3] submitted to the Assembly the observations received from Canada and Colombia in response to the Assembly's renewed request in 1982 for comments on the topic.[4]

By a letter of 5 January 1983 addressed to the Secretary-General,[5] China termed it essential that the Assembly analyse cases of massive refugee flows, rather than speak in generalities; and deal with, and eradicate, the political and ethnic causes that had created the problems.

GENERAL ASSEMBLY ACTION

Acting on the recommendation of the Special Political Committee, the General Assembly, on 15 December, adopted resolution 38/84 without vote.

International co-operation to avert new flows of refugees

The General Assembly,

Reaffirming its resolutions 36/148 of 16 December 1981 and 37/121 of 16 December 1982 on international co-operation to avert new flows of refugees,

Having examined the report of the Secretary-General containing observations received from Governments and the report of the Group of Governmental Experts on International Co-operation to Avert New Flows of Refugees,

Considering the urgency, magnitude and complexity of the task before the Group of Governmental Experts,

Recognizing the necessity of having all the experts participate in the future sessions of the Group, and concerned that, due to financial constraints, experts from least developed countries have been unable to attend,

1. *Takes note* of the report of the Secretary-General containing observations received from Governments;

2. *Welcomes* the report of the Group of Governmental Experts on International Co-operation to Avert New Flows of Refugees, including its programme of work and recommendations, as a constructive step in the fulfilment of its mandate;

3. *Reaffirms and extends* the mandate of the Group of Governmental Experts as defined in General Assembly resolutions 36/148 and 37/121;

4. *Calls upon* the Secretary-General, without prejudice to the rule contained in resolution 36/148, to assist, as far as possible and by way of exception, the experts coming from least developed countries, appointed by the Secretary-General, to participate fully in the work of the Group of Governmental Experts, in order to fulfil its mandate;

5. *Requests* the Secretary-General to prepare a compilation of the comments and suggestions he may receive from Member States on this item;

6. *Calls upon* the Group of Governmental Experts to continue its work in two sessions of two weeks' duration each during 1984, in order to fulfil its mandate;

7. *Requests* the Group of Governmental Experts to submit a report on its work in time for consideration by the General Assembly at its thirty-ninth session;

8. *Decides* to include in the provisional agenda of its thirty-ninth session the item entitled "International co-operation to avert new flows of refugees".

General Assembly resolution 38/84

15 December 1983   Meeting 98   Adopted without vote

Approved by SPC (A/38/593) without vote, 15 November (meeting 29); 34-nation draft (A/SPC/38/L.6/Rev.1), orally revised; agenda item 74.

Sponsors: Austria, Comoros, Costa Rica, Denmark, Djibouti, Egypt, Gambia, Germany, Federal Republic of, Honduras, Iceland, Indonesia, Ireland, Italy, Jordan, Lebanon, Luxembourg, Malaysia, Mali, Norway, Pakistan, Philippines, Rwanda, Samoa, Senegal, Sierra Leone, Singapore, Somalia, Spain, Sudan, Thailand, Togo, United Republic of Cameroon, Upper Volta, Zaire.

Financial implications. 5th Committee, A/38/657; S-G, A/C.5/38/51/Rev.1, A/SPC/38/L.11, A/SPC/38/L.12.

Meeting numbers. GA 38th session: SPC 8, 9, 17, 29; 5th Committee 54; plenary 98.

Prior to its approval by the Special Political Committee, the draft had been orally revised, taking into account amendments submitted, and later withdrawn, by Cuba and Mexico.[6] The proposed amendments concerned the deletion, in paragraph 4, of a phrase qualifying the experts eligible for assistance as those coming from countries "which provide asylum or other significant services to refugees, including returning refugees"; the words "least developed countries", in the same paragraph and in the fourth preambular paragraph, would also have been replaced by "developing countries".

In a related action, the Assembly, in resolution 38/103 on human rights and mass exoduses, recalled having invited the Group of Governmental Experts in 1981[1] to consider the relevant recommendations made on the topic by the Special Rapporteur of the Commission on Human Rights (see Chapter XVIII of this section).

REFERENCES

[1]YUN 1981, p. 1053, GA res. 36/148, 16 Dec. 1981. [2]A/38/273. [3]A/38/274. [4]YUN 1982, p. 1220, GA res. 37/121, 16 Dec. 1982. [5]A/38/66. [6]A/SPC/38/L.9.

Chapter XXII

Drugs of abuse

In 1983, drug abuse—with its health, social and economic consequences—continued to cause concern in many parts of the world. While international controls on psychotropic substances were beginning to work more effectively, there was increasing availability of narcotic raw materials, and multiple use of drugs and the dangerous means of taking them augmented the health hazards.

In May, the Economic and Social Council—acting on the recommendations of the Commission on Narcotic Drugs, which held its thirtieth session at Vienna, Austria, from 7 to 16 February—transmitted to the General Assembly activities proposed for the third and fourth years (1984-1985) of the five-year programme of action (1982-1986) adopted in the context of the 1981 International Drug Abuse Control Strategy (decision 1983/117). It also urged Governments of opiate-producing/consuming countries to dispose of excess stocks (resolution 1983/3).

Further, the Council called for improved international co-operation in the maritime interdiction of illicit drug traffic (resolution 1983/4), recommended that the Commission replace the current task force on the 1981 Strategy (resolution 1983/2), and enlarged the Commission's membership to 40, effective in 1984 (resolution 1983/5). It approved the Commission's recommendation that it would not be appropriate to proclaim an international year against drug abuse (decision 1983/116).

In December, the General Assembly, by resolution 38/93, called for improved co-ordination and co-operation against the illegal production, traffic and abuse of drugs. It outlined, in resolution 38/98, a strategy and policies for drug control and approved the programme of action for 1984-1985, and delineated, in resolution 38/122, an international campaign against traffic in drugs.

The International Narcotics Control Board, composed of 13 members serving in their personal capacities, held two sessions at Vienna—16 to 27 May (thirty-third session) and 4 to 21 October (thirty-fourth session)—at which it discussed drug abuse, drug supply and demand, reduction of illicit demand for psychotropic substances and the international drug control system; in addition, its 1983 report analysed the world situation by region and country.

International control

Implementation of the International Drug Abuse Control Strategy

Activities of the Commission on Narcotic Drugs. In 1983, the 30-member Commission on Narcotic Drugs[1] recommended, through the Economic and Social Council, that the General Assembly entrust the Commission itself, rather than the task force provisionally established in 1982,[2] with reviewing, monitoring and co-ordinating the implementation of the Assembly's 1981 International Drug Abuse Control Strategy[3] and the five-year programme of action (1982-1986). The Commission made the proposal with a view to overcoming what it saw as possible organizational problems, such as the membership and size of the task force, and duplication of work. The recommendation was subsequently endorsed by the Council (resolution 1983/2) and by the Assembly (resolution 38/98).

The task force held its first meeting immediately prior to the Commission's 1983 session, and a further meeting on 14 February, when it reported to the Commission.

The Commission also prepared, and annexed to its report to the Council, a number of projects for 1984-1985, corresponding to the third and fourth years of the five-year programme of action. The Council transmitted the draft projects to the Assembly (decision 1983/117), which approved them in December (resolution 38/98).

Five activities proposed for implementation within regular United Nations budget resources aimed at: reducing excessive stocks of licit opiate raw materials; developing and promoting effective law enforcement; promoting scientific research and providing technical assistance to developing countries; monitoring demand reduction measures; and collecting and disseminating relevant information by the United Nations.

Additional projects, suggested for extrabudgetary financing, focused on: implementing multisectoral country programmes for reducing the illicit supply of narcotic raw materials; preparing drug identification kits for field officers; evaluating the use of community resources in demand reduction; strengthening national narcotics laboratories through provision of equipment and advice by the United Nations Narcotics Laboratory; providing fellowships and study programmes; conducting regional and interregional courses for law enforcement personnel; holding meetings of operational heads of law enforcement agencies; assisting Governments so requesting with the drafting of legislation for national implementation of treaty obligations; and promoting information dissemination.

Report of the Secretary-General. The Secretary-General, in his 1983 report on international co-operation in drug abuse control,[4] stated that activities during the year had focused on developing a network of laboratories with appropriate analytical techniques in areas most affected by drug abuse problems, establishing a computer link between data bases, studying plans for the forfeiture of the proceeds of drug trafficking, researching on the characteristics of seized substances and developing a training programme to curb illicit traffic in transit countries. Although several programmes recommended by the Commission were not implemented due to lack of resources, projects using extrabudgetary resources provided technical assistance on drug law enforcement (Afghanistan, Burma, Egypt, Malaysia, Pakistan, Peru, Turkey), facilitated the preparation of quick-testing kits for field law enforcement officers, provided equipment to national laboratories in over 30 countries, and offered fellowships, study tours and courses for national officials and law enforcement personnel.

ECONOMIC AND SOCIAL COUNCIL ACTION

The Economic and Social Council, in May 1983, adopted a resolution and a decision concerning the International Drug Abuse Control Strategy.

On 24 May, the Council, acting on the recommendation of its Second (Social) Committee, adopted resolution 1983/2 without vote.

Review and implementation of the programme of strategy and policies for drug control
The Economic and Social Council,

Having considered paragraph 3 of General Assembly resolution 36/168 of 16 December 1981, entitled "International Drug Abuse Control Strategy", by which the Assembly requested the Commission on Narcotic Drugs to establish a task force, in the context of that Strategy, to monitor and review the programme of action and to report to the Commission thereon,

Noting that the Commission, in its resolution 1(S-VII) of 8 February 1982, decided, *inter alia*, to establish that task force on a provisional basis, as outlined in paragraph 90 of its report on the seventh special session, and to review the composition of the task force at its thirtieth session,

Noting further the number of representations subsequently made to the Secretary-General concerning the provisional membership of the task force and its possible enlargement,

Aware that a task force with limited participation may prove to be discriminatory in nature,

Recognizing that the original purpose of the task force would be thwarted if the task force were to become too large,

Recognizing also that the monitoring and review procedure, as currently organized, may lead to a duplication of effort between the Commission and its task force,

Concerned that the financial constraints under which the task force was authorized to meet made it necessary for the Commission to renounce its own meeting when its task force was in session, thereby further curtailing the time available to the Commission for examination of its agenda items,

Having taken note of the report of the task force on its discussions held immediately prior to and during the thirtieth session of the Commission,

Recommends to the General Assembly that the Commission on Narcotic Drugs, meeting in plenary during its sessions and in the presence of all interested observers, should in future replace the present task force as provisionally established and thus constitute the task force envisaged in General Assembly resolution 36/168.

Economic and Social Council resolution 1983/2

24 May 1983	Meeting 11	Adopted without vote

Approved by Second Committee (E/1983/64) without vote, 5 May (meeting 3); draft by Commission on Narcotic Drugs (E/1983/15); agenda item 13.
Meeting number. ESC 11.

On the same day, also on the recommendation of its Second Committee, the Council adopted decision 1983/117 without vote.

Strategy and policies for drug control
At its 11th plenary meeting, on 24 May 1983, the Council decided to transmit annex II to the report of the Commission on Narcotic Drugs on its thirtieth session to the General Assembly at its thirty-eighth session. The annex contains the programme for the third and fourth years, corresponding to the biennium 1984-1985, of the basic five-year programme of action adopted by the General Assembly in the context of the International Drug Abuse Control Strategy established by resolution 36/168 of 16 December 1981.

Economic and Social Council decision 1983/117

	Adopted without vote

Approved by Second Committee (E/1983/64) without vote, 5 May (meeting 3); draft by Commission on Narcotic Drugs (E/1983/15); agenda item 13.
Meeting number. ESC 11.

GENERAL ASSEMBLY ACTION

In December, the General Assembly adopted two resolutions concerning drug control.

On the recommendation of the Third (Social, Humanitarian and Cultural) Committee, the Assembly adopted resolution 38/98 without vote on 16 December.

Strategy and policies for drug control
The General Assembly,

Recalling its resolution 32/124 of 16 December 1977, in which it requested the Commission on Narcotic Drugs to study the possibility of launching a meaningful programme of international drug abuse control strategy and policies,

Recalling also its resolution 36/168 of 16 December 1981, by which it adopted the International Drug Abuse Control Strategy and the basic five-year programme of action proposed by the Commission on Narcotic Drugs in its resolution 1(XXIX) of 11 February 1981,

Noting the recommendation contained in Economic and Social Council resolution 1983/2 of 24 May 1983 that the Commission on Narcotic Drugs, meeting in plenary during its sessions and in the presence of all interested observers, should in future replace the current task force provisionally established and thus constitute the task force envisaged in General Assembly resolution 36/168,

Noting also Economic and Social Council decision 1983/117 of 24 May 1983, in which the Council decided to transmit to the General Assembly annex II to the report of the Commission on Narcotic Drugs on its thirtieth session, containing the programme of action for the third and fourth years of the basic five-year programme of action,

1. *Approves* the programme of action for the biennium 1984-1985, the third and fourth years of the basic five-year programme of action, contained in annex II to the report of the Commission on Narcotic Drugs on its thirtieth session;

2. *Decides* that, beginning with its eighth special session, the Commission on Narcotic Drugs, meeting in plenary during its sessions and in the presence of all interested observers, will constitute the task force envisaged in General Assembly resolution 36/168 to review, monitor and co-ordinate the implementation of the International Drug Abuse Control Strategy and the basic five-year programme of action.

General Assembly resolution 38/98

16 December 1983   Meeting 100   Adopted without vote

Approved by Third Committee (A/38/680) without vote, 7 December (meeting 67); 2-nation draft (A/C.3/38/L.60); agenda item 12.
Sponsors: Bahamas, Canada.
Meeting numbers. GA 38th session: 3rd Committee 47, 48, 54, 59, 63, 65, 67; plenary 100.

On 16 December, the Assembly, also on the recommendation of the Third Committee, adopted without vote resolution 38/93.

Measures to improve co-ordination and co-operation in the international struggle against illegal production of drugs, illicit drug traffic and drug abuse

The General Assembly,

Recalling its resolutions 36/168 of 16 December 1981, 37/168 of 17 December 1982 and 37/198 of 18 December 1982,

Recalling also that in paragraph 6 of its resolution 34/177 of 17 December 1979 it urged greater action by the specialized agencies and programmes of the United Nations system, especially the United Nations Educational, Scientific and Cultural Organization, the Food and Agriculture Organization of the United Nations, the International Labour Organisation, the World Health Organization and the United Nations Development Programme, in developing and implementing, within their mandates, programmes aimed at the reduction of illicit production of and demand for drugs, and specifically requested those agencies to make that ac-

tivity a regular item on the agendas of their governing bodies,

Considering that the scourge of drug abuse continues to spread and has reached epidemic proportions, both in developed and in some developing countries,

Considering further that transit States, which have no control over the production of or demand for illicit drugs, are increasingly affected by the illicit drug traffic,

Recognizing that illegal production of drugs, illicit drug traffic and drug abuse are political, security, economic, social and medical problems, in both producing and consuming countries, which must be met with a comprehensive, effective and co-ordinated strategy on the national, regional and international levels,

Acknowledging that constraints of an economic and technical nature are obstacles to many developing countries in their fight against illegal drug cultivation and production, as well as illicit drug traffic and drug abuse,

Aware that the illegal production of drugs must be stopped and that integrated rural development programmes, including crop substitution, combined with control activities are effective measures to curb the production of illicit drugs,

Noting with appreciation the generous contributions made so far and recently pledged to the United Nations Fund for Drug Abuse Control, which should continue, considering the great needs in this field,

Aware of the need to improve regional, interregional and international co-operation and co-ordination in order to intensify the struggle against illegal production of drugs, illicit drug traffic and drug abuse,

Mindful of the decision taken by the Committee for Programme and Co-ordination at its twenty-third session to undertake at its twenty-fifth session, in 1985, an intergovernmental review of drug control on the basis of an in-depth evaluation study to be prepared by the Secretary-General,

1. *Calls upon* Member States that have not yet done so to ratify the international drug control treaties and, until such time, to endeavour to abide by the provisions thereof;

2. *Invites* Member States to make generous contributions to the United Nations Fund for Drug Abuse Control to enable the Fund further to improve and strengthen its activities to reduce the illicit supply of, traffic in and demand for narcotic drugs;

3. *Calls upon* donor countries to allocate an appropriate portion of their development aid resources to programmes aimed at the reduction of illegal production of drugs and to the development of programmes to control drug abuse and drug traffic in the developing countries;

4. *Calls upon* producing countries to identify suitable projects for possible presentation to the Fund, to the specialized agencies and other organizations and programmes of the United Nations system and to international and regional financing institutions;

5. *Urges* the specialized agencies and other organizations and programmes of the United Nations system and other international organizations concerned with assistance to developing countries to initiate and continue, as a matter of priority, within their respective fields and within existing budgetary resources or through voluntarily contributed funds, activities to help developing countries to take the necessary steps to stop the illegal cultivation and production of and trafficking in

drugs, in consultation with and incorporating the experience of the Fund;

6. *Invites* international financing institutions to consider giving financial support to activities in producing countries with a view to stopping the cultivation and production of illicit drugs, and calls upon Member States to encourage regional financing institutions to support such projects;

7. *Urges* the specialized agencies and other organizations and programmes of the United Nations system to identify special drug control activities in their respective fields and to accord higher priority to drug control activities in their programme budgets;

8. *Requests* the Secretary-General to report to the General Assembly at its fortieth session, through the Commission on Narcotic Drugs and the Economic and Social Council, on the drug control activities carried out by the specialized agencies and other organizations and programmes concerned, pursuant to the present resolution;

9. *Also requests* the Secretary-General to take the necessary steps to improve the co-ordination of drug control activities within the United Nations system and among Member States, the specialized agencies and programmes and other international and regional organs and organizations involved in drug control activities, with due consideration for the respective jurisdictions of those bodies, so as to avoid duplication of efforts in this field;

10. *Further requests* the Secretary-General to report to the General Assembly at its fortieth session on measures to improve co-operation and co-ordination of drug control activities within the United Nations system, in the light of the intergovernmental review of drug control to be undertaken by the Committee for Programme and Co-ordination at its twenty-fifth session.

General Assembly resolution 38/93

16 December 1983   Meeting 100   Adopted without vote

Approved by Third Committee (A/38/680) without vote, 7 December (meeting 67); 17-nation draft (A/C.3/38/L.45), orally revised; agenda item 12.

Sponsors: Bahamas, Bolivia, Colombia, Costa Rica, Denmark, Finland, Germany, Federal Republic of, Iceland, Iraq, Italy, Malaysia, Norway, Pakistan, Singapore, Sweden, Thailand, United States.

Meeting numbers. GA 38th session: 3rd Committee 47, 48, 54, 59, 63, 65, 67; plenary 100.

UN Fund for Drug Abuse Control

In 1983, the United Nations Fund for Drug Abuse Control (UNFDAC) devoted 80 per cent of its resources to 21 programmes in 11 countries with major narcotics control problems. Research and training projects carried out by the United Nations Division of Narcotic Drugs, the International Labour Organisation, the United Nations Educational, Scientific and Cultural Organization, the United Nations Social Defence Research Institute and the World Health Organization (WHO) also received UNFDAC funding.

In December, the General Assembly, by resolutions 38/93 and 38/122, urged Member States to contribute to UNFDAC.

In 1983, 43 countries and one Territory contributed some $6.4 million to UNFDAC and 23 countries pledged approximately $3.4 million for 1984 (see table below). In addition, Italy pledged $40,880,503 to be utilized over a five-year period for agreed projects.

CONTRIBUTIONS TO THE UNITED NATIONS FUND
FOR DRUG ABUSE CONTROL, 1983 AND 1984
(as at 31 December 1983; in US dollar equivalent)

Country or Territory	1983 payment	1984 pledge
Argentina	17,300	—
Australia	135,403	138,889
Austria	85,376	81,967
Bahamas	1,000	—
Barbados	250	—
Belgium	25,000	17,371
Brazil	—	5,000
Canada	213,734	—
Chile	5,000	5,000
Denmark	15,969	26,455
Egypt	1,000	1,000
Finland	31,194	—
France	108,377	188,679
Germany, Federal Republic of	1,902,036	1,411,539
Greece	1,997	—
Hong Kong	14,824	—
Iceland	1,500	2,000
India	7,000	7,000
Indonesia	4,000	2,000
Ireland	5,000	—
Italy	196,684	188,679
Ivory Coast	(309)	—
Jamaica	562	344
Japan	294,965	—
Kenya	—	4,089
Liechtenstein	1,000	—
Madagascar	—	2,000
Malaysia	8,500	—
Malta	258	—
Mauritius	351	—
Mexico	969	—
New Zealand	23,580	—
Norway	41,344	816,327
Oman	5,000	—
Pakistan	769	750
Panama	—	2,470
Philippines	1,363	3,300
Portugal	5,000	—
Republic of Korea	2,000	—
Saudi Arabia	150,000	—
South Africa	9,156	—
Sweden	587,243	512,821
Switzerland	73,504	—
Tunisia	1,755	—
Turkey	9,992	10,000
United Kingdom	151,200	—
United Republic of Cameroon	(64)	—
United States	2,270,000	—
Venezuela	2,000	—
Yugoslavia	12,000	—
Zaire	—	500
Total	6,424,782	3,428,180

NOTE: Figures in parentheses indicate negative adjustments to prior pledges.

UN Narcotics Laboratory

The Narcotics Laboratory Section of the United Nations Division of Narcotic Drugs[5] continued to help strengthen national narcotics laboratories in developing countries affected by illicit trafficking. In addition to technical information, it provided, with funds from UNFDAC, chemicals and/or equipment and—with special contributions from Norway—scientific texts and literature. Its reference collection of substances under international control as well as of scientific literature on drugs and drug abuse was further expanded, and preparation continued of a multilingual dictionary,[6] for use by authorities, of narcotic and psychotropic substances. The Laboratory also continued preparing low-cost portable kits to assist law enforcement officials in identifying seized drugs.

The Commission on Narcotic Drugs,[1] in 1983, took note of the report of an expert group to co-ordinate research on the physical and chemical characteristics of heroin to trace its origin and movement in the illicit traffic (Vienna, 28 September–1 October 1982),[7] which had recommended, among other things, the establishment of international facilities for the rapid exchange of samples and data, requesting the Laboratory to procure and distribute statistically significant numbers of heroin samples and recent samples of opium from licit and illicit production.

Drug abuse

The International Narcotics Control Board (INCB), in its 1983 report,[8] observed that the menace of drug abuse—including opiates, cocaine, cannabis and various psychotropic substances—had reached unprecedented dimensions, while there were disquieting signs of the emergence of a permissive attitude towards the use of certain drugs regarded by some to be less harmful than others. It reported that, with traffickers manufacturing heroin and cocaine close to the sources of illicit production, the use of these products was spreading in the producer countries; new sources of cannabis were constantly appearing, including in countries which had been regarded as consumers. Noting that the abuse of psychotropic substances not under international control caused concern to many Governments, INCB observed the importance of the timely placing of particular substances under such control.

The Commission on Narcotic Drugs[1] noted that abuse involving two or more drugs at a time, often in combination with alcohol, was generally increasing and had become the predominant pattern in certain countries. Impairment of health, personal and social dysfunction, accidents, violence and crime were frequently associated with drug abuse; the high profitability of the illicit drug supply, or diversion from licit sources, sustained the spread of abuse.

On 8 February, the Commission adopted a decision[9] on the health, social and economic consequences of drug abuse, and a decision[10] on the report of the Expert Group on Drug Abuse Reduction which had met in September 1982,[11] thereby asking the Division of Narcotic Drugs to publish, in its quarterly *Bulletin on Narcotics*, relevant information supplied by Member States and by the Group.

The General Assembly, in resolution 38/93, called on countries giving development aid to allocate a portion of that aid to drug abuse control in the developing countries.

Proposed international year

In pursuance of an April 1982 resolution of the Economic and Social Council,[12] the Commission on Narcotic Drugs[1] considered in 1983 a proposal to proclaim an international year against drug abuse.

In addition to a note submitted by the Secretary-General, containing replies from 11 Governments, the Commission heard the comments of its members and observers in debate. In the light of the mostly negative views, the Commission recommended against the proposal, adding that the year might even have a negative impact by generating more curiosity than opposition to drug abuse, and that the funds required could be used more wisely to enhance the international strategy for drug control.

ECONOMIC AND SOCIAL COUNCIL ACTION

Acting on the recommendation of its Second Committee, the Economic and Social Council, on 24 May, adopted decision 1983/116 without vote.

International year against drug abuse

At its 11th plenary meeting, on 24 May 1983, the Council took note of, and approved, the recommendation contained in the report of the Commission on Narcotic Drugs on its thirtieth session that it would not be appropriate to proclaim an international year against drug abuse.

Economic and Social Council decision 1983/116

Adopted without vote

Approved by Second Committee (E/1983/64) without vote, 5 May (meeting 3); draft by Commission on Narcotic Drugs (E/1983/15); agenda item 13. *Meeting number.* ESC 11.

Supply and demand

In 1983, INCB reported[8] that the international control system for the licit trade of narcotics generally worked satisfactorily, although there had been increasing diversions of certain narcotic drugs through use of falsified import certificates. It reminded Governments of the their obligation under the 1961 Single Convention on Narcotic Drugs to return copies of export authorizations, endorsed to indicate receipt, to the exporting countries so they could keep track of drug consignments and investigate possible diversions.

Narcotic raw materials for licit use

INCB observed in its 1983 report[8] that, despite a balance achieved in 1982 and 1983 between supply of and demand for opiates for medical and scientific purposes, a return to over-production was anticipated for 1984, and the possibility of an increase in the already excessive raw material stocks, mainly in India and Turkey, could not be excluded. Failing concerted action by the Governments principally concerned, the economic effects of the crisis could worsen still further and lead to consequences unfavourable to the maintenance of effective drug control.

ECONOMIC AND SOCIAL COUNCIL ACTION

On the recommendation of its Second Committee, the Economic and Social Council adopted without vote resolution 1983/3 on 24 May.

Demand and supply of opiates for medical and scientific needs

The Economic and Social Council,

Recalling its resolutions 1979/8 of 9 May 1979, 1980/20 of 30 April 1980, 1981/8 of 6 May 1981 and 1982/12 of 30 April 1982, as well as Commission on Narcotic Drugs resolution 1(XXIX) of 11 February 1981, entitled "Strategy and policies for drug control",

Having considered the report of the International Narcotics Control Board for 1982,

Taking note of the report of the expert group convened by the Division of Narcotic Drugs to explore the feasibility of creation of an international buffer stock of opiate raw materials or transfer of those stocks to the manufacturers' stocks or to special stocks in the consuming countries,

Noting with concern that the traditional supplier countries continue to hold large accumulated stocks of opiate raw materials which constitute a heavy financial and other burden for them,

Recognizing the urgent need to liquidate the accumulated stocks held by the traditional supplier countries, with a view to achieving a lasting world-wide balance between demand and supply of opiates for medical and scientific purposes,

1. *Urges* the Governments of those countries that have not already done so to take urgent and effective steps to implement the above-mentioned resolutions;

2. *Further urges* the Governments of concerned producing and consuming countries to consider, after mutual consultation where necessary, implementing such measures for the disposal of excess stocks recommended in the report of the above-mentioned expert group as may be found feasible and most fruitful, and also to consider other possible measures suggested by the expert group which might contribute to an improvement in the present situation;

3. *Requests* the Secretary-General to transmit the present resolution to all Governments for their consideration and implementation.

Economic and Social Council resolution 1983/3

24 May 1983   Meeting 11   Adopted without vote

Approved by Second Committee (E/1983/64) without vote, 5 May (meeting 3); draft by Commission on Narcotic Drugs (E/1983/15); agenda item 13.
Meeting number. ESC 11.

Illicit traffic

INCB report. In its 1983 report, INCB[8] observed that the enormous criminal profits generated by illicit drug production and trafficking threatened to undermine the economic, social and political stability of the countries concerned. Accordingly, it appealed to Governments to accelerate domestic and international measures to facilitate co-operative investigations to identify and prosecute the criminals who financed organized trafficking. It also advised that manufacturing and exporting countries should exercise special vigilance to prevent the diversion to illicit trafficking of certain narcotics required for medical and scientific purposes.

Action by the Commission on Narcotic Drugs. The Commission on Narcotic Drugs, by a resolution of 16 February 1983,[13] invited Governments to submit suggestions on resolving the problem of deliberate misrepresentation and mislabelling of narcotic drugs and psychotropic substances, and requested the Secretary-General to summarize the information received with a view to developing standards for the clear identification of drugs in international commerce.

ECONOMIC AND SOCIAL COUNCIL ACTION

On 24 May, the Economic and Social Council, on the recommendation of its Second Committee, adopted resolution 1983/4 without vote.

Measures to improve international co-operation in the maritime interdiction of illicit drug traffic

The Economic and Social Council,

Noting the observations made by the expert group to study the functioning, adequacy and enhancement of the Single Convention on Narcotic Drugs, 1961, at its 1982 meeting, particularly with regard to the need for bilateral regional arrangements concerning the boarding of sea-going vessels involved in drug trafficking,

Bearing in mind article 4 of the Single Convention on Narcotic Drugs, 1961, applicable international conventions and the concern of the international community to suppress illegal traffic in narcotic drugs and psychotropic substances,

Noting with concern the alarming number of private vessels transporting illicit drugs on the high seas,

Noting also with concern the large proportion of recidivists among smugglers of illicit drugs by sea,

Recognizing that in many instances illicit drug traffickers also engage in fraudulent practices with respect to the flag State registration of their vessels,

Firmly believing that, in order to be effective in combating illicit maritime traffic, registry information must be readily accessible to and verifiable by law enforcement personnel aboard the vessel and within the claimed flag State,

Convinced that legitimate shipping interests will not be unreasonably hampered by adoption of effective steps by all States to provide, in accordance with relevant domestic constitutional safeguards and legislations, for prompt, positive and unmistaken identification of private vessels registered under their flag,

1. *Appeals* to Governments to inspect closely all requests for registration of private sea-going vessels to ensure that the vessels are those which the applicants are appropriately entitled to register;

2. *Urges* Governments to require their flag vessels to carry on board documents attesting to their registry;

3. *Requests* Governments to explore methods of strengthening international co-operation in combating illicit maritime drug trafficking, and to respond promptly to inquiries made for law enforcement purposes by other States regarding the registry of vessels;

4. *Recommends* that Governments should consider establishing a national centralized vessel registry system for their private flag vessels, to facilitate the international co-ordination needed to implement the present resolution;

5. *Encourages* all States to take prompt action, with due regard to their constitutional, legal and administrative systems, to curtail employment of their flag vessels in the illicit drug trade and to impose significant sanctions on persons convicted of such activity;

6. *Requests* the Secretary-General to transmit the text of the present resolution to all Governments and to invite them to bring it to the attention of their competent authorities for consideration.

Economic and Social Council resolution 1983/4

24 May 1983	Meeting 11	Adopted without vote

Approved by Second Committee (E/1983/64) without vote, 5 May (meeting 3); draft by Commission on Narcotic Drugs (E/1983/15); agenda item 13. *Meeting number.* ESC 11.

Report of the Secretary-General. In pursuance of a December 1982 General Assembly request,[14] the Secretary-General submitted to it in October 1983 a report[15] on activities carried out by the United Nations system in the context of the international campaign against traffic in drugs.

The Secretary-General reported that seven regional seminars were held in 1983—in the Bahamas, Belgium, Bulgaria, India, Malaysia, Peru and Tunisia—with assistance from the drug law enforcement agencies of the Member States, to train enforcement professionals in applying countermeasures to the illicit drug traffic. Study tours were organized for 20 such professionals from Cyprus, Greece, Malaysia, Morocco, Peru, the Syrian Arab Republic, Thailand and Tonga, and a record number of 12 fellows received training from the Narcotics Laboratory Section of the Division of Narcotic Drugs.

The Secretary-General noted that a number of Governments and law enforcement agencies in some regions, such as the Caribbean, where no standing regional co-ordination mechanisms currently existed for drug law enforcement, had expressed the need to remedy the situation. Measures to alleviate the special problems of transit States continued to receive attention, and the Sub-Commission on Illicit Drug Traffic and Related Matters in the Near and Middle East held joint meetings in two regions during the year (see below). The Division was invited to participate in a training seminar for customs officials of the Governments of States members of the League of Arab States (United Arab Emirates, November).

Special issues of the quarterly *Bulletin on Narcotics*,[16] in 1983, focused on forfeiture of the proceeds of drug crimes (No. 2, April-June) and on an analysis of the campaign against drug trafficking (No. 4, October-December).

GENERAL ASSEMBLY ACTION

Acting on the recommendation of the Third Committee, the Assembly, on 16 December, adopted resolution 38/122 without vote.

International campaign against traffic in drugs

The General Assembly,

Recalling its resolutions 36/132 of 14 December 1981, 36/168 of 16 December 1981, 37/168 of 17 December 1982, 37/198 of 18 December 1982 and 38/98 of 16 December 1983,

Recalling also Economic and Social Council resolutions 1982/8 and 1982/9 of 30 April 1982,

Reaffirming the need to improve and maintain regional and interregional co-operation and co-ordination, particularly in the field of law enforcement, to counter drug trafficking and drug abuse,

Noting the growing interest in the development of regional and interregional co-ordination, as indicated by the holding of three meetings in the Bahamas, Greece and India during 1983,

Conscious that while many countries, both developed and developing, continue to divert substantial human, financial and other resources to combat the illicit traffic, the developing countries encounter particular hardships in doing so,

Acknowledging that the illicit production of, demand for and traffic in narcotic drugs and psychotropic substances constitute a serious threat to the development and security of many countries, especially developing countries,

Recognizing, in particular, the dilemma of transit States, which have no control over the production of and demand for illicit narcotic drugs and psychotropic substances yet are seriously affected, both at the domestic and the international levels, by the movement of illicit drugs,

Noting that the international drug control treaties include provisions for the development of effective countermeasures to combat the illicit supply of, demand for and traffic in narcotic drugs and psychotropic substances,

Considering the important role of the United Nations Fund for Drug Abuse Control in supporting various drug control programmes in developing countries, and the necessity of increasing contributions to the Fund to permit it to continue its most valuable work,

Having considered the report of the Secretary-General,

1. *Takes note with appreciation* of the report of the Secretary-General;

2. *Calls upon* Member States that have not yet done so to ratify the international drug control treaties and, until such time, to endeavour to abide by the provisions thereof;

3. *Encourages* Member States to contribute, or to continue to contribute, to the United Nations Fund for Drug Abuse Control to enable it to expand its support for programmes in the field of drug abuse control;

4. *Urges* organizations and programmes within the United Nations system, as well as Member States with available resources and expertise, to continue to grant technical and other forms of assistance, especially in the area of training of law enforcement professionals, to countries most affected by the illicit production of and traffic in drugs and drug abuse and, in this regard, to give appropriate priority to providing the resources and assistance needed to ensure rapid, secure and accurate means of communication and exchange of information;

5. *Expresses its appreciation* to the Governments of the Bahamas, Greece and India for acting as hosts to regional and interregional meetings during 1983;

6. *Requests* the Secretary-General, through the Commission on Narcotic Drugs, to explore all avenues leading to a further improvement of regional and interregional co-ordination of activities against drug trafficking and drug abuse, in particular:

(a) To continue to pursue efforts and initiatives with a view to establishing, on a continuing basis, co-ordination mechanisms for drug law enforcement in regions where these do not yet exist;

(b) To give appropriate priority to measures designed to alleviate the special problems of transit States through co-operative regional and interregional efforts and, in this regard, to bring the present resolution to the attention of all regional and interregional meetings concerned with drug trafficking and drug abuse;

(c) To make every effort to convene, within the resources that may be made available to him, the interregional meeting of heads of national drug law enforcement agencies proposed in paragraph 5 (c) of General Assembly resolution 37/198;

7. *Also requests* the Secretary-General to prepare a report, for review by the General Assembly at its thirty-ninth session, on the progress achieved in the implementation of the present resolution;

8. *Decides* to include in the provisional agenda of its thirty-ninth session the item entitled "International campaign against traffic in drugs".

General Assembly resolution 38/122

16 December 1983   Meeting 100   Adopted without vote

Approved by Third Committee (A/38/689) without vote, 30 November (meeting 57); 21-nation draft (A/C.3/38/L.33); agenda item 99.

Sponsors: Afghanistan, Australia, Bahamas, Barbados, Bolivia, Colombia, Costa Rica, Egypt, Greece, Jamaica, Malaysia, Mexico, Morocco, Pakistan, Peru, Philippines, Saint Lucia, Saint Vincent and the Grenadines, Thailand, Trinidad and Tobago, Vanuatu.

Meeting numbers. GA 38th session: 3rd Committee 47, 48, 54, 57, 59; plenary 100.

Drug law enforcement

The Commission on Narcotic Drugs, by a decision of 8 February 1983[17] on controlled delivery in the fight against the illicit drug traffic, requested the Secretary-General, in co-operation with the International Criminal Police Organization and the Customs Co-operation Council, to prepare and distribute to appropriate national drug law enforcement agencies a comprehensive paper on controlled delivery and on practical ways of applying the technique.

Observing that depriving traffickers of the proceeds of drug crimes would help reduce the illicit traffic, the Commission, by a 15 February reso-

lution,[18] called on Governments and appropriate regional and international organizations to continue improving the ways in which the assets of convicted drug traffickers which had been derived from illicit drug traffic could be made subject to forfeiture.

The Secretary-General reported to the General Assembly in October[15] that consultations had begun, in pursuance of a December 1982 Assembly request,[14] on arrangements for convening an interregional meeting of heads of national drug law enforcement agencies in 1986.

Africa

On 16 February 1983,[19] the Commission on Narcotic Drugs expressed concern at the increasing abuse of, and illicit traffic in, cannabis and psychotropic substances in Africa, and suggested that further domestic and international activities be undertaken for manpower training and solving the problems related to treatment, demand, illicit traffic and availability of drugs of abuse, including khat, in the region. It called for increased international assistance to African countries for research on and prevention and treatment of addiction, and for training drug law enforcement personnel.

Middle East

The Sub-Commission on Illicit Drug Traffic and Related Matters in the Near and Middle East (fifteenth session, Vienna, 4 February 1983)[20] recommended that the Commission on Narcotic Drugs emphasize again the urgent need for Member States to ratify the 1971 Convention on Psychotropic Substances and to reduce over-production, and that it endorse action aimed at developing greater knowledge of measures to deprive drug traffickers of illegally acquired assets. The Sub-Commission also suggested that the Commission promote improved co-ordination for drug law enforcement by encouraging regional meetings in areas where no such mechanisms currently existed.

The Sub-Commission held its sixteenth session at Vienna, on 3 and 4 October.[21]

As authorized by the Commission on 8 February, the Sub-Commission held two joint meetings in 1983, one with the heads of national drug law enforcement agencies in Europe[22] (Greece, October), and another with the Heads of National Narcotics Law Enforcement Agencies, Far East Region[23] (India, November).

1961 Single Convention on Narcotic Drugs and 1972 Protocol

On 16 December 1983, the General Assembly, by resolutions 38/93 and 38/122, called on Member States that had not done so to ratify international drug control treaties and, until that time, to endeavour to abide by them.

In its 1983 report,[8] INCB urged States that had not adhered to the 1961 Single Convention on Narcotic Drugs or its 1972 Protocol to become parties at an early date, and invited the few States not participating in the international drug control system to join in the common effort by developing _de facto_ co-operation.

In 1983, no additional State adhered to the Convention and the total number of parties to that instrument remained at 114. The number of parties to the Convention as amended by the 25 March 1972 Protocol also remained unchanged—at 76.

Psychotropic substances

INCB stated in its 1983 report[8] that the extent of abuse of psychotropic substances—among them, amphetamines—was probably greater than commonly assumed, and that the number of clandestine laboratories producing such substances was increasing, as was diversion from licit channels. The Board asserted that, while the number of parties to the 1971 Convention on Psychotropic Substances remained unchanged and most non-parties complied with its provisions, universal adherence was essential for bringing under control the international licit trade in these substances, thereby dealing effectively with illicit manufacturing and trafficking.

Implementation of the 1971 Convention

In 1983, no additional State adhered to the 1971 Convention on Psychotropic Substances, the number of parties remaining at 76.

On 16 February, the Commission on Narcotic Drugs adopted three resolutions dealing with the Convention—procedures concerning scheduling of benzodiazepines, guidelines for exempting certain preparations, and application of an estimate system to certain scheduled substances.

Scheduling of benzodiazepines

The Commission on Narcotic Drugs, in 1983, discussed the advisability, as recommended by WHO, of scheduling (listing) 26 benzodiazepines under Schedule IV—one of four categories of control—of the 1971 Convention. The Commission recognized that many of the substances were already under various forms of national control, but there were differing views as to whether placing any of them under international control would make for better control at the national level.

At the request of the United States, the Commission voted individually on the inclusion of each substance in the Schedule, including a roll-call vote on diazepam. When none of the substances received the minimum 20 affirmative votes required under the Convention for inclusion, the Commission, at Malaysia's request, voted on the

inclusion of the substances as a whole. That proposal, which was put to a roll-call vote requested by Italy, also failed to receive the minimum affirmative votes.

By a resolution[24] on procedures for it to follow in scheduling the benzodiazepines, the Commission requested WHO, among other things, to review and assess all benzodiazepines on the market as well as amphetamine-type stimulant substances and barbiturates and non-barbiturate sedative-hypnotics, and to provide the Secretary-General with its findings and recommendations.

Guidelines for exemptions

The Commission, having discussed WHO recommendations on establishing guidelines for exempting preparations under article 3 of the Convention, requested the Secretariat to continue reviewing the criteria and guidelines as submitted by WHO and to prepare a refined set for the Commission's consideration and adoption at its next session.[25]

Reporting procedures

The Commission, by a resolution[26] dealing with the application of an estimate system to substances in Schedule II of the 1971 Convention, invited the States parties to that instrument to consider the appropriateness of amending the Convention by introducing a system similar to that used for narcotic drugs under the 1961 Single Convention on Narcotic Drugs and that Convention as amended by the 1972 Protocol.

In making the recommendation, the Commission noted the 1982 conclusions of an expert group on the functioning, adequacy and enhancement of the 1971 Convention[27]—that the time was ripe for instituting obligatory reporting to INCB of estimated requirements of the scheduled substances to enable it to monitor their manufacture, import and export.

Organizational questions
Commission on Narcotic Drugs

In 1983, the Economic and Social Council took action on the membership, periodicity of meetings, agenda for a future session and the 1983 report of the Commission on Narcotic Drugs.

Enlargement of the Commission

ECONOMIC AND SOCIAL COUNCIL ACTION

On 24 May, the Economic and Social Council, on the recommendation of its Second Committee, adopted without vote resolution 1983/5, thereby increasing the membership of the Commission from 30 to 40, effective 1 January 1984.

Enlargement of the Commission on Narcotic Drugs

The Economic and Social Council,

Recalling its resolution 1663(LII) of 1 June 1972, which established the membership of the Commission on Narcotic Drugs at its present size,

Noting that since its fifty-second session the problem of drug traffic and abuse has reached crisis proportions throughout the world,

Taking into consideration the seriousness of the problem, the need for broad international co-operation in seeking solutions and the interest which States have in contributing to efforts to reach solutions,

Decides to enlarge the membership of the Commission on Narcotic Drugs to forty, with effect from 1 January 1984, taking into account the special criteria used in electing members of the Commission and keeping the actual percentage.

Economic and Social Council resolution 1983/5

24 May 1983   Meeting 11   Adopted without vote

Approved by Second Committee (E/1983/64) without vote, 19 May (meeting 15); 14-nation draft (E/1983/C.2/L.2/Rev.1); agenda item 13.
Sponsors: Argentina, Bolivia, Brazil, Colombia, Dominican Republic, Ecuador, Egypt, Mexico, Nicaragua, Peru, Romania, Saint Lucia, Suriname, Venezuela.
Meeting number. ESC 11.

Periodicity of Commission sessions

The Commission on Narcotic Drugs,[1] at its 1983 session, urged the Economic and Social Council to authorize the Commission to hold a five-day special session in 1984 to fulfil its treaty obligations and deal with other urgent matters. It also proposed a provisional agenda for the special session.

The Council, having deferred action on the subject in May 1983 until its second regular session of the year, adopted decision 1983/184 on 29 July, by section IV of which it authorized the Commission to hold the eighth (1984) special session, approved the provisional agenda for that session, and recommended that the Commission should, in the future, adhere to the established biennial cycle of meetings. The Commission, at its seventh (1982) special session,[28] had requested authorization to meet annually in a regular session of no fewer than eight working days, asserting that it had found it necessary to meet annually in regular and special sessions since 1946 (except for 1967 and 1972).

Agenda for the 1985 session

ECONOMIC AND SOCIAL COUNCIL ACTION

Acting on the recommendation of its Second Committee, the Economic and Social Council, on 24 May, adopted without vote decision 1983/115, concerning the thirty-first (1985) session of the Commission.

Provisional agenda and documentation for the thirty-first session of the Commission on Narcotic Drugs

At its 11th plenary meeting, on 24 May 1983, the Council approved the provisional agenda and the list of documents for the thirty-first session of the Commission on Narcotic Drugs set out below.

Provisional agenda and documentation for the thirty-first session of the Commission on Narcotic Drugs

1. Election of officers
2. Adoption of the agenda
3. Situation and trends in drug abuse and the illicit traffic, including reports of subsidiary bodies concerned with the illicit traffic in drugs
   Documentation
   Review of drug abuse and measures to reduce illicit demand
   Review of the illicit traffic
   Reports on the latest sessions of the Sub-Commission on Illicit Drug Traffic and Related Matters in the Near and Middle East
   Reports on the latest Meetings of the Operational Heads of National Narcotics Law Enforcement Agencies, Far East Region
4. Reports on action related to international drug control taken at the international level:
   (a) Report of the Secretary-General on action taken by international drug control bodies of the United Nations;
   (b) Report by the Secretary-General on scientific research, including the work of the Laboratory Section of the Division of Narcotic Drugs;
   (c) Report of the International Narcotics Control Board, with particular reference to world requirements and supply of opiates;
   (d) Report of the United Nations Fund for Drug Abuse Control and reports related to operations financed by it;
   (e) Reports of specialized agencies and international organs and organizations.
   Documentation
   Report of the Secretary-General on international action
   Report of the Secretary-General on scientific research
   Report of the International Narcotics Control Board for 1984
   Report of the United Nations Fund for Drug Abuse Control
   Reports of specialized agencies and international organs and organizations
5. Implementation of the international treaties on the control of narcotic drugs and psychotropic substances
   Documentation
   Implementation of the international drug control treaties
   Status of multilateral treaties
6. Review and implementation of the International Drug Abuse Control Strategy
   Documentation
   Review of the Strategy and programme of action
7. Programme of future work and priorities
   Documentation
   Review of the programme of future work
8. Report of the Commission on its thirty-first session

Economic and Social Council decision 1983/115

Adopted without vote

Approved by Second Committee (E/1983/64) without vote, 5 May (meeting 3); draft by Commission on Narcotic Drugs (E/1983/15); agenda item 13.
Meeting number. ESC 11.

Report of the Commission

ECONOMIC AND SOCIAL COUNCIL ACTION

On 24 May, the Economic and Social Council, on the recommendation of its Second Committee, adopted without vote decision 1983/118.

Report of the Commission on Narcotic Drugs

At its 11th plenary meeting, on 24 May 1983, the Council took note of the report of the Commission on Narcotic Drugs on its thirtieth session.

Economic and Social Council decision 1983/118

Adopted without vote

Approved by Second Committee (E/1983/64) without vote, 5 May (meeting 3); draft by Commission on Narcotic Drugs (E/1983/15); agenda item 13.
Meeting number. ESC 11.

International Narcotics Control Board

ECONOMIC AND SOCIAL COUNCIL ACTION

In 1983, the Economic and Social Council had before it the 1982 report of INCB.[27] Acting on the recommendation of its Second Committee, the Council, on 24 May, adopted decision 1983/114 without vote.

Report of the International Narcotics Control Board

At its 11th plenary meeting, on 24 May 1983, the Council took note of the report of the International Narcotics Control Board for 1982.

Economic and Social Council decision 1983/114

Adopted without vote

Approved by Second Committee (E/1983/64) without vote, 5 May (meeting 3); draft by Commission on Narcotic Drugs (E/1983/15); agenda item 13.
Meeting number. ESC 11

REFERENCES

[1]E/1983/15. [2]YUN 1982, p. 1221. [3]YUN 1981, p. 1058, GA res. 36/168, 16 Dec. 1981. [4]A/38/522. [5]E/CN.7/1983/6. [6]*Multilingual Dictionary of Narcotic Drugs and Psychotropic Substances under International Control* (ST/NAR/1), Sales No. A/C/E/F/R/S.83.XI.5. [7]YUN 1982, p. 1224. [8]*Report of the International Narcotics Control Board for 1983* (E/INCB/1983/1), Sales No. E.83.XI.6. [9]E/1983/15 (dec. 4(XXX)). [10]*Ibid.* (dec. 5(XXX)). [11]YUN 1982, p. 1225. [12]*Ibid.*, ESC res. 1982/10, 30 Apr. 1982. [13]E/1983/15 (res. 3(XXX)). [14]YUN 1982, p. 1227, GA res. 37/198, 18 Dec. 1982. [15]A/38/478. [16]*Bulletin on Narcotics*, vol. XXXV, Nos. 1-4. [17]E/1983/15 (dec. 3(XXX)). [18]*Ibid.* (res. 1(XXX)). [19]*Ibid.* (res. 6(XXX)). [20]E/CN.7/1983/11/Add.1. [21]E/CN.7/1985/4. [22]E/1983/15 (dec. 1(XXX)). [23]*Ibid.* (dec. 2(XXX)). [24]*Ibid.* (res. 4(XXX)). [25]*Ibid.* (res. 5(XXX)). [26]*Ibid.* (res. 2(XXX)). [27]YUN 1982, p. 1230. [28]*Ibid.*, p. 1231.

PUBLICATIONS

Estimated World Requirements of Narcotic Drugs in 1983 (E/INCB/62), Sales No. E/F/S.83.XI.2; *Supplements Nos. 1-12* (E/INCB/62/Supp.1-12), Sales No. E/F/S.83.XI.2/Supp.1-12. *Comparative Statement of Estimates and Statistics on Narcotic Drugs for 1981 Furnished by Governments in accordance with the International Treaties* (E/INCB/65), Sales No. E/F/S.83.XI.3; *1982* (E/INCB/1983/5), Sales No. E/F/S.84.XI.3. *National Laws and Regulations relating to the Control of Narcotic Drugs and Psychotropic Substances: Cumulative Index 1972-1979* (E/NL.1979/Index), Sales No. E.83.XI.4. *Statistics on Narcotic Drugs for 1982* (E/INCB/1983/3), Sales No. E/F/S.83.XI.7. *Statistics on Psychotropic Substances for 1982* (E/INCB/1983/4), Sales No. E/F/S..83.XI.8; *1983* (E/INCB/1984/4), Sales No. E/F/S.84.XI.7.

Chapter XXIII

Statistics

In 1983, the Statistical Commission (twenty-second session, New York, 7-16 March) reviewed the developments, since it last met in 1981, in various fields of economic, social and demographic statistics.

The Statistical Office of the United Nations continued to collect and publish a wide range of statistical data, including those on international trade, industry, transport, energy, national accounts and population.

The Economic and Social Council, in decision 1983/119, authorized the Commission to hold its twenty-third session in 1985.

Economic statistics

Energy statistics

The first edition of a new recurrent publication—*Energy Balances 1977-1980 and Electricity Profiles 1976-1981 for Selected Developing Countries and Areas*[1]—issued in 1983, contained information on energy balances for 26 developing countries and areas, and showed, for the first time, energy flows from the primary source to final consumption; it also presented electricity profiles for 68 developing countries and areas. In view of the special relevance of energy statistics to developing countries, the Statistical Commission, at its 1983 session,[2] agreed that further methodological work should be carried out in that field.

The programme in statistics on new and renewable sources of energy focused in 1983 on assessment of current and planned statistical activities in countries and in international or intergovernmental organizations. The data base on those sources of energy was improved and expanded to include information such as alcohol, vegetable and animal waste, as well as average conversion factors.

Environment statistics

Noting the progress made in the development of methodology for environment statistics, the Statistical Commission, at its 1983 session,[2] expressed regret over the termination as of January 1983 of financial support for that work by the United Nations Environment Programme (UNEP). The Commission requested the Secretariat to continue its methodology work on environment statistics and to promote the results through workshops, seminars and country studies.

The Statistical Office sponsored, together with UNEP, a workshop on natural resources and environment statistics (Abidjan, Ivory Coast, 21-26 November). A *Directory of Environment Statistics*[3] was published, while draft guidelines for freshwater statistics were prepared and reviewed by an expert group (New York, 5-9 December).

Industrial statistics

An updated version[4] of the 1968 *International Recommendations for Industrial Statistics*,[5] dealing with methods for conducting industrial surveys, was issued in 1983, as suggested by the Statistical Commission[2] earlier in the year. A Group of Experts on the Standardization of Definitions and Terminology for Statistics on Mineral Production and Consumption (New York, 11-19 January), meeting in pursuance of a 1979 Economic and Social Council resolution,[6] made recommendations concerning the range of minerals covered by the Statistical Office, mineral consumption statistics, raw material balances and the secondary recovery of metals. Another group of experts (New York, 12-16 December) reviewed draft recommendations for a statistical programme for household and small-scale industries.

National accounts and balances

The Statistical Commission, at its 1983 session,[2] expressed continued support for the revision of the United Nations System of National Accounts (SNA), a task which it agreed should be completed by 1990. It emphasized that what was required was clarification and harmonization of SNA with related statistical systems, rather than its modification or extension, and welcomed the establishment of an intersecretariat working group—involving the United Nations Statistical Office, the Organisation for Economic Co-operation and Development and the European Economic Community—which would plan an overall work programme for SNA revision.

As regards the System of Balances of the National Economy (MPS), the Commission agreed that priority should be given to revising the methodology of intersystem comparisons published by the United Nations in 1977.[7] The Commission also favoured the revision of the SNA/MPS glossary, as well as continuing work on total consumption of the population, on capital formation flows and on the adaptation of the system of indicators of non-material services, which had been developed by the Council for Mutual Economic Assistance for intersystem comparisons.

Price statistics

The Statistical Commission, at its 1983 session,[2] requested the United Nations Statistical Office to continue co-ordinating and producing world-wide comparisons in price statistics (used for assessing the relative economic development of countries) under the International Comparison Project (ICP), and to convene a meeting to complete phase IV of the Project. The Commission endorsed the division of responsibilities between the Statistical Office and the regional commissions, stating that the Statistical Office should play a co-ordinating role and carry out methodological work and analysis on a world-wide basis, while the regional commissions should carry out data collection and adjustments and take account of practical elements of the comparison (see also Chapter VIII of this section).

The Statistical Office computed purchasing power parities linking six main groups of countries. The inter-organizational group on ICP, meeting in June and November, discussed phases IV and V of the Project, and draft chapters were prepared for a manual on ICP.

The Commission decided that the inter-agency price statistics programme should be assigned low priority in view of limited resources.

Trade and shipping statistics

The Commission examined at its 1983 session[2] the third revision prepared by the Statistical Office of the Standard International Trade Classification (SITC), which provided a detailed list of goods moving in international trade, classified in internationally comparable categories, for customs, transport, statistics and other purposes. The Commission requested the Statistical Office to undertake further work on the third revision, bearing in mind the need for harmonization with the International Standard Industrial Classification (ISIC) and with the Integrated System of Classifications of Activities and Products (known as ISCAP or SINAP), while maintaining the character and structure of SITC.

The Commission agreed that further methodological work should be carried out in shipping statistics, which it considered to be of special relevance and interest to developing countries.

International economic classifications

The Commission endorsed the continuing work of the Statistical Office towards harmonization of international economic classifications. It reviewed

a progress report of the Secretary-General on the topic[8] and requested that a draft of the proposed revised International Standard Industrial Classification (ISIC) covering transportable goods-producing activities and a draft of the proposed combined trade/production goods classification should be submitted to the Commission in 1985. The basis for harmonization was formed by ISCAP or SINAP. Draft proposals for SINAP categories of activities and transportable goods were prepared and revised. First drafts of the partial revision of ISIC were prepared.

The fourth session of the Joint Working Group on World Level Classifications, of the United Nations Statistical Office and the Statistical Office of the European Communities, was held in Luxembourg from 16 to 20 May 1983. An expert group on harmonization of international economic classifications met in New York from 12 to 16 December.

Social and demographic statistics

The Statistical Commission, at its 1983 session,[2] expressed support for the continuing work of the Statistical Office in demographic and social statistics. It requested the Secretary-General to revise and expand the information contained in a progress report on population and housing censuses[9] and to keep abreast of national and international work on social statistics and indicators.

An expert group meeting (New York, 5-9 December) discussed a draft of the *Handbook of Vital Statistics Systems and Methods*, while another meeting (New York, 11-15 April), held in co-operation with the International Research and Training Institute for the Advancement of Women, discussed the development of statistics and indicators on the situation of women (see also Chapter XIX of this section). Reports and working papers were issued on the use of population and housing censuses as single-source, multi-subject data bases; population census cost and staffing requirements; development of statistics on disabled persons; integration of social, demographic and related economic statistics; and social indicators.

A revised edition of the *Handbook of Household Surveys*[10] was issued, and data compilation was completed for the *Compendium of Human Settlements Statistics, 1983*.[11]

National Household Survey Capability Programme

The Statistical Commission noted in 1983[2] the considerable progress made in implementing the National Household Survey Capability Programme (NHSCP), a technical co-operation project bringing together national donors and international agencies to assist developing countries in producing socio-economic and demographic statistics needed for their development plans. Recommending that high priority be given to the implementation of country projects, the Commission emphasized the urgency of securing financial support from donor agencies for country programmes, and stressed the importance of continued co-ordination within the United Nations system, as well as with other multilateral and bilateral agencies, in the Programme's execution. As at the end of 1983, 43 countries had officially invited project formulation missions in NHSCP, and project proposals for all of them had been formulated; 34 of those proposals had been approved by the Governments concerned and submitted to interested donor agencies for funding.

Living Standards Measurement Study

In discussing the Living Standards Measurement Study (LSMS)—aimed at identifying ways for Governments to monitor progress in raising living standards—the Statistical Commission, at its 1983 session,[2] endorsed an integrated approach to data collection and analysis designed to provide a conceptual framework for bringing together micro- and macro-data by relating the results of household sample surveys to national accounts statistics. It welcomed the initiative of the World Bank in launching LSMS, emphasized the need for continued co-ordination with NHSCP, and encouraged the Bank to test LSMS methodologies in different developing countries in the light of their needs and capabilities.

Other statistical activities

Technical co-operation

During 1983, the United Nations Department of Technical Co-operation for Development, in co-operation with the Statistical Office, supported country projects in statistics at a cost of $13.5 million. These comprised 80 projects in demographic statistics/population censuses, 14 in vital registration, 40 in statistical organization/multi-sector statistics, 10 in economic statistics and national accounts, 18 in data processing and 4 miscellaneous.

The first edition of the *Directory of Technical Co-operation in Statistics* was published,[12] and the Statistical Commission suggested that an annual update be prepared in a simpler form on a timely basis. Software packages, supplied by a project supported by the United Nations Fund for Population Activities, were installed for a variety of small and large computers in 37 developing countries, and training arrangements were made for fellows from 15 countries in the use of statistical and various demographic analysis packages for processing census and survey data.

A May 1982 report of the Secretary-General on technical co-operation in statistics,[13] submitted to the Commission at its 1983 session,[2] con-

tained information on such programmes during 1979-1982.

Administrative records

Concerning national administrative record systems—which provided vast amounts of information on enterprises and individuals—the Statistical Commission endorsed in broad terms the proposals for further work at the national level, as presented to it by the Secretary-General in an August 1982 report.[14] The report contained summary information on the experience of Canada, France, Israel, the Netherlands and the United States; discussed a number of issues, including increasing accessibility to such records as a result of technological developments; and offered proposals for further work at the national and international level.

The Commission considered that administrative records were not a suitable subject for general treatment at the international level, except for some specific kinds usable for methodological research, such as customs data and taxation and population registers.

Information technology

At its 1983 session,[2] the Statistical Commission discussed the impact of technological innovations on statistical systems, focusing on such issues as the role of meta-data systems for information co-ordination and computerization, the needs of end-users, the exchange of machine-readable data between countries and international agencies, and the selection of technology appropriate to a country's level of statistical development. Among the documentation considered was a September 1982 report of the Secretary-General on implications of new developments in information technology,[15] which outlined relevant developments in computer hardware and software, and assessed current trends and future possibilities.

The Commission agreed on the need for the Statistical Office to give more attention to disseminating generalized statistical software suitable for use on mini- and micro-computers, to assist developing countries. It urged the Office not to expend resources in work towards a global statistical network but to pursue a co-ordinated linking of the data bases of international statistical agencies.

Work programme of the Statistical Office

The Statistical Commission, at its 1983 session,[2] approved the work programme of the Statistical Office for 1984-1985, giving highest priority to the development of SNA and its linkage with MPS, and of concepts, classifications and methods for international trade, transport and related statistics.

Regarding a publication policy for statistics, the Commission endorsed the relevant activities of the Statistical Office, and decided to consider the matter in 1985 on the basis of a comprehensive report to be prepared by that Office.

Co-ordination in the UN system

In 1983, the Statistical Commission endorsed the approach to data collection outlined in a report of the Secretary-General on the co-ordination and integration of international statistical programmes,[16] and asked that special attention be given to reviewing new *ad hoc* questionnaires for maximizing the use of the data already collected and for limiting the burden on respondents.

The Sub-Committee on Statistical Activities, of the Administrative Committee on Co-ordination, at its seventeenth session (Paris, 6-10 June 1983) decided that its members should exchange information on how to measure the informal sector, and agreed that co-ordination was needed on social statistics and indicators, especially in relation to the requirements under the major international strategies and plans of action in the social field. It also reviewed co-ordination of statistics on the environment, migration, women, nutrition, urban poverty, tourism and international trade and transport, industrial and energy data, and price statistics, as well as progress on NHSCP and LSMS.

In pursuance of Economic and Social Council decision 1983/119 of May 1983 (see below), the Working Group on International Statistical Programmes and Co-ordination held its tenth session at Geneva from 26 to 28 September.[17] The Working Group reviewed the statistical programmes of international organizations, discussed special topics for possible consideration by the Statistical Commission, and considered the co-ordination of statistical data-collection activities.

ECONOMIC AND SOCIAL COUNCIL ACTION

In May 1983, the Economic and Social Council, acting on the recommendation of its First (Economic) Committee, adopted without vote decision 1983/119.

Report of the Statistical Commission on its twenty-second session and provisional agenda and documentation for the twenty-third session of the Commission

At its 14th plenary meeting, on 26 May 1983, the Council:

(a) Took note of the report of the Statistical Commission on its twenty-second session;

(b) Decided that the tenth session of the Working Group on International Statistical Programmes and Co-ordination should take place at Geneva from 26 to 28 September 1983;

(c) Approved, in accordance with its resolution 1979/41 of 10 May 1979, the provisional agenda for the twenty-third session of the Commission set out below, together with the documentation listed, bearing in mind the views expressed in chapter XIV of the report of the Commission on the work of its twenty-second session, and the need to reduce documentation in accordance with the relevant resolutions and decisions of the General Assembly and the Council.

Provisional agenda and documentation for the twenty-third session of the Statistical Commission

1. Election of officers
2. Adoption of the agenda and other organizational matters
3. Special issues:

     (a) Meeting user needs for international statistics and improving the dissemination of international statistics;

     (b) Future direction of work on social indicators;

     (c) Publication policy for statistics

     Documentation

     Report on the identification of users and the establishment and development of closer contacts between users and producers of international statistics, including the improvement of dissemination of international statistics

     Report on the future direction of work, including the related issues of co-ordination, methodological development and the international compilation and dissemination of indicators

     Report on the broad aspects of the publication policies of statistical agencies

4. National accounts and balances

     Documentation

     Report on the revision of the System of National Accounts (SNA) and the elaboration of the conceptual framework of SNA and the System of Balances of the National Economy (MPS) comparisons

5. International economic classifications

     Documentation

     Progress report on the harmonization of international economic classifications

     Revised draft of the Standard International Trade Classification, Revision 3

     Draft revision of the part of the International Standard Industrial Classification of All Economic Activities (ISIC) covering transportable goods-producing activities

     Draft of the combined trade/production goods classification

6. Price statistics

     Documentation

     Report on the inter-agency price statistics programme, as well as on phases IV and V of the International Comparison Project (ICP) and the roles of the organizations involved therein

7. Energy and environment statistics

     Documentation

     Report on standards, methods and classifications of energy statistics and on the environment statistics programme, including the methodological work carried out

8. Demographic and social statistics
Documentation
   Report on the development of social indicators and the integration of social, demographic and related statistics
   Report on recent developments in national population registration systems and their statistical use
   Report on national practices in coding country of birth or citizenship in compiling international migration statistics
   Report on the 1985-1994 World Population and Housing Census Programme
9. Technical co-operation
Documentation
   Overall report on technical co-operation in statistics rendered by the United Nations system, other international organizations and countries
   Report on the assessment of the effectiveness of technical co-operation in statistics
   Report on the development of national capabilities in statistics
   Report on several aspects of training in statistics
   Report on several aspects of technical co-operation in statistical data processing
10. Co-ordination and integration of international statistical programmes
Documentation
   Report on the tenth session of the Working Group on International Statistical Programmes and Co-ordination
11. Programme implementation
Documentation
   Overall review of the statistical work of the international organizations for the period 1983-1984
12. Programme objectives and planning
Documentation
   Report on the plans in statistics of the international organizations concentrating on important planned changes and the reasons for them, that is, new activities and activities to be cancelled or significantly modified
   Proposed work programme of the Statistical Office for 1986-1987, including broad resource information, and revisions to the medium-term plan for the period 1984-1989

13. Draft provisional agenda for the twenty-fourth session of the Commission
14. Report of the Commission to the Economic and Social Council

Economic and Social Council decision 1983/119

Adopted without vote

Approved by First Committee (E/1983/56) without vote, 5 May (meeting 3); orally amended by USSR; agenda item 6.
Meeting number. ESC 14.

REFERENCES

[1]*Energy Balances 1977-1980 and Electricity Profiles 1976-1981 for Selected Developing Countries and Areas* (ST/ESA/STAT/SER.W/1), Sales No. 83.XVII.4. [2]E/1983/12 & Corr.1. [3]*Directory of Environment Statistics* (ST/ESA/STAT/SER.M/75), Sales No. E.83.XVII.12. [4]*International Recommendations for Industrial Statistics* (ST/ESA/STAT/SER.M/48/Rev.1), Sales No. E.83.XVII.8. [5]YUN 1968, p. 462. [6]YUN 1979, p. 688, ESC res. 1979/72, 3 Aug. 1979. [7]YUN 1976, p. 490. [8]E/CN.3/1983/15. [9]E/CN.3/1983/16. [10]*Handbook of Household Surveys*, revised edition (ST/ESA/STAT/SER.F/31), Sales No. E.83.XVII.13. [11]*Compendium of Human Settlements Statistics, 1983*, fourth issue (ST/ESA/STAT/SER.N/4), Sales No. E/F.84.XVII.5. [12]*Directory of Technical Co-operation in Statistics* (ST/ESA/STAT/105). [13]E/CN.3/1983/25. [14]E/CN.3/1983/2. [15]E/CN.3/1983/3. [16]E/CN.3/1983/26. [17]E/CN.3/1985/17.

PUBLICATIONS

United Nations Statistical Pocketbook (World Statistics in Brief), Seventh Edition (ST/ESA/STAT/SER.V/7), Sales No. E.83.XVII.2; *Eighth Edition* (ST/ESA/STAT/SER.V/8), Sales No. E.83.XVII.10. *Price and Quantity Measurement in External Trade: Two Studies of National Practice* (ST/ESA/STAT/SER.M/76), Sales No. E.83.XVII.7. *Yearbook of Construction Statistics, 1974-1981* (ST/ESA/STAT/SER.U/16), Sales No. 83.XVII.9. *1983 Energy Statistics Yearbook* (ST/ESA/STAT/SER.J/27), Sales No. E/F.85.XVII.9. *Industrial Statistics Yearbook 1983*, vol. I: *General Industrial Statistics* (ST/ESA/STAT/SER.P/22, vol. I), Sales No. E.85.XVII.10; vol. II: *Commodity Production Statistics, 1974-1983* (ST/ESA/STAT/SER.P/22, vol. II), Sales No. E/F.85.XVII.11. *Construction Statistics Yearbook 1983* (ST/ESA/STAT/SER.U/12), Sales No. E.85.XVII.14. *1983 International Sea-borne Trade Statistics Yearbook (Maritime Transport)* (ST/ESA/STAT/SER.D/83), Sales No. E.86.XVII.25. *Commodity Trade Statistics 1983*, Statistical Papers, Series D, vol. XXXIII, Nos. 5, 20.

Chapter XXIV

Institutional arrangements

In 1983, the Administrative Committee on Co-ordination (ACC) and the Committee for Programme and Co-ordination (CPC) continued their efforts to harmonize the programme activities of the organizations of the United Nations system. Highlights of those efforts included a review of a cross-organizational programme analysis in marine affairs, an evaluation of the technical co-operation activities of the United Nations Industrial Development Organization (UNIDO) in manufactures, and a review of the programme aspects of the proposed United Nations programme budget for 1984-1985. Reviews of the organizations' medium-term plans in selected sectors—food and agriculture, and population—were begun in 1983. Joint Meetings of ACC and CPC centred on economic and technical co-operation among developing countries. Ways of improving the functioning of the Meetings were also pursued.

On the recommendation of the Committee on Non-Governmental Organizations (NGOs), the Economic and Social Council granted consultative status to 40 additional NGOs. A report on prospects for co-operation between the United Nations and the Agency for Cultural and Technical Co-operation, an intergovernmental organization, was noted by the Council and the General Assembly.

Consultations continued on restructuring the economic and social sectors of the United Nations system. Aspects discussed concerned the Council's revitalization, including enlarging its membership, rationalizing its calendar of meetings, and limiting documentation; restructuring issues relating to the Department of International Economic and Social Affairs (DIESA) of the United Nations Secretariat, on which the Joint Inspection Unit (JIU) made recommendations; and rationalizing the work of the Assembly's Second (Economic and Financial) Committee and Third (Social, Humanitarian and Cultural) Committee, on which the Council and the Assembly made a series of recommendations.

Topics related to this chapter. Regional economic and social activities: Africa—restructuring of ECA. United Nations programmes: administrative and budgetary co-ordination.

Co-ordination in the UN system

ACC activities

In 1983, as in previous years, ACC held a general discussion on development and international economic co-operation in keeping with its objective of assisting Governments. It assisted in a comprehensive policy review of operational activities of the United Nations system and considered the question of strengthening the system's capacity to respond to natural disasters and disaster situations. ACC reviewed the state of implementation of the International Development Strategy for the Third United Nations Development Decade (the 1980s), through one of its task forces; the Strategy's implementation system-wide in respect of the environment; and the existing arrangements for inter-agency collaboration at the country level, including arrangements for resident co-ordinators. It also reviewed cross-organizational programme analyses and noted a new series of cross-sectoral reviews of selected sectors in the medium-term plans of United Nations organizations (see below). ACC also acted to strengthen the co-ordination of United Nations information systems, and revised procedures for prior consultations on programme planning documents.[1]

Intensive joint programming was pursued regarding primary health care; aging; research and training in energy assessment, planning and utilization; and energy information systems. Joint programming was also promoted in other areas, such as disarmament and development, science and technology for development, environment, and preparation and support for international conferences (on aging, the Palestine question, the United Nations Decade for Women, population) and years (of disabled persons, world communications) and their follow-up. In addition, ACC took up certain administrative issues involved in regulating and co-ordinating the United Nations common system: staff security, methodology and application of current cost-of-living surveys and staff entitlements at hardship duty stations.

ACC described its activities in annual overview reports for 1982/83[2] and 1983/84.[3] It adopted 18 decisions in 1983—10 at its first regular session (Paris, 30 and 31 March) and 8 at its second (New

York, 26 and 27 October). These decisions concerned a number of the aforementioned topics and matters relating to the ACC machinery; one contained a statement on treaties between States and international organizations or between such organizations. (For details, refer to SUBJECT INDEX or the relevant chapter.)

An organizational session of ACC was held in New York (7-9 February). Its principal subsidiary bodies met during the year as follows:

Consultative Committee on Administrative Questions (CCAQ) (Personnel and General Administrative Questions) (fifty-eighth session, Vienna, Austria, 28 February–18 March; fifty-ninth session, London, 11-15 July, and New York, 18-29 July); CCAQ (Financial and Budgetary Questions) (fifty-eighth session, Geneva, 7-11 March; fifty-ninth session, New York, 12-16 September); Consultative Committee on Substantive Questions (CCSQ) (Operational Activities) (first regular session, Geneva, 4-9 March; second regular session, New York, 3-6 October); Joint Meeting of CCSQ (Programme Matters) and CCSQ (Operational Activities) (Geneva, 9 March); CCSQ (Programme Matters) (first regular session, Geneva, 10-15 March; second regular session, New York, 7-13 October). The ACC Organizational Committee met at Geneva, 16-18 and 31 March, and 4 July; and New York, 14-18 October.

ACC bodies on specific subjects met as follows:

Ad hoc inter-agency meeting on preparations for the International Conference on the Question of Palestine, Geneva, 19 and 20 January and 30 and 31 May; *ad hoc* inter-agency meeting on security matters, Geneva, 24 and 25 January; Task Force on Science and Technology for Development, fourth session, Geneva, 26-28 January; *ad hoc* inter-agency consultations on the cross-organizational programme analysis on human settlements, Geneva, 2 and 3 February; inter-agency meeting to review the cross-organizational programme analysis of the marine affairs activities of the United Nations system, New York, 2-4 February; Inter-Agency Group on New and Renewable Sources of Energy, first and second sessions, New York, 17 and 18 February and 19-28 April; *ad hoc* meeting on co-ordination in matters of international drug control, Vienna, 17 and 18 February, and Geneva, 8-10 August; inter-agency meeting on follow-up to the World Assembly on Aging, Vienna, 17 and 18 February; inter-agency meeting on the preparations for the World Conference to Review and Appraise the Achievements of the United Nations Decade for Women (1985), Vienna, 21 and 22 February; inter-agency consultation on follow-up of the Substantial New Programme of Action for the 1980s for the Least Developed Countries, Geneva, 1 and 2 March; Task Force on Long-Term Development Objectives, eleventh and twelfth sessions, Geneva, 2-4 March, and New York, 10-12 October (a technical working group met at Vienna in July, and a technical energy group met in New York in September), and joint meeting with CCSQ (Programme Matters), New York, 13 October; Joint United Nations Information

Committee, special session, Geneva, 7-9 March, and tenth session, Vienna, 19-22 April; Sub-Committee on Nutrition and its Advisory Group on Nutrition, ninth session, Copenhagen, Denmark, 7-11 March; Task Force on Rural Development, eleventh meeting, Rome, Italy, 11-13 April; inter-agency meeting on the United Nations Decade of Disabled Persons, Geneva, 30 and 31 May; Sub-Committee on Statistical Activities, seventeenth session, Paris, 6-10 June; *Ad Hoc* Task Force on the International Conference on Population (1984), second meeting, Geneva, 15-20 September; Advisory Committee for the Co-ordination of Information Systems, first session, Geneva, 22 and 23 September; inter-agency meeting on outer space activities, Geneva, 4-6 October; Inter-Secretariat Group for Water, fourth session, Rome, 5-9 December.

Following consideration of the ACC 1982/83 annual overview report[2] on 31 May and 1 June, CPC recommended that future reports should emphasize action required from United Nations organizations, rather than from member States, and contain more information on programme management problems, together with proposed solutions. The contributions of organizations to the review process of the Strategy should be consolidated into a synthesized analysis; and an abstract of a survey of their objectives and plans should be submitted to CPC in 1984.

CPC welcomed the Secretary-General's intention to rationalize the work of ACC and to prevent proliferation of its subsidiary machinery.

ECONOMIC AND SOCIAL COUNCIL ACTION

Acting without vote on the recommendation of its Third (Programme and Co-ordination) Committee, the Economic and Social Council adopted decision 1983/175.

Reports considered by the Economic and Social Council in connection with the question of international co-operation and co-ordination within the United Nations system

At its 40th plenary meeting, on 28 July 1983, the Council took note of the following reports:

(a) Annual overview report of the Administrative Committee on Co-ordination for 1982/83;

(b) Report of the Administrative Committee on Co-ordination on the strengthening of the co-ordination of information systems in the United Nations system;

(c) Report of the Secretary-General on the implications of declaring an international year for the mobilization of financial and technological resources for food and agriculture in Africa;

(d) Report of the Secretary-General on co-operation between the United Nations and the Agency for Cultural and Technical Co-operation.

Economic and Social Council decision 1983/175

Adopted without vote

Approved by Third Committee (E/1983/120/Add.1) without vote, 27 July (meeting 19); oral proposal by Chairman; agenda item 19.
Meeting number. ESC 40.

CPC activities

In 1983, CPC met in New York for a series of organizational meetings on 11 and 29 April, and for its twenty-third session, the first part held from 9 May to 4 June, and the second from 29 August to 12 September.[4]

At that session, CPC considered an in-depth evaluation of the work of the Department of Public Information and reviewed the activities of the Joint United Nations Information Committee (see POLITICAL AND SECURITY QUESTIONS, Chapter X). A summary of an evaluation study of the technical co-operation activities of UNIDO in manufactures was considered, as were elements of the UNIDO work programme for 1984-1985 on which CPC made recommendations (see Chapter VI of this section). CPC followed up on implementation of its 1982 recommendations on the mineral resources programme and examined a cross-organizational programme analysis in marine affairs (see Chapter IX of this section). Special attention was given to the evaluation of the performance of the Information Systems Unit in DIESA, especially in terms of its coverage of and services to the regional commissions (see below), and to co-ordination of food and agriculture activities of the Food and Agriculture Organization of the United Nations (FAO) and the Economic and Social Commission for Asia and the Pacific (ESCAP) (see Chapter VIII of this section).

Examination of the programme aspects of the substantive sections of the proposed programme budget for the 1984-1985 biennium, as well as of its foreword and introduction made up the bulk of CPC's work. The Committee also considered various aspects of programme planning, budgeting and evaluation, including proposed rules for planning, changes in the medium-term plan for 1984-1989, statements of programme budget implications for proposed new activities, and institutional arrangements for evaluation within the Secretariat (see ADMINISTRATIVE AND BUDGETARY QUESTIONS, Chapter II).

Two ACC reports, on strengthening the co-ordination of United Nations information systems (see ADMINISTRATIVE AND BUDGETARY QUESTIONS, Chapter IV) and on the Joint Meetings of CPC and ACC (see below), were also examined, in addition to the 1982/83 ACC annual report (see above).

Owing to a delay in the issuance of parts of the proposed 1984-1985 programme budget, the CPC's work was seriously affected. Therefore, on 25 May 1983, it recommended that the Economic and Social Council authorize a resumed session, in August/September. This decision, taken after the Secretariat advised that the costs could be absorbed within existing resources, was conveyed by the Chairman to the Council President on 26 May.[5]

ECONOMIC AND SOCIAL COUNCIL ACTION

On an oral proposal by its President, the Economic and Social Council adopted decision 1983/160 without vote.

Resumed twenty-third session of the Committee for Programme and Co-ordination

At its 15th plenary meeting, on 27 May 1983, the Council decided:

(a) To authorize the Committee for Programme and Co-ordination, on an exceptional basis, to hold a resumed session from 29 August to 9 September 1983;

(b) Further, to authorize the Committee for Programme and Co-ordination to submit the second part of its report, on its resumed twenty-third session, directly to the General Assembly at its thirty-eighth session.

Economic and Social Council decision 1983/160

Adopted without vote

Oral proposal by President; agenda item 1.
Meeting number. ESC 15.

The report of CPC on the first part of its 1983 session was considered at the July session of the Council during the Third Committee's discussion of the agenda item on international co-operation and co-ordination within the United Nations system.

On the Committee's recommendation, the Council adopted resolution 1983/49 without vote on 28 July.

Report of the Committee for Programme and Co-ordination on its twenty-third session

The Economic and Social Council,

Having considered the report of the Committee for Programme and Co-ordination on the first part of its twenty-third session,

I

Endorses the recommendations and conclusions contained therein;

II

Technical co-operation activities of the United Nations Industrial Development Organization financed by the United Nations Development Programme in the field of manufactures

1. *Notes* that the evaluation of the technical co-operation activities of the United Nations Industrial Development Organization financed by the United Nations Development Programme in the field of manufactures was requested by the Committee for Programme and Co-ordination at its twentieth session, in 1980;

2. *Further notes* that the stated design and methodology of the evaluation study was endorsed by the Committee for Programme and Co-ordination at its twenty-second session, in 1982, and was then adopted by the General Assembly at its thirty-seventh session;

3. *Confirms* the importance it attaches to the evaluation procedures;

4. *Regrets* that the comprehensive outcome of the evaluation study was not submitted formally as a report of the Secretary-General to the Committee for Programme and Co-ordination at its twenty-third session,

as requested by the Committee and the General Assembly;

5. *Requests* the Secretary-General to submit formally the evaluation study to the Committee for Programme and Co-ordination at its resumed twenty-third session, on the understanding that his comprehensive report will be submitted to the Committee at its twenty-fourth session;

6. *Requests* the Secretary-General to ensure that the procedure followed on this occasion, namely the submission of an evaluation report to organizations or bodies covered by the evaluation before formal submission to the Committee for Programme and Co-ordination, shall not constitute a precedent for future evaluations;

III

Strengthening the capacity of the United Nations evaluation units and systems and timetable for review of evaluation programmes requested under General Assembly resolutions 36/228 B and 37/234

Requests the Advisory Committee on Administrative and Budgetary Questions to transmit to the General Assembly at its thirty-eighth session its review of the report of the Secretary-General on the strengthening of the capacity of the United Nations evaluation units and systems and a timetable for review of evaluation programmes, requested under General Assembly resolution 36/228 B of 18 December 1981 and section II of Assembly resolution 37/234 of 21 December 1982, pursuant to paragraph 191 of the report of the Committee for Programme and Co-ordination on the first part of its twenty-third session;

IV

Methods and procedures for the provision of statements of programme implications to the General Assembly

1. *Reiterates* the request to the Secretary-General, as contained in paragraph 7 *(b)* of section II of General Assembly resolution 37/234, to take the necessary measures to provide the Assembly at its thirty-eighth session with programme implications of draft resolutions being considered by the Assembly;

2. *Emphasizes* the importance of the recommendation contained in paragraph 166 of the report of the Committee for Programme and Co-ordination, to the effect that the programme budget statement should be an integrated report merging programme, financial and administrative implications of draft resolutions;

V

Proposed programme budget for the biennium 1984-1985: foreword and introduction

Requests the Secretary-General also to ensure the submission of the report on measures for the further integration of the programme planning, budgeting, monitoring and evaluation functions in the Secretariat of the United Nations, requested in paragraph 9 of section II of General Assembly resolution 37/234, to the Assembly at its thirty-eighth session through the Committee for Programme and Co-ordination at its resumed twenty-third session;

VI

Proposed programme budget for the biennium 1984-1985: United Nations Industrial Development Organization

1. *Endorses* the recommendations contained in paragraph 286 *(c)* and *(d)* of the report of the Committee for Programme and Co-ordination, on the understanding that follow-up work on wood and the wood products in-

dustry, industrial financing, and trade and trade-related aspects of industrial collaboration arrangements will be carried out by the United Nations Industrial Development Organization if necessary, in accordance with its programme of work, subject to a decision by the Industrial Development Board;

2. *Requests* the Secretary-General to report to the Committee for Programme and Co-ordination at its twenty-fourth session on questions raised at its twenty-third session concerning the various programme elements, in order to enable the Committee to review the issues relating to the avoidance of duplication and the achievement of a more rational organization of the work programme of the United Nations Industrial Development Organization, in anticipation of the conversion of that organization to specialized agency status.

Economic and Social Council resolution 1983/49

28 July 1983   Meeting 40   Adopted without vote

Approved by Third Committee (E/1983/120) without vote, 22 July (meeting 16); draft by Vice-Chairman (E/1983/C.3/L.14), based on informal consultations; agenda item 19.
Meeting number. ESC 40.

On 29 July, the Council, by section I of decision 1983/184, decided to maintain for two further years discontinuance of summary records for a number of its subsidiary bodies, including CPC.

GENERAL ASSEMBLY ACTION

On 20 December 1983, acting without vote on the recommendation of its Fifth (Administrative and Budgetary) Committee, the General Assembly adopted resolution 38/227 B.

Co-ordination within the United Nations system

The General Assembly,

Recalling its resolution 32/197 of 20 December 1977,

Aware of the need for continuous improvement in the effectiveness of the co-ordination of the activities of the United Nations system,

I

Conclusions and recommendations of the Committee for Programme and Co-ordination

1. *Endorses* the conclusions and recommendations of the Committee for Programme and Co-ordination at its twenty-third session on the annual report of the Administrative Committee on Co-ordination for 1982-1983;

2. *Endorses* the conclusions and recommendations of the Committee for Programme and Co-ordination at its twenty-third session and Economic and Social Council resolution 1983/50 and decision 1983/173 of 28 July 1983 on the Joint Meetings of the Committee for Programme and Co-ordination and the Administrative Committee on Co-ordination;

3. *Requests* the Economic and Social Council to include in its review of the functioning of the Joint Meetings of the Committee for Programme and Co-ordination and the Administrative Committee on Co-ordination, at its organizational session for 1984, consideration of the question of and application of paragraph 12 of General Assembly resolution 31/93 of 14 December 1976;

4. *Endorses* the conclusions and recommendations of the Committee for Programme and Co-ordination at its

twenty-third session on the cross-organizational programme analysis of marine affairs and on future cross-
organizational programme analyses;

5. *Requests* the Committee for Programme and Co-
ordination at its twenty-fourth session and the Economic
and Social Council at its second regular session of 1984
to review the initial report on the cross-organizational
programme analysis of economic and technical co-
operation among developing countries;

6. *Endorses* Economic and Social Council resolutions
1983/76, 1983/77 and 1983/78 of 29 July 1983 relating
to the cross-organizational reviews of selected major sectors in the medium-term plans of the organizations of
the United Nations system;

7. *Endorses* the recommendation of the Committee
for Programme and Co-ordination at its twenty-third
session on the co-ordination of food and agriculture activities in Asia and the Pacific by the Economic and Social Commission for Asia and the Pacific and the Food
and Agriculture Organization of the United Nations;

II

*Other conclusions and recommendations of the
Committee for Programme and Co-ordination*

Notes with satisfaction and endorses the other conclusions
and recommendations of the Committee for Programme
and Co-ordination at its twenty-third session on the programme and plan of activities of the Joint United
Nations Information Committee, on the implementation of the recommendations made on the mineral
resources programme by the Committee for Programme
and Co-ordination at its twenty-second session, and on
the report of the Administrative Committee on Co-
ordination on the strengthening of the co-ordination of
information systems in the United Nations system;

III

*Implications of the recommendations of the
Committee for Programme and Co-ordination*

Takes note of the report of the Secretary-General on
the programme, financial and administrative implications of the recommendations of the Committee for Programme and Co-ordination.

General Assembly resolution 38/227 B

20 December 1983   Meeting 104   Adopted without vote

Approved by Fifth Committee (A/38/727) without vote, 12 December (meeting 61);
    draft by Vice-Chairman (A/C.5/38/L.18, part B), based on informal consultations
    and orally revised, approved together with part A (see resolution 38/227 A);
    agenda item 110.
Financial implications. S-G, EAC.51/1983/L.6.
Meeting numbers. GA 38th session: 5th Committee 7, 12-23, 26-32, 34-37, 39,
    40, 42-44, 46, 52, 54, 60, 61; plenary 104.

In resolution 38/227 A, also of 20 December,
the Assembly requested the Secretary-General to
include, in his review of the operation, structure
and performance of the Secretariat, information
on measures taken to maximize and improve
secretariat support to CPC, taking into account
CPC recommendations calling for substantive servicing to promote effective follow-up to CPC decisions and the Joint Meetings of ACC and CPC;
fostering relations of mutual support between the
work of CPC and that of secretariat and other bodies dealing with programme budgeting and co-

ordination; and rationalizing the current support
structure, including the possibility of setting up
a small CPC secretariat.

Joint Meetings of CPC and ACC

CPC and ACC held the eighteenth in their series of Joint Meetings at Geneva on 4 and 5 July
1983.[6] In accordance with decisions taken by
CPC at the first part of its 1983 session, the Meetings were devoted primarily to an examination of
economic and technical co-operation among developing countries (see Chapter I of this section).
Ways of improving the effectiveness of the Meetings were also examined, in particular the need
for an earlier decision on topics for discussion, a
better structuring of the Meetings and follow-up
of their conclusions.

Unable to give exhaustive treatment to the
primary topic, the Joint Meetings agreed to take
it up at a future date, based on its consideration
by ACC and CPC, at their respective next meetings
during the year, and on a review to be conducted
by United Nations organizations of their work in
this area.

As to improving the functioning of the Joint
Meetings, it was agreed that at least six months
should elapse between the selection of a topic for
discussion and the date of the Meetings, to allow
identification of the crucial issues for debate and
preparation of proper documentation. It was further agreed that a systematic follow-up of recommendations be made to ensure their translation
into action.

ECONOMIC AND SOCIAL COUNCIL ACTION

In resolution 1983/50 of 28 July on the 1983
Joint Meetings, the Economic and Social Council requested the Secretary-General to ensure that
the cross-organizational programme analysis of
United Nations activities in economic and technical co-operation, scheduled for review in 1985,
take account of the system-wide support towards
implementation of the Caracas Programme of Action (adopted by a 1981 High Level Conference
on Economic Co-operation among Developing
Countries convened by the Group of 77 developing countries).[7] The Council recommended that
the initial report on the analysis requested by CPC
be submitted through CPC to the General Assembly in 1984.

On the same date, the Council, acting without
vote on the recommendation of its Third Committee, adopted decision 1983/173.

Joint Meetings of the Committee for Programme and Co-ordination and the Administrative Committee on Co-ordination

At its 40th plenary meeting, on 28 July 1983, the
Council, recalling General Assembly resolution 34/214
of 19 December 1979, paragraph *(c)* of Council deci-

sion 1979/67 of 3 August 1979 and Council decision 1980/185 of 25 July 1980 regarding the improvement of communication between the Administrative Committee on Co-ordination and intergovernmental bodies, decided to review, at its organizational session for 1984, the functioning of the Joint Meetings of the Committee for Programme and Co-ordination and the Administrative Committee on Co-ordination, and to request the Committee for Programme and Co-ordination, at its resumed twenty-third session, and the Administrative Committee on Co-ordination, at its second regular session of 1983, to submit their comments in this regard to the Council at its organizational session for 1984.

Economic and Social Council decision 1983/173

Adopted without vote

Approved by Third Committee (E/1983/120) without vote, 22 July (meeting 16); draft by Vice-Chairman (E/1983/C.3/L.13), based on informal consultations; agenda item 19.
Meeting number. ESC 40.

CPC action. Responding to the Council's request of 28 July, CPC, at the second part of its 1983 session, considered the question of improving the effectiveness of the Joint Meetings.

CPC concluded that the agenda be agreed on at least six months in advance and, if possible, decided on at the previous year's Meetings. The subject of a cross-organizational analysis on the CPC agenda, if one of system-wide concern, should be included in the Meeting's agenda for the same year. At each series of Joint Meetings, ACC should report on measures taken in response to the previous Meetings' recommendations and adequate time should be provided for a complete discussion of such report. CPC also recommended that documents of ACC and its subsidiary bodies be made available to Member States on request.

ACC action. At its October 1983 session, ACC adopted a statement[8] by which it supported the CPC recommendation for an early agreement on the agenda to ensure adequate preparation. It recommended that specific questions be identified and topics defined, to provide a clear focus for discussion. ACC suggested that the Meetings might more usefully explore issues of overall co-ordination and co-operation, rather than examine programmes in detail, a function better served in other forums. An outline of themes for discussion, using the relevant cross-organizational analyses as background, would enhance dialogue on issues of system-wide concern. As to the discussion format, "set-piece" presentation should be avoided in favour of exchanges of views. Response to the Meetings' recommendations could be reported on by the ACC Chairman in his introductory statement, leaving open possible further discussion. To improve on full access to its reports and those of its subsidiary machinery, already provided by existing arrangements, ACC would annex a list of such documents to its annual overview report.

Cross-organizational programme analyses

In its annual report for 1982/83,[2] ACC noted that the final draft of a cross-organizational programme analysis in marine affairs was reviewed by an *ad hoc* inter-agency meeting in February 1983. The Secretary-General submitted a report on the analysis to CPC at its 1983 session (see Chapter IX of this section), as well as a report on co-ordination of ESCAP and FAO activities in food and agriculture in Asia and the Pacific (see Chapter VIII of this section). In preparation for a cross-organizational analysis of human settlements activities, a note outlining the current distribution of such activities was presented to the Commission on Human Settlements for review during the year (see Chapter XVII of this section). ACC had carried out an overall review of results, methodology, effectiveness and evolution of cross-organizational programme analyses since their inception, aimed at making them more useful instruments of programming and co-ordination.

At the first part of its 1983 session,[4] CPC recommended that future cross-organizational programme analyses should bear closer relationship to programme planning, monitoring and evaluation. Suggested areas for analyses, to be presented to CPC in 1984, should take into account the feasibility of scheduling simultaneous consideration of evaluations, analyses and plan reviews on the same subject. Also, the Secretariat should continue to seek the views of States on priorities for action when undertaking an analysis.

These recommendations were endorsed by the General Assembly on 20 December, in resolution 38/227 B, in which it also requested the Economic and Social Council and CPC to review in 1984 an initial report on the cross-organizational analysis of economic and technical co-operation among developing countries.

Medium-term plans

In 1983, a series of cross-sectoral reviews of selected major issues in the medium-term plans of organizations in the United Nations system was initiated. The first two reviews were on food and agriculture, and population, on which the Secretary-General reported to the Economic and Social Council at its July 1983 session (see Chapters IX and XIV of this section). This was in keeping with both a July 1982 Council resolution,[9] by which it decided to review, every six years, selected major issues in the organizations' proposed medium-term plans, and with the Council's work programme for 1983-1984 (see below).

ECONOMIC AND SOCIAL COUNCIL ACTION

Acting without vote on the recommendation of its Third Committee, the Economic and Social Council adopted resolution 1983/78 on 29 July

1983. Prior to adoption, the President stated that the purpose of the resolution was to clarify the nature of the cross-sectoral reviews called for by the 1982 Council resolution.[9] The Committee had approved the text on the understanding that the future reviews would be described as "cross-organizational", instead of "cross-sectoral".

This resolution was endorsed by the General Assembly on 20 December, in resolution 38/227 B.

Cross-organizational review of selected major sectors in the medium-term plans of the organizations of the United Nations system

The Economic and Social Council,

Conscious of its role in co-ordinating the economic and social activities of the United Nations system under the Charter of the United Nations and relevant General Assembly resolutions, particularly resolution 32/197 of 20 December 1977,

Recalling its resolution 1982/50 of 28 July 1982 on the revitalization of the Council, and recognizing the need to clarify the nature of the reviews provided for in paragraph 1 (*f*) of that resolution,

1. *Decides* to review, starting in 1985, on a biennial basis, one or more major sectors, taking account of the medium-term plans of, or equivalent documents and information from, the organs, organizations and bodies of the United Nations system;

2. *Further decides,* in order to allow sufficient lead time for the preparation of documents and necessary financial data, to select the sector or sectors for review in 1985 at its organizational session for 1984, and to follow the same procedure for future reviews, taking into account the topics for cross-organizational programme analyses selected for review by the Committee for Programme and Co-ordination in the respective years;

3. *Requests* the Secretary-General to include in future reports specific conclusions and recommendations, based on an analytical assessment of the activities and programmes of the United Nations system in the selected sectors, in order to enable the Council to enhance its role in co-ordinating the activities and programmes of the system in the economic and social sectors.

Economic and Social Council resolution 1983/78

29 July 1983   Meeting 42   Adopted without vote

Approved by Third Committee (E/1983/128) without vote, 28 July (meeting 20); informal working paper by Chairman, orally revised; agenda item 21. *Meeting number.* ESC 42.

REFERENCES
[1]ACC/1983/INF/1. [2]E/1983/39. [3]E/1984/66. [4]A/38/38. [5]E/1983/81. [6]E/1983/98. [7]YUN 1981, p. 383. [8]ACC/1983/DEC/11-18 (dec. 1983/12). [9]YUN 1982, p. 1241, ESC res. 1982/50, 28 July 1982.

Economic and Social Council

Proposed organizational change

Pursuant to a July 1982 Economic and Social Council resolution,[1] the President gave an oral report to the Council on 22 July 1983 on consultations he had undertaken in preparation for the General Assembly's consideration in 1984 of the restructuring of the economic and social sectors of the United Nations system. The consultations had been held with various heads of delegations or group spokesmen, beginning with representatives of the five permanent members of the Security Council. The report represented the President's assessment of those consultations and included a number of suggestions, some of which he felt would be ripe for action in the near future.

The President stated that the issue of universal membership of the Economic and Social Council had aroused resistance for institutional and practical reasons: it would require an amendment to the Charter of the United Nations, and while the current membership level had been recognized as limiting the use of the Council's machinery, it had been equally recognized as facilitating the negotiating process. No clear view had emerged on the issue of holding special sessions devoted exclusively to certain topics, but it had been strongly felt that, to meet this need, the Council should take advantage of the rule in its rules of procedure providing for such sessions.

Among the suggestions advanced by delegations were: greater use of the Council to alleviate the burden of the Assembly's Second Committee; continuous implementation of the July 1982 Council resolution and the 1977 Assembly resolution on restructuring,[2] and also of the December 1982 Assembly resolution on the Organization's work;[3] strengthening of the Council's co-ordinating role; examination of the usefulness of closer JIU involvement in that role, as well as of the usefulness of the ACC/CPC Joint Meetings as an instrument of co-ordination; and establishment of an open-ended inter-sessional working group to prepare for the deliberations of the Council on its revitalization.

Other suggestions called for pursuing the direct question-and-answer exchange, such as had taken place at the current session between delegations and the executive secretaries of the regional commissions, and widening its scope to include the heads of specialized agencies; eliminating debates on reports already undertaken by the reporting subsidiary bodies, and the general debate at the second regular session; focusing on selected subjects—leaving political issues to the Assembly—and improving the analytical quality of the relevant documentation; and substantially reducing the number of proposed resolutions and decisions. A renewed examination was recommended of the proposed alternatives to the Council's system of holding a spring session in New York and a summer session at Geneva, notably the proposal for a single annual but longer session to be held in New York or alternately between New York and Geneva. A rationalization of the calendar of meetings of the subsidiary bodies of the Council and those of the Assembly reporting through the Council was also advocated.

ECONOMIC AND SOCIAL COUNCIL ACTION

In July, the Economic and Social Council adopted two decisions on the issue of its revitalization: 1983/165, taking note of the President's oral presentation; and 1983/181, requesting him to continue informal consultations.

The Council adopted decision 1983/165 without vote.

Oral report by the President on the revitalization of the Economic and Social Council

At its 38th plenary meeting, on 22 July 1983, the Council took note of the oral report on the revitalization of the Council made by the President in pursuance of Council resolution 1982/50 of 28 July 1982.

Economic and Social Council decision 1983/165

Adopted without vote

Oral proposal by President; agenda item 4.
Meeting number. ESC 38.

The Council adopted decision 1983/181 without vote.

Revitalization of the Economic and Social Council

At its 41st plenary meeting, on 29 July 1983, the Council, bearing in mind the oral report made by the President at its second regular session of 1983, in pursuance of Council resolution 1982/50 of 28 July 1982, decided to request the President to continue his informal consultations with delegations on the question of the revitalization of the Council, and to report to it thereon in 1984.

Economic and Social Council decision 1983/181

Adopted without vote

Draft by Vice-President (E/1983/L.41), based on informal consultations; agenda item 4.
Meeting numbers. ESC 39, 41.

Prior to adopting decision 1983/181, the Council adopted, by a roll-call vote of 30 to 11, with 9 abstentions, a motion by Tunisia not to take action on a revised draft decision introduced by Mexico.[4] By that text, the Council would have requested a report from the Secretary-General on the practical implications of the alternative formats of Council meetings, as orally presented by the President, for its consideration in 1984.

Co-operation with other organizations

Non-governmental organizations

The Economic and Social Council's Committee on Non-Governmental Organizations met three times in 1983—in New York between 7 and 18 February[5] and on 3 May,[6] and at Geneva on 7 July.[7]

In February, the Committee reviewed applications from NGOs for consultative status with the Council, recommending 24 of them for category II consultative status and 16 for the Roster. The reclassification of one organization from the Roster to category II and the withdrawal of consultative status from another were also recommended.

Owing to lack of time, the Committee deferred consideration of the quadrennial reports submitted by 20 NGOs in categories I and II on their United Nations–related activities during 1978-1981,[8] as well as action concerning those that had failed to submit such reports.

In May and July, the Committee heard requests from NGOs with consultative status to address the Council or its committees in connection with items on the Council's agenda. Four organizations in category I and one in category II were recommended to be heard at the Council's May session, and nine in Category I at its July session. In connection with these hearings, the Council received statements submitted in 1983 by seven NGOs[9] concerning specific areas of its work.

ECONOMIC AND SOCIAL COUNCIL ACTION

In May, on the recommendation of the Committee on NGOs, the Economic and Social Council adopted two decisions concerning the consultative status of NGOs.

Decision 1983/109 was adopted without vote.

Applications for consultative status and requests for reclassification received from non-governmental organizations

At its 5th plenary meeting, on 12 May 1983, the Council, having considered the report of the Committee on Non-Governmental Organizations, decided:

(*a*) To grant the following non-governmental organizations consultative status:

Category II

Academy of Criminal Justice Sciences (ACJS)
African Association of Education for Development (AFASED)
African Institute of Private International Law
Children's Own Garden International
Disabled Peoples' International
Elders' Circle of the Four Directions (Elders' Circle)
Federation of Associations of Former International Civil Servants (FAFICS)
Geneva Informal Meeting of International Youth Non-Governmental Organizations (GIM)
Human Rights Internet (HRI)
International Driving Tests Committee (IDTC)
International Federation of Associations of the Elderly
International Federation of Disabled Workers and Civilian Handicapped
International Federation of the Little Brothers of the Poor
International Institute of Humanitarian Law
International Society for Research on Aggression (ISRA)
Inuit Circumpolar Conference

Latin American Association of Development Organizations
Latin American Council of Catholic Women
Parliamentarians for World Order
Prison Fellowship International (PFI)
Stichting Greenpeace Council
World Federation of Development Financing Institutions
World Federation of Methodist Women (WFMW)
Worldview International Foundation

Roster

Asian Cultural Forum on Development (ACFOD)
Brahma Kumaris World Spiritual University
Canadian Comprehensive Auditing Foundation (CCAF)
Defense for Children International Movement
Electoral Reform Society of Great Britain and Ireland
Indian Council of South America (CISA)
Institute of International Education, Inc. (IIE)
International Association of University Presidents
International Halfway House Association (IHHA)
International Human Rights Internship Program
International Institute for Research and Advice on Mental Deficiency (IAMER)
International Organization of Psychophysiology (IOP)
International Women's Anthropology Conference, Inc. (IWAC)
Islamic Chamber of Commerce, Industry and Commodity Exchange (ICCICE)
Soka Gakkai International
SOS-Kinderdorf International

   (b) To reclassify the International Union of Students from the Roster to category II consultative status.

Economic and Social Council decision 1983/109
                                              Adopted without vote
Draft by Committee on NGOs (E/1983/11), orally amended by President; agenda item 3.

Meeting numbers. ESC 4, 5.

The Council adopted decision 1983/110 without vote.

Withdrawal of consultative status

At its 5th plenary meeting, on 12 May 1983, the Council decided to withdraw consultative status from the International Organization—Justice and Development.

Economic and Social Council decision 1983/110
                                              Adopted without vote
Draft by Committee on NGOs (E/1983/11); agenda item 3.
Meeting numbers. ESC 4, 5.

As a result of the Council's decisions and other additions to the Roster, the number of NGOs in consultative status with the Council rose to 692 during the year (see list below).[10] They were divided into three groups: category I, organizations representative of major population segments in a large number of countries, involved with the economic and social life of the areas they represented; category II, international organizations having special competence in a few of the Council's areas of activity; and organizations on the Roster, considered able to make occasional and useful contributions to the Council's work.

On 26 May 1983, the Council, in resolution 1983/28, requested the Secretary-General, the regional commissions and Governments to invite interested NGOs in consultative status with the Council to participate in preparations for the World Conference to Review and Appraise the Achievements of the United Nations Decade for Women, scheduled for 1985.

NGOs in consultative status with the Economic and Social Council

(as at 31 December 1983)

Category I

International Alliance of Women—Equal Rights, Equal Responsibilities
International Association of French-Speaking Parliamentarians
International Chamber of Commerce
International Confederation of Free Trade Unions
International Co-operative Alliance
International Council of Voluntary Agencies (ICVA)
International Council of Women
International Council on Social Welfare
International Federation of Agricultural Producers
International Federation of Business and Professional Women
International Organization for Standardization (IOS)
International Organization of Consumers Unions (IOCU)
International Organization of Employers
International Planned Parenthood Federation
International Social Security Association (ISSA)

International Union of Local Authorities (IULA)
International Youth and Student Movement for the United Nations (ISMUN)
Inter-Parliamentary Union
League of Red Cross Societies
Muslim World League
Organization of African Trade Union Unity (OATUU)
Society for International Development (SID)
United Towns Organization
Women's International Democratic Federation
World Assembly of Youth (WAY)
World Confederation of Labour
World Federation of Democratic Youth (WFDY)
World Federation of Trade Unions (WFTU)
World Federation of United Nations Associations (WFUNA)
World Muslim Congress
World Veterans Federation

Category II

Academy of Criminal Justice Sciences (ACJS)
African Association of Education for Development (AFASED)
African Institute of Private International Law
Afro-Asian Peoples' Solidarity Organization (AAPSO)
AFS International/Intercultural Programs, Inc. (formerly American Field Service)
Agudas Israel World Organization
Airport Associations Co-ordinating Council (AACC)
All-India Women's Conference
All Pakistan Women's Association
Amnesty International
Anti-*Apartheid* Movement, The
Anti-Slavery Society for the Protection of Human Rights, The
Arab Lawyers Union
Associated Country Women of the World
Association for Childhood Education International
Association for the Study of the World Refugee Problem
Bahá'i International Community
Baptist World Alliance
CARE (Cooperative for American Relief Everywhere, Inc.)
Caritas Internationalis (International Confederation of Catholic Charities)
Carnegie Endowment for International Peace
Catholic Relief Services—United States Catholic Conference, Inc.
Chamber of Commerce of the United States of America
Children's Own Garden International
Christian Democratic World Union
Christian Peace Conference
Church World Service, Inc.
Commission of the Churches on International Affairs of the World Council of Churches
Commonwealth Human Ecology Council (CHEC)
Conference of European Churches (CEC)
Consultative Council of Jewish Organizations
Co-ordinating Board of Jewish Organizations (CBJO)
Co-ordinating Committee for International Voluntary Service
Council of European and Japanese National Shipowners Association, The (CENSA)
Democratic Youth Community of Europe
Disabled Peoples' International
Eastern Regional Organization for Public Administration (EROPA)
Environment Liaison Centre
European Association of National Productivity Centres
European Insurance Committee
European League for Economic Co-operation
European Organization for Quality Control (EOQC)
Experiment in International Living, The
Federation for the Respect of Man and Humanity
Federation of Arab Economists, The
Federation of Arab Scientific Research Councils
Federation of Associations of Former International Civil Servants (FAFICS)
Foundation for the Peoples of the South Pacific, Inc., The
Four Directions Council (formerly Elders' Circle of the Four Directions)

Friends World Committee for Consultation
Geneva Informal Meeting of International Youth Non-Governmental Organizations (GIM)
Howard League for Penal Reform
Human Rights Internet (HRI)
Ibero-American Institute of Aeronautic and Space Law and Commercial Aviation
Institute for Policy Studies—Transnational
Institute of Electrical and Electronic Engineers, Inc.
Inter-American Federation of Public Relations Associations (IFPRA)
Inter-American Federation of Touring and Automobile Clubs (FITAC)
Inter-American Planning Society
Inter-American Press Association
Inter-American Statistical Institute
International Air Transport Association
International Association against Painful Experiments on Animals
International Association for Religious Freedom (IARF)
International Association for Social Progress
International Association for the Protection of Industrial Property
International Association for Water Law (IAWL)
International Association of Democratic Lawyers
International Association of Educators for World Peace
International Association of Juvenile and Family Court Magistrates
International Association of Penal Law
International Association of Ports and Harbours (IAPH)
International Association of Schools of Social Work
International Astronautical Federation
International Automobile Federation (FIA)
International Bar Association
International Cargo Handling Co-ordination Association
International Catholic Child Bureau
International Catholic Migration Commission
International Catholic Union of the Press
International Centre for Industry and the Environment (ICIE)
International Centre for Local Credit
International Centre of Social Gerontology
International Chamber of Shipping
International Christian Union of Business Executives (UNIAPAC)
International Civil Airports Association
International College of Surgeons
International Commission of Jurists
International Commission on Irrigation and Drainage
International Committee for European Security and Co-operation
International Committee of the Red Cross
International Co-operation for Socio-Economic Development (CIDSE)
International Co-ordinating Committee of Financial Analysts' Associations
International Council for Adult Education (ICAE)
International Council for Building Research, Studies and Documentation
International Council of Environmental Law
International Council of Jewish Women
International Council of Monuments and Sites (ICOMOS)
International Council of Scientific Unions

International Council of Societies of Industrial Design (ICSID)
International Council on Alcohol and Addictions
International Council on Jewish Social and Welfare Services
International Defence and Aid Fund for Southern Africa
International Driving Tests Committee (IDTC)
International Electrotechnical Commission
International Federation for Home Economics (IFHE)
International Federation for Housing and Planning
International Federation of Associations of the Elderly
International Federation of Beekeepers' Associations
International Federation of Disabled Workers and Civilian Handicapped
International Federation of Human Rights
International Federation of Journalists
International Federation of Landscape Architects
International Federation of Resistance Movements
International Federation of Senior Police Officers
International Federation of Settlements and Neighbourhood Centres
International Federation of Social Workers
International Federation of the Little Brothers of the Poor
International Federation of University Women
International Federation of Women in Legal Careers
International Federation of Women Lawyers
International Federation on Aging
International Fellowship of Reconciliation
International Hotel Association
International Indian Treaty Council
International Institute for Vital Registration and Statistics (IIVRS)
International Institute of Administrative Sciences
International Institute of Humanitarian Law
International Islamic Federation of Student Organizations
International Law Association
International League for Human Rights
International League of Societies for Persons with Mental Handicap
International Movement ATD Fourth World
International Movement for Fraternal Union among Races and Peoples (UFER)
International Organization for the Elimination of All Forms of Racial Discrimination (EAFORD)
International Organization of Journalists
International Organization of Supreme Audit Institutions (INTOSAI)
International Petroleum Industry Environmental Conservation Association (IPIECA)
International Prisoners Aid Association
International Road Federation
International Road Transport Union
International Rural Housing Association
International Savings Banks Institute
International Senior Citizens Association, Inc., The
International Social Service
International Society for Criminology
International Society for Research on Aggression (ISRA)
International Society of Social Defence
International Statistical Institute
International Touring Alliance
International Union for Child Welfare

International Union for Conservation of Nature and Natural Resources
International Union for Inland Navigation
International Union for the Scientific Study of Population
International Union of Architects
International Union of Building Societies and Savings Associations
International Union of Family Organizations
International Union of Latin Notariat
International Union of Lawyers
International Union of Producers and Distributors of Electrical Energy
International Union of Public Transport
International Union of Students
International Union of Young Christian Democrats (IUYCD)
International Young Christian Workers
Inuit Circumpolar Conference
Jaycees International
Latin American Association of Development Organizations
Latin American Association of Finance Development Institutions (ALIDE)
Latin American Council of Catholic Women
Latin American Iron and Steel Institute
Law Association for Asia and the Western Pacific (LAWASIA)
Lions International—The International Association of Lions Clubs
Lutheran World Federation
Mutual Assistance of the Latin American Government Oil Companies (ARPEL)
Organization for International Economic Relations (IER)
OXFAM (Oxford Committee for Famine Relief)
Pan-African Institute for Development
Pan-African Women's Organization
Pan American Federation of Engineering Societies (UPADI)
Pan-Pacific and South-East Asia Women's Association
Parliamentarians for World Order
Pax Christi, International Catholic Peace Movement
Pax Romana
   (International Catholic Movement for Intellectual and Cultural Affairs)
   (International Movement of Catholic Students)
Permanent International Association of Road Congresses (PIARC)
Prison Fellowship International (PFI)
Rädda Barnen International (Save the Children Federation)
Rehabilitation International
St. Joan's International Alliance
Salvation Army, The
Save the Children Federation
Socialist International
Socialist International Women (SIW)
Société internationale de prophylaxie criminelle
Society for Comparative Legislation
Soroptimist International
Stichting Greenpeace Council
Studies and Expansion Society—International Scientific Association (SEC)
Third World Foundation
Union of Arab Jurists

Union of International Associations
Union of International Fairs
United Kingdom Standing Conference on the Second United Nations Development Decade
Universal Federation of Travel Agents Associations
Vienna Institute for Development
War Resisters International
Women's International League for Peace and Freedom
Women's International Zionist Organization
World Alliance of Young Men's Christian Associations
World Association of Former United Nations Interns and Fellows
World Association of Girl Guides and Girl Scouts
World Association of World Federalists
World Confederation of Organizations of the Teaching Profession
World Conference on Religion and Peace
World Council for the Welfare of the Blind
World Council of Credit Unions, Inc. (WOCCU)
World Council of Indigenous Peoples (WCIP)
World Council of Management
World Energy Conference
World Federation for Mental Health
World Federation of Catholic Youth
World Federation of Development Financing Institutions
World Federation of Methodist Women (WFMW)
World Federation of the Deaf
World Jewish Congress
World Leisure and Recreation Association
World Movement of Mothers
World Organization of the Scout Movement (World Scout Bureau)
World Peace Through Law Centre
World Population Society
World Society for the Protection of Animals
World Student Christian Federation
World Trade Centers Association
World Union for the Safeguard of Youth
World Union of Catholic Women's Organizations
World University Service
World Women's Christian Temperance Union
World Young Women's Christian Association
Worldview International Foundation
Zonta International

Roster

Organizations included by action of the Economic and Social Council

African Medical and Research Foundation
Altrusa International, Inc.
American Association of Engineering Societies, Inc. (formerly Engineers Joint Council)
American Foreign Insurance Association
American Foreign Law Association, Inc.
American Society for Engineering Education (ASEE)
Asian Cultural Forum on Development (ACFOD)
Asian Development Center (ADC)
Asian Youth Council
Association for World Education
Battelle Memorial Institute
Brahma Kumaris World Spiritual University
Bureau international de la récupération

Canadian Comprehensive Auditing Foundation (CCAF)
Caribbean Conservation Association
Catholic International Union for Social Service
Center for Inter-American Relations
Commission to Study the Organization of Peace
Committee for Economic Development
Committee for European Construction Equipment (CECE)
Confederation of Asian Chambers of Commerce
Congress of Racial Equality (CORE)
Council of European National Youth Committees (CENYC)
Council on Religion and International Affairs (CRIA)
Data for Development (DFD)
Defense for Children International Movement
Economic Research Committee of the Gas Industry (COMETEC-GAZ)
Electoral Reform Society of Great Britain and Ireland
Environmental Coalition for North America (ENCONA)
European Alliance of Press Agencies
European Association of Refrigeration Enterprises (AEEF)
European Confederation of Woodworking Industries
European Container Manufacturers' Committee
European Federation for the Welfare of the Elderly (EURAG)
European Liquefied Petroleum Gas Association
European Mediterranean Commission on Water Planning
European Union of Women
Ex-Volunteers International
Federation of European Manufacturers of Friction Materials
Federation of National Committees in the International Christian Youth Exchange
Foster Parents Plan International (PLAN)
Foundation for the Establishment of an International Criminal Court, The
Friedrich Ebert Foundation
Gray Panthers
Habitat International Council
Help the Aged
Indian Council of South America (CISA)
Indian Law Resource Centre
Institute of International Container Lessors
Institute of International Education, Inc. (IIE)
International Abolitionist Federation
International Association for Bridge and Structural Engineering
International Association for Community Development
International Association for Housing Science
International Association for Hydrogen Energy
International Association for Research into Income and Wealth
International Association for the Child's Right to Play
International Association for the Defence of Religious Liberty
International Association for the Exchange of Students for Technical Experience
International Association for the Promotion of Democracy under God (Pro Deo)
International Association of Airport and Seaport Police
International Association of Chiefs of Police
International Association of Gerontology
International Association of the Soap and Detergent Industry
International Association of University Presidents
International Board of Co-operation for the Developing Countries (EMCO)
International Bureau of Motor-Cycle Manufacturers
International Center for Dynamics of Development
International Committee against *Apartheid*, Racism and Colonialism in Southern Africa

International Committee of Outer Space Onomastics (ICOSO)
International Confederation for Disarmament and Peace
International Confederation of Associations of Experts and Consultants
International Container Bureau
International Council for Commercial Arbitration
International Council for Game and Wildlife Conservation
International Council of Psychologists
International Federation for Documentation
International Federation of Chemical Energy and General Workers' Unions
International Federation of Free Journalists
International Federation of Freight Forwarders Associations
International Federation of International Furniture Removers
International Federation of Operational Research Societies
International Federation of Pedestrians
International Federation of Rural Adult Catholic Movements
International Federation of Surveyors
International Federation of the Blind
International Fiscal Association
International Halfway House Association (IHHA)
International Human Rights Internship Program
International Hydatidological Association
International Inner Wheel
International Institute for Research and Advice on Mental Deficiency (IAMER)
International Institute of Public Finance
International Institute of Rural Reconstruction (IIRR)
International Iron and Steel Institute
International Juridical Organization (IJO)
International League for the Rights and Liberation of Peoples
International League of Surveillance Societies, The
International Olive Growers Federation
International Organization of Experts (ORDINEX)
International Organization of Psychophysiology (IOP)
International Peace Academy
International Peace Bureau
International Permanent Bureau of Automobile Manufacturers
International Police Association
International Press Institute (IPI)
International Prevention of Road Accidents
International Progress Organization (IPO)
International Public Relations Association (IPRA)
International Real Estate Federation
International Research Institute for Immigration and Emigration Politics
International Schools Association
International Shipping Federation (ISF)
International Society for Prosthetics and Orthotics
International Solar Energy Society
International Textile Manufacturers Federation
International Union of Judges
International Union of Marine Insurance
International Union of Police Federations
International Union of Social Democratic Teachers
International Union of Tenants
International Women's Anthropology Conference, Inc. (IWAC)
International Working Group for the Construction of Sports and Leisure Facilities
Islamic Chamber of Commerce, Industry and Commodity Exchange (ICCICE)

La Leche League International, Inc. (LLLI)
Latin American Confederation of Tourist Organizations (COTAL)
Latin American Official Workers' Confederation (CLATE)
Liberation
Minority Rights Group
Movement against Racism and for Friendship between Peoples
Movement for a Better World
National Organization for Women (NOW)
National Parks and Conservation Association
OISCA International (Organization for Industrial, Spiritual and Cultural Advancement International)
Open Door International (for the Economic Emancipation of the Woman Worker)
Overseas Education Fund of the League of Women Voters
Pan American Development Foundation
Permanent International Association of Navigation Congresses
Pio Mansú International Research Centre for Environmental Structures, The
Planetary Citizens
Population Council, The
Procedural Aspects of International Law Institute— International Human Rights Law Group
Program for the Introduction and Adaptation of Contraceptive Technology (sPIACT)
Quota International Incorporated
Romani Union
Rotary International
SERVAS International
Society for Social Responsibility in Science
Soka Gakkai International
SOS-Kinderdorf International
Survival International Ltd.
Transfrigoroute International (formerly Transfrigoroute Europe)
United Nations of Yoga (UNY)
United Schools International
United Way International
Universal Esperanto Association
World Alliance of Reformed Churches
World Association for Christian Communication
World Confederation for Physical Therapy
World Development Movement
World Environment and Resources Council (WERC)
World Federation of Christian Life Communities
World Federation of Health Agencies for the Advancement of Voluntary Surgical Contraception
World Mining Congress
World Union for Progressive Judaism
Young Lawyers' International Association (AIJA)

Organizations included by action of the Secretary-General

American Association for the Advancement of Science
Asian Environmental Society
Association for the Advancement of Agricultural Sciences in Africa
Center for Research on the New International Economic Order, The
Center of Concern
Committee for International Co-operation in National Research in Demography (CICRED)

Council for Development of Economic and Social Research in Africa, The (CODESRIA)

Fauna Preservation Society, The

Foresta Institute for Ocean and Mountain Studies

Friends of the Earth (FOE)

Institut de la vie

International Association against Noise

International Association on Water Pollution Research (IAWPR)

International Educational Development, Inc.

International Institute for Environment and Development

International Ocean Institute

International Society for Community Development

International Studies Association

International Union of Anthropological and Ethnological Sciences

International Women's Tribune Centre

National Audubon Society

Natural Resources Defence Council, Inc.

Population Crisis Committee

Population Institute

Sierra Club

Trilateral Commission, The

World Education

World Society for Ekistics

Organizations included because of consultative status with specialized agencies or other United Nations bodies

Organization	In consultative status with
African Adult Education Association	UNESCO
African Centre for Monetary Studies	UNCTAD
Arab Federation for Engineering Industries	UNCTAD
Arab Federation of Chemical Fertilizer Producers	UNIDO
Arab Iron and Steel Union (AISU)	UNIDO
Association of African Universities	UNESCO
Association of Arab Universities	UNESCO
Association of European Jute Industries	UNCTAD
Association of Partially and Wholly French-Language Universities	UNESCO
Association of West European Builders, The (AWES)	IMO
Baltic and International Maritime Conference, The	IMO, UNCTAD
B'nai B'rith International Council	UNESCO
Catholic International Education Office	UNESCO
Centre Europe–Tiers Monde (CETIM)	UNCTAD
Centre for Latin American Monetary Studies	UNCTAD

Organization	In consultative status with
Club de Dakar	FAO, UNIDO
Committee on Space Research (COSPAR)	ITU
Confederation of International Trading Houses Associations	UNCTAD
Co-ordination Committee for the Textile Industries in the European Economic Communities (COMITEXTIL)	UNCTAD
Council for International Organizations of Medical Sciences (CIOMS)	UNESCO, WHO
Engineering Committee on Oceanic Resources (ECOR)	IMO
European Academy of Arts, Sciences and Humanities	UNESCO
European Association for Animal Production	FAO
European Broadcasting Union	ITU, UNESCO
European Centre for International Co-operation (CECI)	UNIDO
European Computer Manufacturers Association	ITU
European Confederation of Agriculture	FAO, IAEA, ILO, UNESCO
European Council of Chemical Manufacturers' Federations	IMO, UNCTAD
European Federation of National Associations of Engineers	UNESCO, UNIDO
European Tea Committee	FAO
European Tugowners Association (ETA)	IMO
European Union of Public Relations	UNIDO
Federación Latinoamericana de Periodistas	UNESCO
Federation of Afro-Asian Insurers and Reinsurers	UNCTAD
Federation of Western European Rope and Twine Industries	UNCTAD
General Union of Chambers of Commerce, Industry and Agriculture for Arab Countries	UNCTAD
Institute of Air Transport	ICAO
Institute of International Law	ICAO
Institute on Man and Science	UNESCO
Inter-American Association of Broadcasters	ITU, UNESCO
International Academy of Pathology	WHO
International Aeronautical Federation	ICAO
International Agency for the Prevention of Blindness (Vision International)	WHO
International Amateur Radio Union	ITU
International Association for Cereal Chemistry (ICC)	FAO, UNIDO
International Association for Educational Assessment	UNESCO

Organization	In consultative status with	Organization	In consultative status with
International Association for Mass Communication Research	UNESCO	International Cocoa Trades Federation	UNCTAD
International Association for Suicide Prevention	WHO	International Commission on Illumination	ICAO, ILO
International Association for the Study of the Liver	WHO	International Commission on Radiological Protection (ICRP)	WHO
International Association of Agricultural Economists	UNCTAD	International Committee for Plastics in Agriculture	UNIDO
International Association of Agricultural Librarians and Documentalists	FAO	International Committee for Standardization in Haematology	WHO
International Association of Art (IAA)	UNESCO	International Committee of Catholic Nurses	ILO, WHO
International Association of Cancer Registries	WHO	International Confederation of European Beet Growers	UNCTAD
International Association of Classification Societies	IMO	International Confederation of Midwives	ILO, WHO
International Association of Conference Interpreters	ILO, UNESCO	International Conference of Historians of the Labour Movement	UNESCO
International Association of Crafts and Small and Medium-sized Enterprises	UNIDO	International Copyright Society	UNESCO
International Association of Drilling Contractors (IADC)	IMO	International Council for Distance Education	UNESCO
International Association of Dry Cargo Shipowners	UNCTAD	International Council for Philosophy and Humanistic Studies	UNESCO
International Association of Fish Meal Manufacturers	FAO	International Council of Aircraft Owner and Pilot Associations	ICAO
International Association of Horticultural Producers	FAO	International Council of Marine Industry Associations (ICOMIA)	IMO
International Association of Lighthouse Authorities	IMO, ITU	International Council of Nurses	ILO, UNESCO, WHO
International Association of Literary Critics	UNESCO		
International Association of Logopedics and Phoniatrics	UNESCO, WHO	International Council of Sport and Physical Education	UNESCO
International Association of Medical Laboratory Technologists (IAMLT)	WHO	International Council on Archives	UNESCO
International Association of Microbiological Societies	WHO	International Council on Education for Teaching	UNESCO
International Association of Mutual Insurance Companies	UNCTAD	International Cystic Fibrosis (Mucoviscidosis) Association	WHO
International Association of Students in Economics and Management	ILO, UNESCO	International Dairy Federation	FAO
		International Dental Federation	WHO
International Association of the Third Age Universities	ILO	International Diabetes Federation	WHO
International Association of Universities	UNESCO	International Epidemiological Association	WHO
International Association of University Professors and Lecturers	UNESCO	International Ergonomics Association	ILO, WHO
		International Falcon Movement	UNESCO
International Baccalaureate Office	UNESCO	International Federation for Information Processing	ITU, UNESCO, WHO
International Board on Books for Young People	UNESCO		
International Bureau of Social Tourism	ILO, UNESCO	International Federation for Medical and Biological Engineering	WHO
International Centre of Films for Children and Young People	UNESCO	International Federation for Parent Education	UNESCO

Organization	In consultative status with	Organization	In consultative status with
International Federation of Air Line Pilots Associations	ICAO, WMO	International Fertilizer Industry Association	FAO, IMO, UNCTAD, UNIDO
International Federation of Automatic Control	UNIDO	International Food Policy Research Institute	FAO, UNCTAD
International Federation of Catholic Universities	UNESCO	International Gas Union	ITU
International Federation of Clinical Chemistry	WHO	International Hospital Federation—IHF	WHO
International Federation of Educative Communities (formerly International Federation of Children's Communities)	UNESCO	International Humanist and Ethical Union	UNESCO
International Federation of Film Archives	UNESCO	International Institute for Audio-Visual Communication and Cultural Development (MEDIACULT)	UNESCO
International Federation of Gynecology and Obstetrics	WHO	International Institute for Peace	UNESCO
International Federation of Health Records Organizations	WHO	International League against Rheumatism	WHO
International Federation of Library Associations and Institutions (IFLA)	UNESCO	International Leprosy Association	WHO
International Federation of Margarine Associations	FAO	International Maritime Pilots' Association	IMO
International Federation of Medical Student Associations	WHO	International Organization against Trachoma	WHO
International Federation of Multiple Sclerosis Societies	WHO	International Paediatric Association	WHO
International Federation of Musicians	UNESCO	International Peace Research Association	UNCTAD, UNESCO
International Federation of Newspaper Publishers	UNESCO	International PEN	UNESCO
International Federation of Organizations of School Correspondence and Exchanges	UNESCO	International Pharmaceutical Federation	WHO
International Federation of Pharmaceutical Manufacturers Associations	UNCTAD, UNIDO, WHO	International Phosphate Industry Organization	FAO, IMO, UNCTAD, UNIDO
International Federation of Physical Medicine and Rehabilitation	WHO	International Political Science Association	UNESCO
International Federation of Plantation, Agricultural and Allied Workers	FAO	International Press Telecommunications Council	ITU
International Federation of Popular Travel Organizations	UNESCO	International Publishers Association	UNESCO
International Federation of Purchasing and Materials Management (IFPMM)	UNCTAD	International Radiation Protection Association	WHO
International Federation of Surgical Colleges	WHO	International Round Table for the Advancement of Counselling (IRTAC)	ILO, UNESCO
International Federation of the Periodical Press	UNESCO	International Scientific Film Association	UNESCO
International Federation of Translators	UNESCO	International Secretariat of Catholic Technologists, Agriculturists and Economists	ILO
International Federation of Travel Journalists and Writers	UNESCO	International Shipowners' Association	IMO, UNCTAD
		International Social Science Council	ILO, UNESCO
		International Society and Federation of Cardiology	WHO
		International Society for Burn Injuries	WHO
		International Society for Human and Animal Mycology	WHO

Organization	In consultative status with
International Society for Photogrammetry and Remote Sensing	UNESCO
International Society of Citriculture	FAO
International Society of Endocrinology	WHO
International Society of Haematology	WHO
International Society of Radiographers and Radiological Technicians	WHO
International Society of Soil Science	FAO, UNESCO, WMO
International Sociological Association	UNESCO, WHO
International Time Bureau	ITU
International Transport Workers' Federation	ICAO
International Union against Tuberculosis	ILO, WHO
International Union for Health Education	UNESCO, WHO
International Union of Aviation Insurers	ICAO
International Union of Biological Sciences	WHO
International Union of Forestry Research Organizations (IUFRO)	FAO
International Union of Geodesy and Geophysics	ICAO
International Union of Independent Laboratories	UNIDO
International Union of Nutritional Sciences	FAO, WHO
International Union of Pure and Applied Chemistry	FAO, WHO
International Union of School and University Health and Medicine	UNESCO, WHO
International Water Supply Association	WHO
International Young Catholic Students	UNESCO
International Youth Hostel Federation	UNESCO
Inter-Union Commission on Frequency Allocations for Radio Astronomy and Space Science	ITU
Latin American Federation of Pharmaceutical Industries	UNIDO
Latin American Social Science Council	UNESCO
Liaison Office of the Rubber Industries of the European Economic Community	UNCTAD
Licensing Executives Society International	UNCTAD, UNIDO
Medical Women's International Association	WHO

Organization	In consultative status with
Medicus Mundi Internationalis (International Organization for Co-operation in Health Care)	WHO
Miners' International Federation	UNCTAD
Oil Companies' International Marine Forum (OCIMF)	IMO
Organization for Flora Neotropica	UNESCO
Pacific Science Association	UNESCO, WMO
Permanent Commission and International Association on Occupational Health	ILO, WHO
Société internationale de télécommunications aéronautiques (SITA)	ITU
Sri Aurobindo Society	UNESCO
Standing Conference of Rectors and Vice-Chancellors of the European Universities	UNESCO
Trade Unions International of Agricultural, Forestry and Plantation Workers	FAO
UNDA—Catholic International Association for Radio and Television	UNESCO
Union of Industries of the European Community (UNICE)	UNCTAD, UNIDO
Union of International Technical Associations	UNESCO, UNIDO
United Seamen's Service, Inc.	ILO
United States Trademark Association, The	UNCTAD
World Association for Element Building and Prefabrication	UNIDO
World Association for the School as an Instrument of Peace	UNESCO
World Association of Industrial and Technological Research Organizations	UNIDO
World Association of Societies of Pathology	WHO
World Confederation of Teachers	UNESCO
World Crafts Council	UNESCO
World Education Fellowship, The	UNESCO
World Federation for Medical Education	WHO
World Federation of Agricultural Workers	FAO
World Federation of Associations of Clinical Toxicology Centres and Poison Control Centres	WHO
World Federation of Engineering Organizations	UNESCO, UNIDO
World Federation of Foreign-Language Teachers' Associations	UNESCO
World Federation of Neurosurgical Societies	WHO

Organization	In consultative status with	Organization	In consultative status with
World Federation of Nuclear Medicine and Biology	WHO	World Medical Association	ILO
World Federation of Occupational Therapists	WHO	World Movement of Christian Workers	ILO, UNESCO
World Federation of Public Health Associations	WHO	World Organization for Early Childhood Education	UNESCO
World Federation of Scientific Workers	UNESCO	World Organization of Former Students of Catholic Teaching	UNESCO
World Federation of Societies of Anaesthesiologists	WHO	World ORT Union	ILO
World Federation of Teachers' Unions	UNESCO	World Packaging Organization	UNIDO
World Federation of Workers in Food, Tobacco and Hotel Industries	FAO	World Peace Council	UNCTAD, UNESCO
World Future Studies Federation	UNESCO	World Poultry Science Association	FAO
		World Psychiatric Association	WHO
		World Veterinary Association	FAO, WHO

Calendar of meetings

At its February 1983 meetings,[5] the Committee on NGOs was unable to reach a decision on the applications for consultative status or for reclassification from a number of NGOs, nor was it able to consider applications from 24 others for lack of time. Noting that it would not be able to reconsider these applications until its next biennial session in 1985—thereby depriving the United Nations of the expertise of the organizations concerned—the Committee requested that it be reconvened by the Economic and Social Council, as soon as possible for a period not exceeding one week, in order to complete its work, provided the costs involved were borne by existing resources. A draft text to that effect was submitted to the Council by Kenya.[11] A draft by France, proposing a yearly eight-day session instead of the current two-week session every two years, was not put forward.[12]

ECONOMIC AND SOCIAL COUNCIL ACTION

The Council's action was embodied in decision 1983/108, adopted without vote in May.

Reconvening of the Committee on Non-Governmental Organizations

At its 5th plenary meeting, on 12 May 1983, the Council decided to defer consideration of the draft decision entitled "Reconvening of the Committee on Non-Governmental Organizations" until its second regular session of 1983 in the context of its consideration of the item entitled "Calendar of conferences".

Economic and Social Council decision 1983/108

Adopted without vote

Oral proposal by President; agenda item 3.
Financial implications. S-G, E/1983/L.33.
Meeting numbers. ESC 4, 5.

On 29 July, the Council, having considered the request of the Committee on NGOs to recon-

vene,[5] authorized the Committee to hold a five-day special session in 1984, as an exception, and decided that thereafter it should adhere to the established biennial cycle of meetings. These actions were contained in section V of decision 1983/184.

By section I of the same decision, the Council decided to maintain, for a further period of two years, discontinuance of summary records for a number of its subsidiary bodies, including the Committee on NGOs.

Agenda for 1985

ECONOMIC AND SOCIAL COUNCIL ACTION

In May, on the recommendation of the Committee on NGOs, the Economic and Social Council adopted decision 1983/111 without vote.

Provisional agenda and documentation for the session of the Committee on Non-Governmental Organizations to be held in 1985

At its 5th plenary meeting, on 12 May 1983, the Council approved the provisional agenda set out below, with the documents indicated, for the session of the Committee on Non-Governmental Organizations to be held in 1985.

Provisional agenda and documentation for the session of the Committee on Non-Governmental Organizations to be held in 1985

1. Election of officers
2. Adoption of the agenda and other organizational matters
3. Review of quadrennial reports submitted by non-governmental organizations in consultative status, categories I and II, with the Economic and Social Council
   Documentation
      Report of the Secretary-General containing quadrennial reports on the activities of non-governmental organizations in consultative status, categories I and II, with the Economic and Social Council

4. Applications for consultative status and requests for reclassification received from non-governmental organizations
   (a) Deferred applications
   (b) New applications
   (c) Applications for reclassification
   Documentation
      Note by the Secretary-General on deferred and new applications for consultative status
      Note by the Secretary-General on requests for reclassification
5. Review of future activities
   Documentation
      Note by the Secretary-General on the factual information necessary as a basis for the review of future activities
6. Provisional agenda, documentation and bureau for the session of the Committee to be held in 1987
7. Adoption of the report of the Committee

Economic and Social Council decision 1983/111

Adopted without vote

Draft by Committee on NGOs (E/1983/11); agenda item 3.
Meeting numbers. ESC 4, 5.

Intergovernmental organizations

Agency for Cultural and Technical Co-operation

In response to a December 1982 General Assembly request,[13] the Secretary-General submitted a report[14] to the July session of the Economic and Social Council, detailing the areas of co-operation envisaged by the Agency for Cultural and Technical Co-operation with the United Nations.

The Secretary-General pointed out that, in 1981, the Agency and UNIDO had jointly explored possible collaboration. Since then, UNIDO had provided technical support for the preparation of several Agency seminars on such topics as the creation of enterprises, evaluation and preparation of industrial projects and advanced training of management advisers for small and medium-sized industry. In March 1983, following discussions on prospects for joint activities for 1984-1985, the two organizations agreed to give priority to regional, subregional and interregional projects. The modalities of co-operation could take the form of joint activities, sub-contracting by one organization on behalf of the other and co-ordinated implementation.

The Agency had held a meeting in 1982 with the United Nations Conference on Trade and Development on research projects in the Indian Ocean. Its consultations with the United Nations Financing System for Science and Technology for Development (UNFSSTD) had resulted in a list of projects for possible co-financing. The Agency would consider financial support for training seminars at the UNFSSTD-backed African Regional Centre for Technology at Dakar, Senegal. Consultations with the United Nations Development

Programme had led to some 20 specific projects—ranging from water resources to soil conservation and telecommunications—that could be carried out by the Agency through technical or financial support. Other possible areas of co-operation with the United Nations system were in activities relating to the International Drinking Water Supply and Sanitation Decade (1981-1990); the International Youth Year: Participation, Development, Peace (1985); and the United Nations Children's Fund.

ECONOMIC AND SOCIAL COUNCIL ACTION

In decision 1983/175 of 28 July 1983, the Economic and Social Council took note of, among other reports, that of the Secretary-General.[14]

GENERAL ASSEMBLY ACTION

In December, on the recommendation of its Second Committee, the General Assembly adopted decision 38/431 without vote.

Co-operation between the United Nations and the Agency for Cultural and Technical Co-operation

At its 102nd plenary meeting, on 19 December 1983, the General Assembly, on the recommendation of the Second Committee, took note of the report of the Secretary-General on co-operation between the United Nations and the Agency for Cultural and Technical Co-operation.

General Assembly decision 38/431

Adopted without vote

Approved by Second Committee (A/38/701/Add.1) without vote, 14 December (meeting 56); draft orally proposed by Chairman; agenda item 12.
Meeting numbers. GA 38th session: 2nd Committee 56; plenary 102.

Committee on Negotiations with Intergovernmental Agencies

ECONOMIC AND SOCIAL COUNCIL ACTION

On 4 February 1983, the Economic and Social Council agreed to reconstitute the Committee on Negotiations with Intergovernmental Agencies (see Chapter XXIV of this section and also APPENDIX III), to prepare a relationship agreement between the United Nations and UNIDO as a specialized agency.

Work programme for 1983-1984

At its 1983 organizational session, held in New York from 1 to 4 February, the Economic and Social Council considered the draft basic programme of work for 1983-1984 submitted by the Secretary-General,[15] and a draft text based on informal consultations on the draft work programme and submitted by the President on behalf of the Council's Bureau.[16] Following consideration of both documents, the Council, on 4 February, adopted decision 1983/101 without vote.

By that decision, the Council approved its basic work programme for 1983 and allocated the agenda items for consideration at its sessions. It also decided, among other things, to give priority consideration, at its second regular session, to the world economic situation (under the item on international economic and social policy, including regional and sectoral developments) and to operational activities for development. It assigned for cross-sectoral review, at the same session, two issues in the medium-term plans of the organizations of the United Nations system—food and agriculture, and population—and decided to transmit certain reports without debate to the General Assembly. The Council also noted a list of questions for inclusion in its work programme for 1984.

The Council held its first regular session in New York, from 3 to 27 May 1983, and its second regular session at Geneva, from 6 to 29 July. The First (Economic) Committee met at both sessions; the Second (Social) Committee met at the first session and the Sessional Working Group of Governmental Experts on the Implementation of the International Covenant on Economic, Social and Cultural Rights met prior to and at that session; and the Third (Programme and Co-ordination) Committee met at the second session.

Meeting number. ESC 2.

Agenda of 1983 sessions

The Economic and Social Council considered five items at its February organizational session.[17] The provisional annotated agenda for the first regular session listed 16 items and provided background information on each item.[18] That for the second regular session listed 24 items, with the addition of a question on special assistance to Ghana under item 17, entitled "Special economic, humanitarian and disaster relief assistance".[19] (For lists of agenda items, see APPENDIX IV.)

ECONOMIC AND SOCIAL COUNCIL ACTION

The Economic and Social Council adopted two decisions concerning the work of its 1983 regular sessions.

In February, it adopted decision 1983/107 without vote.

Provisional agenda for the first regular session of 1983 of the Council

At its 2nd plenary meeting, on 4 February 1983, the Council approved the provisional agenda for its first regular session of 1983.

Economic and Social Council decision 1983/107

Adopted without vote

Draft provisional agenda (E/1983/L.14); agenda item 5.
Meeting number. ESC 2.

In May, the Council adopted decision 1983/162 without vote.

Provisional agenda and organization of work for the second regular session of 1983 of the Council

At its 15th plenary meeting, on 27 May 1983, the Council approved the draft provisional agenda for the second regular session of 1983, as orally revised, and the proposed organization of work for that session.

Economic and Social Council decision 1983/162

Adopted without vote

Draft provisional agenda (E/1983/L.29), orally revised; agenda item 16.
Meeting number. ESC 15.

Calendar of meetings

ECONOMIC AND SOCIAL COUNCIL ACTION

The Economic and Social Council, acting without vote in July on the recommendation of its Third Committee, adopted decision 1983/184.

Discontinuance of summary records, and calendar of conferences and meetings

I

Summary records of subsidiary bodies of the Economic and Social Council

At its 42nd plenary meeting, on 29 July 1983, the Council:

(*a*) Recalling its resolutions 1979/69 of 2 August 1979 and 1981/83 of 24 July 1981 and its decision 1980/133 of 2 May 1980, decided to maintain, for a further period of two years, the discontinuance of the provision of summary records for the following subsidiary bodies:

Commission for Social Development;
Commission on the Status of Women;
Commission on Narcotic Drugs;
Economic Commission for Europe;
Economic and Social Commission for Asia and the Pacific;
Economic Commission for Latin America;
Economic Commission for Africa;
Committee on Non-Governmental Organizations;
Committee on Natural Resources;
Committee for Programme and Co-ordination;
Commission on Transnational Corporations;

(*b*) Recalling also its decision 1982/105 of 4 February 1982, decided to maintain, for a further period of two years, the discontinuance of the provision of summary records for its sessional committees (First (Economic) Committee, Second (Social) Committee and Third (Programme and Co-ordination) Committee), and to list the participants in the general discussion held on each agenda item in the report of the Council to the General Assembly, starting in 1984.

II

Calendar of conferences and meetings for 1984 and 1985

At the same meeting, the Council, recalling paragraph 2 (*i*) of its decision 1983/101 of 4 February 1983, and having considered the views expressed by the Human Rights Committee and the letter dated 5 July 1983 from the President of the United Nations Conference on Trade and Development at its sixth session to the President of the Economic and Social Council, decided:

(a) To request the General Assembly, at its thirty-eighth session, in the context of its consideration of the agenda item entitled "Pattern of conferences", to consider, in accordance with paragraph 2 *(i)* of Council decision 1983/101, the possibility of scheduling the meetings of the Human Rights Committee and the Committee on the Elimination of Discrimination against Women so that, starting in 1984, the reports of those Committees can be submitted to the Assembly through the Council at its first regular session, and the possibility of scheduling the meetings of the Trade and Development Board so that, starting in 1984, its report can be submitted to the Assembly through the Council at its second regular session;

(b) To request the General Assembly also to consider the possibility of scheduling the tenth and eleventh sessions of the World Food Council and the thirty-first and thirty-second sessions of the Governing Council of the United Nations Development Programme, with a view to ensuring the timely distribution of the reports of those bodies for consideration by the Economic and Social Council at its second regular session;

(c) To reiterate its request to the Council of the United Nations University to consider the possibility of rescheduling its meetings so that, starting in 1984, its report can be submitted to the General Assembly through the Economic and Social Council at its second regular session.

III
Scheduling of the annual sessions of the Commission on Human Rights

At the same meeting, the Council, recalling its decisions 1982/145 of 7 May 1982 and 1982/156 of 28 July 1982, and having considered the request made by the Commission on Human Rights in its resolution 1982/40 of 11 March 1982, concerning the possibility of rescheduling the annual sessions of the Commission and, if necessary, of the Sub-Commission on Prevention of Discrimination and Protection of Minorities, with a view to enabling the Commission to meet later in the year, decided to continue for the time being the existing pattern of scheduling the annual sessions of the Commission.

IV
Eighth special session of the Commission on Narcotic Drugs

At the same meeting, the Council, having considered the recommendations made by the Commission on Narcotic Drugs, both at its seventh special session and at its thirtieth session, decided:

(a) To authorize the Commission on Narcotic Drugs to hold, on an exceptional basis, a special session of five days' duration in 1984, at a time when it will not overlap with other meetings, within existing United Nations resources;

(b) To approve the provisional agenda and documentation for that session, as proposed by the Commission at its thirtieth session;

(c) To recommend that the Commission should, in the future, pursuant to Council resolution 1768(LIV) of 18 May 1973, adhere to the established biennial cycle of meetings.

V
Special session of the Committee on Non-Governmental Organizations

At the same meeting, the Council, having considered the request made by the Committee on Non-Governmental Organizations concerning the reconvening of the Committee in 1984, decided:

(a) To authorize the Committee on Non-Governmental Organizations to hold, on an exceptional basis, a special session of five days' duration in 1984;

(b) That the Committee should, in the future, pursuant to Council resolution 1768(LIV) of 18 May 1973, adhere to the established biennial cycle of meetings.

VI
Committee on the Review and Appraisal of the Implementation of the International Development Strategy for the Third United Nations Development Decade

At the same meeting, the Council decided:

(a) To request the General Assembly, at its thirty-eighth session, to schedule one session of the Committee on the Review and Appraisal of the Implementation of the International Development Strategy for the Third United Nations Development Decade;

(b) To consider the report of the Committee at its second regular session of 1984, together with the contribution of the subsidiary bodies of the Council in their respective sectors in applying the International Development Strategy as the policy framework in the formulation and implementation of their programmes of work and the medium-term plan, pursuant to paragraph 2 *(e)* and *(f)* of Council decision 1983/101.

Economic and Social Council decision 1983/184

Adopted without vote

Approved by Third Committee (E/1983/119) without vote, 26 July (meeting 18); draft by Council Vice-President (E/1983/C.3/L.12), based on informal consultations, section VI orally revised on proposal by Pakistan, and section I orally amended in Council by Bangladesh, for Group of 77; agenda item 23. *Meeting number.* ESC 42.

The oral amendment by Bangladesh added to section I, paragraph *(b)*, the decision to list the participants in the discussion on each agenda item in the Council's report to the Assembly.

GENERAL ASSEMBLY ACTION

In decision 38/429 of 19 December 1983, the General Assembly invited the Council to request its subsidiary bodies currently meeting annually to consider adopting, on an experimental basis, a biennial cycle of meetings (see below).

Calendar of meetings for 1984 and 1985

During consideration in July 1983 of the provisional calendar of meetings for 1984 and 1985[20] by the Economic and Social Council, a number of States stated their position regarding entries 41, 42 and 51, on each of which a vote had been taken in the Third Committee. These concerned, respectively, the proposed meetings of the Economic Commission for Africa (ECA), the Economic Commission for Latin America (ECLA) and ESCAP away from their headquarters.

Greece, speaking for the 10 member States of the European Economic Community, felt that, because the meetings would incur additional costs of $584,000 at a time of considerable pressure on the United Nations budget, the proposals should be examined against priority needs. The United States agreed, saying the calendar was already overloaded; hence it had proposed reducing the number of meetings by 10 per cent—a proposal it would repeat in due course. Canada regretted its vote in Committee against those entries but stressed that at issue was the justification, in the current period of austerity, for charging additional costs to the regular budget. Portugal had voted similarly because the budgetary implications of the entries had not been taken into account during the Committee's deliberations.

The USSR said it had not objected to the proposed ECA and ECLA meetings to be held at Conakry (Guinea) and Lima (Peru), since the costs involved might be charged to the regular budget when the host countries were developing countries. On that basis, it had been obliged in Committee to vote against the ESCAP meeting to be held in Tokyo and would do so again when the Assembly's Fifth Committee examined the matter. Japan remarked that to make such distinctions between host countries was dangerous; noting its adherence to a strict budgetary policy, it said it had nevertheless invited ESCAP to hold a session in Tokyo to highlight its support for United Nations activities.

Brazil, India and the Sudan—which had voted for the proposed meetings in Committee—held that, as provided for by a 1976 Assembly resolution,[21] most regional commission meetings had been held away from their headquarters and that the practice of charging the expenditures incurred to the United Nations regular budget had always enjoyed general approval.

ECONOMIC AND SOCIAL COUNCIL ACTION

On the recommendation of its Third Committee, the Economic and Social Council adopted decision 1983/185 without vote.

Calendar of conferences and meetings for 1984 and 1985

At its 42nd plenary meeting, on 29 July 1983, the Council approved the calendar of conferences and meetings for 1984 and 1985.

Economic and Social Council decision 1983/185

Adopted without vote

Approved by Third Committee (E/1983/119) without vote, 26 July (meeting 18); provisional calendar of conference and meetings (E/1983/L.20/Add.1), orally revised; agenda item 23.
Financial implications. S-G, E/1983/L.37.
Meeting number. ESC 42.

Prior to adopting the calendar of meetings as a whole, the Council, at Japan's request, took separate roll-call votes on each of the three entries in question. The entries were approved as follows: entries 41 and 42, by 39 votes to 10, with 2 abstentions; entry 51, by 34 votes to 15, with 2 abstentions.

Norway, speaking also on behalf of Denmark, said they had been compelled to abstain—in all three votes—because no discussion had been held on the financial implications of the proposed meetings. Explaining their affirmative votes, Bangladesh said it regarded the practice of holding meetings away from headquarters as important and hoped this would be the only time that the issue was put to a vote; Brazil saw no reason to abandon a well-established practice and said that lengthy informal consultations had indeed been held on the issue.

Limitation of documentation

ECONOMIC AND SOCIAL COUNCIL ACTION

On the question of limitation of documentation, the Economic and Social Council, in July, adopted decision 1983/163 without vote.

Control and limitation of documentation

At its 38th plenary meeting, on 22 July 1983, the Council, recalling the resolutions and decisions adopted by the General Assembly and the Economic and Social Council concerning the control and limitation of documentation, decided to request the Secretary-General:

(a) To bring to the attention of intergovernmental and expert bodies, before decisions are adopted, any request for documentation that exceeds the ability of the Secretariat to prepare and process on time and within its approved resources;

(b) To draw the attention of intergovernmental bodies to areas where duplication of documentation is likely to occur and/or where opportunities for integrating or consolidating documents that deal with related or similar themes might exist, with a view to rationalizing documentation.

Economic and Social Council decision 1983/163

Adopted without vote

Draft by Vice-President (E/1983/L.39), based on informal consultations; agenda item 4.
Meeting number. ESC 38.

By section I of its decision 1983/184 of 29 July, the Council decided to maintain, for a further period of two years, discontinuance of summary records for the following subsidiary bodies: Commission for Social Development, Commission on Narcotic Drugs, Commission on the Status of Women, Commission on Transnational Corporations, Committee on Natural Resources, Committee on NGOs, CPC, ECA, Economic Commission for Europe, ECLA, ESCAP; and for the

Council's First, Second and Third Committees. The Council also decided to list, starting in 1984, the participants in the general discussion held on each agenda item in its report to the Assembly.

Financial implications of resolutions and decisions

In a July 1983 report,[22] the Secretary-General submitted a summary of estimates of programme budget implications of resolutions and decisions adopted by the Economic and Social Council in 1983. The estimated costs for 1982-1983 and 1984-1985, excluding conference servicing, totalled $3,615,600. This figure was subject to change, in the light of a review by the General Assembly to determine how much of the costs might be absorbed.

ECONOMIC AND SOCIAL COUNCIL ACTION

In July, following consideration of the report and acting without vote on an oral proposal by its President, the Economic and Social Council adopted decision 1983/188.

Summary of estimates of programme budget implications of resolutions and decisions adopted by the Economic and Social Council during its first and second regular sessions of 1983

At its 42nd plenary meeting, on 29 July 1983, the Council took note of the report of the Secretary-General containing the summary of estimates of programme budget implications of resolutions and decisions adopted by the Council during its first and second regular sessions of 1983.

Economic and Social Council decision 1983/188

Adopted without vote

Oral proposal by President.
Meeting number. ESC 42.

GENERAL ASSEMBLY ACTION

As later approved by the General Assembly, on the recommendation of the Fifth Committee, a net addition of $382,700 was made to the 1984-1985 budget to cover a number of the 1983 Economic and Social Council actions having financial implications. This amount, requested by the Secretary-General in a report revising his initial submission for the budget as a whole,[23] was approved by the Fifth Committee on 8 December, on the recommendation of the Advisory Committee on Administrative and Budgetary Questions (ACABQ).[24] The financial implications of a number of other items arising from Council resolutions and decisions were dealt with separately by the Fifth Committee when it considered the financial implications of Assembly resolutions on the same topics. Conference servicing costs were also dealt with separately (see ADMINISTRATIVE AND BUDGETARY QUESTIONS, Chapter IV).

An additional $400,000 attributable to Council actions affecting 1983 expenditures was included in the package of budget revisions approved by the Fifth Committee on 19 December 1983 in connection with the Secretary-General's budget performance report for 1982-1983[25] (see ADMINISTRATIVE AND BUDGETARY QUESTIONS, Chapter I).

Meeting number. GA 38th session: 5th Committee 59.

Report for 1983

The work of the Economic and Social Council at its organizational session and two regular sessions in 1983 was summarized in its annual report to the General Assembly.[26] Parts of the report were considered by the plenary Assembly, others by the Fifth Committee and by the Second, Third and Fourth Committees.

GENERAL ASSEMBLY ACTION

On 20 December, the Assembly adopted two decisions on the report: 38/449, taking note of those chapters that had been allocated to the Fifth Committee; and 38/453, taking note of those that had been assigned to plenary meetings.

The Assembly adopted decision 38/449 without vote, on a recommendation of the Fifth Committee.

Report of the Economic and Social Council

At its 104th plenary meeting, on 20 December 1983, the General Assembly, on the recommendation of the Fifth Committee, took note of chapters III (section D), IV (sections A to E and G to O), VI (section D) and IX (section H) of the report of the Economic and Social Council.

General Assembly decision 38/449

Adopted without vote

Approved by Fifth Committee (A/38/747) without vote, 20 December (meeting 75); oral proposal by Chairman; agenda item 12.
Meeting numbers. GA 38th session: 5th Committee 75; plenary 104.

The Assembly adopted decision 38/453 without vote, on an oral proposal by its President.

Report of the Economic and Social Council

At its 104th plenary meeting, on 20 December 1983, the General Assembly took note of chapters I, VI (sections B and E), VIII and IX (sections A to C) of the report of the Economic and Social Council.

General Assembly decision 38/453

Adopted without vote

Oral proposal by President; agenda item 12.
Meeting number. GA 38th session: plenary 104.

REFERENCES

[1]YUN 1982, p. 1241, ESC res. 1982/50, 28 July 1982. [2]YUN 1977, p. 438, GA res. 32/197, 20 Dec. 1977. [3]YUN 1982, p. 1387, GA res. 37/67, 3 Dec. 1982. [4]E/1983/L.40/Rev.1. [5]E/1983/11. [6]E/1983/54. [7]E/1983/109. [8]E/C.2/1983/2 & Add.1. [9]E/1983/NGO/1-7. [10]E/1983/INF.9. [11]E/1983/L.23. [12]E/1983/L.21. [13]YUN 1982, p. 586, GA res. 37/132, 17

Dec. 1982. (14)A/38/236-E/1983/75. (15)E/1983/1 & Add.1.
(16)E/1983/L.12. (17)E/1983/2. (18)E/1983/30. (19)E/1983/100.
(20)E/1983/L.20 & Add.1. (21)YUN 1976, p. 908, GA
res. 31/140, 17 Dec. 1976. (22)E/1983/127. (23)A/C.5/38/32 &
Add.1. (24)A/38/7/Add.15. (25)A/C.5/38/49. (26)A/38/3.

PUBLICATIONS

Index to Proceedings of the Economic and Social Council, Organizational Session, First Regular Session, Second Regular Session—1982 (ST/LIB/SER.B/E.59), Sales No. E.83.I.13; *1983* (ST/LIB/SER.B/E.60 & Corr.1), Sales No. E.84.I.5 & corrigendum. *Terms of Reference of the Subsidiary Machinery of the Economic and Social Council and the Related Organs and Programmes of the United Nations*, E/1983/INF.4.

Organizational structure

In addition to the question of revitalizing the Economic and Social Council (see above), other aspects of the ongoing process of restructuring the economic and social sectors of the United Nations system, initiated in 1977,[1] were considered in 1983. These concerned the organization of work of the Second and Third Committees of the General Assembly, as well as restructuring issues relating to the Department of International Economic and Social Affairs of the United Nations Secretariat.

Work organization of the Second and Third Committees of the General Assembly

Second Committee

ECONOMIC AND SOCIAL COUNCIL ACTION

At its July session, the Council considered a set of draft recommendations on the organization of the Second Committee's work, on the basis of which it adopted without vote decision 1983/164.

Recommendations regarding the organization of the work of the Second Committee of the General Assembly

At its 38th plenary meeting, on 22 July 1983, the Council, pursuant to paragraph 6 of the annex to General Assembly resolution 32/197 of 20 December 1977 and paragraph 1 (*b*) of Council resolution 1982/50 of 28 July 1982, decided to submit to the General Assembly the following recommendations regarding the organization of the work of the Second Committee of the General Assembly:

I. *Structure of the deliberations of the Second Committee*

(*a*) Debates in the Second Committee should be more meaningful, better focused, and action-oriented and should establish a constructive dialogue among delegations and between delegations and executive heads of organs, organizations and bodies of the United Nations system.

(*b*) There is general agreement that the debates in the Committee should be better structured. Recent experience has shown that a general debate in the Committee may perhaps be necessary, but that its relationship to the general debate in plenary, on the one hand, and to the discussion of specific issues in the Committee, on the other, should be further clarified. Such a general debate in the Committee should take place during the first two weeks of the session.

(*c*) Apart from the general debate, the deliberations of the Committee on various questions should be organized around clusters of related issues, focusing on specific reports and proposals submitted. Those deliberations should be as brief and concise as possible.

(*d*) Statements on behalf of organs, organizations and bodies of the United Nations system should henceforth be made in the context of the deliberations on specific reports and should be circulated in advance. In this context, opportunities should be provided for members of the Committee to exchange views with the executive heads of the organs, organizations and bodies of the United Nations system.

II. *Organization of the work of the Second Committee*

(*a*) The General Assembly may consider adopting a biennial programme of work for the Second Committee, apart from the general debate, and identifying questions for substantive consideration in alternate years; in other years, the Assembly will be kept informed of progress on such questions.

(*b*) The subsidiary bodies of the General Assembly in the economic field should ensure that their substantive contributions are made available in time to the Assembly, in the context of its biennial programme of work. Furthermore, those subsidiary bodies may consider adopting, on an experimental basis, a biennial cycle of meetings, in conformity with the biennial programme of work to be established for the Second Committee.

(*c*) The Economic and Social Council shall continue to assist the Second Committee in the organization of work and documentation, and shall make recommendations in this regard to the General Assembly for its consideration.

(*d*) In that context, the Council should also identify:

(i) Those issues on which it would take a final decision, particularly those issues which are considered in depth by its subsidiary bodies and/or those issues which are not included in the agenda of the General Assembly;

(ii) Those issues which should be transmitted without debate to the Assembly for consideration and decisions;

(iii) Those issues in respect of which the Council will substantively prepare the work of the Assembly by defining policy matters requiring special attention by the Assembly, and by formulating recommendations for action by the Assembly;

(*e*) The General Assembly may wish to consider making arrangements to have members of the Bureau of the Second Committee informally agreed upon at least two weeks before the beginning of the work of the Committee, so as to enable them, in consultation with Member States, to begin the preparation of the work of the Committee.

III. *Deadlines for the submission of draft proposals, and consideration thereof by the Second Committee*

(*a*) The Second Committee, in organizing its work, should identify issues which would require lengthy informal consultations, and should, to the extent possible, spread the consideration of those issues evenly throughout the session.

(b)   The deadline for the submission of draft proposals under various items of the agenda should be established when the Second Committee approves its organization of work. Greater efforts should be made to adhere to the deadlines. To this end, the Chairman of the Committee should play an active role, in consultation with delegations, in ensuring the observance of deadlines.

(c)   Efforts should be made to keep to a minimum the number of draft proposals under each item. To the extent possible, the Committee should endeavour to adopt only one draft resolution or decision on each specific issue before it.

(d)   Draft resolutions should be concise and should concentrate on policy recommendations addressed to Member States and organs, organizations and bodies of the United Nations system.

(e)   Informal consultations on draft proposals have proved to be a useful procedure to expedite the work of the Second Committee. Further efforts should be made to improve the working methods and procedures of such informal consultations, including, to the extent possible, the establishment of a weekly programme of work for those consultations.

Economic and Social Council decision 1983/164

Adopted without vote

Draft by Vice-President (E/1983/CRP.2), based on informal consultations; agenda item 4.
Meeting number. ESC 38.

GENERAL ASSEMBLY ACTION

In December, on the recommendation of the Second Committee, the General Assembly adopted decision 38/429 without vote.

Rationalization of the work of the Second Committee
At its 102nd plenary meeting, on 19 December 1983, the General Assembly, on the recommendation of the Second Committee:

(a)   Endorsed the recommendations of the Economic and Social Council regarding the organization of the work of the Second Committee of the General Assembly, as contained in Council decision 1983/164 of 22 July 1983;

(b)   Decided to adopt, beginning at its fortieth session, a biennial programme of work for the Second Committee, apart from its general debate;

(c)   Requested the Economic and Social Council to consider and to recommend for consideration by the General Assembly at its thirty-ninth session a proposed biennial programme of work for the Second Committee, including the identification of questions for substantive consideration by the Assembly in alternate years, taking into account the biennial programme of work of the Council and the invitation already addressed to the Council in Assembly decision 37/442 of 20 December 1982;

(d)   Recommended that the Intergovernmental Committee on Science and Technology for Development should consider adopting, on an experimental basis, a biennial cycle of meetings, in conformity with the biennial programme of work to be established for the Second Committee;

(e)   Invited the Economic and Social Council, pursuant to its resolution 1768(LIV) of 18 May 1973, to request its subsidiary bodies that currently meet on an annual basis to consider adopting, on an experimental basis, a biennial cycle of meetings;

(f)   Requested the Trade and Development Board to consider scheduling its second regular session so that its reports might be available in all the working languages of the General Assembly in time for consideration by the Assembly;

(g)   Decided that the work of the Second Committee should be organized in such a manner as to encourage meaningful and better-focused discussions, leading to action-oriented decisions, and, in that context, that the general debate of the Second Committee should focus on specific major issues of international economic co-operation and development.

General Assembly decision 38/429

Adopted without vote

Approved by Second Committee (A/38/701Add.1) without vote, 14 December (meeting 56); draft orally proposed by Chairman, based on informal consultations held on recommendations in Economic and Social Council decision 1983/164; agenda item 12.
Meeting numbers. GA 38th session: 2nd Committee 56; plenary 102.

Third Committee

At the Economic and Social Council's May session, the Chairman of an informal working group established to formulate recommendations regarding the documentation and organization of work of the Third Committee—in pursuance of the 1977 Assembly[1] and 1982 Council[2] resolutions on restructuring—orally reported to the Council that the group had not been in a position to discharge the task assigned to it. He said the group felt that, if the Council itself did not take up the matter in plenary meetings, it should be left to the Assembly to do so.

ECONOMIC AND SOCIAL COUNCIL ACTION

On an oral proposal by the President, the Council adopted decision 1983/159 without vote.

Documentation and organization of work of the Third Committee of the General Assembly
At its 15th plenary meeting, on 27 May 1983, the Council took note of the oral progress report made by the Chairman of the informal open-ended working group for formulating recommendations to the Council regarding the documentation and organization of work of the Third Committee of the General Assembly, in pursuance of General Assembly resolution 32/197 of 20 December 1977 and Council resolution 1982/50 of 28 July 1982.

Economic and Social Council decision 1983/159

Adopted without vote

Oral proposal by President; agenda item 1.
Meeting number. ESC 15.

Department of International Economic and Social Affairs

In an August 1983 report transmitted by the Secretary-General to the General Assembly,[3] JIU analysed the organization, functions and work programme of the Department of International Economic and Social Affairs, as part of a series of studies to assess implementation of the 1977 Assembly resolution on restructuring.[1] Also analysed were the relationship of DIESA with other departments of the United Nations Secretariat and with the system's organizations, and the problems encountered by it in performing its functions as described by the Secretary-General in 1978 in keeping with the 1977 resolution. As a result of the study, JIU made seven main recommendations, six in respect of DIESA.

The recommendations called for definitive terms of reference to rationalize the Department's work and organization, including the transfer of its Energy Unit, Fiscal and Financial Branch, and Mineral Resources Section to the Department of Technical Co-operation for Development (DTCD). Documents for the use of intergovernmental bodies should be more relevant to the world economic and social situation so as to provide a sound basis for action-oriented recommendations. A review should be made of DIESA's collaborative arrangements with DTCD devised in 1978, aimed at achieving a cross-fertilization between research and technical co-operation. DIESA should work out agreements with main United Nations entities involved in development research to harmonize their work programmes. The Centre for Social Development and Humanitarian Affairs (CSDHA) should be moved back to New York from Vienna, to overcome communication difficulties between it and DIESA, which JIU felt were compounded by overly bureaucratic administrative arrangements.

Other recommendations called for the Secretary-General to present his views to the Assembly on the further integration of programme planning, budgeting, monitoring and evaluation functions in the specific components of the Secretariat, including his views on combining the current evaluation units into a central unit and allowing the Office for Programme Planning and Co-ordination to concentrate on elaborating guidelines for an evaluation system and its implementation; and to formalize the provisional arrangement placing technical co-operation functions in statistics under the Statistical Office.

Commenting on the report,[4] the Secretary-General agreed with JIU that the Department's performance needed strengthening. He welcomed the recognition that improvement had taken place and that DIESA faced a number of constraints outside its control. He concurred with the recommendations for definitive terms of reference, and agreed that the means for integrating research and technical co-operation needed examination, the key issues being the extent to which integration and feedback were required between the two activities. He noted that the organizational arrange-

ments in the area of programme planning and evaluation were under review and that the steps recently initiated to streamline the Organization's management and administration would include treatment of programming and budgeting issues. The recommendation regarding the Statistical Office would be taken into account in his report to the Assembly in 1984.

The Secretary-General could not, however, agree with several of the recommendations. He felt that the units proposed for transfer were appropriately assigned as they were, that a mechanism for co-ordinating development research already existed, and that the problems identified as requiring the relocation of CSDHA were temporary and he was seeking to overcome them.

In its report on the JIU report and the comments of the Secretary-General, ACABQ[5] noted that, in its final report on restructuring to be completed in 1984, JIU would address itself to a number of complex issues and problems with Secretariat or system-wide implications that had been brought to light. That final report and the JIU reports on individual departments or offices would be taken into account by the Secretary-General in his own report to the Assembly in 1984, when he was also to report on the results of an ongoing review of the Secretariat's administration and management by a high-level advisory group on administrative reform. Because of these forthcoming comprehensive reports, ACABQ did not attempt to consider all the JIU recommendations. In noting, however, that the Secretary-General did not adequately address the problems that had led JIU to recommend CSDHA relocation to New York, ACABQ also noted that, for the Assembly to reverse its 1976 decision[6] transferring CSDHA to its current location at Vienna, it should be provided with an analysis more thorough than had been provided by either JIU or the Secretary-General.

GENERAL ASSEMBLY ACTION

Acting without vote on the recommendation of the Fifth Committee, the General Assembly adopted resolution 38/234, section IX, on 20 December 1983.

Report of the Joint Inspection Unit on the Department of International Economic and Social Affairs

[*The General Assembly* . . .]

1. *Takes note* of the relevant paragraphs of the report of the Joint Inspection Unit and the comments thereon of the Secretary-General and of the related report of the Advisory Committee on Administrative and Budgetary Questions;

2. *Reaffirms* the provisions of its resolutions 31/194 of 22 December 1976 and 33/181 of 21 December 1978 as regards the location of the Centre for Social Development and Humanitarian Affairs at Vienna;

. . .

General Assembly resolution 38/234, section IX

20 December 1983   Meeting 104   Adopted without vote

Approved by Fifth Committee (A/38/760 & Corr.1) without vote, 30 November (meeting 51); 13-nation draft (A/C.5/38/L.10/Rev.1); agenda item 109.

Sponsors: Argentina, Austria, Egypt, Germany, Federal Republic of, Greece, Hungary, India, Indonesia, Japan, Kenya, Mexico, Spain, Sweden.

Meeting numbers. GA 38th session: 5th Committee 51, 60; plenary 104.

The Fifth Committee had considered the JIU report, together with the Secretary-General's comments and the related ACABQ report. Following Committee approval of the 13-nation draft text, the United States introduced but later withdrew a draft resolution,[7] by which the Assembly would have, among other things, requested the Secretary-General to provide DIESA and DTCD with definitive terms of reference and to examine arrangements for collaboration between the two Departments.

REFERENCES

[1]YUN 1977, p. 438, GA res. 32/197, 20 Dec. 1977. [2]YUN 1982, p. 1241, ESC res. 1982/50, 28 July 1982. [3]A/38/334. [4]A/38/334/Add.1. [5]A/38/600. [6]YUN 1976, p. 915, GA res. 31/194, 22 Dec. 1976. [7]A/C.5/38/L.15.

Trusteeship and decolonization

General questions relating to colonial countries

During the year, the General Assembly's Special Committee on the Situation with regard to the Implementation of the Declaration on the Granting of Independence to Colonial Countries and Peoples (Committee on colonial countries) continued to consider the implementation by international organizations of the Assembly's 1960 Declaration and foreign interests impeding its implementation, military bases in Non-Self-Governing Territories (NSGTs), dissemination of information on decolonization, and reports on the Territories supplied by their administering Powers and by visiting missions of the Committee.

In addition to the general question of decolonization, the Committee examined situations in the following individual Territories: Trust Territory of the Pacific Islands (see next chapter), Namibia (see Chapter III of this section), Falkland Islands (Malvinas), East Timor, Western Sahara, American Samoa, Anguilla, Bermuda, British Virgin Islands, Brunei, Cayman Islands, Cocos (Keeling) Islands, Gibraltar, Guam, Montserrat, Pitcairn, St. Helena, St. Kitts-Nevis, Tokelau, Turks and Caicos Islands, United States Virgin Islands (see Chapter IV of this section).

The 25-member Committee held two sessions in 1983 at United Nations Headquarters—on 18 May and from 12 to 31 August—and also held an extra-sessional meeting from 1 September to 13 October. The Committee's subsidiary bodies, the Sub-Committee on Petitions, Information and Assistance and the Sub-Committee on Small Territories, met between 20 May and 8 September and between 20 May and 13 October, respectively, and made a number of recommendations for action.

In July, the Economic and Social Council adopted resolution 1983/42 reaffirming the extension of moral and material assistance to the people of Namibia and other colonial territories and their national liberation movements by the United Nations system, and deploring the collaboration of the International Monetary Fund (IMF) with the Government of South Africa.

Acting on the basis of the Committee's recommendations, the General Assembly took action in December on general aspects of colonial countries. By resolution 38/54, it called for the implementation of the 1960 Declaration, approved the recommendations of the Committee in that regard, and requested it to continue its efforts by taking certain measures. States, in particular the administering Powers, and United Nations bodies were urged to give effect to the Committee's recommendations for implementing the Declaration. The Assembly, by resolution 38/51, called for assistance by the specialized agencies and the international institutions associated with the United Nations in order to achieve implementation. The Economic and Social Council made a similar request in July by resolution 1983/42. In resolution 38/50, the Assembly condemned activities of foreign economic and other interests which were impeding the Declaration's implementation, as well as the policies of Governments that continued to collaborate with those foreign interests exploiting the resources of the Territories, and called on States to take measures in respect of their nationals and corporations under their jurisdiction operating in colonial Territories which were detrimental to the inhabitants' interests. The Assembly, by decision 38/419, condemned military activities in colonial Territories which denied the peoples concerned their right to self-determination and independence and which were detrimental to their interests.

By resolution 38/55 on the dissemination of information on decolonization, the Assembly requested the Secretary-General to take measures through the media at his disposal to give publicity to the work of the United Nations in decolonization. Resolution 38/53 included an invitation to States to make offers of study and training facilities to the inhabitants of NSGTs. In resolution 38/49, the Assembly requested the administering Powers to transmit information as prescribed in Article 73 *e* of the United Nations Charter as well as information on political and constitutional developments in the Territories concerned.

Topics related to this chapter. Africa: South Africa and *apartheid*. Namibia. Other colonial territories.

Implementation of the 1960 Declaration on colonial countries

Various aspects of the implementation of the 1960 Declaration on the Granting of Independence to Colonial Countries and Peoples[1] were kept under consideration by the Committee on colonial countries which submitted its annual report to the General Assembly in October 1983.[2]

GENERAL ASSEMBLY ACTION

Following consideration of the report of the Committee on colonial countries, the General Assembly, on 7 December, adopted by recorded vote resolution 38/54 on the implementation of the 1960 Declaration.

Implementation of the Declaration on the Granting of Independence to Colonial Countries and Peoples

The General Assembly,

Having examined the report of the Special Committee on the Situation with regard to the Implementation of the Declaration on the Granting of Independence to Colonial Countries and Peoples,

Recalling its resolutions 1514(XV) of 14 December 1960, containing the Declaration on the Granting of Independence to Colonial Countries and Peoples, 2621(XXV) of 12 October 1970, containing the programme of action for the full implementation of the Declaration, and 35/118 of 11 December 1980, the annex to which contains the Plan of Action for the Full Implementation of the Declaration,

Recalling all its previous resolutions concerning the implementation of the Declaration, in particular resolution 37/35 of 23 November 1982, as well as the relevant resolutions of the Security Council,

Recalling the relevant provisions of the Paris Declaration on Namibia and the Programme of Action on Namibia adopted by the International Conference in Support of the Struggle of the Namibian People for Independence, held in Paris from 25 to 29 April 1983,

Condemning the continued colonialist and racist repression of millions of Africans, particularly in Namibia, by the Government of South Africa through its persistent, illegal occupation of the international Territory and its intransigent attitude towards all efforts being made to bring about an internationally acceptable solution to the situation obtaining in the Territory,

Deeply conscious of the urgent need to take all necessary measures to eliminate forthwith the remaining vestiges of colonialism, particularly in respect of Namibia where desperate attempts by South Africa to perpetuate its illegal occupation have brought untold suffering and bloodshed to the people,

Strongly condemning the policies of those States which, in defiance of the relevant resolutions of the United Nations, have continued to collaborate with the Government of South Africa in its domination of the people of Namibia,

Conscious that the success of the national liberation struggle and the resultant international situation have provided the international community with a unique opportunity to make a decisive contribution towards the total elimination of colonialism in all its forms and manifestations in Africa,

Welcoming the achievement of independence by Saint Christopher and Nevis on 19 September 1983 and noting with satisfaction the imminent accession to independence of Brunei, scheduled for 31 December 1983,

Noting with satisfaction the work accomplished by the Special Committee with a view to securing the effective and complete implementation of the Declaration and the other relevant resolutions of the United Nations,

Noting also with satisfaction the co-operation and active participation of the administering Powers concerned in the relevant work of the Special Committee, as well as the continued readiness of the Governments concerned to receive United Nations visiting missions in the Territories under their administration,

Reiterating its conviction that the total eradication of racial discrimination, *apartheid* and violations of the basic human rights of the peoples of colonial Territories will be achieved most expeditiously by the faithful and complete implementation of the Declaration, particularly in Namibia, and by the speediest possible complete elimination of the presence of the illegal occupying régimes therefrom,

Keenly aware of the pressing needs of the newly independent and emerging States for assistance from the United Nations and its system of organizations in the economic, social and other fields,

1. *Reaffirms* its resolutions 1514(XV), 2621(XXV) and 37/35 and all other resolutions on decolonization and calls upon the administering Powers, in accordance with those resolutions, to take all necessary steps to enable the dependent peoples of the Territories concerned to exercise fully and without further delay their inalienable right to self-determination and independence;

2. *Affirms once again* that the continuation of colonialism in all its forms and manifestations—including racism, *apartheid*, the exploitation by foreign and other interests of economic and human resources and the waging of colonial wars to suppress national liberation movements—is incompatible with the Charter of the United Nations, the Universal Declaration of Human Rights and the Declaration on the Granting of Independence to Colonial Countries and Peoples and poses a serious threat to international peace and security;

3. *Reaffirms its determination* to take all necessary steps with a view to the complete and speedy eradication of colonialism and to the faithful and strict observance by all States of the relevant provisions of the Charter, the Declaration on the Granting of Independence to Colonial Countries and Peoples and the guiding principles of the Universal Declaration of Human Rights;

4. *Affirms once again* its recognition of the legitimacy of the struggle of the peoples under colonial and alien domination to exercise their right to self-determination and independence by all the necessary means at their disposal;

5. *Approves* the report of the Special Committee on the Situation with regard to the Implementation of the Declaration on the Granting of Independence to Colonial Countries and Peoples covering its work during 1983, including the programme of work envisaged for 1984;

6. *Calls upon* all States, in particular the administering Powers, and the specialized agencies and other organizations of the United Nations system to give effect to the recommendations contained in the report of the Special Committee for the speedy implementation of the Declaration and the other relevant resolutions of the United Nations;

7. *Condemns* the continuing activities of foreign economic and other interests which are impeding the implementation of the Declaration with respect to the colonial Territories, particularly Namibia;

8. *Strongly condemns* all collaboration, particularly in the nuclear and military fields, with the Government of South Africa and calls upon the States concerned to cease forthwith all such collaboration;

9. *Requests* all States, directly and through their action in the specialized agencies and other organizations of the United Nations system, to withhold assistance of any kind from the Government of South Africa until the inalienable right of the people of Namibia to self-determination and independence within a united and integrated Namibia, including Walvis Bay, has been restored, and to refrain from taking any action which might imply recognition of the legitimacy of the illegal occupation of Namibia by that régime;

10. *Calls upon* the colonial Powers to withdraw immediately and unconditionally their military bases and installations from colonial Territories and to refrain from establishing new ones;

11. *Urges* all States, directly and through their action in the specialized agencies and other organizations of the United Nations system, to provide all moral and material assistance to the oppressed people of Namibia and, in respect of the other Territories, requests the administering Powers, in consultation with the Governments of the Territories under their administration, to take steps to enlist and make effective use of all possible assistance, on both a bilateral and a multilateral basis, in the strengthening of the economies of those Territories;

12. *Requests* the Special Committee to continue to seek suitable means for the immediate and full implementation of General Assembly resolution 1514(XV) in all Territories that have not yet attained independence and, in particular:

  (a) To formulate specific proposals for the elimination of the remaining manifestations of colonialism and to report thereon to the General Assembly at its thirty-ninth session;

  (b) To make concrete suggestions which could assist the Security Council in considering appropriate measures under the Charter with regard to developments in colonial Territories that are likely to threaten international peace and security;

  (c) To continue to examine the compliance of Member States with the Declaration and with other relevant resolutions on decolonization, particularly those relating to Namibia;

  (d) To continue to pay particular attention to the small Territories, including the sending of visiting missions to them, as appropriate, and to recommend to the General Assembly the most suitable steps to be taken to enable the populations of those Territories to exercise their right to self-determination, freedom and independence;

  (e) To take all necessary steps to enlist world-wide support among Governments, as well as national and international organizations having a special interest in decolonization, for the achievement of the objectives of the Declaration and the implementation of the relevant resolutions of the United Nations, particularly as concerns the oppressed people of Namibia;

13. *Calls upon* the administering Powers to continue to co-operate with the Special Committee in the discharge of its mandate and, in particular, to permit the access of visiting missions to the Territories to secure first-hand information and ascertain the wishes and aspirations of their inhabitants;

14. *Requests* the Secretary-General and the specialized agencies and other organizations of the United Nations system to provide or continue to provide to the newly independent and emerging States all possible assistance in the economic, social and other fields;

15. *Requests* the Secretary-General to provide the Special Committee with the facilities and services required for the implementation of the present resolution, as well as of the various resolutions and decisions on decolonization adopted by the General Assembly and the Special Committee.

General Assembly resolution 38/54

7 December 1983   Meeting 86   141-2-8 (recorded vote)

21-nation draft (A/38/L.33 & Add.1); agenda item 18.
Sponsors: Afghanistan, Algeria, Congo, Cuba, Cyprus, Ethiopia, Guyana, India, Lao People's Democratic Republic, Libyan Arab Jamahiriya, Madagascar, Mongolia, Qatar, Sierra Leone, Syrian Arab Republic, Trinidad and Tobago, Tunisia, United Republic of Tanzania, Viet Nam, Yugoslavia, Zambia.
Financial implications. 5th Committee, A/38/696; S-G, A/C.5/38/72.
Meeting numbers. GA 38th session: plenary 84-86.

Recorded vote in Assembly as follows:

In favour: Afghanistan, Albania, Algeria, Angola, Argentina, Australia, Austria, Bahamas, Bahrain, Bangladesh, Barbados, Belize, Benin, Bhutan, Bolivia, Botswana, Brazil, Bulgaria, Burma, Burundi, Byelorussian SSR, Cape Verde, Central African Republic, Chad, Chile, China, Colombia, Congo, Costa Rica, Cuba, Cyprus, Czechoslovakia, Democratic Kampuchea, Democratic Yemen, Denmark, Djibouti, Dominica, Dominican Republic, Ecuador, Egypt, El Salvador, Equatorial Guinea, Ethiopia, Fiji, Finland, Gabon, Gambia, German Democratic Republic, Ghana, Greece, Guatemala, Guinea, Guinea-Bissau, Guyana, Haiti, Honduras, Hungary, Iceland, India, Indonesia, Iran, Iraq, Ireland, Ivory Coast, Jamaica, Japan, Jordan, Kenya, Kuwait, Lao People's Democratic Republic, Lebanon, Lesotho, Liberia, Libyan Arab Jamahiriya, Madagascar, Malaysia, Maldives, Mali, Malta, Mauritania, Mauritius, Mexico, Mongolia, Morocco, Mozambique, Nepal, Netherlands, New Zealand, Nicaragua, Niger, Nigeria, Norway, Oman, Pakistan, Panama, Papua New Guinea, Peru, Philippines, Poland, Portugal, Qatar, Romania, Rwanda, Saint Lucia, Saint Vincent and the Grenadines, Samoa, Sao Tome and Principe, Saudi Arabia, Senegal, Sierra Leone, Singapore, Solomon Islands, Somalia, Spain, Sri Lanka, Sudan, Suriname, Swaziland, Sweden, Syrian Arab Republic, Thailand, Togo, Trinidad and Tobago, Tunisia, Turkey, Uganda, Ukrainian SSR, USSR, United Arab Emirates, United Republic of Cameroon, United Republic of Tanzania, Upper Volta, Uruguay, Vanuatu, Venezuela, Viet Nam, Yemen, Yugoslavia, Zaire, Zambia, Zimbabwe.

Against: United Kingdom, United States.

Abstaining: Belgium, Canada, France, Germany, Federal Republic of, Italy, Luxembourg, Malawi, Paraguay.

A number of delegations explained that they had reservations on various parts of the text, despite their positive votes. New Zealand could not accept the implication in paragraph 4 that force was legitimate to bring change in Non-Self-Governing Territories, or the assumption in paragraph 10 that the presence of military bases necessarily an impediment to decolonization; it was disappointed that the sponsors had not put forward a draft that could be adopted by consensus.

Denmark, speaking also on behalf of Finland, Iceland, Norway and Sweden, expressed their commitment to the decolonization process but regretted that paragraph 4 contradicted United Nations principles of always encouraging peaceful solutions; they felt paragraph 10 was too categorically formulated and had reservations regarding paragraphs that seemed to run counter to the principle of universality. Austria also expressed reservations on paragraph 4 which it said it understood to mean support for the struggle by peaceful and negotiated means only. Ireland stated that with regard to paragraph 10, its position on specific military bases and installations would be guided by the attitudes, freely expressed, of the inhabitants. Turkey felt that paragraph 10 had not been drafted in a sufficiently balanced manner.

Portugal, which mentioned the need to safeguard such principles as seeking a peaceful solution before resorting to armed struggle, the universality of the Organization, and the exclusion of unrelated matters, said it had particular reservations concerning paragraphs 4, 8 and 10. Japan commended the efforts of the authors in trying to avoid inserting unnecessarily controversial elements, but had reservations on paragraph 5 because it could not support all parts of the report of the Committee on colonial countries, as well as on paragraphs 4, 6 and 10. The Netherlands stressed the need to apply in Namibia the principles of the 1960 Declaration which it saw as the main task remaining in the decolonization process, and it expressed reservations concerning paragraphs 2, 4, 7, 8 and 10.

In other action in December, the Assembly in resolution 38/190 urged the speedy implementation of the 1960 Declaration on colonial countries when it reaffirmed the legitimacy of the struggle of peoples under colonial domination, foreign occupation or racist régimes and their inalienable right to self-determination and independence.

The right of such peoples was also recognized in a resolution adopted by the March/April 1983 United Nations Conference on Succession of States in respect of State Property, Archives and Debts (see LEGAL QUESTIONS, Chapter III).

Implementation by international organizations

In response to a series of calls by the General Assembly for implementation of its 1960 Declaration, including a November 1982 resolution,[3] a number of United Nations specialized agencies and organizations continued providing assistance to peoples of colonial countries and their national liberation movements, particularly in Namibia (see Chapter III of this section). Assistance to such movements in southern Africa was mainly provided by FAO, UNESCO, WHO, UNHCR, UNDP and UNCTAD (see p. 159).

In accordance with the same resolutions, a 1983 report[4] was prepared by the Secretary-General summarizing the replies of 19 United Nations bodies on action taken since the circulation of the Secretary-General's previous report on the subject in 1982.[5]

Among the 1983 activities, the International Labour Organisation (ILO) monitored developments related to *apartheid* and provided assistance to its victims in southern Africa. Following an initiative undertaken by the Workers Group of the International Labour Conference and the United Nations Special Committee against *Apartheid,* an international conference of trade unions on sanctions and other actions against the *apartheid* régime in South Africa was held at Geneva in June 1983 as part of the ILO effort to mobilize public opinion against *apartheid.* The ILO technical cooperation programme in support of the front-line States and the liberation movements recognized by the Organization of African Unity (OAU) was expanded through additional ILO funds, which supplemented funds previously committed by UNDP and the United Nations Fund for Namibia.

The World Food Programme reported that at the beginning of the year it was conducting five projects for liberation movement refugees and displaced persons based on a $19 million budget, including a new commitment of $6.5 million for assistance for Namibians in Angola.

The Universal Postal Union (UPU) provided fellowships to Anguilla, the British Virgin Islands, the Cayman Islands, Montserrat and the Turks and Caicos Islands for a UPU technical meeting of postmasters-general at Bridgetown, Barbados, from 30 May to 4 June, and UPU consultants visited Anguilla and Montserrat in June and July to discuss problems of postal management. In addition, training and other assistance were provided to a number of newly independent countries in Africa, the Caribbean and the Pacific.

The International Telecommunication Union continued to provide training courses in radio programme production and equipment maintenance at the Posts and Telecommunication Corporation's Staff Training College as part of the UNDP Nationhood Programme for Namibia. Consultancy services were provided for planning a telecommunication administration and a broadcasting authority for Namibia.

The International Maritime Organization cooperated with the United Nations Council for Namibia and the United Nations Commissioner for Namibia concerning a transport survey for Namibia and a maritime training and harbour survey. The International Civil Aviation Organization also participated in the Nationhood Programme for Namibia; in that context, an evaluation of the future civil aviation needs of Namibia was completed, and civil aviation training fellowships were provided through a UNDP-funded programme.

The World Intellectual Property Organization (WIPO) provided assistance to refugees from colonial Territories and awarded two fellowships in the fields of industrial property and copyright. The World Bank reported that it was able to consider loans only to member Governments thus precluding any loans to colonies or national liberation groups, but that, in the case of Namibia, once conditions for independence were agreed upon and interest in Bank membership had been indicated by the new authorities, it would take steps in advance of membership to initiate discussions on development policy and assistance.

In accordance with a July 1982 Economic and Social Council request,[6] the President of the Council and the Acting Chairman of the Committee on colonial countries held consultations and reported[7] that the situation in southern Africa as a result of South Africa's policies presented a serious threat to peace and security and that, while several United Nations organizations had continued to assist the peoples of Namibia and South Africa, the assistance to date was far from adequate in terms of acute needs. They called for renewed efforts to secure additional funds and emphasized the role of the executive heads of the institutions concerned. They also noted with satisfaction that, in response to the appeals of the General Assembly, FAO, UN-ESCO and ILO had waived overhead costs for projects, and they expressed the hope that all organizations concerned would act accordingly.

In accordance with the same request,[6] consultations were also held[8] between the Council President and the Acting Chairman of the Special Committee against *Apartheid* on the implementation of the 1960 Declaration on colonial countries. The two presiding officers agreed that the deteriorating conditions resulting from South Africa's policies required urgent action and continued co-operation of the Council, the Committee against *Apartheid* and the Committee on colonial countries. The commitment of the United Nations was a matter of priority for which all United Nations bodies should provide moral and material assistance.

ECONOMIC AND SOCIAL COUNCIL ACTION

On 25 July, the Economic and Social Council, on the recommendation of its Third (Programme and Co-ordination) Committee, adopted resolution 1983/42 by recorded vote.

Implementation of the Declaration on the Granting of Independence to Colonial Countries and Peoples by the specialized agencies and the international institutions associated with the United Nations and assistance to the oppressed people of South Africa and their national liberation movement by agencies and institutions within the United Nations system

The Economic and Social Council,

Having examined the report of the Secretary-General and the reports of the President of the Economic and Social Council concerning the question of the implementation of the Declaration on the Granting of Independence to Colonial Countries and Peoples by the specialized agencies and the international institutions associated with the United Nations and of assistance to the oppressed people of South Africa and their national liberation movement by agencies and institutions within the United Nations system,

Having heard the statements of the Chairman of the Special Committee on the Situation with regard to the Implementation of the Declaration on the Granting of Independence to Colonial Countries and Peoples and the Acting Chairman of the Special Committee against *Apartheid,*

Recalling General Assembly resolution 1514(XV) of 14 December 1960, containing the Declaration on the Granting of Independence to Colonial Countries and Peoples, and all other resolutions adopted by United Nations bodies on this subject, including in particular Assembly resolution 37/32 of 23 November 1982 and Council resolution 1982/47 of 27 July 1982,

Reaffirming the responsibility of the specialized agencies and other organizations within the United Nations system to take all effective measures, within their respective spheres of competence, to ensure the full and speedy implementation of the Declaration on the Granting of Independence to Colonial Countries and Peoples and other relevant resolutions of United Nations bodies,

Noting with deep concern that the situation in southern Africa continues to present a serious threat to peace and security as a result of South Africa's intensified and ruthless repression, its policy and practice of *apartheid* and other gross violations of the human rights of the peoples in Namibia and South Africa and its armed aggression and military, political and economic destabilization directed against independent States in the region,

Deeply conscious of the continuing critical need of the people of Namibia and their national liberation movement, the South West Africa People's Organization, for concrete assistance from the specialized agencies and the international institutions associated with the United Nations in their struggle for liberation from the illegal occupation of their country by the racist minority régime in South Africa,

Deeply concerned that, while progress has been maintained through the continuing efforts of the United Nations High Commissioner for Refugees in the extension of assistance to refugees from southern Africa, the action taken thus far by the organizations and agencies concerned in the provision of assistance generally to the people of Namibia is still far from adequate to meet their urgent and growing needs,

Gravely concerned at the continued collaboration of the International Monetary Fund with the Government of South Africa, in disregard of relevant General Assembly resolutions,

Noting with satisfaction the continuing efforts of the United Nations Development Programme in the extension of assistance to the national liberation movements concerned, and commending the initiative taken by that organization in establishing channels for closer, periodic contacts and consultations between the specialized agencies and United Nations institutions and the Organization of African Unity and the national liberation movements in the formulation of assistance programmes,

Noting further the high-level meetings held at Addis Ababa in April 1983 between representatives of the General Secretariat of the Organization of African Unity and the secretariats of the United Nations and other organizations within the United Nations system, in accordance with General Assembly resolution 37/15 of 16 November 1982 on co-operation between the United Nations and the Organization of African Unity,

Mindful of the Paris Declaration on Namibia and the Programme of Action on Namibia adopted by the International Conference in Support of the Struggle of the Namibian People for Independence, held in Paris from 25 to 29 April 1983,

1.   *Takes note* of the reports of the President of the Economic and Social Council and endorses the observations and suggestions contained therein;

2.   *Reaffirms* that the recognition by the General Assembly, the Security Council and other United Nations organs of the legitimacy of the struggle of colonial peoples to exercise their right to self-determination and independence entails, as a corollary, the extension by the United Nations system of organizations of all the necessary moral and material assistance to the peoples of the colonial territories and their national liberation movements;

3.   *Expresses its appreciation* to those specialized agencies and organizations within the United Nations system which have continued to co-operate in varying degrees with the United Nations and the Organization of African Unity in the implementation of the Declaration on the Granting of Independence to Colonial Countries and Peoples and other relevant resolutions of United Nations bodies, and urges all the specialized agencies and other organizations within the United Nations system to accelerate the full and speedy implementation of the relevant provisions of those resolutions;

4.   *Requests* the specialized agencies and other organizations within the United Nations system, in the light of the intensification of the liberation struggle in Namibia, to do everything possible as a matter of urgency to render, in consultation with the Organization of African Unity and the United Nations Council for Namibia, increased assistance to the people of Namibia, in particular in connection with the Nationhood Programme for Namibia;

5.   *Requests also* the specialized agencies and other organizations within the United Nations system to continue to take, in accordance with the relevant resolutions of the General Assembly and the Security Council, all necessary measures to withhold any financial, economic, technical or other assistance to the Government of South Africa until that Government restores to the people of Namibia their inalienable right to self-determination and independence, and to refrain from taking any action which might imply recognition of, or support for, the illegal occupation of Namibia by that régime;

6.   *Requests further* the specialized agencies and other organizations within the United Nations system, in accordance with the relevant resolutions of the General Assembly and the Security Council on the *apartheid* policy of the Government of South Africa, to intensify their support for the oppressed people of South Africa and to take such measures as will totally isolate the *apartheid* régime and mobilize world public opinion against *apartheid;*

7.   *Strongly condemns* the attacks carried out by South African armed forces on Namibian refugee camps and settlements in Angola, and requests the United Nations High Commissioner for Refugees and other competent organs of the United Nations and international organizations, as a matter of urgency, to use all ways and means to ensure the protection of those refugees and their safety from such attacks;

8.   *Strongly condemns* the blatant aggression of the Pretoria régime in its bombing attack on Mozambique in the spring of 1983 and the frequent acts of destabilization carried out by that régime against the front-line States, which have resulted in heavy loss of life, the creation of large numbers of refugees and massive destruction;

9.   *Deeply deplores* the persistent collaboration of the International Monetary Fund with the Government of South Africa, in disregard of repeated General Assembly resolutions to the contrary, and urgently calls upon the Fund to put an end to such collaboration;

10.   *Recommends* that a separate item on assistance to national liberation movements recognized by the Organization of African Unity should be included in the agenda of future high-level meetings of the General Secretariat of the Organization of African Unity and the secretariats of the United Nations and other organizations within the United Nations system, with a view to strengthening further the existing measures of co-ordination of action to ensure the best use of available resources for assistance to the peoples of the colonial territories;

11.   *Notes with satisfaction* the inclusion of Namibia, represented by the United Nations Council for Namibia, in the membership of the International Atomic Energy Agency and the International Telecommunication Union, in accordance with General Assembly resolution 37/233 C of 20 December 1982, and urges the specialized agencies and other organizations within the United Nations system which have not yet granted full membership to the United Nations Council for Namibia to do so without delay;

12.   *Notes with satisfaction* the arrangements made by several specialized agencies and United Nations institutions which enable representatives of the national liberation movements recognized by the Organization of African Unity to participate fully as observers in the proceedings relating to matters concerning their respective countries, and calls upon those international institutions which have not yet done so to follow that example and make the necessary arrangements without delay, including arrangements to defray the cost of the participation of those representatives;

13.   *Recommends* that all Governments should intensify their efforts in the specialized agencies and other organizations within the United Nations system of which they are members to ensure the full and effective implementation of the Declaration on the Granting of Independence to Colonial Countries and Peoples and other relevant resolutions of United Nations bodies;

14.   *Urges* those specialized agencies and organizations within the United Nations system which have not already done so to include in the agenda of the regular meetings of their governing bodies a separate item on the progress made by those organizations in their implementation of the Declaration on the Granting of Independence to Colonial Countries and Peoples and other relevant resolutions of United Nations bodies;

15. *Further urges* the executive heads of the specialized agencies and other organizations within the United Nations system to formulate, with the active cooperation of the Organization of African Unity, and to submit, as a matter of priority, to their governing and legislative organs concrete proposals for the full implementation of the relevant United Nations decisions;

16. *Draws the attention* of the Special Committee on the Situation with regard to the Implementation of the Declaration on the Granting of Independence to Colonial Countries and Peoples to the present resolution and to the discussions on the subject at the second regular session of 1983 of the Council;

17. *Requests* the President of the Economic and Social Council to continue consultations on these matters with the Chairman of the Special Committee on the Situation with regard to the Implementation of the Declaration on the Granting of Independence to Colonial Countries and Peoples and the Chairman of the Special Committee against *Apartheid* and to report thereon to the Council;

18. *Requests* the Secretary-General to follow the implementation of the present resolution and to report thereon to the Council at its second regular session of 1984;

19. *Decides* to keep these questions under continuous review.

Economic and Social Council resolution 1983/42

25 July 1983   Meeting 39   35-1-13 (roll-call vote)

Approved by Third Committee (E/1983/114) by roll-call vote (29-1-13), 15 July (meeting 11); 25-nation draft (E/1983/C.3/L.2), orally revised and orally amended by Mexico; agenda item 22.

Sponsors: Algeria, Bangladesh, Benin, Bulgaria, Byelorussian SSR, China, Congo, Djibouti, German Democratic Republic, Ghana, India, Kenya, Lebanon, Nigeria, Pakistan, Poland, Saint Lucia, Senegal, Sierra Leone, Somalia, Sudan, Syrian Arab Republic, Tunisia, United Republic of Tanzania, Yugoslavia.

Meeting number. ESC 39.

Roll-call vote in Council as follows:

In favour: Algeria, Argentina, Bangladesh, Benin, Botswana, Brazil, Bulgaria, Byelorussian SSR, China, Colombia, Congo, Djibouti, Ecuador, German Democratic Republic, India, Kenya, Lebanon, Liberia, Malaysia, Mali, Mexico, Pakistan, Peru, Poland, Qatar, Romania, Saint Lucia, Saudi Arabia, Sudan, Suriname, Swaziland, Thailand, Tunisia, USSR, Venezuela.

Against: United States.

Abstaining: Austria, Canada, Denmark, France, Germany, Federal Republic of, Greece, Japan, Luxembourg, Netherlands, New Zealand, Norway, Portugal, United Kingdom.

Prior to the approval of the draft in the Council's Third Committee, Mexico orally proposed amendments to the eighth preambular paragraph, to read "continued collaboration of the International Monetary Fund with the Government of South Africa" in place of "continued collaboration between the International Monetary Fund and the Government of South Africa" and to the ninth operative paragraph to replace "Deeply deplores the persistent collaboration between the International Monetary Fund and South Africa, in disregard of repeated resolutions to the contrary by the General Assembly, and calls upon the International Monetary Fund to put an end to such collaboration" by the text, "Deeply deplores the persistent collaboration of the International Monetary Fund with the Government of South Africa, in disregard of repeated General Assembly reso-

lutions to the contrary, and urgently calls upon the International Monetary Fund to put an end to such collaboration". Mexico also proposed the deletion of the words "the United Nations Council for" between the words "full membership to" and "Namibia" at the end of operative paragraph 11; that proposal was rejected by the sponsors. The Committee adopted the eighth preambular paragraph, as amended, by 26 votes to 2, with 12 abstentions, and operative paragraph 9, as amended, by 27 votes to 2, with 12 abstentions.

Following the vote in the Council, several delegations explained their reservations. Affirming that the best way to negotiate change in South Africa was through peaceful persuasion rather than ostracism, the United Kingdom said it was unable to accept the language in the fifth preambular paragraph and operative paragraph 8; it also rejected the condemnation of IMF in the eighth preambular paragraph and operative paragraph 9 because it supported the principle of the universality and independence of the specialized agencies. Austria and New Zealand agreed with regard to respecting the independence of IMF, and Greece, speaking on behalf of the European Community, said the formulation on paragraphs concerning IMF was not in line with their views, although they commended the humanitarian and economic assistance furnished by specialized agencies and deplored South African attacks against front-line States. Norway, speaking also on behalf of Denmark, noting their increased humanitarian, technical and educational assistance to peoples struggling for self-determination, said that the statutes of the specialized agencies should be taken into account and that those institutions should retain their universal character.

Portugal supported many elements of the resolution but regretted that a number of discriminatory references and the allusion to certain Assembly resolutions prevented its endorsement.

In 1983, several other United Nations bodies were concerned with relations between IMF and South Africa, and the Assembly in several resolutions called for an end to those relations (see p. 146).

Action by the Committee on colonial countries. On 14 September, the Committee on colonial countries adopted a resolution[9] on the role of the specialized agencies and other organizations of the United Nations system which became the basis for a draft resolution recommended to the Assembly.

GENERAL ASSEMBLY ACTION

On 7 December, the General Assembly adopted by recorded vote resolution 38/51 which was based on the text by the Committee on colonial countries and was recommended by the Fourth Committee.

Implementation of the Declaration on the Granting of Independence to Colonial Countries and Peoples by the specialized agencies and the international institutions associated with the United Nations

The General Assembly,

Having examined the item entitled "Implementation of the Declaration on the Granting of Independence to Colonial Countries and Peoples by the specialized agencies and the international institutions associated with the United Nations",

Recalling the Declaration on the Granting of Independence to Colonial Countries and Peoples, contained in its resolution 1514(XV) of 14 December 1960, and the Plan of Action for the Full Implementation of the Declaration, contained in the annex to its resolution 35/118 of 11 December 1980, as well as all other relevant resolutions adopted by the General Assembly on this subject, in particular resolution 36/52 of 24 November 1981 on the item and 37/233 of 20 December 1982 on the question of Namibia,

Having examined the reports submitted on the item by the Secretary-General, the Economic and Social Council and the Special Committee on the Situation with regard to the Implementation of the Declaration on the Granting of Independence to Colonial Countries and Peoples,

Taking into account the relevant provisions of the Paris Declaration on Namibia and the Programme of Action on Namibia adopted at the International Conference in Support of the Struggle of the Namibian People for Independence,

Bearing in mind the relevant provisions of the Political Declaration adopted by the Seventh Conference of Heads of State or Government of Non-Aligned Countries, held at New Delhi from 7 to 12 March 1983, and other documents of the Co-ordinating Bureau of the Non-Aligned Countries,

Aware that the struggle of the people of Namibia for self-determination and independence is in its crucial stage and has sharply intensified as a consequence of the stepped-up aggression by the illegal colonialist régime of Pretoria against the people of the Territory and the increased general support rendered to that régime by certain Western countries, especially the United States of America and Israel, coupled with efforts to deprive the Namibian people of their hard-won victories in the liberation struggle, and that it is therefore incumbent upon the entire international community decisively to intensify concerted action in support of the people of Namibia and their sole and authentic representative, the South West Africa People's Organization, for the attainment of their goal,

Deeply conscious of the critical need of the Namibian people and their national liberation movement, the South West Africa People's Organization, and of the peoples of other colonial Territories for concrete assistance from the specialized agencies and other organizations of the United Nations system in their struggle for liberation from colonial rule and in their efforts to achieve and consolidate their national independence,

Reaffirming the responsibility of the specialized agencies and other organizations of the United Nations system to take all the necessary measures, within their respective spheres of competence, to ensure the full and speedy implementation of the Declaration on the Granting of Independence to Colonial Countries and Peoples and other relevant resolutions of the United Nations, particularly those relating to the provision of moral and material assistance, on a priority basis, to the peoples of the colonial Territories and their national liberation movements,

Deeply concerned that, although there has been progress in the extension of assistance to refugees from Namibia, the action taken hitherto by the organizations concerned in providing assistance to the people of the Territory through their national liberation movement, the South West Africa People's Organization, still remains inadequate to meet the urgent and growing needs of the Namibian people,

Expressing its confident hope that closer contacts and consultations between the specialized agencies and other organizations of the United Nations system and the Organization of African Unity and the national liberation movement concerned will help to overcome procedural and other difficulties which have impeded or delayed the implementation of some assistance programmes,

Recalling its resolution 37/233 C of 20 December 1982, requesting all specialized agencies and other organizations and conferences of the United Nations system to grant full membership to the United Nations Council for Namibia as the legal Administering Authority for Namibia,

Expressing its appreciation to the General Secretariat of the Organization of African Unity for the continued co-operation and assistance extended by it to the specialized agencies and other organizations of the United Nations system in connection with the implementation of the relevant resolutions of the United Nations,

Expressing its appreciation also to the Governments of the front-line States for the steadfast support extended to the people of Namibia and their national liberation movement, the South West Africa People's Organization, in their just and legitimate struggle for the attainment of freedom and independence, despite increased armed attacks by the forces of the racist régime of South Africa, and aware of the particular needs of those Governments for assistance in that connection,

Noting the efforts of the United Nations Development Programme in the extension of assistance to the national liberation movements and commending its initiative in establishing channels for closer periodic contacts and consultations between the specialized agencies and other organizations of the United Nations system and the Organization of African Unity and the national liberation movements in the formulation of assistance programmes,

Noting also the support given by the specialized agencies and other organizations of the United Nations system to the implementation of the Nationhood Programme for Namibia, in accordance with General Assembly resolution 32/9 A of 4 November 1977,

Deploring the continued links with and assistance rendered to South Africa by certain specialized agencies in the financial, economic, technical and other fields, in contravention of the relevant resolutions of the United Nations,

Gravely concerned, in particular, at the continued collaboration between the International Monetary Fund and the Government of South Africa in disregard of relevant General Assembly resolutions, especially resolution 37/2 of 21 October 1982,

Bearing in mind the importance of the activities of non-governmental organizations aimed at putting an end to the assistance which is still being rendered to South Africa by some specialized agencies,

Mindful of the necessity of keeping under continuous review the activities of the specialized agencies and other organizations of the United Nations system in the implementation of the various United Nations decisions relating to decolonization,

1. *Approves* the chapter of the report of the Special Committee on the Situation with regard to the Implementation of the Declaration on the Granting of Independence to Colonial Countries and Peoples relating to the question;

2. *Reaffirms* that the specialized agencies and other organizations and bodies of the United Nations system should continue to be guided by the relevant resolutions of the United Nations in their efforts to contribute, within their spheres of competence, to the full and speedy implementation of the Declaration on the Granting of Independence to Colonial Countries and Peoples, contained in General Assembly resolution 1514(XV);

3. *Reaffirms also* that the recognition by the General Assembly, the Security Council and other United Nations organs of the legitimacy of the struggle of colonial peoples to exercise their right to self-determination and independence entails, as a corollary, the extension by the specialized agencies and other organizations of the United Nations system of all the necessary moral and material assistance to those peoples and their national liberation movements;

4. *Expresses its appreciation* to those specialized agencies and other organizations of the United Nations system which have continued to co-operate in varying degrees with the United Nations and the Organization of African Unity in the implementation of the Declaration and other relevant resolutions of the United Nations and urges all the specialized agencies and other organizations of the United Nations system to accelerate the full and speedy implementation of the relevant provisions of those resolutions;

5. *Expresses its concern* that the assistance extended thus far by certain specialized agencies and other organizations of the United Nations system to the colonial peoples, particularly the people of Namibia and their national liberation movement, the South West Africa People's Organization, is far from adequate in relation to the actual needs of the peoples concerned;

6. *Requests* all specialized agencies and other organizations and bodies of the United Nations system, in accordance with the relevant resolutions of the General Assembly and the Security Council, to take all necessary measures to withhold from the racist régime of South Africa any form of co-operation and assistance in the financial, economic, technical and other fields and to discontinue all support to that régime until the people of Namibia have exercised fully their inalienable right to self-determination, freedom and national independence in a united Namibia and until the inhuman system of *apartheid* has been totally eradicated;

7. *Reiterates its conviction* that the specialized agencies and other organizations and bodies of the United Nations system should refrain from taking any action which might imply recognition of the legitimacy of, or support for, the domination of the Territory by the racist régime of South Africa;

8. *Regrets* that, notwithstanding the statement of the representative of the World Bank on 8 June 1983 that the Bank has terminated business relations with the South African régime, the World Bank and the International Monetary Fund continue to maintain links with the racist régime of Pretoria, as exemplified by the continued membership of South Africa in both agencies, and expresses the view that the two agencies should put an end to all links with the racist régime;

9. *Strongly condemns* the persistent collaboration between the International Monetary Fund and South Africa, in disregard of repeated resolutions to the contrary by the General Assembly, particularly the granting of a loan of $1.1 billion to South Africa in November 1982 in defiance of General Assembly resolution 37/2, and calls upon the International Monetary Fund to rescind the loan and to put an end to such collaboration;

10. *Commends* those non-governmental organizations which, by their activities, as exemplified by the co-operation between the Center for International Policy and the United Nations Council for Namibia, are helping to inform public opinion, in the United States of America and elsewhere, and mobilize it against the assistance rendered by the International Monetary Fund to South Africa, and calls upon all non-governmental organizations to redouble their efforts in this respect;

11. *Urges* the executive heads of the World Bank and the International Monetary Fund to draw the particular attention of their governing bodies to the present resolution, with a view to formulating specific programmes beneficial to the peoples of the colonial Territories, particularly Namibia;

12. *Requests* the specialized agencies and other organizations of the United Nations system to render or continue to render, as a matter of urgency, all possible moral and material assistance to the colonial peoples struggling for liberation from colonial rule, bearing in mind that such assistance should not only meet their immediate needs but also create conditions for development after they have exercised their right to self-determination and independence;

13. *Once again requests* the specialized agencies and other organizations of the United Nations system to continue to provide all moral and material assistance to the newly independent and emerging States;

14. *Reiterates its recommendation* that the specialized agencies and other organizations of the United Nations system should initiate or broaden contacts and co-operation with the colonial peoples and their national liberation movements directly or, where appropriate, through the Organization of African Unity, and review and introduce greater flexibility in their procedures with respect to the formulation and preparation of assistance programmes and projects so as to be able to extend the necessary assistance without delay to help the colonial peoples and their national liberation movements in their struggle to exercise their inalienable right to self-determination and independence in accordance with General Assembly resolution 1514(XV);

15. *Notes with satisfaction* that the South West Africa People's Organization continues to be the beneficiary of a number of programmes established within the framework of the United Nations Institute for Namibia at Lusaka and that the United Nations Council for Namibia, in co-operation with the South West Africa

People's Organization, continues to represent the people of Namibia at meetings of the specialized agencies and other organizations of the United Nations system, and urges those agencies and organizations to increase their assistance to the South West Africa People's Organization, as well as to the United Nations Institute for Namibia and the Nationhood Programme for Namibia;

16. *Urges* the specialized agencies and other organizations of the United Nations system that have not already done so to include in the agenda of the regular meetings of their governing bodies a separate item on the progress they have made in the implementation of the Declaration and the other relevant resolutions of the United Nations;

17. *Notes with satisfaction* the arrangements made by several specialized agencies and other organizations of the United Nations system which enable representatives of the national liberation movements recognized by the Organization of African Unity to participate fully as observers in the proceedings relating to matters concerning their respective countries, and calls upon those agencies and organizations that have not yet done so to follow this example and to make the necessary arrangements without delay;

18. *Notes with satisfaction* the admittance of Namibia, represented by the United Nations Council for Namibia, as a member of the International Atomic Energy Agency and the International Telecommunication Union, in accordance with General Assembly resolution 37/233 C, and urges the specialized agencies and other organizations of the United Nations system that have not so far granted full membership to the United Nations Council for Namibia to do so without delay;

19. *Urges* the specialized agencies and other organizations and institutions of the United Nations system to extend, as a matter of priority, substantial material assistance to the Governments of the front-line States in order to enable them to support more effectively the struggle of the people of Namibia for freedom and independence and to resist the violation of their territorial integrity by the armed forces of the racist régime of South Africa directly or, as in Angola and Mozambique, through puppet traitor groups in the service of Pretoria;

20. *Urges* the specialized agencies and other organizations and institutions of the United Nations system to assist in accelerating progress in all sectors of the national life of the small Territories, particularly in the development of their economies;

21. *Recommends* that all Governments should intensify their efforts in the specialized agencies and other organizations of the United Nations system of which they are members to ensure the full and effective implementation of the Declaration and other relevant resolutions of the United Nations and, in that connection, that they should accord priority to the question of providing assistance on an emergency basis to the peoples of the colonial Territories and their national liberation movements;

22. *Reiterates its proposal*, under article III of the Agreement between the United Nations and the International Monetary Fund, for the urgent inclusion in the agenda of the Board of Governors of the Fund of an item dealing with the relationship between the Fund and South Africa and further reiterates its proposal that, in pursuance of article II of the Agreement, the relevant

organs of the United Nations should participate in any meeting of the Board of Governors called by the Fund for the purpose of discussing the item and urges the Fund to discuss its relationship with South Africa at its annual meeting in September 1984, in compliance with the above-mentioned Agreement;

23. *Recommends* the sending in 1984 of a high-level mission to the International Monetary Fund which, subject to the agreement of the United Nations bodies involved, would be composed of the Chairman of the Special Committee on the Situation with regard to the Implementation of the Declaration on the Granting of Independence to Colonial Countries and Peoples, the President of the United Nations Council for Namibia and the Chairman of the Special Committee against *Apartheid*;

24. *Draws the attention* of the specialized agencies and other organizations of the United Nations system to the Plan of Action for the Full Implementation of the Declaration on the Granting of Independence to Colonial Countries and Peoples, contained in the annex to General Assembly resolution 35/118, in particular to those provisions calling on the agencies and organizations to render all possible moral and material assistance to the peoples of the colonial Territories and their national liberation movements;

25. *Urges* the executive heads of the specialized agencies and other organizations of the United Nations system, having regard to the provisions of paragraphs 14 and 24 above, to formulate, with the active co-operation of the Organization of African Unity where appropriate, and to submit, as a matter of priority, to their governing and legislative organs concrete proposals for the full implementation of the relevant United Nations decisions, in particular specific programmes of assistance to the peoples of the colonial Territories and their national liberation movements;

26. *Requests* the Secretary-General to continue to assist the specialized agencies and other organizations of the United Nations system in working out appropriate measures for implementing the relevant resolutions of the United Nations and to prepare for submission to the relevant bodies, with the assistance of those agencies and organizations, a report on the action taken in implementation of the relevant resolutions, including the present resolution, since the circulation of his previous report;

27. *Requests* the Economic and Social Council to continue to consider, in consultation with the Special Committee on the Situation with regard to the Implementation of the Declaration on the Granting of Independence to Colonial Countries and Peoples, appropriate measures for the co-ordination of the policies and activities of the specialized agencies and other organizations of the United Nations system in implementing the relevant resolutions of the General Assembly;

28. *Requests* the Special Committee to continue to examine this question and to report thereon to the General Assembly at its thirty-ninth session.

General Assembly resolution 38/51

7 December 1983   Meeting 86   117-3-33 (recorded vote)

Approved by Fourth Committee (A/38/609) by recorded vote (101-4-28), 17 November (meeting 19); draft by Committee on colonial countries (A/38/23); agenda items 12 and 104.

Meeting numbers. GA 38th session: 4th Committee 8, 10-19; plenary 86.

Recorded vote in Assembly as follows:

In favour: Afghanistan, Albania, Algeria, Angola, Argentina, Bahrain, Bangladesh, Barbados, Benin, Bhutan, Botswana, Brazil, Bulgaria, Burma, Burundi, Byelorussian SSR, Cape Verde, Chile, China, Colombia, Comoros, Congo, Costa Rica, Cuba, Cyprus, Czechoslovakia, Democratic Kampuchea, Democratic Yemen, Djibouti, Dominican Republic, Ecuador, Egypt, El Salvador, Equatorial Guinea, Ethiopia, Fiji, Gabon, Gambia, German Democratic Republic, Ghana, Greece, Guinea, Guinea-Bissau, Guyana, Haiti, Honduras, Hungary, India, Indonesia, Iran, Iraq, Jamaica, Jordan, Kenya, Kuwait, Lao People's Democratic Republic, Lebanon, Liberia, Libyan Arab Jamahiriya, Madagascar, Malaysia, Maldives, Mali, Malta, Mauritania, Mauritius, Mexico, Mongolia, Morocco, Mozambique, Nepal, Nicaragua, Niger, Nigeria, Oman, Pakistan, Panama, Papua New Guinea, Peru, Philippines, Poland, Qatar, Romania, Rwanda, Saint Vincent and the Grenadines, Samoa, Sao Tome and Principe, Saudi Arabia, Senegal, Sierra Leone, Singapore, Somalia, Sri Lanka, Sudan, Suriname, Syrian Arab Republic, Thailand, Togo, Trinidad and Tobago, Tunisia, Turkey, Uganda, Ukrainian SSR, USSR, United Arab Emirates, United Republic of Cameroon, United Republic of Tanzania, Upper Volta, Uruguay, Vanuatu, Venezuela, Viet Nam, Yemen, Yugoslavia, Zaire, Zambia, Zimbabwe.

Against: Israel, United Kingdom, United States.

Abstaining: Australia, Austria, Bahamas, Belgium, Bolivia,[a] Canada, Central African Republic, Chad, Denmark, Dominica, Finland, France, Germany, Federal Republic of, Guatemala, Iceland, Ireland, Italy, Ivory Coast, Japan, Lesotho, Luxembourg, Malawi, Netherlands, New Zealand, Norway, Paraguay, Portugal, Saint Christopher and Nevis, Saint Lucia, Solomon Islands, Spain, Swaziland, Sweden.

[a]Later advised the Secretariat it had intended to vote in favour.

Prior to approving the text as a whole, the Fourth Committee voted on a United States amendment to the sixth preambular paragraph by which "Western" and "especially the United States of America and Israel" would have been deleted, and a second amendment in paragraph 10, to replace "in the United States of America and elsewhere against the assistance rendered by the International Monetary Fund to South Africa" by "on the situation in South Africa". The first amendment was rejected by a recorded vote of 65 to 40 with 19 abstentions, and the second by a recorded vote of 63 to 39 with 18 abstentions.

Speaking in explanation of vote, the United States said that paragraph 10, which was directed exclusively against the United States, constituted interference in its internal affairs and was therefore inadmissible and contradicted the principles of the Charter. Israel opposed the draft as a whole because of its imbalanced structure and phraseology and because Israel, the United States and "certain Western countries" were singled out for maintaining relations with South Africa when many other countries did so as well.

France recalled the importance it attached to the principles of universality and independence of the specialized agencies and expressed reservations on paragraphs 9 and 10 which it said amounted to unfair criticism of the actions of the World Bank and IMF. Canada had not been able to accept paragraphs 8, 9, 10 and 22 and the sixth preambular paragraph because it was opposed to the politicization of the decision-making processes of organizations such as IMF and the World Bank, United Nations efforts to impose its views on autonomous agencies, and the condemnation of certain States by name. Sri Lanka expressed reservations concerning paragraphs 8, 9 and 10, which it said contained inappropriate references to the role of certain international organizations.

While convinced that United Nations organizations had an obligation to promote decolonization, Uruguay objected to the selective nature of certain condemnatory references which did nothing to assist United Nations efforts to ensure the universal implementation of the 1960 Declaration on colonial countries, as well as certain references to IMF which were incompatible with the apolitical nature that should characterize its management and the implementation of its decisions. Similarly, Fiji and Togo opposed selective condemnation of countries and expressed reservations concerning the sixth preambular paragraph and paragraph 10. For the same reason, Gambia objected to paragraph 9. Greece said it was regrettable that certain countries had been mentioned by name, and for that reason it had voted for the United States amendments.

Although it supported the Special Committee's recommendations, Lesotho considered that it was impossible to implement certain paragraphs of the resolution, particularly those providing for commercial sanctions against South Africa.

Bolivia said it had reservations concerning certain preambular and operative paragraphs of the text.

Foreign interests impeding implementation of the Declaration on colonial countries

In 1983, both the Committee on colonial countries and the General Assembly reaffirmed their concern that the activities of foreign economic, financial and other interests operating in the colonial Territories, particularly in southern Africa, constituted an obstacle to political independence by the indigenous population. The Committee considered the item from August 24 to September 1 including the subject of the profits of transnational corporations from colonial Territories. On 1 September, the Committee adopted a resolution[10] on the activities of foreign economic and other interests which became the basis for a draft resolution recommended to the Assembly.

According to a November 1982 request by the Assembly,[11] the United Nations Centre on Trnnsnational Corporations was to complete a register indicating the profits that transnational corporations derived from their activities in colonial Territories and report to the Committee on colonial countries at its 1983 session, as originally requested in 1981.[12] However, since the report was not ready for the Committee meetings, the report was transmitted to the Assembly's Fourth Committee by a note[13] of 30 September from the Secretary-General. It indicated the profits which transnational corporations derived from their activities in colonial Territories with a list of corporations and their affiliates by home country, host Territory, line of business and major economic sector, as well as data on profits and sales which were verified with or directly provided by the corporations themselves.

On 3 November, the Committee adopted by recorded vote a text as drafted by the Committee on colonial countries and recommended its adoption to the Assembly.

GENERAL ASSEMBLY ACTION

On 7 December, the General Assembly adopted by recorded vote resolution 38/50, which was based on the text by the Committee on colonial countries and recommended by the Fourth Committee.

Activities of foreign economic and other interests which are impeding the implementation of the Declaration on the Granting of Independence to Colonial Countries and Peoples in Namibia and in all other Territories under colonial domination and efforts to eliminate colonialism, *apartheid* and racial discrimination in southern Africa

The General Assembly,

Having considered the item entitled "Activities of foreign economic and other interests which are impeding the implementation of the Declaration on the Granting of Independence to Colonial Countries and Peoples in Namibia and in all other Territories under colonial domination and efforts to eliminate colonialism, *apartheid* and racial discrimination in southern Africa",

Having examined the chapter of the report of the Special Committee on the Situation with regard to the Implementation of the Declaration on the Granting of Independence to Colonial Countries and Peoples relating to this question,

Taking into consideration the relevant chapter of the report of the United Nations Council for Namibia,

Having considered the report of the United Nations Centre on Transnational Corporations, relating to the preparation of a register indicating the profits that transnational corporations derive from their activities in colonial Territories, submitted in pursuance of General Assembly resolution 37/31 of 23 November 1982,

Recalling its resolutions 1514(XV) of 14 December 1960, containing the Declaration on the Granting of Independence to Colonial Countries and Peoples, 2621(XXV) of 12 October 1970, containing the programme of action for the full implementation of the Declaration, and 35/118 of 11 December 1980, the annex to which contains the Plan of Action for the Full Implementation of the Declaration, as well as all other resolutions of the United Nations relating to the item,

Reaffirming the solemn obligation of the administering Powers under the Charter of the United Nations to promote the political, economic, social and educational advancement of the inhabitants of the Territories under their administration and to protect the human and natural resources of those Territories against abuses,

Taking into account the relevant provisions of the Paris Declaration on Namibia and the Programme of Action on Namibia, adopted at the International Conference in Support of the Struggle of the Namibian People for Independence,

Reaffirming that any economic or other activity which impedes the implementation of the Declaration on the

Granting of Independence to Colonial Countries and Peoples and obstructs efforts aimed at the elimination of colonialism, *apartheid* and racial discrimination in southern Africa and other colonial Territories is in direct violation of the rights of the inhabitants and of the principles of the Charter and all relevant resolutions of the United Nations,

Reaffirming that the natural resources of all Territories under colonial and racist domination are the heritage of the peoples of those Territories and that the exploitation and depletion of those resources by foreign economic interests, in particular in Namibia, in association with the occupying régime of South Africa, constitute a direct violation of the rights of the peoples and of the principles of the Charter and all relevant resolutions of the United Nations,

Bearing in mind the relevant provisions of the Economic Declaration and other documents of the Seventh Conference of Heads of State or Government of Non-Aligned Countries, held at New Delhi from 7 to 12 March 1983,

Taking into account the relevant provisions of the Arusha Declaration and Programme of Action on Namibia, adopted by the United Nations Council for Namibia on 13 May 1982 at its extraordinary plenary meeting held at Arusha, United Republic of Tanzania,

Noting with profound concern that the colonial Powers and certain States, through their activities in the colonial Territories, have continued to disregard United Nations decisions relating to the item and that they have failed to implement, in particular, the relevant provisions of General Assembly resolutions 2621(XXV) and 37/31, by which the Assembly called upon all Governments that had not yet done so to take legislative, administrative or other measures in respect of their nationals and the bodies corporate under their jurisdiction that own and operate enterprises in colonial Territories, particularly in Africa, which are detrimental to the interests of the inhabitants of those Territories, in order to put an end to such enterprises and to prevent new investments that run counter to the interests of the inhabitants of those Territories,

Condemning the intensified activities of those foreign economic, financial and other interests which continue to exploit the natural and human resources of the colonial Territories and to accumulate and repatriate huge profits to the detriment of the interests of the inhabitants, particularly in the case of Namibia, thereby impeding the realization by the peoples of the Territories of their legitimate aspirations for self-determination and independence,

Strongly condemning the support which the racist minority régime of South Africa continues to receive from those foreign economic, financial and other interests which are collaborating with it in the exploitation of the natural and human resources of the international Territory of Namibia, in the further entrenchment of its illegal racist domination over the Territory and in the strengthening of its system of *apartheid*,

Strongly condemning the investment of foreign capital in the production of uranium and the collaboration of certain Western States and other States with the racist minority régime of South Africa in the nuclear field which, by providing that régime with nuclear equipment and technology, enable it to develop nuclear and military capabilities and to become a nuclear Power, thereby promoting South Africa's continued illegal occupation of Namibia,

Reaffirming that the resources of Namibia are the inviolable heritage of the Namibian people and that the exploitation of those resources by foreign economic interests under the protection of the illegal colonial administration, in violation of the Charter, of the relevant resolutions of the General Assembly and the Security Council and of Decree No. 1 for the Protection of the Natural Resources of Namibia, enacted by the United Nations Council for Namibia on 27 September 1974, and in disregard of the advisory opinion of the International Court of Justice of 21 June 1971, is illegal and contributes to the maintenance of the illegal occupation régime,

Concerned about the conditions in other colonial Territories, including certain Territories in the Caribbean and the Pacific regions, where foreign economic, financial and other interests continue to deprive the indigenous populations of their rights over the wealth of their countries, and where the inhabitants of those Territories continue to suffer from a loss of land ownership as a result of the failure of the administering Powers concerned to restrict the sale of land to foreigners, despite the repeated appeals of the General Assembly,

Conscious of the continuing need to mobilize world public opinion against the involvement of foreign economic, financial and other interests in the exploitation of natural and human resources, which impedes the independence of colonial Territories and the elimination of racism, particularly in southern Africa,

1. *Reaffirms* the inalienable right of the peoples of dependent Territories to self-determination and independence and to the enjoyment of the natural resources of their Territories, as well as their right to dispose of those resources in their best interests;

2. *Reiterates* that any administering or occupying Power that deprives the colonial peoples of the exercise of their legitimate rights over their natural resources or subordinates the rights and interests of those peoples to foreign economic and financial interests violates the solemn obligations it has assumed under the Charter of the United Nations;

3. *Reaffirms* that, by their depletive exploitation of natural resources, the continued accumulation and repatriation of huge profits and the use of those profits for the enrichment of foreign settlers and the entrenchment of colonial domination and racial discrimination in the Territories, the activities of foreign economic, financial and other interests operating at present in the colonial Territories, particularly in southern Africa, constitute a major obstacle to political independence and racial equality, as well as to the enjoyment of the natural resources of those Territories by the indigenous inhabitants;

4. *Condemns* the activities of foreign economic and other interests in the colonial Territories impeding the implementation of the Declaration on the Granting of Independence to Colonial Countries and Peoples, contained in General Assembly resolution 1514(XV), and the efforts to eliminate colonialism, *apartheid* and racial discrimination;

5. *Condemns* the policies of Governments that continue to support or collaborate with those foreign economic and other interests engaged in exploiting the natural and human resources of the Territories, including, in particular, illegally exploiting Namibia's marine resources, violating the political, economic and social rights and interests of the indigenous peoples and thus obstructing the full and speedy implementation of the Declaration in respect of those Territories;

6. *Strongly condemns* the collusion of the Governments of certain Western States and other States with the racist minority régime of South Africa in the nuclear field and calls upon those and all other Governments to refrain from supplying that régime, directly or indirectly, with installations that might enable it to produce uranium, plutonium and other nuclear materials, reactors or military equipment;

7. *Requests* the Special Committee on the Situation with regard to the Implementation of the Declaration on the Granting of Independence to Colonial Countries and Peoples to continue to monitor closely the situation in other Non-Self-Governing Territories so as to ensure that all economic activities in those Territories are aimed at strengthening and diversifying their economies in the interests of the indigenous peoples and their speedy accession to independence and that those peoples are not exploited for political, military and other purposes detrimental to their interests;

8. *Strongly condemns* those Western States and all other States, as well as the transnational corporations, which continue their investments in, and supply of armaments and oil and nuclear technology to, the racist régime of South Africa, thus buttressing it and aggravating the threat to world peace;

9. *Calls upon* all States, in particular certain Western States, to take urgent, effective measures to terminate all collaboration with South Africa in the political, diplomatic, economic, trade, military and nuclear fields and to refrain from entering into other relations with the racist régime of South Africa in violation of the relevant resolutions of the United Nations and of the Organization of African Unity;

10. *Calls once again upon* all Governments that have not yet done so to take legislative, administrative or other measures in respect of their nationals and the bodies corporate under their jurisdiction that own and operate enterprises in colonial Territories, particularly in Africa, which are detrimental to the interests of the inhabitants of those Territories, in order to put an end to such enterprises and to prevent new investments that run counter to the interests of the inhabitants of those Territories;

11. *Calls upon* all States to terminate, or cause to have terminated, any investments in Namibia or loans to the racist minority régime of South Africa and to refrain from any agreements or measures to promote trade or other economic relations with that régime;

12. *Requests* all States that have not yet done so to take effective measures to end the supply of funds and other forms of assistance, including military supplies and equipment, to the racist minority régime of South Africa, which uses such assistance to repress the people of Namibia and their national liberation movement;

13. *Strongly condemns* South Africa for its continued exploitation and plundering of the natural resources of Namibia, in complete disregard of the legitimate interests of the Namibian people, for the creation in the Territory of an economic structure dependent essentially upon its mineral resources and for its illegal extension of the territorial sea and its proclamation of an economic zone off the coast of Namibia;

14. *Calls upon* those oil-producing and oil-exporting countries that have not yet done so to take effective

measures against the oil companies concerned so as to terminate the supply of crude oil and petroleum products to the racist régime of South Africa;

15. *Reiterates* that the exploitation and plundering of the natural resources of Namibia by South African and other foreign economic interests, including the activities of those transnational corporations which are engaged in the exploitation and export of the Territory's uranium ores and other resources, in violation of the relevant resolutions of the General Assembly and the Security Council and of Decree No. 1 for the Protection of the Natural Resources of Namibia, are illegal and contribute to the maintenance of the illegal occupation régime;

16. *Calls upon* the Governments of all States, particularly those whose corporations are involved in the mining and processing of Namibian uranium, to take all appropriate measures in compliance with the provisions of Decree No. 1 for the Protection of the Natural Resources of Namibia, including the practice of requiring negative certificates of origin, to prohibit and prevent State-owned and other corporations, together with their subsidiaries, from dealing in Namibian uranium and from engaging in uranium prospecting activities in Namibia;

17. *Requests* all States to take legislative, administrative and other measures, as appropriate, in order effectively to isolate South Africa politically, economically, militarily and culturally, in accordance with General Assembly resolutions ES-8/2 of 14 September 1981, 36/121 B of 10 December 1981 and 37/233 A of 20 December 1982;

18. *Calls once again upon* all States to discontinue all economic, financial and trade relations with the racist minority régime of South Africa concerning Namibia and to refrain from entering into any relations with South Africa, purporting to act on behalf of or concerning Namibia, which may lend support to its continued illegal occupation of that Territory;

19. *Invites* all Governments and organizations of the United Nations system, having regard to the relevant provisions of the Declaration on the Establishment of a New International Economic Order, contained in General Assembly resolution 3201(S-VI) of 1 May 1974, and of the Charter of Economic Rights and Duties of States, contained in Assembly resolution 3281(XXIX) of 12 December 1974, to ensure, in particular, that the permanent sovereignty of the colonial Territories over their natural resources is fully respected and safeguarded;

20. *Calls upon* the administering Powers to abolish all discriminatory and unjust wage systems and working conditions prevailing in the Territories under their administration and to apply in each Territory a uniform system of wages to all the inhabitants without any discrimination;

21. *Requests* the Secretary-General to continue, through the Department of Public Information of the Secretariat, a sustained and broad campaign with a view to informing world public opinion of the facts concerning the pillaging of natural resources in colonial Territories and the exploitation of their indigenous populations by foreign monopolies and, in respect of Namibia, the support they render to the racist minority régime of South Africa;

22. *Appeals* to all non-governmental organizations to continue their campaign to mobilize international public opinion for the enforcement of economic and other sanctions against the Pretoria régime;

23. *Takes note* of the register prepared by the United Nations Centre on Transnational Corporations and requests the Special Committee on the Situation with regard to the Implementation of the Declaration on the Granting of Independence to Colonial Countries and Peoples to take due account of the register in connection with its consideration of the related items;

24. *Requests* the Special Committee to continue to examine this question and to report thereon to the General Assembly at its thirty-ninth session.

General Assembly resolution 38/50

7 December 1983   Meeting 86   129-7-16 (recorded vote)

Approved by Fourth Committee (A/38/582) by recorded vote (101-6-16), 3 November (meeting 10); draft by Committee on colonial countries (A/38/23); agenda item 103.

Meeting numbers. GA 38th session: 4th Committee 2-10; plenary 86.

Recorded vote in Assembly as follows:

In favour: Afghanistan, Albania, Algeria, Angola, Argentina, Australia, Bahamas, Bahrain, Bangladesh, Barbados, Belize, Benin, Bhutan, Bolivia, Botswana, Brazil, Bulgaria, Burma, Burundi, Byelorussian SSR, Cape Verde, Central African Republic, Chad, Chile, China, Colombia, Comoros, Congo, Costa Rica, Cuba, Cyprus, Czechoslovakia, Democratic Kampuchea, Democratic Yemen, Djibouti, Dominica, Dominican Republic, Ecuador, Egypt, El Salvador, Equatorial Guinea, Ethiopia, Fiji, Gabon, Gambia, German Democratic Republic, Ghana, Guatemala, Guinea, Guinea-Bissau, Guyana, Haiti, Honduras, Hungary, India, Indonesia, Iran, Iraq, Ivory Coast, Jamaica, Jordan, Kenya, Kuwait, Lao People's Democratic Republic, Lebanon, Liberia, Libyan Arab Jamahiriya, Madagascar, Malaysia, Maldives, Mali, Malta, Mauritania, Mauritius, Mexico, Mongolia, Morocco, Mozambique, Nepal, New Zealand, Nicaragua, Niger, Nigeria, Oman, Pakistan, Panama, Papua New Guinea, Peru, Philippines, Poland, Qatar, Romania, Rwanda, Saint Lucia, Saint Vincent and the Grenadines, Samoa, Sao Tome and Principe, Saudi Arabia, Senegal, Sierra Leone, Singapore, Solomon Islands, Somalia, Sri Lanka, Saint Christopher and Nevis, Sudan, Suriname, Swaziland, Thailand, Togo, Trinidad and Tobago, Tunisia, Turkey, Uganda, Ukrainian SSR, USSR, United Arab Emirates, United Republic of Cameroon, United Republic of Tanzania, Upper Volta, Uruguay, Vanuatu, Venezuela, Viet Nam, Yemen, Yugoslavia, Zaire, Zambia, Zimbabwe.

Against: Belgium, Canada, Germany,[a] Federal Republic of, Luxembourg, Netherlands, United Kingdom, United States.

Abstaining: Austria, Denmark, Finland, France, Greece, Iceland, Ireland, Israel, Italy, Japan, Lesotho, Malawi, Norway, Portugal, Spain, Sweden.

[a]Later advised the Secretariat it had intended to abstain.

In explanation of vote, New Zealand said it had always supported the broad principles in the text and scrupulously observed them in its administration of Tokelau; it could not accept the generally condemnatory tone of the text, the unjustified assertions made about the behaviour of administering Powers nor the assertion that foreign economic interests in colonial Territories were by nature detrimental to the interests of the people, since foreign investment and trade could be a vital spur to development. Italy, the Netherlands and the United Kingdom shared this view. The Netherlands added that economic interests did not necessarily constitute an obstacle to political independence and racial equality, and it could not accept the inclusion of unwarranted and selective criticism of Western countries, or the equation of the situation in South Africa with a colonial one. Speaking similarly, the Federal Republic of Germany felt the draft lacked balance and did not allow an in-depth approach to a solution. Ireland agreed and added that it did not address the complex range of issues which confronted the remaining small Territories for which carefully promoted economic development was an important factor in achieving independence.

Japan appreciated the Fourth Committee's efforts to reach consensus and to avoid accusing any country by name and felt that activities of investors must not deprive Territories of their rights, but it did not subscribe to the idea that all such activities in colonial countries were prejudicial to the interests of the peoples. Denmark said the failure of the draft to distinguish between activities which impeded decolonization and those which were beneficial detracted from its fundamental aims. Canada took the same position and also supported the principle that national Governments in whose territory transnational corporations had their headquarters should not interfere in the activities of such corporations in host countries.

Sweden noted with satisfaction that the draft did not regard all foreign economic activities as negative, but only those impeding decolonization, and felt the text was aimed mainly at the situation in southern Africa; none the less, it had difficulties with certain paragraphs dealing with the division of competence among the principal organs of the United Nations—a position shared by Denmark. Turkey expressed reservations on the naming of a specific region in the text. France noted that the draft had retained improvements over the corresponding 1981 resolution, particularly in having eliminated selective condemnations, but expressed reservations because, although it recognized that the activities of foreign interests could on occasion be harmful, the real problem was the imbalance between developing and industrialized countries.

Australia and New Zealand had reservations about the appropriateness of some of the paragraphs concerning Namibia and South Africa, even though Australia expressed concern about the exploitative practices of many companies in Namibia.

Regarding the situation in other Non-Self-Governing Territories, Australia said there was something contradictory in the wholesale condemnation of foreign economic involvement and the calls made in other resolutions for further economic development of those Territories; it did not consider that the terms of the draft related to the Australian administration of the Cocos (Keeling) Islands. The United Kingdom could not accept that a resolution extrapolating from conditions in Namibia was valid for other Territories, and, as an administering Power in 10 Territories, it took pride in the fact that it had fully complied with its obligations, and was frustrated to be exhorted to accelerate development and to be criticized for encouraging private economic contributions to the fulfilment of that objective in Territories where ex-

ternal trade and an inward flow of investment were crucial. Austria said that measures proposed should genuinely serve the political, economic and social interests of the Territories and should thus leave room for activities clearly benefiting their development. While supporting the basic ideas expressed in the resolution, Chile did not think that all economic activites hampered decolonization and, in this connection, it noted other United Nations resolutions where the administering Powers had been asked to increase investment in order to ensure the economic viability of Territories.

Uruguay supported the inalienable right of peoples to self-determination and to dispose of their natural resources, but had reservations on paragraphs 9, 10, 11 and 18 which could not be fully reconciled with the sovereign right of States to conduct freely their international relations.

Swaziland stressed the importance of independence for Namibia, but stated that owing to its geographical location, it would find difficulty endorsing certain provisions, especially paragraph 14, since oil sanctions against South Africa would have a disastrous effect on Swaziland's economy. Similarly, Botswana expressed reservations on economic sanctions and the oil embargo due to conditions beyond its control in southern Africa. Malawi could not endorse concepts and language in the draft which were not in line with the Charter and international law. Mozambique welcomed the draft and urged that transnational corporations and their affiliates provide the required information.

Military bases in colonial countries

Further to a September 1982 request of the General Assembly,[14] the Committee on colonial countries continued to consider in 1983 military activities and bases in colonial Territories and approved a decision on the subject on 1 September.[15] On the basis of that text, the Committee recommended a draft decision to the Assembly.

GENERAL ASSEMBLY ACTION

Decision 38/419, as recommended by the Fourth Committee, was adopted by the General Assembly by recorded vote in December.

Military activities and arrangements by colonial Powers in Territories under their administration which might be impeding the implementation of the Declaration on the Granting of Independence to Colonial Countries and Peoples
At its 86th plenary meeting, on 7 December 1983, the General Assembly, on the recommendation of the Fourth Committee, adopted the following text:
"1. The General Assembly, having considered the chapter of the report of the Special Committee on the Situation with regard to the Implementation of the

Declaration on the Granting of Independence to Colonial Countries and Peoples relating to an item on the Special Committee's agenda entitled 'Military activities and arrangements by colonial Powers in Territories under their administration which might be impeding the implementation of the Declaration on the Granting of Independence to Colonial Countries and Peoples', and recalling its decision 37/420 of 23 November 1982 on this subject, deplores the fact that the colonial Powers concerned have taken no steps to implement the requests repeatedly addressed to them by the Assembly, most recently in paragraph 10 of its resolution 37/35 of 23 November 1982, to withdraw immediately and unconditionally their military bases and installations from colonial Territories and to refrain from establishing new ones.

"2.   The General Assembly, in reaffirming the inalienable right of the peoples of all colonial and dependent Territories to self-determination and independence in accordance with the Declaration on the Granting of Independence to Colonial Countries and Peoples, contained in its resolution 1514(XV) of 14 December 1960, reiterates its conviction that military activities and arrangements in the Territories concerned constitute, in a great number of instances, a serious impediment to the full and speedy implementation of the Declaration with respect to those Territories.

"3.   The General Assembly deplores the fact that South Africa and the colonial Powers continue to engage in activities and dispositions of a military character and to establish and maintain bases and other military installations in Namibia and other colonial Territories in violation of the purposes and principles of the Charter of the United Nations and of Assembly resolution 1514(XV).

"4.   The General Assembly condemns all military activities and arrangements in colonial Territories which deny the peoples concerned their right to self-determination and independence.

"5.   The General Assembly notes that, in southern Africa in general and in and around Namibia in particular, an extremely serious situation continues to prevail as a result of South Africa's continued illegal occupation of the Territory. The illegal occupying régime has resorted to desperate measures in order to suppress by force the legitimate aspirations of the people and to maintain its control over the Territory. In its escalating war against the people of Namibia and their national liberation movement, the South West Africa People's Organization, struggling for freedom and independence, the régime has repeatedly committed acts of armed aggression against the neighbouring independent African countries, particularly Angola and Zambia, which have caused extensive loss of human life and destruction of the economic infrastructure.

"6.   The General Assembly, noting that in Namibia the South African Government has continued to expand its network of military bases and carried out a massive build-up of its military forces, condemns the continuing co-operation of certain Western States and other States with South Africa in supplying it with arms and military equipment as well as technology, including technology and equipment in the nuclear field capable of being utilized for military purposes. The Assembly condemns South Africa for its massive military build-up in Namibia, its introduction of compulsory military service for Namibians, its recruitment and training of Namibians for tribal armies and its recruitment of mercenaries and other foreign agents in order to carry out its policies of internal repression and its military attacks against independent African States. In this connection, the Assembly calls upon all States to co-operate in taking effective measures to prevent the recruitment, training and transit of mercenaries for service in Namibia. The Assembly is particularly mindful in that regard of the relevant resolutions of the Organization of African Unity, the Political Declaration adopted by the Seventh Conference of Heads of State or Government of Non-Aligned Countries, held at New Delhi from 7 to 12 March 1983, and the Declaration adopted at the International Conference in Solidarity with the Front-line States, held at Lisbon from 25 to 27 March 1983.

"7.   The General Assembly, accordingly, demands the immediate cessation of the war of oppression waged by the racist minority régime against the people of Namibia and their national liberation movement, as well as the urgent dismantling of all military bases in the Territory. Reaffirming the legitimacy of the struggle of the people of Namibia to achieve their freedom and independence, the Assembly appeals to all States to render sustained and increased moral and political support, as well as financial, military and other material assistance, to the South West Africa People's Organization to enable it to intensify its struggle for the liberation of Namibia.

"8.   The General Assembly condemns the continued military collaboration and support which certain Western States and other States render to the Government of South Africa and calls upon all States to cease such collaboration with and support of that Government, particularly the sale of weapons and other matériel, which increases South Africa's capacity to wage wars against neighbouring African States. In particular, the Assembly calls upon all Governments to comply strictly with the provisions of Security Council resolution 418(1977) of 4 November 1977, by which the Council, acting under Chapter VII of the Charter, decided to apply specific sanctions against South Africa. In this connection, the Assembly draws particular attention to the relevant provisions of its resolution 37/233 of 20 December 1982, the Paris Declaration on Namibia and the Programme of Action on Namibia adopted at the International Conference in Support of the Struggle of the Namibian People for Independence and the Declaration adopted at the International Conference in Solidarity with the Front-line States.

"9.   The General Assembly considers that the acquisition of nuclear weapons capability by the racist régime of South Africa, with its record of violence and aggression, constitutes a further effort on its part to terrorize and intimidate independent States in the region into submission while also posing a danger to all mankind. The continuing assistance rendered to the South African régime by certain Western States and other States in the military and nuclear fields belies their stated opposition to the racist practice of the South African régime and makes them willing partners of its hegemonistic and criminal policies. The Assembly accordingly condemns the continued nuclear co-operation by certain Western States and other States with South Africa. It calls upon the States concerned to end all such co-operation and, in particular, to halt the supply to South Africa of equipment, technology, nuclear materials and related training, which increases its nuclear capability.

"10. The General Assembly, noting that the militarization of Namibia has led to the forced conscription of Namibians, to a greatly intensified flow of refugees and to a tragic disorganization of the family life of the Namibian people, strongly condemns the forcible and wholesale displacement of Namibians from their homes for military and political purposes and the introduction of compulsory military service for Namibians and declares that all measures by the illegal occupation régime to enforce military conscription in Namibia are null and void. In this connection, the Assembly urges all Governments, the specialized agencies and other intergovernmental organizations to provide increased material assistance to the thousands of refugees who have been forced by the *apartheid* régime's oppressive policies in Namibia and South Africa to flee into the neighbouring front-line States.

"11. The General Assembly recalls its resolution ES-8/2 of 14 September 1981, by which it strongly urged States to cease forthwith, individually and collectively, all dealings with South Africa in order totally to isolate it politically, economically, militarily and culturally.

"12. The General Assembly strongly deprecates the establishment and maintenance by colonial Powers and their allies of military bases and other installations in the colonial Territories under their administration which impede the implementation of the Declaration on the Granting of Independence to Colonial Countries and Peoples and which are incompatible with the purposes and principles of the Charter of the United Nations and of Assembly resolution 1514 (XV).

"13. The General Assembly reiterates its condemnation of all military activities and arrangements by colonial Powers in Territories under their administration which are detrimental to the interests and rights of the colonial peoples concerned, especially their right to self-determination and independence. The Assembly once again calls upon the colonial Powers concerned to terminate such activities and eliminate such military bases in compliance with its relevant resolutions and in particular with paragraph 9 of the annex to its resolution 35/118 of 11 December 1980, containing the Plan of Action for the Full Implementation of the Declaration on the Granting of Independence to Colonial Countries and Peoples.

"14. The General Assembly deprecates the continued alienation of land in colonial Territories for military installations. While it has been argued that the servicing of such installations creates employment, nevertheless, the large-scale utilization of local economic and manpower resources for this purpose diverts resources which could be more beneficially utilized in promoting the economic development of the Territories concerned and is thus contrary to the interests of their populations.

"15. The General Assembly requests the Secretary-General to continue, through the Department of Public Information of the Secretariat, an intensified campaign of publicity with a view to informing world public opinion of the facts concerning the military activities and arrangements in colonial Territories which are impeding the implementation of the Declaration on the Granting of Independence to Colonial Countries and Peoples, contained in Assembly resolution 1514 (XV).

"16. The General Assembly requests the Special Committee to continue its consideration of the item and to report thereon to the Assembly at its thirty-ninth session."

General Assembly decision 38/419

123-10-16 (recorded vote)

Approved by Fourth Committee (A/38/582) by recorded vote (97-10-15), 3 November (meeting 10); draft by Committee on colonial countries (A/38/23); agenda item 103.
Meeting numbers. GA 38th session: 4th Committee 2-10; plenary 86.

A number of States explained their votes in the Fourth Committee. Greece, speaking on behalf of the 10 member States of the European Economic Community (EEC), expressed concern that a draft on a subject not in the list of items allocated to the Committee was being put to a vote. Australia, the Federal Republic of Germany, Italy and the United Kingdom agreed, as did Canada which added that the recommendation concerning military activities in the report of the Committee on colonial countries was incompatible with the recommendation concerning foreign economic interests and should not be treated as belonging to the same agenda item.

New Zealand could not accept the assertion that military activities in Non-Self-Governing Territories were necessarily detrimental to decolonization, and added that the decision had no relevance to its administration of Tokelau. Turkey felt that the text of the draft decision, particularly paragraphs 2, 4, 12, 13 and 14, could have been drafted in a more balanced manner, and also expressed reservations on the reference to a particular group of States made in several paragraphs of the text.

Mozambique said no one could deny that military activities of colonial Powers deprived the peoples there of the right to self-determination and independence, while Fiji stated that those activities and arrangements by Powers in Territories under their administration should not be detrimental to the people concerned, but did not think that all such activities impeded independence which was a question the inhabitants should be left to decide. Viet Nam would have preferred the word "are" instead of "might be" in paragraph 1 since it firmly believed that such military activities were indeed impeding implementation of the 1960 Declaration.

Also on 7 December, the Assembly called upon the colonial Powers to withdraw their military bases and installations from colonial Territories and to refrain from establishing new ones in resolution 38/54 (see above). In further action the same day, the Assembly, in resolutions 38/42, 38/43 and 38/47 on Guam, Bermuda and the Turks and Caicos Islands, respectively (see Chapter IV of this section), reaffirmed that the administering Powers must ensure that military bases and installations not hinder the population of the Territories from exercising their right to self-determination and independence.

Information dissemination

On 14 September, the Committee on colonial countries considered dissemination of information on decolonization, and approved the recommendations on this subject put forward by its Sub-Committee on Petitions, Information and Assistance. Reiterating the importance of the widest possible dissemination of information on the aims of the 1960 Declaration on colonial countries, the Sub-Committee made a number of recommendations concerning the work of the Information Unit on Decolonization in the Secretariat's Department of Political Affairs, Trusteeship and Decolonization, and of the Department of Public Information (DPI). It considered the studies and monographs published in the *Decolonialization* series a valuable source of information and urged that they be published without delay in various languages and updated more frequently. It noted with satisfaction the intensified efforts of DPI to disseminate information on decolonization and to monitor responses received from United Nations information centres, and urged it to increase its efforts to obtain wider coverage by the mass media, particularly in certain countries in Western Europe and the Americas which received limited coverage. Both Departments were called on to continue speaking engagements at North American universities on decolonization with particular emphasis on Namibia (see Chapter III of this section).

The General Assembly, in decision 38/419 (see above), requested the Secretary-General to continue, through DPI, an intensified campaign to inform world public opinion of the facts concerning military activities in colonial Territories which were impeding the implementation of the 1960 Declaration.

GENERAL ASSEMBLY ACTION

By recorded vote, the General Assembly adopted resolution 38/55 on 7 December.

Dissemination of information on decolonization
The General Assembly,

Having examined the chapter of the report of the Special Committee on the Situation with regard to the Implementation of the Declaration on the Granting of Independence to Colonial Countries and Peoples relating to the dissemination of information on decolonization and publicity for the work of the United Nations in the field of decolonization,

Recalling its resolution 1514(XV) of 14 December 1960, containing the Declaration on the Granting of Independence to Colonial Countries and Peoples, and all other resolutions and decisions of the United Nations concerning the dissemination of information on decolonization, in particular General Assembly resolution 37/36 of 23 November 1982,

Reiterating the importance of publicity as an instrument for furthering the aims and purposes of the Declaration and mindful of the continuing pressing need to take all possible steps to acquaint world public opinion with all aspects of the problems of decolonization with a view to assisting effectively the peoples of the colonial Territories to achieve self-determination, freedom and independence,

Aware of the increasingly important role being played in the widespread dissemination of relevant information by a number of non-governmental organizations having a special interest in decolonization, and noting with satisfaction the intensified efforts of the Special Committee in enlisting the support of those organizations in that regard, including its decision to organize in Europe in 1984 a seminar on decolonization with the non-governmental organizations concerned,

1. *Approves* the chapter of the report of the Special Committee on the Situation with regard to the Implementation of the Declaration on the Granting of Independence to Colonial Countries and Peoples relating to the dissemination of information on decolonization and publicity for the work of the United Nations in the field of decolonization;

2. *Reaffirms* the importance of effecting the widest possible dissemination of information on the evils and dangers of colonialism, on the determined efforts of the colonial peoples to achieve self-determination, freedom and independence and on the assistance being provided by the international community towards the elimination of the remaining vestiges of colonialism in all its forms;

3. *Requests* the Secretary-General, having regard to the suggestions of the Special Committee, to continue to take concrete measures through all the media at his disposal, including publications, radio and television, to give widespread and continuous publicity to the work of the United Nations in the field of decolonization, and, *inter alia*:

(*a*) To continue, in consultation with the Special Committee, to collect, prepare and disseminate basic material, studies and articles relating to the problems of decolonization and, in particular, to continue to publish the periodical *Objective: Justice* and other publications, special articles and studies, including the *Decolonization* series, and to select from them appropriate material for wider dissemination by means of reprints in various languages;

(*b*) To seek the full co-operation of the administering Powers concerned in the discharge of the tasks referred to above;

(*c*) To intensify the activities of all United Nations information centres, particularly those located in Western Europe and the Americas;

(*d*) To maintain a close working relationship with the Organization of African Unity by holding periodic consultations and by systematically exchanging relevant information with that organization;

(*e*) To enlist the support of non-governmental organizations having a special interest in decolonization in the dissemination of the relevant information;

(*f*) To ensure the availability of the necessary facilities and services in this regard;

(*g*) To report to the Special Committee on the measures taken in implementation of the present resolution;

4. *Invites* all States, the specialized agencies and other organizations of the United Nations system and non-governmental organizations having a special interest in decolonization to undertake or intensify, in co-operation

with the Secretary-General and within their respective spheres of competence, the large-scale dissemination of the information referred to in paragraph 2 above;

5. *Requests* the Special Committee to follow the implementation of the present resolution and report thereon to the General Assembly at its thirty-ninth session.

General Assembly resolution 38/55

7 December 1983   Meeting 86   147-0-4 (recorded vote)

26-nation draft (A/38/L.34 & Add.1); agenda item 18.
Sponsors: Afghanistan, Algeria, Congo, Cuba, Cyprus, Czechoslovakia, Ethiopia, German Democratic Republic, Guyana, Hungary, India, Lao People's Democratic Republic, Libyan Arab Jamahiriya, Madagascar, Mali, Mongolia, Qatar, Romania, Sierra Leone, Syrian Arab Republic, Trinidad and Tobago, Tunisia, United Republic of Tanzania, Viet Nam, Yugoslavia, Zambia.
Financial implications. 5th Committee, A/38/696; S-G, A/C.5/38/72
Meeting numbers. GA 38th session: 4th Committee 8-19; plenary 84-86.

Recorded vote in Assembly as follows:

In favour: Afghanistan, Albania, Algeria, Angola, Argentina, Australia, Austria, Bahamas, Bahrain, Bangladesh, Barbados, Belgium, Belize, Benin, Bhutan, Bolivia, Botswana, Brazil, Bulgaria, Burma, Burundi, Byelorussian SSR, Canada, Cape Verde, Central African Republic, Chad, Chile, China, Colombia, Congo, Costa Rica, Cuba, Cyprus, Czechoslovakia, Democratic Kampuchea, Democratic Yemen, Denmark, Djibouti, Dominica, Dominican Republic, Ecuador, Egypt, El Salvador, Equatorial Guinea, Ethiopia, Fiji, Finland, Gabon, Gambia, German Democratic Republic, Ghana, Greece, Guatemala, Guinea, Guinea-Bissau, Guyana, Haiti, Honduras, Hungary, Iceland, India, Indonesia, Iran, Iraq, Ireland, Italy, Ivory Coast, Jamaica, Japan, Jordan, Kenya, Kuwait, Lao People's Democratic Republic, Lebanon, Lesotho, Liberia, Libyan Arab Jamahiriya, Luxembourg, Madagascar, Malawi, Malaysia, Maldives, Mali, Malta, Mauritania, Mauritius, Mexico, Mongolia, Morocco, Mozambique, Nepal, Netherlands, New Zealand, Nicaragua, Niger, Nigeria, Norway, Oman, Pakistan, Panama, Papua New Guinea, Paraguay, Peru, Philippines, Poland, Portugal, Qatar, Romania, Rwanda, Saint Lucia, Saint Vincent and the Grenadines, Samoa, Sao Tome and Principe, Saudi Arabia, Senegal, Sierra Leone, Singapore, Solomon Islands, Somalia, Spain, Sri Lanka, Sudan, Suriname, Swaziland, Sweden, Syrian Arab Republic, Thailand, Togo, Trinidad and Tobago, Tunisia, Turkey, Uganda, Ukrainian SSR, USSR, United Arab Emirates, United Republic of Cameroon, United Republic of Tanzania, Upper Volta, Uruguay, Vanuatu, Venezuela, Viet Nam, Yemen, Yugoslavia, Zaire, Zambia, Zimbabwe.

Against: None.

Abstaining: France, Germany, Federal Republic of, United Kingdom, United States.

Week of Solidarity with peoples of Namibia and all other colonial Territories

The Week of Solidarity with the Peoples of Namibia and All Other Colonial Territories, as well as those in South Africa, Fighting for Freedom, Independence and Human Rights was observed by a series of United Nations activities from 23 to 30 May 1983.

Following the General Assembly's 1982 decision[16] to enlarge the scope of the Week by including the peoples of all the remaining dependent Territories, the name of the Week was changed (formerly the Week of Solidarity with the Colonial Peoples of Southern Africa Fighting for Freedom, Independence and Equal Rights). DPI arranged events at Headquarters and at United Nations information centres, including an exhibition of photographs and publications depicting the struggle of the colonial peoples for independence, the public screening of films on that subject, and the distribution of audio-visual materials to national radio and television stations.

On 23 May, the three presiding officers of the Committee on colonial countries, the Special

Committee against *Apartheid* and the United Nations Council for Namibia issued a joint statement[2] paying tribute to the courageous peoples who had given their lives to the cause of freedom for colonial peoples and urging States to mobilize support for the peoples of southern Africa struggling for freedom and human rights by disseminating information on their cause, organizing publicity programmes, and increasing assistance to oppressed peoples.

Role of NGOs

The Sub-Committee on Petitions, Information and Assistance of the Committee on colonial countries noted that a considerable number of non-governmental organizations (NGOs) were playing an important role in broadening the dissemination of information on decolonization and appealed for further assistance in this regard. In its annual report,[2] the Committee approved the Sub-Committee's conclusions and recommendations.

The Sub-Committee reiterated its appeal to NGOs active in decolonization to intensify their campaigns in support of all colonial peoples, in particular those in southern Africa and their national liberation movements; recommended that they strive to counteract hostile propaganda that liberation movements in southern Africa were terrorists; and proposed that the Secretary-General be requested to maintain an updated list of NGOs active in decolonization so that the Sub-Committee could increase its contacts with them. The Sub-Committee also proposed that a seminar be held in Europe during 1984 with relevant NGOs to improve co-ordination with the Committee in disseminating information on decolonization.

Puerto Rico

In 1983, the Committee on colonial countries reviewed the list of Territories to which the 1960 Declaration on colonial countries[1] was applicable and considered an item based on its August 1982 decision[17] concerning Puerto Rico. At meetings held between 22 and 24 August 1983, the Committee heard the representatives of 20 organizations mainly from Puerto Rico. By a resolution of 24 August,[18] adopted by a vote of 10 to 2, with 10 abstentions, the Committee reaffirmed the inalienable right of the people of Puerto Rico to self-determination and independence in conformity with the Declaration, urged the United States to transfer all sovereign powers to the people of Puerto Rico, requested it to assist the Committee in sending a fact-finding mission there, deplored measures aimed at changing the Latin American character of the Puerto Rican people, deplored decisions to enlarge military installations, demanded the cessation of repressive measures against Puerto Rican independence forces including intimidation by the United States federal Grand Jury, and requested the Committee's Chairman to undertake consultations with respect to the proposed fact-finding mission.

On 26 October, during the Fourth Committee's consideration of the topic, Rafael Anglada-López of the Central Committee of the Puerto Rican Socialist Party, whose request for a hearing had been circulated, made a statement concerning Puerto Rico.

REFERENCES

[1]YUN 1960, p. 49, GA res. 1514(XV), 14 Dec. 1960. [2]A/38/23. [3]YUN 1982, p. 1264, GA res. 37/32, 23 Nov. 1982. [4]A/38/111 & Add. 1-3, Add.3/Corr.1 & Add.4. [5]YUN 1982, p. 1260. [6]*Ibid.*, p. 1263, ESC res. 1982/47, 27 July 1982. [7]E/1983/102. [8]E/1983/106. [9]A/38/23 (res. A/AC.109/759). [10]*Ibid.* (res. A/AC.109/755). [11]YUN 1982, p. 1268, GA res. 37/31, 23 Nov. 1982. [12] YUN 1981, p. 1108, GA res. 36/51, 24 Nov. 1981. [13]A/38/444. [14]YUN 1982, p. 1272, GA dec. 37/420, 23 Nov. 1982. [15]A/38/23 (dec. A/AC.109/757).[16]YUN 1982, p. 1275, GA dec. 37/421, 23 Nov. 1982. [17] *Ibid.*, p. 1275. [18]A/38/23 (res. A/AC.109/751).

Other general questions concerning NSGTs

Fellowships and scholarships

In a report to the General Assembly covering 1 October 1982 to 30 September 1983,[1] the Secretary-General stated that the following 32 States had offered to make scholarships and fellowships available to persons from Non-Self-Governing Territories for secondary, vocational and post-graduate studies: Austria, Brazil, Bulgaria, Cyprus, Czechoslovakia, Egypt, German Democratic Republic, Germany, Federal Republic of, Ghana, Greece, Hungary, India, Iran, Israel, Italy, Libyan Arab Jamahiriya, Malawi, Malta, Mexico, Pakistan, Philippines, Poland, Romania, Sri Lanka, Syrian Arab Republic, Tunisia, Turkey, Uganda, USSR, United Arab Emirates, United States and Yugoslavia. Information about these offers was included in the twenty-third edition of the handbook, *Study Abroad* (1981/82-1982/83), published by UNESCO.

The Secretary-General reported that 150 applications for scholarships were received by the United Nations Secretariat and were transmitted to the offering States for consideration and to the administering Powers for information. Five new fellowships were offered in Bulgaria, two new scholarships in Cyprus and one new scholarship in Pakistan for a Namibian national.

GENERAL ASSEMBLY ACTION

Following the recommendation of the Fourth Committee, the General Assembly adopted without vote resolution 38/53 on 7 December.

Offers by Member States of study and training facilities for inhabitants of Non-Self-Governing Territories

The General Assembly,

Recalling its resolution 37/34 of 23 November 1982,

Having examined the report of the Secretary-General on offers by Member States of study and training facilities for inhabitants of Non-Self-Governing Territories, prepared pursuant to General Assembly resolution 845(IX) of 22 November 1954,

Considering that more scholarships should be made available to the inhabitants of Non-Self-Governing Territories in all parts of the world and that steps should be taken to encourage applications from students in those Territories,

1. *Takes note* of the report of the Secretary-General;

2. *Expresses its appreciation* to those Member States that have made scholarships available to the inhabitants of Non-Self-Governing Territories;

3. *Invites* all States to make or continue to make generous offers of study and training facilities to the inhabitants of those Territories that have not yet attained self-government or independence and, wherever possible, to provide travel funds to prospective students;

4. *Urges* the administering Powers to take effective measures to ensure the widespread and continuous dissemination in the Territories under their administration of information relating to offers of study and training facilities made by States and to provide all the necessary facilities to enable students to avail themselves of such offers;

5. *Requests* the Secretary-General to report to the General Assembly at its thirty-ninth session on the implementation of the present resolution;

6. *Draws the attention* of the Special Committee on the Situation with regard to the Implementation of the Declaration on the Granting of Independence to Colonial Countries and Peoples to the present resolution.

General Assembly resolution 38/53

7 December 1983   Meeting 86   Adopted without vote

Approved by Fourth Committee (A/38/611) without objection, 18 November (meeting 20); 46-nation draft (A/C.4/38/L.6); agenda item 106.

Sponsors: Afghanistan, Algeria, Angola, Australia, Austria, Bangladesh, Barbados, Benin, Bulgaria, Congo, Cuba, Cyprus, Democratic Yemen, Egypt, Ethiopia, Fiji, Greece, Guinea-Bissau, Guyana, India, Ivory Coast, Jamaica, Kenya, Liberia, Madagascar, Mali, Mauritania, New Zealand, Nigeria, Pakistan, Qatar, Romania, Senegal, Sierra Leone, Sudan, Syrian Arab Republic, Togo, Trinidad and Tobago, Tunisia, Turkey, Uganda, United Republic of Cameroon, United Republic of Tanzania, Yugoslavia, Zambia, Zimbabwe.

Meeting numbers. GA 38th session: 4th Committee: 10-18, 20; plenary 86.

Information to the United Nations

Under the terms of Article 73 *e* in Chapter XI of the Charter of the United Nations, States responsible for the administration of Territories which had not attained a full measure of self-government undertook to transmit regularly to the Secretary-General information on their economic, social and educational conditions. In addition, several General Assembly resolutions, including the most recent of November 1982,[2] requested the fullest possible information on political and constitutional developments. In an October 1983 report to the Assembly,[3] the Secretary-General stated that he had received information with respect to the following Non-Self-Governing Territories:

Australia: Cocos (Keeling) Islands
New Zealand: Tokelau
United Kingdom: Bermuda, British Virgin Islands, Cayman Islands, Falkland Islands (Malvinas), Gibraltar, Montserrat, Pitcairn, St. Helena, Turks and Caicos Islands
United States: American Samoa, Guam, United States Virgin Islands

On 28 March,[4] Portugal informed the Secretary-General that it had nothing to add to the information provided in a 1979 note (stating that conditions in East Timor had prevented it from assuming its responsibilities for the Territory's administration).[5]

With respect to Western Sahara, the Secretary-General noted in his October report[3] that Spain had informed him in 1976 that with the termination of its presence in the Territory, it considered itself exempt from any international responsibility in connection with the administration of the Territory.[6]

The Secretary-General also reported that the United Kingdom, as the administering Power for Anguilla, had informed a 14 September meeting of the Committee on colonial countries that it would resume the transmission of information on Anguilla (information was received by the Secretariat in November).[7] As regards Brunei, the United Kingdom considered that the transmission of information was no longer appropriate since it had attained full internal self-government.

GENERAL ASSEMBLY ACTION

On 7 December, the General Assembly adopted by recorded vote resolution 38/49 on the recommendation of the Fourth Committee based on a draft by the Committee on colonial countries.

Information from Non-Self-Governing Territories transmitted under Article 73 *e* of the Charter of the United Nations

The General Assembly,

Having examined the chapter of the report of the Special Committee on the Situation with regard to the Implementation of the Declaration on the Granting of Independence to Colonial Countries and Peoples relating to the information from Non-Self-Governing Territories transmitted under Article 73 *e* of the Charter of the United Nations and the action taken by the Committee in respect of that information,

Having also examined the report of the Secretary-General on the question,

Recalling its resolution 1970(XVIII) of 16 December 1963, in which it requested the Special Committee to study the information transmitted to the Secretary-General in accordance with Article 73 *e* of the Charter and to take such information fully into account in examining the situation with regard to the implementation of the Declaration,

Recalling also its resolution 37/29 of 23 November 1982, in which it requested the Special Committee to continue to discharge the functions entrusted to it under resolution 1970(XVIII),

Noting the decision of the Government of the United Kingdom of Great Britain and Northern Ireland to resume transmission of information with respect to Anguilla, under Article 73 *e* of the Charter,

1. *Approves* the chapter of the report of the Special Committee on the Situation with regard to the Implementation of the Declaration on the Granting of Independence to Colonial Countries and Peoples relating to the information from Non-Self-Governing Territories transmitted under Article 73 *e* of the Charter of the United Nations;

2. *Reaffirms* that, in the absence of a decision by the General Assembly itself that a Non-Self-Governing Territory has attained a full measure of self-government under the terms of Chapter XI of the Charter, the administering Power concerned should continue to transmit information under Article 73 *e* of the Charter with respect to that Territory;

3. *Requests* the administering Powers concerned to transmit, or continue to transmit, to the Secretary-General the information prescribed in Article 73 *e* of the Charter, as well as the fullest possible information on political and constitutional developments in the Territories concerned, within a maximum period of six months following the expiration of the administrative year in those Territories;

4. *Requests* the Special Committee to continue to discharge the functions entrusted to it under General Assembly resolution 1970(XVIII), in accordance with established procedures, and to report thereon to the Assembly at its thirty-ninth session.

General Assembly resolution 38/49

7 December 1983   Meeting 86   147-0-4 (recorded vote)

Approved by Fourth Committee (A/38/608) by recorded vote (121-0-6), 17 November (meeting 19); draft by Committee on colonial countries (A/38/23); agenda item 102.

Meeting numbers. GA 38th session: 4th Committee 8, 10-19; plenary 86.

Recorded vote in Assembly as follows:

In favour: Afghanistan, Albania, Algeria, Angola, Argentina, Australia, Austria, Bahamas, Bahrain, Bangladesh, Barbados, Belgium, Belize, Benin, Bhutan, Bolivia, Botswana, Brazil, Bulgaria, Burma, Burundi, Byelorussian SSR, Canada, Cape Verde, Central African Republic, Chad, Chile, China, Colombia, Comoros, Congo, Costa Rica, Cuba, Cyprus, Czechoslovakia, Democratic Kampuchea, Democratic Yemen, Denmark, Djibouti, Dominican Republic, Ecuador, Egypt, El Salvador, Equatorial Guinea, Ethiopia, Fiji, Finland, Gabon, Gambia, German Democratic Republic, Germany, Federal Republic of, Ghana, Greece, Guatemala, Guinea, Guinea-Bissau, Guyana, Haiti, Honduras, Hungary, Iceland, India, Indonesia, Iran, Iraq, Ireland, Israel, Italy, Ivory Coast, Jamaica, Japan, Jordan, Kenya, Kuwait, Lao People's Democratic Republic, Lebanon, Lesotho, Liberia, Libyan Arab Jamahiriya, Luxembourg, Madagascar, Malawi, Malaysia, Maldives, Mali, Malta, Mauritania, Mauritius, Mexico, Mongolia, Mozambique, Nepal, Netherlands, New Zealand, Nicaragua, Niger, Nigeria, Norway, Oman, Pakistan, Panama, Papua New Guinea, Peru, Philippines, Poland, Portugal, Qatar, Romania, Rwanda, Saint Lucia, Saint Vincent and the Grenadines, Samoa, Sao Tome and Principe, Saudi Arabia, Senegal, Sierra Leone, Singapore, Solomon Islands, Somalia, Spain, Sri Lanka, St. Christopher and Nevis, Sudan, Suriname, Swaziland, Sweden, Thailand, Togo, Trinidad and Tobago, Tunisia, Turkey, Uganda, Ukrainian SSR, USSR, United Arab Emirates, United Republic of Cameroon, United Republic of Tanzania, Upper Volta, Uruguay, Vanuatu, Venezuela, Viet Nam, Yemen, Yugoslavia, Zaire, Zambia, Zimbabwe.

Against: None.

Abstaining: France, Paraguay, United Kingdom, United States.

Visiting missions

In August, the Committee on colonial countries adopted a resolution on the question of sending visiting missions to Territories,[8] stressing the need to continue to dispatch missions to facilitate the full implementation of the 1960 Declaration on colonial countries.[9] The Committee called on the administering Powers concerned to co-operate or continue to co-operate with the United Nations by permitting the missions access to Territories under their administration.

In resolution 38/54 of 7 December (see above), the General Assembly called on the administering Powers to continue to co-operate with the Committee on colonial countries in the discharge of its mandate and, in particular, to permit the access of visiting missions to the Territories to secure first-hand information and ascertain the wishes and aspirations of their inhabitants.

The question of sending visiting missions to other Territories was also dealt with by the Assembly in individual resolutions on these Territories (see Chapter IV of this section).

REFERENCES

[1]A/38/549. [2]YUN 1982, p. 1278, GA res. 37/29, 23 Nov. 1982. [3]A/38/477. [4]A/38/125. [5]YUN 1979, p. 1117. [6]YUN 1976, p. 738. [7]A/39/519. [8]A/38/23 (res. A/AC.109/745 & Corr.1). [9]YUN 1960, p. 49, GA res. 1514(XV), 14 Dec. 1960.

Chapter II

International Trusteeship System

The Trusteeship Council continued during 1983 to supervise, on behalf of the Security Council, the one Trust Territory remaining under the International Trusteeship System—the Trust Territory of the Pacific Islands, a strategic territory administered by the United States.

The Council considered the annual report submitted by the Administering Authority, heard 13 petitioners, and examined 83 written petitions and 29 communications concerning the Territory. After considering the report of a 1982 Visiting Mission sent by the Council to the Trust Territory, the Council invited the Administering Authority to take into account the Mission's recommendations and conclusions as well as comments by the Council members (resolution 2175(L)). It also took note of the report of a February 1983 Visiting Mission to observe a plebiscite in Palau (resolution 2176(L)). Two other visiting missions were dispatched in June and August to observe plebiscites in the Federated States of Micronesia and the Marshall Islands. Following a general debate on conditions in the Territory, the Council adopted a report to the Security Council containing conclusions and recommendations.

The Trusteeship Council held its fiftieth session at United Nations Headquarters from 16 May to 10 June and resumed the session on 28 November. Of the Council's five members (China, France, USSR, United Kingdom, United States), China did not participate in the session.

Trust Territory of the Pacific Islands

Conditions in the Territory

The Trust Territory of the Pacific Islands, designated as a strategic area and administered by the United States under an Agreement approved by the Security Council in 1947,[1] comprised three archipelagos of more than 2,100 islands and atolls scattered over an area of some 7.8 million square kilometres of the western Pacific Ocean, north of the Equator. The Territory, known collectively as Micronesia, had a population of some 133,000 according to the 1980 census.

There were four administrative entities within the Territory—the Federated States of Micronesia, the Marshall Islands, the Northern Mariana Islands and Palau. As a result of referendums, each had its own constitution and popularly elected legislature and executive head.

Trusteeship Council action. The Trusteeship Council, at its 1983 session, adopted its report[2] to the Security Council after considering the annual report for the year ending 30 September 1982, submitted by the United States as Administering Authority for the Trust Territory and transmitted by the Secretary-General in April.[3] The Council's report contained conclusions and recommendations which covered such questions as land and people and war-related damage claims; political, economic, social and educational advancement; and constitutional development and progress towards self-government or independence.

These conclusions and recommendations, drafted on the basis of the Council's discussions, were annexed to a report on conditions in the Trust Territory,[4] prepared by the Drafting Committee (France and the United Kingdom). On 10 June, the Council adopted the conclusions and recommendations, before adopting the Committee's report as a whole. It also adopted, on the Committee's recommendation, a Secretariat working paper on conditions in the Territory[5] as the basic text for the relevant sections of its report to the Security Council. The draft of that report was adopted by the Trusteeship Council on 28 November. All these actions were taken by a vote of 3 to 1.

In explaining its negative vote, the USSR said that the report contained shortcomings and inaccuracies, had not taken account of its comments, did not reflect the actual situation in the Territory or respond to the mandate of the Council, and failed to conclude that, as a result of the Authority's policy, the people of the Territory were deprived of the opportunity to exercise their inalienable right to genuine independence. In addition, the part of the report dealing with constitutional developments was viewed by the USSR as a would-be justification of United States efforts to change the status of the Territory contrary to the Charter of the United Nations.

Action by the Committee on colonial countries. On 13 October, the General Assembly's Special Committee on the Situation with regard to the Implementation of the Declaration on the Granting of Independence to Colonial Countries and Peoples (Committee on colonial countries) adopted, by 19 votes to none, with 4 abstentions, conclusions and recommendations concerning the Trust Territory,[6] made by its Sub-Committee on Small Territories.

The 25-member Committee expressed regret over the repeated refusal of the Administering Authority to co-operate with it and called again on the United States to ensure the presence of its representative at Committee meetings to provide information. It noted that the reports on the strategic Trust Territory were a matter of which the Security Council was seized, and drew the attention of the relevant United Nations bodies to Article 83 of the Charter empowering the Security Council to exercise all United Nations functions relating to strategic areas, with the Trusteeship Council's assistance on political, economic, social and educational matters.

The Committee reaffirmed the inalienable right of the people of the Trust Territory to self-determination and independence, recalled the Administering Authority's duty to transfer all power to the Territory's freely elected representatives and called for increased economic assistance thereto (see below). It also encouraged the local authorities to develop closer relations with regional and international agencies, particularly within the United Nations system, noting with satisfaction the material assistance provided to the Territory by some of them.

In accordance with decisions taken in May and August, the Committee recommended to the General Assembly adoption of a draft resolution, repeating most of its conclusions on the question of the Trust Territory.

The Chairman transmitted the Committee's conclusions to the Security Council by a letter of 13 October.[7]

General Assembly consideration. On 23 September, the Assembly referred to the Fourth Committee the chapter of the report of the Committee on colonial countries relating to the Trust Territory. On 17 November, the Committee Chairman suggested, based on his consultations with the Chairman of the Committee on colonial countries and delegations concerned, that the Fourth Committee should take no action at that stage on the draft resolution. The suggestion was adopted without objection.[8]

In resolution 38/54 (see Chapter I of this section), the Assembly called on the administering Powers to continue to co-operate with the Special Committee in the discharge of its mandate and, in particular, to permit the access of visiting missions to the Territories to secure firsthand information and ascertain the wishes and aspirations of their inhabitants.

Self-determination and independence

The future political status of the Trust Territory was a dominant issue in its relations with the Administering Authority, with the negotiations between the two sides centring on the compact of free association which defined the political status of the Federated States, the Marshall Islands and Palau in the post-Trusteeship period.[9] To enable the people of Micronesia to express their wishes on the proposed option, the Administering Authority held plebiscites in each of the areas to which the compact applied (see below).

Conclusions of the 1982 Visiting Mission. In its March 1983 report,[10] the Council's July 1982 Visiting Mission to the Territory[11] noted that the Micronesian Governments concerned wished to maintain close and preferential relations with the United States after termination of the Trusteeship Agreement, particularly concerning economic development and defence. It believed that during the period of Trusteeship the Authority had fostered the political, social and educational development of the Territory, which, however, remained almost totally dependent economically and financially on the United States. The Visiting Mission felt that Micronesia should receive technical assistance from the United States and the international community, even after termination of the Agreement. The Mission noted at the same time that the Administering Authority had avoided setting any specific date for terminating that Agreement.

Plebiscites in Palau, the Federated
States of Micronesia and the Marshall Islands

By a December 1982 resolution,[12] the Trusteeship Council had decided to send visiting missions in 1983 to observe plebiscites in Palau, the Marshall Islands and the Federated States of Micronesia.

Palau. The Mission to Palau, composed of one representative each from Fiji, France, Papua New Guinea and the United Kingdom, was dispatched to observe the plebiscite on the compact of free association and a number of subsidiary agreements, conducted throughout the area on 10 February 1983. The visit began on 3 February in Koror and lasted until 12 February, with a United Nations Secretariat staff member remaining in Palau until 17 February to observe the counting and tabulation of votes. The Mission held meetings with executive, legislative and community leaders and individuals, groups and the general public in Koror, Babelthuap, Angaur and Peleliu, which together accounted for over 90 per cent of Palau's population, and observed the arrangements and procedures of vote casting and ballot counting and tabulation.

In its April report on the plebiscite,[13] the Mission concluded that, although the compact and its subsidiary agreements were long and complex, the broad issues raised and the wording of the ballot were generally understood by voters due to the political campaign itself and to a political education programme conducted co-operatively by the Administering Authority and the Palau Government. It reiterated the importance of holding political education programmes prior to plebiscites in the Federated States of Micronesia and the Marshall Islands. The Mission observed no irregularities, violence or improper intervention by the Authority during the campaign and plebiscite. Vote counting was carefully carried out by a single team, enabling the Mission and general public to verify the counting's propriety.

Summing up the results, the Mission stated that 88.2 per cent of the 8,213 registered voters took part in the plebiscite, with 4,452 (61.4 per cent) voting for the compact and 2,715 against, the remaining 79 ballots being void. With regard to the subsidiary agreement on the introduction of radioactive, chemical and biological materials into Palau, as provided for by the compact, 3,717 voters (51.3 per cent) approved of it and 3,309 voted against; 220 ballots were void. Thus the compact was approved by the people of Palau but could not enter into force because of the insufficient number of votes in favour of the agreement on radioactive materials (51.3 per cent as against the 75 per cent required by the 1979 Palau Constitution). The Mission concluded that it was for the Governments of Palau and the United States to look for a mutually acceptable solution to reconcile the differences between the relevant sections of the Palau Constitution and the compact. The third question on the ballot, concerning political status arrangements in case the compact was rejected, elicited response from only 56.1 per cent of the voters, 55.5 per cent of whom favoured closer relationship with the United States, while 44.5 per cent preferred independence.

Federated States of Micronesia. The plebiscite in the Federated States of Micronesia, held on 21 June, was observed by another Visiting Mission, composed of one representative each of Fiji and France and two representatives each of Papua New Guinea and the United Kingdom, which began its visit at Kolonia, Ponape, on 15 June and ended it on 26 June at Moen, Truk. During its stay there, the Mission met ministers and officials at national and state levels, as well as traditional leaders and the public in each of the four federated states of Ponape, Truk, Yap and Kosrae.

In its October report,[14] the Mission stated that, although few voters fully grasped the details of the compact, thanks to a public information programme the majority had some idea of the main issues. However, in the Mission's view, the programme's effectiveness was undercut by lack of adequate written teaching aids, and little attention was given in the programme to alternative options to the compact. Further, the Mission noted the unsatisfactory composition of the advisory section of the ballot, which was largely misunderstood by voters.

No systematic political campaign was observed in the Federation, with the exception of Truk, where the plebiscite was boycotted in the Faichuk and Udot islands. Despite inadequate verification of affidavits, and certain irregularities in Truk, vote counting and tabulating were generally professional. Of the 40,538 registered voters, 25,606 (63.2 per cent) took part in the plebiscite, with 20,121 (79 per cent) voting in favour of the compact and 5,348 against. In the advisory part of the ballot, 13,924 voters indicated a preference for independence in case the compact was not approved; 1,319 voted in favour of United States Commonwealth status; 820 opted for "United States territory" and 568 for "state of the United States"; 2,587 indicated a preference for a different status or gave no description of what that status should be; and 4,771 advisory section ballots were rejected or spoilt. The Mission concluded that the compact was thus approved by the voters of the Federated States of Micronesia.

Marshall Islands. To observe the plebiscite in the Marshall Islands, held on 7 September 1983, a Visiting Mission, composed of one representative each of Fiji, France, Papua New Guinea and the United Kingdom, began its visit at Majuro on 31 August and ended it there on 10 September, with a member of the United Nations Secretariat staying behind until 15 September to continue observing the counting and tabulation of votes.

In its report,[15] the Mission stated that the plebiscite had been accompanied by a lively political campaign in which no violence was observed and everyone appeared able to express his or her views freely and openly. The Mission concluded that, as a result of a well-organized and well-executed political education campaign, the Marshallese had a knowledge of the major issues involved and some idea of the alternative constitutional options. The plebiscite was largely dominated by financial considerations related to compensation under the radiation agreement and the scale of payments to the Kwajalein landowners. Other aspects of the compact played little part in the campaign and the alternative constitutional options did not excite much interest.

With the exception of two polling stations on Majuro and Ebeye, the Mission had found polling arrangements to be excellent and the vote counting and tabulating thorough, careful and correct, although unduly long. It noted, however, that same-day registration procedures employed during the plebiscite were open to abuse without foolproof means of voter identification. According to the official results, 6,215 votes had been cast for the compact and 4,509 against, which led the Mission to conclude that it had been approved. Some minor inconsistencies in the totals, in the Mission's view, had not significantly affected the result.

Trusteeship Council action. In its 1983 report,[2] the Trusteeship Council reaffirmed the inalienable right of the people of Micronesia to self-determination, including the right to independence in accordance with the United Nations Charter and the Trusteeship Agreement. It noted that full functional self-government in the Trust Territory would be realized with the termination of the Agreement and noted the wish of the constitutional Governments to maintain links with the Administering Authority after termination. The Council also expressed satisfaction with the Authority's reaffirmation that the people of Micronesia would have the opportunity to choose their future political status from a range of options and the fact that the Palau plebiscite was conducted in complete freedom and without any irregularities. It endorsed the view of the Mission with regard to reconciling conflicting provisions of the Palau Constitution and the compact of free association (see above) and noted establishment of a task force by Palau, and the Authority's readiness to negotiate resolution of the problem.

Refraining, as in previous years, from making recommendations on the future political status of the various Micronesian entities, the Council reiterated its view that free association was not incompatible with the Trusteeship Agreement, provided that it was freely accepted by the populations concerned, and noted that, following approval of the compact, the Administering Authority would take up the matter of terminating the Agreement with the Trusteeship and Security Councils. The Trusteeship Council welcomed the Authority's commitment to provide economic assistance to the constitutional Governments during the initial stage of the free association relationship and expressed hope for speedy termination of the Agreement, noting with interest the formation of an inter-agency group for maintaining liaison with the United States in the post-Trusteeship period. It expressed some regret at the decision of the peoples of Micronesia to seek their future separately and urged all interested parties to co-operate fully in establishing, after the Agreement's termination, the all-Micronesian entity as agreed at Molokai, Hawaii, in 1977.

On 2 June 1983, the Trusteeship Council adopted resolution 2176(L) by vote.

Report of the United Nations Visiting Mission to observe the plebiscite in Palau, Trust Territory of the Pacific Islands, February 1983

The Trusteeship Council,

Having examined at its fiftieth session the report of the United Nations Visiting Mission, dispatched at the in-

vitation of the Administering Authority and pursuant to its resolution 2174(S-XV) of 20 December 1982, to observe the plebiscite in Palau, Trust Territory of the Pacific Islands,

1. *Takes note* of the report of the Visiting Mission;
2. *Expresses its appreciation* of the work accomplished by the Visiting Mission on its behalf.

Trusteeship Council resolution 2176(L)

2 June 1983   Meeting 1559   3-1

Draft by France and United Kingdom (T/L.1237); agenda item 7.
Meeting number. TC 1559.

In explanation of its negative vote, the USSR said that the United States actions, including the organization and holding of a plebiscite in Palau, were aimed at dismembering and annexing the Trust Territory under its administration in violation of the Charter, despite the 1960 Declaration on the Granting of Independence to Colonial Countries and Peoples[16] and in circumvention of the Security Council, without whose decision no change in the status of a strategic territory could be legally binding. The USSR pointed out that sending a Mission to Micronesia to observe the plebiscite was tantamount to United Nations participation in an illegal process. It said that the Mission's report could not prove convincingly that the plebiscite in Palau had been carried out on a free basis and that petitions presented to the Council indicated that it had been held in a politically tendentious atmosphere which had made impossible a proper expression of will by the population.

Action by the Committee on colonial countries. In its conclusions and recommendations,[6] the Committee on colonial countries reaffirmed the inalienable right of the people of the Territory to self-determination and independence in conformity with the Charter and the 1960 Declaration on colonial countries, the speedy implementation of which should not be delayed by the Territory's size, geographical location, population and limited natural resources. It reiterated that the Authority had an obligation to create conditions enabling the people to exercise freely that right with full knowledge of the various options open to them. Calling on the Authority to refrain from any action that might impede the Territory's unity, the Committee said that termination of the Trusteeship Agreement should be in strict conformity with the Charter. It also reaffirmed its strong conviction that the Authority must ensure, by complying fully with United Nations resolutions, that military installations and activities in the Territory should not hinder the population from exercising its rights.

Communications. By a letter dated 15 August,[17] the USSR transmitted to the Secretary-General a 12 August TASS statement, charging that the United States was involved in illegal activities aimed at dismemberment and *de facto* annexation of the Trust Territory of the Pacific Islands. Describing those activities as contrary to the Charter, the statement accused the United States of preventing the creation of an independent viable economy in the Territory, turning parts of it into a testing ground for nuclear weapons, imposing on the inhabitants long-term military agreements, and using the United Nations mandate as a cover to frustrate the exercise of the inalienable right of the people of Micronesia to self-determination, freedom and independence.

In a 29 August statement, transmitted the next day to the Security Council President,[18] the United States said that the USSR description bore little relationship to reality. It pointed out that it acted in accordance with the Charter and the Trusteeship Agreement by improving the quality of life in Micronesia, relinquishing virtually all executive, legislative and judicial functions to the Governments of Palau, the Marshall Islands and the Federated States of Micronesia and signing compacts of free association with them after extensive debate within Micronesia. It also stated that under the Agreement the United States was authorized to establish military facilities and station armed forces in the Territory.

Politics and government

1982 Visiting Mission's conclusions. In its report,[10] the Council's 1982 Visiting Mission noted that since the emergence of new constitutional Governments in Micronesia there had been a reduction in the day-to-day exercise of administrative, legislative and juridical powers over the Territory, which were to be retained formally by the Administering Authority until termination of the Trusteeship Agreement. Apart from legal matters, most functions previously carried out by the Authority were transferred to the new Governments, which emphasized, in their contacts with the Mission, the importance of the interim period for gaining experience. With regard to foreign affairs, the Authority informed the Mission that it was assisting in contacts with foreign countries and international organizations. However, Micronesian leaders had expressed concern over their inability to sign directly the 1982 United Nations Convention on the Law of the Sea[19] or to negotiate with a group of South Pacific States on the establishment of a common fisheries organization. Assessing the role of tradition and traditional authorities, the Mission noted the influence they continued to exert on emerging institutions. It also reported a high level of political awareness and education of the Territory's inhabitants.

In the Mission's view, since 1980 each of the Territory's political components had achieved full functional self-government under the Agreement. In the Federated States of Micronesia, the new state governments, with fully elected executive and legislative branches, carried out their functions in accordance with the terms of their charters. The Palau Constitution provided for observance of democratic principles and local traditions, without being inconsistent with the national Constitution. The Marshall Islands Constitution recognized the right of each populated atoll, or island not a part of an atoll; the Northern Mariana Islands was divided into four municipal jurisdictions, each headed by an elected mayor. The Mission also reported that all the Micronesian entities had established their respective civil services and judicial authorities.

With regard to the political education programme, the Mission characterized it as successful in instructing Micronesians in democratic processes, but noted that the objective of informing them of the political options in the post-Trusteeship period had been overshadowed by preparations for constitutional referendums. During its visit, the Mission found a growing recognition on the part of constitutional leaders for an education programme that would inform the voters about the issues at stake and their political options. Noting a certain diminishing of fear among the population that termination of the Agreement would result in cessation of all financial aid and expert assistance from the United States and the United Nations, the Mission recommended that the political campaign should cover economic as well as political options and urged the Authority and the constitutional leaders to set up new education programmes.

Trusteeship Council action. The Trusteeship Council, in its 1983 report,[2] welcomed the continuing devolution of administrative responsibility for the Territory to fully organized constitutional Governments and noted with satisfaction that the Administering Authority was encouraging its contacts with regional and international organizations and other nations in the region. The Council also reiterated its satisfaction at the performance of legislative bodies in the Trust Territory. Regarding the civil service, a 1981 government employee strike and 1981/82 budgetary problems in Palau were a cause of concern for the Council, which reiterated that the Authority should continue to assist the Governments in stimulating private sector employment. The Council noted the reduction by the Authority of its headquarters staff in 1982 by 200 employees.

Noting with satisfaction the $375,000 for political education provided by the Administering Authority to the three Governments by the end of 1982, the Council welcomed the 1982 Mission's findings that the Territory's population appeared politically well-informed while enjoying complete freedom of expression, and the view of the 1983 Mission to Palau that the political education programme there had been useful and effective. The

Council emphasized the importance of conducting adequate education programmes on economic as well as political issues, prior to plebiscites in the Federated States and the Marshall Islands, and noted with satisfaction that the juridical systems in the Territory were fully established and functioning.

Action by the Committee on colonial countries. In its conclusions and recommendations,[6] the Committee on colonial countries noted that administrative responsibility throughout the Territory was exercised by local authorities but regretted that the High Commissioner still maintained the power, although rarely invoked, to suspend certain legislation. The Committee recalled that the Administering Authority was duty-bound to transfer all power to the Territory's freely elected representatives.

Economic conditions

Conclusions of the 1982 Visiting Mission. While noting in its report[10] the significant efforts by the Administering Authority in preparing for the end of Trusteeship, the 1982 Visiting Mission pointed out the limited impact on the Micronesian economy, which remained structurally imbalanced and dependent on outside financing.

Given Micronesia's great distances and the spread of population over a large number of islands, the Mission was particularly concerned about the problem of transport, which, despite some progress, was exacerbated by the inadequate road network and irregularities of the inter-island shipping service. It called on the Authority to play a galvanizing role in developing an effective transportation system and proposed increased participation in the effort by relevant United Nations agencies.

Micronesian agriculture, although facing a number of serious constraints such as subsistence-type farming, a fragmentary pattern of landholding and dependence on food imports, was viewed as having the potential for development. The Mission noted the encouraging results of the introduction in various parts of the Territory of import taxes on foodstuffs, financial incentives, export promotion and other measures, and made recommendations on improving livestock breeding and production of copra, Micronesia's most important agricultural product. Of crucial importance for its future development were Micronesia's rich marine resources, capable of meeting the entire domestic demand and becoming a major source of export earnings, processing activity, employment and income in most parts of the Territory. In this connection, the Mission found that the Governments in various entities were concerned with the protection of their 200-mile economic zone.

Another priority issue was the neglected state of economic development in the outer islands and the outlying municipalities. The Mission urged the Authority to provide the necessary resources under the second-level capital improvement programme to establish and upgrade the economic infrastructure. It also said that due attention should be given to maintenance of the rapidly deteriorating infrastructure, increase in export earnings and income from tourism, establishment of a viable statistical system and a long-term planning programme, and reduction of administrative expenses.

With regard to public finance and taxation, the Mission reported a steady enhancement of the budgetary powers of the territorial entities, stressing, however, that the taxation system remained heavily dependent on income tax. It also noted numerous requests for greater financial assistance from the Administering Authority, whose appropriations and federal programme grants were the main source of investment capital in the Territory.

Trusteeship Council action. In its 1983 report,[2] the Trusteeship Council noted with regret that Micronesia remained, to a large extent, economically and financially dependent on the Administering Authority and that there had been no significant reduction of the economy's structural imbalances. Emphasizing the need for economic and financial assistance to Micronesian Governments, the Council noted the Authority's efforts in that respect, including an overall 9 per cent increase in budgetary allocations, but regretted the delay in launching the second phase of the capital improvement programme; it was hopeful that the Authority would provide substantial budgetary support through the compact of free association. The Council endorsed the conclusions of the 1982 Visiting Mission, laying stress on the problems of infrastructure, transport and outer island development, and on the pressing need for a viable statistical system. It urged the Administering Authority to give serious consideration to preparing an overall development programme as a prerequisite for inward investment.

Regarding public finance matters, the Council noted that in 1981/82 the constitutional Governments had received $98.6 million from the Administering Authority and $21.3 million from federal categorical grants, and that the number of health and education programmes had increased over that period, while several federal programmes had been, regrettably, reduced or discontinued. The Council also reiterated the Mission's conclusions with regard to the need for early establishment of separate financial management systems in each Micronesian entity and the advisability, in view of the taxation system's heavy dependence on income tax, of introducing import duties on non-essential goods or items competing with local products.

The Council welcomed the continuing development of relations between Micronesian Governments and other regional States, as well as international organizations and regional and international programmes. It also noted with satisfaction that the Economic Development Loan Fund (EDLF) was fully operational through the central banks in each government centre; expressed hope for the speedy resolution of the administrative and legal difficulties encountered in the transfer of public lands and spoke for continuation of the cadastral survey of private lands; and reaffirmed that the Authority had a duty to help the constitutional Governments expand agricultural and livestock production to achieve greater self-sufficiency.

Reiterating that the development of marine resources was a high-priority aspect of the Territory's economic future, the Council noted the Administering Authority's intention to endorse the constitutional Governments' efforts in developing their fishing industries and assist them in ensuring their rights over the 200-mile zones. It also noted the hope of the Governments of the Federated States of Micronesia, the Marshall Islands and Palau to sign the Convention on the Law of the Sea even before the termination of the Trusteeship Agreement and the fact that the Authority had no objection to their signing after the termination of the Agreement.

The Council endorsed the Mission's conclusions that tourism should develop in a gradual and planned manner to avoid overwhelming the small and fragile economies, social structures, environment and cultural traditions of the Territory.

With regard to transport, while noting such positive developments as the construction of new airstrips, road improvements and inauguration of satellite ground stations in Palau and the Marshall Islands and gradual commissioning of all the stations in the Federated States, the Council called for better sea transport to integrate the outer islands into the Territory's economy and increased efforts to provide a minimum road network. It also reiterated its concern at the poor development of small industrial enterprises in the Territory.

Action by the Committee on colonial countries. In its conclusions and recommendations,[6] the Committee on colonial countries called for increased economic assistance to the Trust Territory to help its people gain economic independence and reduce the structural imbalances of the economy.

Noting the overall 9 per cent increase in budgetary allocations for the Territory, an $18.4 million appropriation for the capital improvement programme, the progress in EDLF operation and the encouragement given to investment, exports and tourism, the Committee recalled the Administering Authority's obligation to the Territory's economic

development. It also urged the Authority to safeguard and guarantee, in co-operation with the local authorities, the right of Micronesians to own and dispose freely of the natural resources and to control their future development. In this connection, the Committee noted the work of the Territory's maritime authorities to strengthen the existing legislation on a 200-mile exclusive economic zone, and reaffirmed that the Micronesian people's rights over such a zone should be respected and that they should receive all benefits deriving from it.

Social conditions

Conclusions of the 1982 Visiting Mission. Regarding social advancement, the 1982 Visiting Mission concluded[10] that all aspects of medical and health care services in the Territory were the responsibility of the constitutional Governments, with the Micronesia Health Co-ordinating Council periodically reviewing health plans and their implementation and the Trust Territory Bureau of Health Services providing technical and advisory assistance. The Mission commended the Administering Authority for its efforts to improve health standards, noting its consistently increasing expenditures on public health.

After touring hospitals and dispensaries in various parts of the Territory, the Mission recommended that medical facilities be constructed with due consideration to local weather conditions and that sufficient funds be set aside for regular maintenance. It also hoped that both the Administering Authority and the constitutional Governments would give priority to improving the dispensary services in the Territory, particularly in the outer islands. With regard to medical referrals, the Mission noted the considerable improvement in interisland transportation for carrying patients from outer islands to hospitals within the Territory, but reported numerous complaints about the exorbitant cost of health referring services.

Addressing other aspects of social development, the Mission expressed deep concern over the worsening unemployment problem, observed that there continued to be too much reliance on external aid for financing and carrying out community activities, and described as sensible the approach to the population problem by the Economic and Social Commission for Asia and the Pacific, which was prepared to assist a family planning programme in the Territory. The Mission also questioned the Administering Authority's assumptions that local materials were inadequate for use in the housing construction programme, partly sponsored by the Trust Territory Administration, and that high maintenance costs frequently precluded preventive maintenance.

While noting the legal equality of men and women in the Territory and certain steps taken to put it into practice, the Mission urged the authorities to recognize the importance of women playing a full part in economic, social and political development. Juvenile delinquency continued to be a major concern, its increase caused mainly by a lack of job opportunities, the drift of youth to the urban centres and alcoholism. The Mission commended various youth training programmes for unemployed and potentially delinquent youths and called on the Administering Authority to view sympathetically requests from the Governments for appropriate assistance and technical support.

Trusteeship Council action. The Trusteeship Council, in its 1983 report,[2] took note of the transfer of all health-related activities to the constitutional Governments, an increase in the number of doctors in the Territory and the Governments' encouragement of students to go into the medical field. It also urged the Administering Authority to continue assisting the development of health services in the Territory and welcomed its emphasis on the improvement of hospital facilities and the efforts to improve health standards in the Territory, particularly noting the doubling of health appropriations to $8.1 million per annum between 1970 and 1980, and the Authority's $10 million in assistance to the construction of a new health-care centre in the Northern Mariana Islands. The Council welcomed the combined efforts of the Governments, the Authority, the World Health Organization and the United Nations Children's Fund in containing and eradicating a cholera epidemic in Truk. It also stressed the importance of maintaining and expanding dispensary services in the Territory, especially away from state centres.

Noting that community activities regrettably continued to rely too much on external aid, the Council reiterated the need for the Territory's inhabitants to participate more actively in community projects and urged the Authority to continue assisting various kinds of infrastructure-building undertakings. It also expressed considerable concern over the apparently worsening unemployment and the persevering imbalance between the wage-earners in the public and the private sectors, urging the Authority and the constitutional Governments to give high priority to the problem. The Council was concerned about the discontinuation of a housing loan programme for the Federated States of Micronesia and the increasing incidence of juvenile delinquency. It regretted the phasing out of youth-related programmes, but expressed satisfaction at the increased funding under the Juvenile Justice and Delinquency Prevention Act. With regard to public safety, the Council welcomed the Authority's assurances of continued assistance to the constitutional Governments in maintaining order and training juridical, legal and police agencies.

Education

Conclusions of the 1982 Visiting Mission. Assessing educational advancement in the Territory, the 1982 Visiting Mission reported[10] that responsibility for educational operations had been transferred to the constitutional Governments and commended the Administering Authority for its achievements in laying a sound foundation for future development. There were many problems remaining, however, such as inadequate funds and shortages of qualified teachers, school supplies and accommodation. The Mission observed that there was an urgent need to maintain and restore existing buildings, as well as to construct new ones, and reiterated the importance of providing adequate funds. The Mission also noted various steps taken to train more teachers and provide more schoolbooks in local languages, emphasized the importance of aid for the development of the College of Micronesia and noted the increasing interest by the constitutional Governments in preserving their cultural heritage.

Trusteeship Council action. In its 1983 report,[2] the Trusteeship Council congratulated the Administering Authority for the sound foundations it had laid in the Territory for primary education but noted with regret such remaining problems as inadequate funding and shortages of teachers and supplies. The Council continued to be concerned about the deterioration of school facilities and the spreading of social problems among the unemployed youth, including university graduates and school drop-outs.

Noting the Authority's concern about the deterioration of primary school buildings, the Council urged it to consider funding maintenance programmes after termination of the Trusteeship Agreement. Of particular concern for the Council was the lowering of standards at the College of Micronesia, the Territory's only institution of higher learning, which was overcrowded due to building deterioration and threatened with losing accreditation. The Council recommended speedy implementation of the Authority-funded project for a new College campus, while noting with satisfaction the expanded role of the Northern Mariana Islands Community College.

The Council was pleased to note the interest shown by the constitutional Governments in preserving their cultural heritage, including broadening programmes for preserving indigenous language as well as measures to provide more school-books in local languages. Addressing the problems of vocational training, it indicated the need for its close correlation with job requirements and welcomed the Administering Authority's intention to continue co-operation in training for actual job opportunities in the various jurisdictions of the Territory.

The Council commended the efforts made to overcome the shortage of qualified teachers and drew special attention to the College of Micronesia as the principal teacher training institution.

The Council urged the Authority to co-operate fully with the constitutional Governments and the United Nations Information Centre in Tokyo in ensuring rapid, efficient and comprehensive dissemination of information on the United Nations and the International Trusteeship System in the Trust Territory.

Claims

In its report,[10] the 1982 Visiting Mission reiterated that outstanding claims for damage resulting from Second World War hostilities between Japan and the United States (Title I claims) should be met in full as speedily as possible and before the termination of the Trusteeship Agreement.

This concern was reiterated by the Trusteeship Council,[2] which urged both countries to resume negotiations and welcomed the Administering Authority's statements that all parties were continuing their efforts to settle Title I claims, with nearly 30 per cent of the awarded $34 million already paid, and that all post-war claims against the United States (Title II claims) had been settled.

Radioactive waste management

During its 1982 tour of the Territory,[10] the Visiting Mission noted the expressed opposition of the Trust Territory's public officials and private citizens to the possible disposal of nuclear wastes in the sea by States having Pacific coastlines.

The Trusteeship Council noted this concern in its 1983 report,[2] the United States statement that it did not intend to dispose of nuclear wastes in the Territory or in adjacent waters and the Administering Authority's assurances that the competent agencies continued to take this problem into consideration.

The Council also noted that the Northern Marianas Commonwealth Legislature had passed a law declaring a nuclear-free and chemical-free zone in and around the Northern Mariana Islands.

Resettlement of the Bikini and Enewetak populations

The 1982 Visiting Mission to the Trust Territory[10] examined the situation of the people of Bikini and Enewetak atolls in the Marshall Islands who had relocated to other islands because of radioactive contamination from nuclear-weapon tests three decades earlier. On Ejit Island, the Mission was asked by Bikinians living there to convey to the Administering Authority their request for resettlement on Bikini or Hawaii, or, if that was not possible, to have the United States develop Ejit. During the meetings with the Mission at Majuro, Marshall Islands, representatives of the people of Enewetak spoke of various medical, food, maintenance and youth problems and stressed that the United States should assume responsibility for them, in part in the compact of free association.

In its 1983 report,[2] the Trusteeship Council reiterated its serious concern about the quality of medical care available to the displaced persons of Bikini and Enewetak and regretted that a health programme proposed under United States legislation had not been implemented. While noting the 1982 supplementary appropriation of $21.4 million by the United States for resettlement purposes and the Administering Authority's measures to assist and compensate nuclear test victims, the Council reiterated that resettlement proposals should take fully into account any remaining health hazards and recommended that the Authority continue to remove radiation threats.

The Council recalled the wish of the Bikinians of Ejit to resettle to another island and urged the Administering Authority to develop Ejit in case such resettlement was not feasible. It hoped that the Authority would interpret its obligations generously, particularly regarding health and compensation matters, and that there would be a speedy conclusion to the negotiations between the Authority and the Marshallese authorities on establishing a compensation fund and referral of complaints to the competent courts. The Council also noted that a scientific research mission was studying the possible rehabilitation of Bikini.

Military base

The 1982 Visiting Mission described in its report[10] a sail-in strike held from June to October 1982 by the inhabitants of Ebeye and Third Island who, as owners of the land used for the United States military facility on Kwajalein Atoll, reoccupied it by establishing camps at Kwajalein and Roi-Namir and stationed their boats in the mid-atoll corridor of the Kwajalein lagoon. The Mission concluded that the conflict between the landowners, on the one hand, and the Government of the Marshall Islands and the Administering Authority, on the other, was caused by inadequate compensation for rent provided in the interim agreement and the compact of free association, and the landowners' inability to return to leased ancestral land while having to live in overpopulated conditions, with deteriorating housing and community services. The Mission welcomed the moderation displayed by the parties to the conflict, which occurred without serious incident. It also called on the United States scientific community at Kwajalein and Roi-Namur to improve its knowledge and understanding of the people of the Marshall Islands.

The Trusteeship Council[2] reiterated its concern over the difficulties of the people living on Ebeye arising primarily from over-population. It also urged the Administering Authority to arrive at universally satisfactory solutions to specific problems raised by the United States military installations on Kwajalein Atoll and to avoid a repetition of incidents such as the sail-in.

Visiting missions

The report of the July 1982 Visiting Mission to the Trust Territory of the Pacific Islands[10] was submitted, on 16 May 1983, to the Trusteeship Council for consideration (for the report's conclusions, see above, under subject headings).

Trusteeship Council action. On 2 June 1983, the Trusteeship Council adopted resolution 2175(L) by vote.

Report of the United Nations Visiting Mission to the Trust Territory of the Pacific Islands, 1982

The Trusteeship Council,

Having examined at its fiftieth session the report of the United Nations Visiting Mission to the Trust Territory of the Pacific Islands, 1982,

Having heard the statements made by the representatives of the United States of America concerning the report,

1. *Takes note* of the report of the Visiting Mission and of the observations of the Administering Authority thereon;

2. *Expresses its appreciation* of the work accomplished by the Visiting Mission on its behalf;

3. *Decides* that it will continue to take the recommendations, conclusions and observations of the Visiting Mission into account in future examination of matters relating to the Trust Territory;

4. *Invites* the Administering Authority to take into account the recommendations and conclusions of the Visiting Mission as well as the comments made thereon by the members of the Trusteeship Council.

Trusteeship Council resolution 2175(L)

| 2 June 1983 | Meeting 1559 | 3-0-1 |

Draft by France and United Kingdom (T/L.1236); agenda item 6.
Meeting number. TC 1559.

Explaining its abstention, the USSR said that, while the report indicated the failure by the Administering Authority to fulfil its obligations, the material had not been presented in a way to enable valid conclusions to be drawn and specific proposals to be put forward to alter the situation and compel the Authority to discharge its obligations. The USSR asserted that the report did not give due consideration to the illegal fragmentation of the Territory by the United States, was silent on the planned expansion of its illegal military activity aimed at establishing a military strategic staging-point in the Pacific region, and contained no objective evaluation of the United States responsibility for the catastrophic economic situation in the Territory. The USSR

also noted that the preambular paragraphs of the resolution might have referred also to other statements made in the Council, but did not oppose it because it invited the Administering Authority to take into account the Council members' recommendations.

During 1983, visiting missions of the Council observed plebiscites in Palau, the Marshall Islands and the Federated States of Micronesia (see above).

Hearings

From 18 to 20 May 1983, the Trusteeship Council heard the following 13 petitioners whose requests for oral hearings had been previously circulated: Senator Henchi Balos, of Bikini; Stuart Beck, on behalf of Senator Joshua Koshiba, National Congress of the Republic of Palau; William Butler, Minority Rights Group; Roger S. Clark, International League for Human Rights; Silvestre T. Cruz, Tinian Landowners' Association; Douglas Faulkner, a photographer/writer living in New York; Ibedul Y. M. Gibbons, Mayor, Koror State, Palau; Bernie Tosie Keldermans, of Palau; Julian Riklon, of the Rongelap and Kwajalein Atolls, Marshall Islands; Christopher Roosevelt, on behalf of the Coalition to Support the Palau Constitution; George Wald, Professor Emeritus of Biology at Harvard University, United States; Jonathan M. Weisgall, Legal Counsel, Bikini; and Father William Wood, Focus on Micronesia Coalition.

Meeting numbers. TC 1546-1549.

Petitions, communications and observations

The Trusteeship Council, on 2 and 8 June 1983, examined 83 written petitions and 29 communications it received, and drew the attention of the petitioners to the observations of the Administering Authority, where applicable.

Meeting numbers. TC 1559, 1560.

REFERENCES

[1]YUN 1946-47, p. 398. [2]S/16347. [3]S/15731 (T/1853). [4]T/L.1238. [5]T/L.1235 & Add.1. [6]A/38/23. [7]S/16042. [8]A/38/612. [9]YUN 1981, p. 1121. [10]T/1850. [11]YUN 1982, p. 1286. [12]*Ibid.*, p. 1287, TC res. 2174(S-XV), 20 Dec. 1982. [13]T/1851. [14]T/1860. [15]T/1865. [16]YUN 1960, p. 49, GA res. 1514(XV), 14 Dec. 1960. [17]A/38/340-S/15927. [18]S/15940. [19]YUN 1982, p. 181.

Other aspects of the International Trusteeship System

Fellowships and scholarships

Under a scholarship programme, launched by the General Assembly in 1952,[1] 11 Member States had in the past made scholarships available for students from Trust Territories: Czechoslovakia, Hungary,

Indonesia, Italy, Mexico, Pakistan, Philippines, Poland, Tunisia, USSR, Yugoslavia. In a report to the Trusteeship Council, covering the period from 14 May 1982 to 18 May 1983,[2] the Secretary-General stated that in April 1983 those States had been requested to provide up-to-date information on the scholarships available and the extent of their utilization. As of 18 May, a response had been received from the USSR, which stated that it had no students from the Trust Territory of the Pacific Islands.

On 26 May, the Council, without objection, took note of the report.

Meeting number. TC 1556.

Information dissemination

A report of the Secretary-General covering the period from 1 May 1982 to 30 April 1983[3] described activities by the United Nations Department of Public Information (DPI) in distributing United Nations documents, official records and information materials throughout the Trust Territory, including its legislatures, libraries, offices of administrators, educational institutions and the information media. The United Nations Information Centre in Tokyo, while continuing to mail materials to the Territory, gave wide publicity to the 1983 Visiting Mission to observe the plebiscite in Palau. Its counterpart in Washington, D. C., provided information on developments in the Trusteeship Council to the United States Congress and Departments of State and the Interior, as well as to non-governmental organizations and the media. DPI radio programmes, considered the most effective means of bringing news of United Nations activities to Micronesians, were dispatched weekly to the Territory and played by all local radio stations. Video tape cassettes were widely used by various educational institutions and the library of the College of Micronesia in Ponape kept United Nations films for loan (temporarily suspended during the period under review due to a shortage of staff).

In observance of the 1982 United Nations Day, messages from the President of the Trusteeship Council and the Secretary-General were broadcast throughout Micronesia.

On 26 May, the Council took note of the report without objection.

Meeting number. TC 1555.

Trusteeship Council

The Trusteeship Council held its fiftieth session at United Nations Headquarters from 16 May to 10 June 1983. The agenda of the session[4] was adopted on 16 May (for list of agenda items, see APPENDIX IV).

At its resumed fiftieth session, held on 28 November, the Council adopted its report to the Security Council.[5]

Meeting numbers. TC 1544, 1563.

Co-operation with the
Committee on colonial countries

At its 1983 session,[5] the Trusteeship Council considered together the questions of attainment of self-government or independence by the Trust Territory and co-operation with the Special Committee on the Situation with regard to the Implementation of the Declaration on the Granting of Independence to Colonial Countries and Peoples.

On 10 June, the Council, by 3 votes to 1, decided to draw the Security Council's attention to the conclusions and recommendations adopted at the session, along with the statements by its members, on the attainment of self-government or independence by the Trust Territory in accordance with the Charter's relevant provisions. An amendment proposed by the USSR, which would have added a reference to the implementation of the 1960 Declaration on colonial countries, was rejected by 3 votes to 1.

Meeting numbers. TC 1558, 1561.

Co-operation with CERD and the
Decade against racial discrimination

In 1983, the Trusteeship Council[5] considered together the question of co-operation with the Committee on the Elimination of Racial Discrimination (CERD) and the Decade for Action to Combat Racism and Racial Discrimination (1973-1983). On 26 May, the Council took note, without objection, of the statements made.

Meeting number. TC 1556.

REFERENCES

[1]YUN 1951, p. 788, GA res. 557(VI), 18 Jan. 1952. [2]T/1855. [3]T/1854. [4]T/1852 & Add.1. [5]S/16347.

Chapter III

Namibia

United Nations efforts to achieve independence for Namibia—the largest Territory remaining under colonial rule—continued throughout 1983.

The Security Council convened twice at the request of the African countries and the Non-Aligned Movement to consider the question of Namibia. At each series of meetings it considered a report by the Secretary-General on implementation of the plan for Namibia's independence approved by the Council in 1978. In May 1983, the Secretary-General reported that despite progress in certain areas, issues outside the scope of the United Nations plan were being raised. South Africa had agreed to co-operate, provided that Cuban troops were withdrawn from Angola. After the first set of meetings, the Council, in resolution 532(1983) of 31 May, mandated the Secretary-General to consult with the parties to the proposed cease-fire and requested him to report on the results.

Having visited the front-line States in February and South Africa, Namibia and Angola in August, the Secretary-General stated that further progress had been made on the outstanding questions, but South Africa had not changed its position on linking the two issues, which made it impossible to launch the independence plan. After considering the Secretary-General's report, the Council, in resolution 539(1983) of 28 October, rejected South Africa's linking Namibia's independence to extraneous issues, called on South Africa to decide on the electoral system it preferred for a constituent assembly in an independent Namibia, and requested the Secretary-General to report on progress in implementing the plan for Namibia's independence before the end of the year. In the event of continued obstruction by South Africa, the Council decided to consider the adoption of appropriate measures under the United Nations Charter.

Reporting to the Council in December, the Secretary-General noted that South Africa had not changed its position, nor had it indicated its choice for an electoral system.

At its regular 1983 session, the General Assembly considered the question of Namibia and adopted five resolutions on the subject, including one (resolution 38/36 B) requesting the Security Council to implement the plan for Namibia's independence and urging it to impose comprehensive mandatory sanctions against South Africa.

Resolution 38/36 A dealt with the situation in Namibia resulting from South Africa's illegal occupation. By that text, the Assembly called for action by Member States, the Security Council, other United Nations bodies and intergovernmental organizations, and the United Nations Secretariat to counteract the occupation. The Assembly outlined the work programme of the United Nations Council for Namibia in resolution 38/36 C and requested the Secretariat and the Council to take measures to disseminate information in support of Namibia in resolution 38/36 D. By resolution 38/36 E, the Assembly called for assistance to Namibians, particularly through the United Nations Fund for Namibia.

The International Conference in Support of the Struggle of the Namibian People for Independence, organized by the Council for Namibia, was held in Paris from 25 to 29 April. It adopted the Paris Declaration on Namibia and issued a Programme of Action. In the Declaration, the Conference, expressing concern over South Africa's continued illegal occupation, stated that the repeated use of the veto by the Security Council's Western permanent members to prevent the adoption of sanctions had encouraged South Africa to defy the United Nations. Affirming that the Namibian people were entitled to use all means at their disposal to achieve independence, the Conference expressed solidarity with the people under the leadership of the South West Africa People's Organization (SWAPO), their sole and authentic representative, and called for assistance to them. It stated that sanctions were the only means to ensure South Africa complied with United Nations decisions and called on the Security Council to take such steps.

Namibians outside their country continued to receive assistance from various United Nations programmes, financed primarily by the Fund for Namibia. In 1983, the Fund spent $8.8 million, while contributions to the Fund by States totalled $4.3 million. Funding was also provided from the regular United Nations budget, UNDP and executing agencies. The Assembly, in resolution 38/36 E, allocated $1 million to the Fund from the 1984 United Nations regular budget.

The Fund consisted of three main programmes co-ordinated by the United Nations Council for Namibia—the Nationhood Programme for Namibia; the United Nations Institute for Namibia; and educational, social and relief assistance to

Namibians. Under the Nationhood Programme, which continued to finance training programmes and surveys of the Namibian economic and social sectors in preparation for independence, the United Nations Vocational Training Centre for Namibia in Angola became operational in August 1983 when 100 students were enrolled. Also concerned with developing human resources in preparation for independence, the Institute for Namibia continued its various research, training and planning activities, including studies on agrarian reform, constitutional options, a language policy and manpower requirements. The third programme, administered by the Office of the United Nations Commissioner for Namibia, emphasized the immediate needs and welfare of Namibians.

Topics related to this chapter. Africa. Refugees and displaced persons. Human rights. General questions relating to colonial countries.

Namibia question

Conference on the Namibian people. The International Conference in Support of the Struggle of the Namibian People for Independence, organized by the United Nations Council for Namibia in accordance with a December 1982 resolution of the General Assembly,[1] was held in Paris from 25 to 29 April 1983.[2] Pursuant to the Assembly's resolution, invitations to participate were sent to all States Members of the United Nations and of the specialized agencies; organizations which had been invited to participate as observers in the Assembly; national liberation movements recognized by the Organization of African Unity (OAU); United Nations bodies, organs and offices; the Movement of Non-Aligned Countries; eminent persons; and non-governmental organizations (NGOs). (For list of States Members attending, see APPENDIX III.) The Conference was preceded by a journalists' encounter on 21 and 22 April and followed by a workshop for NGOs on 30 April. The Conference conducted its work in four series of simultaneous meetings—plenary, the Committee of the Whole, the drafting Committee and the Bureau.

At its concluding session on 29 April, the Conference adopted by acclamation the Paris Declaration on Namibia. The Declaration and the Committee's report and a Programme of Action on Namibia were transmitted by a 9 May letter[3] from the President of the United Nations Council for Namibia to the Secretary-General for consideration by the Assembly and the Security Council.

In the Declaration, the Conference affirmed the inalienable right of the people of Namibia to self-determination and national independence in a united Namibia. It expressed concern over South Africa's continued illegal occupation of Namibia in disregard of the international community as expressed in numerous United Nations resolutions. The Conference found that the repeated use of the veto by the Security Council's Western permanent members to prevent the adoption of sanctions against South Africa had not only encouraged the South African régime in its lawlessness but had provoked increased acts of defiance to the authority of the United Nations (see p. 119 *et seq.*). The Conference affirmed that the Namibian people, in the exercise of their right of self-defence, were entitled to use all means at their disposal, including armed struggle, to repel South Africa's aggression and to achieve independence. Expressing solidarity with the people under the leadership of the South West Africa People's Organization (SWAPO), their sole and authentic representative, it called on participants to render increased assistance to the Namibian people and to SWAPO, its liberation movement.

The Conference denounced South Africa's military buildup in Namibia and its use of compulsory military service for Namibians and of mercenaries; it expressed concern about South Africa's nuclear weapons capability, and reports of certain countries' military and nuclear assistance to that country (see p. 135). It strongly condemned the armed aggression and acts of destabilization against independent States of the region (see p. 169) and condemned aggression against Angola (see p. 173). Concern was also expressed about violations of human rights of Namibians, its imprisonment of SWAPO freedom fighters, the rapid depletion of Namibia's natural resources which were the inviolable heritage of its people, assistance provided by international organizations to South Africa (see p. 146), and South Africa's refusal to comply with United Nations resolutions on Namibia.

Calling for the release of Namibian political prisoners, the Conference demanded that all captured freedom fighters be accorded prisoner-of-war status as called for by the 1949 Geneva Convention Relative to the Treatment of Prisoners of War and the 1977 Additional Protocol I.[4] It called for increased material assistance to oppressed Namibians and to SWAPO in the liberation struggle. It called on transnational corporations to terminate their illegal exploitation of Namibia's natural resources and affirmed that South Africa and the foreign economic interests which were illegally exploiting those resources were liable to pay reparations to the Government of an independent Namibia. Denouncing any South African scheme to perpetuate its domination in Namibia, it stated that the United Nations plan for Namibia endorsed by Security Council resolution 435 (1978)[5] remained the only basis for peaceful settlement of the Namibian question, called for its immediate implementation, and rejected the attempts of the United States and South Africa to obstruct implemenation. The Conference also rejected their efforts to link Namibia's independence with irrelevant issues, in particular the withdrawal of Cuban forces from Angola, which constituted interference in the internal affairs of that country.

According to the Conference, South Africa's policies towards Namibia constituted a threat to international peace and security, and expressed dismay at the Security Council's failure to discharge its responsibilities owing to the opposition of Western permament members, and affirmed that sanctions under Chapter VII of the United Nations Charter were the only available means to ensure South Africa's compliance with United Nations decisions. Therefore, the Conference called on the Council to consider further action to implement the independence plan and, pending the imposition of sanctions by the Council (see p. 129), urged the adoption of economic measures against South Africa.

The Committee of the Whole considered assistance to the people of Namibia in their struggle for independence in a united Namibia under the leadership of SWAPO, and to the front-line States so they could sustain support for the cause of Namibia, as well as measures for implementing the United Nations plan for Namibia's independence as provided for in Security Council resolutions 385(1976)[6] and 435(1978).[5] The Committee adopted a report and a Programme of Action on Namibia which were included in the Conference's report.[2]

In the Programme of Action, the Committee agreed that the Council should immediately impose sanctions, in view of its aggression and threat to international peace and security. It requested the Council to implement its resolutions on Namibia's independence, declare Walvis Bay an integral part of Namibia not to be negotiated between an independent Namibia and South Africa, and tighten the 1977 arms embargo against South Africa.[7] States were urged to support resolution 435(1978) and to oppose linking independence with extraneous issues, in particular the withdrawal of Cuban forces from Angola.

It called on Governments to apply sanctions called for by the Assembly in September[8] and December 1981[9] and December 1982;[10] to render political, financial, military and other material support to SWAPO in the liberation struggle and to the front-line States in exercising their right of self-defence *vis-à-vis* South Africa; to contribute to the United Nations Fund for Namibia and the United Nations Institute for Namibia in support of projects for the economic and social development of Namibia once independence was achieved; and to ensure that corporations and individuals within their jurisdiction complied with efforts to protect Namibia's natural resources within the provisions of Decree No. 1 for the Protection of the Natural Resources of Namibia, proclaimed by the Council for Namibia in 1974.[11]

United Nations and other international organizations were urged to provide assistance to SWAPO and the front-line States in supporting Namibia's struggle. Increased assistance for refugees was also urged.

The Committee supported an appeal by the President of the Council for Namibia to the United Kingdom to prohibit the export of radar equipment to South Africa. Taking note of a resolution by the European Parliament concerning aid to Namibians, the Committee requested the Council, in co-operation with SWAPO, to consult with the European Economic Community and the Parliament to ensure that no action was taken implying recognition of South Africa's illegal administration of Namibia.

The Secretary-General was requested to ensure that all companies with which the United Nations had contracts complied with United Nations sanctions policies against South Africa. United Nations bodies were called on to expand the campaign for Namibia's cause and to participate in the Nationhood Programme for Namibia, including providing funds for projects approved by the Council.

NGOs were urged to support the liberation struggle and SWAPO, and to increase public awareness of the issues, especially the campaign for sanctions. An appeal was made to trade unions to organize an embargo on shipments to and from South Africa as well as transport and communication with it. Individuals working in communications and information were urged to promote Namibia's cause.

On 26 April, two countries addressed letters to the Secretary-General concerning the Conference. South Africa, in a letter[12] from its Minister of Foreign Affairs and Information, said that the United Nations, by deciding to hold the Conference, had raised further doubts concerning its fitness to play the role envisaged in resolution 435(1978) by supporting SWAPO's violence, generating propaganda in SWAPO's favour, and undermining the current international negotiations on Namibia. The USSR forwarded a 25 April message[13] from the Presidium of the Supreme Soviet and the Council of Ministers to the Conference's participants, expressing solidarity with peoples struggling against colonialism, condemning South Africa and its imperialist sponsors for attempts to maintain its rule in Namibia, and demanding an end to the manoeuvres of the United States and other Western Powers to frustrate United Nations decisions on Namibia's independence.

Report of the Secretary-General. In May,[14] the Secretary-General reported to the Security Council on developments since 1981 concerning the implementation of its resolutions 435(1978)[5] and 439(1978).[15]

Since the adoption of the independence plan for Namibia, he and the parties concerned had held consultations on setting a date for a cease-fire and the start of the plan, but no progress had been made. In September 1981, Canada, France, the Federal Republic of Germany, the United Kingdom and the United States (the countries known as the Western contact group which had proposed the settlement plan) said that they had developed proposals for a timetable for negotiations with the objective of implementing the independence plan in 1982. The Secretary-General was kept informed of the progress of successive phases of the ensuing negotiations. In consultations with the contact group, the front-line States, OAU, Nigeria and SWAPO, as well as with South Africa, on all aspects of United Nations involvement in implementation of the plan, he had emphasized that resolution 435(1978) must remain the basis for settling the Namibian situation. Despite reports of progress in 1982 on many points,[16] it had become clear that issues outside the scope of that resolution were becoming a factor—South Africa had informed the Secretary-General of its willingness to co-operate, provided that agreement was reached on the withdrawal of Cuban troops from Angola. Issues unrelated to resolution 435(1978) constituted the main reason for delay in its implementation, the Secretary-General said.

As far as the United Nations was concerned, the only outstanding issues were the choice of the electoral system and the settlement of some final problems relating to the United Nations Transition Assistance Group (UNTAG), to be installed in Namibia while a new government was being formed. The views of South Africa on those issues were being awaited.

The Secretary-General, having visited in February 1983 all the front-line States, where he had held discussions on Namibia with African leaders as well as with SWAPO, remained convinced of the necessity of implementing the plan without delay. He noted that the political situation in the region had deteriorated and there had been recurrent fighting; the delay in implementing the independence plan was having an adverse effect on the people of Namibia, on the prospect for a peaceful future of the region, and on international relations. He urged that the Namibia problem be regarded as a primary question in its own right.

SECURITY COUNCIL ACTION

The Security Council debated the question of Namibia at a series of 12 meetings held from 23 May to 1 June. Requests for the Council to convene were made to the President on 12 May by Mauritius,[17] on behalf of the Group of African States, and on 13 May by India,[18] on behalf of the Movement of Non-Aligned Countries.

At their requests, the following States were invited to participate in the discussion: Afghanistan, Algeria, Angola, Argentina, Australia, Bangladesh, Barbados, Benin, Botswana, Bulgaria, Canada, Chile, Colombia, Cuba, Cyprus, Czechoslovakia, Democratic Yemen, Egypt, Ethiopia, Gabon, Gambia, German Democratic Republic, Germany, the Federal Republic of, Ghana, Grenada, Guinea, Hungary, India, Indonesia, Iran, Jamaica, Japan, Kenya, Kuwait, Liberia, Libyan Arab Jamahiriya, Malaysia, Mali, Mauritius, Mexico, Mongolia, Morocco, Mozambique, Niger, Nigeria, Panama, Qatar, Romania, Senegal, Seychelles, Sierra Leone, Somalia, South Africa, Sri Lanka, Syrian Arab Republic, Tunisia, Turkey, Uganda, United Republic of Tanzania, Upper Volta, Venezuela, Viet Nam, Yugoslavia and Zambia. In accordance with a decision by the Seventh Conference of Heads of State or Government of Non-Aligned Countries (New Delhi, India, 7-12 March), which adopted a political declaration[19] on several subjects including Namibia, a number of non-aligned States were represented in the debate by their Minister for Foreign Affairs. Those countries represented at that level were: Angola, Benin, Botswana, Cuba, India, Indonesia, Jamaica, Mozambique, Nigeria, Pakistan, Senegal, Sierra Leone, Uganda, United Republic of Tanzania, Yugoslavia, Zambia and Zimbabwe.

At the request of Council members and another State, certain individuals were invited to participate in conformity with rule 39[a] of the Council's provisional rules of procedure.

On 20 May, Togo, Zaire and Zimbabwe called for such an invitation to Sam Nujoma, President of SWAPO;[20] similar requests were made on 25 May by Jordan concerning Clovis Maksoud, Permanent Observer of the League of Arab States;[21] on 26 May by Togo, Zaire and Zimbabwe concerning Johnstone F. Makatini, representative of the African National Congress of South Africa (ANC),[22] and Lesaoana S. Makhanda, representative of the Pan Africanist Congress of Azania (PAC);[23] and on 26 May by France, the United Kingdom and the United States concerning L. J. Barnes and J. G. A. Diergaardt.[24] In addition,

---

[a]Rule 39 of the Council's provisional rules of procedure states: "The Security Council may invite members of the Secretariat or other persons, whom it considers competent for the purpose, to supply it with information or to give other assistance in examining matters within its competence."

the Council invited representatives of certain other United Nations bodies to participate, in accordance with past practice: the President of the Council for Namibia, a representative of the Chairman of the Special Committee against *Apartheid*, and the Acting Chairman of the Special Committee on the Situation with regard to the Implementation of the Declaration on the Granting of Independence to Colonial Countries and Peoples (Committee on colonial countries).

On 31 May, the Council unanimously adopted resolution 532(1983).

The Security Council,

Having considered the report of the Secretary-General,

Recalling General Assembly resolutions 1514(XV) of 14 December 1960 and 2145(XXI) of 27 October 1966,

Recalling and reaffirming its resolutions 301(1971), 385(1976), 431(1978), 432(1978), 435(1978) and 439(1978),

Reaffirming the legal responsibility of the United Nations over Namibia and the primary responsibility of the Security Council for ensuring the implementation of its resolutions 385(1976) and 435(1978), including the holding of free and fair elections in Namibia under the supervision and control of the United Nations,

Taking note of the results of the International Conference in Support of the Struggle of the Namibian People for Independence, held at UNESCO House in Paris from 25 to 29 April 1983,

Taking note of the protracted and exhaustive consultations which have taken place since the adoption of resolution 435(1978),

Further noting with regret that those consultations have not yet brought about the implementation of resolution 435(1978),

1. *Condemns* South Africa's continued illegal occupation of Namibia in flagrant defiance of resolutions of the General Assembly and decision of the Security Council;

2. *Calls upon* South Africa to make a firm commitment as to its readiness to comply with Council resolution 435(1978) for the independence of Namibia;

3. *Further calls upon* South Africa to co-operate forthwith and fully with the Secretary-General in order to expedite the implementation of resolution 435(1978) for the early independence of Namibia;

4. *Decides* to mandate the Secretary-General to undertake consultations with the parties to the proposed cease-fire, with a view to securing the speedy implementation of resolution 435(1978);

5. *Requests* the Secretary-General to report to the Council on the results of these consultations as soon as possible and not later than 31 August 1983;

6. *Decides* to remain actively seized of the matter.

Security Council resolution 532(1983)

31 May 1983   Meeting 2449   Adopted unanimously

Draft prepared in consultations among Council members (S/15803).
Meeting numbers. SC 2439-2444, 2446-2451.

Speaking after the vote, the United Kingdom said that in regard to the third preambular paragraph listing previous Council resolutions 301(1971)[25] and 439(1978)[15] on which the United Kingdom had abstained, its position remained unchanged; in regard to the results of the international Conference on Namibia (see above), of which the current Council resolution took note, the United Kingdom was not a party to its decisions. The latter view was echoed by the United States, which also pointed out that the third preamublar paragraph referred to resolution 439(1978) which it did not support.

All speakers in the debate supported implementation of resolution 435(1978) and many (Angola, Bangladesh, China, Egypt, Gabon, Gambia, Federal Republic of Germany, Guyana, India, speaking for the Non-Aligned Movement, Indonesia, Kenya, Kuwait, Niger, Poland, Qatar, Romania, Senegal, Sierra Leone, Tunisia, Turkey, Uganda and Venezuela) described it as the sole basis for negotiations on independence for Namibia. Gambia, for example, considered that the framework for a settlement to the question of Namibia existed in resolution 435(1978) and that what was needed at the current juncture was the political will to implement it. Sierra Leone called for its immediate implementation and for resolving the remaining issues; to that end, voter education and registration was needed, as well as free assembly to permit political parties to participate in an electoral process without intimidation, the removal of South Africa from the Territory and increased responsibilities for the Council for Namibia in the electoral process.

Most speakers expressed appreciation for the Secretary-General's report and agreed with his conclusions.

South Africa felt that the Council had been convened to undermine negotiations currently under way. During the previous five years, South Africa, which had never accepted the United Nations view that its presence in the Territory was illegal, had persistently searched for an internationally acceptable settlement and had advised the Secretary-General in 1979 that early implementation of resolution 435(1978) was imperative. Since then, Secretariat officials had altered the independence proposal to remove basic guarantees for the security of Namibians, at the insistence of SWAPO and with the connivance of certain countries. The United Nations, through material and political assistance, had demonstrated its bias in favour of SWAPO. South Africa believed there was a *de facto* linkage between the withdrawal of Cuban forces from Angola and the settlement of the Namibia question since the introduction of hostile surrogates of a super-Power into southern Africa had implications for the region's security. South Africa had attempted to play a constructive role in removing the last major obstacle to a settlement—the withdrawal of Cuban forces from Angola—and was prepared to hold further talks with Angola.

It would not bow to threats nor tolerate the expansion of Soviet imperialism on its borders.

Responding to South Africa's claims, Botswana said that by giving some form of recognition to the role played by the Western contact group, the United Nations had demonstrated its desire to dispel South Africa's concerns regarding bias in favour of SWAPO.

Much of the debate focused on whether Namibia's independence should be linked to security in the region, in particular to the withdrawal of Cuban forces from Angola, as suggested by South Africa. Afghanistan, Algeria, Angola, Benin, China, Cuba, Ethiopia, Gambia, Ghana, Grenada, Guinea, Guyana, India, speaking for the Movement of Non-Aligned countries, Jamaica, Kenya, Kuwait, Mauritius, on behalf of the African Group at the United Nations, Mexico, Mongolia, Mozambique, Nicaragua, Niger, Nigeria, Pakistan, Poland, Qatar, speaking for the Arab group at the United Nations, Romania, Sierra Leone, Sri Lanka, the Syrian Arab Republic, Togo, Tunisia, the United Republic of Tanzania, Upper Volta, Zambia and Zimbabwe rejected the idea of linkage, which many of them described as extraneous or irrelevant to Namibia's independence. According to the United States, if there were to be a lasting settlement, the conditions needed to be created in which all countries in the region, particularly South Africa and Angola, could feel secure; this would involve respect for territorial integrity by all countries and the withdrawal of all foreign forces in the region.

Angola, noting that South African troops had continued occupying southern Angola since 1981, said that the major obstacle to implementation of resolution 435(1978) was the fact that the United States persisted in trying to link the two issues although linkage was incompatible with the letter and spirit of that resolution and constituted unacceptable interference in the internal affairs of Angola. Similarly, Grenada said that Namibia was held hostage because the United States insisted on the withdrawal of Cuban forces from Angola, a policy Grenada rejected because independence could not be predicated on a diminution of Angolan sovereignty. Kenya viewed South Africa's demand as unrealistic, unrelated and unacceptable. Mongolia and Togo stated that Cuban troops were there to protect Angola from South African aggression. Cuba stressed that its forces were there at the request of the Government.

Having participated in negotiations regarding implementation of the United Nations plan, Nigeria said it was not prepared to expand the discussion beyond resolution 435(1978); independence was being sacrificed on the altar of mistaken strategic perceptions by the United States. Sri Lanka noted that the withdrawal of Cuban troops

had been acknowledged by some members of the Western contact group to be irrelevant, as did India, which added that the non-aligned countries regretted that certain countries had supported linkage thus abetting South Africa in delaying Namibia's independence. According to Tunisia, South Africa and its allies were introducing extraneous issues to prolong the illegal occupation of Namibia; the resurgence of East-West tension provided the pretext for prejudicing the negotiating process by trying to establish an unacceptable link between Namibia's independence and the right of States to choose their allies.

While Canada, a member of the contact group, could not accept South Africa's conditions for the implementation of resolution 435(1978), it acknowledged that regional security concerns existed and posed an obstacle, which it hoped could be resolved with respect for the sovereignty of the States concerned.

The United Republic of Tanzania said that linkage, rejected by the front-line States, OAU, the non-aligned summit and the General Assembly, was in defiance of international law because it was interference in the internal affairs of Angola.

Many countries agreed that the question of foreign troops in a country was a matter between sovereign States, pertaining to the right of a State to defend itself, and that raising the issue constituted interference in its internal affairs. Angola, Benin, Botswana, Cuba, Ethiopia, Gabon, Ghana, Grenada, Guyana, Kuwait, the Libyan Arab Jamahiriya, Mozambique, the Netherlands, Sierra Leone, the Syrian Arab Republic, Togo, Uganda and the United Republic of Tanzania shared that view. The Syrian Arab Republic said that South Africa had aborted all efforts to implement the United Nations plan by raising unrelated issues.

Botswana, China, Ghana, Mexico, the Netherlands, Nicaragua, Pakistan, Qatar, speaking for the Arab group, Romania, Togo, Tunisia, Uganda, the USSR, Upper Volta, Yugoslavia and Zimbabwe said that raising the linkage issue was the direct cause for the delay in implementing resolution 435(1978). Uganda said that the only matter holding up Namibia's independence was the injection of that issue into the negotiations. Zimbabwe was among those pointing out that Cuban troops had been in Angola since 1975 but the issue had not been raised at the time resolution 435(1978) was accepted by all sides; it added that pressure should be put on South Africa to withdraw its forces from Angola, since that was the current obstacle to peace in the region.

According to Argentina, Bangladesh, Barbados, Benin, Canada, Chile, China, Cyprus, France, Ghana, Guinea, Indonesia, Kenya, the Libyan Arab Jamahiriya, Nicaragua, Niger, Panama, Romania, Tunisia, Zaire and Zimbabwe, extraneous issues or conditions should not be attached to implementation of the United Nations plan for Namibia's independence. France, a member of the contact group, said that Namibia's independence could not be impeded by such considerations, conditions or prerequisites, and for that reason, the Council should give the Secretary-General a mandate to resume contact with all parties concerned to ensure implementation of resolution 435(1978); as for the future security of Namibia, France was willing to serve as guarantor in the region if requested. Panama said that the Council should not allow Namibia's independence to be made conditional on or linked to the strategic interests of other States, or to the conclusion of international agreements under the doctrines of geographical proximity.

Many countries stressed that it was the responsibility of the Council to implement the resolution in question. Algeria, Angola, Argentina, Benin, Botswana, China, Colombia, Cuba, Cyprus, Egypt, Gambia, the German Democratic Republic, India, on behalf of the Non-Aligned Movement, Jamaica, Jordan, Malaysia, Mozambique, Nicaragua, Pakistan, Panama, Romania, Sri Lanka, the Syrian Arab Republic, Togo, Uganda, United Republic of Tanzania, Viet Nam and Zimbabwe shared this view.

Some States, including Bulgaria, Cuba, China, Ethiopia, Ghana, Guinea, Guyana, India, on behalf of the Non-Aligned Movement, Indonesia, Kenya, Kuwait, the Libyan Arab Jamahiriya, Mongolia, Pakistan, Poland, Qatar, for the Arab group, Romania, Togo, the United Republic of Tanzania, Zambia and Zimbabwe, said that South Africa was using delaying tactics to prolong its occupation by raising obstacles to implementation. Ethiopia said that in negotiations conducted through the contact group, South Africa, using such tactics, had pursued its policy of intransigence and prevarication, and currently insisted on introducing extraneous issues; in addition, the United States was striving to make implementation conditional on some of its strategic objectives.

In a similar vein, Afghanistan, Benin, Bulgaria, China, Ethiopia, the German Democratic Republic, Ghana, Iran, the Libyan Arab Jamahiriya, Mexico, Mozambique, Pakistan, Poland, Romania, Togo, the USSR and Upper Volta believed that South Africa had been able to maintain its intransigent position because of the support it received from certain countries. Bulgaria said that without that assistance provided by some Western countries, particularly the United States, Namibia would have achieved independence; South Africa continued its oppression and aggression through the use of mercenaries whom it recruited from Western countries. China spoke similarly, stating that South Africa would not have been so intran-

sigent had it not been for the support of a super-Power which sought to maintain its vested interests in the region. In Ghana's view, South Africa was emboldened by the support it received from some powerful countries in a position to bring it to heel and which had been entrusted with the responsibility of seeking a peaceful solution to the problem.

The Libyan Arab Jamahiriya said that South Africa and its allies were attempting to bypass SWAPO and to impose a solution that would support their interests. Mexico believed that the presence of South Africa in Namibia was something which had been acquiesced in by those who could have prevailed upon it to cease its occupation. Pakistan expressed a similar view, adding that protection provided by some members of the contact group, as demonstrated by the veto of mandatory sanctions in the Council, had emboldened South Africa to continue its occupation and aggression. Poland said that South Africa's policies would not have been possible without the co-operation of major countries of the North Atlantic Treaty Organization, particularly the United States.

A number of countries mentioned the United States role, in particular, in blocking implementation of resolution 435(1978). They included Afghanistan, Botswana, Bulgaria, Cuba, Ethiopia, the German Democratic Republic, Iran, Kuwait, the Libyan Arab Jamahiriya, Nicaragua, Nigeria, Poland, Qatar, for the Arab group, Uganda, the USSR and Zambia. The German Democratic Republic rejected the United States efforts to interfere in the internal affairs of States through the linkage policy and to raise new obstacles to resolving the Namibia problem. While appreciating the role of the contact group, Zambia noted that the United States had injected the linkage issue just at a time when the parties to the conflict had resolved major misunderstandings.

Algeria, Benin, Ethiopia, Ghana, Guyana, Jamaica, Liberia, Malaysia, Nicaragua, the Syrian Arab Republic, Togo, Tunisia and Uganda were among those questioning the intentions or usefulness of the contact group in trying to negotiate implementation of the United Nations plan on Namibia. Benin said that for political and military as well as economic reasons, the group had refused to exert real pressure on South Africa, and the net result of its efforts was helping South Africa to gain time to consolidate its entrenchment and to exploit Namibian territory. In Ethiopia's view, the contact group had collaborated with South Africa in its attempt to undermine and modify the plan, and the United States was trying to make it conditional on some of its own strategic objectives. Jamaica said there was growing concern within the international community that the contact group had not succeeded in securing South Africa's compliance with resolution 435(1978) and therefore had outlived its usefulness. In Malaysia's view, the discussions initiated by the contact group could have complemented United Nations efforts to seek a negotiated settlement, but it had introduced extraneous issues which served only to prolong South Africa's domination of Namibia.

Some countries, including Australia, Canada, the Federal Republic of Germany, Jordan, Kuwait, Mauritius, the Netherlands, Senegal, the United Kingdom, the United States and Zambia, expressed satisfaction that the contact group had been able to achieve agreement on some elements of the United Nations plan or believed it had the potential to achieve further results. The Federal Republic of Germany, a member of the contact group, pointed out that the group had undertaken to strengthen the confidence between the parties concerned in order to establish the basis for implementation; however, the negotiations had shown that the presence of foreign troops in the region was a matter causing mistrust. Security in the region was also a concern of the United Kingdom, another member, which stressed that a solution on Namibia must assure the security of all States in the region.

Jordan welcomed the co-operation of the front-line States with the contact group in the search for implementation, as well as the realistic spirit shown by SWAPO and its willingness to sign a cease-fire agreement. While recognizing the primary responsibility of the Council to implement the plan, Kuwait emphasized the group's role in making that a reality. Mauritius, speaking for the African group, felt that the contact group members should help by using their influence in a positive manner, particularly through economic, moral and other pressures. In Senegal's view, the group, whose efforts it encouraged, had a special responsibility in settling the Namibia question; however, the members needed to show greater firmness in order to compel South Africa to implement resolution 435(1978). Chile and Romania spoke similarly. In the opinion of the Netherlands, the contact group remained the only viable way to enable the Namibian people to exercise early self-determination. Yugoslavia viewed the group's role as an instrument of implementation, which could influence South Africa to comply with the United Nations plan.

Japan hoped that the talks among the parties concerned, particularly the contact group members, the front-line States, SWAPO and South Africa would resolve the Namibia problem. Malta believed that collective and bilateral efforts should be intensified and that the guidelines in resolution 435(1978) needed to be maintained but added that it was time to concentrate on the most effective practical modalities to achieve those guidelines.

In regard to the contact group, Guyana, Kuwait, Nicaragua, Pakistan, Qatar, speaking for the Arab group, and Uganda praised one of its members—France—for having dissociated itself from the linkage policy.

Bangladesh, Botswana, Egypt, India, speaking for the non-aligned countries, Liberia, Mozambique, Poland, the USSR, Upper Volta and Viet Nam stressed that the United Nations was the proper framework for achieving independence for Namibia. According to Egypt, the Council and the Secretary-General should undertake the main role in achieving a just solution. The USSR pointed out that the United Nations had not mandated anyone to take over its role and responsibility to find a Namibia settlement; it called for strengthening the United Nations role by ensuring effective control by the Security Council, and not some group of States, over all aspects of independence, including UNTAG.

Benin, Malaysia, Mozambique, Tunisia, Uganda, the United Republic of Tanzania, Upper Volta and Zaire expressed concern that the credibility of the United Nations or the Council was at stake if the Council did not take effective action. Angola, Cyprus, France, Indonesia, Jamaica, Kenya, Liberia, Morocco, Mozambique, Uganda, the United Republic of Tanzania, Upper Volta, Viet Nam, Yugoslavia and Zimbabwe believed that the role of the Secretary-General should be strengthened or reaffirmed in regard to implementation of the United Nations plan.

Afghanistan, Benin, Bulgaria, China, Colombia, Cuba, Egypt, the German Democratic Republic, India, for the non-aligned countries, Indonesia, Jamaica, the Libyan Arab Jamahiriya, Mongolia, Morocco, Mozambique, Pakistan, Poland, Qatar, for the Arab group, Uganda, the USSR, Viet Nam, Yugoslavia and Zaire felt that the Council should establish a time-frame for implementing resolution 435(1978). Colombia stated that the Council should shoulder its responsibility by defining specific objectives, particularly in terms of deadlines, so that independence could be achieved. Similarly, Zaire urged the Council to draw up a timetable for implementation.

Many countries either called on the Council to impose comprehensive mandatory sanctions against South Africa, in accordance with Chapter VII of the United Nations Charter, as a means of pressuring it to grant independence, or urged that sanctions be applied if no progress was achieved in implementing the resolution in question. Those countries included Afghanistan, Algeria, Argentina, Benin, Bulgaria, Cuba, Cyprus, Egypt, Ethiopia, Gabon, the German Democratic Republic, Guinea, Guyana, India, for the non-aligned countries, the Libyan Arab Jamahiriya, Malaysia, Mongolia, Niger, Pakistan, Panama,

Poland, Qatar, for the Arab group, Romania, the Syrian Arab Republic, Tunisia, Turkey, Uganda and Viet Nam. Guyana believed that in the event of non-compliance on the part of South Africa, the contact group had an obligation to support the adoption of effective measures to achieve United Nations objectives, and that continued intransigence would warrant mandatory sanctions. In the light of recent experience, Turkey said, only sanctions as envisaged by the Charter would produce the necessary effect.

Iran, Morocco and Nicaragua also called for measures against South Africa. Iran believed that barring South Africa from United Nations membership would guarantee progress in attaining Namibia's independence. In Morocco's view, the Council should adopt concrete measures to compel South Africa to proceed with the settlement plan. Nicaragua believed that if those countries with economic, political and military links with South Africa were to pressure it, the possibilities of a solution would be much greater.

Afghanistan, Argentina, Barbados, Botswana, Cyprus, Indonesia, Pakistan, Sierra Leone, Uganda and Zambia emphasized that Namibia was a decolonization issue, and Afghanistan, Algeria, Pakistan, Qatar, speaking for the Arab group, Zaire and Zambia said the issue should not be viewed as an East-West issue. Qatar, for example, said that the United States was using the linkage issue to serve its national interests and that linkage represented a dimension of the East-West confrontation.

Support was expressed by Afghanistan, Argentina, Barbados, Benin, Gabon, the German Democratic Republic, India, for the non-aligned countries, Indonesia, Nicaragua, Panama, Qatar, for the Arab group, Sierra Leone, Uganda and the USSR for maintaining the territorial integrity of Namibia, including Walvis Bay and the offshore islands, once Namibia became independent.

Algeria, the German Democratic Republic, Kenya, Mongolia, Sierra Leone, Uganda and Viet Nam said that South Africa was using Namibia as a base or springboard for launching aggression against neighbouring States. Viet Nam stated that the enemy of the Namibian people was seeking to hold on to the Territory at all costs and to make it a military base for perpetuating the illegal occupation and a platform for launching such armed attacks. A number of countries expressed the view that South Africa and its allies, frequently through their transnational corporations (TNCs), were exploiting the natural resources of Namibia. They included Afghanistan, Argentina, Benin, Bulgaria, China, Cyprus, Egypt, Ethiopia, Gabon, the German Democratic Republic, Ghana, Guyana, India, for the non-aligned countries, Indonesia, Jamaica, the Libyan Arab Jamahiriya, Mongolia,

Nicaragua, Qatar, for the Arab group, the Syrian Arab Republic, Tunisia, Uganda, Venezuela, Yugoslavia and Zambia. Some added that human resources were being exploited as well. Indonesia said that since South Africa had continued to destroy the territorial integrity and undermine the economic viability of Namibia, the Council must act against the continuing economic collaboration between certain States or their TNCs and South Africa which had accelerated the illicit plundering of Namibia's natural wealth, in violation of the 1974 decree to protect Namibia's natural resources.[11]

Bangladesh, Ethiopia, Mozambique, Pakistan, Romania, Upper Volta and Zaire welcomed the flexible attitude SWAPO had shown in negotiations on Namibia. Afghanistan, Bangladesh, Barbados, Bulgaria, Cyprus, Egypt, the German Democratic Republic, India, for the non-aligned countries, the Libyan Arab Jamahiriya, Malaysia, Mongolia, Qatar, for the Arab group, Romania, the Syrian Arab Republic and Uganda affirmed their support for SWAPO as the sole legitimate representative of the Namibian people, and several of those States called for assistance to SWAPO. Guinea urged increased assistance to Namibian refugees and to the front-line States suffering from South Africa's aggression.

India, Niger and Uganda felt that the use of armed force was justified in the struggle of the Namibian people to obtain independence, while Australia and Chile rejected use of force. Cuba, Jamaica, Pakistan and the Syrian Arab Republic warned that if no progress were made towards a solution, the consequences would include confrontation, bloodshed or armed struggle.

The representative of SWAPO said that the organization had concluded that the contact group, in particular the United States, by injecting the linkage issue, had lost proper contact with the letter and spirit of resolution 435(1978), that the group had ceased to be an honest broker in its implementation, and that the whole exercise had turned out to be a rescue operation for South Africa; the Council should oblige South Africa to make a firm commitment on signing a cease-fire agreement with SWAPO, as provided for in the United Nations plan, and the Secretary-General should initiate contact with the parties to the conflict and report to the Council.

The President of the Council for Namibia also rejected what he said were attempts by the United States and South Africa to obstruct implementation of the resolution and to link independence with extraneous issues, in particular the withdrawal of Cuban forces from Angola; the Council for Namibia believed that the time had come to bring all talks on independence back to the United Nations, which had legal and primary responsibility for the Territory, and for the Security Council to consider appropriate action under the Charter to ensure South Africa's co-operation. Also rejecting the linkage issue, the representative of the Chairman of the Committee against *apartheid* said that it was apparent that attempts to move negotiations away from the United Nations framework had been used by South Africa's trading partners as a means of muting criticism and delaying action towards independence; it was time for the Council to consider sanctions against South Africa as a means of ensuring compliance with United Nations decisions on Namibia. The Acting Chairman of the Committee on colonial countries joined in rejecting linkage and calling for coercive action provided for in the Charter; he welcomed SWAPO's willingness to facilitate the negotiating process and clear the way for elections based on universal suffrage.

Echoing the views of the United Nations bodies, the representative of PAC said that the Council had no alternative but to meet South Africa's intransigence firmly, which required the collective will of all Council members to impose comprehensive mandatory sanctions; should the Council fail to take this action, the people of Namibia, acting through SWAPO, would use every effort to regain their inalienable rights.

Referring to South Africa's statement that it had never accepted the view that its presence in the Territory was illegal, the ANC representative said that statement went to the root of the problem and negated the contact group's assurances that negotiations had reached a crucial stage and Namibia's independence was near.

The Permanent Observer of the Arab League called on the Council to set its resolutions in motion and to restore its effectiveness and credibility.

Communications. During the period the Security Council was debating the question of Namibia, several countries addressed letters to the Council President on the issue. On 20 May,[26] Mauritius, on behalf of the African Group, forwarded to the Council a document entitled "Namibia: The Crisis in United States Policy towards Southern Africa", produced by TransAfrica and 23 other non-governmental organizations in the United States. India, on 23 May,[27] forwarded a message from its Prime Minister, the current Chairman of the Movement of Non-Aligned Countries, stating that the Council must make South Africa comply with the United Nations plan on Namibia by imposing mandatory sanctions, if necessary. Panama forwarded a 26 May letter[28] from its President in which he expressed confidence that the Council would take prompt, decisive action to ensure there was no further delay in independence for Namibia, in accordance with United Nations resolutions. Venezuela, on 31

May,[29] also forwarded a message from its President, expressing support for the struggle of the Namibian people and accusing South Africa of continuing to defy United Nations resolutions on Namibia's independence.

On 1 June,[30] Somalia forwarded a statement calling on the Council to reaffirm the direct responsibility of the United Nations for the independence of Namibia, to condemn South Africa's stalling tactics and its internal arrangements designed to maintain control of Namibia, and to set a date for the implementation of the United Nations plan. Stating its position on 10 June,[31] the Seychelles said that the primary reason for the delay in implementing the plan was the linkage by foreign interests of independence with the withdrawal of Cuban forces in Angola. India forwarded on 5 August[32] the text of a communiqué adopted at a meeting of the Movement of Non-Aligned Countries held that day at United Nations Headquarters. Expressing concern over South Africa's decision to establish a so-called State Council in Namibia to draw up a "constitution" for the Territory, the Movement said this action was another demonstration of South Africa's intention of imposing an "internal settlement" in Namibia and of blocking the plan's implementation.

Report of the Secretary-General. On 29 August,[33] the Secretary-General issued a further report on the implementation of resolutions 435(1978)[5] and 439(1978)[15] concerning Namibia, in accordance with the Council's June 1983 resolution. Exercising his mandate, he said that he had held discussions with South African senior officials at Headquarters and visited South Africa in August for talks with the Prime Minister, the Foreign Minister, the Defence Minister and the Administrator-General of Namibia, among others. At that time, South Africa restated its commitment to seek a settlement based on resolution 435(1978) within the framework reached with the United States and the other members of the Western contact group. South Africa maintained that there was one major issue to be resolved—the withdrawal of foreign troops from Angola, on the understanding that they would not be replaced by any other hostile force. In reply, the Secretary-General said that the United Nations could not accept the linkage precondition for implementation of the independence plan.

In regard to the electoral system for a constituent assembly, South Africa indicated that its choice would be communicated as soon as a date for implementation had been set. At the discussions, South Africa expressed agreement on the proposed composition of UNTAG and said that as far as South Africa was concerned the matter was resolved. The discussions also resulted in the settlement of outstanding issues regarding the Agreement on the Status of UNTAG, which would provide UNTAG with the necessary immunities and privileges to facilitate its work.

The Secretary-General also visited Namibia, where he noted the consequences of the drought which was having a devastating effect on the people, and Angola, for talks with the President of SWAPO. SWAPO reaffirmed that it was ready to sign a cease-fire with South Africa and to cooperate with the Secretary-General and UNTAG in facilitating the speedy implementation of resolution 435(1978). In addition, SWAPO expressed support for recommendations the Secretary-General would make to the Council with regard to UNTAG's composition. On the two proposals for an electoral system, SWAPO was prepared in principle to accept either choice—proportional representation or the single-member constituency system.

The Secretary-General concluded that his consultations had resulted, as far as UNTAG was concerned, in resolving virtually all outstanding issues and that finality on the modalities of implementing resolution 435(1978) had never been so close. However, the position of South Africa regarding the withdrawal of Cuban troops from Angola still made it impossible to launch the United Nations plan. Real progress could not be claimed until an actual date was fixed for the start of implementation and the cease-fire came into force.

SECURITY COUNCIL ACTION

The Security Council considered the Secretary-General's August report[33] at a series of nine meetings held between 20 and 28 October. It convened in response to a 17 October[34] request of Senegal, on behalf of the Group of African States, and an 18 October[35] request of India, on behalf of the Movement of Non-Aligned Countries.

Algeria, Angola, Argentina, Botswana, Bulgaria, Canada, Cuba, Czechoslovakia, Ethiopia, the German Democratic Republic, Germany, the Federal Republic of, Hungary, India, Iran, Kenya, Kuwait, the Libyan Arab Jamahiriya, Mexico, Mozambique, Nigeria, Peru, Senegal, Sierra Leone, South Africa, Sri Lanka, the Sudan, the Syrian Arab Republic, Tunisia, Turkey, Uganda, the United Republic of Tanzania, Venezuela, Yugoslavia and Zambia, at their request, were invited to participate in the Council's discussion without the right to vote.

During the debate, certain individuals were also invited to address the Council, under rule 39[b] of its provisional rules of procedure. On 20 October,[36] Togo, Zaire and Zimbabwe asked that Peter Mueshihange, Secretary for Foreign Relations of SWAPO, be invited to speak, and on 24 October,[37] they made a similar request for John-

stone F. Makatini, representative of ANC. Canada, France, the Federal Republic of Germany, the United Kingdom and the United States, by a letter of 25 October,[38] submitted communications from K. Riruako, President of the Democratic Turnhalle Alliance in Namibia, and L. J. Barnes of the Labour Party of Namibia, presenting their positions on representation of the people of the Namibia. The President of the Council of Namibia, the Acting Chairman of the Committee against *apartheid*, and the Chairman of the Committee on colonial countries were also invited to speak at their request.

On 28 October, the Council adopted resolution 539(1983) by vote.

The Security Council,

Having considered the report of the Secretary-General of 29 August 1983,

Recalling General Assembly resolutions 1514(XV) of 14 December 1960 and 2145(XXI) of 27 October 1966,

Recalling and reaffirming its resolutions 301(1971), 385(1976), 431(1978), 432(1978), 435(1978), 439(1978) and 532(1983),

Gravely concerned at South Africa's continued illegal occupation of Namibia,

Gravely concerned also at the tension and instability prevailing in southern Africa and the mounting threat to the security of the region and its wider implications for international peace and security resulting from continued utilization of Namibia as a springboard for attacks against and destabilization of African States in the region,

Reaffirming the legal responsibility of the United Nations over Namibia and the primary responsibility of the Security Council for ensuring the implementation of its resolutions, in particular, resolutions 385(1976) and 435(1978), which call for the holding of free and fair elections in the Territory under the supervision and control of the United Nations,

Indignant that South Africa's insistence on an irrelevant and extraneous issue of "linkage" has obstructed the implementation of resolution 435(1978),

1. *Condemns* South Africa for its continued illegal occupation of Namibia in flagrant defiance of resolutions of the General Assembly and decisions of the Security Council;

2. *Further condemns* South Africa for its obstruction of the implementation of Security Council resolution 435(1978) by insisting on conditions contrary to the provisions of the United Nations plan for the independence of Namibia;

3. *Rejects* South Africa's insistence on linking the independence of Namibia to irrelevant and extraneous issues as incompatible with resolution 435(1978), other decisions of the Security Council and the resolutions of the General Assembly on Namibia, including General Assembly resolution 1514(XV);

4. *Declares* that the independence of Namibia cannot be held hostage to the resolution of issues that are alien to resolution 435(1978);

[b]See footnote a, p. 1047.

5.   *Reiterates* that resolution 435(1978), embodying the United Nations plan for the independence of Namibia, is the only basis for a peaceful settlement of the Namibian problem;

6.   *Takes note* that the consultations undertaken by the Secretary-General pursuant to paragraph 5 of resolution 532(1983) have confirmed that all the outstanding issues relevant to resolution 435(1978) have been resolved;

7.   *Affirms* that the electoral system to be used for the elections of the Constituent Assembly should be determined prior to the adoption by the Council of the enabling resolution for the implementation of the United Nations plan;

8.   *Calls upon* South Africa to co-operate with the Secretary-General forthwith and to communicate to him its choice of the electoral system in order to facilitate the immediate and unconditional implementation of the United Nations plan embodied in resolution 435(1978);

9.   *Requests* the Secretary-General to report to the Council on the implementation of this resolution as soon as possible and not later than 31 December 1983;

10.   *Decides* to remain actively seized of the matter and to meet as soon as possible following the Secretary-General's report for the purpose of reviewing progress in the implementation of resolution 435(1978) and, in the event of continued obstruction by South Africa, to consider the adoption of appropriate measures under the Charter of the United Nations.

Security Council resolution 539(1983)

28 October 1983   Meeting 2492   14-0-1

8-nation draft (S/16085/Rev.2).
Sponsors: Guyana, Jordan, Malta, Nicaragua, Pakistan, Togo, Zaire, Zimbabwe.
Meeting numbers. SC 2481-2486, 2488, 2490, 2492.
Vote in Council as follows:
    In favour: China, France, Guyana, Jordan, Malta, Netherlands, Nicaragua, Pakistan, Poland, Togo, USSR, United Kingdom, Zaire, Zimbabwe.
    Against: None.
    Abstaining: United States.

Explaining its vote, the United States said it supported the spirit of the resolution; however, it had reservations about the time-frame and warned of unreasonable or unrealistic constraints on the negotiating flexibility required to overcome remaining obstacles, and the resolution's implicit allusions to possible future action under Chapter VII of the Charter which the United States regarded as premature. The United Kingdom was concerned at the burden the Council placed on the Secretary-General by asking him to make a further report in a short period and had reservations about the reference in the fifth preambular paragraph to the use of Namibia as a springboard for destabilization. The USSR supported the resolution because it strengthened the role of the United Nations in settling the question; it regretted, however, that a direct statement that sanctions should be imposed against South Africa was not included. Zimbabwe stated that the resolution used language reflecting the international consensus expressed in the Council and in other places which would be useful to move forward with implementing resolution 435(1978)[5] and to reject obstacles to it.

During the second 1983 Council debate on Namibia, speakers again praised the work of the Secretary-General in pursuing a settlement based on resolution 435(1978) and the conclusions he drew in his latest report.[33] Many noted that the debate was occurring at a time when South Africa was mounting an attack against Mozambique (see p. 179)—an attack which they condemned. A number of countries reiterated the points they had raised earlier, and, in general, States expressed increased concern over South Africa's insistence on linking Namibia's independence with the withdrawal of Cuban troops from Angola. Those setting forth additional points are described below.

South Africa praised the Secretary-General for having accurately reflected its position in his August report. It reaffirmed its commitment to seek a settlement on the basis of resolution 435(1978) and stated that there remained only one major issue to be resolved—the withdrawal of Cuban forces from Angola (which it estimated at 30,000) on the understanding they would not be replaced by other hostile forces. This position had support from within the international community, according to South Africa. SWAPO operated from Angola with Cuban support; therefore, the presence of Cuban forces there was relevant to the search for a peaceful settlement. The introduction of surrogate forces of the USSR into southern Africa was a cause for concern to all countries of the region. South Africa continued to reject the General Assembly's recognition of SWAPO as the sole and authentic representative of the people of Namibia; under no circumstances would it receive United Nations representatives in Namibia on that basis. Certain United Nations bodies remained biased in favour of SWAPO and no settlement plan could be implemented unless the Secretariat acted with strict impartiality. It would be futile for the Council to set deadlines for implementation until the matter of the Cuban presence had been resolved.

Angola, affirming that it had a right to self-defence and to be assisted by friends of its choice, said that if independence were to be achieved peacefully, the next and only step was the immediate implementation of resolution 435(1978), starting with a cease-fire, the emplacement of UNTAG, the withdrawal of South African troops and elections under United Nations supervision; as part of that process, South Africa should immediately announce its choice of electoral system, hold talks to fix a date for the cease-fire and withdraw from Angolan territory. In regard to its troops, Cuba pointed out that under its 1982 declaration with Angola, the two States had agreed that if the resolution were implemented and if South Africa withdrew its occupying troops to the other side of the Orange River, thereby diminishing the danger of aggression against Angola, then Angola and Cuba would consider withdrawing Cuban forces in keeping with a timetable agreed upon by the two Governments.

Czechoslovakia, Ethiopia, speaking for OAU, Hungary, the Libyan Arab Jamahiriya, Nigeria, Uganda and the United Republic of Tanzania stressed that Cuban troops were in Angola because its security was threatened and its territory occupied by South Africa. According to Ethiopia, the Cuban troops were in Angola at its request and in conformity with the Charter for the purpose of repulsing the South African invasion; it was convinced that the withdrawal of Cuban troops from Angola was intended to achieve the occupation of Angola, the overthrow of its Government, its replacement by elements subservient to neo-colonist interests, and the weakening of the liberation struggle of the Namibian people. Uganda added that South Africa was continuing to use Namibia as a launching pad for aggression.

Togo believed that the Cuban troop withdrawal would be greatly facilitated by South Africa's military withdrawal from Namibia and southern Africa. Stressing that measures to build confidence and reduce conflict in the region were urgently needed, Canada said the first step towards a settlement must be the immediate and unconditional withdrawal of South African forces from Angola. Bulgaria, Hungary, Mexico, Senegal, speaking for the African group, the USSR, Zaire and Zimbabwe stressed that the presence of foreign troops in a country was an issue to be decided between the sovereign States; a similar position was held by Venezuela. Nicaragua called on the Council to declare that the presence of Cuban troops was exclusively a sovereign decision of Angola.

Many speakers, including Botswana, Bulgaria, Hungary, Mexico, Mozambique, Nicaragua, Nigeria, Sri Lanka, Togo, Uganda, the United Republic of Tanzania, and Zaire urged the Council to reject linkage of Namibia's independence with the withdrawal of Cuban troops from Angola. In Bulgaria's view, the growing aggressiveness of the United States, motivated by its ambition for world supremacy, could be seen clearly in its attempts to impose such a link arbitrarily. Botswana called on the Council to reject such linkage which challenged its authority. In addition to those speakers and many others in the first series of 1983 Council meetings on Namibia (see above), Czechoslovakia, Ethiopia, for OAU, the German Democratic Republic, the Federal Republic of Germany, the Libyan Arab Jamahiriya, Senegal, the United Kingdom and Venezuela rejected linkage. The United Kingdom stressed that the Council could not accept that the withdrawal of Cuban troops from Angola should be a precondition for implementing a settlement.

Kuwait, Malta, Nigeria, Sierra Leone, Sri Lanka, the Sudan, the Syrian Arab Republic, Tunisia, Uganda and Zambia believed that raising the linkage issue was a tactic to delay implementation of a settlement.

Algeria, Angola, Czechoslovakia, Hungary, Mexico, the Netherlands, Sri Lanka, the Sudan, the United Republic of Tanzania, Yugoslavia and Zambia joined those who had stated at previous meetings that no extraneous issues should be attached to the United Nations plan for Namibia's independence.

While recognizing that the linkage issue was not within the scope of the contact group, the Federal Republic of Germany said the problem would have to be taken into account by those who realistically aimed at implementing resolution 435(1978); as pointed out by the Secretary-General, the problem had to be solved by those directly concerned acting within their sovereign rights.

A number of States offered suggestions for the Council to take as the next steps to achieve implementation of resolution 435(1978). France, the Sudan, the United Republic of Tanzania, Yugoslavia and Zambia said that South Africa should be required to inform the Secretary-General of its choice regarding the electoral system. According to France, all other issues had been completely settled in regard to implementation of the plan; although the situation remained difficult, concessions were possible.

Nicaragua, the United Republic of Tanzania and Yugoslavia, among others, affirmed that resolution 435(1978) remained the sole basis for negotiating Namibia's independence. Nicaragua called on the Council to demand its immediate implementation. In Yugoslavia's view, the Council should confirm the plan as the only basis for a settlement, thus removing any grounds for obstructing its implementation. Argentina, Cuba, Kuwait, Nicaragua, Senegal, speaking for the African group, Togo, the United Republic of Tanzania, and Yugoslavia stressed that the United Nations or the Council was responsible for Namibia's future and was the proper framework for reaching a solution. Mexico, the Netherlands and Nigeria warned that the effectiveness of the Council would be questioned if it could not act decisively.

That an issue outside the scope of that resolution was delaying its implementation was a matter of frustration, the United States said, but implementation would take place only if the fundamental concerns of all parties were addressed; the United States was seeking a solution based on reciprocity with mutual respect for security and sovereignty on all sides and with Namibia's independence as the only acceptable result.

Iran stated that rather than through the United Nations, the issue could be resolved only through the collaboration of African countries, independent of all affiliations with either West or East.

Senegal, for the African group, said that Africa expected the Council to adopt appropriate and specific measures to enable the Namibians to achieve independence. Malta emphasized that a unanimously adopted resolution would confirm to South Africa that it was isolated and would demonstrate the real wishes of the international community. The Netherlands believed that South Africa should be called on to agree to a cease-fire; failing that, the Council was duty-bound to consider appropriate means of applying pressure on South Africa.

In addition to those which had called at the previous series of meetings for sanctions or measures under Chapter VII of the Charter, Angola, China, Czechoslovakia, Hungary, Kenya, Kuwait, Mexico, Mozambique, Nicaragua, Nigeria, Sierra Leone, the Sudan, Togo, the USSR, the United Republic of Tanzania, Yugoslavia and Zimbabwe called for such action either immediately or, if South Africa's position did not change, within a set time-frame. Hungary, Kenya, Kuwait, the Sudan, Tunisia and Zambia joined those advocating a time-frame or deadline.

Peru, the Sudan, the United States and Venezuela agreed that progress had been made at the latest round of discussions held by the Secretary-General.

The German Democratic Republic and India, speaking for the Non-Aligned Movement, on the other hand, felt that there had been no progress in finding a solution. India hoped that the Council members would appreciate the limits to forbearance, and display the necessary political will to implement its own decision without further delay.

The role of the contact group was discussed by several countries. The Libyan Arab Jamahiriya and Pakistan said it was the group's responsibility to bring about implementation of resolution 435(1978). Hungary urged the members of the group to exert pressure on South Africa to ensure its compliance with United Nations resolutions. Kenya stressed that those countries which had assumed responsibility for negotiations and had received the co-operation of SWAPO should stop sending conflicting signals to South Africa. The Sudan felt that the group's mission had been completed and that it was time for the Council to shoulder its responsibilities in accordance with the Charter. Zimbabwe charged that some members of the group, instead of pressuring South Africa to co-operate in implementing resolution 435(1978), had been trying to usurp the role of the United Nations by seeking solutions outside that resolution; the current series of meetings had been convened to protect the plan for Namibia's independence from the newly contrived stratagem

of linkage and to ensure that nothing would delay its launching. The Libyan Arab Jamahiriya and Poland questioned the intentions and seriousness of the group's discussions. In the opinion of the latter, the group had only gained time for South Africa to strengthen its hold over Namibia. China noted that most members of the group had indicated that they did not approve of linkage, but added that it was regrettable that there was still a permanent member of the Council which supported that unreasonable position.

Czechoslovakia, Kenya, Kuwait, Nigeria and Zimbabwe believed that the support of certain countries had encouraged South Africa's intransigence. Czechoslovakia, Kuwait, Sierra Leone, the USSR and the United Republic of Tanzania believed that the United States had played a leading role in blocking progress. According to Czechoslovakia, the United States had been instrumental in putting forward the unjustified and unacceptable demand to link Namibia's independence with withdrawal of Cuban troops from Angola. In the opinion of the USSR, the United States was using excuses for its interference in the affairs of the region and to ensure its strategic interests; together with South Africa, it intended to block a settlement of the Namibia question, to weaken Angola through military threats and to limit its sovereign rights.

Algeria, Mozambique, Senegal, for the African countries, and Togo emphasized that Namibia was a decolonization issue. India, Kuwait and Nicaragua could not accept that the issue should become part of the East-West confrontation. Kuwait stated that the delay in implementing the United Nations plan had opened the way for introducing new, extraneous elements stemming from the escalating tension between the two super-Powers, and the linkage issue was being used by the United States to serve its strategic interests. According to Cuba, Czechoslovakia, Hungary and Poland, South Africa and others were exploiting the natural resources of Namibia through their transnational corporations.

Czechoslovakia, Kuwait, Mexico, Nicaragua, Poland, Togo, Turkey, the USSR, the United Republic of Tanzania, Venezuela, Yugoslavia, Zaire and Zambia joined those expressing support for SWAPO as the sole legitimate representative of the people of Namibia. The German Democratic Republic and the Libyan Arab Jamahiriya called for increased assistance to SWAPO.

Poland and Sierra Leone considered that armed struggle would be justified if the United Nations were unable to achieve Namibia's independence, but the United States rejected the use of force. Poland said that if sanctions were not effective and if the supply of weapons to South Africa continued, there would be no other way for Namibians led by SWAPO but to continue the liberation struggle by all means, including armed struggle, as a legitimate way to achieve independence. In Sierra Leone's view, SWAPO, faced with South Africa's intransigence, was left with no alternative but to intensify the armed struggle. Support for the action of SWAPO and the front-line States was expressed by Argentina.

The representative of SWAPO, who urged the Council to impose sanctions against South Africa, said that linkage was the primary source of the catastrophe in the negotiations and the only obstacle to Namibia's full independence; there was a political will on SWAPO's part to sign a cease-fire agreement and to co-operate with the Secretary-General in implementing the United Nations plan, and SWAPO challenged South Africa to do likewise.

Also calling for sanctions if South Africa did not choose an electoral system within a certain time, the President of the Council for Namibia said that the problems relating to UNTAG's composition had been of South Africa's making; Namibia would continue to be held hostage as long as South Africa linked its independence to other issues. The Chairman of the Committee on colonial countries, explaining the Committee's position, said it had recommended comprehensive mandatory sanctions and rejected the attempts by the United States and South Africa to establish any linkage, attempts which would only retard the decolonization process in Namibia and interfere in Angola's internal affairs. Again calling for sanctions and rejecting linkage, the Acting Chairman of the Committee against *apartheid* said South Africa intended to impose an internal settlement in Namibia through a so-called State Council, or constitutional changes which were to be the subject of a referendum some 10 days hence among whites only; those proposed changes would set up a racially segregated Parliament giving limited representation to coloureds and Indians but excluding the Africans who made up 72 per cent of the population.

The representative of ANC said that the change in the United States administration had resulted in the cancellation of limited positive elements achieved by the contact group and the multiplication of the negative elements; the linkage issue introduced by the United States was a flagrant act of hostility against the liberation cause of Africa and the international community.

Communications. At the time of the Council's October debate, the President received two communications on Namibia. On 17 October,[39] the Chairman of the Committee on colonial countries transmitted parts of a 13 October Committee decision, in which it condemned South Africa for its military buildup in Namibia as well as the collabo-

ration between South Africa and certain States, and recommended that the Council impose comprehensive mandatory sanctions against South Africa, under Chapter VII of the Charter. Guinea transmitted on 20 October[40] a message by its President, stating that resolution 435(1978) had not been implemented because of the opposition of the South African minority régime, supported by certain Member States, and that it was time that all Council members defined their position on Namibia.

After the Council adopted resolution 539(1983) (see above), South Africa forwarded three messages to the Secretary-General, from its Minister of Foreign Affairs and Information. In a 29 October statement,[41] the Minister pointed out that while the choice of an electoral system was not of great importance and should not cause unnecessary problems, what was important was that no settlement plan could be implemented unless a firm agreement was reached on Cuban withdrawal from Angola; he added that South Africa did not intend to succumb to the Council's threat. Two other messages were forwarded in a letter of 15 December.[42] By the first, dated 22 November, the Minister, referring to the Secretary-General's August report,[33] expressed surprise that the relatively inconsequential issue of the electoral system had been resurrected, since South Africa had received the impression that its position was acceptable to the other parties involved; since a decision on the choice of electoral system would involve further consultations with the leaders of the Territory, the Minister suggested that a further exchange of views between the Administrator-General and the Secretary-General's Special Representative might be useful. In a letter of 15 December, the Minister said South Africa was prepared to begin a disengagement of its forces, which from time to time conducted military operations against SWAPO in Angola, on 31 January 1984, on the understanding that Angola would reciprocate by assuring that Angolan forces, SWAPO and the Cubans would not exploit the resulting situation, in particular with regard to the security of the inhabitants of Namibia; South Africa remained prepared to begin implementing resolution 435(1978) when the problem of Cuban forces in Angola was resolved.

Report of the Secretary-General. In accordance with resolution 539(1983) (see above), the Secretary-General, on 29 December,[43] submitted to the Council a further report—his third in 1983—concerning the implementation of resolutions 435(1978)[5] and 439(1978).[15] He reported that during discussions with South African ambassadors to the United Nations, he had pointed out that the Council had already rejected South Africa's insistence on linking the independence of

Namibia to irrelevant issues and that resolution 435(1978) must remain the only basis for a peaceful settlement. He urged South Africa to co-operate and to communicate its choice of the electoral system in order to facilitate implementation of the United Nations plan. The ambassadors informed him that South Africa's position with regard to implementation of resolution 435(1978) had not changed, and they agreed to refer the question of the electoral system to their Government.

At subsequent meetings, the Secretary-General had again asked South Africa for a definitive response with regard to the electoral system. Stressing that it was essential to abide by the Council's decisions, he urged South Africa to reconsider its position and communicate its choice as a matter of urgency in order to facilitate implementation of the United Nations plan. As South Africa had not provided a definitive response, the Secretary-General said he was not in a position to report any further progress.

Activities of the UN Council for Namibia. Throughout 1983, the United Nations Council for Namibia, acting as a policy-making organ of the United Nations and the legal Administering Authority for Namibia until independence under the role assigned to the Council by the General Assembly in 1967,[44] continued to carry out its mandate. The Council reported to the Assembly at its 1983 regular session on developments concerning the Territory and on the Council's activities from 1 September 1982 to 31 August 1983.[45] Later 1983 activities were described in its 1984 report.[46]

As part of the activities assigned to it by the Assembly in December 1982,[47] the Council, in consultation with OAU, organized the International Conference in Support of the Struggle of the Namibian People for Independence (Paris, 25-29 April 1983) (see above).

The Council considered that South Africa's continued illegal occupation of the Territory, its war of repression against the Namibians, its persistent acts of aggression launched from Namibia against neighbouring States, its policy of *apartheid* and development of nuclear weapons seriously threatened international peace and security. It believed that South Africa must be made to comply with the United Nations plan for Namibia without prevarication, dilution or further delay, and it reiterated its position that it was incumbent on the Security Council to impose comprehensive mandatory sanctions in order to compel South Africa to withdraw from Namibia. Those views were expressed not only in the annual report, but also during the Security Council debates on Namibia (see above), in which the Council participated.

As part of its ongoing programme of consultations with Member States, the Council held high-level meetings in 1983, sending two missions to Europe (10-22 April and 15 April-6 May) and one to Latin America (11-22 April). The first mission to Europe visited the USSR, Belgium, Denmark and Czechoslovakia; the second went to Greece, Turkey, Bulgaria, Italy and Switzerland. The mission to Latin America visited Costa Rica, Haiti, the Dominican Republic and Nicaragua. Following those visits, individual statements and joint communiqués were issued.

The Council continued to provide material assistance to Namibians through the United Nations Fund for Namibia, the United Nations Institute for Namibia, and the Nationhood Programme for Namibia (see below). Other activities included meetings and seminars to further the implementation of relevant United Nations resolutions. In 1983, the Council organized its first regional symposium—the Regional Symposium in Support of the Namibian Cause in Latin America (San José, Costa Rica, 16-19 August). The programme of co-operation with non-governmental organizations was strengthened as part of its efforts to mobilize international public opinion in support of the liberation struggle of the Namibians and their representative, SWAPO.

On 26 August, the Council held its annual commemoration of Namibia Day, and on 27 October, it commemorated the Week of Solidarity with the People of Namibia and their Liberation Movement, SWAPO (see below, under INFORMATION DISSEMINATION).

The Council participated in the Second World Conference to Combat Racism and Racial Discrimination, held at Geneva in August 1983 (see p. 802).

The Council continued to co-operate with OAU and to attend its meetings, including the OAU Assembly of Heads of State and Government (Addis Ababa, Ethiopia, 6-12 June) with the status of observer. The OAU Assembly adopted a number of resolutions which were forwarded to the General Assembly on 6 July.[48] In a special resolution on Namibia, OAU expressed concern at the attempt to introduce extraneous elements to resolution 435(1978), declared that that resolution remained the only basis for a negotiated settlement and welcomed the May 1983 report[14] of the Secretary-General on its implementation. As in the past, the Council participated in the meetings of the Movement of Non-Aligned Countries, including the Seventh Conference of Heads of State or Government of Non-Aligned Countries (New Delhi, India, 7-11 March). In its Political Declaration forwarded to the Security Council and the Assembly on 30 March,[49] the Conference pledged to give increased support to SWAPO; expressed concern that South Africa continued to obstruct implementation of resolution 435(1978), rejected the linkage being drawn by the United States on the Namibia issue; called on the Security Council to consider further action with regard to implementation of resolution 435(1978); and reiterated its support for the Council for Namibia in its role as the sole legal administering authority of Namibia until independence. That position was reiterated in a communiqué[50] issued by the Meeting of Ministers and Heads of Delegation of Non-Aligned Countries to the Assembly (4-7 October, New York), in which the Council also participated.

The Council also continued to participate as a full member in the activities of a number of United Nations agencies and other bodies. On 17 February, Namibia, represented by the Council, was granted full membership in the International Atomic Energy Agency.

In its report,[45] the Council described developments and social conditions in Namibia. The economy, based primarily on mining of natural resources (diamonds, uranium, copper, lead, zinc, tin, cadmium, vanadium, silver and lithium), continued to be dominated by South African and Western transnational corporations (TNCs). As in previous years, the bulk of the profits was repatriated to foreign shareholders. There were 88 TNCs operating in Namibia, of which 35 were based in South Africa, 25 in the United Kingdom, 15 in the United States, 8 in the Federal Republic of Germany, 3 in France and 2 in Canada. Agriculture and fishing, the second and third largest sectors of the economy, were also dominated by South African companies.

With regard to the military situation in Namibia, the Council reported that the size of the South African occupation force in Namibia was estimated at 100,000 (approximately 1 soldier for every 12 Namibians), stationed at approximately 85 to 90 South African bases. The number of troops increased considerably when preparations were made for military attacks on neighbouring Angola. Among the forces deployed by South Africa were units consisting largely of mercenaries.

South Africa's *apartheid* policy continued to characterize all spheres of life in Namibia—housing and living conditions, labour and work, education and health facilities. Repressive legislation enacted by South Africa was used to crush the national liberation struggle through arbitrary arrests and maltreatment of political prisoners. Thousands of Namibians had fled their native land to seek refuge in Angola, Botswana and Zambia (see p. 949).

While maintaining its military occupation, South Africa attempted in 1983 to impose internal institutions. Following the collapse in mid-January of the Democratic Turnhalle Alliance "internal administration", South Africa had an-

nounced the creation of what the Council said was another puppet institution, a so-called Council of State; due to lack of support, however, that plan was postponed. In view of its repeated failures at imposing "internal schemes", South Africa had sponsored another political coalition—the Multi-Party Conference—meant to be an alternative to SWAPO.

Activities of the Committee on colonial countries. On 13 October 1983, the Special Committee on the Situation with regard to the Implementation of the Declaration on the Granting of Independence to Colonial Countries and Peoples adopted a decision on Namibia.[51] Noting that the situation continued to deteriorate because of South Africa's refusal to comply with United Nations decisions, the Committee stated that South Africa, by perpetuating its illegal occupation and trying to impose an "internal settlement" on the Namibians, was responsible for a situation which threatened international peace and security. South Africa's intransigence, its continued failure to implement Security Council resolution 435(1978), its military build-up in Namibia and armed aggression against the Namibians, made it imperative for the United Nations to reassert its legal responsibility for Namibia until its independence and to take steps to bring about South Africa's compliance so that the Namibians could exercise their inalienable right to self-determination and independence without further delay.

Reiterating its position in support of the legitimacy of the people's struggle by all means and of the territorial integrity of Namibia, the Committee rejected all manoeuvres by South Africa to bring about a sham independence under a puppet régime, including the establishment of the so-called State Council to draw up a draft constitution. It called on States to deny recognition to and refuse to co-operate with any illegal entity which South Africa might impose.

The Committee rejected attempts by the United States and South Africa to establish linkage between Namibia's independence and extraneous issues, in particular the withdrawal of Cuban forces from Angola. It demanded that South Africa release all Namibian political prisoners, and that all captured Namibian freedom fighters be accorded prisoner-of-war status.

South Africa was condemned for its military build-up in Namibia, its recruitment of Namibians, use of mercenaries in occupying Namibia and in attacks against other States, use of Namibia for aggression against other States and the establishment of military bases. The Committee called on States to prevent recruitment of their nationals to serve as mercenaries in Namibia.

The Committee also condemned South African and other foreign economic interests which exploited the human and natural resources of Namibia, including marine resources off the coast, in disregard of the Council's 1974 Decree No. 1 for the Protection of the Natural Resources of Namibia,[11] and demanded that the exploitation cease. States whose TNCs continued to operate in Namibia were urged to end such co-operation.

The Committee recommended that the Security Council impose comprehensive mandatory sanctions against South Africa. Endorsing the policies and programmes defined by the Council for Namibia in co-operation with SWAPO to promote the self-determination and independence of the Namibians, it again requested the Secretary-General to mobilize world public opinion against South Africa's policy.

The Committee took other action in regard to Namibia. With the assistance of the United Nations information centres, it organized activities in observance of the Week of Solidarity with the Peoples of Namibia and All Other Colonial Territories, as well as those in South Africa, Fighting for Freedom, Independence and Human Rights (see p. 1029).

Action by the Commission on Human Rights. In several February resolutions, the Commission on Human Rights took action relating to human rights violations in Namibia by South Africa. Among other things, it reaffirmed the inalienable right of the Namibians to self-determination, freedom and national independence in a united Namibia; condemned the occupation of Namibia; and demanded that South Africa cease human rights violations there (see p. 836).

ECONOMIC AND SOCIAL COUNCIL ACTION

In resolution 1983/42, the Economic and Social Council requested United Nations agencies and organizations to withhold financial, economic, technical or other assistance to South Africa until it restored to Namibians their right to self-determination and independence, and to refrain from action which might imply support for the illegal occupation of Namibia. It also noted with satisfaction the inclusion of Namibia, represented by the Council for Namibia, in the membership of IAEA and ITU, and urged other United Nations bodies which had not granted full membership to the Council to do so without delay (see p. 1015). In resolution 1983/74, the Council called for action to limit the activities of TNCs in South Africa and Namibia; in particular, it called on home countries of TNCs to terminate the collaboration of their corporations with South Africa, to prevent further investments and reinvestments and to bring about an immediate withdrawal of existing investments in South Africa and Namibia. The Council, by resolution 1983/75, took steps towards organizing public hearings on TNC activities in South Africa and Namibia. (See p. 144.)

GENERAL ASSEMBLY ACTION

Of the five resolutions (38/36 A-E) on Namibia adopted by the General Assembly in December, two dealt with the situation in that country.

On 1 December, the General Assembly adopted resolution 38/36 A by recorded vote.

Situation in Namibia resulting from the illegal occupation of the Territory by South Africa

The General Assembly,

Having examined the report of the United Nations Council for Namibia and the relevant chapters of the report of the Special Committee on the Situation with regard to the Implementation of the Declaration on the Granting of Independence to Colonial Countries and Peoples,

Recalling its resolution 1514(XV) of 14 December 1960 containing the Declaration on the Granting of Independence to Colonial Countries and Peoples,

Recalling, in particular, its resolutions 2145(XXI) of 27 October 1966 and 2248(S-V) of 19 May 1967 and subsequent resolutions of the General Assembly and the Security Council relating to Namibia, as well as the advisory opinion of the International Court of Justice of 21 June 1971, delivered in response to the request addressed to it by the Security Council in its resolution 284(1970) of 29 July 1970,

Recalling also its resolutions 3111(XXVIII) of 12 December 1973 and 31/146 and 31/152 of 20 December 1976, by which it, *inter alia,* recognized the South West Africa People's Organization as the sole and authentic representative of the Namibian people and granted observer status to it,

Recalling further its resolutions ES-8/2 of 14 September 1981 and 36/121 B of 10 December 1981, by which it called upon States to cease forthwith, individually and collectively, all dealings with South Africa in order totally to isolate it politically, economically, militarily and culturally,

Recalling the Political Declaration adopted by the Seventh Conference of Heads of State or Government of Non-Aligned Countries, held at New Delhi from 7 to 12 March 1983,

Recalling the Paris Declaration on Namibia and the report of the Committee of the Whole and the Programme of Action on Namibia adopted at the International Conference in Support of the Struggle of the Namibian People for Independence,

Recalling the debate on the question of Namibia held in the Security Council from 23 May to 1 June 1983,

Recalling the resolution on Namibia adopted by the Assembly of Heads of State and Government of the Organization of African Unity at its nineteenth ordinary session, held at Addis Ababa from 6 to 12 June 1983,

Strongly reiterating that the continuing illegal and colonial occupation of Namibia by South Africa, in defiance of repeated General Assembly and Security Council resolutions, constitutes an act of aggression against the Namibian people and a challenge to the authority of the United Nations, which has direct responsibility for Namibia until independence,

Stressing the grave responsibility of the international community to take all possible measures in support of the Namibian people in their liberation struggle under the leadership of their sole and authentic representative, the South West Africa People's Organization,

Reaffirming its full support for the armed struggle of the Namibian people under the leadership of the South West Africa People's Organization to achieve self-determination, freedom and national independence in a united Namibia,

Indignant at South Africa's refusal to comply with repeated resolutions of the Security Council, in particular resolutions 385(1976) of 30 January 1976, 435(1978) of 29 September 1978, 439(1978) of 13 November 1978 and 532(1983) of 31 May 1983, and at its manoeuvres aimed at perpetuating its brutal domination and exploitation of the Namibian people, as repeatedly manifested in the course of the consultations for the implementation of the United Nations plan for the independence of Namibia,

Commending the front-line States and the South West Africa People's Organization for the statesmanlike and constructive attitude which they have displayed throughout the consultations to implement Security Council resolution 435(1978),

Strongly condemning South Africa's continued illegal occupation of Namibia, its brutal repression of the Namibian people and its ruthless exploitation of the people and resources of Namibia, as well as its attempts to destroy the national unity and territorial integrity of Namibia,

Strongly condemning the racist régime of South Africa for its efforts to develop a nuclear capability for military and aggressive purposes,

Deeply concerned at the increasing militarization of Namibia, the forceful conscription of Namibians, the creation of tribal armies and the use of mercenaries for internal repression and external aggression,

Noting with grave concern that, as a result of the Security Council's failure on 31 August 1981, on account of the veto of the United States of America, to exercise its responsibilities, unprovoked massive armed aggression against Angola continues and recently has escalated to extremely dangerous proportions,

Expressing its strong condemnation of South Africa's continuing acts of aggression against independent African States, particularly Angola, which have caused extensive loss of human life and destruction of economic infrastructures,

Reaffirming that the resources of Namibia are the inviolable heritage of the Namibian people and that the exploitation of those resources by foreign economic interests under the protection of the illegal colonial administration, in violation of the Charter of the United Nations, of the relevant resolutions of the General Assembly and the Security Council and of Decree No. 1 for the Protection of the Natural Resources of Namibia, enacted by the United Nations Council for Namibia on 27 September 1974, and in disregard of the advisory opinion of the International Court of Justice of 21 June 1971, is illegal and contributes to the maintenance of the illegal occupation régime,

Deeply deploring the continued collaboration with South Africa of certain Western States, in particular the United States of America, as well as that of Israel, in disregard of the relevant resolutions of the General Assembly and the Security Council,

Deeply concerned at the continued assistance rendered to the racist Pretoria régime by certain international organizations and institutions, in particular the International Monetary Fund, in disregard of the relevant resolutions of the General Assembly,

Indignant at the continuing arbitrary imprisonment and detention of political leaders and followers of the South West Africa People's Organization, the killing of Namibian patriots and other acts of brutality, including the wanton beating, torture and murder of innocent Namibians, and the arbitrary inhuman measures of collective punishment and measures designed to intimidate the Namibian people and to destroy their will to fulfil their legitimate aspirations for self-determination, freedom and national independence in a united Namibia,

Noting with grave concern that the Security Council has been prevented on several occasions from taking effective action against South Africa in the discharge of its responsibilities under Chapter VII of the Charter on account of the vetoes cast by one or more of the Western permanent members of the Security Council,

Commending the efforts of the United Nations Council for Namibia in the discharge of the responsibilities entrusted to it under the relevant resolutions of the General Assembly as the legal Administering Authority for Namibia until independence,

1. *Approves* the report of the United Nations Council for Namibia;

2. *Takes note* of the Paris Declaration on Namibia and the report of the Committee of the Whole and the Programme of Action on Namibia adopted at the International Conference in Support of the Struggle of the Namibian People for Independence;

3. *Takes note* of the debate on the question of Namibia held in the Security Council from 23 May to 1 June 1983, in which the international community overwhelmingly pronounced itself against the establishment of any linkage or parallelism between Namibian independence and extraneous and irrelevant issues, in particular the withdrawal of Cuban forces from Angola;

4. *Reaffirms* the inalienable right of the people of Namibia to self-determination, freedom and national independence in a united Namibia, in accordance with the Charter of the United Nations and as recognized in General Assembly resolutions 1514(XV) and 2145(XXI) and in subsequent resolutions of the Assembly relating to Namibia, as well as the legitimacy of their struggle by all the means at their disposal, including armed struggle, against the illegal occupation of their territory by South Africa;

5. *Reiterates* that, in accordance with its resolution 2145(XXI), Namibia is the direct responsibility of the United Nations until genuine self-determination and national independence are achieved in the Territory and, for this purpose, reaffirms the mandate given to the United Nations Council for Namibia as the legal Administering Authority for Namibia until independence under resolution 2248(S-V) and subsequent resolutions of the General Assembly;

6. *Reaffirms* that the South West Africa People's Organization, the national liberation movement of Namibia, is the sole and authentic representative of the Namibian people;

7. *Solemnly reaffirms* that the genuine independence of Namibia can be achieved only with the direct and full participation of the South West Africa People's Organization in all efforts to implement resolutions of the United Nations relating to Namibia and further reaffirms that the only parties to the conflict in Namibia are, on the one hand, South Africa, as the illegal oc-

cupying Power, and, on the other, the Namibian people under the leadership of the South West Africa People's Organization, their sole and authentic representative;

8. *Commends* the Namibian people's courage and determination and proclaims its full support for the heroic struggle they are waging under the leadership of the South West Africa People's Organization, their sole and authentic representative, to achieve self-determination, freedom and national independence in a united Namibia;

9. *Strongly condemns* the South African régime for its continued illegal occupation of Namibia in defiance of the resolutions of the United Nations relating to Namibia;

10. *Declares* that South Africa's illegal occupation of Namibia constitutes an act of aggression against the Namibian people in terms of the Definition of Aggression contained in General Assembly resolution 3314(XXIX) of 14 December 1974 and supports the armed struggle of the Namibian people, under the leadership of the South West Africa People's Organization, to repel South Africa's aggression and to achieve self-determination, freedom and national independence in a united Namibia;

11. *Reiterates* that, in accordance with the resolutions of the United Nations, in particular Security Council resolution 432(1978) of 27 July 1978 and General Assembly resolutions S-9/2 of 3 May 1978 and 35/227 A of 6 March 1981, Walvis Bay and the offshore islands of Namibia are an integral part of Namibia and that all attempts by South Africa to annex them are therefore illegal, null and void;

12. *Calls upon* the Security Council to declare categorically that Walvis Bay is an integral part of Namibia and that the question should not be left as a matter for negotiation between an independent Namibia and South Africa;

13. *Reaffirms* that Security Council resolution 435(1978), together with Council resolution 385(1976), is the only basis for a peaceful settlement of the question of Namibia and calls for its immediate and unconditional implementation without qualification or modification;

14. *Firmly rejects* the manoeuvres by the United States of America and South Africa aimed at undermining the international consensus embodied in Security Council resolution 435(1978) and at depriving the oppressed people of Namibia of their hard-won victories in the struggle for national liberation;

15. *Firmly rejects and condemns* the persistent attempts by the United States of America and South Africa to establish a linkage or parallelism between the independence of Namibia and any extraneous issues, in particular the withdrawal of Cuban forces from Angola, and emphasizes unequivocally that all such attempts are designed to delay the decolonization process in Namibia and that they constitute interference in the internal affairs of Angola;

16. *Expresses its appreciation* to the front-line States and the South West Africa People's Organization for their statesmanlike and constructive attitude throughout the consultations to implement Security Council resolution 435(1978);

17. *Strongly condemns* South Africa for obstructing the implementation of Security Council resolutions 385(1976), 435(1978) and 439(1978) and for its manoeuvres, in contravention of those resolutions, designed to consolidate its colonial and neo-colonial interests at the expense of the legitimate aspirations of the Namibian people for genuine self-determination, freedom and national independence in a united Namibia;

18. *Denounces* all fraudulent constitutional and political schemes through which the illegal racist régime of South Africa may attempt to perpetuate its colonial domination of Namibia and, in particular, calls upon the international community, especially all Member States, to continue to refrain from according any recognition or extending any co-operation to any régime which the illegal South African administration may impose upon the Namibian people in disregard of the present resolution, of Security Council resolutions 385(1976), 435(1978) and 439(1978) and of other relevant resolutions of the General Assembly and the Council;

19. *Strongly condemns* the illegal South African administration in Namibia for its manoeuvres, such as the establishment of another puppet institution in the form of the so-called State Council in direct violation of Security Council resolution 439(1978), aimed at perpetuating its domination and exploitation of the people and natural resources of the Territory;

20. *Strongly urges* the Security Council to act decisively against any dilatory manoeuvres and fraudulent schemes of the illegal occupation régime aimed at frustrating the legitimate struggle of the Namibian people, under the leadership of the South West Africa People's Organization, for self-determination and national liberation, as well as at negating the achievements of their just struggle;

21. *Declares* that all so-called laws and proclamations issued by the illegal occupation régime in Namibia are illegal, null and void;

22. *Calls upon* Member States and the specialized agencies and other international organizations associated with the United Nations to render sustained and increased support as well as material, financial, military and other assistance to the South West Africa People's Organization so as to enable it to intensify its struggle for the liberation of Namibia;

23. *Urges* all Governments and the specialized agencies and other intergovernmental organizations to provide increased material assistance to the thousands of Namibian refugees who have been forced by the *apartheid* régime's oppressive policies to flee Namibia, especially into the neighbouring front-line States;

24. *Calls upon* all Governments, especially those which have close links with South Africa, to support, in co-operation with the United Nations Council for Namibia, the actions of the United Nations to defend the national rights of the Namibian people until independence;

25. *Condemns* the increased assistance rendered by the major Western countries and Israel to South Africa in the political, economic, financial and particularly the military fields, expresses its conviction that this assistance constitutes a hostile action against the people of Namibia and the front-line States since it is bound to strengthen the military capability of the racist régime, and demands that such assistance be immediately terminated;

26. *Declares* that the resolution on the need for development aid for Namibia, adopted by the European

Parliament on 13 January 1983, calling upon the European Economic Community to extend aid to occupied Namibia as well as to so-called "refugees from southern Angola" in Namibia, if implemented, would flout international law by implying recognition of South Africa's presence in Namibia and would subsidize Pretoria's illegal administration of the Territory, while encouraging its acts of aggression against Angola and the occupation of a part of Angolan territory;

27. *Notes*, in this connection, the declaration of the European Parliament of 14 November 1983 concerning the resolution on the need for development aid for Namibia, which the Parliament adopted on 13 January 1983, and the letter of 15 November 1983 from the President of the European Parliament to the Secretary-General underlining that the European Parliament and the European Community support and respect the framework established by the United Nations in respect of Namibia;

28. *Condemns*, in this connection, the visit in August 1983 by four members of the European Parliament to Namibia and the parts of Angolan territory occupied by South Africa;

29. *Strongly condemns* South Africa for its military build-up in Namibia, its introduction of compulsory military service for Namibians, its recruitment and training of Namibians for tribal armies, its use of mercenaries to suppress the Namibian people and to carry out its military attacks against independent African States, its threats and acts of subversion and aggression against those States and the forcible displacement of Namibians from their homes;

30. *Strongly condemns* South Africa for its persistent acts of subversion and aggression against Angola, including the occupation of a part of its territory, and calls upon South Africa to cease all acts of aggression against and withdraw all its troops from that country;

31. *Condemns* the use of the territory of Namibia by the racist régime of South Africa as a staging ground from which to launch armed attacks against neighbouring African States, particularly the repeated unprovoked acts of aggression against and invasion of Angola, including occupation of parts of that country, in order to intimidate those States and, *inter alia*, to prevent them from supporting the legitimate struggle of the Namibian and South African peoples for freedom and independence;

32. *Condemns* the continuing military and nuclear collaboration on the part of certain Western States and Israel with the racist régime of South Africa, which is encouraging the Pretoria régime in its defiance of the international community and obstructing efforts to eliminate *apartheid* and bring South Africa's illegal occupation of Namibia to an end, and urges those States to cease and desist forthwith from such collaboration with South Africa, which is in violation of the arms embargo imposed against South Africa under Security Council resolution 418(1977) of 4 November 1977;

33. *Expresses its grave concern* at the acquisition of nuclear weapons capability by the racist régime of South Africa, with its record of violence and aggression, and declares that such acquisition constitutes a further attempt on its part to terrorize and intimidate independent States in the region into submission, while also posing a danger to all mankind;

34. *Strongly condemns* the collusion by the Governments of certain Western and other States, particularly those of the United States of America and Israel, with the racist régime of South Africa in the nuclear field and calls upon France and all other States to refrain from supplying the racist minority régime of South Africa, directly or indirectly, with installations that might enable it to produce uranium, plutonium or other nuclear materials, reactors or military equipment;

35. *Calls upon* the international community to extend, as a matter of urgency, full support and assistance, including military assistance, to the front-line States in order to enable them to defend their sovereignty and territorial integrity against the repeated acts of aggression by South Africa;

36. *Condemns* South Africa's attempts to thwart the work of the Southern African Development Coordination Conference, and calls upon all States to render all possible assistance to the Conference in its efforts to promote regional economic co-operation and development;

37. *Requests* the Secretary-General to continue to develop, in consultation with the United Nations Development Programme, a comprehensive programme of assistance to States that are neighbours of South Africa and Namibia, on the understanding that such assistance should not only envisage the overcoming of short-term difficulties but be designed to enable those States to move towards complete self-reliance, and requests the Secretary-General to report to the General Assembly at its thirty-ninth session on the development of this programme;

38. *Requests* all specialized agencies and other organizations and institutions of the United Nations system to co-operate with the Secretary-General in the development of a comprehensive programme of assistance to States neighbouring South Africa and Namibia;

39. *Reiterates its call* upon all States to take legislative and other appropriate measures to prevent the recruitment, training and transit of mercenaries for service in Namibia;

40. Strongly condemns the illegal South African administration for its massive repression of the people of Namibia and their national liberation movement, the South West Africa People's Organization, with the intention of establishing an atmosphere of intimidation and terror for the purpose of imposing upon the Namibian people a political arrangement aimed at undermining the territorial integrity and unity of Namibia as well as perpetuating the systematic plunder of the natural resources of the Territory;

41. *Demands* that South Africa immediately release all Namibian political prisoners, including all those imprisoned or detained under the so-called internal security laws, martial law or any other arbitrary measures, whether such Namibians have been charged or tried or are being held without charge in Namibia or South Africa;

42. *Demands* that South Africa account for all "disappeared" Namibians and release any who are still alive and declares that South Africa shall be liable for damages to compensate the victims, their families and the future lawful Government of an independent Namibia for the losses sustained;

43. *Reaffirms* that the natural resources of Namibia are the birthright of the Namibian people and expresses its deep concern at the rapid depletion of the natural resources of the Territory, particularly its uranium

deposits, as a result of their reckless plunder by South Africa and certain Western and other foreign economic interests, in violation of the pertinent resolutions of the General Assembly and of the Security Council, of the advisory opinion of the International Court of Justice of 21 July 1971 and of Decree No. 1 for the Protection of the Natural Resources of Namibia;

44. *Declares* that all activities of foreign economic interests in Namibia are illegal under international law and that consequently South Africa and all the foreign economic interests operating in Namibia are liable to pay damages to the future lawful Government of an independent Namibia;

45. *Strongly condemns* the activities of all foreign economic interests operating in Namibia under the illegal South African administration which are illegally exploiting the resources of the Territory and demands that transnational corporations engaged in such exploitation comply with all the relevant resolutions of the United Nations by immediately refraining from any new investment or activities in Namibia, by withdrawing from the Territory and by putting an end to their co-operation with the illegal South African administration;

46. *Requests once again* all Member States to take all appropriate measures, including legislation and enforcement action, to ensure the full application of, and compliance by all corporations and individuals within their jurisdiction with, the provisions of Decree No. 1 for the Protection of the Natural Resources of Namibia;

47. *Declares* that, by their depletive exploitation of natural resources and continued accumulation and repatriation of huge profits, the activities of foreign economic, financial and other interests operating at present in Namibia constitute a major obstacle to its independence;

48. *Calls upon* the Governments of all States, particularly those whose corporations are involved in the mining and processing of Namibian uranium, to take all appropriate measures in the context of the implementation of Decree No. 1 for the Protection of the Natural Resources of Namibia, including the practice of requiring negative certificates of origin, to prohibit and prevent State-owned and other corporations, together with their subsidiaries, from dealing in Namibian uranium and from engaging in any uranium-prospecting activities in Namibia;

49. *Requests* the Governments of the Federal Republic of Germany, the Netherlands and the United Kingdom of Great Britain and Northern Ireland, which operate the Urenco uranium-enrichment plant, to have Namibian uranium specifically excluded from the Treaty of Almelo, which regulates the activities of Urenco;

50. *Deeply deplores* the continued collaboration of the International Monetary Fund with South Africa in disregard of General Assembly resolution 37/2 of 21 October 1982, and calls upon the Fund to put an end to such collaboration;

51. *Reiterates its request* to all States, pending the imposition of mandatory sanctions against South Africa, to take legislative, administrative and other measures unilaterally and collectively, as appropriate, in order effectively to isolate South Africa politically, economically, militarily and culturally, in accordance with General Assembly resolutions ES-8/2 and 36/121 B and 37/233 A of 20 December 1982;

52. *Requests* the United Nations Council for Namibia to continue to follow the implementation of the provi-

sions of paragraph 51 above on the basis of information received from States as well as from other sources;

53. *Requests* the United Nations Council for Namibia, in implementation of paragraph 15 of General Assembly resolution ES-8/2 and of the relevant provisions of Assembly resolutions 36/121 B and 37/233 A, to continue to monitor the boycott of South Africa and to submit to the Assembly at its thirty-ninth session a comprehensive report on all contacts between all States and South Africa, containing an analysis of the information received from Member States and other sources on the continuing political, economic, financial and other relations of States and their economic and other interest groups with South Africa and of measures taken by States to terminate all dealings with the racist régime of South Africa;

54. *Requests* all States to co-operate fully with the United Nations Council for Namibia in the fulfilment of its tasks concerning the implementation of General Assembly resolutions ES-8/2, 36/121 B and 37/233 A and to report to the Secretary-General by the thirty-ninth session of the Assembly on the measures taken by them in the implementation of those resolutions;

55. *Requests* the Secretary-General to seek to ensure that all banks, corporations and other institutions with which the United Nations has contracts are in compliance with United Nations sanctions policies against South Africa;

56. *Declares* that the liberation struggle in Namibia is a conflict of an international character in terms of article 1, paragraph 4, of Additional Protocol I to the Geneva Conventions of 12 August 1949 and, in this regard, demands that the Conventions and Additional Protocol I be applied by South Africa, and in particular that all captured freedom fighters be accorded prisoner-of-war status as called for by the Geneva Convention Relative to the Treatment of Prisoners of War and Additional Protocol thereto;

57. *Declares* that South Africa's defiance of the United Nations, its illegal occupation of the Territory of Namibia, its war of repression against the Namibian people, its persistent acts of aggression launched from bases in Namibia against independent African States, its policies of *apartheid* and its development of nuclear weapons constitute a serious threat to international peace and security;

58. *Strongly urges* the Security Council, in the light of the serious threat to international peace and security posed by South Africa, to respond positively to the overwhelming demand of the international community by immediately imposing comprehensive mandatory sanctions against that country, as provided for in Chapter VII of the Charter of the United Nations;

59. *Calls upon* the Security Council to adopt the necessary measures to tighten the arms embargo imposed against South Africa under Council resolution 418(1977) and to ensure strict compliance with the embargo by all States;

60. *Further calls upon* the Security Council to implement, as a matter of urgency, the recommendations contained in the report of the Committee established by Council resolution 421(1977);

61. *Deplores* the decision of the Government of the United Kingdom of Great Britain and Northern Ireland to supply radar equipment to South Africa and urges the Security Council Committee established in pursu-

ance of resolution 421(1977) to take appropriate action to ensure that the mandatory arms embargo against South Africa is not violated;

62. *Requests* the Secretary-General to report to the General Assembly at its thirty-ninth session on the implementation of the present resolution.

General Assembly resolution 38/36 A

1 December 1983   Meeting 79   117-0-28 (recorded vote)

Draft by Council for Namibia (A/38/24); agenda item 36.

Financial implications. A/38/653, A/C.5/38/54 & Corr.1 & Add. 1.

Meeting numbers. GA 38th session: 5th Committee 52; plenary 72-79.

Recorded vote in Assembly as follows:

In favour: Afghanistan, Albania, Algeria, Angola, Antigua and Barbuda, Argentina, Bahamas, Bahrain, Bangladesh, Barbados, Belize, Benin, Bhutan, Bolivia, Botswana, Brazil, Bulgaria, Burma, Burundi, Byelorussian SSR, Cape Verde, China, Comoros, Congo, Costa Rica, Cuba, Cyprus, Czechoslovakia, Democratic Kampuchea, Democratic Yemen, Djibouti, Dominican Republic, Ecuador, Egypt, El Salvador, Equatorial Guinea, Ethiopia, Fiji, Gabon, German Democratic Republic, Ghana, Greece, Guinea, Guinea-Bissau, Guyana, Haiti, Honduras, Hungary, India, Indonesia, Iran, Iraq, Jamaica, Jordan, Kenya, Kuwait, Lao People's Democratic Republic, Lebanon, Libyan Arab Jamahiriya, Madagascar, Malaysia, Maldives, Mali, Malta, Mauritania, Mauritius, Mexico, Mongolia, Morocco, Mozambique, Nepal, Nicaragua, Niger, Nigeria, Oman, Pakistan, Panama, Papua New Guinea, Peru, Philippines, Poland, Qatar, Romania, Rwanda, Saint Vincent and the Grenadines, Sao Tome and Principe, Saudi Arabia, Senegal, Seychelles, Sierra Leone, Singapore, Sri Lanka, Sudan, Suriname, Swaziland, Syrian Arab Republic, Thailand, Togo, Trinidad and Tobago, Tunisia, Turkey, Uganda, Ukrainian SSR, USSR, United Arab Emirates, United Republic of Cameroon, United Republic of Tanzania, Upper Volta, Uruguay, Vanuatu, Venezuela, Viet Nam, Yemen, Yugoslavia, Zaire, Zambia, Zimbabwe.

Against: None.

Abstaining: Australia, Austria, Belgium, Canada, Central African Republic, Chad, Denmark, Finland, France, Germany, Federal Republic of, Iceland, Ireland, Italy, Ivory Coast, Japan, Luxembourg, Malawi, Netherlands, New Zealand, Norway, Portugal, Saint Lucia, Samoa, Solomon Islands, Spain, Sweden, United Kingdom, United States.

On 1 December, the Assembly also adopted resolution 38/36 B by recorded vote.

Implementation of Security Council resolution 435(1978)

The General Assembly,

Indignant at South Africa's refusal to comply with Security Council resolutions 385(1976) of 30 January 1976, 431(1978) of 27 July 1978, 435(1978) of 29 September 1978, 439(1978) of 13 November 1978 and 532(1983) of 31 May 1983 and at its manoeuvres aimed at gaining international recognition for illegitimate groups which it has installed in Namibia, and which are subservient to Pretoria's interests, in order to maintain its policies of domination and exploitation of the people and natural resources of Namibia,

Reaffirming the imperative need to proceed without any further delay with the implementation of Security Council resolution 435(1978), which, together with Council resolution 385(1976), is the only basis for a peaceful settlement of the question of Namibia,

Condemning the attempts by South Africa and the United States of America to continue to deny the Namibian people their inalienable right to self-determination and independence by linking the independence of Namibia with totally irrelevant and extraneous issues,

Reaffirming that the Cuban forces are in Angola by a sovereign act of the Government of Angola, in accordance with the provisions of the Charter of the United Nations, and that the attempts to link their presence in that country with Namibia's independence constitute interference in the internal affairs of Angola,

Reaffirming that the only parties to the conflict in Namibia are, on the one hand, the Namibian people represented by the South West Africa People's Organization, their sole and authentic representative, and, on the other, the racist régime of South Africa which illegally occupies Namibia,

Recalling its request to the Security Council, in the light of the serious threat to international peace and security posed by South Africa, to respond positively to the overwhelming demand of the international community by immediately imposing comprehensive mandatory sanctions against that country as provided for in Chapter VII of the Charter of the United Nations,

Recalling its call upon all States, in view of the threat to international peace and security posed by South Africa, to impose comprehensive mandatory sanctions against that country in accordance with the provisions of the Charter,

Taking note of the further reports of the Secretary-General dated 19 May 1983 and 29 August 1983 concerning the implementation of Security Council resolutions 435(1978) and 439(1978) concerning the question of Namibia,

1. *Strongly condemns* South Africa for obstructing the implementation of Security Council resolutions 385(1976), 435(1978), 439(1978) and 532(1983) and for its manoeuvres, in contravention of those resolutions, designed to consolidate its colonial and neo-colonial interests at the expense of the legitimate aspirations of the Namibian people for genuine self-determination, freedom and national independence in a united Namibia;

2. *Reaffirms* the direct responsibility of the United Nations for Namibia pending its achievement of genuine self-determination and national independence;

3. *Reiterates* that Security Council resolution 435(1978), in which the Council endorsed the United Nations plan for the independence of Namibia, is the only basis for a peaceful settlement of the question of Namibia and demands its immediate and unconditional implementation without qualification, modification or amendment or the introduction of extraneous and irrelevant issues of "linkage", "parallelism" or "reciprocity" insisted upon by the United States of America and South Africa;

4. *Emphasizes once again* that the only parties to the conflict in Namibia are, on the one hand, the Namibian people represented by the South West Africa People's Organization, their sole and authentic representative, and, on the other, the racist régime of South Africa, which illegally occupies Namibia;

5. *Demands* that South Africa urgently comply fully and unconditionally with the resolutions of the Security Council, in particular resolutions 385(1976) and 435(1978) and subsequent resolutions of the Council relating to Namibia;

6. *Firmly rejects and condemns* the persistent attempts by the United States of America and South Africa to establish a linkage or parallelism between the independence of Namibia and any extraneous and irrelevant issues, in particular the presence of Cuban forces in Angola, and emphasizes unequivocally that all such attempts are designed to delay the decolonization process in Namibia and that they constitute interference in the internal affairs of Angola;

7. *Calls upon* all States to condemn and reject any attempt to link the independence of Namibia with extraneous and irrelevant issues;

8. *Expresses its dismay* at the fact that the Security Council has been prevented by its three Western permanent members from adopting effective measures against South Africa in the discharge of its responsibilities for the maintenance of international peace and security, and considers that comprehensive and mandatory sanctions under Chapter VII of the Charter of the United Nations, if universally and effectively implemented, would ensure South Africa's compliance with the decisions of the United Nations;

9. *Requests* the Security Council to exercise its authority with regard to the implementation of its resolutions 385(1976), 435(1978) and 532(1983) so as to bring about the independence of Namibia without further delay, and to act decisively against any dilatory manoeuvres and fraudulent schemes of the South African administration in Namibia aimed at frustrating the legitimate struggle of the Namibian people for independence;

10. *Urges* the Security Council to impose comprehensive mandatory sanctions against the racist régime of South Africa under Chapter VII of the Charter, in order to ensure the total cessation of all co-operation with that régime, particularly in the military and nuclear fields, by Governments, corporations, institutions and individuals;

11. *Requests* the Secretary-General to report to the General Assembly at its thirty-ninth session on the implementation of the present resolution.

General Assembly resolution 38/36 B

1 December 1983   Meeting 79   121-0-26 (recorded vote)

Draft by Council for Namibia (A/38/24); agenda item 36.
Financial implications. A/38/653.
Meeting numbers. GA 38th session: 5th Committee 52; plenary 72-79.

Recorded vote in Assembly as follows:

In favour: Afghanistan, Albania, Algeria, Angola, Antigua and Barbuda, Argentina, Bahamas, Bahrain, Bangladesh, Barbados, Belize, Benin, Bhutan, Bolivia, Botswana, Brazil, Bulgaria, Burma, Burundi, Byelorussian SSR, Cape Verde, Chile, China, Colombia, Comoros, Congo, Costa Rica, Cuba, Cyprus, Czechoslovakia, Democratic Kampuchea, Democratic Yemen, Djibouti, Dominican Republic, Ecuador, Egypt, El Salvador, Equatorial Guinea, Ethiopia, Fiji, Gabon, German Democratic Republic, Ghana, Greece, Guinea, Guinea-Bissau, Guyana, Haiti, Honduras, Hungary, India, Indonesia, Iran, Iraq, Jamaica, Jordan, Kenya, Kuwait, Lao People's Democratic Republic, Lebanon, Libyan Arab Jamahiriya, Madagascar, Malaysia, Maldives, Mali, Malta, Mauritania, Mauritius, Mexico, Mongolia, Morocco, Mozambique, Nepal, Nicaragua, Niger, Nigeria, Oman, Pakistan, Panama, Papua New Guinea, Peru, Philippines, Poland, Qatar, Romania, Rwanda, Saint Vincent and the Grenadines, Samoa, Sao Tome and Principe, Saudi Arabia, Senegal, Seychelles, Sierra Leone, Singapore, Solomon Islands, Sri Lanka, Sudan, Suriname, Swaziland, Syrian Arab Republic, Thailand, Togo, Trinidad and Tobago, Tunisia, Turkey, Uganda, Ukrainian SSR, USSR, United Arab Emirates, United Republic of Cameroon, United Republic of Tanzania, Upper Volta, Uruguay, Vanuatu, Venezuela, Viet Nam, Yemen, Yugoslavia, Zaire, Zambia, Zimbabwe.

Against: None.

Abstaining: Australia, Austria, Belgium, Canada, Central African Republic, Chad, Denmark, Finland, France, Germany, Federal Republic of, Iceland, Ireland, Italy, Ivory Coast, Japan, Luxembourg, Malawi, Netherlands, New Zealand, Norway, Portugal, Saint Lucia, Spain, Sweden, United Kingdom, United States.

In explanation of vote on the five resolutions on Namibia (38/36 A-E), many countries expressed general reservations which applied to all of them, as well as to specific texts. The Federal Republic of Germany, on behalf of the five members of the Western contact group, said they had reservations about certain aspects, and it had been their custom not to adopt a substantive position on texts on Namibia because of the group's involvement in formulating the United Nations settlement plan and subsequent negotiations aimed at its implementation. Speaking for the 10 member States of the European Community (EC), Greece said they regretted that in certain respects the texts did not take into consideration the on-going efforts to find a solution in accordance with Council resolution 435(1978),[5] implementation of which should not be delayed or made subject to preconditions; they believed that the United Nations had to encourage peaceful solutions and that no one should be designated in advance as the sole representative of the Namibians, reaffirmed their commitment to the Charter and the division of competences of United Nations organs, and rejected all arbitrary and unjustified attacks on individual Member States. With regard to paragraphs 26 and 27 of resolution 38/36 A, they explained that the resolution on development aid to Namibia, adopted by the European Parliament in January 1983, had been in keeping with the United Nations framework.

Australia, Austria, Japan, the Netherlands, Sweden (speaking also for Denmark, Finland, Iceland and Norway) and Uruguay had reservations about designating SWAPO as the sole representative of the Namibians prior to free elections; they did not want to associate themselves with the endorsement of armed struggle and opposed the selective condemnation of certain countries. The concept of armed struggle was also found unacceptable by Ireland, which pointed specifically to the twelfth preambular paragraph and paragraph 4 of resolution 38/36 A, and by New Zealand.

Selective singling out of States and groups of States drew further objections from Burma, Chad, Chile, Costa Rica, the Dominican Republic, Ecuador, Fiji, Honduras, Ireland, Maldives, New Zealand, Oman, Panama, Peru, Singapore, Sri Lanka, Togo and Turkey. In this regard, Turkey mentioned the eighteenth, twenty-first and twenty-fourth preambular paragraphs and paragraphs 14, 15, 25, 31, 33 and 42 of resolution 38/36 A, as well as the third preambular paragraph and paragraphs 6 and 8 of resolution 38/36 B. Botswana and Swaziland specifically expressed reservations on paragraph 57 of resolution 38/36 A which, Swaziland said, would prejudice its relations with the countries concerned; Botswana also had reservations on paragraph 10 of resolution 38/36 B.

Guatemala did not participate in the vote because of serious reservations on certain paragraphs. Reservations on many provisions were expressed by the Bahamas. Malta stated that it did not fully subscribe especially to those paragraphs with operative intent.

While supporting both resolutions, Greece noted that it would have abstained if a separate vote had been taken on the eighteenth, twenty-first and twenty-fourth preambular paragraphs and paragraphs 14, 15, 25, 26, 28, 31, 33 and 60 of resolution 38/36 A, as well as on the third preambular paragraph and paragraphs 3, 6 and 8 of resolution 38/36 B. Uruguay had reservations in particular on paragraphs 26, 27 and 43, and on similar concepts in other resolutions.

The language of some preambular and operative paragraphs of both resolutions 38/36 A and 38/36 B was variously described as extreme, excessive and categorical and was considered to be inappropriate by Austria, the Bahamas, Brazil, Burma, Chile, Ecuador, El Salvador, Ireland, the Ivory Coast, the Philippines and Singapore, while Turkey particularly disagreed with the wording of paragraph 14 of resolution 38/36 A as lacking balance. The Ivory Coast believed that the wording of certain paragraphs was not likely to facilitate a solution, an opinion shared by Brazil and others. Malawi had difficulties in endorsing the language in some paragraphs.

Commitment to the United Nations Charter and the division of competence between the General Assembly and Security Council was expressed by Chile, the Netherlands, Sweden (on behalf of the Nordic countries) and Uruguay, the last two stressing that only the Council could adopt decisions binding on Member States. Austria had strong reservations about the attempt to prejudge and influence the independent work of the Council.

Chile had reservations about the attempt to apply extreme measures, by which, it believed, the Assembly would infringe on the competence of the Council. Japan doubted the effectiveness of comprehensive mandatory sanctions against South Africa. Costa Rica said it had a different opinion about some of the proposed means of exerting pressure on South Africa. The Netherlands believed that selective measures against South Africa would be more effective than total isolation, which would bring hardship to the entire population of South Africa and its neighbouring States.

With regard to the reference to the International Monetary Fund (IMF) in paragraph 50, Chile expressed the view that IMF's autonomy precluded the Assembly's attempt to influence its decisions.

Uruguay said it would have expected a reference in the texts to the progress made in the negotiations between the front-line States, the Western contact group and SWAPO.

A number of other Assembly actions in 1983 were related to issues covered by the two resolutions. In resolution 38/17, the Assembly, reaffirming its condemnation of the illegal occupation of Namibia by South Africa, demanded the immediate implementation of its 1981 call[8] for comprehensive mandatory sanctions against South Africa and for the immediate start of unconditional implementation of Security Council resolution 435(1978), and urged support for the Namibians through their sole representative, SWAPO, in their struggle for independence. In resolution 38/21, it strongly condemned *apartheid* in South Africa and Namibia as the most abhorrent form of racial discrimination and urged Member States to adopt measures to eliminate that policy and to implement the relevant United Nations resolutions.

In resolution 38/50, the Assembly reiterated the illegality of the exploitation and plundering of Namibian natural resources by South Africa and other foreign economic interests, and condemned South Africa and Governments that continued to support economic interests exploiting Namibia's marine resources. It called on all States to end assistance to and discontinue all economic, financial and trade relations with South Africa concerning Namibia, terminate all loans and investments and prevent corporations from dealing in Namibian uranium. In resolution 38/54, the Assembly requested all States to withhold any assistance from South Africa and refrain from any action implying legitimization of its occupation of Namibia.

Noting the extremely serious situation in and around illegally occupied Namibia, the Assembly, in decision 38/419, condemned South Africa for its massive military build-up there and certain Western and other States for their continuing co-operation in that regard. It called on all States to prevent recruitment, training and transit of mercenaries for service in Namibia and demanded the immediate cessation of the racist minority régime's war of oppression against the people of Namibia and its national liberation movement, as well as the urgent dismantling of all military bases there. Noting that the militarization of Namibia had led to forced conscription of Namibians and a flow of refugees, the Assembly strongly condemned the forcible displacement of Namibians from their homes and declared that measures by the régime to enforce military conscription were null and void.

(For full texts, refer to INDEX OF RESOLUTIONS AND DECISIONS).

As requested by the Assembly in December 1982,[52] the Secretary-General submitted a report[53] in May 1983, with two later addenda in July and November containing replies from a total of 17 Governments with regard to action taken or envisaged by them in the implementation of the resolution.

Work programme of the UN Council for Namibia

In December, the General Assembly adopted resolution 38/36 C by recorded vote.

Programme of work of the United Nations Council for Namibia

The General Assembly,

Having examined the report of the United Nations Council for Namibia,

Reaffirming that Namibia is the direct responsibility of the United Nations and that the Namibian people must be enabled to attain self-determination and independence in a united Namibia,

Recalling its resolution 2248(S-V) of 19 May 1967, by which it established the United Nations Council for Namibia as the legal Administering Authority for Namibia until independence,

Taking into consideration the Paris Declaration on Namibia and the report of the Committee of the Whole and the Programme of Action on Namibia adopted at the International Conference in Support of the Struggle of the Namibian People for Independence,

Convinced of the need for continued consultations with the South West Africa People's Organization in the formulation and implementation of the programme of work of the United Nations Council for Namibia, as well as in any matter of interest to the Namibian people,

Deeply conscious of the urgent and continuing need to press for the termination of South Africa's illegal occupation of Namibia and to put an end to its repression of the Namibian people and its exploitation of the natural resources of the Territory,

1. *Approves* the report of the United Nations Council for Namibia, including the recommendations contained therein, and decides to make adequate financial provision for their implementation;

2. *Expresses its strong support* for the efforts of the United Nations Council for Namibia in the discharge of the responsibilities entrusted to it both as the legal Administering Authority for Namibia and as a policy-making organ of the United Nations;

3. *Requests* all Member States to co-operate fully with the United Nations Council for Namibia in the discharge of the mandate entrusted to it under the provisions of General Assembly resolution 2248(S-V) and subsequent resolutions of the Assembly;

4. *Decides* that the United Nations Council for Namibia, in the discharge of its responsibilities as the legal Administering Authority for Namibia until independence, shall:

(*a*) Continue to mobilize international support in order to press for the speedy withdrawal of the illegal South African administration from Namibia in accordance with the resolutions of the United Nations relating to Namibia;

(*b*) Counter the policies of South Africa against the Namibian people and against the United Nations, as well as against the United Nations Council for Namibia as the legal Administering Authority for Namibia;

(*c*) Denounce and seek the rejection by all States of all fraudulent constitutional or political schemes through which South Africa may attempt to perpetuate its presence in Namibia;

(*d*) Ensure non-recognition of any administration or entity installed at Windhoek not issuing from free elections in Namibia conducted under the supervision and control of the United Nations, in accordance with the relevant resolutions of the Security Council, in particular resolution 439(1978) of 13 November 1978;

(*e*) Undertake a concerted effort to counter the attempts to establish linkage or parallelism between the decolonization of Namibia and extraneous issues such as the withdrawal of Cuban forces from Angola;

5. *Decides* that the United Nations Council for Namibia shall:

(*a*) Consult Governments in order to further the implementation of United Nations resolutions on the question of Namibia and to mobilize support for the cause of Namibia;

(*b*) Represent Namibia in United Nations conferences and intergovernmental and non-governmental organizations, bodies and conferences to ensure that the rights and interests of Namibia shall be adequately protected;

6. *Decides* that Namibia, represented by the United Nations Council for Namibia, shall participate as a full member in all conferences and meetings organized by the United Nations to which all States, or, in the case of regional conferences and meetings, all African States are invited;

7. *Requests* all committees and other subsidiary bodies of the General Assembly and of the Economic and Social Council to continue to invite a representative of the United Nations Council for Namibia to participate whenever the rights and interests of Namibians are discussed, and to consult closely with the Council before submitting any draft resolution which may involve the rights and interests of Namibians;

8. *Reiterates its request* to all specialized agencies and other organizations and institutions of the United Nations system to grant full membership to Namibia, represented by the United Nations Council for Namibia, so that the Council may participate as the legal Administering Authority for Namibia in the work of those agencies, organizations and institutions;

9. *Reiterates its request* to all specialized agencies and other organizations of the United Nations system that have not yet done so to grant a waiver of the assessment of Namibia during the period in which it is represented by the United Nations Council for Namibia;

10. *Again requests* all intergovernmental organizations, bodies and conferences to ensure that the rights and interests of Namibia are protected and to invite Namibia, represented by the United Nations Council for Namibia, to participate as a full member whenever such rights and interests are involved;

11. *Takes note* of the ratification by the United Nations Council for Namibia of the United Nations Convention on the Law of the Sea;

12. *Takes note* of the accession by the United Nations Council for Namibia, in its capacity as legal Administering Authority for Namibia, to the Geneva Conventions of 12 August 1949 and the Additional Protocols thereto and requests the Council to accede to such other international conventions as it may deem appropriate;

13. *Takes note* of the signing by the United Nations Council for Namibia, in its capacity as the legal Administering Authority for Namibia, of the Final Act of the United Nations Conference on Succession of States in respect of State Property, Archives and Debts;

14. *Requests* the United Nations Council for Namibia to promote and secure the implementation of the Programme of Action for Namibia adopted at the International Conference in Support of the Struggle of the Namibian People for Independence;

15. *Decides* that the United Nations Council for Namibia shall:

(*a*) Review the progress of the liberation struggle in Namibia in its political, military and social aspects and prepare periodic reports related thereto;

(*b*) Consider the compliance of Member States with the relevant United Nations resolutions relating to Namibia, taking into account the advisory opinion of the International Court of Justice of 21 June 1971;

(*c*) Consider the activities of foreign economic interests operating in Namibia with a view to recommending appropriate policies to the General Assembly in order to counter the support which those foreign economic interests give to the illegal South African administration in Namibia;

(*d*) Continue to examine the exploitation of and trade in Namibian uranium by foreign economic interests and report on its findings to the General Assembly at its thirty-ninth session;

(*e*) Notify the Governments of States whose corporations, whether public or private, operate in Namibia of the illegality of such operations;

(*f*) Send missions of consultation to Governments of States whose corporations have investments in Namibia in order to review with them all possible action to discourage the continuation of such investments;

(*g*) Contact administering and managing bodies of foreign corporations operating in Namibia regarding the illegal basis on which they are operating in the Territory;

(*h*) Contact specialized agencies and international institutions associated with the United Nations, in particular the International Monetary Fund, with a view to protecting Namibia's interests;

(*i*) Draw the attention of the specialized agencies to Decree No. 1 for the Protection of the Natural Resources of Namibia, enacted by the United Nations Council for Namibia on 27 September 1974;

(*j*) Take all measures to ensure compliance with the provisions of Decree No. 1 for the Protection of the Natural Resources of Namibia, including consideration of the institution of legal proceedings in the domestic courts of States and other appropriate bodies;

(*k*) Undertake, in consultation with the South West Africa People's Organization, urgent consultations with the Commission of the European Communities and the European Parliament in order to ensure that no action is taken which implies recognition of South Africa's illegal administration in Namibia;

(*l*) Conduct hearings, seminars and workshops in order to obtain relevant information on the exploitation of the people and resources of Namibia by South African and other foreign interests and to expose such activities;

(*m*) Organize regional symposia on the situation in Namibia with a view to intensifying active support for the Namibian cause;

(*n*) Prepare and publish reports on the political, economic, military, legal and social situation in and relating to Namibia;

(*o*) Secure the territorial integrity of Namibia as a unitary State, including Walvis Bay and the offshore islands of Namibia;

16. *Decides* to make adequate financial provision in the section of the programme budget of the United Nations relating to the United Nations Council for Namibia to finance the office of the South West Africa People's Organization in New York in order to ensure appropriate representation of the people of Namibia at the United Nations through the South West Africa People's Organization;

17. *Decides* to continue to defray the expenses of representatives of the South West Africa People's Organization, whenever the United Nations Council for Namibia so decides;

18. *Requests* the United Nations Council for Namibia to continue to consult with the South West Africa People's Organization in the formulation and implementation of its programme of work, as well as in any matter of interest to the Namibian people;

19. *Requests* the United Nations Council for Namibia, in the discharge of its responsibilities as the legal Administering Authority for Namibia, to hold a series of plenary meetings in Asia during 1984 and to recommend appropriate action to the General Assembly in the light of South Africa's refusal to implement Security Council resolution 435(1978) of 29 September 1978;

20. *Requests* the Secretary-General to defray the cost of the plenary meetings of the United Nations Council for Namibia and to provide the necessary staff and services for them;

21. *Requests* the Secretary-General, in consultation with the President of the United Nations Council for Namibia, to review the requirements in personnel and facilities of all units which service the Council so that the Council may fully and effectively discharge all tasks and functions arising out of its mandate;

22. *Requests* the Secretary-General to provide the Office of the United Nations Commissioner for Namibia with the necessary resources in order for it to strengthen, under the guidance of the United Nations Council for Namibia, the assistance programmes and services for Namibians, the implementation of Decree No. 1 for the Protection of the Natural Resources of Namibia, the preparation of economic and legal studies and the existing activities of dissemination of information undertaken by that Office.

General Assembly resolution 38/36 C

1 December 1983   Meeting 79   144-0-5 (recorded vote)

Draft by Council for Namibia (A/38/24); agenda item 36.
Financial implications. Committee on Conferences, A/C.5/38/54Add.1; 5th Committee, A/38/653; SG, A/C.5/38/54 & Corr.1.
Meeting numbers. GA 38th session: 5th Committee, 52; plenary, 72-29.

Recorded vote in Assembly as follows:

In favour: Afghanistan, Albania, Algeria, Angola, Antigua and Barbuda, Argentina, Australia, Austria, Bahamas, Bahrain, Bangladesh, Barbados, Belgium, Belize, Benin, Bhutan, Bolivia, Botswana, Brazil, Bulgaria, Burma, Burundi, Byelorussian SSR, Cape Verde, Central African Republic, Chad, Chile, China, Colombia, Comoros, Congo, Costa Rica, Cuba, Cyprus, Czechoslovakia, Democratic Kampuchea, Democratic Yemen, Denmark, Djibouti, Dominican Republic, Ecuador, Egypt, El Salvador, Equatorial Guinea, Ethiopia, Fiji, Finland, Gabon, German Democratic Republic, Ghana, Greece, Guatemala, Guinea, Guinea-Bissau, Guyana, Haiti, Honduras, Hungary, Iceland, India, Indonesia, Iran, Iraq, Ireland, Italy, Ivory Coast, Jamaica, Japan, Jordan, Kenya, Kuwait, Lao People's Democratic Republic, Lebanon, Liberia, Libyan Arab Jamahiriya, Luxembourg, Madagascar, Malawi, Malaysia, Maldives, Mali, Malta, Mauritania, Mauritius, Mexico, Mongolia, Morocco, Mozambique, Nepal, Netherlands, New Zealand, Nicaragua, Niger, Nigeria, Norway, Oman, Pakistan, Panama, Papua New Guinea, Peru, Philippines, Poland, Portugal, Qatar, Romania, Rwanda, Saint Lucia, Saint Vincent and the Grenadines, Samoa, Sao Tome and Principe, Saudi Arabia, Senegal, Seychelles, Sierra Leone, Singapore, Solomon Islands, Spain, Sri Lanka, Sudan, Suriname, Swaziland, Sweden, Syrian Arab Republic, Thailand, Togo, Trinidad and Tobago, Tunisia, Turkey, Uganda, Ukrainian SSR, USSR, United Arab Emirates, United Republic of Cameroon, United Republic of Tanzania, Upper Volta, Uruguay, Vanuatu, Venezuela, Viet Nam, Yemen, Yugoslavia, Zaire, Zambia, Zimbabwe.
Against: None.
Abstaining: Canada, France, Germany, Federal Republic of, United Kingdom, United States.

In explanation of their votes, Australia, the Netherlands, New Zealand and Sweden, speaking also for Denmark, Finland, Iceland and Norway, expressed concern about the financial implications of resolution 38/36 C. Australia objected to the Council for Namibia holding plenary meetings away from Headquarters because it was not convinced that the considerable amount of money involved was spent to good advantage. New Zealand spoke similarly, while recognizing the Council as the legally-constituted administering body for Namibia. The Netherlands felt that conference facilities at Headquarters were more than adequate for the Council. Sweden said the Nordic countries had hesitations about some paragraphs containing sweeping financial implications as well as vaguely defined meeting proposals which might not always serve to promote the early independence of Namibia.

Brazil, Ireland and Oman had reservations about certain parts of the Council's 1983 report.[45] Affirming that the report fully justified the confidence vested in the Council by the international community, Brazil nevertheless expressed disappointment that the Council saw fit to refer to press reports in which Brazil was mentioned in the context of a North Atlantic Treaty Organization–style South Atlantic pact, thereby disregarding the Government's official denials. Oman believed that the Council's report was unbalanced because it condemned the dealings of certain groups of countries with South Africa whereas other countries belonging to various groups were not mentioned, even though they too had such dealings, the latest of which were within the framework of the Antarctic Treaty. While it generally supported the activities of the Council and many of its recommendations, Ireland had difficulties with some of them and had reservations about the powers of the Council in regard to certain issues. The Netherlands questioned the need to ensure for the Council the same rights and privileges in international organizations as were reserved for States, and expressed reservations about the Programme of Action adopted by the International Conference in Support of the Struggle of the Namibian People for Independence (see above).

Japan said its affirmative vote on resolution 38/36 C should not be construed as support for all paragraphs.

Information dissemination

In 1983, the Council for Namibia continued to disseminate information to Governments, institutions, NGOs and directly to the public, in order to inform and to mobilize world public opinion in support of independence for Namibia,[45] in accordance with a December 1982 General Assem-

bly request.[54] In this regard, the Council acted through its Standing Committee III, which worked closely with the Department of Public Information (DPI) of the Secretariat and NGOs, and consulted with DPI and the Department of Conference Services to guide them in their efforts.

The Council held its annual commemorations of Namibia Day on 26 August and of the Week of Solidarity with the People of Namibia and their Liberation Movement, SWAPO, on 27 October 1983,[46] at which United Nations officials and representatives of regional groups and organizations spoke. To highlight Namibia Day, the Council, in co-operation with the International Defence and Aid Fund for Southern Africa, organized an art exhibit depicting political prisoners in Namibia and South Africa, at United Nations Headquarters from 26 August to 15 September.

To mark the Week, the three presiding officers of the Council for Namibia, the Special Committee against *Apartheid* and the Special Committee on the Situation with regard to the Implementation of the Declaration on the Granting of Independence to Colonial Countries and Peoples (Committee on colonial countries) issued a joint statement to the effect that the only political and internationally acceptable solution for Namibia should be based on the termination of South Africa's illegal occupation and on the exercise by Namibians of their right to self-determination and independence within a united Namibia. They urged Member States to mobilize support for the peoples of southern Africa struggling for their rights by disseminating information on their cause. In particular, they requested preparation of publicity programmes to encourage support by all media operating under their jurisdiction.

The Council's activities included publicity for and at the International Conference in Support of the Struggle of the Namibian People for Independence (see above). In preparation for the Conference, the Council, with DPI assistance, produced a press kit, a brochure, a poster, a leaflet on the Council's activities and a pamphlet entitled "Namibia: A Unique United Nations Responsibility". Advertisements announcing the Conference were placed in *The Guardian* (Manchester), *Le Monde*, *The New York Times*, *The Times* (London) and *The Washington Post*. A journalists' encounter was held in Paris on 21 and 22 April, at which 40 journalists and media representatives from around the world participated. The television series *World Chronicle* produced a programme featuring the Secretary-General of the Conference. A background press release outlining the issues was widely disseminated, and daily press releases during the Conference were issued.

Additional funds were provided to 33 United Nations information centres for such special activities as organizing information sessions for NGO representatives, student groups and prominent personalities, and translating United Nations publications on Namibia into local languages. Radio coverage in Arabic, Chinese, English, French, Russian and Spanish included feature and magazine programmes, interviews, round-table discussions and excerpts of statements. Film recordings of the Conference were made by DPI for archival purposes and for later use. A total of 386 news releases in three languages were transmitted to the media through the information centres. Daily press briefings were held and special press conferences were organized for the public and NGOs. The Conference was covered by 187 accredited correspondents.

Apart from Conference-related activities, the Council carried out its regular information programme, publicizing its activities through press releases distributed at Headquarters and through the information centres. Material on Namibia was also made available to the centres and to the pool of non-aligned news agencies for dissemination to local media. Radio coverage was provided in Arabic, Chinese, English, French, Greek, Hebrew, Japanese, Pilipino, Portuguese, Russian, Somali, Spanish and Swahili. In addition, some 470 radio programmes were devoted entirely to Namibia, most of which were produced in the daily anti-*apartheid* series in Afrikaans, English, Sotho, Tswana, Xhosa and Zulu. DPI continued to provide film, television and photo coverage of the Council's activities, which was made available to news syndicators and other film producers.

As part of its programme of co-operation with NGOs, the Council, in consultation with SWAPO, made financial contributions to a number of NGOs for special activities to advance the cause of Namibia's independence. DPI held a special commemorative meeting for NGO representatives on 26 May to mark the Week of Solidarity with the Peoples of Namibia and All Other Colonial Territories, as well as those in South Africa, Fighting for Freedom, Independence and Human Rights (see p. 1029).

The Office of the United Nations Commissioner for Namibia assisted the Council in its activities and also disseminated information on the Council's work. It continued preparing the *Namibia Bulletin*, a quarterly review and analysis of events relating to Namibia published in English, French, German and Spanish, and *Namibia in the News*, a weekly newsletter. Both publications were widely distributed.

In a decision adopted on 13 October,[51] the Committee on colonial countries, noting the massive publicity campaign by South Africa to gain support for its occupation of Namibia, reiterated its request to the Secretary-General to intensify ef-

forts, through all available media, to mobilize world public opinion against that Government's policy on Namibia and to increase dissemination of information on the liberation struggle of the Namibian people under the leadership of SWAPO.

GENERAL ASSEMBLY ACTION

On 1 December 1983, the General Assembly adopted resolution 38/36 D by a recorded vote.

Dissemination of information and mobilization of international public opinion in support of Namibia

The General Assembly,

Having examined the report of the United Nations Council for Namibia and the relevant chapters of the report of the Special Committee on the Situation with Regard to the Implementation of the Declaration on the Granting of Independence to Colonial Countries and Peoples,

Recalling its resolutions 2145(XXI) of 27 October 1966, 2248(S-V) of 19 May 1967 and 37/233 of 20 December 1982, as well as all other resolutions of the General Assembly and the Security Council relating to Namibia,

Taking into consideration the Paris Declaration on Namibia and the report of the Committee of the Whole and the Programme of Action on Namibia adopted at the International Conference in Support of the Struggle of the Namibian People for Independence,

Taking into consideration also the conclusions and recommendations adopted at the Regional Symposium in Support of the Namibian Cause in Latin America, held at San José, from 16 to 19 August 1983,

Stressing the urgent need to mobilize international public opinion on a continuous basis with a view to assisting effectively the people of Namibia in the achievement of self-determination, freedom and independence in a united Namibia and, in particular, to intensify the worldwide and continuous dissemination of information on the struggle for liberation being waged by the people of Namibia under the leadership of the South West Africa People's Organization, their sole and authentic representative,

Recognizing the important role that non-governmental organizations are playing in the dissemination of information on Namibia and in the mobilization of international public opinion in support of the Namibian cause,

Reiterating the importance of publicity as an instrument for furthering the mandate given by the General Assembly to the United Nations Council for Namibia and mindful of the pressing need for the Department of Public Information of the Secretariat to intensify its efforts to acquaint world public opinion with all aspects of the question of Namibia, in accordance with policy guidelines formulated by the Council,

1. *Requests* the United Nations Council for Namibia, in pursuance of its international campaign in support of the struggle of the Namibian people for independence, to continue to consider ways and means of increasing the dissemination of information relating to Namibia;

2. *Requests* the Secretary-General to ensure that the Department of Public Information of the Secretariat, in all its activities of dissemination of information on the question of Namibia, follows the policy guidelines laid down by the United Nations Council for Namibia as the legal Administering Authority for Namibia;

3. *Requests* the Secretary-General to direct the Department of Public Information, in addition to its responsibilities relating to southern Africa, to assist, as a matter of priority, the United Nations Council for Namibia in the implementation of its programme of dissemination of information in order that the United Nations may intensify its efforts to generate publicity and disseminate information with a view to mobilizing public support for the independence of Namibia, particularly in the Western States;

4. *Decides* to intensify its international campaign in support of the cause of Namibia and to expose and denounce the collusion of the United States of America, certain other Western States and Israel with the South African racists and, to this end, requests the United Nations Council for Namibia to include in its programme of dissemination of information for 1984 the following activities:

(a) Preparation and dissemination of publications on the political, economic, military and social consequences of the illegal occupation of Namibia by South Africa, as well as on legal matters, on the question of the territorial integrity of Namibia and on contacts between Member States and South Africa;

(b) Production and dissemination of radio programmes in English, French, German and Spanish designed to draw the attention of world public opinion to the current situation in Namibia;

(c) Production of material for publicity through radio and television broadcasts;

(d) Placement of advertisements in newspapers and magazines;

(e) Production of films, film-strips and slide sets on Namibia;

(f) Production and dissemination of posters;

(g) Full utilization of the resources related to press releases, press conferences and press briefings in order to maintain a constant flow of information to the public on all aspects of the question of Namibia;

(h) Production and dissemination of a comprehensive economic map of Namibia;

(i) Preparation and wide dissemination of a booklet containing resolutions of the General Assembly and the Security Council relating to Namibia, together with relevant portions of Assembly resolutions on the activities of foreign economic interests in Namibia and on military activities in Namibia;

(j) Publicity for and distribution of an indexed reference book on transnational corporations involved in Namibia;

(k) Preparation and dissemination of a booklet based on a study on the implementation of Decree No. 1 for the Protection of the Natural Resources of Namibia, enacted by the Council on 27 September 1974;

(l) Acquisition of books, pamphlets and other materials relating to Namibia for further dissemination;

5. *Requests* the United Nations Council for Namibia to organize a symposium to be held at United Nations Headquarters in 1984 with the participation of prominent personalities, scholars, support groups, media personalities and others from all parts of the world, in order to mark the one hundredth anniversary of the heroic struggle of the Namibian people against colonial occupation and the plunder of the natural resources of their country and for self-determination, freedom and independence, and to draw the attention of the world public, particularly in the Western countries, to the question of Namibia, with a view to further mobilizing international support for the just struggle of the Namibian people under the leadership of the South West Africa People's Organization, their sole and authentic representative, to bring about the speedy independence of Namibia;

6. *Requests* the Secretary-General to allocate, in consultation with the United Nations Council for Namibia, sales numbers to publications on Namibia selected by the Council;

7. *Requests* the Secretary-General to provide the United Nations Council for Namibia with the work programme of the Department of Public Information for the year 1984 covering the activities of dissemination of information on Namibia, followed by periodic reports on the programmes undertaken, including details of expenses incurred;

8. *Requests* the Secretary-General to group under a single heading, in the section of the proposed programme budget of the United Nations for the biennium 1984-1985 relating to the Department of Public Information, all the activities of the Department relating to the dissemination of information on Namibia;

9. *Requests* the Secretary-General to direct that the United Nations Day students' leaflet for 1984 be devoted to the question of Namibia;

10. *Requests* Member States to broadcast programmes on their national radio and television networks and to publish material in their official news media, informing their populations about the situation in Namibia and the obligation of Governments and peoples to assist in the struggle of Namibians for independence;

11. *Requests* the United Nations Council for Namibia, in co-operation with the Department of Public Information and the Department of Conference Services of the Secretariat, to continue to inform and provide information material to leading opinion makers, media leaders, academic institutions, trade unions, cultural organizations, support groups and other concerned persons and non-governmental organizations about the objectives and functions of the United Nations Council for Namibia and the struggle of the Namibian people under the leadership of the South West Africa People's Organization and also to hold consultations with, and seek the co-operation of, those personalities and institutions by inviting them on special occasions to participate in the deliberations of the Council, and to establish for this purpose a regular and expeditious pattern of distribution of information material to political parties, universities, libraries, churches, students, teachers, professional associations and others falling into the general categories enumerated above;

12. *Requests* all Member States to commemorate and publicize Namibia Day and to issue special postage stamps for the occasion;

13. *Requests* the Secretary-General to direct the United Nations Postal Administration to issue a special postage stamp on Namibia by the end of 1984 in commemoration of Namibia Day;

14. *Calls upon* the United Nations Council for Namibia to enlist the support of non-governmental organizations in its efforts to mobilize international public opinion in support of the liberation struggle of the Namibian people and of their sole and authentic

representative, the South West Africa People's Organization;

15. *Requests* the United Nations Council for Namibia to prepare, update and continually disseminate lists of non-governmental organizations from all over the world, in particular those in the major Western States, in order to ensure better co-operation and co-ordination among non-governmental organizations working in support of the Namibian cause and against *apartheid*;

16. *Requests* those non-governmental organizations and support groups that are actively engaged in supporting the struggle of the Namibian people under the leadership of the South West Africa People's Organization, their sole and authentic representative, to continue to intensify, in co-operation with the United Nations Council for Namibia, international action in support of the liberation struggle of the Namibian people, including assistance to the Council in the monitoring of the boycott of South Africa called for in General Assembly resolution ES-8/2 of 14 September 1981;

17. *Decides* to allocate the sum of $300,000 to be used by the United Nations Council for Namibia for its programme of co-operation with non-governmental organizations, including support to conferences in solidarity with Namibia arranged by those organizations, dissemination of conclusions of such conferences and support to such other activities as will promote the cause of the liberation struggle of the Namibian people, subject to decisions of the Council in each individual case on the recommendation of the South West Africa People's Organization.

General Assembly resolution 38/36 D

1 December 1983　　　Meeting 79　　　122-0-22 (recorded vote)

Draft by Council for Namibia (A/38/24); agenda item 36.
Financial implications. Committee on Conferences, A/C.5/38/54/Add.1; 5th Committee, A/38/653; S-G, A/C.5/38/54.
Meeting numbers. GA 38th session: 5th Committee 52; plenary 72-79.

Recorded vote in Assembly as follows:

In favour: Afghanistan, Albania, Algeria, Angola, Antigua and Barbuda, Argentina, Bahamas, Bahrain, Bangladesh, Barbados, Belize, Benin, Bhutan, Bolivia, Botswana, Brazil, Bulgaria, Burma, Burundi, Byelorussian SSR, Cape Verde, Chile, China, Colombia, Comoros, Congo, Costa Rica, Cuba, Cyprus, Czechoslovakia, Democratic Kampuchea, Democratic Yemen, Djibouti, Dominican Republic, Ecuador, Egypt, El Salvador, Equatorial Guinea, Ethiopia, Fiji, Gabon, German Democratic Republic, Ghana, Greece, Guinea, Guinea-Bissau, Guyana, Haiti, Honduras, Hungary, India, Indonesia, Iran, Iraq, Ivory Coast, Jamaica, Jordan, Kenya, Kuwait, Lao People's Democratic Republic, Lebanon, Libyan Arab Jamahiriya, Madagascar, Malawi, Malaysia, Maldives, Mali, Malta, Mauritania, Mauritius, Mexico, Mongolia, Morocco, Mozambique, Nepal, Nicaragua, Niger, Nigeria, Oman, Pakistan, Panama, Papua New Guinea, Peru, Philippines, Poland, Qatar, Romania, Rwanda, Saint Lucia, Saint Vincent and the Grenadines, Sao Tome and Principe, Saudi Arabia, Senegal, Seychelles, Sierra Leone, Singapore, Sri Lanka, Sudan, Suriname, Swaziland, Syrian Arab Republic, Thailand, Togo, Trinidad and Tobago, Tunisia, Turkey, Uganda, Ukrainian SSR, USSR, United Arab Emirates, United Republic of Cameroon, United Republic of Tanzania, Upper Volta, Uruguay, Vanuatu, Venezuela, Viet Nam, Yemen, Yugoslavia, Zaire, Zambia, Zimbabwe.

Against: None.

Abstaining: Australia, Austria, Belgium, Canada, Chad, Denmark, Finland, France, Germany, Federal Republic of, Iceland, Ireland, Italy, Japan, Luxembourg, Netherlands, New Zealand, Norway, Portugal, Spain, Sweden, United Kingdom, United States.

In explanation of their votes on resolution 38/36 D, a number of countries expressed reservations in addition to general reservations on the five resolutions on Namibia (38/36 A-E). Most of those countries objected to the specific mention of certain States as in paragraph 4. Austria, Chad,

Greece, Ireland, the Ivory Coast, Japan, the Netherlands, New Zealand, Portugal, Sri Lanka and Turkey made such comments.

Austria did not believe that the arbitrary singling out of certain States for condemnation was either justified or advanced the legitimate interests of the Namibians. Chad stated that such selective condemnation was not likely to facilitate a solution. Similarly, Ireland believed that while it was important for the Council for Namibia to consider ways of mobilizing public opinion in support of the struggle of the Namibians for independence, it objected to paragraph 4 on the grounds that an intensified campaign to expose the collusion of certain Western countries with South Africa would be harmful to the pursuit of common objectives.

Objecting to what it called extravagant assertions about the policies of certain countries, New Zealand said such provisions were not well calculated to reinforce efforts to overcome the final impediments to the implementation of the United Nations settlement plan. The Netherlands feared that if the entire effort of the Council in the field of information was harnessed to a campaign of defamation against certain States, the Council's ability to contribute to Namibia's early and peaceful attainment of independence would inevitably suffer. Portugal was not able to support the resolution because of the language in some of its provisions and because of discriminatory references to certain countries. Sri Lanka would have preferred to have avoided specific condemnation of countries with which it had diplomatic relations.

Greece said if a separate vote had been taken on paragraph 4, it would have abstained because of the wording and because of some elements of the content. The Ivory Coast expressed reservations with regard to paragraph 4, particularly subparagraph 4(*a*).

Japan, attaching importance to the dissemination of information on Namibia, believed that such information must be accurate, fair and balanced, and that close co-operation must be maintained between the Council for Namibia and DPI to ensure that DPI facilities were used effectively and information disseminated in a co-ordinated manner.

Austria and New Zealand were concerned about the financial implications of some of the proposed activities.

Guatemala did not participate in the voting because of serious reservations on certain paragraphs.

In resolution 38/51, the Assembly requested the Secretary-General to continue, through DPI, a broad campaign to inform world public opinion, with respect to Namibia, of the facts concerning the support of the South African régime by foreign monopolies.

UN Commissioner for Namibia

Activities of the Commissioner

In 1983, the Office of the United Nations Commissioner for Namibia continued to collect and analyse information on Namibia and followed internal political, economic and legal developments in South Africa concerning the Territory.[45] It continued to administer assistance programmes for Namibians under the United Nations Fund for Namibia (see below), composed of the General Account, the Nationhood Programme for Namibia and the United Nations Institute for Namibia. It prepared project proposals for consideration by the Fund's Committee and reported on activities financed from the General Account. In addition, the Commissioner participated in several fund-raising missions for the Fund (see below, under INTERNATIONAL ASSISTANCE). Under the Nationhood Programme, consultants were recruited for various sectoral survey projects, and trainees were selected for fellowships. Two consultants were engaged to prepare a document on all aspects of economic planning in an independent Namibia. As in previous years, the Office renewed or issued travel and identity documents to Namibians in Africa and other parts of the world.

To secure universal implementation of the 1974 Decree for the protection of Namibia's natural resources,[11] the Commissioner's Office undertook consultations with Belgium, France, the Federal Republic of Germany, Japan, the United Kingdom and the United States, which indicated, however, that they had not banned trade with Namibia. The Office subsequently engaged lawyers in Belgium, France, the Netherlands, the United Kingdom and the United States to determine the feasibility of instituting legal proceedings in domestic courts against firms or individuals engaged in trade in Namibian products in violation of the Decree.

The Office was preparing a study on transnational corporations (TNCs) operating or investing in Namibia, as requested by the General Assembly in December 1982.[1] The study was to identify the commercial and investment practices of foreign companies and the extent of their exploitation of Namibian resources, and to recommend future action by the Council for Namibia. The first draft of the section on North American companies was completed and sections on Western European and South African companies were planned. A study on assistance to the front-line States was also in preparation, as was a demographic study of the Namibia population that would analyse socio-economic characteristics and make growth projections.

The regional Office of the Commissioner at Luanda, Angola, which opened in August 1982,[55]

became fully operational on 21 January 1983. It served as the liaison between the New York office and the provisional headquarters of SWAPO in Luanda, and assumed new responsibilities when 21 projects were transferred to it from the regional office at Lusaka, Zambia. The Luanda office facilitated the work of a consultant conducting a workshop for Namibian broadcasters and assisted in placing some 100 Namibians in training programmes in various countries. It worked with United Nations bodies in co-ordinating assistance programmes for Namibians in Angola. The regional office at Lusaka served as a centre for political and informational activities, as well as an administrative office for assistance programmes of the Fund for Namibia, providing support to executing agencies and consultants associated with 26 projects remaining in Lusaka. The Lusaka office also co-ordinated placement of Namibians in training programmes in various countries and participated in seminars on health training, TNCs, mineral development and telecommunications planning. Similarly, the office at Gabarone, Botswana, maintained contacts with the host Government, SWAPO and United Nations organizations concerning assistance to Namibian refugees. It made periodic visits to refugee settlements to assess the needs of Namibians, assisted in placing Namibians in educational institutions and helped administer other Fund projects.

Appointment of the Commissioner

The Secretary-General, by a note of 28 November 1983,[56] proposed to the General Assembly that it extend the appointment of Brajesh Chandra Mishra as United Nations Commissioner for Namibia for a one-year term beginning on 1 January 1984. Mr. Mishra had served in that capacity since his appointment on 1 April 1982.[57]

GENERAL ASSEMBLY ACTION

The General Assembly acted on the Secretary-General's recommendation by adopting decision 38/312 without vote.

Appointment of the United Nations Commissioner for Namibia

At its 79th plenary meeting, on 1 December 1983, the General Assembly, on the proposal of the Secretary-General, appointed Mr. Brajesh Chandra Mishra as United Nations Commissioner for Namibia for a further one-year term beginning on 1 January 1984.

General Assembly decision 38/312

Adopted without vote

Proposal by Secretary-General (A/38/614); agenda item 17 *(g)*.
Meeting number. GA 38th session: plenary 79.

REFERENCES
(1)YUN 1982, p. 1304, GA res. 37/233 C, 20 Dec. 1982. (2)A/CONF.120/13. (3)A/38/189-S/15757. (4)YUN 1977, p. 706.

(5)YUN 1978, p. 915, SC res. 435(1978), 29 Sep. 1978. (6)YUN 1976, p. 782, SC res. 385(1976), 30 Jan. 1976. (7)YUN 1977, p. 162, SC res. 421(1977), 9 Dec. 1977. (8)YUN 1981, p. 1153, GA res. ES-8/2, 14 Dec. 1981. (9)*Ibid.*, p. 1157, GA res. 36/121 B, 10 Sep. 1981. (10)YUN 1982, p. 1300, GA res. 37/233 A, 20 Dec. 1982. (11)YUN 1974, p. 152. (12)S/15733. (13)A/38/169-S/15737. (14)S/15776. (15)YUN 1978, p. 916, SC res. 439(1978), 13 Nov. 1978. (16)YUN 1982, p. 1292. (17)S/15760. (18)S/15761. (19)A/38/132-S/15675. (20)S/15779. (21)S/15790. (22)S/15799. (23)S/15800. (24)S/15792. (25)YUN 1971, p. 560, SC res. 301(1971), 20 Oct. 1971. (26)S/15781. (27)S/15784. (28)S/15795. (29)S/15807. (30)S/15811. (31)S/15791. (32)A/38/332-S/15917. (33)S/15943. (34)S/16048. (35)S/16051. (36)S/16055. (37)S/16064. (38)S/16081. (39)S/16050. (40)S/16056. (41)S/16106. (42)S/16219. (43)S/16237. (44)YUN 1967, p. 709, GA res. 2248(S-V), sect. II, 19 May 1967. (45)A/38/24. (46)A/39/24. (47)YUN 1982, p. 1304, GA res. 37/233 C, 20 Dec. 1982. (48)A/38/312. (49)A/38/132-S/15675. (50)A/38/495-S/16035. (51)A/38/23 (dec. A/AC.109/760). (52)YUN 1982, p. 1300, GA res. 37/233 A, 20 Dec. 1982. (53)A/38/183 & Add.1,2. (54)YUN 1982, p. 1307, GA res. 37/233 D, 20 Dec. 1982. (55)*Ibid.*, p. 1310. (56)A/38/614. (57)YUN 1982, p. 1310, GA dec. 36/325, 29 Mar. 1982.

International assistance

United Nations assistance to Namibia continued during 1983 mainly through the United Nations Institute for Namibia and the Nationhood Programme for Namibia, both of which received financing from the United Nations Fund for Namibia and the United Nations Development Programme (UNDP).

In December, the General Assembly outlined the work of the United Nations Council for Namibia in respect of the Fund, the Institute and the Nationhood Programme, called for increased support for the Fund and allocated $1 million to it for 1984 from the Organization's regular budget (resolution 38/36 E).

The International Conference in Support of the Struggle of the Namibian People for Independence, in adopting the Paris Declaration on Namibia,[1] also called for increased international assistance for the Namibian people and to the front-line States (see above). The Conference stated that the United Nations and the international community had to take energetic and concerted action in support of the Namibian people's struggle for self-determination, freedom and national independence. In its Programme of Action on Namibia, the Conference called on the United Nations system to initiate a major programme of assistance to the front-line States enabling them to implement more effectively United Nations resolutions supporting the Namibian people's struggle for liberation and to withstand the economic sabotage perpetrated against them by South Africa. Governments were asked to make or increase their contribution to the Fund (see below) in order to assist the Nationhood Programme and the Institute in formulating and implementing projects in support of the Namibian people.

The Special Committee on the Situation with regard to the Implementation of the Declaration on the Granting of Independence to Colonial Countries and Peoples (Committee on colonial countries), in a 14 September resolution,[2] expressed concern that assistance extended by certain specialized agencies and other United Nations organizations to colonial peoples—particularly the people of Namibia and their national liberation movement, the South West Africa People's Organization (SWAPO)—was far from adequate in relation to their needs (see Chapter I of this section).

The Committee noted with satisfaction that SWAPO continued to benefit from programmes established within the framework of the Institute and that the Council for Namibia, in co-operation with SWAPO, continued to represent the people of Namibia at United Nations meetings. Specialized agencies and other United Nations organizations were urged to increase assistance to SWAPO and to the Institute and the Nationhood Programme, and to extend material assistance to the front-line States.

In an October report,[3] submitted to the Assembly in pursuance of its December 1982 request,[4] the Secretary-General, who had been asked to develop a comprehensive programme of assistance to States bordering Namibia and South Africa to enable them to move towards complete self-reliance, noted that the beginning elements of such a programme were available in the national development plans of those States and in the projects being developed under the Southern African Development Co-ordination Conference (see p. 170); he therefore considered that additional international assistance to ensure their implementation would represent the most realistic approach to the type of assistance envisaged by the Assembly.

GENERAL ASSEMBLY ACTION

In 1983, the General Assembly called for assistance to the Namibians in two resolutions adopted on 7 December (see Chapter I of this section).

By resolution 38/51, it requested United Nations organizations to withhold from South Africa any financial, economic or technical co-operation and assistance until the Namibian people had exercised their right to self-determination and *apartheid* had been totally eradicated. They should also refrain from taking action implying recognition of the legitimacy of or support for South Africa's domination of Namibia. The Assembly again called for increased assistance by those organizations to SWAPO, the Institute and the Nationhood Programme.

By resolution 38/54, the Assembly urged all States, directly and through action in United Nations bodies, to provide moral and material assistance to the oppressed people of Namibia.

Further, the Assembly, by resolution 38/36 A of 1 December, called on Member States and United Nations organizations to increase support and material, financial, military and other assistance to SWAPO to enable it to intensify its struggle for Namibia's liberation. The Assembly declared that implementation of a resolution on the need for development aid to Namibia, adopted by the European Parliament on 13 January, calling on the European Economic Community (EEC) to extend aid to occupied Namibia, as well as to so-called "refugees from southern Angola" in Namibia, would flout international law by implying recognition of South Africa's presence in Namibia and would subsidize Pretoria's illegal administration of the Territory, while encouraging its acts of aggression against Angola and the occupation of a part of Angolan territory. The Assembly noted the 14 November declaration of the European Parliament concerning the January resolution, and a 15 November letter from the President of the Parliament to the Secretary-General underlining that the Parliament and the European Community supported and respected the framework established by the United Nations in respect of Namibia.

By resolution 38/36 C, also of 1 December, the Assembly decided to make adequate financial provision in the United Nations programme budget to finance the SWAPO office in New York to ensure appropriate representation of the Namibian people at the United Nations, and agreed to continue to defray the expenses of SWAPO representatives whenever the Council for Namibia so decided.

UN Fund for Namibia

Activities of the Fund

The United Nations Council for Namibia reported[1] that the United Nations Fund for Namibia, which became operative in 1972[5] and for which the Council was trustee, continued to serve in 1983 as the main vehicle through which the Council channelled its assistance. The Fund financed three main programmes: the United Nations Institute for Namibia (see below); the Nationhood Programme for Namibia (see below); and educational, social and relief assistance to Namibians.

While the first two programmes were set up with particular reference to the future attainment of independence, the establishment of State machinery and the assumption of administrative responsibilities by Namibians, the third programme emphasized their immediate needs and welfare. This programme was administered by the Office of the United Nations Commissioner for Namibia and financed from the Fund's General Account.

Under the scholarship programme, during the period 1 July 1982 to 30 June 1983, 49 new awards

were made and 26 students completed their courses. As of 1 July, 126 awards were being used for various fields of study in 13 countries. In accordance with a December 1982 General Assembly resolution,[6] requesting a study of the Namibian population's educational needs, a consultant was engaged to evaluate the scholarships awarded under the Fund in order to increase their effectiveness. The General Account financed training projects in broadcasting, cinematography and video techniques, journalism and communications, and vocational training. In addition, individual scholarships were provided to 28 Institute graduates and educational materials were provided to Namibian students in SWAPO schools. Individual Namibians in need received emergency medical treatment and other forms of humanitarian assistance.

Fund expenditures for the three programmes in 1983 were: $2,143,192 for the Nationhood Programme; $4,310,471 for the Institute; and $2,332,769 for educational, social and relief assistance.

GENERAL ASSEMBLY ACTION

On 1 December, on the recommendation of the Council for Namibia, the General Assembly adopted by recorded vote resolution 38/36 E.

United Nations Fund for Namibia

The General Assembly,

Having examined the parts of the report of the United Nations Council for Namibia relating to the United Nations Fund for Namibia,

Recalling its resolution 2679(XXV) of 9 December 1970, by which it established the United Nations Fund for Namibia,

Recalling also its resolution 3112(XXVIII) of 12 December 1973, by which it appointed the United Nations Council for Namibia trustee of the United Nations Fund for Namibia,

Recalling its resolution 31/153 of 20 December 1976, by which it decided to launch the Nationhood Programme for Namibia,

Recalling further its resolution 34/92 A of 12 December 1979, by which it approved the Charter of the United Nations Institute for Namibia, and resolution 37/233 E of 20 December 1982, by which it approved amendments to the Charter,

1. *Takes note* of the relevant parts of the report of the United Nations Council for Namibia;

2. *Decides* that the United Nations Council for Namibia shall:

(a) Continue to formulate policies of assistance to Namibians and co-ordinate assistance for Namibia provided by the specialized agencies and other organizations and institutions of the United Nations system;

(b) Continue to act as trustee of the United Nations Fund for Namibia and, in this capacity, administer and manage the Fund;

(c) Continue to provide broad guidelines and formulate principles and policies for the United Nations Institute for Namibia;

(d) Continue to co-ordinate, plan and direct the Nationhood Programme for Namibia in consultation with the South West Africa People's Organization, with the aim of consolidating all measures of assistance by the specialized agencies and other organizations and institutions of the United Nations system into a comprehensive assistance programme;

(e) Continue to consult with the South West Africa People's Organization in the formulation and implementation of assistance programmes for Namibians;

(f) Report to the General Assembly at its thirty-ninth session on activities in respect of the United Nations Fund for Namibia, the United Nations Institute for Namibia and the Nationhood Programme for Namibia;

3. *Decides* that the United Nations Fund for Namibia, including the Trust Funds for the Nationhood Programme for Namibia and the United Nations Institute for Namibia, shall be the primary source of assistance to Namibians;

4. *Expresses its appreciation* to all States, specialized agencies and other organizations of the United Nations system, governmental and non-governmental organizations and individuals that have made voluntary contributions to the United Nations Fund for Namibia, the United Nations Institute for Namibia and the Nationhood Programme for Namibia, and calls upon them to increase their assistance to Namibians through those channels;

5. *Decides* to allocate as a temporary measure to the United Nations Fund for Namibia the sum of $1 million from the regular budget of the United Nations for 1984;

6. *Requests* the Secretary-General and the President of the United Nations Council for Namibia to intensify appeals to Governments, intergovernmental and non-governmental organizations and individuals for generous voluntary contributions to the General Account of the United Nations Fund for Namibia and to the Trust Funds for the Nationhood Programme for Namibia and the United Nations Institute for Namibia and, in this connection, emphasizes the need for contributions in order to increase the number of scholarships awarded to Namibians under the United Nations Fund for Namibia;

7. *Invites* Governments to appeal once more to their national organizations and institutions for voluntary contributions to the United Nations Fund for Namibia;

8. *Urges* the organizations of the United Nations system to waive agency support costs in respect of projects in favour of Namibians financed from the United Nations Fund for Namibia and other sources; and in cases where such costs cannot be waived, urges the organizations to treat contributions from the United Nations Fund for Namibia as government cash counterpart contributions in accordance with decision 83/10 B of 24 June 1983 of the Governing Council of the United Nations Development Programme;

9. *Commends* the progress made in the implementation of the pre-independence components of the Nationhood Programme for Namibia and requests the United Nations Council for Namibia to elaborate and consider in due course policies and contingency plans regarding the transitional and post-independence phases of the Programme;

10. *Commends* the United Nations Institute for Namibia for the effectiveness of its training programmes for Namibians and its research activities on Namibia, which contribute substantially to the struggle for freedom of the Namibian people and to the establishment of an independent State of Namibia;

11. *Requests* the specialized agencies and other organizations and institutions of the United Nations system, when planning and initiating their new measures of assistance to Namibians, to do so within the context of the Nationhood Programme for Namibia and the United Nations Institute for Namibia;

12. *Expresses its appreciation* to those specialized agencies and other organizations and institutions of the United Nations system that have contributed to the Nationhood Programme for Namibia and calls upon them to continue their participation in the Programme by:

(a) Implementing projects approved by the United Nations Council for Namibia;

(b) Preparing new project proposals at the request of the Council;

(c) Allocating funds from their own financial resources for the implementation of the projects approved by the Council;

13. *Requests* the specialized agencies and other organizations and institutions of the United Nations system, in the light of the urgent need to strengthen the programme of assistance to the Namibian people, to make every effort to expedite the execution of Nationhood Programme for Namibia projects and other projects in favour of Namibians and to execute those projects on the basis of procedures which will reflect the role of the United Nations Council for Namibia as the legal Administering Authority for Namibia;

14. *Requests* the United Nations Council for Namibia to complete the preparation of and publish at an early date, through the United Nations Institute for Namibia, a comprehensive reference book on Namibia covering aspects of the question of Namibia as considered by the United Nations since its inception, in accordance with the outline prepared by the Council;

15. *Requests* the United Nations Institute for Namibia to complete the preparation, in co-operation with the South West Africa People's Organization, the Office of the United Nations Commissioner for Namibia and the United Nations Development Programme, of a comprehensive document on all aspects of economic planning in an independent Namibia, and requests the Secretary-General to provide substantive support through the Office of the Commissioner for the preparation of that document;

16. *Requests* the United Nations Council for Namibia to complete the preparation of and publish at an early date, in consultation with the Office of the United Nations Commissioner for Namibia, a demographic study of the Namibian population and a study of its educational needs;

17. *Urges* the specialized agencies and other organizations and institutions of the United Nations system to co-operate closely with the United Nations Institute for Namibia in strengthening its programme of activities;

18. *Expresses its appreciation* to the United Nations Development Programme for its contribution to the financing and administration of the Nationhood Programme for Namibia and the financing of the United Nations Institute for Namibia and calls upon it to continue to allocate, at the request of the United Nations Council

for Namibia, funds from the indicative planning figure for Namibia for the implementation of the projects within the Nationhood Programme and for the United Nations Institute for Namibia;

19. *Calls upon* the United Nations Development Programme to raise the indicative planning figure for Namibia;

20. *Expresses its appreciation* for the efforts of the United Nations High Commissioner for Refugees to assist Namibian refugees and requests him to expand those efforts in view of the substantial increase in the number of Namibian refugees;

21. *Decides* that Namibians shall continue to be eligible for assistance through the United Nations Educational and Training Programme for Southern Africa and the United Nations Trust Fund for South Africa;

22. *Requests* the Secretary-General to continue to provide the Office of the United Nations Commissioner for Namibia with the necessary resources for the performance of the responsibilities entrusted to it by the United Nations Council for Namibia as the co-ordinating authority for the implementation of the Nationhood Programme for Namibia, as well as other assistance programmes.

General Assembly resolution 38/36 E

1 December 1983   Meeting 79   144-0-5 (recorded vote)

Draft by Council for Namibia (A/38/24); agenda item 36.
Financial implications. 5th Committee, A/38/653; S-G, A/C.5/38/54 & Corr.1.
Meeting numbers. GA 38th session: 5th Committee 52; plenary 72, 74-79.

Recorded vote in Assembly as follows:

In favour: Afghanistan, Albania, Algeria, Angola, Antigua and Barbuda, Argentina, Australia, Austria, Bahamas, Bahrain, Bangladesh, Barbados, Belgium, Belize, Benin, Bhutan, Bolivia, Botswana, Brazil, Bulgaria, Burma, Burundi, Byelorussian SSR, Cape Verde, Central African Republic, Chad, Chile, China, Colombia, Comoros, Congo, Costa Rica, Cuba, Cyprus, Czechoslovakia, Democratic Kampuchea, Democratic Yemen, Denmark, Djibouti, Dominican Republic, Ecuador, Egypt, El Salvador, Equatorial Guinea, Ethiopia, Fiji, Finland, Gabon, German Democratic Republic, Ghana, Greece, Guatemala, Guinea, Guinea-Bissau, Guyana, Haiti, Honduras, Hungary, Iceland, India, Indonesia, Iran, Iraq, Ireland, Italy, Ivory Coast, Jamaica, Japan, Jordan, Kenya, Kuwait, Lao People's Democratic Republic, Lebanon, Liberia, Libyan Arab Jamahiriya, Luxembourg, Madagascar, Malawi, Malaysia, Maldives, Mali, Malta, Mauritania, Mauritius, Mexico, Mongolia, Morocco, Mozambique, Nepal, Netherlands, New Zealand, Nicaragua, Niger, Nigeria, Norway, Oman, Pakistan, Panama, Papua New Guinea, Peru, Philippines, Poland, Portugal, Qatar, Romania, Rwanda, Saint Lucia, Saint Vincent and the Grenadines, Samoa, Sao Tome and Principe, Saudi Arabia, Senegal, Seychelles, Sierra Leone, Singapore, Solomon Islands, Spain, Sri Lanka, Sudan, Suriname, Swaziland, Sweden, Syrian Arab Republic, Thailand, Togo, Trinidad and Tobago, Tunisia, Turkey, Uganda, Ukrainian SSR, USSR, United Arab Emirates, United Republic of Cameroon, United Republic of Tanzania, Upper Volta, Uruguay, Vanuatu, Venezuela, Viet Nam, Yemen, Yugoslavia, Zaire, Zambia, Zimbabwe.

Against: None.

Abstaining: Canada, France, Germany, Federal Republic of, United Kingdom, United States.

Japan recalled that the Fund had been established on a voluntary basis and said it had reservations with regard to allocating $1 million from the regular budget. Sweden, on behalf of the five Nordic countries, said they, too, had reservations about sweeping financial implications, a point also raised by Austria. New Zealand also had reservations on certain aspects of the text.

Most of the other States which spoke in explanation of vote indicated their position on resolution 38/36 E when they spoke on all the resolutions (38/36 A-E) adopted concerning Namibia (see above).

Financing of the Fund

In 1983, 43 States made a total contribution of $4,256,412 to the United Nations Fund for Namibia (see table). Other income included $1 million from the United Nations budget, as authorized by the General Assembly in December 1982.[6] Funding for assistance projects was also provided by UNDP and the executing agencies.

Several fund-raising missions were conducted in 1983,[1] in response to the Assembly's 1982 request.[6] Missions composed of the Vice-Chairman/Rapporteur of the Committee on the Fund and the United Nations Commissioner for Namibia visited Austria, Belgium, France, the Federal Republic of Germany, Italy, the Netherlands and the headquarters of EEC (21 January-3 February); and Denmark, Finland, Norway and Sweden(14-17 February). The Commissioner visited Australia and Japan (25 February-2 March). The Vice-Chairman/Rapporteur undertook a mission in Paris, during the International Conference in Support of the Struggle of the Namibian People for Independence (25-29 April), and continued fund-raising efforts with the permanent missions in New York. Finland was visited again on 2 May.

Governments visited unanimously recognized the need to prepare the Namibians for independence and expressed support for the Council's assistance programmes. They further stressed the importance of thorough project evaluation.

In the Programme of Action on Namibia, the Conference on Namibia called on Governments to contribute or to increase contributions to the Fund and to appeal again to their national organizations and institutions for contributions.

By resolution 38/36 E (see above), the General Assembly allocated $1 million to the Fund from the regular budget of the United Nations for 1984 and called for increased contributions to the Fund.

Nationhood Programme

The Nationhood Programme for Namibia, launched by the General Assembly in 1976,[7] continued in 1983 to finance training programmes and surveys of the Namibian economic and social sectors in preparation for independence.

The Council for Namibia[1] reported that, during 1982 and the first half of 1983, one group of students embarked on the fourth phase of training in the administration of public enterprises, while another group commenced training in development planning; groups commenced studies in railway operations and in the mining industry, as well as in maritime economics and management; a group of disabled Namibians began remedial training to be followed by basic trades training; and training continued in agricultural economics, pre-engineering in preparation for

CONTRIBUTIONS TO THE UN FUND FOR NAMIBIA, 1983
(as at 31 December 1983)

	Amount (in US dollar equivalent)		
Country	General Account	Nationhood Programme	Institute for Namibia
Algeria	10,000	—	—
Argentina	7,300	—	—
Australia	69,258	—	—
Austria	16,700	—	—
Bahamas	1,000	—	—
Barbados	500	—	—
Canada	—	—	158,473
Chile	1,300	—	—
China	30,000	—	—
Cyprus	182	182	182
Denmark	—	64,059	437,417
Egypt	—	10,000	2,857
Finland	55,679	379,081	348,897
France	17,319	—	75,501
Germany, Federal Republic of	—	—	64,705
Ghana	2,200	—	2,200
Greece	4,500	—	5,500
Haiti	—	—	1,000
Iceland	2,000	—	—
India	1,000	1,000	2,000
Indonesia	4,000	—	—
Iran	4,000	—	—
Ireland	5,741	5,741	5,741
Italy	—	—	7,334
Japan	10,000	—	210,000
Kuwait	1,000	—	—
Liberia	3,000	—	—
Mexico	5,001	—	—
Netherlands	66,547	—	125,085
New Zealand	3,278	—	—
Norway	—	251,738	315,516
Pakistan	3,000	—	—
Panama	1,000	—	—
Republic of Korea	—	—	1,000
Saudi Arabia	25,000	—	—
Sweden	—	—	486,145
Thailand	—	—	1,000
Trinidad and Tobago	1,493	—	—
Tunisia	20,000	—	5,000
United States	—	—	865,000
Venezuela	2,000	—	1,000
Yugoslavia	10,000	—	—
Zimbabwe	39,060	—	—
Total	423,058	711,801	3,121,553

mining engineering studies, statistics, aircraft maintenance, air traffic control, pilot training and tax administration.

In August 1983, the United Nations Vocational Training Centre for Namibia (Sumbe, Kwanza-Sul province, Angola) became operational when 100 students were enrolled in full-time vocational training courses. The Centre's financing derived from both the Trust Fund for the Nationhood Programme and UNDP, whose contribution from the indicative planning figure (IPF) for Namibia for 1983 was $575,629. The International Labour Organisation was the executing agency.

The fourth meeting of the Centre's Governing Board was held in May 1983 at Luanda, Angola, with the Council's participation.

The Committee on the Fund for Namibia approved a project, drawn up by the Office of the Commissioner in consultation with SWAPO, to provide training in English, mathematics, natural and social sciences and physical education for 100 Namibians

to prepare them to follow more specialized training courses such as those provided under the Nationhood Programme. The Government of Zambia agreed to make teaching facilities available.

Of the sectoral surveys envisaged by the Programme, final reports on transport, health, and land use and human settlements were submitted to the Council, draft reports on mineral resources and mining, transnational corporations and labour legislation were awaiting finalization, and draft reports on agrarian reform, agricultural education, maritime training and harbour survey, civil aviation, telecommunications, energy, protection of food supplies, public administration systems, water resouces, land suitability and the criminal justice system were awaiting further discussion. All sectors had been surveyed to some extent except trade and information, which were to be dealt with in a comprehensive study on all aspects of economic planning to be prepared by the Institute for Namibia as requested by the Assembly in 1982[6] (see below).

By a 25 July resolution (1983/42), the Economic and Social Council requested United Nations organizations to render increased assistance to the Namibian people, particularly in connection with the Nationhood Programme.

By resolution 38/36 E (see above), the General Assembly requested the Council for Namibia to elaborate policies and contingency plans for the transitional and post-independence phases of the Nationhood Programme and called on United Nations organizations to expedite execution of the Programme's projects.

UN Institute for Namibia

The United Nations Institute for Namibia, inaugurated in 1976[8] to undertake research, training, planning and related activities, continued in 1983 to develop human resources in anticipation of Namibia's independence.

In 1983, the Institute, located at Lusaka, Zambia, and open to persons of Namibian origin who fulfilled the requirements of the Institute's 16-member Senate, had a student body of 422.[1] The expanded curriculum of the Institute included teacher training/upgrading courses, secretarial instruction and special preparatory courses in English, statistics and mathematics. In January, the fourth group of students, numbering 62, graduated from the Institute with diplomas in management and development studies, bringing the total number of graduates to 282. A group of 76 students also graduated from the secretarial course, to which 86 new ones were admitted.

As part of its continuing applied research programme, intended to make available basic documentation for policy formulation by the future Government of an independent Namibia, the

Institute published studies on agrarian reform, constitutional options, a language policy, a legal system, and manpower requirements and development implications. Studies on health, education and mining had been completed and readied for publication. Work continued on a comprehensive reference book covering aspects of the Namibia question as considered by the United Nations since its inception.

By a December 1982 resolution,[6] the Institute had been requested to prepare a comprehensive study on all aspects of economic planning in an independent Namibia. Inter-agency meetings were held in May and November 1983 to discuss details of the study and the work carried out by consultants and specialized agencies, as well as by other organizations.

In 1983, the Institute's Namibian Extension Unit, which became operational in November 1981, was serving some 40,000 Namibians in Angola and Zambia who had limited access to formal education.

UNDP, which had provided assistance to the Institute since its establishment, continued in 1983 with financing for various research and training activities. The UNDP contribution of $968,592 for 1983 financed the services of the Institute's deputy director, three assistant directors, six lecturers, a senior librarian and a publications editor. There was also provision for administrative support, stipends and maintenance costs for 400 students, equipment and supplies.

In the Programme of Action on Namibia, the Conference on Namibia urged States and United Nations organizations to contribute to the Institute in the form of scholarship grants and other assistance.

By resolution 38/36 E (see above), the General Assembly commended the Institute for the effectiveness of its training programmes and research activities, requested early completion of the Namibia reference book and comprehensive document on economic planning, and urged United Nations organizations to co-operate with the Institute in strengthening its activities.

Other UN assistance

UN Educational and Training Programme for Southern Africa. In an October 1983 report to the General Assembly,[9] the Secretary-General stated that for the 1982/83 academic year, the United Nations Educational and Training Programme for Southern Africa granted 18 new scholarship awards to Namibians and extended 5, making a total of 23 scholarship holders studying in seven countries. The scholarships did not include awards financed by the United Nations Fund for Namibia. (For details of other scholarships granted and contributions to the Programme in 1983, see p. 190.)

In resolution 38/36 E, the Assembly decided that Namibians should continue to be eligible for assistance through the Programme, and, in resolution 38/52, it appealed for greater financial and other support to the Programme.

UNIDO activities. In a report on technical assistance to the Namibian people in 1983,[10] the Executive Director of the United Nations Industrial Development Organization (UNIDO) stated that UNIDO undertook a mission to Zambia in July to discuss implementation of a pre-independence assistance project, for which it had approved $103,960 from the United Nations Industrial Development Fund. Designed to lead to industrial and technological co-operation with the Institute for Namibia, the project was to award fellowships for the acquisition of skills to meet the tasks that independence would entail. Also discussed was the possible UNIDO contribution to a comprehensive document—under preparation by the Institute in co-operation with SWAPO, the Office of the Commissioner for Namibia and UNDP—on all aspects of economic planning in an independent Namibia, as requested by the Assembly in December 1982.[6] For this purpose, UNIDO revised its project to consist of assistance in the preparation of that document.

Implementation of the project began in December 1983 and it was expected to be completed in 1984. Approval of three project proposals of assistance to SWAPO, submitted to UNDP for financing in 1982,[11] remained in abeyance in 1983 for lack of funds.

On 13 May 1983,[12] the Industrial Development Board took note of the Executive Director's report on technical assistance to Namibians in 1982.[13] It emphasized the need for effective delivery of such assistance, taking account of the priority areas within the industrial sector as defined in the programme for the Industrial Development Decade for Africa (1980-1990) and the Nationhood Programme for Namibia. The Board reiterated its request to UNDP to approve the technical co-operation projects submitted by UNIDO and release funds for implementation of those already approved. It also reiterated the importance of close co-operation between UNIDO, UNDP, the Institute, the Council for Namibia and SWAPO.

UNDP assistance. In 1983, UNDP financed three projects for Namibia, in the amount of $1,545,721.[14] This covered assistance for: establishment of the Vocational Training Centre for Namibia in Angola; various research and training activities of the Institute for Namibia; and preparation of the report on a project completed in 1982, under which advisory services on labour legislation had been provided.

On 18 June 1983,[15] the UNDP Governing Council decided that information on assistance to

Namibia should be submitted in a separate report, and not as theretofore part of the Administrator's annual report on assistance to national liberation movements. On 24 June,[16] the Council requested the Administrator, in consultation with the executing agencies, to examine the feasibility and financial implications of waiving agency support costs of projects financed from the United Nations Fund for Namibia, as called for by the Assembly in 1982.[6] To ensure that contributions from the Fund were used mainly for project, rather than for administrative, support costs, the Council also requested that those contributions be treated as government cash counterpart contributions so that executing agencies would not charge more than 3.5 per cent as reimbursement of their support costs.

In resolution 38/36 E of 1 December (see above), the General Assembly called on UNDP to continue to allocate, at the request of the Council for Namibia, funds from the Namibia IPF for implementation of projects within the Nationhood Programme and for the Institute and to raise the IPF for Namibia.

UNCTAD activities. Following consideration of a report on UNCTAD assistance to national liberation movements recognized by regional intergovernmental organizations,[17] UNCTAD VI on 2 July adopted resolution 147(VI) on assistance to the peoples of Namibia and South Africa[18] (see also p. 160). By that resolution, the Conference urged the UNCTAD Secretary-General to cooperate with the Institute for Namibia, by providing technical expertise, in preparing the comprehensive document on all aspects of economic planning in an independent Namibia.

REFERENCES

[1]A/38/24. [2]A/38/23. [3]A/38/525. [4]YUN 1982, p. 1300, GA res. 37/233 A, 20 Dec. 1982. [5]YUN 1972, p. 616. [6]YUN 1982, p. 1314, GA res. 37/233 E, 20 Dec. 1982. [7]YUN 1976, p. 791, GA res. 31/153, 20 Dec. 1976. [8]*Ibid.*, p. 779. [9]A/38/469. [10]ID/B/314. [11]YUN 1982, p. 1317. [12]A/38/16 (conclusion 1983/10). [13]ID/B/293 & Corr.1. [14]A/39/293. [15]E/1983/20 (dec. 83/10 A). [16]*Ibid.* (dec. 83/10 B). [17]TD/282. [18]*Proceedings of the United Nations Conference on Trade and Development, Sixth Session, Belgrade, 6 June–2 July 1983*, vol. I, *Report and Annexes* (TD/326, vol. I), Sales No. E.83.II.D.6.

Chapter IV

Other colonial Territories

Progress towards self-determination and independence in individual Non-Self-Governing Territories continued to be closely examined in 1983 by the General Assembly and its Special Committee on the Situation with regard to the Implementation of the Declaration on the Granting of Independence to Colonial Countries and Peoples (Committee on colonial countries).

The Assembly adopted resolution 38/12 requesting Argentina and the United Kingdom to resume negotiations for a peaceful solution to their sovereignty dispute over the Falkland Islands (Malvinas) and asking the Secretary-General to continue his renewed mission of good offices to assist the parties. By resolution 38/40, the Assembly urged Morocco and the Frente Popular para la Liberación de Saguia el-Hamra y de Río de Oro to conduct cease-fire negotiations and to create the necessary conditions for a referendum among the people of Western Sahara on their future. In decision 38/402, it decided to defer the item on East Timor to its 1984 session. Human rights issues in Western Sahara and East Timor were taken up by the Commission on Human Rights and in the latter by the Sub-Commission on Prevention of Discrimination and Protection of Minorities (see ECONOMIC AND SOCIAL QUESTIONS, Chapter XVIII).

For most of the Territories, the United Nations Secretariat prepared working papers for the 25-member Committee on colonial countries, outlining recent developments. The Committee, and usually its Sub-Committee on Small Territories, examined the situation in each Territory and adopted conclusions and recommendations for the Assembly's consideration; these were discussed mainly in the Fourth Committee.

The Assembly adopted resolutions on American Samoa (38/41), Guam (38/42) and the United States Virgin Islands (38/48), under United States administration, and on Bermuda (38/43), the British Virgin Islands (38/44), the Cayman Islands (38/45), Montserrat (38/46) and the Turks and Caicos Islands (38/47), under United Kingdom administration.

Because of a United Kingdom decision to resume transmitting information on Anguilla to the Committee on colonial countries, the Assembly by decision 38/418 deferred consideration of the Territory to its 1984 session. In decision 38/417, it took note with satisfaction of the imminent accession to independence of Brunei. It noted in decision 38/412 that Australia, as the administering Power, had discussed with representatives of the Cocos (Keeling) Islands the holding of an act of self-determination to determine their future status, and that Australia was ready to receive visiting missions in that regard. It urged in decision 38/415 that the United Kingdom and Spain initiate negotiations to settle the Gibraltar problem. The Assembly called on the United Kingdom in decision 38/414 to continue to safeguard the interests of the people of Pitcairn. It also adopted decisions 38/416 and 38/413, declaring that the dispatch of visiting missions to St. Helena and Tokelau, respectively, should be kept under review.

Topics related to this chapter. General questions relating to colonial countries—information to the United Nations—visiting missions.

Question of the Falkland Islands (Malvinas)

Communications (January-August). A number of letters were addressed to the President of the Security Council and the Secretary-General by Argentina and the United Kingdom on the question of the Falkland Islands (Malvinas) between January and August 1983.

On 3 January,[1] Argentina reiterated its claim to sovereignty over the Malvinas, protested against measures by the United Kingdom, such as a so-called protection zone and militarization of the Territory, which, it said, constituted a source of serious tension in the South Atlantic, and expressed readiness to implement immediately the General Assembly's November 1982 resolution[2] calling for negotiations for a peaceful solution. On 12 January,[3] Argentina added that a visit to the Malvinas by the Prime Minister of the United Kingdom had aggravated tension in the region and that the British Government had shown no readiness to implement the 1982 resolution. Argentina, on 24 January,[4] denounced international press reports about an alleged Argentine military build-up in the South Atlantic, and declared it was scrupulously observing the existing *de facto* cessation of hostilities and was committed to a peaceful settlement of the dispute.

Referring to the three Argentine letters, the United Kingdom, on 27 January,[5] stated that its position on the sovereignty issue remained unchanged and added that the criticism of "militarization" ignored the unprovoked Argentine invasion of the Islands in 1982 and the need to defend them from further attacks.

On 30 March,[6] Argentina drew attention to continuous public pronouncements by the highest British authorities that the United Kingdom was not prepared to negotiate on the sovereignty of the territories and asserted that that attitude was a challenge to the decisions of the Security Council and the Assembly.

Replying, the United Kingdom said on 18 May[7] that the continuing tension in the South Atlantic lay in the refusal of Argentina to declare a definitive cessation of hostilities and to renounce the use of force as a means of resolving the dispute. Argentina declared on 28 June[8] that study of the 18 May letter and other statements by the British authorities indicated that the United Kingdom was not ready to seek a definitive negotiated solution to the sovereignty question but seemed bent on consolidating its illegal colonial presence in Argentine territory.

On 16 July,[9] Argentina called attention to the United Kingdom's decision to build a new airfield for civil and military use in the Malvinas at March Ridge about 30 kilometres from Puerto Argentino (Port Stanley), and declared that its construction, combined with the intention of establishing a naval base in the islands capable of accommodating nuclear submarines, showed that the United Kingdom planned to introduce nuclear weapons into the region as part of its global strategic design. The United Kingdom, on 9 November,[10] declared that the military facilities were strictly limited to the scale required to meet the current threat to the Islands.

On 26 July,[11] Argentina transmitted a resolution adopted by the General Assembly of the Organization of American States (OAS) on 20 November 1982, expressing support for the 1982 Assembly resolution and exhorting Argentina and the United Kingdom to carry it out.

On 10 August,[12] Argentina charged that on 1 August two fishing vessels, the *Rivera Vasca* and the *Arcos*, flying the Argentine flag and fishing in what it described as Argentine jurisdictional waters, were forced by British helicopters and a missile frigate to leave the area where the United Kingdom had illegally established a so-called exclusion zone. On 7 November,[13] the United Kingdom stated that repeated incursions by the two vessels into the protection zone on 1, 5 and 6 August were attempts to bolster Argentine claims to sovereignty over the Falklands and to jurisdiction over their surrounding waters; it also reported an incursion

on 5 August by an Argentine naval aircraft and its interception by two British aircraft, pointing out that such actions created the risk of a serious incident.

Responding on 25 August[14] to the Argentine letters of 28 June and 16 July, the United Kingdom rejected the allegations that it was maintaining a climate of confrontation and militarizing the Falklands; it added that recent incursions by both Argentine military aircraft and unauthorized civilian vessels had demonstrated the continuing need for measures to defend the Islands.

Action by the Committee on colonial countries. The question of the Falkland Islands (Malvinas) was considered by the Committee on colonial countries on 31 August and 1 September.[15] The Committee heard statements by the United Kingdom as the administering Power, by representatives of the Falklands Executive and Legislative Councils, by Argentina and by Committee members. On 1 September, the Committee requested Argentina and the United Kingdom to resume negotiations, expressing support for a renewed good offices mission by the Secretary-General based on the 1982 Assembly resolution,[2] and deciding to continue examining the question, subject to any directives by the Assembly.

Report of the Secretary-General. In pursuance of the 1982 Assembly resolution,[2] the Secretary-General submitted in October 1983 a report on the Falkland Islands (Malvinas) question.[16] Recalling that he had been requested to assist Argentina and the United Kingdom to resume negotiations, he said that he had had extensive exchanges with the two Governments, including meetings with the President of Argentina and the Prime Minister of the United Kingdom as well as with their respective Foreign Ministers. It was his belief that a resumption of negotiations could open the way towards a solution of the problem in the South Atlantic, and he stood ready to assist both parties in that process.

Communications (October-December). Further letters on the Falkland Islands (Malvinas) question were received by the President of the General Assembly and the Secretary-General from October to December.

Twelve Latin American and Caribbean countries transmitted in a letter dated 3 October[17] a resolution adopted on 19 May by the General Conference of the Agency for the Prohibition of Nuclear Weapons in Latin America (OPANAL) on the alleged introduction of nuclear weapons by the United Kingdom into the Falklands Islands (Malvinas) region. The Conference took note of the allegations by Argentina. It also took note of a statement by the United Kingdom that it was upholding its obligations under Additional Protocols I and II of the 1967 Treaty for the Prohibition of Nuclear Weapons in Latin America (Treaty of Tlatelolco)[18] and had not deployed nuclear weapons in areas for which it was internationally responsible. The Conference expressed concern that nuclear-propelled submarines had been used in warlike actions within the geographical zone defined by the Treaty, and reaffirmed the commitment of all States bound by the Treaty and its Protocols to refrain from activities which might endanger the military nuclear-free status of Latin America (see also p. 42).

On 3 November,[19] Argentina stated that the military base being constructed by the United Kingdom was not only a provocation against Argentina but also a source of growing concern for Latin America, and that its characteristics and cost left no doubt as to the global nature and long-term thrust of the United Kingdom's current policy in the South Atlantic. By another letter of the same date,[20] Argentina transmitted a document summarizing and discussing the consideration given to the Malvinas question during 1982 and 1983 by the General Assembly, the Movement of Non-Aligned Countries, OAS and OPANAL; resolutions adopted by those bodies were included in a series of appendices.

On 9 November,[21] Argentina transmitted an 8 November statement by the President-elect of Argentina in which he said that negotiations, with the good offices of the Secretary-General in the context of the 1982 Assembly resolution, were the proper way to settle the Malvinas dispute.

On 8 December,[22] Argentina conveyed the text of a resolution adopted by the OAS General Assembly on 17 November, expressing concern at the lack of progress in complying with the 1982 resolution and resolution 38/12 (see below) and urging that they be complied with.

GENERAL ASSEMBLY ACTION

On 16 November, the General Assembly adopted resolution 38/12 by recorded vote.

Question of the Falkland Islands (Malvinas)

The General Assembly,

Having considered the question of the Falkland Islands (Malvinas),

Aware that the maintenance of colonial situations is incompatible with the United Nations ideal of universal peace,

Recalling its resolutions 1514(XV) of 14 December 1960, 2065(XX) of 16 December 1965, 3160(XXVIII) of 14 December 1973, 31/49 of 1 December 1976 and 37/9 of 4 November 1982,

Recalling also Security Council resolutions 502(1982) of 3 April 1982 and 505(1982) of 26 May 1982,

Having received the report of the Secretary-General on his mission of good offices,

Regretting the lack of progress in the implementation of resolution 37/9,

Aware of the interest of the international community in the resumption by the Governments of Argentina and

the United Kingdom of Great Britain and Northern Ireland of their negotiations in order to find as soon as possible a peaceful and just solution to the sovereignty dispute relating to the question of the Falkland Islands (Malvinas),

Taking into account the existence of a *de facto* cessation of hostilities in the South Atlantic and the expressed intention of the parties not to renew them,

Reaffirming the need for the parties to take due account of the interests of the population of the Falkland Islands (Malvinas) in accordance with the provisions of General Assembly resolutions 2065(XX), 3160(XXVIII) and 37/9,

Reaffirming also the principles of the Charter of the United Nations on the non-use of force or the threat of force in international relations and the peaceful settlement of international disputes,

1. *Reiterates* its request to the Governments of Argentina and the United Kingdom of Great Britain and Northern Ireland to resume negotiations in order to find as soon as possible a peaceful solution to the sovereignty dispute relating to the question of the Falkland Islands (Malvinas);

2. *Takes note* of the report of the Secretary-General on the implementation of General Assembly resolution 37/9;

3. *Requests* the Secretary-General to continue his renewed mission of good offices in order to assist the parties in complying with the request made in paragraph 1 above, and to take the necessary measures to that end;

4. *Requests* the Secretary-General to submit a report to the General Assembly at its thirty-ninth session on the progress made in the implementation of the present resolution;

5. *Decides* to include in the provisional agenda of its thirty-ninth session the item entitled "Question of the Falkland Islands (Malvinas)".

General Assembly resolution 38/12

16 November 1983   Meeting 59   87-9-54 (recorded vote)

20-nation draft (A/38/L.12); agenda item 25.

Sponsors: Argentina, Bolivia, Brazil, Chile, Colombia, Costa Rica, Cuba, Dominican Republic, Ecuador, El Salvador, Guatemala, Haiti, Honduras, Mexico, Nicaragua, Panama, Paraguay, Peru, Uruguay, Venezuela.

Meeting numbers. GA 38th session: plenary 54, 57, 59.

Recorded vote in Assembly as follows:

In favour: Afghanistan, Albania, Algeria, Angola, Argentina, Austria, Benin, Bolivia, Botswana, Brazil, Bulgaria, Burundi, Byelorussian SSR, Cape Verde, Central African Republic, Chile, China, Colombia, Comoros, Congo, Costa Rica, Cuba, Czechoslovakia, Democratic Kampuchea, Democratic Yemen, Dominican Republic, Ecuador, Egypt, El Salvador, Equatorial Guinea, Ethiopia, Gabon, German Democratic Republic, Ghana, Guatemala, Guinea, Guinea-Bissau, Guyana, Haiti, Honduras, Hungary, India, Indonesia, Iran, Iraq, Ivory Coast, Japan, Lao People's Democratic Republic, Libyan Arab Jamahiriya, Madagascar, Malaysia, Mali, Malta, Mauritania, Mexico, Mongolia, Morocco, Nicaragua, Nigeria, Pakistan, Panama, Papua New Guinea, Paraguay, Peru, Philippines, Poland, Romania, Rwanda, Spain, Suriname, Syrian Arab Republic, Togo, Tunisia, Uganda, Ukrainian SSR, USSR, United Republic of Cameroon, United Republic of Tanzania, United States, Upper Volta, Uruguay, Venezuela, Viet Nam, Yemen, Yugoslavia, Zambia, Zimbabwe.

Against: Belize, Dominica, Gambia, Malawi, New Zealand, Oman, Solomon Islands, Sri Lanka, United Kingdom.

Abstaining: Australia, Bahamas, Bahrain, Bangladesh, Barbados, Belgium, Bhutan, Burma, Canada, Chad, Denmark, Fiji, Finland, France, Germany, Federal Republic of, Greece, Iceland, Ireland, Israel, Italy, Jamaica, Jordan, Kenya, Kuwait, Lebanon, Lesotho, Liberia, Luxembourg, Maldives, Mauritius, Nepal, Netherlands, Niger, Norway, Portugal, Qatar, Saint Christopher and Nevis, Saint Lucia, Saint Vincent and the Grenadines, Samoa, Saudi Arabia, Senegal, Sierra Leone, Singapore, Somalia, Sudan, Swaziland, Sweden, Thailand, Trinidad and Tobago, Turkey, United Arab Emirates, Vanuatu, Zaire.

Following adoption of the resolution, several countries explained their votes. Austria said it voted in favour because the resolution was founded on the principles of non-use of force and the right of peoples to self-determination, while in no way prejudging the sovereignty question. Guyana, Japan, Malaysia and Papua New Guinea supported the resolution's call for negotiations which could lead to a settlement of the dispute.

Greece averred that its abstention should be construed as a reflection of its desire to see a negotiated settlement. Italy declared that it abstained to keep alive the possibility of pursuing its efforts to re-establish a dialogue between the parties. The Netherlands said it had close ties with both and that it could not support a text that described their negotiations in a prejudicial manner. Maldives held that, although the resolution contained a number of welcome elements, it also lacked certain principles necessary to finding a solution to the conflict. Turkey said it abstained because it was not possible to agree on a consensus text that would have facilitated the resumption of negotiations.

Fiji, Qatar and Samoa said they abstained because the resolution failed to provide the population adequate opportunity to express their wishes about the future.

Earlier, on 15 November, the Assembly adopted without vote decision 38/405. The following petitioners had requested hearings[23] and made statements before the Fourth Committee on 14 November:[24] Anthony T. Blake and John E. Cheek, members of the Falkland Islands Legislative Council; Alexander Jacob Betts, a native of the Falkland Islands (Malvinas); and Derek William Rozee, a native currently residing in Argentina.

Question of the Falkland Islands (Malvinas)

At its 57th plenary meeting, on 15 November 1983, the General Assembly took note of the report of the Fourth Committee.

General Assembly decision 38/405

Adopted without vote

Oral proposal by President; agenda item 25.
Meeting numbers. GA 38th session: 4th Committee 8, 12, 16; plenary 57.

REFERENCES
[1]A/38/71 (S/15547). [2]YUN 1982, p. 1347, GA res. 37/9, 4 Nov. 1982. [3]A/38/72. [4]A/38/81. [5]A/38/83 (S/15575). [6]A/38/130-S/15668. [7]A/38/208-S/15774. [8]A/38/287-S/15849. [9]A/38/301-S/15873. [10]A/38/577-S/16135. [11]A/38/320. [12]A/38/355 (S/15918). [13]S/16136. [14]A/38/362-S/15938. [15]A/38/23. [16]A/38/532. [17]A/38/496. [18]YUN 1967, p. 832. [19]A/38/567-S/16125. [20]A/38/563. [21]A/38/578-S/16137. [22]A/38/722-S/16210. [23]A/C.4/38/5 & Add.1,2. [24]A/38/584.

East Timor question

In a note dated 19 August 1983,[1] regarding implementation of the General Assembly's November 1982 resolution on East Timor,[2] the Secretary-General said that in view of developments in the situation he did not consider it opportune to submit a substantive report on his efforts to achieve a comprehensive settlement of the problem to the Assembly at its 1983 session. He proposed to submit the report in 1984.

The Secretary-General had held consultations with Indonesia and Portugal throughout 1982 and in the first half of 1983; as a result, contacts were initiated between the two States in July 1983.

On 23 September, the Assembly adopted decision 38/402 in which it decided to defer the East Timor question to its 1984 session.

Action by the Committee on colonial countries. The question of East Timor was considered by the Committee on colonial countries on 2 September 1983.[3] The Committee examined the military developments, the human rights situation, the food situation and economic, social and educational conditions.

After hearing statements by Portugal as the administering Power, Indonesia, Amnesty International, Human Rights Advocates International, and the Frente Revolucionária de Timor Leste Independente (FRETILIN), the Committee decided to continue consideration of the question in 1984, subject to any directives by the General Assembly.

Communications. The President of the Security Council and the Secretary-General received four letters on the question of East Timor between October and December.

Two of the letters were from Angola, Cape Verde, Guinea-Bissau, Mozambique, and Sao Tome and Principe. On 7 October,[4] they forwarded a letter of the same date from FRETILIN, charging that a major Indonesian military offensive was currently under way in East Timor, giving a report from church sources on the massacre of 200 East Timorese villagers, commending the Secretary-General for his efforts to find a solution to the East Timor problem, and declaring that the FRETILIN leadership welcomed any peace initiative and was available for consultations with him and Indonesia and Portugal. On 24 October,[5] they transmitted a 20 October letter from FRETILIN, providing additional information on what it described as the extremely grave situation and alleging widespread violations of human rights in East Timor; excerpts of an interview given in September to a London-based human rights organization by the former Bishop of East Timor; and excerpts of a 25 July FRETILIN report on the human rights and social and humanitarian situation.

Referring to the 7 October letter from FRETI-LIN, Indonesia on 8 November[6] charged that it was an attempt to transform an earlier orchestrated media campaign of deception into a more respectable exposition of so-called facts; it stated that no major military offensive was under way, that the only security activity during the year took place in an area where a band of FRETILIN diehards attacked an army engineering unit on 8 August, and that the one major development in East Timor was the significant progress being made by the East Timorese, with the assistance of some humanitarian organizations, in the reconstruction of their province.

On 9 December,[7] Vanuatu forwarded a 30 November letter from its Prime Minister, enclosing an August report by Amnesty International; the report reviewed the conduct of Indonesian forces in East Timor and said evidence had been received indicating that official policy condoned torture, extrajudicial executions, disappearances, and the transportation of people to Atauro island and elsewhere, where they were held without charge or trial.

REFERENCES

[1]A/38/352. [2]YUN 1982, p. 1349, GA res. 37/30, 23 Nov. 1982. [3]A/38/23. [4]S/16034. [5]S/16083. [6]S/16132. [7]S/16215.

Western Sahara question

Co-operation with OAU. On 2 November 1983, the Secretary-General submitted to the General Assembly a report on the question of Western Sahara,[1] pursuant to the Assembly's November 1982 resolution[2] and decision[3] requesting him to co-operate closely with the Organization of African Unity (OAU) and the OAU Implementation Committee on Western Sahara in organizing a referendum on self-determination in the Territory.

The Secretary-General reported that on 6 January 1983 he had informed the OAU Secretary-General that he was ready to provide assistance and to co-operate with him. On 28 June, the OAU Secretary-General transmitted the text of a resolution on Western Sahara adopted by the OAU Assembly of Heads of State and Government (nineteenth session, Addis Ababa, Ethiopia, 6-12 June). In a further message, on 29 June, he requested United Nations assistance in implementing the resolution, by which OAU urged the parties to the conflict in Western Sahara—Morocco and the Frente Popular para la Liberación de Saguia el-Hamra y de Río de Oro (POLISARIO Front)—to undertake cease-fire negotiations;

directed the Implementation Committee to work out the details of the cease-fire and the conduct of the referendum in December 1983; requested the United Nations in conjunction with OAU to provide a peace-keeping force for Western Sahara; and decided to remain seized of the question.

The United Nations Secretary-General replied on 30 June that he had noted the resolution and would co-operate closely with the OAU Secretary-General. A United Nations team was sent to Addis Ababa to meet with an OAU secretariat task force on 19 and 20 September and to attend meetings of the Implementation Committee on 21 and 22 September.

Co-operation between the United Nations and OAU continued in a number of other political and economic areas in 1983 (see p. 191).

Action by the Committee on colonial countries. Western Sahara was considered by the Committee on colonial countries on 2 and 8 September.[4] The Committee discussed recent developments in the Territory and heard statements by a representative of POLISARIO, Cuba, Iran and Mali. It decided to continue consideration of the question in 1984, subject to any directives by the General Assembly.

GENERAL ASSEMBLY ACTION

On 7 December, following the recommendation of the Fourth Committee, the General Assembly adopted without vote resolution 38/40.

Question of Western Sahara

The General Assembly,

Having considered in depth the question of Western Sahara,

Taking account of decision AHG/Res.103(XVIII) on the question of Western Sahara, adopted unanimously by the Assembly of Heads of State and Government of the Organization of African Unity at its eighteenth ordinary session, held at Nairobi from 24 to 27 June 1981, as well as all the relevant resolutions of the Organization of African Unity, and reaffirming all the relevant resolutions of the United Nations on the question of Western Sahara,

1. *Takes note* of resolution AHG/Res.104(XIX) on Western Sahara, adopted unanimously by the Assembly of Heads of State and Government of the Organization of African Unity at its nineteenth ordinary session, held at Addis Ababa from 6 to 12 June 1983, which reads as follows:

"*The Assembly of Heads of State and Government of the Organization of African Unity*, meeting in its nineteenth ordinary session in Addis Ababa, Ethiopia, from 6 to 12 June 1983,

"*Having examined* the report of the Implementation Committee of Heads of State on Western Sahara,

"*Recalling* the solemn commitment made by His Majesty King Hassan II at the eighteenth ordinary session to accept the holding of a referendum in Western Sahara to enable the people of that territory to exercise their right to self-determination,

"*Recalling with appreciation* His Majesty King Hassan's acceptance of the recommendation of the sixth session of the *Ad Hoc* Committee of Heads of State on Western Sahara contained in document AHG/103(XVIII) B, annex I, as well as his pledge to co-operate with the *Ad Hoc* Committee in the search for a just, peaceful and lasting solution,

"*Reaffirming* its previous resolutions and decisions on the question of Western Sahara, and in particular AHG/Res.103(XVIII) of 27 June 1981,

"1. *Takes note* of the report of the Implementation Committee of Heads of State on Western Sahara;

"2. *Urges* the parties to the conflict, the Kingdom of Morocco and the POLISARIO Front, to undertake direct negotiations with a view to bringing about a cease-fire to create the necessary conditions for a peaceful and fair referendum for self-determination of the people of Western Sahara, a referendum without any administrative or military constraints, under the auspices of the Organization of African Unity and the United Nations, and calls on the Implementation Committee to ensure the observance of the cease-fire;

"3. *Directs* the Implementation Committee to meet as soon as possible and, in collaboration with the parties to the conflict, to continue to work out the modalities and all other details relevant to the implementation of the cease-fire and the conduct of the referendum in December 1983;

"4. *Requests* the United Nations, in conjunction with the Organization of African Unity, to provide a peace-keeping force to be stationed in Western Sahara to ensure peace and security during the organization and conduct of the referendum;

"5. *Mandates* the Implementation Committee, with the participation of the United Nations, to take all necessary measures to ensure the proper implementation of this resolution;

"6. *Requests* the Implementation Committee to report to the Assembly of Heads of State and Government at its twentieth session on the result of the referendum with a view to enabling the Assembly at that session to reach a final decision on all aspects of the question of Western Sahara;

"7. *Decides* to remain seized with the question of Western Sahara;

"8. *Requests* the Implementation Committee in the discharge of its mandate to take account of the proceedings of the eighteenth and nineteenth ordinary sessions on the question of Western Sahara and to this end invites the Secretary-General of the Organization of African Unity to make available the full records of the said proceedings to the Committee;

"9. *Welcomes* the constructive attitude of the Sahrawi leaders in making it possible for the nineteenth ordinary session to meet by withdrawing from it voluntarily and temporarily."

2. *Requests* the Secretary-General to take the necessary steps to ensure that the United Nations participates effectively in the organization and conduct of the referendum and to report to the General Assembly and the Security Council on this subject and on the measures requiring a decision by the Council;

3. *Urges* the Secretary-General to co-operate closely with the Secretary-General of the Organization of African Unity with a view to the implementation of the pertinent decisions of the Organization of African Unity and of the present resolution;

4. *Requests* the Special Committee on the Situation with regard to the Implementation of the Declaration on the Granting of Independence to Colonial Countries and Peoples to continue to consider the situation in Western Sahara as a matter of priority and to report thereon to the General Assembly at its thirty-ninth session.

General Assembly resolution 38/40

7 December 1983   Meeting 86   Adopted without vote

Approved by Fourth Committee (A/38/612 & Corr.1) without objection, 17 November (meeting 18); 41-nation draft (A/C.4/38/L.2), orally amended by Chairman, based on consultations on amendments by Equatorial Guinea (A/C.4/38/L.7) and sub-amendments by Sao Tome and Principe (A/C.4/38/L.8); agenda item 18.

Sponsors: Afghanistan, Algeria, Angola, Belize, Benin, Bolivia, Botswana, Burundi, Cape Verde, Congo, Costa Rica, Cuba, Cyprus, Democratic Yemen, Gambia, Ghana, Guinea-Bissau, Guyana, Iran, Lao People's Democratic Republic, Lesotho, Madagascar, Malawi, Mali, Mauritania, Mexico, Mozambique, Nicaragua, Panama, Rwanda, Sao Tome and Principe, Senegal, Seychelles, Uganda, United Republic of Tanzania, Upper Volta, Vanuatu, Viet Nam, Yugoslavia, Zambia, Zimbabwe.

Financial implications. S-G, A/C.4/38/L.4.

Meeting numbers. GA 38th session: 4th Committee 8-11, 13, 15, 17, 18; plenary 86.

The oral amendment by the Fourth Committee Chairman added the second preambular paragraph, which took into account amendments by Equatorial Guinea and sub-amendments by Sao Tome and Principe. Equatorial Guinea had suggested taking note of the 1981 OAU resolution[5] and annexing it to the text which became Assembly resolution 38/40; Sao Tome and Principe would have had the Assembly refer to all resolutions adopted by OAU on the Western Sahara question.

During its consideration, the Fourth Committee heard the following petitioners:[6] Biadillah Mohamed Cheikh, Secretary-General, Front de libération du Sahara; Chabihanna Hamdati, President, and Mohamed Takiou Allah Maoul Ainine, Association of Former Members of the Moroccan Liberation Army in the Saharan Provinces; Khatri Ould Said Ould Joummani, President, Sahrawi Assembly; Bohoy Sidi Ahmed, Secretary-General, Mouvement révolutionnaire des hommes bleus; Ahmed Rachid, Secretary-General, Association des originaires du Sakiat el-Hamra et du Río de Oro; Malika Brahim and M'Barka Bent Mahmoud, Union des femmes marocaines; Leili Mohamed Salem, on behalf of the nationals of Moroccan Western Sahara detained at Tindouf; Zerouali Breika, on behalf of those elected by the communes and the occupational chambers of the southern provinces of Morocco; Ali H. Kentaoui, deputy representative of POLISARIO in New York; Dakhil Khalil, Secretary-General, Parti de l'Union nationale sahraouie; and Douihi Rachid, Secretary-General, Front de libération et de l'unité.

In related action on 22 November, the Assembly adopted resolution 38/17, in which it reaffirmed the 1981 and 1983 OAU resolutions on organizing a referendum.

REFERENCES
(1)A/38/555. (2)YUN 1982, p. 1352, GA res. 37/28, 23 Nov. 1982. (3)*Ibid.*, p. 1353, GA dec. 37/411, 23 Nov. 1982. (4)A/38/23. (5)YUN 1981, p. 1193. (6)A/C.4/38/6 & Add.1-12.

Other Territories

American Samoa

GENERAL ASSEMBLY ACTION

On 7 December 1983, the General Assembly adopted without vote resolution 38/41, as approved by the Fourth Committee.

Question of American Samoa

The General Assembly,

Having considered the question of American Samoa,

Having examined the relevant chapters of the report of the Special Committee on the Situation with regard to the Implementation of the Declaration on the Granting of Independence to Colonial Countries and Peoples,

Recalling its resolution 1514(XV) of 14 December 1960, containing the Declaration on the Granting of Independence to Colonial Countries and Peoples, and all other resolutions and decisions of the United Nations relating to American Samoa,

Taking into account the statement of the representative of the administering Power relating to developments in American Samoa,

Conscious of the need to promote progress towards the full implementation of the Declaration in respect of American Samoa,

Noting with appreciation the continued participation of the administering Power in the work of the Special Committee in regard to American Samoa, thereby enabling it to conduct a more informed and meaningful examination of the situation in the Territory,

Reiterating the view that it remains the obligation of the administering Power to carry out a thorough programme of political education so as to ensure that the people of American Samoa are made fully aware of their inalienable right to self-determination and independence in accordance with General Assembly resolution 1514(XV),

Noting that the Office of Economic Development and Planning of the Government of American Samoa is implementing a five-year economic development plan, focusing on economic diversification, land use, housing, banking and tourism, for the benefit of the people of the Territory,

Aware of the special circumstances of the geographical location and economic conditions of American Samoa and stressing the necessity of diversifying the economy of the Territory as a matter of priority in order to reduce its dependence on fluctuating economic activities,

Mindful that United Nations visiting missions provide an effective means of ascertaining the situation in the small Territories and expressing its satisfaction at the willingness of the administering Power to receive visiting missions in the Territories under its administration,

1. *Approves* the chapter of the report of the Special Committee on the Situation with regard to the Im-

plementation of the Declaration on the Granting of Independence to Colonial Countries and Peoples relating to American Samoa;

2. *Reaffirms* the inalienable right of the people of American Samoa to self-determination and independence in conformity with the Declaration on the Granting of Independence to Colonial Countries and Peoples, contained in General Assembly resolution 1514(XV);

3. *Reiterates* the view that such factors as territorial size, geographical location, size of population and limited natural resources should in no way delay the speedy implementation of the Declaration contained in General Assembly resolution 1514(XV), which fully applies to American Samoa;

4. *Calls upon* the Government of the United States of America, as the administering Power, to take all necessary steps, taking into account the freely expressed wishes of the people of American Samoa, to expedite the process of decolonization of the Territory in accordance with the relevant provisions of the Charter of the United Nations and the Declaration;

5. *Reaffirms* that it is the responsibility of the administering Power to ensure that the people of American Samoa are kept fully informed of their inalienable right to self-determination and independence, in accordance with General Assembly resolution 1514(XV);

6. *Reiterates its recommendation* that, in accordance with the expressed wishes of the people of American Samoa, as reflected in the report of the second Political Status Commission, the Chief Justice and Associate Justices be appointed by the Governor and approved by the Legislature, a procedure which could be facilitated by the fact that a growing number of American Samoans are qualified lawyers;

7. *Reaffirms* the responsibility of the administering Power, under the Charter, for the economic and social development of the Territory;

8. *Calls upon* the administering Power, in co-operation with the territorial Government and within the framework of the five-year economic development plan covering the period 1979-1984, to continue to help to strengthen and diversify the economy of American Samoa in the interests of the people of the Territory;

9. *Urges* the administering Power to continue to facilitate close relations and co-operation between the people of the Territory and their neighbours and between the territorial Government and the regional institutions to enhance further the economic welfare of the people of American Samoa;

10. *Urges* the administering Power, in co-operation with the freely elected representatives of American Samoa, to safeguard the inalienable right of the people of the Territory to the enjoyment of their natural resources by taking effective measures to ensure their right to own and dispose of those resources and to establish and maintain control of their future development;

11. *Considers* that the possibility of sending a further visiting mission to American Samoa at an appropriate time should be kept under review;

12. *Requests* the Special Committee to continue the consideration of this question at its next session, including the possible dispatch of a further visiting mission to American Samoa at an appropriate time and in consultation with the administering Power, and to report thereon to the General Assembly at its thirty-ninth session.

General Assembly resolution 38/41

7 December 1983   Meeting 86   Adopted without vote

Approved by Fourth Committee (A/38/612 & Corr.1) without objection, 17 November (meeting 19); draft by Committee on colonial countries (A/38/23); agenda item 18.

Meeting numbers. GA 38th session: 4th Committee 8-19; plenary 86.

The draft was recommended by the Committee on colonial countries on 12 August, following its approval of the conclusions and recommendations of its Sub-Committee on Small Territories.[1]

Anguilla

GENERAL ASSEMBLY ACTION

The Assembly, on the recommendation of the Fourth Committee, decided without vote in December 1983 to defer consideration of the question of Anguilla until 1984.

Question of Anguilla

At its 86th plenary meeting, on 7 December 1983, the General Assembly, on the recommendation of the Fourth Committee, decided to defer until its thirty-ninth session consideration of the question of Anguilla and requested the Special Committee on the Situation with regard to the Implementation of the Declaration on the Granting of Independence to Colonial Countries and Peoples to continue to keep the situation in the Territory under review.

General Assembly decision 38/418

Adopted without vote

Approved by Fourth Committee (A/38/612 & Corr.1) without vote, 17 November (meeting 19); oral proposal by Chairman; agenda item 18.

Meeting numbers. GA 38th session: 4th Committee 8-19; plenary 86.

The Committee on colonial countries decided without objection on 14 September to consider the question of Anguilla at its 1984 session, subject to any directives by the Assembly.[1] The United Kingdom, as the administering Power, had informed the Committee that it would resume transmission of information on the Territory. The Committee had also considered Anguilla's constitutional and political developments, and economic, social and educational conditions.

Bermuda

GENERAL ASSEMBLY ACTION

Acting on the recommendation of the Fourth Committee, the General Assembly adopted without vote on 7 December resolution 38/43.

Question of Bermuda

The General Assembly,

Having considered the question of Bermuda,

Having examined the relevant chapters of the report of the Special Committee on the Situation with regard to the Implementation of the Declaration on the Granting of Independence to Colonial Countries and Peoples,

Recalling its resolution 1514(XV) of 14 December 1960, containing the Declaration on the Granting of Independence to Colonial Countries and Peoples, and all other resolutions and decisions of the United Nations relating to Bermuda,

Taking into account the statement of the representative of the administering Power relating to the Territory, in which he said that his Government would fully respect the wishes of the people of Bermuda in determining the future constitutional status of the Territory,

Conscious of the need to ensure the full and speedy implementation of the Declaration in respect of the Territory,

Noting with appreciation the continued active participation of the administering Power in the work of the Special Committee in regard to Bermuda, which contributes to informed consideration of conditions in the Territory, with a view to accelerating the process of decolonization for the purpose of the full implementation of the Declaration,

Recalling all relevant resolutions of the United Nations relating to military bases and installations in colonial and Non-Self-Governing Territories,

Noting that the economy of the Territory continues to be based on revenue generated from tourism and the registration of foreign companies, which creates a heavy dependence on those activities,

Aware of the special circumstances of the geographical location and economic conditions of the Territory and bearing in mind the necessity of diversifying and strengthening further its economy as a matter of priority in order to promote economic stability,

Mindful that United Nations visiting missions provide an effective means of ascertaining the situation in the small Territories,

1. *Approves* the chapter of the report of the Special Committee on the Situation with regard to the Implementation of the Declaration on the Granting of Independence to Colonial Countries and Peoples relating to Bermuda;

2. *Reaffirms* the inalienable right of the people of Bermuda to self-determination and independence in conformity with the Declaration on the Granting of Independence to Colonial Countries and Peoples, contained in General Assembly resolution 1514(XV);

3. *Reiterates* the view that such factors as territorial size, geographical location, size of population and limited natural resources should in no way delay the speedy exercise by the people of the Territory of their inalienable right to self-determination and independence, in conformity with the Declaration contained in General Assembly resolution 1514(XV), which fully applies to Bermuda;

4. *Urges* the administering Power, taking into account the freely expressed will and desire of the people of Bermuda, to continue to take all necessary steps to ensure the full and speedy implementation of General Assembly resolution 1514(XV);

5. *Reiterates* that it is the obligation of the administering Power to create such conditions in the Territory as will enable the people of Bermuda to exercise freely and without interference their inalienable right to self-determination and independence in accordance with General Assembly resolution 1514(XV) and, in that connection, reaffirms the importance of fostering an awareness among the people of Bermuda of the possibilities open to them in the exercise of that right;

6. *Reaffirms* that, in accordance with the relevant provisions of the Charter of the United Nations and the

Declaration contained in General Assembly resolution 1514(XV), it is ultimately for the people of Bermuda themselves to decide on their future political status;

7. *Notes* that general elections were held in the Territory in February 1983 and also notes with interest that the Government of the Territory has expressed its intention to revive discussion of the 1979 White Paper on Independence and to promote public debate on Bermuda's future status;

8. *Reaffirms* the importance of the need to foster national unity and a national identity and takes note of the steps taken by the local authorities in that regard, such as the establishment of an institution with a view to preventing discrimination among the people of the Territory on racial, religious, social or political grounds;

9. *Reaffirms its strong conviction* that the administering Power must ensure that military bases and installations do not hinder the people of the Territory from exercising their right to self-determination and independence in conformity with the purposes and principles of the Charter and urges the administering Power to take all necessary measures to comply fully with the relevant resolutions of the United Nations relating to military bases and installations in colonial and Non-Self-Governing Territories;

10. *Urges once again* the administering Power, in co-operation with the territorial Government, to continue to take all effective measures to guarantee the right of the people of Bermuda to own and dispose of their natural resources and to establish and maintain control of their future development;

11. *Strongly urges* the administering Power, in consultation with the Government of Bermuda, to make every effort to diversify the economy of Bermuda, including increased efforts to promote agriculture and fisheries and the manufacturing sector for the benefit of the people of the Territory;

12. *Welcomes* the role being played in the Territory by the United Nations Development Programme in providing assistance in the fields of agriculture, forestry and fisheries and urges the specialized agencies and all other organizations of the United Nations system to continue to pay special attention to the development needs of Bermuda;

13. *Reiterates its call* upon the administering Power, in co-operation with the local authorities, to continue to expedite the process of "bermudianization" in the Territory and, in that connection, urges that particular attention be paid to greater localization of the public service;

14. *Calls upon* the Government of the United Kingdom of Great Britain and Northern Ireland to receive a visiting mission in the Territory at an appropriate time;

15. *Requests* the Special Committee to continue the examination of this question at its next session, including the possible dispatch of a visiting mission to Bermuda at an appropriate time and in consultation with the administering Power, and to report thereon to the General Assembly at its thirty-ninth session.

General Assembly resolution 38/43

7 December 1983   Meeting 86   Adopted without vote

Approved by Fourth Committee (A/38/612 & Corr.1) without objection, 17 November (meeting 19); draft by Committee on colonial countries (A/38/23); agenda item 18.

Meeting numbers. GA 38th session: 4th Committee 8-19; plenary 86.

The draft was recommended by the Committee on colonial countries on 12 August, following its approval of the conclusions and recommendations of its Sub-Committee on Small Territories.[1] The Committee had considered the Territory's population, property development, tourism and financial developments.

British Virgin Islands

GENERAL ASSEMBLY ACTION

The General Assembly adopted without vote on 7 December resolution 38/44, as approved by the Fourth Committee.

Question of the British Virgin Islands

The General Assembly,

Having considered the question of the British Virgin Islands,

Having examined the relevant chapters of the report of the Special Committee on the Situation with regard to the Implementation of the Declaration on the Granting of Independence to Colonial Countries and Peoples,

Recalling its resolution 1514(XV) of 14 December 1960, containing the Declaration on the Granting of Independence to Colonial Countries and Peoples, and all other resolutions and decisions of the United Nations relating to the British Virgin Islands,

Taking into account the statement of the representative of the administering Power relating to the Territory, in which he said that his Government would fully respect the wishes of the people of the British Virgin Islands in determining the future political status of the Territory,

Conscious of the need to ensure the full and speedy implementation of the Declaration in respect of the Territory,

Noting with appreciation the continued active participation of the administering Power in the work of the Special Committee in regard to the British Virgin Islands, thereby enabling it to conduct a more informed and meaningful examination of the situation in the Territory, with a view to accelerating the process of decolonization for the purpose of the full implementation of the Declaration,

Reaffirming the responsibility of the administering Power for the economic and social development of the Territory,

Taking note of the fact that the economy of the Territory has continued to grow during the period under review, particularly in the fields of real estate and construction industries, tourism and banking,

Aware of the special circumstances of the geographical location and economic conditions of the Territory and bearing in mind the necessity of diversifying and strengthening further its economy as a matter of priority in order to promote economic stability,

Recalling the recommendation of the United Nations visiting mission dispatched to the British Virgin Islands in 1976 that the administering Power should facilitate the participation of the Territory as an associate member in various organizations within the United Nations system as part of the overall strategy of accelerating the decolonization process, and the continuing assistance provided by the United Nations Development Programme in the development of the Territory,

Mindful that United Nations visiting missions provide an effective means of ascertaining the situation in the small Territories and expressing its satisfaction at the willingness of the administering Power to receive visiting missions in the Territories under its administration,

1.   *Approves* the chapter of the report of the Special Committee on the Situation with regard to the Implementation of the Declaration on the Granting of Independence to Colonial Countries and Peoples relating to the British Virgin Islands;

2.   *Reaffirms* the inalienable right of the people of the British Virgin Islands to self-determination and independence in conformity with the Declaration on the Granting of Independence to Colonial Countries and Peoples, contained in General Assembly resolution 1514(XV);

3.   *Reiterates* the view that such factors as territorial size, geographical location, size of population and limited natural resources should in no way delay the speedy implementation of the Declaration contained in General Assembly resolution 1514(XV), which fully applies to the British Virgin Islands;

4.   *Reiterates* that it is the responsibility of the administering Power to create such conditions in the Territory as will enable the people of the British Virgin Islands to exercise freely and without interference their inalienable right to self-determination and independence in accordance with General Assembly resolution 1514(XV), as well as all other relevant resolutions of the Assembly;

5.   *Reaffirms* that it is ultimately for the people of the British Virgin Islands themselves to determine their future political status in accordance with the relevant provisions of the Charter of the United Nations and the Declaration and reaffirms the importance of fostering an awareness among the people of the Territory of the possibilities open to them in the exercise of their right to self-determination;

6.   *Calls upon* the administering Power, in consultation with the freely elected authorities of the territorial Government, to take all necessary steps to ensure the full and speedy attainment of the objectives of decolonization set out in the Charter and the Declaration and all other relevant resolutions of the United Nations;

7.   *Notes* the continuing commitment of the territorial Government to the goal of economic diversification, particularly in the areas of agriculture, fisheries and small industries, and reiterates its call upon the administering Power, in consultation with the local authorities, to intensify its efforts in this regard;

8.   *Urges* the administering Power, in co-operation with the territorial Government, to safeguard the inalienable right of the people of the Territory to the enjoyment of their natural resources by taking effective measures to ensure their right to own and dispose of those resources and to establish and maintain control of their future development;

9.   *Urges* the specialized agencies and other organizations of the United Nations system, as well as regional institutions such as the Caribbean Development Bank, to take measures to accelerate progress in the social and economic life of the British Virgin Islands;

10.   *Notes with satisfaction* the request of the British Virgin Islands, through the administering Power, for associate membership in the Economic Commission for Latin America and, in that connection, requests the administering Power to facilitate the participation of the

Territory in various organizations within the United Nations system in an appropriate capacity;

11.   *Considers* that the possibility of sending a further visiting mission to the British Virgin Islands at an appropriate time should be kept under review;

12.   *Requests* the Special Committee to continue the examination of this question at its next session, including the possible dispatch of a visiting mission to the British Virgin Islands at an appropriate time and in consultation with the administering Power, and to report thereon to the General Assembly at its thirty-ninth session.

General Assembly resolution 38/44

7 December 1983   Meeting 86   Adopted without vote

Approved by Fourth Committee (A/38/612 & Corr.1) without objection, 17 November (meeting 19); draft by Committee on colonial countries (A/38/23); agenda item 18.
Meeting numbers. GA 38th session: 4th Committee 8-19; plenary 86.

The draft was recommended by the Committee on colonial countries on 12 August, following its endorsement of the conclusions and recommendations of its Sub-Committee on Small Territories.[1] The Committee had taken up constitutional and political developments, and economic, social and educational conditions in the Territory.

Brunei

GENERAL ASSEMBLY ACTION

Acting on the recommendation of the Fourth Committee, the General Assembly in December adopted without vote decision 38/417.

Question of Brunei

At its 86th plenary meeting, on 7 December 1983, the General Assembly, on the recommendation of the Fourth Committee, took note with satisfaction of the imminent accession of Brunei to independence and extended to the Government and people of Brunei its warm congratulations on their achievement and its best wishes for peace, happiness and prosperity in the years ahead. In welcoming the declared intention of the Government, upon attaining independence, to apply for membership in the United Nations, the Assembly appealed to the United Nations and the organizations of the United Nations system to render all possible assistance to the emerging nation for the consolidation of its independence.

General Assembly decision 38/417

Adopted without vote

Approved by Fourth Committee (A/38/612 & Corr.1) without vote, 17 November (meeting 19); oral proposal by Chairman; agenda item 18.
Meeting numbers. GA 38th session: 4th Committee 8-19; plenary 86.

The Committee on colonial countries took note with satisfaction on 14 September of the scheduled accession to independence of Brunei on 31 December 1983.[1] It had considered Brunei's constitutional and political developments, and its economic, social and educational conditions.

Cayman Islands

GENERAL ASSEMBLY ACTION

The General Assembly, on the recommendation of the Fourth Committee, adopted without vote resolution 38/45 on 7 December.

Question of the Cayman Islands

The General Assembly,

Having considered the question of the Cayman Islands,

Having examined the relevant chapters of the report of the Special Committee on the Situation with regard to the Implementation of the Declaration on the Granting of Independence to Colonial Countries and Peoples,

Recalling its resolution 1514(XV) of 14 December 1960, containing the Declaration on the Granting of Independence to Colonial Countries and Peoples, and all other resolutions and decisions of the United Nations relating to the Cayman Islands,

Taking into account the statement of the representative of the administering Power relating to the Territory, in which he said that his Government would fully respect the wishes of the people of the Cayman Islands in determining the future constitutional status of the Territory,

Conscious of the need to ensure the full and speedy implementation of the Declaration in respect of the Territory,

Noting that, in the period under review, the economy of the Territory has continued to sustain sound rates of growth, especially in the tourist, international finance and real estate industries,

Mindful that United Nations visiting missions provide an effective means of ascertaining the situation in the small Territories and expressing its satisfaction at the willingness of the administering Power to receive visiting missions in the Territories under its administration,

Aware of the special circumstances of the geographical location and economic conditions of the Territory and bearing in mind the necessity of diversifying and strengthening further the economy as a matter of priority in order to promote economic stability,

1. *Approves* the chapter of the report of the Special Committee on the Situation with regard to the Implementation of the Declaration on the Granting of Independence to Colonial Countries and Peoples relating to the Cayman Islands;

2. *Reaffirms* the inalienable right of the people of the Cayman Islands to self-determination and independence in conformity with the Declaration on the Granting of Independence to Colonial Countries and Peoples, contained in General Assembly resolution 1514(XV);

3. *Reiterates* the view that such factors as territorial size, geographical location, size of population and limited natural resources should in no way delay the speedy implementation of the process of self-determination in accordance with the Declaration contained in General Assembly resolution 1514(XV), which fully applies to the Cayman Islands;

4. *Notes with appreciation* the participation of the administering Power in the work of the Special Committee in regard to the Cayman Islands, thereby enabling it to conduct a more informed and meaningful examination of the situation in the Territory, with a view to accelerating the process of decolonization for the purpose of the full implementation of the Declaration;

5. *Reiterates* that it is the responsibility of the administering Power to create such conditions in the Cayman Is-

lands as will enable the people of the Territory to exercise freely and without interference their inalienable right to self-determination and independence in accordance with General Assembly resolution 1514(XV), as well as all other relevant resolutions of the Assembly;

6. *Reaffirms* that it is ultimately for the people of the Cayman Islands themselves to determine their future political status in accordance with the relevant provisions of the Charter of the United Nations and the Declaration and reaffirms the importance of fostering an awareness among the people of the Territory of the possibilities open to them in the exercise of their right to self-determination;

7. *Reaffirms* the responsibility of the administering Power for the economic and social development of the Territory and urges it, in co-operation with the territorial Government, to render continuing support, to the fullest extent possible, to the development of programmes of economic diversification which will benefit the people of the Territory;

8. *Urges* the administering Power, in co-operation with the territorial Government, to safeguard the inalienable right of the people of the Territory to the enjoyment of their natural resources by taking effective measures to ensure their right to own and dispose of those resources and to establish and maintain control of their future development;

9. *Urges* the specialized agencies and other organizations of the United Nations system, as well as regional institutions such as the Caribbean Development Bank, to take all the necessary measures to accelerate progress in the social and economic life of the Cayman Islands;

10. *Notes* the continuing assistance provided to the Territory by the United Nations Development Programme;

11. *Considers* that the possibility of sending a further visiting mission to the Cayman Islands at an appropriate time should be kept under review;

12. *Requests* the Special Committee to continue the examination of this question at its next session, including the possible dispatch of a visiting mission to the Cayman Islands at an appropriate time and in consultation with the administering Power, and to report thereon to the General Assembly at its thirty-ninth session.

General Assembly resolution 38/45

7 December 1983   Meeting 86   Adopted without vote

Approved by Fourth Committee (A/38/612 & Corr.1) without objection, 17 November (meeting 19); draft by Committee on colonial countries (A/38/23); agenda item 18.

Meeting numbers. GA 38th session: 4th Committee 8-19; plenary 86.

The draft was recommended by the Committee on colonial countries on 12 August, following its endorsement of the conclusions and recommendations of its Sub-Committee on Small Territories.[1] The Committee had considered consitutional and political developments, and economic, social and educational conditions in the Cayman Islands.

Cocos (Keeling) Islands

GENERAL ASSEMBLY ACTION

The General Assembly, on the recommendation of the Fourth Committee, adopted without vote decision 38/412 in December.

Question of the Cocos (Keeling) Islands

At its 86th plenary meeting, on 7 December 1983, the General Assembly, on the recommendation of the Fourth Committee, adopted the following text as representing the consensus of the members of the Assembly:

"The General Assembly, having examined the relevant chapters of the report of the Special Committee on the Situation with regard to the Implementation of the Declaration on the Granting of Independence to Colonial Countries and Peoples and having heard the statement of the representative of Australia regarding the Cocos (Keeling) Islands, notes with appreciation the continuing co-operation of the Government of Australia, as the administering Power, with regard to the implementation of the Declaration on the Granting of Independence to Colonial Countries and Peoples, contained in Assembly resolution 1514(XV) of 14 December 1960, in respect of the Territory. The Assembly reaffirms that it is the responsibility of the administering Power to create conditions under which the people of the Cocos (Keeling) Islands will be able to determine freely their own future in conformity with resolution 1514(XV) as well as other relevant resolutions of the Assembly. In this respect, the Assembly notes the positive and continuing commitment of the administering Power to the political, social and economic advancement of the people of the Territory to enable them to exercise fully their inalienable rights as quickly as possible. It notes in particular that the administering Power has directly discussed with the representatives of the Cocos (Keeling) community the question of the holding of an act of self-determination to determine their future status. The Assembly welcomes the continuing willingness of the administering Power to receive visiting missions in the Cocos (Keeling) Islands and, in this regard, reaffirms that the need to send further missions as appropriate should be kept under review."

General Assembly decision 38/412

Adopted without vote

Approved by Fourth Committee (A/38/612 & Corr.1) without objection, 17 November (meeting 19); draft by Committee on colonial countries (A/38/23); agenda item 18.
Meeting numbers. GA 38th session: 4th Committee 8-19; plenary 86.

The draft had been recommended on 14 September by the Committee on colonial countries, following its approval of a draft consensus submitted by its Sub-Committee on Small Territories.[1] The Committee had considered constitutional and political developments, and economic, social and educational conditions in the Cocos (Keeling) Islands.

By a letter of 6 December,[2] Australia transmitted a letter of 8 November from its Foreign Minister to the Secretary-General, stating that the people of the Cocos (Keeling) Islands had indicated that they were ready to participate in an act of self-determination. The islanders would choose between independence, free association with Australia and integration with Australia during 1984. Accordingly, a United Nations mission was invited to visit the Islands to observe the act.

On 7 December, the General Assembly adopted without vote decision 38/420.

Appointment and dispatch of a United Nations visiting mission to the Cocos (Keeling) Islands

At its 86th plenary meeting, on 7 December 1983, the General Assembly:

(*a*) Authorized the Secretary-General, on the basis of his consultations, to appoint and dispatch a United Nations mission to visit the Cocos (Keeling) Islands in 1984;

(*b*) Requested the Secretary-General to submit a report on the findings of the visiting mission to the General Assembly at its thirty-ninth session.

General Assembly decision 38/420

Adopted without vote

Oral proposal by President; agenda item 18.
Meeting number. GA 38th session: plenary 86.

Gibraltar

GENERAL ASSEMBLY ACTION

In December, on the recommendation of the Fourth Committee, the General Assembly adopted without vote decision 38/415.

Question of Gibraltar

At its 86th plenary meeting, on 7 December 1983, the General Assembly, on the recommendation of the Fourth Committee, adopted the following text as representing the consensus of the members of the Assembly:

"The General Assembly, noting that the Governments of Spain and the United Kingdom of Great Britain and Northern Ireland signed a Declaration on 10 April 1980 at Lisbon, intending, in accordance with the relevant resolutions of the United Nations, to resolve the problem of Gibraltar, agreeing to that end to start negotiations aimed at overcoming all the differences between them on Gibraltar, agreeing also to the re-establishment of direct communications in the region, the Government of Spain having decided to suspend the application of the measures at present in force, and both Governments agreeing to base future co-operation on reciprocity and full equality of rights, noting that both Governments agreed on 8 January 1982 in London to fix the date of 20 April 1982 for the full implementation of the Lisbon Declaration, including the initiation of negotiations and the simultaneous re-establishment of direct communications in the region, and noting that, when it was subsequently agreed to postpone these arrangements, both Governments expressed their determination to keep alive the process initiated by the Lisbon Declaration of April 1980 and their intention to set a new date for its implementation, urges both Governments to make possible the initiation of the negotiations as envisaged in the consensus adopted by the Assembly on 14 December 1973, with the object of reaching a lasting solution to the problem of Gibraltar in the light of the relevant resolutions of the Assembly and in the spirit of the Charter of the United Nations."

General Assembly decision 38/415

Adopted without vote

Approved by Fourth Committee (A/38/612 & Corr.1) without objection, 17 November (meeting 19); draft (A/C.4/38/L.10); agenda item 18.
Meeting numbers. GA 38th session: 4th Committee 8-19; plenary 86.

On 14 September, the Committee on colonial countries, taking into account the continuing negotiations between the parties on the question of Gibraltar, decided to continue consideration of the item at its 1984 session, subject to any directives of the Assembly.[1] The Committee had considered political developments and economic, social and educational conditions in Gibraltar.

Guam

On 7 December, on the recommendation of the Fourth Committee, the General Assembly adopted without vote resolution 38/42.

Question of Guam

The General Assembly,

Having considered the question of Guam,

Having examined the relevant chapters of the report of the Special Committee on the Situation with regard to the Implementation of the Declaration on the Granting of Independence to Colonial Countries and Peoples,

Recalling its resolution 1514(XV) of 14 December 1960, containing the Declaration on the Granting of Independence to Colonial Countries and Peoples, and all other resolutions and decisions of the United Nations relating to Guam,

Having heard the statement of the representative of the administering Power,

Noting with appreciation the continued active participation of the administering Power in the work of the Special Committee in regard to Guam, thereby enabling it to conduct a more informed and meaningful examination of the situation in the Territory with a view to accelerating the process of decolonization towards the full and speedy implementation of the Declaration,

Noting that a referendum on political status was organized in the Territory, the final phase of which was held on 4 September 1982,

Recalling all relevant resolutions of the United Nations relating to military bases and installations in colonial and Non-Self-Governing Territories,

Noting the great potential for diversifying and developing the economy of Guam offered by commercial fishing, agriculture and the development of the transportation industry,

Bearing in mind that an obstacle to the economic development of the Territory has been the uncertainty concerning land held by the federal authorities,

Aware of the special circumstances of the geographical location and economic conditions of Guam and the necessity of diversifying the economy of the Territory as a matter of priority and noting the great potential for diversification offered by commercial fishing, agriculture and the development of the transportation industry,

Mindful that United Nations visiting missions provide an effective means of ascertaining the situation in the small Territories and expressing its satisfaction at the willingness of the administering Power to receive visiting missions in the Territories under its administration,

1. *Approves* the chapter of the report of the Special Committee on the Situation with regard to the Implementation of the Declaration on the Granting of Independence to Colonial Countries and Peoples relating to Guam;

2. *Reaffirms* the inalienable right of the people of Guam to self-determination and independence in con-

formity with the Declaration on the Granting of Independence to Colonial Countries and Peoples, contained in General Assembly resolution 1514(XV);

3. *Reaffirms its conviction* that such factors as territorial size, geographical location, size of population and limited natural resources should in no way delay the implementation of the Declaration contained in General Assembly resolution 1514(XV), which fully applies to Guam;

4. *Takes note* of the fact that in the referendum on political status, held on 4 September 1982, 75 per cent of the voters voted in favour of Commonwealth status in association with the United States of America and, in that connection, mindful of the principles contained in the Charter of the United Nations and in the Declaration, calls upon the administering Power, in cooperation with the territorial Government, to expedite the process of decolonization in accordance with the expressed wishes of the people of the Territory;

5. *Reaffirms its strong conviction* that the administering Power must ensure that military bases and installations do not hinder the population of the Territory from exercising its right to self-determination and independence in conformity with the purposes and principles of the Charter and urges the administering Power to take all necessary measures to comply fully with the relevant resolutions;

6. *Reaffirms* the responsibility of the administering Power, under the Charter, for the economic and social development of Guam and calls upon the administering Power to take all necessary steps to strengthen and diversify the economy of the Territory, with a view to reducing the Territory's economic dependence on the administering Power;

7. *Reiterates its call* upon the administering Power, in co-operation with the territorial Government, to remove the constraints which limit growth in the economic development of the Territory, particularly with regard to commercial fishing, agriculture and the transportation industry;

8. *Calls upon* the administering Power, in co-operation with the local authorities, to accelerate the transfer of land to the people of the Territory;

9. *Urges* the administering Power, in co-operation with the territorial Government, to continue to take effective measures to safeguard and guarantee the right of the people of Guam to their natural resources and to establish and maintain control over their future development and requests the administering Power to take all necessary steps to protect the property rights of the people of the Territory;

10. *Takes note* of the steps taken by the administering Power to strengthen its efforts to develop and promote the language and culture of the Chamorro people, who comprise more than half of the population of the Territory, and reaffirms the importance of further efforts in that field;

11. *Considers* that the possibility of sending a further visiting mission to Guam at an appropriate time should be kept under review;

12. *Requests* the Special Committee to continue the consideration of this question at its next session, including the possible dispatch of a further visiting mission to Guam at an appropriate time and in consultation with the administering Power, and to report thereon to the General Assembly at its thirty-ninth session.

General Assembly resolution 38/42

7 December 1983   Meeting 86   Adopted without vote

Approved by Fourth Committee (A/38/612 & Corr.1) without objection, 17 November (meeting 19); draft by Committee on colonial countries (A/38/23); agenda item 18.

Meeting numbers. GA 38th session: 4th Committee 8-19; plenary 86.

The Committee on colonial countries recommended the draft on 14 September,[(1)] after adopting the report and endorsing the conclusions and recommendations of its Sub-Committee on Small Territories. The Committee had considered Guam's constitutional and political developments, and economic, social and educational conditions.

Montserrat

GENERAL ASSEMBLY ACTION

The General Assembly, on the recommendation of the Fourth Committee, adopted without vote resolution 38/46 on 7 December.

Question of Montserrat

The General Assembly,

Having considered the question of Montserrat,

Having examined the relevant chapters of the report of the Special Committee on the Situation with regard to the Implementation of the Declaration on the Granting of Independence to Colonial Countries and Peoples,

Recalling its resolution 1514(XV) of 14 December 1960, containing the Declaration on the Granting of Independence to Colonial Countries and Peoples,

Recalling also its resolution 37/27 of 23 November 1982 on the question of Montserrat,

Recalling the dispatch, in 1975 and 1982, of United Nations visiting missions to the Territory,

Taking into account the statement of the representative of the administering Power, in which he said that the policy of his Government was to respect the wishes of the people of the Territory in determining their future political status,

Reaffirming the responsibility of the administering Power for the economic and social development of the Territory,

Noting that during the period under review the economy of Montserrat grew in real terms and that in recent years no budgetary grant-in-aid from the administering Power has been considered necessary to balance the regular budget of the Territory,

Noting that an in-service review of the organization and training needs of the public service was undertaken in 1982 and that priority would be given to the establishment of a civil service training centre,

Mindful of the responsibility of the United Nations to help the people of Montserrat to realize their aspirations in accordance with the objectives set forth in the Declaration,

Noting the assistance being rendered by those organizations of the United Nations system operating in the Territory,

Aware of the special problems facing the Territory by virtue of its isolation, small size, limited resources and lack of infrastructure,

Mindful that United Nations visiting missions provide an effective means of ascertaining the situation in the Territories visited,

1. *Approves* the chapter of the report of the Special Committee on the Situation with regard to the Implementation of the Declaration on the Granting of Independence to Colonial Countries and Peoples relating to Montserrat;

2. *Reaffirms* the inalienable right of the people of Montserrat to self-determination and independence in conformity with the Declaration on the Granting of Independence to Colonial Countries and Peoples, contained in General Assembly resolution 1514(XV) of 14 December 1960;

3. *Reiterates* the view that such factors as territorial size, geographical location, size of population and limited natural resources should in no way delay the speedy exercise by the people of the Territory of their inalienable right to self-determination and independence in conformity with the Declaration, which fully applies to Montserrat;

4. *Notes with appreciation* the continued participation of the administering Power in the work of the Special Committee, which enables it to conduct a more meaningful examination of the situation in the Territory with a view to accelerating the process of decolonization for the purpose of the full implementation of the Declaration;

5. *Reiterates* that it is the responsibility of the administering Power to create such conditions in Montserrat as will enable its people to exercise freely and without interference their inalienable right to self-determination and independence in accordance with General Assembly resolution 1514(XV), as well as all other relevant resolutions of the Assembly;

6. *Reaffirms* that it is ultimately for the people of Montserrat themselves to determine their future political status in accordance with the relevant provisions of the Charter of the United Nations and the Declaration and reiterates its call upon the administering Power to launch, in co-operation with the territorial Government, programmes of political education so that the people of Montserrat may be fully informed of the options available to them in the exercise of their right to self-determination and independence;

7. *Calls upon* the administering Power to continue, in co-operation with the territorial Government, to strengthen the economy and to increase its assistance to programmes of diversification;

8. *Takes note* of the growth of the manufacturing, construction and tourist industries and urges the administering Power, in co-operation with the territorial Government, to intensify the development of other sectors of the economy, in particular agriculture, livestock and fisheries, for the benefit of the people of the Territory;

9. *Urges* the administering Power, in co-operation with the territorial Government, to continue to take effective measures to safeguard, guarantee and ensure the rights of the people of Montserrat to own and dispose of their natural resources and to establish and maintain control of their future development;

10. *Also urges* the administering Power, in co-operation with the territorial Government, to continue to render the assistance necessary for the localization of the civil service, particularly at senior levels;

11. *Takes note* of the continued participation of the Territory in the work of the Caribbean Group for Co-operation and Economic Development, as well as such

regional organizations as the Caribbean Community and the Caribbean Development Bank, and calls upon the organizations of the United Nations system, as well as donor Governments and regional organizations, to intensify their efforts to accelerate progress in the economic and social life of the Territory;

12. *Requests* the Special Committee to continue the examination of this question at its next session, including the possible dispatch of a further visiting mission to Montserrat at an appropriate time and in consultation with the administering Power, and to report thereon to the General Assembly at its thirty-ninth session.

General Assembly resolution 38/46

7 December 1983   Meeting 86   Adopted without vote

Approved by Fourth Committee (A/38/612 & Corr.1) without objection, 17 November (meeting 19); draft by Committee on colonial countries (A/38/23); agenda item 18.
Meeting numbers. GA 38th session: 4th Committee 8-19; plenary 86.

The Committee on colonial countries recommended the draft on 12 August,[1] following its adoption of the report and endorsement of the conclusions and recommendations of its Sub-Committee on Small Territories. The Committee had considered the constitutional and political developments, and economic, social and educational conditions in Montserrat.

Pitcairn

GENERAL ASSEMBLY ACTION

In December, on the recommendation of the Fourth Committee, the General Assembly adopted without vote decision 38/414.

Question of Pitcairn

At its 86th plenary meeting, on 7 December 1983, the General Assembly, on the recommendation of the Fourth Committee, adopted the following text as representing the consensus of the members of the Assembly:

"The General Assembly, having examined the relevant chapters of the report of the Special Committee on the Situation with regard to the Implementation of the Declaration on the Granting of Independence to Colonial Countries and Peoples, takes note of the statement of the representative of the United Kingdom of Great Britain and Northern Ireland affirming the policy of his Government to encourage as much local initiative and enterprise as possible, so that the people of Pitcairn can make the most of their own way of life. The Assembly takes note of the willingness of the administering Power to discuss any change of constitutional status with the people of the Territory whenever the latter so desire. It notes that the present size of the population continues to raise the question of the capacity of the islanders to maintain the essential services such as education and medical welfare and their ability to launch long boats on which, in the absence of adequate dock facilities, trade with passing ships depends. In that connection, the Assembly calls once again upon the administering Power to continue to take the necessary measures to safeguard the interests of the people of Pitcairn. The Assembly requests the Special Committee

to continue to examine the question at its next session and to report thereon to the Assembly at its thirty-ninth session."

General Assembly decision 38/414

Adopted without vote

Approved by Fourth Committee (A/38/612 & Corr.1) without objection, 17 November (meeting 19); draft by Committee on colonial countries (A/38/23); agenda item 18.
Meeting numbers. GA 38th session: 4th Committee 8-19; plenary 86.

The draft was recommended by the Committee on colonial countries on 12 August,[1] following approval of a draft consensus submitted by the Sub-Committee on Small Territories. The Committee had considered Pitcairn's constitutional and political developments, and economic, social and educational conditions.

St. Helena

In a letter of 22 August 1983[3] to the Chairman of the Committee on colonial countries, the United Kingdom enclosed excerpts from an address by the Governor of St. Helena to its Legislative Council on the work of a commission set up in 1981 to consider changes in the St. Helena Constitution. The Governor stated that every reasonable effort had been made to obtain people's views on the question, but that little interest was shown and no positive proposals had emerged. He suggested that the Council might prepare changes, or improvements, as a modest step in St. Helena's constitutional development.

GENERAL ASSEMBLY ACTION

In December, on the recommendation of the Fourth Committee, the General Assembly adopted decision 38/416 by recorded vote.

Question of St. Helena

At its 86th plenary meeting, on 7 December 1983, the General Assembly, on the recommendation of the Fourth Committee, having examined the relevant chapters of the report of the Special Committee on the Situation with regard to the Implementation of the Declaration on the Granting of Independence to Colonial Countries and Peoples and having heard the statement of the representative of the United Kingdom of Great Britain and Northern Ireland, as the administering Power, reaffirmed the inalienable right of the people of St. Helena to self-determination and independence in conformity with the Declaration on the Granting of Independence to Colonial Countries and Peoples, contained in Assembly resolution 1514(XV) of 14 December 1960. The Assembly noted the commitment of the Government of the United Kingdom to respect the wishes of the people of the Territory and, in that regard, urged the administering Power, in consultation with the freely elected representatives of the people of St. Helena, to continue to take all necessary steps to ensure the speedy implementation of the Declaration in respect of that Territory. The Assembly expressed the hope that the administering Power would continue to implement infrastructure and community development projects aimed at improving the general welfare of the community and to encourage local initiative and enterprise, particularly in the areas of forestry, fisheries and the handicrafts industry. The Assembly reaffirmed that continued development assistance from the administering Power, together with any assistance that the international community might be able to provide, constituted an important means of developing the economic potential of the Territory and of enhancing the capacity of its people to realize fully the goals set forth in the relevant provisions of the Charter of the United Nations for the improvement of economic conditions in the Territory. The Assembly noted with concern the presence of a military base on the dependency of Ascension and, in that regard, recalled all the relevant United Nations resolutions and decisions concerning military bases and installations in colonial and Non-Self-Governing Territories. Noting the positive attitude of the administering Power with respect to the question of receiving United Nations visiting missions in the Territories under its administration, the Assembly considered that the possibility of dispatching such a mission to St. Helena at an appropriate time should be kept under review. The Assembly requested the Special Committee to continue to examine the question at its next session, including the possible dispatch of a visiting mission to St. Helena, at an appropriate time and in consultation with the administering Power, and to report thereon to the Assembly at its thirty-ninth session.

General Assembly decision 38/416

114-2-31 (recorded vote)

Approved by Fourth Committee (A/38/612 & Corr.1) by recorded vote (95-2-26), 17 November (meeting 19); draft by Committee on colonial countries (A/38/23); agenda item 18.

Meeting numbers. GA 38th session: 4th Committee 8-19; plenary 86.

Recorded vote in Assembly as follows:

In favour: Afghanistan, Albania, Algeria, Angola, Argentina, Bahamas, Bahrain, Bangladesh, Barbados, Benin, Bhutan, Bolivia, Botswana, Brazil, Bulgaria, Burma, Burundi, Byelorussian SSR, Cape Verde, Chad, China, Colombia, Congo, Costa Rica, Cuba, Cyprus, Czechoslovakia, Democratic Kampuchea, Democratic Yemen, Djibouti, Dominican Republic, Ecuador, Egypt, El Salvador, Equatorial Guinea, Ethiopia, Gabon, German Democratic Republic, Ghana, Greece, Guatemala, Guinea, Guinea-Bissau, Guyana, Haiti, Honduras, Hungary, India, Indonesia, Iran, Iraq, Ivory Coast, Jamaica, Jordan, Kuwait, Lao People's Democratic Republic, Lebanon, Lesotho, Libyan Arab Jamahiriya, Madagascar, Malawi, Malaysia, Maldives, Mali, Malta, Mauritania, Mauritius, Mexico, Mongolia, Mozambique, Nepal, Nicaragua, Niger, Nigeria, Oman, Pakistan, Panama, Paraguay, Peru, Philippines, Poland, Qatar, Romania, Rwanda, Saint Vincent and the Grenadines, Sao Tome and Principe, Saudi Arabia, Senegal, Sierra Leone, Singapore, Somalia, Spain, Sri Lanka, Sudan, Suriname, Thailand, Togo, Trinidad and Tobago, Tunisia, Uganda, Ukrainian SSR, USSR, United Arab Emirates, United Republic of Cameroon, United Republic of Tanzania, Upper Volta, Uruguay, Venezuela, Viet Nam, Yemen, Yugoslavia, Zaire, Zambia, Zimbabwe.

Against: United Kingdom, United States.

Abstaining: Australia, Austria, Belgium, Belize, Canada, Comoros, Denmark, Dominica, Fiji, Finland, France, Germany, Federal Republic of, Iceland, Ireland, Israel, Italy, Japan, Kenya, Liberia, Luxembourg, Netherlands, New Zealand, Norway, Papua New Guinea, Portugal, Saint Christopher and Nevis, Saint Lucia, Samoa, Solomon Islands, Sweden, Turkey.

The draft was recommended by the Committee on colonial countries on 14 September,[1] following adoption of a draft decision submitted by its Sub-Committee on Small Territories. The Committee had considered St. Helena's constitutional arrangements and economic, social and educational conditions, as well as its dependencies—Tristan da Cunha and Ascension Island.

Before the Fourth Committee approved the draft, it took a vote, requested by the United Kingdom, on the fifth sentence of the text, which was retained by a recorded vote of 72 to 27, with 17 abstentions.

Explaining its vote on that sentence, the United Kingdom said it felt that the reference to Ascension Island was out of place; that the island and St. Helena were legally distinct, 1,000 miles apart and connected only for administrative reasons; and that the military facilities there were not an obstacle to the self-determination of a people, since there was no local population on that island. Australia, voting for the sentence's omission, agreed that the two islands were separate entities.

Voting in favour of the sentence, Czechoslovakia pointed out that it did not mention that the military facilities on Ascension had been used by British invasion forces during the South Atlantic conflict or that the United Kingdom had used a colonial Territory to restore its rule over another Non-Self-Governing Territory. Venezuela said the fact that Ascension Island did not have an indigenous population did not justify the installation or use of military bases on colonial Territories; since the Falkland Islands (Malvinas) conflict, Ascension Island had been used as a supply and refuelling centre for naval and air units going to the South Atlantic. Cuba said it had voted for the draft for the same reasons as Venezuela and Czechoslovakia and because, as a member of the Committee on colonial countries, it felt that decisions adopted there by consensus should be respected by the Fourth Committee.

Norway, on behalf of the Nordic countries, stated that they considered that Ascension Island was not covered by the Assembly's 1960 Declaration on the Granting of Independence to Colonial Countries and Peoples,[4] under which the question of St. Helena was being considered. Canada agreed and said it regretted that the controversial sentence had not been withdrawn. Nepal said it had abstained because the text covered two separate issues, decolonization and the question of military bases; it would have been preferable for the Committee to discuss the question of demilitarization separately.

St. Kitts–Nevis

The Committee on colonial countries took note on 14 September 1983 of the scheduled accession to independence of St. Kitts–Nevis on 19 September 1983.[1] The Committee also welcomed the declared intention of the Government, upon attaining independence (as Saint Christopher and Nevis), to apply for United Nations membership (see p. 388).

Tokelau

In December, the General Assembly adopted without vote decision 38/413 as recommended by the Fourth Committee.

Question of Tokelau

At its 86th plenary meeting, on 7 December 1983, the General Assembly, on the recommendation of the Fourth Committee, adopted the following text as representing the consensus of the members of the Assembly:

"The General Assembly, having examined the relevant chapters of the report of the Special Committee on the Situation with regard to the Implementation of the Declaration on the Granting of Independence to Colonial Countries and Peoples and having heard the statement of the representative of New Zealand with regard to Tokelau, notes with appreciation the willingness of the administering Power to maintain its close co-operation with the United Nations in the exercise of its responsibility towards Tokelau. The Assembly reaffirms the inalienable right of the people of Tokelau to self-determination and independence in conformity with the Declaration on the Granting of Independence to Colonial Countries and Peoples, contained in Assembly resolution 1514(XV) of 14 December 1960, and reaffirms further that it is the responsibility of the administering Power to keep the people of Tokelau fully informed of this right. In this regard, the Assembly notes that the people of the Territory have expressed the view that, at the present time, they do not wish to review the nature of the existing relationship between Tokelau and New Zealand. The Assembly welcomes the assurances of the administering Power that it will continue to be guided solely by the wishes of the people of Tokelau as to the future status of the Territory. The Assembly notes that the administering Power has assured the people of Tokelau of its continuing assistance in the event that they should desire to change their status. The Assembly calls upon the administering Power to continue its programme of political education within the context of its efforts to ensure the preservation of the identity and cultural heritage of the people of Tokelau. The Assembly recognizes that the economic development of Tokelau is an important element in the process of self-determination. The Assembly notes the continuing efforts of the administering Power to promote the economic development of the Territory and the measures it has taken to safeguard and guarantee the rights of the people of Tokelau to all their natural resources and the benefits derived therefrom. The Assembly is of the opinion that the administering Power should continue to expand its programme of budgetary support and development aid to the Territory. The Assembly notes with appreciation the continuing efforts of the administering Power to make improvements in the fields of public health, public works and education. The Assembly reiterates its expression of appreciation to the specialized agencies and other organizations of the United Nations system, as well as to the regional organizations, for their assistance to Tokelau and calls upon those bodies to continue providing assistance to the Territory. Mindful of the effective means provided by United Nations visiting missions to assess the situation in the Territories, the Assembly is of the opinion that the possibility of sending another visiting mission to the Territory at an appropriate time should be kept under review, taking into account, in particular, the wishes of the people of Tokelau. The Assembly requests the Special Committee to continue to examine this question at its next session, including the possible dispatch of a further visiting mission to Tokelau, at an appropriate time and in consultation with the administering Power, and to report thereon to the Assembly at its thirty-ninth session."

General Assembly decision 38/413
Adopted without vote

Approved by Fourth Committee (A/38/612 & Corr.1) without objection, 17 November (meeting 19); draft by Committee on colonial countries (A/38/23); agenda item 18.
Meeting numbers. GA 38th session: 4th Committee 8-19; plenary 86.

The draft was recommended by the Committee on colonial countries on 12 August,[1] following approval of a draft consensus submitted by its Sub-Committee on Small Territories. The Committee had considered constitutional and political developments, and economic, social and educational conditions in Tokelau.

Turks and Caicos Islands

On the recommendation of the Fourth Committee, the General Assembly adopted without vote resolution 38/47 on 7 December.

Question of the Turks and Caicos Islands
The General Assembly,

Having considered the question of the Turks and Caicos Islands,

Having examined the relevant chapters of the report of the Special Committee on the Situation with regard to the Implementation of the Declaration on the Granting of Independence to Colonial Countries and Peoples,

Recalling its resolution 1514(XV) of 14 December 1960, containing the Declaration on the Granting of Independence to Colonial Countries and Peoples, and all other resolutions and decisions of the United Nations relating to the Turks and Caicos Islands,

Taking into account the statement of the representative of the administering Power relating to the Territory, in which he said that his Government would fully respect the wishes of the people of the Turks and Caicos Islands in determining the future constitutional status of the Territory, and bearing in mind the importance of fostering an awareness among the people of the Territory of the possibilities open to them,

Conscious of the need to ensure the full and speedy implementation of the Declaration in respect of the Territory,

Noting with appreciation the participation of the administering Power in the work of the Special Committee in regard to the Turks and Caicos Islands, thereby enabling it to conduct a more meaningful examination of the situation in the Territory,

Aware of the special circumstances of the geographical location and economic conditions of the Territory and bearing in mind the necessity of diversifying and strengthening further its economy as a matter of priority in order to promote economic stability and to develop a wider economic base for the Territory,

Recalling all relevant resolutions of the United Nations relating to military bases and installations in colonial and Non-Self-Governing Territories,

Noting the assistance rendered by the United Nations Development Programme in the development of the Territory and welcoming the attendance of a delegation from the Turks and Caicos Islands at the Fifth Annual Conference of the Caribbean Group for Co-operation and Economic Development, held under the auspices of the World Bank,

Noting the arrangements made for university training abroad and for vocational training in the Territory,

Mindful that United Nations visiting missions provide an effective means of ascertaining the situation in the small Territories and expressing its satisfaction at the willingness of the administering Power to receive visiting missions in the Territories under its administration,

1. *Approves* the chapter of the report of the Special Committee on the Situation with regard to the Implementation of the Declaration on the Granting of Independence to Colonial Countries and Peoples relating to the Turks and Caicos Islands;

2. *Reaffirms* the inalienable right of the people of the Turks and Caicos Islands to self-determination and independence in conformity with the Declaration on the Granting of Independence to Colonial Countries and Peoples, contained in General Assembly resolution 1514(XV);

3. *Reiterates* the view that such factors as territorial size, geographical location, size of population and limited natural resources should in no way delay the speedy exercise by the people of the Territory of their inalienable right as set out in the Declaration contained in General Assembly resolution 1514(XV), which fully applies to the Turks and Caicos Islands;

4. *Reiterates* that it is the obligation of the administering Power to create such conditions in the Turks and Caicos Islands as will enable the people of the Territory to exercise freely and without interference their inalienable right to self-determination and independence in accordance with General Assembly resolution 1514(XV), as well as all other relevant resolutions of the Assembly;

5. *Reaffirms* that it is the responsibility of the administering Power under the Charter of the United Nations to develop its dependent Territories economically and socially and urges the administering Power, in consultation with the territorial Government, to take the necessary measures to promote the economic and social development of the Turks and Caicos Islands and, in particular, to intensify and expand its programme of assistance in order to accelerate the development of the economic and social infrastructure of the Territory;

6. *Emphasizes* that greater attention should be paid to diversification of the economy, particularly in the promotion of agriculture and fisheries, for the benefit of the people of the Territory;

7. *Recalls* that it is the responsibility of the administering Power, in accordance with the freely expressed wishes of the people of the Territory, to safeguard, guarantee and ensure the inalienable right of the people to the enjoyment of their natural resources by taking effective measures to guarantee their right to own and dispose of those resources and to establish and maintain control of their future development;

8. *Urges* the specialized agencies and other organizations of the United Nations system, as well as regional institutions such as the Caribbean Development Bank, to continue to pay special attention to the development needs of the Turks and Caicos Islands;

9. *Reaffirms its strong conviction* that the administering Power must ensure that military bases and installa-

tions do not hinder the people of the Territory from exercising their right to self-determination and independence in conformity with the purposes and principles of the Charter and urges the administering Power to take all necessary measures to comply fully with the relevant resolutions of the United Nations relating to military bases and installations in colonial and Non-Self-Governing Territories;

10. *Requests* the administering Power, in consultation with the territorial Government, to continue to provide the assistance necessary for the training of qualified local personnel in the skills essential to the development of various sectors of society in the Territory;

11. *Considers* that the possibility of sending a further visiting mission to the Turks and Caicos Islands at an appropriate time should be kept under review;

12. *Requests* the Special Committee to continue the examination of this question at its next session, including the possible dispatch of a further visiting mission to the Turks and Caicos Islands at an appropriate time and in consultation with the administering Power, and to report thereon to the General Assembly at its thirty-ninth session.

General Assembly resolution 38/47

7 December 1983   Meeting 86   Adopted without vote

Approved by Fourth Committee (A/38/612 & Corr.1) without objection, 17 November (meeting 19); draft by Committee on colonial countries (A/38/23); agenda item 18.

Meeting numbers. GA 38th session: 4th Committee 8-19; plenary 86.

The draft was recommended by the Committee on colonial countries on 12 August, following endorsement of the conclusions and recommendations of the Sub-Committee on Small Territories. The Committee had considered constitutional and political developments, and economic, social and educational conditions in the Turks and Caicos Islands.

United States Virgin Islands

On 7 December, the General Assembly adopted without vote resolution 38/48, on the recommendation of the Fourth Committee.

Question of the United States Virgin Islands

The General Assembly,

Having considered the question of the United States Virgin Islands,

Having examined the relevant chapters of the report of the Special Committee on the Situation with regard to the Implementation of the Declaration on the Granting of Independence to Colonial Countries and Peoples,

Recalling its resolution 1514(XV) of 14 December 1960, containing the Declaration on the Granting of Independence to Colonial Countries and Peoples, and all other resolutions and decisions of the United Nations relating to the United States Virgin Islands,

Noting with appreciation the continued participation of the administering Power in the work of the Special Committee in regard to the United States Virgin Islands, thereby enabling it to conduct a more informed and meaningful examination of the situation in the Territory, and expressing its satisfaction at the willingness of the administering Power to receive visiting missions in the Territories under its administration,

Having heard the statement of the representative of the administering Power,

Recalling that it had urged the administering Power to expedite the passage of legislation placed before the Congress of the United States of America concerning the problem of aliens in the Territory,

Noting that the territorial Government has intensified its efforts to expand and diversify the economy and noting also with concern that the international recession has adversely affected the main sectors of the Territory's economy,

Reiterating the view that the participation of Territories as associate members in organizations of the United Nations system is a part of the overall strategy of accelerating the decolonization process,

Noting with satisfaction the efforts to revitalize health care programmes and to discourage juvenile delinquency, the measures to improve crime prevention and the action taken to expand and upgrade school facilities,

1. *Approves* the chapter of the report of the Special Committee on the Situation with regard to the Implementation of the Declaration on the Granting of Independence to Colonial Countries and Peoples relating to the United States Virgin Islands;

2. *Reaffirms* the inalienable right of the people of the United States Virgin Islands to self-determination and independence in conformity with the Declaration on the Granting of Independence to Colonial Countries and Peoples, contained in General Assembly resolution 1514(XV);

3. *Reiterates* the view that such factors as territorial size, geographical location, size of population and limited natural resources should in no way delay the speedy implementation of the Declaration contained in General Assembly resolution 1514(XV), which fully applies to the United States Virgin Islands;

4. *Reiterates* that it is the responsibility of the administering Power to create such conditions in the United States Virgin Islands as will enable the people of the Territory freely to exercise without interference their inalienable right to self-determination and independence in conformity with General Assembly resolution 1514(XV);

5. *Calls upon* the administering Power, taking into account the freely expressed wishes of the people of the United States Virgin Islands, to take all necessary steps to expedite the process of decolonization in accordance with the relevant provisions of the Charter of the United Nations and the Declaration, as well as all other relevant resolutions and decisions of the General Assembly;

6. *Welcomes* the enactment by the Congress of the United States of America of the Virgin Islands Alien Adjustment Act;

7. *Takes note* of the fact that the Governor of the United States Virgin Islands has introduced legislation to provide for a constitutional convention to discuss political status alternatives and has recommended that a referendum on the Convention's proposals be held simultaneously with the general election in 1984;

8. *Reaffirms* the responsibility of the administering Power under the Charter for the economic and social development of the Territory;

9. *Urges* the administering Power, in co-operation with the territorial Government, to strengthen the economy of the Territory by taking additional measures of diversification in all fields and developing an adequate infrastructure with a view to reducing its economic dependence on the administering Power;

10. *Notes with satisfaction* the recommendation of the Virgin Islands Status Commission that the Territory become an associate member of the Economic Commission for Latin America and calls upon the administering Power to facilitate the application of the Territory for associate membership in the Economic Commission for Latin America and its subsidiary bodies, including the Caribbean Development and Co-operation Committee;

11. *Urges* the administering Power, in co-operation with the Government of the United States Virgin Islands, to safeguard the inalienable right of the people of the Territory to the enjoyment of their natural resources by taking effective measures which guarantee the right of the people to own and dispose of those resources and to establish and maintain control of their future development;

12. *Urges* the administering Power, in co-operation with the territorial Government, to continue to improve social conditions and to pay particular attention to overcoming problems of unemployment, public housing, health care, education and crime and, in that connection, notes with satisfaction the efforts to revitalize health care programmes and to discourage juvenile delinquency, the measures to improve crime prevention and the action taken to expand and upgrade school facilities;

13. *Considers* that the possibility of sending a further visiting mission to the United States Virgin Islands at an appropriate time should be kept under review;

14. *Requests* the Special Committee to continue the examination of this question at its next session, including the possible dispatch of a further visiting mission to the United States Virgin Islands at an appropriate time and in consultation with the administering Power, and to report thereon to the General Assembly at its thirty-ninth session.

General Assembly resolution 38/48

7 December 1983   Meeting 86   Adopted without vote

Approved by Fourth Committee (A/38/612 & Corr.1) without objection, 17 November (meeting 19); draft by Committee on colonial countries (A/38/23); agenda item 18.

Meeting numbers. GA 38th session: 4th Committee 8-19; plenary 86.

The draft was recommended by the Committee on colonial countries on 14 September,[1] following its endorsement of the conclusions and recommendations of the Sub-Committee on Small Territories. The Committee had considered the military installations, constitutional and political developments, and economic, social and educational conditions in the United States Virgin Islands.

REFERENCES

[1]A/38/23. [2]A/38/695. [3]A/AC.109/753. [4]YUN 1960, p. 49, GA res. 1514(XV), 14 Dec. 1960.

Legal questions

International Court of Justice

In 1983, the International Court of Justice continued to deal with two contentious cases. A third dispute was referred to it in October.

In December, the General Assembly amended the Pension Scheme Regulations for members of the Court, with effect from the beginning of 1984 (resolution 38/239).

Judicial work of the Court

In 1983, the International Court of Justice—meeting at The Hague, Netherlands, from 23 February to 2 March[1] and on 13 October[2]—continued to deal with cases concerning the continental shelf delimitation between the Libyan Arab Jamahiriya and Malta, and the maritime boundary delimitation between Canada and the United States. In October, a case concerning a frontier dispute between Mali and the Upper Volta was submitted to the Court.

Continental shelf delimitation between the Libyan Arab Jamahiriya and Malta

On 26 July 1982, the Libyan Arab Jamahiriya and Malta had instituted proceedings by joint notification to the Court of a Special Agreement signed on 23 May 1976 and in force since an exchange on 20 March 1982 of instruments of ratification. The Agreement requested the Court to indicate the principles and rules applicable to delimitation of the continental shelf between the parties and the practical method for their application.

In 1983, the parties filed Memorials, in compliance with the Court's 1982 Order[3] setting 26 April 1983 as the time-limit. By an Order made that day,[4] the Court fixed 26 October as the time-limit for the filing of Counter-Memorials; the pleadings were duly filed.

Since the Court did not include on the Bench a Judge of Libyan or of Maltese nationality, each of the parties exercised its right under Article 31 of the Statute of the Court to choose a person to sit as Judge *ad hoc*. The Libyan Arab Jamahiriya chose Eduardo Jiménez de Aréchaga and Malta chose Jorge Castañeda.

On 24 October, Italy filed an application for permission to intervene pursuant to Article 62 of the Statute, explaining that it wished to take part in the proceedings to defend its rights over certain areas claimed by the parties. On 5 December, the Libyan Arab Jamahiriya and Malta submitted written observations on Italy's request.

Maritime boundary delimitation between Canada and the United States

On 25 November 1981, Canada and the United States had notified the Court of a Special Agreement, signed on 29 March 1979 and in force as from 20 November 1981, by which they submitted to the Court a question concerning the course of the maritime boundary dividing the continental shelf and fisheries zones in the Gulf of Maine area.

Memorials were filed by the parties in 1982[3] and by 28 June 1983, the date fixed by the Court, Counter-Memorials were filed. A five-member Chamber, formed in January 1982 to deal with the case, met from 18 to 20 October 1983. In accordance with an Order of 27 July[5] by the President of the Chamber fixing 12 December as the time-limit for the filing of Replies, the parties submitted to the Chamber documentation—some 9,500 pages—in support of their contentions.

Frontier dispute between Mali and the Upper Volta

On 14 October 1983, Mali and the Upper Volta jointly notified to the Registrar of the Court a Special Agreement concluded by them on 16 September, having entered into force on that day and registered with the United Nations, by which they submitted to a chamber of the Court the question of the delimitation of part of the land frontier between them.[2]

Organizational questions

ICJ pension scheme

In December 1983, the Advisory Committee on Administrative and Budgetary Questions (ACABQ),[6] in response to a request by the General Assembly's Fifth (Administrative and Budgetary) Committee, considered proposals on post-retirement benefits for members of the International Court of Justice as put forward in a report of the Secretary-General.[7]

ACABQ concurred with the Secretary-General's suggestions for: changing from 65 to 60 the normal minimum age at which pension might be payable; reducing from five to three years the minimum period of service requirement for payment of a retirement pension; amending the provisions for disability pension; introducing a provision on benefit for an incapacitated child, and amending another provision regarding the ceiling to child's benefit; and revising those concerning pension payment and adjustment procedure.

GENERAL ASSEMBLY ACTION

Acting on the recommendation of the Fifth Committee, the Assembly adopted resolution 38/239 on 20 December by recorded vote.

Pension scheme for the members of the International Court of Justice

The General Assembly,

Recalling its resolutions 1562(XV) of 18 December 1960, 1925(XVIII) of 11 December 1963, 2367(XXII) of 19 December 1967, 2890 A (XXVI) of 22 December 1971, 3193 A (XXVIII) of 18 December 1973 and 3537 A (XXX) of 17 December 1975, on the pension scheme for members of the International Court of Justice,

Having considered the report of the Secretary-General and the related report of the Advisory Committee on Administrative and Budgetary Questions,

Decides to amend the Pension Scheme Regulations for members of the International Court of Justice as indicated in the annex to the present resolution, with effect from 1 January 1984.

ANNEX
Amendments to the Pension Scheme Regulations of the International Court of Justice

Article I
Retirement pension
Replace "the age of sixty-five" by "the age of sixty" wherever the term appears.
In paragraph 1 *(a)*, replace "five years of service" by "three years of service".

Article II
Disability pension
Replace paragraph 2 by the following text:
"2. The amount of the disability pension shall be equal to the amount of the retirement pension which would have been payable to the member of the Court concerned had he, at the time of leaving office, completed the term for which he had been elected, pro-

vided that it shall not be less than one quarter of the annual salary."

Article III
Widow's pension
In paragraph 3 *(b)* and *(c)*, replace "the age of sixty-five" by "the age of sixty".

Article IV
Child's benefit
In paragraph 1 *(a)*, last line, replace "1,200 dollars a year" by "one thirty-sixth of the annual base salary".
Add the following new paragraph 3:
"3. The age-limit mentioned in paragraph 1 above shall be waived if the child is incapacitated by illness or injury, and the benefit shall continue to be paid for as long as the child remains incapacitated."

Article V
Special provisions
To be deleted.

Article VI
Definitions
Renumber as article V.
Replace paragraph 2 by the following text:
"2. 'Annual salary' means the annual base salary, exclusive of any allowances, fixed by the General Assembly and received by the member at the time he ceased to hold office."

Article VII
Miscellaneous provisions
Renumber as article VI.
Replace paragraph 3 by the following text:
"3. The President of the Court and the Secretary-General shall determine conditions for the application of article IV, paragraph 3, and, on the advice of a qualified actuary or actuaries, establish a table of actuarial reduction factors."

Article VIII
Application and effective date
Renumber as article VII.
Replace the entire article by the following text:
"1. The present Regulations shall be applicable as from 1 January 1984 to all who are members of the Court on or after that date, to their eligible beneficiaries and to recipients of pensions or benefits under article III or IV of the Regulations adopted on 19 December 1967.
"2. Pensions in payment shall be automatically revised by the same percentage and at the same date as pension entitlements.
"3. Former members of the Court who left office prior to 1 January 1968, or their eligible beneficiaries, shall continue to have their entitlements governed by the Regulations approved in General Assembly resolution 1562(XV) or 1925(XVIII), except that in their case the revised provisions of article III approved in General Assembly resolution 2367(XXII) and the consequential changes in article IV shall continue to be applicable to all relevant entitlements, regardless of the date on which the said entitlements first became payable."

General Assembly resolution 38/239
20 December 1983   Meeting 104   124-10-7 (recorded vote)

Approved by Fifth Committee (A/38/760 & Corr.1) by vote (64-1-17), 18 December (meeting 70); oral proposal by Chairman on ACABQ recommendation; agenda item 109.

Meeting numbers. GA 38th session: 5th Committee 70; plenary 104.

Recorded vote in Assembly as follows:

In favour: Afghanistan, Algeria, Argentina, Australia, Austria, Bahamas, Bahrain, Bangladesh, Barbados, Belize, Benin, Bhutan, Bolivia, Botswana, Brazil, Burma, Burundi, Canada, Central African Republic, Chad, Chile, China, Colombia, Congo, Costa Rica, Cuba, Cyprus, Democratic Kampuchea, Democratic Yemen, Denmark, Djibouti, Dominican Republic, Ecuador, Egypt, El Salvador, Ethiopia, Fiji, Finland, Gabon, Gambia, Ghana, Greece, Guatemala, Guinea, Guinea-Bissau, Guyana, Haiti, Honduras, Iceland, India, Indonesia, Iran, Iraq, Ireland, Israel, Ivory Coast, Jamaica, Japan, Jordan, Kenya, Kuwait, Lebanon, Lesotho, Libyan Arab Jamahiriya, Luxembourg, Madagascar, Malawi, Malaysia, Maldives, Mali, Malta, Mauritania, Mauritius, Mexico, Morocco, Mozambique, Nepal, Netherlands, Nicaragua, Niger, Nigeria, Norway, Oman, Pakistan, Panama, Papua New Guinea, Paraguay, Peru, Philippines, Portugal, Qatar, Romania, Rwanda, Saint Lucia, Saint Vincent and the Grenadines, Samoa, Sao Tome and Principe, Saudi Arabia, Senegal, Sierra Leone, Singapore, Solomon Islands, Spain, Sudan, Suriname, Swaziland, Sweden, Syrian Arab Republic, Thailand, Togo, Trinidad and Tobago, Tunisia, Turkey, Uganda, United Arab Emirates, United Republic of Cameroon, United Republic of Tanzania, Upper Volta, Uruguay, Vanuatu, Venezuela, Yemen, Yugoslavia, Zambia.

Against: Bulgaria, Byelorussian SSR, Czechoslovakia, German Democratic Republic, Hungary, Mongolia, Poland, Ukrainian SSR, USSR, United States.

Abstaining: Belgium, France, Germany, Federal Republic of, Italy, Liberia, Sri Lanka, United Kingdom.

In the Fifth Committee, the vote was taken at the request of the United States, which feared creating a precedent of setting the Court members apart by providing them with benefits greater than those enjoyed by Secretariat officials, in view of the possibility that the latter would in future demand equal treatment.

The Under-Secretary-General for Administration and Management pointed out that the Court's pension scheme was completely different from the United Nations Joint Staff Pension Fund in origin, development, modalities, amounts and timing.

Orally proposing that the Fifth Committee recommend to the Assembly approval of the Secretary-General's proposals on the question, the Committee Chairman stated that the action entailed direct financial implications of $63,500, but that no appropriation was currently required.

Reports of the Court

The 1983 activities of the International Court of Justice were contained in two reports to the General Assembly, covering the periods 1 August 1982 to 31 July 1983[8] and 1 August 1983 to 31 July 1984.[9]

GENERAL ASSEMBLY ACTION

On 5 December 1983, on an oral proposal by its President, the Assembly adopted decision 38/411 without vote, thus taking note of the 1982-1983 report.

Report of the International Court of Justice

At its 82nd plenary meeting, on 5 December 1983, the General Assembly took note of the report of the International Court of Justice.

General Assembly decision 38/411

Adopted without vote

Oral proposal by President; agenda item 13.
Meeting number. GA 38th session: plenary 82.

REFERENCES

[1]*International Court of Justice Yearbook 1982-1983*, No. 37, I.C.J. Sales No. 488. [2]*International Court of Justice Yearbook 1983-1984*, No. 38, I.C.J. Sales No. 502. [3]YUN 1982, p. 1367. [4]*Case concerning the Continental Shelf* (Libyan Arab Jamahiriya/Malta), *Order of 26 April 1983*, I.C.J. Sales No. 485. [5]*Case concerning Delimitation of the Maritime Boundary in the Gulf of Maine Area* (Canada/United States of America), *Order of 27 July 1983*, I.C.J. Sales No. 486. [6]A/38/7/Add.23. [7]A/C.5/38/27. [8]A/38/4. [9]A/39/4.

PUBLICATIONS

The International Court of Justice (ST/DPI/780), Sales No. E.83.I.20. *International Court of Justice: Reports of Judgments, Advisory Opinions and Orders, Index 1983*, I.C.J. Sales No. 485. *Bibliography of the International Court of Justice*, Nos. 36, 37, *1982/1983*, I.C.J. Sales No. 495. *Judgements of the United Nations Administrative Tribunal, Nos. 231 to 300, 1978-1982* (AT/DEC/231 to 300), Sales No. E.83.X.1.

Chapter II

Legal aspects of international political relations

In 1983, the United Nations continued to explore effective legal measures for promoting friendly relations among States as well as for combating mercenary activities and international terrorism.

In December, the General Assembly adopted several resolutions calling for continued work towards the legal codification of: good-neighbourliness (38/126), peaceful settlement of disputes (38/131), non-use of force in international relations (38/133), and the banning of mercenary activities (38/137). States were also invited to take measures for the speedy and final elimination of international terrorism (38/130).

Further, the Assembly invited the International Law Commission (ILC) to continue elaborating the 1954 draft Code of Offences against the Peace and Security of Mankind (resolution 38/132), as well as draft articles on non-navigational uses of international watercourses.

Topic related to this chapter. International peace and security.

Peaceful settlement of disputes between States

In 1983, the question of peaceful settlement of disputes between States was considered by the General Assembly, in pursuance of a November 1982 decision,[1] and by the Special Committee on the Charter of the United Nations and on the Strengthening of the Role of the Organization. In December 1983, the Assembly requested the Special Committee to continue work on the question and to consider elaborating a handbook on the topic.

Following Assembly approval in November 1982 of the Manila Declaration on the Peaceful Settlement of International Disputes,[2] the Secretary-General, on 14 January 1983,[3] transmitted the text to the President of the Security Council, as requested by the Assembly. The Declaration—based on work by the Special Committee and the Assembly's Sixth (Legal) Committee—set out principles for States' observance, such as good-faith action for avoiding disputes or the use of direct negotiations, and discussed the United Nations role in dispute settlement.

Special Committee consideration. The Special Committee, at its April/May 1983 session,[4] continued work on the peaceful settlement of disputes, as called for by the Assembly in December

1982.[5] This was one of three main questions considered by the Committee, the others being proposals on rationalizing the existing procedures of the United Nations and ways to maintain international peace and security (see Chapter IV of this section).

An open-ended Working Group of the Committee held eight meetings on the question between 25 and 28 April, devoting three of them to consideration of an oral proposal by the Philippines and Romania—later joined by Nigeria, and submitted as a working paper to the Assembly in August[6]—for the creation of a United Nations permanent commission on good offices, mediation and conciliation for the settlement of disputes and the prevention of conflicts among States. The proposed commission was to be composed of all Member States and established by the Assembly, for preventing situations of tension from degenerating into armed conflict and for the mediation of disputes. The commission would be seized of a dispute at the request of a State party concerned, on the Assembly's decision or that of the Security Council, or on the Secretary-General's recommendation. The proposal met with varied responses.

The Working Group also reviewed 21 other proposals, contained in a list prepared by the Special Committee in 1979,[7] and agreed that the Assembly should call on the Secretary-General to prepare a preliminary outline of a handbook on the pacific settlement of disputes, which was to contain all existing means and mechanisms available for that purpose.

GENERAL ASSEMBLY ACTION

On 19 December 1983, the General Assembly, on the recommendation of the Sixth Committee, adopted resolution 38/131 without vote.

Peaceful settlement of disputes between States
The General Assembly,
Having examined the item entitled "Peaceful settlement of disputes between States",
Recalling its resolution 37/10 of 15 November 1982, by which it approved the Manila Declaration on the Peaceful Settlement of International Disputes, annexed thereto,
Deeply concerned at the continuation of conflict situations and the emergence of new sources of disputes and tension in international life, and especially at the growing tendency to resort to force or the threat of force and to intervention in internal affairs, and at the escalation

of the arms race, which gravely endanger the independence and security of States as well as international peace and security,

Taking into account the need to exert the utmost effort in order to settle any situations and disputes between States exclusively by peaceful means and to avoid any military action and hostilities against other States, which can only make more difficult the solution of existing problems,

Considering that the question of the peaceful settlement of disputes should represent one of the central concerns for States and for the United Nations, and that efforts for strengthening the process of the peaceful settlement of disputes should be continued,

Taking note of the working paper on the establishment of a permanent commission on good offices, mediation and conciliation for the settlement of disputes and the prevention of conflicts among States, submitted to the General Assembly by Nigeria, the Philippines and Romania,

1. *Again urges* all States to observe and promote in good faith the provisions of the Manila Declaration on the Peaceful Settlement of International Disputes in the settlement of their international disputes;

2. *Stresses* the need to continue efforts to strengthen the process of the peaceful settlement of disputes through the progressive development and codification of international law and through enhancing the effectiveness of the United Nations in this field;

3. *Requests* the Special Committee on the Charter of the United Nations and on the Strengthening of the Role of the Organization, during its session in 1984, to continue its work on the question of the peaceful settlement of disputes between States and, in this context:

(a) To consider the proposal contained in the above-mentioned working paper;

(b) To continue, in conformity with the agreement reached by the Special Committee, consideration of the proposal concerning the elaboration of a handbook on the peaceful settlement of disputes between States;

4. *Requests* the Secretary-General, in the light of the report of the Special Committee, to prepare a preliminary outline of the possible content of a handbook on the peaceful settlement of disputes between States, which will comprise all the existing means and mechanisms available for the purpose, and to submit this outline to the Special Committee at its session in 1984;

5. *Decides* to include in the provisional agenda of its thirty-ninth session the item entitled "Peaceful settlement of disputes between States".

General Assembly resolution 38/131

19 December 1983   Meeting 101   Adopted without vote

Approved by Sixth Committee (A/38/664) without vote, 8 December (meeting 70); 33-nation draft (A/C.6/38/L.9); agenda item 124.

Sponsors: Australia, Bangladesh, Bolivia, Chile, Congo, Costa Rica, Cyprus, Dominican Republic, Ecuador, Egypt, Ethiopia, Guinea, Guyana, Ivory Coast, Madagascar, Mali, Mexico, Morocco, Nigeria, Philippines, Romania, Rwanda, Senegal, Sierra Leone, Singapore, Sudan, Togo, Uganda, United Republic of Cameroon, Upper Volta, Uruguay, Yugoslavia, Zambia.

Meeting numbers. GA 38th session: 6th Committee 51, 53, 55, 57-62, 64, 65, 70; plenary 101.

When the Sixth Committee approved the text, its Chairman announced that the peaceful settlement of disputes between States would be considered, at the 1984 Assembly session, in conjunction with the Special Committee's report.

In explanation of position, the Federal Republic of Germany expressed concern at what it said was a trend to deal with various aspects of the report of a subsidiary body under separate agenda items, thereby leading to separate draft resolutions. Sharing that view, the United Kingdom added that if procedural questions such as the combining of agenda items were to become political and prestige matters, the Sixth Committee might lose control of the organization of its work.

Somalia felt that the United Nations would be strengthened if the preparation of a handbook led to the actual observance of human rights. The USSR, which favoured a handbook, opposed the establishment of a permanent commission, considering it to be contrary to the Charter and likely to undermine the prerogatives of the Security Council. Peru said its views as regards paragraph 1 remained unchanged from those it had expressed in 1982.

The Assembly's call for consideration of proposals for a permanent commission on good offices and for a handbook was repeated in resolution 38/141 (see Chapter IV of this section). Explaining its position on that text, Viet Nam said the proposal for a commission would impinge on the right of States under the Charter to choose freely among the various means of dispute settlement; the lack of political will, rather than of mechanisms and procedures, accounted for impasses in settlement, and it preferred mediation by regional organizations of direct negotiations between the parties.

Good-neighbourliness between States

In 1983, the General Assembly called again for developing good-neighbourly relations between States and declared it appropriate to start clarifying and formulating the elements of good-neighbourliness as part of a process of elaborating an international document on the subject.

GENERAL ASSEMBLY ACTION

The Secretary-General submitted to the Assembly in September 1983, in follow-up to its December 1982 request,[8] a report with a later addendum,[9] containing the views and suggestions on good-neighbourliness as received from 12 States in 1982 and from 14 States in 1983, along with those received from organizations within the United Nations system in the same two years.

In addition, Romania transmitted to the Secretary-General on 21 September a working paper[10] suggesting an outline for an international document on good-neighbourliness, as first suggested by the Assembly in 1981.[11] The proposed outline dealt with the elements and legal content of good-neighbourliness, ways of strengthening and developing the concept, and the role of international organizations in its promotion.

On 19 December 1983, the General Assembly, on the recommendation of the Sixth Committee, adopted resolution 38/126 without vote.

Development and strengthening of good-neighbourliness between States

The General Assembly,

Bearing in mind the determination of the peoples of the United Nations, as expressed in the Charter, to practise tolerance and live together in peace with one another as good neighbours,

Recalling the Declaration on Principles of International Law concerning Friendly Relations and Co-operation among States in accordance with the Charter of the United Nations, approved by its resolution 2625(XXV) of 24 October 1970,

Recalling its resolutions 1236(XII) of 14 December 1957, 1301(XIII) of 10 December 1958, 2129(XX) of 21 December 1965, 34/99 of 14 December 1979, 36/101 of 9 December 1981 and 37/117 of 16 December 1982,

Bearing in mind that, owing to geographic proximity and to other relevant reasons, there are particularly favourable opportunities for co-operation and mutual advantage between neighbouring countries, in many fields and various forms, and that the development of such co-operation may have a positive influence on international relations as a whole,

Considering that the great changes of a political, economic and social nature, as well as the scientific and technological progress which have taken place in the world and led to unprecedented interdependence of nations, have given new dimensions to good-neighbourliness in the conduct of States and increased the need to develop and strengthen it,

Taking into account the working paper concerning the development and strengthening of good-neighbourliness between States, as well as the written replies sent by States and international organizations on the content of good-neighbourliness and on ways and means to enhance it and the views expressed by States in 1981 and 1982 on this subject,

Recalling its opinion that it is necessary to continue to examine the question of good-neighbourliness in order to strengthen and develop its content, as well as ways and modalities to enhance its effectiveness, and that the results of this examination could be included, at an appropriate time, in a suitable international document,

1. *Reaffirms* that good-neighbourliness fully conforms with the purposes of the United Nations and shall be founded upon the strict observance of the principles of the Charter and of the Declaration on Principles of International Law concerning Friendly Relations and Co-operation among States in accordance with the Charter of the United Nations, and so presupposes the rejection of any acts seeking to establish zones of influence or domination;

2. *Calls once again upon* States, in the interest of the maintenance of international peace and security, to develop good-neighbourly relations, acting on the basis of these principles;

3. *Reaffirms* that the generalization of the long practice of good-neighbourliness and of principles and rules pertaining to it is likely to strengthen friendly relations and co-operation among States in accordance with the Charter;

4. *Deems it appropriate*, on the basis of the working paper concerning the development and strengthening of good-neighbourliness between States mentioned above, as well as of other proposals and ideas which have been or will be submitted by States, and the replies and views of States and international organizations, to start clarifying and formulating the elements of good-neighbourliness as part of a process of elaboration of a suitable international document on the subject;

5. *Requests* the Sixth Committee to decide, at the thirty-ninth session of the General Assembly, on the appropriate framework to accomplish the above-mentioned tasks;

6. *Decides* to include in the provisional agenda of its thirty-ninth session the item entitled "Development and strengthening of good-neighbourliness between States".

General Assembly resolution 38/126

19 December 1983   Meeting 101   Adopted without vote

Approved by Sixth Committee (A/38/659) without vote, 8 December (meeting 70); 31-nation draft (A/C.6/38/L.20); agenda item 64.

Sponsors: Bangladesh, Bolivia, Burundi, Chile, Colombia, Congo, Costa Rica, France, Guinea, Guyana, Indonesia, Iraq, Ivory Coast, Kenya, Liberia, Madagascar, Mali, Niger, Nigeria, Panama, Philippines, Portugal, Romania, Rwanda, Senegal, Singapore, Spain, Sudan, Turkey, Yugoslavia, Zaire.

Meeting numbers. GA 38th session: 6th Committee 61, 63-66, 70; plenary 101.

Non-use of force in international relations

The General Assembly, in 1983 as in previous years, requested the Special Committee on Enhancing the Effectiveness of the Principle of Non-Use of Force in International Relations to continue its work with the goal of drafting a world treaty on that principle.

In the course of 1983, the Secretary-General received a number of communications concerning alleged incidents of the use of force in international relations (see specific conflicts discussed in POLITICAL AND SECURITY QUESTIONS).

Special Committee consideration. In response to a December 1982 Assembly resolution,[12] the 35-member Special Committee—established in 1977[13] to consider proposals and suggestions with the goal of drafting a world treaty as well as the peaceful settlement of disputes or such other recommendations as the Committee deemed appropriate—met at United Nations Headquarters from 31 January to 25 February 1983.[14]

The Committee had before it a draft world treaty on the non-use of force submitted in 1976 by the USSR;[15] a 1979 working paper by Belgium, France, the Federal Republic of Germany, Italy and the United Kingdom;[16] and a 1981 revised working paper from 10 non-aligned countries (Benin, Cyprus, Egypt, India, Iraq, Morocco, Nepal, Nicaragua, Senegal, Uganda).[17] Also before the Committee was an informal paper by the Chairman of the Committee's 1982 session,[18] which had been discussed in a preliminary manner at that session. The informal paper grouped the suggestions made in the Committee under the headings of: manifestations, scope and dimensions of the threat or use of force; general prohibition of the threat or use of force; consequences of the threat or use of force; legitimate use of force; peaceful settlement of disputes; role of the United Nations; and disarmament and confidence-building measures.

Also before the Committee was a report of the Secretary-General,[19] containing comments submitted by five Member States in reply to a renewed Assembly invitation in 1982 for States' observations.[12]

An open-ended Working Group, re-established by the Committee, held 13 meetings between 8 and 18 February and considered one by one the headings contained in the 1982 Chairman's informal paper.

On 25 February, the Committee approved the Working Group's report as well as its own report. Since the Committee had not completed its work, it generally recognized the desirability of further considering the question before it. While the majority was in favour of renewing the Committee's mandate, some delegations were not; others thought the mandate should be reviewed.

GENERAL ASSEMBLY ACTION

On the recommendation of the Sixth Committee, the General Assembly adopted resolution 38/133 by recorded vote on 19 December. In the Sixth Committee, the recorded vote was requested by France.

Report of the Special Committee on Enhancing the Effectiveness of the Principle of Non-Use of Force in International Relations

The General Assembly,

Recalling its resolution 31/9 of 8 November 1976, in which it invited Member States to examine further the draft World Treaty on the Non-Use of Force in International Relations as well as other proposals made during the consideration of this item,

Recalling also its resolution 32/150 of 19 December 1977, by which it established the Special Committee on Enhancing the Effectiveness of the Principle of Non-Use of Force in International Relations,

Recalling, in particular, its resolutions 33/96 of 16 December 1978, 34/13 of 9 November 1979, 35/50 of 4 December 1980, 36/31 of 13 November 1981 and 37/105 of 16 December 1982, in which it decided that the Special Committee should continue its work,

Taking note of the statement made by the Chairman of the Special Committee at its session in 1983, based on the informal working paper presented by the Chairman of the Special Committee at its session in 1982,

Having considered the report of the Special Committee,

Taking note of the prospects of progress in the work of the Special Committee registered during its session in 1983,

Taking into account that the Special Committee has not completed the mandate entrusted to it,

Reaffirming the need for effectiveness in the universal application of the principle of non-use of force in inter-

national relations and for assistance by the United Nations in this endeavour,

Expressing the hope that the Special Committee will, on the basis of the proposals before it, complete the mandate entrusted to it as soon as possible,

1. *Takes note* of the report of the Special Committee on Enhancing the Effectiveness of the Principle of Non-Use of Force in International Relations;

2. *Decides* that the Special Committee shall continue its work with the goal of drafting, at the earliest possible date, a world treaty on the non-use of force in international relations as well as the peaceful settlement of disputes or such other recommendations as the Committee deems appropriate;

3. *Requests* the Special Committee, in order to ensure further progress in its work, to continue at its session in 1984 the elaboration of the formulas of the working paper containing the main elements of the principle of non-use of force in international relations, taking duly into account the proposals submitted to it and the efforts undertaken at its session in 1983;

4. *Invites* Governments to communicate their comments or suggestions or to bring them up to date, in accordance with General Assembly resolution 31/9;

5. *Requests* the Special Committee to be mindful of the importance of reaching general agreement whenever it has significance for the outcome of its work;

6. *Decides* that the Special Committee shall accept the participation of observers of Member States, including participation in the meetings of its working group;

7. *Requests* the Special Committee to concentrate its work in the framework of its working group;

8. *Requests* the Secretary-General to provide the Special Committee with the necessary facilities and services;

9. *Invites* the Special Committee to submit a report on its work to the General Assembly at its thirty-ninth session;

10. *Decides* to include in the provisional agenda of its thirty-ninth session the item entitled "Report of the Special Committee on Enhancing the Effectiveness of the Principle of Non-Use of Force in International Relations".

General Assembly resolution 38/133

19 December 1983   Meeting 101   119-15-8 (recorded vote)

Approved by Sixth Committee (A/38/666) by recorded vote (88-14-9), 29 November (meeting 57); 32-nation draft (A/C.6/38/L.7); agenda item 126.

Sponsors: Afghanistan, Angola, Benin, Bulgaria, Byelorussian SSR, Cuba, Cyprus, Czechoslovakia, Democratic Yemen, Egypt, Ethiopia, German Democratic Republic, Guinea, Hungary, India, Iraq, Lao People's Democratic Republic, Libyan Arab Jamahiriya, Madagascar, Mali, Mongolia, Morocco, Mozambique, Nicaragua, Poland, Romania, Syrian Arab Republic, Uganda, Ukrainian SSR, USSR, Venezuela, Viet Nam.

Financial implications. 5th Committee, A/38/709; S-G, A/C.5/38/63, A/C.6/38/L.12.

Meeting numbers. GA 38th session: 5th Committee 58; 6th Committee 12-20, 57; plenary 101.

Recorded vote in Assembly as follows:

In favour: Afghanistan, Algeria, Angola, Argentina, Bahamas, Bahrain, Bangladesh, Barbados, Belize, Benin, Bhutan, Bolivia, Brazil, Bulgaria, Burma, Burundi, Byelorussian SSR, Cape Verde, Chad, Chile, China, Colombia, Congo, Costa Rica, Cuba, Cyprus, Czechoslovakia, Democratic Kampuchea, Djibouti, Dominican Republic, Ecuador, Egypt, El Salvador, Ethiopia, Fiji, Finland, Gabon, Gambia, German Democratic Republic, Ghana, Greece, Guatemala, Guinea, Guinea-Bissau, Guyana, Haiti, Honduras, Hungary, India, Indonesia, Iran, Iraq, Jamaica, Jordan, Kenya, Kuwait, Lao People's Democratic Republic, Lebanon, Lesotho, Liberia, Libyan Arab Jamahiriya, Madagascar, Malawi, Malaysia, Maldives, Mali, Malta, Mauritania, Mauritius, Mexico, Mongolia, Morocco, Mozambique, Nepal, Nicaragua, Niger, Nigeria, Oman, Pakistan, Panama, Papua New Guinea, Paraguay, Peru, Philippines, Poland, Qatar, Romania, Rwanda, Saint Lucia, Sao Tome and Principe, Saudi Arabia, Senegal, Sierra Leone, Singapore, Somalia,

Sri Lanka, Sudan, Suriname, Swaziland, Syrian Arab Republic, Thailand, Togo, Trinidad and Tobago, Tunisia, Uganda, Ukrainian SSR, USSR, United Arab Emirates, United Republic of Cameroon, United Republic of Tanzania, Upper Volta, Uruguay, Vanuatu, Venezuela, Viet Nam, Yemen, Yugoslavia, Zaire, Zambia.
Against: Belgium, Canada, Denmark, France, Iceland, Israel, Italy, Japan, Luxembourg, Netherlands, Norway, Portugal, Spain, United Kingdom, United States.
Abstaining: Australia, Austria, Germany, Federal Republic of, Ireland, Ivory Coast, New Zealand, Sweden, Turkey.

In explanation of vote, Norway and Spain felt that elaborating a treaty could raise doubts with regard to the legally binding character, and interpretation, of the provisions in the Charter of the United Nations, which already prohibited the use of force in international relations. Sharing that view, Sweden also observed that the only exception allowed under the Charter was the use of force in legitimate self-defence (Article 51). Spain and Sweden asserted that the non-use of force could be strengthened through better observance by all States of the relevant Charter provisions.

Australia regretted that the text continued to place undue emphasis on drafting a new treaty and that the suggestions by many States about future work on the subject had not been taken into account.

Draft code of offences against peace and security

In December 1983, the General Assembly invited the International Law Commission to continue work on the draft Code of Offences against the Peace and Security of Mankind by first elaborating an introduction as well as a list of offences. The Assembly took this action after ILC had continued working on the draft Code at its 1983 session,[20] in response to a 1982 Assembly invitation.[21]

Prepared by ILC in 1954[22] in response to a 1947 Assembly request,[23] the draft Code defined offences which were crimes under international law and for which the responsible individual was to be punished.

ILC consideration. The Commission, at its 1983 session, considered, and held a general debate based on, the first report submitted by its Special Rapporteur on the topic, Doudou Thiam (Senegal).[24] The report focused on the scope and methodology as well as implementation of the draft Code.

ILC also had before it a compendium of relevant international instruments[25] and an analytical paper containing the written or oral comments of Member States,[26] both prepared by the Secretariat at the Commission's 1982 request. According to the analytical paper, divergent views had been expressed, among other things, on: the advisability of elaborating a code; implications, and relationship with the proposed Code, of the Assembly's 1974 Definition of Aggression;[27] and the status of the 1954 draft as a possible basis for further United Nations work on the topic.

The Secretary-General submitted to ILC comments received from three Member States[28] in response to a December 1982 Assembly invitation;[21] he also submitted these replies in a September report to the Assembly.[29]

The Commission, concluding that the draft Code should cover only the most serious international offences, solicited the Assembly's views on: the subjects of law to which international criminal responsibility could be attributed; whether the ILC mandate extended to the preparation of the statute of an international criminal jurisdiction for individuals; and whether such jurisdiction should also apply to States. ILC considered it advisable to include in the draft Code an introduction recalling the general principles of criminal law, such as the non-retroactivity of such law and the theories of aggravating or mitigating circumstances, complicity, preparation and justified acts.

GENERAL ASSEMBLY ACTION

On 19 December, the General Assembly, acting on the recommendation of the Sixth Committee, adopted by recorded vote resolution 38/132.

Draft Code of Offences against the Peace and Security of Mankind

The General Assembly,

Mindful of Article 13, paragraph 1 *a*, of the Charter of the United Nations, which provides that the General Assembly shall initiate studies and make recommendations for the purpose of encouraging the progressive development of international law and its codification,

Recalling its resolution 177(II) of 21 November 1947, by which it directed the International Law Commission to prepare a draft code of offences against the peace and security of mankind,

Having considered the draft Code of Offences against the Peace and Security of Mankind prepared by the International Law Commission and submitted to the General Assembly in 1954,

Recalling its belief that the elaboration of a code of offences against the peace and security of mankind could contribute to strengthening international peace and security and thus to promoting and implementing the purposes and principles set forth in the Charter of the United Nations,

Recalling its resolution 36/106 of 10 December 1981, in which it invited the International Law Commission to resume its work with a view to elaborating the draft Code and to examine it with the required priority in order to review it, taking into account the results achieved by the process of the progressive development of international law,

Taking into account the views expressed during the debate on this item at the current session,

Taking note of the report of the Special Rapporteur,

Taking into account the importance and the urgency of the subject,

1. *Invites* the International Law Commission to continue its work on the elaboration of the draft Code of Offences against the Peace and Security of Mankind by elaborating, as a first step, an introduction in conformity with paragraph 67 of its report on the work of its thirty-fifth session, as well as a list of the offences in conformity with paragraph 69 of that report;

2. *Requests* the Secretary-General to seek the views of Member States and intergovernmental organizations regarding the questions raised in paragraph 69 of the report of the International Law Commission and to include them in a report to be submitted to the General Assembly at its thirty-ninth session with a view to adopting, at the appropriate time, the necessary decision thereon;

3. *Decides* to include in the provisional agenda of its thirty-ninth session the item entitled "Draft Code of Offences against the Peace and Security of Mankind", to be considered in conjunction with the consideration of the report of the International Law Commission.

General Assembly resolution 38/132

19 December 1983   Meeting 101   128-0-13 (recorded vote)

Approved by Sixth Committee (A/38/665) by vote (104-0-13), 8 December (meeting 70); 27-nation draft (A/C.6/38/L.19 & Corr.1); agenda item 125.

Sponsors: Algeria, Benin, Bolivia, Congo, Cuba, Cyprus, Democratic Yemen, Egypt, Gabon, German Democratic Republic, Ivory Coast, Lao People's Democratic Republic, Liberia, Mali, Mongolia, Morocco, Nigeria, Philippines, Poland, Rwanda, Senegal, Sudan, Thailand, Togo, Tunisia, Viet Nam, Zaire.

Meeting numbers. GA 38th session: 6th Committee 43, 49, 50, 52-54, 63, 65, 70; plenary 101.

Recorded vote in Assembly as follows:

In favour: Afghanistan, Algeria, Angola, Argentina, Australia, Austria, Bahamas, Bahrain, Bangladesh, Barbados, Belize, Benin, Bhutan, Bolivia, Brazil, Bulgaria, Burundi, Byelorussian SSR, Canada, Cape Verde, Chad, Chile, China, Colombia, Congo, Costa Rica, Cuba, Cyprus, Czechoslovakia, Democratic Kampuchea, Denmark, Djibouti, Dominican Republic, Ecuador, Egypt, El Salvador, Ethiopia, Fiji, Finland, Gabon, Gambia, German Democratic Republic, Ghana, Greece, Guatemala, Guinea, Guinea-Bissau, Guyana, Haiti, Honduras, Hungary, Iceland, India, Indonesia, Iran, Iraq, Ireland, Ivory Coast, Jamaica, Jordan, Kenya, Kuwait, Lao People's Democratic Republic, Lebanon, Lesotho, Liberia, Libyan Arab Jamahiriya, Madagascar, Malawi, Malaysia, Maldives, Mali, Malta, Mauritania, Mauritius, Mexico, Mongolia, Morocco, Mozambique, Nepal, New Zealand, Nicaragua, Niger, Nigeria, Norway, Oman, Pakistan, Panama, Papua New Guinea, Paraguay, Peru, Philippines, Poland, Portugal, Qatar, Romania, Rwanda, Saint Lucia, Sao Tome and Principe, Saudi Arabia, Senegal, Sierra Leone, Singapore, Somalia, Sri Lanka, Sudan, Suriname, Swaziland, Sweden, Syrian Arab Republic, Thailand, Togo, Trinidad and Tobago, Tunisia, Uganda, Ukrainian SSR, USSR, United Arab Emirates, United Republic of Cameroon, Upper Volta, Uruguay, Vanuatu, Venezuela, Viet Nam, Yemen, Yugoslavia, Zaire, Zambia.

Against: None.

Abstaining: Belgium, Burma, France, Germany, Federal Republic of, Israel, Italy, Japan, Luxembourg, Netherlands, Spain, Turkey, United Kingdom, United States.

Before acting on the text as a whole, the Sixth Committee approved paragraph 3 by a vote, requested by Norway and the United States, of 89 to 2, with 26 abstentions.

In explanation of vote in the Sixth Committee, Canada, France, Ireland, Norway (on behalf also of Denmark, Finland, Iceland and Sweden), Spain and the United States asserted that the draft Code should be considered in conjunction with the ILC report, rather than constitute a separate agenda item. Canada, which abstained in the vote on paragraph 3 but voted in favour of the text as a whole, said steps should be taken first to rationalize the work of the Sixth Committee through either the joint discussion or the combining of various items which had points in common. Further, France, Ireland and Norway (on behalf of the five Nordic countries) saw no reason to assign special priority to preparing a draft Code.

Spain, which abstained in the vote on the whole text because it could not accept paragraph 3, had

doubts about the methods adopted for elaborating the draft Code and about its scope. Abstaining in both Committee votes, Israel said it would have voted against the penultimate preambular paragraph had it been put to a vote; that paragraph implied that the Assembly would take note of the report of the Special Rapporteur, which the Sixth Committee had neither considered nor approved.

Also abstaining in the votes, the United Kingdom felt that the political pressure implied in the last preambular paragraph, along with paragraph 3, could give the impression that the Sixth Committee was not confident of ILC's ability to carry out the task entrusted to it. It also observed that, while paragraph 1 referred to a list of offences, the ILC report made no such mention; it would be premature to elaborate such a list until ILC had specified general criteria for application.

The USSR supported the text and stressed its support for paragraph 3, saying that separate consideration of important questions produced better results.

Draft convention against mercenaries

In 1983, the General Assembly decided that its *Ad Hoc* Committee on the Drafting of an International Convention against the Recruitment, Use, Financing and Training of Mercenaries should continue its work towards that goal, with a view to completing its mandate in 1984.

Work of the Committee against mercenaries. Responding to a December 1982 Assembly resolution,[30] the Committee against mercenaries held its third session at United Nations Headquarters from 2 to 26 August 1983.[31] Established in 1980,[32] the Committee, which was to be composed of 35 Member States, continued to have one vacancy during 1983 (see APPENDIX III).

The Committee re-established two Working Groups: Group A to deal with issues of definition and the convention's scope, and Group B to deal with all other issues relevant to the future convention. In addition to the Committee's 1982 report to the Assembly[33] and the documents and proposals annexed thereto, Group A had, for its consideration, an 18-article draft convention submitted by France, which was subsequently annexed to the Committee's 1983 report to the Assembly. Following discussions, the Chairman of Group A introduced as a basis for future work six draft articles (articles 1 to 6) relating to definition of "mercenary", scope of the convention and the obligations of States, which were included as paragraph 56 of the Committee's report. Group B had before it a draft convention submitted by Nigeria in 1981[34] and subsequently revised,[33] and the draft convention submitted by France in 1983. It resumed consideration of a provision on preventive measures on which the debate in 1982 had remained inconclusive. It decided to discuss, subsequently, damage reparation, status of mercenaries and settlement of disputes, it being understood that the questions of jurisdiction and extradition would be examined at a later stage in view of their close links with matters being dealt with in Group A.

The Committee also had before it a 5 August communication from Angola,[35] forwarding the text of its Revolutionary Council Law of 1977 on the prevention and repression of the crime of mercenary conduct, and a note by the Secretariat[36] listing documents relevant to the topic.

Other action. A number of other actions were taken in 1983 with regard to mercenaries.

In July, the Security Council agreed that the Commission of Inquiry, established in 1981 to investigate the mercenary aggression of 25 November 1981 against Seychelles, had fulfilled its mandate (see POLITICAL AND SECURITY QUESTIONS, Chapter V).

On the right of peoples to self-determination, the Commission on Human Rights, on 15 February,[37] and the General Assembly, by resolution 38/17 of 22 November, reaffirmed that the practice of using mercenaries against sovereign States and national liberation movements constituted a criminal act. They called on all Governments to enact legislation declaring the recruitment, financing and training of mercenaries in their territories and the transit of mercenaries through their territories to be punishable offences, and prohibiting their nationals from serving as mercenaries, and to report on such legislation to the Secretary-General. By a 17 November report,[38] the Secretary-General transmitted to the Commission the summaries of replies received from 13 Governments as of 15 November on the status of such legislation.

In 1983, Mexico submitted to the Assembly's Sixth Committee, for referral also to the Committee against mercenaries, an informal working paper[39] containing elements for a draft convention, such as the definition of mercenaries, obligations as to prevention and suppression, co-operation among States, international responsibility, dispute settlement and final clauses.

GENERAL ASSEMBLY ACTION

On 19 December 1983, the General Assembly, on the recommendation of the Sixth Committee, adopted resolution 38/137 without vote.

Drafting of an international convention against the recruitment, use, financing and training of mercenaries

The General Assembly,

Bearing in mind the need for strict observance of the principles of sovereign equality, political independence,

territorial integrity of States and self-determination of peoples, enshrined in the Charter of the United Nations and developed in the Declaration on Principles of International Law concerning Friendly Relations and Co-operation among States in accordance with the Charter of the United Nations,

Recalling its resolutions, particularly resolutions 2395(XXIII) of 29 November 1968, 2465(XXIII) of 20 December 1968, 2548(XXIV) of 11 December 1969, 2708(XXV) of 14 December 1970, 3103(XXVIII) of 12 December 1973 and its resolution 1514(XV) of 14 December 1960, as well as Security Council resolutions 405(1977) of 14 April 1977, 419(1977) of 24 November 1977, 496(1981) of 15 December 1981 and 507(1982) of 28 May 1982, in which the United Nations denounced the practice of using mercenaries, in particular against developing countries and national liberation movements,

Recalling in particular its resolution 37/109 of 16 December 1982, by which it renewed the mandate of the *Ad Hoc* Committee on the Drafting of an International Convention against the Recruitment, Use, Financing and Training of Mercenaries, composed of thirty-five Member States,

Having considered the report of the *Ad Hoc* Committee on its third session,

Recognizing that the activities of mercenaries are contrary to fundamental principles of international law, such as non-interference in the internal affairs of States, territorial integrity and independence, and seriously impede the process of self-determination of peoples struggling against colonialism, racism and *apartheid* and all forms of foreign domination,

Bearing in mind the pernicious impact that the activities of mercenaries have on international peace and security,

Considering that the progressive development and codification of the rules of international law on mercenaries would contribute immensely to the implementation of the purposes and principles of the Charter,

Taking account of the fact that, although the *Ad Hoc* Committee has made substantial progress, it has not yet fulfilled its mandate,

Reaffirming the need for the elaboration, at the earliest possible date, of an international convention against the recruitment, use, financing and training of mercenaries,

1. *Takes note* of the report of the *Ad Hoc* Committee on the Drafting of an International Convention against the Recruitment, Use, Financing and Training of Mercenaries and the progress made by the *Ad Hoc* Committee, especially during its third session;

2. *Decides* that the *Ad Hoc* Committee shall continue its work, with the goal of drafting, at the earliest possible date, an international convention against the recruitment, use, financing and training of mercenaries;

3. *Requests* the *Ad Hoc* Committee, in the fulfilment of its mandate, to consider the suggestions and proposals of Member States, bearing in mind the views and comments submitted to the Secretary-General and those expressed at the thirty-eighth session of the General Assembly during the debate in the Sixth Committee devoted to the consideration of the report of the *Ad Hoc* Committee, including the various views expressed on the definition of the term "mercenary";

4. *Invites* the *Ad Hoc* Committee to take into account the draft articles contained in paragraph 56 of its report for the elaboration of the provisions relating to the scope of the convention, the definition of the term "mercenary" and the obligations of States, as well as the proposals which

have been made and which may be submitted at its next session;

5. *Requests* the Secretary-General to make available to the *Ad Hoc* Committee at its fourth session any up-to-date and relevant documentation on the subject;

6. *Also requests* the Secretary-General to provide the *Ad Hoc* Committee with any assistance and facilities it may require for the performance of its work, such as preparing a topical summary of the discussions that have taken place in the Sixth Committee during the thirty-eighth session of the General Assembly;

7. *Decides* that the *Ad Hoc* Committee shall hold its fourth session for four weeks, from 30 July to 24 August 1984;

8. *Requests* the *Ad Hoc* Committee to make every effort to complete its mandate at its fourth session;

9. *Also requests* the *Ad Hoc* Committee to submit its report to the General Assembly at its thirty-ninth session;

10. *Decides* to include in the provisional agenda of its thirty-ninth session the item entitled "Report of the *Ad Hoc* Committee on the Drafting of an International Convention against the Recruitment, Use, Financing and Training of Mercenaries".

General Assembly resolution 38/137

19 December 1983   Meeting 101   Adopted without vote

Approved by Sixth Committee (A/38/669) by consensus, 1 December (meeting 60); 54-nation draft (A/C.6/38/L.5), orally revised; agenda item 129.

Sponsors: Afghanistan, Algeria, Angola, Bangladesh, Barbados, Benin, Burundi, China, Congo, Cuba, Cyprus, Democratic Yemen, Egypt, Equatorial Guinea, Ethiopia, German Democratic Republic, Ghana, Guyana, India, Iraq, Jamaica, Kenya, Lao People's Democratic Republic, Liberia, Libyan Arab Jamahiriya, Madagascar, Malawi, Mali, Mauritania, Mexico, Mongolia, Morocco, Mozambique, Nicaragua, Nigeria, Pakistan, Panama, Romania, Rwanda, Sao Tome and Principe, Senegal, Sudan, Swaziland, Syrian Arab Republic, Togo, Trinidad and Tobago, Turkey, Uganda, Ukrainian SSR, United Republic of Cameroon, Viet Nam, Yugoslavia, Zaire, Zambia.

Financial implications. 5th Committee, A/38/739; S-G, A/C.5/38/98 & Add.1, A/C.6/38/L.10/Rev.1.

Meeting numbers. GA 38th session: 5th Committee 66; 6th Committee 19, 21-29, 50, 51, 54, 57, 60, 61; plenary 101.

In explanation of position, Greece (on behalf of the 10 States members of the European Community (EC)), Japan, Norway (on behalf also of Denmark, Finland and Iceland) and the United States felt that the statement in the fifth preambular paragraph was far-reaching; the misdeeds of private individuals acting in a personal capacity could not be imputed to States or regarded as breaches of international law.

Further, the EC members believed that the term mercenary should be defined on the basis of the only existing definition of universal character, as contained in article 47, paragraph 2, of Additional Protocol I to the 1949 Geneva Conventions (relating to the protection of victims of international armed conflicts), although the scope of the draft convention need not be restricted to cases covered by that Protocol. While in favour of a speedy finalization of a draft convention, the EC members asserted that the request in paragraph 8 should not be interpreted as fixing a rigid time-limit for the completion of negotiations, and that the Committee against mercenaries should continue to work on the basis of consensus.

The United States said it would have been more accurate to state in the second preambular paragraph that the Security Council, in resolutions mentioned therein, denounced the use of mercenaries to destabilize States or violate their territorial integrity, sovereignty and independence; as to the sixth preambular paragraph, the United States condemned the illegal use of force by mercenaries, but considered that a future convention should recognize Governments' legitimate need for assistance to ensure their self-defence.

Prevention of terrorism

Deep concern about continuing acts of international terrorism and the need for closer international co-operation for its prevention and elimination were expressed by the General Assembly when, in 1983, it re-endorsed the 1979 recommendations of the *Ad Hoc* Committee on International Terrorism.[40]

Report of the Secretary-General. Pursuant to a 1981 Assembly resolution,[41] the Secretary-General submitted to the Assembly in September 1983 a report, with later addenda,[42] containing the views and other information on the topic received from nine Governments, one United Nations specialized agency and two other international organizations.

Annexed to the report was information on the state of signatures, ratifications of or accessions to, as at 19 August 1983, a number of relevant international conventions, including the following, for which the Secretary-General was the depositary: the Convention on the Prevention and Punishment of Crimes against Internationally Protected Persons, including Diplomatic Agents,[43] and the International Convention against the Taking of Hostages.[44]

On 1 December,[45] Chile transmitted to the Secretary-General a press release issued on 7 November by its Ministry of Foreign Affairs, in which it denounced as an act of international terrorism an attack of 9 October in Rangoon, Burma, that had killed four ministers and other officials of the Republic of Korea.

GENERAL ASSEMBLY ACTION

The General Assembly, on the recommendation of the Sixth Committee, adopted without vote resolution 38/130 on 19 December.

Measures to prevent international terrorism which endangers or takes innocent human lives or jeopardizes fundamental freedoms and study of the underlying causes of those forms of terrorism and acts of violence which lie in misery, frustration, grievance and despair and which cause some people to sacrifice human lives, including their own, in an attempt to effect radical changes

The General Assembly,

Recalling its resolutions 3034(XXVII) of 18 December 1972, 31/102 of 15 December 1976, 32/147 of 16 December 1977, 34/145 of 17 December 1979 and 36/109 of 10 December 1981,

Recalling also the Declaration on Principles of International Law concerning Friendly Relations and Co-operation among States in accordance with the Charter of the United Nations, the Declaration on the Strengthening of International Security, the Definition of Aggression and the Protocols Additional to the Geneva Conventions of 1949,

Deeply concerned about continuing acts of international terrorism which take a toll of innocent human lives,

Convinced of the importance of international co-operation for dealing with acts of international terrorism,

Reaffirming the principle of self-determination of peoples enshrined in the Charter of the United Nations,

Reaffirming the inalienable right to self-determination and independence of all peoples under colonial and racist régimes and other forms of alien domination, and upholding the legitimacy of their struggle, in particular the struggle of national liberation movements, in accordance with the purposes and principles of the Charter and of the Declaration on Principles of International Law concerning Friendly Relations and Co-operation among States in accordance with the Charter of the United Nations,

Taking note of the report of the Secretary-General,

1. *Deeply deplores* the loss of innocent human lives and the pernicious impact of acts of international terrorism on friendly relations among States as well as on international co-operation, including co-operation for development;

2. *Urges* all States, unilaterally and in co-operation with other States, as well as relevant United Nations organs to contribute to the progressive elimination of the causes underlying international terrorism;

3. *Invites* all States to take all appropriate measures at the national level with a view to the speedy and final elimination of the problem of international terrorism, such as the harmonization of domestic legislation with international conventions, the implementation of assumed international obligations and the prevention of the preparation and organization in their territory of acts directed against other States;

4. *Calls upon* all States to fulfil their obligations under international law to refrain from organizing, instigating, assisting or participating in acts of civil strife or terrorist acts in another State, or acquiescing in organized activities within their territory directed towards the commission of such acts;

5. *Appeals* to all States that have not yet done so to consider becoming parties to the existing international conventions relating to various aspects of the problem of international terrorism;

6. *Urges* all States to co-operate with one another more closely, especially through the exchange of relevant information concerning the prevention and combating of international terrorism, the apprehension and prosecution of the perpetrators of such acts, the conclusion of special treaties and/or the incorporation into appropriate bilateral treaties of special clauses, in particular regarding the extradition or prosecution of international terrorists;

7. *Re-endorses* the recommendations submitted by the *Ad Hoc* Committee on International Terrorism in its report to the General Assembly at its thirty-fourth session relating to practical measures of co-operation for the speedy elimination of the problem of international terrorism;

8. *Calls upon* all States to observe and implement the recommendations submitted by the *Ad Hoc* Committee;

9. *Requests* the Secretary-General to follow up, as appropriate, the implementation of the present resolution and, in particular, of the recommendations submitted by the *Ad Hoc* Committee and to submit a report to the General Assembly at its fortieth session;

10. *Decides* to include the item in the provisional agenda of its fortieth session.

General Assembly resolution 38/130

19 December 1983   Meeting 101   Adopted without vote

Approved by Sixth Committee (A/38/663) by consensus, 8 December (meeting 71); 4-nation draft (A/C.6/38/L.21), orally revised, and orally amended by France and by Romania; agenda item 123.

Sponsors: Cuba, Czechoslovakia, Lao People's Democratic Republic, Mongolia.

Meeting numbers. GA 38th session: 6th Committee 63, 66-69, 71, 72; plenary 101.

The Sixth Committee approved the text as orally revised and amended. Revisions by the sponsors included deleting a paragraph by which the Assembly would have unequivocally condemned all acts of international terrorism. Amendments by France and by Romania resulted in rearranging some paragraphs in what they felt was a more logical order.

Statements in explanation of position were made by a number of States.

Asserting that it would not have supported the text, had a vote been taken, and calling the *Ad Hoc* Committee's report sterile, Israel said the Sixth Committee, by deleting the paragraph condemning all acts of international terrorism, had rendered possible interpretation of some provisions as encouraging such acts. For Israel, the text's call to United Nations organs included prohibition of the abuse of the United Nations flag, asserting that the Security Council had agreed to that abuse by allowing Yasser Arafat of the Palestine Liberation Organization to leave Tripoli, Lebanon, in December 1983 (see also POLITICAL AND SECURITY QUESTIONS, Chapter IX).

The United States said the rights and duties mentioned in the text should be interpreted in the light of the United Nations Charter and the 1970 Declaration on Principles of International Law concerning Friendly Relations and Co-operation among States in accordance with the Charter of the United Nations;[46] some acts were so barbarous that not even Charter Article 51, concerning the right of self-defence, could justify them.

Ethiopia, Indonesia, the Philippines and Thailand said they joined in the consensus on the understanding that the national liberation movements referred to in the preamble were those recognized by the United Nations and the relevant regional organizations.

Draft articles on non-navigational uses of international watercourses

Pursuant to a December 1982 General Assembly recommendation,[47] the International Law

Commission, at its May-July 1983 session,[20] continued work on the law of the non-navigational uses of international watercourses. ILC took up the first report submitted by Jens Evensen (Norway),[48] who had been appointed in 1982[49] as the new Special Rapporteur. The report, the fourth on the topic, contained, as a basis for discussion, a tentative draft of a convention, consisting of 39 articles divided into six chapters: an introduction (articles 1 to 5); general principles (rights and duties of system States) (articles 6 to 9); co-operation and management in regard to international watercourse systems (articles 10 to 19); environmental protection, pollution, health or natural hazards, regulation and safety, use preferences, and national or regional sites (articles 20 to 30); settlement of disputes (articles 31 to 38); and final provisions (article 39).

ILC focused attention on the approach suggested by the Special Rapporteur on the definition of "international watercourse system", on the question of such a system as a shared natural resource, and on other general principles to be reflected in the draft. It also had before it a note[50] submitted by a Commission member concerning a set of draft principles of conduct in the field of the environment for the guidance of States in the conservation and harmonious utilization of natural resources shared by two or more States, as approved in 1978 by the Governing Council of the United Nations Environment Programme[51] and taken note of by the General Assembly in 1979.[52]

In its 1983 resolution (38/138) on the work of ILC, the Assembly recommended that, taking into account government comments, ILC should continue preparing the draft articles (see Chapter VII of this section).

REFERENCES

[1]YUN 1982, p. 1374, GA dec. 37/407, 15 Nov. 1982. [2]*Ibid.*, p. 1372, GA res. 37/10, annex, 15 Nov. 1982. [3]S/15565. [4]A/38/33. [5]YUN 1982, p. 1389, GA res. 37/114, 16 Dec. 1982. [6]A/38/343. [7]YUN 1979, p. 160. [8]YUN 1982, p. 251, GA res. 37/117, 16 Dec. 1982. [9]A/38/336 & Add.1. [10]A/38/440. [11]YUN 1981, p. 152, GA res. 36/101, 9 Dec. 1981. [12]YUN 1982, p. 1375, GA res. 37/105, 16 Dec. 1982. [13]YUN 1977, p. 118, GA res. 32/150, 19 Dec. 1977. [14]A/38/41. [15]YUN 1976, p. 105. [16]YUN 1979, p. 153. [17]YUN 1981, p. 1204. [18]YUN 1982, p. 1374. [19]A/38/357 & Add.1,2. [20]A/38/10. [21]YUN 1982, p. 1377, GA res. 37/102, 16 Dec. 1982. [22]YUN 1954, p. 411. [23]YUN 1947-48, p. 215, GA res. 177(II), 21 Nov. 1947. [24]A/CN.4/364. [25]A/CN.4/368 & Add.1. [26]A/CN.4/365. [27]YUN 1974, p. 847, GA res. 3314(XXIX), annex, 14 Dec. 1974. [28]A/CN.4/369 & Add.1,2. [29]A/38/356. [30]YUN 1982, p. 1378, GA res. 37/109, 16 Dec. 1982. [31]A/38/43. [32]YUN 1980, p. 1145, GA res. 35/48, 4 Dec. 1980. [33]YUN 1982, p. 1377. [34]YUN 1981, p. 1215. [35]A/AC.207/L.16. [36]A/AC.207/L.14 & Add.1. [37]E/1983/13 (res. 1983/4). [38]E/CN.4/1984/16. [39]A/C.6/38/L.2. [40]YUN 1979, p. 1146. [41]YUN 1981, p. 1221, GA res. 36/109, 10 Dec. 1981. [42]A/38/355 & Add.1-3. [43]YUN 1973, p. 775, GA res. 3166(XXVIII), annex, 14 Dec. 1973. [44]YUN 1979, p. 1144, GA res. 34/146, annex, 17 Dec. 1979. [45]A/C.6/38/7. [46]YUN 1970, p. 789, GA res. 2625(XXV), annex, 24 Oct. 1970. [47]YUN 1982, p. 1407, GA res. 37/111, 16 Dec. 1982. [48]A/CN.4/367 & Corr.1. [49]YUN 1982, p. 1379. [50]A/CN.4/L.353. [51]YUN 1978, p. 537. [52]YUN 1979, p. 697, GA res. 34/186, 18 Dec. 1979.

Chapter III

States and international law

In 1983, a United Nations Conference, held in Austria, adopted the Vienna Convention on Succession of States in respect of State Property, Archives and Debts, the draft of which had been finalized by the International Law Commission (ILC) in 1981.

ILC at its May-July 1983 session (see Chapter VII of this section) continued preparing draft articles with a view to elaborating legal instruments on the status of the diplomatic courier and the diplomatic bag not accompanied by courier, jurisdictional immunities of States and their property, international liability for injurious consequences arising from acts not prohibited by international law, and State responsibility for internationally wrongful acts.

In December, the General Assembly, by resolution 38/136, condemned acts of violence against diplomatic and consular missions and representatives, and urged States to ensure their protection.

Topics related to this chapter. International organizations and international law: host country relations. Other legal questions: International Law Commission.

Diplomatic relations

Throughout the year, the United Nations continued to receive reports of incidents which threatened the security and safety of diplomatic and consular missions and representatives. The General Assembly, by resolution 38/136 adopted in December, urged States to protect those missions and representatives. Also in 1983, ILC continued preparing draft articles on the status of the diplomatic courier and the diplomatic bag not accompanied by courier.

Protection of diplomats

As at 31 December 1983, the number of parties to the various international instruments relating to the protection of diplomats and to diplomatic and consular relations[1] was as follows: 141 States were parties to the 1961 Vienna Convention on Diplomatic Relations,[2] Sao Tome and Principe having acceded in 1983; 40 States were parties to the Optional Protocol concerning acquisition of nationality;[3] and 51 States were parties to the

Optional Protocol concerning the compulsory settlement of disputes.[3]

The 1963 Vienna Convention on Consular Relations[4] had 108 States parties, Japan, Mozambique, Sao Tome and Principe, and Togo having acceded in 1983; 33 States were parties to the Optional Protocol concerning the acquisition of nationality;[5] and 40 States were parties to the Optional Protocol concerning the compulsory settlement of disputes,[5] Japan having acceded in 1983.

The 1973 Convention on the Prevention and Punishment of Crimes against Internationally Protected Persons, including Diplomatic Agents,[6] had 59 States parties, Guatemala and the Republic of Korea having adhered in 1983.

Report of the Secretary-General. Pursuant to a December 1982 General Assembly resolution,[7] the Secretary-General submitted to that body in September 1983 a report, with later addenda,[8] containing information from States on serious violations of the protection, security and safety of diplomatic and consular missions and representatives as well as on subsequent action taken by them to bring offenders to justice and prevent a repetition.

Turkey gave information about a February discovery and defusion of an explosive device at its Embassy in Luxembourg; a May bomb explosion at its Embassy's Culture and Information Office at Brussels, Belgium, and a July killing of a Turkish diplomat there; and a July attack on its Embassy in Portugal, which resulted in the death of seven persons, including the wife of a Turkish diplomat. Luxembourg and Portugal informed of their actions in connection with those attacks, as did the Netherlands and the United Kingdom on the sentencing of the perpetrators of actual or attempted attacks, respectively, against Turkish diplomats in 1982.

Lebanon reported that, in April 1983, an attack using explosives perpetrated against the United States Embassy in Beirut had killed 63 people and wounded some 100 others; also, an attempt was made on the life of a Libyan diplomat in June for which the perpetrator was arrested. Other 1983 incidents were reported by: El Salvador, a January occupation of its Consulate at Granada, Spain; France, an April shooting incident at the USSR Consulate-General and indictment of the perpetrator; the Netherlands, a February bomb explosion at the Consulate-General of France in Amsterdam and the resultant ongoing investigation;

Nicaragua, aggressive acts against its diplomats by the authorities of Honduras; the USSR, offences against its diplomatic and consular representatives and property in the United States; and the United Kingdom, a March sentencing of three men accused of a 1982 assassination attempt against Israel's Ambassador to the United Kingdom.

While Austria, El Salvador and Nicaragua also reported on several incidents that had taken place in 1982, Denmark, Finland, the Federal Republic of Germany, Kenya, Kuwait and the Sudan informed the Secretary-General that they had no incidents to report; the United States said it had had no major incidents.

The Secretary-General's report also contained the views of 13 States (Austria, Denmark, El Salvador, Finland, France, Nicaragua, Portugal, Sudan, Sweden, Tunisia, USSR, United States, Uruguay) on measures needed to enhance the protection of diplomatic missions and representatives.

Communications. By a letter of 4 January to the Secretary-General,[9] Israel reported on two bombing incidents of 23 December 1982 at Sydney, Australia; one resulted in serious injury to an employee and damage to the building housing its Consulate-General. In the same letter, Israel listed six other 1982 incidents against its diplomatic missions or representatives in Colombia, Ecuador, France, Guatemala and the United Kingdom.

In a letter of 30 November to the Secretary-General,[10] the USSR charged that the United States had committed criminal acts against its diplomatic mission and citizens in Grenada in October by, among other things, blockading the USSR Embassy and firing at those premises, thereby wounding an employee.

GENERAL ASSEMBLY ACTION

On 19 December 1983, the General Assembly adopted without vote resolution 38/136, as recommended by the Sixth (Legal) Committee.

Consideration of effective measures to enhance the protection, security and safety of diplomatic and consular missions and representatives

The General Assembly,

Having considered the report of the Secretary-General,

Emphasizing the important role of diplomatic and consular missions and representatives, as well as of missions and representatives to international intergovernmental organizations and officials of such organizations, in the maintenance of international peace and the promotion of friendly relations among States,

Emphasizing also the duty of States to take all appropriate steps, as required by international law:

(*a*) To protect the premises of diplomatic and consular missions, as well as of missions to international intergovernmental organizations;

(*b*) To prevent any attacks on diplomatic and consular representatives, as well as on representatives to international intergovernmental organizations and officials of such organizations;

(*c*) To bring the offenders to justice;

Deeply concerned about the continued large number of failures to respect the inviolability of diplomatic and consular missions and representatives, and about the serious threat presented by such violations to the maintenance of normal and peaceful international relations, which are necessary for co-operation among States,

Expressing its sympathy for the victims of illegal acts against diplomatic and consular representatives and missions as well as against representatives and missions to international intergovernmental organizations and officials of such organizations,

Convinced that respect for the principles and rules of international law governing diplomatic and consular relations, in particular those aimed at ensuring the inviolability of diplomatic and consular missions and representatives, is a basic prerequisite for the normal conduct of relations among States and for the fulfilment of the purposes and principles of the Charter of the United Nations,

Noting that only a small number of States have so far, in response to the call by the General Assembly at its thirty-fifth, thirty-sixth and thirty-seventh sessions, become parties to the relevant conventions concerning the inviolability of diplomatic and consular missions and representatives,

Convinced that the reporting procedures established under General Assembly resolution 35/168 of 15 December 1980 and further elaborated in Assembly resolutions 36/33 of 13 November 1981 and 37/108 of 16 December 1982 are important steps in the efforts to enhance the protection, security and safety of diplomatic and consular missions and representatives,

Desiring to maintain and further strengthen those reporting procedures,

1. *Takes note* of the report of the Secretary-General;

2. *Strongly condemns* acts of violence against diplomatic and consular missions and representatives, as well as against missions and representatives to international intergovernmental organizations and officials of such organizations;

3. *Emphasizes* the importance of enhanced awareness throughout the world of the necessity of ensuring the protection, security and safety of such missions, representatives and officials, as well as of the role of the United Nations in this regard;

4. *Urges* States to observe and to implement the principles and rules of international law governing diplomatic and consular relations and, in particular, to take all necessary measures in conformity with their international obligations to ensure effectively the protection, security and safety of all diplomatic and consular missions and representatives officially present in territory under their jurisdiction, including practicable measures to prohibit in their territories illegal activities of persons, groups and organizations that encourage, instigate, organize or engage in the perpetration of acts against the security and safety of such missions and representatives;

5. *Recommends* that States should co-operate closely through, *inter alia*, contacts between the diplomatic and consular missions and the receiving State, with regard to practical measures designed to enhance the protection, security and safety of diplomatic and consular mis-

sions and representatives and with regard to exchange of information on the circumstances of all serious violations thereof;

6. _Calls upon_ States that have not yet done so to consider becoming parties to the instruments relevant to the protection, security and safety of diplomatic and consular missions and representatives;

7. _Calls upon_ States, in cases where a dispute arises in connection with a violation of the principles and rules of international law concerning the inviolability of diplomatic and consular missions and representatives, to make use of the means for peaceful settlement of disputes, including the good offices of the Secretary-General;

8. _Requests:_

(_a_) All States to report to the Secretary-General as promptly as possible serious violations of the protection, security and safety of diplomatic and consular missions and representatives;

(_b_) The State in which the violation took place—and, to the extent applicable, the State where the alleged offender is present—to report as promptly as possible on measures taken to bring the offender to justice and eventually to communicate, in accordance with its laws, the final outcome of the proceedings against the offender, and on measures adopted with a view to preventing a repetition of such violations;

9. _Requests_ the Secretary-General to circulate to all States, upon receipt, the reports received by him pursuant to paragraph 8 above, unless the reporting State requests otherwise;

10. _Requests_ the Secretary-General to invite States to inform him of their views with respect to any measures needed to enhance the protection, security and safety of diplomatic and consular missions and representatives;

11. _Also requests_ the Secretary-General, when a serious violation has been reported pursuant to paragraph 8 (_a_) above, to draw the attention, when appropriate, of the States directly concerned to the reporting procedures provided for in paragraph 8 above;

12. _Further requests_ the Secretary-General to submit to the General Assembly at its thirty-ninth session a report on the state of ratification of, and accessions to, the instruments referred to in paragraph 6 above, as well as the reports received and views expressed pursuant to paragraphs 8 and 10 above, and invites him to submit any views he may wish to express on these matters;

13. _Decides_ to include in the provisional agenda of its thirty-ninth session the item entitled "Consideration of effective measures to enhance the protection, security and safety of diplomatic and consular missions and representatives: report of the Secretary-General".

General Assembly resolution 38/136

19 December 1983   Meeting 101   Adopted without vote

Approved by Sixth Committee (A/38/668) without vote, 28 November (meeting 56); 18-nation draft (A/C.6/38/L.13); agenda item 128.

Sponsors: Argentina, Australia, Austria, Canada, Denmark, Ecuador, Finland, Germany, Federal Republic of, Iceland, Ivory Coast, Japan, Nigeria, Norway, Philippines, Sierra Leone, Sweden, Turkey, Uruguay.

Meeting numbers. GA 38th session: 6th Committee 8-11, 53, 56; plenary 101.

The USSR explained its position by saying that, while it supported the resolution's condemnation of failure to protect diplomats, the text did not go far enough and could be improved.

Status of diplomatic bags and couriers

Responding to a December 1982 General Assembly recommendation,[11] ILC, at its 1983 session, continued preparing draft articles on the status of the diplomatic courier and the diplomatic bag not accompanied by courier, with a view to elaborating a legal instrument on the topic.[12]

The Commission had before it a fourth report by the Special Rapporteur, Alexander Yankov (Bulgaria).[13] Due to lack of time, it considered only those parts of the report containing draft articles 15 to 23 of part II (status of the diplomatic courier, the diplomatic courier _ad hoc_ and the captain of a commerical aircraft or the master of a ship carrying a diplomatic bag): general facilities (article 15), entry into the territory of the receiving State and the transit State (article 16), freedom of movement (article 17), freedom of communication (article 18), temporary accommodation (article 19), personal inviolability (article 20), inviolability of temporary accommodation (article 21), inviolability of the means of transport (article 22) and immunity from jurisdiction (article 23).

The Commission referred articles 15 to 19 to its Drafting Committee, while deciding to resume debate on articles 20 to 23 at its 1984 session.

On the recommendation of the Drafting Committee, ILC provisionally adopted in 1983 eight draft articles and commentaries concerning: scope of the articles (article 1), couriers and bags not within such scope (article 2), use of terms (article 3), freedom of official communications (article 4), duty to respect the laws and regulations of the receiving State and the transit State (article 5), non-discrimination and reciprocity (article 6), documentation of the diplomatic courier (article 7), and appointment of the diplomatic courier (article 8). Draft articles 1 to 6 belonged to part I, on general provisions, and 7 and 8 belonged to part II (see above).

The texts of these articles were transmitted to the Assembly in an August note by the Secretary-General.[14]

REFERENCES

[1]_Multilateral Treaties Deposited with the Secretary-General, Supplement: Actions from 1 January to 31 December 1983_ (ST/LEG/SER.E/2/Add.1), Sales No. E.84.V.4. [2]YUN 1961, p. 512. [3]_Ibid._ p. 516. [4]YUN 1963, p. 510. [5]_Ibid._ p. 512. [6]YUN 1973, p. 775. GA res. 3166 (XXVIII), annex, 14 Dec. 1973. [7]YUN 1982, p. 1381, GA res. 37/108, 16 Dec. 1982. [8]A/38/379 & Corr.1 & Add.1-3. [9]A/38/60-S/15548. [10]A/38/655. [11]YUN 1982, p. 1407, GA res. 37/111, 16 Dec. 1982. [12]A/38/10. [13]A/CN.4/374 & Corr.1 & Add.1 & Add.1/Corr.1 & Add.2 & Add.2/Corr.1 & Add.3 & Add.3/Corr.1 & Add.4 & Add.4/Corr.1,2. [14]A/38/148.

State succession in respect of property, archives and debts

The United Nations Conference on Succession of States in respect of State Property, Archives and Debts—convened at Vienna, Austria, from 1 March to 8 April 1983 in pursuance of 1981[1] and 1982[2] General Assembly resolutions—adopted on 7 April a Convention on the subject, on the basis of a text finalized by ILC in 1981.[3]

Known as the Vienna Convention on Succession of States in respect of State Property, Archives and Debts,[4] the instrument dealt with various aspects of State succession—the replacement of one State by another in the responsibility for the international relations of a territory. In addition to general provisions, the Convention covered such topics as State property; the preservation of the unity of State archives; the effects of the passing of State debts with regard to creditors; and the transfer of part of a State's territory, newly independent States, uniting of States, separation of part(s) of a State's territory and dissolution of a State.

The Convention was opened for signature on 8 April at Vienna, and subsequently in New York, with the Secretary-General serving as its depositary from 1 January 1984. As at 31 December 1983, Algeria, Argentina, Peru and Yugoslavia had signed the Convention.

Among the resolutions adopted by the Conference, which were annexed to the Final Act,[5] was one recognizing that the Convention's provisions would not impair the exercise of the right to self-determination and independence, in accordance with the Charter of the United Nations, for peoples struggling against colonialism, alien domination or occupation, racial discrimination and *apartheid;* and recognizing also their permanent sovereignty over their resources and their rights to development, information concerning their history and the conservation of their cultural heritage. In another action, the Conference resolved that the articles of the Convention should be interpreted, in the case of Namibia, in conformity with relevant United Nations resolutions and that all the rights of the future independent State of Namibia should be reserved.

Ninety States participated in the Conference in response to the Assembly's 1982 invitation[2] (for participating States and officers, see APPENDIX III). Also participating were a number of organizations and intergovernmental bodies invited by the Assembly. Mohammed Bedjaoui (Algeria), Judge of the International Court of Justice and former ILC Special Rapporteur on the topic, acted as the Expert Consultant.

Among the documentation before the Conference were the draft articles by ILC and an analytical compilation, prepared by the Secretariat,[6] of comments of Governments on the draft articles, as submitted in writing or made orally in the Assembly's Sixth Committee in 1981 and 1982. Comments were made on the value of the draft and usefulness of a convention, the general approach and basic principles reflected in the draft and its scope and structure.

REFERENCES

[1]YUN 1981, p. 1230, GA res. 36/113, 10 Dec. 1981. [2]YUN 1982, p. 1383, GA res. 37/11, 15 Nov. 1982. [3]YUN 1981, p. 1227. [4]A/CONF.117/14. [5]A/CONF.117/15. [6]A/CONF.117/5 & Add.1.

State immunities, liability and responsibility

In response to a December 1982 General Assembly resolution,[1] ILC, at its 1983 session,[2] continued drafting articles on three aspects of international law concerning States: jurisdictional immunities of States and their property; international liability for injurious consequences arising from acts not prohibited by international law; and State responsibility for internationally wrongful acts.

In its resolution 38/138 adopted in December, the Assembly recommended that, taking into account government comments, ILC should continue its work on the topics in its current programme.

Draft articles on State immunities

In 1983, ILC continued preparing draft articles on the jurisdictional immunities of States and their property. Its work, detailed in its annual report,[2] was based on a fifth report by the Special Rapporteur, Sompong Sucharitkul (Thailand),[3] which dealt with part III (to comprise articles 11 to 20) of the draft articles concerning exceptions to State immunity and contained articles on contracts of employment (article 13), personal injuries and damage to property (article 14), and ownership, possession and use of property (article 15).

While the Commission members generally supported draft article 15, they suggested improving draft articles 13 and 14 by either enlarging or restricting the scope of the possible exceptions. In so doing, many recognized that draft article 13 covered a completely new area, while some saw few cases for application of, and hence doubted justification for, draft article 14. Based on the discussion, the Special Rapporteur subsequently submitted to the Drafting Committee a revised version of draft articles 13 and 14.

On the recommendation of the Drafting Committee, the Commission provisionally adopted in 1983 draft articles and commentaries on counterclaims (article 10), commercial contracts (article 12), and ownership, possession and use of property (article 15), as well as two paragraphs belonging to draft articles 2 (use of terms) and 3 (interpretative provisions).

The texts of these articles were transmitted to the Assembly in an August note by the Secretary-General.[(4)]

Draft articles on State liability

In 1983, ILC continued its work on international liability for injurious consequences arising out of acts not prohibited by international law.[(2)] It had before it a fourth report by the Special Rapporteur, Robert Q. Quentin-Baxter (New Zealand),[(5)] containing a single chapter entitled "The delineation of the topic", intended to re-evaluate the topic's schematic outline—which was annexed to the report—in the light of the views expressed in the Commission and in the Assembly's Sixth Committee in 1982 and to provide a more complete commentary. The Special Rapporteur also suggested that the Commission should decide in 1984 on the future of the topic.

The Commission agreed, among other things, that those parts of a Secretariat study, dealing, respectively, with multilateral and bilateral treaty practice, and with settlements and claims practice, should be made widely available; and that the Special Rapporteur, with the Secretariat's assistance, should prepare a questionnaire to be addressed to selected international organizations, in view of the fact that the mutual obligations of States as members of such organizations might fulfil or replace some of the procedures indicated in the schematic outline.

Draft articles on State responsibility

In 1983, ILC[(2)] continued preparing draft articles on State responsibility for internationally wrongful acts, and had before it a fourth report by the Special Rapporteur, Willem Riphagen (Netherlands),[(6)] which focused on an outline of the possible contents of part II (dealing with the content, forms and degrees of international responsibility) and part III (concerning the implementation of such responsibility and the settlement of disputes) of the draft articles. Four draft articles were presented for inclusion in part II. The first of these (article 1) marked the transition and the link between part I, dealing with the conditions under which the international responsibility of a State arose, and part II, determining the legal consequences of the internationally wrongful act. Draft articles 2 and 3 dealt with limitations and rules of customary international law, respectively. Draft article 5 stipulated that the legal consequences set out in part II were subject to the provisions and procedures of the Charter of the United Nations relating to the maintenance of international peace and security.

The Commission provisionally adopted the four draft articles and commentaries thereto, on the recommendation of the Drafting Committee, and the Secretary-General transmitted these texts to the General Assembly in an August note.[(4)] The Commission, at its 1983 session, had before it, comments and observations submitted by Czechoslovakia[(7)] on the draft articles contained in chapters IV and V of part I, in pursuance of a 1980 Assembly resolution.[(8)]

REFERENCES

[(1)]YUN 1982, p. 1407, GA res. 37/111, 16 Dec. 1982. [(2)]A/38/10. [(3)]A/CN.4/363 & Corr.1 & Add.1 & Add.1/Corr.1. [(4)]A/38/148. [(5)]A/CN.4/373 & Corr.1, 2. [(6)]A/CN.4/366 & Add.1 & Add.1/Corr.1. [(7)]A/CN.4/362. [(8)]YUN 1980, p. 1129, GA res. 35/163, 15 Dec. 1980.

Chapter IV

International organizations and international law

In 1983, at its April/May session, the Special Committee on the Charter of the United Nations and on the Strengthening of the Role of the Organization continued work to that end, and, in December, the General Assembly, by resolution 38/141, asked it to devote more time to considering the maintenance of international peace and security and to complete its work on rationalizing the Organization's existing procedures.

The United Nations remained concerned with the security of missions and their personnel accredited to Headquarters and, by resolution 38/140 adopted in December, the Assembly called on all countries to make the public aware of the role of the United Nations and its accredited missions in strengthening international peace and security.

The Assembly deferred, until its 1984 regular session, consideration of draft standard rules of procedure for United Nations conferences (decision 38/427), and agreed to consider, when its current session resumed, an item on the implementation of United Nations resolutions (decision 38/456).

Topics related to this chapter. International peace and security. Legal aspects of international political relations.

Strengthening the role of the United Nations

The Committee on the Charter of the United Nations and on the Strengthening of the Role of the Organization, in 1983, continued its consideration of the maintenance of international peace and security in order to strengthen the role of the United Nations, in particular the Security Council, and to enable it to discharge fully its responsibilities under the Charter.

Report of the Secretary-General for 1982/83

The Secretary-General, in his annual report to the General Assembly on the work of the Organization (p. 3), observed that the weakening of universal commitment to the Charter of the United Nations, perhaps more than any other factor, had led to the partial paralysis of the United Nations as the guardian of international peace and security. Instead of bypassing the Organization or

using it as a forum for polemical exchanges, parties to international disputes should co-operate with the Security Council and the Secretary-General in suitable forms of conflict control. At the same time, the willingness of the parties to co-operate with the United Nations was contingent upon the capacity of the Organization to act as an effective and impartial instrument of peace.

Activities of the Special Committee

The Special Committee on the Charter of the United Nations and on the Strengthening of the Role of the Organization met in New York from 11 April to 6 May 1983 to consider Member States' proposals on rationalizing the existing procedures of the United Nations, and submitted a report on its work[1] to the General Assembly. The 47-member Committee, meeting in response to a December 1982 Assembly resolution,[2] also continued consideration of ways of maintaining international peace and security, and the peaceful settlement of disputes (see Chapter II of this section).

An open-ended Working Group of the Committee held eight meetings between 14 and 18 April at which it discussed rationalization of United Nations procedures on the basis of a draft list, prepared jointly by the Philippines and Romania. Of 31 proposals relating to the General Assembly, it found that general agreement on most of them was unlikely, except for a few such as the one on streamlining the Assembly's agenda. Due to lack of time, the Committee was unable to complete consideration of the list. Working papers containing proposals on the topic were also submitted, individually by Egypt (two), France (two), Greece, Mexico, the Philippines, Romania, the United Kingdom, the United States and Yugoslavia, and jointly by Mexico and El Salvador, and by Romania and Turkey.

Concerning the maintenance of international peace and security, including suggestions on the functioning of the Security Council, the Working Group took up a revised draft recommendation presented by Egypt on behalf of Committee members belonging to the Movement of Non-Aligned Countries, two proposals submitted by France and a draft list of proposals prepared by Romania (see POLITICAL AND SECURITY QUESTIONS, Chapter XI).

During its consideration of the question, the General Assembly had before it the comments of Ecuador, Senegal, Suriname and Uruguay, submitted in response to a 1982 invitation[2] and forwarded to it in September 1983 by the Secretary-General.[3] The Nordic countries (Denmark, Finland, Iceland, Norway, Sweden), by a letter of 10 June, also transmitted to the Secretary-General their views on the strengthening of the United Nations.[4]

On the recommendation of the Sixth (Legal) Committee, the General Assembly adopted resolution 38/141 on 19 December without vote.

Report of the Special Committee on the Charter of the United Nations and on the Strengthening of the Role of the Organization
The General Assembly,

Reaffirming its support for the purposes and principles set forth in the Charter of the United Nations,

Recalling its resolutions 686(VII) of 5 December 1952, 992(X) of 21 November 1955, 2285(XXII) of 5 December 1967, 2552(XXIV) of 12 December 1969, 2697(XXV) of 11 December 1970, 2968(XXVII) of 14 December 1972 and 3349(XXIX) of 17 December 1974,

Recalling also its resolutions 2925(XXVII) of 27 November 1972, 3073(XXVIII) of 30 November 1973 and 3282(XXIX) of 12 December 1974 on the strengthening of the role of the United Nations,

Recalling especially its resolution 3499(XXX) of 15 December 1975, by which it established the Special Committee on the Charter of the United Nations and on the Strengthening of the Role of the Organization, and its resolutions 31/28 of 29 November 1976, 32/45 of 8 December 1977, 33/94 of 16 December 1978, 34/147 of 17 December 1979, 35/164 of 15 December 1980, 36/122 of 11 December 1981 and 37/114 of 16 December 1982,

Taking note of the report of the Secretary-General on the work of the Organization submitted to the General Assembly at its thirty-seventh session, as well as of the views and comments expressed on it by Member States,

Having considered the report of the Special Committee on the Charter of the United Nations and on the Strengthening of the Role of the Organization on the work of the session it held in 1983,

Noting the importance that pre-session consultations among the members of the Special Committee and other interested States may have in facilitating the fulfilment of its task,

Considering that the Special Committee has not yet fulfilled the mandate entrusted to it,

1. *Takes note* of the report of the Special Committee on the Charter of the United Nations and on the Strengthening of the Role of the Organization;

2. *Decides* that the Special Committee shall convene its next session from 2 to 27 April 1984;

3. *Requests* the Special Committee at its next session:

   (a) To accord priority by devoting more time to the question of the maintenance of international peace and security in all its aspects in order to strengthen the role of the United Nations, in particular the Security Council, and to enable it to discharge fully its responsibilities under the Charter in this field; this necessitates the examination, *inter alia*, of the prevention and removal of threats to the peace and of situations which may lead to international friction or give rise to a dispute; the Special Committee will work on all questions with the aim of submitting its conclusions to the General Assembly, in accordance with paragraph 4 below, for the adoption of such recommendations as the Assembly deems appropriate;

   (b) To continue its work on the question of the peaceful settlement of disputes between States and in this context:

   (i) To consider the proposal contained in the working paper on the establishment of a permanent commission on good offices, mediation and conciliation for the settlement of disputes and the prevention of conflicts among States;

   (ii) To continue, in conformity with the agreement reached by the Special Committee, the consideration of the proposal concerning the elaboration of a handbook on the peaceful settlement of disputes between States;

   (c) To finalize its present work on the question of the rationalization of existing procedures, with a view to submitting its conclusions to the General Assembly at its thirty-ninth session;

4. *Also requests* the Special Committee to be mindful of the importance of reaching general agreement whenever that has significance for the outcome of its work;

5. *Urges* members of the Special Committee to participate fully in its work in fulfilment of the mandate entrusted to it;

6. *Decides* that the Special Committee shall accept the participation of observers of Member States, including in the meetings of its working groups;

7. *Invites* Governments to submit or to bring up to date, if they deem it necessary, their observations and proposals, in accordance with General Assembly resolution 3499(XXX);

8. *Requests* the Secretary-General to render all assistance to the Special Committee;

9. *Requests* the Special Committee to submit a report on its work to the General Assembly at its thirty-ninth session;

10. *Decides* to include in the provisional agenda of its thirty-ninth session the item entitled "Report of the Special Committee on the Charter of the United Nations and on the Strengthening of the Role of the Organization".

General Assembly resolution 38/141

19 December 1983   Meeting 101   Adopted without vote

Approved by Sixth Committee (A/38/674) without vote, 9 December (meeting 72); 49-nation draft (A/C.6/38/L.24); agenda item 134.

Sponsors: Antigua and Barbuda, Argentina, Australia, Bangladesh, Barbados, Belgium, Bolivia, Brazil, Chile, Colombia, Congo, Cyprus, Dominican Republic, Ecuador, Egypt, El Salvador, Germany, Federal Republic of, Ghana, Guyana, Indonesia, Italy, Ivory Coast, Japan, Kenya, Liberia, Madagascar, Malaysia, Mexico, Nepal, New Zealand, Nigeria, Papua New Guinea, Paraguay, Philippines, Romania, Rwanda, Samoa, Senegal, Sierra Leone, Singapore, Somalia, Spain, Thailand, Trinidad and Tobago, Uruguay, Venezuela, Yugoslavia, Zaire, Zambia.

Financial implications. 5th Committee, A/38/740; S-G, A/C.5/38/97, A/C.6/38/L.30.

Meeting numbers. GA 38th session: 6th Committee 51, 55, 57-62, 64, 65, 68, 72, 73; plenary 101.

Before approving the 49-nation draft, the Sixth Committee Chairman stated his understanding that it would be for the Special Committee to decide, in accordance with paragraph 4, whether conclusions for submission to the Assembly should be of a comprehensive character or should deal with successive phases of its work.

In explanation of position, the United Kingdom said the Special Committee should accord priority to consideration of the proposals on which agreement seemed possible; it was pleased that the consensus rule laid down in the Assembly's 1982 resolution[2] was reiterated more flexibly in paragraph 4 and that the three major issues in the work programme had been retained. France and the United States supported the text for its commitment, though implicit, to the idea that the Committee should give priority to areas where general agreement seemed possible.

Algeria welcomed paragraph 3 *(a)* for giving priority to international peace and security and for encouraging the Committee to move away from the listing of relevant proposals; however, the Assembly should have asked the Committee for recommendations in its next report. The USSR felt that efforts should be directed not at trying to amend the Charter but at ensuring universal adherence to its obligations and compliance with Security Council resolutions. Viet Nam said that direct negotiations between parties concerned in a dispute and mediation by regional organizations were preferable to mediation by an international body as envisaged in the draft. The Libyan Arab Jamahiriya saw the text as an encouragement to broader participation in the Committee, and urged further consideration of an increase in its membership.

Acting on a proposal by the Netherlands, the Sixth Committee decided—by a recorded vote, requested by France, of 58 to 45, with 23 abstentions—not to act on another draft on the Special Committee's report, sponsored by Benin, Iran and the Libyan Arab Jamahiriya.[5] That draft would have had the Assembly decide to have the Special Committee examine what the sponsors called the adverse effects of the abuse of the unanimity rule (the right of veto) on the maintenance of international peace and security, taking into account, among other things, the need to restrict the rule's use on matters relating to the rights of peoples struggling for self-determination.

Publication of repertories of practice

Pursuant to a 1981 General Assembly resolution[6] requesting that high priority be given to the preparation and publication of supplements to the *Repertoire of the Practice of the Security Council* and the *Repertory of Practice of United Nations Organs* in order to bring both up to date, Supplement No. 7 to the *Repertoire* covering 1972-1974 was published in 1983 in French,[7] and volumes I and II

of Supplement No. 4 to the *Repertory*, covering 1 September 1966 to 31 December 1969, were published in English.[8]

Implementation of UN resolutions

GENERAL ASSEMBLY ACTION

The General Assembly—which, in pursuance of a December 1982 decision,[9] had retained on its agenda an item on implementation of the resolutions of the United Nations for consideration at its resumed thirty-seventh session—adopted decision 37/457, on an oral proposal by its President, at the closing of that session on 19 September 1983.

Implementation of the resolutions of the United Nations

At its 122nd plenary meeting, on 19 September 1983, the General Assembly decided to include in the draft agenda of its thirty-eighth session the item entitled "Implementation of the resolutions of the United Nations".

General Assembly decision 37/457

Adopted without vote

Oral proposal by President; agenda item 141.
Meeting number. GA 37th session: plenary 122.

By decision 38/456 of 20 December, the Assembly decided to resume its thirty-eighth session, at a date to be announced, for the sole purpose of considering six agenda items, one of which was the implementation of the resolutions of the United Nations (see POLITICAL AND SECURITY QUESTIONS, Chapter XI).

REFERENCES

[1]A/38/33. [2]YUN 1982, p. 1389, GA res. 37/114, 16 Dec. 1982. [3]A/38/358. [4]A/38/271-S/15830. [5]A/C.6/38/L.14/Rev.1. [6]YUN 1981, p. 1240, GA res. 36/123, 11 Dec. 1981. [7]*Repertoire of the Practice of the Security Council, Supplement No. 7* (ST/PSCA/1/Add.7), Sales No. F.79.VII.1. [8]*Repertory of Practice of United Nations Organs, Supplement No. 4* (covering the period 1 September 1966 to 31 December 1969), vol. I: *Articles 1-54 of the Charter*, Sales No. E.80.V.13; vol. II: *Articles 55-111 of the Charter*, Sales No. E.82.V.7. [9]YUN 1982, p. 583, GA dec. 37/452, 21 Dec. 1982.

Host country relations

Improving the relations between New York City's diplomatic community and the local population continued to be a major concern of the Committee on Relations with the Host Country in 1983, and the Committee's recommendations to that end were endorsed by the General Assembly.

Consideration by the Committee on host country relations. The 15-member Committee on Relations with the Host Country met seven times in 1983, in pursuance of a December 1982 Assembly resolution.[1] Details of its work on various aspects of relations between the Headquarters diplomatic community and the host country—the United States—were contained in its 1983 report to the Assembly.[2]

In the course of the year, several communications, summarized in the Committee's report, were received by the Committee or the Secretary-General, concerning the security of Member States' missions accredited to the United Nations.

In March and April, the USSR complained of anti-USSR "telephone hooliganism"—numbering 845 calls in January and 1,795 in February, many of them containing bomb threats—and asserted as insufficient a United States proposal to place a "tap" on the Mission telephone. While strongly condemning the irresponsible and illegal activities directed against the Mission, the United States said the USSR refusal to co-operate with the law enforcement authorities had hampered investigations and police records did not reflect the great number of calls reported by the Mission.

Responding to a USSR protest that a group of people had trespassed on its Riverdale (New York City) residential complex grounds in May, the United States reported that an investigation had revealed the trespassers to be college students playing pranks, and that the USSR refusal to sign a complaint had led to the dismissal of the charges.

The USSR also protested[3] that, in September, the United States authorities failed to prevent an enraged crowd of some 100 people, accompanied by United States journalists and camera-equipped television correspondents, from breaking into the grounds of the Glen Cove, New York, residence of its Permanent Representative to the United Nations. It asserted that the presence of journalists attested to the pre-planning and organization of the criminal action. Recounting the incident, the United States reported that about 75 persons, breaking away from a peaceful demonstration by some 500 members and supporters of the Korean Association of New York, had entered the grounds but that order was restored by the additional police force summoned to the scene; no arrests were made due to the confusion resulting from the disturbance. The United States rejected the USSR assertion of the authorities' failure to safeguard the residence and of their connivance in criminal actions; it asserted that the Soviet diplomatic premises in New York City and suburbs continued to receive a large protective security force on a 24-hour basis, and that the Soviet authorities' refusal to co-operate with the law enforcement authorities, by not presenting themselves as witnesses or documenting alleged damage or losses, demonstrated the Mission's lack of co-operation. Subsequently, the USSR denied misrepresentation of

facts in the Glen Cove incident and stated that it co-operated according to the principles and norms of diplomatic immunity, including questions of court jurisdiction.

The Committee also considered communications concerning the safety of Member States' mission personnel. In January 1983, the United States and the USSR exchanged notes concerning the latter's protest against New Jersey police authorities in apprehending the wife of a Mission member for alleged shoplifting in December 1982.

The Democratic People's Republic of Korea protested as unjust, in communications of July and August, a 1982 sexual assault charge by the host country against one of its Mission members,[4] the United States subsequent charge against the Mission for allegedly harbouring that person as a fugitive from justice, and its refusal to issue visas to some Mission members. The Committee Chairman subsequently noted that an arrangement had been found and that the person in question had left the United States.

In June, the Libyan Arab Jamahiriya stated that the host country had violated the norms of international law by authorizing the use of property, acquired at Englewood, New Jersey, as its Ambassador's residence, solely for his and his immediate family's recreational purposes.

In the Committee, the USSR asserted that the United States refusal to create normal conditions and guarantee the safety of its Foreign Minister who was heading its delegation to the thirty-eighth (1983) session of the General Assembly as well as to provide for the proper arrival and handling of the USSR plane at either Kennedy or Newark airport violated the 1947 Agreement between the United Nations and the United States of America regarding the Headquarters of the United Nations.[5] In reponse, the United States said that normal conditions had ceased to exist when the USSR shot down a civilian airliner belonging to the Republic of Korea (see POLITICAL AND SECURITY QUESTIONS, Chapter VII, and PART II, Chapter X); that its proposal for the USSR Foreign Minister's plane to land at a military airfield in New Jersey was reasonable; and that it would continue to fulfil its obligations as long as delegations conducted legitimate business in the United States.

The Committee also considered, and agreed to keep under review, questions relating to the application of the United States Foreign Missions Act which had become effective on 1 October 1982, particularly section 205, pertaining to the acquisition of real estate by foreign missions, which had been extended to United Nations missions. At the Committee's request, the Legal Counsel of the United Nations prepared a note, in which he examined the Act and stated that he intended to seek from the host country the assurances that its application of section 205 would conform to that country's international obligations.

Other questions considered by the Committee included issuance of entry visas to representatives of non-governmental organizations and liberation movements, tax exemption, diplomatic vehicle parking problems, public relations, and organization of the Committee's work. It also took note of the establishment of child-care facilities for members of the United Nations community in New York.

By recommendations approved on 18 November, the Committee, among other things, urged the host country to continue preventing acts violating the security of missions and the safety of their personnel or property, and to ensure normal conditions for their functioning. It urged the host country to continue punishing those responsible for criminal acts against missions and called on missions to co-operate fully with United States authorities in cases affecting security. It also called on the host country to avoid actions not consistent with its international obligations regarding Member States' privileges and immunities.

The Committee also welcomed the diplomatic community's readiness to co-operate with local authorities in solving traffic problems, and appealed to the host country to review its diplomatic parking measures. It expressed the hope that the host country could ameliorate the housing situation causing problems for the diplomatic community and that efforts would be intensified to acquaint the people of New York City with the privileges and immunities of mission personnel and the importance of their international functions. It suggested that the Secretariat and others concerned work together to solve difficulties regarding unpaid bills of certain missions and their diplomats. Further, it expressed appreciation to the New York City Commission for the United Nations and the Consular Corps and those bodies, particularly the New York City Police, contributing to its efforts to help the diplomatic community, provide hospitality and promote mutual understanding between the community and the local population.

GENERAL ASSEMBLY ACTION

On 19 December, the General Assembly, on the recommendation of the Sixth Committee, adopted resolution 38/140 without vote.

Report of the Committee on Relations with the Host Country

The General Assembly,

Having considered the report of the Committee on Relations with the Host Country,

Recalling Article 105 of the Charter of the United Nations, the Convention on the Privileges and Immunities of the United Nations and the Agreement between the United Nations and the United States of America regarding the Headquarters of the United Nations,

Recalling further that the problems related to the privileges and immunities of all missions accredited to the United Nations, the security of the missions and the safety of their personnel are of great importance and concern to Member States, as well as the primary responsibility of the host country,

Noting with deep concern the continued acts violating the security and the safety of the personnel of those missions accredited to the United Nations,

Recognizing that effective measures should continue to be taken by the competent authorities of the host country, in particular to prevent any acts violating the security of missions and the safety of their personnel,

1. *Endorses* the recommendations of the Committee on Relations with the Host Country contained in paragraph 60 of its report;

2. *Strongly condemns* any acts violating the security of missions accredited to the United Nations and their personnel;

3. *Urges* the host country to continue to take all necessary measures to ensure effectively the protection, security and safety of the missions accredited to the United Nations and their personnel, including practicable measures to prohibit illegal activities of persons, groups and organizations that encourage, instigate, organize or engage in the perpetration of acts and activities against the security and safety of such missions and representatives;

4. *Recalls* that continued adherence to the Agreement between the United Nations and the United States of America regarding the Headquarters of the United Nations remains an indispensable condition for the normal functioning of the Organization;

5. *Calls upon* all countries to build up public awareness by explaining the importance of the role played by the United Nations and all missions accredited to it in the strengthening of international peace and security;

6. *Requests* the Secretary-General to remain actively engaged in all aspects of the relations of the United Nations with the host country and to continue to stress the importance of effective measures to avoid acts of terrorism and violence against the missions and their personnel;

7. *Requests* the Committee on Relations with the Host Country to continue its work, in conformity with General Assembly resolution 2819(XXVI) of 15 December 1971;

8. *Decides* to include in the provisional agenda of its thirty-ninth session the item entitled "Report of the Committee on Relations with the Host Country".

General Assembly resolution 38/140

19 December 1983   Meeting 101   Adopted without vote

Approved by Sixth Committee (A/38/673) without vote, 9 December (meeting 73); 9-nation draft (A/C.6/38/L.31); agenda item 133.
Sponsors: Benin, Bulgaria, Byelorussian SSR, Cuba, Cyprus, Lao People's Democratic Republic, Madagascar, Nicaragua, Syrian Arab Republic.
Meeting numbers. GA 38th session: 6th Committee 68, 71, 73; plenary 101.

REFERENCES

[1]YUN 1982, p. 1392, GA res. 37/113, 16 Dec. 1982. [2]A/38/26. [3]A/38/384. [4]YUN 1982, p. 1391. [5]YUN 1947-48, p. 199, GA res. 169(II), 31 Oct. 1947.

Draft standard rules of procedure for conferences

Since asking the Secretary-General in 1980[1] to propose draft standard rules of procedure for special conferences of the United Nations, the General Assembly had twice deferred consideration of the reports he submitted in 1981[2] and 1982.[3]

In August 1983, the Secretary-General resubmitted his 1982 report,[4] offering a set of draft rules of procedure which followed closely those of United Nations conferences convened during the previous decade. The report was followed by two addenda[5] containing the comments and observations of 12 Member States and three international intergovernmental organizations on the proposed rules, submitted in response to a December 1982 Assembly decision.[6]

GENERAL ASSEMBLY ACTION

The General Assembly, on the recommendation of the Sixth Committee, adopted decision 38/427 without vote.

Draft standard rules of procedure for United Nations conferences

At its 101st plenary meeting, on 19 December 1983, the General Assembly, on the recommendation of the Sixth Committee:

(a) Decided to defer to its thirty-ninth session consideration of the report of the Secretary-General on draft standard rules of procedure for United Nations conferences;

(b) Again invited Governments and the international organizations concerned to communicate to the Secretary-General, by 1 May 1984, their observations on the above-mentioned report;

(c) Requested the Secretary-General to submit to the General Assembly at its thirty-ninth session a report on draft standard rules of procedure for United Nations conferences.

General Assembly decision 38/427

Adopted without vote

Approved by Sixth Committee (A/38/677) by consensus, 9 December (meeting 72); draft by Chairman (A/C.6/38/L.27); agenda item 137.
Meeting numbers. GA 38th session: 6th Committee 72; plenary 101.

REFERENCES
[1]YUN 1980, p. 1225, GA res. 35/10 C, 3 Nov. 1980. [2]YUN 1981, p. 1370. [3]YUN 1982, p. 1393. [4]A/38/298. [5]A/38/298/Add.1,2. [6]YUN 1982, p. 1394, GA dec. 37/428, 16 Dec. 1982.

Chapter V

Treaties and agreements

In 1983, the General Assembly decided, by resolution 38/139, to convene not earlier than 1985 a conference of plenipotentiaries on the law of treaties between States and international organizations or between such organizations. The International Law Commission (ILC) resumed consideration of the relations between States and international organizations as they related to the status, privileges and immunities of such bodies and their representatives. By decision 38/425, the Assembly agreed that work on reviewing the multilateral treaty-making process should continue in 1984.

As in previous years, several multilateral treaties, concluded under United Nations auspices, were deposited with the Secretary-General. The Assembly approved additional appropriations aimed at eliminating the backlog in publishing the *Treaty Series*.

Drafting process for multilateral treaties

In December 1983, the General Assembly decided that in 1984 it would establish a working group of the Sixth (Legal) Committee to try to complete work on the review of the multilateral treaty-making process.

Earlier, the Sixth Committee reconvened, as decided in 1982,[1] the Working Group on the Review of the Multilateral Treaty-making Process, which held 10 meetings between 28 October and 7 December.[2] The Group completed the first reading of a working paper prepared by the Chairman in 1982,[3] dealing with initiating a treaty-making process, formulating and adopting a multilateral treaty and post-adoption and entry into force. Further proposals were submitted in 1983—by the Chairman, on draft rules of procedure of treaty-making conferences convened within the Assembly framework; and jointly by Australia, Egypt and Mexico, on establishing an advisory drafting committee of the Assembly.

The Working Group discussed, among other things, the role of a drafting committee, provision of legal advisory services through technical assistance, determination of readiness for treaty adoption and choice of forum, follow-up action on adoption, preparation and publication of records and commentaries, and monitoring of treaty implementation. Due to lack of time, it did not consider in detail proposals submitted by its members on various aspects of the topic.

GENERAL ASSEMBLY ACTION

The General Assembly, on the recommendation of the Sixth Committee, adopted decision 38/425 without vote.

Review of the multilateral treaty-making process

At its 101st plenary meeting, on 19 December 1983, the General Assembly, on the recommendation of the Sixth Committee:

(*a*) Took note with appreciation of the report of the Working Group on the Review of the Multilateral Treaty-making Process, established in accordance with General Assembly resolution 36/112 of 10 December 1981 to determine whether the current methods of multilateral treaty-making were as efficient, economical and effective as they could be to meet the needs of the Member States;

(*b*) Decided to establish at its thirty-ninth session an open-ended working group of the Sixth Committee with the aim of completing the work on the review of the multilateral treaty-making process;

(*c*) Requested the Secretary-General to circulate to Member States the report of the Working Group on the Review of the Multilateral Treaty-making Process established at the thirty-seventh session and reconvened at the thirty-eighth session;

(*d*) Decided to include in the provisional agenda of its thirty-ninth session the item entitled "Review of the multilateral treaty-making process".

General Assembly decision 38/425

Adopted without vote

Approved by Sixth Committee (A/38/670) without vote, 9 December (meeting 73); draft by Australia (A/C.6/38/L.29); agenda item 130.
Meeting numbers. GA 38th session: 6th Committee 73; plenary 101.

Treaties involving international organizations

In December 1983, the General Assembly decided to convene not earlier than 1985 a conference of plenipotentiaries for the final consideration of the draft articles, adopted by ILC in 1982,[4] on the law of treaties between States and international organizations or between such organizations.

Report of the Secretary-General. In response to a December 1982 Assembly request,[5] the Secretary-General transmitted to it in September 1983 a report with a later addendum,[6] containing the written comments and observations on the final draft articles submitted by 13 Governments, the United Nations, six agencies and organizations within the United Nations system and two other international intergovernmental organizations.

ACC action. The Administrative Committee on Co-ordination (ACC), at its October 1983 session,

considered the procedural and substantive matters relating to the draft articles and adopted a decision, which was presented to the Sixth Committee by the Secretariat.[7] ACC suggested that the
Assembly, without precluding the eventual conclusion of a convention, consider the possibility of
first incorporating the draft articles in a declaration, endorsing them as principles or guidelines
to be applied by all intergovernmental organizations. It further observed that, whichever approach
the Assembly chose in respect of the instrument
to incorporate the draft articles, and whether it
decided to have such incorporation accomplished
at a conference or by the Sixth Committee, the
process should involve the widest possible
representation of those actively concluding treaties.
ACC deemed it prudent to allow sufficient time to
elucidate the serious substantive questions raised
by the draft articles, meanwhile perhaps convening one or more working groups.

GENERAL ASSEMBLY ACTION.

On the recommendation of the Sixth Committee, the General Assembly, on 19 December 1983,
adopted resolution 38/139 without vote.

**United Nations Conference on the Law of Treaties
between States and International Organizations
or between International Organizations**

The General Assembly,

Recalling its resolution 37/112 of 16 December 1982,
by which it decided that an international convention
should be concluded on the basis of the draft articles
on the law of treaties between States and international
organizations or between international organizations,
adopted by the International Law Commission at its
thirty-fourth session,

Recalling further that, by its resolution 37/112, it agreed
to decide at its thirty-eighth session upon the appropriate forum for the adoption of the convention in the light
of the comments received in accordance with that resolution,

Having received the report of the Secretary-General
which contains the comments and observations submitted by a number of States and principal international
intergovernmental organizations, in accordance with
General Assembly resolution 37/112, and having further
received the statement adopted by the Administrative
Committee on Co-ordination,

1. *Decides* that the appropriate forum for the final
consideration of the draft articles on the law of treaties
between States and international organizations or between international organizations, adopted by the International Law Commission at its thirty-fourth session,
shall be a conference of plenipotentiaries to be convened
not earlier than 1985;

2. *Agrees* to decide at its thirty-ninth session upon
the question of the date and place for the convening of
the United Nations Conference on the Law of Treaties
between States and International Organizations or between International Organizations, as well as upon the
question of participation in the Conference;

3. *Invites* States that have not already done so to submit, not later than 1 July 1984, their written comments
and observations on the final draft articles on the law
of treaties between States and international organizations or between international organizations prepared
by the International Law Commission, as well as on the
questions referred to in paragraph 60 of the report of
the Commission on the work of its thirty-fourth session;

4. *Invites also* the principal international intergovernmental organizations that have not already done so to
submit, within the same period, their written comments
and observations on the subject;

5. *Requests* the Secretary-General to circulate such
comments so as to facilitate the discussion on the subject at the thirty-ninth session of the General Assembly;

6. *Appeals* to potential participants in the Conference to undertake consultations on the draft articles concerned and other related questions prior to the thirty-
ninth session of the General Assembly, in order to facilitate the successful conclusion of the work of the Conference;

7. *Decides* to include in the provisional agenda of its
thirty-ninth session an item entitled "United Nations
Conference on the Law of Treaties between States and
International Organizations or between International
Organizations".

General Assembly resolution 38/139

19 December 1983   Meeting 101   Adopted without vote

Approved by Sixth Committee (A/38/672) by consensus, 8 December (meeting 70);
    26-nation draft (A/C.6/38/L.23); agenda item 132.
Sponsors: Algeria, Angola, Argentina, Australia, Austria, Bolivia, Cape Verde, Chile,
    Colombia, Ecuador, Egypt, El Salvador, Germany, Federal Republic of, Ghana,
    Guatemala, Guyana, Iraq, Kuwait, Liberia, Libyan Arab Jamahiriya, Oman, Qatar,
    Sierra Leone, Sudan, Thailand, United Kingdom.
Meeting numbers. GA 38th session: 6th Committee 31-33, 35, 70; plenary 101.

Speaking in explanation of position, Israel, the
USSR and the United States believed that the subject would be more appropriately dealt with by the
Sixth Committee, rather than by a conference of
plenipotentiaries, because of the financial implications involved. Recalling that a recent similar
conference had cost more than $3 million, the
United States said it would have abstained had a
vote been taken on the text. Israel dissociated itself from the consensus and asked the Secretariat
to submit in 1984 a memorandum on the organization of the work of the proposed conference, after
consulting ILC. Both the USSR and the United
States stressed that the question of financial implications would have to be settled in due course.

Relations between States
and international organizations

In 1983, ILC resumed consideration of the relations between States and international organizations,[8] which it had last dealt with in 1979,[9]
taking up a preliminary report[10] of the Special
Rapporteur on the second part of the topic,
Leonardo Díaz-González (Venezuela). Work on
the first part of the topic, dealing with the status,
privileges and immunities of representatives of
States to international organizations, had been

completed with the adoption in 1975 of the Vienna Convention on the Representation of States in Their Relations with International Organizations of a Universal Character.[11] Work on the second part of the topic—relating to the status, privileges and immunities of international organizations and persons engaged in their activities who were not representatives of States—had commenced in 1976 and was suspended between 1980 and 1982 while ILC focused on other studies with respect to which the process of preparing draft articles was already advanced. The second part of the topic had also been the subject of two previous reports submitted by a former Special Rapporteur.

The Commission agreed in 1983 to adopt a broad outlook and include regional organizations in the study, and to request the Secretariat to revise and update the 1967 Secretariat study on the practice of the United Nations, the specialized agencies and the International Atomic Energy Agency concerning their status, privileges and immunities. It also agreed to request the United Nations Legal Counsel to gather relevant information through questionnaires addressed to legal counsels of regional organizations.

On 19 December, the General Assembly, in resolution 38/138 on the ILC report, recommended that the Commission continue its work on the subject (see Chapter VII of this section).

Registration and publication of treaties by the United Nations

During 1983, some 1,273 international agreements and 588 subsequent actions were received by the Secretariat for registration or filing and recording. In addition, there were 259 registrations of formalities concerning agreements for which the Secretary-General performs depositary functions.

The texts of international agreements registered or filed and recorded are published in the United Nations *Treaty Series* in the original languages with translations into English and French where necessary. In 1983, the following volumes of the *Treaty Series* covering treaties registered or filed and recorded in 1973, 1974, 1975 and 1976 were issued:

883/884, 901/902, 942, 949, 950, 955, 958, 960, 961, 964, 965, 966, 968, 969, 970, 971, 972, 973, 974, 975, 977, 978, 979, 981, 982, 983, 986, 987, 988, 989, 994, 995, 997, 998, 999, 1000, 1001, 1002, 1003, 1007, 1009.

Elimination of the backlog in publication

In November 1983, the Secretary-General submitted to the Assembly his second biennial report[12] on his plan for eliminating the backlog in publishing the United Nations *Treaty Series*.

The report reviewed the plan since its inception in 1980[13] and gave the overall situation as at 31 July 1983. The Secretary-General estimated the

number of depositary formalities in 1983 at 738, and noted that an increasing number of legal opinions had been provided, particularly with regard to final clauses of multilateral treaties. He reported that, while marked progress had been achieved in 1982-1983 in eliminating the backlog, delays still experienced at various stages warranted some adjustments, requiring an additional appropriation of $994,000 for 1984-1985. On the basis of its examination of the report, the Advisory Committee on Administrative and Budgetary Questions (ACABQ) recommended that the Assembly provide $938,400.[14]

GENERAL ASSEMBLY ACTION

On 20 December, the Assembly adopted, by recorded vote, resolution 38/236 A on the programme budget for the 1984-1985 biennium, in which it approved, on the recommendation of the Fifth (Administrative and Budgetary) Committee, the additional appropriations recommended by ACABQ (see ADMINISTRATIVE AND BUDGETARY QUESTIONS, Chapter I).

In explanation of vote in the Fifth Committee, the USSR said it could not support the appropriation requested, as savings could be made through greater efficiency and co-ordination. The United Kingdom also considered the funds requested to be excessive and felt that more might have been done through redeployment of resources. Sharing that view, the Byelorussian SSR felt that the publication of the *Treaty Series* could be speeded up by such measures as having some Member States provide English and French translations of treaties concluded in other languages; it saw no need to publish in the *Treaty Series* those treaties which had already been published in other United Nations documents. Japan had difficulty understanding why the requests had been made in the form of revised estimates rather than in the original budget submission.

In addition, the Assembly, by section XII of resolution 38/234 of 20 December, invited the Committee on Conferences to examine, at its substantive session in 1984, the question of backlogs in documentation (*ibid.*). The proposal was made in the Fifth Committee by the United States, which noted the recurrence of requests for additional appropriations to eliminate other publication backlogs. Australia supported the United States proposal.

Multilateral treaties

New multilateral treaties concluded under United Nations auspices

The following treaties, concluded under United Nations auspices, were deposited with the Secretary-General during 1983:[15]

International Convention on the Harmonization of Frontier Control of Goods, concluded at Geneva on 21 October 1982

International Sugar Agreement, 1977, concluded at Geneva on 7 October 1977, as extended until 31 December 1984 by the International Sugar Council in decisions No. 13 of 20 November 1981 and 14 of 21 May 1982

Regulation No. 56: Uniform provisions concerning the approval of headlamps for mopeds and vehicles treated as such; Regulation No. 57: Uniform provisions concerning the approval of headlamps for motor cycles and vehicles treated as such; Regulation No. 58: Uniform provisions concerning the approval of goods vehicles, trailers and semi-trailers with regard to their rear underrun protection; Regulation No. 59: Uniform provisions concerning the approval of replacement silencing systems; all annexed to the *Agreement concerning the Adoption of Uniform Conditions of Approval and Reciprocal Recognition of Approval for Motor Vehicle Equipment and Parts*, done at Geneva on 20 March 1958

Statutes of the International Centre for Genetic Engineering and Biotechnology, concluded at Madrid on 13 September 1983

Vienna Convention on Succession of States in respect of State Property, Archives and Debts, concluded at Vienna on 8 April 1983

Multilateral treaties
deposited with the Secretary-General

The number of multilateral treaties for which the Secretary-General performed depositary functions stood at 672 at the end of 1983. During the year, 138 signatures were affixed to treaties for which the Secretary-General performed depositary functions and 445 instruments of ratification, accession, acceptance and approval or notifications were transmitted to him. In addition, the Secretary-General received 89 communications from States expressing observations or declarations and reservations made by certain States at the time of signature, ratification or accession.

The following multilateral treaties,[15] in respect of which the Secretary-General acts as depositary, came into force during 1983:

Charter of the Asian and Pacific Development Centre, adopted by the United Nations Economic and Social Commission for Asia and the Pacific on 1 April 1982

Regulation No. 56: Uniform provisions concerning the approval of headlamps for mopeds and vehicles treated as such; Regulation No. 57: Uniform provisions concerning the approval of headlamps for motor cycles and vehicles treated as such; Regulation No. 58: Uniform provisions concerning the approval of goods vehicles, trailers and semi-trailers with regard to their rear underrun protection; Regulation No. 59: Uniform provisions concerning the approval of replacement silencing systems; all annexed to the *Agreement concerning the Adoption of Uniform Conditions of Approval and Reciprocal Recognition of Approval for Motor Vehicle Equipment and Parts*, done at Geneva on 20 March 1958

Convention on a Code of Conduct for Liner Conferences, concluded at Geneva on 6 April 1974

International Convention against the Taking of Hostages, adopted by the General Assembly of the United Nations on 17 December 1979

International Sugar Agreement, 1977, concluded at Geneva on 7 October 1977, as extended until 31 December 1984 by the International Sugar Council in decisions No. 13 of 20 November 1981 and 14 of 21 May 1982

International Coffee Agreement, 1983, adopted by the International Coffee Council on 16 September 1982

Convention on Prohibitions or Restrictions on the Use of Certain Conventional Weapons Which May Be Deemed to Be Excessively Injurious or to Have Indiscriminate Effects, concluded at Geneva on 10 October 1980

REFERENCES

[1]YUN 1982, p. 1395, GA res. 37/110, 16 Dec. 1982. [2]A/C.6/38/L.28. [3]YUN 1982, p. 1395. [4]*Ibid.*, p. 1396. [5]*Ibid.*, p. 1397, GA res. 37/112, 16 Dec. 1982. [6]A/38/145 & Corr.1 & Add.1. [7]A/C.6/38/4. [8]A/38/10. [9]YUN 1979, p. 1125. [10]A/CN.4/370 & Corr.1 [11]YUN 1975, p. 880. [12]A/C.5/38/46. [13]YUN 1980, p. 1141. [14]A/38/7/Add.12. [15]*Multilateral Treaties Deposited with the Secretary-General, Supplement: Actions from 1 January to 31 December 1983* (ST/LEG/SER.E/2/Add.1), Sales No. E.84.V.4.

PUBLICATIONS

United Nations Juridical Yearbook 1980 (ST/LEG/SER.C/18), Sales No. E.83.V.1. *United Nations Legislative Series No. 21*, (ST/LEG/SER.B/21, vol. I), Sales No. E/F.83.V.8 (vol. I). *Statement of Treaties and International Agreements*, registered or filed and recorded with the Secretariat during 1983, ST/LEG/SER.A/431-442 (monthly).

Chapter VI

International economic law

Various legal aspects of international economic relations continued to be dealt with in 1983 by the United Nations Commission on International Trade Law (UNCITRAL) and the General Assembly's Sixth (Legal) Committee.

In December, the Assembly, by resolution 38/135, recommended that States implement the Uniform Rules on Contract Clauses for an Agreed Sum Due upon Failure of Performance, which UNCITRAL had adopted at its May/June session. In taking note of its report, the Assembly, in resolution 38/134, called on UNCITRAL to continue work on the topics in its work programme and reaffirmed the importance of training and assistance in international trade law. On legal aspects of the new international economic order, the Assembly, by resolution 38/128, requested the United Nations Institute for Training and Research to complete an analytical study on the topic for submission in 1984. In resolution 38/127, it again invited States and interested organizations to comment on, among other things, draft articles on most-favoured-nation clauses, which the International Law Commission had adopted in 1978.

Topics related to this chapter. Development and international economic and social policy: economic rights and duties of States. Industrial development: industrial co-operation contracts.

General aspects

Report of UNCITRAL

At its sixteenth session, held at Vienna, Austria, from 24 May to 3 June 1983,[1] UNCITRAL considered such legal aspects of international commerce as contract practices, payments and commercial arbitration. It also considered legal aspects of the new international economic order, as well as training and assistance.

The 1983 report of UNCITRAL was considered and taken note of by the Trade and Development Board of the United Nations Conference on Trade and Development (UNCTAD) on 4 October (see ECONOMIC AND SOCIAL QUESTIONS, Chapter IV)—an action which the Secretary-General reported to the General Assembly in November.[2]

GENERAL ASSEMBLY ACTION

By resolution 38/134 adopted without vote on 19 December, the Assembly, on the recommendation of the Sixth Committee, also took note of the UNCITRAL report.

Report of the United Nations Commission on International Trade Law

The General Assembly,

Having considered the report of the United Nations Commission on International Trade Law on the work of its sixteenth session,

Recalling that the object of the United Nations Commission on International Trade Law is the promotion of the progressive harmonization and unification of international trade law,

Recalling in this regard its resolutions 2205(XXI) of 17 December 1966, 3108(XXVIII) of 12 December 1973, 34/142 of 17 December 1979, 36/32 of 13 November 1981, 36/111 of 10 December 1981 and 37/106 of 16 December 1982, as well as its previous resolutions concerning the reports of the United Nations Commission on International Trade Law on the work of its annual sessions,

Recalling also its resolutions 3201(S-VI) and 3202(S-VI) of 1 May 1974, 3281(XXIX) of 12 December 1974 and 3362(S-VII) of 16 September 1975,

Reaffirming its conviction that the progressive harmonization and unification of international trade law, in reducing or removing legal obstacles to the flow of international trade, especially those affecting the developing countries, would significantly contribute to universal economic co-operation among all States on a basis of equality, equity and common interests and to the elimination of discrimination in international trade and, thereby, to the well-being of all peoples,

Having regard for the need to take into account the different social and legal systems in harmonizing and unifying the rules of international trade law,

Stressing the usefulness and importance of sponsoring symposia and seminars, including those organized on a regional basis, for promoting a better knowledge and understanding of international trade law and, especially, for the training of lawyers from developing countries in this field,

1. *Takes note with appreciation* of the report of the United Nations Commission on International Trade Law on the work of its sixteenth session;

2. *Commends* the United Nations Commission on International Trade Law for the progress made in its work and for having reached decisions by consensus;

3. *Calls upon* the United Nations Commission on International Trade Law, in particular its Working Group on the New International Economic Order, to continue to take account of the relevant provisions of the resolutions concerning the new international economic order,

as adopted by the General Assembly at its sixth and seventh special sessions;

4. *Takes note with appreciation* of the commencement by the United Nations Commission on International Trade Law, through its Working Group on the New International Economic Order, of work on drafting a legal guide on drawing up contracts for the supply and construction of industrial works, identifying the legal issues involved in such contracts and suggesting possible solutions to assist parties, in particular from developing countries, in their negotiations;

5. *Notes* that the United Nations Commission on International Trade Law has adopted Uniform Rules on Contract Clauses for an Agreed Sum Due upon Failure of Performance;

6. *Notes with appreciation* the progress made by the Working Group on International Contract Practices of the United Nations Commission on International Trade Law in the preparation of a draft model law on international commercial arbitration for adoption by the Commission;

7. *Reaffirms* the mandate of the United Nations Commission on International Trade Law, as the core legal body within the United Nations system in the field of international trade law, to co-ordinate legal activities in this field in order to avoid duplication of effort and to promote efficiency, consistency and coherence in the unification and harmonization of international trade law, and, in this connection:

(*a*) Recommends that the Commission should continue to maintain close co-operation with the other international organs and organizations active in the field of international trade law, in particular the United Nations Conference on Trade and Development, the International Law Commission, the United Nations Industrial Development Organization, the Commission on Transnational Corporations, the International Institute for the Unification of Private Law and the Hague Conference on Private International Law;

(*b*) Welcomes the close co-operation with the Commission of regional organizations active in the field of international trade law;

(*c*) Reaffirms the importance of the participation of observers from all States and interested international organizations at sessions of the Commission and its Working Groups;

8. *Reaffirms* the importance of bringing into effect the conventions emanating from the work of the United Nations Commission on International Trade Law for the global unification and harmonization of international trade law;

9. *Reaffirms also* the importance, in particular for the developing countries, of the work of the United Nations Commission on International Trade Law concerned with training and assistance in the field of international trade law and the desirability for the Commission to sponsor symposia and seminars, in particular those organized on a regional basis, to promote training and assistance in the field of international trade law, and, in this connection:

(*a*) Notes with appreciation the collaboration of regional organizations with the secretariat of the Commission in organizing regional seminars including, in particular, the Asian-African Legal Consultative Committee, the Council for Mutual Economic Assistance and the Organization of American States, reaffirms the im-

portance of this co-operation and recommends that the Commission should continue to maintain such close co-operation;

(*b*) Welcomes the additional initiatives being undertaken by the Commission and its secretariat to collaborate with other organizations and institutions in the organization of regional seminars;

(*c*) Expresses its appreciation to Governments and institutions for arranging seminars or symposia in the field of international trade law, in particular the Government of Australia for assisting in the organization of an Asian/Pacific regional trade law seminar and for making available fellowships, and invites such Governments and institutions to supply the secretariat of the Commission with copies of papers or proceedings in connection with these seminars or symposia in order to assist in the planning of future regional seminars;

(*d*) Invites Governments, relevant United Nations organs, organizations, institutions and individuals to assist the secretariat of the Commission in financing and organizing symposia and seminars;

10. *Recommends* that the United Nations Commission on International Trade Law should continue its work on the topics included in its programme of work;

11. *Reaffirms* the importance of the programme of work of the United Nations Commission on International Trade Law;

12. *Reaffirms also* the importance of the growing role of the International Trade Law Branch of the Office of Legal Affairs of the Secretariat, as the substantive secretariat of the United Nations Commission on International Trade Law, in assisting in the implementation of the work programme of the Commission and takes note with appreciation of its valuable services in the performance of this role;

13. *Requests* the Secretary-General to forward to the United Nations Commission on International Trade Law the records of the discussion at the thirty-eighth session of the General Assembly relating to the report of the Commission on the work of its sixteenth session.

General Assembly resolution 38/134

19 December 1983   Meeting 101   Adopted without vote

Approved by Sixth Committee (A/38/667) by consensus, 30 November (meeting 59); 30-nation draft (A/C.6/38/L.15); agenda item 127.

Sponsors: Argentina, Australia, Austria, Belgium, Brazil, Canada, Chile, Cyprus, Egypt, Finland, France, Germany, Federal Republic of, Greece, Hungary, Italy, Jamaica, Japan, Kenya, Morocco, Netherlands, Nigeria, Philippines, Senegal, Singapore, Spain, Sweden, Thailand, Trinidad and Tobago, Turkey, Yugoslavia.

Meeting numbers. GA 38th session: 6th Committee 2-8, 59; plenary 101.

REFERENCES

[1]A/38/17. [2]A/C.6/38/L.18.

PUBLICATION

United Nations Commission on International Trade Law Yearbook, vol. XIV: *1983* (A/CN.9/SER.A/1983), Sales No. E.85.V.3.

International trade law

In December 1983, the General Assembly, by resolution 38/135, recommended that States give serious consideration to, and implement, the Uniform Rules on Contract Clauses for an Agreed Sum Due upon Failure of Performance, which UN-CITRAL had adopted earlier in the year. It again invited Member States, United Nations organs and intergovernmental organizations to comment on the 1978 draft of the International Law Commission on most-favoured-nation clauses (38/127).

In addition, UNCITRAL continued considering a draft model law on international commercial arbitration and the draft Conventions on bills of exchange and promissory notes and on international cheques; took note of progress made in preparing a legal guide on electronic funds transfers; and supported continued co-operation in harmonizing international trade law.

Unification of trade law

International commercial arbitration

Draft model law

At its May/June 1983 session,[1] UNCITRAL—which in 1981 had requested its Working Group on International Contract Practices to prepare a draft model law on international commercial arbitration for use in modernizing and harmonizing national laws and practices on the subject—took note of two reports by the Group (fourth session, Vienna, 4-15 October 1982;[2] fifth session, New York, 22 February–4 March 1983[3]) and requested it to proceed with its work expeditiously. The sixth session of the Group was held at Vienna from 29 August to 9 September;[4] the Group requested the UNCITRAL secretariat to redraft the articles it had discussed at the session.

The Commission agreed that the model law could help to facilitate arbitration as an appropriate method of settling disputes in international trade transactions.

Suggestions made in UNCITRAL concerned: exploring suitable means by which the Commission and its secretariat could assist regional arbitration centres and similar institutions in developing countries; including in the model law some provisions on conciliation; and having the Group study all aspects of the relationship between courts and arbitral tribunals.

In resolution 38/134 of 19 December on the work of UNCITRAL, the General Assembly noted with appreciation the progress made by the Working Group in preparing the draft model law.

International payments

Draft Conventions on international bills of exchange and promissory notes and on international cheques

In 1983, UNCITRAL[1] agreed to devote not more than two weeks at its seventeenth (1984) session to discussing main features and controversial issues which might be identified in written comments—expected from Governments and international organizations by 30 September 1983—on the draft Conventions on international bills of exchange and promissory notes (mainly credit instruments) and on international cheques (mainly payment instruments).

These draft Conventions, adopted in 1981 by UNCITRAL's Working Group on International Negotiable Instruments,[5] would establish comprehensive sets of uniform rules applicable to international instruments for optional use in international payments; UNCITRAL was to decide in 1984 on future action on the draft texts.

Electronic funds transfer

UNCITRAL[1] took note in 1983 of a progress report that its secretariat and its Study Group on International Payments—a consultative body composed of representatives of banking and trade institutions—had begun preparing a legal guide on electronic funds transfers, which would identify the legal issues, describe the various approaches, point out the advantages and disadvantages of each approach and suggest alternative solutions. The Study Group was expected to continue its work, and several draft chapters of the legal guide were to be submitted to UNCITRAL's 1984 session.

Draft uniform rules on international trade contracts

UNCITRAL adopted in 1983[1] draft uniform rules on contract clauses for an agreed sum due upon failure of performance, which specified the circumstances and conditions under which a party to an international contract was entitled to recover or forfeit an agreed sum in the event of a failure or delay in performance. The rules, prepared in 1981 by UNCITRAL's Working Group on International Contract Practices,[6] were to apply to both liquidated damages (where a contract sought to pre-estimate compensation payable on its breach) and penalty clauses. The draft rules, which had been revised by the secretariat at the Commission's 1982 request,[7] were discussed in 1983 by UNCITRAL and a six-member Drafting Group. The Commission agreed to change provisionally the title of the rules from that previously used—"uniform rules on liquidated damages and penalty clauses". It took this action because in civil law systems the term "penalty clauses" covered both penalty clauses and liquidated damages clauses as understood in common law. The draft rules, as adopted, were annexed to the Commission's 1983 report.

The Commission also considered, as in 1982, whether the draft rules should be in the form of a convention, a model law or general contract conditions. A fourth possibility, suggested as a compromise, was a convention with the draft rules annexed, thus allowing those States not wishing to adhere to a convention the option of using the annex as a model law; a sample draft convention prepared by the UNCITRAL secretariat for that eventuality was also annexed to the Commission's 1983 report.

UNCITRAL noted a greater preference in favour of a model law as well as considerable support for the approach based on a convention with the rules annexed. In the absence of a consensus and in view of the importance of the issue, the Commission felt that the General Assembly's Sixth Committee should decide on the final form of the rules.

GENERAL ASSEMBLY ACTION

On 19 December, the General Assembly, on the recommendation of the Sixth Committee, adopted resolution 38/135 without vote.

Uniform Rules on Contract Clauses for an Agreed Sum Due upon Failure of Performance

The General Assembly,

Recognizing that a wide range of international trade contracts contain clauses obligating a party that fails to perform an obligation under the contract to pay an agreed sum to the other party,

Noting that the effect and validity of such clauses are often uncertain owing to disparities in the treatment of such clauses in various legal systems,

Believing that these uncertainties constitute an obstacle to the flow of international trade,

Being of the opinion that it would be desirable for the legal rules applicable to such clauses to be harmonized so as to reduce or eliminate the uncertainties concerning such clauses and remove these uncertainties as a barrier to the flow of international trade,

Noting that the United Nations Commission on International Trade Law has adopted Uniform Rules on Contract Clauses for an Agreed Sum Due upon Failure of Performance,

Recognizing that there are various ways in which the Uniform Rules on Contract Clauses for an Agreed Sum Due upon Failure of Performance could be implemented by States, and being of the opinion that a recommendation by the General Assembly to States that they should implement the Uniform Rules in an appropriate manner would not prejudice the Assembly from making a further recommendation or taking further action with respect to the Uniform Rules if circumstances so warrant,

Recommends that States should give serious consideration to the Uniform Rules on Contract Clauses for an Agreed Sum Due upon Failure of Performance adopted by the United Nations Commission on International Trade Law and, where appropriate, implement them in the form of either a model law or a convention.

General Assembly resolution 38/135

19 December 1983   Meeting 101   Adopted without vote

Approved by Sixth Committee (A/38/667) without vote, 30 November (meeting 59); 13-nation draft (A/C.6/38/L.16); agenda item 127.

Sponsors: Australia, Austria, Chile, Cyprus, Egypt, Finland, Germany, Federal Republic of, Greece, Japan, Nigeria, Philippines, Singapore, Thailand.
Meeting numbers. GA 38th session: 6th Committee 2-8, 59; plenary 101.

Also on 19 December, in resolution 38/134 on the work of UNCITRAL, the Assembly noted the adoption of the Uniform Rules.

In explanation of position on the draft that became resolution 38/135, Algeria and Tunisia said Governments should be given time to study the substance of the rules and comment on their form; for Algeria, the text ignored the preference expressed by many States for other ways of implementing the rules, while Tunisia felt that it was ambiguous. The United Kingdom believed it was unlikely that the rules could be implemented in the form adopted by UNCITRAL.

Co-ordination of trade law activities

In 1983, UNCITRAL[1] continued to consider the co-ordination of trade law activities. It took note of a report of the Secretary-General on current activities of international organizations related to the harmonization and unification of international trade law, and urged its secretariat to continue co-operating and co-ordinating work with those bodies. The secretariat was requested to report to the Commission's 1984 session on action taken to create closer co-operation between UNCTAD and UNCITRAL.

Among other things, the Commission noted that the Governing Council of the International Institute for the Unification of Private Law, in adopting a preliminary draft Convention on Operators of Transport Terminals in May 1983, had stated that it would forgo further work on the topic if UNCITRAL were to decide to pursue it. The draft Convention sought to fill in the gaps in the liability régime for the international transport of goods by unifying the disparate legal rules on the liability of international terminal operators. The Commission decided to include the topic in its work programme, asked the Institute for the draft text, and requested the secretariat to submit in 1984 a study of important issues arising from the preliminary draft Convention and of the possibility of broadening the scope of the rules to cover storage and safekeeping of goods not involved in transport.

The Commission had before it a report on legal aspects of automatic data processing by the Working Party of the Economic Commission for Europe and UNCTAD on Facilitation of International Trade Procedures. The Party had identified UNCITRAL as the appropriate forum to undertake and co-ordinate activities in the field, and the secretariat planned to submit to the Commission in 1984 a report on actions that might be taken in that regard.

UNCITRAL was informed that the Council of the International Chamber of Commerce (ICC)

expected to adopt in June 1983 a new version of the 1974 Uniform Customs and Practice for Documentary Credits, being prepared by the ICC Commission on Banking Technique and Practice, for submission to UNCITRAL in 1984 with a request for endorsement.

Most-favoured-nation clauses

As it had decided in 1981,[8] the General Assembly, in 1983, resumed consideration of a set of draft articles on the scope and application of most-favoured-nation clauses in international agreements, adopted by the International Law Commission (ILC) in 1978[9] with a recommendation that they be submitted to Member States as the basis for a convention. Since then, the Assembly had solicited—in 1978,[10] 1980[11] and 1981[8]—the views of Member States, United Nations organs and intergovernmental organizations on the ILC draft. Pursuant to the 1981 Assembly invitation, the Secretary-General submitted a report in September 1983,[12] containing the comments and observations received from Ecuador, Spain and Venezuela as well as from the World Intellectual Property Organization.

The ILC draft on most-favoured-nation clauses dealt with: the scope of the articles and definitions, including the definition of the most-favoured-nation clause and the definition, legal basis, source and scope of most-favoured-nation treatment (articles 1 to 8); the general application, including the scope and acquisition of rights under such a clause, and compliance with the laws and regulations of the granting State (articles 9 to 22); and exceptions to the application—in relation to a generalized system of preferences, arrangements between developing States, frontier traffic, and rights and facilities extended to land-locked States (articles 23 to 26). The final four articles dealt with, among other things, the establishment of new rules of international law in favour of developing countries and a provision on the residual character of the articles.

GENERAL ASSEMBLY ACTION

At the Assembly's 1983 session, two draft resolutions on the topic were submitted and later withdrawn in the Sixth Committee, in favour of a third draft submitted by the Committee Chairman which was based on informal consultations on the two texts. The Committee subsequently approved the Chairman's draft and submitted it for Assembly action.

One draft, sponsored by 11 Eastern European and other socialist States, would have had the Assembly establish at its fortieth (1985) session a working group of the Sixth Committee to conclude elaboration of the draft articles with a view to their submission for the Assembly's final consideration. The other draft, sponsored by 10 Western European States, would have had the Assembly bring the draft articles adopted by ILC and the proposals for amendment thereto to the attention of Member States for their consideration and use, where appropriate, in concluding agreements bearing on most-favoured-nation treatment or in dealing with questions concerning their interpretation and application.

On 19 December, the Assembly, on the recommendation of the Sixth Committee, adopted resolution 38/127 without vote.

Consideration of the draft articles on most-favoured-nation clauses

The General Assembly,

Recalling its resolution 33/139 of 19 December 1978 relating to the report of the International Law Commission on the work of its thirtieth session, in particular section II of that resolution,

Recalling also its resolutions 35/161 of 15 December 1980 and 36/111 of 10 December 1981, entitled "Consideration of the draft articles on most-favoured-nation clauses",

Reaffirming its appreciation of the high quality of the work done by the International Law Commission in elaborating a series of draft articles on most-favoured-nation clauses,

Bearing in mind the importance of facilitating international trade and the development of economic co-operation among all States on the basis of equality, mutual advantage and non-discrimination in the establishment of the new international economic order,

Bearing in mind also the complexity of codification or progressive development of international law on most-favoured-nation clauses at a time of rapid development of new forms of economic co-operation, notably those in favour of developing countries,

Taking note of the comments and observations submitted and of the statements made in the Sixth Committee at the thirty-fifth, thirty-sixth and thirty-eighth sessions of the General Assembly, including the proposals for amendment of the draft articles adopted by the International Law Commission,

1. *Requests* the Secretary-General to reiterate his invitation to Member States and interested organs of the United Nations, as well as interested intergovernmental organizations, to submit or bring up to date, not later than 31 March 1985, any written comments and observations which they deem appropriate on chapter II of the report of the International Law Commission on the work of its thirtieth session, in particular on:

(a) The draft articles on most-favoured-nation clauses adopted by the International Law Commission;

(b) Those provisions relating to such clauses on which the International Law Commission was unable to take a decision;

(c) Any other aspects of problems relating to most-favoured-nation clauses that Governments may consider relevant in view of recent developments of international practice, including the recommendation of the International Law Commission on the conclusion of a convention;

2. *Also requests* the Secretary-General to invite Member States to comment on the most appropriate procedure for completing work on most-favoured-nation clauses and on the forum for future discussion, bearing in mind the suggestions and proposals made in the Sixth Committee, including the suggestion to establish a working group of the Sixth Committee after one of the existing working groups accomplishes its mandate;

3. *Further requests* the Secretary-General to submit to the General Assembly at its fortieth session a report containing the comments and observations received pursuant to paragraphs 1 and 2 above with a view to taking a final decision on the procedure to be followed;

4. *Decides* to include in the provisional agenda of its fortieth session the item entitled "Consideration of the draft articles on most-favoured-nation clauses".

General Assembly resolution 38/127

19 December 1983   Meeting 101   Adopted without vote

Approved by Sixth Committee (A/38/660) by consensus, 30 November (meeting 59); draft by Chairman (A/C.6/38/L.17), based on informal consultations on drafts by 11 (A/C.6/38/L.3) and 10 (A/C.6/38/L.4) nations; agenda item 120.

Meeting numbers. GA 38th session: 6th Committee 18, 20-23, 25, 41, 59; plenary 101.

Training and assistance

Throughout 1983, the UNCITRAL secretariat continued to promote training and assistance and to publicize the work of UNCITRAL, through association with several regional seminars dealing with international trade law. Regional seminars and symposia dealing with the 1980 United Nations Convention on Contracts for the International Sale of Goods[13] were held in 1983, by: the Council for Mutual Economic Assistance (Moscow, April); the Austrian Ministry of Justice, the Economic University in Vienna and the Osterreichische Kontrollbank A. G. (Vienna, April); the International Law Section of the American Bar Association (Atlanta, Georgia, United States, August); and the Law Association for Asia and the Western Pacific (Manila, Philippines, September). Other meetings included the eighth Inter-American Conference on Commercial Arbitration (Santiago, Chile, April) and an international conference on the techniques of international commerce, organized by the Chamber of Industry of the Ivory Coast, the Economic Community of West Africa and the International Chamber of Commerce (Abidjan, Ivory Coast, November).

The Commission[1] approved the general approach taken by the secretariat in training and assistance activities, but suggested that more specific mention should be made in future regarding the secretariat's involvement in the various projects, and that university-level teaching material on international trade law should be developed.

In resolution 38/134 of 19 December on the work of UNCITRAL, the General Assembly reaffirmed the importance of training and assistance in international trade law, particularly for developing

countries, and invited Governments, United Nations bodies and individuals to help finance and organize seminars.

REFERENCES
[1]A/38/17.   [2]YUN 1982, p. 1401.   [3]A/CN.9/233.
[4]A/CN.9/245. [5]YUN 1981, p. 1254. [6]*Ibid.*, p. 1256.
[7]YUN 1982, p. 1403. [8]YUN 1981, p. 1259, GA res. 36/111,
10 Dec. 1981. [9]YUN 1978, p. 945. [10]*Ibid.*, p. 950, GA
res. 33/139, 19 Dec. 1978. [11]YUN 1980, p. 1130, GA
res. 35/161, 15 Dec. 1980. [12]A/38/344. [13]YUN 1980, p. 1131.

Legal aspects of the new international economic order

Consideration of legal aspects of the new international economic order continued in 1983 in UNCITRAL[1] and in the General Assembly's Sixth Committee, while other aspects were considered in other United Nations forums (see ECONOMIC AND SOCIAL QUESTIONS, Chapter I). In December, the Assembly, by resolution 38/128, requested the United Nations Institute for Training and Research (UNITAR) to complete and submit in 1984 an analytical study on the legal aspects.

UNCITRAL Working Group action. In 1983, the UNCITRAL Working Group on the New International Economic Order (fourth session, Vienna, 16-20 May) began considering the draft structure and sample draft chapters of a legal guide on drawing up contracts for the supply and construction of industrial works (see ECONOMIC AND SOCIAL QUESTIONS, Chapter VI).

UNCITRAL agreed with the Working Group on the need for expeditious preparation of the guide. The view was expressed that other legal aspects of the new international economic order were also important and that consideration should be given to the Group's long-term work programme.

UNITAR study. Pursuant to a December 1982 Assembly resolution,[2] the Secretary-General submitted in September 1983 a report with an addendum,[3] containing a progress report by UNITAR on its analytical study on the progressive development of the principles and norms of international law relating to the new international economic order—a study requested by the Assembly in 1980.[4] The addendum gave the views of Bulgaria and Madagascar, while an annex carried a report of a Panel of Experts (New York, 6-8 July), convened in response to the Assembly's 1982 invitation[2] to assist in the third and final phase of the study. The first phase of the study—a compendium listing all possible sources of norms and principles evolving in the direction of law—had been forwarded to the Assembly in 1981.[5] As part of the second phase, UNITAR had completed in 1982 analytical papers on three principles—preferential treatment for developing countries, stabilization of their export earnings, and permanent sovereignty over natural resources. The Institute engaged, in 1983, four consultants to assist in the preparation of papers dealing with four other principles—entitlement of developing countries to development assistance, right of every State to benefit from science and technology, participatory equality of developing countries in economic relations, and common heritage of mankind. The Panel of Experts recommended that, in view of the complexity of the task and of the need for the consultants and UNITAR to revise some papers, UNITAR should submit to the Assembly a progress report in 1983, and the completed study in 1984 or, more realistically, in 1985.

Reporting that it could not meet the deadline for completing the study in 1983, UNITAR requested the Assembly to extend its mandate to accomplish the task which, it asserted, dealt with a vast and complex question encompassing all aspects of international economic relations.

GENERAL ASSEMBLY ACTION

On the recommendation of the Sixth Committee, the General Assembly, on 19 December, adopted resolution 38/128 by recorded vote.

Progressive development of the principles and norms of international law relating to the new international economic order

The General Assembly,

Bearing in mind that, in accordance with the Charter of the United Nations, the General Assembly is called upon to initiate studies and make recommendations for the purpose of encouraging the progressive development of international law and its codification,

Recalling its resolutions 3201(S-VI) and 3202(S-VI) of 1 May 1974, containing the Declaration and the Programme of Action on the Establishment of a New International Economic Order, 3281(XXIX) of 12 December 1974, containing the Charter of Economic Rights and Duties of States, 3362(S-VII) of 16 September 1975 on development and international economic co-operation and 35/56 of 5 December 1980, the annex to which contains the International Development Strategy for the Third United Nations Development Decade,

Recalling its resolutions 34/150 of 17 December 1979 and 35/166 of 15 December 1980, entitled "Consolidation and progressive development of the principles and norms of international economic law relating in particular to the legal aspects of the new international economic order", and its resolutions 36/107 of 10 December 1981 and 37/103 of 16 December 1982, entitled "Progressive development of the principles and norms of international law relating to the new international economic order",

Taking note of the report of the Secretary-General, particularly of the progress report prepared by the United Nations Institute for Training and Research, of the analytical papers and analysis of texts of relevant instruments, prepared by the consultants and the Institute in accordance with paragraph 4 of General Assembly resolution 37/103, of the views submitted by States in response to resolution 37/103 and of the report of the Panel of Experts,

Taking note, in particular, of the recommendation of the Panel of Experts that the United Nations Institute for Training and Research should complete, in 1984, the analytical study on the progressive development of the principles and norms of international law relating to the new international economic order,

Recognizing the need for a systematic and progressive development of the principles and norms of international law relating to the new international economic order,

1. *Requests* the United Nations Institute for Training and Research to continue preparing the third and final phase of the analytical study and to complete it in time for the Secretary-General to submit it to the General Assembly at its thirty-ninth session;

2. *Also requests* the United Nations Institute for Training and Research to prepare a summary and an outline of the study in order to facilitate debate on the item;

3. *Urges* Member States to submit, not later than 31 May 1984, relevant information with respect to the study, including proposals concerning further action to be taken on the final study to be submitted to the General Assembly at its thirty-ninth session;

4. *Requests* the United Nations Commission on International Trade Law, the United Nations Conference on Trade and Development, the United Nations Industrial Development Organization, the regional commissions, the United Nations Centre on Transnational Corporations and other relevant intergovernmental and non-governmental organizations active in this field, as determined by the United Nations Institute for Training and Research, to submit relevant information and to co-operate fully with the Institute in the implementation of the present resolution;

5. *Requests* the Secretary-General to submit to the General Assembly at its thirty-ninth session a report on the final study prepared by the United Nations Institute for Training and Research for its consideration, on a priority basis, under the item entitled "Progressive development of the principles and norms of international law relating to the new international economic order" to be included in the provisional agenda of that session.

General Assembly resolution 38/128

19 December 1983   Meeting 101   110-1-30 (recorded vote)

Approved by Sixth Committee (A/38/661) by recorded vote (79-1-30), 28 November (meeting 56); 14-nation draft (A/C.6/38/L.6); agenda item 121.

Sponsors: Colombia, Ecuador, Jamaica, Kenya, Mexico, Nigeria, Pakistan, Philippines, Romania, Thailand, Tunisia, Venezuela, Zaire, Zambia.

Financial implications. 5th Committee, A/38/698; S-G, A/C.5/38/62, A/C.6/38/L.11.

Meeting numbers. GA 38th session: 5th Committee 56; 6th Committee 25, 27, 29-33, 35, 56; plenary 101.

Recorded vote in Assembly as follows:

In favour: Afghanistan, Algeria, Angola, Austria, Bahamas, Bahrain, Bangladesh, Barbados, Belize, Benin, Bhutan, Bolivia, Brazil, Burma, Burundi, Cape Verde, Chad, China, Colombia, Congo, Costa Rica, Cuba, Cyprus, Democratic Kampuchea, Democratic Yemen, Djibouti, Dominican Republic, Ecuador, Egypt, El Salvador, Ethiopia, Fiji, Finland, Gabon, Gambia, Ghana, Greece, Guatemala, Guinea, Guyana, Haiti, Honduras, India, Indonesia, Iran, Iraq, Ivory Coast, Jamaica, Jordan, Kenya, Kuwait, Lebanon, Lesotho, Liberia, Libyan Arab Jamahiriya, Madagascar, Malawi, Malaysia, Maldives, Mali, Malta, Mauritania, Mauritius, Mexico, Morocco, Mozambique, Nepal, Netherlands, Nicaragua, Niger, Nigeria, Oman, Pakistan, Panama, Papua New Guinea, Paraguay, Peru, Philippines, Qatar, Romania, Rwanda, Saint Lucia, Sao Tome and Principe, Saudi Arabia, Senegal, Sierra Leone, Singapore, Somalia, Sri Lanka, Sudan, Suriname, Swaziland, Syrian Arab Republic, Thailand, Togo, Trinidad and Tobago, Tunisia, Turkey, Uganda, United Arab Emirates, United Republic of Cameroon, United Republic of Tanzania, Upper Volta, Uruguay, Venezuela, Viet Nam, Yemen, Yugoslavia, Zaire, Zambia.

Against: United States.
Abstaining: Argentina, Australia, Belgium, Bulgaria, Byelorussian SSR, Canada, Chile, Czechoslovakia, Denmark, France, German Democratic Republic, Germany, Federal Republic of, Hungary, Iceland, Ireland, Israel, Italy, Japan, Lao People's Democratic Republic, Luxembourg, Mongolia, New Zealand, Norway, Poland, Portugal, Spain, Sweden, Ukrainian SSR, USSR, United Kingdom.

In related action, the Assembly, by resolution 38/134 on the work of UNCITRAL, noted with appreciation that the Working Group on the New International Economic Order had commenced work on drafting a legal guide on industrial works contracts, and called on the Group to continue taking into account the Assembly resolutions relevant to the new international economic order.

In explanation of vote on the text that became resolution 38/128, Chile observed that, during the debate, one group of States had criticized with severity the outcome of UNITAR's work, another group had proposed that the item be referred to UNCITRAL, while a third, despite its special interest in the new international economic order, had said that the study fell short of expectations; under the circumstances, it was doubtful that current efforts would result in a satisfactory legal instrument.

The Netherlands considered the study lacking in desired analytical structure and legal clarity. Belgium felt the methodology used by UNITAR was neither scientific nor politically appropriate. Similarly, the United Kingdom, which had expressed the fear that the study could result in an *ex post facto* justification of predetermined conclusions, felt the composition of the Panel of Experts did not guarantee a balanced and representative character of legal systems or political approaches. For the United States, the authors of the study had dealt with extraneous questions in the erroneous belief that they could thus compensate for the lack of juridical material pertinent to the subject.

Along with the United Kingdom, which expressed dismay at UNITAR's request for further financial subvention, the United States found it perplexing that the study, which originally was to have had no financial implications, should require additional expenditures chargeable to the regular budget.

Apart from finances, Belgium doubted that UNITAR could achieve the task in the time allotted; it would have preferred giving that body two years to complete the study. Austria, even though it did not fully agree with all aspects of the procedures followed nor with the total content of the studies carried out, believed the work had been useful.

Czechoslovakia, on behalf also of Bulgaria, the Byelorussian SSR, the German Democratic Republic, Hungary, Poland, the Ukrainian SSR and the USSR, continued to consider UNCITRAL, especially its Working Group on the New International Economic Order, as the most appropriate body to consider the subject; apart from financial implications, asking UNITAR to undertake a study affecting the interests of States in various spheres of international relations was unjustified and unacceptable. The socialist States felt that if the obligatory legal norms were to be based on the recommendations mentioned in the second preambular paragraph, their practical application would have to be analysed carefully, bearing in mind the diversity of economic relations between States.

While supporting the establishment of a new international economic order, Spain abstained because the text was subjected to a vote, and because it doubted the appropriateness of the progressive development of the principles in question.

Argentina—which had serious reservations about the sytematization used by UNITAR in its analytical study—and Chile considered it inappropriate to introduce an item on Antarctica under the heading "Common heritage of mankind", terming the views of the Panel of Experts as ignoring the characteristics of the system established by the Antarctic Treaty and incompatible with the rights of the countries exercising sovereignty in Antarctica (see also POLITICAL AND SECURITY QUESTIONS, Chapter X).

REFERENCES

[1]A/38/17. [2]YUN 1982, p. 1405, GA res. 37/103, 16 Dec. 1982. [3]A/38/366 & Corr.1,2 & Add.1. [4]YUN 1980, p. 532, GA res. 35/166, 15 Dec. 1980. [5]YUN 1981, p. 1261.

Chapter VII

Other legal questions

In 1983, the International Law Commission (ILC), which held its thirty-fifth session at Geneva from 3 May to 22 July, continued work on the progressive development and codification of international law. By resolution 38/138, the General Assembly recommended that ILC continue work on all the topics in its current programme.

During the year, activities under the United Nations Programme of Assistance in the Teaching, Study, Dissemination and Wider Appreciation of International Law included the granting of fellowships and the holding of seminars, lectures and training and refresher courses. In December, the Assembly, by resolution 38/129, authorized further activities for 1984 and 1985.

By resolution 38/37 adopted in December, the Assembly requested the Secretary-General to continue strengthening co-operation between the United Nations and the Asian-African Legal Consultative Committee.

International Law Commission

ILC work programme

The 1983 ILC session (Geneva, 3 May–22 July)[1] was devoted mainly to considering draft articles on the following aspects of international law: jurisdictional immunities of States and their property (see Chapter III of this section); State responsibility (*ibid.*); status of the diplomatic courier and the diplomatic bag not accompanied by courier (*ibid.*); non-navigational uses of international watercourses (Chapter II); and international liability for injurious consequences arising out of acts not prohibited by international law (Chapter III). It also continued work on elaborating the draft Code of Offences against the Peace and Security of Mankind, which it had prepared in 1954 (Chapter II), and resumed consideration of relations between States and international organizations (Chapter V).

The Secretary-General, by an August note,[2] transmitted to the General Assembly the texts of the draft articles which had been provisionally adopted by ILC on the first three topics.

The 34-member Commission also maintained co-operation with other juridical bodies such as the Inter-American Juridical Committee, the Asian-African Legal Consultative Committee (see below), the European Committee on Legal Co-

operation and the Arab Commission for International Law.

The Commission's programme and methods of work were examined at four meetings of a planning group set up for the 1983 ILC session. The group, whose recommendations were included in the Commission's report to the Assembly, observed that interest was shown among members to the idea of staggering annually the major consideration of topics on the ILC work programme, and the need was expressed for further expanding and intensifying research and studies undertaken by the Codification Division of the Secretariat's Office of Legal Affairs. ILC emphasized the importance of timely preparation and distribution of documentation, and decided to give priority in 1984 to the work of its Drafting Committee and to continue preparing draft articles on all topics in its current programme.

GENERAL ASSEMBLY ACTION

On the recommendation of the Sixth (Legal) Committee, the General Assembly, on 19 December, adopted resolution 38/138 without vote.

Report of the International Law Commission
The General Assembly,
Having considered the report of the International Law Commission on the work of its thirty-fifth session,
Emphasizing the need for the progressive development of international law and its codification in order to make it a more effective means of implementing the purposes and principles set forth in the Charter of the United Nations and in the Declaration on Principles of International Law concerning Friendly Relations and Co-operation among States in accordance with the Charter of the United Nations and to give increasing importance to its role in relations among States,
Recognizing the importance of referring legal and drafting questions to the Sixth Committee, including topics which might be submitted to the International Law Commission, and of enabling the Sixth Committee and the Commission further to enhance their contributions to the progressive development of international law and its codification,
Recalling the need to keep under review those topics of international law which, given their new or renewed interest for the contemporary international community, may be suitable for progressive development and codification of international law and therefore may be included in the future programme of work of the International Law Commission,
1. *Takes note* of the report of the International Law Commission on the work of its thirty-fifth session;

2. *Expresses its appreciation* to the International Law Commission for the work accomplished at that session;

3. *Recommends* that, taking into account the comments of Governments, whether in writing or expressed orally in debates in the General Assembly, the International Law Commission should continue its work on all the topics in its current programme;

4. *Expresses its satisfaction* with the conclusions and intentions of the International Law Commission concerning its procedures and methods of work, as reflected in paragraphs 305 to 307 and 310 to 314 of its report;

5. *Reaffirms* its previous decisions concerning the increased role of the Codification Division of the Office of Legal Affairs of the Secretariat and those concerning the documentation of the International Law Commission and endorses the request of the Commission contained in paragraph 310 of its report;

6. *Appeals* to Governments and, as appropriate, to international organizations to respond as fully and expeditiously as possible to the requests of the International Law Commission for comments, observations and replies to questionnaires and for materials on topics in its programme of work;

7. *Reaffirms its wish* that the International Law Commission continue to enhance its co-operation with intergovernmental legal bodies whose work is of interest for the progressive development of international law and its codification;

8. *Expresses the wish* that seminars will continue to be held in conjunction with sessions of the International Law Commission and that an increasing number of participants from developing countries will be given the opportunity to attend those seminars;

9. *Requests* the Secretary-General to forward to the International Law Commission, for its attention, the records of the debate on the report of the Commission at the thirty-eighth session of the General Assembly and to prepare and distribute a topical summary of the debate.

General Assembly resolution 38/138

19 December 1983   Meeting 101   Adopted without vote

Approved by Sixth Committee (A/38/671) by consensus, 8 December (meeting 70); 61-nation draft (A/C.6/38/L.22); agenda item 131.

Sponsors: Algeria, Angola, Argentina, Australia, Austria, Belgium, Bolivia, Brazil, Canada, Cape Verde, Chile, China, Colombia, Cyprus, Dominican Republic, Ecuador, Egypt, El Salvador, Ethiopia, Fiji, France, Germany, Federal Republic of, Ghana, Greece, Guatemala, Guyana, India, Iraq, Italy, Jamaica, Japan, Kenya, Kuwait, Liberia, Libyan Arab Jamahiriya, Madagascar, Mauritania, Morocco, Nepal, Netherlands, New Zealand, Nigeria, Norway, Oman, Papua New Guinea, Philippines, Qatar, Romania, Saudi Arabia, Sierra Leone, Spain, Sudan, Thailand, United Arab Emirates, United Kingdom, United States, Venezuela, Yemen, Yugoslavia, Zaire, Zambia.

Meeting numbers. GA 38th session: 6th Committee 34, 36-50, 54, 70; plenary 101.

In explanation of position in the Sixth Committee, Bulgaria felt that the text should have included specific reference to the ILC recommendations and that consideration needed to be given to priorities of topics and the progress made in each one. Sharing that view, the USSR hoped ILC would take into account the comments made concerning the allocation of priority to various topics; along with Turkey, it could not accept all of the Commission's conclusions.

UN Programme for the teaching and study of international law

The 1982-1983 activities of the United Nations Programme of Assistance in the Teaching, Study, Dissemination and Wider Appreciation of International Law, along with recommendations for the Programme's future implementation, were outlined by the Secretary-General in a biennial report,[3] submitted to the General Assembly in accordance with its 1981 request.[4] As in previous years, the report gave an account of steps taken or planned by the United Nations as well as a description of those of the United Nations Institute for Training and Research (UNITAR) and the United Nations Educational, Scientific and Cultural Organization (UNESCO).

International Law Seminar

Pursuant to a December 1982 Assembly wish,[5] the nineteenth session of the International Law Seminar—intended for advanced students and junior government officials dealing with international law—was held at Geneva from 24 May to 10 June 1983 with 24 participants, all of different nationality and a majority from developing countries.[1] The participants followed the work of ILC at its 1983 session and heard lectures given by its members and other eminent jurists. As in the past, none of the Seminar's costs fell on the United Nations. Austria, Denmark, Finland, the Federal Republic of Germany, the Netherlands and Viet Nam made fellowships available to participants from developing countries, and a private body, the Dana Fund for International and Comparative Legal Studies (United States), also made funds available.

In its December 1983 resolution 38/138 (see above), the Assembly expressed the wish that seminars would continue to be held in conjunction with ILC sessions and that an increasing number of participants from developing countries would be given the opportunity to attend.

Fellowships

Under the joint fellowship programme of the United Nations and UNITAR, which continued to be administered by the latter,[3] 17 fellows in 1982 and 15 in 1983—middle-grade governmental legal officers and young teachers of international law—attended courses at the Hague Academy of International Law (Netherlands), participated in lectures, seminars and courses organized by UNITAR, and, in some cases, received practical training at legal offices of the United Nations and related organizations.

The Secretary-General reported that the late receipt of voluntary contributions had prevented the launching, during the 1982-1983 reporting period, of the Hamilton Shirley Amerasinghe Fellowship on the Law of the Sea, established in 1981[6] as a memorial to the Sri Lankan diplomat who was President of the Third United Nations Conference on the Law of the Sea until his death in 1980. The Assembly had called for contributions to the Fellowship in 1981.[7]

Other activities

UNITAR organized and financed regional training and refresher courses in international law—one for Asia (Seoul, Republic of Korea, 18-29 October 1982) and another for Latin America and the Caribbean (Buenos Aires, Argentina, 26 September–7 October 1983).[3] The United Nations Commission on International Trade Law also collaborated in organizing, or participated in, a number of activities and trained four interns at its secretariat during 1982-1983 (see Chapter VI of this section).

UNESCO continued, among other things, to develop university-level teaching materials, provide fellowships and training, and organize seminars and expert meetings, including consultations on the teaching of international law in Africa (Yaoundé, United Republic of Cameroon, 28 November–2 December 1983).

The Secretary-General—following consultation with the 13-member Advisory Committee on the United Nations Programme of Assistance in the Teaching, Study, Dissemination and Wider Appreciation of International Law (seventeenth session, 11 January; eighteenth session, 27 October)—recommended the continuation, in 1984 and 1985, as in previous years, of fellowship programmes and other training activities in international law.

Noting that the four-year term of membership on the Advisory Committee was to expire at the end of 1983, the Secretary-General, by a November note,[8] drew the the Assembly's attention to the need to appoint new members for 1984-1987.

GENERAL ASSEMBLY ACTION

On the recommendation of the Sixth Committee, the General Assembly, on 19 December, adopted resolution 38/129 without vote.

United Nations Programme of Assistance in the Teaching, Study, Dissemination and Wider Appreciation of International Law
The General Assembly,
Noting with appreciation the report of the Secretary-General on the implementation of the United Nations Programme of Assistance in the Teaching, Study, Dissemination and Wider Appreciation of International Law and the recommendations made to the Secretary-General by the Advisory Committee on the United Nations Programme of Assistance in the Teaching,

Study, Dissemination and Wider Appreciation of International Law, which are contained in that report,
Considering that international law should occupy an appropriate place in the teaching of legal disciplines at all universities,
Noting with appreciation the efforts made by States at the bilateral level to provide assistance in the teaching and study of international law,
Convinced, nevertheless, that States and international organizations and institutions should be encouraged to give further support to the Programme and to increase their activities to promote the teaching, study, dissemination and wider appreciation of international law, in particular those activities which are of special benefit to persons from developing countries,
Recalling that, in the conduct of the Programme, it is desirable to use as far as possible the resources and facilities made available by Member States, international organizations and others,
Noting that, following the request for voluntary contributions made to Member States by the Assembly in its resolution 36/108 of 10 December 1981, the fund of the Hamilton Shirley Amerasinghe Fellowship on the Law of the Sea has not yet become operational and consequently no fellowships have yet been awarded,
1. *Authorizes* the Secretary-General to carry out in 1984 and 1985 the activities specified in his report, including the provision of:
(*a*) A minimum of fifteen fellowships each in 1984 and 1985, at the request of Governments of developing countries;
(*b*) A minimum of one scholarship each in 1984 and 1985 under the Hamilton Shirley Amerasinghe Fellowship on the Law of the Sea to be financed by the voluntary contributions specifically made for the Fellowship as a result of the requests set out in paragraphs 9 and 10 below;
(*c*) Assistance in the form of a travel grant for one participant from each developing country who will be invited to the regional courses to be organized in 1984 and 1985; and to finance the above activities from provisions in the regular budget and also from voluntary financial contributions which would be received as a result of the requests set out in paragraphs 9 and 10 below;
2. *Expresses its appreciation* to the Secretary-General for his constructive efforts to promote training and assistance in international law within the framework of the United Nations Programme of Assistance in the Teaching, Study, Dissemination and Wider Appreciation of International Law in 1982 and 1983;
3. *Expresses its appreciation* to the United Nations Educational, Scientific and Cultural Organization for its participation in the Programme, in particular for the efforts made to support the teaching of international law;
4. *Expresses its appreciation* to the United Nations Institute for Training and Research for its participation in the Programme, particularly in the organization of regional courses and in the conduct of the fellowship programme in international law sponsored jointly by the United Nations and the Institute;
5. *Also expresses its appreciation* to the States which provided host facilities for the regional training and refresher courses held in 1982 and 1983;
6. *Further expresses its appreciation* to the Hague Academy of International Law for the valuable contri-

butions it has made to the Programme by enabling international law fellows under the sponsorship of the United Nations and the United Nations Institute for Training and Research to attend its annual international law courses and by providing facilities for seminars organized by the Institute in conjunction with the Academy courses, and for its constructive efforts in organizing the regional training and refresher courses held at Tunis in 1982;

7. *Notes with appreciation* the contributions made by the Hague Academy of International Law to the teaching, study, dissemination and wider appreciation of international law and calls upon Member States and interested organizations to give favourable consideration to the appeal of the Academy for a continuation of and, if possible, an increase in their financial contributions in order to enable the Academy to go on with the above-mentioned activities;

8. *Urges* all Governments to encourage the inclusion of courses on international law in the programmes of legal studies offered at institutions of higher learning;

9. *Requests* the Secretary-General to continue to publicize the Programme and to invite periodically Member States, universities, philanthropic foundations and other interested national and international institutions and organizations, as well as individuals, to make voluntary contributions towards the financing of the Programme or otherwise to assist in its implementation and possible expansion;

10. *Reiterates its request* to Member States and to interested organizations and individuals to make voluntary contributions towards the financing of the Programme and expresses its appreciation to those Member States that have made voluntary contributions for this purpose;

11. *Requests* the Secretary-General to report to the General Assembly at its fortieth session on the implementation of the Programme during 1984 and 1985 and, following consultations with the Advisory Committee on the United Nations Programme of Assistance in the Teaching, Study, Dissemination and Wider Appreciation of International Law, to submit recommendations regarding the execution of the Programme in subsequent years;

12. *Decides* to appoint thirteen Member States as members of the Advisory Committee on the United Nations Programme of Assistance in the Teaching, Study, Dissemination and Wider Appreciation of International Law, for a period of four years beginning on 1 January 1984;

13. *Decides* to include in the provisional agenda of its fortieth session the item entitled "United Nations Programme of Assistance in the Teaching, Study, Dissemination and Wider Appreciation of International Law".

General Assembly resolution 38/129

19 December 1983   Meeting 101   Adopted without vote

Approved by Sixth Committee (A/38/662) by consensus, 9 December (meeting 73); draft by Chairman (A/C.6/38/L.32); agenda item 122.
Meeting numbers. GA 38th session: 6th Committee 49, 54, 73; plenary 101, 104.

On 20 December, the Assembly entrusted its President with the task of appointing 13 Member States as members of the Advisory Committee.

Co-operation between the United Nations and the Asian-African Legal Consultative Committee

In pursuance of an October 1982 General Assembly resolution,[9] the Secretary-General submitted to that body in 1983 a report[10] on co-operation between the United Nations and the Asian-African Legal Consultative Committee— an organization to which the Assembly had accorded permanent observer status in 1980.[11]

By a letter of 9 December,[12] Iraq submitted to the Secretary-General, on behalf of 64 delegations, the views and suggestions of the Legal Advisers of the member States of the Consultative Committee, which met in New York in November, for rationalizing the work of the Assembly's Sixth Committee. The Legal Advisers concluded that several matters needed urgent consideration: amalgamation of items on similar subjects for discussion in the Sixth Committee; identification of items for resolutions of formal or carry-forward character; consideration of items referred to *ad hoc* committees in appropriate stages; allocation of sufficient time to working groups at the beginning of sessions or between sessions; restricting debate on ILC reports to such issues where discussions were essential for policy guidelines, method of approach or acceptance of draft articles; and mechanisms for consultations on inscription of items of a legal character on the Assembly's agenda as well as other legal issues referred to the Sixth Committee.

GENERAL ASSEMBLY ACTION

On 5 December 1983, the General Assembly adopted without vote resolution 38/37.

Co-operation between the United Nations and the Asian-African Legal Consultative Committee

The General Assembly,

Recalling its resolutions 36/38 of 18 November 1981 and 37/8 of 29 October 1982,

Having considered the report of the Secretary-General on co-operation between the United Nations and the Asian-African Legal Consultative Committee,

Having heard the statement of the Secretary-General of the Asian-African Legal Consultative Committee on the continuing close and effective co-operation between the two organizations,

1. *Takes note with appreciation* of the report of the Secretary-General;

2. *Notes with deep satisfaction* the ongoing close and effective co-operation between the United Nations and the Asian-African Legal Consultative Committee in the field of progressive development and codification of international law and other areas of common interest;

3. *Requests* the Secretary-General to continue to take steps to strengthen the co-operation between the United Nations and the Asian-African Legal Consultative Committee in the field of progressive development and codification of international law and other areas of common interest;

4. *Requests* the Secretary-General to submit to the General Assembly at its thirty-ninth session a report on co-operation between the United Nations and the Asian-African Legal Consultative Committee;

5. *Decides* to include in the provisional agenda of its thirty-ninth session the item entitled "Co-operation between the United Nations and the Asian-African Legal Consultative Committee".

General Assembly resolution 38/37

5 December 1983   Meeting 82   Adopted without vote

25-nation draft (A/38/L.32 & Add.1); agenda item 24.

Sponsors: Australia, Bangladesh, Cyprus, Egypt, India, Indonesia, Iraq, Japan, Jordan, Kenya, Mauritius, Mongolia, Nepal, New Zealand, Nigeria, Pakistan, Philippines, Sierra Leone, Somalia, Sri Lanka, Syrian Arab Republic, Thailand, Turkey, United Arab Emirates, United Republic of Tanzania.

Meeting number. GA 38th session: plenary 82.

REFERENCES

[1]A/38/10. [2]A/38/148. [3]A/38/546. [4]YUN 1981, p. 1268, GA res. 36/108, 10 Dec. 1981. [5]YUN 1982, p. 1407, GA res. 37/111, 16 Dec. 1982. [6]YUN 1981, p. 139. [7]*Ibid.*, p. 130, GA res. 36/79, 9 Dec. 1981; and p. 1268, GA res. 36/108, 10 Dec. 1981. [8]A/C.6/38/5. [9]YUN 1982, p. 1408, GA res. 37/8, 29 Oct. 1982. [10]A/38/491. [11]YUN 1980, p. 469, GA res. 35/2, 13 Oct. 1980. [12]A/C.6/38/8.

PUBLICATIONS

Yearbook of the International Law Commission, 1983, vol. I: *Summary Records of the Meetings of the Thirty-fifth Session, 3 May–22 July 1983* (A/CN.4/SER.A/1983), Sales No. E.84.V.6; vol. II Part One: *Documents of the Thirty-fifth Session (Excluding the Report of the Commission to the General Assembly)* & *Part Two: Report of the Commission to the General Assembly on the Work of Its Thirty-fifth Session* (A/CN.4/SER.A/1983/Add.1, Parts I, II), Sales No. E.84.V.7 (Parts I, II).

Administrative and budgetary questions

Chapter I

United Nations financing

A United Nations programme budget for 1984-1985 containing appropriations of $1,587,159,800 was adopted by the General Assembly in December 1983 (resolution 38/236 A). This was $117,520,300, or 7.4 per cent, above the $1,469,639,500 in final appropriations for 1982-1983, also approved by the Assembly in December (resolution 38/226 A). Excluding inflation and foreign exchange rate movements, the real budgetary growth between the two bienniums was calculated by the Secretariat at 0.9 per cent.

Most of the budget was to be financed by assessed contributions from Member States. Assembly-approved estimates of income from other sources totalled $256,685,700 for 1982-1983 (resolution 38/226 B) and $283,892,800 for 1984-1985 (resolution 38/236 B).

The Committee on Contributions began a study on possible changes in the criteria for determining the share of each United Nations Member in future budgets, with a view to making the scale of assessments more equitable.

The Secretary-General reported in August 1983 that the cash position of the United Nations had improved, due in large measure to the fact that many Members were responding to the Assembly's 1982 appeal for expeditious payment of their budget contributions. However, the overall deficit increased by $19.8 million, to a total of $326.4 million, because of withheld contributions relating to activities which some Members regarded as illegal or unjustified.

In November, the Assembly, by decision 38/408, approved a change in the auditing terms of reference, specifying matters on which the United Nations Board of Auditors was asked to give its opinion when reviewing the Organization's financial management.

Approval of the two budgets and action on other financial matters was taken by the Assembly on the recommendation of its Fifth (Administrative and Budgetary) Committee.

UN budget

Budget for 1982-1983

Appropriations

The final appropriations under the United Nations programme budget for the biennium 1982-1983 were fixed by the General Assembly in December 1983 at $1,469,639,500. This was the second reduction since the initial budget was approved in 1981,[1] the first having been made in December 1982 when the Assembly approved the mid-biennium budget adjustment.[2]

The $3,322,200 reduction in 1983 was due in large part to lower inflation rates than had been foreseen when the initial budget was adopted in 1981, permitting savings which exceeded increases due to other factors. The reduction was based on figures supplied by the Secretary-General in his budget performance report of December 1983,[3] which put the net savings resulting from lower inflation at $5 million. Further savings, in a net amount of $1.6 million, arose from the fact that the staff vacancy rate was higher than had been anticipated and actual salary and common staff (fringe benefit) costs were lower than standard figures used in the initial budget calculations. The vacancy factor was the main cause of reductions in certain areas, notably conference and library services ($6.9 million), public information ($2.1 million) and human settlements ($1 million). Unused appropriations for meetings serviced by the United Nations Conference on Trade and Development accounted for savings of $1 million.

These savings were partly offset by increases due to other factors. The largest of these, totalling $5.6 million, were for general services at Headquarters, notably steam for heating and cooling ($1.6 million), office alterations in a recently occupied building ($1.4 million) and increased use of the diplomatic pouch for carrying mail ($1.2 million). Higher than anticipated staff costs were the prime factor in increases of $2.8 million for the United Nations Industrial Development Organization and $1.1 million for the Economic Commission for Latin America. The relocation to Baghdad, Iraq, of the secretariat of the Economic Commission for Western Asia (ECWA) (see ECONOMIC AND SOCIAL QUESTIONS, Chapter VIII) cost $1.3 million more than had been appropriated. Less favourable foreign exchange rates for non-dollar expenditures resulted in net additional requirements of $1.6 million. Decisions of policy-making organs led to a $1.4 million gross increase.

The United Nations Controller informed the Fifth Committee that the 1982-1983 budget as revised by the Assembly showed a real growth rate of 4.4 per cent over that of the previous biennium.

After analysing the increases and decreases proposed by the Secretary-General, the Advisory Committee on Administrative and Budgetary Questions (ACABQ) recommended in a report to the Assembly that his figures be approved.[4]

GENERAL ASSEMBLY ACTION

On the recommendation of the Fifth Committee, the Assembly on 20 December adopted by recorded vote resolution 38/226 A based on the Secretary-General's figures but with two additional appropriations approved by the Committee earlier in December: $886,000 as an advance to the United Nations Institute for Training and Research (UNITAR) (see ECONOMIC AND SOCIAL QUESTIONS, Chapter XV) and $240,000 for grants for emergency disaster assistance (see ECONOMIC AND SOCIAL QUESTIONS, Chapter III). The UNITAR appropriation was in a new temporary section of the budget.

Final budget appropriations for the biennium 1982-1983

The General Assembly

Resolves that for the biennium 1982-1983:

1.   The amount of $US 1,472,961,700 appropriated by its resolution 37/243 A of 21 December 1982 shall be decreased by $US 3,322,200 as follows:

Section	Amount appropriated by resolution 37/243 A	Increase or (decrease) (US dollars)	Final appropriation
Part I. *Overall policy-making, direction and co-ordination*			
1. Overall policy-making, direction and co-ordination	38,849,500	(610,300)	38,239,200
Total, PART I	38,849,500	(610,300)	38,239,200
Part II. *Political and Security Council affairs; peace-keeping activities*			
2A. Political and Security Council affairs; peace-keeping activities	76,918,600	(385,300)	76,533,300
2B. Department for Disarmament Affairs	7,408,200	(22,100)	7,386,100
Total, PART II	84,326,800	(407,400)	83,919,400
Part III. *Political affairs, trusteeship and decolonization*			
3. Political affairs, trusteeship and decolonization	21,106,700	(1,244,500)	19,862,200
Total, PART III	21,106,700	(1,244,500)	19,862,200
Part IV. *Economic, social and humanitarian activities*			
4. Policy-making organs (economic and social activities)	2,597,500	(67,200)	2,530,300
5A. Office of the Director-General for Development and International Economic Co-operation	3,280,500	(49,800)	3,230,700
5B. Centre for Science and Technology for Development	3,615,600	20,100	3,635,700
6. Department of International Economic and Social Affairs	43,669,700	126,000	43,795,700
7. Department of Technical Co-operation for Development	15,647,300	913,400	16,560,700
8. Office of Secretariat Services for Economic and Social Matters	3,200,500	(235,700)	2,964,800
9. Transnational corporations	9,000,300	(541,600)	8,458,700
10. Economic Commission for Europe	23,749,200	787,100	24,536,300
11. Economic and Social Commission for Asia and the Pacific	29,155,700	1,088,000	30,243,700
12. Economic Commission for Latin America	44,863,000	(443,900)	44,419,100
13. Economic Commission for Africa	37,302,500	337,100	37,639,600
14. Economic Commission for Western Asia	19,502,500	1,595,000	21,097,500
15. United Nations Conference on Trade and Development	52,411,700	(547,400)	51,864,300
16. International Trade Centre	8,293,700	(140,800)	8,152,900
17. United Nations Industrial Development Organization	71,782,400	2,825,500	74,607,900
18. United Nations Environment Programme	11,404,600	(416,900)	10,987,700
19. United Nations Centre for Human Settlements (Habitat)	9,131,300	(1,482,700)	7,648,600
20. International drug control	5,881,000	(287,200)	5,593,800
21. Office of the United Nations High Commissioner for Refugees	28,939,900	(1,395,300)	27,544,600
22. Office of the United Nations Disaster Relief Co-ordinator	4,856,200	171,800	5,328,000
23. Human rights	10,789,600	415,000	11,204,600
24. Regular programme of technical co-operation	30,843,900	(414,300)	30,429,600
Total, PART IV	469,918,600	2,556,200	472,474,800
Part V. *International justice and law*			
25. International Court of Justice	8,956,700	461,900	9,418,600
26. Legal activities	13,061,800	(338,900)	12,722,900
Total, PART V	22,018,500	123,000	22,141,500
Part VI. *Public information*			
27. Public information	64,635,000	(2,316,800)	62,318,200
Total, PART VI	64,635,000	(2,316,800)	62,318,200
Part VII. *Common support services*			
28. Administration and management	265,778,500	5,721,300	271,499,800
29. Conference and library services	245,223,500	(6,942,600)	238,280,900
Total, PART VII	511,002,000	(1,221,300)	509,780,700

Section	Amount appropriated by resolution 37/243 A	Increase or (decrease) (US dollars)	Final appropriation
Part VIII. *Special expenses*			
30. United Nations bond issue	17,220,300	(302,000)	16,918,300
Total, PART VIII	17,220,300	(302,000)	16,918,300
Part IX. *Staff assessment*			
31. Staff assessment	207,802,500	(684,100)	207,118,400
Total, PART IX	207,802,500	(684,100)	207,118,400
Part X. *Capital expenditures*			
32. Construction, alteration, improvement and major maintenance of premises	36,081,800	(101,000)	35,980,800
Total, PART X	36,081,800	(101,000)	35,980,800
Part XI. *Special grants*			
33. Advance to the United Nations Institute for Training and Research	—	886,000	886,000
Total, PART XI	—	886,000	886,000
GRAND TOTAL	1,472,961,700	(3,322,200)	1,469,639,500

2. The Secretary-General shall be authorized to transfer credits between sections of the budget with the concurrence of the Advisory Committee on Administrative and Budgetary Questions;

3. The total net provision made under the various sections of the budget for contractual printing shall be administered as a unit under the direction of the United Nations Publications Board;

4. The appropriations for the regular programme of technical co-operation under section 24, part IV, shall be administered in accordance with the Financial Regulations of the United Nations, except that the definition of obligations and the period of validity of obligations shall be subject to the following procedures:

(a) Obligations for personal services established in the current biennium shall be valid for the succeeding biennium, provided that appointments of the experts concerned are effected by the end of the current biennium and that the total period to be covered by obligations established for these purposes against the resources of the current biennium shall not exceed twenty-four work-months;

(b) Obligations established in the current biennium for fellowships shall remain valid until liquidated, provided that the fellow has been nominated by the requesting Government and accepted by the Organization and that a formal letter of award has been issued to the requesting Government;

(c) Obligations in respect of contracts or purchase orders for supplies or equipment recorded in the current biennium will remain valid until payment is effected to the contractor or vendor, unless they are cancelled;

5. In addition to the appropriations voted under paragraph 1 above, an amount of $19,000 is appropriated for each year of the biennium 1982-1983 from the accumulated income of the Library Endowment Fund for the purchase of books, periodicals, maps and library equipment and for such other expenses of the Library at the Palais des Nations as are in accordance with the objects and provisions of the endowment;

6. The Secretary-General shall be authorized to enter into commitments of up to $1 million in 1984, to be drawn from the savings reported in respect of the biennium 1982-1983, for the resources required to initiate the activities called for in section II, paragraph 5, of General Assembly resolution 38/192 of 20 December 1983.

General Assembly resolution 38/226 A

20 December 1983   Meeting 104   120-14-9 (recorded vote)

Approved by Fifth Committee (A/38/742) by vote (58-13-8) on revised appropriations and revised income estimates together, 19 December (meeting 73); draft prepared by Rapporteur after vote; agenda item 108.
Meeting numbers. GA 38th session: 5th Committee 22, 61, 69, 73; plenary 104.

Recorded vote in Assembly as follows:

In favour: Afghanistan, Algeria, Argentina, Austria, Bahamas, Bahrain, Bangladesh, Barbados, Belize, Benin, Bhutan, Bolivia, Botswana, Brazil, Burma, Burundi, Central African Republic, Chad, Chile, China, Colombia, Congo, Costa Rica, Cuba, Cyprus, Democratic Kampuchea, Democratic Yemen, Denmark, Djibouti, Dominican Republic, Ecuador, Egypt, El Salvador, Ethiopia, Fiji, Finland, Gabon, Gambia, Ghana, Greece, Guatemala, Guinea, Guinea-Bissau, Guyana, Haiti, Honduras, Iceland, India, Indonesia, Iran, Iraq, Ireland, Ivory Coast, Jamaica, Jordan, Kenya, Kuwait, Lebanon, Lesotho, Liberia, Libyan Arab Jamahiriya, Madagascar, Malawi, Malaysia, Maldives, Mali, Malta, Mauritania, Mauritius, Mexico, Morocco, Mozambique, Nepal, Nicaragua, Niger, Nigeria, Norway, Oman, Pakistan, Panama, Papua New Guinea, Paraguay, Peru, Philippines, Portugal, Qatar, Rwanda, Saint Lucia, Saint Vincent and the Grenadines, Samoa, Sao Tome and Principe, Saudi Arabia, Senegal, Sierra Leone, Singapore, Somalia, Spain, Sri Lanka, Sudan, Suriname, Swaziland, Sweden, Syrian Arab Republic, Thailand, Togo, Trinidad and Tobago, Tunisia, Turkey, Uganda, United Arab Emirates, United Republic of Cameroon, United Republic of Tanzania, Upper Volta, Uruguay, Vanuatu, Venezuela, Viet Nam, Yemen, Yugoslavia, Zambia.

Against: Bulgaria, Byelorussian SSR, Czechoslovakia, German Democratic Republic, Germany, Federal Republic of, Hungary, Israel, Japan, Mongolia, Poland, Ukrainian SSR, USSR, United Kingdom, United States.

Abstaining: Australia, Belgium, Canada, France, Italy, Luxembourg, Netherlands, New Zealand, Romania.

The USSR, the United Kingdom and the United States, explaining their negative votes on the draft and that on income (see below), said the savings were largely the result of unexpectedly lower rates of inflation, while the rate of real growth had risen unacceptably. The United States thought the savings should be passed on to Member States by reducing their assessments, a position shared by the Netherlands, which noted that its abstention was a break from its tradition of voting for revised budgets and felt that many opportunities to save money through redeployment had been missed. The USSR also criticized the Secretariat for not saving more by eliminating obsolete activities. Israel based its opposition on what it called anti-Israeli activities financed by the budget.

Chile, while voting in favour, reiterated its reservations on the financing of the Special Rapporteur on human rights in Chile. Egypt commended the Secretariat for producing savings and expressed the view that there was no such thing as zero real growth.

Income sources

Final income estimates under the United Nations programme budget for 1982-1983, covering income other than that derived from assessments of Member States, were approved by the General Assembly in December 1983 in the amount of $256,685,700. This was $374,200 below the total approved when the budget was revised in December 1982.[5] According to the Secretary-General's December 1983 budget performance report[3] and the analysis of that report by ACABQ,[4] an increase of $3.5 million in items classified as general income was more than offset by reductions of $2.9 million and $1 million in income from sales revenue and staff assessment, respectively.

The increase in general income was the net effect of several changes. The largest positive ones—rises of $2.9 million in miscellaneous income including gains on foreign exchange, and $1 million in bank interest—were due to actual receipts exceeding projections. Offsetting shortfalls in general income included $1.7 million due to a postponed reimbursement of an advance by the United Nations to the Common Fund for Commodities (see ECONOMIC AND SOCIAL QUESTIONS, Chapter IV), and $1.3 million due to lower reimbursement by the International Atomic Energy Agency for its space in the Vienna International Centre, a consequence of reduced buildings management costs there.

Most sales revenue showed net decreases in income, notably from the Souvenir Shop at Headquarters, whose net revenue was $1.1 million below the original projection of $1.8 million. Also, ACABQ noted that a net deficit of $1.3 million was projected for catering in United Nations buildings. Staff assessment, a kind of income tax levied by the United Nations on its employees, produced less income as a consequence of lower staff costs (see above).

GENERAL ASSEMBLY ACTION

The income estimates were approved by the Assembly on 20 December in resolution 38/226 B adopted by recorded vote, in the amount submitted by the Secretary-General, as recommended by ACABQ and the Fifth Committee. In both the Fifth Committee and the Assembly, the appropriations and income resolutions were voted on together (see above, under resolution 38/226 A, for recorded vote in the Assembly).

Final income estimates for the biennium 1982-1983

The General Assembly

Resolves that for the biennium 1982-1983:

1.   The estimates of income other than assessments on Member States in the amount of $US 257,059,900 approved by its resolution 37/243 B of 21 December 1982 shall be decreased by $US 374,200 as follows:

Income section	Amount approved by resolution 37/243 B	Increase or (decrease)	Final approved estimates
		(US dollars)	
Part I. *Income from staff assessment*			
1. Income from staff assessment	211,123,800	(978,700)	210,145,100
Total, PART I	211,123,800	(978,700)	210,145,100
Part II. *Other income*			
2. General income	32,194,500	3,464,400	35,658,900
3. Revenue-producing activities	13,741,600	(2,859,900)	10,881,700
Total, PART II	45,936,100	604,500	46,540,600
GRAND TOTAL	257,059,900	(374,200)	256,685,700

2.   The income from staff assessment shall be credited to the Tax Equalization Fund in accordance with the provisions of General Assembly resolution 973(X) of 15 December 1955;

3.   Direct expenses of the United Nations Postal Administration, services to visitors, catering and related services, garage operations, television services and the sale of publications, not provided for under the budget appropriations, shall be charged against the income derived from those activities.

General Assembly resolution 38/226 B

20 December 1983   Meeting 104   120-14-9 (recorded vote)

Approved by the Fifth Committee (A/38/742) by vote (58-13-8) on revised appropriations and revised income estimates together, 19 December (meeting 73); draft prepared by Rapporteur after vote; agenda item 108.

Meeting numbers. GA 38th session: 5th Committee 22, 61, 69, 73; plenary 104.

See explanations of vote following resolution 38/226 A, above.

Budget for 1984-1985

The United Nations programme budget for 1984-1985, in a net amount of $1,303,267,000, was adopted by the General Assembly in December 1983. This total—essentially the amount to be paid by Member States—consisted of appropriations of $1,587,159,800 less $283,892,800 in estimates of income expected from sources other than Members' contributions.

The Secretary-General initially proposed a budget calling for gross expenditures of $1,605,568,000, of which $284,565,400 was to be financed from income sources other than Members.[6] Recommendations for reductions of $17,714,200 in expenditures and $1,887,900 in income estimates were made by ACABQ in its first report on the proposed budget.[7] Following a general debate in October on the budget and related matters, the Fifth Committee examined the proposed budget's 32 expenditure and 3 income sections, taking also into account revised estimates presented by the Secretary-General subsequent to his initial submission, along with the financial implications of actions taken by the Assembly during the session and ACABQ recommendations on each of these proposed changes. The result, as recommended by the Fifth Committee and approved by the Assembly, was a gross budget $18,408,200 less than the Secretary-General had initially proposed, with income estimates $672,600 below the initial estimate.

The programme contents of the budget were reviewed by the Committee for Programme and Co-ordination (CPC)[8] and its recommendations were incorporated into the programme descriptions contained in the budget document.[9]

The major factor in the reduction from the initial level was a recalculation of costs, done by the Secretary-General in December,[10] based on a drop in the assumed annual inflation rate from 5.5 to 5 per cent and an increase in the value of the United States dollar relative to other currencies. This recosting lowered expenditure estimates by a total of $35,129,000 and income estimates by $5,745,200. The Fifth Committee approved these changes in two separate actions on 18 and 19 December, the first (covering the bulk of the amount) by a vote of 80 to 9 and the second without vote.

These reductions were partly offset by the Committee's action on some 27 sets of revised estimates and 48 statements of administrative and financial implications of resolutions and decisions proposed during the session by the Assembly's Main Committees or directly in plenary meetings. Most of these involved additions to the budget, of which two exceeded $1 million each: common services at the United Nations offices at Nairobi, Kenya, $1,398,300 in expenditures and $1,295,600 in income[11] (see Chapter IV of this section), and preparations for the Common Fund for Commodities, $942,000 in expenditures and $1,750,500 in income from repayment by the Fund[12] (see ECONOMIC AND SOCIAL QUESTIONS, Chapter IV). Both actions were taken without vote.

The estimated additional cost of servicing all conferences and meetings approved by the Assembly during the 1983 session, totalling $7,340,000, was added to the budget by the Committee on 18 December by 64 votes to 17 (see Chapter IV of this section).

The Secretary-General stated in the foreword to his proposed budget that he had asked programme managers to exercise maximum restraint in their budgetary requests, while ensuring that provision was made for fulfilling their objectives. Considerable effort had been expended in determining priorities and redeploying resources. The resulting real growth rate of less than 1 per cent might not arouse marked enthusiasm from the proponents of either contraction or expansion.

However, he hoped examination of the budget would not be dominated by the question of growth, since growth was a concept not satisfactorily defined.

In the introduction to the proposed budget, the Secretary-General noted that this was the first programme budget based on a medium-term plan approved by the Assembly—the 1984-1989 plan, adopted in December 1982—and prepared within the framework of programme planning and budgeting regulations adopted by the Assembly when it approved the medium-term plan.[13]

Analysing the budget's main features, the Secretary-General attributed most of the increase over the 1982-1983 level to inflation. He estimated the real growth rate of his proposed budget at 0.7 per cent, but pointed out that the rate was higher in the areas of disarmament, regional commissions, energy resources, law of the sea and refugees. A policy of containment was in effect for political programmes other than disarmament, for legal and public information activities, and for common (administrative and conference) services. He observed that much of the proposed growth was offset by a decrease in extrabudgetary funds available to the United Nations.

In its report on the Secretary-General's budget proposals, ACABQ noted that the regular budget represented only part of the funds available to the United Nations.[7] It cited estimates of $1,873 million anticipated in voluntary contributions for United Nations programmes during 1984-1985, excluding the costs of peace-keeping operations and funds contributed to other organizations in the United Nations system.

Analysing its own recommendations for cuts totalling $17.7 million, ACABQ said that $11.1 million of this represented "real" reductions. The rest consisted of $2.7 million resulting from an increased "turnover deduction" (a percentage subtracted from staff costs to take account of likely vacancies), $2.2 million due to deletion of provisional budget estimates that were to be updated during the Assembly session, and $1.7 million resulting from a recalculation of the cost of certain staff allowances and inflation rates.

The approved budget included provision for 11,904 established and 271 temporary posts. This represented an increase of 182 established and 55 temporary posts over the authorized strength in 1982-1983. (A section-by-section breakdown of approved posts appears in the table "UN programme budgets, 1982-1983 and 1984-1985" (see below).

The budget adopted by the Assembly was set out in three resolutions, detailing appropriations (38/236 A), income estimates (38/236 B) and the financing of 1984 appropriations (38/236 C) (see below). Other resolutions relating to the budget biennium concerned unforeseen costs (38/237) and Working Capital Fund financing (38/238) (see these headings below). In addition, a 23-section resolution (38/234) dealt with miscellaneous matters relating to the budget, and two others concerned health insurance contributions for the international civil service (38/235) and pensions for members of the International Court of Justice (38/239) (refer to INDEX OF RESOLUTIONS AND DECISIONS).

Appropriations

The $1,587,159,800 in appropriations approved by the General Assembly under the expenditure sections of the 1984-1985 budget were divided among major fields of activity as follows: common support services, 36 per cent; economic, social and humanitarian activities, 32.3 per cent; staff assessment, 14.2 per cent; political and Security Council affairs and peace-keeping activities, 5.7 per cent; public information, 4.5 per cent; overall policy-making, direction and co-ordination, 2.5 per cent; international justice and law, 1.5 per cent; trusteeship and decolonization, 1.5 per cent; interest and repayment of principal on the 1961 United Nations bond issue, 1.1 per cent; buildings, 0.8 per cent.

According to an analysis by the Secretariat included in its published breakdown of the approved budget,[9] real growth of the 1984-1985 budget over the 1982-1983 level amounted to 0.9 per cent. (Real growth excludes inflation, foreign exchange rate movements and non-recurrent expenditures for such matters as special conferences.) Programme support and common services together, which made up the bulk of the budget, rose by 1.2 per cent in real terms, while appropriations for buildings (other than routine maintenance) fell by 39.2 per cent. The main growth areas (above 10 per cent) were political policy-making organs (70.4 per cent, mainly for printing of records), CPC travel costs (21.8 per cent), Namibia (11.9 per cent) and the Executive Office of the Secretary-General (10.3 per cent). Declines greater than 10 per cent were recorded for ACABQ (16.2 per cent) and conference services at Vienna (13.4 per cent). A subsection for the new Information Service at Vienna was added to the budget.

(Growth rates of individual budget sections and subsections can be found in the table "UN programme budgets, 1982-1983 and 1984-1985".)

Several activities provided for in 1982-1983 were dropped from the initial 1984-1985 budget: activities relating to the situation in Afghanistan and its implications for international peace and security (amalgamated with the provision for the Under-Secretaries-General for Special Political Affairs), the situation in Kampuchea, missing persons in Cyprus, special identification cards to all Palestine refugees, the proposed University of Jerusalem for Palestine refugees, Israel's decision to build a canal linking the Mediterranean Sea to the Dead Sea, the International Conference on the Question of Palestine, the International Conference for Assistance to Chad, and the Office of the Special Representative for the Co-ordination of Humanitarian Operations in Kampuchea (superseded by the Office of the Co-ordinator of the Programme of Assistance to the Kampuchean People).

GENERAL ASSEMBLY ACTION

The expenditures sections of the 1984-1985 budget, comprising the appropriations for the biennium, were adopted by recorded vote by the General Assembly on 20 December in resolution 38/236 A, on the Fifth Committee's recommendation.

Budget appropriations for the biennium 1984-1985
The General Assembly
Resolves that for the biennium 1984-1985:
1. Appropriations totalling $US 1,587,159,800 are hereby voted for the following purposes:

Section	(US dollars)
PART I. *Overall policy-making, direction and co-ordination*	
1. Overall policy-making, direction and co-ordination	39,960,500
Total, PART I	39,960,500
PART II. *Political and Security Council affairs; peace-keeping activities*	
2A. Political and Security Council affairs; peace-keeping activities	81,866,700
2B. Department for Disarmament Affairs	8,893,000
Total, PART II	90,759,700
PART III. *Political affairs, trusteeship and decolonization*	
3. Political affairs, trusteeship and decolonization	23,052,300
Total, PART III	23,052,300
PART IV. *Economic, social and humanitarian activities*	
4. Policy-making organs (economic and social activities)	3,823,700
5A. Office of the Director-General for Development and International Economic Co-operation	3,655,600
5B. Centre for Science and Technology for Development	3,872,500
5C. Regional Commissions Liaison Office	597,400
6. Department of International Economic and Social Affairs	48,900,000
7. Department of Technical Co-operation for Development	17,493,700
8. Office of Secretariat Services for Economic and Social Matters	3,774,800
9. Transnational corporations	9,608,200
10. Economic Commission for Europe	25,109,300
11. Economic and Social Commission for Asia and the Pacific	34,818,600
12. Economic Commission for Latin America	46,929,700
13. Economic Commission for Africa	46,312,300
14. Economic Commission for Western Asia	26,408,600
15. United Nations Conference on Trade and Development	56,459,000
16. International Trade Centre	8,627,100
17. United Nations Industrial Development Organization	72,149,500
18. United Nations Environment Programme	10,761,100
19. United Nations Centre for Human Settlements (Habitat)	9,429,000
20. International drug control	5,808,900
21. Office of the United Nations High Commissioner for Refugees	30,025,000
22. Office of the United Nations Disaster Relief Co-ordinator	5,236,400
23. Human rights	10,247,700
24. Regular programme of technical co-operation	32,910,900
Total, PART IV	512,959,000

	PART V. *International justice and law*	
25.	International Court of Justice	9,048,600
26.	Legal activities	14,750,600
	Total, PART V	23,799,200

	PART VI. *Public information*	
27.	Public information	71,649,400
	Total, PART VI	71,649,400

	PART VII. *Common support services*	
28.	Administration and management	304,707,200
29.	Conference and library services	266,012,300
	Total, PART VII	570,719,500

	PART VIII. *Special expenses*	
30.	United Nations bond issue	16,769,100
	Total, PART VIII	16,769,100

	PART IX. *Staff assessment*	
31.	Staff assessment	224,869,600
	Total, PART IX	224,869,600

	PART X. *Capital expenditures*	
32.	Construction, alteration, improvement and major maintenance of premises	12,621,500
	Total, PART X	12,621,500
	GRAND TOTAL	1,587,159,800

2. The Secretary-General shall be authorized to transfer credits between sections of the budget with the concurrence of the Advisory Committee on Administrative and Budgetary Questions;

3. The total net provision made under the various sections of the budget for contractual printing shall be administered as a unit under the direction of the United Nations Publications Board;

4. The appropriations for the regular programme of technical co-operation under part IV, section 24, shall be administered in accordance with the Financial Regulations of the United Nations, except that the definition of obligations and the period of validity of obligations shall be subject to the following procedures:

(a) Obligations for personal services established in the current biennium shall be valid for the succeeding biennium, provided that appointments of the experts concerned are effected by the end of the current biennium and that the total period to be covered by obligations established for these purposes against the resources of the current biennium shall not exceed twenty-four work-months;

(b) Obligations established in the current biennium for fellowships shall remain valid until liquidated, provided that the fellow has been nominated by the requesting Government and accepted by the Organization and that a formal letter of award has been issued to the requesting Government;

(c) Obligations in respect of contracts or purchase orders for supplies or equipment recorded in the current biennium shall remain valid until payment is effected to the contractor or vendor, unless they are cancelled;

5. In addition to the appropriations voted under paragraph 1 above, an amount of $19,000 is appropriated for each year of the biennium 1984-1985 from accumulated income of the Library Endowment Fund for the purchase of books, periodicals, maps and library equipment and for such other expenses of the Library at the Palais des Nations as are in accordance with the objects and provisions of the endowment.

General Assembly resolution 38/236 A

20 December 1983   Meeting 104   122-9-13 (recorded vote)

Approved by Fifth Committee (A/38/760 & Corr.1, draft resolution III A) by recorded vote (81-9-13), 20 December (meeting 74); agenda item 109.
Meeting numbers. GA 38th session: 5th Committee 7, 12-23, 26-32, 34-37, 39, 40, 42, 43, 46, 52, 63, 74, 75; plenary 104.

Recorded vote in Assembly as follows:

In favour: Afghanistan, Algeria, Argentina, Australia, Austria, Bahamas, Bahrain, Bangladesh, Barbados, Belize, Benin, Bhutan, Bolivia, Botswana, Brazil, Burma, Burundi, Canada, Central African Republic, Chad, Chile, China, Colombia, Congo, Costa Rica, Cuba, Cyprus, Democratic Kampuchea, Democratic Yemen, Denmark, Djibouti, Dominican Republic, Ecuador, Egypt, El Salvador, Ethiopia, Fiji, Finland, Gabon, Gambia, Ghana, Greece, Guatemala, Guinea, Guinea-Bissau, Guyana, Haiti, Honduras, Iceland, India, Indonesia, Iran, Iraq, Ireland, Ivory Coast, Jamaica, Jordan, Kenya, Kuwait, Lebanon, Lesotho, Liberia, Libyan Arab Jamahiriya, Madagascar, Malawi, Malaysia, Maldives, Mali, Malta, Mauritania, Mauritius, Mexico, Morocco, Mozambique, Nepal, New Zealand, Nicaragua, Niger, Nigeria, Norway, Oman, Pakistan, Panama, Papua New Guinea, Paraguay, Peru, Philippines, Portugal, Qatar, Rwanda, Saint Lucia, Saint Vincent and the Grenadines, Samoa, Sao Tome and Principe, Saudi Arabia, Senegal, Sierra Leone, Singapore, Solomon Islands, Somalia, Sri Lanka, Sudan, Suriname, Swaziland, Sweden, Syrian Arab Republic, Thailand, Togo, Trinidad and Tobago, Tunisia, Turkey, Uganda, United Arab Emirates, United Republic of Cameroon, United Republic of Tanzania, Upper Volta, Uruguay, Vanuatu, Venezuela, Yemen, Yugoslavia, Zambia.

Against: Bulgaria, Byelorussian SSR, Czechoslovakia, German Democratic Republic, Hungary, Mongolia, Poland, Ukrainian SSR, USSR.

Abstaining: Belgium, France, Germany, Federal Republic of, Israel, Italy, Japan, Luxembourg, Netherlands, Romania, Spain, United Kingdom, United States, Viet Nam.

Explaining its vote against the appropriations, the USSR said the budget authorized unjustified expenditures and included appropriations for illegal activities violating the Charter of the United Nations; the USSR would not pay for costs related to the United Nations bond issue or for posts previously financed from voluntary funds.

Among those abstaining, Belgium commended the Secretary-General's efforts to limit real growth but said the rise in its 1984 contribution, which might reach 35 per cent in terms of Belgian currency, was too heavy a burden. France said that although the Secretariat had produced a markedly improved budget, necessary decisions on redeployment among programmes had not been taken and there had been excessive use of the budget to offset reductions in voluntary funding.

The Federal Republic of Germany said it had abstained rather than voting against, as it had done on past budgets, because the current one was moderate and balanced, though a zero-growth budget would have been preferable. Israel announced that it would continue to withhold its share of the costs of activities directed against it. Italy called for continued restraint and voiced reservations about higher administrative and staff costs, but noted that it had substantially increased its voluntary contributions to United Nations activities. Japan also expressed concern at rising administrative costs and the increase in staff, particularly for posts transferred from extrabudgetary funding.

The Netherlands, though pleased with the Secretary-General's restraint and the improved format and programme content of the budget, considered the growth rate too high and said supporting future budgets would be difficult if there were further growth. Spain explained that, as in 1982, it had been unable to vote in favour because of the enormous amounts requested and the unfair and arbitrary increase in its contribution.

The United Kingdom, while welcoming the restraint shown in the Secretary-General's proposed budget, preferred zero growth to maximum restraint as the best way of imposing discipline and redeploying resources to priority areas. The United States believed that much progress had been achieved in reconciling divergent interests, and commended the Secretary-General's efforts at budgetary restraint and his commitment to administrative reform; however, it was concerned at the dramatic increases in expenditures on activities for whose costs Members should not be assessed and those contrary to the Charter, and felt that unrestrained increases in assessments might lead to lower voluntary contributions. Viet Nam said it could not accept expenditures relating to the *Ad Hoc* Committee of the International Conference on Kampuchea.

Of the States which voted for the appropriations, Austria regarded the budget as a realistic compromise between the aspirations of the majority and the position of major contributors; it believed that both redeployment and growth were needed. Canada said it had cast a positive vote to enable the United Nations to carry out its mandate; however, priority-setting was necessary if the Organization was to be dynamic. Iceland, speaking for the five Nordic countries, said they had no difficulty with the rate of real growth but felt that broader application of a programme approach would have produced a better budget.

Mexico, noting that the developing countries had voted positively, said they were concerned at the inadequacy of available resources for carrying out the increasingly complex tasks of the United Nations; they rejected such concepts as zero growth, freezes and maximum restraint. Cuba, while endorsing the views of the developing countries on the budget, said it had reservations on various items, including the bond issue. Iraq, pointing to unimplemented programmes of ECWA, opposed savings achieved by terminating activities which, although authorized, had never been implemented for justifiable reasons.

Turkey, though voting in favour of the appropriations, opposed expenditures relating to the law of the sea and said it would withhold the part of its contribution related to such items. The United Republic of Cameroon said it would be strange to curtail or terminate priority activities provided for in the current budget just because the Assembly later decided to authorize new ones; the Secretary-General must request sufficient resources to carry out the increasing tasks called for by Members.

Income sources

The appropriations approved by the General Assembly in December 1983 under the 1984-1985 budget were to be financed from three main income sources: assessments on Member States, 82.1 per cent (see "Budget contributions" below); staff assessment (an income tax levied by the United Nations on staff salaries), 14.3 per cent, and sales revenues (mainly from postage stamps), 1.3 per cent. The remaining 2.3 per cent was to come from miscellaneous sources classified as "general income", about half of which consisted of reimbursement for services provided to specialized agencies and others.

GENERAL ASSEMBLY ACTION

Estimates of income other than Members' assessments, in a total amount of $283,892,800, were approved by the General Assembly on 20 December 1983, when it adopted resolution 38/236 B without vote, as part of the 1984-1985 budget. The approval process was the same as that for appropriations—involving proposals by the Secretary-General, analysis by ACABQ and recommendation by the Fifth Committee (see BUDGET FOR 1984-1985 above).

Income estimates for the biennium 1984-1985
The General Assembly
Resolves that for the biennium 1984-1985:

1. Estimates of income other than assessments on Member States totalling $US 283,892,800 are approved as follows:

Income section	(US dollars)
PART I. *Income from staff assessment*	
1. Income from staff assessment	226,751,400
Total, PART I	226,751,400
PART II. *Other income*	
2. General income	36,639,300
3. Revenue-producing activities	20,502,100
Total, PART II	57,141,400
GRAND TOTAL	283,892,800

2. The income from staff assessment shall be credited to the Tax Equalization Fund in accordance with the provisions of General Assembly resolution 973(X) of 15 December 1955;

3. Direct expenses of the United Nations Postal Administration, services to visitors, catering and related services, garage operations, television services and the sale of publications, not provided for under the budget appropriations, shall be charged against the income derived from those activities.

General Assembly resolution 38/236 B

20 December 1983   Meeting 104   Adopted without vote

Approved by Fifth Committee (A/38/760 & Corr.1, draft resolution III B) without vote, 20 December (meeting 74); agenda item 109.
Meeting numbers. GA 38th session: 5th Committee 7, 12-18, 22, 36, 37, 46, 74, 75; plenary 104.

Financing 1984 appropriations

GENERAL ASSEMBLY ACTION

Acting on the recommendation of the Fifth Committee, the General Assembly on 20 December 1983 adopted by recorded vote resolution 38/236 C, specifying the amounts to be obtained from each of the major income sources in order to finance appropriations during the first year of the 1984-1985 biennium (see APPROPRIATIONS above). Member States were to be assessed $649,685,500 for 1984, net of staff assessment.

Financing of appropriations for the year 1984
The General Assembly
Resolves that for the year 1984:

1. Budget appropriations totalling $US 791,257,700, consisting of $US 793,579,900, being one half of the appropriations approved for the biennium 1984-1985 under resolution A above, together with revised appropriations for 1982-1983 decreased by $US 2,322,200 shall be financed in accordance with regulations 5.1 and 5.2 of the Financial Regulations of the United Nations as follows:

(a) $28,570,700 being half of the estimated income other than staff assessment approved for the biennium 1984-1985 under resolution B above;

(b) $604,500 being the increase in the revised income other than staff assessment for the biennium 1982-1983;

(c) $762,082,500 being the assessment on Member States in accordance with General Assembly resolution 37/125 A of 17 December 1982 on the scale of assessments for the years 1983, 1984 and 1985;

2. There shall be set off against the assessment on Member States, in accordance with the provisions of General Assembly resolution 973(X) of 15 December 1955, their respective share in the Tax Equalization Fund in the total amount of $US 112,397,000 consisting of:

(a) $113,375,700 being half of the estimated staff assessment income approved for the biennium 1984-1985 under resolution B above;

(b) Less $978,700 being the decrease in the revised income from staff assessment for the biennium 1982-1983.

General Assembly resolution 38/236 C

20 December 1983   Meeting 104   119-9-14 (recorded vote)

Approved by Fifth Committee (A/38/760 & Corr.1, draft resolution III C) by vote (82-9-13), 20 December (meeting 74); agenda item 109.
Meeting numbers. GA 38th session: 5th Committee 74, 75; plenary 104.

Recorded vote in Assembly as follows:

In favour: Afghanistan, Algeria, Argentina, Australia, Austria, Bahamas, Bahrain, Bangladesh, Barbados, Belize, Benin, Bhutan, Bolivia, Botswana, Brazil, Burma, Burundi, Canada, Chad, Chile, China, Colombia, Congo, Costa Rica, Cuba, Cyprus, Democratic Kampuchea, Democratic Yemen, Denmark, Djibouti, Dominican Republic, Ecuador, Egypt, El Salvador, Ethiopia, Fiji, Finland, Gabon, Gambia, Ghana, Greece, Guatemala, Guinea, Guinea-Bissau, Guyana, Haiti, Honduras, Iceland, India, Indonesia, Iran, Iraq, Ireland, Ivory Coast, Jamaica, Jordan, Kenya, Kuwait, Lebanon, Lesotho, Libyan Arab Jamahiriya, Madagascar, Malawi, Malaysia, Maldives, Mali, Malta, Mauritania, Mauritius, Mexico, Morocco, Mozambique, Nepal, New Zealand, Nicaragua, Niger, Nigeria, Norway, Oman, Pakistan, Panama, Papua New Guinea, Paraguay, Peru, Philippines, Portugal, Qatar, Rwanda, Saint Lucia, Saint Vincent and the Grenadines, Samoa, Sao Tome and Principe, Saudi Arabia, Senegal, Sierra Leone, Singapore, Somalia, Sri Lanka, Sudan, Suriname, Swaziland, Sweden, Syrian Arab Republic, Thailand, Togo, Trinidad and Tobago, Tunisia, Turkey, Uganda, United Arab Emirates, United Republic of Cameroon, United Republic of Tanzania, Upper Volta, Uruguay, Vanuatu, Venezuela, Yemen, Yugoslavia, Zambia.

Against: Bulgaria, Byelorussian SSR, Czechoslovakia, German Democratic Republic, Hungary, Mongolia, Poland, Ukrainian SSR, USSR.

Abstaining: Belgium, France, Germany, Federal Republic of, Israel, Italy, Japan, Liberia, Luxembourg, Netherlands, Romania, Spain, United Kingdom, United States, Viet Nam.

Unforeseen costs

GENERAL ASSEMBLY ACTION

As recommended by the Fifth Committee, the General Assembly on 20 December 1983 adopted resolution 38/237 by recorded vote, authorizing the Secretary-General to enter into commitments during 1984-1985 to meet unforeseen and extraordinary expenses, under specified limitations. The provisions were substantially the same as in the corresponding resolution for 1982-1983, adopted in 1981,[14] except for small increases in allowable extra costs of the International Court of Justice and an additional clause permitting commitments of up to $100,000 for Court sessions away from its seat at The Hague, Netherlands.

Unforeseen and extraordinary expenses for the biennium 1984-1985
The General Assembly

1. *Authorizes* the Secretary-General, with the prior concurrence of the Advisory Committee on Administrative and Budgetary Questions and subject to the Financial Regulations of the United Nations and the provisions of paragraph 3 below, to enter into commitments in the biennium 1984-1985 to meet unforeseen and extraordinary expenses arising either during or subsequent to that biennium, provided that the concurrence of the Advisory Committee shall not be necessary for:

(a) Such commitments, not exceeding a total of $US 2 million in any one year of the biennium 1984-1985, as the Secretary-General certifies relate to the maintenance of peace and security;

(b) Such commitments as the President of the International Court of Justice certifies relate to expenses occasioned by:

(i) The designation of *ad hoc* judges (Statute of the Court, Article 31), not exceeding a total of $200,000;

(ii) The appointment of assessors (Statute, Article 30), or the calling of witnesses and the appointment of experts (Statute, Article 50), not exceeding a total of $50,000;

(iii) The maintenance in office of judges who have not been re-elected (Statute, Article 13, paragraph 3), not exceeding a total of $200,000;

(iv) The payment of pensions and travel and removal expenses of retiring judges, and travel and removal expenses and the installation grant of members of the Court, not exceeding a total of $250,000;

(v) The holding of sessions of the Court away from The Hague (Statute, Article 22), not exceeding a total of $100,000;

(c) Such commitments, in an amount not exceeding $300,000, in the biennium 1984-1985, as the Secretary-General certifies are required for interorganizational security measures pursuant to section IV of General Assembly resolution 36/235 of 18 December 1981;

2. *Resolves* that the Secretary-General shall report to the Advisory Committee on Administrative and Budgetary Questions and to the General Assembly at its thirty-ninth and fortieth sessions all commitments made under the provisions of the present resolution, together with the circumstances relating thereto, and shall submit supplementary estimates to the Assembly in respect of such commitments;

3. *Decides* that if, as a result of a decision of the Security Council, commitments relating to the maintenance of peace and security should arise in an estimated total exceeding $10 million either before the thirty-ninth session or between the thirty-ninth and fortieth sessions of the General Assembly, a special session of the Assembly shall be convened by the Secretary-General to consider the matter.

General Assembly resolution 38/237

20 December 1983   Meeting 104   131-9-1 (recorded vote)

Approved by Fifth Committee (A/38/760 & Corr.1, draft resolution IV) by vote (92-9-1), 20 December (meeting 74); agenda item 109.

Meeting numbers. GA 38th session: 5th Committee 74, 75; plenary 104.

Recorded vote in Assembly as follows:

In favour: Afghanistan, Algeria, Argentina, Australia, Austria, Bahamas, Bahrain, Bangladesh, Barbados, Belgium, Belize, Benin, Bhutan, Bolivia, Botswana, Brazil, Burma, Burundi, Canada, Chad, Chile, China, Colombia, Congo, Costa Rica, Cuba, Cyprus, Democratic Kampuchea, Democratic Yemen, Denmark, Djibouti, Dominican Republic, Ecuador, Egypt, El Salvador, Ethiopia, Fiji, Finland, France, Gabon, Gambia, Germany, Federal Republic of, Ghana, Greece, Guatemala, Guinea, Guinea-Bissau, Guyana, Haiti, Iceland, India, Indonesia, Iran, Iraq, Ireland, Israel, Italy, Ivory Coast, Jamaica, Japan, Jordan, Kenya, Kuwait, Lebanon, Lesotho, Liberia, Libyan Arab Jamahiriya, Luxembourg, Madagascar, Malawi, Malaysia, Maldives, Mali, Malta, Mauritania, Mauritius, Mexico, Morocco, Mozambique, Nepal, Netherlands, New Zealand, Nicaragua, Niger, Nigeria, Norway, Oman, Pakistan, Panama, Papua New Guinea, Paraguay, Peru, Philippines, Portugal, Qatar, Rwanda, Saint Lucia, Saint Vincent and the Grenadines, Samoa, Sao Tome and Principe, Saudi Arabia, Senegal, Sierra Leone, Singapore, Solomon Islands, Somalia, Spain, Sri Lanka, Sudan, Suriname, Swaziland, Sweden, Syrian Arab Republic, Thailand, Togo, Trinidad and Tobago, Tunisia, Turkey, Uganda, United Arab Emirates, United Kingdom, United Republic of Cameroon, United Republic of Tanzania, United States, Upper Volta, Uruguay, Vanuatu, Venezuela, Yemen, Yugoslavia, Zambia.

Against: Bulgaria, Byelorussian SSR, Czechoslovakia, German Democratic Republic, Hungary, Mongolia, Poland, Ukrainian SSR, USSR.

Abstaining: Romania.

Working Capital Fund financing

GENERAL ASSEMBLY ACTION

Establishment of the Working Capital Fund at a level of $100 million during 1984-1985 was authorized by the General Assembly on 20 December 1983 by resolution 38/238, adopted by recorded vote, as recommended by the Fifth Committee. The provisions of this resolution corresponded to those approved in 1981 for the previous biennium, when the Assembly raised the level of the Fund from $40 million.[15] As in the past, the Fund was to be used to finance appropriations pending the receipt of Members' contributions, and to pay unforeseen costs.

Working Capital Fund for the biennium 1984-1985

The General Assembly

Resolves that:

1. The Working Capital Fund shall be established for the biennium 1984-1985 in the amount of $US 100 million;

2. Member States shall make advances to the Working Capital Fund in accordance with the scale adopted by the General Assembly for contributions of Member States to the budget for the year 1984;

3. There shall be set off against this allocation of advances:

(*a*) Credits to Member States resulting from transfers made in 1959 and 1960 from surplus account to the Working Capital Fund in an adjusted amount of $1,025,092;

(*b*) Cash advances paid by Member States to the Working Capital Fund for the biennium 1982-1983 under General Assembly resolution 36/231 B of 18 December 1981;

4. Should the credits and advances paid by any Member State to the Working Capital Fund for the biennium 1982-1983 exceed the amount of that Member State's advance under the provisions of paragraph 2 above, the excess shall be set off against the amount of the contributions payable by the Member State in respect of the biennium 1984-1985;

5. The Secretary-General is authorized to advance from the Working Capital Fund:

(*a*) Such sums as may be necessary to finance budgetary appropriations pending the receipt of contributions; sums so advanced shall be reimbursed as soon as receipts from contributions are available for the purpose;

(*b*) Such sums as may be necessary to finance commitments which may be duly authorized under the provisions of the resolutions adopted by the General Assembly, in particular resolution 38/237 of 20 December 1983 relating to unforeseen and extraordinary expenses; the Secretary-General shall make provision in the budget estimates for reimbursing the Working Capital Fund;

(*c*) Such sums as, together with net sums outstanding for the same purpose, do not exceed $200,000, to continue the revolving fund to finance miscellaneous self-liquidating purchases and activities; advances in excess of the total of $200,000 may be made with the prior concurrence of the Advisory Committee on Administrative and Budgetary Questions;

(*d*) With the prior concurrence of the Advisory Committee on Administrative and Budgetary Questions, such sums as may be required to finance payments of advance insurance premiums where the period of insurance extends beyond the end of the biennium in which payment is made; the Secretary-General shall make provision in the budget estimates of each biennium, during the life of the related policies, to cover the charges applicable to each biennium;

(*e*) Such sums as may be necessary to enable the Tax Equalization Fund to meet current commitments pending the accumulation of credits; such advances shall be repaid as soon as credits are available in the Tax Equalization Fund;

6. Should the provision in paragraph 1 above prove inadequate to meet the purposes normally related to the Working Capital Fund, the Secretary-General is authorized to utilize, in the biennium 1984-1985, cash from special funds and accounts in his custody, under the conditions approved in General Assembly resolution 1341(XIII) of 13 December 1958, or the proceeds of loans authorized by the Assembly.

General Assembly resolution 38/238

20 December 1983   Meeting 104   133-9 (recorded vote)

Approved by Fifth Committee (A/38/760 & Corr.1, draft resolution V) by vote (93-9), 20 December (meeting 74); agenda item 109.

Meeting numbers. GA 38th session: 5th Committee, 74, 75; plenary, 104.

Recorded vote in Assembly as follows:

In favour: Afghanistan, Algeria, Argentina, Australia, Austria, Bahamas, Bahrain, Bangladesh, Barbados, Belgium, Belize, Benin, Bhutan, Bolivia, Botswana, Brazil, Burma, Burundi, Canada, Chad, Chile, China, Colombia, Congo, Costa Rica, Cuba, Cyprus, Democratic Kampuchea, Democratic Yemen, Denmark, Djibouti, Dominican Republic, Ecuador, Egypt, El Salvador, Ethiopia, Fiji, Finland, France, Gabon, Gambia, Germany, Federal Republic of, Ghana, Greece, Guatemala, Guinea, Guinea-Bissau, Guyana, Haiti, Honduras, Iceland, India, Indonesia, Iran, Iraq, Ireland, Israel, Italy, Ivory Coast, Jamaica, Japan, Jordan, Kenya, Kuwait, Lebanon, Lesotho, Liberia, Libyan Arab Jamahiriya, Luxembourg, Madagascar, Malawi, Malaysia, Maldives, Mali, Malta, Mauritania, Mauritius, Mexico, Morocco, Mozambique, Nepal, Netherlands, New Zealand, Nicaragua, Niger, Nigeria, Norway, Oman, Pakistan, Panama, Papua New Guinea, Paraguay, Peru, Philippines, Portugal, Qatar, Romania, Rwanda, Saint Lucia, Saint Vincent and the Grenadines, Samoa, Sao Tome and Principe, Saudi Arabia, Senegal, Sierra Leone, Singapore, Solomon Islands, Somalia, Spain, Sri Lanka, Sudan, Suriname, Swaziland, Sweden, Syrian Arab Republic, Thailand, Togo, Trinidad and Tobago, Tunisia, Turkey, Uganda, United Arab Emirates, United Kingdom, United Republic of Cameroon, United Republic of Tanzania, United States, Upper Volta, Uruguay, Vanuatu, Venezuela, Yemen, Yugoslavia, Zambia.

Against: Bulgaria, Byelorussian SSR, Czechoslovakia, German Democratic Republic, Hungary, Mongolia, Poland, Ukrainian SSR, USSR.

UN PROGRAMME BUDGETS, 1982-1983 AND 1984-1985
(appropriations and income estimates in thousands of US dollars)

PART/SECTION/SUBSECTION	1982-1983 Appropri-ations	1982-1983 Established posts	1984-1985 Initial estimates	1984-1985 Appropri-ations	1984-1985 Established posts	Real growth	Vote
PART I. _Overall policy-making, direction and co-ordination_							
1. Overall policy-making, direction and co-ordination	38,239.2	219	40,259.3	39,960.5	226	1.7%	101-2-0
A. Policy-making organs	14,984.8	47	16,369.5	15,996.7	47	-1.1%	—
B. Executive direction and management	23,254.4	172	23,889.8	23,963.8	179	3.6%	—
PART II. _Political and Security Council affairs; peace-keeping activities_							
2A. Political and Security Council affairs; peace-keeping activities	76,533.3	741	82,650.7	81,866.7	775	1.1%	101-1-0
A. Policy-making organs	374.7	—	483.6	455.3	—	70.4%	—
B. Department of Political and Security Council Affairs	9,906.1	94	10,365.8	10,434.9	94	0.7%	—
C. Secretariat of the Third United Nations Conference on the Law of the Sea	4,310.6	—	5,427.3	5,402.2	30	3.9%	—
D. Special missions	50,741.9	559	55,066.5	54,461.9	559	-0.2%	—
E. United Nations Relief and Works Agency for Palestine Refugees in the Near East	11,200.0	88	11,307.5	11,112.4	92	5.2%	—
2B. Department for Disarmanent Affairs	7,386.1	46	8,297.6	8,893.0	57	6.9%	94-7-1
A. Policy-making organs	317.5	—	358.1	357.1	—	0.0%	—
B. Department for Disarmanent Affairs	7,068.6	46	7,939.5	8,535.9	57	7.3%	—
PART III. _Political affairs, trusteeship and decolonization_							
3. Political affairs, trusteeship and decolonization	19,862.2	130	19,708.5	23,052.3	131	3.2%	99-1-0
A. Policy-making organs	1,564.5	—	1,901.2	2,499.9	—	0.1%	—
B. Department of Political Affairs, Trusteeship and Decolonization	5,940.7	60	6,951.5	6,797.2	60	-3.5%	—
C. Namibia	8,869.2	32	7,329.2	9,949.1	33	11.9%	—
D. Centre against _Apartheid_	3,487.8	38	3,526.6	3,545.3	38	1.1%	—
E. Office of the Co-ordinator of the Programme of Assistance to the Kampuchean People	—	—	—	260.8	—	—	—
PART IV. _Economic, social and humanitarian activities_							
4. Policy-making organs (economic and social activities)	2,530.3	—	2,354.1	3,823.7	—	1.0%	93-0-9
A. Economic and Social Council and its functional commissions and committees and other recurrent meetings	1,209.0	—	1,607.3	1,382.0	—	1.0%	—
B. Special conferences	1,321.3	—	746.8	2,461.7	—	0.0%	—
5A. Office of the Director-General for Development and International Economic Co-operation	3,230.7	27	3,460.6	3,655.6	27	-2.0%	86-1-17
5B. Centre for Science and Technology for Development	3,635.7	32	3,892.1	3,872.5	32	0.0%	95-0-9
5C. Regional Commissions Liaison Office	—	—	—	597.4	6	0.3%	95-0-9
6. Department of International Economic and Social Affairs	43,795.7	516	49,450.3	48,900.0	518	-0.6%	94-0-8
7. Department of Technical Co-operation for Development	16,560.7	199	17,596.5	17,493.7	199	-0.7%	95-9-0
8. Office of Secretariat Services for Economic and Social Matters	2,964.8	36	3,792.2	3,774.8	39	8.1%	no vote
9. Transnational corporations	8,458.7	81	9,765.3	9,608.2	83	-0.5%	no vote
10. Economic Commission for Europe	24,536.3	233	25,089.1	25,109.3	233	-0.1%	no vote
11. Economic and Social Commission for Asia and the Pacific	30,243.7	555	36,093.7	34,818.6	554	3.9%	no vote
12. Economic Commission for Latin America	44,419.1	581	54,092.9	46,929.7	586	1.5%	no vote
13. Economic Commission for Africa	37,639.6	609	45,726.2	46,312.3	618	2.9%	no vote
14. Economic Commission for Western Asia	21,097.5	310	29,584.5	26,408.6	313	3.3%	98-1-4
15. United Nations Conference on Trade and Development	51,864.3	448	54,505.5	56,459.0	454	1.1%	84-11-9
16. International Trade Centre	8,152.9	—	8,627.1	8,627.1	—	-1.1%	no vote
17. United Nations Industrial Development Organization	74,607.9	740	74,524.9	72,149.5	735	-0.7%	no vote
18. United Nations Environment Programme	10,987.7	113	12,585.6	10,761.1	104	-3.9%	94-10-0
19. United Nations Centre for Human Settlements (Habitat)	7,648.6	88	10,901.9	9,429.0	87	0.0%	no vote
20. International drug control	5,593.8	59	5,953.4	5,808.9	59	0.6%	93-9-0
21. Office of the United Nations High Commissioner for Refugees	27,544.6	297	32,274.3	30,025.0	290	3.8%	90-10-0
22. Office of the United Nations Disaster Relief Co-ordinator	5,328.0	34	5,241.5	5,236.4	36	3.4%	no vote
23. Human rights	11,204.6	81	9,714.3	10,247.7	80	-1.3%	no vote
24. Regular programme of technical co-operation	30,429.6	—	34,519.2	32,910.9	—	0.0%	84-14-5

PART/SECTION/SUBSECTION	1982-1983		1984-1985				
	Appropri-ations	Established posts	Initial estimates	Appropri-ations	Established posts	Real growth	Vote
PART V. *International justice and law*							
25. International Court of Justice	9,418.6	39	8,911.7	9,048.6	41	4.6%	no vote
26. Legal activities	12,722.9	108	14,072.5	14,750.6	108	4.5%	95-0-9
A. Policy-making organs	1,980.3	2	2,127.2	2,081.4	2	-5.4%	—
B. Office of Legal Affairs	10,742.6	106	11,945.3	12,669.2	106	6.3%	—
PART VI. *Public information*							
27. Public information	62,318.2	732	69,959.3	71,649.4	750	2.9%	81-16-7
A. Headquarters	40,769.4	315	43,122.3	44,281.0	320	2.0%	—
B. Geneva	3,744.0	35	3,728.9	3,716.9	34	-1.4%	—
C. Information centres	17,804.8	382	23,108.1	22,920.4	385	2.0%	—
D. Information Service, Vienna	—	—	—	731.1	11		—
PART VII. *Common support services*							
28. Administration, management and general services	271,499.8	2,048	312,307.1	304,707.2	2,082	2.2%	83-10-10
A. Office of the Under-Secretary-General for Administration, Finance and Management	857.4	8	888.4	886.2	8	1.2%	—
B. Office of Financial Services	13,272.1	173	14,950.1	14,877.1	174	0.9%	—
C. Office of Personnel Services	14,343.1	168	15,980.7	15,784.8	170	0.8%	—
D. Office of General Services, Headquarters	114,865.8	765	135,607.9	130,987.8	764	1.9%	—
E. Administrative Management Service	1,914.0	20	2,183.6	2,180.9	20	0.0%	—
F. Internal Audit Division	3,545.4	42	3,936.8	3,948.0	42	-0.5%	—
G. Electronic Data Processing and Information Systems Division	14,081.4	57	15,327.4	15,129.1	55	1.1%	—
H. Division of Administration, Geneva	10,991.1	107	11,399.0	11,271.9	108	1.8%	—
I. General Services Division, Geneva	43,054.5	374	48,971.3	47,185.6	389	-2.4%	—
J. Staff training activities (Headquarters, Geneva, and the regional commissions)	7,041.6	43	7,949.7	8,050.8	43	3.8%	—
K. Miscellaneous expenses	6,196.6	—	5,755.2	5,605.2	—	0.9%	—
L. Jointly financed administrative activities	10,717.9	70	11,538.6	11,981.2	71	1.2%	—
M. Administrative Services, Vienna	30,618.9	221	37,818.4	34,496.2	221	5.6%	—
N. Common services, Nairobi	—	—	—	2,322.4	17		—
29. Conference and library services	238,280.9	2,418	262,267.5	266,012.3	2,477	-0.4%	82-2-20
A. Department of Conference Services, Headquarters	123,946.4	1,437	141,390.4	143,641.7	1,437	0.8%	—
B. Conference Services, Geneva	86,201.7	781	93,156.4	93,628.2	800	-0.8%	—
C. Conference Services, Vienna	12,048.0	—	10,330.0	11,602.5	42	-13.4%	—
D. Library, Headquarters	11,086.4	152	12,229.4	12,066.9	150	-0.4%	—
E. Library, Geneva	4,448.1	48	4,525.4	4,486.4	48	0.0%	—
F. Library, Vienna	550.3	—	635.9	586.6	—	2.5%	—
PART VIII. *Special expenses*							
30. United Nations bond issue	16,918.3	—	16,769.1	16,769.1	—	-2.6%	87-13-1
PART IX. *Staff assessment*							
31. Staff assessment	207,118.4	—	227,511.1	224,869.6	—	1.4%	no vote
PART X. *Capital expenditures*							
32. Construction, alteration, improvement and major maintenance of premises	35,980.8	—	13,108.4	12,621.5	—	-39.2%	92-9-0
PART XI. *Special grants*							
33. United Nations Institute for Training and Research	886.0	—	—	—	—	—	—
TOTAL APPROPRIATIONS (gross)	1,469,639.5	11,520	1,605,568.0	1,587,159.8	11,700	0.9%	81-9-13

INCOME SECTION	Approved income estimates	Established posts	Initial income estimates	Approved income estimates	Established posts	Real growth	Vote
1. Income from staff assessment	210,145.1	—	229,787.9	226,751.4	—	—	no vote
2. General income	35,658.9	—	34,129.3	36,639.6	—	—	no vote
3. Revenue-producing activities	10,881.7	202	20,648.2	20,502.1	204	—	no vote
TOTAL INCOME ESTIMATES	256,685.7	202	284,565.4	283,892.8	204	—	no vote
GRAND TOTAL NET BUDGET	1,212,943.8	11,722	1,321,002.6	1,303,267.0	11,904	—	—

NOTES:

1982-1983: Appropriations: Approved by the General Assembly on 20 December 1983 (resolution 38/226 A); subsection figures from the budget performance report (A/C.5/38/49 & Add.1-33) as revised by the Fifth Committee on 19 December 1983 in respect of UNDRO and UNITAR (see APPROPRIATIONS in text). *Approved income estimates:* Approved by the General Assembly on 20 December 1983 (resolution 38/226 B). *Established posts:* Number of established (non-temporary) staff posts authorized under the 1982-1983 regular budget.

1984-1985: Initial estimates: Contained in the Secretary-General's proposed programme budget (A/38/6 (vol.I & Corr.1)). *Appropriations:* Approved by the General Assembly on 20 December 1983 (resolution 38/236 A). *Approved income estimates:* Approved by the General Assembly on 20 December 1983 (resolution 38/236 B). *Established posts:* Number of established (non-temporary) staff posts authorized under the 1984-1985 regular budget. *Real growth:* Percentage increase (or decrease) in appropriations from 1982-1983 to 1984-1985, excluding inflation and non-recurrent items, as calculated by the United Nations Secretariat (dash signifies not applicable). *Vote:* Totals of recorded section-by-section votes (in favour–against–abstaining) in the Fifth Committee during the second reading of the budget and the Committee vote on the appropriations as a whole, 20 December 1983; the vote in the Assembly on the appropriation resolution was 122-9-13. Dashes in the final column indicate subsections not put separately to the vote; "no vote" refers to sections approved without vote.

SOURCE for subsection appropriations (1984-1985), established posts (1982-1983 and 1984-1985) and real growth: A/38/6/Add.1.

REFERENCES

[1]YUN 1981, p. 1278, GA res. 36/240 A, 18 Dec. 1981.
[2]YUN 1982, p. 1412, GA res. 37/243 A, 21 Dec. 1982.
[3]A/C.5/38/49 & Add.1-33. [4]A/38/748. [5]YUN 1982, p. 1414,
GA res. 37/243 B, 21 Dec. 1982. [6]A/38/6 (vols. I-III) & Corr.1.
[7]A/38/7 & Corr.1. [8]A/38/38. [9]A/38/6/Add.1. [10]A/C.5/38/102
& Add.1. [11]A/C.5/38/35. [12]A/C.5/38/12. [13]YUN 1982,
p. 1430, GA res. 37/234, 21 Dec. 1982. [14]YUN 1981, p. 1280,
GA res. 36/241, 18 Dec. 1981. [15]Ibid., p. 1282, GA
res. 36/242, 18 Dec. 1981.

Budget contributions

The General Assembly's Committee on Contributions began a detailed study during 1983 of ways to improve the calculation of the share payable by each United Nations Member towards the Organization's budget. The Assembly, which in December 1982 had approved a scale of assessments for 1983-1985 setting out the percentage of each Member's budget contribution,[1] requested the Committee in December 1983 (resolution 38/33) to carry out the mandate the Assembly had given it in 1982[2] to propose methods for determining future scales.

Report of the Committee on Contributions. Following its forty-third session (New York, 3-27 May 1983), the Committee submitted to the Assembly a report describing the initial results of its study on possible refinements of, and alternatives to, the current methods of calculating Members' capacity to pay their share of the budget.[3]

The Committee considered four alternatives:

I. To divide Members into three groupings—developed market economies, centrally planned economies, and others, mainly developing countries—then negotiate the share to be borne by each group, and have the groups themselves, or the Committee, establish individual shares. The Committee agreed to study this idea further in 1984.

II. To replace the capacity-to-pay principle by "personnel and sovereignty factors", according to which a fourth of each country's share would be the same in recognition of their equal sovereignty, and the remainder would depend on the number of their nationals in the Secretariat and possibly on other factors, such as the size of the Member's permanent mission to the United Nations, supplements for the host country and for permanent members of the Security Council, and reductions for least developed countries. The Committee agreed to consider this further, along with a possible link between assessment rates and benefits derived by States from their membership.

III. To use national wealth as the primary criterion in place of national income. The Committee decided not to pursue this alternative on the ground that statistical methodology, and the availability and comparability of national wealth statistics, had not progressed sufficiently.

IV. To vary the current methodology. In this respect the Committee focused on three main areas:

(1) Tempering national income statistics by the use of socio-economic indicators. The Committee experimented with several formulae that took account of such factors as the share of manufacturing in gross domestic product, manufactured exports as a percentage of total exports, dependence on a few export commodities, agricultural employment as a share of total employment, telephones per capita, literacy and per capita cereal production. However, agreement was not reached on which indicators would best reflect development or on the weights to assign them. The Committee decided to study the matter further, based on a detailed assessment of the effects on individual rates.

(2) Adjustments for inflation and changes in foreign exchange rates. Various methods were examined to correct over- or underestimation of changes in the United States dollar value of a State's national income due to these monetary factors, but the Committee reached no conclusion.

(3) Other elements, including a different statistical base period for measuring changes in national income, a revised upper limit of the low per capita income allowance formula used to lower the rates of the poorest countries, and a limit for increases between two successive assessment scales. The Committee agreed to study these matters again in 1984.

An addendum to the Committee's report contained a table showing the assessed and voluntary contributions of countries to organizations and programmes of the United Nations system in 1981 and 1982.[4]

GENERAL ASSEMBLY ACTION

By resolution 38/33, adopted without vote on 25 November 1983 on the recommendation of the Fifth Committee, the Assembly requested the Committee on Contributions to carry out the mandate given it in 1982, taking account of the views of Member States expressed to the Assembly in 1982 and 1983.

Scale of assessments for the apportionment of the expenses of the United Nations

The General Assembly,

Recalling its resolution 37/125 B of 17 December 1982,

Having examined the report of the Committee on Contributions,

Recognizing the need for an improved methodology to assess the real capacity to pay of Member States, in order to increase the fairness and equity of the scale of assessments,

Mindful of the obligation of Member States to bear the expenses of the Organization as apportioned by the General Assembly according to the real capacity to pay,

1. *Takes note* of the report of the Committee on Contributions on the work in progress, as requested in General Assembly resolution 37/125 B;

2. *Requests* the Committee on Contributions to carry out the mandate entrusted to it by resolution 37/125 B, taking into account the views expressed by Member States

during the thirty-seventh and thirty-eighth sessions of the General Assembly;

3. *Invites* the Secretary-General to provide the Committee on Contributions with the facilities it requires to carry out its work and, if requested by the Committee, necessary supplementary assistance;

4. *Requests* the Secretary-General in particular to forward to the members of the Committee on Contributions the studies prepared by the Statistical Office of the Secretariat as soon as possible after each study has been completed.

General Assembly resolution 38/33

25 November 1983   Meeting 71   Adopted without vote

Approved by Fifth Committee (A/38/583) without vote, 11 November (meeting 35); 3-nation draft (A/C.5/38/L.5), amended by France (A/C.5/38/L.8); agenda item 115.
Sponsors: Canada, Morocco, Poland.
Meeting numbers. GA 38th session: 5th Committee 4, 8-12, 14, 19, 35, 36; plenary 71.

The wording of the request to the Committee on Contributions (paragraph 2) came from an amendment by France which replaced a paragraph in the original text asking the Committee, in carrying out its 1982 mandate, simply to take account of the views of Member States. The amendment, approved without vote by the Fifth Committee, also deleted a paragraph containing requests that the Committee on Contributions submit in 1984 a completed study on alternative methods to assess capacity to pay together with suggestions for methods to determine future assessment scales, and guidelines for the collection and presentation of data.

Budget contributions in 1983

Of the $760.7 million in budget contributions payable as at 1 January 1983, $590.2 million had been collected from Member States by 31 December, leaving $170.5 million outstanding[5] (see table, "Status of contributions to the UN regular budget"). Of the total payable, net assessments for 1983, due early in the year, totalled $612.6 million; the remaining $148.1 million related to prior years. In addition, nine non-member States were assessed a total of $2.3 million for their share of United Nations activities in which they participated[6] (see table, "Assessment of non-member States for 1983 expenses of UN activities in which they participated"). Assessments of Members and non-members for the regular budget were in accordance with scales for 1983-1985 approved by the General Assembly in 1982.[1]

The continuing shortfall in collections was among the matters dealt with in a report to the Assembly by the Secretary-General on the Organization's financial situation (see below).

At the resumption of the thirty-seventh session of the Assembly on 10 May 1983, the Secretary-General, in a letter of that date, informed the Assembly President that eight Members (Central African Republic, Chad, Comoros, El Salvador, Grenada, Guinea-Bissau, Mauritania, South Africa) were more than two years in arrears in the payment of their budget contributions.[7] By 19 September, the Central African Republic, Chad, El Salvador, Guinea-Bissau and Mauritania had made payments bringing their arrears below the two-year limit.[8]

When the Assembly opened its thirty-eighth session on 20 September, the Secretary-General reported that only two Members (Comoros, South Africa) were more than two years in arrears.[9] By a letter of 29 September, he reported that the Comoros had paid enough to reduce its arrears below the two-year limit.[10] Consequently, only South Africa remained in arrears throughout 1983; it would have had to pay $14,773,229 to remove itself from this category.

This information was conveyed by the President to the Assembly, which took note of it at both of its sessions in 1983.

Under Article 19 of the Charter of the United Nations, a Member in arrears to the extent of contributions due for the preceding two full years shall have no vote in the Assembly, but the Assembly can permit such a Member to vote if it is satisfied that failure to pay was due to conditions beyond the State's control.

Meeting numbers. GA 37th session: plenary 116, 122. GA 38th session: plenary 1, 13.

REFERENCES

[1]YUN 1982, p. 1418, GA res. 37/125 A, 17 Dec. 1982.
[2]*Ibid.*, p. 1421, GA res. 37/125 B, 17 Dec. 1982.
[3]A/38/11.   [4]A/38/11/Add.1   &   Add.1/Corr.2.
[5]ST/ADM/SER.B/271.   [6]ST/ADM/SER.B/277.
[7]A/37/807.   [8]A/37/807/Add.1.   [9]A/38/430.
[10]A/38/430/Add.1.

Financial situation

Report of the Secretary-General. An improved cash position for 1983 was reported by the Secretary-General in an analysis of the United Nations financial situation. In an August 1983 report,[1] requested by the General Assembly in November 1982,[2] he attributed the improvement to the higher percentage of budget contributions paid by mid-year, the increase in the Working Capital Fund authorized by the Assembly in 1982 (see WORKING CAPITAL FUND FINANCING above) and the retention of unspent appropriations under previous budgets.

(continued on p. 1160)

STATUS OF CONTRIBUTIONS TO THE UN REGULAR BUDGET

(amounts in US dollars)

Member State	1983-1985 scale of assessments (per cent)	Collections in 1983	Contributions outstanding as at 31 Dec. 1983	Net assessment for 1984	Member State	1983-1985 scale of assessments (per cent)	Collections in 1983	Contributions outstanding as at 31 Dec. 1983	Net assessment for 1984
Afghanistan	0.01	6,000	58,834	64,969	Iraq	0.12	657,208	774,195	779,623
Albania	0.01	—	94,834	64,969	Ireland	0.18	1,059,027	—	1,169,434
Algeria	0.13	805,051	—	844,591	Israel	0.23	1,428,199	2,864,417	1,494,276
Angola	0.01	—	164,905	64,969	Italy	3.74	22,004,208	—	24,298,237
Antigua and Barbuda	0.01	65,000	60,631	64,969	Ivory Coast	0.03	134,532	200,404	194,905
Argentina	0.71	6,188,593	299,271	4,612,766	Jamaica	0.02	117,670	—	129,937
Australia	1.57	9,237,061	—	10,200,062	Japan	10.32	60,717,492	—	67,047,543
Austria	0.75	4,412,610	—	4,872,640	Jordan	0.01	58,834	—	64,969
Bahamas	0.01	58,834	—	64,969	Kenya	0.01	—	71,452	64,969
Bahrain	0.01	58,834	—	64,969	Kuwait	0.25	1,470,870	—	1,624,214
Bangladesh	0.03	176,504	—	194,905	Lao People's Democratic				
Barbados	0.01	65,866	14,417	64,969	Republic	0.01	—	58,834	64,969
Belgium	1.28	9,606,732	30,853	8,315,974	Lebanon	0.02	481,731	—	129,937
Belize	0.01	125,631	—	64,969	Lesotho	0.01	125,411	—	64,969
Benin	0.01	51,587	118,003	64,969	Liberia	0.01	58,834	47,056	64,969
Bhutan	0.01	58,834	—	64,969	Libyan Arab				
Bolivia	0.01	44,000	110,769	64,969	Jamahiriya	0.26	—	1,529,705	1,689,182
Botswana	0.01	60,694	—	64,969	Luxembourg	0.06	353,010	—	389,811
Brazil	1.39	4,366,177	12,250,833	9,030,627	Madagascar	0.01	—	104,846	64,969
Bulgaria	0.18	1,196,600	724,923	1,169,434	Malawi	0.01	58,834	—	64,969
Burma	0.01	58,834	—	64,969	Malaysia	0.09	529,514	—	584,717
Burundi	0.01	—	119,283	64,969	Maldives	0.01	57,128	74,077	64,969
Byelorussian SSR	0.36	2,048,926	1,850,942	2,338,867	Mali	0.01	29,301	121,753	64,969
Canada	3.08	18,121,113	—	20,010,313	Malta	0.01	58,834	—	64,969
Cape Verde	0.01	66,449	110,040	64,969	Mauritania	0.01	24,000	187,310	64,969
Central African					Mauritius	0.01	—	58,834	64,969
Republic	0.01	61,920	127,361	64,969	Mexico	0.88	5,177,461	—	5,717,232
Chad	0.01	50,000	191,366	64,969	Mongolia	0.01	57,112	57,672	64,969
Chile	0.07	411,843	—	454,780	Morocco	0.05	294,544	—	324,843
China	0.88	5,101,692	4,179,092	5,717,232	Mozambique	0.01	58,834	—	64,969
Colombia	0.11	1,312,118	—	714,654	Nepal	0.01	58,834	—	64,969
Comoros	0.01	22,297	194,777	64,969	Netherlands	1.78	10,472,592	—	11,571,822
Congo	0.01	81,866	38,762	64,969	New Zealand	0.26	1,529,705	—	1,689,182
Costa Rica	0.02	141,553	160,919	129,937	Nicaragua	0.01	116,128	116,283	64,969
Cuba	0.09	451,707	742,742	584,717	Niger	0.01	—	134,688	64,969
Cyprus	0.01	58,834	—	64,969	Nigeria	0.19	1,841,498	129,845	1,234,402
Czechoslovakia	0.76	4,406,007	2,355,235	4,937,609	Norway	0.51	3,000,575	—	3,313,395
Democratic					Oman	0.01	58,834	—	64,969
Kampuchea	0.01	45,700	177,997	64,969	Pakistan	0.06	375,311	—	389,811
Democratic Yemen	0.01	58,834	—	64,969	Panama	0.02	117,670	—	129,937
Denmark	0.75	4,412,610	—	4,872,640	Papua New Guinea	0.01	59,024	—	64,969
Djibouti	0.01	—	110,040	64,969	Paraguay	0.01	—	172,411	64,969
Dominica	0.01	91,408	104,575	64,969	Peru	0.07	285,684	810,535	454,780
Dominican Republic	0.03	280,057	267,177	194,905	Philippines	0.09	566,822	208,271	584,717
Ecuador	0.02	83,115	122,100	129,937	Poland	0.72	3,400,000	18,187,666	4,677,735
Egypt	0.07	411,843	—	454,780	Portugal	0.18	1,059,027	—	1,169,434
El Salvador	0.01	33,883	193,734	64,969	Qatar	0.03	176,504	—	194,905
Equatorial Guinea	0.01	—	166,926	64,969	Romania	0.19	500,000	2,180,581	1,234,402
Ethiopia	0.01	58,834	—	64,969	Rwanda	0.01	58,834	—	64,969
Fiji	0.01	58,834	—	64,969	Saint Lucia	0.01	—	120,283	64,969
Finland	0.48	2,824,070	—	3,118,490	Saint Vincent and the				
France	6.51	38,301,442	4,357,157	42,294,525	Grenadines	0.01	58,834	—	64,969
Gabon	0.02	132,125	193,084	129,937	Samoa	0.01	42,290	134,121	64,969
Gambia	0.01	—	89,397	64,969	Sao Tome and				
German Democratic					Principe	0.01	58,834	—	64,969
Republic	1.39	7,850,000	3,043,005	9,030,627	Saudi Arabia	0.86	5,059,792	—	5,587,294
Germany, Federal					Senegal	0.01	58,834	—	64,969
Republic of	8.54	50,245,432	—	55,483,141	Seychelles	0.01	58,834	—	64,969
Ghana	0.02	117,670	—	129,937	Sierra Leone	0.01	—	75,785	64,969
Greece	0.40	2,563,392	—	2,598,741	Singapore	0.09	529,514	—	584,717
Grenada	0.01	49,732	194,174	64,969	Solomon Islands	0.01	58,834	—	64,969
Guatemala	0.02	117,670	—	129,937	Somalia	0.01	104,868	2,543	64,969
Guinea	0.01	57,623	1,211	64,969	South Africa	0.41	—	19,122,404	2,663,710
Guinea-Bissau	0.01	51,206	176,411	64,969	Spain	1.93	17,135,704	—	12,538,929
Guyana	0.01	—	124,290	64,969	Sri Lanka	0.01	58,834	—	64,969
Haiti	0.01	—	100,654	64,969	Sudan	0.01	168,602	—	64,969
Honduras	0.01	61,607	57,676	64,969	Suriname	0.01	58,834	—	64,969
Hungary	0.23	1,313,499	1,906,039	1,494,276	Swaziland	0.01	56,639	2,195	64,969
Iceland	0.03	176,504	—	194,905	Sweden	1.32	7,766,192	—	8,575,848
India	0.36	1,828,053	337,662	2,338,867	Syrian Arab Republic	0.03	163,340	194,510	194,905
Indonesia	0.13	764,853	—	844,591	Thailand	0.08	470,680	—	519,749
Iran	0.58	7,341,578	4,611,441	3,768,175					

STATUS OF CONTRIBUTIONS*(cont.)*

Member State	1983-1985 scale of assess-ments (per cent)	Collections in 1983	Contri-butions outstanding as at 31 Dec. 1983	Net assessment for 1984
Togo	0.01	79,715	85,997	64,969
Trinidad and Tobago	0.03	176,504	—	194,905
Tunisia	0.03	188,760	—	194,905
Turkey	0.32	228,834	1,660,575	2,084,594
Uganda	0.01	—	59,334	64,969
Ukrainian SSR	1.32	7,512,583	5,907,493	8,575,848
USSR	10.54	61,229,636	41,171,584	68,476,851
United Arab Emirates	0.16	941,358	—	1,039,497
United Kingdom	4.67	27,475,843	—	30,340,312
United Republic of Cameroon	0.01	—	124,962	64,969
United Republic of Tanzania	0.01	65,751	70,143	70,094
United States	25.00	147,297,515	27,434,157	190,520,626
Upper Volta	0.01	61,659	57,933	64,969
Uruguay	0.04	—	477,135	259,875
Vanuatu	0.01	125,631	—	64,969
Venezuela	0.55	2,810,338	932,515	3,573,269
Viet Nam	0.02	271,288	117,670	129,937
Yemen	0.01	54,135	64,834	64,969
Yugoslavia	0.46	2,661,079	3,964,985	2,988,552
Zaire	0.01	88,000	193,054	64,969
Zambia	0.01	58,834	—	64,969
Zimbabwe	0.02	—	117,670	129,937
Total	100.00	590,237,893	170,516,259	677,802,899

SOURCES: ST/ADM/SER.B/264, 270, 271.

ASSESSMENT OF NON-MEMBER STATES FOR 1983 EXPENSES OF UN ACTIVITIES IN WHICH THEY PARTICIPATED
(amounts in US dollars)

Non-member State	Rate of assessment	Amount
Democratic People's Republic of Korea	0.05	42,266
Holy See	0.01	9,634
Liechtenstein	0.01	6,153
Monaco	0.01	310
Nauru	0.01	1,796
Republic of Korea	0.18	190,992
San Marino	0.01	1,352
Switzerland	1.10	2,017,724
Tonga	0.01	2,106
Total		2,272,333

NOTE: Activities, conferences and subsidiary bodies for which non-member States were assessed were: International Court of Justice; ESCAP; ECE; international drug control; UNCTAD; UNIDO; formal meeting on the conversion of UNIDO into a special-ized agency; UNEP; transnational corporations; UNHCR; human rights; Second World Conference to Combat Racism and Racial Discrimination; Preparatory Commission for the International Sea-Bed Authority and for the International Tribunal for the Law of the Sea; Intergovernmental Committee on Science and Technology for De-velopment; Tenth United Nations Regional Cartographic Conference for Asia and the Pacific; International Conference on the Question of Palestine; United Nations Conference on Succession of States in Respect of State Property, Archives and Debts; International Conference in Support of the Struggle of the Namibian Peo-ple for Independence; and Second Review Conference of the Parties to the Treaty on the Prohibition of the Emplacement of Nuclear Weapons and Other Weapons of Mass Destruction on the Sea-Bed and the Ocean Floor and in the Subsoil Thereof.

SOURCE: ST/ADM/SER.B/277.

CUMULATIVE WITHHOLDINGS OF ASSESSED CONTRIBUTIONS BY MEMBER STATES
(estimated as at end of 1983 financial periods; in thousands of US dollars)

Member State	Regular budget	UNEF/ UNDOF	UNIFIL
Albania	36.9	20.8	15.5
Algeria	—	—	178.7
Benin	—	10.2	7.4
Bulgaria	619.2	27.5	242.5
Byelorussian SSR	1,310.6	605.7	3,030.6
China	4,178.9	—	—
Cuba	—	—	166.1
Czechoslovakia	1,824.9	397.7	6,371.6

Member State	Regular budget	UNEF/ UNDOF	UNIFIL
Democratic Kampuchea	70.6	20.8	—
Democratic Yemen	—	4.9	7.4
France	4,357.1	—	—
German Democratic Republic	2,919.9	1,223.7	10,615.4
Hungary	1,060.4	—	490.6
Iraq	—	100.2	167.8
Lao People's Democratic Republic	—	—	7.4
Libyan Arab Jamahiriya	—	199.0	330.5
Mongolia	55.1	9.3	15.5
Poland	2,618.8	—	9,411.5
Romania	902.1	—	—
South Africa	19,122.4	2,859.4	3,237.9
Syrian Arab Republic	—	29.0	41.9
Ukrainian SSR	5,854.4	2,261.4	11,307.5
USSR	42,922.3	20,116.7	103,214.5
United States	995.3	—	—
Viet Nam	9.6	12.0	44.4
Yemen	—	9.8	—
Total	88,858.5	27,908.1	148,904.7

NOTE: Estimated withholdings from the regular budget, projected to 31 December 1983, consisted of $43,102,100 relating to the 1961 United Nations bond issue, $19,918,700 relating to the regular programme of technical assistance and $25,837,700 relating to other budget items. Estimated withholdings in regard to the Middle East peace-keeping forces related to (1) the second United Nations Emergency Force (UNEF) from its inception in 1973 through its liquidation in 1979 and the inception of the United Nations Disengagement Observer Force (UNDOF) in 1974 to 30 Novem-ber 1983; and (2) the United Nations Interim Force in Lebanon (UNIFIL) from its inception in 1978 to 18 July 1983.

SOURCE: A/C.5/38/9.

The Secretary-General reported that a sub-stantial number of States had heeded the Assem-bly's 1982 appeal for expeditious and full pay-ment of contributions. By 30 June 1983, 42 Members had paid their 1983 assessment in full and 50 others had made partial payments. A small number of others had indicated the date and approximate amount of payments. On the other hand, more than 50 Members had neither paid nor replied to the Organization's written communications on the subject. As at 30 Sep-tember,[3] $308.2 million had been collected, representing 50.3 per cent of 1983 assessments, compared to 48.6 per cent at the corresponding time in 1982. By 31 December, collections had risen to $486 million, or 79.3 per cent of 1983 as-sessments.

(A table showing the status of contributions to the regular budget appears in the preceding sub-chapter. This lists contributions outstanding for 1983 and prior years.)

The Secretary-General reported that a provi-sional saving of $14 million had resulted from the Assembly's 1981 decision[4] to suspend financial regulations requiring unspent appropriations to be returned to Members. This saving related to 1980-1981 appropriations; no' figures pertaining to the 1982-1983 budget were available.

Although the cash flow situation had im-proved, the Secretary-General stated that the short-term deficit of the United Nations, projected to 31 December 1983, had risen by $19.8 million during the year, to $326.4 million. This increase was due to continued withholding by Members in regard to expenditures for activities to which they objected in principle. The withholdings consisted of $19.8 million relating to peace-keeping operations and $6.3 million relating to the regular budget. The net impact on the deficit was lessened by $6.2 million in interest income. Cumulative withholdings totalled $265.7 million (see table above).

The Secretary-General estimated that net revenue of $1.25 million would be derived from the sale of postage stamps on the subject of nature conservation, issued by the United Nations Postal Administration in November 1982 (see Chapter IV of this section).

GENERAL ASSEMBLY ACTION

By resolution 38/228 B of 20 December 1983 adopted without vote, the General Assembly, on the recommendation of the Fifth Committee, requested the Negotiating Committee on the Financial Emergency of the United Nations to keep the financial situation under review and report as and when appropriate. The Negotiating Committee, established by the Assembly in 1975,[5] had not met since 1976.[6]

Financial situation of the United Nations

The General Assembly,

Having considered the report of the Secretary-General on the analysis of the financial situation of the United Nations and the report of the Advisory Committee on Administrative and Budgetary Questions on administrative and budgetary co-ordination of the United Nations with the specialized agencies and the International Atomic Energy Agency,

Taking note of the relevant statements of Member States in the Fifth Committee on the item entitled "Financial emergency of the United Nations",

1. *Requests* the Negotiating Committee on the Financial Emergency of the United Nations to keep the financial situation of the Organization under review and to report, as and when appropriate, to the General Assembly;

2. *Requests* the Secretary-General to submit to the General Assembly at its thirty-ninth session detailed information relating to the extent, rate of increase and composition of the deficit of the Organization, as well as voluntary contributions received from Member States and other sources;

3. *Decides* to include in the provisional agenda of its thirty-ninth session the item entitled "Financial emergency of the United Nations: report of the Negotiating Committee on the Financial Emergency of the United Nations".

General Assembly resolution 38/228 B

20 December 1983   Meeting 104   Adopted without vote

Approved by Fifth Committee (A/38/743) without vote, 19 December (meeting 73); draft by Vice-Chairman (A/C.5/38/L.26, part B); agenda item 111.

Meeting numbers. GA 38th session: 5th Committee 3-6, 8, 73; plenary 104.

The draft resulted from informal consultations with Committee members.

Along with this text, the Assembly adopted resolution 38/228 A, by which it decided to allocate to the United Nations Special Account half of the revenue from the 1982 postage stamps on nature conservation (see Chapter IV of this section). The Special Account, originally set up for voluntary contributions aimed at resolving the Organization's financial difficulties, recorded no such contributions from States during 1983.

REFERENCES

[1]A/C.5/38/9 & Corr.1. [2]YUN 1982, p. 1424, GA res. 37/13, 16 Nov. 1982. [3]A/C.5/38/9/Add.1. [4]YUN 1981, p. 1298, GA res. 38/116 B, 10 Dec. 1981. [5]YUN 1975, p. 957, GA res. 3538(XXX), 17 Dec. 1975. [6]YUN 1976, p. 889.

PUBLICATION

United Nations: Image and Reality (DPI/789).

Accounts and auditing

Accounts for 1982

GENERAL ASSEMBLY ACTION

The 1982 accounts and financial statements of six voluntarily financed United Nations development and humanitarian assistance programmes were accepted by the General Assembly, along with reports on those programmes by the United Nations Board of Auditors.[1] The Assembly also concurred with the recommendations of ACABQ on the subject.[2] These actions were incorporated into resolution 38/30, adopted without vote on 25 November 1983, as recommended by the Fifth Committee.

Financial reports and audited financial statements and reports of the Board of Auditors

The General Assembly,

Having considered the financial reports and audited financial statements for the year ended 31 December 1982 of the United Nations Development Programme, the United Nations Children's Fund, the United Nations Relief and Works Agency for Palestine Refugees in the Near East, the United Nations Institute for Training and Research, the voluntary funds administered by the United Nations High Commissioner for Refugees and the United Nations Fund for Population Activities, the audit opinions of the Board of Auditors and the report of the Advisory Committee on Administrative and Budgetary Questions,

Taking into account the views expressed by delegations during the debate in the Fifth Committee,

1. *Accepts* the financial reports and audited financial statements and the audit opinions of the Board of Auditors;

2. *Concurs* with the observations and comments made by the Advisory Committee on Administrative and Budgetary Questions in its report;

3.   *Requests* the Board of Auditors and the Advisory Committee on Administrative and Budgetary Questions to continue to give greater attention to areas regarding which they have made observations and comments, including the problems relating to the use of experts and consultants, where appropriate;

4.   *Requests* the executive heads of the organizations and programmes concerned within the United Nations system to take such remedial action in areas falling within their competence as may be required by the observations and comments made by the Board of Auditors in its reports;

5.   *Invites* the governing bodies of the organizations concerned to consider each year at their regular sessions the remedial action taken by the respective executive heads in response to the observations and comments made by the Board of Auditors in its reports.

General Assembly resolution 38/30

25 November 1983   Meeting 71   Adopted without vote

Approved by Fifth Committee (A/38/492) without vote, 10 October (meeting 8); draft by Chairman (A/C.5/38/L.3), orally amended by Benin, and by Greece for EC members; agenda item 107.
Meeting numbers. GA 38th session: 5th Committee 3, 5-8; plenary 71.

The Fifth Committee considered the Board of Auditors' observations and the administration's response on various aspects of the financial management of each programme (see the headings ACCOUNTS FOR 1982 in the chapters of this book pertaining to individual programmes).

The draft resolution was adopted with two oral amendments approved in Committee without vote. The first, by Greece on behalf of the European Community members, added paragraph 5. The second, by Benin, added a call for greater attention to "problems relating to the use of experts and consultants, where appropriate". Benin had originally proposed a new paragraph requesting the Board and ACABQ to consider the use of experts and consultants in project execution, but withdrew that proposal in favour of the addition of a phrase to paragraph 3.

Accounts and financial statements for 1983 relating to the United Nations and other programmes were submitted to the Assembly in 1984.[3]

Auditing terms of reference

The General Assembly in November 1983 amended the terms of reference for the audit by the Board of Auditors of the United Nations and related programmes and funds.

The amendments, as proposed by the Board, were intended to deal with situations which had prevented it from expressing a clear opinion on the financial statements prepared by programme administrations. They added two matters on which the Board would henceforth be required to express an opinion: that the statements accorded with stated accounting principles of the Organi-

zation and that those principles had been consistently applied. They retained two matters on which the Board was already mandated to express an opinion: whether the statements presented fairly the financial position and the results of operations, and whether transactions were in accordance with the Financial Regulations of the United Nations and with legislative authority.

The Board also sought to remove from the terms of reference a clause specifying language to be placed in each audit opinion, describing the scope of audit coverage as including a general review of accounting procedures and tests of records and other evidence. However, the Fifth Committee accepted the view of ACABQ that this language was an important part of the audit opinion which should be retained.

The proposed amendments by the Board were included in an August note by the Secretary-General in which he stated that he had no objection to them.[4] The ACABQ comments were made in its annual report on United Nations financial reports and statements.[2]

GENERAL ASSEMBLY ACTION

The Assembly, on the recommendation of the Fifth Committee, adopted decision 38/408 without vote.

Additional terms of reference governing the audit of the United Nations: amendments to the annex to the Financial Regulations of the United Nations

At its 71st plenary meeting, on 25 November 1983, the General Assembly, on the recommendation of the Fifth Committee, decided to amend paragraphs 5, 6 and 8 of the annex to the Financial Regulations of the United Nations, entitled "Additional terms of reference governing the audit of the United Nations", to read as follows:

Paragraph 5
"5.   The Board of Auditors (or such of its officers as it may designate) shall express and sign an opinion on the financial statements which shall read as follows:
" 'We have examined the following appended financial statements, numbered . . . to . . ., properly identified, and relevant schedules of (name of the body) for the financial period ended 31 December 19 . . . Our examination included a general review of the accounting procedures and such tests of the accounting records and other supporting evidence as we considered necessary in the circumstances.'
and which shall state, as appropriate, whether:
"(a)   The financial statements present fairly the financial position as at the end of the period and the results of its operations for the period then ended;
"(b)   The financial statements were prepared in accordance with the stated accounting principles;
"(c)   The accounting principles were applied on a basis consistent with that of the preceding financial period;

"*(d)* Transactions were in accordance with the Financial Regulations and legislative authority."

Paragraph 6

"6. The report of the Board of Auditors to the General Assembly on the financial operations of the period should mention:

". . ."

Paragraph 8

"8. Whenever the scope of audit of the Board of Auditors is restricted, or whenever the Board is unable to obtain sufficient evidence, it shall refer to the matter in its opinion and report, making clear in its report the reasons for its comments and the effect on the financial position and the financial transactions as recorded."

and to add a new paragraph 10, as follows:

"10. The Board is not required to mention any matter referred to in the foregoing that, in its opinion, is insignificant in all respects."

General Assembly decision 38/408

Adopted without vote

Approved by Fifth Committee (A/38/492) without vote, 10 October (meeting 8); draft by Chairman (A/C.5/38/L.4); agenda item 107.
Meeting numbers. GA 38th session: 5th Committee 3, 5-8; plenary 71.

REFERENCES

[1]A/38/5/Add.1-3 & Add.3/Corr.1 & Add.4 & Add.4/Corr.1 & Add.5,7. [2]A/38/433. [3]A/39/5 & Corr.1 & Add.1-5 & Add.5/Corr.1 & Add.6-8 & Add.8/Corr.1 & Add.9. [4]A/38/313 & Corr.1.

Chapter II

United Nations programmes

Further steps were taken in 1983 to improve programme planning, budgeting and evaluation in the United Nations, so that its activities could have greater coherence and impact.

A Programme Planning and Budgeting Board (PPBB), established within the Secretariat in 1982, guided the preparation of the proposed United Nations programme budget for 1984-1985, which the General Assembly adopted in December 1983. In a resolution on programme planning and evaluation (38/227 A), the Assembly requested the Secretary-General to strengthen the capacity of United Nations programme planning units and systems. It also asked him to issue as soon as possible rules to implement the Regulations Governing Programme Planning, the Programming Aspects of the Budget, the Monitoring of Implementation and the Methods of Evaluation adopted by the Assembly in 1982.

The Secretary-General's draft rules, originally requested by the Assembly at the time it adopted the Regulations, were examined in 1983 by the Committee for Programme and Co-ordination (CPC) and the Joint Inspection Unit (JIU). Both bodies recommended changes.

Also by resolution 38/227 A, the Assembly adopted revised versions of two portions of the United Nations medium-term plan for 1984-1989 which it had asked to be reformulated when it adopted the bulk of the plan in 1982. It also asked the Secretary-General to submit to it a statement of programme implications every time proposals for new United Nations activities were made. At the request of the Economic and Social Council in July (resolution 1983/51), the Secretary-General submitted to the Assembly a report on experience gained in preparing the 1984-1985 budget.

Plans to strengthen programme evaluation units in the Secretariat, involving the addition of a few posts, were approved by the Assembly in its programme planning resolution.

JIU submitted a number of reports in 1983, most of which evaluated specific programmes. The Assembly requested those bodies to bear in mind a JIU recommendation that they specify which points of each JIU report they approved and disapproved.

The annual report on administrative and budgetary co-ordination in the United Nations system, prepared by the Advisory Committee on Administrative and Budgetary Questions

(ACABQ), concentrated in 1983 on cash flow and liquidity problems.

Topics related to this chapter. Operational activities for development—programme evaluation; UNDP programme planning. Science and technology—programme evaluation. Institutional arrangements (economic and social)—co-ordination in the UN system. UN budget.

Programme planning

Integration of programme planning, budgeting, monitoring and evaluation functions in the United Nations Secretariat was the subject in 1983 of recommendations by CPC and of the General Assembly.

In an August report on this subject considered by both bodies,[1] the Secretary-General said the most significant step taken during the previous year to integrate these functions had been preparation of the proposed programme budget for 1984-1985 (see Chapter I of this section) under the guidance of PPBB (see next subchapter). The Secretary-General considered that the effect of the Board and the new planning methods had been an improvement in the quality of the programme budget proposals and a more satisfactory correlation between programme and financial aspects.

He also mentioned plans for a Central Monitoring Unit, work on the preparation of programme planning rules and steps towards a procedure for providing information on programme implications of proposals before the Assembly. A separate report analysed the Secretariat's preparations for the 1984-1985 budget. (Details of these subjects can be found under relevant subject headings in this Chapter.)

The August report had been called for by the Assembly in a December 1982 resolution on programme planning.[2] The Economic and Social Council, in resolution 1983/49 of 28 July 1983 concerned with work done by CPC at the first part of its 1983 session in May/June, asked the Secretary-General to ensure that the report was submitted as requested.

Noting this report in September at its resumed session,[3] CPC agreed that integration of programme planning, budgeting, monitoring and evaluation was an evolving process and that judgement on the new institutional arrangements should be reserved for the time being. It recommended improved co-ordination between the Secretariat and intergovernmental bodies in determining programme priorities. It also recommended further study of how the Secretariat could better assist CPC in programme planning matters.

In a recommendation concerned with programme planning throughout the United Nations system, CPC asked that ACC pursue progress in joint planning and report the results in 1984. According to the overall ACC report for 1983-1984,[4] joint planning, which involved co-operation between organizations on the planning of activities in selected programme areas, was under review in four areas: primary health care, aging persons, energy information systems, and research and training of personnel in energy assessment, planning and utilization.

In its annual report on administrative and budgetary co-ordination in the United Nations system[5] (see subchapter below under that heading), ACABQ concluded that the varying arrangements in different agencies for programme planning, budgeting and evaluation lent support to the idea that institutional arrangements for this purpose should be tailored to meet the needs and size of each organization. Consequently, it cautioned that harmonizing arrangements among agencies in this area might not be desirable or feasible.

GENERAL ASSEMBLY ACTION

Acting on the recommendation of the Fifth Committee, the General Assembly, on 20 December 1983, adopted without vote resolution 38/227 A on various matters related to programme planning, including the medium-term plan, programme evaluation (see under those headings) and the evaluation of technical co-operation in regard to manufactures (see ECONOMIC AND SOCIAL QUESTIONS, Chapter VI). It was adopted along with resolution 38/227 B on co-ordination in the United Nations system.

Programme planning

The General Assembly,

Recalling its resolution 3043(XXVII) of 19 December 1972, in which it approved the new form of presentation of the United Nations budget,

Recalling also its resolutions 3199(XXVIII) of 18 December 1973, 3534(XXX) of 17 December 1975, 31/93 of 14 December 1976, 32/197 of 20 December 1977, 32/206 of 21 December 1977, 33/118 of 19 December 1978, 34/224 of 20 December 1979, 35/9 of 3 November 1980, 36/228 of 18 December 1981 and 37/234 of 21 December 1982, in which it elaborated further on the establishment of an integrated programme planning, budgeting, monitoring and evaluation system in the United Nations,

Having considered the report of the Committee for Programme and Co-ordination on the work of its twenty-third session, the report of the Economic and Social Council and the reports of the Advisory Committee on Administrative and Budgetary Questions on the proposed programme budget for the biennium 1984-1985,

Having also considered the proposed programme budget for the biennium 1984-1985, the reports of the Secretary-General on the set of rules governing programme planning, the programme aspects of the budget, the monitoring of implementation and methods of evaluation, on the integration of the programme planning, budgeting, monitoring and evaluation functions in the Secretariat of the United Nations, on the methods, procedures and timetable followed in the preparation of the proposed programme budget for the biennium 1984-1985, and on strengthening the capacity of the United Nations evaluation units and systems and timetable for review of the evaluation programmes, as well as the second report of the Joint Inspection Unit on the elaboration of regulations for the planning, programming and evaluation cycle of the United Nations,

Concerned by the delay in the submission of the proposed programme budget for the biennium 1984-1985 to the Committee for Programme and Co-ordination and the Advisory Committee on Administrative and Budgetary Questions,

Recalling the intention expressed by the Secretary-General to take the necessary measures to improve the effectiveness of the programme planning, budgeting, monitoring and evaluation system of the United Nations,

Stressing that the budgetary policy of maximum restraint should not adversely affect the efficient and effective implementation of the activities and programmes of the Organization,

Taking note with satisfaction of the improvements in the quality of the presentation of programmes in various sections of the proposed programme budget for the biennium 1984-1985,

I
Medium-term plan

Adopts subprogramme 5 of programme 1 of chapter 21 (Social development and humanitarian affairs) and chapter 25 (Marine affairs) of the medium-term plan for the period 1984-1989, as revised by the recommendations of the Committee for Programme and Co-ordination at its twenty-third session and the Economic and Social Council in its resolutions 1983/48 and 1983/49 of 29 July 1983, and subject to any observations with regard to that subprogramme that may be formulated by the Third Committee of the General Assembly;

II
Programme planning, programme aspects of the budget, monitoring of implementation and methods of evaluation

1. *Requests* the Secretary-General to improve the programme analyses of all the sections of the programme budget and to strengthen the capacity of United Nations programme planning units and systems;

2. *Takes note* of the assurance given by the Secretary-General that he will take appropriate measures in order to avoid delays in the future in the issuance of documentation regarding the programme budget;

3. *Takes note further* of the intention expressed by the Secretary-General to review the operation, structure and performance of the Secretariat in 1984;

4. *Requests* the Secretary-General, in undertaking the review referred to in paragraph 3 above, to take fully into account General Assembly resolution 32/197, in particular section VIII of the annex thereto, as well as the related views expressed by Member States during the thirty-eighth session, and to submit his proposals on organizational changes, if any, to the General Assembly at its thirty-ninth session;

5. *Also requests* the Secretary-General to include in his review of the Secretariat information on the measures taken to maximize and improve secretariat support to the Committee for Programme and Co-ordination, taking into account the recommendations contained in paragraphs 413 to 415 of the report of the Committee for Programme and Co-ordination, and to report to the General Assembly at its thirty-ninth session, through the Committee for Programme and Co-ordination at its twenty-fourth session;

6. *Urges* the Secretary-General to issue as soon as possible the rules in implementation of the Regulations Governing Programme Planning, the Programming Aspects of the Budget, the Monitoring of Implementation and the Methods of Evaluation, adopted by the General Assembly at its thirty-seventh session, as requested by the Assembly in section II of its resolution 37/234, taking fully into account the recommendations of the Committee for Programme and Co-ordination at its twenty-third session;

7. *Reaffirms its request* to the Secretary-General to provide the General Assembly with programme implications of draft resolutions being considered by the Assembly in accordance with the following general guidelines:

(*a*) Each statement should be an integrated statement of programme, financial and administrative implications;

(*b*) Each statement should indicate how the activities proposed in the draft resolution fulfil or reinforce the objectives and strategies of the current legislative mandate;

(*c*) Each statement should provide, for decision by the General Assembly:

(i) An analysis and recommendation of the Secretary-General for the funding of the proposed activities;

(ii) An analysis of alternative solutions to the funding of the proposed activities through existing or additional appropriations;

(iii) Further indications of clear implications of the draft resolution with regard to the existing programmes within the relevant sections of the programme budget, in the case of possible funding through existing resources;

8. *Decides* that the adoption of new resolutions by the General Assembly will not imply the elimination of existing activities or programmes carried out as a result of legislative mandates, nor the elimination or reduction of resources appropriated to them by the Assembly, unless the Assembly expressly decides otherwise;

9. *Decides* that the fact that the Committee for Programme and Co-ordination will not normally be in a position to review the programme implications statements during the General Assembly should not prevent or delay their adoption by the Assembly, and their subsequent implementation by the Secretariat, unless the Assembly decides otherwise;

10. *Decides* that the review of integrated programme, financial and administrative implications statements shall be subject to the same procedures as specified in rule 153 of the rules of procedure of the General Assembly for the review of administrative and financial implications statements by the Assembly;

11. *Decides* that the new methods and procedures for the provision of programme, financial and administrative implications statements should apply initially only to draft resolutions and decisions submitted to the General Assembly during its sessions;

12. *Requests* the Secretary-General to report to the General Assembly at its fortieth session, through the Committee for Programme and Co-ordination at its twenty-fifth session, on the experience gained in implementing paragraph 7 above, in order for the Assembly to review the situation;

III

Strengthening of the capacity of United Nations evaluation units and systems and timetable for review of evaluation programme, requested under General Assembly resolutions 36/228 B and 37/234, section II

1. *Reaffirms* its resolution 36/228 B and deplores the continuing failure to implement its provisions;

2. *Reiterates* the need to strengthen the capacity of the United Nations evaluation units and systems, in particular those in the regional commissions, in accordance with the estimates of the Secretary-General contained in his report;

3. *Requests* the Secretary-General to review all the possibilities available to strengthen the capacity of the United Nations evaluation units and systems, including a timetable for the adequate establishment of such units in all departments, as called for in General Assembly resolution 36/228 B, and measures for redeployment of resources, prior to the thirty-ninth session of the General Assembly, and to report to the Assembly thereon at that session;

4. *Takes note with satisfaction* of the progress made in improving the quality of the in-depth evaluation studies in specific programme areas and stresses the need to develop a comprehensive evaluation system along the lines of the recommendations contained in paragraphs 189 to 197 of the report of the Committee for Programme and Co-ordination;

5. *Endorses* the conclusions and recommendations of the Committee for Programme and Co-ordination at its twenty-third session on the in-depth evaluation of the work of the Department of Public Information of the Secretariat and on the timetable for intergovernmental review of in-depth and triennial evaluation studies;

IV

Technical co-operation activities of the United Nations Industrial Development Organization financed by the United Nations Development Programme in the field of manufactures

1. *Endorses* the recommendations of the Committee for Programme and Co-ordination at its twenty-third session and Economic and Social Council resolution 1983/49, section II, on the above topic;

2. *Requests* the Secretary-General to submit his comprehensive report to the Committee for Programme and Co-ordination at its twenty-fourth session, taking into account the views of the Permanent Committee of the Industrial Development Board at its twentieth session

and of the Governing Council of the United Nations Development Programme at its next organizational session.

General Assembly resolution 38/227 A

20 December 1983   Meeting 104   Adopted without vote

Approved by Fifth Committee (A/38/727) without vote, 12 December (meeting 61); draft by Vice-Chairman (A/C.5/38/L.18, part A), based on informal consultations and orally revised, approved together with part B (see resolution 38/227 B); agenda item 110.
Financial implications. S-G, A/C.5/38/11.
Meeting numbers. GA 38th session: 5th Committee 7, 12-23, 26-32, 34-37, 39, 40, 42-44, 46, 52, 54, 60, 61; plenary 104.

Rules and regulations

The Secretariat continued work in 1983 on the drafting of rules to supplement the Regulations Governing Programme Planning, the Programme Aspects of the Budget, the Monitoring of Implementation and the Methods of Evaluation adopted by the General Assembly in December 1982.[2] The proposed rules, and implementation of the Regulations, were the subject of reports by the Secretary-General and JIU, and of recommendations by CPC and the Assembly.

In an April 1983 report to the Assembly[6] which was first examined by CPC, the Secretary-General submitted a revised set of draft rules which he said he intended to promulgate. They differed in several respects from a 1982 draft which the Assembly asked him to bring into line with with the new Regulations.[7]

The proposed rules, to be implemented by the new PPBB (see "Programme budgeting" below), contained details on the preparation of the medium-term plan (see next section) and on programme aspects of the budget, including links between budget and plan. They also covered monitoring of programme implementation by a central monitoring unit and included two new rules on programme evaluation. An annex to the 1983 report contained definitions of programming and planning terms.

The report also contained the Secretary-General's comments on 1982 recommendations by JIU made in a report on programme planning rules and regulations.[8] Referring to a JIU suggestion that all planned activities be placed in one of three categories: plannable, partly plannable and unplannable, the Secretary-General acknowledged that some United Nations activities were less amenable to planning than others, but he did not think it possible to envisage the formal distinctions proposed by JIU.

Maurice Bertrand, the JIU inspector responsible for the 1982 report on this topic, submitted a second report on the programme planning rules and regulations which was also circulated to the Assembly in April 1983.[9] Criticizing the Secretary-General's redrafted rules as based on the idea that the medium-term plan was purely a management tool for the Secretariat, he suggested changes which he said were intended to enable intergovernmental bodies to examine the design of programmes and select between various types of activity to attain their objectives (see next section). Additional changes were suggested to strengthen programme evaluation.

After considering these divergent views in May,[3] CPC recommended a number of changes to the draft rules. One of them was a proposed new rule specifying a five-stage process for programme planning by the Secretariat, applicable to both the medium-term plan and the proposed budget. These stages consisted of: *(a)* formulation of policy guidelines; *(b)* issuance of instructions incorporating the guidelines; *(c)* submission of proposals by the heads of Secretariat units; *(d)* revisions of original submissions within the concept of the medium-term plan or programme budget; and *(e)* finalization and approval of the proposed plan or budget by the Secretary-General. The Secretary-General would be responsible for establishing a timetable for this procedure and for ensuring that his plan and budget proposals reached CPC and ACABQ on time.

The General Assembly, in resolution 38/227 A of 20 December on programme planning, urged the Secretary-General to issue the rules as soon as possible, taking full account of the CPC recommendations.

Medium-term plan

Following General Assembly adoption in December 1982 of the United Nations medium-term plan for 1984-1989,[2] CPC and the Assembly examined in 1983 proposals by the Secretary-General and JIU to codify procedures for preparing future plans. In addition, the Assembly adopted reformulated versions of the two segments of the plan which it had failed to approve in 1982 (see next section).

Procedures for future plans were considered in the context of proposed rules for programme planning (see preceding section). The set of rules which the Secretary-General proposed to the Assembly and CPC in April 1983[6] spelled out the requirement that activities included in the plan must have a legislative mandate, in the form of a decision by a United Nations intergovernmental body. Assembly adoption of the plan would give a mandate for new activities proposed in it by the Secretary-General. Objectives and strategies would be specified for each subprogramme, subprogrammes being defined as activities within a programme aimed at achieving one or a few closely related objectives, such as the subprogramme on traffic facilities in the programme on transport.

Medium-term plan proposals for substantive services would be submitted to the Assembly through CPC and ACABQ, for common (administrative) services through ACABQ, and for conference services through the Committee on Conferences and ACABQ. The proposed rules spelled out the types of information to be included in the plan's descriptions of substantive and servicing activities, the circumstances under which revisions to the plan would be required and an outline of the kinds of documents to be submitted. The Secretary-General would indicate, for Assembly action, the subprogrammes he considered as having highest and lowest priority, based on recommendations by intergovernmental bodies.

The JIU report on the proposed rules,[9] also submitted in April, suggested a number of changes in the section on the medium-term plan. They would have required objectives and strategies to be defined for programmes rather than subprogrammes, in line with the author's belief that this would better enable intergovernmental bodies to choose among various possible objectives for achieving the aims of Member States. They would also have placed additional emphasis on the introduction to the plan, as a vehicle for allowing the Economic and Social Council and the Assembly to define the Organization's priorities.

In May, CPC recommended its own set of changes.[3] One of these, in line with the JIU emphasis on programmes, would require the Secretariat to include, for each programme in the medium-term plan, an analysis of the rationale for selecting objectives and the subprogrammes intended to attain them. Another would require achievement indicators to be included in subprogramme descriptions as an aid to evaluation. The policy nature of the plan's introduction would be detailed and its inter-agency co-ordination aspect elaborated. The responsibility of PPBB for formulating the draft plan would be specified, as would the Secretary-General's responsibility for recommending priorities among subprogrammes.

No action to promulgate the rules was taken in 1983.

In July 1983 the Economic and Social Council decided by resolution 1983/78 to initiate biennial reviews of selected major sectors in the medium-term plans of organizations in the United Nations system. In addition, the medium-term plans of the United Nations Conference on Trade and Development (UNCTAD), the International Trade Centre and the United Nations Children's Fund were considered in the bodies concerned with those areas (see ECONOMIC AND SOCIAL QUESTIONS, Chapters IV and XX).

Medium-term plan for 1984-1989

On the recommendation of CPC and the Economic and Social Council, the General Assembly adopted on 20 December 1983 the two portions of the United Nations medium-term plan for 1984-1989 which it had recommended for reformulation when adopting the plan as a whole in December 1982.[2] These were a subprogramme on "Participation of women in promoting international peace and co-operation" (see p. 922) and a major programme on marine affairs, comprising a new chapter of the plan. The new major programme covered activities formerly included under the major programme on natural resources as well as those carried out in connection with the United Nations Convention on the Law of the Sea (see p. 104, and p. 657).

The reformulated portions of the plan included a number of revisions recommended in May by CPC.[3] These were endorsed by the Economic and Social Council in resolution 1983/48, on marine affairs, and resolution 1983/49, on the work of CPC. The Assembly adopted them in resolution 38/227 A of 20 December, on programme planning.

REFERENCES

(1)A/C.5/38/6 & Corr.1. (2)YUN 1982, p. 1430, GA res. 37/234, 21 Dec. 1982. (3)A/38/38. (4)E/1984/66. (5)A/38/515 and Corr.1. (6)A/38/126. (7)YUN 1982, p. 1437. (8)*Ibid.*, p. 1438. (9)A/38/160.

Programme budgeting

Arrangements for informing the General Assembly of the programme implications of proposed new activities at the same time that it was given information on the financial implications were approved by the Assembly in December 1983. In addition, CPC, the Economic and Social Council and the Assembly examined the methods, procedures and timetable followed in the preparation of the proposed budget for 1984-1985 which the Assembly adopted in December (see previous Chapter), and CPC considered procedures for future programme budgeting in the context of rules for programme planning.

Programme implications

Following consideration by CPC, the General Assembly in December, by resolution 38/227 A, adopted guidelines to be followed by the Secretary-General in presenting it with information on the programme implications of draft resolutions being considered by the Assembly.

A report on the methods and procedures for the provision of such statements was submitted in May to CPC,[1] in response to a December 1982 request by the Assembly.[2] In it, the Secretary-General suggested that the statements should describe the effects of each draft resolution on the medium-term plan and on existing work programmes, cite the output expected from the proposed activities, analyse the full costs of work-months and other resource requirements, propose activities that could be terminated or curtailed if resources were redeployed for the new tasks, and set out funding alternatives through redeployment or new appropriations. Each statement would go to the Main Committee of the Assembly which was considering the related draft resolution. That Committee would recommend whether the Assembly should add the proposed activities to the existing work programme or help pay for them by terminating or curtailing other projects.

In his April report proposing rules for programme planning (see previous subchapter),[3] the Secretary-General suggested a rule specifying three types of information to be presented in his statements on the programme budget implications of draft resolutions: what changes to the work programme would be required, what similar work was being done by the Secretariat or in the United Nations system, and what would have to be cut if resources were redeployed from another activity.

In June, CPC noted the Secretary-General's report on programme implications after a brief discussion.[4] With regard to the proposed rule, it expressed the view that the programme budget statement should merge programme, financial and administrative implications.

In resolution 1983/49 of 28 July, concerned with the work of CPC, the Economic and Social Council reiterated the Assembly's 1982 request for information on programme implications of proposals, and emphasized the CPC recommendation for an integrated statement on the implications of draft resolutions.

The guidelines approved by the Assembly, in resolution 38/227 A of 20 December 1983 on programme planning, called for programme information to be integrated with the statements on financial and administrative implications previously supplied. These statements would include the Secretary-General's recommendation for funding of the proposed activities, an analysis of alternative funding through existing or additional appropriations and the implications for existing programmes. Review procedures would be the same as those for financial implications statements, namely, submission of statements to both the Fifth Committee and the Main Committee considering the related draft resolution, with only the Fifth Committee required to make a recommendation to the Assembly on programme and financial implications.

Programme budgeting methods and procedures

A report by the Secretary-General[5] analysing the methods, procedures and timetable followed in preparing the proposed budget for 1984-1985 was considered in 1983 by CPC and the General Assembly. As noted in the report, this was the first budget prepared with the assistance of the new PPBB.

This Secretariat Board, set up with effect from 7 April 1982, was chaired by the Secretary-General or, in his absence, the Director-General for Development and International Economic Co-operation. Other members were the Under-Secretaries-General for Administration and Management, for International Economic and Social Affairs, and for Political Affairs, Trusteeship and Decolonization; the Controller; the Assistant Secretary-General for Programme Planning and Co-ordination, and the Executive Assistant to the Secretary-General. During 25 meetings between 15 June 1982 and 4 May 1983, the Board evaluated programme proposals and made recommendations to the Secretary-General on the programme content and financial level of the proposed budget.

Programme aspects of the budget were also dealt with in a number of rules proposed by the Secretary-General in April (see previous subchapter). In his report on this subject,[3] he proposed rules spelling out the link between the medium-term plan and the budget, the budget structure, standards for programme narratives, and criteria for identifying obsolete and marginal activities which might be dropped. Also included was a proposed rule on programme implications statements (see previous section).

After considering these proposed rules in May,[4] CPC recommended several changes, including a new paragraph requiring the Secretary-General, in the context of budget preparation, to submit to the Assembly, through CPC, information on activities he considered obsolete, marginal or ineffective, and an estimate of resources that might be released by terminating or curtailing them.

ECONOMIC AND SOCIAL COUNCIL ACTION

The report on programme budgeting methods and procedures was requested by the Economic and Social Council in resolution 1983/51 of 28 July 1983, adopted without vote on the recommendation of the Council's Third (Programme and Co-ordination) Committee.

Situation with regard to the preparation and submission of the proposed programme budget for the biennium 1984-1985

The Economic and Social Council,

Having considered the situation with regard to the preparation and submission of the proposed programme budget, within the context of Council decision 1983/160 of 27 May 1983, and the report of the Committee for Programme and Co-ordination thereon,

Noting the statement made at the second regular session of 1983 of the Council by the representative of the Secretary-General,

1. *Deeply regrets* that the Council is not in a position to carry out a thorough review of the proposed programme budget for the biennium 1984-1985, in accordance with Council resolution 1982/50 of 28 July 1982, as a result of the serious delays in the preparation and submission of the sections of the budget to the Committee for Programme and Co-ordination;

2. *Affirms* that this situation is untenable and, in this context, endorses the conclusions of the Committee for Programme and Co-ordination that the present grave situation is unrelated to the schedule established for the meetings of the Committee and that therefore no modification of that schedule should be contemplated;

3. *Requests* the Secretary-General:

(a) To take the necessary measures to ensure that complete and final texts of all sections of the proposed programme budget for the biennium 1984-1985, in particular sections 7, 15 and 25, shall be submitted to the members of the Committee for Programme and Co-ordination in good time prior to its resumed twenty-third session;

(b) To ensure that there shall be no repetition of the present situation in connection with the preparation and submission of future proposed programme budgets;

(c) To this end, to submit to the General Assembly at its thirty-eighth session, through the Committee for Programme and Co-ordination at its resumed twenty-third session, an analytical report on the methods, procedures and timetable followed in the preparation of the programme budget, with a view to identifying deficiencies and shortcomings.

Economic and Social Council resolution 1983/51

28 July 1983   Meeting 40   Adopted without vote

Approved by Third Committee (E/1983/117) without vote, 22 July (meeting 16); draft by Chairman (E/1983/C.3/L.9/Rev.1), orally revised; agenda item 20.
Meeting number. ESC 40.

The request for a report was added to the initial draft by the Chairman, taking account of an oral amendment by Pakistan, not pressed to a vote, that would have had the Council call for the submission to the Assembly of an analytical table showing the time-frame and preparation stages of the 1984-1985 budget.

Reports of the Secretary-General and CPC action. Submitted in August, the Secretary-General's report[5] identified seven shortcomings and deficiencies in the preparation of the 1984-1985 budget: a late decision on budget priorities, delays and inadequacies in revaluating the 1982-1983 resource base (used to project budget growth in real terms), difficulties in reconciling data on extrabudgetary resources, provision of excessive detail on programmes to PPBB, difficulties in consulting programme managers on changes the Board proposed to make in their requests, late issuance of budget instruction forms and delays in the submission of budget proposals by departments. According to the report, five of those

problems were being corrected but two—the timing of departmental submissions and the need for extensive consultations with programme managers—raised more complex issues and efforts to resolve them were continuing.

Noting this report in September,[4] CPC requested the Secretary-General to keep each phase of budget preparation under constant review in order to avoid delays in issuing documents, and to report to it in 1984.

GENERAL ASSEMBLY ACTION

In resolution 38/227 A of 20 December on programme planning, the General Assembly noted an assurance by the Secretary-General that he would act to avoid delays in issuing documents on future budgets.

REFERENCES

[1]E/AC.51/1983/11. [2]YUN 1982, p. 1430, GA res. 37/234, 21 Dec. 1982. [3]A/38/126. [4]A/38/38. [5]A/C.5/38/7.

Programme evaluation

Plans to strengthen Secretariat machinery for evaluating the efficiency and impact of United Nations programmes and activities were drawn up in 1983, and possibilities for further action were examined by JIU, CPC and the General Assembly.

In April the Secretary-General circulated to the Assembly a report proposing steps to strengthen the capacity of United Nations evaluation units and systems, and a timetable for intergovernmental review of evaluation studies.[1] Submitted in response to Assembly requests in 1981[2] and December 1982,[3] the report detailed provisions in the Secretary-General's proposed 1984-1985 budget to increase the staff of evaluation units in the regional commissions for Africa and for Asia and the Pacific as well as in the United Nations Centre for Human Settlements (UNCHS).

Rules for programme evaluation and for monitoring programme implementation were included in the set of rules proposed by the Secretary-General in April[4] (see PROGRAMME PLANNING above). They provided for both periodic self-evaluation of programmes by their managers and *ad hoc* evaluations, internal or external, conducted at the initiative of intergovernmental bodies or the Secretariat. A central evaluation unit would set standards for self-evaluation.

The proposed rules also covered procedures for monitoring ongoing activities. Under the guidance of PPBB (see PROGRAMME BUDGETING above), a central monitoring unit would keep track of changes in the work programme, determine programme delivery in comparison with commitments made in the budget document, and prepare a report to the General Assembly every second year. Procedures were also set out for monitoring within departments.

The Secretary-General informed the Fifth Committee, in his August report on intergration of programme planning, budgeting, monitoring and evaluation[5] (see PROGRAMME PLANNING above), that PPBB had been designated as a steering committee for all evaluation studies.

In its April report commenting on the draft rules,[6] JIU proposed additional provisions requiring evaluation of all major programmes once every six years (the length of each medium-term plan), with the resulting reports to be considered either by CPC or by the intergovernmental or expert body directly concerned. Three major programmes would be covered each year by the central evaluation unit and CPC, according to a list and timetable that would be drawn up by the Secretary-General for Assembly approval. Another list and timetable would identify all other programmes due for self-evaluation.

JIU also suggested that more specific guidelines for report preparation be added to the rules, including a requirement that evaluation reports identify alternative subprogrammes to help achieve the major programme's objectives. Other provisions spelled out how policy-making bodies, making use of evaluation reports, might recommend changes in Secretariat structure, procedures and programme contents.

Commenting on the Secretary-General's report on evaluation machinery,[1] JIU criticized it for not indicating clearly whether there should be a central evaluation unit and for reflecting a decentralized concept of evaluation, with each department or regional commission left to decide whether to set up its own unit. The author favoured a central unit staffed by at least six Professionals, and a network of 22 evaluation officers in the departments.

After reviewing these reports in May,[7] CPC expressed concern that more had not been done to strengthen evaluation units and recommended ways in which the Secretary-General might continue to strengthen them. These included studying the possibility of merging central evaluation units, ensuring that sectoral and regional units drew on the experience of central ones, developing mechanisms for disseminating evaluation findings to intergovernmental bodies and programme managers, emphasizing to programme managers the significance of incorporating those findings into decision-making, and monitoring implementation. The Committee suggested nine functions for central evaluation units, in the areas of evaluation policy, standards, methods, monitoring, co-ordination, training of personnel and information services.

The Committee established a timetable for in-depth evaluations to be reviewed by CPC at the rate of one topic a year, and for reviews of what had been done to implement decisions taken by CPC as a result of earlier evaluations. New evaluations would alternate between economic and social sectors one year and political, legal, humanitarian and other sectors the next. The first topics selected were technical co-operation in manufactures (1984) and drug control (1985). A tentative timetable for 1986-1992 listed population, electronic data processing and information systems, development issues and policies, human rights, human settlements, political and Security Council affairs, and science and technology for development.

Reviews of implementation were to begin in 1985 with the three topics on which evaluations had been conducted since 1979—manufactures (examined in 1980), transnational corporations and mineral resources. Thereafter, the reviews were to take place three years after the evaluations.

In 1983 CPC made recommendations with regard to four areas previously chosen for evaluation. Two concerned public information: Department of Public Information activities (see p. 383) and the work programme of the Joint United Nations Information Committee (see p. 385). The other two were on economic subjects: technical co-operation in manufactures financed by the United Nations Development Programme (UNDP) and executed by the United Nations Industrial Development Organization (see ECONOMIC AND SOCIAL QUESTIONS, Chapter VI), and mineral resources development (*Ibid.*, Chapter IX).

Two JIU reports circulated in 1983 dealt with programme and project evaluation of operational activities for development. One of these concerned inter-agency co-operation to encourage evaluation by Governments, and the other dealt with the UNDP evaluation system (see ECONOMIC AND SOCIAL QUESTIONS, Chapter II). JIU also performed its own evaluation of a number of programmes (see next section).

On the matter of resources needed to implement the CPC recommendations for strengthening evaluation in the Secretariat, the Committee, at its May/June session, called its views to the attention of ACABQ and requested the Secretariat to prepare a statement of programme and financial implications.

The Economic and Social Council, in resolution 1983/49 of 28 July on the work of CPC, requested ACABQ to transmit to the General Assembly its review of the Secretary-General's report on evaluation.

In September, the CPC Chairman informed the Committee that, at a meeting with its other officers to clarify the Committee's intentions, it had been reaffirmed that CPC had recommended that the reinforcement proposed for strengthening evaluation units and systems would be required.

In a statement of the financial and other implications of the CPC call for strengthening evaluation in the Secretariat, submitted to the Fifth Committee in September,[8] the Secretary-General suggested that six additional Professional posts would be needed. One of these, the Evaluation Unit of the Department of International Economic and Social Affairs, would help perform the central evaluation functions identified by CPC. The others would be for the regional commissions for Asia and the Pacific, Latin America and Africa, UNCTAD and UNCHS. However, the Secretary-General asked for no additional funds pending a review of possibilities for redeploying staff, the results of which would be reported to the Assembly in 1984.

The ACABQ Chairman told the Fifth Committee that his Committee would await the results of the Secretary-General's review before commenting.

The Assembly, in resolution 38/227 A of 20 December 1983 on programme planning, reiterated the need to strengthen the capacity of evaluation units and systems, particularly in the regional commissions, in accordance with the Secretary-General's estimates. It requested him to report on possibilities in that regard, including a timetable for establishing units in all departments and redeployment measures. It stressed the need to develop a comprehensive evaluation system along the lines recommended by CPC and endorsed the CPC timetable for intergovernmental review of evaluation studies.

Joint Inspection Unit

JIU activities. During 1983 the Joint Inspection Unit (JIU) submitted 10 reports, most of them evaluating selected programmes of the United Nations and the United Nations system. Eight were circulated to the General Assembly and two to the Economic and Social Council. In most cases the reports were the subject of written comments by the Secretary-General or, on reports affecting more than one organization, by ACC.

Five of the reports covered specific organizational units: the United Nations Relief and Works Agency for Palestine Refugees in the Near East[9] (see p. 345), the Office for Projects Execution of the United Nations Development Programme[10] (circulated in 1984), the Department of Technical Co-operation for Development[11] (see p. 478), the United Nations Sudano-Sahelian Office[12] (see p. 526) and the Department of International Economic and Social Affairs[13] (see ECONOMIC AND SOCIAL QUESTIONS, Chapter XXIV).

The other reports were studies of activities in which more than one unit was involved. One concerned the UNDP programme and project evaluation system[14] (see p. 460). Another dealt with cultural property preservation and environmental protection in Latin America[15]. A report circulated for consideration in 1984 by the Economic and Social Council concerned wildlife conservation in Africa[16] and cultural property preservation and environmental protection in Asia and the Pacific.[17] One report contained JIU comments on programme planning rules and regulations in the United Nations[6] (see RULES AND REGULATIONS above).

During 1983 the UNDP Governing Council considered a 1982 JIU report on inter-agency co-operation regarding programme evaluation by Governments of operational activities for development[18] (see p. 453).

The activities of JIU from 1 July 1982 to 30 June 1983 were described in its fifteenth report to the Assembly.[19] The rest of the year was covered in the 1983-1984 report.[20] Each document included summaries of all JIU topical reports during the period covered.

In its 1983 report,[19] JIU stressed the need for renewed efforts to comply with established time-limits for comments on its reports by the executive heads of the United Nations system or ACC. Those limits were three months for the reports addressed to one organization and six months for those addressed to more than one. It observed that, between January 1980 and June 1982, the time-limits had been met for only 32 per cent of its 32 reports.

On another matter, it reported that arrangements had been made to list its reports as separate sub-items on the Assembly's agenda wherever they related to existing items. The aim was to enable Main Committees of the Assembly to consider the reports individually.

In paragraph 12 of its report, JIU suggested a form of wording by which the Assembly or other intergovernmental body could state precisely which JIU recommendations that body approved or disapproved. It would then become standard practice for JIU to follow up, a year later, on action taken on each report by the organizations concerned.

The Secretary-General submitted to the Fifth Committee in October his annual report on implementation of past JIU recommendations, with explanations for why certain of them had not been carried out.[21] The report dealt with recommendations on: organizational change in the Economic Commission for Africa (see p. 634); the United Nations University (see p. 765); relationships between the Director-General for Development and International Economic Co-operation and other Secretariat units (see ECONOMIC AND SOCIAL QUESTIONS, Chapter XXIV); geographical distribution in the Secretariat, consultants, and travel of officials (see next Chapter); and organizational structure of conference secretariats and documents limitation (see Chapter IV of this section).

On 20 December 1983, acting without vote, the General Assembly adopted resolution 38/229 on the recommendation of the Fifth Committee.

Joint Inspection Unit

The General Assembly

1. *Takes note* of the annual report of the Joint Inspection Unit and of the report of the Secretary-General on the implementation of the recommendations of the Unit;

2. *Confirms* the importance it attaches to the proper consideration of the reports of the Joint Inspection Unit;

3. *Invites* United Nations organs, when considering reports of the Joint Inspection Unit, to bear in mind the recommendation contained in paragraph 12 of the 1983 annual report of the Unit;

4. *Requests* the Secretary-General to issue his comments on individual reports of the Joint Inspection Unit as well as his report on the implementation of the recommendations of the Unit as early as possible before the opening of the session of the General Assembly at which such reports are to be considered.

General Assembly resolution 38/229

20 December 1983   Meeting 104   Adopted without vote

Approved by Fifth Committee (A/38/692) without vote, 30 December (meeting 51); draft by Chairman (A/C.5/38/L.9/Rev.1); agenda item 113.
Meeting numbers. GA 38th session: 5th Committee 19, 24, 36, 51; plenary 104.

REFERENCES

[1]A/38/133 & Corr.1. [2]YUN 1981, p. 1312. GA res. 36/228 B, 18 Dec. 1981. [3]YUN 1982, p. 1430. GA res. 37/234, 21 Dec. 1982. [4]A/38/126. [5]A/C.5/38/6 & Corr.1. [6]A/38/160. [7]A/38/38. [8]A/C.5/38/11. [9]A/38/143 & Add.1. [10]A/39/80 & Add.1. [11]A/38/172 & Add.1. [12]A/38/180 & Add.1. [13]A/38/334 & Add.1. [14]DP/1983/68. [15]A/38/170. [16]E/1984/3 & Add.1. [17]E/1984/52. [18]A/38/333 & Add.1. [19]A/38/34. [20]A/39/34. [21]A/C.5/38/8.

Administrative and budgetary co-ordination in the UN system

In its annual report to the General Assembly on administrative and budgetary co-ordination in the United Nations system,[1] submitted in October 1983, ACABQ reviewed financial problems of the specialized agencies and the International Atomic Energy Agency related to cash flow and liquidity. It observed that, as in the case of the United Nations (see previous Chapter), a serious problem existed regarding the collection of contributions from member States. For most specialized agencies, only between 37 and 62 per cent of 1983 contributions had been received by 30 June. As an exception, the two agencies that charged interest on late payments (International Telecommunication Union, Universal Postal Union) had received over 90 per cent of their contributions by mid-year.

The report described measures taken to speed the payment of arrears and encourage the timely receipt of contributions, as well as to cope with the cash flow problem through the use of working capital and reserve funds, and internal borrowing. ACABQ emphasized the serious nature of the cash flow problem throughout the system.

The report also dealt with programme planning, budgeting and evaluation in the United Nations system (see PROGRAMME PLANNING above).

According to the report, which covered organizations other than the international financial institutions with headquarters in Washington, D. C., the regular budgets of the United Nations system, excluding the International Fund for Agricultural Development, would total $1.76 billion in 1984, of which $1.64 billion was to be paid by member States' assessments. Including voluntary funds, States paid over $3.9 billion to United Nations organizations in 1982. Staff totals were also provided in the report (see next Chapter).

After the ACABQ report had been considered in the Fifth Committee, the General Assembly, on 25 November 1983, adopted resolution 38/31 without vote, as recommended by the Committee.

Administrative and budgetary co-ordination of the United Nations with the specialized agencies and the International Atomic Energy Agency

The General Assembly

1. *Notes with appreciation* the report of the Advisory Committee on Administrative and Budgetary Questions on the administrative and budgetary co-ordination of the United Nations with the specialized agencies and the International Atomic Energy Agency;

2. *Refers* to the organizations concerned the report of the Advisory Committee as well as the comments and observations made in the course of its consideration in the Fifth Committee;

3. *Transmits* the report of the Advisory Committee to the Board of Auditors, the Panel of External Auditors, the Committee for Programme and Co-ordination and the Joint Inspection Unit for their information;

4. *Invites* the Advisory Committee to continue, in odd-numbered years, to conduct special studies and report thereon, as necessary, in accordance with the provisions of paragraph 5 (*b*) of General Assembly resolution 36/229 of 18 December 1981.

General Assembly resolution 38/31

25 November 1983   Meeting 71   Adopted without vote

Approved by Fifth Committee (A/38/587) without vote, 10 November (meeting 33); draft by Chairman (A/C.5/38/L.7); agenda item 112 *(a)*.
Meeting numbers. GA 38th session: Fifth Committee 16, 24, 33; plenary 71.

Also in relation to co-ordination in the United Nations system, the Assembly adopted resolution 38/227 B, concerned with programme co-ordination, and decision 38/409, on the possibility of establishing a single administrative tribunal. In addition, it acted on a number of personnel questions affecting the system as a whole (see next Chapter).

REFERENCE

[1]A/38/515 & Corr.1.

Chapter III

United Nations officials

Staff in organizations of the United Nations system belonging to the common system of salaries and fringe benefits of the international civil service totalled 50,799 as at 31 December 1983, according to figures compiled for the inter-agency Administrative Committee on Co-ordination (ACC). This total consisted of 26,719 in the United Nations Secretariat and 24,080 in specialized agencies and other related intergovernmental organizations. The common system encompassed the entire United Nations system except for the international financial institutions with headquarters at Washington, D. C.

Of the total in the system, 21,113, or 41 per cent, were stationed at the organizations' headquarters, 20,269, or 39 per cent, were at other established offices, and 9,417, or 18 per cent, were project staff, working on technical co-operation and other operational activities in the field. By category, 19,315 were Professionals and 31,484 were in the General Service or related categories.

Salaries and benefits for the international civil service of the common system were for the most part determined by the General Assembly, guided by advice from the International Civil Service Commission (ICSC), which in turn consulted the administrations and staff representatives of participating intergovernmental organizations. The Assembly also determined certain personnel management policies to be followed by the central Secretariat, encompassing United Nations staff in units financed mainly under the regular budget. Such staff numbered 16,159 as at 31 December.

In 1983, ICSC held its seventeenth and eighteenth sessions, 7 to 24 March at Vienna and 18 July to 5 August in New York, and a special session, 21 to 23 November in New York. After considering its activities and recommendations, the Assembly in December, by resolution 38/232, urged all organizations concerned to implement ICSC decisions, and took a number of actions affecting salaries and benefits. Among them, it asked to be kept informed annually of the difference between international civil service pay and that of the best-paid national civil service, using a new comprehensive method of assessing total compensation; approved an increase in the education grant paid to internationally recruited staff to help them meet the expenses involved in their childrens' schooling while the staff served outside their home

country; and acted on matters relating to job classification, language incentives, field staff, post adjustment (the cost-of-living component of salaries), miscellaneous allowances and a cost-of-living index for pensioners.

By decision 38/451, the Assembly requested consultations on a proposal to remove a prohibition on the recruitment of ICSC members by a United Nations organization within three years of leaving the Commission.

Also in December, by resolution 38/231, the Assembly requested special efforts to meet previously established goals aimed at improving the balance among nationalities and women's status in the Secretariat. It accepted the Secretary-General's proposals on job classification of General Service staff at Geneva (resolution 38/284, section XIX). Regarding steps to promote better linguistic balance, it noted a report by the Secretary-General proposing that no limitation be placed on the number of languages a United Nations staff member could study free of charge in the Organization's language-training programme (section VIII). The language teachers in that programme were to be given the contractual status of staff members, the Assembly decided (section XIII).

Acting on proposed amendments to the Staff Rules of the United Nations, the Assembly, by decision 38/450, requested a review of provisions relating to staff/management relations.

An expression of concern about what the Assembly called continuing neglect of principles relating to respect for the privileges and immunities of the international civil service was contained in resolution 38/230. It acted after examining a report on further incidents adversely affecting staff security.

Acting on recommendations by the United Nations Joint Staff Pension Board, the Assembly, by resolution 38/233, decided to raise, for the first time, the contribution rates of staff and their employing organizations to the United Nations Joint Staff Pension Fund, so as to improve its financial situation. By the same resolution, the Regulations of the Fund were amended to alter certain benefits and a 1984 budget was approved. A report on the Fund's improved investment picture was noted by the Assembly in decision 38/452.

By resolution 38/235, the Assembly approved the experimental use of an ICSC formula authorizing the United Nations to pay a larger share of the health insurance premiums of Secretariat staff.

As the United Nations Administrative Tribunal delivered 20 judgements during 1983 in cases involving labour contracts of the international civil service, work proceeded on ways to improve co-ordination with the Administrative Tribunal of the International Labour Organisation (ILO). In November, by decision 38/409, the Assembly asked that these consultations be accelerated.

The Assembly noted reports on steps to improve United Nations machinery for handling its officials' travel and on savings achieved by using economy-class travel where first-class had once been the norm (resolution 38/234, section IV). It urged maximum restraint on staff travel to attend Assembly sessions (section XVI) and deferred action on proposals to increase certain allowances payable to the officers of two United Nations bodies (section XVII).

Personnel management

The General Assembly dealt in 1983 with a number of personnel questions, some affecting the international civil service as a whole and others confined to the United Nations Secretariat. It acted after considering reports and other documents from the Secretary-General and the bodies principally concerned, namely ICSC, the Advisory Committee on Administrative and Budgetary Questions (ACABQ), and three organizations representing groups of staff in the United Nations system.

Some of these questions concerned personnel management issues such as United Nations staff composition, career development, staff representation, field staff, the Staff Rules of the United Nations, and privileges and immunities. Other questions involved staff costs (see next subchapter). A question pertaining to certain non-Secretariat officials was also raised (see under OTHER UN OFFICIALS below).

The 1983 ICSC report to the General Assembly covered its two regular sessions and one special session held during the year (for places and dates see the introduction to this chapter).[1] Recommendations regarding ICSC proposals were made by ACABQ.[2]

The Secretary-General submitted reports on seven United Nations personnel and related questions: staff composition,[3] Staff Rules,[4] privileges and immunities,[5] staff security in the United Nations Relief and Works Agency for Palestine Refugees in the Near East (UNRWA),[6] health insurance,[7] travel,[8] and allowances and pensions of non-Secretariat officials.[9]

Three staff organizations submitted comments on various personnel matters which were circu-

lated by the Secretary-General to the Assembly's Fifth (Administrative and Budgetary) Committee. Two of the organizations, the Federation of International Civil Servants' Associations (FICSA)[10] and the Staff Unions and Associations of the United Nations Secretariat,[11] commented in October. The third, the Co-ordinating Committee for Independent Staff Unions and Associations of the United Nations System (CCISUA),[12] conveyed its views in November.

GENERAL ASSEMBLY ACTION

On 20 December 1983, the General Assembly, on the recommendation of the Fifth Committee, adopted by recorded vote resolution 38/232, covering various matters pertaining to the international civil service and ICSC.

United Nations common system: report of the International Civil Service Commission

The General Assembly,

Having considered with appreciation the report of the International Civil Service Commission for the year 1983,

Reaffirming the central role of the Commission within the United Nations common system in the development of a single unified international civil service through the application of common personnel standards and arrangements,

Reaffirming the importance of respect for these common standards and arrangements by all organizations members of the common system,

I

1. *Urges* all organizations concerned to implement the decisions of the International Civil Service Commission and to act positively on the recommendations of the Commission in accordance with its statute;

2. *Urges* the executive heads of organizations concerned, after consultation with the Commission, to report to their respective governing bodies such decisions or proposals as would modify the recommendations of the Commission;

3. *Calls upon* all organizations of the United Nations common system to bring to the attention of the Commission all matters relating to salaries, allowances, benefits and other conditions of employment so as to ensure their uniform application throughout the common system;

4. *Reaffirms* the principles embodied in the statute of the Commission as approved in General Assembly resolution 3357(XXIX) of 18 December 1974, in particular article 6 thereof, and requests Governments, secretariats and staff associations to co-operate in this regard;

5. *Approves* the development of the special index for pensioners as recommended by the Commission in paragraph 15 *(a)* of its report;

6. *Takes note* of the current status of the margin between the remuneration of the United States federal civil service and that of the United Nations system;

7. *Requests* the Commission to complete, in close consultation with the United States authorities concerned, the study of the equivalency between the higher grade levels of the United Nations system and the Senior

Executive Service of the United States federal civil service and to report thereon to the General Assembly at its thirty-ninth session;

8. *Notes* the progress made to date concerning the comparison of total compensation based on non-expatriate benefits applicable on both sides and requests the Commission to inform the General Assembly, on an annual basis, of the margin between the remuneration of United Nations employees and those of the United States federal civil service on this total compensation basis;

II

1. *Expresses concern* that the International Civil Service Commission was unable to make corrections in the current post adjustment classification at certain duty stations in spite of the fact that the post adjustments were found to be higher than those which the results of the new cost-of-living survey could justify;

2. *Notes* the efforts by the Commission to improve the post adjustment system and requests the Commission in this regard to expedite, in particular, the application of the revised methodology for cost-of-living measurement, called for in General Assembly resolution 34/165 of 17 December 1979, in order to improve the mechanism for adjusting United Nations remuneration to reflect more accurately the differences in cost of living at various duty stations;

3. *Calls upon* the executive heads and the staff of organizations of the United Nations common system to co-operate fully with the Commission in the application of the post adjustment system;

4. *Notes* the introduction by the Commission, with effect from 1 April 1983, of a rental subsidy scheme for staff in the Professional and higher categories at Headquarters and other duty stations not previously covered by a subsidy scheme;

5. *Requests* the Commission to monitor this rental subsidy scheme with a view to ensuring both its equity and its effectiveness;

III

1. *Recalls* its resolution 2480 B (XXIII) of 21 December 1968 concerning language incentives in the United Nations;

2. *Requests* the Secretary-General to submit to the General Assembly at its thirty-ninth session a report on the status of the linguistic skills of United Nations staff, including the effects of the language incentive programme, and to propose, if necessary, further measures to improve the present situation;

3. *Decides* that:

(a) The education grant for eligible staff members shall be set at a level of 75 per cent of the cost of attendance at an educational institution in respect of expenses up to a maximum of $6,000 per year, with a maximum reimbursement of $4,500 per child per year;

(b) The reimbursement rate for disabled children shall be set at 100 per cent of a maximum of $6,000 for expenses at an educational institution;

(c) The limit of allowable boarding costs within the overall maximum allowable expenditure of $6,000 shall be raised to $1,500 per year;

(d) Provision shall be made to use a currency floor for this grant, using exchange rates effective 1 March 1983, to ensure the maintenance of equitable reimbursement of education costs among duty stations;

4. *Requests* the International Civil Service Commission to conduct a study of the education grant, the purpose of which was to facilitate a child's reassimilation in the staff member's home country, and to report on the results of the study to the General Assembly at its thirty-ninth session;

IV

1. *Takes note* of the decision of the International Civil Service Commission to modify, with effect from 1 September 1983, the non-resident's allowance provisions to make the allowance payable for a fixed duration of five years at designated duty stations and to make it non-pensionable, subject to the protection of acquired rights as set out in paragraph 63 of the report of the Commission;

2. *Requests* the United Nations Joint Staff Pension Board to review article 54 (a) of the Regulations of the United Nations Joint Staff Pension Fund in the light of the Commission's decision and to make appropriate recommendations to the General Assembly at its thirty-ninth session;

3. *Decides* that, in the mean time, the modified non-resident's allowance shall not be pensionable;

V

1. *Requests* the International Civil Service Commission to undertake a comprehensive review of after-service health-care coverage with particular attention to locally recruited field staff;

2. *Approves* the Commission's recommendation that the present non-contributory system of death-grant benefits be continued inasmuch as it provides benefits in the most cost-effective manner;

VI

1. *Recalls* section IV of its resolution 37/126 of 17 December 1982 and reaffirms its support for the overall approach envisaged by the International Civil Service Commission, which aims at the development of policies for an integrated personnel management system, based on human resources planning, to assist organizations in achieving their programme objectives in an efficient manner, while providing improved conditions for career development;

2. *Welcomes* the decision taken by the Commission to establish job classification standards, under article 13 of its statute, for locally recruited staff in field offices where several of the organizations employ staff in common areas of work;

3. *Expresses its satisfaction* that job classification standards have been developed for the General Service and related categories in New York and requests the organizations concerned to co-ordinate their implementation of these standards in order to utilize fully the opportunities they provide for improved job design, recruitment, career planning and training;

4. *Welcomes* the Commission's efforts to develop a common approach to skills inventories on an inter-organizational basis;

5. *Recommends* that the organizations normally dispense with the requirement for a probationary appointment as a prerequisite for a career appointment following a period of five years' satisfactory service on fixed-term contracts;

6. *Again requests* the Commission to pursue its mandate under article 14 of its statute, in consultation with

organizations and staff, with regard to the development of common training, recruitment and promotion policies for the organizations and to report thereon to the General Assembly as each phase of its studies is completed;

VII

Notes the progress made to date by the International Civil Service Commission in its review of conditions of service in the field and requests the Commission to keep the General Assembly informed of further developments in its review;

VIII

Requests the International Civil Service Commission to report to the General Assembly at its thirty-ninth session on the question of longevity and merit steps in the various grade levels.

General Assembly resolution 38/232

20 December 1983   Meeting 104   128-10-2 (recorded vote)

Approved by Fifth Committee (A/38/745) by vote (91-9-5), 15 December (meeting 66); 9-nation draft (A/C.5/38/L.17), amended by United States (A/C.5/38/L.20, paras. 1 and 2, orally revised); agenda item 117.

Sponsors: Australia, Austria, Canada, Denmark, Egypt, Norway, Pakistan, Sweden, Venezuela.

Financial implications. ACABQ, A/38/7/Add.7; S-G, A/C.5/38/37.

Meeting numbers. GA 38th session: 5th Committee 28, 31, 33, 38, 41, 42, 49, 50, 61, 62, 65-67; plenary 104.

Recorded vote in Assembly as follows:

In favour: Algeria, Argentina, Australia, Austria, Bahamas, Bahrain, Bangladesh, Barbados, Belgium, Belize, Benin, Bhutan, Bolivia, Botswana, Brazil, Burma, Burundi, Canada, Central African Republic, Chad, Chile, China, Colombia, Congo, Costa Rica, Cyprus, Democratic Kampuchea, Democratic Yemen, Denmark, Djibouti, Dominican Republic, Ecuador, Egypt, El Salvador, Ethiopia, Fiji, Finland, France, Gabon, Gambia, Germany, Federal Republic of, Ghana, Greece, Guatemala, Guinea, Guyana, Haiti, Honduras, Iceland, India, Indonesia, Iran, Iraq, Ireland, Israel, Italy, Ivory Coast, Jamaica, Japan, Jordan, Kenya, Kuwait, Lebanon, Lesotho, Liberia, Libyan Arab Jamahiriya, Luxembourg, Madagascar, Malawi, Malaysia, Maldives, Mali, Malta, Mauritania, Mauritius, Mexico, Morocco, Nepal, Netherlands, New Zealand, Nicaragua, Niger, Nigeria, Norway, Oman, Pakistan, Panama, Papua New Guinea, Paraguay, Peru, Philippines, Portugal, Qatar, Rwanda, Saint Lucia, Saint Vincent and the Grenadines, Samoa, Sao Tome and Principe, Saudi Arabia, Senegal, Sierra Leone, Singapore, Somalia, Spain, Sri Lanka, Sudan, Suriname, Swaziland, Sweden, Syrian Arab Republic, Thailand, Togo, Trinidad and Tobago, Tunisia, Turkey, Uganda, United Arab Emirates, United Kingdom, United Republic of Cameroon, United Republic of Tanzania, United States, Upper Volta, Uruguay, Vanuatu, Venezuela, Yemen, Yugoslavia, Zambia.

Against: Bulgaria, Byelorussian SSR, Czechoslovakia, German Democratic Republic, Hungary, Mongolia, Poland, Romania, Ukrainian SSR, USSR.

Abstaining: Afghanistan, Cuba.

Before approving the draft as a whole, the Fifth Committee approved two amendments by the United States by separate votes. The amendments added paragraphs on post adjustment (section II, paragraph 1) and the education grant (section III, paragraph 4) (see those topics under STAFF COSTS below). The United States withdrew a third amendment, on extensions of appointment beyond retirement age (see STAFF COMPOSITION below).

A Moroccan amendment to change the ICSC statute in regard to the duties of Commission members[13] was withdrawn in favour of a separate draft decision on the matter (see next section).

Among those voting against the resolution, the USSR objected to ICSC recommendations which, in its view, would result in unjustified pay increases for the international civil service. The German

Democratic Republic also spoke of the need to reduce excessive salaries and added that career development should apply as well to staff members holding fixed-term contracts and should not affect equitable geographical distribution among nationalities in the staff.

Abstaining in the vote, Cuba said it had reservations on a number of paragraphs and regretted that there had not been more consultations among delegations on the text.

Voting for the resolution, Mexico opposed the United States amendments but thought they did not alter the basic thrust of the text. Bolivia also had reservations on the amendment concerning post adjustment. Venezuela described the text as balanced.

In addition to this resolution, the Assembly adopted others dealing with specific personnel questions (see the introduction to this chapter). A draft decision[14] on the staffing of regional commissions was withdrawn by its sponsor, Iraq. By that text, the Assembly would have called on the Secretary-General to make special efforts to solve the problem of vacancies in certain regional commissions.

In resolution 38/231 on the composition of the Secretariat, the Assembly requested the Secretary-General to strengthen the role of the Office of Personnel Services in all personnel matters throughout the Secretariat.

ICSC statute

In December 1983, the General Assembly asked for consultations with other United Nations organizations and with ICSC on a Moroccan proposal to amend the ICSC statute by removing a restriction that prevented any former Commission member from working for an organization in the United Nations system within three years of leaving ICSC. The request was made in decision 38/451, adopted by recorded vote on the recommendation of the Fifth Committee.

Statute of the International Civil Service Commission

At its 104th plenary meeting, on 20 December 1983, the General Assembly, on the recommendation of the Fifth Committee, requested the Secretary-General to consult with the organizations members of the common system of the United Nations and the International Civil Service Commission, bringing to their attention, *inter alia*, the discussions in the Fifth Committee on the draft decision annexed to the present decision and to report on the results of those consultations to the Assembly at its thirty-ninth session.

ANNEX
Draft decision on the statute of the International Civil Service Commission
The General Assembly decides to amend article 6, paragraph 2, of the statute of the International Civil Service Commission to read:

"2. No member of the Commission may participate in the deliberations of any organ of the organizations on any matter within the competence of the Commission unless the Commission has requested him or her to do so as its representative; nor shall a member of the Commission serve as an official or consultant of any such organization during his or her term of office."

General Assembly decision 38/451

82-31-13 (recorded vote)

Approved by Fifth Committee (A/38/745) by vote (24-6-37), 15 December (meeting 67); draft orally proposed by Egypt, amended by United States; agenda item 117.

Meeting numbers. GA 38th session: 5th Committee 28, 31, 33, 38, 41, 42, 49, 50, 61, 62, 65-67; plenary 104.

Recorded vote in Assembly as follows:

In favour: Algeria, Austria, Bahrain, Bangladesh, Belize, Benin, Bhutan, Bolivia, Botswana, Brazil, Burma, Burundi, Central African Republic, Chad, Chile, China, Colombia, Costa Rica, Democratic Kampuchea, Djibouti, Dominican Republic, Egypt, Fiji, Gabon, Gambia, Ghana, Guatemala, Guinea, Iran, Jamaica, Jordan, Kenya, Kuwait, Lebanon, Lesotho, Liberia, Libyan Arab Jamahiriya, Madagascar, Malawi, Malaysia, Maldives, Malta, Mauritania, Mauritius, Morocco, Nepal, Niger, Nigeria, Oman, Pakistan, Papua New Guinea, Paraguay, Peru, Philippines, Portugal, Qatar, Romania, Rwanda, Saint Lucia, Saudi Arabia, Senegal, Sierra Leone, Singapore, Somalia, Sri Lanka, Sudan, Suriname, Swaziland, Syrian Arab Republic, Thailand, Togo, Trinidad and Tobago, Tunisia, Turkey, Uganda, United Arab Emirates, United Republic of Cameroon, United Republic of Tanzania, Upper Volta, Vanuatu, Yemen, Zambia.

Against: Australia, Belgium, Bulgaria, Byelorussian SSR, Canada, Czechoslovakia, Denmark, Finland, France, German Democratic Republic, Germany, Federal Republic of, Greece, Hungary, Iceland, India, Ireland, Israel, Italy, Japan, Luxembourg, Mongolia, Netherlands, New Zealand, Norway, Poland, Spain, Sweden, Ukrainian SSR, USSR, United Kingdom, United States.

Abstaining: Afghanistan, Argentina, Barbados, Congo, Cuba, Ecuador, Haiti, Ivory Coast, Mali, Mexico, Uruguay, Venezuela, Yugoslavia.

The ICSC statute, adopted by the Assembly in 1974,[15] provided that no Commission member could serve as an official or consultant with any United Nations organization that accepted the statute. This restriction applied "during his or her term of office or within three years of ceasing to be a member of the Commission".

During the Fifth Committee's discussion of the ICSC report in December 1983, Morocco proposed that the Assembly adopt an amendment that would in effect delete from the statute the reference to a three-year period.[13] Morocco explained that it wished to give the organizations broader options in the choice of experts.

This proposal was originally presented as an amendment to what became resolution 38/232 on the international civil service. However, Morocco withdrew this amendment in favour of an oral proposal by Egypt for a separate decision to have the Secretary-General consult on the proposed amendment with the other organizations involved.

On an oral proposal by the United States, the Committee approved the addition of two points to the Egyptian proposal: to involve ICSC in the consultations and to call attention to the Committee's discussion. The United States amendment was adopted by 37 votes to 10, with 14 abstentions.

Voting against the amended text in Committee but in favour in the Assembly, Morocco objected to prior consultation with other organizations and with ICSC. The USSR and the United States

voted against on the ground that the proposed amendment of the statute could jeopardize the independence of ICSC members.

In the Assembly, the Bahamas said it wished to record its non-participation in the vote.

ICSC budget for 1984-1985

On 10 November 1983, by 74 votes to 8, the Fifth Committee approved revised ICSC budget estimates totalling $366,200 (gross) for 1984-1985,[16] raising total appropriations for the Commission to $7,107,100. The increase over the initial estimates submitted by the Secretary-General was attributed by him to a recosting of office space requirements and to the need for an additional clerk, raising the Commission's staff to 52.[17] As a consequence of this increase, the Committee also approved revised income estimates, representing the 59.8 per cent share of the ICSC budget to be paid by other organizations of the United Nations system that helped finance the Commission. The Secretary-General's revised estimates were endorsed by ACABQ.[18]

Later Fifth Committee actions, including approval of pension contributions for the ICSC Chairman and Vice-Chairman (see below, under OTHER UN OFFICIALS), brought the Commission's total appropriation for 1984-1985 to $7,187,000.

Staff composition

Various matters affecting the composition of the international civil service, with special reference to geographical distribution and women's advancement and status, were considered during 1983. In addition to the treatment of these matters in the Secretary-General's annual report on the composition of the United Nations Secretariat,[3] ICSC examined aspects of recruitment, staff contracts and retirement affecting the entire international civil service—topics also commented on by staff organizations. In December, the General Assembly called for special efforts to meet previously established goals on Secretariat composition.

In his September 1983 report to the Assembly,[3] the Secretary-General presented statistical data showing changes in the composition of the Secretariat during the year ended 30 June, with respect to the geographical distribution of staff among nationalities and the proportion of men and women. The report stated that the number of nationalities unrepresented in the Secretariat among the 157 Member States had fallen from 17 to 14, as a result of the appointment of nationals of Equatorial Guinea, Samoa and Suriname. Unrepresented were Albania, Bahrain, Djibouti, Gabon, Guinea-Bissau, Kuwait, Maldives, Mongolia, Papua New Guinea, Qatar, Saint Lucia, Sao Tome and Principe, Solomon Islands and Vanuatu.

Twenty-five Members were underrepresented, in the sense that the number of their nationals was less than the lower limit of their desirable ranges of representation, calculated according to a formula based largely on budget contributions. This constituted a net increase of one underrepresented nationality. Eighty-seven Members were within range, down from 90, while 31 were above range, up from 26. The States which moved from adequately represented to slightly overrepresented (by one to three posts) were Kenya, Morocco, Peru, Poland, and Trinidad and Tobago. Those remaining above range were Algeria, Argentina, Australia, Austria, Bangladesh, Chile, China, Egypt, Ethiopia, Ghana, Guyana, India, Iraq, Jamaica, Lebanon, Nigeria, Pakistan, Philippines, Sierra Leone, Sri Lanka, Thailand, Tunisia, Uganda, United Kingdom, United Republic of Tanzania and Zaire.

These figures were limited to the 3,077 posts subject to geographical distribution. They thus excluded staff in posts with special language requirements (mainly interpreters and translators) and certain other staff among the total of 4,251 Professional posts in the Secretariat.

During the year covered, 277 appointments were made to these "geographical" posts, of which 98 were of unrepresented or underrepresented nationalities, 151 were of those within range and 26 were of overrepresented nationalities.

Another table in the report showed that the proportion of women in geographical posts had risen from 16.3 per cent in 1973 to 22.3 per cent in 1983, falling short of the 25 per cent target first set by the Assembly in 1978.[19] During the year covered, 15.9 per cent of appointees to geographical posts were women.

The report stated that, in compliance with a 1980 Assembly request,[20] an annual work plan of recruitment had been drawn up for 1983, corresponding to the first stage of a medium-term recruitment plan for 1983-1985.

Steps taken in regard to recommendations on geographical distribution made by the Joint Inspection Unit (JIU) in 1981[21] and 1982[22] were reported to the Assembly in an October 1983 report of the Secretary-General[23] on the implementation of various JIU recommendations (see preceding chapter). He stated that 6 of the 10 recommendations made in 1981 were either being implemented or were the subject of Assembly decisions that were being implemented.

He reported that progress had been achieved towards bringing unrepresented and underrepresented nationalities within their desirable ranges. However, he considered that the JIU recommendation for an interruptible fixed-term staff contract, permitting rotation of persons seconded from their national service and others holding fixed-term contracts, would interrupt the continuity of the Secretariat's work and create difficulties for career development. Secondment arrangements could be systematized, he felt, without introducing a new type of appointment. With regard to top echelon staff, he said the Secretariat's efforts were directed towards an objective fixed by the Assembly in 1982[24]—to have the largest possible number of Member States represented at the higher levels.

ICSC acted in 1983 on three matters affecting staff composition throughout the international civil service—recruitment, types of appointment, and retirement.[1] Regarding the first, it established at its July/August session a three-year timetable for its consideration of various aspects of recruitment, beginning in 1984 with selection interviews and reviews of candidates' prior education and experience.

On the matter of types of appointment (staff contracts), ICSC instructed its secretariat in March 1983 to continue consultations with United Nations organizations and staff representatives, with the goal of reporting back in 1984 with proposals on the subject. The Commission suggested that there be three basic types of appointment: short-term, fixed-term and career. It requested its secretariat to propose criteria to harmonize the granting of career appointments, while allowing for the reappointment of fixed-term staff such as those on secondment from government service. It recommended that organizations normally dispense with the requirement that staff who had satisfactorily served on fixed-term contracts undergo further probationary appointment before becoming eligible for career appointment.

After considering proposals to raise the mandatory age of separation from service from 60 to 62 years, ICSC decided by a majority at its July/August session not to recommended any change. It recommended that organizations facilitate the transition of their staff to retirement, ensure that they received full information on retirement provisions well before their departure, and provide pre-retirement training on such matters as material problems, health issues and the use of time.

The United Nations Joint Staff Pension Board, in July 1983, reiterated its 1982 recommendation[25] that the retirement age be raised to 62 while maintaining the right to full pension at 60 for those who chose to leave earlier. (See also PENSIONS below.)

With regard to recruitment, FICSA, in its comments to the Fifth Committee on various personnel matters,[10] expressed disappointment at what it called the low priority assigned in the ICSC work programme to aspects of recruitment which should have higher priority, such as underrepresentation of some countries. Criticizing what it called the proliferation of fixed-term contracts in the United Nations system, FICSA reiterated its view that at least 75 per cent of the international civil service should have career appointments and asked the Assembly to commend to other organizations its 1982 decision[26] that United Nations staff, after five years of fixed-term contracts, be given every reasonable consideration for career appointment. It also hoped the Assembly would reiterate that political considerations should not be allowed to affect recruitment.

On retirement, FICSA said it would not oppose giving the staff the option of working until age 62, provided that this applied to staff at all levels, that it was exercised solely at the staff member's discretion, and that existing rights to retirement at 60 and early retirement at 55 were not affected.

Commenting on personnel questions,[12] CCISUA stated with regard to staff contracts that excessive reliance on fixed-term appointments should be avoided.

Staff representatives of the United Nations Secretariat, in their written comments to the Fifth Committee,[11] observed with concern that the proportion of women in geographical posts had risen by only 0.1 per cent since mid-1982. They believed that fixed- or short-term staff contracts must not replace the notion of a career staff. While taking no position on proposals to raise the retirement age, they insisted on maintaining the right to retire on full pension at age 60 and with reduced benefits at 55.

Geographical distribution in the Department of Public Information was the subject of an April 1983 report by the Secretary-General to the Committee on Information.[27] The Committee, in a recommendation approved by the General Assembly in resolution 38/82 B of 15 December 1983, said the Department should intensify efforts to redress the imbalance in its staff, particularly in the Radio and Visual Services Division.

GENERAL ASSEMBLY ACTION

On 20 December 1983, the General Assembly adopted without vote resolution 38/231. The Assembly took this action on the recommendation of the Fifth Committee following its consideration of the Secretary-General's report.

Composition of the Secretariat

The General Assembly,

Reaffirming its previous resolutions on personnel policy and in particular resolutions 33/143 of 20 December 1978, 35/210 of 17 December 1980 and 37/235 of 21 December 1982,

Noting that some limited progress has been made with respect to the situation of unrepresented and under-represented Member States and towards a balanced and equitable geographical distribution of staff in the Secretariat,

Concerned by the lack of progress, especially in the past year, towards increasing the proportion of women in the Secretariat and, in particular, the failure to reach the target set in section III of resolution 33/143,

Recognizing the central role of the Office of Personnel Services in the implementation of personnel policies,

1. *Takes note* of the report of the Secretary-General on the composition of the Secretariat;

2. *Calls upon* the Secretary-General to continue to make every effort to ensure the implementation of the provisions of the previous resolutions of the General Assembly, in particular of resolutions 33/143, 35/210 and 37/235;

3. *Requests* the Secretary-General to make special efforts to meet the goals and objectives established with respect to:

(a) The situation of unrepresented and under-represented Member States;

(b) The recruitment, career development and promotion of women;

(c) The achievement of a balanced and equitable geographical distribution of staff throughout the Secretariat;

4. *Requests* the Secretary-General to strengthen the role of the Office of Personnel Services of the Department of Administration and Management in all personnel matters throughout the Secretariat;

5. *Reaffirms its request* to the Secretary-General in paragraph 8 of resolution 37/235 A to report to the General Assembly at its thirty-ninth session on progress made in the implementation of all aspects of personnel policy reform.

General Assembly resolution 38/231

20 December 1983   Meeting 104   Adopted without vote

Approved by Fifth Committee (A/38/744) without vote, 19 December (meeting 73); draft by Barbados (A/C.5/38/L.27); agenda item 116.

Meeting numbers. GA 38th session: 5th Committee 41, 45-48, 50, 53, 60, 73; plenary 104.

An amendment by the United States relating to retirement age,[28] proposed to the draft resolution on the international civil service (resolution 38/232), was withdrawn by its sponsor. It would have had the Assembly invite executive heads in the United Nations system to make greater use of their authority to extend appointments beyond normal retirement age when that was in the Organization's interest.

Career development

Various aspects of career development in the international civil service were dealt with by ICSC in 1983.[1] The General Assembly acted on two aspects, job classification and language instruction (see following sections). In addition, ICSC briefly considered human resources planning, promotion and training (see below) as well as recruitment and types of appointment (see preceding section).

In March, welcoming initiatives by United Nations organizations to integrate human resources management, ICSC assigned three tasks to its secretariat: to continue work on a common approach to inter-agency skills inventories aimed at fostering career development and staff exchange, to explore the possibility of a seminar for personnel management specialists on human resources planning for General Service staff and to serve as a focal point for information exchange on human resources matters.

At its July/August session, the Commission postponed substantive discussion of promotion policy until 1984. It also adopted a work programme on staff training and asked its secretariat to report on progress.

Comments on career development were included in the documents submitted to the Fifth Committee in 1983 by the three main organizations of staff representatives (see PERSONNEL MANAGEMENT above).

Welcoming ICSC initiatives on human resources planning, FICSA suggested that the Assembly recommend the development of an integrated approach to such planning, with a view to enhancing career development opportunities.[10] For its part, CCISUA thought that ICSC could co-ordinate activities in this area, starting with the creation of a computerized roster of staff skills that could be matched with each organization's long-term planning.[12]

Staff representatives of the United Nations Secretariat favoured a unified personnel structure to eliminate the distinctions between Professional and General Service staff, comprehensive career development planning through a career development service, strengthened staff training and greater opportunities for promotion from the General Service to the Professional category by competitive examination.[11]

Job classification

As part of a continuing process of developing job classification standards for occupational groups throughout the international civil service, ICSC established standards during 1983 for civil engineers (March session) and for purchasing and contracting specialists (July/August session).[1]

With regard to non-Professional categories, ICSC promulgated standards for some 600 positions in New York, covering Headquarters tour guides, security officers, printers, buildings maintenance workers, and shipping, transportation and receiving workers. These had been prepared by the Co-ordination Committee for Development of Classification Standards for the General Service Category in New York, established in 1981 by the United Nations, the United Nations Development Programme and the United Nations Children's Fund. They covered jobs other than the 3,200 General Service positions for which standards had been promulgated in 1982.[29] At the Commission's request, the standards for printers and for

the two manual workers groups, developed separately, were merged into a combined standard defining eight grade levels.

ICSC also became involved, at the request of the United Nations, in the development of standards for the General Service and related categories at Addis Ababa, Ethiopia. Welcoming the initiative of the organizations concerned in establishing a Joint Committee on Job Classification, the Commission requested that Committee to take account of standards and guidelines established for New York and asked for a final report in 1984.

The Sub-Committee on Job Classification, a sub-committee of the Consultative Committee on Administrative Questions (CCAQ) ACC, held two sessions in 1983—its ninth (New York, 24-27 May)[30] and tenth (Geneva, 5-8 December)[31]—at which it continued work on developing standards for various occupational groups of the international civil service. In December, it approved a procedure for testing standards proposed for General Service posts in non-headquarters duty stations and approved a standard for auditors' jobs that was to be placed before ICSC in 1984.

Staff representatives of the United Nations Secretariat, in their comments to the Fifth Committee on various personnel questions,[11] felt that, before the new job classification systems were implemented, agreement should be reached on all aspects of career development planning through joint staff/management machinery.

In a December report to the Fifth Committee,[32] the Secretary-General made several proposals to complete implementation of a job classification scheme for General Service staff at the United Nations Office at Geneva. With implementation under way since 1982 for the six lower levels, he asked for authority to complete the process at the principal level (G-7) by converting 11 General Service posts to the Professional category, shifting the 72 existing principal-level posts among budget sections and assigning a temporary G-7 level to 29 staff members already at that level but whose posts had been downgraded. He announced the intention of absorbing the additional costs, estimated at $410,200 for 1984-1985, without an additional appropriation.

GENERAL ASSEMBLY ACTION

The Secretary-General's proposals on job classification for General Service staff at Geneva, which had the endorsement of ACABQ, were accepted by the General Assembly without vote on 20 December 1983 in section XIX of resolution 38/234, on miscellaneous matters relating to the 1984-1985 budget. The action was recommended by the Fifth Committee.

Job classification of the General Service category at Geneva

[*The General Assembly . . .*]

Accepts the proposals of the Secretary-General as reflected in his report on the job classification of the General Service category at Geneva;

. . .

General Assembly resolution 38/234, section XIX

20 December 1983   Meeting 104   Adopted without vote

Approved by Fifth Committee (A/38/760 & Corr.1) without vote, 16 December (meeting 69); oral proposal by Chairman on ACABQ recommendation; agenda item 109.
Meeting numbers. GA 38th session: 5th Committee 69; plenary 104.

In related action, the Assembly, in resolution 38/232, welcomed the ICSC decision to establish job classification standards for local recruits in field offices where several organizations employed staff in common areas of work. With regard to the standards developed for the General Service and related categories at Headquarters, the Assembly requested the organizations concerned to co-ordinate their implementation in order to utilize the opportunities they provided for improved job design, recruitment, career planning and training.

Language instruction and incentives

Language instruction

The Secretary-General, in an August 1983 report to the Fifth Committee,[33] proposed that no limitation be placed on the number of languages a staff member could learn free of charge in the United Nations language-training programme. Tables in the report showed that 125 students in 1981 and 142 in 1982 who had studied two of the six official languages taught in the programme (Arabic, Chinese, English, French, Russian, Spanish) subsequently studied a third. The Secretary-General concluded that this number was so low that limiting the number of languages would not result in substantial cost savings. The idea of a limit had been advanced by the Secretary-General in 1981, in a package of four proposals for making the language programme more effective, but the Assembly at that time requested a further report on the matter while approving the three other proposals.[34]

GENERAL ASSEMBLY ACTION

On 20 December 1983, on the recommendation of the Fifth Committee, the Assembly adopted without vote section VIII of resolution 38/234.

United Nations language-training programme

[*The General Assembly . . .*]

Takes note of the report of the Secretary-General on the United Nations language-training programme;

. . .

General Assembly resolution 38/234, section VIII

20 December 1983   Meeting 104   Adopted without vote

Approved by Fifth Committee (A/38/760 & Corr.1) without vote, 29 November (meeting

49); oral proposal by Chairman; agenda item 109.
Meeting numbers. GA 38th session: 5th Committee 49; plenary 104.

Language teachers

In December 1983, the General Assembly approved proposals by the Secretary-General to grant staff member status to the 48 full-time teachers conducting language instruction for the Secretariat at Headquarters and major United Nations offices overseas.

The proposals were made in a November report to the Fifth Committee[35] in which the Secretary-General explained why he and the teachers favoured changing their status from that of hourly paid employees to locally recruited staff. He recalled the objectives of a similar proposal he had made in December 1982:[36] to improve the language-training programme through greater participation of full-time teachers, and to give the teachers greater security of tenure, pension coverage, and benefits and allowances available to locally recruited staff. He proposed that they be paid on a scale, varying by duty station, that took account of their current pay, the salaries of other locally recruited staff and the pay received by outside teachers. He put the cost at $532,200 for 1984-1985, covering a contribution to the United Nations Joint Staff Pension Fund, the salary difference and fringe benefits.

A similar approach, to rectify what they described as an injustice, was endorsed by staff representatives of the United Nations Secretariat in their comments to the Fifth Committee on personnel questions.[11]

In a December 1983 report to the Assembly,[37] ACABQ reiterated its December 1982 recommendation that the teachers' status not be changed. It suggested that a new one- to three-year contract be devised, providing for the same pay they currently received, requiring them to teach at least 15 hours a week for no less than 10 months a year, and allowing for sick and maternity leave as well as post-employment benefits. No appropriation would be required other than the $225,900 already included in the Secretary-General's initial budget proposals for 1984-1985, earmarked for post-employment benefits.

GENERAL ASSEMBLY ACTION

The General Assembly accepted the Secretary-General's proposals when it adopted by recorded vote section XIII of resolution 38/234, on the recommendation of the Fifth Committee.

Staff training activities (Headquarters, Geneva and the regional commissions): contractual status of language teachers

[*The General Assembly . . .*]

Approves the proposals of the Secretary-General on the contractual status of language teachers contained in his report;

. . .

General Assembly resolution 38/234, section XIII

20 December 1983   Meeting 104   106-16-16 (recorded vote)

Approved by Fifth Committee (A/38/760 & Corr.1) by vote (46-16-24), 15 December (meeting 67); oral proposal by Egypt; agenda item 109.
Meeting numbers. GA 38th session: 5th Committee 57, 59, 61, 67; plenary 104.

Recorded vote in Assembly as follows:

In favour: Algeria, Australia, Bahrain, Bangladesh, Barbados, Belgium, Belize, Benin, Bhutan, Bolivia, Botswana, Brazil, Burma, Burundi, Chad, Chile, China, Colombia, Congo, Cyprus, Democratic Kampuchea, Democratic Yemen, Denmark, Djibouti, Dominican Republic, Ecuador, Egypt, El Salvador, Ethiopia, Fiji, Finland, France, Gabon, Gambia, Ghana, Greece, Guatemala, Guinea, Guinea-Bissau, Guyana, Haiti, Honduras, Iceland, Iran, Iraq, Ireland, Ivory Coast, Jamaica, Jordan, Kenya, Kuwait, Lebanon, Lesotho, Liberia, Libyan Arab Jamahiriya, Luxembourg, Madagascar, Malawi, Malaysia, Maldives, Mali, Malta, Mauritania, Mauritius, Morocco, Nepal, New Zealand, Niger, Nigeria, Norway, Oman, Papua New Guinea, Paraguay, Peru, Qatar, Rwanda, Saint Lucia, Saint Vincent and the Grenadines, Samoa, Sao Tome and Principe, Saudi Arabia, Senegal, Sierra Leone, Singapore, Solomon Islands, Somalia, Sri Lanka, Sudan, Suriname, Swaziland, Sweden, Syrian Arab Republic, Thailand, Togo, Trinidad and Tobago, Tunisia, Turkey, Uganda, United Arab Emirates, United Republic of Cameroon, United Republic of Tanzania, Upper Volta, Vanuatu, Yemen, Yugoslavia, Zambia.

Against: Bulgaria, Byelorussian SSR, Canada, Czechoslovakia, German Democratic Republic, Germany, Federal Republic of, Hungary, India, Italy, Japan, Mongolia, Poland, Ukrainian SSR, USSR, United Kingdom, United States.

Abstaining: Afghanistan, Argentina, Austria, Bahamas, Costa Rica, Cuba, Israel, Mexico, Netherlands, Pakistan, Panama, Portugal, Romania, Spain, Uruguay, Venezuela.

Among those voting in favour, Belgium thought the Secretary-General's proposals offered a more comprehensive solution. Benin, France and Morocco saw a need to promote an equitable geographical balance; Benin added that there should be no second-class employees. The United Republic of Cameroon also spoke in favour.

Voting against, the USSR suggested that the ACABQ proposals be implemented experimentally for two years, allowing the Secretary-General to recommend a longer-term solution. This suggestion was supported by India and the United Kingdom, and by Cuba, which abstained in the vote. It was opposed by New Zealand, which voted for the Egyptian proposal. Canada viewed the ACABQ proposals as the best solution for the teachers and the United Nations.

The Bahamas abstained because it was not satisfied about career development aspects and the ultimate status of the teachers.

Language incentives

Following discussion by ICSC at its July/August 1983 session of the scheme of financial and other incentives applied to encourage the broader use of languages in the United Nations Secretariat,[1] a majority of its members concluded that the scheme was not achieving its objective. They felt that the scheme as currently applied should not continue, that it would be desirable to harmonize, among organizations in the United Nations system, practices to encourage and recognize language knowledge, and that a solution should be found as soon as possible. ICSC instructed its secretariat to examine alternative approaches, such as enhanced training facilities, and to report back with recommendations.

The extension of language incentives to additional organizations in the United Nations system, including accelerated salary increments and other payments in recognition of language skills, was advocated by FICSA in its comments to the Fifth Committee on personnel matters.[10]

In resolution 38/232, the Assembly requested the Secretary-General to report in 1984 on the status of the linguistic skills of United Nations staff, including the effects of the language incentive programme, and to propose further measures if necessary to improve the situation.

Staff representation

Following consideration by its CCAQ Working Party on Staff Representation (Geneva, 26 and 27 January 1983),[38] ACC decided in April to invite CCISUA to address it at future sessions when issues of concern to the international civil service were on the agenda.[39] It also reaffirmed its past invitation, couched in similar terms, to FICSA, which had previously been the sole staff organization heard by ACC and ICSC.

At its July/August session,[1] ICSC approved three criteria to determine whether to invite staff bodies to attend and address its meetings and those of its subsidiary bodies: the constituent organizations of such a body should meet specified criteria of recognition, the body should represent staff preferably in more than one United Nations organization and it should represent at least 25 per cent of the international civil service within the common system. On the basis of those criteria, the Commission invited CCISUA to participate but decided not to invite the Federation of Associations and Unions of the International Civil Service.

Staff representatives of the United Nations Secretariat, in their written comments to the Fifth Committee on personnel questions,[11] stressed the importance of staff representation and expressed the view that the staff had an important role in contributing to administrative efficiency, streamlining personnel procedures and making the United Nations more responsive to its Members' needs.

Provisions on staff representative bodies and joint staff/management machinery were included in provisional amendments to the Staff Rules of the United Nations acted on by the General Assembly in December (see below).

Field staff

At its July/August 1983 session,[1] ICSC authorized a review of duty stations and of the allowances and benefits received by staff. This was to be conducted by its tripartite Working Group on the Classification of Duty Stations according to Conditions of Life and Work, composed of representatives of the Commission, United Nations organizations and staff. ICSC also requested other information on conditions of service in the field, with emphasis on health and security.

The Commission also authorized additional reimbursements for field staff relating to departure expenses and family medical expenses (see "Other allowances" below, under STAFF COSTS).

The concerns of field staff were dealt with in comments by the three groups of staff representatives which submitted written statements to the Fifth Committee. Declaring that conditions of service in the United Nations system compared unfavourably with those offered by other development assistance organizations, FICSA called for the elaboration of a methodology to set benefit levels and review them periodically, and asked that ICSC complete its studies without further delay.[10] Better security arrangements (see PRIVILEGES AND IMMUNITIES below), the possible introduction of hazardous duty pay, and improved rotation policies that would encourage training were urged by CCISUA.[12] Staff representatives of the United Nations Secretariat stressed staff security concerns, adequate briefing about local conditions, the provision of housing in areas where the local market was limited and expanded medical coverage.[11]

In resolution 38/232, the General Assembly noted the progress by ICSC in its review of conditions of service in the field and asked to be kept informed of developments. It also welcomed the ICSC decision to establish job classification standards for local recruits in field offices where several organizations of the United Nations system employed staff in common areas of work.

Staff Rules of the United Nations

Provisionally amended staff rules designed to update and improve the Secretariat machinery for handling staff appeals of administrative decisions were prepared by the Secretary-General in 1983. The rules covered the establishment of Joint Appeals Boards and detailed the appeals procedure.

Two other rules changes were also prepared and reported to the General Assembly. One, concerning payment of the installation grant to compensate staff for expenses they incurred as a result of transfer to a different duty station, provided for full payment as long as the staff member had not served at that duty station during the previous year; under the previous rule, the full grant was not paid unless the absence had been for at least two years. The second change amended the rule on suspension of staff pending investigation of alleged misconduct, so as to provide for suspension with pay as the norm.

All these changes were reported in September 1983 in the Secretary-General's annual report to the Fifth Committee[4] on amendments to the Staff Rules of the United Nations since the previous report in 1982.[40] In accordance with revisions to the Staff Regulations approved by the Assembly in December 1982,[41] the provisional amendments were to take effect on 1 January 1984, the beginning of the year following their submission to the Assembly. The report also covered changes in salary scales and certain allowances for the General Service and related categories, put into effect under the Secretary-General's authority.

The Secretary-General also submitted provisional amendments to the Staff Rules pertaining to staff/management relations, made to implement amendments to the Staff Regulations approved by the Assembly in December 1982.[41]

GENERAL ASSEMBLY ACTION

The General Assembly, by decision 38/450, requested the Secretary-General to review two subparagraphs of the provisional amendments to the Staff Rules in the light of amendments proposed by the USSR. The Assembly acted without vote on the recommendation of the Fifth Committee.

Amendments to the Staff Rules

At its 104th plenary meeting, on 20 December 1983, the General Assembly, on the recommendation of the Fifth Committee:

(a) Took note of the report of the Secretary-General on the amendments to the Staff Rules;

(b) Requested the Secretary-General to review the text of staff rules 108.1, subparagraph (d), and 108.2, subparagraph (c), in the light of the amendments submitted by the delegation of the Union of Soviet Socialist Republics.

General Assembly decision 38/450

Adopted without vote

Approved by Fifth Committee (A/38/744) without vote, 19 December (meeting 73); oral proposal by Chairman, based on informal consultations on proposal by USSR, amended by German Democratic Republic; agenda item 116.
Meeting numbers. GA 38th session: 5th Committee 41, 45-48, 50, 53, 60, 73; plenary 104.

The two rules referred to in the Assembly decision concerned staff/management relations. Rule 108.1, on staff representative bodies, defined the scope of action of staff councils and similar bodies elected by the staff at each duty station. According to subparagraph (d), they could participate in identifying, examining and resolving staff welfare issues, including conditions of work, general conditions of life and other personnel policies, and could make proposals to the Secretary-General on behalf of the staff. Rule 108.2, on joint staff/management machinery, provided for joint advisory committees at each duty station, composed of equal numbers of representatives of the staff and the Secretary-General, and a similarly constituted Secretariat-wide body. According to subparagraph (c), instructions or directives embodying the joint bodies' recommendations, if made with the staff representatives' concurrence, would be regarded as satisfying the requirements of rule 108.1 *(d)*.

The USSR proposed orally in the Fifth Committee the deletion of "and other personnel policies" from rule 108.1 *(d)* and subparagraph *(c)* from rule 108.2. It described the purpose of the proposal as the elimination of provisions that might be interpreted as giving staff representatives powers that ran counter to the Secretary-General's role as chief administrative officer.

The Committee accepted an oral motion by the German Democratic Republic, made after informal consultations, to have the Assembly request the Secretary-General to review the two subparagraphs in the light of the USSR amendments.

Privileges and immunities of the international civil service

Measures to safeguard staff security and encourage respect for the privileges and immunities of officials of the United Nations, the specialized agencies and related intergovernmental organizations were called for by the General Assembly in December 1983.

ACC activities. Administrative measures to clarify and safeguard the privileges and immunities of the international civil service, especially of field staff, were discussed at an ACC *Ad Hoc* Inter-Agency Meeting on Security Matters held at Geneva on 24 and 25 January 1983.[42] Among those attending were designated officials responsible for security co-ordination in the various organizations.

Report of the Secretary-General. In October 1983, the Secretary-General, on behalf of ACC, submitted to the Fifth Committee the third in a series of annual reports originally requested by the General Assembly in 1980[43] on problems that had arisen in regard to the exercise by international officials of the privileges and immunities necessary for the independent exercise of their functions. The report[5] gave information as of 31 August 1983 on 98 cases of officials from 13 organizations or units in the United Nations system who had been arrested and detained in 21 countries or areas. Twenty-three of these, involving four organizations and five countries or areas, were listed as cases in which the Secretary-General or other organization head had not been able, during the year covered, to exercise fully his responsibility for protecting officials. Of the latter group, 20 were officials of UNRWA, including 15 in Lebanon.

The chief difficulties, according to the report, concerned the arrest and detention of locally recruited nationals whose status as "officials" for purposes of privileges and immunities was not always readily accepted and understood by local authorities.

The report also detailed other cases in which the safety or security of officials had been affected, as well as problems arising over tax exemption for locally recruited international officials, and travel restrictions in territories occupied by Israel. It stated that a problem relating to the duty-free importation of furniture and effects of certain officials serving in Thailand had been resolved.

The Secretary-General mentioned the issuance in December 1982 of two Secretariat documents (annexed to the report) outlining procedures to be followed in the event of arrest and detention, and clarifying for all staff the nature and scope of their privileges and immunities. He said he would give favourable consideration to proposals by the United Nations Staff-Management Co-ordination Committee, including one for an interdepartmental advisory committee in the Secretariat to report to him on each case of arrest and detention, and another for a co-ordinator to act as a focal point for reporting cases. He would also consider the wider use of sending a special representative to the country concerned when other channels were not productive. He concluded by calling for the full observance by all concerned—Member States, organizations and officials—of the law and practice of international immunities.

The Secretary-General submitted an addendum to this report in November, updating information on UNRWA staff, and a separate report in October on UNRWA staff detained in Lebanon by Israeli authorities (see p. 347).

Comments of staff representatives. Staff security was also addressed by the three bodies of staff representatives in their written comments on personnel questions to the Fifth Committee.

The first of these, FICSA,[10] pointed out that the steady stream of cases of arrest, detention, disappearance or death of staff members had continued unabated. It appealed to the States concerned to grant immediate access by United Nations officials to any staff member arrested or detained, to provide full details of facts and charges, to ensure due legal process, to release those against whom no charges had been made, to find humane solutions to pending cases, and to respect international conventions.

Urging the Assembly to endorse strong measures, CCISUA[12] stated that the growing tendency by some Members to interfere in the independent role of the international civil service by actions against locally recruited staff must be discontinued.

Staff representatives of the United Nations Secretariat[11] presented a proposal calling on Member States to recognize their obligation to report immediately to the Secretary-General any arrest or detention of a staff member, disclose charges, grant access by United Nations authorities and allow the Organization to be represented in legal proceedings. States would also be asked to recognize the primacy of the Charter of the United Nations over national legislation where staff members' rights were concerned, respect the independence of United Nations officials in their own countries and elsewhere, recognize an obligation not to interfere with appointments and other personnel actions, honour compensation claims in cases of staff members killed or injured as a result of detention, and commit themselves to collective measures against Governments that had not respected the privileges and immunities of the international civil service.

GENERAL ASSEMBLY ACTION

Further measures to safeguard the privileges and immunities of the international civil service were called for by the Assembly in resolution 38/230 of 20 December 1983, adopted without vote on the recommendation of the Fifth Committee.

Respect for the privileges and immunities of officials of the United Nations and the specialized agencies and related organizations

The General Assembly,

Recalling its resolutions 35/212 of 17 December 1980, 36/232 of 18 December 1981 and 37/236 of 21 December 1982,

Recalling that, under Article 105 of the Charter of the United Nations, officials of the Organization shall enjoy in the territory of each of its Member States such privileges and immunities as are necessary for the independent exercise of their functions in connection with the Organization, which is indispensable for the proper discharge of their duties,

Recalling the obligation of the staff in the conduct of their duty to observe fully the laws and regulations of Member States,

1. *Takes note with concern* of the reports submitted to the General Assembly by the Secretary-General on behalf of the Administrative Committee on Co-ordination, which show a continuing neglect of the observance of the principles related to respect for the privileges and immunities of officials of the United Nations and the specialized agencies and related organizations;

2. *Expresses particular concern* at the detention of a great number of officials of the United Nations Relief and Works Agency for Palestine Refugees in the Near East and about the cases in which full exercise of the right of functional protection was impossible, as mentioned in the reports of the Secretary-General;

3. *Reaffirms* the above-mentioned resolutions;

4. *Welcomes* the measures already taken by the Secretary-General to enhance the safety and protection of international civil servants, as outlined in paragraph 7 of his report;

5. *Calls upon* the Secretary-General, as chief administrative officer of the Organization, to continue personally to act as the focal point in promoting and ensuring the observance of the privileges and immunities of officials of the United Nations and the specialized agencies and related organizations by using such means as are available to him;

6. *Welcomes* the designation by the Secretary-General of officials to take on special responsibilities for the security and protection of the Organization's personnel and property;

7. *Urges* the Secretary-General to give priority through his designated officials, as mentioned in annex III to his report, to the reporting and prompt follow-up of cases of arrest, detention and possible other matters relating to the security of officials of the United Nations and the specialized agencies and related organizations;

8. *Calls upon* the staff of the United Nations to comply with the obligations arising from the Staff Regulations of the United Nations, in particular regulation 1.8;

9. *Requests* the Secretary-General, as Chairman of the Administrative Committee on Co-ordination, to suggest in his annual report to be submitted to the General Assembly at its thirty-ninth session further measures to be taken with regard to the safety and protection of international civil servants.

General Assembly resolution 38/230

20 December 1983	Meeting 104	Adopted without vote

Approved by Fifth Committee (A/38/744) without vote, 19 December (meeting 73); 13-nation draft (A/C.5/38/L.19); agenda item 116.

Sponsors: Australia, Bahamas, Belgium, Canada, Denmark, Germany, Federal Republic of, Ireland, Netherlands, New Zealand, Norway, Sierra Leone, Spain, Sweden.

Meeting numbers. GA 38th session: 5th Committee 41, 45-48, 50, 53, 60, 73; plenary 104.

In resolution 38/83 I of 15 December 1983, on the protection of Palestine refugees, the Assembly called on Israel to release forthwith all detained Palestine refugees, including UNRWA employees.

REFERENCES

[1]A/38/30 & Add.1. [2]A/38/7/Add.7. [3]A/38/347 & Corr.1. [4]A/C.5/38/10 & Corr.1. [5]A/C.5/38/17 & Corr.1 & Add.1. [6]A/C.5/38/18. [7]A/C.5/38/16. [8]A/C.5/38/14 and 22. [9]A/C.5/38/27. [10]A/C.5/38/23. [11]A/C.5/38/29. [12]A/C.5/38/40. [13]A/C.5/38/L.23. [14]A/C.5/38/L.28. [15]YUN 1974, p. 876, GA res. 3357(XXIX), annex, 18 Dec. 1974. [16]A/38/760 & Corr.1. [17]A/C.5/38/28. [18]A/38/7/Add.4. [19]YUN 1978, p. 988, GA res. 33/143, 20 Dec. 1978. [20]YUN 1980, p. 1164, GA res. 35/210, 17 Dec. 1980. [21]YUN 1981, p. 1318. [22]YUN 1982, p. 1447. [23]A/C.5/38/8. [24]YUN 1982, p. 1449, GA res. 37/235 A, 21 Dec. 1982. [25]Ibid., p. 1466. [26]Ibid., p. 1455, GA res. 37/126, 17 Dec. 1982. [27]A/AC.198/66. [28]A/C.5/38/L.20. [29]YUN 1982, p. 1461. [30]ACC/1983/PER/21. [31]ACC/1984/PER/1. [32]A/C.5/38/92 & Corr.1. [33]A/C.5/38/5. [34]YUN 1981, p. 1331, GA res. 36/235, sect. II, 18 Dec. 1981. [35]A/C.5/38/41. [36]YUN 1982, p. 1463. [37]A/38/7/Add.13. [38]ACC/1983/PER/10. [39]ACC/1983/DEC/1-10 (dec. 1983/3). [40]YUN 1982, p. 1464. [41]Ibid., GA res. 37/235 C, 21 Dec. 1982. [42]ACC/1983/2. [43]YUN 1980, p. 1142, GA res. 35/212, 17 Dec. 1980.

Staff costs

Salaries and allowances

Salaries

ICSC activities. In its 1983 report,[1] ICSC informed the General Assembly that the average net remuneration of international civil service Professional staff in the period from 1 October 1982 to 30 September 1983 was 16.5 per cent above that of matching grades in the United States federal civil service, down from an 18.2 per cent difference 12 months earlier. This calculation of the pay margin between the two services, performed annually at the behest of the Assembly in order to relate international civil service salaries to those of a comparator representing the best-paying national civil service, took into account net salaries and post adjustment payable to United Nations staff in New York, adjusted for the cost-of-living differential between New York and Washington, D. C. (In the international civil service, net salaries are those received by the staff after deduction of staff assessment; they correspond to after-tax salaries in national services.)

ICSC attributed the decrease in the margin since 1982 to a 4 per cent salary increase for the United States civil service in October 1982, lower United States federal tax rates, and bonuses and performance awards received by the United States Senior Executive Service. The only pay increase for the international civil service in New York during the period was a post adjustment increase in May 1983, raising average salaries by 5.9 per cent in response to a rise in the cost of living.

After several years of work on a methodology for comparing total compensation under the two systems, a majority of ICSC members agreed at its July/August session to submit two sets of margin calculations in future: the traditional one based on salary alone and a new one comparing all benefits, including pensions and insurance subsidies, except for expatriate benefits paid specifically for service outside the employees' home country. This action was taken after a majority endorsed a proposal covering the last outstanding issue in regard to the comparison. This was a formula to adjust for the fact that United States government employees, who had no mandatory retirement age, could earn higher pension benefits by remaining in service beyond 60 years whereas international civil servants had to retire at that age, thus limiting their pension entitlements.

With regard to General Service staff, ICSC surveyed best prevailing conditions of employment in Paris and in Montreal, Canada, and then recommended salary scales for employees in those cities of the United Nations Educational, Scientific and Cultural Organization and the International Civil Aviation Organization, respectively.

Comments of staff representatives. In its written comments on personnel issues submitted to the Fifth Committee in October 1983,[2] FICSA urged a 10 per cent increase in Professional staff salaries, on the ground that their purchasing power had declined substantially since the previous increase, approved in 1974[3] with effect from 1975.

With regard to the comparison of total compensation, FICSA expressed the view that the methodology would not be complete until a comparison was made of the benefits paid by the two civil services to employees serving outside their home country. In November, CCISUA urged that a review of total compensation be completed for Assembly consideration in 1984.[4]

GENERAL ASSEMBLY ACTION

In resolution 38/232 of 20 December 1983 on the international civil service, the General Assembly noted the pay margin between that service and the United States federal civil service, requested ICSC to complete the study of grade equivalents between the higher grades of the United Nations system and the United States Senior Executive Service, and asked it to report annually on the margin of total compensation. The Assembly also asked for an ICSC report in 1984 on longevity and merit steps in the various grade levels.

By decision 38/450 of 20 December, the Assembly took note of amendments to the Staff Rules of the United Nations reported by the Secretary-General in September, including revised salary scales for General Service staff at Headquarters, effective 1 October 1982, and Geneva, effective 1 February 1983.[5]

Post adjustment

By consensus, ICSC agreed at a special session in November 1983[6] to take no decision on post adjustment classifications of the main duty stations in the United Nations system. It thus left frozen the levels at which various locations were classified for purposes of determining how much post adjustment the staff serving there would receive as a supplement to base salaries in response to cost-of-living changes over time and purchasing power differentials between duty stations.

The operation of the post adjustment system, and specifically the results of cost-of-living surveys at six headquarters locations and Washington, D. C., were examined at the eighth session of the ICSC Advisory Committee on Post Adjustment Questions (ACPAQ), held at Rome, Italy, from 30 May to 10 June and resumed in New York from 31 October to 10 November. The ICSC secretariat had found the current post adjustment indices higher than the surveys justified. However, ACPAQ was unable to verify those results and asked the secretariat to reprocess them. As ACPAQ had not found the technical justification for making recommendations, ICSC concluded at its November session that it was not in a position to take specific decisions. Instead, it requested ACPAQ to make final recommendations in 1984 on the survey results, after which the Commission would again take up post adjustment classifications at the six duty stations.

The General Assembly, in resolution 38/232 of 20 December, expressed concern that ICSC had been unable to correct post adjustment classifications despite the fact that post adjustments had been found higher than justified by the cost-of-living surveys. It requested ICSC to expedite the application of revised methodology so as to improve the mechanism for adjusting remuneration to reflect more accurately the cost-of-living differences at various duty stations. Organization heads and their staff were asked to co-operate fully with ICSC in the application of the post adjustment system.

The expression of concern in section II, paragraph 1, of this resolution was added on an amendment by the United States, orally revised by the sponsor, which the Fifth Committee accepted by 32 votes to 21, with 32 abstentions.

Allowances

Education grant

On the recommendation of ICSC, the General Assembly, in December 1983, increased the maximum of the education grant payable to internationally recruited staff of the international civil service serving outside their home country. The grant was designed to reimburse such staff for a substantial share of the tuition and boarding costs they incurred in sending their children to schools, universities or colleges.

The level of the grant was fixed at 75 per cent of the cost of attending an educational institution, up to an annual maximum grant of $4,500 per child (increased from $3,000). In the case of disabled children, all costs would be reimbursed up to a $6,000 maximum (formerly $3,750). The limit of allowable boarding costs in cases where the institution did not provide board was fixed at $1,500 (formerly $1,100).

In recommending these increases, ICSC estimated their cost to the United Nations system at $1.7 million a year.[1] It agreed to review the level of the grant again in 1986.

In its written comments on personnel questions submitted to the Fifth Committee,[2] FICSA urged the extension of the grant to all international recruits, including those serving in their home country, and eventually to all staff regardless of category. It also favoured continuous monitoring by ICSC to ensure that the grant remained in line with educational fees.

Assembly approval of the increased education grant was included in section III of resolution 38/232. On an amendment by the United States, orally revised by the sponsor, a paragraph was added by which the Assembly requested ICSC to study the grant and to report in 1984. The amendment was approved in the Fifth Committee by 63 votes to 13, with 15 abstentions.

Other allowances

Decisions were taken during 1983 on four allowances and fringe benefits payable to the international civil service: secondary dependant's allowance, death grant, non-resident's allowance and housing rent subsidy. In addition, certain additional reimbursements for field staff were authorized.

Secondary dependant's allowance. At its July/August session,[1] ICSC confirmed existing rules on eligibility for this allowance, which was payable to all Professional staff, as well as to General Service staff at many duty stations, when a father, mother, brother or sister received substantial financial support from the staff member. In so doing, it did not accept the position of staff representatives that, for General Service staff, this should be considered as a social benefit applicable at all duty stations whether or not a similar benefit was paid by outside employers at a given location. Instead, the Commission decided that it should be paid only at duty stations where local practice called for such payment, in amounts determined by surveys of local pay scales. It also decided to study variations in eligibility criteria among outside employers at different duty stations, but in the mean time to apply universal criteria for all categories of staff everywhere. In cases where the allowance was currently being paid at duty stations where no local practice existed, or for persons not meeting universal eligibility standards, payments would continue to staff already receiving them but new staff, joining on 1 September 1983 or later, would have the entitlement only within the framework of local practice and the criteria decided by ICSC.

Death grant. Regarding this grant, payable to a survivor when a staff member died in service, ICSC, at its July/August session, recommended to the General Assembly the retention of the current scheme, whereby all costs (averaging $897,188 a year for the United Nations system) were met by the employing organization. It concluded that this would be more cost-effective than two other options—a 50-50 sharing of costs by organizations and staff, and a scheme arranged through an insurance company.

The Assembly, which in 1980 had requested ICSC to review the possibility of establishing a cost-effective contributory scheme,[7] approved the ICSC recommendation in resolution 38/232 of 20 December 1983.

Non-resident's allowance. Also in resolution 38/232, the Assembly noted an ICSC decision to modify the non-resident's allowance, payable to internationally recruited General Service staff at selected duty stations in Africa and Asia. As decided by ICSC at its July/August session, this allowance was to be granted for a fixed duration of five years from time of arrival and was to be non-pensionable. The amount, set in comparison with the assignment allowance received by Professional staff in similar circumstances, was to be $3,000 a year for staff with dependants and $2,400 a year for others. To protect acquired rights, allowances already being paid would not be reduced, but a staff member who opted for the new scheme in order to receive a higher allowance would have to accept the conditions of duration and non-pensionability.

The Assembly decided that the allowance, formerly pensionable, would be made non-pensionable for the time being, pending the outcome of a review by the United Nations Joint Staff Pension Board.

Housing rent subsidy. With effect from 1 April 1983, ICSC decided in March to extend the existing rent subsidy scheme for Professional staff to Headquarters and other duty stations not previously covered. Under the expanded scheme, applicable to newly appointed staff and those transferred from other duty stations, the United Nations or other employing organization would pay, for up to five years, a share of the amount by which the staff member's rent exceeded a "threshold rent". The subsidy would also be paid, but only for three years, when a staff member was obliged to rent new housing for reasons beyond his or her control, such as building demolition, eviction, or conversion of the dwelling to co-operative or condominium. The subsidy would decrease from 80 per cent of the difference the first year to 20 per cent in the fifth year. ICSC noted that the scheme would not cost the organizations extra money and might even result in savings, because the subsidies would tend to keep post adjustment rates down.

Noting this scheme in resolution 38/232, the Assembly requested ICSC to monitor it so as to ensure equity and effectiveness.

At its July/August session, ICSC agreed on a trial basis to grant a housing rent subsidy to internationally recruited General Service staff at high-rent duty stations where no non-resident's allowance was being paid. The annual subsidy would not exceed the limits fixed for that allowance—$3,000 for staff with dependants and $2,400 for others. ICSC instructed its secretariat to study the problem and report back with proposals in 1984.

Field staff. Also at that session, ICSC decided that, effective 1 September, United Nations organizations should reimburse their field staff for pre-departure hotel expenses incurred when they left a non-headquarters duty station. Reimbursement was to be limited to 10 days and to 60 per cent of the daily subsistence allowance payable at that duty station, and to half of that rate for dependants. The Commission also approved reimbursement of the costs of basic medical examinations for family members accompanying staff

assigned to countries where the majority of duty stations were classified as having adverse health conditions, up to a limit of $150 per staff member every two years. The annual cost of these two measures for the United Nations system was estimated at $200,000 for the first and $150,000 for the second.

Pensions

To improve the financial situation of the United Nations Joint Staff Pension Fund, the General Assembly decided in 1983 to raise the contribution rates of organizations of the United Nations system and their staff. The change, recommended by the United Nations Joint Staff Pension Board, marked the first increase in contribution rates since the Fund was established in 1946.[8]

The Assembly also decided to defer any increase in pensionable remuneration which might become due in 1984 as a result of the operation of the automatic formula that adjusted pension entitlements of serving staff to cost-of-living changes. The effect was to freeze such entitlements for Professional and top echelon staff of the international civil service until the Assembly re-examined the matter in 1984, following consideration by the Pension Board and ICSC.

As at 31 December 1983, the number of participants in the Pension Fund had risen by 1,466 since the same date in 1982, to 52,432. The increase was due in part to the impact of an amendment to the Regulations of the Fund approved by the General Assembly in December 1982, whereby participation in the Fund began upon commencing six months rather than one year of service with a participating organization.[9]

During 1983, the principal of the Fund increased by $352,363,028, to $3,115,548,779. On 31 December, the Fund was paying 7,001 retirement benefits, 7,065 early and deferred retirement benefits, 2,402 widows' and widowers' benefits, 3,937 children's benefits, 454 disability benefits and 40 secondary dependants' benefits. In the course of the year, it also paid 3,579 lump-sum withdrawal and other settlements.

Pension Board activities. The United Nations Joint Staff Pension Board held its thirty-first session in London from 4 to 14 July 1983.[10] Its Standing Committee met in New York from 4 to 6 October to make recommendations to the General Assembly on certain adjustments in the pension scheme for the international civil service.[11] These tripartite bodies—composed of representatives of the international civil service (participants), administrations of organizations in the United Nations system (employers) and intergovernmental bodies of the organizations—continued to oversee the Fund's operations.

The major item dealt with by the Board was the financial situation of the Fund, as measured by the actuarial balance, comparing projections of future income and anticipated benefit payments. The Board made recommendations to improve the existing imbalance, going beyond economy measures approved by the Assembly in December 1982.[9] It also devoted considerable attention to the management of the Fund's investments. In addition, it recommended a 1984 administrative budget and an addition to the 1983 budget, and dealt with miscellaneous matters pertaining to the functioning of the pension system, including the development of a cost-of-living index for pensioners.

GENERAL ASSEMBLY ACTION

On the recommendation of the Fifth Committee, the General Assembly, on 20 December 1983, adopted by recorded vote resolution 38/233.

Report of the United Nations Joint Staff Pension Board

The General Assembly,

Having considered the report of the United Nations Joint Staff Pension Board for 1983 to the General Assembly and to the member organizations of the United Nations Joint Staff Pension Fund, and the related report of the Advisory Committee on Administrative and Budgetary Questions,

Welcoming the improvement in the actuarial situation of the Fund as a result of the economy measures applied with effect from 1 January 1983,

Concerned at the continuing actuarial imbalance of the Fund and the mounting cost of the pension system,

Desirous of bringing about a further improvement in the actuarial situation of the Fund,

Concerned at the different evolution over the years of the levels of pensionable remuneration for staff in the Professional and higher categories and those of the comparator civil service,

Recalling its resolutions 3526(XXX) of 16 December 1975, 31/196 of 22 December 1976, 33/120 of 19 December 1978, 34/221 of 20 December 1979, 35/215 of 17 December 1980, 36/118 of 10 December 1981 and 37/131 of 17 December 1982,

Bearing in mind earlier General Assembly resolutions which stated, *inter alia,* that changes in the pension adjustment system should not lead to increases in the liabilities of Member States,

Conscious that a number of factors have combined to make necessary the consideration and adoption of significant remedial actions on the problem of the actuarial imbalance, including the raising of the rate of contributions hereinafter referred to,

Mindful of the social aspects of the pension system,

Aware that a co-operative effort by member organizations, participants and beneficiaries is required if the actuarial imbalance is to be reduced or eliminated, thereby securing an adequate level of benefits under the Fund,

I
Amendments to the Regulations of the United Nations Joint Staff Pension Fund

1. *Decides* that, with effect from 1 January 1984, the rate of contributions shall be raised from 21 to 21.75 per

cent of pensionable remuneration, of which the employing member organization shall pay 14.5 per cent and the participant 7.25 per cent;

2. *Amends* the Regulations of the United Nations Joint Staff Pension Fund, without retroactive effect, as set forth in the annex to the present resolution;

II
Measures to improve the actuarial balance of the Fund

Requests the United Nations Joint Staff Pension Board, with the assistance of the Committee of Actuaries, to consider, early in 1984, the various proposals discussed at the thirty-eighth session of the General Assembly with a view to reducing or eliminating the actuarial imbalance of the United Nations Joint Staff Pension Fund, including the following measures:

(a) Increasing to a realistic level the interest rate used to calculate the amount of the lump-sum commutation;

(b) Determination of the lump sum in net equivalent terms, subject to the reimbursement of any taxes payable thereon;

(c) Re-examination of the early retirement provisions, taking into account, *inter alia,* the observations made by the Committee of Actuaries;

(d) Imposition of a ceiling on the highest levels of pensions;

(e) Review of the two-track system followed to determine the initial amount of the pension and its subsequent adjustment;

(f) Re-examination of the survivor benefits under the Regulations of the Fund, together with alternative ways of financing them;

and to submit its findings and recommendations thereon and on such other measures as may be deemed appropriate, through the Advisory Committee on Administrative and Budgetary Questions, to the General Assembly at its thirty-ninth session;

III
Pensionable remuneration for the Professional and higher categories

1. *Decides* to review at its thirty-ninth session the pensionable remuneration for the Professional and higher categories;

2. *Requests* the International Civil Service Commission, in co-operation with the United Nations Joint Staff Pension Board, to submit to the General Assembly at its thirty-ninth session recommendations on the appropriate level of pensionable remuneration for the Professional and higher categories;

3. *Further requests* the International Civil Service Commission, in examining the comparative levels of pensionable remuneration in co-operation with the Board, to compare the levels of pension entitlements in the light of all the factors it brought to the attention of the General Assembly in its fifth annual report, as part of the total compensation comparisons to be carried out within the framework of the Noblemaire principle, and to report thereon to the Assembly by the beginning of its thirty-ninth session on the basis of the latest data available in 1984;

4. *Decides* that the implementation of any adjustment which may become due in 1984 on the basis of article 54 *(b)* of the Regulations of the United Nations Joint Staff Pension Fund shall be deferred until the General Assembly, at its thirty-ninth session, has considered the recommendations of the International Civil Service

Commission and the Board on the level of pensionable remuneration;

5. *Decides further* that, if the General Assembly is unable to take a decision on the level of pensionable remuneration at its thirty-ninth session, it will re-examine at that session the question of the deferment of implementation of adjustments which become due under article 54 *(b)* of the Regulations of the Fund;

6. *Requests* the Board, in the light of the recommendations on the level of pensionable remuneration, to recommend to the General Assembly, at its thirty-ninth session, consequential amendments to article 54 *(b)* of the Regulations of the Fund;

IV
Complementary Pension Scheme of the International Labour Organisation

Draws the attention of the International Labour Organisation to the strong concern expressed during the thirty-eighth session of the General Assembly about the need to maintain the unity, cohesion and integrity of the United Nations Joint Staff Pension system and to avoid any action which may have an adverse effect on the said system;

V
Emergency Fund

Authorizes the United Nations Joint Staff Pension Board to supplement the voluntary contributions to the Emergency Fund, for a further period of one year, by an amount not exceeding $100,000;

VI
Administrative expenses

Approves expenses, chargeable directly to the United Nations Joint Staff Pension Fund, totalling $6,723,100 (net) for 1984 and additional expenses of $17,700 (net) for 1983 for the administration of the Fund.

ANNEX
Amendments to the Regulations of the United Nations Joint Staff Pension Fund

Article 1
Definitions

(n) "Own contributions" shall mean the contributions, not exceeding the percentage of his pensionable remuneration specified in column B in article 25 *(a)*, made to the Fund by or on behalf of a participant in respect of contributory service under article 22, with interest, provided that, in respect of service in a member organization prior to its admission to membership in the Fund, which has been recognized as contributory, it shall mean:

Subparagraphs (i) and (ii) remain unchanged.

Article 21
Participation

(b) Participation shall cease when the organization by which the participant is employed ceases to be a member organization, or when he dies or separates from such member organization, except that participation shall not be deemed to have ceased where a participant resumes his contributory service with a member organization within twelve months after separation, without a benefit having been paid to him.

Article 22
Contributory service

(a) Contributory service shall accrue to a participant in pay status from the date of commencement to the date of cessation of his participation. For purposes of each of the articles 28 *(b)*, 28 *(c)* and 29 *(b)* separate periods of contributory service shall be aggregated except that in such aggregation no account shall be taken of periods of service in respect of which a withdrawal settlement was paid and which were not subsequently restored.

Article 25
Contributions

(a) Contributions by the participant and by the employing member organization shall be payable to the Fund concurrently with the accrual of contributory service under article 22 *(a)*, at the percentage rates of pensionable remuneration specified below:

A *For periods of contributory service*	B *By participants (per cent)*	C *By employing member organization (per cent)*
Before 1984	7.00	14.00
As from 1984	7.25	14.50

(b) (i) Contributions for the purpose of article 22 *(b)* in respect of a period of leave without pay shall be at a percentage rate of the pensionable remuneration of the participant equal to the applicable rates specified in *(a)* above payable by the participant and by the employing member organization, combined. Such contributions shall be payable concurrently with such leave by the participant in full or by the organization in full, or in part by the participant and in part by the organization;

Subparagraph (ii) remains unchanged.

(c) Contributions for the purpose of validation under article 23 shall be payable, with interest, by the participant and the organization in the amounts which would have been payable respectively by each, had service during the period been contributory.

Article 28
Retirement benefit

(b) The benefit shall, subject to *(d)* and *(e)* below, in respect of a period or periods of participation commencing on or after 1 January 1983, be payable at the standard rate obtained by multiplying:

Subparagraphs (i), (ii) and (iii) remain unchanged. However, in respect of a participant with a prior period of contributory service of five years or longer ending between 1 January 1978 and 31 December 1982, the standard annual rate specified above shall be calculated by taking into account as periods of contributory service for the purpose of subparagraphs (i), (ii) and (iii) above the period of contributory service before 1 January 1983.

(c) The benefit shall, subject to *(d)* and *(e)* below, in respect of any period of participation commencing prior to 1 January 1983, be payable at the standard annual rate obtained by multiplying:

(i) The first thirty years of the participant's contributory service, by 2 per cent of his final average remuneration, and

(ii) The years of his contributory service in excess of thirty, but not exceeding five, by 1 per cent of his final average remuneration.

Article 32
Deferment of payment or choice of benefit

(a) The payment to a participant of a withdrawal settlement, or the exercise by a participant of a choice available to him between one benefit and another, or between a form of benefit involving payment in a lump sum and

another form, may be deferred at his request at the time of separation for a period of twelve months.

Article 40
Effect of re-entry into participation

(b) Such a participant, who again becomes a participant and is again separated after at least five years of additional contributory service, shall also be entitled, at the time of such subsequent separation, in respect of such service and subject to *(d)* below, to a retirement, early retirement or deferred retirement benefit, or a withdrawal settlement under article 28, 29, 30 or 31, as the case may be.

(c) Such a participant, who again becomes a participant and is again separated after less than five years of additional contributory service, shall, in respect of such service, become entitled to:

(i) A withdrawal settlement under article 31; or

(ii) If he is at least age fifty-five at such separation, and subject to *(d)* below, a retirement, early retirement or deferred retirement benefit, as the case may be, under article 28, 29 or 30, based on the length of such additional contributory service; such benefit may not be commuted into a lump sum, in whole or in part, and shall not be subject to any minimum provisions.

(d) Payment of benefits under *(b)* or *(c)* (ii) above shall commence on the date of the resumption or commencement, as the case may be, of payment of benefits suspended under *(a)* above. In no event shall the total benefits payable to or on account of a former participant in respect of separate periods of contributory service exceed the benefits which would have been payable had his participation in the Fund been continuous.

General Assembly resolution 38/233

20 December 1983   Meeting 104   127-10-2 (recorded vote)

Approved by Fifth Committee (A/38/746) by vote (78-9-2), 16 December (meeting 68); draft by Vice-Chairman (A/C.5/38/L.24), based on informal consultations; agenda item 118.

Meeting numbers. GA 38th session: 5th Committee 28, 33, 36, 38, 45, 68; plenary 104.

Recorded vote in Assembly as follows:

In favour: Algeria, Argentina, Australia, Austria, Bahamas, Bahrain, Bangladesh, Barbados, Belgium, Belize, Benin, Bhutan, Bolivia, Botswana, Brazil, Burma, Burundi, Canada, Chad, Chile, China, Colombia, Congo, Costa Rica, Cyprus, Democratic Kampuchea, Democratic Yemen, Denmark, Djibouti, Dominican Republic, Ecuador, Egypt, El Salvador, Ethiopia, Fiji, Finland, France, Gabon, Gambia, Germany, Federal Republic of, Ghana, Greece, Guatemala, Guinea, Guinea-Bissau, Guyana, Haiti, Honduras, Iceland, India, Indonesia, Iran, Iraq, Ireland, Israel, Italy, Ivory Coast, Jamaica, Japan, Jordan, Kenya, Kuwait, Lebanon, Lesotho, Liberia, Libyan Arab Jamahiriya, Luxembourg, Madagascar, Malawi, Malaysia, Maldives, Mali, Malta, Mauritania, Mauritius, Mexico, Morocco, Nepal, Netherlands, New Zealand, Niger, Nigeria, Norway, Oman, Pakistan, Panama, Papua New Guinea, Paraguay, Peru, Philippines, Portugal, Qatar, Rwanda, Saint Lucia, Saint Vincent and the Grenadines, Samoa, Sao Tome and Principe, Saudi Arabia, Senegal, Sierra Leone, Singapore, Somalia, Spain, Sri Lanka, Sudan, Suriname, Swaziland, Sweden, Syrian Arab Republic, Thailand, Togo, Trinidad and Tobago, Tunisia, Turkey, Uganda, United Arab Emirates, United Kingdom, United Republic of Cameroon, United Republic of Tanzania, United States, Upper Volta, Uruguay, Vanuatu, Venezuela, Yemen, Yugoslavia, Zambia.

Against: Bulgaria, Byelorussian SSR, Czechoslovakia, German Democratic Republic, Hungary, Mongolia, Poland, Romania, Ukrainian SSR, USSR.

Abstaining: Afghanistan, Cuba.

Explaining its negative vote, the USSR disagreed in principle with any increase in Member States' contributions to the pension scheme and stated that the economy measures proposed were inadequate to eliminate the actuarial imbalance.

Though voting in favour, Argentina voiced reservations regarding the decision to defer adjustments in pensionable remuneration. Benin was pleased that the text omitted mention of a higher retirement age and hoped the Pension Board would not reopen the subject. Kenya reserved its position on the specific issues which the Pension Board and ICSC were asked to study and which the Assembly was to consider in 1984.

The United Nations Under-Secretary-General for Administration and Management told the Fifth Committee that representatives of the administrations and staff of organizations participating in the pension system were profoundly concerned at, and regarded as undesirable, unjustified and legally contestable, the decision to defer adjustments in pensionable remuneration. Expressing similar concern, the ICSC Chairman said the decision amounted to an amendment of the Regulations of the Pension Fund without consulting the participating organizations and without prior study.

The Fifth Committee annexed to its report to the Assembly on this item a paper[12] containing statistical data on the evolution since 1971 of the levels of pensionable remuneration and retirement benefits of staff in the Professional and higher categories under the United Nations system and those of the United States federal civil service.

In other action pertaining to pensions, the Assembly, in resolution 38/239 of 20 December, amended the Pension Scheme Regulations of the International Court of Justice (ICJ), affecting members of the Court. Retirement income of certain other non-Secretariat officials was dealt with in a report by the Secretary-General (see under OTHER UN OFFICIALS below).

Pension Fund financing

Financial situation and amendments to the Regulations

An actuarial valuation of the Pension Fund as at 31 December 1982, performed by the Board's Consulting Actuary (George B. Buck Consulting Actuaries, Inc.), showed an improvement in the Fund's financial situation since the last such valuation two years previously. This was attributed largely to the latest economy measures, which took effect on 1 January 1983. However, calculations based on seven different sets of assumptions about salaries, interest earnings and inflation rates for pensions after retirement all indicated that the current contribution rates would be insufficient to meet the Fund's long-run obligations to pensioners.

Using a "regular valuation basis" designated by the Board's Committee of Actuaries, the Fund's imbalance was found to be 4.79 per cent, down from 7.32 per cent two years previously. This figure represented the amount by which contributions to the Fund by participants and their employing organizations would have to be increased above the current rate of 21 per cent of pensionable remuneration (14 per cent by organizations and 7 per cent by staff) in order to restore the balance.

After reviewing these results, the Committee of Actuaries recommended three steps to improve the Fund's financial situation: a gradual increase in the contribution rate to 24 per cent of pensionable remuneration, a higher age for mandatory retirement and consideration of further reducing early retirement benefits.

The Board accepted the first two of these proposals. It recommended that the Assembly approve a 3 per cent increase in the contribution rate, to take place in four equal stages of 0.75 per cent each, starting on 1 January 1984 and continuing every two years until 1 January 1990, by which time it would reach 24 per cent. The organizations would pay two thirds of the increase (about $8.6 million a year for the first round) and the employees one third (about $4.3 million). The Board also reaffirmed its 1981 recommendation that the mandatory retirement age be raised from 60 to 62 years[13] (see also STAFF COMPOSITION above). However, it decided not to endorse the Committee's third recommendation, citing the advantages of the Fund's liberal early retirement provisions for the organizations and staff alike.

Commenting on these proposals in its November 1983 report to the Assembly on pensions,[14] ACABQ agreed in principle that the contribution rate should be increased, in view of what it saw as the likelihood that the imbalance would progressively worsen if left uncorrected. However, it recommended that the Assembly initially approve only the first of the proposed increases and request the Board to review the situation on the basis of the December 1984 actuarial valuation, making any further increases subject to prior Assembly confirmation.

The Assembly, in resolution 38/233, decided on a 0.75 rise in the contribution rate with effect from 1 January 1984 but made no reference to possible future increases. It requested the Board to review various proposals to improve the actuarial situation and to report back in 1984 .

The Assembly also approved several amendments to the Regulations of the Fund intended to correct anomalies resulting from the package of economy measures it had adopted in 1982. These changes were recommended by the Pension Board's Standing Committee, which met in October at the Board's request to study this problem.[11] The Consulting Actuary informed the Standing Committee that these adjustments would have an extremely small financial impact.

The amendments provided for clarification or corrective action in three areas.

The first related to the reduced annual rate of accumulation of pension benefits for persons entering the Fund on or after 1 January 1982—1.5 per cent during the first five years of service, 1.75 during the next five and 2 per cent thereafter up to a career maximum of 25 years. For those entering prior to 1 January 1983, the rate was 2 per cent during the first 30 years and 1 per cent thereafter up to a career maximum of 35 years. Under the new amendments, participants with broken service periods, such as technical assistance experts rehired for a series of projects, would have those periods added together for the purpose of determining the accumulation rate, rather than having to stay indefinitely at the 1.5 per cent rate until they had five years of continuous service. However, persons who had not been participants during the five years following 1 January 1978 would be treated as new entrants if they rejoined after 1 January 1983.

The second change related to the provision limiting to five years the length of prior service which a person returning to the United Nations system after a break could have restored to his or her service record for pension purposes. The new amendments provided that, if the break in service was no more than 12 months, service would not be deemed to have been interrupted.

The third change related to a provision that, if persons leaving the system before age 50 elected to receive a deferred pension instead of withdrawing their full entitlement in a lump sum, cost-of-living adjustments would not be applied to the value of that pension until the prospective recipients reached 50 years of age. The new amendments allowed all persons affected by this provision, and who had been separated before 1 January 1983, to choose again between a deferred benefit and a withdrawal settlement. If they chose the latter, they would receive the amount they would have been given on separation plus 6.5 per cent compounded interest, corresponding to the Fund's average investment return.

Investments

The market value of Pension Fund investments stood at $3,519,891,000 as at 31 December 1983, compared to $2,975,117,000 a year earlier. Income of the Fund from interest and dividends during 1983, less investment management costs, was $203,670,000.

According to a report of the Secretary-General on the Fund's investments for the 12 months ended 31 March, submitted to the Fifth Committee in October,[15] the investment return for the year was 27.05 per cent, the highest ever recorded for the Fund. Over the preceding 33 years, the book value of the investment portfolio had risen from $13 million to $2,790 million, a compound increase of

18 per cent a year. The report said that a turn-around in investment market conditions, sparked by falling interest rates, had been largely responsible for the high rate of return in 1982/83.

During the preceding two years, the report stated, emphasis had been placed on investments in the United States, where yields had been higher than elsewhere. The non-dollar portion of the Fund's portfolio, which had stood at 40 per cent in 1982, had declined to 38 per cent by 31 March 1983. Investment in equities (stocks) amounted to 52 per cent of the portfolio's market value, compared with 47 per cent a year earlier, the shift from bonds having been made in response to the sharp rebound in the equity market.

In a section of the report on implementation of General Assembly resolutions, the Secretary-General said that funds from investment income and contributions were sufficient to cover increasing investment in developing countries without resorting to sale of transnational corporation stocks. As at 30 June 1983, development-related investments had reached $554 million at cost, up from $481 million a year earlier, and represented 19.2 per cent of total investments. Most of these ($344 million in 1982, rising to $421 million in 1983) were in international development institutions rather than directly invested in specific countries. Investments in Africa had risen to $50.2 million from $27.6 million.

The Pension Board reviewed the investments picture in July. During the discussion, according to its report to the Assembly,[10] particular emphasis was placed on diversification as a means of ensuring the integrity of the Fund's assets and on the requirement that all investments meet strict criteria. In deciding to recommend a gradual increase in the rates of contribution to the Fund (see above), the Board took note of the fact that the inflation-adjusted rate of return over the previous 23 years had been only 1.3 per cent annually.

Following a recommendation by the Board of Auditors that the administration make maximum use of the latest technology for portfolio analysis, provision for subscriptions to computerized economic data services was included in the Fund's 1984 administrative budget, as approved by the Assembly in December 1983 (see next section).

GENERAL ASSEMBLY ACTION

Decision 38/452 was adopted without vote by the General Assembly on a recommendation of the Fifth Committee.

Investments of the United Nations Joint Staff Pension Fund

At its 104th plenary meeting, on 20 December 1983, the General Assembly, on the recommendation of the Fifth Committee, took note of the report of the Secretary-General on the investments of the United Nations Joint Staff Pension Fund.

General Assembly decision 38/452

Adopted without vote

Approved by Fifth Committee (A/38/746) without vote, 16 December (meeting 68); oral proposal by Chairman; agenda item 118.
Meeting numbers. GA 38th session: 5th Committee 28, 33, 36, 38, 45, 68; plenary 104.

Budgets for 1983 and 1984

In resolution 38/233 of 20 December 1983, the General Assembly approved an additional $17,700 in regard to the administrative expenses of the Pension Fund in 1983, and a total of $6,723,100 for 1984. These two amounts, net of staff assessment, were recommended by the Pension Board[10] and endorsed by ACABQ.[14] The 1983 increase, raising estimated expenses for the year to $5,973,000, was attributed to a rise in investment costs, partly offset by administrative savings due to vacant posts. The $750,100 increase between 1983 and 1984 was attributed mainly to an increase in advisory and custodial fees due to the assumed higher market value of the Fund's investment portfolio.

The Fund's secretariat was to be increased to 84 posts by the conversion of 5 temporary positions to established posts. In addition, one new post, for a data collection and management information supervisor, was to be added to the Investment Management Section of the Office of the United Nations Controller, raising its complement to 11.

Accounts for 1982

The Board of Auditors, in its report on the 1982 accounts of the Pension Fund annexed to the Pension Board's 1983 report,[10] made several recommendations to improve financial and administrative management, including a suggestion that the Fund strengthen procedures to verify that beneficiaries were still alive. The Pension Board, though concluding that existing verification arrangements were adequate, requested its Secretary to keep the matter under review. On another point, it accepted the Auditors' suggestion that the Fund's Administrative Manual be amended to specify the responsibility of the United Nations Internal Audit Service for internal audit of all operational and financial aspects of the Fund.

Cost-of-living index

In resolution 38/232 of 20 December 1983, the General Assembly approved the development of a special index for pensioners to replace the post adjustment index used since 1981 to determine cost-of-living adjustments to benefits paid to retired staff members living at different locations.

A method for applying such an index was recommended in 1983 by both the Pension

Board[10] and ICSC,[1] in response to a 1980 Assembly request that the matter be given high priority.[16] The purpose was to have an index reflecting the expenditure patterns of retirees, rather than to rely for pension adjustments on the post adjustment index, which was designed to measure the purchasing power of the salaries of serving staff.

According to the approach recommended by the two bodies and accepted by the Assembly, the special index would initially exclude the impact of national income tax. However, for locations where the index indicated the need to raise pension payments, the cost-of-living differential would be lowered where pension income was not taxed or was taxed at a substantially lower rate than in New York. ICSC found that this approach would be less costly to the Pension Fund than if the special index automatically took account of national income tax along with costs relating to consumables, housing and similar factors.

Work on developing a special index for pensioners continued in ACPAQ, which at its May/June session expressed the view that more case studies were needed to judge the effects of such an index. Initial studies by the ICSC secretariat, based on four high-cost locations, showed few differences between the results given by the special index and the post adjustment index, but ACPAQ felt that it could not draw conclusions from such a small sample.

Other pension questions

The Pension Board, in its 1983 report,[10] responded to 1982 requests by the Assembly[9] that it consider two types of problems relating to the financial obligations of pensioners to their spouses or former spouses: the absence of effective measures within the pension scheme for dealing with such obligations, and the effects of the dissolution of a marriage on survivors' entitlements. The Board expressed the view that such questions should be left to national tribunals. This view was endorsed by ACABQ in its report on pensions.[14]

In response to another 1982 request by the Assembly,[9] the Board informed it that few persons employed by United Nations organizations for periods of at least six months were expressly excluded, by the terms of their appointment, from participation in the Pension Fund. Consequently, it saw no need to change the Fund regulation allowing such exclusion.

The Board also reported that it had discussed a proposal being considered by ILO for a complementary pension scheme to provide additional coverage for ILO Professional staff. The balance of opinion in the Board was that the Board could not support the proposal, primarily because nothing should be done to jeopardize efforts to improve the Pension Fund's actuarial status. The Board's concern was shared by ACABQ,[14] which stated that, if organizations participating in the Fund adopted complementary schemes, the costs to both organizations and participants would be significantly higher.

In written comments on personnel questions circulated to the Fifth Committee,[2] FICSA urged flexibility that would allow individual organizations to resolve local issues.

In resolution 38/233 of 20 December, the Assembly drew the attention of ILO to the strong concern expressed in the Assembly about the need to maintain the unity, cohesion and integrity of the existing pension system and to avoid any action that might adversely affect it.

Other fringe benefits

Health insurance

In December 1983, the General Assembly, responding to rising health insurance costs which especially affected staff at United Nations Headquarters, approved the experimental use of a formula devised by ICSC authorizing the Organization to pay a larger share of the premiums than the 50-50 ratio between employer and employee payments which had been the previous norm.

ICSC considered this issue in March and July/August,[1] in response to a December 1982 request by the Assembly that it examine the need to raise the ratio of the organizations' contributions for the health insurance of their staff.[17] It agreed that the matter should be considered from the point of view of all staff of the United Nations system at all duty stations. On behalf of the organizations, the Chairman of CCAQ had taken the position that, as several organizations had no problem with the 50-50 share in effect at most locations while others proposed a 2 to 1 ratio, the matter should not be pursued on an inter-agency basis.

ICSC noted that the 50-50 ratio had produced satisfactory results in most instances, but that some organizations had experienced serious difficulties because of high health-care costs at one or more locations. The health insurance contribution was a relatively small part of total compensation for all categories of staff. Nevertheless, whereas the staff contribution amounted to about 3 per cent of net salary for staff with dependants at Geneva and Vienna, it was above 6 per cent in New York, indicating apparent difficulties with the 50-50 formula at that location.

ICSC decided to supply organization heads with figures showing average staff contributions for health insurance as a proportion of total remuneration, weighted by the number of staff at the seven headquarters locations of the United Nations system. Where the ratio was above average, it said, those officials might wish to propose to their legislative bodies cost-sharing formulae that would reduce the staff share to a level in line with the average.

The Secretary-General, in an October note to the Fifth Committee,[18] endorsed the ICSC recommendations, while observing that he would have preferred the world-wide application of a 2 to 1 ratio. He proposed that the new rate take effect on 1 January 1983 rather than 1 January 1984 as recommended by ICSC. He estimated the additional cost, for the United Nations regular budget and extrabudgetary programmes, at $1.8 million in 1983, $3.8 million in 1984 and $4.9 million in 1985. He also proposed, with the Assembly's concurrence, to liberalize eligibility requirements for after-service health insurance.

In support of the argument for an increase in the organizations' contributions, he noted that between May 1978 and April 1983, while the cost of living had risen by 49 per cent in New York, the cost of health insurance under the commercially insured Headquarters plans had gone up by an average of 123 per cent. A similar increase had occurred in respect of the world-wide plan for United Nations system staff, while smaller increases had been recorded at Geneva and Vienna. At Headquarters, staff were paying an average of 2.9 per cent of their net remuneration for health insurance to cover themselves alone or 6.4 per cent for family coverage, compared to a world-wide average for United Nations staff of 1.9 per cent for individual coverage and 3.8 per cent for families.

In a November report to the Assembly on this subject,[19] ACABQ endorsed the ICSC cost-sharing formula with effect from January 1984. It further recommended that ICSC be invited to review the formula's application and report in 1985 on any required modifications.

As to the Secretary-General's proposals to implement the ICSC formula by raising the United Nations health insurance contribution for Headquarters staff, ACABQ concurred with his intention to report on the costs after they occurred rather than to seek additional appropriations immediately. It recommended that the method of charging Headquarters staff—on a sliding scale whereby the United Nations paid between 10 and 90 per cent of a given staff member's insurance premium depending on salary level—be re-examined to keep a constant average ratio between salary and health insurance payments by staff. It offered no objection to the Secretary-General's proposals on after-service insurance but suggested that the financing of the scheme be kept under review.

In written comments on personnel questions circulated to the Fifth Committee, FICSA supported

steps to alleviate the problems experienced by New York staff, stressed the need for equal representation by staff and administration in the management of health insurance schemes, and urged a thorough review of health insurance questions, including benefits and after-service coverage.[2] The Staff Unions and Associations of the United Nations Secretariat welcomed the Secretary-General's initiative and expressed the view that the Organization should bear 75 per cent of health insurance costs.[20]

GENERAL ASSEMBLY ACTION

The ICSC formula and ACABQ recommendations were approved by the General Assembly in resolution 38/235 of 20 December 1983, adopted by recorded vote on the Fifth Committee's recommendation.

Health insurance contributions by the organizations of the United Nations common system

The General Assembly,

Having considered the report of the International Civil Service Commission on health insurance contributions by the organizations of the United Nations common system as well as the note by the Secretary-General and the related report of the Advisory Committee on Administrative and Budgetary Questions,

1. *Takes note* of the report of the International Civil Service Commission and the note by the Secretary-General;

2. *Approves* the recommendations of the Advisory Committee on Administrative and Budgetary Questions contained in paragraphs 23 to 25 of its report;

3. *Decides* that, in applying the formula recommended by the International Civil Service Commission and the Advisory Committee on Administrative and Budgetary Questions, a maximum ratio of 2 to 1 between the share of the organization and the contributor, respectively, will be used, on an experimental basis, until the study requested in paragraph 5 below is submitted to the General Assembly;

4. *Requests* the International Civil Service Commission, as a matter of priority, to study the possibility of providing a range of health insurance plans, including practices in the comparator service, both basic and comprehensive, with deductible clauses, as well as health maintenance organization plans, which could be made available, at lower costs, to contributors, and to report thereon to the General Assembly at its thirty-ninth session;

5. *Further requests* the International Civil Service Commission to study the following related matters and to report thereon to the General Assembly, preferably at its thirty-ninth session and not later than at its fortieth session:

(a) Fixing a maximum rate for the share to be borne by the organization and by the contributor;

(b) Making participation in a health insurance plan or plans of the organization mandatory, especially to those who are not covered by other plans.

General Assembly resolution 38/235

20 December 1983   Meeting 104   126-9-7 (recorded vote)

Approved by Fifth Committee (A/38/760 & Corr.1) by vote (70-7-12), 7 December (meeting 58); draft by Egypt (A/C.5/38/L.16); agenda item 109.
Meeting numbers. GA 38th session: 5th Committee 49, 58; plenary 104.

Recorded vote in Assembly as follows:

In favour: Afghanistan, Algeria, Argentina, Australia, Austria, Bahamas, Bahrain, Bangladesh, Barbados, Belgium, Belize, Benin, Bhutan, Bolivia, Botswana, Brazil, Burma, Burundi, Canada, Central African Republic, Chad, Chile, China, Colombia, Congo, Costa Rica, Cuba, Cyprus, Democratic Kampuchea, Democratic Yemen, Denmark, Djibouti, Dominican Republic, Ecuador, Egypt, El Salvador, Ethiopia, Fiji, Finland, Gabon, Gambia, Ghana, Greece, Guatemala, Guinea, Guinea-Bissau, Guyana, Haiti, Honduras, Iceland, India, Indonesia, Iran, Iraq, Ireland, Israel, Ivory Coast, Jamaica, Jordan, Kenya, Kuwait, Lebanon, Lesotho, Liberia, Libyan Arab Jamahiriya, Luxembourg, Madagascar, Malawi, Malaysia, Maldives, Mali, Malta, Mauritania, Mauritius, Mexico, Morocco, Nepal, Netherlands, New Zealand, Nicaragua, Niger, Nigeria, Norway, Oman, Pakistan, Panama, Papua New Guinea, Paraguay, Peru, Philippines, Portugal, Qatar, Rwanda, Saint Lucia, Saint Vincent and the Grenadines, Samoa, Sao Tome and Principe, Saudi Arabia, Senegal, Sierra Leone, Singapore, Solomon Islands, Somalia, Spain, Sri Lanka, Sudan, Suriname, Swaziland, Sweden, Syrian Arab Republic, Thailand, Togo, Trinidad and Tobago, Tunisia, Turkey, Uganda, United Arab Emirates, United Republic of Cameroon, United Republic of Tanzania, Upper Volta, Uruguay, Vanuatu, Venezuela, Yemen, Yugoslavia, Zambia.

Against: Bulgaria, Byelorussian SSR, Czechoslovakia, German Democratic Republic, Hungary, Mongolia, Poland, Ukrainian SSR, USSR.

Abstaining: France, Germany, Federal Republic of, Italy, Japan, Romania, United Kingdom, United States.

After the Fifth Committee approved the draft, the United States withdrew a draft it had submitted.[21] Rather than approving the ICSC formula, the United States proposal would have had the Assembly request the Commission to follow United States federal civil service practice on the employer-employee contribution ratio, study the experience of that service in providing a range of health insurance plans and report back in 1984 with advice on the possible application of its studies to the United Nations system.

The USSR expressed preference for the United States draft and said the matter should be studied further before the contribution ratio was altered. The United States said the Assembly decision to approve the ACABQ recommendations should not take precedence over its approval of a 2-to-1 ratio on an experimental basis. Canada voiced satisfaction that the Assembly had faced the problem of the high cost of health insurance and was moving towards agreement on a ratio.

In another action relating to health insurance, the Assembly, in resolution 38/232 of 20 December, requested ICSC to review after-service health-care coverage with particular attention to locally recruited field staff.

REFERENCES

[1]A/38/30. [2]A/C.5/38/23. [3]YUN 1974, p. 889, GA res. 3358 A (XXIX), 18 Dec. 1974. [4]A/C.5/38/40. [5]A/C.5/38/10 & Corr.1. [6]A/38/30/Add.1. [7]YUN 1980, p. 1175, GA res. 35/214 A, 17 Dec. 1980. [8]YUN 1946-47, p. 226, GA res. 82(I), 15 Dec. 1946. [9]YUN 1982, p. 1478, GA res. 37/131, 17 Dec. 1982. [10]A/38/9 & Corr.2. [11]A/38/9/Add.1 & Add.1/Corr.1,2. [12]A/C.5/38/L.25. [13]YUN 1981, p. 1344. [14]A/38/547. [15]A/C.5/38/19. [16]YUN 1980, p. 1186, GA dec. 35/447, 17 Dec. 1980. [17]YUN 1982, p. 1455, GA res. 37/126, 17 Dec. 1982. [18]A/C.5/38/16. [19]A/38/7/Add.9. [20]A/C.5/38/29. [21]A/C.5/38/L.12.

UN Administrative Tribunal

Activities of the Tribunal

The United Nations Administrative Tribunal delivered 20 judgements during 1983 in cases brought by staff members against the Secretary-General or the executive heads of other organizations in the United Nations system with respect to claims arising under labour contracts. They concerned such personnel management matters as compensation, disability, promotion and tax reimbursement on pensions.

The Tribunal met in special plenary session on 9 June at Geneva and in annual plenary session on 26 October in New York. It also held two panel sessions, 16 May to 10 June (Geneva) and 3 to 28 October (New York). In accordance with past practice, it submitted a note to the General Assembly outlining its activities for the year.[1]

The Assembly's Committee on Applications for Review of Administrative Tribunal Judgements, at the final meeting of its twenty-second session (New York, 14 December 1982 and 4-16 February 1983),[2] adopted rules of procedure incorporating a number of amendments designed to meet concerns about some Tribunal procedures expressed by ICJ in its July 1982 advisory opinion reviewing Tribunal Judgement No. 273 of 1981 (Ivor Peter Mortished v. the United Nations Secretary-General).[3] Three new rules required the Committee to work in closed session except for public meetings at which its decisions were to be announced, to elect a Chairman and a Rapporteur, and to have its Secretary prepare verbatim records of its proceedings on any case on which it decided to request an advisory opinion. Other changes concerned details of the form and processing of applications by staff members.

Co-ordination with the ILO Administrative Tribunal

Consultations continued in 1983 among legal advisers of organizations in the United Nations system on proposals to improve co-ordination between the United Nations Administrative Tribunal and the ILO Administrative Tribunal. According to a report by the Secretary-General submitted to the General Assembly's Fifth Committee in October,[4] considerable agreement was reached on a number of proposed reforms designed to improve and/or harmonize the proceedings of the two Tribunals. He proposed to prepare proposals on the instruments governing the Tribunals and their practices, consult on them with organization and staff representatives, and submit the proposed reforms in 1984 to the Assembly and ILO.

GENERAL ASSEMBLY ACTION

The General Assembly acted on this report by adopting without vote decision 38/409, as recommended by the Fifth Committee.

Feasibility of establishing a single administrative tribunal

At its 71st plenary meeting, on 25 November 1983, the General Assembly, on the recommendation of the Fifth Committee:

(a) Took note of the report of the Secretary-General on the feasibility of establishing a single administrative tribunal;

(b) Requested the Secretary-General to accelerate the necessary consultations and to report thereon to the Assembly at its thirty-ninth session.

General Assembly decision 38/409

Adopted without vote

Approved by Fifth Committee (A/38/587) without vote, 10 November (meeting 33); oral proposal by Chairman, orally amended by Spain; agenda item 112 *(b)*.
Meeting numbers. GA 38th session: 5th Committee 16, 24, 33; plenary 71.

Paragraph *(b)* of this decision was added in Committee on an oral proposal by Spain, accepted without vote.

REFERENCES
[1]A/INF/38/5. [2]A/AC.86/28. [3]YUN 1982, p. 1367.
[4]A/C.5/38/26.

PUBLICATION
Judgements of the United Nations Administrative Tribunal Numbers 231 to 300, 1978-1982 (AT/DEC/231-300), Sales No. E.83.X.1.

Travel

The Secretary-General reported to the General Assembly's Fifth Committee in October 1983[1] on actions taken regarding 1982 JIU recommendations[2] to improve the organization and methods for United Nations–financed travel by its staff and other officials. The report had been requested by the Assembly in December 1982.[3]

The principal step was the selection, on a competitive basis, of a new agency to handle official travel arrangements at United Nations Headquarters. As a result, Don Travel Services replaced Thomas Cook Travel, with a three-year contract effective 1 November 1983. The United Nations Development Programme and the United Nations Children's Fund joined in the contract. The agent was to reimburse the three organizations a total of $350,000 a year for facilities and services they provided to it.

On related matters, the Secretary-General reported that: negotiations with national airlines on fare discounts had been mentioned as a possibility by six States in response to a Secretariat questionnaire sent to all permanent missions of

United Nations Member States and non-members; obstacles to establishing a United Nations travel agency remained but the situation would continue to be monitored; action was being initiated to review contracts with travel agencies at United Nations offices overseas; revised administrative instructions on staff travel had been issued, introducing the use of business class in place of first class for certain flights and making greater use of excursion fares; and recommendations on travel procedures were being studied.

In another October report,[4] the Secretary-General informed the Fifth Committee of 81 cases in which first-class air travel had been allowed in exercise of his discretion during the year ended 30 June 1983, under circumstances in which a less costly mode was not considered appropriate. According to the report, the latest in an annual series, $372,623 had been saved during the year covered, through implementation of a 1977 Assembly resolution limiting first-class travel of United Nations officials.[5]

Further information on these matters was furnished by ACABQ in a November report to the Assembly.[6]

GENERAL ASSEMBLY ACTION

The General Assembly adopted section IV of resolution 38/234 without vote on 20 December 1983, on the recommendation of the Fifth Committee.

First-class travel and organization and methods for official travel

[The General Assembly . . .]
Takes note of the reports of the Secretary-General on first-class travel and on the organization and methods for official travel and of the related report of the Advisory Committee on Administrative and Budgetary Questions;

. . .

General Assembly resolution 38/234, section IV

20 December 1983   Meeting 104   Adopted without vote

Approved by Fifth Committee (A/38/760 & Corr.1) without vote, 22 November (meeting 44); oral proposal by Chairman; agenda item 109.
Meeting numbers. GA 38th session: 5th Committee 44; plenary 104.

Staff travel to General Assembly sessions

At the request of Poland, the Secretary-General submitted to the Fifth Committee in December 1983[7] a breakdown and brief explanation of all staff travel to attend the 1983 regular session of the General Assembly. The paper indicated that 46 staff members had travelled to New York for this purpose from overseas United Nations offices.

GENERAL ASSEMBLY ACTION

The General Assembly adopted without vote on 20 December 1983, on the recommendation of the Fifth Committee, section XVI of resolution 38/234.

Travel of United Nations officials to attend sessions of the General Assembly

[*The General Assembly* . . .]

1. *Takes note* of the information provided by the Secretary-General on the travel of staff members to attend the current session of the General Assembly;

2. *Requests* the Secretary-General to ensure that maximum restraint is exercised concerning such travel;

3. *Requests* the Secretary-General to inform the General Assembly at its thirty-ninth session on action taken in this regard;

. . .

General Assembly resolution 38/234, section XVI

20 December 1983   Meeting 104   Adopted without vote

Approved by Fifth Committee (A/38/760 and Corr.1) without vote, 15 December (meeting 66); draft by Poland (A/C.5/38/L.22); agenda item 109.
Meeting numbers. GA 38th session: 5th Committee 66; plenary 104.

REFERENCES

[1]A/C.5/38/22. [2]YUN 1982, p. 1490. [3]*Ibid.*, p. 1493, GA res. 37/241, 21 Dec. 1982. [4]A/C.5/38/14. [5]YUN 1977, p. 1004, GA res. 32/198, 21 Dec. 1977. [6]A/38/7/Add.6. [7]A/C.5/38/L.29.

Other UN officials

Allowances and pensions

The General Assembly decided in December 1983 to defer until 1984 consideration of proposals by the Secretary-General to increase certain allowances payable to the Chairman of ACABQ and the Chairman and Vice-Chairman of ICSC.

The proposals were made by the Secretary-General in a November report to the Fifth Committee reviewing the compensation and fringe benefits paid to these three officials and to ICJ members.[1] They called for: a $3,000 increase in the special allowance for the two Chairmen, currently $5,000 a year, and a $2,000 allowance for the ICSC Vice-Chairman, who currently did not receive one; reimbursement of education costs and related travel of the children of the three officials, similar to the education grant for staff; a relocation allowance payable on completion of their appointment; and an installation allowance for newly appointed officials.

Also, as the three officials had joined the United Nations Joint Staff Pension Fund with effect from 1 January 1983 under a change in the Regulations of the Fund approved by the Assembly in December 1982,[2] the Secretary-General proposed a United Nations contribution to the Fund representing the Organization's share of the pension entitlements related to the officials' service prior to that date.

The Secretary-General estimated the total cost of these measures at $379,100 for 1984-1985, of which the other organizations sharing the cost of ICSC would pay $128,600 in relation to its officers.

Although recommending that action be deferred on those aspects of the Secretary-General's proposals pertaining to increased benefits for the three officials, the Fifth Committee, on 15 December, approved without vote appropriations in the 1984-1985 budget to cover the pension contributions he had proposed. These amounted to $160,100 for the ICSC officials and $81,300 for the ACABQ Chairman, with $95,700 of the former figure to be reimbursed by other organizations.

GENERAL ASSEMBLY ACTION

The General Assembly adopted section XVII of resolution 38/234 without vote on 20 December 1983, on the recommendation of the Fifth Committee.

Conditions of service and compensation for officials other than Secretariat officials

[*The General Assembly* . . .]

Decides to defer until its thirty-ninth session consideration of the recommendations of the Secretary-General with regard to which no action has been taken during the current session;

. . .

General Assembly resolution 38/234, section XVII

20 December 1983   Meeting 104   Adopted without vote

Approved by Fifth Committee (A/38/760 and Corr.1) without vote, 18 December (meeting 70); oral proposal by Chairman; agenda item 109.
Meeting numbers. GA 38th session: 5th Committee 67, 70; plenary 104.

By resolution 38/239 of 20 December, the Assembly amended the Pension Scheme Regulations of ICJ in accordance with the Secretary-General's recommendations, to improve the pension benefits available to members of the Court (see LEGAL QUESTIONS, Chapter I).

REFERENCES

[1]A/C.5/38/27. [2]YUN 1982, p. 1478, GA res. 37/131, 17 Dec. 1982; *ibid.*, p. 1489.

Chapter IV

Other administrative and management questions

The General Assembly, in 1983, adopted a number of resolutions on matters related to conferences, meetings and documentation. It approved the calendar of conferences and meetings of the United Nations for 1984-1985 (38/32 A), approving a change of venue for the 1984 regular sessions of three of the regional commissions; and requested the Secretary-General to bring to the attention of the Committee on Conferences the summary of the discussion in the Fifth (Administrative and Budgetary) Committee on the pattern of conferences (38/32 C). By other resolutions, it dealt with the shortening of sessions or adoption of a biennial cycle for sessions of United Nations organs (38/32 D) and with control and limitation of documentation (38/32 E). In addition, it requested information on conference-servicing resources (38/32 F). With the three-year term of the members of the Committee on Conferences expiring at the end of 1983, the Assembly President was requested to appoint 22 Member States for the term starting 1 January 1984 (38/32 B). Most of these actions were taken on the recommendation of the Committee on Conferences.

In December, the Fifth Committee approved additional appropriations for conference services in 1984 totalling $7,340,000.

Improvements to United Nations premises in various parts of the world—notably the office accommodation and common services at Nairobi, Kenya—were considered, and actions taken, by the Assembly in December.

As part of continuing efforts to strengthen co-ordination of information systems in United Nations organizations and agencies, an inter-agency Advisory Committee for the Co-ordination of Information Systems was established in March. The Committee on Information and the Assembly's Special Political Committee reviewed an interim report on acquiring a United Nations communications satellite, and the 1984 budget estimates for the International Computing Centre at Geneva were approved.

Gross revenue from the sale of philatelic items totalled over $6 million in 1983. In December, the Assembly allocated half of the net revenues from the sale of a special issue of postage stamps to the United Nations Environment Programme (UNEP) to finance projects to conserve and protect nature and endangered species (38/228 A).

Topics related to this chapter: Institutional machinery. Institutional arrangements.

Conferences and meetings

The work of the 22-member Committee on Conferences in 1983 focused on five main areas: calendar of conferences; control and limitation of documentation; utilization of conference resources; further improvements in conference services facilities in 1984-1985; and evaluation of the preparation and holding of United Nations special conferences.

In 1983, the Committee held two series of five meetings each, between 2 and 6 May and between 24 and 31 August. In its report on the session,[1] it submitted five draft resolutions to the General Assembly. The Assembly, on 25 November, adopted without vote six resolutions (38/32 A-F) relating to various aspects of the work of the Committee (see below).

Calendar of meetings

By a note of 21 April 1983 to the Committee on Conferences,[2] the United Nations Secretariat submitted data on the utilization of conference resources by subsidiary bodies of the Assembly in 1980-1982, with the recommendation that the Committee might wish to identify those for which adjustments in the duration of their sessions appeared to be appropriate.

After considering the matter at its 1983 session, the Committee recommended two draft resolutions on the subject for the Assembly's consideration (see below).

GENERAL ASSEMBLY ACTION

On 25 November 1983, on the recommendation of the Fifth Committee, the General Assembly adopted resolution 38/32 C without vote.

Pattern of conferences

The General Assembly

1. *Requests* the Committee on Conferences to examine the provisions of section I of General Assembly resolution 31/140 of 17 December 1976, as well as all other provisions relating to the pattern of conferences, and to report to the Assembly at its thirty-ninth session;

2. *Requests* the Secretary-General to bring to the attention of the Committee on Conferences the summary of the discussion in the Fifth Committee during the current session on the item entitled "Pattern of conferences", including the text of all amendments proposed

to draft resolution C recommended by the Committee on Conferences in paragraph 4 of its report.

General Assembly resolution 38/32 C

25 November 1983   Meeting 71   Adopted without vote

Approved by Fifth Committee (A/38/585) without vote, 2 November (meeting 25); draft by Chairman (A/C.5/38/L.6, para. 2), based on informal consultations on draft by Committee on Conferences (A/38/32); agenda item 114.
Meeting numbers. GA 38th session: 5th Committee 4, 8, 9, 25; plenary 71.

On the same date, again on the recommendation of the Fifth Committee, the Assembly adopted resolution 38/32 D without vote.

Shortening of sessions or adoption of a biennial cycle for sessions of United Nations organs

The General Assembly,

Reaffirming its resolutions 32/71, section IV, and 32/72 of 9 December 1977 and 35/10 A of 3 November 1980,

Concerned at the serious under-utilization of conference resources by United Nations organs,

1. *Takes note* of the proposals submitted by the Committee on Conferences designed to relieve the overloading of conference services;

2. *Invites* the Committee on Conferences to pursue further its consultations with the officers of those organs which have over the past three years utilized 75 per cent or less of the conference resources made available to them, with a view to adjusting the length of their sessions accordingly;

3. *Requests* its subsidiary organs to consider, in the interests of greater efficiency, meeting and reporting on a biennial basis;

4. *Requests* United Nations organs, especially those which have over the past few years under-utilized the meeting time allocated to them, to consider at their organizational sessions the question of improving the organization of their work in order to secure a more effective use of conference resources and to put forward concrete proposals on this matter, including, where feasible, the shortening of sessions;

5. *Invites* United Nations organs to hold informal consultations with the aim of reaching agreement on organizational questions as well as on the composition of the bureaux before the opening of their substantive sessions.

General Assembly resolution 38/32 D

25 November 1983   Meeting 71   Adopted without vote

Approved by Fifth Committee (A/38/585) without vote, 2 November (meeting 25); draft by Committee on Conferences (A/38/32), amended by Chairman (A/C.5/38/L.6, para. 3), based on informal consultations; agenda item 114.
Meeting numbers. GA 38th session: 5th Committee 4, 8, 9, 25; plenary 71.

By the original draft on the pattern of conferences, as proposed by the Committee on Conferences, the Assembly would have reaffirmed the general principle that, in drawing up the schedule of conferences and meetings, United Nations bodies should plan to meet at their respective established headquarters, with the exception of sessions and meetings of the following: the Governing Council of the United Nations Development Programme; the International Law Commission; the United Nations Commission on International Trade Law; the Economic and Social Council (second regular session) and its functional commissions; the regional commissions (regular sessions), except for the Economic Commission for Europe, and their subsidiary bodies; the International Civil Service Commission; the Legal Sub-Committee of the Committee on the Peaceful Uses of Outer Space; and the Committee on Disarmament.

The Assembly further would have: decided that United Nations bodies might hold sessions away from their headquarters when a Government issuing an invitation had agreed to defray the actual additional costs, and that, as a general principle, invitations from specialized agencies to United Nations bodies should not be encouraged; reaffirmed its instruction to all its subsidiary organs to complete their reports for the following Assembly session not later than 1 September; requested the Secretary-General to provide interpretation services for informal meetings on an *ad hoc* basis as resources permitted and authorized him to apply maximum overprogramming of meetings to achieve better utilization of conference resources.

The Assembly would have requested the Committee on Conferences and the Secretary-General to take account of the following principles in drawing up the draft calendar of conferences: the biennial calendar approved by the Assembly should govern the meetings programme; all United Nations meetings should be carried out within the resources allocated; between Assembly sessions, departures from the calendar might in special circumstances be approved by the Committee; subsidiary organs should not without Assembly approval create new standing bodies or *ad hoc* sessional or inter-sessional bodies requiring additional resources; an adequate time interval should be allowed between sessions of the same bodies to permit Member States to derive maximum benefit from the activities and to provide sufficient time for preparation of future activities; United Nations bodies should in general meet at their headquarters; only one United Nations special conference should be convened at any one time; and, in one year, no more than five special conferences, i.e. no more than one in each of the five fields of activity (political, scientific, economic, social, legal), should be convened.

The original draft resolution on shortening of sessions or a biennial cycle for sessions of United Nations organs, as proposed by the Committee on Conferences, did not contain paragraph 5. The original paragraph 4 differed from that adopted in that the phrases "especially those" and "this matter, including, where feasible" were not included.

Calendar for 1983

In 1983, the Committee on Conferences approved two inter-sessional departures from the calendar of conferences and meetings for 1983 which involved financial implications. The changes concerned the venue and dates of the International Conference on the Question of Palestine (see p. 275), and an additional session in New York in September of the Group of Experts on All Aspects of the Conventional Arms Race and on Disarmament relating to Conventional Weapons and Armed Forces (see p. 65).

By approving these changes, the Committee followed requests by the United Nations Secretariat in notes of 20 June[3] and 2 August.[4]

By letters of 15, 19 and 23 September,[5] the Chairman of the Committee on Conferences informed the President of the General Assembly that he had received requests from a number of subsidiary organs of the Assembly asking to meet at United Nations Headquarters during the regular 1983 Assembly session in order to finalize their reports. He stated that the Committee did not object to those requests on the clear understanding that any meetings would have to be accommodated as facilities and services became available, so that the activities of the Assembly itself would not be adversely affected. He asked that the Assembly authorize additional meetings for the bodies which had requested them.

GENERAL ASSEMBLY ACTION

The General Assembly adopted decision 38/403 without vote.

Meetings of subsidiary organs during the thirty-eighth session

At its 3rd and 11th plenary meetings on 23 and 29 September 1983, the General Assembly, on the recommendations of the Committee on Conferences and of the General Committee, decided that the following subsidiary organs should be authorized to hold meetings during the thirty-eighth session:

(a) _Ad Hoc_ Committee on the Indian Ocean;
(b) Advisory Committee on the United Nations Educational and Training Programme for Southern Africa;
(c) Committee on Relations with the Host Country;
(d) Committee on the Exercise of the Inalienable Rights of the Palestinian People;
(e) Group of Experts on the Supply of Oil and Oil Products to South Africa;
(f) Intergovernmental Committee on Science and Technology for Development;
(g) International Civil Service Commission;
(h) Meeting of permanent representatives to the United Nations of the oil-producing and oil-exporting countries committed to the oil embargo against South Africa;
(i) Special Committee against _Apartheid_;
(j) Special Committee on the Situation with regard to the Implementation of the Declaration on the Granting of Independence to Colonial Countries and Peoples;
(k) United Nations Council for Namibia;
(l) Working Group on the Financing of the United

Nations Relief and Works Agency for Palestine Refugees in the Near East.

General Assembly decision 38/403

Adopted without vote

Approved by General Committee (A/38/250) without vote, 21 September (meeting 1); proposals by Committee on Conferences (A/38/414 & Add.1,2) (Add.2 approved by Assembly); agenda item 8.
Meeting numbers. GA 38th session: General Committee 1; plenary 3, 11.

Calendar for 1984-1985

A draft calendar of conferences and meetings of United Nations bodies for 1984-1985 was recommended by the Committee on Conferences at its 1983 session and was annexed to the Committee's report.[1] The General Assembly, by resolution 38/32 A, approved the calendar subject to later modifications it might make. Before adopting the resolution, the Assembly changed the venues for the 1984 regular sessions of three of the regional commissions—the Economic Commission for Africa (ECA), the Economic Commission for Latin America (ECLA) and the Economic and Social Commission for Asia and the Pacific (ESCAP).

The Economic and Social Council, by decision 1983/185, approved the calendar for its subsidiary and related bodies. Various aspects of the 1984-1985 calendar were also dealt with by the Council in decision 1983/184.

The Trade and Development Board of the United Nations Conference on Trade and Development (UNCTAD) took similar action with regard to the UNCTAD calendars for the remainder of 1983, and for 1984-1985 (see p. 568).

GENERAL ASSEMBLY ACTION

On 25 November 1983, on the recommendation of the Fifth Committee, the General Assembly adopted resolution 38/32 A without vote.

Report of the Committee on Conferences
The General Assembly,

Having considered the report of the Committee on Conferences,

1. _Takes note with appreciation_ of the report of the Committee on Conferences;

2. _Approves_ the calendar of conferences and meetings of the United Nations for 1984-1985 as submitted by the Committee on Conferences, subject to any amendments as a result of subsequent decisions taken by the General Assembly at its thirty-eighth session;

3. _Requests_ the Secretary-General to take all appropriate measures with a view to achieving maximum efficiency and effectiveness in the use of conference resources when implementing the calendar of conferences and meetings for 1984-1985.

General Assembly resolution 38/32 A

25 November 1983   Meeting 71   Adopted without vote

Approved by Fifth Committee (A/38/585) without vote, 2 November (meeting 25); draft by Committee on Conferences (A/38/32), amended by Chairman (A/C.5/38/L.6, para. 1), based on informal consultations; agenda item 114.

Financial implications. ACABQ, A/38/7/Add.10; 5th Committee, A/38/585/Add.1; S-G, A/C.5/38/31.
Meeting numbers. GA 38th session: 5th Committee 4, 8, 9, 25, 46; plenary 71.

An amendment by the Chairman of the Fifth Committee replaced paragraph 3 of the draft proposed by the Committee on Conferences, by which the Assembly would have authorized the Committee on Conferences to make within approved resources adjustments to the calendar that might become necessary as a result of action and decisions by the Assembly at its 1983 session.

Before adopting the resolution, the Assembly approved the proposed venues of the 1984 regular sessions of ECA, ECLA and ESCAP by a recorded vote of 106 to 21, with 9 abstentions.

Recorded vote in Assembly as follows:

In favour: Afghanistan, Algeria, Angola, Argentina, Austria, Bahrain, Bangladesh, Barbados, Benin, Bhutan, Bolivia, Botswana, Brazil, Burma, Burundi, Central African Republic, Chad, Chile, China, Comoros, Congo, Costa Rica, Cuba, Cyprus, Democratic Kampuchea, Democratic Yemen, Djibouti, Dominican Republic, Ecuador, Egypt, El Salvador, Ethiopia, Fiji, Gabon, Gambia, Ghana, Guatemala, Guinea, Guyana, Honduras, India, Indonesia, Iraq, Ivory Coast, Jamaica, Japan, Jordan, Kenya, Kuwait, Lebanon, Lesotho, Libyan Arab Jamahiriya, Madagascar, Malawi, Malaysia, Maldives, Mali, Mauritania, Mauritius, Mexico, Morocco, Mozambique, Nepal, Nicaragua, Niger, Nigeria, Oman, Pakistan, Panama, Papua New Guinea, Peru, Philippines, Qatar, Romania, Rwanda, Saint Lucia, Samoa, Saudi Arabia, Senegal, Sierra Leone, Singapore, Solomon Islands, Somalia, Spain, Sri Lanka, Sudan, Suriname, Swaziland, Syrian Arab Republic, Thailand, Trinidad and Tobago, Tunisia, Turkey, Uganda, United Arab Emirates, United Republic of Cameroon, United Republic of Tanzania, Upper Volta, Uruguay, Venezuela, Viet Nam, Yemen, Yugoslavia, Zaire, Zambia, Zimbabwe.

Against: Australia, Belgium, Bulgaria, Byelorussian SSR, Canada, Czechoslovakia, France, German Democratic Republic, Germany, Federal Republic of, Hungary, Italy, Luxembourg, Mongolia, Netherlands, New Zealand, Poland, Portugal, Ukrainian SSR, USSR, United Kingdom, United States.

Abstaining: Bahamas, Denmark, Finland, Greece, Iceland, Ireland, Israel, Norway, Sweden.

In taking that action, the Assembly followed the recommendation of the Fifth Committee which, on an oral proposal of its Chairman, had approved the venues on 2 November, by 65 votes to 18, with 14 abstentions. The venues, proposed by the Commissions concerned, were reflected in the report of the Committee on Conferences and endorsed by the Economic and Social Council (see p. 1005). On 23 November, by 69 votes to 19, with 12 abstentions, the Committee approved additional resources of $611,900 required for holding the sessions of those Commissions away from their headquarters. The Committee made these appropriations on the recommendation of the Advisory Committee on Administrative and Budgetary Questions (ACABQ).

Speaking in the Committee, the United States, which had requested the vote, took strong exception to the implications of the changed venues for the budget and said the way in which those implications had been submitted to the Committee was equally regrettable; the matter should have been referred to the Second (Economic and Financial) Committee first. Austria,

however, said the changes had been approved by the Economic and Social Council and their financial implications were within the Fifth Committee's competence.

The USSR pointed out that host countries were required to defray the additional costs. A similar position was taken by the Netherlands and New Zealand. The Federal Republic of Germany thought it inconsistent to appropriate funds for expanding conference facilities on the one hand and for holding sessions of regional commissions away from their headquarters on the other. In a similar vein, Canada pointed out that new conference facilities were shortly to be installed at a number of headquarters; it intended to request the Economic and Social Council to review exceptions to the calendar of meetings in the light of that situation.

The Bahamas said it did not understand the way in which the 1976 Assembly resolution on conference matters[6] was to be applied with regard to those exceptions. Trinidad and Tobago explained that it had voted for ACABQ's recommendation based on that resolution. Japan pointed out that the Assembly had followed that practice of approving exceptions since 1969;[7] also, the meetings of the regional commissions should not be confused with those of other United Nations bodies for which the Assembly did not authorize exceptions.

Original estimates of the additional costs were $584,800. They were submitted by the Secretary-General in a 20 July statement to the Economic and Social Council.[8]

On 21 October,[9] the Secretary-General submitted revised estimates of $637,400 for the additional costs; he noted that while the amounts for ECLA and ESCAP remained the same as those included in the proposed 1984-1985 programme budget, the estimate for ECA was $136,600 higher than the $150,700 originally estimated because at the time of the budget preparation it had been planned to hold the ECA session at Maputo, Mozambique, but the Commission changed the venue subsequently to Conakry, Guinea. He noted that the revised estimates were at the same level as the resources requested in the proposed programme budget, which ACABQ had recommended to be provisionally deleted until the Council and the Assembly had approved the venues.

In a 22 November report,[10] ACABQ recommended acceptance of the Secretary-General's estimates of additional resources for ECA ($287,300) and ECLA ($143,300); with regard to the additional requirements for ESCAP, however, it recommended a reduction of the estimate of $206,800 to $181,300, thereby reducing the overall additional allocation requested to $611,900.

Conference and meeting services

By a resolution of 25 November 1983, the General Assembly requested the Secretary-General to provide information on conference-servicing resources (see below).

In the context of the 1984-1985 United Nations programme budget (see Chapter I of this section), the Fifth Committee approved on 18 December 1983, by 64 votes to 17, additional appropriations totalling $7,340,000 for conference services in 1984. The Committee followed the recommendation of ACABQ to reduce the Secretary-General's estimates by $1,233,000.

In a 14 December statement,[11] the Secretary-General estimated conference-servicing requirements for 1984, calculated on a full-cost basis, at $18,972,100, comprising $15,293,200 for Headquarters, $2,751,000 for Geneva and $927,900 for Vienna. Taking into account existing resources available, he requested appropriations totalling $8,573,000, of which $4,133,000 related to Headquarters, $2,340,000 to Geneva and $2,100,000 to Vienna. The additional Headquarters conference-servicing requirements were based on a comparison of weekly work-load capacity as against actual requirements, whereas requirements for Geneva and Vienna were based on overall work-load requirements for the year. The appropriations requested reflected the application of over-programming of 13 per cent under temporary assistance requirements for interpretation at Headquarters and 10 and 11.8 per cent overall at Geneva and Vienna, respectively.

In an oral report to the Committee, ACABQ expressed the opinion that a slight increase in the percentage of over-programming in a number of areas, combined with an increase in productivity, could result in a reduction of $1,233,000. Accordingly, it recommended a total appropriation of $7,340,000 broken down as follows: $3,500,000 for Headquarters ($633,000 less than estimated by the Secretary-General); $1,940,000 for Geneva ($400,000 less than his estimate); and $1,900,000 for Vienna (a reduction of $200,000).

Improvement of conference resources

GENERAL ASSEMBLY ACTION

On 25 November 1983, on the recommendation of the Fifth Committee, the General Assembly adopted resolution 38/32 F without vote.

Improved organization of work and effective use of conference resources

The General Assembly,

1.   *Requests* the Secretary-General to provide the Committee on Conferences with data in summary form on:

(*a*)   The physical and human conference-servicing resources for United Nations Headquarters and United

Nations offices generally, including rooms available and documentation, interpretation and translation capacity, in a format enabling comparison of the demand and the conference-servicing capacity for all categories of meetings of United Nations organs—scheduled, anticipated to the extent possible, and held—grouped according to subject-matter;

(*b*)   External conference servicing available to the United Nations in case of urgent or unforeseen demands on the calendar;

2.   *Requests* the Secretary-General to submit to all United Nations bodies the relevant information requested under paragraph 1 above as supplementary data for their implementation of the present resolution.

General Assembly resolution 38/32 F

25 November 1983   Meeting 71   Adopted without vote

Approved by Fifth Committee (A/38/585) without vote, 2 November (meeting 25); draft by Chairman (A/C.5/38/L.6, para. 5), based on informal consultations; agenda item 114.

Meeting numbers. GA 38th session: 5th Committee 4, 8, 9, 25; plenary 71.

Membership of Committee on Conferences

As recommended by the Committee on Conferences, the General Assembly requested its President to appoint 22 Member States to serve on the Committee for a three-year term. The term of the current Committee members was to expire on 31 December 1983.

GENERAL ASSEMBLY ACTION

On 25 November, on the recommendation of the Fifth Committee, the General Assembly adopted resolution 38/32 B without vote.

Membership of the Committee on Conferences

The General Assembly,

Recalling its resolutions 3351(XXIX) of 18 December 1974, 32/72 of 9 December 1977 and 35/10 A of 3 November 1980,

Requests the President of the General Assembly, after consultations with the chairmen of the regional groups, to appoint twenty-two Member States, on the basis of an equitable geographical balance, to serve on the Committee on Conferences for a three-year term.

General Assembly resolution 38/32 B

25 November 1983   Meeting 71   Adopted without vote

Approved by Fifth Committee (A/38/585) without vote, 2 November (meeting 25); draft by Committee on Conferences (A/38/32); agenda item 114.

Meeting numbers. GA 38th session: 5th Committee 4, 8, 9, 25; plenary 71.

Guidelines for conferences

In its draft resolution on the pattern of conferences (see above), submitted to the General Assembly in its 1983 report,[1] the Committee on Conferences recommended that only one United Nations special conference should be convened at any one time and that annually no more than five special conferences, i.e. not more than one in each of the five different fields of United Nations activity (political, scientific, economic, social, legal), should be convened.

In an October report, on implementation of recommendations of the Joint Inspection Unit (JIU)[12] the Secretary-General referred to its 1982 recommendations on the organization and preparation of United Nations special conferences. On the basis of those recommendations and his comments on them,[13] the Committee on Conferences had recommended a set of guidelines which the General Assembly adopted in November 1982.[14] The Secretary-General noted, however, that in the guidelines the following three recommendations were not reflected: that the function of Conference Secretary be merged with that of Executive or Administrative Officer; that the new preparatory mechanism be supplemented by standard guidelines and by the development of basic servicing requirements and costing rates; and that the Economic and Social Council and the Assembly consider adopting guidelines for the formulation and evaluation of future special conferences, similar to those adopted in 1980 for international years.[15] The reasons for non-implementation of those recommendations had been explained in the Secretary-General's 1982 comments.[13]

Draft rules of procedure for conferences

By decision 38/427, the General Assembly decided to defer consideration of a report of the Secretary-General on draft standard rules of procedure for United Nations conferences (see p. 1126) to its 1984 session, and requested him to submit another report at that time.

Smoking in conference rooms

By decision 38/401, the General Assembly adopted several recommendations made by the General Committee concerning the organization of its 1983 regular session (see p. 392), among them a recommendation that smoking should be prohibited in small conference rooms and be discouraged in large ones.

REFERENCES

[1]A/38/32. [2]A/AC.172/88 & Add.1,2. [3]A/AC.172/89. [4]A/AC.172/90. [5]A/38/414 & Add.1,2. [6]YUN 1976, p. 908, GA res. 31/140, 17 Dec. 1976. [7]YUN 1969, p. 834, GA res. 2609(XXIV), 16 Dec. 1969. [8]E/1983/L.37. [9]A/C.5/38/31. [10]A/38/7/Add.10. [11]A/C.5/38/104. [12]A/C.5/38/8. [13]YUN 1982, p. 1497. [14]*Ibid.*, p. 1498, GA res. 37/14 B, 16 Nov. 1982. [15]YUN 1980, p. 1030, ESC res. 1980/67, annex, 25 July 1980; and p. 1031, GA dec. 35/424, 5 Dec. 1980.

Documents

Documents limitation

Report of the Secretary-General. In an October 1983 report to the Fifth Committee on implementation of JIU recommendations on various operational aspects of the United Nations system,[1] the Secretary-General recalled that the 1981 JIU report on documents limitation[2] had contained 18 specific recommendations, of which 10 required decisions by the legislative organs of the United Nations organizations and 8 could be implemented by their executive heads. Of the latter group, 7 had been or were being implemented. The Secretary-General recalled that he had considered the remaining recommendation—suggesting introduction of a documents quota system—as unworkable where the nature and volume of documentation were determined largely by Member States. Any attempt to administer the provision of central services, such as those for documentation, in the same way as budgetary appropriations would substantially detract from the flexibility of those services to respond to the Organization's priority needs as they arose.

The Secretary-General stated that the main purpose of a quota system, namely, to limit the volume of documentation originating in the Secretariat, was being sought through the application of a maximum-length rule to individual documents. On 24 February 1982,[3] he had directed that documents submitted to United Nations organs and bodies in the name of the Secretary-General or of the Secretariat should not exceed 24 single-spaced pages in length; exceptions to that rule must be authorized by the Under-Secretary-General for Conference Services and Special Assignments.

Activities of the Committee on Conferences. In 1983, the Committee on Conferences[4] discussed various aspects of the question of documents control and limitation. The basis for the Committee's consideration were Secretariat notes on: documents for treaty bodies[5] and subsidiary organs;[6] recurrent United Nations publications;[7] identification of documents that might be discontinued, shortened or consolidated;[8] and compliance by subsidiary organs with the 32-page limit for reports,[9] the desirability for which was reiterated by the General Assembly in November 1982.[10] The Committee also considered comparative costs of the preparation of meeting records.

In the light of its consideration of these documents, the Committee made a series of recommendations in a draft resolution on documents control and limitation, which it submitted to the Assembly.

ECONOMIC AND SOCIAL COUNCIL ACTION

In July, the Economic and Social Council adopted two decisions designed to control and limit documentation (see p. 1005): decision 1983/163, by which the Council requested the Secretary-General to draw to the attention of intergovernmental and expert bodies any request for documentation exceeding the Secretariat's ability to process on time and within approved resources, and areas where duplication was likely to occur or where opportunities for consolidating documents might exist; and decision 1983/184, by section I of which the Council extended, for another two years, discontinuance of summary records for 11 of its subsidiary bodies and for its sessional committees.

GENERAL ASSEMBLY ACTION

On 25 November 1983, acting on the recommendation of the Fifth Committee, the General Assembly adopted resolution 38/32 E without vote.

Control and limitation of documentation

The General Assembly,

Recalling its resolutions 2292(XXII) of 8 December 1967, 2538(XXIV) of 11 December 1969, 2732(XXV) of 16 December 1970, 31/140, section II, of 17 December 1976, 33/56, section II, of 14 December 1978, 34/50 of 23 November 1979, 36/117 of 10 December 1981 and 37/14 C and D of 16 November 1982 and its decision 34/401 of 21 September, 25 October, 29 November and 12 December 1979,

1. *Recommends* to Member States that they take into consideration the aim of limiting to a minimum requests for the preparation of reports or the circulation of documents;

2. *Recommends* to Member States and specialized agencies that, when preparing their replies to questionnaires or submissions of organizations and programmes of the United Nations system, they take into consideration the aim of achieving maximum brevity in setting out their positions;

3. *Requests* the Secretary-General, when sending out such questionnaires, to attach to them a reference to the present resolution;

4. *Invites* its subsidiary organs to include in their agenda an item on control and limitation of documentation with a view to ensuring the production of concise reports;

5. *Commends* the Secretary-General for his efforts in reducing the length and number of reports originating in the Secretariat and requests him to continue with these measures;

6. *Requests* the Secretary-General to examine ways of improving the drafting skills of Secretariat officials who are involved in the various phases of preparing final reports of United Nations bodies with a view to ensuring the production of more concise reports;

7. *Calls upon* its subsidiary organs not to reproduce in their reports the full text of earlier resolutions relevant to their work, but instead, as a frame of reference, to include a list of relevant documents in their reports, giving the exact titles and symbols;

8. *Decides* that the practice of reproducing statements *in extenso* as separate documents shall be discontinued for all its subsidiary organs that are entitled to summary records;

9. *Decides further* that any exceptions to this rule may be made by the body concerned only if the statements are to serve as bases for discussion and if, after hearing

a statement of the relevant financial implications, the body decides that one or more statements *in extenso* may be included in the summary record, or reproduced as separate documents or as annexes to authorized documents;

10. *Requests* the Committee on Conferences to undertake a study of the feasibility of instituting an abbreviated form of summary record;

11. *Requests* the Committee on Conferences to examine the various causes of the late issuance of documents in the different official and working languages and to consider possible solutions to this problem;

12. *Urges* all treaty bodies to review their documentation requirements, with particular reference to the possible reduction of their need for summary records;

13. *Invites* the Committee on Conferences to examine the report to be issued by the Joint Inspection Unit on publications policy and practice in the United Nations system;

14. *Requests* its subsidiary organs responsible for the issuance of recurrent publications to review them with the objective of identifying and discontinuing those which no longer serve a useful purpose;

15. *Invites* the Economic and Social Council similarly to request its subsidiary organs responsible for recurrent publications to undertake such a review;

16. *Requests* the Committee for Programme and Coordination to review recurrent publications in the context of the medium-term plan or the programme budget, as appropriate;

17. *Recommends* that, in conducting their reviews, intergovernmental bodies bear in mind the following criteria:

(*a*) Usefulness to the end-user of the publication as gauged from end-user response or from the sales record of a publication;

(*b*) Filling of a need;

(*c*) High standard of analysis or data;

(*d*) Promotion of the principles and purposes of the Organization;

(*e*) Continued validity of the original mandate;

(*f*) Recommendations of the Joint Inspection Unit in its report on publications policy and practice in the United Nations system, if applicable.

General Assembly resolution 38/32 E

25 November 1983   Meeting 71   Adopted without vote

Approved by Fifth Committee (A/38/585) without vote, 2 November (meeting 25); draft by Committee on Conferences (A/38/32), amended by Chairman (A/C.5/38/L.6, para. 4, following informal consultations, and further orally amended by Vice-Chairman); agenda item 114.

Meeting numbers. GA 38th session: 5th Committee 4, 8, 9, 25; plenary 71.

In the version recommended by the Committee on Conferences, the Assembly would have: called on Member States to limit requests to a minimum, in paragraph 1; proposed to Member States and specialized agencies that they strive for maximum brevity, in paragraph 2; requested Secretariat officials (instead of the Secretary-General), in paragraph 3; referred to improving the drafting skills of Secretariat officials who assisted rapporteurs in their work with a view to producing more concise reports, in paragraph 6; and referred only to the late issuance of documentation (without mentioning official and working languages), in paragraph 11. A drafting change was also made to the preambular paragraph. The recommended version and the adopted text were the same in all other respects.

Documents production

During discussion by the Fifth Committee of a report on the depositary functions of the Secretary-General and registration and publication of treaties (see p. 1129) in connection with its examination of the proposed programme budget for 1984-1985, the question of backlogs in documentation arose as a result of the request for additional resources required during that biennium to implement the Secretary-General's 10-year (1980-1989) plan to eliminate the backlog in the publication of the United Nations *Treaty Series*. Stating that it could not support that request and in view of the recurrence of such requests, the United States proposed that the Fifth Committee should recommend that the Assembly invite the Committee on Conferences to examine the whole question of backlogs in documentation at its next substantive session.

GENERAL ASSEMBLY ACTION

On 20 December, on the recommendation of the Fifth Committee, the General Assembly adopted section XII of resolution 38/234 without vote.

Question of backlogs in documentation
[*The General Assembly . . .*]
Invites the Committee on Conferences, at its next substantive session, to examine the question of backlogs in documentation;

. . .

General Assembly resolution 38/234, section XII

20 December 1983   Meeting 104   Adopted without vote

Approved by Fifth Committee (A/38/760 & Corr.1) without vote, 5 December (meeting 55); oral proposal by United States; agenda item 109.
Meeting numbers. GA 38th session: 5th Committee 55; plenary 104.

REFERENCES
(1)A/C.5/38/8. (2)YUN 1981, p. 1370. (3)ST/AI/189/Add.20/ Rev.1. (4)A/38/32. (5)A/AC.172/86 & Corr.1. (6)A/AC.172/87. (7)A/AC.172/87/Add.1. (8)A/AC.172/87/Add.2. (9)A/AC.172/87/ Add.3. (10)YUN 1982, p. 1500, GA res. 37/14 C, 16 Nov. 1982.

UN premises

Addis Ababa

After considering in 1983 the adequacy of the conference facilities of ECA at Addis Ababa, Ethiopia, the General Assembly approved a programme of maintenance and alterations (see

p. 634). It deferred, until 1984, consideration of a proposal for constructing new conference facilities at ECA headquarters.

Bangkok

The Assembly considered, in 1983, a proposal to expand the conference facilities of ESCAP at Bangkok, Thailand (see p. 641).

Nairobi

Construction

In a November 1983 report to the Fifth Committee,[1] the Secretary-General described the progress made in constructing at Nairobi permanent headquarters facilities for UNEP and the United Nations Centre for Human Settlements, also known as Habitat, and accommodation in that complex for other United Nations offices. The report also contained information on the status of appropriations, disbursements and obligations in connection with the construction.

The report stated that, following approval in June 1983 by ACABQ, additional construction of an office block and a visitors and tours pavilion was incorporated in the building work programme in pursuance of a December 1982 Assembly resolution.[2] Completion of all construction work was projected for May/June 1984, while occupancy of a number of buildings began in September 1983. Further negotiations were being planned with the potential occupants with a view to reducing the projected office space deficit. Security requirements were identified by a Headquarters Security Service mission in September.

In December, ACABQ[3] recommended that the Assembly take note of the Secretary-General's report.

GENERAL ASSEMBLY ACTION

On 20 December, on the recommendation of the Fifth Committee, the General Assembly adopted section XXII of resolution 38/234 without vote.

United Nations accommodation at Nairobi
[*The General Assembly . . .*]
Takes note of the report of the Secretary-General on United Nations accommodation at Nairobi and of the related report of the Advisory Committee on Administrative and Budgetary Questions;

. . .

General Assembly resolution 38/234, section XXII

20 December 1983   Meeting 104   Adopted without vote

Approved by Fifth Committee (A/38/760 & Corr.1) without vote, 18 December (meeting 70); oral proposal by Chairman; agenda item 109.
Meeting numbers. GA 38th session: 5th Committee 70; plenary 104.

Common services

The Secretary-General, in a December 1983 report to the Fifth Committee,[4] stated that agreement had been reached between interested parties at Nairobi and at Headquarters on the organizational structure, general procedures and the staffing for common services and the related functions of the administrative offices of UNEP and Habitat. Accordingly, he proposed setting up a United Nations Common Services Unit (UNCS) at Nairobi, effective 1 June 1984, to be funded mainly through redeployment of existing regular budget and extrabudgetary resources. UNCS would provide all tenants with common services (utilities, security, local transportation of some staff, buildings and grounds management), while providing only UNEP and Habitat with joint services covering finances, personnel, computers, conferences, library, procurement, legal liaison, local transportation and communications. The net additional cost to the regular budget was estimated at $109,500 for 1984-1985.

After considering the Secretary-General's report, ACABQ[3] recommended, among other things, that no fixed date should yet be set for the implementation of the joint services, that the proposed budgetary transfer in respect of joint services should not be made at the 1983 Assembly session, and that the Secretary-General should report to the Assembly at its 1985 session on the progress made in integrating administrative services at Nairobi. With regard to common services, ACABQ made a number of observations and recommendations on staffing requirements and financial aspects of the occupancy of the United Nations accommodation, and recommended that the Assembly approve a revised appropriation of $102,700.

GENERAL ASSEMBLY ACTION

Acting on the recommendation of the Fifth Committee, the General Assembly, on 20 December, adopted section XXI of resolution 38/234 without vote.

Common services at the United Nations accommodation at Nairobi

[*The General Assembly . . .*]

1. *Takes note* of the report of the Secretary-General and of the related report of the Advisory Committee on Administrative and Budgetary Questions;

2. *Endorses* the recommendations of the Advisory Committee as contained in its report;

. . .

General Assembly resolution 38/234, section XXI

20 December 1983   Meeting 104   Adopted without vote

Approved by Fifth Committee (A/38/760 & Corr.1) without vote, 18 December (meeting 70); oral proposal by Chairman; agenda item 109.
Meeting numbers. GA 38th session: 5th Committee 70; plenary 104.

Other premises

In an April 1983 report to the Committee for Programme and Co-ordination (CPC),[5] the Secretary-General summarized the results of a 1982 review by the Administrative Management Service (AMS) of the efficiency of maintaining the United Nations Supply Depot—in operation at Pisa, Italy, since 1958, as a central point for the delivery of equipment, materials and supplies to United Nations peace-keeping operations. AMS had concluded that maintaining the Depot would be in the best interests of United Nations peace-keeping missions.

As regards the ECLA Subregional Office for the Caribbean, at Port-of-Spain, Trinidad, the Secretary-General, in a December report[6] to the Assembly's Fifth Committee, requested an additional appropriation of $242,500 for 1984-1985 for the leasing of an additional office space of 6,000 square feet in order to relieve overcrowding of staff and to provide sufficient conference facilities.

REFERENCES

[1]A/C.5/38/36. [2]YUN 1982, p. 1504, GA res. 37/237, sect. IX, 21 Dec. 1982. [3]A/38/7/Add.22 and Corr.1. [4]A/C.5/38/35. [5]E/AC.51/1983/9. [6]A/C.5/38/100.

Computerized information systems and communications

Co-ordination of information systems

ACC activities. In an April 1983 report to the Economic and Social Council, on strengthening co-ordination of information systems in the United Nations system[1]—prepared according to a November 1982 Council resolution[2] and submitted through CPC—the Administrative Committee on Co-ordination (ACC) reported on the establishment, at its first regular session of 1983 (Paris, 30 and 31 March),[3] of an Advisory Committee for the Co-ordination of Information Systems (ACCIS).

By the 1982 resolution, the Council had urged setting up a small central mechanism in ACC, as replacing the Inter-Organization Board for Information Systems (IOB), to ensure more efficient operation of United Nations information systems from the perspective of users at the national level and to enhance the capacity of the United Nations system to process information. The question of establishing such a body was discussed at a joint meeting, held at Geneva on 9 March 1983, of the ACC Consultative Committees on Substantive

Questions—one on programme matters and the other on operational activities.[4]

ACC stated in the report that ACCIS—an inter-secretariat body, composed of representatives of each of the participating organizations and guided by a steering committee—would focus its work programme on: information needs of Member States, tools for accessing United Nations system information, a register of development activities, proposals for new information systems, and basic co-ordination services. It would monitor and orient the work of technical panels of specialists from interested organizations, which would carry out projects under a lead agency able and willing to make its expertise and guidance available.

In May, CPC[5] noted with satisfaction the ACC report, recommended that ACC continue its work, and decided to keep under close review progress made by ACCIS.

The ACC report was also taken note of by the Economic and Social Council, in decision 1983/175 of 28 July; the General Assembly, in section II of resolution 38/277 B of 20 December, endorsed the CPC conclusions and recommendations on the ACC report.

ACCIS activities. At its first session (Geneva, 22 and 23 September),[6] ACCIS drew up its work programme, established a procedure for recruitment of its secretariat staff, and approved guidelines for its technical panels. Panels were set up on: computer-based communication services, a register of development activities, and access to United Nations data bases.

In preparing its 1984-1985 budget estimates, which had previously been reviewed by the ACC Consultative Committee on Administrative Questions (CCAQ) (Financial and Budgetary Questions) (New York, 12-16 September),[7] ACCIS noted that, in accordance with the directives given by the Council[2] and ACC,[3] they were not to exceed the level previously approved for IOB. It estimated that some $1.3 million would be required for the biennium, to be financed by the participating organizations.

In a November report to the Fifth Committee,[8] the Secretary-General said the United Nations share of ACCIS's 1984-1985 estimated budget, representing approximately 43 per cent of the total, would be $561,600, or $288,200 in excess of the provisional amount included in the proposed programme budget for the period. However, no additional appropriation was requested since related expenditures during 1982-1983 had been below the approved estimates.

In October, ACCIS prepared a report on the performance of the Information Systems Unit of the United Nations Department of International Economic and Social Affairs (see p. 427).

On 20 December, on the recommendation of the Fifth Committee, the General Assembly adopted section III of resolution 38/234 without vote.

Advisory Committee for the Co-ordination of Information Systems

[*The General Assembly . . .*]

Approves the programme of work and budget estimates for the Advisory Committee for the Co-ordination of Information Systems for the biennium 1984-1985;

. . .

General Assembly resolution 38/234, section III

20 December 1983　　　Meeting 104　　　Adopted without vote

Approved by Fifth Committee (A/38/760 & Corr.1) without vote, 22 November (meeting 44); oral proposal by Chairman; agenda item 109.
Meeting numbers. GA 38th session: 5th Committee 44; plenary 104.

Budget estimates of the International Computing Centre for 1984

In November 1983, the Secretary-General submitted to the Fifth Committee 1984 budget estimates for the International Computing Centre (ICC) at Geneva,[9] as had been reviewed by the United Nations and 12 other participating organizations and programmes in the system which used and financed ICC services.

The United Nations share of ICC's 1984 estimated budget stood at $1.6 million against a total of $5.5 million.

On 20 December, on the recommendation of the Fifth Committee, the General Assembly adopted section II of resolution 38/234 without vote.

International Computing Centre

[*The General Assembly . . .*]

Approves the budget estimates for the International Computing Centre for the year 1984;

. . .

General Assembly resolution 38/234, section II

20 December 1983　　　Meeting 104　　　Adopted without vote

Approved by Fifth Committee (A/38/760 & Corr.1) without vote, 22 November (meeting 44); oral proposal by Chairman; agenda item 109.
Meeting numbers. GA 38th session: 5th Committee 44; plenary 104.

Revised programme budget estimates for word-processing equipment

In a December 1983 report to the Fifth Committee,[10] the Secretary-General recommended introduction of word-processing equipment in the Conference Services Division of the United Nations Office at Geneva. The non-recurrent costs for 1984-1985—of acquiring and installing the equipment and furniture as well as preparing the site—were estimated at $1.8 million, while recurring costs per biennium for maintenance, supplies and staff were estimated at $470,000. The Secretary-General requested an additional appropriation of $975,600, with the balance to be met from within existing resources.

Acting on the recommendation of ACAQB, the Fifth Committee approved the additional appropriations, on 18 December, by 74 votes to 1, with 8 abstentions.

UN communications

In 1983—observed as World Communications Year: Development of Communications Infrastructures (see p. 576)—ways to improve communications within the United Nations system and with those outside it were discussed in various forums. The Committee on Information considered among other things, at its June/July session,[11] the viability of a United Nations communications satellite (see below) and a world-wide short-wave network involving the regional commissions (see p. 378).

At its February/March session, CCAQ considered a January note[12] by its Secretary on improving telecommunications between its secretariat and United Nations organizations, annexing basic information on the possibilities offered by ICC at Geneva (see above).

In an April report to CPC,[13] the Secretary-General discussed the measures taken to improve the coverage and services of the Development Information System and the co-operative activities with the information systems of the regional commissions (see p. 427).

Communications satellite

The question of the acquisition and operation by the United Nations of its own communications satellite was again discussed in 1983 by the Committee on Information (see p. 362),[11] in pursuance of a December 1982 General Assembly resolution.[14] It heard an oral summary of an interim report prepared by the International Telecommunication Union at the Secretary-General's request, which examined the technical and financial implications of a single-satellite system to cover most major United Nations locations in North and South America, Africa, the Middle East and Europe, as well as a two-satellite system which would also cover Asia. The report concluded that, currently, other alternatives appeared preferable, as the financing of either system would involve major budgetary increases and would significantly impinge on other allocations.

The Committee's suggestion that the Secretary-General should submit a final report on the subject to the Assembly in 1983 was subsequently included in the annex to Assembly resolution 38/82 B of 15 December, as one of 62 recommendations made by the Committee.

The interim report was submitted to the Assembly's Special Political Committee through a note by the Secretary-General[15] in lieu of the final report, which was still under preparation during the Committee's consideration of questions relating to information. It was understood that the Committee on Information would receive the final report at its 1984 substantive session.

REFERENCES

[1]E/1983/48. [2]YUN 1982, p. 1506, ESC res. 1982/71, 10 Nov. 1982. [3]ACC/1983/DEC/1-10 (dec. 1983/9). [4]ACC/1983/10. [5]A/38/38. [6]ACC/1983/26. [7]ACC/1983/21. [8]A/C.5/38/42. [9]A/C.5/38/39. [10]A/C.5/38/79. [11]A/38/21 & Corr.1. [12]ACC/1983/PER/15-ACC/1983/FB/4. [13]E/AC.51/-1983/6. [14]YUN 1982, p. 567, GA res. 37/94 B, 10 Dec. 1982. [15]A/SPC/38/L.3 & Corr.1.

UN Postal Administration

In 1983, gross revenue of the United Nations Postal Administration (UNPA) from the sale of philatelic items at United Nations Headquarters and at overseas offices totalled over $6 million. Revenue from the sale of stamps for philatelic purposes was retained by the United Nations; revenue from stamps used for postage from Headquarters was retained by the United States Postal Service under an agreement between the United Nations and the United States Government. Similarly, revenue from stamps used for postage from the Palais des Nations, Geneva, and from the Vienna International Centre was retained by the Swiss and Austrian postal authorities, respectively, in accordance with agreements between the Organization and the Swiss and Austrian Governments.

Six commemorative stamps and two souvenir cards were issued during the year.

On 28 January, the first commemorative stamp, on the subject of "World Communications Year", was issued in denominations of 20 and 40 United States cents, 1.20 Swiss francs (SwF) and 4 Austrian schillings (S).

The theme of the second commemorative, issued on 18 March, was "Safety at Sea". Stamps were issued in denominations of 20 and 37 cents, SwF 0.40 and 0.80, and S 4 and 6. A souvenir card was also issued.

The third stamp, issued on 22 April in denominations of 20 cents, SwF 1.50 and S 5 and 7, commemorated the "World Food Programme".

On 6 June, the fourth stamp was issued on the theme "Trade and Development", in denominations of 20 and 28 cents, SwF 0.80 and 1.10 and S 4 and 8.50. A souvenir card accompanied the issue.

On 23 September, the fourth group of 16 stamps was issued in the commemorative "Flag Series", in denominations of 20 cents each. This was the fifth commemorative issue for the year.

The sixth and final commemorative, issued on 9 December, honoured the "Thirty-fifth Anniversary of the Universal Declaration of Human Rights". The stamps were issued in denominations of 20 and 40 cents, SwF 0.40 and 1.20 and S 5 and 7.

The number of first day covers serviced for the various issues in 1983 was as follows:

World Communications Year	465,115
Safety at Sea	638,672
World Food Programme	512,109
Trade and Development	530,661
Flag Series	2,214,134
Thirty-fifth Anniversary of the Universal Declaration of Human Rights	737,761

Issue of special postage stamps

As requested by the General Assembly in November 1982,[1] the Secretary-General, in August 1983,[2] provided an analysis of the financial situation of the United Nations (see Chapter I of this section), which included the status of the project to issue special postage stamps. At the Assembly's request, he was to include proposals to use a portion of the revenues to further the cause of the protection of nature.

A total of 10.9 million stamps on the subject of conservation and protection of nature were issued simultaneously in New York, Geneva and Vienna on 19 November 1982.[3] In order to publicize the stamp, UNPA, in co-operation with UNEP, printed brochures, information folders, photographs and press releases for use by the general public, the press and collectors and at stamp shows. An information circular was sent to delegations and staff. Two television programmes were produced and advertisements were taken in specialized European and United States magazines. Special exhibitions were held in the three UNPA offices on conserving and protecting nature and the stamp issue.

As at 31 March 1983, gross sales amounted to $1,867,183, which yielded a net revenue of $1,133,687 after expenses. Income on the issue was expected to be about $1.25 million when the stamps were withdrawn from sale on 19 November.

GENERAL ASSEMBLY ACTION

On 20 December, the General Assembly, on the recommendation of the Fifth Committee, adopted resolution 38/228 A by recorded vote.

Issue of special postage stamps

The General Assembly,

Having considered the report of the Secretary-General on the analysis of the financial situation of the United Nations,

Recalling its resolution 35/113 of 10 December 1980 and, in particular, paragraphs 1 to 3 thereof, according to which the provisions of regulations 5.2 and 7.1 of the Financial Regulations of the United Nations shall not apply to the sale proceeds of postage stamps on the conservation and protection of nature so that a portion of the revenues so earned, after deduction of the cost of producing the stamps, shall be earmarked for promoting, under United Nations auspices, the noble cause of the conservation and protection of nature and endangered species, and the remainder of the net proceeds shall be placed in a special account,

Recalling also its resolution 37/13 of 16 November 1982,

1. *Decides* to allocate one half of the net revenues from the sale of the above-mentioned postage stamps to the United Nations Environment Programme for financing projects which promote conservation and protection of nature and endangered species;

2. *Decides* to allocate the remaining one half of the net proceeds to the United Nations Special Account;

3. *Requests* the Executive Director of the United Nations Environment Programme to submit a report to the Governing Council of the United Nations Environment Programme, at an appropriate time, on the results of the projects and their impact on conservation and protection of nature and endangered species;

4. *Requests* the Secretary-General to submit to the General Assembly at its thirty-ninth session a financial report on the project to issue special postage stamps.

General Assembly resolution 38/228 A

20 December 1983   Meeting 104   132-9 (recorded vote)

Approved by Fifth Committee (A/38/743) by vote (73-8), 19 December (meeting 73); draft by Vice-Chairman (A/C.5/38/L.26, part A), based on informal consultations and orally revised; agenda item 111.

Meeting numbers. GA 38th session: 5th Committee 3-6, 8, 73; plenary 104.

Recorded vote in Assembly as follows:

In favour: Afghanistan, Algeria, Argentina, Australia, Austria, Bahamas, Bahrain, Bangladesh, Barbados, Belgium, Belize, Benin, Bhutan, Bolivia, Botswana, Brazil, Burma, Burundi, Canada, Central African Republic, Chad, Chile, China, Congo, Costa Rica, Cuba, Cyprus, Democratic Kampuchea, Democratic Yemen, Denmark, Djibouti, Dominican Republic, Ecuador, Egypt, El Salvador, Ethiopia, Fiji, Finland, France, Gabon, Gambia, Germany, Federal Republic of, Ghana, Greece, Guatemala, Guinea, Guinea-Bissau, Guyana, Haiti, Honduras, Iceland, India, Indonesia, Iran, Ireland, Israel, Italy, Ivory Coast, Jamaica, Japan, Jordan, Kenya, Kuwait, Lebanon, Lesotho, Liberia, Libyan Arab Jamahiriya, Luxembourg, Madagascar, Malawi, Malaysia, Maldives, Mali, Malta, Mauritania, Mauritius, Mexico, Morocco, Mozambique, Nepal, Netherlands, New Zealand, Nicaragua, Niger, Nigeria, Norway, Oman, Pakistan, Panama, Papua New Guinea, Paraguay, Peru, Philippines, Portugal, Qatar, Romania, Rwanda, Saint Lucia, Saint Vincent and the Grenadines, Samoa, Sao Tome and Principe, Saudi Arabia, Senegal, Sierra Leone, Singapore, Somalia, Spain, Sri Lanka, Sudan, Suriname, Swaziland, Sweden, Syrian Arab Republic, Thailand, Togo, Trinidad and Tobago, Tunisia, Turkey, Uganda, United Arab Emirates, United Kingdom, United Republic of Cameroon, United Republic of Tanzania, United States, Upper Volta, Uruguay, Vanuatu, Venezuela, Viet Nam, Yemen, Yugoslavia, Zambia.

Against: Bulgaria, Byelorussian SSR, Czechoslovakia, German Democratic Republic, Hungary, Mongolia, Poland, Ukrainian SSR, USSR.

REFERENCES

[1]YUN 1982, p. 1424, GA res. 37/13, 16 Nov. 1982. [2]A/C.5/38/9 & Corr.1 & Add.1. [3]YUN 1982, p. 1509.

PART TWO

Intergovernmental organizations related to the United Nations

Chapter I

International Atomic Energy Agency (IAEA)

In 1983, the International Atomic Energy Agency (IAEA) continued to assist research on and practical application of atomic energy for peaceful purposes and to ensure that the assistance provided was not used for military purposes.

Continued emphasis was placed on safeguards, the safety of nuclear power stations, nuclear fuel-cycle services and the management of nuclear wastes, and on providing technical assistance to member States, particularly developing countries.

At the end of 1983, the Treaty on the Non-Proliferation of Nuclear Weapons[a] (Non-Proliferation Treaty (NPT)) had 118 non-nuclear-weapon States parties and 98 per cent of the world's nuclear facilities outside the nuclear-weapon States were under IAEA safeguards. The Agency continued its efforts to improve the effectiveness and efficiency of its international safeguards system, which aimed at deterring the proliferation of nuclear weapons by early detection, while respecting States' sovereign rights. Work also continued on assuring supplies of nuclear material, equipment and technology and fuel-cycle services, on possible schemes for international storage of plutonium and on the international management of spent fuel.

Further progress was made during the year towards completion of an up-to-date set of internationally agreed safety standards for nuclear power plants—IAEA's Nuclear Safety Standards (NUSS)—and the Agency assisted member States in implementing NUSS recommendations through advisory missions and training courses. Increased emphasis was also given to an exchange of information in such fields as safety research, nuclear-plant operating experience and emergency preparedness.

During 1983, IAEA continued to assist in preparations for the United Nations Conference for the Promotion of International Co-operation in the Peaceful Uses of Nuclear Energy which, the General Assembly decided by resolution 38/60, would be held in 1986 (see ECONOMIC AND SOCIAL QUESTIONS, Chapter X).

Membership of IAEA rose to 111 in 1983 when Namibia, represented by the United Nations Council for Namibia, became a member on 17 February. China's application for membership was unanimously approved by the IAEA General Conference on 11 October. China was to become a member on 1 January 1984.

The twenty-seventh session of the IAEA General Conference was held at Vienna, Austria, from 10 to 14 October. The Conference decided, among other things: to declare that armed attacks against nuclear installations devoted to peaceful purposes should be prohibited and to urge member States to adopt binding international rules prohibiting such attacks; to demand that South Africa submit its nuclear installations and facilities to IAEA inspection, and to call on member States which had not done so to end nuclear co-operation with South Africa and, in particular, to terminate transfers of fissionable material and technology to South Africa which could be used to develop nuclear arms; and to call on Israel to withdraw forthwith its threat to attack and destroy nuclear facilities in Iraq and other countries, to withhold Agency research contracts to Israel, to discontinue the purchase of equipment and materials from Israel and to refrain from holding seminars and scientific and technical meetings there if, by the 1984 General Conference, Israel had not complied with the call to withdraw its threat.

The Board of Governors met four times during 1983, in February and June, and twice in October, at Vienna.

Agency safeguards responsibilities

As at 31 December 1983, 118 non-nuclear-weapon States and three nuclear-weapon States (USSR, United Kingdom, United States) had ratified or acceded to NPT. Safeguards agreements with IAEA, concluded under article III of the Treaty, had entered into force for 76 non-nuclear-weapon States parties. Negotiation of an agreement with the USSR under which IAEA might apply safeguards to certain nuclear material in civil nuclear facilities in the USSR commenced. Similar agreements were in force with France (1981), the United Kingdom (1978) and the United States (1980).

Agency safeguards were applied under other agreements in 10 non-nuclear-weapon States not party to either NPT or the Treaty for the Prohibition of Nuclear Weapons in Latin America (Treaty of Tlatelolco) but which have significant nuclear activities—Argentina, Brazil, Chile, Cuba, the Democratic People's Republic of Korea, India,

[a]YUN 1968, p. 17, GA res. 2373(XXII), annex, 12 June 1968.

Israel, Pakistan, South Africa and Spain—as well as in Viet Nam (which is a party to NPT).

At the end of 1983, safeguards applied by IAEA in non-nuclear-weapon States covered material in 147 power reactors, 177 research reactors and critical assemblies, 7 conversion, 40 fuel fabrication, 6 reprocessing and 4 enrichment plants, and in some 500 other installations.

Technical assistance

During 1983, more than 70 countries received IAEA technical assistance in the form of expert services or equipment or both. A total of 631 fellows were carrying out individual field studies, and 891 persons participated in 35 group training projects. Technical assistance provided by IAEA in 1983 exceeded $26 million in value, some 16 per cent higher than in 1982.

The Agency served as the executing agency for 29 large-scale projects financed by the United Nations Development Programme (UNDP). Among these were: nuclear engineering (Argentina); nuclear minerals exploration (Bangladesh, Chile, Colombia, Madagascar); nuclear manpower training, and development of agriculture through nuclear technology (Brazil); centre for isotope applications (Bulgaria); introduction of nuclear techniques (Cuba, Senegal); national centre for radiation technology (Egypt); nuclear techniques in animal production (Nigeria); nuclear energy (Peru); training in nuclear power plant safety analysis, engineering and public information, and manpower development (Philippines); nuclear technology (Romania); radioactive tracer techniques for studying coastal sedimentation (Sri Lanka); industrial application of high-energy ionizing radiation (Yugoslavia); strengthening the regional centre for nuclear studies at Kinshasa (Zaire); industrial application of isotopes and radiation technology, and nuclear techniques training in the mineral industry (regional, Asia and the Pacific); and Rift Valley fever control and modern techniques in physics (interregional).

The Agency also continued to provide large-scale assistance to projects in Bangladesh and India for the use of nuclear techniques in agricultural research, financed by Sweden.

The target for member States' voluntary contributions to IAEA's regular programme was $19 million in 1983, of which $17.6 million was pledged. Other sources of support for the technical assistance programme were UNDP funds ($3.7 million), extrabudgetary contributions ($9.4 million) and assistance in kind ($2.2 million).

Nuclear power

At the end of 1983, 317 nuclear power plants with a total capacity of some 191,000 megawatts (electrical) accounted for around 12 per cent of the world's electricity-generating capacity. The record of operating nuclear power plants continued to be excellent; 3,150 reactor years had accumulated without any significant spread of radioactivity to the environment or any radiation-induced fatality.

The Agency continued to assist developing member States to introduce nuclear-powered electricity-generating plants with planning surveys, feasibility studies and development of manpower and infrastructure. It also continued preparing a series of guidebooks on, for example, manpower development for nuclear power, bid specifications for nuclear power plants, technical and economic evaluation of bids for nuclear power plants, introduction of nuclear power, the interaction of grid characteristics with design and performance of nuclear power plants, nuclear power plant instrumentation and control, qualification of nuclear power plant operations personnel, expansion planning for electrical generation systems, and energy planning in developing countries with special attention to nuclear energy.

In 1983, six interregional training courses, three of which focused on special aspects of nuclear power plant safety, were attended by about 200 participants from developing countries.

IAEA continued to develop its energy and economy data bank and to collect and disseminate information on nuclear technology and the reliability of nuclear power plants. A computerized power-reactor information system containing nuclear power plant operating-experience data provided by member States since 1971 had been in use since 1982.

Environment

In co-operation with the United States Department of Energy, the International Conference on Radioactive Waste Management was held at Seattle, Washington, United States, in May 1983. The Conference brought together 528 participants from 29 member States and eight international organizations. It covered the entire spectrum of radioactive waste management, including technological, environmental, regulatory, institutional, legal, economic, social and policy issues. In general, the Conference confirmed that nuclear power could be harnessed for mankind without creating an unmanageable waste disposal problem.

In the area of handling and treatment of radioactive waste, six reports were published dealing with off-gas treatment, managing waste from nuclear plants, conditioning of wastes and decommissioning of nuclear power plants. Two coordinated research programmes were initiated—on the retention of iodine and other airborne radio-nuclides during abnormal and accident conditions, and the decommissioning and decontamination of nuclear facilities—and three were completed—on the evaluation of solidified high-level waste forms, the treatment of spent ion exchange resins and the testing of particulate filters.

In 1983, IAEA's underground disposal programme organized three technical committee meetings and one advisory group meeting on regulatory, safety, technological and other aspects of underground disposal of radioactive wastes. Publications included a guidebook on disposal of low- and intermediate-level solid radioactive wastes in rock cavities, and reports on concepts and examples of safety analysis for radioactive waste repositories in continental geological formations, and criteria for underground disposal of solid radioactive wastes.

Among material published in 1983 relating to environmental aspects of nuclear energy were a bibliography of information and data for a review of the scientific and technical considerations related to the dumping of radioactive wastes at sea, and reports on an oceanographic model for the dispersion of wastes disposed of in the deep sea, environmental assessment methodologies for sea dumping, *de minimis* concepts in radioactive waste disposal, and the regional and global environmental behaviour of radio-nuclides.

Two co-ordinated research programmes were in progress: one on the role of sediments in the transport and accumulation of radioactive pollutants in rivers and estuaries, and one on the environmental migration of radium and other contaminants present in solid and liquid wastes from the mining and milling of uranium.

Nuclear safety

The development stage of the NUSS programme neared its end in 1983 with the completion of 52 safety codes and guides for nuclear power plants. As part of a new activity aimed at increasing the safety of operating nuclear installations, an operational safety review team was sent to a member State. This activity was to be expanded with teams going to several other member States in 1984.

A revised code of practice on radiation protection in the mining and milling of radioactive ores, jointly prepared by the International Labour Organisation, the World Health Organization (WHO) and IAEA, was published in 1983. Work continued on implementing the revised Basic Safety Standards for Radiation Protection, through publication of documents on occupational safety, radiation protection of the public and the environment, and radiation safety during transport.

Information exchange continued to be emphasized. Safety information was transmitted through training courses and seminars given by IAEA throughout the world, and through visits of individual experts to member States.

The Agency made final preparations in 1983 to initiate a reporting system to collect information on incidents occurring at nuclear power plants. Its purpose would be to provide information to plant operators, designers and regulatory bodies in order to aid in preventing or mitigating the consequences of similar accidents.

To assist member States in emergency planning and preparedness for radiological emergencies, guidelines for mutual emergency assistance in connection with nuclear accidents were prepared. An interregional training course which included instruction in the use of computers in accident assessment was developed. Missions to assess emergency planning arrangements visited three countries, and a report was prepared on a full-scale emergency exercise carried out in Yugoslavia.

Nuclear information

The International Nuclear Information System, with 72 participating countries and 14 international organizations, in 1983 enlarged its bibliographic data base on nuclear literature to some 807,000 records.

Life sciences

In co-operation with WHO and several other international organizations, IAEA continued in 1983 to assist member States—especially the developing countries—with the application of nuclear techniques in medicine, biology and health-related environmental research, and in improving the accuracy of radiation dosimetry for medical and industrial purposes.

A symposium was held jointly with WHO in April on the biological effects of low-level ionizing radiation with special regard to stochastic and non-stochastic effects (Venice, Italy). A training seminar was conducted in June on calibration procedures in Secondary Standard Dosimetry Laboratories (SSDLs) (IAEA Laboratory, Seibersdorf, Austria). Co-sponsored by WHO, advisory group meetings dealt with the future of the dose intercomparison service for radiation therapy, and with radiation sterilization practices for tissue grafts and tissue banking of sterile grafts in the developing countries of Asia and the Far East.

In 1983, Venezuela nominated a dosimetry laboratory for membership in the IAEA/WHO network of SSDLs, bringing the number of member laboratories to 46, 31 of which were in developing countries.

Nineteen co-ordinated research programmes were carried out during 1983. These included: maintenance of nuclear instruments; data processing for internal quality control for radioimmunoassay; optimization of nuclear medicine procedures; comparative methods for studying trace elements in human nutrition; application of nuclear-related techniques in occupational health; high dose standardization and intercomparison for industrial radiation processing; nuclear techniques for determining parasitic antigens in body fluids; possible use of high-LET (linear energy transfer) radiation in cancer therapy; improvement of cancer therapy by combining conventional radiation and physical or chemical means; comparative biological hazards from low-level radiation and major chemical pollutants; analysis of radiation-induced chromosomal aberration for genetic risk evaluation in occupationally exposed workers; radiation sterilization of medical supplies including tissue graft sterilization; and health-related environmental research using nuclear techniques.

Efforts were made to assist the Agency's technical co-operation programme in the relevant areas, particularly for developing member States, including an IAEA/WHO project on the use of brachy-therapy in treating cancer of the cervix, which was started in Egypt. The first training/demonstration course was attended by 33 participants. A training course on nuclear techniques for dealing with parasitic infections, organized by IAEA in collaboration with the United States Department of Energy, was attended by 30 clinicians and biomedical researchers.

Physical sciences and laboratories

IAEA's role in co-ordinating the international effort in controlled fusion continued through the International Tokamak Reactor Workshop, in which scientists from the major fusion laboratories of the European Atomic Energy Community, Japan, the USSR and the United States participated. Work on optimization of the design and cost/benefit/risk analysis of design alternatives was under way in 1983. Problems facing developing countries in their plasma physics and fusion work were addressed at several informal meetings, and assistance was provided in a number of cases.

Support was given by IAEA to a large-scale UNDP project on the industrial application of radioisotopes and radiation technology in Asia and the Pacific, conducted within the framework of the Regional Co-operative Agreement for Research, Development and Training Related to Nuclear Science and Technology. Under this project, construction of an irradiation facility and the commissioning of an associated rubber vulcanization plant were completed in September. Obstacles to the wider use of industrial radiation processing and priorities for international action to overcome them were reviewed by an advisory group.

The Agency continued to support the transfer of isotope hydrology techniques to its member States through 24 technical co-operation projects. Research was also promoted through 18 research contracts. A new co-ordinated programme on isotope application in ground-water hydrology in Latin America was initiated with funding from the Federal Republic of Germany. The current status of isotope hydrology was reviewed at an international symposium at Vienna in September. The symposium was followed by an interregional training course attended by participants from 25 countries.

The Agency continued to provide nuclear data services to member States, responding in 1983 to some 700 requests for data and associated information from more than 60 countries. Expert groups were convened to review the status of basic nuclear properties of reactor materials and to identify requirements associated with the use of nuclear techniques in geological exploration. In line with its general policy of transferring nuclear data technology to developing member States, the Agency organized an interregional training course and study tour in the USSR on neutron physics and nuclear data measurements with accelerators and research reactors, in which 20 scientists from developing countries participated.

The Seibersdorf Laboratory provided support services for the Agency's food and agriculture, life sciences, physical sciences and safeguards programmes. Work in biotechnology in 1983 included producing sterile insects for biological methods of control, developing genetic techniques for rearing only male Mediterranean fruit flies, and developing controlled-release insecticide. Work in the environment and nutrition field focused on applications of nuclear analytical techniques in studies of trace elements in the human diet. In the physical sciences, the Laboratory's work was concerned mainly with instrumentation for nuclear measurements and chemical analysis. The Safeguards Analytical Laboratory, also at Seibersdorf, analysed nuclear fuel-cycle samples collected by IAEA safeguards inspectors.

The International Laboratory of Marine Radioactivity in Monaco continued to evaluate the impact of radio-nuclides released into the marine environment, with particular attention paid to problems connected with the deep-sea disposal of radioactive wastes. During 1983, the Laboratory increased the number of trainees, mostly from developing countries, accepted for training in measuring radioactive and non-radioactive marine pollutants. The Laboratory also continued to organize intercalibrations of measurements of radio-nuclides in marine samples and to develop methods for low-level measurements. In collaboration with the United Nations Environment Programme (UNEP) and the Intergovernmental Oceanographic Commission of the United Nations Educational, Scientific and Cultural Organization, the Laboratory provided scientific and technical expertise in non-nuclear marine pollution for the UNEP action plans for the Mediterranean, Kuwait, and West and Central Africa.

The International Centre for Theoretical Physics at Trieste, Italy, continued research and training-for-research in plasma and nuclear physics, non-conventional energy, elementary particle physics and fundamental theory, applications of physics in medicine and biology, atomic molecular and laser physics, geophysics and mathematics. Among its

1983 activities, the Centre held, for the first time, a workshop/college on the physics of communications, with particular emphasis on significant advances made in space research; 62 scientists took part, 51 of them from developing countries.

Food and agriculture

Under joint programmes of the Food and Agriculture Organization of the United Nations and IAEA, work continued through 27 co-ordinated research programmes on the application of isotope and radiation techniques to increase agricultural production, improve food quality, reduce food losses and minimize pollution of food and the environment. Support was given to about 140 technical assistance projects in 46 developing member States during the year.

Work continued on insect control, particularly of the Mediterranean fruit fly in Peru and Egypt and the tsetse fly in Nigeria. Other projects were designed to improve crop and livestock production.

Secretariat

As at the end of 1983, 1,756 staff members were employed by IAEA. Of these, 619—drawn from 74 countries—were in the Professional and higher categories and 1,137 were in the General Service and Maintenance and Operatives Service categories.

Budget

The General Conference of IAEA at its October 1983 session adopted a regular budget of $96,830,000 for 1984. The target for voluntary contributions to finance the Agency's technical assistance and co-operation programme for 1984 was set at $22,500,000.

Annex I. MEMBERSHIP OF THE INTERNATIONAL ATOMIC ENERGY AGENCY AND CONTRIBUTIONS

(Membership as at 31 December 1983; contributions as assessed for 1983 and 1984)

MEMBER	CONTRIBUTION FOR 1983 Percentage	CONTRIBUTION FOR 1983 Net amount (in US dollars)	CONTRIBUTION FOR 1984 Percentage	CONTRIBUTION FOR 1984 Net amount (in US dollars)
Afghanistan	0.00731	5,924	0.00720	6,396
Albania	0.00731	5,924	0.00720	6,396
Algeria	0.07995	64,790	0.08571	76,096
Argentina	0.54047	437,973	0.48445	430,122
Australia	1.91762	1,553,965	1.62330	1,441,264
Austria	0.74632	604,788	0.77546	688,501
Bangladesh	0.02976	24,113	0.02293	20,359
Belgium	1.27496	1,033,177	1.32346	1,175,044
Bolivia	0.00731	5,924	0.00720	6,396
Brazil	0.85056	689,258	0.91427	811,740
Bulgaria	0.10844	87,873	0.12019	106,709
Burma	0.00765	6,199	0.00751	6,671
Byelorussian SSR	0.41462	335,991	0.37222	330,481
Canada	3.44136	2,788,740	3.19490	2,836,625
Chile	0.05101	41,340	0.05028	44,644
China*	—	—	0.77187	685,310
Colombia	0.07738	62,708	0.07648	67,900
Costa Rica	0.01369	11,095	0.01356	12,039
Cuba	0.07484	60,648	0.06145	54,556
Cyprus	0.00731	5,924	0.00720	6,396
Czechoslovakia	0.87071	705,585	0.78580	697,680
Democratic Kampuchea	0.00731	5,924	0.00720	6,396
Democratic People's Republic of Korea	0.03487	28,254	0.03448	30,614
Denmark	0.77741	629,986	0.77546	688,501
Dominican Republic	0.02007	16,265	0.01992	17,681
Ecuador	0.01369	11,095	0.01356	12,039
Egypt	0.04974	40,311	0.04912	43,615
El Salvador	0.00731	5,924	0.00720	6,396
Ethiopia	0.00731	5,924	0.00720	6,396
Finland	0.50791	411,591	0.49630	440,642
France	6.56139	5,317,087	6.74135	5,985,372
Gabon	0.02073	16,800	0.02068	18,359
German Democratic Republic	1.46154	1,184,374	1.43719	1,276,023
Germany, Federal Republic of	8.70706	7,055,850	8.84026	7,848,916
Ghana	0.02084	16,884	0.01426	12,658
Greece	0.23729	192,288	0.26696	237,019
Guatemala	0.01403	11,370	0.01387	12,314
Haiti	0.00731	5,924	0.00720	6,396
Holy See	0.01037	8,400	0.01034	9,179
Hungary	0.24598	199,333	0.17850	158,486
Iceland	0.03110	25,200	0.03102	27,539
India	0.44172	357,951	0.27672	245,686
Indonesia	0.11056	89,590	0.09035	80,215
Iran	0.44298	358,975	0.38856	344,988
Iraq	0.07868	63,760	0.07819	69,424
Ireland	0.16585	134,398	0.18611	165,242
Israel	0.25914	209,997	0.23781	211,140
Italy	3.61757	2,931,538	3.87731	3,442,506
Ivory Coast	0.02007	16,265	0.01992	17,681
Jamaica	0.01392	11,284	0.01377	12,228
Japan	10.04421	8,139,427	10.68070	9,482,961
Jordan	0.00731	5,924	0.00720	6,396
Kenya	0.00731	5,924	0.00720	6,396
Kuwait	0.20731	167,997	0.25849	229,500
Lebanon	0.02041	16,540	0.01387	12,314
Liberia	0.00731	5,924	0.00720	6,396
Libyan Arab Jamahiriya	0.23841	193,197	0.26883	238,682
Liechtenstein	0.01037	8,400	0.01034	9,179
Luxembourg	0.05183	42,000	0.06204	55,081
Madagascar	0.00731	5,924	0.00720	6,396
Malaysia	0.06039	48,935	0.05990	53,183
Mali	0.00731	5,924	0.00720	6,396
Mauritius	0.00731	5,924	0.00720	6,396
Mexico	0.52898	428,662	0.59364	527,071
Monaco	0.01037	8,400	0.01034	9,179
Mongolia	0.00731	5,924	0.00720	6,396
Morocco	0.03444	27,911	0.03410	30,271
Namibia†	—	—	—	—
Netherlands	1.71032	1,385,971	1.84043	1,634,042
New Zealand	0.27987	226,796	0.26883	238,682
Nicaragua	0.00731	5,924	0.00720	6,396

MEMBER	CONTRIBUTION FOR 1983		CONTRIBUTION FOR 1984	
	Percentage	Net amount (in US dollars)	Percentage	Net amount (in US dollars)
Niger	0.00731	5,924	0.00720	6,396
Nigeria	0.10632	86,157	0.12461	110,636
Norway	0.52864	428,390	0.52731	468,181
Pakistan	0.05101	41,340	0.04393	39,002
Panama	0.01369	11,095	0.01356	12,039
Paraguay	0.00731	5,924	0.00720	6,396
Peru	0.04125	33,424	0.04719	41,898
Philippines	0.07185	58,225	0.06454	57,303
Poland	0.93405	756,919	0.58216	516,877
Portugal	0.12800	103,728	0.12058	107,053
Qatar	0.03110	25,200	0.03102	27,539
Republic of Korea	0.10036	81,330	0.11864	105,336
Romania	0.14711	119,216	0.13273	117,844
Saudi Arabia	0.61157	495,589	0.88920	789,483
Senegal	0.00731	5,924	0.00720	6,396
Sierra Leone	0.00731	5,924	0.00720	6,396
Singapore	0.05274	42,735	0.05874	52,154
South Africa	0.29638	240,172	0.28066	249,183
Spain	1.78287	1,444,768	1.99553	1,771,746
Sri Lanka	0.01403	11,370	0.00751	6,671
Sudan	0.00754	6,113	0.00742	6,585
Sweden	1.37862	1,117,176	1.36481	1,211,763
Switzerland	1.09875	890,380	1.13734	1,009,802

MEMBER	CONTRIBUTION FOR 1983		CONTRIBUTION FOR 1984	
	Percentage	Net amount (in US dollars)	Percentage	Net amount (in US dollars)
Syrian Arab Republic	0.02007	16,265	0.01992	17,681
Thailand	0.06846	55,478	0.05509	48,913
Tunisia	0.02007	16,265	0.01992	17,681
Turkey	0.20411	165,406	0.21496	190,851
Uganda	0.00731	5,924	0.00720	6,396
Ukrainian SSR	1.53410	1,243,173	1.36481	1,211,763
USSR	11.63014	9,424,600	10.90816	9,684,921
United Arab Emirates	0.10366	83,999	0.16543	146,880
United Kingdom	4.67486	3,788,320	4.83888	4,296,248
United Republic of Cameroon	0.00731	5,924	0.00720	6,396
United Republic of Tanzania	0.00731	5,924	0.00720	6,396
United States	25.91386	20,999,553	25.84873	22,950,050
Uruguay	0.02806	22,740	0.02774	24,628
Venezuela	0.33937	275,012	0.36228	321,654
Viet Nam	0.02168	17,570	0.01503	13,344
Yugoslavia	0.28918	234,336	0.30586	271,559
Zaire	0.01392	11,284	0.00742	6,585
Zambia	0.01369	11,095	0.00720	6,396
Total	100.00000	81,036,000	100.00000	89,471,310

*Membership effective 1 January 1984.

†United Nations organizations were requested by the General Assembly in resolution 36/121 D of 10 December 1981 "to grant a waiver of the assessment of Namibia during the period in which it is represented by the United Nations Council for Namibia".

Annex II.   OFFICERS AND OFFICES OF THE INTERNATIONAL ATOMIC ENERGY AGENCY

BOARD OF GOVERNORS
(For period October 1983 — September 1984)

OFFICERS

Chairman: Roberto Rosenzweig-Díaz (Mexico).
Vice-Chairmen: André Ernemann (Belgium), Ivan Pandev (Bulgaria).

MEMBERS

Argentina, Australia, Austria, Belgium, Brazil, Bulgaria, Canada, Chile, Cuba, Denmark, Egypt, France, Germany, Federal Republic of, Hungary, India, Iraq, Italy, Japan, Kenya, Libyan Arab Jamahiriya, Mexico, Nigeria, Pakistan, Philippines, Portugal, Syrian Arab Republic, Thailand, Tunisia, USSR, United Kingdom, United States, Venezuela, Yugoslavia, Zaire.

MAIN COMMITTEES OF THE BOARD OF GOVERNORS

ADMINISTRATIVE AND BUDGETARY COMMITTEE

Participation in the Administrative and Budgetary Committee is open to all members of the Board of Governors.

TECHNICAL ASSISTANCE COMMITTEE

Participation in the Technical Assistance Committee is open to all members of the Board of Governors.

SCIENTIFIC ADVISORY COMMITTEE

K. Beckurts (Federal Republic of Germany), D. Beninson (Argentina), A. Bennini (Algeria), Floyd L. Culler (United States), H. Dunster (United Kingdom), G. Fernández de la Garza (Mexico), L. Gutiérrez Jodra (Spain), J. Jennekens (Canada), Malu wa Kalenga (Zaire), J. Minczewski (Poland), H. Murata (Japan), R. Ramanna (India), I. Ursu (Romania), A. A. Vasiliev (USSR), G. Vendryes (France).

SENIOR SECRETARIAT OFFICERS

Director General: Hans Blix.
Deputy Director General for Safeguards: Hans Gruemm.
Deputy Director General for Nuclear Energy and Safety: Leonard Konstantinov.

Deputy Director General for Administration: Nelson F. Sievering, Jr.
Deputy Director General for Technical Co-operation: Carlos Vélez Ocón.
Deputy Director General for Research and Isotopes: Maurizio Zifferero.

HEADQUARTERS AND OTHER OFFICE

HEADQUARTERS
International Atomic Energy Agency
Vienna International Centre
Wagramerstrasse 5, P. O. Box 100
A-1400 Vienna, Austria
  Cable address: INATOM VIENNA
  Telephone: (222) 2360-1270
  Telex: 1-12645

LIAISON OFFICE
International Atomic Energy Agency
  Liaison Office at the United Nations
United Nations Headquarters, Room DC1-1155
New York, N. Y. 10017, United States
  Telephone: (212) 754-6010, 754-6011

Chapter II

International Labour Organisation (ILO)

During 1983, the International Labour Organisation (ILO) continued activities in its six major programme areas: promotion of policies to create employment and satisfy basic human needs; development of human resources; improvement of working and living conditions and environment; promoting social security; strengthening of industrial relations and tripartite (government/employer/worker) co-operation; and the advancement of human rights in the social and labour fields. The main instruments of action continued to be standard-setting, technical co-operation activities, research and publishing.

The ILO membership remained at 150 during the year.

Meetings

The sixty-ninth session of the International Labour Conference, held at Geneva from 1 to 22 June 1983, was attended by some 1,850 delegates and advisers from 138 countries. The Conference had before it the annual report of the ILO Governing Body, the report of the Director-General, focusing on child labour, and the nineteenth special report on the effect of *apartheid* on labour and employment in South Africa.

The Conference adopted an International Labour Convention and Recommendation on vocational rehabilitation and employment (disabled persons), and a Recommendation on maintenance of rights in social security. It held a first discussion on employment policy with a view to adopting an instrument on this theme at its 1984 session.

A general discussion was held on the social aspects of industrialization.

In accordance with usual practice, a tripartite Conference committee examined the application by member States of the 158 Conventions and 166 Recommendations adopted since 1919 and reviewed the application of ILO standards concerning freedom of association, the right to organize, collective bargaining and rural workers' organizations.

A resolution was adopted on young people and the ILO contribution to International Youth Year (1985). In another resolution, the Conference decided to place on the agenda of its seventieth (1984) session all questions examined by its Committee on Structure relating to amendment of the ILO Constitution.

Ratifications of ILO Conventions registered during the Conference raised their total to 5,103.

Special sittings of the Conference were addressed by President Hosni Mubarak of Egypt, Prime Minister Robert Hawke of Australia and Prime Minister Robert Mugabe of Zimbabwe.

The Sixth African Regional Conference, held at Tunis, Tunisia, from 4 to 12 October, was attended by some 230 delegates from 40 countries. A general discussion was held on the Director-General's report on social aspects of development in Africa. Conclusions were adopted on the application of the Declaration of Principles and Programme of Action of the 1976 World Employment Conference,[a] and on conditions of work and the working environment. The Conference also reviewed the ratification and implementation of international labour standards, and adopted resolutions on standards, action against *apartheid* and aid to refugees.

Reviews of technical co-operation programmes and the application of international labour standards in Asia and the Pacific were carried out by the eighteenth session of the Asian Advisory Committee (Geneva, 21-24 November). It decided that rural and urban vocational training and rehabilitation of the disabled should be included on the agenda of the next ILO Asian Regional Conference.

Two sets of conclusions on improving working conditions and the working environment in the construction industry and on management training for the industry in developing countries were adopted at the tenth session of the Building, Civil Engineering and Public Works Committee (Geneva, 12-21 April). Resolutions were adopted on future ILO activities, measures to expand employment, collective bargaining, labour-leasing and labour-contracting.

Technical discussions at the eleventh session of the Metal Trades Committee (Geneva, 20-29 September) led to the adoption of conclusions on collective bargaining, and training and retraining. Resolutions were adopted on employment and social policies, freedom of association, multinational enterprises and occupational safety and health.

Among issues examined at the tenth session of the Advisory Committee on Rural Development (Geneva, 22 November–1 December) were the promotion of rural employment through non-farm activities, aspects of rural labour markets and employment policies, and labour utilization, remuneration and the position of women. ILO rural development activities since 1979 were also reviewed.

[a]YUN 1976, pp. 346 and 942.

Social problems and employment in developing countries and the need to adapt training to changing needs were considered by the Third Tripartite Technical Meeting for Hotels, Restaurants and Similar Establishments (Geneva, 6-15 December). The meeting adopted conclusions on these items, as well as resolutions on other aspects of the hotel and catering sector.

Working environment

The International Programme for the Improvement of Working Conditions and Environment (PIACT) continued to encourage member States to set definite objectives. The Programme used all means of action at ILO's disposal, including standard-setting, studies and research, tripartite meetings, technical co-operation and the dissemination of information. In addition to the wide range of activities carried out within PIACT during 1983, preparatory work began for its evaluation by the International Labour Conference at its 1984 session.

A number of technical co-operation activities were designed to assist member States in establishing policies for the improvement of working conditions and environment through the organization of national tripartite seminars or multidisciplinary team missions. Activities included a large-scale project to assist Angola; a national tripartite seminar on occupational safety and health in Bolivia; and support for tripartite national workshops in Indonesia and Thailand. Some 20 technical advisory missions were carried out and preparatory work was undertaken for forthcoming missions and national tripartite meetings.

Training activities were increased and an innovative consultancy and training programme was organized for the benefit of small-scale enterprises in Asia, which included the development of training materials.

Continued emphasis was placed on disseminating technical information. The Clearing-house for the Dissemination of Information on Conditions of Work published two issues of *Conditions of work: A cumulative digest*, containing fact sheets on law and practice, information about research in progress and forthcoming meetings, and selected bibliographies in occupational safety and health.

Collaboration with the World Health Organization (WHO) and other United Nations agencies in occupational safety and health continued, and included participation in the United Nations Environment Programme/WHO/ILO International Programme on Chemical Safety, as well as close co-operation with the International Atomic Energy Agency and WHO in protecting workers against ionizing radiation.

In 1983, the International Occupational Safety and Health Information Centre added two new centres to its network of national centres, bringing the total to 46.

World Employment Programme

The World Employment Programme (WEP) was launched in 1969 to assist Governments to promote an increase in employment and income, alleviate poverty and satisfy basic needs. The Declaration of Principles and Programme of Action adopted by the 1976 World Employment Conference, endorsed by the 1979 International Labour Conference, reinforced ILO's central role in the world-wide attack on unemployment and poverty.

During 1983, through its action-oriented research, technical advisory services and other field activities, WEP continued to address employment and development problems of the rural poor, of disadvantaged groups such as women and youth, and of the rapidly growing urban informal sector. Among other important elements comprising this major programme were employment, manpower and basic needs planning, population and labour-market policy, appropriate and new technologies, special public works programmes, participatory organizations, and international aspects of employment and adjustment policy. Much of this work was carried out by WEP regional employment teams in Africa and southern Africa, Asia and Latin America.

Field activities

During 1983, ILO spent almost $94.7 million on technical co-operation activities (about 8.5 per cent less than in 1982) to promote employment, development of human resources and social institutions, and improvement in living and working conditions.

Most of this expenditure ($44 million) continued to be financed by the United Nations Development Programme (UNDP). The ILO regular programme provided $9.1 million, while expenditure funded from multi-bilateral arrangements and other special programmes was $36.4 million. Activities financed by the United Nations Fund for Population Activities (UNFPA) accounted for $5.1 million.

Training received the largest share of funds ($34.8 million), followed by employment planning and promotion ($30.8 million), sectoral activities ($13.2 million), industrial relations and labour administration ($3.8 million), working conditions and environment ($3.1 million), workers' activities ($2.9 million), regional and other services ($1.4 million), personnel, budget and finance, and internal administration ($1.2 million) and social security ($1.1 million); other activities received $2.5 million.

A breakdown of expenditure on technical co-operation by field of activity and source of funds, and country, territory, region or organization is shown in the following tables.

ASSISTANCE IN 1983 BY ACTIVITY AND SOURCE OF FUNDS
(Excluding programme support costs; in US dollars)

Activity	Regular budget	UNDP	Trust funds (including UNFPA)	Total
Training	2,088,222	22,900,831	9,826,155	34,815,208
Employment and development	2,219,458	10,380,024	18,155,122	30,754,604
Sectoral activities	336,896	6,352,982	6,461,752	13,151,630
Industrial relations and labour administration	1,239,821	1,109,436	1,475,634	3,824,891
Working conditions and environment	861,445	1,859,103	370,366	3,090,914
Workers' activities	1,093,757	—	1,839,537	2,933,294
Regional and other services		169,755	1,216,854	1,386,609
Personnel, budget and finance, internal administration	—	29,700	1,124,304	1,154,004
Social security	124,714	667,801	300,876	1,093,391
Employers' activities	381,791	—	170,472	552,263
Promotion of equality	225,921	1,500	311,385	538,806
Statistics and special studies	356,456	102,933	62,091	521,480
International Institute for Labour Studies	53,303	430,364	35,774	519,441
International labour standards	159,618	—	—	159,618
Programming and management	—	—	95,931	95,931
General analysis of labour problems	2,208	14,916	51,952	69,076
Total	9,143,610	44,019,345	41,498,205	94,661,160

COUNTRIES, TERRITORIES, REGIONS AND ORGANIZATIONS AIDED BY ILO IN 1983

EXPENDITURES ON AID GIVEN BY SOURCE OF FUNDS
(in US dollars)

COUNTRY, TERRITORY OR OTHER	No. of experts provided	No. of fellowships awarded	ILO regular programme	UNDP*	UNFPA	Trust funds	Total
Afghanistan	—	5	—	14,189	26,229	—	40,418
Algeria	15	47	7,068	533,166	—	—	540,234
Angola	6	16	22,320	943,071	—	—	965,391
Antigua and Barbuda	2	1	3,932	180,141	—	—	184,073
Argentina	4	22	11,717	295,596	—	—	307,313
Austria	—	1	—	—	—	—	—
Bahamas	3	2	—	77,042	—	143,096	220,138
Bahrain	1	2	1,240	97,460	—	—	98,700
Bangladesh	32	17	43,458	1,276,296	160,363	1,045,642	2,525,759
Barbados	1	1	7,321	—	—	—	7,321
Belgium	—	3	—	—	—	—	—
Belize	—	2	17,896	(223)†	—	—	17,673
Benin	17	10	16,727	827,664	—	298,531	1,142,922
Bhutan	1	1	938	44,697	—	—	45,635
Bolivia	3	8	51,413	—	(2,350)†	—	49,063
Botswana	18	6	15,147	325,976	—	643,592	984,715
Brazil	9	35	95,653	567,521	—	13,101	676,275
Bulgaria	—	11	23,806	75,746	—	—	99,552
Burma	17	18	12,330	1,155,375	—	14,688	1,182,393
Burundi	21	6	167,972	827,714	—	930,010	1,925,696
Canada	—	1	—	—	—	—	—
Cape Verde	5	1	—	298,296	—	423,315	721,611
Caribbean islands	—	—	179,081	24,345	—	—	203,426
Cayman Islands	—	3	—	7,933	—	—	7,933
Central African Republic	3	3	—	367,778	—	—	367,778
Chad	1	—	—	28,037	—	—	28,037
Chile	1	7	13,768	9,377	—	49,853	72,998
China	—	12	31,271	—	—	—	31,271
Colombia	3	15	33,368	3,114	—	55,867	92,349
Comoros	3	1	8,069	(910)†	—	—	7,159
Congo	9	17	1,907	781,745	17,708	77,732	879,092
Cook Islands	—	—	2,706	—	—	—	2,706
Costa Rica	6	15	72,070	90,209	—	201,064	363,343
Cuba	2	3	11,335	69,493	—	—	80,828
Cyprus	4	4	49,983	75,632	—	—	125,615
Democractic Yemen	13	6	40,328	351,188	114,975	606,961	1,113,452
Djibouti	3	5	7,733	248,665	—	—	256,398
Dominica	3	—	22,010	30,568	—	214,660	267,238
Dominican Republic	8	7	9,865	234,300	—	197,929	442,094
Ecuador	1	15	27,491	251,363	—	—	278,854
Egypt	21	79	14,948	345,259	99,051	893,866	1,353,124
El Salvador	—	3	14,568	16,724	—	(1,415)†	29,877

			EXPENDITURES ON AID GIVEN BY SOURCE OF FUNDS (in US dollars)				
COUNTRY, TERRITORY OR OTHER	No. of experts provided	No. of fellowships awarded	ILO regular programme	UNDP*	UNFPA	Trust funds	Total
Equatorial Guinea	2	4	—	87,720	—	—	87,720
Ethiopia	23	40	31,481	826,518	—	184,810	1,042,809
Fiji	8	6	20,583	138	187,701	244,252	452,674
France	—	17	—	—	—	—	—
Gabon	4	3	2,136	188,443	1,626	172,024	364,229
Gambia	11	11	6,262	254,749	—	286,603	547,614
German Democratic Republic	—	2	—	—	—	—	—
Germany, Federal Republic of	—	2	—	—	—	—	—
Ghana	2	6	7,558	—	—	231,363	238,921
Greece	—	1	889	—	—	—	889
Grenada	—	2	1,700	—	—	—	1,700
Guatemala	2	2	5,468	307	258,817	—	264,592
Guinea	5	12	—	353,147	—	—	353,147
Guinea-Bissau	5	2	12,524	245,938	—	152,262	410,724
Guyana	—	5	3,529	—	—	—	3,529
Haiti	16	1	41,917	1,269,361	—	98,217	1,409,495
Honduras	3	11	14,401	370,439	—	7,028	391,868
Hong Kong	—	5	—	14,299	17,304	—	31,603
Hungary	—	—	945	—	—	—	945
India	23	68	167,803	1,214,049	334,861	1,120,209	2,836,922
Indonesia	33	68	81,564	1,065,320	—	436,676	1,583,560
Iran	2	8	—	2,576,620	—	—	2,576,620
Iraq	25	12	1,118	393,849	—	1,648,215	2,043,182
Israel	—	—	1,129	—	—	—	1,129
Italy	—	365	—	—	—	—	—
Ivory Coast	7	13	10,967	—	—	476,827	487,794
Jamaica	3	2	25,737	—	—	15,403	41,140
Japan	—	1	2,225	—	—	—	2,225
Jordan	10	6	36,430	341,061	8,673	—	386,164
Kenya	21	30	15,695	647,303	—	520,528	1,183,526
Kiribati	—	1	—	11,264	32,579	—	43,843
Kuwait	4	3	29,222	186,144	—	991	216,357
Lao People's Democratic Republic	11	4	7,557	442,813	—	18,070	468,440
Lebanon	1	5	19,513	13,972	—	—	33,485
Lesotho	4	—	17,941	41,392	—	208,193	267,526
Liberia	1	15	2,363	57,494	—	(1,556)†	58,301
Libyan Arab Jamahiriya	3	31	5,010	375,862	—	14,338	395,210
Madagascar	7	30	16,523	298,049	—	209,792	524,364
Malawi	16	6	9,549	1,068,711	—	17,611	1,095,871
Malaysia	5	63	59,075	137,889	—	153,753	350,717
Maldives	2	—	4,149	314,139	—	—	318,288
Mali	7	11	12,134	179,121	109,042	436,100	736,397
Malta	1	2	6,566	24,892	—	—	31,458
Mauritania	10	7	18,369	564,387	—	371,492	954,248
Mauritius	2	3	18,031	13,886	—	—	31,917
Mexico	10	13	18,035	464,260	—	104,458	586,753
Mongolia	2	—	6,262	(1,292)†	—	—	4,970
Morocco	6	8	14,578	55,614	—	2,271	72,463
Mozambique	4	3	6,262	—	—	235,675	241,937
Namibia	5	—	160	377,652	—	1,122,890	1,500,702
National liberation movements‡	—	22	122,753	(20,318)†	—	—	102,435
Nepal	13	17	90,363	876,080	17,156	331,480	1,315,079
Netherlands	—	6	—	—	—	—	—
Netherlands Antilles	10	1	3,422	376,879	—	—	380,301
New Caledonia	—	—	—	—	—	3,326	3,326
New Zealand	—	1	—	—	—	—	—
Nicaragua	2	7	12,182	24,250	—	238,981	275,413
Niger	10	19	591	252,460	—	195,754	448,805
Nigeria	11	36	—	570,648	—	34,560	605,208
Niue	—	—	—	9,917	—	—	9,917
Oman	—	2	—	—	—	—	—
Pakistan	22	26	89,598	646,336	46,326	694,543	1,476,803
Panama	4	6	29,032	199,823	—	109,064	337,919
Papua New Guinea	3	2	8,405	39,105	—	164,787	212,297
Paraguay	5	4	4,816	216,648	—	262,150	483,614
Peru	11	13	65,569	64,898	188,190	172,826	491,483
Philippines	5	31	158,263	4,356	—	259,033	421,652
Poland	—	5	—	8,400	—	—	8,400
Portugal	1	165	72,130	264,231	—	—	336,361
Qatar	—	2	—	—	—	—	—
Republic of Korea	1	12	21,224	396	—	—	21,620
Romania	—	3	27,591	—	—	—	27,591
Rwanda	3	2	70,534	143,230	—	40,701	254,465
St. Kitts-Nevis-Anguilla	—	1	638	—	—	—	638
Saint Lucia	2	1	28,805	—	—	—	28,805
Saint Vincent and the Grenadines	—	2	—	(8,439)†	—	—	(8,439)†
Samoa	—	1	2,000	—	—	—	2,000

COUNTRY, TERRITORY OR OTHER	No. of experts provided	No. of fellowships awarded	ILO regular programme	UNDP*	UNFPA	Trust funds	Total
			EXPENDITURES ON AID GIVEN BY SOURCE OF FUNDS (in US dollars)				
Saudi Arabia	2	65	5,740	99,866	—	53,051	158,657
Senegal	16	29	4,289	684,837	—	1,284,137	1,973,263
Seychelles	—	1	—	—	—	—	—
Sierra Leone	3	3	10,081	5,846	51,740	132,602	200,269
Singapore	—	12	75	246	—	—	321
Solomon Islands	3	2	3,396	192,978	—	—	196,374
Somalia	16	12	26,405	586,221	93,596	413,981	1,120,203
Spain	—	3	—	—	—	—	—
Sri Lanka	9	24	24,042	355,669	49,206	130,821	559,738
Sudan	21	40	67,507	947,403	156,971	1,049,732	2,221,613
Suriname	—	—	—	2,587	—	—	2,587
Swaziland	5	3	39,360	151,330	—	—	190,690
Switzerland	4	4	—	—	—	38,558	38,558
Syrian Arab Republic	4	9	6,709	180,283	—	—	186,992
Thailand	29	44	55,760	1,129,891	—	604,056	1,789,707
Togo	7	1	17,245	460,094	—	712,892	1,190,231
Tokelau	—	—	—	14	—	—	14
Tonga	—	—	3,000	15,486	—	—	18,486
Trinidad and Tobago	5	7	—	113,321	—	54,267	167,588
Trust Territory of the Pacific Islands	—	—	3,635	—	—	—	3,635
Tunisia	3	19	—	24,261	—	20,879	45,140
Turkey	2	33	93,146	88,703	—	—	181,849
Tuvalu	1	—	3,662	38,382	15,348	—	57,392
Uganda	23	12	68,496	1,068,913	—	—	1,137,409
United Arab Emirates	4	2	—	278,601	—	5,178	283,779
United Kingdom	—	2	—	—	—	—	—
United Republic of Cameroon	25	23	30,345	758,253	153,959	413,071	1,355,628
United Republic of Tanzania	11	48	51,435	432,261	—	1,684,316	2,168,012
United States	—	2	—	—	—	—	—
Upper Volta	9	7	3,131	269,768	—	465,563	738,462
Uruguay	2	6	1,980	10,851	—	383	13,214
Vanuatu	2	—	4,994	115,641	—	7,988	128,623
Venezuela	2	12	16,789	132,835	—	—	149,624
Viet Nam	—	1	7,305	—	—	—	7,305
Yemen	—	10	10,400	—	—	—	10,400
Yugoslavia	—	1	—	—	—	—	—
Zaire	12	66	5,415	582,269	—	161,499	749,183
Zambia	15	13	41,577	—	17,157	352,539	411,273
Zimbabwe	7	4	40,779	332,864	—	45,490	419,133
Subtotal	887	2,228	3,257,413	37,678,631	2,156,228	24,435,195	67,527,467
INTERCOUNTRY REGIONAL PROJECTS+							
Africa	56	—	1,252,267	1,358,329	340,991	5,242,071	8,193,658
Asia	46	—	1,775,208	1,526,777	613,728	1,875,448	5,791,161
Europe	2	—	496	236,133	—	4,740	241,369
Latin America and the Caribbean	31	—	1,601,731	724,120	260,776	1,556,988	4,143,615
Arab States in the Middle East	7	—	89,385	128,159	—	33,883	251,427
Subtotal	142	—	4,719,087	3,973,518	1,215,495	8,713,130	18,621,230
INTERREGIONAL PROJECTS	62	—	1,167,110	2,457,034	1,754,427	7,199,538	12,578,109
Total	1,091	2,228	9,143,610	44,109,183	5,126,150	40,347,863	98,726,806
Deduct programme support costs	—	—	—	(89,838)	—	(3,975,808)	(4,065,646)
GRAND TOTAL	1,091	2,228	9,143,610	44,019,345	5,126,150	36,372,055	94,661,160

*Includes projects for which ILO acted as executing and associated agency.

†Adjustment on figures previously reported.

‡Liberation movements of South Africa.

+Number of fellowships awarded included in the list above by country or territory.

Educational activities

The International Institute for Labour Studies at Geneva, an ILO centre for advanced labour and social studies, held its eighteenth annual international internship course on active labour policy development from 19 April to 1 June 1983 in Spanish. Of the 22 participants, 20 came from Latin America, one from Spain and one from the Ukrainian SSR. The four major topics studied were: processes of economic and social change;

manpower and population policies; labour-management relations; and the role of ILO in formulating and implementing labour and social policy. The Institute also organized a UNDP-supported training programme for officials to be attached to the Office of the President of Benin.

During 1983, the ILO International Centre for Advanced Technical and Vocational Training at Turin, Italy, organized 83 courses and seminars involving 1,680 participants from 138 countries, as well as administering and executing 482 fellowships and study tours. There was increased demand for the training of trainers and managers, particularly in the energy, small enterprises and rural co-operatives sectors. Management courses and seminars represented one third of total activity. Four seminars and workshops were completed: one in Africa, on interaction between Governments and employers' and workers' organizations in planning and programming vocational training; another in Asia, on the management of welfare facilities for women workers; and two in Latin America, on collective bargaining and international labour standards.

Publications

ILO's published research covered a wide range of topical social and labour questions. New volumes issued in 1983 included: *Accident prevention: A workers' education manual*; *Collective bargaining: A response to the recession in industrialised market economy countries*; *Economics: A workers' education manual*; *Employment and manpower problems and policy issues in Arab countries: Proposals for the future*; *International conflicts of labour law: A survey of the law applicable to the international employment relation*; *Labour co-operatives: Retrospect and prospects*; *Microelectronics and office jobs: The impact of the chip on women's employment*; *Occupational safety and health in the iron and steel industry: An ILO code of practice*;

Rural small-scale industries and employment in Africa and Asia; and *Strategic management of development programmes*.

A new, completely revised edition of the *Encyclopaedia of occupational health and safety* was published, in two volumes, and the forty-third (1983) issue of the *Year Book of Labour Statistics* appeared. Regular periodicals and technical series continued to be published, including the bimonthly *International Labour Review*, the quarterly *Social and Labour Bulletin* and the biannual *Legislative Series*.

Secretariat

As at 31 December 1983, the total number of full-time staff under permanent, fixed-term and short-term appointments at ILO headquarters and elsewhere was 2,982. Of these, 1,465 were in the Professional and higher categories (drawn from 114 nationalities), and 1,517 were in the General Service or Maintenance categories. Of the Professional staff, 636 were assigned to technical co-operation projects.

Budget

The International Labour Conference in June 1983 adopted a budget of $254.7 million for the 1984-1985 biennium.

MAIN CATEGORIES OF EXPENDITURE IN 1983

	Amount (in US dollars)
Staff costs	72,432,156
Refund to the Working Capital Fund	12,175,608
General operating expenses	9,717,288
Operational activities	9,143,610
Fellowships, grants and contributions	5,114,598
Contractual services	4,975,580
Travel on official business	4,755,748
Acquisition and improvement of premises	2,568,370
Acquisition of furniture and equipment	2,206,672
Joint activities within the United Nations system	971,704
Supplies and materials	869,156
Total	124,930,990

Annex I.   MEMBERSHIP OF THE INTERNATIONAL LABOUR ORGANISATION AND CONTRIBUTIONS

(Membership as at 31 December 1983; contributions as assessed for 1984)

MEMBER	CONTRIBUTION Percentage	Gross amount (in US dollars)	MEMBER	CONTRIBUTION Percentage	Gross amount (in US dollars)	MEMBER	CONTRIBUTION Percentage	Gross amount (in US dollars)
Afghanistan	0.01	12,737	Belize	0.01	12,737	Chad	0.01	12,737
Algeria	0.13	165,584	Benin	0.01	12,737	Chile	0.07	89,160
Angola	0.01	12,737	Bolivia	0.01	12,737	China	0.87	1,108,137
Antigua and Barbuda	0.01	12,737	Botswana	0.01	12,737	Colombia	0.11	140,109
Argentina	0.70	891,604	Brazil	1.38	1,757,734	Comoros	0.01	12,737
Australia	1.56	1,987,003	Bulgaria	0.18	229,270	Congo	0.01	12,737
Austria	0.74	942,553	Burma	0.01	12,737	Costa Rica	0.02	25,475
Bahamas	0.01	12,737	Burundi	0.01	12,737	Cuba	0.09	114,635
Bahrain	0.01	12,737	Byelorussian SSR	0.36	458,539	Cyprus	0.01	12,737
Bangladesh	0.03	38,212	Canada	3.05	3,884,846	Czechoslovakia	0.75	955,290
Barbados	0.01	12,737	Cape Verde	0.01	12,737	Democratic Kampuchea	0.01	12,737
Belgium	1.27	1,617,625	Central African Republic	0.01	12,737	Democratic Yemen	0.01	12,737

MEMBER	CONTRIBUTION Percentage	CONTRIBUTION Gross amount (in US dollars)	MEMBER	CONTRIBUTION Percentage	CONTRIBUTION Gross amount (in US dollars)	MEMBER	CONTRIBUTION Percentage	CONTRIBUTION Gross amount (in US dollars)
Denmark	0.74	942,553	Lao People's Democratic Republic	0.01	12,737	Saudi Arabia	0.85	1,082,662
Djibouti	0.01	12,737	Lebanon	0.02	25,475	Senegal	0.01	12,737
Dominica	0.01	12,737	Lesotho	0.01	12,737	Seychelles	0.01	12,737
Dominican Republic	0.03	38,212	Liberia	0.01	12,737	Sierra Leone	0.01	12,737
Ecuador	0.02	25,475	Libyan Arab Jamahiriya	0.26	331,167	Singapore	0.09	114,635
Egypt	0.07	89,160	Luxembourg	0.06	76,423	Somalia	0.01	12,737
El Salvador	0.01	12,737	Madagascar	0.01	12,737	Spain	1.91	2,432,805
Equatorial Guinea	0.01	12,737	Malawi	0.01	12,737	Sri Lanka	0.01	12,737
Ethiopia	0.01	12,737	Malaysia	0.09	114,635	Sudan	0.01	12,737
Fiji	0.01	12,737	Mali	0.01	12,737	Suriname	0.01	12,737
Finland	0.48	611,386	Malta	0.01	12,737	Swaziland	0.01	12,737
France	6.46	8,228,231	Mauritania	0.01	12,737	Sweden	1.31	1,668,573
Gabon	0.02	25,475	Mauritius	0.01	12,737	Switzerland	1.09	1,388,355
German Democratic Republic	1.38	1,757,734	Mexico	0.87	1,108,137	Syrian Arab Republic	0.03	38,212
Germany, Federal Republic of	8.47	10,788,409	Mongolia	0.01	12,737	Thailand	0.08	101,898
Ghana	0.02	25,475	Morocco	0.05	63,686	Togo	0.01	12,737
Greece	0.40	509,488	Mozambique	0.01	12,737	Trinidad and Tobago	0.03	38,212
Grenada	0.01	12,737	Namibia	0.01	12,737	Tunisia	0.03	38,212
Guatemala	0.02	25,475	Nepal	0.01	12,737	Turkey	0.32	407,590
Guinea	0.01	12,737	Netherlands	1.76	2,241,747	Uganda	0.01	12,737
Guinea-Bissau	0.01	12,737	New Zealand	0.26	331,167	Ukrainian SSR	1.31	1,668,573
Guyana	0.01	12,737	Nicaragua	0.01	12,737	USSR	10.45	13,310,374
Haiti	0.01	12,737	Niger	0.01	12,737	United Arab Emirates	0.16	203,795
Honduras	0.01	12,737	Nigeria	0.19	242,007	United Kingdom	4.63	5,897,324
Hungary	0.23	292,956	Norway	0.50	636,860	United Republic of Cameroon	0.01	12,737
Iceland	0.03	38,212	Pakistan	0.06	76,423	United Republic of Tanzania	0.01	12,737
India	0.36	458,539	Panama	0.02	25,475	United States	25.00	31,843,000
Indonesia	0.13	165,584	Papua New Guinea	0.01	12,737	Upper Volta	0.01	12,737
Iran	0.57	726,021	Paraguay	0.01	12,737	Uruguay	0.04	50,949
Iraq	0.12	152,846	Peru	0.07	89,160	Venezuela	0.54	687,809
Ireland	0.18	229,270	Philippines	0.09	114,635	Viet Nam	0.02	25,475
Israel	0.23	292,956	Poland	0.71	904,341	Yemen	0.01	12,737
Italy	3.71	4,725,501	Portugal	0.18	229,270	Yugoslavia	0.46	585,911
Ivory Coast	0.03	38,212	Qatar	0.03	38,212	Zaire	0.01	12,737
Jamaica	0.02	25,475	Romania	0.19	242,007	Zambia	0.01	12,737
Japan	10.23	13,030,156	Rwanda	0.01	12,737	Zimbabwe	0.02	25,475
Jordan	0.01	12,737	Saint Lucia	0.01	12,737			
Kenya	0.01	12,737	San Marino	0.01	12,737	Total	100.00	127,372,000
Kuwait	0.25	318,430	Sao Tome and Principe	0.01	12,737			

Annex II. OFFICERS AND OFFICES OF THE INTERNATIONAL LABOUR ORGANISATION

(As at 31 December 1983)

MEMBERSHIP OF THE GOVERNING BODY OF THE INTERNATIONAL LABOUR OFFICE

Chairman: Dr. Robert Ouko (Kenya).

Vice-Chairmen: Jean-Jacques Oechslin (France), Employers' Group; Gerd Muhr (Federal Republic of Germany), Workers' Group.

REGULAR MEMBERS

Government members
Australia, Bahrain, Bangladesh, Barbados, Brazil,* Bulgaria, China,* Colombia, Ecuador, Egypt, France,* German Democratic Republic, Germany, Federal Republic of,* India,* Italy,* Japan,* Kenya, Mali, Mexico, Mozambique, Netherlands, Nigeria, Philippines, Senegal, USSR,* United Kingdom,* United States,* Venezuela.

Employers' members
Frank Bannerman-Menson (Ghana), Murat Eurnekian (Argentina), Daniel J.Flunder (United Kingdom), Henri Georget (Niger), Abderrahim Gharbaoui (Morocco), David L. Grove (United States), Wolf-Dieter Lindner (Federal Republic of Germany), Marwan Nasr (Lebanon), Jean-Jacques Oechslin (France), George Polites (Australia), Naval H. Tata (India), Albert Verschueren (Belgium), Horatio G. Villalobos (Venezuela), Koh Yoshino (Japan).

Workers' members
Irving Brown (United States), Shirley Carr (Canada), J. J. Delpino (Venezuela), Cliff O. Dolan (Australia), Abdul M. Issifu (Ghana), Glynn Lloyd (United Kingdom), Elias Mashasi (United Republic of Tanzania), Kanti Mehta (India), Gerd Muhr (Federal Republic of Germany), Vassily I. Prokhorov (USSR), Alfonso Sánchez Madariaga (Mexico), Moussa D. Sow (Mauritania), John Svenningsen (Denmark), Yoshikazu Tanaka (Japan).

DEPUTY MEMBERS

Government deputy members
Algeria, Angola, Argentina, Belgium, Burma, Cuba, Denmark, Ethiopia, Ghana, Hungary, Indonesia, Madagascar, Mongolia, Panama, Portugal, Ukrainian SSR, Uruguay, Zimbabwe.

Employers' deputy members
Agil Al-Jassem (Kuwait), Sidney B. Chambers (Jamaica), Albert Deschamps (Canada), Jairo Escobar Padrón (Colombia), Johan von Holten (Sweden), J. M. Lacasa Aso (Spain), Felix Moukoko Kingue (United Republic of Cameroon), Munga-wa-Nyasa (Zaire), Tom D. Owuor (Kenya), Aurelio Periquet (Philippines), Najib Said (Tunisia), Lucia Sasso-Mazzufferi (Italy), Fanuel C. Sumbwe (Zambia), Fernando Yllanes Ramos (Mexico).

Workers' deputy members
Jerome Abondo (United Republic of Cameroon), Nangbog Barnabo (Togo), Gideon Ben-Israel (Israel), Marc Blondel (France), Youcef Briki (Algeria), Tulio E. Cuevas (Colombia), V. David (Malaysia), Heribert Maier (Austria), Democrito T. Mendoza (Philippines), Agus Sudono (Indonesia), Jozsef Timmer (Hungary), Raffaele Vanni (Italy), Frank Walcott (Barbados), Newstead Zimba (Zambia).

*Member holding a non-elective seat as a State of chief industrial importance.

SENIOR OFFICIALS OF THE INTERNATIONAL LABOUR OFFICE

Director-General: Francis Blanchard.
Deputy Directors-General: Bertil Bolin, Surendra K. Jain, David P. Taylor.

Assistant Directors-General: Vladimir G. Chkounaev, Fuyao Jin, Elimane Kane, Shigeru Nakatani, Franz von Mutius, Francis Wolf.

HEADQUARTERS, REGIONAL, LIAISON AND OTHER OFFICES

HEADQUARTERS

International Labour Office
4 Route des Morillons
1211 Geneva 22, Switzerland
  Cable address: INTERLAB GENEVA
  Telephone: (022) 99 61 11
  Telex: 22271

REGIONAL OFFICES

International Labour Organisation Regional
Office for Africa
P. O. Box 2788
Addis Ababa, Ethiopia
  Cable address: INTERLAB ADDISABABA

International Labour Organisation Regional
Office for the Americas
Apartado Postal 3638
Lima 1, Peru
  Cable address: INTERLAB LIMA

International Labour Organisation Regional
Office for Asia and the Pacific
P. O. Box 1759
Bangkok 2, Thailand
  Cable address: INTERLAB BANGKOK

International Labour Organisation Regional
Office for Europe
1211 Geneva 22, Switzerland
  Cable address: INTERLAB GENEVA

LIAISON OFFICES

International Labour Organisation Liaison
Office with the European Communities and
the Benelux
40 Rue Aimé Smekens
B-1040 Brussels, Belgium

International Labour Organisation Liaison
Office with the United Nations
300 East 44th Street, 18th floor
New York, N. Y. 10017, United States

International Labour Organisation Liaison
Office with the United Nations Economic
Commission for Latin America
Casilla de Correo 2353
Santiago, Chile

OTHER OFFICES

International Labour Organisation Office
01-Boîte Postale 3960
Abidjan 01, Ivory Coast

International Labour Organisation Office
Boîte Postale 226
Alger-Gare, Algeria

International Labour Organisation Office
P. K. 407
Ankara, Turkey

International Labour Organisation Office
Boîte Postale 683
101-Antananarivo, Madagascar

International Labour Organisation Office
Boîte Postale 114-5096
Beirut, Lebanon

OTHER OFFICES *(cont.)*

International Labour Organisation Office
Hohenzollernstrasse 21
D-5300 Bonn 2, Federal Republic of Germany

International Labour Organisation Office
Caixa Postal 04-401-403
70 312-Brasilia DF, Brazil

International Labour Organisation Office
Avenida Julio A. Roca 710 (3er piso)
Buenos Aires, Argentina

International Labour Organisation Office
9 Dr. Taha Hussein Street
11561 Zamalek
Cairo, Egypt

International Labour Organisation Office
Boîte Postale 414
Dakar, Senegal

International Labour Organisation Office
P. O. Box 9212
Dar es Salaam, United Republic of Tanzania

International Labour Organisation Office
P. O. Box 2061
Dhaka, Bangladesh

International Labour Organisation Office
P. O. Box 1047
Islamabad, Pakistan

International Labour Organisation Office
P. O. Box 75
Jakarta 10001, Indonesia

International Labour Organisation Office
Boîte Postale 7248
Kinshasa 1, Zaire

International Labour Organisation Office
P. O. Box 20275 SAFAT
Kuwait, Kuwait

International Labour Organisation Office
P. O. Box 2331
Lagos, Nigeria

International Labour Organisation Office
96/98 Marsham Street
London SW1P 4LY, England

International Labour Organisation Office
P. O. Box 2181
Lusaka, Zambia

International Labour Organisation Office
P. O. Box 7587 ADC/MIA
Metro Manila, Philippines

International Labour Organisation Office
Apartado Postal 12-992
Mexico 03000, D. F., Mexico

International Labour Organisation Office
Petrovka 15, Apt. 23
Moscow 103 031, USSR

International Labour Organisation Office
7 Sardar Patel Marg
Chanakyapuri
New Delhi 110021, India

OTHER OFFICES *(cont.)*

International Labour Organisation Office
Fuller Building, Suite 202
79 Albert Street
Ottawa K1P 5E7, Ontario, Canada

International Labour Organisation Office
205 Boulevard Saint-Germain
F-75340 Paris Cedex 07, France

International Labour Organisation Office
P. O. Box 1201
Port of Spain, Trinidad

International Labour Organisation Office
Villa Aldobrandini
Via Panisperna 28
I-00184 Rome, Italy

International Labour Organisation Office
Apartado Postal 10170
1000 San José, Costa Rica

International Labour Organisation Office
P. O. Box 1546
Government Buildings
Suva, Fiji

International Labour Organisation Office
5th floor, Nippon Press Center Building
2-1, Uchisaiwai-cho 2-Chome
Chiyoda-Ku
Tokyo 100, Japan

International Labour Organisation Office
1750 New York Avenue, N. W., Suite 330
Washington, D. C. 20006, United States

International Labour Organisation Office
Boîte Postale 13
Yaoundé, United Republic of Cameroon

International Labour Organisation Office for Iran
CH-1211 Geneva 22, Switzerland

INSTITUTE

International Institute for Labour Studies
4 Route des Morillons
1211 Geneva 22, Switzerland

TRAINING CENTRES

Jobs and Skills Programme for Africa
  (JASPA)
P. O. Box 2532
Addis Ababa, Ethiopia

Asian Regional Project for Strengthening
  Labour/Manpower Administration (ARPLA)
c/o ILO Regional Office for Asia
  and the Pacific
P. O. Box 1759
Bangkok 2, Thailand

Asian Regional Team for Employment
  Promotion (ARTEP)
P. O. Box 2-146
Bangkok 2, Thailand

Asian and Pacific Skill Development
  Programme (APSDEP)
P. O. Box 1423
Islamabad, Pakistan

TRAINING CENTRES *(cont.)*

Inter-American Labour Administration Centre
    (CIAT)
Apartado Postal 3638
Lima 1, Peru

Inter-American Centre of Research and
    Documentation on Vocational Training
    (CINTERFOR)
Casilla de Correo 1761
Montevideo, Uruguay

TRAINING CENTRES *(cont.)*

African Regional Labour Administration
    Centre (ARLAC)
P. O. Box 59672
Nairobi, Kenya

Regional Employment Programme for Latin
    America and the Caribbean (PREALC)
Casilla de Correo 618
Santiago, Chile

TRAINING CENTRES *(cont.)*

International Centre for Advanced Technical
    and Vocational Training
Via Ventimiglia 201
I-10127 Turin, Italy

African Regional Labour Administration
    Centre (CRADAT)
Boîte Postale 1055
Yaoundé, United Republic of Cameroon

Chapter III

Food and Agriculture Organization of the United Nations (FAO)

The twenty-second biennial session of the Conference of the Food and Agriculture Organization of the United Nations (FAO) was held at Rome, Italy, from 5 to 23 November 1983. The Conference unanimously approved FAO's programme of work and budget for 1984-1985 and adopted far-reaching resolutions concerning world food security, rural development, plant genetic resources and the African food crisis.

The Conference reviewed the world food situation and the overall global economy and found both critical. It noted with concern that preliminary assessments indicated a decline of 1 per cent in world food and agricultural production in 1983 after an increase of about 3 per cent in the preceding two years. Moreover, the Conference noted that production in developing countries had increased at a rate well below that of the previous two years and was also lower than the average for 1978-1982. In the developed countries, food production had declined by 8 per cent overall. Cereal output, including coarse grains, had fallen by 13 or 14 per cent, notably in North America.

The Conference noted that the budget of some $421 million for the 1984-1985 programme of work provided for a net increase of 3.6 per cent in resources for FAO's technical and economic programmes of direct development impact, while limiting the overall net programme growth to only 0.5 per cent.

The Conference expressed special concern about the situation in Africa where as many as 22 sub-Saharan countries were threatened by grave food shortages. It stressed the need for additional immediate food and agricultural aid.

The Conference adopted the International Undertaking on Plant Genetic Resources, which sought to ensure that the world's plant genetic resources were better identified, preserved and made available for breeding and scientific purposes. (Plant genetic resources are drawn upon by breeders in the search for new crop varieties better suited to local conditions.) The Conference, which launched the Undertaking as a moral instrument rather than as a legally-binding convention, also resolved that a Commission on Plant Genetic Resources should be set up to guide FAO policy and to monitor implementation of the Undertaking. The Commission was established by the FAO Council on 24 November.

On 7 November, the Conference admitted four new members to FAO—Antigua and Barbuda, Be-

lize, Saint Christopher and Nevis, and Vanuatu—bringing its membership to 156. Monkombu Sambasivan Swaminathan of India was re-elected as Independent Chairman of the FAO Council—FAO's governing body between sessions of the Conference—for a further two years.

Funding

FAO funds come from three main sources: contributions by member nations, national trust funds and the United Nations Development Programme (UNDP).

The regular programme, financed by members according to a scale of contributions set by the Conference, supports field work and enables FAO to advise Governments, to provide a neutral forum for discussing issues related to food and agriculture and to provide the international farming community with information.

In 1983, slightly less than half the expenditure under FAO field programmes was funded by UNDP. National trust funds provided a similar share, while slightly less than 10 per cent was provided by FAO's regular programme budget through the Technical Co-operation Programme (TCP), which allows FAO to respond quickly to unforeseen demands for emergency assistance and to provide training, investment project preparation and specialized advice.

Preliminary figures suggested that UNDP funding fell by 16 per cent in 1983 following a fall of some 27 per cent in 1982. The impact of the reduction was cushioned to some extent by the increasingly important role of trust funds, both bilateral and unilateral. Even so, total FAO field programme expenditure fell by about 7 per cent in 1983.

Activities in 1983

Food emergency in Africa

In early 1983, reports from the FAO Global Information and Early Warning System indicated that famine threatened almost 150 million people in sub-Saharan Africa. In April, the Director-General established a task force to review and monitor the food and crop situation and on 3 May he appealed for extra food and other aid for the affected countries.

Prospects for the 1983/84 harvest worsened as the year progressed. In August, satellite pictures showed that the northern edge of the "green belt", which normally appears across the Sahel during the most critical period of the growing season, had moved south by an average of 200 kilometres. A huge and normally productive area was left parched and useless.

On 27 October, the Director-General reported to the United Nations General Assembly on the scale of the problem and the measures necessary to overcome it. Special meetings of affected countries, donors and international organizations at Rome in October and November resulted in a threefold increase in pledges of food aid by the end of 1983. Total food aid pledged to the 24 affected countries amounted to 1.75 million tonnes, compared with estimated requirements for the 1983/84 season of 5.3 million tonnes.

In addition to co-ordinating food aid supplied bilaterally or through the World Food Programme (WFP)—a joint venture of FAO and the United Nations—FAO gave direct help to farmers, including supplying them with seeds and fertilizers, so that they could resume production. The FAO Office for Special Relief Operations co-ordinated more than 20 emergency projects in sub-Saharan Africa, with a total budget of some $15 million. Many of them were small-scale operations financed through TCP: seven were designed to rehabilitate crop production affected by drought; four provided assistance to control rinderpest (in cattle) and other animal diseases; and four helped to resettle refugees in their home countries by providing them with essential inputs such as seeds and hand tools.

Field programmes

FAO devotes a large proportion of its field and regular programme resources to increasing production of crops, livestock and foodfish. Activities include research support, the supply of seeds and semen, and the provision of technical advice and assistance to field projects. Emphasis is placed on assisting developing countries to plan and carry out their own programmes and on encouraging technical co-operation among those countries.

Crops. About a third of FAO's field programme expenditure in 1983 was devoted to increasing crop production, with more than 600 field projects under way. The emphasis was on demonstrating to small farmers techniques for increased production, particularly of staple foods and oil crops, without high risk of failure. Governments were advised on conserving genetic resources, improving the supply of seeds and protecting crops from diseases and pests.

Livestock. By mobilizing greater resources in 1983 to deal with animal diseases, FAO responded to the advance southwards in Africa of the cattle disease rinderpest and the continuing outbreaks of African swine fever in many countries of Latin America and the Caribbean. More than 200 field projects, involving expenditure of almost $13 million, were concerned with animal health. Some $4 million in emergency assistance was provided through TCP to help more than 20 African countries control rinderpest, and a long-term Pan-African Rinderpest Campaign was planned.

An Italian trust fund project to strengthen veterinary services to prevent African swine fever in five South American countries became operational in July. Some 700,000 doses of foot-and-mouth disease vaccine were supplied to Bulgaria, Greece and Turkey during the year to maintain a buffer zone in south-eastern Europe, while Morocco was supplied with 1.5 million doses through TCP to control a serious outbreak of the disease.

Swedish funding for the International Meat Development Scheme (IMDS) ended in 1983 after nine years, during which missions had visited 45 countries to advise on meat and livestock sector development. IMDS identified $400-million worth of technical assistance and investment projects, resulting in $250 million of funding. Altogether, some 250 field projects involving expenditure of more than $25 million during 1983 were concerned with animal production.

Fisheries. The FAO Committee on Fisheries met in October to consider an overall strategy for fisheries management and development and associated action programmes, with final proposals to be submitted to the 1984 FAO World Conference on Fisheries Management and Development. The Conference would represent the first major initiative to examine the practical implications for fisheries of exclusive economic zones claimed by many coastal States.

Some 50 FAO fisheries projects under way in 1983 centred on small-scale fisheries and aquaculture. The Bay of Bengal Programme, one of the first and most successful of the regional programmes directed specifically at artisanal fisheries, was extended until 1986. The Programme, which began in 1979, was funded largely by Sweden.

Other projects helped member countries to improve marketing and distribution of fish catches and foodfish handling and processing. FAO operated 352 fisheries projects with expenditure of almost $30 million in 1983.

Food security, distribution and marketing. In April 1983, the FAO Committee on World Food Security adopted a new concept of food security proposed by the Director-General, which recognized that food security should have three specific aims: to ensure production of adequate food supplies; to maximize stability in the flow of supplies; and to secure access to available supplies by those who need them.

Much of FAO's direct help to improve distribution and marketing was channelled through its Programme for the Prevention of Food Losses and its Food Security Assistance Scheme, designed to help vulnerable countries strengthen their basic food security measures.

FAO technical assistance for marketing and trade led to significant investment by Governments and financing institutions. In 1983, financing institutions approved five marketing and credit projects prepared by the FAO Investment Centre worth some $484 million.

Land and water management. Greater awareness of the importance of soil conservation for agricultural production was reflected in the increasing number of requests from countries for assistance to control erosion and desertification and to reclaim degraded lands. In 1983, some 40 field projects with an expenditure of more than $2 million and involving some 50 resident experts were either entirely or partly concerned with soil conservation. Almost 140 projects worth some $11 million dealt with water development and irrigation.

FAO Fertilizer Programme activities expanded considerably during 1983 with projects under way in 19 African, Asian and Latin American countries. Increasing emphasis was given to integrated plant nutrition, combining the use of chemical fertilizers, locally available organic wastes such as crop residues and dung, and the biological "capture" of atmospheric nitrogen (nitrogen fixation).

Rural development. In accordance with the Programme of Action of the 1979 World Conference on Agrarian Reform and Rural Development (WCARRD),[a] FAO continued to support national policies to alleviate rural poverty and to promote rural development.

Twenty-nine country studies on the causes of rural poverty and the impact of government programmes formed the basis of the first of a series of progress reports on rural development, called for by WCARRD.

An important part of WCARRD follow-up was a programme to support women's roles in food production. In 1983, projects were under way in 12 countries, mostly in Africa. They concentrated on involving women in identifying what they needed to increase food production while making their other activities more efficient.

The People's Participation Programme was FAO's main vehicle for carrying out specific field elements of the WCAARD Programme of Action. In 1983, projects were under way in seven countries in Africa, six in Asia and the Pacific and one in the Near East.

Technical co-operation in rural development was encouraged through regional centres for integrated rural development, two of which were operating in Africa and in Asia and the Pacific. In October,

Amman, Jordan, was selected as the site for the Near East centre.

Forestry. In forestry, FAO concentrated on training, curriculum development and institution building in member countries and was involved in 1983 in more than 300 projects costing almost $27 million.

The role of forestry in rural development was supported through programmes such as the Forestry for Local Community Development Programme supported by Sweden, which in 1983 approved funding for a three-year second phase. Sixteen projects remaining in operation from the first phase were concerned with increasing fuelwood supplies through village or farm woodlots, introducing and strengthening agro-forestry systems and increasing income through small-scale forest-based activities.

FAO helped the World Bank's Economic Development Institute to prepare and teach a course on project planning in forestry and forest industries. A comprehensive study was completed in 1983 on *Foreign Investment in the Forest-based Sector in Africa*, and work was begun on updating a similar study for Latin America.

Nutrition. A long-term strategy to improve nutrition by introducing the subject into all agricultural development projects became fully operational in 1983.

During the year, FAO was involved in some 80 field projects, with a total expenditure of almost $3 million, directed specifically at improving nutrition surveillance, education and food standards. Activities included assisting 16 countries to strengthen their food quality-control systems—with advice on food laws and their enforcement, assistance in setting up laboratories and food inspection systems, and training programmes.

Popular participation. The FAO-sponsored Freedom from Hunger Campaign/Action for Development (FFHC/AD) programme encourages non-governmental organizations (NGOs) in developing countries to find partner organizations in the developed world. In 1983, FAO helped NGOs in developed countries to allocate more than $2 million to projects run by partners in developing countries. FFHC/AD projects encouraged the rural poor to identify and satisfy their own needs.

Each year, World Food Day (16 October) provides a major opportunity for people to reflect on the importance of food. In 1983, the day was observed in more than 150 countries.

Investment in agriculture. FAO continued to help developing countries prepare agricultural investment projects to attract external capital. In 1983, financing institutions and Governments approved 38 projects worth $2,053 million prepared by the

[a]YUN 1979, p. 500.

FAO Investment Centre. Besides continuing its co-operation with major multilateral institutions such as the World Bank, FAO negotiated new agreements with three financing institutions: the United Nations Capital Development Fund, the East African Development Bank and the Central American Bank for Economic Integration.

By the end of 1983, FAO was responsible for carrying out more than $60-million worth of technical assistance in 36 investment projects, 29 of which were funded by the World Bank. FAO's work in this area was financed by host Governments, which recovered the costs from the investment funds.

World Food Programme. In 1983, 400 projects in 88 countries valued at $3,500 million were operational through WFP, which began operations in 1963.[b] By the end of 1983, pledges in food aid and cash to WFP for 1983-1984 totalled $961.4 million—80 per cent of the target for the period and more than the total pledged during any previous biennium.

The 1983 FAO Conference established a pledging target of $1,350 million for WFP for 1985-1986.

WFP committed $696 million to development projects in 1983, a record for any one year. The projects were designed to increase food production, improve nutrition standards, promote human development and reduce rural poverty. Projects approved in 1983 included three totalling $84 million for forestry activities in the Indian states of Bihar, Madhya Pradesh and Orissa, three projects totalling $30 million to improve drainage and irrigation in three provinces of China, and multi-purpose projects for rural development in Mali ($31 million) and the Central African Republic ($10 million).

Much of the food aid for projects was supplied in the form of "food for work" paid to landless agricultural workers who would otherwise be unemployed. Food aid was also given to improve the nutritional standards of vulnerable groups such as pregnant women and children.

In 1983, the food crisis in sub-Saharan Africa absorbed a large part of WFP's emergency relief resources. Some 382,380 tonnes of cereals were shipped to the 24 African countries most affected by food shortages, mostly from the International Emergency Food Reserve (IEFR), which WFP managed on behalf of the international community.

All IEFR and WFP resources set aside for emergency purposes in 1983 were used. Apart from sub-Saharan Africa, WFP shipped emergency food aid to refugees along the Thai/Kampuchean border, to Afghan refugees in Pakistan and to refugees in Lebanon and Central America.

Secretariat

At end of 1983, the total number of staff employed by FAO at its headquarters was 3,265, of whom 1,098 were in the Professional and higher categories. Field project personnel working in 113 countries numbered 1,112 in the Professional and higher categories and 726 in the General Service category. Regional office, joint division and country representation staff numbered 241 in the Professional and higher categories and 717 in the General Service category. Of the 293 associate experts working with FAO, 246 were in the field, 16 in regional and country offices and 31 at headquarters. In addition, WFP employed 120 Professional and higher category staff and 184 General Service personnel at headquarters and 197 staff in the field.

Budget

The November 1983 session of the FAO Conference approved a budget of some $421 million for 1984-1985.

[b]YUN 1963, p. 211.

Annex I.   MEMBERSHIP OF THE FOOD AND AGRICULTURE ORGANIZATION AND CONTRIBUTIONS

(Membership as at 31 December 1983; contributions as assessed for 1984 and 1985)

MEMBER	CONTRIBUTION Percentage	CONTRIBUTION Net amount (in US dollars)	MEMBER	CONTRIBUTION Percentage	CONTRIBUTION Net amount (in US dollars)	MEMBER	CONTRIBUTION Percentage	CONTRIBUTION Net amount (in US dollars)
Afghanistan	0.01	19,729	Bahamas	0.01	19,729	Bolivia	0.01	19,729
Albania	0.01	19,729	Bahrain	0.01	19,729	Botswana	0.01	19,729
Algeria	0.16	315,664	Bangladesh	0.04	78,916	Brazil	1.68	3,314,472
Angola	0.01	19,729	Barbados	0.01	19,729	Bulgaria	0.22	434,038
Antigua and Barbuda	0.01	19,729	Belgium	1.55	3,057,995	Burma	0.01	19,729
Argentina	0.86	1,696,694	Belize	0.01	19,729	Burundi	0.01	19,729
Australia	1.90	3,748,510	Benin	0.01	19,729	Canada	3.72	7,339,188
Austria	0.91	1,795,339	Bhutan	0.01	19,729	Cape Verde	0.01	19,729

MEMBER	CONTRIBUTION Percent-age	Net amount (in US dollars)	MEMBER	CONTRIBUTION Percent-age	Net amount (in US dollars)	MEMBER	CONTRIBUTION Percent-age	Net amount (in US dollars)
Central African Republic	0.01	19,729	Israel	0.28	552,412	Rwanda	0.01	19,729
Chad	0.01	19,729	Italy	4.52	8,917,508	Saint Christopher and		
Chile	0.08	157,832	Ivory Coast	0.04	78,916	Nevis	0.01	19,729
China	1.06	2,091,274	Jamaica	0.02	39,458	Saint Lucia	0.01	19,729
Colombia	0.13	256,477	Japan	12.46	24,582,334	Saint Vincent and the		
Comoros	0.01	19,729	Jordan	0.01	19,729	Grenadines	0.01	19,729
Congo	0.01	19,729	Kenya	0.01	19,729	Samoa	0.01	19,729
Costa Rica	0.02	39,458	Kuwait	0.30	591,870	Sao Tome and Principe	0.01	19,729
Cuba	0.11	217,019	Lao People's Democratic			Saudi Arabia	1.04	2,051,816
Cyprus	0.01	19,729	Republic	0.01	19,729	Senegal	0.01	19,729
Czechoslovakia	0.92	1,815,068	Lebanon	0.02	39,458	Seychelles	0.01	19,729
Democratic Kampuchea	0.01	19,729	Lesotho	0.01	19,729	Sierra Leone	0.01	19,729
Democratic People's			Liberia	0.01	19,729	Somalia	0.01	19,729
Republic of Korea	0.06	118,374	Libyan Arab Jamahiriya	0.31	611,599	Spain	2.33	4,596,857
Democratic Yemen	0.01	19,729	Luxembourg	0.07	138,103	Sri Lanka	0.01	19,729
Denmark	0.91	1,795,339	Madagascar	0.01	19,729	Sudan	0.01	19,729
Djibouti	0.01	19,729	Malawi	0.01	19,729	Suriname	0.01	19,729
Dominica	0.01	19,729	Malaysia	0.11	217,019	Swaziland	0.01	19,729
Dominican Republic	0.04	78,916	Maldives	0.01	19,729	Sweden	1.59	3,136,911
Ecuador	0.02	39,458	Mali	0.01	19,729	Switzerland	1.33	2,623,957
Egypt	0.08	157,832	Malta	0.01	19,729	Syrian Arab Republic	0.04	78,916
El Salvador	0.01	19,729	Mauritania	0.01	19,729	Thailand	0.10	197,290
Equatorial Guinea	0.01	19,729	Mauritius	0.01	19,729	Togo	0.01	19,729
Ethiopia	0.01	19,729	Mexico	1.06	2,091,274	Tonga	0.01	19,729
Fiji	0.01	19,729	Mongolia	0.01	19,729	Trinidad and Tobago	0.04	78,916
Finland	0.58	1,144,282	Morocco	0.06	118,374	Tunisia	0.04	78,916
France	7.86	15,506,994	Mozambique	0.01	19,729	Turkey	0.39	769,431
Gabon	0.02	39,458	Namibia	0.01	19,729	Uganda	0.01	19,729
Gambia	0.01	19,729	Nepal	0.01	19,729	United Arab Emirates	0.19	374,851
Germany, Federal			Netherlands	2.15	4,241,735	United Kingdom	5.64	11,127,156
Republic of	10.31	20,340,599	New Zealand	0.31	611,599	United Republic of		
Ghana	0.02	39,458	Nicaragua	0.01	19,729	Cameroon	0.01	19,729
Greece	0.48	946,992	Niger	0.01	19,729	United Republic of		
Grenada	0.01	19,729	Nigeria	0.23	453,767	Tanzania	0.01	19,729
Guatemala	0.02	39,458	Norway	0.62	1,223,198	United States	25.00	49,972,500
Guinea	0.01	19,729	Oman	0.01	19,729	Upper Volta	0.01	19,729
Guinea-Bissau	0.01	19,729	Pakistan	0.07	138,103	Uruguay	0.05	98,645
Guyana	0.01	19,729	Panama	0.02	39,458	Vanuatu	0.01	19,729
Haiti	0.01	19,729	Papua New Guinea	0.01	19,729	Venezuela	0.66	1,302,114
Honduras	0.01	19,729	Paraguay	0.01	19,729	Viet Nam	0.02	39,458
Hungary	0.28	552,412	Peru	0.08	157,832	Yemen	0.01	19,729
Iceland	0.04	78,916	Philippines	0.11	217,019	Yugoslavia	0.56	1,104,824
India	0.43	848,347	Poland	0.87	1,716,423	Zaire	0.01	19,729
Indonesia	0.16	315,664	Portugal	0.22	434,038	Zambia	0.01	19,729
Iran	0.70	1,381,030	Qatar	0.04	78,916	Zimbabwe	0.02	39,458
Iraq	0.15	295,935	Republic of Korea	0.22	434,038			
Ireland	0.22	434,038	Romania	0.23	453,767	Total	100.00	197,940,000*

*The total sum for the 1984-1985 biennium was $395,880,000.

Annex II. MEMBERS OF THE COUNCIL OF THE FOOD AND AGRICULTURE ORGANIZATION

Holding office until conclusion of twenty-second session of the FAO Conference, November 1983: Afghanistan, Angola, Barbados, Brazil, Canada, Colombia, Congo, Cuba, Ireland, Kenya, Lebanon, Mexico, Morocco, Nigeria, Poland, Romania, United States.

Holding office until 31 December 1984: Cape Verde, Ecuador, Egypt, Ethiopia, France, India, Italy, Lesotho, New Zealand, Norway, Pakistan, Philippines, Saudi Arabia, Sudan, United Kingdom, Upper Volta.

Holding office until conclusion of twenty-third session of the FAO Conference, November 1985: Argentina, Bangladesh, Benin, China, Cyprus, Germany, Federal Republic of, Indonesia, Iraq, Japan, Malawi, Malaysia, Panama, Rwanda, Spain, Thailand, Venezuela.

Annex III. OFFICERS AND OFFICES OF THE FOOD AND AGRICULTURE ORGANIZATION

OFFICERS

OFFICE OF THE DIRECTOR-GENERAL
Director-General: Edouard Saouma.
Deputy Director-General: Edward M. West.
Executive Director, World Food Programme: James C. Ingram.

DEPARTMENTS
Assistant Director-General, Administration and Finance Department: Dean K. Crowther.
Assistant Director-General, Agriculture Department: D. F. R. Bommer.
Assistant Director-General, Development Department: R. S. Lignon.
Assistant Director-General, Forestry Department: M. A. Flores Rodas.
Assistant Director-General, Department of General Affairs and Information: P. Savary.
Assistant Director-General, Economic and Social Department: N. Islam.

Assistant Director-General, Fisheries Department: J. E. Carroz.

REGIONAL REPRESENTATIVES OF THE DIRECTOR-GENERAL
Assistant Director-General and Regional Representative for Africa: J. A. C. Davies.
Assistant Director-General and Regional Representative for Asia and the Pacific: S. S. Puri.
Assistant Director-General and Regional Representative for Latin America and the Caribbean: M. E. Jalil.
Assistant Director-General and Regional Representative for the Near East: S. Jum'a.
Regional Representative for Europe: S. Stampach.

HEADQUARTERS AND REGIONAL OFFICES

HEADQUARTERS

Food and Agriculture Organization
Via delle Terme di Caracalla
Rome 00100, Italy
 Cable address: FOODAGRI ROME
 Telephone: 57971
 Telex: 610181

REGIONAL AND OTHER OFFICES

Food and Agriculture Organization Regional
 Office for Africa
United Nations Agency Building
North Maxwell Road
P. O. Box 1628
Accra, Ghana

REGIONAL AND OTHER OFFICES *(cont.)*

Food and Agriculture Organization Regional
 Office for Asia and the Pacific
Maliwan Mansion
Phra Atit Road
Bangkok 10200, Thailand

Food and Agriculture Organization Regional
 Office for the Near East
Via delle Terme di Caracalla
Rome 00100, Italy

Food and Agriculture Organization Regional
 Office for Europe
Via delle Terme di Caracalla
Rome 00100, Italy

REGIONAL AND OTHER OFFICES *(cont.)*

Food and Agriculture Organization Regional
 Office for Latin America and the Caribbean
Avenida Providencia 871
Casilla de Correo 10095
Santiago, Chile

Food and Agriculture Organization Liaison
 Office with the United Nations
United Nations Headquarters, Room DC1-1125
New York, N. Y. 10017, United States

Food and Agriculture Organization Liaison
 Office for North America
1001 22nd Street, N. W., Suite 300
Washington, D. C. 20437, United States

Chapter IV

United Nations Educational, Scientific and Cultural Organization (UNESCO)

During 1983, the United Nations Educational, Scientific and Cultural Organization (UNESCO) continued to promote collaboration among nations through education, natural and social sciences, culture and communication.

Three States joined UNESCO during 1983—Saint Vincent and the Grenadines (15 February), Fiji (14 July) and Saint Christopher and Nevis (26 October)—bringing the membership to 161. The Netherlands Antilles and the British Virgin Islands were admitted as associate members of UNESCO on 26 October and 24 November, respectively, raising the associate membership to three.

The twenty-second session of the UNESCO General Conference was held at UNESCO headquarters, Paris, from 25 October to 26 November.

Education

The 1983 UNESCO education programme continued to emphasize literacy, the elimination of all forms of inequality and discrimination, improvement of the quality of education, while assuring its relevance with respect to the advancement of knowledge and of the needs of a multidimensional endogenous development, and its contribution to strengthening peace, disarmament, international understanding and co-operation, the promotion of human rights and the elimination of all forms of oppression.

An international conference on education for international understanding, co-operation and peace and education relating to human rights and fundamental freedoms, with a view to developing a climate of opinion favourable to the strengthening of security and disarmament, was held in Paris from 12 to 20 April. Attended by representatives from 122 member States, the conference took stock of their efforts to implement UNESCO's 1974 recommendation on the subject.

On the thirtieth anniversary of the Associated Schools Project, an international congress (Sofia, Bulgaria, 12-16 September), attended by more than 200 people from 69 countries, reviewed three decades of activities and drew up a strategy to reinforce the Associated Schools network. By 1983, there were 1,730 schools in 85 member States belonging to the network.

The fifth regional conference of Arab education ministers and those responsible for economic planning, scheduled for 1983, was postponed until 1984 for technical reasons.

In science and technology education, a regional consultation was held in 1983 as a follow-up to a recommendation of the 1982 conference of African education ministers and ministers for economic planning. The meeting suggested establishing a regional consultative committee to advise on formulating a programme for renewal of science and technology education in Africa. Among publications produced during 1983 to improve science and technology education were *New Trends in Primary School Science Education* and *New Trends in School Science Equipment*, published in English; French, Spanish and Arabic versions were under preparation. A number of books on physics teaching and mathematics education were also ready for publication.

During the 1981-1983 triennium, there was an increase in aid given to member States under UNESCO's regular programme to support national efforts in the fight against illiteracy, with 60 countries (including 15 of the least developed) benefiting from this co-operation, compared with 35 during the previous biennium. Projects were divided among the regions as follows: Africa, 20, including one regional; Asia and the Pacific, 11 (one regional); Arab States, 9; Latin America and the Caribbean, 13 (one regional and one subregional). Some activities were carried out within large campaigns for literacy (Ethiopia, Nicaragua and Yemen). Efforts to rally world opinion and stimulate international co-operation to combat illiteracy were principally directed towards intensifying activities related to International Literacy Day (8 September). In 1983 there were 32 candidates for literacy prizes.

UNESCO's activities in higher education, aimed at improving the mobility of students, teachers and research workers, included the adoption by an international conference of States (Bangkok, Thailand, 12-16 December) of a Regional Convention on the Recognition of Studies, Diplomas and Degrees in Higher Education in Asia and the Pacific. Co-operation with member States in developing higher education continued during 1983 with assistance provided in the form of missions and advisory services. Study grants were allocated under the regular programme and the Participation Programme.

Activities of UNESCO's regional and subregional educational innovation programmes and networks were further developed and expanded during the year. The Asian Programme of Educational Innovation for Development and the Network of Educational Innovation for Development in Africa held regional advisory meetings at Bangkok and Kano, Nigeria, respectively, and an agreement was signed with Kuwait to set up a regional co-ordination centre for the educational innovation programme for development in Arab member States.

Other efforts by UNESCO during 1983 to develop co-operation with member States in education included: training educational personnel; building schools; financing education; promoting equality of educational opportunity; improving educational structures, content, methods and techniques; promoting technical, vocational and adult education; and integrated rural development.

The International Institute for Educational Planning (IIEP) in Paris continued to organize workshops, seminars and fellowship programmes in educational planning and administration. Its annual training programme had 44 participants in 1983. Workshops and seminars dealt mainly with educational reform and the new role of educational planning; special emphasis was given to microplanning, education and employment, administration and communication. IIEP continued to conduct research and publications programmes.

The International Bureau of Education at Geneva and the UNESCO Institute for Education at Hamburg (Federal Republic of Germany) strengthened research and training activities at all levels.

During 1983, UNESCO took part in some 300 national, regional and subregional education projects with financial assistance from the United Nations Development Programme (UNDP), the United Nations Fund for Population Activities (UNFPA), the World Bank, regional banks and funds-in-trust. Over 100 missions were fielded to identify and prepare projects and to provide technical backstopping.

Natural sciences

During 1983, UNESCO strengthened its efforts to use the resources of science and technology for the benefit of developing countries by assisting member States in planning, training and research activities. Following a meeting in March, a group of eminent scientists and engineers made final proposals concerning the draft programme and budget for 1984-1985 in implementation of the second medium-term plan (1984-1989).

Increased co-operation between UNESCO and the International Council of Scientific Unions (ICSU) led to the launching of a joint fellowship programme with stipends of $50,000 each. The two organizations also collaborated in creating the new ICSU Press.

The International Geological Correlation Programme (IGCP) continued to undertake projects in geological sciences. At its 1983 session, the UNESCO General Conference endorsed the IGCP Scientific Committee's recommendation that the name of the Programme be changed to International Geological Co-operation Programme in order to accommodate disciplines such as geophysics. During the year, IGCP published a second bibliographic catalogue of more than 14,000 titles. A conference of Central and East African countries on the study of the Kibarian chain (Bujumbura, Burundi) enabled those countries to pool their contribution to the study of a major structure. Studies of the metallogeny of various pre-Cambrian formations of West Africa were carried out in Togo and the Upper Volta.

The year 1983 marked the end of the implementation of the second phase (1981-1983) of the International Hydrological Programme. Through projects co-ordinated by its Intergovernmental Council, improvements were made in understanding hydrological processes, in surveying and assessing water resources, in computing hydrological parameters, in analysing and predicting changes in the hydrological régime due to human activities, and in developing procedures for managing water resources.

In the area of ocean and coastal-marine systems, a major interregional project of research and training leading to integrated management of coastal-marine systems saw, in 1983, its first research schemes financed from extrabudgetary sources.

Social sciences

During 1983, UNESCO continued to support the development of the social sciences in all regions, both directly and indirectly, through international professional non-governmental organizations, regional centres and associations. Activities involved training, research, theory and methodology, information and documentation services, international exchanges and publications.

Concerning development planning, several studies were undertaken on the endogenous development process, bearing mainly on factors favourable to it or prerequisites in respect of various aspects—social, economic, administrative, cultural—of endogenous development. A meeting of some 15 experts was held in Paris in October on the exchange of knowledge for an endogenous development—a study of the conditions for North-South and South-South co-operation. An important UNESCO publication devoted to the study of development was issued in 1983 entitled *Towards a new philosophy of development*. Other studies on development were concerned with: socio-cultural inequalities between and within nations; new styles of development and participation of populations in the development process; socio-cultural aspects of rural development; the socio-cultural impact of the activities of transnational corporations; and the situation and role of children in different cultural and environmental contexts.

Socio-economic analysis and development planning activities were aimed at elaborating and applying social science methods of analysis, planning and evaluation, with a view to strengthening national capacity in those skills. They dealt with: the practical use of socio-economic indicators at the national and subnational levels for analysis and planning; research on planning methods, including modelling, and the strengthening of national capacity to use the UNESCO Educational Simulation Model; and studies on evaluation methods and their use in different countries.

Environmental activities were directed towards research on rural habitat and public participation—rehabilitation of historic centres, the broader ecosystem in which people lived, the integrated training of planners and administrators of human settlements, the training of "barefoot" architects, and the UNESCO mass media programme to inform the public of environmental issues which concerned them. A second seminar on setting up a training programme for specialists wishing to help inhabitants of precarious human settlements to improve their physical living conditions was held at Bangkok from 30 May to 4 June. A third seminar on possible solutions to urban problems was held at the end of December at New Delhi, India. The third in a series of meetings organized in conjunction with the International Association of City and Regional Planners was held at Amsterdam, Netherlands, during the year on the theme "Implementation of town-planning: the partners".

Population activities dealt with the demographic, socio-cultural and economic aspects of internal and international migration; the interrelationship between population, resources and development; assistance to member States to develop strategies for peoples' participation and involvement in development and in implementing population policies and programmes; the integration of human rights and development considerations in population communication programmes; the training of personnel in social communication techniques; and the training of journalists. The research network in three key areas—internal and international migration, effects of demographic trends and development on the status of women, and family structure and socio-economic change—was extended to a large number of universities and research institutions in all regions. An international symposium was held in October 1983 to investigate migration problems which needed to be studied as a basis for future action. Technical documents issued in 1983 contained: a descriptive analysis of the pilot experiments integrating human rights factors in

population communication programmes; an analysis of research on population communication and its implications for population policies and programmes in West Africa; the role of folk media and mass media in population communication; and analysis of communication for population and development programmes in Egypt. A study on the attitudes of Chinese youth to family formation was published in Chinese.

In continuing its work on an analysis of human rights violations and the conditions for a constructive peace, UNESCO collaborated more closely with the United Nations, the United Nations University and an increasing number of universities and research institutions. The second and third in a series of regional meetings of experts on ethno-development and ethnocide were held during 1983. The participants at a meeting on Africa (Ouagadougou, Upper Volta) emphasized the need to maintain an African cultural identity rather than isolate specific ethnic identities within Pan-Africanism. The European regional meeting (Karasjok, Norway) was held with the assistance of the Norwegian National Commission for UNESCO, the Nordic Sami Institute and the University of Troms. A meeting of experts on improving the exercise of human rights in urban areas was held at Cairo, Egypt, in April with the support of the Arab Regional Centre for Social Sciences.

Regarding disarmament education, the third in a series of regional training seminars took place in 1983 at Dakar, Senegal. An international symposium on the role of the media concerning disarmament (Nairobi, Kenya, April) revealed divergent positions held by specialists on the question of the relationship between the media and society and the conditions required for disarmament. The 1983 UNESCO Prize for Peace Education was awarded to Pax Christi, International Catholic Peace Movement.

The UNESCO programme on the status of women, their participation in development and their role in strengthening peace involved studies and analyses on the implications of certain social phenomena for the status of women. Interdisciplinary research was conducted on the role of women in society and forms of discrimination and mechanisms conducive to discrimination against them. Women's participation in political and public life was the subject of an expert meeting (Lisbon, Portugal) and a workshop (Ottawa, Canada).

UNESCO's youth programme evolved national operational projects in developing countries through: analysis and dissemination of information concerning youth; enlistment of young people in the service of international co-operation, development and peace; and action on behalf of disadvantaged young people. During the year UN-ESCO participated in planning activities for International Youth Year (1985), both within and outside the United Nations system. To promote subregional co-operation in youth affairs, a meeting of senior officials from Indian Ocean countries was organized in Réunion.

Culture

In 1983, preparations began on the *General History of Latin America* and the *General History of the Caribbean*, and work continued on the *General History of Africa* and the *History of the Civilizations of Central Asia*. Historical studies and research were carried out on various aspects of Islamic culture, on Asian, Pacific, Celtic, Slav, South-East European and Arctic cultures.

New literary works, translated from a number of languages into others, both widely spoken and less widely spoken, were added to the UNESCO collection of representative works. Radio programmes based on these translations were produced for broadcasting services in different parts of the world.

In the field of artistic creativity, a UNESCO collection of dance films, kept at the Stockholm Dance Museum, Sweden, was started in 1983 with the assistance of the International Dance Council. Four important meetings, organized with the assistance of various bodies, took place in Africa in 1983: a seminar on oral tradition as a source of literary inspiration, International PEN (Dakar); a symposium on musical traditions, International Music Council (Kinshasa, Zaire); a meeting of experts on cinema education, International Film and Television Council (Upper Volta); and a workshop on utilizing theatrical traditions as an aid to social development, International Theatre Institute (Harare, Zimbabwe).

The third UNESCO/International Music Council Prize was awarded in 1983 to Claudio Arrau, Herbert von Karajan and the Royal Academy of Music of Sweden in recognition of their efforts in the cause of international co-operation and their contribution to the enrichment and development of music. The International Simón Bolívar Prize was awarded for the first time on 24 July 1983, the bicentenary of Bolívar's birth.

During 1983, there was an increase in activities to implement international campaigns for the protection of cultural heritage. By the end of the year, 29 international campaigns approved by the UNESCO General Conference were being conducted or were in preparation and $2.9 million had been collected. New campaigns were launched to safeguard the historic quarters of Istanbul and the site of Göreme (Turkey), as well as for the Plaza Vieja at Havana (Cuba). A second appeal was launched for the preservation of the monumental site of Moenjodaro (Pakistan).

The World Heritage Committee, established under the 1972 International Convention concerning the Protection of the World Cultural and Natural Heritage, held its seventh session at Florence, Italy, from 5 to 9 December 1983. The Committee inscribed 29 additional sites on the World Heritage List, making a total of 165 cultural and natural properties in 45 countries protected by the Convention, to which 78 States were party as at 31 December 1983. Efforts continued to promote public awareness of the Convention's objectives and to encourage contributions to the World Heritage Fund which provided assistance for training activities and restoration work at World Heritage sites.

Communications

During 1983, UNESCO continued to promote a free flow and wider and better-balanced dissemination of information and to conduct research on the social role of communication. Work was expanded in communication policy and planning to bridge the gap between research and action to improve communication systems in developing countries.

Studies and analyses were undertaken to frame proposals for the establishment of a new world information and communication order. A major event was a round-table meeting held at Innsbruck, Austria, in September, in conjunction with the United Nations.

Work continued on defining and analysing the concept of the right to communicate and the findings of studies carried out under this programme were published, in English and French, under the title *The right to communicate*. Assistance was provided for a conference on the role of information in the realization of the human rights of migrant workers (Tampere, Finland).

Studies on the flow of information included a global survey of the flow of television news and programmes, carried out by a network of institutions, which supplied data from 57 countries. A report on the circulation of world news in the early 1980s was prepared for publication.

Information flow activities included renewed efforts to lower telecommunication tariffs for the mass media (in co-operation with the International Telecommunication Union), co-operation with journalists' and broadcasters' organizations, and proposals to establish a network for the exchange of television films and documentaries. The exchange of news by satellite was a specific concern, and an experiment in the regular exchange of televised news by satellite among broadcasting services of 25 African, Arab, Asian and Pacific countries was successfully carried out during March.

Communication research work was undertaken on the role of communication media in combating racism, racial discrimination and *apartheid*. An international symposium was held at Nairobi on the theme of the media and disarmament. Communication technologies were examined at three 1983 symposia organized with UNESCO assistance. The economic and socio-cultural impact of such technologies was the central topic of a fourth symposium, held in Rome.

A meeting of documentation centres belonging to the International Network of Documentation Centres on Communication Research and Policies was held at Cracow, Poland, in 1983, and plans were made for further expansion of the network and for its progressive automation.

Preparations were intensified for the Intergovernmental Conference on Communication Policies in the Arab States (1984), and follow-up activities to earlier meetings held in Africa, Asia and Latin America were pursued. Preliminary discussions were held with member States on a possible European region conference.

The Intergovernmental Council of the International Programme for the Development of Communication (IPDC) held its fourth session at Tashkent, USSR, in September. The Council recommended 32 interregional, regional and national projects for financial support, ranging from the training of communicators to providing electronic field production facilities for rural television. Of these, 13 national and six interregional and regional projects were approved for immediate funding.

Development of communication infrastructures continued to be one of the most important IPDC objectives. Operational activities were centred on the creation or development of regional news exchange organizations, the Pan-African News Agency, the Latin American Features Agency and the Asian News Network. A project to expand the Caribbean News Agency, including creating a specialized radio news bulletin service, was also launched.

Many training projects were also organized, such as the establishment of a national training centre in Bangladesh and assistance to regional training programmes in Africa, Asia, the Arab States and the Caribbean.

Two in a series of regional consultations to coordinate follow-up action to the 1982 World Congress on Books[a] were held in June 1983: one for Africa at Yaoundé, United Republic of Cameroon, and the other for Asia and the Pacific in Singapore.

General Information Programme

The UNESCO General Information Programme was concerned with developing and promoting national, regional and international information systems in scientific and technological information, documentation, libraries and archives.

The Programme continued to emphasize socio-economic information and the special needs of developing countries. It aimed to facilitate member States' choice, use and adaptation of advanced information and communication technology and to strengthen UNESCO's information role in the United Nations system.

Publications included the quarterly *Journal of Information Science, Librarianship and Archives Administration*, as well as guidelines, studies, technical reports, state-of-the-art reviews and directories.

Technical assistance

Participation Programme

As at 31 December 1983, allocations approved by the Director-General for 1981-1983 under the UNESCO Participation Programme, through which member States and organizations participate in technical assistance activities, amounted to $15,788,818. In view of the fact that the budget provisions, approved by the UNESCO General Conference at its twenty-first (1980) session, were for three years, distribution of the funds was made in two instalments.

The amounts (in United States dollars) by sector and by region were as follows:

Sector	Allocation
Culture	4,648,845
Education	4,007,832
Social sciences	2,156,100
Natural sciences	1,605,020
General Information Programme	1,201,617
Training abroad and national commissions	1,075,780
Communication	969,874
Programme support	123,750
Total	15,788,818

Region	
Africa	4,658,674
Latin America and the Caribbean	2,780,699
Interregional	2,525,960
Asia and the Pacific	2,230,865
Europe	2,070,240
Arab States	1,522,380
Total	15,788,818

Extrabudgetary programmes

Expenditure incurred in 1983 in respect of projects for which UNESCO served as executing agency, financed by UNDP, UNFPA and other extrabudgetary sources, amounted to $79.9 million as shown below:

Source	Amount (in millions of US dollars)
UN sources:	
UNDP	42.0
UNFPA	4.9
Others	7.2
Subtotal	54.1

[a]YUN 1982, p. 1535.

Source	Amount (in millions of US dollars)
Other programmes:	
World Bank technical assistance	2.5
Regional banks and funds	1.8
Self-benefiting funds	11.6
Donated funds	7.4
Associate experts	2.5
Subtotal	25.8
Total	79.9
Sector	
Education	39.5
Natural sciences	21.6
Culture	8.6
Communication	3.6
General Information Programme	3.4
Social sciences	2.3
Others	0.9
Total	79.9
Region	
Africa	28.6
Arab States	19.3
Asia and the Pacific	17.1
Latin America and the Caribbean	7.4
Interregional and global	5.7
Europe and North America	1.8
Total	79.9

Secretariat

As at 31 December 1983, the total number of full-time staff employed by UNESCO on permanent, fixed-term and short-term appointments was 3,448 drawn from 130 nationalities. Of these, 1,382 were in the Professional or higher categories and 2,066 in the General Service and Maintenance Worker categories.

Of the Professional staff, 467 were serving in the field, as were 444 General Service and Maintenance Worker staff.

Budget

The 1983 session of the UNESCO General Conference approved a budget of $374.4 million for the period 1984-1985. The Conference fixed the level of the Working Capital Fund at $20 million and approved a total assessment on member States (after reducing miscellaneous income) of $344.7 million. Amounts allocated (in thousands of United States dollars) are shown in the table below:

UNESCO REGULAR BUDGET

	Amount
Programme operations and services	255,070
Programme support services	54,292
General administrative services	30,916
Common services	30,748
Appropriation reserve	29,387
General policy and direction	25,780
Capital expenditure	4,845
Negative provision for currency fluctuation	(46,145)
Subtotal	348,893
Less overall budget reduction approved by the General Conference	(10,483)
Total	374,410

Annex I. MEMBERSHIP OF THE UNITED NATIONS EDUCATIONAL, SCIENTIFIC AND CULTURAL ORGANIZATION AND CONTRIBUTIONS

(Membership as at 31 December 1983; annual contributions as assessed for 1984 and 1985)

MEMBER	CONTRIBUTION Percentage	CONTRIBUTION Amount (in US dollars)	MEMBER	CONTRIBUTION Percentage	CONTRIBUTION Amount (in US dollars)	MEMBER	CONTRIBUTION Percentage	CONTRIBUTION Amount (in US dollars)
Afghanistan	0.01	17,235	Cape Verde	0.01	17,235	Fiji	0.01	17,235
Albania	0.01	17,235	Central African Republic	0.01	17,235	Finland	0.47	810,045
Algeria	0.13	224,055	Chad	0.01	17,235	France	6.43	11,082,105
Angola	0.01	17,235	Chile	0.07	120,645	Gabon	0.02	34,470
Antigua and Barbuda	0.01	17,235	China	0.67	1,499,445	Gambia	0.01	17,235
Argentina	0.70	1,206,450	Colombia	0.11	189,585	German Democratic		
Australia	1.55	2,671,425	Comoros	0.01	17,235	Republic	1.37	2,361,195
Austria	0.74	1,275,390	Congo	0.01	17,235	Germany, Federal		
Bahamas	0.01	17,235	Costa Rica	0.02	34,470	Republic of	8.44	14,546,340
Bahrain	0.01	17,235	Cuba	0.09	155,115	Ghana	0.02	34,470
Bangladesh	0.03	51,705	Cyprus	0.01	17,235	Greece	0.39	672,165
Barbados	0.01	17,235	Czechoslovakia	0.75	1,292,625	Grenada	0.01	17,235
Belgium	1.26	2,171,610	Democratic Kampuchea	0.01	17,235	Guatemala	0.02	34,470
Belize	0.01	17,235	Democratic People's			Guinea	0.01	17,235
Benin	0.01	17,235	Republic of Korea	0.05	86,175	Guinea-Bissau	0.01	17,235
Bhutan	0.01	17,235	Democratic Yemen	0.01	17,235	Guyana	0.01	17,235
Bolivia	0.01	17,235	Denmark	0.74	1,275,390	Haiti	0.01	17,235
Botswana	0.01	17,235	Dominica	0.01	17,235	Honduras	0.01	17,235
Brazil	1.37	2,361,195	Dominican Republic	0.03	51,705	Hungary	0.23	396,405
Bulgaria	0.18	310,230	Ecuador	0.02	34,470	Iceland	0.03	51,705
Burma	0.01	17,235	Egypt	0.07	120,645	India	0.36	620,460
Burundi	0.01	17,235	El Salvador	0.01	17,235	Indonesia	0.13	224,055
Byelorussian SSR	0.36	620,460	Equatorial Guinea	0.01	17,235	Iran	0.57	982,395
Canada	3.04	5,239,440	Ethiopia	0.01	17,235	Iraq	0.12	206,820

MEMBER	Percent-age	Amount (in US dollars)	MEMBER	Percent-age	Amount (in US dollars)	MEMBER	Percent-age	Amount (in US dollars)
		CONTRIBUTION			CONTRIBUTION			CONTRIBUTION
Ireland	0.18	310,230	Norway	0.50	861,750	Thailand	0.08	137,880
Israel	0.23	396,405	Oman	0.01	17,235	Togo	0.01	17,235
Italy	3.69	6,359,715	Pakistan	0.06	103,410	Tonga	0.01	17,235
Ivory Coast	0.03	51,705	Panama	0.02	34,470	Trinidad and Tobago	0.03	51,705
Jamaica	0.02	34,470	Papua New Guinea	0.01	17,235	Tunisia	0.03	51,705
Japan	10.19	17,562,465	Paraguay	0.01	17,235	Turkey	0.31	534,285
Jordan	0.01	17,235	Peru	0.07	120,645	Uganda	0.01	17,235
Kenya	0.01	17,235	Philippines	0.09	155,115	Ukrainian SSR	1.30	2,240,550
Kuwait	0.25	430,875	Poland	0.71	1,223,685	USSR	10.41	17,941,635
Lao People's Democratic Republic	0.01	17,235	Portugal	0.18	310,230	United Arab Emirates	0.16	275,760
Lebanon	0.02	34,470	Qatar	0.03	51,705	United Kingdom	4.61	7,945,335
Lesotho	0.01	17,235	Republic of Korea	0.18	310,230	United Republic of Cameroon	0.01	17,235
Liberia	0.01	17,235	Romania	0.19	327,465	United Republic of Tanzania	0.01	17,235
Libyan Arab Jamahiriya	0.26	448,110	Rwanda	0.01	17,235	United States	25.00	43,087,500
Luxembourg	0.06	103,410	Saint Christopher and Nevis	0.01	17,235	Upper Volta	0.01	17,235
Madagascar	0.01	17,235	Saint Lucia	0.01	17,235	Uruguay	0.04	68,940
Malawi	0.01	17,235	Saint Vincent and the Grenadines	0.01	17,235	Venezuela	0.54	930,690
Malaysia	0.09	155,115	Samoa	0.01	17,235	Viet Nam	0.02	34,470
Maldives	0.01	17,235	San Marino	0.01	17,235	Yemen	0.01	17,235
Mali	0.01	17,235	Sao Tome and Principe	0.01	17,235	Yugoslavia	0.45	775,575
Malta	0.01	17,235	Saudi Arabia	0.85	1,464,975	Zaire	0.01	17,235
Mauritania	0.01	17,235	Senegal	0.01	17,235	Zambia	0.01	17,235
Mauritius	0.01	17,235	Seychelles	0.01	17,235	Zimbabwe	0.02	34,470
Mexico	0.87	1,499,445	Sierra Leone	0.01	17,235			
Monaco	0.01	17,235	Singapore	0.09	155,115	Total†	100.02	172,384,470
Mongolia	0.01	17,235	Somalia	0.01	17,235			
Morocco	0.05	86,175	Spain	1.91	3,291,885	ASSOCIATE MEMBER		
Mozambique	0.01	17,235	Sri Lanka	0.01	17,235			
Namibia*	—	—	Sudan	0.01	17,235	British Eastern Caribbean Group	0.01	17,235
Nepal	0.01	17,235	Suriname	0.01	17,235	British Virgin Islands	0.01	17,235
Netherlands	1.76	3,033,360	Swaziland	0.01	17,235	Netherlands Antilles	0.01	17,235
New Zealand	0.26	448,110	Sweden	1.30	2,240,550	Total	0.03	51,705
Nicaragua	0.01	17,235	Switzerland	1.09	1,878,615			
Niger	0.01	17,235	Syrian Arab Republic	0.03	51,705			
Nigeria	0.19	327,465						

*Namibia's assessment remained suspended in 1983.

†Includes contributions assessed for Fiji and Saint Christopher and Nevis, admitted as members after assessments for the period 1984-1985 had been established.

Annex II.   OFFICERS AND OFFICES OF THE UNITED NATIONS EDUCATIONAL, SCIENTIFIC AND CULTURAL ORGANIZATION

(As at 31 December 1983)

MEMBERS OF THE EXECUTIVE BOARD

Chairman: Patrick K. Seddoh (Ghana).

Vice-Chairmen: Jean B. S. Gerard (United States), Mamadi Keita (Guinea), Mahmoud Messadi (Tunisia), Ladislav Smid (Czechoslovakia), José Israel Vargas (Brazil), Yang Bozhen (China).

Members: Eid Abdo (Syrian Arab Republic), José Luis Abellán (Spain), Camille Aboussouan (Lebanon), Daniel Arango (Colombia), Alphonse Blagué (Central African Republic), Mario Cabral (Guinea-Bissau), Estrella Z. de Carazo (Costa Rica), Ian Christie Clark (Canada), Dimitri Cosmadopoulos (Greece), Jean-Pierre Cot (France), Buyant Dashtseren (Mongolia), William A. Dodd (United Kingdom), Georges-Henri Dumont (Belgium), Dmitri V. Ermolenko (USSR), Pierre Foulani (Niger), Carmen Guerrero-Nakpil (Philippines), Alfredo Guevara (Cuba), Abdul Aziz Hussein (Kuwait), Attiya Inayatullah (Pakistan), Andri Isaksson (Iceland), Osman Sid Ahmed Ismail (Sudan), Ben Kufakunesu Jambga (Zimbabwe), Takaaki Kagawa (Japan), Triloki Nath Kaul (India), A. Majeed Khan (Bangladesh), Donald M. Kusenha (United Republic of Tanzania), Jean-Félix Loung (United Republic of Cameroon), Edward Victor Luckhoo (Guyana), Ivo Margan (Yugoslavia), Karl Moersch (Federal Republic of Germany), Musa Justice Nsibande (Swaziland), A. Bola Olaniyan (Nigeria), Demodetdo Y. Pendje (Zaire), Jean Ping (Gabon), Gian Franco Pompei (Italy), Abdellatif Rahal (Algeria), Guy A. Rajaonson (Madagascar), Jesús Reyes Heroles (Mexico), Hubert de Ronceray (Haiti), Saeed Abdullah Salman (United Arab Emirates), Kaw Swasdi Panich (Thailand), Alfredo Tarre Murzi (Venezuela), Gleb N. Tsvetkov (Ukrainian SSR), Hector L. Wynter (Jamaica).

PRINCIPAL OFFICERS OF THE SECRETARIAT

Director-General: Amadou-Mahtar M'Bow.

Assistant Director-General, Director of the Executive Office: Chikh Békri.

Assistant Directors-General: Gérard Bolla, John Borema Kaboré (acting), Abdul-Razzak Kaddoura, Jean Knapp, Henri Lopes, Makaminan Makagiansar, Zala Lusibu N'Kanza (acting), George Saddler, Sema Tanguiane, Tien-Chang Young.

HEADQUARTERS AND OTHER OFFICE

HEADQUARTERS
UNESCO House
7 Place de Fontenoy
75700 Paris, France
  Cable address: UNESCO PARIS
  Telephone: 568-10-00
  Telex: 204461

NEW YORK OFFICE
United Nations Educational, Scientific and
  Cultural Organization
2 United Nations Plaza
New York, N. Y. 10017, United States
  Cable address: UNESCORG NEWYORK
  Telephone: (212) 754-5995

Chapter V

World Health Organization (WHO)

The thirty-sixth World Health Assembly met at Geneva from 2 to 16 May 1983 and approved a wide-ranging programme of activities in support of the plan of action for attaining health for all by the year 2000, approved in 1982.[a] The Assembly also endorsed the findings of an international committee of experts on the probable effects of nuclear war. The committee had concluded that it was impossible to prepare health services to deal in any systematic way with a catastrophe resulting from nuclear warfare, and that nuclear weapons constituted the greatest immediate threat to the health and welfare of mankind. Members of the committee included physicists, physicians, geneticists, epidemiologists, and experts in public health, nuclear medicine and biology, radiopathology, radiation protection, burn injuries and plastic surgery. The Assembly urged the member States of the World Health Organization (WHO) to give careful consideration to the committee's conclusions, and requested the Director-General to publish the committee's report to ensure that it received wide publicity.

Dr. Halfdan Mahler was reappointed as WHO Director-General by the Assembly for a third five-year term beginning in July 1983.

Among other programme and operational topics considered by the Executive Board and the Assembly in 1983 were: infant and child nutrition; alcohol-related health problems; cardiovascular diseases; tuberculosis control; African human trypanosomiasis; oral health; progress towards the goals of the International Drinking Water Supply and Sanitation Decade (1981-1990); and the role of nursing/midwifery personnel in health-for-all strategies.

In 1983, responding to an Executive Board resolution, the Director-General outlined a framework for the optimal use of WHO's resources in direct support of member States. Such resources would be used to help Governments build up their health systems, emphasizing the creation of sound infrastructures to carry out health programmes using appropriate technology.

Three countries became members of WHO during 1983—Vanuatu on 7 March, Solomon Islands on 4 April and Saint Vincent and the Grenadines on 2 September—which brought its membership to 161 and one associate member.

Emergency assistance

WHO continued to participate fully in providing emergency assistance in 1983, its work being carried out in close collaboration with United Nations agencies and other institutions and non-governmental organizations active in disaster work. WHO undertook over 50 emergency actions in connection with earthquakes, hurricanes, cyclones, volcanoes, epidemics, the plight of refugees, post-war conditions and civil strife. WHO also took part in all major United Nations multi-agency missions on disaster situations.

Health system infrastructure

Health system development

Information, training, research and legislative activities related to health system development were carried out by WHO during 1983.

A meeting of regional advisers (Geneva, December) examined the global implications of WHO's programme to assess health situations and trends, set up in 1982.[b]

WHO assisted 13 countries to perform morbidity and mortality surveys and health studies: four in South-East Asia, three in Europe and six in the Eastern Mediterranean. Assistance was also given in investigating epidemics, including an outbreak of illness on the West Bank of the Jordan.

Four students graduated from the field epidemiology training programme in Thailand, which was supported by WHO and the Centers for Disease Control in Atlanta, Georgia (United States).

Courses on health statistics and health records were given in many countries, and a number of teaching manuals and aids were prepared for publication. Guidelines were drafted for those teaching the collection, analysis and use of health information to primary health care workers.

A systematic attempt was made to strengthen national health research capabilities in the African region. Numerous workshops, short courses and courses on research methodology and management were arranged for participants from English- and French-speaking countries. At the same time, the region's network of national research centres was expanded with the establishment of institutions in Ethiopia, the Ivory Coast, Kenya, Mozambique, Nigeria, Zaire and Zambia.

In the region of the Americas, WHO co-operated with Peru and Uruguay in general sur-

---

[a]YUN 1982, p. 1538.
[b]*Ibid.*

veys of health services with a view to their reorganization. The surveys were aided financially by the World Bank in Peru and by the United Nations Development Programme (UNDP) in Uruguay.

In the South-East Asia region, a health services research information system was being developed and linked with the health literature, library and information services network. Guidelines for the standardization of information were tested in some countries. A conceptual description of health systems research, as recommended by the Advisory Committee on Medical Research (ACMR), was circulated to all countries.

In the European region, ACMR recommended that WHO activate and support health services research wherever it was lacking. Reviewing the recommendations of a regional study group (Mürren, Switzerland, January), ACMR discussed a programme on social equity and health. The programme had started in 1982 and focused initially on migrants and the unemployed. ACMR stressed that equity in health was a research priority of increasing importance. An advisory committee on the programme met in October to examine national experience in the field.

Workshops supported by WHO were held on drug legislation in Nepal in April and on food safety laws in China in October.

A study on trends in health legislation in Europe was completed. It attempted to demonstrate the importance of such legislation in the reorientation of national health systems and the implementation of specific health programmes. Two meetings were held at Brussels, Belgium, to prepare for an international course on health legislation; the course was to be held in 1984 (in English) and in 1985 (in French).

Primary health care systems

Translating the primary health care approach into tangible programmes that national health services could implement in such varied places as remote rural villages and crowded urban slums remained one of the greatest challenges facing WHO. As a means of diverting resources away from undue emphasis on sophisticated, hospital-based technologies, WHO developed in 1983 guiding principles to demonstrate what might be accomplished through alternative methods. The principles were intended to help reorient health delivery systems to primary care and overcome the dearth of information available to those responsible for system planning, implementation and evaluation.

A project for the joint control of diabetes and cardiovascular diseases within the primary health care system was begun in the United Republic of Tanzania in 1983, while workshops at Lomé, Togo, and Arusha, United Republic of Tanzania, discussed ways of improving malaria control.

With support from the Swedish International Development Authority and the Swedish Agency for Research Co-operation with Developing Countries, co-ordinated efforts to strengthen primary health care were begun in Ethiopia, Sri Lanka, the United Republic of Tanzania, and Zambia. Often focused on specific districts, activities included decentralized planning, practical research, management and other training, and evaluation. The needs common to most countries were found to be logistic support, information system development, drug supply, integration of services and promotion of teamwork. Areas for further action were identified at an interregional meeting held in Zambia in December.

An interregional consultation (Dubrovnik, Yugoslavia, April), which brought together participants from national and regional health and management training institutions in 14 developed and developing countries, identified three areas for future collaboration: strengthening of training capabilities; development of teaching/learning modules; and research on the roles of middle-level managers.

Health manpower

The motive power behind the concept of health for all comes primarily from trained personnel, each with the necessary training and understanding of the tasks he or she is to perform, whether at the ministry level or the rural health centre, whether highly trained medical specialist or part-time community health worker. To bring about a broader comprehension of the tasks to be performed, WHO conducted workshops and study groups in 1983, dealing with intersectoral co-operation, manpower planning, administration of fellowship programmes, continuing education and resources deployment.

In November/December, an interregional consultation at Bangalore, India, assessed health manpower management and proposed ways to improve it. In support of the International Drinking Water Supply and Sanitation Decade, a workshop was held (Geneva, November) to form a global team to explore ways to implement the strategies for the Decade. Fellowship officers from the Western Pacific region met at Manila, Philippines, in October to discuss improving the planning of fellowships and the selection of fellows.

Public information and education for health

Topics related to public information and health education were the focus of technical discussions at the World Health Assembly and regional committee meetings in 1983. The Assembly considered new policies for health education in primary health care. The consensus was that new policies must include unequivocal recognition of the need to involve the community in health planning, and awareness that health was not merely a medical issue, but involved environmental, cultural, political, social and economic factors. In the regions, the concept of community participation was emphasized. The importance of providing children and youth with adequate information and education for health and the use of appropriate technology, including traditional methods of communication, were also high on the list of priorities.

World Health Day 1983 (7 April) warned of the need for drastic and immediate action, with the slogan "Health for all by the year 2000: the countdown has begun".

General health protection

During 1983, WHO prepared a monograph on nutritional surveillance and an updated set of guidelines for the measurement of change in nutritional status.

An interregional WHO meeting at Geneva in June reviewed the strengthening of national capabilities in nutrition and stressed the importance of filling manpower gaps through the training of senior staff. The training of staff was explored in detail and a plan of action drawn up at a meeting in September of representatives of training institutions, the United Nations and bilateral agencies.

A common strategy for oral health was outlined by the World Health Assembly in 1983. The strategy was based on the recognition that all national oral health situations were really variations on a single theme. Whatever the prevalence of oral disease, the key to its reduction was the well-managed prevention of periodontal disease and dental caries. The role of WHO was to help countries to analyse the situation, establish policies and goals, plans and programmes, and identify obstacles to their achievement.

The accident prevention programme was expanded beyond its initial focus on motor vehicle mishaps. Children and the aged were given special attention in the overall programme. Information was collected on accident risks in domestic surroundings in different socio-cultural settings. A consultation was held in October to examine the types of accidents and injuries encountered in agricultural work.

The first interregional post-graduate course on injury prevention in developing countries was held in June at Baltimore, Maryland (United States), in co-operation with Johns Hopkins University. Seventeen countries from five WHO regions sent participants.

Health of specific population groups

The wide gap between maternal mortality rates in developed and developing countries reflected differences in health, the availability of care, socio-economic conditions and the status of women. Data were being collected and analysed at the global level on the incidence and causes of maternal mortality, with particular reference to women who received no qualified care during childbirth. In the Eastern Mediterranean region, a system of confidential inquiries was promoted to improve understanding of avoidable maternal deaths, with a view to modifying health workers' training and service.

In 1983, 70 countries, 44 of which were developing countries, took part in the WHO Special Programme of Research, Development and Research Training in Human Reproduction. Some 600 research projects were carried out, 36 research training courses and workshops were held, and 120 research training grants were awarded to scientists from 25 countries.

The study of two practical problems associated with aging was undertaken in 1983 by WHO. The first was senile dementia, an intractable problem causing widespread suffering. A WHO scientific group (Paris, August/September) reviewed biomedical and health services research on senile brain disorders. Its report, containing an integrated plan for collaborative research, was submitted to ACMR in October. The second problem concerned the consequences for health of longevity, raising the question of whether disabling diseases might increase with the life-span. This was discussed by the WHO Scientific Group on the Epidemiology of Aging (Geneva, January), which recommended epidemiological investigations directed to the maintenance of function.

Mental health

The mental health programme of WHO comprised three interrelated activities: psychosocial factors in promoting health and human development; preventing and controlling alcohol and drug abuse; and preventing and treating mental and neurological disorders.

Collaboration with countries in formulating national mental health programmes and policies remained a central concern of WHO in 1983. To this end numerous symposia, meetings and workshops were held in various regions.

Environmental health

During 1983, WHO co-operated with member States to provide safe drinking-water and sanitation to people still unserved or underserved as part of the International Drinking Water Supply and Sanitation Decade. The World Health Assembly, noting that countries were encountering difficulties in achieving the goals that they had set for the Decade, recommended that member States promote safe drinking-water and sanitation as an essential component of primary health care.

With the support of 17 member States and more than 100 institutions, the International Programme on Chemical Safety spearheaded a global effort to reduce existing environmental hazards and to anticipate the possibly adverse effects of new substances. The first phase of an international study on short-term, *in vitro* tests for genotoxicity and carcinogenicity was completed in 1983.

Environmental pollution control in relation to development was considered by a WHO expert committee (Geneva, November). It reviewed problems associated with agrochemicals, urbanization and industrial operations, and offered recommendations on prevention and control measures.

In the Western Pacific region, a WHO-sponsored intercountry workshop on environmental mutagenesis, carcinogenesis and teratogenesis (Shanghai, China, May) was attended by experts from 11 countries.

Traditional medicine

A WHO survey of traditional medicine, completed in 1983, provided information on some national activities. Member States showed increasing interest in utilizing traditional and indigenous resources in implementing primary health care programmes. Legislation was adopted by Burma, Malawi, Mexico, Sri Lanka, the Sudan, Thailand, the United Republic of Tanzania, Viet Nam and Zambia. WHO collaborating centres for traditional medicine continued to aid national efforts. By the end of 1983, 16 centres had been designated: four in Africa, three in the Americas, two in South-East Asia, one in Europe and six in the Western Pacific. Guidelines were developed on the recognition, use, preparation and quality control of the most commonly used medicinal plants and their extracts.

Disease prevention and control

Acute respiratory infections

The mortality rate from respiratory infections was still very high in developing countries. The situation for children was particularly disturbing, with a mortality rate some 50 times greater than in developed countries.

A newly appointed technical advisory group on acute respiratory infections held its first meeting at Geneva in March 1983. It concluded that there was enough knowledge and technology available to enable countries to introduce programmes for the control of such infections. Programmes should be carried out in the context of primary health care and include early discrimination between mild and severe infections, antimicrobial treatment, criteria for referral of cases to a higher health care level, health education of families, and immunization against measles, diphtheria, pertussis and childhood tuberculosis.

Blindness

The WHO programme advisory group on the prevention of blindness met at Manila in 1983 and focused on the development of prevention strategies within a framework of primary health care. Collaborative efforts with non-governmental organizations also were explored.

A working group met at Geneva in November/December to recommend methods for the prevention and treatment of ophthalmia neonatorum, with particular reference to primary health care.

Cancer

The three programme priorities in cancer control were prevention, early detection coupled with efficient therapy, and pain relief. National cancer policies being formulated were based on those principles. The use of primary health care systems for delivery of control measures was explored and the cost-effectiveness of those measures and existing knowledge taken into account.

A clearer division of work between WHO and the International Agency for Research on Cancer (IARC) was established with WHO concentrating on cancer control, including developing national policies, prevention, early detection, therapy, aftercare and operational research. IARC efforts were directed towards the identification of carcinogenic factors in the environment, the definition of risk groups, and the description of the epidemiological situation throughout the world, including related laboratory and field research.

The list of essential drugs for cancer chemotherapy was reviewed at a consultation (Geneva, October). Therapeutic clinical trials were conducted at 12 cancer institutes in Latin America and 10 centres in the United States, as part of the collaborative cancer treatment research programme.

The African Organization for Research and Training in Cancer was established with the help of WHO in 1983. Among its objectives were the development of regional training facilities and the formulation of a regional curriculum in oncology.

An international case-control study of cancer of the pancreas, with emphasis on the role of known stimulators of cholecystokinin release, currently involved centres at Adelaide, Australia; Toronto, Canada; Utrecht, Netherlands; and Warsaw, Poland. The analysis of occupational histories in case-control studies was also being sponsored.

Cardiovascular diseases

In 1983, the World Health Assembly concurred with recommendations of the Executive Board that additional funds be allocated to the programme on cardiovascular diseases, with particular reference to the prevention of coronary heart disease. The Assembly urged member States to give special attention to the wide possibilities for prevention and control of cardiovascular diseases as part of their national health plans.

The chief investigators of community control programmes in developing countries met at Manila in June to consider the possibilities for the prevention of cardiovascular diseases in primary health care. They recommended that for the time being projects be restricted to a defined area and a few priority problems. Such programmes were being developed in the Philippines, Sri Lanka, Thailand and the United Republic of Tanzania.

Heart muscle disease of obscure or unknown etiology was an important cause of cardiovascular morbidity and death in many parts of the world. In some Latin American countries, for example, mortality from involvement of the heart due to Chagas' disease accounted for more than 40 per cent of all cardiovascular deaths. Many questions remained unanswered in this area of cardiology and there was still much confusion in terminology. In April, the Expert Committee on Cardiomyopathies met at Geneva to review current knowledge and propose action and research, including epidemiological studies which might be undertaken.

Diarrhoeal diseases

By the end of 1983, of the 71 developing countries that had completed plans for national programmes of diarrhoeal disease control, 50 were operational. Much of the planning had been facilitated by the WHO training course for programme managers which had been given 20 times and had been attended by 678 senior staff from 117 developing countries.

Forty-three morbidity and mortality surveys were carried out in 19 countries to provide baseline data for national programmes. They showed that, on average, children under the age of five had three episodes of diarrhoea annually and that about one third of all deaths in this age-group were associated with diarrhoea.

An International Conference on Oral Rehydration Therapy (Washington, D. C., June), attended by more than 500 participants, was sponsored by the United States Agency for International Development in co-operation with the International Centre for Diarrhoeal Disease Research (Bangladesh), the United Nations Children's Fund (UNICEF) and WHO.

Malaria

The UNICEF/WHO Joint Committee on Health Policy, at its twenty-fourth session in February 1933, recognized that malaria continued to be a major problem in many countries, with serious effects on the health of mothers and children. A study group on malaria control as part of primary health care (Geneva, November) met to identify practical approaches that could be applied at various levels and those which needed to be further developed.

A regional workshop on drug-resistant malaria (Jakarta, Indonesia, May) was devoted to research on the monitoring, epidemiology and control of drug-resistant falciparum malaria. The development of new antimalarial drugs had become a major need for the global malaria programme and field trials of new drugs were being conducted. The largest such field trial, using a combination of mefloquine, sulfadoxine and pyrimethamine and involving 100,000 people, was conducted in Thailand by the Government, industry and WHO.

Other parasitic diseases

Multicentre clinical trials of the new, effective, orally administered antischistosomal drug, praziquantel, co-ordinated by WHO and the manufacturers, were completed by the end of 1983. Long-term toxicity and carcinogenicity studies also co-ordinated by WHO did not reveal untoward effects. Extensive experience with use of the drug was gained, particularly in the Blue Nile health project in the Sudan, whose most important achievement to date was the prevention of the introduction of schistosomiasis into the Rahad zone. Other countries showed interest in the large-scale use of the drug; in the Philippines, striking reductions in the prevalance of infection were seen after field trials.

Emphasis was placed on the use of diethylcarbamazine (DEC) to control acute manifestations of lymphatic filariasis and thus prevent the development of chronic disabling lesions such as elephantiasis and hydrocele. This approach, using relatively small doses of DEC given at intervals of a week, a month or a year, was being followed with success, and was sometimes being extended to treatment of asymptomatic microfilariae carriers, as in China, French Polynesia, Indonesia and Samoa. It was being considered for use in India as a supplement to existing mosquito control measures.

Technical co-operation continued for the control of onchocerciasis, using larvicides against *Simulium*, nodulectomy and chemotherapy. Participating countries in Africa were Malawi, Nigeria, the Sudan and the United Republic of Tanzania, as well as those involved in the Onchocerciasis Control Programme in the Volta River basin area and its proposed western extension. Similar work in the Americas involved Brazil, Ecuador, Guatemala, Mexico and Venezuela. In Mexico a WHO collaborating centre was designated, and in Ecuador the distribution and delineation of the endemic foci were assessed. Research to find new drugs for treatment of onchocerciasis included clinical trials of mebendazole, flubendazole and ivermectin, preclinical toxicity testing of new macrofilaricides, and expansion of basic research on biochemistry, chemical synthesis and screening to find new active compounds.

Accurate data on the prevalence and distribution of Chagas' disease were scarce, but current estimates suggested that some 65 million people lived under conditions favouring transmission and that the number of infected people probably was about 25 million. For control, large-scale insecticide spraying was being carried out in Argentina, Brazil and Venezuela. A cause of concern was the apparent spread of the disease through the migration of people from rural areas to the cities and through blood transfusion from infected donors. Research concentrated on the prevention of transmission by blood transfusion, development of new therapeutic drugs, and exploration of various epidemiological methods including serological tests.

The public health importance of the leishmaniases had been re-emphasized during the past few years. Severe outbreaks in India and Kenya were brought under control, but new active foci were suspected, for instance in Afghanistan and Nepal. In South America, the leishmaniases were on the increase, often as a result of movements of temporary labourers in sandfly-infested areas such as the Amazonian forest. In general, control efforts were insufficient and hampered by the wide diversity of transmission situations. *Ad hoc* technical support continued to be provided where needed by WHO.

Sexually transmitted diseases

A meeting at Geneva in November 1983 synthesized global knowledge of acquired immune deficiency syndrome (AIDS), whose aetiology and therapy remained unknown. It examined risk factors, possible causes, and the clinical and immunological picture. It made preliminary recommendations for prevention, diagnostic and screening tests, and clinical management of cases, and indicated promising areas for research.

The WHO Expert Committee on Venereal Diseases and Treponematoses also met at Geneva in November and reviewed complex changes which had taken place in the perspectives and dynamics of sexually transmitted infections. The Committee outlined an adaptation of technologies and priorities to improve control.

Smoking and health

Co-sponsored by WHO, the Fifth World Conference on Smoking and Health (Winnipeg, Canada, July 1983) was attended by more than 1,000 people from about 80 countries. Emphasis was given to issues relating to developing countries; smoking among women and young people; and the social and economic aspects of tobacco consumption. An important recommendation was that non-smoking—and the right to a smoke-free atmosphere—should be established as the social norm.

Tuberculosis

In view of the fact that tuberculosis hardly seemed to be declining in developing countries and of the unexpected finding from a study in south India that BCG (Bacillus Calmette-Guérin) vaccination might not afford the protection against the disease formerly thought to be the case, the World Health Assembly directed the WHO tuberculosis programme to develop more effective control strategies. To achieve nation-wide coverage, it was suggested that tuberculosis programmes be integrated into comprehensive health systems. An epidemiological breakthrough might come from the judicious extension of programme activities towards early detection and better case-holding (retaining patients on long-term therapy). Technological developments in immunology and molecular biology indicated that well coordinated research in these fields could produce more effective control measures in a relatively short time.

Vector control

Resistance to pesticides remained the greatest technical impediment to the control of arthropod vectors, rodent reservoirs and snail intermediate hosts of disease. Continual monitoring of the susceptibility status of target vector species was required to determine the necessity of shifting to an alternative pesticide or control method. Results of more than 1,000 susceptibility tests, received between January 1982 and June 1983, were passed on to investigators. The appearance of resistance to temephos in one member of the *Simulium damnosum* complex in the Ivory Coast had given rise to particularly serious concern. Within the framework of the Onchocerciasis Control Programme, the area in which resistance had been detected was immediately treated with the biological control agent *Bacillus thuringiensis H-14* and the infestation was eliminated.

More than 60 representatives of the world's leading pesticide producers attended a meeting in June 1983 on insecticide resistance problems with the aim of encouraging industry to direct research towards the needs of vector control.

Zoonoses

The zoonoses receiving high priority in WHO's programme were rabies, hydatidosis, leptospirosis, and major food-borne diseases related to animals and animal products, such as salmonellosis and brucellosis.

A consultation organized by WHO, the International Committee on Food Microbiology and Hygiene, and the International Union of Microbiological Societies (Budapest, Hungary, July 1983) discussed current international problems in food microbiology and recommended future action for better protection of the consumer against food-borne infections.

Two centres—one at Madison, Wisconsin (United States), the other at Brno, Czechoslovakia—collaborated in the food virology programme. Up-to-date knowledge was summarized in a manual on food virology, in which measures for preventing human viral infections by way of food were proposed for the veterinary and public health services at the national level.

Secretariat

As at 31 December 1983, the total number of full-time staff employed by WHO stood at 4,444 on permanent and fixed-term contracts. Of these, 1,521 staff members, drawn from 119 nationalities, were in the Professional and higher categories and 2,923 were in the General Service category. Of the total number of staff, 155 were in posts financed by UNDP, the United Nations Environment Programme, the United Nations Fund for Drug Abuse Control and the United Nations Fund for Population Activities.

Budget

The thirty-fourth (1981) World Health Assembly had approved a working budget of $468,900,000 for 1982-1983.[c]

The thirty-sixth Assembly approved a working budget of $520,100,000 for the biennium 1984-1985.

The budget was divided into allocations for WHO's programme of work as follows: health system infrastructure, 33 per cent; health science and technology, 32 per cent; programme support, 23 per cent; and direction, co-ordination and management, 12 per cent.

INTEGRATED INTERNATIONAL HEALTH PROGRAMME OBLIGATIONS BY
SOURCE OF FINANCING FOR THE TWO-YEAR PERIOD 1982-1983

Source	Amount (in thousands of US dollars)
Regular budget	468,900
Pan American Health Organization	165,411
International Agency for Research on Cancer	23,040
Other sources	
Voluntary Fund for Health Promotion	84,353
Sasakawa Health Trust Fund	5,563
United Nations sources	
UNICEF	315
UNDP	53,133
UNEP	2,439
UNFDAC	628
UNFPA	36,911
Trust funds	108,061
Special Account for Servicing Costs	7,384
Total	956,138

[c]YUN 1982, p. 1542.

SERVICES AND CO-OPERATION EXTENDED BY WHO IN THE TWO-YEAR PERIOD 1982-1983, BY REGION AND COUNTRY OR TERRITORY

(in US dollars)

	Regular budget	Other sources	Total		Regular budget	Other sources	Total
Africa				*Africa* (cont.)			
Angola	1,154,900	470,000	1,624,900	St. Helena	26,600	—	26,600
Benin	892,000	660,000	1,552,000	Sao Tome and Principe	512,000	860,000	1,372,000
Botswana	518,300	259,500	777,800	Senegal	800,300	1,280,200	2,080,500
Burundi	1,085,200	623,800	1,709,000	Seychelles	374,700	129,600	504,300
Cape Verde	782,500	—	782,500	Sierra Leone	814,700	130,000	944,700
Central African Republic	1,054,200	299,800	1,354,000	Swaziland	413,900	—	413,900
Chad	1,113,000	—	1,113,000	Togo	867,900	—	867,900
Comoros	1,238,200	—	1,238,200	Uganda	1,101,300	315,800	1,417,100
Congo	779,900	590,900	1,370,800	United Republic of Cameroon	660,200	21,200	681,400
Equatorial Guinea	191,700	986,000	1,177,700	United Republic of Tanzania	1,106,100	388,700	1,494,800
Ethiopia	2,649,600	4,149,100	6,798,700	Upper Volta	1,209,700	—	1,209,700
Gabon	676,100	—	676,100	Zaire	1,574,000	600,000	2,174,000
Gambia	781,800	1,102,400	1,884,200	Zambia	1,181,700	389,900	1,571,600
Ghana	830,100	—	830,100	Zimbabwe	900,000	—	900,000
Guinea	1,209,800	835,000	2,044,800	Intercountry			
Guinea-Bissau	844,500	205,800	1,050,300	programmes	25,965,000	42,611,600	68,576,600
Ivory Coast	647,600	180,000	827,600				
Kenya	995,800	95,600	1,091,400	Subtotal	66,871,500	67,433,800	134,305,300
Lesotho	757,800	677,800	1,435,600				
Liberia	1,047,500	—	1,047,500	*The Americas*			
Madagascar	730,000	1,827,600	2,557,600				
Malawi	782,300	856,700	1,639,000	Argentina	1,059,600	682,100	1,741,700
Mali	1,185,100	82,000	1,267,100	Bahamas	335,800	211,800	547,600
Mauritania	968,300	506,100	1,474,400	Barbados	320,900	287,100	608,000
Mauritius	339,900	44,600	384,500	Belize	319,900	35,000	354,900
Mozambique	1,042,000	339,000	1,381,000	Bolivia	318,200	2,369,800	2,688,000
Namibia	232,200	—	232,200	Brazil	1,978,200	6,155,200	8,133,400
Niger	1,177,700	177,200	1,354,900	Canada	32,400	33,700	66,100
Nigeria	2,304,600	5,067,400	7,372,000	Chile	604,700	1,098,400	1,703,100
Réunion	24,100	—	24,100	Colombia	876,900	3,119,000	3,995,900
Rwanda	1,326,700	670,500	1,997,200				

	Regular budget	Other sources	Total		Regular budget	Other sources	Total
The Americas (cont.)				**Europe** (cont.)			
Costa Rica	354,600	1,014,700	1,369,300	USSR	50,600	—	50,600
Cuba	594,800	653,100	1,247,900	United Kingdom	23,000	—	23,000
Dominican Republic	276,200	1,053,200	1,329,400	Yugoslavia	31,000	—	31,000
Ecuador	1,342,400	467,100	1,809,500				
El Salvador	779,900	551,700	1,331,600	Intercountry			
French Guiana	—	36,000	36,000	programmes	16,165,100	5,229,100	21,394,200
Grenada	—	61,400	61,400				
Guatemala	501,500	2,318,300	2,819,800	Subtotal	18,084,000	6,507,600	24,591,600
Guyana	734,800	480,700	1,215,500				
Haiti	669,000	2,992,800	3,661,800	**Eastern Mediterranean**			
Honduras	524,000	2,200,800	2,724,800				
Jamaica	650,900	746,500	1,397,400	Afghanistan	4,005,100	933,800	4,938,900
Mexico	617,000	2,927,700	3,544,700	Bahrain	126,500	34,500	161,000
Netherlands Antilles	39,100	19,900	59,000	Cyprus	521,000	—	521,000
Nicaragua	947,700	396,200	1,343,900	Democratic Yemen	2,927,000	1,551,000	4,478,000
Panama	596,100	723,600	1,319,700	Djibouti	401,500	—	401,500
Paraguay	298,800	877,800	1,176,600	Egypt	1,741,800	161,300	1,903,100
Peru	601,900	1,242,500	1,844,400	Iran	429,500	—	429,500
Suriname	254,300	371,400	625,700	Iraq	633,000	91,300	724,300
Trinidad and Tobago	705,800	490,100	1,195,900	Israel	416,000	—	416,000
United States	267,000	324,900	591,900	Jordan	1,042,900	323,700	1,366,600
Uruguay	480,500	416,200	896,700	Kuwait	116,000	66,700	182,700
Venezuela	672,800	987,700	1,660,500	Lebanon	1,045,800	222,900	1,268,700
West Indies	525,800	438,900	964,700	Libyan Arab Jamahiriya	100,000	1,405,700	1,505,700
				Oman	793,300	716,300	1,509,600
Intercountry				Pakistan	2,686,600	222,600	2,909,200
programmes	19,510,200	69,865,600	89,375,800	Qatar	58,800	63,300	122,100
				Saudi Arabia	152,000	2,584,700	2,736,700
Subtotal	37,791,700	105,650,900	143,442,600	Somalia	3,681,300	854,300	4,535,600
				Sudan	2,772,100	8,266,900	11,039,000
South-East Asia				Syrian Arab Republic	1,605,000	129,300	1,734,300
Bangladesh	5,438,000	688,400	6,126,400	Tunisia	1,560,000	366,500	1,926,500
Bhutan	—	640,800	640,800	United Arab Emirates	50,700	93,600	144,300
Burma	3,548,200	3,451,900	7,000,100	Yemen	2,809,300	2,581,800	5,391,100
Democratic People's							
Republic of Korea	1,150,100	—	1,150,100	Intercountry			
India	8,593,300	11,040,000	19,633,300	programmes	12,503,800	3,955,700	16,459,500
Indonesia	6,216,000	1,492,300	7,708,300				
Maldives	669,200	8,000	677,200	Subtotal	42,179,000	24,625,900	66,804,900
Mongolia	1,307,100	447,100	1,754,200				
Nepal	3,863,400	4,963,100	8,826,500	**Western Pacific**			
Sri Lanka	2,830,200	666,200	3,496,400	American Samoa	115,000	—	115,000
Thailand	3,334,500	140,700	3,475,200	Australia	100,000	—	100,000
				China	2,500,000	—	2,500,000
Intercountry				Cook Islands	447,300	70,000	517,300
programmes	10,423,600	3,354,500	13,778,100	Democratic Kampuchea	500,000	—	500,000
				Fiji	944,800	6,600	951,400
Subtotal	47,373,600	26,893,000	74,266,600	French Polynesia	70,000	—	70,000
				Guam	80,000	—	80,000
Europe				Hong Kong	110,000	—	110,000
Albania	27,600	—	27,600	Japan	100,000	—	100,000
Algeria	330,000	314,200	644,200	Kiribati	547,300	90,000	637,300
Austria	20,700	—	20,700	Lao People's Democratic			
Belgium	17,200	—	17,200	Republic	1,267,700	716,000	1,983,700
Bulgaria	77,000	—	77,000	Macao	50,000	—	50,000
Czechoslovakia	20,700	—	20,700	Malaysia	1,127,500	163,300	1,290,800
Denmark	17,200	—	17,200	New Zealand	60,000	—	60,000
Finland	17,200	—	17,200	Niue	50,000	11,000	61,000
France	23,000	—	23,000	Papua New Guinea	1,889,700	864,800	2,754,500
German Democratic				Philippines	1,624,900	1,072,800	2,697,700
Republic	25,300	—	25,300	Republic of Korea	1,498,000	—	1,498,000
Germany, Federal				Samoa	694,600	230,000	924,600
Republic of	23,000	—	23,000	Singapore	415,700	314,400	730,100
Greece	25,300	45,200	70,500	Solomon Islands	744,600	906,600	1,651,200
Hungary	30,000	—	30,000	Tokelau	10,000	—	10,000
Iceland	17,200	—	17,200	Tonga	547,300	340,000	887,300
Ireland	20,700	—	20,700	Trust Territory of the			
Italy	25,300	—	25,300	Pacific Islands	647,300	90,000	737,300
Luxembourg	12,600	—	12,600	Tuvalu	75,000	26,500	101,500
Malta	20,700	—	20,700	Vanuatu	794,600	453,000	1,247,600
Monaco	2,500	—	2,500	Viet Nam	3,333,600	—	3,333,600
Morocco	385,000	229,100	614,100				
Netherlands	20,700	230,400	251,100	Intercountry			
Norway	17,200	—	17,200	programmes	13,168,600	1,469,000	14,637,600
Poland	38,000	—	38,000				
Portugal	60,000	305,600	365,600	Subtotal	33,513,500	6,824,000	40,337,500
Romania	38,000	—	38,000				
San Marino	2,500	—	2,500	**Global and interregional**			
Spain	25,300	—	25,300	activities	30,732,200	162,992,100	193,724,300
Sweden	17,200	—	17,200				
Switzerland	17,200	—	17,200	Total	276,545,500	400,927,300	677,472,800
Turkey	440,000	154,000	594,000				

ASSISTANCE RENDERED BY WHO IN THE PERIOD 1982-1983, BY SECTOR AND REGION
(in US dollars)

				REGION				
SECTOR	*Headquarters/ global/interregional activities*	*Africa*	*The Americas*	*South-East Asia*	*Europe*	*Eastern Mediter- ranean*	*Western Pacific*	*Total*
Policy organs	8,116,100	685,500	675,900	55,000	212,200	65,000	280,000	10,089,700
General programme de- velopment, manage- ment and co- ordination	24,869,000	13,010,300	14,875,700	7,225,000	4,501,900	6,175,300	7,033,100	77,690,300
Development of com- prehensive health services	69,769,400	36,994,400	54,057,900	22,260,900	7,744,900	18,284,100	13,597,300	222,708,900
Disease prevention and control	124,870,600	53,601,100	34,744,000	27,932,400	3,097,400	21,831,200	7,808,500	273,885,200
Promotion of environ- mental health	19,914,300	6,695,700	12,837,000	8,065,800	4,930,400	7,191,100	4,280,700	63,915,000
Health manpower de- velopment	3,457,600	25,221,300	23,272,300	9,043,500	3,782,800	12,479,200	8,445,500	85,702,200
Health information	31,368,800	3,038,900	12,044,000	1,512,900	4,972,900	2,299,700	1,288,500	56,525,700
General services and support programmes	56,920,500	9,524,900	16,946,500	3,700,700	9,558,100	2,888,300	3,705,300	103,244,300
Total	339,286,300	148,772,100	169,453,300	79,796,200	38,800,600	71,213,900	46,438,900	893,761,300

Annex I.   MEMBERSHIP OF THE WORLD HEALTH ORGANIZATION AND CONTRIBUTIONS
(Membership as at 31 December 1983; contributions as assessed for 1984)

	CONTRIBUTION			CONTRIBUTION			CONTRIBUTION	
MEMBER	*Percent- age*	*Amount* (in US dollars)*	*MEMBER*	*Percent- age*	*Amount* (in US dollars)*	*MEMBER*	*Percent- age*	*Amount* (in US dollars)*
Afghanistan	0.01	23,730	Democratic Yemen	0.01	26,230	Ivory Coast	0.03	71,190
Albania	0.01	23,730	Denmark	0.74	1,755,990	Jamaica	0.02	47,460
Algeria	0.15	355,945	Djibouti	0.01	23,730	Japan	10.14	24,061,810
Angola	0.01	23,730	Dominica	0.01	23,730	Jordan	0.01	23,730
Argentina	0.69	1,637,340	Dominican Republic	0.03	71,190	Kenya	0.01	23,730
Australia	1.50	3,559,440	Ecuador	0.03	71,190	Kuwait	0.27	640,700
Austria	0.74	1,755,990	Egypt	0.08	189,835	Lao People's Democratic		
Bahamas	0.01	23,730	El Salvador	0.01	23,730	Republic	0.01	23,730
Bahrain	0.02	47,460	Equatorial Guinea	0.01	23,730	Lebanon	0.02	47,460
Bangladesh	0.03	71,190	Ethiopia	0.01	23,730	Lesotho	0.01	23,730
Barbados	0.01	23,730	Fiji	0.01	23,730	Liberia	0.01	23,730
Belgium	1.26	2,989,930	Finland	0.47	1,115,290	Libyan Arab Jamahiriya	0.27	640,700
Benin	0.01	23,730	France	6.39	15,638,210	Luxembourg	0.06	142,375
Bhutan	0.01	23,730	Gabon	0.03	71,190	Madagascar	0.01	23,730
Bolivia	0.01	23,730	Gambia	0.01	23,730	Malawi	0.01	23,730
Botswana	0.01	23,730	German Democratic			Malaysia	0.09	213,565
Brazil	1.44	3,417,060	Republic	1.36	3,227,225	Maldives	0.01	23,730
Bulgaria	0.18	427,130	Germany, Federal			Mali	0.01	23,730
Burma	0.01	23,730	Republic of	8.39	19,909,130	Malta	0.01	23,730
Burundi	0.01	23,730	Ghana	0.02	47,460	Mauritania	0.01	23,730
Byelorussian SSR	0.35	830,530	Greece	0.39	925,455	Mauritius	0.01	23,730
Canada	2.96	7,043,960	Grenada	0.01	23,730	Mexico	0.95	2,254,310
Cape Verde	0.01	23,730	Guatemala	0.02	47,460	Monaco	0.01	23,730
Central African Republic	0.01	23,730	Guinea	0.01	23,730	Mongolia	0.01	23,730
Chad	0.01	23,730	Guinea-Bissau	0.01	23,730	Morocco	0.06	142,375
Chile	0.08	189,835	Guyana	0.01	23,730	Mozambique	0.01	23,730
China	0.79	1,874,635	Haiti	0.01	23,730	Nepal	0.01	23,730
Colombia	0.11	261,025	Honduras	0.01	23,730	Netherlands	1.75	4,152,680
Comoros	0.01	23,730	Hungary	0.20	474,590	New Zealand	0.25	593,240
Congo	0.01	38,230	Iceland	0.03	71,190	Nicaragua	0.01	23,730
Costa Rica	0.02	47,460	India	0.31	735,615	Niger	0.01	23,730
Cuba	0.09	213,565	Indonesia	0.13	308,485	Nigeria	0.21	498,320
Cyprus	0.01	23,730	Iran	0.57	1,352,585	Norway	0.50	1,186,480
Czechoslovakia	0.73	1,732,260	Iraq	0.15	355,945	Oman	0.02	47,460
Democratic Kampuchea	0.01	23,730	Ireland	0.18	427,130	Pakistan	0.06	142,375
Democratic People's			Israel	0.22	522,050	Panama	0.02	47,460
Republic of Korea	0.05	118,645	Italy	3.68	8,732,490	Papua New Guinea	0.01	23,730

MEMBER	CONTRIBUTION Percent-age	CONTRIBUTION Amount* (in US dollars)	MEMBER	CONTRIBUTION Percent-age	CONTRIBUTION Amount* (in US dollars)	MEMBER	CONTRIBUTION Percent-age	CONTRIBUTION Amount* (in US dollars)
Paraguay	0.01	23,730	Somalia	0.01	23,730	United Republic of Cameroon	0.02	47,460
Peru	0.09	213,565	South Africa	0.35	830,530	United Republic of Tanzania	0.01	23,730
Philippines	0.09	213,565	Spain	1.91	4,532,350	United States	25.00	62,473,975
Poland	0.61	1,447,505	Sri Lanka	0.01	23,730	Upper Volta	0.01	23,730
Portugal	0.18	427,130	Sudan	0.01	23,730	Uruguay	0.05	118,645
Qatar	0.04	94,920	Suriname	0.01	23,730	Vanuatu+	—	—
Republic of Korea	0.21	498,320	Swaziland	0.01	23,730	Venezuela	0.57	1,352,585
Romania	0.19	450,860	Sweden	1.30	3,084,840	Viet Nam	0.02	47,460
Rwanda	0.01	23,730	Switzerland	1.08	2,562,795	Yemen	0.01	23,730
Saint Lucia	0.01	23,730	Syrian Arab Republic	0.04	94,920	Yugoslavia	0.47	1,115,290
Saint Vincent and the Grenadines†	—	—	Thailand	0.08	189,835	Zaire	0.01	23,730
			Togo	0.01	23,730	Zambia	0.01	23,730
Samoa	0.01	23,730	Tonga	0.01	23,730	Zimbabwe	0.02	47,460
San Marino	0.01	23,730	Trinidad and Tobago	0.04	94,920			
Sao Tome and Principe	0.01	23,730	Tunisia	0.03	71,190	ASSOCIATE MEMBER		
Saudi Arabia	0.89	2,111,935	Turkey	0.32	759,345	Namibia	0.01	23,730
Senegal	0.01	23,730	Uganda	0.01	23,730			
Seychelles	0.01	23,730	Ukrainian SSR	1.30	3,084,840			
Sierra Leone	0.01	23,730	USSR	10.15	24,085,540	Total	100.00	240,957,900
Singapore	0.10	237,295	United Arab Emirates	0.19	450,860			
Solomon Islands‡	—	—	United Kingdom	4.59	10,891,880			

*Adjusted to take into account the actual amounts paid to staff as reimbursement for taxes levied by member countries on the WHO emoluments of their nationals.

†Became a member on 2 September; assessment was to be established by the thirty-seventh (1984) World Health Assembly.

‡Became a member on 4 April; assessed at the rate of 0.01 per cent for the financial period 1984-1985.

+Became a member on 7 March; assessed at the rate of 0.01 per cent for the financial period 1984-1985.

Annex II.   OFFICERS AND OFFICES OF THE WORLD HEALTH ORGANIZATION
(As at 31 December 1983)

OFFICERS OF THE THIRTY-SIXTH WORLD HEALTH ASSEMBLY

President: Tan Sri Chong Hon Nyan (Malaysia).
Vice Presidents: Dr. J. de D. Lisboa Ramos (Cape Verde), C. Maynard (Dominica), Dr. T. Mork (Norway), A. Mroueh (Lebanon), S. Ranasinghe (Sri Lanka).
Chairman, Committee A: Dr. U. Frey (Switzerland).
Chairman, Committee B: Dr. D. B. Sebina (Botswana).

MEMBERS OF THE EXECUTIVE BOARD*

Chairman: M. M. Hussain (Maldives).
Vice-Chairmen: Dr. J. M. Borgoño (Chile), G. Thomas (Seychelles), Dr. Xu Shou-ren (China).
Rapporteurs: Dr. D. G. Makuto (Zimbabwe), J. Roux (France).

Other members were designated by: Argentina, Belgium, Bulgaria, Djibouti, Ethiopia, Ghana, Guinea-Bissau, Iceland, Iraq, Japan, Malaysia, Morocco, Mozambique, Nepal, Pakistan, Panama, Sao Tome and Principe, Spain, Syrian Arab Republic, Trinidad and Tobago, USSR, United Arab Emirates, United States, Venezuela.

*The Board consists of 30 persons designated by as many member States which have been elected for such purpose by WHO.

SENIOR OFFICERS OF THE SECRETARIAT

Director-General: Dr. Halfdan Mahler.

Deputy Director-General: Dr. T. A. Lambo.
Assistant Directors-General: Warren W. Furth, Dr. J. Hamon, Dr. S. K. Litvinov, Dr. Lu Rushan, Dr. F. Partow, Dr. David Tejada-de-Rivero.
Director, Regional Office for Africa: Dr. Comlan A. A. Quenum.

Director, Regional Office for the Americas (Pan American Sanitary Bureau): Dr. C. Guerra de Macedo.
Director, Regional Office for South-East Asia: Dr. U Ko Ko.
Director, Regional Office for Europe: Dr. Leo A. Kaprio.
Director, Regional Office for the Eastern Mediterranean: Dr. Hussein A. Gezairy.
Director, Regional Office for the Western Pacific: Dr. Hiroshi Nakajima.

HEADQUARTERS AND OTHER OFFICES

HEADQUARTERS
World Health Organization
20 Avenue Appia
1211 Geneva 27, Switzerland
Cable address: UNISANTE GENEVE
Telephone: 91 21 11
Telex: 27821

LIAISON OFFICE WITH THE
UNITED NATIONS
World Health Organization
New York, N. Y. 10017, United States
Cable address: UNISANTE NEWYORK
Telephone: (212) 754-6004, 754-6005
Telex: 234292

REGIONAL OFFICE FOR THE EASTERN
   MEDITERRANEAN
World Health Organization
P. O. Box 1517
Alexandria 21511, Egypt
Cable address: UNISANTE ALEXANDRIA
Telephone: 802318, 807843
Telex: 54028

REGIONAL OFFICE FOR EUROPE
World Health Organization
8 Scherfigsvej
DK-2100 Copenhagen O, Denmark
Cable address: UNISANTE COPENHAGEN
Telephone: 29 01 11
Telex: 15348

REGIONAL OFFICE FOR SOUTH-EAST ASIA
World Health Organization
World Health House
Indraprastha Estate, Mahatma Gandhi Road
New Delhi 110002, India
Cable address: WHO NEWDELHI
Telephone: 27 01 81 88
Telex: 312241, 312195

REGIONAL OFFICE FOR AFRICA
World Health Organization
P. O. Box No. 6
Brazzaville, Congo
Cable address: UNISANTE BRAZZAVILLE
Telephone: 81 38 60-65
Telex: 5217, 5278

REGIONAL OFFICE FOR THE WESTERN
   PACIFIC
World Health Organization
P. O. Box 2932
Manila, Philippines 2801
Cable address: UNISANTE MANILA
Telephone: 59 20 41, 59 37 21
Telex: 27652, 40365, 63260

REGIONAL OFFICE FOR THE AMERICAS/
   PAN AMERICAN SANITARY BUREAU
World Health Organization
525 23rd Street, N. W.
Washington, D. C. 20037, United States
Cable address: OFSANPAN WASHINGTON
Telephone: (202) 861-3200
Telex: 248338

Chapter VI

International Bank for Reconstruction and Development (World Bank)

During the fiscal year 1 July 1982 to 30 June 1983, the International Bank for Reconstruction and Development (World Bank) and its affiliate, the International Development Association (IDA), continued to help developing countries to raise their standards of living by channelling to them financial resources from developed countries.

Lending commitments by the Bank, credit approvals from IDA, and investment commitments by a second affiliate, the International Finance Corporation (IFC), amounted to $15,322 million—up $1,694 million from the previous fiscal year.

Membership in the Bank rose to 146 in 1983, with the admission of Antigua and Barbuda (22 September) and Malta (26 September).

Lending operations

In the fiscal year ending 30 June 1983, the World Bank made 137 loans amounting to $11,136 million to 43 countries, an increase of $806 million over fiscal 1982. This brought the cumulative total of loan commitments by the Bank since its inception in 1946 to $89,616.2 million.

The following table summarizes World Bank lending in fiscal 1983 by region or country and by purpose.

WORLD BANK LOANS APPROVED BY REGION/COUNTRY AND PURPOSE
1 JULY 1982–30 JUNE 1983
(in millions of US dollars)

REGION/COUNTRY	Agriculture and rural development	Development finance companies	Education	Energy	Industry	Non-project	Population, health and nutrition	Small-scale enterprises	Technical assistance	Transportation	Urbanization	Water supply and sewerage	Total
Eastern Africa													
Botswana	—	—	—	32.5	—	—	—	—	—	—	—	—	32.5
Kenya	—	—	—	12.0	—	60.9	—	—	—	—	7.0	—	79.9
Mauritius	—	—	—	—	—	—	—	—	—	—	—	12.2	12.2
Zimbabwe	—	70.6	—	105.0	—	—	—	—	—	26.4	—	—	202.0
Subtotal	—	70.6	—	149.5	—	60.9	—	—	—	26.4	7.0	12.2	326.6
Western Africa													
Congo	—	—	—	—	12.0	—	—	11.0	12.7	—	—	—	35.7
Ivory Coast	32.2	—	—	—	—	—	—	—	—	—	—	—	32.2
Nigeria	—	120.0	—	—	—	—	—	—	—	—	—	—	120.0
United Republic of Cameroon	—	—	—	—	—	—	—	—	—	22.5	20.0	—	42.5
Western Africa region	—	6.1	—	—	—	—	—	—	—	—	—	—	6.1
Subtotal	32.2	126.1	—	—	12.0	—	—	11.0	—	35.2	20.0	—	236.5
East Asia and Pacific													
China	35.3	40.6	—	263.2	—	—	—	—	—	124.0	—	—	463.1
Indonesia	319.1	208.9	137.4	579.0	5.5	—	27.0	—	—	—	—	53.0	1,329.9
Malaysia	56.9	—	—	—	—	—	—	—	—	86.2	—	—	143.1
Papua New Guinea	14.1	—	—	—	—	—	—	—	—	31.0	—	—	45.1
Philippines	—	—	24.4	73.5	—	302.3	—	—	—	—	67.0	35.5	502.7
Republic of Korea	—	255.0	—	—	—	—	—	70.0	—	247.0	100.0	—	672.0
Thailand	87.0	—	—	30.6	—	175.5	—	—	—	100.0	—	—	393.1
Subtotal	512.4	504.5	161.8	946.3	5.5	477.8	27.0	70.0	—	588.2	167.0	88.5	3,549.0

REGION/COUNTRY	Agriculture and rural development	Development finance companies	Education	Energy	Industry	Non-project	Population, health and nutrition	Small-scale enterprises	Technical assistance	Transportation	Urbanization	Water supply and sewerage	Total
South Asia													
India	68.9	—	—	794.9	—	—	—	—	—	200.0	24.1	—	1,087.9
Pakistan	20.2	—	—	43.0	12.0	—	—	—	—	—	—	—	75.2
Subtotal	89.1	—	—	837.9	12.0	—	—	—	—	200.0	24.1	—	1,163.1
Europe, the Middle East and North Africa													
Cyprus	16.0	—	—	10.2	—	—	—	—	—	—	—	—	26.2
Egypt	122.7	—	38.0	—	165.3	—	—	—	—	24.0	—	—	350.0
Hungary	130.4	—	—	—	109.0	—	—	—	—	—	—	—	239.4
Jordan	—	—	18.8	—	—	—	—	—	—	—	—	17.0	35.8
Morocco	72.0	16.0	—	75.2	—	—	—	—	—	85.0	60.0	—	308.2
Portugal	—	40.3	—	126.4	—	—	—	—	—	—	—	—	166.7
Tunisia	16.5	—	27.0	—	16.8	—	—	—	4.5	—	25.0	59.0	148.8
Turkey	150.4	—	—	218.2	—	300.8	—	—	—	—	—	—	669.4
Yugoslavia	215.0	—	—	—	—	275.0	—	—	—	—	—	30.0	520.0
Subtotal	723.0	56.3	83.8	430.0	291.1	575.8	—	—	4.5	109.0	85.0	106.0	2,464.5
Latin America and the Caribbean													
Argentina	—	—	—	—	—	—	—	—	—	100.0	—	—	100.0
Barbados	—	—	—	—	—	—	—	10.5	—	—	—	—	10.5
Belize	—	—	—	—	—	—	—	—	—	5.3	—	—	5.3
Brazil	467.8	—	—	—	304.5	—	—	220.0	—	154.0	8.9	302.3	1,457.5
Chile	—	—	—	—	—	—	—	—	—	128.0	—	—	128.0
Colombia	63.4	—	15.0	—	—	—	—	—	—	—	—	—	78.4
Costa Rica	—	25.2	—	—	—	—	—	—	—	—	—	—	25.2
Dominican Republic	—	—	—	—	—	—	—	—	—	—	7.1	—	7.1
Ecuador	—	—	—	—	—	—	—	40.6	—	—	—	—	40.6
Guatemala	—	—	18.5	—	—	—	—	—	—	—	—	—	18.5
Honduras	45.0	—	—	—	—	—	—	—	—	—	—	—	45.0
Jamaica	—	45.2	—	—	—	60.2	—	—	—	15.0	—	—	120.4
Mexico	253.4	350.0	—	—	—	—	—	175.0	—	—	9.2	100.3	887.9
Panama	—	—	—	63.4	—	—	—	—	—	—	—	21.6	85.0
Paraguay	40.0	—	—	—	—	—	—	—	—	—	—	—	40.0
Peru	160.0	—	17.3	81.2	—	—	33.5	—	10.2	—	—	—	302.2
Uruguay	—	—	—	—	—	—	—	—	—	45.0	—	—	45.0
Subtotal	1,029.6	420.4	50.8	144.6	304.5	60.2	33.5	446.1	10.2	447.3	25.2	424.2	3,396.6
Total	2,386.3	1,177.9	296.4	2,508.3	625.1	1,174.7	60.5	516.1	25.7	1,406.1	328.3	630.9	11,136.3
NUMBER OF LOANS	32	12	9	22	7	6	2	5	3	18	10	11	137

Agriculture and rural development

The Bank continued its commitment to agriculture and rural development, making 32 loans in fiscal 1983 amounting to $2,386 million in 21 countries. Brazil received $467.8 million, of which $400 million went for an agro-industries credit project to finance plants and to help industries processing agricultural products and inputs. Indonesia received a total of $319.1 million, of which $154.6 million went to establish about 50,000 hectares of tree crops, thereby assisting government estates, providing employment for 4,000 estate workers and benefiting 19,000 smallholder families. A total of $253.4 million was provided to Mexico, of which $138.4 million went to a rainfed development project to increase crop production, benefiting more than 17,000 families.

Development finance companies

The Bank made 12 loans totalling nearly $1,178 million in fiscal 1983 to assist development finance companies in 10 countries and the Western Africa region. The largest borrowers were Mexico ($350 million to help expand non-petroleum exports), the Republic of Korea ($255 million to finance high-priority investment projects, technical assistance and training) and Indonesia ($208.9 million for foreign exchange to finance medium-sized and large industrial projects).

Education

During fiscal 1983, the Bank granted nine loans totalling $296.4 million for education projects in eight countries. Indonesia received a total of $137.4 million, of which $107.4 million went to expand existing polytechnic schools and construct new ones. Egypt received $38 million to build and equip vocational schools for construction and industry and provide technical assistance and training. Tunisia received $27 million to improve the country's agricultural-education and training system, strengthen the Ministry of Agriculture and assist in expanding and improving primary teacher-training capacity.

Energy

Twenty-two projects in the energy field—oil, gas, coal and power—were assisted in 15 countries during fiscal 1983 at a total cost of $2,508.3 million.

Four loans totalling $794.9 million were made to India, of which $250.7 million went to provide a major transmission capability to the southern region and interregional transmission links. Indonesia received two loans for a total of $579 million, of which $300 million was to diversify electricity production sources, improve national distribution networks, reduce system losses and provide training and consultant services. China received a total of $263.2 million for two loans; $162.4 million went to develop a new reservoir in an oilfield and introduce modern technology into the petroleum industry. Of two loans totalling $218.2 million to Turkey, one for $163 million was to construct about 1,500 kilometres of 380-kilovolt transmission lines to accommodate new generating capacity.

Other loans went for: improvement of electricity services; energy policy and conservation programmes; hydroelectric power plants and storage dams; geothermal power projects; and petroleum exploration and appraisal.

Industry

The Bank made seven loans to seven countries for the industry sector, amounting to $625.1 million during fiscal 1983. A $304.5-million loan went to Brazil to develop and export iron ore. Egypt received $165.3 million to construct an integrated reinforcing bar plant. Hungary received $109 million to help contain its import of energy by institution building.

Non-project

Six non-project loans amounting to $1,174.7 million were made to six countries during the fiscal year. The Philippines received $302.3 million to finance essential imports and improve the allocation and efficiency of investment over the medium term. A $300.8-million loan to Turkey went to finance imports in support of redirecting its economy towards a more outward-oriented strategy. Yugoslavia received $275 million to finance essential imports and improve the balance of payments and the efficiency of investment selection and resource allocation.

Other loans went to finance high-priority import requirements and assist government structural-adjustment programmes.

Population, health and nutrition

Two loans totalling $60.5 million were made to two countries in fiscal 1983. Peru received $33.5 million to establish a primary health-care system benefiting 3.5 million people by providing staff training and constructing health facilities in four regions. Indonesia received $27 million to increase the effectiveness of health-care services and reduce malaria.

Small-scale enterprises

Five loans totalling $516.1 million were made to five countries for small-scale enterprises during the fiscal year. Brazil received $220 million to reduce distortions affecting trade and industrial development, to provide resources to small and medium enterprises, to strengthen State development banks and to undertake studies for industrial policy change. A $175-million loan to Mexico was to provide credit and technical assistance to small and medium-sized enterprises for maintaining or expanding production and employment levels. The Republic of Korea received $70 million for technical assistance to about 660 individual enterprises and training in manufacturing processes and management techniques for 3,300 managers, engineers and supervisors.

Technical assistance

Three countries received a total of $25.7 million for technical assistance in fiscal 1983. The Congo received $11 million to improve the quality of government public-finance management and its urban infrastructural-investment programme through institution building. A $10.2-million loan went to Peru to design and implement a programme-budgeting system and a compensation system for the central Government and to support public-sector, management-training programmes. Tunisia received $4.5 million to promote investment projects in agriculture, industry and energy, and to strengthen local project-preparation capabilities in the public and private sectors.

More than 90 per cent of loans had some provision for technical assistance; in fiscal 1983, these components totalled $1,275.3 million in 219 operations. Among the larger amounts financed as components of Bank loans were $74 million for a transmigration project in Indonesia, $30 million in a power loan to Zimbabwe and $24.9 million in a water and sewerage loan to Brazil.

The Bank continued to serve as executing agency for projects financed by the United Nations Development Programme (UNDP). The number of such projects in progress at the end of fiscal 1983 stood at 127—down from 132 a year earlier—while 33 new projects involving commitments of $33.1 million were approved during the year, compared to 37 projects with commitments of $41.8 million previously. With the Bank as executing agency, UNDP financed a number of large and innovative projects, one being the preparation of a water sector master plan in Bangladesh which utilized one of the largest grants ($6.6 million) UNDP had ever made. About one third of Bank-executed UNDP projects involved some form of cost-sharing, most of which was provided by Governments out of the proceeds of Bank loans and IDA credits.

To enhance economic management and assist in investment projects in the Caribbean, the Bank agreed to serve as executing agency for a $2.4-million inter-agency resident mission programme, involving cost-sharing contributions from the Bank, UNDP and other sources. Continuing its work on global and interregional projects, in March the Bank and UNDP inaugurated an energy sector management programme, an outgrowth of the 1980 energy assessment programme, expected to cost $47 million over four years.

The Bank's technical co-operation extended to capital-surplus developing countries in Europe, the Middle East and North Africa on a reimbursable basis when the annual programme exceeded one staff-year of Bank input, such as in the case of Oman, Saudi Arabia and the United Arab Emirates, and on a non-reimbursable basis in response to *ad hoc* requests for programmes requiring less than one staff-year. In fiscal 1983, about 29 staff-years of reimbursable technical assistance were provided by the Bank, of which Saudi Arabia received more than 86 per cent. The Bank also provided non-reimbursable technical assistance to Bahrain for an energy policies study and to the United Arab Emirates for a general economic review.

Transportation

Eighteen loans totalling $1,406.1 million were made to 17 countries during fiscal 1983 to help develop their transportation systems. India received $200 million to upgrade existing diesel electric locomotives, to continue a modernization programme for electric locomotives, to improve fuel efficiency and to upgrade the operation of bulk freight movements. A $154-million loan to Brazil went to construct, improve and rehabilitate about 8,000 kilometres of feeder roads in order to expand and diversify agricultural production by providing rural communities with all-weather access to storage, marketing and processing facilities. Chile received $128 million for road reconstruction and maintenance, including the purchase of road-maintenance vehicles.

Other loans were for highway and railroad maintenance and improvement, and port operations and management.

Urbanization

Ten countries received loans totalling $328.3 million to aid the urban poor. The Republic of Korea received $100 million to develop 22,000 low- and middle-income urban-housing plots, 10,000 housing units for low-income families and 10,000 middle-income serviced lots. A $67-million loan went to the Philippines to reduce infrastructure bottle-necks to economic development in targeted cities, provide basic urban services and improve the project-management capabilities of the cities and participating government agencies. Morocco received $60 million for 13,000 new housing units affordable to households in the lower half of the urban income-distribution scale.

Water supply and sewerage

In fiscal 1983, the Bank made 11 loans amounting to $630.9 million for water supply and sewerage projects in nine countries. Brazil received $302.3 million to finance investments in support of a national plan to provide 90 per cent of the urban population with piped water and 65 per cent with sewerage services by 1990. A $100.3-million loan to Mexico went for water supply and sewerage services in small and medium-sized cities throughout the country. The Philippines received $35.5 million for the Government's rural water supply and sanitation programme, benefiting more than 6 million people.

Economic Development Institute

The fiscal 1983 programme of the Economic Development Institute (EDI), designed to train senior officials of the Bank's developing member countries in economic management and investment, included 17 seminars at Washington, D. C., and 52 activities in countries other than the United States for about 1,500 participants. The emphasis in the EDI programme began to shift during the fiscal year towards increased training activities for trainers in other institutions; improvement and expansion of training materials for EDI and other institutions' use; and more policy-oriented seminars for high-level officials. At Washington, D. C., the sixth annual seminar on world development issues, co-sponsored by the United Nations Institute for Training and Research, was held for senior delegates assigned to United Nations Headquarters. EDI co-operated with other United Nations bodies in offering seminars in Africa, Asia and Latin America.

Six seminars were held in China on several topics, including two held under an expanded training programme financed by UNDP, for which the Bank was the executing agency. Assistance was given to the Arab countries through seminars and by helping the Arab Organization for Agricultural Development to organize regional seminars on agricultural project planning and implementation. In Latin America and the Caribbean, seminars were co-sponsored for the first time with the Caribbean Agricultural Credit Association and the Inter-American Institute for Co-operation in Agriculture. Other EDI activities in fiscal 1983 included seminars on costs, efficiency and strategies in education; industrial development for small economies; forestry projects; management of the project cycle; and telecommunications.

To guide future objectives and programmes, EDI's Executive Directors established new priorities: an institutional development programme in developing countries; direct training efforts; and a programme of seminars on national and sectoral policy issues. By emphasizing institutional development, EDI hoped to enable more officials to benefit from Bank experience than would be possible with direct training activities. The 10 per cent of training activities for trainers during fiscal 1983 was projected to increase to 50 per cent by fiscal 1989. Despite the planned reduction in direct training in Asia and Latin America (where the largest growth of training institutions had occurred), direct training was to increase in sub-Saharan Africa and institutionally least developed countries in other regions, as well as those with special training needs.

Co-financing

During fiscal 1983, three new co-financing instruments were introduced which permitted the Bank, for the first time, to participate directly in commercial loans, supplementing its methods of co-financing with the private sector and providing a wider range of options for co-financing. Approved by the Bank's Executive Directors in January 1983, these were: direct financial participation by the Bank in the later maturities of a commercial loan; guarantees of the later maturities of a private loan instead of direct funding; and contingent participation in the later maturities of a commercial loan initially financed by commercial lenders. These options were to be tested for one or two years to see if they proved attractive to co-lenders and advantageous to borrowers. During the pilot phase, the Bank was authorized to provide up to $500 million for participation in about 15 to 20 commercial loans; assuming its share of each transaction was 20 per cent, $2.5 billion could be raised.

Special Assistance Programme

In February 1983, the Executive Directors approved a Special Assistance Programme, aimed at helping developing countries restore their development efforts despite adverse external circumstances. The Programme's objectives were to: emphasize high-priority operations supporting policy change; expand lending to help maintain infrastructure and fuller use of existing capacity, especially in export-oriented activities; expand Bank advisory services in the design and implementation of appropriate policies; maintain the impetus of project activities by increasing the share of Bank financing; and accelerate disbursements out of existing loans and credits, where feasible, urging other lenders to do the same. The Programme's major elements were expanded structural-adjustment lending, sector-adjustment support, financing an increased share of project costs, enhanced policy dialogue and co-ordination with other donors.

The Programme was established for two years in the expectation that the world economy would have begun to recover in that period; if recovery took longer, an extension would be considered. The estimated increase in Bank disbursements resulting from the Programme was $2 billion over the fiscal period 1983-1985, an 8 per cent increase in

total projected disbursements. Net transfers (disbursements less interest and amortization) were expected to increase by nearly 25 per cent. The Programme's major impact would be on Bank borrowings, which would have to increase by $1.6 billion— a slight increase over the $30.2 billion previously anticipated for this period—to accommodate its needs.

Financing activities

During fiscal 1983, the World Bank borrowed the equivalent of $10,292 million: $3,536.9 million in United States dollars; $2,514 million in Swiss francs; $1,518.8 million in deutsche mark; $1,325.9 million in Japanese yen; $810.7 million in Netherlands guilders; $320.5 million in pounds sterling; $130.7 million in Canadian dollars; $92.3 million in Austrian schillings; and $42.1 million in Belgian francs. Of these borrowings, $9,224 million were new funds and $1,068 million represented refinancing of outstanding medium- and long-term borrowings. This record amount of borrowings—some $1,771 million over fiscal 1982 totals—reflected the Bank's desire to maintain substantial liquidity.

Of the 86 medium- and long-term borrowing operations conducted by the Bank, 70 were public issues or private placements throughout the world and accounted for $6,994 million, or 68 per cent of total funds borrowed. The other 16 issues, totalling $1,780 million, or 17 per cent of the funds raised, were placed with official sources such as member Governments of the Bank, central banks and government institutions. Short-term borrowings outstanding as at 30 June amounted to $1,501 million. At the end of fiscal 1983, the Bank's outstanding obligations had increased $7,567 million to $39,407 million, denominated in 18 different currencies placed with investors in over 100 countries.

The Bank continued to engage in currency swaps, initiated in fiscal 1982 to increase its access to Swiss francs, deutsche mark and other currencies. In fiscal 1983, the Bank executed 49 currency swaps, aggregating $1,731 million: $1,116 million was swapped into Swiss francs, $324 million into deutsche mark, $152 million into pounds sterling, $108 million into Netherlands guilders, and $31 million into Austrian schillings. In fiscal 1982, currency swaps amounted to $758 million. In a currency swap, the Bank, having borrowed in a particular currency (usually United States dollars), converts the currency into another while entering into a long-term, forward-exchange contract with a counter-party. The Bank agrees to repurchase the borrowed currency from the counter-party in exchange for the currency obtained through the swap. The amounts repurchased correspond to the Bank's debt-service obligations on the swapped borrowing. Thus the Bank effectively borrows the swapped-for currency on a fully hedged basis at a known cost, no greater, and frequently less, than it would have paid had it borrowed the currency directly.

Capitalization

In the Bank's Articles of Agreement, the institution's capital stock is expressed in terms of 1944 dollars—the United States dollar of the weight and fineness in effect on 1 July 1944. On 1 April 1978, when the Second Amendment of the Articles of Agreement of the International Monetary Fund (IMF) became effective, currencies no longer had par values, and the basis for translating the 1944 dollar into current United States dollars no longer existed.

Thus, for the fiscal year ended 30 June 1983, the value of the Bank's capital stock was expressed on the basis of special drawing rights (SDRs) in terms of the United States dollar as computed by IMF on 30 June. On that date, the value of the SDR was set at $1.06835.

The subscribed capital of the Bank totalled SDR 48,756 million as at 30 June, an increase of over SDR 9,200 million from fiscal 1982.

Income, expenditures and reserves

The Bank's gross revenues, generated primarily from its loans and investments, increased by $860 million—26 per cent—to a record level of $4,232 million in fiscal 1983. Net income was $752 million, an increase of $154 million or 26 per cent from fiscal 1982, largely due to high rates of return on the Bank's liquidity.

Total expenses amounted to $3,480 million, up 25 per cent from the previous fiscal year. Administrative costs totalled $322 million, up $32 million.

The General Reserve of the Bank amounted to $3,134 million at the end of fiscal 1983.

Secretariat

As at 30 June 1983, the staff of the World Bank numbered 5,587, of whom 2,821 were in Professional or higher categories, drawn from 106 nationalities.

STATEMENT OF INCOME AND EXPENSES
(for the fiscal year ended 30 June 1983)

Income	Amount (in thousands of US dollars)
Income from investments*	1,417,113
Income from loans	
Interest	2,486,728
Commitment charges	212,674
Front-end fees	97,451
Other income†	18,491
Total income	4,232,457
Expenses	
Administrative expenses‡	321,919
Interest on borrowings	3,085,065
Bond issuance and other financial expenses	49,972
Contributions to special programmes	23,500
Total expenses	3,480,456
Net income	752,001

*Includes net gains of $174,239,000 resulting from sales of investments.
†Includes net gains of $16,190,000 resulting from repurchases of obligations of the Bank prior to maturity pursuant to the terms of the respective borrowing agreements.
‡All administrative expenses of the Bank and IDA and a portion of those of IFC are paid by the Bank. The administrative expenses are net of a management fee of $213,727,000 charged to IDA and of a service and support fee of $3,660,000 charged to IFC.

Annex I. MEMBERS OF THE WORLD BANK, SUBSCRIPTIONS AND VOTING POWER

(As at 30 June 1983)

MEMBER	SUBSCRIPTION Amount (in SDRs)	SUBSCRIPTION Percentage of total	VOTING POWER Number of votes	VOTING POWER Percentage of total	MEMBER	SUBSCRIPTION Amount (in SDRs)	SUBSCRIPTION Percentage of total	VOTING POWER Number of votes	VOTING POWER Percentage of total
Afghanistan	30,000	0.06	550	0.11	Comoros	1,600	†	266	0.05
Algeria	475,500	0.98	5,005	0.96	Congo	10,000	0.02	350	0.07
Argentina	470,100	0.96	4,951	0.95	Costa Rica	13,100	0.03	381	0.07
Australia	1,273,700	2.61	12,987	2.48	Cyprus	78,800	0.16	1,038	0.20
Austria	546,900	1.12	5,719	1.09	Democratic Kampuchea	21,400	0.04	464	0.09
Bahamas	17,100	0.04	421	0.08	Democratic Yemen*	24,800	0.05	498	0.10
Bahrain	56,600	0.12	816	0.16	Denmark	513,600	1.05	5,386	1.03
Bangladesh*	124,200	0.25	1,492	0.28	Djibouti	3,100	0.01	281	0.05
Barbados	51,900	0.11	769	0.15	Dominica	1,600	†	266	0.05
Belgium	1,051,800	2.16	10,768	2.06	Dominican Republic	58,900	0.12	839	0.16
Belize	3,900	0.01	289	0.06	Ecuador	36,800	0.08	618	0.12
Benin	10,000	0.02	350	0.07	Egypt	344,400	0.71	3,694	0.71
Bhutan	900	†	259	0.05	El Salvador*	12,000	0.02	370	0.07
Bolivia	26,400	0.05	514	0.10	Equatorial Guinea	6,400	0.01	314	0.06
Botswana	33,100	0.07	581	0.11	Ethiopia	11,400	0.02	364	0.07
Brazil	1,070,600	2.20	10,956	2.09	Fiji	42,500	0.09	675	0.13
Burma*	59,100	0.12	841	0.16	Finland	339,200	0.70	3,642	0.70
Burundi	15,000	0.03	400	0.08	France	2,356,700	4.83	23,817	4.55
Canada*	1,396,200	2.86	14,212	2.71	Gabon	12,000	0.02	370	0.07
Cape Verde	1,600	†	266	0.05	Gambia	5,300	0.01	303	0.06
Central African Republic	10,000	0.02	350	0.07	Germany, Federal Republic of	3,434,700	7.04	34,597	6.61
Chad	10,000	0.02	350	0.07	Ghana	85,600	0.18	1,106	0.21
Chile	124,000	0.25	1,490	0.28	Greece	94,500	0.19	1,195	0.23
China	2,348,200	4.82	23,732	4.53	Grenada	1,700	†	267	0.05
Colombia	117,500	0.24	1,425	0.27	Guatemala	16,700	0.03	417	0.08

MEMBER	SUBSCRIPTION Amount (in SDRs)	SUBSCRIPTION Percent-age of total	VOTING POWER Number of votes	VOTING POWER Percent-age of total	MEMBER	SUBSCRIPTION Amount (in SDRs)	SUBSCRIPTION Percent-age of total	VOTING POWER Number of votes	VOTING POWER Percent-age of total
Guinea	20,000	0.04	450	0.09	Philippines	359,800	0.74	3,848	0.73
Guinea-Bissau	2,700	0.01	277	0.05	Portugal	132,400	0.27	1,574	0.30
Guyana*	57,900	0.12	829	0.16	Qatar	32,700	0.07	577	0.11
Haiti	15,000	0.03	400	0.08	Republic of Korea	294,700	0.60	3,197	0.61
Honduras*	8,400	0.02	334	0.06	Romania	200,100	0.41	2,251	0.43
Hungary	204,200	0.42	2,292	0.44	Rwanda*	17,400	0.04	424	0.08
Iceland	22,200	0.05	472	0.09	Saint Lucia	2,900	0.01	279	0.05
India	2,263,300	4.64	22,883	4.37	Saint Vincent and the				
Indonesia	388,800	0.80	4,138	0.79	Grenadines	1,300	†	263	0.05
Iran	158,000	0.32	1,830	0.35	Samoa	1,700	†	267	0.05
Iraq	95,600	0.20	1,206	0.23	Sao Tome and Principe	1,400	†	264	0.05
Ireland	270,100	0.55	2,951	0.56	Saudi Arabia*	489,900	1.00	5,149	0.98
Israel	110,800	0.23	1,358	0.26	Senegal	36,200	0.07	612	0.12
Italy	1,959,200	4.02	19,842	3.79	Seychelles	1,100	†	261	0.05
Ivory Coast	58,400	0.12	834	0.16	Sierra Leone	15,000	0.03	400	0.08
Jamaica	44,600	0.09	696	0.13	Singapore	32,000	0.07	570	0.11
Japan	3,420,600	7.02	34,456	6.58	Solomon Islands*	1,700	†	267	0.05
Jordan	23,300	0.05	483	0.09	Somalia	18,900	0.04	439	0.08
Kenya*	40,000	0.08	650	0.12	South Africa	346,300	0.71	3,713	0.71
Kuwait	645,100	1.32	6,701	1.28	Spain	455,100	0.93	4,801	0.92
Lao People's Democratic					Sri Lanka*	96,100	0.20	1,211	0.23
Republic	10,000	0.02	350	0.07	Sudan	60,000	0.12	850	0.16
Lebanon	9,000	0.02	340	0.06	Suriname	16,200	0.03	412	0.08
Lesotho*	4,300	0.01	293	0.06	Swaziland	44,000	0.09	690	0.13
Liberia	21,300	0.04	463	0.09	Sweden	736,700	1.51	7,617	1.45
Libyan Arab Jamahiriya	195,100	0.40	2,201	0.42	Syrian Arab Republic	123,300	0.25	1,483	0.28
Luxembourg	71,400	0.15	964	0.18	Thailand	311,100	0.64	3,361	0.64
Madagascar	21,900	0.04	469	0.09	Togo	15,000	0.03	400	0.08
Malawi*	15,000	0.03	400	0.08	Trinidad and Tobago*	53,500	0.11	785	0.15
Malaysia*	206,600	0.42	2,316	0.44	Tunisia	37,300	0.08	623	0.12
Maldives	600	†	256	0.05	Turkey	340,800	0.70	3,658	0.70
Mali	17,300	0.04	423	0.08	Uganda	33,300	0.07	583	0.11
Mauritania	10,000	0.02	350	0.07	United Arab Emirates*	98,000	0.20	1,230	0.23
Mauritius	22,100	0.05	471	0.09	United Kingdom	2,600,000	5.33	26,250	5.01
Mexico	315,600	0.65	3,406	0.65	United Republic of Cameroon	20,000	0.04	450	0.09
Morocco	261,200	0.54	2,862	0.55	United Republic of Tanzania*	35,000	0.07	600	0.11
Nepal	53,300	0.11	783	0.15	United States	10,223,900	20.97	102,489	19.58
Netherlands	1,511,700	3.10	15,367	2.94	Upper Volta	10,000	0.02	350	0.07
New Zealand	272,500	0.56	2,975	0.57	Uruguay	41,100	0.08	661	0.13
Nicaragua	9,100	0.02	341	0.07	Vanuatu	32,300	0.07	573	0.11
Niger	10,000	0.02	350	0.07	Venezuela	197,200	0.40	2,222	0.42
Nigeria	294,100	0.60	3,191	0.61	Viet Nam	54,300	0.11	793	0.15
Norway*	241,000	0.49	2,660	0.51	Yemen	10,600	0.02	356	0.07
Oman	19,200	0.04	442	0.08	Yugoslavia*	150,900	0.31	1,759	0.34
Pakistan*	251,900	0.52	2,769	0.53	Zaire	96,000	0.20	1,210	0.23
Panama	21,600	0.04	466	0.09	Zambia*	115,100	0.24	1,401	0.27
Papua New Guinea	24,600	0.05	496	0.09	Zimbabwe	81,700	0.17	1,067	0.20
Paraguay	38,600	0.08	636	0.12					
Peru	93,800	0.19	1,188	0.23	Total	48,756,100	100.00‡	523,561	100.00‡

NOTE: Antigua and Barbuda, and Malta became members on 22 and 26 September, respectively.

*Amounts aggregating the equivalent of $102,599,000, in current United States dollars, had been received from members on account of increases in subscriptions which were in process of completion: Bangladesh $412,000, Burma $936,000, Canada $2,000, Democratic Yemen $1,071,000, El Salvador $253,000, Guyana $308,000, Honduras $31,000, Kenya $984,000, Lesotho $588,000, Malawi $250,000, Malaysia $1,750,000, Norway $4,022,000, Pakistan $19,388,000, Rwanda $1,472,000, Saudi Arabia $56,933,000, Solomon Islands $116,000, Sri Lanka $3,748,000, Trinidad and Tobago $1,594,000, United Arab Emirates $1,082,000, United Republic of Tanzania $130,000, Yugoslavia $517,000 and Zambia $7,012,000.

†Less than 0.005 per cent.

‡May differ from the sum of the individual percentages because of rounding.

Annex II.   EXECUTIVE DIRECTORS AND ALTERNATES OF THE WORLD BANK
(As at 30 June 1983)

Appointed Director	Appointed Alternate	Casting the vote of
James B. Burnham	George R. Hoguet	United States
Reinhard Münzberg	Norbert Schmidt-Gerritzen	Federal Republic of Germany
Kenji Yamaguchi	Toshihiro Yamakawa	Japan
Nigel L. Wicks	Derek F. Smith	United Kingdom
Bruno de Maulde	Robert Hudry*	France

Elected Director	Elected Alternate	Casting the votes of
H. N. Ray (India)	Gholam Kibria (Bangladesh)	Bangladesh, Bhutan, India, Sri Lanka
Said E. El-Naggar (Egypt)	Abdulrahman M. Sehaibani (Saudi Arabia)	Bahrain, Egypt, Iraq, Jordan, Kuwait, Lebanon, Maldives, Oman, Pakistan, Qatar, Saudi Arabia, Syrian Arab Republic, United Arab Emirates, Yemen

Elected Director	Elected Alternate	Casting the votes of
Wang Liansheng (China)	Fei Lizhi (China)	China
Jacques de Groote (Belgium)	Herbert A. Lust (Austria)	Austria, Belgium, Hungary, Luxembourg, Turkey
Giorgio Ragazzi (Italy)	Rodrigo M. Guimarães (Portugal)	Greece, Italy, Portugal
Ferdinand van Dam (Netherlands)	Riza Sapunxhiu (Yugoslavia)	Cyprus, Israel, Netherlands, Romania, Yugoslavia
Morris Miller (Canada)	George L. Reid (Barbados)	Bahamas, Barbados, Belize, Canada, Dominica, Grenada, Guyana, Ireland, Jamaica, Saint Lucia, Saint Vincent and the Grenadines
Ronald H. Dean (Australia)	You Kwang Park (Republic of Korea)	Australia, New Zealand, Papua New Guinea, Republic of Korea, Samoa, Solomon Islands, Vanuatu
Pekka Korpinen (Finland)	Ole L. Poulsent (Denmark)	Denmark, Finland, Iceland, Norway, Sweden
Antonio V. Romuáldez (Philippines)	Héctor Echeverri (Colombia)	Brazil, Colombia, Dominican Republic, Ecuador, Haiti, Philippines
Mourad Benachenhou (Algeria)	Salem Mohamed Omeish (Libyan Arab Jamahiriya)	Afghanistan, Algeria, Democratic Yemen, Ghana, Iran, Libyan Arab Jamahiriya, Morocco, Tunisia
Phaichitr Uathavikul (Thailand)	Vacant	Burma, Fiji, Indonesia, Lao People's Democratic Republic, Malaysia, Nepal, Singapore, Thailand, Viet Nam
William Smith (Liberia)	Astère Girukwigomba (Burundi)	Botswana, Burundi, Ethiopia, Gambia, Guinea, Kenya, Lesotho, Liberia, Malawi, Nigeria, Seychelles, Sierra Leone, Sudan, Swaziland, Trinidad and Tobago, Uganda, United Republic of Tanzania, Zambia, Zimbabwe
Patricio Ayala-González (Mexico)	Roberto Mayorga-Cortés (Nicaragua)	Costa Rica, El Salvador, Guatemala, Honduras, Mexico, Nicaragua, Panama, Spain, Suriname, Venezuela
Nicéphore Soglo (Benin)	André Milongo (Congo)	Benin, Cape Verde, Central African Republic, Chad, Comoros, Congo, Djibouti, Equatorial Guinea, Gabon, Guinea-Bissau, Ivory Coast, Madagascar, Mali, Mauritania, Mauritius, Niger, Rwanda, Sao Tome and Principe, Senegal, Somalia, Togo, United Republic of Cameroon, Upper Volta, Zaire
Eduardo Zalduendo (Argentina)	Pedro O. Montórfano (Paraguay)	Argentina, Bolivia, Chile, Paraguay, Peru, Uruguay

NOTE: Democratic Kampuchea and South Africa did not participate in the 1982 regular election of Executive Directors. Antigua and Barbuda, and Malta became members after that election.

*Resigned effective 31 August; succeeded by Francis Mayer.

†Resigned effective 7 July; succeeded by Per Taxell (Sweden).

Annex III. PRINCIPAL OFFICERS AND OFFICES OF THE WORLD BANK

(As at 1 July 1983)

PRINCIPAL OFFICERS*

President: A. W. Clausen.
Senior Vice-President, Finance: Moeen A. Qureshi.
Senior Vice-President, Operations: Ernest Stern.
Regional Vice-President, Latin America and the Caribbean: Nicolás Ardito Barletta.
Vice-President, External Relations: Munir P. Benjenk.
Regional Vice-President, Europe, Middle East and North Africa: Roger Chaufournier.
Vice-President, Pension Fund: K. Georg Gabriel.

Vice-President and Controller: Masaya Hattori.
Regional Vice-President, South Asia: W. David Hopper.
Vice-President, Operations Policy: S. Shahid Husain.

Regional Vice-President, East Asia and Pacific: Attila Karaosmanoglu.
Regional Vice-President, Western Africa: A. David Knox.
Vice-President, Economics and Research: Anne O. Krueger.
Vice-President, Co-financing: Teruyuki Ohuchi.
Vice-President, Personnel and Administration: Martijn J. W. M. Paijmans.
Vice-President and Treasurer: Eugene H. Rotberg.
Vice-President and General Counsel: Hugh N. Scott (acting).
Vice-President, Energy and Industry: Ernest Stern (acting).
Vice-President and Secretary: Timothy T. Thahane.
Regional Vice-President, Eastern Africa: Willi A. Wapenhans.
Director-General, Operations Evaluation: Mervyn L. Weiner.

*The World Bank and IDA had the same officers and staff.

HEADQUARTERS AND OTHER OFFICES

HEADQUARTERS
The World Bank
1818 H Street, N. W.
Washington, D. C. 20433, United States
  Cable address: INTBAFRAD WASHINGTONDC
  Telephone: (202) 477-1234
  Telex: RCA 248423 WORLDBK,
    WUI 64145 WORLDBANK

NEW YORK OFFICE
The World Bank Mission to the United Nations
747 Third Avenue, 26th floor
New York, N. Y. 10017, United States
  Cable address: INTBAFRAD NEWYORK
  Telephone: (212) 754-6008

EUROPEAN OFFICE
The Wold Bank
66 Avenue d'Iéna
75116 Paris, France
  Cable address: INTBAFRAD PARIS
  Telephone: (1) 723-54-21
  Telex: 620628

LONDON OFFICE
The World Bank
New Zealand House, 15th floor
Haymarket
London SW1 Y4TE, England
  Cable address: INTBAFRAD LONDON
  Telephone: (01) 930-8511
  Telex: 919462

REGIONAL MISSION IN EASTERN AFRICA
The World Bank
Reinsurance Plaza, 5th and 6th floors
Taifa Road
(P. O. Box 30577)
Nairobi, Kenya
  Cable address: INTBAFRAD NAIROBI
  Telophone: 24391
  Telex: 22022

GENEVA OFFICE
The World Bank
ITC Building
54 Rue de Montbrillant
(P. O. Box 104)
1211 Geneva 20, Switzerland
  Telephone: 33 21 20
  Telex: 28883

REGIONAL MISSION IN WESTERN AFRICA
The World Bank
Immeuble Shell, 64 Avenue Lamblin
(Boîte Postale 1850)
Abidjan 01, Ivory Coast
  Cable address: INTBAFRAD ABIDJAN
  Telephone: 32-24-01, 32-42-40
  Telex: 3533

TOKYO OFFICE
The World Bank
Kokusai Building, Room 916
1-1 Marunouchi 3-chome, Chiyoda-ku
Tokyo 100, Japan
  Cable address: INTBAFRAD TOKYO
  Telephone: (03) 214-5001, 5002
  Telex: 26838

REGIONAL MISSION IN THAILAND
The World Bank
Udom Vidhya Building, 956 Rama IV Road
Sala Daeng
Bangkok 5, Thailand
  Cable address: INTBAFRAD BANGKOK
  Telephone: 235-9115-9
  Telex: 82817

Chapter VII

International Finance Corporation (IFC)

The International Finance Corporation (IFC) was established in 1956 as an affiliate of the International Bank for Reconstruction and Development (World Bank) to assist developing member countries by helping them to promote the private sector of their economies. The principal objectives of IFC are: to provide risk capital for productive private enterprise, in association with private investors and management; to encourage the development of local capital markets; and to stimulate the international flow of private capital.

In the fiscal year ending on 30 June 1983, the IFC Board of Directors approved 58 projects in 36 countries, with investments totalling $844.5 million, an increase of 38 per cent over the previous year. Fewer projects were approved than in the previous year (65) and several were cancelled or postponed due to the unfavourable investment climate. Of the total approvals, $789.2 million was for loans made at prevailing commercial rates, including four subordinated loans totalling $20.4 million. The typical loan was for seven years with a grace period of three years.

Operating income for fiscal 1983 was $137.4 million, up from $126.5 million in 1982. Equity investments in 41 companies totalled $55.3 million, the highest in IFC's history. In January 1983, Saudi Arabia agreed to make $100 million available to be used in parallel with IFC for equity investments. Net income was $23 million compared with the previous year's $21.6 million. Syndications—a measure of IFC's ability to attract others to help finance projects in which it is involved—reached a record level of $418.9 million, representing a greater total and percentage of total approved investments (about 50 per cent) than ever before. Among the 18 transactions was a $73.2 million syndication for Pakistan Petroleum Limited which attracted 12 commercial banks.

The estimated total cost of approved investments—$2,894 million—and the investment ratio of IFC to other financial institutions—one dollar to six—were about the same in fiscal 1983 as in the previous year. More than 57 per cent of project financing was raised from domestic sources. Most of the funds from foreign sources were in the form of suppliers' credits or government funding. Of the $599.2 million from foreign commercial banks, 70 per cent was raised through the syndication of IFC loans.

Manufacturing, which in the past accounted for about two thirds of the number of projects, was less than 38 per cent of the total and fewer fertilizer, chemical and petrochemical projects were approved than previously. Fourteen agribusiness projects, accounting for 24 per cent of all investments, were approved at a cost of almost $55 million. Developing country financial institutions received 13 investments totalling $198 million, and seven mining enterprises were supported with $126 million of investments. Among the 58 projects approved were five cement plants, four leasing companies and two pulp and paper mills. IFC diversified its operations into new types of business: coconut growing and processing in Brazil, the production of mini-hydroelectric plants in Colombia, ornamental plants for export in Costa Rica, diamond mining in Guinea, and industrial packages, arranged through commercial banks, in Mexico and Yugoslavia.

Reflecting an emphasis on projects in low-income countries, 22 projects totalling $324 million, 38 per cent of both the total approved projects and the year's total dollar volume, were in countries with a per capita income of less than $730. Although projects in low-income countries tended to be small, two large projects were supported: a steel bar production project in Egypt for over $102 million and a natural gas project in Pakistan for some $90 million.

Projects approved were located in 36 countries, up from 31 countries in fiscal 1982. In six of these countries (Botswana, Costa Rica, Malaysia, Uganda, Yemen, Zaire), IFC had not undertaken investments during the previous three years and in three (Fiji, Gabon, Guinea), investments were undertaken for the first time. About 28 per cent of the projects approved were in Africa; particular attention was given to sub-Saharan Africa where 12 projects with a total cost of $275 million were located in 10 countries. Sixteen investments were made in Asia, 19 in Latin America and the Caribbean and seven in the Middle East and Europe.

Membership in IFC increased to 124, with the admission of Guinea and Maldives.

IFC COMMITMENTS BY TYPE OF BUSINESS
(as at 30 June 1983)

Sector	Amount (in millions of US dollars)
Cement and construction materials	844.4
Mining and energy	467.0
General manufacturing	427.1
Chemicals and petrochemicals	420.0
Pulp and paper products	371.9
Iron and steel	358.2
Textiles and fibres	263.3
Development financing	249.4
Food and agribusiness	241.4
Fertilizers	217.9
Motor vehicles and accessories	217.1
Money and capital markets	191.3
Tourism	121.1
Non-ferrous metals	46.9
Utilities	36.0
Machinery	33.5
Others	41.0

IFC INVESTMENTS
(1 July 1982-30 June 1983)

Recipient	Sector	Amount (in thousands of US dollars)
Argentina	Food and agribusiness	480
Bangladesh	Shoe manufacturing and leather	3,920
Botswana	Development financing	460
Brazil	Cement and construction materials	50,000
	Chemicals and petrochemicals	21,000
	Food and agribusiness	5,500
	Iron and steel	640
	Mining and energy	400
Chile	Mining and energy	44,510
Colombia	Cement and construction materials	28,600
	Utilities	200
Costa Rica	Food and agribusiness	1,460
Dominican Republic	Food and agribusiness	10,450
Ecuador	Cement and construction materials	50
Egypt	Iron and steel	102,400
	Food and agribusiness	8,500
Fiji	Food and agribusiness	6,000
Gabon	Mining and energy	10
Guinea	Mining and energy	16,110
India	Money and capital markets	10,910
	Cement and construction materials	4,300
Indonesia	Cement and construction materials	25,000
Ivory Coast	Textiles and fibres	3,550
Kenya	Development financing	4,760
	Leather	2,670
Madagascar	Food and agribusiness	7,430
Malaysia	Lumber	11,500
Mexico	Export/import financing	100,000
	Cement and construction materials	76,000
	Pulp and paper products	3,200
Morocco	Development financing	40,000
Pakistan	Chemicals and petrochemicals	90,210
Peru	Mining and energy	8,000
Philippines	Pulp and paper products	5,640
Portugal	Money and capital markets	310
Republic of Korea	Money and capital markets	2,160
Spain	Money and capital markets	400
Sri Lanka	Tourism	7,100
	Development financing	300
Thailand	Chemicals and petrochemicals	57,670
	Glass containers	5,110
Turkey	Food and agribusiness	3,900
	Development financing	1,440
Uganda	Food and agribusiness	9,720

Recipient	Sector	Amount (in thousands of US dollars)
United Republic of Cameroon	Food and agribusiness	1,290
Uruguay	Food and agribusiness	2,780
Yemen	Batteries	4,010
Yugoslavia	Export/import financing	35,400
Zaire	Mining and energy	240
Zambia	Tourism	18,820
Total		844,510

Financial operations

IFC's total operating income in fiscal 1983 was $137.4 million. After administrative expenses and charges on borrowings, income from operations amounted to almost $49 million. Net income was $23 million.

STATEMENT OF INCOME AND EXPENDITURE
(for fiscal year ending 30 June 1983)

Income	Amount (in thousands of US dollars)
Income from obligations of Governments	3,031
Income from loan and equity investments	
Interest	111,596
Dividends and profit participations	11,213
Commitment charges	5,210
Realized gain on equity sales	5,090
Commissions	1,098
Other operating income	132
Total income	137,370
Expenditure	
Charges on borrowings	45,539
Administrative expenses*	43,081
Total expenditure	88,620
Income from operations	48,750
Provision for losses	(25,700)
Net income—transferred to accumulated earnings	23,050

*The World Bank charges IFC an annual service and support fee which for the year ending 30 June 1983 was fixed at $3,660,000.

Capital and reserves

The terminal payment date for subscriptions to IFC's capital increase—approved by its Board of Governors in November 1977—was 1 August 1982. Of the $468.8 million allocated for subscription, $420.9 million had been paid for. Seven countries, representing an additional $1.8 million, were granted a payment extension. After the terminal date, five other countries subscribed to $8.2 million additional capital which had been allocated but not subscribed by others. By the end of fiscal 1983, $435.3 million—93 per cent of the total allocated—had been subscribed.

With a paid-in capital of $543.8 million, the total paid-in capital and accumulated earnings was $747.6 million, as at 30 June 1983, up from $678.1 million at the end of fiscal 1982. Accumulated earnings amounted to $203.8 million, including the $23 million net income. Reserve against losses was increased to $99.6 million, including a provision of $25.7 million made from operating income.

city of skills. IFC staff also took part in several technical seminars to discuss the problems of appraising, financing, implementing and operating projects in developing countries.

Technical assistance

IFC provided technical assistance that, in many cases, resulted in conceptual and fundamental technical restructuring of projects. It also provided industry and sectoral technical assistance. Greater emphasis was placed on technology for small industrial units, designed to use available natural resources and promote import substitution, in developing countries with limited markets and scar-

Secretariat

As at 30 June 1983, IFC staff numbered 410, drawn from 68 nationalities. In order to strengthen administrative procedures and serve IFC investment priorities better, one vice-presidency and one investment division were created and an overseas representation was established in India.

Annex I.   MEMBERS OF THE INTERNATIONAL FINANCE
CORPORATION, SUBSCRIPTIONS AND VOTING POWER
(As at 30 June 1983)

MEMBER	SUBSCRIPTION Amount (in thousands of US dollars)	Percent-age of total	VOTING POWER Number of votes	Percent-age of total	MEMBER	SUBSCRIPTION Amount (in thousands of US dollars)	Percent-age of total	VOTING POWER Number of votes	Percent-age of total
Afghanistan	111	0.02	361	0.06	Ireland	332	0.06	582	0.10
Argentina	9,821	1.81	10,071	1.75	Israel	550	0.10	800	0.14
Australia	12,191	2.24	12,441	2.16	Italy	19,114	3.52	19,364	3.37
Austria	5,085	0.94	5,335	0.93	Ivory Coast	913	0.17	1,163	0.20
Bangladesh	2,328	0.43	2,578	0.45	Jamaica	1,103	0.20	1,353	0.24
Barbados	93	0.02	343	0.06	Japan	25,546	4.70	25,796	4.49
Belgium	13,723	2.52	13,973	2.43	Jordan	429	0.08	679	0.12
Belize	26	*	276	0.05	Kenya	1,041	0.19	1,291	0.22
Bolivia	490	0.09	740	0.13	Kuwait	4,533	0.83	4,783	0.83
Botswana	29	0.01	279	0.05	Lebanon	50	0.01	300	0.05
Brazil	10,169	1.87	10,419	1.81	Lesotho	18	*	268	0.05
Burma	666	0.12	916	0.16	Liberia	83	0.02	333	0.06
Burundi	100	0.02	350	0.06	Libyan Arab Jamahiriya	55	0.01	305	0.05
Canada	20,952	3.85	21,202	3.69	Luxembourg	551	0.10	801	0.14
Chile	2,328	0.43	2,578	0.45	Madagascar	111	0.02	361	0.06
China	4,154	0.76	4,404	0.77	Malawi	368	0.07	618	0.11
Colombia	2,083	0.38	2,333	0.41	Malaysia	3,921	0.72	4,171	0.73
Congo	67	0.01	317	0.06	Maldives	4	*	254	0.04
Costa Rica	245	0.05	495	0.09	Mali	116	0.02	366	0.06
Cyprus	551	0.10	801	0.14	Mauritania	55	0.01	305	0.05
Denmark	4,779	0.88	5,029	0.87	Mauritius	429	0.08	679	0.12
Djibouti	21	*	271	0.05	Mexico	6,004	1.10	6,254	1.09
Dominica	11	*	261	0.05	Morocco	2,328	0.43	2,578	0.45
Dominican Republic	306	0.06	556	0.10	Nepal	306	0.06	556	0.10
Ecuador	674	0.12	924	0.16	Netherlands	14,458	2.66	14,708	2.56
Egypt	3,124	0.57	3,374	0.59	New Zealand	923	0.17	1,173	0.20
El Salvador	11	*	261	0.05	Nicaragua	184	0.03	434	0.08
Ethiopia	33	0.01	283	0.05	Niger	67	0.01	317	0.06
Fiji	74	0.01	324	0.06	Nigeria	5,575	1.03	5,825	1.01
Finland	4,043	0.74	4,293	0.75	Norway	4,533	0.83	4,783	0.83
France	29,528	5.43	29,778	5.18	Oman	306	0.06	556	0.10
Gabon	429	0.08	679	0.12	Pakistan	4,411	0.81	4,661	0.81
Germany, Federal Republic of	33,204	6.11	33,454	5.82	Panama	344	0.06	594	0.10
Ghana	1,306	0.24	1,556	0.27	Papua New Guinea	490	0.09	740	0.13
Greece	1,777	0.33	2,027	0.35	Paraguay	123	0.02	373	0.06
Grenada	21	*	271	0.05	Peru	1,777	0.33	2,027	0.35
Guatemala	306	0.06	556	0.10	Philippines	3,247	0.60	3,497	0.61
Guinea	134	0.02	384	0.07	Portugal	2,144	0.39	2,394	0.42
Guinea-Bissau	18	*	268	0.05	Republic of Korea	2,450	0.45	2,700	0.47
Guyana	368	0.07	618	0.11	Rwanda	306	0.06	556	0.10
Haiti	306	0.06	556	0.10	Saint Lucia	19	*	269	0.05
Honduras	184	0.03	434	0.08	Samoa	9	*	259	0.05
Iceland	11	*	261	0.05	Saudi Arabia	9,251	1.70	9,501	1.65
India	19,788	3.64	20,038	3.49	Senegal	707	0.13	957	0.17
Indonesia	7,351	1.35	7,601	1.32	Seychelles	7	*	257	0.04
Iran	372	0.07	622	0.11	Sierra Leone	83	0.02	333	0.06
Iraq	67	0.01	317	0.06	Singapore	177	0.03	427	0.07

MEMBER	SUBSCRIPTION		VOTING POWER		MEMBER	SUBSCRIPTION		VOTING POWER	
	Amount (in thousands of US dollars)	Percentage of total	Number of votes	Percentage of total		Amount (in thousands of US dollars)	Percentage of total	Number of votes	Percentage of total
Solomon Islands	11	*	261	0.05	United Kingdom	37,900	6.97	38,150	6.64
Somalia	83	0.02	333	0.06	United Republic of Cameroon	490	0.09	740	0.13
South Africa	4,108	0.76	4,358	0.76	United Republic of Tanzania	724	0.13	974	0.17
Spain	6,004	1.10	6,254	1.09	United States	146,661	26.97	146,911	25.56
Sri Lanka	1,838	0.34	2,088	0.36	Upper Volta	245	0.05	495	0.09
Sudan	111	0.02	361	0.06	Uruguay	919	0.17	1,169	0.20
Swaziland	184	0.03	434	0.08	Vanuatu	25	*	275	0.05
Sweden	6,923	1.27	7,173	1.25	Venezuela	7,106	1.31	7,356	1.28
Syrian Arab Republic	72	0.01	322	0.06	Viet Nam	166	0.03	416	0.07
Thailand	2,818	0.52	3,068	0.53	Yemen	184	0.03	434	0.08
Togo	368	0.07	618	0.11	Yugoslavia	2,422	0.45	2,672	0.46
Trinidad and Tobago	1,059	0.19	1,309	0.23	Zaire	1,929	0.35	2,179	0.38
Tunisia	919	0.17	1,169	0.20	Zambia	1,286	0.24	1,536	0.27
Turkey	3,063	0.56	3,313	0.58	Zimbabwe	546	0.10	796	0.14
Uganda	735	0.14	985	0.17					
United Arab Emirates	1,838	0.34	2,088	0.36	Total	543,746	100.00†	574,746	100.00†

*Less than 0.005 per cent.

†May differ from the sum of the individual percentages because of rounding.

Annex II. EXECUTIVE DIRECTORS AND ALTERNATES OF THE INTERNATIONAL FINANCE CORPORATION
(As at 30 June 1983)

Appointed Director	Appointed Alternate	Casting the vote of
James B. Burnham	George R. Hoguet	United States
Nigel L. Wicks	Derek F. Smith	United Kingdom
Reinhard Münzberg	Norbert Schmidt-Gerritzen	Federal Republic of Germany
Bruno de Maulde	Robert Hudry*	France
Kenji Yamaguchi	Toshihiro Yamakawa	Japan

Elected Director	Elected Alternate	Casting the votes of
Said E. El-Naggar (Egypt)	Abdulrahman M. Sehaibani (Saudi Arabia)	Egypt, Iraq, Jordan, Kuwait, Lebanon, Maldives, Oman, Pakistan, Saudi Arabia, Syrian Arab Republic, United Arab Emirates, Yemen
Morris Miller (Canada)	George L. Reid (Barbados)	Barbados, Belize, Canada, Dominica, Grenada, Guyana, Ireland, Jamaica, Saint Lucia
H. N. Ray (India)	Gholam Kibria (Bangladesh)	Bangladesh, India, Sri Lanka
Giorgio Ragazzi (Italy)	Rodrigo M. Guimarães (Portugal)	Greece, Italy, Portugal
Jacques de Groote (Belgium)	Herbert A. Lust (Austria)	Austria, Belgium, Luxembourg, Turkey
Patricio Ayala-González (Mexico)	Roberto Mayorga-Cortés (Nicaragua)	Costa Rica, El Salvador, Guatemala, Honduras, Mexico, Nicaragua, Panama, Spain, Venezuela
Pekka Korpinen (Finland)	Ole L. Poulsen (Denmark)†	Denmark, Finland, Iceland, Norway, Sweden
Ferdinand van Dam (Netherlands)	Riza Sapunxhiu (Yugoslavia)	Cyprus, Israel, Netherlands, Yugoslavia
Antonio V. Romuáldez (Philippines)	Héctor Echeverri (Colombia)	Brazil, Colombia, Dominican Republic, Ecuador, Haiti, Philippines
Ronald H. Dean (Australia)	You Kwang Park (Republic of Korea)	Australia, New Zealand, Papua New Guinea, Republic of Korea, Samoa, Solomon Islands, Vanuatu
Phaichitr Uathavikul (Thailand)	Vacant	Burma, Fiji, Indonesia, Malaysia, Nepal, Singapore, Thailand, Viet Nam
Eduardo Zalduendo (Argentina)	Pedro O. Montórfano (Paraguay)	Argentina, Bolivia, Chile, Paraguay, Peru, Uruguay
William Smith (Liberia)	Astère Girukwigomba (Burundi)	Botswana, Burundi, Ethiopia, Guinea, Kenya, Lesotho, Liberia, Malawi, Nigeria, Seychelles, Sierra Leone, Sudan, Swaziland, Trinidad and Tobago, Uganda, United Republic of Tanzania, Zambia, Zimbabwe
Nicéphore Soglo (Benin)	André Milongo (Congo)	Congo, Djibouti, Gabon, Guinea-Bissau, Ivory Coast, Madagascar, Mali, Mauritania, Mauritius, Niger, Rwanda, Senegal, Somalia, Togo, United Republic of Cameroon, Upper Volta, Zaire
Mourad Benachenhou (Algeria)	Salem Mohamed Omeish (Libyan Arab Jamahiriya)	Afghanistan, Ghana, Iran, Libyan Arab Jamahiriya, Morocco, Tunisia
Wang Liansheng (China)	Fei Lizhi (China)	China

NOTE: South Africa did not participate in the 1983 regular election of Executive Directors.
*Resigned effective 31 August; succeeded by Francis Mayer.
†Resigned effective 7 July; succeeded by Per Taxell (Sweden).

Annex III.   PRINCIPAL OFFICERS AND OFFICES
              OF THE INTERNATIONAL FINANCE CORPORATION
              (As at 1 July 1983)

PRINCIPAL OFFICERS

President: A. W. Clausen.*
Executive Vice-President: Hans A. Wuttke.
Vice President, Finance and Planning: K. Georg Gabriel.
  Director, Accounting and Administration Department: Marshall Burkes.
  Director, Planning, Budgeting and Analysis Department: Richard H. Frank.
Vice-President, Asia, Europe and Middle East: Judhvir Parmar.
  Director, Department of Investments, Asia: Torstein Stephansen.
  Director, Department of Investments, Europe and Middle East: Douglas Gustafson.
Vice-President, Latin America and the Caribbean: Jose M. Ruisanchez.
  Director, Department of Investments, Latin America and Caribbean I: Giovanni Vacchelli.
  Director, Department of Investments, Latin America and Caribbean II: Daniel F. Adams.
Vice-President, Africa: Sven K. Riskaer.
  Director, Department of Investments, Africa I: Gunter H. Kreuter.
  Director, Department of Investments, Africa II: M. Azam K. Alizai.
Vice-President and General Counsel: Jose E. Camacho.
  Deputy General Counsel: Walter F. Norris.
  Director, Capital Markets Department: David Gill.
  Deputy Director, Capital Markets Department: Wilfried E. Kaffenberger.
  Director, Syndications: Rolf Th. Lundberg.

    *Held the same position in the World Bank.

Vice-President, Engineering and Technical Assistance: Makarand V. Dehejia.
  Deputy Director: Robert D. King.
Secretary: Timothy T. Thahane.*
Director-General, Operations Evaluation: Mervyn L. Weiner.*
  Economic Adviser and Director, Development Department: Richard W. Richardson.
  Director, Compensation Department: R. A. Clarke.*
  Director, Administrative Services Department: William J. Cosgrove.*
  Director, Personnel Management Department: Gautam S. Kaji.*
  Director, Internal Auditing Department: Lawrence N. Rapley.*
  Director, Programming and Budgeting Department: Heinz Vergin.*
  Chief, Information Office: Carl T. Bell.
  Special Representative, Middle East: Cherif Hassan.
  Special Representative, Far East: Naokado Nishihara.
  Special Representative, Europe: Hans Pollan.
  Regional Mission in East Asia: Vijay K. Chaudhry.
  Regional Mission in Eastern Africa: V. S. Raghavan.
  Regional Mission in India: Athishdam Tharmaratnam.
  Regional Mission in Western Africa: Guy C. Antoine.
  Special Adviser for African Affairs: Pierre-Claver Damiba.
  Special Advisor: James M. Kearns.

HEADQUARTERS AND OTHER OFFICES

HEADQUARTERS
International Finance Corporation
1818 H Street, N. W.
Washington, D. C. 20433, United States
  Cable address: CORINTFIN
  WASHINGTONDC
  Telephone: (202) 477-1234
  Telex: ITT 440098, RCA 248423, WU 64145

NEW YORK OFFICE
International Finance Corporation
747 Third Avenue, 26th floor
New York, N. Y. 10017, United States
  Cable address: CORINTFIN NEWYORK
  Telephone: (212) 754-6008

EUROPEAN OFFICE
International Finance Corporation
New Zealand House, 15th floor
Haymarket, London SW1 Y4TE, England
  Cable address: CORINTFIN LONDON
  Telephone: (01) 930-8741
  Telex: 851-919462

PARIS OFFICE
International Finance Corporation
66 Avenue d'Iéna
75116 Paris, France
  Cable address: CORINTFIN PARIS
  Telephone: (1) 723-54-21
  Telex: 842-620628

TOKYO OFFICE
International Finance Corporation
5-1 Nibancho, Chiyoda-ku
Tokyo 102, Japan
  Cable address: SPCORINTFIN TOKYO
  Telephone: (03) 261-3626
  Telex: 781-26554

REGIONAL MISSION IN EAST ASIA
World Bank Group
Central Bank of the Philippines
Manila, Philippines
  Cable address: CORINTFIN MANILA
  Telephone: 58-93-12
  Telex: 742-40541

REGIONAL MISSION IN EASTERN AFRICA
International Finance Corporation
Reinsurance Plaza, 5th Floor
Taifa Road
(P. O. Box 30577)
Nairobi, Kenya
  Cable address: CORINTFIN NAIROBI
  Telephone: 24726
  Telex: 963-22022

REGIONAL MISSION IN INDIA
International Finance Corporation
55 Lodi Estate
New Delhi 3, India
  Telephone: 617241
  Telex: 953-313150

REGIONAL MISSION IN THE MIDDLE EAST
International Finance Corporation
3 Elbergas Street, Garden City
Cairo, Egypt
  Cable address: IFCAI CAIRO
  Telephone: 982914
  Telex: 927-93110

REGIONAL MISSION IN WESTERN AFRICA
International Finance Corporation
Immeuble Alpha 2000, Rue Gourgas
01-P. O. Box 1748
Abidjan-01, Ivory Coast
  Cable address: CORINTFIN ABIDJAN
  Telephone: 32-65-97, 33-11-51
  Telex: 969-3533

Chapter VIII

International Development Association (IDA)

Established in 1960 as an affiliate of the International Bank for Reconstruction and Development (World Bank), the International Development Association (IDA) promotes economic development primarily in poorer developing countries.

IDA lends for the same purposes as the World Bank and uses the same staff and appraisal criteria, but its capital and assets are entirely separate from those of the Bank.

The funds used by IDA, called credits to distinguish them from World Bank loans, come mostly from subscriptions, general replenishments from its more industrialized and developed members and transfers from the net earnings of the Bank. Credits are lent to the poorest countries on more flexible terms that bear less heavily on their balance of payments than World Bank loans.

In general, a country eligible to receive IDA credits must have an annual per capita gross national product of less than $796 (in 1981 dollars); thus, in the fiscal year ending on 30 June 1983, more than 50 countries were eligible. Credits are interest-free, with a service charge of 0.75 per cent on disbursed and 0.5 per cent on undisbursed balances. The credits have an initial grace period of 10 years before repayment begins and then are repayable over 50 years.

Unlike the Bank, which may lend to public and private entities with government guarantees, IDA lends only to Governments. In the case of revenue-producing projects, IDA credits are relent by the Governments on terms reflecting the local cost of capital. In this way, IDA terms assist Governments to finance economic development without distorting the local credit structure.

At the end of fiscal 1983, IDA's resources totalled $27,967 million.

The bulk of IDA funds for lending is provided by its Part I (richer) member countries and several Part II (developing) countries under a series of replenishment agreements.

The sixth replenishment of IDA was negotiated at a level of $12 billion at October 1979 exchange rates and it was envisaged that these contributions would be committed in the fiscal period 1981-1983. However, reductions in the United States appropriations for the sixth replenishment resulted in a 13-month delay in its effectiveness, a substantial reduction in its fiscal

1982-1984 programme and a delay in negotiations for the seventh replenishment, originally expected to have become effective in fiscal 1984. A meeting of IDA Deputies (The Hague, Netherlands, 5 and 6 July 1982) reviewed the status of IDA's commitment authority and discussed ways to increase such authority in fiscal 1983 and, especially, in fiscal 1984. At another meeting (Toronto, Canada, 4-8 September), donors—other than the United States—agreed to provide special contributions, in general equivalent to one third of their total contributions to the sixth replenishment through either a Fiscal Year 1984 Account or a Special Fund. It was agreed that these two schemes should operate in parallel, permitting donors to choose the mechanism accommodating their concerns and facilitating approval for such special contributions in their respective legislatures.

Negotiations for the seventh IDA replenishment were launched with a meeting of Deputies on 22 and 23 November 1982 (Washington, D. C.). Resources contributed would provide funds for credit commitments in the fiscal period 1985-1987. Deputies met on two other occasions in fiscal 1983: in Paris (February) to discuss IDA's allocation criteria; and at Copenhagen, Denmark (March), to discuss burden-sharing arrangements. Donors' sixth replenishment releases, a Special Fund contribution by France—representing the equivalent of its sixth replenishment release beyond the *pro rata* level—and other IDA resources brought the level of commitment authority for fiscal 1983 to about $3.3 billion (3.1 billion special drawing rights).

Membership of IDA rose to 131 in fiscal 1983, with the admission of Saint Vincent and the Grenadines on 30 August 1982.

Lending operations

By 30 June 1983, IDA had made cumulative net commitments totalling $30,078.9 million. Commitments in fiscal 1983 amounted to $3,340.7 million, of which $1,816.1 million went to seven countries in South Asia and $803.2 million to 15 countries in Eastern Africa. India was the largest borrower during the year with seven credits amounting to $1,063 million, followed by Bangladesh with seven credits of $367.3 million and Pakistan with five credits totalling $228.8 million.

The following table summarizes IDA lending in fiscal 1983 by region or country and by purpose.

IDA CREDITS APPROVED BY REGION/COUNTRY AND PURPOSE
1 JULY 1982–30 JUNE 1983
(including IDA share of joint Bank/IDA operations; in millions of US dollars)

REGION/COUNTRY	Agriculture and rural development	Development finance companies	Education	Energy	Industry	Non-project	Population, health and nutrition	Small-scale enterprises	Technical assistance	Telecommunications	Transportation	Urbanization	Water supply and sewerage	Total
Eastern Africa														
Burundi	—	—	15.8	—	—	—	—	—	—	—	—	—	—	15.8
Comoros	—	2.3	—	—	—	—	—	—	—	—	—	—	—	2.3
Djibouti	—	—	—	—	—	—	—	—	—	—	6.4	—	—	6.4
Ethiopia	—	—	—	7.0	—	—	—	—	—	—	—	20.0	—	27.0
Kenya	15.0	—	—	—	—	70.0	—	—	6.0	—	—	22.0	—	113.0
Madagascar	18.0	—	—	11.5	—	—	—	—	—	—	45.0	—	—	74.5
Malawi	15.6	—	34.0	—	—	—	6.8	—	—	—	—	—	—	56.4
Rwanda	16.3	7.0	—	—	—	—	—	—	—	—	—	—	13.0	36.3
Somalia	—	—	—	—	—	—	—	—	—	—	23.0	—	—	23.0
Sudan	130.0	—	—	—	—	—	—	—	—	—	—	—	—	130.0
Uganda	70.0	—	32.0	—	—	—	—	—	—	22.0	—	—	—	124.0
United Republic of Tanzania	—	—	—	6.3	18.0	—	—	—	—	—	—	—	22.5	46.8
Zaire	13.0	—	—	—	7.0	—	—	—	—	—	68.5	—	—	88.5
Zambia	—	—	—	—	4.3	—	—	—	—	—	—	—	16.0	20.3
Zimbabwe	37.7	—	—	—	1.2	—	—	—	—	—	—	—	—	38.9
Subtotal	315.6	9.3	81.8	24.8	30.5	70.0	6.8	—	6.0	22.0	142.9	42.0	51.5	803.2
Western Africa														
Benin	20.0	—	—	—	—	—	—	—	—	—	—	—	—	20.0
Cape Verde	—	—	—	—	—	—	—	—	—	—	7.2	—	—	7.2
Central African Republic	10.4	—	11.0	—	—	—	—	—	—	—	—	—	—	21.4
Equatorial Guinea	—	—	—	2.4	—	—	—	—	—	—	—	—	—	2.4
Ghana	—	—	—	11.0	—	40.0	—	9.3	—	—	—	—	13.0	73.3
Guinea	—	—	11.0	—	—	—	—	—	—	—	13.0	—	—	24.0
Guinea-Bissau	—	—	—	13.1	—	—	—	—	—	—	16.0	—	—	29.1
Liberia	—	—	13.5	—	—	—	—	—	—	—	1.8	—	—	15.3
Mali	—	—	—	24.0	—	—	—	—	10.4	—	—	—	—	34.4
Mauritania	—	—	—	—	—	—	—	—	4.6	—	—	—	—	4.6
Niger	—	—	—	—	—	—	—	—	—	—	23.6	—	6.5	30.1
Senegal	—	—	—	9.5	7.7	—	15.0	—	—	—	—	—	—	32.2
Sierra Leone	—	—	20.0	—	—	—	—	—	—	—	—	—	—	20.0
Togo	23.5	—	—	—	—	40.0	—	5.7	—	—	—	—	12.0	81.2
Upper Volta	18.5	—	—	—	—	—	—	—	—	—	—	—	—	18.5
Western Africa region	—	14.0	—	—	—	—	—	—	—	—	—	—	—	14.0
Subtotal	72.4	14.0	55.5	60.0	7.7	80.0	15.0	15.0	15.0	—	61.6	—	31.5	427.7
East Asia and Pacific														
China	45.0	30.0	75.4	—	—	—	—	—	—	—	—	—	—	150.4
Lao People's Democratic Republic	6.2	—	—	—	—	—	—	—	—	—	—	—	—	6.2
Papua New Guinea	—	—	—	3.0	—	—	—	—	—	—	—	—	—	3.0
Subtotal	51.2	30.0	75.4	3.0	—	—	—	—	—	—	—	—	—	159.6
South Asia														
Bangladesh	168.0	—	19.8	—	28.5	110.0	—	—	—	35.0	6.0	—	—	367.3
Burma	42.0	—	—	—	—	—	—	—	—	—	50.0	—	—	92.0
India	474.0	—	—	170.0	—	—	—	—	—	—	200.0	147.0	72.0	1,063.0
Maldives	5.0	—	—	—	—	—	—	—	—	—	—	—	—	5.0
Nepal	22.0	—	—	—	—	—	—	—	6.0	—	—	—	—	28.0
Pakistan	112.8	—	—	7.0	—	—	18.0	—	—	—	50.0	16.0	25.0	228.8
Sri Lanka	32.0	—	—	—	—	—	—	—	—	—	—	—	—	32.0
Subtotal	855.8	—	19.8	177.0	28.5	110.0	18.0	—	6.0	35.0	306.0	163.0	97.0	1,816.1
Europe, the Middle East and North Africa														
Democratic Yemen	9.0	—	—	—	—	—	7.6	—	—	—	7.0	—	—	23.6
Yemen	8.0	—	10.0	19.0	—	—	10.5	—	—	—	—	—	—	47.5
Subtotal	17.0	—	10.0	19.0	—	—	18.1	—	—	—	7.0	—	—	71.1

REGION/COUNTRY	Agriculture and rural development	Development finance companies	Education	Energy	Industry	Non-project	Population, health and nutrition	Small-scale enterprises	Technical assistance	Telecommunications	Transportation	Urbanization	Water supply and sewerage	Total
Latin America and the Caribbean														
Haiti	—	—	9.0	26.0	—	—	—	—	—	—	—	21.0	—	56.0
Caribbean region	—	7.0	—	—	—	—	—	—	—	—	—	—	—	7.0
Subtotal	—	7.0	9.0	26.0	—	—	—	—	—	—	—	21.0	—	63.0
Total	1,312.0	60.3	251.5	309.8	66.7	260.0	57.9	15.0	27.0	57.0	517.5	226.0	180.0	3,340.7
NUMBER OF CREDITS	39	5	12	13	6	4	5	2	4	2	13	5	8	118

Agriculture and rural development

As in previous years, in fiscal 1983 credits for agriculture and rural development accounted for the largest amount of IDA lending—39.3 per cent. Thirty-nine credits totalling $1,312 million were committed in 23 countries.

Of credits totalling $474 million made to India, one of $150 million went to modernize canals and waterways by lining about 2,900 kilometres of canals and about 7 million metres of watercourses, and installing 325 augmentation tubewells to supplement irrigation water.

Bangladesh received two credits amounting to $168 million, of which $100 million went to a rural development project to provide credit, institution-building measures, expansion of an irrigation management programme and assistance to the Bangladesh Rural Development Board.

Other credits went to agricultural credit, irrigation and drainage, agro-industry, area development, fisheries, forestry, livestock and research and extension.

Development finance companies

Five credits totalling $60.3 million were made to development finance companies in fiscal 1983. A credit of $30 million went to China to establish the China Investment Bank, a new institution providing investment loans for small and medium-sized industries in three cities. The Western Africa region received $14 million to be re-lent for projects in IDA-eligible countries that were members of the West African Development Bank, a regional institution furthering its six member States' national development objectives. The Caribbean region received $7 million to finance small projects too costly and difficult for the World Bank to appraise and supervise. Rwanda received $7 million to develop a small-scale enterprise programme, and a $2.3-million credit was made to the Comoros to strengthen a newly created development bank.

Education

Eleven countries received 12 credits totalling $251.5 million for educational projects during fiscal 1983.

China received $75.4 million to strengthen higher education and research in the agricultural sciences by providing assistance to agricultural colleges and research institutes and a new national rice research institute. A $34-million credit was made to Malawi to improve primary education, expand secondary education, increase the number of trained accountants and strengthen the management of education and audit systems. Uganda received $32 million to assist its education system with such items as books, teachers' guides and classroom equipment, roofing materials, spare parts and tools.

Other purposes for which credits were committed included public administration, business administration and primary-teacher training, educational materials, and construction and equipping of facilities.

Energy

Thirteen countries received credits totalling $309.8 million for energy-related projects. India received $170 million to build a hydroelectric power plant, increasing power-generating capacity in Orissa State by about 600 megawatts. A credit of $26 million was made to Haiti to construct a diesel power station at Port-au-Prince, rehabilitate 10 kilometres of the distribution network, and undertake repairs, surveys and a feasibility study. Mali received $24 million for technical assistance to help alleviate major managerial and operational constraints in the Energie du Mali, and to construct a 2-megawatt biomass power plant and distribution-system works.

Other credits went for strengthening the management of national petroleum industries, geothermal energy development, evaluation of hydrocarbon potential, petroleum and mineral research and exploration, and an electrification programme.

Industry

Six countries received credits totalling $66.7 million for industrial development projects in fiscal 1983. Bangladesh received a credit of $28.5 million to rehabilitate refinery facilities, provide technical assistance to the Bangladesh Petroleum Corporation, conduct a feasibility study on export projects, and develop energy conservation/diversification programmes and the uses of methanol. A credit of $18 million went to the United Republic of Tanzania for management services to operate a pulp and paper mill and to market its output, and convert the mill's power boiler to use fuelwood as well as coal and oil. Senegal received a $7.7-million credit for studies and tests to help maximize the efficiency of the phosphate mining and processing operations and orient the country's development efforts to exploit its phosphate resources. Other countries received credits for technical and economic feasibility studies of the mining and petroleum industries.

Non-project

In the non-project sector, four credits totalling $260 million were made to four countries during fiscal 1983. Bangladesh received $110 million for essential imports in support of improvements in public financial-resource mobilization and budgetary management, agricultural and food policies, and trade and industrial policies. A $70-million credit was made to Kenya for a structural-adjustment programme to rationalize the trade régime, promote exports, stimulate agricultural output, encourage conservation and efficient production of energy and reduce population growth. Ghana received $40 million to meet priority import requirements of an economic-recovery programme and Togo received $40 million to aid a structural-adjustment programme by financing imports of raw materials, intermediate goods, capital equipment and spare parts.

Population, health and nutrition

During fiscal 1983, five countries received credits amounting to $57.9 million for projects in population, health and nutrition. Pakistan received $18 million to implement its new population welfare plan and establish an effective long-term population-planning effort. A $15-million credit to Senegal went for better health-care services, especially maternal and child health care, to the rural population by strengthening basic services and the Ministry of Public Health, in-service training of personnel, improved drug utilization

and developing health education services. Yemen received $10.5 million for technical assistance, training, civil works, equipment and supplies for infrastructure development for the Ministry of Health in order to strengthen and expand the country's health-care system.

Other credits were made to establish and strengthen primary health-care systems.

Small-scale enterprises

Two countries received credits totalling $15 million for small-scale enterprises. Ghana received $9.3 million and Togo $5.7 million to assist Ciments de l'Afrique de l'Ouest, a clinker-producing firm, to improve its operations and finances, by providing technical assistance, equipment and spare parts, financing fuel oil and restoring the level of its working capital.

Technical assistance

Credits totalling $27 million went to four countries for technical assistance in fiscal 1983. Mali received $10.4 million for a project assisting cereals marketing, rural development agencies, State enterprises, economic-policy analysis and data management, the civil service bureau and other local agencies. Kenya received $6 million to provide technical assistance in grain pricing and marketing, land policy and management and budget in support of a structural-adjustment programme in the agriculture sector. Another $6 million went to Nepal to provide assistance for a number of high-priority projects suitable for financing by the Government and external donors. Mauritania received $4.6 million to assist the Ministry of Planning to formulate and monitor macro-economic policy, implement a national investment plan, support technical ministries and sectoral planning, and continue the rehabilitation of key public enterprises.

Telecommunications

Two credits totalling $57 million were granted for telecommunications during the fiscal year. Bangladesh received $35 million to provide equipment, transmission facilities and technical assistance as well as to increase telephone service to rural areas. A credit of $22 million went to Uganda to finance part of the rehabilitation and investment programme of its Posts and Telecommunications Corporation, including rehabilitation of telecommunications and postal and common services, technical assistance and imported spare parts and materials.

Transportation

Thirteen credits totalling $517.5 million were awarded to 12 countries for transportation projects in fiscal 1983. India received $200 million to upgrade existing diesel electric locomotives, continuing a programme of modernization of electric locomotives, improving fuel efficiency and upgrading the operation of bulk freight movements. A $50-million credit to Burma would enable the port of Rangoon to handle the projected growth in international breakbulk and facilitate containerized traffic by improving port efficiency and basic port services. Pakistan received $50 million for its railways system to improve locomotive maintenance, install a management-information system, facilities and equipment for an international container service and provide spare parts, technical assistance and training.

Credits approved for other countries went to improve highways, ports, railways and transportation.

Urbanization

Five countries received credits amounting to $226 million for urban development during fiscal 1983. India received $147 million to improve urban management in Calcutta through a comprehensive approach, including institutional and financial reforms and physical improvements. Kenya received $22 million to benefit about 29,000 lower- and middle-income urban households by land and construction loans for residential and small-enterprise development, community facilities, support of urban-sector projects and policy studies. Haiti received $21 million—its first IDA credit for urban development—to rehabilitate and upgrade the Port-au-Prince central market area, a sites-and-services scheme for families displaced by that upgrading, and measures for institutional development. Other purposes for which credits were awarded included housing construction, upgrading of settlements, and the provision of services, technical assistance and training.

Water supply and sewerage

Of eight credits totalling $180 million, $72 million went to India to expand water supply and sewerage facilities in eight urban areas by constructing reservoirs, transmission lines and treatment plants, and to build tubewells for safe water to more than 300 villages. A $25-million credit to Pakistan was to expand the Karachi water supply system, improve service for as many as half a million low-income consumers and provide technical assistance. The United Republic of Tanzania received $22.5 million to develop low-cost, on-plot sanitation and services, institutions and management practices for the first phase of a long-range programme rehabilitating the sewerage system and developing basic sanitation services in Dar es Salaam. Other credits were for institution building and strengthening, improved sewerage systems, safe drinking water, studies, technical assistance and training.

Secretariat

The principal officers, staff, headquarters and other offices of IDA are the same as those of the World Bank.

STATEMENT OF INCOME AND EXPENSES
(for the fiscal year ended 30 June 1983)

	Amount (in thousands of US dollars)
Income	
From development credits:	
Service charges	121,757
Commitment charges	6,725
From investments	17,793
Exchange adjustments	(1,127)
Total income	145,148
Expenses	
Management fee to World Bank	213,727
Operating loss (income less expenses)	(68,579)
Translation adjustments as a result of currency fluctuations	(22,066)
Net loss	(90,645)

Annex I. MEMBERS OF THE INTERNATIONAL DEVELOPMENT ASSOCIATION, SUBSCRIPTIONS, VOTING POWER AND SUPPLEMENTARY RESOURCES

(As at 30 June 1983)

MEMBER	TOTAL SUBSCRIPTIONS AND SUPPLEMENTARY RESOURCES (in thousands of US dollars)		VOTING POWER		MEMBER	TOTAL SUBSCRIPTIONS AND SUPPLEMENTARY RESOURCES (in thousands of US dollars)		VOTING POWER	
	Amount (in current US dollars)*	Percentage of total	Number of votes	Percentage of total		Amount (in current US dollars)*	Percentage of total	Number of votes	Percentage of total
Part I countries					*Part I countries (cont.)*				
Australia	528,378	1.87	69,115	1.46	Canada	1,493,460	5.28	165,730	3.51
Austria	186,914	0.66	29,657	0.63	Denmark	285,069	1.01	45,928	0.97
Belgium	398,245	1.41	58,076	1.23	Finland	132,012	0.47	25,939	0.55

MEMBER	TOTAL SUBSCRIPTIONS AND SUPPLEMENTARY RESOURCES (in thousands of US dollars)		VOTING POWER		MEMBER	TOTAL SUBSCRIPTIONS AND SUPPLEMENTARY RESOURCES (in thousands of US dollars)		VOTING POWER	
	Amount (in current US dollars)*	Percentage of total	Number of votes	Percentage of total		Amount (in current US dollars)*	Percentage of total	Number of votes	Percentage of total
Part I countries (cont.)					*Part II countries* (cont.)				
France	1,355,329	4.79	175,147	3.71	Israel	2,392	0.01	9,386	0.20
Germany, Federal					Ivory Coast	1,155	0.01	7,771	0.16
Republic of	3,232,701	11.43	342,586	7.26	Jordan	393	†	10,982	0.23
Iceland	2,282	0.01	10,658	0.23	Kenya	1,966	0.01	15,047	0.32
Ireland	30,688	0.11	13,702	0.29	Lao People's Democratic				
Italy	809,633	2.86	123,671	2.62	Republic	568	†	11,723	0.25
Japan	3,488,684	12.33	338,756	7.18	Lebanon	521	†	8,562	0.18
Kuwait	446,704	1.58	54,021	1.14	Lesotho	188	†	10,487	0.22
Luxembourg	12,865	0.04	11,397	0.24	Liberia	910	†	12,227	0.26
Netherlands	782,504	2.76	96,098	2.04	Libyan Arab				
New Zealand	27,304	0.09	13,410	0.28	Jamahiriya	1,171	0.01	7,771	0.16
Norway	279,218	0.99	42,759	0.91	Madagascar	1,093	0.01	702	0.01
South Africa	47,274	0.17	15,065	0.32	Malawi	896	†	12,667	0.27
Sweden	819,851	2.90	114,958	2.44	Malaysia	3,015	0.01	18,254	0.39
United Arab Emirates	136,464	0.48	18,132	0.38	Maldives	35	†	10,008	0.21
United Kingdom	2,918,660	10.32	336,440	7.13	Mali	1,014	0.01	12,559	0.27
United States	9,642,646	34.08	873,571	18.51	Mauritania	577	†	6,685	0.14
					Mauritius	1,035	0.01	13,055	0.28
Subtotal	27,056,885	95.64	2,974,816	63.02	Mexico	13,684	0.05	15,896	0.34
Part II countries					Morocco	4,124	0.01	22,789	0.48
					Nepal	591	†	11,723	0.25
Afghanistan	1,210	0.01	13,557	0.29	Nicaragua	396	†	10,982	0.23
Algeria	4,698	0.02	18,481	0.39	Niger	585	†	11,723	0.25
Argentina	46,656	0.16	81,053	1.72	Nigeria	3,836	0.01	4,057	0.09
Bangladesh	6,238	0.02	29,522	0.63	Oman	383	†	10,985	0.23
Belize	216	†	540	0.01	Pakistan	12,010	0.04	46,750	0.99
Benin	541	†	600	0.01	Panama	26	†	5,657	0.12
Bhutan	54	†	510	0.01	Papua New Guinea	1,020	0.01	13,050	0.28
Bolivia	1,199	0.01	13,136	0.28	Paraguay	353	†	8,124	0.17
Botswana	188	†	10,487	0.22	Peru	1,915	0.01	854	0.02
Brazil	52,658	0.19	81,496	1.73	Philippines	5,913	0.02	16,583	0.35
Burma	2,380	0.01	17,284	0.37	Republic of Korea	4,014	0.01	14,959	0.32
Burundi	907	†	12,667	0.27	Rwanda	907	†	12,667	0.27
Cape Verde	87	†	516	0.01	Saint Lucia	167	†	10,445	0.22
Central African					Saint Vincent and				
Republic	578	†	9,720	0.21	the Grenadines	75	†	514	0.01
Chad	562	†	2,093	0.04	Samoa	103	†	7,537	0.16
Chile	3,979	0.01	17,113	0.36	Sao Tome and Principe	76	†	514	0.01
China	35,173	0.12	91,311	1.93	Saudi Arabia	774,004	2.74	106,443	2.25
Colombia	10,427	0.04	23,784	0.50	Senegal	1,958	0.01	16,021	0.34
Comoros	92	†	5,774	0.12	Sierra Leone	898	†	12,667	0.27
Congo	572	†	6,685	0.14	Solomon Islands	98	†	518	0.01
Costa Rica	230	†	7,844	0.17	Somalia	872	†	10,506	0.22
Cyprus	893	†	12,667	0.27	Spain	61,140	0.22	57,788	1.22
Democratic Kampuchea	1,152	0.01	7,826	0.17	Sri Lanka	3,495	0.01	20,940	0.44
Democratic Yemen	1,388	0.01	10,591	0.22	Sudan	1,174	0.01	12,975	0.27
Djibouti	175	†	532	0.01	Swaziland	376	†	11,073	0.23
Dominica	88	†	516	0.01	Syrian Arab Republic	1,101	0.01	7,651	0.16
Dominican Republic	548	†	11,379	0.24	Thailand	3,601	0.01	20,940	0.44
Ecuador	902	†	12,273	0.26	Togo	886	†	12,667	0.27
Egypt	5,966	0.02	28,424	0.60	Trinidad and Tobago	1,461	0.01	770	0.02
El Salvador	369	†	6,244	0.13	Tunisia	1,697	0.01	2,793	0.06
Equatorial Guinea	359	†	1,967	0.04	Turkey	6,609	0.02	23,450	0.50
Ethiopia	620	†	11,727	0.25	Uganda	1,894	0.01	15,047	0.32
Fiji	629	†	2,130	0.05	United Republic				
Gabon	565	†	2,093	0.04	of Cameroon	1,161	0.01	7,771	0.16
Gambia	314	†	10,722	0.23	United Republic				
Ghana	2,740	0.01	15,362	0.33	of Tanzania	1,965	0.01	16,021	0.34
Greece	5,811	0.02	19,656	0.42	Upper Volta	578	†	9,720	0.21
Grenada	107	†	10,211	0.22	Vanuatu	205	†	538	0.01
Guatemala	479	†	11,367	0.24	Viet Nam	1,703	0.01	8,889	0.19
Guinea	1,200	0.01	13,557	0.29	Yemen	515	†	11,468	0.24
Guinea-Bissau	152	†	528	0.01	Yugoslavia	21,004	0.07	29,446	0.62
Guyana	957	†	12,859	0.27	Zaire	3,403	0.01	12,164	0.26
Haiti	910	†	12,667	0.27	Zambia	2,911	0.01	19,730	0.42
Honduras	361	†	10,982	0.23	Zimbabwe	4,507	0.02	1,324	0.03
India	50,859	0.18	157,108	3.33					
Indonesia	12,875	0.05	50,392	1.07	Subtotal	1,232,102	4.36	1,745,830	36.98
Iran	5,822	0.02	15,455	0.33					
Iraq	893	†	9,407	0.20	Total	28,288,987	100.00‡	4,720,646	100.00‡

*Includes amounts aggregating $2,389,997,000 equivalent in current United States dollars receivable from members, of which at 30 June 1983 $272,547,00 equivalent was past due and $2,117,450,000 equivalent was not yet due.

†Less than 0.005 per cent.

‡May differ from the sum of the individual percentages because of rounding.

Annex II. EXECUTIVE DIRECTORS AND ALTERNATES OF THE INTERNATIONAL DEVELOPMENT ASSOCIATION
(As at 30 June 1983)

Appointed Director	*Appointed Alternate*	*Casting the vote of*
James B. Burnham	George R. Hoguet	United States
Reinhard Münzberg	Norbert Schmidt-Gerritzen	Federal Republic of Germany
Kenji Yamaguchi	Toshihiro Yamakawa	Japan
Nigel L. Wicks	Derek F. Smith	United Kingdom
Bruno de Maulde	Robert Hudry*	France

Elected Director	*Elected Alternate*	*Casting the votes of*
Said E. El-Naggar (Egypt)	Abdulrahman M. Sehaibani (Saudi Arabia)	Egypt, Iraq, Jordan, Kuwait, Lebanon, Maldives, Oman, Pakistan, Saudi Arabia, Syrian Arab Republic, United Arab Emirates, Yemen
Pekka Korpinen (Finland)	Ole L. Poulsen† (Denmark)	Denmark, Finland, Iceland, Norway, Sweden
Morris Miller (Canada)	George L. Reid (Barbados)	Belize, Canada, Dominica, Grenada, Guyana, Ireland, Saint Lucia, Saint Vincent and the Grenadines
H. N. Ray (India)	Gholam Kibria (Bangladesh)	Bangladesh, Bhutan, India, Sri Lanka
William Smith (Liberia)	Astère Girukwigomba (Burundi)	Botswana, Burundi, Ethiopia, Gambia, Guinea, Kenya, Lesotho, Liberia, Malawi, Nigeria, Sierra Leone, Sudan, Swaziland, Trinidad and Tobago, Uganda, United Republic of Tanzania, Zambia, Zimbabwe
Nicéphore Soglo (Benin)	André Milongo (Congo)	Benin, Cape Verde, Central African Republic, Chad, Comoros, Congo, Djibouti, Equatorial Guinea, Gabon, Guinea-Bissau, Ivory Coast, Madagascar, Mali, Mauritania, Mauritius, Niger, Rwanda, Sao Tome and Principe, Senegal, Somalia, Togo, United Republic of Cameroon, Upper Volta, Zaire
Antonio V. Romuáldez (Philippines)	Héctor Echeverri (Colombia)	Brazil, Colombia, Dominican Republic, Ecuador, Haiti, Philippines
Ferdinand van Dam (Netherlands)	Riza Sapunxhiu (Yugoslavia)	Cyprus, Israel, Netherlands, Yugoslavia
Giorgio Ragazzi (Italy)	Rodrigo M. Guimarães (Portugal)	Greece, Italy
Phaichitr Uathavikul (Thailand)	Vacant	Burma, Fiji, Indonesia, Lao People's Democratic Republic, Malaysia, Nepal, Thailand, Viet Nam
Patricio Ayala-González (Mexico)	Roberto Mayorga-Cortés (Nicaragua)	Costa Rica, El Salvador, Guatemala, Honduras, Mexico, Nicaragua, Panama, Spain
Jacques de Groote (Belgium)	Herbert A. Lust (Austria)	Austria, Belgium, Luxembourg, Turkey
Eduardo Zalduendo (Argentina)	Pedro O. Montórfano (Paraguay)	Argentina, Bolivia, Chile, Paraguay, Peru
Ronald H. Dean (Australia)	You Kwang Park (Republic of Korea)	Australia, New Zealand, Papua New Guinea, Republic of Korea, Samoa, Solomon Islands, Vanuatu
Mourad Benachenhou (Algeria)	Salem Mohamed Omeish (Libyan Arab Jamahiriya)	Afghanistan, Algeria, Democratic Yemen, Ghana, Iran, Libyan Arab Jamahiriya, Morocco, Tunisia
Wang Liansheng (China)	Fei Lizhi (China)	China

NOTE: Democratic Kampuchea and South Africa did not participate in the 1982 regular election of Executive Directors.

*Resigned effective 31 August; succeeded by Francis Mayer.

†Resigned effective 7 July; succeeded by Per Taxell (Sweden).

Annex III. PRINCIPAL OFFICERS AND OFFICES OF THE INTERNATIONAL DEVELOPMENT ASSOCIATION
(As at 1 July 1983)

PRINCIPAL OFFICERS*

President: A. W. Clausen.
Senior Vice-President, Finance: Moeen A. Qureshi.
Senior Vice-President, Operations: Ernest Stern.
Regional Vice-President, Latin America and the Caribbean: Nicolás Ardito Barletta.
Vice-President, External Relations: Munir P. Benjenk.
Regional Vice-President, Europe, Middle East and North Africa: Roger Chaufournier.
Vice-President, Pension Fund: K. Georg Gabriel.
Vice-President and Controller: Masaya Hattori.
Regional Vice-President, South Asia: W. David Hopper.
Vice-President, Operations Policy: S. Shahid Husain.
Regional Vice-President, East Asia and Pacific: Attila Karaosmanoglu.

Regional Vice-President, Western Africa: A. David Knox.
Vice-President, Economics and Research: Anne O. Krueger.
Vice-President, Co-financing: Teruyuki Ohuchi.
Vice-President, Personnel and Administration: Martijn J. W. M. Paijmans.
Vice-President and Treasurer: Eugene H. Rotberg.
Vice-President and General Counsel: Hugh N. Scott (acting).
Vice-President, Energy and Industry: Ernest Stern (acting).
Vice-President and Secretary: Timothy T. Thahane.
Regional Vice-President, Eastern Africa: Willi A. Wapenhans.
Director-General, Operations Evaluation: Mervyn L. Weiner.

*The World Bank and IDA had the same officers and staff.

HEADQUARTERS AND OTHER OFFICES

HEADQUARTERS
International Development Association
1818 H Street, N. W.
Washington, D. C. 20433, United States
  Cable address: INDEVAS WASHINGTONDC
  Telephone: (202) 477-1234
  Telex: RCA 248423 INDEVAS,
      WUI 64145 INDEVAS

LONDON OFFICE
International Development Association
New Zealand House, 15th floor,
Haymarket
London SW1 Y4TE, England
  Cable address: INDEVAS LONDON
  Telephone: (01) 930-8511
  Telex: 919462

REGIONAL MISSION IN EASTERN AFRICA
International Development Association
Reinsurance Plaza, 5th & 6th floors
Taifa Road
(P. O. Box 30577)
Nairobi, Kenya
  Cable address: INDEVAS NAIROBI
  Telephone: 24391
  Telex: 22022

NEW YORK OFFICE
International Development Association
747 Third Avenue, 26th floor
New York, N. Y. 10017, United States
  Cable address: INDEVAS NEWYORK
  Telephone: (212) 754-6008

GENEVA OFFICE
International Development Association
ITC Building
54 Rue de Montbrillant
(P. O. Box 104)
1211 Geneva 20, Switzerland
  Telephone: 33 21 20
  Telex: 28883

REGIONAL MISSION IN WESTERN AFRICA
International Development Association
Immeuble Shell, 64 Avenue Lamblin
(Boîte Postale 1850)
Abidjan 01, Ivory Coast
  Cable address: INDEVAS ABIDJAN
  Telephone: 32-24-01, 32-42-40
  Telex: 3533

EUROPEAN OFFICE
International Development Association
66 Avenue d'Iéna
75116 Paris, France
  Cable address: INDEVAS PARIS
  Telephone: (1) 723-54-21
  Telex: 620628

TOKYO OFFICE
International Development Association
Kokusai Building, Room 916
1-1 Marunouchi 3-chome, Chiyoda-ku
Tokyo 100, Japan
  Cable address: INDEVAS TOKYO
  Telephone: (03) 214-5001, 5002
  Telex: 26838

REGIONAL MISSION IN THAILAND
International Development Association
Udom Vidhya Building, 956 Rama IV Road
Sala Daeng
Bangkok 5, Thailand
  Cable address: INDEVAS BANGKOK
  Telephone: 235-9115-9
  Telex: 82817

Chapter IX

International Monetary Fund (IMF)

Financial assistance by the International Monetary Fund (IMF) to its member countries rose sharply in 1983 in response to the continuing deterioration in world trade and payments positions and to the increasing difficulties experienced by developing countries in servicing their external debt. Total purchases—measured in special drawing rights (SDRs), the unit of account of IMF—amounted to a record SDR 12.6 billion in 1983, or 69.4 per cent above the 1982 peak of SDR 7.4 billion, with all drawings representing financial assistance by IMF to its developing member countries. The total did not include reserve tranche drawings, which were not regarded as uses of IMF credit but rather as drawings by members on reserve assets deposited by them with IMF. Reserve tranche drawings, which are subject neither to conditionality nor to repurchase requirements, rose moderately in 1983 and amounted to SDR 1.5 billion, compared with SDR 1.3 billion in 1982.

New loan commitments under stand-by and extended arrangements, which had amounted to only SDR 2.4 billion in 1982, rose fourfold in 1983 to SDR 10.5 billion. At the end of 1983, there were 33 stand-by arrangements and 10 extended arrangements in effect with an approved value of SDR 22.9 billion and an undrawn balance of SDR 12.4 billion.

Purchases made available in support of economic adjustment programmes and subject to relatively strong conditionality requirements accounted for about 75 per cent of the drawings of SDR 12.6 billion in 1983, up about 13 per cent on 1982. This reflected almost a doubling of drawings under stand-by arrangements (typically made over a one-year period) to SDR 4.6 billion and more than a doubling of drawings under extended arrangements (usually made over three years) also to SDR 4.6 billion; first credit tranche purchases that were made under stand-by arrangements amounted to SDR 259.1 million.

Conditionality requirements, linking financial assistance by IMF to the adoption of economic adjustment policies by members, were less rigorous for drawings under the first credit tranche, which may be made outright or through a stand-by arrangement. Purchases in the upper credit tranches, almost always made under a stand-by or extended arrangement, required substantial justification and were subject to phased disbursements and to fulfilment of specific performance criteria.

Drawings under the compensatory financing facility, designed to compensate for temporary shortfalls in export earnings of member countries or for excessive increases in cereal import costs and entailing less restrictive conditionality, rose by 8 per cent in 1983 to SDR 2.8 billion. Purchases under the buffer stock financing facility, which assists members in making contributions to Fund-approved international buffer stocks, rose to around SDR 352 million in 1983.

In contrast to the rise in total drawings, repurchases (repayments by IMF members) grew only slightly in 1983 to SDR 2 billion, from SDR 1.8 billion in 1982. This small increase resulted in an increase in net purchases of more than 82 per cent to a record SDR 10.6 billion, compared with the previous record of SDR 5.9 billion in 1982.

Use of SDRs also increased substantially in 1983, largely because of payments in SDRs by participants of all or part of the reserve asset portion of their quota increases under the Eighth General Review of Quotas (see below). These payments, made in December 1983 by 120 member countries and amounting to SDR 6 billion, helped to increase total SDR transfers to SDR 20.7 billion, from SDR 12.2 billion in 1982. Transactions "by agreement", voluntary transfers in exchange for currencies, grew to a record SDR 2.7 billion in 1983, compared with the previous record of SDR 1.8 billion in 1978. This was the first time since 1978 that the level of transactions "by agreement" exceeded that of transactions "with designation", which totalled SDR 2.1 billion. Under transactions "with designation", participants whose international financial position was sufficiently strong were designated by IMF to exchange their usable currencies for the SDRs of participants requiring balance-of-payments assistance.

IMF liquidity

Several important decisions were reached in 1983 with the purpose of effectively doubling the usable resources of IMF so that it could continue to provide adequate financial assistance to its members. These decisions included an increase of about 50 per cent in the level of IMF quotas, an almost threefold enlargement in the total amount of commitments under the General Arrangements to Borrow (GAB) and the extension of this facility to finance purchases by any member, as well as the establishment of a separate credit facility by Saudi Arabia to provide financial assistance to IMF under the same conditions as GAB.

The increase in Fund quotas from the current level of about SDR 61 billion to SDR 90 billion under the Eighth General Review of Quotas was agreed by the Interim Committee of the IMF Board of Governors, meeting at Washington, D. C., in February. The Committee agreed that 40 per cent of the overall increase was to be distributed to all members in proportion to their existing individual quotas and that the balance should be distributed in the form of selective adjustments reflecting members' relative positions in the world economy.

A resolution authorizing the increase in quotas was adopted by the Board of Governors on 31 March. The new quotas were to become effective when members having at least 70 per cent of total quotas had consented to their individual increases and paid them in full. IMF said that this provision had been met on 30 November. As at 2 December, 132 member countries (of a total membership of 146, unchanged in 1983), representing 96.55 per cent of total Fund quotas, had notified IMF of their consent to the increases.

Another measure to improve the liquidity of IMF was adopted on 18 January by the Group of 10—the original industrial member countries participating in GAB—when it agreed to increase the aggregate commitments available under GAB from SDR 6.4 billion to SDR 17 billion and to make the resources available for drawings by any member of IMF if needed to forestall or cope with an impairment of the international monetary system. Previously, use of GAB had been limited to financing drawings by participants in GAB. The revision, which was approved by the Fund's Executive Board on 24 February and entered into force on 26 December, also authorized the participation of Switzerland in GAB and permitted IMF to enter into GAB-associated borrowing arrangements with lenders other than GAB participants. One such borrowing arrangement with Saudi Arabia for up to SDR 1.5 billion was approved by the Executive Board on 20 May.

Access to IMF resources

In addition to augmenting the resources of IMF, the increase in quotas was to raise the levels of members' access to these resources. The enlarged access policy, which was to replace the supplementary financing facility, would enable IMF to provide supplementary financing to all members facing payments imbalances that were large in relation to their quotas. No funds were to be disbursed by the supplementary financing facility after 22 February 1984.

Because of the continuing high demand for IMF financial assistance, a review of access limits was undertaken in 1983. At a meeting in Washington, D. C., on 25 September, the Interim Committee recommended that the enlarged access policy should continue for 1984.

Access to the Fund's resources under the policy during the extension was to be subject to annual limits of 102 or 125 per cent of quota, three-year limits of 306 or 375 per cent of quota, and cumulative limits of 408 or 500 per cent of quota, depending on the seriousness of the balance-of-payments needs and the strength of the adjustment effort. These limits were to be examined periodically in conjunction with reviews of the enlarged access policy itself.

Debt renegotiation

In 1983, a number of developing countries continued to face major debt-servicing difficulties owing to high interest payments and to a further contraction of their export markets that reflected the recession in the industrial countries and their recourse to protectionist measures. With Governments, central and commercial banks, and the Bank for International Settlements, IMF helped to put together financing arrangements for the major debtor countries. An important aspect of the Fund's role was to explain the thrust of Fund-supported adjustment policies, to identify the immediate financing requirements of the debtor countries, and to encourage commercial banks to reschedule payments due on their loans to these countries and to make new loans.

Exchange rate policies

Under its Articles of Agreement, the Fund was charged with overseeing the international monetary system. Article IV, Section 3 (*b*), provided that "the Fund shall exercise firm surveillance over the exchange rate policies of members, and shall adopt specific principles for the guidance of all members with respect to those policies". The timing and timeliness of Article IV consultations were of considerable importance. In principle, consultations were to take place annually, but in practice even the operational guideline that had been adopted—covering three fourths of the membership annually—had not been met in the early 1980s. This slippage led the Executive Board in 1983 to implement a stricter adherence to an annual consultation cycle for most members, particularly those whose policies had a significant impact on other economies, those that had Fund-supported programmes, and those for which there were substantial doubts about the medium-term viability of the balance-of-payments situation.

IMF also strengthened its surveillance activities in 1983 to encompass in-depth analyses of debt policies of individual countries, including debt developments and debt-servicing prospects. The analyses were to cover all members engaged in significant external borrowing operations.

Another decision in 1983 initiated a system whereby the Executive Board would be notified regularly of all sizeable changes in real effective exchange rates. A large change in a country's exchange rate would result in the issuance of an information notice to the Board. The notice would include a discussion of developments in the member's exchange rate and its costs and prices, together with a statement of how they were related to changes in the balance of payments and other developments in the economy.

Other developments

The Executive Board adopted a decision on the SDR interest rate, effective 1 August 1983. The general purpose of the decision was to enhance further the role of the SDR as an international reserve asset by bringing its yield closer in line with yields on other reserve assets included in the SDR interest basket. The SDR interest rate and charges and the rate of remuneration that IMF pays on members' creditor positions were to be calculated weekly instead of quarterly; payments of SDR interest and charges, as well as those of remuneration, were to be made quarterly rather than annually.

IMF made the final payments from its oil facility subsidy account on 23 August. Disbursements to 25 members amounting to SDR 11.7 million brought the amount of total payments under the subsidy account to SDR 186.8 million. The account had been established in 1975 to assist Fund members most seriously affected by oil price increases to meet part of the cost of using the IMF oil facility, which was in operation from June 1975 until May 1976.

Publications

Publications issued by IMF in 1983 included the *Annual Report, Summary Proceedings* of the annual meeting of the Board of Governors, the *Annual Report on Exchange Arrangements and Exchange Restrictions, World Economic Outlook, International Financial Statistics* (including supplements on international reserves and on money), *Direction of Trade Statistics, Balance of Payments Statistics,* and *Government Finance Statistics Yearbook.* Periodicals included the quarterlies *Staff Papers* and *Finance and Development* (published jointly with the World Bank), the *IMF Survey,* published 23 times a year, and the monthly *IMF Memorandum.* Also published were explanatory pamphlets on the workings of the Fund and papers on wide-ranging subjects of interest to the international financial community.

Secretariat

As at 31 December 1983, the total full-time staff of IMF, including permanent, fixed-term and tem-

porary employees, was 1,734, drawn from 101 nationalities. On 12 May, the Managing Director of IMF, Jacques de Larosière, was appointed to a second five-year term.

DRAWINGS AND REPURCHASES IN 1983
(in millions of SDRs)

	Drawings	Repurchases
World	14,132.5	2,032.8
Industrial countries	87.2	106.9*
Australia	—	32.5
Finland	—	14.4
Iceland	—	0.9
Luxembourg	7.6	—
Netherlands	79.6	—
New Zealand	—	2.9
Spain	—	4.8
United Kingdom	—	51.6
Developing countries	832.8	—
Oil exporting countries	643.5*	—
Iran	111.9	—
Iraq	77.4	—
Non-oil developing countries	13,212.6*	1,925.9*
Africa	1,862.6*	425.6
Benin	1.8	—
Burundi	—	4.8
Central African Republic	5.7	0.3
Chad	3.3	—
Congo	3.3	—
Equatorial Guinea	1.4	—
Ethiopia	—	18.0
Gabon	—	7.5
Gambia	0.9	2.6
Ghana	275.0	15.4
Guinea	4.7	—
Guinea-Bissau	0.4	0.4
Ivory Coast	167.8	—
Kenya	132.6	43.0
Liberia	62.0	10.3
Madagascar	15.2	3.7
Malawi	34.2	10.3
Mali	17.6	1.8
Mauritania	2.1	4.4
Mauritius	31.6	14.5
Morocco	134.8	23.3
Niger	30.8	—
Senegal	37.0	10.5
Seychelles	0.7	—
Sierra Leone	23.6	2.0
Somalia	47.4	—
South Africa	—	50.0
Sudan	193.0	41.6
Swaziland	10.0	—
Togo	21.9	—
Uganda	112.7	11.9
United Republic of Cameroon	13.0	0.5
United Republic of Tanzania	6.1	25.1
Zaire	130.3	10.4
Zambia	188.4	113.6
Zimbabwe	153.6	—
Asia	2,855.7*	867.0*
Afghanistan	15.1	—
Bangladesh	68.4	21.1
Burma	44.2	18.2
China	—	450.0
India	1,500.0	33.3
Malaysia	113.0	46.2
Nepal	2.2	4.9
Pakistan	285.0	24.3
Philippines	319.9	144.6
Republic of Korea	192.0	40.9
Samoa	3.2	0.9
Solomon Islands	1.0	—
Sri Lanka	35.8	46.2
Thailand	265.5	35.2
Viet Nam	10.5	1.3

	Drawings	Repurchases
Europe	1,859.2	414.9
Cyprus	—	6.8
Hungary	332.5	—
Portugal	403.5	9.8
Romania	222.9	60.9
Turkey	346.3	168.3
Yugoslavia	554.0	169.1
Middle East	26.3*	30.8
Democratic Yemen	—	0.9
Egypt	—	2.7
Israel	—	27.2
Jordan	16.6	—
Yemen	9.8	—
Western hemisphere	6,608.9*	187.6*
Antigua and Barbuda	0.4	—
Argentina	1,289.3	—
Barbados	14.5	0.9
Belize	3.6	—
Bolivia	23.7	10.8
Brazil	2,402.7	—
Chile	678.3	5.7
Costa Rica	116.5	11.7
Dominica	2.7	0.7
Dominican Republic	179.1	8.1
Ecuador	203.5	—
El Salvador	21.6	—
Grenada	1.5	—
Guatemala	38.3	—
Guyana	2.9	4.1
Haiti	31.9	0.3
Honduras	45.9	—
Jamaica	116.0	41.5
Mexico	1,003.1	—
Nicaragua	—	4.3
Panama	108.9	0.9
Peru	165.0	87.5
Saint Lucia	0.5	—
Suriname	7.9	—
Uruguay	151.2	11.2

*Differs from sum of individual figures because of rounding.

CURRENCIES DRAWN AND REPURCHASES BY CURRENCY OF REPURCHASE IN 1983
(in millions of SDRs)

	Currencies drawn	Repurchases by currency of repurchase
World	14,132.5	2,032.8
Industrial countries	8,887.3*	1,445.7
Austrian schillings	130.6	20.9
Canadian dollars	25.8	21.9
Danish kroner	45.7	1.9
Deutsche mark	1,182.8	260.7
French francs	21.1	—
Irish pounds	12.8	—
Italian lire	70.5	18.1
Japanese yen	603.7	167.2
Netherlands guilders	239.4	51.5
Norwegian kroner	142.6	34.1
Pounds sterling	344.6	107.0
United States dollars	6,067.8	762.4
Developing countries		
Oil-exporting countries	2,162.7*	163.3*
Algerian dinars	—	2.1
Kuwaiti dinars	211.3	15.1
Omani rials	1.8	0.3
Qatar riyals	5.6	—
Saudi Arabian riyals	1,808.7	127.3
United Arab Emirates dirhams	5.8	—
Venezuelan bolívares	129.4	18.4

	Currencies drawn	Repurchases by currency of repurchase
Non-oil developing countries	105.5	18.4
Asia	22.5	1.7
Chinese yuan	20.0	—
Singapore dollars	2.5	1.7
Europe	—	0.7
Maltese pounds	—	0.7
Middle East	3.0	—
Bahrain dinars	3.0	—
Western hemisphere	80.0	16.0*
Colombian pesos	70.1	9.4
Paraguayan guaraníes	2.1	1.0
Trinidad and Tobago dollars	7.8	5.7
SDRs	2,977.0	405.4

*Differs from sum of individual figures because of rounding.

STAND-BY AND EXTENDED FACILITY ARRANGEMENTS
(as at 31 December 1983, in thousands of SDRs)

Member	Amount agreed	Undrawn balance
Stand-by arrangements	8,180,500	4,470,460
Argentina	1,500,000	899,490
Barbados	31,875	7,800
Central African Republic	18,000	13,500
Chile	500,000	216,000
Ecuador	157,500	39,375
Ghana	238,500	95,400
Guatemala	114,750	76,500
Haiti	60,000	53,000
Hungary	475,000	—
Kenya	175,950	46,150
Liberia	55,000	27,000
Mali	40,500	30,500
Mauritius	49,500	24,750
Morocco	300,000	270,000
Niger	18,000	11,200
Panama	150,000	100,000
Philippines	315,000	215,000
Portugal	445,000	348,250
Republic of Korea	575,775	383,775
Romania	1,102,500	468,600
Samoa	3,375	1,685
Senegal	63,000	31,500
Solomon Islands	2,400	1,440
Somalia	60,000	—
Sri Lanka	100,000	70,000
Sudan	170,000	25,500
Togo	21,375	1,995
Turkey	225,000	168,750
Uganda	95,000	51,000
Uruguay	378,000	226,800
Zaire	228,000	228,000
Zambia	211,500	135,000
Zimbabwe	300,000	202,500
Extended arrangements	14,755,500	7,948,731
Brazil	4,239,375	2,992,500
Dominica	8,550	476
Dominican Republic	371,250	247,500
Grenada	13,500	12,375
India	5,000,000	1,700,000
Ivory Coast	484,500	38,475
Jamaica	477,700	74,900
Malawi	100,000	90,000
Mexico	3,410,625	2,407,505
Peru	650,000	385,000
Total	22,936,000	12,419,191

Annex I. MEMBERSHIP OF THE INTERNATIONAL MONETARY FUND, QUOTAS AND VOTING POWER
(As at 1 February 1984)

MEMBER	QUOTA Amount (in millions of SDRs)	QUOTA General and SDR Departments percentage of total*	VOTING POWER Number of votes†	VOTING POWER General and SDR Departments percentage of total
Afghanistan	86.70	0.10	1,117	0.12
Algeria	623.10	0.70	6,481	0.70
Antigua and Barbuda	5.00	0.01	300	0.03
Argentina	1,113.00	1.26	11,380	1.23
Australia	1,619.20	1.83	16,442	1.78
Austria	775.60	0.88	8,006	0.87
Bahamas	66.40	0.08	914	0.10
Bahrain	48.90	0.06	739	0.08
Bangladesh	287.50	0.32	3,125	0.34
Barbados	34.10	0.04	591	0.06
Belgium	2,080.40	2.35	21,054	2.28
Belize	9.50	0.01	345	0.04
Benin	31.30	0.04	563	0.06
Bhutan	2.50	0.002	275	0.03
Bolivia	90.70	0.10	1,157	0.13
Botswana	22.10	0.02	471	0.05
Brazil	1,461.30	1.65	14,863	1.61
Burma	137.00	0.15	1,620	0.18
Burundi	42.70	0.05	677	0.07
Canada	2,941.00	3.32	29,660	3.22
Cape Verde	4.50	0.01	295	0.03
Central African Republic	30.40	0.03	554	0.06
Chad	30.60	0.03	556	0.06
Chile	440.50	0.50	4,655	0.51
China	2,390.90	2.70	24,159	2.62
Colombia	394.20	0.45	4,192	0.45
Comoros	3.50	0.003	285	0.03
Congo	37.30	0.04	623	0.07
Costa Rica	84.10	0.10	1,091	0.12
Cyprus	69.70	0.08	947	0.10
Democratic Kampuchea	25.00	0.03	500	0.05
Democratic Yemen	77.20	0.09	1,022	0.11
Denmark	711.00	0.80	7,360	0.80
Djibouti	5.70	0.01	307	0.03
Dominica	4.00	0.004	290	0.03
Dominican Republic	112.10	0.13	1,371	0.15
Ecuador	150.70	0.17	1,757	0.19
Egypt	463.40	0.52	4,884	0.53
El Salvador	89.00	0.10	1,140	0.12
Equatorial Guinea	18.40	0.02	434	0.05
Ethiopia	70.60	0.08	956	0.10
Fiji	36.50	0.04	615	0.07
Finland	574.90	0.65	5,999	0.65
France	4,482.80	5.06	45,078	4.89
Gabon	73.10	0.08	981	0.11
Gambia	17.10	0.02	421	0.05
Germany, Federal Republic of	5,403.70	6.10	54,287	5.89
Ghana	204.50	0.23	2,295	0.25
Greece	399.90	0.45	4,249	0.46
Grenada	6.00	0.01	310	0.03
Guatemala	108.00	0.12	1,330	0.14
Guinea	57.90	0.07	829	0.09
Guinea-Bissau	7.50	0.01	325	0.04
Guyana	49.20	0.06	742	0.08
Haiti	44.10	0.05	691	0.07
Honduras	67.80	0.08	928	0.10
Hungary	530.70	0.60	5,557	0.60
Iceland	59.60	0.07	846	0.09
India	2,207.70	2.49	22,327	2.42
Indonesia	1,009.70	1.14	10,347	1.12
Iran	660.00	0.75	6,850	0.74
Iraq	234.10	0.26	2,591	0.28
Ireland	343.40	0.39	3,684	0.40
Israel	446.60	0.50	4,716	0.51
Italy	2,909.10	3.29	29,341	3.18
Ivory Coast	165.50	0.19	1,905	0.21
Jamaica	111.00	0.13	1,360	0.15
Japan	4,223.30	4.77	42,483	4.61
Jordan	73.90	0.08	989	0.11
Kenya	142.00	0.16	1,670	0.18
Kuwait	635.30	0.72	6,603	0.72
Lao People's Democratic Republic	24.00	0.03	490	0.05
Lebanon	78.70	0.09	1,037	0.11
Lesotho	15.10	0.02	401	0.04
Liberia	71.30	0.08	963	0.10
Libyan Arab Jamahiriya	298.40	0.34	3,234	0.35
Luxembourg	77.00	0.09	1,020	0.11
Madagascar	66.40	0.08	914	0.10
Malawi	37.20	0.04	622	0.07
Malaysia	550.60	0.62	5,756	0.62
Maldives	2.00	0.002	270	0.03
Mali	50.80	0.06	758	0.08
Malta	45.10	0.05	701	0.08
Mauritania	33.90	0.04	589	0.06
Mauritius	53.60	0.06	786	0.09
Mexico	1,165.50	1.32	11,905	1.29
Morocco	306.60	0.35	3,316	0.36
Nepal	37.30	0.04	623	0.07
Netherlands	2,264.80	2.56	22,898	2.48
New Zealand	461.60	0.52	4,866	0.53
Nicaragua	51.00	0.06	760	0.08
Niger	33.70	0.04	587	0.06
Nigeria	849.50	0.96	8,745	0.95
Norway	699.00	0.79	7,240	0.79
Oman	63.10	0.07	881	0.10
Pakistan	546.30	0.62	5,713	0.62
Panama	102.20	0.12	1,272	0.14
Papua New Guinea	65.90	0.07	909	0.10
Paraguay	48.40	0.05	734	0.08
Peru	246.00	0.28	2,710	0.29
Philippines	440.40	0.50	4,654	0.50
Portugal	376.60	0.43	4,016	0.44
Qatar	114.90	0.13	1,399	0.15
Republic of Korea	462.80	0.52	4,878	0.53
Romania	523.40	0.59	5,484	0.60
Rwanda	43.80	0.05	688	0.07
Saint Lucia	7.50	0.01	325	0.04
Saint Vincent and the Grenadines	4.00	0.004	290	0.03
Samoa	6.00	0.01	310	0.03
Sao Tome and Principe	3.00	0.003	280	0.03
Saudi Arabia	3,202.40	3.62	32,274	3.50
Senegal	85.10	0.10	1,101	0.12
Seychelles	3.00	0.003	280	0.03
Sierra Leone	57.90	0.07	829	0.09
Singapore	92.40	0.10	1,174	0.13
Solomon Islands	5.00	0.01	300	0.03
Somalia	44.20	0.05	692	0.08
South Africa	915.70	1.03	9,407	1.02
Spain	1,286.00	1.45	13,110	1.42
Sri Lanka	223.10	0.25	2,481	0.27
Sudan	169.70	0.19	1,947	0.21
Suriname	49.30	0.06	743	0.08
Swaziland	24.70	0.03	497	0.05
Sweden	1,064.30	1.20	10,893	1.18
Syrian Arab Republic	94.50	0.11	1,195	0.13
Thailand	386.60	0.44	4,116	0.45
Togo	38.40	0.04	634	0.07
Trinidad and Tobago	170.10	0.19	1,951	0.21
Tunisia	138.20	0.16	1,632	0.18
Turkey	429.10	0.48	4,541	0.49
Uganda	99.60	0.11	1,246	0.14
United Arab Emirates	202.60	0.23	2,276	0.25
United Kingdom	6,194.00	7.00	62,190	6.75
United Republic of Cameroon	92.70	0.10	1,177	0.13
United Republic of Tanzania	107.00	0.12	1,320	0.14
United States	17,918.30	20.24	179,433	19.47
Upper Volta	31.60	0.04	566	0.06
Uruguay	163.80	0.19	1,888	0.20
Vanuatu	9.00	0.01	340	0.04

MEMBER	QUOTA		VOTING POWER		MEMBER	QUOTA		VOTING POWER	
	Amount (in millions of SDRs)	General and SDR Departments percentage of total*	Number of votes†	General and SDR Departments percentage of total		Amount (in millions of SDRs)	General and SDR Departments percentage of total*	Number of votes†	General and SDR Departments percentage of total
Venezuela	1,371.50	1.55	13,965	1.52	Zaire	291.00	0.33	3,160	0.34
Viet Nam	176.80	0.20	2,018	0.22	Zambia	270.30	0.31	2,953	0.32
Yemen	43.30	0.05	683	0.07	Zimbabwe	150.00	0.17	1,750	0.19
Yugoslavia	613.00	0.69	6,380	0.69	Total	88,517.30	100.00‡	921,673	100.00‡

*All members were participants in the SDR Department.

†Voting power varies on certain matters pertaining to the General Department with use of the Fund's resources in that Department, which comprised four accounts: the General Resources Account, the Borrowed Resources Suspense Account, the Special Disbursement Account and the Investment Account.

‡May differ from the sum of the individual percentages because of rounding.

Annex II. EXECUTIVE DIRECTORS AND ALTERNATES OF THE INTERNATIONAL MONETARY FUND
(As at 31 December 1983)

Appointed Director	*Appointed Alternate*	*Casting the vote of*
Richard D. Erb	Mary K. Bush	United States
Nigel L. Wicks	T. A. Clark	United Kingdom
Gerhard Laske	Guenter Grosche	Federal Republic of Germany
Bruno de Maulde	Xavier Blandin	France
Teruo Hirao	Tadaie Yamashita	Japan
Yusuf A. Nimatallah	Jobarah E. Suraisry	Saudi Arabia

Elected Director	*Elected Alternate*	*Casting the votes of*
Miguel A. Senior (Venezuela)	José L. Feito (Spain)	Costa Rica, El Salvador, Guatemala, Honduras, Mexico, Nicaragua, Spain, Venezuela
J. J. Polak (Netherlands)	Tom de Vries (Netherlands)	Cyprus, Israel, Netherlands, Romania, Yugoslavia
Jacques de Groote (Belgium)	Heinrich G. Schneider (Austria)	Austria, Belgium, Hungary, Luxembourg, Turkey
Giovanni Lovato (Italy)	Costa P. Caranicas (Greece)	Greece, Italy, Malta, Portugal
Robert K. Joyce (Canada)	Luke Leonard (Ireland)	Antigua and Barbuda, Bahamas, Barbados, Belize, Canada, Dominica, Grenada, Ireland, Jamaica, Saint Lucia, Saint Vincent and the Grenadines
A. R. G. Prowse (Australia)	Kerry G. Morrell (New Zealand)	Australia, New Zealand, Papua New Guinea, Philippines, Republic of Korea, Samoa, Seychelles, Solomon Islands, Vanuatu
John Tvedt (Norway)	Arne Linda (Sweden)	Denmark, Finland, Iceland, Norway, Sweden
Mohamed Finaish (Libyan Arab Jamahiriya)	Tariq Alhaimus (Iraq)	Bahrain, Democratic Yemen, Iraq, Jordan, Kuwait, Lebanon, Libyan Arab Jamahiriya, Maldives, Oman, Pakistan, Qatar, Somalia, Syrian Arab Republic, United Arab Emirates, Yemen
R. N. Malhotra (India)	A. S. Jayawardena (Sri Lanka)	Bangladesh, Bhutan, India, Sri Lanka
Alexandre Kafka (Brazil)	César Robalino (Ecuador)	Brazil, Colombia, Dominican Republic, Ecuador, Guyana, Haiti, Panama, Suriname, Trinidad and Tobago
J. E. Ismael (Indonesia)	Jaafar Ahmad (Malaysia)	Burma, Fiji, Indonesia, Lao People's Democratic Republic, Malaysia, Nepal, Singapore, Thailand, Viet Nam
N'Faly Sangare (Guinea)	E. I. M. Mtei (United Republic of Tanzania)	Botswana, Burundi, Ethiopia, Gambia, Guinea, Kenya, Lesotho, Liberia, Malawi, Nigeria, Sierra Leone, Sudan, Swaziland, Uganda, United Republic of Tanzania, Zambia, Zimbabwe
Zhang Zicun (China)	Wang Enshao (China)	China
Alvaro Donoso (Chile)	Mario Teijeiro (Argentina)	Argentina, Bolivia, Chile, Paraguay, Peru, Uruguay
Ghassem Salehkhou (Iran)	Omar Kabbaj (Morocco)	Afghanistan, Algeria, Ghana, Iran, Morocco, Tunisia
Abderrahmane Alfidja (Niger)	wa Bilenga Tshishimbi (Zaire)	Benin, Cape Verde, Central African Republic, Chad, Comoros, Congo, Djibouti, Equatorial Guinea, Gabon, Guinea-Bissau, Ivory Coast, Madagascar, Mali, Mauritania, Mauritius, Niger, Rwanda, Sao Tome and Principe, Senegal, Togo, United Republic of Cameroon, Upper Volta, Zaire

NOTE: Democratic Kampuchea, Egypt and South Africa did not participate in the 1982 regular election of Executive Directors.

Annex III. PRINCIPAL OFFICERS AND OFFICES OF THE INTERNATIONAL MONETARY FUND
(As at 31 December 1983)

PRINCIPAL OFFICERS

Managing Director: Jacques de Larosière.
Deputy Managing Director: William B. Dale.
Counsellor: Walter O. Habermeier.*
Economic Counsellor: William C. Hood.*
Counsellor: L. A. Whittome.*
Director, Administration Department: Roland Tenconi.
Director, African Department: J. B. Zulu.
Director, Asian Department: Tun Thin.
Director, Central Banking Department: P. N. Kaul.
Director, European Department: L. A. Whittome.
Director, Exchange and Trade Relations Department: C. David Finch.
Director, External Relations Department: Azizali F. Mohammed.
Director, Fiscal Affairs Department: Vito Tanzi.

Director, IMF Institute: Gérard M. Teyssier.
Director, Legal Department: George Nicoletopoulos.
Director, Middle Eastern Department: A. Shakour Shaalan.
Director, Research Department: William C. Hood.
Secretary, Secretary's Department: Leo Van Houtven.
Treasurer, Treasurer's Department: Walter O. Habermeier.
Director, Western Hemisphere Department: Eduardo Wiesner.
Director, Bureau of Computing Services: Warren N. Minami.
Director, Bureau of Language Services: Andrew J. Beith.
Director, Bureau of Statistics: Werner Dannemann.
Director, Office in Europe (Paris): Aldo Guetta.
Director, Office in Geneva: Carlos A. Sansón.
Internal Auditor: Peter A. Whipple.
Special Representative to the United Nations: Jan-Maarten Zegers.

*Alphabetical listing.

HEADQUARTERS AND OTHER OFFICES

HEADQUARTERS

International Monetary Fund
700 19th Street N. W.
Washington, D. C. 20431, United States
  Cable address: INTERFUND WASHINGTONDC
  Telephone: (202) 477-7000
  Telex: (RCA) 248331 IMF UR, (ITT) 440040 UI,
    (TRT) 197677 FUND UT, (WU) 89524 INTERFUND WSH,
    (WUI) 64111 INTERFUND WSH

OTHER OFFICES

International Monetary Fund
European Office
64-66 Avenue d'Iéna
75116 Paris, France
  Cable address: INTERFUND PARIS
  Telephone: 723-54-21
  Telex: 610712 INTERFUND

International Monetary Fund
58, Rue de Moillebeau
1209 Geneva, Switzerland
  Cable address: INTERFUND GENEVA
  Telephone: 34-30-00
  Telex: 23503 IMF CH

International Monetary Fund Office
United Nations Headquarters, Room DC1-1146
New York, N. Y. 10017, United States
  Telephone: (212) 754-6009

Chapter X

International Civil Aviation Organization (ICAO)

The International Civil Aviation Organization (ICAO) estimated total traffic of the world's scheduled airlines to be close to 146 billion tonne-kilometres during 1983, an increase of almost 6 per cent over 1982. The airlines carried over 780 million passengers at a load factor of 64 per cent, as in 1982. Air freight increased by 10 per cent to some 34 billion tonne-kilometres, the second highest annual increase during the past decade. Airmail traffic amounted to 4 billion tonne-kilometres, an increase of about 4 per cent, close to the average rate of increase in 10 years.

In 1983, in addition to three regular sessions, the ICAO Council—at the request of Canada and the Republic of Korea—held an extraordinary session (15 and 16 September) to consider the destruction of a Korean Air Lines civil aircraft, on 1 September, by USSR military aircraft. The Council directed the ICAO Secretary-General to investigate the incident. The ICAO Assembly, which meets triennially, held its twenty-fourth session at Montreal, Canada, from 20 September to 7 October and referred to the Council for further consideration a Canadian proposal for a convention on the interception of civil aircraft. (For further details, see below, under AIR NAVIGATION and LEGAL MATTERS.)

During 1983, membership of ICAO rose to 152 with the admission of Vanuatu on 16 September and Saint Vincent and the Grenadines on 15 December.

The official opening ceremonies of ICAO's new Eastern African Regional Office took place on 1 December at Nairobi, Kenya.

Activities in 1983

Air navigation

At its 1983 extraordinary session, the ICAO Council requested the Air Navigation Commission to examine ways to improve the co-ordination of communication systems between aircraft and air traffic control services and to improve procedures in cases involving identification and interception of civil aircraft, and to consider possible amendments to the Convention on International Civil Aviation (Chicago, United States, 1944) to prevent a recurrence of such an incident as that involving the Korean aircraft (see also below, under LEGAL MATTERS).

During 1983, ICAO's efforts in air navigation continued to be directed mainly towards updat-

ing and implementing ICAO Specifications and Regional Plans. The Specifications consisted of International Standards and Recommended Practices contained in 17 technical annexes to the Chicago Convention, and of Procedures for Air Navigation Services (PANS) contained in three PANS documents. Regional Plans set forth air navigation facilities and services required for international air navigation in the nine ICAO regions.

During the year, the Specifications in eight annexes and in two PANS documents were amended. Amendments were also made to Regional Plans.

Eight air navigation meetings were held in 1983. They covered a wide range of subjects and made recommendations for changes to ICAO Specifications; to promote their uniform application, ICAO made available guidance material—new and revised technical manuals and ICAO circulars—to assist States in establishing and maintaining up-to-date and effective aeronautical infrastructures.

ICAO regional offices helped States to implement Regional Plans and experts were sent to advise on installing new facilities and services and on operating existing ones.

Special attention was given to: aircraft airworthiness, operations, noise and accident investigation and prevention; aerodromes; air traffic control; aeronautical charts, communications, information services and meteorology; helicopter operations; personnel licensing and training; search and rescue; aviation medicine and security; and transport of dangerous goods.

Air transport

Concerning air transport during 1983, ICAO continued its programmes of economic studies, collecting and publishing air transport statistics and promoting greater facilitation in international air transport. Air transport meetings convened during the year included three meetings of panels of experts and nine regional workshops.

Panel meetings considered the regulation of international non-scheduled air services (Montreal, March), guidelines on route facility cost accounting and cost allocation (Montreal, June), and international air transport fares and rates (Montreal, November/December). Workshops were held on aviation forecasting and economic planning (Bangkok, Thailand, February; Dakar, Senegal,

November), airport and route facility economics (Rome, Italy, March), international fares and rates (Dakar, January; Lima, Peru, July; Bangkok, November), and statistics (Addis Ababa, Ethiopia, August; Lima, November; Mexico City, November).

ICAO publications in 1983 included a study of air passenger and freight development for Latin America and the Caribbean, the regular series of digests of civil aviation statistics, the yearbook on world civil aviation statistics, the triennial review of the economic situation of air transport covering the period 1972-1982, a manual on the establishment of international air carrier tariffs, a manual of airport and air navigation facility tariffs, two studies, covering 1980 and 1981, of regional differences in fares, rates and costs for international air transport and a survey of international air transport fares and rates in 1982.

ICAO continued to co-operate closely with other international organizations such as the International Air Transport Association, the Airport Associations Co-ordinating Council, the Customs Co-operation Council, the World Tourism Organization and the Universal Postal Union. It also continued to provide secretariat services to three independent regional civil aviation bodies—the African Civil Aviation Commission, the European Civil Aviation Conference and the Latin American Civil Aviation Commission.

Following a 1982 conference to amend a 1956 joint financing agreement for air navigation services in Greenland and the Faeroe Islands, and another for Iceland, the two agreements as amended were provisionally applied from 1 January 1983.

Legal matters

The Legal Committee held its twenty-fifth session at Montreal from 12 to 25 April 1983 to review its general work programme. In the light of a decision of the twenty-third (1980) session of the ICAO Assembly that only problems of sufficient magnitude and practical importance requiring urgent international action should be included, the Committee's work programme contained the following three items: implications of the 1982 United Nations Convention on the Law of the Sea[a] for the application of the Chicago Convention; liability of air traffic control agencies; and study of the legal instruments of the Warsaw System (the 1929 Warsaw Convention for the Unification of Certain Rules relating to International Carriage by Air, as amended by the Protocols of 1955, 1971 and 1975). In connection with the last item, the Committee urged all member States to ratify the Protocols as soon as possible.

The ICAO Council, at its extraordinary session, decided to examine the question of an amendment

to the Chicago Convention involving an undertaking to abstain from recourse to the use of force against civil aircraft, and to convene an extraordinary session of the ICAO Assembly to examine and adopt that amendment. This decision was endorsed by the Assembly and it was decided to hold the session from 24 April to 11 May 1984. By the end of 1983, specific proposals for an amendment were received from Austria and France (joint proposal), the USSR and the United States.

On 9 December, the Council decided to include in the work programme of the Legal Committee an item, proposed by Canada, on the preparation of a draft instrument on the interception of civil aircraft and to accord the item high priority. A sub-committee was to consider the matter from 25 September to 5 October 1984.

The Committee on Unlawful Interference with International Civil Aviation and its Facilities held six meetings during the year. It reviewed proposals of the Air Navigation Commission related to the authority and responsibility of the pilot-in-command.

The following conventions and protocols on international air law concluded under ICAO auspices were ratified, adhered to or denounced during 1983:

Convention on International Civil Aviation (Chicago, 1944)
Saint Vincent and the Grenadines, Vanuatu

International Air Services Transit Agreement of the Convention on International Civil Aviation (Chicago, 1944)
Ecuador

International Air Transport Agreement of the Convention on International Civil Aviation (Chicago, 1944)
Sweden (denunciation)

Convention on Damage Caused by Foreign Aircraft to Third Parties on the Surface (Rome, 1952)
Guatemala

Protocol to Amend the Convention for the Unification of Certain Rules relating to International Carriage by Air signed at Warsaw on 12 October 1929 (The Hague, 1955)
Trinidad and Tobago, Viet Nam, Yemen

Convention, Supplementary to the Warsaw Convention, for the Unification of Certain Rules relating to International Carriage by Air Performed by a Person other than the Contracting Carrier (Guadalajara, 1961)
Byelorussian SSR, Ukrainian SSR, USSR

Convention on Offences and Certain Other Acts Committed on Board Aircraft (Tokyo, 1963)
Democratic People's Republic of Korea, Jamaica, Mauritius, Monaco, Saint Lucia, United Republic of Tanzania, Venezuela

Convention for the Suppression of Unlawful Seizure of Aircraft (The Hague, 1970)
Democratic People's Republic of Korea, Jamaica, Mauritius, Saint Lucia, United Republic of Tanzania, Venezuela

[a]YUN 1982, p. 181.

Protocol to Amend the Convention for the Unification of Certain Rules relating to International Carriage by Air signed at Warsaw on 12 October 1929, as amended by the Protocol done at The Hague on 28 September 1955 (Guatemala City, 1971) (not in force)
Netherlands

Convention for the Suppression of Unlawful Acts against the Safety of Civil Aviation (Montreal, 1971)
Jamaica, Mauritius, Saint Lucia, United Republic of Tanzania

Additional Protocol No. 1 to Amend the Convention for the Unification of Certain Rules relating to International Carriage by Air signed at Warsaw on 12 October 1929 (Montreal, 1975) (not in force)
Denmark, Netherlands, Norway

Additional Protocol No. 2 to Amend the Convention for the Unification of Certain Rules relating to International Carriage by Air signed at Warsaw on 12 October 1929, as amended by the Protocol done at The Hague on 28 September 1955 (Montreal, 1975) (not in force)
Denmark, Netherlands, Norway

Additional Protocol No. 3 to Amend the Convention for the Unification of Certain Rules relating to International Carriage by Air signed at Warsaw on 12 October 1929, as amended by the Protocols done at The Hague on 28 September 1955 and at Guatemala City on 8 March 1971 (Montreal, 1975) (not in force)
Netherlands

Montreal Protocol No. 4 to Amend the Convention for the Unification of Certain Rules relating to International Carriage by Air signed at Warsaw on 12 October 1929, as amended by the Protocol done at The Hague on 28 September 1955 (Montreal, 1975) (not in force)
Netherlands

Technical assistance

During 1983, ICAO provided technical assistance to 99 States; in 58 of these, there were resident missions consisting of one or more experts. In addition to resident expertise, assistance was provided in the form of equipment, fellowships and scholarships and through short missions by experts.

Fifteen new large-scale projects, each costing more than $500,000, for which ICAO was to be the executing agency, were approved by the Administrator of the United Nations Development Programme (UNDP). Three large-scale projects were financed under trust fund assistance.

ICAO employed 626 experts from 51 countries during all or part of 1983, 337 on assignments under UNDP and 301 on trust fund projects (including 18 under the associate experts programme). There were also 28 United Nations Volunteers. The number of experts in the field at the end of 1983 was 373 as compared with 411 at the end of 1982.

A total of 985 fellowships were awarded in 1983 (compared with 1,014 in 1982), of which 945 were implemented.

Equipment purchases and sub-contracts were

a substantial proportion of the technical assistance programme in 1983. Thirty-three Governments or organizations had registered with ICAO under the Civil Aviation Purchasing Service. The total equipment and sub-contracts committed during the year amounted to almost $13 million.

The following countries and territories were aided:

Africa: Angola, Benin, Botswana, Cape Verde, Chad, Equatorial Guinea, Ethiopia, Gabon, Ghana, Guinea, Guinea-Bissau, Ivory Coast, Kenya, Lesotho, Liberia, Madagascar, Malawi, Mali, Mauritania, Mauritius, Mozambique, Niger, Nigeria, Senegal, Seychelles, Sierra Leone, Swaziland, Togo, Uganda, United Republic of Cameroon, United Republic of Tanzania, Upper Volta, Zaire, Zambia, Zimbabwe.

Americas: Argentina, Bahamas, Bolivia, Brazil, Cayman Islands, Chile, Colombia, Ecuador, El Salvador, Guatemala, Haiti, Honduras, Netherlands Antilles, Panama, Peru, Saint Lucia, Suriname, Trinidad and Tobago, Turks and Caicos Islands, Uruguay, Venezuela.

Asia/Pacific: Afghanistan, Bangladesh, Burma, China, Democratic People's Republic of Korea, India, Indonesia, Kiribati, Lao People's Democratic Republic, Malaysia, Maldives, Nepal, Pakistan, Philippines, Republic of Korea, Singapore, Sri Lanka, Thailand, Viet Nam.

Europe, Mediterranean and Middle East: Algeria, Democratic Yemen, Djibouti, Egypt, Greece, Iraq, Jordan, Kuwait, Lebanon, Libyan Arab Jamahiriya, Morocco, Oman, Poland, Qatar, Romania, Saudi Arabia, Somalia, Sudan, Syrian Arab Republic, Turkey, Yemen.

Included in the above were the following, aided during the year under trust fund arrangements: Argentina, Bolivia, Cape Verde, Iraq, Ivory Coast, Jordan, Libyan Arab Jamahiriya, Nigeria, Peru, Qatar, Saudi Arabia, Suriname, Trinidad and Tobago, Venezuela, Yemen.

Secretariat

As at 31 December 1983, the total number of staff members employed in the ICAO secretariat stood at 889: 316 in the Professional and higher categories drawn from 65 nationalities, and 573 in the General Service and related categories. In addition, 208 persons were employed in regional offices and 173 in the Professional category served as technical experts on UNDP projects in the field.

Budget

At its twenty-fourth session, the ICAO Assembly adopted the ICAO budget for 1984, 1985 and 1986. Annual amounts authorized for expenditure were to be financed as follows (in United States dollars):

	1984	1985	1986
By assessments on contracting States	27,090,000	28,362,000	30,124,000
By miscellaneous income	8,105,000	8,555,000	8,983,000
Total	35,195,000	36,917,000	39,107,000

The revised appropriations for the 1983 financial year totalled $32,879,000. Modifications were approved by the ICAO Council and are reflected below (in United States dollars):

	Appropriations	Revised appropriations	Actual obligations
Meetings	530,000	844,000	668,758
Secretariat	21,744,000	26,478,800	26,478,211
General services	3,377,000	4,026,300	4,025,618
Equipment	184,000	359,700	359,606
Other budgetary provisions	126,000	329,000	328,902
Contingencies	5,418,000	805,000	—
Establishment of new regional office	300,000	36,200	—
Total	31,679,000	32,879,000	31,861,095

Annex I. MEMBERSHIP OF THE INTERNATIONAL CIVIL AVIATION ORGANIZATION AND CONTRIBUTIONS

(Membership as at 31 December 1983; contributions as assessed for 1983)

MEMBER	CONTRIBUTION Percentage	CONTRIBUTION Net amount (in US dollars)	MEMBER	CONTRIBUTION Percentage	CONTRIBUTION Net amount (in US dollars)	MEMBER	CONTRIBUTION Percentage	CONTRIBUTION Net amount (in US dollars)
Afghanistan	0.06	14,514	Guatemala	0.06	14,514	Paraguay	0.06	14,514
Algeria	0.15	36,285	Guinea	0.06	14,514	Peru	0.09	21,771
Angola	0.06	14,514	Guinea-Bissau	0.06	14,514	Philippines	0.21	50,799
Antigua and Barbuda	0.06	14,514	Guyana	0.06	14,514	Poland	0.90	217,710
Argentina	0.74	179,006	Haiti	0.06	14,514	Portugal	0.30	72,570
Australia	1.94	469,286	Honduras	0.06	14,514	Qatar	0.06	14,514
Austria	0.56	135,464	Hungary	0.27	65,313	Republic of Korea	0.50	120,950
Bahamas	0.06	14,514	Iceland	0.08	19,352	Romania	0.21	50,799
Bahrain	0.06	14,514	India	0.65	157,235	Rwanda	0.06	14,514
Bangladesh	0.06	14,514	Indonesia	0.24	58,056	Saint Lucia	0.06	14,514
Barbados	0.06	14,514	Iran	0.63	152,397	Saint Vincent and the Grenadines*	—	—
Belgium	1.15	278,185	Iraq	0.17	41,123	Sao Tome and Principe	0.06	14,514
Benin	0.06	14,514	Ireland	0.19	45,961	Saudi Arabia	0.50	120,950
Bolivia	0.06	14,514	Israel	0.37	89,503	Senegal	0.06	14,514
Botswana	0.06	14,514	Italy	3.02	730,538	Seychelles	0.06	14,514
Brazil	1.38	333,822	Ivory Coast	0.06	14,514	Sierra Leone	0.06	14,514
Bulgaria	0.14	33,866	Jamaica	0.07	16,933	Singapore	0.46	111,274
Burma	0.06	14,514	Japan	8.31	2,010,189	Somalia	0.06	14,514
Burundi	0.06	14,514	Jordan	0.09	21,771	South Africa	0.52	125,788
Canada	3.25	786,175	Kenya	0.06	14,514	Spain	1.88	454,772
Cape Verde	0.06	14,514	Kiribati	0.06	14,514	Sri Lanka	0.06	14,514
Central African Republic	0.06	14,514	Kuwait	0.23	55,637	Sudan	0.06	14,514
Chad	0.06	14,514	Lao People's Democratic Republic	0.06	14,514	Suriname	0.06	14,514
Chile	0.12	29,028	Lebanon	0.25	60,475	Swaziland	0.06	14,514
China	0.74	179,006	Lesotho	0.06	14,514	Sweden	1.16	280,604
Colombia	0.21	50,799	Liberia	0.06	14,514	Switzerland	1.22	295,118
Congo	0.06	14,514	Libyan Arab Jamahiriya	0.20	48,380	Syrian Arab Republic	0.07	16,933
Costa Rica	0.06	14,514	Luxembourg	0.06	14,514	Thailand	0.22	53,218
Cuba	0.11	26,609	Madagascar	0.06	14,514	Togo	0.06	14,514
Cyprus	0.06	14,514	Malawi	0.06	14,514	Trinidad and Tobago	0.06	14,514
Czechoslovakia	0.64	154,816	Malaysia	0.14	33,866	Tunisia	0.06	14,514
Democratic Kampuchea	0.06	14,514	Maldives	0.06	14,514	Turkey	0.30	72,570
Democratic People's Republic of Korea	0.06	14,514	Mali	0.06	14,514	Uganda	0.06	14,514
Democratic Yemen	0.06	14,514	Malta	0.06	14,514	USSR	10.85	2,624,615
Denmark	0.67	162,073	Mauritania	0.06	14,514	United Arab Emirates	0.10	24,190
Djibouti	0.06	14,514	Mauritius	0.06	14,514	United Kingdom	4.96	1,199,824
Dominican Republic	0.06	14,514	Mexico	0.77	186,263	United Republic of Cameroon	0.06	14,514
Ecuador	0.06	14,514	Monaco	0.06	14,514	United Republic of Tanzania	0.06	14,514
Egypt	0.16	38,704	Morocco	0.12	29,028	United States	25.00	6,047,500
El Salvador	0.06	14,514	Mozambique	0.06	14,514	Upper Volta	0.06	14,514
Equatorial Guinea	0.06	14,514	Nauru	0.06	14,514	Uruguay	0.06	14,514
Ethiopia	0.06	14,514	Nepal	0.06	14,514	Vanuatu	0.06	3,629
Fiji	0.06	14,514	Netherlands	1.85	447,515	Venezuela	0.55	133,045
Finland	0.42	101,598	New Zealand	0.37	89,503	Viet Nam	0.06	14,514
France	5.86	1,417,534	Nicaragua	0.06	14,514	Yemen	0.06	14,514
Gabon	0.06	14,514	Niger	0.06	14,514	Yugoslavia	0.41	99,179
Gambia	0.06	14,514	Nigeria	0.15	36,285	Zaire	0.06	14,514
Germany, Federal Republic of	6.95	1,681,205	Norway	0.50	120,950	Zambia	0.06	14,514
Ghana	0.06	14,514	Oman	0.06	14,514	Zimbabwe	0.06	14,514
Greece	0.48	116,112	Pakistan	0.27	65,313			
Grenada	0.06	14,514	Panama	0.06	14,514	Total†	100.30	24,251,685
			Papua New Guinea	0.06	14,514			

*Saint Vincent and the Grenadines became a contracting State of ICAO on 15 December 1983.

†Includes assessments for Antigua and Barbuda, Grenada, Kiribati, Vanuatu and Zimbabwe, which became contracting States after current assessment rates were set.

Annex II.   OFFICERS AND OFFICES OF THE INTERNATIONAL CIVIL AVIATION ORGANIZATION

(As at 31 December 1983)

ICAO COUNCIL

OFFICERS

President: Assad Kotaite (Lebanon).
First Vice-President: G. B. Morris (Jamaica).
Second Vice-President: A. Sciolla-Lagrange (Italy).
Third Vice-President: A. Djunaedi (Indonesia).
Secretary: Yves Lambert (France).

MEMBERS

Algeria, Argentina, Australia, Belgium, Brazil, Canada, China, Colombia, Czechos-lovakia, Egypt, France, Germany, Federal Republic of, Guatemala, India, Indo-nesia, Iraq, Italy, Jamaica, Japan, Kenya, Lebanon, Madagascar, Mexico, Nigeria, Norway, Pakistan, Senegal, Spain, USSR, United Kingdom, United Republic of Tanzania, United States, Venezuela.

PRINCIPAL OFFICERS OF THE SECRETARIAT

Secretary-General: Yves Lambert.
Director, Air Navigation Bureau: D. W. Freer.
Director, Air Transport Bureau: R. A. Bickley.

Director, Legal Bureau: B. S. Gidwani.
Director, Technical Assistance Bureau: M. J. Challons.
Chief, Public Information Office: Eugene Sochor.

OFFICES

HEADQUARTERS

International Civil Aviation Organization
1000 Sherbrooke Street West, Suite 400
Montreal, Quebec, Canada H3A 2R2
   Cable address: ICAO MONTREAL
   Telephone: (514) 285-8219
   Telex: 05-24513

REGIONAL OFFICES

International Civil Aviation Organization
African Office
Boîte Postale 2356
Dakar, Senegal
   Cable address: ICAOREP DAKAR
   Telephone: 21-42-13, 22-47-86
   Telex: 3348 ICAO/SG

International Civil Aviation Organization
North American and Caribbean Office
Apartado Postal 5-377
Mexico 5, D. F., Mexico
   Cable address: ICAOREP MEXICO
   Telephone: 250-32-11
   Telex: 1777598 ICAO ME

International Civil Aviation Organization
South American Office
Apartado 4127
Lima 100, Peru
   Cable address: ICAOREP LIMA
   Telephone: 51-5414, 51-5325, 51-5497
   Telex: 25689 PE ICAO

International Civil Aviation Organization
European Office
3 bis, Villa Emile-Bergerat
92522 Neuilly-sur-Seine (Cedex)
France
   Cable address: ICAOREP PARIS
   Telephone: 745-13-26
   Telex: 610075 ECAC NLLSN

International Civil Aviation Organization
Asia and Pacific Office
P. O. Box 614
Bangkok, Thailand
   Cable address: ICAOREP BANGKOK
   Telephone: 281-5366, 281-5571, 281-0138
   Telex: 87969 ICAOBKK TH

International Civil Aviation Organization
Middle East Office
16 Hassan Sabri
Zamalek
Cairo, Egypt
   Cable address: ICAOREP CAIRO
   Telephone: 698163, 698344, 698463, 698532
   Telex: 92459 ICAOR UN

International Civil Aviation Organization
Eastern African Office
P. O. Box 46 294
Nairobi, Kenya
   Cable address: ICAOREP NAIROBI
   Telephone: 333 930
   Telex: 22068 UNITERRA (FOR ICAO)

Chapter XI

Universal Postal Union (UPU)

The Universal Postal Union (UPU), established at Berne, Switzerland, in 1874 for the reciprocal exchange of postal services between nations, is one of the oldest international intergovernmental organizations. Its aim is to promote the organization and improvement of postal services and to further the development of international collaboration in this sphere. It also participates in various forms of postal technical assistance requested by its member States.

In 1983, the membership of UPU remained unchanged at 166.

Activities of UPU organs

Universal Postal Congress

The Universal Postal Congress, composed of all member States, is the supreme legislative authority of UPU. The Congress, which normally meets every five years, met most recently at Rio de Janeiro, Brazil, in 1979; the next (the nineteenth) was due to be held at Hamburg, Federal Republic of Germany, in 1984. The work of the Congress consists mainly of examining and revising the Acts of the Union based on proposals submitted by member States, the Executive Council or the Consultative Council for Postal Studies, and of making administrative arrangements for UPU activities. The Acts in force since 1 July 1981 were those of the 1979 Congress.

Executive Council

The 40-member Executive Council, which carries out the work of UPU between sessions of the Congress, held its annual session at Berne from 28 April to 13 May 1983. It considered administrative matters and examined studies concerning international mail referred to it by the 1979 Congress.

Among questions examined by the Council in 1983 were: technical assistance for developing countries; relations with the United Nations and other international organizations and with restricted postal unions; the organization, functioning and work methods of the Congress and Executive Council, including the delimitation of powers between the Council and the Consultative Council for Postal Studies; UPU finances; international high-speed mail (Datapost, Express Mail, Postadex, etc.); measures to ease payment of international accounts; customs treatment of postal items; calculation of basic airmail conveyance rates; maximizing air conveyance of mail; the situation of the international parcel-post service in UPU member countries; the development of postal financial services; and preparations for the 1984 Congress.

The Council approved measures taken or envisaged by the International Bureau of UPU in connection with the observance of 1983 as World Communications Year: Development of Communications Infrastructures, proclaimed by the General Assembly in 1981[a] (see below and ECONOMIC AND SOCIAL QUESTIONS, Chapter V), and took note of activities planned by postal administrations for that occasion.

Consultative Council for Postal Studies

The 35-member Consultative Council for Postal Studies continued studying problems in the technical, operational and economic fields and technical co-operation problems of interest to the postal administrations of UPU member States, including matters of particular interest to new and developing countries.

During its annual meeting held at Berne from 10 to 21 October 1983, the Council took note of progress made in studies undertaken by its committees and finalized its draft work programme for 1984-1989, to be submitted to the 1984 Congress. Two colloquia were held during the Council's session—one on the future of the postal services and the other on the promotion of savings banks in developing countries.

International Bureau

The Berne-based International Bureau, the secretariat of UPU, continued to serve the postal administrations of UPU member States as an organ for liaison, information and consultation. The Bureau's responsibilities included collecting, co-ordinating, publishing and distributing information of interest to the international postal service. At the request of postal administrations, it also conducted inquiries and acted as a clearing-house for settling certain accounts betweeen them.

With regard to the 1983 World Communications Year, the Bureau provided postal administrations with information and materials concern-

[a]YUN 1981, p. 573, GA res. 36/40, 19 Nov. 1981.

ing the Year and invited them to apply the programme of activities prepared for that purpose, including measures, such as issuing postage stamps, to make the public aware of the Year's objectives.

As at 31 December 1983, the total number of permanent and temporary staff members employed at the Bureau was 138, of whom 57 were in the Professional and higher categories (drawn from 48 countries) and 81 were in the General Service category. Also, 14 officials were employed in the Arabic, English, Portugese, Russian and Spanish translation services.

Technical co-operation

In 1983, technical co-operation provided by UPU was financed for the most part by the United Nations Development Programme (UNDP); UNDP/UPU project expenditures amounted to some $1.6 million.

The Union furnished complementary assistance from its own resources: the UPU Special Fund, financed by voluntary contributions from member States in cash and kind, and the UPU regular budget. Total expenditures from these two sources in 1983 amounted to approximately $998,000. In addition, postal administrations provided assistance on a bilateral basis.

Training of postal instructors continued to be given priority with training courses held in France and the United Kingdom, as well as at regional training centres; four interregional courses were organized in developing countries (Angola, Ivory Coast, Kenya, Malawi).

During the year, 46 national and regional projects relating to postal services were carried out under UNDP auspices. Forty-nine expert missions were undertaken and 134 scholarships were awarded, two thirds of which were for students to participate in study courses or tours. Several projects received assistance in the form of equipment. Projects dealt with all main branches of the postal service, including national or regional vocational training centres.

The UPU Special Fund and regular budget funded various projects such as expert missions, training scholarships, instruction materials and equipment, and also financed individual expert missions and scholarships. During 1983, 48 consultants, four of whom were financed by the United Nations Educational, Scientific and Cultural Organization and two by the World Bank, carried out technical missions in 41 postal administrations. Also, 164 fellowships were granted, most of which were used to attend courses, study cycles, seminars and technical meetings.

In addition, the Special Fund programme included a contribution by Belgium to continue a project to assist the drought-stricken Sahelian region of Africa. Several countries also offered contributions in kind within the framework of the Special Fund, mainly in the form of scholarships and the organization of workshops.

UPU continued its programme of technical assistance subject to payment, by which member States could finance assistance themselves by funds on deposit. It also continued its efforts to promote technical co-operation among developing countries, particularly by furnishing assistance to regional training centres.

Budget

The 1983 financial year was the third year of UPU's self-financing system introduced by the 1979 Universal Postal Congress, by which contributions were payable in advance on the basis of the following year's budget. At its April/May 1983 session, the Executive Council approved a budget of 23,451,200 Swiss francs for 1984 (see table).

Income	Amount (in Swiss francs)
Contributions from member States	18,637,500
Taken from reserve funds	2,905,000
Contribution allocated by UNDP for support of technical co-operation projects	963,000
Sale of publications	210,500
Other	735,200
Total	23,451,200*

Expenditure	
Staff	16,953,100
General expenses	4,641,500
Expenditure relating to the nineteenth Congress	1,856,600
Total	23,451,200*

*Equal to $10,757,431 on the basis of 2.18 Swiss francs = $US 1.00.

Each member State of UPU chooses its class of contribution, on a scale of 1 to 50 units. For 1984, the Executive Council fixed the amount of the contributory unit at 17,500 Swiss francs on the basis of a total of 1,065 units. The following table gives assessments in Swiss francs by class of contribution:

	ASSESSMENTS	
CLASS OF CONTRIBUTION	Swiss francs	US dollar equivalents*
50 units	875,000	401,376
25 units	437,500	200,688
20 units	350,000	160,550
15 units	262,500	120,413
10 units	175,000	80,275
5 units	87,500	40,138
3 units	52,500	24,083
1 unit	17,500	8,028

*Calculated on the basis of 2.18 Swiss francs = $US $1.00.

Annex I.   MEMBERSHIP OF THE UNIVERSAL POSTAL UNION AND CLASS OF CONTRIBUTION

(Membership as at 31 December 1983; contributions as assessed for 1984)

Member	Class of contribution;* no. of units	Member	Class of contribution;* no. of units	Member	Class of contribution;* no. of units	Member	Class of contribution;* no. of units	Member	Class of contribution;* no. of units	Member	Class of contribution;* no. of units
Afghanistan	1	Congo	1	Germany,		Libyan Arab		Peru	3	Togo	1
Albania	1	Costa Rica	1	Federal		Jamahiriya	5	Philippines	1	Tonga	1
Algeria	5	Cuba	3	Republic of	50	Liechtenstein	1	Poland	10	Trinidad and	
Angola	1	Cyprus	1	Ghana	3	Luxembourg	3	Portugal	5	Tobago	1
Argentina	20	Czecho-		Greece	3	Madagascar	3	Qatar	5	Tunisia	5
Australia	25	slovakia	10	Grenada	1	Malawi	1	Republic of		Turkey	5
Austria	5	Democratic		Guatemala	3	Malaysia	3	Korea	1	Tuvalu	1
Bahamas	1	Kampuchea	1	Guinea	1	Maldives	1	Romania	5	Uganda	1
Bahrain	1	Democratic		Guinea-Bissau	1	Mali	1	Rwanda	1	Ukrainian SSR	10
Bangladesh	15	People's		Guyana	1	Malta	1	Saint Lucia	1	USSR	25
Barbados	1	Republic		Haiti	3	Mauritania	1	Saint Vincent		United Arab	
Belgium	15	of Korea	5	Honduras	1	Mauritius	1	and the		Emirates	1
Belize	1	Democratic		Hungary	10	Mexico	15	Grenadines	1	United	
Benin	1	Yemen	1	Iceland	1	Monaco	1	San Marino	1	Kingdom	50
Bhutan	1	Denmark	10	India	25	Mongolia	1	Sao Tome		United Kingdom	
Bolivia	1	Djibouti	1	Indonesia	10	Morocco	5	and Principe	1	Overseas	
Botswana	1	Dominica	1	Iran	5	Mozambique	1	Saudi Arabia	25	Territories	5
Brazil	25	Dominican		Iraq	5	Nauru	1	Senegal	1	United Republic	
Bulgaria	3	Republic	3	Ireland	10	Nepal	3	Seychelles	1	of Cameroon	1
Burma	3	Ecuador	3	Israel	3	Netherlands	15	Sierra Leone	1	United Republic	
Burundi	1	Egypt	15	Italy	25	Netherlands		Singapore	1	of Tanzania	1
Byelorussian		El Salvador	1	Ivory Coast	3	Antilles	1	Somalia	1	United States	50
SSR	3	Equatorial		Jamaica	1	New Zealand	20	South Africa	1	Upper Volta	1
Canada	50	Guinea	3	Japan	50	Nicaragua	1	Spain	25	Uruguay	3
Cape Verde	1	Ethiopia	1	Jordan	1	Niger	1	Sri Lanka	5	Vanuatu	1
Central		Fiji	1	Kenya	3	Nigeria	10	Sudan	1	Vatican	1
African		Finland	10	Kuwait	10	Norway	10	Suriname	1	Venezuela	3
Republic	1	France	50	Lao People's		Oman	1	Swaziland	1	Viet Nam	1
Chad	1	Gabon	1	Democratic		Pakistan	15	Sweden	15	Yemen	1
Chile	5	Gambia	1	Republic	1	Panama	1	Switzerland	15	Yugoslavia	5
China	50	German		Lebanon	1	Papua New		Syrian Arab		Zaire	3
Colombia	3	Democratic		Lesotho	1	Guinea	1	Republic	1	Zambia	3
Comoros	1	Republic	15	Liberia	1	Paraguay	1	Thailand	3	Zimbabwe	3

NOTE: The UPU official nomenclature differs from that of the United Nations.

*For amount of contributions from members, see table under BUDGET above.

ANNEX II.   ORGANS, OFFICERS AND OFFICE OF THE UNIVERSAL POSTAL UNION

EXECUTIVE COUNCIL

(Elected to hold office until the nineteenth (1984) Universal Postal Congress)

Chairman: Brazil.
Vice-Chairmen: China, Liberia, Spain, USSR.
Secretary-General: Mohamed I. Sobhi, Director-General of the International Bureau.
Members: Algeria, Argentina, Bangladesh, Barbados, Brazil, Canada, Chile, China, Cuba, Czechoslovakia, Denmark, Egypt, France, Gabon, Germany, Federal Republic of, Guinea, Honduras, India, Iraq, Ireland, Ivory Coast, Jordan, Kenya, Liberia, Libyan Arab Jamahiriya, Malaysia, Mali, Mexico, Mongolia, Saudi Arabia, Senegal, Spain, Sri Lanka, Sudan, Syrian Arab Republic, Thailand, USSR, United Kingdom, United States, Yugoslavia.

CONSULTATIVE COUNCIL FOR POSTAL STUDIES

(Elected to hold office until the nineteenth (1984) Universal Postal Congress)

Chairman: United Kingdom.
Vice-Chairman: Tunisia.
Secretary-General: Mohamed I. Sobhi, Director-General of the International Bureau.
Members: Algeria, Argentina, Australia, Austria, Bangladesh, Belgium, Brazil, China, Colombia, Egypt, France, German Democratic Republic, Germany, Federal Republic of, India, Indonesia, Iraq, Italy, Japan, Mexico, Morocco, Netherlands, New Zealand, Nigeria, Pakistan, Poland, Romania, Spain, Sweden, Switzerland, Thailand, Tunisia, USSR, United Kingdom, United Republic of Cameroon, United States.

INTERNATIONAL BUREAU

OFFICERS

Director-General: Mohamed I. Sobhi.
Deputy Director-General a.i.: Félix Cicéron.
Assistant Directors-General: Félix Cicéron, Abdel Kader Baghdadi, El Mostafa Gharbi.
Assistant Director-General a.i.: Sven Backström.

HEADQUARTERS

Bureau international de l'Union postale universelle
Weltpoststrasse 4
Berne, Switzerland
  Postal address: Union postale universelle
              Case postale
              3000 Berne 15 (Suisse)
  Cable address: UPU BERNE
  Telephone: (031) 43 22 11
  Telex: 32 842 UPU CH

Chapter XII

International Telecommunication Union (ITU)

As at 31 December 1983, 158 countries were members of the International Telecommunication Union (ITU), Saint Vincent and the Grenadines having become a member on 25 March.

Administrative Council

The thirty-eighth session of the Administrative Council of ITU was held from 2 to 20 May 1983 at ITU headquarters, Geneva. It reviewed administrative matters, approved a revised schedule of conferences, and drew up the agenda for the second (1984) session of the Regional Administrative Conference for FM (frequency modulation) sound broadcasting in the VHF (very high frequency) band (Region 1—Africa and Europe—and certain countries in Region 3—Asia and Australasia) and for a 1985 Regional Administrative Radio Conference for the Maritime Mobile Service and the Aeronautical Radionavigation Service in certain parts of the MF (medium frequency) band in Region 1.

Administrative radio conferences

The World Administrative Radio Conference for the Mobile Services was held at Geneva from 23 February to 18 March 1983. It adopted a partial revision of the Radio Regulations, notably with regard to frequency allocations, the notification and recording of frequency assignments, distress and safety communications, and aeronautical and maritime mobile-satellite services.

The Regional Administrative Conference for the Planning of the Broadcasting-Satellite Service in Region 2 (the Americas), held at Geneva from 13 June to 17 July, adopted provisions for the broadcasting-satellite service in the frequency band 12.2-12.7 gigahertz.

International consultative committees

The International Radio Consultative Committee (CCIR) made further important progress in the study of standards for satellite broadcasting, high definition television, digital television transmission and recording. An improved and simplified propagation calculation method was developed for HF (high frequency) broadcast planning, and a comprehensive set of technical criteria and characteristics for HF broadcasting was presented to an HF broadcasting conference. Improvements of compatibility were studied between aeronautical radionavigation reception in the band above 108 megahertz and broadcasting in the band below it. Further studies were to be carried out in a joint interim working party of two study groups. Technical preparatory work was under way for the World Administrative Radio Conference (scheduled for 1985 and 1988) on the use of the geostationary satellite orbit and the planning of the space services using it. Seminars were held on propagation in tropical regions (Lomé, Togo) and domestic satellite communications (Shanghai, China).

Study groups of the International Telegraph and Telephone Consultative Committee (CCITT) concentrated on preparing the final drafts of recommendations and replies to questions assigned to them by the 1980 CCITT plenary assembly. Topics covered in the principal study groups included: transmission systems; telephone operation and quality, data transmission on the public-switched telephone network and public data networks; digital networks; switching and signalling; maintenance and protection; and general tariff principles. Special study groups produced manuals and case studies of interest to developing countries on subjects such as: general network planning; primary sources of energy; rural telecommunications; regional satellite communications; transition from analogue to digital telecommunication networks; effects of inflation on telecommunications organizations; allocation of scarce resources and application of information technology; and socioeconomic implications of teleprocessing.

The CCITT Regional Plan Committee for Africa met during 1983 (Libreville, Gabon, 1-8 June) to co-ordinate development of telecommunications facilities and to prepare a plan for 1983-1987 and forecasts for 1987-1990. The Plan Committee for Europe and the Mediterranean Basin (Nicosia, Cyprus, 28 September–4 October) drew up a plan for 1983-1986.

International Frequency Registration Board

The International Frequency Registration Board continued to implement the decisions taken at the 1979 World Administrative Radio Conference, including a review of the Master International Frequency Register (MIFR), activities related to computer analysis and the search for replacement frequencies, conversion and transfer of MIFR resulting from revision of the International Frequency List, and conversion of MIFR to a new method of designating emissions.

Among the Board's other activities were follow-up actions to the 1981 Regional Administrative MF Broadcasting Conference (Region 2) and to the first (1982) session of the Regional Administrative Conference for FM sound broadcasting in the VHF band (Region 1 and certain countries in Region 3); assistance to member administrations in applying the provisions and obligatory procedures of the Radio Regulations; and examining frequency assignment notices received from member countries, recording them in MIFR and applying co-ordination procedures.

Technical co-operation

In 1983, ITU continued its technical co-operation activities. However, there was a certain slowing down during the course of the year in the United Nations Development Programme (UNDP) mainly due to financial stringency, which gave rise to delays in the authorization of certain expenditures. The same constraints were experienced with trust fund projects. Since ITU is the executing agency in the telecommunications sector for UNDP and the bulk of ITU funds for technical co-operation are provided by or through UNDP, this reflected adversely on the implementation of many projects.

Under ITU programmes of technical co-operation in developing countries, 583 expert missions were carried out, 827 fellows were trained abroad and equipment valued at $5,643,999 was delivered for various field projects. The total cost of this assistance amounted to $28,335,851. Countries and territories aided were the following:

Africa: Algeria, Angola, Botswana, Burundi, Central African Republic, Chad, Congo, Djibouti, Egypt, Equatorial Guinea, Ethiopia, Gambia, Ivory Coast, Lesotho, Malawi, Mauritania, Mozambique, Namibia, Nigeria, Rwanda, Senegal, Somalia, Sudan, Swaziland, Tunisia, Uganda, United Republic of Cameroon, Zaire.

The Americas: Argentina, Brazil, Cuba, Ecuador, El Salvador, Guatemala, Haiti, Honduras, Jamaica, Nicaragua, Panama, Saint Christopher and Nevis, Trinidad and Tobago, Uruguay.

Asia and the Pacific: Afghanistan, Bangladesh, Burma, China, India, Indonesia, Iran, Lao People's Democratic Republic, Malaysia, Mongolia, Nepal, Pakistan, Papua New Guinea, Philippines, Republic of Korea, Samoa, Singapore, Sri Lanka, Tokelau, Tonga.

Europe and the Middle East: Albania, Bulgaria, Cyprus, Czechoslovakia, Democratic Yemen, Greece, Jordan, Kuwait, Oman, Poland, Qatar, Romania, Saudi Arabia, Turkey, United Arab Emirates, Yemen.

The main objectives of ITU technical co-operation continued to be: promoting development of regional telecommunications networks in Africa, the Americas, Asia, the Pacific, the Middle East and the Mediterranean Basin; strengthening telecommunication technical and administrative services in developing countries; and vocational training.

ITU continued to promote development of regional telecommunication networks and their integration into the world-wide telecommunication system, in accordance with objectives established by the World Plan Committee and regional plan committees.

The Pan-African Telecommunications Network continued to be extended across the African continent; the most important activities of the project remained the development of the principal international arteries and the resolution of interface problems, mainly in the western subregion of Africa.

Special attention was paid to the question of tariffs, especially in central African countries, in order to promote a tariff structure that could be applied to all countries of the continent. Work was started in the area of international accounting procedures with a survey of English-speaking countries and publication of a draft manual on international telecommunication accounting.

With regard to maintenance, a global strategy was finalized and elaborated in a manual, the *National Plan for Improvement of Maintenance*, distributed to all countries. Three seminars on this subject were organized at Lomé, Dakar (Senegal) and Addis Ababa (Ethiopia).

Regional assistance was provided by ITU to the Panafrican News Agency to establish a news collection and dissemination network.

Progress was made in formulating the Inter-American Plan for Telecommunications Development, with increased co-ordination between the Steering Committee of the Inter-American Telecommunication Conference and CCITT.

In Central America, all activities related to telecommunications development were carried out by the Central American Telecommunications Commission (COMTELCA) through its supervisory group, assisted by the ITU regional adviser. Activities included: preparation of general technical specifications for international digital telephone exchanges to be used by the administrations of the five member countries of COMTELCA; opening of two telex transit centres in Guatemala and Costa Rica; and the integration of telex service into the regional network, progressively abandoning the facilities provided by international carriers.

ITU collaborated with the Asia-Pacific Telecommunity on preparations for a development survey with a view to extending and upgrading the regional network. It prepared proposals for a regional telecommunications network, including various options—terrestrial, satellite and submarine cable—for consideration by the Economic and Social Commission for Asia and the Pacific. It assisted the least developed countries of the region in developing rural networks, and the Organization of Asian News Agencies to develop a news network.

A UNDP/ITU regional project for the development of telecommunications helped Fiji, Kiribati, Papua New Guinea and Tuvalu to assess tender bids and provided technical back-up and contract management. These countries were receiving grants and loans from the European Economic Community to fund satellite earth stations and to extend telex exchanges and equipment.

Activities continued in the Middle East and Mediterranean Basin to develop the regional network, under the 1978 Middle East and Mediterranean telecommunication network master plan. This included assistance to implement a subregional microwave network and the international switching centres in Aden, Djibouti and Nouakchott (Mauritania); some additional links within the region also were completed. Assistance also was given in drawing up equipment supply contracts and sub-contracting agreements for ARABSAT earth stations to be installed in Democratic Yemen, Djibouti, Mauritania, Somalia and the Sudan. Mauritania received assistance to set up its "Standard A" earth station. A study of the Maghreb-Machrek submarine cable system was carried out, with Arab Telecommunication Union experts.

In collaboration with GULFVISION, ITU conducted a study of radio propagation in the area in Bands III, IV and V. The results of the study will enable the countries of the region to make the best use of the allocated bands for television and sound/FM broadcasting services.

Through an ITU European regional project for developing international telecommunications, UNDP agreed to finance assistance to 12 countries in East Europe and the Mediterranean Basin to introduce new technology and modernize planning and maintenance systems.

World Communications Year

World Communications Year: Development of Communications Infrastructures was observed in 1983 and ITU, as the lead agency for the Year, maintained close contacts with numerous organizations, particularly the Food and Agriculture Organization of the United Nations (FAO), the Universal Postal Union, the United Nations Educational, Scientific and Cultural Organization and the World Meteorological Organization. Together with FAO, ITU prepared a special issue of the *World Communications Year Bulletin* dealing with the frequently neglected role of telecommunications in the development of agriculture. The basic objectives for the Year as laid down by the United Nations General Assembly in 1981[a] were to provide the opportunity for all countries to undertake an in-depth review and analysis of their policies on communications development and stimulate the accelerated development of communications infrastructures. (See ECONOMIC AND SOCIAL QUESTIONS, Chapter V.)

Publications

Publications issued by ITU in either trilingual or separate English, French and Spanish editions during 1983 included:

> *Report on the Activities of the Union, 1982*
> *Financial Operating Report for 1982*
> *Twenty-second Report by the International Telecommunication Union on Telecommunication and the Peaceful Uses of Outer Space*, Information Booklet No. 31
> *International Telecommunication Convention adopted by the Plenipotentiary Conference* (Nairobi, 1982)
> *Final Acts of the World Administrative Radio Conference for the Mobile Services* (Geneva, 1983)
> *Final Acts of the Regional Administrative Broadcasting Conference, Region 2* (Rio de Janeiro, 1981)
> *Yearbook of Common Carrier Telecommunication Statistics*, 10th ed., 1983
> *List of Coast Stations*, 9th ed., 1983, and Supplement No. 1
> *List of Ship Stations*, 23rd ed., 1983, and Supplement Nos. 1-3
> *List of Radiodetermination and Special Service Stations*, 8th ed., 1983, and Supplement No. 1
> *Alphabetical List VIIA of Call Signs of Stations Used by the Maritime Mobile Service*, 11th ed., 1983 and Supplement Nos. 1 and 2
> *Catalogue of Telecommunication Training Opportunities*, Publication No. 1
> *Spectrum Management and Computer-Aided Techniques*, 1983 ed.
> *Satellite Broadcasting Systems*
> *General Network Planning*, Special Autonomous Group 3 (GAS 3), 1983 ed.
> *Methods Used in Long-Term Forecasting of Domestic Telecommunications Demand and Required Resources (Overall and by Main Sector)* (GAS 5/2)
> *Conditions Required for the Establishment of a National Industry for the Manufacture of Telecommunication Equipment (Especially Switching Equipment)* (GAS 5/3)
> *Special Aspects of Telecommunications Development in Isolated and/or Underprivileged Areas of Countries* (GAS 5/4)
> *Procedure for Establishing a Budget Model for a Telecommunication Undertaking* (GAS 5/5)
> *Data Transmission and New Telematic Services: Studies and Results in CCITT*

Secretariat

As at 31 December 1983, the total staff of ITU numbered 699 officials (excluding staff on short-term contracts). Of these, nine were elected

---

[a]YUN 1981, p. 573, GA res. 36/40, 19 Nov. 1981.

officials, 546 had permanent contracts and 144 had fixed-term contracts; 51 nationalities were represented in posts subject to geographical distribution.

Budget

The budget for 1983 shown in the opposite column was adopted by the Administrative Council's session in 1982.

Each member of ITU chooses the class of contribution in which it wishes to be included and pays in advance its annual contributory share to the budget on the basis of the budgetary provision. In accordance with the 1982 International Telecommunication Convention, new classes of contribution were chosen by ITU members with effect from 1 January 1984. The classes of contribution for 1984 for members are listed in ANNEX I below.

As at the end of 1983, the total of units for members was 427 5/8. The contributory unit for 1983 was

176,600 Swiss francs; the contributory unit for 1984 was to be 209,000 Swiss francs.

	Amount (in Swiss francs)
Income	
Contribution by members and private operating agencies	85,861,000
Contribution by UNDP for technical co-operation administrative expenses	9,450,000
Sales of publications	7,258,000
Miscellaneous	85,000
Total	102,654,000
Expenditures	
Administrative Council	669,000
Common headquarters expenditure	69,992,000
Miscellaneous	85,000
Conferences and meetings	13,800,000
Other expenses	1,400,000
Total general expenses	85,946,000
Technical co-operation	9,450,000
Publications	7,258,000
Total	102,654,000

Annex I.   MEMBERSHIP OF THE INTERNATIONAL
TELECOMMUNICATION UNION AND CONTRIBUTIONS

(Membership as at 31 December 1983; contributions as assessed for 1984)

MEMBER	Class of contribution; no. of units	In Swiss francs*	MEMBER	Class of contribution; no. of units	In Swiss francs*	MEMBER	Class of contribution; no. of units	In Swiss francs*
Afghanistan	1/8	26,125	Ecuador	1/2	104,500	Liberia	1/4	52,250
Albania	1/4	52,250	Egypt	1	209,000	Libyan Arab		
Algeria	1	209,000	El Salvador	1/4	52,250	Jamahiriya	1 1/2	313,500
Angola	1/4	52,250	Equatorial Guinea	1/8	26,125	Liechtenstein	1/2	104,500
Argentina	3	627,000	Ethiopia	1/8	26,125	Luxembourg	1/2	104,500
Australia	18	3,762,000	Fiji	1/4	52,250	Madagascar	1/4	52,250
Austria	1	209,000	Finland	5	1,045,000	Malawi	1/8	26,125
Bahamas	1/2	104,500	France	30	6,270,000	Malaysia	3	627,000
Bahrain	1/2	104,500	Gabon	1/2	104,500	Maldives	1/8	26,125
Bangladesh	1/8	26,125	Gambia	1/8	26,125	Mali	1/8	26,125
Barbados	1/4	52,250	German Democratic			Malta	1/4	52,250
Belgium	5	1,045,000	Republic	3	627,000	Mauritania	1/4	52,250
Belize	1/8	26,125	Germany, Federal			Mauritius	1/4	52,250
Benin	1/4	52,250	Republic of	30	6,270,000	Mexico	1	209,000
Bolivia	1/4	52,250	Ghana	1/4	52,250	Monaco	1/4	52,250
Botswana	1/2	104,500	Greece	1	209,000	Mongolia	1/4	52,250
Brazil	3	627,000	Grenada	1/8	26,125	Morocco	1	209,000
Bulgaria	1	209,000	Guatemala	1/4	52,250	Mozambique	1/4	52,250
Burma	1/2	104,500	Guinea	1/8	26,125	Nauru	1/8	26,125
Burundi	1/8	26,125	Guinea-Bissau	1/8	26,125	Nepal	1/8	26,125
Byelorussian SSR	1/2	104,500	Guyana	1/4	52,250	Netherlands	10	2,090,000
Canada	18	3,762,000	Haiti	1/8	26,125	New Zealand	2	418,000
Cape Verde	1/8	26,125	Honduras	1/4	52,250	Nicaragua	1/2	104,500
Central African			Hungary	1	209,000	Niger	1/8	26,125
Republic	1/8	26,125	Iceland	1/4	52,250	Nigeria	2	418,000
Chad	1/8	26,125	India	10	2,090,000	Norway	5	1,045,000
Chile	1	209,000	Indonesia	1	209,000	Oman	1/2	104,500
China	10	2,090,000	Iran	1	209,000	Pakistan	2	418,000
Colombia	1	209,000	Iraq	1/4	52,250	Panama	1/2	104,500
Comoros	1/8	26,125	Ireland	2	418,000	Papua New Guinea	1/2	104,500
Congo	1/2	104,500	Israel	1	209,000	Paraguay	1/2	104,500
Costa Rica	1/4	52,250	Italy	10	2,090,000	Peru	1/2	104,500
Cuba	1/2	104,500	Ivory Coast	1	209,000	Philippines	1	209,000
Cyprus	1/4	52,250	Jamaica	1/4	52,250	Poland	2	418,000
Czechoslovakia	2	418,000	Japan	30	6,270,000	Portugal	1	209,000
Democratic Kampuchea	1/2	104,500	Jordan	1/2	104,500	Qatar	1/2	104,500
Democratic People's			Kenya	1/4	52,250	Republic of Korea	1	209,000
Republic of Korea	1/4	52,250	Kuwait	1	209,000	Romania	1/2	104,500
Democratic Yemen	1/8	26,125	Lao People's			Rwanda	1/8	26,125
Denmark	5	1,045,000	Democratic Republic	1/2	104,500	Saint Vincent and the		
Djibouti	1/8	26,125	Lebanon	1/4	52,250	Grenadines	1/8	26,125
Dominican Republic	1/2	104,500	Lesotho	1/8	26,125	San Marino	1/4	52,250

MEMBER	CONTRIBUTION Class of contribution; no. of units	CONTRIBUTION In Swiss francs*	MEMBER	CONTRIBUTION Class of contribution; no. of units	CONTRIBUTION In Swiss francs*	MEMBER	CONTRIBUTION Class of contribution; no. of units	CONTRIBUTION In Swiss francs*
Sao Tome and Principe	1/8	26,125	Syrian Arab Republic	1/2	104,500	United Republic of		
Saudi Arabia	10	2,090,000	Thailand	1	209,000	Tanzania	1/8	26,125
Senegal	1	209,000	Togo	1/4	52,250	United States	30	6,270,000
Sierra Leone	1/8	26,125	Tonga	1/8	26,125	Upper Volta	1/8	26,125
Singapore	1	209,000	Trinidad and Tobago	1	209,000	Uruguay	1/2	104,500
Somalia	1/8	26,125	Tunisia	1	209,000	Vatican City State	1/4	52,250
South Africa	1	209,000	Turkey	1	209,000	Venezuela	2	418,000
Spain	3	627,000	Uganda	1/8	26,125	Viet Nam	1/2	104,500
Sri Lanka	1/2	104,500	Ukrainian SSR	1	209,000	Yemen	1/4	52,250
Sudan	1/8	26,125	USSR	30	6,270,000	Yugoslavia	1	209,000
Suriname	1/4	52,250	United Arab Emirates	1	209,000	Zaire	1/2	104,500
Swaziland	1/4	52,250	United Kingdom	30	6,270,000	Zambia	1/4	52,250
Sweden	10	2,090,000	United Republic of			Zimbabwe	1/2	104,500
Switzerland	10	2,090,000	Cameroon	1/2	104,500	Total	392 1/4	81,980,250

NOTE: The ITU nomenclature differs from that of the United Nations.

*For the equivalent amounts in United States dollars, the rate of exchange that was to be applicable on 1 January 1984 was 2.18 Swiss francs = $US 1.00.

Annex II.   OFFICERS AND OFFICE OF THE INTERNATIONAL TELECOMMUNICATION UNION

ADMINISTRATIVE COUNCIL, INTERNATIONAL FREQUENCY REGISTRATION BOARD AND PRINCIPAL OFFICERS

PRINCIPAL OFFICERS OF THE UNION
Secretary-General: Richard E. Butler.
Deputy Secretary-General: Jean Jipguep.

ITU ADMINISTRATIVE COUNCIL
Algeria (Vice-Chairman), Argentina, Australia, Benin, Brazil, Canada, China, Colombia, Egypt, Ethiopia, France, German Democratic Republic, Germany, Federal Republic of, India, Indonesia, Italy, Japan, Kenya, Kuwait, Lebanon, Mexico, Morocco, Nigeria, Pakistan, Peru, Philippines, Romania, Saudi Arabia, Senegal, Spain (Chairman), Sweden, Switzerland, Thailand, USSR, United Kingdom, United Republic of Cameroon, United Republic of Tanzania, United States, Venezuela, Yugoslavia, Zambia.

INTERNATIONAL FREQUENCY REGISTRATION BOARD
(from 1 January until 30 April 1983)

Chairman: Charles William Sowton (United Kingdom).
Vice-Chairman: Yoshitaka Kurihara (Japan).
Members: Abderrazak Berrada (Morocco), Petr S. Kurakov (USSR), Francis G. Perrin (Canada).
(from 1 May until 31 December 1983)
Chairman: Yoshitaka Kurihara.
Vice-Chairman: Abderrazak Berrada.
Members: William H. Bellchambers (United Kingdom), Gary C. Brooks (Canada), Petr S. Kurakov.

OFFICERS OF THE INTERNATIONAL CONSULTATIVE COMMITTEES
Director, International Radio Consultative Committee (CCIR): Richard C. Kirby (United States).
Director, International Telegraph and Telephone Consultative Committee (CCITT): Léon Burtz (France).

HEADQUARTERS

General Secretariat of the International Telecommunication Union
Place des Nations
1211 Geneva 20, Switzerland
   Cable address: BURINTERNA GENEVA
   Telephone: 99 51 11
   Telex: 421000 UIT CH

Chapter XIII

World Meteorological Organization (WMO)

In 1983, the Ninth World Meteorological Congress, which convenes at least once every four years as the highest body of the World Meteorological Organization (WMO), met at Geneva from 2 to 27 May and established the organization's programme and budget for the ninth financial period (1984-1987), approving a maximum expenditure of $77.5 million. It appointed G. O. P. Obasi (Nigeria) as Secretary-General of WMO for a four-year period beginning on 1 January 1984.

By amendments to the WMO Convention, the Ninth Congress changed the name of the WMO Executive Committee to Executive Council and increased its membership from 29 to 36. The Council, which supervises implementation of Congress resolutions and regulations, held its thirty-fifth session, also at Geneva, from 30 May to 3 June 1983.

The Congress decided to introduce long-term planning for the scientific and technical programmes of WMO so as to provide guidance to the Executive Council and to other WMO bodies, as well as to help members in developing and planning their meteorological and hydrological services. It agreed that long-term plans should cover a 10-year period, but be replaced at four-year intervals, each Congress adopting a new plan for the decade following the Congress. The Ninth Congress adopted the first part of the long-term plan for 1984-1993 and requested the Executive Council to prepare the second part of the plan.

The Congress, deciding to give the highest priority to the World Weather Watch (WWW) Programme, agreed that other major programmes of WMO were those concerned with world climate, research and development, applications of meteorology, hydrology and water resources, education and training, and regional activities.

It revised the terms of reference of WMO's eight technical commissions—composed of experts nominated by members and working on a voluntary basis—and decided that the commission presidents should participate more actively in the work of the Congress and the Executive Council. The presidents subsequently met at Geneva from 26 to 28 October to consider the follow-up action on relevant Congress decisions, including those relating to the long-term plan.

WMO carried out its 1983 programmes in accordance with the programme and budget as approved for 1980-1983 by the Eighth (1979) Congress. WMO's membership remained at 157 in 1983, composed of 152 States and five territories.

The twenty-eighth annual International Meteorological Organization Prize, which commemorates the non-governmental organization which preceded WMO, was awarded jointly to M. F. Taha (Egypt), WMO President from 1971 to 1979, and J. J. Burgos (Argentina), President of the WMO Commission for Agricultural Meteorology from 1951 to 1958, for their outstanding contributions to meteorology, operational hydrology and international co-operation.

Activities in 1983

World Weather Watch

As the basic programme of WMO, WWW continued to provide in 1983 the observational data and processed information required by members for operational and research purposes. Its essential elements were: the Global Observing System (GOS), whereby observational data were obtained; the Global Data-processing System (GDPS), which provided for processing, storage and retrieval of observational data and made available processed information; and the Global Telecommunication System (GTS), which offered telecommunication facilities and arrangements for rapid and reliable collection, exchange and distribution of observational data and processed information.

During 1983, operations of GOS, consisting of surface-based and space-based sub-systems, continued to be maintained and improved. The surface-based sub-system provided conventional basic data from regional basic synoptic networks, other observational networks of stations on land and at sea, and aircraft meteorological observations required for operations and research. In the space-based system, meteorological satellites in near-polar orbiting and geostationary systems took direct observations and provided data collection and dissemination. GOS provided member States with both quantitative information, such as measurements of atmospheric pressure, humidity, air temperature and wind velocity, and qualitative information which described the state of the sky, forms of clouds and types of precipitation. Progress was achieved in developing the Aircraft to Satellite Data Relay system and the Automated Shipboard Aerological Programme for meteorological observations, two important elements for an improved GOS in the future.

With regard to GDPS, a number of WWW processing centres installed new-generation electronic computers, thus improving their capability to produce analysis and forecast products for global and regional exchange in real-time.

Upgrading to high-speed data transmission was accomplished on many GTS circuits during 1983, in particular those of the Main Telecommunication Network, and a number of radio point-to-point circuits were converted to satellite communications, thus making the system more reliable.

The Instruments and Methods of Observation Programme emphasized standardization of instruments and observing methods. The fifth edition of the *WMO Guide to Meteorological Instruments and Methods of Observation* was published, and efforts continued to develop performance specifications for instruments and regulatory and guidance material.

Ocean affairs

In 1983, the Ninth Congress urged all WMO members to strengthen their marine meteorological services programmes, to develop improved observing systems, and to make full use of modern telecommunication means involving satellites, for the timely acquisition of the data. It also decided that the United Nations and members of WMO should be informed of the relevant implications of the United Nations Convention on the Law of the Sea.[a]

Efforts continued to promote the use of drifting buoys as a source of meteorological data from ocean areas and for collecting data using satellite communication techniques. A second edition of the "Guide to Marine Meteorological Services", which was expected to be particularly useful to developing countries in the process of organizing a marine meteorology programme, was issued. A seminar on Marine Meteorological Services was organized in December at Bombay, India, for member countries in the Asian and South-West Pacific regions.

The Integrated Global Ocean Services System, a joint WMO/Intergovernmental Oceanographic Commission programme, continued to collect and exchange oceanic data for operational and research activities. WMO maintained support to the meteorological component of the investigation of the phenomenon known as "El Niño" on the Pacific coast of equatorial South America.

Aviation

The Ninth Congress recognized the importance of aeronautical meteorology in the day-to-day ac-

tivities of national meteorological services and adopted an outline of the Aeronautical Meteorology Programme for 1984-1987. The Programme's 1983 activities focused on improving meteorological services to ensure the safety, efficiency and economy of air navigation. The WMO Commission for Aeronautical Meteorology paid particular attention to the provision of meteorological information before and during flight and the implementation of the World Area Forecast System.

World Climate Programme

The Ninth Congress decided that the World Climate Programme (WCP), instituted in 1979 to aid nations in applying climate information to human activities, should continue to receive high priority; it approved the institutional arrangements for coordinating the Programme and defined the division of responsibilities within WCP, which comprised: the World Climate Applications Programme (WCAP), the World Climate Data Programme (WCDP), the World Climate Impact Studies Programme (WCIP) and the World Climate Research Programme (WCRP). The Congress also renamed the Commission for Climatology and Applications of Meteorology as the Commission for Climatology, with the lead role, under its revised terms of reference, for activities in WCAP and WCDP.

As part of the WCAP activities under the WMO Plan of Action in the Field of Energy Matters, endorsed by the Ninth Congress, short-term missions of experts were undertaken in 1983 to assist several developing countries in applying climate data to energy-related questions, mainly the development of solar and wind energy.

In 1983, action was taken under WCDP to establish climate data requirements, set up data banks, and assist countries in strengthening national and subregional climate data banks; the Ninth Congress endorsed a project involving the use of a relatively low-cost microcomputer system for processing and using climate data. Progress was made in developing a World Climate Data Information Referral Service; some components of the Climate Applications Referral System project, for information on operationally used methods in applied climatology, were completed.

Activities within WCIP, carried out by the United Nations Environment Programme (UNEP) in collaboration with WMO, focused on reduction of the vulnerability of food systems to climate, anticipation of impacts of man-induced climatic changes (especially increased atmospheric carbon dioxide), improvement of the methodology for cli-

---

[a]YUN 1982, p. 181.

mate impact studies, and identification of climate-sensitive sectors of human activity.

Research under WCRP, conducted jointly by WMO and the International Council of Scientific Unions to determine the extent of climate predictability and of man's influence on climate, dealt with prediction of short-term climate anomalies, inter-annual variability and long-term climate trends.

Research and development

The Research and Development Programme continued to focus on weather prediction, tropical meteorology, environmental pollution monitoring and weather modification research. Future activities of the WMO Commission for Atmospheric Sciences (CAS), responsible for promoting and co-ordinating research activities, were examined by its Advisory Working Group (sixth session, Hamburg, Federal Republic of Germany, 10-12 August 1983).

In 1983, the CAS Co-ordinating Group on Experimentation in Numerical Weather Prediction was established at the request of the Ninth Congress to oversee the relevant research on all time scales. The Congress also approved a programme for long-range forecasting research, as well as an expanded plan prepared by the CAS Working Group on Short- and Medium-range Weather Prediction Research (Geneva, 24-28 January) involving research on applying high-resolution quantitative satellite data, limited-area weather prediction modelling, objective interpretation methods, and very short-range forecasting. The Symposium on Maintenance of the Quasi-stationary Components of the Flow in the Atmosphere and in Atmospheric Models (Paris, 29 August–2 September), co-sponsored by WMO and the International Association of Meteorology and Atmospheric Physics, examined research results aimed at improving weather forecasting techniques. Informal meetings of experts were held at Reading, United Kingdom (September), and at Sofia, Bulgaria (November/December), concerning new study projects on phenomenological studies and on Mediterranean cyclones.

Under the research programme in tropical meteorology, a long-term Asian monsoon study project commenced with the participation of States in monsoon-affected regions; activity centres were established in India and Malaysia for the summer and winter monsoon studies, respectively. Ongoing projects included radiation flux studies, with pilot studies in Australia and India, and moisture budget studies in the Sahelian region of Africa.

The Ninth Congress stressed the importance of WMO's involvement in environmental pollu-

tion monitoring and research, recognized the need for a permanent environmental and climate-related monitoring system of adequate global coverage, and observed that member States were soon likely to study problems caused by chemical contaminants in the atmosphere. The WMO Technical Conference on Observation and Measurement of Atmospheric Contaminants (Vienna, Austria, 17-21 October) established the current state of knowledge of man-induced climate and environment-related chemical and physical variables and their possible future developments.

By the end of the year, 98 countries operated or were planning to operate Background Air Pollution Monitoring Network stations, and data were reported by 47 countries. With funds supplied partially or entirely by UNEP, sampling equipment was provided for new stations in China and the Dominican Republic, and expert assistance was provided to 10 countries. An expert meeting on quality assurance in the Network discussed quality assurance procedures used in national networks.

WMO also continued to collaborate in projects on long-range transmission of air pollutants in Europe, assessment of air pollutants' contribution to the contamination of the Mediterranean Sea and global ozone research and monitoring.

A major component of the weather modification programme—field activity involving seeding experiments in Spain, under the Precipitation Enhancement Project—was discontinued by the Ninth Congress, which decided that the site was unsuitable for achieving the project's objectives; analysis of data collected was to be completed, however, and options were to be explored for an alternative demonstration project. Other 1983 activities included a meeting of experts on cumulus (single) cloud modification (Mexico City) and a planning session for the International Cloud Modelling Conference/Workshop (Aspen, Colorado, United States).

Hydrology and water resources development

The Ninth Congress re-established the Hydrology and Water Resources Programme as a major programme for the 1984-1987 period, to be composed of the Operational Hydrology Programme, applications and services to water resources, and co-operation with water-related programmes of other international organizations.

The first phase of the Hydrological Operational Multi-purpose Subprogramme, for transferring operational hydrological technology and integrating techniques for data collection and processing, was completed in 1983 and the Ninth Congress approved the second phase for further strengthening the Subprogramme's institutional and technical aspects.

Technical support to the hydrological components of other programmes, such as WCP and the Tropical Cyclone Programme, continued to be provided. In addition to technical conferences and meetings of working groups, WMO, in the framework of a WMO/United Nations Development Programme (UNDP) regional project, organized a nine-week regional training course (Niamey, Niger, August-October) for hydrological supervisors and senior technicians to enable them, in turn, to train hydrological technicians in their own countries.

Education and training

The main activities of the Education and Training Programme in 1983 were the awarding of fellowships, strengthening of regional meteorological training centres, organization and co-sponsorship of courses, seminars and workshops, preparation of training publications and other training aids, surveys of training needs, provision of advice and information on education and training, and collaboration with other organizations.

Twenty-eight training events organized or co-sponsored by WMO during 1983 covered: hydrological forecasting, hydrologic techniques, satellite data for operational purposes, advances in tropical meteorology, and remote sensing (United States); a course for hydrological technicians, and remote sensing applications to operational agrometeorology in semi-arid countries (Niger); agrometeorology, and applied statistics (Belgium); background air pollution measurements (Hungary); understanding climate (United Kingdom); Mediterranean cyclogenesis and Alpex, climatological aspects of desertification, and satellite applications to flood monitoring and forecasting (Italy); mesometeorology (Sweden); application of satellite remote sensing to disaster preparedness, and a course for agrometeorological technicians (Colombia); management and applications of meteorological data, and a course for meteorological instrumentation inspectors (Brazil); real-time river flow forecasting and hierarchical modelling of agricultural production, weather, soils and crops (Netherlands); application of radar data to tropical cyclone forecasting (Thailand); marine meteorological services (India); archiving, storage, quality control and retrieval functions of national meteorological centres in Africa (Algeria); a regional training seminar for national instructors (Senegal); a roving seminar on satellite meteorology (Bangladesh and Burma); and utilization of satellite cloud pictures in weather analysis and forecasting (Iraq).

Some 470 participants, mainly from developing countries, participated in WMO training events, and 227 fellowships were awarded and commenced during the year; financial assistance was also provided to 56 participants in various WMO-supported training events.

Technical co-operation

In 1983, WMO's technical co-operation activities continued through UNDP, the Voluntary Co-operation Programme (VCP), trust-fund arrangements and the WMO regular budget.

Under UNDP, assistance was provided to 94 countries in 1983 to a value of approximately $11.3 million, compared to $11.8 million in 1982; developing countries received assistance in meteorological and hydrological services development and for personnel training. Under UNDP sectoral support in meteorology and operational hydrology, missions were undertaken to 10 countries for the formulation of new UNDP projects.

The total value of assistance provided under VCP in 1983 amounted to some $4.9 million; support was given mainly to WWW's GOS and to the establishment or updating of automatic picture transmission/weather facsimile and upper-air stations. Fellowships for training meteorological personnel were also awarded.

Under WMO's technical co-operation programme, 494 fellows received meteorological or hydrological training during the year: 248 under UNDP, 183 under VCP, 42 under the WMO regular budget and 21 under trust funds. Under the associate expert programme, five young professionals with limited experience worked in association with, and under the guidance of, senior experts. Nine United Nations Volunteers served in WMO-executed projects during the year—seven in Yemen, one in Bangladesh and one in Botswana.

Secretariat

As at 31 December 1983, the total number of full-time staff employed by WMO (excluding 69 professionals on technical assistance projects) on permanent and fixed-term contracts stood at 303. Of these, 128 were in the Professional and higher categories (drawn from 57 nationalities) and 175 in the General Service and related categories.

Budget

The year 1983 was the fourth and final year of the eighth financial period (1980-1983), for which the Eighth (1979) Congress had established a maximum expenditure of $74.4 million, and authorized additional expenditures of not more than $1 million to provide for such circumstances as losses resulting from currency exchange rate changes or urgent unforeseen programme activities.

The regular budget for 1983 amounted to $18,558,700; the budget for technical co-operation activities, financed from overhead allocations and other extrabudgetary sources, amounted to an additional $2,401,700.

In a resolution on members' contributions for the ninth financial period (1984-1987), the Ninth Congress decided that, with effect from 1 January 1984, a combination of the United Nations assessment for 1983-1985 and the WMO scale of assessments for the eighth financial period would be used.

At its May/June 1983 session, the Executive Council approved the following regular budget of $18,750,000 for 1984.

	Amount (in US dollars)
Income	
Contributions	18,750,000
Total	18,750,000
Expenditure	
Policy-making organs	424,100
Executive management	967,900
Scientific and technical programmes	
World Weather Watch	2,979,300
World Climate Programme	2,142,300
Education and training	1,420,300
Regional programme	1,230,800
Research and development	1,208,600
Hydrology and water resources	958,800
Overall co-ordination	217,400
Technical co-operation activities	210,000
Programme supporting activities	3,539,500
Administration	2,968,100
Other budgetary provisions	482,900
Total	18,750,000

Annex I.   MEMBERSHIP OF THE WORLD
METEOROLOGICAL ORGANIZATION AND CONTRIBUTIONS
(Membership as at 31 December 1983; contributions as assessed for 1984)

MEMBER	Percent-age	Net amount (in US dollars)	MEMBER	Percent-age	Net amount (in US dollars)	MEMBER	Percent-age	Net amount (in US dollars)
Afghanistan	0.04	7,500	Ecuador	0.09	16,875	Luxembourg	0.09	16,875
Albania	0.04	7,000	Egypt	0.40	75,000	Madagascar	0.04	7,500
Algeria	0.09	16,875	El Salvador	0.04	7,500	Malawi	0.04	7,500
Angola	0.08	15,000	Ethiopia	0.04	7,500	Malaysia	0.33	61,875
Argentina	1.26	236,250	Fiji	0.04	7,500	Maldives	0.04	7,500
Australia	1.76	330,000	Finland	0.53	99,375	Mali	0.04	7,500
Austria	0.60	112,500	France	4.87	913,125	Malta	0.04	7,500
Bahamas	0.04	7,500	Gabon	0.04	7,500	Mauritania	0.04	7,500
Bahrain	0.04	7,500	Gambia	0.04	7,500	Mauritius	0.04	7,500
Bangladesh	0.04	7,500	German Democratic Republic	1.38	258,750	Mexico	0.86	161,250
Barbados	0.04	7,500				Mongolia	0.04	7,500
Belgium	1.26	236,250	Germany, Federal Republic of	5.37	1,006,875	Morocco	0.17	31,875
Belize	0.04	7,500				Mozambique	0.08	15,000
Benin	0.04	7,500	Ghana	0.11	20,625	Nepal	0.04	7,500
Bolivia	0.17	31,875	Greece	0.29	54,375	Netherlands	1.20	225,000
Botswana	0.04	7,500	Guatemala	0.09	16,875	New Zealand	0.51	95,625
Brazil	1.35	253,125	Guinea	0.04	7,500	Nicaragua	0.04	7,500
Bulgaria	0.33	61,875	Guinea-Bissau	0.04	7,500	Niger	0.04	7,500
Burma	0.14	26,250	Guyana	0.04	7,500	Nigeria	0.26	48,750
Burundi	0.04	7,500	Haiti	0.04	7,500	Norway	0.62	116,250
Byelorussian SSR	0.48	90,000	Honduras	0.04	7,500	Oman	0.04	7,500
Canada	2.69	504,375	Hungary	0.50	93,750	Pakistan	0.20	37,500
Cape Verde	0.04	7,500	Iceland	0.09	16,875	Panama	0.09	16,875
Central African Republic	0.04	7,500	India	1.65	309,375	Papua New Guinea	0.04	7,500
Chad	0.04	7,500	Indonesia	0.57	106,875	Paraguay	0.04	7,500
Chile	0.33	61,875	Iran	0.43	80,625	Peru	0.29	54,375
China	3.48	652,500	Iraq	0.09	16,875	Philippines	0.37	69,375
Colombia	0.29	54,375	Ireland	0.26	48,750	Poland	1.23	230,625
Comoros	0.04	7,500	Israel	0.26	48,750	Portugal	0.26	48,750
Congo	0.04	7,500	Italy	2.43	455,625	Qatar	0.29	16,875
Costa Rica	0.09	16,875	Ivory Coast	0.09	16,875	Republic of Korea	0.09	16,875
Cuba	0.25	46,875	Jamaica	0.09	16,875	Romania	0.38	71,250
Cyprus	0.04	7,500	Japan	3.49	654,375	Rwanda	0.04	7,500
Czechoslovakia	0.92	172,500	Jordan	0.04	7,500	Saint Lucia	0.04	7,500
Democratic Kampuchea	0.04	7,500	Kenya	0.04	7,500	Sao Tome and Principe	0.04	7,500
Democratic People's Republic of Korea	0.09	16,875	Kuwait	0.16	30,000	Saudi Arabia	0.26	48,750
			Lao People's Democratic Republic	0.04	7,500	Senegal	0.04	7,500
Democratic Yemen	0.04	7,500				Seychelles	0.04	7,500
Denmark	0.72	135,000	Lebanon	0.09	16,875	Sierra Leone	0.04	7,500
Djibouti	0.04	7,500	Lesotho	0.04	7,500	Singapore	0.09	16,875
Dominica	0.04	7,500	Liberia	0.04	7,500	Somalia	0.04	7,500
Dominican Republic	0.09	16,875	Libyan Arab Jamahiriya	0.12	22,500	South Africa*	0.76	142,500

MEMBER	CONTRIBUTION		MEMBER	CONTRIBUTION		MEMBER	CONTRIBUTION	
	Percent-age	Net amount (in US dollars)		Percent-age	Net amount (in US dollars)		Percent-age	Net amount (in US dollars)
Spain	1.33	249,375	Uganda	0.04	7,500	Yemen	0.04	7,500
Sri Lanka	0.17	31,875	Ukrainian SSR	1.58	296,250	Yugoslavia	0.53	99,375
Sudan	0.11	20,625	USSR	10.33	1,936,875	Zaire	0.14	26,250
Suriname	0.04	7,500	United Kingdom	5.57	1,044,375	Zambia	0.08	15,000
Swaziland	0.04	7,500	United Republic of			Zimbabwe	0.04	7,500
Sweden	1.38	258,750	Cameroon	0.04	7,500			
Switzerland	1.16	217,500	United Republic of Tanzania	0.04	7,500	British Caribbean Territories	0.04	7,500
Syrian Arab Republic	0.16	30,000	United States	24.51	4,595,625	French Polynesia	0.04	7,500
Thailand	0.28	52,500	Upper Volta	0.04	7,500	Hong Kong	0.04	7,500
Togo	0.04	7,500	Uruguay	0.27	50,625	Netherlands Antilles	0.04	7,500
Trinidad and Tobago	0.09	16,875	Vanuatu	0.04	7,500	New Caledonia	0.04	7,500
Tunisia	0.09	16,875	Venezuela	0.54	101,250			
Turkey	0.51	95,625	Viet Nam	0.09	16,875	Total	100.00	18,750,000

*Suspended by the Seventh (1975) WMO Congress from exercising the rights and privileges of a member.

Annex II.   OFFICERS AND OFFICE OF THE WORLD METEOROLOGICAL ORGANIZATION

MEMBERS OF THE WMO EXECUTIVE COUNCIL

President: R. L. Kintanar (Philippines).
First Vice-President: Ju. A. Izrael (USSR).
Second Vice-President: Zou Jingmeng (China).
Third Vice-President: J. P. Bruce (Canada).
Members: S. P. Adhikary (Nepal), S. Aguilar Anguiano* (Mexico), L.-K. Ahialeg-bedzi (Togo), S. Alaimo (Argentina), M. A. Badran (Egypt), A. Bensari (Morocco), C. E. Berridge (British Caribbean Territories), S. K. Das (India), J. Delmar Correa (Peru), Workineh Degefu* (Ethiopia), J. Djigbenou (Ivory Coast), P. Gonzalez-

Haba Gonzalez (Spain), J. Gonzalez-Montoto (Cuba), C. A. Grezzi* (Uruguay), R. E. Hallgren (United States), J. T. Houghton (United Kingdom) (acting), E. J. Jatila (Finland), A. W. Kabakibo* (Syrian Arab Republic), J. P. N. Labrousse (France), E. Lingelbach (Federal Republic of Germany), G. Mankedi (Congo), J. K. Murithi (Kenya), A. Nania (Italy), C. Padilha (Brazil), V. Richter (Czechoslova-kia), R. M. Romaih (Saudi Arabia), M. Seck (Senegal), V. A. Simango (Zambia), S. Suyehiro (Japan), U Thu Ta* (Burma), Ho Tong Yuen* (Malaysia), J. W. Zillman (Australia).

NOTE: The Executive Council is composed of four elected officers, the six Presidents of the regional associations (indicated by an asterisk), who are *ex-officio* members, and 26 elected members. Members serve in their personal capacities, not as representatives of Governments.

SENIOR MEMBERS OF THE WMO SECRETARIAT

Secretary-General: A. C. Wiin-Nielsen.
Deputy Secretary-General: R. List.
Director, Scientific and Technical Programmes: R. Czelnai.
Director, World Weather Watch Department: G. K. Weiss.
Director, Research and Development Department: A. Zaitsev.
Director, Hydrology and Water Resources Department: J. Nemec.
Director, Technical Co-Operation Department: G. Gosset.
Director, Education and Training Department: G. O. P. Obasi.
Director, Administration Department: M. J. Connaughton.

Director, Languages, Publications and Conferences Department: H. Tabatabay.
Director, World Climate Programme Department: T. D. Potter.
Director, World Climate Research Programme: P. Morel.
Regional Director for Africa: S. Mbele-Mbong.
Regional Director for Latin America: I. G. Meira-Filho.
Regional Director for Asia: K. Rajendram.
Special Assistant for Regional Affairs: A. K. Elamly.
Executive Assistant to the Secretary-General: J. B. L. Breslin.

PRESIDENTS OF REGIONAL ASSOCIATIONS AND TECHNICAL COMMISSIONS

REGIONAL ASSOCIATIONS

I.   Africa: Workineh Degefu (Ethiopia).
II. Asia: U Thu Ta (Burma).
III. South America: C. A. Grezzi (Uruguay).

IV. North and Central America: S. Aguilar Anguiano (Mexico).
V.   South-West Pacific: Ho Tong Yuen (Malaysia).
VI. Europe: A. W. Kabakibo (Syrian Arab Republic).

TECHNICAL COMMISSIONS

Aeronautical Meteorology: J. Kastelein (Netherlands).
Agricultural Meteorology: M. N. Gerbier (France).
Atmospheric Sciences: F. Mesinger (Yugoslavia).
Basic Systems: J. R. Neilon (United States).

Climatology: J. L. Rasmussen (United States).
Hydrology: R. H. Clark (Canada).
Instruments and Methods of Observation: S. Huovila (Finland).
Marine Meteorology: K. P. Vasiliev (USSR).

HEADQUARTERS

World Meteorological Organization
41, Avenue Giuseppe-Motta
Case Postale No. 5
1211 Geneva 20, Switzerland
Cable address: METEOMOND GENEVA
Telephone: 34 64 00
Telex: 23260

Chapter XIV

International Maritime Organization (IMO)

On 17 March 1983, the International Maritime Organization (IMO) celebrated its twenty-fifth anniversary. The thirteenth regular session of the IMO biennial Assembly was held from 7 to 18 November at its new headquarters at 4 Albert Embankment on the south bank of the River Thames in London. The 45 resolutions adopted by the Assembly dealt with the prevention of marine pollution and improving maritime safety and included amendments to the International Convention on Load Lines, 1966. The Assembly also adopted the budget and work programme of IMO for 1984-1985 and took decisions regarding the future of the World Maritime University (see below) and the IMO long-term work plan.

In other action, the Assembly elected 24 States to serve on the IMO Council, the organization's governing body between Assembly sessions (see ANNEX II). In anticipation of the entry into force, on 10 November 1984, of the 1979 amendments to the IMO Convention, the Assembly elected another eight member States to serve on the Council as of that date when the Council's membership would be increased from 24 to 32. The eight States elected were Argentina, Bulgaria, Chile, Gabon, Ghana, India, Italy and Liberia.

Membership of IMO as at 31 December 1983, stood at 125, plus one associate member. New members admitted during the year were Fiji (14 March), Guatemala (16 March) and Togo (20 June).

Activities in 1983

The World Maritime University, established by IMO, was opened on 4 July 1983 at Malmö, Sweden. Its purpose was to provide high-level training in various maritime subjects for students from developing countries and the 72 students who joined at the start of its operations came from 42 countries. The University received financial assistance from Sweden, the United Nations Development Programme and a number of IMO member States.

The new IMO headquarters was officially opened by Her Majesty Queen Elizabeth II at a ceremony attended by 800 guests on 17 May. World Maritime Day was celebrated by IMO on 29 September with the theme "Maritime telecommunications for safety, efficiency and seafarers' welfare".

At a special ceremony held on 18 November, George A. Maslov (USSR) was presented with the International Maritime Prize for 1982. The Prize is awarded annually to the individual or organization judged by the IMO Council to have made the most significant contribution to the organization's aims.

Intervention Protocol

The 1973 Protocol to the International Convention relating to Intervention on the High Seas in Cases of Oil Pollution Casualties, 1969, entered into force on 30 March 1983. The Protocol establishes the circumstances under which, and the procedures by which, States may act when threatened by pollution following major maritime accidents. The 1969 Convention applied only to incidents threatening pollution by oil. The 1973 Protocol extends the application to other substances listed in an annex to the Protocol.

Collision regulations

Amendments to the Convention on the International Regulations for Preventing Collisions at Sea, 1972, entered into force on 1 June 1983. These amendments had been adopted by the IMO Assembly in November 1981.

Safety of life at sea

On 17 June 1983, the IMO Maritime Safety Committee adopted further amendments to the International Convention for the Safety of Life at Sea, 1974. These amendments, expected to enter into force on 1 July 1986, mainly affected Chapter III on life-saving appliance and arrangements, which was completely rewritten, and Chapter VII on the carriage of dangerous goods, under which the International Bulk Chemical Code and the International Gas Carrier Code were to become mandatory to all States parties to the Convention.

Prevention of pollution

The International Convention for the Prevention of Pollution from Ships, 1973, as modified by the 1978 Protocol (MARPOL 73/78), entered into force on 2 October 1983. The instrument contained measures designed to combat pollution from shipborne substances such as oil, liquid noxious substances, harmful substances in packaged forms, sewage and garbage.

Standards of training, certification and watchkeeping

The conditions for entry into force of the International Convention on Standards of Training, Certification and Watchkeeping for Seafarers, 1978, were fulfilled on 27 April 1983 when the twenty-fifth ratification was received. The Convention, generally regarded as the first attempt to establish minimum international professional standards for seafarers, was to enter into force on 28 April 1984.

Publications

Among publications issued by IMO during 1983 were the following: amendments 20-82 to the *International Maritime Dangerous Goods Code; Official Records of the International Conference on Limitation of Liability for Maritime Claims, 1976;* amendments to the *Convention on the International Regulations for Preventing Collisions at Sea, 1972; Basic Documents—Volume 1;* amendment No. 4 to *Ships' Routeing; Guidelines for Surveys under Annex I of MARPOL* 73/78; *Recommendations on the Safe Transport, Handling and Storage of Dangerous Substances in Port Areas; Crude Oil Washing Systems; Fresh Water Tanker Ballasting; Inert Gas Systems;* and amendment No. 10 to the *Code for the Construction and Equipment of Ships Carrying Dangerous Chemicals in Bulk.*

Secretariat

As at 31 December 1983, the IMO secretariat consisted of 238 full-time staff members (excluding those on technical assistance projects). Of these, 82 were in the Professional and higher categories (drawn from 34 nationalities) and 156 were in the General Service and related categories. There were 39 Professional staff employed on technical assistance projects in the field.

Budget

In November 1983, the IMO Assembly adopted a budget of $25,772,000 for the 1984-1985 biennium, with $12,593,800 allocated to 1984 and $13,178,200 to 1985.

Annex I. MEMBERSHIP OF THE INTERNATIONAL MARITIME ORGANIZATION AND CONTRIBUTIONS

(Membership as at 31 December 1983; contributions as assessed for 1983)

MEMBER	Percentage of total	Net amount (in US dollars)	MEMBER	Percentage of total	Net amount (in US dollars)	MEMBER	Percentage of total	Net amount (in US dollars)
Algeria	0.34	37,710	France	2.55	285,780	Mauritania	0.02	2,209
Angola	0.04	4,355	Gabon	0.04	4,041	Mauritius	0.03	2,811
Argentina	0.54	61,019	Gambia	0.02	2,078	Mexico	0.31	34,754
Australia	0.46	51,052	German Democratic Republic	0.35	39,646	Morocco	0.11	12,307
Austria	0.04	4,642	Germany, Federal Republic of	1.83	205,623	Mozambique	0.03	3,073
Bahamas	0.12	13,328	Ghana	0.08	8,723	Nepal	0.02	2,000
Bahrain	0.02	2,523	Greece	9.35	1,049,357	Netherlands	1.28	143,086
Bangladesh	0.11	12,752	Guatemala†	—	—	New Zealand	0.08	8,540
Barbados	0.03	3,177	Guinea	0.02	2,157	Nicaragua	0.02	2,549
Belgium	0.55	61,412	Guinea-Bissau	0.02	2,105	Nigeria	0.13	14,113
Benin	0.02	2,105	Guyana	0.02	2,549	Norway	5.11	573,932
Brazil	1.34	150,542	Haiti	0.02	2,052	Oman	0.02	2,235
Bulgaria	0.31	34,649	Honduras	0.07	8,122	Pakistan	0.15	17,173
Burma	0.04	4,302	Hungary	0.04	4,145	Panama	7.62	854,850
Canada	0.78	88,055	Iceland	0.06	6,735	Papua New Guinea	0.02	2,654
Cape Verde	0.02	2,288	India	1.47	164,538	Peru	0.21	23,871
Chile	0.13	14,950	Indonesia	0.45	50,319	Philippines	0.66	74,571
China	1.90	212,779	Iran	0.32	36,349	Poland	0.87	97,514
Colombia	0.09	10,215	Iraq	0.37	41,791	Portugal	0.34	38,678
Congo	0.02	2,209	Ireland	0.07	8,253	Qatar	0.07	8,122
Costa Rica	0.02	2,602	Israel	0.18	19,685	Republic of Korea	1.31	146,644
Cuba	0.24	26,827	Italy	2.45	275,421	Romania	0.53	59,633
Cyprus	0.52	58,246	Ivory Coast	0.05	5,977	Saint Lucia	0.02	2,052
Czechoslovakia	0.06	6,840	Jamaica	0.02	2,262	Saint Vincent and the Grenadines	0.02	2,680
Democratic Kampuchea	0.02	2,105	Japan	9.79	1,098,142	Saudi Arabia	1.02	114,545
Democratic Yemen	0.02	2,366	Jordan	0.02	2,549	Senegal	0.03	3,046
Denmark	1.23	138,404	Kenya	0.02	2,131	Seychelles	0.02	2,026
Djibouti	0.02	2,078	Kuwait	0.49	54,688	Sierra Leone	0.02	2,105
Dominica	0.02	2,026	Lebanon	0.10	11,627	Singapore	1.69	189,915
Dominican Republic	0.03	2,916	Liberia	16.50	1,852,056	Somalia	0.02	2,471
Ecuador	0.10	11,261	Libyan Arab Jamahiriya	0.23	25,859	Spain	1.91	214,715
Egypt	0.17	18,638	Madagascar	0.04	4,014	Sri Lanka	0.05	5,270
El Salvador	0.02	2,078	Malaysia	0.30	33,262	Sudan	0.04	4,433
Equatorial Guinea	0.02	2,157	Maldives	0.07	7,703	Suriname	0.02	2,392
Ethiopia	0.02	2,759	Malta	0.12	13,145	Sweden	0.90	101,098
Fiji*	—	—				Switzerland	0.09	10,241
Finland	0.57	64,185						

MEMBER	CONTRIBUTION Percent-age of total	CONTRIBUTION Net amount (in US dollars)	MEMBER	CONTRIBUTION Percent-age of total	CONTRIBUTION Net amount (in US dollars)	MEMBER	CONTRIBUTION Percent-age of total	CONTRIBUTION Net amount (in US dollars)
Syrian Arab Republic	0.03	3,125	United Kingdom	5.28	592,754	Yemen	0.02	2,078
Thailand	0.12	13,563	United Republic of			Yugoslavia	0.61	68,240
Togo‡	—	—	Cameroon	0.03	2,994	Zaire	0.04	4,407
Trinidad and Tobago	0.02	2,497	United Republic of					
Tunisia	0.05	5,558	Tanzania	0.03	3,544	ASSOCIATE MEMBER		
Turkey	0.51	57,671	United States	4.54	509,963			
USSR	5.64	632,345	Uruguay	0.06	7,285	Hong Kong	0.42	46,756
United Arab Emirates	0.07	8,043	Venezuela	0.23	25,833	Total	100.00	11,221,400

*Became a member on 14 March 1983.

†Became a member on 16 March 1983.

‡Became a member on 20 June 1983.

Annex II. OFFICERS AND OFFICE OF THE INTERNATIONAL MARITIME ORGANIZATION

(As at 31 December 1983)

IMO COUNCIL AND MARITIME SAFETY COMMITTEE

IMO COUNCIL

Chairman: William A. O'Neill (Canada).

Members: Algeria, Bangladesh, Brazil, Canada, China, Cuba, Egypt, France, Germany, Federal Republic of, Greece, Indonesia, Japan, Kuwait, Lebanon, Morocco, Nigeria, Netherlands, Norway, Saudi Arabia, Spain, Trinidad and Tobago, USSR, United Kingdom, United States.

MARITIME SAFETY COMMITTEE

Chairman: Per Eriksson (Sweden)

Membership in the Maritime Safety Committee is open to all IMO member States.

OFFICERS AND OFFICES

PRINCIPAL OFFICERS OF IMO SECRETARIAT

Secretary-General: Chandrika Prasad Srivastava.

Assistant Secretary-General: Thomas A. Mensah.

Secretary, Maritime Safety Committee: G. P. Kostylev.

HEADQUARTERS

International Maritime Organization

4 Albert Embankment

London, SE1 7SR, England

Cable address: INTERMAR LONDON, SE1

Telephone: 01-735-7611

Telex: 23588

Chapter XV

World Intellectual Property Organization (WIPO)

During 1983, membership of the World Intellectual Property Organization (WIPO) rose to 105 with the admission of Guatemala, Haiti, Honduras, Panama and the United Republic of Tanzania. Berne Union membership increased to 75 as a result of the accession by Barbados to the Berne Convention for the Protection of Literary and Artistic Works. Mauritania deposited its instrument of accession to the Patent Co-operation Treaty (PCT), thus bringing PCT Union membership to 33. At the end of the year, total membership in WIPO and its various Unions, taken together, was 123.

Sixteen intergovernmental Unions in the two main fields of intellectual property were administered by WIPO in 1983. They were founded on the multilateral treaties, conventions and agreements listed below in order of adoption:

> *Industrial property:* Paris Convention for the Protection of Industrial Property; Madrid Agreement for the Repression of False or Deceptive Indications of Source on Goods; Madrid Agreement concerning the International Registration of Marks; The Hague Agreement concerning the International Deposit of Industrial Designs; Nice Agreement concerning the International Classification of Goods and Services for the Purpose of the Registration of Marks; Lisbon Agreement for the Protection of Appellations of Origin and Their International Registration; Locarno Agreement establishing an International Classification for Industrial Designs; Patent Co-operation Treaty; International Patent Classification (IPC) Agreement; Trademark Registration Treaty; Budapest Treaty on the International Recognition of the Deposit of Micro-organisms for the Purposes of Patent Procedure; Nairobi Treaty on the Protection of the Olympic Symbol.
>
> *Copyright and neighbouring rights:* Berne Convention for the Protection of Literary and Artistic Works; Rome Convention for the Protection of Performers, Producers of Phonograms and Broadcasting Organizations; Geneva Convention for the Protection of Producers of Phonograms against Unauthorized Duplication of Their Phonograms; Brussels Convention relating to the Distribution of Programme-Carrying Signals Transmitted by Satellite.

At the fourteenth series of meetings, held at Geneva in September/October 1983, the governing bodies of WIPO and the Unions administered by it approved reports on activities, and the programme and budget for 1984-1985.

The one hundredth anniversary of the signing of the Paris Convention was celebrated in 1983, with WIPO representation, at a ceremony organized in Paris (May) by France and the International Association for the Protection of Industrial Property, and at a solemn meeting held at Geneva (September).

Activities in 1983

Development co-operation activities

Two WIPO permanent programmes, supervised by intergovernmental permanent committees, provided the framework for development co-operation relating to industrial property and to copyright and neighbouring rights.

In the field of industrial property, WIPO organized a Round Table on the Promotion of Indigenous Inventive and Innovative Activity in Asia and the Pacific, and a Workshop on Industrial Property Licences and Technology Transfer Arrangements, both at Manila, Philippines; a Seminar on the Roles of Government Industrial Property Authorities and the Legal Profession in Administering Industrial Property Rights in Asia and the Pacific, at Bangkok, Thailand; a High-Level Meeting of Government Officials of South Pacific Countries to Consider Co-operation in the Field of Industrial Property, at Suva, Fiji; a Seminar on Trademarks and Patents in ASEAN (Association of South-East Asian Nations) Countries, at Kuala Lumpur, Malaysia; and a Workshop on Patents in the Service of Development, at Harare, Zimbabwe.

Medals and prizes for inventors were awarded by WIPO at exhibitions or contests held in Bulgaria, France, Japan, the Philippines, the Republic of Korea and the USSR.

In continuation of a programme started in 1975, 287 state-of-the-art search reports on technology disclosed in patent documents and related literature were provided to developing countries free of charge under agreements concluded between WIPO and contributing industrial property offices in developed countries. Most of the reports were prepared by the Austrian, German Democratic Republic and Swedish Patent Offices.

Development co-operation activities in copyright and neighbouring rights included the convening, jointly or in co-operation with other organizations—notably the United Nations

Educational, Scientific and Cultural Organization (UNESCO)—of regional committees (Africa, Asia) of experts on means of implementation of model provisions on intellectual property aspects of protection of expressions of folklore, at Dakar, Senegal, and New Delhi, India, respectively; a Consultative Committee on the Access by Developing Countries to Works Protected by Copyright, at Geneva; a Congress on the Intellectual Property Rights of Performers, at Buenos Aires, Argentina; and a Committee of Governmental Experts on the Drafting of Model Statutes for Institutions Administering Authors' Rights in Developing Countries, at Geneva.

The WIPO training programmes in industrial property and in copyright continued to grow, with 210 fellowships granted in 1983 to nationals of 75 developing countries or individuals recommended by various organizations. Twenty-eight countries, including nine developing countries, and three intergovernmental organizations provided individual training, in addition to study opportunities and courses for groups organized at Berlin (West), Budapest (Hungary), Geneva, The Hague (Netherlands), Lyon (France), Madrid (Spain), Moscow, Munich (Federal Republic of Germany), Paris, Quito (Ecuador), Rio de Janeiro (Brazil), Stockholm (Sweden), Strasbourg (France), Vienna (Austria) and Zurich (Switzerland). Regional and national meetings and seminars were organized by WIPO in Argentina, China, Colombia, Costa Rica, the Democratic People's Republic of Korea, El Salvador, Fiji, Guatemala, India, Malaysia, Peru, the Philippines, Senegal, Thailand, Trinidad and Tobago, Uruguay, Viet Nam and Zimbabwe.

During 1983, WIPO co-operated with Governments of 66 developing countries and with seven intergovernmental organizations in their development projects relating to intellectual property, by providing assistance in the preparation of legislation, or establishment or modernization of national or regional institutions, including patent documentation and information services.

Industrial property

An extraordinary session of the Paris Union Assembly in February 1983 decided that the fourth session of the Diplomatic Conference on the Revision of the Paris Convention would take place at Geneva from 27 February to 24 March 1984. The objective of the revision was to introduce provisions to meet the needs of developing countries more effectively and to incorporate new provisions giving full recognition to inventors' certificates, a form of protection of inventions existing in several socialist countries.

In resolution 143(VI) on the technological transformation of developing countries (see ECONOMIC AND SOCIAL QUESTIONS, Chapter XII), UNCTAD VI invited countries attending the Conference to co-operate in concluding the revision, taking fully into account the interests particularly of the developing countries.

Work continued on keeping up to date IPC and other classifications relating to industrial designs or registration of trade marks and service marks. As in the past, WIPO assisted the International Patent Documentation Centre and remained on its Supervisory Board, while efforts continued towards early conclusion of the Computerized Administration of Patent Documents Reclassified According to IPC. The revised (fourth) edition of the *Guide to the International Patent Classification* was prepared for publication.

At the end of 1983, thirty-three States were party to PCT. During the year, 5,050 international applications were filed in 19 receiving offices. Twenty-nine issues of the *PCT Gazette* were published during the year, containing information on 4,466 published international applications.

The Committees of Experts on Joint Inventive Activity (Geneva, May) examined a draft guide to the legal regulation of questions concerning the results of joint inventive activity in the course of international scientific, technological and economic co-operation. The Committee of Experts on the Legal Protection of Computer Software (second session, Geneva, June) discussed the question on the basis of a draft treaty and model provisions for national legislation, as prepared by WIPO, but concluded it premature to decide on such international protection.

Publications in the industrial property field included those on industrial property statistics, industrial property laws and treaties, the monthly review *Industrial Property*, *The Role of Industrial Property in the Protection of Consumers* and the third volume of the *WIPO Handbook on Patent Information and Documentation*. A special publication on industrial property statistics, 1883-1982, was issued on the occasion of the Paris Convention centenary.

Copyright and neighbouring rights

A Consultants' Meeting on Television by Cable, convened jointly with ILO and UNESCO (Geneva, March) dealt with the protection of various interests relating to the cable distribution of programmes. WIPO also held at Geneva a World-Wide Forum on the Piracy of Broadcasts and of the Printed Word.

Publications in the copyright field included the *WIPO Glossary of Terms of the Law of Copyright and Neighboring Rights* in a three-language edition (English, French, Portuguese) and the monthly periodicals *Copyright* and *Le Droit d'auteur*.

Secretariat

As at 31 December 1983, WIPO employed 250 full-time staff members. Of these, 91 were in the Professional and higher categories (drawn from 39 member States) and 159 were in the General Service category. In addition, 110 experts were employed by WIPO on technical assistance projects during the year.

Budget

The principal sources of the WIPO budget—expected to approximate 86 million Swiss francs for the biennium 1984-1985—are ordinary and special contributions from member States and income derived from international registration services.

Ordinary contributions are paid on the basis of a class-and-unit system by members of the Paris, Berne, Nice and Locarno Unions and by member States of WIPO that are not members of any of the Unions.

States members of those four Unions are placed in seven classes (I to VII) to determine the amounts of their ordinary contributions. States members of WIPO not members of any of the Unions are placed in three classes (A, B or C) for the same purpose. States in Class I or A pay the highest contributions of their group and those in Class VII or C the lowest. The class in which a State is placed is decided solely by the State. The rights of each State are the same, irrespective of class chosen.

The contribution class for each member State of WIPO and of the Paris or Berne Unions, together with the amount of the ordinary contribution of each State, is given in ANNEX I below (the class indicated for the Paris Union also applies to the Nice, Locarno and IPC Unions). Members of one or more Unions do not pay separate contributions to WIPO; the Unions themselves contribute towards the costs of WIPO's International Bureau.

The amounts of ordinary contributions payable for 1983 are given in the table below.

Income and expenditure

Summary figures for income and expenditure for 1983 are as follows:

	In thousands of Swiss francs	Equivalent in thousands of US dollars*
Income		
Contributions	18,658	8,559
Income from registration services	15,673	7,189
Publications and miscellaneous	4,566	2,094
Total	38,897	17,842
Expenditure		
Staff	24,077	11,044
Publications	5,509	2,527
Buildings†	4,981	2,285
Travel	1,573	722
Meetings	647	297
Other	2,682	1,230
Total	39,469	18,105

*At the United Nations rate of exchange for December 1983: 2.18 Swiss francs = $US 1.00.
†Includes maintenance, rental and amortization of the building loan.

CONTRIBUTION SCALES FOR 1984

(2.18 Swiss francs = $US 1.00: United Nations rate as at 31 December 1983)

	In Swiss francs	Equivalent in US dollars		In Swiss francs	Equivalent in US dollars
*WIPO**			II	†	†
Class			III	10,764	4,938
A	75,000	34,403	IV	7,176	3,292
B	22,500	10,321	V	3,589	1,646
C	7,500	3,440	VI	2,153	988
PARIS UNION			VII	†	†
Class			*BERNE UNION*		
I	507,828	232,949	*Class*		
II	†	†	I	296,273	135,905
III	304,698	139,770	II	237,018	108,724
IV	203,131	93,179	III	177,764	81,543
V	101,565	46,589	IV	118,509	54,362
VI	60,939	27,954	V	59,255	27,181
VII	20,313	9,318	VI	35,553	16,309
NICE UNION			VII	11,851	5,436
Class			*IPC UNION*		
I	46,301	21,239	*Class*		
II	†	†	I	242,479	111,229
III	27,781	12,744	II	†	†
IV	18,521	8,496	III	145,488	66,738
V	9,259	4,247	IV	96,991	44,491
VI	5,556	2,549	V	†	†
VII	1,853	850	VI	29,097	13,347
LOCARNO UNION			VII	9,699	4,449
Class			Total	2,914,345	1,336,856
I	17,941	8,230			

NOTE: There were no contributions to the PCT Union for 1984.
*The amounts indicated are payable by those States members of WIPO which are not members of any of the Unions (see Annex I).
†No State currently belonged to this class.

Annex I. MEMBERSHIP OF THE WORLD INTELLECTUAL PROPERTY ORGANIZATION AND UNIONS ADMINISTERED TO WHICH CONTRIBUTIONS ARE PAYABLE

(As at 31 December 1983; ordinary contributions payable in 1984)

STATE	MEMBER						CLASS W	CLASS P	CLASS B	CONTRIBUTION In Swiss francs	CONTRIBUTION Equivalent in US dollars*
Algeria	W	P	—	N	—	—	—	VI	—	66,495	30,502
Argentina	W	P	B	—	—	—	—	VI	VI	96,492	44,262
Australia	W	P	B	N	—	IPC	—	III	III	655,731	300,794
Austria	W	P	B	N	—	IPC	—	IV	VI	354,196	162,475
Bahamas	W	P	B	—	—	—	—	VII	VII	32,164	14,754
Barbados	W	—	B	—	—	—	—	—	VII	11,851	5,436
Belgium	W	P	B	N	—	IPC	—	III	III	655,731	300,794
Benin	W	P	B	N	—	—	—	VII	VII	34,017	15,604
Brazil	W	P	B	—	—	IPC	—	IV	IV	418,631	192,032
Bulgaria	W	P	B	—	—	—	—	VI	VI	96,492	44,262
Burundi	W	P	—	—	—	—	—	VII	—	20,313	9,317
Byelorussian SSR	W	—	—	—	—	—	C	—	—	7,500	3,440
Canada	W	P	B	—	—	—	—	III	III	482,462	221,312
Central African Republic	W	P	B	—	—	—	—	VII	VII	32,164	14,754
Chad	W	P	B	—	—	—	—	VII	VII	32,164	14,754
Chile	W	—	B	—	—	—	—	—	VI	35,553	16,308
China	W	—	—	—	—	—	B	—	—	22,500	10,321
Colombia	W	—	—	—	—	—	C	—	—	7,500	3,440
Congo	W	P	B	—	—	—	—	VII	VII	32,164	14,754
Costa Rica	W	—	B	—	—	—	—	—	VII	11,851	5,436
Cuba	W	P	—	—	—	—	—	VI	—	60,939	27,953
Cyprus	—	P	B	—	—	—	—	VI	VII	72,790	33,389
Czechoslovakia	W	P	B	N	LO	IPC	—	IV	IV	444,328	203,820
Democratic People's Republic of Korea	W	P	—	—	—	—	—	VII	—	20,313	9,317
Denmark	W	P	B	N	LO	IPC	—	IV	IV	444,328	203,820
Dominican Republic	—	P	—	—	—	—	—	VI	—	60,939	27,953
Egypt	W	P	B	—	—	IPC	—	VI	VII	101,887	46,737
El Salvador	W	—	—	—	—	—	C	—	—	7,500	3,440
Fiji	W	—	B	—	—	—	—	—	VII	11,851	5,436
Finland	W	P	B	N	LO	IPC	—	IV	IV	444,328	203,820
France	W	P	B	N	LO	IPC	—	I	I	1,110,822	509,551
Gabon	W	P	B	—	—	—	—	VII	VII	32,164	14,754
Gambia	W	—	—	—	—	—	C	—	—	7,500	3,440
German Democratic Republic	W	P	B	N	LO	IPC	—	III	V	547,986	251,369
Germany, Federal Republic of	W	P	B	N	—	IPC	—	I	I	1,092,881	501,321
Ghana	W	P	—	—	—	—	—	VII	—	20,313	9,317
Greece	W	P	B	—	—	—	—	V	VI	137,118	62,898
Guatemala	W	—	—	—	—	—	C	—	—	7,500	3,440
Guinea	W	P	B	—	—	—	—	VII	VII	32,164	14,754
Haiti	W	P	—	—	—	—	—	VII	—	20,313	9,317
Holy See	W	P	B	—	—	—	—	VII	VII	32,164	14,754
Honduras	W	—	—	—	—	—	C	—	—	7,500	3,440
Hungary	W	P	B	N	LO	—	—	V	VI	149,966	68,791
Iceland	—	P	B	—	—	—	—	VI	VI	96,492	44,262
India	W	—	B	—	—	—	—	—	IV	118,509	54,361
Indonesia	W	P	—	—	—	—	—	VI	—	60,939	27,953
Iran	—	P	—	—	—	—	—	VI	—	60,939	27,953
Iraq	W	P	—	—	—	—	—	VI	—	60,939	27,953
Ireland	W	P	B	N	LO	IPC	—	IV	IV	444,328	203,820
Israel	W	P	B	N	—	IPC	—	VI	VI	131,145	60,158
Italy	W	P	B	N	LO	IPC	—	III	III	666,495	305,731
Ivory Coast	W	P	B	—	—	—	—	VII	VI	55,866	25,626
Jamaica	W	—	—	—	—	—	C	—	—	7,500	3,440
Japan	W	P	B	—	—	IPC	—	I	II	987,325	452,901
Jordan	W	P	—	—	—	—	—	VII	—	20,313	9,317
Kenya	W	P	—	—	—	—	—	VI	—	60,939	27,953
Lebanon	—	P	B	N	—	—	—	VI	VI	102,048	46,810
Libyan Arab Jamahiriya	W	P	B	—	—	—	—	VI	VI	96,492	44,262
Liechtenstein	W	P	B	N	—	—	—	VII	VII	34,017	15,604
Luxembourg	W	P	B	N	—	IPC	—	VII	VII	43,716	20,053
Madagascar	—	P	B	—	—	—	—	VII	VI	55,866	25,626
Malawi	W	P	—	—	—	—	—	VII	—	20,313	9,317
Mali	W	P	B	—	—	—	—	VII	VII	32,164	14,754
Malta	W	P	B	—	—	—	—	VII	VII	32,164	14,754
Mauritania	W	P	—	—	—	—	—	VII	—	20,313	9,317
Mauritius	W	P	—	—	—	—	—	VII	—	20,313	9,317
Mexico	W	P	B	—	—	—	—	IV	IV	321,640	147,541
Monaco	W	P	B	N	—	IPC	—	VII	VII	43,716	20,053
Mongolia	W	—	—	—	—	—	C	—	—	7,500	3,440
Morocco	W	P	B	N	—	—	—	VI	VI	102,048	46,810
Netherlands	W	P	B	N	LO	IPC	—	III	III	666,495	305,731
New Zealand	—	P	B	—	—	—	—	V	V	160,820	73,770
Niger	W	P	B	—	—	—	—	VII	VII	32,164	14,754
Nigeria	—	P	—	—	—	—	—	VI	—	60,939	27,953

STATE	MEMBER						CLASS			CONTRIBUTION	
							W	P	B	In Swiss francs	Equivalent in US dollars*
Norway	W	P	B	N	LO	IPC	—	IV	IV	444,328	203,820
Pakistan	W	—	B	—	—	—	—	—	VI	35,553	16,308
Panama	W	—	—	—	—	—	C	—	—	7,500	3,440
Peru	W	—	—	—	—	—	C	—	—	7,500	3,440
Philippines	W	P	B	—	—	—	—	VI	VI	96,492	44,262
Poland	W	P	B	—	—	—	—	V	VI	137,118	62,898
Portugal	W	P	B	N	—	IPC	—	IV	V	377,898	173,347
Qatar	W	—	—	—	—	—	B	—	—	22,500	10,321
Republic of Korea	W	P	—	—	—	—	—	VI	—	60,939	27,953
Romania	W	P	B	—	—	—	—	V	VI	137,118	62,898
San Marino	—	P	—	—	—	—	—	VI	—	60,939	27,953
Saudi Arabia	W	—	—	—	—	—	A	—	—	75,000	34,403
Senegal	W	P	B	—	—	—	—	VII	VI	55,866	25,626
Somalia	W	—	—	—	—	—	C	—	—	7,500	3,440
South Africa	W	P	B	—	—	—	—	IV	IV	321,640	147,541
Spain	W	P	B	N	LO	IPC	—	IV	II	562,837	258,182
Sri Lanka	W	P	B	—	—	—	—	VII	VII	32,164	14,754
Sudan	W	—	—	—	—	—	C	—	—	7,500	3,440
Suriname	W	P	B	N	—	IPC	—	VII	VII	43,716	20,053
Sweden	W	P	B	N	LO	IPC	—	III	III	666,495	305,731
Switzerland	W	P	B	N	LO	IPC	—	III	III	666,495	305,731
Syrian Arab Republic	—	P	—	—	—	—	—	VI	—	60,939	27,953
Thailand	—	—	B	—	—	—	—	—	VII	11,851	5,436
Togo	W	P	B	—	—	—	—	VII	VII	32,164	14,754
Trinidad and Tobago	—	P	—	—	—	—	—	VI	—	60,939	27,953
Tunisia	W	P	B	N	—	—	—	VI	VI	102,048	46,810
Turkey	W	P	B	—	—	—	—	VI	VI	96,492	44,262
Uganda	W	P	—	—	—	—	—	VII	—	20,313	9,317
Ukrainian SSR	W	—	—	—	—	—	C	—	—	7,500	3,440
USSR	W	P	—	N	LO	IPC	—	I	—	814,549	373,646
United Arab Emirates	W	—	—	—	—	—	B	—	—	22,500	10,321
United Kingdom	W	P	B	N	—	IPC	—	I	I	1,092,881	501,321
United Republic of Cameroon	W	P	B	—	—	—	—	VII	VI	55,866	25,626
United Republic of Tanzania	W	P	—	—	—	—	—	VII	—	20,313	9,317
United States	W	P	—	N	—	IPC	—	I	—	796,608	365,416
Upper Volta	W	P	B	—	—	—	—	VII	VII	32,164	14,754
Uruguay	W	P	B	—	—	—	—	VII	VII	32,164	14,754
Venezuela	—	—	B	—	—	—	—	—	V	59,255	27,181
Viet Nam	W	P	—	—	—	—	—	VII	—	20,313	9,317
Yemen	W	—	—	—	—	—	C	—	—	7,500	3,440
Yugoslavia	W	P	B	N	LO	—	—	VI	VI	104,201	47,798
Zaire	W	P	B	—	—	—	—	VI	VI	96,492	44,262
Zambia	W	P	—	—	—	—	—	VII	—	20,313	9,317
Zimbabwe	W	P	B	—	—	—	—	VII	VII	32,164	14,754
Total	105	92	75	32	15	27				20,036,500	9,191,003

NOTE: Membership in WIPO is indicated by "W"; in the Paris Union by "P"; in the Berne Union by "B"; in the Nice Union by "N"; in the Locarno Union by "LO"; in the Strasbourg (IPC) Union by "IPC". The class indicated for the Paris Union applies equally to the Nice, Locarno and IPC Unions. In addition, the following five States, not members of WIPO, are party to one or more of the treaties administered by WIPO: Ecuador, Equatorial Guinea, Ethiopia, Nicaragua, Paraguay.

*Calculated on the basis of the United Nations rate of exchange for December 1983: 2.18 Swiss francs = $US 1.00.

Annex II.   OFFICERS AND OFFICES OF THE WORLD INTELLECTUAL PROPERTY ORGANIZATION
(As at 31 December 1983)

CO-ORDINATION COMMITTEE

OFFICERS
Chairman: Paul Braendli (Switzerland).
First Vice-Chairman: Fernando Jiménez Dávila (Argentina).
Second Vice-Chairman: Ibrahima Sy (Senegal).

MEMBERS
Algeria, Argentina, Australia, Austria, Benin, Brazil, Bulgaria, Canada, Chile, China, Colombia, Congo, Costa Rica, Czechoslovakia, Egypt, France, German Democratic Republic, Germany, Federal Republic of, Guatemala,* Hungary, India, Italy, Ivory Coast, Japan, Lebanon, Mexico, Mongolia, Morocco, Netherlands, Norway, Poland, Portugal, Qatar,† Senegal, Sudan, Switzerland, Trinidad and Tobago, Tunisia, Turkey, USSR, United Kingdom, United Republic of Tanzania, United States, Uruguay, Viet Nam, Yugoslavia, Zaire, Zambia.

*With effect from the date on which the number of members of WIPO, not members of any of the Unions, becomes 20.
†With effect from the date on which the number of members of WIPO, not members of any of the Unions, becomes 24.

SENIOR OFFICERS OF THE INTERNATIONAL BUREAU

Director General: Arpad Bogsch.
Deputy Directors General: Klaus Pfanner, Marino Porzio, Lev Kostikov.
Director, Public Information and Copyright Department: Claude Masouyé.
Director, Copyright Law Division: Gyorgy Boytha.
Director, Developing Countries Division (Copyright): Shahid Alikhan.
Director, Public Information Division: Roger Harben.

Director, Industrial Property Division: Ludwig Baeumer.
Director, Classifications and Patent Information Division: Paul Claus.
Director, Patent Co-operation Treaty Division: François Curchod.
Director, Administrative Division: Thomas Keefer.
Legal Counsel: Gust Ledakis.

HEADQUARTERS AND OTHER OFFICE

HEADQUARTERS
World Intellectual Property Organization
34 Chemin des Colombettes
1211 Geneva 20, Switzerland
  Cable address: WIPO Geneva *or* OMPI Genève
  Telephone: 999111
  Telex: 22376 OMPI CH

LIAISON OFFICE WITH THE UNITED NATIONS IN NEW YORK
World Intellectual Property Organization
2 United Nations Plaza, Room 560
New York, N. Y. 10017, United States
  Telephone: (212) 754-6813
  Telex: 420544 UNH UI

Chapter XVI

International Fund for Agricultural Development (IFAD)

The International Fund for Agricultural Development (IFAD), which completed its sixth year of operation in 1983, continued to provide concessional-term resources for agricultural development and reduction of rural poverty in its developing member States. As in previous years, the Fund's lending policies reflected its conviction that food problems could be solved only if the rural poor were enabled to participate in the development process. In 1983, emphasis continued to be on projects which were quick-maturing and based on increased and improved use of water, fertilizers and pest control.

The 18-member Executive Board of IFAD met three times in 1983 (20-22 April, 12-15 September, 12-14 December) and approved 24 projects. At the seventh session of the Governing Council (6-9 December), the term of IFAD President Abdelmuhsin M. Al-Sudeary was extended until December 1984. Meetings on the replenishment of IFAD's resources were held on 25 and 26 July and on 18 and 19 October. All meetings were held at Rome, Italy.

Membership of IFAD remained at 139 countries during 1983. Of these, 20 were in Category I (developed countries), 12 in Category II (oil-exporting developing countries) and 107 in Category III (other developing countries).

With the approval of 24 additional projects in 1983, the total assistance provided by the Fund to some 80 member countries since 1978 amounted to about $1,656 million, of which approximately $1,580 million was committed for 135 projects, and $76 million was provided as technical assistance grants.

Of the 135 loans provided since 1978, 46 were for projects in Africa, 40 in Asia, 27 in Latin America and the Caribbean, and 22 in the Near East and North Africa. Most of the Fund's loans (66 per cent) were made on highly concessional terms, with a service charge of 1 per cent per annum, a 50-year maturity period and a 10-year grace period. Another 28 per cent of the loans were made available on intermediate terms (at 4 per cent, 20 years maturity and a five-year grace period) and the remaining 6 per cent were on ordinary terms (8 per cent, 15-18 years maturity and a three-year grace period). The Fund paid particular attention to the needs of the poorest developing countries—some 67 per cent of total loan commitments since 1978 went to those countries with

a per capita income of less than $300 (in 1976 terms); about 32 per cent went to those countries classified as least developed.

Since 1979, approved loans were denominated in special drawing rights (SDRs), an international unit of account. Dollar figures in this chapter are based on the SDR/United States dollar conversion rate at 31 December 1983 (SDR 1 = $US 1.04695).

Resources

The Fund was faced with growing resource difficulties in 1983. The first replenishment contribution payments which should have been completed by the end of 1983 were considerably delayed. Contributions pledged by Category I and II members towards the first replenishment amounted to $1,050 million at the valuation date, 11 December 1980. As a result of changes in exchange rates, these pledges totalled $948,566,000 at 31 December 1983; payments towards these pledges by Category I and II countries totalled $623,972,392. Payments by Category III countries as of 31 December 1983 totalled $31,151,733, against pledges totalling $32,409,363. Consultations began in 1983 on the second replenishment to cover the 1984-1986 programmes.

Investments

Investment of the Fund's liquid assets, which totalled $587 million at the end of 1983, continued to be restricted to obligations (bonds) issued or fully guaranteed by Governments and to time deposits with major banks. Of these assets, $14.5 million was held on demand deposit, and $274.9 million was held on time deposit with, or in obligations issued by, commercial banks, while the balance of $297.6 million was in bonds and similar securities issued or guaranteed by member Governments. While the maximum maturity for any of these investments was five years, the average length of an investment in the Fund's portfolio was 16 months.

At 31 December 1983, the Fund had a total of $188 million, or 32 per cent of its total liquid assets, deposited with banks of developing countries or in bonds or similar securities issued by their Governments and international development institutions.

Interest rates, which had dropped in the second half of 1982, stabilized somewhat in 1983.

However, the average rate of return on the Fund's investments in 1983 was about 11 per cent, compared to 12.4 per cent in 1982.

Activities in 1983

During 1983, IFAD approved 24 new loans totalling some $260 million and technical assistance grants of about $19 million, bringing the total financial assistance provided in 1983 to $279 million, compared with $322 million in 1982.

Because of the Fund's difficult resource position in 1983, the work programme, initially projected and approved for $422 million, was reduced to $300 million. In addition, the Executive Board decided to limit new loans and grants to resources actually available. These measures had a significant impact on operations throughout the year: efforts to mobilize resources from external donors, through co-financing, were increased; priority was given to countries which had not previously received loans, and to other countries, particularly in Africa, facing chronic food shortages; and the size of loans was reduced in cases in which the Government or other co-financiers could increase their contribution.

Overall, in 1983, IFAD contributed about 27 per cent of total investment costs, the balance being financed by external donors (39 per cent) and recipient countries (34 per cent). In 1980 and 1981, IFAD had contributed some 31 per cent of project costs; the 1983 reduction emphasized the mobilizing of external resources and efforts to protect IFAD's lending programme.

In 1983, the emphasis on Africa continued, with 11 projects, involving loans of some $108.6 million, approved. Of these projects, three emphasized rural development and two agricultural production, two would provide credit to co-operatives and small farmers for agricultural production, marketing and processing, two pertained to national research and extension, one was to assist in developing an inland fisheries area, and one would finance fertilizer imports and widen their distribution.

Six projects emphasizing food production in Asia involving loans of $96.2 million were approved in 1983: five were selected for co-financing from co-operating institutions; the other was to be financed exclusively by IFAD. Since land was scarce in Asia, irrigation was emphasized. Two projects were for irrigation, one was for agricultural development including irrigation, and the remaining three were credit projects, the outcome of the success of similar ones enabling the poor to gain access to credit.

Of four loans totalling some $21.3 million approved for Latin America and the Caribbean, three were for rural development and the fourth was for agricultural development.

In the Near East and North Africa, three projects involving loans of $33.6 million were approved, all for irrigation to increase agricultural production.

One was for northern Sudan, an area which had not previously benefited from public investments.

As regards technical assistance, IFAD provided some $1.7 million to assist 12 member States in project preparation activities. Grant financing also continued for elements of technical assistance included in projects such as training, agricultural extension and special studies, with Guinea-Bissau, the Lao People's Democratic Republic and Malawi receiving some $2.4 million. In support of international agricultural research, IFAD made grants totalling $8.6 million to research centres co-ordinated by the Consultative Group on International Agricultural Research (CGIAR). Grants amounting to $5.4 million were also made to institutions outside the CGIAR network.

The tables below show technical assistance grants approved during 1983 for project preparation and for research. Technical assistance grants as components within loans are shown in the table on project loans.

IFAD also organized programming missions to selected member countries to assist Governments to analyse the constraints and potentials of the agricultural sector in expanding food production. By the end of 1983, the Fund had organized 22 such missions, including two in 1983 to the Dominican Republic and Pakistan.

Income and expenditures

Total revenue in 1983 was $70.2 million, of which $65.2 million was investment income and $5 million was income from interest and service charges on loans. Expenses amounted to $18.6 million compared with the budget of $22.7 million approved by the Governing Council in December 1982. The excess of revenue over expenses for the year was $51.6 million.

Secretariat

As at 31 December 1983, the secretariat of IFAD totalled 160, of whom 68 were executive or technical staff (Professional category and above) drawn from 42 countries, and 92 were support staff (General Service category).

PROJECT PREPARATION GRANTS

Country	Amount (in thousands of US dollars)
Belize	200
Bolivia	157
Cape Verde	240
Congo	80
Cuba	180
Ethiopia	195
Malawi	80
Nepal	250
Papua New Guinea	200
Philippines	150
Total	1,732

RESEARCH GRANTS

Recipient	Amount (in thousands of US dollars)
Arab Centre for the Study of Arid Zones and Dry Lands, Damascus, Syrian Arab Republic	954
Centro Agronómico Tropical de Investigación y Ensenanza, Turrialba, Costa Rica	1,246
Centro Internacional de Agricultura Tropical, Cali, Colombia	1,150
International Centre for Agricultural Research in the Dry Areas, Aleppo, Syrian Arab Republic	2,150
International Centre for Insect Physiology and Ecology, Nairobi, Kenya	1,100
International Crops Research Institute for the Semi-Arid Tropics, Hyderabad, India	350
International Fertilizer Development Centre, Alabama, United States	1,100
International Food Policy Research Institute, Washington, D. C., United States	160
International Institute for Tropical Agriculture, Ibadan, Nigeria	1,500
International Livestock Centre for Africa, Addis Ababa, Ethiopia	600
International Potato Centre, Lima, Peru	700
International Rice Research Institute, Los Baños, Philippines	1,700
Scientific, Technical and Research Commission of the Organization of African Unity, Ouagadougou, Upper Volta	1,000
West African Rice Development Association, Monrovia, Liberia	300
Total	14,010

PROJECT LOANS APPROVED AND TECHNICAL ASSISTANCE GRANTED DURING 1983

COUNTRY	Purpose	AMOUNT* (in thousands of US dollars) Loan	Technical assistance
Bangladesh	Small-scale flood control, drainage and irrigation	11,000	—
Congo	La Cuvette artisanal fisheries	4,600†	—
Ecuador	Sur de Loja integrated rural development	5,400†	—
Ethiopia	Agricultural credit	11,000	—
Guinea-Bissau	Tombali rice development	7,000	1,000
Haiti	Northern region rural development	5,000	—
India	Uttar Pradesh public tubewells	35,300	—
Kenya	National extension	6,000	—
Lao People's Democratic Rep.	Agricultural production	7,400	390
Madagascar	Highlands rice	13,800	—
Malawi	Smallholder fertilizer supply	9,300	1,050
Mali	Mali Sud rural development	13,000	—
Morocco	Central Haouz irrigation	17,000†	—
Pakistan	Small farmers' credit	25,000	—
Panama	Rural development for the Guaymi communities	9,000‡	—
Saint Lucia	Small farmers' agricultural development	2,000†	—
Sudan	Northern region agricultural rehabilitation	10,000	—
Swaziland	Smallholder credit and marketing	6,200†	—
Thailand	Agricultural credit	20,200†	—
Togo	Notse rural development	8,000	—
Tonga	Agricultural credit	1,000	—
Tunisia	Sidi Bouzid irrigation	7,300‡	—
United Republic of Cameroon	Western Province rural development	14,500†	—
Zimbabwe	National agricultural extension and research	18,000†	—
Total		267,000	2,440

*Dollar equivalent based on SDR/United States dollar exchange rate effective at the time of loan negotiations.

NOTE: Loans are on highly concessional terms except for those marked †, which are on intermediate terms, and ‡, which are on ordinary terms.

Annex I. MEMBERSHIP OF THE INTERNATIONAL FUND FOR AGRICULTURAL DEVELOPMENT AND CONTRIBUTIONS PLEDGED AND PAID

(As at 31 December 1983)

MEMBER	INITIAL CONTRIBUTIONS (in US dollar equivalents) Pledged	Paid	FIRST REPLENISHMENT CONTRIBUTIONS (in US dollar equivalents) Pledged	Paid
Category I				
Australia	7,207,207	7,207,207	8,076,577	8,076,577
Austria	4,800,000	4,800,000	3,860,694	3,860,694
Belgium	9,986,341	9,986,341	8,361,610	7,704,888
Canada	26,612,903	26,612,903	33,870,968	22,580,645
Denmark	7,500,000	7,500,000	6,079,027	6,079,027
Finland	2,065,404	2,065,404	4,130,809	4,130,809
France	15,269,461	15,269,461	27,477,844	22,898,204
Germany, Federal Republic of	55,000,000	55,000,000	42,948,530	28,643,383
Ireland	827,286	827,286	720,772	720,772
Italy	25,000,000	25,000,000	38,700,000	38,700,000
Japan	55,000,000	55,000,000	54,785,909	36,523,939
Luxembourg	335,024	335,024	234,220	153,343
Netherlands	35,679,739	35,679,739	32,101,307	32,101,307
New Zealand	1,307,189	1,307,189	1,361,961	1,361,961
Norway	16,883,117	16,883,117	23,550,357	23,550,357
Spain	2,000,000	2,000,000	2,000,000	2,000,000
Sweden	14,375,000	14,375,000	18,535,000	18,535,000
Switzerland	10,091,743	10,091,743	13,045,872	13,045,872
United Kingdom	26,124,819	26,124,819	18,724,422	12,482,949
United States	200,000,000	200,000,000	180,000,000	40,000,000
Subtotal	516,065,233	516,065,233	518,565,879	323,149,727

MEMBER	INITIAL CONTRIBUTIONS (in US dollar equivalents) Pledged	Paid	FIRST REPLENISHMENT CONTRIBUTIONS (in US dollar equivalents) Pledged	Paid
Category II				
Algeria	10,000,000	10,000,000	15,580,000	15,580,000
Gabon	500,000	500,000	801,000	801,000
Indonesia	1,250,000	1,250,000	1,909,000	1,909,000
Iran	124,750,000	41,583,333	—	—
Iraq	20,000,000	20,000,000	31,099,000	31,099,000
Kuwait	36,000,000	36,000,000	56,041,000	56,041,000
Libyan Arab Jamahiriya	20,000,000	20,000,000	—	—
Nigeria	26,000,000	26,000,000	40,459,000	13,498,333
Qatar	9,000,000	9,000,000	13,980,000	13,980,000
Saudi Arabia	105,500,000	105,500,000	155,618,000	103,745,332
United Arab Emirates	16,500,000	16,500,000	25,680,000	25,680,000
Venezuela	66,000,000	66,000,000	38,489,000	38,489,000
Subtotal	435,500,000	352,333,333	379,656,000	300,822,665
Category III				
Afghanistan	8,000	8,000	—	—
Angola*	—	—	—	—
Argentina	1,032	1,032	900,000	900,000
Bangladesh	300,000	300,000	681,040	681,040
Barbados	1,000	1,000	—	—
Belize	—	—	—	—

MEMBER	INITIAL CONTRIBUTIONS (in US dollar equivalents)		FIRST REPLENISHMENT CONTRIBUTIONS (in US dollar equivalents)	
	Pledged	Paid	Pledged	Paid
Category III (cont.)				
Benin	—	—	10,000	10,000
Bhutan	—	—	1,000	1,000
Bolivia	—	—	50,000	—
Botswana	—	—	15,000	15,000
Brazil	—	—	9,741,413	9,741,413
Burundi	—	—	85,324	—
Cape Verde	1,000	1,000	—	—
Central African Republic	2,395	2,395	—	—
Chad	—	—	—	—
Chile	50,000	50,000	—	—
China	903,030	903,030	1,300,000	1,300,000
Colombia	—	—	—	—
Comoros	23,960	11,980	—	—
Congo	—	—	66,415	66,415
Costa Rica	—	—	—	—
Cuba	—	—	100,000	82,800
Cyprus	25,000	25,000	12,000	12,000
Democratic Yemen	—	—	50,000	50,000
Djibouti	—	—	3,000	3,000
Dominica	—	—	10,987	10,987
Dominican Republic	25,000	25,000	—	—
Ecuador	25,047	25,047	50,946	50,946
Egypt	171,429	171,429	257,143	257,143
El Salvador	40,000	40,000	—	—
Equatorial Guinea	—	—	—	—
Ethiopia	23,623	23,623	23,623	—
Fiji	10,000	10,000	10,000	10,000
Gambia	—	—	—	—
Ghana	100,000	100,000	—	—
Greece	150,000	150,000	200,000	200,000
Grenada	—	—	—	—
Guatemala	—	—	—	—
Guinea	1,058,425	1,058,425	60,000	—
Guinea-Bissau	—	—	10,000	—
Guyana	—	—	30,000	10,000
Haiti	60,000	—	—	—
Honduras	25,000	25,000	50,000	50,000
India	5,000,000	5,000,000	6,500,000	6,500,000
Israel	150,000	150,000	150,000	—
Ivory Coast	—	—	—	—
Jamaica	4,495	4,495	15,000	15,000
Jordan	30,000	30,000	75,000	75,000
Kenya	572,464	572,464	943,419	943,419
Lao People's Democratic Republic	2,886	2,886	—	—
Lebanon	—	—	25,000	25,000
Lesotho	15,000	15,000	50,000	16,841
Liberia	10,000	10,000	10,000	10,000
Madagascar	—	—	—	—
Malawi	5,000	5,000	14,205	14,205
Maldives	—	—	—	—
Mali	—	—	10,000	10,000
Malta	—	—	—	—
Mauritania	—	—	—	—
Mauritius	—	—	—	—
Mexico	5,000,000	5,000,000	7,000,000	6,374,152

MEMBER	INITIAL CONTRIBUTIONS (in US dollar equivalents)		FIRST REPLENISHMENT CONTRIBUTIONS (in US dollar equivalents)	
	Pledged	Paid	Pledged	Paid
Category III (cont.)				
Morocco	268,248	268,248	107,299	107,299
Mozambique	28,867	28,867	86,601	86,601
Nepal	5,000	5,000	5,000	5,000
Nicaragua	28,571	28,571	—	—
Niger	35,928	35,928	—	—
Oman	—	—	75,000	75,000
Pakistan	870,370	870,370	1,207,358	1,207,358
Panama	—	—	25,000	25,000
Papua New Guinea	20,000	20,000	—	—
Paraguay	—	—	—	—
Peru	—	—	60,000	60,000
Philippines	250,000	250,000	—	—
Portugal	—	—	—	—
Republic of Korea	165,716	165,716	287,014	287,014
Romania	271,140	271,140	—	—
Rwanda	—	—	—	—
Saint Lucia	—	—	—	—
Saint Vincent and the Grenadines*	—	—	—	—
Samoa	10,000	10,000	—	—
Sao Tome and Principe	—	—	—	—
Senegal	10,000	10,000	11,980	—
Seychelles	5,000	5,000	—	—
Sierra Leone	18,296	18,296	18,430	18,430
Solomon Islands	—	—	10,000	—
Somalia	10,000	10,000	—	—
Sri Lanka	810,800	810,800	1,000,000	1,000,000
Sudan	10,000	10,000	10,000	—
Suriname	—	—	—	—
Swaziland	—	—	8,980	8,980
Syrian Arab Republic	127,226	127,226	127,226	—
Thailand	100,000	100,000	100,000	100,000
Togo	7,186	7,186	—	—
Tonga	—	—	—	—
Tunisia	68,776	68,776	300,000	300,000
Turkey	12,230	12,230	74,533	74,533
Uganda	719	719	67,986	67,986
United Republic of Cameroon	50,000	50,000	47,919	24,649
United Republic of Tanzania	24,077	24,077	38,941	38,941
Upper Volta	10,000	10,000	—	—
Uruguay	—	—	—	—
Viet Nam	50,454	50,454	—	—
Yemen	50,000	50,000	—	—
Yugoslavia	42,970	42,970	136,894	136,894
Zaire	30,000	—	—	—
Zambia	32,515	32,515	92,687	92,687
Zimbabwe	—	—	—	—
Subtotal	17,217,875	17,115,895	32,409,363	31,151,733
Total	968,783,108	885,514,461	930,631,242	655,124,125
Special contributions				
OPEC Fund	—	—	20,000,000	20,000,000
Other	101,157	101,157	—	—

NOTE: According to article 4, section 2 *(c)*, of the Agreement establishing IFAD, members' initial contributions are payable in cash or promissory notes, either in a single sum or in three annual instalments. Contributions have been translated on the basis of International Monetary Fund exchange rates as at 31 December 1983.

*Had not completed the required membership formalities.

Annex II. OFFICERS AND OFFICES OF THE INTERNATIONAL FUND FOR AGRICULTURAL DEVELOPMENT

EXECUTIVE BOARD

Chairman: Abdelmuhsin M. Al-Sudeary.

MEMBERS
Category I: (until 14 December 1983) France, Germany, Federal Republic of, Japan, Netherlands, Sweden, United States. *Alternates:* Austria, Canada, Denmark, Switzerland, United Kingdom; (from 15 December) Belgium, Denmark, Germany, Federal Republic of, Italy, Japan, United States. *Alternates:* Canada, Finland, France, Netherlands, United Kingdom.

Category II: (until 14 December 1983) Iran, Kuwait, Libyan Arab Jamahiriya, Nigeria, Saudi Arabia, Venezuela. *Alternates:* Algeria, Gabon, Indonesia, Iraq, Qatar, United Arab Emirates; (from 15 December) Algeria, Iraq, Kuwait, Nigeria, Saudi Arabia, Venezuela. *Alternates:* Gabon, Indonesia, Iran, Libyan Arab Jamahiriya, Qatar, United Arab Emirates.

Category III: (until 14 December 1983) Bangladesh, Brazil, Jamaica, Kenya, Thailand, Tunisia. *Alternates::* Colombia, Ghana, Lesotho, Panama, Republic of Korea, Turkey; (from 15 December) Brazil, India, Jamaica, Kenya, Thailand, United Republic of Cameroon. *Alternates:* Colombia, Egypt, Ghana, Pakistan, Panama, Turkey.

SENIOR SECRETARIAT OFFICERS

President: Abdelmuhsin M. Al-Sudeary.
Vice-President: Donald S. Brown.
Assistant President, Head of Economic and Planning Department: Sartaj Aziz.
Assistant President, Head of Project Management Department: Moise Mensah.
Assistant President, Head of General Affairs Department: Vacant.

Controller, Financial Services Division: Desmond Saldanha.
Treasurer, Financial Services Division: My Huynh Cong.
Officer-in-Charge, Personnel Services Division: Surangani W. Marian.
Director, Legal Services Division: Mohammed Nawaz.

HEADQUARTERS AND OTHER OFFICE

HEADQUARTERS
International Fund for Agricultural Development
107 Via del Serafico
00142 Rome, Italy
  Cable address: IFAD ROME
  Telephone: 54591
  Telex: 614160, 614162

ACTING LIAISON OFFICE WITH THE UNITED NATIONS IN NEW YORK
International Fund for Agricultural Development
Room S-2955
United Nations Headquarters
New York, N. Y. 10017, United States
  Telephone: (212) 754-4245, 4246, 4248

Chapter XVII

Interim Commission for the International Trade Organization (ICITO) and the General Agreement on Tariffs and Trade (GATT)

The United Nations Conference on Trade and Employment, held at Havana, Cuba, between November 1947 and March 1948, drew up a charter for an International Trade Organization (ITO) and established an Interim Commission for the International Trade Organization (ICITO). Since the charter itself was never accepted, ITO was not established. However, while drawing up the charter, the Preparatory Committee's members negotiated on tariffs among themselves, and also drew up the General Agreement on Tariffs and Trade (GATT). The Agreement—a multilateral treaty embodying reciprocal rights and obligations—is the only multilateral instrument that lays down agreed rules for international trade. It entered into force on 1 January 1948 with 23 contracting parties. Since then, ICITO has provided the GATT secretariat.

By the end of 1983, the number of contracting parties to GATT had risen to 90 with the addition of Maldives (April) and Belize (October). One other country, Tunisia, had acceded provisionally. The contracting parties conducted about 85 per cent of all international trade while 31 other countries applied the rules of GATT.

Multilateral trade negotiations

Implementation of the Tokyo Round agreements

Of two distinct strands of the multilateral work programme pursued within GATT during 1983, the first was the continuation of work resulting from the conclusion of the Tokyo Round of multilateral trade negotiations in 1979.[a] The agreements of the Tokyo Round, the seventh "round" of multilateral trade negotiations in the 36-year history of GATT, provided an improved framework for the conduct of world trade and were adopted as an integral part of the rules of GATT.

Tariff negotiations during the Tokyo Round resulted in agreement on import duty reductions to be effected in eight annual cuts by the industrialized countries. With the fourth of such cuts being made on 1 January 1983, the half-way point in the Tokyo Round reductions was reached.

During 1983, the GATT Committee on Tariff Concessions continued work on establishing a loose-leaf system of tariff schedules to permit easier and more systematic access to changes made during rounds of tariff negotiations. In February, the Committee adopted procedures for renegotiating tariff schedules in the light of the decision of the 1982 ministerial session of GATT member States to adopt the Harmonized Commodity Description and Coding System developed by the Customs Co-operation Council in Brussels, Belgium. This system would facilitate analysis of trade statistics and monitor and protect the value of tariff concessions.

The Committee on Subsidies and Countervailing Measures agreed on the need to achieve greater transparency in the area of subsidies and to settle outstanding differences of interpretation between the various signatories to the Agreement on the subject. The Committee also considered two panel reports on complaints by the United States on alleged subsidies by the European Community (EC) on exports of wheat flour and pasta products. A further panel was established to examine a complaint by EC relating to United States subsidies on exports of wheat flour to Egypt.

The Committee on Government Procurement continued to examine laws, procedures and regulations relating to implementation of the Agreement on Government Procurement and set up its first dispute panel to consider a complaint by the United States against exclusion by EC of value added tax from the contract price of government purchases in its member States.

During 1983, the Committee on Trade in Civil Aircraft recommended the inclusion of a further 32 categories of products in the Agreement on such trade as from 1 January 1985 and the conditions for the elimination of duties and other charges relating to aircraft repairs were agreed.

The Arrangement regarding Bovine Meat and the International Dairy Arrangement were the multilateral agreements relating to trade in agricultural products negotiated during the Tokyo Round. The 25 signatories to the bovine meat Arrangement accounted for approximately 90 per cent of the world's exports of fresh, chilled and frozen beef and veal. The International Dairy

[a]YUN 1979, p. 1328.

Products Council, which supervised the International Dairy Arrangement, met three times during 1983. Its work included consideration of a complaint by EC arising from United States sales of dairy products to Egypt. A report on the world market for dairy products was published in October.

Work continued in committees overseeing the agreements on anti-dumping practices, technical barriers to trade, customs valuation and import licensing. The updating of the inventory of non-tariff measures affecting industrial products also proceeded. By the end of 1983, the inventory, which was originally prepared as an information base for the Tokyo Round negotiations, included over 600 measures.

Ministerial work programme

The second strand of the 1983 multilateral work programme of GATT was continuation of the plan set out by the 1982 GATT Ministerial Meeting. The ministerial declaration had called for new efforts to achieve a comprehensive understanding on safeguards. In this context, safeguards referred to the right of GATT contracting parties to impose temporary trade restrictions on imports which seriously injured a domestic industry or threatened to do so. Consultations took place throughout 1983 but did not progress sufficiently for a comprehensive understanding to be presented to the session of contracting parties in November.

The Committee on Trade in Agriculture, established by the Ministerial Meeting, held four meetings in 1983. It compiled information on measures affecting agricultural trade in 45 countries and went on to examine trade measures of 36 of them, including EC. The Committee considered, in particular, measures affecting market access and supplies, the operation of GATT with respect to agricultural subsidies and measures maintained under exceptions or derogations from GATT.

In 1983, the Committee on Trade and Development initiated the first five of a series of consultations with individual developed countries aimed at reviewing their trade policies in the context of Part IV of the General Agreement, which envisaged special treatment for developing countries. The Committee also set in motion a new round of consultations covering trade in tropical products, and a sub-committee began a programme of consultations aimed at examining barriers affecting the trading prospects of the least developed countries.

Other aspects of the ministerial work programme included the establishment of a group to examine quantitative restrictions and other non-tariff measures with a view to eliminating those not in conformity with GATT, and a review of the adequacy and effectiveness of the Tokyo Round

agreements and obstacles to their acceptance by non-signatories.

Other GATT activities

Contracting parties session

In November 1983, GATT contracting parties met at senior official level and heard first progress reports on the ministerial work programme.

Council of Representatives

The Council of Representatives, GATT's highest body between sessions of the contracting parties, in 1983 acted on many international trade policy issues and trade disputes between GATT parties. Four new dispute panels were set up during the year. Two reports were adopted by such panels and seven other disputes were considered further.

Consultative Group of Eighteen

At its two meetings held in 1983, the Consultative Group of Eighteen reviewed developments in trade policy since the 1982 GATT Ministerial Meeting and discussed the relationship between trade policy and the international financial system. It also discussed dispute settlement in the light of the 1982 ministerial declaration.

Committee on Trade and Development

During 1983, the Committee on Trade and Development continued to review trade issues affecting the developing countries, as did its two sub-committees: the sub-committee on trade of the least developed countries and the sub-committee on protective measures. The latter sub-committee continued to examine new measures implemented by developed countries which affected the exports of developing countries. Among measures considered were restrictions and other actions against steel, footwear, tableware, sugar, meat and quartz watches.

Balance-of-payments restrictions

During 1983, the GATT Committee on Balance-of-Payments Import Restrictions held full consultations with Brazil, Ghana, Hungary, Israel and Portugal, whose balance-of-payments difficulties had led them to restrict imports. Consultations under a simplified procedure took place with Egypt, Peru, the Republic of Korea, Sri Lanka, Tunisia and Turkey.

Textiles Arrangement

By the end of 1983, the second extension of the Arrangement regarding International Trade in Textiles,[b] known as the Multifibre Arrangement

[b]YUN 1981, p. 1484.

(MFA), had been operating for two years. Agreements under MFA covered most of the textiles and clothing exported by MFA members in the developing world to those in the developed world (worth approximately $15 billion annually).

In December, the Textiles Committee conducted the second annual review of the second extension, which was due to expire on 31 July 1986.

Technical assistance

In 1983, the GATT secretariat's Technical Co-operation Division organized missions to, or seminars in, the following developing countries: Argentina, Burundi, Haiti, Indonesia, Malaysia, Maldives, Paraguay, Peru, the Philippines, Rwanda, Senegal, Thailand and Venezuela. GATT officials also participated in seminars sponsored by a number of regional organizations.

Training programme

Two commercial policy training courses with a total of 44 participants were held at Geneva during 1983. These were the fifty-fifth and fifty-sixth in the series which began in 1955 and which, by the end of 1983, had been attended by 882 officials from 109 countries and six regional organizations. The courses were held in French and English but were to be supplemented, as from 1984, by a course in Spanish.

International Trade Centre

Established by GATT in 1964 and jointly operated by GATT and the United Nations Conference on Trade and Development since 1968, the International Trade Centre continued to provide trade information and trade promotion advisory services for developing countries. The Centre's work was directed towards helping developing countries to formulate and implement trade promotion programmes and activities. The value of its technical co-operation programme in 1983 was estimated at $15 million.

Publications

Publications issued in 1983 included the annual volumes of *GATT Activities* and *International Trade*, and the monthly newsletter *GATT Focus*.

Secretariat

As at 31 December 1983, the GATT secretariat employed 284 staff members; of these, 123 were in the Professional and higher categories and 161 were in the General Service category. They were drawn from 43 nationalities.

Financial arrangements

Member countries of GATT contribute to the budget in accordance with a scale assessed on the basis of each country's share in the total trade of the contracting parties and associated Governments. The budget for 1983 was 48,538,000 Swiss francs. The scale of contributions for 1983 is given below. (The United Nations rate of exchange for December 1983 was SwF 2.18 = $US 1.00.)

Annex I.   CONTRACTING PARTIES TO THE GENERAL AGREEMENT ON TARIFFS AND TRADE AND SCALE OF CONTRIBUTIONS FOR 1983

(As at 31 December 1983)

Contracting party	Net contribution (in Swiss francs)	Contracting party	Net contribution (in Swiss francs)	Contracting party	Net contribution (in Swiss francs)
Argentina	218,420	Finland	407,720	Malawi	58,250
Australia	655,260	France	3,533,560	Malaysia	330,050
Austria	582,450	Gabon	58,250	Maldives	58,250
Bangladesh	58,250	Gambia	58,250	Malta	58,250
Barbados	58,250	Germany, Federal Republic of	5,329,470	Mauritania	58,250
Belgium	1,732,800	Ghana	58,250	Mauritius	58,250
Belize	58,250	Greece	213,560	Netherlands	2,213,330
Benin	58,250	Guyana	58,250	New Zealand	160,170
Brazil	645,550	Haiti	58,250	Nicaragua	58,250
Burma	58,250	Hungary	266,960	Niger	58,250
Burundi	58,250	Iceland	58,250	Nigeria	553,330
Canada	1,965,790	India	310,640	Norway	490,230
Central African Republic	58,250	Indonesia	461,110	Pakistan	111,630
Chad	58,250	Ireland	281,520	Peru	92,220
Chile	145,610	Israel	208,710	Philippines	199,000
Colombia	116,490	Italy	2,499,700	Poland	519,350
Congo	58,250	Ivory Coast	67,950	Portugal	203,860
Cuba	155,320	Jamaica	58,250	Republic of Korea	621,280
Cyprus	58,250	Japan	3,941,280	Romania	368,890
Czechoslovakia	461,110	Kenya	58,250	Rwanda	58,250
Denmark	529,060	Kuwait	383,450	Senegal	58,250
Dominican Republic	58,250	Luxembourg	150,460	Sierra Leone	58,250
Egypt	131,050	Madagascar	58,250	Singapore	446,550

Contracting party	Net contribution (in Swiss francs)	Contracting party	Net contribution (in Swiss francs)	Contracting party	Net contribution (in Swiss francs)
South Africa	495,080	Turkey	160,170	Zaire	58,250
Spain	766,900	Uganda	58,250	Zambia	58,250
Sri Lanka	58,250	United Kingdom	3,470,460	Zimbabwe	58,250
Suriname	58,250	United Republic of Cameroon	58,250	*Associated Government*	
Sweden	902,800	United Republic of Tanzania	58,250		
Switzerland	912,510	United States	7,042,860	Democratic Kampuchea	58,250
Thailand	228,130	Upper Volta	58,250	Tunisia	87,370
Togo	58,250	Uruguay	58,250	Total	48,654,500*
Trinidad and Tobago	82,510	Yugoslavia	354,320		

*Total includes contributions assessed on contracting parties (Belize, Maldives) subsequent to adoption of scale of contributions.

Annex II.   OFFICERS AND OFFICE OF THE GENERAL AGREEMENT ON TARIFFS AND TRADE

(As at 31 December 1983)

OFFICERS

OFFICERS OF THE CONTRACTING PARTIES*

Chairman of the Contracting Parties: Hans V. Ewerlöf (Sweden).

Vice-Chairmen of the Contracting Parties: Mahmoud Abdel-Bari Hamza (Egypt), Kazimir Vidas (Yugoslavia), Dame Anne Warburton (United Kingdom).
Chairman of the Council of Representatives: Felipe Jaramillo (Colombia).
Chairman of the Committee on Trade and Development: Tai Soo Chew (Singapore).

SENIOR OFFICERS OF THE SECRETARIAT
Director-General: Arthur Dunkel.
Deputy Directors-General: Madan G. Mathur, William B. Kelly.

SENIOR OFFICERS OF THE
INTERNATIONAL TRADE CENTRE UNCTAD/GATT
Executive Director: Goran M. Engblom.
Deputy Executive Director: Said T. Harb.

*Elected at the end of the November 1983 session, to hold office until the end of the next session.

HEADQUARTERS

GATT Secretariat
Centre William Rappard
Rue de Lausanne 154
1211 Geneva 21, Switzerland
   Cable address: GATT GENEVA
   Telephone: 31 02 31
   Telex: 28787

Appendices

Appendix I

Roster of the United Nations

(As at 31 December 1983)

MEMBER	DATE OF ADMISSION	MEMBER	DATE OF ADMISSION	MEMBER	DATE OF ADMISSION
Afghanistan	19 Nov. 1946	Ghana	8 Mar. 1957	Philippines	24 Oct. 1945
Albania	14 Dec. 1955	Greece	25 Oct. 1945	Poland	24 Oct. 1945
Algeria	8 Oct. 1962	Grenada	17 Sep. 1974	Portugal	14 Dec. 1955
Angola	1 Dec. 1976	Guatemala	21 Nov. 1945	Qatar	21 Sep. 1971
Antigua and Barbuda	11 Nov. 1981	Guinea	12 Dec. 1958	Romania	14 Dec. 1955
Argentina	24 Oct. 1945	Guinea-Bissau	17 Sep. 1974	Rwanda	18 Sep. 1962
Australia	1 Nov. 1945	Guyana	20 Sep. 1966	Saint Christopher	
Austria	14 Dec. 1955	Haiti	24 Oct. 1945	and Nevis	23 Sep. 1983
Bahamas	18 Sep. 1973	Honduras	17 Dec. 1945	Saint Lucia	18 Sep. 1979
Bahrain	21 Sep. 1971	Hungary	14 Dec. 1955	Saint Vincent and	
Bangladesh	17 Sep. 1974	Iceland	19 Nov. 1946	the Grenadines	16 Sep. 1980
Barbados	9 Dec. 1966	India	30 Oct. 1945	Samoa	15 Dec. 1976
Belgium	27 Dec. 1945	Indonesia[2]	28 Sep. 1950	Sao Tome and Principe	16 Sep. 1975
Belize	25 Sep. 1981	Iran (Islamic		Saudi Arabia	24 Oct. 1945
Benin	20 Sep. 1960	Republic of)	24 Oct. 1945	Senegal	28 Sep. 1960
Bhutan	21 Sep. 1971	Iraq	21 Dec. 1945	Seychelles	21 Sep. 1976
Bolivia	14 Nov. 1945	Ireland	14 Dec. 1955	Sierra Leone	27 Sep. 1961
Botswana	17 Oct. 1966	Israel	11 May 1949	Singapore[3]	21 Sep. 1965
Brazil	24 Oct. 1945	Italy	14 Dec. 1955	Solomon Islands	19 Sep. 1978
Bulgaria	14 Dec. 1955	Ivory Coast	20 Sep. 1960	Somalia	20 Sep. 1960
Burma	19 Apr. 1948	Jamaica	18 Sep. 1962	South Africa	7 Nov. 1945
Burundi	18 Sep. 1962	Japan	18 Dec. 1956	Spain	14 Dec. 1955
Byelorussian Soviet		Jordan	14 Dec. 1955	Sri Lanka	14 Dec. 1955
Socialist Republic	24 Oct. 1945	Kenya	16 Dec. 1963	Sudan	12 Nov. 1956
Canada	9 Nov. 1945	Kuwait	14 May 1963	Suriname	4 Dec. 1975
Cape Verde	16 Sep. 1975	Lao People's		Swaziland	24 Sep. 1968
Central African		Democratic Republic	14 Dec. 1955	Sweden	19 Nov. 1946
Republic	20 Sep. 1960	Lebanon	24 Oct. 1945	Syrian Arab Republic[1]	24 Oct. 1945
Chad	20 Sep. 1960	Lesotho	17 Oct. 1966	Thailand	16 Dec. 1946
Chile	24 Oct. 1945	Liberia	2 Nov. 1945	Togo	20 Sep. 1960
China	24 Oct. 1945	Libyan Arab		Trinidad and Tobago	18 Sep. 1962
Colombia	5 Nov. 1945	Jamahiriya	14 Dec. 1955	Tunisia	12 Nov. 1956
Comoros	12 Nov. 1975	Luxembourg	24 Oct. 1945	Turkey	24 Oct. 1945
Congo	20 Sep. 1960	Madagascar	20 Sep. 1960	Uganda	25 Oct. 1962
Costa Rica	2 Nov. 1945	Malawi	1 Dec. 1964	Ukrainian Soviet	
Cuba	24 Oct. 1945	Malaysia[3]	17 Sep. 1957	Socialist Republic	24 Oct. 1945
Cyprus	20 Sep. 1960	Maldives	21 Sep. 1965	Union of Soviet	
Czechoslovakia	24 Oct. 1945	Mali	28 Sep. 1960	Socialist Republics	24 Oct. 1945
Democratic Kampuchea	14 Dec. 1955	Malta	1 Dec. 1964	United Arab Emirates	9 Dec. 1971
Democratic Yemen	14 Dec. 1967	Mauritania	27 Oct. 1961	United Kingdom of	
Denmark	24 Oct. 1945	Mauritius	24 Apr. 1968	Great Britain and	
Djibouti	20 Sep. 1977	Mexico	7 Nov. 1945	Northern Ireland	24 Oct. 1945
Dominica	18 Dec. 1978	Mongolia	27 Oct. 1961	United Republic	
Dominican Republic	24 Oct. 1945	Morocco	12 Nov. 1956	of Cameroon	20 Sep. 1960
Ecuador	21 Dec. 1945	Mozambique	16 Sep. 1975	United Republic	
Egypt[1]	24 Oct. 1945	Nepal	14 Dec. 1955	of Tanzania[4]	14 Dec. 1961
El Salvador	24 Oct. 1945	Netherlands	10 Dec. 1945	United States	
Equatorial Guinea	12 Nov. 1968	New Zealand	24 Oct. 1945	of America	24 Oct. 1945
Ethiopia	13 Nov. 1945	Nicaragua	24 Oct. 1945	Upper Volta	20 Sep. 1960
Fiji	13 Oct. 1970	Niger	20 Sep. 1960	Uruguay	18 Dec. 1945
Finland	14 Dec. 1955	Nigeria	7 Oct. 1960	Vanuatu	15 Sep. 1981
France	24 Oct. 1945	Norway	27 Nov. 1945	Venezuela	15 Nov. 1945
Gabon	20 Sep. 1960	Oman	7 Oct. 1971	Viet Nam	20 Sep. 1977
Gambia	21 Sep. 1965	Pakistan	30 Sep. 1947	Yemen	30 Sep. 1947
German Democratic		Panama	13 Nov. 1945	Yugoslavia	24 Oct. 1945
Republic	18 Sep. 1973	Papua New Guinea	10 Oct. 1975	Zaire	20 Sep. 1960
Germany, Federal		Paraguay	24 Oct. 1945	Zambia	1 Dec. 1964
Republic of	18 Sep. 1973	Peru	31 Oct. 1945	Zimbabwe	25 Aug. 1980

(footnotes on next page)

(footnotes for preceding page)

[1]Egypt and Syria, both of which became Members of the United Nations on 24 October 1945, joined together—following a plebiscite held in those countries on 21 February 1958—to form the United Arab Republic. On 13 October 1961, Syria, having resumed its status as an independent State, also resumed its separate membership in the United Nations; it changed its name to the Syrian Arab Republic on 14 September 1971. The United Arab Republic continued as a Member of the United Nations and reverted to the name of Egypt on 2 September 1971.

[2]By a letter of 20 January 1965, Indonesia informed the Secretary-General that it had decided to withdraw from the United Nations. By a telegram of 19 September 1966, it notified the Secretary-General of its decision to resume participation in the activities of the United Nations. On 28 September 1966, the General Assembly took note of that decision and the President invited the representatives of Indonesia to take their seats in the Assembly.

[3]On 16 September 1963, Sabah (North Borneo), Sarawak and Singapore joined with the Federation of Malaya (which became a United Nations Member on 17 September 1957) to form Malaysia. On 9 August 1965, Singapore became an independent State and on 21 September 1965 it became a Member of the United Nations.

[4]Tanganyika was admitted to the United Nations on 14 December 1961, and Zanzibar, on 16 December 1963. Following ratification, on 26 April 1964, of the Articles of Union between Tanganyika and Zanzibar, the two States became represented as a single Member: the United Republic of Tanganyika and Zanzibar; it changed its name to the United Republic of Tanzania on 1 November 1964.

Appendix II

Charter of the United Nations and Statute of the International Court of Justice

Charter of the United Nations

NOTE: The Charter of the United Nations was signed on 26 June 1945, in San Francisco, at the conclusion of the United Nations Conference on International Organization, and came into force on 24 October 1945. The Statute of the International Court of Justice is an integral part of the Charter.

Amendments to Articles 23, 27 and 61 of the Charter were adopted by the General Assembly on 17 December 1963 and came into force on 31 August 1965. A further amendment to Article 61 was adopted by the General Assembly on 20 December 1971, and came into force on 24 September 1973. An amendment to Article 109, adopted by the General Assembly on 20 December 1965, came into force on 12 June 1968.

The amendment to Article 23 enlarges the membership of the Security Council from 11 to 15. The amended Article 27 provides that decisions of the Security Council on procedural matters shall be made by an affirmative vote of nine members (formerly seven) and on all other matters by an affirmative vote of nine members (formerly seven), including the concurring votes of the five permanent members of the Security Council.

The amendment to Article 61, which entered into force on 31 August 1965, enlarged the membership of the Economic and Social Council from 18 to 27. The subsequent amendment to that Article, which entered into force on 24 September 1973, further increased the membership of the Council from 27 to 54.

The amendment to Article 109, which relates to the first paragraph of that Article, provides that a General Conference of Member States for the purpose of reviewing the Charter may be held at a date and place to be fixed by a two-thirds vote of the members of the General Assembly and by a vote of any nine members (formerly seven) of the Security Council. Paragraph 3 of Article 109, which deals with the consideration of a possible review conference during the tenth regular session of the General Assembly, has been retained in its original form in its reference to a "vote of any seven members of the Security Council," the paragraph having been acted upon in 1955 by the General Assembly, at its tenth regular session, and by the Security Council.

WE THE PEOPLES
OF THE UNITED NATIONS
DETERMINED
to save succeeding generations from the scourge of war, which twice in our lifetime has brought untold sorrow to mankind, and
to reaffirm faith in fundamental human rights, in the dignity and worth of the human person, in the equal rights of men and women and of nations large and small, and
to establish conditions under which justice and respect for the obligations arising from treaties and other sources of international law can be maintained, and
to promote social progress and better standards of life in larger freedom,

AND FOR THESE ENDS
to practice tolerance and live together in peace with one another as good neighbours, and
to unite our strength to maintain international peace and security, and
to ensure, by the acceptance of principles and the institution of methods, that armed force shall not be used, save in the common interest, and
to employ international machinery for the promotion of the economic and social advancement of all peoples,

HAVE RESOLVED TO
COMBINE OUR EFFORTS TO
ACCOMPLISH THESE AIMS
Accordingly, our respective Governments, through representatives assembled in the city of San Francisco, who have exhibited their full powers found to be in good and due form, have agreed to the present Charter of the United Nations and do hereby establish an international organization to be known as the United Nations.

Chapter I
PURPOSES AND PRINCIPLES

Article 1
The Purposes of the United Nations are:

1. To maintain international peace and security, and to that end: to take effective collective measures for the prevention and removal of threats to the peace, and for the suppression of acts of aggression or other breaches of the peace, and to bring about by peaceful means, and in conformity with the principles of justice and international law, adjustment or settlement of international disputes or situations which might lead to a breach of the peace;

2. To develop friendly relations among nations based on respect for the principle of equal rights and self-determination of peoples, and to take other appropriate measures to strengthen universal peace;

3. To achieve international co-operation in solving international problems of an economic, social, cultural, or humanitarian character, and in promoting and encouraging respect for human rights and for fundamental freedoms for all without distinction as to race, sex, language, or religion; and

4. To be a centre for harmonizing the actions of nations in the attainment of these common ends.

Article 2
The Organization and its Members, in pursuit of the Purposes stated in Article 1, shall act in accordance with the following Principles.

1. The Organization is based on the principle of the sovereign equality of all its Members.

2. All Members, in order to ensure to all of them the rights and benefits resulting from membership, shall fulfil in good faith the obligations assumed by them in accordance with the present Charter.

3. All Members shall settle their international disputes by peaceful means in such a manner that international peace and security, and justice, are not endangered.

4. All Members shall refrain in their international relations from the threat or use of force against the territorial integrity or political independence of any state, or in any other manner inconsistent with the Purposes of the United Nations.

5. All Members shall give the United Nations every assistance in any action it takes in accordance with the present Charter, and shall refrain from giving assistance to any state against which the United Nations is taking preventive or enforcement action.

6. The Organization shall ensure that states which are not Members of the United Nations act in accordance with these Principles so far as may be necessary for the maintenance of international peace and security.

7. Nothing contained in the present Charter shall authorize the United Nations to intervene in matters which are essentially within the domestic jurisdiction of any state or shall require the Members to submit such matters to settlement under the present Charter; but this principle shall not prejudice the application of enforcement measures under Chapter VII.

Chapter II
MEMBERSHIP

Article 3

The original Members of the United Nations shall be the states which, having participated in the United Nations Conference on International Organization at San Francisco, or having previously signed the Declaration by United Nations of 1 January 1942, sign the present Charter and ratify it in accordance with Article 110.

Article 4

1. Membership in the United Nations is open to all other peace-loving states which accept the obligations contained in the present Charter and, in the judgment of the Organization, are able and willing to carry out these obligations.

2. The admission of any such state to membership in the United Nations will be effected by a decision of the General Assembly upon the recommendation of the Security Council.

Article 5

A Member of the United Nations against which preventive or enforcement action has been taken by the Security Council may be suspended from the exercise of the rights and privileges of membership by the General Assembly upon the recommendation of the Security Council. The exercise of these rights and privileges may be restored by the Security Council.

Article 6

A Member of the United Nations which has persistently violated the Principles contained in the present Charter may be expelled from the Organization by the General Assembly upon the recommendation of the Security Council.

Chapter III
ORGANS

Article 7

1. There are established as the principal organs of the United Nations: a General Assembly, a Security Council, an Economic and Social Council, a Trusteeship Council, an International Court of Justice, and a Secretariat.

2. Such subsidiary organs as may be found necessary may be established in accordance with the present Charter.

Article 8

The United Nations shall place no restrictions on the eligibility of men and women to participate in any capacity and under conditions of equality in its principal and subsidiary organs.

Chapter IV
THE GENERAL ASSEMBLY

Composition

Article 9

1. The General Assembly shall consist of all the Members of the United Nations.

2. Each Member shall have not more than five representatives in the General Assembly.

Functions and powers

Article 10

The General Assembly may discuss any questions or any matters within the scope of the present Charter or relating to the powers and functions of any organs provided for in the present Charter, and, except as provided in Article 12, may make recommendations to the Members of the United Nations or to the Security Council or to both on any such questions or matters.

Article 11

1. The General Assembly may consider the general principles of co-operation in the maintenance of international peace and security, including the principles governing disarmament and the regulation of armaments, and may make recommendations with regard to such principles to the Members or to the Security Council or to both.

2. The General Assembly may discuss any questions relating to the maintenance of international peace and security brought before it by any Member of the United Nations, or by the Security Council, or by a state which is not a Member of the United Nations in accordance with Article 35, paragraph 2, and, except as provided in Article 12, may make recommendations with regard to any such questions to the state or states concerned or to the Security Council or to both. Any such question on which action is necessary shall be referred to the Security Council by the General Assembly either before or after discussion.

3. The General Assembly may call the attention of the Security Council to situations which are likely to endanger international peace and security.

4. The powers of the General Assembly set forth in this Article shall not limit the general scope of Article 10.

Article 12

1. While the Security Council is exercising in respect of any dispute or situation the functions assigned to it in the present Charter, the General Assembly shall not make any recommendation with regard to that dispute or situation unless the Security Council so requests.

2. The Secretary-General, with the consent of the Security Council, shall notify the General Assembly at each session of any matters relative to the maintenance of international peace and security which are being dealt with by the Security Council and shall similarly notify the General Assembly, or the Members of the United Nations if the General Assembly is not in session, immediately the Security Council ceases to deal with such matters.

Article 13

1. The General Assembly shall initiate studies and make recommendations for the purpose of:
   a. promoting international co-operation in the political field and encouraging the progressive development of international law and its codification;
   b. promoting international co-operation in the economic, social, cultural, educational, and health fields, and assisting in the realization of human rights and fundamental freedoms for all without distinction as to race, sex, language, or religion.

2. The further responsibilities, functions and powers of the General Assembly with respect to matters mentioned in paragraph 1(b) above are set forth in Chapters IX and X.

Article 14

Subject to the provisions of Article 12, the General Assembly may recommend measures for the peaceful adjustment of any situation, regardless of origin, which it deems likely to impair the general welfare or friendly relations among nations, including situations resulting from a violation of the provisions of the present Charter setting forth the Purposes and Principles of the United Nations.

Article 15

1. The General Assembly shall receive and consider annual and special reports from the Security Council; these reports shall include an account of the measures that the Security Council has decided upon or taken to maintain international peace and security.

2. The General Assembly shall receive and consider reports from the other organs of the United Nations.

Article 16

The General Assembly shall perform such functions with respect to the international trusteeship system as are assigned to it under Chapters XII and XIII, including the approval of the trusteeship agreements for areas not designated as strategic.

Article 17

1. The General Assembly shall consider and approve the budget of the Organization.

2. The expenses of the Organization shall be borne by the Members as apportioned by the General Assembly.

3. The General Assembly shall consider and approve any financial and budgetary arrangements with specialized agencies referred to in Article 57 and shall examine the administrative budgets of such specialized agencies with a view to making recommendations to the agencies concerned.

Voting

Article 18

1. Each member of the General Assembly shall have one vote.

2. Decisions of the General Assembly on important questions shall be made by a two-thirds majority of the members present and voting. These questions shall include: recommendations with respect to the maintenance of international peace and security, the election of the non-permanent members of the Security Council, the election of the members of the Economic and Social Council, the election of members of the Trusteeship Council in accordance with paragraph 1(c) of Article 86, the admission of new Members to the United Nations, the suspension of the rights and privileges of membership, the expulsion of Members, questions relating to the operation of the trusteeship system, and budgetary questions.

3. Decisions on other questions, including the determination of additional categories of questions to be decided by a two-thirds majority, shall be made by a majority of the members present and voting.

Article 19

A Member of the United Nations which is in arrears in the payment of its financial contributions to the Organization shall have no vote in the General Assembly if the amount of its arrears equals or exceeds the amount of the contributions due from it for the preceding two full years. The General Assembly may, nevertheless, permit such a Member to vote if it is satisfied that the failure to pay is due to conditions beyond the control of the Member.

Procedure

Article 20

The General Assembly shall meet in regular annual sessions and in such special sessions as occasion may require. Special sessions shall be convoked by the Secretary-General at the request of the Security Council or of a majority of the Members of the United Nations.

Article 21

The General Assembly shall adopt its own rules of procedure. It shall elect its President for each session.

Article 22

The General Assembly may establish such subsidiary organs as it deems necessary for the performance of its functions.

Chapter V
THE SECURITY COUNCIL

Composition

Article 23[1]

1. The Security Council shall consist of fifteen Members of the United Nations. The Republic of China, France, the Union of Soviet Socialist Republics, the United Kingdom of Great Britain and Northern Ireland, and the United States of America shall be permanent members of the Security Council. The General Assembly shall elect ten other Members of the United Nations to be non-permanent members of the Security Council, due regard being specially paid, in the first instance to the contribution of Members of the United Nations to the maintenance of international peace and security and to the other purposes of the Organization, and also to equitable geographical distribution.

2. The non-permanent members of the Security Council shall be elected for a term of two years. In the first election of the non-permanent members after the increase of the membership of the Security Council from eleven to fifteen, two of the four additional members shall be chosen for a term of one year. A retiring member shall not be eligible for immediate re-election.

3. Each member of the Security Council shall have one representative.

Functions and powers

Article 24

1. In order to ensure prompt and effective action by the United Nations, its Members confer on the Security Council primary responsibility for the maintenance of international peace and security, and agree that in carrying out its duties under this responsibility the Security Council acts on their behalf.

2. In discharging these duties the Security Council shall act in accordance with the Purposes and Principles of the United Nations. The specific powers granted to the Security Council for the discharge of these duties are laid down in Chapters VI, VII, VIII, and XII.

3. The Security Council shall submit annual and, when necessary, special reports to the General Assembly for its consideration.

Article 25

The Members of the United Nations agree to accept and carry out the decisions of the Security Council in accordance with the present Charter.

Article 26

In order to promote the establishment and maintenance of international peace and security with the least diversion for armaments of the world's human and economic resources, the Security Council shall be responsible for formulating, with the assistance of the Military Staff Committee referred to in Article 47, plans to be submitted to the Members of the United Nations for the establishment of a system for the regulation of armaments.

---

[1]Amended text of Article 23 which came into force on 31 August 1965. (The text of Article 23 before it was amended read as follows:

1. The Security Council shall consist of eleven Members of the United Nations. The Republic of China, France, the Union of Soviet Socialist Republics, the United Kingdom of Great Britain and Northern Ireland, and the United States of America shall be permanent members of the Security Council. The General Assembly shall elect six other Members of the United Nations to be non-permanent members of the Security Council, due regard being specially paid, in the first instance to the contribution of Members of the United Nations to the maintenance of international peace and security and to the other purposes of the Organization, and also to equitable geographical distribution.

2. The non-permanent members of the Security Council shall be elected for a term of two years. In the first election of non-permanent members, however, three shall be chosen for a term of one year. A retiring member shall not be eligible for immediate re-election.

3. Each member of the Security Council shall have one representative.)

Voting

Article 27[2]

1. Each member of the Security Council shall have one vote.
2. Decisions of the Security Council on procedural matters shall be made by an affirmative vote of nine members.
3. Decisions of the Security Council on all other matters shall be made by an affirmative vote of nine members including the concurring votes of the permanent members; provided that, in decisions under Chapter VI, and under paragraph 3 of Article 52, a party to a dispute shall abstain from voting.

Procedure

Article 28

1. The Security Council shall be so organized as to be able to function continuously. Each member of the Security Council shall for this purpose be represented at all times at the seat of the Organization.
2. The Security Council shall hold periodic meetings at which each of its members may, if it so desires, be represented by a member of the government or by some other specially designated representative.
3. The Security Council may hold meetings at such places other than the seat of the Organization as in its judgment will best facilitate its work.

Article 29

The Security Council may establish such subsidiary organs as it deems necessary for the performance of its functions.

Article 30

The Security Council shall adopt its own rules of procedure, including the method of selecting its President.

Article 31

Any Member of the United Nations which is not a member of the Security Council may participate, without vote, in the discussion of any question brought before the Security Council whenever the latter considers that the interests of that Member are specially affected.

Article 32

Any Member of the United Nations which is not a member of the Security Council or any state which is not a Member of the United Nations, if it is a party to a dispute under consideration by the Security Council, shall be invited to participate, without vote, in the discussion relating to the dispute. The Security Council shall lay down such conditions as it deems just for the participation of a state which is not a Member of the United Nations.

Chapter VI
PACIFIC SETTLEMENT OF DISPUTES

Article 33

1. The parties to any dispute, the continuance of which is likely to endanger the maintenance of international peace and security, shall, first of all, seek a solution by negotiation, enquiry, mediation, conciliation, arbitration, judicial settlement, resort to regional agencies or arrangements, or other peaceful means of their own choice.
2. The Security Council shall, when it deems necessary, call upon the parties to settle their dispute by such means.

Article 34

The Security Council may investigate any dispute or any situation which might lead to international friction or give rise to a dispute, in order to determine whether the continuance of the dispute or situation is likely to endanger the maintenance of international peace and security.

Article 35

1. Any Member of the United Nations may bring any dispute, or any situation of the nature referred to in Article 34, to the attention of the Security Council or of the General Assembly.
2. A state which is not a Member of the United Nations may bring to the attention of the Security Council or of the General Assembly any dispute to which it is a party if it accepts in advance, for the purposes of the dispute, the obligations of pacific settlement provided in the present Charter.
3. The proceedings of the General Assembly in respect of matters brought to its attention under this Article will be subject to the provisions of Articles 11 and 12.

Article 36

1. The Security Council may, at any stage of a dispute of the nature referred to in Article 33 or of a situation of like nature, recommend appropriate procedures or methods of adjustment.
2. The Security Council should take into consideration any procedures for the settlement of the dispute which have already been adopted by the parties.
3. In making recommendations under this Article the Security Council should also take into consideration that legal disputes should as a general rule be referred by the parties to the International Court of Justice in accordance with the provisions of the Statute of the Court.

Article 37

1. Should the parties to a dispute of the nature referred to in Article 33 fail to settle it by the means indicated in that Article, they shall refer it to the Security Council.
2. If the Security Council deems that the continuance of the dispute is in fact likely to endanger the maintenance of international peace and security, it shall decide whether to take action under Article 36 or to recommend such terms of settlement as it may consider appropriate.

Article 38

Without prejudice to the provisions of Articles 33 to 37, the Security Council may, if all the parties to any dispute so request, make recommendations to the parties with a view to a pacific settlement of the dispute.

Chapter VII
ACTION WITH RESPECT TO THREATS TO THE PEACE, BREACHES OF THE PEACE, AND ACTS OF AGGRESSION

Article 39

The Security Council shall determine the existence of any threat to the peace, breach of the peace, or act of aggression and shall make recommendations, or decide what measures shall be taken in accordance with Articles 41 and 42, to maintain or restore international peace and security.

Article 40

In order to prevent an aggravation of the situation, the Security Council may, before making the recommendations or deciding upon the measures provided for in Article 39, call upon the parties concerned to comply with such provisional measures as it deems necessary or desirable. Such provisional measures shall be without prejudice to the rights, claims, or position of the parties concerned. The Security Council shall duly take account of failure to comply with such provisional measures.

Article 41

The Security Council may decide what measures not involving the use of armed force are to be employed to give effect to its decisions, and it may call upon the Members of the United Nations to apply such measures. These may include complete or partial interruption of economic relations and of rail, sea, air, postal, telegraphic, radio, and other means of communication, and the severance of diplomatic relations.

---

[2]Amended text of Article 27 which came into force on 31 August 1965. (The text of Article 27 before it was amended read as follows:

1. Each member of the Security Council shall have one vote.
2. Decisions of the Security Council on procedural matters shall be made by an affirmative vote of seven members.
3. Decisions of the Security Council on all other matters shall be made by an affirmative vote of seven members including the concurring votes of the permanent members; provided that, in decisions under Chapter VI, and under paragraph 3 of Article 52, a party to a dispute shall abstain from voting.)

Article 42

Should the Security Council consider that measures provided for in Article 41 would be inadequate or have proved to be inadequate, it may take such action by air, sea, or land forces as may be necessary to maintain or restore international peace and security. Such action may include demonstrations, blockade, and other operations by air, sea, or land forces of Members of the United Nations.

Article 43

1.   All Members of the United Nations, in order to contribute to the maintenance of international peace and security, undertake to make available to the Security Council, on its call and in accordance with a special agreement or agreements, armed forces, assistance, and facilities, including rights of passage, necessary for the purpose of maintaining international peace and security.

2.   Such agreement or agreements shall govern the numbers and types of forces, their degree of readiness and general location, and the nature of the facilities and assistance to be provided.

3.   The agreement or agreements shall be negotiated as soon as possible on the initiative of the Security Council. They shall be concluded between the Security Council and Members or between the Security Council and groups of Members and shall be subject to ratification by the signatory states in accordance with their respective constitutional processes.

Article 44

When the Security Council has decided to use force it shall, before calling upon a Member not represented on it to provide armed forces in fulfilment of the obligations assumed under Article 43, invite that Member, if the Member so desires, to participate in the decisions of the Security Council concerning the employment of contingents of that Member's armed forces.

Article 45

In order to enable the United Nations to take urgent military measures, Members shall hold immediately available national air-force contingents for combined international enforcement action. The strength and degree of readiness of these contingents and plans for their combined action shall be determined, within the limits laid down in the special agreement or agreements referred to in Article 43, by the Security Council with the assistance of the Military Staff Committee.

Article 46

Plans for the application of armed force shall be made by the Security Council with the assistance of the Military Staff Committee.

Article 47

1.   There shall be established a Military Staff Committee to advise and assist the Security Council on all questions relating to the Security Council's military requirements for the maintenance of international peace and security, the employment and command of forces placed at its disposal, the regulation of armaments, and possible disarmament.

2.   The Military Staff Committee shall consist of the Chiefs of Staff of the permanent members of the Security Council or their representatives. Any Member of the United Nations not permanently represented on the Committee shall be invited by the Committee to be associated with it when the efficient discharge of the Committee's responsibilities requires the participation of that Member in its work.

3.   The Military Staff Committee shall be responsible under the Security Council for the strategic direction of any armed forces placed at the disposal of the Security Council. Questions relating to the command of such forces shall be worked out subsequently.

4.   The Military Staff Committee, with the authorization of the Security Council and after consultation with appropriate regional agencies, may establish regional sub-committees.

Article 48

1.   The action required to carry out the decisions of the Security Council for the maintenance of international peace and security shall be taken by all the Members of the United Nations or by some of them, as the Security Council may determine.

2.   Such decisions shall be carried out by the Members of the United Nations directly and through their action in the appropriate international agencies of which they are members.

Article 49

The Members of the United Nations shall join in affording mutual assistance in carrying out the measures decided upon by the Security Council.

Article 50

If preventive or enforcement measures against any state are taken by the Security Council, any other state, whether a Member of the United Nations or not, which finds itself confronted with special economic problems arising from the carrying out of those measures shall have the right to consult the Security Council with regard to a solution of those problems.

Article 51

Nothing in the present Charter shall impair the inherent right of individual or collective self-defence if an armed attack occurs against a Member of the United Nations, until the Security Council has taken measures necessary to maintain international peace and security. Measures taken by Members in the exercise of this right of self-defence shall be immediately reported to the Security Council and shall not in any way affect the authority and responsibility of the Security Council under the present Charter to take at any time such action as it deems necessary in order to maintain or restore international peace and security.

Chapter VIII
REGIONAL ARRANGEMENTS

Article 52

1.   Nothing in the present Charter precludes the existence of regional arrangements or agencies for dealing with such matters relating to the maintenance of international peace and security as are appropriate for regional action, provided that such arrangements or agencies and their activities are consistent with the Purposes and Principles of the United Nations.

2.   The Members of the United Nations entering into such arrangements or constituting such agencies shall make every effort to achieve pacific settlement of local disputes through such regional arrangements or by such regional agencies before referring them to the Security Council.

3.   The Security Council shall encourage the development of pacific settlement of local disputes through such regional arrangements or by such regional agencies either on the initiative of the states concerned or by reference from the Security Council.

4.   This Article in no way impairs the application of Articles 34 and 35.

Article 53

1.   The Security Council shall, where appropriate, utilize such regional arrangements or agencies for enforcement action under its authority. But no enforcement action shall be taken under regional arrangements or by regional agencies without the authorization of the Security Council, with the exception of measures against any enemy state, as defined in paragraph 2 of this Article, provided for pursuant to Article 107 or in regional arrangements directed against renewal of aggressive policy on the part of any such state, until such time as the Organization may, on request of the Governments concerned, be charged with the responsibility for preventing further aggression by such a state.

2.   The term enemy state as used in paragraph 1 of this Article applies to any state which during the Second World War has been an enemy of any signatory of the present Charter.

Article 54

The Security Council shall at all times be kept fully informed of activities undertaken or in contemplation under regional arrangements or by regional agencies for the maintenance of international peace and security.

Chapter IX
INTERNATIONAL ECONOMIC
AND SOCIAL CO-OPERATION

Article 55

With a view to the creation of conditions of stability and well-being which are necessary for peaceful and friendly relations among nations based on respect for the principle of equal rights and self-determination of peoples, the United Nations shall promote:

a.   higher standards of living, full employment, and conditions of economic and social progress and de-velopment;

b.   solutions of international economic, social, health, and related problems; and international cultural and educational co-operation; and

c.   universal respect for, and observance of, human rights and fundamental freedoms for all without distinction as to race, sex, language, or religion.

Article 56

All Members pledge themselves to take joint and separate action in co-operation with the Organization for the achievement of the purposes set forth in Article 55.

Article 57

1.   The various specialized agencies, established by intergovernmental agreement and having wide international responsibilities, as defined in their basic instruments, in economic, social, cultural, educational, health, and related fields, shall be brought into relationship with the United Nations in accordance with the provisions of Article 63.

2.   Such agencies thus brought into relationship with the United Nations are hereinafter referred to as specialized agencies.

Article 58

The Organization shall make recommendations for the co-ordination of the policies and activities of the specialized agencies.

Article 59

The Organization shall, where appropriate, initiate negotiations among the states concerned for the creation of any new specialized agencies required for the accomplishment of the purposes set forth in Article 55.

Article 60

Responsibility for the discharge of the functions of the Organization set forth in this Chapter shall be vested in the General Assembly and, under the authority of the General Assembly, in the Economic and Social Council, which shall have for this purpose the powers set forth in Chapter X.

Chapter X
THE ECONOMIC AND SOCIAL COUNCIL

Composition

Article 61[3]

1.   The Economic and Social Council shall consist of fifty-four Members of the United Nations elected by the General Assembly.

2.   Subject to the provisions of paragraph 3, eighteen members of the Economic and Social Council shall be elected each year for a term of three years. A retiring member shall be eligible for immediate re-election.

3.   At the first election after the increase in the membership of the Economic and Social Council from twenty-seven to fifty-four members, in addition to the members elected in place of the nine members whose term of office expires at the end of that year, twenty-seven additional members shall be elected. Of these twenty-seven additional members, the term of office of nine members so elected shall expire at the end of one year, and of nine other members at the end of two years, in accordance with arrangements made by the General Assembly.

4.   Each member of the Economic and Social Council shall have one representative.

Functions and powers

Article 62

1.   The Economic and Social Council may make or initiate studies and reports with respect to international economic, social, cultural, educational, health, and related matters and may make recommendations with respect to any such matters to the General Assembly, to the Members of the United Nations, and to the specialized agencies concerned.

2.   It may make recommendations for the purpose of promoting respect for, and observance of, human rights and fundamental freedoms for all.

3.   It may prepare draft conventions for submission to the General Assembly, with respect to matters falling within its competence.

4.   It may call, in accordance with the rules prescribed by the United Nations, international conferences on matters falling within its competence.

Article 63

1.   The Economic and Social Council may enter into agreements with any of the agencies referred to in Article 57, defining the terms on which the agency concerned shall be brought into relationship with the United Nations. Such agreements shall be subject to approval by the General Assembly.

2.   It may co-ordinate the activities of the specialized agencies through consultation with and recommendations to such agencies and through recommendations to the General Assembly and to the Members of the United Nations.

Article 64

1.   The Economic and Social Council may take appropriate steps to obtain regular reports from the specialized agencies. It may make arrangements with the Members of the United Nations and with the specialized agencies to obtain reports on the steps taken to give effect to its own recommendations and to recommendations on matters falling within its competence made by the General Assembly.

2.   It may communicate its observations on these reports to the General Assembly.

Article 65

The Economic and Social Council may furnish information to the Security Council and shall assist the Security Council upon its request.

Article 66

1.   The Economic and Social Council shall perform such functions as fall within its competence in connexion with the carrying out of the recommendations of the General Assembly.

2.   It may, with the approval of the General Assembly, perform services at the request of Members of the United Nations and at the request of specialized agencies.

3.   It shall perform such other functions as are specified elsewhere in the present Charter or as may be assigned to it by the General Assembly.

Voting

Article 67

1.   Each member of the Economic and Social Council shall have one vote.

2.   Decisions of the Economic and Social Council shall be made by a majority of the members present and voting.

Procedure

Article 68

The Economic and Social Council shall set up commissions in economic and social fields and for the promotion of human rights, and such other commissions as may be required for the performance of its functions.

---

[3]Amended text of Article 61, which came into force on 24 September 1973. (The text of Article 61 as previously amended on 31 August 1965 read as follows:

1.   The Economic and Social Council shall consist of twenty-seven Members of the United Nations elected by the General Assembly.

2.   Subject to the provisions of paragraph 3, nine members of the Economic and Social Council shall be elected each year for a term of three years. A retiring member shall be eligible for immediate re-election.

3.   At the first election after the increase in the membership of the Economic and Social Council from eighteen to twenty-seven members, in addition to the members elected in place of the six members whose term of office expires at the end of that year, nine additional members shall be elected. Of these nine additional members, the term of office of three members so elected shall expire at the end of one year, and of three other members at the end of two years, in accordance with arrangements made by the General Assembly.

4.   Each member of the Economic and Social Council shall have one representative.)

Article 69

The Economic and Social Council shall invite any Member of the United Nations to participate, without vote, in its deliberations on any matter of particular concern to that Member.

Article 70

The Economic and Social Council may make arrangements for representatives of the specialized agencies to participate, without vote, in its deliberations and in those of the commissions established by it, and for its representatives to participate in the deliberations of the specialized agencies.

Article 71

The Economic and Social Council may make suitable arrangements for consultation with non-governmental organizations which are concerned with matters within its competence. Such arrangements may be made with international organizations and, where appropriate, with national organizations after consultation with the Member of the United Nations concerned.

Article 72

1. The Economic and Social Council shall adopt its own rules of procedure, including the method of selecting its President.

2. The Economic and Social Council shall meet as required in accordance with its rules, which shall include provision for the convening of meetings on the request of a majority of its members.

Chapter XI
DECLARATION REGARDING NON-SELF-GOVERNING TERRITORIES

Article 73

Members of the United Nations which have or assume responsibilities for the administration of territories whose peoples have not yet attained a full measure of self-government recognize the principle that the interests of the inhabitants of these territories are paramount, and accept as a sacred trust the obligation to promote to the utmost, within the system of international peace and security established by the present Charter, the well-being of the inhabitants of these territories, and, to this end:

a. to ensure, with due respect for the culture of the peoples concerned, their political, economic, social, and educational advancement, their just treatment, and their protection against abuses;

b. to develop self-government, to take due account of the political aspirations of the peoples, and to assist them in the progressive development of their free political institutions, according to the particular circumstances of each territory and its peoples and their varying stages of advancement;

c. to further international peace and security;

d. to promote constructive measures of development, to encourage research, and to co-operate with one another and, when and where appropriate, with specialized international bodies with a view to the practical achievement of the social, economic, and scientific purposes set forth in this Article; and

e. to transmit regularly to the Secretary-General for information purposes, subject to such limitation as security and constitutional considerations may require, statistical and other information of a technical nature relating to economic, social, and educational conditions in the territories for which they are respectively responsible other than those territories to which Chapters XII and XIII apply.

Article 74

Members of the United Nations also agree that their policy in respect of the territories to which this Chapter applies, no less than in respect of their metropolitan areas, must be based on the general principle of good-neighbourliness, due account being taken of the interests and well-being of the rest of the world, in social, economic, and commercial matters.

Chapter XII
INTERNATIONAL TRUSTEESHIP SYSTEM

Article 75

The United Nations shall establish under its authority an international trusteeship system for the administration and supervision of such territories as may be placed thereunder by subsequent individual agreements. These territories are hereinafter referred to as trust territories.

Article 76

The basic objectives of the trusteeship system, in accordance with the Purposes of the United Nations laid down in Article 1 of the present Charter, shall be:

a. to further international peace and security;

b. to promote the political, economic, social, and educational advancement of the inhabitants of the trust territories, and their progressive development towards self-government or independence as may be appropriate to the particular circumstances of each territory and its peoples and the freely expressed wishes of the peoples concerned, and as may be provided by the terms of each trusteeship agreement;

c. to encourage respect for human rights and for fundamental freedoms for all without distinction as to race, sex, language, or religion, and to encourage recognition of the interdependence of the peoples of the world; and

d. to ensure equal treatment in social, economic, and commercial matters for all Members of the United Nations and their nationals, and also equal treatment for the latter in the administration of justice, without prejudice to the attainment of the foregoing objectives and subject to the provisions of Article 80.

Article 77

1. The trusteeship system shall apply to such territories in the following categories as may be placed thereunder by means of trusteeship agreements:

a. territories now held under mandate;

b. territories which may be detached from enemy states as a result of the Second World War; and

c. territories voluntarily placed under the system by states responsible for their administration.

2. It will be a matter for subsequent agreement as to which territories in the foregoing categories will be brought under the trusteeship system and upon what terms.

Article 78

The trusteeship system shall not apply to territories which have become Members of the United Nations, relationship among which shall be based on respect for the principle of sovereign equality.

Article 79

The terms of trusteeship for each territory to be placed under the trusteeship system, including any alteration or amendment, shall be agreed upon by the states directly concerned, including the mandatory power in the case of territories held under mandate by a Member of the United Nations, and shall be approved as provided for in Articles 83 and 85.

Article 80

1. Except as may be agreed upon in individual trusteeship agreements, made under Articles 77, 79, and 81, placing each territory under the trusteeship system, and until such agreements have been concluded, nothing in this Chapter shall be construed in or of itself to alter in any manner the rights whatsoever of any states or any peoples or the terms of existing international instruments to which Members of the United Nations may respectively be parties.

2. Paragraph 1 of this Article shall not be interpreted as giving grounds for delay or postponement of the negotiation and conclusion of agreements for placing mandated and other territories under the trusteeship system as provided for in Article 77.

Article 81

The trusteeship agreement shall in each case include the terms under which the trust territory will be administered and designate the authority which will exercise the administration of the trust territory. Such authority, hereinafter called the administering authority, may be one or more states or the Organization itself.

Article 82

There may be designated, in any trusteeship agreement, a strategic area or areas which may include part or all of the trust territory to which the agreement applies, without prejudice to any special agreement or agreements made under Article 43.

Article 83

1.   All functions of the United Nations relating to strategic areas, including the approval of the terms of the trusteeship agreements and of their alteration or amendments, shall be exercised by the Security Council.

2.   The basic objectives set forth in Article 76 shall be applicable to the people of each strategic area.

3.   The Security Council shall, subject to the provisions of the trusteeship agreements and without prejudice to security considerations, avail itself of the assistance of the Trusteeship Council to perform those functions of the United Nations under the trusteeship system relating to political, economic, social, and educational matters in the strategic areas.

Article 84

It shall be the duty of the administering authority to ensure that the trust territory shall play its part in the maintenance of international peace and security. To this end the administering authority may make use of volunteer forces, facilities, and assistance from the trust territory in carrying out the obligations towards the Security Council undertaken in this regard by the administering authority, as well as for local defence and the maintenance of law and order within the trust territory.

Article 85

1.   The functions of the United Nations with regard to trusteeship agreements for all areas not designated as strategic, including the approval of the terms of the trusteeship agreements and of their alteration or amendment, shall be exercised by the General Assembly.

2.   The Trusteeship Council, operating under the authority of the General Assembly, shall assist the General Assembly in carrying out these functions.

Chapter XIII
THE TRUSTEESHIP COUNCIL

Composition

Article 86

1.   The Trusteeship Council shall consist of the following Members of the United Nations:
   a.   those Members administering trust territories;
   b.   such of those Members mentioned by name in Article 23 as are not administering trust territories; and
   c.   as many other Members elected for three-year terms by the General Assembly as may be necessary to ensure that the total number of members of the Trusteeship Council is equally divided between those Members of the United Nations which administer trust territories and those which do not.

2.   Each member of the Trusteeship Council shall designate one specially qualified person to represent it therein.

Functions and powers

Article 87

The General Assembly and, under its authority, the Trusteeship Council, in carrying out their functions, may:
   a.   consider reports submitted by the administering authority;
   b.   accept petitions and examine them in consultation with the administering authority;
   c.   provide for periodic visits to the respective trust territories at times agreed upon with the administering authority; and
   d.   take these and other actions in conformity with the terms of the trusteeship agreements.

Article 88

The Trusteeship Council shall formulate a questionnaire on the political, economic, social, and educational advancement of the inhabitants of each trust territory, and the administering authority for each trust territory within the competence of the General Assembly shall make an annual report to the General Assembly upon the basis of such questionnaire.

Voting

Article 89

1.   Each member of the Trusteeship Council shall have one vote.

2.   Decisions of the Trusteeship Council shall be made by a majority of the members present and voting.

Procedure

Article 90

1.   The Trusteeship Council shall adopt its own rules of procedure, including the method of selecting its President.

2.   The Trusteeship Council shall meet as required in accordance with its rules, which shall include provision for the convening of meetings on the request of a majority of its members.

Article 91

The Trusteeship Council shall, when appropriate, avail itself of the assistance of the Economic and Social Council and of the specialized agencies in regard to matters with which they are respectively concerned.

Chapter XIV
THE INTERNATIONAL COURT OF JUSTICE

Article 92

The International Court of Justice shall be the principal judicial organ of the United Nations. It shall function in accordance with the annexed Statute, which is based upon the Statute of the Permanent Court of International Justice and forms an integral part of the present Charter.

Article 93

1.   All Members of the United Nations are *ipso facto* parties to the Statute of the International Court of Justice.

2.   A state which is not a Member of the United Nations may become a party to the Statute of the International Court of Justice on conditions to be determined in each case by the General Assembly upon the recommendation of the Security Council.

Article 94

1.   Each Member of the United Nations undertakes to comply with the decision of the International Court of Justice in any case to which it is a party.

2.   If any party to a case fails to perform the obligations incumbent upon it under a judgment rendered by the Court, the other party may have recourse to the Security Council, which may, if it deems necessary, make recommendations or decide upon measures to be taken to give effect to the judgment.

Article 95

Nothing in the present Charter shall prevent Members of the United Nations from entrusting the solution of their differences to other tribunals by virtue of agreements already in existence or which may be concluded in the future.

Article 96

1.   The General Assembly or the Security Council may request the International Court of Justice to give an advisory opinion on any legal question.

2.   Other organs of the United Nations and specialized agencies, which may at any time be so authorized by the General Assembly, may also request advisory opinions of the Court on legal questions arising within the scope of their activities.

Chapter XV
THE SECRETARIAT

Article 97

The Secretariat shall comprise a Secretary-General and such staff as the Organization may require. The Secretary-General shall be appointed by the General Assembly upon the recommendation of the Security Council. He shall be the chief administrative officer of the Organization.

Article 98

The Secretary-General shall act in that capacity in all meetings of the General Assembly, of the Security Council, of the Economic and Social Council, and of the Trusteeship Council, and shall perform such other functions as are entrusted to him by these organs. The Secretary-General shall make an annual report to the General Assembly on the work of the Organization.

Article 99

The Secretary-General may bring to the attention of the Security Council any matter which in his opinion may threaten the maintenance of international peace and security.

Article 100

1. In the performance of their duties the Secretary-General and the staff shall not seek or receive instructions from any government or from any other authority external to the Organization. They shall refrain from any action which might reflect on their position as international officials responsible only to the Organization.

2. Each Member of the United Nations undertakes to respect the exclusively international character of the responsibilities of the Secretary-General and the staff and not to seek to influence them in the discharge of their responsibilities.

Article 101

1. The staff shall be appointed by the Secretary-General under regulations established by the General Assembly.

2. Appropriate staffs shall be permanently assigned to the Economic and Social Council, the Trusteeship Council, and, as required, to other organs of the United Nations. These staffs shall form a part of the Secretariat.

3. The paramount consideration in the employment of the staff and in the determination of the conditions of service shall be the necessity of securing the highest standards of efficiency, competence, and integrity. Due regard shall be paid to the importance of recruiting the staff on as wide a geographical basis as possible.

Chapter XVI
MISCELLANEOUS PROVISIONS

Article 102

1. Every treaty and every international agreement entered into by any Member of the United Nations after the present Charter comes into force shall as soon as possible be registered with the Secretariat and published by it.

2. No party to any such treaty or international agreement which has not been registered in accordance with the provisions of paragraph 1 of this Article may invoke that treaty or agreement before any organ of the United Nations.

Article 103

In the event of a conflict between the obligations of the Members of the United Nations under the present Charter and their obligations under any other international agreement, their obligations under the present Charter shall prevail.

Article 104

The Organization shall enjoy in the territory of each of its Members such legal capacity as may be necessary for the exercise of its functions and the fulfilment of its purposes.

Article 105

1. The Organization shall enjoy in the territory of each of its Members such privileges and immunities as are necessary for the fulfilment of its purposes.

2. Representatives of the Members of the United Nations and officials of the Organization shall similarly enjoy such privileges and immunities as are necessary for the independent exercise of their functions in connexion with the Organization.

3. The General Assembly may make recommendations with a view to determining the details of the application of paragraphs 1 and 2 of this Article or may propose conventions to the Members of the United Nations for this purpose.

Chapter XVII
TRANSITIONAL SECURITY ARRANGEMENTS

Article 106

Pending the coming into force of such special agreements referred to in Article 43 as in the opinion of the Security Council enable it to begin the exercise of its responsibilities under Article 42, the parties to the Four-Nation Declaration, signed at Moscow, 30 October 1943, and France, shall, in accordance with the provisions of paragraph 5 of that Declaration, consult with one another and as occasion requires with other Members of the United Nations with a view to such joint action on behalf of the Organization as may be necessary for the purpose of maintaining international peace and security.

Article 107

Nothing in the present Charter shall invalidate or preclude action, in relation to any state which during the Second World War has been an enemy of any signatory to the present Charter, taken or authorized as a result of that war by the Governments having responsibility for such action.

Chapter XVIII
AMENDMENTS

Article 108

Amendments to the present Charter shall come into force for all Members of the United Nations when they have been adopted by a vote of two thirds of the members of the General Assembly and ratified in accordance with their respective constitutional processes by two thirds of the Members of the United Nations, including all the permanent members of the Security Council.

Article 109[4]

1. A General Conference of the Members of the United Nations for the purpose of reviewing the present Charter may be held at a date and place to be fixed by a two-thirds vote of the members of the General Assembly and by a vote of any nine members of the Security Council. Each Member of the United Nations shall have one vote in the conference.

2. Any alteration of the present Charter recommended by a two-thirds vote of the conference shall take effect when ratified in accordance with their respective constitutional processes by two thirds of the Members of the United Nations including all the permanent members of the Security Council.

3. If such a conference has not been held before the tenth annual session of the General Assembly following the coming into force of the present Charter, the proposal to call such a conference shall be

---

[4]Amended text of Article 109 which came into force on 12 June 1968. (The text of Article 109 before it was amended read as follows:

1. A General Conference of the Members of the United Nations for the purpose of reviewing the present Charter may be held at a date and place to be fixed by a two-thirds vote of the members of the General Assembly and by a vote of any seven members of the Security Council. Each Member of the United Nations shall have one vote in the conference.

2. Any alteration of the present Charter recommended by a two-thirds vote of the conference shall take effect when ratified in accordance with their respective constitutional processes by two thirds of the Members of the United Nations including all the permanent members of the Security Council.

3. If such a conference has not been held before the tenth annual session of the General Assembly following the coming into force of the present Charter, the proposal to call such a conference shall be placed on the agenda of that session of the General Assembly, and the conference shall be held if so decided by a majority vote of the members of the General Assembly and by a vote of any seven members of the Security Council.)

placed on the agenda of that session of the General Assembly, and the conference shall be held if so decided by a majority vote of the members of the General Assembly and by a vote of any seven members of the Security Council.

Chapter XIX
RATIFICATION AND SIGNATURE

Article 110

1. The present Charter shall be ratified by the signatory states in accordance with their respective constitutional processes.

2. The ratifications shall be deposited with the Government of the United States of America, which shall notify all the signatory states of each deposit as well as the Secretary-General of the Organization when he has been appointed.

3. The present Charter shall come into force upon the deposit of ratifications by the Republic of China, France, the Union of Soviet Socialist Republics, the United Kingdom of Great Britain and Northern Ireland, and the United States of America, and by a majority of the other signatory states. A protocol of the ratifications deposited shall thereupon be drawn up by the Government of the United States of America which shall communicate copies thereof to all the signatory states.

4. The states signatory to the present Charter which ratify it after it has come into force will become original Members of the United Nations on the date of the deposit of their respective ratifications.

Article 111

The present Charter, of which the Chinese, French, Russian, English, and Spanish texts are equally authentic, shall remain deposited in the archives of the Government of the United States of America. Duly certified copies thereof shall be transmitted by that Government to the Governments of the other signatory states.

IN FAITH WHEREOF the representatives of the Governments of the United Nations have signed the present Charter.

DONE at the city of San Francisco the twenty-sixth day of June, one thousand nine hundred and forty-five.

Statute of the International Court of Justice

Article 1

THE INTERNATIONAL COURT OF JUSTICE established by the Charter of the United Nations as the principal judicial organ of the United Nations shall be constituted and shall function in accordance with the provisions of the present Statute.

Chapter I
ORGANIZATION OF THE COURT

Article 2

The Court shall be composed of a body of independent judges, elected regardless of their nationality from among persons of high moral character, who possess the qualifications required in their respective countries for appointment to the highest judicial offices, or are jurisconsults of recognized competence in international law.

Article 3

1. The Court shall consist of fifteen members, no two of whom may be nationals of the same state.

2. A person who for the purposes of membership in the Court could be regarded as a national of more than one state shall be deemed to be a national of the one in which he ordinarily exercises civil and political rights.

Article 4

1. The members of the Court shall be elected by the General Assembly and by the Security Council from a list of persons nominated by the national groups in the Permanent Court of Arbitration, in accordance with the following provisions.

2. In the case of Members of the United Nations not represented in the Permanent Court of Arbitration, candidates shall be nominated by national groups appointed for this purpose by their governments under the same conditions as those prescribed for members of the Permanent Court of Arbitration by Article 44 of the Convention of The Hague of 1907 for the pacific settlement of international disputes.

3. The conditions under which a state which is a party to the present Statute but is not a Member of the United Nations may participate in electing the members of the Court shall, in the absence of a special agreement, be laid down by the General Assembly upon recommendation of the Security Council.

Article 5

1. At least three months before the date of the election, the Secretary-General of the United Nations shall address a written request to the members of the Permanent Court of Arbitration belonging to the states which are parties to the present Statute, and to the members of the national groups appointed under Article 4, paragraph 2, inviting them to undertake, within a given time, by national groups, the nomination of persons in a position to accept the duties of a member of the Court.

2. No group may nominate more than four persons, not more than two of whom shall be of their own nationality. In no case may the number of candidates nominated by a group be more than double the number of seats to be filled.

Article 6

Before making these nominations, each national group is recommended to consult its highest court of justice, its legal faculties and schools of law, and its national academies and national sections of international academies devoted to the study of law.

Article 7

1. The Secretary-General shall prepare a list in alphabetical order of all the persons thus nominated. Save as provided in Article 12, paragraph 2, these shall be the only persons eligible.

2. The Secretary-General shall submit this list to the General Assembly and to the Security Council.

Article 8

The General Assembly and the Security Council shall proceed independently of one another to elect the members of the Court.

Article 9

At every election, the electors shall bear in mind not only that the persons to be elected should individually possess the qualifications required, but also that in the body as a whole the representation of the main forms of civilization and of the principal legal systems of the world should be assured.

Article 10

1. Those candidates who obtain an absolute majority of votes in the General Assembly and in the Security Council shall be considered as elected.

2. Any vote of the Security Council, whether for the election of judges or for the appointment of members of the conference envisaged in Article 12, shall be taken without any distinction between permanent and non-permanent members of the Security Council.

3. In the event of more than one national of the same state obtaining an absolute majority of the votes both of the General Assembly and of the Security Council, the eldest of these only shall be considered as elected.

Article 11

If, after the first meeting held for the purpose of the election, one or more seats remain to be filled, a second and, if necessary, a third meeting shall take place.

Article 12

1. If, after the third meeting, one or more seats still remain unfilled, a joint conference consisting of six members, three appointed by the General Assembly and three by the Security Council, may be formed at any time at the request of either the General Assembly or the Security Council, for the purpose of choosing by the vote of an absolute majority one name for each seat still vacant, to submit to the General Assembly and the Security Council for their respective acceptance.

2. If the joint conference is unanimously agreed upon any person who fulfils the required conditions, he may be included in its list, even though he was not included in the list of nominations referred to in Article 7.

3. If the joint conference is satisfied that it will not be successful in procuring an election, those members of the Court who have already been elected shall, within a period to be fixed by the Security Council, proceed to fill the vacant seats by selection from among those candidates who have obtained votes either in the General Assembly or in the Security Council.

4. In the event of an equality of votes among the judges, the eldest judge shall have a casting vote.

Article 13

1. The members of the Court shall be elected for nine years and may be re-elected; provided, however, that of the judges elected at the first election, the terms of five judges shall expire at the end of three years and the terms of five more judges shall expire at the end of six years.

2. The judges whose terms are to expire at the end of the above-mentioned initial periods of three and six years shall be chosen by lot to be drawn by the Secretary-General immediately after the first election has been completed.

3. The members of the Court shall continue to discharge their duties until their places have been filled. Though replaced, they shall finish any cases which they may have begun.

4. In the case of the resignation of a member of the Court, the resignation shall be addressed to the President of the Court for transmission to the Secretary-General. This last notification makes the place vacant.

Article 14

Vacancies shall be filled by the same method as that laid down for the first election, subject to the following provision: the Secretary-General shall, within one month of the occurrence of the vacancy, proceed to issue the invitations provided for in Article 5, and the date of the election shall be fixed by the Security Council.

Article 15

A member of the Court elected to replace a member whose term of office has not expired shall hold office for the remainder of his predecessor's term.

Article 16

1. No member of the Court may exercise any political or administrative function, or engage in any other occupation of a professional nature.

2. Any doubt on this point shall be settled by the decision of the Court.

Article 17

1. No member of the Court may act as agent, counsel, or advocate in any case.

2. No member may participate in the decision of any case in which he has previously taken part as agent, counsel, or advocate for one of the parties, or as a member of a national or international court, or of a commission of enquiry, or in any other capacity.

3. Any doubt on this point shall be settled by the decision of the Court.

Article 18

1. No member of the Court can be dismissed unless, in the unanimous opinion of the other members, he has ceased to fulfil the required conditions.

2. Formal notification thereof shall be made to the Secretary-General by the Registrar.

3. This notification makes the place vacant.

Article 19

The members of the Court, when engaged on the business of the Court, shall enjoy diplomatic privileges and immunities.

Article 20

Every member of the Court shall, before taking up his duties, make a solemn declaration in open court that he will exercise his powers impartially and conscientiously.

Article 21

1. The Court shall elect its President and Vice-President for three years; they may be re-elected.

2. The Court shall appoint its Registrar and may provide for the appointment of such other officers as may be necessary.

Article 22

1. The seat of the Court shall be established at The Hague. This, however, shall not prevent the Court from sitting and exercising its functions elsewhere whenever the Court considers it desirable.

2. The President and the Registrar shall reside at the seat of the Court.

Article 23

1. The Court shall remain permanently in session, except during the judicial vacations, the dates and duration of which shall be fixed by the Court.

2. Members of the Court are entitled to periodic leave, the dates and duration of which shall be fixed by the Court, having in mind the distance between The Hague and the home of each judge.

3. Members of the Court shall be bound, unless they are on leave or prevented from attending by illness or other serious reasons duly explained to the President, to hold themselves permanently at the disposal of the Court.

Article 24

1. If, for some special reason, a member of the Court considers that he should not take part in the decision of a particular case, he shall so inform the President.

2. If the President considers that for some special reason one of the members of the Court should not sit in a particular case, he shall give him notice accordingly.

3. If in any such case the member of the Court and the President disagree, the matter shall be settled by the decision of the Court.

Article 25

1. The full Court shall sit except when it is expressly provided otherwise in the present Statute.

2. Subject to the condition that the number of judges available to constitute the Court is not thereby reduced below eleven, the Rules of the Court may provide for allowing one or more judges, according to circumstances and in rotation, to be dispensed from sitting.

3. A quorum of nine judges shall suffice to constitute the Court.

Article 26

1. The Court may from time to time form one or more chambers, composed of three or more judges as the Court may determine, for dealing with particular categories of cases; for example, labour cases and cases relating to transit and communications.

2. The Court may at any time form a chamber for dealing with a particular case. The number of judges to constitute such a chamber shall be determined by the Court with the approval of the parties.

3. Cases shall be heard and determined by the chambers provided for in this Article if the parties so request.

Article 27

A judgment given by any of the chambers provided for in Articles 26 and 29 shall be considered as rendered by the Court.

Article 28

The chambers provided for in Articles 26 and 29 may, with the consent of the parties, sit and exercise their functions elsewhere than at The Hague.

Article 29

With a view to the speedy dispatch of business, the Court shall form annually a chamber composed of five judges which, at the request of the parties, may hear and determine cases by summary procedure. In addition, two judges shall be selected for the purpose of replacing judges who find it impossible to sit.

Article 30

1. The Court shall frame rules for carrying out its functions. In particular, it shall lay down rules of procedure.
2. The Rules of the Court may provide for assessors to sit with the Court or with any of its chambers, without the right to vote.

Article 31

1. Judges of the nationality of each of the parties shall retain their right to sit in the case before the Court.
2. If the Court includes upon the Bench a judge of the nationality of one of the parties, any other party may choose a person to sit as judge. Such person shall be chosen preferably from among those persons who have been nominated as candidates as provided in Articles 4 and 5.
3. If the Court includes upon the Bench no judge of the nationality of the parties, each of these parties may proceed to choose a judge as provided in paragraph 2 of this Article.
4. The provisions of this Article shall apply to the case of Articles 26 and 29. In such cases, the President shall request one or, if necessary, two of the members of the Court forming the chamber to give place to the members of the Court of the nationality of the parties concerned, and, failing such, or if they are unable to be present, to the judges specially chosen by the parties.
5. Should there be several parties in the same interest, they shall, for the purpose of the preceding provisions, be reckoned as one party only. Any doubt upon this point shall be settled by the decision of the Court.
6. Judges chosen as laid down in paragraphs 2, 3 and 4 of this Article shall fulfil the conditions required by Articles 2, 17 (paragraph 2), 20, and 24 of the present Statute. They shall take part in the decision on terms of complete equality with their colleagues.

Article 32

1. Each member of the Court shall receive an annual salary.
2. The President shall receive a special annual allowance.
3. The Vice-President shall receive a special allowance for every day on which he acts as President.
4. The judges chosen under Article 31, other than members of the Court, shall receive compensation for each day on which they exercise their functions.
5. These salaries, allowances, and compensation shall be fixed by the General Assembly. They may not be decreased during the term of office.
6. The salary of the Registrar shall be fixed by the General Assembly on the proposal of the Court.
7. Regulations made by the General Assembly shall fix the conditions under which retirement pensions may be given to members of the Court and to the Registrar, and the conditions under which members of the Court and the Registrar shall have their travelling expenses refunded.
8. The above salaries, allowances, and compensation shall be free of all taxation.

Article 33

The expenses of the Court shall be borne by the United Nations in such a manner as shall be decided by the General Assembly.

Chapter II
COMPETENCE OF THE COURT

Article 34

1. Only states may be parties in cases before the Court.
2. The Court, subject to and in conformity with its Rules, may request of public international organizations information relevant to cases before it, and shall receive such information presented by such organizations on their own initiative.

3. Whenever the construction of the constituent instrument of a public international organization or of an international convention adopted thereunder is in question in a case before the Court, the Registrar shall so notify the public international organization concerned and shall communicate to it copies of all the written proceedings.

Article 35

1. The Court shall be open to the states parties to the present Statute.
2. The conditions under which the Court shall be open to other states shall, subject to the special provisions contained in treaties in force, be laid down by the Security Council, but in no case shall such conditions place the parties in a position of inequality before the Court.
3. When a state which is not a Member of the United Nations is a party to a case, the Court shall fix the amount which that party is to contribute towards the expenses of the Court. This provision shall not apply if such state is bearing a share of the expenses of the Court.

Article 36

1. The jurisdiction of the Court comprises all cases which the parties refer to it and all matters specially provided for in the Charter of the United Nations or in treaties and conventions in force.
2. The states parties to the present Statute may at any time declare that they recognize as compulsory *ipso facto* and without special agreement, in relation to any other state accepting the same obligation, the jurisdiction of the Court in all legal disputes concerning:
   a. the interpretation of a treaty;
   b. any question of international law;
   c. the existence of any fact which, if established, would constitute a breach of an international obligation;
   d. the nature or extent of the reparation to be made for the breach of an international obligation.
3. The declarations referred to above may be made unconditionally or on condition of reciprocity on the part of several or certain states, or for a certain time.
4. Such declarations shall be deposited with the Secretary-General of the United Nations, who shall transmit copies thereof to the parties to the Statute and to the Registrar of the Court.
5. Declarations made under Article 36 of the Statute of the Permanent Court of International Justice and which are still in force shall be deemed, as between the parties to the present Statute, to be acceptances of the compulsory jurisdiction of the International Court of Justice for the period which they still have to run and in accordance with their terms.
6. In the event of a dispute as to whether the Court has jurisdiction, the matter shall be settled by the decision of the Court.

Article 37

Whenever a treaty or convention in force provides for reference of a matter to a tribunal to have been instituted by the League of Nations, or to the Permanent Court of International Justice, the matter shall, as between the parties to the present Statute, be referred to the International Court of Justice.

Article 38

1. The Court, whose function is to decide in accordance with international law such disputes as are submitted to it, shall apply:
   a. international conventions, whether general or particular, establishing rules expressly recognized by the contesting states;
   b. international custom, as evidence of a general practice accepted as law;
   c. the general principles of law recognized by civilized nations;
   d. subject to the provisions of Article 59, judicial decisions and the teachings of the most highly qualified publicists of the various nations, as subsidiary means for the determination of rules of law.
2. This provision shall not prejudice the power of the Court to decide a case *ex aequo et bono*, if the parties agree thereto.

Chapter III
PROCEDURE

Article 39

1. The official languages of the Court shall be French and English. If the parties agree that the case shall be conducted in French, the

judgment shall be delivered in French. If the parties agree that the case shall be conducted in English, the judgment shall be delivered in English.

2. In the absence of an agreement as to which language shall be employed, each party may, in the pleadings, use the language which it prefers; the decision of the Court shall be given in French and English. In this case the Court shall at the same time determine which of the two texts shall be considered as authoritative.

3. The Court shall, at the request of any party, authorize a language other than French or English to be used by that party.

Article 40

1. Cases are brought before the Court, as the case may be, either by the notification of the special agreement or by a written application addressed to the Registrar. In either case the subject of the dispute and the parties shall be indicated.

2. The Registrar shall forthwith communicate the application to all concerned.

3. He shall also notify the Members of the United Nations through the Secretary-General, and also any other states entitled to appear before the Court.

Article 41

1. The Court shall have the power to indicate, if it considers that circumstances so require, any provisional measures which ought to be taken to preserve the respective rights of either party.

2. Pending the final decision, notice of the measures suggested shall forthwith be given to the parties and to the Security Council.

Article 42

1. The parties shall be represented by agents.

2. They may have the assistance of counsel or advocates before the Court.

3. The agents, counsel, and advocates of parties before the Court shall enjoy the privileges and immunities necessary to the independent exercise of their duties.

Article 43

1. The procedure shall consist of two parts: written and oral.

2. The written proceedings shall consist of the communication to the Court and to the parties of memorials, counter-memorials and, if necessary, replies; also all papers and documents in support.

3. These communications shall be made through the Registrar, in the order and within the time fixed by the Court.

4. A certified copy of every document produced by one party shall be communicated to the other party.

5. The oral proceedings shall consist of the hearing by the Court of witnesses, experts, agents, counsel, and advocates.

Article 44

1. For the service of all notices upon persons other than the agents, counsel, and advocates, the Court shall apply direct to the government of the state upon whose territory the notice has to be served.

2. The same provision shall apply whenever steps are to be taken to procure evidence on the spot.

Article 45

The hearing shall be under the control of the President or, if he is unable to preside, of the Vice-President; if neither is able to preside, the senior judge present shall preside.

Article 46

The hearing in Court shall be public, unless the Court shall decide otherwise, or unless the parties demand that the public be not admitted.

Article 47

1. Minutes shall be made at each hearing and signed by the Registrar and the President.

2. These minutes alone shall be authentic.

Article 48

The Court shall make orders for the conduct of the case, shall decide the form and time in which each party must conclude its arguments, and make all arrangements connected with the taking of evidence.

Article 49

The Court may, even before the hearing begins, call upon the agents to produce any document or to supply any explanations. Formal note shall be taken of any refusal.

Article 50

The Court may, at any time, entrust any individual, body, bureau, commission, or other organization that it may select, with the task of carrying out an enquiry or giving an expert opinion.

Article 51

During the hearing any relevant questions are to be put to the witnesses and experts under the conditions laid down by the Court in the rules of procedure referred to in Article 30.

Article 52

After the Court has received the proofs and evidence within the time specified for the purpose, it may refuse to accept any further oral or written evidence that one party may desire to present unless the other side consents.

Article 53

1. Whenever one of the parties does not appear before the Court, or fails to defend its case, the other party may call upon the Court to decide in favour of its claim.

2. The Court must, before doing so, satisfy itself, not only that it has jurisdiction in accordance with Articles 36 and 37, but also that the claim is well founded in fact and law.

Article 54

1. When, subject to the control of the Court, the agents, counsel, and advocates have completed their presentation of the case, the President shall declare the hearing closed.

2. The Court shall withdraw to consider the judgment.

3. The deliberations of the Court shall take place in private and remain secret.

Article 55

1. All questions shall be decided by a majority of the judges present.

2. In the event of an equality of votes, the President or the judge who acts in his place shall have a casting vote.

Article 56

1. The judgment shall state the reasons on which it is based.

2. It shall contain the names of the judges who have taken part in the decision.

Article 57

If the judgment does not represent in whole or in part the unanimous opinion of the judges, any judge shall be entitled to deliver a separate opinion.

Article 58

The judgment shall be signed by the President and by the Registrar. It shall be read in open court, due notice having been given to the agents.

Article 59

The decision of the Court has no binding force except between the parties and in respect of that particular case.

Article 60

The judgment is final and without appeal. In the event of dispute as to the meaning or scope of the judgment, the Court shall construe it upon the request of any party.

Article 61

1. An application for revision of a judgment may be made only when it is based upon the discovery of some fact of such a nature as to be a decisive factor, which fact was, when the judgment was given, unknown to the Court and also to the party claiming revision, always provided that such ignorance was not due to negligence.

2. The proceedings for revision shall be opened by a judgment of the Court expressly recording the existence of the new fact, recognizing

that it has such a character as to lay the case open to revision, and declaring the application admissible on this ground.

3. The Court may require previous compliance with the terms of the judgment before it admits proceedings in revision.

4. The application for revision must be made at latest within six months of the discovery of the new fact.

5. No application for revision may be made after the lapse of ten years from the date of the judgment.

Article 62

1. Should a state consider that it has an interest of a legal nature which may be affected by the decision in the case, it may submit a request to the Court to be permitted to intervene.

2. It shall be for the Court to decide upon this request.

Article 63

1. Whenever the construction of a convention to which states other than those concerned in the case are parties is in question, the Registrar shall notify all such states forthwith.

2. Every state so notified has the right to intervene in the proceedings; but if it uses this right, the construction given by the judgment will be equally binding upon it.

Article 64

Unless otherwise decided by the Court, each party shall bear its own costs.

Chapter IV
ADVISORY OPINIONS

Article 65

1. The Court may give an advisory opinion on any legal question at the request of whatever body may be authorized by or in accordance with the Charter of the United Nations to make such a request.

2. Questions upon which the advisory opinion of the Court is asked shall be laid before the Court by means of a written request containing an exact statement of the question upon which an opinion is required, and accompanied by all documents likely to throw light upon the question.

Article 66

1. The Registrar shall forthwith give notice of the request for an advisory opinion to all states entitled to appear before the Court.

2. The Registrar shall also, by means of a special and direct communication, notify any state entitled to appear before the Court or international organization considered by the Court, or, should it not be sitting, by the President, as likely to be able to furnish information on the question, that the Court will be prepared to receive, within a time limit to be fixed by the President, written statements, or to hear, at a public sitting to be held for the purpose, oral statements relating to the question.

3. Should any such state entitled to appear before the Court have failed to receive the special communication referred to in paragraph 2 of this Article, such state may express a desire to submit a written statement or to be heard; and the Court will decide.

4. States and organizations having presented written or oral statements or both shall be permitted to comment on the statements made by other states or organizations in the form, to the extent, and within the time limits which the Court, or, should it not be sitting, the President, shall decide in each particular case. Accordingly, the Registrar shall in due time communicate any such written statements to states and organizations having submitted similar statements.

Article 67

The Court shall deliver its advisory opinions in open court, notice having been given to the Secretary-General and to the representatives of Members of the United Nations, of other states and of international organizations immediately concerned.

Article 68

In the exercise of its advisory functions the Court shall further be guided by the provisions of the present Statute which apply in contentious cases to the extent to which it recognizes them to be applicable.

Chapter V
AMENDMENT

Article 69

Amendments to the present Statute shall be effected by the same procedure as is provided by the Charter of the United Nations for amendments to that Charter, subject however to any provisions which the General Assembly upon recommendation of the Security Council may adopt concerning the participation of states which are parties to the present Statute but are not Members of the United Nations.

Article 70

The Court shall have power to propose such amendments to the present Statute as it may deem necessary, through written communications to the Secretary-General, for consideration in conformity with the provisions of Article 69.

Appendix III

Structure of the United Nations

General Assembly

The General Assembly is composed of all the Members of the United Nations.

SESSIONS
Resumed thirty-seventh session: 10-13 May and 19 September 1983.
Thirty-eighth session:[1] 20 September–20 December 1983 (suspended).

OFFICERS
Resumed thirty-seventh session
President: Imre Hollai (Hungary).
Vice-Presidents: Austria, China, Congo, Cyprus, Democratic Yemen, France, Haiti, Jamaica, Kuwait, Libyan Arab Jamahiriya, Mali, Nicaragua, Philippines, Qatar, Turkey, Uganda, USSR, United Kingdom, United States, Upper Volta, Zambia.

Thirty-eighth session
President: Jorge Enrique Illueca (Panama).[a]
Vice-Presidents:[b] Algeria, Belgium, Bhutan, Burundi, Canada, China, Czechoslovakia, France, Guyana, Lebanon, Liberia, Nepal, Pakistan, Sierra Leone, Singapore, Sudan, Swaziland, USSR, United Kingdom, United States, Venezuela.

[a]Elected on 20 September 1983 (decision 38/302).
[b]Elected on 20 September 1983 (decision 38/304).

The Assembly has four types of committees: (1) Main Committees; (2) procedural committees; (3) standing committees; (4) subsidiary and *ad hoc* bodies. In addition, it convenes conferences to deal with specific subjects.

Main Committees

Seven Main Committees have been established as follows:

Political and Security Committee (disarmament and related international security questions) (First Committee)
Special Political Committee
Economic and Financial Committee (Second Committee)
Social, Humanitarian and Cultural Committee (Third Committee)
Trusteeship Committee (including Non-Self-Governing Territories) (Fourth Committee)
Administrative and Budgetary Committee (Fifth Committee)
Legal Committee (Sixth Committee)

The General Assembly may constitute other committees, on which all Members of the United Nations have the right to be represented.

OFFICERS OF THE MAIN COMMITTEES

Resumed thirty-seventh session

Special Political Committee[a]
Chairman: Abduldayem M. Mubarez (Yemen).
Vice-Chairmen: Turkia Ould Daddah (Mauritania), Ernesto Rodríguez-Medina (Colombia).
Rapporteur: Osman Faruk Logoglu (Turkey).

[a]The only Main Committee which met at the resumed thirty-seventh session.

Thirty-eighth session[a]

[a]Chairmen elected by the Main Committees; announced by the Assembly President on 20 September 1983 (decision 38/303).

First Committee
Chairman: Tom Eric Vraalsen (Norway).
Vice-Chairmen: Elfaki Abdalla Elfaki (Sudan), Gheorghe Tinca (Romania).
Rapporteur: Humberto Y. Goyén Alvez (Uruguay).

Special Political Committee
Chairman: Ernesto Rodríguez-Medina (Colombia).
Vice-Chairman: Feodor Starcevic (Yugoslavia).
Rapporteur: Edouard H. Lingani (Upper Volta).

Second Committee
Chairman: Peter Dietze (German Democratic Republic).
Vice-Chairmen: Phillip H. Gibson (New Zealand), Faruq S. Ziada (Iraq).
Rapporteur: Policarpo Arce-Rojas (Colombia).

Third Committee
Chairman: Saroj Chavanaviraj (Thailand).
Vice-Chairmen: Roderick L. Bell (Canada), María de los Angeles Flórez Prida (Cuba).
Rapporteur: Moussokoro Sangaré-Kaba (Guinea).

Fourth Committee
Chairman: Ali A. Treiki (Libyan Arab Jamahiriya).
Vice-Chairmen: Jaime Hermida Castillo (Nicaragua), Ralph Karepa (Papua New Guinea).
Rapporteur: Rudolph Yossiphov (Bulgaria).

Fifth Committee
Chairman: Sumihiro Kuyama (Japan).
Vice-Chairmen: Henrik Amneus (Sweden), Tommo Monthe (United Republic of Cameroon).
Rapporteur: Even Fontaine Ortiz (Cuba).

Sixth Committee
Chairman: Elies Gastli (Tunisia).
Vice-Chairman: Eladio Knipping-Victoria (Dominican Republic).
Rapporteur: Soud Mohamad Zedan (Saudi Arabia).

Procedural committees

General Committee
The General Committee consists of the President of the General Assembly, as Chairman, the 21 Vice-Presidents and the Chairmen of the seven Main Committees.

Credentials Committee
The Credentials Committee consists of nine members appointed by the General Assembly on the proposal of the President.

Resumed thirty-seventh session
Bahamas *(Chairman)*, China, Dominican Republic, Nepal, New Zealand, Nigeria, Seychelles, USSR, United States.

Thirty-eighth session
China, Colombia, Indonesia, Jamaica, Mali, Portugal, Uganda *(Chairman)*, USSR, United States.[a]

[a]Appointed on 20 September 1983 (decision 38/301).

[1]The thirty-eighth session of the General Assembly resumed in 1984 on 26 June and 17 September.

Standing committees

The two standing committees consist of experts appointed in their individual capacity for three-year terms.

Advisory Committee on Administrative and Budgetary Questions

Members:

To serve until 31 December 1983: Henrik Amneus (Sweden); Michel Brochard (France); Ernesto C. Garrido (Philippines); Sumihiro Kuyama (Japan); Samuel Pinheiro-Guimarães (Brazil); Tang Jianwen (China).

To serve until 31 December 1984: Enrique Ferrer Vieyra (Argentina); A. V. Grodsky (USSR);[a] Virginia C. Housholder (United States); Rachid Lahlou (Morocco); Carl C. Pedersen (Canada).

To serve until 31 December 1985: Traian Chebeleu (Romania); Mohamed Malloum Fall (Mauritania); Mohammad Samir Mansouri (Syrian Arab Republic); C. S. M. Mselle, *Chairman* (United Republic of Tanzania); Christopher R. Thomas (Trinidad and Tobago).

[a]Resigned on 19 September 1983; I. V. Khalevinski (USSR) was appointed by the General Assembly on 4 October (decision 38/305 A) to fill the resultant vacancy.

On 20 December 1983 (decision 38/305 B), the General Assembly appointed the following six members for a three-year term beginning on 1 January 1984 to fill the vacancies occurring on 31 December 1983: Henrik Amneus (Sweden), Ma Longde (China), Andrew Robin Murray (United Kingdom), Samuel Pinheiro-Guimarães (Brazil), Banbit A. Roy (India), Yukio Takasu (Japan).

Committee on Contributions

Members:

To serve until 31 December 1983: Hélio de Burgos Cabal (Brazil); Leoncio Fernández Maroto (Spain); Lance Louis E. Joseph (Australia); Japhet Gideon Kiti, *Vice-Chairman* (Kenya); Rachid Lahlou (Morocco); Atilio Norberto Molteni (Argentina).

To serve until 31 December 1984: Syed Amjad Ali, *Chairman* (Pakistan); A. S. Chistyakov (USSR); Miguel Angel Dávila Mendoza (Mexico);[a] Wilfried Koschorreck (Federal Republic of Germany); Yang Hushan (China); Philippe Zeller (France).

To serve until 31 December 1985: Andrzej Abraszewski (Poland); Nobutoshi Akao (Japan); Mohammed Sadiq Al-Mahdi (Iraq); Hamed Arabi El-Houderi (Libyan Arab Jamahiriya); Richard Vognild Hennes (United States); Zoran Lazarevic (Yugoslavia).

[a]Resigned on 22 September 1983; Javier Castillo Ayala (Mexico) was appointed by the General Assembly on 25 November (decision 38/308) to fill the resultant vacancy.

On 25 November 1983 (decision 38/308), the General Assembly appointed the following six members for a three-year term beginning on 1 January 1984 to fill the vacancies occurring on 31 December 1983: Marco Antônio Diniz Brandão (Brazil), Leoncio Fernández Maroto (Spain), Lance Louis E. Joseph (Australia), Atilio Norberto Molteni (Argentina), Aluseye D. Oduyemi (Nigeria), Omar Sirry (Egypt).

Subsidiary, *ad hoc* and related bodies

The following subsidiary, *ad hoc* and related bodies were in existence or functioning in 1983, or were established during the General Assembly's thirty-eighth session, held from 20 September to 20 December 1983. (For other related bodies, see p. 1364.)

Ad Hoc Committee of the General Assembly for the Announcement of Voluntary Contributions to the 1984 Programme of the United Nations High Commissioner for Refugees

As soon as practicable after the opening of each regular session of the General Assembly, an *ad hoc* committee of the whole of the Assembly meets, under the chairmanship of the President of the session, to enable Governments to announce pledges of voluntary contributions to the programme of UNHCR for the following year. Also invited to announce their pledges are States which are members of specialized agencies but not Members of the United Nations. In 1983, the *Ad Hoc* Committee met on 18 November.

Ad Hoc Committee of the General Assembly for the Announcement of Voluntary Contributions to the United Nations Relief and Works Agency for Palestine Refugees in the Near East

As soon as practicable after the opening of each regular session of the General Assembly, an *ad hoc* committee of the whole of the Assembly meets, under the chairmanship of the President of the session, to enable Governments to announce pledges of voluntary contributions to the programme of UNRWA for the following year. Also invited to announce their pledges are States which are members of specialized agencies but not Members of the United Nations. In 1983, the *Ad Hoc* Committee met on 22 November.

Ad Hoc Committee of the International Conference on Kampuchea

The *Ad Hoc* Committee of the International Conference on Kampuchea held five meetings between 24 January and 20 September 1983, at United Nations Headquarters.

Members: Belgium, Japan, Malaysia, Nepal, Nigeria, Peru, Senegal, Sri Lanka, Sudan, Thailand.

Chairman: Massamba Sarré (Senegal).
Vice-Chairman: Edmonde Dever (Belgium).
Rapporteur: Zainal Abidin bin Sulong (Malaysia).

Ad Hoc Committee on the Drafting of an International Convention against *Apartheid* in Sports

The *Ad Hoc* Committee on the Drafting of an International Convention against *Apartheid* in Sports, which was to consist of 25 members, had a membership of 24 in 1983. It held two meetings during the year, at United Nations Headquarters, on 20 January and 29 August.

Members: Algeria, Barbados, Canada, Congo, German Democratic Republic, Ghana, Guinea, Haiti, Hungary, India, Indonesia, Jamaica, Malaysia, Nepal, Nigeria, Peru, Philippines, Somalia, Sudan, Syrian Arab Republic, Trinidad and Tobago, Ukrainian SSR, United Republic of Tanzania, Yugoslavia.

Chairman: Ernest Besley Maycock (Barbados).
Vice-Chairmen: Keshav Raj Jha (Nepal), Janos Matus (Hungary), George K. Mwanjabala (United Republic of Tanzania).
Rapporteur: Stafford Oliver Neil (Jamaica).

Ad Hoc Committee on the Drafting of an International Convention against the Recruitment, Use, Financing and Training of Mercenaries

The *Ad Hoc* Committee on the Drafting of an International Convention against the Recruitment, Use, Financing and Training of Mercenaries, which was to be composed of 35 members, had a membership of 34 in 1983. It held its third session at United Nations Headquarters from 2 to 26 August.

Members: Algeria, Angola, Bahamas, Bangladesh, Barbados, Benin, Bulgaria, Canada, Democratic Yemen, Ethiopia, France, German Democratic Republic, Germany, Federal Republic of, Guyana, India, Italy, Jamaica, Japan, Mongolia, Nigeria, Portugal, Seychelles, Spain, Suriname, Togo, Turkey, Ukrainian SSR, USSR, United Kingdom, United States, Uruguay, Yugoslavia, Zaire, Zambia.

Chairman: Mohamed Sahnoun (Algeria).
Vice-Chairmen: Luigi Ferrari Bravo (Italy), Ernest Besley Maycock (Barbados), B. I. Tarasyuk (Ukrainian SSR).
Rapporteur: Moritaka Hayashi (Japan).

Ad Hoc Committee on the Implementation of the Collective Security Provisions of the Charter of the United Nations

On 20 December 1983, the General Assembly established an *ad hoc* committee to explore ways and means of implementing the collective security provisions of the Charter of the United Nations; it was to report to the Security Council and to the Assembly. The Committee, whose members were to be appointed by the Assembly President, had not been constituted by the end of 1983.

Ad Hoc Committee on the Indian Ocean

In 1983, the membership of the *Ad Hoc* Committee on the Indian Ocean rose from 46 to 47, pursuant to a 1979 General Assembly decision to enlarge it.[2]

The Committee, undertaking the preparatory work for the Conference on the Indian Ocean (scheduled for 1986 at Colombo, Sri Lanka), held three sessions during the year—from 31 January to 9 February, from 11 to 22 April and from 12 to 22 July—with additional meetings on 15 and 30 November, all at United Nations Headquarters.

Members: Australia, Bangladesh, Bulgaria, Canada, China, Democratic Yemen, Djibouti, Egypt, Ethiopia, France, German Democratic Republic, Germany, Federal Republic of, Greece, India, Indonesia, Iran, Iraq, Italy, Japan, Kenya, Liberia, Madagascar, Malaysia, Maldives, Mauritius, Mozambique, Netherlands, Norway, Oman, Pakistan, Panama, Poland, Romania, Seychelles, Singapore, Somalia, Sri Lanka, Sudan, Thailand, USSR, United Arab Emirates,[a] United Kingdom, United Republic of Tanzania, United States, Yemen, Yugoslavia, Zambia.

Sweden, a major maritime user of the Indian Ocean, continued to participate in the meetings as an observer.

[a]Appointed by the President of the General Assembly's thirty-seventh session, on the basis of a Committee recommendation, as stated in his communication of 11 May 1983 to the Secretary-General.

Chairman: Ignatius Benedict Fonseka (Sri Lanka).
Vice-Chairmen: Susan Jennifer Boyd (Australia); Izhar Ibrahim (Indonesia); Siegfried Kahn (German Democratic Republic); José Carlos Lobo (Mozambique) (until 19 July), Daniel Assa Nhaguilunguana (Mozambique) (from 19 July).
Rapporteur: Henri Rasolondraibe (Madagascar) (until 11 April), André Tahindro (Madagascar) (from 11 April).

Ad Hoc Committee on the World Disarmament Conference

The 40-member *Ad Hoc* Committee on the World Disarmament Conference held two sessions in 1983, at United Nations Headquarters: the first from 4 to 7 April; and the second from 5 to 8 July.

Members: Algeria, Argentina, Austria, Belgium, Brazil, Bulgaria, Burundi, Canada, Chile, Colombia, Czechoslovakia, Egypt, Ethiopia, Hungary, India, Indonesia, Iran, Italy, Japan, Lebanon, Liberia, Mexico, Mongolia, Morocco, Netherlands, Nigeria, Pakistan, Peru, Philippines, Poland, Romania, Spain, Sri Lanka, Sweden, Tunisia, Turkey, Venezuela, Yugoslavia, Zaire, Zambia.

The USSR participated in the work of the *Ad Hoc* Committee, while China, France, the United Kingdom and the United States maintained contact with it through its Chairman, pursuant to a 1973 General Assembly resolution.[3]

Chairman: Ignatius Benedict Fonseka (Sri Lanka).
Vice-Chairmen: Ryszard Krystosik (Poland), Celso Pastor de la Torre (Peru) (from 4 April to 5 July).
Rapporteur: Arturo Laclaustra (Spain).

WORKING GROUP
Members: Burundi, Egypt, Hungary, India, Iran, Italy, Mexico, Peru, Poland, Spain *(Chairman)*, Sri Lanka.

Advisory Committee for the International Youth Year

The 24-member Advisory Committee for the International Youth Year did not meet in 1983.

Members: Algeria, Chile, Costa Rica, Democratic Yemen, Germany, Federal Republic of, Guatemala, Guinea, Indonesia, Ireland, Jamaica, Japan, Lebanon, Morocco, Mozambique, Netherlands, Nigeria, Norway, Poland, Romania, Rwanda, Sri Lanka, USSR, United States, Venezuela.

Advisory Committee on the United Nations Educational and Training Programme for Southern Africa

Members: Byelorussian SSR, Canada, Denmark, India, Japan, Liberia, Nigeria, Norway, United Republic of Tanzania, United States, Venezuela, Zaire, Zambia.

Chairman: Tom Eric Vraalsen (Norway).
Vice-Chairman: Love Kunda M'tesa (Zambia).

Advisory Committee on the United Nations Programme of Assistance in the Teaching, Study, Dissemination and Wider Appreciation of International Law

The Advisory Committee on the United Nations Programme of Assistance in the Teaching, Study, Dissemination and Wider Appreciation of International Law held two sessions in 1983, at United Nations Headquarters: its seventeenth on 11 January; and its eighteenth on 27 October.

Members (until 31 December 1983):[a] Barbados, Cyprus, Egypt, El Salvador, France, Ghana, Hungary, Netherlands, Sierra Leone, Syrian Arab Republic, Turkey, USSR, United Kingdom.

[a]The succeeding members had not been appointed by the end of 1983.

Chairman: Kofi Darko Asante (Ghana) (seventeenth session), Yaw Konadu-Yiadom (Ghana) (eighteenth session).

Board of Auditors

The Board of Auditors consists of three members appointed by the General Assembly for three-year terms.

Members:
To serve until 30 June 1984: Comptroller and Auditor-General of Bangladesh.
To serve until 30 June 1985: Auditor-General of Ghana.
To serve until 30 June 1986: Senior President of the Audit Office of Belgium.

On 25 November 1983 (decision 38/309), the General Assembly appointed the Chairman of the Commission of Audit of the Philippines for a three-year term beginning on 1 July 1984.

Collective Measures Committee

Established in 1950 under the General Assembly's "Uniting for Peace" resolution,[4] the Collective Measures Committee reported three times to the Assembly. In noting the third report, to its ninth (1954) session, the Assembly directed the Committee to remain in a position to pursue such further studies as it may deem desirable to strengthen the capability of the United Nations to maintain peace and to report to the Security Council and to the Assembly as appropriate.[5]

Members: Australia, Belgium, Brazil, Burma, Canada, Egypt, France, Mexico, Philippines, Turkey, United Kingdom, United States, Venezuela, Yugoslavia.

Commission on Human Settlements

The Commission on Human Settlements reports to the General Assembly through the Economic and Social Council.

For details of the Commission's membership and session in 1983, see p. 1361.

Committee for Programme and Co-ordination

The Committee for Programme and Co-ordination is the main subsidiary organ of the Economic and Social Council and of the General Assembly for planning, programming and co-ordination; it reports to both.

For details of the Committee's membership and session in 1983, see p. 1361.

Committee for the United Nations Population Award

The Committee for the United Nations Population Award is composed of: *(a)* 10 representatives of United Nations Member States elected by the Economic and Social Council for a three-year period, with due regard for equitable geographical representation and the need to in-

---

[2]Resolution 34/80 B, 11 December 1979 (YUN 1979, p. 67).
[3]Resolution 3183(XXVIII), 18 December 1973 (YUN 1973, p. 18).
[4]Resolution 377(V), part A, para. 11, 3 November 1950 (YUN 1950, p. 194).
[5]Resolution 809(IX), 4 November 1954 (YUN 1954, p. 23).

clude Member States that had made contributions for the Award; *(b)* the Secretary-General and the UNFPA Executive Director, to serve *ex officio;* and *(c)* five individuals eminent for their significant contributions to population-related activities, selected by the Committee, to serve as honorary members in an advisory capacity for a renewable three-year term.

In 1983, the Committee held six meetings between 20 January and 8 September, at United Nations Headquarters.

Members (until 31 December 1985): Australia, Bangladesh, Burundi, China, Colombia, Egypt, Japan, Mexico, Tunisia, Yugoslavia.
Ex-officio members: The Secretary-General and the UNFPA Executive Director.
Honorary members:[a] Kenneth K. S. Dadzie, Nobusuke Kishi, Alva Myrdal, Raúl Prebisch, Theodore W. Schultz.[b]

[a]Selected by the Committee on 18 March 1983.
[b]Resigned on 18 July; no replacement was selected during 1983.

Chairman: Anwarul Karim Chowdhury (Bangladesh).

Committee of Trustees of the United Nations Trust Fund for South Africa
Members: Chile, Morocco, Nigeria, Pakistan, Sweden.

Chairman: Anders Ferm (Sweden).
Vice-Chairman: Alhaji Yusuff Maitama-Sule (Nigeria).

Committee on Applications for Review of Administrative Tribunal Judgements
The Committee on Applications for Review of Administrative Tribunal Judgements held the second part of its twenty-second session from 4 to 16 February 1983.

Members (until 19 September 1983) (based on the composition of the General Committee at the General Assembly's thirty-seventh session): Austria, Brazil, Canada, China, Congo, Cuba, Cyprus, Democratic Yemen, France, Ghana, Haiti, Hungary, Jamaica, Kuwait, Libyan Arab Jamahiriya, Mali, Nicaragua, Nigeria, Philippines, Poland, Qatar, Turkey, Uganda, USSR, United Kingdom, United States, Upper Volta, Yemen, Zambia.

Chairman: Philippe Kirsch (Canada).
Rapporteur: Franklin D. Berman (United Kingdom).

Members (from 20 September 1983) (based on the composition of the General Committee at the General Assembly's thirty-eighth session): Algeria, Belgium, Bhutan, Burundi, Canada, China, Colombia, Czechoslovakia, France, German Democratic Republic, Guyana, Japan, Lebanon, Liberia, Libyan Arab Jamahiriya, Nepal, Norway, Pakistan, Panama, Sierra Leone, Singapore, Sudan, Swaziland, Thailand, Tunisia, USSR, United Kingdom, United States, Venezuela.

Committee on Arrangements for a Conference for the Purpose of Reviewing the Charter
All Members of the United Nations are members of the Committee on Arrangements for a Conference for the Purpose of Reviewing the Charter.
The Committee, established in 1955, last met in 1967, following which the General Assembly decided to keep it in being.[6]

Committee on Conferences
The Committee on Conferences consists of 22 Member States appointed by the President of the General Assembly on the basis of equitable geographical balance, to serve for a three-year term.

Members (until 31 December 1983):[a] Algeria, Austria, Chile, Cyprus, France, Germany, Federal Republic of, Honduras, Hungary, Indonesia, Japan, Kenya, Mexico, New Zealand, Nigeria, Peru, Senegal, Sri Lanka, Tunisia, USSR, United Kingdom, United States, Yugoslavia.

[a]The succeeding members had not been appointed by the end of 1983.

Chairman: Michael George Okeyo (Kenya).
Vice-Chairmen: Bernard A. B. Goonetilleke (Sri Lanka), Tibor Gubcsi (Hungary), Alberto Yoacham (Chile).
Rapporteur: Wilfried Almoslechner (Austria).

Committee on Information
In 1983, the 67-member Committee on Information held, at United Nations Headquarters, an organizational session on 28 and 29 March and its fifth session from 20 June to 9 July.

Members: Algeria, Argentina, Bangladesh, Belgium, Benin, Brazil, Bulgaria, Burundi, Chile, Colombia, Congo, Costa Rica, Cuba, Cyprus, Denmark, Ecuador, Egypt, El Salvador, Ethiopia, Finland, France, German Democratic Republic, Germany, Federal Republic of, Ghana, Greece, Guatemala, Guinea, Guyana, India, Indonesia, Italy, Ivory Coast, Japan, Jordan, Kenya, Lebanon, Mongolia, Morocco, Netherlands, Niger, Nigeria, Pakistan, Peru, Philippines, Poland, Portugal, Romania, Singapore, Somalia, Spain, Sri Lanka, Sudan, Syrian Arab Republic, Togo, Trinidad and Tobago, Tunisia, Turkey, Ukrainian SSR, USSR, United Kingdom, United Republic of Tanzania, United States, Venezuela, Viet Nam, Yemen, Yugoslavia, Zaire.

Chairman: Luis Moreno-Salcedo (Philippines).
Vice-Chairmen: Miguel A. Albornoz (Ecuador), Rachid Lahlou (Morocco), Willi Schlegel (German Democratic Republic).
Rapporteur: Mario Bondioli Osio (Italy).

Committee on Relations with the Host Country
Members: Bulgaria, Canada, China, Costa Rica, Cyprus, France, Honduras, Iraq, Ivory Coast, Mali, Senegal, Spain, USSR, United Kingdom, United States (host country).

Chairman: Constantine Moushoutas (Cyprus).
Vice-Chairmen: Bulgaria, Canada, Ivory Coast.
Rapporteur: Emilia Castro de Barish (Costa Rica).

Committee on the Development and Utilization of New and Renewable Sources of Energy
The Committee on the Development and Utilization of New and Renewable Sources of Energy, open to the participation of all States as full members, held its first session at United Nations Headquarters from 18 to 29 April 1983. Thereafter it was to meet once every two years in even years.

Chairman: Porfirio Muñoz Ledo (Mexico).
Vice-Chairmen: Mihail Bushev (Bulgaria), Habib M. Kaabachi (Tunisia), Krister Kumlin (Sweden).
Rapporteur: Qazi Shaukat Fareed (Pakistan).

Committee on the Exercise of the Inalienable Rights of the Palestinian People
Members: Afghanistan, Cuba, Cyprus, German Democratic Republic, Guinea, Guyana, Hungary, India, Indonesia, Lao People's Democratic Republic, Madagascar, Malaysia, Mali, Malta, Nigeria, Pakistan, Romania, Senegal, Sierra Leone, Tunisia, Turkey, Ukrainian SSR, Yugoslavia.

Chairman: Massamba Sarré (Senegal).

Vice-Chairmen: Raúl Roa Kouri (Cuba), Mohammad Farid Zarif (Afghanistan).
Rapporteur: Victor J. Gauci (Malta).

WORKING GROUP
Members: Afghanistan, Cuba, German Democratic Republic, Guinea, Guyana, India, Malta *(Chairman)*, Pakistan, Senegal, Tunisia, Turkey, Ukrainian SSR; Palestine Liberation Organization.

Committee on the Peaceful Uses of Outer Space
The 53-member Committee on the Peaceful Uses of Outer Space held its twenty-sixth session at United Nations Headquarters from 20 June to 1 July 1983.

Members: Albania, Argentina, Australia, Austria, Belgium, Benin, Brazil, Bulgaria, Canada, Chad, Chile, China, Colombia, Czechoslovakia, Ecuador, Egypt, France, German Democratic Republic, Germany,

---

[6]Resolution 2285(XXII), 5 December 1967 (YUN 1967, p. 291).

Federal Republic of, Greece, Hungary, India, Indonesia, Iran, Iraq, Italy, Japan, Kenya, Lebanon, Mexico, Mongolia, Morocco, Netherlands, Niger, Nigeria, Pakistan, Philippines, Poland, Romania, Sierra Leone, Spain, Sudan, Sweden, Syrian Arab Republic, USSR, United Kingdom, United Republic of Cameroon, United States, Upper Volta, Uruguay, Venezuela, Viet Nam, Yugoslavia.

Chairman: Peter Jankowitsch (Austria).
Vice-Chairman: Teodor Marinescu (Romania).
Rapporteur: Henrique Rodrigues Valle (Brazil).

LEGAL SUB-COMMITTEE
The Legal Sub-Committee, a committee of the whole, held its twenty-second session at United Nations Headquarters from 21 March to 8 April 1983.

Chairman: Ludek Handl (Czechoslovakia).

SCIENTIFIC AND TECHNICAL SUB-COMMITTEE
The Scientific and Technical Sub-Committee, a committee of the whole, held its twentieth session at United Nations Headquarters from 7 to 17 February 1983.

Chairman: J. H. Carver (Australia).

Committee on the Review and Appraisal of the Implementation of the International Development Strategy for the Third United Nations Development Decade
The Committee on the Review and Appraisal of the Implementation of the International Development Strategy for the Third United Nations Development Decade, open to the participation of all States as full members, held an organizational session on 16 December 1983 at United Nations Headquarters.

Chairman: Kenneth K. S. Dadzie (Ghana).
Vice-Chairmen:[a] Per Jodahl (Sweden), Oscar R. de Rojas (Venezuela).
Rapporteur: Yousif Gewaily (Qatar).

[a]The Committee postponed until its next session the election of a third Vice-Chairman, on the understanding that he would be a representative of Bulgaria.

Disarmament Commission
In 1983, the Disarmament Commission, composed of all the Members of the United Nations, held a series of meetings between 9 May and 3 June and organizational meetings on 1 and 8 December, all at United Nations Headquarters.

Chairman: Celso Antonio de Souza e Silva (Brazil).
Vice-Chairmen: Bangladesh, Czechoslovakia, Germany, Federal Republic of, Romania, Sierra Leone, Sweden, Tunisia.
Rapporteur: Abdul Mou'men Al-Atassi (Syrian Arab Republic).

High-level Committee on the Review of Technical Co-operation among Developing Countries
The High-level Committee on the Review of Technical Co-operation among Developing Countries, composed of all States participating in UNDP, held its third session from 31 May to 8 June 1983, at United Nations Headquarters.

President: José Luis Pardos (Spain).
Vice-Presidents: Anton Baramov (Bulgaria), Francis R. C. Blain (Gambia).
Rapporteur: Norma G. Shalhoub (Jordan).

Intergovernmental Committee on Science and Technology for Development
During 1983, the Intergovernmental Committee on Science and Technology for Development, open to the participation of all States as full members, held two sessions, at United Nations Headquarters: a special session from 25 April to 4 May; and its fifth session from 6 to 20 June.

Chairman: Juan Carlos Blanco (Uruguay).
Vice-Chairmen: Olagoke Aderemi Esan (Nigeria), Anton Greber (Switzerland), Georges Matache (Romania) (fifth session only).

Rapporteur: Yousif Gewaily (Qatar) (fifth session only).

ADVISORY COMMITTEE ON SCIENCE
AND TECHNOLOGY FOR DEVELOPMENT
The 28-member Advisory Committee on Science and Technology for Development held its third session at United Nations Headquarters from 1 to 8 February 1983.

Members:
To serve until 31 December 1983: Daniel Adzei Bekoe (Ghana); Umberto Colombo, *Vice-Chairman* (Italy); Bernard M. J. Delapalme (France); Jan Gabel (Czechoslovakia); Henri Hogbe-Nlend, *Vice-Chairman* (United Republic of Cameroon); Jorge Katz (Argentina); Abdelsalam Majali (Jordan); Cyril Agodi Onwumechili (Nigeria); Keichi Oshima (Japan); Armando Samper (Colombia); Sitali Mundia Silangwa (Zambia); M. S. Swaminathan, *Chairman* (India); José Israel Vargas, *Vice-Chairman* (Brazil); Rudolf Wittenzellner (Federal Republic of Germany).
To serve until 31 December 1984: Sadak Ben Jamaa, *Vice-Chairman* (Tunisia); Just Faaland (Norway); Edmundo Flores (Mexico); Peter Gacii (Kenya); Dennis Irvine (Jamaica); Lu Jing-ting (China); Loretta Makasiar-Sicat (Philippines); Rodney W. Nichols (United States); V. I. Popkov (USSR); Hamida Radouane (Algeria); Bachtiar Rifai (Indonesia); Leopold Schmetterer (Austria); Adnan Shihab-Eldin (Kuwait); Klaus Stubenrauch, *Vice-Chairman* (German Democratic Republic).

On 16 June 1983, the Intergovernmental Committee appointed the following members of the Advisory Committee for a three-year term beginning on 1 January 1984 to fill the vacancies occurring on 31 December 1983: Oscar Aguero Wood (Chile), Umberto Colombo (Italy), Etienne Cracco (Belgium); Djibril Fall (Senegal); Essam El Din Galal (Egypt); Henri Hogbe-Nlend (United Republic of Cameroon); Mumtaz Ali Kazi (Pakistan); Lydia Makhubu (Swaziland); James Mullin (Canada); Tiberiu Muresan (Romania); Keichi Oshima (Japan); Francisco R. Sagasti (Peru); M. S. Swaminathan (India); José Israel Vargas (Brazil).

Interim Committee of the General Assembly
The Interim Committee of the General Assembly, on which each Member of the United Nations has the right to appoint one representative, was originally established by the General Assembly in 1947 to function between the Assembly's regular sessions. It was re-established in 1948 for a further year and in 1949[7] for an indefinite period. The Committee has not met since 1961.[8]

International Civil Service Commission
The International Civil Service Commission consists of 15 members who serve in their personal capacity as individuals of recognized competence in public administration or related fields, particularly in personnel management. They are appointed by the General Assembly, with due regard for equitable geographical distribution, for four-year terms.
The Commission held three sessions in 1983: its seventeenth at Vienna, Austria, from 7 to 24 March; its eighteenth at United Nations Headquarters from 18 July to 5 August; and a special session at United Nations Headquarters from 21 to 23 November.

Members:
To serve until 31 December 1984: Syed Amjad Ali (Pakistan); Michael O. Ani (Nigeria); A. S. Chistyakov (USSR);[a] M. A. Vellodi (India); Halima Embarek Warzazi (Morocco).
To serve until 31 December 1985: Ralph Enckell (Finland); Jean-Claude Fortuit (France);[a] Masao Kanazawa (Japan); Helmut Kitschenberg (Federal Republic of Germany); Antonio Fonseca Pimentel (Brazil).
To serve until 31 December 1986: Richard M. Akwei, *Chairman* (Ghana); Gastón de Prat Gay, *Vice-Chairman* (Argentina); Moulaye El Hassen (Mauritania); Dayton W. Hull (United States); Jiri Nosek (Czechoslovakia).

[a]Resigned in December 1983; V. V. Tsybukov (USSR) and Michel Auchère (France) were appointed by the General Assembly on 20 December (decision 38/321) to fill the resultant vacancies.

[7]Resolution 295(IV), 21 November 1949 (YUN 1948-49, p. 411).
[8]YUN 1961, p. 705.

ADVISORY COMMITTEE ON
POST ADJUSTMENT QUESTIONS

The Advisory Committee on Post Adjustment Questions consists of six members, of whom five are chosen from the geographical regions of Africa, Asia, Latin America, Eastern Europe, and Western Europe and other States; and one, from ICSC, who serves *ex officio* as Chairman. Members are appointed by the ICSC Chairman to serve for four-year terms.

In 1983, the Advisory Committee held its eighth session in two parts: at Rome, Italy, from 30 May to 10 June; and at United Nations Headquarters from 31 October to 10 November.

Members:

To serve until 31 December 1983: A. F. Revenko (USSR).
To serve until 31 December 1984: G. K. Nair (Malaysia).
To serve until 31 December 1985: Nana Wereko Ampem II (also known as Emmanuel Noi Omaboe) (Ghana), Janes A. de Souza (Brazil).[a]
To serve until 31 December 1986: Hugues Picard (France).[b]
Ex-officio member: Jiri Nosek, *Chairman* (Czechoslovakia).

[a]Resigned as of July 1983; Carmen McFarlane (Jamaica) was appointed in October to serve until 31 December 1986.
[b]Appointed in April 1983.

International Law Commission

The International Law Commission consists of 34 persons of recognized competence in international law, elected by the General Assembly to serve in their individual capacity for a five-year term. Vacancies occurring within the five-year period are filled by the Commission.

The Commission held its thirty-fifth session at Geneva from 3 May to 22 July 1983.

Members (until 31 December 1986): Richard Osuolale A. Akinjide (Nigeria); Riyadh Mahmoud Sami Al-Qaysi (Iraq); Balanda Mikuin Leliel (Zaire); Julio Barboza (Argentina); Boutros Boutros-Ghali (Egypt); Carlos Calero Rodrigues (Brazil); Jorge Castañeda (Mexico); Leonardo Díaz-González (Venezuela); Khalafalla El Rasheed Mohamed-Ahmed (Sudan); Jens Evensen (Norway); Constantin Flitan (Romania); Laurel B. Francis, *Chairman* (Jamaica); Jorge Enrique Illueca (Panama); Andreas J. Jacovides (Cyprus); Satya Pal Jagota, *Rapporteur* (India); Abdul G. Koroma (Sierra Leone); José Manuel Lacleta Muñoz (Spain); Ahmed Mahiou (Algeria); Chafic Malek (Lebanon); Stephen C. McCaffrey (United States); Ni Zhengyu (China); Frank X. J. C. Njenga (Kenya); Motoo Ogiso (Japan); Syed Sharifuddin Pirzada (Pakistan); Robert Q. Quentin-Baxter (New Zealand); Edilbert Razafindralambo, *Second Vice-Chairman* (Madagascar); Paul Reuter (France); Willem Riphagen (Netherlands); Sir Ian Sinclair (United Kingdom); Constantin A. Stavropoulos (Greece); Sompong Sucharitkul (Thailand); Doudou Thiam (Senegal); N. A. Ushakov (USSR); Alexander Yankov, *First Vice-Chairman* (Bulgaria).

Investments Committee

The Investments Committee consists of nine members appointed by the Secretary-General, after consultation with the United Nations Joint Staff Pension Board and ACABQ, subject to confirmation by the General Assembly. Members serve for three-year terms.

Members:

To serve until 31 December 1983: David Montagu; Yves Oltramare; Emmanuel Noi Omaboe (also known as Nana Wereko Ampem II).
To serve until 31 December 1984: Jean Guyot; George Johnston; Michiya Matsukawa.
To serve until 31 December 1985: Aloysio de Andrade Faria; Braj Kumar Nehru, Chairman; Stanislaw Raczkowski.

In addition, during 1983, Juergen Reimnitz served in an *ad hoc* consultative capacity.

On 25 November 1983 (decision 38/310), the General Assembly confirmed the appointment by the Secretary-General of David Montagu, Yves Oltramare and Emmanuel Noi Omaboe as members for a three-year term beginning on 1 January 1984.

Joint Advisory Group on the International
Trade Centre UNCTAD/GATT

The Joint Advisory Group was established in accordance with an agreement between UNCTAD and GATT with effect from 1 January 1968, the date on which their joint sponsorship of the International Trade Centre commenced.

Participation in the Group is open to all States members of UNCTAD and to all Contracting Parties to GATT.

The Group held its sixteenth session at Geneva from 21 to 28 March 1983.

Chairman: Wiebo J. Rijpma (Netherlands).
Vice-Chairman: V. Petrov (USSR).
Rapporteur: J. A. D. de Lanerolle (Sri Lanka).

TECHNICAL COMMITTEE

The Technical Committee of the Joint Advisory Group on the International Trade Centre UNCTAD/GATT, which is open to the participation of experts, as well as officials responsible for national trade promotion activities, from any country represented in the Joint Advisory Group, reviews the Centre's work programme and organizational structure and reports to the Group.

In 1983, for the first year of a two-year experiment, meetings of the Committee and the Group were combined in a single meeting—the Group's sixteenth session.

Joint Inspection Unit

The Joint Inspection Unit consists of not more than 11 Inspectors appointed by the General Assembly from candidates nominated by Member States following appropriate consultations, including consultations with the President of the Economic and Social Council and with the Chairman of ACC. The Inspectors, chosen for their special experience in national or international administrative and financial matters, with due regard for equitable geographical distribution and reasonable rotation, serve in their personal capacity for five-year terms.

Members:

To serve until 31 December 1985: Maurice Bertrand (France); Alfred Nathaniel Forde, *Vice-Chairman* (Barbados); Moustapha Ould Khalifa (Mauritania); Earl D. Sohm (United States); Miljenko Vukovic, *Chairman* (Yugoslavia).
To serve until 31 December 1987: Mark E. Allen (United Kingdom); A. S. Efimov (USSR); Toman Hutagalung (Indonesia); Mohamed Salah Eldin Ibrahim (Egypt); Nasser Kaddour (Syrian Arab Republic); Norman Williams (Panama).

Negotiating Committee on the Financial Emergency
of the United Nations

Established in 1975 by the General Assembly[9] to consist of 54 Member States appointed by its President on the basis of equitable geographical balance, the Negotiating Committee on the Financial Emergency of the United Nations has a membership of 48. It has not met since 1976.[10]

Members: Argentina, Austria, Bangladesh, Bolivia, Canada, Chad, Colombia, Cuba, Ecuador, Egypt, Finland, France, Gabon, German Democratic Republic, Germany, Federal Republic of, Ghana, Greece, Grenada, India, Indonesia, Iran, Ireland, Italy, Jamaica, Japan, Jordan, Kenya, Kuwait, Libyan Arab Jamahiriya, Malawi, Mexico, Morocco, Nigeria, Pakistan, Philippines, Poland, Spain, Sudan, Swaziland, Sweden, Trinidad and Tobago, Tunisia, Turkey, USSR, United Kingdom, United States, Upper Volta, Venezuela.

Office of the United Nations High Commissioner
for Refugees (UNHCR)

*EXECUTIVE COMMITTEE OF THE HIGH
COMMISSIONER'S PROGRAMME*

The Executive Committee held its thirty-fourth session at Geneva from 10 to 20 October 1983.

Members: Algeria, Argentina, Australia, Austria, Belgium, Brazil, Canada, China, Colombia, Denmark, Finland, France, Germany, Federal Republic of, Greece, Holy See, Iran, Israel, Italy, Japan, Lebanon, Lesotho, Madagascar, Morocco, Netherlands, Nicaragua,

[9]Resolution 3538(XXX), 17 December 1975 (YUN 1975, p. 957).
[10]YUN 1976, pp. 889 and 1064.

Nigeria, Norway, Sudan, Sweden, Switzerland, Thailand, Tunisia, Turkey, Uganda, United Kingdom, United Republic of Tanzania, United States, Venezuela, Yugoslavia, Zaire; Namibia (represented by the United Nations Council for Namibia).

Chairman: Hans V. Ewerlof (Sweden).
Vice-Chairman: F. Mebazaa (Tunisia).
Rapporteur: Erika Feller (Australia).

United Nations High Commissioner for Refugees: Poul Hartling.
Deputy High Commissioner: William Richard Smyser.

SUB-COMMITTEE OF THE WHOLE
ON INTERNATIONAL PROTECTION
The Sub-Committee of the Whole on International Protection held its eighth meeting at Geneva from 3 to 6 and on 11 October 1983.

Chairman: Ibrahim Kharma (Lebanon).

SUB-COMMITTEE ON
ADMINISTRATIVE AND FINANCIAL MATTERS
The Sub-Committee on Administrative and Financial Matters, which is composed of all members of the Executive Committee, held its third meeting at Geneva concurrently with the eighth meeting of the Sub-Committee of the Whole on International Protection.

Chairman: Hans V. Ewerlof (Sweden).

Panel for Inquiry and Conciliation
The Panel for Inquiry and Conciliation was created by the General Assembly in 1949[11] to consist of qualified persons, designated by United Nations Member States, each to serve for a term of five years. Information concerning the Panel's composition had from time to time been communicated to the Assembly and the Security Council; the last consolidated list was issued by the Secretary-General in a note of 20 January 1961.

Panel of External Auditors
The Panel of External Auditors consists of the members of the United Nations Board of Auditors and the appointed external auditors of the specialized agencies and IAEA.

Panel of Military Experts
The General Assembly's "Uniting for Peace" resolution[12] called for the appointment of military experts to be available, on request, to United Nations Member States wishing to obtain technical advice on the organization, training and equipment of elements within their national armed forces which could be made available, in accordance with national constitutional processes, for service as a unit or units of the United Nations upon the recommendation of the Security Council or the Assembly.

Peace Observation Commission
The Peace Observation Commission ceased to exist on 23 September 1983 (decision 38/402), when the General Assembly adopted the General Committee's recommendation that the Assembly conclusively clarify its intention to abolish the Commission by deleting sub-item *(f)* on the appointment of the members of the Commission from item 17 of the draft agenda of its thirty-eighth session.
Established in 1950 by the Assembly's "Uniting for Peace" resolution,[13] the Commission was at the time of its abolition composed of the following members: Czechoslovakia, France, Honduras, India, Maldives, New Zealand, Pakistan, Sweden, USSR, United Kingdom, United States, Uruguay.

Preparatory Committee for the Fortieth Anniversary of the United Nations
On 20 December 1983 (decision 38/455), the General Assembly established a Preparatory Committee for the Fortieth Anniversary of the United Nations (in 1985), to consider and recommend to the Assembly at its thirty-ninth (1984) session proposals for suitable activities in connection with the observance of the anniversary. The Committee was to consist of the members of the General Committee at the Assembly's thirty-eighth session (p. 1369) and to be open to the participation of all Member States on an equal basis.

Preparatory Committee for the International Conference on the Question of Palestine
The Committee on the Exercise of the Inalienable Rights of the Palestinian People (p. 1342) was designated by the General Assembly as the Preparatory Committee for the International Conference on the Question of Palestine (p. 1354).
The Preparatory Committee held its second and final session at United Nations Headquarters from 4 February to 27 July 1983 and at Geneva on 29 August.

Chairman: Massamba Sarré (Senegal).
Vice-Chairmen: Raúl Roa Kouri (Cuba), Mohammad Farid Zarif (Afghanistan).
Rapporteur: Victor J. Gauci (Malta).

Preparatory Committee for the United Nations Conference for the Promotion of International Co-operation in the Peaceful Uses of Nuclear Energy
In 1983, the Preparatory Committee for the United Nations Conference for the Promotion of International Co-operation in the Peaceful Uses of Nuclear Energy (rescheduled for 1986), which was to be composed of 70 Member States and, on an equal footing, other Member States which might express interest in participating in the Committee's work, had a membership of 66. It held its fourth session at United Nations Headquarters from 28 March to 8 April.

Members: Algeria, Argentina, Australia, Austria, Belgium, Brazil, Bulgaria, Byelorussian SSR, Canada, Chile, China, Colombia, Costa Rica, Cuba, Czechoslovakia, Denmark, Ecuador, Egypt, Finland, France, German Democratic Republic, Germany, Federal Republic of, Ghana, Greece, Guatemala, Hungary, India, Indonesia, Iran,[a] Iraq, Ireland, Italy, Ivory Coast, Japan, Libyan Arab Jamahiriya, Malaysia, Mauritania, Mexico, Morocco, Netherlands, Niger, Nigeria, Norway, Pakistan, Peru, Philippines, Poland, Romania, Saudi Arabia,[a] Senegal, Spain, Sri Lanka, Sweden, Syrian Arab Republic, Thailand, Turkey, Ukrainian SSR, USSR, United Arab Emirates, United Kingdom, United Republic of Cameroon, United States, Uruguay, Venezuela, Yugoslavia, Zaire.

[a]Appointed by the President of the General Assembly's thirty-seventh session on 8 July and 11 February 1983, respectively.

Chairman: Novak Pribicevic (Yugoslavia).
Vice-Chairmen: F. K. A. Allotey (Ghana), Augusto Arzubiaga Rospigliosi (Peru), Essam El-Din Hawas (Egypt), Suror Merza Mahmoud (Iraq), L. A. Olivieri (Argentina), Miroslav Oplt (Czechoslovakia), B. Skala (Sweden), Frans J. A. Terwisscha van Scheltinga (Netherlands).
Rapporteur: Dalindra Aman (Indonesia).

Special Committee against *Apartheid*
The Special Committee against *Apartheid* has a membership of 18. Additional members remained to be appointed by the end of 1983 in pursuance of a 1979 General Assembly request[14] to increase that number.

Members: Algeria, German Democratic Republic, Ghana, Guinea, Haiti, Hungary, India, Indonesia, Malaysia, Nepal, Nigeria, Peru, Philippines, Somalia, Sudan, Syrian Arab Republic, Trinidad and Tobago, Ukrainian SSR.

Chairman: Alhaji Yusuff Maitama-Sule (Nigeria).
Vice-Chairmen: Uddhav Deo Bhatt (Nepal), V. A. Kravets (Ukrainian SSR).
Rapporteur: Gervais Charles (Haiti).

SUB-COMMITTEE ON PETITIONS AND INFORMATION
Members: Algeria *(Chairman)*, German Democratic Republic, Nepal, Somalia, Trinidad and Tobago.

---

[11]Resolution 268 D (III), 28 April 1949 (YUN 1948-49, p. 416).
[12]Resolution 377(V), part A, para. 10, 3 November 1950 (YUN 1950, p. 194).
[13]*Ibid.*, para. 3.
[14]Resolution 34/93 R, 17 December 1979 (YUN 1979, p. 201).

SUB-COMMITTEE ON THE IMPLEMENTATION
OF UNITED NATIONS RESOLUTIONS
AND COLLABORATION WITH SOUTH AFRICA
Members: Ghana *(Chairman)*, Hungary, India, Peru, Sudan.

Special Committee on Enhancing the Effectiveness of the Principle of Non-Use of Force in International Relations

The 35-member Special Committee on Enhancing the Effectiveness of the Principle of Non-Use of Force in International Relations held one series of meetings at United Nations Headquarters between 31 January and 25 February 1983.

Members: Argentina,[a] Belgium, Benin, Brazil,[a] Bulgaria, Chile,[a] Cyprus, Egypt, Finland, France, Germany, Federal Republic of, Greece, Guinea, Hungary, India, Iraq, Italy, Japan, Mongolia, Morocco, Nepal, Nicaragua, Panama, Peru, Poland, Romania, Senegal, Somalia, Spain, Togo, Turkey, Uganda, USSR, United Kingdom, United States.

[a]Replaced Cuba, Ecuador and Mexico, in accordance with a system of rotation agreed upon by the Latin American States when the Special Committee was constituted.

Chairman: Ivan Garvalov (Bulgaria).
Vice-Chairmen: Ahmed Amin Fathalla (Egypt), Moritaka Hayashi (Japan), Ricardo Sateler (Chile).
Rapporteur: Agustín Font (Spain).

Special Committee on Peace-keeping Operations

During 1983, the 33-member Special Committee on Peace-keeping Operations held meetings at United Nations Headquarters on 23 June, 1 August and 1 September.

Members: Afghanistan, Algeria, Argentina *(Vice-Chairman)*, Australia, Austria, Canada *(Vice-Chairman)*, Denmark, Egypt *(Rapporteur)*, El Salvador, Ethiopia, France, German Democratic Republic, Guatemala, Hungary *(Vice-Chairman)*, India, Iraq, Italy, Japan *(Vice-Chairman)*, Mauritania, Mexico, Netherlands, Nigeria *(Chairman)*, Pakistan, Poland, Romania, Sierra Leone, Spain, Thailand, USSR, United Kingdom, United States, Venezuela, Yugoslavia.

WORKING GROUP
Members: France, India, Mexico, Pakistan, USSR, United Kingdom, United States, and the officers of the Special Committee.

Special Committee on the Charter of the United Nations and on the Strengthening of the Role of the Organization

The 47-member Special Committee on the Charter of the United Nations and on the Strengthening of the Role of the Organization held a series of meetings at United Nations Headquarters between 11 April and 6 May 1983.

Members: Algeria, Argentina, Barbados, Belgium, Brazil, China, Colombia, Congo, Cyprus, Czechoslovakia, Ecuador, Egypt, El Salvador, Finland, France, German Democratic Republic, Germany, Federal Republic of, Ghana, Greece, Guyana, India, Indonesia, Iran, Iraq, Italy, Japan, Kenya, Liberia, Mexico, Nepal, New Zealand, Nigeria, Pakistan, Philippines, Poland, Romania, Rwanda, Sierra Leone, Spain, Tunisia, Turkey, USSR, United Kingdom, United States, Venezuela, Yugoslavia, Zambia.

Chairman: Nabil A. Elaraby (Egypt).
Vice-Chairmen: Bengt H. G. A. Broms (Finland), Ion Diaconu (Romania), Moritaka Hayashi (Japan).
Rapporteur: Domingo S. Cullen (Argentina).

Special Committee on the Situation with regard to the Implementation of the Declaration on the Granting of Independence to Colonial Countries and Peoples

Members: Afghanistan, Australia, Bulgaria, Chile, China, Congo, Cuba, Czechoslovakia, Ethiopia, Fiji, India, Indonesia, Iran, Iraq, Ivory Coast, Mali, Norway,[a] Sierra Leone, Syrian Arab Republic, Trinidad and Tobago, Tunisia, USSR, United Republic of Tanzania, Venezuela, Yugoslavia.

[a]Withdrew from membership as from 31 December 1983, as stated in a letter of 30 September to the President of the General Assembly. On 7 December (decision 38/313), the Assembly confirmed the nomination by its President of Sweden, effective 1 January 1984, to fill the resultant vacancy.

Chairman: Abdul G. Koroma (Sierra Leone).
Vice-Chairmen: Ole Peter Kolby (Norway), Jiri Pulz (Czechoslovakia), Raúl Roa Kouri (Cuba).
Rapporteur: Mohamed Farouk Adhami (Syrian Arab Republic).

SUB-COMMITTEE ON PETITIONS,
INFORMATION AND ASSISTANCE
Members: Afghanistan, Bulgaria, Congo, Cuba, Czechoslovakia *(Chairman)*, Indonesia, Iran, Iraq, Mali, Norway, Sierra Leone, Syrian Arab Republic, Tunisia, United Republic of Tanzania.

SUB-COMMITTEE ON SMALL TERRITORIES
Members: Afghanistan, Australia *(Rapporteur)*, Bulgaria, Chile, Cuba, Czechoslovakia, Ethiopia, Fiji, India, Indonesia, Iran, Iraq, Ivory Coast *(Chairman)*, Mali, Norway, Trinidad and Tobago, United Republic of Tanzania, Venezuela, Yugoslavia.

WORKING GROUP
In 1983, the Working Group of the Special Committee, which functions as a steering committee, consisted of: Congo, Iran, Tunisia; the five officers of the Special Committee; and the Chairman and the Rapporteur of the Sub-Committee on Small Territories.

Special Committee to Investigate Israeli Practices Affecting the Human Rights of the Population of the Occupied Territories

Members: Senegal, Sri Lanka *(Chairman)*, Yugoslavia.

Special Committee to Select the Winners of the United Nations Human Rights Prize

The Special Committee to Select the Winners of the United Nations Human Rights Prize was established pursuant to a 1966 resolution of the General Assembly[15] recommending that a prize or prizes in the field of human rights be awarded not more often than at five-year intervals. Prizes were awarded for the third time on 11 December 1978.[16]

Members: The President of the General Assembly, the President of the Economic and Social Council, the Chairman of the Commission on Human Rights, the Chairman of the Commission on the Status of Women and the Chairman of the Sub-Commission on Prevention of Discrimination and Protection of Minorities.

United Nations Administrative Tribunal

Members:
To serve until 31 December 1983: Arnold Wilfred Geoffrey Kean, *Second Vice-President* (United Kingdom); Herbert K. Reis (United States).
To serve until 31 December 1984: Luis María de Posadas Montero (Uruguay); Endre Ustor, *President* (Hungary).
To serve until 31 December 1985: Mutuale Tshikankie (Zaire); Roger Pinto (France); Samarendranath Sen, *First Vice-President* (India).

On 25 November 1983 (decision 38/311), the General Assembly appointed Arnold Wilfred Geoffrey Kean (United Kingdom) and Herbert K. Reis (United States) for a three-year term beginning on 1 January 1984 to fill the vacancies occurring on 31 December 1983.

United Nations Capital Development Fund

The United Nations Capital Development Fund was set up as an organ of the General Assembly to function as an autonomous organization within the United Nations framework, with the control of its policies and operations to be exercised by a 24-member Executive Board elected by the General Assembly from Members of the United Nations or members of the specialized agencies or of IAEA. The chief executive officer of the Fund, the Managing Director, exercises his functions

---

[15]Resolution 2217 A (XXI), annex, recommendation C, 19 December 1966 (YUN 1966, p. 458).
[16]YUN 1978, p. 721.

under the general direction of the Executive Board. The Executive Board reports to the General Assembly through the Economic and Social Council.

EXECUTIVE BOARD

The UNDP Governing Council (p. 1365) acts as the Executive Board of the Fund—and the UNDP Administrator as its Managing Director (see below)—in conformity with measures the General Assembly adopted provisionally in 1967[17] and reconfirmed yearly until 1980.[18] In 1981 the Assembly decided that UNDP continue to provide the Fund with, among other things, all headquarters administrative support services;[19] the Fund thus continued to operate under the same arrangements, which remained unchanged in 1983.

Managing Director: F. Bradford Morse (UNDP Administrator).

United Nations Children's Fund (UNICEF)

EXECUTIVE BOARD

The Executive Board of UNICEF (p. 1364) reports to the Economic and Social Council and, as appropriate, to the General Assembly.

United Nations Commission on International Trade Law (UNCITRAL)

The United Nations Commission on International Trade Law consists of 36 members elected by the General Assembly, in accordance with a formula providing equitable geographical representation and adequate representation of the principal economic and legal systems of the world. Members serve for six-year terms. The Commission held its sixteenth session at Vienna, Austria, from 24 May to 3 June 1983.

Members:

To serve until the day preceding the Commission's regular annual session in 1986: Cuba, Cyprus, Czechoslovakia, Germany, Federal Republic of, Guatemala, Hungary, India, Iraq, Italy, Kenya, Peru, Philippines, Senegal, Sierra Leone, Spain, Trinidad and Tobago, Uganda, United States, Yugoslavia.

To serve until the day preceding the Commission's regular annual session in 1989: Algeria, Australia, Austria, Brazil, Central African Republic, China, Egypt, France, German Democratic Republic, Japan, Mexico, Nigeria, Singapore, Sweden, USSR, United Kingdom, United Republic of Tanzania.

Chairman: M. H. Chafik (Egypt).
Vice-Chairmen: M. J. Bonell (Italy), T. Sawada (Japan), J. Vilus (Yugoslavia).
Rapporteur: Jorge Barrera Graf (Mexico).

WORKING GROUP ON
INTERNATIONAL CONTRACT PRACTICES

The Working Group on International Contract Practices held two sessions in 1983: its fifth at United Nations Headquarters from 22 February to 4 March; and its sixth at Vienna, Austria, from 29 August to 9 September.

Members:[a] Austria, Czechoslovakia, France, Ghana, Guatemala, Hungary, India, Japan, Kenya, Philippines, Sierra Leone, Trinidad and Tobago, USSR, United Kingdom, United States.

[a]On 2 June 1983, the Commission expanded the Working Group's membership to include all States members of UNCITRAL.

Chairman: I. Szasz (Hungary).
Rapporteur: Peter Kihara Mathanjuki (Kenya) (fifth session), M. Mwagiru (Kenya) (sixth session).

WORKING GROUP ON THE
NEW INTERNATIONAL ECONOMIC ORDER

The Working Group on the New International Economic Order, which is composed of all States members of UNCITRAL, held its fourth session at Vienna, Austria, from 16 to 20 May 1983.

Chairman: Leif Sevon (Finland).
Rapporteur: Stephen K. Muchui (Kenya).

United Nations Conciliation Commission for Palestine
Members: France, Turkey, United States.

United Nations Conference on Trade and Development (UNCTAD)

Members of UNCTAD are Members of the United Nations or members of the specialized agencies or of IAEA.

The Conference held its sixth session at Belgrade, Yugoslavia, from 6 June to 2 July 1983.

Following are the States members of UNCTAD:

Part A. Afghanistan, Algeria, Angola, Bahrain, Bangladesh, Benin, Bhutan, Botswana, Burma, Burundi, Cape Verde, Central African Republic, Chad, China, Comoros, Congo, Democratic Kampuchea, Democratic People's Republic of Korea, Democratic Yemen, Djibouti, Egypt, Equatorial Guinea, Ethiopia, Fiji, Gabon, Gambia, Ghana, Guinea, Guinea-Bissau, India, Indonesia, Iran, Iraq, Israel, Ivory Coast, Jordan, Kenya, Kuwait, Lao People's Democratic Republic, Lebanon, Lesotho, Liberia, Libyan Arab Jamahiriya, Madagascar, Malawi, Malaysia, Maldives, Mali, Mauritania, Mauritius, Mongolia, Morocco, Mozambique, Nepal, Niger, Nigeria, Oman, Pakistan, Papua New Guinea, Philippines, Qatar, Republic of Korea, Rwanda, Samoa, Sao Tome and Principe, Saudi Arabia, Senegal, Seychelles, Sierra Leone, Singapore, Solomon Islands, Somalia, South Africa, Sri Lanka, Sudan, Swaziland, Syrian Arab Republic, Thailand, Togo, Tonga, Tunisia, Uganda, United Arab Emirates, United Republic of Cameroon, United Republic of Tanzania, Upper Volta, Vanuatu,[a] Viet Nam, Yemen, Yugoslavia, Zaire, Zambia, Zimbabwe;[a] Namibia.[a]

Part B. Australia, Austria, Belgium, Canada, Cyprus, Denmark, Finland, France, Germany, Federal Republic of, Greece, Holy See, Iceland, Ireland, Italy, Japan, Liechtenstein, Luxembourg, Malta, Monaco, Netherlands, New Zealand, Norway, Portugal, San Marino, Spain, Sweden, Switzerland, Turkey, United Kingdom, United States.

Part C. Antigua and Barbuda,[a] Argentina, Bahamas, Barbados, Belize,[a] Bolivia, Brazil, Chile, Colombia, Costa Rica, Cuba, Dominica,[a] Dominican Republic, Ecuador, El Salvador, Grenada, Guatemala, Guyana, Haiti, Honduras, Jamaica, Mexico, Nicaragua, Panama, Paraguay, Peru, Saint Christopher and Nevis,[b] Saint Lucia,[a] Saint Vincent and the Grenadines,[a] Suriname, Trinidad and Tobago, Uruguay, Venezuela.

Part D. Albania, Bulgaria, Byelorussian SSR, Czechoslovakia, German Democratic Republic, Hungary, Poland, Romania, Ukrainian SSR, USSR.

[a]Became members of UNCTAD after the fifth (1979) session of the Conference. By decision of the Board, they were subsequently included in Parts A (Namibia, Vanuatu, Zimbabwe) and C (Antigua and Barbuda, Belize, Saint Lucia, Saint Vincent and the Grenadines) for the purpose of elections, pending approval by the Conference at its sixth session. The Conference granted its approval on 6 June 1983.
[b]Became a Member of the United Nations and, *ipso facto*, of UNCTAD on 23 September 1983, after the sixth session of the Conference. On 3 October 1983, the Board decided that it should be associated with the countries in Part C for the purpose of elections, pending approval by the Conference at its seventh session.

President: Lazar Mojsov (Yugoslavia).
Vice-Presidents: Algeria, Australia, Chile, China, Cuba, Gabon, German Democratic Republic, Germany, Federal Republic of, Greece, Guinea, Haiti, Hungary, Indonesia, Iraq, Jamaica, Mexico, Nicaragua, Pakistan, Portugal, Sri Lanka, Sudan, Sweden, Syrian Arab Republic, Thailand, Tunisia, USSR, United Kingdom, United States, Zimbabwe.
Rapporteur: Gabriel O. Martínez (Argentina).

Chairmen of committees:
Committee I: Shunji Kobayashi (Japan).
Committee II: Georgi Pirinski (Bulgaria).
Committee III: G. O. Nwankwo (Nigeria).
Committee IV: Kamran Inan (Turkey).
Credentials Committee: Davidson L. Hepburn (Bahamas).

[17]Resolution 2321(XXII), para. 1 *(a)* & *(b)*, 15 December 1967 (YUN 1967, p. 372).
[18]Decision 35/422, para. *(c)*, 5 December 1980 (YUN 1980, p. 607).
[19]Resolution 36/196, para. 6, 17 December 1981 (YUN 1981, p. 469).

TRADE AND DEVELOPMENT BOARD
The Trade and Development Board is a permanent organ of UNCTAD.

BOARD MEMBERS AND SESSIONS
The membership of the Board is open to all UNCTAD members. Those wishing to become members of the Board communicate their intention to the Secretary-General of UNCTAD for transmittal to the Board President, who announces the membership on the basis of such notifications.

The Board held the following sessions in 1983, at Geneva: its twenty-sixth from 18 to 28 April; its twelfth special session from 25 to 30 April and on 6 May; and its twenty-seventh session from 3 to 20 October and on 2 November.

Members: Afghanistan, Algeria, Angola, Argentina, Australia, Austria, Bahrain, Bangladesh, Barbados, Belgium, Benin, Bolivia, Brazil, Bulgaria, Burma, Burundi, Byelorussian SSR, Canada, Central African Republic, Chad, Chile, China, Colombia, Congo,[a] Costa Rica, Cuba, Cyprus, Czechoslovakia, Democratic People's Republic of Korea, Democratic Yemen, Denmark, Dominican Republic, Ecuador, Egypt, El Salvador, Ethiopia, Finland, France, Gabon, German Democratic Republic, Germany, Federal Republic of, Ghana, Greece, Grenada, Guatemala, Guinea, Guyana, Haiti, Honduras, Hungary, India, Indonesia, Iran, Iraq, Ireland, Israel, Italy, Ivory Coast, Jamaica, Japan, Jordan, Kenya, Kuwait, Lebanon, Liberia, Libyan Arab Jamahiriya, Liechtenstein, Luxembourg, Madagascar, Malaysia, Mali, Malta, Mauritania, Mauritius, Mexico, Mongolia, Morocco, Nepal,[b] Netherlands, New Zealand, Nicaragua, Nigeria, Norway, Oman, Pakistan, Panama, Papua New Guinea, Peru, Philippines, Poland, Portugal, Qatar, Republic of Korea, Romania, Saudi Arabia, Senegal, Sierra Leone, Singapore, Somalia, Spain, Sri Lanka, Sudan, Suriname, Sweden, Switzerland, Syrian Arab Republic, Thailand, Togo, Trinidad and Tobago, Tunisia, Turkey, Uganda, Ukrainian SSR, USSR, United Arab Emirates, United Kingdom, United Republic of Cameroon, United Republic of Tanzania, United States, Upper Volta, Uruguay, Venezuela, Viet Nam, Yemen, Yugoslavia, Zaire, Zambia.

[a]Became a member on 3 October 1983.
[b]Became a member on 18 April 1983.

OFFICERS (BUREAU) OF THE BOARD
Twenty-sixth and twelfth special sessions
President: Richard Hlavaty (Czechoslovakia).
Vice-Presidents: Mansur Ahmad (Pakistan), Omer Yousif Birido (Sudan), K. Chiba (Japan), I. Darsa (Indonesia), Martin J. Huslid (Norway), N. Kombot-Naguemon (Central African Republic), José Luis Lovo-Castelar (El Salvador), A. Manjoulo (USSR), G. Streeb (United States), Hans-Günther Sulimma (Federal Republic of Germany).
Rapporteur: J. Dupouy (Chile).

Twenty-seventh session
President: Abdullahi Said Osman (Somalia).
Vice-Presidents: S. H. Ahmad (Bangladesh), K. Al-Shakar (Bahrain), W. Carrasco (Chile), A. de la Serna (Spain), A. Fajardo-Maldonado (Guatemala), M. S. Pankine (USSR), A. Petropoulos (Greece), Alioune Sène (Senegal), G. Streeb (United States), T. Takala (Finland).
Rapporteur: G. Philipp (German Democratic Republic).

SUBSIDIARY ORGANS OF THE TRADE AND DEVELOPMENT BOARD
The main committees of the Board are open to the participation of all interested UNCTAD members, on the understanding that those wishing to attend a particular session of one or more of the main committees communicate their intention to the Secretary-General of UNCTAD during the preceding regular session of the Board. On the basis of such notifications, the Board determines the membership of the main committees.

COMMITTEE ON COMMODITIES
The Committee on Commodities held its tenth session at Geneva from 26 January to 8 February 1983.

Members: Algeria, Argentina, Australia, Austria, Bahrain,[a] Bangladesh, Belgium, Bolivia, Brazil, Bulgaria, Burma, Burundi, Canada, Central African Republic, Chad, Chile, China, Colombia, Costa Rica, Cuba, Czechoslovakia, Democratic People's Republic of Korea, Democratic Yemen, Denmark, Dominican Republic, Ecuador, Egypt, El Salvador, Ethiopia, Finland, France, Gabon, German Democratic Republic, Germany, Federal Republic of, Ghana, Greece, Guatemala, Guinea, Haiti,[a] Honduras, Hungary, India, Indonesia, Iran, Iraq, Ireland, Israel, Italy, Ivory Coast, Jamaica, Japan, Jordan, Kenya, Kuwait,[a] Liberia, Libyan Arab Jamahiriya, Madagascar, Malaysia, Malta, Mauritius, Mexico, Morocco, Netherlands, New Zealand, Nicaragua, Nigeria, Norway, Pakistan, Panama, Peru, Philippines, Poland, Qatar, Republic of Korea, Romania, Rwanda, Saudi Arabia, Senegal, Somalia, Spain, Sri Lanka, Sudan, Sweden, Switzerland, Syrian Arab Republic, Thailand, Togo, Trinidad and Tobago, Tunisia, Turkey, Uganda, USSR, United Kingdom, United Republic of Cameroon, United Republic of Tanzania, United States, Upper Volta, Uruguay, Venezuela, Viet Nam, Yemen, Yugoslavia, Zaire.

[a]Declared elected by the Trade and Development Board on 18 April (Bahrain, Kuwait) and 3 October 1983 (Haiti), raising the Committee's membership to 103.

Chairman: Shunji Kobayashi (Japan).
Vice-Chairmen: L. Denisov (USSR), A. Fajardo-Maldonado (Guatemala), T. O. Oseni (Nigeria), R. Rasmusson (Sweden), Suwit Thatphitakkul (Thailand).
Rapporteur: Kifle Shenkoru (Ethiopia).

COMMITTEE ON TUNGSTEN
The Committee on Tungsten held its fifteenth session at Geneva from 12 to 16 December 1983.

Members: Argentina, Australia, Austria, Belgium, Bolivia, Brazil, Canada, China, Cyprus, France, Gabon, Germany, Federal Republic of, Italy, Japan, Mexico, Netherlands, Peru, Poland, Portugal, Republic of Korea, Romania, Rwanda, Spain, Sweden, Thailand, Turkey, USSR, United Kingdom, United States.

Chairman: J. Denison Cross (United Kingdom).
Vice-Chairman/Rapporteur: F. Laschinger (Canada).

PERMANENT GROUP ON SYNTHETICS AND SUBSTITUTES
The Permanent Group on Synthetics and Substitutes did not meet in 1983.

Members: Argentina, Brazil, Canada, Chad, Egypt, France, Germany, Federal Republic of, Indonesia, Italy, Japan, Malaysia, Mexico, Netherlands, Nigeria, Philippines, Poland, Senegal, Sri Lanka, Sudan, Uganda, USSR, United Kingdom, United States, Viet Nam.

PERMANENT SUB-COMMITTEE ON COMMODITIES
The Permanent Sub-Committee on Commodities, whose membership is identical to that of the Committee on Commodities, held its third session at Geneva from 17 to 26 January 1983.

Chairman: John J. Noble (Canada).
Vice-Chairmen: D. Dimitrov (Bulgaria), H. Malky (Syrian Arab Republic), A. M. Najib (Somalia), M. S. Pompeu Brasil Frota (Brazil), Jean Poswick (Belgium).
Rapporteur: Kifle Shenkoru (Ethiopia).

COMMITTEE ON ECONOMIC CO-OPERATION AMONG DEVELOPING COUNTRIES
The Committee on Economic Co-operation among Developing Countries held its third session at Geneva from 12 September to 5 October 1983.

Members: Algeria, Argentina, Australia, Austria, Bahrain,[a] Bangladesh, Belgium, Benin,[a] Bolivia, Brazil, Bulgaria, Burma, Canada, Central African Republic, Chile, China, Colombia, Costa Rica, Cuba, Czechoslovakia, Democratic People's Republic of Korea, Democratic Yemen, Denmark, Dominican Republic,[a] Ecuador, Egypt, El Salvador, Ethiopia, Finland, France, Gabon, German Democratic Republic, Germany, Federal Republic of, Ghana, Greece, Guatemala, Guyana, Haiti,[a] Honduras, Hungary,[a] India, Indonesia, Iran, Iraq, Ireland, Israel, Italy, Ivory Coast,[a] Jamaica, Japan, Jordan, Kenya, Kuwait, Lebanon, Liberia,

Libyan Arab Jamahiriya, Madagascar, Malaysia, Malta, Mauritius, Mexico, Morocco, Netherlands, New Zealand, Nicaragua, Nigeria, Norway, Oman, Pakistan, Panama, Peru, Philippines, Poland, Qatar, Republic of Korea, Romania, Saudi Arabia, Senegal, Singapore,[a] Somalia, Spain, Sri Lanka, Sudan, Suriname, Sweden, Switzerland, Syrian Arab Republic, Thailand, Togo, Trinidad and Tobago, Tunisia, Turkey, Uganda, USSR, United Arab Emirates, United Kingdom, United Republic of Cameroon, United Republic of Tanzania, United States, Uruguay, Venezuela, Viet Nam, Yemen, Yugoslavia, Zaire, Zambia.

[a]Declared elected by the Trade and Development Board on 18 April (Bahrain), 3 October (Benin, Dominican Republic, Haiti, Hungary, Ivory Coast) and 4 October 1983 (Singapore), raising the Committee's membership 106.

Chairman: Tahsin Tarlan (Turkey).
Vice-Chairmen: Ivan Anastassov (Bulgaria), N. Contreras-Saravia (Guatemala), Salah Fellah (Algeria), Khalid Mahmood (Pakistan), T. Tanabe (Japan).
Rapporteur: R. G. Torres (Brazil).

COMMITTEE ON INVISIBLES AND FINANCING RELATED TO TRADE
The Committee on Invisibles and Financing related to Trade held the second part of its tenth session at Geneva from 1 to 17 March 1983.

Members: Algeria, Argentina, Australia, Austria, Bahrain,[a] Bangladesh, Belgium, Bolivia, Brazil, Bulgaria, Burundi, Canada, Central African Republic, Chad, Chile, China, Colombia, Costa Rica, Cuba, Czechoslovakia, Democratic People's Republic of Korea, Democratic Yemen, Denmark, Dominican Republic, Ecuador, Egypt, El Salvador, Ethiopia, Finland, France, German Democratic Republic, Germany, Federal Republic of, Ghana, Greece, Guatemala, Guinea, Honduras, Hungary, India, Indonesia, Iran, Iraq, Ireland, Israel, Italy, Ivory Coast, Jamaica, Japan, Jordan, Kenya, Kuwait, Lebanon, Liberia, Libyan Arab Jamahiriya, Madagascar, Malaysia, Mali, Malta, Mexico, Morocco, Netherlands, New Zealand, Nicaragua, Nigeria, Norway, Pakistan, Panama, Peru, Philippines, Poland, Qatar, Republic of Korea, Romania, Saudi Arabia, Senegal, Somalia, Spain, Sri Lanka, Sudan, Sweden, Switzerland, Syrian Arab Republic, Thailand, Trinidad and Tobago, Tunisia, Turkey, Uganda, USSR, United Kingdom, United Republic of Cameroon, United Republic of Tanzania, United States, Upper Volta, Uruguay, Venezuela, Viet Nam, Yemen, Yugoslavia, Zaire, Zimbabwe.[a]

[a]Declared elected by the Trade and Development Board on 18 April and 3 October 1983, respectively, raising the Committee's membership to 100.

Chairman: Mario Alemán (Ecuador).
Vice-Chairmen: J. Dupouy (Chile), M. Mirdass (Saudi Arabia), D. Popov (Bulgaria), Raymond Raoelina (Madagascar), Michel Rougé (France).
Rapporteur: Christian du Plessis (Switzerland).

COMMITTEE ON MANUFACTURES
The Committee on Manufactures held its tenth session at Geneva from 14 to 22 March 1983.

Members: Algeria, Argentina, Australia, Austria, Bahrain,[a] Bangladesh, Belgium, Bolivia, Brazil, Bulgaria, Canada, Central African Republic, Chile, China, Colombia, Costa Rica, Cuba, Czechoslovakia, Democratic People's Republic of Korea, Democratic Yemen, Denmark, Dominican Republic, Ecuador, Egypt, El Salvador, Ethiopia, Finland, France, German Democratic Republic, Germany, Federal Republic of, Ghana, Greece, Guatemala, Haiti,[a] Honduras, Hungary, India, Indonesia, Iran, Iraq, Ireland, Israel, Italy, Ivory Coast, Jamaica, Japan, Jordan, Kenya, Kuwait,[a] Liberia, Libyan Arab Jamahiriya, Madagascar, Malaysia, Mali, Malta, Mauritius, Mexico, Morocco, Netherlands, New Zealand, Nicaragua, Nigeria, Norway, Pakistan, Panama, Peru, Philippines, Poland, Qatar, Republic of Korea, Romania, Saudi Arabia, Senegal, Singapore, Somalia, Spain, Sri Lanka, Sudan, Sweden, Switzerland, Syrian Arab Republic, Thailand, Trinidad and Tobago, Tunisia, Turkey, USSR, United Kingdom, United Republic of Cameroon, United Republic of Tanzania, United States, Upper Volta, Uruguay, Venezuela, Viet Nam, Yemen, Yugoslavia, Zaire.

[a]Declared elected by the Trade and Development Board on 18 April (Bahrain, Kuwait) and 3 October 1983 (Haiti), raising the Committee's membership to 97.

Chairman: Abdullahi Said Osman (Somalia).
Vice-Chairmen: M. S. El Din Abbas (Sudan), Sergio Delgado Lecourtois (Mexico), E.-A. Hörig (Federal Republic of Germany), M. Pullinen (Finland), H. Rahman (Bangladesh).
Rapporteur: L. Petrov (Bulgaria).

COMMITTEE ON SHIPPING
The Committee on Shipping did not meet in 1983.

Members: Algeria, Argentina, Australia, Bahrain,[a] Bangladesh, Belgium, Benin, Bolivia, Brazil, Bulgaria, Canada, Central African Republic, Chile, China, Colombia, Costa Rica, Cuba, Cyprus, Czechoslovakia, Democratic People's Republic of Korea, Democratic Yemen, Denmark, Dominican Republic, Ecuador, Egypt, El Salvador, Ethiopia, Finland, France, Gabon, German Democratic Republic, Germany, Federal Republic of, Ghana, Greece, Guatemala, Guinea, Honduras, Hungary, India, Indonesia, Iran, Iraq, Israel, Italy, Ivory Coast, Jamaica, Japan, Jordan, Kenya, Kuwait, Lebanon, Liberia, Libyan Arab Jamahiriya, Madagascar, Malaysia, Malta, Mauritius, Mexico, Morocco, Netherlands, New Zealand, Nicaragua, Nigeria, Norway, Pakistan, Panama, Peru, Philippines, Poland, Portugal, Qatar, Republic of Korea, Romania, Saudi Arabia, Senegal, Somalia, Spain, Sri Lanka, Sudan, Sweden, Switzerland, Syrian Arab Republic, Thailand, Trinidad and Tobago, Tunisia, Turkey, Uganda, USSR, United Kingdom, United Republic of Cameroon, United Republic of Tanzania, United States, Upper Volta, Uruguay, Venezuela, Viet Nam, Yemen, Yugoslavia, Zaire.

[a]Declared elected by the Trade and Development Board on 18 April 1983, raising the Committee's membership to 99.

WORKING GROUP ON INTERNATIONAL SHIPPING LEGISLATION
The Working Group on International Shipping Legislation, whose membership is identical to that of the Committee on Shipping, held its ninth session at Geneva from 31 January to 18 February 1983.

Chairman: Jorge T. Pereira (Argentina).
Vice-Chairmen: A. Denekew (Ethiopia), A. Kokin (USSR), Rifaat Izzat Rifaat (Iraq), J. M. Ritter (Honduras), J. Van Den Esch (France).
Rapporteur: James O. Lynch (Canada).

COMMITTEE ON TRANSFER OF TECHNOLOGY
The Committee on Transfer of Technology did not meet in 1983.

Members: Algeria, Argentina, Australia, Austria, Bahrain,[a] Belgium, Bolivia, Brazil, Bulgaria, Canada, Chile, China, Colombia, Costa Rica, Cuba, Czechoslovakia, Democratic People's Republic of Korea, Democratic Yemen, Denmark, Ecuador, Egypt, El Salvador, Ethiopia, Finland, France, German Democratic Republic, Germany, Federal Republic of, Ghana, Greece, Guatemala, Haiti,[a] Honduras, Hungary, India, Indonesia, Iran, Iraq, Ireland, Israel, Italy, Ivory Coast, Jamaica, Japan, Jordan, Kenya, Kuwait, Liberia, Libyan Arab Jamahiriya, Madagascar, Malaysia, Malta, Mauritius, Mexico, Morocco, Netherlands, New Zealand, Nicaragua, Nigeria, Norway, Pakistan, Panama, Peru, Philippines, Poland, Qatar, Republic of Korea, Romania, Saudi Arabia, Senegal, Sierra Leone, Somalia, Spain, Sri Lanka, Sudan, Sweden, Switzerland, Syrian Arab Republic, Thailand, Trinidad and Tobago, Tunisia, Turkey, USSR, United Arab Emirates, United Kingdom, United Republic of Cameroon, United Republic of Tanzania, United States, Upper Volta, Venezuela, Viet Nam, Yemen, Yugoslavia, Zaire.

[a]Declared elected by the Trade and Development Board on 18 April and 3 October 1983, respectively, raising the Committee's membership to 93.

SPECIAL COMMITTEE ON PREFERENCES
The Special Committee on Preferences, which is open to the participation of all UNCTAD members, did not meet in 1983.

PREPARATORY COMMITTEE FOR THE UNITED NATIONS CONFERENCE ON CONDITIONS FOR REGISTRATION OF SHIPS
Pursuant to a 1982 General Assembly resolution,[20] the Trade and De-

---

[20]Resolution 37/209, 20 December 1982 (YUN 1982, p. 748).

velopment Board, by virtue of the adoption on 28 April 1983 of its calendar of meetings, approved the establishment of the Preparatory Committee for the United Nations Conference on Conditions for Registration of Ships (scheduled for 1984).

The Preparatory Committee, open to the participation of all States, held its only series of meetings at Geneva from 7 to 18 November 1983.

Chairman: Abderrahman Bouayad (Morocco).
Vice-Chairmen: M. Wasfy Abbas (Egypt), Jon Blaslid (Norway), Hortencio J. Brillantes (Philippines), Tadeusz Lodykowski (Poland), Hugo Torrijos (Panama).
Rapporteur: Rudi Okken (Netherlands).

United Nations Council for Namibia
Members: Algeria, Angola, Australia, Bangladesh, Belgium, Botswana, Bulgaria, Burundi, Chile, China, Colombia, Cyprus, Egypt, Finland, Guyana, Haiti, India, Indonesia, Liberia, Mexico, Nigeria, Pakistan, Poland, Romania, Senegal, Turkey, USSR, United Republic of Cameroon, Venezuela, Yugoslavia, Zambia.

President: Paul John Firmino Lusaka (Zambia).
Vice-Presidents: Ignac Golob (Yugoslavia), A. Coskun Kirca (Turkey), Natarajan Krishnan (India), Mohamed Sahnoun (Algeria), Noel G. Sinclair (Guyana).

United Nations Commissioner for Namibia: Brajesh Chandra Mishra.[a]

[a]Reappointed by the General Assembly on 1 December 1983 (decision 38/312) for a one-year term beginning on 1 January 1984.

COMMITTEE ON THE UNITED NATIONS FUND FOR NAMIBIA
Members: Australia, Finland, India, Nigeria, Romania, Senegal, Turkey, Venezuela *(Vice-Chairman/Rapporteur)*, Yugoslavia, Zambia; the President of the Council *(ex-officio Chairman)*.

STANDING COMMITTEE I
Members: Algeria, China, Colombia, Finland, Haiti, Indonesia, Nigeria, Poland, Senegal, Turkey *(Vice-Chairman)*, USSR, United Republic of Cameroon *(Chairman)*, Venezuela, Zambia.

STANDING COMMITTEE II
Members: Angola, Australia, Bangladesh, Botswana, Bulgaria, Chile, Colombia, Cyprus, Finland, Guyana, Liberia *(Vice-Chairman)*, Mexico, Pakistan *(Chairman)*, Romania, Zambia.

STANDING COMMITTEE III
Members: Algeria, Angola, Australia, Belgium, Bulgaria *(Chairman)*, Burundi, Colombia, Cyprus, Egypt, India, Mexico *(Vice-Chairman)*, Nigeria, Pakistan, Romania, Venezuela, Yugoslavia, Zambia.

STEERING COMMITTEE
In 1983, the Steering Committee consisted of the Council's President and five Vice-Presidents, the chairmen of its three standing committees and the Vice-Chairman/Rapporteur of the Committee on the United Nations Fund for Namibia.

United Nations Development Programme (UNDP)

GOVERNING COUNCIL
The Governing Council of UNDP (p. 1365) reports to the Economic and Social Council and through it to the General Assembly.

United Nations Environment Programme (UNEP)

GOVERNING COUNCIL
The Governing Council of UNEP consists of 58 members elected by the General Assembly for three-year terms.
Seats on the Governing Council are allocated as follows: 16 to African States, 13 to Asian States, 6 to Eastern European States, 10 to Latin American States, and 13 to Western European and other States.
The Governing Council, which reports to the Assembly through the Economic and Social Council, held its eleventh session at Nairobi, Kenya, from 11 to 24 May 1983.

Members:
To serve until 31 December 1983: Brazil, Egypt, Germany, Federal Republic of, Ghana, Haiti, Iceland, Japan, Kenya, Libyan Arab Jamahiriya, Malaysia, Netherlands, Pakistan, Sri Lanka, Switzerland, Ukrainian SSR, USSR, United States, Venezuela, Zaire.
To serve until 31 December 1984: Afghanistan, Botswana, Burundi, Byelorussian SSR, Canada, Colombia, Greece, Guinea, India, Jamaica, Mexico, Morocco, Oman, Poland, Senegal, Spain, Thailand, United Kingdom, United Republic of Tanzania, Uruguay.
To serve until 31 December 1985: Argentina, Australia, Chile, China, Finland, France, Hungary, Indonesia, Italy, Ivory Coast, Lesotho, Nigeria, Papua New Guinea, Peru, Philippines, Saudi Arabia, Uganda, United Republic of Cameroon, Yugoslavia.

President: M. Holdgate (United Kingdom).
Vice-Presidents: Juan Carlos Arlía (Argentina), T. Khoshoo (India), E. Szenes (Hungary).
Rapporteur: F. Matholoane (Lesotho).

Executive Director of UNEP: Mostafa Kamal Tolba.
Deputy Executive Director: Peter Shaw Thacher (until 31 May), Joseph C. Wheeler (from 1 June).

On 15 December 1983 (decision 38/316), the General Assembly elected the following 19 members for a three-year term beginning on 1 January 1984 to fill the vacancies occurring on 31 December 1983: Algeria, Austria, Belgium, Brazil, Germany, Federal Republic of, Haiti, Japan, Kuwait, Malaysia, Nepal, Norway, Rwanda, Sudan, Togo, Ukrainian SSR, USSR, United States, Venezuela, Zaire.

United Nations Financing System for Science and Technology for Development
The United Nations Financing System for Science and Technology for Development finances, at the request of Governments, a broad range of activities intended to strengthen the endogenous scientific and technological capacities of developing countries. Its policy-making body is the Intergovernmental Committee on Science and Technology for Development (p. 1343) and the overall supervision of its management is entrusted to the UNDP Administrator, who was to be accountable to an Executive Board responsible for the System's operation and conduct. The Administrator, in consultation with the Director-General for Development and International Economic Co-operation, reports annually to the Intergovernmental Committee.
On 19 December 1983, the General Assembly decided that the existing operating procedures of the Financing System should continue until the sixth (1984) session of the Intergovernmental Committee.

EXECUTIVE BOARD
The Executive Board was to be composed of 21 directors elected by the Intergovernmental Committee on Science and Technology for Development for three-year terms, one third to be drawn from developed countries and two thirds from developing countries reflecting an appropriate balance between donors and recipients.
The Board had not been constituted by the end of 1983.

United Nations Fund for Population Activities (UNFPA)
The United Nations Fund for Population Activities, a subsidiary organ of the General Assembly, plays a leading role within the United Nations system in promoting population programmes and in providing assistance to developing countries at their request in dealing with their population problems. It operates under the overall policy guidance of the Economic and Social Council and under the financial and administrative policy guidance of the Governing Council of UNDP.

Executive Director: Rafael M. Salas.
Deputy Executive Director: Heino E. Wittrin.

United Nations Industrial Development Organization (UNIDO)

INDUSTRIAL DEVELOPMENT BOARD
The Industrial Development Board, the principal organ of UNIDO, consists of 45 States elected by the General Assembly, on the basis of equitable geographical distribution, to serve for three-year terms.

States eligible for election to the Board are those which are Members of the United Nations or members of the specialized agencies or of IAEA.

The Board reports annually to the Assembly through the Economic and Social Council.

The Board's membership is drawn from the following four groups of States:

List A. 18 of the following States: Afghanistan, Algeria, Angola, Bahrain, Bangladesh, Benin, Bhutan, Botswana, Burma, Burundi, Cape Verde, Central African Republic, Chad, China, Comoros, Congo, Democratic Kampuchea, Democratic People's Republic of Korea, Democratic Yemen, Djibouti, Egypt, Equatorial Guinea, Ethiopia, Fiji, Gabon, Gambia, Ghana, Guinea, Guinea-Bissau, India, Indonesia, Iran, Iraq, Israel, Ivory Coast, Jordan, Kenya, Kuwait, Lao People's Democratic Republic, Lebanon, Lesotho, Liberia, Libyan Arab Jamahiriya, Madagascar, Malawi, Malaysia, Maldives, Mali, Mauritania, Mauritius, Mongolia, Morocco, Mozambique, Nepal, Niger, Nigeria, Oman, Pakistan, Papua New Guinea, Philippines, Qatar, Republic of Korea, Rwanda, Sao Tome and Principe, Saudi Arabia, Senegal, Seychelles, Sierra Leone, Singapore, Solomon Islands, Somalia, South Africa, Sri Lanka, Sudan, Swaziland, Syrian Arab Republic, Thailand, Togo, Tunisia, Uganda, United Arab Emirates, United Republic of Cameroon, United Republic of Tanzania, Upper Volta, Vanuatu, Viet Nam, Yemen, Yugoslavia, Zaire, Zambia, Zimbabwe.

List B. 15 of the following States: Australia, Austria, Belgium, Canada, Cyprus, Denmark, Finland, France, Germany, Federal Republic of, Greece, Iceland, Ireland, Italy, Japan, Liechtenstein, Luxembourg, Malta, Monaco, Netherlands, New Zealand, Norway, Portugal, Spain, Sweden, Switzerland, Turkey, United Kingdom, United States.

List C. 7 of the following States: Antigua and Barbuda, Argentina, Bahamas, Barbados, Belize, Bolivia, Brazil, Chile, Colombia, Costa Rica, Cuba, Dominica, Dominican Republic, Ecuador, El Salvador, Grenada, Guatemala, Guyana, Haiti, Honduras, Jamaica, Mexico, Nicaragua, Panama, Paraguay, Peru, Saint Christopher and Nevis,[a] Saint Lucia, Saint Vincent and the Grenadines, Suriname, Trinidad and Tobago, Uruguay, Venezuela.

List D. 5 of the following States: Albania, Bulgaria, Byelorussian SSR, Czechoslovakia, German Democratic Republic, Hungary, Poland, Romania, Ukrainian SSR, USSR.

[a]Included in list C by a General Assembly resolution of 20 December 1983.

The Industrial Development Board held its seventeenth session at Vienna, Austria, from 26 April to 13 May 1983.

BOARD MEMBERS

To serve until 31 December 1983: Brazil, Denmark, Ecuador, France, German Democratic Republic, Guinea, India, Japan, Mongolia, Netherlands, Pakistan, Romania, Sri Lanka, United States, Zambia.

To serve until 31 December 1984: Australia, China, Germany, Federal Republic of, Iraq, Lesotho, Liberia, Malaysia, Mexico, Panama, Sierra Leone, Spain, Turkey, Ukrainian SSR, United Kingdom, Venezuela.

To serve until 31 December 1985: Austria, Belgium, Bulgaria, Chad, Chile, Finland, Indonesia, Italy, Libyan Arab Jamahiriya, Peru, Rwanda, Sudan, Switzerland, Uganda, USSR.

President: Gerrit Willem van Barneveld Kooy (Netherlands).
Vice-Presidents: Carlos Derpsch Bartsch (Chile), C. Popov (Bulgaria), C. E. Zambia Liberty (Liberia).
Rapporteur: A. A. Khan (Pakistan).

Executive Director of UNIDO: Abd-El Rahman Khane.
Deputy Executive Director: Philippe Jacques Farlan Carré.

On 19 December 1983 (decision 38/320), the General Assembly elected the following 15 members of the Industrial Development Board for a three-year term beginning on 1 January 1984 to fill the vacancies occurring on 31 December 1983: Argentina, Brazil, Democratic Yemen, France, Ghana, Hungary, India, Japan, Malawi, Netherlands, Norway, Pakistan, Romania, United Arab Emirates, United States.

PERMANENT COMMITTEE

The Permanent Committee has the same membership as the Industrial Development Board and normally meets twice a year.

During 1983, the Committee held its nineteenth session on 25 and 29 April and its twentieth from 28 November to 2 December, both at Vienna, Austria. Its officers were the same as those of the seventeenth session of the Industrial Development Board.

United Nations Institute for Disarmament Research (UNIDIR)

BOARD OF TRUSTEES

The Secretary-General's Advisory Board on Disarmament Studies, composed in 1983 of 22 eminent persons selected on the basis of their personal expertise and taking into account the principle of equitable geographical representation, functions as the Board of Trustees of UNIDIR; the Director of UNIDIR reports to the General Assembly.

Members: Oluyemi Adeniji, *Chairman* (Nigeria); Hadj Benabdelkader Azzout (Algeria); O. N. Bykov (USSR); James E. Dougherty (United States); Omran El-Shafei (Egypt); Constantin Ene (Romania); Edgar Faure (France); Alfonso García Robles (Mexico); Ignac Golob (Yugoslavia); A. C. Shahul Hameed (Sri Lanka); Liang Yufan (China); Sir Ronald Mason (United Kingdom); Akira Matsui (Japan); William Eteki Mboumoua (United Republic of Cameroon); Manfred Mueller (German Democratic Republic); Carlos Ortiz de Rozas (Argentina); Maharajakrishna K. Rasgotra (India); Friedrich Ruth (Federal Republic of Germany); Agha Shahi (Pakistan); Tadeusz Strulak (Poland); José A. Tabares del Real (Cuba); Oscar Vaernö (Norway).

Director of UNIDIR: Liviu Bota.

United Nations Institute for Training and Research (UNITAR)

The Executive Director of UNITAR, in consultation with the Board of Trustees of the Institute, reports through the Secretary-General to the General Assembly and, as appropriate, to the Economic and Social Council and other United Nations bodies.

BOARD OF TRUSTEES

Until 23 May 1983, the Board of Trustees of UNITAR was composed of: *(a)* up to 24 members, which might include one or more officials of the United Nations Secretariat, appointed on a broad geographical basis by the Secretary-General, in consultation with the Presidents of the General Assembly and the Economic and Social Council; and *(b)* four *ex-officio* members. With effect from 24 May, the UNITAR statute was amended by the Secretary-General, providing that the Board was to be composed of not less than 11 and not more than 30 members.

The Board held a special session at United Nations Headquarters from 11 to 14 April 1983.

Members (until 30 June 1983):
To serve until 30 June 1983: Margaret Joan Anstee (Secretariat); Wahbi El-Bouri (Libyan Arab Jamahiriya); Lai Ya-li (China); Donald O. Mills (Jamaica); Bibiano F. Osorio-Tafall (Mexico); Agha Shahi, *Chairman* (Pakistan); Victor Umbricht (Switzerland); Anton Vratusa (Yugoslavia).
To serve until 30 June 1984: Siméon Aké (Ivory Coast); William H. Barton, *Vice-Chairman* (Canada); Ademar M. A. d'Alcantara (Belgium); Roberto E. Guyer (Argentina); K. Natwar-Singh (India); Shizuo Saito (Japan); Joel Segall (United States); Rüdiger von Wechmar (Federal Republic of Germany).
To serve until 30 June 1985:[a] Ole Algard (Norway); Stephane Hessel (France); Johan Kaufmann (Netherlands); Olara A. Otunnu (Uganda); Taieb Slim (Tunisia); Anders I. Thunborg (Sweden); B. S. Vaganov (USSR).

[a]One seat remained vacant.

The Secretary-General appointed the following eight members for a three-year term beginning on 1 July 1983 to fill the vacancies occurring on 30 June: Margaret Joan Anstee (Secretariat), Mohamed Omar Madani (Saudi Arabia), Donald O. Mills (Jamaica), Pei Monong (China), Agha Shahi (Pakistan), Ali A. Treiki (Libyan Arab Jamahiriya), Victor Umbricht (Switzerland), Anton Vratusa (Yugoslavia). He also appointed Porfirio Muñoz Ledo (Mexico) and José Luis Pardos (Spain) for a two-year term beginning on 1 July.

Members (from 1 July 1983):

To serve until 30 June 1984: Siméon Aké (Ivory Coast), William H. Barton (Canada), Ademar M. A. d'Alcantara (Belgium), Roberto E. Guyer (Argentina), K. Natwar-Singh (India), Shizuo Saito (Japan), Joel Segall (United States), Rüdiger von Wechmar (Federal Republic of Germany).

To serve until 30 June 1985: Ole Algard (Norway), Stephane Hessel (France), Johan Kaufmann (Netherlands), Porfirio Muñoz Ledo (Mexico), Olara Otunnu (Uganda), José Luis Pardos (Spain), Taieb Slim (Tunisia), Anders I. Thunborg (Sweden), B. S. Vaganov (USSR).

To serve until 30 June 1986: Margaret Joan Anstee (Secretariat), Mohamed Omar Madani (Saudi Arabia), Donald O. Mills (Jamaica), Pei Monong (China), Agha Shahi (Pakistan), Ali A. Treiki (Libyan Arab Jamahiriya), Victor Umbricht (Switzerland), Anton Vratusa (Yugoslavia).

Ex-officio members: The Secretary-General, the President of the General Assembly, the President of the Economic and Social Council and the Executive Director of UNITAR.

Executive Director of UNITAR: Michel Doo Kingué.

United Nations Joint Staff Pension Board

The United Nations Joint Staff Pension Board is composed of 21 members, as follows:

Six appointed by the United Nations Staff Pension Committee (two from members elected by the General Assembly, two from those appointed by the Secretary-General, two from those elected by participants).

Fifteen appointed by Staff Pension Committees of other member organizations of the United Nations Joint Staff Pension Fund, as follows: two each by WHO, FAO, UNESCO; and one each by ILO, ICAO, IAEA, WMO, IMO, ITU, ICITO/GATT, WIPO, IFAD.

The Board held its thirty-first session in London from 4 to 14 July 1983.

Members:

United Nations

Representing the General Assembly: Representatives: Mario Majoli (Italy); Michael George Okeyo (Kenya). Alternates: Sol Kuttner (United States); Jobst Holborn (Federal Republic of Germany); Yukio Takasu, *Rapporteur* (Japan); Eduardo César Añón Noceti (Uruguay).

Representing the Secretary-General: Representatives: J. Richard Foran (Canada); Louis-Pascal Nègre (Mali). Alternates: Clayton C. Timbrell (United States); Raymond Gieri (United States); Shing-yi Huang (China); Paul C. Szasz (United States).

Representing the Participants: Representatives: Susanna H. Johnston (United States); Rosa María Vicien-Milburn (Argentina). Alternates: Bruce C. Hillis (Canada); Gualtiero Fulcheri (Italy); Sergio Zampetti (Italy); Anders Tholle (Denmark).

International Labour Organisation

Representing the Participants: Representative: Gerald F. Starr (Canada). Alternates: Edmond Ryser (Switzerland); H. Leydier (France).

World Health Organization

Representing the Governing Body: Representative: Dr. Arnold Sauter, *Chairman* (Switzerland). Alternates: Dr. A. Tanaka (Japan); Georgette Thomas (Seychelles); Dr. N. Jogezai (Pakistan); A. Narasingha (Nepal); Dr. H. Rodriguez Castells (Argentina).

Representing the Participants: Representative: G. Dazin (France). Alternates: Ram L. Rai (India); Dr. Alain Vessereau (France); A. Piel (United States); Dr. D. Ray (India); Vincent Bambinelli (United States).

Food and Agriculture Organization of the United Nations

Representing the Executive Head: Representative: Mohsen Bel Hadj Amor (Tunisia). Alternate: Maria Grazia Iuri (Italy).

Representing the Participants: Representative: Aurelio Marcucci, *First Vice-Chairman* (Italy). Alternate: Massimo Arrigo (Italy).

United Nations Educational, Scientific and Cultural Organization

Representing the Governing Body: Representative: Gollerkery Vishvanath Rao (India). Alternate: Robert Brulard (Belgium).

Representing the Participants: Representative: Witold Zyss (Israel). Alternate: E. S. Solomon (United States).

International Civil Aviation Organization

Representing the Governing Body: Representative: O. Ogunbiyi (Nigeria). Alternate: Alan R. Boyd (Canada).

International Atomic Energy Agency

Representing the Governing Body: Representative: M. Ugalde (Chile).

World Meteorological Organization

Representing the Governing Body: Representative: Bernhard Ziese (Federal Republic of Germany).

International Maritime Organization

Representing the Executive Head: Representative: Marcel Landey (Canada). Alternates: Kaare Stangeland (Norway); Denis G. Aitken, *Second Vice-Chairman* (United Kingdom).

International Telecommunication Union

Representing the Participants: Representative: C. Glinz (Switzerland). Alternate: Jacques Bacaly (France).

Interim Commission for the International Trade Organization / General Agreement on Tariffs and Trade

Representing the Executive Head: Representative: Cyril F. Johnson (United Kingdom). Alternate: R. Blackhurst (United States).

World Intellectual Property Organization

Representing the Executive Head: Representative: Thomas A. J. Keefer (Canada).

International Fund for Agricultural Development

Representing the Executive Head: Representative: Tor Myrvang (Norway).

STANDING COMMITTEE OF THE PENSION BOARD

Members (elected at the Board's thirty-first session):

United Nations (Group I)

Representing the General Assembly: Representative: Mario Majoli. Alternates: Michael George Okeyo, Sol Kuttner, Jobst Holborn, Yukio Takasu, Eduardo César Añón Noceti.

Representing the Secretary-General: Representative: J. Richard Foran. Alternates: Louis-Pascal Nègre, Clayton C. Timbrell, Raymond Gieri, V. Elissejev, Paul C. Szasz.

Representing the Participants: Representative: Susanna H. Johnston. Alternates: Rosa María Vicien-Milburn, Bruce C. Hillis, Gualtiero Fulcheri, Sergio Zampetti, Anders Tholle.

Specialized agencies (Group II)

Representing the Governing Body: Representative: Dr. Arnold Sauter (WHO). Alternates: Dr. A. Tanaka (WHO), Georgette Thomas (WHO), Dr. N. Jogezai (WHO), A. Narasingha (WHO), Dr. H. Rodriguez Castells (WHO).

Representing the Executive Head: Representative: M. Fellague (WMO). Alternates: Michel Bardoux (ITU), Luis Alonso de Huarte (IAEA), Denis G. Aitken (IMO).

Representing the Participants: Representative: Edmond Ryser (ILO). Alternate: Gerald F. Starr (ILO).

Specialized agencies (Group III)

Representing the Governing Body: Representative: Gollerkery Vishvanath Rao (UNESCO). Alternate: Robert Brulard (UNESCO).

Representing the Executive Head: Representative: Shelton E. Jayasekera (ICAO). Alternates: Tor Myrvang (IFAD), Cyril F. Johnson (ICITO), Thomas A. J. Keefer (WIPO).

Representing the Participants: Representative: Aurelio Marcucci (FAO). Alternates: Massimo Arrigo (FAO), C. Cherubini (FAO), E. Paardekooper (FAO), Pietro E. Buttinelli (FAO).

COMMITTEE OF ACTUARIES

The Committee of Actuaries consists of five members, each representing one of the five geographical regions of the United Nations.

Members: Ajibola O. Ogunshola (Nigeria), *Region I* (African States); Kunio Takeuchi (Japan), *Region II* (Asian States); E. M. Chetyrkin (USSR), Region III (Eastern European States); Dr. Gonzalo Arroba (Ecuador), *Region IV* (Latin American States); Robert J. Myers (United States), *Region V* (Western European and other States).

United Nations Relief and Works Agency for Palestine Refugees in the Near East (UNRWA)

ADVISORY COMMISSION OF UNRWA

The Advisory Commission of UNRWA met at Vienna, Austria, on 25 August 1983.

Members: Belgium, Egypt, France, Japan *(Chairman)*, Jordan, Lebanon, Syrian Arab Republic, Turkey, United Kingdom, United States.

WORKING GROUP ON THE FINANCING OF UNRWA
Members: France, Ghana *(Vice-Chairman)*, Japan, Lebanon, Norway *(Rapporteur)*, Trinidad and Tobago, Turkey *(Chairman)*, United Kingdom, United States.

Commissioner-General of UNRWA: Olof Rydbeck.
Deputy Commissioner-General: Alan J. Brown.

United Nations Scientific Advisory Committee
Established by the General Assembly in 1954 as a seven-member advisory committee on the International Conference on the Peaceful Uses of Atomic Energy (1955), the United Nations Scientific Advisory Committee was so renamed and its mandate revised by the Assembly in 1958,[21] retaining its original composition. The Committee has not met since 1956.[22]

Members: Brazil, Canada, France, India, USSR, United Kingdom, United States.

United Nations Scientific Committee on
the Effects of Atomic Radiation
The 20-member United Nations Scientific Committee on the Effects of Atomic Radiation held its thirty-second session at Vienna, Austria, from 20 to 24 June 1983.

Members: Argentina, Australia, Belgium, Brazil, Canada, Czechoslovakia, Egypt, France, Germany, Federal Republic of, India, Indonesia, Japan, Mexico, Peru, Poland, Sudan, Sweden, USSR, United Kingdom, United States.

Chairman: D. Beninson (Argentina).
Vice-Chairman: T. Kumatori (Japan).
Rapporteur: A. Hidayatalla (Sudan).

United Nations Special Fund
(to provide emergency relief and development assistance)

BOARD OF GOVERNORS
The activities of the United Nations Special Fund were suspended, *ad interim,* in 1978 by the General Assembly, which assumed the functions of the Board of Governors of the Fund. In 1981,[23] the Assembly decided to continue performing those functions, within the context of its consideration of the item on development and international economic co-operation, pending consideration of the question in 1983. However, no action was taken in 1983.

United Nations Special Fund for Land-locked
Developing Countries
The General Assembly established the United Nations Special Fund for Land-locked Developing Countries in 1975[24] and approved its statute in 1976.[25] The Special Fund was to operate as an organ of the Assembly, with its policies and procedures to be formulated by a Board of Governors.
The chief executive officer of the Special Fund, the Executive Director, to be appointed by the Secretary-General subject to the confirmation of the Assembly, was to discharge his functions under the guidance and supervision of the Board of Governors and an Executive Committee, if established.
Pending appointment of the Executive Director, the Administrator of UNDP, in close collaboration with the Secretary-General of UNCTAD, manages the Fund.

BOARD OF GOVERNORS
A 36-member Board of Governors of the United Nations Special Fund for Land-locked Developing Countries was to be elected by the General Assembly from among Members of the United Nations or members of the specialized agencies or of IAEA, keeping in view the need for a balanced representation of the beneficiary land-locked developing countries and their transit neighbours, on the one hand, and potential donor countries on the other.
Members were to serve three-year terms, except that at the first election the terms of one third of the members were to be for one year and those of a further third for two years.
The Board was to report annually to the Assembly through the Economic and Social Council.

On 15 December 1983 (decision 38/319), the Assembly deferred election of the Board to its thirty-ninth (1984) session.

United Nations Staff Pension Committee
The United Nations Staff Pension Committee consists of three members elected by the General Assembly, three appointed by the Secretary-General and three elected by the participants in the United Nations Joint Staff Pension Fund. The term of office of the elected members is three years, or until the election of their successors.

Members:
Elected by Assembly (to serve until 31 December 1985): *Members:* Sol Kuttner *(Chairman)*; Mario Majoli; Michael George Okeyo. *Alternates:* Eduardo César Añón Noceti; Jobst Holborn; Yukio Takasu.
Appointed by Secretary-General (to serve until further notice):[a] *Members:* J. Richard Foran; Louis-Pascal Nègre; Clayton C. Timbrell. *Alternates:* Raymond Gieri; V. Elissejev; Paul C. Szasz.
Elected by Participants (to serve until 31 December 1985):[b] *Members:* Susanna H. Johnston; Rosa María Vicien-Milburn; Bruce C. Hillis. *Alternates:* Gualtiero Fulcheri; Sergio Zampetti; Anders Tholle.

[a]Appointed on 10 January 1983.
[b]Elected on 19 May 1983.

United Nations University

COUNCIL OF THE UNITED NATIONS UNIVERSITY
The Council of the United Nations University, the governing board of the University, consists of: *(a)* 24 members appointed jointly by the Secretary-General and the Director-General of UNESCO, in consultation with the agencies and programmes concerned including UNITAR, who serve in their personal capacity for six-year terms; *(b)* the Secretary-General, the Director-General of UNESCO and the Executive Director of UNITAR, who are *ex-officio* members; and *(c)* the Rector of the University, who is normally appointed for a five-year term.
The Council held two sessions in 1983, at Tokyo, Japan: its twenty-first from 27 June to 1 July; and its twenty-second from 5 to 9 December.

Members:
To serve until 2 May 1986: Ungku Abdul Aziz (Malaysia); Daniel Adzei Bekoe, *Vice-Chairman* (Ghana); Elise M. Boulding (United States); Satish Chandra, *Vice-Chairman* (India); Valy Charles Diarrassouba (Ivory Coast);[a] Dennis H. Irvine, *Vice-Chairman* (Guyana); André Louis Jaumotte (Belgium); Reimut Jochimsen, *Vice-Chairman* (Federal Republic of Germany); F. S. C. P. Kalpage (Sri Lanka); Sir John Kendrew, *Chairman* (United Kingdom); Karl Eric Knutsson (Sweden); Shizuo Saito (Japan); Víctor Luis Urquidi, *Vice-Chairman* (Mexico).
To serve until 2 May 1989:[b] Bakr Abdullah Bakr (Saudi Arabia); Bashir Bakri (Sudan); Marie-Thérèse Basse (Senegal); André Blanc-Lapierre (France); Mercedes B. Concepcion (Philippines); Walter Joseph Kamba (Zimbabwe); Maria de Lourdes Pintasilgo (Portugal); Y. M. Primakov (USSR); Alberto Wagner de Reyna (Peru); Zhao Dihua (China).
Ex-officio members: The Secretary-General, the Director-General of UNESCO and the Executive Director of UNITAR.
Rector of the United Nations University: Mr. Soedjatmoko.

[a]Changed his name to Charles Valy Tuho as of December 1983.
[b]Appointed in May 1983, except for Y. M. Primakov (USSR) who was appointed in November; one seat remained unfilled in 1983.

The Council maintained two standing committees during 1983: the Committee on Finance and Budget; and the Committee on Institutional and Programmatic Development. In addition, at its twenty-second session it made the *Ad Hoc* Committee on Statutes and Rules a standing Committee on Statutes, Rules and Guidelines, and established a standing Committee on the Report of the Council.

[21]Resolution 1344(XIII), 13 December 1958 (YUN 1958, p. 31).
[22]YUN 1956, p. 108.
[23]Decision 36/424, 4 December 1981 (YUN 1981, p. 418).
[24]Resolution 3504(XXX), 15 December 1975 (YUN 1975, p. 387).
[25]Resolution 31/177, annex, 21 December 1976 (YUN 1976, p. 356).

United Nations Voluntary Fund for Victims of Torture

BOARD OF TRUSTEES

The Board of Trustees to advise the Secretary-General in his administration of the United Nations Voluntary Fund for Victims of Torture was to consist of five members with wide experience in the field of human rights, appointed in their personal capacity by the Secretary-General with due regard for equitable geographical distribution and in consultation with their Governments. In 1983, however, it had a membership of four.

The Board held two sessions in 1983: its first from 21 to 25 March at Geneva; and its second from 24 to 28 October at United Nations Headquarters.

Members (to serve until 31 December 1985): Hans Danelius, *Chairman* (Sweden); Elizabeth Odio Benito (Costa Rica); Waleed M. Sadi (Jordan); Amos Wako (Kenya).

World Food Council

The World Food Council, at the ministerial or plenipotentiary level, functions as an organ of the United Nations and reports to the General Assembly through the Economic and Social Council. It consists of 36 members, nominated by the Economic and Social Council and elected by the Assembly according to the following pattern: nine members from African States, eight from Asian States, seven from Latin American States, four from socialist States of Eastern Europe and eight from Western European and other States. Members serve for three-year terms.

During 1983, the World Food Council held its ninth session at United Nations Headquarters from 27 to 30 June. It was preceded by a series of preparatory meetings held at Rome, Italy, from 10 to 13 May.

Members:

To serve until 31 December 1983: Argentina, Egypt, France, Haiti, Hungary, Indonesia, Italy, Japan, Norway, Pakistan, Rwanda, Zaire.

To serve until 31 December 1984: Botswana, Canada, China, Colombia, Gambia, Greece, India, Mexico, Thailand, United Republic of Tanzania, United States, Yugoslavia.

To serve until 31 December 1985: Australia, Bangladesh, Ecuador, Ethiopia, German Democratic Republic, Germany, Federal Republic of, Ghana, Nicaragua, Nigeria, USSR, United Arab Emirates, Venezuela.

President: Francisco Merino Rábago (Mexico).
Vice-Presidents: Ahmad Affandi (Indonesia), Robert Sagna (Senegal), Dumitru Vsiliu (Romania).
Rapporteur: Aage Bothner (Norway).

Executive Director: Maurice J. Williams.
Deputy Executive Director: Diogo A. N. de Gaspar.

On 25 May and 28 July 1983 (decisions 1983/161 and 1983/179), the Economic and Social Council nominated the following 15 States, 12 of which were to be elected by the General Assembly, for a three-year term beginning on 1 January 1984 to fill the vacancies occurring on 31 December 1983: Argentina, Burundi, Central African Republic, Chile, Finland, France, Hungary, Indonesia, Iraq, Italy, Japan, Morocco, Pakistan, Philippines, Sri Lanka. All except Indonesia, the Philippines and Sri Lanka were elected by the Assembly on 15 December 1983 (decision 38/317).

Conferences

International Conference in Support of the Struggle of the Namibian People for Independence

The International Conference in Support of the Struggle of the Namibian People for Independence was held in Paris from 25 to 29 April 1983. Participating were the following 137 States and the United Nations Council for Namibia:

Afghanistan, Albania, Algeria, Angola, Argentina, Australia, Austria, Bahrain, Bangladesh, Belgium, Benin, Bhutan, Botswana, Brazil, Bulgaria, Burma, Burundi, Byelorussian SSR, Canada, Cape Verde, Central African Republic, Chad, Chile, China, Colombia, Comoros, Congo, Costa Rica, Cuba, Cyprus, Czechoslovakia, Democratic Kampuchea, Democratic People's Republic of Korea, Democratic Yemen, Denmark, Dominican Republic, Ecuador, Egypt, Equatorial Guinea, Ethiopia, Finland, France, Gabon, Gambia, German Democratic Republic, Germany, Federal Republic of, Ghana, Greece, Grenada, Guatemala, Guinea, Guinea-Bissau, Guyana, Haiti, Holy See, Honduras, Hungary, Iceland, India, Indonesia, Iran, Iraq, Ireland, Italy, Ivory Coast, Jamaica, Japan, Jordan, Kenya, Kuwait, Lao People's Democratic Republic, Lebanon, Lesotho, Liberia, Libyan Arab Jamahiriya, Madagascar, Malaysia, Mali, Mauritania, Mauritius, Mexico, Mongolia, Morocco, Mozambique, Nepal, Netherlands, New Zealand, Nicaragua, Niger, Nigeria, Norway, Oman, Pakistan, Panama, Peru, Philippines, Poland, Portugal, Qatar, Republic of Korea, Romania, Rwanda, San Marino, Saudi Arabia, Senegal, Seychelles, Sierra Leone, Singapore, Somalia, Spain, Sri Lanka, Sudan, Swaziland, Sweden, Switzerland, Syrian Arab Republic, Thailand, Togo, Trinidad and Tobago, Tunisia, Turkey, Uganda, Ukrainian SSR, USSR, United Arab Emirates, United Kingdom, United Republic of Cameroon, United Republic of Tanzania, United States, Upper Volta, Uruguay, Venezuela, Viet Nam, Yugoslavia, Zaire, Zambia, Zimbabwe.

President: Moustapha Niasse (Senegal).
Vice-Presidents: Botswana, Bulgaria, Cuba, Finland, India.
Rapporteur-General: Mohamed Sahnoun (Algeria).

Chairmen of committees:

Committee of the Whole: Francisco Paparoni (Venezuela).
Credentials Committee: Susan Nancy Gordon (Trinidad and Tobago).
Drafting Committee: Oladapo Olusola Fafowora (Nigeria).

International Conference on the Question of Palestine

The International Conference on the Question of Palestine was held at Geneva from 29 August to 7 September 1983. Participating were the following 117 States and the United Nations Council for Namibia:

Afghanistan, Albania, Algeria, Angola, Argentina, Austria, Bahrain, Bangladesh, Barbados, Benin, Bhutan, Bolivia, Brazil, Bulgaria, Burma, Burundi, Byelorussian SSR, Central African Republic, Chile, China, Colombia, Comoros, Congo, Cuba, Cyprus, Czechoslovakia, Democratic Kampuchea, Democratic People's Republic of Korea, Democratic Yemen, Djibouti, Dominican Republic, Ecuador, Egypt, El Salvador, Ethiopia, Finland, Gabon, Gambia, German Democratic Republic, Ghana, Greece, Grenada, Guinea, Guinea-Bissau, Guyana, Hungary, India, Indonesia, Iran, Iraq, Ivory Coast, Jamaica, Jordan, Kenya, Kuwait, Lao People's Democratic Republic, Lebanon, Liberia, Libyan Arab Jamahiriya, Madagascar, Malaysia, Maldives, Mali, Malta, Mauritania, Mexico, Mongolia, Morocco, Mozambique, Nepal, Nicaragua, Niger, Nigeria, Oman, Pakistan, Panama, Papua New Guinea, Peru, Philippines, Poland, Portugal, Qatar, Republic of Korea, Romania, Rwanda, San Marino, Saudi Arabia, Senegal, Seychelles, Sierra Leone, Singapore, Somalia, Spain, Sri Lanka, Sudan, Suriname, Sweden, Syrian Arab Republic, Thailand, Trinidad and Tobago, Tunisia, Turkey, Uganda, Ukrainian SSR, USSR, United Arab Emirates, United Republic of Cameroon, United Republic of Tanzania, Upper Volta, Uruguay, Venezuela, Viet Nam, Yemen, Yugoslavia, Zaire, Zambia, Zimbabwe.

The Palestine Liberation Organization participated in the Conference as the representative of the party most directly concerned. The Conference decided that it should be placed among the full participants in the Conference.

The following 20 States were represented by observers: Australia, Belgium, Canada, Costa Rica, Denmark, France, Germany, Federal Republic of, Guatemala, Holy See, Honduras, Iceland, Ireland, Italy, Japan, Luxembourg, Netherlands, New Zealand, Norway, Switzerland, United Kingdom.

President: Moustapha Niasse (Senegal).
Vice-Presidents: Algeria, Austria, Bangladesh, Benin, Burundi, Cuba, Ecuador, Egypt, Finland, German Democratic Republic, India, Malaysia, Nicaragua, Palestine Liberation Organization, Sudan, Turkey, Ukrainian SSR, United Arab Emirates, United Republic of Tanzania, Venezuela, Yugoslavia.
Rapporteur-General: Victor J. Gauci (Malta).

Officers of committees:

Main Committee: Abdullah Kamil (Indonesia), *Chairman*.
Credentials Committee: Lolita Janet Applewhaite (Barbados), *Presiding Officer*.

Second World Conference to Combat Racism and Racial Discrimination

The Second World Conference to Combat Racism and Racial Discrimination was held at Geneva from 1 to 12 August 1983. Participating were the following 128 States and the United Nations Council for Namibia:

Afghanistan, Albania, Algeria, Angola, Argentina, Australia, Austria, Bahrain, Bangladesh, Barbados, Belgium, Benin, Bhutan, Bolivia, Botswana, Brazil, Bulgaria, Burma, Burundi, Byelorussian SSR, Canada, Central African Republic, Chad, Chile, China, Colombia, Congo, Costa Rica, Cuba, Cyprus, Czechoslovakia, Democratic Kampuchea, Democratic People's Republic of Korea, Democratic Yemen, Denmark, Djibouti, Dominican Republic, Ecuador, Egypt, El Salvador, Ethiopia, Finland, France, Gabon, German Democratic Republic, Germany, Federal Republic of, Ghana, Greece, Guinea-Bissau, Haiti, Holy See, Honduras, Hungary, Iceland, India, Indonesia, Iran, Iraq, Ireland, Italy, Ivory Coast, Jamaica, Japan, Jordan, Kenya, Kuwait, Lebanon, Lesotho, Liberia, Libyan Arab Jamahiriya, Luxembourg, Madagascar, Malaysia, Mali, Mauritania, Mexico, Mongolia, Morocco, Mozambique, Nepal, Netherlands, New Zealand, Nicaragua, Nigeria, Norway, Oman, Pakistan, Panama, Peru, Philippines, Poland, Portugal, Qatar, Republic of Korea, Romania, Rwanda, Saint Lucia, Saudi Arabia, Senegal, Seychelles, Sierra Leone, Singapore, Somalia, Spain, Sri Lanka, Sudan, Sweden, Switzerland, Syrian Arab Republic, Thailand, Togo, Tunisia, Turkey, Uganda, Ukrainian SSR, USSR, United Arab Emirates, United Kingdom, United Republic of Cameroon, United Republic of Tanzania, Uruguay, Venezuela, Viet Nam, Yemen, Yugoslavia, Zaire, Zambia, Zimbabwe.

President: Héctor Charry Samper (Colombia).
Vice-Presidents: Bahrain, Burundi, Cuba, Italy, Nicaragua, Norway, Philippines, Somalia, USSR, Yugoslavia.
Rapporteur-General: A. K. H. Morshed (Bangladesh).
Secretary-General: James O. C. Jonah.

Chairmen of committees:
General Committee: Héctor Charry Samper (Colombia).
First Committee: Gerhard Richter (German Democratic Republic).

Second Committee: Francis Mahon Hayes (Ireland).
Credentials Committee: Oladapo Olusola Fafowora (Nigeria).

United Nations Conference on Succession of States in Respect of State Property, Archives and Debts

The United Nations Conference on Succession of States in Respect of State Property, Archives and Debts was held at Vienna, Austria, from 1 March to 8 April 1983. Participating were the following 90 States and the United Nations Council for Namibia:

Algeria, Angola, Argentina, Australia, Austria, Bangladesh, Belgium, Brazil, Bulgaria, Byelorussian SSR, Canada, Chile, Congo, Costa Rica, Cuba, Cyprus, Czechoslovakia, Democratic People's Republic of Korea, Democratic Yemen, Denmark, Ecuador, Egypt, Finland, France, Gabon, German Democratic Republic, Germany, Federal Republic of, Greece, Guatemala, Holy See, Honduras, Hungary, India, Indonesia, Iran, Iraq, Ireland, Israel, Italy, Ivory Coast, Japan, Jordan, Kenya, Kuwait, Lebanon, Libyan Arab Jamahiriya, Luxembourg, Malaysia, Mali, Mauritania, Mexico, Morocco, Mozambique, Netherlands, Nicaragua, Nigeria, Norway, Oman, Pakistan, Panama, Peru, Philippines, Poland, Portugal, Qatar, Republic of Korea, Romania, San Marino, Saudi Arabia, Senegal, Seychelles, Spain, Suriname, Sweden, Switzerland, Syrian Arab Republic, Thailand, Tunisia, Turkey, Ukrainian SSR, USSR, United Arab Emirates, United Kingdom, United States, Uruguay, Venezuela, Viet Nam, Yemen, Yugoslavia, Zaire.

President: Ignaz Seidl-Hohenveldern (Austria).
Vice-Presidents: Algeria, Bulgaria, Chile, Ecuador, Egypt, France, German Democratic Republic, India, Indonesia, Italy, Morocco, Nigeria, Norway, Pakistan, Suriname, Switzerland, USSR, United Arab Emirates, United Kingdom, United States, Uruguay, Zaire.

Chairmen of committees:
General Committee: Ignaz Seidl-Hohenveldern (Austria).
Committee of the Whole: Milan Sahovic (Yugoslavia).
Drafting Committee: Sompong Sucharitkul (Thailand).
Credentials Committee: Geraldo Eulálio do Nascimento e Silva (Brazil).

Security Council

The Security Council consists of 15 Member States of the United Nations, in accordance with the provisions of Article 23 of the United Nations Charter as amended in 1965.

MEMBERS

Permanent members: China, France, USSR, United Kingdom, United States.
Non-permanent members: Guyana, Jordan, Malta, Netherlands, Nicaragua, Pakistan, Poland, Togo, Zaire, Zimbabwe.

On 31 October 1983 (decision 38/306), the General Assembly elected Egypt, India, Peru, the Ukrainian SSR and the Upper Volta for a two-year term beginning on 1 January 1984, to replace Guyana, Jordan, Poland, Togo and Zaire, whose terms of office were to expire on 31 December 1983.

PRESIDENTS

The presidency of the Council rotates monthly, according to the English alphabetical listing of its member States. The following served as Presidents during 1983:

Month	Member	Representative
January	Togo	Atsu-Koffi Amega
February	USSR	O. A. Troyanovsky
March	United Kingdom	Sir John Adam Thomson
April	United States	Jeane J. Kirkpatrick
May	Zaire	Kamanda wa Kamanda
		Umba di Lutete
June	Zimbabwe	Elleck Kufakunesu Mashingaidze
July	China	Ling Qing
August	France	Luc de La Barre de Nanteuil
September	Guyana	Noel G. Sinclair
October	Jordan	Abdullah Salah
November	Malta	Victor J. Gauci
December	Netherlands	Max van der Stoel

Collective Measures Committee

The Collective Measures Committee (p. 1341) reports to both the General Assembly and the Security Council.

Military Staff Committee

The Military Staff Committee consists of the chiefs of staff of the permanent members of the Security Council or their representatives. It met fortnightly throughout 1983; the first meeting was held on 13 January and the last on 29 December.

Standing committees

Each of the two standing committees of the Security Council is composed of representatives of all Council members:

Committee of Experts (to examine the provisional rules of procedure of the Council and any other matters entrusted to it by the Council)
Committee on the Admission of New Members

In addition, the Council maintains an *ad hoc* Committee on Council Meetings Away from Headquarters.

Ad hoc bodies

Ad Hoc Committee established under resolution 507(1982)
Members: France *(Chairman)*, Guyana, Jordan, Uganda.[a]

[a]Not a Council member in 1983.

Ad Hoc Sub-Committee on Namibia
The *Ad Hoc* Sub-Committee on Namibia consists of all the members of the Security Council. It did not meet in 1983.

Committee of Experts established by the Security Council at its 1506th meeting
(on the question of micro-States)

The Committee of Experts consists of all the members of the Security Council. The chairmanship is rotated monthly in the English alphabetical order of the member States.

The Committee did not meet in 1983.

Committee on the Exercise of the Inalienable Rights of the Palestinian People

The Committee (p. 1342) reports to the General Assembly, which has also drawn the attention of the Security Council to the need for urgent action on the recommendations of the Committee.

Security Council Commission established under resolution 446(1979)
(to examine the situation relating to settlements in the Arab territories occupied since 1967, including Jerusalem)

Members:[a] Bolivia, Portugal *(Chairman)*, Zambia.

[a]Not Council members in 1983.

Security Council Commission of Inquiry established under resolution 496(1981)

Members: Ireland, Japan, Panama *(Chairman)*.

On 8 July 1983, the Council agreed that the Commission had fulfilled its mandate (p. 189).

Security Council Committee established by resolution 421(1977) concerning the question of South Africa

The Committee consists of all the members of the Security Council.

Special Committee against *Apartheid*

The Special Committee against *Apartheid* (p. 1345) reports to the General Assembly and, as appropriate, to the Security Council.

PEACE-KEEPING OPERATIONS AND SPECIAL MISSIONS

United Nations Truce Supervision Organization (UNTSO)
Chief of Staff: Lieutenant-General Emmanuel Alexander Erskine.

United Nations Disengagement Observer Force (UNDOF)
Force Commander: Major-General Carl-Gustav Stahl.

United Nations Interim Force in Lebanon (UNIFIL)
Force Commander: Lieutenant-General William Callaghan.

United Nations Peace-keeping Force in Cyprus (UNFICYP)
Special Representative of the Secretary-General in Cyprus: Hugo J. Gobbi.
Force Commander: Major-General Günther G. Greindl.

United Nations Military Observer Group in India and Pakistan (UNMOGIP)
Chief Military Observer: Brigadier-General Thor A. Johnsen.

United Nations Transition Assistance Group (UNTAG)
Authorized by the Security Council in 1978,[26] the United Nations Transition Assistance Group had not been emplaced in Namibia by the end of 1983.

Special Representative of the Secretary-General: Martti Ahtisaari.
Commander-designate: Lieutenant-General Dewan Prem Chand.

---

[26]Resolution 435(1978), 29 September 1978 (YUN 1978, p. 915).

Economic and Social Council

The Economic and Social Council consists of 54 Member States of the United Nations, elected by the General Assembly, each for a three-year term, in accordance with the provisions of Article 61 of the United Nations Charter as amended in 1965 and 1973.

MEMBERS

To serve until 31 December 1983: Argentina, Bangladesh, Burundi, Byelorussian SSR, Canada, China, Denmark, Fiji, India, Kenya, Nicaragua, Norway, Peru, Poland, Sudan, USSR, United Kingdom, United Republic of Cameroon.

To serve until 31 December 1984: Austria, Benin, Brazil, Colombia, France, Germany, Federal Republic of, Greece, Japan, Liberia, Mali, Pakistan, Portugal, Qatar, Romania, Saint Lucia, Swaziland, Tunisia, Venezuela.

To serve until 31 December 1985: Algeria, Botswana, Bulgaria, Congo, Djibouti, Ecuador, German Democratic Republic, Lebanon, Luxembourg, Malaysia, Mexico, Netherlands, New Zealand, Saudi Arabia, Sierra Leone, Suriname, Thailand, United States.

On 31 October and 21 November 1983 (decision 38/307), the General Assembly elected the following States for a three-year term beginning on 1 January 1984 to fill 17 of the 18 vacancies occurring on 31 December 1983: Argentina, Canada, China, Costa Rica, Finland, Indonesia, Papua New Guinea, Poland, Rwanda, Somalia, Sri Lanka, Sweden, Uganda, USSR, United Kingdom, Yugoslavia, Zaire. No further election was held in 1983 to fill the remaining seat, allocated to a member from Latin American States.

SESSIONS

Organizational session for 1983: United Nations Headquarters, 1-4 February.
First regular session of 1983: United Nations Headquarters, 3-27 May.
Second regular session of 1983: Geneva, 6-29 July.

OFFICERS
President: Sérgio Corrêa da Costa (Brazil).
Vice-Presidents: Peter Dietze (German Democratic Republic); Awad Mohamed Elhassan (Sudan); Adolf J. Kuen (Austria); Kesrouan Labaki (Lebanon) (until 11 July), Ibrahim Kharma (Lebanon) (from 11 July).

Subsidiary and other related organs

SUBSIDIARY ORGANS

In addition to three regular sessional committees, the Economic and Social Council may, at each session, set up other committees or working groups, of the whole or of limited membership, and refer to them any items on the agenda for study and report.

Other subsidiary organs reporting to the Council consist of functional commissions, regional commissions, standing committees, expert bodies and *ad hoc* bodies.

The inter-agency Administrative Committee on Co-ordination also reports to the Council.

Sessional bodies

SESSIONAL COMMITTEES

Each of the sessional committees of the Economic and Social Council consists of the 54 members of the Council.

First (Economic) Committee. Chairman: Adolf J. Kuen (Austria).
  Vice-Chairmen: Habib M. Kaabachi (Tunisia); Enrique de la Torre (Argentina) (until 7 July), Alberto Dumont (Argentina) (from 7 July).
Second (Social) Committee. Chairman: Kesrouan Labaki (Lebanon).
  Vice-Chairmen: Karl Borchard (Federal Republic of Germany); Kalin Mitrev (Bulgaria).

Third *(Programme and Co-ordination) Committee. Chairman:* Awad Mohamed Elhassan (Sudan). *Vice-Chairmen:* Konstantin Kolev (Bulgaria); Yukio Takasu (Japan).

SESSIONAL WORKING GROUP OF GOVERNMENTAL EXPERTS
ON THE IMPLEMENTATION OF THE INTERNATIONAL
COVENANT ON ECONOMIC, SOCIAL AND CULTURAL RIGHTS
The Sessional Working Group of Governmental Experts on the Implementation of the International Covenant on Economic, Social and Cultural Rights, which was to consist of 15 members elected by the Council from among the States parties to the Covenant, met at United Nations Headquarters from 18 April to 5 May 1983.

Members:
To serve until 31 December 1983: Colombia, Denmark, German Democratic Republic, Japan, Tunisia.
To serve until 31 December 1984: Bulgaria, Ecuador,[a] Jordan, Libyan Arab Jamahiriya, Spain.
To serve until 31 December 1985:[b] France, Kenya, Peru, USSR.

[a]Elected on 4 February 1983 (decision 1983/106).
[b]One seat allocated to a member from Asian States remained unfilled in 1983.

Chairman: Hisami Kurokochi (Japan).
Vice-Chairmen: Néjib Bouziri (Tunisia), Edwin Johnson (Ecuador), Ulrich Kords (German Democratic Republic).
Rapporteur: María de los Angeles Jiménez Butragueño (Spain).

On 25 May 1983 (decision 1983/161), the Economic and Social Council elected the following States for a three-year term beginning on 1 January 1984 to fill four of the five vacancies occurring on 31 December 1983: Denmark, German Democratic Republic, Japan, Tunisia. No further election was held in 1983 to fill the remaining seat, allocated to a member from Latin American States.
On 27 May 1983 (decision 1983/134), the Council decided that the Group's 1984 Bureau be constituted as follows: Chairman—Western European and other States; Vice-Chairmen—African States, Asian States, Eastern European States; Rapporteur—Latin American States.

Functional commissions and subsidiaries

Commission for Social Development
The Commission for Social Development consists of 32 members, elected for four-year terms by the Economic and Social Council according to a specific pattern of equitable geographical distribution.

Members:
To serve until 31 December 1983: Costa Rica, El Salvador, France, Indonesia, Kenya, Mongolia, Morocco, Netherlands, Ukrainian SSR, USSR, United States.
To serve until 31 December 1984: Chile, Italy, Madagascar, Panama, Philippines, Poland, Sudan, Sweden, Thailand, Turkey.
To serve until 31 December 1986: Argentina, Austria, Byelorussian SSR, Central African Republic, Cyprus, Ecuador, Finland, Ghana, India, Liberia, Togo.

The Commission held its twenty-eighth session at Vienna, Austria, from 7 to 16 February 1983. The members were represented as follows:
Argentina: Juan Carlos Beltramino. Austria: Udo Ehrlich-Adam, *Rapporteur.* Byelorussian SSR: A. V. Lyutsko. Chile: María Teresa Infante Barros. Costa Rica: Jorge Arturo Montero-Castro, *Chairman.* Cyprus: Mikis Demetriou Sparsis. Ecuador: Gladys Pozo de Ruiz. El Salvador: José Roberto Andino-Salazar. Finland: Pekka Harttila. France: Antoine Lion. Ghana: J. B. Amoako. India: Mir Nasrullah. Indonesia: Mr. Dradjat. Italy: Anna Maria Cavallone. Kenya: Joseph Muliro. Liberia: Francis B. S. Dunbar, *Vice-Chairman.* Mongolia: Luvsandanzangyn Ider. Morocco: Aicha Kabbaj. Netherlands: R. G. Deible. Panama: Lourdes C. Vallarino. Philippines: Leandro I. Verceles. Poland: Michal Dobroczynski, *Vice-Chairman.* Sudan: Rashida Abdel Mutalib. Sweden: Eva Nauckhoff. Thailand: Kosit Panpiemras, *Vice-Chairman.* Togo: Folly Glidjito Akakpo. Turkey: Istiklal Alpar. Ukrainian SSR: N. N. Varvartzev. USSR: A. P. Biryukova. United States: Roger Kirk.

On 25 May 1983 (decision 1983/161) and (with respect to Haiti) on 28 July (decision 1983/179), the Economic and Social Council elected

the following 11 members for a four-year term beginning on 1 January 1984 to fill the vacancies occurring on 31 December 1983: Canada, El Salvador, France, Haiti, Kenya, Malaysia, Mongolia, Morocco, Romania, USSR, United States.

Commission on Human Rights
The Commission on Human Rights consists of 43 members, elected for three-year terms by the Economic and Social Council according to a specific pattern of equitable geographical distribution.

Members:
To serve until 31 December 1983: Australia, Brazil, Fiji, France, Ghana, Jordan, Mexico, Philippines, Poland, Senegal, Uganda, United States, Yugoslavia, Zaire.
To serve until 31 December 1984: Argentina, Bulgaria, Canada, China, Cuba, Gambia, Germany, Federal Republic of, Italy, Japan, Pakistan, Rwanda, Togo, United Kingdom, Uruguay, Zimbabwe.
To serve until 31 December 1985: Bangladesh, Colombia, Costa Rica, Cyprus, Finland, India, Ireland, Libyan Arab Jamahiriya, Mozambique, Netherlands, Nicaragua, Ukrainian SSR, USSR, United Republic of Tanzania.

The Commission held its thirty-ninth session at Geneva from 31 January to 11 March 1983. The members were represented as follows:
Argentina: Gabriel O. Martínez. Australia: Pierre N. Hutton. Bangladesh: Abu Sayeed Chowdhury. Brazil: Carlos Calero Rodrigues. Bulgaria: Borislav Konstantinov. Canada: Yvon Beaulne. China: Li Luye. Colombia: Héctor Charry Samper. Costa Rica: Elías Soley Soler. Cuba: Luis Solá Vila. Cyprus: Andreas V. Mavrommatis. Fiji: Ross I. V. Ligairi. Finland: Heikki Talvitie. France: Claude-Albert Colliard. Gambia: Francis R. C. Blain. Germany, Federal Republic of: Wolfgang Behrends. Ghana: Jonas Kwami Dotse Foli. India: B. R. Bhagat. Ireland: Francis Mahon Hayes, *Vice-Chairman.* Italy: Giuseppe Walter Maccotta. Japan: Sadako Ogata. Jordan: Ghaleb Z. Barakat, *Vice-Chairman.* Libyan Arab Jamahiriya: Ali A. Treiki. Mexico: Antonio González de León, *Vice-Chairman.* Mozambique: Murade Isaac Murargy. Netherlands: Peter H. Kooijmans. Nicaragua: Leonte Herdocia Ortega. Pakistan: Agha Hilaly. Philippines: Armando D. Manalo. Poland: Adam Lopatka. Rwanda: Alphonse Sebazungu. Senegal: Alioune Sène. Togo: Koffi Adjoyi. Uganda: Olara A. Otunnu, *Chairman.* Ukrainian SSR: I. S. Khmel; V. P. Koutchinsky, *Rapporteur.* USSR: V. A. Zorin. United Kingdom: Viscount Colville of Culross. United Republic of Tanzania: Wilbert Kumalija Chagula. United States: Richard Schifter. Uruguay: Carlos Giambruno. Yugoslavia: Aleksandar Bozovic. Zaire: Bagbeni Adeito Nzengeya. Zimbabwe: Stephen Cletus Chiketa.

On 25 May 1983 (decision 1983/161), the Economic and Social Council elected the following 14 members for a three-year term beginning on 1 January 1984 to fill the vacancies occurring on 31 December 1983: Brazil, France, German Democratic Republic, Jordan, Kenya, Mauritania, Mexico, Philippines, Senegal, Spain, Syrian Arab Republic, United Republic of Cameroon, United States, Yugoslavia.

AD HOC WORKING GROUP OF EXPERTS
(established by Commission on Human Rights resolution 2(XXIII) of 6 March 1967)
Members: Balanda Mikuin Leliel (Zaire); Annan Arkyin Cato, *Chairman/Rapporteur* (Ghana); Humberto Díaz-Casanueva (Chile); Felix Ermacora (Austria); Branimir M. Jankovic, *Vice-Chairman* (Yugoslavia); Mulka Govinda Reddy (India).

GROUP OF THREE ESTABLISHED UNDER THE
INTERNATIONAL CONVENTION ON THE SUPPRESSION
AND PUNISHMENT OF THE CRIME OF *APARTHEID*
Members: Bulgaria, Mexico, Zaire.

The Group of Three held its sixth session at Geneva from 24 to 28 January 1983. The members were represented as follows:
Bulgaria: Emile Golemanov. Mexico: Alberto Székely, Francisco Cruz González, Patricia Espinosa. Zaire: Lisembe Elebe, *Chairman/Rapporteur.*

SUB-COMMISSION ON PREVENTION OF
DISCRIMINATION AND PROTECTION OF MINORITIES
The Sub-Commission consists of 26 members elected by the Commission on Human Rights from candidates nominated by Member States

of the United Nations, in accordance with a scheme to ensure equitable geographical distribution. Members serve in their individual capacity as experts, rather than as governmental representatives, each for a three-year term.

The Sub-Commission held its thirty-sixth session at Geneva from 15 August to 9 September 1983.

Members (until March 1984): Marc Bossuyt, *Vice-Chairman* (Belgium); John Carey (United States);[a] Dumitru Ceausu, *Vice-Chairman* (Romania); Abu Sayeed Chowdhury (Bangladesh); Erica-Irene A. Daes (Greece); Asbjorn Eide (Norway); Raúl Ferrero Costa, *Vice-Chairman* (Peru); Jonas Kwami Dotse Foli (Ghana); Riyadh Aziz Hadi (Iraq); Ibrahim Sulaiman Jimeta (Nigeria); Louis Joinet (France); Nasser Kaddour (Syrian Arab Republic); Ahmed Mohamed Khalifa (Egypt), Antonio Martínez Báez (Mexico); Syed S. A. Masud, *Rapporteur* (India); Chama L. C. Mubanga-Chipoya (Zambia); Mohamed Yousif Mudawi (Sudan); Elizabeth Odio Benito (Costa Rica); Julio Oyhanarte (Argentina); Syed Sharifuddin Pirzada (Pakistan); Jorge Eduardo Ritter (Panama); V. N. Sofinsky (USSR); Ivan Tosevski (Yugoslavia); Halima Embarek Warzazi, *Chairman* (Morocco); Benjamin Charles George Whitaker (United Kingdom); Fisseha Yimer (Ethiopia).

[a]Elected on 11 March 1983 to replace W. Beverly Carter, Jr. (United States), who had died in 1982.

Working Group
(established by resolution 2(XXIV) of 16 August 1971 of the Sub-Commission on Prevention of Discrimination and Protection of Minorities pursuant to Economic and Social Council resolution 1503(XLVIII))

The Working Group on Communications concerning human rights held its twelfth session at Geneva from 1 to 12 August 1983.

Members: Marc Bossuyt (Belgium); Raúl Ferrero Costa (Peru); Syed S. A. Masud (India); V. N. Sofinsky (USSR); Fisseha Yimer, *Chairman/Rapporteur* (Ethiopia).

Working Group
(established on 21 August 1974 by resolution 11(XXVII) of the Sub-Commission on Prevention of Discrimination and Protection of Minorities)

The Working Group on Slavery held its ninth session at Geneva from 8 to 12 August 1983.

Members: Dumitru Ceausu (Romania);IAbu Sayeed Chowdhury, *Chairman/Rapporteur* (Bangladesh); Chama L. C. Mubanga-Chipoya (Zambia); Elizabeth Odio Benito (Costa Rica); Benjamin Charles George Whitaker (United Kingdom).

Working Group on Indigenous Populations

The Working Group on Indigenous Populations held its second session at Geneva from 8 to 12 and on 23 August 1983.

Members: Asbjorn Eide, *Chairman/Rapporteur* (Norway); Mohamed Yousif Mudawi (Sudan); Jorge Eduardo Ritter (Panama); Ahmed Saker (Syrian Arab Republic); Ivan Tosevski (Yugoslavia).

WORKING GROUP OF GOVERNMENTAL EXPERTS ON THE RIGHT TO DEVELOPMENT

The Working Group of Governmental Experts on the Right to Development held two sessions in 1983, at Geneva: its sixth from 13 to 24 June; and its seventh from 31 October to 11 November.

Members: Luís Aguirre Gallardo (Panama); Juan Alvarez Vita (Peru); Peter L. Berger (United States); D. V. Bykov (USSR); Paul J. I. M. de Waart (Netherlands); Georges Gautier, *Rapporteur* (France); Riyadh Aziz Hadi (Iraq); Julio Heredia Pérez, *Vice-Chairman* (Cuba); Fatma Z. Ksentini (Algeria); Viswanathan Ramachandran, *Vice-Chairman* (India); Ahmed Saker (Syrian Arab Republic); Alioune Sène, *Chairman* (Senegal); Kongit Sinegiorgis (Ethiopia); Henryk J. Sokalski (Poland); Danilo Turk, *Vice-Chairman* (Yugoslavia).

WORKING GROUP ON ENFORCED OR INVOLUNTARY DISAPPEARANCES

During 1983, the mandate of the Working Group on Enforced or Involuntary Disappearances was extended for one year by a Commission on Human Rights resolution of 22 February, as approved by the Economic and Social Council on 27 May (decision 1983/141).

The Working Group held three sessions in 1983: its tenth, at United Nations Headquarters, from 13 to 17 June; and its eleventh and twelfth, both at Geneva, from 26 to 30 September and from 5 to 9 December, respectively.

Members: Viscount Colville of Culross, *Chairman/Rapporteur* (United Kingdom); Jonas Kwami Dotse Foli (Ghana); Agha Hilaly (Pakistan); Ivan Tosevski (Yugoslavia); Luis Alberto Varela Quirós (Costa Rica).

WORKING GROUPS
(to study situations revealing a consistent pattern of gross violations of human rights)

Working Group established by Commission on Human Rights decision 1982/103 of 5 March 1982:
Members: Ivon Beaulne, *Chairman/Rapporteur* (Canada); Borislav Konstantinov (Bulgaria); E. E. E. Mtango (United Republic of Tanzania); Andreas C. Pouyouros (Cyprus); Luis Solá Vila (Cuba).

Working Group established by Commission on Human Rights decision 1983/110 of 28 February 1983:
Members: Francis Mahon Hayes (Ireland); Borislav Konstantinov (Bulgaria); E. E. E. Mtango (United Republic of Tanzania); Sadako Ogata (Japan); Luis Solá Vila (Cuba).

WORKING GROUPS (OPEN-ENDED)

Working Group established by Commission on Human Rights resolution 1982/39 of 11 March 1982 (to draft a convention on the rights of the child):
Chairman/Rapporteur: Adam Lopatka (Poland).

Working Group established by Commission on Human Rights resolution 1982/44 of 11 March 1982 (to draft a convention against torture and other cruel, inhuman or degrading treatment or punishment):
Chairman/Rapporteur: Jan Herman Burgers (Netherlands).

Commission on Narcotic Drugs

The Commission on Narcotic Drugs consisted of 30 members, elected for four-year terms by the Economic and Social Council from among the Members of the United Nations and members of the specialized agencies and the parties to the Single Convention on Narcotic Drugs, 1961, with due regard for the adequate representation of *(a)* countries which are important producers of opium or coca leaves, *(b)* countries which are important in the manufacture of narcotic drugs, and *(c)* countries in which drug addiction or the illicit traffic in narcotic drugs constitutes an important problem, as well as taking into account the principle of equitable geographical distribution.

Members:
To serve until 31 December 1983: Argentina, Colombia, France, Germany, Federal Republic of, Hungary, India, Italy, Madagascar, Malawi, Norway, Pakistan, Spain, Thailand, United States, Yugoslavia.
To serve until 31 December 1985: Australia, Bahamas, Belgium, Bulgaria, Japan, Malaysia, Mexico, Nigeria, Panama, Republic of Korea, Senegal, Turkey, USSR, United Kingdom, Zaire.

The Commission held its thirtieth session at Vienna, Austria, from 7 to 16 February 1983. The members were represented as follows:
Argentina: Juan Carlos García Fernández, *Chairman*. Australia: Duncan Campbell. Bahamas: Missouri A. Sherman-Peter. Belgium: B. J. A. Huyghe-Braeckmans. Bulgaria: Alexandrina Nentcheva. Colombia: Gustavo Rodriguez Vargas. France: François Colcombet. Germany, Federal Republic of: Oskar Schroeder (until 13 February), Wolfgang Hoffmann (from 14 February). Hungary: Istvan Bayer, *First Vice-Chairman*. India: Maruthi Vasudev Narayan Rao. Italy: Raffaele Costa. Japan: Tsutomu Shimomura. Madagascar: Maurice Randrianame, *Second*

Vice-Chairman. Malaysia: Rozhan Kuntom. Mexico: Luis Alberto Barrero Stahl. Nigeria: P. O. Emafo. Norway: Torbjorn Mork. Pakistan: Mairaj Husain, *Rapporteur*. Panama: Laura Torres de Rodríguez. Republic of Korea: Dongsoon Park. Senegal: Mounirou Ciss. Spain: Enrique Suárez de Puga y Villegas. Thailand: Chavalit Yodmani. Turkey: Ecmel Barutcu. USSR: E. A. Babayan. United Kingdom: Brian Oliver Bubbear. United States: Dominick L. DiCarlo. Yugoslavia: Petar Dzundev. Zaire: Bintou-a Tshiabola.

On 24 May 1983, the Economic and Social Council decided to enlarge the Commission's membership from 30 to 40, with effect from 1 January 1984.

On 25 May (decision 1983/161) and (with respect to Algeria, the German Democratic Republic and the Ivory Coast) on 28 July (decision 1983/179), the Council elected the following 25 members, for terms beginning on 1 January 1984 and expiring on 31 December of the year indicated, to fill the vacancies occurring on 31 December 1983 and the 10 additional seats: 1985—Argentina, Austria, Hungary, India, Ivory Coast; 1987—Algeria, Brazil, Canada, Colombia, Finland, France, German Democratic Republic, Germany, Federal Republic of, Greece, Iran, Italy, Madagascar, Morocco, Netherlands, Pakistan, Peru, Sri Lanka, Thailand, United States, Yugoslavia.

SUB-COMMISSION ON ILLICIT DRUG TRAFFIC AND
RELATED MATTERS IN THE NEAR AND MIDDLE EAST
Members: Afghanistan, Iran, Pakistan, Sweden, Turkey.

During 1983, the Sub-Commission held two sessions at Vienna, Austria: its fifteenth on 4 February, and its sixteenth on 3 and 4 October. The members were represented as follows:

Afghanistan: Abdullah Hamkar, Enayatullah Nabiel (fifteenth session); Gul Mohammed Andar, Mohammed Naim (sixteenth session). Iran: Dr. Ahmad Mohit, Dr. Seyed Ahmad Vaezi (fifteenth session). Pakistan: Mairaj Husain, *Vice-Chairman;* Aziz Ahmad Khan. Sweden: Lars Hultstrand; Staffan Vangby (fifteenth session). Turkey: Ecmel Barutcu, *Chairman;* Hilal Baskal, Fugen Ok.

MEETING OF OPERATIONAL HEADS
OF NATIONAL NARCOTICS LAW ENFORCEMENT
AGENCIES, FAR EAST REGION (HONLEA)
A meeting to co-ordinate regional activities directed against illicit drug traffic has been convened annually in one of the region's capitals following endorsement on 15 May 1974 by the Economic and Social Council of a recommendation by the *Ad Hoc* Committee on Illicit Traffic in the Far East Region to hold such a meeting.[27]

The meeting is open to any country or territory in the region approved by the Commission, as well as to observers from the Association of South-East Asian Nations, the Colombo Plan Bureau, the Customs Co-operation Council, the International Criminal Police Organization and the International Narcotics Control Board. Any interested Government outside the region may be invited by the Secretary-General to send an observer at its own expense.

The tenth meeting of HONLEA was held at New Delhi, India, on 7 and 8 November 1983. It was followed on 9 and 10 November by the first joint meeting between HONLEA and the Sub-Commission on Illicit Drug Traffic and Related Matters in the Near and Middle East with the aim of further improving co-ordinated drug law enforcement action between the two regions.

Commission on the Status of Women
The Commission on the Status of Women consists of 32 members, elected for four-year terms by the Economic and Social Council according to a specific pattern of equitable geographical distribution.

The Commission was designated by the Council as the preparatory body for the World Conference to Review and Appraise the Achievements of the United Nations Decade for Women (p. 1363), scheduled for 1985.

The Commission did not hold a regular session in 1983.

Members:
To serve until 31 December 1983: China, Cuba, France, German Democratic Republic, Guatemala, Honduras, Lesotho, Nigeria, Norway, Pakistan.

To serve until 31 December 1984: Canada, Egypt, India, Italy, Japan, Spain, Sudan, Trinidad and Tobago, Ukrainian SSR, Venezuela, Zaire.
To serve until 31 December 1986: Australia, Czechoslovakia, Indonesia, Kenya, Liberia, Mexico, Philippines, Sierra Leone, USSR, United Kingdom, United States.

On 25 May 1983 (decision 1983/161), the Economic and Social Council elected the following 10 members for a four-year term beginning on 1 January 1984 to fill the vacancies occurring on 31 December 1983: China, Cuba, Denmark, Ecuador, German Democratic Republic, Germany, Federal Republic of, Nicaragua, Pakistan, Togo, Zambia.

Population Commission
The Population Commission consists of 27 members, elected for four-year terms by the Economic and Social Council according to a specific pattern of equitable geographical distribution. The Commission was designated by the Council as the Preparatory Committee for the International Conference on Population (p. 1363), scheduled for 1984.
The Commission did not meet in 1983.

Members:
To serve until 31 December 1983: Ecuador, Finland, France, Indonesia, Morocco, Nigeria, Sierra Leone, Sri Lanka, Ukrainian SSR.
To serve until 31 December 1984: Greece, Honduras, Hungary, Netherlands, Norway, Peru, Rwanda, Thailand, Zaire.
To serve until 31 December 1985: Bolivia, China, Japan, Mexico, Sudan, USSR, United Kingdom, United States, Zambia.

On 25 May 1983 (decision 1983/161) the Economic and Social Council elected the following nine members for a four-year term beginning on 1 January 1984 to fill the vacancies occurring on 31 December 1983: Bulgaria, Costa Rica, Egypt, France, India, Malaysia, Nigeria, Sweden, Togo.

Statistical Commission
The Statistical Commission consists of 24 members, elected for four-year terms by the Economic and Social Council according to a specific pattern of equitable geographical distribution.

Members:
To serve until 31 December 1983: Austria, Czechoslovakia, Ecuador, Ghana, Hungary, India, Iraq, Kenya.
To serve until 31 December 1984: Australia, Brazil, Finland, Japan, Malaysia, Mexico, Ukrainian SSR, United Kingdom.
To serve until 31 December 1985: Argentina, France, Ireland, Libyan Arab Jamahiriya, Nigeria, Spain, Togo, USSR.

The Commission held its twenty-second session at United Nations Headquarters from 7 to 16 March 1983. The members were represented as follows:
Argentina: Lelia Boeri de Cervetto, *Vice-Chairman*. Australia: Roy James Cameron. Austria: Josef Schmidl. Brazil: Jessé de Souza Montello. Czechoslovakia: Vladimir Micka. Ecuador: Wilson Ruales. Finland: Olavi E. Niitamo. France: Edmond Malinvaud. Ghana: Emmanuel Oti Boateng, *Vice-Chairman*. Hungary: Vera Nyitrai, *Chairman*. India: Kiron Chandra Seal. Iraq: Wisam Jamel Tawfik. Ireland: Thomas Patrick Linehan, *Vice-Chairman*. Japan: Saburo Kawai. Libyan Arab Jamahiriya: Mohamed Shellid. Malaysia: Khoo Teik Huat, *Rapporteur*. Mexico: Jaime Alatorre. Spain: Francisco Azorín Poch. Togo: Dzigbodi Bouaka. Ukrainian SSR: A. I. Troyan. USSR: V. I. Guryev. United Kingdom: Sir John Boreham.

On 25 May 1983 (decision 1983/161) the Economic and Social Council elected the following eight members for a four-year term beginning on 1 January 1984 to fill the vacancies occurring on 31 December 1983: Bulgaria, China, Cuba, Czechoslovakia, Ghana, Kenya, Pakistan, United States.

WORKING GROUP ON INTERNATIONAL
STATISTICAL PROGRAMMES AND CO-ORDINATION
The Working Group consists of the Bureau of the Statistical Commission; the representatives to the Commission of the two major contributors to the United Nations budget, unless these are already represented

---

[27]Resolution 1845(LVI) (YUN 1974, p. 615).

in the Bureau; and one representative to the Commission from a developing country from among members of each of the following: ECA, ECLA, ECWA and ESCAP, unless these are also already represented in the Bureau. Members serve two-year terms.

The Working Group held its tenth session at Geneva from 26 to 28 September 1983. Attending were:

Emmanuel Oti Boateng (Ghana); V. I. Guryev (USSR); Khoo Teik Huat (Malaysia); Thomas Patrick Linehan (Ireland); Vera Nyitrai, *Chairman* (Hungary).

Regional commissions

Economic and Social Commission for Asia and the Pacific (ESCAP)

The Economic and Social Commission for Asia and the Pacific held its thirty-ninth session at Bangkok, Thailand, from 19 to 29 April 1983.

Members: Afghanistan, Australia, Bangladesh, Bhutan, Burma, China, Democratic Kampuchea, Fiji, France, India, Indonesia, Iran, Japan, Lao People's Democratic Republic, Malaysia, Maldives, Mongolia, Nauru, Nepal, Netherlands, New Zealand, Pakistan, Papua New Guinea, Philippines, Republic of Korea, Samoa, Singapore, Solomon Islands, Sri Lanka, Thailand, Tonga, USSR, United Kingdom, United States, Viet Nam.

Associate members: Brunei, Cook Islands, Guam, Hong Kong, Kiribati, Niue, Trust Territory of the Pacific Islands, Tuvalu, Vanuatu.[a]

Switzerland, not a Member of the United Nations, participates in a consultative capacity in the work of the Commission.

[a]Retained associate membership in 1983 although admitted to the United Nations on 15 September 1981.

Chairman: A. M. A. Muhith (Bangladesh).

Vice-Chairmen: J. Cecil Cocker (Tonga), Ha Van Lau (Viet Nam), He Ying (China), Dong Whie Kim (Republic of Korea), Toshio Kimura (Japan), Mochtar Kusumaatmadja (Indonesia), Dennis Lulei (Solomon Islands), M. H. M. Naina Marikkar (Sri Lanka), Mohan Man Sainju (Nepal), Siddhi Savetsila (Thailand), Vishwanath Pratap Singh (India), Soubanh Srithirath (Lao People's Democratic Republic).

Following are the main subsidiary bodies of the Commission:

For advice on policy and direction: Advisory Committee of Permanent Representatives and Other Representatives Designated by Members of the Commission.

For sectoral review and project formulation and programming: Committee on Agricultural Development; Committee on Development Planning; Committee on Industry, Technology, Human Settlements and the Environment; Committee on Natural Resources; Committee on Population; Committee on Shipping, and Transport and Communications; Committee on Social Development; Committee on Statistics; Committee on Trade; Special Body on Land-locked Countries. *Ad hoc* conferences are convened for issues not dealt with by the committees.

For project implementation: Advisory Council, Statistical Institute for Asia and the Pacific; Committee for Co-ordination of Joint Prospecting for Mineral Resources in Asian Offshore Areas; Committee for Co-ordination of Joint Prospecting for Mineral Resources in South Pacific Offshore Areas; Governing Board, Regional Co-ordination Centre for Research and Development of Coarse Grains, Pulses, Roots and Tuber Crops in the Humid Tropics of Asia and the Pacific; Governing Council, Regional Mineral Resources Development Centre; Interim Committee for Co-ordination of Investigations of the Lower Mekong Basin; Management Board, Asian and Pacific Development Centre; Typhoon Committee.

Economic Commission for Africa (ECA)

The Economic Commission for Africa meets in annual session at the ministerial level known as the Conference of Ministers.

The Commission held its eighteenth session (ninth meeting of the Conference of Ministers) at Addis Ababa, Ethiopia, from 27 April to 2 May 1983.

Members: Algeria, Angola, Benin, Botswana, Burundi, Cape Verde, Central African Republic, Chad, Comoros, Congo, Djibouti, Egypt, Equatorial Guinea, Ethiopia, Gabon, Gambia, Ghana, Guinea, Guinea-Bissau, Ivory Coast, Kenya, Lesotho, Liberia, Libyan Arab Jamahiriya, Madagascar, Malawi, Mali, Mauritania, Mauritius, Morocco, Mozambique, Niger, Nigeria, Rwanda, Sao Tome and Principe, Senegal, Seychelles, Sierra Leone, Somalia, South Africa,[a] Sudan, Swaziland, Togo, Tunisia, Uganda, United Republic of Cameroon, United Republic of Tanzania, Upper Volta, Zaire, Zambia, Zimbabwe.

Switzerland, not a Member of the United Nations, participates in a consultative capacity in the work of the Commission.

[a]On 30 July 1963, the Economic and Social Council decided that South Africa should not take part in the work of ECA until conditions for constructive co-operation had been restored by a change in South Africa's racial policy (resolution 974 D IV (XXXVI), YUN 1963, p. 274).

Chairman: Hailu Yimenu (Ethiopia).
First Vice-Chairman: Ambroise Mulindangabo (Rwanda).
Second Vice-Chairman: Taieb Ben Cheik (Morocco).
Rapporteur: Ebun Oyagbola (Nigeria).

The Commission has established the following principal legislative organs:

Conference of Ministers; sectoral ministerial conferences, each assisted by an appropriate committee of technical officials; Council of Ministers of each Multinational Programming and Operational Centre, assisted by its committee of officials.

The Commission has also established the following subsidiary bodies:

Joint Conference of African Planners, Statisticians and Demographers, and Technical Preparatory Committee of the Whole (two standing technical bodies); Governing Council, African Institute for Economic Development and Planning; Intergovernmental Committee of Experts for Science and Technology Development; Joint Intergovernmental Regional Committee on Human Settlements and Environment; Regional Institute for Population Studies.

Economic Commission for Europe (ECE)

The Economic Commission for Europe held its thirty-eighth session at Geneva from 12 to 23 April 1983.

Members: Albania, Austria, Belgium, Bulgaria, Byelorussian SSR, Canada, Cyprus, Czechoslovakia, Denmark, Finland, France, German Democratic Republic, Germany, Federal Republic of, Greece, Hungary, Iceland, Ireland, Italy, Luxembourg, Malta, Netherlands, Norway, Poland, Portugal, Romania, Spain, Sweden, Switzerland, Turkey, Ukrainian SSR, USSR, United Kingdom, United States, Yugoslavia.

The Holy See, Liechtenstein and San Marino, which are not Members of the United Nations, participate in a consultative capacity in the work of the Commission.

Chairman: Fernando Reino (Portugal).
Vice-Chairman: Lyuben Gotsev (Bulgaria).
Rapporteurs: Jan Bielawski (Poland), Philip McDonagh (Ireland).

Following are the principal subsidiary bodies of the Commission:

Chemical Industry Committee; Coal Committee; Committee on Agricultural Problems; Committee on Electric Power; Committee on Gas; Committee on Housing, Building and Planning; Committee on the Development of Trade; Committee on Water Problems; Conference of European Statisticians; Inland Transport Committee; Senior Advisers to ECE Governments on Environmental Problems; Senior Advisers to ECE Governments on Science and Technology; Senior Economic Advisers to ECE Governments; Steel Committee; Timber Committee.

Other subsidiary bodies are: Senior Advisers to ECE Governments on Energy; Working Party on Engineering Industries and Automation.

Ad hoc meetings of experts are convened for sectors of activity not dealt with by these principal bodies.

Economic Commission for Latin America (ECLA)

The Economic Commission for Latin America and its Committee of the Whole did not meet in 1983.

Members: Antigua and Barbuda, Argentina, Bahamas, Barbados, Belize, Bolivia, Brazil, Canada, Chile, Colombia, Costa Rica, Cuba, Dominica, Dominican Republic, Ecuador, El Salvador, France, Grenada, Guatemala, Guyana, Haiti, Honduras, Jamaica, Mexico, Netherlands, Nicaragua, Panama, Paraguay, Peru, Saint Christopher and Nevis,[a] Saint Lucia, Saint Vincent and the Grenadines, Spain, Suriname, Trinidad and Tobago, United Kingdom, United States, Uruguay, Venezuela.
Associate members: Montserrat, Netherlands Antilles.

Switzerland, not a Member of the United Nations, participates in a consultative capacity in the work of the Commission.

[a]Became a full member on 23 September 1983.

The Commission has established the following principal subsidiary bodies: Caribbean Development and Co-operation Committee; Central American Economic Co-operation Committee and its Inter-agency Committee; Committee of High-level Government Experts; Committee of the Whole; Technical Committee, Latin American Institute for Economic and Social Planning; Trade Committee.

Economic Commission for Western Asia (ECWA)

The Economic Commission for Western Asia held its tenth session at Baghdad, Iraq, from 7 to 11 May 1983.

Members: Bahrain, Democratic Yemen, Egypt, Iraq, Jordan, Kuwait, Lebanon, Oman, Qatar, Saudi Arabia, Syrian Arab Republic, United Arab Emirates, Yemen; Palestine Liberation Organization.

Chairman: Walid Asfour (Jordan).
Vice-Chairmen: Haidar Abu Bakr Al-Attas (Democratic Yemen), Ali Hassan Khalaf (Qatar).
Rapporteur: Hammam Radi Al Shama'a (Iraq).

The Commission has one main subsidiary organ, the Standing Committee for the Programme, composed of all ECWA members.

Standing committees

Commission on Human Settlements

The Commission on Human Settlements consists of 58 members elected by the Economic and Social Council for three-year terms according to a specific pattern of equitable geographical distribution; it reports to the General Assembly through the Council.

The Commission held its sixth session at Helsinki, Finland, from 25 April to 6 May 1983.

Members:
To serve until 31 December 1983: Argentina, Barbados, Bulgaria, Burundi, Denmark, Finland, Guinea, Jamaica, Japan, Mexico, Pakistan, Philippines, Somalia, Spain, Swaziland, Syrian Arab Republic, USSR, United Republic of Tanzania, United States, Zambia.
To serve until 31 December 1984: Bangladesh, Bolivia, Byelorussian SSR, Chile, Cyprus, El Salvador, Germany, Federal Republic of, Greece, India, Italy, Jordan, Kenya, Liberia, Morocco, New Zealand, Romania, Sri Lanka, Sudan, Zimbabwe.
To serve until 31 December 1985: Algeria, Canada, Colombia, Cuba, France, German Democratic Republic, Hungary, Indonesia, Lebanon,[a] Libyan Arab Jamahiriya, Malaysia,[a] Netherlands, Nigeria, Norway, Papua New Guinea, Peru, Sierra Leone, Sweden, Uganda.

[a]Elected on 25 May (decision 1983/161) and on 4 February 1983 (decision 1983/106), respectively.

Chairman: Arno Hannus (Finland).
Vice-Chairmen: Juan Carlos Arlía (Argentina), Marvis Muyunda (Zambia), Stefan Staynov (Bulgaria).
Rapporteur: Amir Ali Mondal (Bangladesh).

On 25 May 1983 (decision 1983/161) and (with respect to Turkey) on 28 July (decision 1983/179), the Economic and Social Council elected the following 20 members for a three-year term beginning on 1 January 1984 to fill the vacancies occurring on 31 December 1983: Bulgaria, Central African Republic, Finland, Gabon, Ghana, Guinea, Honduras, Iraq, Japan, Nicaragua, Pakistan, Philippines, Rwanda, Spain, Turkey, USSR, United Republic of Tanzania, United States, Venezuela.

Commission on Transnational Corporations

The Commission on Transnational Corporations consists of 48 members, elected from all States for three-year terms by the Economic and Social Council according to a specific pattern of geographical distribution.

During 1983, the Commission held a special session, open to the participation of all States, from 7 to 18 March and from 9 to 21 May, and its ninth session from 20 to 30 June, both at United Nations Headquarters.

Members:
To serve until 31 December 1983:[a] Argentina, Bangladesh,[b] China, Costa Rica, Egypt, France, German Democratic Republic, Germany, Federal Republic of, Guatemala, Guinea, Japan, Libyan Arab Jamahiriya, Romania, Sierra Leone, Switzerland.
To serve until 31 December 1984: Algeria, Canada, Congo, Ghana, India, Iran, Italy, Jamaica, Pakistan, Peru, Republic of Korea, Swaziland, Turkey, Ukrainian SSR, Venezuela, Yugoslavia.
To serve until 31 December 1985: Bahamas, Brazil, Central African Republic, Cuba, Cyprus, Indonesia, Kenya, Mexico, Netherlands, Nigeria, Norway, Thailand, Uganda, USSR, United Kingdom, United States.
Expert advisers (to serve through the tenth (1984) session): Michael A. Ajomo (Nigeria), Friedrich Dribbusch (Federal Republic of Germany), Wim Kok (Netherlands), Elias Mashasi (United Republic of Tanzania), Charles Albert Michalet (France), Zuhayr Mikdashi (Lebanon), Carlos Omar Navarro Carrasco (Venezuela), Jones Santos Neves (Brazil), Mario Joel Ramos da Silva (Portugal), Bogdan Sosnowski (Poland), David Sycip (Philippines), Louis von Planta (Switzerland), Branko Vukmir (Yugoslavia), Nat Weinberg (United States), Ralph A. Weller (United States), Eduardo White (Argentina).

[a]One seat allocated to a member from Asian States remained unfilled in 1983.
[b]Elected on 4 February 1983 (decision 1983/106).

Special session
Chairman: Sergio González-Gálvez (Mexico).
Vice-Chairmen: Horst Heininger (German Democratic Republic), Jürgen Kühn (Federal Republic of Germany), Nitish Kumar Sengupta (India).
Rapporteur: Raouf A. Saad (Egypt).

Ninth session
Chairman: Hassan Gadel Hak (Egypt)
Vice-Chairmen: Luigi Ferrari Bravo (Italy), Horst Heininger (German Democratic Republic), Irtiza Husain (Pakistan).
Rapporteur: Peter D. Maynard (Bahamas).

On 25 May 1983 (decision 1983/161) and (with respect to Czechoslovakia and the Philippines) on 28 July (decision 1983/179), the Economic and Social Council elected the following 16 members for a three-year term beginning on 1 January 1984 to fill the vacancies occurring on 31 December 1983: Bangladesh, China, Colombia, Costa Rica, Czechoslovakia, Egypt, France, German Democratic Republic, Germany, Federal Republic of, Guinea, Japan, Morocco, Philippines, Switzerland, Togo, Trinidad and Tobago.

INTERGOVERNMENTAL WORKING GROUP OF EXPERTS ON INTERNATIONAL STANDARDS OF ACCOUNTING AND REPORTING

The Intergovernmental Working Group of Experts on International Standards of Accounting and Reporting (p. 1363) reports to the Commission on Transnational Corporations.

Committee for Programme and Co-ordination

The Committee for Programme and Co-ordination is the main subsidiary organ of the Economic and Social Council and of the General Assembly for planning, programming and co-ordination and reports directly to both. It consists of 21 members nominated by the Council and elected by the Assembly for three-year terms according to a specific pattern of equitable geographical distribution.

During 1983, the Committee held organizational meetings on 11 and 29 April, and its twenty-third session from 9 May to 4 June, resumed from 29 August to 12 September, all at United Nations Headquarters.

Members:
To serve until 31 December 1983: Brazil, India, Japan, Morocco, Philippines, Senegal, United Republic of Cameroon.
To serve until 31 December 1984: Germany, Federal Republic of, Netherlands, Pakistan, Romania, Trinidad and Tobago, United Kingdom, Yugoslavia.
To serve until 31 December 1985: Argentina, Chile, Ethiopia, France, Nigeria, USSR, United States.

Chairman: Angel María Oliveri López (Argentina).
Vice-Chairmen: Jan Berteling (Netherlands), Ion Goritza (Romania), Tommo Monthe (United Republic of Cameroon).
Rapporteur: Banbit A. Roy (India).

On 25 May 1983 (decision 1983/161), the Economic and Social Council nominated the following eight Member States of the United Nations, seven of which were to be elected by the General Assembly, for a three-year term beginning on 1 January 1984 to fill the vacancies occurring on 31 December 1983: Brazil, Egypt, India, Indonesia, Iraq, Japan, Liberia, United Republic of Cameroon. All but Iraq were elected by the Assembly on 15 December 1983 (decision 38/318).

Committee on Natural Resources

The Committee on Natural Resources consists of 54 members, elected by the Economic and Social Council for four-year terms in accordance with the geographical distribution of seats in the Council.

The Committee held its eighth session at United Nations Headquarters from 8 to 17 June 1983.

Members:
To serve until 31 December 1984:[a] Bangladesh, Belgium, Botswana, Brazil, Canada, Colombia, Dominican Republic, Greece, Guinea, India, Jamaica, Japan, Kenya, Morocco, Niger, Paraguay, Peru, Sierra Leone, Sudan, Ukrainian SSR, USSR, United Kingdom, Uruguay, Venezuela, Zaire.
To serve until 31 December 1986:[b] Algeria, Australia, Bolivia, Central African Republic, Czechoslovakia,[c] Denmark, France, German Democratic Republic, Germany, Federal Republic of, Italy, Liberia, Mexico, Norway, Pakistan, Philippines, Spain, Thailand, Turkey, Uganda, United States, Upper Volta, Yugoslavia, Zimbabwe.

[a]Two seats allocated to members from Asian States remained unfilled in 1983.
[b]The seats allocated to three members from Asian States and one member from Eastern European States remained unfilled in 1983.
[c]Elected on 28 July 1983 (decision 1983/179).

Chairman: Daniel D. C. Don Nanjira (Kenya).
Vice-Chairmen: Wolfgang Jung (German Democratic Republic), Yannis Kinnas (Greece), S. K. Mukerjee (India).
Rapporteur: Makoto Wakasugi (Japan).

Committee on Negotiations with Intergovernmental Agencies

The Committee on Negotiations with Intergovernmental Agencies was originally established by the Economic and Social Council in 1946.

On 4 February 1983 (decision 1983/105), the Council authorized its President, in consultation with the Chairmen of the regional groups, to appoint the members of the Committee from among the States members of the Council, in pursuance of a General Assembly request[28] that the Council arrange for the negotiation with UNIDO of an agreement to constitute it as a specialized agency.

The members remained to be appointed as of the end of 1983.

Committee on Non-Governmental Organizations

The Committee on Non-Governmental Organizations consists of 19 members, elected by the Economic and Social Council for a four-year term according to a specific pattern of equitable geographical representation.

In 1983, the Committee met at United Nations Headquarters between 7 and 18 February and on 3 May, and at Geneva on 7 July.

Members (until 31 December 1986): Chile, Costa Rica, Cuba, Cyprus, France, Ghana, India, Kenya, Libyan Arab Jamahiriya, Nicaragua, Nigeria, Pakistan, Rwanda, Sweden, Thailand, USSR, United Kingdom, United States, Yugoslavia.

Chairman: Emilia Castro de Barish (Costa Rica).
Vice-Chairman: Rose Adhiambo Arungu-Olende (Kenya).
Rapporteur: Simone Poudade (France).

Expert bodies

Ad Hoc Group of Experts on International Co-operation in Tax Matters

The membership of the *Ad Hoc* Group of Experts on International Co-operation in Tax Matters—to consist of 25 members drawn from 15 developing and 10 developed countries, appointed by the Secretary-General to serve in their individual capacity—remained at 24 in 1983, with one member from a developing country still to be appointed.

The *Ad Hoc* Group held its second meeting at Geneva from 5 to 16 December 1983.

Members: Maurice Hugh Collins (United Kingdom), Jean François Court (France), T. Dekker (Netherlands), Francisco O. N. Dornelles (Brazil), Hussein M. El Baroudi (Egypt), Mordecai S. Feinberg (United States), José Ramón Fernández Pérez (Spain), Antonio H. Figueroa (Argentina), Mayer Gabay (Israel), R. R. Khosla (India), Marwan Koudsi (Syrian Arab Republic), Felipe Lamarca (Chile), Daniel Luthi (Switzerland), Mohamed Medaghri-Alaoui (Morocco), Thomas Menck (Federal Republic of Germany), Canute R. Miller (Jamaica), Muhammad Wasim Mirza (Pakistan),[a] Alberto Navarro Rodríguez (Mexico), I. O. Oni (Nigeria), Alfred Philipp (Austria), Rainer Söderholm (Finland), Sutadi Sukarya (Indonesia), Tetsuo Takikawa (Japan),[a] André Titty (United Republic of Cameroon).

[a]Appointed in November 1983 to replace Abdul Waheed (Pakistan), who died in August, and Yasuyuki Kawahara (Japan), respectively.

Committee for Development Planning

The Committee for Development Planning is composed of 24 experts representing different planning systems. They are appointed by the Economic and Social Council, on nomination by the Secretary-General, to serve in their personal capacity for a term of three years.

The Committee held its nineteenth session at United Nations Headquarters from 18 to 27 April 1983.

Members (until 31 December 1983):[a] Ismail-Sabri Abdalla (Egypt); Khatijah Ahmad (Malaysia); Abdlatif Y. Al-Hamad (Kuwait); Maria Augusztinovics, *Vice-Chairman* (Hungary); Hendricus Cornelis Bos (Netherlands); Robert Cassen (United Kingdom); William Gilbert Demas, *Chairman* (Trinidad and Tobago); José Encarnacion, Jr. (Philippines); Celso Furtado (Brazil); Robert K. A. Gardiner (Ghana); Shinichi Ichimura (Japan); V. N. Kirichenko (USSR); John P. Lewis (United States); Li Zong (China); Gabriel Mignot (France); J. M. Mwanza (Zambia); Joseph Elenga Ngaporo (Congo); G. O. Nwankwo (Nigeria); Goran Ohlin, *Rapporteur* (Sweden); Jozef Pajestka (Poland); I. G. Patel (India); Germánico Salgado (Ecuador); Leopoldo Solís (Mexico).

[a]The vacancy created by the resignation in 1982 of Gerhard Fels (Federal Republic of Germany) remained unfilled in 1983.

Committee of Experts on the Transport of Dangerous Goods

The Committee of Experts on the Transport of Dangerous Goods is composed of experts from countries interested in the international transport of dangerous goods. The experts are made available by their Governments at the request of the Secretary-General. The membership, to be increased to 15 in accordance with a 1975 resolution of the Economic and Social Council,[29] remained at 13 in 1983. The Committee did not meet during the year.

---

[28]Resolution 34/96, 13 December 1979 (YUN 1979, p. 622).
[29]Resolution 1973(LIX), 30 July 1975 (YUN 1975, p. 734).

Members: Canada, France, Germany, Federal Republic of, Iran,[a] Iraq,[a] Italy, Japan, Norway, Poland, Thailand,[a] USSR, United Kingdom, United States.

[a]Inactive member.

The Committee may alter, as required, the composition of its subsidiary bodies. In addition, any Committee member may participate in the work of and vote in those bodies provided such member notify the United Nations Secretariat of the intention to do so.

GROUP OF EXPERTS ON EXPLOSIVES

The Group of Experts on Explosives held its twenty-third session at Geneva from 12 to 16 September 1983. The following experts attended the session:

J. des Rivières (Canada); J. Engeland (Federal Republic of Germany); O. Hakenstad (Norway); P. Marrec (France); A. Ostrovski (USSR); C. Schultz (United States); R. R. Watson, *Chairman* (United Kingdom).

GROUP OF RAPPORTEURS OF THE COMMITTEE OF
EXPERTS ON THE TRANSPORT OF DANGEROUS GOODS

The Group of Rapporteurs of the Committee of Experts on the Transport of Dangerous Goods held its thirtieth session at Geneva from 1 to 12 August 1983. The following experts attended the session:

L. P. Andronov, *Chairman* (USSR); T. Austerheim (Norway); J. Engeland, *Vice-Chairman* (Federal Republic of Germany); L. Grainger, *Vice-Chairman* (United Kingdom); K. Kumagai (Japan); P. Marrec (France); H. Morton (Canada); A. I. Roberts (United States).

Committee on Crime Prevention and Control

The Committee on Crime Prevention and Control consists of 27 members elected for four-year terms by the Economic and Social Council, according to a specific pattern of equitable geographical representation, from among experts nominated by Member States.

The Committee did not meet in 1983.

Members:

To serve until 31 December 1984: A. Adeyemi (Nigeria), Anthony John Edward Brennan (United Kingdom), Ronald L. Gainer (United States), Jozsef Godony (Hungary), Aura Guerra de Villaláz (Panama), Ds. Hudioro (Indonesia), Abdul Meguid Ibrahim Kharbit (Kuwait), Mawik-Ndi-Muyeng (Zaire), Juan Manuel Mayorca (Venezuela), Albert Metzger (Sierra Leone), Gioacchino Polimeni (Italy), Abdel Aziz Abdalla Shiddo (Sudan), Ramananda Prasad Singh (Nepal).

To serve until 31 December 1986: Amadou Racine Ba (Mauritania), André Bissonnette (Canada), S. V. Borodin (USSR), Dusan Cotic (Yugoslavia), Ahmed Mohamed Khalifa (Egypt), Robert Linke (Austria), Manuel López-Rey y Arrojo (Bolivia), Charles Alfred Lunn (Barbados), Jorge Arturo Montero-Castro (Costa Rica), Mphanza Patrick Mvunga (Zambia), Simone Andrée Rozes (France), Yoshio Suzuki (Japan), Mervyn Patrick Wijesinha (Sri Lanka), Wu Han (China).

United Nations Group of Experts on Geographical Names

The United Nations Group of Experts on Geographical Names represents various geographical/linguistic divisions, of which there were 17 in 1983, as follows: Africa Central; Africa East; Africa West; Arabic; Asia East (other than China); Asia South-East and Pacific South-West; Asia South-West (other than Arabic); China; Dutch- and German-speaking; East Central and South-East Europe; India; Latin America; Norden; Romano-Hellenic; Union of Soviet Socialist Republics; United Kingdom; United States of America and Canada.

The Group of Experts did not meet in 1983.

Ad hoc bodies

Ad Hoc Committee on the Preparations for the Public Hearings on the Activities of Transnational Corporations in South Africa

On 4 February 1983, the Economic and Social Council decided that the membership of the *Ad Hoc* Committee on the Preparations for the Public Hearings on the Activities of Transnational Corporations in South Africa should include one member from each of the regional groups and authorized its President to appoint the members on the nomination of each group.

The Committee had not been constituted by the end of 1983.

Commission on the Status of Women acting as the Preparatory Body for the World Conference to Review and Appraise the Achievements of the United Nations Decade for Women

The Commission on the Status of Women (p. 1359) acting as the Preparatory Body for the World Conference to Review and Appraise the Achievements of the United Nations Decade for Women, scheduled for 1985, held its first session at Vienna, Austria, from 23 February to 4 March 1983. The Commission members were represented as follows:

Australia: Kathleen Joan Taperell. Canada: Maureen O'Neil. China: Huang Ganying. Cuba: Olga Finlay Saavedra. Czechoslovakia: Dagmar Molkova, *Vice-Chairman*. Egypt: Farida Abou El-Fetouh. France: Cécile Goldet. German Democratic Republic: Helga Hoerz. Guatemala: Jorge F. Gonzales. India: Prabha Rao, *Vice-Chairman*. Indonesia: Artati Sudirdjo. Italy: Paola Gaiotti de Biase. Japan: Yoko Nuita. Kenya: Esther Ondipo Jonathan Wandeka. Mexico: Olga Pellicer de Brody. Nigeria: Olajumoke Oladayo Obafemi, *Chairman*. Norway: Grethe Vaernoe, *Vice-Chairman*. Pakistan: Salima Raisuddin Ahmed. Philippines: Rosario G. Manalo. Spain: Enrique Suárez de Puga y Villegas. Ukrainian SSR: V. I. Sivolob. USSR: T. N. Nikolaeva. United Kingdom: R. T. Gardner of Parkes. United States: Nancy Clark Reynolds. Venezuela: María Esperanza de Furter, *Rapporteur*. Zaire: Luanghy Mangaza.

Intergovernmental Working Group of Experts on International Standards of Accounting and Reporting

The Intergovernmental Working Group of Experts on International Standards of Accounting and Reporting, which reports to the Commission on Transnational Corporations (p. 1361), consists of 34 members, elected for three-year terms by the Economic and Social Council according to a specific pattern of equitable geographical distribution. Each State elected appoints an expert with appropriate experience in accounting and reporting.

The Group held its first session at United Nations Headquarters from 22 February to 4 March 1983.

Members:

To serve until 31 December 1984:[a] Argentina, Brazil, Canada, China, Egypt, France, Grenada, Liberia, Netherlands, Nigeria, Norway, Pakistan, Philippines, Spain, Swaziland, Zaire.

To serve until 31 December 1985:[b] Algeria, Cyprus, Ecuador, Germany, Federal Republic of, India, Italy, Japan, Morocco, Panama, Saint Lucia, Tunisia, Uganda, United Kingdom, United States.

[a]One seat allocated to a member from Eastern European States remained unfilled in 1983.
[b]The seats allocated to one member from Asian States and two members from Eastern European States remained unfilled in 1983.

Chairman: Jaime C. Laya (Philippines).
Vice-Chairmen: Mohamed Adel El-Safty (Egypt), Pieter A. Wessel (Netherlands).
Rapporteur: Irtiza Husain (Pakistan).

Preparatory Committee for the International Conference on Population

The Population Commission (p. 1359) was designated by the Economic and Social Council as the Preparatory Committee for the International Conference on Population, to be held in 1984.

The Preparatory Committee, to convene in open-ended session with the participation of any other State, did not meet in 1983.

Preparatory Sub-Committee for the Second World Conference to Combat Racism and Racial Discrimination

The Preparatory Sub-Committee for the Second World Conference to Combat Racism and Racial Discrimination (p. 1355), which consisted of 23 members appointed by the Economic and Social Council President on the basis of equitable geographical distribution, held its second and final session at United Nations Headquarters from 21 to 25 March 1983.

Members: Bulgaria, Congo, Costa Rica, Cuba, Egypt, France,[a] German Democratic Republic, Ghana, Greece,[a] India, Iraq, Italy,[a] Mexico, Nigeria, Pakistan, Philippines, Sudan, Syrian Arab Republic, USSR, United Kingdom,[a] Venezuela, Yugoslavia, Zimbabwe.

ªAppointed by the Council President as stated in his letter to the Secretary-General of 28 February 1983.

Chairman: Elleck Kufakunesu Mashingaidze (Zimbabwe).
Vice-Chairmen: Javid Husain (Pakistan), Willi Schlegel (German Democratic Republic), Maria Zografou (Greece).
Rapporteur: Miguel Ruíz Cabañas (Mexico).

Administrative Committee on Co-ordination

The Administrative Committee on Co-ordination held three sessions in 1983: an organizational session at United Nations Headquarters from 7 to 9 February; its first in Paris on 30 and 31 March; and its second at United Nations Headquarters on 26 and 27 October.

The membership of ACC, under the chairmanship of the Secretary-General of the United Nations, also includes the executive heads of ILO, FAO, UNESCO, WHO, the World Bank, IMF, ICAO, UPU, ITU, WMO, IMO, WIPO, IFAD, IAEA and the secretariat of the Contracting Parties to GATT.

Also taking part in the work of ACC are the United Nations Director-General for Development and International Economic Co-operation; the Under-Secretaries-General for International Economic and Social Affairs, for Administration, Finance and Management, for Technical Co-operation for Development, and for Legal Affairs; and the executive heads of UNCTAD, UNDP, UNEP, UNFPA, UNHCR, UNICEF, UNIDO, UNITAR, UNRWA and WFP.

ACC has established subsidiary bodies on organizational, administrative and substantive questions.

Other related bodies

Human Rights Committee

The Human Rights Committee (p. 1368) reports annually to the General Assembly through the Economic and Social Council.

Intergovernmental Committee on Science and Technology for Development

The Intergovernmental Committee on Science and Technology for Development (p. 1343) reports annually to the General Assembly through the Economic and Social Council.

International Research and Training Institute for the Advancement of Women (INSTRAW)

The International Research and Training Institute for the Advancement of Women, a body of the United Nations financed through voluntary contributions, functions under the authority of a Board of Trustees.

BOARD OF TRUSTEES

The Board of Trustees of INSTRAW is composed of a President appointed by the Secretary-General; 10 members serving in their individual capacity, appointed by the Economic and Social Council on the nomination of the Secretary-General; and *ex-officio* members. Members serve for three-year terms, with a maximum of two terms.

The Board, which reports annually to the Council, held its third session at United Nations Headquarters from 24 to 28 January 1983.

Members (until 30 June 1983):
To serve until 30 June 1983: Emmanuel T. Esquea-Guerrero (Dominican Republic); Lily Monze (Zambia); Irene Tinker (United States).
To serve until 30 June 1984: Marcelle Devaud (France); Aziza Hussein, *Rapporteur* (Egypt); Nobuko Takahashi (Japan).
To serve until 30 June 1985: Gulzar Bano (Pakistan); Ester Boserup (Denmark); Vilma Espín de Castro, *Vice-President* (Cuba); Vida Tomsic (Yugoslavia).

On 25 May 1983 (decision 1983/161), the Economic and Social Council appointed Suad Ibrahim Eissa (Sudan), María Lavalle Urbina (Mexico) and Helen Arnopoulos Stamiris (Greece) for a three-year term beginning on 1 July 1983 to fill the vacancies occurring on 30 June.

Members (from 1 July 1983):
To serve until 30 June 1984: Marcelle Devaud (France), Aziza Hussein (Egypt), Nobuko Takahashi (Japan).
To serve until 30 June 1985: Gulzar Bano (Pakistan), Ester Boserup (Denmark), Vilma Espín de Castro (Cuba), Vida Tomsic (Yugoslavia).

To serve until 30 June 1986: Suad Ibrahim Eissa (Sudan), María Lavalle Urbina (Mexico), Helen Arnopoulos Stamiris (Greece).

President: Delphine Tsanga (United Republic of Cameroon).ª
Ex-officio members: The representative of the Secretary-General, the Director of the Institute and the directors of the centres and programmes for women of the regional commissions.

ªReappointed in June 1983 for a term expiring on 30 June 1985.

Director of the Institute: Dunja Pastizzi-Ferencic.

Office of the United Nations High Commissioner for Refugees (UNHCR)

The United Nations High Commissioner for Refugees (p. 1344) reports annually to the General Assembly through the Economic and Social Council.

United Nations Capital Development Fund

EXECUTIVE BOARD

The Executive Board of the United Nations Capital Development Fund (p. 1346) reports annually to the General Assembly through the Economic and Social Council.

United Nations Children's Fund (UNICEF)

EXECUTIVE BOARD

The UNICEF Executive Board consists of 41 members elected by the Economic and Social Council from Member States of the United Nations or members of the specialized agencies or of IAEA, for three-year terms.

In 1983, the Executive Board held a series of meetings between 9 and 20 May and (with its composition as of 1 August) two organizational meetings on 20 May and 30 June, all at United Nations Headquarters.

Members (until 31 July 1983):
To serve until 31 July 1983: Barbados, Belgium, Botswana, Brazil, Canada, China, Germany, Federal Republic of, Norway, Thailand, Yugoslavia.
To serve until 31 July 1984: Austria, German Democratic Republic, India, Ivory Coast, Pakistan, Sweden, Switzerland, Togo, United Arab Emirates, Venezuela.
To serve until 31 July 1985: Algeria, Bahrain, Bangladesh, Central African Republic, Chad, Chile, France, Hungary, Italy, Japan, Madagascar, Mexico, Nepal, Netherlands, Panama, Somalia, Swaziland, USSR, United Kingdom, United States, Upper Volta.

Chairman: Hugo Scheltema (Netherlands).
First Vice-Chairman: Dr. Haydee Martínez de Osorio (Venezuela).
Second Vice-Chairman: Mihaly Simai (Hungary).
Third Vice-Chairman: Amara Essy (Ivory Coast).
Fourth Vice-Chairman: Basharat Jazbi (Pakistan).

On 17 May 1983 (decision 1983/161), the Economic and Social Council elected the following 10 members for a three-year term beginning on 1 August 1983 to fill the vacancies occurring on 31 July: Australia, Canada, China, Colombia, Cuba, Finland, Germany, Federal Republic of, Lesotho, Thailand, Yugoslavia.

Members (from 1 August 1983):
To serve until 31 July 1984: Austria, German Democratic Republic, India, Ivory Coast, Pakistan, Sweden, Switzerland, Togo, United Arab Emirates, Venezuela.
To serve until 31 July 1985: Algeria, Bahrain, Bangladesh, Central African Republic, Chad, Chile, France, Hungary, Italy, Japan, Madagascar, Mexico, Nepal, Netherlands, Panama, Somalia, Swaziland, USSR, United Kingdom, United States, Upper Volta.
To serve until 31 July 1986: Australia, Canada, China, Colombia, Cuba, Finland, Germany, Federal Republic of, Lesotho, Thailand, Yugoslavia.

Chairman: Dr. Haydee Martínez de Osorio (Venezuela).
First Vice-Chairman: Umberto La Rocca (Italy).
Second Vice-Chairman: Mihaly Simai (Hungary).
Third Vice-Chairman: Atsu-Koffi Amega (Togo).
Fourth Vice-Chairman: Richard Manning (Australia).

Executive Director of UNICEF: James P. Grant.

COMMITTEE ON ADMINISTRATION AND FINANCE

The Committee on Administration and Finance is a committee of the whole of the UNICEF Executive Board.

Chairman: François Nordmann (Switzerland) (until 31 July), Jassim Buallay (Bahrain) (from 1 August).
Vice-Chairman: Hisami Kurokochi (Japan) (from 1 August).

PROGRAMME COMMITTEE

The Programme Committee is a committee of the whole of the UNICEF Executive Board.

Chairman: Dr. N. N. Mashalaba (Botswana)[a] (until 31 July), Anwarul Karim Chowdhury (Bangladesh) (from 1 August).
Vice-Chairman: Ngaré Kessely (Chad) (from 1 August).

[a]Elected by the Executive Board on 9 May 1983 to replace Serla Grewal (India), who was unable to complete her term.

UNICEF/WHO Joint Committee on Health Policy

The UNICEF/WHO Joint Committee on Health Policy consists of: six members of the UNICEF Executive Board, among whom are the chairmen of the Executive Board and the Programme Committee who serve *ex officio;* and six members of the WHO Executive Board.

The Joint Committee, which meets biennially, held its twenty-fourth session at Geneva on 1 and 2 February 1983.

Members:
UNICEF ex-officio members: Hugo Scheltema (Netherlands); Serla Grewal (India).
Elected by UNICEF: Dr. John J. Hutchings, *Rapporteur* (United States); Dr. Haydee Martínez de Osorio (Venezuela); Dr. N. N. Mashalaba (Botswana); Abdul Shakoor H. Tahlak (United Arab Emirates).
Appointed by WHO: K. Al-Sakkaf, *Rapporteur* (Yemen); Dr. J. M. Borgoño (Chile); Dr. A. J. R. Cabral (Mozambique); M. M. Hussain (Maldives); Y. F. Isakov (USSR); Dr. Maureen M. Law, *Chairman* (Canada).

United Nations Conference on Trade and Development (UNCTAD)

TRADE AND DEVELOPMENT BOARD

The Trade and Development Board (p. 1348) reports to UNCTAD; it also reports annually to the General Assembly through the Economic and Social Council.

United Nations Development Programme (UNDP)

GOVERNING COUNCIL

The Governing Council of UNDP consists of 48 members, elected by the Economic and Social Council from Member States of the United Nations or members of the specialized agencies or of IAEA.

Twenty-seven seats are allocated to developing countries as follows: 11 to African countries, 9 to Asian countries and Yugoslavia, and 7 to Latin American countries.

Twenty-one seats are allocated to economically more advanced countries as follows: 17 to Western European and other countries, and 4 to Eastern European countries.

The term of office is three years, one third of the members being elected each year.

During 1983, the Governing Council held an organizational meeting on 14 February, a special meeting from 14 to 18 February and its thirtieth session from 6 to 24 June, all at United Nations Headquarters.

Members:
To serve until 31 December 1983: Argentina, Bulgaria, Germany, Federal Republic of, Guinea, India, Netherlands, Niger, Pakistan, Poland, Somalia, Sweden, Switzerland, Trinidad and Tobago, Turkey, Venezuela, Yemen.
To serve until 31 December 1984: Austria, Barbados, Bhutan, China, Ecuador, Fiji, Italy, Japan, Mali, Mexico, Spain, Tunisia, USSR, United Kingdom, United States, Zambia.
To serve until 31 December 1985: Australia, Belgium, Brazil, Canada, Central African Republic, Chad, Denmark, Finland, France, German

Democratic Republic, Lesotho, Mauritania, Nepal, Philippines, United Republic of Tanzania, Yugoslavia.

President: Taieb Slim (Tunisia).
First Vice-President: Erich Maximilian Schmid (Austria).
Second Vice-President: Leandro I. Verceles (Philippines).
Third Vice-President: Miguel A. Albornoz (Ecuador).
Fourth Vice-President: Jerzy W. Szeremeta (Poland).

On 25 May 1983 (decision 1983/161), the Economic and Social Council elected the following 16 members for a three-year term beginning on 1 January 1984 to fill the vacancies occurring on 31 December 1983: Argentina, Bahrain, Bangladesh, Ethiopia, Gambia, Germany, Federal Republic of, Hungary, India, Jamaica, Netherlands, Norway, Poland, Switzerland, Togo, Turkey, Venezuela.

Administrator of UNDP: F. Bradford Morse.
Deputy Administrator: G. Arthur Brown.

BUDGETARY AND FINANCE COMMITTEE

The Budgetary and Finance Committee, a committee of the whole, held one series of meetings in 1983, at United Nations Headquarters, between 31 May and 24 June.

Chairman: Erich Maximilian Schmid (Austria) (until 15 June), Franz Schmid (Austria) (from 15 June).
Rapporteur: Achyut Bhandari (Bhutan).

INTER-SESSIONAL COMMITTEE OF THE WHOLE

During 1983, the Inter-sessional Committee of the Whole held its second session from 9 to 11 February and its third and final session from 6 to 8 April, both at United Nations Headquarters.

Chairman: Douglas P. Lindores (Canada).
First Vice-Chairman: Habib M. Kaabachi (Tunisia).
Second Vice-Chairman: B. M. Oza (India) (second session), Shri Vatsa Purushottam (India) (third session).
Third Vice-Chairman: Stoyan Bakalov (Bulgaria).
Fourth Vice-Chairman: Miguel A. Albornoz (Ecuador).
Rapporteur: Qazi Shaukat Fareed (Pakistan).

On 24 June 1983, the Governing Council decided that, for a three-year trial period, it would, in the context of regularly scheduled sessions, resolve itself into a Committee of the Whole to consider matters related to programme planning and evaluation.

United Nations Environment Programme (UNEP)

GOVERNING COUNCIL

The Governing Council of UNEP (p. 1350) reports to the General Assembly through the Economic and Social Council.

United Nations Industrial Development Organization (UNIDO)

INDUSTRIAL DEVELOPMENT BOARD

The Industrial Development Board (p. 1350), the principal organ of UNIDO, reports annually to the General Assembly through the Economic and Social Council.

United Nations Institute for Training and Research (UNITAR)

The Executive Director of UNITAR (p. 1351) reports to the General Assembly and, as appropriate, to the Economic and Social Council.

United Nations Research Institute for Social Development (UNRISD)

BOARD OF DIRECTORS

The Board of Directors of UNRISD reports to the Economic and Social Council through the Commission for Social Development.
The Board consists of:

The Chairman, appointed by the Secretary-General: (vacant);
Seven members, nominated by the Commission for Social Development and confirmed by the Economic and Social Council (to serve until

30 June 1983): Paul-Marc Henry (France), Karl Eric Knutsson (Sweden), Vera Nyitrai (Hungary), Achola Pala Okeyo (Kenya), K. N. Raj (India), Eugene B. Skolnikoff (United States); (to serve until 30 June 1985): Gustavo Esteva (Mexico);[a]

Eight other members, as follows: a representative of the Secretary-General, the Director of the Latin American Institute for Economic and Social Planning, the Director of the Asian and Pacific Development Centre, the Director of the African Institute for Economic Development and Planning, the Executive Secretary of ECWA, the Director of UNRISD *(ex officio),* and the representatives of two of the following specialized agencies appointed as members and observers in annual rotation: ILO and FAO (members); UNESCO and WHO (observers).

[a]Acting Chairman, pending appointment of the Chairman.

On 26 May 1983 (decision 1983/122), the Economic and Social Council confirmed the nomination by the Commission for Social Development on 15 February of the following six members for terms beginning on 1 July to fill the vacancies occurring on 30 June: for a four-year term, Ulf Hannerz (Sweden); for a two-year term, Paul-Marc Henry (France), Vera Nyitrai (Hungary), Achola Pala Okeyo (Kenya), K. N. Raj (India), Eugene B. Skolnikoff (United States).

United Nations Special Fund

BOARD OF GOVERNORS

The Board of Governors of the United Nations Special Fund (p. 1353) reports annually to the General Assembly through the Economic and Social Council.

United Nations Special Fund for Land-locked Developing Countries

BOARD OF GOVERNORS

A Board of Governors of the United Nations Special Fund for Land-locked Developing Countries (p. 1353), when constituted, was to report to the General Assembly through the Economic and Social Council.

United Nations University

COUNCIL OF THE UNITED NATIONS UNIVERSITY

The Council of the United Nations University (p. 1353), the governing board of the University, reports annually to the General Assembly, to the Economic and Social Council and to the UNESCO Executive Board through the Secretary-General and the UNESCO Director-General.

World Food Council

The World Food Council (p. 1354), an organ of the United Nations at the ministerial or plenipotentiary level, reports to the General Assembly through the Economic and Social Council.

World Food Programme

COMMITTEE ON FOOD AID
POLICIES AND PROGRAMMES

The Committee on Food Aid Policies and Programmes, the governing body of WFP, consists of 30 members, of which 15 are elected by the Economic and Social Council and 15 by the FAO Council, from Member States of the United Nations or from members of FAO. Members serve for three-year terms.

The Committee reports annually to the Economic and Social Council, the FAO Council and the World Food Council.

The Committee held two sessions during 1983, at Rome, Italy: its fifteenth from 16 to 27 May; and its sixteenth from 20 to 28 October.

Members:
To serve until 31 December 1983:
  Elected by Economic and Social Council: Denmark, Greece, Hungary, India, Morocco.
  Elected by FAO Council: Australia, Bangladesh, Canada *(Second Vice-Chairman),* Saudi Arabia, United States.
To serve until 31 December 1984:
  Elected by Economic and Social Council: Belgium, Finland, Japan, Pakistan, Somalia.
  Elected by FAO Council: Brazil, Congo, Mali, Netherlands *(Chairman),* Thailand.
To serve until 31 December 1985:
  Elected by Economic and Social Council: Colombia *(First Vice-Chairman),* Mexico, Sweden, United Kingdom, Upper Volta.
  Elected by FAO Council: Cuba, France, Germany, Federal Republic of, Nigeria, Zambia.

On 25 May 1983 (decision 1983/161) and (with respect to India) on 28 July (decision 1983/179), the Economic and Social Council elected Egypt, Hungary, India, Italy and Norway; and, on 24 November, the FAO Council elected Australia, Bangladesh, Canada, Saudi Arabia and the United States, all for a three-year term beginning on 1 January 1984 to fill the vacancies occurring on 31 December 1983.

Executive Director of WFP: James Charles Ingram.
Deputy Executive Director: Salahuddin Ahmed.

Trusteeship Council

Article 86 of the United Nations Charter lays down that the Trusteeship Council shall consist of the following:

Members of the United Nations administering Trust Territories;
Permanent members of the Security Council which do not administer Trust Territories;
As many other members elected for a three-year term by the General Assembly as will ensure that the membership of the Council is equally divided between United Nations Members which administer Trust Territories and those which do not.[a]

[a]During 1983, only one Member of the United Nations was an administering member of the Trusteeship Council, while four permanent members of the Security Council continued as non-administering members. Therefore, the parity called for by Article 86 of the Charter was not maintained.

MEMBERS
Member administering a Trust Territory: United States.
Non-administering members: China, France, USSR, United Kingdom.

SESSIONS
Fiftieth session: United Nations Headquarters, 16 May–10 June 1983.
Resumed fiftieth session: United Nations Headquarters, 28 November 1983.

OFFICERS
President: John W. D. Margetson (United Kingdom).
Vice-President: Paul Poudade (France).

United Nations Visiting Mission to Observe the Plebiscite in Palau, Trust Territory of the Pacific Islands, February 1983
Members: Marrack I. Goulding (United Kingdom); Stephen Igo (Papua New Guinea); Paul Poudade, *Chairman* (France); Bal Ram (Fiji).

United Nations Visiting Mission to Observe the Plebiscite in the Federated States of Micronesia, Trust Territory of the Pacific Islands, June 1983
Members: Stephen Igo (Papua New Guinea); Ralph Karepa (Papua New Guinea); John W. D. Margetson, *Chairman* (United Kingdom); Hugh R. Mortimer (United Kingdom); Paul Poudade, *Vice-Chairman* (France); Bal Ram (Fiji).

United Nations Visiting Mission to Observe the Plebiscite in the Marshall Islands, Trust Territory of the Pacific Islands, September 1983
Members: David Anggo (Papua New Guinea); John W. D. Margetson, *Chairman* (United Kingdom); Paul Poudade, *Vice-Chairman* (France); Muneshwar Sahadeo (Fiji).

International Court of Justice

Judges of the Court

The International Court of Justice consists of 15 Judges elected for nine-year terms by the General Assembly and the Security Council, each voting independently.

The following were the Judges of the Court serving in 1983, listed in the order of precedence:

Judge	Country of nationality	End of term[a]
Taslim Olawale Elias, *President*	Nigeria	1985
José Sette Câmara, *Vice-President*	Brazil	1988
Manfred Lachs	Poland	1985
Platon D. Morozov	USSR	1988
Nagendra Singh	India	1991
José María Ruda	Argentina	1991
Hermann Mosler	Federal Republic of Germany	1985
Shigeru Oda	Japan	1985
Roberto Ago	Italy	1988
Abdullah Fikri El-Khani	Syrian Arab Republic	1985
Stephen M. Schwebel	United States	1988
Sir Robert Y. Jennings	United Kingdom	1991
Guy Ladreit de Lacharrière	France	1991
Kéba M'Baye	Senegal	1991
Mohammed Bedjaoui	Algeria	1988

[a]Term expires on 5 February of the year indicated.

Registrar: Santiago Torres Bernárdez.
Deputy Registrar: Alain Pillepich.

Chamber formed in the case concerning *Delimitation of the maritime boundary in the Gulf of Maine area*

Members: Roberto Ago *(President)*, André Gros,[a] Hermann Mosler, Stephen M. Schwebel.
Ad hoc member: Maxwell Cohen.[b]

[a]Member of the Court whose term of office expired on 5 February 1982, but who continued to sit as a member of the Chamber in accordance with Article 13, paragraph 3, of the Statute.
[b]As the Court noted in its Order constituting the Chamber, one of the members of the Court elected to the Chamber gave place to the Judge *ad hoc* chosen by one of the parties (Canada) in accordance with Article 31, paragraph 4, of the Statute.

Chamber of Summary Procedure
(as constituted by the Court on 23 February 1983)

Members: Taslim Olawale Elias *(ex officio)*, José Sette Câmara *(ex officio)*, Nagendra Singh, Abdullah Fikri El-Khani, Guy Ladreit de Lacharrière.

Substitute members: Kéba M'Baye, Mohammed Bedjaoui.

Parties to the Court's Statute

All Members of the United Nations are *ipso facto* parties to the Statute of the International Court of Justice. Also parties to it are the following non-members: Liechtenstein, San Marino, Switzerland.

States accepting the compulsory jurisdiction of the Court

Declarations made by the following States accepting the Court's compulsory jurisdiction (or made under the Statute of the Permanent Court of International Justice and deemed to be an acceptance of the jurisdiction of the International Court) were in force at the end of 1983:

Australia, Austria, Barbados, Belgium, Botswana, Canada, Colombia, Costa Rica, Democratic Kampuchea, Denmark, Dominican Republic, Egypt, El Salvador, Finland, Gambia, Haiti, Honduras, India, Israel, Japan, Kenya, Liberia, Liechtenstein, Luxembourg, Malawi, Malta, Mauritius, Mexico, Netherlands, New Zealand, Nicaragua, Nigeria, Norway, Pakistan, Panama, Philippines, Portugal, Somalia, Sudan, Swaziland, Sweden, Switzerland, Togo, Uganda, United Kingdom, United States, Uruguay.

United Nations organs and specialized and related agencies authorized to request advisory opinions from the Court

Authorized by the United Nations Charter to request opinions on any legal question: General Assembly, Security Council.
Authorized by the General Assembly in accordance with the Charter to request opinions on legal questions arising within the scope of their activities: Economic and Social Council, Trusteeship Council, Interim Committee of the General Assembly, Committee on Applications for Review of Administrative Tribunal Judgements, ILO, FAO, UNESCO, WHO, World Bank, IFC, IDA, IMF, ICAO, ITU, WMO, IMO, WIPO, IFAD, IAEA.

Committees of the Court

BUDGETARY AND ADMINISTRATIVE COMMITTEE
Members: Taslim Olawale Elias *(ex officio)*, José Sette Câmara *(ex officio)*, Manfred Lachs, Nagendra Singh, Stephen M. Schwebel.

COMMITTEE ON RELATIONS
Members: Platon D. Morozov, Guy Ladreit de Lacharrière, Kéba M'Baye.

LIBRARY COMMITTEE
Members: José María Ruda, Hermann Mosler, Shigeru Oda, Sir Robert Y. Jennings.

RULES COMMITTEE
Members: Manfred Lachs, Platon D. Morozov, José María Ruda, Hermann Mosler, Shigeru Oda, Roberto Ago, Sir Robert Y. Jennings.

Other United Nations-related bodies

The following bodies are not subsidiary to any principal organ of the United Nations but were established by an international treaty instrument or arrangement sponsored by the United Nations and are thus related to the Organization and its work. These bodies, often referred to as "treaty organs", are serviced by the United Nations Secretariat and may be financed in part or wholly from the Organization's regular budget, as authorized by the General Assembly, to which most of them report annually.

Committee on Disarmament

The Committee on Disarmament, the multilateral negotiating forum on disarmament, reports annually to the General Assembly and is serviced by the United Nations Secretariat. It was composed of 40 members in 1983.

The Committee met at Geneva in 1983 from 1 February to 29 April and from 14 June to 30 August.

Members: Algeria, Argentina, Australia, Belgium, Brazil, Bulgaria, Burma, Canada, China, Cuba, Czechoslovakia, Egypt, Ethiopia, France, German Democratic Republic, Germany, Federal Republic of, Hungary, India, Indonesia, Iran, Italy, Japan, Kenya, Mexico, Mongolia, Morocco, Netherlands, Nigeria, Pakistan, Peru, Poland, Romania, Sri Lanka, Sweden, USSR, United Kingdom, United States, Venezuela, Yugoslavia, Zaire.

The chairmanship, which rotates in English alphabetical order among the members, was held by the following in 1983: February, Mongolia; March, Morocco; April and the recess between the first and second parts of the 1983 session, Netherlands; June, Nigeria; July, Pakistan; August and the recess until the 1984 session, Peru.

Committee on the Elimination of Discrimination against Women

The Committee on the Elimination of Discrimination against Women was established under the Convention on the Elimination of All Forms of Discrimination against Women.[30] It consists of 23 experts elected by the States parties to the Convention to serve in their personal capacity, with due regard for equitable geographical distribution and for representation of the different forms of civilization and principal legal systems. Members serve for four-year terms.

The Committee, which reports annually to the General Assembly through the Economic and Social Council, held its second session at United Nations Headquarters from 1 to 12 August 1983.

Members:

To serve until 15 April 1984: Desirée P. Bernard, *Rapporteur* (Guyana); Marie Caron, *Vice-Chairman* (Canada); Graciela Escudero-Moscoso (Ecuador); Aida Gonzalez Martínez (Mexico); Vanda Lamm (Hungary); Maria Margarida de Rego da Costa Salema Moura Ribeiro (Portugal); Nguyen Ngoc Dung (Viet Nam); Johan Nordenfelt (Sweden); Edith Oeser (German Democratic Republic); Lia Patiño de Martínez (Panama); Esther Véliz Díaz de Villalvilla (Cuba).

To serve until 15 April 1986: A. P. Biryukova (USSR); Irene R. Cortes (Philippines); Farida Abou El-Fetouh (Egypt);[a] Guan Minqian (China); Luvsandanzangyn Ider, *Chairman* (Mongolia); Zagorka Ilic, *Vice-Chairman* (Yugoslavia); Vinitha Jayasinghe (Sri Lanka); Raquel Macedo de Sheppard (Uruguay); Landrada Mukayiranga, *Vice-Chairman* (Rwanda); Vesselina Peytcheva (Bulgaria); Maria Regent-Lechowicz (Poland); Lucy Smith (Norway).[a]

[a]Appointment approved by the Committee on 1 August 1983 to replace, respectively: Mervat Tallawy (Egypt), who had been elected in 1982 but, having become a United Nations staff member, was ineligible; and Rakel Surlien (Norway), who resigned.

Committee on the Elimination of Racial Discrimination

The Committee on the Elimination of Racial Discrimination was established under the International Convention on the Elimination of All Forms of Racial Discrimination.[31] It consists of 18 experts elected by the States parties to the Convention to serve in their personal capacity, with due regard for equitable geographical distribution and for representation of the different forms of civilization and principal legal systems. Members serve for four-year terms.

The Committee held two sessions in 1983, at United Nations Headquarters: its twenty-seventh from 7 to 25 March; and its twenty-eighth from 11 to 29 July.

Members:

To serve until 19 January 1984: Eugenio Carlos José Aramburu (Argentina); Pedro Brin Martínez (Panama); André Dechezelles (France); Silvo Devetak (Yugoslavia); José D. Ingles, *Chairman* (Philippines); Matey Karasimeonov (Bulgaria);[a] Erik Nettel (Austria); Shanti Sadiq Ali (India); G. B. Starushenko, *Vice-Chairman* (USSR).

To serve until 19 January 1986: Jean-Marie Apiou (Upper Volta); Dimitrios J. Evrigenis (Greece); Oladapo Olusola Fafowora (Nigeria); Abdel Moneim M. Ghoneim (Egypt); George O. Lamptey, *Vice-Chairman* (Ghana); Karl Josef Partsch, *Rapporteur* (Federal Republic of Germany); Agha Shahi (Pakistan); Michael E. Sherifis (Cyprus); Luis Valencia Rodríguez, *Vice-Chairman* (Ecuador).

[a]Appointment approved by the Committee on 8 March 1983 to replace Yuli Bahnev (Bulgaria), who resigned by a letter of 14 January.

Human Rights Committee

The Human Rights Committee was established under the International Covenant on Civil and Political Rights.[32] It consists of 18 experts elected by the States parties to the Covenant to serve in their personal capacity for four-year terms.

The Committee, which reports annually to the General Assembly through the Economic and Social Council, held three sessions in 1983: its eighteenth at United Nations Headquarters from 21 March to 8 April; and its nineteenth and twentieth at Geneva from 11 to 29 July and from 24 October to 11 November, respectively.

Members:

To serve until 31 December 1984: Andrés Aguilar (Venezuela); Mohammed Abdullah Ahmed Al Douri (Iraq); Felix Ermacora (Austria); Sir Vincent Evans (United Kingdom); Vladimir Hanga (Romania); Leonte Herdocia Ortega (Nicaragua);[a] Andreas V. Mavrommatis, *Chairman* (Cyprus); A. P. Movchan (USSR); Walter Surma Tarnopolsky, *Rapporteur* (Canada).[b]

To serve until 31 December 1986: Néjib Bouziri, *Vice-Chairman* (Tunisia); Joseph A. L. Cooray (Sri Lanka); Vojin Dimitrijevic (Yugoslavia); Roger Errera (France); Bernhard Graefrath, *Vice-Chairman* (German Democratic Republic); Birame Ndiaye (Senegal);[c] Torkel Opsahl (Norway); Julio Prado Vallejo, *Vice-Chairman* (Ecuador); Christian Tomuschat (Federal Republic of Germany).

[a]On 28 October 1983, the Committee was informed of his death; no replacement was elected in 1983.
[b]Resigned with effect from 1 August 1983; Gisèle Côté-Harper (Canada) was elected on 18 November to fill the resultant vacancy.
[c]Elected on 21 July 1983 to fill the vacancy created by the death of Abdoulaye Diéye (Senegal), of which the Committee was informed on 21 March.

International Narcotics Control Board (INCB)

The International Narcotics Control Board, established under the Single Convention on Narcotic Drugs, 1961, as amended by the 1972 Protocol, consists of 13 members, elected by the Economic and Social Council for five-year terms, three from candidates nominated by WHO and 10 from candidates nominated by Members of the United Nations and parties to the Single Convention.

The Board held two sessions in 1983, at Vienna, Austria: its thirty-third from 16 to 27 May; and its thirty-fourth from 4 to 21 October.

Members:

To serve until 1 March 1985: Dr. Bela Bolcs (Hungary); Dr. John C. Ebie, *Rapporteur* (Nigeria);[a] Dr. Diego Garcés-Giraldo (Colombia); Dr. Mohsen Kchouk (Tunisia); Dr. Victorio V. Olguín, *President* (Argentina); Jasjit Singh, *First Vice-President* (India).

To serve until 1 March 1987: Dr. Ramón de la Fuente Muñiz (Mexico);[a] Betty C. Gough (United States); Dr. Sukru Kaymakcalan, *Second Vice-President* (Turkey);[a] Paul Reuter (France); Dr. Bror Anders Rexed (Sweden); Adolf-Heinrich von Arnim (Federal Republic of Germany); Sir Edward Williams (Australia).

[a]Elected from candidates nominated by WHO.

Preparatory Commission for the International Sea-Bed Authority and for the International Tribunal for the Law of the Sea

The Preparatory Commission for the International Sea-Bed Authority and for the International Tribunal for the Law of the Sea, established by the Third United Nations Conference on the Law of the Sea, consists of the States which have signed or acceded to the United Nations Convention on the Law of the Sea, which numbered 130 as at 31 December 1983, as well as the Cook Islands and Namibia, represented by the United Nations Council for Namibia.

In 1983, the Commission held its first session at Kingston, Jamaica, from 15 March to 8 April (first part) and from 15 August to 9 September (resumed).

Members: Afghanistan, Algeria, Angola, Antigua and Barbuda, Australia, Austria, Bahamas, Bahrain, Bangladesh, Barbados, Belize, Benin, Bhutan, Brazil, Bulgaria, Burma, Burundi, Byelorussian SSR, Canada, Cape Verde, Chad, Chile, China, Colombia, Congo, Cook Islands, Costa Rica, Cuba, Cyprus, Czechoslovakia, Democratic Kampuchea, Democratic People's Republic of Korea, Democratic Yemen, Denmark, Djibouti, Dominica, Dominican Republic, Egypt, Ethiopia, Fiji, Finland, France, Gabon, Gambia, German Democratic Republic, Ghana, Greece, Grenada, Guatemala, Guinea-Bissau, Guyana, Haiti, Honduras, Hungary, Iceland, India, Indonesia, Iran, Iraq, Ireland, Ivory Coast, Jamaica, Japan, Kenya, Kuwait, Lao Peo-

[30]General Assembly resolution 34/180, annex, article 17, 18 December 1979 (YUN 1979, p. 898).
[31]General Assembly resolution 2106 A (XX), annex, article 8, 21 December 1965 (YUN 1965, p. 443).
[32]General Assembly resolution 2200 A (XXI), annex, part IV, 16 December 1966 (YUN 1966, p. 427).

ple's Democratic Republic, Lesotho, Liberia, Madagascar, Malaysia, Maldives, Mali, Malta, Mauritania, Mauritius, Mexico, Monaco, Mongolia, Morocco, Mozambique, Namibia (United Nations Council for), Nauru, Nepal, Netherlands, New Zealand, Niger, Nigeria, Norway, Oman, Pakistan, Panama, Papua New Guinea, Paraguay, Philippines, Poland, Portugal, Republic of Korea, Romania, Rwanda, Saint Lucia, Saint Vincent and the Grenadines, Sao Tome and Principe, Senegal, Seychelles, Sierra Leone, Singapore, Solomon Islands, Somalia, Sri Lanka, Sudan, Suriname, Sweden, Thailand, Togo, Trinidad and Tobago, Tunisia, Tuvalu, Uganda, Ukrainian SSR, USSR, United Arab Emirates, United Republic of Cameroon, United Republic of Tanzania, Upper Volta, Uruguay, Vanuatu, Viet Nam, Yemen, Yugoslavia, Zaire, Zambia, Zimbabwe.

Chairman: Joseph S. Warioba (United Republic of Tanzania).
Vice-Chairmen: Algeria, Australia, Brazil, Chile, China, France, India, Iraq, Japan, Liberia, Nigeria, Sri Lanka, USSR, United Republic of Cameroon.
Rapporteur-General: Kenneth O. Rattray (Jamaica).

CREDENTIALS COMMITTEE

Members: Austria, China, Colombia, Costa Rica, Hungary, Ireland, Ivory Coast, Japan, Somalia.
Chairman: Karl Wolf (Austria).

GENERAL COMMITTEE

The General Committee consists of the Commission's Chairman, the 14 Vice-Chairmen, the Rapporteur-General and the 20 officers of the four Special Commissions.

SPECIAL COMMISSIONS

The four Special Commissions, each composed of all the members of the Commission, were established on 8 September 1983.

Special Commission 1 (on the problem of land-based producers)
Chairman: Hasjim Djalal (Indonesia).
Vice-Chairmen: Austria, Cuba, Romania, Zambia.

Special Commission 2 (on the Enterprise)
Chairman: Lennox Ballah (Trinidad and Tobago).
Vice-Chairmen: Canada, Mongolia, Senegal, Yugoslavia.

Special Commission 3 (on the mining code)
Chairman: Hans H. M. Sondaal (Netherlands).
Vice-Chairmen: Gabon, Mexico, Pakistan, Poland.

Special Commission 4 (on the International Tribunal for the Law of the Sea)
Chairman: Gunter Goerner (German Democratic Republic).
Vice-Chairmen: Colombia, Greece, Philippines, Sudan.

Principal members of the United Nations Secretariat
(as at 31 December 1983)

Secretariat

The Secretary-General: Javier Pérez de Cuéllar

Executive Office of the Secretary-General
Under-Secretary-General, Chef de Cabinet: Virendra Dayal

Office of the Director-General for Development and International Economic Co-operation
Director-General: Jean L. Ripert

Office of the Under-Secretaries-General for Special Political Affairs
Under-Secretaries-General: Diego Cordovez, Brian E. Urquhart
Assistant Secretary-General: Fou-Tchin Liu

Office for Special Political Questions
Under-Secretary-General, Co-ordinator, Special Economic Assistance Programmes: Abdulrahim Abby Farah
Assistant Secretary-General, Joint Co-ordinator, Unit for Special Economic Assistance Programmes: Sotirios Mousouris

Office of the Under-Secretary-General for Political and General Assembly Affairs
Under-Secretary-General: William B. Buffum

Office of Secretariat Services for Economic and Social Matters
Assistant Secretary-General: Robert G. Muller

Office for Field Operational and External Support Activities
Assistant Secretary-General: James O. C. Jonah

Office of Legal Affairs
Under-Secretary-General, the Legal Counsel: Carl-August Fleischhauer

Department of Political and Security Council Affairs
Under-Secretary-General: Viacheslav A. Ustinov

Assistant Secretary-General, Centre against Apartheid: Enuga S. Reddy

Department of Political Affairs, Trusteeship and Decolonization
Under-Secretary-General: Rafeeuddin Ahmed

Department for Disarmament Affairs
Under-Secretary-General: Jan Martenson

Department of International Economic and Social Affairs
Under-Secretary-General: Shuaib Uthman Yolah
Assistant Secretary-General for Development Research and Policy Analysis: P. N. Dhar
Assistant Secretary-General for Programme Planning and Co-ordination: Peter Hansen
Assistant Secretary-General for Social Development and Humanitarian Affairs: Leticia R. Shahani

Department of Technical Co-operation for Development
Under-Secretary-General: Bi Jilong
Assistant Secretary-General: Margaret Joan Anstee

Economic Commission for Europe
Under-Secretary-General, Executive Secretary: Klaus Aksel Sahlgren

Economic and Social Commission for Asia and the Pacific
Under-Secretary-General, Executive Secretary: Shah A. M. S. Kibria

Economic Commission for Latin America
Under-Secretary-General, Executive Secretary: Enrique V. Iglesias

Economic Commission for Africa
Under-Secretary-General, Executive Secretary: Adebayo Adedeji

Economic Commission for Western Asia
Under-Secretary-General, Executive Secretary: Mohamed Said Al-Attar

Centre for Science and Technology for Development
Assistant Secretary-General, Executive Director: Amilcar F. Ferrari

United Nations Centre for Human Settlements
Under-Secretary-General, Executive Director: Arcot Ramachandran

United Nations Centre on Transnational Corporations
Assistant Secretary-General, Executive Director: Sydney Dell

Department of Administration and Management
Under-Secretary-General: Patricio Ruedas

OFFICE OF FINANCIAL SERVICES
Assistant Secretary-General: J. Richard Foran

OFFICE OF PERSONNEL SERVICES
Assistant Secretary-General: Louis-Pascal Nègre

OFFICE OF GENERAL SERVICES
Assistant Secretary-General: Clayton C. Timbrell

Department of Conference Services
Under-Secretary-General for Conference Services and Special Assignments: Eugeniusz Wyzner

Department of Public Information
Under-Secretary-General: Yasushi Akashi

United Nations Office at Geneva
Under-Secretary-General, Director-General of the United Nations Office at Geneva: Erik Suy
Assistant Secretary-General, Personal Representative of the Secretary-General, Secretary of the Committee on Disarmament: Rikhi Jaipal

Centre for Human Rights
Assistant Secretary-General: Kurt Herndl

United Nations Office at Vienna
Assistant Secretary-General, Director-General: Mowaffak Allaf

International Court of Justice Registry
Registrar: Santiago Torres Bernárdez

Secretariats of subsidiary organs, special representatives and other related bodies

Office of the Special Representative of the Secretary-General for Namibia
Under-Secretary-General, Special Representative of the Secretary-General: Martti Ahtisaari

Office of the United Nations Disaster Relief Co-ordinator
Under-Secretary-General, Disaster Relief Co-ordinator: M'Hamed Essaafi

Office of the Special Representative of the Secretary-General for Humanitarian Affairs in South-East Asia
Under-Secretary-General: Rafeeuddin Ahmed

Office of the United Nations High Commissioner for Refugees
High Commissioner: Poul Hartling
Deputy High Commissioner: William Richard Smyser

International Conference on the Question of Palestine
Under-Secretary-General, Secretary-General of the Conference: Lucille M. Mair

United Nations Conference for the Promotion of International Co-operation in the Peaceful Uses of Nuclear Energy
Assistant Secretary-General, Secretary-General of the Conference: Amrik S. Mehta

Office of the Special Representative of the Secretary-General for the Law of the Sea
Assistant Secretary-General, Special Representative of the Secretary-General: Satya N. Nandan

Office of the United Nations Co-ordinator of Assistance for the Reconstruction and Development of Lebanon
Assistant Secretary-General, Co-ordinator: Iqbal A. Akhund

Office of the United Nations Commissioner for Namibia
Assistant Secretary-General, Commissioner for Namibia: Brajesh Chandra Mishra

United Nations Children's Fund
Under-Secretary-General, Executive Director: James P. Grant
Assistant Secretary-General, Deputy Executive Director, Operations: Karl-Eric Knutsson
Assistant Secretary-General, Deputy Executive Director, Programmes: Richard Jolly
Assistant Secretary-General, Deputy Executive Director for External Relations: Varindra T. Vittachi

United Nations Conference on Trade and Development
Under-Secretary-General, Secretary-General of the Conference: Gamani Corea
Assistant Secretaries-General, Deputy Secretaries-General of the Conference: Alister McIntyre, Johannes Pronk

United Nations Development Programme
Administrator: F. Bradford Morse
Deputy Administrator: G. Arthur Brown
Assistant Administrator, Bureau for Finance and Administration: Pierre Vinde
Assistant Administrator, Bureau for Special Activities: Paul Thyness
Assistant Administrator and Director, Bureau for Programme Policy and Evaluation: Horst P. Wiesebach
Executive Director, United Nations Fund for Population Activities: Rafael M. Salas
Deputy Executive Director, United Nations Fund for Population Activities: Heino E. Wittrin
Assistant Executive Director, United Nations Fund for Population Activities: Nafis I. Sadik
Assistant Administrator and Regional Director, Regional Bureau for Africa: Pierre-Claver Damiba
Assistant Administrator and Regional Director, Regional Bureau for Arab States: Mustapha Zaanouni
Assistant Administrator and Regional Director, Regional Bureau for Asia and the Pacific: Andrew J. Joseph
Assistant Administrator and Regional Director, Regional Bureau for Latin America: Hugo Navajas-Mogro
Assistant Administrator and Director, European Office, Geneva: Pierre Bourgois

United Nations Disengagement Observer Force
Force Commander: Major-General Carl-Gustav Stahl

United Nations Environment Programme
Executive Director: Mostafa Kamal Tolba
Assistant Secretary-General, Deputy Executive Director: Joseph Wheeler
Assistant Secretary-General, Assistant Executive Director, Office of the Environment Programme: Gennady N. Golubev
Assistant Secretary-General, Assistant Executive Director, Office of the Environment Fund and Administration: Rudolf Schmidt

United Nations Fund for Drug Abuse Control
Assistant Secretary-General, Executive Director: Giuseppe di Gennaro

United Nations Industrial Development Organization
Under-Secretary-General, Executive Director: Abd-El Rahman Khane
Assistant Secretary-General, Deputy Executive Director: Philippe Jacques Farlan Carré

United Nations Institute for Training and Research
Under-Secretary-General, Executive Director: Michel Doo Kingué

United Nations Interim Force in Lebanon
Force Commander: Lieutenant-General William Callaghan

United Nations Peace-keeping Force in Cyprus
Force Commander: Major-General Günther G. Greindl
Special Representative of the Secretary-General: Hugo J. Gobbi

United Nations Relief and Works Agency for Palestine Refugees in the Near East
Commissioner-General: Olof Rydbeck

United Nations Truce Supervision Organization
Assistant Secretary-General, Chief of Staff: Lieutenant-General Emmanuel Alexander Erskine

United Nations University
Rector: Mr. Soedjatmoko

World Food Council
Assistant Secretary-General, Executive Director: Maurice J. Williams

---

On 31 December 1983, the total number of staff of the United Nations holding permanent, probationary and fixed-term appointments with service or expected service of a year or more was 26,993. Of these, 9,100 were in the Professional and higher categories and 17,893 were in the General Service, Manual Worker and Field Service categories. Of the same total, 24,036 were regular staff serving at Headquarters or other established offices and 2,957 were assigned as project personnel to technical co-operation projects. In addition, UNRWA had some 17,000 local area staff.

Appendix IV

Agenda of United Nations principal organs in 1983

This appendix lists the items on the agenda of the General Assembly, the Security Council, the Economic and Social Council and the Trusteeship Council during 1983. For the Assembly and the Economic and Social Council, the column headed "Allocation" indicates the assignment of each item to plenary meetings or committees.

Agenda item titles have been shortened by omitting mention of reports following the subject of the item. Thus, "Question of Cyprus: report of the Secretary-General" has been shortened to "Question of Cyprus". Where the subject-matter of the item is not apparent from its title, the subject is identified in square brackets; this is not part of the title.

General Assembly

Agenda items considered at the resumed thirty-seventh session
(10-13 May and 19 September 1983)

Item No.	Title	Allocation
2.	Minute of silent prayer or meditation.	Plenary
8.	Adoption of the agenda and organization of work.	Plenary
27.	Preparation of the United Nations Conference for the Promotion of International Co-operation in the Peaceful Uses of Nuclear Energy.	Plenary
37.	Question of Cyprus.	Plenary, SPC[1]
38.	Launching of global negotiations on international economic co-operation for development.	Plenary
110.	Scale of assessments for the apportionment of the expenses of the United Nations.	2
141.	Implementation of the resolutions of the United Nations.	Plenary

Agenda of the thirty-eighth session
(first part, 20 September–20 December 1983)

Item No.	Title	Allocation
1.	Opening of the session by the Chairman of the delegation of Hungary.	Plenary
2.	Minute of silent prayer or meditation.	Plenary
3.	Credentials of representatives to the thirty-eighth session of the General Assembly: (a) Appointment of the members of the Credentials Committee; (b) Report of the Credentials Committee.	Plenary Plenary
4.	Election of the President of the General Assembly.	Plenary
5.	Election of the officers of the Main Committees.	Plenary
6.	Election of the Vice-Presidents of the General Assembly.	Plenary
7.	Notification by the Secretary-General under Article 12, paragraph 2, of the Charter of the United Nations.	Plenary
8.	Adoption of the agenda and organization of work.	Plenary
9.	General debate.	Plenary
10.	Report of the Secretary-General on the work of the Organization.	Plenary
11.	Report of the Security Council.	Plenary
12.	Report of the Economic and Social Council.	Plenary, 2nd, 3rd, 4th, 5th
13.	Report of the International Court of Justice.	Plenary
14.	Report of the International Atomic Energy Agency.	Plenary
15.	Elections to fill vacancies in principal organs: (a) Election of five non-permanent members of the Security Council; (b) Election of eighteen members of the Economic and Social Council.	Plenary Plenary
16.	Elections to fill vacancies in subsidiary organs: (a) Election of fifteen members of the Industrial Development Board;	Plenary

---

[1]Hearings of Cypriot representatives.
[2]Allocated to the Fifth Committee at the first part of the session in 1982 but considered only in plenary meetings at the resumed session.

Item No.	Title	Allocation
(b)	Election of nineteen members of the Governing Counccil of the United Nations Environment Programme;	Plenary
(c)	Election of twelve members of the World Food Council;	Plenary
(d)	Election of seven members of the Committee for Programme and Co-ordination;	Plenary
(e)	Election of the members of the Board of Governors of the United Nations Special Fund for Land-locked Developing Countries.	Plenary
17.	Appointments to fill vacancies in subsidiary organs and other appointments:	
(a)	Appointment of six members of the Advisory Committee on Administrative and Budgetary Questions;	5th
(b)	Appointment of six members of the Committee on Contributions;	5th
(c)	Appointment of a member of the Board of Auditors;	5th
(d)	Confirmation of the appointment of three members of the Investments Committee;	5th
(e)	Appointment of two members of the United Nations Administrative Tribunal;	5th
(f)	Confirmation of the appointment of the Administrator of the United Nations Development Programme;	Plenary
(g)	Appointment of the United Nations Commissioner for Namibia;	Plenary
(h)	Confirmation of the appointment of the Executive Director of the United Nations Special Fund for Land-locked Developing Countries;	Plenary
(i)	Appointment of a member of the International Civil Service Commission.	5th
18.	Implementation of the Declaration on the Granting of Independence to Colonial Countries and Peoples.	Plenary, 4th
19.	Admission of new Members to the United Nations.	Plenary
20.	Return or restitution of cultural property to the countries of origin.	Plenary
21.	Thirty-five years of the Universal Declaration of Human Rights: international co-operation for the promotion and observance of civil, political, economic, social and cultural rights.	Plenary
22.	Co-operation between the United Nations and the Organization of the Islamic Conference.	Plenary
23.	The situation in Kampuchea.	Plenary
24.	Co-operation between the United Nations and the Asian-African Legal Consultative Committee.	Plenary
25.	Question of the Falkland Islands (Malvinas).	Plenary, 4th[3]
26.	Co-operation between the United Nations and the Organization of African Unity.	Plenary
27.	Co-operation between the United Nations and the League of Arab States.	Plenary
28.	Armed Israeli aggression against the Iraqi nuclear installations and its grave consequences for the established international system concerning the peaceful uses of nuclear energy, the non-proliferation of nuclear weapons and international peace and security.	Plenary
29.	The situation in Afghanistan and its implications for international peace and security.	Plenary
30.	Question of the Comorian island of Mayotte.	Plenary
31.	Third United Nations Conference on the Law of the Sea.	Plenary
32.	Policies of *apartheid* of the Government of South Africa.	Plenary, SPC[3]
33.	Question of Palestine.	Plenary
34.	The situation in the Middle East.	Plenary
35.	United Nations Conference for the Promotion of International Co-operation in the Peaceful Uses of Nuclear Energy.	Plenary
36.	Question of Namibia.	Plenary, 4th[3]
37.	Question of peace, stability and co-operation in South-East Asia.	Plenary
38.	Launching of global negotiations on international economic co-operation for development.	Plenary
39.	Question of equitable representation on and increase in the membership of the Security Council.	Plenary
40.	Observance of the quincentenary of the discovery of America.	Plenary
41.	Question of Cyprus.	4
42.	Implementation of the resolutions of the United Nations.	Plenary
43.	Implementation of General Assembly resolution 37/71 concerning the signature and ratification of Additional Protocol I of the Treaty for the Prohibition of Nuclear Weapons in Latin America (Treaty of Tlatelolco).	1st
44.	Cessation of all test explosions of nuclear weapons.	1st
45.	Urgent need for a comprehensive nuclear-test-ban treaty.	1st
46.	Implementation of the Declaration on the Denuclearization of Africa.	1st
47.	Establishment of a nuclear-weapon-free zone in the region of the Middle East.	1st
48.	Establishment of a nuclear-weapon-free zone in South Asia.	1st

---

[3]Hearings of organizations.

[4]On 23 September 1983, the General Assembly adopted the General Committee's recommendation that the allocation of item 41 should be deferred until an appropriate time in the future.

Item No.	*Title*	*Allocation*
49.	Prohibition of the development and manufacture of new types of weapons of mass destruction and new systems of such weapons.	1st
50.	Review of the implementation of the recommendations and decisions adopted by the General Assembly at its tenth special session:	
	(a) Report of the Disarmament Commission;	1st
	(b) Report of the Committee on Disarmament;	1st
	(c) Bilateral nuclear-arms negotiations;	1st
	(d) Cessation of the nuclear-arms race and nuclear disarmament;	1st
	(e) Disarmament Week;	1st
	(f) Prohibition of the nuclear neutron weapon;	1st
	(g) Implementation of the recommendations and decisions of the tenth special session;	1st
	(h) Prevention of nuclear war;	1st
	(i) Proposal for the establishment of an international satellite monitoring agency;	1st
	(j) Advisory Board on Disarmament Studies.	1st
51.	United Nations Conference on Prohibitions or Restrictions of Use of Certain Conventional Weapons Which May Be Deemed to Be Excessively Injurious or to Have Indiscriminate Effects.	1st
52.	Conclusion of an international convention on the strengthening of the security of non-nuclear-weapon States against the use or threat of use of nuclear weapons.	1st
53.	Conclusion of effective international arrangements to assure non-nuclear-weapon States against the use or threat of use of nuclear weapons.	1st
54.	Israeli nuclear armament.	1st
55.	Prevention of an arms race in outer space.	1st
56.	Relationship between disarmament and development.	1st
57.	Immediate cessation and prohibition of nuclear-weapon tests.	1st
58.	Reduction of military budgets.	1st
59.	Implementation of the Declaration of the Indian Ocean as a Zone of Peace.	1st
60.	World Disarmament Conference.	1st
61.	Chemical and bacteriological (biological) weapons.	1st
62.	General and complete disarmament:	
	(a) Report of the Disarmament Commission;	1st
	(b) Report of the Committee on Disarmament;	1st
	(c) Study on conventional disarmament;	1st
	(d) Non-stationing of nuclear weapons on the territories of States where there are no such weapons at present;	1st
	(e) Independent Commission on Disarmament and Security Issues;	1st
	(f) Prohibition of the development, production, stockpiling and use of radiological weapons;	1st
	(g) Prevention of an arms race in outer space and prohibition of anti-satellite systems;	1st
	(h) Prohibition of the production of fissionable material for weapons purposes;	1st
	(i) Measures to provide objective information on military capabilities;	1st
	(j) Institutional arrangements relating to the process of disarmament.	1st
63.	Review and implementation of the Concluding Document of the Twelfth Special Session of the General Assembly:	
	(a) Freeze on nuclear weapons;	1st
	(b) Implementation of General Assembly resolution 37/100 B on a nuclear-arms freeze;	1st
	(c) Convention on the Prohibition of the Use of Nuclear Weapons;	1st
	(d) Consideration of guidelines for confidence-building measures;	1st
	(e) Regional disarmament;	1st
	(f) United Nations programme of fellowships on disarmament;	1st
	(g) World Disarmament Campaign.	1st
64.	Development and strengthening of good-neighbourliness between States.	6th
65.	Strengthening of security and co-operation in the Mediterranean region.	1st
66.	Review of the implementation of the Declaration on the Strengthening of International Security.	1st
67.	Implementation of the collective security provisions of the Charter of the United Nations for the maintenance of international peace and security.	1st
68.	Effects of atomic radiation.	SPC
69.	Report of the Special Committee to Investigate Israeli Practices Affecting the Human Rights of the Population of the Occupied Territories.	SPC
70.	International co-operation in the peaceful uses of outer space:	
	(a) Report of the Committee on the Peaceful Uses of Outer Space;	SPC
	(b) Implementation of the recommendations of the Second United Nations Conference on the Exploration and Peaceful Uses of Outer Space.	SPC
71.	Comprehensive review of the whole question of peace-keeping operations in all their aspects.	SPC
72.	Questions relating to information.	SPC
73.	United Nations Relief and Works Agency for Palestine Refugees in the Near East.	SPC

Item No.	Title	Allocation
74.	International co-operation to avert new flows of refugees.	SPC
75.	Israel's decision to build a canal linking the Mediterranean Sea to the Dead Sea.	SPC
76.	Question of the Malagasy islands of Glorieuses, Juan de Nova, Europa and Bassas da India.	SPC
77.	Question of the composition of the relevant organs of the United Nations.	SPC
78.	Development and international economic co-operation:	
	(a) International Development Strategy for the Third United Nations Development Decade;	2nd
	(b) Trade and development;	2nd
	(c) Industrialization;	2nd
	(d) Science and technology for development;	2nd
	(e) Food problems;	2nd
	(f) Economic and technical co-operation among developing countries;	2nd
	(g) Environment;	2nd
	(h) Human settlements;	2nd
	(i) International Year of Shelter for the Homeless;	2nd
	(j) Effective mobilization and integration of women in development;	2nd
	(k) United Nations Special Fund;	2nd
	(l) New and renewable sources of energy;	2nd
	(m) Implementation of the Substantial New Programme of Action for the 1980s for the Least Developed Countries;	2nd
	(n) New international human order: moral aspects of development.	2nd
79.	Operational activities for development:	
	(a) Operational activities of the United Nations system;	2nd
	(b) United Nations Development Programme;	2nd
	(c) United Nations Capital Development Fund;	2nd
	(d) United Nations Fund for Population Activities;	2nd
	(e) United Nations Volunteers programme;	2nd
	(f) United Nations Special Fund for Land-locked Developing Countries;	2nd
	(g) United Nations Children's Fund;	2nd
	(h) World Food Programme;	2nd
	(i) Technical co-operation activities undertaken by the Secretary-General.	2nd
80.	Training and research:	
	(a) United Nations Institute for Training and Research;	2nd
	(b) United Nations University;	2nd
	(c) Unified approach to development analysis and planning.	2nd
81.	Special economic and disaster relief assistance:	
	(a) Office of the United Nations Disaster Relief Co-ordinator;	2nd
	(b) Special programmes of economic assistance;	2nd
	(c) Implementation of the medium-term and long-term recovery and rehabilitation programme in the Sudano-Sahelian region.	2nd
82.	Implementation of the Programme for the Decade for Action to Combat Racism and Racial Discrimination.	3rd
83.	Second World Conference to Combat Racism and Racial Discrimination.	3rd
84.	International Youth Year: Participation, Development, Peace.	3rd
85.	World social situation:	
	(a) Implementation of General Assembly resolution 37/54;	3rd
	(b) National experience in achieving far-reaching social and economic changes for the purpose of social progress;	3rd
	(c) Popular participation in its various forms as an important factor in development and in the realization of human rights.	3rd
86.	Importance of the universal realization of the right of peoples to self-determination and of the speedy granting of independence to colonial countries and peoples for the effective guarantee and observance of human rights.	3rd
87.	Elimination of all forms of racial discrimination:	
	(a) Report of the Committee on the Elimination of Racial Discrimination;	3rd
	(b) Status of the International Convention on the Elimination of All Forms of Racial Discrimination;	3rd
	(c) Status of the International Convention on the Suppression and Punishment of the Crime of *Apartheid*.	3rd
88.	Policies and programmes relating to youth.	3rd
89.	Question of aging.	3rd
90.	World Programme of Action concerning Disabled Persons.	3rd
91.	United Nations Decade for Women: Equality, Development and Peace:	
	(a) Implementation of the Programme of Action for the Second Half of the United Nations Decade for Women;	3rd
	(b) Preparations for the World Conference to Review and Appraise the Achievements of the United Nations Decade for Women;	3rd
	(c) International Research and Training Institute for the Advancement of Women;	3rd
	(d) Voluntary Fund for the United Nations Decade for Women.	3rd
92.	Elimination of all forms of discrimination against women:	

Item No.	Title	Allocation
	(a) Report of the Committee on the Elimination of Discrimination against Women;	3rd
	(b) Status of the Convention on the Elimination of All Forms of Discrimination against Women.	3rd
93.	Elimination of all forms of religious intolerance.	3rd
94.	Human rights and scientific and technological developments.	3rd
95.	Question of a convention on the rights of the child.	3rd
96.	International Covenants on Human Rights:	
	(a) Report of the Human Rights Committee;	3rd
	(b) Status of the International Covenant on Economic, Social and Cultural Rights, the International Covenant on Civil and Political Rights and the Optional Protocol to the International Covenant on Civil and Political Rights.	3rd
97.	Torture and other cruel, inhuman or degrading treatment or punishment.	3rd
98.	Office of the United Nations High Commissioner for Refugees:	
	(a) Report of the High Commissioner;	3rd
	(b) Assistance to refugees in Africa.	3rd
99.	International campaign against traffic in drugs.	3rd
100.	Alternative approaches and ways and means within the United Nations system for improving the effective enjoyment of human rights and fundamental freedoms:	
	(a) Study on international conditions and human rights;	3rd
	(b) National institutions for the promotion and protection of human rights.	3rd
101.	New international humanitarian order.	3rd
102.	Information from Non-Self-Governing Territories transmitted under Article 73 *e* of the Charter of the United Nations.	4th
103.	Activities of foreign economic and other interests which are impeding the implementation of the Declaration on the Granting of Independence to Colonial Countries and Peoples in Namibia and in all other Territories under colonial domination and efforts to eliminate colonialism, apartheid and racial discrimination in southern Africa.	4th
104.	Implementation of the Declaration on the Granting of Independence to Colonial Countries and Peoples by the specialized agencies and the international institutions associated with the United Nations.	4th
105.	United Nations Educational and Training Programme for Southern Africa.	4th
106.	Offers by Member States of study and training facilities for inhabitants of Non-Self-Governing Territories.	4th
107.	Financial reports and audited financial statements, and reports of the Board of Auditors:	
	(a) United Nations Development Programme;	5th
	(b) United Nations Children's Fund;	5th
	(c) United Nations Relief and Works Agency for Palestine Refugees in the Near East;	5th
	(d) United Nations Institute for Training and Research;	5th
	(e) Voluntary funds administered by the United Nations High Commissioner for Refugees;	5th
	(f) United Nations Fund for Population Activities.	5th
108.	Programme budget for the biennium 1982-1983.	5th
109.	Proposed programme budget for the biennium 1984-1985.	5th
110.	Programme planning.	5th
111.	Financial emergency of the United Nations.	5th
112.	Administrative and budgetary co-ordination of the United Nations with the specialized agencies and the International Atomic Energy Agency:	
	(a) Report of the Advisory Committee on Administrative and Budgetary Questions;	5th
	(b) Feasibility of establishing a single administrative tribunal.	5th
113.	Joint Inspection Unit.	5th
114.	Pattern of conferences.	5th
115.	Scale of assessments for the apportionment of the expenses of the United Nations.	5th
116.	Personnel questions:	
	(a) Composition of the Secretariat;	5th
	(b) Respect for the privileges and immunities of officials of the United Nations and the specialized agencies and related organizations;	5th
	(c) Other personnel questions.	5th
117.	United Nations common system.	5th
118.	United Nations pension system.	5th
119.	Financing of the United Nations peace-keeping forces in the Middle East:	
	(a) United Nations Disengagement Observer Force;	5th
	(b) United Nations Interim Force in Lebanon.	5th
120.	Consideration of the draft articles on most-favoured-nation clauses.	6th
121.	Progressive development of the principles and norms of international law relating to the new international economic order.	6th

Item No.	Title	Allocation
122.	United Nations Programme of Assistance in the Teaching, Study, Dissemination and Wider Appreciation of International Law.	6th
123.	Measures to prevent international terrorism which endangers or takes innocent human lives or jeopardizes fundamental freedoms and study of the underlying causes of those forms of terrorism and acts of violence which lie in misery, frustration, grievance and despair and which cause some people to sacrifice human lives, including their own, in an attempt to effect radical changes.	6th
124.	Peaceful settlement of disputes between States.	6th
125.	Draft Code of Offences against the Peace and Security of Mankind.	6th
126.	Report of the Special Committee on Enhancing the Effectiveness of the Principle of Non-Use of Force in International Relations.	6th
127.	Report of the United Nations Commission on International Trade Law on the work of its sixteenth session.	6th
128.	Consideration of effective measures to enhance the protection, security and safety of diplomatic and consular missions and representatives.	6th
129.	Report of the *Ad Hoc* Committee on the Drafting of an International Convention against the Recruitment, Use, Financing and Training of Mercenaries.	6th
130.	Review of the multilateral treaty-making process.	6th
131.	Report of the International Law Commission on the work of its thirty-fifth session.	6th
132.	Convention on the Law of Treaties between States and International Organizations or between International Organizations.	6th
133.	Report of the Committee on Relations with the Host Country.	6th
134.	Report of the Special Committee on the Charter of the United Nations and on the Strengthening of the Role of the Organization.	6th
135.	Draft Declaration on Social and Legal Principles relating to the Protection and Welfare of Children, with Special Reference to Foster Placement and Adoption Nationally and Internationally.	6th
136.	Draft Body of Principles for the Protection of All Persons under Any Form of Detention or Imprisonment.	6th
137.	Draft standard rules of procedure for United Nations conferences.	6th
138.	Consequences of the prolongation of the armed conflict between Iran and Iraq.	Plenary
139.	Implementation of the conclusions of the Second Review Conference of the Parties to the Treaty on the Non-Proliferation of Nuclear Weapons and establishment of a preparatory committee for the Third Review Conference.	1st
140.	Question of Antarctica.	1st
141.	Conclusion of a treaty on the prohibition of the use of force in outer space and from space against the Earth.	1st
142.	The situation in Central America: threats to international peace and security and peace initiatives.	Plenary
143.	Condemnation of nuclear war.	1st
144.	Nuclear-weapon freeze.	1st
145.	The situation in Grenada.	Plenary
146.	Commemoration of the fortieth anniversary of the United Nations in 1985.	Plenary

Security Council

Agenda items considered during 1983[5]

Item No.	Title
1.	The situation in the Middle East.
2.	The situation in the occupied Arab territories.
3.	Letter dated 19 February 1983 from the Permanent Representative of the Libyan Arab Jamahiriya to the United Nations addressed to the President of the Security Council (complaint against the United States).
4.	Letter dated 16 March 1983 from the Permanent Representative of Chad to the United Nations addressed to the President of the Security Council (complaint against the Libyan Arab Jamahiriya).
5.	Letter dated 22 March 1983 from the representative of Nicaragua on the Security Council addressed to the President of the Security Council (complaint against Honduras and the United States).
6.	Letter dated 5 May 1983 from the representative of Nicaragua on the Security Council addressed to the President of the Security Council (complaint against Honduras and the United States).
7.	The situation in Namibia.
8.	The question of South Africa.
9.	The situation in Cyprus.
10.	Complaint by Lesotho against South Africa.

[5]Numbers indicate the order in which items were taken up in 1983.

Item No.	Title

11. Letter dated 2 August 1983 from the Permanent Representative of Chad to the United Nations addressed to the President of the Security Council (complaint against the Libyan Arab Jamahiriya).

12. Letter dated 8 August 1983 from the Chargé d'affaires a.i. of the Permanent Mission of the Libyan Arab Jamahiriya to the United Nations addressed to the President of the Security Council (complaint against the United States).

13. Letter dated 1 September 1983 from the Acting Permanent Representative of the United States of America to the United Nations addressed to the President of the Security Council; letter dated 1 September 1983 from the Permanent Observer for the Republic of Korea to the United Nations addressed to the President of the Security Council; letter dated 1 September 1983 from the Chargé d'affaires a.i. of the Permanent Mission of Canada to the United Nations addressed to the President of the Security Council; letter dated 1 September 1983 from the Permanent Representative of Japan to the United Nations addressed to the President of the Security Council; letter dated 2 September 1983 from the Acting Permanent Representative of Australia to the United Nations addressed to the President of the Security Council (Korean Air Lines incident).

14. Letter dated 12 September 1983 from the representative of Nicaragua on the Security Council addressed to the President of the Security Council (complaint against Honduras and the United States).

15. Admission of new Members.

16. The situation in Grenada.

17. The situation between Iran and Iraq.

18. Consideration of the draft report of the Security Council to the General Assembly.

19. Complaint by Angola against South Africa.

Economic and Social Council

Agenda of the organizational session for 1983
(1-4 February 1983)

Item No.	Title	Allocation
1.	Election of the Bureau.	Plenary
2.	Adoption of the agenda and other organizational matters.	Plenary
3.	Basic programme of work of the Council for 1983 and 1984.	Plenary
4.	Elections to subsidiary bodies of the Council and confirmation of representatives on the functional commissions and on the Sessional Working Group of Governmental Experts on the Implementation of the International Covenant on Economic, Social and Cultural Rights.	Plenary
5.	Provisional agenda for the first regular session of 1983 and organizational matters.	Plenary

Agenda of the first regular session of 1983
(3-27 May 1983)

Item No.	Title	Allocation
1.	Adoption of the agenda and other organizational matters.	Plenary
2.	Decade for Action to Combat Racism and Racial Discrimination.	Plenary
3.	Non-governmental organizations.	Plenary
4.	Implementation of the International Covenant on Economic, Social and Cultural Rights.	6
5.	Preparations for the International Conference on Population in 1984.	1st
6.	Statistical questions.	1st
7.	Unified approach to development analysis and planning.	1st
8.	Transport of dangerous goods.	1st
9.	Cartography.	1st
10.	Human rights.	2nd
11.	Social development.	2nd
12.	Activities for the advancement of women: United Nations Decade for Women: Equality, Development and Peace.	2nd
13.	Narcotic drugs.	2nd

---

[6]Allocated to the Sessional Working Group of Governmental Experts on the Implementation of the International Covenant on Economic, Social and Cultural Rights.

Item No.	Title	Allocation
14.	Convention on the Elimination of All Forms of Discrimination against Women.	Plenary
15.	Elections and nominations.	Plenary
16.	Consideration of the provisional agenda for the second regular session of 1983.	Plenary

Agenda of the second regular session of 1983
(6-29 July 1983)

Item No.	Title	Allocation
1.	Opening of the session.	Plenary
2.	Adoption of the agenda and other organizational matters.	Plenary
3.	General discussion of international economic and social policy, including regional and sectoral developments.	Plenary
4.	Revitalization of the Economic and Social Council.	Plenary
5.	Permanent sovereignty over national resources in the occupied Palestinian and other Arab territories.	Plenary
6.	Report of the United Nations High Commissioner for Refugees.	Plenary
7.	Regional co-operation.	1st
8.	Transnational corporations.	1st
9.	Natural resources.	1st
10.	Development of the energy resources of the developing countries.	1st
11.	Development and utilization of new and renewable sources of energy.	1st
12.	Science and technology for development.	1st
13.	Industrial development co-operation.	1st
14.	International co-operation on the environment.	1st
15.	International co-operation in the field of human settlements.	1st
16.	Food problems.	1st
17.	Special economic, humanitarian and disaster relief assistance.	3rd
18.	Operational activities for development.	Plenary, 3rd
19.	International co-operation and co-ordination within the United Nations system.	3rd
20.	Proposed programme budget for the biennium 1984-1985.	3rd
21.	Cross-sectoral review of selected major issues in the medium-term plans of the organizations of the United Nations system.	3rd
22.	Implementation of the Declaration on the Granting of Independence to Colonial Countries and Peoples by the specialized agencies and the international institutions associated with the United Nations.	3rd
23.	Calendar of conferences.	3rd
24.	Elections and nominations.	Plenary

Trusteeship Council

Agenda of the fiftieth session
(16 May-10 June 1983)

Item No.	Title
1.	Adoption of the agenda.
2.	Report of the Secretary-General on credentials.
3.	Election of the President and the Vice-President.
4.	Examination of the annual report of the Administering Authority for the year ended 30 September 1982: Trust Territory of the Pacific Islands.
5.	Examination of petitions listed in the annex to the agenda.
6.	Report of the United Nations Visiting Mission to the Trust Territory of the Pacific Islands, 1982.
7.	Report of the United Nations Visiting Mission to Observe the Plebiscite in Palau, Trust Territory of the Pacific Islands, February 1983.
8.	Offers by Member States of study and training facilities for inhabitants of Trust Territories.
9.	Dissemination of information on the United Nations and the International Trusteeship System in Trust Territories.
10.	Co-operation with the Committee on the Elimination of Racial Discrimination.
11.	Decade for Action to Combat Racism and Racial Discrimination.

---

[7]Item considered at the resumed fiftieth session on 28 November 1983.

Appendix V

United Nations Information Centres and Services

(As at 31 December 1983)

ACCRA. United Nations Information Centre
Liberia and Maxwell Roads
(P. O. Box 2339)
Accra, Ghana
  Serving: Ghana, Sierra Leone

ADDIS ABABA. United Nations Information
  Service, Economic Commission for Africa
Africa Hall
(P. O. Box 3001)
Addis Ababa, Ethiopia
  Serving: Ethiopia

ALGIERS. United Nations Information Centre
19 Avenue Chahid El Waly Mustapha Sayed
Algiers, Algeria
  Serving: Algeria

ANKARA. United Nations Information Centre
197 Ataturk Bulvari
(P. K. 407)
Ankara, Turkey
  Serving: Turkey

ANTANANARIVO. United Nations Information
  Centre
22 Rue Rainitovo
Antsahavola
(Boîte Postale 1348)
Antananarivo, Madagascar
  Serving: Madagascar

ASUNCION. United Nations Information
  Centre
Calle Estrella y Chile
Edificio City (3er piso)
(Casilla de Correo 1107)
Asunción, Paraguay
  Serving: Paraguay

ATHENS. United Nations Information Centre
36 Amalia Avenue
GR-105, 58 Athens, Greece
  Serving: Cyprus, Greece, Israel

BAGHDAD. United Nations Information Serv-
  ice, Economic Commission for Western Asia
Amiriya, Airport Street
(P. O. Box 27)
Baghdad, Iraq
  Serving: Iraq

BANGKOK. United Nations Information Serv-
  ice, Economic and Social Commission for
  Asia and the Pacific
United Nations Building
Rajdamnern Avenue
Bangkok 10200, Thailand
  Serving: Brunei, Democratic Kam-
  puchea, Hong Kong, Lao People's Demo-
  cratic Republic, Malaysia, Singapore,
  Thailand, Viet Nam

BEIRUT. United Nations Information Centre
Apt. No. 1, Fakhoury Building
Montée Bain Militaire, Ardati Street
(P. O. Box 4656)
Beirut, Lebanon
  Serving: Jordan, Kuwait, Lebanon,
  Syrian Arab Republic

BELGRADE. United Nations Information
  Centre
Svetozara Markovica 58
(P. O. Box 157)
Belgrade, Yugloslavia YU-11001
  Serving: Albania, Yugoslavia

BOGOTA. United Nations Information Centre
Calle 61 No. 13-23 (piso 5)
(Apartado Aéreo 058964)
Bogotá 2, Colombia
  Serving: Colombia, Ecuador, Venezuela

BRAZZAVILLE. United Nations Information
  Centre
Boîte Postale 465
Brazzaville, Congo
  Serving: Congo

BRUSSELS. United Nations Information
  Centre and Liaison Office
108 Rue d'Arlon
1040 Brussels, Belgium
  Serving: Belgium, Luxembourg, Netherlands; liaison with European Communities

BUCHAREST. United Nations Information
  Centre
16 Aurel Vlaicu Street
(P. O. Box 1-701)
Bucharest, Romania
  Serving: Romania

BUENOS AIRES. United Nations Information
  Centre
Junin 1940, 1er piso
1113 Buenos Aires, Argentina
  Serving: Argentina, Uruguay

BUJUMBURA. United Nations Information
  Centre
Avenue de la Poste 7
Place de l'Indépendance
(Boîte Postale 2160)
Bujumbura, Burundi
  Serving: Burundi

CAIRO. United Nations Information Centre
1 Osiris Street
Tagher Building (Garden City)
(Boîte Postale 262)
Cairo, Egypt
  Serving: Egypt, Saudi Arabia, Yemen

COLOMBO. United Nations Information
  Centre
202-204 Bauddhaloka Mawatha
(P. O. Box 1505)
Colombo 7, Sri Lanka
  Serving: Maldives, Sri Lanka

COPENHAGEN. United Nations Information
  Centre
37 H. C. Andersen Boulevard
DK-1553 Copenhagen V, Denmark
  Serving: Denmark, Finland, Iceland, Nor-
  way, Sweden

DAKAR. United Nations Information Centre
9 Allée Robert Delmas
(Boîte Postale 154)
Dakar, Senegal
  Serving: Cape Verde, Gambia, Guinea,
  Guinea-Bissau, Ivory Coast, Mauritania,
  Senegal

DAR ES SALAAM. United Nations Informa-
  tion Centre
Samora Machel Avenue
Matasalamat Building (1st floor)
(P. O. Box 9224)
Dar es Salaam, United Republic of Tanzania
  Serving: United Republic of Tanzania

DHAKA. United Nations Information Centre
House 12, Road 6
Dhanmondi
(G. P. O. Box 3658)
Dhaka, Bangladesh
  Serving: Bangladesh

GENEVA. United Nations Information Service,
  United Nations Office at Geneva
Palais des Nations
1211 Geneva 10, Switzerland
  Serving: Bulgaria, Hungary, Poland,
  Spain, Switzerland

HARARE. United Nations Information Centre
Lenbern House, Moffat Street
(P. O. Box 4408)
Harare, Zimbabwe
    Serving: Zimbabwe

ISLAMABAD. United Nations Information
Centre
House No. 26
88th Street, Ramna 6/3
(P. O. Box 1107)
Islamabad, Pakistan
    Serving: Pakistan

KABUL. United Nations Information Centre
Shah Mahmoud Ghazi Watt
(P. O. Box 5)
Kabul, Afghanistan
    Serving: Afghanistan

KATHMANDU. United Nations Information
Centre
P. O. Box 107
Lazimpat
Kathmandu, Nepal
    Serving: Nepal

KHARTOUM. United Nations Information
Centre
Al Qasr Avenue, Street No. 15
Block 3, House 3 East
Khartoum East
(P. O. Box 1992)
Khartoum, Sudan
    Serving: Somalia, Sudan

KINSHASA. United Nations Information
Centre
Bâtiment Deuxième République
Boulevard du 30 Juin
(Boîte Postale 7248)
Kinshasa, Zaire
    Serving: Zaire

LAGOS. United Nations Information Centre
17 Kingsway Road, Ikoyi
(P. O. Box 1068)
Lagos, Nigeria
    Serving: Nigeria

LA PAZ. United Nations Information Centre
Avenida Arce No. 2529
Edificio Santa Isabel
Bloque C, 2º Mezzanine
(Apartado Postal 686)
La Paz, Bolivia
    Serving: Bolivia

LIMA. United Nations Information Centre
Mariscal Blas Cerdeña 450
San Isidro
(Apartado Postal 11199)
Lima, Peru
    Serving: Peru

LISBON. United Nations Information Centre
Rua Latino Coelho No. 1
Edificio Aviz, Bloco A1-10º
1000 Lisbon, Portugal
    Serving: Portugal

LOME. United Nations Information Centre
Rue Albert Sarraut
  coin Avenue de Gaulle
(Boîte Postale 911)
Lomé, Togo
    Serving: Benin, Togo

LONDON. United Nations Information Centre
14/15 Stratford Place
London, W1N 9AF, England
    Serving: Ireland, United Kingdom

LUSAKA. United Nations Information Centre
P. O. Box 32905
Lusaka, Zambia
    Serving: Botswana, Malawi, Swaziland,
Zambia

MANAMA. United Nations Information Centre
King Faisal Road, Gufool
(P. O. Box 26004)
Manama, Bahrain
    Serving: Bahrain, Qatar, United Arab
Emirates

MANILA. United Nations Information Centre
NEDA Building (ground floor)
106 Amorsolo Street
Legaspi Village, Makati
(P. O. Box 7285 (ADC), MIA Road, Pasay City)
Metro Manila, Philippines
    Serving: Philippines

MASERU. United Nations Information Centre
Corner Hilton Road
  opposite Sanlam Centre
Kingsway
(P. O. Box 301)
Maseru, 100 Lesotho
    Serving: Lesotho

MEXICO CITY. United Nations Information
Centre
Presidente Masaryk 29 (7º piso)
México 11570, D. F., Mexico
    Serving: Cuba, Dominican Republic,
Mexico

MONROVIA. United Nations Information
Centre
LBDI Building
Main Road, Congotown
(P. O. Box 274)
Monrovia, Liberia
    Serving: Liberia

MOSCOW. United Nations Information Centre
4/16 Ulitsa Lunacharskogo
Moscow 121002, USSR
    Serving: Byelorussian SSR, Ukrainian
SSR, USSR

NAIROBI. United Nations Information Centre
Electricity House
Harambee Avenue
(P. O. Box 30218)
Nairobi, Kenya
    Serving: Kenya, Seychelles, Uganda

NEW DELHI. United Nations Information
Centre
55 Lodi Estate
New Delhi 110 003, India
    Serving: Bhutan, India

OUAGADOUGOU. United Nations Information
Centre
218 Rue de la Gare
(Boîte Postale 135)
Ouagadougou, Upper Volta
    Serving: Chad, Mali, Niger, Upper Volta

PARIS. United Nations Information Centre
4 et 6 Avenue de Saxe
75700 Paris, France
    Serving: France

PORT MORESBY. United Nations Information
Centre
Towers Building (ground floor)
Musgrave Street, Ela Beach
(P. O. Box 472)
Port Moresby, Papua New Guinea
    Serving: Papua New Guinea, Solomon
Islands

PORT OF SPAIN. United Nations Information
Centre
15 Keate Street
(P. O. Box 130)
Port of Spain, Trinidad
    Serving: Antigua and Barbuda, Ba-
hamas, Barbados, Belize, Dominica,
Grenada, Guyana, Jamaica, Netherlands
Antilles, Saint Christopher and Nevis, Saint
Lucia, Saint Vincent and the Grenadines,
Suriname, Trinidad and Tobago

PRAGUE. United Nations Information Centre
Panska 5
11000 Prague 1, Czechoslovakia
    Serving: Czechoslovakia, German Demo-
cratic Republic

RABAT. United Nations Information Centre
Angle Charia Moulay Hassan et Zankat Assafi
(Casier ONU)
Rabat-Chellah, Morocco
    Serving: Morocco

RANGOON. United Nations Information
Centre
28A Manawhari Road
(P. O. Box 230)
Rangoon, Burma
    Serving: Burma

RIO DE JANEIRO. United Nations Information
Centre
Rua Cruz Lima 19, Grupo 201
22230 Rio de Janeiro, Brazil RJ
    Serving: Brazil

ROME. United Nations Information Centre
Palazzetto Venezia
Piazza San Marco 50
Rome, Italy
    Serving: Holy See, Italy, Malta

SAN SALVADOR. United Nations Information
Centre
Edificio Escalón (2º piso)
Paseo General Escalón y 87 Avenida Norte
Colonia Escalón
(Apartado Postal 2157)
San Salvador, El Salvador
Serving: Costa Rica, El Salvador,
Guatemala, Honduras, Nicaragua, Panama

SANTIAGO. United Nations Information Serv-
ice, Economic Commission for Latin
America
Edificio Naciones Unidas
Avenida Dag Hammarskjold
(Casilla 179-D)
Santiago, Chile
Serving: Chile

SYDNEY. United Nations Information Centre
National Mutual Centre
44 Market Street (16th floor)
(P. O. Box 4045, Sydney 2001, N. S. W.)
Sydney 2000, N. S. W., Australia
Serving: Australia, Fiji, Kiribati, Nauru,
New Zealand, Samoa, Tonga, Tuvalu,
Vanuatu

TEHERAN. United Nations Information Centre
Avenue Gandhi
43 Street No. 3
(P. O. Box 1555)
Teheran, Iran
Serving: Iran

TOKYO. United Nations Information Centre
Shin Aoyama Building Nishikan (22nd floor)
1-1 Minami Aoyama 1-chome, Minato-ku
Tokyo 107, Japan
Serving: Japan, Trust Territory of the Pa-
cific Islands

TRIPOLI. United Nations Information Centre
Zawia Street
(P. O. Box 286)
Tripoli, Libyan Arab Jamahiriya
Serving: Libyan Arab Jamahiriya

TUNIS. United Nations Information Centre
61 Boulevard Bab-Benat
(Boîte Postale 863)
Tunis, Tunisia
Serving: Tunisia

VIENNA. United Nations Information Service
Vienna International Centre
(P. O. Box 500)
A-1400 Vienna, Austria
Serving: Austria, Federal Republic of
Germany

WASHINGTON, D. C. United Nations Information Centre
1889 F Street, N. W.
Washington, D. C. 20006, United States
Serving: United States

YAOUNDE. United Nations Information Centre
Immeuble Kamden
Rue Joseph Clerc
(Boîte Postale 836)
Yaoundé, United Republic of Cameroon
Serving: Central African Republic,
Gabon, United Republic of Cameroon

Indexes

USING THE SUBJECT INDEX

The subject index to the *Yearbook of the United Nations 1983* is designed to assist the reader to find information on specific subjects. The designations employed and the presentation of entries in the index do not imply the expression of any opinion by the Department of Public Information of the United Nations. The subject index contains four types of entries:

Subject terms, including geographical names, are in bold face and, in most cases, are based on the subject descriptors used in the United Nations Bibliographical Information System (UNBIS), published in the *UNBIS Thesaurus* (United Nations Publication: Sales No. E.85.I.20). In order to minimize subentries, the index lists broad and narrow terms in their separate alphabetical positions; for example, "human rights", "racial discrimination" and "right to development". Subjects pertaining to the United Nations or the system as a whole, such as "contributions (UN)", "finances (UN)" and "staff (UN/UN system)", are indexed separately, with cross-references under "United Nations".

NAMES of organizations and subsidiary bodies, conferences, United Nations Secretariat departments and offices, programmes, and special decades and observances, are given in full in capitals and small capitals and are alphabetized in either of two ways: (1) Names of bodies, units and programmes that are part of the United Nations, names of subsidiary bodies of specialized agencies and of their affiliated institutions, and titles of special decades and observances, are indexed under their key word: APARTHEID, SPEC. CT. AGAINST; DEVELOPMENT DECADE, 3RD UN; LAW OF THE SEA, 3RD UN CF. ON THE; MARITIME DAY, WORLD; TECHNICAL CO-OPERATION FOR DEVELOPMENT, DEPARTMENT OF. (2) Names of specialized agencies and of non–United Nations organizations are alphabetized under the first word of their title: INTER-AMERICAN CS. ON HUMAN RIGHTS; WORLD METEOROLOGICAL ORGANIZATION.

Names of publications are italicized, with only those receiving relatively extensive treatment in *Yearbook* articles, such as *Development Forum* and the *World Economic Survey 1983*, being listed.

Cross-references are not given to entries in close proximity; for example, there is a cross-reference to "economic development" under "development" but not "development assistance".

Entries are alphabetized word by word. Examples: **human rights**; HUMAN RIGHTS, CS. ON; **humanitarian assistance**.

Within most entries, the organization, body or unit dealing with the subject is indicated (by abbreviation or short title) in parentheses, preceded or followed by the appropriate page number(s). Bold-face numbers refer to resolution or decision texts. Thus, the entry

cardiovascular diseases, 1245, 1247-48 (WHO)

indicates that WHO activities relating to cardiovascular diseases are described on the pages cited. The entry

Ecuador: disaster relief 529-32 (ECLA, 529; ESC, 530, **530-31**; GA, 531, **531-32**; SG/UN, 530)

indicates that information on disaster relief assistance to Ecuador appears on pages 529 to 532 and that the subject was considered by the Economic Commission for Latin America, on page 529, the Economic and Social Council, on page 530, and the General Assembly, on page 531. The texts of one or more resolution(s)/decision(s) (or provisions thereof) adopted by the Council is/are on pages 530 and 531; that/those of the Assembly is/are on pages 531 and 532. The activities of the Secretary-General and United Nations bodies are described on page 530.

Abbreviations

In addition to the abbreviations contained in the list on pp. xiv-xv, the subject index uses the following:

CD	Committee on Disarmament
cf(s).	conference(s)
cl(s).	council(s)
cs(s).	commission(s)
ct(s).	committee(s)
DC	Disarmament Commission
DG	Director-General
mtg(s).	meeting(s)
sess.	session
spec.	special
UNCLS	United Nations Conference on the Law of the Sea
UNJSPB	United Nations Joint Staff Pension Board

Subject index

Page numbers in boldface type indicate resolutions and decisions

WOMEN, UN DECADE FOR *(1976-1985)*, 907-13

Action Programme, Second Half: implementation, 907 (SG)

Review Cf. *(1985)*, 908-12 (Cs. on Status of Women, 908-9; GA, **909-10**, 910; Inter-Agency Meeting, 908; SG, 908); financing, 910-11 (ACABQ, 910-11; ESC, **910**, SG, 910); NGO participation, 911 (GA, **909**, 911; ESC/SG, 910, **911**); Preparatory Body for, 908-9, **909** (ESC), 1363 (members)

Voluntary Fund, 911-13 (Consultative Ct./ SG, 911-12; GA, 912, **912-13**); contributions, 911, 913 (GA), 912 *(table)*; Technical Advisory Group, 912; & UNDP, 912

WOMEN AND *APARTHEID*, INTERNATIONAL CF. ON *(1982)*: implementation, 156

women and society, 920-23

in development, 427-28 (JUNIC/CSDHA); **438**, **916** (GA); 477 (DCTD); **909** (ESC); 920-22 (ESC, 920; GA, **922**; JUNIC/CSDHA, 920; UNDP, 920-21; Voluntary Fund, 921); world survey, 920; Inter-Agency mtg., 908; SG, 920; & TCDC High-Level Ct., 922

education, 921, 1238 (UNESCO)

food problems, 916 (FAO/INSTRAW), 921 (FAO)

industrialization, 916 (INSTRAW/UNDP/ UNIDO), 921 (UNIDO)

international economic relations, 915 (INSTRAW/UNCTAD)

peace/co-operation, participation in promoting, Declaration on, 376, 922, **922** (GA)

population programmes, 745, 921 (UNFPA)

& science and technology, 922 (Advisory/Intergovernmental cts. on science/technology)

technical co-operation, 921 (DTCD)

see also) regional entries

WOMEN IN DEVELOPMENT, INTERAGENCY CT. ON (ESCAP): spec. sess., 640

WOMEN IN DEVELOPMENT, INTER-DIVISIONAL WORKING GROUP ON (FAO), 921

WOMEN IN INDUSTRIAL DEVELOPMENT, INTERDIVISIONAL WORKING GROUP ON INTEGRATION OF (UNIDO), 921

WOMEN IN SOUTH AFRICA AND NAMIBIA, INTERNATIONAL DAY OF SOLIDARITY WITH THE STRUGGLE OF, 156 (*Apartheid* Ct.), 920 (Cf. against discrimination)

WOMEN INTO DEVELOPMENT PLANNING, INCORPORATION OF, seminar, 915 (INSTRAW)

WOMEN'S DAY, INTERNATIONAL, 156 (*Apartheid* Ct.)

wood/wood products industry: 1st consultation, 592, 600 (FAO/UNIDO)

working conditions, 1216-17 (IAEA); occupational safety, 1222 (ILO); radiation, protection (IAEA/ILO/WHO), 1217

WORKING CONDITIONS AND ENVIRONMENT, INTERNATIONAL PROGRAMME FOR (PIACT): implementation, 1222 (ILO)

World Bank Economic Development Institute, *see* Economic Development Institute (World Bank)

World Charter for Nature, *see under* nature

World Disarmament Campaign, *see* Disarmament Campaign, World

World Economic Survey 1983, 402, 420-21, **422** (ESC/GA): on energy balance, 673-74

World Employment Programme, see Employment Programme, World

World Food Council (WFC), *see* Food Council, World

WORLD HEALTH ORGANIZATION (WHO), 1244-54; Assembly (36th), 1244, 1253; budget, 1250 *(tables)*; contributions, 1252-53 *(table)*; DG, reappointment, 1244; Executive Board, 1252-53 *(list)*; headquarters/regional offices, 1254; members, 1244, 1252-53 *(table)*; & NGOs, 997-1001 *(list)*; officers, 1253; secretariat, 1250; technical co-operation, 1250-53 *(tables)*

WORLD INTELLECTUAL PROPERTY ORGANIZATION (WIPO), 1306-11; anniversary observance, 1306; budget, 1308 *(table)*; contributions, 1309-10 *(tables)*; Coordination Ct., 1309; headquarters/liaison office, 1310; International Bureau, officers, 1310; members, 1306, 1309-10 *(table)*; multilateral treaties, 1306 *(list)*; publications, 1307; Secretariat, 1307-8; training programmes, 1307

WORLD METEOROLOGICAL ORGANIZATION (WMO), 1297-1302; budget, 1297, 1300-1, 1301 *(table)*; Congress (9th), 1297; contributions, 1301-2 *(table)*; Executive Cl. (Executive Ct.), 1297, 1302; headquarters, 1302; members, 1297, 1301-2 *(table)*; & NGOs, 998, 1000 *(list)*; Prize, 1297; publication, 1298; regional associations, 1302; secretariat, 1300, 1302; SG, appointment, 1297; technical co-operation, 1300; technical css., 1297, 1302

World Newspaper Supplement, 373, 385 (Information Ct.)

WORLD WAR II: end of, 40th anniversary, 376, 818, **819** (GA/Human Rights Cs.)

Yearbook of the United Nations, 380-81 (ACABQ/SG, 380; GA, **380-81**, 381)

Yemen: earthquake relief, 533, **533** (GA/UNCTAD VI/UNDP), 653-54 (ECWA)

youth, 938-45 (ESC, 938, **938-39**; SG, 938); & aging, joint activities, 944, **947** (GA); communication channels with UN, 941-42 (GA, 941, **941-42**; SG, 941); coordination/information, 939-41 (ESC, 940, **940**; GA, 941, **944**; SG, 939-40); in development, 640 (ESCAP); & human rights, 938, **939** (ESC/Social Development Cs.), 902 (Human Rights Cs.), 902-3, **944** (GA); participation in social/economic development, 938-39 (ESC, **939**, 939; SG, 938); UNESCO programmes, 1238-39; & UN Volunteers Programme, **483**, 944 (GA); world population, 938

YOUTH YEAR, ADVISORY CT. FOR THE INTERNATIONAL, **938** (ESC); members/officers, 1341

YOUTH YEAR, INTERNATIONAL *(1985)*: preparations, 482, **483** (GA/UNV), 942-45 (GA, 942-43, **943**; SG, 942), 1221 (ILO), 1239 (UNESCO); contributions, 942, **944** (GA/SG); Specific Programme of Measures for, **939**, 940, **940** (ESC), **944**, 944 (GA); 942 (SG); public information, 376 (GA), 377 (Information Ct.)

Zaire: transport/trade problems, 630-31 (ECA, 630; ESC, **631**; GA, **631**; SG, 630-31)

zones of peace (proposed): South-East Asia, 79, **228** (GA); *see also* Indian Ocean

zoonoses, 1249-50 (WHO)

Index of names

Page numbers in bold-face type indicate resolutions and decisions

Index of resolutions and decisions

[a]Adopted on 15 December to confirm the appointment of the Administrator of UNDP.

[b]Adopted on 4 February to approve the basic programme of work of the Economic and Social Council for 1983 and 1984.

[c]Adopted on 27 May to approve the draft provisional agenda for the second regular session of 1983.

How to obtain previous volumes of the *Yearbook*

Volumes of the *Yearbook of the United Nations* published previously may be obtained in many bookstores throughout the world and also from the Sales Section, United Nations, New York, N. Y. 10017, or from United Nations Publications, Palais des Nations, 1211 Geneva 10, Switzerland. Volumes listed below with an asterisk (*) are special reprints of editions out of print.

Yearbook of the United Nations, 1982
Vol. 36. Sales No. E.85.I.1 $75.

Yearbook of the United Nations, 1981
Vol. 35. Sales No. E.84.I.1 $75.

Yearbook of the United Nations, 1980
Vol. 34. Sales No. E.83.I.1 $72.

Yearbook of the United Nations, 1979
Vol. 33. Sales No. E.82.I.1 $72.

Yearbook of the United Nations, 1978
Vol. 32. Sales No. E.80.I.1 $60.

Yearbook of the United Nations, 1977
Vol. 31. Sales No. E.79.I.1 $50.

Yearbook of the United Nations, 1976
Vol. 30. Sales No. E.78.I.1 $42.

Yearbook of the United Nations, 1975
Vol. 29. Sales No. E.77.I.1 $35.

Yearbook of the United Nations, 1974
Vol. 28. Sales No. E.76.I.1 $35.

Yearbook of the United Nations, 1973
Vol. 27. Sales No. E.75.I.1 $35.

Yearbook of the United Nations, 1972
Vol. 26. Sales No. E.74.I.1 $35.

Yearbook of the United Nations, 1971
Vol. 25. Sales No. E.73.I.1 $35.

Yearbook of the United Nations, 1970*
Vol. 24. Sales No. E.72.I.1 $35.

Yearbook of the United Nations, 1969
Vol. 23. Sales No. E.71.I.1 $35.

Yearbook of the United Nations, 1968
Vol. 22. Sales No. E.70.I.1 $35.

Yearbook of the United Nations, 1967
Vol. 21. Sales No. E.68.I.1 $35.

Yearbook of the United Nations, 1966*
Vol. 20. Sales No. E.67.I.1 $50.

Yearbook of the United Nations, 1965*
Vol. 19. Sales No. 66.I.1 $50.

Yearbook of the United Nations, 1964*
Vol. 18. Sales No. 65.I.1 $58.

Yearbook of the United Nations, 1963
Vol. 17. Sales No. 64.I.1 $35.

Yearbook of the United Nations, 1962
Vol. 16. Sales No. 63.I.1 $35.

Yearbook of the United Nations, 1961
Vol. 15. Sales No. 62.I.1 $35.

Yearbook of the United Nations, 1960
Vol. 14. Sales No. 61.I.1 $35.

Yearbook of the United Nations, 1959*
Vol. 13. Sales No. 60.I.1 $58.

Yearbook of the United Nations, 1958
Vol. 12. Sales No. 59.I.1 $35.

Yearbook of the United Nations, 1957*
Vol. 11. Sales No. 58.I.1 $58.

Yearbook of the United Nations, 1956*
Vol. 10. Sales No. 57.I.1 $40.

Yearbook of the United Nations, 1955*
Vol. 9. Sales No. 56.I.20 $40.

Yearbook of the United Nations, 1954*
Vol. 8. Sales No. 55.I.25 $46.

Yearbook of the United Nations, 1953*
Vol. 7. Sales No. 54.I.15 $50.

Yearbook of the United Nations, 1952*
Vol. 6. Sales No. 53.I.30 $50.

Yearbook of the United Nations, 1951*
Vol. 5. Sales No. 52.I.30 $50.

Yearbook of the United Nations, 1950*
Vol. 4. Sales No. 1951.I.24 $75.

Yearbook of the United Nations, 1948-49*
Vol. 3. Sales No. 1950.I.11 $75.

Yearbook of the United Nations, 1947-48
Vol. 2. Sales No. 1949.I.13 $35.

Yearbook of the United Nations, 1946-47*
Vol. 1. Sales No. 1947.I.18 $75.

Yearbook Volumes 1-34 (1946-1980) are now also available in microfiche at the cost of US$ 1,198.90 for silver halide or US$ 1,041.15 for diazo duplication. Orders for microfiche sets should be sent either to the Sales Section, United Nations, New York, N. Y. 10017, or to United Nations Publications, Palais des Nations, 1211 Geneva 10, Switzerland.

NOTES

NOTES

NOTES

NOTES

NOTES

HORACE BARKS
REFERENCE LIBRARY

STOKE-ON-TRENT